The Good Pub Guide 1990

The Good Pub Guide 1990

Edited by Alisdair Aird

Deputy editor: Fiona May

PUBLISHED BY CONSUMERS' ASSOCIATION
AND HODDER & STOUGHTON

The Good Pub Guide operates on the same principle as *The Good Food Guide,* also published by Consumers' Association, but is independently owned and edited. Consumers' Association is not involved in the choice of hotels/pubs in this *Guide* nor in its awards, and *The Good Pub Guide* has no say in the hotels/pubs chosen by other Consumers' Association publications.

Which? Books are commissioned and researched by
The Association for Consumer Research
and published by Consumers' Association,
2 Marylebone Road, London NW1 4DX, and
Hodder & Stoughton, 47 Bedford Square,
London WC1B 3DP

Designed by Trevor Vincent and Tim Higgins
Illustrations by Trevor Vincent from photographs by the editor
Cover artwork by Julie Tennent
Maps by Eugene Fleury

Copyright © 1989 Alisdair Aird and Consumers' Association Ltd
Illustrations copyright © 1982, 1983, 1984, 1985, 1986 and 1987
Trevor Vincent
Maps copyright © 1989 Consumers' Association Ltd

The Good Pub Guide.—1990.
   1. Hotels, taverns, etc.—Great Britain—
   Directories   2. Restaurants, lunchrooms etc.
   —Great Britain—Directories
   I. Aird, Alisdair   II. Consumers' Association
   647'.9541'05   TX910.G7

ISBN 0 340 51144 3

Typeset by Precise Printing & Communications Ltd
Leatherhead, Surrey
Printed and bound in Great Britain by
BPCC Hazell Books Ltd
Aylesbury, Bucks

Contents

Introduction

This has been a momentous year for pubs. English and Welsh pubs have begun to get used to all-day opening, which became legal in 1988. In a special survey conducted by the *Guide* of pubs throughout England and Wales, we've found that only one in four or five are now staying open right through the afternoon. This is rather fewer than the one in three that told us they hoped to open all day when the new law first came into force – and far fewer than the two-thirds which now stay open all day in Scotland (where the law has allowed them to since 1976). The proportion's highest in London and the other big cities (around two-thirds), lowest in Bedfordshire, Cambridgeshire, the Midland counties, Essex, Suffolk and Oxfordshire. In country areas, all-day opening at least in summer is most common in Cornwall, the Lake District, and (surprisingly – perhaps it's the Scottish influence) the North. A checklist at the back of the book includes all pubs which do open all day.

All-day opening is clearly accelerating the trend towards the civilisation of pubs. Generally speaking, they are getting much more hospitable – and thinking much harder about how they can please all sorts of customers, including families. But there are still some serious problems. In particular, too many pubs go on the *Guide*'s black list because they aren't clean enough; too high a proportion of the complaints made to us by readers are about hygiene problems. Which brings us to the second major event of the year – the Government's announcement that it is to tighten up the rules about food sales, including pubs. This is good news; there's no doubt that dirt in pubs is their most serious weakness. As the new rules and procedures are worked out, the *Guide* will be trying to focus attention on some particular problems. We'd very much like your help in the next few months: please let us know of individual pubs that either score high for hygiene or cause worry (and say why); and tell us about any general practices that you think need attention.

The biggest event of all has been the report by the Monopolies and Mergers Commission on the Supply of Beer. It showed clearly that the six big national brewers – Allied, Bass, Courage, Scottish & Newcastle (McEwans/Youngers), Grand Metropolitan (Watneys) and Whitbreads – have kept up drinks prices and varied them unfairly throughout the country. There's nothing new about that – we've been saying it for years. In response to the report, *The Good Pub Guide* has passed the results of its own research to the Government, based on the many thousands of reports received from readers (over 25,000 reports for this edition), and on our systematic records of price changes and so forth. As we've told the Government, a vital point is that our research shows that the MMC proposals to break the big brewers' complex monopoly pose no threat to the future of The British Pub as a thriving institution. The *Guide* strongly supported the MMC recommendations, and in particular showed that pub-goers don't see a range of beers from one brewer that dominates the pubs in any one area as a decent substitute for a true choice of beers from a variety of different brewers; that the monopoly also hurts pub-goers by restricting their choice of wines, soft drinks and other drinks; that by and large the pubs tied to the smaller brewers are more than twice as likely to be good pubs (in the sense that they might find their way into this *Guide*) as those tied to the national megabrewers; and (of course) that you, the readers, have been very concerned about undue regional variations in beer prices, and about beer price rises. We reported our experience that tied pubs don't make use of the limited freedom given them by a recent EEC regulation to buy some non-beer drinks from suppliers other than their tied brewery – and urged the Government to give tenants greater security of tenure, so that they won't be scared of using their legal rights to break their brewery-landlords' monopoly powers. On a small but important point, the *Guide* took up a recommendation that the MMC had made – that tied pubs should have the right to stock a guest beer. It looked for a while as if this might be interpreted as a lager or other mass-selling fizzy beer. We were able to report to the Government that in each of the several hundred and perhaps thousands of cases where readers have told us about guest beers, they've invariably meant cask-conditioned real ales.

Although it is not yet certain what the final outcome will be, it is clear that action to break the monopoly will be taken only against the big six national brewers. It is also clear that guest beer will mean guest real ale; and it looks quite likely that tenants will be given enough security of tenure to allow them to stand up to their landlord breweries. Whatever happens, the *Guide* will continue to fight for a fairer price deal – on beer and on soft drinks – for pub-goers, and for a wider choice of beers, wines and other drinks. And we'll keep a special eye on what happens in those areas where the stranglehold of the big six is particularly tight, as it is in London and the South-East, Yorkshire and Humberside, and the West Midlands, where the big six have controlled half or more of the pubs.

THE BEST BREWERIES

The *Guide* has analysed what proportion of each brewer's pubs get into its pages as main entries. We've then compared this figure with the average of all pubs, to see whether that brewer's pubs have done better or worse than average. None of the big six national brewers matches the average. Of course, these big beer producers may well be scoring a huge commercial success by pouring the beers down the regulars at their thousands of tied locals. But when it comes to true Good Pubs – places worth making a trip to – it's a different story. According to the analysis, the *best big brewer* for good tied pubs is Whitbreads. Even so, its score of good pubs is only about three-quarters of the national average. Bass scores only about a quarter as well as the national average, for good pubs. The other four score only about half as well as the national average – that is, only about half as many of their pubs get in as main entries as would do if they were as good as other brewer's pubs and free houses.

Devenish is the *best regional brewer* for good pubs, doing considerably better than the national average, or the typical free house. Robinsons and Greene King also have more good pubs than average. But the real success stories come with the smaller local breweries. The three *best brewers of all* for good tied pubs are Harveys (Sussex), Brakspears (Oxfordshire) and Adnams (Suffolk). Other local breweries that are outstandingly good for tied pubs are, in rough order, Wadworths (Wiltshire), King & Barnes (Sussex), Hook Norton (Oxfordshire), St Austell (Cornwall), Palmers (Dorset), Gibbs Mew (Wiltshire), Youngs (London), Sam Smiths (Yorkshire) and Badger (Dorset). Their pubs do at least three times better than average. And we'd rate as the *beer-consumer's friend* Holts (Manchester) and Burts (Isle of Wight), for their continuing policy of holding down prices in their pubs.

THE YEAR'S TOP FOOD PUBS

Sifting through the more than 25,000 reports from readers which have gone into this edition, and going through hundreds of the editorial inspection records made by the Editor and the Deputy Editor, we've come up with some clear winners. On the food side, standards have been rising so markedly that this year we've remodelled the food award, raising the standard pubs must meet. Pubs qualifying for the new award – and dozens of them have – are truly exceptional. Among this elite, the top rank includes some places that are very special indeed.

For *best all-round bar food*, the Notley Arms at Monksilver in Somerset comes top. Close on its heels – all showing a good value combination of imaginative touches with honest straightforward cooking – come the Walnut Tree at Fawley (Buckinghamshire), Cholmondeley Arms near Bickley Moss (Cheshire), Moorcock above Blacko (Lancashire), Druid at Birchover (Derbyshire), Wenlock Edge Inn (Shropshire), Angel at Hetton (North Yorkshire), Royal Oak at Appleby (Cumbria) and New Inn at Dowlish Wake (Somerset). The *Guide*'s best new *food discovery of the year* is the Wheatsheaf at Swinton (Scottish Borders). And the prize for the *best cold table* goes to the Red Lion at Newton (Lincolnshire).

There are of course the specialists. For us and a great many readers, the most important pub food specialists are those that give proper honour to simple snacks. One of the most common complaints readers make is that many pubs have switched off snacks, boosting their turnover by turning themselves into restaurants, offering nothing to eat under £3. Even worse, some don't even sell nuts or crisps. This year the tide seems to be turning. The honest bar snack is making a strong comeback. Among hundreds of fine examples, this year's joint winners of the award for *first-class simple pub food* are the Cock at Broom (Bedfordshire) and Harrow at Steep (Hampshire).

Lots of pubs this year have been giving particularly good value with variations on the ploughman's lunch (not in fact as traditional as many people think – it was first dreamed up some thirty years ago). Essentials are of course good ingredients (in generous amounts for the price), with butter served as a pat or in a pot – not wrapped in sticky finger-traps. This past year, many more pubs have been adding to these basic requirements really good home-baked bread and their own home-made pickles and chutneys. There have been too many good examples of these to note here – they're described in detail in the text. But *tops for cheese* are two Manchester pubs that have a splendid range, at prices that seem too good to be true: the Royal Oak in Didsbury and Mark Addy in Salford. Other marvellous cheese specialists are the Nobody Inn at Doddiscombsleigh (Devon), La Galoche in Tunbridge Wells (Kent) and Sportsmans Arms at Wath-in-Nidderdale (North Yorkshire).

A marvellous northern pub snack is Yorkshire pudding with a richly nourishing filling. The *foremost Yorkshire pudding specialist* is the Half Moon at Skidby (Humberside). The Yorkshire pudding sandwich at the Bulls Head above Linthwaite (West Yorkshire) gives unbeatable value.

This year's *super sandwichmen* are the licensees of the Star at Harome (North Yorkshire) – not cheap, but well worth the pilgrimage – and Old Howgate Inn at Howgate (Lothian, Scotland) – exciting Danish-style finger-sandwiches.

Fish is becoming a prize bargain in many pubs. *Fish pub of the year* is the Sloop at Bantham (Devon), run very close by the Morefield Motel in Ullapool (Scottish Highlands). For people with huge appetites, the Waterford Arms at Seaton Sluice (Northumberland) is splendid value, and Pearsons Crab and Oyster House in Whitstable (Kent) has great fish bargains, too. If you're on the relevant island, you shouldn't miss the Rocquaine Bistro (Guernsey) or New Inn at Shalfleet (Isle of Wight) – super fresh local fish. Top marks for fresh fish well inland go to Sankeys at the Gate in Tunbridge Wells (Kent) and Frog & Parrot in Sheffield (South Yorkshire).

There is a top elite of pubs which beat top restaurants at their own game – serving really imaginative delicious food which, admittedly not cheap, still gives streets better value than you could find in comparable restaurants. The Walnut Tree Inn at Llandewi Skirrid (Gwent) is tops for *luxury pub food*, no expense spared. The Royal Oak at Yattendon (Berkshire) and Silver Plough at Pitton (Wiltshire) are also hard to beat for luxury pub meals, and in this elite group the best pub for classy fish cooking is the Three Horseshoes at Powerstock (Dorset).

A real find for *unusual pub food* is the Black Horse at Walcote (Leicestershire); the landlady, from Thailand, does nothing but Thai food.

TOPS FOR DRINKS

Drinks pub of the year is the Nobody Inn, Doddiscombsleigh (Devon): they keep interesting real ales, usually over fifteen good wines by the glass, a remarkably rich collection of several hundred wines by the bottle, over two hundred whiskies including great rarities (with helpful tasting notes), and plenty of other interesting drinks.

Cellarman of the year is a lady – Mrs Phyllis Cheffers, who keeps up to sixteen real ales at a time in fine condition, at the Bridge in Topsham (Devon). The Hoop at Stock (Essex), Ringlestone Inn at Ringlestone (Kent) and Bon Accord in Glasgow also keep an exceptional range of fine beers. But the *best beer pub* is the Richmond Arms at West Ashling (West Sussex) – a wide range of real ales, a most ambitious programme of quickly changing guest beers, and interesting bottled beers. *Best pub for bottled beers* is the Masons Arms on Cartmel Fell (Cumbria) – this is where you'll find that there's much more to bottled beer than fuel for lager louts. Instead of keeping lots of beers, some pubs concentrate on just one, learning the intricacies of its character so well that they can always serve it in tip-top condition; of these, the *best one-beer pub* is the Athletic Arms (the Diggers) in Edinburgh – a shrine to McEwans 80/-. A great many pubs now brew their own beer; the *best range of home-brews* comes from the Sair in Linthwaite (West Yorkshire), a remarkable choice that now includes one of the only genuine low-alcohol real ales.

Whisky is, with beer, the great indigenous staple of pub drinking. Like beer, it's a fascinating drink with subtleties of taste and style which can take a lifetime to discover. More and more pubs are now stocking unusual blends, or better still a good range of single malts. The *best pub for whisky* is the Cragg Lodge at Wormald Green (North Yorkshire); their comprehensive collection of many hundreds must be the finest in the world. To get into the spirit with a swing, try the Inverarnan Inn at Inverarnan (Central, Scotland): kilted barmen and the skirl of pipes. The Pot Still in Glasgow has a superb collection, and further south the George at Leadenham (Lincolnshire), Cadeby Inn at Cadeby (South Yorkshire) and Crown & Horns at East Ilsley (Berkshire) are excellent for whisky choice. The Hotel Eilean Iarmain at Isle Ornsay (Skye) has produced, enterprisingly, two fine blends.

Wine is at least slowly climbing out of the pub doldrums. *Outstanding for wines by the glass* are the Plough at Blackbrook (Surrey), New Inn in Cerne Abbas (Dorset), La Galoche in Tunbridge Wells (Kent), Crown in Southwold (Suffolk) and Wykeham Arms in Winchester (Hampshire). The Green Man at Toot Hill (Essex) – specialising in champagne – and Red Lion at Steeple Aston (Oxfordshire) have notable wine cellars. The new licensees at the Cornish Arms at Pendoggett (Cornwall) look out for interesting bin-ends. And the Royal Oak at Yattendon (Berkshire) and Beetle & Wedge at Moulsford (Oxfordshire) have a splendid system: anyone wanting a half-bottle can choose from their list of full bottles, and the rest of that bottle is then sold fresh by the glass in the bar. This practice deserves to be taken up much more widely.

GREAT PUBS – AND PUBLICANS

Whatever the food and drink, it's the pub itself that counts above all. We'd rate as the *finest unspoilt country pub* the Three Horseshoes on the downs above Petersfield (Hampshire), with the Falkland Arms at Great Tew (Oxfordshire) hard on its heels.

Our award for *perfectly preserved antiquity* goes to the Fleece at Bretforton (Hereford & Worcester), with others to consider including the Royal Standard of England at Forty Green (Buckinghamshire), Bull i' th' Thorn south of Buxton (Derbyshire) and (for furnishings) Eagle & Child at Wharles (Lancashire). For *Victorian/Edwardian magnificence* you can't beat the Philharmonic in Liverpool, though the Barton Arms in Birmingham and Black Friar in London EC4 should not be missed. Hollands in London E1 is a *unique Victorian survivor*, hardly changed since it was opened by the present landlord's great-grandfather.

The most *spectacularly unusual pub* is the Yew Tree at Cauldon (Staffordshire), stuffed full of remarkable collections. Other fascinating pubs are the George & Dragon at Potterne (Wiltshire), for its unique antique indoor shooting gallery; the Crooked House at Himley (West Midlands) – it really is crooked; the Beehive in

Grantham (Lincolnshire), for its centuries-old living inn-sign; the Olde Trip to Jerusalem in Nottingham for its inner bar – literally a cavern; the Monkey House at Defford (Hereford & Worcester) – the only pub we know where you stand *outside* to be served; and the Abbey at Llanthony (Gwent) – part of a romantically isolated ruined Norman priory. Everybody's favourite station buffet must be the Stalybridge Station Buffet (Greater Manchester); quite delightful.

Theme pubs have had a bad press. But when they are done individually (rather than as a string of carbon copies) they can be exhilarating good fun. Our award for the *most high-spirited theme pub* goes to the Little Tumbling Sailor at Kidderminster (Hereford & Worcester); runner-up is the extravagantly Disneyesque Highwayman at Sourton (Devon) – not for the weak-spirited.

Often, hotels and the larger inns have pretty dreadful bars – at best dull, at worst downright grotty. But the bars of some well run hotels can easily hold their own with the warmth and interest of any really good pub. Our award for the *best hotel bar* goes to the Bear at Crickhowell (mid-Wales), with strong competition from the Pheasant at Bassenthwaite and Dove & Olive Bar of the Wordsworth Hotel at Grasmere (both Cumbria), the George III at Penmaenpool (also Wales), and two fine old inns under the same ownership – the George in Stamford (Lincolnshire) and Haycock at Wansford (Cambridgeshire).

Pub restoration and extension has now become quite an art. This year we've seen some splendid examples. The Smugglers at Osmington Mills (Dorset) is the *best-extended pub* we've seen this year – so well done that it's hard to tell the new from the old. Morlands, local brewers based in Abingdon, have done the *best pub refurbishment*, at the Swan at East Ilsley (Berkshire), an object-lesson in breaking up a spacious bar into welcoming smaller areas. A close runner-up is Marstons, with their showpiece Albion, just round the corner from the brewery in Burton-on-Trent (Staffordshire). Another local brewers, Wadworths of Devizes, earns top marks for *best pub rehabilitation* for their lovely work on the formerly virtually derelict Barge at Seend (Wiltshire). The *best conversion of another building* is the independently done Station at Broadbottom (Greater Manchester); formerly a derelict station house, it's now a smashing pub. The Tadcaster brewers Sam Smiths haven't quite finished their work on the Abbey Inn in Derby (it was the ruined remnant of an ancient abbey) – but it's looking very promising.

Manchester wins the prize for *Britain's best-pubbed city* – a fascinating collection of pubs for all tastes in the city itself, and many more delights tucked away in the moors just outside. Edinburgh runs it close. The *best pub countryside* is Wharfedale in Yorkshire – at every turn there seems to be yet another lovely pub.

Our *discovery of the year* is the Cap & Feathers at Tillingham in Essex. Two other marvellous finds are the Stables near Hope (Shropshire) and Strode Arms at Cranmore (Somerset).

Behind every good pub's bar is a good landlord or landlady. And no matter how interesting the pub, how good the drink or food, what makes a pub enjoyable is the welcome. Striking the right balance is a very fine art: too effusive a welcome for a perfect stranger can be as off-putting as the traditional cold shoulder. We found our *welcome of the year* from the Hawkins family at the Halfway Bridge at Lodsworth (West Sussex), with notably welcoming and helpful licensees and staff also at the Britannia at Elterwater (Cumbria), Bull Terrier at Croscombe (Somerset) and Griffin at Llyswen (mid-Wales). Gregg and Angela Worrall have transformed the Crown at Bathford (Avon) into an interesting, relaxing and welcoming place with good drink and interesting healthy food, outstandingly well run – they earn the accolade of *licensees of the year*.

Alisdair Aird

Using the *Guide*

THE COUNTIES

England has been split alphabetically into counties, mainly to make it easier for people scanning through the book to find pubs near them. Each chapter starts by picking out pubs that are specially attractive for one reason or another.

Occasionally, counties have been grouped together into a single chapter, and metropolitan areas have been included in the counties around them – for example, Merseyside in Lancashire. When there's any risk of confusion, we have put a note about where to find a county at the place in the book where you'd probably look for it. But if in doubt, check the Contents: note that this year the north-eastern chapter, grouping together Durham, Northumberland, Cleveland and Tyne & Wear, has been called Northumbria.

Scotland and Wales have each been covered in single chapters, and London appears immediately before them at the end of England. Except in London (which is split into Central, North, South, West and East), pubs are listed alphabetically under the name of the town or village where they are. If the village is so small that you probably wouldn't find it on a road map, we've listed it under the name of the nearest sizeable village or town instead. The maps use the same town and village names, and additionally include a few big cities that don't have any listed pubs – for orientation.

We always list pubs in their true locations – so if a village is actually in Buckinghamshire that's where we list it, even if its postal address is via some town in Oxfordshire. Just once or twice, while the village itself is in one county the pub is just over the border in the next-door county. We then use the village county, not the pub one.

STARS

Specially good pubs are picked out with a star after the name. In a few cases, pubs have two stars: these are outstanding pubs, really worth going out of your way to find. And just three pubs have three stars – the real aristocrats. The stars do *not* signify extra luxury or specially good food. The detailed description of each pub shows what its special appeal is, and it's that that the stars refer to.

FOOD AWARD (NEW THIS YEAR): 🍴

The knife-and-fork rosette shows those pubs where food is particularly good. This symbol is new in this year's edition. Because of the continuing improvement in the quality of pub food, we've been able to set a higher standard for this award than for the plain knife-and-fork symbol used in previous editions. So the rosette distinguishes pubs where the food is a special attraction.

STAY AWARD: 🛏

The bed symbol shows pubs which we know to be good as places to stay in – bearing in mind the price of the rooms (obviously you can't expect the same level of luxury at £10 a head as you'd get for £40 a head).

RECOMMENDERS

At the end of each main entry we include the names of readers who have recently recommended that pub (unless they've asked us not to). Important note: the description of the pub and the comments on it are the editor's or the deputy editor's and *not* the recommenders'; they are based on our own personal inspections and on

12

later verification of facts with each pub. As some recommenders' names appear quite often, you can get an extra idea of what a pub is like by seeing which other pubs those recommenders have approved.

LUCKY DIPS

At the end of each county chapter are included brief descriptions of pubs that have been recommended by readers, with the readers' names in brackets. They give pointers to thousands of pubs well worth trying, with descriptions often reflecting the balanced judgement of a number of different readers. They haven't usually been inspected by us, unless the recommenders include the initials LYM or BB. LYM means the pub was in a previous edition of the *Guide*. The usual reason that it's no longer a main entry is that, although we've heard nothing really condemnatory about it, we've not had enough favourable reports to be sure that it's still ahead of the local competition. BB means that, although the pub has never been a main entry, we have inspected it, found nothing against it, and reckon it's useful to know of – and perhaps worth a closer look. In both these cases, the description is our own; in others, it's based on the readers' reports.

As we get hundreds of these reports each week, many from an inner core of 500 or so readers whose judgement we have learned to respect particularly highly, we can give firm recommendations for many Lucky Dip pubs even though we haven't inspected them personally. Such pubs are marked with a ☆. Roughly speaking, we'd say that these pubs are as much worth considering, at least for the virtues described for them, as many of the main entries themselves.

The Lucky Dips (particularly, of course, the starred ones) are under consideration for inspection for a future edition – so please let us have any comments you can make on them. You can use the report forms at the end of the book, the report card included in it, or just write direct (no stamp needed if posted in the UK). Our address is *The Good Pub Guide*, FREEPOST, London SW10 0BR.

MAP REFERENCES

All pubs are given a four-figure map reference. On the main entries it looks like this: SX5678 Map 1. Map 1 means that the town or village is on the first map at the end of the book. SX means it's in the square labelled SX on that map. The first figure, 5, tells you to look along the grid at the top and bottom of the SX square for the figure 5. The *third* figure, 7, tells you to look down the grid at the side of the square to find the figure 7. Imaginary lines drawn down and across the square from these figures should intersect near the pub itself.

The second and fourth figures, the 6 and the 8, are for more precise pin-pointing, and are really for use with larger-scale maps such as road atlases or the Ordnance Survey 1:50,000 maps, which use exactly the same map reference system. On the relevant Ordnance Survey map, instead of finding the 5 marker on the top grid you'd find the 56 one; instead of the 7 on the side grid you'd look for the 78 marker. This makes it very easy to locate even the smallest village.

Where a pub is exceptionally difficult to find, we include a six-figure reference in the directions, such as OS Sheet 102 reference 654783. This refers to Sheet 102 of the Ordnance Survey 1:50,000 maps, which explain how to use the six-figure references to pinpoint a pub to the nearest 100 metres.

MOTORWAY PUBS

If a pub is within four or five miles of a motorway junction, and reaching it doesn't involve much slow traffic, we give special directions for finding it from the motorway. And the Special Interest Lists at the end of the book include a list of these pubs, motorway by motorway.

PRICES AND OTHER FACTUAL DETAILS

The *Guide* went to press during the summer of 1989. As late as possible before that, each pub was sent a checking sheet to provide up-to-date food, drink and bedroom prices and other factual information. In the last two or three years, we've found that prices tend to increase by about 10 per cent over the year – so you should expect that sort of increase by summer 1990. But if you find a significantly different price (with a few pubs this last year, some prices have jumped by over 30 per cent) *please let us know*. Not every pub returned the sheet to us (if it didn't, we don't show a licensee's name after the brewery name at the end of the entry), and in some cases those that did omitted some prices. In such cases we ourselves were usually able to gather the information – especially prices – anyway. But where details are missing, that is the explanation. Again, this is something we'd particularly welcome readers' reports on.

Breweries to which pubs are 'tied' are named at the beginning of the italic-print rubric after each main entry. That means the pub has to get most if not all of its drinks from that brewery. If the brewery is not an independent one but just part of a combine, we name the combine in brackets. (This year, we've used Allied as the name for the pubs we previously described as Ind Coope; we've been reluctant to do this, as the name Allied misleadingly implies some free alliance of independent breweries, instead of the single conglomerate which in fact it is.)

Free house are pubs not tied to a brewery, so in theory they can shop around to get the drinks their customers want, at the best prices they can find. But in practice many free houses have loans from the big brewers, on terms that bind them to sell those breweries' beers – indeed, about half of all the beer sold in free houses is supplied by the big national brewery combines to free houses that have these loan ties. So don't be too surprised to find that so-called free houses may be stocking just as restricted a range of beers as openly tied pubs.

Real ale is used to mean beer that has been maturing naturally in its cask. We do not count as real ale beer which has been pasteurised or filtered to remove its natural yeasts. If it is kept under a blanket of carbon dioxide ('blanket pressure') to preserve it, we still generally mention it – as long as the pressure is too light for you to notice any extra fizz, it's hard to tell the difference. But we say that the carbon dioxide blanket is there.

Other drinks: this year we've made a special effort to gather more information about other drinks worth noting – and we'd very much welcome more help from readers in this. We've paid particular attention to picking out those pubs where the quality or range of *wines* is above the general pub average (gradually improving, though still well below what it should be). We've also looked out particularly for pubs doing enterprising non-alcoholic drinks (including good tea or coffee), interesting spirits (especially malt whiskies), country wines (elderflower and the like) and good farm ciders. So many pubs now stock one of the main brands of draught cider that we normally mention cider only if the pub keeps quite a range, or one of the less-common farm-made ciders.

Meals refers to what is sold in the bar, not in any separate restaurant. It means that the pub sells food in its bar substantial enough to do as a proper meal – something you'd sit down to with knife and fork. It doesn't necessarily mean you can get three separate courses.

Snacks means sandwiches, ploughman's, pies and so forth, rather than pork scratchings or packets of crisps. We always mention sandwiches in the text if we know that a pub does them – if you don't see them mentioned, assume you can't get them.

The food listed in the description of each pub is an example of the sort of thing you'd find served in the bar on a normal day. We try to indicate any difference we know of between lunchtime and evening, and between summer and winter (on the whole stressing summer food more). In winter, many pubs tend to have a more restricted range, particularly of salads, and tend then to do more in the way of filled baked potatoes, casseroles and hot pies. We always mention barbecues if we know a pub does them. Food quality and variety may be affected by holidays – particularly in a small pub, where the licensees do the cooking themselves (May and early June seems to be a popular time for licensees to take their holidays).

Any separate restaurant is mentioned, and we give a telephone number if tables can be booked (for London, we give the new 071- and 081- prefixes, which take effect in May 1990, as well as the 01-). We also note any pubs which told us they'd be keeping their restaurant open into Sunday afternoons (when, in England and Wales, they have to close their bars). But in general all comments on the type of food served, and in particular all the other details about meals and snacks at the end of each entry, relate to the pub food and not to the restaurant food.

Children under 14 are now allowed into at least some part of most of the pubs included in this *Guide* (there is no legal restriction on 14-year-olds going into the bar, though only 18-year-olds can get alcohol there). As we went to press, we asked pubs a series of detailed questions about their rules. *Children welcome* means the pub has told us that it simply lets them come in, with no special restrictions. In other cases we report exactly what arrangements pubs say they make for children. However, we have to note that in readers' experience some pubs set a time-limit (say, no children after 8pm) that they haven't told us about, while others may impose some other rule (children only if eating, for example). If you come across this, please let us know, so that we can clarify the information for the pub concerned in the next edition. Even if we don't mention children at all, it is worth asking: one or two pubs told us frankly that they do welcome children but don't want to advertise the fact for fear of being penalised. All but one or two pubs (we mention these in the text) allow children in their garden or on their terrace, if they have one.

Dogs, cats and other animals are mentioned in the text if we know either that they are likely to be present or that they are specifically excluded – we depend chiefly on readers and partly on our own inspections for this information.

If an entry says something like 'on *Good Walks Guide* Walk 22' (or, in the Lucky Dips, 'on GWG 22'), the pub is on one of the walks described in the book of that name by Tim Locke, also published by Consumers' Association and Hodder & Stoughton.

Parking is not mentioned if you should normally be able to park outside the pub, or in a private car par, without difficulty. But if we know that parking space is limited or metered, we say so.

Opening hours are for summer weekdays. If these show a pub stays open until 11pm, it will close at 10.30pm in winter unless we say *all year*. And in winter some pubs open an hour or so later, too: we mention this where we know of it. In the country, many pubs may open rather later and close earlier than their details show unless there are plenty of customers around (if you come across this, please let us know – with details). Unless we say otherwise for a particular county or pub, pubs generally stay open until 11pm on Friday and Saturday evening. Since 1988, pubs in England and Wales have been allowed to stay open all day Mondays to Saturdays, from 11am (earlier, if the area's licensing magistrates have permitted) till 11pm; Scottish pubs have been allowed to do this since 1976, and all-day opening is far more generally common there – outside cities, it's still quite rare in England and Wales, where pubs are still experimenting with the new hours. Again, we'd be very grateful to hear of any differences from the hours we quote. You are allowed 20 minutes' drinking-up time after the quoted hours – half an hour if you've been having a meal in the pub.

Sunday hours are standard for all English and Welsh pubs that open on that day: 12–3, 7–10.30. In Scotland a few pubs close on Sundays (we specify those that we know of), most are open 12.30–2.30 and 6.30–11, and some stay open all day. If we know of a pub closing for any day of the week or part of the year, we say so. The few pubs which we say stay closed on Monday do open on Bank Holiday Mondays.

Bedroom prices normally include full English breakfasts (if these are available, which they usually are), VAT and any automatic service charge that we know about. If we give just one price, it is the total price for two people sharing a double or twin-bedded room for one night. Otherwise, prices before the '/' are for single occupancy, prices after it for double. A capital B against the price means that it inlcudes a private bathroom, a capital S a private shower. As all this coding packs in quite a lot of information, some examples may help to explain it:

    £20 on its own means that's the total bill for two people sharing a twin or double room without private bath; the pub has no rooms with private bath, and a single person might have to pay that full price

    £20B means exactly the same – but all the rooms have private bath

    £20 (£24B) means rooms with private baths cost £4 extra

    £15/£20(£24B) means the same as the last example, but also shows that there are single rooms for £15, none of which have private bathrooms

If there's a choice of rooms at different prices, we normally give the cheapest. If there are seasonal price variations, we give the summer price (the highest). This winter – 1989–90 – many inns, particularly in the country, will have special cheaper rates. And at other times, especially in holiday areas, you will often find prices cheaper if you stay for several nights. On weekends, inns that aren't in obvious weekending areas often have bargain rates for two- or three-night stays.

MEAL TIMES (NEW THIS YEAR)

As bar food service has become such a normal part of a pub's operations, pubs have become more consistent in the times at which they serve it. Commonly, it's served from 12–2 and 7–9, at least from Monday to Saturday (food service often stops a bit earlier on Sundays). If we don't give a time against the Meals and Snacks note at the bottom of a main entry, that means that you should be able to get bar food at those times. However, we spell out the times if we know that bar food service starts after 12.15 or after 7.15; if it stops before 2 or before 8.45; or if food is served for significantly longer than usual (say, until 2.30 or 9.45).

    Though we note days when pubs have told us they don't do food, experience suggests that you should play safe on Sundays and check first with any pub before planning an expedition that depends on getting a meal there. Also, out-of-the-way pubs often cut down on cooking during the week if they're quiet – as they tend to be, except at holiday times. Please let us know if you find anything different from what we say.

CHANGES DURING THE YEAR – PLEASE TELL US

Changes are inevitable during the course of a year. Landlords change, and so do their policies. And, as we've said, not all returned our fact-checking sheets. We very much hope that you will find everything just as we say. But if you find anything different, please let us know, using the tear-out card in the middle of the book (which doesn't need an envelope), and report forms at the end, or just a letter. you don't need a stamp: the address is *The Good Pub Guide*, FREEPOST, London SW10 0BR.

Author's acknowledgements

Particular thanks to Bridget Warrington who has kept our research on track; and to Martin Hamilton, who stepped in with editorial assistance in the summer.

Thanks too to the publicans who have taken such trouble over filling in our very detailed fact sheets – and thanks to them, also, for making and running so many friendly and attractive places.

We owe a great deal to the many hundreds of readers who report, often regularly, on pubs – thanks to you all. Special thanks to the people who have given most help to this new edition (in rough order of the volume of reports they've sent):
Ian Phillips, Jon Wainwright, Gwen and Peter Andrews, Roger Huggins, Tom McLean and Ewan McCall, Nick Dowson and Alison Hayward, Lyn and Bill Capper, WHBM, Wayne Brindle, Richard Houghton, Graham Gibson, Derek and Sylvia Stephenson, Richard Sanders, E G Parish, John Evans, Thomas Nott, Peter Griffiths, Graham Bush, Syd and Wyn Donald, Heather Sharland, Joan Olivier, David and Flo Wallington, Steve Mitcheson and Anne Collins, S J A Velate, S V Bishop, Frank Cummings, Dr and Mrs A K Clarke, Brian and Anna Marsden, AE, GRE, M A and W R Proctor, A T Langton, Peter Corris, Jenny and Brian Seller, PLC, TBB, PADEMLUC, Dr John Innes, Brian Jones, Len Beattie, Dave Braisted, Simon Collett-Jones, Mr and Mrs J H Adam, Michael and Alison Sandy, Rob and Gill Weeks, John Baker, Gordon and Daphne, BKA, Pamela and Merlyn Horswell, Joy Heatherley, Peter and Rose Flower, Shirley Pielou, Steve and Carolyn Harvey, Patrick Young, Phil and Sally Gorton, E J Alcock, Tom Evans, John Tyzack, Steve Waters, Ted George, D L Johnson, Paul McPherson, Dave Butler and Lesley Storey, Lee Goulding, A J Skull, Chris Raisin, Jenny Cantle, Robert and Vicky Tod, Howard and Sue Gascoyne, Robert Lester, T Mansell, John Oddey, Col G D Stafford, Sheila Keene, Jon Dewhirst, Grahame Archer, Jane Maclean, Richard Gibbs, and my uncle, W T Aird.

And a special word of thanks to Joel Dobris who has done so much to keep us abreast of pub and beer developments in the USA.

England

Avon *see* Somerset

Bedfordshire *see* Cambridgeshire

Berkshire

Even with the new, higher standards we've been able to introduce this year for the Guide food award, a good many pubs in this privileged area have already shown that they are worthy of it. The elegant Royal Oak at Yattendon, an attractive place to stay, has perhaps the most inventive food of any pub in the county, and readers who've enjoyed it will want to know that the owners have now also taken over the Beetle & Wedge at Moulsford (see Oxfordshire main entries). Stylish food may also be had at the White Hart in Hamstead Marshall (a new main entry; authentic Italian cooking and good fish, in a charming small English village inn), the Swan at Inkpen (interesting Singapore-Chinese dishes in the evenings; another new main entry) and the Little Angel at Remenham (particularly strong on fish dishes). Along more traditional pub-food lines, the Four Points at Aldworth's vast helpings have beaten so many customers that they've now added scaled-down cut-price versions of their best sellers, and earns the award primarily on value; the Pheasant near Great Shefford, also new to the main entries this year, offers excellent just-off-the-motorway value; at Knowl Hill, the Bird in Hand's excellent buffet is a great standby, and the recent extensions have if anything added to the appeal of this popular old pub; and the Old Boot at Stanford Dingley is relied on by many for a relaxed meal out. Changes at some favourite pubs in the area include new

Bel & the Dragon, Cookham

21

licensees at the Swan in Great Shefford, the civilised old Bear in Hungerford and the Red House at Marsh Benham; the new conservatory and restaurant at the Belgian Arms in Holyport is proving popular. Besides the three pubs already mentioned, several pubs newly promoted to the main entries, or back among them after an absence, include the pleasantly idiosyncratic Blue Boar at Chieveley, the cosy Swan Uppers in Cookham Rise, the Swan at East Ilsley (a remarkably fine example of careful refurbishment – the brewers are Morlands), the Cricketers at Littlewick Green (licensees who've taken over since it was last in the main entries are doing well), the Fox & Hounds tucked away at Peasemore on the downs north of Newbury, the neatly modernised and friendly Bull in Wargrave and the cheerful New Inn in its pretty village location at Winterbourne. The Dew Drop in the woods above Hurley deserves a special mention: delightfully placed, it's built up such a following among those readers who've tracked it down that this year we've awarded it a star. Other starred pubs not so far mentioned are the unpretentious Bell up on the downs at Aldworth (excellent fresh filled crusty rolls, incidentally; if you like this rustic pub, you should also try the Pot Kiln tucked away in lovely countryside at Frilsham) and the splendidly old-fashioned Bel & the Dragon in Cookham. The Crown & Horns at East Ilsley deserves high marks for its collection of whiskies – over 170 the last time we counted. And the Bull not far from the Thames at Sonning is a must for the collector of picturesque pubs. Among Lucky Dip entries at the end of the chapter, we'd particularly note the anachronistic and determinedly rustic Old Hatch Gate at Cockpole Green, the Horns at Crazies Hill (it's had good south-east Asian cooking), the Union at Old Windsor, the White Hart at Sonning for its Thames-side elegance, both Waltham St Lawrence entries, the Horse & Groom and perhaps the Royal Oak in Windsor and the Slug & Lettuce at Winkfield.

ALDWORTH   SU5579 Map 2

Bell ★

Popular with walkers on Sundays, this cheerful, old-fashioned pub is perhaps at its best on weekday lunchtimes. There are benches built around the panelled walls and into the gaps left by a big disused fireplace and bread oven (though there's still a wood-burning stove), and beams in the shiny ochre ceiling. Perfectly kept Arkells BBB and Kingsdown, Badger Best and Morrells (all on handpump) are handed through a small hatch in the central servery. Fresh hot crusty rolls are filled with Cheddar, ham, pâté or Stilton (60p), turkey or tongue (70p) and smoked salmon (£1.20); darts, shove-ha'penny, dominoes, chess and Aunt Sally (the local single-pin version of skittles). At Christmas time steaming jugs of hot punch and mince pies are handed round after the local mummers perform in the road outside by the ancient well-head (the shaft is sunk 400 feet through the chalk). In summer, there are seats in the quiet garden among roses, mallows and lavender. The path by the pub joins the nearby Ridgeway. *(Recommended by Dr Stewart Rae, Neville Burke, A T Langton, Gordon and Daphne)*

Free house   Licensee Mrs H E Macaulay   Real ale   Snacks (not Mon)   Children in tap-room   Open 11–2.30, 6–11 all year; closed Mon (not bank hols) and 25 Dec

Four Points ✪

B4009 towards Hampstead Norreys

The helpings at this low thatched seventeenth-century pub have been so gargantuan that the friendly licensees have introduced optional smaller helpings. Depending on what Mrs Gillas fancies cooking that day, this might include sandwiches (from

75p), soup (£1), ploughman's with imaginatively presented salads (£2.25), curried prawn mayonnaise or stuffed tomato, cheese and peppers (£2.25), avocado cheesy bake salad, ox-tongue and egg pie or lasagne (£2.70), roast lamb, beef or pork or steak and kidney pie (£2.95) and venison or rabbit pies (£3.20); there are croûtons set out on the thick-topped wooden tables and on Sundays nibbles such as prawns, cheese and celery and poppadums. Well kept Charringtons, Courage Directors, Morlands and Wadworths 6X on handpump, and a thoughtful choice of wines. There's simple red leatherette furniture on the red-tiled floor, china in a corner cupboard, a big log fire, and vases of flowers. A partly panelled carpeted side room has sensibly placed darts. The young barman uses a cash register with an odd combination of ancient and modern (a set of cups, one for each denomination of money, with an electronic calculator). In summer, the hanging baskets and flower tubs are very pretty, and the garden across from the pub has climbing-frames, a little-old-lady shoe house and so forth. *(Recommended by David Wallington, Gordon and Daphne, Lyn and Bill Capper, HNJ, PEJ, Richard and Dilys Smith, Stan Edwards, John Bell, Dave Braisted)*

Free house   Licensees John and Audrey Gillas   Real ale   Meals and snacks   Children welcome   Open 11–2.30, 6–11 all year

BRAY   SU9079 Map 2

Crown

1¾ miles from M4 junction 9; A308 towards Windsor, then left at Bray signpost on to B3028

The softly lit and partly panelled main bar in this fourteenth-century timbered pub has low beams, old timbers conveniently left at elbow height where walls have been knocked through, leather-backed seats around copper-topped or wooden tables, and a cosy winter fire; decorations include caricatures by Spy and his competitors, guns, pistols and stuffed animals. Good bar food includes sandwiches on request, a choice of well filled rolls (70p), ploughman's (£2.50) and main dishes such as cheese and asparagus flan (£3), summer salads (from £3), steak and kidney pie, chilli con carne or lasagne (from £3.50) and popular home-made puddings like treacle tart, mousses or apple pie (£1.85); vegetables are grown in their kitchen garden; summer Sunday barbecues. Courage Best tapped from the cask and a fair choice of wines; piped music. There are tables under cocktail parasols here, with more tables and benches on flagstones, shaded by a well trained vine. *(Recommended by JMC, W J Wonham, W A Gardiner, Alison Hayward, Nick Dowson)*

Courage   Licensee Hugh Whitton   Real ale   Meals (12.30–2, 7.30–10; not Sat lunchtime, or Sun, but see above for barbecues) and lunchtime snacks   Children welcome   Restaurant tel Maidenhead (0628) 21936; closed Sun   Open 10.30–2.30, 5.30–11

BRIMPTON COMMON   SU5662 Map 2

Pineapple

B3051, W of Heath End

Old enough in itself, this very popular thatched country pub stands on the site of a building mentioned in Domesday Book. There are low and heavy black medieval beams, furniture mainly hewn from shiny golden tree-trunks (which suits the quarry-tiled floor and stripped brick and timbering), a rocking-chair by the fire, wheel-back chairs around neater tables in a side eating area, and a thriving, chatty atmosphere. Bar food includes sandwiches, salads (from £2.85), a very wide range of baked potatoes with enterprising fillings, and a choice of several home-made pies. A lino-floored side area has sensibly placed darts, shove-ha'penny, fruit machine, trivia, and there may be piped pop music. Well kept Flowers Original, Wethereds and Whitbreads Pompey Royal on handpump, and a better than usual choice of other drinks. There are lots of picnic-table sets under cocktail parasols on a well hedged side lawn, with swings and a slide. *(Recommended by R M Sparkes; more reports please)*

Whitbreads   Licensee John Lay   Real ale   Meals and snacks (12–2, 5–9; sandwiches through afternoon; no food Sun evenings)   Children in eating area of bar   Open 11–11 all year

CHIEVELEY   SU4774 Map 2

Blue Boar

4 miles from M4 junction 13; A34 N towards Abingdon, first left into Chieveley, bear left and keep on until T-junction with B4494 – turn right towards Wantage, pub on right

The three rooms of the beamed bar in this well kept sixteenth-century thatched inn are attractively decorated with a variety of heavy harness (including a massive collar), hunting prints and photographs, and furnished with plush or brocaded cushioned stools, old-fashioned high-backed settles, Windsor chairs and polished tables. The middle room has an unusual inglenook seat, and the left-hand room has a seat built into the sunny bow window with a fine view over unspoilt fields, and a roaring log fire. Good bar food includes soup (£1.50), sandwiches (from £2; fillet steak £4.95), an excellent ploughman's (£3.25), pasta of the day (£3.45), home-made burger (£3.75), grilled ham with sauté potatoes, mushroom, tomato and fried egg (£4.50), kedgeree (£4.75), salads (from £4.95), beef curry (£5.75), beef kebabs (£7.95) and puddings (from £2); three-course Sunday lunch (£8.95). Well kept Arkells BBB and Wadworths 6X on handpump, 60 types of whisky, cocktails, and several liqueur coffees; piped music. Recently, most readers have found friendly and helpful service. There are tables among tubs and flower beds on the rough front cobbles and standing on the picturesquely stunted ancient oak is the Blue Sandstone Boar, presented to the inn by Cromwell who stayed here in 1644, the night before the Battle of Newbury. With their own stables, they do riding weekends. *(Recommended by C R Ball, L G and D L Smith, Jill Field, S Matthews, John Hill, Mr and Mrs F H Stokes, Sheila Keene, RAB, Patrick Stapley, Bobby Goodale, Peter Sutton)*

Free house   Licensee Noel Morton   Real ale   Meals and snacks (12–2, 7–10)   Restaurant (until 4 Sun)   Children (no babies) welcome   Open 10.30–3, 6–11   Bedrooms tel Chieveley (0635) 248236; £28B/£38B

COOKHAM   SU8884 Map 2

Bel & the Dragon ★ [illustrated on page 21]

High Street; B4447

The atmosphere in the three communicating lounge rooms of this comfortable old pub is quietly civilised: oak panelling, old oak settles, and deep, comfortable leather chairs, and pewter tankards hanging from heavy Tudor beams. A gravely friendly blue-coated barman behind the very low zinc-topped bar counter serves well kept Brakspears and Youngs tapped from the cask, wines including decent ports and champagne, and all the ingredients necessary for proper cocktails. There are often free peanuts and so forth, as well as home-made soup or quiche (£2), sandwiches (from £2.25, prawn £3.75, smoked salmon £5.25; toasties £3), home-made pizza (£3.50), slimmer's salad (£4.50), steak and kidney pie (£5.50) and puddings (£2). The Stanley Spencer Gallery is almost opposite. *(Recommended by BKA, Richard Houghton, John Day, TBB, Ian Phillips, Mr and Mrs T F Marshall, AE)*

Free house   Licensee F E Stuber   Real ale   Bar snacks   Restaurant tel Bourne End (062 85) 21263   Children in eating area of bar only   Open 11–2.30, 6–10.30; closed evening 25 Dec

---

Post Office address codings confusingly give the impression that some pubs are in Berkshire when they're really in Oxfordshire or Hampshire (which is where we list them).

COOKHAM RISE   SU8984 Map 2
Swan Uppers
B4447 Cookham–Maidenhead

Heavy black beams in the cream ceiling, broad worn flagstones throughout, shiny black woodwork, flowery-curtained latticed windows and log fires – one of them pretty vast – in stripped brick fireplaces: it adds up to a good deal of cosy character, and the noticeable piped music (anything from Ella Fitzgerald to funk and soul) isn't what you'd expect. There are cushioned wall benches and stools, with two or three quieter dark blue plush booths around on the left, and the restaurant area rambling off on the right. Good bar food includes sandwiches (from £1.20), soup (£1.60), ploughman's (from £1.75), macaroni cheese (£3.75), popular fresh haddock (£3.75) and curry (£3.95), liver and bacon (£4.75) and steaks (from £5.95), with home-made gateaux (£1.50). Well kept Huntsman Best and Royal Oak, Marstons Pedigree and Palmers Best on handpump, with a dozen or so decent malts; tables out on a fairy-lit back terrace, and in front by the village road. The poodles are called Lanson (from the colour as well as the effervescence) and Podge. *(Recommended by St John Sandringham, TBB, Simon Collett-Jones, Roger Baskerville)*

Free house   Licensee J Waring   Real ale   Meals and snacks (12–2, 7–10; not Sun evening)   Restaurant (not Sun evening; late supper licence)   Children welcome   Open 11–3, 6–11 all year, probably 11–11 Sats and bank hols; closed evening 25 Dec   Bedrooms tel Bourne End (062 85) 21324; £20/£33

EAST ILSLEY   SU4981 Map 2
Crown & Horns
The fine range of sensibly priced real ales at this friendly pub may, at any one time, include Arkells BBB, Bass, Brakspears SB, Morlands, Ruddles County, Theakstons Old Peculier and Wadworths 6X, on handpump. There's also a collection of 170 whiskies from all over the world – Moroccan, Korean, Japanese, Chinese, Spanish and New Zealand. As this is horse-training country, there are racing prints and photographs on the walls in the partly panelled and beamed main bar, and the TV is on for the racing in a side bar. Bar food includes sandwiches (from 85p), filled baked potatoes (from £1.50), and main meals such as good value, tasty venison pie or trout with walnut and celery sauce (£2–£6); friendly service. There's a skittle alley, as well as darts, pool, bar billiards, dominoes, cribbage, pinball, fruit machine, juke box and piped music. The pretty paved stableyard has tables under two chestnut trees. *(Recommended by Mr and Mrs D A P Grattan, Philip King, I R Hewitt, A M Kelly, Joan Olivier)*

Free house   Licensees Chris and Jane Bexx   Real ale   Meals and snacks (12–2, 6–10) Children in eating area and restaurant   Open 10.30–2.30 (3 Sat), 6–11 all year Bedrooms tel East Ilsley (063 528) 205; £17.50/£27.50(£37.50B)

Swan 🛏

Since refurbishment finished here in late summer 1988, we've been getting very warm reports on this well contrived Morlands house. The bar is open-plan, but the way it's been divided into irregularly shaped nooks and corners should be an object-lesson to pub designers. The dividers are low walls, topped with broad polished woodwork; one area down by an elegantly arched 1930s fireplace is mainly for drinkers – the fact that the serving-counter's right over on the opposite side somehow seems to help the quietly thriving overall atmosphere, as does the elegant combination of bentwood chairs and tables with the pastel patterned carpet. Good value home-made bar food includes sandwiches (from £1.10), soup such as minestrone (£1.50), several ploughman's (from £1.90), spaghetti (£2.85), cottage pie (£2.90) and steak and onions braised in beer (£3.40), with half a dozen dishes of the day such as pâté with hot wholemeal bread and herb butter (£2.50) or fresh

sixteen-ounce lemon sole (£5.10) and several home-made puddings; well kept
Morlands Bitter and Old Masters on handpump; an unobtrusive silenced fruit
machine, faint piped music; good friendly service. There are picnic-table sets on a
prettily trellised back terrace and on a sheltered lawn with a play area.
(Recommended by Stan Edwards, S A Starkey, A T Langton)

*Morlands   Licensees Michael and Jenny Connolly   Real ale   Meals and snacks (11.45–2.15,
6.30–10)   Restaurant   Children allowed in some areas   Open 10.30–2.30, 6–11 all year;
closed evening 25 Dec   Bedrooms tel East Ilsley (063 528) 238; £26S/£40S*

FRILSHAM   SU5473 Map 2

Pot Kiln

From Yattendon follow Frilsham signpost, but just after crossing motorway go straight on
towards Bucklebury when Frilsham is signposted right

Surrounded by sheltering woods and peaceful pastures, this simple brick house has a
friendly and timeless old-fashioned atmosphere, as well as bare benches and pews,
wooden floorboards and a good log fire. Well kept Arkells BBB, Morlands and
Ringwood Fortyniner, all on handpump, are served from a hatch in the panelled
entrance lobby – which just has room for one bar stool. Good bar food includes filled
hot rolls (from 70p), home-made soup (£1.10), ploughman's (£1.95), lots of vegetarian
dishes like spinach and mushroom lasagne or vegetable curry (around £2.40), pheasant
pie in season (£3.85), smoked trout salad (£5.25) and steak (£5.45); there may be
delays at busy times. The public bar has darts, dominoes, shove-ha'penny and
cribbage. Outside, there are sun-trap tables and folding garden chairs. *(Recommended by
Gordon and Daphne, TBB, Jon Wainwright, H N and P E Jeffery, Richard and Dilys Smith)*

*Free house   Licensee Mrs Gent   Real ale   Meals (not Sun) and snacks   Children welcome if
well behaved   Folksinging Sun   Open 12–2.30, 6.30–11*

GREAT SHEFFORD   SU3875 Map 2

Pheasant ⊗

Under half a mile from M4 junction 14; A338 towards Wantage, then first left (pub visible
from main road and actually at Shefford Woodland, S of the village itself)

Connected as it is to the Royal Oak at Wootton Rivers (see Wiltshire), this new
main entry can be relied on for good value home-made bar food such as sandwiches
(from £1), soups (from £1, with speciality ones such as courgette and coriander or
carrot with citrus and ginger £1.50), ravioli (£1.95), ploughman's (from £2.25 –
their winter bargain of soup and ploughman's for £2.75 is a good idea), omelettes
(£2.75), curry (£3.75), steak and kidney pie (£5), steaks (from £7.95) and fresh fish
such as red mullet (£8.25), with popular puddings (£2). The four neat
communicating room areas have cut-away cask seats, wall pews and other chairs on
their Turkey carpet, and racehorse prints on the walls; there are rustic tables in a
smallish garden beside the white-painted tile-hung house, looking over the fields.
Well kept Courage Best and Wadworths IPA and 6X on handpump, and decent
coffee; friendly service, and a pleasant country atmosphere; the public bar has
darts, cribbage, dominoes, ring the bull and trivia; maybe unobtrusive piped music.
(Recommended by Graham and Glenis Watkins, John and Pat Smyth)

*Free house   Licensees John Jones and Mrs Barbara Brooker   Real ale   Meals and snacks
Small restaurant tel Great Shefford (0488) 39284   Children in eating area and restaurant
Open 11–3, 5.30–11 all year*

Swan

2 miles from M4 junction 14; on A338 towards Wantage

Especially pleasant in summer, this low-ceilinged, friendly pub has barbecues then,
and tables on a terrace by a big willow and sycamore overhanging the stream, with

more on an attractive quiet lawn with a swing. It's a popular place for lunch: sandwiches (from 80p), ploughman's (£2.25), filled baked potatoes (from £2.50) and home-made lasagne (£3.25); well kept Courage Best and Directors on handpump. The public bar has darts, pool, a fruit machine, juke box and piped music. The pub is a base for the local football, cricket and rugby teams, and where the Vine and Craven hunt often meet. *(Recommended by TBB, Pat and Dennis Jones, Joan Olivier; more reports on new regime, please)*

Courage   Licensee Noel Bennett   Real ale   Meals and snacks (12–2, 7–10; not Sun evening)   Children in eating areas   Restaurant tel Great Shefford (048 839) 271 (not Sun evenings)   Open 11–3, 6–11 (maybe longer Sat afternoons) all year

HAMPSTEAD NORREYS   SU5376 Map 2

New Inn

Yattendon Road

The comfortable and friendly back lounge here has horsebrasses on the low black beams, horses and reproduction coaching prints and pictures of World War II military aircraft from the local Air Gunners Association on the walls, and a log fire. Good value bar food ranges from sandwiches (from 80p, open prawn sandwich £2.75), ploughman's, home-made cottage pie (£1.50), chilli con carne (£2.50), steak and kidney pie (£3) and seafood platter (£3.20); in the evening there is a more elaborate menu with dishes such as chicken Kiev (£5), Japanese prawns (£5.50) or rump steak (£6.90). Well kept Morlands Mild, Bitter and Best on handpump under light blanket pressure. The lively and simply furnished public bar, decorated with early 1950s local photographs, has darts, dominoes, cribbage, juke box and fruit machine. The fine garden has well spaced seats among roses, conifers and fruit trees, a sheltered terrace overlooking matured woodlands, and a big lawn with swings, children's play area and goldfish pond with a floodlit waterfall. *(Recommended by Gordon and Daphne, Dave Braisted, A T Langton; more reports please)*

Morlands   Licensee David Reid   Real ale   Meals and snacks (not Mon or Tues evenings) Children welcome   Open 10.30–2.30 (3 Sat), 5.30–11; opens 6 in winter   Bedrooms tel Hermitage (0635) 201301; £16/£26

HAMSTEAD MARSHALL   SU4165 Map 2

White Hart 🏵 🛏

Village signposted from A4 W of Newbury

The charming balance between civilised comforts and the unpretentious country atmosphere of the L-shaped bar makes this inn popular all the year round. Around Christmas, the old-fashioned decorations are a bonus, while in summer the interestingly planted garden with tables on its terrace and lawn has great appeal. The low-ceilinged bar has red plush seats built into its bow windows, red-cushioned chairs around oak and other tables, steeplechasing and other horse prints on its ochre walls, and a central log fire. Home-made bar food includes soup (£2), pâté with bread they bake themselves (£2.20), authentic pasta (from £4.50) such as lasagne, cannelloni, fettuccine, gnocchi and a tasty vegetarian lasagne, speciality spare ribs (£6.20), an unusual variety of children's dishes, and a lot of fish brought fresh from Billingsgate, from calamari (£3.50 or so) to bass or turbot (£7.20); they make their own cassata (Mr Aronado, from Italy, does most of the cooking; his wife, who is English and holds the licence, does the puddings, including a popular concoction called tirami su). Well kept Badger Best and Wadworths 6X on

We mention bottled beers and spirits only if there is something unusual about them – imported Belgian real ales, say, or dozens of malt whiskies; so do please let us know about them in your reports.

handpump; politely friendly service; maybe unobtrusive piped music. No dogs (their own Welsh setter's called Sam and the pony's called Solo). The four bedrooms are very comfortable indeed. *(Recommended by John Tyzack, Chris Ensor, GB, CH)*

Free house   Licensee Nicola Aronado   Real ale   Meals (12–2.30, 7–9), not Sun Restaurant   Children allowed if well behaved   Open 12–2.30, 6.30–11 all year; closed Sun and 25–26 Dec

HOLYPORT   SU8977   Map 2
Belgian Arms

1½ miles from M4 junction 8/9; take A308(M) then at terminal roundabout follow Holyport signpost along A330 towards Bracknell; in village turn left on to big green, then left again at War Memorial shelter

The garden here is delightful, with plenty of tables looking over a flag-iris pond to the green, a climbing-frame and slide, and a pen of goats and hens. Inside, the L-shaped bar has varied homely chairs around the few small tables on the carpet, good prints and framed postcards of Belgian military uniform on the walls, a china cupboard in one corner, a low ceiling, and a winter log fire. Good, simple bar food includes sandwiches, plain or toasted (from £1; the open prawn one is excellent and the toasted 'special' is very popular: ham, cheese, sweetcorn, peppers, onion and mushroom £1.50), ploughman's (from £2, with home-cooked ham £2.50), pizzas (from £2.75), seafood platter or home-cooked ham and eggs (£4) and eight-ounce steak (£7.50); at lunchtime you can eat in the new conservatory (which acts as a restaurant in the evening). Well kept Brakspears PA and SB on handpump; friendly service. *(Recommended by Peter Blood, TBB, Simon Collett-Jones, John Day, Richard Houghton, G Shannon, Lyn and Bill Capper)*

Brakspears   Licensee Alfred Morgan   Real ale   Meals and snacks (not Fri–Sun evenings)   Small conservatory restaurant tel Maidenhead (0628) 34468   Open 11–2.30, 5.30–11; closed evening 25 Dec

HUNGERFORD   SU3368   Map 2
Bear 📷

3 miles from M4 junction 14; town signposted at junction

Big French windows at one end of the spacious main bar in this civilised old coaching-inn open on to a charming enclosed courtyard with a pergola and fountain. It's a place appreciated most by our older readers, with nice touches like the day's newspapers (including the *FT, Sporting Life* and *Herald Tribune*) hanging on reading sticks, spirits served in ¼-gill measures (instead of the usual ⅙-gill) and properly mixed Kirs; there's a huge black and gold wall clock by Marsh of Highworth, and several readers have mentioned the ornate lavatories. Well kept Arkells John's Bitter (BB) and BBB, and Morlands on handpump. Bar meals brought to your table by waitresses include home-made soup (£1.75), garlic-fried prawns with crusty bread (£2.25), delicious home-made taramosalata (£2.50), toasted muffin with ham, avocado, poached egg and hollandaise (£4.50), tagliatelle with a four-cheese sauce (£4.75), prawn and cucumber salad (£5.50), fried fresh fish of the day (£5.60) and sirloin steak with café de Paris butter (£7.50); puddings (£2.50). There is a courtyard, with a terrace above the River Dun, and a small garden (most of the former garden is now a discreet housing estate). No dogs. *(Recommended by Sheila Keene, J F Estdale, Neville Burke, Ian Phillips, M E Lawrence, GB, CH; more reports please)*

Free house   Licensee Stephen Swire   Real ale   Meals and snacks   Restaurant   Children in restaurant   Open 11 (though coffee served in bar from 10.30)–2.30, 6–11   Bedrooms tel Hungerford (0488) 82512; £55.95B/£75.40B

nr HURLEY SU8283 Map 2
Dew Drop ★

Just W of Hurley on A423 turn left up Honey Lane – look out for the IGAP sign; at small red post-box after large farm, fork right – the pub is down a right-hand turn-off at the first cluster of little houses

One reader with exacting tastes who managed to track this pub down with his new copy of the 1989 *Guide* reckoned – when he found it – that the *Guide* had already paid for its keep. It's a welcoming place with friendly locals, simple furnishings that include a log fire at each end of the main bar, and a landlord with a passion for golf (evident in his conversation and in the golfing pictures on the wall). Generous helpings of good bar food includes sandwiches (from 50p), thick, hot, tasty mushroom soup (£1.10), ploughman's (£1.80), pâté (£2), deep-fried courgettes with garlic mayonnaise (£2.25), moussaka (£3.25), seafood platter (£3.50), massive, juicy gammon with egg (£3.70) and puddings such as jam roly-poly or pecan pie (from £1.40). Well kept Brakspears PA and Old on handpump and some good malt whiskies; shove-ha'penny. It's a lovely place in summer when you can sit on seats in the attractively wild sloping garden, looking down to where white doves strut on the pub's red tiles, above tubs of bright flowers; there's a children's play area. *(Recommended by Chris Raisin, Graham Doyle, Ian Phillips, Richard Houghton, David Wallington, Nick Dowson, Simon Collett-Jones)*

Brakspears   Licensee Michael Morris   Real ale   Meals (not Mon evening or Sun) and snacks (not Mon evening or Sun)   Open 11–2.30, 6–11

HURST SU7972 Map 2
Green Man

Hinton Road; off A321 Twyford–Wokingham, turning NE just S of filling station in village centre

This relaxed pub has tapestried wall seats and wheel-back chairs around brass-topped tables on the green carpet, lots of alcoves and country pictures, black standing timbers, dark oak beams hung with horsebrasses and brass stirrups, and an open fire at both ends (neatly closed in summer by black-and-brass folding doors). The servery, which dispenses well kept Brakspears PA and SB and Old tapped from the cask, has some black japanned milkchurns as seats. Dominoes, cribbage and piped music (maybe Radio 1). Good bar food includes rolls (from 90p), superb Stilton ploughman's (£2.25), burgers (from £1.20), good prawn curry (£3.25), home-made pies like steak and kidney, pigeon or game (all £4.25), evening vegetarian dishes like nut roast Portuguese (£6.25), steaks (from £8); best to get there early. Trivia on Mondays, boules, Aunt Sally and a golf society; pleasant back garden. *(Recommended by S J Curtis, Chris Raisin, Graham Doyle, Ian Phillips, Mrs Caroline Gibbins, Simon Collett-Jones, Nick Dowson)*

Brakspears   Licensee Allen Hayward   Real ale   Meals and snacks (12–2, 7–10; not Sun, not Mon evening)   Marquee restaurant (not Sun) tel Reading (0734) 342599   Children in restaurant   Open 11–2.30 (3 Sat), 6–11 all year

INKPEN SU3564 Map 2
Swan 🏵

Lower Inkpen; coming from A338 in Hungerford, take Park Street (first left after railway bridge, coming from A4); Inkpen is then signposted from Hungerford Common

In the evenings, Mrs Scothorne's Singapore-Chinese background shows in the fresh and fragrantly flavoured food: a spicy seafood soup (£2.30), prawns marinated in beer and wine then deep-fried (£2.50), satay (£3.75), nasigoreng (£4.20), Singapore noodles (£4.50), her very popular chicken with cashew-nuts (£5.10) and pork in ginger and pineapple sauce (£6.20), besides western-style lamb cutlets (£6.50) and steaks (from £8.50). (At lunchtime it's all western-style, with home-made pâté (£2.50), quiche (£2.80) and beef and venison pie or big scampi (£4.50) as well as the cutlets and steaks and children's helpings.) The Singapore connection shows in one or two other ways, too: a wicked gin sling, for instance, and deeply chilled foreign lagers (as well as well kept Brakspears, Flowers IPA and Original and Hook Norton Best on handpump, and a decent house claret château-bottled for them by a friend with a house in Bordeaux); a dice game called balut (as well as darts, shove-ha'penny and a fruit machine); and the magazines in one snug alcove up a couple of steps. The pub has a long row of rooms opening into one another, with well waxed flowery-cushioned pews and tables on the muted beige and brown carpet, some traditional black-painted wall settles, log fires, and at the bottom end (which is heavily beamed) neat blond dining-chairs and tables with a wood-burning stove; service is friendly. There are picnic-table sets on the tarmac in front, by the quiet village road, and in the garden behind. (*Recommended by Wg Cdr R M Sparkes, Ian Meredith, Chris Payne, Joan and John Calvert, Michael Thomson, Mr and Mrs C Austin*)

Free house   Licensees John and Esther Scothorne   Real ale   Meals and snacks (12–1.45, 7–9.30; not Sun evening or Mon)   Evening restaurant (not Sun) tel Inkpen (048 84) 326 Children in restaurant and bottom end of bar   Open 11.30–2.30, 6.30–11 all year; closed Mon

KINTBURY   SU3866 Map 2

Dundas Arms 🍺

Set between a quiet pool of the River Kennet and the Kennet and Avon Canal, this old-fashioned inn was put up in the early nineteenth century for the canal builders. There's a remarkable collection of blue and white plates on one cream wall in the partly panelled and carpeted bar, and a juke box with rather a nostalgic repertoire. Food includes sandwiches, home-made soup (£1.40), smoked salmon pâté or crab au gratin (£2.60), smoked salmon quiche (£3.50), gammon and egg (£4), mixed seafood platter (£4.25), steak and kidney pie (£4.45) and steak (£7.50); good breakfasts. Well kept Adnams, Huntsman Dorset and Morlands on handpump. The restaurant has a notable range of wines – particularly clarets. Bedrooms have French windows opening on to a secluded waterside terrace, and there's an attractive lock just the other side of the hump-backed bridge. (*Recommended by Mr and Mrs D A P Grattan, Philip Lewis Williams, AE*)

Free house   Licensee David Dalzell-Piper   Real ale   Lunchtime meals and snacks (not Sun)   Restaurant   Children in eating area of bar   Open 11–2.30, 6–11 all year; closed Christmas to New Year   Bedrooms tel Kintbury (0488) 58263; £46B/£52B

KNOWL HILL   SU8279 Map 2

Bird in Hand 🍺

A4

The big, recently refurbished main bar here has cosy alcoves, beams, some attractive Victorian stained glass in one big bow window, dark brown panelling with a high shelf of willow-pattern plates, a red Turkey carpet on polished oak parquet, a log fire, and a stylishly civilised but relaxed atmosphere – no doubt owing a lot to the fact that Mr Shone celebrated 30 years here in 1989. There's a centuries-older side bar, and a snug, well padded back cocktail bar. Generous helpings of good home-made food includes an excellent buffet (£4.75 for as much as you want), with good cold salt beef, salami, ham, three other cold meats, four or five fish and shellfish dishes, and lots of fresh and imaginative salads such as apple, celery and peanut, or carrot and leek strips in a lemon juice dressing. There are also sandwiches (from £1.75, smoked salmon or prawn open sandwich on home-made brown bread £3.75), filled baked potatoes (from £2), chicken and beef satay (£3.25), daily changing hot dishes such as popular steak and kidney pudding, ham shanks, fish pie, half a shoulder of lamb, curry or pasta (from £4.75) and good home-made puddings such as sherry trifle or lemon meringue pie (£2). Well kept Brakspears PA and Old, and Youngs Special on handpump, and several wines. Efficient, helpful service; a few good malt whiskies, including the Macallan. There are tables in the roomy and neatly kept tree-sheltered side garden. *(Recommended by Gary Scott, Hilary Robinson, Peter Maden, Lindsey Shaw Radley, Simon Collett-Jones, Nick Dowson)*

Free house   Licensee Jack Shone   Real ale   Meals and snacks   Children in eating area of bar   Restaurant   Open 11–3, 6–11; 11–11 in summer   Bedrooms tel Littlewick Green (062 882) 2781; £55B/£75B

LITTLEWICK GREEN   SU8379 Map 2

Cricketers

3¾ miles from M4 junction 9; A423(M) then on to A4, from which village is signposted on left

An enormous old factory clocking-in clock dominates the friendly, refurbished lounge in this neatly kept, sway-backed old pub: maroon plush window seats and stools, lots of Windsor chairs, and a pretty painting of the pub by a local artist, cricketing prints and cartoons on the walls. Bar food includes sandwiches (from £1; toasties from £1.25), ploughman's (from £2), good filled pancakes (£2.50), vegetarian or meaty lasagne or chicken curry (£3.50), home-made steak and kidney pie (£3.75), tasty smoked haddock pasta with prawns and mushrooms (£4), and puddings like hot treacle tart (£1.25); dishes are archly given cricketing pun names. Adnams, Brakspears PA, Huntsman Dorset and Wadworths 6X on handpump; cribbage, a fruit machine and piped music. In summer, the landlord captains his cricket team (matches every weekend, some weekdays) on the attractive village green opposite. The National Trust's Maidenhead Thicket, just east on the A4, and the woods along the A404 towards Marlow, have good walks. *(Recommended by TBB, J P Day, Ian Phillips, Simon Collett-Jones, David Young)*

Free house   Licensees John and Adrienne Hammond   Real ale   Meals and snacks   Children welcome   Open 11–3, 5.30–11 all year; 11–11 Sat; closed 26 Dec

MARSH BENHAM   SU4267 Map 2

Red House

Village signposted from A4 W of Newbury

This busy thatched brick pub has lots of glossily varnished tables set for diners in the two rooms of the comfortable bar, with deeply carved Victorian Gothic settles (and some older ones), and attractive prints (including nice Cecil Aldin village scenes) on the leafy green and gold flock wallpaper; they are separated by an arch with a fine formal flower arrangement. Old faithfuls will have noticed quite a change in the food since new licensees have taken over: still well presented and brought to your table by uniformed waitresses, it now includes home-made soup (£1), sandwiches (from £1.25), steak and kidney pie or moussaka (£2.25), ploughman's (from £2.25), home-cooked gammon (£3), leek and almond or seafood crêpes (from £3), liver and bacon casserole (£3.25), spicy lamb with mango chutney (£3.95) and fresh salmon mayonnaise (£5.50); home-made puddings (£1.75). Well kept Arkells BBB, Brakspears PA and SPA, and Flowers Original on handpump, and good wines by the glass. An attractive side garden has a wooden sun house and a butterfly reserve. *(Recommended by HNJ, PEJ, Sheila Keene, Stephen Goodchild, Aubrey and Margaret Saunders, John Bell, Mrs E M Brandwood, Prof A N Black, Lyn and Bill Capper, Henry Midwinter)*

Free house   Licensees J Goodman and M Hoskins   Real ale   Meals and snacks (12–2, 6.30–9.30)   Restaurant tel Newbury (0635) 41637   Children in restaurant   Open 10.30–3, 6–11 all year

PEASEMORE   SU4577 Map 2

Fox & Hounds

Village signposted from B4494 Newbury–Wantage

Just outside the village, this downland pub is popular with people working in one of the local industries: training racehorses. Appropriately, it's decorated with the full set of Somerville's entertaining *Slipper's ABC of Fox-Hunting* prints, and one stripped-brick wall has a row of flat-capped fox masks. On our visit in early summer, work was going ahead on a side extension which will effectively shift the L-shaped bar over to the left, making more space for the restaurant. It should be much as before in style: brocaded, stripped wall settles, chairs and stools around shiny wooden tables, log-effect gas fires, and an unaffected country atmosphere. Good home-made bar food includes soups such as celery and tomato (£1.50), a proper ploughman's with real, as opposed to plastic-wrapped, butter (from £2.25), filled baked potatoes (from £2.95), vegetarian lasagne (£3.95), several pies such as beef in beer or tuna and sweetcorn (£3.95), chicken breast marinated in yoghurt and charcoal-grilled (£4.95) and steaks (from eight-ounce rump £7.50); they even do lunch on Christmas Day. Well kept Courage Best, John Smiths and Palmers on handpump, with a reasonable choice of wines; quick, friendly service; sensibly placed darts, unobtrusive piped music; picnic-table sets in front. *(Recommended by C Matthews; more reports please)*

Free house   Licensees David and Loretta Smith   Real ale   Meals and snacks   Restaurant tel Chieveley (0635) 248252   Children welcome   Open 11–3, 6–11 all year, maybe longer summer afternoons; closed evening 25 Dec

REMENHAM   SU7683 Map 2

Little Angel 🏮

A423, just over bridge E of Henley

The main attraction here is the wide choice of food, which from the bar menu might typically include home-made soup (£2), chicken liver pâté or pan-fried soft roes on toast (£3), steamed fresh haddock Mornay (£3.50), steak and kidney pie or stir-fried chicken with cashew-nuts (£4.50), six jumbo prawns (£6.50), calf's liver and bacon or ten-ounce Dijon rump steak (£8.50); they add a ten per cent service charge. The restaurant is particularly strong on seafood – they collect from Billingsgate several times a week, and there are special food events, particularly over Henley Regatta week when it's best to book well ahead. The bar – which has a feeling of trendiness (accentuated by the celebrity photos on the wall) – has big bay window seats and some built-in cushioned grey wall seats, and the main part is decorated in deep glossy red and black, which matches the little tiles of the bar counter and the carpet; this leads through to the Garden Room (and restaurant) with deep pink furnishings, cosy alcoves, candlelight and fresh flowers, and is given over more to eating. The terrace behind (its name, the Champagne Garden, gives some idea of the style of this pub) has tables and pink umbrellas and is floodlit at night. Brakspears PA and Old on handpump, a wide range of attractive and reasonably priced wines and Kirs; piped music. It can get very crowded at peak times (when even the big car park overflows into a tricky narrow side lane); there are some wooden tables and benches outside. *(Recommended by Lindsey Shaw Radley; more reports please)*

Brakspears   Licensee Paul Southwood   Real ale   Meals and snacks (12–2, 7–10)   Children in eating area of bar   Restaurant tel Henley-on-Thames (0491) 574165   Open 11–2.30, 6–10.30 (11 Sat) all year

---

Children: if the details at the end of an entry don't mention them, you should assume that the pub does not allow them inside.

SONNING SU7575 Map 2
Bull
Off B478, in village

Quaint without being pretentious, this picturesque old pub has a warm, friendly atmosphere in the two communicating rooms of the bar. There are beams in the low ceilings, cosy alcoves (one with a set of books), cushioned antique settles and low wooden chairs, newspapers on racks, an inglenook fireplace in each room, and even a penny-farthing. Lunchtime bar food includes a good cold buffet with salads such as pork pie and mixed meats (£3.80); well kept Flowers Original, Marstons Pedigree and Wethereds SPA on handpump. Chatty staff; soft piped music. The courtyard outside is particularly attractive with wistaria cascading over the black and white timbered pub, and tubs of flowers and a rose pergola – though, unfortunately, at busy times you may find it packed with cars. If you bear left through the churchyard opposite (taken over by Russian ivy), then turn left along the bank of the River Thames, you come to a very pretty lock. *(Recommended by Chris Raisin, Graham Doyle, Margaret Dyke, Brian and Jenny Seller, TBB, JMC, Dick Brown, Mr and Mrs H L Malhotra, Ian Phillips, Lindsey Shaw Radley, Alison Hayward, Nick Dowson, John Knighton, Simon Collett-Jones, M C Howells)*

Wethereds (Whitbreads)   Licensee Dennis Catton   Real ale   Meals (evenings, not Sun or Mon) and lunchtime snacks   Restaurant   Children in restaurant   Open 10–2.30, 5.30–11 all year; closed evening 25 Dec   Bedrooms tel Reading (0734) 693901; £25.30/£50.60

STANFORD DINGLEY SU5771 Map 2
Old Boot 🏶

Neatly kept and quietly friendly, this beamed pub has fine old pews, settles, country chairs and tables, bunches of fresh flowers, attractive fabrics for the old-fashioned wooden-ring curtains, thoughtfully chosen pictures and an inglenook fireplace. A good choice of bar food includes sandwiches, home-made soup (£1.30), garlic mushrooms with bacon and granary toast (£2.65), home-made eight-ounce burgers (from £2.70), chilli con carne (£2.50), various omelettes (from £3.10), smoked salmon and scrambled eggs on croûtons (£3.15), scallops provençale (£3.75), ham and egg (£4.25), lemon sole stuffed with crabmeat (£4.85), changing daily specials such as home-made cottage pie, chicken and Stilton roulade or roast pork (£3–£4) and vegetarian dishes such as home-made, deep-fried cheese and herb 'sausage' (£4.25). Well kept Arkells, Ind Coope Burton, Tetleys and Wadworths 6X on handpump; attentive staff; darts and piped music. There are tables outside in front, with more on a secluded back terrace and in its sloping country garden. *(Recommended by Dr Stewart Rae, Comus Elliott, Barry and Anne, H N and P E Jeffery, Richard and Dilys Smith, Calum and Jane, Lyn and Bill Capper)*

Free house   Licensee Anthony Howells   Real ale   Meals and snacks (12–2, 5.30–10.30) Restaurant tel Bradfield (0734) 744292   Children in restaurant   Open 11–3, 5.30–11 all year

WARGRAVE SU7878 Map 2
Bull
High Street

This small and neatly modernised fifteenth-century brick inn has a low-beamed comfortable bar that opens out into one room with French windows to a sheltered back terrace, and another area with a huge log fireplace; there are lots of simple chairs and tables and collections of baseball caps, horsebrasses and – in a corner cupboard – china bulls. Well kept Brakspears Mild, PA and SB on handpump, and a decent collection of other drinks including several wines by the glass and Pimms by the half-pint. Good value bar food at lunchtime includes sandwiches (from 80p), home-made soup (£1.25), ploughman's (£2.25), vegetarian lasagne (£3), salads (from £3), fresh grilled trout (£4.50), and daily specials like steak and kidney pie, curry or vol-au-vent (£2.75–£3.50); in the evening this changes to savoury crêpes or scallops with bacon (£2.50), marinated Barnsley chop in a red wine sauce (£4.50), Norfolk duckling with almonds and orange (£6.50) and steaks (from £6.25); friendly, speedy service. The attractive terrace has rustic tables and benches among flowering shrubs, below a fairy-lit pergola of hanging baskets. *(Recommended by K H Miller, TBB, Ian Phillips, Simon Collett-Jones, Comus Elliott, Jane and Calum)*

Brakspears   Licensee Noel Harman   Real ale   Meals and snacks (not Sun evening)
Children in restaurant   Open 11–2.30, 6–11   Bedrooms tel Wargrave (073 522) 3120;
£18/£30

WEST ILSLEY   SU4782 Map 2

Harrow

Village signposted at East Ilsley slip road off A34 Newbury–Abingdon

On the edge of a racing village, this homely and warmly welcoming little downland inn is simply furnished with red leatherette wall seats and bucket chairs, and decorated with the cricket team and other local photographs that mark a true village pub. It's a place where there always seems to be something happening, especially on show days. Besides snacks like filled granary French bread (from £1.30), spiced tomato and red lentil soup (£1.50), ploughman's (from £2), creamed lambs' kidneys (£2.45), main dishes like home-made steak and kidney pie (£3.25), Somerset honeyed pork casserole (£4.75), poached chicken breast with ginger, lemon and yoghurt (£5.25), steaks (from £6.50) and home-made puddings like fudge tart or carrot cake with cream cheese, honey and lemon juice topping (£1.75), there are things that reflect the area's sporting interests: a good game pie in season, or rabbit (off the downs) with lemon, bacon and herbs (£3). Vegetables are fresh and nicely cooked. The well kept beer is Morlands Bitter and Old Masters, on handpump; they started brewing in this village before they moved to Abingdon. Darts, piped music. Picnic-table sets and other tables under cocktail parasols look out over the duck pond and cricket green, and a spacious children's garden has a notable play area with a big climber, swings, rocker and so forth – not to mention ducks, fowls, canaries, rabbits, goats and a donkey. There are lots of walks from the village, with the Ridgeway just a mile away. *(Recommended by A T Langton, TBB, Dr and Mrs A K Clarke, R C Watkins)*

Morlands   Licensee Mrs Heather Humphreys   Real ale   Meals and snacks   Restaurant (not Sun evening)   Children in restaurant   Open 10.30–2.30 (3 Sat), 6–11 all year   Bedrooms tel East Ilsley (063 528) 260; £13/£26

WICKHAM   SU3971 Map 2

Five Bells 🍺

3 miles from M4 junction 14; A338 towards Wantage, then first right into B4000

As most of the pictures on the walls demonstrate, this partly thatched pub is in horse-racing country, and there's a separate TV room to keep up with the latest results. At one end of the long, open-plan carpeted bar (with a stripped brick dado along each side) there are wheel-back chairs around polished tables, and patio doors that lead out to the garden, which has plenty more tables, outdoor games and even a swimming-pool. At the other end, beyond brick pillars, there's a huge log fire, with tables set for meals. The servery extends back into the low eaves, which are hung with all sorts of bric-à-brac: brass blowlamps, an antique muller, copper whisking bowl, old bottles, fox brush, tug-o'-war trophies, even a Saudi camel-goad. Home-made bar food includes sandwiches (from £1.20), good soup (£1.50), pâté (£2.50), good ploughman's (£2.50), jumbo sausages or vegetarian spring roll (£3), steak and kidney pie or gammon with egg or pineapple (£4.50), a choice of salads (from £5) and grilled steak (£7.50); daily specials (from £4.50) and a choice of puddings (£2.25). Well kept Ushers Best, Ruddles County and Websters Yorkshire on handpump, and a good choice of spirits; pool, dominoes, juke box, fruit machine. Outside, there's a children's play area with new equipment. *(Recommended by HNJ, PEJ, John and Pat Smyth, John Bell)*

Ushers (Watneys) Licensee Mrs Dorothy Channing-Williams Real ale Meals and snacks Children in eating area of bar Restaurant Open 10.30–2.30, 5.30–11 all year Bedrooms tel Boxford (048 838) 242; £30/£40

WINTERBOURNE SU4572 Map 2
New Inn
Village signposted from B4494 Newbury–Wantage

Though the tables outside are picnic-sets, this pretty black and white brick house and its surroundings take you back to the 1930s, with lawn on both sides of the village lane, a big weeping willow, a fingerpost pointing out a path across a stream and off through the rolling cornfields, a nearby studio pottery, even the ancient AA Safety First village sign opposite. There's a cheerful welcome in the bar, given a cottagey feeling both by the peaceful view from the big windows and by the pleasantly cluttered decoration (old bottles on strings, plates, smoothing-irons and lots of small pictures on the cream walls, the slow-ticking wall clock). Changing home-made bar food, presented quickly and well in generous helpings, includes filled rolls (£1.25), soup (£1.75), pâté including a popular smoked mackerel pâté (£2.75), ham with baked potato (£4.25), chilli (£4.50), chicken provençale or beef and onion pie (£5.25), salmon (£5.75) and sirloin steak (£7.75), with a useful winter combination of soup and ploughman's (£3.75); well kept Flowers Original, Marstons Pedigree and Wethereds Bitter and SPA on handpump. It's comfortably furnished with brocaded small settles, chairs and stools on the flowery red carpet, and a log fire; off on the right you can find bar billiards (the pub has strong players), darts, shove-ha'penny, cribbage, dominoes, shut-the-box and a tucked-away fruit machine; maybe unobtrusive piped music. The elderly cat's name, Shreer, is Moroccan for 'tiny one'. *(Recommended by Duncan Bruce, HNJ, PEJ)*

Free house Licensees A T and J P Tratt Real ale Meals and snacks (12–2, 6–10) Restaurant Children in restaurant Open 11.30–2.30, 6–11; may open slightly later in winter, closed evening 25 Dec

WOOLHAMPTON SU5767 Map 2
Rising Sun
A4, nearly a mile E of village

A good, regularly changing range of real ales on handpump in this small and friendly pub might include Archers Best, Arkells BBB, Gales HSB, Morlands, Ringwood Old Thumper, Theakstons XB and Youngers Scotch and IPA; several malts. Popular, reasonably priced bar food includes sandwiches (from 95p), cottage pie (£1.75), curry (£2.25), home-made steak pie (£2.35), lasagne (£2.55), scampi (£2.85), chicken Kiev (£4.75) and steaks (from £7.45). The red and black lounge is decorated with small reproduction coaching prints, and the public bar has darts, bar billiards, dominoes, cribbage, fruit machine and piped music. You can sit out behind, where there's a swing. *(Recommended by Phil Smith, John Baker, L G and D L Smith)*

Free house Licensee Peter Head Real ale Meals and snacks (12–2, 7–10) Restaurant tel Woolhampton (0734) 712717 (not Sun evening) Children in restaurant Open 11.15–2.30 (3 Sat), 6–11 all year

Pubs brewing their own beers are listed at the back of the book.

YATTENDON   SU5572 Map 2
Royal Oak ★ ⦿ ⇥
The Square

The very wide choice of interesting food is obviously what draws the great majority of customers here, though this handsome old inn has other firm attractions too. The stylishly old-fashioned and comfortable lounge and prettily decorated panelled bar have an extremely pleasant atmosphere, and good log fires in winter. Changing daily, the food includes filled rolls (if they're not too busy – they don't like to do them unless they've time to make them really good), home-made soups such as creamy mushroom (£2.50), rollmop herrings with sour cream and chives (£2.75), salad of warm ducks' livers with spring onions or grilled calves' kidneys with black pudding with green herb mustard sauce (£3.75), avocado and squid salad (£4), ploughman's with an unusual selection of farmhouse cheeses (£4.50), salad with honey-baked ham or cold roast beef (£6.25), crispy duck and salad frisée (£6.95), suprême of chicken with oyster mushrooms and creamy curry sauce (£8.25), grilled fillet of monkfish with scallops and saffron sauce (£9.75) and medallions of venison with pink peppercorn sauce (£10.25); home-made puddings such as apple and raspberry crumble and good vegetables. For bar lunches you have to book a table. Well kept Adnams Bitter, Badger Tanglefoot and Wadworths 6X on handpump; they will also open any bottle of wine on their bar wine list if customers wish to have half a bottle. The pretty garden is primarily for the use of residents and restaurant guests, but is available on busy days for those in the bar. The village – where Robert Bridges lived for many years – is very attractive. *(Recommended by Henry Midwinter, A T Langton, Dr Stewart Rae, TBB, Mr and Mrs D A P Grattan, S D Samuels, Nancy Witts, A Pearce, Jaine Redmond, J E Thompson)*

Free house   Licensees Richard and Kate Smith   Real ale   Meals and snacks (12.30–2, 7.30–10)   Well behaved children welcome   Restaurant (closed Sun evenings)   Occasional jazz evenings   Open 11–2.30, 6–11 all year   Bedrooms tel Hermitage (0635) 201325; £50B/£70B

Lucky Dip

Besides the fully inspected pubs, you might like to try these Lucky Dips recommended to us and described by readers (if you do, please send us reports):

Ascot [High St; SU9268], *Stag*: Traditional, unspoilt pub with lots of pictures and crockery; busy and lively under new regime, well kept Friary Meux and Tetleys, piped music, slick service *(Simon Collett-Jones)*

☆ **Aston** [Ferry Lane, on back road through Remenham; SU7884], *Flower Pot*: Warm welcome in recently redecorated comfortable lounge of Edwardian hotel a short stroll from Thames; well kept Brakspears, well presented ploughman's and other bar food, friendly service; on GWG68; definitely a place to watch, with the newish owners clearly implementing their well-thought-out plans with great care *(Brian and Jenny Seller, John Hayward, Ian Philips)*

☆ **Binfield** [B3034 from Windsor; SU8471], *Stag & Hounds*: Partly medieval Courage pub with cosy, relaxed atmosphere in nice collection of rambling low-beamed rooms – the last one of which is a bistro with quite reasonably priced food; well kept Best and Directors, real fires, friendly service

and pub cat *(Simon Collett-Jones, Alan Symes, Nick Dowson)*

Binfield [Terrace Rd North], *Victoria Arms*: Cleverly laid out Fullers pub with good choice of seating areas, well kept real ales, reasonably priced bar food; children's room, summer barbecues in quiet garden *(LYM)*

Bradfield [A4; SU6072], *Queens Head*: Well worth knowing, well run with good atmosphere *(Comus Elliott)*

Bray [SU9079], *Hinds Head*: Lovely building, smart and beautifully kept with leather armchairs, high-backed settles, early Tudor beams, oak panelling and handsome upstairs restaurant *(LYM, TBB)*; [High St] *Ringers*: Old free house, comfortable inside with pleasant, relaxed atmosphere, varying real ales such as Fullers ESB, Marstons and Youngers IPA, generous helpings of straightforward bar food *(TBB, Alison Hayward, Nick Dowson)*

Bucklebury [Chapel Row; SU5570], *Blade Bone*: Comfortable pub, piped music in public bar, friendly service and good bar food *(Lyn and Bill Capper)*

☆ **Chaddleworth** [SU4177], *Ibex*: Friendly licensee and staff in attractively laid out and comfortably old-fashioned village pub, usual range of bar food including good choice of daily specials such as beef and orange casserole or their own pies, all attractively presented and quite quickly served, well kept Courage *(HNJ, PEJ, A T Langton and others)*

Chieveley [East Lane; SU4774], *Hare & Hounds*: Excellent beer, very friendly atmosphere, good food at remarkably low prices in low-beamed bar; enjoyable skittle evenings (with food, by arrangement) *(A T Langton, Thomas Newton)*; [East Lane] *Red Lion*: Refurbished and upgraded free house with Courage real ales and usual bar food *(Ian Phillips)*

Cippenham [Lower Cippenham Lane; SU9480], *Kings Head*: Pleasantly refurbished to retain 'old ale house' atmosphere; friendly service, excellent choice of lunchtime bar food, large garden and car park *(Richard Houghton)*; [Cippenham Lane; next to modern housing estate] *Long Barn*: Classily converted barn full of ancient beams, Courage Best and John Smiths on handpump, cheerful atmosphere (it's popular with young people – the fruit machines are prominent), separate upstairs restaurant, picnic-table sets on pleasant terrace *(Nick Dowson, Alison Hayward)*

☆ **Cockpole Green** [SU7981], *Old Hatch Gate*: A very basic anachronism, where one is almost surprised that they have electricity: genuinely rustic, with cheap well kept Brakspears beers in its beamed and flagstoned tap-room – the carpeted saloon seems always closed; no cash register – pencil and paper, with a jug for the money; opening hours can be a bit erratic, though if the landlord's out feeding the pigs one of the regulars (and it's decidedly them that it's run for) will usually serve you *(Gordon and Daphne, Simon Collett-Jones, Nick Dowson, TBB, LYM)*

Compton [SU5279], *Swan*: Lively atmosphere and good food *(Mrs K Godley)*

Cookham [SU8884], *Ferry*: Included for its splendid riverside position with big terrace, walk-through windows for stripped-décor waterside bar, upstairs restaurant, much older original pub behind, choice of real ales *(LYM)*; [High St] *Royal Exchange*: Cosy old village pub with pleasant staff, good choice of food, Ind Coope real ale, decent wines; not one of the cheapest *(P S Yeoman)*

Cookham Dean [Church Lane; SU8785], *Jolly Farmer*: Eighteenth-century brick and flint cottage pub, bought from Courage when it came up for sale in 1987 by a consortium of regulars, to keep it as they like it; tastefully redecorated, with snug, bar with low beams, brasses and fireplace and small separate restaurant; good bar food, Courage beers

still, new lavatories, garden with village views from this beautiful spot opposite church *(Anon)*

Cookham Dean Common [SU8785], *Hare & Hounds*: Included for its position by the peaceful green, with tables among rose and fruit trees on its well kept lawn; well kept Wethereds, bar food, polite and helpful licensee; lots of walks nearby *(LYM)*; [Harding Green] *Uncle Toms Cabin*: Quaint and basic small bars with numerous oil lamps, home-made bar food, well kept Benskins Best, friendly licensee and locals, pleasant atmosphere *(Richard Houghton)*

Cox Green [Kimbers Lane – handy for M4 junction 9, via A423(M); SU8779], *Shepherds Hut*: Welcoming locals, caring and jovial landlord, well kept Bass, Charrington IPA and in winter Fullers ESB; separate food bar, fast and agreeable service, small car park but plenty of street parking *(R Houghton)*

☆ **Crazies Hill** [from A4, take Warren Row Rd at Cockpole Green signpost just E of Knowl Hill, then past Warren Row follow Crazies Hill signposts; also signposted – OS Sheet 175 reference 799809; SU7980], *Horns*: The speciality here has been authentic south-east Asian cooking – dishes from Madras through Burma to Thailand, using carefully chosen fresh ingredients, alongside more orthodox pub cooking; well kept Brakspears PA and SB on handpump, decent wines, good collection of spirits, yet a thoroughly unassuming village-pub atmosphere, with basic furnishings; some seats outside, meals limited Sun and Mon evenings, and during Henley week; piped music from jazz to Vivaldi; children in small bistro area until 7.30 *(Ian Phillips, Mrs N P North, Jack Lalor, Jane and Calum, TBB, Janet Kingsbury, Simon Collett-Jones, LYM)*

Curridge [OS Sheet 174 reference 492723; SU4871], *Bunk*: Popular pub with a choice of good value bar food and – under new owners – new restaurant behind; real ales such as Arkells, Boddingtons and Morlands; the name's said to be a Berkshire word for a single-track railway line *(A T Langton)*

Datchet [The Green – not far from M4 junction 5; SU9876], *Royal Stag*: Very friendly locals' pub with good mix of customers and lovely atmosphere; interesting wood panelling, pictures and knick-knacks, good service and well kept Ind Coope beers; lunchtime and evening food (not tried), small car park; overlooks churchyard *(Richard Houghton, Dr and Mrs A K Clarke)*

East Ilsley, *Star*: Friendly, olde-worlde atmosphere in 500-year-old listed building of character, with beams, lots of black woodwork, inglenook log fire, simple traditional furnishings and big windows overlooking village; well kept Morlands Best, Ruddles County and Ushers Best, attractively priced food from sandwiches through fry-ups to scampi and salads, faint piped music, garden behind with picnic-table sets and big play boot-house; plans for bedrooms *(Lyn and Bill Capper, Chris and Liz Norman, BB)*

Eton [Bridge St; SU9678], *Watermans Arms*: Striking rowing and other decorations in lively local near the Thames (and near Eton College rowing club), well kept Courage Best and Directors on handpump, straightforward bar food *(LYM)*

Grazeley [SU6966], *Wheatsheaf*: Welcoming, clean and efficient little one-room pub with the original half-timbered building behind it in cornfields; tweed-covered stools and benches on the carpet, a few farm tools on the plain walls; Courage Best, straightforward bar food; nice people, no machines, open fire, quiet piped music, spotless lavatories *(Ian Phillips)*

Hampstead Norreys [SU5376], *White Hart*: Pleasant spotless pub in pretty village, warm welcome from landlord, well kept Wethereds and good choice of competitively priced food *(Shirley Fluck)*

☆ **Hare Hatch** [just N of A4 Reading–Maidenhead; SU8077], *Queen Victoria*: Good local atmosphere in well kept low-beamed pub, comfortable, warm and welcoming; good range of attractively priced food from excellent soup with lovely crusty bread to pheasant casserole, Brakspears real ales, lots of games, very popular landlord *(Ian Phillips, Nick Dowson, BB)*

Hermitage [2½ miles from M4 junction 13; village slip road off A34 just N of exit roundabout; SU5073], *Fox*: Handily placed, with prettily decorated plush lounge, wide choice of bar food from sandwiches, burgers, baked potatoes and many other snacks through pies and vegetarian dishes to steaks; Morlands, Eldridge Pope Royal Oak and Websters Yorkshire on handpump, with a guest beer which readers suggest may be the one to try; nicely laid out terrace and garden; children welcome; open all day Fri–Sat; a former main entry, well worth knowing – especially when the new owner has sorted out what in spring 1989 seemed to be some teething problems *(Jon Wainwright, Tom Evans, LYM; more reports please)*

Holyport [The Green; SU8977], *George*: Exceptional roast beef and Yorkshire pudding, plain cooking at its best, in open-plan Courage pub *(TBB)*

Hungerford [Bridge St; A338; SU3368], *John o' Gaunt*: Considerable character, good reasonably priced bar food, well kept Courage Best and Wadworths 6X; bedrooms *(Chris Payne, Prof A N Black, LYM)*; [Charnham St – on A4/A338 roundabout] *Red Lion*: Basic pub with good helpings of simple food and good beers; juke box can be loud; bedrooms *(Jenny and Michael Back)*; [top of High St] *Tuttiman*: Pleasant refurbished pub with canal/agricultural theme and really friendly new landlord

(Dr and Mrs A K Clarke)

Hurley [SU8283], *Olde Bell*: Civilised and old-fashioned partly beamed bar with cosy atmosphere and friendly, efficient service in handsome timbered inn with Norman doorway and window, fine gardens, restaurant; not cheap; bedrooms *(Simon Collett-Jones, LYM)*

☆ **Hurst** [opp church; SU7972], *Castle*: Fine old village inn with warm welcome, excellent simple home-cooked food including wonderful puddings, well kept Courage and good open fires in its three bars; bedrooms *(Comus Elliott, Ian Phillips)*

Hurst [Davis St], *Jolly Farmer*: Intimate little pub, comfortable rather than smart, with tables under cocktail parasols on its spacious lawn; reasonable choice of bar food *(IP)*

Knowl Hill [A4 Reading–Maidenhead; SU8279], *Old Devil*: Free house with spacious bar sensibly divided to create comfortable, relaxed atmosphere; smartly dressed bar staff, obliging service, several real ales, extensive range of cheap bar food and separate restaurant *(Richard Houghton)*; *Royal Oak*: Simple friendly pub with excellent service and very good home-made steak and kidney pie – very inexpensive; spotless gents, good parking *(Brian Barefoot)*; *Seven Stars*: Well run and friendly partly panelled pub with well kept Brakspears, pleasant atmosphere, simple food at sensible prices; tables outside, children's play house *(Alison Hayward, Nick Dowson, LYM)*

Littlewick Green [3 miles from M4 junction 9; A423(M) then left on to A4; SU8379], *Shire Horse*: Well worth visiting for Courage's adjoining Shire Horse Centre (open Mar–Oct); comfortable open-plan lounge bar, well kept Courage ales, tea house, play area by big side lawn, food *(LYM)*

nr Maidenhead [Pinkneys Green – A308 N of town; SU8582], *Golden Ball*: Much refurbished in plush comfort, though low-ceilinged part by open fire still has a rustic air; friendly and clean, with well kept Wethereds, winter mulled wine, changing choice of traditional bar food, no piped music, seats on peaceful lawn *(Ian Phillips, TBB, Simon Collett-Jones, LYM)*; [Marion Rd – A308 N] *Robin Hood*: Old pub with low ceilings, excellent service, friendly atmosphere, well kept Courage beer and bar food, garden with slide and swings; parking can be difficult *(Richard Houghton)*; [Pinkneys Green – A308 N] *Stag & Hounds*: Rather basic two-room pub with excellent range of simple, home-cooked food, Courage ales and a welcoming atmosphere; children welcome *(Ian Phillips)*

Maidens Green [SU8972], *Stirrups*: Country house hotel, though bar is quite pub-like – with good if fairly expensive food *(TBB)*

Midgham [Bath road (N side); SU5567], *Coach & Horses*: Comfortably refurbished

Wethereds pub with wide range of bar food, tables in back garden *(BB)*

Moneyrow Green [B3024 – OS Sheet 175 reference 889768; SU8977], *Jolly Gardener*: Expensively refurbished, pleasant décor with old brick and timber alcoves, relaxing atmosphere, decent bar food, good service, Youngers real ales *(R Houghton, Nick Dowson)*; [OS Sheet 175 reference 892774], *White Hart*: Pleasant, friendly pub; 1930s lounge bar with panelled walls, prints, plates and large mounted butterfly, serving hatch at one end of bar, Gothic fireplace, sizeable public bar; Morlands ales on handpump *(Alison Hayward, Nick Dowson)*

Newbury [Market Pl; SU4666], *Old Waggon & Horses*: Included for its sunny flower-filled waterside terrace and perhaps the big upstairs family dining bar *(LYM)*; [Stroud Green; SU4766] *Plough*: Small refurbished and extended pub with servery for outdoor tables, Courage Directors on handpump, partitioned-off darts area *(Paul Corbett)*

Oakley Green [B3024; SU9276], *Olde Red Lion*: Cosy old pub with pink button-back banquettes, log-effect gas fire, well kept Friary Meux, pleasant service, separate restaurant *(R Houghton, Alison Hayward, Nick Dowson)*

☆ **Old Windsor** [17 Crimp Hill – between River Thames and Savill Gardens; SU9874], *Union*: Very picturesque outside, open-plan bar inside with tables, settles and stools, film-star photographs, fresh ingredients cooked well in bar and beamed evening restaurant, friendly efficient staff; Flowers, John Smiths, Theakstons, Websters Yorkshire, Wethereds and Murphys Stout on handpump *(Lyn and Bill Capper, H Foster, Mrs Shirley Pielou, TBB)*

Paley Street [SU8675], *Bridge*: Well kept pub with fires in both bars, friendly and helpful staff, Wethereds real ale, wide range of reasonably priced food and good mix of customers giving a nice, relaxed atmosphere; good-sized car park *(Richard Houghton)*

Pangbourne [opp Church; SU6376], *Cross Keys*: Comfortable lounge with aviation photographs and intimate, friendly atmosphere; Courage ales and decent bar food, two interconnecting family rooms with suitable furniture, little stream with decorative Japanese bridge running through back terrace *(Ian Phillips)*; [Shooters Hill] *Swan*: Comfortable and welcoming genuinely old pub in lovely setting by Thames, good atmosphere, popular restaurant – the bar food is pricey *(IP, A Goodman)*

☆ **Reading** [Kennetside; SU7272], *Fishermans Cottage*: Currently the Reading pub that's most enjoyed by readers, particularly for its position by a lock on the Kennet, and lovely back garden; pretty stone-built Victorian cottage core with crenellated front, modern extension including conservatory; pleasant stone snug behind fireplace with wood-burning cast-iron range, brisk efficient service, short and rather pricey menu, Fullers ales; busy at lunchtime, more relaxed in the evening *(Ian Phillips, Stephen King, Richard Houghton)*

☆ **Reading** [8 Gt John St; SU7272], *Retreat*: Epitome of a 1960s local – a good, honest no-nonsense pub, full of atmosphere and people enjoying their well kept Flowers and Wethereds; no airs and graces, but plenty of chat and humour; narrow benches and genuine old pub tables in two smallish bars with boarded dado and Anaglypta walls, darts, local notices, bar billiards, very cheap basic food, really warm welcome; very much a man's pub – the lounge bar would count as a public bar in most places *(Ian Phillips, Richard Houghton, I D Norris)*

Reading [Chatham St; SU7272], *Butler*: Smart barmen serving very good Fullers London Pride, tasty food served by ticket number; gets crowded before Reading football matches *(R G Ollier)*; [29 Market Pl] *Coopers*: The one spacious area includes a big alcove with two fully panelled walls and the third filled by a vast carved oak fireplace, also an upper gallery; Courage ales and short choice of straightforward bar food; wine bar on far side of original coach entry *(Ian Phillips)*; [316 Kennetside] *Jolly Anglers*: Right on canal, looking over to gasworks and railway beyond, with couple of picnic-table sets on towpath; warm welcome, simple décor (a few stuffed fish), very reasonable food, Courage beers *(Ian Phillips)*; [88 Queens Rd] *Lyndhurst Arms*: Clean, comfortable and efficiently run pub with Wethereds beer and good food *(Ian Phillips)*; [Castle St] *Sun*: Large, many-roomed pub with two bars and various levels; good decorative order, carpeted throughout and some genuine as well as reproduction beams; Courage Bitter and quite a range of straightforward snacks *(Ian Phillips)*; [London Rd (low number)] *Turks Head*: Free house on main road with plain chairs and floorboards, well kept Tetleys and Wadworths 6X, good reasonably priced food, young, pleasant and efficient staff *(Richard Houghton)*; [Abbey St] *White Lion*: Modern Morlands house among modern office blocks but with impressive carved limestone heraldic lion as its sign; spotless interior is striking mixture of Byzantine pillars, stainless steel girders, wooden trellises and plastic ivy; calm and comfortable atmosphere, limited but well presented bar food, piped music, pleasant terrace *(Ian Phillips)*; [110 Kings Rd] *Wynford Arms*: Clean and welcoming with efficient service and reasonable prices; one bar with pool-table, juke box and fruit machine, the other serving good, simple, well prepared bar food – especially the doorstep sandwiches; no parking *(Ian Phillips)*

☆ **Remenham** [Wargrave Rd; SU7683], *Two*

Brewers: Comfortable, rambling rooms with wooden beams around central bar, oldest part dating back 600 years; log fire, darts, fruit machine, friendly service; good range of fresh and well presented reasonably priced bar food, and above all a really friendly atmosphere; children's room at back *(Lyn and Bill Capper, Ian Phillips)*

☆ Sindlesham [Bearwood Rd – signposted Sindlesham from B3349; SU7769], *Walter Arms*: Comfortable dining pub – not a place for just a drink – with wide choice of good quickly served bar food, well kept Courage Best and Directors, cheerful welcome; pleasant bedrooms, with substantial well cooked breakfasts *(William Main, LYM)*

Slough [Church St; SU9779], *Coachmakers*: Lovely town-centre local with one bar, well kept Courage, friendly and efficient service *(RH)*; [Stoke Rd] *Printers Devil*: Comfortably refurbished, with well kept Benskins Best, polite uniformed bar staff *(Richard Houghton)*; [Parkstreet] *Queen of England*: Back-street town pub with public and lounge areas separated by an arch, giving the feeling of two bars; pleasant welcome and good Wethereds *(RH)*; [Windsor Rd] *Rising Sun*: Long pub with pleasant atmosphere and wide age range of customers; Charrington IPA, good choice of bar food, polite service *(Richard Houghton)*

☆ Sonning [SU7575], *White Hart*: Spacious Thames-side hotel with oak settles, log fires and bow windows in heavily timbered main bar, expensive sandwiches and other bar snacks (some interesting), well kept Brakspears, comfortable garden chairs, awnings and canopies on lovely riverside lawn and spacious restaurant *(Ian Phillips, LYM)*

Stanford Dingley [SU5771], *Bull*: Proper English village pub with friendly and welcoming licensees, good choice of home-made bar food at reasonable prices *(Keith and Dorothy Pickering, Comus Elliott)*

☆ Streatley [SU5980], *Bull*: Real pub with well kept Watneys-related real ales on handpump, popular for good sensibly priced bar food (it can get crowded), good restaurant; nr GWG97 *(E J Cutting, A T Langton, Mike Tucker)*

Streatley [SU5980], *Swan*: This smart Thames-side hotel, a former main entry, has now become part of a substantial timeshare complex where comfortable and big-windowed boathouse-theme bar adjoins fitness centre; original bar now an adjunct to restaurant; well kept real ales, smartly served and well made if rather pricey bar food, traditional games; attractive riverside grounds include play area; maybe light evening meals (not Sun) in college rowing club state barge; children welcome; jazz club Weds; bedrooms luxurious, many with river views and own terraces *(LYM)*

Three Mile Cross [A33, just S of M4 junction 11; SU7167], *Swan*: Welcoming pub with well kept beer *(Dr and Mrs A K Clarke)*

Twyford [High St; SU7876], *Duke of Wellington*: Congenial, with noisy, friendly bar and quiet lounge; well kept Brakspears SB *(John Baker)*; [A4] *Horse & Groom*: Substantial old place recently renovated as steak pub with other straightforward but good bar food, comfortable and friendly atmosphere, and Brakspears ales; good parking *(Ian Phillips)*

Upper Basildon [village signposted from Pangbourne and A417 Pangbourne–Streatley; SU5976], *Beehive*: Blond furniture in knocked-through black-beamed bar with cushioned booths around tables, good range of real ales on handpump, straightforward bar food, swings and seats in small garden *(LYM)*

☆ Waltham St Lawrence [SU8276], *Bell*: Handsome sixteenth-century pub in lovely village setting by gate to church; two nicely restored bars, open fires, oak beams, longcase clock and other antiques, plainish home-cooked bar food (not Sun), choice of well kept real ales such as Brakspears and Tetleys, wide choice of whiskies; piped music, outside lavatories *(Simon Collett-Jones, JMC, Margaret Dyke, LYM)*

☆ Waltham St Lawrence [West End – well outside village], *Plough*: Calm and civilised old country pub, unchanging for years, with almost a living-room atmosphere, good (if a bit pricey) food, well kept Morlands tapped from the cask and devoted regulars, some of whom arrive on horseback; usually quiet, relaxing and welcoming – very much a reflection of the long-serving landlady's personality *(Nick Dowson, Richard Houghton, Sarah and Jamie Allan, Simon Collett-Jones, LYM)*

Warfield [Cricketers Lane; SU8872], *Cricketers*: Warm and cosily old-fashioned three-bar pub notable (and very popular) for at least half a dozen real ales; nice garden, food in bar and prettily decorated restaurant *(Steve Huggins, TBB)*; [Church Lane] *Plough & Harrow*: Vivacious landlady, well kept Morlands Best, good value food *(Stephen King)*; [Church Lane] *Yorkshire Rose*: Decent pub – with super gents lavatory *(TBB)*

☆ Wargrave [High St; SU7878], *White Hart*: Spacious but cheerfully bustling low-beamed lounge bar decorated to suit its eighteenth-century character, good value bar food, well kept Wethereds and Flowers real ale; restaurant *(TBB, Richard Houghton, LYM)*

Wargrave [Upper Wargrave], *Queen Victoria*: Good atmosphere, decent food and well kept Brakspears *(Comus Elliott)*; *St George & Dragon*: Now a Harvester restaurant rather than a pub, but still worth knowing for its Thames-side position with décor blended tastefully into surroundings, and charming garden *(TBB)*

☆ **Windsor** [Castle Hill – opp Henry VIII Gate; SU9676], *Horse & Groom*: Small pub dating from 1520, with excellent cheap food, really imaginative, well kept Courage ales and a surprisingly nice and uncrowded atmosphere for this tourist town; staff friendly, relaxed and helpful *(Derek House, Dr and Mrs A K Clarke, Gary Scott)*

☆ **Windsor** [opp stn, nr Castle], *Royal Oak*: Friendly well run pub with excellent bar food; under the same ownership as the Greyhound in Chalfont St Peter, a popular main entry in Bucks – and some say this is even better *(TBB)*

Windsor [Thames St], *Adam & Eve*: Bustling pub by theatre, usually crowded with teenagers, with loud piped music; occasional barbecues in little back yard, well kept Bass and Charrington IPA; virtually no nearby parking *(LYM)*; [Thames St] *Donkey House*: Unrenovated pub of great potential in superb riverside spot, with Friary Meux Best and Ind Coope Burton, plain food *(Peter Kitson, Bridgett Sarsby)*; [Dedworth Green; SU9476] *Nags Head*: Comfortably furnished Courage pub with two bars, friendly atmosphere and large garden with Wendy house; piped music *(Simon Collett-Jones)*; [Park St; off High St next to Mews] *Two Brewers*: Courage house in Georgian street close to Castle; Armoury bar to left, lounge furnished with Windsor chairs to right, and food servery near entrance; good, home-made lunchtime bar food, wooden benches on pavement outside; open all day in summer *(JMC)*

☆ **Winkfield** [Lovel Rd; A330 just W of junction with B3034, turning off at Fleur de Lis – OS Sheet 175 reference 921715; SU9071], *Slug & Lettuce*: Attractive pastiche of old-world tavern – all bare bricks, low beams, black oak timbers and cottagey furnishings; decent if not cheap bar food (in evenings may be served only if you have seat in restaurant, and at lunchtime food service stops sharply at 2), barbecues, restaurant (not Sun), well kept real ales such as Boddingtons, Brakspears, Courage Best and Theakstons Old Peculier; friendly Labrador and Siamese cats; particularly at weekends is very much a place for young Radio 1 fans, but quiet weekday lunchtimes; children in restaurant *(Richard Houghton, Simon Collett-Jones, Nick Dowson, TBB, RH, LYM)*

Winkfield [Woodside Rd], *Duke of Edinburgh*: Pleasant, cosy atmosphere, well kept Arkells, good if a little pricey bar food, friendly service *(R Houghton)*; [towards Windsor on B3022] *Hernes Oak*:

Welcoming well run local with enterprising choice of spirits; bar food, children allowed in back room *(LYM)*; [Church Rd – A330] *White Hart*: Neatly modernised Tudor pub with ex-bakery bar and ex-courthouse weekend restaurant, bar food, Courage real ale, relaxed atmosphere, good décor including grandfather clock, friendly and efficient service, sizeable garden *(SCCJ, LYM)*

☆ **Wokingham** [Gardeners Green; from Wokingham inner ring rd turn left into Easthampstead Rd just after A329 Bracknell turnoff, then right at White Horse, then left into Honey Hill –- OS Sheet 175 reference 826668; SU8068], *Crooked Billet*: Jolly and homely atmosphere in sprucely furnished country pub – pews, tiles, brick serving-counter, crooked black joists; well kept Brakspears PA, SB, Mild and Old on handpump, good simple cheap food from sandwiches to gammon and egg, nice mix of customers from farm-workers to doctors and computer people, communicating restaurant area (not Sun – bar food very limited Sun evening); seats and swings outside ; children in restaurant; has been open all day *(Steve Waters, LYM)*

Wokingham [Milton Rd, behind theatre] *Penguin & Vulture*: Watneys pub in converted stables – an adjunct to Cantley House Hotel; genuine low beams, Websters Yorkshire on handpump, bar food, separate attractive restaurant, sheltered seats outside *(Ian Phillips)*

Woolhampton [off A4; SU5767], *Rowbarge*: Country pub near canal with friendly beamed bar, panelled family room, big French-windowed dining-room, tables in cottage garden; bar food *(LYM)*

Wraysbury [29 Wraysbury Rd; TQ0174], *George*: Two bars with light wood beams and panelling, stripped pine and farmhouse-style furniture; friendly service, Courage Best and Directors and John Smiths, and extensive range of continental-style bar food *(Simon Collett-Jones)* [Coppermill Rd] *Green Man*: Fairly old pub with bright interior, very popular for food; well kept Friary Meux Best and Ind Coope Burton, welcoming and obliging staff, big car park *(Richard Houghton)*

Yattendon [Burnt Hill; take Pangbourne rd, then 3rd turn right signed Bradfield, Burnt Hill; SU5574], *Nut & Bolt*: Generous helpings of good value food in quietly placed country pub with comfortably refurbished open-plan bar; summer barbecues *(S P Jeffries, LYM)*

Buckinghamshire

Several contrasting new entries here include the Bottle & Glass listed under Aylesbury (sophisticatedly traditional, with interesting food and particularly good wines), the Pheasant looking out from the hilltop village of Brill (a good ploughman's here), the friendly Old Red Lion at Great Brickhill (another pub with a remarkable view), the Red Lion in Great Missenden (long evening bar food service), the cosy Old Sun at Lane End, the well run Dog & Badger at Medmenham and the outstandingly pretty Clifden Arms at Worminghall (again, long food service). The best pub food in the area's probably to be found at the Walnut Tree at Fawley, and food is also a notable attraction at the Peacock at Bolter End, the charming old Chequers at Fingest, the suave Austrian-run Yew Tree at Frieth (good drinks, including enterprising non-alcoholic ones), the very popular George in Great Missenden (particularly good vegetarian dishes), the Rising Sun by the woods at Little Hampden, the snug little Old Crown at Skirmett, the rambling Old Swan near The Lee (particularly strong on fish), the beautifully placed Bull & Butcher at Turville (one of the very few pubs prepared to take the minimal trouble needed to produce freshly squeezed orange juice), the grand old George & Dragon in West Wycombe (long evening food service) and the homely White Swan in Whitchurch (which this year wins a star award for its warm friendliness). New licensees to note are those at the Red Lion near Princes Risborough

The Kings Arms, Amersham

(emphasising its period style) and the White Hart at Northend (proving particularly popular). Pubs for connoisseurs include the old Lions of Bledlow on its dramatic Chilterns escarpment, the Royal Standard of England at Forty Green (oozing with character), the quite unspoilt Full Moon on Hawridge Common, and the Pink & Lily at Lacey Green (for its Rupert Brooke room – though it's a perfectly good pub in other ways). Notable pubs in the Lucky Dip at the end of the chapter include the Old Hare in Beaconsfield, Plough at Cadsden, Red Lion at Chenies, Dinton Hermit at Ford, Hit or Miss at Penn Street, Cock & Rabbit at The Lee and Falcon at Wooburn Moor.

ADSTOCK   SP7330 Map 4

Old Thatched Inn

Just N of A413, 4 miles SE of Buckingham

Kept neat and spotless, this cosy and comfortable country pub has wheel-back chairs and bays of green plush button-back banquettes in carpeted areas leading off the flagstoned bar. There are stripped beams and timbers, antique hunting prints, copper and brassware, potted plants and fresh flowers, and a log-effect gas fire. The wide-ranging, reasonably priced bar food includes open sandwiches (from £1), home-made soup (£1.50), huge toasted sandwiches (from £2.25), ploughman's (from £2.50), chilli con carne or vegetable curry (£4), a hefty plate of gammon and eggs or home-made steak and kidney pie (£4.50) and eight-ounce sirloin steak (£7); good friendly service. Well kept Adnams, Marstons Pedigree, Ruddles County and a guest beer on handpump, with Morrells under light blanket pressure – and as a useful alternative as much tea or coffee as you can drink for 75p; dominoes, piped music. The countryside around this pretty village thatched pub is rolling farmland – with a gentle wash of farm noises in the sheltered back garden, which has tables under fruit trees and a sycamore. *(Recommended by M O'Driscoll, Lyn and Bill Capper, Mr and Mrs G D Amos, Nick Dowson, Alison Hayward)*

Free house   Licensee Ian Tring   Real ale   Meals and snacks (12–2, 7–10; not Sun evening) Restaurant tel Winslow (029 671) 2584   Children in restaurant   Open 12–2.30, 6–11 all year; closed 25 Dec

AKELEY   SP7037 Map 4

Bull & Butcher

The Square; just off A413

Popular for reliable food, this friendly village pub also serves well kept Hook Norton Best, Marstons Pedigree and a guest beer from handpump, and good value wines by the bottle. At lunchtime, when typical food prices run from £3 to £4.40, their most popular dish is home-cooked honey-baked ham; other things include generous baked potatoes served with a wedge of granary bread, and a wide range of decently made help-yourself salads served from a buffet in the small dining-room. There's an evening steak bar (from eight-ounce sirloin, £9, including pudding and coffee; other dishes too). The long open-plan bar has fires on each side of a massive central stone chimney, with a third down at the end; the curved beams in this wood-floored lower bar area are unusual. There are red plush button-back banquettes, and the rough-cast walls are decorated with drawings of well known customers; darts, shove-ha'penny, cribbage, dominoes, Sunday evening bridge club, piped music. Pleasant beer garden. *(Recommended by B A Law, Dr T MacLennan, B M Eldridge, HKR, Alison Hayward, Nick Dowson)*

Free house   Licensee Harry Dyson   Real ale   Meals (lunchtime, not Sun) and snacks (not Sun)   Steak bar tel Lillingstone Dayrell (028 06) 257 (not Sun–Mon)   Children in eating areas   Open 12–2.30 (3 Sat), 6–11 all year

AMERSHAM   SU9597   Map 4

Kings Arms   [*illustrated on page 42*]

High Street; A413

The two big pluses at this Tudor inn are its striking appearance (expectations raised by the elaborately timbered façade aren't at all let down in the rambling, heavily beamed bar, which oozes character), and its unusually warm and friendly atmosphere. There are lots of snug alcoves with high-backed antique settles, quaint old-fashioned chairs and other seats – you can usually find a seat even though it tends to get busy at lunchtime. Simple bar food includes home-made soup (£1.25), good sandwiches, ploughman's (£2), cauliflower cheese, garlic mushrooms or smoked salmon pâté (£2.50), potted prawns and salad or fish pie (£3) and daily specials. Benskins Best and Tetleys on handpump, with Ind Coope Burton tapped from the cask behind the bar counter; friendly efficient service; a big inglenook fireplace. There are seats behind in an attractive little flower-filled courtyard and coachyard, with more tables and a climbing-frame beyond, on a tree-sheltered lawn. *(Recommended by M J Dyke, Mr and Mrs D M Norton, Simon Collett-Jones, Lindsey Shaw Radley, John Tyzack, M C Howells)*

Benskins (Allied)   Licensee John Jennison   Real ale   Meals and snacks   Restaurant (not Sun evening or Mon – no pipes or cigars, and they ask other smokers to be considerate) tel Amersham (0494) 726333   Children in restaurant and eating area   Open 11–11 (but may well close 2.30–6 in winter)

nr AMERSHAM   SU9495   Map 4

Queens Head

Whielden Gate; pub in sight just off A404, 1½ miles towards High Wycombe at Winchmore Hill turn-off; OS Sheet 165 reference 941957

This pretty little fairy-lit brick and tile eighteenth-century cottage is almost alone in the countryside. It's refreshingly unassuming, with low beams and flagstones, a big inglenook fireplace with lots of brass spigots (and a stuffed bird) on its mantelbeam, simple traditional furnishings, a good cigarette card collection, horsebrasses and old guns. Home-made bar food includes soup (£1), ploughman's (from £1.75), omelettes, popular chicken and ham or steak and kidney pies (£3.50), salmon steak (£4), eight-ounce sirloin (£6.50) and lots of pizzas (from £2.50; a £6 monster is named after Monty, their friendly Dalmatian); in winter there's often game, bagged by the landlord or by customers. Well kept Benskins Best and Ind Coope Burton on handpump; darts, shove-ha'penny, dominoes, cribbage, fruit machine, space game, trivia and piped music. There are often summer barbecues in the recently tidied up garden behind – plump conifers, a small pond, attractive tubs of flowers on the terrace, swings and a climber. *(Recommended by Simon Collett-Jones, J H Walker, Nick Dowson, Lyn and Bill Capper)*

Benskins (Allied)   Licensee Les Robbins   Real ale   Meals and snacks   Children in family-room   Live music once a month or so   Open 11–2.30, 5.30–11 all year (opens 6 Sat evening)

ASTWOOD   SP9547   Map 4

Swan

Main Road; village signposted from A422 Milton Keynes–Bedford

With so many Swans in the area, the owners have recently decided to rechristen this the 'Swan at Astwood' (though of course, in line with our usual policy, we don't ourselves include the place-name in the title we use). But don't worry: this entails no change of policy. Business is still very much as before, in this partly thatched early seventeenth-century pub. Bar food includes good home-made soup (£1), a choice of ploughman's (from £1.75), good quiche (£2.50), harvest pie (£2.80), steak sandwich in a freshly baked roll (£2.95), salads (from £2.95), roast chicken or scampi (£2.95) and eight-ounce steak (£6 – in the restaurant their steaks run up to two pounds); service is friendly rather than coldly efficient. Though it's open-plan, the low-beamed bar has a thoroughly old-fashioned atmosphere, with logs burning in its handsome inglenook, and antique seats and tables. Well kept Brakspears SB, Flowers Original, Marstons Pedigree, Wethereds and Whitbreads Castle Eden on handpump; darts, shove-ha'penny, cribbage, dominoes, maybe piped pop music. The quiet lawn at the back has tables under old fruit trees, and there are more seats out in front. *(Recommended by Mr and Mrs H W Clayton, TBB, Mr and Mrs G D Amos, Paul and Margaret Baker)*

Free house Licensees Jim and Diane Niklen and Paul Cribb Real ale Meals and snacks (not Sun evening) Restaurant Children in one part of bar and restaurant Open 11–2.30, 6–11 all year, maybe all day on bank hols and special occasions Two bedrooms tel North Crawley (023 065) 272; £25S/£30S

nr AYLESBURY SP8213 Map 4

Bottle & Glass 😊

Gibraltar – A418 some miles towards Thame, beyond Stone; OS Sheet 165 reference 758108

Most of the space in this thatched white pub is given over to eating, though on the right there's a very snug little alcovey bar, all deep green – walls, ceiling, Lloyd Loom-style chairs and other seats, even the former fireplace where a sofa nestles; only the flooring tiles are red. The green mood does filter through to the left side, too (as do the red tiles), but stops short of the main dining-room. This has well spaced tables, big old photographs on its panelled walls, and a high Delft shelf; it opens into an airy extension, which itself leads out to a terrace and neat lawn with more tables. Enterprising food includes soup (£1.75), vegetarian lasagne (£2.50), open sandwiches (£3), pork casserole (£4.50), fish crumble (£4.75) and generous salads (£5.50), with additional lunchtime main courses such as chicken marinated with fresh lime (£4.95) and evening dishes such as vegetarian filo-pastry parcels (£5.95), steaks (from £6.95) and brill done with chervil (£7.50). Besides well kept ABC and Wadworths 6X on handpump, they do notably good wines; well reproduced pop music; no dogs. *(Recommended by Mr and Mrs T F Marshall; more reports please)*

ABC (Allied) Licensees Jes Davies and Dave Berry Real ale Meals and snacks (12–2.15, 7–10; not Sun evening) Children welcome Open 12–2.30, 6–11 all year

BLEDLOW SP7702 Map 4

Lions of Bledlow ★

From B4009 from Chinnor towards Princes Risborough, the first right turn about 1 mile outside Chinnor goes straight to the pub; from the second, wider right turn, turn right through village

Over the last year or two the range of freshly cooked food in this old-fashioned sixteenth-century Chilterns pub has swollen to include around eight dishes of the day such as vegetarian hot-pot (£2.50), liver and bacon (£2.75) and seafood crumble (£2.95), alongside soup (£1.25), huge open sandwiches (from £1.25), ploughman's (from £1.95), burgers, salads (from £2.25), chilli con carne (£2.50), plaice or haddock (£2.75), steak and kidney pie (£2.95), lasagne (£3.50), scampi (£3.75), a tender mixed grill and good puddings such as lemon meringue pie. The heavily beamed inglenook bar has attractive oak stalls built into one partly panelled wall, other seats including an antique settle on its deeply polished ancient tiles, and among the best views in the county from its bay windows. Well kept Courage Directors, Wadworths 6X, Wethereds and Youngs on handpump, with a guest beer such as Morlands Old Masters; log fires; one of the two cottagey side rooms has a space game. There are picnic-table sets behind, on a sheltered crazy-paved terrace and a series of small sloping lawns; you can walk straight up into the hills and the steep beech woods beyond. *(Recommended by Gwen and Peter Andrews, Lyn and Bill Capper, Mary Claire, Mick and Hannah Jones, Nick Dowson, Alison Hayward, Colin Donald, Simon Collett-Jones, Brian and Rosemary Wilmot, Maureen Hobbs, Peter Hitchcock)*

Free house Licensee F J McKeown Real ale Meals and snacks (not Sun evening) Restaurant (not Sun evening) tel Princes Risborough (084 44) 3345 Children in side rooms and restaurant Open 11–2.30 (3 Sat), 6–11 all year; closed evening 25 Dec

BOLTER END SU7992 Map 4
Peacock ⊛

Just over 4 miles from M40 junction 5; A40 to Stokenchurch, then B482

In summer the prettily kept front garden has some seats around a low stone table, as well as picnic-table sets; inside in winter, it's the seats by the log fire that go first. All year, though, the main attraction is the wide range of good bar food, such as ploughman's (£2.30), two sizes of deep-pan pizzas (from £2.60 or £3.50, depending on filling), vegetarian dishes with Basmati rice (from £2.75), locally smoked ham and melon (£3.50), steak and kidney or curried beef and vegetable pies (£3.50), seafood Mornay or prawn fritters with a sweet-and-sour dip (£3.95), steaks from twelve-ounce rump (£7.25), lots of popular puddings (£1.50), and dishes of the day such as pork satay done for them by a Thai cook, or fish fresh from Billingsgate on Thursdays. The rambling series of modernised rooms and alcoves have rugs on the polished brick and tile floor and much wrought-ironwork. ABC and Bass on handpump, decent wines, good cider; darts, piped music; with food cooked to order, there may be a delay if they're busy. *(Recommended by Ian Phillips, M V Saunders, W A Lund; more reports please)*

ABC (Allied) Licensee Peter Hodges Real ale Meals and snacks (12–2, 7–11, not Sun evening) Open 11–2.30, 6–11 all year

BRILL SP6513 Map 4
Pheasant

Windmill Road; village signposted from B4011 Bicester–Long Crendon

Picnic-table sets in the small, sheltered garden behind look down towards Oxfordshire fading into a great distance, with one of the oldest post windmills still in working order in the foreground. The quietly modernised and neatly kept bar has comfortable russet leatherette button-back banquettes in bays around its tables, with a step up to a dining area which is decorated with attractively framed Alken hunting prints – and which has the view. Bar food includes sandwiches (served from 1 o'clock), winter soup (£1.40), popular burgers (£2.60), chilli con carne or ham and eggs (£3.40), a notable ploughman's (£3.60 – but that does include home-baked ham as well as three different cheeses, an apple, coleslaw and pickle, and chunks of both good white and brown bread), trout with prawns (£5.95), steaks (from £7.80), daily specials such as spaghetti bolognese (£2.95) and home-made puddings (from £1.60). Well kept Ind Coope Burton on handpump, wood-burning stove; no dogs (they have a friendly golden retriever themselves). *(Recommended by Joan Olivier, Mike O'Driscoll, Mrs M E Lawrence; more reports please)*

Halls (Allied) Licensees Mike and Pam Carr Real ale Meals and snacks (12–2, 7–10) Children in dining area Open 11–3, 5.30–11 all year; 11–4, 6.30–11.30 Sat; closed 25 Dec

CHALFONT ST PETER SU9990 Map 3
Greyhound

High Street; A413

The long and low-beamed open-plan bar in this handsome old coaching-inn has a friendly and informal atmosphere, with younger people drawn down to one end by the piped pop music there, and plenty of deep red plush seats for quieter chat in the main part. There are brasses on the lantern-lit dark panelling, and, in winter, a huge log fire in a handsome fireplace. Bar food includes home-made soup (£1), sandwiches (from £1.10 – a choice of four breads), ploughman's (from £1.95), filled baked potatoes (from £2.25), chilli con carne (£2.50), home-made shepherd's pie (£2.95), salads (from £3.75), daily specials such as lasagne, and a roast of the day from their carvery (£4.20); readers like the restaurant, too. Well kept Courage Best, Directors and John Smiths on handpump, from a good long counter; fruit machine. There are tables among flower tubs in the pretty front courtyard, with more on a sheltered lawn by the little River Misbourne. Fans of this pub might like to know that the same people also run the Royal Oak in Windsor – and think it even better. *(Recommended by D C Horwood, J F and M I Wallington, John Tyzack; more reports please)*

Courage   Real ale   Meals and snacks (12–2.30, 7–9.30)   Restaurant (midnight supper licence)   Children in eating area and restaurant   Open 11–3, 5.30–11 all year; 11–11 Sat Bedrooms tel Gerrards Cross (0753) 883404; £33/£44

CHESHAM   SP9502 Map 4
Black Horse
The Vale; leaving Chesham on A416 towards Berkhamsted fork left at Hawridge 3, Colesbury 3½ signpost

In the last year or two lots of pubs have filled shelves with old books. Mostly, they're just for show – the sort no one would dream of reading. In this much-extended dining pub, though, they're considerably more interesting. An inglenook takes up much of the small black-beamed low-ceilinged original core; the seating's mainly in a separate heavy-raftered barn and an airy side extension. They specialise in pies, with eight from steak and kidney to rabbit and tarragon or chicken with leeks and walnuts (£4.25); other generously served bar food includes sandwiches (from 95p), soup (95p), filled baked potatoes (from £1.95), ploughman's (£1.95), salads (from £3.50), scampi or gammon and egg (£4.25) and sirloin steak (£5.75). Well kept Benskins Best, Friary Meux Best, Ind Coope Burton and Taylor-Walker Best on handpump; pleasant quick service; piped music. There are lots of well spaced picnic-table sets and a climbing-frame on the big back lawn, with more tables under cocktail parasols in front. *(Recommended by TBB; more reports please)*

Benskins (Allied)   Licensee Roger Wordley   Real ale   Meals and snacks (12–2, 6–9.30) Open 11.30–3, 6–11 all year

COLNBROOK   TQ0277 Map 3
Ostrich
1¼ miles from M4 junction 5; A4 towards Hounslow, then first right on to B3378 – at start of village where main road bends sharply to right keep straight on into Access Only village High Street

If you had a foreign friend flying through who wanted to see a traditional English pub and had just an hour or two between flights at Heathrow, this would be an obvious choice. Its striking Elizabethan timbered façade, jettied out over the village street, still has a coach entry, and inside there are heavy beams, big log fireplaces, a grandfather clock, and timbered ochre walls decorated with guns, swords and old pictures of the pub; though the present building is mainly sixteenth century, there's been an inn here since Norman times. They specialise in fresh seafood to some extent, running up to shark steak (£6.95), parrot fish (£8.95) and lobsters or langoustines, with other bar food from Camembert fritters (£1.95) or cheeses with hot granary bread (£2.30), through home-made steak and kidney pie, salads and vegetarian dishes, to venison (£7.95), and old-fashioned puddings such as bread-

and-butter pudding (£2.25); Sunday roast is £6.95. Well kept if rather pricey Courage Best and Directors and Youngs on handpump; some interesting wines; maybe discreet piped music. There are picnic-table sets under cocktail parasols in the back car park. *(Recommended by Graham Bush, Simon Collett-Jones)*

Free house   Licensees Derek Lamont and Mervyn Parrish   Real ale   Meals and snacks (11.30–2.30, 6–10.30)   Restaurant tel Slough (0753) 682628   Children in restaurant (and on Sun in bar's eating area)   Open 11–2.30, 6–11 all year; closed 25–26 Dec

FAWLEY   SU7586 Map 2

Walnut Tree   ★   🏵

Village signposted off A4155 and off B480 N of Henley

The good range of imaginative bar food in this friendly Chilterns pub includes soup (£1.30) and plenty of other starters or light snacks such as pâté or nut-stuffed mushrooms with garlic mayonnaise (£2.25), deep-fried Camembert with a gooseberry dip or giant mussels grilled with pesto (£2.95), avocado with prawns (£3.10, baked or plain) and smoked trout with a home-made horseradish dip (£3.15). These are served as generously as some pubs' main dishes, but they also do big servings of such things as mushroom and tarragon burgers (£4.25), home-made eight-ounce hamburgers or home-cooked ham and parsley sauce (£4.50), chicken Kiev or lamb kleftiko (£5.95), duck en croûte or baked scallops (£6.95) and sirloin steak (£7.25); the puddings are good, too. Well kept Brakspears PA and SB on handpump, a good range of wines (including local English ones), decent malt whiskies; pleasant and helpful service. The bar is snug and simply furnished, with a log fire in winter and a warm welcome for walkers – though not a great deal of room; darts, dominoes, cribbage, fruit machine, juke box. Rustic tables are spaced well apart on the big lawn around the front car park; there are some seats in a covered terrace extension – and a hitching rail for riders. *(Recommended by TBB, Margaret Dyke, Roger and Lynda Pilgrim, Gordon Hewitt, June Clark, JMC, CGB, Stanley Matthews, Barbara Hatfield)*

Brakspears   Licensee G W Knight   Real ale   Meals and snacks (12–2 (2.30 weekends), 7–10)   Restaurant tel Turville Heath (049 163) 360/617   Children in public bar's eating area and restaurant   Open 11–3, 6–11; 11–2.30, 6–11 in winter

FINGEST   SU7791 Map 2

Chequers   🏵

Village signposted off B482 Marlow–Stokenchurch

Dating from the fifteenth century, this white-shuttered brick and flint pub is charmingly placed, with views right down the Hambleden valley. Outside, there are lots of new tables under cocktail parasols on spacious lawns flanked by flower beds, with the pastures beyond sloping up to beech woods, and over the road is a unique Norman twin-roofed church tower – probably the nave of the original church. Food from an efficiently run servery gets universal praise from readers, and includes sandwiches (from £1.10), ploughman's (from £1.85), home-made soup or local spicy sausages (£1.95), cottage pie or lasagne (£3.95), chicken and game pie (£4.50), steak and kidney pie (£4.75 – a special favourite here), roast lamb or liver and bacon (£4.95), hot avocado and prawns in cheese sauce (£5) and freshly caught trout (£6.50); there's also a romantic restaurant. The central room of the bar has an eighteenth-century oak settle, some seats built into its black-painted wooden dado, and other chairs of varying ages from ancient to modern; it's decorated with pistols, antique guns and swords, toby jugs, pewter mugs and decorative plates, and has a big log fire. There are comfortable easy chairs in a sunny lounge with French windows leading to the garden. Well kept Brakspears PA, SB and in season Old Ale on handpump; dominoes, cribbage, backgammon. *(Recommended by Dr and Mrs James Stewart, John Day, Roger and Lynda Pilgrim, TBB, Dr Paul Kitchener, Doug Kennedy)*

Brakspears   Licensee Bryan Heasman   Real ale   Meals and snacks (cold buffet only, Sun evening)   Restaurant tel Turville Heath (049 163) 335   Children in eating area and restaurant   Open 11–3, 6–11 all year; closed evening 25 Dec

FORTY GREEN   SU9292 Map 2
Royal Standard of England

3½ miles from M40 junction 2, via A40 to Beaconsfield, then follow sign to Forty Green, off B474 ¾ mile N of New Beaconsfield

One of the most striking pubs in this part of the world, the Royal Standard is justifiably a magnet for tourists, though recently service has been consistently friendly and helpful even when it's packed. Even so, weekday lunchtimes are best if you want to explore the treasures in this ancient, rambling warren: oak settles, finely carved antique panelling, stained glass, old rifles, powder-flasks and bugles, ancient pewter and pottery tankards, lots of brass and copper, needlework samplers, and fine decorated iron firebacks for the open fires – including one from Edmund Burke's old home nearby. The food bar (Charles II, on the run in 1651, is supposed to have hidden in its rafters) does a good soup of the day (£1.25), ploughman's with a good choice of cheeses (£2.50), sausages and chips (£3.50), chicken (£4), a range of home-made pies including venison or pigeon (from £4.25), hot dishes such as plaice, fritto misto or vegetarian flan (£4.50), crab (£4.50) and salmon (£5.50). Well kept Brakspears SB, Huntsman Royal Oak and Marstons Pedigree and Owd Rodger (the beer was originally brewed here, until the pub passed the recipe on to Marstons), and another beer brewed for the pub, on handpump. There are seats outside in a neatly hedged front rose garden, or in the shade of a tree. *(Recommended by Lindsey Shaw Radley, Mr and Mrs D Norton, BKA, Chris Raisin, Graham Doyle, Richard Houghton, Mrs E M Thompson, George and Chris Miller, Nick Dowson, Brian and Rosemary Wilmot, Ewan McCall, Roger Huggins, Tom McLean, Gary Scott)*

Free house   Licensees Philip Eldridge and Alan Wainwright   Real ale   Meals and snacks (12–2.30, 6–10)   Children in area alongside Candle Bar   Open 11–3, 5.30–11 all year; closed evening 25 Dec

FRIETH   SU7990 Map 2
Yew Tree ✪

Village, signposted off B482 N of Marlow, is in Buckinghamshire though it has an Oxfordshire postal address

The Continental touch – Mr Aitzetmuller comes from Austria – shows not just in the good food here, but also in a more thoughtful approach than usual to the drinks side. Besides well kept Arkells, Ruddles County, Theakstons Old Peculier and Websters Yorkshire on handpump, they do gluhwein and several interesting punches, maybe including schnapps, honey and spices in the hot winter ones, and squeezing fresh fruit for delightful cold ones in summer – including non-alcoholic ones; their wines and coffee are good. The bar food might include potato and watercress soup (£1.75), pâté or vegetarian pancakes (£2.65), home-made sausages or bacon pie made with suet pastry (£2.95), stuffed peppers (£3.15), ham and mushroom strudel (£3.50), steamed skate in cheese sauce (£3.95), wiener brathuhn (£4.95) and a dish of the day like stuffed shoulder of veal (around £4.50). The neatly furnished beamed bar has log fires in stripped brick fireplaces at each end – the one on the left's an inglenook, flanked by china cabinets and surmounted by guns; among the animal and sporting pictures, look out for the entertaining fishing engravings by F Naumann. The neat front garden has tables on its lawn and small terrace — they serve out here too. *(Recommended by David Wallington, Mr and Mrs D Norton, V H Balchin, R F Llewellyn*

Free house   Licensees Franz Aitzetmuller and Annie Beckett   Real ale   Meals   Children welcome   Restaurant tel High Wycombe (0494) 882330   Open 11–2.30, 5.30–11 all year; opens 6 in winter

GREAT BRICKHILL   SP9030 Map 4

Old Red Lion

Picnic-table sets in the prettily kept walled back garden have a superb view over Buckinghamshire and far beyond; the Ouzel Valley falls away steeply below. Inside, the two carpeted bars have been gently refurbished, with fresh flowers on the tables and a log fire in the smaller one; there's a comfortable villagey atmosphere. Attractively presented freshly made bar food includes sandwiches (steak sandwich £2.50), ploughman's (£2), basket meals (from £2), cottage pie (£3.50), steak and kidney pie (£4.25), steaks (from £4.65), chicken Kiev (£4.95) and home-made puddings (£1.25); well kept Flowers Original and Wethereds on handpump, decent wines and coffee; dominoes, fruit machine, unobtrusive piped music. There are swings in the garden. *(Recommended by Lyn and Bill Capper, Mrs M E Lawrence)*

Whitbreads   Licensee Andrew McCollin   Real ale   Meals and snacks (not Sun evening) Children in eating area   Open 11–2.30, 5.30–11 all year

GREAT MISSENDEN   SP8900 Map 4

George ★ ⊛

94 High Street

There's usually a thriving, busy atmosphere in the bar itself, where you'll find the most signs of this fifteenth-century pub's age — small alcoves, attractively moulded heavy beams, timbered walls decorated with prints, a high mantelpiece holding Staffordshire and other figurines over the big log fire, a small carved settle under a handsome oak panel. A snug inner room has a sofa, little settles and a smaller coal fire. But it's really the food that attracts most people — and that's served in a more straightforward (but spaciously comfortable) room. It runs from crab filo-pastry parcels (£2.45) through pasta (£3.35) or seafood platter (£4.05) to eight-ounce gammon (£4.95), several curries (around £5.45) and ten-ounce rump steak (£6.90), with children's dishes (from £1.50) and good puddings; the menu changes frequently. Vegetarian dishes include thick vegetable soup (£1.10), crunchy mixed vegetables (£1.50, weekday lunchtimes), deep-fried Brie or mushrooms (£2.25), fresh pasta or homity (£3.25), spinach and cheese strudel (£4.45) and vegetable Stroganoff (£5.20). On weekday lunchtimes there are also chips with a dip (75p), sandwiches (from £1), filled baked potatoes (from £1.25) and ploughman's (£2.25). They do two sittings in the evenings (you should now book a few days before for Friday and Saturday evening, and for Sunday lunchtime — when you can order a whole joint to carve yourself, and take home anything left). ABC, Bass, Chiltern Beechwood and Wadworths 6X on handpump (well kept under a light carbon dioxide blanket), mulled wine in winter, tea, coffee and so forth; obliging service; bar billiards, shove-ha'penny, fruit machine and piped light music. *(Recommended by BKA, Mr and Mrs T F Marshall, Richard Houghton, Douglas Bail, Mrs J Kingsbury, E J and J W Cutting, J N Phillips, J P Day, Hugh Morgan, Alison Hayward, Nick Dowson, Pat and Dennis Jones)*

ABC (Allied)   Licensees Guy and Sally Smith   Real ale   Snacks (weekday lunchtimes) and meals (12–2, 7–9.45; not Sun evening)   Restaurant Fri–Sat evenings, Sun lunch tel Great Missenden (024 06) 2084   Children in eating area and restaurant   Open 11–2.30 (3 Sat), 6–11 all year

Red Lion

62 High Street

On Tuesdays and Fridays the fish arrives fresh from Billingsgate, giving a wide choice from fried sardines (£1.95) or squid (£2.75) to poached salmon (£5.95); helpings here are big, and their snacks such as home-made pâté, mushrooms and bacon or black pudding with bacon fried in garlic butter (£1.95 – their bacon is good) are quite enough for many people, though other dishes include lambs' kidneys (£3.95), pork chop (£4.50) and lots of steaks (from £5.95). A row of comfortable rooms open into each other, with brocaded wall settles, stools and other seats, sturdy pub tables, an ochre Anaglypta ceiling, varnished wooden dado, small engravings on the papered walls, and in the spacious end dining-room shelves of books and a pretty Victorian fireplace. Well kept Brakspears, Charles Wells Bombardier and Thwaites on handpump; quite well reproduced pop music, fruit machine, space game; cheerful young staff. *(Recommended by Quentin Williamson, G A Farmer)*

Free house   Licensee Andrew Holden   Real ale   Meals and snacks (12–2, 6.30–10; no food 26 Dec)   Restaurant   Well behaved children welcome   Open 11–3, 5.30–11 all year; closed evening 25 Dec   Bedrooms tel Great Missenden (024 06) 2208; £22/£35

HAMBLEDEN   SU7886 Map 2

Stag & Huntsman

Village signposted from A4155

The pretty and neatly kept country garden here backs directly on to the Chilterns beech woods, and in both summer and winter the two small and simply furnished bars fill quickly – especially the low-ceilinged and closely furnished lounge. Though some prices are up quite a bit since last year, most readers still find good value in the home-made bar food, which includes soup (£1.95), ploughman's (from £2.35), smoked salmon pâté (£2.50), chilli nachos (£3), lasagne or steak and kidney pie (£4.25), crab salad (£4.75), fresh scallops in ginger and onion sauce (£5.50), evening steaks from the good village butcher (£8) and puddings (from £1.95); at really busy times the choice may be much curtailed. Brakspears PA and SPA, Flowers Original, Huntsman Royal Oak and Wadworths 6X on handpump, with a guest beer such as Wadworths Farmers Glory; helpful landlord; fruit machine in public bar. *(Recommended by Margaret Dyke, Margaret and Trevor Errington, Alison Hayward, Nick Dowson, J Maloney, Lindsey Shaw Radley, G B Longden)*

Free house   Licensees Mike and Janet Matthews   Real ale   Meals and snacks (not Sun evening)   Restaurant   Children no longer allowed   Open 11–2.30, 6–11 all year; closed evening 25 Dec   Bedrooms tel Henley (0491) 571227; £35S/£35S

HAWRIDGE COMMON   SP9406 Map 4

Full Moon

Follow Hawridge sign off A416 N of Chesham and keep on towards Cholesbury; OS Sheet 165 reference 945062

While so many country pubs nosedive into refurbished uniformity, this unspoilt heavy-beamed tavern by the common still keeps its shiny black built-in floor-to-ceiling settles and ancient polished flagstones and flooring tiles, with real logs

The Post Office makes it virtually impossible for people to come to grips with British geography by using a system of post towns which are often across the county boundary from the places they serve. So the postal address of a pub often puts it in the wrong county. We use the correct county – the one the pub is actually in. Lots of pubs which the Post Office alleges are in Oxfordshire are actually in Berkshire, Buckinghamshire, Gloucestershire or the Midlands.

instead of a log-effect gas fire burning in its inglenook; the hunting prints are genuine, and have been there a good long time. Service is old-fashioned, too, in the best sense. Simple but wholesome food includes pasties (£1.20), ploughman's (from £1.90), salads (from £2.60) and maybe one or two hot dishes such as soup (90p), lasagne or steak and kidney pudding (£2.50). Well kept Flowers and Wethereds SPA on handpump, with Winter Royal when it's available; well priced Rombouts coffee, friendly service. A couple of more modern little rooms lead off; it can get smoky if it's busy. Picnic-table sets and rustic seats are set out among fruit trees on a spacious side lawn with roses along its low flint wall. *(More reports please)*

Whitbreads   Licensee Wally Pope   Real ale   Meals (weekday lunchtimes) and snacks (lunchtime, not Sun)   Open 11.30–2.30, 6–11 all year; closed evening 25 and 26 Dec

IBSTONE   SU7593 Map 4

Fox   🏨

1¾ miles from M40 junction 5: unclassified lane leading S from motorway exit roundabout; pub is on Ibstone Common

Now describing itself – quite properly – as a country hotel, this seventeenth-century inn has been considerably extended and refurbished over the last few years, but still has its log fires and low beams, with high-backed settles, country seats and old village photographs in the comfortable lounge, and pine settles and tables on the wood-block floor of the public bar. Home-made bar food includes generous sandwiches (from £1.20), several substantial ploughman's (from £2.50), vegetarian dishes or fish (from £3.75), home-made steak and kidney pie or turkey and leek pie (£4.50), popular seasonal game casseroles, and puddings such as bread-and-butter or treacle tart (£1.50); there's also a smart restaurant. In summer there are decent cook-it-yourself barbecues in the rose garden, which is prettily lit by old lamps. Well kept Brakspears PA and SB, Flowers Original, Greene King Abbot and in season Wethereds Winter Royal on handpump, with several imported bottled lagers, Westons farm cider, and decent wines by the glass; friendly service; darts, shove-ha'penny, dominoes and cribbage in the public bar, maybe unobtrusive piped music. The pub overlooks the village common and its cricket ground, with good Chilterns walking nearby. *(Recommended by AP, Joan Olivier, V H Balchin; more reports please)*

Free house   Licensees Ann and David Banks   Real ale   Meals and snacks (12–2, 7–10) Restaurant   Children in eating area   Open 11–3, 6–11   Bedrooms tel Turville Heath (049 163) 289/722; £48S/£60S

LACEY GREEN   SP8100 Map 4

Pink & Lily

Parslow's Hillock; from A4010 High Wycombe–Princes Risborough follow Loosley Row signpost, and in that village follow Great Hampden, Great Missenden signpost; OS Sheet 165 reference 826019

This spaciously extended and modernised dining pub is popular for good value simple home-cooked food including filled baked potatoes (£2.50), open sandwiches (from £2.50, steak £2.95), steak and kidney or cod and prawn pie (£3.25), lasagne (£3.50), goulash (£3.75) and Sunday roast beef (£3.95). The airy main bar has low pink plush seats, with more intimate side areas and an open fire; a quite separate little tap-room is preserved very much as it used to be in the days when this was a favourite pub of Rupert Brooke's, with traditional furniture and a big inglenook fireplace – not to mention shove-ha'penny, dominoes and cribbage. Well kept Adnams, Brakspears PA and SB, Flowers Original, Glenny Hobgoblin, Wadworths 6X and Wethereds on handpump; good friendly service. The sizeable garden has lots of rustic tables and seats; boules in summer. *(Recommended by Mr and Mrs T F Marshall, Nick Dowson, Alison Hayward, Roger and Lynda Pilgrim, A D Button, CGB)*

Free house Licensees Clive and Marion Mason Real ale Meals and snacks Well behaved children in eating area until 7.30 Open 11.45 (11 Sat)–3, 6–11 all year

LANE END SU7991 Map 2

Old Sun

B482 Marlow–Stokenchurch

Pretty outside, this village pub is firmly traditional inside: three communicating areas with snug side recesses, cushioned wooden wall seats, a low shiny ochre ceiling, brasses, old prints and cartoons on the walls and a big log fire towards the back. The atmosphere's lively and warmly welcoming. Good value simple bar food includes toasted sandwiches (£1.10), ploughman's (£2.50; with several cheeses £3), deep-fried Brie or fettuccine romana (£2.75), burgers (£2.95), spinach and mushroom lasagne (£3.25) and prawns or a giant helping of filled potato skins (£3.50); well kept Flowers Original, Wethereds and a guest beer such as Marstons Pedigree on handpump; darts, shove-ha'penny, table skittles, cribbage, dominoes, unobtrusive piped pop music. Picnic-table sets under cocktail parasols on grass at the side look out over the nearby woods. *(Recommended by Nick Dowson, Alison Hayward, Algis and Lesley Kuliukas, Richard Houghton)*

Wethereds Licensee Malcolm Raven Real ale Meals and snacks (12–2, 6–9) Children welcome Singer fortnightly, Thurs or Fri Open 11–2.30, 6–11 (11–3, 5.30–11 Sat) all year; closed 25 Dec

LEY HILL SP9802 Map 4

Swan

Village signposted from A416 in Chesham

This last year, the wall of the separate no-smoking room has been knocked through. It's still no-smoking, but now forms part of the main carpeted bar – making that even more rambling: low heavy black beams, black oak props, snugs and alcoves with cushioned window and wall seats around country tables, an old kitchen range with a club fireguard, another big fireplace flanked by signposted cricket bats, and fresh flowers on the neat bar counter. Besides four or five dishes of the day served with fresh vegetables, such as smoked halibut with prawns or baked curried crab, bar food has included home-made French onion soup, sandwiches, ploughman's, filled baked potatoes, vegetarian pancake or lasagne, salads, several enterprising pies such as cod with prawns, mussels and crab (most main dishes around £3.25 to £4), rump steak; new licensees took over in summer 1989, so there may well be changes. Well kept Ind Coope Burton on handpump, with a couple of guest beers such as Adnams and Youngs Special. Outside is pretty, with hanging baskets and tubs of flowers; picnic-table sets on the front terrace and side lawn face the common, and the back garden has now been opened up, with more tables on a terrace there, and a climbing-frame. *(Recommended by Stephen King, D C Bail, Mr and Mrs T F Marshall, Mr and Mrs F W Sturch, Lyn and Bill Capper, John Tyzack, David Tench)*

Benskins (Allied) Licensees Matthew and Teresa Lock Real ale Meals and snacks (until 8.30; not Sun evening or 25 Dec; set Sun lunch) Open 11–2.30, 5.30 (6 Sat)–11 all year

LITTLE HAMPDEN SP8503 Map 4

Rising Sun 🏵

Village signposted from back road (ie W of A413) Great Missenden–Stoke Mandeville; pub at end of village lane; OS Sheet 165 reference 856040

Since being taken over late last year by people who'd earned a high reputation for good food at the nearby Plough at Hyde Heath, this comfortable and isolated

Chilterns pub has won a good deal of praise for imaginative cooking – even on Sundays. The menu changes every quarter; in summer, for instance, it might include home-made soup (£1.35), sandwiches (from £1.75 – though one reader found nothing cheaper than prawns, at £2.45), ploughman's (£2.75), crab and cucumber mousse (£2.95), chicory and watercress salad with chicken livers (£3.95), scallops with bacon, fresh anchovy fillets and garlic bread (£4.95), salmon with wine and dill (£6.95), steaks (from £7.50) and sweet-and-sour king prawns (£8.45), with specials such as spinach and mushroom pancakes (£4.95) and puddings such as mango and banana almond crumble (£1.75). Hardly surprisingly, dining-tables now dominate the bar – smarter now, with new stripped pine panelling, and carpeting throughout; it's been opened up to include the former restaurant extension. There's an attractive inglenook fireplace at the front. Well kept Adnams, Sam Smiths OP and King & Barnes Festive on handpump, with guest beers such as Batemans XXXB or another King & Barnes beer, and Hacker-Pschorr lager from Munich; the bar games have all gone now. There are tables out on the terrace by the sloping front grass. At weekends it attracts walkers (as long as they leave their boots – and dogs – outside), who reach it by the tracks leading on through the woods in various directions; the pub's on *Good Walks Guide* Walk 71, which takes in Hampden House and Coombe Hill (National Trust – with fine views). *(Recommended by Michael and Alison Sandy, Colin Price, Asher and Sarah Rickayzen, BKA, Lindsey Shaw Radley, Lyn and Bill Capper, Mr and Mrs T F Marshall, Stephen King, D J Cooke, Ken and Barbara Turner, J N Phillips, Mark Evans, Nick Dowson, Alison Hayward)*

Free house   Licensee Rory Dawson   Real ale   Meals and snacks (not Sun evening, Mon) Children in eating area   Open 11.30–2.30, 6.30–11 all year; closed Sun evening, all day Mon (exc bank hol lunchtimes); opens 7 in winter; may close over/after Christmas

LITTLE HORWOOD   SP7930 Map 4

Shoulder of Mutton

Back road 1 mile S of A421 Buckingham–Bletchley

At weekends and in the evenings the atmosphere positively buzzes in this half-timbered partly thatched medieval pub. The T-shaped quarry-tiled bar has been recently redecorated; it has a huge fireplace at one end, and sturdy seats around chunky rustic tables. Bar food includes sandwiches and hot light snacks (from £1.30), a decent ploughman's, and main dishes (from £3.50) such as lamb cooked in beer, steak and kidney pie, beef in Guinness with hazelnut-stuffed prunes, and T-bone steak (£8.50). Well kept ABC Best and Everards Tiger on handpump; pleasant service; darts, shove-ha'penny, cribbage, dominoes and fruit machine in the games area; piped music. The pub, crowned by a striking arched chimney, is backed by a garden with plenty of tables, and is prettily set beside the churchyard. *(Recommended by Nick Dowson, Alison Hayward; more reports please)*

ABC (Allied)   Licensee June Fessey   Real ale   Meals and snacks (not Mon or Sun evenings)   Dining-room tel Winslow (029 671) 2514   Children in dining-room until 9 Open 11–2.30, 6–11 all year; 11–11 Sat

MARLOW   SU8586 Map 2

Ship

West Street (A4155 towards Henley)

Cosy and interesting, this traditional town local has a fine collection of warship photographs and sundry pieces of nautical hardware in its twin very low-beamed communicating rooms. Bar food includes sandwiches (from 95p), toasties (from £1.10), salads (from £1.75), ploughman's (£2), filled baked potatoes (£2.15), home-made lasagne, pizzas and steak and oyster pie (£3.50). Well kept Marstons Pedigree and Wethereds and SPA on handpump, with Winter Royal in season; fruit machine, piped music. A back courtyard terrace, smartened up recently, has tables among tubs of flowers. *(Recommended by Jon Wainwright, TBB, Quentin Williamson; more reports please)*

Wethereds (Whitbreads)   Licensees Peter Miller and Mr and Mrs Harpur   Real ale Lunchtime meals and snacks   Evening restaurant tel Marlow (062 84) 4360   Children in restaurant   Nearby parking may be difficult in daytime   Open 11–3, 5.30–11; open all day Fri and Sat

Two Brewers

St Peter Street; at double roundabout approaching bridge turn into Station Road, then first right

On a quiet evening you can hear the swish of a Thames weir from the front benches – though the stretch of water you see at the end of the alley is calm. There are more rustic seats in a sheltered back courtyard. Inside, shiny black woodwork, nautical pictures and gleaming brassware give the low-beamed T-shaped bar a traditional air. A wide choice of bar food includes sandwiches (from £1.20), ploughman's (£2.50), filled baked potatoes (£2.60), chilli con carne (£3.40), decent salads (£4.50), plaice fingers (£4.60) and good moules marinière (£4.80). Well kept Flowers Original, Marstons Pedigree and Wethereds on handpump, traditional cider, decent wines, tea and coffee; maybe piped music. They've converted the former functions room into a second, no-smoking restaurant area. *(Recommended by Jon Wainwright, Richard Houghton, W J G Wingate, J P Day, TBB, IP)*

Whitbreads   Licensee F W J Boxall   Real ale   Meals and snacks   Restaurant (not Sun evening in winter)   Children in restaurant unless pub too busy   Open 11–3, 5.30–11 all year; may open all day Sat and bank hols   Bedrooms tel Marlow (062 84) 4140; /£38

MARSH GIBBON   SP6423 Map 4

Greyhound

Back road about 4 miles E of Bicester; pub SW of village, towards A41 and Blackthorn

In front of this stone-built, largely eighteenth-century pub is a neat flower-filled garden with silvery stone tables; there's a more spacious garden at the back, too, with swings and a climbing-frame tucked among the trees – children like the ponies looking out of their stables. Inside is quietly old-fashioned, with comfortable heavy armed seats on the unusual hexagonal flooring tiles, stripped beams and masonry, and a finely ornamented iron stove. Home-made food includes sandwiches, soup, burgers (from £1.95) and salads; some current favourites are meat ploughman's (£2.75), lasagne, Cumberland sausages in red wine and onions, and home-made steak and kidney pie (all £3.75); well kept Fullers London Pride and Greene King Abbot and IPA on handpump; shove-ha'penny, dominoes, cribbage, piped music. *(Recommended by Brian and Anna Marsden, Janet and Gary Amos, Alan Skull, P J Taylor, Nick Dowson)*

Free house   Real ale   Meals and snacks (not Sun evening)   Restaurant tel Stratton Audley (086 97) 365   Children allowed   Open 11–3, 6–11 all year

MARSWORTH   SP9114 Map 4

Red Lion

Vicarage Road; follow village signpost off B489 Dunstable–Aylesbury

Partly thatched, this unspoilt and relaxed eighteenth-century pub is close to an impressive flight of locks on the Grand Union Canal. Inside, there's quite a contrast between the attractively basic tiled-floor main bar (pews, an ancient curved and high-backed settle, two open fires, a lively games area) and the small genteel parlour, up a step or two (pretty china corner cupboard, big pictures of boats). The rambling layout also includes a little front snug bar, and a back buttery which serves sandwiches (£1.20), a choice of ploughman's (£2), salads, a curry

(£3–£4.50), a home-made pie (£3–£4.50) and sirloin steak (£7). Well kept ABC Best, Bass, Everards Tiger and Wadworths 6X on handpump, Westons vintage cider, a good clutch of malt whiskies and decent house wines; friendly service; darts, bar billiards, shove-ha'penny, cribbage, dominoes, fruit machine, space game. A small sheltered back garden has picnic-table sets, and more face the quiet lane in front. There is a nearby nature reserve. We had some rather mixed reports from readers as we went to press in summer 1989 – more reports please.
(Recommended by Janet and Gary Amos, Dr Paul Kitchener)

ABC (Allied)   Licensee Peter Goodwin   Real ale   Meals and snacks (not Sun)   Children in games area until 8.30   Open 11–3, 6–11 all year

MEDMENHAM   SU8084 Map 2
Dog & Badger
A4155 Henley–Marlow

A pleasant short walk takes you down to the Thames from here; inside, the pub is comfortably modernised, welcoming and neatly kept. The big, busy bar has banquettes and stools around the tables, low oak beams, some dating back to the fifteenth century, soft lighting, brasses, patterned carpet and an open fire (as well as an illuminated oven). Reasonably priced and attractively presented straightforward bar food includes good sandwiches, enterprising filled baked potatoes, ploughman's, pizza, ham and egg and steak and kidney pie; well kept Flowers Original, Wethereds and Whitbreads Pompey Royal on handpump; unobtrusive piped pop music, cribbage, dominoes, trivia; efficient service. *(Recommended by Ian Meredith, Lyn and Bill Capper, Don Mather, Alison Hayward, Nick Dowson)*

Whitbreads   Licensee W F Farrell   Real ale   Meals and snacks   Restaurant tel Henley-on-Thames (0491) 571362   Children in eating area and restaurant   Open 11–3, 5.30–11 all year

NORTHEND   SU7392 Map 4
White Hart

Recent reports speak promisingly for the couple who've taken over this snug and largely unspoiled Chilterns pub. Their food includes sandwiches (£1), soup (from £1), a choice of pâtés (from £1.50), ploughman's with home-made chutney (£1.50), and hot dishes changing from day to day, such as lentil crumble (£3.75), stufatina alla romana (an Italian beef dish, £4.25), steak and kidney pie done with Old Ale (£4.75) and sirloin steak (£6.50); puddings (£1.50) are firmly traditional – spotted dick, bread-and-butter. The partly panelled bar has good log fires (one in a vast fireplace), with handsomely carved low oak beams in the cosy older part. A hatch serves the attractive sheltered garden, which has a play area. Well kept Brakspears PA, SB and Old on handpump; friendly service; good walking nearby.
(Recommended by Roger and Lynda Pilgrim, BHP, Michael Thomson, I Meredith, Lyn and Bill Capper, Dr and Mrs E G W Bill)

Brakspears   Licensees Frank and Barbara Nolan   Real ale   Meals and snacks (12–2, 7–10)   Children welcome (lunchtime only)   Open 11–2.30, 6–11 all year; all day Sat

PENN   SU9193 Map 4
Crown
B474

Neat and comfortable, this Chef & Brewer pub has kept quite an individual layout, with well preserved medieval flooring tiles in one room, and an olde-worlde décor; they've even shifted the serving-bar back to its original position, after an experiment with a more streamlined layout. The gardens are a particular attraction: tables among pretty roses facing the fourteenth-century church in front, more tables among tubs of flowers on a series of back terraces which have fine views out over rolling pastures, and slides, swings, climbing-frames and a wooden horse and cart for children; in summer they've had mid-week barbecues. Efficiently served bar food includes sandwiches, ploughman's (£2.25) and hot dishes such as lasagne, chicken in lemon sauce, steak and mushroom pie, chilli con carne and a vegetarian dish (all £3.45); the carvery is popular. Well kept Ruddles Best and County, Trumans Best and Websters Yorkshire on handpump; fruit machine, trivia, juke box or piped music; can be busy evenings and weekend lunchtimes. *(Recommended by Nick Dowson, Mr and Mrs Bain, Mr and Mrs F W Sturch, Mr and Mrs G D Amos, Lindsey Shaw Radley, M C Howells; more reports please)*

Trumans (Watneys)   Manager Peter Holloway   Real ale   Bar meals and snacks (lunchtime; also evening July–Aug)   Restaurant (open noon–10 Sun)   tel Penn (049 481) 2640   Children in eating area and restaurant – also weekday family-room   Open 11.30–2.30, 6–11 all year

nr PRINCES RISBOROUGH   SP8003 Map 4
Red Lion

Upper Icknield Way, Whiteleaf; village signposted off A4010 towards Aylesbury; OS Sheet 165 reference 817040

Dating from the seventeenth century, this quietly placed inn has been modernised in a simple, unfussy style; the new licensees have been adding period furnishings to the low-ceilinged small bar, to join its alcove of cream-painted antique winged settles. There are vases of flowers, small prints on the walls, and a rack of magazines by the log fire. Home-cooked bar food includes sandwiches, filled baked potatoes, ploughman's, lasagne, cottage pie and so forth; the four-course Sunday lunch (£7.95) is popular. Well kept Brakspears PA and SB, Morlands PA and Hook Norton Best on handpump; cribbage, dominoes. Tucked up a quiet village lane close to Whiteleaf Fields (National Trust), the pub attracts walkers at weekends; it has a couple of rustic tables on the neat little side lawn. *(Recommended by Gordon Leighton; more reports please)*

Free house   Licensee R T Howard   Real ale   Meals and snacks (not Sun)   Restaurant Children in restaurant   Open 11.30–3, 5.30–11 all year   Bedrooms tel Princes Risborough (084 44) 4476; £20/£30

SKIRMETT   SU7790 Map 2
Old Crown   ★   ✪

High Street; from A4155 NE of Henley take Hambleden turn and keep on; or from B482 Stokenchurch–Marlow take Turville turn and keep on

The two main rooms of this small village pub are delightfully unspoilt, and quiet during the week; tankards hang from the beams, logs burn in the big fireplace. At weekends all the tables here may be booked, though you may then find room to eat in the little white-painted side room, which has trestle tables, and an old-fashioned settle by its smaller coal fire. The reason for the popularity is the interesting, efficiently served home-cooked bar food, including enterprising soups, ploughman's with good cheeses (from £2.85), well filled baked potatoes (£3.65), chilli con carne (£4.75), chicken done with sherry, ginger and cream (£5.95), a pair of boned pork chops in calvados, herbs and cream (£6.35), salmon poached in white wine, cream and herbs (£6.75), seafood gratin (£6.95), and prawns cooked in garlic butter (£9.25); there's a good choice of puddings such as apple, cinnamon and raisin pie (£1.75) or cheesecake (£1.85). Well kept Brakspears PA, SB and Old Ale are tapped from casks in a still-room and served though a hatch; good value wine; dominoes, cribbage, trivia, shut-the-box. A sheltered front terrace has old oak cask tables and flower tubs; there are picnic-table sets under cocktail parasols on the big back lawn. Note that children under 10 are no longer allowed even in the garden (and they don't serve food out here). The alsatian's called Bruno. *(Recommended by Norman Foot, John Day, J Maloney, Dennis and Pat Jones, Lindsey Shaw Radley, BKA, Geoffrey Griggs)*

Brakspears   Licensees Peter and Liz Mumby   Real ale   Meals and snacks (12–1.45, 7–9.30; not Mon)   Restaurant (not Mon) tel Turville Heath (049 163) 435   Children over 10 may be allowed in tap-room or restaurant   Open 11.30–2.30, 6–11 all year; closed 25 Dec

STOKE GREEN   SU9882 Map 2

Red Lion ⊗

1 mile S of Stoke Poges, off B416 signposted to Wexham and George Green; OS Sheet 175 reference 986824

The friendly New Zealand licensees and staff make for a warm and welcoming atmosphere for everyone – babies and all – in this rambling seventeenth-century former farmhouse. Sturdy high-backed settles form alcoves in the main bar, which has inglenook seats, lots of bric-à-brac, big antique prints and mezzotints including a good Alken steeplechasing series, and fresh flowers. Good value bar lunches served in a no smoking pantry bar include sandwiches, a choice of ploughman's (from £2.20), and hot dishes among which current favourites are lasagne, chilli con carne, chicken casserole done with marmalade, pork with cream and mushrooms and turkey and mushroom pancakes (all £3.50); in the evening food is served only in the back Stables restaurant, decorated in a lively rustic style, and connected to the main pub by a covered walkway. Well kept Charrington IPA and Bass from a chest-high bar counter, lots of lagers, a good choice of wines, winter hot toddies, and tea or coffee; dominoes, cribbage, fruit machine, maybe piped music. There are picnic-table sets under cocktail parasols on the roundel of lawn in front of this attractive wistaria-covered tiled house, and they have summer barbecues on the sheltered back terrace. *(Recommended by Nick Dowson, Lindsey Shaw Radley, TBB and others; more reports please)*

Charringtons   Licensees Brian and Denize O'Connor   Real ale   Meals and snacks (11.30–2.30)   Restaurant (not Sun evening; open until 3.30 Sun afternoon) tel Slough (0753) 21739   Children in pantry bar (not evening) and restaurant   Open 11–2.30, 5.30–11 all year; 11–11 Thurs–Sat; closed evening 25 Dec

nr THE LEE   SP8904 Map 4

Old Swan ⊗

Swan Bottom; back road ¾ mile N of The Lee; OS map 165 reference 902055

The four low-beamed interconnecting rooms of this relaxed country dining pub have an attractive mixture of carpet and flooring tiles, high-backed antique settles and window seats as well as more modern dining-chairs; there's a melodious wall clock, and in winter logs burn in the old iron cooking-range of the sixteenth-century inglenook fireplace. The former stables are now a cosy dining area. In summer the spreading back garden, with plenty of tables among shrubs and flower beds (and a play area) is a particular attraction, with more seats in front of the pretty tiled white pub; they have weekend barbecues then. The main draw, however, is obviously the food: not cheap but very popular, it includes lunchtime sandwiches (from £1.30), soup (£1.60), ploughman's (£2.75 – there's a good honey-roast ham version, too), bangers and mash (£3.25) and chicken and mushroom pie (£3.75); chef Kevin Davis specialises in fish, such as big grilled sardines with crusty bread or plump moules marinière (£3.25), dressed crab (£3.95), seafood pancake (£4), plaice or trout (£4.50), and his puddings (£1.95) are imaginative – lime and mint cheesecake, for instance, or rhubarb and orange pie. In winter there's been a set lunch (around £10) on Sunday, with no bar food then. Particularly well kept Adnams, Morlands and Wadworths 6X on handpump; friendly service, usually but not always quick.

Muddy boots are unwelcome, though the pub's dogs may appear. *(Recommended by Gordon Davico, Richard Houghton, Alan Skull, David Wallington, Gordon Leighton, BKA, DBB; more reports please)*

Free house Licensee Sean Michaelson-Yeates Real ale Meals and snacks Restaurant tel The Lee (024 020) 239 Children in restaurant Open 12–3, 6–11 all year; 12–11 Sat

TURVILLE   SU7690 Map 4

Bull & Butcher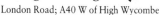

In a glorious Chilterns valley crowned by a white windmill, this black and white timbered cottage is picturesquely set among ancient cottages. Its comfortable low-ceilinged two-room bar has cushioned wall settles, and an old-fashioned high-backed settle by one log fire; a stable half-door lets in a breeze on warm summer days, and walkers are welcome. It's liberally decorated with big motor-racing prints, other photographs, and yachting and photographic bric-à-brac. Good bar food includes a choice of four home-made pies such as fish, chicken and ham, beef in ale (from £3), baked potatoes with a range of fillings (winter, £3.50), summer salads (from £3.50), chicken and asparagus pasta bake (£3.75) and chicken breast with marmalade and coriander (£4.50). Well kept Brakspears PA, SB and Old Ale on handpump, freshly squeezed orange juice, Coates farm cider, decent wines, mulled wine in winter; darts, dominoes, cribbage – with a locals' cards and dice school on Tuesday evenings. There are tables in the pretty garden, among fruit trees and a neatly umbrella-shaped hawthorn; Sunday barbecues out here when it's fine (£3.95), with a weekend children's kiosk. It can get hectic on fine weekends. *(Recommended by Ian Phillips, Chris Raisin, Graham Doyle, John Day, Michael Thomson, Lindsey Shaw Radley, Barbara Hatfield, Martin and Jane Bailey, Nick Dowson)*

Brakspears Licensees Peter Wright and Sandy Watson Real ale Meals and snacks Well behaved children in eating area Guirria – gipsy jazz – every other Thurs Open 11–2.30 (3 or 3.30 Sat), 6–11 all year; closed evening 25, 26 Dec

WEST WYCOMBE   SU8394 Map 4

George & Dragon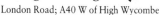
London Road; A40 W of High Wycombe

One of the most striking buildings in this handsome National Trust village, the George & Dragon still has a rare and elegantly mounted lead inn-sign spanning much of the street. Inside, it's comfortably modernised, but the rambling bar still has its massive Tudor beams, sloping walls and a big log fire – and it's reputed to have kept its ghosts, including a wronged girl who haunts the magnificent oak staircase. Consistently good home-cooked bar food using fresh ingredients includes sandwiches (from 80p), soup (£1.30), ploughman's with a choice of cheeses (£2.25), potted Stilton (£2.35), savoury mushrooms and courgettes (£2.95), baked avocado and crab with a cheese sauce (£3.45), interesting home-made pies such as lamb with beer, rum and fruit, or sole and grape in a white wine sauce (£3.55), lamb cutlets (£4.75) and sirloin steak (£5.95); dishes of the day might include pheasant casserole (£3.85) or wild duck breast in pastry with good orange gravy (£5.95), and there are homely puddings (£1.50). It's very popular at weekends – you have to get there early for a seat, though the cheerful service is still usually fairly prompt. Courage Best and Directors on handpump (by the jug, if you want), a good range of whiskies; dominoes, cribbage; the back-to-front clock, in spite of appearances, keeps good time. The arched and cobbled coach entry leads to a spacious, peaceful garden with picnic-table sets, a climbing-frame and slides; the pub is on *Good Walks Guide* Walk 70. We'd be particularly grateful for reports on the bedrooms here – we've no reason to think that the inn does not deserve our place-to-stay award, but have never heard from readers who've stayed here.

(Recommended by Hilarie Miles-Sharp, Ian Phillips, Barbara Hatfield, Prof and Mrs Keith Patchett, Simon Collett-Jones, Lyn and Bill Capper, Mr and Mrs T F Marshall, Mrs M J Dyke, Dennis Jones, Maureen Hobbs, J P Day)

Courage   Licensee Philip Todd   Real ale   Meals and snacks (12–2, 6–10; not Sun evening)   Children in separate room   Open 11–2.30, 5.30–11 all year; all day Sat; closed evening 25, 26 Dec   Bedrooms tel High Wycombe (0494) 464414; £33S(£36B)/£43S(£46B)

WHITCHURCH   SP8020 Map 4

White Swan   ★   ✪

10 High Street; A413 Aylesbury–Buckingham

Owing a great deal to the warm personalities of its licensees, the White Swan is one of the most cheerily relaxed pubs in the county. And though there's nothing fancy about the wide and flexible choice of bar food, it's wholesome and generously good value, including soup (90p), a fine choice of well made sandwiches and toasties (from 70p, triple-deckers from £1.35, good hot salt beef with dill £1.35), ploughman's in wide variety (from £1.50), salads (from £2.25), breakfast grill (£2.50), good omelettes virtually any way you want them (from £2.50), steak and kidney pie or seafood au gratin (£3.50), good gammon and eggs (£4), rump steak (£6.75) and fine puddings (from only 75p); the chunky chips are excellent (they do croquette potatoes too), and service is quick. The irregularly shaped and partly oak-panelled saloon bar has an unaffected mix of seats including old leather-seated dining-chairs and a carved Gothick settle around its chunky elm tables; there are pretty wall lamps, fresh flowers, a longcase clock and a small open fire. This room's named after Charlie, the pub's yellow labrador – alas Sam, the golden retriever who gave his name to the little beamed front bar, has now died after a peaceful old age, though Bertie the budgerigar in the kitchen still sounds in fine fettle. Well kept ABC Best, Bass and Wadworths 6X on handpump, cheap help-yourself coffee; sensibly placed darts, shove-ha'penny, dominoes, cribbage and (in Sam's bar) piped music. Behind the partly thatched old building, a rambling informal garden has picnic-table sets under trees. *(Recommended by Lyn and Bill Capper, Alan Skull, Nick Dowson, Alison Hayward, Michael and Alison Sandy, D L Johnson, M J Morgan, Dr Paul Kitchener, J A Jennings)*

ABC (Allied)   Licensees Rex and Janet Tucker   Real ale   Meals and snacks (12–2, 6–9.45; 12–1.45 Sun, not Sun evening)   Children in separate room   Open 11–2.30, 6–11 all year

WINSLOW   SP7627 Map 4

Bell   🍽

Market Square

The most interesting bar (unfortunately not always open) in this striking black and white timbered inn is a snug little traditional tap-room, so carefully preserved that it still has ancient market documents hanging from the ceiling, as well as leather armchairs on oak floor, and dark wood serving shelves. The two main rooms are comfortably modernised, with plush banquettes and upholstered settles and stools, but still have dark and heavy beams, a good log fire, and seats in a bow window looking out on the bustling square. Bar food includes soup (£1.10), sandwiches (from £1.25, steak £3.95), filled baked potatoes (from £2.25), ploughman's (from £2.50), quiche (£3), basket meals (from £3) and pizzas (£3.95), with daily specials like a roast and steak and kidney pudding (£3.95); the Sunday lunch is good. Well kept Adnams, Hook Norton Best and Old Hookey and Marstons Pedigree on handpump, decent wines, attentive service; unobtrusive piped music. There are

---

Places with gardens or terraces usually let children sit there; we note in the text the very, few exceptions that don't.

tables on the pleasant front terrace. *(Recommended by S V Bishop, M J Morgan, Alison Hayward, Nick Dowson, Lyn and Bill Capper; more reports please)*

*Free house   Licensee William Alston   Real ale   Meals and snacks (not Sun evening)
Restaurant   Children in eating area (and they're planning a children's bar)   Open 10.30–2.30
(3 Sat), 6–11 all year   Bedrooms tel Winslow (029 671) 2741; £45S(£50B)/£50S(£50B)*

WORMINGHALL   SP6308 Map 4

Clifden Arms

Off A40 E of Oxford; take Wheatley turn-off, then Old London Road off A418 (sign easiest to see heading east) on outskirts of Wheatley; pub signposted off road in village

The prettiest pub we know in the county, this black and white sixteenth-century timbered cottage has a profusion of creeper climbing into its steep thatch, and is set by a neat orchard, with fields behind. Inside, a snug little lounge has old-fashioned seats, squint-timbered ochre walls, quite a forest of interesting bottles, brass powder-flasks, black iron vices and tools (it's worth asking the landlord what the unfamiliar ones are for), milk-yokes and so forth hanging from its heavy beams, and a roaring log fire in its big fireplace. A cheerful lino-floored bar, also beamed, has a second fire, and opens into a pool-room; darts, shove-ha'penny, fruit machine, space game, ring the bull (with real horns), maybe unobtrusive piped radio. Good value bar food includes sandwiches (from £1.20; steak £2.25, a monumental club sandwich named after a neighbouring American £4), home-made soup (£1.50), burger (£2), filled baked potatoes (from £2), salmon fishcakes (£2.50), a breakfast grill (£2.95), a hefty ploughman's with five cheeses (£3.50), salads (from £3.50), plaice or omelettes (£4), trout (£5.50) and steaks (from £5.50), with specials such as mushroom and nut fettuccine or lasagne (£3), children's helpings on request, and puddings such as blackberry and apple pancake (£1.55). Well kept Halls Harvest, Ind Coope Burton and Tetleys on handpump, decent coffee. Everyone seems to be friendly – not just the staff, but Porty the Jack Russell, the turtle in the pond, and even the ornamental poultry, ducks, geese and donkeys outside. The attractive garden has a big play area with slides, a boot house, log fort and giant Red Indian, and the village is picturesque and interesting. *(Recommended by Lyn and Bill Capper, Gordon and Daphne; more reports please)*

*Halls (Allied)   Licensees Bob and Gwen Spencer   Real ale   Meals and snacks (11–3, 6–10)
Children in lounge   Open 10.30–3 (4 Sat), 6–11 all year; closed 25 Dec*

Lucky Dip

Besides the fully inspected pubs, you might like to try these Lucky Dips recommended to us and described by readers (if you do, please send us reports):

Amersham [High St (A413); SU9597], *Elephant & Castle*: Low beams, china, velvet and brasses in popular Whitbreads food pub with fine U-shaped bar counter, efficient service, piped music; Wethereds on handpump *(Simon Collett-Jones, LYM)*; [A404], *Saracens Head*: Fifteenth-century Courage pub which has been popular with young people and has had a moderately priced bistro, with efficient service and a pleasant landlord; but restructured and refurnished early 1989 – reports on the new layout and style, please *(LYM)*
Asheridge [SP9404], *Blue Ball*: Excellent play area behind pub; very good food such as chicken curry and lasagne, well kept

Brakspears and other real ales, quiet country location; piped music *(Nigel Paine)*
Ashley Green [A416 Chesham–Berkhamsted; SP9705], *Golden Eagle*: Pleasant, timbered bars with clean and welcoming bars, Ind Coope Burton, good bar food at reasonable prices; pet rabbits in small inner courtyard *(Douglas Bail)*
☆ **Beaconsfield** [Aylesbury End, Old Beaconsfield; SU9490], *Old Hare*: Well kept and increasingly popular pub with low, dark rooms, old beams, high-backed settles, one enormous fireplace with log-effect gas fire and one smaller electric fire; extensive and quite exciting range of lunchtime and evening bar food with three or four

imaginative daily specials, well kept Ind Coope Burton on handpump, small but brightly flowery garden with lots of tables *(Tony Marshall, Pat and Dennis Jones, Ian Phillips)*; [A40, a mile from M40 junction 2] *George*: Smallish bar with friendly service and good bar food that's popular with local office and shop workers; well kept Ind Coope real ales; bedrooms *(John Tyzack, LYM)*; [also A40] *Royal Saracens Head*: Striking timbered facade and, in one corner of the spreading open-plan much-modernised bar, massive beams and timbers; Wethereds real ale, lots of artificial plants, books and knick-knacks, Beefeater steak bar, attractive sheltered courtyard, long history *(Simon Collett-Jones, LYM)*

Botley [Tylers Hill Rd; SP9702], *Five Bells*: Remote, clean and pleasant country pub with inglenook fireplaces, wide choice of real ales, good value lunchtime food – now owned by Sandy Lyle, the golfer; children in eating area *(Mr and Mrs F W Sturch, LYM)*

Bourne End [Hedsor Rd; SU8985], *Old Red Lion*: Pleasant little pub with generous helpings of good bar food, relaxed atmosphere, friendly service, old beams and Courage real ales; often known by the name of its separate restaurant – Masons *(Brian and Rosemary Wilmot, Simon Collett-Jones)*

Butlers Cross [SP8406], *Russell Arms*: Small, clean pub, welcoming and efficient staff, consistently good bar food with light flaky pastry on the pies and decent vegetables – the puddings are well made, too *(Joan Chenhalls)*

Cadmore End [OS Sheet 175 reference 785927; SU7892], *Old Ship*: Unspoilt and old-fashioned simple little country pub *(Roger and Lynda Pilgrim)*

☆ **Cadsden** [Lower Cadsden – OS Sheet 165 reference 825045; SP8204], *Plough*: Good, rustic atmosphere, warm welcome (provided walkers remove their boots), attractively refurbished in old-fashioned style with Turkey carpet, chintz curtains, dark oak tables; Benskins Best, Friary Meux Best and Ind Coope Burton on handpump, wide choice of wines including mulled wine, and good range of well presented food; friendly, efficient service – new landlord previously did well at the Black Horse, Chesham Vale; on GWG71 *(D J Cooke, R M Savage)*

Chalfont Common [TQ0092], *Dumb Bell*: Comfortably refurbished country pub with good value simple food and well kept Courage *(LYM)*

Chalfont St Giles [High St; village signposted off A413; SU9893], *Feathers*: Cosy and cheerful low-beamed local, handy for Milton's cottage, with well kept Whitbreads-related real ales, lunchtime food, comfortable settees, good open fires, friendly service and seats outside – in summer it's beautifully decked out with flower baskets and boxes *(Alison Hayward, Nick Dowson, TBB, Simon Collett-Jones, LYM)*; [Silver Hill;

SU9893] *Fox & Hounds*: Local with limited range of good value lunchtime food including well filled sandwiches and ploughman's, and atmosphere made by dry-humoured landlord *(Alison Hayward, Nick Dowson)*; [A413] *Pheasant*: Friendly place with good, simple food (not Mon evening) *(John Tyzack)*

Chalfont St Peter [Copthall Lane; SU9990], *Waggon & Horses*: Comfortable, spotlessly clean local with small single bar, making considerable efforts on the food side (home-roasted gammons, home-made pastry), with well kept beer *(Anon)*

Cheddington [Station Rd; by stn, about a mile from village; SP9217], *Rosebery Arms*: Solid former railway-junction hotel, clean and tidy, sympathetically refurbished rather in the style of an Edwardian chop-house, with old pictures and so forth; decent food (runner-up in *PubCaterer* 1988 steak and kidney pie competition), reasonably priced beer and house wine; children welcome *(John Francis)*

☆ **Chenies** [Chesham Rd; TQ0198], *Red Lion*: Lavishly refurbished pub with lots of character in U-shaped main bar (look out for the long step which rather merges into the brown carpet), small back snug, dining-room with wide and interesting choice of good value well presented bar food, well kept Benskins Best, Ind Coope Burton and Tetleys; no piped music or fruit machines, good atmosphere, friendly landlord; convenient for Chenies Manor which is open 2–5 Weds, Thurs Apr–Oct *(Lyn and Bill Capper, R M Savage, Mr and Mrs R P Begg, David Wallington, B R Shiner)*

Chesham [SP9501], *George & Dragon*: Extensively refurbished seventeenth-century pub with thick beams in the low ceilings, little alcoves, period pictures and fine fireplace; Benskins Best, Ind Coope Burton and Tetleys, standard bar food and copies of *Beano* in the gents lavatories; pity about the piped music in such a characterful pub *(Gwen and Peter Andrews)*; [Waterside; SP9502] *Pheasant*: Well kept beer and good value bar food (pretty simple at weekends) in pleasant and popular Benskins conversion – log-effect gas fires, areas where once there were rooms; garden by River Chess *(John Tyzack, David Wallington)*; [Church St] *Queens Head*: Neat, warm local with coal fire in each bar, excellent Brakspears, well presented basic pub food from separate servery *(David and Flo Wallington)*

Coleshill [SU9495], *Magpies*: Real welcome from licensee, mixed clientele creating warm, lively atmosphere, no juke box; well kept Benskins Best, reasonably priced bar food *(Richard Houghton)*; *Red Lion*: Good food in bar and restaurant *(Lyn and Bill Capper)*

Colnbrook [High St – nr M4 junction 5; TQ0277], *Red Lion*: Great atmosphere and service, with genuine welcome even for strangers; good helpings of nicely prepared reasonably priced food, well kept Courage Best, log fire in cosy, low-ceilinged bar *(R Houghton)*

☆ **Cuddington** [Upper Church St (village signposted from A418 Thame–Aylesbury); SP7311], *Red Lion:* Olive-green plush chairs, stools and sofa and dimpled copper tables in discreetly chintzy small lounge with big inglenook fireplace, well kept ABC Best and maybe Bass or Tetleys on handpump, and – under new licensees – rewarding restaurant food including a good choice of vegetarian, fish, chicken and steak dishes; also lots of starters, and bar food such as soup, sandwiches, ploughman's and hot dishes; piped music, friendly efficient service, garden with play area *(Don and Margaret Wrattan, Lyn and Bill Capper, Mike O'Driscoll, I Meredith, BB)*

Denham [¾ mile from M40 junction 1; follow Denham Village signs; TQ0486], *Falcon:* One-roomed pub with character and style *(B R Shiner)*; *Swan:* Neatly renovated bar with friendly staff, well kept Courage real ales, bar food often including interesting daily specials and good hot salt beef rolls, coal fire, maybe piped music; extensive floodlit garden with children's play house *(Henry Midwinter, Ian Phillips, TBB, Michael and Alison Sandy, LYM)*

☆ **Dinton** [Stars Lane; take New Road signposted Dinton off A418 SW of Aylesbury at Gibraltar; SP7611], *Seven Stars:* Pretty white pub tucked away in quiet village, popular for attractively priced bar food from soup, sandwiches and ploughman's to home-made pies and salads, with specials such as ham and egg or pork schnitzel; neat modernised lounge, more interesting public bar with glossily varnished ancient built-in settles by vast stone inglenook, well kept ABC Best and maybe Tetleys on handpump, tables on sheltered terrace and lawn, restaurant *(Lyn and Bill Capper, BB)*

Dorney [Village Rd; SU9179], *Palmers Arms:* Adventurous lunchtime and evening bar food with emphasis on fish, in popular pine and stripped brick bar with big eating area, discreet piped music, friendly service, well kept Bass and Charrington IPA, reasonable wine list, restaurant; attractive garden behind *(Simon Collett-Jones, Ian Phillips)*

Downley [OS Sheet 165 reference 849959; SU8594], *Le De Spencer:* Unpretentious pub hidden away on common, fairy-lit loggia overlooking lawn, friendly landlord, Wethereds SPA on handpump, snacks *(LYM)*

Eton Wick [17 Eton Wick Rd; SU9478], *Shepherds Hut:* Welcoming licensees, simple but comfortable bar, well kept Friary Meux Best, good bar food, reasonable prices *(R Houghton)*

Farnham Common [A355 opposite Saab garage; SU9684], *Royal Oak:* Welcoming and comfortable pub with well kept Courage ales, large wine list, good value bar food, garden *(R M Savage)*

Farnham Royal [Farnham Rd; SU9583], *Dukes Head:* Pleasant atmosphere inside, well kept Courage ales, good food at acceptable prices, friendly service *(R Houghton)*

Flackwell Heath [SU8988], *Green Man:* Popular, with friendly service (may be slow Sat), good value food from wide-ranging menu (even fish-and-chip takeaways); children's room *(Peter Powrie)*

☆ **Ford** [village signposted between A418 and B4009, SW of Aylesbury; SP7709], *Dinton Hermit:* Good atmosphere in snug stone cottage with good value food (not Sun or Mon) such as soup, sandwiches, ploughman's, baked potatoes, salads and fish and other main-course dishes, well kept ABC Best and Ind Coope Burton on handpump, friendly service; comfortable log-fire lounge on right, more interesting scrubbed-table public bar with wood-burning stove in huge inglenook on left, attractive sheltered country garden with play area *(Lyn and Bill Capper, BB; more reports on this nice pub please)*

Fulmer [Windmill Rd; SU9985], *Black Horse:* Simple but remarkably popular Courage pub; real ales, bar food, small garden *(I Meredith)*

Gayhurst [B526; SP8446], *Sir Francis Drake:* Charmingly incongruous Gothick traceried and pinnacled building, cosy inside, strong on spirits and cocktails (beers are keg); not cheap *(LYM)*

Gerrards Cross [A40 E; TQ0087], *Apple Tree:* Comfortable atmosphere and pleasant, attentive staff; usual Whitbreads ales and good variable range of bar snacks; Beefeater restaurant *(AP)*

Great Hampden [on corner of Hampden Common – OS Sheet 165 reference 845015; SP8401], *Hampden Arms:* Small pub by common with cricket green; two cosy bars, pleasant young licensees, wide choice of food at prices that are reasonable for the area; cats seem to go where they like *(Mr and Mrs F W Sturch, Mrs Olive Way)*

Great Horwood [SP7731], *Swan:* Friendly and comfortable old pub, good bar food – especially ploughman's, steak and kidney pie, chilli con carne *(Mrs M E Lawrence)*

Great Linford [4½ miles from M1, junction 14; from Newport Pagnell take Wolverton Rd towards Stony Stratford; SP8542], *Black Horse:* Genuinely pubby atmosphere in spacious rambling pub just below the Grand Union Canal embankment, well kept ABC Best, Ind Coope Burton and another beer such as Everards Tiger on handpump, good range of popular bar food, garden including biggish play area; children allowed in restaurant *(Dave Braisted, LYM)*

Great Missenden [Mobwell; SP8900], *Black*

Horse: Decent food, well kept Morrells *(J N Phillips)*; *Cross Keys*: Pleasant bar with good choice of beers and adjoining eating area with buffet and hot dishes such as lasagne and pizza *(Norman Foot)*

Hawridge [The Vale; village signposted from A416 N of Chesham – OS Sheet 165 reference 960050; SP9505], *Rose & Crown*: Around eight well kept real ales on handpump (attracting lots of young people in the evening), masses of whiskies, bar food (no evening hot dishes); big log fire in spaciously refurbished open-plan bar, broad terrace with lawn dropping down beyond, play area ; children allowed *(LYM)*

☆ **Hedgerley** [SE of M40 junction 2, at junction Parish Lane and Collum Green Rd – OS Sheet 175 reference 968863; SU9686], *One Pin*: Cheerfully welcoming family-run pub with good value, straightforward and freshly prepared bar food, consistently good service, well kept Courage ales *(AP, Nick Dowson)*

Hedsor [SU9187], *Garibaldi*: Lovely pub, pleasant owner, good food with superb pizzas *(Mrs R Wilmot)*; [Cores End Rd] *Heart in Hand*: Pleasant, vibrant atmosphere with predominantly young customers, comfortable interior and well kept Whitbreads *(Richard Houghton)*

Holmer Green [SU9097], *Bat & Ball*: Small pub overlooking village green and football pitch; friendly landlord, wide range of excellent bar food, garden *(W A Lund)*; [Earl Howe Rd] *Earl Howe*: Honest down-to-earth local, friendly and spotlessly clean; acceptable real ale, simple good value food *(Anon)*; [New Pond Rd] *Valiant Trooper*: Cosy pub in village centre; well kept ales, good attractively priced bar food including home-made pies, restaurant *(J N Phillips)*

Hyde Heath [village signposted off B485 Great Missenden–Chesham; SU9399], *Plough*: Prettily placed little pub with chatty local atmosphere in freshly furnished long bar, well kept Benskins Best and Ind Coope Burton, open fires; has been very popular for exceptionally interesting food, but since the licensee moved to the Rising Sun at Little Hampden we've had too few reports to judge current state of affairs *(LYM – more news please)*

Iver [146 Swallow St; TQ0381], *Oddfellows Arms*: Large old free house divided into small areas, roaring fire and cosy atmosphere; obliging licensee, well kept Courage and Youngs beers, extensive lunchtime bar food *(Richard Houghton)*

Ivinghoe [SP9416], *Kings Head*: Comfortable, well organised pub with attentive, polished service; good bar food *(Anon)*

☆ **Kingswood** [A41; SP6919], *Crooked Billet*: Well kept ABC Best, maybe other real ales, and good value bar food served efficiently in picturesque pub near Waddesdon Manor;

well kept carpeted lounge, low-ceilinged public bar with inglenook, restaurant, garden with swings *(Mrs P J Pearce)*

Little Kingshill [Hare La; SU8999], *Full Moon*: Spacious and reasonably comfortable, given a thoroughgoing brasses-copper-and-riding-crops refurbishment but quiet and homely, which has had friendly service and cheap but traditional bar food (not Sun evening), very popular with older people *(Mr and Mrs T F Marshall, J N Phillips)*

Little Marlow [Church Rd; off A4155 about two miles E of Marlow, pub signposted off main rd; SU8786], *Kings Head*: Quiet, relaxing and cosy lounge with dark oak panelling, low beams, real fire, settles, wooden chairs, brass gongs and keg taps on walls – used virtually wholly as dining area weekday lunchtime; welcoming licensees, well kept Wethereds and other Whitbreads-related beers, quick service *(Richard Houghton, Nick Dowson)*

Little Missenden [SU9298], *Red Lion*: Simple country pub with large coal fire and attractive old kitchen range, friendly staff, real ales and fresh, home-cooked bar food at reasonable prices – genuine dishes, such as liver and bacon, roast lamb, plum and apple pie *(R J Groves)*

Littleworth Common [2 miles from M40 junction 2 – off A355; SU9487], *Jolly Woodman*: Alone on the edge of Burnham Beeches, and handy for Cliveden (NT); beamed and cottagey yet pleasantly extended, with good atmosphere, clean surroundings and wide range of hot and cold bar food served efficiently, including well presented puddings; the real ale has not been one of its particular points of appeal *(R Houghton, Mr and Mrs F W Sturch, P Gillbe, LYM)*

Long Crendon [Bicester Rd (B4011); SP6808], *Angel*: Attractively refurbished partly seventeenth-century pub with bar food and real ales such as Brakspears, Flowers, Wethereds and Worthington *(Roger and Lynda Pilgrim, Revd Brian Andrews)*; [Bicester Rd] *Chandos Arms*: Small elaborately thatched country pub with well presented reasonably priced food from sandwiches, filled baps and salads to particularly good steaks, in two low-beamed communicating bars with lots of brass and copperware; log fire, darts and shove ha'penny; Wethereds and Whitbreads real ales, friendly and efficient service *(Lyn and Bill Capper, D S Kennedy)*

Loudwater [Derchams Lane; SU8990], *Blacksmiths Arms*: Tiny pub, friendly atmosphere, 1960s piped music, bar food, good barbecues; bedrooms *(Brian and Rosemary Wilmot)*; *General Havelock*: Pleasant little pub with old-fashioned décor, huge helpings of good bar food, lots of bar nibbles Sun *(Mrs R Wilmot)*

☆ **Marlow** [Henley Rd; SU8586], *Hare &*

Hounds: Ivy-clad cottage on outskirts, with calm, almost club-like atmosphere but warm welcome for strangers, dove-grey carpeted bar on different levels, two log-effect gas fires; charming licensee, Wethereds Bitter, wide choice of bar food, popular restaurant, small garden *(Ian Phillips)*

Marlow [Quoiting Sq], *Clayton Arms*: Splendidly eccentric local with excellent Brakspears and really friendly clientele comprised of local farmers, pensioners and archetypal darts players; side lounge harks back to pre-war times, and licensee has been here for over half a century *(Jon Wainwright)*; *Coach & Horses*: Large choice of good freshly cooked food at reasonable prices *(Anon)*; *Donkey*: Useful for decent food, lots of space and big garden; comfortable modern décor *(Lindsey Shaw Radley)*; [Mill Rd], *Prince of Wales*: Welcoming, comfortably renovated Wethereds pub with good well prepared bar food including some unusual dishes served impeccably in lounge; bar with pool-table, darts, fruit machine and juke box; seats outside *(Ian Phillips)*

Marsworth [Startops Ends; SP9114], *White Lion*: Busy pub beside Grand Union Canal, well kept Marstons Pedigree, good food in bar and restaurant; on GWG110 *(Jill Field)*

☆ **Mentmore** [SP9119], *Stag*: Small but civilised carpeted lounge bar with sturdy green leatherette seats around low oak tables, attractive fresh flower arrangements, open fire, and restaurant leading off; sturdily furnished public bar; good value bar food from sandwiches to main dishes, with wider choice in the evenings; well kept if rather pricey Charles Wells Eagle, polite well dressed staff, charming sloping garden with floodlit pear tree *(BB)*

New Bradwell [2 Bradwell Rd; SP8341], *New*: On bank of Grand Union Canal; well kept Charles Wells Eagle and competently produced bar food *(John Baker)*

☆ **Oving** [off A413 Whitchurch–Winslow; SP7821], *Black Boy*: Early seventeenth-century pub at end of superb green with panoramic view from terrace over plain towards Buckingham; warm and comfortable atmosphere, well kept Ind Coope Burton, good choice of well prepared food in bar and (evenings Tues–Sat) restaurant *(Brian Law, J N Phillips)*

Penn [SU9193], *Horse & Jockey*: Pleasant local with fairly varied good value menu and Ind Coope Burton on handpump *(Mike Tucker)*; [Elm Rd], *Red Lion*: Overlooks pleasant well kept green with large duck pond; comfortable lounge, separate games-room, unobtrusive piped music; Flowers, Wethereds and Whitbreads, good range of hot and cold bar food from sandwiches upwards, efficient service *(Lyn and Bill Capper)*

☆ **Penn Street** [SU9295], *Hit or Miss*: Well furnished eighteenth-century low-beamed

pub with open fire, no piped music or fruit machines; Hook Norton and Marstons Pedigree, decent wines by the glass, promising hot and cold bar food from sandwiches upwards, big inglenook fireplaces, large restaurant; cricket memorabilia, and own cricket ground; friendly new owners since 1988 *(Lyn and Bill Capper, R M Savage, Lindsey Shaw Radley, David Gaunt)*

Saunderton [SU8198], *Rose & Crown*: Feels (and looks) more like someone's lounge with helpful, friendly and somewhat eccentric service; well kept Morlands, Morrells and Wethereds, good choice of whiskies, bar food with an emphasis on seafood; jolly atmosphere, separate restaurant *(Simon Collet-Jones)*

Shabbington [SP6607], *Old Fisherman*: Unpretentious, white Morrells riverside pub by bridge; clean, comfortable bar with dart board, landlord with strong local accent, excellent filled cottage rolls; seats on waterside lawns ; children's playground *(Ian Phillips)*

Skirmett [SU7790], *Kings Arms*: Inglenook fireplace and log fire in traditionally furnished high-beamed bar, bar food (not Sun evening) often enterprising, using fresh vegetables and maybe herbs from the garden, and including summer cold buffet in lofty-raftered side room, well kept Brakspears and Whitbreads-related real ales, seats on side lawn; has had jazz Weds ; children in eating area and restaurant ; attractive bedrooms *(Mr and Mrs T F Marshall, LYM)*

Speen [Hampden Rd; SU8399], *King William IV*: Though it has Watneys-related and other real ales and a comfortable atmosphere, this is moving towards being a restaurant rather than a pub (one room has been a no-smoking restaurant for some time, and other bar earmarked in 1989 for refurbishment into further dining area); food well cooked, but meals rather than snacks now, and not cheap by pub standards *(Mr and Mrs T F Marshall)*; [Flowers Bottom Lane; road from village towards Lacey Green and Saunderton Stn – OS Sheet 165 reference 835995; SU8399] *Old Plow*: Pretty and crisply cottagey little country inn, in attractive surroundings; since a change of ownership in summer 1988 bar food including freshly made sandwiches and ploughman's has been back on the scene – it had been through a spell when it was really best thought of as a restaurant (and the restaurant is still a main focus); friendly and welcoming, with summer barbecues; bedrooms *(JMC, Michael Thomson, LYM; up-to-date reports please)*

☆ **St Leonards** [edge of Buckland Common – village signposted off A4011 Wendover–Tring; SP9107], *White Lion*: Unpretentious charm in tile and pink-washed rose-covered Chilterns pub, no frills in simple but neat open-plan bar with old black beams, cushioned seats, log-effect gas fire; good value simple home cooking from sandwiches, filled baked potatoes and ploughman's to salads, chilli, sausage and egg, gammon, shepherd's pie and so forth; well kept Benskins Best, Friary Meux Best and Ind Coope Burton on handpump, friendly service, unobtrusive piped music, small but attractive sheltered garden; no hot main dishes Sat, no food Sun; provision for children *(David Wallington, BB)*

Stewkley [High St South; junction of Wing and Dunton rds; SP8526], *Carpenters Arms*: Nice old building with jolly little public bar and bookcases and wood-burning stove in more homely lounge, also small restaurant in converted railway carriage; Benskins Best on handpump, bar meals *(AB, SV Bishop, LYM)*; *Swan*: Large but cosy and popular open-plan local with lots of old beams and huge freestanding fireplace; good bar food, small restaurant; bar billiards and other games, tables in garden *(AB, Stephen and Helen Doole)*

Stoke Goldington [SP8348], *White Hart*: Thatched pub with beams and quarry tiles in saloon, comfortable plush lounge, lively public bar and games-room; enterprising choice of drinks including well kept Charles Wells real ale, friendly staff, sheltered back lawn *(LYM)*

Stoke Hammond [SP8829], *Three Locks*: Neat canal pub with full range of bar food from counter at one end of its big carpeted bar, reasonably priced restaurant; garden overlooks a flight of locks on the Grand Union Canal and across to distant fields – a popular spot, can get packed at holiday times *(Lyn and Bill Capper, David Crafts)*

Stoke Poges [B416, Stoke Common – OS Sheet 175 reference 982857; SU9885], *Fox & Pheasant*: Recently refurbished, with well appointed and welcoming bar and a good range of beers and spirits; pleasant and obliging staff and straightforward, good quality bar food; restaurant is now Chef & Brewer carvery *(AP)*

Stokenchurch [nr M40 junction 5; SU7695], *Kings Arms*: Popular, with generous bar snacks throughout opening hours; occasional evening entertainment *(Roger and Lynda Pilgrim)*

Stone [Hartwell; A418 SW of Aylesbury; SP7812], *Bugle Horn*: Long low whitewashed stone building with lovely trees in pretty garden, horses grazing in meadows beyond; warm and friendly, with open fire and prettily planted well furnished conservatory; food in bar and restaurant *(Ian Phillips)*

Stony Stratford [High St; SP7840], *Bull*: Basic public bar popular with lively young regulars for good range of well kept guest beers, and Sun folk music; separate hotel bar too ; bedrooms *(Nick Dowson, LYM)*; [72 High St] *Cock*: Quiet, old-fashioned and unpretentious hotel with handsome old oak

settles in otherwise straightforward bar, Adnams and Courage Directors, lunchtime bar food; bedrooms *(LYM)*; [High St] *George*: Well kept real ale, decent food, friendly staff, comfortable and inviting; good value bedrooms *(D K and H M Brenchley)*

Taplow [Station Rd; SU9082], *Oak & Saw*: Lovely pub in quiet village with old photographs of area and good atmosphere created by mixture of customers; pleasant staff, well kept Courage, separate eating area *(R Houghton)*

☆ **The Lee** [back roads 2½ miles N of Great Missenden, E of A413; SP8904], *Cock & Rabbit*: Stylish and comfortable, with a strong Italian flavour – Italian-owned, with attractively served food, all home-made, using local produce; well kept real ales such as Flowers, Morlands and Wethereds, and big garden with tables on verandah, terraces and lawn; well worth knowing, though bar food prices (not Sun or Mon evening) are rather high for a pub, and the character of the place is closer to a country restaurant; children in eating area and restaurant *(AE, AP, LYM)*

Wavendon [not far from M1 junctions 13 and 14; SP9137], *Plough*: Pretty pub with foliage-covered walls and interesting painting on garage doors; pleasant atmosphere, imaginative and reasonably priced bar food (not Sun, nor Mon and Tues evening) *(Rita Horridge)*

Wheelerend Common [just off A40; SU8093], *Brickmakers Arms*: Well refurbished, with efficient staff, huge garden with play area and lines of picnic-table sets, upstairs carvery restaurant, Watneys-related beers; a Chef & Brewer *(Nick Dowson, Alison Hayward)*; [about ½ mile from Lane End] *Chequers*: Pleasant old free house, welcoming licensee, well kept if limited range of beers, wide range of bar food *(R Houghton)*

Winchmore Hill [The Hill; SU9394], *Plough*: Clean and comfortably modernised spacious bar overlooking green, several interconnecting areas, some interesting knick-knacks, wide choice of reasonably priced bar food, real ales including Youngers Scotch and IPA, neat helpful staff, piped music, tables on lawn with wishing well; restaurant named after landlady Barbara Windsor *(Nick Dowson, BB)*

Wooburn Common [Kiln Lane; SU9387], *Chequers*: Beams, comfortable sofas, pleasant bar food even Sun lunchtime, well kept real ales such as Badger – though the other customers may be tucking into champagne; can get crowded *(Brian and Rosemary Wilmot)*; [Wooburn Common Rd, about 3½ miles from M40 junction 2] *Royal Standard*: Squeaky-clean and brightly redecorated pub with well kept Whitbreads-related real ales, pleasant atmosphere, reasonably priced bar food, seats out behind

– a useful standby ; children welcome *(C J Cuss, Nick Dowson, Alison Hayward, LYM)*
Wooburn Green [The Green; SU9188], *Red Lion*: Building formerly an old forge, now a Roast Inn with separate restaurant; old photographs around bar, well kept beer, pleasant uniformed bar staff *(Richard Houghton)*

☆ **Wooburn Moor** [Watery Lane – OS Sheet 175 reference 913898; SU9189], *Falcon*: Wonderful, relaxing atmosphere in friendly little low-beamed local with good mix of customers, welcoming landlord and staff, well kept Flowers Original, Wethereds and a Whitbreads-related guest beer, bar food including super sandwiches and good hot specials; attractive well kept garden *(Brian and Rosemary Wilmot, R Houghton, Nick Dowson, Alison Hayward)*
Woughton on the Green [SP8737], *Olde Swan*: Village pub with good value bar food and large garden; children's play area *(H Rust)*

Cambridgeshire and Bedfordshire

*Early this year we were shocked to hear of a bad fire at the Olde Plough in
Bolnhurst, just as very long drawn out refurbishments to this popular and
unassuming old place were coming to an end; many readers will want to join
us in wishing the Horridges well – they've been living in a caravan on the site
while the extensive damage has been put right (we hope all will be well by the
time this edition is published). Among pubs that have come through the year
less eventfully, food deserving our new higher-standard award rosette can be
found at the Cock at Broom (a marvellously traditional country pub proving
that cheeses and simple pies can be ideal pub food), the Plough at Coton (the
much fuller range of what has now come to be thought of as pub food, in easy
reach of the M11), the Kings Head at Dullingham (almost the feel of a
restaurant, though an easy-going one – particularly when there's racing at
Newmarket), the Three Tuns at Fen Drayton (simple home cooking, but done
well, with plenty of choice), the Plough & Fleece at Horningsea (often using
interesting antique recipes), the Pheasant at Keyston (reliably good, including
imaginative dishes), the Queens Head at Newton (very simple stuff, but
thoughtful – using good materials), the gaslit Anchor at Sutton Gault (people
like their versions of pub standbys such as steak and kidney pie, as well as their
more individual dishes) and the Haycock at Wansford (particularly its smart
buffet; this grand old place, nice but expensive to stay at, has a successfully
enlarged bar area this year). Cheese lovers should also note the Bell at Stilton –
where they use the cheese which got its name from the village in all sorts of
ways; the gradual refurbishment of this interesting old inn has made quite a bit
of progress this year and bedrooms should be open by late autumn. A new
entry this year, the Crafty Fox on the fens south of Chatteris, has straight away
won an award for its food – nothing pretentious, but very carefully produced,
using good fresh ingredients; it's a most attractive place, too. Other new main*

The Three Tuns, Fen Drayton

entries are the Royal Oak at Barrington (heavily beamed, timbered and
thatched, on a charming village green), the Boathouse by the river in
Cambridge (a very successful Whitbreads refurbishment) and the relaxed
Golden Pheasant up at Etton (looks more like a rectory than a pub, with
particularly well kept real ales). Among other main entries, some changes or
developments to note include new licensees at the King William IV in Heydon
(though some of the Austrian dishes have remained on the menu), the White
Horse, Southill (the miniature railway is still running), the Black Horse,
Woburn, and the Olde Ferry Boat at Holywell (in the Guinness Book of
Records as one of Britain's oldest inns). In the Lucky Dip section, Cambridge
itself is a notable hunting-ground for good pubs; the standard of pubs in the
city has certainly risen in the last few years, with lots happening on the pub
scene (and this is the year which will show whether an old favourite there, the
Eagle, which has been submerged in a massive surrounding rebuilding scheme
for the last couple of years, will as promised once again see the light of day).
Other Lucky Dips to mention particularly are the Crown in Eaton Socon, the
beautifully situated Pike & Eel at Needingworth (which has bedrooms), that
remarkable pub the Tickell Arms at Whittlesford and – particularly valuable in
their own areas – the Bell at Odell, John o' Gaunt at Sutton near Biggleswade
and Red Lion at Studham (which has changed hands yet again).

BARRINGTON (Cambs)   TL3949 Map 5

Royal Oak

From M11 junction 11, take A10 to Newton and turn right

The heavily beamed and timbered rambling rooms in this friendly, thatched
fourteenth-century pub have openings knocked between them and are decorated
with brass, copper, antlers and harness. The huge central chimney (which has some
fine Tudor brickwork above one mantelbeam) has also been knocked through and
is now a sort of connecting lobby. Good popular bar food includes sandwiches
(from £1.10), soup (£1.40), ploughman's (from £2.10), omelettes (£2.85), salads
(from £3), kidney Stroganoff (£3.60), home-made steak and kidney pie (£3.75),
vegetarian dishes like walnut roulade with a sweet-and-sour sauce (£3.75) or
Challis cottage crumble (£3.85) and eight-ounce sirloin steak (£6.50); puddings
such as home-made apple strudel (£1.60). Well kept Adnams and Greene King IPA
and Abbot on handpump; fruit machine, piped music and skittle alley. The pub
faces the attractive and unusually long village green where you can sit under
cocktail parasols in summer. Barrington Court (National Trust) is nearby.
(Recommended by Gordon Theaker, Nigel Gibbs, NAC, Mr and Mrs P J Barrett)
Free house   Licensees Robert and Elizabeth Nicholls   Real ale   Meals and snacks (12–2,
6.30–10.30)   Restaurant tel Cambridge (0223) 870791   Children in eating areas   Open
11.30–2.30, 6.30–11 all year

BIDDENHAM (Beds)   TL0249 Map 5

Three Tuns

57 Main Road; village signposted from A428 just W of Bedford

The public bar of this well kept thatched stone village pub is a lively, popular place,
with table skittles as well as darts, dominoes, fruit machine and piped music. The
low-beamed comfortable lounge has country paintings on the walls and a little
jungle of pot plants in its stone fireplace. There are twenty-seven different dishes on
the menu: sandwiches (from 80p), excellent home-made celery soup (95p; they also
do soup and a choice of sandwich for £1.45 – an idea it would be nice if other pubs

copied), pâté (£1.40), several ploughman's (£1.60), burgers (from £2.20), salads (from £2.30), various hot dishes such as quiche, lasagne or chilli con carne (£2.90), home-made chicken casserole or steak and kidney pie (£3.20), evening steaks (£5.50) and specials such as excellent seafood gratin; children's menu (£1.20). Well kept Greene King IPA and Abbot on handpump. The big garden, which is good for families, has doves and a dovecote. *(Recommended by Wayne Brindle, Pete Storey, Dr and Mrs B D Smith; more reports please)*

*Greene King   Licensees Alan and Tina Wilkins   Real ale   Meals and snacks (not Sun)
Children in small dining-room   Open 11.30–2.30, 6–11 all year; closed evening 25 Dec*

BOLNHURST (Beds)   TL0859 Map 5
Olde Plough

B660 Bedford–Kimbolton

We're keeping our fingers crossed that by the time this edition is published, this friendly fifteenth-century cottage will have re-opened after the oldest part was gutted by fire. The licensees plan to refurbish the place much as before: a carpeted lounge bar with black beams, little armchairs around low tables, a leather sofa and a leather armchair and a log fire in the big stone fireplace, a room leading off here has some dining-tables. Well kept Paines XXX and EG, plus a guest beer on handpump; good mulled wine in cold weather. Bar food has included home-made soup, burgers, toasted French bread with cheese and herbs, ploughman's, meat or vegetarian lasagne, cod Kiev or gamekeeper's pie; they hope to open a restaurant. The public bar had two refectory tables, a pair of settles and other seats on the flagstones, a big wood-burning stove and darts, dominoes, cribbage, card games, Trivial Pursuit, pool, hood skittles and fruit machine; the cats are called Chubbs, Blacky and Titch. The garden is very pretty, with rustic seats and tables, a long crazy-paved terrace by rose beds, a lawn and the remains of a moat under trees by a rock bank. *(Recommended by Steve Waters, R L Turnham, Chris Hill, Roger Danes; more reports please)*

Free house   Licensee M J Horridge   Real ale   Meals and snacks   Children welcome until 9pm, if well behaved   Open 12–2.30 (3 Sat), 7–11 all year; closed 25 Dec

BROOM (Beds)   TL1743 Map 5
Cock ★ ⊗

23 High Street; from A1 opposite northernmost Biggleswade turnoff follow Old Warden 3, Aerodrome 2 signpost and take first left signposted Broom

Exceptionally friendly, this lovingly run and beautifully kept village pub has four small rooms with low ochre ceilings, antique tile floors, stripped panelling and old-fashioned stripped built-in furnishings – cupboards, uncushioned wall benches, simple latch doors. There are only two or three tables in each room, some with neat gingham tablecloths. Though they also serve a good filling game soup (65p), filled baked potato (75p), sandwiches (from 75p, toasties from 60p), salads (£2.50), pork and rabbit, game or shepherd's pies (from £1.20), they keep around twenty different cheeses in fine condition – mostly English. These come in sandwiches, in variations on the ploughman's theme, from the simplest (£1.35) to several tailored to the taste of an individual cheese (£1.60–£2.50). A central corridor runs down the middle of the pub, with the sink for washing glasses on one side (pewter mugs hang over it) and on the other steps down to the cellar where very well kept Greene King IPA and Abbot are tapped straight from the cask – there's no bar counter; service is most friendly. There are log fires in winter, hood skittles, darts, shove-ha'penny, cribbage and dominoes in one front room, unobtrusive piped music. A terrace by the back lawn has some picnic-table sets. Though it's usually very quiet on weekday lunchtimes, weekends can be extremely busy. *(Recommended by Roger Danes, Nigel Paine, Janet and Gary Amos, M J Horridge, S J Curtis, Trevor Rule, John Baker, G Farmelo, Pete Storey)*

Greene King Licensees Martin and Brenda Murphy Real ale Snacks (not evenings Sun or bank hols) Children welcome Open 12–2.30, 6–11 all year; closed evening 25 Dec

CAMBRIDGE TL4658 Map 5

Boathouse

14 Chesterton Road; one-way section of ring road, by A10 Ely turnoff

Formerly the Rob Roy, this was closed and virtually derelict until Whitbreads reopened it a couple of years ago. It's been thoroughly reworked in an old-fashioned style, with little partitioned snugs by net-curtained etched-glass windows on the roadside, a U-shaped bar counter, paisley-pattern wallpaper and dark Anaglypta, bookshelves and small prints and steps up to an airier part – hung with oars and inverted sections of boats – with big windows looking down on the picnic-table sets in a smallish riverside garden. This is a most attractive spot in summer, looking across to Jesus Green, with barges moored between the pub and a nearby lock; besides the garden itself, there are benches on a platform cantilevered out above it. The clientele is as you'd expect, predominantly youngish and it can get very busy in good weather. Good value bar food quickly served from a side counter includes soup (£1.25), filled baked potatoes (from £1.65), hot beef sandwiches (£1.75), salads (from £2), steak and kidney pie (£3.50) and eight-ounce rump steak (£5.45), with four or five specials such as aubergine and Parmesan bake (£3.25) and chicken Madras (£3.50), with Sunday lunches and filled rolls normally available through the afternoon. Well kept Adnams, Boddingtons, Flowers IPA and Original, Greene King Abbot, Marstons Pedigree and Whitbreads Castle Eden on handpump; well reproduced jazz, two fruit machines. *(Recommended by Howard and Sue Gascoyne, Alan and Ruth Woodhouse, John Bromell, Steve Waters)*

Whitbreads Licensees J N Riddell and R Shearer Real ale Meals and snacks Jazz Sun evening Open 11–11 all year

Cambridge Blue

85 Gwydir Street

Simply furnished and with a warm and supportive atmosphere, this popular pub has a range of well kept real ales on handpump: Banks & Taylors Shefford, SOS, SOD, Elgoods, Nethergate and two guest beers. The two small rooms, one of them no-smoking, have been redecorated, though still have stripped kitchen chairs and some cushioned built-in wall benches around a medley of tables on dark red linoleum, lots of university sports photographs on the buttery Anaglypta walls and low ceilings (but the big windows brighten it up). French windows open on to a sheltered terrace, with picnic-table sets among some shrubs; in summer there are boules and Thursday evening barbecues. Food includes a good choice of home-made pies and cold meats served with as many salads as you like (from £3), home-made soups such as a good fish chowder (£1.10) and hot dishes such as spicy hot sausage, barbecued chicken breast or broccoli and cauliflower au gratin (£2–£3.20); Sunday roast lunch (£3.75). The pub is now leased to Banks & Taylors by the same people running our long-standing main entry the Free Press. *(Recommended by Steve Waters, Yvonne Lahaise, John Bromell, Alan and Ruth Woodhouse, Catherine Allerton)*

Banks & Taylors Manager Tony Shelvington Real ale Meals and snacks Children welcome Open 12–2.30, 6–11 all year; closed 25 Dec

Free Press

Prospect Row

Well off the beaten track, this unspoilt, busy pub is traditionally furnished throughout and one room is even served from a hatch. Tasty wholesome bar food includes soup such as curried parsley or iced yoghurt and cucumber (£1), filled baked potatoes (from £1.20), cold dishes with interesting salads such as pear with mayonnaise and a dash of tabasco or marinated carrot and parsnip, good smoked ham and hot dishes like navarin of lamb or home-made chicken and ham pie (£2.85), spiced beef and spinach (£2.95) and fresh salmon (£3.50); puddings such as hot treacle or pear tart (£1.30); there's a permanent no-smoking area and No Smoking signs on the tables where people are eating (get there early if you want a seat). Well kept Greene King IPA and Abbot on handpump; iced coffee in hot weather; dominoes. Though many pubs in Cambridge sport oars and rowing photographs, this one has the perfect right to them, as it's the only one here – or indeed anywhere – which is registered as a boat club; the rabbit in the garden is called Gismo. The licensees own the Cambridge Blue, which they've leased out to Banks & Taylors. *(Recommended by Steve Waters, Nigel Gibbs, Dave Butler, Lesley Storey, Alan and Ruth Woodhouse)*

Greene King   Licensees Chris and Debbie Lloyd   Real ale   Meals and snacks (12–2, 6–8.30)   Children welcome   Open 12–2.30, 6–11 all year

Old Spring

Ferry Path (pub's car park is on Chesterton Road)

As a rule, places recently kitted out to look old are a disappointment. This one, however, works well, with its bare boards, cushioned small settles, pews and stools around cast-iron and other traditional tables and soft gas lighting, its dimness accentuated by the earth-coloured rough plaster walls. Electricity's virtually confined to lighting some of the countryside and romantic pictures and there are a couple of open fires. The new conservatory/restaurant has now opened. Bar food includes ploughman's (£2.50), Greek dips with pitta bread (£3.25), sausage and tomato pie, chilli con carne or vegetarian pasta bake (all £3.45), steak (£5.95) and fish such as shark or swordfish; Sunday roast £3.95, and barbecues on request. Well kept Greene King IPA and Abbot and Rayments on handpump, two fruit machines and maybe piped 1930s jazz. Given the method of lighting, it can get quite hot if crowded. *(Recommended by Steve Waters, T E Cheshire, Howard and Sue Gascoyne, R D Norman, Alan and Ruth Woodhouse)*

Greene King   Licensees Adrian and Bernardette Brown   Real ale   Meals and snacks (11–3, 5.30–9.30)   Restaurant tel Cambridge (0223) 357228   Children in conservatory   Open 11–3, 5.30–11 all year; open all day Sat

CATWORTH (Cambs)   TL0873 Map 5

Racehorse

B660, between A45 (Kimbolton) and A604

The spacious well kept lounge in this popular pub has red cloth stools, wall banquettes and small easy chairs, as well as lots of photographs and genealogies of Derby winners and flat-racing prints; an airy extension with a rug on its parquet floor opens off. Bar food includes soup (95p), sandwiches (from 95p), deep fried mushrooms with garlic (£2.20), ploughman's (£2.95), lamb moussaka (£3.50), steak, kidney and Guinness pie (£3.75), rump steak (£5.25) and mixed grill (£5.85); three-course lunchtime special (£4.25, not Sunday). Well kept Adnams and Courage Directors on handpump, a good choice of some ninety whiskies, log fire and piped classical music. The red-tiled public bar has sensibly placed darts, table skittles and fruit machine. There are tables by flowers on a side terrace, with stables behind. *(Recommended by Fiona and Chris Brown, L F Turner, Dr A V Lewis)*

Free house Licensees Christopher Watson and Kay Owen Real ale Meals and snacks Restaurant tel Bythorn (080 14) 262 Children welcome Open 11.30–2.30, 6–11 all year

nr CHATTERIS (Cambs) TL3883 Map 5

Crafty Fox 🍺

Pickle Fen; B1050 towards St Ives

Under a new owner for the last couple of years, this isolated fenland house has developed a charming atmosphere that combines the unassuming personal friendliness of a genuine country pub with snug comfort and food that's a decided cut above the average without being at all fussy or pretentious. There's only enough space by the serving-counter for a few chatting drinkers, but the buzz of conversation percolating over from that corner is an important ingredient in the relaxed character of the main part of the bar – the dining area. This has soft lighting (some candles at night), fresh flowers and a mix of country kitchen chairs around its half-dozen tables, with attractive pictures and a log fire set in one stripped-stone wall. The short choice of quickly served food, changing day by day, might include fresh vegetable soup (£1.10), cockles and garlic bread (£1.50), mushrooms in wine (£1.95), vegetarian moussaka (£3.50), chicken goulash (£3.95), venison and orange chilli (£4.95), succulent pieces of honey-roast gammon in a thin creamy mustard sauce (£4.50) and steak (£7.25; with king prawns £9.25), with crisp zestily dressed side salads; puddings like butterscotch pudding (£1.50); best to book. Well kept Adnams Bitter and a guest such as Wadworths 6X or Youngs on handpump, decent wines; cribbage, dominoes, draughts, backgammon, chess and faint piped music. In summer the pub's great pride is an extensive conservatory terrace shaded by properly cared-for grape vines, with a small fountain, coloured lights and a barbecue for Sunday lunchtimes (though if you book in advance, they will arrange a do-it-yourself barbecue in the week); the shade netting is a useful idea. *(Recommended by Frank Gadbois)*

Free house Licensees Tim Lough and David Skeggs Real ale Meals and snacks (bookings tel Chatteris (035 43) 2266; after 9.30pm if booked in advance; no food 25 or 26 Dec, 1 Jan or bank hol evenings) Well behaved children in eating area (not after their bedtime) Open 11.30–2.30, 6–11 all year

COTON (Cambs) TL4058 Map 5

Plough 🍺

Under a mile from M11 junction 13; left on to A1303, then village signposted left – once on this side road don't turn off right at the Village, Church signpost; though this junction is exit only northbound and entrance only southbound, you can quickly get back to the motorway by heading straight on past the pub to the nearby junction 12 – which also gives signposted access to the village if you're heading south on the M11

It's not so much the choice of food as the careful cooking and presentation which draws readers to this popular pub. To some extent it concentrates on the restaurant (which occupies the handsomely beamed front part), with the bar in a spacious modern back extension: comfortable seats and long machine tapestry-upholstered banquettes around polished tables on either side of an arched dividing wall and a wood-burning stove. Bar food includes sandwiches (from £1.20), decent home-made soups (£1.30), ploughman's (£2.20), salads (from £4.10), quite a lot of fish such as grilled trout (£4.20) or fresh Scotch salmon (£5.80), gammon (£5) and steaks (from £7.60), with specials such as excellent dressed Cromer crab (£4.40).

There are report forms at the back of the book.

Well kept Flowers Original on handpump; pleasant, attentive service; inoffensive piped music. The back garden's attractive, with seats in smallish groups divided by trees and shrubs – and some in a summerhouse. Part of the Wimpole Way footpath runs from the pub to the centre of Cambridge. *(Recommended by Frank Cummins, Mrs E M Thompson, G F Scott, R C Wiles)*

Whitbreads Licensees Mr and Mrs Barrie Ashworth Real ale Meals and snacks (12–2, 7–10 Tues–Sat, until 9.30 Sun and Mon) Restaurant tel Madingley (0954) 210489 Well behaved children welcome Open 10.30–2.30, 6–11 all year; closed 25 and 26 Dec

DULLINGHAM (Cambs)   TL6357 Map 5

Kings Head 🏵

50 Station Road

Except when Newmarket racegoers crowd in, the two connecting carpeted rooms here have a cosy, old-fashioned atmosphere. There are small button-back leatherette bucket seats, Windsor chairs, hunting prints, some more private booths around sturdy wooden tables and a coal fire at each end in winter. Freshly made bar food – perhaps the feel of the place is more that of a restaurant now – includes sandwiches, home-made soup (80p), home-made pâté (£1.75), ploughman's (from £1.75), filled baked potatoes (from £2.15), lasagne (£2.50), various omelettes (from £2.50), celery and cashew-nut risotto or grilled ham with two fried eggs (£2.95), schnitzels (from £3.75), chicken Kiev (£4.75), roast peppered duck with Grand Marnier cream sauce (£6.95) and steaks (from £5.75); lots of puddings (from £1.10) and children's meals (from £1.45). Well kept Tolly Bitter and Original on handpump; friendly staff. The family/functions room is called the Loose Box. Under fairy lights on the grass above the car park there are sheltered seats, with more on a terrace overlooking the big sloping village green; also swings. *(Recommended by Alison Findlay, Cdr G R Roantree, Frank W Gadbois)*

Tolly Licensee Erich Kettenacker Real ale Meals and snacks Restaurant tel Newmarket (0638) 76486; closed Sun Children in eating area of bar Open 11–2.30, 6–11 all year

ELTISLEY (Cambs)   TL2659 Map 5

Leeds Arms 🛏

The Green; village signposted off A45

This well kept, tall white brick house has a friendly beamed lounge bar with red plush stools, pew-like cushioned wall benches and a huge log fire in winter with brass hunting horns and decorative plates on the mantelpiece; it's basically two rooms knocked together, with a third down some steps and dominated by tables with cushioned wheel-back chairs. Good value bar food includes sandwiches (from 85p, not Saturday evenings), home-made soup (90p), ploughman's (£1.60, not Saturday evenings), curry (£2.75), salads (from £3), home-made steak and kidney pie (£3.45), lasagne (£3.75), scampi (£3.60) and steaks (from £6.80); puddings include home-made apple pie (£1). Well kept Greene King IPA on handpump; good service; darts, a fruit machine sensibly set aside in an alcove, and piped music. There are picnic-table sets, swings and a slide set among the silver birches on the lawn. *(Recommended by M D Hare, G D Howard, Jamie and Sarah Allan, Stephen McKenzie)*

Free house Licensee George Cottrell Meals and snacks (12–2, 7–9.45) Restaurant Children in restaurant Open 11.30–2.30, 6.30–11 all year; closed 25 Dec Bedrooms tel Croxton (048 087) 283; £27.50B/£35B

Please tell us if the décor, atmosphere, food or drink at a pub is different from our description. We rely on readers' reports to keep us up to date. No stamp needed: *The Good Pub Guide*, FREEPOST, London SW10 0BR.

ETTON (Cambs)   TF1406 Map 5

Golden Pheasant

Village just off B1443, just E of Helpston level crossing; and will no doubt be signposted from near N end of new A15 Peterborough bypass

Like a square stone-built rectory among its tall trees, this rather surprises you with its comfortable but properly pubby bar – with well kept Adnams, Batemans XXXB, Courage Directors, Greene King IPA, Marstons Pedigree and two guest beers each week on handpump and some decent malt whiskies. It has high-backed button-back maroon plush settles built against the walls and around the corners, prints of birds and racing cars on its light brown rose-patterned wallpaper and a friendly atmosphere which can verge on the hilarious. Good value bar food includes French onion soup (£1.25), ploughman's (from £2.25), chicken tikka (£3.85), beef Stroganoff (£4.85) and pork massala or rump steak (£6.50); barbecues on Sunday lunchtimes in summer (from £3.50); open fire, fruit machine, well reproduced and chosen piped pop music. An airily furnished glass-walled side room looks out on the stone-walled garden where they play pétanque in summer; the big paddock is safe for children. The cats are called Cid and Timid. *(Recommended by John Baker)*

Free house   Licensees C M Phillips and M E Allingham   Real ale   Meals and snacks (12–2, 6–9.30; not Sun evening)   Restaurant tel Peterborough (0733) 252387   Children in conservatory   Open 11.30–3.30, 5.30–11 (all day Fri and Sat) all year

FEN DRAYTON (Cambs)   TL3368 Map 5

Three Tuns 🏵   [illustrated on page 68]

High Street

The inn sign outside this pretty, friendly thatched pub is unusual – three tiny barrels sitting on a pole. Inside, there are cushioned settles and an interesting variety of chairs, big portraits and old photographs of local scenes and brass plates on the timbered walls, attractively moulded very heavy early Tudor beams, old crockery in a corner dresser and two inglenook fireplaces (one is always alight). Bar food includes sandwiches with a choice of brown, white or French bread (from 90p), home-made soup (£1.10), home-made chicken liver and bacon pâté (£1.80), Greek dips (£2), ploughman's (from £2), various big fluffy omelettes (£2.50), home-made dishes such as cottage pie (£2.80) or steak and kidney pie with light pastry (£3), salads (from £2.80), gammon with pineapple (£4), chicken Kiev (£4.80), eight-ounce rump steak (£5.80) and puddings like home-made apple pie or maple syrup pancakes (from £1); Sunday roast beef (£3.95) and lovely garlic bread; pleasant service. Seven malt whiskies; sensibly placed darts, shove-ha'penny, dominoes, cribbage and fruit machine. Behind the pub there are tables under cocktail parasols on the neat flower-edged lawn, with apple and flowering cherry trees; also some children's play equipment. *(Recommended by M D Hare, Wayne Brindle, Frank Cummins, Mrs E M Thompson, Gordon Theaker, Alan and Ruth Woodhouse, Rob and Gill Weeks, J Gaudern, M D Hare)*

Greene King   Licensee Michael Nugent   Meals and snacks (12–2, 7–10; not Sun evening) Children in eating area   Open 11–2.30, 6.30–11 all year

FOWLMERE (Cambs)   TL4245 Map 5

Chequers

B1368

There's a discreet, civilised atmosphere in the two comfortably furnished communicating bar rooms here. The upper room has beams, some wall timbering and some notable moulded plasterwork above the fireplace and the lower room has prints and photographs of Spitfires and Mustangs flown from Fowlmere aerodrome. If you ask, they will point out to you the priest's hole above the bar. There have been one or two disappointments with the food in this last year, with consequent doubts about value for money. Though we can't therefore guarantee absolute consistency at the moment, we can say that most readers have recently enjoyed a high standard of unusual and well presented food: watercress soup (£2.40), salad of hot pigeon breast with pine kernels (£2.80), marinated chicken with avocado dip and tortilla chips (£4.95) and crab au gratin with whisky and ginger (£5.60). Besides Tolly on handpump, there is usually a choice of vintage and late-bottled ports by the glass and an excellent range of fine brandies and liqueurs, and there's a Cruover machine so that fine wines can be kept in perfect condition for serving by the glass; freshly squeezed orange juice. Waitress service extends to the white tables under cocktail parasols among the flowers and shrub roses of the attractive and neatly kept garden. *(Recommended by M Fisher, Joy Heatherley, Henry Midwinter, George Little, G and J Halphide, Mr and Mrs R Gammon, David Gaunt, JMC, Barbara Hatfield)*

Tolly   Licensee Norman Rushton   Real ale   Meals and snacks (12–2, 7–10)   Children welcome   Restaurant tel Fowlmere (076 382) 369   Open 12–2.30, 6–11 all year; closed 25 Dec

HEYDON (Cambs)   TL4340 Map 5

King William IV   🛏

Village signposted from A505 W of M11 junction 10; bear right in village

Although this friendly village inn has new licensees, the rambling rooms have changed little. The standing props, wall timbers and dark oak beams are very nearly covered with ploughshares, yokes, iron tools, cowbells, beer steins, samovars, cut-glass brass or black wrought-iron lamps, copper-bound casks and milk ewers, harness, horsebrasses, smiths' bellows, decorative plates and stuffed birds and animals (or rococo full-size models of them); the furnishings are the same as well – Liberty-cushioned housekeeper's chairs, carved pews (one with a lectern) and some tables made of great slabs of wood slung on black chains from the ceiling. The new chef still does a few Austrian dishes, as well as soup (£1.20), sandwiches (from £1.95), mushrooms in lager batter (£2.40), filled baked potatoes (from £2.50), ploughman's (£2.95), steak and mushroom pie, goulash or wiener schnitzel (£3.60); well kept Adnams, Flowers Original and IPA, Greene King IPA, Ruddles and Wethereds on handpump; fruit machine, trivia and piped music. The pretty garden has pieces of old farming machinery and there's a paddock with Jacob sheep, a donkey, geese, rabbit, guinea-pigs and fan-tail doves. The Wood Green Animal Shelter further along the road is worth a visit. *(Recommended by GP, N Barker, Dennis Royles, Derek and Sylvia Stephenson, Christopher Knowles-Fitton, T D Underwood, T Nott, Joy Heatherley, M C Howells, Gordon Theaker)*

Free house   Licensee Mrs Mary Kirkham   Real ale   Meals and snacks   Restaurant Children in restaurant and eating area of bar   Open 12–3, 7–11 all year   Bedrooms tel Royston (0763) 838773; £30S/£55(£60S)

HOLYWELL (Cambs)   TL3370 Map 5

Olde Ferry Boat

Village and pub both signposted (keep your eyes skinned!) off A1123 in Needingworth

New licensees have taken over this thousand-year-old building – one of Britain's oldest inns. In the middle of the rambling beamed bar there's a stone that marks the site of a 900-year-old grave (and even a resident ghost called Juliette). Steps between timbered or panelled walls create different areas, each with a distinct character, though all are cosy and old-fashioned and there are four open fires – one with a fish and an eel among rushes moulded on its chimney beam; a good mix of seats include rush ones with big cushions, red leather settees, river-view window seats and a pretty little carved settle. Bar food is imaginative: a daily home-made soup (£1.20), home-made chicken liver pâté (£2.50), sandwiches (from £1.50), ploughman's (£2.25), omelettes (from £3.50), sauté of lamb's liver lyonnaise (£4.50), home-made lasagne or scampi (£4.95), venison burgers (£4.50), home-made steak and kidney pie (£4.90), smoked wild boar in red wine sauce (£5.50), seafood pilaff (£5.75), chicken Maori (a mild curry with fruit, £5.55), escalope of pork (£7.95), steaks (from £8.50) and a wide choice of puddings. Well kept Adnams, Bass, Greene King IPA and Abbot on handpump; friendly staff; piped music. On a flower-edged front terrace by the old thatched building there are tables under cocktail parasols and more on a side rose lawn along the edge of the Great Ouse. (*Recommended by Simon Scott, Frank W Gadbois, E Kinnersly, John Baker, Nigel Gibbs, Kelvin Lawton, Sue and Tim Kinning, R Robinson, Paul and Margaret Baker, J C Proud, Alan and Ruth Woodhouse, Gordon Theaker*)

Free house   Licensee Richard Jeffrey   Real ale   Meals and snacks (12–2, 7–10)   Children welcome   Restaurant (not Sun evening)   Open 11–3, 6–11 all year; closed evening 25 Dec Bedrooms tel St Ives (0480) 63227; £33(£37B)/£37(£44B)

HORNINGSEA (Cambs)   TL4962 Map 5

Plough & Fleece ★ ✿

Although there is a comfortable lounge, readers prefer the friendly public bar in this homely village pub: high-backed settles and plain seats on the red tiled floor, plain wooden tables – including an enormously long slab of elm (with an equally long pew to match it) – black beams in the red ceiling, butter-yellow walls, a stuffed parrot and a stuffed fox by the lovely log fire. An unusual point about the home-cooked food is that they often use imaginatively recast antique recipes: soup (£1.25), home-made pâté (£1.90), devilled crab (£2.20), cottage pie (£2.60), omelettes (£3.50), salads such as home-cooked ham (£3.50), Suffolk ham hot-pot (£3.70), fish pie (£4.50), Romany rabbit (£5.75), honey-roast guinea-fowl (£6.25), Scotch salmon poached in white wine and topped with a smoked salmon and prawn sauce (£7.50), sirloin steak (£7.75) and beef Wellington (£8.50). In the evenings, when the menu also includes hot garlic cockles (£2), a vegetarian dish with asparagus, eggs, cheese and almonds (£4.80) and giant prawns (£6), these hot dishes all cost about 80p extra, with extra vegetables. At lunchtimes only there are also sandwiches (from £1, toasties from £1.25), ploughman's or hot snacks such as sausage and bacon flan (£1.90) and home-cooked ham and egg (£2.80). Good puddings include Norfolk treacle tart or home-made ginger and brandy ice-cream and a potent chocolate pudding (£1.50); efficient service. Well kept Greene King IPA and Abbot on handpump, half a dozen good malt whiskies and a couple of vintage ports. Dominoes and cribbage. There are picnic-table sets (with table service) beyond the car park, and beyond a herbaceous border is a children's play area with a rope ladder climbing into an old pear tree. (*Recommended by Mrs R Green, Mrs E M Thompson, Nigel Gibbs, Gordon Theaker, R C Vincent, Alan and Ruth Woodhouse*)

Greene King   Licensee Kenneth Grimes   Real ale   Meals (not Mon evening or Sun) and snacks (not Mon evening)   Open 11.30–2.30, 7–11 all year; closed evenings 25 and 26 Dec

KENNETT (Cambs)   TL6968 Map 5

Bell

Bury Road; crossroads B1506/B1085, through Kentford on the Newmarket slip-road just off A45 Bury St Edmunds–Cambridge

Rambling back behind the free-standing fireplace, the spacious and cheery Turkey-carpeted bar in this fifteenth-century inn has a mass of heavy oak beams, plenty of stripped country tables with Windsor armchairs and cushioned dining-chairs and a brick inglenook; it's a shame that the servery and tables in the eating area aren't really in keeping. A wide choice of tasty bar food from an attractive and efficient servery includes good leek and onion soup (£1.25), filled baked potatoes (from £1.25), good filled French bread (£1.75), Newmarket jumbo sausage (£1.95), smoked salmon sandwich (£2.75), ploughman's (from £2.75), a choice of pies (£3.75), salads (from £3.50), daily specials such as steak and kidney pie and twice-weekly roasts (from £3.50) and several more expensive dishes such as steaks (from £8.95) and Dover sole (£9.95). Leading off is a tiled-floor room serving as a wine and oyster bar where there are occasional 'special' evenings. Well kept Adnams, Charles Wells Bombardier, Courage Directors, Flowers Original, Greene King IPA, Marstons Owd Rodger, Nethergate and Sam Smiths all on handpump; fruit machine, juke box and piped music. *(Recommended by Rona Murdoch, Paul Sexton, Sue Harrison, Mr and Mrs H W Clayton, Frank W Gadbois)*

Free house   Licensee Colin Knighton Hayling   Real ale   Meals and snacks (12–2, 7–9.45) Restaurant   Children in restaurant at lunchtime   Jazz Tues evenings   Open 11.30–2.30, 6–11 all year; closed evenings 25 and 26 Dec   Bedrooms tel Newmarket (0638) 750286; £25B/£35B

KEYSOE (Beds)   TL0762 Map 5

Chequers

B660

Comfortably modernised, the two beamed rooms in this very popular, well kept village pub are divided by an unusual stone-pillared log fireplace. Good bar food includes home-made courgette and parsley soup (£1.10), sandwiches (from £1.10), ploughman's (£2.75), various omelettes (£3.25), home-made steak pie or scampi (£3.75), salads (from £3.95), chicken stuffed with Stilton and chives (£4.50), glazed lamb cutlets (£4.75), steaks (from £5.95), huge mixed grill (£6.50) and puddings (£1.75); Sunday roast lunch (£3.25); children's helpings (from £1.40). Well kept Adnams and Mansfield Riding and guest beers such as McEwans, Sam Smiths Old Brewery and Websters from handpumps on the stone bar counter, and Kellercup – a blend of stawberries and hock; darts, a fruit machine, a space game and piped music. Outside, there's a terrace, tables on the small front lawn among flowers (with more on the grass around the car park behind), swings, a Wendy house and a fairy-tale play tree. *(Recommended by M and J Back, Roger Danes, J K Clark; more reports please)*

Free house   Licensee Jeffrey Kearns   Real ale   Meals and snacks (12–2, 7–9.45; not Mon) Children welcome   Open 11–2.30, 6.30–11 all year; closed Mon, exc bank hols

KEYSTON (Cambs)   TL0475 Map 5

Pheasant 🏅

Village loop road

Consistently good and very popular, the fresh home-cooked food in this well run old village pub includes filled rolls (from £1.10), soup (£1.25), pâté (£1.95), Paris mushrooms (£2.95), crab Mornay (£3.25), cold ham salad (£3.95), lasagne (£4.25), loin of pork with orange sauce (£4.50), lamb sweetbreads (£4.75), whole grilled plaice, trout or tandoori spring chicken (£4.95), king prawn salad (£6.95) and rump steak (£6.95); home-made puddings such as bread-and-butter pudding or crème brûlée (£2). In season local pheasant is used in pâtés and casseroles. Just off the comfortable and low-beamed main bar is a room that was once the village smithy: high rafters are hung with heavy-horse harness and an old horse-drawn harrow, and there are leather slung stools and a heavily carved wooden armchair among the Windsor chairs. Well kept Adnams and Tolly on handpump; friendly, efficient service. Tables under cocktail parasols in front of this attractive thatched white house are laid with tablecloths – a pleasant, quiet spot. One of Ivo Vannocci's Poste Hotels. No dogs. *(Recommended by P Miller, Dr M V Jones, Rita Horridge, C R Cooke, John Baker)*

Free house   Licensee William Bennett   Meals and snacks   Children welcome   Restaurant tel Bythorn (080 14) 241   Open 10.30–2.30, 6–11 all year

NEWTON (Cambs)   TL4349 Map 5

Queens Head 🏮

2½ miles from M11 junction 11; A10 towards Royston, then left on to B1368

Our award here recognises that there's nothing to beat really good simple ingredients presented well, for a pub meal. Freshly prepared, this includes a good choice of sandwiches (from £1.20, smoked salmon £1.60), superb soup (£1.30) or baked potato with cheese (£1.30); in the evening and on Sunday lunchtime they serve plates of excellent quality cold meat, smoked salmon, cheeses and pâté (from £1.90). The traditionally furnished main bar has bare wooden benches and seats built into its walls and bow windows, a curved high-backed settle on the yellow tiled floor of the main bar, unusual seats in the fireplace, a loudly ticking clock and paintings on its cream walls. The little carpeted saloon is broadly similar but more cosy. Well kept Adnams Bitter and Broadside tapped from the cask, with Old Ale in winter; elderflower wine; efficient service. Darts in a side room, with shove-ha'penny, table skittles, dominoes, cribbage, nine men's morris and a fruit machine. There are seats in front of the pub, with its vine trellis and unusually tall chimney. Belinda the goose, who adopted the pub in summer 1987, still patrols the car park day and night (and features on the newly painted pub sign – one side done by the landlord's father, the other by his son). *(Recommended by Dr Mark Stocker, Steve Waters, GP, Dave Butler, Lesley Storey, Tony Beaulah, Joy Heatherley)*

Free house   Licensee David Short   Real ale   Snacks (12–2, 7–10)   Children in games-room   Open 11.30 (11 Sat)–2.30, 6–11 all year; closed 25 Dec

SOUTHILL (Beds)   TL1542 Map 5

White Horse

More or less alone in quiet countryside, this popular pub has a comfortable and well kept main lounge with 1930s cigarette picture cards, framed old English currency notes and cricketing prints on the cream walls; a smaller public bar has plain seats and settles in front of a big wood-burning stove, and comic railway pictures and prints among the harness on the terracotta-coloured walls. The new licensees may have changed the menu by the time this book is published, but as we went to press it included sandwiches (from £1.10), ploughman's (from £2.50), sausages or ham and egg (£2.85), burgers (£3.25), salads (from £4.50), scampi (£3.75) and children's meals (£1.40); they do Sunday roasts. Flowers IPA and Wethereds on handpump. There's an interesting spotlit well in the dining-room; darts, shove-ha'penny, dominoes, cribbage, table skittles, fruit machine and piped music. The big garden includes a garden shop, a children's games and play area and, most importantly, a 7¼-inch gauge railway with both steam and diesel engines, bridges and a tunnel. Children's rides are 20p, and steam enthusiasts are encouraged to bring their own locomotives. Big car park. The pub is handy for the Shuttleworth Collection of old cars and early aeroplanes. *(Recommended by Mrs E M Thompson, Lyn and Bill Capper, Mr and Mrs G D Amos)*

Whitbreads   Licensees Tony and Brenda Tafari   Meals and snacks (12–2.30, 6.30–10; not Sun evening)   Children in eating areas   Restaurant tel Hitchin (0462) 813364; closed Sun evening   Open 11–3, 6.30–11 all year

STILTON (Cambs) TL1689 Map 5

Bell

High Street; village signposted from A1 S of Peterborough

With a fine coach-arch (distances to cities are carved on the courtyard side) and curlicued gantry for its heavy sign, this handsome seventeenth-century inn is being gradually restored by its enthusiastic owners. The two opened-up rooms of the attractive bar have flagstones, floor tiles, big prints of sailing and winter coaching scenes on the partly stripped walls, plush-cushioned button-back banquettes built around the walls and bow windows, other sturdy upright wooden seats, and a large log fire in the fine stone fireplace. A new extension for the bedrooms has just been completed. The Stilton is quite something here: soup (£1.20), excellent pâté (£1.70), ploughman's (£2.40) and with plum bread (£2.50); the cheese got its name originally from being sold to the inn's coaching customers and thus widely travelled around the country, though until then it had been known as the Quenby cheese and was actually made in Little Dalby and Wymondham up near Melton Mowbray. Other bar food from a menu that changes daily includes sandwiches (from £1.10), steak and kidney pie (£3.75), Cajan prawns (£3.95), salmon en croûte (£4.50) and sixteen-ounce rib steak (£7.50); well kept Bass, Courage Directors, Marstons Pedigree, Tetleys and guest beers on handpump, under light blanket pressure; friendly staff. Dominoes, backgammon, cards, Mastermind. The sheltered cobbled and flagstoned back courtyard has some tables. *(Recommended by Dr J R Hamilton, Byrne Sherwood, Comus Elliott, Mrs C S Smith)*

Free house Licensees John and Liam McGivern Real ale Meals and snacks Children in eating area lunchtimes only Restaurant Open 11–2.30, 6–11 all year Bedrooms tel Peterborough (0733) 242626; £50B/£65B

SUTTON GAULT (Cambs) TL4279 Map 5

Anchor 🍺

Village signposted off B1381 in Sutton

At the time of going to press, the cheerful licensee was aiming to place the emphasis in this riverside pub firmly on the food, without changing the relaxed, old-fashioned atmosphere. A new room has been created from the old kitchen (which has moved into an extension, along with new lavatories) in the same style as the other three beamed rooms: antique settles (including one elaborately Gothick, and another with an attractively curved high back), dining- or kitchen chairs, well spaced stripped deal tables, good lithographs and big prints, candles and gas lighting (from swan's-neck gas lamps) and three log fires. Home-made bar food comes with salad and new potatoes or granary bread and includes chicken liver and brandy pâté (£1.95), egg and prawn in garlic mayonnaise (£2.25), tagliatelle with bacon, mushrooms and cream (£3.50), vegetarian curried nut loaf with tomato and basil sauce or chilli con carne (£4.50), seafood bake, chicken Elizabeth (cold chicken in a lightly curried mayonnaise with grapes) or really rare roast beef (£5.50), fresh salmon salad with hollandaise (£7) and rump steak with brandy and cream (£7.50); home-made puddings such as lemon soufflé, mixed fruit crumble or chocolate roulade (£1.50 with cream). Well kept Tolly Bitter, Original and XXXX tapped from the cask and in winter hot punch; they also do freshly squeezed orange juice (90p a glass); attentive service. Shove-ha'penny, dominoes, cribbage, well reproduced classical music at lunchtime, middle-of-the-road in the evening; there's a rough-haired dachshund. There are tables out by the swans on the Old Bedford River. *(Recommended by Wayne Brindle, Julian Holland, S Simon, Michael Thomson, R C Wiles, Dr P D Smart)*

Free house Licensees A P and J R F Stretton-Downes Real ale Meals (not Sun evening) Restaurant tel Ely (0353) 778537 Children in restaurant until 9pm Open 12–2.30, 6–11 all year

SWAVESEY (Cambs)   TL3668 Map 5

Trinity Foot

A604, N side; to reach it from the westbound carriageway, take Swavesey, Fen Drayton turnoff

A friendly, well kept pub in a pleasantly enclosed garden of shrubs, trees and lawns. Inside, it's comfortable and the well set out tables have fresh flowers. The wide choice of consistently good and nicely presented bar food includes sandwiches, ploughman's or pâté, fish dishes, lamb cutlets, mixed grill, daily specials which might include oysters as well as steak and kidney pie and good Sunday roasts. Well kept Flowers Original and Wethereds on handpump; nicely made Pimms with bergamot flower; quick, efficient service even when busy. *(Recommended by Annette and John Kenny, Wayne Brindle, Mrs E M Thompson, Janet Goodjohn, F Oliveira-Pinto)*

Whitbreads   Licensee H J Mole   Real ale   Meals and snacks (12–2, 6–9.30; not Sun evening)   Children in eating area   Open 11–2.30, 6–11 all year; closed 25 and 26 Dec

TURVEY (Beds)   SP9452 Map 4

Three Fyshes

A428 NW of Bedford; pub at W end of village

A charming squint-walled stone corridor in this determinedly traditional and friendly pub links the cosy flagstoned public bar (which has a big inglenook) with the main room: heavy beams, a carpet and flagstone floor, a collection of seats around the close-set tables, a large box window seat and another stone inglenook fireplace. From their brewery called Nix Wincott (set up with help from Banks & Taylors), they brew their own beer – Old Nix and Two Henrys; other real ales on handpump include Banks & Taylors, Marstons Pedigree and Owd Rodger and a guest beer; also farm cider. Food includes good sandwiches (from £1.25), big crusty rolls (from £1.65; £2.50 for Dynamic – steak with fried egg and cheese – or Thermodynamic – similar, but with ham and pineapple), salads (from £3.25), mung bean and mushroom biriani (£3.25), trout (£4.75), rabbit in mustard sauce (£5.25), steak (£6.50) and grilled venison (£6.95). Hood skittles, dominoes, cribbage and fruit machine. The dogs and cats make their presence felt and there's rather a rough-and-ready feel to the place. A room by the small back garden has barbecues in summer – weather permitting. *(Recommended by Roger Danes, Michael and Alison Sandy, Mr and Mrs G D Amos)*

Free house   Licensee Charles Wincott   Real ale   Meals and snacks   Children welcome Open 11.30–3, 5.30–11 all year; open all day Sat

UFFORD (Cambs)   TF0904 Map 5

Olde White Hart

A farm until 1847, this attractive old pub is half-way up the only hill for miles. There's a sunny terrace with white metal seats and an electric canopy (for theme nights in summer and on wet days) and a big, pretty garden with two tethered goats and a children's play area with swings, slides and so forth. Inside, the well kept and carpeted lounge bar is divided into two by a stone chimney and there are pewter tankards hanging from the beam over the bar counter, wheel-back chairs around dark tripod tables, and Boris the stuffed tarantula. The public bar has been refurbished with old-fashioned settles, dark tables and a new carpet and food is now served here. Good, substantial and home-made, this includes very good value rolls (80p), steak and mushroom pie or lasagne (£3.95) and weekly changing specials such as chicken goujons with garlic sauce (£3.95), vegetarian tortellini (£4), fresh Cromer crab salad (£4.25), poached salmon (£5.50) and fillet steak Torpel (stuffed with Stilton, with a herb and port sauce, £8); on Sunday lunchtime they do hot roast beef rolls (£1.20) and Sunday roast lunch; barbecues Thursday, Friday and Saturday evenings. Well kept Home Bitter, Theakstons XB and Old Peculier, Youngers Scotch and guest beers on handpump, and several wines by the glass; darts, cribbage and dominoes. *(Recommended by Dr A V Lewis; more reports please)*

Home (S&N)   Licensee Christopher Hooton   Real ale   Meals and snacks (12–2, 6–9.30; not Sun evening or Mon)   Restaurant tel Stamford (0780) 740250   Children in eating area   Open 11–3 (4 Sat), 6–11 all year; closed 25 Dec

WANSFORD (Cambs)   TL0799 Map 5

Haycock ★ 🏵 🍺

Village clearly signposted from A1 W of Peterborough

The old-fashioned and well kept walled garden of this civilised, dark golden stone inn opens on to its own cricket field by the stately bridge over the River Nene; there's also an extensive pétanque court and fishing. Inside, the lively panelled main bar – reached through a flagstoned entry hall with antique seats and a longcase clock – has been slightly enlarged and refurbished in dark blue and deep pink; it overlooks tables in a charming cobbled courtyard. On the other side of the servery is a quieter lounge with plush sofas and easy chairs, hunting or steeplechasing prints, wallpaper to match the long flowery curtains, and a good log fire in winter. Though you can eat here, it's another lounge, overlooking the attractive and spacious formal garden, which has the buffet table. This, spick and span with gleaming copper on clean white linen, has a good range of cold meats and salads (from £4.95 for home-made turkey and pork pie or vegetarian quiche, £6.25 for fresh roast turkey, £7.95 for poached salmon). Other waitress-served home-made food includes soup (£1.95), chicken liver pâté (£3.25), home-made lasagne (£4.95), poached fillet of plaice stuffed with spinach topped with tomato and cheese sauce or grilled gammon and egg (£5.25), beef curry with rice (£5.45) and roast duck legs and pease pudding with gravy (£5.95); a good choice of puddings (£2.95) and barbecues (weather permitting, from £4.95). Well kept Bass, Ruddles Best and County and Tolly Original on handpump, with a good range of other drinks extending to properly mature vintage ports by the glass; the Cruover machine allows them to keep a dozen or so decent wines for sale by the glass in perfect condition; courteous service. One of Ivo Vannocci's Poste Hotels. *(Recommended by Philip Orbell, Rosalind Russell, Wayne Brindle, John Baker, Roger Bellingham, Syd and Wyn Donald, Mr and Mrs B Amos, R C Wiles)*

Free house   Manager Richard Neale   Real ale   Meals and snacks (12–2.30, 6.30–10.30) Children welcome   Restaurant   Open 10–2.30 (3 Sat), 5.30–11 all year   Bedrooms tel Stamford (0780) 782223; £65B/£80B

WOBURN (Beds)   SP9433 Map 4

Black Horse

This pretty brick ex-coaching-inn has a carefully decorated, L-shaped main bar with lots of neat tables and Windsor chairs, terracotta-coloured half-panelling and sporting prints on the buff walls; a back room has pine panelling and Liberty prints. New licensees have introduced a different menu: home-made soup (80p), sandwiches, home-made pâté (£1.75), filled baked potatoes (from £2.40), burgers (from £2.50), vegetarian lasagne (£2.75), venison pie or Mexican tostados (£2.95), gammon steak with pineapple (£3.95) and sirloin steak (£5.95); children's meals (from £1.50) and summer barbecues, lunchtimes and early evenings. Well kept Arkells BBB, Banks & Taylors Shefford and Marstons Burton and Pedigree on handpump and a range of wines by the glass; pleasant, efficient service. Through the coach entry there are several tables in a sheltered garden, looking down to a small lawn and then on to the church. No car park, and parking in the village is limited. The pub is close to Woburn Abbey. *(Recommended by David Shillitoe, Michael and Alison Sandy, Gordon Theaker, Alison Gurr, J K Clark, Wayne Brindle, Lyn and Bill Capper, Mr and Mrs G D Amos)*

Free house Licensee John Cambell Real ale Meals and snacks Restaurant tel *Woburn (0525) 290210 Children in eating area and restaurant Open 11–3, 6–11; open all day Sat in summer and bank hols*

WOODDITTON (Cambs) TL6659 Map 5
Three Blackbirds
Village signposted off B1063 at Cheveley

Deservedly popular bar food in this pretty thatched village pub includes sandwiches (from 85p), home-made soup (£1.10), lunchtime ploughman's (£2.25), potted shrimps (£2.35), home-cooked ham (£3.75), home-made lasagne (£3.95), escalope of pork (£4.25), beef in Guinness (£4.95), seafood gratin (£5.75), good steaks (from £6.55), with specials such as chicken bonne femme (£3.75); and good Sunday roasts (£3.55 one course, £7.50 three courses), with a choice of rare or well done beef. The two snug bars have high winged settles or dining-chairs around fairly closely spaced neat tables, cigarette cards, Derby Day photographs, little country prints, and fires in winter – the room on the left has the pubbier atmosphere. Well kept Tolly Bitter and Original on handpump; service stays friendly and efficient, even when busy; piped music. The front lawn, sheltered by an ivy-covered flint wall, has flowers, roses and a flowering cherry, with a muted chorus of nearby farm noises. *(Recommended by Graham and Glenis Watkins, W T Aird)*

Tolly Licensee Edward Spooner Real ale Meals and snacks Restaurant tel *Newmarket (0638) 730811; open Tues–Sat Children in restaurant Open 11–3, 5.30–11 all year*

Lucky Dip
(Besides the fully inspected pubs, you might like to try these Lucky Dips recommended to us and described by readers (if you do, please send us reports):

Abbots Ripton, Cambs [TL2378], *Three Horseshoes*: Lovely pink-washed, thatched pub with warm, low-beamed lounge and good food *(Wayne Brindle)*

Abbotsley, Cambs [High St/St Neots Rd; TL2356], *Jolly Abbot*: Wide choice of food is the reason for including this refurbished pub – button-back leatherette settles, rough painted plaster, choice of real ales *(Anon)*

Alwalton, Cambs [Oundle Rd; TL1396], *Wheatsheaf*: Popular village pub with well kept Ind Coope real ales and good food *(T Mansell)*

☆ **Arrington**, Cambs [TL3250], *Hardwicke Arms*: Recent reports mention promisingly imaginative and well prepared lunchtime bar food in this quaint creeper-covered coaching inn with quiet beamed and panelled lounge, high-ceilinged food bar, Adnams and Greene King real ales, games-room, tables outside; next to Wimpole Hall; bedrooms *(Mrs D M Llewellyn, LYM)*

☆ **Babraham**, Cambs [just off A1307; TL5150], *George*: Pleasant old pub with friendly landlord and range of interesting bar food, well cooked and served; the restaurant is well liked, too *(Gordon Theaker, Tom, Lorna, Audrey and Alan Chatting)*

☆ **Balsham**, Cambs [High St; TL5850], *Black Bull*: Attractive, beamed interior with cheerful log fire, spacious eating area by bar serving wide range of food including interesting daily specials, well kept Sam Smiths OB, separate evening restaurant *(Philip and Diana Nicholson, Stuart Watkinson)*

☆ **Barnack**, Cambs [Millstone Lane; off B1443 SE of Stamford – turn off School Lane nr the Fox; TF0704], *Millstone*: Well kept Adnams, Everards Tiger and Old Original and Fullers ESB in strongly traditional bar with wall timbers and high beams weighed down with harness and a really good wood-burning stove; good choice of simple but decent bar food from soup and sandwiches through omelettes and pies to gammon and trout in side area with pews; fruit machine, piped music; not far from Burghley House *(A V Lewis, M V Jones, M J Morgan, BB)*

Bartlow, Cambs [TL5845], *Three Hills*: Excellent rural pub with Greene King IPA and Abbot, good home-cooked food, log fire; very friendly *(Graham Tuthill)*

Bedford [Goldington Rd; TL0449], *Cricketers*: Pleasant two-bar pub with oak panelling, well kept Greene King Abbot and Charles Wells, good bar food and entertaining banter between licensees and locals *(Patrick Godfrey)*; [St Mary's St] *Kings Arms*: Well kept open-plan town-centre pub, recently given the barrels-and-floorboards treatment, with a huge pubby painting in a smaller carpeted area off to the right; popular for lunchtime food, well kept Greene King real ales *(Roger Danes, Steve Waters, LYM)*

Bletsoe, Beds [TL0258], *Falcon*: Very pleasant main-road coaching-inn dating from seventeenth century, bar, lounge, Charles Wells real ale, sandwiches, bar food and restaurant; big garden leading down to river *(Keith Garley, Mrs E M Thompson)*

Boxworth, Cambs [TL3464], *Golden Ball*: Very popular eating place – booking is advisable at weekends; ten or so real ales from an overall rotating stock of more than three dozen, friendly atmosphere; good parking *(E and G Slater)*

Brampton, Cambs [Broomholme Lane; TL2170], *Old Mill*: Beautiful spot, old converted watermill, attractively floodlit at night; busy though not really pubby atmosphere, wide range of real ales including Badger Best, excellent farm cider and upper-level restaurant *(Wayne Brindle)*

Bythorn, Cambs [on A604; TL0575], *White Hart*: Relaxed and friendly atmosphere, well kept real ales including Adnams Bitter and winter Old and Marstons Pedigree, bar food *(John Baker)*

☆ **Cambridge** [19 Bridge St; TL4658], *Baron of Beef*: Unspoilt pub with one of longest bars in city, panelled partition dividing two bars with traditional atmosphere, wide range of customers, Greene King kept under pressure, simple good value food from help-yourself buffet, friendly service *(Barry and Anne, Howard and Sue Gascoyne)*

☆ **Cambridge** [Tenison Rd], *Salisbury Arms*: It's the dozen or so well kept real ales which attract crowds of predominantly under-thirty customers to the high-ceilinged back bar of this Tardis-like pub, with its brewing posters and lively chatty atmosphere; generously served lunchtime bar food including ploughman's and hot dish, pub games, smaller front public bar – one bar is no-smoking *(Steve Waters, Nigel Gibbs, LYM)*

☆ **Cambridge** [Dover St (off East Rd)], *Tram Depot*: Part of the old tram depot with a built-in glazed mezzanine, a central skylight that runs the length of the building, bare brick walls and bare stone floor and old furniture that fits in nicely; popular home-made bar food; from same stable as Victoria, Earl Soham (see Suffolk main entries), and its own-brewed beers are also served here *(Howard and Sue Gascoyne)*

Cambridge [Napier St – next to Grafton Centre], *Ancient Druids*: Recently built pub with street windows showing its own brewery to passing pedestrians – it produces Kite, Merlin and Druids Special and does bar food (not Sun evening) *(Anon)*; [4 King St] *Cambridge Arms*: Spacious modern conversion of what used to be the Scales Brewery, giving unusual interesting layout; Greene King IPA and Abbot, rather good food, sheltered courtyard, maybe jazz nights *(LYM)*; [Bene't St] *Eagle*: Closed at the beginning of 1988 while the surrounding buildings were being reconstructed for Corpus Christi College, this formerly fine pub – perhaps the most atmospheric in Cambridge – was originally scheduled to reopen early in 1990, though we've had no hard news recently; [Elm St] *Elm Tree*: Pleasant, back-street pub with unusual Thai bar food *(P A Jennings)*; [Thoday St], *Empress*: Good, traditional local with customers of all ages, friendly licensee and staff, lounge, bar and games-room with pool and darts; superbly kept Whitbreads beer, terraced garden *(Nigel Gibbs)*; [Midsummer Common] *Fort St George*: Consistently good atmosphere and character in well refurbished pub in charming waterside position on Midsummer Common, interesting old-fashioned Tudor core, Greene King real ales, bistro-style bar food, games in public bar, enthusiastic licensees; outside bar serving terrace, garden with more seating and picnic-table sets *(Howard and Sue Gascoyne, LYM)*; [Barton Rd, corner Kings Rd], *Hat & Feathers*: Friendly local with good atmosphere, long, low bar, three rooms, one raised, galleried and with plenty of tables; Tolly ales, popular lunchtime and evening bar food, garden *(JMC)*; [nr Grafton Centre] *Hop Bine & Barley Ear*: Well kept Greene King and Mild and imaginative but reasonably priced lunchtime food in modernised end-of-terrace pub *(Peter Corris, Sue and Tim Kinning)*; [Mawson Rd] *Live & Let Live*: Pleasant side-street free house with old pine interior, antiques and knick-knacks on walls and cosy atmosphere; good range of well kept beers including Marstons Pedigree and Owd Rodger, Nethergate, Theakstons Old Peculier and Wadworths 6X *(Nigel Gibbs)*; [Mill Lane – nr Queens' Coll and Garden House Hotel] *Mill*: Most beautiful surroundings on River Cam and a useful respite from shopping or sightseeing; Tolly on handpump, sandwiches and other bar food; beware – they have been charging extra for non-returnable 'glasses' if you sit outside *(Graham and Glenis Watkins)*; [205 Milton Rd] *Milton*: Large and extensively refurbished open-plan Greene King dining pub with home-cooked food using local produce in bar's eating area, including vegetarian dishes; also restaurant *(Anon)*; [Magdelene St] *Pickerel*: Olde-worlde, very atmospheric street; spacious free house with several adjoining areas, friendly staff, juke box and fruit machines; Greene King, Ruddles Best and County, hot dishes and salad bar *(Alan and Ruth Woodhouse)*; [110

Water St, Chesterton; TL4660], *Pike & Eel*:
Substantially refurbished Greene King dining
pub with airy open-plan split-level bar and
restaurant overlooking one of the main
rowing reaches of the River Cam and cattle
and horses grazing on Stourbridge Common;
buffet lunches, more substantial evening
food, well chilled bottled drinks, pleasant
terrace and garden with play area; jazz some
evenings *(Howard and Sue Gascoyne)*; [Regent
St] *University Arms*: Spacious and
comfortable if simply decorated hotel bar
with windows overlooking cricket pitches on
Parker's Piece, friendly, cheerful licensees
and locals, good range of well kept real ales,
good value bar lunches including sandwiches
and quite an original range of meat and other
salads; good fire in octagonal lounge which
serves afternoon teas; bedrooms *(John Baker,
Liz and Ian Phillips)*

☆ **Castor**, Cambs [24 Peterborough Rd;
TL1298], *Royal Oak*: Good value home
cooking, well kept Ind Coope Bitter and
Burton and open fires in old thatched main-
road inn with several small traditional bar
areas; pretty village *(T Mansell, LYM)*
Castor, *Fitzwilliam Arms*: Long, thatched
pub on same main road; well kept Ind Coope
beers and varied range of good food
(T Mansell)
Caxton Gibbet, Cambs [junction A45/A14;
TL2960], *Caxton Gibbet*: Former coaching-
inn with well kitted out bar, open all day at
least for coffee; usefully placed *(Rob and Gill
Weeks)*
Chatteris, Cambs [High St – A141 towards
March; TL3986], *Ship*: Unpretentious free
house, good roaring fires at each end of bar,
darts and cribbage; lounge bar with flowers
on tables and pleasant atmosphere; well kept
Adnams and Tetleys on handpump *(Roger
Broadie)*

☆ **Clayhithe**, Cambs [TL5064], *Bridge*:
Idiosyncratic enough to generate mixed
reports from readers, this is at its best a
beautiful place to unwind at, with a serene
and interestingly furnished beamed and
timbered bar and a pretty garden by the
River Cam; good log fire, well kept Everards,
maybe whelk and prawn nibbles on the bar,
bar food that can be good value – especially
the popular buffet, service that may be casual
but seems mostly obliging and friendly;
bedrooms in motel extension, some with
attractive river outlook and hearty breakfasts
*(P G Evans, James Douglas, A D Fisher,
E Kinnersly, LYM)*
Conington, Cambs [Boxworth Rd; TL3266],
White Swan: Friendly pub with good
atmosphere, consistently good bar food
(Gordon Theaker)
Croxton, Cambs [TL2459], *Spread Eagle*:
Welcoming haven, Greene King ales, good
hot and cold bar food *(R Aitken)*
Croydon, Cambs [TL3149], *Queen Adelaide*:
Cosy free house in rural spot; large bar, with

pleasant décor, relaxing atmosphere, quiet
piped music, friendly service, consistently
well kept Adnams, Marstons Pedigree,
Youngers IPA and guest beers such as Hook
Norton; children's room, big paddock with
climbing-frames *(Mr and Mrs Geoffrey
Perryman)*
Downham, Cambs [Main St; sometimes
known as Little Downham – the one near
Ely; TL5283], *Plough*: Superbly cheerful
rough-and-ready fenland atmosphere in
unspoilt pub with wide choice of whiskies
and good home-made bar food – the oxtail
soup is particularly recommended *(John
Baker)*
nr **Dunstable**, Beds [handy for M1 junction 9
– A5, S of town; TL0221], *Horse & Jockey*:
Particularly notable for its big garden with
lots of attractions for children, this plushly
comfortable food pub has a popular buttery
and well kept beer; picnic-table sets in shady
back courtyard *(LYM)*; [also A5 S, by
Kensworth turn] *Packhorse*: Good
atmosphere in simple but welcoming local
(Margaret and Trevor Errington)
Duxford, Cambs [Moorfield Rd; TL4745],
John Barleycorn: Large bar with low and
heavily beamed ceiling, log fire, hunting
prints and plates, divided into more intimate
sections by high oak settles; well kept Greene
King, good wines, good value bar food,
splendidly quick service; barbecues in
summer, attractive garden *(Joy Heatherley)*
Earith, Cambs [TL3874], *Riverview*:
Excellent reasonably priced food in bar and
restaurant, very friendly staff *(E G Passant)*
East Hyde, Beds [Lower Luton Rd (B653);
TL1217], *Leather Bottle*: Small Whitbreads
house with rather brown-Windsor décor,
two bars, character landlord and large
alsatian; Flowers beer and bar food including
fresh fish and a weekday meat special
(D L Johnson)

☆ **Eaton Socon**, Cambs [Old Great North Rd;
village signposted from A1 nr St Neots;
TL1658], *Crown*: Small and cosy low-beamed
pub with two connecting bars and a fine
choice of real ales such as Brains SA,
Felinfoel, Hook Norton, Sam Smiths, Tetleys
and Wadworths Farmers Glory, good value
home-made bar food including large range of
fish, separate little restaurant, pleasant
welcoming atmosphere – note that T-shirts
are forbidden though open-necked shirts are
OK *(Genie and Brian Smart, Wayne Brindle,
Rita Horridge)*

☆ **Eaton Socon**, *White Horse*: Popular
straightforward food served quickly in
rambling series of well kept low-beamed
rooms including one with high-backed
traditional settles around fine log fire, several
well kept Whitbreads-related real ales on
handpump, relaxed chatty atmosphere, play
area (maybe with guinea-pigs) in pretty back
garden ; children in eating areas; bedrooms
(Wayne Brindle, LYM)

Eaton Socon, *Waggon & Horses*: Traditional pub with comfortable roomy bar, good range of moderately priced hot and cold bar food and Tolly and John Paines on handpump *(G T Rhys)*

☆ **Elsworth**, Cambs [TL3163], *George & Dragon*: Pleasantly idiosyncratic pub with attractively furnished and decorated panelled main bar and quieter back dining area by garden, good atmosphere, wide choice of decent food, Tolly real ales, nice terraces, play area in garden, restaurant *(Wayne Brindle, LYM)*

Elsworth, *Poacher*: Small, cosy, thatched pub with friendly welcome and good atmosphere *(Wayne Brindle)*

☆ **Elton**, Cambs [Duck St; TL0893], *Crown*: Opposite green in small, beautiful village, rebuilt and modernised with taste and real character since 1984 fire; well kept real ales including Greene King IPA and Marstons Pedigree, delicious and varied food in bar, new conservatory-style extension and upstairs restaurant *(T Mansell and others)*

Elton [A605], *Black Horse*: Old stone pub with very comfortable low basket chairs in homely carpeted lounge, stripped stone walls, beams and brasses, well kept Sam Smiths OB, bar food in separate dining area *(T Mansell, Tom Evans)*

Ely, Cambs [Annesdale; TL5380], *Cutter*: Riverside pub with view of moorings and boatyard from narrow terrace and spacious public bar (where the juke box may be loud); lounge with close-set tables, Watneys-related real ales on handpump, wide range of sensibly priced bar food in generous helpings from servery shaped like a boat hull; good parking – and moorings *(Howard and Sue Gascoyne, Peter and Jacqueline Petts)*; [2 Lynn Rd] *Lamb*: Free house with formal but comfortable panelled lounge bar, friendly and less formal Fenman bar in old stabling block with pleasant rural atmosphere and large collection of ties behind bar; good range of real ales on handpump, car park with picnic-table sets; bedrooms *(Howard and Sue Gascoyne)*

☆ **Fen Ditton**, Cambs [High St; TL4860], *Ancient Shepherds*: Very pleasant welcome in small and friendly well run country pub with excellent food, easy chairs and open fire in comfortable lounge, well kept Tolly on handpump (and perfectly served Worthington White Shield); small convivial public bar, small restaurant *(John Hibbs, R Wiles, J A Jennings)*

Fen Ditton [Green End], *Plough*: Whitbreads Brewers Fayre food pub, comfortably refurbished, notable for its attractive riverside garden with gazebo; big car park, nice walk across meadows from town *(Howard and Sue Gascoyne, LYM)*

Fenstanton, Cambs [High St – off A604 nr St Ives; TL3168], *King William IV*: Attractive cottage-style pub with big round tables, wide range of generously served bar food, separate restaurant *(Alan and Ruth Woodhouse)*

Fowlmere, Cambs [High St; TL4245], *Swan House*: Helpful friendly landlord, excellent bar food, separate varied restaurant menu, proper wine cellar; handy for the RSPB reserve and not far from Duxford war museum *(Anon)*

☆ **Godmanchester**, Cambs [London Rd; TL2470], *Exhibition*: Interesting décor and good choice of excellent bar food – new licensees are consolidating this pub's high reputation *(E Robinson, Dr and Mrs R J Ashleigh)*

Gorefield, Cambs [TF4111], *Woodmans Cottage*: Spacious modernised open-plan bar rambling around central servery, leatherette stools and banquettes, beams and open fires, welcoming staff and lively atmosphere, good value bar food, tables on front verandah; rather late evening opening, welcoming Australian landlady *(John Honnor, BB)*

Grantchester, Cambs [TL4354], *Green Man*: Attractively laid-out pub in pretty village with individual furnishings; unusual salad bar with wide variety, not cheap but generous helpings (readers have not been unanimous about food value – nor about service quality); Tolly ales; short stroll to beautiful riverside meadows *(E Kinnersly, M C Howells, LYM)*; *Red Lion*: Big food pub with sheltered terrace and good-sized lawn (which has had animals to entertain the many children that have come here); has been comfortable and spacious, with busy food counter and popular restaurant, though as this edition went to press there was a longish closure for refurbishment *(Wayne Brindle, LYM – up-to-date reports please)*; [junction Coton rd with Cambridge–Trumpington rd – OS Sheet 154 reference 433557] *Rupert Brooke*: Tastefully refurbished Whitbreads pub recently done out with beamery, stripped brickwork, farm and forestry tools, bric-à-brac and so forth – and framed extracts of Rupert Brooke poems; lobby leads to central bar with cheerful fire and two further raised areas, with round stained-wood tables and brocaded chairs; well kept Flowers IPA and Original and Wethereds on handpump, good plentiful bar food including vegetarian dishes served quickly, cheerful young bar staff along with attentive Italian catering manager, separate restaurant, unobtrusive piped pop music in main bar; back lawn and shrubbery; the old Cadbury's Cocoa clock stands permanently at ten to three *(Frank Cummins, Gordon Theaker, Alan and Ruth Woodhouse)*

☆ **Great Chishill**, Cambs [TL4239], *Pheasant*: Good atmosphere in unassuming but interestingly furnished pub, good food (not Sun lunchtime or Mon), well kept Adnams and Greene King IPA, charming garden; closed Mon lunchtime *(LYM)*

Great Eversden, Cambs [off A603; TL3653],
Hoops: Country pub, good atmosphere,
friendly landlord, pool-table and darts,
Charles Wells beers, simple and well
prepared bar food *(Gordon Theaker)*
Guyhirn, Cambs [High Rd; TF3903], *Oliver
Twist*: Free house with wide choice of beers,
reasonably priced bar food and separate
dining-room serving excellent evening meals;
a good place to stay at *(E Robinson)*
Harrold, Beds [SP9456], *Oakley Arms*: Large
thatched village pub, comfortable and
welcoming; real ale and varied choice of
unusually interesting home-made bar food
(F M Williams)
Harston, Cambs [48 Royston Rd (A10) – nr
M11 junction 11; TL4251], *Queens Head*:
Attractive, friendly and efficient, with well
kept Greene King ale and decent house wine;
good bar food that specialises in home-made
pies with crisp chips; the glass engraver
around the corner is worth a visit *(Joy
Heatherley)*
nr **Hexton**, Beds [Pegsdon – B655 a mile E of
Hexton; TL1030], *Live & Let Live*: Snug
little pub with lovely garden below the
Chilterns, two rooms opening off tiled and
panelled tap-room, Greene King ales and
usual pub food, amiable dog *(John and
Margaret Estdale, LYM)*
Hildersham, Cambs [High St; TL5448], *Pear
Tree*: Friendly little village local, good if a
little pricey bar food *(Stuart Watkinson)*
Hinxton, Cambs [High St; TL4945], *Red
Lion*: Clean and cosy, some real beams, well
kept Brakspears PA and interesting choice of
freshly prepared food *(John Baker)*
☆ **Histon**, Cambs [TL4363], *Red Lion*: Super
pub with clean, warm and friendly bar;
excellent food (especially the seafood pie)
and several real ales such as Adnams, Greene
King and superb Timothy Taylors Landlord
(Graham and Glenis Watkins)
Holme, Cambs [Station Rd; TL1987],
Admiral Wells: Large, characterful pub very
popular with commuters; ale brewed for the
pub by Woodfordes; restaurant is well
spoken of *(John Baker)*
Houghton, Cambs [TL2872], *Jolly Butchers*:
Traditional black and white pub with beams
and brasses; quiet, family atmosphere, good
bar food including Sun lunches, outside
seating and occasional barbecues ; children's
play area *(Simon Scott)*; *Three Horseshoes*:
French windows into garden from extended
refurbished lounge, locals' bar with black
beams and inglenook, well kept Watneys-
related real ales, bar food (not Sun evening)
including lunchtime cold buffet *(Wayne
Brindle, LYM)*
Houghton Conquest, Beds [3 miles from M1
junction 11; TL0441], *Knife & Cleaver*: Old
and well furnished dining pub (more of a
restaurant really) with well kept Banks &
Taylors Shefford Bitter, excellent wines,
superb food in lovely conservatory

restaurant and friendly staff *(Brian and Jenny
Seller)*
Huntingdon, Cambs [TL2371], *George*:
Elegant and spacious Georgian lounge bar in
comfortable THF hotel, popular for bar food
(Sun traditional lunch only); restaurant;
bedrooms overlook galleried central
courtyard where Shakespeare play
performed during last fortnight or so of June;
bedrooms *(LYM)*; *Old Bridge*: Quite
individual but quite splendid in the Poste
Hotels manner, with same kind of buffet as
at George, Stamford (see Leics/Lincs/Notts
main entries); bedrooms *(Syd and Wyn
Donald)*; [Victoria Sq] *Victoria*: Welcoming
local, well kept beers including Paines, farm
cider excellent value, imaginative bar food –
perhaps the best of the pubs as opposed to
hotels here *(Wayne Brindle)*
Isleham, Cambs [TL6474], *Griffin*: Pleasant,
local atmosphere, well kept Adnams
(Graham and Glenis Watkins)
Kirtling, Cambs [TL6857], *Queens Head*:
Matter-of-fact but very civilised small village
inn in attractive country setting which has
had short choice of food including good
home-cooked main dishes and well kept
Tolly Original, but as this edition went to
press we heard of plans for its closure and
conversion to a private house *(LYM)*
Leighton Bromswold, Cambs [TL1175],
Green Man: Neatly modernised open-plan
village pub with hundreds of good
horsebrasses on heavy low beams, bar food,
well kept Tolly Original, sensible games area
(LYM)
Linton, Cambs [TL5646], *Dog & Duck*: Old
village local with bustling, homely
atmosphere; low-beamed bar, fireplace, old
prints and brasses on walls, Greene King on
handpump, lunchtime and evening bar food;
pleasant garden at rear by babbling river and
waterfall, lots of tame ducks *(Howard and Sue
Gascoyne)*
☆ **Madingley**, Cambs [TL3960], *Three
Horseshoes*: Smart thatched pub with
comfortable furnishings and elegant garden,
rather pricey but usually good food including
popular summer buffet, restaurant-like
starters and appetising choice of puddings;
Tolly and Original on handpump and usually
a good range of wines; restaurant; in recent
years service has not been a consistently
strong point here and we'd like more reports
on this aspect, as the pub has otherwise been
a candidate for the main entries; children
welcome *(Mrs E M Thompson, R Wiles, Mary
and Edward Fisher, JMC, Rita Horridge,
S Lowherd, LYM)*
☆ **March**, Cambs [Acre Rd; turn off B1101
opp Royal Exchange pub on corner of
Market Sq; TL4195], *Acre*: Busy at lunchtime
for its good value food, this pub separated by
a narrow stretch of meadow from the River
Nene has an airy main bar with blond
captain's chairs and blue plush stools around

the tables, more tables in a smaller side bar with unusual horizontal planks for the backs of its wall seats and tables out on a verandah and terrace; keg Greene King; can be very quiet in the evenings *(John Honnor, R H Inns, BB)*

March, *Golden Lion*: Tidied up (though not modernised overmuch) and serves well kept Greene King IPA; caters well for young families *(John Baker)*

Marholm, Cambs [TF1402], *Fitzwilliam Arms*: Old floodlit thatched pub in small village, reasonably large front, well filled bar with tables and upholstered seats and three open fires; well kept Ind Coope real ale on handpump, food including home-made pizzas in bar and back extension, friendly service; also known as Green Man because of the way the tree by the front entrance has been shaped *(T Mansell, Mike Prentice)*

Melchbourne, Beds [Knotting Rd; TL0265], *St John Arms*: Friendly rambling country pub with bar food, well kept Greene King real ales, peaceful cottagey garden *(LYM)*

Milton, Cambs [TL4762], *White Horse*: Free house with choice of real ales and good atmosphere; good value food *(Sue and Tim Kinning)*

Molesworth, Cambs [TL0775], *Cross Keys*: Well kept Adnams, good service, good value food; bedrooms *(A V Lewis)*

Needingworth, Cambs [Overcote Lane; pub signposted from A1123; TL3472], *Pike & Eel*: Marvellous peaceful riverside location, with spacious lawns and marina; extensive glass-walled restaurant (food confined to this, but earning warm reports from knowledgeable readers – it includes well liked daily specials, a cold buffet with help-yourself salads and excellent puddings), snugger areas as well as big plush bar in original core; altogether there's lots of room, including provision for children (one reader with a baby was treated with exceptional kindness); the only drawback for some is that especially if you do go for the food the style of the place is more that of a restaurant than of a pub; pleasant bedrooms *(Mr and Mrs J D Cranston, Betsy Coury, Frank W Gadbois, Sue and Tim Kinning, LYM)*

Northill, Beds [TL1546], *Crown*: Consistently high standard in Greene King pub with welcoming staff, reasonably priced varied and interesting bar food (the ploughman's is noted as good value), spacious garden with seats and tables; quite handy both for the A1 and the Shuttleworth collection *(R H Inns, P Devitt)*

☆ **Odell**, Beds [Horsefair Lane; SP9658], *Bell*: Lovely old pub with good Greene King beer and excellent value bar food including home-cooked pies, decent range of vegetarian dishes and children's dishes; garden backing on to River Ouse *(Mrs E M Thompson)*

Odsey, Cambs [A505 NE of Baldock, by Ashwell & Morden stn; TL2938], *Jester*:

Rural spot by railway, large, comfortable, open-plan pub with carpets throughout, variety of seating including banquettes, chairs and stools; pleasant atmosphere, friendly licensees, three real ales, bar food, restaurant with interesting menu *(Jim Froggatt, Denise Plummer)*

☆ **Old Warden**, Beds [TL1343], *Hare & Hounds*: Cosy and friendly old local in charming village, with comfortable lounge, subdued piped music, public bar with darts and fruit machine; Charles Wells beers, large choice of hot and cold food generously served, restaurant, garden with children's play area; handy for the Shuttleworth collection *(Lyn and Bill Capper, BMS)*

Old Weston, Cambs [SP7560], *Swan*: Low-ceilinged old pub with big inglenook, Adnams and Greene King real ale, bar food *(LYM – more reports please)*

Peterborough, Cambs [465 Oundle Rd; off A605 in Woodston; TL1999], *Botolph Arms*: Sam Smiths house with interesting interior including predominantly stone floors and a medley of seating; popular with business people at lunchtime *(Wayne Brindle)*; [Ham Lane, Orton Meadows] *Granary*: Beefeater steakhouse on edge of golf course and short walk from Nene Valley Railway; elaborate modern building with mixed décor, spacious lounge bar with comfortable family area; good choice of bar food, restaurant, maybe Whitbreads Castle Eden on handpump, tables outside behind, overlooking greens *(Howard and Sue Gascoyne)*

☆ **Ridgmont**, Beds [2½ miles from M1 junction 13: towards Woburn Sands, then left towards Ampthill on A418; SP9736], *Rose & Crown*: Old brick house with comfortable low-ceilinged public bar, smarter lounge with Rupert annual cover prints, straightforward bar food, well kept Charles Wells Eagle and Bombardier on handpump; two dogs and maybe rabbits in attractive back garden, restaurant *(A T Langton, L M Miall, Michael and Alison Sandy, Lyn and Bill Capper)*

☆ **nr Sandy**, Beds [Deepdale; B1042 towards Potton and Cambridge; TL1749], *Locomotive*: Open-plan bar with lots of railway memorabilia, big garden with views and summer Sunday barbecues, bar food (not Sun and Mon evenings), new restaurant area, well kept Charles Wells Eagle and Bombardier; handy for RSPB headquarters; children allowed in eating area *(Edward Barber, NBM, LYM)*

Sawston, Cambs [TL4849], *University Arms*: Ordinary building but good choice of real ales including Adnams, Boddingtons, Marstons and Sam Smiths and attractive bar food *(Alan and Ruth Woodhouse)*

Sharnbrook, Beds [SP9959], *Swan With Two Nicks*: Popular locals' pub in picturesque H E Bates-style village; friendly welcome and well kept Charles Wells Eagle *(John Baker)*

St Ives, Cambs [Ramsey Rd; TL3171], *Slepe Hall*: Plush hotel bar with friendly service and reasonably priced food; bedrooms *(Wayne Brindle)*

Stanbridge, Beds [pub signposted off A5 N of Dunstable; SP9623], *Five Bells*: Large low-beamed bar, very comfortable, smart, quiet and friendly, with well kept Charles Wells; though most customers seem to be on their way to the rather nice restaurant, there's as much welcome for people just having a drink *(Michael and Alison Sandy)*

☆ **Stretham**, Cambs [Cambridge Rd (off A10); TL5174], *Lazy Otter*: Riverside spot with boat moorings; family pub, large bar and conservatory with homely décor, pleasant atmosphere, helpful staff, well kept Adnams and Greene King, fairly priced and imaginative bar food including Fenman's lunch, restaurant; waterside garden with terrace, moorings on River Cam, swings, family theme days with games and evening barbecues; big car park *(Nigel Gibbs, E and G Slater)*

Studham, Beds [TL0215], *Bell*: Warm welcome from licensees and staff, well presented drinks and excellent bar food *(Karen Elton)*; *Red Lion*: Handily placed for Whipsnade Zoo, in attractive spot with tables outside by climbing roses, looking up to grassy common; peaceful and civilised plushly modernised lounge bar with cheerful décor including attractive prints, small alcove room with bar billiards, good range of well kept beer including Adnams, Hook Norton Best and Old Hookey, Marstons Pedigree, Youngers IPA and Brakspears or Wadworths 6X, wide choice of whiskies; changed hands at the end of 1988 – promising initial reports on the friendly new regime and lunchtime bar food including a wide range of excellent value lunchtime 'bloomers' *(Michael and Alison Sandy, E G Parish, R Simmonds, LYM – more reports please)*

Stuntney, Cambs [Soham Rd (A142 Ely–Newmarket); TL5578], *Fenlands Lodge*: Warm, friendly atmosphere in lounge bar, well kept Bass on handpump, wide range of good value bar food from sandwiches to grills and including a cold table, excellent service, restaurant ; luxuriously modern bedrooms *(John and Margaret Harvey)*

☆ **Sutton**, Beds [village signposted off B1040 Biggleswade–Potton; TL2247], *John o' Gaunt*: Lovely pink-washed low building framed by larch and apple trees; cosy low-beamed bar with easy chairs and low settles around copper-topped tables, enterprising bar food including imaginative seafood dishes, well kept Greene King IPA, pretty flowers; close to fine fourteenth-century packhorse bridge with shallow ford taking cars past it; service normally friendly and attentive, but can be very quiet *(Joan and Tony Walker, Alison Hayward, Nick Dowson, GB, CH, LYM)*

☆ **Swaffham Prior**, Cambs [B1102 NE of Cambridge; TL5764], *Red Lion*: Welcoming and very friendly staff in pleasant small village pub with Tolly Original and Old Strong tapped from cask on bar, wide range of decent food from ploughman's through ham and eggs to steaks in separate dining lounge *(M and J Back, K R Harris)*

☆ **Tempsford**, Beds [TL1652], *Anchor*: Extensive road-house with lots for children, included as a useful break from A1 and notable for its big riverside gardens with outdoor chess and draughts, boules, fishing on the River Ouse; quickly served straightforward food, restaurant *(Wayne Brindle, LYM)*

Toddington, Beds [64 High St; TL0028], *Bedford Arms*: Well preserved and not over-decorated Tudor pub with well kept Charles Wells Eagle; good provision for families with children *(John C Baker)*

Totternhoe, Beds [SP9821], *Cross Keys*: Very small, friendly bar in picturesque black and white pub with lovely garden and orchard views *(Stephen and Helen Doole, BB)*

Trumpington, Cambs [High St; TL4454], *Coach & Horses*: Big helpings of good bar food such as curries, lasagne and excellent choice of cold platters in large rambling roadside free house with Adnams, Greene King and Marstons Pedigree; very friendly staff *(Alan and Ruth Woodhouse)*

☆ **Turvey**, Beds [off A428, by church; SP9452], *Three Cranes*: Well kept and tastefully furnished old pub with attractive window boxes, several good real ales such as Batemans (including Mild) and Hook Norton, choice of decent bar food such as ploughman's, pizza, pies and lasagne, restaurant, friendly licensees, seats outside *(F M Williams)*

Turvey, Beds, *Laws*: Superb hotel bar with really good reasonably priced food, especially Sun lunch; bedrooms *(R H Sawyer)*

Upware, Cambs [village signposted off A1123 Stretham–Wicken; TL5370], *Five Miles From Anywhere, No Hurry*: Riverside free house with spacious modern layout – almost more that of a town hotel than of a country pub which really is as isolated as its name implies; friendly and attentive service, good value bar food and a splendid stretch of moorings on the River Cam *(R Robinson, LYM)*

Weston Colville, Cambs [Weston Green; TL6153], *Fox & Hounds*: Very welcoming and friendly, comfortably refurbished, with excellent unusual food including huge pieces of garlic bread with really good fillings *(Alan and Ruth Woodhouse)*

☆ **Whipsnade**, Beds [B4540 E; TL0117], *Old Hunters Lodge*: Smallish bar with very good food from sandwiches up, particularly including fish dishes, well kept Greene King Abbot, nice character; good restaurant;

children welcome *(Mr and Mrs G D Amos, D L Johnson)*

Whittlesey, Cambs [B1040 N; TL2696], *Old Dog in a Doublet*: Isolated fenland spot by River Nene, close to Bronze Age site at Flag Fen; large, comfortably furnished bar with good range of beer including Adnams and Greene King, generous helpings of good reasonably priced bar food, restaurant, tables outside; much changed since the days when it was a hangout of the great fenland skaters who invented bandy, the even rougher precursor of ice hockey *(R D Norman)*

☆ **Whittlesford,** Cambs [off B1379 S of Cambridge – handy for M11 junction 10, via A505; TL4748], *Tickell Arms*: This idiosyncratic and flamboyantly theatrical pub delights many readers (and indeed ourselves), who enjoy its exuberant panache, individual furnishings, flower-filled conservatory, formal garden, distinctive food and classical music; but the owner – who never masks his feelings – comes down hard on T-shirts (a harmless enough sumptuary regulation in a pub of this type) and on people he sees as long-haired lefties or as bad parkers; though some would say this is perhaps the most enjoyable pub in the area, others have felt so uncomfortable with the style of management that we hesitate to list it among the main entries – but if you don't know it, do try it (and tell us what you think)! *(Peter Hall, AE, GRE, Dr P D Smart, M A and C R Starling, Barbara Hatfield, Frank W Gadbois, George Little, LYM)*

Woburn, Beds [18 Bedford St; SP9433], *Magpie*: Friendly atmosphere and jovial landlord in village local with well kept Watneys-related real ales, good value bar food (not Sun), restaurant, tables outside; bedrooms *(R Q Hepherd, Sue Bourke)*

Cheshire

New main entries to mention particularly here are the civilised old Spinner &
Bergamot at Comberbatch and engagingly relaxed Dog at Peover Heath (both
with particularly good food), the attractively reconstructed old Boot in
Chester, the handsome Alvanley Arms at Cotebrook (also popular for food
and a comfortable place to stay), the picturesque Tollemache Arms at Faddiley
(new licensees doing well), and the poised and comfortable Smoker at Plumley
(again, a place where new licensees have been earning praise). One of the
county's most popular pubs, Bells of Peover, also has new licensees; they were
formerly well known to many readers at the Maypole in Acton Bridge (and are
closely related to the licensees of the Spinner & Bergamot), and we have high
hopes of Bells in their hands. Pubs that seem to have been gaining even
stronger support than before this last year include the Cholmondeley Arms at
Bickley Moss (the food at this imaginatively converted schoolhouse earns high
praise), the Stanley Arms up in the Macclesfield Forest at Bottom of the Oven
(fresh flowers, friendly atmosphere, good value), the smart Bears Head at
Brereton Green (long-serving continental staff give it a distinctive blend of
style and informality – a nice place to stay), the Crown at Goostrey (the family
in charge give it a really warm atmosphere), the Chetwode Arms at Lower
Whitley (the hard-working licensee keeps this nice old-fashioned country pub
spick and span), the Bird in Hand at Mobberley (a fine example of a good all-
rounder), and the Sutton Hall Hotel at Sutton (an elegant old place, nice to
stay at, with good food and a warmly welcoming bar). Connoisseurs of
Cheshire pubs (and the county is very rich in pubs of real character) should not
miss the Pheasant perched on the Peckforton Hills at Higher Burwardsley, the
Holly Bush at Little Leigh (a real throwback – part farm, part pub), and the
Highwayman looking out over the Cheshire Plain from Rainow; each is quite
unique. In the Lucky Dip, pubs to note include lots in Chester itself,

The White Lion, Barthomley

particularly the newish Telfords Warehouse; the Lamb in Nantwich; the Ferry at Fiddlers Ferry near Warrington; the White Lion at Weston (very handy for the M6 now); the Ship at Wincle; and the Swan at Wybunbury.

ALVANLEY   SJ4974 Map 7
White Lion
2½ miles from M56, junction 14; A5117 towards Helsby, bear left into A56 then quickly turn right, following village signpost; in village, turn right into Manley Road

Opposite the church on a quiet lane, this pretty black-shuttered white pub has decorative plates on the walls of the cosy lounge, as well as softly cushioned red plush seats and wall banquettes and beer-steins, pistols, copper jugs and so forth hanging from its nicely moulded black beams; piped music. Generous helpings of tasty food include soup (90p), sandwiches (from £1, toasties from £1.10, steak barm-cake £1.50), quite a wide variety of ploughman's (from £1.70), home-made hot-pot or cottage pie (£1.60), salads (from £2.80), and specials like home-made steak pie (£3) or chicken chasseur (£3.50); puddings (£1.20). Well kept Greenalls Mild and Bitter on handpump; friendly staff. The smaller public bar has darts, dominoes, fruit machine and space game. Outside, there are rustic picnic-table sets on the grass by the play area (which has an assault course and sand-floored fortress), white tables and chairs under cocktail parasols, and attractive hanging baskets; an adjacent field has various ducks, geese and sheep. *(Recommended by Brian and Anna Marsden, BHP, Geoff Halson, J J Kennedy, E Lee)*

*Greenalls   Licensees Keith and Brenda Morris   Real ale   Meals and snacks (12–2, 6–9.30)
Children welcome   Open 11.30–3, 5.30–11 all year*

BARTHOMLEY   SJ7752 Map 7
White Lion ★   [illustrated on page 91]
Under a mile from M6 junction 16; village signposted from Crewe exit

One of the most attractive buildings in a pretty village, this early seventeenth-century pub has a marvellously friendly, unspoilt atmosphere. The simply furnished main room has heavy oak beams in the low ceiling (one big enough to house quite a collection of plates), attractively moulded black panelling, Cheshire watercolours and prints, an open fire and latticed windows; up some steps, a second room has more oak panelling, a high-backed winged settle, a paraffin lamp hinged to the wall, another open fire and sensibly placed darts, shove-ha'penny and dominoes. Limited, cheap bar snacks run to hot pies, excellent ham, beef or cheese salad rolls, and soup at lunchtime; well kept Burtonwood Bitter and Mild on handpump. Tables under the old yew tree beside the black and white timbered and thatched pub or on the front cobbles, have a peaceful view of the village and the early fifteenth:-century red sandstone church of St Bertiline just opposite. *(Recommended by William Rodgers, Martin Aust, Denis Mann, Theo Schofield, Ewan McCall, Wayne Brindle, S D Samuels, Graham Gibson)*

*Burtonwood   Real ale   Snacks (not Sun evening)   Children at lunchtime only
Open 11–3, 6–11*

BARTON   SJ4554 Map 7
Cock o' Barton
A534 E of Farndon

The separate snug areas in the more or less open-plan bar of this handsome sandstone pub have old-fashioned furnishings that include high-backed built-in cushioned settles; also, prints of ornamental fowls and newer ones of game birds on the bobbly white walls, log fires, black beams and joists, and old carpet squares on the ancient black slate tiles of the older small-roomed part, with green Turkey carpet in the most spacious area (closest to the entry). There's a gun above the door and hunting scene prints in the entrance hall. Well kept McEwans 80/- (called Draught here) on handpump, Youngers Scotch on electric; friendly, welcoming service. Bar food includes home-made soup, sandwiches, ploughman's, cannelloni, gammon and eight-ounce rump steak, with a wider lunchtime choice on Tuesdays to Fridays. There are some teak seats by a little lily pool in a dwarf shrubbery; in summer they sell snacks and soft drinks from an outside servery. (*Recommended by Jon Wainwright, Philip Riding, Graham Gibson, Laurence Manning, Peter Corris, Lee Goulding*)

Free house   Real ale   Meals and snacks   Open 12–2.15, 7.30–11; closed Mon lunchtime

BICKLEY MOSS   SJ5549   Map 7

Cholmondeley Arms ★ ⊗

Cholmondeley; A49 5½ miles N of Whitchurch

An unusual conversion of what was formerly a Victorian schoolhouse, this fresh and airy cross-shaped pub has a warm, friendly atmosphere, first-class drinks and a wide range of good imaginative food. Furnishings range from cane and bentwood to pews and carved oak, there are masses of Victorian pictures (especially portraits and military subjects), patterned paper on the shutters that matches the curtains, high ceilings, an open fire, and a great stag's head over one of the side arches; unobtrusively well reproduced taped music. Besides changing specials, bar food includes freshly made soup (£1.25), sandwiches (from £1.50), several children's dishes (from £1.50), a complicated terrine or ploughman's (£2.75), garlic mushrooms with bacon (£2.95), hot crab pâté (£3), omelettes (£3.50), good stuffed pancakes (£3.75), a tasty home-made pie of the day (£3.95), devilled kidneys (£4.25), salads with home-made mayonnaise, gammon or hot beef curry (£4.50), chicken breast wrapped in bacon, grilled and coated with a chilli and honey sauce (£5.75), steaks (from £7) and grilled king prawns and chicken with satay sauce (£7.95); a very wide choice of home-made puddings such as fantastic syrup sponge and ice-creams (from £1.50). Even the table settings have obviously been carefully thought out. Well kept Marstons Burton and Pedigree on handpump, with a guest such as Border; big (four cup) pot of coffee. Up over the bar a gantry carries some of the old school desks, but more importantly the old blackboard listing ten or so interesting and often uncommon wines by the glass, including a decent champagne. There are seats out on a lawn. The Manager, John Radford, was with the licensees in their days at the Crown in Hopton Wafers. (*Recommended by Philip Williams, Martin Aust, Philip Riding, M A and W R Proctor, C F Walling, M and J Godfrey, Graham Gibson, W C M Jones, Laurence Manning, Jon Wainwright*)

Free house   Licensees Julian and Ginney Harrison   Real ale   Meals and snacks (12–2.15, 7–10)   Children welcome   Bedrooms tel Cholmondeley (0829) 720300; £30S/£40S   Open 11–3, 6.30–11 all year; winter evening opening 7; closed 25 Dec

BOLLINGTON   SJ9377   Map 7

Vale

29 Adlington Road; off B5091 on road heading N by railway viaduct; OS Sheet 118 reference 931781

This quietly modernised, friendly pub – close to a bowling-green, cricket field, play-park and tennis courts – has tapestried wall seats all the way round the open-plan bar, wheel-back chairs, and tables set with cheery red tablecloths at lunchtime. Also, heavy dark green velvet curtains, brass platters on the end stripped-stone wall, some racehorse prints and 1936 Gallaghers cricketer cigarette cards, a log fire in the stone fireplace (as well as central heating), and a couple of big stone supporting pillars with internal arches. Food includes home-made soup or sandwiches (90p), ploughman's (£3), home-made dishes such as chilli con carne (£3) and steak and kidney pie or lasagne (£3.20), seafood platter (£3.30), and half a chicken or scampi (£3.70); they are aiming to increase their fish dishes which at the moment include cod, plaice or haddock (£2.70) and lemon sole (£3.20); the beef and ham are home-cooked, and the chips are home-made. Well kept Thwaites Bitter and Mild and Timothy Taylors Landlord on handpump from the substantial heavily timber-topped stone-built corner counter. Fruit machine, good pop music. The garden is a neat little lawn with picnic-table sets, by the edge of a wood, and there are swings, a slide, a rocking horse, climbing-frame and paddling pool. The charming village is being well preserved as a conservation area. Nearby is the start of *Good Walks Guide* Walk 73. (*Recommended by Brian and Anna Marsden, Paul Wreglesworth, Dr and Mrs C D E Morris*)

Free house   Licensee Mrs Patricia Capper   Real ale   Lunchtime meals and snacks (12–2, 6.30–9.30; not Mon lunchtime exc bank hols)   Open 11.30–3, 5.30–11; closed Mon lunchtime exc bank hols

BOTTOM OF THE OVEN   SJ9872 Map 7

Stanley Arms 🏮

From A537 Buxton–Macclesfield heading towards Macclesfield, take first left turn (not signposted) after Cat & Fiddle; OS Sheet 118 reference 980723

With big bunches of flowers in summer, open fires in winter, little landscape watercolours on the ochre walls and piped Vivaldi, the atmosphere in this isolated moorland pub is warmly friendly. Two of the three snug rooms, notable for their shiny black lacquered woodwork, have muted red and black flowery plush wall settles and stools, some dark blue seats, and low dimpled copper tables on the grey carpets; the third is laid out as a dining-room, with pretty pastel tablecloths. Excellent value-for-money bar food (served in remarkably generous helpings) includes at lunchtime, sandwiches (from £1, not Sunday), home-made soup (£1.20), ploughman's (£3) and lasagne (£3.80); in the evening there are more substantial dishes such as outstanding salads (from £3.95), chicken in a bacon, mushroom and wine sauce (£4.95), beef cooked in Guinness (£5.20), halibut steak (£6.95) and half a duckling with orange sauce (£7.30); also, a daily special. Well kept Marstons Burton and Pedigree on handpump, and a good range of spirits. There are some picnic-table sets on the grass behind. Quiet during the week, it can get very busy at weekends. (*Recommended by Paul Wreglesworth, Philip Riding, Mr and Mrs B Hobden, Alan Skull, Graham Gibson, Lee Goulding, Dr and Mrs R J Ashleigh*)

Marstons   Licensee Alan Harvey   Real ale   Lunchtime snacks and meals (12–2.30, 7–10) Restaurant tel Sutton (026 05) 2414   Children in eating area and restaurant   Open 11.30–3, 7–11

BRERETON GREEN   SJ7864 Map 7

Bears Head 🛏️

1¾ miles from M6 junction 17; fork left from Congleton road almost immediately, then left on to A50; also from junction 18, via Holmes Chapel

Courteous and smartly uniformed staff set the tone in this friendly and civilised black and white timbered inn. There's a series of open-plan communicating rooms – served by two bar counters – with masses of heavy black beams and timbers, antique panelled settles, big Windsor armchairs and more modern but quite harmonious ladder-back seats, a corner cupboard full of Venetian glass, and a large brick inglenook fireplace full of gleaming copper pots (with a winter coal fire). A section of wall in one room (under glass for protection) has had the plaster removed to show the construction of timber underneath. Bar food consists of home-made soup (£1.25), sandwiches (from £1.45, excellent steak and onion £4.20), home-made pâtés (from £2.75), salads (£3.95, poached fresh Scotch salmon £4.25), and daily hot dishes such as gammon with egg or pineapple, roast chicken or fried fillet of plaice (all £3.95) and sirloin steak (£6.95); home-made puddings like chocolate roulade (£1.75). Bass and Burtonwood Bitter on handpump, well kept in fine deep cellars; fruit machine, soothing piped music. A pretty side terrace has white cast-iron tables and chairs under Hawaiian-style rustling parasols, big black cast-iron lamp clusters and a central fountain, and is sheltered by a little balconied brick building. *(Recommended by David Shillitoe, Laurence Manning, Charles and Mary Winpenny, John and Pat Smyth, Robert and Vicky Tod, AE, Graham Gibson, E G Parish)*

Free house   Licensee Roberto Tarquini   Real ale   Meals and snacks (not Sun evening) Restaurant (closed Sun evening)   Children in eating area, restaurant, Italian trattoria (closed Sun and Mon evenings)   Open 11–3, 6–11 all year   Bedrooms tel Holmes Chapel (0477) 35251; £41.50S(£43.50B)/£49.50B

CHESTER   SJ4166   Map 7

Boot

Eastgate Row North

This pub used to be just the upstairs part when it opened via a long corridor off the balconied shopping arcade above the street. Now, the main part is downstairs, opened at the end of 1988 after a long spell of rebuilding. It's been carefully done on two floors, using good materials – oak flooring and flagstones, solidly built-in wooden furniture, heavy beams and woodwork, the brewery's Yorkshire-rose emblem worked into stained-glass panels, in the latticed windows, ancient wattle and daub exposed behind glass panels, and there are a couple of framed Victorian newspapers; fruit machine, piped music. A handsome staircase takes you to an oak-panelled function room; there is a further lounge beyond the food serving room. Well kept Sam Smiths OB (delivered bright from the brewery) and Museum tapped from cask downstairs; excellent service from seven bar staff. Bar food includes filled rolls (90p), soup (£1), pâté or hot beef sandwich (£2), and ploughman's, filled baked potatoes and quiche (all £2.25). The attractively landscaped zoo to the north of the city is good. *(Recommended by Mr and Mrs J H Adam, Jon Wainwright, Graham Gibson, Dennis Royles)*

Sam Smiths   Licensees Anne and Peter Kinsey   Real ale   Snacks (not evenings)   No nearby parking   Open 11–4, 5–11; Sat evening opening 7; closed 25 and 26 Dec

Falcon

Lower Bridge Street

This splendidly ornamental timbered building dates mainly from around 1600, though the massive stone blocks of the base and the cellars go back some 700 years or more. Inside, it's been carefully decorated and the bar staff wear uniforms; upstairs, the quiet, airy room has a fine range of latticed windows looking over the street (it's available for functions in the early part of the week). Bar food includes open sandwiches (£2), various salads (£2.95) and daily hot dishes such as casseroles, steak and kidney pie or moussaka (from £2.95); well kept Sam Smiths OB and Museum on handpump; fruit machine, piped music. It can get very crowded on Friday and Saturday evenings. This whole area of Chester – centring particularly on this handsome pub – has been well restored and brought back to life. *(Recommended by Jon Wainwright, Dennis Royles)*

Sam Smiths   Licensees Gail and Andrew Waller   Real ale   Meals and snacks (lunchtime, not Sun)   Children in upstairs bar lunchtime only   Parking may be difficult   Jazz (Thurs evening and occasionally Sat lunchtime)   Open 11–4, 5–11

COMBERBATCH   SJ6477 Map 7

Spinner & Bergamot 🏮

Village signposted from A553 and A559 NW of Northwich; pub towards Great Budworth

The hottest tip here is for the scampi (£5.50); the home-made batter makes them quite special. Other home-cooked bar food, in generous helpings, includes sandwiches (from £1.20), soup (£1), several other starters such as deep-fried mushrooms filled with pâté (£1.80), steak and kidney pie (£3.60), gammon and egg (£4), steaks (from eight-ounce rump £6.50) and dishes of the day such as potted shrimps (£2), lasagne (£4) or fresh salmon salad (£5.50). Readers think nothing of a 30-mile drive for the Sunday lunch. The back dining-room is attractive and softly lit, with country-kitchen furniture (some of oak), pretty curtains and a big inglenook. The Turkey-carpeted front bar has similar furniture, with red plush button-back built-in wall banquettes too, some toby jugs hanging from the beams, and one or two hunting prints. The neat red-tiled public bar has darts. Well kept Greenalls Bitter and Mild on handpump, friendly licensees, efficient service. A hatch in the front lobby serves the white tables out on a sloping lawn, which has swings and a climber; there are lots of flower tubs and hanging baskets outside, bunches of fresh flowers inside. (*Recommended by Syd and Wyn Donald, Jon Wainwright, D P Manchett, G Eyre-Rodger*)

Greenalls   Licensees Doug and Mavis Hughes   Real ale   Meals and snacks (not Sun evening)   Open 11.30–3.30, 5.30–11 all year

COTEBROOK   SJ5765 Map 7

Alvanley Arms 🛏

Junction A49/B5152, N of Tarporley

The only complaint about the food in this handsome old creeper-covered Georgian inn seems to be that the helpings are too big for some readers. Served by waitresses, it includes home-made soup (£1.15), other starters or light snacks from melon (£1.60) to potted shrimps (£2.85) or pâté (£2.95), ploughman's (£3.50), salads (from £3.75), fresh plaice (£3.60), good home-made steak and kidney pie (£3.95), lamb chops (£4.95) and eight-ounce sirloin steak (£6.95); the vegetables are fresh. The main bar has fairly close-set tables, dining-height by the red plush wall banquettes around the sides, and lower ones with plush stools in the middle; there are a few hunting and sporting prints, brasses, neat high beams and a big open fire. On the other side of a pleasantly chintzy small hall is a quieter but broadly similar room, with more interesting prints and a Delft shelf of china. Well kept Robinsons Mild, Best and Old Tom on handpump, prompt and friendly service, faint piped music, fruit machine tucked away in a lobby. A side lawn by a pond with geese looks out over rolling fields and has fairy-lit picnic-table sets under a small cedar, and swings; food is not normally served out here. (*Recommended by Geoff Halson, C F Walling, Dr P Webb, G T Jones, W C M Jones, Mr and Mrs J H Adam*)

Robinsons   Licensee Kenneth Moulton   Real ale   Meals and snacks (12–2, 6–10 Tues–Sat; 12–2, 6–9.30 Sun, Mon)   Candlelit restaurant   Children in eating area   Open 11.30–3, 5.30–11 all year   Bedrooms tel Little Budworth (082 921) 200; £25B/£50B

FADDILEY   SJ5753 Map 7

Tollemache Arms

A534 Nantwich–Wrexham

The friendly new licensees had been in for only a few weeks when we called, but already there was a warmly well established atmosphere in this prettily thatched and timbered fifteenth-century cottage. The two little connecting rooms on the right are particularly nice, with green cloth built-in wall settles and leatherette-cushioned cask seats around gleaming copper tables, dark glossy beams and an open fire; the inner room, up a couple of steps, is the snugger of the two, with flowery-curtained windows looking out over fields and cows. The room on the left is laid out more conventionally, but like the others has lots of brass and copper, and shiny beams. Bar food includes sandwiches (£1), home-made soup (£1), ploughman's (£1.75), omelettes (£2.50), plaice (£2.55), steak and kidney pie (£2.95), salads (starting from home-made quiche Lorraine £3) and gammon and egg (£3.40), with lots of dishes of the day that might run from a bargain hot beef bap with Yorkshire pudding and baked potato (£1.60) or cottage pie with red cabbage (£1.75) to rump steak (£5.95). Well kept Greenalls Cask on handpump; darts and dominoes in the back public bar; maybe piped music. The neat small lawn, with a couple of substantial yew trees guarding the gate in its picket fence, has picnic-table sets. *(Recommended by P Corris, Graham Gibson)*

Greenalls Licensees Andy Babbington and Mrs J Brindley Real ale Meals and snacks (12–2, 7–10; 9 Sun) Children in eating area Open 12–3, 7–11 all year

FULLERS MOOR SJ4954 Map 7
Copper Mine

A534 Wrexham–Nantwich, just under two miles E of A41 junction

The prettily papered walls of the two low-ceilinged rooms here are covered with masses of copper-mining mementoes – blasting explosives and fuses, old lamps, and photographic tableaux of more or less tense moments in local mining history. It's friendly and neatly kept, with well broken up separate seating areas, stripped beams and timbering, blacked stove doors set into the dividing wall, and soft lighting. Good bar food includes soup (95p), pancake rolls (£1.95), cottage pie (£3.75), steak and mushroom pie (£3.95), curry of the day (£4.25), a good few help-yourself salads (from £4.50), vegetarian lasagne or chilli con carne (£4.25), honey-grilled pork ribs (£4.95), steaks (from eight-ounce sirloin £7.25) and specials like fresh salmon or seafood platter (£4.25); well kept Boddingtons Bitter and Mild and Burtonwood on handpump. Juke box, rack of magazines, good open fires. You can watch the house martins nesting in the eaves from the picnic-table sets under cocktail parasols on the side lawn, where they have summer barbecues. There are good walks to Bickerton and Larkton Hills. *(Recommended by Mr and Mrs J H Adam, Dr P Webb, BHP, Peter Corris, Laurence Manning)*

Boddingtons Licensees Dave and Gill Furmston Real ale Meals and snacks Children in eating area (lunchtime) Open 11.30–3, 6.30–11 all year

GOOSTREY SJ7870 Map 7
Crown

111 Main Road; village signposted from A50 and A535

This very friendly, homely village pub has a lounge bar made up of two communicating rooms with a chaise-longue and cushioned settles as well as more conventional seats, decorations that include a couple of Lowry prints – not the usual ones – and open fires. Get there reasonably early to be sure of a place, particularly towards the end of the week. The smaller and brighter tap-room is plain and traditional, with darts, dominoes and cribbage; also pool and piped music. An upstairs room can be booked for dinner parties, preferably not on Saturdays, and is otherwise available for diners. Popular, freshly prepared food includes sandwiches (from 85p, delicious open prawn with lots of prawns £2.95; toasties such as ham and pineapple £1.10), excellent Stilton ploughman's (£1.95), chilli con carne (£2.55), Southern fried chicken (£2.95) and a lunchtime special (£2.75); in the evening, there are extra dishes such as fresh fried fish (£3.95), Barnsley chop (£4.95), sirloin steak (£5.75) or honey roast duckling (£5.95) in the back bistro dining-room. Well kept Marstons Burton, Mild and Pedigree on handpump. Seats on the front terrace face the village road. *(Recommended by Roger Huggins, Laurence Manning, Robert and Vicky Tod, Dennis Royles, David Young, Graham Gibson, Wayne Brindle)*

Marstons   Licensee Peter McGrath   Real ale   Meals and snacks (12–2, 7–10; not Mon, not Sun evening – and not Sat evening if restaurant fully booked)   Restaurant   Children in eating area of bar   Jazz or folk Sun evening   Open 11.30–3, 5.30–11 all year   Bedrooms tel Holmes Chapel (0477) 32128; £12/£18

Olde Red Lion

Main Road; closer to A535

New licensees have taken over this comfortably modernised pub, which has been refurbished since our last edition. The open-plan bar has cushioned banquettes built in against the floral wallpapered walls, and the easy chairs now have floral covers. Bar food has changed as well: home-made soup (£1.05), sandwiches (from £1.45), gammon and egg (£3.15), roast chicken (£3.50), peppered steak (£5.75) and daily specials like sweet-and-sour chicken wings (£1.55), 15-ounce T-bone steak (£8.50); children's menu (£1.35), and puddings (£1.40). Tetleys on handpump; darts, fruit machine and piped music. The garden has white tables on a small lawn at the bottom of an attractive steep dell. *(Recommended by Wayne Brindle; more reports please)*

Tetleys (Allied)   Manager Michael Reavey   Real ale   Meals and snacks   Children in eating area of bar and restaurant   Restaurant tel Holmes Chapel (0477) 32033   Open 11.30–3, 5.30 (may be 6.30 early in the week)–11 all year; closed evening 25 Dec

GREAT BUDWORTH   SJ6778 Map 7

George & Dragon

4½ miles from M6 junction 19; from A556 towards Northwich, turn right into B5391 almost at once; then fork right at signpost to Aston-by-Budworth, Arley Hall & Gardens

This seventeenth-century pub was solidly refaced in old-fashioned style in 1875 and goes well with the very pretty village and with the eleventh-century church and village stocks opposite it. The rambling, panelled lounge has red plush button-back banquettes and older settles on its Turkey carpet, plenty of nooks and alcoves, copper jugs hanging from the beams, and a fine big mirror with horsebrasses on the wooden pillars of its frame. The lively and simply furnished public bar has darts, dominoes and fruit machine; the music may sometimes be loud. Ind Coope Burton, Tetleys Mild and Bitter on handpump; bar food such as sandwiches (from £1.20), ploughman's (£2.75), vegetarian lasagne (£3), a lunchtime cold table on the bar counter (from £3.25), and steaks (from £5.95); children's menu (£1.20), and Sunday roast (£3.75). *(Recommended by C F Walling, Dr P Webb, PAB, Brenda Gentry, Wayne Brindle, AE, GRE)*

Tetleys (Allied)   Licensees Malcolm and Lynne Curtin   Real ale   Meals and snacks   Upstairs restaurant tel Comberbach (0606) 891317   Children in eating area at lunchtimes, in restaurant in evenings   Open 11.30–3, 7–11 all year

HIGHER BURWARDSLEY   SJ5256 Map 7

Pheasant 🛏

Burwardsley signposted from Tattenhall (which itself is signposted off A41 S of Chester) and from Harthill (reached by turning off A534 Natnwich–Holt at the Copper Mine); follow pub's signpost on up hill from post office; OS Sheet 117 reference 523566

A conservatory aimed primarily at families is to be built on what was the terrace of this popular, seventeenth-century inn, while the existing dining-room will become the Highland beef and salmon room, specialising in these and game dishes only. The pub's own Highland cattle herd has won several prizes at the Royal Show and other major shows. The beamed and timbered bar has large and attractive colour engravings of Victorian officials of the North Cheshire Hunt, a stuffed pheasant (as well as a picture of one), a set of whimsical little cock-fighting pictures done in real feathers, foreign banknotes on the beams, and plates over the high stone mantelpiece of the see-through fireplace – said to house the biggest log fire in the county. The window with the best view of the Cheshire Plain and the Wirral houses a laconic blue-fronted amazon parrot, and this faintly seafaring note is underlined by a brass ship's barometer, some ship photographs and the licensee's own 1958 Merchant Navy apprenticeship papers. There's a tall leather-cushioned fender around the fire and a fine variety of other seats on its Turkey carpet, ranging from red leatherette or plush wall seats to one or two antique oak settles. Good bar food from a constantly changing menu includes home-made soup (£1.50), nicely presented sandwiches (from £1.20, home-cooked topside £1.50, smoked Scotch salmon £2.50), ploughman's (£2.60), several salads (from £2.20 for Scotch egg, £3 for game pie, £4.50 prawn), lasagne or home-made steak and kidney pie (£3), chicken and Stilton roulades (£4.50), and sirloin steak (£6.50); children's menu (£1.50). Well kept Marstons Burton and Pedigree on handpump and quite a few wines; friendly staff. Darts (winter only), fruit machine (not in main bar) and piped music. There are picnic-table sets on a big side lawn that makes the most of this very peaceful spot. The bedrooms, all with views, are in an attractively and very comfortably converted sandstone-built barn; there are some self-catering flats as well. The inn is well placed for walks along the Peckforton Hills, and is at the start of *Good Walks Guide* Walk 72; in summer the nearby candle factory is a big draw. *(Recommended by Laurence Manning, Martin Aust, David and Eloise Smaylen, Mark Evans, David Waterhouse, Neil and Angela Huxter, G T Jones, Graham Gibson, Jon Wainwright)*

Free house   Licensee David Greenhaugh   Real ale   Meals and snacks   Restaurant Children in eating area and in restaurant   Horses welcomed, and horse-and-trap rides can be arranged   Bedrooms tel Tattenhall (0829) 70434; £40B/£40B   Open 12–3, 7–11 all year; 12–2.30, 7–11 in winter

HIGHER WHITLEY   SJ6280 Map 7

Birch & Bottle

1¼ miles from M56 junction 10; A559 towards Northwich

Steps, alcoves and surviving sections of knocked-through wall break this spacious and Turkey-carpeted pub up into cosier areas, with interesting decorations such as lots of miniature oil lamps, little country pictures, hunting prints, old engravings, lots of repoussé brass platters, a stuffed pheasant, guns and even a case of pistols. There are plenty of dark rustic tables under the heavy beams, with dark red plush button-back wall settles and wheel-back chairs, and open fires in winter. Bar food includes home-made soup (85p), lunchtime sandwiches (from £1.05), ploughman's (£2.25), cold platters (from £2.75), salads (from £2.70), lasagne (£3.25), pan-fried trout or ham with egg or pineapple (£3.50), mixed grill (£5.35) and steaks (from £5.50); lunchtime carvery (£3.50), daily specials like shark or swordfish steaks, and puddings such as After Eight delight (£1.75); the steak and kidney pie has, however, disappointed several readers. The dining area is separated from the bar by attractive leaded-light windows, and a new conservatory/restaurant was being built as we went to press. Very well kept Greenalls Mild, Bitter and Original on handpump, and fresh orange juice; fruit machine, piped music; three anti-smoke air-cleaners. They have Fivewin, a 2p seaside glass-cased game where you try to flick a ballbearing into a winning cup. Outside, there are brick-built seats and tables on a terrace under an appropriate fairy-lit silver birch. *(Recommended by C F Walling, Wayne Brindle, Mike Tucker, Dr and Mrs S G Donald, P J Atkin, L A Stead, G T Jones, C F Walling, Lee Goulding, Mr and Mrs Hendry)*

Greenalls   Licensee Ian Holt   Real ale   Meals and snacks (12–2, 6–10)   Conservatory restaurant tel Norcott Brook (092 573) 225   Children in eating area and restaurant if eating, but must leave by 8.30   Open 11–3, 5.30–11 all year nr LANGLEY   SJ9471 Map 7

Hanging Gate

Higher Sutton; follow Langley signpost from A54 beside Fourways Motel, and that road passes the pub; from Macclesfield, heading S from centre on A523 turn left into Byrons Lane at Langley, Wincle signpost; in Sutton (half-mile after going under canal bridge, i.e. before Langley) fork right at Church House Inn, following Wildboarclough signpost, then two miles later turning sharp right at steep hairpin bend; OS Sheet 118 reference 952696

Known locally as Tom Steele's, this friendly country pub has cosy little low-beamed rooms that look out beyond a patchwork of valley pastures to distant moors (and the tall Sutton Common transmitter above them); they are simply furnished with small seats and modern settles by the big coal fires, a stuffed otter, and some attractive old photographs of Cheshire towns. Down stone steps an airier garden-room has much the same view from its picture window; cribbage, dominoes, jukebox and sitting space game. Reasonably priced bar food includes soup, sandwiches and specials such as steak and kidney pie, pigeon, venison, rabbit, vegetarian dishes or curry (£3.50). Well kept Border Bitter and Marstons Pedigree on handpump, with mulled wine in winter. There is a crazy-paved terrace outside. *(Recommended by Dr and Mrs R J Ashleigh, M A and W R Proctor; more reports please)*

Free house   Licensees John and Lyn Vernon   Real ale   Meals and snacks (12–3, 7–10.30)
Children in garden-room or upper small room   Open 12–3, 7–11; closed 25 Dec

Leathers Smithy

Follow directions from Macclesfield as for previous entry, but keeping on into Langley; in Langley follow main road forking left at church into Clarke Lane – keep on towards the moors; OS Sheet 118 reference 952715

The atmosphere is liveliest (and most popular with walkers) in the right-hand bar of this isolated, friendly pub: flagstones as you go in, bow window seats or wheel-back chairs, and gin-traps, farrier's pincers, a hay basket and other ironwork on the roughcast cream walls. On the left, there are more wheel-back chairs around cast-iron-framed tables on Turkey carpet, little country pictures and drawings of Cheshire buildings, Wills steam-engine cigarette cards and a locomotive name-plate curving over one of the two open fires, and faint piped music. Good, reasonably priced bar food includes sandwiches (from £1.10), beef pie (£1.80), king rib steaklet (£1.90), ploughman's (from £2.10), lasagne or vegetarian mung-bean biriani (£2.70), tasty steak and kidney pie (£3.25) and gammon and egg (£3.70); delicious puddings such as butterscotch and walnut fudge cake (£1.20). Well kept Ind Coope Burton, Jennings Bitter, and Tetleys Bitter and Mild on handpump, hot mulled wine in winter (imported from Germany) served from a polished copper salamander, and a decent collection of spirits, including several malt whiskies; dominoes, fruit machine. The pub is backed by the steep mass of Teggs Nose (a country park) and surrounded by rich upland sheep pastures, hills and pinewoods; a couple of benches in front look across to Ridgegate Reservoir. *(Recommended by Lee Goulding, Mr and Mrs J H Adam, Dr and Mrs R J Ashleigh, M A and W R Proctor)*

Tetleys (Allied)   Licensee Paul Hadfield   Real ale   Meals and snacks (not Mon evening)
Children in own room Sat and Sun lunchtime only   Occasional pianola music
Open 12–3, 7–11 all year

LITTLE LEIGH   SJ6276 Map 7

Holly Bush

4½ miles from M56 junction 10: A49 towards Northwich, pub just S of A533 junction

It would be easy to drive straight past this pub with its sign almost hidden in a holly tree and no car park to speak of. It stands in a farmyard, and the atmosphere is wonderfully unspoilt and old-fashioned (the licensee is increasingly leaving the running of the pub to his son, so it will be in good hands). The heavy-beamed parlour has varnished wall benches with sloping panelled backs around waxed and polished country tables, two naval pictures on the wall, and a warm open fire; there's also a little upstairs snug. Well kept Greenalls and Mild (on handpump) is served from the open doorway of a little back tap-room, and there are pork pies (50p), hot pies with gravy (55p) and sandwiches (from 70p); darts, dominoes. A separate overflow room has much more space, less atmosphere; you can also sit outside. *(Recommended by Graham Gibson; more reports please)*

Greenalls   Licensee Albert Cowap   Real ale   Snacks   Children in small snug, not after 9pm   Open 11–3, 5.30–11 all year

LOWER PEOVER   SJ7474 Map 7

Bells of Peover ★

From B5081 take short cobbled lane signposted to church

This graceful wistaria-covered building – a long-standing favourite of many readers in Cheshire and much further afield – has new licensees this year. In a sense, it's the wheel coming full circle: it was Mrs Barker's great-grandfather George Bell, running the place for half a century, who gave the place its name. And the pub is certainly in good hands, as Mr Barker was rated his brewery's top inn-keeper at his last pub, the Maypole at Acton Bridge, which we included as a popular main entry. As you'd expect, the Barkers are very keen to preserve and even enhance the pub's timeless atmosphere. Much is unchanged: the little tiled bar with toby jugs, comic Victorian prints, and side hatches for its serving counter, and the general style of the original lounge with its antique settles, high-backed Windsor armchairs, spacious window seat, pictures above the panelling, and log fire (they've added a new club fender for this, filled the dresser with some of their antique china, and laid a Turkey carpet). The former kitchen is being changed into a second similar lounge (allowing useful housekeeping changes – new kitchen and lavatories); the dining-room is even more elegant than before. Bar food has included soup, potted shrimps, lasagne and steak and kidney pie; as we went to press the Barkers were still uncertain about future menus, but early reports have been promising (particularly mentioning the good sandwiches), and the Barkers' food at the Maypole was noted for value, good fresh ingredients and particularly good salads. Well kept Greenalls Best on handpump; dominoes. The sheltered crazy-paved terrace in front of the pub faces a beautiful black and white timbered church (mainly fourteenth-century, with lovely woodwork inside; the stone tower is sixteenth-century). A spacious lawn beyond the old coachyard at the side spreads down through trees and rose pergolas to a little stream. *(Recommended by Chris Cooke, Paul Wreglesworth, Graham Gibson, J H M Broughton, Laurence Manning, Tim Halstead, J C Proud, Mr and Mrs J A Hendry, Barbara Hatfield, Simon Turner)*

Greenalls   Licensee Dave Barker   Real ale   Meals and snacks   Restaurant tel Lower Peover (056 581) 2269 (closed Sun evening, Mon)   Open 11–3, 5.30–11

LOWER WHITLEY   SJ6179 Map 7

Chetwode Arms

2¼ miles from M 56 junction 10; village signposted from A49 Whitchurch road

By the small central servery in this friendly country pub is a snug little room with a settle and some chairs, and two more carpeted rooms leading off – one with a handsome heavy seat built right around its walls. The locals' bar is on the right, served by a hatch, with old green-cushioned settles, heavy mahogany tables, and darts and dominoes. There's some farm equipment such as a miniature harrow and plough, little country pictures on the walls, a collection of china teapots and so forth, horsebrasses, and cosy winter fires. Wholesome, tasty food includes home-made soup (95p), sandwiches (from £1), kofta curry or vegetarian quiche (£2.95), salads (from £2.95), fresh fillet of plaice or steak and kidney pie (£3.25) and steaks (£5.95); also specials like chicken tikka or tandoori (£4.25); well kept Greenalls Mild and Bitter on electric pump; darts, pool, dominoes, piped music. The bowling-green is beautifully kept. (Recommended by Syd and Wyn Donald, C F Walling, Dennis Royles, Wayne Brindle, Graham Gibson, A T Langton)

Greenalls   Licensee Robert Southerton   Real ale   Meals and snacks   Children welcome   Open 11–3, 5.30–11

MOBBERLEY   SJ7879 Map 7
Bird in Hand

B5085 towards Alderley

On Sundays, there are chunks of strong Cheddar cheese and bowls of biscuits on the bar in this redecorated, partly sixteenth-century building. Several atmospheric low-ceilinged little rooms open through wide arches off the friendly central servery: small pictures on the attractive Victorian wallpaper, Toby jugs and other china on a high shelf, comfortably cushioned heavy wooden seats and so forth, wood panelling in the cosy snug, and a blazing winter fire. Very well kept Sam Smiths OB and Museum on handpump and several malt whiskies; darts, dominoes and fruit machine. Good bar food includes home-made soup (£1.20), sandwiches (from £1.20; open sandwiches such as home-cooked ham with peach £2.50 or fresh crab £3.15), ploughman's (£2.75), home-made pâté (£3), salads (from £3.25, fresh crab £4.50), with home-made specials like steak and onion pie, gammon and eggs or fresh battered haddock (£3.90); puddings such as home-made pie or cheesecake (from £1.25); filled rolls only on Sunday. The atmosphere is pleasantly relaxed, though it does get crowded. There are seats outside. The new inn-sign is as attractive as the old one. (Recommended by Paul Wreglesworth, David and Karina Stanley, Alan Skull, E V Walder, AE, GRE, Brian and Anna Marsden, David Waterhouse, Jon Wainwright)

Sam Smiths   Licensee Andrew Bentley   Real ale   Meals (not Mon evening or Sun) and snacks (not Mon or Sun evenings)   Children in eating area of bar   Open 11.30–3, 5.30–11

OLLERTON   SJ7877 Map 7
Dun Cow

A537 SE of Knutsford

Once you're past the curve of the old-fashioned wooden draught screen sheltering the lounge from the outside world, this comfortable and genuine place has a warm, timeless welcome. There's a little alcove where an oak settle with an unusually broad seat just manages to slot in, a low wicker-seat chair by the fire (like a nursing chair with arms), traditional dark wood built-in seats, a couple of longcase clocks, a polished chest by the entry and some large embroidered panels (particularly the one on the way through to the restaurant). The corner snug has small pictures and nice little oak chairs and tables, the lounge has two blazing fires, and there's a sawfish snout in the hall. Bar food includes soup (95p), sandwiches (from 95p; on Sunday this is all they do in the bar), home-made steak and kidney pie (£3), deep fried plaice (£3.70), steaks (from £4) and daily specials; the small tap-room has darts, dominoes and bar billiards; well kept Greenalls Bitter and Original on handpump. Under the oak trees in front of the building there are a few picnic-table sets on the

---

Cribbage is a card game using a block of wood with holes for matchsticks or special pins to score with; regulars in cribbage pubs are usually happy to teach strangers how to play.

grass. *(Recommended by Ian Blackwell, Roger Huggins, Graham Gibson, Peter and Moyna Lynch, J H M Broughton, Jon Wainwright, Laurence Manning)*

Greenalls *Licensee Geoffrey Tilling* *Real ale* *Meals and snacks (not Sun–Tues evenings)* *Restaurant tel Knutsford (0565) 3093* *Children in eating area and in restaurant* *Open 11–11 all year; closed evening 25 Dec*

OVERTON SJ5277 Map 7
Ring o' Bells

Just over 2 miles from M56 junction 12; 2 Bellemonte Road – from A56 in Frodsham take B5152 and turn right (uphill) at Parish Church signpost

A couple of the small cosy rambling rooms in this early seventeenth-century pub have plush seats, with windows giving a view past the stone church to the Mersey far below; one at the back has brass-and-leather fender seats by the log fire, old hunting prints on its butter-coloured walls and some antique settles. Yet another small room, with beams, antique dark oak panelling and stained glass, leads through to a darts-room (there's also shove-ha'penny, dominoes and cribbage) liberally adorned with pictures of naked ladies. As we went to press, the licensees told us they were about to redecorate the bars (in keeping with the style of the pub) and re-cover the seats and stools. Well cooked, waitress-served lunchtime bar food (popular with businessmen) includes sandwiches, home-made steak and mushroom pie, various quiches, lasagne or chilli con carne (all £2.50), breast of chicken in tarragon sauce (£2.95), prawn and mushroom filled plaice (£3) and daily specials. Well kept Greenalls Bitter and Original on handpump from the old-fashioned hatch-like central servery; 84 different malt whiskies; piped music. The cats are called Basil and Blackberry India. *(Recommended by G J Lewis, Mary Anne Cameron, G J Lewis, RJH)*

Greenalls *Licensee Shirley Wroughton-Craig* *Real ale* *Lunchtime meals and snacks* *Children welcome (not in bar)* *Restaurant tel Frodsham (0928) 32068* *Open 11.30–3, 5.30 (6 Sat)–11 all year*

PEOVER HEATH SJ7973 Map 7
Dog 🏵

Off A50 N of Holmes Chapel at the Whippings Stocks, keep on past Parkgate into Wellbank Lane; OS Sheet 118 reference 794735; note that this village is called Peover Heath on the OS map and shown under that name on many road maps, but the pub is often listed under Over Peover instead

Enterprising and attractively priced food in this friendly country pub includes interesting soups (£1.10), a good choice of sandwiches (from £1.15), ploughman's with good cheeses (£2), lots of starters or light snacks such as black pudding with fried apple, mushroom crumble or fresh crab pancake (all around £1.95–£2.25), and main dishes such as steak pie, ham shank or kidneys done in a cider and cream sauce (around £3), a whole lemon sole (£3.25), rabbit done with herbs and mustard or poached salmon (£3.25) and sirloin steak (£4.75). The main bar rambles engagingly around various small areas, with logs burning in one old-fashioned black grate, and a coal fire opposite it flanked by two wood-backed built-in fireside seats. Other seats range from a little rocking chair, through rust-coloured cloth wall seats (one built into a snug alcove around an oak table), to the handsome ribbed banquettes in the quiet and spacious dining-room on the left; the atmosphere's relaxed and chatty. There is something of a dog motif, especially in the big dog cartouches on the red carpet, and the Staffordshire dogs in the china cupboard. Well kept Chesters, Flowers IPA, Marstons Pedigree, Thwaites and Whitbreads Castle Eden on handpump; darts, pool and a juke box in the tap-room, a tucked-away fruit machine; notably quick and friendly service – though you should get there by 12.15 to be sure of a lunchtime table. There are picnic-table sets out on the quiet lane. We have not yet had reports from readers who've stayed here, but would expect the inn from its performance in other respects to deserve our place-to-stay award. *(Recommended by G T Jones, Mrs T A Uthwatt)*

Free house   Licensee Harry Carney   Real ale   Meals and snacks (12–2.30, 7–9.30; lunch stops 2 at weekends; not Mon or Sun evenings)   Children in eating area   Open 11.30–3, 5.30–11 all year (opens an hour later Sat)   Bedrooms tel Chilford (0625) 861421; £20.70B/ £41.40B

PLUMLEY   SJ7175 Map 7

Smoker

2½ miles from M6 junction 19: A556 towards Northwich and Chester

This 400-year-old thatched pub has a cobbled frontage and dismounting block, and the quite spacious side lawn is prettily broken up by roses and flower beds. Inside, the three communicating comfortable rooms have deep sofas, well cushioned settles, Windsor chairs, some rush-seat dining-chairs and open fires. Decorations include military prints on dark panelling in one room, a glass case containing a remnant from the Houses of Parliament salvaged after it was hit by a bomb in World War II, and an Edwardian print by Goodwin Kilburne of a hunt meeting outside the pub. The licensees who took over at the end of 1988 have brought with them the thriving friendly atmosphere which readers liked at their previous pub, the Shrewsbury Arms at Little Budworth. Bar food includes sandwiches, lasagne or kofta curry (£2.95), fresh plaice or beef Stroganoff (£3.25), home-made steak and kidney pie (£3.50), gammon (£3.60), roast sirloin of beef (£3.75) and rump steak (£5.25). Well kept Robinsons Best and Mild on electric pump; 20 single malt whiskies and a decent choice of wines by the bottle; good service. *(Recommended by J H M Broughton, W C M Jones, Mr and Mrs J H Adam, W D Horsfield, Simon Barber, Graham Gibson)*

Robinsons   Licensees John and Diana Bailey   Meals and snacks (12–2, 7–10; sandwiches only until 8 Sat and Sun)   Restaurant tel Lower Peover (056 581) 2338   Children in eating area and restaurant   Open all day

RAINOW   SJ9576 Map 7

Highwayman ★

Above village, a mile along A5002 towards Whaley Bridge

From the small windows – and the front terrace – of this friendly early seventeenth-century pub there are fine views over the Cheshire Plain. Inside, the low-beamed cosy little rooms (each with its own winter coal fire) have some antique settles as well as simpler cushioned seats around rustic wooden tables. A high copper-covered bar counter serves the well kept Thwaites on handpump. Good value food includes sandwiches and filled barm-cakes, home-made soup, black pudding, savoury pancake rolls, a choice of half a dozen freshly made pizzas, breaded plaice, freshly roasted chicken and scampi; darts, fruit machine. On fine summer evenings or weekends it gets quite crowded (when parking nearby may not be easy). *(Recommended by M A and W R Proctor, Dennis Royles, Doug Kennedy, Ian Briggs, Bob and Val Collman, Dr and Mrs R J Ashleigh)*

Thwaites   Real ale   Meals and snacks   Children in snug   Open 12–3, 6–11

SANDBACH   SJ7661 Map 7

Old Hall

1¼ miles from M6 junction 17; Sandbach signposted from junction exit, hotel in Newcastle Road just outside centre

This handsome black and white timbered hotel has remarkably big windows for its age – over three centuries old – and fine carved gable-ends. The comfortable Jacobean oak-panelled lounge has a solidly carved fireplace with Staffordshire statuettes on its mantelpiece, a soft low button-back sofa, wall banquettes and tapestried chairs, black beams, books in the bookshelves, and attractive pictures. A Turkey carpet sweeps through from here into the communicating bar, which has comfortable but more modern furnishings, a cheery atmosphere and piped music. Bar food includes soup (£1), sandwiches (£1.20), ploughman's, spaghetti or cauliflower cheese (£2.50), lamb stew (£2.95) and plaice (£3.25); well kept Boddingtons and Youngers Scotch on handpump; friendly service. The big garden has some tables and chairs. *(Recommended by Richard Phillips, Brian and Anna Marsden)*

Free house   Licensee Frank Ribeiro   Real ale   Meals and snacks (lunchtime only, not Sun)
Handsome Jacobean restaurant (lunchtime only on Sun)   Children welcome   Open all day
Bedrooms tel Crewe (0270) 761221; £32.50B/£45B

SUTTON   SJ9271 Map 7

Sutton Hall Hotel ★ 🏵 🛏

Leaving Macclesfield southwards on A523, turn left into Byrons Lane signposted Langley, Wincle, then just before canal viaduct fork right into Bullocks Lane; OS Sheet 118 reference 925715

Several unusual touches in the civilised, though stylishly pubby, bar of this secluded country hotel give it a good deal of character: an enormous bronze bell for calling time, the brass cigar-lighting gas taper on the bar counter itself, antique squared oak panelling, lightly patterned art nouveau stained glass windows, and an open fire, raised a couple of feet, at the end of the bar counter (which is surrounded by broad flagstones – there's carpet elsewhere); also, a longcase clock, a suit of armour by another substantial stone fireplace, and raj fans circling slowly in the lofty ceiling. Tall black timbers divide the separate areas, and furnishings are mainly straightforward ladder-back chairs around sturdy thick-topped cast-iron-framed tables; the atmosphere is warmly welcoming. A limited but good range of bar food (prices haven't changed since last year), kindly served by neatly uniformed waitresses, might include home-made soup (£1.25), open sandwiches (from £1.55), smoked mackerel or chicken liver pâté (£2.75 starter, £3.65 main course), big ploughman's (£3.65), tagliatelle with ham, mushrooms, tomatoes and cream or vegetable kebabs with yoghurt, cucumber and mint dip (£3.95), steak and kidney pie, kebabs or seafood bake (£4.55), and puddings (£1.75). Well kept Bass and Mild, Marstons Burton and Stones Best on handpump, decent wines. There are tables on a tree-sheltered lawn, overlooked by the worn black figures carved into the timbering of one black and white wing – the rest of the house is stone-built. *(Recommended by Brian and Anna Marsden, Leith Mills, Laurence Manning, Dr and Mrs R J Ashleigh)*

Free house   Licensee Robert Bradshaw   Real ale   Meals and snacks   Restaurant   Children
welcome weekend and bank hol lunchtimes only   Four-poster bedrooms tel Sutton
(026 05) 3211; £49.95B/£66B   Open all day

TARPORLEY   SJ5563 Map 7

Rising Sun

High Street; village signposted off A51 Nantwich–Chester

Popular with the local cricketers or bowls team, this cosy village pub has low ceilings with a good few beams (especially in the front room), character seats including creaky nineteenth-century mahogany and oak settles around the well chosen tables, an attractively blacked iron kitchen range, a big oriental rug in the back room, and sporting and other old-fashioned prints. Lunchtime bar food includes sandwiches (from £1.10), filled baked potatoes (from £1.15), home-made cottage pie (£1.65), steak and kidney pie (£2.50), scampi (£2.95), salads (from £2.25), gammon and egg (£3.20) and chicken chasseur (£3.45); in the evening they concentrate more on full meals, with starters such as pâté-stuffed mushrooms (£1.70) and main dishes like seafood platter (£3.25), game casserole (£4.95), steaks (from £4.95) and a huge mixed grill (£5.75). Well kept Robinsons Best and Mild on handpump, friendly service; fruit machine, maybe unobtrusive background music, three open fires. *(Recommended by KC, Jon Wainwright, David and Eloise Smaylen, E G Parish, Laurence Manning, Wayne Brindle)*

Robinsons   Licensee Alec Robertson   Real ale   Meals and snacks (12–2, 6–9.30; not in back bar evenings)   Children in restaurant (lunchtime)   Restaurant tel Tarporley (082 93) 2423   Open 11.30–3, 5.30–11 all year

WRENBURY   SJ5948   Map 7
Dusty Miller

Village signposted from A530 Nantwich–Whitchurch

A handsome conversion of an early nineteenth-century mill, this comfortably modern place has a series of tall glazed arches facing the water with russet velvet curtains, long low hunting prints on the white walls, and tapestried banquettes and wheel-back chairs flanking dark brown rustic tables in the carpeted main area. At the back, there's a quarry-tiled standing-only area by the bar counter, which has well kept Robinsons Best and Mild on handpump; piped music. A wide choice of bar food includes soup (95p), open sandwiches (from £1.85), salads (from £2.85), smoked oysters (£2.95), vegetarian cucumber and mint cheesecake (£3.25), chilli con carne (£3.85), chicken tarragon (£4.25), gammon with peach (£4.85), steaks (from £7.55) and home-made puddings (£1.45); also, daily specials such as pork in apple and cider (£4.45) or coulibiac of salmon (£5.95) and children's dishes (from £1.35); several liqueur coffees; very good service. The picnic-table sets outside are on a gravel terrace among rose bushes by the Llangollen Canal; they're reached either by the towpath or by a high wooden catwalk above the little River Weaver which used to drive the mill's side wheel (and before that drove the underpass wheel of a sixteenth-century mill built over the stream for Combermere Abbey). *(Recommended by Laurence Manning, Dawn and Phil Garside, Catherine and Andrew Brian, Wayne Brindle)*

Robinsons   Licensee Robert Lloyd-Jones   Real ale   Meals and snacks   Upstairs restaurant tel Nantwich (0270) 780537 (not Sun evening)   Children in restaurant   Open noon–11; shorter in winter

Lucky Dip

Besides the fully inspected pubs, you might like to try these Lucky Dips recommended to us and described by readers (if you do, please send us reports):

☆ **Acton Bridge** [Hilltop Rd; take B5153 off A49 in Weaverham; then right towards Acton Cliff; SJ5975], *Maypole*: Spacious and comfortably refurbished beamed bar with some antique settles as well as more modern furnishings, two coal fires, Greenalls Bitter and Mild on handpump, gentle piped music, seats outside, orchard behind; has been very popular, particularly among older people, for impeccable housekeeping and good value lunchtime bar food, but the long-serving licensees moved to Bells of Peover, Lower Peover early 1989 – too soon to tell about new regime, though preliminary reports are favourable; there has not been provision for children *(G T Jones, Geoff Halson, LYM)*

Adlington [Wood Lanes; by Middlewood Way linear park, and Macclesfield Canal – OS Sheet 109 reference 936818; SJ9180], *Miners Arms*: Popular extended pub in nice canalside spot, reliably well kept Boddingtons Mild and Bitter, bar food lunchtime and evening – particularly popular with families at Sun lunchtime *(Brian and Anna Marsden)*

Alderley Edge [about 250 yds past Royal Oak, off Heyes Lane (which is off A34); SJ8478], *Moss Rose*: Tucked-away terraced pub down an alley, enlarged a few years ago by incorporating some neighbouring cottages, and with its own bowling-green; bar food, Robinsons real ale *(Graham Gibson)*; [The Sidings, London Rd – off A34 by stn], *Queensgate*: Recently refurbished Chef & Brewer in mock-Victorian shopping arcade; fine wood panelling and ornate ceiling, although the viewing area of cellar has now gone; Ruddles Best and County on handpump, bar food, spotless lavatories *(Graham Gibson)*

Alsager [Crewe Rd; SJ7956], *Lodge*: Friendly, well run local with separate public and lounge bars; good atmosphere and decent mix of customers; well kept Tetleys Bitter and Ansells or Tetleys Mild on handpump, snack lunches including generously filled rolls, good coffee *(Dave Webster, Sue Holland)*

Appleton [not far from M6 junction 20 – B5356 Stretton Rd, junction with Arley Rd; SJ6484], *Thorn*: Pleasant, modern, clean roadside pub, comfortable furnishings, wide choice of bar food *(Tim Brierly)*

Ashley [SJ7784], *Greyhound*: More or less open-plan village pub with smashing atmosphere and fox heads and stagecoach pictures on the wall; lunchtime snacks, Greenalls on handpump *(Graham Gibson)*

Ashton [B5393; SJ5169], *Golden Lion*: Pleasant village pub appealing to all ages, well furnished three-tiered lounge with many pictures for sale, well kept Greenalls Original (though not served at all the counters), friendly golden labrador, public bar *(Jon Wainwright)*

Audlem [The Square (junction A529/A525); SJ6644], *Lord Combermere*: Interesting pub full of bric-à-brac; well kept McEwans 70/- on handpump, good range of spirits *(Graham Gibson)*; [Audlem Wharf – OS Sheet 118 reference 658436] *Shroppie Fly*: Named after the narrowboats using the Shropshire Union Canal, and included for its position looking out over one of the long flights of locks here; mainly modern furnishings, one bar shaped like a barge, good canal photographs, collection of brightly painted bargees' china and bric-à-brac, seats on waterside terrace; simple food, well kept Boddingtons and Marstons Pedigree on handpump, children in room off bar and in restaurant *(Graham Gibson, LYM)*

Barbridge [by A51 to Chester, some ¾ mile N of Nantwich; SJ6156], *Barbridge*: Popular canalside pub with Boddingtons, Higsons and maybe Oldham Mild on handpump; get there early on fine summer evenings or at weekends *(Peter Corris, Graham Gibson, Martin Aust)*

Beeston [Bunbury Heath (A49 S of Tarporley); SJ5459], *Beeston Castle*: Though the pub itself is perhaps not remarkable, the range of food is – including heavenly smoked goose breast, enormous open sandwiches, Greek dishes and interesting specials; jolly licensee, country and western and quiz evenings *(M and J Godfrey)*

Bell o' th' Hill [signposted from A41 Whitchurch–Chester; SJ5245], *Bluebell*: Oomfortable series of rooms in Greenalls pub with one main bar, popular for food including vegetarian dishes, lunchtime and evening; pleasant young licensees, cheap house wine *(Jane Kearley)*

☆ **Bickerton** [Bulkeley – A534 E of junction with A41; SJ5052], *Bickerton Poacher*: Attractive sheltered barbecue courtyard (summer Fri and Sat evenings, Sun lunchtime), with lots of live music and special events; good atmosphere in traditionally furnished rambling rooms inside, up to five Border and Marstons real ales kept well, bar food; children welcome *(Graham Gibson, Martin Aust, Peter Corris, LYM)*

Bollington [SJ9377], *Church House*: Small, friendly and cosy local with well kept Theakstons and Wadworths 6X and good simple bar food *(Dr and Mrs R J Ashleigh, Graham Gibson)*

Boothdale [OS Sheet 117 reference 530673; SJ5367], *Boot*: Nice relaxing country pub tucked away on hillside, good views of lush farmland and hedgerows, well kept Greenalls, model of penny-farthing made from pennies set into one wall, bar food *(Jon Wainwright)*

Bosley [Leek Rd (A523); SJ9266], *Harrington Arms*: Spacious and comfortable former Yates wine lodge with Robinsons Best Mild and Best Bitter on handpump; grandfather clock, roaring fires, bar food, rock-and-roll nights *(Graham Gibson)*

Buglawton [A54 Congleton–Buxton; SJ8763], *Church House*: Agricultural and horticultural theme with scythes and sickles; bar snacks and Robinsons Mild and Bitter on electric pump; plenty of room outside, with lawn mower used as a flower box, hay trough, doves on roof *(Graham Gibson)*; *Robin Hood*: Friendly landlord and staff, well kept Marstons and excellent food from sandwiches to steaks; children in dining-room *(ATC)*

Burleydam [A525 Whitchurch–Audlem; SJ6143], *Combermere Arms*: Rural pub, supposedly 450 years old and haunted; lots of fine woodwork, leaded windows, comfortable wall seating and other chairs and pretty carpet; Bass, Marstons Pedigree, Springfield and Youngers on handpump, bar food from sandwiches to steaks, restaurant *(Graham Gibson, M A and W R Proctor)*

☆ **Butley Town** [A523 Macclesfield–Stockport; SJ9177], *Ash Tree*: As we went to press we were told that this slate-roofed white pub, previously a popular main entry, was to be turned into a 'Henry's Table'; these are Boddington's pub/restaurants designed to cater more for families, and we've had promising reports on one or two others; the management were hoping that the small-roomed layout would be kept, and aimed to keep on a proper drinking area – the Bitter's well kept (Brian and Anna Marsden, Paul Wreglesworth, Dr and Mrs R J Ashleigh, LYM – reports on the changes, please)

☆☆ Chester [Tower Wharf, Raymond St – behind Northgate St, nr rly], Telfords Warehouse: Popular converted warehouse credited architecturally to Thomas Telford, with big windows overlooking Shropshire Union Canal basin – a must for cheese lovers, with up to three dozen different cheeses at lunchtime including interesting ones from Scotland, Wales and England as well as the Continent; pleasing new-wood furniture, well kept Matthew Browns and Theakstons Old Peculier, bar food served at tables when your name is called by loudspeaker; steps down to cellar wine bar (with decent wines), steps up to restaurant area; uniformed staff with name badges, working red telephone box inside (Jon Wainwright, Graham Gibson, Peter Corris)

Chester [Park St – by Roman Walls, off Albion St], Albion: Charismatic if smoky pub with character landlord, good bar food and Greenalls real ales (Jon Wainwright); [Lower Bridge St] Bear & Billet: Small black and white timbered pub by river, Wilsons/Websters real ales (John Gould, Jon Wainwright); [Garden Lane (off A540)] Bouverie: Bustling, friendly local, Greenalls beers on handpump (Jon Wainwright); [Foregate St/Frodsham St] City Arms: Bright, clean interior set out in three themes – bookshop, toys and apothecary and haberdashers behind the bar; well kept Greenalls and Davenports, good range of hot and cold bar food (Mr and Mrs J H Adam); [Lower Bridge St] Clavertons: Lees pub/wine bar, nicely furnished and open all day; popular with young people (piped music or juke box to match), quick service from young staff, Bitter and Moonraker on handpump and interesting choice of bar food including vegetarian dishes; rather pricier than some other pubs here (John Gould, Peter Corris, Jon Wainwright); [Watergate St] Custom House: Consistently lively and popular, with plenty of big wooden tables and high-backed settles, well kept Border and Marstons Pedigree, reasonably priced lunches in back dining-room crammed with brass and porcelain (Jon Wainwright, Mr and Mrs J H Adam); [Westgate Row N] Deva: Pleasantly renovated – one long lounge bar, carpeted throughout, with windows partly plain, partly coloured (Graham Gibson); [Lower Bridge St] Kings Head: Black and white timbered Greenalls house dating back to seventeenth century; original woodwork, Davenports on handpump, open all day – can get crowded in evenings; eight bedrooms, some with four-posters (John Gould); [99 Boughton (A51, 10 minutes' walk from centre)] Little Oak: Quaint and

narrow eighteenth-century pub with slightly partitioned lounge bar and tap-room; wall seating, brasses, bellows and a nice fire; Greenalls beers on handpump, lunchtime sandwiches (Graham Gibson, Jon Wainwright); [Sandy Lane – B5130, Dee banks] Red House: Bright and comfortable pub with garden sloping down to the Dee; inside has raj fans, an oak bar counter and pictures of Chester on the walls; Bass on handpump, bar snacks (Graham Gibson); [George St] Ship Victory: Pleasant, simple décor, well kept Jennings and Tetleys (not that cheap here), lunchtime food (Jon Wainwright); [Watergate St] Watergates: Wine bar which also sells pricey lagers and Murphys Stout, recently fitted into interesting medieval vaulted cellar formerly used for storing wines; closed Sun, best lunchtime; bouncers (Jon Wainwright)

Christleton [Plough Lane – OS Sheet 117 reference 454653; SJ4466], Plough: Curious window seat (the former entrance) in older part, with clocking-on timepiece, wooden partitioning and lots of horsebrasses; new part with tapestried wall seats and benches on stone floor; ebullient landlord, darts, connect-4, good lunchtime food, tables on terrace, children's play area (Jon Wainwright, Mr and Mrs J H Adam); [Laneside (off A41)] Ring o' Bells: Comfortably refurbished pub in attractive village, with settees, old prints, grandfather clock; Bass and Stones Best on handpump; good range of hot and cold bar food lunchtimes and evenings, tables on terrace; some car park spaces reserved for disabled drivers (Graham Gibson, Mr and Mrs J H Adam)

Church Minshull [B5074 Winsford–Nantwich; SJ6661], Badger: Small, spotless pub in quiet village setting, with varied choice of food in popular restaurant, and tables in garden behind; licensee/chef also owns adjoining post office (C F Walling)

Churton [Farndon Rd (B5130); SJ4256], White Horse: Small village pub with fine atmosphere, friendly service, Bass on handpump, lunchtime and evening bar food; three connecting bars, copper-topped tables and chairs, pool table, masses of bric-à-brac including brasses and lots of miners' lamps (Peter Corris, Graham Gibson)

Congleton [off A34 S; SJ8663], Great Moreton Hall: Beautifully kept hotel and restaurant in marvellous handsomely restored building with high ceilings, reproduction Old Masters, and lots of seasonal festivities; attractive spacious grounds, comfortable bedrooms (Graham Gibson)

Crewe [Nantwich Rd (A534, nr rly stn); SJ7056], Crewe Arms: Handsome hotel with marble tables and fireplaces, comfortable furnishings, alabaster nudes, Tetleys on handpump; bedrooms (Graham Gibson);

[Sydney – just off A534 towards M6 junction 17; SJ7256] *Hunters Lodge*: Comfortable bar in attractive hotel, a former farmhouse; well kept Tetleys and Peter Walkers on handpump, good bar food at moderate prices, first-class service, Tudor-style restaurant; bedrooms *(E G Parish)*; [Middlewich Rd (A530)] *Rising Sun*: Popular pub recently refurbished to high standard with log fires, well kept Wem Best on handpump, good bar food, well organised bar service, warm atmosphere and good mix of customers; bedrooms comfortable *(E G Parish, Martin Aust)*

Croft [left just after the Noggin, right at next T-junction; SJ6393], *Horseshoe*: Friendly staff and good lunchtime food – especially the fish and chips, though there's a tremendous choice of other things; keg beers now *(Simon Turner)*

Dean Row [SJ8781], *Unicorn*: Generous helpings of good home-cooked food, well kept Boddingtons, pleasant staff and comfortable seating *(Mr and Mrs B Hobden)*

Delamere [A54/B5152; SJ5669], *Fishpool*: Bright and comfortable, with good range of bar food and Greenalls real ale; pleasantly placed near Delamere Forest *(Mr and Mrs J H Adam)*

Disley [Buxton Rd – E end of village, opp school; SJ9784], *Crescent*: Homely local on busy main road; well kept Robinsons on handpump, good lunchtime and evening bar food generously served, small garden overlooking railway *(Keith Mills)*; [Buxton Rd] *Dandy Cock*: Remarkably clean pub with lots of brass and militaria; Robinsons ales and good value food; restaurant; children welcome *(John Hayward)*; [Mudhurst Lane – Higher Disley, off old Buxton rd] *Moorside*: Isolated hotel with superb views across to Stockport and Manchester; tiled bar, fruit machines, compartment seating, Watneys-related real ales on handpump, bar food and restaurant; bedrooms *(Graham Gibson)*; [up side rd by Rams Head Hotel] *White Horse*: Well kept Robinsons on handpump, excellent food using fresh ingredients *(A F C Young)*

Dodleston [turn right on A483 from Chester at Pulford – then 1½ miles; SJ3661], *Red Lion*: A listed building, most attractive inside and out *(Peter Corris)*

Duddon [SJ5265], *Headless Woman*:Pleasant Greenalls pub with good varied bar food *(R H Sawyer)*

Eaton [A536 Congleton–Macclesfield; SU8765], *Plough*: Nicely renovated with leaded windows and beams, Banks's Bitter and Mild on handpump, good bar food including steak done in lots of different ways *(Graham Gibson)*; [Manchester Rd – A34 Congleton–Wilmslow; SU8765] *Waggon & Horses*: Roaring log fire, Robinsons Best Mild and Best on handpump, changing bar food, children's room *(Graham Gibson)*

Elworth [London Rd; SJ7462], *Fox*: Rare example of well modernised village pub; open-plan, with old prints, Marstons Burton on handpump and enterprising bar food *(Jon Wainwright)*

Farndon [High St – A534 E of Wrexham; SJ4254], *Greyhound*: Bright, clean pub with model ships, open fire, pictures of cats as customers; Greenalls Best, Mild and Original on handpump, good bar food (not Sat evening or Sun lunchtime); cats and dogs, and two donkeys in field behind; bedrooms *(Graham Gibson)*

Farnworth [Lunts Heath Rd – nr Black Horse roundabout; SJ5187], *Church View*: Brick and wood bar in attractive pub with nicely varnished beams, log-effect gas fires and brasses; Greenalls Bitter and Mild on handpump *(Graham Gibson)*

Fivecrosses [B5152 Frodsham–Kingsley; SJ5376], *Travellers Rest*: Superb views across the Weaver Valley from pub with nautical theme, two coal fires, dining area, Greenalls Mild and Bitter on handpump *(Anon)*

Gawsworth [SJ8969], *Harrington Arms*: Basic farm pub with tree-trunk tables outside and rudimentary comforts inside; well kept Robinsons Best and Best Mild on handpump *(LYM)*

Glazebury [opp Bents Garden Centre – OS Sheet 109 reference 672976; SJ6796], *Foresters Arms*: Spotlessly clean, snug little place with lots of brass, jugs, and so forth, attractively priced bar food, well kept Tetleys, good atmosphere *(G T Jones, Alan and Marlene Radford)*

Grappenhall [Church Lane (off A50); SJ6486], *Rams Head*: Attractive sandstone building a short distance from Bridgewater Canal with elaborate wrought-iron sign and sundial; lots of fine panelling, leaded windows, wall seats and carved heads; Greenalls Bitter on handpump *(Graham Gibson)*

Guilden Sutton [SJ4568], *Bird in Hand*: Recently refurbished Whitbreads village local, tastefully decorated; well kept Castle Eden on handpump, good value bar food; children allowed until 8pm *(Peter Corris)*

Halton [Castle Rd; SJ5482], *Castle*: Built on a rocky crag near ruined Halton Castle, with fine views over Widnes and Runcorn – they say that on a clear day you can see seven counties; prints of rural scenes, live music upstairs, Greenalls real ale, tables outside *(Graham Gibson)*

Hankelow [Audlem Rd (A529 Audlem–Nantwich); SJ6745], *White Lion*: Well organised, comfortable pub with open fires, pool-table at one end and clean, friendly atmosphere; good food with fresh vegetables *(Dr G B Whitaker)*

Hartford [Chester Rd – opp stn; SJ6472], *Coachmans*: Three-hundred-year-old local on main road with friendly regulars, darts, dominoes and Greenalls Mild and Bitter on handpump *(Graham Gibson)*

Haslington [A534; SJ7456], *Hawk*: Old timbered pub with lots of brasses, two guns behind the bar, some swords, an original oak door and a log fire; charming low-ceilinged dining-room and bar snacks with lunchtime specials; Robinsons Best and Mild on electric pump *(Graham Gibson)*

☆ **Hatchmere** [B5152, off A556 at Abbey Arms; SJ5672], *Carriers*: One of Cheshire's friendliest landlords, always has a pleasant word for both locals and strangers, in pleasantly placed pub overlooking Hatchmere Lake (where pike can be caught); tap-room and two-level lounge, Burtonwood Bitter and Mild on handpump, food including good value Sun lunch *(Graham Gibson, Mr and Mrs J H Adam)*

Heatley [Rushgreen Rd; SJ7088], *Farmers Arms*: Very friendly and well kept, excellent range of cheap bar food *(David and Amanda Watts)*

High Legh [A50; SJ7084], *Bears Paw*: Left-hand bar in small rural pub has open fire, two settles, old prints, horns and stuffed fox; Greenalls Bitter, bar food, really good atmosphere; outside drinking/barbecue area in semi-marquee *(Graham Gibson, G T Jones)*

Hollins Green [just off A57 Manchester–Warrington, 3 miles from M6 junction 21; SJ6991], *Black Swan*: Single bar full of nooks and crannies with low ceiling, collection of clocks and good atmosphere; lots of whiskies, lunchtime bar food, no juke box or piped music *(Peter Corris)*

☆ **Holmes Chapel** [Station Rd (A54 – handy for M6 junction 18); SJ7667], *Swan*: Bright, clean, comfortably furnished with red plush seating, lots of bric-à-brac including horseshoes, plates, old prints and photos; open-plan, but with impression of small rooms; well kept Sam Smiths OB on handpump, friendly atmosphere, attractively priced bar food lunchtime and evening, darts; pretty outside, with window boxes, shutters and arched coach entry *(Graham Gibson, John Hayward, Jon Wainwright)*

Holmes Chapel [19 London Rd], *Olde Red Lion*: Welcoming, comfortable and warm pub with home-cooked food; the popular landlord moved in 1989 to the Olde Red Lion at Goostrey – reports on the new regime, please *(John Shirley)*

Hooton [A41; SJ3678], *Chimneys*: Fine gothic-style hotel, giant fork and spoon hanging from beams and clock shaped like key in public bar; Bass, Stones Best and Boddingtons on handpump, grill-room, dining-room for residents; bedrooms *(Graham Gibson)*

☆ **Kelsall** [SJ5268], *Morris Dancers*: Unspoilt, delightful and good value pub with a tremendous friendly atmosphere; well kept Greenalls Local and Original, plain, wholesome food, lots of keys hanging from black beams, maybe morris dancers or folk

music (which can sometimes verge on the bawdy); darts and pool in back room, dogs and cockatiel; going from strength to strength since the bypass has removed the heavy traffic *(G T Jones, Jon Wainwright)*

Knutsford [Mobberley Rd; SJ7578], *Builders Arms*: Tremendously lively pub on edge of town; attractive, whitewashed terraced building with good windows; Marstons Burton and Pedigree *(Jon Wainwright)*; [Tatton St (off A50 at White Bear roundabout)] *Lord Eldon*: Two or three interconnected bars, cosy and low-ceilinged, with very affable licensees and Wilsons real ale – traditional town pub, deservedly popular locally *(H G and C J McCafferty)*

☆ **Little Bollington** [2 miles from M56 junction 7; A56 towards Lymm, then first right at Stamford Arms into Park Lane – use A556 to get back on to M56 westbound; SJ7286], *Swan With Two Nicks*: Village pub richly decorated with brass and copperware and other bric-à brac, antique settles in back room, snug alcoves, log fire, good home-cooked bar food (lunchtime, not Sun), well kept Whitbreads-related real ales at fair prices, tables outside, attractive surroundings including Dunham Hall deer park; no dogs or children *(Dr P Webb, G T Jones, Jon Wainwright, GRE, AE, LYM)*

Little Budworth [SJ5966], *Red Lion*: Pleasant little pub with clean and comfortable lounge bar and decent bar food; Robinsons real ales, quick and cheerful service *(Mr and Mrs P W Dryland)*; [A54] *Shrewsbury Arms*: Clean and comfortable pub with pleasant outside area for summer drinking; has been popular for well kept Robinsons beer and well presented and generously served bar food, though we've had no reports since the licensees moved to the Smoker at Plumley *(C F Walling; more reports please)*

☆ **Little Leigh** [A49 by swing bridge; SJ6276], *Leigh Arms*: Popular very mock-Tudor pub in pleasant waterside setting with limited choice of tasty and inexpensive bar food including vegetarian dishes and steaks; friendly service, well kept Burtonwood, country wines; organ music Sun, quiz night Weds, country and western duo Thurs; children allowed in eating area *(C F Walling, G T Jones, Wayne Brindle)*

Lower Peover [Crown Lane; SJ7474], *Crown*: Pleasant country pub with good mix of customers, bar food *(Wayne Brindle)*

☆ **Lymm** [Eagle Brow – nr M6 junction 20; SJ6787], *Spread Eagle*: Big, well furnished village pub with Lees Bitter and winter Moonraker, lots of friendly regulars, good range of bar food; quiet midweek, and small room near entrance has no piped music; weekly jazz; parking may be difficult *(Simon Turner, G T Jones, David and Amanda Watts)*

Lymm [A6144 – OS Sheet 109 reference 684874; SJ6787], *Bulls Head*: Spotlessly clean, friendly and well run pub; well kept

Hydes Mild and Bitter and straightforward reasonably priced lunchtime bar meals; gets crowded in summer and weekends as it's so handy for the canal boats; has been open all day *(Dennis Royles, Geoff Lee)*

Macclesfield [Congleton Rd; junction Pack Lane/Ivy Lane; SJ9273], *Flower Pot*: Good choice of lunchtime hot and cold food laid out on counter, well kept Robinsons; in the evenings gets very popular with young people *(Paul Wreglesworth)*

☆ **nr Macclesfield** [A537 some miles out towards Buxton – OS Sheet 119 reference 001719; SK0071], *Cat & Fiddle*: Britain's 2nd-highest pub, surrounded by spectacular moorland (though on a trunk road), with magnificent views across Cheshire; spacious lounge, roomy flagstoned public bar, Robinsons real ales, bar food; gets busy at lunchtime in summer *(Ian Briggs, Graham Gibson, Bob and Val Collman, LYM)*

Malpas [High St; SJ4947], *Red Lion*: Hotel with pool-room and even a sauna; Bass and Oak Best on handpump, juke box; bedrooms *(Graham Gibson)*

Marbury [OS Sheet 117 reference 562457; SJ5645], *Swan*: Pleasant, rustic pub with good bar food including interesting daily specials and fantastic choice of puddings; friendly service, Greenalls real ale *(W C M Jones)*

Marton [Manchester Rd (A34 N of Congleton); SJ8568], *Davenport Arms*: Recently refurbished pub with Watneys-related real ales on handpump and well prepared bar menu of good value set meals and snacks; two open fires, darts *(Gerald Hixon)*

Mobberley [Wilsons Mill Lane; SJ7879], *Bulls Head*: Friendly and comfortable low-beamed village pub with soft lighting, well kept Tetleys real ale, folk-singing landlord and own immaculate bowling-green *(BB)*; [Faulkners Lane – OS Sheet 118 reference 782802] *Frozen Mop*: Beefeater food pub with Chesters on handpump and lots of reproductions of paintings; good newish furnishings *(Jon Wainwright)*; [Town Lane – down hill from sharp bend on B5185 at E edge of 30mph limit; SJ7879] *Roebuck*: Spacious and popular open-plan bar with long pews on richly polished floorboards, well kept Watneys-related real ales from the handsome bar counter, generously served bar food, restaurant, seats in cobbled court-yard and garden behind, play area; the licensee is French, his Cheshire wife does the cooking, and the cat's called Tiger; children welcome *(Neil and Elspeth Fearn, LYM)*

Moore [Runcorn Rd (A558); SJ5784], *Red Lion*: Nice Greenalls village pub shaded by great beech tree, in attractive Bridgewater Canal village; very popular annual folk day – usually St George's Day (23 Apr) *(Jon Wainwright)*

Moulton [SJ6569], *Travellers Rest*: Very popular three-room pub in centre of village; welcoming atmosphere, Chesters and Whitbreads Castle Eden on handpump and separate restaurant *(Peter Corris)*

Mow Cop [Station Rd – OS Sheet 118 reference 854574; SJ8557], *Cheshire View*: What marks out this friendly and simply furnished pub is its tremendous bird's-eye view of the Cheshire Plain; Marstons real ales, bar food *(LYM)*

☆ **Nantwich** [Hospital St – by side passage to central church; SJ6552], *Lamb*: Fine flower-decked old pub with pillared entrance, lamb etched in glass just through the door; comfortably sedate bar with lots of seating, real ale, and standards of service that readers who've known the pub for over 40 years say are as high as ever *(E G Parish, Graham Gibson, W C M Jones)*

Nantwich [High St, almost opp W end of church], *Crown*: Striking timbered Elizabethan inn with rambling beamed and timbered bar, comfortably modernised; Tetleys and related real ales, maybe Marstons Pedigree, reasonable bar food, restaurant; quiet at lunchtime but can get very busy in the evenings (when young people appreciate the video juke box if not the bouncers); bedrooms very comfortable and characterful, if a bit aged *(Wayne Brindle, LYM)*

Neston [19 Quayside; SW of town – OS Sheet 117 reference 290760; SJ2978], *Harp*: Great potential, lovely Deeside position (despite nearby housing estate) with uninterrupted saltmarsh views to distant mountains, very pleasant licensee, Whitbreads-related real ale, cheap bar snacks – though interior unremarkable *(Anon)*

☆ **Over Peover** [Stocks Lane, A50 – OS Sheet 118 reference 767746; SJ7674], *Whipping Stocks*: Recently extended rustic pub with attractive panelling, leaded windows, comfortable seats, pleasant and welcoming new licensee (who used to work at the well kept Bird in Hand at Mobberley), Sam Smiths OB on handpump, bar meals and snacks, children's room and play area; pleasant walk to church and sixteenth-century hall *(Graham Gibson, G T Jones)*

Over Tabley [Chester Rd (A556, by M6 junction 19); SJ7280], *Windmill*: Little rooms to explore and an ideal meeting place with good beer and fires *(Denis Mann)*

Parkgate [The Parade; SJ2878], *Boathouse*: Tastefully restored in 1989 – bright interior with views over Dee estuary to N Wales; good range of bar food, evening restaurant, Greenalls real ale *(Mr and Mrs J H Adam)*; [The Parade] *Red Lion*: Old-fashioned pub with charming landlady, well kept Tetleys and Walkers, good bar food; lounge, men's bar and darts-room with fruit machine; hasn't moved with the times – which is part of its charm *(D P Manchett)*

Plumley [Plumley Moor Lane; signposted

Plumley off A556 by the Smoker; SJ7175], *Golden Pheasant*: Spacious series of comfortably modernised open-plan rooms with one or two antiques among more conventional furnishings, open fire, games-room with pool-table, bar food, restaurant; thriving atmosphere, well priced Lees Bitter and Mild; neat bowling-green and climbing-frame in sizeable garden; new licensees late 1988, and not enough reports since for us to form a clear impression yet; bedrooms *(Mr and Mrs J A Hendry, LYM)*

☆ Pott Shrigley [from B5091 out of Bollington at Turners Arms fork straight ahead into Ingersley Rd towards Rainow, then up hill turn left at Pott Shrigley sign; OS Sheet 118 reference 945782; SJ9479], *Cheshire Hunt*: Rambling small rooms in stone-built former farmhouse, giving a feel of rustic snugness, with quite a few hunting pictures; formerly popular for interesting range of bar food running up to hefty steaks, but too soon to tell about standard under new licensees who took over 1988; well kept Stones, decent wines, lots of liqueurs; tables on flagstoned terrace with pasture views, play area *(Graham Gibson, M A and W R Proctor, Dr and Mrs R J Ashleigh, David Waterhouse, LYM; more reports on the new regime please)*

Prestbury [SJ9077], *Admiral Rodney*: Welcoming, comfortable pub with well kept Robinsons ales and good range of bar food *(Mr and Mrs J H Adam)*

Puddington [A540 nr A550; SJ3373], *Yacht*: Good choice of bar food and pleasant atmosphere in nicely decorated lounge bar *(Mr and Mrs J H Adam)*

Rainow [SJ9576], *Rising Sun*: Comfortable décor, wooden tables and a central bar; Burtonwood and Marstons on handpump, reasonable bar food from sandwiches, soup or ploughman's through burgers, vegetarian dishes and omelettes to scampi or curry *(Simon Turner)*

Risley [Gorse Covert Shopping Precinct – nr M62 junction 11; SJ6592], *Poacher*: Large, modern but comfortable Tetleys house, good lunchtime bar food including help-yourself salad bar; very busy Fri lunchtime (close to BNFLQ Risley); Tues quiz night *(Simon Turner)*

Sandbach [Market Sq – handy for M6 junction 17; SJ7661], *Lower Chequer*: Picturesque market-square pub, comfortably modernised, good bar food and accommodating staff *(Wayne Brindle)*

Stoak [OS Sheet 117 reference 423734; SJ4273], *Bunbury Arms*: Pleasant flagstoned main bar decorated with stuffed fish, good value bar lunches, well kept Boddingtons and Higsons, handy for Chester Zoo *(Jon Wainwright)*

Sutton [Higher Sutton – outside Macclesfield; SJ9271], *Ryles Arms*: Attractive stone pub by picturesque country lane, variety of comfortable chairs and settees,

always welcoming, very popular range of reasonably priced food; pretty garden *(M A and W R Proctor)*

Swettenham [off A54 Congleton–Holmes Chapel or A535 Chelford–Holmes Chapel; SJ8067], *Swettenham Arms*: Included for its very pretty position behind the church of a tucked-away village, and its carefully restored big beamed family bar with old-fashioned furnishings; Websters and other real ales, bar food; may be closed weekday lunchtimes *(Simon Turner, LYM; more reports on service and so forth, please)*

☆ Tarporley [High St – village signposted off A49; SJ5563], *Swan*: Georgian inn with engaging traditionally furnished flagstoned bar (formerly the kitchen – there's still a bread oven by the log fire); Greenalls Local on handpump, restaurant; children in eating area and restaurant; have been ups and downs in last couple of years or so, though most recently we've had reports of new management with a cosy, relaxed atmosphere again, shining brassware, attractive new furnishings, and a good choice of reasonably priced bar food (not Sun lunchtime); bedrooms *(Laurence Manning, Wayne Brindle, KC, W C M Jones, I Coburn, LYM; more reports please)*

Tattenhall [Whitchurch Rd, Broxton – nr junction A41/A534, 3 miles S; SJ4959], *Broxton Hall*: Well run hotel with comfortable residents' lounge, pictures depicting the months hanging in the bar, Websters Yorkshire on handpump, interesting food in spotless dining-room; bedrooms *(Graham Gibson)*; [Broxton; junction A41/A534] *Egerton Arms*: Popular black and white pub with good food and beer; cosy atmosphere, excellent restaurant; bedrooms *(E G Parish)*

Tiverton [Wharton's Lock (Bates Mill Lane) – OS Sheet 117 reference 532603; SJ5660], *Shady Oak*: Now a Chef & Brewer pub, with reasonable choice of meals (not cheap) and cold snacks, and lovely position in open countryside by Shropshire Union Canal; plenty of seats and good play area in waterside garden and terrace; airy inside, with lounge opening into carpeted conservatory; well kept Watneys-related real ales, fine views of the Peckforton Hills; juke box may be rather loud; summer barbecues; bar food service can come under strain at busy times *(Wayne Brindle, Graham Gibson, LYM)*

Tushingham [old A41; SJ5346], *Blue Bell*: Striking fifteenth-century black and white pub with lots of old beams, Greenalls on handpump *(Graham Gibson)*

Walker Barn [A537 Macclesfield–Buxton; SJ9573], *Setter Dog*: Extended pub with fine bleak and windswept view; plain but pleasant inside, with well kept Marstons, reasonable choice of food in small bar and restaurant; roaring fire *(M A and*

W R Proctor)

Walleys Green [Wimboldsley; A530 Middlewich–Crewe, about 200 yds from main rly line – OS Sheet 118 reference 684621; SJ6861], *Verdin Arms*: Tastefully modernised country pub with relaxing atmosphere, Robinsons Best Mild and Best Bitter on electric pump, open fires, and archways leading to different areas; recent new management *(Graham Gibson)*

Warmingham [Middlewich Rd; SJ7161], *Bears Paw*: Country pub with well kept Chesters Best, Marstons Pedigree and Whitbreads on handpump, solid wooden bar counter, nicely varnished wooden ceiling; usual bar food *(Graham Gibson)*

☆ **Warrington** [Golden Sq; SJ6188], *Barley Mow*: Lovely fifteenth-century building in modern shopping precinct, open all day for coffee, tea and so forth, and a place where a woman on her own can feel quite at home; low beams, nooks and crannies, Tetleys ales on handpump, hot bar food from servery; can get crowded *(G T Jones, Graham Gibson, Peter Corris)*

Warrington [Old Hall Rd, Bewsey; off A57/A574 NW of town; SJ5989], *Bewsey Farm*: Attractive open-plan bar, part carpeted and part flagstones, with Boddingtons and Higsons on handpump, sensibly placed darts, tables outside *(Graham Gibson)*; [Ballater Dr, Cinnamon Brow, New Town] *Millhouse*: Modern estate pub with traditional layout of public bar and large lounge, lunchtime meals, garden for children, Holts Mild and Bitter at prices to make southerners green with envy *(P Corris)*; [Church St] *Ring o' Bells*: Fine old seventeenth-century pub by church, with low beams, friendly atmosphere and good lunchtime bar food *(Peter Corris)*

☆ nr **Warrington** [Fiddlers Ferry; leaving Warrington on A562 towards Widnes, keep eyes open as you pass Harris Carpets in Penketh then turn left by Red Lion Cavalier Restaurant (Tetleys); in Tannery Lane turn left again into Station Rd, park by rly and walk across – about 50 yds; OS Sheet 108 reference 560863; SJ6188], *Ferry*: Picturesquely isolated between Manchester Ship Canal and Mersey, with comfortable easy chairs, old-fashioned settle and sofa as well as more modern seats in nautically decorated low-beamed bar, buffet bar food lunchtimes and Fri–Sat evenings, good river views, tables outside; provision for children, well kept Watneys-related real ales on handpump *(Graham Gibson, LYM)*

Weaverham [SJ6274], *Maypole*: Pleasant food under new regime – promises well when they've settled in properly *(Syd and Wyn Donald)*

☆ **Weston** [the one nr Crewe – very handy for M6 junction 16; SJ7352], *White Lion*: Classic black and white seventeenth-century Cheshire inn, expertly managed, with old low beams and comfortable chairs and settles

in network of rooms, good bar food from sandwiches to Dee salmon and steaks, restaurant, excellent service by polite staff, well kept Tetleys and related beers tapped from the cask, pleasant atmosphere; lovely garden with bowling-green *(E G Parish, Laurence Manning, Martin Aust)*

☆ **Whiteley Green** [OS Sheet 118 reference 924789; SJ9278], *Windmill*: Big lawn prettily planted with shrub and flower borders, summer bar and barbecues – idyllic on a fine afternoon, in attractive countryside; comfortable seats around well spaced tables in spaciously modernised lounge with friendly helpful staff, good lunchtime bar food (children allowed in new carvery/bistro area, which has stayed open on Sun afternoons), well kept Boddingtons and Marstons Burton and Pedigree, cappuccino coffee, fruit machine; close to Middlewood Way *(Brian and Anna Marsden, Paul Corbett, Mrs S Corrigan, BB)*

Wildboarclough [SJ9868], *Crag*: Sheltered valley pub surrounded by moorland, bar food, Burtonwood real ale on handpump, restaurant, pretty terrace *(LYM)*

☆ **Willaston** [OS Sheet 117 reference 329777; SJ3378], *Pollards*: Striking building with two sandstone wings, central whitewashed part, biggish lawns and gardens – originally a fourteenth-century farmhouse; comfortable stone-floored bar on left has beams and high shelves, nice cushioned wall seats with some stone armrests, French windows to garden, Greenalls Original on handpump; wide choice of excellent bar food, restaurant on right *(Jon Wainwright, Mr and Mrs J C MacGregor)*

Willaston [87 Wistaston Rd], *Nags Head*: Old pub with typical atmosphere, bar where dominoes and cribbage are regularly played, comfortable lounge and superb beer *(K H Miller)*

Wilmslow [Altrincham Rd; SJ8481], *Boddington Arms*: Spacious and comfortably refurbished Boddingtons house with helpful young staff, well kept ales on handpump, good value 'Henry's Table' bar food and separate restaurant, outside seating; close to Lindon Common *(John Gould, David Waterhouse)*; [Chapel Lane (off A34); SJ8481] *Farmers Arms*: Small multi-roomed pub with fine collection of brass, plates, guns, clocks and barometers, and beautiful etched windows; Boddingtons Mild and Bitter on handpump, lunchtime bar food (not Sun) *(Graham Gibson)*; [Swan St (a stroll from rly stn); SJ8481] *Swan*: Seventeenth-century pub, lounge divided into sections with names linked to swans – Pen Parlour, Cob Bar; lunchtime bar food, separate Swannery Restaurant (meals from 7pm), good friendly service, well kept Boddingtons on handpump, decent wines *(John Gould)*

☆ **Wincle** [SU9666], *Ship*: Friendly sixteenth-century free house tucked away in scenic

countryside; small, quaint and cosy lounge and bar, stone walls some 18 inches thick, well kept Marstons Pedigree, good value bar food, coal fire and tables in garden; get there early for a seat at weekends; nr start GWG103 *(Jon Wainwright, John Gould, Dr and Mrs R J Ashleigh, M A and W R Proctor)*
Wrenbury [SJ5948], *Cotton Arms*: On Shropshire Canal, with reasonably priced food and pleasant garden by bowling-green; children allowed in family room *(DMM)*
Wrinehill [Main Rd; SJ7547], *Hand & Trumpet*: Welcoming and comfortable, with large back room for families; well cooked,

excellent value food, splendid garden with duck pond *(Joy Heatherley)*
☆ **Wybunbury** [B5071; SJ6950], *Swan*: Fine whitewashed village inn with prominent bay window facing elegant church tower (all that's left after storm collapse) in beautiful sloping churchyard with great lime trees; interesting, tasteful décor and lots to entertain inside, good beers including McEwans 80/- and Youngers Scotch, bar food, huge open fire, friendly landlord, relaxed atmosphere; bedrooms comfortable *(Jon Wainwright, Graham Gibson, D P Bagnall, Mr and Mrs J H Adam, Martin Aust)*

Cleveland *see* Northumbria

Cornwall

A good many new main entries here (or pubs reappearing in these pages after a break) include the Maltsters Arms at Chapel Amble (some most unusual dishes among a wide range of popular food), attractively old-fashioned Carpenters Arms at Metherell (with a pleasantly enthusiastic landlord), the Ship down by the water at Mousehole (bags of character), the London Inn near the harbour in Padstow (a spick-and-span seaman's pub – very rewarding for visitors), the Victoria at Perranuthnoe on Mounts Bay (popular food in unspoilt surroundings), the rookery-nookery Royal Oak at Perranwell (excellent lunchtime buffet), the Stag Hunt at Ponsanooth (Colin Gilham, one of Cornwall's really crack landlords, is making great strides at this unassuming village pub), the ancient yet thoroughly cheerful Cornish Arms on its scenic coast road at St Merryn, the friendly Fox & Hounds at Scorrier (good value food) and the remarkably stylish new Inn for all Seasons at Treleigh near Redruth (opened by the team who've made such a long-standing success of the Rising Sun at St Mawes, which they continue to run). Many other changes here include new licensees at the Coachmakers Arms in Callington, the Cornish Arms at Pendoggett (winning very warm praise already, for food, atmosphere and an excellent choice of wines), the lively Admiral Benbow in Penzance (he's suitably friendly), the beautifully situated Rashleigh Inn at Polkerris and the Mill House just up from the sea at Trebarwith. Old favourites doing particularly well at the moment are the Old Ferry at Bodinnick (what a lovely situation, too – if you can manage to get your car's handbrake to hold it on that hill down to the river), the Cobweb in Boscastle (lots of atmosphere), the Shipwrights Arms in Helford (another waterside position that's hard to beat; really good food, too), the Blue Anchor at Helston (the epitome of a basic local brewing its own beer), the delightful New Inn at Manaccan, the happily informal Bullers Arms at Marhamchurch, the particularly friendly Miners Arms at Mithian, the Jubilee at Pelynt (good food and a most comfortable

The Pandora, near Mylor Bridge

place to stay at), the ever-friendly Turks Head in Penzance, the Blue Peter at Polperro (good food and a charming harbourside position), the Ship at Porthleven (doing so well that we've given it a star award this year), and the Logan Rock at Treen, so popular with both visitors and locals. The Roseland at Philleigh, too, has been earning really warm reports this last year, but we've just heard that its tenant for 21 years has been given 12 months' notice to quit by the Devenish brewery chain. Devenish/Cornish Brewery have recently been giving notice to a good many other of their tenants and this is having a significant impact on the Cornish pub scene. In parallel, quite a few of the larger Cornish Brewery pubs, now under management, have been given a broadly similar refurbishment: several room areas around a central bar servery, with a more or less parlourish atmosphere, comfortable old-fashioned furnishings and lots of old pictures and bric-à-brac. These refurbishments seem invariably successful and enjoyable (the Kings Head in Falmouth, Norway at Perranarworthal and Globe at Truro are fine examples). But there is a certain sameness about them which makes one turn with some relief to the more genuinely idiosyncratic Cornish pub instead – places such as the Crows Nest at the village of the same name, up on the moors; or the Bush at Morwenstow; or, above all, the idyllic Pandora on Restronguet Creek near Mylor Bridge. Among the Lucky Dips, we'd pick out as particularly promising the Napoleon at Boscastle, Fishermans Arms at Golant, Crown at Lanlivery and Top House at Lizard; Falmouth and to a less extent Padstow are both rich hunting-grounds for pub lovers. In the Isles of Scilly the Turks Head at St Agnes sounds outstanding, if you are out on the islands.

BODINNICK   SX1352 Map 1
Old Ferry Inn

Following the slope down towards the River Fowey, this old inn has a friendly and traditionally furnished public bar with sea photographs on the panelled walls and a very large stuffed salmon. The comfortable lounge bar has a 'Parliament' clock, aquarium, and sea photographs and prints; piped music. Bar food includes sandwiches, home-made pasties (98p), ploughman's (from £2.25), pâté (£2.75) and home-cured ham (£3.15); good breakfasts; well kept Flowers Original and St Austell Tinners on handpump (light top pressure may be used). A games-room at the back – that actually burrows into rock at one end – has a stag's head on one wall, and darts, pool (in winter), shove-ha'penny, dominoes and fruit machine. Make sure your brakes work well if you park on the steep lane outside. *(Recommended by David Wallington, Mrs D M Gray; more reports please)*

Free house   Licensee Simon Farr   Real ale   Snacks   Evening restaurant (closed Nov–Mar) Children in eating area of bar   Open 11–2.30, 6–11; opens 11.30 in winter   Bedrooms tel Polruan (072 687) 237; £22.50(£25B)/£45(£50B)

BOSCASTLE   SX0990 Map 1
Cobweb

B3263, just E of harbour

This popular village pub takes its name from cobwebs belonging to spiders that were used to kill off the wine flies. The big, friendly flagstoned bar has hundreds of old bottles hanging from the heavy beams, two or three curved high-backed winged settles against the dark stone walls, a few leatherette dining-chairs, and a log fire in cool weather. Good value bar food includes sandwiches, roast beef (£2.50), and vegetarian or meaty lasagne (£2.75). Well kept St Austell Tinners, HSD and Wadworths 6X on handpump, with occasional guest beers and Inch's cider. There's a good juke box, darts, dominoes, pool-table (keen players here) and a fruit machine; the big communicating family-room has an enormous armchair carved out of a tree trunk as well as its more conventional Windsor armchairs, and another cosy fire in winter. Opening off this a good-sized children's room has a second pool-table and more machines. The tiny steeply cut harbour nearby is very attractive, as is the main village climbing up above. *(Recommended by P Miller, John Branford, Linda Duncan, Tim and Lynne Crawford, Steve Dark, Roger Huggins, Robin and Bev Gammon, J Harvey Hallam)*

Free house   Licensee Alfred 'Ivor' Bright   Real ale   Meals and snacks   Restaurant tel (not Sun evening) Boscastle (084 05) 278   Children in own room   Folk, country and western or modern music Sat   Open 11–11 (midnight Sat)

CALLINGTON   SX3669 Map 1
Coachmakers Arms 🍴

Newport Square (A388 towards Launceston)

The timbered butter-coloured walls of the irregularly shaped bar in this friendly seventeenth-century inn are decorated with reproductions of old local advertisements (particularly for coaching and coachbuilding), and there are black beams, and little winged settles and stools made from polished brass-bound casks; one more comfortably carpeted end has a log-effect electric fire in its stone fireplace. Good bar food at lunchtime includes sandwiches, soup (£1.25), home-made pâtés (from £1.65, crab or salmon £1.85), ham and eggs (£2.50), vegetable curry or cauliflower and broccoli gratin (£2.85), omelettes (from £3.45), salads (from £3.65), scampi (£4.95), gammon poached in honey, mustard and pineapple (£5.75) and mixed grill (£8.25); Sunday roast lunch. Bass on handpump; efficient service; trivia machine and euchre. *(Recommended by H W and A B Tuffill, John Kirk, Ceri Jarr, Revd Stephen Pakenham, Roy and Barbara Longman)*

Free house   Licensees Bryan and Sylvia Wilkinson   Meals and snacks   Restaurant   Children in eating area and restaurant   Open 11.30–3, 6.30–11 all year   Bedrooms tel Liskeard (0579) 82567; £22.50B/£35B

CHAPEL AMBLE   SW9975 Map 1
Maltsters Arms 🏵

Village signposted from A39 NE of Wadebridge; and from B3314

Attractively knocked together, the rooms of the busy main bar in this friendly sixteenth-century village pub have black oak joists in the white ceiling, heavy wooden tables on the partly carpeted big flagstones, partly panelled stripped stone walls, and a large stone fireplace; there's a family-room and a side room with Windsor chairs. A wide choice of interesting bar food includes home-made leek and watercress or mange-tout and bacon soup (£1.25), home-made burger or lambs' sweetbreads in marsh mint and tarragon sauce (£1.95), salads (from £2.50), kidney-bean and vegetable bake (£2.95), baked local mackerel with grain mustard sauce (£3.45), rabbit in cider and sorrel (£3.75), steak and mushroom pie with port (£3.85), monkfish, apricot and bacon kebab (£4.75) and steaks (from £7.25); specials like baked dogfish with wild garlic (£4.75), puddings such as magnificent home-made treacle tart (from £1.30), three-course Sunday roast lunch (£5.25) and children's meals (£1.25 – until 7.30 in the evening). Well kept St Austell Tinners and HSD and Ruddles County tapped from the cask. Benches outside in a sheltered sunny corner overlook the village green. The local hunt meets here twice a year. During the Children in Need appeal, they donate the evening's proceeds to charity. *(Recommended by C L Ives, Tim and Lynne Crawford, Giles and Fiona Ebbutt, R F Warner, Roger Huggins, Mr and Mrs G R Salt)*

Free house   Licensees Mike and Gill Staples   Real ale   Meals and snacks (12–2.30, 6.30–10)   Children in eating areas   Open 11–3, 5.30–11

CROWS NEST SX2669 Map 1
Crows Nest

Signposted off B3264 N of Liskeard; or pleasant drive from A30 by Siblyback/St Cleer road from Bolventor, turning left at Common Moor, Siblyback signpost, then forking right to Darite; OS Sheet 201 reference 263692

Lots of stirrups, bits and spurs hang from the bowed dark oak beams in this snug stripped stone seventeenth-century pub. It's charmingly old-fashioned but comfortable, with an unusually long black wall settle by the big fireplace as well as other more orthodox seats around the polished tables. There are old local photographs and maybe flowers on the tablecloths, down past the balustered dividing partition, and a children's room has been opened. Good value bar food includes sandwiches, ploughman's (£2), paella (£2.20), tagliatelle or tandoori chicken (£2.45), a home-made daily special such as steak and kidney pie, beef curry or chilli con carne, and puddings like home-made rhubarb crumble or apple pie with clotted cream (£1.20). Well kept St Austell Tinners and HSD on handpump or tapped from the cask; darts, dominoes, euchre, juke box, fruit machine and piped music; quick and pleasant service. On the terrace by the quiet village lane there are picnic-table sets. *(Recommended by Charles Gurney; more reports please)*

St Austell   Licensee T W C Rosser   Real ale   Meals and snacks   Children in own room Open 11–11

HELFORD SW7526 Map 1
Shipwrights Arms ★ 🏵

The terraces which drop down from this very friendly thatched pub to the water's edge give a lovely view of this beautiful wooded creek. On summer evenings there are barbecues among flowers and palm trees: early evening burgers for children, and prawns and steaks. The top part of the terrace is roofed over with Perspex. Inside, the atmosphere is easy-going, with lots of ship models and navigation lamps, sea pictures, drawings of lifeboat coxwains, and yachtsmen congregating under the low shiny ochre ceiling by the bar counter. At the other end there are oak settles and tables in a dining area with good waitress service; an open fire in winter. Home-made bar food includes pasties (£1.20), home-made soup (£1.30), ploughman's (from £2.30, with crab £3.95), a winter home-made daily special (£3.75), and very good summer salads (from £4; fresh local crab £5.50), with evening dishes like mushrooms in garlic butter or pâté (£2.25), lasagne (£3.75), crab salad (£5.50), beef curry or beef cooked in red wine (£5.25), local scallops or monkfish provençale in white wine (£6.50), sirloin steak (£6.50) and lobster (from £7.50); home-made puddings (from £1.75). Well kept John Devenish and Cornish Original on handpump; chilled white wine. Courteous, efficient staff; dominoes, cribbage, euchre, piped music. *(Recommended by David Wallington, G Smith, S A Robbins, David Pearman, Gwen and Peter Andrews, Stephen McNees, Clifford Blakemore, Roy and Shirley Bentley, Audrey and Alan Chatting, GB, CH, Jon Wainwright, Hazel Morgan, R Trigwell, N J Cutter)*

Cornish Brewery   Licensees Brandon Flynn and Charles Herbert   Real ale   Meals and snacks (not Mon evening in winter, not Sun evening) tel Manaccan (032 623) 235   Children in eating area   Parking only right outside the village in summer   Open 11–2.30, 6–11 all year

HELSTON SW6527 Map 1
Blue Anchor

50 Coinagehall Street

The ancient brewhouse in this medieval thatched town pub (mainly popular with locals) still produces the Medium, Best, 'Spingo' Special and Extra Special ales at very reasonable prices. Opening off the central corridor, there's a series of small, flagstoned and low-ceilinged rooms with simple old-fashioned furniture, interesting old prints, some bared stone walls, and in one room a fine inglenook fireplace; a family-room has several space games and a fruit machine. Past this, and an old stone bench in the sheltered little garden, is a skittle alley which has its own bar at busy times. The nearby Cornwall Aero Park has a lot of family attractions, and Godolphin House is well worth visiting. (*Recommended by Cliff Blakemore, Theo Schofield, Gwen and Peter Andrews*)

Own brew   Real ale   Snacks   Children in family-room   Parking sometimes difficult   Open 10.30–2.30, 6–11

LAMORNA   SW4424 Map 1

Lamorna Wink

This neatly kept and simply furnished place has one of the best collections of warship mementoes, sea photographs and nautical brassware in the county. Bar food (which stops at 2pm) includes sandwiches, home-made quiches (£2.25), vegetarian dishes (from £2.25), locally smoked mackerel and trout (from £3), and home-made fruit pies with clotted cream (£1.50). Well kept Devenish Cornish Original tapped from the cask; piped music. Darts, pool, dominoes, cribbage, fruit machine, space game, trivia and juke box are in a connected but quite separate building. Sitting on the front benches outside, you can just hear the sound of the sea in the attractive sandy cove down the lane, joining the birdsong and the burble of the stream behind – where you can catch trout; near *Good Walks Guide* Walk 3. (*Recommended by James and Marion Seeley, Gwen and Peter Andrews, Russell and Christina Jones, Patrick Stapley, Richard Gibbs, RAB*)

Cornish Brewery   Licensee Bob Drennan   Real ale   Meals and snacks (not Sun evening) Children in own room   Open 11–11; 11–3, 6–11 in winter

LANNER   SW7240 Map 1

Fox & Hounds

Comford; junction A393/B3293

Though this pretty white house has been comfortably modernised inside, with greeny gold plush or deep pink cloth banquettes, it's kept a good deal of character. Several red-carpeted areas ramble around, with black beams and joists, some stripped stonework and some dark panelling, comical 1920s prints by Lawson Wood, and a wood-burning stove in one granite fireplace with logs burning in another. A good range of bar food, served quickly except at peak times, includes sandwiches, good soup, salads (from £2.95; local crab in season), plaice (£3.25), gammon (£5.75), sirloin steak (£6.25) and daily specials (£3.50); a new restaurant area spreads out at the back. Well kept Bass and St Austell BB and HSD tapped from the cask; darts, fruit machine, space game, juke box and piped music. There are hanging baskets and tubs of flowers with the picnic-table sets on the front terrace, with more by swings and a climber on a sheltered and neatly kept back lawn. (*Recommended by TBB, Charles and Mary Winpenny and others; more reports please*)

St Austell   Licensee Coral Snipp   Real ale   Meals and snacks (12–2, 7–10)   Children in eating area of bar and restaurant   Restaurant (not Sun evening) tel St Day (0209) 820251 Open 11–3, 6–11; all day Aug–Sept; closed evening 25 Dec

LANREATH   SX1757 Map 1

Punch Bowl 🏠

Village signposted off B3359

This 400-year-old inn has been a court house, coaching-inn and smugglers' distribution house. The two-roomed flagstoned Farmers' Kitchen has a big stone fireplace, built-in red leatherette wall seats and sturdy wooden tables. The Turkey-carpeted Visitors' Kitchen, its atmosphere reminding some of an Alpine inn, has a couple of flamboyant red velveteen chaises-longues, some high-backed antique black settles, a Delft shelf above the squared black panelling, and a longcase clock; piped music. Bar food includes filled eight-inch brown baps (£1.25) and home-made curry or leek and bacon pie (£3.25); very well kept Bass, Charringtons IPA and Courage Directors on handpump, and local farm cider. The games-bar has darts, pool, dominoes, fruit machine, space game and juke box. The tucked-away village has a farm museum and an attractive church with a fine set of bells. *(Recommended by J C Proud, Charles and Mary Winpenny, Steve and Carolyn Harvey, J D Mackay)*

Free house   Licensee Harvey Frith   Real ale   Meals and snacks   Restaurant (not Sun evening)   Children in restaurant and own room   Open 11–11; 11–3, 6–11 in winter Bedrooms tel Lanreath (0503) 20218; £17.50(£21.50B)/£35(£43B)

LERRYN   SX1457 Map 1
Ship
Village signposted from A390 in Lostwithiel

With a good local atmosphere, this friendly pub has a cheerful open-plan bar with small yachting pictures, brasses on beams, a grandfather clock, and is part carpeted, part big slate flagstones. Bar food includes sandwiches, home-made soups (£1), ploughman's (£2.45), home-made pies such as steak and Guinness or venison (£4), a variety of vegetarian dishes like pumpkin crumble or fennel pie, and local fresh fish and shellfish. Well kept Bass, Flowers Original and IPA (known here as Bilge Water) on handpump from the central servery, and local farm cider; a separate room has sensibly placed darts, pool, dominoes, cribbage, fruit machines, space game and piped music. A sheltered back lawn has a children's play area and some picnic-table sets, with a couple more in front of the stone building by the flower borders, tubs and hanging baskets. In December they hold a race for small craft using seagull engines, the winner being the first back to the pub to ring the ship's bell. *(Recommended by J C Proud, Patrick Young, A B Sykes, Ted George, Gwen and Peter Andrews, Steve and Carolyn Harvey, J D Mackay, Mr and Mrs D A P Grattan)*

Free house   Licensee Ted Bealey   Real ale   Meals and snacks   Restaurant tel Bodmin (0208) 872374   Children welcome   Open 11.30–3, 6–11; 12–2.30, 6–10.30 in winter

LOSTWITHIEL   SX1059 Map 1
Royal Oak
Duke Street; pub easily visible from A390 in centre

This ancient and cosy town-centre pub has an unusual range of real ales for Cornwall: Bass, Flowers Original and IPA, Fullers London Pride, Huntsman Royal Oak, and two guest beers such as Batemans and Hook Norton Old Hookey on handpump; they also have a good choice of bottled beers and draught ciders. The well kept lounge has captain's chairs and brown leatherette button-back banquettes on its patterned carpet, a couple of wooden armchairs by the gas-effect log fire, and walls stripped back to the old reddish granite. There's a Delft china shelf, with a small dresser in one inner alcove; piped music. Generous helpings of bar food include sandwiches (from 90p), soup (£1), pâté (£1.90), ploughman's (from £2), basket meals (from £2.50), very good scallops in cheese and white wine sauce (£2.70), curries (from £2.75), summer salads (from £2.95) and specials; children's menu (from £1.50). The flagstoned back public bar has darts, dominoes, cribbage, fruit machine and juke box, and younger customers. A raised terrace by the car park, lined with cordylines, has picnic-table sets. An underground tunnel is reputed to connect the pub's cellar to the dungeons in the courtyard of Restormel Castle.

(Recommended by S A Robbins, Ian Shaw, Lindsey Shaw Radley, JM, PM, Mrs Fennell, Roger Davies, Andrew Hudson)

Free house   Licensees Malcolm and Eileen Hine   Real ale   Meals and snacks (12–2, 7–10)
Restaurant   Children in eating area of bar   Open 11–3, 5.30–11   Bedrooms tel Bodmin
(0208) 872552; £22B/£38B

MALPAS   SW8442 Map 1
Heron
Village signposted from A39 at main Truro roundabout

On the walls of the long, comfortable rectangular bar here is an excellent collection of late-nineteenth-century photographs of Truro and the surrounding countryside; also, re-upholstered seats and carpets, brasses, bric-à-brac, and log fires in winter. Good bar food includes generously filled sandwiches (from £1.25; fresh crab £2.45), filled baked potatoes (from £2.25), liver, bacon and mushroom kebab (£2.55), ploughman's (from £2.60), home-made steak pie (£3.25), lasagne (£3.95) and hot seafood platter (£4.15), with evening dishes like gammon with egg and pineapple (£5.75), whole trout with celery and walnut stuffing (£6.50), and ten-ounce sirloin steak (£7.25); children's menu (from £1.65). Well kept St Austell Tinners and HSD on handpump; dominoes, fruit machine, space game, and a quiz night on winter Wednesdays. In summer, much of its appeal lies in the sunny slate-paved front terrace with a good view over the creek. At weekends and in other busy periods the pub can get exceedingly crowded – when nearby parking may not be easy (especially as there are now double yellow lines outside the building); service still copes well then. *(Recommended by Patrick Young, Peter Corris, S A Robbins, Roger Mallard)*

St Austell   Licensees Calvin and Anne Kneebone   Real ale   Meals and snacks (12–2, 7–10)   Restaurant tel Truro (0872) 72773   Children in eating area of bar   Ballad/country duo every other Sat evening   Open 11–3, 6–11; 11.30–2.30, 7–10.30 in winter

MANACCAN   SW7625 Map 1
New   ★ ✪
Down hill signposted to Gillan and St Keverne

Lively and friendly, the snug double-room bar in this thatched pub is simply furnished with individually chosen chairs, traditional built-in wall seats, pictures on the walls, and a beam and plank ceiling; attractive touches include hops around the windows, freshly cut flowers and oriental rugs. Bar food is good, with dishes like very good home-made soup such as purée local vegetable and curry or chilled pea and mint (£1.50), home-made pasty (winter only, £1), sandwiches (£1, delicious crab £2), good crab or smoked salmon pâté, ploughman's (£2.50), home-made steak and kidney pie or casseroles (£4.50), king prawns in garlic, kidney turbigo, and the house speciality, treacle tart (£1.50); they may have home-cooked locally caught fish dishes (depending on availability, from £5). Well kept Devenish JD and Cornish Original tapped from the cask; dominoes, cribbage, euchre, chess, backgammon and yahtzee. A sheltered lawn with picnic-table sets slopes up behind the pub. The outside lavatories are not the place to linger on a cold day. *(Recommended by Ian Shaw, Lindsey Shaw Radley, David Wallington, Cliff Blakemore, JM, PM, Clifford Blakemore, Sue Carlyle, Dr and Mrs A K Clarke, Russell and Christina Jones, Audrey and Alan Chatting, C S Trevor, Gwen and Peter Andrews, Jon Wainwright)*

Cornish Brewery   Licensee Patrick Cullinan   Real ale   Meals and snacks   Children welcome, though not too late in evenings   Parking may be difficult in summer   Open 11–3, 6–11

MARHAMCHURCH SS2203 Map 1
Bullers Arms

Opposite this happy, friendly pub, where the village road joins the A39, is a mile-long footpath that leads to the cliffy coves just north of Widemouth Sand. Inside, the L-shaped bar has comfortable little settles forming booths around its walls, local hunting trophies mounted above the stone fireplace, and a good long bar counter. Bar food includes soup (85p), sandwiches (£1, toasties £1.25), ploughman's (from £1.80), omelette (£2.30), vegetarian fruit and nut pilaff (£2.75), lasagne (£2.95), very fresh cod, steak and kidney pie (£3.20), ham or chicken salad (£3.50), local Tamar trout (£3.95), very hot curry, gammon (£4) and steaks (from £5.95); pudding of the day (85p), traditional Sunday roast and children's meals. Well kept Bass, Devenish Cornish Original, Greene King Abbot, Halls Plympton Best, Marstons Pedigree and guest beers on handpump, or tapped from casks in a back still-room; piped music, cribbage; quick service. Darts in a flagstone-floored back part, and beyond that a separate pool-room. The cocktail bar is decorated in 1930s style. *(Recommended by Richard Cole, Dr R Trigwell, Doug Kennedy, Mr and Mrs J M Elden, Stephen Davies, Charles and Mary Winpenny)*

Free house Licensees Keith Hendry and Christine Nesbitt Real ale Meals and snacks (12–2, 6.30–9.30) Restaurant open Weds–Sat evenings in summer, Thurs–Sat evenings in winter; Sun lunch all year Children welcome Open 11–3, 5.30–11; 11–2.30, 6–11 in winter Bedrooms tel Widemouth Bay (028 885) 277; £18B/£36B

METHERELL SX4069 Map 1
Carpenters Arms

Village signposted from Honicombe, which is signposted from St Ann's Chapel, just W of Gunnislake on A390; pub signposted in village; OS Sheet 201 reference 408694

Relaxed and friendly fourteenth-century village inn with huge polished flagstones, massive stone walls with tiny windows, and horsebrasses on a few heavy black beams. Winged high-backed red leatherette settles fill the various alcoves, together with lots of succulent plants, and a large slowly ticking clock. There are easy chairs in the simply furnished separate lounge. A wide choice of bar food includes home-made soup (£1.10), sandwiches (from £1.10; toasties from £1.20), filled baked potatoes (from £1.40), ploughman's (from £2), excellent omelettes (from £2.50), salads (from £2.60), home-made pizzas (from £2.75), fresh cod in batter (£3.20), vegetarian dishes (£3.50), good home-made steak and kidney pie (£3.75), gammon with egg or pineapple (£3.80) and steaks (from £5.50); puddings like home-made blackcurrant cake (£1.20), and children's meals (from 50p). Well kept Bass, Cotleigh Tawny, Flowers Original and Wadworths 6X tapped from casks behind the bar, as well as good farm ciders and decent house white wine; piped music, sensibly placed darts and fruit machine. Outside, by an old well, there are some sheltered tables. Cotehele, the lovely National Trust Tudor house by the head of the Tamar estuary, is a couple of miles further on through these narrow lanes. *(Recommended by Mrs B Barnes, John Kirk, Ewan and Moira McCall, Theo Schofield, Charles and Mary Winpenny, J C Proud)*

Free house Licensees Douglas and Jill Brace Real ale Meals and snacks Children in eating area of bar Open 11.30–3, 6.30–11; 12–2.30, 7–11 in winter; closed 25 Dec Bedrooms tel Liskeard (0579) 50242; /£25

MITCHELL SW8654 Map 1
Plume of Feathers

A natural spring well has been uncovered in the large, rambling horseshoe bar of this comfortable and friendly roadside pub. There's plenty of bric-à-brac on the

walls, such as kitchen and farm tools, and dark wooden chairs and settles, stripped old beams, and an enormous open fire at the back (that once belonged to the old kitchen). Bar food includes sandwiches (from £1.10), a range of ploughman's (from £2.15) and daily specials like home-made steak and vegetable pie, curries or casseroles (£3.25). Cornish Original and Devenish JD on handpump; good coffee; darts, a pool-table in winter, piped music. The raised lawn at the back has an adventure playground and lots of farm animals. There are two car parks.
(Recommended by Gwen and Peter Andrews, R Trigwell, Lyn and Bill Capper, Derek and Jennifer Taylor, Mr and Mrs Pocock, Alan and Julie Wear)

Cornish Brewery   Licensees Maureen and Peter Fowler   Real ale   Meals and snacks
Children welcome   Open 11–2.30, 6–11 all year; closed evening 25 Dec

MITHIAN   SW7450 Map 1
Miners Arms ★

In a secluded spot – with benches on the sheltered front cobbled terrace – this very friendly, well run pub has a little back bar full of atmosphere: irregular beam and plank ceiling, woodblock floor, and bulging squint walls (one has a fine old wall painting of Elizabeth I). A lot of this character spills over into the comfortable and spacious main lounge; there's also a stone-built cellar lounge and darts-room. Good, popular bar food includes plain or toasted sandwiches, soup (from 75p, wonderful home-made tomato soup with toasted garlic bread £1.65), tasty locally made pasty (£1.85), exceptionally good ploughman's (from £2.30), a pot of pâté with tomato bread (£1.95), home-made cottage pie or basket meals (£2.95), seafood lasagne (£3.05), steak and kidney pie (£3.50), prawn salad with home-made mayonnaise (£4.95) and rump steak (£5.95); specials such as home-made beef curry with poppadums and mango chutney (£3.45), home-made puddings like traditional English trifle or date and banana cake topped with chocolate cream, children's menu (from £1.10), three-course Sunday lunch (booking essential), and afternoon teas with snacks and fancy teacakes. Well kept Cornish Original and Devenish JD on handpump; may be loud piped music; good fire in winter.
(Recommended by M P Hallewell, JM, PM, James and Marion Seeley, Mr and Mrs J M Elden, Mrs L Cantelo, Steve Dark, D G Nicolson, Mr and Mrs G R Salt, Denis Waters, Charles and Mary Winpenny, Roy and Barbara Longman)

Cornish Brewery   Licensee Peter Andrew   Real ale   Meals and snacks   Restaurant
Children in cellar lounge   Open 12–3, 6–11   Bedrooms tel St Agnes (087 255) 2375;
£12/£18

MORWENSTOW   SS2015 Map 1
Bush

Village signposted off A39 N of Kilkhampton

Part of this delightful old-fashioned pub dates back just over 1000 years (a Celtic piscina carved from serpentine stone is still set in one wall), and it has a strong claim to be one of the very oldest in Britain. The small main bar has ancient built-in settles, a big stone fireplace, and a cosy side area with antique seats, a lovely old elm trestle table, and a wooden propeller from a 1930 De Havilland Gipsy. Well kept Bass and St Austell HSD on handpump or tapped from a wooden cask behind the wood-topped stone bar counter (with pewter tankards lining the beams above it), and St Austell Tinners, kept under a light blanket pressure; half a dozen malt whiskies and Bulmer's cider. Simple bar food includes sandwiches, soup (90p), quiche or steak and kidney pie (£1.50), and stew or ploughman's with a bowl of home-made pickle (£1.75), and good pasties. An upper bar, opened at busy times, has built-in settles and is decorated with antique knife-grinding wheels, miners' lamps, casks, funnels and so forth. Darts, fruit machine; the landlord is firmly against piped music and dogs in the bar. Seats outside shelter in the slightly sunken yard. Vicarage Cliff, one of the grandest parts of the Cornish coast – with 400-foot precipices – is a ten-minute walk away. *(Recommended by R Del Mar; more reports please)*

Free house   Licensee J H Gregory   Real ale   Meals and snacks (not Sun)   Open 12–2.30, 7–11 all year; closed Mon Oct–Mar (readers have found it closed at other times; to be safe, ring Morwenstow (028 883) 242)

MOUSEHOLE   SW4726   Map 1

Ship

Right in the heart of this close-knit village, this is the obvious port of call not just for the young fishermen but for their grandmothers too. Yet visitors are also welcome in the L-shaped main bar with its black beams and panelling, rough granite and bare board floor, built-in wooden wall benches and stools around low tables, sailors' fancy ropework, and open fire. A communicating bar has a pool-table in winter, when there are darts too; windows overlook the harbour. Bar food includes fisherman's lunch (£2.20), sandwiches (crab £2.50), smoky fish bake or lasagne (£3.20) and crab salad (£5.50). Well kept St Austell HSD on handpump and several malt whiskies; lively young bar staff. The beautiful village gets packed in summer and over the Christmas period (when people come to visit the harbour lights). On 23 December they bake Star Gazy pie to celebrate Tom Bawcock's Eve: some 200 years ago Tom braved a fierce storm to catch his Christmas meal and returned with seven types of fish which were cooked in a pie, with their heads and tails protruding through the pastry crust. *(Recommended by Gwyneth and Salvo Spadaro-Dutturi, Les King, John Branford, Linda Duncan, Steve Mitcheson, Anne Collins, Patrick Stapley, RAB, Annie Taylor)*

St Austell   Licensees Michael and Tracey Maddern   Meals and snacks (12–2, 6–9.30; not winter evenings)   Children in eating area of bar   Summer parking can be difficult   Open 10.30–11; 10.30–2.30, 6–11 in winter   Bedrooms tel Penzance (0736) 731234; /£24

nr MYLOR BRIDGE   SW8036   Map 1

Pandora ★ ★ [*illustrated on page 116*]

Restronguet Passage: from A39 in Penryn, take turning signposted Mylor Church, Mylor Bridge, Flushing and go straight through Mylor Bridge following Restronguet Passage signs; or from A39 further N, at or near Perranarworthal, take turning signposted Mylor, Restronguet, then follow Restronguet Weir signs, but turn left down hill at Restronguet Passage sign

This lovely medieval thatched pub – on a sheltered tidal waterfront – has several interconnecting rooms rambling about under low wooden ceilings (mind your head on some of the beams): cosy alcoves with leatherette benches built into the medieval walls, beautifully polished big flagstones, a kitchen range, and a log fire in a high hearth (to protect it against tidal floods). Lunchtime bar food includes home-made soup (£1 or £1.20), sandwiches (from £1.75 for creamcheese, nuts, lettuce, tomato and cucumber, £3.50 for chicken, bacon, lettuce, tomato and mayonnaise with chips, £3.75 for local crab with cucumber and lettuce), ploughman's (from £2.25), home-made quiche of the day (£3.25), burger (£3.50) and salads (from £3.95), with evening dishes such as home-made pâté (£2.25), crab cocktail (£3.25), fish pie (£3.75), marinated beef fillet in chive and tomato sauce (£4.75) and char-grilled steak (£7.95); puddings like very good treacle tart (£1.60) and children's menu (from £1.25). Bass, St Austell Tinners, HSD and Bosun on handpump, and malt whiskies; pool in winter. There are lots of picnic-table sets in front, by a long floating jetty – where food and drink are served (weather permitting); showers for visiting yachtsmen. It can get very crowded in summer, and parking is difficult at peak times. *(Recommended by David Wallington, Annie Taylor, Patrick Young, Joy*

Heatherley, R L Turnham, David Pearman, Gwen and Peter Andrews, Bill Hendry, Steve Dark, Michael Beckley, Mrs N W Neill, Ted George, Roger Mallard, J C Proud, D S Beeson, Charles and Mary Winpenny, Jon Wainwright, H J Stirling, Roger Broadie, Malcolm Ramsay, Tom Evans)

St Austell Licensees Roger and Helen Hough Real ale Meals and snacks (noon–10pm in summer, normal hours in winter) Restaurant tel Falmouth (0326) 72678; closed Sun evenings in winter Children in eating area of bar and restaurant Open 11–11; 11–2.30, 6.30–11 weekdays in winter

PADSTOW SW9175 Map 1

London

Lanadwell Street

Just a short stroll away from the interesting working harbour, this friendly side-street inn has two neatly nautical rooms: brass ships' instruments and sea photographs, lots of red and cream woodwork, oak parquet floor, and red curtains and cushions. Bar food includes sandwiches (from £1, good crab), omelettes, roasts (£3.50), gammon (£5), steaks (£8.50) and a variety of fresh seafood like scallops, langoustines, crab and prawns (from £5). Well kept St Austell BB, Tinners and HSD on handpump, and quite a few malts and other whiskies; darts, dominoes, cribbage, euchre and fruit machine. For vigorous walks you might try the old railway line as well as the Coast Path. It can get very busy in summer. There is a good bird garden nearby. *(Recommended by J C Proud, Dave Butler, Lesley Storey, Ted George, W S D Hendry, TBB)*

St Austell Licensee Clive Lean Real ale Meals and snacks Restaurant Children in restaurant at lunchtime and until 8.30 Open 11–4, 6–11 Three bedrooms (not Christmas week) tel Padstow (0841) 532554; £12/£24

PELYNT SX2055 Map 1

Jubilee 🏵 🛏

B3359 NW of Looe

The main part of the lounge in this rather smart, well kept old inn has neatly squared oak beams, an early-eighteenth-century Derbyshire oak armchair, brown leather and red fabric cushioned wall and window seats, Windsor armchairs, magazines stacked under the oak tables, and, in winter, a good log fire under a copper hood in the big stone fireplace; an inner area is decorated with mementoes of Queen Victoria. The flagstoned entry is separated from this room by an attractively old-fangled glass-paned partition. There are handsome flagstones in the public bar, and pool, sensibly placed darts, dominoes, fruit machine, space game and juke box. Good bar food – served quickly by neat and friendly waitresses – includes a good choice of sandwiches (from £1.30, local crab £2.40), home-made soup (£1.40), ploughman's (£2.20), vegetarian lasagne or mushrooms in batter with a devilled sauce (£3.30), home-baked ham and eggs (£4.10), salads (from £4.15, £5.55 for local crab), steaks (from £7.60), and a daily special such as good roast lamb with home-made mint sauce, sweet-and-sour pork, local scallops or curries (around £3.80); the choice may be different at lunchtime. Well kept Ferguson Dartmoor Pride (known as Jubilee Original here) on handpump. A crazy-paved central courtyard has weekend barbecues (weather permitting, during the week also), and there's a well equipped children's play area. *(Recommended by J C Proud, Joy Heatherley, Mrs Shirley Pielou, R F Warner, Charles Gurney, Steve and Carolyn Harvey, J D Mackay)*

Free house Licensee Frank Williams Real ale Meals and snacks (12–2.30, 7–10) Restaurant Children welcome Open 11–3, 6–11 all year; will open longer in the afternoon according to demand by trade Bedrooms tel Lanreath (0503) 20312; £24.40B/£39.80B

PENDOGGETT   SX0279 Map 1

Cornish Arms 🏵 🛏

B3314

This fine old inn has been lucky in the people who've taken it over: in less than a
year they've given most readers a lot of pleasure. The atmosphere is warm and
friendly, the food very good, and the range of drinks is splendid. The two panelled
rooms of the front bar have high-backed built-in oak settles surrounding solid old
wooden tables on the Delabole slate floor, and fresh flowers. The big, lively locals'
bar has high-backed settles around stripped deal tables, a big wood-burning stove,
and darts, dominoes, cribbage, euchre, a fruit machine, maybe a portable television,
and occasional piped music. As well as sandwiches (from £1) and ploughman's
(£2.15), the lunchtime buffet (not Sunday) includes a wide choice of salads with
meat cut from home-cooked joints of delicious beef, pork, ham, chicken and duck,
as well as quiche (from £3), hot dishes such as king prawns in garlic (£2.60),
chicken breast stuffed with garlic, Brie and chives or grilled swordfish (£4.50), trout
(£5.25), a half lobster (£6), and home-made summer pudding, fruit pies or crumbles
and treacle tart (from £1.25). Although they do more straightforward bar food in
the evenings, you can eat from the restaurant menu: soup (£1.65, crab bisque
£1.95), crab claws (£2.95), Japanese breaded prawns (£3.25), lemon sole (£5.85),
roast duck (£6.95), poached sole fillets coated with Mornay sauce and topped with
king prawns and asparagus (£7.25), and big steaks (from £8.25; tail of fillet stuffed
with mushrooms and smoked oysters £8.50); Sunday lunch (£7). Well kept Bass
tapped from the cask, and Pendoggett Special brewed for the pub on handpump.
Good wines – the extensive list is carefully thought out and strong on bin-ends;
farm ciders, a dozen malt whiskies and lots of liqueurs. There are tables out on a
corner terrace with a sea view down the valley. *(Recommended by Paul Smith, C Vallely,
Rosalind Russell, Charles and Mary Winpenny, Steve Dark, Graham Tayar, W J Hallett,
J C Proud, D S Beeson, Mike Hallewell)*

*Free house   Licensees Mervyn Gilmour, John Robinson and Paul Stewart   Real ale   Meals
and snacks (12.15–2.30, 6–10.30)   Restaurant   Children in coffee-room lunchtimes and
restaurant Sun lunch and evenings   Sat evening pianist and other live entertainment   Open
11–11 all year   Bedrooms tel Port Isaac (0208) 880263; £27(£33B)/£43(£48B)*

PENZANCE   SW4730 Map 1

Admiral Benbow

Chapel Street; turn off top of main street, by big domed building (Lloyds Bank)

Upstairs, the low-beamed bar here has elaborate balustered pillars, fancy carving,
figureheads, lots of shiny paintwork, engine-room telegraphs, model ships in glass
cases, wreck charts (including a nice one with Gillespie drawings), a lovely brass
cannon, navigation lanterns and so forth, with ropes neatly wound in and out all
over the place. The various alcoves have red plush seats around the tables, and there
are lots of mirrors and plants. A plainer back room – with less atmosphere – has a
pool-table and lots of seats. The new licensee uses only fresh food, and nothing is
frozen: sandwiches (from £1), baked potatoes (from 1.20), various ploughman's
(from £2.50), fresh fish of the day (around £2.65), meaty or vegetarian lasagne
(£2.95), and chicken curry with poppadums or steak and Guinness pie (£3.50).
They stock country wines and keep Ruddles County and Ushers Best on handpump.
Friendly staff; darts, fruit machine and piped music. The pub is popular with young
people in the evenings. *(Recommended by Peter Corris, WMS, Deryck and Mary Wilson)*

*Free house   Licensee Colin Dennis   Real ale   Meals and snacks (12–2, 6–9.30)   Restaurant
tel Penzance (0736) 63448   Children welcome   Open 10.30–3, 6–11; may open longer in
summer*

Turks Head

At top of main street, by big domed building (Lloyds Bank), turn left down Chapel Street

There's a relaxed, friendly atmosphere in this popular pub. The busy main bar has wall seats and tables, a couple of elbow rests around central pillars, old flat irons, jugs and so forth hanging from the beams, and old pottery above the wood-effect panelling; a smaller side room is set out for eating, as is the downstairs cellar room. A wide choice of seafood includes crab soup (£1), excellent grilled sardines, crevettes (from £3.30), fisherman's pie (£3.50), mussels in wine (£3.65), crab salad (mixed meat £3.95, white meat £4.75), scallops in wine, cream and garlic (£5.50), cold seafood platter (£5.95), crab and prawn thermidor (£5.85) and whole lobster thermidor (£14.50); there's also plenty of non-seafood variety such as lunchtime sandwiches (from 95p), filled baked potatoes (from £1.50) and ploughman's (from £2.50), as well as home-made soup (from 80p), ratatouille topped with cheese (£2.20), good chilli con carne (£2.65), meaty or vegetarian lasagne (£3.40), gammon steak (£4.75) and very good charcoal-grilled steaks (from £5.85) using English steer beef. Devenish Royal Wessex, Cornish Original and Steam on handpump, and country wines, with sangria in summer and hot punch in winter; pleasant, helpful service; fruit machine, and a good juke box which attracts a lively young crowd in the evening. The sun-trap back garden has big urns of flowers. *(Recommended by Mr and Mrs M A Smith, Roger Chisnall, Audrey and Alan Chatting, Dr and Mrs M F Greaves, Simon Turner, Caroline Bailey, Patrick Stapley, Richard Gibbs, RAB, Bobby Goodale, Pat and Malcolm Rudlin)*

Cornish Brewery   Licensee William Morris   Real ale   Meals and snacks (11–2.30, 6–9.30) *Restaurant* tel Penzance (0736) 63093   *Children in cellar dining-room*   Open 11–11 all year

PERRANUTHNOE   SW5329   Map 1

Victoria

Village signposted off A394 Penzance–Helston

A couple of minutes' stroll from the beaches of Mounts Bay, this village pub's large bar has brocaded settles along its walls (some stripped to stone) and around polished wooden tables, exposed joists in its dark ochre ceiling, local coastal and wreck photographs, a neat coal fire and a friendly, lively atmosphere. It's L-shaped, and angles around at the back on the left to a snug alcove; on the right there's a more spacious family area with some higher-backed settles forming booths, a pool-table, darts, dominoes, fruit machine and juke box. Bar food, not cheap but generously served, includes sandwiches (£1.20), soup (£1.60), filled baked potatoes (from £2.85), smoked chicken breast (£3.95), smoked mussels or lasagne (£4.45), salads (from £4.95) and steaks (£8.50); well kept Courage Best and Directors and John Smiths on handpump. There are picnic-table sets under cocktail parasols in a sheltered stone-walled garden and by flower beds across the lane; the inn sign shows a very young Queen Victoria. *(Recommended by Cliff Blakemore, Charles Spicer, Theo Schofield, Charlie Salt, Rod Elwood, Jim Turnbull)*

Courage   Licensee C J Martin   Real ale   Meals and snacks (12–2, 6.30–9.30, not Sun evening)   *Children in family-room*   Open 11–3, 6–11 all year, maybe longer in summer if busy   *Bedrooms* tel Penzance (0736) 710309; /£32B

Children welcome means the pub says it lets children inside without any special restriction. If it allows them in, but to restricted areas such as an eating area or family-room, we specify this. Places with separate restaurants usually let children use them; hotels usually let them into public areas such as lounges. Some pubs impose an evening time-limit – let us know if you find this.

PERRANWELL   SW7839 Map 1

Royal Oak

Village signposted off A393 Redruth–Falmouth and A39 Falmouth–Truro

Cosy and warm, this pretty stone-built village pub is notable for its attractively laid-out lunchtime cold buffet, giving generous helpings of such things as smoked mackerel or quiche (£2.80), home-cooked gammon (£3.75), roast beef (£4.75) or crab and prawn (£5.20); they also do soup (£1), filled baked potatoes (£1.50), ploughman's (from £1.80), omelettes (from £2), plaice (£2.50) and scampi (£3.50), with similar hot dishes in the evening running up to steaks. There are red-cushioned seats around the tables on the red carpet, with horsebrasses and pewter and china mugs on black beams and joists, foxhunting decorations, and lots of brassware around the stone fireplace – the bar rambles around into a snug little nook of a room behind this. Well kept Devenish JD and Royal Wessex on handpump, fruit machine, piped pop music, and, in winter, evening quizzes. There are some picnic-table sets outside. *(Recommended by M P Hallewell, C A Foden, G Atkinson, NM)*

Cornish Brewery   Licensees Adrian Dighton and Desmond Fitzgerald   Real ale   Meals and snacks   Children in area behind fireplace   Open 11–2.30, 5–11 all year; maybe 11–11 in summer if busy

PHILLEIGH   SW8639 Map 1

Roseland ★ ✪

As we went to press, there was a questionmark over this well kept and friendly pub's future, as Mr Sinnott, who has run it as a tenant so well for 21 years, was given 12 months' notice by his brewery; how sad it will be if the pub does indeed lose him. It's a charming place both outside and in, with a lovely oak settle and old-fashioned seats around the sturdy tables on the flagstones, lots of old sporting prints and other pictures under its low beams, an old wall clock and attractive bunches of fresh flowers; a good fire in winter. Home-made bar food includes sandwiches (from £1.10, fresh local crab £2.30), generous ploughman's (£2.75), home-made quiche or lasagne (£3.25), tasty seafood Mornay, egg mayonnaise and prawns with salad or beef casserole (£3.50), kedgeree or fruity pork curry (£4), coquilles St Jacques (£4.50), and puddings like apricot and banana crumble or teacle tart with cream (£1.50). Well kept Devenish JD and Cornish Original on handpump, from a temperature-controlled cellar; dominoes, cribbage. The pretty paved courtyard in front of the pub has flowers among its attractive tables. The quiet lane leads on to the little half-hourly King Harry car ferry across a pretty wooded channel, with Trelissick Gardens on the far side. *(Recommended by JM, PM, Dr C J Weir, Dr and Mrs I W Muir, Mary Rayner, Russell and Christina Jones, S A Robbins, Steve and Carolyn Harvey, Mrs J H Aston, N C Rose, Patrick Young, Peter Argent, Ian Blackwell, Mrs N W Neill)*

Cornish Brewery   Licensee Desmond Sinnott   Real ale   Lunchtime snacks (evenings also June–Sept)   Children in lounge   Open 11.30–2.30, 6–11 all year; opens 7 in winter

POLKERRIS   SX0952 Map 1

Rashleigh

New licensees have taken over this marvellously placed pub, which has tables by a figurehead on the stone terrace overlooking an isolated beach and attractively restored jetty; there are barbecues here in summer. Inside, the front part of the bar has comfortably cushioned seats, with local photographs on the brown panelling of a more simply furnished back area. Food includes an extensive lunchtime cold buffet with home-cooked meats and fish (£5.20); also soup (£1), sandwiches (from £1, fresh local crab £3, open sandwiches £3.50), ploughman's (£3), scampi (£3.95), pies such as fish or cottage (from £4), prawns (£6) and charcoal steaks (£8).

Fergusons Dartmoor and Tetleys on handpump; dominoes, cribbage, euchre, fruit machine and piped music. This section of the Cornish Coast Path includes striking scenery, and there are safe moorings for small yachts in the cove. *(Recommended by David Wallington, Joy Heatherley, Barbara Want, Steve and Carolyn Harvey, R Inns, A R Friedl, Charles Gurney)*

Free house   Licensee Bernard Smith   Real ale   Meals and snacks   Restaurant tel Par (072 681) 3991   Children welcome in winter, in eating area of bar in summer   Pianist Fri and Sat evenings   Open 11–2.30, 6–11; 11–11 July and Aug

POLPERRO   SX2051 Map 1

Blue Peter ★ ✿

The Quay; on the right-hand side as you go around the harbour – a brisk ten-minute walk from the public car park

The food is a good deal better than the simplicity of this cosy, friendly pub suggests: fresh pizzas are baked every morning, the curries are Burmese and the home-made burgers are 100 per cent meat. Other dishes include sandwiches and baps (from 90p, hand-picked local crab £1.85), pasty (95p), home-made soup (£1), sausage casserole (£1.75), platters (a mixture between a ploughman's and a salad, from £2.15, home-made pâté £2.35, local crab £3.25), burgers or pizzas (from £2.15), home-made beef and Guinness pie (£2.25), home-made Rangoon chicken curry with side dishes (£3.50), deep ocean bake (cod, prawn, tuna and crab in a light cheese sauce topped with potato £3.25), fresh seafood platter (£6), and specials such as monkfish kebabs (£3.15), scallops in cream and white wine or fresh local trout grilled with garlic (£3.50); puddings (from £1) and children's menu (from £1.20). Well kept St Austell Tinners and HSD, and a beer brewed for the pub on handpump, as well as strong farm cider. One window seat in the low-beamed bar looks down on the harbour, another looks out past rocks to the sea. Besides more ordinary seats, there's a small winged settle, a polished pew and a seat cut from a big cask, as well as a big naval shell by the coal fire, fishing nets and some boat pictures. Darts, fruit machine, space game, trivia and piped jazz and blues. The small V-shaped terrace at the top of the flight of steps up to the door has some slat seats. Near *Good Walks Guide* Walk 9. *(Recommended by Ian Shaw, Lindsey Shaw Radley, Rosalind Russell, John Branford, Linda Duncan, Tim and Lynne Crawford, Colin Gooch, Charles Gurney, Pete Storey, Steve and Carolyn Harvey)*

Free house   Licensees Tim Horn and Jennie Craig-Hallam   Real ale   Meals and snacks (12–2.30, 6–9.30)   Children in upstairs family-room   Light rock/blues/jazz Sat June–Sept, Thurs Oct–May   Open 11–11 all year; closed evening 25 Dec

PONSANOOTH   SW7537 Map 1

Stag Hunt

A393 Redruth–Penryn; turn off into the village back road to find parking behind the pub, as the little main-road car park is very tricky to use

Straightforwardly refurbished (perhaps too straightforwardly, we'd say, for a building of considerable underlying age and potential) and simply furnished, this village pub owes its great charm to the atmosphere generated by its landlord, who scored such a hit with readers in his time at the Miners Arms, Mithian. Here since just a year ago, he is the very model of a good licensee: good-humoured, with flexible concern for all his customers, both regular and casual, and a firm eye on giving real value in food and drink. Home-cooked bar food includes sandwiches (from 70p), soup (95p), filled baked potatoes (from 95p), ploughman's (from £1.75), lasagne (£2.25), salads including home-baked ham (£2.50), mussels cooked with smoky bacon and garlic (£2.50), steak and kidney pie (£2.60), eight-ounce rump steak (£4.95) and a dish of the day such as curry (£2.25); there's an attractive stone-walled back dining-room, where the three-course Sunday lunch has to be a notable bargain at £3.95. Well kept Devenish JD and Cornish Original on handpump; darts, dominoes, euchre, fruit machine, piped music; there's a big wood-burning stove. *(Recommended by C A Foden, G Atkinson)*

Cornish Brewery   Licensee Colin Gilham   Real ale   Meals and snacks (12–2, 6–9.30 (9.45 in summer); not Sun or Mon evenings)   Well behaved children in dining-room Open 11.30–2.30 or 3, 6.30–11 all year; opens 7 weekdays in winter, opens 6 Sat; closed evening 25 Dec

nr PORT ISAAC   SX0080 Map 1

Port Gaverne Hotel ★ ⌂

Port Gaverne signposted from Port Isaac, and from B3314 E of Pendoggett

The style of the well kept bars in this civilised and popular early-seventeenth-century inn fits in well here, with low beams, some exposed stone, flagstones where they're not carpeted, a collection of antique cruets, an enormous marine chronometer, and big log fires. In spring the lounge is filled with pictures from the local art society's annual exhibition in aid of the Royal National Lifeboat Institution (they also take part in the annual costumed four-legged race in aid of the same organisation); at other times there are interesting antique local photographs. Many people praise the bar food, though the choice is not wide: sandwiches (from 95p, excellent crab £1.90), home-made soup (from £1.25, crab £1.75), pâté (£1.65), ploughman's (from £1.75), home-made cottage pie (£2.10), salads (from £3, half a lobster £7.75), home-made steak and kidney pie or a daily special (£4.25), and a winter home-made curry (£3.75) and six-ounce sirloin steak (£4.95); Sunday roast lunch and cream teas in summer. From spring Bank Holiday until the end of September the food is served buffet-style in the dining-room at lunchtime, and there is the same arrangement for Sunday lunchtime (when food stops at 1.30 sharp) throughout the year, but otherwise it's served in the bar or Captain's Cabin – a little room where everything except its antique admiral's hat is shrunk to scale (old oak chest, model sailing ship, even the prints on the white stone walls). As well as well kept Flowers IPA and St Austell HSD on handpump, there is a very good choice of whiskies and other spirits such as ouzo, east Friesian schnapps, and akvavit. There's a good bin-end wine list, with fifty wines; dominoes and cribbage, with darts, pool and a fruit machine in the renovated Green Door Club across the lane. A raised terrace outside has a good sea view (the bar does not). Splendidly unspoilt, the land around the cove a few yards away is owned by the National Trust; a costumed raft race is held here each year, as is the National Jet Ski Sea Championships. *(Recommended by Mr and Mrs M V Melling, Paul Smith, Mr and Mrs D M Norton, Sue Carlyle, David Pearman, Peter Corris, George Jonas, Graham Tayar, Charles and Mary Winpenny, Mr and Mrs J M Elden, WHBM, Professor A N Black, Lyn and Bill Capper, Robin and Bev Gammon)*

Free house   Licensee Frederick Ross   Real ale   Meals and snacks (12–2, 6–10) Restaurant   Children in Captain's Cabin (please reserve; children under 10 until 9pm) or restaurant   Open 11–3.30, 5.30–11; closed 8 Jan to 17 Feb   Bedrooms tel Bodmin (0208) 880244; £34B/£68B; canine guests £2, food not provided; restored eighteenth-century self-contained cottages as well

PORTHLEVEN   SW6225 Map 1

Ship ★

Readers have been so warmly enthusiastic that we've decided to award this old fisherman's pub a star this year. It's in a fine position, set into steep rocks above a working harbour which is lit up at night, and to get into the pub you have to climb a flight of rough stone steps. Though the bar and lounge have been knocked into one room, the old seafaring style has been retained: cosy alcove window seats with good sea views, a huge log fire in a big stone fireplace, and a friendly atmosphere. There's also a summer cellar bar. Very good, nicely presented bar food – served in the candle-lit dining-room with excellent views – includes filled hot crusty bread (£1.20), tasty fish pie or lasagne (£3.50), salads (from £3.75, crab claws £4.95, crab £5.25), smoked haddock (£4.75), sweet-and-sour chicken (£4.95), tuna steak (£5.25), and a summer seafood platter (£8.95), with specials like fresh mackerel cooked in cider and stuffed with apple (£2.50); well kept Courage Best and Directors and John Smiths Bitter on handpump; good, fast service; dominoes, cribbage and piped music. Terraced garden. *(Recommended by Tom McLean, Clifford Blakemore, Annie Taylor, Tim and Lynne Crawford, S A Robbins, Patrick Young, Tom Evans)*

Courage   Licensee Colin Oakden   Real ale   Meals and snacks   Children in own room Parking can be difficult in summer   Open 11.30–11; 11.30–2.30, 7–11 in winter

ST AGNES   SW7250   Map 1

Railway

Vicarage Road; from centre follow B3277 signs for Porthtowan and Truro

Almost like a museum, this busy little pub has some splendid brasswork and a notable collection of naval memorabilia from model sailing-ships and rope fancywork to the texts of Admiralty messages at important historical moments. Also, a remarkable collection of shoes – minute or giant, made of strange skins, fur, leather, wood, mother-of-pearl, or embroidered with gold and silver, from Turkey, Persia, China or Japan and worn by ordinary people or famous men. Bar food includes burger (£1.10), home-made soup (£1.20), sandwiches (from £1.20), ploughman's (from £2.20), chicken (£2.90), scampi (£3.40) and a home-made special (£2.90). Well kept Devenish JD and GBH tapped from the cask; darts, shove-ha'penny, dominoes, fruit machine and piped music. When the locals are there in force it can get pretty crowded. *(Recommended by JM, PM, Peter Corris, W S D Hendry)*

Cornish Brewery   Licensee Christopher O'Brien   Real ale   Meals and snacks   Children in family-room   Open all day

ST EWE   SW9746   Map 1

Crown

Village signposted from B3287; easy to find from Mevagissey

In a pretty village setting, this old-fashioned cottage has a warm welcome for the visitors who come here to dine. Traditional furniture includes sixteenth-century flagstones, one very high-backed curved old settle with flowery cushions, long shiny wooden tables, and, in winter, a roaring log fire with an ancient weight-driven working spit; shelves beside the fire have plates, a brass teapot and jug. The eating area has a burgundy-coloured carpet, velvet curtains and matching cushions to go on the old church pews. Good bar food includes good pasties (65p), traditional and open sandwiches (from 80p, local crab £2.50), home-made soup or egg mayonnaise (£1), pâté (£1.70), ploughman's (£2.10), filled baked potatoes (from £2.30), scampi (£4.50), gammon and pineapple (£5.10), tasty steaks (from £6), and home-made puddings like banana, mincemeat and brandy pie (£1.10). Well kept St Austell BB on handpump; darts, pool, dominoes, fruit machine and space game. There are several picnic-table sets on a raised back lawn, with a family-room out at the back too. *(Recommended by Mark Evans, Mrs Fennell, Gwen and Peter Andrews, Peter Corris, Harry Stirling, D Godden, Joy Heatherley)*

St Austell   Licensee Norman Jeffery   Real ale   Meals and snacks (12.30–2, 7.30–9.45) Restaurant   Children in eating areas and family-room   Open 11–3, 6–11; closed evening 25 Dec   Bedrooms tel Mevagissey (0726) 843322; £10/£20

ST KEW SX0276 Map 1

St Kew Inn

Village signposted from A39 NE of Wadebridge

Close to the church of this peaceful hamlet, the old village inn has a friendly bar
with winged high-backed settles and varnished rustic tables on the lovely dark
Delabole flagstones, a Windsor armchair and a handsome window seat; an open
kitchen range under a high mantelpiece is decorated with earthenware flagons, and
there are black wrought-iron rings for hanging lamps or hams from the high ceiling.
Well kept St Austell Tinners and HSD tapped from wooden casks behind the
counter (lots of tankards hang from the beams above it); fruit machine. The local
sirloin steaks cooked in the evening (not Sunday) are highly recommended. Picnic-
table sets shelter between the wings of the pub, by a stone-trough pump on the front
cobbles, and parking in what must have been a really imposing stableyard. *(Recommended by Roger Huggins, Steve Dark, Roy and Barbara Longman, Iain and Penny Muir)*

St Austell   Real ale   Meals and snacks   Open 10.30–2.30, 5.30–11

ST MAWES SW8537 Map 1

Rising Sun 🏵 🍺

An attractive new conservatory bar with cane furniture, lots of brass and white
boarding has been built on to the front of this busy small hotel, overlooking the
little harbour. The friendly and pubby front bar – still popular with locals – hasn't
changed, furnishings are simple and there's a big window seat overlooking the sea.
Imaginative home-made bar food includes cauliflower and dill or mushroom and
sherry soup (£1.20), filled baked potatoes (from £1.85), sandwiches with home-
made bread (tuna and gherkin £2, prawn and caper mayonnaise £2.80, crab £2.95;
open sandwiches from £2.95), ploughman's (from £2.75), salads (from £2.95,
smoked ham with home-made apricot chutney £3.85), veal and tomato casserole
(£3.65), guinea-fowl provençale (£3.95), curried chicken with mango and pawpaw
(£4.35), steak and kidney pie (£4.25), and scallops Mornay (£4.85), with puddings
like honey and cardamom or prune and armagnac ice-creams (£1.10) and
strawberry roulade (£1.25). Well kept St Austell BB and HSD on handpump; good
service and darts, fruit machine. The crazy-paved terrace has sturdy slate-topped
tables, with a low stone wall to sit on when those are full. *(Recommended by David
Wallington, John Tyzack, Mary Rayner, Stephen R Holman, A J Bright, Mrs N W Neill,
St John Sandringham)*

*St Austell   Licensees Frank Atherley and John Milan   Real ale   Lunchtime meals and
snacks   Restaurant   Children in eating area of bar   Open 11–11; 11–2.30, 6–10.30 in
winter   Bedrooms tel St Mawes (0326) 270233; £30(£35B)/£60(£70B)*

ST MERRYN SW8874 Map 1

Cornish Arms

Church Town; B3276 towards Padstow

The bar by the sturdy mahogany serving-counter dates from the twelfth or
thirteenth century, and though of course it's been substantially modernised there is
still neatly exposed ancient stonework and a floor of fine Delabole slate flagstones –
set off neatly by the shining copper of the foot rail. It's simply furnished, with
leatherette-cushioned oak wall settles and dining-chairs around wooden tables, and
photographs of local lighthouses facing a striking print of a lifeboat launch. Simple
bar food includes good pasties (95p), ploughman's (£1.85), home-made cottage pie
(£2.45), chicken (£2.75) and steaks (from rump £6.85); well kept St Austell Bosun
tapped from casks behind the bar, Tinners on handpump, and most attractively
priced wines; coal-effect gas fire, maybe piped music; quietly friendly service. On
the left there's a thickly carpeted ply-panelled games-bar with pool, darts, shove-

ha'penny, cribbage, dominoes, fruit machines and a juke box. Picnic-table sets under cocktail parasols in front of this pretty cottage face the stone-built church; this can be a breezy spot. *(Recommended by David Wallington, Bill Hendry)*

St Austell   Licensees Mr and Mrs Peter Fitter   Real ale   Meals and snacks (served all day in high summer, not Sun–Tues evenings in winter unless arranged)   Children eating with parents in side room   Open 11–3, 6–11 all year; 11–11 July–Aug

ST TEATH   SX0680 Map 1

White Hart

This rambling village pub has a fine Delabole flagstone floor in the main bar, with a snug little high-backed settle between the counter and the coal fire; decorations include sailor hat-ribands and ships' pennants from all over the world, swords, a cutlass, and coins embedded in the ceiling over the serving-counter. A carpeted room, mainly for eating, leads off, with modern chairs around neat tables, and brass and copper jugs on its stone mantelpiece; piped music. Simple bar food includes sandwiches, half a chicken (£3.75), and gammon steak with pineapple or good, tender ten-ounce rump steak (£6.30); well kept Ruddles County and Ushers Best on handpump. The games-bar has darts, two pool-tables, dominoes, fruit machine, space game and satellite TV with three screens. *(Recommended by Dr and Mrs I W Muir, Roy and Barbara Longman)*

Free house   Licensees Barry and Rob Burton   Real ale   Meals and snacks (12–2, 7–10.30)   Children welcome   Open 11–3, 6–11   Bedrooms tel Bodmin (0208) 850281; £12.50/£25

SCORRIER   SW7244 Map 1

Fox & Hounds

Village signposted from A30; B3298 Falmouth road

Well set back from the road, this long, low white building is prettily decorated with hanging baskets and window boxes, and has picnic-table sets under cocktail parasols in front. The bar itself is long, too, but divided into sections by a partition wall and low screens. It's comfortably furnished, with red plush seats around dimpled copper tables, some vertical panelling, some stripped stonework, big log fires, hunting prints, a stuffed fox and a fox's mask. There are creaky joists in the red ceiling. Good and often inventive bar food includes soup (£1.50), filled rolls (from £1.85), filled baked potatoes or open sandwiches (from £2.10), ploughman's (£2.15), several vegetarian dishes (from £2.45), mussels in a creamy garlic and wine sauce (£3.25), lasagne, plaice or Lebanese kofta (£3.30) and eight-ounce sirloin steak (£6.10); well kept Devenish JD and Cornish Original on handpump, fruit machine, piped nostalgic music, warmly friendly service. The food is locally so popular that it's wise to get there early for a table – there are more in a front extension, formerly a verandah. *(Recommended by Pat and Malcolm Rudlin, M P Hallewell)*

Devenish   Licensees Mr and Mrs Halfpenny   Real ale   Meals and snacks (12–2, 7–9.30; snacks until 10)   Open 11–2.30, 6–11 all year; closed 26 Dec

TREBARWITH   SX0585 Map 1

Mill House Inn

Signposted from B3263 and B3314 SE of Tintagel

New licensees have taken over this charmingly placed inn and have been working hard in the garden. As we went to press they were planning to add another terrace, build waterfalls and create a children's play area. Inside, the big main bar has pews, handle-back chairs around oak tables, some stripped pine settles on its Delabole slate floor; an airy communicating extension has pine tables in side stalls. Home-made bar food includes sandwiches (from 85p), home-made soup (£1.20), basket meals (from £1.50), pâté (£1.85), ploughman's (from £2.50), salads (from £2.50), fish platter (£3.75), smoked salmon (£4.50), gammon (£4.95), and eight-ounce steak (£6.75), with daily specials like vegetable bake, Turkish lamb or beef in beer (£3.95); home-made puddings (£1.20), and they do children's helpings for two-thirds of the adult price. Well kept Flowers IPA and Original on handpump; darts, pool, shove-ha'penny, dominoes, cribbage, fruit machine, ring the bull, draughts and piped music. The beach, a few minutes' walk away through a secluded wooded valley, is good for surfing. (*Recommended by Mr and Mrs D M Norton, Stephen McNees, John Branford, Linda Duncan, Charles and Mary Winpenny, Mr and Mrs D A P Grattan, Mike Hallewell, Iain and Penny Muir; more reports on the new regime please, as there have been some mixed early experiences*)

Free house Licensee Kevin Howard Real ale Meals and snacks (12–2.30, 6.30–10) Evening restaurant Children in family-room Open 11–3, 6–11; 11–midnight Tues and Sat Bedrooms tel Camelford (0840) 770200; £21.80B/£43.70B

TREEN SW3824 Map 1

Logan Rock

Busy, friendly pub with high-backed modern oak settles, wall seats and tables, a really warm fire, and old prints on the partly panelled walls of the low beamed bar telling the story of the Logan Rock – an eighty-ton teetering boulder which someone once tipped from its clifftop fulcrum to show off his strength, and then had to pay a small fortune to have it hauled up the cliff again. Very popular home-made food includes sandwiches (from 85p, local crab £2.25), good pasties (£1), filled baked potatoes (from £1.25), wholesome soup (£1.35), vegetarian quiche (£1.80), salads (from £2.95, crab £4.50), lasagne or a popular fish and egg dish they call the Seafarer (£3), scampi (£4) and good charcoal-grilled steaks (from £5.95); specials such as seafood pasta or leek and potato pie (£3), and home-made blackberry and apple pie (£1.75). They will heat baby foods on request. Well kept St Austell BB, Tinners and HSD on handpump; helpful, efficient service. Darts, dominoes, cribbage, fruit machine and piped music, with space game, juke box, pool-table and another fruit machine in the family-room; in winter they play Trivial Pursuit and have quiz games. Dogs are allowed in on a lead. There are some tables in a small but attractive wall-sheltered garden, looking over fields, with more in the front court. (*Recommended by Ewan and Moira McCall, Patrick Stapley, Richard Gibbs, RAB, Bobby Goodale, Philip Haggar, D G Nicolson, Roger Chisnall, C S Trevor*)

St Austell Licensees Peter and Anita George Real ale Meals and snacks Restaurant tel St Buryan (0736) 810495 Children in family-room Open 10.30–3, 5.30–11

TRELEIGH SW7043 Map 1

Inn for all Seasons

From A30, take easternmost Scorrier turnoff, then immediate right on A3047 towards Camborne

Very new and quite different from all the other places we include in Cornwall, this has a spacious and stylish lounge bar with a muted décor of deep purples, soft pinks and gentle greys and browns – very restful after the toils of the trunk road. There are plush banquettes, small easy chairs and black-lacquered chairs well spaced around solid dark tables, in carefully staggered booths along the walls, in separate islands, or in quiet recesses; lighting (and the well reproduced piped music) is gentle, and the few old prints on the textured walls are carefully chosen. The whole venture is under the same control as the Rising Sun down in St Mawes – a long-standing favourite: so, though it's so far too soon for us to be certain, we have hopes that the bar food here too will merit our new food rosette. It includes soup (£1.25), sandwiches (from £1.20, local crab £2.95, steak £3.25), filled baked potatoes (from £1.95), ploughman's (£2.35), vegetable and nut Mornay (£2.65), fish pie or pork and bean casserole (£3.25), salads (from £3.75), char-grilled monkfish provençale(£4.75) and sirloin steak (£6.95). Wadworths 6X served under light pressure, and a wide range of drinks from the long and elegant bar counter; good coffee; friendly, correct service. Broad windows, and white tables under cocktail parasols in front, look beyond the busy dual carriageway a couple of hundred yards away to distant rolling hills. *(More reports please)*

Free house   Licensees John Milan and Frank Atherley   Meals and snacks (12–2.30, 7–9.30) Restaurant (evenings Mon-Sat, Sun lunch) tel Redruth (0209) 219511   Open 11–2.30, 5.30–11 all year

---

Lucky Dip

Besides the fully inspected pubs, you might like to try these Lucky Dips recommended to us and described by readers (if you do, please send us reports):

Albaston [SX4270], *Queens Head*: Friendly welcome, folk evenings Fri *(Phil Gorton)*

Blackwater [SW7346], *Chiverton Arms*: Friendly country local with U-shaped bar, wood-burning stove in winter, subdued lighting; piped music, fruit machine, space game and darts; consistently well kept Devenish Wessex, Cornish Original and Dry Hop on handpump, good lunchtime and evening bar food; busy in summer – nearby campsite *(Charles and Mary Winpenny)*

Bodmin [SX0767], *Hole in the Wall*: Busy local with helmets, swords, model ships and other militaria in dark-beamed bar, two other bars, fruit machines; can seem full of smokers *(Bill Hendry)*

Bolingey [Penwartha Rd (off B3284); SW7653], *Bolingey*: Quiet, picturesque pub in small village; cosy atmosphere, Devenish on handpump, lunchtime bar food, outside seating *(Peter Corris)*

Bolventor [A30 on Bodmin Moor; SX1876], *Jamaica Inn*: Highly commercialised, but well worth knowing for its atmosphere, good efficient service, reasonably priced bar food including good pasties, well kept St Austell HSD and Tinners, Flowers IPA and Whitbreads; large family eating area *(Roger Huggins, Tom McLean)*

☆ **Boscastle** [SX0990], *Napoleon*: Small-roomed sixteenth-century pub at top of village, good mainly home-cooked bar food including vegetarian dishes (service may not be brisk), lots of interesting Napoleon prints including rare ones, Bass and St Austell real ale, decent wines, darts, pool, sheltered terrace; has had Celtic folk music Mon and Weds; children allowed in eating area *(Louise Donovan, R Del Mar, LYM)*

Botallack [SW3633], *Queens Arms*: Friendly pub with large open fireplace, Devenish ales, excellent huge pasties; garden, wonderful clifftop walks – it's nr start GWG4 *(Charlie Salt)*

Botusfleming [SX4061], *Rising Sun*: Interesting unspoilt pub, improving under current brother and sister regime (for instance, there's a proper lawn now) *(Phil Gorton)*

Camborne [B3303 towards Helston; SW6440], *Old Shire*: Comfortable, homely pub with friendly staff, good range of beers, interesting good value bar food, barbecues in summer, popular help-yourself carvery/buffet, children's area, garden; five bedrooms *(Gwen Cranfield, Pat and Malcolm Rudlin)*

Chilsworthy [OS Sheet 201 reference 415722; SX4172], *White Hart*: Pleasant, well restored village pub – friendly welcome, good choice of well kept beer, lots of local activities *(Phil Gorton)*

Constantine [Nancenoy – village signposted from B3291 Penryn–Gweek; in village turn right just before minimarket (towards Gweek); in nearly a mile pub signposted left; OS Sheet 204 reference 731282; SW7229], *Trengilly Wartha*: Quietly pleasant small country hotel with quite a modern feel to its décor, spacious games-room including darts and pool, comfortable lounge, bar food (perhaps including a cold buffet in summer), real ales such as Courage Directors, John Smiths and Tinners; evening restaurant, good provision for children, seats outside, folk music Fri; bedrooms comfortable and good value *(M D Velzeboer, Cliff Blakemore, Jon Wainwright, M P Hallewell, H J Stirling, J C Proud, Charles and Mary Winpenny, Ray Y Bromell, LYM)*

Crafthole [village signposted off A574; SX3654], *Finnygook*: Good friendly welcome in much modernised spacious lounge bar with wide choice of good value straightforward food, efficient service; pleasant restaurant, good sea views from residents' lounge; bedrooms small but very comfortable, beautifully warm – good value *(Mrs Shirley Pielou, Geoffrey Thompson, BB)*

Crantock [SW7960], *Old Albion*: Pleasantly placed thatched and pink-washed village pub with old-fashioned dark-beamed bars, Courage Best and Directors on handpump, good bar lunches; smuggling background *(Mike Dick, LYM)*

Cremyll [SX4553], *Mount Edgecombe*: Good Courage real ales in unrefurbished pub *(J C Proud)*

Cripples Ease [SW5036], *Engine*: Former counting house of old tin mine, popular with locals, with well kept beer and bar food; superb moorland location with views of the sea on all sides from nearby hill; bedrooms good value *(John Branford, Linda Duncan)*

Cubert [Trebellan; SW7858], *Smugglers Den*: Picturesque old beamed pub with inglenook, two bars, pool-room with juke box and space games; good value bar food and separate restaurant; weekend discos; can be crowded in summer *(Charles and Mary Winpenny)*

Dunmere [A389 W of Bodmin; SX0467], *Borough Arms*: Partly panelled stone-walled long single bar, brown leather banquettes and plush stools around pine tables, wood-burning stove, farm tools, Cornish Original and Dry Hop on handpump, good food from sandwiches and ploughman's to main dishes; family-room, tables outside *(Patrick Young)*

☆ **Falmouth** [Prinslow Lane; SW8032], *Boslowick*: Fine old black and white beamed and panelled manor house, well kept Courage Best and Directors, log-effect gas fires, courteous bar staff, plenty of seats including plush sofas; good reasonably priced bar food; children's playpark *(M P Hallewell, J C Proud)*

☆ **Falmouth** [Custom House Quay], *Chain Locker*: Strongly nautical décor and atmosphere, friendly and welcoming, with consistently good atmosphere under new regime; many customers from the inner harbour which it overlooks; well kept Devenish JD and Cornish Original, bar food, waterside tables outside, occasional pianist *(Les King, Jon Wainwright, LYM)*

☆ **Falmouth** [Church St], *Kings Head*: Well kept Devenish real ales and engagingly furnished bar rambling around long thin serving-counter that's done out like the front of an old-fashioned shop – pleasant mix of soft settees, easy chairs and firmer dining-chairs, old plates and engravings, lots of hat boxes, winter log fire, comfortable atmosphere; bar food, efficient service, piped music; popular with young people in the evenings *(M P Hallewell, Roy and Barbara Longman, Jon Wainwright, LYM)*

Falmouth [Boslowick Rd], *Clipperway*: Local with character, bar with pool-table, off-licence, large lounge with distinctive fireplace, Ushers *(M P Hallewell)*; [Church St] *Grapes*: Recently renovated open-plan bar on two levels with views over the harbour and docks, Cornish beer and Wadworths 6X, pool-table, juke box, trendy bar food, young clientele *(M P Hallewell)*; [Killgrew St] *Kimberley Arms*: Devenish town-centre pub with cosy atmosphere, low ceiling, stone walls, maritime artefacts, ships' lights, model boats; one room with small bar, good choice of food *(M P Hallewell)*; [Maenporth Beach] *Seahorse*: Very promising and popular

recently refurbished free house overlooking beach, with smoked glass façade and a continental cafe/bar feel; good reasonably priced bar food including fine paella and other seafood, well kept Watneys-related real ales, lots of chilled foreign beers, big waterside terrace, upstairs restaurant *(M P Hallewell)*; [The Moor] *Seven Stars*: Warmly welcoming old-fashioned local with well kept Bass, Flowers Original and St Austell HSD tapped from the cask, simple snacks, tables on courtyard behind flower tubs; run as it has been for generations *(Phil Gorton, J C Proud, BB)*; [Trevethan Hill – from centre follow High St straight on up hill] *Sportsmans Arms*: Worthy and relatively quiet local with exceptional harbour views and well kept Cornish ales; darts, and euchre's particularly here *(Jon Wainwright, LYM)*; [Killgrew St] *Wodehouse Arms*: Well kept popular St Austell local, warm and cosy, HSD, darts, juke box, bar food *(M P Hallewell)*

☆ **Fowey** [SX1252], *Ship*: Interesting building with well worn atmosphere, cosy fire and lighting, friendly licensee and good mix of customers; the popular bar food includes good daily specials such as lentil and bacon soup, scallops in garlic butter, gammon with parsley sauce and leek and ham pie; can be more than quiet out of season *(David Wallington, J D Mackay)*

Fowey [Town Quay], *King of Prussia*: Splendid spot, with harbour view from bow windows of upstairs bar; St Austell real ales, largely home-cooked food, juke box (which can be loud), popular downstairs restaurant *(John Branford, Linda Duncan, LYM)*; [from centre follow Car Ferry signs] *Riverside*: Comfortable hotelish lounge with fine view over river and boats, more workmanlike streetside public bar; bedrooms comfortable *(BB)*

Fraddon [SW9158], *Blue Anchor*: Large roadside pub with attractive lounge bar, well kept St Austell HSD and Tinners, big range of bar food, darts and fruit machine in public bar *(Bill Hendry, Roger Huggins)*

Gerrans [SW8735], *Royal Standard*: Pleasant friendly pub with cosy and well furnished rambling rooms, Cornish ales and pool-table; opposite church *(Mark Evans)*

☆ **Golant** [SX1155], *Fishermans Arms*: Superb spot with view of lovely stretch of Fowey estuary from bar window, and terrace looking down on garden; pleasant atmosphere, interesting copper, brass and old photographs; great staff (the landlord comes from Lancashire), well kept Courage ales and St Austell Tinners, bar food including excellent sandwiches with thick-cut roast beef *(David Wallington, W HBM, Caroline Gibbins)*

Goldsithney [SW5430], *Trevelyan Arms*: Comfortable, very friendly place with excellent, reasonably priced food served in generous helpings; good ales, too; children welcome *(Mr and Mrs R W Mair)*

Gunnislake [The Square; SX4371], *Cornish Inn*: Good food and well kept St Austell beers; bedrooms bright and comfortable *(J C Proud)*; [lower Calstock rd] *Rising Sun*: Unspoilt seventeenth-century pub overlooking upper Tamar valley, with pretty terraced garden – beautiful and peaceful on a summer's evening *(H G and C J McCafferty)*

☆ **Hayle** [Bird Paradise Park; SW5536], *Bird in Hand*: Converted coach-house notable for its home-brewed Paradise, Artists and maybe Victory Bobber ales, as well as well kept guest beers; salad bar and other food aimed at family groups visiting the Bird Park (lunchtime Easter–end Oct, evenings not Sun July–early Sept); four-table pool-room, garden, play area, summer evening do-it-yourself barbecues; children in food bar and pool-room *(M P Hallewell, Tom McLean)*

Helford Passage [SW7627], *Ferry Boat*: Big modernised open-plan bar where fruit machines and so forth have some prominence, but there's decent bar food (at a price) and afternoon teas, the St Austell BB, HSD and Tinners are well kept, the atmosphere is friendly, and above all it's excellently placed to overlook the boating estuary; children welcome; can get packed in summer (when parking's difficult); worth walking along waterside lane to small private beach *(Ian Shaw, Lindsey Shaw Radley, Les King, BB)*

nr **Helston** [Gunwalloe – signposted off A3083; SW7627], *Halzephron*: Pleasant and relatively unspoilt communicating bars looking over clifftop fields to Mounts Bay; well kept Devenish beers, standard pub food, log fire, friendly landlord, tables with cocktail parasols outside; children welcome; bedrooms *(Cliff Blakemore, Gwen and Peter Andrews, LYM)*

Hessenford [A387 Looe–Torpoint; SX3057], *Copley Arms*: Lovely riverside spot, comfortably furnished pub with St Austell Tinners on handpump, lunchtime and evening bar food, restaurant, garden *(Peter Corris)*

Kilkhampton [SS2511], *New*: Spacious well kept local with rambling interconnecting rooms, some traditional furnishings, fine wood-burner, bar food, well kept Bass; children in good games-room *(LYM)*

☆ **Kingsand** [Fore St; towards Cawsand – OS Sheet 201 reference 434505; SX4350], *Halfway House*: Cosy, dimly lit, neat and clean free house with low ceilings, huge central fireplace, simple furnishings, unobtrusive piped music, popular with locals but with warm welcome for visitors; Bass and Charrington IPA, reasonable house wines, excellent value food including generous mixed grill; handy for Mount Edgcumbe and marvellous cliff walks on Rame Head *(Joy Heatherley)*

Lands End [SW3425], *Lands End*: Rather smart (but obviously new) bar with efficient young barman; big picture windows overlooking terrace and sea beyond, light and airy conservatory with light cane chairs and cushioned seats (children allowed here) *(Anon)*; *State House*: Remarkable transformation since De Savary bought Lands End – excellent bar with Theakstons Old Peculier and a beer named for the pub, food particularly good value considering the setting; bedrooms good value too *(HEG)*

☆ **Lanlivery** [SX0759], *Crown*: Spick-and-span ancient whitewashed building with connecting rooms all painted black and white, carpets and flagstones, church pews, painted settles, armchairs and sofas, separate lounge with ornate stained-glass window; cosy atmosphere throughout, well kept Bass and Hancocks HB on handpump, good choice of reasonably priced waitress-served lunchtime bar food, evening restaurant, friendly efficient staff; bedrooms in separate accommodation by garden (no dogs allowed in these) *(A J Skull, Steve and Carolyn Harvey, David Wallington, Mr and Mrs Owen)*

Liskeard [Two Waters Foot – off A38 towards Bodmin; SX2564], *Halfway House*: Free house next to river with lots of outside seating; pleasant bar staff, no-smoking area and well kept St Austell Tinners; lots of parking space *(Simon Turner, Caroline Bailey)*

☆ **Lizard** [SW7712], *Top House*: Comfortable and genuine village pub, with strong maritime theme including photographs, maps and equipment from Lizard lifeboats, exposed timber rafters and log fire; pleasant efficient service, well kept real ales including Devenish Steam; very wide range of attractively presented, quickly served and often creative bar food including notable ploughman's, crab sandwiches and vegetarian dishes; fruit machine; tables on attractive terrace *(Cliff Blakemore, Stephen McNees, Colin Gooch, George and Chris Miller)*

Longrock [old coast rd Penzance–Marazion; SW5031], *Mexico*: Bustling pub, popular with young people; Bass and St Austell ales, imaginative and reasonably priced range of bar food with most dishes prepared to order so service not fast, but worth waiting for – especially the 'work and rest' pudding; local paintings *(Pat and Malcolm Rudlin, HEG)*

Looe [West Looe quayside, nr main bridge; SX2553], *Harbour Moon*: Mixture of old and new, the new being the picture windows overlooking the harbour; Courage Best on handpump, good lunchtime and evening bar food; children's room; bedrooms *(Peter Corris)*; *Jolly Roger*: Dimly lit lounge bar, flagstoned floor, pool-table; friendly bar staff, simple bar food *(Steve and Carolyn Harvey)*; [West Looe, just off quayside] *Jolly Sailors*: Old, unusually planned pub with various nooks and crannies; Watneys-related real ales on handpump, good value bar food *(Peter Corris)*

Mabe Burnthouse [SW7634], *New*: Friendly and informal atmosphere, small public bar, cosy lounge with stone masonry tools and old photographs; Cornish Original and Steam Bitter on tap, good choice of reasonably priced bar food *(M P Hallewell)*

Madron [SW4532], *King William IV*: Pleasant and cheerful, good food *(Alan and Audrey Chatting)*

Marazion [The Square; SW5231], *Cutty Sark*: Simple place with big helpings of food, Theakstons Old Peculier, easy-going service, friendly owner; bedrooms very reasonably priced – excellent breakfast and evening meal *(C H Beaumont, C S Trevor, Rosalind Russell)*

Mawgan [SW7125], *Ship*: Simple Devenish pub down a steep lane with welcoming Cornish landlord, popular with locals; well kept beer and good, piping hot pasties *(Gwen and Peter Andrews, Patrick Young)*; [at Trelowarren House; off B3293 towards Coverack] *Trelowarren Yard Bistro*: More wine bar than pub, but Devenish on handpump as well as a good choice of wines including Australian ones; converted stable, with tiled floor, panelled bar, ladder-back chairs, red tablecloths; very good food – light lunches and more ambitious evening meals, with good fresh fish and very frequent menu changes *(Patrick Young)*

Mawnan Smith [SW7728], *Red Lion*: Good value simple food, served quickly, and Devenish real ales in friendly thatched village pub with warm wood-burning stove in high-ceilinged lounge (pianist Fri), spacious public bar which can be lively in the evenings, well kept Devenish real ales; children in big family-room *(Ewan and Moira McCall, J C Proud, BB)*

Mevagissey [Fore St – nr harbour; SX0145], *Ship*: Old stone building recently modernised on nautical theme; St Austell Bosuns and HSD on handpump, wide range of good value lunchtime and evening bar food with seafood specials and children's dishes, friendly service, good atmosphere; children welcome *(Peter Corris, S J Abrahams)*

Mullion [SW6719], *Old*: Shipwreck mementoes and crabbing pictures in long lantern-lit bar of thatched village inn, big inglenook fireplace, Cornish Original, Devenish JD and Steam on handpump, wide range of home-cooked bar food including choice of pizzas and often local fish, summer barbecues Tues–Sat, good games area (pool in winter), TV and small aviary in children's room, seats outside; bedrooms and self-catering cottages *(Alan Sillitoe, R Trigwell, LYM)*

Newbridge [A3071 Penzance–St Just; SW4232], *Fountain*: Welcoming, friendly local with simple, comfortable alcoves, armchairs and a fire in winter *(WMS)*

Newlyn [SW4628], *Tolcarne*: Traditional

Cornish local with two rooms; well kept Courage, extensive hot and cold bar food at reasonable prices *(Clifford Blakemore)*

Newquay [Bank St – up alley by Newquay Arms; SW8161], *Malt & Hops*: Spacious pub with rustic-style décor, non-stop surfing videos on several screens accompanied by not too noisy pop music and attentive staff serving a wide range of local beers; surprisingly quiet atmosphere and popular with families *(Colin Gooch)*

Padstow [The Quay; SW9175], *Blue Lobster*: Good, clean welcoming pub facing the harbour with chairs and tables on a terrace; attractive, clean upstairs restaurant; excellent, original bar snacks *(Anon)*; [Lanadwell St] *Golden Lion*: Friendly local with pleasant black-beamed front bar, high-raftered back lounge with russet plush banquettes against the ancient white stone walls; good value lunches from soup and sandwiches including fresh crab to ham and egg, scampi and so forth; evening steaks and fresh seafood; well kept Devenish JD and Cornish Original on handpump, piped music, juke box, fruit machines, skittle alley; live entertainment Sat; three decently equipped bedrooms *(Bill Hendry, BB)*; [South Quay] *Old Custom House*: St Austell real ale in spacious and comfortably modernised split-level bar; pub food, steak bar; pretty spot on waterfront; bedrooms *(LYM)*; [Mill Sq; just off North Quay/Broad St] *Old Ship*: Tables on front courtyard of simple hotel tucked away behind harbour, bustling open-plan bar with well kept Flowers IPA on handpump, usual bar food, fruit machines, juke box or piped music, more tables in Perspex-roofed inner courtyard; children's room; open all day summer; live music Weds and Sat; dogs allowed; fifteen bedrooms *(Bill Hendry, BB)*

Pendeen [SW3834], *Radjel*: Local photographs on stripped walls of simple local with bar food, St Austell Tinners, darts, pool, juke box; nr GWG4; children in eating area; bedrooms *(LYM)*

Penryn [SW7834], *Seven Stars*: Cosy and popular Devenish pub notable for its exceptional collection of sparkling-clean brass platters and ornaments – perhaps the biggest in the country *(BB)*

Penzance [Barbican; Newlyn rd, opp harbour after swing-bridge; SW4730], *Dolphin*: Extensively refurbished pub with big windows overlooking harbour, maritime theme, quickly served bar food, St Austell ales under light CO2 blanket, limited choice of well presented and quickly served food, big pool-room with juke box, tables outside; children in room off main bar *(Deryck and Mary Wilson, LYM)*; [Market Jew St] *Star*: Low beams, red plush wall seats, ship pictures and nautical memorabilia, some stripped stone and panelling; notable for splendid new two-storey indoor children's play area overlooked by family-room; home-made bar food *(Anon)*

Perranarworthal [A39 Truro–Penryn; SW7839], *Norway*: Elaborately refurbished in old-fashioned style, with a more or less parlourish mood in most of the little beamed room-areas that ramble around the central bar, and lots of country bygones, china, stuffed birds and fish, fishing-rods and so forth, with masses of pictures; lunchtime bar food – soup, ploughman's, big filled rolls, a few hot dishes; restaurant (evenings too); Devenish real ales; tables outside *(Lt Cdr G J Cardew, BB)*

Phillack [SW5638], *Bucket of Blood*: Cheerfully busy, with well kept St Austell ales and entertaining ghost stories *(LYM)*

Pityme [Pityme Farm Rd; SW9576], *Pityme*: Former seventeenth-century farmhouse, extended to give a modern bar, restaurant and pool-room; friendly, welcoming and relaxed atmosphere, dartboard and fruit machine, St Austell HSD and Tinners, wide choice of good bar food, pleasant garden with tables and chairs; children welcome *(Peggy and John Tucker, Roy and Barbara Longman)*

Polgooth [SW9950], *Polgooth*: Lively rustic inn with own farmyard, well kept St Austell real ales; bedrooms *(LYM)*

Polperro [by harbour; SX2051], *Three Pilchards*: Good, basic, informal pub serving varied imaginative bar food, pleasant service by young staff – one to watch *(Ian Shaw, Lindsey Shaw Radley, K and E Leist)*

Polruan [SX1251], *Russell*: Warm pub sheltering in a village of closely built cottages; match-boarded walls, coal fire, genial landlord and customers, St Austell Tinners *(J D Mackay)*

Polzeath [SW9378], *Doom*: Excellent views all year, cosy atmosphere *(J D Shaw)*

Port Isaac [SX0080], *Golden Lion*: Old pub high over harbour in lovely steep village, nice view from the seat by the window, snacks maybe including a fine local crab ploughman's, well kept St Austell Tinners, good atmosphere *(Roger Huggins, John and Jane Horn, LYM)*

Porthallow [SW7923], *Five Pilchards*: Decent, friendly country pub with good range of lunchtime snacks *(George and Chris Miller)*

☆ **Porthleven** [Peverell Terr; SW6225], *Atlantic*: Reopened after major structural changes and refurbishment in 1988; pleasant open log fire in Cornish granite fireplace, large, open-plan lounge with alcoves; well kept Devenish ales, extensive range of bar food with emphasis on local seafood, stunning setting overlooking sea *(Cliff Blakemore, Patrick Young)*

Porthleven , *Harbour*: Cleanly and spaciously modernised harbourside pub with pine furniture, St Austell Bosuns and HSD on handpump; children allowed in restaurant; bedrooms *(Peter Corris)*

Portloe [SW9339], *Lugger*: Not really a pub,

but a welcome refuge on the coast path with its good crab sandwiches and sea views; keg beers; bedrooms *(St John Sandringham)*

Portmellon Cove [closed Oct–Mar; SX0144], *Rising Sun*: Small lower bar and big upper summer bar overlooking sandy cove near Mevagissey, bar food, St Austell real ales; open for morning coffee and afternoon cream teas; some live music; children in restaurant and family-room *(LYM)*

Portscatho [SW8735], *Plume of Feathers*: Friendly local with good value quickly served food, including takeaways, from hatch in corner of main bar – beware the garlic with the excellent steaks; small eating area, side locals' bar, well reproduced loudish pop music; very popular; children's room *(Mrs Shirley Pielou, LYM)*

Poughill [SS2207], *Preston Gate*: Attractive partly flagstoned bar with pews, mahogany tables and log fires in fairly recent conversion of two cottages; reasonably priced bar food, Watneys-related real ales, friendly landlord, some seats outside; village is pronounced 'Poffle' *(Stephen McNees, Robin and Bev Gammon, LYM)*

Roche [SW9860], *Victoria*: Useful A30 stop with popular food including excellent home-made pasties in softly lit character bar, well kept St Austell ales, panelled children's room, cheery service, restaurant *(C A Foden, John Hayward, G Atkinson, Patrick Young, LYM)*

Rosudgeon [SW5529], *Coach & Horses*: Busy pub, open fires, wide choice of good home-made bar and restaurant food *(Fiona Carrey)*

St Breward [SX0977], *Old*: One of highest pubs in Cornwall, with warm welcome from licensees, slate floors, comfortable dining-room; Ushers on handpump, good well cooked bar food at reasonable prices *(Mr and Mrs R P Begg)*

St Columb Major [Market Sq – Bank St; SW9163], *Ring o' Bells*: Friendly town pub with simple food in several simply furnished rooms going back from narrow road frontage *(BB)*

☆ **St Dominick** [Saltash; SX3967], *Who'd Have Thought It*: Beautifully kept pub with flock wallpaper, tasselled plush seats, Gothick tables, gleaming pottery and copper, good bar food, well kept Bass and Courage Directors, friendly Jack Russell terriers *(John Kirk, LYM)*

St Issey [SW9271], *Ring o' Bells*: Cheerful and well modernised village inn with well kept Courage real ale and good value food; bedrooms *(LYM)*

St Ive [A390 Liskeard–Callington; SX3167], *Butchers Arms*: Old inn set back from main road, well kept Courage Directors, good value meals, large tastefully furnished bar and lounge, friendly staff, big gardens *(Ted George)*

☆ **St Just In Penwith** [SW3631], *Star*: Dimly lit and cosy L-shaped flagstoned bar and smaller family TV lounge in relaxed but well kept local with very friendly landlord, efficient staff, popular with local arts and crafts people; well kept St Austell real ale tapped from the cask, limited but decent bar food including good steak rolls, open fire, nostalgic juke box, piano, fruit machine; bedrooms comfortable with huge breakfast served in delightful snug *(Steve Waters, R Fieldhouse, Charlie Salt, Tim and Lynne Crawford, RAB, LYM)*

St Mawes [SW8537], *Victory*: Lots of sailing and other sea photographs in unpretentious and friendly local with well kept Devenish JD on handpump, simple bar lunches; seats out in the alley, a few steep yards up from the harbour; bedrooms cheap (maybe serenaded late by fishermen's songs – but the breakfasts are good) *(LYM)*

St Mawgan [signposted from A30; SW8765], *Falcon*: Stone-built local inn with well kept St Austell Bosuns and Tinners, bar food and most attractive sheltered garden with sun-trap seating area; nice village; bedrooms *(Charles and Mary Winpenny, LYM)*

St Neot [SX1867], *London*: Pretty pub with excellent service and wide choice of well presented and unusual bar food *(Mr Edwicker)*

Sennen [SW3525], *First & Last*: Good atmosphere and genuine warm welcome from licensees; bar food including good pasties and local seafood bake; dogs allowed if on lead; children's room *(Gwyneth and Salva Spadaro-Dutturi)*

☆ **Sennen Cove** [SW3526], *Old Success*: Seventeenth-century fisherman's local in glorious spot beside long beach, giving lovely sea views; friendly staff, good range of real ales including Bass, excellent food including local seafood; nr GWG2; recently decorated bedrooms good value – especially out of season *(Gwyneth and Salvo Spadaro-Dutturi)*

nr **Stithians** [Frogpool – off A393; SW7366], *Cornish Arms*: Good value bar food and steak dinners in friendly village pub with well kept Devenish real ales, cheerful local atmosphere and comfortable sitting areas *(BB)*

Stratton [SS2406], *Tree*: Rambling, seventeenth-century building with arched entrance, pleasant lounge with flagstone floor, log fire in open fireplace, genuine old furniture and beamed ceiling; Bass and St Austell Tinners, reasonable range of bar food; this used to be the home of Antony Payne, the last Cornish giant *(Prof H G Allen)*

Threemilestone [SW7844], *Victoria*: Friendly, comfortable pub, well kept St Austell Tinners on handpump, lunchtime and evening restaurant; children welcome *(Peter Corris)*

Tideford [SX3459], *Rod & Line*: Unspoilt, single-roomed pub with low, bowed, ochre ceiling and Victorian cash register; children welcome *(Phil Gorton)*

Tintagel [SX0588], *Min Pin*: Neatly kept

newish pub named after the miniature pinschers bred by the licensees, and notable for the Brown Willy and Legend beers brewed here by their daughter – malt-extract, but good *(Tim and Lynne Crawford)*

Trebarwith [Trebarwith Strand; SX0585], *Port William*: Unpretentious-looking pub with magnificent sea views, friendly atmosphere and service, good value bar food; self-catering flat above pub *(Mrs Margaret Dyke)*

Tregadillett [A30; SX2984], *Eliot Arms*: Busy, friendly, comfortable pub with well kept Devenish beers and outstanding food such as creamy curried prawns; hundreds of horsebrasses, pleasant atmosphere *(Dr and Mrs I W Muir)*

☆ **Trelights** [village signposted off B3314; SW9979], *Longcross*: Pleasant, clean bars behind small hotel; lounge with central ornamental fountain, well kept St Austell HSD and Tinners, good reasonably priced wines, good value and varied home-made bar food and cream teas, excellent family-room, friendly staff, beautifully laid out gardens with view of sea and play area; bedrooms comfortable *(R F Warner, Roger Huggins)*

Trelissick [Feock Downs; B3291; SW8339], *Punch Bowl & Ladle*: Large Cornish Brewery house decorated with old farm implements, carpentry tools and other bric-à-brac; cosy lounge with armchairs, lively and interesting atmosphere, real ales; children allowed if eating; very handy for Trelissick Gardens *(Charles and Mary Winpenny, Peter Corris)*

☆ **Tresillian** [A39 Truro–St Austell; SW8646], *Wheel*: Smartly renovated and neatly thatched low-beamed Devenish pub with good value food from ploughman's to prawn salad, gammon and steaks, Devenish real ales; efficient service, cosy atmosphere, horsebrasses, rope fancywork; reasonable access for the disabled *(C A Foden, G Atkinson, Philip King, Jon Wainwright, BB)*

☆ **Truro** [Francis St; SW8244], *Globe*: Interesting recent conversion with several rooms around central serving area; full of atmosphere with lots of old panelling and beams, deep button-back leather armchairs and sofas, red plush banquettes, oak tables and chairs, lots of Christies hat boxes, stuffed fish, hunting trophies and old prints; particularly good value bar food including excellent help-yourself salad bar; well kept Devenish JD, Royal Wessex and Steam and a guest such as Marstons Pedigree *(Patrick Young, Pat and Malcolm Rudlin, Les King)*

☆ **Truro** [Kenwyn St], *William IV*: Busy, popular bar with dark oak panelling, slightly secluded raised areas, lots of chamberpots, bottles, scales, ewers and basins; attractively done conservatory dining-room opening into garden; good value buffet food including daily hot specials, well kept St Austell beers, maybe large-screen music video on weekday lunchtimes in main bar *(Patrick Young, Ian Shaw, Lindsey Shaw Radley, B H Stamp)*

Truro [Lemon St], *Daniel Arms*: Prints on cork-lined walls, padded banquettes with upper brasswork, food mainly salads with some hot dishes, Devenish Cornish Original and GBH; old stone building popular with young businessmen at lunchtime *(Patrick Young)*; [Lemon Quay – by central car park] *Market*: Refurbished with oak-boarded floor, stained oak panelling with inset prints, timbered ceiling including some mirror panels, cast-iron-framed oak tables, bentwood chairs, Devenish Cornish Original and GBH on handpump, intimate cosy atmosphere, simple home-made food *(Patrick Young, LYM)*; [Frances St] *Old Globe*: Given the full Devenish refurbishment treatment, with three or four low-beamed rooms around a central bar; old panelling, bottle-glass window screens, part carpeted, part flagstones, oak tables and chairs, leather Chesterfields and armchairs, prints, a clock and a huge collection of hat boxes; well kept Cornish Brewery and Steam on handpump, good bar food *(Patrick Young)*

Tywardreath [off A3082; SX0854], *New*: Well kept Bass and St Austells ales in friendly pub with nice village setting; bedrooms *(BB)*

Veryan [SW9139], *New*: Good food, attractively served, in traditional village inn with real ale, open fire, friendly locals; bedrooms good value *(Mrs Shirley Pielou)*

West Pentire [SW7760], *Bowgie*: Modernised inn with rolling lawns on magnificent headland, good play area for children; one of the two lounge bars has fine beach and sea view; well kept Flowers IPA and Original, decent bar food, games-room, family-room; friendly atmosphere; bedrooms *(S P Bobeldijk, LYM)*

Zennor [SW4538], *Tinners Arms*: Well kept St Austell real ales in comfortable stripped-panelling pub near fine part of Coast Path, bar food (somewhat pricey, considering), useful new terrace *(John Branford, Linda Duncan, Roy and Barbara Longman, LYM)*

ISLES OF SCILLY

Bryher [SV8715], *Hell Bay*: Comfortable hotel worth mentioning in this context for its small stone-walled bar; friendly service, good range of snacks including good crab sandwiches and delicious gateau, decent drinks and good cappuccino coffee, very nice garden *(John Evans)*

Hugh Town [The Quay; SV9010], *Mermaid*: Has been entertaining and relaxed pub in lovely tranquil quayside surroundings, looking out to the island of Samson – memorable sunsets; lots of woodwork and naval artefacts from flags to figureheads; upstairs picture-window dining-room has had good food, with popular local fish; Devenish real ales, live music some nights, and particularly lively atmosphere on gig-racing days; as we went to press in summer 1989, though, doubts were raised about atmosphere and restyling, even including a video juke box, under new regime *(Peter and Rose Flower, Graeme Smalley, Dave and Angie Parkes, Jon Wainright – up-to-date reports please)*

Hugh Town [The Strand], *Atlantic*: Two bars decorated with shipwreck pictures, perhaps worth mentioning for sun-trap bay-view terrace (view too from back bar) and well kept Marstons Pedigree *(Jon Wainwright)*; *Bishop & Wolf*: Renovations in progress have caused mixed reports, but as things settled down in summer 1989 we had promising news of good crab sandwiches, friendly efficient management – more news please *(TBB)*

☆ **St Agnes** [The Quay; SV8807], *Turks Head*: Idyllic surroundings when sunny (and romantically desolate in poor weather); small converted whitewashed stone boathouse just above the quiet beach, lovely view over Porth Conger from terrace, with simple wall benches inside, low ceilings, sea pictures and charts – ideal stop-off after trip to Bishop Rock; good big local crab rolls or sandwiches, consistently outstanding pasties; in winter open only one day a week, by special provision of its lease from the Duchy of Cornwall; welcoming licensees, Thurs and Sun evening singsongs, with one of the island's two councillors on the piano; one couple of readers love their annual pilgrimages here so much that they've had a replica of the inn-sign made as a memento *(Peter and Rose Flower, John Evans, P and M Rudlin)*

St Martins [SV9215], *Seven Stones*: This is still the closest thing to a real pub on the island; very plain inside (doubles as village hall), but wonderful views, cheery service, decent crab sandwiches *(John Evans and others)*; *St Martins Hotel*: This luxury hotel, with splendid views to Tresco, has now opened a bar in very modern Laura Ashley style; service very friendly, reasonable choice of bar food – not over-priced *(John Evans)*

Cumbria

One of the most attractive things about Lakeland and Pennine pubs is that
they don't change hands quite as briskly as ones further south. This makes for
a pleasant sense of continuity that goes well with the timeless character of
many of them. There are of course some new faces at familiar favourites: new
licensees at the cheerful Queens Head in Askham, the comfortable Barbon Inn
at Barbon (early reports speak promisingly of the food and atmosphere), the
strikingly placed Queens Arms at Biggar on the Isle of Walney, and the gently
traditional Blue Bell at Heversham (taken over by Sam Smiths – so far there's
been no real change in style, though). The people who last year we reported
had taken on the Middleton Fells Inn at Middleton are continuing their
ambitious renovations, incorporating an adjacent barn, and those who took
on the delightfully placed Sun in Dent are on the point of opening their own
brewery; this may also be the year that sees fruition of the long-cherished plans
of the Stevensons to do the same at their Masons Arms on Cartmel Fell – very
highly rated by most readers. (A slightly longer-established pub brewery here,
included as a promising Lucky Dip at the end of the chapter, is the Old Crown
at Hesket Newmarket.) The warmly friendly old Royal Oak at Appleby is
having a new conservatory/restaurant added, and some more bedrooms – it's a
nice place to stay at, with good food; the Drunken Duck in its attractive spot
up above Hawkshead has been making some changes on the bedroom side,
too. The White Horse at Scales has been making changes – including freeing
itself from its former tie to Jennings brewery; changes and all, it's still one of
the area's best pubs for food. New main entries, or pubs back in these pages
after a break, include the pleasantly traditional New Inn at Brampton near
Appleby, the Mill Inn in a dramatic setting up in Mungrisdale, the Ship looking
out across the water from Sandside, and the Queens Arms at Warwick on
Eden. Even pubs that don't superficially change of course have their ups and
downs, and, apart from some already mentioned, ones currently at the crest of
the food wave include the friendly Sun overlooking Coniston, the imaginative
Snooty Fox in Kirkby Lonsdale, the Hare & Hounds at Levens, the

The Hare & Hounds, Levens

143

consistently good Shepherds up at Melmerby, and (best of all, though expensive) the imaginatively reconstructed Bay Horse on the sea just outside Ulverston. The civilised and unchanging Pheasant at Bassenthwaite (a good place to stay at) keeps a particularly warm place in readers' affections, as does the Britannia at Elterwater (always friendly, with a smashing atmosphere), and the chummy Hare & Hounds at Talkin. It's worth noting that about four out of every ten main entries here are worth knowing as good places to stay at – a far higher proportion than in most parts of England. Among the Lucky Dip entries at the end of the chapter, some to note as particularly promising include the Hole in t' Wall in Bowness, the George & Dragon at Garrigill, the George in Keswick, the Outgate Inn at Outgate, the Yew Tree at Seatoller (hardly a pub, but well worth knowing for its food) and the Tarn End at Talkin.

AMBLESIDE   NY3804 Map 9

Golden Rule

Smithy Brow; follow Kirkstone Pass signpost from A591 on N side of town

The golden rule here is a brass measuring yard, mounted over the bar counter. The three friendly rooms have lots of local country pictures and a few foxes' masks on their butter-coloured walls, horsebrasses on the black beams, built-in leatherette wall seats, cast-iron-framed tables, and a busy atmosphere. The room on the left has darts, a fruit machine, trivia, and dominoes; the one down a few steps on the right is a quieter sitting-room. Very well kept Hartleys Mild and XB on handpump; good baps, filled French sticks and some meals. The pub is a fine sight in summer, with its window boxes full of colour, and is near start of *Good Walks Guide* Walk 130. *(Recommended by H K Dyson, Steve Waters, Peter Corris)*

Hartleys   Licensee John Lockley   Real ale   Lunchtime meals and snacks   Children welcome   Nearby parking virtually out of the question   Open all day

APPLEBY   NY6921 Map 10

Royal Oak 🏵 🛏

Bongate; B6542 on S edge of town

As we went to press, there were plans for some changes to this friendly country-town inn; a new conservatory/restaurant will be added, some extra bedrooms opened, and some sensitive refurbishment will take place. The comfortable lounge has some armchairs and a carved settle, as well as other furniture, beams, old pictures on the timbered walls, and a panelling and glass snug enclosing the bar counter. The smaller oak-panelled public bar has a good open fire. Well kept McEwans 70/- and local Yates on handpump, with guest beers like Brakspears, Broughton Merlins, Huntsman and Wadworths; several malt whiskies, and a carefully chosen wine list; dominoes. Well presented and reasonably priced, the fresh home-made bar food includes superb soup with home-made bread (90p), sandwiches (lunchtime) such as home-cooked ham and beef (85p), Cumberland sausage or traditional ploughman's (£1.95), potted shrimps (£2.65), vegetarian dishes such as leek and fresh tomato crustade (£2.95) or savoury crumble (£3.45), fresh white fish or salads (from £2.95), fish and meat hors-d'oeuvre or pie of the day (£3.25), local lamb cutlets (£3.95), Loch Fyne langoustines (which they buy fresh from creel fishermen off the West Coast of Scotland, £4.45), and daily specials such as Cevapcici (a Yugoslavian kebab dish in a pitta bread pocket, £2.95) or Kotopoulo Kapama (chicken breast in a gently spiced Greek tomato sauce, £3.45); puddings (from £1.20), local cheeses (£1.50) and children's meals (from £1.30); the breakfasts are gigantic. The front terrace has seats among masses of flowers in tubs, troughs and hanging baskets that look over to the red stone church.

(Recommended by Mike Beiley, R F Plater, A C and S J Beardsley, Jill and Paul Ormrod, John Honnor, David Young, Carol and Philip Seddon, Sara Cundy, AHNR, PLC, David and Ruth Hollands, Carol Wright)

Free house Licensees Colin and Hilary Cheyne Real ale Meals and snacks Restaurant Children in eating area of bar Open 11–3, 6–11 all year Bedrooms tel Appleby (0930) 51463; £16.50(£27B)/£33(£40B)

ASKHAM NY5123 Map 9

Queens Head

The two comfortably furnished rooms of the main carpeted lounge in this friendly, well kept pub have some old calico printing blocks on the red flock wallpaper, beams hung with gleaming copper, brass and horsebrasses, and an open fire. Good waitress-served bar food includes lunchtime sandwiches (from £1.20), cottage pie (£2.75), salads (from £3), and steak in ale pie (£3.50); the steaks and fish are served on sizzling platters. Well kept Vaux Samson and Wards Sheffield Best on handpump; darts, dominoes and piped music. The new licensees have added a pond with a waterfall, fountain and fish. The pub is handy for the Lowther Wildlife Park. *(Recommended by Fiona Carrey, T Nott, Jon Wainwright, Syd and Wyn Donald, Brian Randall, J Pearson, Roger Stephenson, R C Wiles, Michael Williamson, JFH, Roger Broadie)*

Vaux Licensee Graham Ferguson Real ale Meals and snacks Restaurant Children in back bar until 9 Occasional live entertainment Open 11.30–3, 6.30–11 Bedrooms tel Hackthorpe (093 12) 225; £17/£34

BARBON SD6385 Map 10

Barbon Inn ★ ⌂

Village signposted off A683 Kirkby Lonsdale–Sedbergh; OS Sheet 97 reference 628826

Close below the fells – tracks and paths lead up to them – this comfortable inn is warmly welcoming. The individually furnished small rooms that open off the main bar are attractively furnished with carved eighteenth-century oak settles, deep chintzy sofas and armchairs, and lots of fresh flowers. Home-made bar food includes tasty soup (£1.10), sandwiches (from 95p), superb Morecambe Bay potted shrimps (£2.85), ploughman's (from £2.50), duck and chicken liver pâté (£2.50), Cumberland sausage (£2.95), home-baked ham (£3.75), home-made steak and kidney pie (£3.95), sirloin steak (£6.95), and puddings like home-made fruit pie (£1.20); well kept Theakstons Best and Old Peculier on handpump, and quite a few wines; dominoes and piped music. The neatly kept, sheltered garden is very prettily planted and floodlit at night. *(Recommended by Jill and Paul Ormrod, Mike Tucker, John and Joan Wyatt, Mr and Mrs J E Rycroft, Steve Dark, Col G D Stafford, Mr and Mrs D C Leaman, AE, GRE)*

Free house Licensee L MacDiarmid Real ale Meals and snacks (not Sat evening) Restaurant Children welcome Open 12–11 all year Bedrooms tel Barbon (046 836) 233; £22.55/£42.90

BASSENTHWAITE LAKE NY2228 Map 9

Pheasant ★ ⌂

Follow Wythop Mill signpost at N end of dual carriageway stretch of A66 by Bassenthwaite Lake

The pubby bar in this civilised hotel has two cosy rooms linked by a fine wood-framed arch: a low serving-counter has a hatch to the entry corridor through a traditional wood and glass partition, and there are rush-seat chairs, library seats, and hunting prints and photographs on the tobacco-coloured walls. A large and airy beamed lounge at the back (overlooking the garden, from which you can walk up into the beech woods) has easy chairs on its polished parquet floor and a big log fire on cool days; there are also attractively chintzy sitting-rooms with antique furniture. Good, freshly made lunchtime bar food includes soup (95p), ploughman's or pâté (£2.25), quails' eggs with hazel-nut mayonnaise (£2.55), vegetable and nut terrine (£2.45), cold Cumberland sausage platter (£2.65), smoked lamb with melon or prawns with lobster sauce (£3.10), sweet smoked chicken (£3.25), and smoked Scotch salmon (£4.80); they do main dishes in the dining-room (which is non-smoking). Well kept Bass and Theakstons Best on handpump; helpful, friendly service. The wooded surroundings are lovely. *(Recommended by J E Rycroft, Lord Evans of Claughton, Dr R H M Stewart, M A and W R Proctor, PLC, Dr J R Hamilton, Miss A Tress, G Smith, BKA, D Thornton, Syd and Wyn Donald, Sue Braisted, D G Nicolson, Pat and Dennis Jones)*

Free house   Licensee W E Barrington Wilson   Real ale   Lunchtime snacks (11–2) Restaurant   Children welcome weekdays (not Sun)   Open 11–3, 5.30–10.30; closed 25 Dec   Bedrooms tel Bassenthwaite Lake (059 681) 234; £38B/£68B

BEETHAM   SD5079 Map 7

Wheatsheaf 🛏️

Village (and inn) signposted just off A6 S of Milnthorpe

This warmly old-fashioned place has a comfortably conversational lounge bar – neatly exposed beams and joists, a massive antique carved oak armchair, attractive built-in wall settles, tapestry-cushioned chairs, a cabinet filled with foreign costume dolls, a fox's mask and brush, and a calm old golden labrador. The one counter serves this, a little central snug, then beyond that is a tiled-floor bar with darts, dominoes and fruit machine. Bar food includes home-made soup (75p), sandwiches (from 90p), home-made cheese pie (£1.95), good cottage pie with cheesy topping (£2.05), home-made steak and onion pie (£2.80), fresh fish of the day (£3), salads (from £3), and steaks (from £5.50), with daily specials such as good sausage, liver and bacon (£2.05); well kept Thwaites Bitter on handpump, and quite a few malt whiskies and wines. The black and white timbered cornerpiece is very striking – a glorified two-storey set of gabled oriel windows jettied out from the corner and peeking down what is now the very quiet village street. *(Recommended by JM, PM, Mrs H D Astley, A T Langton)*

Free house   Licensee Mrs Florence Miller   Real ale   Meals and snacks (12–2, 6–9) Restaurant   Open 11–3, 6–11 all year   Children welcome   Bedrooms tel Milnthorpe (044 82) 2123; £18(£20.50)/£26.50(£32)

BIGGAR   SD1965 Map 7

Queens Arms

On Isle of Walney; follow A590 or A5087 into Barrow-in-Furness centre, then Walney signposted through Vickerstown – bear left on the island

In what looks like a little huddle of black-trimmed white farm buildings is a snug little bar with a good deal of brown varnish, wheel-back chairs and tapestried built-in banquettes, a Delft shelf, and an open fire in its stone fireplace; well kept Hartleys XB and Whitbreads Castle Eden and Trophy on handpump, kept under light top pressure; piped music. Rustic seats and tables shelter in the yard, and opening off this there's a smallish eating-room with high-backed settles forming booths around the tables, and a more spacious restaurant. Bar food includes sandwiches, drunken prawns (£2.95), seafood Mornay (£4.20), Cumberland game pie (£4.50), trout Cleopatra (£6.95), and steak (£7.95). Tracking down this pub is an entertaining expedition: the road threads past a series of gigantic shipyard gates, weaves across a couple of great drawbridges, then tracks down the island.

There are broad sandy beaches practically on the doorstep, with a nature reserve to the south (the air's full of the liquid pipings of curlews and wading birds). *(Recommended by Brian Jones, Paul Corbett; more reports please)*

Whitbreads   Licensee Cyril Whiteside   Real ale   Meals and snacks   Restaurant tel Barrow-in-Furness (0229) 41113   Children in eating area of bar and restaurant   Open 11.30–3, 6.30–11 all year

BOOT   NY1801 Map 9

Burnmoor

Village signposted just off the Wrynose/Hardknott Pass road; OS Sheet 89 reference 175010

Even in summer, the surroundings here are more peaceful than much of Lakeland, and the landlord who shepherded for years on these hills is expert at suggesting good walks. There are lots of attractive tracks such as the one up along Whillan Beck to Burnmoor Tarn, and *Good Walks Guide* Walk 125 is nearby. Inside, the beamed and carpeted white-painted bar has an open fire, red leatherette seats and small metal tables; the snug and restaurant can be traced back to 1578. Generous helpings of quickly served bar food include delicious soup (80p), ploughman's (£2.20), cheese and onion flan (£2.40), breaded haddock or cold beef or ham (£2.90), Cumberland game pie (£4), wiener schnitzel (£4.40), sirloin steak (£5.70), and puddings (£1); children's menu (£1.90); they grow a lot of the vegetables themselves, and keep hens and pigs. Well kept Jennings on handpump; dominoes, juke box, pool-room. There are seats outside on the sheltered front lawn. *(Recommended by Roger Huggins, P Lloyd, Syd and Wyn Donald, Charles and Mary Winpenny, AE, GRE, W P P Clarke)*

Free house   Licensee Tony Foster   Real ale   Meals and snacks (12–2, 5.45–9)   Restaurant Children welcome until 8.45   Open 11–3, 4.45–11; 11–2.30, 5–11 in winter   Bedrooms tel Eskdale (094 03) 224; £14.50(£16.25B)/£29(£32.50B)

BOWLAND BRIDGE   SD4289 Map 9

Hare & Hounds 🏠

Village signposted from A5074; OS Sheet 97 reference 417895

Down by the bridge, this pretty white building has geraniums in hanging baskets and climbing roses on the walls. Inside, it's friendly and comfortably modernised, and the spacious open-plan lounge bar has ladder-back chairs around dark wood tables on its Turkey carpet, open fires, and is divided into smaller areas by surviving stub walls; decorations include blue and white china, reproduction hunting prints, a stuffed pheasant, and England caps and a Liverpool team photograph (the landlord is the former Anfield favourite and England wing). Besides sandwiches (from £1.30), bar food includes soup (£1.10), pâté (£2.25), ploughman's (£2.95), pizzas (from £3.25), salads (from £3.50), roast chicken (£4.25), chilli con carne (£4.75), and evening steaks (from £7.50); prompt service; well kept Greenalls on handpump, from a long bar counter with a comfortably cushioned red leatherette elbow rest for people using the sensible back-rest-type bar stools; the Stable Bar is now a residents' lounge. *(Recommended by Carol and Richard Glover, H K Dyson, Brian Jones, A T Langton, David Heath, Lee Goulding, Diane Hall, J Howard)*

Free house   Licensee Peter Thompson   Real ale   Meals and snacks   Children welcome Open 11–3, 5.30–11   Bedrooms tel Crosthwaite (044 88) 333; £28S/£36S

BRAMPTON   NY6723 Map 10

New Inn

Off A66 N of Appleby – follow Long Marton 1 signpost then turn right at church; village also signposted off B6542 at N end of Appleby

It's the dining-room that appeals most in this attractive traditional village inn

– a well proportioned flagstoned room with horsebrasses on its low black beams, well spaced tables, and a splendid original black cooking range at one end, separated from the door by an immensely sturdy old oak built-in settle. During the Appleby Horse Fair (second week in June), this room is still the special preserve of the gipsy ladies – but at other times it's noted for good value home cooking. Bar food includes soup (90p), garlic mushrooms (£1.35), potted shrimps (£2) and lots of other starters, with main dishes such as Cumberland sausage (£2.50), curry nut roast (£2.95), tandoori chicken or steak and kidney pie (£3.25) and ten-ounce sirloin steak (£6.20). They also do children's dishes (from 80p), and at lunchtime sandwiches (90p) and ploughman's (£2.25). On Sundays, besides three-course lunches, there's a more limited choice. The two small rooms of the bar have lots of local pictures, mainly sheep and wildlife; a stuffed fox is curled on top of the corner TV, and a red squirrel pokes out of a little hole in the dividing wall. A medley of seats includes panelled oak settles and a nice little oak chair. Well kept Whitbreads Castle Eden and Youngers Scotch on handpump; a good choice of whiskies with some eminent malts; friendly service, and no games other than dominoes. No dogs in bedrooms. *(Recommended by Gwen and Peter Andrews and others; more reports please)*

Free house   Licensees Roger and Anne Cranswick   Real ale   Meals and snacks   Restaurant   Children welcome   Open 11–3, 6–11 all year (closes 2–7 afternoons Dec–Feb); closed 25 Dec   Bedrooms tel Kirkby Thore (0930) 51231; £17/£30

CARTMEL FELL   SD4288 Map 9

Masons Arms ★ ★

Strawberry Bank, a few miles S of Windermere between A592 and A5074; perhaps the simplest way of finding the pub is to go uphill W from Bowland Bridge (which is signposted off A5074) towards Newby Bridge and keep right then left at the staggered crossroads – it's then on your right, below Gummer's How; OS Sheet 97 reference 413895

The unrivalled fellside setting, looking over the Winster Valley to the woods below Whitbarrow Scar, the preservation of the old-fashioned bars, and the exceptional and unusual range of some two hundred bottled beers from all over the world are reasons this country pub is one of the most popular in the country. The main bar has country chairs and plain wooden tables on polished flagstones, low black beams in a bowed ceiling, needlework samplers and country pictures, a big log fire, and by it a grandly Gothick seat with snarling dogs as its arms. A small lounge has oak tables and settles to match its fine Jacobean panelling, and a plain little room beyond the serving-counter has more pictures and a fire in an open range. Food, plentiful though not cheap, is often imaginative, and might include soup (from £1.20), sandwiches (from £1.60), ploughman's (£3.25), lamb koftas or fisherman's pie (£4.25), Waberthwaite dried ham (£4.95), and beef casserole (£5.50), with specials (several for vegetarians) such as fennel and cashew-nut crumble (£3.50), Stilton and apple pancakes (£3.95), or lamb and prune pie (£4.50); puddings like lemon chiffon pie (£1.75). The splendid choice of bottled beers is helpfully narrowed down by a fine descriptive list (£1); thirty or so are from all over Britain and have their own separate list. Besides these, they keep Batemans XB, Thwaites Bitter and Yates Bitter, with guest beers from all over the country (last year they had around a hundred); a small building at the end of the car park is to be their own micro-brewery. They also have Furstenburg Export and Antonio, and Weizenthaler from West Germany – some of the first German real beers we've come across a British pub serving on draught. A house red and white wine, plus two guests, interesting farm ciders and perrys, and there are usually country wines; filter, espresso and cappuccino coffee; dominoes. The outside has been terraced, with rustic benches and tables to make the most of the view (which is shared by comfortable self-catering flats in an adjoining stone barn). They sell a book outlining local walks of varying lengths and difficulty, each linked to a page of recipes. The car park is to be expanded. *(Recommended by Jill and Paul Ormrod, Mr and Mrs D M Norton, Dennis Royles, Steve and Carolyn Harvey, P Lloyd, K Bamford, A T Langton, Carol and Richard Glover, Brian and Anna Marsden, Roger Bellingham, J E Rycroft, M A and W R Proctor, David Heath, S J Willmot, Steve Dark, Lee Goulding, Laurence Manning, Lynn Stevens, Gill Quarton, R C Wiles, Mr and Mrs Jon Payne, JH, Margaret and Roy Randle, Miss A Tress, G Smith, Rob and Gill Weeks, S D Samuels, Gwynne Harper, NIP, J L Thompson, Syd and Wyn Donald, Ashley Madden)*

Free house   Licensees Helen and Nigel Stevenson   Meals and snacks (12–2, 6–8.45)
Children welcome until 9   Open 11–3, 6–11 all year; may open longer Sat afternoon
Self-catering flats tel Crosthwaite (044 88) 486

CASTERTON   SD6379 Map 7

Pheasant

A683 about a mile N of junction with A65, by Kirkby Lonsdale

The two neatly modernised rooms of the main bar in this well kept village inn have been refurbished with ladder-back chairs and antique tables, there are newspapers and magazines to read, and an open log fire in a nicely arched bare stone fireplace. A wide choice of bar food includes home-made soup (£1.25), sandwiches (from £1.50), black pudding with mustard (£1.75), ploughman's (£3), steak and kidney pie (£3.75), omelettes (£4), seafood crêpe Mornay (£4.50), gammon with cheese and pineapple or eggs (£5), seafood platter (£5.50), and eight-ounce minute steak (£7.50), with puddings like apricot and almond pancakes with brandy (£1.50). Well kept Jennings, Tetleys and Youngers Scotch on handpump, and several wines; friendly staff; dominoes. Tables with cocktail parasols shelter in the front of the white building, by the road. There are attractive Pre-Raphaelite stained glass and paintings in the nearby church, built for the girls' school of Brontë fame here. *(Recommended by Jill and Paul Ormrod, Wayne Brindle, Jon Wainwright, Mrs Margaret Cross)*

Free house   Licensee David Seed Hesmondhalgh   Real ale   Meals and snacks
Restaurant   Children welcome   Open 11.30–2.30, 6–11 all year   Bedrooms tel Kirkby Lonsdale (0468) 71230; £30B(£45B)

CONISTON   SD3098 Map 9

Sun 🏷 🛏

Inn signposted from centre

At the foot of the mountains, this substantial white-walled stone house has pretty window boxes and hanging baskets, white tables out on the terrace, and a big garden that runs down to a steep little beck. Inside, the back bar has some cask seats (one pair remarkably heavy) as well as cushioned spindle-back chairs and brown plush built-in wall benches around the traditional cast-iron-framed tables, lots of Lakeland colour photographs, some recalling Donald Campbell (this was his HQ during his final attempt on the world water speed record), and a small but very warm log fire; the floors are part carpeted, part handsome polished flagstones. Home-made bar food includes a soup of the day such as cucumber and mint or thick, fresh celery (£1), excellent sandwiches (from £1), two baked potatoes with interesting daily fillings or Cumberland sausage (£2.75), ploughman's (from £2.75), home-cooked gammon salad (£3.95), and several dishes of the day such as cheese and herb pâté (£2.75), lamb moussaka (£3.75), beef and prune ragout (£3.95), delicious beef casserole, and prawns in a lightly curried cream sauce (£4.25); lots of wonderful puddings such as sticky toffee or real bread-and-butter pudding. The restaurant specialises in local ingredients – Herdwick lamb, Esthwaite trout. Well kept Jennings, Marstons Pedigree and Tetleys on handpump, from the deep sixteenth-century granite cellar, and lots of rare malt whiskies; friendly, efficient staff; darts. The inn (which serves as a mountain rescue post) looks across its neat tree-sheltered lawn to the spectacular bare fells around, and tracks from the lane lead straight up to the Old Man of Coniston. Fishing, riding and shooting can be arranged for residents, and the start of *Good Walks Guide* Walk 126 is nearby. Being out of the centre, it's a good deal less touristy than most places here. *(Recommended by Doug Kennedy, Heather Sharland, Nicola Plummer, Grahame Archer, Ned Edwards, AE, GRE, Linda and Carl Worley)*

Free house   Licensees Joan LeLong and Karen Farmer   Real ale   Meals and snacks Restaurant   Children welcome until 8.30   Open 11–11; in winter only open 6–11 Bedrooms tel Coniston (053 94) 41258; £30B/£60B

DENT   SD7187 Map 10

Sun

Village signposted from Sedbergh; and from Barbon, off A683

By the time this book is published, this friendly and popular little whitewashed inn should be on the point of opening its own brewery, the Dent Brewery. As we went to press, the plans were that it was to be set up in a converted barn some three miles up in the dale, with a production of a thousand gallons a week – which they hope to sell to other pubs in the area. The cheerful modernised carpeted bar still has quite a traditional feel, with some fine old oak timbers and beams (studded with coins), dark armed chairs, brown leatherette wall benches, and a coal fire; the walls are decorated with lots of local snapshots and old Schweppes advertisements. Through the arch to the left are banquettes upholstered to match the carpet (as are the curtains). Generous helpings of bar food include sandwiches, home-made pasties (£2.35), chilli con carne (£2.55), vegetarian or meaty lasagne (£2.85), twelve-ounce Cumberland sausage (£2.95), ten-ounce gammon steak with pineapple (£3.25), and steaks (from £3.75); enormous breakfasts. Well kept Theakstons XB and Youngers Scotch and No 3 on handpump, and some of their own brew; darts, pool, dominoes, fruit machine and juke box (in the pool-room). There are rustic seats and tables outside, and barbecues in summer. *(Recommended by Helena and Arthur Harbottle, Alan Hall, Jenny Cantle, Jonathan Williams)*

Free house   Licensees Jacky and Martin Stafford   Real ale   Meals and snacks   Children in eating area of bar   Open 11–2.30, 6.15–11; 11–2, 7–11 in winter   Bedrooms tel Dent (058 75) 208; £11/£22

ELTERWATER   NY3305 Map 9

Britannia Inn ★ 🛏

Off B5343

In a beautiful part of Cumbria, this busy and old-fashioned walkers' pub has a particularly friendly welcome. The front bar has a couple of window seats looking across the pretty village green to glimpses of Elterwater itself through the trees on the far side (a view shared by seats in the garden above the front of the pub), as well as settles, oak benches, Windsor chairs and, in winter, coal fires. At the back, the traditionally furnished, small beamed bar doesn't turn up its nose at walking boots; there's also a comfortable lounge. Good home-cooked bar food includes home-made soup (90p), filled wholemeal baps (95p), cheeseburger (£1.40), filled baked potato (from £1.40), hot potted shrimps on granary roll (£1.95), lunchtime ploughman's (£2.75), salads, steak and kidney pie or cheese and broccoli flan (all £3.70), and rainbow trout (£4.25); daily specials such as Lancashire hot-pot, spinach roulade or lasagne (£3.70), puddings (from £1.30), children's dishes (from £1.40), and good breakfasts. Well kept Hartleys XB and Bitter, Jennings Bitter and Mild, and Marstons Pedigree on handpump, Bulmers cider, several malt whiskies, a well chosen, good value wine list, and country wines; darts, dominoes and cribbage. The pub is well placed for Langdale and the central lakes, with tracks over the fells to Grasmere and Easedale, and is near the start of *Good Walks Guide* Walk 128. It can get quite crowded here in summer, but readers find the service unruffled even when people flock here to watch morris and step and garland dancers on the green. *(Recommended by Mike Beiley, Rosalind Russell, Steve Waters, Steve and Carolyn Harvey, KC, Alun and Eryl Davies, P Lloyd, K Bamford, D J Cooke, M J Lawson, Brian Jones, Dr and Mrs Peter Dykes, Ewan McColl, C A Holloway, JH, J L Thompson, Robert Gartery, Michael Thomson, Wayne Brindle, John Atherton, S C Beardwell, J Stacey, David and Christine Foulkes)*

Free house   Licensee David Fry   Real ale   Meals and snacks   Restaurant   Occasional morris dancing   Summer parking may be difficult   Open 11–11; closed 25 Dec and evening 26 Dec   Bedrooms tel Langdale (096 67) 210 or 382 ; £19.75/£39.50(£44.50B)

ESKDALE GREEN   NY1400 Map 9

Bower House 🛏

½ mile W of village towards Santon Bridge

The sheltered lawn and garden, very pretty and well kept, are an unusual bonus for the Lake District. They lead out directly behind the comfortable lounge bar, which has cushioned settles and Windsor chairs that blend in well with the original beamed and alcoved nucleus around the serving-counter; there's a good fire in winter too. Good bar food includes sandwiches, pâté (£1.95), lasagne or steak and kidney pie (£3.75), gammon and egg (£3.95), guinea-fowl in cranberry sauce (£5), steak (£7.50), and home-made puddings such as raspberry and ginger russe or cherry pudding (£1.20). Well kept Hartleys, Theakstons and Youngers on handpump; good, reasonably priced wine list. There's also a separate comfortable lounge with easy chairs and sofas. Some bedrooms are in the annexe across the garden. The pub is near *Good Walks Guide* Walk 125. *(Recommended by Nick Poole, J A Edwards, Steve Dark, G Bloxsom, P Lloyd, Miss A Tress, G Smith, Ian Briggs)*

Free house   Licensee D J Connor   Real ale   Meals and snacks   Restaurant   Children welcome   Open 11–3, 6–11   Bedrooms tel Eskdale (094 03) 244; £29.75B/£45B

FAUGH   NY5155 Map 9

String of Horses 🛏

From A69 in Warwick Bridge, turn off at Heads Nook, Castle Carrock signpost, then follow Faugh signs – if you have to ask the way, it's pronounced Faff

The walls of the several cosy communicating rooms of the open-plan bar in this seventeenth-century inn are now panelled or covered with Laura Ashley wallpaper. There are heavy beams, fine old settles and elaborately carved Gothick seats and tables, as well as simpler Windsor and other chairs, and log fires in cool weather (which may even mean a summer evening); decorations include brass pots and warming-pans, and some interesting antique prints on the walls. Bar food includes sandwiches (from £1.20), home-made smoked mackerel pâté (£1.50), mushroom and nut fettuccine (£1.95), Cumberland sausage (£3.25), home-made steak and mushroom pie or chilli con carne (£3.50), salads (from £3.50), a good lunchtime buffet or gammon with pineapple (£3.85), and sirloin steak (£5.75); also, daily specials like Hungarian goulash (£3.75) or sweet-and-sour pork fillet (£3.95), good home-made puddings (£1.50), and Sunday roast lunch. Several malt whiskies and an extensive wine list; fruit machine, trivia and piped music. Outside, it's pretty, with Dutch blinds and lanterns, and more lanterns and neat wrought-iron among the greenery of the sheltered terrace. Residents have the use of a jacuzzi, sauna, solarium and small outdoor heated pool. *(Recommended by Dr R H M Stewart, Steve Dark, R Wiles, J H Tate, Nigel Furneaux, Debbie Pratt)*

Free house   Licensee Anne Tasker   Meals and snacks (12–2.30, 7–10.15)   Restaurant Children welcome   Occasional music in restaurant Sat   Open 11.30–3, 5.30–11 all year Bedrooms tel Hayton (022 870) 297 or 509; £46B/£54B

GRASMERE NY3406 Map 9

Wordsworth Hotel 🛏

In the village itself

Off to the left of the main entrance in this luxurious hotel is the unpretentious little
Dove & Olive bar. It's decorated with stuffed fish, foxes' masks and brushes, sea
and sporting prints, and photographs of the local fell races; also, a good log fire in
winter, big bare beams with nice plates, and mate's chairs and attractively
cushioned built-in seats around cast-iron-framed tables on the slate floor. Good
value, simple bar food includes home-made soup (95p), filled wheatmeal rolls
(£1.10), generously filled baked potatoes (£1.50), a pot of home-made smoked fish
pâté (£2.50), shepherd's pie or ploughman's (£2.75), and home-made puddings
(90p); well kept Bass Special on handpump, and a good hot toddy; lively staff.
There are sturdy old teak seats in a slate-floored verandah leading out of the cleanly
kept bar, and the hotel gardens are very neat; near the start of *Good Walks Guide*
Walk 129. *(Recommended by Mary Ann Cameron; more reports please)*

*Free house   Licensee Robin Lees   Real ale   Meals and snacks (evening food July–Oct only,
from 6.30–8.30)   Restaurant   Open 11–3 (4 Sat), 5.30–11; opens 6 in winter   Bedrooms
tel Grasmere (096 65) 592; £31B/£77B*

HAWKSHEAD SD3598 Map 9

Kings Arms 🛏

A delightful bonus to this picturesque old inn is the terrace out in the pretty central
square, with old-fashioned teak seats and oak cask tables around the roses. Inside,
the relaxed and cheerful low-ceilinged bar has an open fire, red-cushioned wall and
window seats and red plush stools on the Turkey carpet, and most tables of a height
to suit drinkers rather than eaters (you can have bar meals at the same price in the
restaurant, too). Bar food includes home-made soup (£1), sandwiches (from £1.15),
ploughman's (from £2.90), Cumberland sausage (£3.30), salads (from £3.45),
home-made steak and kidney pie (£3.65), baked local trout (£4.15), chicken Kiev
(£4.95), and eight-ounce sirloin steak (£6.10), with specials like mushroom
Stroganoff (£3.50) or honey-roast ham with peaches (£3.95); puddings (£1.55) and
children's meals (£1.95). Well kept Matthew Browns Mild, Tetleys and Theakstons
Best on handpump, open fire; darts, dominoes, and unobtrusive piped pop music.
Some of the bedrooms have ancient coins embedded in the oak beams. They supply
free permits to guests for nearby public car park. *(Recommended by H K Dyson, Brian
and Anna Marsden, Gary Scott, Charles and Mary Winpenny, Margaret and Roy Randle,
Michael Thomson, Wayne Brindle, AE, GRE)*

*Free house   Licensee Rosalie Johnson   Real ale   Meals and snacks (12–2, 5.30–9.30 in
summer)   Restaurant   Children welcome until 9   Open 11–11   Bedrooms tel Hawkshead
(096 66) 372; £18.50(£21B)/£30(£37B)*

Queens Head

This popular food pub has an open-plan refurbished bar with heavy bowed black
beams in the low ceiling, red leatherette wall seats and plush stools around heavy
traditional tables – mostly used by diners – on the discreetly patterned red carpet, a
few plates decorating one panelled wall, and a snug little room leading off. Bar food
includes home-made soup (£1.10), lunchtime sandwiches (from £1.10, bacon and
egg brunch bap £2.25, open sandwiches from £2.75), pâté (£2.75), salads (from
£3.25), ploughman's (£3.50), Cumberland sausage (£3.75), home-made beef and
mushroom pie (£4.25), grilled gammon with egg or pineapple or tagliatelle (£4.50),
lamb korma (£4.75) and sirloin steak (£6.75); puddings (£1.75). Well kept Hartleys
Bitter and Mild and Robinsons Bitter on handpump; dominoes, cribbage, piped
classical music. The village is a charming and virtually car-free network of stone-

paved alleys winding through huddles of whitewashed cottages. *(Recommended by May Ann Cameron, H K Dyson, Gary Scott, S J Willmot, Ewan McCall, E J Knight, R H Sawyer, Charles and Mary Winpenny, A T Langton, Wayne Brindle, AE, GRE, Peter Race, PAB, Brenda Gentry, M G Hart, R P Taylor, Pat and Dennis Jones)*

Hartleys   Licensee Tony Merrick   Real ale   Meals and snacks (12–2.15, 6.15–9.30); closed 25 Dec   Restaurant   Children in eating area of bar   Open 11–11   Bedrooms tel Hawkshead (096 66) 271; £22(£24.50B)/£36(£43B)

nr HAWKSHEAD   SD3598 Map 9
Drunken Duck

Barngates; hamlet signposted from B5286 Hawkshead–Ambleside, opposite Outgate Inn; OS Sheet 90 reference 350013

Though the several busy pubby rooms in this remote white pub remain unchanged, quite a few alterations have taken place in other parts of the building. The kitchen has been completely re-done, three extra bedrooms have been added (all bedrooms now have private bathrooms and have been redecorated in a cottagey style), and the beer garden has been moved slightly further down the road (a new reception area for residents was built on to the old one); they've also installed a manager and his wife. Furnishings include ladder-back country chairs, blond pews, cushioned old settles, and tapestried stools on fitted Turkey carpet, and there are beams, good fires, lots of landscapes, Cecil Aldin prints, and a big longcase clock. Popular home-made bar food is chalked up on a board and changes daily: sandwiches (£1), soup such as carrot and coriander or goulash (£1.50), pâtés such as mushroom and nut or port and Stilton (£2.50), ploughman's (from £2.75), spicy mushroom and courgette crumble or tortellini in a basil and bacon sauce (£3.75), chicken, cashew-nut and ginger pie, lamb and watercress lasagne or steak and kidney pie (£4.25), pork schnitzel (£5), mixed grill (£7.50), and puddings like jam or syrup roly-poly pudding or sticky toffee pudding (£1.50); there are now two people in the kitchen, which should cut down on delays at peak times. Well kept Jennings, Marstons Pedigree and Merrie Monk, Tetleys Bitter, Theakstons XB and Old Peculier, and Yates Bitter on handpump; over sixty whiskies and their own-label wine. Darts, dominoes. There are seats under the bright hanging baskets on the front verandah with views of distant Lake Windermere; to the side there are quite a few rustic wooden chairs and tables, sheltered by a stone wall with alpine plants along its top, and the pub has fishing in two private tarns behind. Dogs welcome. *(Recommended by P Lloyd, K Bamford, Brian and Anna Marsden, Steve and Carolyn Harvey, Greg Parston, Lynn Stevens, Gill Quarton, Charles and Mary Winpenny, JH, Syd and Wyn Donald, Mike Stables, Mr and Mrs Evelyn Cribb)*

Free house   Licensee Peter Barton   Real ale   Meals and snacks   Children welcome (not in bar)   Open 11.30–3, 6–11; 12–3, 6.30–11 in winter   Bedrooms tel Hawkshead (096 66) 347; £25B/£44.50B

HEVERSHAM   SD4983 Map 9
Blue Bell

A6 (now a relatively very quiet road here)

Sam Smiths have taken over this friendly and well kept place. As we went to press no changes had been made, though there were possible plans for some refurbishment. The bay-windowed lounge bar has pewter platters hanging from one of the black beams, small antique sporting prints on the partly panelled walls, and an antique carved settle, comfortable cushioned Windsor armchairs and upholstered stools on its flowery carpet; in cool weather there's an open fire. One big bay-windowed area has been divided off as a children's room, and the long, tiled-floor, quieter public bar has darts and dominoes. Good value bar food includes home-made soup (£1), open sandwiches (from £1), Morecambe Bay potted shrimps or locally baked steak and kidney pie (£2), home-made quiche (£2.20), home-made cottage pie (£2.45) and salads (from £4.50, fresh salmon £4.75). Well kept Sam Smiths OB and Museum on handpump; helpful staff; darts, dominoes and cribbage. *(Recommended by Roger Bellingham, D Singleton, D J Cooke, R H Sawyer, Jonathan Williams, Raymond Palmer)*

Sam Smiths   Licensee Christopher Bates   Real ale   Meals and snacks   Restaurant Children in own room   Occasional live music   Open 11–3, 6–11 all year   Bedrooms tel Milnthorpe (044 82) 2018; £30(£40S)/£55B

KESWICK   NY2624 Map 9

Dog & Gun

Lake Road; off top end of Market Square

Changes to this lively old tavern include the knocking down of a wall to create an open-plan bar and the installation of a new long bar counter (which has a slate floor in front of it); one room has low beams studded with coins (the lanterns have gone), wheel-back chairs and upholstered, high-backed settles on the new bare floorboards, and an open fire; what was the back room now has a new carpet, more upholstered settles, a cast-iron stove, and old beams taken from a local pub undergoing renovation. A fine collection of striking mountain photographs by the local firm G P Abrahams are hung on the walls. Good, reasonably priced food includes home-made French onion soup (90p), sandwiches (from £1.15), hot home-roasted ham with garlic bread, fresh Borrowdale trout, home-made Hungarian goulash and hot roast chicken (all £3.95). Well kept Theakstons Best, XB and Old Peculier on handpump; dominoes, cribbage, fruit machine and piped music. On Friday and Saturday evenings they have a doorman who may turn away groups of young men. *(Recommended by Steve Waters, R F Plater, David Gwynne Harper, Rita Horridge, David Millar)*

Matthew Browns (S&N)   Licensee Frank Hughes   Real ale   Meals and snacks (12–2.30, 6–9.30)   Children in eating area of bar   Open 11–11; 11–3, 6–11 in winter; closed 25 Dec

KIRKBY LONSDALE   SD6278 Map 7

Snooty Fox 🏮

Main Street (B6254)

Especially popular for the good value bar food (get there early, especially on Thursday – market day), this attractively de-modernised old inn has several rambling rooms: bar counters made from English oak, some oak panelling, flagstones, country kitchen chairs, pews, one or two high-backed settles, marble-topped sewing-trestle tables, and two coal fires and shutters. There are mugs hanging from beams, eye-catching coloured engravings, stage gladiator costumes, stuffed wildfowl and falcons, a mounted badger and foxes' masks, guns and a powder-flask, horse-collars and stirrups, and so forth. Bar food includes home-made soup (£1), filled baked potatoes (from £1.60), bacon ribs in a sweet-and-sour sauce (£1.95), filled pancakes (£2.95), stuffed mushrooms (£2.25), Mexican tacos filled with prawns cooked in ginger garlic butter (£2.55), cheese platter (£2.65), Cumberland sausage with local black pudding and apple sauce (£3.35), a cold platter called Fox's Farmhouse Forage – which also includes a bowl of farmhouse broth (£3.75) – steak and kidney pudding (£3.95), guinea-fowl (£4.75), haunch of venison marinated in ale (£4.95), daily specials, and home-made puddings (£1.65); they use British Charolais beef – excellent – for Sunday lunch and steaks; huge breakfasts. Well kept Hartleys XB and Youngers Scotch on handpump, and country wines; friendly service. Dominoes, fruit machine, and good juke box. There are tables out on a small terrace beside the biggish back cobbled stableyard.

(Recommended by Jill and Paul Ormrod, Jon Wainwright, Wayne Brindle, Hayward Wane, Colin Hall, Professor S Barnett, Col G D Stafford)

Free house   Licensees Andrew Walker and Jack Shone   Real ale   Meals and snacks Restaurant   Children welcome   Jazz band third Tues of month   Open 11–11; 11–3, 6–11 in winter   Bedrooms tel Kirkby Lonsdale (0468) 71308; £17/£30(£38S)

Sun 🍺

Market Street (B6254)

Turner stayed in this atmospheric little inn in 1818 when painting *Ruskin's view*. The several neatly kept and comfortably modernised interconnecting rooms have low beams, green plush cushioned seats, captain's and spindle-back chairs on the red carpet, and fires in winter; also, a large collection of some three hundred banknotes, maps, old engravings, and battleaxes on the walls – some are stripped to bare stone, others have panelled dados. They were refurbishing the dining-room as we went to press, with hopes to incorporate the sixteenth-century arched cellar. Generous helpings of homely bar food include sandwiches, local Cumberland sausage or haddock (£2.95), home-made lasagne (£3.25), pizzas (from £3.25), and beef and Guinness casserole or chicken (£3.95). Well kept Theakstons Best and Youngers Scotch and No 3 on handpump, and several malt whiskies (the stools by the long bar counter in the front room have good back rests); quick, cheerful service; dominoes and piped music. The pub is by a cobbled alley to the churchyard. *(Recommended by Jill and Paul Ormrod, Mr and Mrs R P Begg, Jon Wainwright, Ray and Jenny Colquhoun)*

Free house   Licensees Andrew and Belinda Wilkinson   Real ale   Meals and snacks (11–2, 6–10)   Restaurant   Children welcome   Open 11–11   Bedrooms tel Kirkby Lonsdale (0468) 71965; £17.50(£17.50B)/£30(£35B)

LANGDALE   NY2906   Map 9

Old Dungeon Ghyll 🍺

B5343

The cosy, friendly bar in this marvellously situated place is simply furnished with a particular view to the needs of the walkers and climbers who use it most, with window seats cut into the enormously thick stone walls, a huge fire, and a grand view of the Pike of Blisco rising behind Kettle Crag. Well kept Hartleys Mild, Marstons Burton, Pedigree, Merrie Monk and Owd Rodger, Yates Bitter and guest beers on handpump; Bulmers cider and a choice of snuffs. Good value bar food includes home-made soup with home-made bread (£1), and Cumberland sausage, home-made steak and kidney pie, lasagne or chilli con carne (£3); book if you want a full evening meal. Darts, shove-ha'penny and dominoes. It can get really lively on a Saturday night. The inn is surrounded by towering fells, including the Langdale Pikes flanking Dungeon Ghyll Force waterfall (which inspired Wordsworth's poem 'The Idle Shepherd Boys'). *(Recommended by A C and S J Beardsley, Steve Waters, Steve and Carolyn Harvey, M J Lawson, Brian and Anna Marsden, Andrew McKeand, Dick Brown, David White)*

Free house   Licensee Neil Walmsley   Real ale   Meals and snacks   Evening restaurant Children welcome   Folk music Weds   Open 11–11; closed 24, 25 and 26 Dec   Bedrooms tel Langdale (096 67) 272; £17.75(£20.50B)/£35.50(£41B)

LEVENS   SD4886   Map 9

Hare & Hounds [illustrated on page 143]

Village signposted from A590; since completion of dual carriageway link, best approach is following route signposted for High Vehicles

Good value simple food in this busy, friendly village pub includes soup (75p), sandwiches (from 75p, toasties from £1.05, shrimp open sandwich £1.95), ploughman's (£1.75), plaice (£2.45), flan (£2.70), beef or scampi (£2.90), properly served, delicious Morecambe Bay shrimps, and in the evening steaks (from £3.60) and griddled ham (£4.60). Well kept Vaux Samson on handpump with Wards Bitter on electric pump. Angling around the servery, the low-beamed, carpeted lounge bar has a wicker-backed Jacobean-style armchair and antique settle on its sloping floor, as well as old-fashioned brown leatherette dining-seats and red-cushioned seats built into the partly panelled walls. The snug front public bar, with a shelf of game-bird plates above its serving-counter, has darts, dominoes and a fruit machine. A separate pool-room, down steps, has golden oldies on its juke box. *(Recommended by Steve Waters, A T Langton, Roger Bellingham, Margaret and Roy Randle, Jon and Jacquie Payne, A T Langton, Peter Race)*

Vaux   Licensee Jim Stephenson   Real ale   Meals and snacks; no food Sun or Mon evenings Nov–Mar   Children in eating area of bar lunchtimes only   Open 11.15–2.30, 6–11 all year

LITTLE LANGDALE   NY3204 Map 9

Three Shires 🏠

From A593 3 miles W of Ambleside take small road signposted The Langdales, Wrynose Pass; then bear left at first fork

Seats on the verandah outside this family-run stone-built house have a lovely view out over the valley to the partly wooded hills below Tilberthwaite Fells, and there are more seats on a well kept lawn behind the car park, backed by a small oak wood. The pub is on *Good Walks Guide* Walk 128. Inside, it's comfortable, and the carefully extended back bar has antique oak carved settles, country kitchen chairs and stools on its big dark slate flagstones, local photographs on the walls, and a coal fire in cool weather. Good value, generously served bar food includes soup (£1.10), lunchtime sandwiches (from £1), excellent ploughman's (from £2.75), salads (from £2.85), Cumberland pie (£3.20), home-made steak and kidney pie (£3.60), local trout (£4.50), and sirloin steak (£6.25) – in the evening, dishes are slightly more expensive; children's menu (£1.50), and daily specials; good breakfasts. Ruddles County and Websters Yorkshire on handpump, and lots of malt whiskies; friendly staff; darts, dominoes. *(Recommended by H W and A B Tuffill, Lt G I Mitchell, David Goldstone, R C Watkins, TOH, Peter Race)*

Free house   Licensee Neil Stephenson   Real ale   Meals and snacks (no food Dec and Jan) Restaurant   Children in eating area of bar if eating until 9   Open 11–11; 12–2, 8–10.30 in winter; closed 25 Dec   Bedrooms tel Langdale (096 67) 215; £20/£40(£48B)

LOWESWATER   NY1222 Map 9

Kirkstile

From B5289 follow signs to Loweswater Lake; OS Sheet 89 reference 140210

It's the position, close to Loweswater and Crummock Water, with striking peaks and fells on all sides, that draws people here. The low-beamed carpeted main bar has partly stripped stone walls, comfortably cushioned small settles and pews, and a big log fire; an adjoining room has big windows overlooking the beck and the fells. Bar food includes sandwiches (from £1), home-made soup (£1.25), omelettes (from £2.95), vegetarian casserole (£3), and steaks (from £7.50), with weekend specials; good breakfasts, morning coffee. Well kept Jennings on handpump, and a good choice of malt whiskies. Darts, dominoes and a slate shove-ha'penny board; a side games-room called the Little Barn has pool, fruit machine, space game and juke box. There are new picnic-table sets on the lawn. *(Recommended by Jon and Jacquie Payne, C M T Johnson, C A Hood)*

Free house   Licensees Ken and Shirley Gorley   Real ale   Meals and snacks   Restaurant Children welcome   Open all day (even for breakfast)   Bedrooms tel Lorton (090 085) 219; £22.50(£29.50B)/£29.50(£36.50B)

LOWICK GREEN   SD2985 Map 9
Farmers Arms
A595

Not far from Coniston Water, this busy, rambling old hotel has a heavy beamed public bar with huge flagstones and a handsome fireplace with a big open fire; some seats are in cosy side alcoves. Bar food includes soup (75p), sandwiches, ploughman's (from £2.50), salads (from £2.50), home-made steak and kidney pie in stout (£3), gammon with egg or pineapple (£3.75), and sirloin steak (£6.25), with specials such as cheese and onion pie (£2.50), sweet-and-sour pork (£3), and fresh salmon (£3.95). Youngers IPA and Scotch on handpump; a computerised till displays a list of purchases, prices and even the barmaid's name on a VDU above the bar; dominoes, fruit machine, juke box and piped music; also a pool-room and darts alley. Across the courtyard, the hotel is attractively furnished, and has its own plusher lounge bar, as well as a preserved spinning-gallery. *(Recommended by M A and W R Proctor, Brian Jones, A T Langton)*

Scottish & Newcastle   Licensee Alan Lockwell   Real ale   Meals and snacks   Restaurant Children welcome until 8.30   Open 11–3, 6–11   Bedrooms tel Greenodd (022 986) 376; £18.50(£26B)/£40B

MELMERBY   NY6237 Map 10
Shepherds 🏮
A686

There's a consistency about this spacious eating pub, both in the warmth of the welcome and in the high quality of the food. There are cushioned wall seats, sunny window seats, sensible tables and chairs, light panelling, lots of pot plants, and an open fire. A wide choice of home-made food (using local produce where possible, and local butchers) is brought to your table: home-made rolls to order, home-made pasties (80p), soup (£1), pork and port pâté (£2), ploughman's with some fourteen good cheeses to choose from – the mature Cheddar is *really* mature (£2.30) – or home-cooked ham (£2.80), plaice (£3.15), flavoursome Cumberland sausage and egg (£3.30), salads with delicious garlic mayonnaise, chicken curry or lasagne (£3.90), steak and kidney or very good ham and mushroom pie (£4), beef goulash (£4.30), very tender spiced lamb with yoghurt or chicken breast Leoni (£4.50), and steaks (from £6.50); lots of daily specials, vegetarian dishes such as chestnut and mushroom pie or hot-pots (£3.90), surprise starters like chicken wings in sherry and ginger, Sunday roast lunch (£3.50) and home-made puddings (£1.20). Very well kept Marstons Burton, Pedigree, Merrie Monk and Owd Rodger on handpump, as well as quite a few malt whiskies; happy staff. A games-bar has darts, pool, dominoes and fruit machine. Hartside Nursery Garden, a noted alpine and primula plant specialist, is just over the Hartside Pass. The pub looks across the green of the unspoilt red sandstone village to the Pennines climbing immediately behind. *(Recommended by Simon Ward, L D Rainger, G Bloxsom, Mr and Mrs M Wall, PLC, E V Walder, Comus Elliott, Grahame Archer, Dewi and Linda Jones, R C Wiles, R J Yates)*

Marstons   Licensee Martin Baucutt   Real ale   Meals and snacks (11–2.30, 6–9.45) Children in eating area until 9   Open 11–3, 6–11 all year; closed 25 Dec

MIDDLETON   SD6397 Map 10
Middleton Fells
A683 Kirkby Lonsdale–Sedbergh

The alterations here were almost completed by the time we went to press. The open-plan bar – which incorporates the old barn, where there's a pool-table, dartboard and bar stools – has green plush wall banquettes and stools, oak beams and leaning posts from the old cow stalls, local photographs on the walls, lots of horsebrasses and brass ornaments (some made by the landlord), and a fireplace in local stone; the eating area has upholstered fiddle-back chairs, more green plush banquettes and settles. Home-made, popular bar food from a menu that changes weekly includes warm crusty rolls (from £1.35, hot roast beef on Sundays £2.20), breaded mushrooms with garlic dip (£1.95), dressed crab (£2.95), spare ribs, beef or vegetarian curries (£3.25), salads, chicken and broccoli lasagne (£3.40), seafood tagliatelle (£3.65), duck in Grand Marnier or ten-ounce gammon with local free-range egg (£4.25), and twelve-ounce rump steak (£5.85); Sunday roast lunch (£3.95 main course, £5.75 three courses). Service is friendly; well kept Tetleys Bitter and Youngers Scotch on handpump; darts, pool, dominoes, fruit machine and juke box. The neatly kept and attractive garden has pretty shrub and flower borders with sturdy old-fashioned teak benches and more modern tables and seats out on the back terrace. The pub is surrounded by the quiet countryside of the Lune valley below the great fells that lead up to Calf Top. *(Recommended by Col G D Stafford; more reports please)*

Free house   Licensee John O'Neill   Real ale   Meals and snacks (not Mon in winter exc bank hols)   Children welcome until 8.30   Open 12–2.30 (3 Sat), 7 (6 Sat in summer)–11 all year; closed Mon lunchtime Oct–Apr (exc bank hols)

MUNGRISDALE   NY3630 Map 10

Mill Inn 🛏

Village signposted off A66 Penrith–Keswick, a bit over a mile W of A5091 Ullswater turn-off

In one of the nicest spots of any Cumbrian pub, this neatly modernised inn nestles among trees in a high, secluded valley below soaring fells that climb eventually to Blencathra. There are picnic-table sets under cocktail parasols and rustic tables and benches on a gravel forecourt, and down on a neat and very sheltered lawn that slopes down towards the little river. The main bar is simply furnished, with leatherette banquettes, dark tables and chairs, and a modern stone through fireplace, with photographs of local huntsmen, and prints of sheepdogs and wildlife. Generously served simple bar food includes sandwiches (from 85p), soup (85p), pâté (£1.50), ploughman's (£2.50), salads (from £2.75), prawns with smoked salmon (£3.50) and poached salmon (£4.50), with hot dishes of the day and admirable puddings served with lots of cream (£1); friendly staff; well kept Theakstons Best on handpump, lots of malt whiskies; a side room is shared by a cold cabinet and pool-tables and fruit machine; keen local dominoes school. Note that there is a separate Mill Hotel in this same hamlet. *(Recommended by Dick Brown, David Heath, Mr and Mrs M Wall)*

Free house   Licensees Mike and Penny Sutton   Real ale   Meals and snacks (12–1.45, 7–8.30; also afternoon teas)   Restaurant   Children allowed if sitting with parents   Open 11–2.30 (3 in high season), 6–11 all year; closes 2–7 afternoons in winter; during the afternoon the receptionist should be able to find you refreshments   Bedrooms tel Threlkeld (059 683) 632; £14.50(£17B)/£29(£34B)

NEAR SAWREY   SD3796 Map 9

Tower Bank Arms

B5285 towards the Windermere ferry

Backing on to Beatrix Potter's farm and owned by the National Trust, this quaint black and white cottage has an enjoyable, relaxed atmosphere. The traditionally furnished main bar has local hunting photographs under the low beams, a grandfather clock, high-backed settles on the rough slate floor, a big cooking-range with a lovely log fire, and maybe Emma, Maxwell or Nelson the pub's labradors. Lunchtime bar food includes home-made soup (£1), filled brown rolls (from £1), good ploughman's (from £2.50), potted shrimps (£2.75), pâté (£3.10), home-made quiche (£3.25), tasty chicken and ham pie (£3.50), and scampi (£4); in the evening there are more substantial main meals such as grilled gammon and eggs or good Esthwaite trout (£4.50), and steaks (from £6.25). Well kept Matthew Browns Mild, Theakstons Best and XB, and Youngers Scotch and No 3 on handpump, as well as several malt whiskies and wine bottled for the pub; darts, shove-ha'penny, dominoes and cribbage. Seats outside have a view of the wooded Claife Heights. It does get crowded in summer. (*Recommended by Steve and Carolyn Harvey, Steve Waters, A T Langton, Gary Scott, Wayne Brindle, Miss A Tress, G Smith, Michael and Alison Sandy, Simon and Sally Boxall, Brian Jones, Margaret and Roy Randle*)

Free house   Licensee Philip Broadley   Real ale   Meals and lunchtime snacks (not 25 Dec)
Restaurant   Children in eating area of bar lunchtime, in restaurant evening   Open 11–3,
5.30 (6 in winter)–11   Bedrooms tel Hawkshead (096 66) 334; £20B/£30B

SANDSIDE   SD4981 Map 7

Ship

On a bend of the shoreside road, this extensive modernised pub has glorious views over the Kent estuary to the Lakeland hills. The water is about half a mile wide here, but dries to sand and a very narrow channel at low tide. The softly lit open-plan bar has red button-back banquettes down one side, old-fashioned armchairs, upholstered stools and wheel-back chairs, dark wood panelling, and several big stormy seascapes. An end section, bare-boarded, has bar billiards, darts and a juke box, and there are two fruit machines; well kept Youngers IPA on handpump. Good value bar food includes home-made soup (85p), good ploughman's (from £1.90), and hot dishes such as vegetable flan (£2.80), steak and kidney pie (£2.95), gammon and egg or scampi (£3.25), sirloin steak (£5.80), and specials like curries or lasagne; there is a quiet back dining section (away from the views). The big car park has a cluster of picnic-table sets under cocktail parasols, and there's an excellent children's play area with a slide and assault course. (*Recommended by Matthew Waterhouse, Brian Jones, Comus Elliott*)

Scottish & Newcastle   Licensee Alan Hurst   Real ale   Meals and snacks (12–2, 6.30–8.30)
Children in eating area of bar   Open 11–3, 6–11   Bedrooms tel Milnthorpe
(044 82) 3113; £15/£28(£33B)

SCALES   NY3427 Map 9

White Horse ⊗

A66 1½ miles E of Threlkeld: keep your eyes skinned – it looks like a farmhouse up on a slope

At the end of 1988 the Slatterys bought this friendly pub from Jennings. Since then, they've repainted the outside of the building in traditional style, and added wooden settles, flower boxes and tubs. Inside, the old kitchen has been incorporated into the spotlessly clean, beamed bar, and fitted with dark oak high-backed settle-style seating upholstered in deep red; the rest of the bar has been re-upholstered to match, extra hunting pictures have been added to the local hunting cartoons and unusual textured wall hanging showing a white horse on the fells, and there are warm fires in winter, candles on the tables, and a growing range of attractive locally mounted animals and birds native to the area. There's also a cosy little snug (in what used to be the dairy). Local produce is used in the consistently good cooking here as much as possible – no chips or convenience foods – and at lunchtime (when it's best to get there early) this includes home-made carrot and coriander soup (£1), Lancashire cheese and spinach flan, peach halves filled with garlic and herb creamcheese or a good ploughman's (£2.95), potted shrimps with hot garlic bread or prawn open sandwich (£3.75), Waberthwaite Cumberland sausage with mushrooms (£3.75), and superb Waberthwaite Cumberland ham with two eggs (£4.50); in the evenings (when booking is essential – Threlkeld (059 683) 241) there are dishes like good poached Borrowdale trout (£5.50), pork fillet with sherry and mushroom sauce (£6.95), steaks (from £7.75), and seasonal specials like local salmon, grouse, venison and muscovy duck; puddings such as home-made brown bread and honey ice-cream or fresh strawberry cheesecake (from £1.50). Well kept Jennings on handpump; cheery, efficient service; dominoes. From this isolated cluster of pub and farm buildings, tracks lead up into the splendidly daunting and rocky fells around Blencathra – which have names like Foule Crag and Sharp Edge. *(Recommended by Sue Holland, Dave Webster, Graham Bush, Hayward Wane, Mr and Mrs M Wall, H W and A B Tuffill, PLC, Miss A Tress, G Smith, V P Prentice, H A R Saunders, Andy Tye, Sue Hill)*

Jennings   Licensees Laurence and Judith Slattery   Real ale   Meals and lunchtime snacks; from Nov–Easter not Mon–Thurs evening; no food 25 Dec   Children in eating area until 8.30   Open 11–3, 6–11; 12–2, 7–11 in winter

STAINTON   NY4928 Map 9
Kings Arms

1¾ miles from M6 junction 40: village signposted from A66 towards Keswick, though quickest to fork left at A592 roundabout then turn first right

Fairly quiet on weekday lunchtimes, this comfortably modernised old pub is more lively in the evenings when it's full of local people and visitors. The open-plan bar has leatherette wall banquettes, stools and armchairs, wood-effect tables, brasses on the black beams and swirly cream walls; piped music. Good value bar food includes soup (70p), sandwiches (from 80p, open sandwiches from £1.20), filled baked potatoes (£1), Cumberland sausage with egg or steak and kidney pie (£2.40), salads (from £2.40), home-roast ham (£2.80), local trout or spinach and walnut lasagne (£2.90), delicious farmhouse gammon with egg or pineapple (£3.20), and sirloin steak (£4.80); children's menu (£1.30). Well kept Whitbreads Castle Eden on handpump; pleasant staff. Sensibly placed darts, dominoes, fruit machine, fairly quiet juke box. There are tables outside on the side terrace and a small lawn. *(Recommended by R F Plater, Richard Dolphin, Mr and Mrs J H Adam, Cdr J W Hackett, H A R Saunders, Neil and Angela Huxter, Sue Braisted, L D Rainger)*

Whitbreads   Licensee Raymond Tweddle   Real ale   Meals and snacks (not weekday evenings in winter)   Children welcome if eating   Country and western Sun evening once a month   Open 11–3, 6–11 all year

TALKIN   NY5557 Map 10
Hare & Hounds ★ 🍺

Village signposted from B6413 S of Brampton

This well kept, small eighteenth-century village inn appeals very strongly to the many readers who like being put at once on first name terms with staff and maybe fellow guests (that's what happens if you're staying), and appreciate the way the landlord makes sure diners are enjoying each course of their meal. The two knocked-through rooms, one black-beamed and timbered, the other with a shiny white plank ceiling, have big antique prints over the two open fires, a fine longcase clock (made in Brampton), settles, wicker armchairs and red-cushioned country chairs around the close-set dark elm rustic tables, and stained-glass municipal coats of arms over the serving-counter. Big helpings of good food include home-made soup (75p), baked potatoes with six interesting fillings (from 85p), burgers (£1.10), double-decker sandwich (£1.75), and steak sandwich (£2.25), with main dishes such as plaice with ratatouille (£3.60), scampi or venison in red wine (£5.25), good local fillet steak (£6.25); home-made specials such as lasagne (£1.95), and beef in beer, steak and kidney pie or minty lamb pie (£2.45), puddings (from 85p), and cheap children's dishes (under £1). Tables in the main bar – which can be booked – may all be reserved for diners, so you might find yourself in a quieter back room with stalls around rustic tables. People are asked the night before what they'd like

for breakfast – which is served at ten-minute intervals between 8 and 9. Well kept
Hartleys XB and Theakstons Best, XB and Old Peculier on handpump, and country
wine, Bulmers cider and malt whisky; darts and dominoes; no dogs. There are a few
tables on a gravel side terrace, and they have acquired a red telephone box for the
use of customers – it had been in the village for 45 years before being replaced by a
more modern one. You can walk straight from the small village into fine
countryside (Talkin Tarn is a lovely spot for boating, fishing or just sitting, and
there's a golf course virtually on the doorstep, which has reduced green fees for
residents). The RSPB have designated an area of 90,000 acres nearby as a Bird
Reserve. *(Recommended by Simon Ward, David and Flo Wallington, Alan Hall, John
Townsend, Lynn Stevens, Gill Quarton, Mrs J Frost, Mrs B M Kinnell, R Wiles, Mrs M
Wettern, P H S Wettern)*

*Free house   Licensees Les and Joan Stewart   Real ale   Meals and snacks   Children in family
lounge   Open 12–3, 7–11 all year   Bedrooms tel Brampton (069 77) 3456; £16(£18B)/
£27(£30B)*

ULVERSTON   SD2978 Map 7

Bay Horse ✪

Canal Foot; in Ulverston follow Industrial Estate signpost off A596 and keep on down North
Lonsdale Road, bearing left at T-junction and skirting vast Glaxo plant – the pub's name is
painted in huge letters on its slate roof; OS Sheet 96 reference 314777

A small wall in the restaurant which divided the conservatory and little back bar in
this charmingly renovated pub has been removed, giving all diners the marvellous
view across Morecambe Bay. The civilised but pubby smallish bar has black beams
and props with lots of horsebrasses, attractive wooden armchairs, glossy hardwood
traditional tables, some pale green plush built-in wall banquettes, blue plates on a
Delft shelf, and a huge but elegant stone horse's head. The short choice of
imaginative food (which we should stress is restaurant food – none is served in the
bar itself) changes weekly and may include five starters such as chilled black cherry
and kirsch soup with cream and toasted almonds (£2), fresh duck leg fried with
lemon, honey and thyme on a salad with pink grapefruit (£3.85), and chicken, veal
and pistachio-nut terrine with garlic and herb bread (£4.10), and five main courses
such as fried skate wings with lemon, capers and parsley butter (£10.80) and
medallions of wild boar pan-fried with strips of bacon, apple and black cherries
with cream and calvados (£13.75); the puddings (£2.45) are sumptuous; three-
course Sunday lunch (£11.55); we've included the ten per cent service in our prices.
They do sandwiches in the bar. Besides well kept Mitchells Best and ESB on
handpump, there's a decent choice of spirits, and a wine list with a strong emphasis
on New World wines (we can firmly recommend the Morris Old Liqueur Muscat
from Australia as a sweet wine, by the glass); they serve these wines by the glass in
the bar. Magazines are dotted about, there's a handsomely marbled green granite
fireplace, and well chosen decently reproduced piped music. A small room by the
entrance has a pool-table and darts, dominoes. There are picnic-table sets out on
the terrace. The owners also run an outstanding restaurant at their Miller Howe
hotel on Windermere. *(Recommended by GRE, AE, Martin Rayner, and others)*

*Mitchells   Licensee Robert Lyons   Real ale   Meals (not Sun evening or Mon)   Restaurant
tel Ulverston (0229) 53972 (not Sun evenings and Mon)   Children welcome   Open 11–3,
6–11 all year*

WARWICK ON EDEN   NY4657 Map 9

Queens Arms

2 miles from M6 junction 43: A69 towards Hexham, then village signposted

There's a cheery atmosphere in the two-roomed bar of this well kept old pub, with
its roaring winter log fires and model cars, trains, vintage car pictures and so forth.

Bar food includes lentil soup (90p), good sandwiches (from £1 – not Sunday lunchtime), filled baked potatoes (from £1.50), burger (£1.95), home-made pizzas or salads (from £3.30), and gammon and egg (£4.50); home-made puddings and Sunday roast beef lunch. Well kept Marstons Pedigree, Tetleys and Theakstons on handpump, with several malt whiskies, Australian wines (and some French – even up here they manage to get Beaujolais Nouveau on the first evening) and farm cider. The neat side garden, with roses, marigolds and other flowers, has rustic tables and seats, and a new well equipped play area. *(Recommended by Mr and Mrs L D Rainger, Michael Davis, Neil and Angela Huxter, T A Hoyle, J F M West, Syd and Wyn Donald)*

Free house   Licensees Tony and Angela Wood   Real ale   Meals and snacks (12–2, 6–8.30; not Sun evenings Nov–Mar)   Restaurant   Children welcome until 9.30   Open 11–3, 5.30–11; 11–11 Sat   Bedrooms tel Wetheral (0228) 60699; £25B/£34B

WASDALE HEAD   NY1808 Map 9

Wasdale Head Inn 🛏

As it's well away from the main tourist areas and surrounded by steep fells, this gabled old hotel makes an excellent base for walking and climbing. The big main bar has a polished slate floor, high ceilings, shiny panelling, cushioned settles, fine George Abraham photographs on the walls, and a log-effect gas fire; there's an adjoining pool-room, as well as a panelled and comfortably old-fashioned residents' bar and lounge. Home-made bar food includes soup (95p), locally potted shrimps or cheese and onion flan (£1.90), steak and kidney pie (£2.45), ploughman's (from £2.50), chicken casserole (£2.90) and mixed locally smoked meat salad (£3.80); also daily specials and huge breakfasts. Well kept Jennings, Theakstons Best and Old Peculier and Yates on handpump, and a good selection of malt whiskies; dominoes, cribbage. The main bar is named after the inn's first landlord, Will Ritson, who for his tall stories was reputed to be the world's biggest liar, and in his memory they still hold liar competitions here towards the end of November. There's a self-catering cottage and two flats in converted inn buildings nearby. *(Recommended by Graham Bush, A C and S J Beardsley, R K Smith, Doug Kennedy, Heather Sharland, R H Sawyer, Tony Pounder, M A and W R Proctor)*

Free house   Licensee Jasper Carr   Real ale   Meals and snacks (11–3, 6–10)   Restaurant Children in own room   Open 11–11; mid-Nov–mid-Mar open only Fri evening, Sat, and Sun lunchtime 11–3, 6 (5.30 Sat)–11   Bedrooms (they do only dinner, bed and breakfast; no accommodation mid-Nov–mid-Mar (exc New Year period) tel Wasdale (094 06) 229; £39B/£74B

Lucky Dip

Besides the fully inspected pubs, you might like to try these Lucky Dips recommended to us and described by readers (if you do, please send us reports):

☆ **Alston** [Main St; NY7246], *Angel*: Lively seventeenth-century pub with good jolly atmosphere and excellent Drybroughs 80/-; village is close to long-distance Pennine Way; bedrooms *(Len Beattie)*
nr **Ambleside** [NY3804], *Kirkstone Pass*: Remote roadside mountain inn – the highest in Lakeland – with wide choice of whiskies, lively amusements, cheery atmosphere, all-day summer cafe, fine surrounding scenery; a useful shelter in bad weather; bedrooms *(Steve Waters, LYM)*
Appleby [Boroughgate; NY6921], *Crown & Cushion*: Unpretentious town local, useful for cheap lunches, with Jennings and Tetleys on handpump; busy in the evening, with loud music *(D Stokes)*; [B6542, about 2 miles SE, nr junction with A66] *Gate*: Good food very pleasantly served in comfortable surroundings, excellent atmosphere – much nicer than you might imagine from outside *(D Tinbergen)*
☆ **Askham** [NY5123], *Punch Bowl*: A mix of interesting furnishings in the rambling beamed bar, log fire, Whitbreads Castle Eden on handpump, bar food and games in separate public bar; very popular under its previous licensees, but changed hands summer 1988 – recent reports suggest the food (from sandwiches to pheasant) and beer are still reliable; has been open all day Sat – attractive position by lower village green;

nice bedrooms; children welcome *(Sue Holland, Dave Webster, PLC, Alan Franck, LYM – more reports on the new regime please)*

☆ **Bampton** [NY5118], *St Patricks Well*: Friendly welcome, well kept beer, high standard of home-cooked bar food served quickly; bedrooms excellent value, with basic facilities and good breakfasts *(Dr and Mrs R J Ashleigh, Mrs P Cardy)*

Bampton Grange [NY5120], *Crown & Mitre*: Elegant small white house with portico and balcony above, spacious through lounge, pleasant chatty landlady, usual range of food and drink; useful for Haweswater and – with the church opposite – worth the small detour *(Anon)*

Bardsea [SD3074], *Bradylls Arms*: Popular, pleasant village pub overlooking Morecambe Bay, bar food in extended dining lounge *(AE, GRE)*

Barrow in Furness [Holbeck Park Av, Roose; SD2069], *Crofters*: Converted farmhouse with well kept Thwaites on handpump, bar food, barbecue *(Anon)*

Bassenthwaite [NY2228], *Sun*: Very good food and service *(L D Rainger)*

Borrowdale [Ravenscraig; NY2515], *Sca Fell*: Remote hotel with good Riverside Bar; walkers in scruffy gear won't be frowned on *(Graham Bush)*

☆ **Bowness on Windermere** [SD4097], *Hole in t' Wall*: Ancient pub with farm tools, smith's bellows, ploughshares, etc. in slate-floored lower bar (which can get crowded), handsome if simply furnished panelled upper room with fine plaster ceiling, simple good value lunchtime food, well kept Hartleys XB on handpump, quick service; tables in nice flagstoned courtyard; very popular with youngsters in summer *(Steve Waters, E J Knight, A J Foote, LYM)*

Bowness on Windermere [Queens Sq], *Albert*: This always has its firm local supporters, and the beer's good, though the pop music certainly makes itself heard; bar food, and bedrooms said to be large, clean and comfortable *(A J Hartley)*

Braithwaite [NY2324], *Coledale*: Popular pub with busy lounge bar and dining-room and friendly, efficient service; wide range of food from sandwiches, home-made soup and potted shrimps to gammon and egg, with children's dishes (they're allowed until 9.30) *(Mr and Mrs D J Nash)*

Brampton [Market Pl; this is the one E of Carlisle; NY5361], *Nags Head*: Attractive frontage, conventionally decorated bar and lounge, obliging prompt service, good bar food *(Anon)*

Brigsteer [OS Sheet 97 reference 481896; SD4889], *Wheatsheaf*: Whitbreads pub with well kept Castle Eden, good bar food – especially the soups, gammon sandwiches and Cumberland sausages with proper sauce *(A T Langton)*

☆ **Brough Sowerby** [A685; NY7913], *Black*

Bull: Well kept beer and good, decent food in quiet pub with separate dining area; very clean, with welcoming licensees *(K H Frostick, J E Rycroft)*

Broughton in Furness [Princes St; SD2187], *Black Cock*: Pleasant pub with character, friendly service, cosy fireside, good but limited menu including particularly good ploughman's, well kept Watneys-related real ales on handpump; bedrooms *(D B Haunch, GRE, AE)*; [Foxfield Rd] *Eccle Riggs*: Whitbreads Castle Eden on handpump, good value bar food, extensive Sun lunchtime buffet, children's menu (they can use the small but pleasant indoor swimming-pool free if they eat here); food service may be leisurely; bedrooms *(GRE, AE)*; [Church St] *Old Kings Head*: Delightful old-world pub with stone fireplace, chintz and knick-knacks; mouthwatering choice of moderately priced food in separate restaurant area, as well as sandwiches, snacks and children's dishes; bedrooms *(Raymond Palmer)*

☆ **Buttermere** [NY1817], *Bridge*: Robust lunchtime bar food in simply furnished but comfortable lounge bar of extended stone hotel, well kept Theakstons Best, XB and Old Peculier on handpump, tables on flagstoned terrace; handy for Crummock Water and Buttermere – the pretty little village, at the start of GWG135, fills with walkers in summer (though they don't allow boots or walking gear here), and it's the location that appeals most to readers; evening restaurant; prices not low; bedrooms *(C M T Johnson, D Rowlatt, Graham Bush, TOH, Cynthia McDowall, Miss A Tress, G Smith, LYM)*

Buttermere, *Fish*: Decent food and pleasant landlady, though décor is rather pedestrian and un-pub-like; at start GWG135; bedrooms *(C A Hood)*

☆ **Cark in Cartmel** [SD3776], *Engine*: Friendly and comfortably modernised with lots of brasses and flowers, good open fire, friendly and attentive newish landlord, well kept Bass, good range of whiskies, piped music; tables out by little stream *(A T Langton, Pete Storey, LYM)*

Carlisle [Lowther St; NY4056], *Post*: Large Victorian-style pub in former post office building, full of mahogany and stained-glass dividers between banquettes; helpful cheerful staff, locally popular at lunchtime for wide choice of good food from soup and sandwiches to hot dishes such as steak pie; Matthew Browns and Theakstons Old Peculier *(Raymond Palmer)*; [St Nicholas St] *Theakston*: Rather basic town pub with open fires, well kept Matthew Browns and remarkable value food including superb cold ham *(Mr and Mrs Hendry)*

Cartmel [off main sq; SD3879], *Cavendish Arms*: Spacious, dark and cosy inside, well kept Bass, good bar food from cheap sandwiches (including excellent ham) to

Aberdeen Angus steaks in variety, helpful service *(A T Langton, Pete Storey)*; [The Square] *Kings Arms*: Picturesque pub nicely placed at the head of the attractive town square – rambling bar with heavy beams but clean and bright décor, bar food (they're generous with the prawns, and soup's been enjoyed), well kept Whitbreads Castle Eden; children welcome *(AE, GRE, Pete Storey, Mrs H D Astley, LYM)*; *Pig & Whistle*: Stone exterior, long bar with old photographs of interesting local scenes; pleasant landlady, well kept Hartleys, good coffee, occasional local folk music *(Pete Storey)*; *Royal Oak*: Roomy, with pleasant local paintings, good atmosphere, friendly and helpful staff, well kept Whitbreads Castle Eden *(Pete Storey)*

☆ **Chapel Stile** [B5343; NY3205], *Wainwrights*: Decent pub with generous helpings of good value food including children's dishes, served quickly and personally by landlady; well kept Theakstons XB and Old Peculier on handpump, good friendly atmosphere *(N B Pritchard, J A Edwards, N F Doherty)*

Cockermouth [Main St; NY1231], *Globe*: Eighteenth-century pub decorated with old music hall posters, big marble tables in main bar, good choice of malt whiskies; bedrooms *(Dave Braisted)*; *Trout*: Chintz and red plush in comfortable bar of solid old hotel, consistently good food in bar and well kept restaurant, really friendly licensee and staff, garden by River Cocker; bedrooms *(Mr and Mrs L D Rainger, BB)*

Coniston [SD3098], *Crown*: Swiftly served food including Sun lunches, Hartleys on handpump and pictures of the late Sir Donald Campbell in lounge; bedrooms *(Roger Huggins)*

Crook [SD4695], *Sun*: Friendly straightforward pub which has had basic chippy food, welcoming fire, Websters and Wilsons real ales; children welcome; very recent reports suggest improvements – more news please *(Denzil Taylor, LYM)*

☆ **Crosby Ravensworth** [NY6215], *Butchers Arms*: Simple village pub with really friendly young licensees (and spaniel), decent home cooking including splendidly sticky puddings, well kept Marstons Pedigree, Yates and Youngers Scotch on handpump, interesting mountain photographs; picnic-table sets in small, sheltered back courtyard; children welcome; this village like its neighbour Maulds Meaburn is most attractive *(Martin Rayner, Penelope Willink, BB)*

Crosthwaite [off A5074 Levens–Windermere; SD4491], *Punch Bowl*: Idyllic spot in Lythe Valley; spacious pub with large staircase to minstrels' gallery, assorted old farming equipment on walls, comfortable furnishings, good bar food generously served, excellent service *(C Trows)*

Dalton in Furness [Goose Green; SD2273], *Brown Cow*: Lively and busy locals' pub with sensibly knocked together rooms, some tables outside *(Brian Jones)*

Dean [just off A5086 S of Cockermouth; NY0825], *Royal Yew*: Comfortable and pleasantly furnished village pub with good evening atmosphere, Theakstons and Youngers real ales, good reasonably priced bar food *(R D Norman)*

Dufton [NY6925], *Stag*: Small, basic pub in lovely village, well worth a visit despite having no food and keg beer *(Len Beattie)*

Eaglesfield [just off village road, on right coming from A5086; NY0928], *Blackcock*: Simple country local, spick and span, with cheap Jennings real ales and uncommon version of ring the bull; no bar food *(LYM)*

Eamont Bridge [handy for M6 junction 40; NY5328], *Beehive*: Eighteenth-century pub with excellent homely service, Whitbreads ales, varied and interesting bar food from ploughman's to steaks, including children's helpings; dogs welcome, children's play area *(E R Thompson)*; *Crown*: Very welcoming pubby lounge bar, well cooked, fairly priced food – even a choice of mustards; bedrooms *(Alan Jones)*

Eskdale [Bleabeck – mid-way between Boot and Hard Knott Pass; NY1400], *Woolpack*: Comfortable roadside inn with small lounge and larger bar with pool-table; well kept Youngers IPA on handpump, limited choice of bar food running up to very good value sirloin steak; handily placed for walkers; bedrooms *(P Lloyd, K Bamford)*

☆ **Eskdale Green** [NY1400], *George IV*: Many-roomed, oak-beamed pub with good value food, well kept Marstons Pedigree, McEwans 70/-, Theakstons XB and Youngers No 3 on handpump; over 100 malt whiskies – some over 50 years old; on GWG125; bedrooms *(P Lloyd, K Bamford)*

☆ **Far Sawrey** [SD3893], *Sawrey*: Interesting if basic Claife Crier stable bar with wooden stalls dividing tables and harness on rough white walls, good simple food including wide choice of sandwiches and fine ploughman's, well kept Jennings and Theakstons real ales; seats on nice lawn look up to Claife Heights, which have good views of Lake Windermere; bedrooms; nr GWG127 *(Greg Parston, AE, GRE, Doug Kennedy, N Burrell, LYM)*

Flookburgh [SD3676], *Hope & Anchor*: Large and relaxing pub in small, pleasant village with friendly landlord, darts, pool, well kept Hartleys Mild and Bitter *(Pete Storey)*

☆ **Garrigill** [NY7441], *George & Dragon*: Seventeenth-century village pub with friendly and informal welcome in flagstoned bar of genuine character, good ale, good value bar food, unexpectedly comprehensive menu in part stripped stone, part panelled dining-room, running up to duck and pheasant but all freshly cooked; on a dead-end road in beautiful scenery; bedrooms small but comfortable – good value *(Mr and Mrs*

C R Bryant, R A Hall – more reports please)
Glenridding [back of main car park, top of road; NY3917], *Travellers Rest*: Friendly welcome, good value food in simple bar, wonderful view of fells across Ullswater from terrace; nr GWG132, nr start GWG138 *(Charles and Mary Winpenny)*
Gosforth [off A595 and unclassified rd to Wasdale; NY0703], *Gosforth Hall*: Lovely old Jacobean building, fine plaster coats of arms over fireplaces; has had attentive service and excellent bar food, though we've heard nothing since reports of sale plans; bedrooms *(AE, GRE – more reports please)*
☆ **Grasmere** [main bypass rd; NY3406], *Swan*: Good home-made bar food in relaxing and attractively old-fashioned lounge of spacious THF hotel, popular with walkers even though it's short on 'local' feel – certainly a comfortable base for the fells which rise behind; darts in small public bar, Tetleys on handpump (in good condition, though it may be rather cold), decent range of simple but well prepared bar food including fine sandwiches, staff usually friendly; bedrooms *(Steve Dark, Col G D Stafford, Laurence Manning, LYM)*
Grasmere [main bypass rd; NY3406], *Travellers Rest*: Main-road pub in outstanding Lakeland scenery, with fitted carpet stretching from games-room through plainly furnished lounge to family dining-room, real ale, gentle piped music, tables in small area outside; since its sale in 1988 we've had promising reports of good lunchtime bar food (meals rather than snacks) and a friendly new licensee giving a pleasant homely atmosphere; nr start GWG129; bedrooms comfortable *(Phil Taylor, Steve and Carolyn Harvey, BB – more news please)*; *Tweedies*: Young theme bar named after local character, very friendly welcome even for bedraggled hikers; large games-room, lots of chatter – it's assumed you'll join in *(David Gwynne Harper)*
Great Urswick [SD2775], *General Burgoyne*: Small village pub overlooking small tarn; bar and lounge with open log fires, Hartleys ale and basic bar food including cheap specials *(N M Williams)*
Haverthwaite [A590 Barrow rd – OS Sheet 97 reference 328842; SD3484], *Dicksons Arms*: Well kept Bass on draught, good lunchtime bar food *(A T Langton)*
Hawkshead [SD3598], *Red Lion*: Friendly and comfortable modernised inn with lively atmosphere, well kept Websters and Wilsons on handpump, good value bar food, restaurant; bedrooms *(Charles and Mary Winpenny, A T Langton, H K Dyson, Wayne Brindle, LYM)*
☆ **Hesket Newmarket** [NY3438], *Old Crown*: Small and outstandingly friendly, with wide range of bar games from shove-ha'penny and dominoes to modern, three-dimensional wooden puzzles, and small lending library

(10p a book, for benefit of guide dogs for the blind); well kept beer, especially the Blencathra Bitter from their own new malt-extract barn brewery; wide range of food; bedrooms *(Nicola MacLeod)*
High Newton [just off A590 Lindale–Newby Bridge, towards Cartmel Fell; SD4082], *Crown*: Good bar food including quickly served Sun lunch *(A T Langton)*
Hoff [NY6718], *New*: Friendly straightforward pub with good value bar food; children welcome *(Anon of Dartford)*
Ireby [NY2439], *Sun*: Plentiful helpings of wholesome food, including a very filling mixed grill; out-of-the-way village on the fringe of the northern fells *(N J Neil-Smith)*
Kendal [SD5293], *Globe*: Civilised place in daytime, with bar food, pleasant décor and separate dining-room upstairs (where children welcome); but loud music at night, with live jazz and folk music two nights a week *(MGBD)*; [Main St] *Olde Fleece*: Smart pub with character, tastefully refurbished without destroying its olde-worlde atmosphere, well kept real ales and bar food *(R A Nelson)*
☆ **Keswick** [St John's St; NY2624], *George*: Interesting inside, with well worn flagstones, old beams, old-fashioned furnishings as well as modern banquettes, snug black-panelled side bar with log fire, well kept Theakstons and Yates, good if sometimes rather noisy atmosphere; good value bar food – which may be served in music-free restaurant; trout fishing; bedrooms comfortable *(Dick Brown, P Miller, Graham Bush, LYM)*
Keswick [Lake Rd], *Four in Hand*: Small and cosy hotel bar with warm welcome, open fire in winter, walls covered with bric-à-brac such as horsebrasses and bridles, foreign and UK bank notes, old local pictures; good range of reasonably priced bar food; bedrooms *(Carol and Richard Glover)*; [off Market Sq, behind Queens Hotel] *Old Queens Head*: Modernised, olde-worlde pub, large and open-planned downstairs bar with low beams, exposed stone walls, half flagstoned floor, large open fire, atmospheric wall lights, bric-à-brac on walls, pool-table and red plush seating, juke box in upstairs attic-style room; warm welcome and good range of bar food *(Carol and Richard Glover)*; [off Market Sq, behind Lloyds Bank] *Pack Horse*: Snug and likeable low-beamed town pub in attractive alley courtyard, well kept Jennings *(LYM)*
☆ nr **Keswick** [Newlands Valley – OS Sheet 90 reference 242217], *Swinside*: Friendly and unpretentious country inn, quiet and clean, in peaceful valley surrounded by marvellous crags and fells – tables outside, and picture-window upstairs dining-room, make the most of the view; wide choice of bar food from good sandwiches and massive ploughman's to main dishes which people say they can scarcely move after; Jennings

Mild and Bitter; bedrooms *(Margaret and Roy Randle, R D Norman, Rita Horridge, Dave and Sue Braisted, LYM)*

Kirkby Lonsdale [SD6278], *Red Dragon*: Wide choice of good reasonably priced bar food in well kept pub with very courteous service *(W P Haigh)*

☆ **Kirkby Stephen** [NY7808], *Kings Arms*: Solid comfort in cosy if rather formal oak-panelled lounge bar, darts and dominoes in easy-going if sometimes smoky main bar, very friendly welcome for strangers, pleasant service, bar food including well filled sandwiches with local cheese and maybe enterprising evening dishes, restaurant allowing children, well kept Whitbreads Trophy, walled garden; children welcome; bedrooms *(Anne Morris, W D Horsfield, LYM)*

Kirkby Stephen, *Pennine*: Colin and Maureen Porter, who made the Kings Head at Ravenstonedale so popular with readers for good value food and a friendly atmosphere moved here in late 1988 – plainly furnished saloon, small public bar (the Mon and Weds pin-ball competitions are popular), well kept Marstons Pedigree and Whitbreads Trophy on handpump, simple attractively priced bar food, upstairs restaurant; some tables out in front, facing the square of this attractive hill town *(BB)*

Lane End [A595 Bootle–Ravenglass; SD1093], *Brown Cow*: Plain pub, good for simple unpretentious bar food – useful for the West Cumbrian coast road *(AE, GRE)*

Langdale [NY2906], *New Dungeon Ghyll*: Large barn with dim lighting and tiled floor, open all day and very welcome after a long day's walking over the Langdale Pikes; bar food at standard times *(Ewan McCall)*

nr Levens [Sedgwick Rd, nr entrance to Sizergh Castle – OS Sheet 97 reference 500872; SD5087], *Strickland Arms*: Pleasant and comfortable local, warm welcome, well kept Theakstons Best, good if not imaginative bar food, piped music *(A T Langton, Roger Bellingham)*

Lindale [OS Sheet 97 reference 419805; SD4280], *Lindale Inn*: Decent real ale, good bar food *(A T Langton)*

Little Bampton [NY2755], *Tam o' Shanter*: Good village pub with decent and attractively priced lunchtime and evening bar food (not Thurs) from soup and omelettes to steaks *(P R Rainger)*

Loweswater [unclassified Loweswater rd off B5289 Cockermouth–Buttermere; NY1421], *Scale Hill*: Peaceful hotel where non-residents welcome; entrance lounge with comfortable sofas and armchairs, old-fashioned fireplace and inviting snug; drinks served through small hatch, bar food; bedrooms *(AE, GRE)*

Moresby [attached to Rosehill Theatre, though run separately; NX9921], *Rosehill*: A good small restaurant rather than a pub, but enterprising snacks in the bar too *(Syd and Wyn Donald)*

☆ **Nether Wasdale** [between Gosforth and Wasdale Head; NY1808], *Screes*: Comfortable and relaxed pub well placed in spectacular valley, off the usual tourist track; well kept Theakstons Best and Old Peculier and Yates, good choice of malt whiskies, decent food; five bedrooms *(P Lloyd)*

Nether Wasdale, *Strands*: Comfortable and very quiet, with well kept Hartleys and Robinsons, good choice of food – another place with a lovely setting; bedrooms *(P Lloyd, K Bamford)*

Newby Bridge [SD3786], *Swan*: Cosy fire, friendly atmosphere and well kept Theakstons in straightforward lounge of large hotel; bedrooms *(Brian Marsden)*

☆ **Outgate** [B5286 Hawkshead–Ambleside; SD3699], *Outgate Inn*: Well run and tastefully modernised pub with friendly landlord and staff, good atmosphere, popular bar food, well kept Hartleys, no juke box but restrained piped music and Fri jazz night; currently doing well for more mature customers including many from nearby villages; families allowed in two rooms away from bars *(MGBD, H Carline, A T Langton, Denzil Taylor)*

Oxen Park [OS Sheet 97 reference 316873; SD3287], *Manor House*: Quiet beamed pub, extensively modernised with plush carpets and seating, raging fire, welcoming licensees, good reasonably priced bar food, Hartleys real ales; children welcome; bedrooms *(Brian and Anna Marsden)*

Patterdale [NY3916], *White Lion*: Friendly and comfortable atmosphere, if a bit brash at times, well kept beer, rather ordinary food; worth knowing – nr GWG132; bedrooms basic *(Dr and Mrs R J Ashleigh)*

☆ **Penrith** [NY5130], *George*: Well run and substantial hotel with old-fashioned lounge hall – oak panelling and beams, handsome plasterwork, oak settles and easy chairs around good open fire, big bow windows; reasonably priced lunchtime bar food, well kept Marstons Pedigree, lively back bar, restaurant; bedrooms *(Heather Sharland, LYM)*

Penrith [Cromwell Rd], *Agricultural*: Friendly, dicky-bowed landlord, well kept Marstons, large helpings of bar food *(R G Ollier)*

Piel Island [accessible by ferry from Roa Island, nr Rampside SE of Barrow; SD2364], *Piel Island Inn*: Unique island setting, shared with castle ruins – sparsely decorated, ideal for unusual evening; hosts finish of annual coastal raft race *(Paul Corbett)*

Pooley Bridge [NY4724], *Sun*: Warm, cosy bar with well kept Marstons Pedigree on handpump, good value, generously served bar food and restaurant *(Mike Beiley)*

Ravenglass [SD0996], *Ratty Arms*: Ex-railway bar (terminus for England's oldest narrow-gauge steam railway) with bustling public bar, good value restaurant *(LYM)*

Ravenstonedale [just off A685 W of Kirkby Stephen; NY7204], *Black Swan*: Rather sombre hotel bar with comfortable seats, polished copper-topped tables, some stripped stonework and panelling-effect walls, tables in tree-sheltered streamside garden over road; quickly served bar food, Youngers No 3 on handpump; bedrooms *(BB)*; *Kings Head*: Friendly beamed bar with log fires in each of its two rooms, button-back banquettes and dining-chairs, well kept Tetleys, decent bar food, separate games-room; the licensees who made the inn so popular for its cheerful atmosphere and quick service moved in late 1988 to the Pennine in Kirkby Stephen – and we'd like more reports on the new regime here; children welcome; bedrooms *(LYM)*

Rockcliffe [NY3661], *Crown & Thistle*: Good lunchtime bar food in huge helpings, including good soup and home-cooked ham, served quickly even when it's busy *(Mr and Mrs L Rainger)*

Rosthwaite [NY2615], *Scafell*: Plain riverside bar suitable even for muddy boots and waterproofs, though it's tucked away behind kitchens of smart hotel; well kept Jennings or Theakstons, cheap food, friendly Geordie barman, simple terrace over river; bedrooms *(Graham Bush, Doug Kennedy)*

Rydal [NY3706], *Glen Rothay*: Small hotel with boats for residents on nearby Rydal Water, armchairs around fire in beamed hotel bar, stuffed animals in Badger Bar with bar food, Bass and Hartleys XB on handpump, piped music, seats in pretty garden; nr GWG129; bedrooms comfortable *(LYM)*

☆ **Seathwaite** [Duddon Valley, nr Ulpha (ie *not* Seathwaite in Borrowdale); SD2396], *Newfield*: Friendly welcome in good clean local, popular with walkers; good service, good bar food – particularly steaks *(Mrs P Brown, G L Daltry, Peggie Ellwood)*

☆ **Seatoller** [NY2414], *Yew Tree*: More restaurant than pub, and busy – our excuse for including it is the fact that the back bar does serve well kept Jennings; but the reason for knowing it is the lovely low-ceilinged seventeenth-century Lakeland dining-room with pictures, old photographs and cigarette cards, outstanding food such as home-made broth, smoked eel, real Cumberland sausage, steaks and jugged hare – you really have to book; at foot of Honister Pass, nr start GWG134; lunches simpler than dinners *(Lord Evans of Claughton, Dick Brown)*

☆ **Sedbergh** [Main St; SD6692], *Dalesman*: Well renovated free house with attractive bar, good service, friendly staff, good choice of excellent food; bedrooms superb value *(Col G D Stafford, DJF)*

Sedbergh [Finkle St (A683)], *Red Lion*: Cheerful local bar with stuffed game birds

and sporting dog prints, Marstons Mild, Burton and Pedigree on handpump, bar food from sandwiches through cottage pie and omelettes to steak; bedrooms *(BB)*

☆ nr **Sedbergh** [A683 half-way between Sedbergh and Kirkby Stephen], *Fat Lamb*: Alone on the moors, pews and piped music in two-room bar with some red flock wallpaper and brightly patterned carpet, but also open fire in traditional black kitchen range and good photographs of steam trains and local beagles; filled baked potatoes, ploughman's, lasagne, Cumberland ham and other bar food, restaurant, seats outside by sheep pastures; bedrooms *(BB)*

Silecroft [SD1382], *Miners Arms*: Pleasant surprise to find this extended old inn in an area where there are few pubs; barnacle-encrusted anchor by front entrance and battleship crests over the bar; attractive moderately priced lunchtime and evening bar food (takeaway too), paved back garden with shrubs and barbecue *(Mrs M Brown, Dick Brown)*

Southwaite [Broad Field – away from village, at NY4244], *Crown*: Welcoming and friendly new licensees making improvements and developing a cheerful atmosphere, well kept Theakstons and a guest beer, good value food well served *(Charles Holloway)*

Spark Bridge [SD3185], *Royal Oak*: Large riverside food pub with vaulted beams in upper bar, large pool-room; well kept Hartleys XB and Thwaites Mild and Bitter; children allowed *(Brian and Anna Marsden)*

☆ **Staveley** [SD4798], *Eagle & Child*: Very good value simple food including cheap steak-in-a-bun and nice home-cooked ham or Cumberland sausage – generous helpings; bright but comfortable little modern front lounge and more spacious carpeted bar; well kept, with small neat garden; bedrooms quite cheap *(BB)*

Swarthmoor [Fox St; SD2777], *Miners Arms*: Small village pub, well kept Hartleys tapped from the cask, good bar food, friendly service, live music every other Weds *(M W Woodburn)*

☆ **Talkin** [Talkin Tarn; NY5557], *Tarn End*: Nineteenth-century family-run farmhouse on banks of lake, with two boats for residents; good fresh food in bar and evening restaurant includes unusual dishes such as venison sausages, mussels and scallops, splendid puddings; Tennents ales, afternoon teas, really friendly service, good welcome for children; bedrooms well equipped and good value *(E R Thompson, Nigel Furneaux, Debbie Pratt)*

Talkin, *Blacksmiths Arms*: Clean, bright and cheerful-looking pub, which has pleased a good few readers with its friendly staff, cosy and comfortable atmosphere, good varied food, McEwans and Youngers real ales and decent wines – but up for sale in 1989, so more news please; bedrooms well appointed

(Alan Hall, L D and G E Rainger, Mr and Mrs R G Ing)

Tebay [A685 N of village – nr M6 junction 38; NY6204], *Barnaby Rudge*: Large pub on two levels including restaurant; Victorian décor, friendly service, separate pool-room, good bar food *(M V Fereday)*

Temple Sowerby [NY6127], *Kings Arms*: Cosily comfortable hotelish lounge and bigger L-shaped lounge bar with lots of window seats, in handsome well run red sandstone inn; bedrooms *(M J Morgan, LYM)*

Thirlspot [A591 Grasmere–Keswick; NY3217], *Kings Head*: Long refurbished bar with unpretentious bar food (stops 9pm sharp), Marstons Pedigree and Yates on handpump, games end with pool, piped music; popular with hikers, picnic-table sets outside; closes 2pm winter lunchtimes; children welcome; bedrooms, with generous breakfasts (the hotel part and restaurant is quite separate) *(N Burrell, N B Pritchard, LYM)*

☆ **Threlkeld** [old main road, bypassed by A66; NY3325], *Salutation*: Friendly small village local used by fell-walkers, with lots of connecting rooms; open fire, cards and dominoes; big helpings of excellent food, well kept Matthew Browns and Theakstons Old Peculier on handpump, welcoming staff; can get crowded *(Simon Barber, C A Holloway)*

Tirril [3½ miles from M6 junction 40 – A66 towards Brough, A6 towards Shap, then B5320 towards Ullswater; NY5126], *Queens Head*: Still a core of low beams, black panelling, old-fashioned settles and inglenook fireplace, but the atmosphere's mainly much more modern – there's even a pizzeria besides more standardised bar food; Matthew Browns and Theakstons on handpump, noticeable fruit machine and juke box, has had live entertainment Thurs; bedrooms *(LYM)*

Torver [A593 S of Coniston; SD2894], *Wilsons Cottage*: Period furniture, log fires, helpful licensees, well kept Tetleys, good bar food; bedrooms comfortable and well equipped but quite cheap *(Phil Ridgewell)*

☆ **Troutbeck** [NY4103], *Mortal Man*: Warm,

clean inn with wide choice of bar food – dishes that have been praised include soup, sandwiches, buttered shrimps, salads, salmon and smoked meats; the main bar is more attractive than the rather sombre second room; friendly welcoming service, well kept Youngers Scotch, reasonable prices; restaurant meals too; on GWG130; bedrooms *(M J Morgan, JH, Syd and Wyn Donald, MGBD, K W Schofield, Mr and Mrs David M Jones, Eileen Broadbent)*

Troutbeck [NY4103], *Queens Head*: Busily popular heavily beamed tourist pub with rambling alcoves – lots of oddities and antique carvings (even a massive Elizabethan four-poster as bar counter); lively atmosphere, fine views from seats outside, Watneys-related real ales, bar food (not cheap), darts; nr GWG130; bedrooms *(Len Beattie, LYM)*

☆ **Ulverston** [King St; SD2978], *Rose & Crown*: Interesting old building with a wide choice of food and well kept Hartleys *(Mrs P Brown, AE, GRE)*

Underbarrow [SD4792], *Punchbowl*: Attractive outside and clean inside, with friendly staff, well kept beer, good bar food *(Denzil Taylor)*

Wigton [West St; NY2648], *Hare & Hounds*: Busy pub, attentive and helpful licensees, excellent food – really worth knowing, in this under-represented area *(Mr and Mrs L D Rainger)*

☆ **Windermere** [SD4109], *Greys*: Exceptional food in both quality and quantity, including a good range of pizzas and running up to steaks and gigantic good value mixed grills; pool, darts, dominoes, juke box and fruit machine; adjoins hotel *(Steve and Carolyn Harvey)*

☆ **Winton** [just off A683; NY7810], *Bay Horse*:
Friendly little village local in lovely moorland setting, two low-ceilinged rooms decorated with Pennine photographs and local fly-tying, good value bar food running up to local pheasant, well kept McEwans 80/-, Youngers and guest real ales; pool in games-room; clean bedrooms *(Alan Hall, LYM)*

Derbyshire and Staffordshire

Quite an influx of new main entries in this area includes two highly praiseworthy but sharply contrasting approaches by different regional breweries to the challenge of bringing old buildings right up to date, as really satisfying pubs. In Burton-on-Trent, Marstons have turned the Albion, right by their brewery, into a spacious showpiece of how much can be done to please a wide variety of customers in a single comfortable pub – and its garden. Over in Derby, Sam Smiths (based in Tadcaster) have taken in hand the derelict remains of a Norman abbey and turned it into a neat little combination of unpretentious pubbiness with considerable architectural interest; it's called the Abbey Inn. Another interesting new venture in Derby, opened in late 1987, is the Brunswick, where people flock for the widest choice of well kept real ales in the area, in a pub that's also an enjoyable place in its own right. Other new entries include the delightfully traditional Olde Gate in Brassington, the cosily welcoming Coach & Horses in Fenny Bentley, the Jervis Arms with its pretty riverside garden in Onecote, the stately fifteenth-century Olde Dog & Partridge in Tutbury (a very comfortable if not cheap place to stay at – with food served long into the evening), the Greyhound in Warslow (also good to stay at, in a more accommodating price-range), and the relaxing Crown at Wrinehill. Changes in other longer-standing main entries include the restaurant opened by the new landlord at the Crown

The Black Lion, Consall

in Abbots Bromley, the Pullman coach at long last converted into unusual bedrooms at the Little Mill up at Rowarth, the brewery opened at the cheerful Rising Sun at Shraleybrook (worth knowing they stay open until midnight), and the new licensees at the Seven Stars at Sandonbank (considerable refurbishments) and the Three Stags Heads at Wardlow Mires – they're trying to keep it as firmly traditional as ever, but now do food (all day). The area's most interesting pub, by a long margin, is still the Yew Tree at Cauldon, one of the country's most idiosyncratic pubs, packed with unusual things. And it exemplifies the unfussy receptiveness which distinguishes so many of the area's licensees: two campers, short of a place to pitch their tent, told us the landlord offered them his lawn – then, when it deluged with rain, let them sleep in the bar, left the heating on for them, and even woke them with a cup of tea. For food, pubs that stand out here include the Druid at Birchover, the Cavalier at Grindon, the Lathkil at Over Haddon (a good place to stay at, too, in fine countryside), the Holly Bush at Seighford and the Malt Shovel overlooking the canal at Shardlow. It's worth knowing, too, about the fine Yorkshire puddings done at the civilised Maynard Arms in Grindleford (another good place to stay at), the generously filled hot meat baps from the Packhorse at Little Longstone, and the low-priced grills and toasted sandwiches that the cheerful Royal Oak at Millthorpe has made rather a speciality. The area has a good many pubs of real character, including the George at Alstonefield, the little Coopers Tavern in Burton-on-Trent, the rambling Black Lion in Butterton (a nice place to stay at), the striking Bull i' th' Thorn a few miles south of Buxton, the Barrel looking out from its ridge near Foolow, the civilised Chequers on Froggatt Edge, the spick-and-span Old Bulls Head at Little Hucklow (with its fine collection of agricultural machinery outside; though it was put on the market in 1989, as we went to press in the summer the latest indications were that it wasn't likely to change hands before well into 1990), and the handsome Peacock at Rowsley (a comfortable place to stay at). Among the Lucky Dip entries at the end of the chapter we'd pick out as particularly promising, in Staffordshire, the Burton Bridge Brewery in Burton-on-Trent (for its own-brewed beers), Green Man at Clifton Campville and Red Lion in Ipstones; and in Derbyshire itself, the Devonshire Arms at Beeley, Cheshire Cheese at Hope, Red Lion at Litton (especially for food), Wanted Inn at Sparrowpit, Chequers at Ticknall and Bulls Head at Wardlow; two places that seem to stand out for spawning good pubs are Shardlow and the area around Chinley and Hayfield.

ABBOTS BROMLEY (Staffs)   SK0724 Map 7

Crown 🏠

The change of licensee in this welcoming village inn doesn't seem to have affected standards adversely; readers are still warm in their praise, in particular, of the accommodation and the breakfasts. The modernised lounge bar has soft lighting and carpets, comfortable plush button-back banquettes, modern panelling, and fresh flowers. In the public bar there are darts, dominoes, cribbage and a fruit machine; piped music. The bar food includes soup (95p), sandwiches, vegetarian dishes, salmon steak (£5.95), and steaks (from £6.25); well kept Bass on electric pump. They now have a separate restaurant. (*Recommended by S G Game, David Barnes, Jon Wainwright, S M Shaw, M J How*)

Bass   Licensee Philip Barnes   Real ale   Meals and snacks (until 10 evenings) Restaurant   Children welcome   Open 11–3, 6–11; 11–2.30, 7–11 in winter Bedrooms tel Burton-on-Trent (0283) 840227; £15/£27.50

ALREWAS (Staffs)   SK1714 Map 7
George & Dragon 🛏
High Street; bypassed village signposted from A38 and A513

The warm, low-beamed rooms which lead off the central servery of this attractive village inn are furnished in a simple but homely way, with flagstones and a large number of brass candlesticks; the photographs hanging above the remarkably long inglenook mantelpiece testify to the family's forty-year ownership. There's a splendid collection of commemorative Royal china in the large room at one side. Bar food includes sandwiches (from 90p), ploughman's (£2), cold meat with crusty bread (£2), a wide choice of hot dishes such as omelettes (from £2), salads (from £2.40), vegetarian dishes (from £2.60), home-made pies (£2.80), gammon with egg or pineapple (£4.20) and sirloin steak (£7), with a choice of baked potatoes or chips; efficient service. Well kept Marstons Pedigree on handpump; dominoes, cribbage, fruit machine, piped music. The attractive, partly covered garden has a terrace (where there are occasional barbecues) and a well serviced children's play area, with a swing, playboat and aviary with cockatiels and other birds, white doves strutting along the tops of the walls and roofs, and a play elephant called Eric. The modern bedrooms are in a separate block. *(Recommended by Christopher Knowles-Fitton, Tim and Lynne Crawford, Pamela and Merlyn Horswell, Mandy and Michael Challis, Nigel Hopkins)*

Marstons   Licensees Ray and Mary Stanbrook   Real ale   Meals and snacks (until 10 evenings, not Sun or 25 Dec)   Restaurant (evenings)   Children welcome if eating Open 11–2.30, 6–11 all year   Bedrooms tel Burton-on-Trent (0283) 790202; £28B/£38B

ALSTONEFIELD (Staffs)   SK1355 Map 7
George
Village signposted from A515 Ashbourne–Buxton

The atmosphere in this snug, unspoilt sixteenth-century inn is pleasant and friendly; the popular low-beamed bar has darkening cream walls, a fine collection of old Peak District photographs and drawings, a good many foreign banknotes, pewter tankards hanging by the copper-topped bar counter and a good winter fire. In the spacious family-room there are lots of wheel-back chairs around tables. The simple but much appreciated food is ordered at the kitchen door – so you can cast an approving eye over the hygiene yourself; it includes soup or sandwiches (£1.10), ploughman's (£2.45), home-made Spanish quiche (£3.20), and meat and potato pie or lasagne (£3.30); considerate service. Well kept Ansells and Ind Coope Burton on handpump; darts, dominoes, fruit machine. The pretty rockery in the sheltered and spacious back stableyard has picnic seats, and beneath the pretty inn sign at the front there are some stone seats looking on to the stone-built farming hamlet. It's good walking territory, and you can arrange with the landlord to camp on the croft. *(Recommended by C McDowall, Peter Walker, Jon Wainwright, Keith Mills, E J Alcock, P Miller, Jenny Seller, BKA, Lee Goulding, Dr and Mrs R J Ashleigh, D Stephenson, M A and W R Proctor, Brian and Anna Marsden)*

Free house   Licensees Richard and Sue Grandjean   Real ale   Meals and snacks (until 10 evenings)   Open 11–2.30, 6–11; opens 7 in winter; closed 25 Dec

BAMFORD (Derbys)   SK2083 Map 7
Derwent 🛏
Main Street (A6013)

The relaxed and spacious atmosphere in this quiet pub is partly due to its unusual layout: the servery is in a central carpeted hall, from where several rooms lead off. One of these has an airy feel, with lots of wooden tables, big pictures on its wood-effect panelling, and big sunny windows; another has an old-fashioned green plush wall seat curving all around it (including two more bay windows), and its partly panelled walls are hung with yokes, heavy-horse harness and trace shafts; there are usually lots of fresh flowers and potted plants. The games bar (with its local team photographs) has darts, table skittles, pool, fruit machine, shove-ha'penny, cribbage, shut-the-box; piped music. Well kept Stones Best, Wards Sheffield Best and Tetleys on handpump. Bar food ranges from sandwiches (from £1.25), soup (£1.20) and ploughman's (£2.75), through steak and kidney pie or lasagne (£3) and chicken breast in a wine sauce (£4.25), to steaks (from £5.25); home-made puddings (95p). The charming little dining-room has stripped-pine panelling. There are seats in the garden. *(Recommended by Lee Goulding, Diane Hall, Steve Mitcheson, Anne Collins, KC, Mr and Mrs H Hearnshaw, Brian and Anna Marsden, W P P Clarke, Michael Lloyd, M A and W R Proctor, Jon Wainwright)*

Free house   Licensees David and Angela Ryan   Real ale   Meals and snacks   Children welcome   Restaurant   Open 11–11 all year   Bedrooms tel Hope Valley (0433) 51395; £21(£25B)/£31(£37B)

BIRCH VALE (Derbys)   SK0287   Map 7

Sycamore 🛏

From A6015 take Station Road towards Thornsett

The main bar area in this food-orientated pub is divided into two areas – upstairs is primarily for eaters (you can book except on Saturday evening and Sunday lunchtime, and there's a sensible table-queue system with a 'waiting board' for busy times), the downstairs one for drinkers; there's an indoor fountain down here. Four warmly welcoming connecting carpeted rooms have some stripped brick walls, and a variety of seats including wheel-back chairs, pews, button-back red plush wall banquettes, mate's chairs, high seats by eating-ledges, and settees. There's a wide choice of bar food, including soup (95p), sandwiches (£1.55), ploughman's (£2.35), lasagne or moussaka (£2.95), home-made steak and kidney pie (£3.35), curry (£3.65), vegetable Stroganoff (£3.95), a good range of steaks (£6.95), with children's dishes (from £1.15) and lots of rich puddings (from £1.55). The pub also has its own sun and sauna fitness room. Below the pub (where you can also find the main car park), there are some attractively spacious valley gardens by a stream; these have good solid swings, seesaw, and a climbing-frame made of trunks and logs, a play-tree, canaries in an aviary, and rabbits; also a summer drinks-and-ice-cream bar. There are do-it-yourself summer barbecues on a terrace up above. Disco in downstairs bar on Fridays and Sundays; no dogs. *(Recommended by Alan Skull, David Waterhouse, Brian and Anna Marsden)*

Free house   Licensees Malcolm and Christine Nash   Meals and snacks (12–2.30, 5.30–10.30)   Children welcome   Open 12–3, 5.30–11 all year; all day Sat in summer Bedrooms tel New Mills (0663) 42715; £27.50B/£37.50B

BIRCHOVER (Derbys)   SK2462   Map 7

Druid 🍺

Village signposted from B5056

In this off-the-beaten-track, creeper-covered gritstone house the emphasis is very much on the food side of things; it's not the sort of place one visits just for a casual drink. The unusually wide range of, in some cases, award-winning food is chalked up on three large blackboards, and includes soups (£1.30), fillet of herring in sour cream sauce or walnut pâté (£2.40), prawns in hot garlic butter with apple and celery or melon filled with prawns and mayonnaise (£2.80) and a generous three-cheese ploughman's (£3.40); main courses can include such dishes as steak and mussel pie (£4.24), lasagne, Greek moussaka or spaghetti bolognese (£3.90), grilled pork chop with chilled cream, apple and French mustard (£4.80), lamb curry with yoghurt, a dish of nuts, mango chutney and a poppadum (£4.90), lamb cooked Turkish-style with apricot, almonds, cumin, cardamom, garlic and yoghurt or chicken cooked in lemon, lime, ginger and banana (£5.90), chicken Kiev (£6.40), and sirloin steak (from £6.60); there's also a decent range of vegetarian dishes like casserole with red kidney beans (£3.40), fruit and vegetable curry or steamed Chinese vegetables in a sweet-and-sour sauce (£4.20) and almond risotto (£4.40); enterprising puddings such as bakewell pudding and chocolate roulade (all at £2); half-price helpings for children. At weekends, when it can get very crowded, it may be advisable to book for meals. The bar itself is strikingly simple, with green plush-upholstered wooden wall benches, small dining-chairs and stools around straightforward tables and a little coal fire. The spacious and airy two-storey dining-extension, candle-lit at night, has pink plush seats on olive-green carpet and pepper-grinders and sea salt on all the tables. Well kept Marstons Pedigree on handpump and a good collection of malt whiskies; a small public bar has darts, dominoes, cribbage and fruit machine; well reproduced classical music. The pub's name was reputedly inspired, during the eighteenth-century craze for druids, by a strange cave behind it, among the beech trees sprouting from the Row Tor. There are picnic-table sets in front. *(Recommended by Pat and Norman Godley, Alan Skull, A F C Young, Keith Bloomfield, Jim Wiltshire, Brian and Genie Smart, M A and W R Proctor, Paul and Margaret Baker, Roger Broadie, Mrs P Cardy, BKA, Dr and Mrs R J Ashleigh, K G A Lewis, AE)*

Free house   Licensee Brian Bunce   Real ale   Meals and snacks (not evening 26 Dec)
Bookings tel Winster (062 988) 302   Children in bar until 8, and must be eating
Open 12–3, 7–11 all year; closed 25 Dec

BRASSINGTON (Derbys)   SK2354 Map 7
Olde Gate

Village signposted off B5056 and B5035 NE of Ashbourne

The public bar on the right has a lovely old kitchen range with lots of gleaming copper pots, and stone-mullioned windows that look across the garden to small silvery-walled pastures; though the date outside is 1874, it was built in 1616, of magnesian limestone and timbers salvaged from Armada wrecks exchanged for lead mined here. Traditional furnishings include antique settles, pewter mugs hang from one beam, embossed Doulton stoneware flagons on a side shelf, and an ancient wall clock; the atmosphere's pleasantly relaxed. On the left of a small hatch-served lobby, another beamed room has tables with scrubbed tops, stripped panelled settles, and a fire under a huge mantelbeam. Good value bar food changing day by day includes open sandwiches (from £2.25), salads (from £3.25), home-made hot dishes such as lasagne (£3.25) and Madras curry (£3.50), and traditional English puddings with custard – they don't do chips; well kept Marstons Pedigree on handpump; darts, cribbage, dominoes. The small front yard has a couple of benches – a nice spot in summer to listen to the village bell-ringers practising on Friday evenings (best from 8 to 9, as it's learners earlier). *(Recommended by Alastair Campbell, Tim and Lynne Crawford, Derek and Sylvia Stephenson)*

Marstons   Licensee Paul Scott Burlinson   Real ale   Meals and snacks (not Mon evening)
Children in room on left until 9   Open 11.30–3, 6–11 all year

BURTON-ON-TRENT (Staffs)   SK2423 Map 7
Albion

Shobnall Road (close to Marstons Brewery, out by A38 flyover)

The huge carpeted lounge of this attractively modernised family pub has good solid furnishings, nice Victorian reproductions on the flowery-papered walls, deep maroon swagged velvet curtains, a long and efficiently staffed bar counter, and a side area, slightly raised behind a balustrade, with a button-back leather settee, great winged armchair and other more parlourish furnishings. It opens into a conservatory with cane chairs around marble-topped tables, which in turn leads out into a spacious fairy-lit garden with swings, a children's bar, a yew walk and a fenced-off stream. The big public bar is comfortable and well decorated too, with pool, darts, fruit machine and juke box. As you'd expect from the position, the Marstons Pedigree on handpump here is in excellent condition. Bar food includes rolls (from 70p, hot meat ones £1.45), ploughman's (from £1.70), salads (£2.65), curry or steak and kidney pie (£2.75) and a roast of the day (£3.30). *(Recommended by Richard Sanders, Colin Gooch, Dr and Mrs C D E Morris)*

Marstons   Licensee Malcolm Wink   Real ale   Meals and snacks (lunchtime)   Children's room   Open 11–2.30, 5.30–11 all year

Coopers Tavern

Cross Street; off Station Street but a No Entry – heading N down High Street then Station Road from centre, pass Bass brewery and turn left into Milton Street (from which the pub has a back entrance)

Executives from the brewery across the road enjoy their lunch breaks here too much to be keen on any real change, so plans for more whole-hearted refurbishment have been dropped in favour of a gentle clean-up. This leaves the back tap-room unspoilt and old fashioned, with simple tables, stools, settles and now an old fireplace, as well as the pub's showpiece, an ancient gas meter which is still in working order; there's no counter here, but Bass is tapped straight from a row of splendid casks. The front bar is similarly decorated in cream and burgundy, and has a piano, and barrels on the serving-counter; darts, dominoes, table skittles and a fruit machine; piped music. Bar food includes filled cobs (50p, sausage or bacon 70p), toasties (from 70p), hot pork, stuffing and apple sauce baps (75p), and pie and chips or ploughman's (£1.65). The museum in the nearby gleaming Bass brewery is well worth a visit. *(Recommended by Rob and Gill Weeks, Angus Lindsay, A V Lewis, Richard Sanders, Pete Storey)*

Bass   Licensees Barry and Helen Knight   Real ale   Meals and snacks (11.30–2.30, 5.30–10.30)   Children welcome   Open 11–2.30, 5–11

BUTTERTON (Staffs)   SK0756 Map 7

Black Lion ★ ⌂

Village signposted from B5053

The layout of the several rooms in this eighteenth-century stone village inn is intriguing, rambling and unspoilt: one, with a low black beam-and-board ceiling, has a fine old red leatherette settle around its good log fire, well polished mahogany tables, and comfortable old bar stools with backrests. An inner room has a lively parakeet called Sergeant Bilko, a Liberty-print sofa and a fine old kitchen range. A third has red plush button-back banquettes around sewing-machine tables; the dining-room has a good log fire. There are attractive Victorian prints throughout. Picnic-table sets and rustic seats on the prettily planted terrace have a quiet view of the surrounding hills. Bar food includes sandwiches (95p), ploughman's or salads (£2.70), roast chicken or steak and kidney pie (£2.95), lasagne, moussaka or vegetarian lasagne (£3.15), liver, bacon and onions (£3.20), beef in red wine (£3.85) and rump steak (£4.95), as well as daily specials such as chicken provençal (£3.45) and steak and mushroom casserole (£3.65); friendly service. McEwans 70/- and 80/- and Youngers No 3 on handpump; darts, shove-ha'penny, dominoes, table skittles, juke box, space game, fruit machine, and separate well lit pool-room; piped music. The local church, with its tall and elegant spire, is nearby, as is the Manifold

---

The opening hours we quote are for weekdays; in England and Wales, Sunday hours are now always 12–3, 7–10.30.

Valley. *(Recommended by Steve Mitcheson, Anne Collins, D R and J A Munford, Graham Bush, David Eversley, E J Waller, M A and W R Proctor, AHNR, BKA, Nick Dowson, Alison Hayward, Lee Goulding)*

Free house   Licensees Ron, Derek and Marie-Pierre Smith   Real ale   Meals and snacks Restaurant   Children welcome   Open 11–3, 7–11 all year; may open longer afternoons; closed lunchtime Weds   Bedrooms tel Onecote (053 88) 232; £19.55B/£32.20B

nr BUXTON (Derbys)   SK0673 Map 7

Bull i' th' Thorn ★

Ashbourne Road (A515) 6 miles S of Buxton, nr Hurdlow; OS Sheet 119 reference 128665

This attractive roadside farmhouse was first known as the Bull in 1472, then as Hurdlow House of Hurdlow Thorn in the seventeenth century; its present title seems to be a combination of the two. A lively carving over the main entrance depicts a bull caught in a thornbush; there are others of an eagle with a freshly caught hare, and some spaniels chasing a rabbit. The interior very much lives up to its interesting exterior: the main bar is a striking Tudor hall, the oldest part of the inn and sufficiently authentically decorated for one reader to feel transported back in time; it's full of oak beams, joists, and squared panelling, and furnished with ancient carved and panelled seats cut into the thick walls, a longcase clock, armour, swords, blunderbusses and so forth, and old flagstones stepping shallowly down to a big open fire. The straightforward bar food includes sandwiches (from 50p), soup (70p), ploughman's (£1.70), hot dishes such as sausages (£1.50), cottage pie and peas (£2), steak and kidney pie, roast beef or scampi (£2.75), salads (from £2; prawn £3) and sirloin steak (£4.75); children's dishes (£1) and a Sunday roast lunch (£3); friendly service. An adjoining room has darts, pool, dominoes, fruit machine and a juke box; well kept Robinsons Best on handpump. The family-room opens on to a terrace and big lawn, with swings, and there are more tables in a sheltered angle in front. *(Recommended by Steve Mitcheson, Anne Collins, Roy and Margaret Randle, Mrs M Price, J E Rycroft, R F Moat, M A and W R Proctor)*

Robinsons   Licensees Bob and Judith Haywood   Real ale   Meals and snacks   Children in family- and games-rooms   Open 11–3, 6–11 all year   Two bedrooms tel Longnor (029 883) 348; £20

CASTLETON (Derbys)   SK1583 Map 7

Castle Hotel 🛏

High Street at junction with Castle Street

The atmosphere inside this Peak District inn has a distinctly historical feel: in the plush bars there are stripped stone walls with built-in cabinets, an open fire, finely carved early seventeenth-century beams and, in one room, ancient flagstones. Bar food includes soup or Yorkshire pudding with onion gravy (95p), sandwiches (from £1.25), fresh crudités (£1.85), club sandwich (£1.95), ploughman's or macaroni cheese (£1.95), stuffed pancakes (£2.35), Madras curry (£2.95), gammon (£3.55), seafood Mornay (£3.95), and steak (£4.95); darts. The haunted feel to which some readers testify may (or may not) be borne out by the fact that a woman is said to have been buried under its threshold – a throwback to pagan rites designed to bring prosperity to a new building; or that the passage to the restaurant is said to have the ghost of a bride who, instead of enjoying her planned wedding breakfast here, died broken-hearted when she was left at the altar. The village is just below the ruins of Peveril Castle and handy for some of Derbyshire's most spectacular caves; on *Good Walks Guide* Walk 81. Seats outside. *(Recommended by Steve Mitcheson, Anne Collins, Mike Tucker, Alistair Campbell)*

Bass   Licensee Jose Rodriguez   Meals and snacks   Restaurant   Children welcome   Open 11–11; 11–3, 6–11 in winter   Bedrooms tel Hope Valley (0433) 20578; £35B/£45B

CAULDON (Staffs) SK0749 Map 7
Yew Tree ★ ★ ★

Village signposted from A523 and A52 about 8 miles W of Ashbourne; OS Sheet 119 reference 075493

Don't expect any airs and graces here: this unashamedly basic yet fascinating pub wins its top rating chiefly on the strength of the extraordinary collections which Alan East has filled it with (we can never understand where he finds the space to go on adding to them). The most unusual things are the working Polyphons and Symphonions – a couple more of these this year. They're the nineteenth-century culmination of the musical box, often taller than a person, each with quite a repertoire of tunes and of the most elaborate sound-effects; go with plenty of 2p pieces to work them. On the hour, strong competition comes from the fine set of longcase clocks in the gallery just above the entrance, and when Mr East can be tempted from behind the bar the pianola chimes in happily, too (we've not heard of his medieval leather serpent being played yet, but on one visit we found the ancient valve radio set struggling to make itself heard). Here and there you'll find several penny-farthings, an old sit-and-stride boneshaker, a rocking horse, swordfish blades, ancient guns and pistols, even a fine marquetry cabinet crammed with notable early Staffordshire pottery – and above the bar an odd iron dog-carrier (don't ask how it works!). Furnishings range from soggily sprung sofas to heavy eighteenth-century carved settles; dim lamps hang from the beams. The atmosphere is down to earth but exceptionally friendly, and prices for the hot sausage rolls (25p), big pork pies (40p), big filled baps (from 60p), quiche (£1) and smoked mackerel (£1.20) are remarkably low, as they are for the drinks – including well kept Bass, Burton Bridge and M&B Mild on handpump or tapped from the cask, and some interesting malt whiskies such as overproof Glenfarclas. Darts, shove-ha'penny, table skittles (taken very seriously here), dominoes and cribbage. This last year, the old brick pub hiding behind its big yew tree has been easier to spot, as a 1929 Dennis bus has often been parked outside. Dovedale and the Manifold Valley are not far away. (*Recommended by Chris Raisin, Graham Doyle, Hazel Morgan, Steve Mitcheson, Anne Collins, Margaret and Roy Randle, WHBM, David and Flo Wallington, Steve and Carolyn Harvey, Alan Skull, Klaus and Elizabeth Leist, Rob and Gill Weeks, David Barnes, Nick Dowson, Alison Hayward, Angus Lindsay, Jenny Seller, M A and W R Proctor, Dr Aristos Markantonakis, BKA, JV, Laurence Manning, Gordon and Daphne, Richard Sanders*)

Free house Licensee Alan East   Real ale   Snacks (generally something to eat any time they're open)   Children in Polyphon room   Open 10–3 (4 if needed on Sat), 6–11 all year

CHEDDLETON (Staffs) SJ9651 Map 7
Boat

Basford Bridge Lane; off A520

Not unlike the barges with which the surrounding canals are populated, this pub's interior is long and narrow, with low plank ceilings to match. The furnishings are simple, with upholstered wall benches and wooden tables at one end, copper ones at the other. There are good moorings for barges, and it's close to the little Caldon Canal, with its attractive, brightly painted boats. Bar food includes baps (50p), sandwiches (from 70p), basket meals (from £1.50), cheese salad (£3), gammon (£4) and steak (£5). Marstons Burton and Pedigree on handpump, and a decent range of malts; darts, dominoes, fruit machine, space game, piped music. There are benches at the front, and tables and seats under the new canopy; occasional barbecues out here. The pub is handy for the North Staffordshire Steam Railway museum. (*Recommended by Jon Wainwright, Janet Williams; more reports please*)

Marstons   Licensees Mr and Mrs Wooliscroft   Real ale   Meals and snacks (12–2, 6–8; only sandwiches Sun lunchtime)   Children in eating area   Open 11.30–3, 6–11 all year

CONSALL (Staffs)   SJ9748 Map 7

Black Lion   [*illustrated on page 169*]

Consallforge; from A522 just S of Wetley Rocks (which is E of Stoke-on-Trent) follow Consall turn-off right through village, then turn right into Nature Park, with easy access to the pub from its car park; OS Sheets 118 and 119 reference 000491

This charmingly down-at-heel, unspoilt and welcoming canalside pub has cafe seats and Formica tables, plain brick walls, a good coal fire on cool days, and straightforward bar food. It's attractively situated near the Caldon Canal and the weir on the River Churnet, and, although the new access road means it no longer has quite such a distinctive sense of isolation in this deep wooded valley, it's still pleasantly remote; the two traditional walks to it – from the footpath sign just past the Old Hall on the village road, or along the canal from Cheddleton – are still well worth making. Marstons Pedigree and Ruddles County on handpump; sensibly placed darts at one end, also table skittles, dominoes, cribbage, maybe piped music. *(Recommended by Richard Sanders, G C Hixon; more up-to-date reports please)*

Free house   Real ale   Meals and snacks   Children welcome   Open 10.30–2.30, 6–11 all year

DERBY   SK3438 Map 7

Abbey Inn

Darley Street; coming in from A38/A6 roundabout, take first left signposted Darley Abbey, then left into Old Road signposted to toll bridge, turning right just before the bridge itself

This smallish pub earns high marks for its sensitive rehabilitation of the derelict remains of an eleventh-century monastery. As we went to press changes were still under way – for instance, the kitchens had not yet been completed, though by the time this book is published there should be a full range of bar food from sandwiches to lasagne, curry, steak pies and so forth. And the downstairs bar was still due for some development, though already it was attractive for its mix of brickwork and massive stone (leaning, in the case of the outer wall), deep inglenook, studded oak doors and so forth. A new spiral stone staircase leads up to a bigger and quieter bar where the restored stonework is more notable, especially in the modelling of the windows; there are handsome reconstructed high oak rafters and trusses, and neat cushioned pews are built into stalls around the tables. Besides a couple of sturdy teak seats outside, there are stone side-steps to sit on, and a stone well-head; customers tend to stray into the park opposite, by a weir on the Derwent. Well kept Sam Smiths Museum and Old Brewery on handpump; darts, cribbage, dominoes, cards, piped music (reproduced much better upstairs than down on our visit); maybe quiz nights; quietly relaxed atmosphere. *(Recommended by Chris Raisin)*

Sam Smiths   Licensees Chris and Simon Meyers   Real ale   Meals and snacks (probably lunchtime, not Sun)   Children in eating area at lunchtime   Open 11–2.30, 6 (7 in winter)–11 all year; open all day Sat if fine

Brunswick

1 Railway Terrace; close to Derby Midland railway station

Very much what we think of as a CAMRA (Campaign for Real Ale) pub, this serves a remarkable range of real ales in good condition: on our visit they had Bass, Batemans Mild, Burton Bridge Bitter, Hook Norton Old Hooky, Marstons Pedigree, Morrells Varsity, Ringwood Old Thumper, Timothy Taylors Landlord, Wadworths 6X and Wards Kirby and experimental Weizenbier on handpump or tapped from the cask, as well as a couple of farm ciders. Over four days around 3 October (anniversary of their opening in 1987) they have a beer festival, with many more on offer, and around March 1990 they hope their own new brewery will have come on stream. The pub, originally one of England's oldest railway pubs (it was built in 1842), has been thoughtfully renovated, making the most of its rather unusual floor-plan. There are original flagstones throughout downstairs, with heavy railway-reminiscent furniture in the high-ceilinged panelled serving bar, high-backed wall settles in a no-smoking room with swan's-neck lamps and little old-fashioned prints, and, behind a curved glazed partition wall, a quietly chatty family parlour narrowing to the apex of the triangular building. Darts, cribbage, dominoes, fruit machine, occasional piped music; good friendly atmosphere, coal fires. Filled rolls only are served downstairs; bar lunches such as salads and beef in Old Hooky (£2.25) are served in the upstairs dining-room. There are seats in the yard behind. *(Recommended by Carl Southwell, Angie and Dave Parkes, Chris Raisin)*

Free house   Licensee Trevor Harris   Real ale   Meals and snacks (11.30–2.30; only rolls Sun)   Children in dining-room and parlour   Upstairs folk club alternate Suns   Open 11–11 all year

FENNY BENTLEY (Derbys)   SK1750 Map 7
Coach & Horses
A515 N of Ashbourne

Quietly welcoming, this former seventeenth-century coaching-inn has a nice little back room with dark green leafy Victorian wallpaper, old prints and engravings, and comfortable wall seats. There are more old prints in the black-beamed front bar, which has flowery-cushioned wall settles and library chairs around the dark tables on its Turkey carpet; there's a huge mirror. Under the popular new licensees, quickly served good value bar food includes filled baps (85p), soup (90p), sandwiches (£1.20), choice of ploughman's (£1.50), burgers or filled baked potatoes (from £1.50), home-made pies such as steak and kidney (£2.95), salads (£3.20), gammon and egg (£4.25) and steaks running up to generously accompanied sixteen-ounce ones (£7.95 – they give you a free pint if you eat your plate clean). Well kept Bass on handpump, good coffee, unobtrusive piped music. There are picnic-table sets on the back grass by an elder tree, with rustic benches and white tables and chairs under cocktail parasols on the terrace in front of this pretty rendered stone house. *(Recommended by A J Woodhouse, Denzil Taylor)*

Bass   Licensee Edward Anderson   Real ale   Meals and snacks   Restaurant tel Thorpe Cloud (033 529) 246   Open 11–2.30, 6.30–11 all year

nr FOOLOW (Derbys)   SK1976 Map 7
Barrel
Bretton; signposted from Foolow, which itself is signposted from A623 just E of junction with B6465 to Bakewell

There are fine views from the breezy front terrace of this tradional pub to the pastures below the high ridge. Its welcoming, beamed bar is a series of rooms divided by the stubs of massive knocked-through stone walls; the varied seating includes some old barrels, a Delft shelf has lots of old glass and china bottles, and the cream walls are decorated with local maps, an aerial photograph, a rack of clay pipes, poems about the pub and a clock which moves in an anti-clockwise direction. Its far end is very snug, with a leather-cushioned settle and built-in corner wall-bench by an antique oak table in front of the open fire. Straightforward food includes sandwiches (from 80p), ploughman's (£1.65) and open prawn baps or poacher's pie (£2.10). Well kept Stones and Bass Mild on electric pump, and a good choice of whiskies. *(Recommended by Brian and Anna Marsden, Peter and Moyna Lynch, M A and W R Proctor, Keith and Sheila Baxter, Jon Wainwright)*

Bass   Real ale   Snacks (not Thurs evening)   Children in eating area   Open 12–3, 6.30–11 all year

FROGGATT EDGE (Derbys) SK2477 Map 7

Chequers

B6054, off A623 N of Bakewell; OS Sheet 119 reference 247761

In this partly sixteenth-century, old fashioned and comfortable inn there are antique prints on the white walls (partly stripped back to big dark stone blocks), a big solid-fuel stove and library chairs or small high-backed winged settles on its well waxed floorboards. One corner has a big grandfather clock, another a nicely carved oak cupboard; the richly varnished beam-and-board ceiling is very attractive. Outside there are white benches at the front, and tables on the back terrace. Well kept Wards Sheffield Best on handpump, and a good range of wines and whiskies. Bar food includes a generous soup (90p), home-cooked meat sandwiches (from 95p; prawn £2.25), ploughman's (£2.35), quiche or plaice (£2.75) and salads (from £2.95); there are 'international nights' – Chinese say, or, on a less nationalist note, a seafood-and-strawberry theme – in the restaurant on the last Thursday and Friday of each month. It's close to a striking Peak District edge, and looks out over an attractive valley. Note that they have quite a strict policy towards children. *(Recommended by Tim and Lynne Crawford, E J Waller, Alan Skull, A B Garside, G and M Brooke-Williams, William Rodgers, Jon Wainwright)*

Wards   Licensee Ian McLeod   Real ale   Meals and snacks (not Sat or Sun evening) Restaurant   Children in restaurant only   Open 11–3, 6–11 all year Bedrooms tel Hope Valley (0433) 30231; £18/£26

GRINDLEFORD (Derbys) SK2478 Map 7

Maynard Arms 🍺

B6521 N of village

The bar food in this stately stone-built small hotel includes a Yorkshire pudding filled with roast beef and gravy, turkey or stew (£3.25, not Sunday lunchtime), as well as soup (80p), filled cobs or sandwiches (90p), pâté (£1.95), a traditional breakfast (£2.50, served lunchtime and evening), ploughman's or fish and chips (£2.50), curry (£3.25), rabbit casserole or gammon (£3.25), home-made steak and oyster pie (£3.50, with a twenty-minute wait), and eight-ounce steaks (£5.50); when it's busy there can be considerable delays, and it's often advisable to book. The main bar is spacious, and has comfortable rust-coloured plush seats on the brown patterned carpet, some dark panelling, silver tankards above the bar, tapestry wall hangings and a high ceiling. Off the hall there's a smaller green plush bar. Stones on handpump; piped music, darts and dominoes. The restaurant looks out over the neatly kept garden to the valley. *(Recommended by Peter and Moyna Lynch, WTF, Brian and Anna Marsden, G and M Brooke-Williams, Jon Wainwright)*

Stones (Bass)   Licensees Bob Graham and Helen Siddall   Real ale   Meals and snacks (5.30–9.30 evenings)   Restaurant   Children in eating area   Open 11–3, 5.30–11 all year; all day Sat   Bedrooms tel Hope Valley (0433) 30321; £41B/£52B

GRINDON (Staffs) SK0854 Map 7

Cavalier ⊛

Village signposted from B5033 just over 2 miles N of junction with A523

The sixteenth-century building which houses this friendly village-edge pub has been used variously as a farmhouse, smithy and undertakers' (the ghost's said to be most active in summer). It's pleasantly placed in open country, just a mile from the Manifold Valley, and its two rooms are decorated with old guns and other ancient weapons, including cuirasses, breastplates and so forth; there are also decorative plates on the walls, tiny shoes, lots of brass round one of the open fires, iron tools, and harness with horsebrasses. Furnishings are simple and traditional, with some Turkey carpet on the old flooring tiles, and a high beam-and-plank ceiling. The short choice of good bar food comes in decent helpings, including ploughman's (from £2.40), a hot chilli con carne (£3.25), lasagne or lamb and apricot pie (£3.50), trout (£4.95), charcoal-grilled steaks (from £6.95), and prawn creole (£7.50), with a good choice of often interesting dishes of the day. Well kept Marstons Burton and Pedigree, Wards Sheffield Best and a selection of guest beers on handpump, as well as a wide range of malt whiskies, unusual bottled beers and a decent wine list; darts, pool, dominoes, piped music. There's an engaging rustic garden, with swings, and the area is popular with walkers and cyclists. *(Recommended by Chris Raisin, Lee Goulding, Diane Hall, Tim and Lynne Crawford)*

Free house   Licensee Lynda Blunden   Real ale   Meals and snacks (not Mon evening) Restaurant tel Onecote (0538) 8285 (not Mon evening)   Children in side family-room and restaurant   Live entertainment Fri evening and some Sun lunchtimes   Open 12–3.30, 7–11; closed Mon lunchtime in summer, Mon–Weds lunchtime in winter

HARDWICK HALL (Derbys)   SK4663 Map 7
Hardwick Inn

4½ miles from M1 junction 29: A617 towards Mansfield, then in Glapwell turn right at Hardwick Hall signpost and keep on to the far side of the park; can also be reached from A6010 via Stainsby

This seventeenth-century golden stone house was originally the lodge for the nearby Elizabethan Hall; it's now owned, along with its splendid park, by the National Trust. For one reader the atmosphere in the popular bar is that of an old-fashioned, comfortable town pub, depite its rural position; certainly there's an easy-going and welcoming feel in the several separate rooms. The carpeted lounge has varnished wooden tables, comfortably upholstered wall settles, tub chairs and stools, and stone-mullioned latticed windows. Bar food includes sandwiches, soup (85p), pâté (£1.40), ploughman's (from £2.20), Lincolnshire sausage (£2.25), home-made steak and kidney pie (£2.85), plaice or haddock (£2.95), gammon and egg or pineapple (£3.60) and steaks (from £5.65); carvery and salad bar (Wednesday to Sunday); well kept Youngers Scotch and IPA on handpump. There are extensive lawns all around. *(Recommended by Alan Skull, Dr Keith Bloomfield, Mike and Mandy Challis, Thomas Nott, Richard Sanders, B M Eldridge, Jane and Niall, Tim and Lynne Crawford, M A and W R Proctor, Roger Bellingham)*

Free house   Licensees Peter and Pauline Batty   Real ale   Meals and snacks (not Sun evening)   Restaurant tel Chesterfield (0246) 850245   Children in restaurant and family-room   Open 11.30–3, 6.30–11 all year

nr HARTINGTON (Derbys)   SK1360 Map 7
Jug & Glass

Newhaven; on A515 about 1 mile N of junction with A5012; OS Sheet 119 reference 156614

The cosy bar in this stikingly isolated pub has a warm and welcoming atmosphere; its furnishings are simple, and there's lots of flowery china hanging from low beams, a cuckoo clock and winter coal fires (as well as central heating). Another room with flock wallpaper takes the overflow when the small main bar gets too crowded. In the attractive dining-room there's a stone-pillared fireplace with an old oak mantelbeam. The emphasis is very much on the fine range of beers: Hardys and Hansons Best, Marstons Pedigree and Owd Rodger, Ruddles Best and County, Theakstons XB and a weekly guest beer on handpump; on the second Wednesday of July they hold a mini-beer festival, with all beers at half price. Bar food includes home-made soup (90p), ploughman's (£2.25), Cornish pasty (£2.50), haddock or vegetable lasagne (£3), gammon (£5) and steaks (from seven-ounce sirloin £5.50); weekend specials, and possibly a range of curries; they use local meat, and at 24 hours' notice will do a full leg of lamb, loin of pork or rib of beef to carve yourself (£6.50 each including starters, puddings and coffee, minimum four people – you can take home what's left). Darts, dominoes, cribbage, fruit machine, juke box; piped music. There are tables outside under cocktail parasols on the recently enlarged patio. The exterior has been repainted with highly durable paint to protect it from the wildness of its lonely moorland position. *(Recommended by JMC, M A and W R Proctor, Richard Sanders, Jon Wainwright, Jenny Seller, Rob and Gill Weeks)*

Free house   Licensee John Bryan   Real ale   Meals and snacks (11–2.30, 7–10)   Restaurant   tel Hartington (0298) 84224   Children welcome   Open 11–4, 6–11 all year

LITTLE HUCKLOW (Derbys)   SK1678 Map 7
Old Bulls Head ★
Pub signposted from B6049

This highly praised little pub can be surprisingly popular, considering its isolated position on upland sheep pastures. The two immaculate small oak-beamed rooms have interesting collections of locally mined semi-precious stones and of antique brass and iron household tools; the built-in settles are comfortably cushioned, and there's a coal fire in a neatly restored stone hearth. One room is served from a hatch, the other over a polished bar counter. Well kept Wards Sheffield Best from carved handpumps; bar snacks are simple and consist of sandwiches (£1) and ploughman's (£2); well reproduced classical music, dominoes. In the well tended, dry-stone-walled garden there's a fine collection of well restored and attractively painted old farm machinery. Note the restricted winter opening hours. *(Recommended by H K Dyson, W P P Clarke, Steve Mitcheson, Anne Collins, Steve and Sandra Hampson, Brian and Anna Marsden, M A and W R Proctor, Jon Wainwright)*

Free house   Licensee Geoff Hawketts   Real ale   Snacks (lunchtime)   Children welcome   Open 12–2 (3 Sat), 7–11; closed weekday lunchtimes in winter

LITTLE LONGSTONE (Derbys)   SK1971 Map 7
Packhorse
Monsal Dale and Ashford Village signposted off A6 NW of Bakewell; follow Monsal Dale signposts, then turn right into Little Longstone at Monsal Head Hotel

Good value bar food in this traditional village tavern typically includes soup (90p), sandwiches (from 90p), baps spread with dripping and generously filled with hot well hung beef or with hot pork, apple sauce and stuffing (£1), ploughman's with a selection of cheeses (£2.65), vegetarian bakes such as cauliflower and leek (£2.85), meat salad, chilli con carne or steak and kidney pie (£2.95) and casseroles (£3.25). The pub itself is cosily placed in a village terrace, and its two small rooms have open fires, beam-and-plank ceiling, simple furnishings from country-kitchen chairs and cloth-cushioned settles to an odd almost batwinged corner chair, and decorations that are distinctive but discreet – attractive landscape photographs by Steve Riley, blow-ups of older local photographs, prettily hung decorative mugs, the odd cornet or trumpet, and a collection of brass spigots. Well kept Marstons Burton and Pedigree on handpump; darts, dominoes, cribbage. In the steep little garden there's a variable population of lambs, goats and rabbits. The little cottage was first mentioned as a pub in a census of 1787. *(Recommended by Dennis and Janet Johnson, Derek and Sylvia Stephenson, Mrs D M Everard, Lynda Brown)*

Marstons   Licensees Sandra and Mark Lythgoe   Real ale   Meals and snacks   Well behaved children in eating area until 9   Open 11–3, 5–11 all year; closed evening 25 Dec   Bedrooms   tel Great Longstone (062 987) 471; £10/£20

Real ale may be served from handpumps, electric pumps (not just the on-off switches used for keg beer) or, common in Scotland, tall taps called founts (pronounced 'fonts') where a separate pump pushes up the beer under air pressure. The landlord can adjust the force of the flow – a tight spigot gives the good creamy head that Yorkshire lads like.

nr MELBOURNE (Derbys)   SK3825 Map 7
John Thompson
Ingleby; village signposted from A514 at Swarkestone

The surroundings of this large and modernised farmhouse are attractive; it has well kept lawns and flowerbeds running down to the rich watermeadows along the River Trent (for which they have fishing rights), lots of tables on the upper lawn, and a partly covered outside terrace with its own serving bar. In the spacious lounge there are button-back leather seats, sturdy oak tables, some old oak settles and antique prints and paintings, also a log-effect gas fire; a couple of smaller cosier rooms open off. The pub takes its name from the man who both owns it and brews its highly praised beer; there's also Marstons Pedigree on handpump. Bar food is straightforward, consisting of sandwiches (nothing else on Sundays), a cold buffet, hot roast beef (£4, not Mondays) and puddings. *(Recommended by Jon Wainwright, Richard Sanders, Dave Butler, Lesley Storey, Pete Storey)*

Own brew   Licensee John Thompson   Real ale   Meals (lunchtime, not Sun; only cold buffet Mon) and snacks   Children in separate room   Open 10.30–2.30, 7–11 all year

MILLTHORPE (Derbys)   SK3276 Map 7
Royal Oak
B6051

This atmospherically intimate seventeenth-century stone pub is robustly furnished with old oak beams, bare stone walls and a warm winter fire. The main room opens into a small, more comfortable and quieter lounge. The crazy-paved terrace is partly shaded by hawthorn, ash and other trees, and has picnic-table sets, as does a side lawn further up. Well kept and well priced Darleys Thorne and Wards Sheffield Best on handpump; selection of malt whiskies. The home-made food includes sandwiches and filled rolls (from 80p – toasted ham and cheese and black pudding and bacon, £1.15–£1.25), cottage pie (£2.30), a wide choice of ploughman's (£2–£2.50), chilli con carne (£2.50) and seafood Mornay or chicken and vegetable pie (£2.75), with Cumberland sausage (£2.50) and mixed grill or eight-ounce steak (£3.95) on winter evenings. *(Recommended by Peter Mitchell, Lynn Higginson, Jon Wainwright, Sue Cleasby, Mike Ledger, W P P Clarke)*

Free house   Licensees Harry and Elaine Wills   Real ale   Meals and snacks (not Sat–Sun evenings)   Open 11.30–3, 5.30–11 (11.30–4, 6–11 Sat); closed Mon lunchtime exc bank hols

MONSAL HEAD (Derbys)   SK1871 Map 7
Monsal Head Hotel
B6465

Its marvellous position above the steep valley of the River Wye gives this stone inn good views from its balconies and the big windows of its lounge – perhaps the best place for them is the terrace by the front car park. The old stables now house an attractive all-day bar; it's a lively flagstoned room with a big wood-burning stove in an inglenook and cushioned oak pews around flowery-clothed tables in the stripped timber horse-stalls, which are decked out with harness and horsy brassware; steps lead up into a crafts gallery. The spacious high-ceilinged main front bar is set out more as a wine bar, with dining-chairs around big tables; it's partitioned off from the restaurant area. Simple bar food includes a highly praised soup (£1), sandwiches (from £1) and a selection of pizzas (from £2.95); there's now a carvery in the lounge, with a decent range of dishes such as scampi (£2.50), lasagne or salad (£2.75), home-made steak and kidney pie or Lancashire hot-pot (£2.95), and in the evenings gammon (£4.25), steak (£5.25) and chicken Kiev (£5.75). Well kept John Smiths, Theakstons Best and Old Peculier, a beer brewed for the pub and a regularly changing guest beer on handpump; darts, shove-ha'penny, table skittles, dominoes and cribbage; quiet (and free) juke box. Both the restaurant and the bedrooms are decorated in authentically Victorian style. The back garden has a play area and animals; on *Good Walks Guide* Walk 82. *(Recommended by L G and D L Smith, Wayne Brindle, Derek and Sylvia Stephenson, Peter and Moyna Lynch, M J Steward, Steve Waters, BKA, David Heath, Tim and Lynne Crawford, M A and W R Proctor)*

Free house Licensee Nicholas Smith Real ale Meals and snacks Restaurant Children in eating area and restaurant Open 11–11 all year; closed 25 Dec Bedrooms tel Great Longstone (062 987) 250; £25B/£37.50B

ONECOTE (Staffs) SK0555 Map 7
Jervis Arms
B5053, off A523 Leek–Ashbourne

In a moorland-valley village by the River Hamps, this seventeenth-century pub has white planks over shiny black beams in its irregularly shaped main bar, with toby jugs and decorative plates on the high mantelpiece of its big stone fireplace; there are window-seats, wheel-back chairs, two or three unusually low plush chairs, and little hunting prints on the walls. A similar if slightly simpler inner room has a fruit machine, and there are two family-rooms. Quickly served bar food includes ham, beef or cheese rolls (£1), soup (80p), home-made shepherd's pie (£1.85), ploughman's (£2), roast chicken (quarter £2.75, half £4), generous home-cooked ham (£2.75), vegetarian dishes such as curried nut, fruit and vegetable pie or nut roast (£3.75) and twelve-ounce sirloin steak (£6); children's helpings from 75p. Bass, Marstons Pedigree, Ruddles County, Theakstons Best, XB and Old Peculier on handpump; dominoes, cribbage, fruit and trivia machine and juke box or piped pop music. The neat riverside lawn has picnic-table sets under cocktail parasols, a slide, assault climber and trolley-on-rails, a little shrubby rockery behind, and lots of sheltering ash trees; a footbridge leads to the car park. A spacious barn behind the pub has recently been converted to self-catering accommodation. There are lovely moorland pastures above the village. *(Recommended by John Beeken, Steve Mitcheson, Anne Collins, Jon Wainright)*

Free house Licensees Peter and Julie Wilkinson Real ale Meals and snacks (until 10 evenings) Children welcome Open 12–3, 7–11 all year; closed 25 and 26 Dec Self-catering barn (with two bedrooms) tel Onecote (053 88) 206; £20 for the whole unit

OVER HADDON (Derbys) SK2066 Map 7
Lathkil 🛇 🛏
Village and inn signposted from B5055 just SW of Bakewell

This friendly, informal inn is popular with walkers from Lathkill Dale and the moors (there's even a place in the lobby to leave muddy boots). The room on the right is pleasant, with black beams, big windows, a cheery fire in the attractively carved fireplace, leatherette seats, old-fashioned settles, a Delft shelf of blue and white plates on one white wall, original prints and photographs. On the left is the spacious and sunny family dining area, which doubles as a restaurant in the evenings; at lunchtime the highly praised bar food is served here and includes filled cobs (from 95p), home-made soup (£1.10), smoked mackerel salad (£2.80), lamb curry or quiche (£3.20), lasagne (£3.40), steak and kidney pie or beef and mushroom casserole (£3.40), smoked trout (£3.75), and a help-yourself cold buffet (£3.95); home-made sweets (from £1.25). Well kept Darleys Thorne and Wards Sheffield Best on handpump; piped classical jazz, shove-ha'penny, dominoes,

Most pubs in the *Guide* sell draught cider. We mention it specifically only if they have unusual farm-produced 'scrumpy', or even specialise in it.

cribbage. There are attractive panoramic views. *(Recommended by D J Milner, Kelvin and Janet Lawton, F C Price, Brian and Anna Marsden, M A and W R Proctor, Richard Sanders, A D Lealan, C F Walling, Patrick Young, Dr and Mrs R J Ashleigh, P and H B, R A Hutson, Dr John Innes, R F Moat, Dr and Mrs B D Smith)*

Free house   Licensee Robert Grigor-Taylor   Real ale   Meals and snacks (lunchtime)
Evening restaurant (not Sun)   Children in eating area (lunchtime; evening if dining in
restaurant with adults)   Open 11.30–3, 6–11 all year; closed evening 25 Dec
Bedrooms tel Bakewell (0629) 812501; £27.50B/£50B

PENKHULL (Staffs)   SJ8644 Map 7
Greyhound

Leaving Newcastle centre on A34 for Stafford, look out for first left turn after two hospital signposts and a stretch of parkland; turn into this Newcastle Lane to find village centre at top of hill; pub in Manor Court Street, opposite church; OS Sheet 118 reference 868448

This friendly, pretty Potteries pub is thoroughly authentic (it's one of the oldest in the area), and serves a decent range of simple bar food, including filled baps (from 50p), soup (70p), ploughman's (£1.95), lasagne, curry or chilli con carne (£2.25), home-made pies (£1.95) and a traditional Potteries winter stew called lobby (£1.20). Both of its rooms are traditionally furnished: one has red plush seats around massive old-fashioned gilt tables, tiny pictures on its white walls and a neat and cosy inglenook fireplace; the other has more of a 1940s atmosphere, with seats built into its darkening Anaglypta walls, elaborate gas-style wall lamps, a piano with placards perched along its top, and dark panelling elsewhere. Ansells Bitter and Mild, Ind Coope Burton and usually a guest beer on handpump; table skittles, darts, cribbage, dominoes, CD juke box. A couple of picnic-table sets on the front pavement face the churchyard of the charming village, with more behind.
(Recommended by Nick Dowson; more reports please)

Ansells (Allied)   Licensees Mr and Mrs John Chadwick   Real ale   Meals and snacks
(lunchtime, not Sun)   Children if eating, lunchtime   Open 12–3, 6–11 (all day Sat) all year;
closed evening 25 Dec

ROWARTH (Derbys)   SK0189 Map 7
Little Mill

Turn off A626 at Mellor signpost (in steep dip at Marple Bridge); fork left at Rowarth signpost, then follow Little Mill signpost; OS Sheet 110 reference 011889

The 1932 Pullman railway dining car, which one so unexpectedly finds in the landscaped garden of this remote but surprisingly popular pub, has finally been converted into three well appointed bedrooms. The open-plan bar is Turkey carpeted, with comfortable little settees and armchairs, and has stub walls, bare brick pillars, and a welcoming atmosphere, particularly for families. The front terrace is decorated with tubs of flowers, roses and honeysuckle, and there are little lawns with ash trees, seats, swings and a climbing-frame. Bar food includes soup (65p), black pudding (95p), sandwiches (from £1), ploughman's (£2.25), and home-made dishes such as chicken and mushroom pie (£2.35), lasagne or steak and kidney pie (£2.95). Banks's, Hansons, Hartleys, Robinsons Best Mild and Ruddles County on handpump; darts, pool, dominoes, cribbage, fruit machine and juke box. The pub is tucked away down tricky roads in good walking country.
(Recommended by David Waterhouse, GP; more reports please)

Free house   Licensee Christopher Barnes   Real ale   Meals and snacks (all day until around
10)   Upstairs restaurant   Children welcome   Open 11–11 all year; may close winter
afternoon if weather bad   Bedrooms tel New Mills (0663) 43178; £25B/£32B

We accept no free drinks or payment for inclusion. We take no advertising, and are not sponsored by the brewing industry or by anyone else. So all reports are independent.

ROWSLEY (Derbys)   SK2566 Map 7

Peacock 🛏

A6 Bakewell–Matlock

More of a hotel than a pub, this was originally built as a dower house for Haddon Hall in 1652, and became an inn in 1828; its atmosphere is decidedly civilised and up-market, and its clientele tend to be smartly dressed. However the softly lit inner bar is worth a visit; it has an old-fashioned feel, with oak beams, stripped stone walls, a copper-topped bar counter, antique settles, a nineteenth-century cockfighting chair (with an arm swollen into a little table, like a fiddler crab's fat claw), and an alcove seat for the red-coated lounge waiter. The lounge is quiet and more spacious, with comfortable Windsor chairs and more antique settles; it has a help-yourself lunchtime buffet (£4, not Sundays), and snacks like celery and swede soup with generous helpings of bread and butter (£1.60), sandwiches, and a hot winter dish (£4); puddings (£1.65). Well kept Ind Coope Burton on handpump; afternoon teas. Its attractive gardens run down to the River Derwent, where trout fishing is available; near *Good Walks Guide* Walk 79. You can buy their popular home-made marmalade with rum flavour from the reception. *(Recommended by J Wiltshire, Cynthia McDowall, Miles Kington, Mr and Mrs M C Jaffé, R A Hutson)*

Embassy Hotels (Allied)   Licensee G M Gillson   Lunchtime bar food (not Sun) Restaurant   Children may be allowed under certain circumstances; very young children discouraged in restaurant   Open 11–3, 6–11 all year   Bedrooms tel Matlock (0629) 733518; £38.50(£48.50B)/£45(£69B)

SANDONBANK (Staffs)   SJ9428 Map 7

Seven Stars

4½ miles from M6 junction 14; A34 link road towards Stone, but at first roundabout continue on A513 ring road, then turn left on to B5066; alternatively, from A51 in Sandon, follow B5066, Stafford signpost

The open-plan bar in this popular white house has recently been attractively refurbished, though the layout and décor remain much as ever: several cosy corners, little country prints, lots of polished brass, two large open fires and an array of pink plush stools and cushioned captain's chairs. Steps lead down to a lower wood-panelled lounge with comfortable chairs and thick-pile carpet. Bar food includes sandwiches, ploughman's (lunchtime only), plaice (£3.20), a selection of chicken dishes (from £3.50; with crabmeat and prawns £4.75), beef curry (£3.50), vegetarian dishes (£3.95), lamb cutlets (£4), scampi, gammon or seafood provençale (£4.50) and steaks (from £6.75) – the new licensee who took over in summer 1989 has kept the menu unchanged. They only take credit cards for orders over £10. Burtonwood and Dark Mild on handpump; two pool-tables (used in winter only), piped music. Outside there are picnic-table sets at the front, and a swing on the grass at the back. *(Recommended by Paul and Margaret Baker, Laurence Manning, Dave Braisted, AMcK; reports on the new regime please)*

Burtonwood   Licensee Mrs A D Jackson   Real ale   Meals and snacks (until 10 evenings)   Restaurant tel Sandon (088 97) 316   Children welcome   Open 11–3, 6–11 (11.30 Sat) all year

SEIGHFORD (Staffs)   SJ8725 Map 7

Holly Bush 🏵

3 miles from M6 junction 14: A5013 towards Eccleshall, left on to B5405 in Great Bridgeford, then first left signposted Seighford

After a drop in the degree of warmth of readers' praise for the quality and service of the bar food in this friendly country pub, things seem to have re-established themselves on a more even keel; the enterprising range includes sandwiches (from

85p), soup (95p, seafood or French onion £1.40), Gruyère and Edam cheese fritters (£1.75), devilled whitebait (£1.95), ploughman's (£1.95), devilled lambs' kidneys with rice (£2.95), highly praised hot croissants filled with chicken and mushroom in a creamy sauce (£3.25), home-made vegetarian lasagne or chilli con carne (£3.50), salads (from £4.25), gammon (£4.50), curried prawns and mushrooms (£4.75) and steaks (from £5.95); there are puddings like sherry trifle or home-made apple pie (95p), chocolate and Grand Marnier mousse (£1.45) and hot figs in brandy (£1.85). The spotlessly clean, spacious and airy black-beamed bar has big windows, ivy-leaf chintz curtains, and light modern prints of poppies and landscapes; there are wheel-back chairs and comfortable settles around the varnished rustic tables, and an interesting collection of antique bric-à-brac, brass cooking instruments and foreign coins – these are stuck on the mirrors around the attractively carved inglenook fireplace. Well kept Tetleys on handpump and good vintage ports, as well as an above-average selection of non-alcoholic drinks, including cocktails; darts, trivia machine, piped music. The neat back rose garden has seats on a terrace, in a vine arbour, and on the spacious lawn. *(Recommended by Philip Riding, Mrs E M Bartholomew, Dave Braisted, J K Cunneen, Paul and Margaret Baker, TBB, W D Horsfield, K and R Markham, Mr and Mrs B Amos, G Bloxsom, Dick Brown)*

Ansells (Allied)   Licensee Mrs Louise Fowden   Real ale   Meals and snacks (until 10 evenings)   Restaurant tel Seighford (0785) 282280   Children welcome   Open 12–3, 7–11 all year

SHARDLOW (Derbys)   SK4330 Map 7

Malt Shovel 🏵

3½ miles from M1 junction 24; A6 towards Derby, then in Shardlow turn down Wilne Lane at Great Wilne signpost, then left after crossing canal

This eighteenth-century canalside pub has an atmospheric bar with an interesting layout – all odd angles and varying ceiling heights – and a good winter log fire; it's filled with intriguing mementoes, such as brewery and tobacco mirrors and advertisements, cigarette cards, cartoons and other pictures, jugs, mugs, plates and swords. Good window seats overlook the busy Trent and Mersey canal, with more tables out beside it. Readers continue to enthuse about the lunchtime bar food, which includes sandwiches (from 65p), soup (70p), ploughman's (£1.75), basket meals (from £1.60), sausage and egg (£1.95), chilli con carne (£2.25), steak and kidney pie or beef casserole (£2.35), salads (from £2.70), ham and pineapple (£3.60), with more unusual daily specials like salmon and leek pie (£3.60), lambs' kidneys and sherry casserole (£3.80), and lamb chops in a blue cheese sauce (£4.20); steaks (from £5); puddings (90p); friendly, attentive service. Well kept Marstons Burton, Pedigree and Mercian Mild on handpump; piped music. The nearby marina has a museum of canalboat life, and the Castle Donington collection of historic racing cars is not far. No motor-cyclists. *(Recommended by Ted George, Roger Bellingham, Steve Waters, Jon Wainwright, Genie and Brian Smart, Richard Sanders, Wayne Brindle, Jane and Niall, G Bloxsom, RJH, Derek and Sylvia Stephenson, T Houghton, Tim and Lynne Crawford, Dr and Mrs B D Smith, M A and W R Proctor)*

Marstons   Licensee Peter Morton-Harrison   Real ale   Meals and snacks (lunchtimes, not Sun)   Children welcome   Open 11–3.30, 5.30–11 (all day Sat) all year

SHRALEYBROOK (Staffs)   SJ7850 Map 7

Rising Sun

3 miles from M6 junction 16; from A500 towards Stoke, take first right turn signposted Alsager, Audley; in Audley turn right on the road still shown on many maps as A52, but now in fact a B, signposted Balterley, Nantwich; pub then signposted on left (at the T-junction look out for the Watneys Red Barrel)

Last summer the licensee started producing her own beer in a newly built brewery behind the pub – Rising and Setting bitter and a more powerful brew appropriately called Total Eclipse. This is very much developing the interest that's taken in real ale; half a dozen are kept on handpump, rotating weekly from a cellar of around thirty, and typically including Burton Bridge, Flowers IPA, Holdens Special, Ruddles County, Theakstons Old Peculier and Titanic; they also have 109 malts and over 100 liqueurs. Despite its position near the rush of the motorway, it's welcomingly tranquil and relaxed in the gently lit bar, which is decorated with shiny black panelling and beams and timbers in the ochre walls; there are red leatherette seats tucked into cosy alcoves, and a warm open fire. A wide choice of bar food includes soup (80p), sandwiches or burgers (80p), filled baked potatoes (£1), smoked cod or breaded plaice (£2.75), specials such as lasagne (£2.75), lots of vegetarian dishes (£3.25) and chicken Kiev or sirloin steak (£5). *(Recommended by Martin Aust; more reports please)*

Own brew   Licensee Mrs Gillian Holland   Real ale   Meals and snacks (until 10.30 evenings)   Children welcome   Occasional live entertainment   Open 12–3, 6–12 (all day Sat) all year

TUTBURY (Staffs)   SK2028 Map 7
Olde Dog & Partridge 🛏

A444 N of Burton-on-Trent

The main focus of attention in this handsome extended Tudor coaching-inn is now its very spacious new carvery, where food includes soup (£1.25), a pair of pâtés (£1.85) and lots of other starters, steak pie done in Owd Rodger (£4.40), curry (£4.90), salads (from £4.95), roasts (from £5.50) and spit-roasted local duck (£6.95); a pianist performs here each evening. The well kept and civilised bar has two warm Turkey-carpeted rooms, one with a plush-cushioned oak settle, an attractive built-in window seat, brocaded stools and a couple of Cecil Aldin hunting prints, the other with red plush banquettes and rather close-set studded leather chairs, sporting pictures, stags' heads and a sizeable tapestry. Well kept Marstons Pedigree from the small oak bar counter; lunchtime snacks, including sandwiches; efficient service. The neat garden has white cast-iron seats and tables under cocktail parasols, with stone steps between its lawns, bedding plants, roses and trees. The bedrooms are very comfortable. *(Recommended by Graham Bush, Angus Lindsay, Stephen Goodchild)*

Free house   Licensee Mrs Yvette Martindale   Real ale   Snacks (lunchtime) and meals (12–2, 6.15–10)   Carvery and (not Sun) small restaurant   Children welcome   Evening pianist Open 10.30–3, 5–11 all year   Bedrooms tel Tutbury (0283) 813030; £50B/£62B

WARDLOW (Derbys)   SK1875 Map 7
Three Stags Heads

Wardlow Mires; A623 by junction with B6465

When we heard that this white-painted stone cottage had been sold for the first time in 150 years, we were naturally apprehensive that its unspoilt simplicity would be submerged in refurbishment; there has been some gentle modernisation, and the grandfather clock has gone, but on the whole things seem to be as ever. The small parlour bar has a couple of antique settles with flowery cushions, two high-backed Windsor armchairs, old leathercloth seats and simple oak tables on the flagstone floor, a double rack of willow pattern plates and a petrified cat in a glass case. The cast-iron kitchen range, kept alight in winter, has a gleaming copper kettle. They've started doing food all day and have added a car park – both of which we hope will encourage more readers to investigate and report back to us. Home-made dishes include hummus or crudités (£1), black pudding (£1.25), chicken wings (£1.50), a range of vegetarian meals (£2.50), spaghetti bolognese or lasagne (£2.75), tandoori chicken (£3.50) and lamb curry (£4.50). Theakstons Old Peculier and Youngers Scotch and No 3 on handpump; cribbage, dominoes. The barn has been made into a pottery workshop, which provides the dishes and so forth used by the pub. The front terrace outside looks across the main road to farmland rising gently into the distant hills. Walkers – and their boots – are still welcome. *(Recommended by P and H B, Keith and Sheila Baxter)*

Free house   Licensees Geoff and Pat Fuller   Real ale   Meals and snacks (12–10.30) Children welcome   Live folk/traditional blues Sun lunchtime and occasional Sat evening Open 11–11 all year

WARSLOW (Staffs)   SK0858 Map 7

Greyhound 🛏

B5053 S of Buxton

This simple village is just a short stroll from the Manifold Valley, and quite well placed for other Peak District features. The stone-built pub's long beamed bar has elm-topped stools and cushioned oak antique settles, some quite elegant, on its carpet, with quietly restrained landscapes on the cream walls; the windows, with both curtains and net curtains, are decorated with houseplants. Home-made bar food includes sandwiches or home-baked rolls (from 90p), soup (95p), steak sandwich (£1.85), basket meals (from £1.95), cheesy vegetable flan (£2.15), salads or ploughman's (from £2.15, local Stilton £2.25), steak and kidney pie (£2.95), gammon (£3.50) and steaks (from six-ounce sirloin £4.25); you should get there early on Saturday evenings if you want to eat. Well kept Bass on handpump (they've changed from Marstons), log fire, friendly service; pool-room, with darts, dominoes, fruit machine; piped music from Bros to Beethoven. There are rustic seats out in front, with picnic-table sets under ash trees in the side garden. The homely bedrooms are comfortable and clean. *(Recommended by Gerald Hixon, Mrs A Trustman, Mr and Mrs M Knowles, Mr and Mrs R Armit)*

Free house   Licensees Bob Charlton and Colin Cook   Real ale   Meals and snacks (12–2.30, 6.30–10 (9.30 Sat))   Children in pool-room and tap-room until 9   Live music Sat (usually singer and guitarist)   Open 11.30–3, 6.30–11 (6–11.45 Sat) all year; opens 12 and 7 in winter   Bedrooms tel Buxton (0298) 84249; £12/£24

WETTON (Staffs)   SK1055 Map 7

Olde Royal Oak

The decent range of bar food in this white-painted and shuttered village pub includes sandwiches (from 90p, good prawn £1.50), home-made tomato soup (£1.10), ploughman's (from £2.25 – the cheese for the Stilton version is made in nearby Hartington), omelettes (£2.25), and main dishes (for which they allow 25 minutes' cooking time) like home-made steak and kidney pie or veal Cordon Bleu (£3.50), grilled fresh trout (£4.25), rump steak (£5) and whole lemon sole (£5.50); three-course roast Sunday lunch (£5); friendly atmosphere. The simple original core has a relaxed atmosphere, a log fire in its stone fireplace, black beams supporting white ceiling boards, and an oak corner cupboard. In the small dining-room there are chairs and built-in wall settles around the rustic tables; it extends into a more modern-feeling area, with another fire and a door into a carpeted sun lounge, which looks on to the small garden. Well kept Ruddles Best and County and Theakstons XB on handpump; darts, dominoes, cribbage, and, allegedly, regular toe-wrestling (though one camera-equipped reader was disappointed). It's set in National Trust and walking country, with places like Wetton Hill and the Manifold Valley nearby. *(Recommended by JMC, Dennis Royles, A C and S J Beardsley, Jon Wainwright, Jenny Seller, Lee Goulding)*

Free house   Licensees Roger and Trisha Probert   Real ale   Meals and snacks   Children in sun lounge   Open 11.30–2.30, 7 (6.30 Sat) –11 all year

WHITMORE (Staffs)   SJ8141 Map 7

Mainwaring Arms ★

3 miles from M6 junction 15; follow signposts for Market Drayton, Shrewsbury, on to A53

This attractive Staffordshire stone pub is named after the family that has owned it (and most other things around here) since the eleventh century; it's a charming series of rambling, interconnecting oak-beamed rooms, with some old-fashioned settles among comfortable, more modern seats and reproduction memorial brasses on the walls, and three open fires, one in a capacious stone fireplace in the lower room. Bar food includes sandwiches (from 80p), soup (90p), ploughman's (£2), a cold buffet with salads and a choice of meats (£3), and hot dishes such as cottage or steak and kidney pie, vegetarian or meaty lasagne or chicken in a tomato sauce (all at £3.50); Boddingtons, Davenports and Marstons Pedigree on handpump. The local hunt may use it for gatherings. There are seats outside, opposite the lovely village church. *(Recommended by Laurence Manning, D J Braisted, JM, PM, Jon Wainwright, R G Ollier, C F Walling, J L Thompson)*

Free house   Licensee E Chadwick   Real ale   Meals and snacks (lunchtime)   Children in eating area lunchtime   Open 11–2.30 (3 Sat), 5.30–11 all year

WRINEHILL (Staffs)   SJ7547 Map 7

Crown

Den Lane; pub signposted just off A531 Newcastle-under-Lyme–Nantwich

Imaginatively refurbished and pleasantly decorated, this spick-and-span yet relaxed oak-beamed country pub spreads comfortably around the brick-built serving bar, with red plush wall settles, banquettes and stools around the dark cast-iron-framed tables on its carpet, and attractive pictures ranging from little etchings of pottery kilns to big landscapes and old prints. An open fire in a neatly stripped brick fireplace with black-iron side oven at one end faces a second in a flagstoned inglenook with plush side seats at the other. Generously served good value bar food includes lasagne or plaice (£2.95), scampi (£3.50), vegetarian dishes and steaks from sirloin (£5.50) to sixteen-ounce T-bone (£6.50), with good home-made ice-creams; well kept Bass and Marstons Pedigree on handpump; dominoes, well reproduced pop music, friendly service. *(Recommended by D P Bagnall, Catherine and Andrew Brian, Laurence Manning)*

Free house   Licensees Charles and Sue Davenhill   Real ale   Meals (not Sun, not weekday lunchtimes)   Children in eating area early evening only   Open 6–11 (closed lunch) weekdays, 12–3, 7–11 Sat, all year; usual Sun hours

Lucky Dip

Besides the fully inspected pubs, you might like to try these Lucky Dips recommended to us and described by readers (if you do, please send us reports):

Abbots Bromley, Staffs [SK0724], *Bagots Arms*: Popular local *(M A Robinson)*; [High St] *Coach & Horses*: Attractive low-beamed bar with friendly atmosphere, wide range of customers; lunchtime food, well kept Ind Coope Burton; three comfortable bedrooms *(M A Robinson)*; *Goats Head*: Appealing old timbered building overlooking centre of picturesque village, pleasant inside, with reasonable choice of good reasonably priced bar food, well kept Ind Coope Burton *(M A and W R Proctor, Jon Wainwright)*; [High St] *Royal Oak*: Busier than ever under newish

licensee – rather chic in some ways now, with friendly welcome and high standard of cheap, varied bar food, well kept Wadworths 6X; popular, interesting Oak Room restaurant *(Fiona Carrey, M A Robinson)*
Alrewas, Staffs [King William IV Rd; SK1714], *King William IV*: Particularly good pub food with standard menu and weekly changing specials in separate raised eating area – gets busy, but tables can be reserved (no food Sun–Weds evenings) *(Mike and Mandy Challis)*
Alstonefield, Staffs [Hopedale; SK1355],

Watts Russell Arms: Simple welcoming pub, light and airy, with usual range of bar food decently prepared, well kept Marstons Pedigree on handpump, open fire, chatty staff, piped radio; tables on small terrace by quiet lane, handy for Dovedale and Manifold valleys *(Douglas Bail, Jon Wainwright)*

Amington, Staffs [Tamworth Rd; SK2304], *Gate*: Generously refurbished and extended, with lots of wood and prints, and new family room; wide range of bar food all week, well kept Marstons beers including Pedigree, darts, fruit machine; canalside garden, with limited moorings *(Colin Gooch)*

☆ **Anslow**, Staffs [Bramhill Rd; SK2125], *Brickmakers Arms*: Small and unpretentiously friendly local, well kept Marstons Pedigree, good value bar lunches in generous helpings, including home-made puddings like jam roly-poly and spotted dick *(Eric Locker, M A and W R Proctor)*

Ashbourne, Derbys [Ashbourne Green; top of hill on way to Matlock; SK1846], *Bowling Green*: Good friendly atmosphere, well kept Bass with guest beer each week, good value home-cooked bar food including vegetarian dishes; bedrooms clean and pleasant *(P Da Silva, Richard Sanders)*

Ashbourne, Derbys [St Johns St; SK1846], *Smiths*: Homely sixteenth-century beamed local with nicely decorated interior, well kept Marstons, good range of malt whiskies, well presented home-made food and friendly welcome from pleasant young licensees *(J Yorke, Richard Sanders, Mr and Mrs J L J Songhurst)*

Ashford in the Water, Derbys [SK1969], *Ashford Inn*: Formerly the Devonshire Arms, renamed after recent refurbishment – well kept and comfortable stone pub (with Stones on handpump too), pleasant staff, bar food; in picturesque village with trout in nearby stream, village cricket *(Cdr H R Spedding, BB)*; *Black Bull*: Small and comfortably smart lounge in village pub with friendly licensee and locals, open fires, well kept Marstons, imaginative rather than cheap home-made bar food; in attractive spot *(David Heath, Mrs Carolyn Smith)*

☆ **Ashley**, Staffs [signposted from A53 NE of Market Drayton; SJ7636], *Peel Arms*: Well run refurbished pub in pretty village, with interconnecting rooms, plush seating and large cooking-range fire; well kept Marstons Pedigree, attractive garden overlooking fields *(Laurence Manning, Philip Williams)*

Ashley, *Meynell Arms*: Village pub with deep sofa, cast-iron stove and other old-fashioned touches in timbered, panelled and stripped stone lounge, games including darts and table skittles in comfortable public bar, well kept Bass on handpump, bar food, children in eating area *(Laurence Manning, LYM)*

Ashover, Derbys [SK3564], *Red Lion*: Spacious and gracious pub on windy corner of unspoilt village – a glorious rural spot;

free house with Mansfield and Youngs and good food *(Robert Caldwell)*

Bagnall, Staffs [SJ9251], *Stafford Arms*: Picturesque pub close to village green, open fires in pleasant beamed bar and in stripped stone lounge converted from former stables, friendly welcome, back restaurant extension specialising in steaks *(M A and W R Proctor)*

Bakewell, Derbys [Market Pl; SK2168], *Peacock*: Clean, bright, cheerful and comfortable modernised pub; Wards ales *(R A Hutson)*; [Market Pl] *Red Lion*: Panelled lounge with atmosphere of a market town pub; excellent Marstons Pedigree *(R A Hutson)*

Balterley, Staffs [Newcastle Rd; SJ7650], *Broughton Arms*: Pleasant licensees and staff, clean and airy bar, small choice of good quality, well presented bar food including good value steaks; tables can be booked up to 7.30 *(S R Lear)*

☆ **Bamford**, Derbys [Taggs Knoll – main road; SK2083], *Anglers Rest*: Large, spotlessly clean pub with revolving door and warm atmosphere; wide choice of good value bar food, quick service *(Steve Mitcheson, Anne Collins, T Houghton)*

Bamford, *Marquis of Granby*: Derwentside garden and cocktail bar furnished with sumptuous panelling etc salvaged from Titanic's sister-ship distinguish this old inn; bedrooms *(Steve Mitcheson, Anne Collins, LYM)*

Barlborough, Derbys [SK4878], *Dusty Miller*: Comfortable local with delightful licensees and friendly regulars; John Smiths and Stones, and Tues quiz evenings *(Robert Caldwell)*; *Rose & Crown*: Polite service, elegant dining-room, lots of crimson plush; snooker room *(Robert Caldwell)*; *Royal Oak*: Worth visiting for the 1920s room with cane seating, nostalgic silhouettes and black and white photographs *(Robert Caldwell)*

Barton under Needwood, Staffs [Main St; SK1818], *Red Lion*: Small but friendly Marstons house with well kept Pedigree on handpump; cosy lounge, larger bar with darts and dominoes, separate pool-table upstairs; good atmosphere, bar food *(B M Eldridge)*; [The Green] *Royal Oak*: Marstons house with recently refurbished church pews around walls, original stained glass in partitions, beams and timbers from old sailing-ship, scrubbed tables; well kept Pedigree on handpump, friendly service; children's room *(B M Eldridge)*

Baslow, Derbys [SK2572], *Rutland Arms*: Refurbished, and more restaurant than pub, but very pleasant and efficient *(PB, HB)*

☆ **Beeley**, Derbys [SK2667], *Devonshire Arms*: Black oak beams and stripped stone- and slate-work in spacious pub handy for Chatsworth with well kept Theakstons and Wards real ales, big log fires, good value straightforward food in bar and nice separate dining-room – best to arrive early for good seats; attractive rolling scenery; children welcome, with upstairs family-room and own menu *(Keith Bloomfield, Derek and Sylvia Stephenson, Jon Wainwright, Mark and Shirley Elvin, R A Hutson, Brian and Anna Marsden, LYM)*

Betley, Staffs [OS Sheet 118 reference 753486; SJ7548], *Black Horse*: Friendly old-fashioned, stone-floored pub with good service, Boddingtons on handpump, good value straightforward bar food and Sun lunches, efficient service; restaurant; children welcome if eating *(D P Cartwright, G C Hixon)*

Bobbington, Staffs [A458 Bridgnorth–Stourbridge; SO8090], *Six Ashes*: Pleasant low pub with friendly staff, Banks's, good bar food *(Dave Braisted)*

Bradley, Staffs [SJ8718], *Red Lion*: Friendly welcome at sixteenth-century pub with good food and drink; really good garden centre nearby *(Derrick Turner, Nigel Hopkins)*

Bradwell, Derbys [Smalldale – off B6049; SK1781], *Bowling Green*: Good views from terrace outside much-modernised village pub with lots of malt whiskies *(LYM)*

Brewood, Staffs [SK8808], *Admiral Rodney*: Welcoming pseudo-Victorian atmosphere, good selection of well kept ales and good value food – especially steaks *(Patrick and Mary McDermott)*

Brocton, Staffs [Cannock Rd; SJ9619], *Chetwyn Arms*: Excellent, reasonably priced bar food from a wide-ranging menu, good Banks's ale, cordial atmosphere *(G C Hixon)*

Burnhill Green, Staffs [Snowdon Rd; SJ7900], *Dartmouth Arms*: Charming pub at end of village street, tastefully extended, with good food and service *(Dave Braisted)*

Burslem, Staffs [Newcastle St; M6 junction 15; SJ8749], *Travellers Rest*: Has been lively and busy, with attentive and friendly service, good bar food, well kept beers and lots of local events, though we've heard nothing since earlier in 1989 when as a result of financial or rather fiscal troubles the own-brew Titanic Ales were hived off as a separate operation *(Jon Wainwright, Peter Griffiths – more news please)*

☆ **Burton-on-Trent**, Staffs [23 Bridge St (A50); SK2423], *Burton Bridge Brewery*: The fine real ales brewed on the premises are the reason for seeking out this firmly unpretentious local, its plain tap-room filled with enthusiasts for their XL, Bridge, unusual Porter and Festival; snacks from cheap filled cobs and chip butties to filled Yorkshire puddings, open fire, friendly atmosphere, upstairs skittle alley with occasional folk music *(Iain Anderson, Matt Pringle, A V Lewis, Richard Sanders, Colin Dowse, T R G Alcock, BB)*

Burton-on-Trent [Moor St], *Black Horse*: Quiet but friendly Marstons house with landlady's collection of plates from around the world in lounge; comfortable seating,

piped music and pool-table in bar; well kept Pedigree on handpump, good value filled rolls *(B M Eldridge)*; [349 Anglesey Rd], *New Talbot*: Friendly Marstons pub with well kept Pedigree on handpump, juke box and pool-table in bar, piped music in lounge, wide range of lunchtime and evening bar food (not Sun evening), Sat organ singalong *(B M Eldridge)*

Buxton, Derbys [West Rd; SK0673], *Bakers Arms*: Good, homely, terraced local; struck on entering by friendliness of welcome, relaxed, comfortable atmosphere and good mix of customers *(Jon Wainwright)*

☆ **Buxton**, Derbys [High St; SK0673], *Cheshire Cheese*: Pleasant, open pub with interesting décor including stained-glass panelling, well kept Hardys & Hansons, decent malt whisky, warm welcome and excellent cooking by landlord, yet prices low in bar and restaurant *(Jon Wainwright, Nick and Jean Norton)*

nr **Buxton** [A515 about 6 miles towards Ashbourne], *Duke of York*: Friendly, helpful landlord and good bar food – soups and steak sandwich particularly recommended; also children's menu; Robinsons real ale; can get very busy on holidays *(Ian D Coburn, Steve Mitcheson, Anne Collins)*

☆ **Castleton** Derbys [SK1583], *Olde Cheshire Cheese*: Two comfortable communicating bar areas in slated white timbered pub; well kept Wards real ale, generously served bar food (the daily specials – and the chips – are particularly recommended, sensibly placed darts, leatherette seats around wooden tables, particularly friendly licensee – his laughter's most infectious; popular with young people; bedrooms *(Lorna Koskela, Peter and Moyna Lynch, Steve Mitcheson, Anne Collins, BB)*

☆ **Castleton** [Cross St], *Olde Nags Head*: Village hotel renovated to preserve character, warm and welcoming with open fires, antique furniture, good bar food and service, separate restaurant; bedrooms warm and comfortable *(Angela Nowill, J J Hansen, Peter and Moyna Lynch)*

Castleton [Cross St], *Bulls Head*: Unpretentious place with welcoming, friendly landlord, Robinsons ales (including Old Tom) and reasonably priced varied bar food; big log fire in large lounge; walkers welcome *(Yvonne and Don Johnson)*; *George*: Well kept Bass *(Steve Mitcheson, Anne Collins)*; *Peak*: Tetleys local with two bar areas, one comfortable and tidy, the other more homely and welcoming *(Steve Mitcheson, Anne Collins)*

Cheslyn Hay, Staffs [Moon Lane; SJ9706], *Mary Rose*: Small country pub with nautical décor, well kept beer, excellent value bar meals, friendly service *(M V Fereday)*

Chesterfield, Derbys [Baslow Rd; SK3871], *Highwayman*: Steakhouse-type pub with good, cheap food and friendly service; good well equipped bedrooms in small reasonably priced hotel wing *(MN)*; *Nelson*: Friendly staff, excellent lunchtime bar food including vegetarian dishes *(Lorna Koskela)*; [Lond Shambles], *Royal Oak*: Interesting little pub with high medieval ceiling in tiny lounge, more basic bar, good value lunchtime bar food, Stones on handpump *(G P Dyall, Richard Sanders)*

☆ **Chinley**, Derbys [A624 towards Hayfield; SK0482], *Lamb*: Interesting old stone-built moorland free house, long and low, with row of three small rooms, the middle containing bar counter and chess table; fine stone fireplace; since it's been taken over by Noel Burrows, former crown green bowls champion, we've been getting promising reports on a good friendly atmosphere and on well prepared reasonably priced bar food, Bass and Chesters on handpump *(Steve Mitcheson, Anne Collins, David Waterhouse, Wayne Brindle)*

Chunal, Derbys [A624 1 mile S of Glossop; SK0391], *Grouse*: Pleasant, cosy moorland pub with spectacular views of Glossop, open-plan interior with real fires, old photographs of surrounding countryside, traditional furnishings and candlelit tables; friendly service, well kept Thwaites, bar food *(Lee Goulding)*

Clayton, Staffs [Westbury Rd; Westbury Park; very near M6 junction 15; SJ8542], *Westbury*: Good atmosphere and service under new regime, with even better, good value, well presented bar food *(Catherine and Andrew Brian)*

☆ **Clifton Campville**, Staffs [SK2510], *Green Man*: Spick-and-span fifteenth-century village pub with low beams, inglenook and chubby armchair in public bar, airy lounge, kind service, well kept Ind Coope Bitter and reasonably priced bar meals; children in snug and family-room, garden with donkeys, rabbits, fishpond, aviary and swings *(LYM – more reports please)*

Colton, Staffs [SK0520], *Plough*: Little gem of a pub, with well kept Banks's, courteous and efficient service, bar food such as salmon in pastry so good that you have to book for it *(G C Hixon)*

Combs, Derbys [SK0478], *Beehive*: Big old pub in lovely Dale village with streamside garden, big fire and rugs on boards of main bar, good helpings of interesting home-cooked food (tables set as a restaurant), Wilsons ales; bedrooms *(Doug Kennedy)*

Coven, Staffs [A449 S of Stafford; SJ9006], *Harrows*: Attractive, well furnished and friendly roadside pub with well kept beer and good bar food *(Denzil Taylor)*

Cowers Lane, Derbys [junction A517/B5023; SK3047], *Railway*: Very wide choice of excellent bar food – well cooked, well presented and reasonably priced; Ind Coope beers, comfortable furnishings, polite service *(Tim and Lynne Crawford)*

Cromford, Derbys [SK2956], *Greyhound*: Attractive, spacious old-style bars in centre of pleasant market town made famous by Arkwright's pioneer cotton spinning mill; well kept Home Bitter *(Robert Caldwell)*

Derby, Derbys [Harington St; SK3435], *Baseball*: Good value food and reasonably priced drinks in local close to baseball ground – particularly lively too on football match days *(Ekbal Rai)*; [13 Exeter Pl] *Exeter Arms*: End-terrace town pub recently extended, worth knowing for its hidden treasure – to left of entrance is a small, beautifully preserved snug with built-in settles, black and white tiled floor, black lead and brass range, glowing fire and wonderfully cosy atmosphere; Marstons Pedigree on handpump, memorable sandwiches *(Carl Southwell, Chris Raisin)*; [Arleston La, Sinfin; SK3532] *Ferrers Arms*: Modern, purpose-built pub with split-level carpeted bar (surely Derby's most plush), open fires in lounge during winter; Everards on handpump and occasional guest beer – useful for relaxing drink after shopping in nearby Gateway *(Carl Southwell)*; [Becket St] *Flamingo & Firkin*: New free house done up in traditional style, brewing its own real ales as well as keeping guest beers; bar food, summer garden barbecues, live music most evenings and weekend lunchtimes; has been open all day *(Anon)*; [Queen St] *Olde Dolphin*: In shadow of Cathedral, Derby's oldest pub, with sixteenth-century beams; small cosy snug, lounge, basic bar with darts, a fourth room with memorabilia from former local brewery, and tea-room upstairs; well kept Bass, wide choice of good bar food, friendly service *(Carl Southwell, Richard Green, Steve Waters)*; [204 Abbey St] *Olde Spa*: Friendly old local built on spa, favourably refurbished a few years ago to retain tiled floor and cast-iron fireplace (with coal-effect gas fire) alongside comfortable new built-in settles; refreshing mixture of young and old customers, locals and visitors; Ind Coope Burton on handpump, separate games-room, garden with fountain *(Chris Raisin, Carl Southwell)*; [The Morlege] *Wardwick*: Atmospheric town pub in early eighteenth-century listed building; basic furnishings and floorboards, separate eating area on raised level; ABC Best, Ind Coope Burton and Tetleys on handpump, good value food; often heaving with youngsters in the evening *(Carl Southwell)*

Dilhorne, Staffs [Draycott Cross Lane (A521 Cheadle–Longton, opp turn to village at Boundary); SJ9743], *Red Lion*: Traditional long bar in country pub with settles, padded stools and pottery mugs; Bass and M&B ales and bar food; on ridge overlooking the wooded Cheadle Hills with plenty of country walks, handy for Foxfield Light Railway and Dilhorne Park *(Anon)*

Dovedale, Staffs [Thorpe–Ilam rd; Ilam signposted off A52, Thorpe off A515, NW of Ashbourne; SK1452], *Izaak Walton*: Low-beamed bar with some distinctive antique oak settles and chairs and massive central stone chimney for the good log fire; Ind Coope Burton on handpump, good service, bar food and restaurant, morning coffee and afternoon tea; seats outside; this quite sizeable hotel has to itself a splendid position on the peaceful sloping pastures of Bunster Hill, nr start GWG84; bedrooms comfortable *(M A and W R Proctor, Dr Keith Bloomfield, AE, LYM)*

Draycott in the Clay, Staffs [SK1528], *Roebuck*: Simple roadside Marstons pub with big inglenook and well kept beer *(BB);* *Swan*: Basic village local, friendly staff, well kept Ind Coope tapped from the cask *(Jon Wainwright)*

Eckington, Derbys [SK4379], *White Hart*: Pleasant, cosy and friendly bars with no piped music; particularly well kept Home Bitter and Youngers No 3 *(Robert Caldwell)*

Edale, Derbys [SK1285], *Old Nags Head*: Popular and spaciously high-raftered walkers' pub at start of Pennine Way (and therefore nr start GWG83), with efficiently served substantial basic cheap food, open fire, well kept Marstons and Youngers real ales; children in airy back family-room with several space games; can get busy during walking season – lovely countryside around this village *(Len Beattie, MN, Steve Mitcheson, Anne Collins, W P P Clarke, LYM)*

Ednaston, Derbys [SK2442], *Yew Tree*: Unusual pub with four separate rooms served from central bar, separate games-room out by car park; best room overlooks garden through large bay window and has wall seats, large round table, dark beams and open fire; Bass on handpump, good bar food *(Chris Raisin)*

Egginton, Derbys [SK2628], *White Swan*: Warm welcome, well kept beer and excellent value for money food; children's play area *(P Da Silva)*

Elvaston, Derbys [5 miles W of M1 junction 24, ½ mile N of A6; SK4132], *Harrington Arms*: Friendly country pub with good real ale, good value simple bar food and separate eating rooms *(Mandy and Mike Challis)*

Etruria, Staffs [Etruria Rd (A53); SJ8647], *Rose & Crown*: Warm and friendly atmosphere in local with lots of old photographs and radios; well kept Ansells, Ind Coope and other real ales, pool-room, reasonably priced food in dining lounge; pleasant licensee and staff *(M A and W R Proctor)*

Eyam, Derbys [Water Lane; SK2276], *Miners Arms*: Cheerful and helpful service and nice atmosphere in comfortably modernised dining pub, with pleasant and unhurried set lunch – good fresh ingredients *(Dr and Mrs J W McClenahan, LYM); Rose & Crown*:

Clean and organised, popular with locals, well kept beer, excellent food and obliging service *(G C Hixon)*

☆ **Farnah Green,** Derbys [follow Hazelwood signpost off A517 in Blackbrook, W edge of Belper; SK3346], *Bluebell*: Good meals from omelettes, home-baked ham salads and steak and kidney pies to steaks in smartly kept dining pub with plushly furnished and discreetly decorated small rooms, and sturdy tables out on terrace and in quiet gently sloping spacious side garden; watchful staff, smart restaurant with inventive cooking; well kept Bass *(Wendy and Ian Phillips, BB)*

Flash, Staffs [A53 Buxton–Leek; SK0267], *Travellers Rest*: Isolated hill pub on main road – Britain's third-highest; astonishing array of beers with probably the largest number of pumps and taps in the country (most keg, not all on); old pennies embedded in table-tops are fun; juke box and/or TV can be loud, and there's no shortage of amusement machines; nice views over Longnor and beyond from back terrace, simple snacks; has been open all day *(Patrick Godfrey, Lee Goulding, Diane Hall, LYM)*

Foolow, Derbys [SK1976], *Lazy Landlord*: Very old and popular pub with cosy bar and open fire; good range of bar food with unusual dishes and fresh local trout; friendly, accommodating service, with a welcome for walkers (so long as boots are left outside); nice small restaurant *(Colin Price, Norman Battle)*

Glossop, Derbys [Manor Park Rd; SK0394], *Commercial*: Welcoming and reliably friendly local, attentive licensees and first-class bar service; darts, pool-table, juke box and well kept Chesters; new dining area serving good food including hot roast beef sandwiches cut from joint on Sat evenings *(Steve Mitcheson, Anne Collins)*; [Arundel St (off A57)] *Friendship*: Pleasant and lively atmosphere, with friendly welcoming landlord *(R A Hutson, Steve Mitcheson, Anne Collins)*; [High St West] *Grapes*: Refurbished pub, particularly welcoming to strangers *(Steve Mitcheson, Anne Collins)*; [High St E] *Manor*: Recently refurbished and extended, with happy atmosphere, well kept Boddingtons, bar food, live music Thurs; unwary pool players should beware the sloping floor; bedrooms *(Steve Mitcheson, Anne Collins)*; [Milltown (off High St East)] *Prince of Wales*: Fine modernisation – retains 1940s atmosphere but has all the up-to-date facilities you'd want *(R A Hutson, Steve Mitcheson, Anne Collins)*; [Norfolk St (opp rly stn)] *Winston*: Busy, but warm and friendly pub with pleasant tropical fish tank; well kept Watneys-related real ales, good, competitively priced bar food; bedrooms *(Steve Mitcheson, Anne Collins)*

Hartington, Derbys [The Square; SK1360], *Devonshire Arms*: Large pub in two adjoining buildings, one stone/brick, the other rendered; snug beamed lounge with real fires, popular with locals, food served in more spacious second lounge, well kept Ind Coope Burton; seats outside looking over village square; nr start GWG77 *(Lee Goulding)*

Hathersage, Derbys [SK2381], *George*: Substantial old inn, picturesque outside, comfortable modernity in; a nice place to stay – they look after you well (the back bedrooms are the quiet ones); popular lunchtime bar food, neat flagstoned back terrace by rose garden; nr start GWG80 *(Mr and Mrs M C Jaffé, LYM)*; *Scotsmans Pack*: Spacious and pleasant separate rooms with attractive woodwork, opposite interesting school building – off the main road, so attracts locals and walkers, with darts in back room, bar food lunchtime and evening, Bass on handpump and Stones on electric pump; near Little John's reputed grave *(Matt Pringle)*

nr **Hathersage** [A625 about 6 miles S of Sheffield, and 2½ miles E of village)], *Fox House*: Handsome eighteenth-century stone moorland pub with cheap food, piped mainstream music, simple furnishings *(BB)*

Hayfield, Derbys [Church St; SK0387], *George*: Unspoilt pub with lots of interesting memorabilia; welcoming landlord *(M A and W R Proctor)*; [Little Hayfield (A625 N); SK0388] *Lantern Pike*: Impressive small, friendly village inn, cosy and homely, bar food, fine views of hills from back garden; now under the Blezards banner (the Blezards ale is brewed by Tetley-Walker, but the chain is linked to Belhaven); good value bedrooms *(Steve Mitcheson, Anne Collins)*; [Market St (off A624)] *Pack Horse*: Generous helpings of well presented bar food in pleasant stone-built Peak District pub with good range of drinks including John Smiths real ales; panelled walls, brasses and other knick-knacks; well behaved children allowed until 8pm *(David Waterhouse, N Hesketh)*; [Kinder Rd] *Sportsman*: Solid comfortable olde-worlde atmosphere with fine stone fireplaces in spacious bar with Thwaites on handpump, good bar food, traditional Sun lunch, piped music; in quiet beautiful wooded Sett Valley below Kinder Scout; children welcome *(John Gould)*

Hednesford, Staffs [Hill St; SJ9913], *Queens Arms*: Spotless pub with superb, cosy atmosphere in both lounge and bar; subdued lighting, extensive array of horsebrasses and mining memorabilia, consistently well kept Bass, darts *(Tony Southall)*

High Offley, Staffs [Grub Street Village; SJ7826], *Royal Oak*: Old building modernised in and out, lovely country setting, good traditional bar food and Sun lunches; busy weekends *(M V Fereday)*

Hilton, Derbys [Egginton Rd (A5132); SK2430], *White Swan*: Late seventeenth-century building with original beams, modern facilities; well kept Bass, good value grill-type bar food, garden with quite a menagerie of very friendly animals willing to try any food; children's play area *(Roger Ife)*

Hoar Cross, Staffs [SK1323], *Meynell Ingram Arms*: Fine views from big windows, open fires, relaxed atmosphere, well kept Marstons Pedigree, simple food *(Angus Lindsay)*

☆ **Holmesfield**, Derbys [Lydgate; B6054 towards Hathersage; SK3277], *Robin Hood*: Wide choice of popular food (not Sun evening) and well kept Wards Sheffield Best and Darleys Best in friendly rambling moorland pub with open fires, beams, flagstones, plush banquettes, and a high-raftered restaurant with big pictures; piped music, stone tables out on cobbled front courtyard *(Mike Tucker, LYM)*

☆ **Hope**, Derbys [Edale Rd; SK1783], *Cheshire Cheese*: Little up-and-down oak-beamed rooms – though not a lot of space when it's busy – in sixteenth century stone-built village pub with lots of old local photographs and prints, abundant coal fires, well kept Wards Sheffield Best and Darleys Best, decent wines and other drinks, friendly welcome (for walkers too) and popular home cooking (not Sun evening – some readers would like the chance of simpler and cheaper snacks, others particularly like the Yorkshire puddings which are still a speciality under the new regime); children allowed in eating area; nr start GWG81; bedrooms *(Patrick Godfrey, Derek and Sylvia Stephenson, Ken and Barbara Turner, Jon Wainwright, Alan Skull, M A and W R Proctor, PB, HB, LYM; more reports on the current regime, please)*

Hope [Castleton Rd], *Poachers Arms*: Village pub with several bars, good décor, efficient service, good cooked food including adventurous vegetarian dishes; children welcome; bedrooms *(Anon)*

Hopwas, Staffs [SK1704], *Chequers*: Well kept open-plan pub near canal; frequent discos and live music *(LYM)*

Horse Bridge, Staffs [Denford (off A53 Stoke–Leek); SJ9553], *Holly Bush*: Canalside Ansells pub with log fires, well kept ales and bar food including regional dishes *(G C Hixon)*

Huddlesford, Staffs [SK1509], *Plough*: Extended old brick free house alongside canal and railway; good bar food such as tasty spiced lamb casserole, tables by water *(Dave Braisted)*

Hulme End, Staffs [SK1059], *Manifold Valley*: Well kept Darleys and Wards real ales, generous helpings of good home-cooked food, genuine local atmosphere – used to be named the Light Railway *(BB)*

☆ **Ipstones**, Staffs [B5053 (village signposted from A52 and from A523); SK0249], *Red Lion*: Gentle colour scheme and comfortable seats in friendly and well run pub overlooking valley, well kept Burtonwood

Best on handpump, reliably good value bar food, games area, piped music; the landlord's a fishing man *(Jon Wainwright, Patrick Godfrey, M A and W R Proctor, Wayne Brindle, Nick Dowson, Alison Hayward, G C Hixon, Mike Tucker, AMcK, LYM)*

Kings Bromley, Staffs [SK1216], *Royal Oak*: Basic but cosy bar with very enjoyable atmosphere, pleasant dining-room and good choice of food – nothing fancy, but well prepared and agreeably presented; may be donkeys behind garden *(E J Alcock)*

☆ **Kinver**, Staffs [A449; SO8483], *Whittington*: Striking black and white timbered Tudor house built by Dick Whittington's family, fine garden with pétanque, old-fashioned bar, good choice of lunchtime bar food (soup almost a meal in itself), attentive staff, roaring fire, Marstons Pedigree *(Dr and Mrs C D E Morris, LYM)*

☆ **Kirk Ireton**, Derbys [SK2650], *Barley Mow*: Range of well kept real ales tapped from the cask in unspoilt and basic series of interconnecting rooms – no frills, lots of woodwork *(Richard Sanders)*

Knockerdown, Derbys [1½ miles S of Brassington; SK2352], *Knockerdown*: Pleasant pub with really well kept Marstons Pedigree – popular in the evening with the local farming community *(Alastair Campbell)*

☆ **Ladybower Reservoir**, Derbys [A57 Sheffield–Glossop, at junction with A6013; SK1986], *Ladybower*: Impressive hardy stone pub nestling in sharp-sided valley with menacing boulders perched above; clean and comfortable open-plan layout inside, with well kept Tetleys, Theakstons and Wilsons, popular food in eating area, fox masks; stone settles outside, good views of reservoir and surrounding moorlands (many walks nearby) *(Steve Mitcheson, Anne Collins, Lee Goulding, J L Thompson)*

Lea, Derbys [SK3357], *Coach House*: Cosy converted coachhouse with fire in old cooking range, lots of old harness and so forth; simple informal and friendly atmosphere, nicely presented straightforward food; close to Lea rhododendron gardens *(Dr and Mrs J W McClenahan)*

Lichfield, Staffs [Market St; one of the central pedestrian-only streets; SK1109], *Scales*: Old-fashioned two-room pub with big etched window, Delft shelf over dark oak panelling, Bass and M&B Springfield on electric pump, attractively planted suntrap back courtyard; bar food (lunchtime, not Sun) has been efficiently and kindly served, with attractive cold table and good coffee; small restaurant; children welcome *(K and E Leist, Wayne Brindle, LYM)*

Little Bridgeford, Staffs [nr M6 junction 14; turn right off A5013 at Little Bridgeford; SJ8727], *Worston Mill*: Fine building – former watermill, with wheel and gear still preserved, ducks on millpond and millstream

in well laid out garden with play area and nature trails, attractive conservatory; bar food with an American slant, well kept Whitbreads-related real ales, restaurant *(Tom McLean, Roger Huggins, Dave Braisted, Roger Taylor, David Young, R P Taylor, Wayne Brindle, LYM)*

☆ **Litton**, Derbys [SK1675], *Red Lion*: Food – a mixture of solid provincial and bistro French with British country cooking – is the main thing at this cosy and pretty partly panelled village pub almost wholly given over to close-set bookable tables (reservations Tideswell (0298) 871458 – not open weekday lunchtimes); snug low-ceilinged front rooms with warm open fires, bigger back room with stripped stone and antique prints; good service *(Lynda Brown, Gordon Theaker, LYM)*

Longlane, Derbys [SK2538], *Three Horseshoes*: Unusual in that when it closed after lack of custom a consortium of locals bought it early in 1989, to reopen it as a traditional village pub with open fire, real ale on handpump, no juke box *(Reports please)*

Longnor, Staffs [SK0965], *Olde Cheshire Cheese*: Country inn with several rooms, warm atmosphere, well kept Robinsons ales; under new regime the home-cooked bar meals are wide ranging and well prepared *(G C Hixon)*

Lullington, Derbys [SK2513], *Colvile Arms*: Characterful old village pub with hatch service to unspoilt public bar, two serving areas, good beer; excellent atmosphere, popular with local farmers; new landlord doing well *(David Gaunt)*

Mackworth, Derbys [Ashbourne Rd; on A52 Ashbourne–Derby; SK3137], *Mundy Arms*: Refurbished main-road pub, recently extended with new restaurant and comfortable chalet-type bedrooms, built to match original stableblock; comfortable bar with plush banquettes and framed prints, good food generously served *(Chris Raisin)*

Makeney, Derbys [Holly Bush Lane; SK3544], *Holly Bush*: Traditional flagstoned and stone-walled free house, real ale served by jug, open fire, small games-room, terrace behind; quiet village *(Richard Sanders)*

Marchington, Staffs [Church Lane; SK1330], *Dog & Partridge*: Attractive setting in peaceful village; long, handsome building by brook, warm inside with simple bar and traditional lounge; well kept Ind Coope Burton, bar food (kitchen closes promptly by 2pm) *(Jon Wainwright)*

Matlock Bath, Derbys [Matlock Rd; SK2958], *County & Station*: Particularly well kept Marstons Pedigree, and guest beers; popular with bikers in season, can get smoky *(J D Shaw)*

☆ **Melbourne**, Derbys [SK3825], *White Swan*: Strikingly restored to show ancient structure though interestingly there's a slightly modern feel to it – ambitious food including good

Sun lunch and popular puddings, attractive decorations, comfortable seats, chatty landlord, well kept Marstons Pedigree; pleasant narrow garden; children welcome *(Jon Wainwright, LYM)*

Morley, Derbys [SK3940], *Rose & Crown*: Pleasant country setting, good ploughman's *(HKR)*

Muckley Corner, Staffs [A5/A461; SK0806], *Muckley Corner*: Well run, friendly atmosphere and service, pleasant décor, separate dining area, sensibly priced food, well kept beer; children allowed in dining-room *(M V Fereday)*

Mugginton, Derbys [SK2843], *Cock*: Friendly place with good beer and food, cheerful service; honest good value *(D P Cartwright)*

Newborough, Staffs [SK1325], *Red Lion*: This simple and unpretentious though comfortable local facing the quiet village square has been a main entry for its good value home-cooked bar food and well kept Marstons Burton and Pedigree (children have been allowed in the eating area), but the friendly licensees left in autumn 1989 *(LYM – reports on the new regime please)*

Newcastle under Lyme, Staffs [Gallowstree Lane; off Keele Rd, a mile W of centre; SJ8445], *Dick Turpin*: Welcoming, busy pub with pleasant atmosphere, spacious refurbished beamed lounge with mock windows of highway scenes, well kept Bass, reliably good lunchtime bar food including wide choice of particularly good salads *(Laurence Manning)*; [High St] *Stones*: Good choice of food, well kept Bass, mock-up of Victorian street scene in covered back courtyard; popular with young people in the evening *(D P Bagnall)*

Norbury Junction, Staffs [SJ7922], *Junction*: Picturesquely placed with relaxing canalside garden; clean and friendly, excellent beer, good value bar food; very popular *(Paul and Margaret Baker)*

Oaken, Staffs [A41 just E of A464 junction; SJ8502], *Foaming Jug*: Interesting inside with collection of jugs, nice fireplace, well kept Bass, Springfield and Highgate Mild *(Dave Braisted)*

Ockbrook, Derbys [SK4236], *White Swan*: Small, clean and pretty pub, friendly licensee, well kept real ale *(Brian and Genie Smart)*

Old Glossop, Derbys [SK0494], *Wheatsheaf*: Impressively renovated Whitbreads pub, with friendly landlord, comfortable and cosy surroundings and decent food including good value Sun lunch *(Deborah Clark)*

Osmaston, Derbys [off A52 SE of Ashbourne; SK1944], *Shoulder of Mutton*: Warm welcome, good choice of beers and comfortable rooms *(Alan Robertson)*

Owler Bar, Derbys [A621 2 miles S of Totley; SK2978], *Peacock*: Worth knowing for its attractive moorland setting; keg beers, wide choice of popular food *(Anon)*

Padfield, Derbys [SK0396], *Peels Arms*: Stone

village pub with split-level lounge and cosy public bar, three real fires, games-room, well kept Youngers real ales; the big test here is to squeeze through the tiny hole in the lounge wall – there is a technique *(Steve Mitcheson, Anne Collins, Lee Goulding)*

Penkridge, Staffs [Filiance Bridge (off A449 – easy diversion between junctions 12 and 13 of M6); SJ9214], *Cross Keys*: By Staffordshire and Worcestershire canal with garden next to towpath; bar snacks, hot meals, keg beers *(Patrick and Mary McDermott)*; [village centre] *Star*: Recently refurbished, with friendly atmosphere and excellent food; single bar with lots of old beams and nooks; very busy at lunchtime *(Colin Chattoe)*

Pilsley, Derbys [SK2471], *Devonshire Arms*: Very friendly welcome at small, cosy free house with Mansfield and Stones on electric pump, short choice of quickly served good food including hot dishes and sandwiches served with chips *(Syd and Wyn Donald)*

Renishaw, Derbys [2 miles from M1 junction 30 – A616 towards Sheffield; SK4578], *Sitwell Arms*: Food in comfortable high-ceilinged bar, restaurant, bedrooms in comfortable hotel extension behind *(LYM)*

Rugeley, Staffs [Lichfield Rd; SK0418], *Eaton Lodge*: Reliably good imaginative food in bar and restaurant, using local ingredients; bedrooms *(G C Hixon)*

Rushton Spencer, Staffs [Congleton Rd (off A523 Leek–Macclesfield at Ryecroft Gate); SJ9462], *Crown*: Friendly simple local in attractive scenery, on useful cross-country minor road – busy front snug, bigger back lounge, games-room; has been popular for home-made food and well kept Youngers real ales, but we've had no news since it came up for sale earlier in 1989 *(BB – more reports please)*

Ryecroft Gate, Staffs [Congleton Rd – OS Sheet 118 reference 923618; SJ9461], *Fox*: Cosy pub with real fire, comfortable chairs and sofas in small, partitioned areas; well kept Ind Coope Burton, pleasant atmosphere *(Jon Wainwright)*

☆ **Sawley**, Derbys [Trentlock (off B6540, not far from M1 junction 25 via Long Eaton slip road – OS Sheet 129 reference 490313); SK4731], *Steamboat*: Character pub in attractive spot at junction of Erewash Canal and River Trent, nautical décor inside; brews own beers including Seamans Mild, Frigate, Bosuns and the explosive Broadside, huge log fire, wide choice of quickly served good value food in bar and restaurant, electric organ weekend singalongs; may stay open afternoons on request; can be very busy summer weekends; children welcome *(Andrew Stephenson)*

☆ **Shardlow** [London Rd (A6); SK4330], *Hoskins Wharf*: Eighteenth-century canalside building attractively developed by Hoskins, preserving original beams and brick floors, with very simple furnishings and canal memorabilia; good views over canal, bar food and separate steakhouse-style restaurant; besides the full range of reasonably priced Hoskins ales they have a guest beer; busy atmosphere, very popular in summer; reached by drawbridge from its big car park; children's play area *(Carl Southwell, Dave Butler, Lesley Storey, Derek and Sylvia Stephenson, Jon Wainwright, Stewart Argyle, Steve Waters, Quentin Williamson)*

☆ **Shardlow**, Derbys [Aston Rd (A6)], *Dog & Duck*: Pleasant and cosy old pub with central serving area opening into large lounge with open fire and small low-beamed games room; warm, cosy atmosphere, well kept Marstons ales on handpump, marvellous collection of cigarette cards, children allowed in simply furnished extension; spacious back garden with play equipment, big aviary, geese, a donkey and picnic-table sets; traffic does rather thunder past in front *(Howard and Sue Gascoyne, Carl Southwell, Jon Wainwright)*

Shardlow [London Rd (A6 about ½ mile E)], *Cavendish Arms*: Wards, Darleys and Vaux, bar food *(Dave Braisted)*; [A6] *Shakespeare*: Home ales and exceptionally good value filled rolls *(Dave Braisted)*

Somercotes, Derbys [Nottingham Rd (B600); SK4253], *Royal Tiger*: Friendly pub, Kimberley ales, good choice of attractively priced bar food, snooker and other competitive teams *(Ian Crickmer)*

South Normanton, Derbys [a mile from M1 junction 28; B6019; SK4457], *Hawthorne*: Extended and refurbished pub with very popular carvery *(T Houghton)*

Sparrowpit, Derbys [nr Chapel en le Frith; SK0980], *Wanted Inn*: Marvellous, rugged stone building with two real fires, liberally decorated with photographs of spectacular surrounding countryside and aerial shot of pub; friendly, welcoming licensees and good home-cooked food *(Steve Mitcheson, Anne Collins, PB, HB)*

Stafford, Staffs [Greengate St; SJ9223], *Bear*: Bustling town-centre pub popular with both shoppers and local businessmen; juke box and fruit machine, well kept beer (and tea or coffee), bar food served attractively, separate eating area *(Colin Gooch)*; [Mill St] *Bird in Hand*: Popular town-centre pub, well kept Courage Directors, games and snooker room, good range of bar food, garden with plenty of sheltered seating *(Paul and Margaret Baker)*; *Garth*: Good value fresh hot and cold buffet, friendly service *(John and Ruth Roberts)*

Stafford, Staffs [A34/A449 central roundabout (take Access Only rd past service stn); SJ9223], *Malt & Hops*: Lively rambling pub with real ales such as Holdens, Marstons Pedigree and McEwans 80/-, popular at lunchtime for low-priced food, though in the evenings the clientele's much younger, concentrating more on the lagers and the loud video juke box – with Thurs–Sat discos when it stays open until 1am (midnight other nights); provision for children *(LYM)*; [Forebridge (Lichfield rd, opp Borough Library)] *Sun*: Family-run pub with good if not cheap Bass, food in bar and restaurant *(GCH)*

Stone, Staffs [21 Stafford St; A520; SJ9034], *Star*: Canal photographs and exposed joists in intimate public bar, snug lounge and family-room of simple eighteenth-century pub in attractive canalside setting; well kept Bass and M&B Springfield, friendly welcome, basic food, open fire in one room *(Jon Wainwright, Maureen Hobbs, Jill Hadfield, Tony Gallagher, LYM)*

Stourton, Staffs [Bridgnorth Rd; SO8585], *Fox*: Interesting building with conservatory; Banks's and Bathams real ales, bar food *(Dave Braisted)*

Sudbury, Derbys [off A50; SK1632], *Vernon Arms*: Seventeenth-century free house named for the builder of Sudbury Hall opposite, well kept Marstons, good value bar food *(Richard Sanders)*

Taddington, Derbys [SK1472], *Queens Arms*: Good food in well kept comfortable pub *(G C Hixon)*

Tamworth, Staffs [Albert Rd/Victoria Rd; SK2004], *Tweeddale Arms*: Traditional and homely local with well kept Bass, limited range of bar food, fruit machine and good if somewhat dated juke box *(Colin Gooch)*

Tansley, Derbys [A615 Matlock–Mansfield; SK3259], *Royal Oak*: Well kept Hardys & Hansons, limited choice of excellent value plain and unpretentious food including Sun roast *(Dr and Mrs B D Smith)*

Tatenhill, Staffs [off A38 W of Burton; SK2021], *Horseshoe*: Large and tastefully decorated with friendly service, well kept Marstons Pedigree, well prepared and reasonably priced bar food including good home-made puddings *(Eric Locker)*

☆ **Ticknall**, Derbys[B5006 towards Ashby de la Zouch; SK3423], *Chequers*: Good fire in enormous inglenook fireplace of attractively renovated, clean and cosy sixteenth-century pub with well kept Bass tapped from the cask, unusual spirits, good value bar food (not Sun), friendly service, seats in sizeable garden; nearby Calke Abbey is worth visiting *(Mrs D M Everard, Angus Lindsay, Dave Butler, Lesley Storey, LYM)*

Tideswell, Derbys [SK1575], *George*: Old coaching-inn with good food in spacious main bar, lots of prints and watercolours on painted panelling, old settles, oak chairs and tables, Hardys & Hansons Best on handpump; pool-room, small locals' bar; bedrooms *(Patrick Young)*

Trentham, Staffs [A34 about 5 miles S; SJ8640], *Yesterdays*: Comfortable, well refurbished and tastefully cluttered pub set on large traffic island with good selection of bar meals; Trentham Gardens are worth visiting *(E J Alcock)*

Uttoxeter, Staffs [Dove Bank (A518); SK0933], *Roebuck*: Snug pub with well kept Burton Bridge *(Jon Wainwright)*

nr **Uttoxeter**, Staffs [Stowe-by-Chartley; SK0027], *Cock*: Strangely shaped free house with excellent choice of food and Ind Coope Burton, Tetleys and maybe ABC Best on handpump *(Ned Edwards)*

☆ **Wardlow**, Derbys [B6465; SK1874], *Bulls Head*: Friendly service and good food still under new licensees, in attractively furnished pub with open fire in one of its two cosy bars, well kept Wards on handpump, lots of olde-worlde bric-à-brac and stripped stonework; must book Fri and Sat – gets very busy; has been closed weekday lunchtimes, but they may open then; bedrooms *(Mrs D M Everard, Dennis Royles, MP)*

Wessington, Derbys [The Green; SK3758], *Three Horseshoes*: Comfortable pub by green, friendly service, good lunchtime bar food *(Wayne Brindle)*

Whittington, Staffs [the one nr Lichfield, at SK1608], *Dog*: Pleasant, rambling building, friendly service, Ind Coope ales, bar food *(Dave Braisted)*

☆ **Whittington Moor**, Derbys [Sheffield Rd (off A61 1½ miles N of Chesterfield centre)], *Derby Tup*: Friendly no-frills basic pub with small snug, large lounge, and emphasis on wide range of superbly kept real ales such as Batemans XXXB, Ruddles County, Timothy Taylors Landlord, Tetleys, Theakstons XB and Old Peculier, Wards Sheffield Best and Whitbreads Castle Eden; range of pub games, but no food *(Dave and Angie Parkes, Richard Sanders)*

Willington, Derbys [The Green; SK2928], *Green Dragon*: Pleasant pub with attractive L-shaped bar and friendly, relaxed atmosphere *(Jon Wainwright)*

Windley, Derbys [Nether Lane (B5023); SK3045], *Puss in Boots*: Isolated olde-worlde pub with low beams, brasses, two open fires, sandwiches made to order, Bass on handpump, hot punch, their own home-made chutney for sale; children's play area and seats outside *(Tim and Lynne Crawford)*

Wirksworth, Derbys [Cromford Rd; SK2854], *Lime Kiln*: Tastefully decorated local with Bass on handpump and large helpings of good value food including Sun roasts *(David Stonier)*

Woolley, Derbys [White Horse Lane (off B6014, Woolley Moor); SK3661], *White Horse*: Friendly pub in quiet part of country handy for Ogston Reservoir, with good views and playground for children; Bass and Springfield Bitter on handpump, occasional summer guest beers, wide choice of home-cooked food (not Sun evening) *(Angie and Dave Parkes)*

Wyaston, Derbys [OS Sheet 119 reference 184426; SK1842], *Shire Horse*: Peaceful spot, good food, outside seating; friendly, welcoming staff – they even hunted around for a small Canadian flag to put on dinner table for us *(Bev Prentice, Bill Russell)*

Yarnfield, Staffs [SJ8632], *Labour in Vain*: Well run pub with good décor, M&B on handpump, popular quickly served food *(Anon)*

Yoxall, Staffs [Main St; SK1319], *Crown*: Marstons house, recently refurbished; large bar with pool-table, cosy lounge with log-effect gas fire in large open fireplace, separate raised dining-room; well kept Pedigree on handpump, wide choice of bar food, friendly service *(B M Eldridge)*

Devon

A good few new entries here include the rambling old Harbour Inn in Axmouth, the Fountain Head at Branscombe (an ancient place, of quiet but considerable character), the pleasantly informal Tuckers Arms at Dalwood (good food), the Church House at Harberton (full of antiquity, doing well under its current licensees), the Palk Arms at Hennock in its fine position above the Teign Valley (another pub which seems on an upswing with its new licensees), the friendly Warren House on the moors near Postbridge, the unusual little Sandy Park Inn in the hamlet of that name, the civilised Sea Trout at Staverton, the Kings Arms at Stockland (a smart place to eat at), the friendly Black Horse in the pleasant market town of Torrington, and the warmly welcoming Cridford Inn tucked away at Trusham. There's been quite a bit happening recently at longer-standing main entries, too: with a swing in this county towards long bar food service (even all through the day, as at the Royal Castle in Dartmouth, the delightfully idiosyncratic Double Locks near Exeter, and – right through till midnight – the Inn on the Green in Paignton). And interesting local cheeses, and of course that Devon speciality farm cider, seem to be getting more of a look-in in the area's pubs. Specific changes to mention include the extensive renovations at the Durant Arms in Ashprington (with a good new range of food, including fresh local fish); the new bedrooms at the Coach & Horses at Buckland Brewer and Kings Arms at Winkleigh; new licensees at the Coombe Cellars on the water at Combeinteignhead (whether they stay open through the afternoon depends on the state of the tide), the Church House at Rattery and the Anchor at Ugborough (it's now letting bedrooms, and has opened a restaurant); upgraded bedrooms and restaurant at the Church House at Holne; and perhaps the new goats – called

Rising Sun, Lynmouth

Moët and Chandon – at the New Fountain at Whimple. This pub, changing into a smart yet pleasantly informal restaurant in the evenings, is one of the county's better pubs for food; others include the Waterman's Arms at Ashprington, the Butterleigh Inn (with those lovely Cotleigh beers), the Old Thatch at Cheriton Bishop, the Exmoor Sandpiper up at Countisbury (smoking hams in its great bar chimney), the thatched Cott at Dartington, the Nobody Inn at Doddiscombsleigh (a champion pub on the drinks side too, with a remarkable range of wines – and comfortable bedrooms), the Pyne Arms at East Down, the spacious Swans Nest at Exminster, the Rock on the edge of Dartmoor at Haytor Vale, the Church House at Holne, the Elephant's Nest at Horndon on Dartmoor (for many people, one of Devon's most enjoyable pubs), the quaint Old Rydon at Kingsteignton, the Masons Arms at Knowstone on the edge of Exmoor (another contender for the title of Devon's top pub), the cosy Who'd Have Thought It at Miltoncombe (up to sixteen daily specials), the Ring of Bells at North Bovey (another Dartmoor pub), the Peter Tavy Inn (yet another – particularly good vegetarian food), the notably friendly Blue Ball at Sidford and the stately old Oxenham Arms at South Zeal (both these, in their different ways, are nice places to stay at). Fresh seafood is a special draw at the friendly Sloop at Bantham (a nice place to stay at), the pretty little Cherub in Dartmouth, and the Start Bay on the sea at Torcross. Three main entries brew their own beer: the Royal over on the Cornish border at Horsebridge, the Beer Engine at Newton St Cyres (they've set up an offshoot bar at the Royal Clarence in Seaton) and the London Hotel in Ashburton. But beer drinkers will also want to note the exceptional range of real ales carried by the old Church House at Holne and the delightfully old-fashioned Bridge at Topsham. Pubs to note as specially promising among the Lucky Dip entries at the end of the chapter are the Pickwick near Bigbury, Chichester Arms at Bishops Tawton, Normandy Arms at Blackawton, Hunters Lodge at Cornworthy, Whiteleaf at Croyde (not in fact a pub at all, but a guest-house – the only one in the country which we feel the book would suffer from leaving out), Anglers Rest near Drewsteignton, Sir Walter Raleigh at East Budleigh, Rock at Georgeham, Duke of York at Iddesleigh, Crabshell at Kingsbridge, the two entries outside Lynton, Royal Oak at Meavy, Journeys End at Ringmore, New Inn at Sampford Courtenay, Maltsters Arms at Tuckenhay (Keith Floyd's new venture), Sidmouth Arms at Upottery, Old Smithy at Welcombe and (at least out of season) Olde Inn at Widecombe.

ASHBURTON   SX7569 Map 1

London Hotel

11 West Street

Contrary to the indications of its name, you can't actually stay at this imposing old three-storey coaching-inn; however, they'll make your visit comfortable enough in the spacious and Turkey-carpeted lounge, which is furnished with little brocaded or red leatherette armchairs as well as other seats around the copper-topped casks they use as tables; it spreads back into a softly lit dining area with one wall curtained in red velvet. The clean white walls are largely stripped back to stone, and there's a central fireplace; fruit machine. The distinctive beers that are brewed here, Bitter and IPA (served on handpump under light blanket pressure), can also be sampled in Plymouth at the Mutton Cove, which Mr Thompson also runs. Bar food includes

---

Places with gardens or terraces usually let children sit there; we note in the text the very, very few exceptions that don't.

original soups (£1), sandwiches, ploughman's (from £1.50), shepherd's pie (£2.75), omelettes (from £3), whole plaice (£5), Dart salmon (£7), steaks (from eight-ounce sirloin, £7) and chicken Cordon Bleu (£7.40). *(Recommended by Richard and Dilys Smith, J R Carey, Philip and Trisha Ferris, David Fisher, Dr and Mrs R Wright, B Chapman, SC)*

Own brew   Licensee D F Thompson   Real ale   Meals and snacks (not 25 Dec)   Restaurant tel Ashburton (0364) 52478   Children in eating area and restaurant   Open 11–2.30, 5–11 all year

ASHPRINGTON   SX8156 Map 1

Durant Arms

Village signposted off A381 S of Totnes; OS Sheet 202 reference 819571

The new licensees, now in their second year, go from strength to strength in this pretty gable-ended cottage. Extensive renovations have improved the facilities and attracted more of the tourist trade; although some feel that the price for this has been a diminution of its village atmosphere, the welcome is still on the warm side and the service friendly. A new carpeted lounge, popular with families, has been opened downstairs, with settles, tables, chairs, red velvet curtains and a fire in winter. The old-fashioned upstairs bar has idiosyncratic cutaway barrel seats, newly upholstered, and a bay window overlooking the village street. In the simply furnished games-bar there are darts, dominoes, shove-ha'penny, cribbage and a fruit machine. The bar menu has altered substantially; the prize dish is the Brown Pot – filled with bacon, kidney and vegetables, cooked in stout and topped with pastry (£2.75); there's also a wide range of fresh fish, delivered every other day from Plymouth, from a prawn dip (£2.75) to whole lemon sole (£6.95), as well as sandwiches (from £1.10), ploughman's (from £2.30), vegetarian casserole (£2.40) or flans (around £2.50), and local steaks (from £6.95). Bass, Fergusons Dartmoor and Halls Harvest on handpump, a decent choice of wines and maybe Luscombe cider; tables in the sheltered back garden. George, the black labrador, is the epitome of the pub dog, and an oil painting of him now occupies pride of place in one of the bars. *(Recommended by G and M Stewart, Robert and Linda Carew, Col G D Stafford, Mr and Mrs G W Keddie, David and Flo Wallington, Brian Marsden, Jon Wainwright)*

Free house   Licensees Jill and John Diprose   Real ale   Meals and snacks (11.30–2.30, 6–11)   Children welcome in downstairs bar   Open 11–2.30, 6–11 all year

Watermans Arms

Bow Bridge, on Tuckenhay road

This attractive waterside pub has high-backed settles and built-in black wall benches in the flagstoned front area, and more tables in a comfortable carpeted oak-beamed inner area. It's possible to sit across the road by the little Harbourne River and watch the ducks pottering about, and maybe a heron in the tidal creek to the right. On the food side, there's quite an emphasis on fresh local fish, with in particular a highly praised seafood platter (£5.50); there's also soup (different ones each day, £1.30), sandwiches (from £1.50, generous crab £1.75), ploughman's with a choice of cheeses (from £2.35), lunchtime hot dishes such as cottage pie, lasagne or trout (around £2.95), salads (from £4.50) and steaks (from £7.95): people have found it useful to be able to ring ahead with their bar food order – a short cut given service delays at busy times. Oakhill Farmers on handpump; piped music. *(Recommended by Miss J A Harvey, J K Cuneen, T R Norris, S V Bishop, David and Flo Wallington, Pamela and Merlyn Horswell, Jon Wainwright)*

Free house   Licensee Terry Wing   Meals and snacks (6.30–10 evenings)   Children in family-room   Restaurant tel Harbertonford (080 423) 214   Open 11–2.30, 6–11 all year

AXMOUTH   SY2591 Map 1

Harbour

The Harbour Bar of this thatched pub evokes the days when smugglers must have posted lookouts on the tower of the handsome church opposite, with its fine stone gargoyles: there's a huge inglenook fireplace with fat pots hanging from pot-irons, a high-backed oak settle, brass-bound cask seats and black oak beams and joists. A central lounge has more cask seats and settles, and over on the left another room is divided from the dining-room by a two-way log fireplace. At the back, a big flagstoned lobby with sturdy seats leads on to a very spacious simply furnished family bar, and there are tables in the neat flower garden behind. Simple bar food includes home-made soup (£1.10), sandwiches (from £1.10), a good few other snacks or starters such as garlic bread and cheese (£1.50), ploughman's (from £2), home-cooked ham and egg (£3.45), steak and kidney pie (£3.50), salads (from £3.50), and evening grills running up to rump steak (£6.25), with children's helpings of many dishes, and specials such as fresh local crab. Well kept Bass and Devenish Royal Wessex on handpump, farm cider; darts, winter skittle alley, cribbage, maybe unobtrusive piped music. They have a lavatory for disabled people, and general access is good. *(Recommended by Mrs Caroline Ginnins, Andrew and Michele Wells, Joan and Ian Wilson)*

Free house   Licensees Dave and Pat Squire   Real ale   Meals and snacks (not 25 Dec) Children in family area   Open 11–2.30, 6–11 all year

BANTHAM   SX6643 Map 1

Sloop 🍷 🏠

There's near-universal praise from readers for the fresh fish that's served in this sixteenth-century village inn; it includes crab claws (£2.60), skate or whole plaice (£4.80) and giant cod (£4.85); there are also pasties (80p), home-made turkey soup (£1), granary-bread sandwiches (from £1.15, fresh crab £2.10), basket meals (from £1.80), ploughman's (£2.10), a good range of salads (from £3.80, seafood £5.25) and good steaks (£5.85); puddings like hot chocolate fudge cake (£1.40) or raspberry Pavlova (£1.60); hearty breakfasts for residents. The beamed and flagstoned bar is lively and atmospheric, with stripped stone walls, country chairs around wooden tables, and easy chairs in a quieter side area – this part has quite a nautical atmosphere, with lots of varnished marine ply. The Bass, Flowers IPA and Ushers Best are well kept on handpump, as is Churchward's cider from Paignton; decent range of malts. Darts, dominoes, cribbage, table skittles, fruit machine, space game, piped music. The sandy beach – one of the best for surfing on the South Coast – is only a few hundred yards over the dunes; the Coast Path runs past here. There are seats around a wishing-well in the yard behind. The inn has long associations with local smuggling, and indeed was once owned by John Widdon, one of the more notorious smugglers and wreckers of the South Hams; these days the licensees are more respectable, however. *(Recommended by W C M Jones, Paul and Janet Waring, JS, BS, John Tyzack, Col G D Stafford, David Barnes, John Barker, Amanda Dauncey, Ann and David Stranack, D P Barby, Ian and Daphne Brownlie, F A and J W Sherwood, W C M Jones, Brian and Anna Marsden)*

Free house   Licensee Neil Girling   Real ale   Meals and snacks (until 10 evenings) Restaurant   Children in eating area   Open 11–2.30, 6–11; opens 6.30 in winter Bedrooms tel Kingsbridge (0548) 560489/560215; £16.50(£17B)/£33(£34B)

BERRYNARBOR   SS5646 Map 1

Olde Globe ★

Village signposted from A399 E of Ilfracombe

This interesting seventeenth-century pub (converted from three thirteenth-century cottages) consists of a series of rambling, dimly lit and low-ceilinged homely rooms and alcoves; the curved walls, darkened to a deep ochre, bulge unevenly in places, the floors are of flagstones or of ancient lime-ash (with silver coins embedded in them), and there are old high-backed oak settles (some carved) and red leatherette cushioned cask seats around antique tables. The attention to detail in the decoration is considerable: genuinely old local pictures, a profusion of sheep shears, thatchers' knives, priests (fish-coshes), gin-traps, pitchforks, antlers, copper warming-pans and lots of cutlasses, swords, shields and fine powder flasks. Bar food includes sandwiches (from 60p), pasties, steak and kidney pie (£1.70), ploughman's (£1.80), pizza (£2.25), salads (from £2.50), lasagne or spaghetti bolognese (£2.75), plaice (£2.80), scampi (£3.15), gammon (£3.90) and rump steak (£5.50), with children's meals (£1.40); traditional Sunday lunch (you have to book). Well kept Ushers Best on handpump, and some unusual country wines, such as parsnip or cherry; sensibly placed darts, skittle alley, pool-room, dominoes, shove-ha'penny, cribbage, fruit machine, piped music. The crazy-paved front terrace has old-fashioned garden seats, with an attractive garden beside it – a contributory factor to this pretty little higgledy-piggledy village's winning of the local Best Kept Village Award last year. *(Recommended by Leonard Tivey; more reports please)*

Free house   Licensees Lynne and Phil Bridle   Real ale   Meals and snacks (until 10 evenings)   Gaslit restaurant tel Combe Martin (027 188) 2465   Children in kitchen bar and family-room   Children's night Thurs   Open 11.30–2.30, 6–11 all year; opens 7 in winter

BLAGDON   SX8960 Map 1

Barton Pines

Blagdon Road, Higher Blagdon; pub signposted with Aircraft Museum on right, leaving Paignton on A385 Totnes road

This spacious Elizabethan-style nineteenth-century mansion has a carpeted lounge bar on the left, with oak window seats in the tall stone-mullioned windows, squared oak panelling, a coffered ceiling, wheel-back chairs and round tables, and a handsome stone fireplace with a grandiose carved chimneypiece; the right side is more modern, and has dominoes, darts, cribbage and a fruit machine. There's also a simpler picture-window family extension and (in the rambling back area) a carpeted pool-room with pin-table, juke box and space game, and a children's room with more space games. The decent range of bar food includes home-made soup (95p), sandwiches (£1.65 for home-cooked meats, local crab £2.45), home-made pâté (£1.75), ploughman's (from £1.95), pasty (£2.15), vegetable or meaty lasagne (£2.75), home-made steak, kidney and Guinness pie (£3.15), roast chicken with barbecue sauce (£3.25), plaice or cod in cheese sauce (£3.50), salads (from £4.15) and steak (£5.75), with additional evening dishes such as local rainbow trout (£4.95), a large mixed grill (£6.25), and half a roast duckling in an orange and Grand Marnier sauce (£7.95); several children's dishes or puddings (from £1.40); Halls Harvest on handpump, piped music. The attractive garden looks down over the sea beyond Paignton, and over the countryside to Dartmoor, and consists of a series of stepped lawns with old pines and plenty of flowers; out here are a heated outdoor swimming-pool, skittle alley and a play area (with a tractor to scramble over). The inn is right next to the museum, which has an extensive model railway and fine rose garden. *(Recommended by Brian and Anna Marsden; more reports please)*

Free house   Licensees Mr and Mrs Peter Devonshire   Real ale   Meals and snacks Restaurant tel Paignton (0803) 553350   Children in eating area, family- and games-room Live music Fri and Sat in summer   Open 12–3.30, 6.30–1am; 12–2.30, 7–11 in winter Self-catering flats

Bedroom prices normally include full English breakfast, VAT and any inclusive service charge that we know of.

BRANSCOMBE   SY1988 Map 1

Fountain Head 📭

Upper village, above the robust old church; village signposted off AA3052 Sidmouth–Seaton

Looking down a lane lined by thatched cottages, with the steep pastures of the combe beyond, this medieval tiled stone house has one room, on the left, that was formerly a smithy. So its oak beams – hung with horseshoes and forge tools – are a good deal higher than usual. There are cushioned pews and mates' chairs around wooden tables, walls of stripped uncoursed stone, and a log fire in the original raised firebed with its tall central chimney. A more orthodox snug room on the right, irregularly shaped and with another log fire, has brown-varnished panelled walls, rugs on its flagstone and lime-ash floor, and a white-painted plank ceiling with an unusual carved ceiling-rose. But in summer the best place to sit is out on the front loggia and terrace, with a little stream rustling under the flagstoned path. Good value home-made bar food includes cockles or mussels (75p), soup (£1), sandwiches, often including fresh local crab (£1.25), a choice of ploughman's (£1.50), shepherd's or fish pie (£2.25), vegetarian quiche (£2.75) and other salads, steak and kidney pie (£2.95), kebabs (£3.75) and steaks (from eight-ounce rump or sirloin, £5.75), with children's dishes (from £1.25), and lobster if you order a day ahead. Well kept Badger Best and Tanglefoot and Devenish Royal Wessex on handpump; friendly quick service, with a pleasantly relaxed and unforced local atmosphere – and an amiable dog; darts, cribbage, dominoes. Our place-to-stay award is for the self-catering flat and adjacent cottage; they don't have ordinary letting bedrooms. *(Recommended by A S Clements, Philip and Sheila Hanley, E G Parish, Jenny and Michael Back, A C Earl)*

Free house   Licensee Mrs Catherine Luxton   Real ale   Meals and snacks (Sun lunchtime service stops 1.30; no food evenings in winter unless arranged ahead)   Children in small children's room   Open 11–2.30, 6.30–11; closes half-hour earlier in winter   Self-catering tel Branscombe (029 780) 359

Masons Arms 📭

This busy, creeper-covered fourteenth-century inn has a wide range of lunchtime bar food, including soup (£1), ploughman's (£2.50), filled baked potato (£2.50), salads (from £3.50), venison sausages (£3.75), pork kebab (£3.85) and home-made steak and kidney pie (£4.50); in the evening there are half a dozen main dishes such as smoked pork loin with pineapple and ginger (£3.50), chicken curry with poppadums (£4.25) and braised pigeon breast in a port and pickled walnut sauce (£5.75); set Sunday lunch in the restaurant. The rambling, low-beamed main bar is pleasantly old-fashioned, with chairs and cushioned wall benches, and a grandfather clock; there are settles on the flagstones around the massive central hearth, with its roaring log fire, which is used on Thursday lunchtimes, and on request in the evenings, to spit-roast joints. Outside, the quiet flower-filled front terrace has tables with little thatched roofs, extending into a side garden. Well kept Bass, Badger Best and Tanglefoot on handpump; darts, shove-ha'penny, dominoes. The sea is half a mile down the lane, and the village is surrounded by little wooded hills in National Trust territory. There were management changes towards the end of 1988, and in the first few months following, though many people enjoyed their visits, there was no unanimity among readers about standards and service here, so we'd be particularly glad of more reports. *(Recommended by A C Earl, Mrs Caroline Gibbins, Philip and Sheila Hanley, Graham and Glenis Watkins, D Baddeley, E G Parish, Wayne Brindle, R D Jolliff, DMF, G and M Brooke-Williams, William Rodgers, J F Estdale, WFL, P Conrad Russell, Mrs J M Aston)*

Free house   Licensee Mrs Janet Inglis   Real ale   Meals and snacks   Restaurant Open 11–2.30 (3 Sat), 6–11 all year   Bedrooms (some in cottage across road) tel Branscombe (029 780) 300; £22.50(£32.50B)/£45(£69B)

BRATTON FLEMING SS6437 Map 1
White Hart

This bustling pub is pleasantly situated in the hills above the River Yeo; its home-made food is welcomingly unpretentious and attractively priced: good bread and cheese (£1.50) and generous dishes such as cottage pie (£1.90), steak and kidney pie, home-cooked ham, chilli con carne or lasagne (all £2), and steaks (£6.35). The traditionally furnished rambling low-ceilinged bar is divided into several cosy nooks and alcoves by steps, corners, and even the pillars protected by draymen's leather aprons; there are robust cushioned chairs and wooden stools on flagstones or parquet floors, with a refectory table in one area, and lots of cartoons and Guinness advertisements as decoration. The big stone inglenook has a fine log fire; friendly atmosphere. A decent selection of games includes shove-ha'penny, dominoes, cribbage, darts, pool, fruit machine, space game and juke box in one side section. Well kept Bass and Flowers IPA on handpump, draught cider from a big earthenware jug. There is a separate skittle alley and a small flagstoned courtyard with seats. *(Recommended by WTF, Roger Brennan, B M Eldridge, Christopher and Heather Barton, D B Delaney, Jack Taylor)*

Free house   Licensees Timothy Nicholls and M Doyle   Real ale   Meals and snacks (not Sun lunchtime)   Children welcome   Occasional live entertainment   Open 11–3, 5–11 all year

BRAYFORD SS6834 Map 1
Poltimore Arms

Yarde Down – three miles from village, towards Simonsbath; OS Sheet 180 reference 724356

The decent range of bar food in this friendly, straightforward Exmoor pub includes tasty home-made soup (80p), sandwiches (from 80p, toasties 10p extra), good curried eggs, omelettes (£1.25), ploughman's (from £1.80), home-made steak and kidney pie or lasagne (£2), vegetarian nut croquette (£2.50), salads (from £2.50) and tender steaks (from £4.80), with extra evening dishes such as their speciality noisettes of lamb (£4), fresh fish (from £4) and mixed grills (£6.50). In the main bar there are old leather-seated chairs with carved or slatted backs, wooden wall settles with flowery cushions, a little window seat, old sewing-machine and other interesting tables, a beam in the slightly sagging cream ceiling with another over the small serving-counter, and an inglenook fireplace with a wood-burning stove, old saws and a kettle; there are copper jugs and kettles on the mantelpiece. There's also a hunting theme, with photographs of hunt meetings, hunting cartoons, and on the menu an illustration of a hunt meeting under the antlers outside the pub's front door; Ushers on handpump, Cotleigh Tawny tapped from the cask. The lounge bar has a small brick open fire, a mix of chairs and a settle, Guinness and Fry's Chocolate prints and plants; a plainly decorated games-room has pool, darts, shove-ha'penny, cribbage, fruit machine and juke box. In the side garden there are picnic-table sets and a grill for barbecues. The pub has its own cricket team. *(Recommended by B M Eldridge, Steve and Carolyn Harvey, H Butterworth)*

Free house   Licensees Mike and Mella Wright   Real ale   Meals and snacks   Children's room   Open 11.30–2.30, 6.30 (6 Sat) –11 all year

BUCKLAND BREWER SS4220 Map 1
Coach & Horses

This friendly thatched house serves sandwiches, soup or pasty (£1.10), ploughman's (£1.75), with main dishes like chicken or cod (£2.50), chilli con carne or scampi (£2.75), vegetarian dishes (£2.75–£3.75), local trout (£3.50), beef curry with poppadum and chutney (£3.70), local trout (£3.25) and steak (£5.50); Sunday lunch (£3.50); obliging service. The cosy bar has heavy beams, antique settles and attractive furnishings, with logs burning in the big stone inglenook fireplace; the extension at the back also serves as a family-room. Flowers IPA on handpump; darts, dominoes, shove-ha'penny, cribbage, fruit machine, space game and juke box. There's a stone-walled terrace at the front, and a pretty little garden at the side, with tables, swings and slides. They now do bedrooms. *(Recommended by John Bowdler, Peter Cornall, J E F Rawlins, David and Flo Wallington, Charles and Mary Winpenny)*

Free house   Licensees K A Wolfe and R E Willis   Real ale   Meals and snacks Restaurant   Children in eating area   Occasional live music   Open 11–2.30, 5–11 all year; closed evening 25 Dec   Bedrooms tel Horns Cross (023 75) 395; £22/£35

BURGH ISLAND   SX6443   Map 1
Pilchard

Park in Bigbury-on-Sea and walk about 300 yards across the sands, which are covered for between six and eight hours of the twelve-hour tide; in summer use the Tractor, a unique bus-on-stilts which beats the tide by its eight-foot-high 'deck'

This basic but atmospheric twelfth-century pub is included primarily for its isolated island location. The small L-shaped bar, protected by thick-walled embrasures and storm-shuttered windows, is lit by big ships' lamps hanging from the beam and plank ceiling, and has lots of bare wood and stripped stone, with low chairs, settles edged with rope, others with high backs forming snug booths, and a good – though not always lit – log fire. The white-plastered back bar has darts, shove-ha'penny and dominoes. Bar food (sporadically available) might include soup (80p), home-made pasties (£1), filled baked potatoes (£1.20), open sandwiches (from £2.45) and salads (from around £3); Palmers IPA, Ruddles County and Ushers Founders on handpump, farm cider; maybe piped music. It can be very popular in season, and both its charm and basicness should be more apparent on, say, a quiet April lunchtime. Also on this small island (owned by the licensees) is an attractive art deco hotel, where Agatha Christie used to write and which the Duke of Windsor reputedly visited. *(Recommended by Peter Adcock, Doug Kennedy, Dennis Jones, Graeme Smalley, Jon Wainwright; more reports please)*

Free house   Real ale   Meals and snacks   Evening seafood and salad bistro, bookings only tel Kingsbridge (0548) 810344   Children in back bar and bistro   £1 car parking in Bigbury Open 11–11

BUTTERLEIGH   SS9708   Map 1
Butterleigh Inn   🏵

Village signposted off A398 in Bickleigh; or in Cullompton take turning by Manor House Hotel – it's the old Tiverton road, with the village eventually signposted off on the left

Attractive bar food in this sixteenth-century village inn includes large granary rolls (from £1.75), home-made burgers (£1.90), two or three dishes of the day such as aubergine and red bean casserole (£2.75), chilli con carne or venison sausages (£2.95), fillet steak glazed with Stilton (£6.20) and a formidable mixed grill (£7.45); tempting puddings. The atmosphere in the unpretentious series of little rooms is pleasantly local; they're all interestingly furnished, with old dining-chairs around country kitchen tables in one, sensibly placed darts and an attractive elm trestle table in another, and prettily upholstered settles around the four tables that just fit into the cosy back snug. Plates hang by one big fireplace, there are topographical prints and watercolours, pictures of birds and dogs and a fine embroidery of the Devonshire Regiment's coat of arms. Well kept Cotleigh Tawny, Harrier and Old Buzzard on handpump; darts, shove-ha'penny, cribbage, dominoes, piped music; jars of snuff on the bar. There are tables on a sheltered terrace and lawn with a log cabin for children. *(Recommended by Graham and Glenis Watkins, Steve and Carolyn Harvey, J R Carey, J Stronach, Mr and Mrs C France, Giles Bullard)*

Free house   Licensees Mike and Penny Wolter   Real ale   Meals and snacks (until 9.45 evenings)   Open 12–3, 6 (5 Fri)–11 all year   Bedrooms tel Bickleigh (088 45) 407; £14.50/£21; also cottage sleeping four, from £150 a week

CHERITON BISHOP   SX7793   Map 1
Old Thatch ✹
Village signposted from A30

The wide range of home-made bar food in this relaxed sixteenth-century inn is worth the scenic detour from the A30; it includes home-made soup (80p), sandwiches (toasted from £1.20), imaginative starters such as prawns, tomato and egg in cheese sauce served in a scallop shell (£1.60), ploughman's (£1.80), salads (from £2.75), and good hot dishes like sausage and mash (£2.20), cauliflower moussaka (£2.95), steak and kidney pudding (£3.10), a daily curry with mango chutney and a poppadum (£3.20), scampi (£3.30), jugged rabbit (£3.75), sole Véronique (£4.50), wiener schnitzel (£4.90), steak (£5.95), and enterprising puddings such as Cointreau lemon sorbet (£1), spiced bread pudding made with Guinness, or peach trifle (£1.20); polite, unobtrusive service. The rambling, beamed bar is separated from the lounge by a large open stone fireplace, lit in the cooler months. Ruddles County and Ushers Best on handpump; dominoes, cribbage, piped music. It's actually in Dartmoor's sprawling National Park. *(Recommended by Dr Sheila Smith, Nigel Paine, JS, BS, D Godden)*

Free house   Licensee Brian Bryon-Edmond   Real ale   Meals and snacks   Open 12 (11.30 Sat)–3, 6–11 all year; opens 7 in winter; closed for food and accommodation 5–11 Nov Bedrooms tel Cheriton Bishop (064 724) 204; £25.50B/£36B

CHITTLEHAMHOLT   SS6521   Map 1
Exeter Inn ⇌
Village signposted from A377 Barnstaple–Crediton and from B3226 SW of South Molton

On the old Barnstaple packhorse road, this welcoming sixteenth-century thatched inn serves a straightforward but attractive range of bar food, including plain or toasted sandwiches (from £1), ploughman's (from £2), basket meals (from £2.50), home-made steak and mushroom pie (£3.95) and grilled local trout (£4.25); good value breakfasts for residents; courteous service. The beamed main bar has cushioned mate's chairs and stools, settles, a couple of big cushioned cask armchairs by the open wood-burning stove in a huge stone fireplace, and a collection of matchboxes and foreign coins. In the side area there are seats set out as booths around the tables under the sloping ceiling. Well kept Ushers Best and Websters Yorkshire on handpump, Hancock's Devon cider; shove-ha'penny, dominoes, cribbage, fruit machine and juke box or piped music. It's close to Exmoor National Park, and there are local facilities for fishing, golf and horse-riding. *(Recommended by Tessa Stuart, Rita Horridge, John and Heather Dwane, Mrs P C Clarke, Peter Cornall, Mrs J M Scott, J S Evans)*

Free house   Licensees Norman and Kim Glenister   Real ale   Meals and snacks Restaurant   Children in eating area   Open 11.30–2.30, 6–11 all year   Bedrooms tel Chittlehamholt (076 94) 281; £18.20B/£30.80B

CHURCHSTOW   SX7145   Map 1
Church House
A379 NW of Kingsbridge

The bar in this former Benedictine hospice has plenty of character, with low and heavy black oak beams, a great stone fireplace with side bread oven, and stripped stone walls with cushioned seats cut into the deep window embrasures. The long, cosy room is neatly kept and comfortable, with an antique curved high-backed settle as well as the many smaller red-cushioned ones by the black tables on its Turkey carpet, and a line of stools – each with its own brass coathook – along the long glossy black serving-counter. Just inside the back entrance there's a new conservatory area, with a newly discovered and floodlit well in the centre. Bass, Ruddles County and Ushers Best on handpump; dominoes, darts, cribbage, fruit machine. Bar food, served at the curtained-off end of the bar, includes sandwiches, ploughman's (from £1.50), haddock (£2.45 or £2.75, depending on size), home-made dishes such as cottage pie, curry or chilli con carne (£2.50), devilled chicken or steak and kidney pie (£2.95), trout (£4.25), mixed grill (£4.75) and rump steak (£5.75); the carvery – fine roasts, help-yourself vegetables – is good value (£5.95 including home-made puddings), and you're advised to book. There are seats outside. *(Recommended by Ann and David Stranack, John Barker, Harry Stirling, Jon Wainwright, Margaret and Trevor Errington, Sue Cleasby, Mike Ledger, Mrs Carol Mason, Derek McGarry, Alan and Ruth Woodhouse)*

Free house   Licensee H (Nick) Nicholson   Real ale   Meals and snacks (not 25 or 26 Dec) Carvery Weds–Sat evenings, Sun lunch tel Kingsbridge (0548) 2237; to change to (0548) 852237   Children welcome   Open 11–2.30, 6–11 all year

COCKWOOD   SX9780 Map 1
Anchor

Off, but visible from, A379 Exeter–Torbay

The popular bar here, where tourists and locals seem to mingle happily enough, is a series of communicating small rooms, with low ceilings, black panelling, good-sized tables in various alcoves and a cheerful winter coal fire in the snug. On the food side the emphasis is very much on exceptionally fresh fish (sometimes with shellfish from the River Exe just a couple of hundred yards away); the enterprising range of dishes includes crab, cream and brandy soup (£2.55) or seafood chowder (£3.50), half a pint of prawns with a dip (£4.50), grilled whole plaice or prawns in garlic butter (£4.65), seafood in cheese sauce (£5.95) and Torbay crab salad (£6.95); there are also sandwiches (from £1.25), beef and Stilton pasty (£1.25), home-made soup (£1.35), ploughman's (from £2.85) and cottage pie (£3.95). Well kept Bass, Flowers IPA and Original and Huntsman Royal Oak on handpump, with quite a few wines by the glass; darts, dominoes, cribbage, fruit machine. Tables on a sheltered verandah look over a quiet lane to yachts and crabbing boats in the landlocked harbour. Nearby parking may be difficult on a busy evening. *(Recommended by D J and K Cooke, George Jonas, Tom Evans, Jon Wainwright, S Matthews)*

Heavitree (who no longer brew)   Licensee P Reynolds   Real ale   Meals and snacks Restaurant tel Starcross (0626) 890203   Children in eating area and restaurant Open 11–11; 11–2.30 6–11 in winter

COLEFORD   SS7701 Map 1
New Inn 🍺

Just off A377 Crediton–Barnstaple

The spaciously rambling bar in this thatched fourteenth-cenutry inn has a central servery with modern settles forming stalls around tables on the russet carpet, and a solid-fuel stove; the four areas that spiral around it are interestingly furnished with settles ancient and modern, spindle-back chairs, low dark green velour armchairs and plush-cushioned stone wall seats. There are some character tables – a pheasant worked into the grain of one – carved dressers and chests, paraffin lamps, antique prints and old guns on the white walls, landscape plates on one of the beams and pewter tankards hanging from another. Since taking it over a couple of years ago, the licensees have expanded their food range, which now typically includes home-made soup (£1.15), Stilton and walnut pâté (£1.95), open sandwiches or filled baked potatoes (£2.50), home-made curry, chilli, lasagne and pies (all £2.95), salads (£4), lamb with garlic and ginger, beef in Guinness or tandoori chicken (£5.50), steaks (from £7.25) and home-made puddings (from £1.50). Flowers IPA and Original, Wadworths 6X and a summer guest beer on handpump, and a decent range of wines by the glass; fruit machine (out of the way up by the door), shove-ha'penny and piped music. *(Recommended by Lawrence Manning, Ian Blackwell, Joseph Melling, Theo Schofield)*

Free house Licensee Paul Butt Real ale Meals and snacks Restaurant Children in eating area and restaurant Open 11.30–2.30, 6–11 all year Bedrooms tel Copplestone (0363) 84242; £22(£26B)/£30(£32B)

COLYTON SY2493 Map 1

Kingfisher

Dolphin Street; village signposted off A35 and A3052 E of Sidmouth; in village follow Axminster, Shute, Taunton signpost

This straightforward village pub (very much a local, but also warmly welcoming to strangers) stands out for its range of well kept beers: Badger Best, Flowers IPA, Huntsman Royal Oak and guests such as Cotleigh Kingfisher and Old Buzzard in winter, Wadworths 6X and Wiltshire Old Grumble on handpump; they also have Farmer John's cider, from along the Exeter road a bit (the cider farm's open for visits). The bar has walls stripped back to stone, blue plush cushioned window seats, stools, sturdy elm wing settles and rustic tables, and a big open fireplace. Glasses slotted into the two waggon-wheels hanging above the bar swing in unison when someone in the upstairs family-room (where there's a useful box of toys) walks above the beamed ceiling. Bar food includes sandwiches (from 75p, prawn £2), filled baked potatoes (from £1.60), plaice or gammon (around £3), with children's dishes; sensibly placed darts, shove-ha'penny, dominoes, cribbage, fruit machine, trivia and skittle alley. The garden has a climbing-frame for children and a terrace with tables under cocktail parasols. *(Recommended by Brian and Anna Marsden, John and Heather Dwane, Dr D M Forsyth, Dr Stewart, J R Carey, DMF)*

Free house Licensees Graeme and Cherry Sutherland Real ale Meals and snacks (until 10 evenings) Children in family-room Open 11–2.30, 6–11 all year

COMBEINTEIGNHEAD SX9071 Map 1

Coombe Cellars

Pub signposted off B3195 Newton Abbot–Shaldon

This estuary pub is popular with naturalists, particularly when the tide's out and innumerable busy wading birds join the shelducks, mergansers, herons, cormorants and gulls to pick over the shiny mudflats. The long main bar, recently redecorated by the new licensees, has very large windows along its left-hand side, offering a superb view up the River Teign, and is decorated with nautical bric-à-brac and captain's chairs, with compasses set into the couches. There's a family area off one end, three fire-effect gas fires and lots of patio area outside; the summerhouse, which also overlooks the river, doubles as a restaurant in the evening. Bar food includes soup (95p), sandwiches (from £1), ploughman's (from £2.20), ham and egg (£2.95), steak and kidney pie (£3.45), curry, chicken tikka, lasagne, sweet-and-sour pork and vegetarian dishes (all £3.95), fresh plaice (£4.25) and steaks (from £6.95). Courage Best and Directors on handpump; fruit machine and piped music. There's a play area outside, and lots of watersports facilities – the pub is the base for the South Devon Water Sports Association, runs its own water skiing club and

---

Pubs with outstanding views are listed at the back of the book.

has a landing-stage. *(Recommended by Steve Huggins; reports on the new regime please)*
*Free house   Licensees Mr and Mrs Gooderhan   Real ale   Meals and snacks (until 10
evenings)   Children in family-room   Open 11–3, 6–11 all year; tends to open all day if the
tide is in*

COUNTISBURY   SS7449 Map 1
Exmoor Sandpiper 🏮 🛏

A39, 2 or 3 miles E of Lynton on the Porlock road

Tucked into the hillside opposite a moorland church, and still known to many as
the Blue Boar (a name it carried for more than 300 years), this spaciously rambling
low white inn has four or five welcoming rooms, with ancient bumpy plaster walls,
low ceilings, some heavy black beams and antique dining-chairs and settles; the
unusual collection of paraphernalia here includes an antique fortune-telling
machine and aggressive-looking badger and foxes' masks; darts, pool, dominoes,
board games and fruit machine in the games area; piped music. Particularly
recommended on the food side is their ham, smoked on the premises in the
chimneys of the four log fires – look out for the ones hanging among the pots,
cauldrons and kettles of the great central fire. It features prominently in the good
range of large salads (£4.95); other dishes include sandwiches (£1.10), soup (£1.25)
and ploughman's (£2.50). Well kept Bass, Charringtons IPA and Courage Directors
on handpump, and a good range of unusual whiskies. It's well placed for Exmoor
and the National Trust Watersmeet estate; on *Good Walks Guide* Walk 22.
*(Recommended by Maj and Mrs I McKillop, Henry Midwinter, Wayne Brindle, Wilfred
Plater-Shellard, Lynne Sheridan, Bob West, Steve and Carolyn Harvey)*
*Free house   Licensee A Vickery   Real ale   Meals and snacks   Book-lined restaurant
Children welcome   Open 11–3, 5.30–11 (may open longer afternoons) all year
Bedrooms tel Brendon (059 87) 263; £28.75B/£57.50B*

DALWOOD   ST2400 Map 1
Tuckers Arms 🏮

Village signposted off A35 Axminster–Honiton

Down narrow high-hedged lanes through this rich, gently hilly pasture country, the
Tuckers Arms is a cream-washed thatched medieval longhouse of great age, prettily
decked with hanging baskets and big pots of flowers. A wide choice of enterprising
bar food includes soup such as clear beef and mushroom (£1.05), potato skins with
interesting dips (from £1.95), salmon and cucumber with dill sauce (£2.25), lasagne
(£3.45), steak and kidney pie (£3.95), good salads (from £3.95), duck with smoky
bacon or grilled rack of lamb (£5.95) and steaks (from £5.95), with a good few
specials such as pressed beef brisket with mustard sauce (£3.15), vegetarian
tagliatelle (£3.35) and a plate of continental meats and cheeses (£3.45); good
children's dishes (from £1.55, served until 7.30), rich puddings (from £1.55).
Perhaps their most popular dish is their 'tiddy': a big puff pastry with a changing
savoury filling, such as salmon with lemon and asparagus or veal with mushrooms
and cheese (£4.25). The oak-beamed bar, partly flagstoned and with both a big
inglenook log fireplace and a wood-burning stove, is rather informally furnished: a
random mixture of dining-chairs, a funky armchair, window-seats, a pew and a
high-backed winged black settle. A side lounge with shiny black woodwork has a
couple of cushioned oak armchairs and other comfortable but unpretentious seats.
Well kept Bass, Courage Best and Directors, Palmers IPA and Wadworths 6X on
handpump; skittle alley; picnic-table sets outside. Careful parking will keep the
villagers happy. *(Recommended by W L B Reed, Major and Mrs J V Reed, J R Carey)*
*Free house   Licensees David and Kate Beck   Real ale   Meals and snacks (until 10
evenings)   Children in side room until 9   Open 12–3, 6.30–11 all year   Bedrooms should be
ready late 1989 tel Stockland (040 488) 342; £22B/£32B*

DARTINGTON SX7762 Map 1
Cott

In hamlet with the same name, signposted off A385 W of Totnes opposite A384 turn-off

As we went to press in August 1989 this fine pub burnt down; we wish the owners luck with their rebuilding and look forward to its re-opening

DARTMOUTH SX8751 Map 1
Cherub ✪

Higher Street

This charming and welcoming fourteenth-century Grade-I-listed pub changes hands more frequently than any other we know (three times in as many years), but remarkably manages to maintain the standards of food and service that first brought it to our attention. The unanimously praised range of bar food includes sandwiches, soup (£1.25, French onion £1.35), filled baked potatoes (from £1.25), ploughman's (from £2.25), smoked haddock in white wine and cheese sauce (£2.50), spaghetti bolognese (£2.95), celery hearts baked with ham in a cheese sauce, chilli con carne or ratatouille (£3.25), smoked chicken with broccoli and ham (£3.75), seafood pasta (£4.50) and seven fresh local fish dishes. Bass, Blackawton and Flowers IPA and Original on handpump, and forty-two malt whiskies. Originally a fourteenth-century wool merchant's house, it has shown a resilient attitude to the progress of time: it survived an 1864 fire which destroyed the southern end of the street, and the Second World War bombing which destroyed the north side; hence it's the oldest building around here. Each of the two heavily timbered upper floors juts further out than the one below; inside, the snug bar has tapestried seats under creaky heavy beams, red-curtained leaded-light windows and an open stove in the big stone fireplace. *(Recommended by A E Melven, H K Dyson, Margaret and Trevor Errington, Sue Carlyle, George Jonas, Paul and Janet Waring, AE, GRE, David and Ann Stranack, C A Foden and G Atkinson, Jon Wainwright, R Sinclair Taylor, Simon Turner, Paul and Margaret Baker, CED)*

Free house   Licensees Mr and Mrs J Hill   Real ale   Meals and snacks   Restaurant tel Dartmouth (080 43) 2571   Children in restaurant   Open 11–3, 5–11 all year

Royal Castle 🛏

11 The Quay

The range of generously served bar food in this attractive seventeenth-century waterside hotel was in the process of expanding as we went to press; at present it includes lunchtime sandwiches (from 95p, prawn or crab £2.25), and a choice of ploughman's (from £2.25), as well as home-made soup (£1.10), filled baked potatoes (from £1.75), half a pint of prawns (£2.75), vegetarian dishes (£2.75), steak and kidney pie or fish casserole (£3.75), whole plaice (£3.95), salads (from £3.95), turkey curry with poppadums and chutney (£4.25) and rump steak (£5.85). The bar on the left is a lively local place, with stripped pine country kitchen chairs and stools, mate's chairs and a couple of interesting old settles around a mix of tables, from scrubbed deal through traditional, cast-iron-framed ones to polished mahogany. One wall is stripped to the original stonework, there's a big log fire, and decorations include navigation lanterns, glass net-floats and old local ship photographs. Big windows overlook the inner harbour and beyond to the bigger boats in the main one. On the right in the more sedate, Turkey-carpeted bar, they spit-roast joints on the range at lunchtime; there's also a Tudor fireplace with copper jugs and kettles (beside which are the remains of a spiral staircase) and plush furnishings, including some Jacobean-style chairs, and in one alcove swords and heraldic shields on the wall; some of its oak beams reputedly come from the wreckage of the Spanish Armada. Both bars lead off an attractively sunny nineteenth-century staircase at the centre of the hotel. Well kept Bass, Courage Best and Marstons Pedigree on handpump; backgammon, Trivial Pursuit, cribbage, fruit and trivia machines, piped music. *(Recommended by John Knighton, J E F Rawlins, Jon Wainwright, Pamela and Merlyn Horswell)*

Free house   Licensees Nigel and Anne Way   Real ale   Meals and snacks (12–10) Restaurant   Children in eating areas   Live music Weds, Thurs and Sun evenings in winter   Open 11–11 all year   Bedrooms tel Dartmouth (080 43) 4004; £36B/£68B

DITTISHAM   SX8654 Map 1

Ferry Boat

Follow Ferry sign (*sharp* right turn), park in main car park and walk down narrow steep lane to water's edge; or at low tide keep straight on past Ferry sign, park down by playing fields and walk along foreshore to pub; or even come up on the little passenger ferry from Dartmouth

The position of this straightforward, pleasant pub is particularly idyllic, at the bottom of the quiet thatched village, and looking out over the boats on the wide river. The bar has various nautical accoutrements, including a ship's bell (there's another outside which you can use to call the ferry to take you across the river to Dartmouth), brass gear and a ship's clock over the coal fire, ship's badges over the serving-counter, and photographs of boats and ships; they chalk up the tide times on the wall. There are simple seats in the big picture window (which has fine views over the river), and a few others outside. Bar food includes filled rolls (£2), mussels in garlic butter (£3), salads (from £4), gammon (£6.25) and steak (£6.50); Courage Best and Directors on handpump; shove-ha'penny, darts, table skittles, dominoes, cribbage, piped music. *(Recommended by Helen Emmitt, David and Ann Stranack, Margaret and Trevor Errington, K and R A Markham, AE, Jon Wainwright)*

Courage   Licensee Nicholas Treldar   Real ale   Meals and snacks (not Tues)   Occasional folk music   Open 11–3, 6–11 (all day Sat) all year

DODDISCOMBSLEIGH SX8586 Map 1

Nobody Inn ★ ★ 🏵 🛏

Village signposted off B3193, opposite northernmost Christow turn-off

There's a range of entertaining stories about the origins of the name of this attractive and welcoming sixteenth-century village inn – our favourite this year is of the undertaker who once owned it; a local rumour that he had buried an empty coffin was confirmed when it was exhumed and nobody found in it. However, the two rooms of the lounge bar here are liable to be anything but empty; they're particularly atmospheric, with carriage lanterns hanging from the beams (some of which are original), handsomely carved antique settles, Windsor and wheel-back chairs, red leatherette benches and a Turkey carpet, with guns and hunting prints decorating a snug area by one of the big inglenook fireplaces. A major distinction is the inn's preoccupation with alcoholic gourmandise – it's probably the best pub for wines in the country, with a remarkable choice of 700 well cellared wines by the bottle, a good range by the glass, properly mulled wine in winter, and twice-monthly tutored tastings in winter (they also do a retail trade, and the good tasting-notes in their detailed list are worth the £2 it costs – anyway refunded if you buy more than £10-worth); there's also a choice of 220 whiskies and usually well kept Bass, Flowers IPA, Huntsman Royal Oak and occasional guest beers on handpump or tapped straight from the cask. The wide range of highly praised, efficiently served bar food includes sandwiches (from 90p, made to order), home-made soup (£1.10), coarse home-made calves' liver pâté (£1.20), hot smoked mackerel (£2), sausage and mash (£2.10), hot pitta salad (£2.20), ploughman's or butter-bean casserole (£2.30), and lasagne with a lamb sauce or vegetable pie (£2.90); interesting puddings include ice-cream sprinkled with raisins and marinated in Australian Muscat wine (£1.50), fruit flan (£1.70), chocolate fudge cake (£1.90) and a selection of six local cheeses (£2.30) from a wide range. They also sell local honey and clotted Jersey cream. There are picnic-table sets in the charming garden, with views of the surrounding wooded hill pastures. The medieval stained glass in the local church is some of the best in the West Country. *(Recommended by Lyn and Bill Capper, Sybil Baker, C Vallely, WTF, David and Jane Russell, Gwen and Peter Andrews, Peter Donahue, Christopher Knowles-Fitton, D Rowden, S Matthews, Mr and Mrs J C Dwane, Alan and Ruth Woodhouse, G F Couch, Dave Butler, Lesley Storey, WFL, M W Barratt, J C Proud, W C M Jones, Tom Evans, Stephen McNees, David and Flo Wallington, T B B, WHBM, CED, Roger and Kathy, Mrs E M Brandwood, Richard Balkwill)*

Free house Licensee Nicholas Borst-Smith Real ale Meals and snacks (until 10 evenings) Open 12–2.30, 6–11 (7–10.30 in winter); closed evening 25 Dec Restaurant (closed Sun) Bedrooms (some in distinguished eighteenth-century house 150yds away) tel Christow (0647) 52394; £13(£25B)/£33(£39B) Restaurant and bedrooms closed second week Jan

DREWSTEIGNTON SX7390 Map 1

Drewe Arms

The charm of this thatched village local alehouse lies in its unchanged and unaffected basicness, resolutely maintained by the landlady Mabel Mudge, the oldest licensee in the country. Its atmosphere is pre-war: basic built-in wooden benches face each other across plain tables, ochre walls have local team photographs and advertisements tacked to them, and there's no serving-counter – the well kept real ale (typically Wadworths 6X and Whitbreads) and draught cider, which you can draw yourself, are kept on racks in the tap-room at the back. There's a third room which is used occasionally; friendly locals. Note the herringbone-pattern Elizabethan brick floor. Though nearby Castle Drogo (open for visits) looks medieval, it was built earlier this century. Near the start of *Good Walks Guide*

Walk 19. *(Recommended by Chris Raisin, Graham Doyle, Phil and Sally Gorton, Joseph Melling, Henry Hooper, Mrs Thompson, WFL)*

Free house   Real ale   Snacks   Open 10.30–2.30, 6–11 all year

EAST DOWN   SS5941 Map 1

Pyne Arms 🏆

Off A39 Barnstaple–Lynton; OS sheet 180 reference 600415

Popular and generously served helpings of food in this well maintained old pub, close to Arlington Court, include home-made soup (90p), filled rolls and sandwiches (from £1), ploughman's or home-made pâté (£2), home-cooked ham and egg (£2.95), salads (from £2.45), mussels in season prepared in five different ways (£4.85), beef Stroganoff (£6.85) and several veal dishes (£6.95); the range of puddings (from £1.75) are made by the new pastry chef. The dimly lit and pleasantly rural L-shaped bar has a low beamed ceiling, lots of nooks and crannies, a very high-backed curved settle by the door (as well as more ordinary pub seating), and horse-racing prints and Guinness and Martell placards on the red walls; there's a wood-burning stove with horse harness and farm tools on the wall above it, some copper jugs, and big barrels standing around. Up some steps is a small galleried loft with more tables and chairs. A flagstoned games area has pine-plank wall benches, a shelf with old soda syphons, handbells, and a clock, some swan-necked wall lamps, antlers, racing and hunting prints and a piano; pool-table, darts, shove-ha'penny, cribbage, dominoes and fruit machine; juke box. Well kept Flowers IPA on handpump, several wines by the glass or bottle. The boisterous Dobermann is popular with visitors, though he isn't allowed in the bar. If you like the sound of this pub, you'll probably also like the Black Venus at Challacombe – under the same management. *(Recommended by Mr and Mrs P C Clark, H J Hooper, Paul and Joanna Pearson, Maj and Mrs I McKillop, Alan Symes, Steve and Carolyn Harvey, Wilfred Plater-Shellard, D J Wallington, Wayne Brindle)*

Free house   Licensees Mr and Mrs Kemp   Real ale   Meals and snacks   Children under 14 in small eating area   Open 11–2.30, 6–11 all year; closed evening 25 Dec

EXETER   SX9292 Map 1

Double Locks ★

Canal Banks, Alphington; from A30 take main Exeter turn-off (A377/396) then next right into Marsh Barton Industrial Estate and follow Refuse Incinerator signs; when road bends round in front of the factory-like incinerator, take narrow dead-end track over humpy bridge, cross narrow canal swing bridge and follow track along canal; much quicker than it sounds, and a very worthwhile diversion from the final M5 junction

This remote canal lockhouse, probably one of the oldest in the country, has a lively but easy-going and welcoming bar which resembles the interior of a retired seafarer's cottage, with nautical impedimenta including ships' lamps and model ships. The imaginative, good value food ranges from sandwiches (from 80p), soup (90p), large filled baked potatoes (from £1.50), and generous mushrooms on toast (£1.70), through hot dishes such as fish, chilli con carne or turkey and mushroom pie (£2), vegetarian dishes like stuffed peppers or leek and macaroni bake (£2) and lasagne (£2.20), ploughman's (from £2.15), and salads (from £3), to good puddings (from 80p). Well kept Everards Old Original, Exmoor, Greene King Abbot, Huntsman Royal Oak, Marstons Pedigree and Owd Rodger, Mitchells and Wadsworth 6X on handpump or tapped from the cask, and a decent range of Irish whiskies; darts, shove-ha'penny, dominoes and cribbage in the main bar, bar billiards in another; piped music. There are picnic-table sets and a well provisioned

If we know a pub does summer barbecues, we say so.

play area, with an old steam train and swings, out on the grass. *(Recommended by Ian Phillips, Dr and Mrs B D Smith, Steve and Carolyn Harvey, David Pearman, Patrick Young, Byrne Sherwood, Jon Wainwright, Ruth Humphrey, Patrick Young, J Figueira, B G Steele-Perkins, D Pearman, Hugh Butterworth)*

Free house   Licensee Jamie Stuart   Real ale   Meals and snacks (all day)   Children in two of the bars   Open 11–11 all year

White Hart ★ 🏠

South Street; 4 rather slow miles from M5 junction 30; follow City Centre signs via A379, B3182; straight towards centre if you're coming from A377 Topsham Road

This fine, well kept fourteenth-century inn is exceptionally atmospheric, particularly in the rambling main bar, where the walls are decorated with pictorial plates, old copper and brass platters (on which the antique lantern lights glisten), silver and copper in a wall cabinet, and long-barrelled rifles above the log fire in one great fireplace. There are big Windsor armchairs and built-in winged settles with latticed glass tops to their high backs around oak tables on the bare oak floorboards (carpet in the quieter lower area); big copper jugs hang from heavy bowed beams in the dark ochre terracotta ceiling; and a set of fine old brass beer engines resides in one of the bay windows. From the latticed windows, with their stained-glass coats of arms, one can look out on the cobbled courtyard – lovely when the wistaria is flowering in May. The Tap Bar, across the yard, with flagstones, candles in bottles and a more wine-barish feel, serves soup (£1.25), sandwiches (from £1.60), smoked mackerel (£2), plate of prawns (£2.10), cold-table meats (from £3.85), burgers (£3.95), chicken and chestnut pie (£4.75), steak and kidney pie (£4.95), rib of beef (£7.25) and steak (£7.85). There is yet another bar, called Bottlescreu Bill's, even more dimly candlelit, with bare stone walls and sawdust on the floor. It serves much the same food, as well as a respectable range of Davy's wines and pint jugs of vintage port from the wood or tankards of buck's fizz, and in summer does lunchtime barbecue grills in a second, sheltered courtyard. On Sundays both these bars are closed. Bass and Davy's Old Wallop on handpump. Bedrooms are in a separate modern block. *(Recommended by Steve and Carolyn Harvey, Jon Wainwright, Dr J R Hamilton; more reports please)*

Free house   Licensee Brian Wilkinson   Real ale   Meals and snacks (not Sun) Restaurant   Children welcome   Open 11–3, 5–11 (all day Thurs–Sat); closed 25 and 26 Dec   Bedrooms tel Exeter (0392) 79897; £27(£40B)/£58B

EXMINSTER   SX9487 Map 1

Swans Nest ★ 🚫

Pub signposted from A379 S of village

This is a decidedly rambling place – so much so that the softly lit and genuinely atmospheric bar never seems to end; under the heavy beams there are groups of sofas and armchairs, some carved old-fashioned settles, lots of wheel-back chairs, high-backed winged settles (upholstered in button-back green leather or flock red plush, and set out as booths around the tables), grandfather clocks, high shelves of willow-pattern platters and so on. There's a very strong emphasis on food, for which reason it tends to be very popular – though any delays are generally bearable, and service stays both friendly and efficient. As well as an attractive carvery, the wide range of food from the no-smoking servery includes soup (95p), sandwiches (from £1.60 – not Saturday evening or Sunday lunchtime), chicken chasseur or ham omelette (£3.85), home-made steak, kidney and mushroom pie (£4.25), a good choice of salads (from £3.25), chef's specials such as rabbit stew or braised oxtail (£3.85) or roast haunch of venison in a red wine sauce (£4.05), and an interesting choice of puddings like chocolate Pavlova or brandy and cognac crunch (£1.60); children's menu (£2.25). Bass, Flowers Original and Wadworths 6X on handpump, and some unusual country wines such as apricot or parsnip. It's air-conditioned throughout and has a sensible non-smoking area. In the vast but charmingly landscaped car park they ask you to drive forwards into the bays to prevent exhaust damage to their fine shrubs. *(Recommended by Gerald Gilling, Patrick Young, Mr and Mrs Jon Payne, M P Hallewell)*

Free house   Licensees the Major family   Real ale   Meals and snacks (6–10 evenings)   Live entertainment Thurs–Sat evenings   Open 11–2.30, 6–11 all year

Turf ★

Continue past the Swans Nest (previous entry) to end of track, by gates; park, and walk right along canal towpath – nearly a mile

This attractively isolated inn is peacefully situated by the last lock of the Exeter Canal before the estuary of the River Exe; you can reach the canal basin by a forty-minute ride from Countess Wear in their own boat, the *Water Mongoose* (bar on board; £2 return, charter for up to 56 people £80). The bar itself is a connected series of airy high-ceilinged rooms furnished with flagstones or broad bare floorboards, a wood-burning stove, fresh flowers on low varnished tables, canal photographs and big bright shorebird prints by John Tennent on the white walls. The straightforward bar food is generous and fresh, and includes sandwiches (from 80p, toasted from 95p), pasties (85p), soup (£1), baked potato (from 80p), cottage pie (£1.45), ploughman's (from £2), ham and eggs (£2.10), salads (£2.60); in summer there's a well run cook-yourself barbecue; friendly, efficient service. Well kept Flowers IPA and Huntsman Royal Oak on handpump or tapped from the cask, and Inch's cider; darts, shove-ha'penny. Below, on the big lawn running down to the shore, you can play French boules; there are also log seats, picnic-table sets and a beached cabin boat for children to play in. In summer 1989 the inn was up for sale, so the licensee may well have changed – please let us know if there have been any changes. *(Recommended by Chris Raisin, Graham Doyle, D J and K Cooke, Jon Wainwright, Alan and Audrey Chatting)*

Free house   Licensee Kenneth William Stuart   Real ale   Meals and snacks   Children welcome   Open 11–11; 11–2.30, 6–11 in winter   Bedrooms tel Exeter (0392) 833128; £12/£24

HARBERTON   SX7758 Map 1
Church House

Village signposted from A381 just S of Totnes

We've been getting promising reports of a warm welcome and friendly service at this ancient village pub since it changed hands in early 1988. Parts of it may in fact be Norman, when it was probably used as a chantry-house for monks connected with the church, and some of the oldest sections have benefited from being hidden for centuries – for example the latticed glass on the back wall of the bar by the entrance was in a window which had been walled off (probably to evade window tax) until Victorian times; it's almost 700 years old, and one of the earliest examples of non-ecclesiastical glass in the country. Similarly, the magnificent medieval oak panelling in the other bar was discovered behind some plaster only when renovations were carried out in 1950. Both bars are furnished with attractive seventeenth- and eighteenth-century seats and settles, and connected by a small stone-floored lobby with snugly built-in black settles. The wide range of popular bar food (there may be delays on a busy evening) includes sandwiches (from £1), home-made soup (£1.20, crab £1.70), sausages (£1.75), ploughman's (from £1.95), fillet of plaice (£2.75, whole £4.75), scampi (£3.90), half a chicken or chicken curry with a poppadum (£3.95), gammon or three lamb cutlets (£4.75) and steaks (from £5.75); puddings (from 95p). Courage Best and Directors, Marstons Pedigree and a guest beer such as Blackawton Bitter, Exmoor, Youngs or Wadsworths 6X on handpump, as well as Inch's or another local cider; dominoes. The pub is in a steep little twisting village, pretty and surrounded by hills. *(Recommended by WS, John Walker, Roy Scott, Ken Peet, Jon Wainwright)*

Free house Licensee Mrs J E Wright Real ale Meals and snacks Restaurant tel Totnes (0803) 863707 Children in family-room Local morris team second Thurs of month Open 11.30–2.30 (3 Sat), 6–11 all year

HATHERLEIGH SS5404 Map 1

George 🍺

The main bar in this recently rethatched, welcoming fifteenth-century inn was built from the wreck of the inn's old brewhouse and coachmen's loft; it's a spacious L-shaped affair, with beams, a wood-burning stove and antique settles around sewing-machine treadle tables; a quieter extension, with more modern furnishings, leads off this. The little front bar – mainly for residents – in the original part of the building has easy chairs, sofas and antique cushioned settles, an enormous fireplace, tremendous oak beams and stone walls two or three feet thick. Across the corridor from this there's an even smaller and very simple bar, which is open only on market day (Tuesday). Straightforward, efficiently served bar food ranges from sandwiches (from £1.20, club £2), soup (£1.25), filled baked potatoes (from £1.75) and ploughman's (£1.90), through lasagne (£2.75), spinach and mushroom roulade or plaice (£3), steak and kidney pie (£3), fry-ups (£3.50) and steaks (£6), to puddings (£1.75); Sunday roast lunch (£3.75). Well kept Bass, Flowers Original, Wadworths 6X and a guest beer on handpump; darts, pool, piped music. In the floodlit courtyard there are hanging baskets and window boxes on the black and white timbering, and rustic wooden seats and tables on its cobblestones. A small heated swimming-pool is well screened by the car park. *(Recommended by David Wallington, Roy and Barbara Wallington, J Harvey Hallam, Juliet Streatfield, Neil Evans, Dexter Masters, David Sawyer, Mrs Pamela Roper)*

Free house Licensees Veronica Devereux and John Dunbar-Ainley Real ale Meals and snacks Restaurant (closed Sun) Children in lower room of main bar Occasional live bands and folk music Open 11–11; 11–3.30, 6–11 in winter Bedrooms tel Okehampton (0837) 810454; £27(£35B)/£35(£46B)

HAYTOR VALE SX7677 Map 1

Rock ★ 🏵 🍺

Haytor signposted off B3344 just W of Bovey Tracey, on good moorland road to Widecombe

The bar in this civilised Dartmoor inn is a charming surprise in comparison with its straightforward exterior; it's partly panelled, and has polished antique tables, easy chairs, oak Windsor armchairs and high-backed settles. In the two communicating rooms there are flowers in summer, good log fires in winter (the main fireplace has a fine Stuart fireback), and old-fashioned prints and decorative plates on the walls; Bass, Huntsman Dorchester and Royal Oak on handpump. The wide choice of highly praised bar food includes pasty (95p), sandwiches (from £1, ham, asparagus and pineapple £2.95), home-made soup (£1.20), filled baked potato (£1.95), omelettes made with local free-range eggs (£2.75), ploughman's (£2.75), vegetarian dishes (from £2.75), lasagne (£2.95), curries (£3.75), rabbit and cider casserole (£3.95), crab and mushroom bake or grilled lamb chops (£4.25), fish casserole (£4.95), local trout or plaice (£5.95), steaks (from £5.95) and a good range of puddings such as apple cheesecake, treacle tart or bread-and-butter pudding (all £1.25); they warn of delays at busy periods. The winter Friday-night break – you pay for a meal for two in the restaurant and get free overnight accommodation – is good value. The village itself is just inside the National Park, and the inn is well positioned for golf, horse-riding and fishing. The big garden is pretty and well kept.

(Recommended by J A Harrison, Peter Donahue, D K and H M Brenchley, Steve Huggins, Hilary Robinson, Peter Maden, W A Gardiner, David and Flo Wallington, William Rodgers, Mr and Mrs P W Dryland, SC, Roger Huggins, Tom McLean, Ewan McCall, Paul and Margaret Baker, Alan and Audrey Chatting)

Free house   Licensee Christopher Graves   Real ale   Snacks (not Sun or bank hols) Restaurant (residents only on Sun)   Children in eating area and restaurant   Open 11–2.30, 6 (6.30 in winter)–11   Bedrooms tel Haytor (036 46) 305; £18.50(£30.50B)/£37(£45B)

HENNOCK   SX8380 Map 1

Palk Arms

Village signposted from B3193; also good road first right turn after leaving Chudleigh Knighton on B3344 for Bovey Tracey

Eating in comfort around the low rustic tables of the dining lounge, you have the Teign Valley spread out far below you, with a big picture window for the view. Food includes sandwiches, salads (from £3.50), hot dishes such as steak and kidney pie, curries or pasta (£3.50–£3.95) and fresh plaice (£4.25). Downstairs from the lounge bar is an attractive bread oven. Halls Harvest on handpump; darts, dominoes, cribbage, fruit machine, piped music. Picnic-table sets on the back lawn look down over the valley. The sixteenth-century inn is close to the Hennock reservoirs, good for fly-fishing. *(Recommended by Julia Bowder, J R Carey; more reports please)*

Free house   Licensees Jim and Judith Young   Real ale   Meals and snacks   Restaurant (closed Sun evening)   Children in restaurant   Open 11–2.30, 7–11 (12–2.30, 7–11 in winter)   Bedrooms tel Bovey Tracey (0626) 833027; £12.50/£25

HOLNE   SX7069 Map 1

Church House   🏮 🛏

Originally built as a resting-place for visiting clergy and worshippers at the church, and to brew ale for religious feast days, this Grade-II-listed medieval Dartmoor inn has a fine lower bar with stripped pine panelling, and an atmospheric carpeted lounge bar with a sixteenth-century heavy oak partition and an eighteenth-century curved elm settle. The highly praised bar food ranges from ploughman's (from £1.85), omelettes (from £2.75) and cauliflower cheese (£2.75), through lasagne, shallow-fried plaice, chicken fricassee or moussaka (all £3.25), casseroles (from £3.50) and a large steak and kidney pie (£3.75), to roasts (from £3.75) and grills (from £4.25). Blackawton Bitter and Forty-four and Fergusons Dartmoor on handpump, and local cider; darts, dominoes, table skittles and cribbage in the public bar. The village is surprisingly untouristy; perhaps the nicest way of getting here is the quarter-hour walk from the Newbridge National Trust car park, and there are many other attractive walks nearby, up on to Dartmoor as well as along the wooded Dart valley. There are fine moorland views from the pillared porch (popular with regulars). *(Recommended by Mrs J Fellowes, Mr and Mrs I Blackwell, David and Flo Wallington, Steve Huggins, Philip and Trisha Ferris, Jon Wainwright, A N Martin, WHBM, Mrs J A Trotter, Pat and Malcolm Rudlin, Prof A N Black)*

Free house   Licensees N E and W J Bevan   Real ale   Snacks (not evening) and meals Restaurant   Children in eating area and restaurant   Local folk groups and accordionist last Fri in month   Open 11.30–2.30, 6.30–11; 12–2.30, 7–10.30 in winter (11 Fri and Sat) Bedrooms tel Poundsgate (036 43) 208; £12.50 (£17.50B)/ £25(£35B)

People named as recommenders after the main entries have told us that the pub should be included. But they have not written the report – we have, after anonymous on-the-spot inspection.

HORNDON SX5280 Map 1

Elephant's Nest ★ ★ ⊗

If coming from Okehampton on A386 turn left at Mary Tavy Inn, then left after about ½ mile; pub signposted beside Mary Tavy Inn, then Horndon signposted; on the OS Outdoor Leisure Map it's named as the New Inn

This welcoming sixteenth-century Dartmoor inn (named after a previous licensee's nickname) has an attractively local atmosphere in its flagstoned bar, which has cushioned stone seats built into the windows looking out on the moor, captain's chairs around the tables, large rugs, a beam and board ceiling, a large entertaining elephant mural and a good log fire on cool days. Well kept Palmers IPA, Ruddles Best and County, St Austell HSD and Websters Yorkshire on handpump; sensibly placed darts, cribbage, dominoes, shut-the-box and fruit machine. Bar food (particularly popular in the evening) includes good home-made soup (£1), sandwiches, a good ploughman's with an interesting salad (from £2), chilli con carne (£2.45), a generous home-made steak and kidney pie (£3.45), local trout (£4.75) and steaks (£7.65); they also have a range of specials and three vegetarian dishes; efficient, friendly service. Though you can walk from here straight on to the moor or Black Down, a better start (army exercises permitting) might be to drive past Wapsworthy to the end of the lane, at OS Sheet 191 reference 546805. The spacious flower-bordered lawn has assorted white tables and chairs. The new licensees now do bedrooms. *(Recommended by Heather Sharland, Doug Kennedy, Richard Cole, TBB, Hilary Robinson, Peter Maden, Dennis Heatley, C H and W A Harbottle, Simon Turner, Caroline Bailey, Dr G M Stephenson, R C Vincent, Jill Hampton, Mr and Mrs G J Packer, P and M Rudlin)*

Free house Licensees Nick and Gill Hamer and Peta Hughes Real ale Meals and snacks (until 10 evenings) Children in restaurant Open 11.30–2.30 (3 Sat), 6.30–11 Bedrooms tel Mary Tavy (082 281) 273; £15/£25

HORSEBRIDGE SX3975 Map 1

Royal ★

Village signposted off A384 Tavistock–Launceston

Originally called the Packhorse, this cordial place got its present name for services rendered to Charles I (whose seal is carved in the doorstep). The simple and old-fashioned bar has an unchanging atmosphere; in the right-hand room there are vertically panelled cushioned stall seats around neat old tables, some mate's chairs and wheel-back chairs, and harness and brasses on the stripped stone walls; the one on the left has cushioned casks and benches around three tables on the slate floor, and bar billiards, sensibly placed darts and piped music. There's another small room, called the Drip Tray, for the overflow at busy times. Besides the beers brewed on the premises – Tamar, Horsebridge Best and the more powerful Heller – they also keep Barrons Exe Valley, Bass and Marstons Pedigree on handpump. Bar food includes a wide choice of lunchtime ploughman's (£1.80, with home-made herby bread), pot meals like moussaka or sausage (£2), beef and oyster pie (£2.75), tandoori drumsticks (£3), venison in port (£4) and duck in orange (£4.50), a decent range of vegetarian dishes such as nut roast, onion bhaji or samosa (£2.75) and some unusual puddings (£1.25). There's a covered area in the garden, presided over by Fred, the resident jackdaw. The bridge from which the village takes its name has remarkably exact unmortared masonry, and was the first over the River Tamar, built by monks in 1437 – not long before they built this inn, which is about fifty yards away. *(Recommended by Charles and Mary Winpenny, H W and A B Tuffill, John and Pat Smyth, PB, HB, Phil Gorton, Simon Turner, Caroline Bailey, WFL)*

Own brew Licensees T G and J H Wood Real ale Meals and snacks (not Sun evening) Open 12–2.30, 7–11 all year

KINGSKERSWELL   SX8767   Map 1

Barn Owl

Aller Road; just off A380 Newton Abbot–Torquay – inn-sign on main road opposite RAC post

The wide choice of bar food in this seventeenth-century farmhouse ranges from soup (90p), sandwiches (from £1.35), filled baked potatoes (from £1.65) and whitebait (£1.75), through fresh plaice (£3.25) and sole (£3.50), salads (from £3.25), lamb chops (£4) and steak (from £6.25), to lots of daily specials such as home-made veal pie or lamb vindaloo. Two rooms have been stripped back to low black oak beams, with polished flagstones and a kitchen range in one. A third room is more grandly furnished, with an elaborate ornamental plaster ceiling, antique dark oak panelling, a decorative wooden chimneypiece, a couple of carved oak settles and old-fashioned dining-chairs around the handsome polished tables on its flowery carpet. Courage Directors and Janners on handpump; log fires throughout. There are picnic-table sets in a small sheltered garden. *(Recommended by D Baddeley, Mrs B G Francis; more reports please)*

Free house   Licensees Derek and Margaret Warner   Real ale   Meals and snacks (until 10 evenings)   Restaurant (Mon–Sat evenings and Sun lunchtime) tel Kingskerswell (080 47) 2130   Open 11.30–2.30, 7–11 all year   New bedrooms should now be ready

KINGSTEIGNTON   SX8773   Map 1

Old Rydon   ★   ⊗

From A381 Teignmouth turn off A380, take first real right turn (Longford Lane), go straight on to bottom of hill, then next right turn into Rydon Road following Council Office signpost; pub at end of the straight part of this lane; OS Sheet 192 reference 872739

The food in this little farmhouse pub is surprisingly cosmopolitan; the menu changes daily depending on what fresh ingredients they've bought, but typically includes soup (95p), an interesting Mexican avocado dip with tortilla chips (£1.45), chicken liver and green peppercorn pâté (£1.65), with main dishes like vegetable flan (£2.85), cauliflower and prawn Mornay (£3.40), beef and mushroom pie in Stilton and port sauce (£3.40), beef and vegetable stir-fry with ginger and soy sauce, chicken tandoori or seafood risotto (£3.85), and marinated monkfish, crab claw and Norwegian prawns (£5.25); local game and fresh mussels in winter; good puddings, all with clotted cream (£1.35). The atmospherically snug bar has a heavy beam and plank ceiling with lots of beer mugs hanging from it, a big log fire in winter in a raised fireplace, and cask seats and upholstered seats built against the white-painted stone walls. There are a few more seats in an upper former cider loft, now a gallery facing the antlers and antelope horns on one high white wall. Well kept Bass, Janners Devon Special (called Old Rydon Ale here) and Wadworths 6X on handpump. There are seats on a covered side terrace and in a nice biggish sheltered garden, which has a swing. *(Recommended by Tom Evans, Rita Horridge, MKW, JMW, P Miller, Steve Higgins, Alan Sillitoe, Gordon Hewitt, CED, Jon Wainwright)*

Free house   Licensees Hermann and Miranda Hruby   Real ale   Meals and snacks   Restaurant tel Newton Abbot (0626) 54626   Children in restaurant, lunchtime, upstairs until 8   Open 11–3, 6–11 all year; closed 25 Dec

KINGSTON   SX6347   Map 1

Dolphin

Near the imposing village church, this yellow-shuttered sixteenth-century house has a cheerfully informal bar which consists of a series of knocked-through beamed rooms, with rustic tables and cushioned seats and settles around their bared stone walls; well kept Courage Best and Directors on handpump. There's a good choice of food, more limited at lunchtime, when they serve soup (£1), sandwiches (from £1.35, local crab £2.25), basket meals (from £1.85), cottage pie, quiche or ham and egg (£2.50), ploughman's (from £2.50) and steak and kidney pie or chicken curry (£3.50), with additional evening dishes like salads (from £3.95), a range of fish dishes (from £3.95), and charcoal grills such as steak and gammon kebab or lamb chops (£4.95) and steaks (from £6.95); home-made puddings like treacle tart or chocolate truffle cake (£1.95) and children's helpings (£1.50); the menu is more limited on Sunday and Monday evenings, when the prices are lower. There are tables, swings, a children's summer snack bar and summer barbecues in the garden. Half a dozen tracks lead down to the sea, and unspoilt Wonwell Beach, about a mile and a half away. *(Recommended by Sue Cleasby, Mike Ledger, Ian and Daphne Brownlie, J M Soanes, Jon Wainwright, Mr and Mrs J C Dwane; more reports please)*

Courage   Licensees Barry and Dee Fryer   Real ale   Meals and snacks   Restaurant tel Bigbury-on-Sea (0548) 810314   Children in family-room   Open 11.30–11; 12–2.30, 7–11 in winter

KNOWLE   SS4938 Map 1

Ebrington Arms

Pub signposted just off A361, in village two miles N of Braunton

The atmospheric carpeted lounge here (actually two rooms opened together) has red plush stools around low tables, some pews, cushioned seats built into the stripped-stone outer walls (the inner ones are white) and a copper-plated chimney breast. The walls and black joists are decorated with lots of brass, prints, plates and pewter mugs. There's a candle-lit dining area up one or two steps at one end. The wide-ranging bar menu includes filled baked potatoes (95p), soup (£1), ploughman's (from £2.15), chilli con carne or cottage pie (£2.15), leek, ham and cheese gratin (£2.50), smoked trout or vegetable Stroganoff (£2.95), cockles or mussels (£3.50) and steak casserole in Guinness (£3.95). A snug bar has darts, shove-ha'penny, cribbage, space game and a fruit machine; separate pool-room. Bass on handpump; juke box and piped music. Note that if you choose something from the dining-room menu, you can't eat it in the bar (and vice versa). *(Recommended by Alan P Carr, Pamela and Merlyn Horswell, Mrs Nina Elliott, David and Flo Wallington, Chris Fluck)*

Free house   Licensees Alex and Nancy Coombs   Real ale   Meals and snacks   Restaurant area tel Braunton (0271) 812166   Children in eating area   Open 11–2.30, 6–11 all year

KNOWSTONE   SS8223 Map 1

Masons Arms ★ ★ 🕭 🍺

This charmingly unpretentious thatched thirteenth-century stone inn (quite popular with tourists) is attractively placed opposite the church and over the hilly pastures leading up to Exmoor. The good and often imaginative bar food, genuinely farmhousey, includes home-made soup (£1.10), home-made pâté (£1.50), ploughman's (from £1.60), plaice (£2.65), home-made pies varying from day to day, like cheese and leek or rabbit and venison (£2.90), chicken curry with chutney and a poppadum (£2.90), meat salads (from £2.90), fritto misto (£4.65) and puddings (£1.25). The atmospheric bar area is traditionally furnished; the small stone-floored main room has settles and benches around slab-top tables, farm tools on the walls, ancient bottles of all shapes and sizes hanging from the heavy medieval black beams, and a fine open fireplace with a big log fire and side bread oven. A small lower sitting-room has cosy easy chairs, bar billiards and table skittles. Badger Best, Boddingtons Bitter and Wadworths 6X or Youngs tapped from the cask, farm cider and a small but well chosen wine list; several snuffs on the counter; darts, shove-ha'penny, dominoes, cribbage, shut-the-box, board games, jigsaws and children's games and toys. For many, Mr Todd is the model landlord – a cornucopia of local information and likely to remember your name on a second visit. Charlie the collie is friendly in a more enthusiastically canine way, and liable to sit in the middle of the road outside, to the amused infuriation of some car-driving readers. The kittens Rob and Flora have moved on to a dairy farm, and have been replaced by some more Highlanders, Archie and Allie. *(Recommended by Shirley Allen, Mrs S Andrews, T J Maddison, Sarah Vickers, John Evans, Mr and Mrs D M Norton, Ann and David Stranack, Rita Horridge, Chris Raisin, Graham Doyle, Peter Adcock, Brian and Anna Marsden, Dennis Jones, Pat and Malcolm Rudlin, Peter Cornall, Simon Townend, Nigel Paine)*

Free house Licensees David and Elizabeth Todd Real ale Meals and snacks Restaurant Children in restaurant and eating areas Occasional live entertainment – on Burns Night, say Open 11–3, 7–11; closed evening 25 Dec, maybe evening 26 Dec Bedrooms tel Ansety Mills (039 84) 231; £16(£22S)/£32(£44S)

LUSTLEIGH SX7881 Map 1

Cleave

Village signposted off A382 Bovey Tracey–Moretonhampstead

This deceptively spacious, thatched white fifteenth-century inn is set in a charmingly remote village, and surrounded by a neat and pretty sheltered garden, where you may meet strolling peacocks. The welcomingly cosy low-ceilinged lounge bar is furnished with attractive antique high-backed settles, pale leatherette bucket chairs, red-cushioned wall seats and wheel-back chairs around the tables on its patterned carpet; fresh flowers in summer and big log fires in winter. A traditionally furnished second bar has darts, pool, dominoes, euchre and a fruit machine; piped music. The real ale changes regularly, typically including Bass, Flowers IPA and Marstons Pedigree on handpump. Good bar food includes soup (£1.30), large baps (£2.25), ploughman's (from £2.50), home-made cheese and onion flan (£2.45), home-cooked ham (£2.75), coq au vin (£3.50) and home-made steak, kidney and Guinness pie (£4.75); generous breakfasts for residents; friendly service. It's near *Good Walks Guide* Walk 18. *(Recommended by Paul and Janet Waring, Ann and David Stranack, Hilary Robinson, Peter Maden, Rita Horridge, Henry Hooper, John Knighton, Mr and Mrs B Hobden, W A Gardiner, Alan and Ruth Woodhouse, Mrs E M Brandwood, G and M Stewart, C A Foden, G Atkinson, S Matthews, Eileen Broadbent, Philip and Trisha Ferris)*

Heavitree (who no longer brew) Licensees A and A Perring Real ale Meals and snacks Restaurant Open 11–11; 11–2.30, 7–11 in winter; closed 25 Dec Children in family-room Parking may be difficult Three bedrooms tel Lustleigh (064 77) 223; £32 (doubles only)

LUTTON SX5959 Map 1

Mountain

Pub signposted from Cornwood–Sparkwell road

Looking over the lower slopes of Dartmoor, this atmospheric pub has a rustic beamed bar with a window seat, rugs on the flagstones, some walls stripped back to the bare stone, a high-backed settle by the log fire and Windsor chairs around old-fashioned polished tables in a larger connecting room. Well kept Burton Ind Coope, Butcombe, Fergusons Dartmoor and Exmoor on handpump, and local farm cider; darts, dominoes, cribbage, fruit machine. Straightforward bar food includes French bread filled generously with beef and ham (£3), as well as sandwiches (from £1.30, prawn £2.25), chilli con carne or curries (£2.20), soup with cheese and a roll (£2.50) and ploughman's (£3). There are seats at the front. *(Recommended by Dr and Mrs D N Jones, R Sinclair Taylor, Roger Mallard; more reports please)*

Free house Licensees Charles and Margaret Bullock Real ale Meals and snacks (until 10 evenings) Children in eating area and small family-room Open 11–3 (2.30 in winter), 6–11 all year

LYDFORD   SX5184 Map 1

Castle ★ 🛏

Close to a beautiful river gorge (owned by the National Trust), and next to the village's daunting ruined twelfth-century castle, this charming pink-washed Tudor inn has a twin-roomed bar; in one, where the bar food is served, there are low lamp-lit beams, masses of brightly decorated plates, some Hogarth prints, an attractive grandfather clock, a sizeable open fire and near the serving-counter seven Lydford pennies hammered out in the Saxon mint in the reign of Ethelred the Unready in the tenth century; the second room has an interesting collection of antique stallion posters. Both are furnished with old captain's chairs, country kitchen chairs and high-backed winged settles around mahogany tripod tables on big slate flagstones; unusual stained-glass doors. Bass and Courage Best on handpump; sensibly placed darts, shove-ha'penny, dominoes, cribbage, piped music. The imaginative lunchtime cold buffet table, available every day in summer and at weekends in winter, has a good choice of salads with the meats, home-made pies and scotch eggs, salmon, trout, cold tandoori chicken and so forth; other bar food typically includes chicken, poultry pie, seafood risotto, daily fresh fish or curry (all £3.75) and steak and kidney pie (£4). The well kept garden has an adventure playground and barbecue area. A Jack Russell puppy called Podge has now joined the two cats, Harvey and JR. *(Recommended by Col G D Stafford, Doug Kennedy, David Wallington, Henry Hooper, Mrs K Currie, TBB, Frances Mansbridge, Phil and Sally Gorton, Charles and Mary Winpenny, Janet and Paul Waring, Brian and Genie Krakowska Smart, Verney and Denis Baddeley, Jill Hampton, P and M Rudlin, Mrs J Green)*

Free house   Licensees David and Susan Grey   Real ale   Snacks (not Sun) and meals (12–2.30, 6–9.30)   Restaurant   Children welcome (under 5s until 8 only)   Open 11.30–3, 6–11 all year; closed 25 Dec   Bedrooms tel Lydford (082 282) 242; £25(£30B)/£33(£38B)

LYNMOUTH   SS7249 Map 1

Rising Sun 🛏 [illustrated on page 199]

Mars Hill; down by harbour

This thatched fourteenth-century inn has a welcoming modernised panelled bar, with stripped stone at the fireplace end, black beams in the crooked ceiling, uneven oak floors and cushioned built-in stall-seats, and latticed windows facing the harbour. Bar food is generally available every lunchtime and evening, though one or two readers have been disappointed in the past; it includes sandwiches (£1.25, crab £1.75), home-made soup (£1.50), pork and ham or tomato and chilli sausages (£2.75), ploughman's (£2.95) and a range of dishes at £3.50 such as lasagne, fisherman's pie or salads; the best place to eat in is the small oak-panelled dining-room; friendly service. Its setting is most attractive, near a fine stretch of coast (with Foreland Point in the distance) and with its own residential garden. The steep walk up the Lyn valley to Watersmeet (National Trust) and Exmoor is particularly pleasant; near *Good Walks Guide* Walk 20. The bedrooms are mostly up the hill in the adjoining cottages, in one of which Shelley reputedly spent his honeymoon with his sixteen-year-old bride, Harriet. *(Recommended by Dr R Trigwell, Steve Dark, Rita Horridge, Mrs J R T Mosesson, E G Parish, P Bacon, W A Harbottle, Mr and Mrs Darlow, J C Smith; more reports please)*

Free house   Licensee Hugo Jeune   Meals and snacks   Restaurant   Children in eating area Open 11–2.30, 6–11; closed 3 Jan–10 Feb   Bedrooms tel Lynton (0598) 53223; £27.50B/£55B

Anyone claiming to be able to arrange or prevent inclusion of a pub in the *Guide* is a fraud. Pubs are included only if recommended by genuine readers and if our own anonymous inspection confirms that they are suitable.

MILTONCOMBE SX4865 Map 1
Who'd Have Thought It ★ 🏵
Village signposted from A386 S of Tavistock

Efficiently served and unanimously praised bar food in this friendly valley pub includes granary bread sandwiches (from £1.10, good crab £1.60), home-made soup (£1.40), generous ploughman's (from £2.10), half a chicken (£3), mixed seafood (£3.50), salads (from £3.50), gammon (£4.75) and a large sirloin steak (£7.75), with up to sixteen home-made daily specials and lots of puddings with clotted cream (from £1.20). The wood-panelled and atmospheric bar has cushioned high-backed winged settles around a wood-burning stove in the big stone fireplace, colourful plates on a big black dresser, and rapiers and other weapons on its walls; two other rooms have seats made from barrels. Well kept Blackawton, Exmoor, Huntsman Royal Oak, Palmers IPA and Wadworths 6X on handpump and Inch's cider; darts, dominoes, cribbage, fruit machine, piped music; picnic-table sets on a terrace with hanging baskets, by the little stream. It's handy for the lovely gardens of the Garden House at Buckland Monachorum and for Buckland Abbey. *(Recommended by Heather Sharland, Tom Evans, John Barker, Jutta Whitley, Simon Turner, John Knighton, K and E Leist, Chris Hill, H F and J Hobbs, P and M Rudlin, Ted George)*

Free house   Licensees Keith Yeo and Gary Rager   Real ale   Meals and snacks   Folk club Sun evening   Open 11.30–2.30 (3 Sat), 6.30–11 all year

MORETONHAMPSTEAD SX7585 Map 1
White Hart 🛏

Decent bar food in this friendly hotel includes soup or home-made pasty (£1.50), quiche, home-cooked ham or lasagne (£2.60), home-made chicken and ham pie or curry (£3.25), salads (£3.50), scampi (£3.95) and evening grills such as local trout (£6.25), lamb chops or steak (£7.25); at lunchtime there are also pasties (£1), sandwiches (from £1.25; prawn £2.25) and various ploughman's (£2.35); several puddings such as good treacle tart with clotted cream (£1.55). The meticulously kept, spacious Turkey-carpeted lounge bar has armchairs, plush seats, stools and oak pews from the parish church; the hall has a splendidly large-scale 1827 map of Devon by Greenwood. The lively public bar has leatherette seats and settles under a white beam and plank ceiling; darts, cribbage, dominoes and fruit machine. Well kept Bass and Fergusons Dartmoor on handpump, and farm cider. You can sit on a pew among the flowers in the small back courtyard. Comfortable bedrooms. *(Recommended by David Wallington, Henry Hooper, P Miller, Bernard Phillips, G and M Stewart, Sue Jenkins, Robert Olsen, B C Head)*

Free house   Licensee Peter Morgan   Real ale   Meals and snacks (12–2, 6–8.30); afternoon cream teas   Restaurant and evening grill-room   Children in eating area (not restaurant) May have to park in the public car park a short walk away   Open 11–2.30, 6–11 all year   Bedrooms tel Moretonhampstead (0647) 40406; £30B/£48B

nr NEWTON ABBOT SX8671 Map 1
Two Mile Oak
A381 Newton Abbot–Totnes, 2 miles S of Newton Abbot

Very much a popular local, this pub has a beamed lounge with a handsome old settle, romantically secluded candle-lit alcoves and a fine log fire in winter. The beams of the black-panelled and traditionally furnished public bar are decorated with old beer-mats and lots of horsebrasses; this too has a good log fire on cool days. Darts, cribbage, fruit machine; Flowers IPA on handpump, Bass and Huntsman Royal Oak tapped from the cask. Straightforward but generous and good value helpings of food include soup (90p), large wholemeal rolls (from £1.40), tuna fish and herb loaf (£2.40), ploughman's with local cheeses (from £2.40), king prawns (£2.70), cod and prawn Mornay (£3.10), lasagne or Cumberland sausage (£3.50), scampi or smoked ham (£3.90) and rump steak (£6.80). There are seats on a back terrace, with more on a sheltered lawn broken up by tubs of flowers and well grown shrubs. *(Recommended by Charlie Salt, Steve Huggins, K and E Leist, CED, Jon Wainwright)*

Heavitree (who no longer brew)   Licensee Helen Peers   Real ale   Meals and snacks (12–2, 6.30–10.30)   Children in small lobby area only   Open 11–2.30 (3 Sat), 6–11.30 all year

NEWTON ST CYRES   SX8798   Map 1

Beer Engine

Sweetham; from Newton St Cyres on A377 follow St Cyres Station, Thorverton signpost

This own-brew pub, unusually located in an old railway station, has a lively young clientele, particularly at the weekend. It's possible to see from the cellar bar the Rail Ale, Piston Bitter, and the very strong Sleeper being produced in the stainless brewhouse. There's a simple range of food, including speciality sausages (£2.35), steak and kidney pie or lasagne (£2.45), cod in pineapple and pepper sauce (£3.65) and rump steak (£5.85). The spacious main bar has partitioning alcoves, Windsor chairs and some button-back banquettes around dark varnished tables on its red carpet; darts, shove-ha'penny, dominoes and cribbage; fruit machine and space game in the downstairs lobby. There's a real ale/real train link-up with Exeter at the weekends. The licensee has recently opened a new venture, the Sleeper, at the Royal Clarence Hotel in Seaton. *(Recommended by Charlie Salt, P A Jennings)*

Own brew   Licensee Peter Hawksley   Real ale   Meals and snacks (12–2, 6.30–10)   Children in eating area   Live music Fri and Sat evenings   Open 11.30–3, 6–11 (11.30–11 Sat) all year (cellar bar closes midnight Fri and Sat)

NORTH BOVEY   SX7483   Map 1

Ring of Bells   🏵

The ploughman's in this remote thirteenth-cenututy village inn has come in for particular praise from readers – generously served, it can include more than half a pound of Cheddar; other food ranges from a summer salad bar (£2.50–£4.50) to main dishes like curry (£3.75), steak and kidney pie (£4.50) and specials such as king prawns, pheasant, quail or local trout (£5–£6). The simply furnished carpeted main bar, recently opened up by the removal of some stonework, has bulgy white walls and horsebrasses on its beams, and a good range of real ales tapped from the cask or on handpump: Butcombe Bitter, Fergusons Dartmoor, Eldridge Pope Royal Oak, Flowers IPA and regular guest beers; also Gray's farm cider and a selection of wines; darts, cribbage, pool in winter, fruit machine and piped music. It's set back from the village green – a lively place during the traditional mid-July Saturday fair – and has seats on a terrace well sheltered by the mossily thatched white buildings around it. There are summer lawn skittles and a good children's play area on the attractively bordered lawn; fishing, shooting and ponytrekking can be arranged for guests, and the inn is well placed for some of the most interesting parts of Dartmoor. *(Recommended by John Knighton, Helena and Arthur Harbottle, Steve Huggins, PB, HB, Hilary Robinson, Peter Maden, Henry Hooper, Shirley Allen, P A King-Fisher, Mrs Pamela Roper, Paul and Margaret Baker, Pete Bolsover, Mrs Joan Harris)*

Free house   Licensee Anthony Rix   Real ale   Meals and snacks   Restaurant   Children welcome   Open 11–11; 11–3, 6–11 in winter   Bedrooms tel Moretonhampstead (0647) 40375; £20B/£35B

Remember, this is not just a food guide. Pubs earn their place in it for a variety of virtues. If good food is what you want, look for the rosette award or for specific praise of the food.

PAIGNTON SX8960 Map 1

Inn on the Green

27 Esplanade Road

The lounge bar in this popular family inn spreads spaciously around the enormously long serving-counter through a succession of arches, where lots of blond cane chairs and cane-framed tables match the soft colour-scheme of peachy beige plush banquettes, pink and buff swagged curtains in the many bay windows, and marbled creamy-yellow wallpaper. There's a small dancefloor and a pool-table in the family-room; fruit machine in lobby; Ruddles County, Ushers Best and Websters Yorkshire on handpump, and some non-alcoholic wines and beers. The wide choice of bar food includes soup (95p), sandwiches (from £1.65), filled baked potatoes (£1.65), ploughman's (from £2.15), home-made jumbo sausages (£2.25), steak and kidney or mushroom and Guinness pie (£3.45), a range of fish dishes like cod Mornay (£3.80) or local poached halibut (£4.95), several vegetarian dishes such as mung-bean and mushroom biriani or aubergine and mushroom lasagne (£3.45), charcoal grills (from £3.95, steaks from £5.95); Sunday carvery; there are children's dishes (from 95p), and puddings served with clotted cream (£1.60). Seats on the front terrace among cordylines, pampas grass and hydrangeas look out over the green towards the sea. *(Recommended by Brian and Anna Marsden, M Harris; more reports please)*

Free house Licensees Brian Shone and John Stride Real ale Meals and snacks (11–3, 6.30–12) Restaurant Children in eating area and family-room Live music nightly (George Melly to Acker Bilk) Open 11–midnight all year Self-catering apartments tel Paignton (0803) 557841; from £8.50B a night

PETER TAVY SX5177 Map 1

Peter Tavy ★ 🏵

Close to Dartmoor forest and the River Tavy, this diminutive but popular pub has a particularly atmospheric low-beamed bar, simply furnished with high-backed settles on the black flagstones by the big stone fireplace (which usually has a good log fire on cold days), smaller settles in stone-mullioned windows and a snug side dining area; darts. Bar food is distinguished by the range of vegetarian options, with dishes like creamy cashew-nut fingers (£1.05), pancakes stuffed with spinach and garlic (£2.20) and moussaka (£3.15), with a choice of unusual salads; on the meat side there's beef pepper pot (£4.15) and pork fillet stuffed with sage and onion (£7); friendly service. The good range of real ales is tapped from the cask and includes Bass, Blackawton Forty-four, Courage Best, Eldridge Pope Royal Oak and Exmoor Gold. Picnic-table sets among fruit trees in a small raised garden have peaceful views of the moor rising above nearby pastures. *(Recommended by Simon Turner, Annie Taylor, Helen Crookston, Jackie and Jon Payne, C H and W A Harbottle, Steve Huggins, Ceri Jarr, J D Mackay, Mr and Mrs D A P Grattan, Alan and Ruth Woodhouse, R C Vincent, Cynthia Pollard, Jutta Brigitta Whitley, J M Soanes, P and M Rudlin)*

Free house Licensees Mr and Mrs P J Hawkins Real ale Meals and snacks Children in eating area Nearby parking often difficult Open 11.30–2.30 (3 Sat), 6.30–11 all year; closed evening 25 Dec

nr POSTBRIDGE SX6579 Map 1

Warren House

B3212 1¼ miles NE of Postbridge

Alone on a rugged part of Dartmoor, this isolated pub is included for its position (there are lovely views) and its value as a refuge after a walk or on a cold grey day. A fire at one end is said to have been kept continuously alight since 1845. The dimly lit bar (fuelled by the pub's own generator) is friendly rather than smart, simply furnished with easy chairs and rustic settles under a beamed ochre ceiling; the partly panelled stone walls are decorated with wild animal pictures. It gets busy in the high season, but even then keeps quite a local atmosphere as it's something of a focus for this scattered moorland community. Bar food is simple, including soup, sandwiches, ploughman's and fish and chips; Flowers IPA and Original and Marstons Pedigree on handpump, farm cider and a range of country wines; darts, dominoes, cribbage, pool, space game, fruit machine, piped music. This road is worth knowing as a good little-used route westward through fine scenery. *(Recommended by WMS, J R Carey, H and P B, Alan and Ruth Woodhouse, Helen Crookston, P and M Rudlin)*

Free house   Licensee Peter Parsons   Real ale   Meals and snacks   Children in family-room   Open 11–11; 11–2.30, 5.30–11 in winter

RATTERY   SX7461 Map 1
Church House

Village signposted from A385 W of Totnes, and A38 S of Buckfastleigh

This highly praised, partly eleventh-century pub changed hands in the summer of 1989, but all the most recent indications are that the praise is likely to continue at the same level. The two interesting bar rooms have massive oak beams and standing timbers, large fireplaces (one with a little cosy nook partitioned off around it), Windsor armchairs, comfortable leather bucket seats and window seats, and prints on the plain white walls. Courage Best and Directors and a weekly guest beer on handpump, wines, forty malt whiskies and farm cider. Bar food still includes home-made soup (£1.50), filled granary rolls (£2.25), ploughman's (£2.50), grilled plaice (£3.50), smoked chicken (£3.75), steak and kidney pie (£4.25), seafood lasagne (£4.95), steaks (from £5.50), with local fish and game, and fresh, organically grown vegetables; Sunday roast (£4.25); there may be some delays when it's busy. Outside, there are peaceful views of the partly wooded surrounding hills from picnic-table sets on a hedged courtyard by the churchyard – the building has always been connected with the Norman church, and originally may have housed the craftsmen who built it, before serving as a hostel for passing monks. *(Recommended by Heather Sharland, John Evans, C A Gurney, W A Gardiner, Jean and Roger Davis, Ann and David Stranck, Paul and Janet Waring, Colin Way, J C Proud, Charles Gurney, Neville Burke, S V Bishop, Mrs T Salisbury, Steve and Caroline Harvey, Jon Wainwright, Theo Schofield, Philip and Trisha Ferris, David and Flo Wallington, P J Derrington, Simon Turner, Caroline Bailey, Andy Tye and Sue Hill, Desmond Simpson)*

Free house   Licensees Mr and Mrs Evans   Real ale   Meals and snacks (12–2.30, 7–10.30)   Tables can be booked tel Buckfastleigh (0364) 42220   Children welcome   Open 11–2.30, 6–11 all year; closed evening 25 and 26 Dec

SAMPFORD PEVERELL   ST0214 Map 1
Globe

1 mile from M5 junction 27; village signposted from Tiverton turn-off

This is a comfortably modernised place with a spacious bar which has green plush built-in settles and wheel-back chairs around heavy cast-iron tables, a log fire and some stripped stone. The range of food, which tends towards frying and chips, includes sandwiches (from 90p), hot pies (£1.20), ploughman's (from £2), salads (from £2.60), smoked chicken (£3), omelettes or a big fry-up (£3), whole plaice (£4.60) and a mixed grill; Sunday lunch (£3.30 – as it can get very crowded then they recommend booking). Well kept Flowers Original and IPA; piped music; sensibly placed darts, dominoes, cribbage, draughts, juke box and two fruit machines in the public bar; also a pool-room with two space games, and a full skittle alley. There are picnic-table sets in front by the quiet road. *(Recommended by Richard Dolphin, K R Harris, Steve and Carolyn Harvey, Margaret Dyke, Gwynne Harper, Wendy Healiss, Wayne Brindle)*

Whitbreads   Real ale   Meals and snacks   Bookings tel Tiverton (0884) 821214   Children in eating area and family-room   Open 11–11 all year

SANDY PARK   SX7189   Map 1

Sandy Park Inn

Just off A382 N of Moretonhampstead

Don't let the rustic simplicity of the décor and furnishings mislead you: this small black-beamed bar's regulars are indeed country folk – but decidedly more Brian Aldridge than Eddie Grundy. It's an inviting place: sturdy benches beside the honeysuckle outside the thatched white house look out to the pretty surrounding wooded hills; inside, there are two or three stripped tables on the composition floor, with built-in varnished wall seats, lots of postcards pinned above the crackling log fire, and attractively arranged fresh flowers. The original doorway is blocked by the greyhound's huge wicker basket. Lunchtime bar food consists of pasties (95p), pâté (£1.80), ploughman's (from £1.95), turkey pie salad (£2.50), lasagne (£2.90), smoked trout or duck and orange pie (£3); in the evening they do a dish of the day such as bangers and mash or a casserole (£3.50), and a roast (up to £5.50). Well kept Everards Old Original, Exe Valley and Marstons Pedigree on handpump, and Palmers IPA tapped from the cask; decent wines, a good selection of spirits, a relaxed and chatty atmosphere – absolutely no intrusions by machines or music. *(Recommended by Peter Donahue, Charlie Salt, Martin and Rob Jones)*

Free house   Licensee Marion Weir   Real ale   Meals and snacks (not Mon evening)   Small restaurant   Open 11–3, 5–11 all year; all day Sat   Bedrooms tel Chagford (064 73) 3538; £10.50/£12.50

SHEEPWASH   SS4806   Map 1

Half Moon 🛏

This buff-painted and civilised inn takes up one whole side of the colourful village square – blue, pink, white, cream and olive thatched or slate-roofed cottages. The welcoming beamed and carpeted main bar has white walls, solid old furniture, lots of fishing pictures and a big log fire fronted by slate flagstones. Bass and Courage Best on handpump (well kept in a temperature-controlled cellar), a fine choice of spirits and a good wine list; darts, fruit machine and a separate pool-room. Lunchtime bar food is attractively straightforward, including sandwiches (£1, toasted £1.30), soup or pasty (£1.30), ploughman's (£2.40) and salads (£3.50); friendly service. The fine inn-sign (a curving salmon neatly interlocking with a crescent moon) hints at the inn's fishing reputation: it can arrange salmon or trout fishing on the Torridge for non-residents as well as residents. *(Recommended by P M Bisby, David Wallington, Doug Kennedy, J W Dixon, Mrs Pamela Roper, David Sawyer, Mrs N Lawson, D B Delany, Dr John Innes)*

Free house   Licensees Benjamin Robert Inniss and Charles Inniss   Real ale   Snacks (lunchtime)   Evening restaurant (must book)   Children until 7.30   Open 11.30–2.30 (3.30 Sat), 6–11 all year   Bedrooms tel Black Torrington (040 923) 376; £28B/£48B

SIDFORD   SY1390   Map 1

Blue Ball ★ 🏵 🛏

A3052 just N of Sidmouth

This welcoming fourteenth-century thatched village inn displays its food (particularly fresh local fish on crushed ice) enticingly at the back of the bar area; it includes good crusty bread sandwiches (from £1, crab £1.80), a very generous ploughman's (£2.25), cheese and asparagus flan (£3.25), home-made steak and kidney pie (£3.75), salads (from £3) and good steaks (from eight-ounce rump, £6.25); puddings (from £1.15); friendly, efficient service. The low- and heavy-beamed, partly panelled lounge bar has Windsor chairs and upholstered wall benches and a lovely winter log fire in the stone fireplace. Devenish JD, Royal Wessex and Steam on handpump, kept well in a temperature-controlled cellar; a plainer public bar has darts, dominoes, cribbage and a fruit machine; piped music. Tables on a terrace look out over a colourful walled front flower garden, with more on a bigger back lawn, where there are summer barbecues. The inn has been in the same family for over seventy-five years. *(Recommended by Brian and Anna Marsden, E A George, Gwen Cranfield, JAH, Philip and Sheila Hanley, W C M Jones, A C Earl, Jane and Calum, Stephen R Holman, Mr and Mrs Jon Payne, WFL, DMF)*

Devenish   Licensee R H Newton   Real ale   Meals and snacks (10.30–2, 6.30–10)
Children in eating area and family-room   Open 10.30–2.30, 5.30–11 all year
Bedrooms tel Sidmouth (0395) 514062; £17/£26

SLAPTON   SX8244 Map 1
Tower

Reached by a tortuous narrow lane at the top of the village hill, this fine fourteenth-century inn stands out for its tradition of fine ales; there are usually ten on handpump – Badger Tanglefoot, Blackawton, Gibbs Mew Bishops Tipple, Exe Valley, Exmoor, Eldridge Pope Royal Oak, Palmers IPA, Ruddles County and Best and Wadworths 6X. A second attractive feature is the food, particularly the Italian licensee's pasta dishes, such as lasagne, broccoli pasta or spaghetti bolognese (£3.25) or al mare (£4.50); there are also sandwiches, basket meals (from £1), fresh sole (£5) and chicken and mushrooms (£5.25); they're planning a buffet for the summer. The flagstoned and low-ceilinged bar has an unaffected atmosphere, with small armchairs, low-backed settles, some furniture made from casks, and on cool days a wood-burning stove and a log fire in one stripped stone wall; bar billiards, space game and piped music. There are picnic-table sets on the quiet back lawn, which is overhung by the ivy-covered ruin of a fourteenth-century chantry. *(Recommended by Amanda Dauncey, David and Ann Stranack, Richard and Dilys Smith, John Knighton, J Coles, B Richardson, J Overton, A Mitchell, Jon Wainwright, Sue Cleasby, Mike Ledger, Ruth Humphrey, G F Couch)*

Free house   Licensees Keith and Kim Romp, Jan Khan and Carlo Cascianelli   Real ale Meals and snacks   Restaurant   Children in games-room and restaurant   Open 11.30–2.30, 6–11 (11.30–11 Sat) all year   Bedrooms tel Kingsbridge (0548) 580216; £15.50/£31

SOURTON   SX5390 Map 1
Highwayman ★

A386 SW of Okehampton; a short detour from the A30

This is the best embodiment of sheer fantasy in pub design that we have found anywhere. The owners have taken the twin themes of olde-worldiness and pirate haunts, and injected lots of unrestrained imagination as well as the undoubtedly enormous sums of money that must have been involved in getting meticulously detailed workmanship and first-class materials. The result far outclasses other 'theme pubs' and places done up to look old-fashioned. A nobleman's carriage of a porch leads into a warren of dimly lit stonework and flagstone-floored burrows and alcoves, richly fitted out with red plush seats discreetly cut into the higgledy-piggledy walls, elaborately carved pews, a leather porter's chair, Jacobean-style wicker chairs, and seats in quaintly bulging small-paned bow windows; the ceiling in one part, where there's an array of stuffed animals, gives the impression of being underneath a tree, roots and all. The separate Rita Jones' Locker is a make-believe sailing galleon, full of intricate woodwork and splendid timber baulks, with red-check tables in the embrasures that might have held cannons. The licensees themselves have character to match this exuberant décor, and Mr Jones has also created a play area in similar style outside for children (who aren't allowed in the pub itself); there are little black and white roundabouts like a Victorian fairground, a fairy-tale pumpkin house and an old-lady-who-lived-in-the-shoe house. They don't do real ale, but specialise in farm cider; food is confined to pasties made by Mrs Jones; old-fashioned penny fruit machine. *(Recommended by Jutta Whitley, J C Proud, Gwynne Harper, J Overton, A Mitchell, Charlie Salt)*

Free house   Licensees Buster and Rita Jones   Snacks   Open 10–2, 6–10.30 all year; closed 25 and 26 Dec   Bedrooms tel Bridestowe (083 786) 243; £13.80/£27.60

SOUTH POOL   SX7740   Map 1
Millbrook

A few minutes' stroll from the River Millbrook brings you to this eponymous pub, one of the smallest you're likely to come across; the welcome is much what you'd expect from such an intimate place – particularly in the little back bar, which has a chintz easy chair, handsome Windsor chairs, fresh flowers, a coal fire, and drawings and paintings (and a chart) on its cream walls. Readers express enthusiasm for the bar food, which includes home-made soup (90p), sandwiches (from 90p, crab £2.25), pasties (£1), cottage pie (£1.85), quiche (£1.95), salads such as smoked mackerel (£1.95) or prawn (£2.80), and ploughman's (from £2), with filled baked potatoes and toasted sandwiches in winter, and, for pudding, apple cider cake (75p) or treacle tart (85p). Bass tapped from the cask, and Churchward's cider; darts in the public bar; piped music. There are seats out in front, on a sheltered flowery terrace; you can get here in forty-five minutes by hired boat from Salcombe. Not surprisingly, it can get very crowded at holiday times – it's a small place, and service can slow right down then. *(Recommended by Margaret and Trevor Errington, Major and Mrs J V Rees, David and Ann Stranack, Jon Wainwright, ACMM)*

Free house   Licensees Michael and Christine Jones   Real ale   Snacks   Children in front bar   Nearby parking may be difficult   Open 11–3, 6–11; may open longer in summer to cover high tide

SOUTH ZEAL   SX6593   Map 1
Oxenham Arms ★ ⊘ ⇤

Village signposted from A30 at A382 roundabout and B3260 Okehampton turn-off

The stately exterior of this grand building makes the welcoming homeliness of the beamed and partly panelled bar something of a surprise; it has Windsor armchairs around low oak tables and built-in wall seats, as well as elegant mullioned windows and Stuart fireplaces. Universally praised bar food includes soup (95p), sandwiches (£1.25), a generous ploughman's (£2.25), fish and chips (from £2.50), home-made steak, kidney, mushroom and Guinness pie (£3.15), salads (from £2.75), grilled trout (£3.75), and good daily specials such as lamb, apple, onion and sultana pie (£3.15) or coq au vin (£3.75). St Austell Tinners and HSD tapped from the cask, Gray's farm cider and wines; darts, shove-ha'penny, dominoes and cribbage. The inn was originally a Norman monastery, built here to combat the pagan power of the neolithic standing stone that still forms part of the wall in the family TV room behind the bar (there are actually twenty more feet of stone below the floor). There's further monastic evidence in the imposing curved stone steps leading up to

---

Please keep sending us reports. We rely on readers for news of new discoveries, and particularly for news of changes, however slight, at the fully described pubs. No stamp needed: *The Good Pub Guide*, FREEPOST, London SW10 0BR.

the garden, and a sloping spread of lawn. *(Recommended by Neil and Anita Christopher, William Rodgers, Mary Rayner, Ian Shaw, Lindsay Shaw Radley, Andrew and Michel Wells, Col G D Stafford, Paul Smith, R H Inns, Sue Carlyle, Peter Donahue, Henry Hooper, HEG, Roy and Shirley Bentley)*

Free house   Licensee James Henry   Real ale   Meals and snacks   Restaurant   Children in eating area and separate room near bar   Open 11–2.30, 6–11 all year   Bedrooms tel Okehampton (0837) 840244; £28(£34.50B)/£36(£45B)

STAVERTON   SX7964 Map 1

Sea Trout

Village signposted from A384 NW of Totnes

Not far from a station for the Torbay Steam Railway, this modernised and friendly village inn has a neatly kept, rambling beamed lounge bar with cushioned settles and stools on its carpet, salmon and sea-trout flies, stuffed fish on the walls (some of which are stripped back to bare granite) and a stag's head above the fireplace; the main bar has low banquettes, soft lighting and an open fire. There's also a public bar, popular with locals, with a pool-table, darts, trivia machine and juke box. Bar food includes sandwiches (from £1.35), burgers (from £1.65), ploughman's (from £2.15), local trout or gammon (£4), salads (from £4) and steaks (from around £6). A pretty garden has seats and tables on crazy paving among stone-walled flower borders, with a rock pool under a weeping willow. They can arrange fishing for you on the River Dart. *(Recommended by Charlie Salt, Ann and David Stranack, Miss J A Harvey, Geoffrey Thompson, S V Bishop)*

Free house   Licensee Andrew Mooford   Real ale   Meals and snacks (12–2, 7–10)   Children in eating area   Open 11–3, 6–11 all year   Bedrooms tel Staverton (080 426) 274; £19.50(£25B)/£34(£40B)

STOCKLAND   ST2404 Map 1

Kings Arms 🌑

Village signposted from A30 Honiton–Chard

The small but elegant dining-lounge of this ancient inn is a soothingly civilised place to embark on what can be an elaborate dinner, starting with grilled sardines (£2), trecolori salad (£2.50) or Pacific prawns in garlic and white wine sauce (£4); going on to beef Stroganoff (but using cream and pickled dill cucumber instead of soured cream; £5.50), chicken suprême flamed in brandy, poached in sherry, and reduced with thick cream (£6.50), darne of wild salmon in lobster and dill sauce (£7.50) or crispy slow-roasted duck (£7.50); then wondering if you've room for apple strudel (£1.50) or zabaglione (£2). The choice is very wide, and the manager describes the niceties of each dish (a mouth-watering ritual); booking is essential. At lunchtime there are simpler snacks as well, including a basket of chips (75p), sandwiches (from £1), ploughman's or burger (£2.50), omelettes (£3), steak and kidney pie (£3.50) and salads (£4); on Sundays there's a traditional lunch instead (£7.50, small children half-price). This lounge has dark beams, attractive landscapes, solid refectory tables, a medieval oak screen dividing it into two, and a great stone fireplace across almost the whole width of one end. A flagstoned back bar has leatherette chairs and seats built into the stripped high dado of its bare stone walls; it leads on to a carpeted darts room with two boards, another recently refurbished room with dark beige plush armchairs and settees (and a fruit machine), and a neat ten-pin skittle alley (the pub fields six teams, Monday, Wednesday and Friday in winter; on Thursdays there's a keep-fit class). There are tables under cocktail parasols on the terrace in front of the cream-faced thatched pub, with more by a weeping willow in the sheltered back garden. The pervasive piped classical music (if there is pop, it's pre-1968) reflects the owners' long spell of previous work, at the

London Coliseum (home of English National Opera). Well kept Badger Best and Exmoor, decent wines and brandies, a good choice of whiskies – particularly strong on island single malts; cribbage, dominoes, space game; well behaved dogs allowed. We have no reason to doubt that this would be a nice place at which to stay – but have not heard from any readers who've stayed under this new regime. *(Recommended by W L B Reed, David Gaunt, J W and E K Scropes, Mr and Mrs F E Dethbridge)*

Free house   Licensees Heinz Kiefer and Paul Diviani   Real ale   Snacks (lunchtime, not Sun) and meals (not Sun evening)   Well behaved children welcome   Open 12–3, 6.30 (7 in winter)–11 all year; virtually closed 25 Dec   Bedrooms tel Stockland (040 488) 361; £20B/£30B

STOKE GABRIEL   SX8457 Map 1
Church House ★

Village signposted from A385 just W of junction with A3022, in Collaton St Mary; can also be reached from nearer Totnes; nearby parking not easy

Just above the River Dart, this fourteenth-century, flower-covered pub serves generously priced bar food, including home-made soup (£1), sandwiches (from £1), baked potato filled with prawns (£2), a variety of ploughman's (from £2), home-made cottage pie (£2.75) and Dart salmon (£5.50, possibly caught by the licensee's son-in-law). Of particular interest in the bar is a case containing a mummified cat, probably about 200 years old, found during restoration of the roof space in the verger's cottage three doors up the lane – one of a handful found in the West Country and believed to have been a talisman against evil spirits. Other decorations in the beam and plank ceilinged lounge, which still has a black oak partition wall, include decorative plates and vases of flowers on a dresser, a huge fireplace still used in winter to cook the stew, and window seats cut into the thick butter-coloured walls. Darts, dominoes, cribbage, euchre and fruit machine in the little public bar; piped music. The Bass on handpump is particularly well kept, unusually fed from a temperature-controlled cellar at a higher level. There are picnic-table sets on the little terrace in front of the pub. Relations with the Church of England (which still owns it) go back a long way – witness the priest hole, dating from the Reformation, visible from outside the pub. *(Recommended by W A Gardiner, H K Dyson, Hugh P Patterson, John and Margaret Harvey, Pamela and Merlyn Horswell, Graham and Glenis Watkins)*

Bass   Licensee G W Bradford   Real ale   Meals and snacks (11–2.30, 6–10); cream teas in summer   Open 11–11 all year

TIPTON ST JOHN   SY0991 Map 1
Golden Lion 🛏

Pub signposted off B3176 Sidmouth–Ottery St Mary

A wide choice of reasonably priced home-cooked bar food here includes soup (95p), sandwiches (from £1.65), filled baked potato (£1.90), ploughman's (from £2.20), quiche or lasagne (£2.90) and salads (from £3.50), with grills (not Sunday lunchtime) such as gammon (£5.50) and eight-ounce rump steak (£6.50); friendly service. It's a small, comfortable village inn, with a softly lit, atmospheric bar, liberally decorated with guns, little kegs, a brass cauldron and other brassware, bottles and jars along a Delft shelf, and in summer plenty of fresh flowers; there are also red leatherette built-in wall banquettes, an attractive Gothick carved box settle, a comfortable old settee, a carved dresser and a longcase clock; well kept Bass and Flowers IPA and Original on handpump; dominoes, open fire. There are a few picnic-table sets on the side lawn. It was originally a railway inn, refurbished to give its present form when the line closed. *(Recommended by Shirley Pielou, John and Ruth Roberts, Graham and Glenis Watkins, J R Carey, DMF, JH, Gordon Smith)*

Heavitree (who no longer brew)   Real ale   Meals and snacks   Small restaurant (not Sun evening), best to book   Open 11–2.30, 6–11 all year   Two bedrooms tel Ottery St Mary (040 481) 2881; £16.10S/£32.20S

TOPSHAM   SX9688 Map 1

Bridge ★

2¼ miles from M5 junction 30: Topsham signposted from exit roundabout; in Topsham follow (A376) Exmouth signpost on the Elmgrove Road

A major attraction in this thoroughly unchanging, eccentric sixteenth-century ex-maltings, positioned just above the river, is the outstanding range of real ales, tapped from the cask by Mrs Cheffers herself in the cosy inner sanctum where only the most regular of regulars sit; as well as less common ones, such as Blackawton Headstrong, Gibbs Mew Bishops Tipple, Marstons Owd Rodger, Theakstons Old Peculier, Wadworths Old Timer and Wiltshire Old Devil, there are Badger Tanglefoot, Bass, Blackawton, Courage Directors, Eldridge Pope Royal Oak, Exmoor Bitter and Gold, Fullers ESB, Marstons Pedigree, Wadworths 6X and Youngs Special. The bar itself is a cosy little parlour of a place, particularly atmospheric and decorated with a booming grandfather clock, crossed guns, swords, country pictures and rowing cartoons, and mugs hanging from the beams. The inner corridor, off which a bigger room is opened at busy times, has leaded lights let into the curved high back of one settle. Food is confined to pasties (70p), sandwiches (90p) and ploughman's (from £1.50, ham or Stilton £1.75). *(Recommended by Mrs Caroline Gibbins, Annie Taylor, Dennis Heatley, Jon Wainwright)*

Free house   Licensee Mrs Phyllis Cheffers   Real ale   Snacks   Children in room across corridor   Open 12–2, 6–10.30 (11 Fri and Sat) all year

Globe 🛏

In Topsham, keep straight on into Fore Street, where the inn has a small car park

Traditionally the meeting-place for this pretty little waterside town, this sixteenth-century coaching-inn has a heavy-beamed bar comfortably furnished with red leatherette seats around the big bow window, and traditional décor including a big panel-back settle, heavy wooden armchairs, and good sporting prints on the dark oak panelling, with an open fire under the attractive wooden mantelpiece. Good value bar food includes smokies (£1.20), ploughman's (£1.75), whitebait, egg and kidneys or home-made pies such as rabbit or steak and kidney (£2.75); beside the main restaurant there's a snug little eating room with its own fire; friendly service. Well kept Bass and Ushers Best on handpump; piped classical music. There are seats out in a small sheltered and partly covered courtyard. *(Recommended by Gethin Lewis, Graham and Glenis Watkins, Jon Wainwright, E G Parish, AE)*

Free house   Licensee D G L Price   Real ale   Meals and snacks   Restaurant   Children in eating area   Open 11–11 all year   Bedrooms tel Topsham (0392) 873471; £26B/£35B

Passage

In Topsham, turn right into Follett Road just before centre, then turn left into Ferry Road

The attractively straightforward food in this waterside pub includes soup (£1.15), lunchtime sandwiches (from £1, crab £3.25), ploughman's with a good chunk of cheese (£2.25, lunchtime), four-ounce steak sandwich (£3.15), salads (from £4.50, Exe salmon £7.75), gammon, egg and sausage (£4.95) and steaks (from £5.75). The traditional bar has leatherette wall pews and bar stools and is decorated with electrified oil lamps hanging from big black oak beams in the ochre ceiling; plank panelling and crazy-paving flagstones in one room. Bass and Flowers IPA and

Original on handpump; darts and fruit machine in the public bar. The front courtyard has benches and tables, and there are more seats down on the quiet shoreside terrace. *(Recommended by Jon Wainwright; more reports please)*

Heavitree (who no longer brew)   Licensees R G and D R Evans   Real ale   Meals and snacks (12–2, 7.30–11; not Sun evenings)   Restaurant tel Topsham (0392) 87363   Small car park Open 11–3, 5–11 (all day Sat) all year

TORBRYAN   SX8266   Map 1
Old Church House
Most easily reached from A381 Newton Abbot–Totnes via Ipplepen

An outstanding feature of this white thatched pub (which is separated from the church by a short stretch of lawn) is the range of around twenty real ales, typically including Badger Best, Cotleigh Tawny and winter Old Buzzard, Devenish Cornish Original, Exmoor Dark, Flowers Original, Gibbs Mew Bishops Tipple, Janners Bitter, Old Original and (carrying the name of the pub here) Devon Special, Marstons Merrie Monk, Pedigree and Owd Rodger, Palmers Tally Ho and Wadworths Farmers Glory. The bar on the right is particularly attractive, and has benches built into Tudor panelling as well as the red plush cushioned high-backed settle and leather-backed small seats around its big log fire. On the left there is a series of comfortable and discreetly lit lounges, one with a splendid deep Tudor inglenook fireplace with a side bread oven; piped music. Well presented bar food ranges from sandwiches (from £1), ploughman's (£1.80) and pies (£3.25), to curries or various salads (from £3.45, with a very generous chicken one), and trout (£3.80). *(Recommended by J A Harrison, Steve Huggins, Phil Gorton, Jon Wainwright; more reports please)*

Free house   Licensee Eric Pimm   Real ale   Meals and snacks (11.30–2.30, 7–10.30) Evening restaurant tel Ipplepen (0803) 812372   Children in family-room   Open 11–3, 5.30–11 all year; closed evening 25 Dec

TORCROSS   SX8241   Map 1
Start Bay   ★   🅢
A379 S of Dartmouth

The simple, unpretentious but relaxing main bar in this fourteenth-century thatched pub, which looks on to the pebbled beach, has wheel-back chairs around plenty of dark tables or (around a corner) back-to-back settles forming booths, photographs of storms buffeting the pub and country pictures on its cream walls, and a coal fire in winter; a small chatty drinking area by the counter has a brass ship's clock and barometer. The good winter games-room has pool, darts, shove-ha'penny, dominoes, cribbage, euchre and two space games; there's more booth seating in a family-room with sailing-boat pictures. It's popular virtually all the year round for its large selection of very fresh and generously served seafood; cod and haddock come in three sizes – medium (£2.60), large (£3.20) and jumbo (£3.95 – truly enormous); plaice and lemon sole are served in medium (£2.65) and large (£3.50) varieties; there are also skate (£3.50) and a much praised seafood platter, with prawns or crab, shrimps, cockles, mussels and smoked mackerel (£5.50); other food includes sandwiches (from £1), ploughman's (from £2.20), home-made vegetarian lasagne or spinach, leek and mushroom pie (£2.95), gammon (£3.90) and steaks (from £5.70); children's helpings. Well kept Whitbreads PA and a guest beer, which changes every two months, on handpump, and Addlestones cider; fruit machine in the lobby, piped music. Picnic-table sets on the terrace look out over the pebble beach, and the wildlife lagoon of Slapton Ley is just behind the pub.

It's very helpful if you let us know up-to-date food prices when you report on pubs.

(Recommended by S V Bishop, David and Ann Stranack, Helena and Arthur Harbottle, JAH, Gordon Hewitt, CED, Eileen Broadbent, Verney and Denis Baddeley, Brian and Anna Marsden, Alan and Ruth Woodhouse)

Heavitree (who no longer brew) Licensee Paul Stubbs Real ale Meals and snacks (11.30–2, 6–10) Children in family-room Open 11–2.30, 6–11 all year; no food 25 Dec and open only 11.30–1.30

TORRINGTON SS4919 Map 1

Black Horse 🛏

High Street

Though the pretty twin-gabled building with its overhanging upper storeys is dated 1616, it goes back to the fifteenth century, and over the years is reputed to have collected at least one ghost (though the licensees – a notably friendly couple – haven't seen anything, they're convinced their dogs have). It's good and solid inside: the bar on the left has a comfortable seat running right along its full-width window, chunky elm tables, an oak counter and a couple of fat black beams. A lounge on the right has a striking ancient black oak partition wall, a couple of attractive oak seats, muted plush easy chairs and a settee; the restaurant is oak-panelled. Generously served home-cooked bar food includes sandwiches (from 65p) and a wide choice of other dishes, among which current favourites are the chicken and mushroom pie (£2) and steak and kidney pie (£2.30); well kept Ushers Best and Ruddles County on handpump; darts, shove-ha'penny, cribbage; well reproduced piped music. Handy for the RHS Rosemoor garden. *(Recommended by Miss J Metherell, A R Gale, D J Wallington, K R Harris; more reports please)*

Ushers Licensees David and Val Sawyer Real ale Meals and snacks (not Sun evening) Restaurant Children in lounge and restaurant (no young children in restaurant, evening) Open 11–3, 6 (6.30 in winter)–11 all year Bedrooms tel Torrington (0805) 22121; £14B/£24B

TOTNES SX8060 Map 1

Kingsbridge Inn

Leechwell Street; going up the old town's main one-way street, bear left into Leechwell Street approaching the top

This is Totnes' oldest pub, with parts of it dating from the ninth century – it even gets a mention in the Domesday Book. Bar food includes home-baked filled rolls (from £1.10, prawn £1.85), home-made soup (£1.25), filled baked potatoes (from £2.25), ploughman's (from £2.50), steak and kidney pie or curry with mango chutney and a poppadum (£3.25), chicken chasseur (£4.10) and steaks (from £5.50). The bar is a rambling affair, with broad stripped plank panelling, bare stone or black and white timbering, low heavy beams in a dark ochre ceiling, and comfortable peach plush seats around rustic tables on the dark carpet. There's an elaborately carved bench in one intimate little alcove, an antique waterpump and a log-effect gas fire; Burton Bridge and Courage Best on handpump. *(Recommended by Ann and David Stranack, R F Warner, Ceri Jarr, SC, Jon Wainwright, AE, Mrs Joan Harris, S V Bishop)*

Free house Licensees Timothy and Susan Langsford Real ale Meals and snacks (11.30–2, 6–10) Children in eating area Open 11.30–2.30, 6–11 all year

TRUSHAM SX8582 Map 1

Cridford Inn

Village and pub signposted from B3193 NW of Chudleigh, just N of big ARC works; 1½ very narrow miles

Tucked away in pretty countryside, in a little otherwise largely modern hamlet, this fourteenth-century oak-beamed longhouse has a delightfully relaxed atmosphere, and charming service. There are rugs on flagstones, old hunting prints and a couple of guns on white-painted uncoursed stone walls, stout standing timbers, and cushioned window seats, pews and chapel chairs around kitchen and pub tables, with some stained glass in the windows, and a big wood-burning stove in the stone fireplace. Good value bar food includes sandwiches (from £1), filled baked potatoes (from £1.20), big home-made pasties (£1.50), garlic mushrooms with Stilton (£1.85), sweet-and-sour pork or southern fried chicken (£2.50), speciality sausages (£2.80), casseroles (from £3.25), and dishes from the restaurant menu such as trout (£5.50), venison casserole (£5.95) and steak (£7.95); well kept Exmoor on handpump, Bass, Cotleigh Old Buzzard and an interesting weekly guest beer such as Smiles Best tapped from the cask, and Reddaway's farm ciders from over near Ideford (a first and second prize at Devon County Show, 1989); darts, cribbage, dominoes, fruit machine, trivia and juke box in the end family-room. The sun-trap front terrace has sturdy rustic benches and tables under cocktail parasols, and a small play area has a pool, swing, seesaw, vintage Fordson tractor and maybe pet rabbits. *(Recommended by WHBM, Sarah and David Read; more reports please – we've heard nothing yet about the bedrooms)*

Free house   Licensees Tony and Mick Shepherd   Real ale   Meals and snacks (until 9.45 evenings)   Children in eating area   Open 11–3 (2.30 winter weekdays), 6–11 all year Bedrooms tel Chudleigh (0626) 853694; £20B/£30B

UGBOROUGH   SX6755   Map 1

Anchor

On B3210; village signposted from Ivybridge (just off A38 E of Plymouth)

The oak-beamed public bar in this well kept pub has wall settles and seats around the wooden tables on the polished wood-block floor, and a log fire in its stone fireplace. There are Windsor armchairs in the comfortable carpeted lounge; well kept Bass and Wadworths 6X tapped from the cask; darts and piped music. The straightforward food includes sandwiches (from 95p, toasted from £1.10, prawn £2.10), ploughman's (from £1.95), basket meals (from £1.75), salads (from £3), gammon (£3.20), squid (£3.50), seafood platter (£3.75) and steaks (from £6.50). It's set in an attractive village, unusual for its spacious central square. They now do bedrooms. *(Recommended by F J Robinson, John Bowdler, J S Evans, H F and J Hobbs, Jon Wainwright, Mr and Mrs J C Dwane)*

Free house   Licensee Paul Harding   Real ale   Meals and snacks   Restaurant   Children in restaurant   Open 11–2.30, 5.30–11 all year   Double bedroom tel Plymouth (0752) 892283; £25B

WHIMPLE   SY0497   Map 1

New Fountain 🏵

Village signposted 5 miles off A30 Exeter–Honiton

The atmosphere in the small carpeted lounge bar of this village pub is civilised and snug, with simple chairs around the sturdy wooden tables, fresh flowers, a collection of Dickens cigarette cards from Players, and a log-effect gas fire. Well kept Devenish Royal Wessex on handpump and an interesting range of wines; piped classical music. The licensee's emphasis on food is not something you might remark upon at lunchtime, when what's offered is pleasantly simple – sandwiches (£1.10), soup (£1.30), ploughman's (from £2.20), local pork sausages (£2.20), peppered smoked mackerel (£2.25) and good specials; but in the evenings (not Sunday), the place is transformed into a serious restaurant, with starters such as deep-fried breaded mushrooms (£1.95) and brandy and orange pâté (£2.30), and main courses such as pan-fried kidneys with mushrooms and onion (£5.95), local lamb (£6.25), chicken in Stilton, walnut and port sauce (£6.65) and steak (£8.50);

fresh fish and game in season, and absolutely no frozen products. Every six weeks or so they have special food evenings – Chinese New Year, say – which tend to get booked up very quickly. The garden is actively populated by some angora rabbits, two cats called Corky and Felix, and Moët and Chandon, the nanny goats. *(Recommended by Theo Schofield, John Kirk, Mrs P Powis, M E Dormer, David and Flo Wallington)*

Devenish Licensee Patrick Jackson Real ale Meals and snacks (not Sun evening); booking advised Fri, Sat evenings, essential Sun lunch tel Whimple (0404) 822350 Children in eating area Open 11–2.30ish, 6.30–11 all year

WINKLEIGH SS6308 Map 1
Kings Arms
Off B3220, in village centre

They emphasise that all the bar food in this old-fashioned, thatched pub is home made, and includes vegetable soup (£1.50), ploughman's (£2.55), omelette or lasagne (£3.25), a help-yourself lunchtime summer salad bar (£3.50), game pie (£3.50), plaice (£3.75) and venison pie (£4.50); friendly service. The unspoilt, dimly lit beamed bar, more or less divided into two by the staircase, has some old-fashioned built-in wall settles, scrubbed pine tables and benches on its tiles and flagstones, a log fire in a cavernous fireplace, and a couple of large fish tanks (with some real rarities) over by the lunchtime salad bar. It opens out on one side into an area with a neat row of tables and booth seating; Ruddles County and Ushers Best on handpump, Inch's cider, decent wines; friendly service; well reproduced piped pop music. There are a couple of white tables by a small pool in the little side courtyard, sheltered by large shrubs. It's attractively placed on the edge of the village square. *(Recommended by John Evans, J and A Thurston, Mrs Thompson, David and Flo Wallington)*

Free house Licensee Nigel Rickard Meals and snacks (11.30–2.15, 6–10.30, not Mon) Restaurant Tues–Sat evenings, Sun lunch Children over 6 in eating area and restaurant Open 11–2.30, 6–11 all year; closed Mon exc bank hol evenings Bedrooms in self-contained cottage tel Winkleigh (0837) 83384; £12.50B/£25B

WOODBURY SALTERTON SY0189 Map 1
Digger's Rest ★
3½ miles from M5 junction 30: A3052 towards Sidmouth, village signposted on right about ½ mile after Clyst St Mary; also signposted from B3179 SE of Exeter

The main bar of this welcoming thatched Tudor pub has comfortable old-fashioned country chairs and settles around polished antique tables under its heavy black oak beams, a grandfather clock, plates decorating the walls of one alcove, a dark oak Jacobean screen, a log fire at one end, and an ornate solid-fuel stove at the other. Families can entertain themselves in the big skittles alley and games-room. Bass and Charrington IPA on ancient handpumps, and a good selection of farmhouse ciders; sensibly placed darts, and dominoes, in the small brick-walled public bar. Bar food, not the main attraction here, includes soup (£1.05), sandwiches, ploughman's (from £2) and a daily special (around £3). The terrace garden has views of the countryside. The pub is named after a wandering Australian who finally settled here as the landlord. *(Recommended by Heather Sharland, Brian and Anna Marsden, Peter Finzi, Brian Jones, Bernard Phillips, Graham and Glenis Watkins, Pamela and Merlyn Horswell)*

Free house Real ale Meals and snacks Children in family-room Open 11–2.30, 6.30–11

Lucky Dip

Besides the fully inspected pubs, you might like to try these Lucky Dips recommended to us and described by readers (if you do, please send us reports):

☆ **Alswear** [A373 South Molton–Tiverton; SS7222], *Butchers Arms*: Neat village pub with uncluttered public bar – exposed stone walls, beams, flagstones, chiming grandmother clock, huge inglenook log fire, simple furniture; pool-room with juke box, fruit machine, sensibly placed darts; skittle alley; plusher lounge with log fire; bar food including generously filled sandwiches, hot dishes, small restaurant; Bass and Flowers, regular music nights; bedrooms *(Steve and Carolyn Harvey, J R Carey)*

Ashburton [West St; SX7569], *Exeter*: Immediately appealing old pub, cheerful licensee, Watneys-related real ales, good value simple bar food *(Phil Stone)*

Avonwick [B3210 ½ mile from A38; SX7157], *Mill*: Friendly service and big helpings of reasonably priced light meals in recently extended popular dining pub; Bass on handpump, attractive surroundings, busy restaurant, children's area *(J S Evans, PEG, Geoffrey Thompson)*

Axmouth [SY2591], *Ship*: Attractive garden (a sort of convalescent home for owls and other birds from Newbury Wildlife Hospital), Devenish real ales, log fires, pleasant service; bar meals, evening buttery bar concentrating on fish (has been closed Fri) *(LYM)*

Aylesbeare [A3052 Exeter–Sidmouth, junction with B3180; SY0392], *Halfway*: Very friendly with good, quickly served bar snacks and restaurant area; marvellous views westwards *(Michael Thomson)*

Beer [Fore St; ST2389], *Anchor*: Clean and friendly with well kept beer and good bar food served in separate area, including excellent freshly caught fish; well kept Badger and other real ales; bedrooms *(P Gillbe)*; [B3174 2 miles N] *Bovey House*: Sixteenth-century Inglenook Bar in former manor house, with three-acre garden, which belonged to Katherine Parr; beamed ceiling, flagstone floor, outstanding hospitality, Flowers on handpump, fine wines; bedrooms *(E G Parish)*

Beesands [SX8140], *Cricket*: Friendly local on beach of fishing village, with amiable landlord *(WMS)*

Belstone [SX6293], *Tors*: Enjoyable country pub on the edge of Dartmoor; very good reasonably priced food, well kept beer, local atmosphere *(PB, WMS)*

Berry Head [SX9456], *Berry Head*: Well furnished bars, reasonably priced Bass on handpump, good range of bar food, excellent cliff-top terrace *(P L Jackson)*

Bickington [SX7972], *Dartmoor Half Way*: Warm welcome, good Flowers, wide range of bar food *(J S Evans, Steve Huggins)*

Bickleigh [A396, N of junction with A3072; SS9407], *Trout*: Comfortable and individual furnishings in remarkably spacious dining lounge with wide choice from efficient food counter, including good help-yourself salads; well kept real ales such as Ruddles County, restaurant, tables on pretty lawn, provision for children; bedrooms *(Verney and Denis Baddeley, PHF, LYM)*

☆ **nr Bigbury** [St Ann's Chapel; B3392; SX6544], *Pickwick*: Main bar with traditionally rustic feel, well kept Bass, Flowers and Palmers, local Stancombe cider tapped from the cask, usual bar food including marvellously fresh prawn sandwiches, friendly bar staff, piped music; pool and other games in spacious newer and plainer family extension which brings lots of children to the pub; restaurant; bedrooms *(Amanda Dauncey, Mr and Mrs J C Dwane, John Drummond, R J Whitney, Ian and Daphne Brownlie, Mr and Mrs G J Lewis, Jon Wainwright, LYM)*

☆ **Bishops Tawton** [A377 S of Barnstaple; SS5630], *Chichester Arms*: Picturesque fifteenth-century cob and thatch pub with small windows, almost perilous sagging beams just over six feet above floor, large stone fireplace, splendid set of antlers, fine photographs of life here in the 1920s, pleasant and homely olde-worlde atmosphere; well kept Ushers on handpump, good range of bar food, small garden with terrace by village green *(J R Carey, K R Harris)*

☆ **Blackawton** [SX8050], *Normandy Arms*: Quaint and pleasant fifteenth-century pub in remote, pretty village, Second World War memorabilia, log fire, well kept Bass and Blackawton ales, excellent bar food, restaurant featuring local seafood, friendly staff; bedrooms *(Gordon Hewitt, Dr C I Haines, Allan Wright)*

Bovey Tracey [High St; SX8278], *King of Prussia*: Traditional unpretentious pub, friendly landlady and son, amiable locals, fruit machine, darts, well kept Bass and farm cider *(Charlie Salt)*

Brandis Corner [A3072 Hatherleigh–Holsworthy; SS4103], *Bickford Arms*: Flowers IPA and Original on handpump and good, reasonably priced bar food; games in separate building; good mix of locals and visitors *(Keith Houlgate)*

Braunton [A361; SS4836], *Agricultural*: Pleasant atmosphere, jolly staff even under pressure, Bass and good value, well prepared bar food *(Chris Fluck)*; *New*: Small pub in pretty part of village with helpful service,

well kept Ushers and good bar food (not
normally on Sun) *(Chris Fluck)*
Bridestowe [A386 Okehampton –
Tavistock; SX5189], *Fox & Hounds*: Simple
red leatherette bar in roadside Dartmoor
pub, well kept Flowers real ales, open fires,
good value food, games-room, skittle alley;
children and animals welcome; bedrooms
good value *(BB)*
Brixham [SX9255], *Quayside*: Well kept
beer, good wines, enterprising range of bar
food; may be packed Sun lunchtime when it
has live jazz; bedrooms *(George Jonas)*
☆ **Broadclyst** [SX9897], *New Inn*: Especially
good bar food using fresh ingredients and
home-made bread, with particularly good
vegetables and unusual dishes such as
chicken and mushroom pancakes with
tomato stuffed with Stilton and garlic; did
particularly well in 1989 national cookery
competition run by *PubCaterer* magazine
(J D Acland, Mrs Barbara Andrews)
Broadclyst [adjoining church on B3121],
Red Lion: Semi-rustic free house renovated
to expose old bricks and beams; log fire,
good choice of hot and cold bar food, well
kept Bass, Eldridge Pope and maybe other
real ales, locals' bar, seats outside *(E
V M Whiteway)*
☆ **Broadhembury** [ST1004], *Drewe Arms*:
Unpretentiously friendly fifteenth-century
thatched local separated from the quiet and
picturesque village's church by a flower-filled
lawn; well kept Bass and maybe other real
ales tapped from the cask, plain home-
cooked bar food including good daily
specials, basic bedrooms *(WFL, K R Harris,
Mrs Pamela Roper, LYM)*
Buckfast [100yds up rd to Buckfast from
B3380; SX7467], *Black Rock*:Note that this is
a hotel, not a pub, but visitors are welcome
in its very small, friendly bar next to the
River Dart; obliging staff, real ale, adjacent
dining area where children welcome, decent
home-cooked food, pleasant riverside
terrace, afternoon cream teas; bedrooms
(Brian and Anna Marsden, N F Calver)
Buckfastleigh [SX7366], *Dartbridge*:
Excellent family facilities, indoors and out,
and very popular in summer as opposite Dart
Valley Railway and not far from the abbey;
ten letting chalets *(Rodney Coe)*
☆ **Buckland Monachorum** [SX4868], *Drakes
Manor*: Cosy old beamed pub full of copper
and china, with log fire, well kept Courage,
farm cider, simple reasonably priced home-
cooked bar food such as a generous and
interesting ploughman's, gammon and chips,
good Sun specials; orange banquettes in
lounge, plain public bar with friendly locals
and juke box; handy for the lovely nearby
Garden House *(Jutta Whitley, Dorothy and
Charles Morley, PB, HB, Helen Crookston;
more reports please)*
Budleigh Salterton [High St; SY0682], *King
William*: Attractive exterior with hanging

baskets; Devenish Royal Wessex on
handpump, wide choice of bar food, good
welcoming service; bedrooms *(E G Parish)*;
[Chapel St] *Salterton Arms*: Well kept
comfortable L-shaped bar recently
completely remodelled, with upper gallery
(where children allowed and tables can be
reserved), wide choice of food including
marvellous crab sandwiches, quick friendly
service, Courage Best and Directors on
handpump *(Jim Matthews, Brian Jones)*
Burlescombe [A38 some way E of village
turning; ST0716], *Poachers Pocket*: Simple
food in quiet and comfortably modernised
lounge bar of well kept inn, handy for M5
junction 27, with children's dishes, well kept
real ale, restaurant, skittle alley *(Alan Carr,
LYM)*
Chagford [SX7087], *Ring o' Bells*: Large old
black and white local in long terrace with
comfortable seating and log-effect gas fire;
popular, friendly licensee, well kept
Wadworths 6X and farm cider on
handpump, good home-made bar food,
restaurant *(Peter Donahue)*
☆ **Challacombe** [off B3358 Blackmoor Gate–
Simonsbath – OS Sheet 180 reference
695411; SS6941], *Black Venus*: Under same
ownership as Pyne Arms, East Down (see
main entries); broadly similar good food
(including locally caught fish), layout and
atmosphere; darts, pool and juke box in side
room, well kept Exmoor, Flowers and
Whitbreads real ales; reasonable prices,
friendly staff, occasional live entertainment;
set in beautiful valley; bedrooms *(Steve and
Carolyn Harvey, B M Eldridge, Mrs J Fellowes)*
Cheriton Bishop [SX7793], *Sir John
Devenish*: Good food including Sun lunch,
well kept Boddingtons, Exe Valley, Marstons
Pedigree and Wadworths, decent wines, bar
billiards, children's room – one of the rare
pubs that has reversed general trends by
having its formerly open-plan bar divided
into two *(CS)*
Cheriton Fitzpaine [The Hayes, SS8706],
Ring of Bells: Fourteenth-century thatched
country pub with log fires, old oak settles,
well kept real ales, good choice of bar food,
small restaurant; comfortable well equipped
bedrooms, self-catering holiday flat *(Simon
Boulter)*
☆ **Christow** [Village Rd; SX8385], *Artichoke*:
Quiet, traditional thatched pub in attractive
village, simple flagstoned bar with log fire
and fruit machine, well kept beers and home-
cooked bar food; bedrooms comfortable
(Charlie Salt)
Chudleigh [B3344, off A38; SX8679],
Highwaymans Haunt: Well appointed
carvery restaurant popular for evening meals
and Sun lunch (subject to seasonal change),
good range of bar snacks and specials at
other times; they serve Perrier instead of
plain water *(K Peet)*
Chudleigh Knighton [SX8477], *Clay Cutters*

Arms: Big helpings of simple food in thatched village local with big winter log fires, well kept Flowers IPA and Eldridge Pope Royal Oak, popular games area with loud juke box, seats on side terrace and in orchard; has had live music Sat; basic but warm bedrooms *(St John Sandringham, LYM)*

Chulmleigh [South Molton Rd; SS6814], *Fortescue Arms*: Fishing inn with fresh flowers in simple, pleasant bar, bass, home-cooked food that may include game or freshly caught fish, dining-room; service may not be the briskest; bedrooms *(BB)*

Clayhidon [ST1615], *Half Moon*: Miles from anywhere, with magnificent position and views; interesting reasonably priced food with excellent Sun spread, well kept beers; recent extensions; children welcome *(Alastair and Alison Riley)*; *Harriers*: Friendly pub, full range of local real ales, good bar food, large garden; good picnic/walking area *(K R Harris)*

Clyst St Mary [Sidmouth Rd; SX9790], *Cat & Fiddle*: Wide variety of reasonably priced food served efficiently in comfortable dining lounge; children's play area *(DMF)*

Cockington [SX8963], *Drum*: Thatched pub (though it's not old) in idyllic spot in rustic village; large bar with piped music, juke box, skittle alley, exposed beams and settles, stools and Windsor chairs around tables; Fergusons Dartmoor and Halls Plympton, front terrace and lovely gardens; there can be a long wait for bar food when it's busy *(Steve Huggins)*

Coffinswell [SX8968], *Linhay*: Very relaxed atmosphere in traditional longhouse with friendly staff and tasty food including vegetarian lasagne *(J and J Payne)*

Colyford [A3052 Sidmouth–Lyme Regis – OS Sheet 192 reference 253925; SY2492], *Wheelwright*: Clean and friendly pub with well kept Boddingtons and Marstons Pedigree; good lunchtime bar snacks, restaurant *(W L B and J Reed)*

Combe Martin [SS5847], *Dolphin*: Large cosy front lounge bar overlooking bay, with big lanterns and ship's wheels on walls; good value food including children's dishes, served quickly by pleasant staff; space games and pool in back room *(Derek and Jennifer Taylor)*; *Old Sawmill*: Pleasant outlook on stream from small bar with well kept Exmoor ale, good if not cheap bar food in generous helpings, restaurant *(Steve and Carolyn Harvey)*

☆ **Cornworthy** [SX8255], *Hunters Lodge*: Pleasant and comfortable genuine country local, snug and appealing, with a remarkable range of really good interesting food including delicious home-made Dart salmon gravadlax, with excellent vegetables and salads; friendly alsatian (and staff), well kept Ushers Best on handpump, local Beenleigh farm cider, good service with free lumps of cheese and other snacks on bar *(S V Bishop,*

Brian and Anna Marsden, Jon Wainwright)

Crediton [High St; SS8300], *Swan*: Jolly market-town pub, well kept real ales, extensive lunchtime and evening menus, skittle alley *(Charlie Salt)*

☆ **Croyde** [off B3231 NW of Braunton; SS4439], *Whiteleaf*: Not a pub but a guest-house – included here because it's where readers have been glad to track down the Wallingtons, who previously made the Rhydspence at Whitney on Wye (Hereford & Worcester) outstandingly popular for civilised character and interesting food, using prime ingredients; they're doing the same sort of thing here – as readers say, a culinary experience, and excellent value if you want to be pampered for a few days, with truly imaginative all-fresh food and good wines in comfortable surroundings; dogs accepted *(Miss J A Harvey, Mr and Mrs Norman Edwardes)*

☆ **Croyde**, *Thatched Barn*: Extended thatched inn near fine surfing beach (so busily seasidey in summer, when it's a bustling commercial operation), interesting original features still to be found in rambling but largely modernised bar, well kept Courage ales, largely home-made bar food including local fish and good puddings, loud piped music, provision for children, morning coffee served from 10am, restaurant *(Pamela and Merlyn Horswell, Rita Horridge, Prof H G Allen, Dr and Mrs B D Smith, LYM)*

Croyde, *Manor*: Friendly local with well kept Flowers and quickly served decent bar food; bar billiards, darts, shove-ha'penny, skittles, attractive terraced garden – a good summer family pub *(David and Flo Wallington)*

Cullompton [½ mile from M5 junction 28: enter town and turn left at T-junction; ST0107], *Manor House*: Has been well worth knowing as a spacious and relaxing place off motorway with Flowers Original on handpump and hot and cold bar food. In the winter of 1989–90 it will be going through extensive remodelling which means we cannot keep it in the main entries for this edition; the changes should be completed by early summer 1990, when it will be known as Beryards. We would be very grateful for readers' views *(LYM)*

☆ **Dartmouth** [Smith St; SX8751], *Seven Stars*: Good atmosphere in long black-beamed oak-panelled bar with leatherette settles around rustic elm tables, well kept Courage Best and Directors, piped pop music and fruit machine; upstairs restaurant, children's room, efficiently served and well priced popular food, pleasant staff *(Paul and Margaret Baker, John Barker, David and Ann Stranack, Jon Wainwright, BB)*

Dartmouth [Sandquay], *Floating Bridge*: Pleasant, airy atmosphere, large windows with good view, efficient service *(Jon Wainwright)*;[Mayors Ave] *George &*

Dragon: Cosy pub with naval theme and young licensees; Bass and Flowers Original, bar snacks and meals, children catered for, fishing parties arranged; good value well equipped bedrooms *(Leslie Campbell)*; [Henborough Post; B3207 3 miles outside]
Sportsmans Arms: Recently extended place with pleasant atmosphere, imaginative and extensive bar menu, well kept Bass *(Dr and Mrs D N Jones)*

Dawlish [Beach St; SX9676], *Exeter*: Tucked away down small alley near railway station, lively local, long and narrow with Eldridge Pope Royal Oak and various local ciders *(Jon Wainwright)*; [Strand] *Prince Albert*: Good, warm, friendly local known as Hole in the Wall, well kept Bass and Flowers IPA *(Jon Wainwright)*

☆ **Denbury** [SX8268], *Union*: Good, clean, welcoming fifteenth-century village pub with well kept Flowers and Whitbreads, excellent value home-cooked food including unusual puddings, stripped stonework, log fires, live music three times a week; big garden *(J Rachkind, Mrs S Higgins, W H Anderson)*

Dittisham [The Level; SX8654], *Red Lion*: Attractively placed unspoilt local looking down over village to River Dart, bar food and two real ales; under new regime 1989, apparently no longer doing bedrooms *(P G A Lewis)*

Dog Village [B3185; SX9896], *Hungry Fox*: Large and comfortable mock-Tudor pub with wide range of beers (including well kept Flowers), wines and low-alcohol drinks, and extensive choice of good well priced hot and cold bar food; efficient friendly service *(E V M Whiteway, Theo Schofield)*

☆ *nr* **Drewsteignton** [Fingle Bridge – OS Sheet 191 reference 743899; SX7390], *Anglers Rest*: Sprucely airy and spacious bar in outstanding scenery – picturesque forested valley by sixteenth-century packhorse bridge over River Dart; reliable pub food, well kept Cotleigh and Courage Directors on handpump, Thomas Hardys bottled real ale, real cider, brisk summer business in tourist souvenirs; winter opening times more restricted; present licensee's grandmother started trading here in Queen Victoria's Jubilee year, originally with just a stall and then an open-fronted tea pavilion; handy for Drogo Castle, nr GWG19 *(Helena and Arthur Harbottle, Verney and Denis Baddeley, LYM)*

Dunsford [OS Sheet 191 reference 813891; SX8189], *Royal Oak*: Good value bar food including choice of vegetarian dishes in light and airy lounge bar of village inn, well kept Ushers real ales, games in public bar, small restaurant, provision for children; good value bedrooms *(LYM)*

East Budleigh [SY0684], *Sir Walter Raleigh*: Attractive thatched local in picturesque village; cosy, clean and welcoming, well kept Devenish Royal Wessex on handpump, excellent bar food including huge steaks cut by licensee from bone and splendid home-made steak and kidney pie, friendly and attentive service, restaurant; nearby church has unique collection of bench ends *(J R Carey, P Gillbe, AE)*

East Prawle [SX7836], *Pigs Nose*: Cheerful pubby atmosphere, good home-made food, coal fire, decent beers, interesting 'piggy' theme, family-room; nr start GWG12 and lovely stretch of Coast Path *(D Pearman, Sue Cleasby, Mike Ledger)*

Ermington [SX6353], *Crooked Spire*: Good, friendly service, decent substantial food in restaurant including excellent steaks *(John Evans)*

Exeter [Topsham Rd; on B3181 ring rd roundabout; SX9292], *Countess Wear Lodge*: The bar here has well kept Ushers, decent hot and cold food (also a restaurant), quick service; good value comfortable bedrooms *(E V M Whiteway)*; [59 Magdalen St] *Milestone*: The no-alcohol 'pub' here closed in early 1989; [Martins Lane] *Ship*: Photogenic fourteenth-century pub just off the Cathedral Close, with well kept Bass, Flowers IPA and Original and Sam Whitbreads on handpump; convenient, with quickly served good value food until 9 *(HEG, Pamela and Merlyn Horswell, LYM)*; [High St North] *Turks Head*: City-centre Beefeater pub with wide choice of bar food, Flowers Original on handpump and welcoming polite staff; long two-level lounge bar with bookshelves, restaurant *(E G Parish)*; [Union Rd, Pennsylvania] *Victoria*: City-suburb pub, recently completely rejigged using genuine old timbers, furniture and pictures; good choice of beers including Devenish, wide range of bar food such as pizzas and fish, decent coffee *(E Whiteway)*

Exmouth [The Beacon; SY0080], *Beacon Vaults*: Pleasant and well run *(Graham and Glenis Watkins)*

☆ **Filleigh** [just off A361 Barnstaple–South Molton; SS6627], *Stags Head*: Sixteenth-century thatched pub by lake, single bar with one side devoted to good bar food from speciality ploughman's to steaks, with good home-made puddings; Bass and Websters Yorkshire, picnic-table sets outside; comfortable bedrooms *(Steve and Carolyn Harvey, J R Carey)*

Folly Gate [A386 Hatherleigh–Okehampton; SX5797], *Crossways*: Small, well run pub with Bass and Charrington IPA on handpump; food is well worth the wait, but it can be difficult to find a table during the tourist season; children allowed in quieter parts *(Keith Houlgate)*

Fremington [SS5132], *New Inn*: Good value tasty food *(John Naylor)*

Galmpton [Maypool; off A3022 at Greenway Quay signpost, then bear left to Maypool; SX8856], *Lost & Found*: Idyllic setting overlooking Torbay Steam Railway, with well kept Flowers and good bar food including fine sandwiches – but note that it has a hotel/restaurant licence, so you can drink only if you eat; the restaurant has an attractive dining terrace; comfortable bedrooms *(Margaret and Trevor Errington, S V Bishop, Pamela and Merlyn Horswell);* [OS Sheet 202 reference 889563] *Manor:* Friendly local with excellent value neatly presented food including locally landed fish, well spaced tables in restaurant area *(Verney and Denis Baddeley)*

☆ **Georgeham** [Rock Hill; above village – OS Sheet 180 reference 466399; SS4639], *Rock:* Oak beams, wood-burning stove, old settles and pleasant atmosphere, with well kept Watneys-related real ales and limited but good range of home-made bar food including good soup and superb filled French bread; pool-table at lower end, tables on terrace; doing well under new regime *(David Wallington, Henry Midwinter, J R Carey)*

Gittisham [Gittisham Common; SY1398], *Hare & Hounds:* Convenient spot; spacious pub with warm, friendly welcome and good choice of great ales *(Graham and Glenis Watkins)*

Hartland Quay [SS2522], *Hartland Quay:* Remarkable, isolated spot at foot of cliffs by derelict quay, with waves crashing over the rocks; St Austell Tinners and moderately priced straightforward bar food; room off bar with odd collection of clocks *(Prof H G Allen)*

Hatherleigh [Market St; SS5404], *Tally Ho:* Attractive bar with decorative plates on the walls, log fires, real ales including Eldridge Pope Royal Oak, IPA and Dorchester and Wadworths 6X, wide choice of good food in bar and restaurant, with excellent wines – particularly Italian ones; friendly licensee, attentive staff; children welcome, nice garden; three cosy and prettily furnished bedrooms *(Juliet Streatfield, Neil Evans, J R Carey, Verney and Denis Baddeley, Mrs Pamela Roper)*

Hawkchurch [ST3400], *Fairwater Head:* Not really a pub, but a small and very well appointed hotel – worth knowing for its excellent food and service, and really magnificent views; comfortable bedrooms *(Dr D M Forsyth)*

Hawkchurch [ST3400], *Old Inn:* Charming old pub at centre of lovely village; thoughtfully modernised and maintained, keeping a village atmosphere; simple food in informal surroundings, dogs allowed, picnic-table sets outside *(Anon)*

Haytor Vale [SX7677], *Moorlands:* Excellent, friendly Agatha Christie bar, good food in beautiful dining-room overlooking south-facing gardens with extensive further views; opposite open moor and path to Haytor; comfortable bedrooms *(Philip and Trisha Ferris)*

Hemerdon [SX5657], *Miners Arms:* Excellent pub with low beams, well kept beer, good service *(C A Gurney)*

Hemyock [ST1313], *Catherine Wheel:* Pleasantly appointed, with wide choice of good food *(Mrs Shirley Pielou)*

Hexworthy [village signposted off B3357 Tavistock–Ashburton, 3¾ m E of B3212; SX6572], *Forest:* Extensive knocked-together lounge with separate quite distinctively furnished seating areas, walkers' bar, sheltered tables outside; children welcome, restaurant; main attraction is the location, isolated in the middle of Dartmoor, with fishing available on the Dart; nr GWG17; bedrooms *(John Evans, LYM)*

Heybrook Bay [SX4948], *Eddystone:* Clean, bright pub with good service and good value lunchtime and evening bar food at reasonable prices *(Geoffrey Thompson)*

Higher Ashton [off B3193; SX8584], *Manor:* Small but popular, two bars, friendly atmosphere, well kept Flowers and Wadworths 6X tapped from the cask, simple home-made bar food at reasonable prices, garden overlooking Teign Valley *(David and Flo Wallington)*

Holbeton [Fore St; SX6150], *Dartmoor Union:* Traditional village pub, tastefully modernised, excellent fresh fish delivered daily from Plymouth and other good home-cooked bar food *(J J Hansen); Mildmay Colours:* Popular pub in picturesque village, good cheerful service, lots of atmosphere, large choice of good value bar food (including vegetarian dishes), upstairs restaurant with evening carvery about three times a week and Sun lunch (best to book); front terrace has lovely views *(Susan and Derek Lockyer)*

nr **Honiton** [Fenny Bridges (A30 4 miles W); ST1500], *Fenny Bridges:* Pleasant well kept bar with kindly, quick bar staff; good range of real ales and good choice of decent bar food lunchtime and evening; restaurant, garden *(W R Porter, Ninka Sharland);* [also at Fenny Bridges] *Greyhound:* Big thatched roadhouse, now a Chef & Brewer, with droves of red plush dining-chairs and banquettes in its heavily beamed rambling bar, and a deliberately old-fashioned style; quickly served good value straightforward food, separate carvery (generous helpings), Ushers on handpump, comfortable well equipped games-room; bedrooms *(J S Clements, Dr D M Forsyth, LYM)*

Hope Cove [SX6640], *Hope & Anchor:* Simple seaside inn with local flavour, good open fire, plain good value food, welcoming staff, and basic but clean and cheap bedrooms – generous breakfasts *(Margaret and Trevor Errington, Leslie Dawes, P A King-Fisher, LYM); Lobster Pot:* Pleasant, comfortable atmosphere, good, cheap food; run by popular local family *(W M Sharpe)*

Horns Cross [A39 Clovelly–Bideford – OS Sheet 190 reference 385233; SS3823], *Hoops:*

Neatly refurbished thatched and oak-beamed inn, popular with older people; home-made bar food, piped classical music, Flowers IPA and Original, Inch's cider, log fire in big inglenook; bedrooms *(Mr and Mrs J M Elden, Shirley Allen, Wayne Brindle, LYM)*

☆ **Iddesleigh** [SS5708], *Duke of York*: Unspoilt thatched cob-and-whitewash pub, very much the heart of this isolated farming village, with a warm welcome for strangers too; two log fires (one in an inglenook with side bread oven), flagstones, oak and scrubbed deal tables and benches, well kept Bass and Wadworths 6X tapped from the cask, attractive dining-room, enormous helpings of good wholesome food with children's helpings and excellent puddings, friendly service *(Mrs S Andrews, David and Flo Wallington, J R Carey)*

Ideford [SX8977], *Royal Oak*: Small, olde-worlde, thatched local with one bar crammed with Victorian and turn-of-the-century regalia including dummy dressed in Victorian naval uniform and flags draped from ceiling; friendly character landlord, particularly well kept Bass, raised log fire *(Steve Huggins)*

Ilfracombe [Broad St; just by harbour; SS5147], *Royal Britannia*: Pleasant, friendly and comfortable pub/hotel with low seats, armchairs, copper tables and lots of prints; very reasonably priced bar food including fresh local fish, well kept Courage, John Smiths and Websters Yorkshire; well worth knowing for its attractive position above the harbour, in the quaint part of the town; bedrooms *(B M Eldridge, D J Wallington)*

Instow [SS4730], *Quay*: Single-bar waterfront pub in attractive spot looking up Torridge estuary to Bideford; friendly and obliging, with generous helpings of good simple bar food including freshly caught fish; well kept Flowers Original and a guest beer *(Richard Fawcett, Hugh Butterworth)*

Ipplepen [Poplar Terrace; SX8366], *Plough*: Lively, friendly modernised village local with interesting photographs, well kept Halls Harvest on handpump *(Jon Wainwright)*

Ivybridge [Western Rd; SX6356], *Imperial*: Good value bar meals, especially curry, seafood and steaks in small, busy pub with friendly staff, Courage Best and Directors, garden behind; children welcome *(R J Whitney, Peter and Sue Darling)*

Kenn [not far off A38; SX9285], *Ley Arms*: Dark, cosy old bars, more modern eating area with popular carvery and good choice of reasonably priced hot and cold food, well kept real ales including Bass and Blackawton, friendly efficient service; attractive village surroundings *(WAG, Mrs Joan Harris)*

Kentisbeare [ST0608], *Wyndham Arms*: Comfortable, welcoming pub with good beer and food *(David Gaunt)*

Kilmington [A35; SY2797], *Old Inn*:

Friendly and welcoming thatched inn with character bar, comfortable inglenook lounge, good value bar food, restaurant, Bass and Hancocks, traditional games and skittle alley, children's play area; tables outside *(David Gaunt, LYM)*

Kings Nympton [SS6819], *Grove*: Simple village inn with cream teas, bar food, Tues fish-and-chips night, well kept Ushers Best, lots of games and skittle alley; provision for children *(LYM)*

☆ **Kingsbridge** [edge of town; SX7344], *Crabshell*: Pleasant estuary-side spot, friendly atmosphere, delightful view, well kept Bass and Charringtons IPA, and good bar food – particularly ploughman's and crab sandwiches *(Amanda Dauncey, Ann and David Stranack, R J Whitney)*

Kingskerswell [SX8767], *Hare & Hounds*: Whitbreads food pub extended to house a carvery and dining room; good extensive menu, gets very busy *(M P Hallewell)*

Kingsteignton [below A38; SX8773], *Passage House*: In a creek on the River Teign this friendly pub has a two-tiered bar with a relaxed atmosphere and lots of comfortable chairs; restaurant *(M P Hallewell)*

Kingswear [SX8851], *Ship*: Genuine local, warm welcome for visitors, Flowers real ales, bar food *(John Knighton)*

Landscove [OS Sheet 202 reference 778661; SX7766], *Live & Let Live*: Unassuming village pub with homely open-plan bar, popular food, well kept Courage Best and Flowers IPA, country wines, tables in small orchard *(LYM)*

Lee [SS4846], *Grampus*: Attractive fourteenth-century pub with nice quiet garden, just a stroll up through the village from the sea; well kept Flowers, bar food including a good sheep's-cheese ploughman's *(C Elliott, LYM)*

Lifton [SX3885], *Arundell Arms*: Substantial fishing hotel (can arrange tuition – also shooting, deer-stalking and riding), rich décor, good evening restaurant cooking, good lunchtime cold buffet in hotel bar *(Patrick Young)*

Littleham [SS4323], *Crealock Arms*: Well kept, modern pub with good, friendly service and wide choice of bar food from sandwiches to steaks *(Anon)*

Littlehempston [A381; SX8162], *Pig & Whistle*: Large no-smoking area, good food and service, Bass and Wadworths 6X and Farmers Glory on handpump *(JAH)*; *Tally Ho!*: Off beaten track, with warm welcome, well kept Palmers Tally Ho and good food *(Alan Merricks)*

Lower Ashton [SX8484], *Manor*: Austere but homely Teign Valley village pub with open fires, friendly dog and shove-ha'penny; Bass and good home-cooked food, reasonably priced – particularly good garlic bread *(Charlie Salt)*

Luppitt [OS Sheet 192 reference 169067;

ST1606], *Luppitt*: Unspoilt farm pub – one cosy room by the kitchen, a second sparser games-room; lavatories across the yard *(Phil Gorton, MM)*

Luton [Haldon Moor; SX9076], *Elizabethan*: Comfortable place with conscientious staff, popular for wide choice of good attractively priced food; Devenish and other real ales, unobtrusive piped music *(Mr and Mrs M A Garraway, G Marchant)*

Lynmouth [SS7249], *Rock House*: Small warm and cosy hotel bar with lots of ship/naval memorabilia, good range of simple bar food, friendly, efficient bar staff; piped music; bedrooms *(Prof H G Allen, Wilfred Plater-Shellard)*

☆ **Lynton** [Rockford; Lynton–Simonsbath rd, off B2332 – OS Sheet 180 reference 755477], *Rockford Inn*: Traditional village local in beautiful spot in the heart of Doone country, with split-level seating, local prints and farm tools, well kept Cotleigh Tawny, Courage Best and Directors, evening bar meals, good service, darts; NT walks (Watersmeet) nearby, on GWG22; fishing on the River Exe; bedrooms *(Steve and Carolyn Harvey, Mr and Mrs J R Aylmer)*

☆ **nr Lynton** [Martinhoe, towards Heddon's Mouth – OS Sheet 180 reference 654482; SS7249], *Hunters*: Popular pub, well kept Eldridge Pope Dorset, bar meals (rather than snacks) including help-yourself salads, cheerful service, garden with peacocks; good parking point for walk to coast through NT land – start of GWG21 *(Lynne Sheridan, Bob West)*

☆ **Malborough** [SX7039], *Old Inn*: Full of life yet relaxing, with mixture of young and older customers; wide choice of good reasonably priced bar food including fine mussels and impressive puddings; cheerful service *(Michael Halsted, Mr Forester, Margaret and Trevor Errington)*

Manaton [SX7581], *Kestor*: Gorgeous spot, large and pleasant interior, sun lounge, varied bar food served lunchtimes and evenings, tables in garden; children welcome *(Mrs Shirley Pielou)*

Mary Tavy [A386; SX5079], *Mary Tavy*: Genial licensee, good bar food with help-yourself buffet, well kept real ales including Bass and St Austell HSD; open-plan lounge bar without juke box or fruit machines, restaurant; children's room with video *(R C Vincent, N F Calver)*

☆ **Meavy** [SX5467], *Royal Oak*: Uniquely owned by the parish – attractive spot on green of Dartmoor village, comfortable L-shaped main bar with rustic tables, smaller attractively traditional public bar, good simple home-made food, Bass and Blackawton real ales on handpump, cheerful service, good atmosphere; popular with walkers *(PB, HB, W M Sharpe, Jutta Whitley, Simon Turner, LYM)*

Merrivale [SX5475], *Dartmoor*: Heavy

beams, open fire, Courage Best and Directors and Wadworths 6X on handpump, maybe early morning coffee, good reasonably priced lunchtime bar food, efficient service; start GWG15 *(Margaret and Trevor Errington, Geoffrey Thompson)*

Molland [SS8028], *London*: Long white pub by church on edge of Exmoor, much as it might have been in the 1950s or earlier (it's been in the same family for ages); three small, basic rooms, the main one lit largely by its roaring log fire; no airs or graces, Cotleigh Tawny, pasties in display case; small pretty garden with tables and chairs on flagstone terrace *(Stephen and Carolyn Harvey)*

Monkton [A30 NE of Honiton; ST1803], *Monkton Court*: Imposing stone house, handy for the trunk road, with extensive beamed main bar and snug little inner bar, usual bar food, restaurant, Courage real ales, games-room, provision for children, spacious relaxing garden; we've had no reports since it closed for refurbishment earlier in 1989; bedrooms *(S A and P J Barrett, LYM; more reports please)*

Mortehoe [free parking by church; village signposted with Woolacombe from A361 Ilfracombe–Braunton; SS4545], *Ship Aground*: Village pub by church, in good coastal walking country (Morte Point, Bull Point, Lee, Woolacombe Warren); open-plan, with leatherette wall seating, massive tree-trunk tables, lots of nautical brassware, log fire; well kept Flowers Original, Exmoor and a guest beer, bar food from sandwiches and ploughman's to hot dishes such as haddock with prawns, cockles and mussels; children in restaurant and games-room; has been open all day in summer *(D Godden, P Miller, LYM)*

Newton Abbot [East St; SX8671], *Olde Cider Bar*: Very basic and unspoilt locals' cider house – the only one left in Devon; choice of farm ciders from 40-gallon wooden barrels behind the bar – not licensed to sell other drinks *(David Fisher)*

No Mans Land [SS8313], *Mountpleasant*: Warm welcome, good choice of beers and wines, good food served in bar and restaurant *(Colin Williamson)*

North Bovey [SX7483], *Manor House*: Well kept and comfortable *(Henry Hooper)*

North Tawton [SS6601], *Copper Key*: Comfortably furnished pub with local atmosphere; friendly new licensees, well kept Marstons Pedigree *(Andrew and Michele Wells)*

☆ **Noss Mayo** [SX5447], *Old Ship*: Picturesque pub with good village view, waterside garden, efficient happy service, wide choice of good bar food from toasted bacon and mushroom sandwiches to steak and kidney pie, well kept Bass and Courage on handpump; attractive upstairs restaurant overlooking small harbour; children's bar

(G S and W P Pocock, J R Carey)

Ottery St Mary [The Square; SY0995],
London: Well kept old pub with plenty of
tables, quick service, Ushers and two ciders
on draught, good range of hot and cold bar
food, friendly staff and locals
(E V M Whiteway, JAH)

Parkham [SS3821], *Bell*: Comfortably
refurbished simple thatched village pub with
good local feel, warm welcome, Bass and
Flowers IPA and Original tapped from the
cask and reasonably priced, good simple
meals *(Steve and Carolyn Harvey, LYM)*

Plymouth [Derrys Cross, behind Theatre
Royal; SX4755], *Bank*: Renovated Lloyds
Bank full of mahogany and brass, with oak
staircase to upstairs bar, tasteful Edwardian
décor; well kept Halls Plympton beers, good
cheap food *(W M Sharpe, H Paulinski)*;
[Barbican] *Distillery*: Previous gin distillery,
nicely converted to slick modern town pub
with wrought iron and palm trees in the main
bar, children welcome in more rustic stone-
floored entrance area, good basic pub food
(H G and C J McCafferty, J R Carey); [Mutley
Plain] *Fortescue*: Popular for good value
lunchtime salads and hot dishes; well kept
Halls Plympton Best and Pride and
Fergusons Dartmoor, lovely outside roof
garden *(Amanda Dauncey)*; [West Hoe Rd,
corner of Millbay Rd] *Sippers*: Friendly
Whitbreads pub close to centre, on three
levels; quick service, straightforward bar
food, juke box (not too loud), space game
and fruit machine; gets its name from the
naval way of drinking rum *(Colin Gooch)*;
[Saltram Pl, back of Plymouth Hoe] *Yard
Arm*: Warm welcome from friendly licensees
at naval theme pub, with decent food and
choice of real ales *(George Jonas)*

Plympton [Station Rd; SX5356], *Joshua
Reynolds*: Busy pub in central shopping area,
good value food generously served *(Royal
Bromell)*

☆ **Postbridge** [B3212; SX6579], *East Dart*:
Chummy roadside family bar in central
Dartmoor hotel which has some 30 miles of
fishing; efficiently served bar food, choice of
real ales on handpump, farm cider; children
welcome; bedrooms *(BB)*

Poundsgate [SX7072], *Tavistock*: Well kept
Courage real ales, good value food from
ploughman's and soup to seafood lasagne
and steaks; service normally quick and
friendly, but one reader faced very long Bank
Holiday delay; ancient flagstones and
fireplaces, attractive garden *(Philip and
Trisha Ferris)*

Princetown [SX5873], *Devils Elbow*:
Welcoming landlord, pool-table, Bass,
Courage Best and Directors, bar food *(Simon
Turner)*; *Prince of Wales*: Good value food at
candle-lit tables, Flowers and Wadworths 6X
on handpump, huge fires in two rooms, lots
of rugs draped on the walls; cheerful warders
from Dartmoor Prison chatting and joking;

actually owned by the Prince of Wales
(Simon Turner, GB, CH, BB)

Rackenford [SS8518], *Stag*: Friendly
atmosphere and interesting layout, with
thick thirteenth-century walls; well kept
Cotleigh Tawny, farm cider, bar food,
provision for children *(BB)*

☆ **Ringmore** [SX6545], *Journeys End*:
Interesting old-fashioned furnishings in
panelled lounge of friendly and unusual
partly medieval inn with wide range of bar
food, good choice of well kept real ales and
farm cider, helpful service, homely garden,
evening restaurant; not far from the sea;
bedrooms comfortable and well equipped
(Jon Wainwright, JAH, W C M Jones, LYM)

Salcombe [off Fore St nr Portlemouth Ferry;
SX7338], *Ferry*: It's the setting which attracts
here, with three storeys of stripped-stone
bars looking out over the sheltered
flagstoned waterside terrace to the
picturesque estuary; well kept Palmers real
ales (at a price), bar food, restaurant, games
bar – and of course holiday crowds, which
can slow food service and give it a very
seaside atmosphere in summer, though it
tends to be quiet out of season; the many
steps make it unsuitable for disabled people
*(Tim and Lynne Crawford, S J Curtis, Jon
Wainwright, R H Inns, J S Evans, LYM)*; [Fore
St] *Kings Arms*: Good family pub, Courage
ales, good budget-priced food in restaurant
(Amanda Dauncey); [Fore St] *Shipwrights*:
Good town-centre pub, long and thin with
strong nautical theme, clean, tidy and
comfortable, good service, well kept Courage
Best, good value bar food, pleasant back
courtyard with hanging baskets, table skittles
(Jon Wainwright, S J Curtis); [Fore St]
Victoria: Decent Bass, good value bar
lunches in comfortable lounge; bedrooms
(Pamela and Merlyn Horswell)

Sampford Courtenay [A3072 Crediton–
Tavistock; SS6301], *New Inn*: Charming
sixteenth-century pub, friendly and
comfortable, with three bars, settles, well
kept Flowers IPA, cheerful staff, decent
straightforward bar food including good
toasties, ploughman's, reasonably priced
buffet and puddings; children's room
(Charlie Salt, Tessa Stuart, K R Harris)

Scorriton [SX7068], *Tradesmans Arms*:
Decided local atmosphere, but the large
open-plan bar (with an end snug) has good
views of the Dartmoor-edge hills; friendly
landlord, real ale, farm cider, good value
food, basic but large children's room;
bedrooms *(Ted George)*

Seaton [Queen St; SY2490], *Old George*:
Large, open-plan and on various levels
connected by ramps; black-beamed ceiling,
pine dado, lots of seats and tables, Victorian
pictures and prints, some of fishing scenes;
Devenish and Websters Yorkshire on
handpump, good range of bar food; open all
day in summer and on Sat throughout year

(Michael and Alison Sandy, M and J Back)

☆ **Shaldon** [SX9372], *Ness House*: Elegant, colonial-style, nineteenth-century hotel in lovely spot on Ness headland, attractively furnished; Bass, Flowers and Eldridge Pope Royal Oak on handpump, good bar food, faultless service; restaurant; bedrooms *(E G Parish, J R Carey)*

Shaldon [just past harbour], *Ferryboat*: Rough and ready, slightly brash fisherman's pub with lively, talkative locals crowded at bar, all on first-name terms with licensee; well kept Courage on handpump, wholesome food – a happy place *(Tom Evans)*; [Ringmore Rd (B3195 to Newton Abbot)] *Shipwrights Arms*: Friendly village local with good reasonably priced food, pleasantly chatty atmosphere, well kept Courage Best and Directors; river views from back garden *(LYM)*

Shebbear [SS4409], *Devils Stone*: Friendly country village pub with simple bar food, well kept Flowers Original; bedrooms simple but cheap *(Dr John Innes, Peter Cornall, LYM)*

Sidmouth [ST1386], *Anchor*: Attractive town pub with Devenish ales and decent all-day food; comfortable seating, children's play area and garden *(E G Parish, Elizabeth Lloyd)*; [Fore St] *Black Horse*: Attractive town pub covered in flowers; well designed and spacious bar, good comfortable furnishings, Whitbreads on handpump, good range of reasonably priced bar food *(E G Parish)*; [Old Fore St] *Olde Shippe*: Good, clean, town-centre pub full of locals, with warm, friendly atmosphere, well kept Marstons Pedigree and other real ales, good food *(Graham and Glenis Watkins)*

☆ **nr Sidmouth** [Bowd Cross; junction B3176/ A3052; ST1386], *Bowd*: Thatched pub with one of the best gardens in the region, clean, warm and comfortable inside, with soft lighting, an expanse of Turkey carpet, soothing piped music and nice family-room; well kept Devenish and a guest beer such as Marstons Pedigree, plenty of space for diners and a more up-market feel than many Devon pubs; some interesting furnishings, though character is not perhaps its strong suit *(E G Parish, P Gillbe, LYM)*

Silverton [SS9502], *New Inn*: High standards in warm, welcoming pub with good modestly priced food and Wadworths 6X, friendly service *(Cdr G F Barnett)*; [14 Exeter Rd] *Three Tuns*: Picturesque, 500-year-old thatched pub, long bar with pleasant window alcoves in the thick walls, beams, crackling log fire, saddles, pottery, rifles, prints, cartoons and old photographs; welcoming atmosphere, excellent choice of real ales including Exe Valley, Eldridge Pope Dorchester and Wadworths 6X, decent home-made bar food *(J R Carey)*

South Brent [Exeter Rd; SX6960], *London*: Strong local presence, good value food, well kept Courage, young friendly licensees;

bedrooms quiet, clean, comfortable – good value *(Pat and Malcolm Rudlin)*; [Plymouth Rd] *Pack Horse*: Pleasant interior, friendly service, well kept Flowers IPA on handpump *(Jon Wainwright)*

South Tawton [off A30 at Whiddon Down or Okehampton, then signposted from Sticklepath; SX6594], *Seven Stars*: Unpretentious village pub in quiet countryside, good helpings of simple bar food from sandwiches or steak and kidney pie to Sun roast lunches, Ind Coope Burton, Palmers and Wadworths 6X, farm cider; pool and other bar games, a couple of good-natured dogs, folk club last Sun in month; restaurant (closed Sun and Mon evenings in winter); welcoming licensees still rather feeling their way; children welcome; bedrooms *(HEG, LYM)*

Spreyton [SX6996], *Tom Cobbley*: Good local, busy at weekends, with open fireplace in small, friendly bar, well kept Cotleigh Tawny and one or two other real ales, good home-cooked food including special curry evenings (need to book!) and barbecues in summer *(Charlie Salt)*

St Budeaux [Saltash Passage; SX4458], *Royal Albert Bridge*: Breathtaking views of Royal Albert railway and Tamar road bridges; nautical theme to lounge; good bar food, well cooked and presented – very clean pub *(A R Prout, M Hunt)*

St Giles In The Wood [SS5319], *Cranford*: Pleasant staff and good, nicely served food *(John Naylor)*

Starcross [SX9781], *Atmospheric Railway*: Friendly local with well kept Eldridge Pope Royal Oak on handpump, generous ploughman's and toasted sandwiches, Exe estuary beyond road and railway; nearby museum has working model of Brunel's original 1830s atmospheric railway, drawn by pumping stations every few miles *(Jon Wainwright, Mrs Joan Harris)*

Sticklepath [village signposted from A30 at A382 roundabout and B3260 Okehampton turn-off; SX6494], *Devonshire*: Sixteenth-century thatched village inn with big log fire in friendly beamed bar, easy chairs in cosy sitting-room, well kept Courage and Ushers real ale with a guest such as Wadworths 6X, traditional games, usual bar food served quickly, restaurant, provision for children; bedrooms *(Mayur Shah, LYM)*

Stoke Fleming [SX8648], *Green Dragon*: Very friendly with good service and lots of excellent food *(RS, AS)*; *London*: Good reasonably priced bar food (especially the pasties) in pleasant surroundings, efficient service, friendly dog, maybe pet duck *(Sue Jenkins)*

Stokeinteignhead [SX9170], *Chasers Arms*: Delightful, thatched seventeenth-century pub, new licensees doing good food *(Anon)*

☆ **Stokenham** [opposite church, N of A379 towards Torcross; SX8042], *Church House*:

Popular food pub with wide range of well presented bar food, especially local fish and seafood, with own-grown vegetables; steak, curries and gammon also praised; tables in small dining-room can be booked *(M J Chapman, Derek McGarry, Ann and David Stranack, A R Tingley)*

☆ **Stokenham** [just off A379 Dartmouth–Kingsbridge], *Tradesmans Arms*: Noted for a fine range of malt whiskies, with Bass and a couple of other real ales, this pretty thatched cottage has plenty of neatly set antique tables, piped classical music, and bar food strong on fresh fish – the honey-baked gammon and Madras curry are popular, too; picnic-table sets outside (nice surroundings), restaurant; standards have varied quite a bit recently, though, so we'd like more reports *(Ann and David Stranack, Sue Cleasby, Mike Ledger, Jon Wainwright, Ian and Daphne Brownlie, G F Couch, S J Curtis, Steve Huggins, LYM)*

Talaton [B3176 N of Ottery St Mary; SY0699], *Talaton*: Taken over by keen family from Essex as their first pub venture; no longer tied to Devenish though they still have the beer; promising food, nice caring service, big garden behind *(Doug Kennedy)*

Tamerton Foliot [Seven Stars Lane; SX4761], *Seven Stars*: Rambling old pub with climbing roses and trees in tubs in its walled courtyard, small public/food bar with flagstones and upholstered window seats; big helpings of good value food *(Mrs Pamela Roper)*

Tedburn St Mary [village signposted from A30 W of Exeter; SX8193], *Kings Arms*: Line of knocked-together rooms form long cosy open-plan bar with big log fire, eating area at one end (no bar food Sun evening), games area around corner at other end, well kept Bass and another real ale, a good clutch of malt whiskies, local cider; children allowed in eating area; bedrooms *(Gwen and Peter Andrews, LYM)*

☆ **Thelbridge Cross** [OS Sheet 180 reference 790120; SS7912], *Thelbridge Cross Inn*: Cosy and tastefully traditional old pub, cleanly kept, with well kept Bass and Wadworths 6X tapped from the cask, Inch's farm cider, good changing home-made food in bar and restaurant, friendly service, plenty of loyal local supporters *(John Dubarry, Mr and Mrs F Elliott, Mrs A Byles)*

Thorverton [SS9202], *Dolphin*: Dating from seventeenth century, the wistaria being over 250 years old; white building with black facings and shutters and pillared porch, in most attractive village; sumptuous settees and chairs in lounge, delightful restaurant, colourful approach to festive occasions such as 14 Feb *(J R Carey)*; *Ruffwell Arms*: Excellent food, marvellous value for money *(Tom Gondris)*

Thurlestone [SX6743], *Village Inn*: Interesting building with several homely and friendly modernised rooms; inventive menu with home-made puddings; several well kept real ales, good wine *(Sue Cleasby, Mike Ledger)*

Topsham [SX9688], *Lighter*: Spacious and well kept comfortably refurbished waterside pub with red plush seats, efficient food bar, well kept Badger real ales, lots of board games; long windows looking out on Exminster Marshes and lock-keepers' cottage; bedrooms *(J R Carey, Klaus and Elizabeth Leist, BB)*; [High St] *Lord Nelson*: Delightful atmosphere, attentive service, attractively priced good food, good car park *(Jim Beesley)*; [68 Fore St] *Salutation*: Good value bar food – especially their well presented and generously served hot chicken curry *(Mr and Mrs P A Jones)*; [Monmouth Hill] *Steam Packet*: Attractive old-world restoration with flagstones, scrubbed boards, panelling, stripped stonework and brick, bar food, real ales; on boat-builders' quay *(LYM)*

Torquay [Pavilion; SX9264], *Boulevard*: Cafe/bar/restaurant in up-market redevelopment of Victorian Assembly Rooms with opulent décor, bijou shops on the ground floor, big helpings of very good value food; efficient service; children in restaurant and on terrace *(Sue Jenkins)*; [Park Lane; SX9264] *Devon Arms*: Bustling little pub up a short steep hill, away from the main shopping area; well kept real ale, good value straightforward pub food *(Colin Gooch)*

Totnes [Fore Street, The Plains; SX8060], *Royal Seven Stars*: Ex-coaching-inn, vibrant and likeable, good service, Courage and Ushers Best; river on other side of busy main road; bedrooms *(Jon Wainwright, W A Lund)*

☆ **Tuckenhay** [SX8156], *Maltsters Arms*: Marvellous position by peaceful wooded creek, with picture windows in snug and comfortably extended upstairs lounge bar, family-room in ground-level former wine cellar; it's had Courage real ales and Churchward's cider; taken over summer 1989 by Keith Floyd the cookery writer and broadcaster, so should definitely be one to watch, though as we went to press it was still closed for refurbishment – a lot will of course depend on whom he has put in to manage it *(LYM – more reports please)*

Two Bridges [B3357/B3212 across Dartmoor; SX6175], *Two Bridges*: Well kept real ales including Flowers, good value bar food – especially soup and ploughman's, with cheap helpings of salad; bedrooms *(Andrew Hudson, J E F Rawlins)*

Tytherleigh [A358 Chard–Axminster; ST3103], *Tytherleigh Arms*: Comfortable food pub with big fireplace, well kept Eldridge Pope Dorset on handpump, wide range of bar food, pleasant atmosphere, popular small restaurant *(Anon)*

☆ **Upottery** [ST2007], *Sidmouth Arms*: Fine old friendly Devon pub, tastefully furnished without spoiling its character; good choice of tasty food, all home cooked, from sandwiches to hot dishes (with a choice of potatoes); well kept real ale *(PB, HB, Mrs Shirley Pielou)*

☆ **Welcome** [SS2218], *Old Smithy*: Pretty thatched country pub with charming garden – a good choice for meals outside on a sunny day; good bar food from sandwiches and home-made pasties to steaks, well kept Cornish ales, comfortable open-plan bar with log fires, juke box and so forth; nearby Welcombe Mouth is an attractive rocky cove; comfortable modern good value bedrooms are a particular plus-point *(Peter Cornall, C H Beaumont, W A Harbottle, Mr and Mrs G J Lewis, LYM)*

Wembury [SX5248], *Odd Wheel*: Friendly pub with good value food and garden; facilities for children inside and out *(D J Fisher)*

Westleigh [½ mile off A39 Bideford–Instow; SS4628], *Westleigh Inn*: Friendly village pub included chiefly for the gorgeous views down over the Torridge estuary from its neatly kept garden; straightforward food, service may be slow *(LYM)*

Weston [ST1200], *Otter*: Quite large with pleasant atmosphere, log fire and oak beams; customers of all ages, wide range of bar food *(Dr D M Forsyth)*

☆ **Widecombe** [SX7176], *Olde Inn*: Lovely old pub, comfortably refurbished, with good friendly service, good beer (especially the Widecombe Wallop), interesting reasonably priced food including enormous salads, vegetarian and children's dishes; good garden; the beauty-spot village is a magnet for visitors, so in summer the pub's very busy

indeed – out of season the lovely open fire's an added attraction *(B C Head, Henry Hooper, Sue and John Brumfitt, Pat and Malcolm Rudlin, J and M Larrive, LYM)*

Winkleigh [SS6308], *Winkleigh Inn*: Varied choice of food, well prepared and presented and pleasantly served *(W A Lund)*

Woolacombe [Ossaborough; unclassified rd signposted off B3343 and B3231; SS4543], *Mill*: Seventeenth-century mill barn recently converted to a pub; long narrow bar with flagstone floor and spacious main bar, separated from second bar by large wood-burning stove; well kept Courage Directors, generously served bar food, good service; tables in walled courtyard; lots of potential *(M W Barratt, Steve and Carolyn Harvey)*

Wrafton [A361 just SE of Braunton; SS4935], *Williams Arms*: Pleasant, large pub, busy in evenings, with spacious main bar, good value bar food, restaurant *(Chris Fluck)*

Yealmpton [SX5751], *Rose & Crown*: Good décor and very generous helpings of freshly cooked, tasty food *(Mr and Mrs C D Mason)*

Yelverton [A386 roundabout half-way between Plymouth and Tavistock; SX5267], *Rock*: Consistently good pub, warm welcome from friendly barman, comfortable wall seats, well kept Flowers and St Austell HSD, attractive food including enormous puddings (in evening not served until 8), fruit machine; can get quite smoky when packed; bedrooms *(Simon Turner, P and M Rudlin)*

Yeoford [SX7898], *Mare & Foal*: Friendly Edwardian-looking pub with wide choice of beer, reasonable sandwiches, good value steak, comfortable lounge, parquet-floored games-bar, good log fires, upstairs sauna; good parking *(BB)*

Dorset

Several notable changes here include new licensees at the Royal Oak in Cerne Abbas (in fact a former landlord – very popular indeed in his time at this Tudor inn – back after a gap of a few years), the pretty little Fox in Corfe Castle, the traditional Fox at Corscombe (we were impressed on a visit shortly after they'd taken over), the Blackmore Vale at Marnhull (very promising reports from readers) and the Ship in Shaftesbury (a long-standing favourite for well kept real ale in old-fashioned surroundings). Several new main entries, or pubs back in these pages after an absence, include the Anchor in its lovely seaside location near Chideock, the Smugglers at Osmington Mills (also in a beautiful coastal spot – a lot bigger than the Anchor but very quaint), the Mitre tucked away at Sandford Orcas (an engaging combination of real rusticity with enterprising food) and the Ilchester Arms at Symondsbury (a popular dining pub, strong on fish). When we think of Dorset pubs, we have a vivid image of a warm and unpretentious country welcome in cosy little stone-built cottages, usually thatched and in picturesque surroundings – quite unspoilt places, like the Square & Compass at Worth Matravers, scarcely changed in the eighty years it's been in the same family, or that great favourite, the warm and friendly Spyway at Askerswell. But in fact there's a good deal

The Ilchester Arms, Symondsbury

more to the county's pubs than that. A surprising number are now doing really good, thoughtful food, generally using fresh local ingredients: we'd note particularly the friendly old White Lion at Bourton, the civilised George in Bridport, the Winyards Gap with its remarkable views at Chedington, the oak-panelled Fleur-de-Lys in Cranborne, the idiosyncratic Weld Arms at East Lulworth, the Acorn up at Evershot, the Elm Tree not far from the Coast Path at Langton Herring, the Pilot Boat just across the road from the sea in Lyme Regis, the Marquis of Lorne at Nettlecombe (winter breaks are good value here), the Three Horseshoes at Powerstock (outstanding for fish), the Shave Cross Inn at Shave Cross (a perfect ploughman's), and the comfortable Manor Hotel at West Bexington. The New Inn in Cerne Abbas deserves special mention for its enterprising approach to wines – usually at least a dozen by the glass, and dozens by the bottle. A good few notably promising pubs among the Lucky Dip entries at the end of the chapter include the Inn in the Park at Branksome, the Red Lion in Cerne Abbas (one of those fortunate villages abounding in good pubs), the Saxon at Child Okeford, the New Inn at Church Knowle, the Hambro Arms at Milton Abbas, the Brace of Pheasants at Plush, the Bankes Arms at Studland, the Ship at West Stour, the Coach & Horses at Winterbourne Abbas and, particularly, the Museum at Farnham. Regular readers will note that the Dorset beers and brewery we've previously called Huntsman are called Eldridge Pope in this edition. For decades, both Eldridge Pope and Tetleys have used an identical jovial huntsman design, originally sold to both of them by a London agency. There was no confusion, as the two breweries operated in quite distinct areas. Now though, with both breweries extending their territories, there is the risk of overlap. So Tetleys have paid Eldridge Pope to give up their rights to the name; though the changeover is to be gradual and will not be complete until 1992, for clarity we've switched from Huntsman to Eldridge Pope now.

ABBOTSBURY   SY5785 Map 2

Ilchester Arms

B3157

The new licensees have added a conservatory to this busy, handsome old inn, and built a barbecue area to cater for walkers at lunchtimes. The three cosy main areas – connected by rambling corridors – have red plush button-back seats around cast-iron-framed tables on the Turkey carpet, and lots of pictures in which swans figure strongly (hundreds nest at the nearby swannery, which is closed for visits during the nesting season). Bar food includes soup (£1), a good choice of ploughman's with several pickles (from £2.50), haddock (£2.95), curry (£3.50), salads (from £3.75), scampi (£3.95), sirloin steak (£7.95), and daily specials such as home-made pimento and asparagus quiche (£3.45), roast lamb (£3.95) or monkfish provençale (£4.50). Well kept Devenish Cornish Original, Royal Wessex and Steam, and Wadworths 6X on handpump; darts, fruit machine and piped music. You can see the sea from the windows of the comfortable and attractive back bedrooms, and lanes lead from behind the pub into the countryside; the nearby abbey and its subtropical gardens are well worth visiting. *(Recommended by Richard Dolphin, Heather Sharland, Maggie and Bruce Clarke, I R Hewitt, John Nash, Derek and Sylvia Stephenson)*

Devenish   Licensee T R Hulme   Real ale   Meals and snacks   Restaurant   Children welcome   Open 11–11 all year   Bedrooms tel Dorchester (0305) 871243; £30B/£40B

ASKERSWELL   SY5292 Map 2
Spyway ★
Village signposted N of A35 Bridport–Dorchester; inn signposted locally; OS Sheet 194 reference 529933

The cosiest of the small carpeted bars in this friendly, well run pub has old-fashioned high-backed settles, a grandfather clock, rows of delicately made cups and plates, and old printed notices and local bills on its ochre walls; another has beams, an attractive window seat, cushioned seats built into its walls, and a milkmaid's yoke and harness. Very good value, quickly served home-cooked food includes three-egg omelettes (£1.75), a good choice of excellent ploughman's such as generous helpings of good quality ham and sweet pickle or locally made sausage (from £1.75), haddock or plaice (£2.10), salads (from £2.20, home-cooked ham £3.10), and evening grills such as lamb cutlets (£3.75), gammon (£3.95) and steaks (£5.75); home-made daily specials like filled baked potatoes (£1.95), steak pie or good savoury quiche (£2.20), good puddings such as trifle or pineapple cheesecake (£1.10), and children's dishes; get there early if you want a seat. Well kept Ruddles County, Ushers Best and Websters Yorkshire on handpump, as well as country wines and quite a few whiskies; quick, pleasant service. Darts, shove-ha'penny, table skittles, dominoes and cribbage. Outside, there's a quiet and neatly kept garden, with a small duck pool, pets' corner, swings and climbing-frame. The views over these steep downs just in from the coast are lovely, and the lane past the pub opens on to many paths and bridleways (not to mention badger tracks).
(Recommended by Y M Healey, Shirley Pielou, Mrs L Saumarez Smith, Mrs S A Bishop, Mr and Mrs M Woodger, Alan Skull, Margaret and Trevor Errington, Freddy Costello, David Pearman, P J Hanson, Peter and Rose Flower, Richard Cole, R D Jolliff, Peter Hitchcock, Gwen and Peter Andrews, Mrs E B Robinson, John and Joan Nash, J S Clements, Dr A V Lewis)

Free house   Licensees Don and Jackie Roderick   Real ale   Meals and snacks   Children in family-room   Open 10–3, 6–11 all year

BISHOPS CAUNDLE   ST6913 Map 2
White Hart
A3030

This popular dining pub has a big irregularly shaped lounge bar with some very old black panelling, low beams (some attractively moulded), dark wood furniture and deep red curtains. Good, home-made bar food includes sandwiches, ploughman's, cottage pie (£2.70), curry (£2.90), Somerset or fisherman's pie (£3.20), chicken Kiev (£4.95), local trout (£5.60) and steaks (from £4.95). Well kept Badger Best and Tanglefoot on handpump; darts, dominoes, cribbage, chess, draughts, fruit machine, alley skittles and piped music. The garden – floodlit at night – has a children's play area with trampolines, a playhouse with slides, and some rabbits.
(Recommended by John Kirk, Nigel Paine, Mark Walpole; more reports please)
Badger   Licensee Stephen Symonds   Real ale   Meals and snacks (11–2, 6.30–10)   Children in eating area of bar   Occasional live entertainment   Open 11–2.30, 6.30–11 all year

BOURTON   ST7430 Map 2
White Lion ✿
Pub signposted off A303

In front of this old stone pub – partly covered with climbing roses and clematis – there are a couple of picnic-table sets, with two more in a small enclosed garden across the lane; the back garden has a two-tiered lawn, trees and shrubs, a thatched well with water pump, a swing and a couple more picnic-table sets; regular barbecues with live local music. Inside, it's friendly and relaxed, and the beamed and flagstoned main bar opens into an attractive room with Turkey rugs on its old stone floor, a longish settle by the old oak table in front of the big fireplace, and a curved bow-window seat. Across the entrance corridor a tiny bar, popular with locals, has cushioned wall seats, wheel-back chairs around nice old tables, military hats on the ceiling, and yet another open fire; up a couple of steps, a top room is set out for eating with built-in wooden plank settles and a medley of tables and chairs. Good bar food (they use fresh local produce where possible) includes sandwiches (from 85p), home-made soup (£1.20), burger (£1.95), lots of ploughman's (from £1.95), good home-cooked ham and egg (£2.55), home-made steak and kidney or pork and Stilton pie (£2.95), a daily curry (from £2.95), vegetarian dishes like spinach and walnut lasagne or beans and peppers simmered in a coconut spicy sauce (£3.25), game pie (£3.45), outsize salads (from £3), gammon steak with egg and pineapple (£3.75), fresh local trout (£4.50), and quite special evening Scotch steak and brandy sauce (£7.60); also, daily specials that include at least three fresh fish dishes, and puddings such as jam roly-poly (95p); excellent three-course Sunday roast lunch (£5.50), booking advisable. Well kept Ruddles Best and County and Ushers Best on handpump, five ciders, and local wines; darts, shove-ha'penny, dominoes, fruit machine and quiet piped music. Stourhead is a few minutes away. In 1989 the licensee became a leaseholder under the brewery's Inntrepreneur scheme – tied to sell their beers and cider, but with considerably more freedom of operation in other ways than usual for a tied house. A car park is being built. *(Recommended by John and Joan Nash, WHBM, S V Bishop, Patrick Stapley, RAB, Richard Gibbs, Martin and Rob Jones, David Allsop)*

Ushers (Watneys)   Licensee C M Frowde   Real ale   Meals and snacks (11–2, 6.15–9) Restaurant tel Gillingham (0747) 840866   Children in eating areas (until 7.30 unless over 12)   Occasional live entertainment Sat evenings or special events   Open 11–3 (2.30 in winter), 6–11; 11–11 Sat

BRIDPORT   SY4692 Map 1

George 🏮

South Street

Cooked by the licensee, the good home-made food in this consistently friendly, old-fashioned town local includes soup (£1), sandwiches (from £1, toasted bacon and mushroom £1.75), crudités (£1.50), smoked fish pâté, omelettes or ploughman's with a choice of English cheeses (£2), Welsh rarebit and bacon (£2.50), home-made daily pies, kipper (£2.75), excellent sauté kidneys (£4), home-cooked ham or beef or Finnan haddock (£5.50), fresh fish daily such as local eel fried in garlic, and steaks (from £6); home-made puddings like lemon meringue pie or bread-and-butter pudding (from £1.25). Well kept Palmers Bridport, IPA and Tally Ho on handpump, a good range of spirits, and freshly squeezed orange or grapefruit juice and apple juice from a local cider farm (70p); an ancient pre-fruit machine ball game and Radio 3 or maybe classical or jazz tapes. There are country seats and wheel-back chairs set around the sturdy wooden tables on the flowery carpet, upholstered seats in knobby green cloth built against the gold and green papered walls, and a log fire in winter. *(Recommended by Ian Phillips, C M Whitehouse, Jim Matthews, Gary Scott)*

Palmers   Licensee John Mander   Real ale   Meals and snacks (12–3, 7–9; not Sun lunchtime, bank hol Mons, Good Fri lunchtime or 25–26 Dec and 1 Jan)   Children in dining-room Open 10am–11pm; open 8.30 for coffee and croissants; closed evening 25 Dec Bedrooms tel Bridport (0308) 23187; £15/£30

Though lunchtime closing time is now 3 on Sundays in England and Wales (with 20 minutes' drinking-up time), some pubs hope to close a bit earlier; please let us know if you find this happening.

CERNE ABBAS ST6601 Map 2

New Inn 🛏

14 Long Street

Built in the fifteenth century, supposedly as a guest-house for the abbey (which was built by Benedictine monks), this friendly, well kept inn has a stone roof estimated to weigh over 200 tons. The comfortable L-shaped lounge bar has oak beams in its high ceiling, seats in the mullioned windows that overlook the main street of this pretty village, and chatty locals. Generous helpings of good food include sandwiches (from £1.25), home-made soup (£1.30), French bread with meats from the carvery (£1.65), ploughman's (from £1.95), home-made quiche (from £2.10), sausages and egg (£2.70), three-egg omelette (from £2.75), a vegetarian dish (£3.50), meats, fish and cheese from the good cold carvery and help-yourself salads (£4.50), lamb with garlic and dill (£5), grilled gammon with egg or pineapple (£5.55), steaks (from £7.25), and two daily specials. Well kept Eldridge Pope Dorset, Royal Oak, Best and Dorchester on electric pump, kept under light blanket pressure, and an excellent range of wines by the glass (the landlord was voted Vintner of the Year by his brewery); piped music. Past the old coachyard (which still has its pump and mounting block) is a sheltered back lawn; a good track leads up on to the hills above the village, where the prehistoric (and rather rude) Cerne Giant is cut into the chalk, and the pub is on *Good Walks Guide* Walk 29. *(Recommended by Joanna and Ian Chisholm, Wayne Brindle, Mea Horler, Peter and Rose Flower, WFL, Pamela and Merlyn Horswell)*

Eldridge Pope   Licensee P D Edmunds   Real ale   Meals and snacks (12–2, 6.30–9.30 (10 Fri and Sat)   Children in eating area of bar   Open 11–11; 11–2.30, 6–11 in winter; all day Sat   Bedrooms tel Cerne Abbas (030 03) 274; £17.50/£30

Royal Oak

Long Street

After a two- or three-year gap, Mr Holmes, an ex-merchant seaman, is back at this sturdy and welcoming Tudor inn – which is very good news indeed; it was while he was running the pub before that readers' reports to us were warmest. The three attractive communicating rooms of the bar have black oak beams, lots of dark panelling, flagstones by the long serving-counter (which has a useful foot rail), stripped stonework, farm tools, old plates, china and brasses, and good log fires in winter. Good, home-made bar food includes winter soup, sandwiches (from £1), omelettes (from £2), steak and kidney pie (£2.95), lasagne (£3.25), cold roast beef (£3.50), minute steak (£4.50), gammon (£4.75) and sirloin steak (£6.25), with specials such as seafood Mornay. Well kept Devenish JD and Royal Wessex, and Marstons Pedigree on handpump; piped music. There are seats outside. The pub is on *Good Walks Guide* Walk 29. *(Recommended by A and K D Stansfield, John Nash, Gordon and Daphne)*

Devenish   Licensee Barry Holmes   Real ale   Meals and snacks   Open 11–2.30, 6–11 all year; may open longer lunchtimes in summer; closed evening 25 Dec

CHEDINGTON ST4805 Map 1

Winyards Gap 🌀

A356 Dorchester–Crewkerne

Seats by windows in this modernised inn have a glorious view (described at length in Thomas Hardy's *At Winyard's Gap*) over the little rolling fields far below. It's a comfortably furnished place with beams, plenty of seating, brasses, copper and lots of pottery. Bar food includes home-made soup (£1), ploughman's (from £2.20), filled baked potatoes (from £2), kedgeree (£2.95), curries (from £3.20), several pies (from £3.95 for fish with egg and mushroom, £5.85 for steak and oyster in

Guinness), local trout stuffed with almonds, or pork chop with orange and cranberry sauce (£4.25) and steaks (from £6.25); vegetables are fresh. They also do vegetarian dishes and daily specials such as Hardington fidget bake (local ham cooked in thick cheesy sauce) or locally smoked haddock and mushroom bake, and specialise in about twenty changing home-made puddings chalked up on a blackboard (from £1.50); Sunday roast lunch (£3.50). Locally made pottery is used to serve real butter and cream. Well kept Bass, Golden Hill Exmoor, Eldridge Pope Dorchester and a guest ale on handpump, and country wines; pleasant staff. Darts, pool, a spacious and comfortably furnished skittle alley, fruit machine and piped music. Outside, the terrace (also with good views) has cast-iron furniture, and there's an attractively planted garden. The old barn has been converted into two self-catering flats which can be booked on a daily or weekly basis (telephone Corscombe (093 589) 244. Behind the pub there's a nice walk to the monument, then through the woods to Chedington village. *(Recommended by Heather Sharland, J L Simpson)*

Free house   Licensees Alan and June Pezaro   Real ale   Meals (not Sun evening) and snacks   Children in family-room   Live music Sun evenings   Open 11.30–3, 7–11 all year

CHESIL   SY6873 Map 2
Cove House
Entering Portland on A354, bear right: keep eyes skinned for pub, up Big Ope entry on right

Seats and parasols on the promenade outside this typical Devenish pub overlook the sea, with the pebble beach on the right curling away for mile after mile. Inside, furnishings are simple though comfortable, and the room on the right has dark settles and benches on the polished boards, little lantern lights strung along its beams, photographs of local shipwrecks, and darts, dominoes, cribbage, trivia, fruit machine and lots of board games; the room on the left past the servery has now been furnished as a restaurant. Bar food (which can be eaten anywhere in the pub) includes sandwiches (from 70p, crab or prawn £1.35), soup like tomato and fennel or winter vegetable (£1.25), stuffed mushrooms with spicy dip (£2.20), ploughman's (from £1.95), cottage pie (£2.95), turkey and fruit curry or lasagne (£3.50), turkey, sweetcorn and leek pie (£3.75), chicken provençale (£4.50), savoury baked crab or smoked turkey and avocado salad (£4.75), fresh crab salad (£4.75) and fresh fish (from £4.95). Well kept Devenish JD, Royal Wessex and Steam on handpump; friendly, helpful service, piped music. The two friendly golden retrievers are called Ben and Sam. *(Recommended by Denise Plummer, Jim Froggatt, Ian Phillips, Jack Taylor, D Pearman, Dr A V Lewis, K and D E Worrall)*

Devenish   Licensee Sean Durkin   Real ale   Meals and snacks (12–2, 6.30–10)   Restaurant tel Portland (0305) 820895   Children welcome   Open 12–3, 6–11; 11–11 Sat in summer; 11–2.30, 6–11 in winter

nr CHIDEOCK   SY4292 Map 1
Anchor
Seatown; signposted off A35 from Chideock

This busy, friendly pub is in a lovely position – alone by a seaside cove and almost straddling the Dorset Coast Path. There are new tables by the small windows and on the front terraces that look over a stream to seaside sheep pasture rising by cliffs towards Doghouse Hill and Thorncombe Beacon, and picnic-table sets on the low cliff overlooking the beach. Inside, the two cosy bars have comfortable seats and neat tables, some sailing pictures under the low white-planked ceilings, and log fires in winter. Bar food includes sandwiches (from 95p), home-made soup (£1.20), ploughman's (from £1.85), ham and egg (£2.45), curry (£2.55), pizzas (from £2.75) and steak and mushroom pie (£2.95), with daily specials such as garlic prawns (£3.45) or venison pie (£4.25), and evening extras like rump steak or seafood platter (£6.50); several puddings. Palmers IPA and Tally Ho on handpump, with BB kept under light top pressure; darts, table skittles, dominoes, fruit machine and piped music. The thatched cottage next door can be rented (telephone Bridport (0308) 22396). *(Recommended by Heather Martin, Ian Phillips, David Pearman, Fiona Easeman)*

Palmers   Licensee David Miles   Real ale   Snacks (served all afternoon in summer) and meals (no food Sun evenings in winter)   Children in eating area of bar   Occasional folk/blues Sat evenings in winter   Open 11–11; 11–2.30, 7–11 in winter

nr CHRISTCHURCH   SZ1696 Map 2
Fishermans Haunt 🏠

Winkton: B3347 Ringwood road nearly 3 miles N of Christchurch

The modernised and extended series of interconnecting bars in this creeper-covered hotel – decked with fairy lights at night – has a variety of furnishings and moods: stuffed fish and fishing pictures, oryx and reindeer heads, and some copper, brass and plates; at one end of the chain of rooms big windows look out on the neat front garden, and at the other there's a fruit machine and a space game. Bar food includes ploughman's (from £1), sandwiches (from £1.50, toasties from £1.60), pâté (£2), chicken and ham pie (£2.50) and hot dishes chalked on a board; children's meals (£1.50). Well kept Bass, Courage Directors, Devenish Steam and Ringwood Fortyniner on handpump or electric pump, cheerful staff; piped music. You can sit on the back lawn among shrubs, roses, other flowers and a swing. *(Recommended by Christopher Knowles-Fitton, Dr James Haworth, Ken and Dorothy Worrall; more reports please)*

Free house   Licensee James Bochan   Real ale   Meals and snacks (12–2, 7–10) Restaurant   Children in eating area and restaurant   Open 10–2.30 (3 Sat), 6–11; closed 25 Dec   Bedrooms tel Christchurch (0202) 484071; £21(£28B)/£41(£44B)

COLEHILL   SU0201 Map 2
Barley Mow

Village signposted from A31 E of Wimborne Minster, and also from Wimborne Minster itself; in village take Colehill Lane opposite big church among pine trees; OS Sheet 195 reference 032024

One of the better country pubs within easy reach of Bournemouth, this popular thatched building has a comfortably carpeted and furnished main bar. There are some old beams, nicely moulded oak panelling, Hogarth prints on the walls, and a winter fire in the huge brick fireplace. Bar food includes home-made soup (80p), sandwiches (£1), filled baked potatoes (£1.55), ploughman's with warm French bread (from £1.80), cottage pie or excellent moussaka (£2), home-made steak and kidney pie (£2.50), six-ounce gammon steak (£3.60) and steaks (from £5.20). Badger Best and Tanglefoot, and Gales BBB on handpump; darts, pool, fruit machine, juke box and maybe piped music. There are tables among the tubs of flowers in front, or on the back grass (sheltered by oak trees). *(Recommended by John Nash; more reports please)*

Badger   Licensee David Parker   Real ale   Meals and snacks (12–2, 6–9.30)   Children in family-room   Open 11–3, 5.30–11

CORFE CASTLE (Isle of Purbeck)   SY9681 Map 2
Fox

West Street, off A351; from town centre, follow dead-end Car Park sign behind church

There's scarcely room for the single heavy oak table and the cushioned wall benches which surround it in the tiny front bar of this cosy and unspoilt old pub; it's served by a hatch, lit by one old-fashioned lamp, and among other pictures above the ochre panelling is a good old engraving of the ruined castle. A back lounge is more comfortable, though less atmospheric. Generous helpings of fresh bar food include sandwiches, ploughman's (£1.90), spinach and sweetcorn or Stilton and celery quiche (£2) and fresh crab (when available). Well kept Fremlins tapped from the cask; good dry white wine. The attractive sun-trap garden at the back – divided into secluded areas by flower beds and a twisted pear tree – is reached by a pretty flower-hung side entrance, and has good views of the ruined castle; the surrounding countryside is very fine and the pub is on *Good Walks Guide* Walk 25. There's a local museum opposite. *(Recommended by Steve and Carolyn Harvey, Ian Phillips, Steve Huggins, Phil and Sally Gorton, Alan and Ruth Woodhouse, Peter Hitchcock, Gwen and Peter Andrews)*

Whitbreads   Licensee Miss A L Brown   Real ale   Lunchtime snacks   Open 11–2.30, 6–11; opens 7 in winter; closed 25 Dec

Greyhound

A351

The three small low-ceilinged areas of the main bar in this old-fashioned pub – well placed just below the castle – has mellowed oak panelling and old photographs of the town on the walls; the family area is no-smoking and has been recently refurbished. Fresh local seafood is the speciality here: Poole cockles (£1.80), Mediterranean prawns sauté in garlic (£3.80), fresh crab salad (£5) and fresh lobster or mixed seafood platter (£7); other bar food includes large filled rolls (from 80p, local crab £1.80), home-made soup (£1), a good choice of filled baked potatoes (from £1.50) ploughman's (£2), lasagne or steak and kidney pie (from £2.50) and salads (from £3); daily specials and seafood are chalked up on a blackboard. Well kept Flowers Original, Whitbreads Strong Country and a guest beer on handpump; friendly service; darts sensibly placed in the back room, pool (winter only), fruit machine, trivia, juke box and piped music. There are benches outside. *(Recommended by Klaus and Elizabeth Leist, WHBM, Mrs A M Viney, Wayne Brindle, Alan and Audrey Chatting, A P Carr, Dr R Fuller)*

Whitbreads   Licensee R A Wild   Real ale   Meals and snacks (not 25 Dec)   Children in family area   Open 11–3 (4 Sat; 2.30 in winter), 6–11 all year; occasionally open all day

CORSCOMBE   ST5105   Map 2

Fox

On outskirts, towards Halstock

Mrs Lee and her son (who is a Master of Foxhounds at Cattistock) have taken over this cosy, thatched white pub and are making a few changes – one being the slate-topped bar counter that's made up of coping stones reversed, brought from their last pub in Exmoor; they also plan to add a skittle alley and conservatory, and as we went to press a new kitchen was being installed. The room on the right has lots of beautifully polished copper pots, pans and teapots, harness hanging from the beams, small Leech hunting prints and Snaffles prints, Spy cartoons of fox-hunting gentlemen, a long scrubbed pine table (a highly polished smaller one is tucked behind the door), an open fire and a newly laid old floor. In the left-hand room there are built-in wall benches, candles in champagne bottles on the cloth-covered or barrel tables, an assortment of chairs, lots of horse prints, antlers on the beams, two glass cabinets with a couple of stuffed owls in each, and an L-shaped wall settle by the stove in the fireplace. The atmosphere is relaxed and friendly. Home-made bar food (no chips or microwaved dishes) depends on what Mrs Lee feels like cooking that morning: sandwiches with home-made bread (from 95p), soup (£1.10), omelettes (from £1.25), ploughman's with home-made chutney (from £1.75), half-pint of prawns with home-made roll (£2), steak and kidney, fish or shepherd's pies or spaghetti bolognese (£2.95) and home-made puddings such as apple crumble (£1.25). Well kept Devenish JD and Exmoor tapped from the cask;

darts, dominoes, cribbage. You can sit across the quiet village lane, on a lawn by the little stream which just down the road serves an unusual moated farmhouse.

(Recommended by MCG, Gary Scott, Heather Sharland, Peter and Rose Flower, Mr and Mrs D E Salter, H and P B, Pamela and Merlyn Horswell, Nigel Paine, Gordon and Daphne)

Free house   Licensees M R H and D S Lee   Real ale   Meals and snacks Open 11.30–2.30, 7–11 all year; may open longer in afternoon

CRANBORNE   SU0513 Map 2
Fleur-de-Lys 🏮 🍺
B3078 N of Wimborne Minster

Thomas Hardy stayed here for part of the time that he was writing *Tess of the d'Urbervilles*, and if you fork left past the church you can follow the downland track that Hardy must have visualised Tess taking home to 'Trentridge' (actually Pentridge) after dancing here. There's an attractively modernised, oak-panelled lounge bar and a more simply furnished beamed public bar. Bar food includes sandwiches (from £1.15, toasties 20p extra), home-made soup with home-made wholemeal roll (£1.35), ploughman's (from £2.15, ham cooked in cider and honey £2.35), basket meals (from £1.95), smoked trout (£2.65), vegetarian dishes like nutty mushroom layer or creamcheese cannelloni (£3.95), home-made steak pie (£3.95), salads (from £3.95; the mayonnaise, cocktail sauce and tartare sauce are all home made and free from additives and preservatives), grilled local trout (£5.75), grilled gammon with egg or pineapple (£5.85) and eight-ounce rump steak (£7.45); there are home-made puddings such as blackcurrant cheesecake or raspberry Pavlova (from £1.40), daily specials, and in the evening (not Saturdays) they also do a special three-course meal (£9.45, which includes wine and coffee – must be booked in advance). Well kept Badger Best and Tanglefoot on handpump, and farm cider; darts, shove-ha'penny, dominoes, cribbage, fruit machine, juke box and piped music. There are swings and a slide on the lawn behind the car park. The attractive rolling farmland around the village marks its closeness to the New Forest with occasional ancient oaks and yews. *(Recommended by Roy McIsaac, Hank Hotchkiss, G Shannon, E G Parish, E V Palmer-Jeffery, Steve Dark, C Williams)*

Badger   Licensee Charles Hancock   Real ale   Meals and snacks (not 25 Dec or evening 26 Dec)   Restaurant   Children in restaurant   Open 10.30–3, 6–11 all year; closed 25 Dec Bedrooms tel Cranborne (072 54) 282; £24B/£36B

EAST CHALDON   SY7983 Map 2
Sailors Return
Village signposted from A352 Wareham–Dorchester; from village green, follow Dorchester, Weymouth signpost; note that the village is also known as Chaldon Herring; OS Sheet 194 reference 790834

This extensively renovated old pub has carefully kept its original character – the low-ceilinged stone-floored core now serves as a coffee house. The newer part has open beams showing the roof above, uncompromisingly plain and simple furnishings, and old notices for decoration; the dining area has solid old tables in nooks and crannies. Bar food includes filled rolls (from 75p), home-made soup (£1), filled baked potatoes (from £1.60), ploughman's (from £2.15), home-cooked ham and egg (£2.30), home-made steak and kidney pie (£2.45), salads (from £2.50), scampi (£3.40), and steaks (from £5.75); also, fresh local fish, daily specials and children's meals (£1). Well kept Eldridge Pope Royal Oak, Wadworths 6X, Whitbread Strong Country and guest beers on handpump, and country wines; pleasant service. Darts, bar billiards, shove-ha'penny, table skittles, dominoes and piped music. Benches, picnic-table sets and log seats on the grass in front look down over cow pastures to the village, which is set in a wide hollow below Chaldon Down: a very pretty, peaceful spot, and from nearby West Chaldon a bridleway

leads across to join the Dorset Coast Path by the National Trust cliffs above
Ringstead Bay. *(Recommended by A V Lewis, Mrs K Cooper, P and M Rudlin, J Roots)*

*Free house   Licensees Mr and Mrs L E Groves   Real ale   Meals and snacks (11–2, 7–10)
Restaurant tel Dorchester (0305) 853847   Children in restaurant   Open 11–2.30, 7–11*

EAST LULWORTH   SY8581 Map 2

Weld Arms 🏮

B3070

The licensee here is a single-handed Transatlantic man, and the ensigns which drape
the yellowing ceiling, and the newspaper sailing clippings, yacht pennants and
nautical charts behind the bar reflect his enthusiasm. Up by the fireplace in the
homely and relaxed main bar – where there are likely to be fresh flowers from the
rambling garden in summer, and where you may be able to roast your own
chestnuts in winter (donations to RNLI) – are some assorted easy chairs; also, big
oak tables, a couple of long oak-panelled settles, and a pair of pews as well as more
regular seats. Lunchtime bar food includes home-made soup, home-made cottage
pie (£1.80), prawn or crab sandwiches (£2), steak rolls (£2.10), and delicious chick-
pea and fennel casserole or steak and kidney pie; the changing but distinctive
evening menu may include pizzas (from £1.60), mushroom fritters (£2.20),
pheasant pieces casseroled in red wine (£2.50), crevettes (£3.30), pigeon casseroled
with bacon, celery, mushrooms and sultanas (£5.90), half rack of lamb in an Asian
marinade, roasted and served with a nutty sauce (£6.50), sea-trout (£7.10) and
good home-made puddings. Well kept Devenish JD and Royal Wessex on
handpump; courteous service. There's a smaller, more snug bar on the left (not
always open) and a back family-room, with darts, table skittles, shove-ha'penny,
dominoes, cribbage, fruit machine, juke box and decent unobtrusive piped music.
There are picnic-table sets behind the thatched white house, as well as swings and a
climbing-frame. *(Recommended by Anna Jeffery, Christopher Draper, Denise Plummer, Jim
Froggatt, Gavin Udall, J N Hanson, J F Pritchard, Mr and Mrs D G W Reakes, Dr
R B Crail, R Inns, Barry and Anne, K C D Mitchell, Sian Mitchell)*

*Devenish   Licensee Peter Crowther   Real ale   Meals and snacks   Open 11–2.30, 6.30–11
all year; opens 11.30 in winter   Bedrooms tel West Lulworth (092 941) 211; £12/£22*

EVERSHOT   ST5704 Map 2

Acorn 🏮 🛏

Village signposted from A37 8 miles S of Yeovil

A constantly changing range of real ales is chalked up on a board in this friendly
village inn, and might include well kept Batemans XXXB, Greene King Abbot,
Marstons Pedigree, Palmers IPA, Ringwood Old Thumper and Charles Wells
Bombardier (some are kept under light blanket pressure); a decent wine list. The
comfortable L-shaped lounge bar has tapestry covered wooden benches, two fine
old fireplaces, and copies of the inn's deeds going back to the seventeenth century
on the partly hessian-covered bare stone walls. The carpeted public bar has sensibly
placed darts, pool, shove-ha'penny, table skittles, dominoes, cribbage, fruit
machine, space game and juke box; maybe piped music. Home-made bar food
includes soup (£1.40), sandwiches (from £1.25, toasties 25p extra), burger (£2.65),
various ploughman's (from £2.95), salads (from £4.25, home-cooked ham £4.75),
lasagne (£4.95), fresh breaded seafood platter (£5.45), steak and kidney pie
(£5.55), game pie (£6.95) and steaks (from £8.95); they specialise in fresh fish, with
deliveries three times a week, and have changing daily specials like curries, Somerset
pork chops, several vegetarian dishes, fish crêpes and fresh game in season.
Children's meals are available (£2.15); very good breakfasts and hard-working,
polite staff. Outside, there's a terrace with dark oak furniture. A nice village to stay
in, 600 feet up in real Hardy country – the inn was the model for Evershead's Sow

and Acorn in *Tess of the d'Urbervilles*. There are lots of good walks around. *(Recommended by Roy McIsaac, David Pearman, John Nash, Heather Sharland, Shirley Pielou, Max Rankin, Peter and Rose Flower, Jack Taylor, Mea Horler, M S Hancock, A Cook, Heather Sharland, D Pearman, A and K D Stansfield, P H S Wettern)*

Free house   Licensees Keith and Denise Morley   Real ale   Meals and snacks (12–2, 6.30–9.45)   Restaurant   Children in refurbished skittle alley and restaurant Open 11–2.30, 6.30–11 all year   Bedrooms tel Evershot (093 583) 228; £24B/£32B

GODMANSTONE   SY6697 Map 2

Smiths Arms

A352 N of Dorchester

In the fifteenth century this was a blacksmith's shop, and Charles II is supposed to have stopped here to have his horse shod. The little bar has some antique waxed and polished small pews around the walls, one elegant little high-backed settle, high leather bar stools with comfortable back rests, National Hunt racing pictures, and a warm atmosphere. Well kept Devenish Royal Wessex tapped from casks behind the bar; polite, helpful staff; darts, dominoes, backgammon and shut-the-box. Food includes sandwiches, home-made steak and kidney pie or spaghetti marinara, home-cooked ham and home-made bread pudding. You can sit outside on a crazy-paved terrace or on a grassy mound by the narrow River Cerne – and from here you can walk over Cowdon Hill to the River Piddle, one of the rivers the devil is supposed to have pissed around Dorchester. *(Recommended by Gethin Lewis, Wayne Brindle, Peter and Rose Flower)*

Free house   Licensees John and Linda Foster   Real ale   Meals and snacks (12–2, 6–9.30) Open 11–3, 6–11; opens 6.30 in winter

HURN   SZ1397 Map 2

Avon Causeway 🏵 🛏

Hurn signposted off A338, then at Hurn roundabout follow Avon, Sopley, Mutchams signpost

Though it's now virtually entirely rebuilt, this was once the Station Master's house. An expansively comfortable and spacious lounge bar is divided into several separate rambling areas by the layout of the button-back plush seats, with sturdy pale wood tables and substantial standard-lamp globes standing sentinel here and there. Interesting decorations include old local timetables and scale drawings of steam locomotives, posters, uniforms and photographs, and the bar spreads into an airy Moroccan-theme family-room complete with palm trees. There's a fine range of well kept real ales on handpump – up to eleven, such as Adnams, Marstons Pedigree, Merrie Monk and Owd Rodger, Ringwood Best, Fortyniner and Old Thumper, Wadworths 6X and Farmers Glory and Youngers IPA. Generous helpings of bar food include sandwiches (from £1), filled baked potatoes (£1.80), basket meals (from £1.90), ploughman's (from £2.15), salads (from £3.15, crab £4.25), fish from cod (£3.25) to salmon (£5.45), steak and kidney pie (£3.57), home-cooked ham and egg (£3.80), braised pigeon in walnut and date sauce, weekend roasts (£3.85), steaks (from £6.75) and children's dishes (£1.35). Unobtrusive piped music, fruit machine, space game, trivia. Outside (surrounded by quiet woodland) is fun: they've kept the old platform, with its traditional toothed-edge canopy supporting bright hanging baskets, where sturdy old mahogany station seats face a Pullman carriage (to be a restaurant). There are also lots of picnic-table sets under cocktail parasols. *(Recommended by Tony Triggle, WHBM, Hazel Morgan; more reports please)*

Free house   Licensees John Ricketts and Paul DuBock   Real ale   Meals and snacks Children in family-room   Open 11–2.30, 6–11   Bedrooms tel Christchurch (0202) 482714; £35B/£55B

LANGTON HERRING   SY6182 Map 2

Elm Tree 🏵

Village signposted off B3157

A traditionally furnished extension, giving more room for diners, has been added on to the front of this very popular food pub. The two main carpeted rooms have cushioned window seats, red leatherette stools, Windsor chairs, lots of tables, and beams and walls festooned with copper, brass and bellows; there is a central circular modern fireplace in one room, an older inglenook (and some old-fashioned settles) in the other. A wide choice of very good, inventive home-made food includes sandwiches (from 95p), home-made soup (£1.50), ploughman's (from £2.50), tuna and lemon pâté (£2.95), chestnut and red wine loaf (£3.75), spinach and mushroom roulade or excellent spicy beef casserole (£3.95), home-made cheese and pineapple or crab and avocado quiches (from £4.25), prawn-stuffed garlic bread (£4.50), salads with home-cooked ham or beef (from £4.65), Indian chicken curry (£4.95), mixed grill (£5.50), steaks (from £5.75) and home-made ice-creams like marshmallow or banana and butterscotch (from £1.50), with puddings chalked up on a board (£2.25); they also do cream teas. Devenish Royal Wessex on handpump kept under light top pressure; special liqueur coffees, piped music. There are colourful hanging baskets and flower tubs, and tables out in the pretty flower-filled sunken garden; a track leads down to the Dorset Coast Path, which here skirts the eight-mile lagoon enclosed by Chesil Beach. (*Recommended by K Leist, John and Joan Nash, P J Hanson, Peter and Rose Flower, Robin Armstrong, Gary Scott, W J Wonham*)

Devenish   Licensees Anthony and Karen Guarraci   Real ale   Meals and snacks (all afternoon in summer)   Children welcome   Open 11–11; 11–2.30, 6.30–11 in winter

LYME REGIS   SY3492 Map 1

Pilot Boat 🏵

Bridge Street

Consistently popular for the warm welcome and very good food, this old smugglers' haunt has a light, airy bar with comfortable blue plush seating and an atmosphere that does reflect people's special interest in the food here. Decorations include local pictures, Navy and helicopter photographs, lobster-pot lamps, sharks' heads, an interesting collection of local fossils, a model of one of the last sailing-ships to use the harbour, and a notable collection of sailors' hat ribands. At the back there's a long and narrow lounge bar overlooking the little River Lym. Waitress-served bar food includes sandwiches (from £1, delicious crab £1.95; open sandwiches from £2.25), home-made soup (£1.20), huge ploughman's or a popular Norwegian mushroom dish (£2.50), steak and kidney pie or vegetable moussaka (£3.95), salads (from £4.50, home-cooked ham £4.75, local crab £5.95), mixed grill (£6.50), steaks (from £6.95), puddings such as lemon meringue pie, treacle tart or bread pudding, and a children's menu (from £1.95); specials and fresh fish are chalked up on a blackboard. Well kept Palmers Bridport, IPA and Tally Ho on handpump, and a decent wine and liqueur list. Darts, dominoes, cribbage.

(*Recommended by Peter Argent, Steve and Carolyn Harvey, Dr D M Forsyth, E G Parish, Stan Edwards, Peter and Rose Flower, Alan and Ruth Woodhouse, Peter Lake, Mrs R Thornton, Derek and Sylvia Stephenson*)

Palmers   Licensee W C Wiscombe   Meals and snacks (12–2.30, 6–10 in summer) Restaurant tel Lyme Regis (029 74) 3157   Children in eating area of bar and restaurant if sitting down   Occasional live entertainment   Open 11–3, 6–11; 11–2.30, 7–11 in winter

---

Please tell us if any Lucky Dips deserve to be upgraded to a main entry, and why. No stamp needed: *The Good Pub Guide*, FREEPOST, London SW10 0BR.

LYTCHETT MINSTER SY9593 Map 2

Bakers Arms

Dorchester Road

It's a surprise to find a roomy sprawl of Turkey-carpeted comfort behind the misleadingly small thatched white façade here. There are army badges, some antique Dorset buttons, cigarette cards, models, watches, holograms, a good collection of English stamps, and a run of annual statistics on some sixty items from 1900 onwards; also birds' eggs (shown with pictures of the birds), and even a glass beehive with working bees. The walls show a complete set of £5, £1 and 10/- English notes and of English silver and copper coins since 1837. New this year is the 1940s Wurlitzer juke box (previously owned by Elton John) with the original records. Video displays tell you when you can collect your order from the efficient food counter: home-made soup (£1), ploughman's (from £1.90), pâtés (from £1.85), basket meals (from £1.95), a range of help-yourself salads (from £3, home-cooked meats from £4.35), home-made steak and kidney pie (£4.15), gammon and pineapple (£4.85), a carvery (from £5.25) and eight-ounce rump steak (£6.75); also, daily specials, vegetarian dishes and puddings like home-made fruit pies (from £1). Well kept Flowers Original and Wadworths 6X; fast, efficient service; piped music, fruit machine, trivia, space game and communicating skittle alley. Behind the pub, with tables beside it, is an adventure playground. *(Recommended by Denise Plummer, Jim Froggatt, Jenny and Michael Back, Clifford Blakemore, Ken and Dorothy Worrall, WHBM)*

Free house (part tie to Whitbreads)   Licensee Roy Forrest   Real ale   Meals and snacks (12–2, 6.30–10)   Children in eating area   Open 11–2.30, 6–11; may open longer in afternoon if trade demands; closed 25 Dec

MARNHULL ST7718 Map 2

Blackmore Vale 🏵

Burton Street; quiet side street

The carpeted and comfortably modernised lounge bar in this friendly pub has cushioned wrought-iron and wooden seats built out from the stripped stone wall at the end that has the log fire; it's decorated with a gun, keys, a few horsebrasses and old brass spigots on the beams. Bar food, quickly brought to your table (or to the garden), includes a range of several home-made pies (from £2.25) including an unusual crab pie done with whisky, cheese and cream (£5.60), with a wide choice of other bar food such as home-made soup (£1.10), sandwiches (from £1.10), ploughman's (from £2.40), vegetarian dishes like spinach and mushroom lasagne (£2.99), home-cooked ham and egg or lasagne (£2.99), lambs' kidneys in rich sherry sauce (£4.20), gammon and pineapple (£4.75), shark steak (£4.95) and steaks (from £6.50; 26-ounce T-bone £9.75); also, children's dishes. Well kept Badger Best and Tanglefoot and Gales BBB on handpump, farm cider and a decent wine list; darts, cribbage, dominoes, shove-ha'penny, fruit machine, piped music and a skittle alley. The new licensees are adding a dovecote and new garden furniture. There's an extensive range of purpose-built wooden children's play equipment. *(Recommended by H Richard Dolphin, J Stirling, Lyn and Bill Capper, WHBM, J P Copson, Nigel Paine, Mr and Mrs P W Dryland)*

Badger   Licensees Roger and Marion Hiron   Real ale   Meals and snacks (12–2, 7–10)   Children in small bar only   Open 11–2.30, 6–11 all year; 11–3, 5.30–11 Fri and Sat

Crown 🍺

B3092

You can sit outside this thatched inn by the rose-covered lichened walls looking across to the church or at picnic-table sets on the lawn (where there's a swing).

Inside, the oak-beamed public bar has old settles and elm tables on the huge flagstones, window seats cut into thick stone walls, and logs burning in a big stone hearth. The small and comfortable lounge bar has more modern furniture. Good, reasonably priced bar food includes sandwiches, generous omelettes, three or four daily set lunches chalked on a blackboard (from £3), steak (£6.25), and puddings such as bread-and-butter pudding (£1.35). Well kept Badger Best and Tanglefoot on handpump – appropriately enough, a stuffed badger lurks half-way up the stairs to the bedrooms. Darts, cribbage, dominoes, a skittle alley and fruit machine. This was 'The Pure Drop' at 'Marlott' in Thomas Hardy's *Tess of the d'Urbervilles*. *(Recommended by Roger Huggins, WFL; more reports please)*

Badger   Licensee Thomas O'Toole   Real ale   Meals and snacks   Restaurant   Children in eating area of bar   Open 11–3, 6–11 all year   Bedrooms tel Marnhull (0258) 820224; £14/£28

NETTLECOMBE   SY5195 Map 2

Marquis of Lorne 🏮 🛏

Close to Powerstock and can be found by following the routes described under the entry included for that village – see below

In quiet and peaceful countryside, this popular sixteenth-century inn has a genuinely friendly atmosphere, good food, and very good value weekday bed and breakfast in winter. The main bar has green plush button-back small settles, round green stools and highly varnished tables on a flowery blue carpet, Dobermann and Rottweiler photographs, and a log fire; a similar side room decorated in shades of brown opens off it. Generous helpings of bar food include sandwiches (from £1.10), home-made soup such as lemon and lentil (£1.35), filled, deep-fried mushrooms with mayonnaise dip (£1.75 starter, £2.95 main course), pâté (£2.50), basket meals (from £2.50), ploughman's (£2.75), home-cooked ham and egg (£3.50), salads (from £3.75), chicken in barbecue sauce (£3.95), vegetarian moussaka (£6.75), steaks (from £7.25), half honey-roasted duck (£8.25) and puddings such as home-made sherry trifle (£1.75); daily specials such as rabbit fillets or lobster, and superb Sunday lunch. Well kept Palmers Bridport and IPA on handpump; darts, shove-ha'penny, dominoes, cribbage, table skittles, trivia and piped music. The big garden has masses of swings, climbing-frames and so forth among the picnic-table sets under its apple trees. The earth-fort of Eggardon Hill is close by. *(Recommended by Stephen Goodchild, Gordon Hewitt, Freddy Costello, John Nash, R C Blatch, Joan and John Calvert, Peter and Rose Flower, Mr and Mrs F W Sturch, Jon Dewhirst, Gordon and Daphne, John Clements, Derek and Sylvia Stephenson, Roger and Kathy)*

Palmers   Licensee Robert Bone   Real ale   Meals and snacks   Restaurant   Children welcome   Open 11–2.30, 6–11 all year; closed 25 Dec   Bedrooms tel Powerstock (030 885) 236; £16(£19B)/£32(£38B)

OSMINGTON MILLS   SY7381 Map 2

Smugglers

Village signposted off A353 NE of Wareham

The sea is just moments away – a stroll down through the pretty combe. The partly thatched stone-built pub nestles prettily into this setting, and though it's been extended to cope with lots of summer visitors (there's a holiday settlement just up the lane) the work's been done with great sensitivity, using massive timbers salvaged from Mudeford quay. It's well run, too: Mr Bishop scored high marks with us and with readers when he ran the Black Dog at Broadmayne, before moving here. Inside is big, but still seems really snug and friendly, divided into lots of cosy areas with shiny black panelling and woodwork, soft red lantern-light and logs burning in an open stove. Some seats are tucked into alcoves and window embrasures, and one is part of an upended boat; there are stormy sea pictures, and big wooden blocks and tackle. Good value and efficiently served bar food includes soup (£1), filled French bread (£2), ploughman's (£2.75), lasagne or filled baked potatoes (£3), a changing vegetarian dish (£3.50), steak and kidney pie (£4) and children's dishes (£2), with more elaborate main dishes in a pleasantly cottagey dining area which opens off on the right: seafood terrine with raspberry coulis (£1.75), Cambozola fritters (£2.20), steaks (from £7) and seafood platter (£15). Darts, pool, fruit machine and space game are well segregated, dominoes and card games, and the piped music (the Carpenters on our visit) well reproduced. Well kept Courage Best and Directors and Ringwood Old Thumper on handpump, with a good choice of liqueurs. There are picnic-table sets out on crazy paving by a little stream, with a thatched summer bar and a good play area over on a steep lawn; the Coast Path goes by. *(Recommended by C D Gill, WHBM, Alan and Janet Pearson, H W and A B Tuffill)*

Free house   Licensees William Bishop and K J Slater   Real ale   Meals and snacks Restaurant   Children in family-room and eating areas   Open 10am–11pm; 11–2.30, 6–11 in winter   Bedrooms tel Preston (0305) 833125; £25/£45

POOLE   SZ0190 Map 2

Angel

28 Market Street; opposite Guildhall, which is signposted off A348 in centre – parking at the pub

This well run, comfortable place has a spacious relaxed lounge with cushioned banquettes forming bays around pale wood tables, and a couple of sofas; the carefully decorated green walls are hung with turn-of-the-century prints, magazine covers and advertisements including ones by Toulouse-Lautrec and Mocha, naughty 1920s seaside postcards and some interesting old local photographs. Bar food from a separate efficient servery includes sandwiches (from £1.20), cauliflower and almond au gratin (£2.50), several hot dishes such as fisherman's pie, pork chop in cider or home-made steak and kidney pie (£2.95) and various salads (from £2.95), with children's menu (£1.50). As we went to press there were plans for a restaurant extension. Well kept Ushers Best and Ruddles Best and County on handpump (with spirits half-price 6–7 Monday to Friday); fruit machine, trivia, piped music, winter Sunday quiz league; cricket team, football team (who have a Sunday meat and spirit draw), and Tuesday and Thursday disc jockey. There are picnic-table sets in the back courtyard, with summer barbecues. The handsome eighteenth-century Guildhall is a museum of the town's development. *(Recommended by WHBM)*

Ushers (Watneys)   Licensee D McGuigan   Real ale   Meals and snacks (not evenings in winter)   Children in family-room   Live music twice a month Weds evenings   Open 11–11 all year

POWERSTOCK   SY5196 Map 2

Three Horseshoes 🏚 🍺

Can be reached by taking Askerswell turn off A35 then keeping uphill past the Spyway Inn, and bearing left all the way round Eggardon Hill – a lovely drive, but steep narrow roads; a better road is signposted West Milton off the A3066 Beaminster–Bridport, then take Powerstock road

Rebuilt in local stone after a fire in 1906, this busy, secluded stone and thatch pub has country-style chairs around the polished tables in the comfortable L-shaped bar, pictures on the stripped panelled walls, warm fires, and a friendly atmosphere. Good bar food concentrates on fresh fish, such as a properly made fresh fish soup (£3.50), moules marinière (£3.95), good grilled Lyme Bay plaice (£5), squid risotto (£5.50), baked red gurnard (£6), wing of skate with black butter (£7.50) and scallops in lovely sauce (£10.50); other food includes sandwiches, cream of artichoke soup (£2), an interesting hors d'oeuvre trolley (£3.95), wholewheat pancakes with spinach and cheese sauce (£3.25), lasagne (£3.95), beef carbonnade with a garlic crust (£4.75), pan-fried pork chops with capers, wine and cream (£5.50), and rump steak (£8.50). Good breakfasts with home-made marmalade; the dining-room is no-smoking. Well kept Palmers Bridport and IPA on handpump. On the neat lawn perched steeply above the pub there are charming views as well as swings and a climbing-frame. Our stay award is for the larger rooms, which have their own bathrooms (note that the village church nearby strikes on the quarter all through the night). You can book six-hour fishing trips, there are nearby trout ponds, and plenty of beach casting. *(Recommended by Mrs M T Garden, Rosemary Flower, John and Joan Nash, Jackie and Jon Payne, Amelia Thorpe, Ken and Barbara Turner, H W and A B Tuffill, David Pearman, Freddy Costello, Jim Matthews, J Roots, Derek and Sylvia Stephenson, Peter and Rose Flower)*

Palmers   Licensee P W Ferguson   Real ale   Meals and snacks   Restaurant   Children welcome   Open 11–3, 6–11 all year   Bedrooms tel Powerstock (030 885) 328; £15/£30(£40B)

RAMPISHAM   ST5602 Map 2

Tigers Head 🍺

Pub (and village) signposted off A356 Dorchester–Crewkerne; OS Sheet 194 reference 561023

People from all walks of life in this pretty valley village meet here to catch up on each other's news – making sure also that strangers don't feel excluded – and the atmosphere is delightfully old-fashioned. Two little rooms have comfortable old settles and a sofa, carefully chosen hunting prints of all ages, and photographs of ships brought in by ex-Navy locals; countless competition award rosettes above the bar confirm that riding's a particular interest of the licensees (Mrs Austin judges at horse shows, too), who with notice can arrange riding, clay-pigeon shooting or fishing for residents. The Siamese cat is friendly, though customers' favourite is Gladys the bulldog (a seasoned TV personality). Bar food, all home made and largely using local ingredients and fresh vegetables, includes carrot, tomato and orange soup or sandwiches (£1), steak and kidney pie, excellent rabbit pie or a range of vegetarian dishes (£3.75), venison casserole (£5.75) and steaks (from £7.25 to £12.90 for a 24-ounce rump); well kept Bass, Butcombe, Greene King Abbot and Wadworths 6X tapped from casks behind the bar, local farm cider, and country wines. There are darts, shove-ha'penny, dominoes, table skittles and a skittle alley. An attractive sheltered back garden has picnic-table sets; this is pleasant walking country. *(Recommended by D K and H M Brenchley, Heather Sharland, Charles Bardswell, Michael and Alison Sandy, MCG, Peter Jones, Bill Hendry, Peter and Rose Flower, Angie and Dave Parkes)*

Free house   Licensees Mike and Pat Austin   Real ale   Meals and snacks   Children's room Restaurant   Open 11–3, 7–11 all year; closed Tues lunchtimes in mid-winter   Two bedrooms tel Evershot (093 583) 244; £15/£30

SANDFORD ORCAS   ST6220 Map 2

Mitre 🍺

Village signposted off B3148 and B3145 N of Sherborne

At first sight, tucked into its very quiet hamlet, the Mitre seems the epitome of a remote rustic pub. On our inspection the landlady was out tending to her new-born lambs: they have Hebridean, Manx and Jacobs sheep that were originally just to keep their own steep acre under control, but have now expanded to other pastures such as the cricket green at Over Compton and an orchard at Trent. Other readers have found wool being spun in the simply furnished flagstoned bar, and the pub's four unusually personable whippets and three amiable cats add to the country feel.

Even the dining-room carries through this mood, with plain tables on the flagstones, cream walls, and a big wood-burning stove set in the stripped brick end wall. Against this background, it's a surprise to find such enterprising food. On our visit, the day's specials were chicken and ham pie (£2.95), hot game pie (£3.95), shark steak (£4.25) and guinea-fowl in champagne sauce (£6.25). Other food includes ploughman's or omelettes (£2.25), home-roast ham with egg (£2.95), steak and kidney pie (£3.25), salads (from £3.75), crumbly nut loaf or vegetarian stuffed peppers (£3.95), noisettes of lamb (£5.15), salmon steak with dill and cream (£5.50), steaks (from £5.85) and puddings (from £1). They cook everything themselves, except pâtés and ices (they do make their own sorbets). This is one place you can be sure the venison isn't a freezer pack, as they themselves joint all the venison they use; they also butcher their own sheep, though they're killed elsewhere. Charrington IPA (in summer) and unusually well kept Bass (in winter) on handpump, and decent house wines; fruit machine, piped music. There are picnic-table sets up on grass above the car park. *(Recommended by John Nash, Nigel Paine)*

Free house   Licensees Philip and Brenda Hayes   Real ale   Meals and snacks (12–2, 7–10) Restaurant tel Corton Denham (096 322) 271   Children welcome   Open 11.30–2.30, 7–11 all year

SHAFTESBURY   ST8622 Map 2
Ship

Bleke Street; you pass pub on main entrance to town from N

New licensees have taken over this unpretentious seventeeth-century pub, and as we went to press they were in the process of turning what was the pool-room into a comfortable dining lounge; they've also replanted the small beer garden. Facing the main bar counter, there are seats built into the snug black-panelled alcove, and on the left is a panelled but similarly furnished room. Well kept Badger Best and Tanglefoot on handpump; darts, fruit machine and piped music. Bar food cooked by Mr Lilley includes deep-fried Brie or mushrooms filled with pâté (£3), home-made pies and beef curry (£4), a buffet with hot and cold food, and daily specials. *(Recommended by Alan Skull, Barry and Anne)*

Badger   Licensee Mrs Elizabeth Lilley   Real ale   Meals and snacks (11–2.15, 6.30–10.15) Well behaved children – no prams   Open 11–3, 6.30–11 all year; may open longer in afternoon if weather is good

SHAVE CROSS   SY4198 Map 1
Shave Cross Inn ★ ✿

On back lane Bridport–Marshwood, sigposted locally; OS Sheet 193 reference 415980

The original timbered bar in this attractive cottagey pub is a lovely flagstoned room with one big table in the middle, a smaller one by the window seat, a row of chintz-cushioned Windsor chairs, and an enormous inglenook fireplace with plates hanging from the chimney breast. The larger carpeted side lounge has a dresser at one end set with plates, and modern rustic light-coloured seats making booths around the tables. Apart from an excellent ploughman's (£1.65), good bar food includes soup (45p), pâté (£1.65), basket meals (from £2.10), steak sandwich (£2.75), daily specials like lamb and apricot pie, lasagne, chicken, ham and leek pie or vegetarian chilli (all £2.95), salads that include fresh crab or lobster (from £2.75), evening char-grilled steaks (from £6.85), puddings such as Dorset apple cake (from 85p), and children's meals (from £1.55). Well kept Badger Best, Bass and Eldridge Pope Royal Oak on handpump; friendly, polite staff. Darts, table skittles, dominoes, cribbage and space game. The pretty flower-filled garden, sheltered by the thatched partly fourteenth-century pub and its long skittle alley, has a thatched wishing-well and a goldfish pool. There's a children's adventure playground, and a small secluded campsite for touring caravans and campers.

(Recommended by Dr Stewart Rae, Margaret and Trevor Errington, Gordon and Daphne, Peter and Rose Flower, J E F Rawlins, A and K D Stansfield, Mrs Joan Harris, Paul and Margaret Baker, Derek and Sylvia Stephenson, E A George)

Free house   Licensees Bill and Ruth Slade   Real ale   Meals and snacks (not Mon, exc bank hols)   Children in two family-rooms   Open 12–3, 7–11 all year; closed Mon (exc bank hols)

STOKE ABBOTT   ST4500 Map 1

New Inn

Village signposted from B3162 and B3163 W of Beaminster

The redecorated black-beamed carpeted bar in this friendly place has wheel-back chairs and cushioned built-in settles around its simple wooden tables, a settle built into a snug stripped stone alcove beside the big log fireplace, old coins framed on the walls, and the licensee's own collection of over 200 horsebrasses on the beams. Bar food includes ploughman's or basket meals (from £1.95), home-made pizza or quiches (£2.95), salads or vegetarian dishes (from £2.95), plaice or home-made chicken curry (£3.50), excellent home-made steak and kidney pie (£3.50), ten-ounce sirloin steak (£7.25), mixed grill (£7.50), puddings (£1.25) and daily specials. Well kept Palmers Bridport and IPA on handpump kept under light blanket pressure; table skittles, and pleasant, helpful service. Sheltering behind a golden stone wall which merges into an attractively planted rockery, the well kept garden here has long gnarled silvery logs to sit on, wooden benches by the tables, and swings. *(Recommended by Charlie Salt, C S Kirk, D G Nicolson, Gordon Lane; more reports please)*

Palmers   Licensee Graham Gibbs   Real ale   Meals and snacks (not Mon evenings, exc bank hols)   Children in dining-room   Open 12–2.30, 7–11 all year   Bedrooms tel Broadwindsor (0308) 68333; £12.50/£20

SYMONDSBURY   SY4493 Map 1

Ilchester Arms 🕲 🛏️   [illustrated on page 249]

Village signposted from A35 just W of Bridport

This neatly kept and friendly old thatched inn was becoming more of a dining pub even under the previous licensees. The trend has continued, and readers are certainly pleased with the food: locally caught fresh fish, such as crab, lobster, scallops and whole fresh baby shark (when available), has been warmly praised, game in season, and there's an excellent range of other food chalked up on all available beams and woodwork, such as home-made chicken pâté or marsh samphire with smoked bacon and crispy croûtons (£2.95), pan-fried calamares (£2.95 or £4.95), fresh sardines with a lime sauce (£3.25), thali of fresh vegetables with hot garlic bread (£4.50), roast beef and Yorkshire pudding or roast English lamb with redcurrant, orange and mint sauce (£5.50), whole plaice (£6.95), roast quail with light orange sauce (£8.95), and puddings like home-made Dorset apple cake or banana and caramel crunch (£1.95); booking essential. Very good breakfasts. One side of the open-plan bar has rustic benches and tables, seats in the mullioned windows, and a high-backed settle built into the bar counter next to the big inglenook fireplace; the other side, also with an open fire, has candle-lit tables and is used mainly for dining in the evening and at weekends. Well kept Devenish JD and Royal Wessex on handpump, and ten wines and champagne by the glass; quick, helpful service. Darts, pool, dominoes, cribbage, backgammon, chess and a separate skittle alley (with tables). The friendly Great Dane is called Oliver, and the Burmese cats are called Eric and George. There are tables outside in a quiet back garden by a stream. The high-hedged lanes which twist deeply through the sandstone behind this village of pretty stone houses lead to good walks through the wooded low hills above Marshwood Vale. *(Recommended by Mr and Mrs R G Ing, Freddy Costello, Don Easton, C S Kirk, Mr and Mrs M Woodger, Denis Waters, Steve Huggins, Peter and Rose Flower, Jim Matthews, R D Jolliff, D G Nicolson, Gordon and Daphne)*

Devenish   Licensees Terry and Margaret Flenley   Real ale   Meals and snacks (not Mon evening)   Restaurant   Well behaved children welcome   Open 11–3, 7–11 all year   Bedrooms tel Bridport (0308) 22600; £16/£29

TARRANT MONKTON   ST9408 Map 2
Langton Arms

Village signposted from A354, then head for church

In attractive countryside and next to the village church, this friendly, pretty seventeenth-century thatched pub is reached by driving through a shallow ford; there are tracks leading up to Crichel Down above the village. Inside, the main bar has settles forming a couple of secluded booths around tables at the carpeted end, window seats, and another table or two at the serving end where the floor's tiled. Bar food includes ploughman's (£1.95), steak and kidney pudding or mushroom florentine (£2.60), gammon steak (£4.25), steaks (from £5.75), puddings (£1.10) and specials such as smoked trout mousse, braised lamb's heart or beef madras (all £2.60); most evenings have special food themes – Chinese, French, pizza and curry. To be sure of a table, it's best to get there early. The public bar, with a big inglenook fireplace, has darts, pool, shove-ha'penny, dominoes, cribbage and juke box, while a skittle alley with its own bar and more tables has a space game and fruit machine. Well kept Bass, and Wadworths 6X, with guest beers such as Adnams, Eldridge Pope or Ringwoods on handpump or tapped from the cask; sangria and Pimms in summer, mulled wine in winter, quite a few wines. There's a barbecue in the pretty garden. On the end of the building, they have opened a village/craft/delicatessen shop. Badbury Rings, a hill fort by the B3082 just south of here, is very striking. *(Recommended by E M Brandwood, Bernard Phillips, M D Hare, Gavin Udall, R F K Hutchings, Charles and Mary Winpenny, Richard Cole, David Jones, Alison Kerruish, Roger and Kathy, Gwen and Peter Andrews)*

Free house   Licensees Chris and Diane Goodinge   Real ale   Meals and snacks (11–2, 6–10.30)   Restaurant   Children welcome   Occasional live music   Open 11–2.30, 6–11 all year   Bedrooms tel Tarrant Hinton (025 889) 225; £25B/£38B

WEST BEXINGTON   SY5387 Map 2
Manor Hotel 🕲 ⛭

Village signposted off B3157 SE of Bridport, opposite the Bull in Swyre

The popular, pubby Cellar Bar in this well kept hotel is reached down a flight of steps from the handsome flagstoned and Jacobean carved-oak-panelled hall, and is on a level with the spreading south-sloping garden: picnic-table sets on a small lawn with flower beds line the low sheltering walls, and there's a much bigger side lawn with a children's play area. The bar has black beams and joists, heavy harness over the log fire, small country pictures and good leather-mounted horsebrasses on the walls, red leatherette stools, low-backed chairs (with one fat seat carved from a beer cask) and soft lighting. A handsome Victorian-style conservatory has airy furnishings and lots of plants. Very good bar food includes sandwiches, vegetarian pancakes (£4.65), roast quail stuffed with chestnuts, lamb cutlets with herb sauce, game or home-made steak and kidney pies or liver and bacon (all £4.85), poached salmon in lemon sauce (£6.55) and fish thermidor (£6.65). Well kept Eldridge Pope Royal Oak, Palmers Bridport (which here carries the pub's name) and Wadworths 6X on handpump; skittle alley, trivia and piped music. The sea is just a stroll away (past the bungalows which make up most of this village), and the walks along the cliff are bracing. *(Recommended by M Aston, Heather Sharland, K Leist, Nigel Williamson, Bernard Phillips, TOH, Mrs M C Gray, Derek and Sylvia Stephenson, John and Joan Nash, Heather Sharland, Jon Dewhirst, Gwen and Peter Andrews)*

Free house   Licensee Richard Childs   Real ale   Meals and snacks (12–2, 7–10) Restaurant   Children welcome   Open 11–2.30, 6.30–11 all year   Bedrooms tel Burton Bradstock (0308) 897616; £28.95B/£51B

WEST LULWORTH   SY8280 Map 2

Castle 🛏

B3070

Button-back leatherette seats form a maze of booths around the tables on the polished flagstones in the lively public bar of this thatched white house. The comfortably furnished lounge bar is cosy, though more modern-feeling, with blue banquettes under the countryside prints on the walls, and pewter tankards hanging from one beam. Good, popular bar food includes sandwiches, ploughman's with good ham, chilli con carne (£3), home-made pies or beef Stroganoff (£3.80), and rabbit and pork casserole with apple or pigeon and bacon casserole (£4); excellent breakfasts. Well kept Devenish JD, Royal Wessex and Steam on handpump, and cocktails; friendly, helpful staff; darts, shove-ha'penny, table skittles, dominoes, cribbage, fruit machine, trivia, outdoor chess and piped music. On the lawn above steeply terraced rose beds, there's a barbecue area. Best to walk down to Lulworth Cove from here, as the car park at the bottom is expensive; there are lots of fine walks in the area (the inn is near the start of *Good Walks Guide* Walk 27), usually with splendid views. *(Recommended by Jenny and Michael Back, Richard Dolphin, Fiona Holt, Denise Plummer, Jim Froggatt, W C M Jones, Steve and Carolyn Harvey, David Pearman, Sue Corrigan, Ian Phillips, Alan and Ruth Woodhouse, Barry and Anne)*

Devenish   Licensee Graham Halliday   Real ale   Meals and snacks, served all the time pub open   Restaurant   Children in restaurant and eating area of bar   Very occasional live music   Open 11–2.30, 7–11 all year, though may open longer on fine afternoons   Bedrooms tel West Lulworth (092 941) 311; £15(£20B)/£30(£36B)

WORTH MATRAVERS (Isle of Purbeck)   SY9777 Map 2

Square & Compass

At fork of both roads signposted to village from B3069

With no concessions to stylised comfort, this defiantly traditional pub has an old-fashioned main bar with wall benches around the elbow-polished old tables on the flagstones, and interesting local pictures under its low ceilings. Whitbreads Pompey Royal and Strong Country are tapped from a row of casks behind a couple of hatches in the flagstoned corridor (local fossils back here, and various curios inside the servery), which leads to a more conventional summer bar. Reasonably priced bar snacks include crab sandwiches, home-made pasties or filled rolls and ploughman's. There are seats outside on a side lawn that looks down over the village rooftops to the sea showing between the East Man and the West Man (hills that guard the sea approach); on summer evenings you can watch the sun set beyond Portland Bill. The pub is at the start of an OS Walkers Britain walk and on *Good Walks Guide* Walk 25. *(Recommended by Phil and Sally Gorton, Steve and Carolyn Harvey, David Pearman, Peter Hitchcock, C Gray, Alan and Audrey Chatting, Barry and Anne, Jane and Calum)*

Whitbreads   Licensee Ray Newman   Real ale   Snacks   Children welcome   Occasional live music   Open 10.30–3, 6–11 all year; closes 2.30 lunchtime in winter

Lucky Dip

Besides the fully inspected pubs, you might like to try these Lucky Dips recommended to us and described by readers (if you do, please send us reports):

Alderholt [back rd Fordingbridge–Cranborne; SU1212], *Churchill Arms*: Unusually well furnished local with pub games, quick and friendly service, Badger beer, wide range of reasonably priced bar food, garden, swimming-pool; children's room *(Canon G Hollis)*

☆ **Almer** [just off A31 Wimborne Minster–Bere Regis; SY9097], *Worlds End*: Charming fifteenth-century L-shaped thatched pub with Badger real ales, well renovated red tiles, horsebrasses, wide choice of good value food in eating area decorated with hats and fans (children allowed here), friendly atmosphere; tables out in former stone sheep pen, big well equipped play area; very handy for this stretch of the road *(WHBM, Gwen and Peter Andrews)*

☆ **Ansty** [Higher Ansty – not to be confused with the Ansty in Wilts; ST7603], *Fox*: Intriguingly decorated place, with some 800 toby jugs and lots of colourful plates, and considerable energy being put into ancillaries like the little swimming-pool, elaborate curtains and fixtures; generous cold buffet (now around £6), char-grill, well equipped children's bar with games and pool-table, skittle alley with own bar, pop music in one room; bedrooms (generous breakfasts); adjacent caravan site *(Steve Dark, H W and A B Tuffill, Robert Crail, R Sinclair Taylor, LYM)*

☆ **Bere Regis** [West St; SY8494], *Royal Oak*: Cheerful local atmosphere in well kept open-plan modernised bar, good range of low-priced and well made bar food, Flowers Original and Whitbreads Strong Country on handpump, wood-burning stove, sensibly placed darts, cribbage, fruit machine; dining-room; open all day Fri and Sat; bedrooms *(R Wilson, Nigel Williamson, Mrs Nina Elliott, BB)*

Bournemouth [SZ0991], *Broadway*: Good enough for at least one customer (Snowy, the old gentleman in the corner) to have been going every day since the pub opened in 1935 *(WHBM)*; [423 Charminster Rd] *Fiveways*: Well updated pre-war pub – the brewers have injected some interest without extravagant expenditure; good games-room with two pool-tables and efficent built-in ventilation; wide range of fair-priced standard food including a good ploughman's, three Eldridge Pope beers on handpump, decent wines by the glass, no-smoking area, efficient friendly service *(WHBM, Nigel Williamson, Ian Phillips)*

☆ **Branksome** [Pinewood Rd; SZ0590], *Inn in the Park*: Attractive and popular free house in converted Victorian house, quiet and well ventilated, a few minutes from sea in pleasant residential area by Branksome Dene Chine; well kept real ales such as Wadworths IPA and 6X on handpump, very reasonably priced food such as sandwiches, ploughman's, home-made quiche and cold meats; five bedrooms – clean, comfortable and inexpensive *(WHBM, Bernard Phillips, Steve J Pratt)*

Bridport [34 East St (A35); SY4692], *Bull*: Small, busy but comfortable bar with open fire in winter and good atmosphere – popular with locals; charming efficient service, wide variety of well kept ales, over 50 malt whiskies, wines (and shellfish) imported direct from France; bedrooms *(Cdr W S D Hendry)*

Broadstone [Waterloo Rd (junction A349/B3074); SZ0095], *Darbys Corner*: Completely refurbished a few years ago, this large pub has three areas (one non-smoking) radiating from the central bar; comfortable, well ventilated and clean; good food, if rather pricey, with several hot dishes; Badger Best and Tanglefoot; atmosphere pleasant for a large pub *(WHBM)*

Buckhorn Weston [ST7524], *Stapleton Arms*: Spacious pub with piped classical music in lounge, eating area with wide choice of reasonably priced bar food including children's helpings and Sun lunches, carpeted games-bar with pool-tables and fruit machine; friendly efficient young landlord, Exmoor, Palmers, Wadworths 6X and Wethereds on handpump, plenty of tables in back garden *(Nigel Paine)*

Burton Bradstock [SY4889], *Anchor*: Friendly pub in good setting in unspoilt village with large helpings of home-made food *(R Wilson)*; *Three Horseshoes*: Attractive thatched inn with comfortable carpeted lounge, Palmers real ales including Tally Ho, sandwiches, ploughman's, good range of hot and cold dishes including children's ones, puddings, coffee, also separate restaurant; clean lavatories, no piped music, pleasant shingle beach a few minutes' drive away (with NT car park); nice atmosphere; bedrooms *(Lyn and Bill Capper)*

Cashmoor [A354 6 miles E of Blandford; ST9713], *Cashmoor*: Small former coaching-inn, not greatly modernised; Badger house, experienced friendly licensees, fair-sized bar with central wishing-well, over 60 whiskies, wide range of reasonably priced bar food, restaurant (where children allowed) *(WHBM)*

☆ **Cerne Abbas** [Main St; ST6601], *Red Lion*: Cosy, picturesque and friendly oak-beamed pub, pleasantly refurbished, with friendly and amusing licensee; well kept real ales such as Wadworths 6X, good atmosphere and food (some concentration on this), quick service; good value accommodation *(D K and H M Brenchley, WFL, Chris Raisin)*

Charlton Marshall [A350 Poole–Blandford; ST9004], *Charlton*: Attractively refurbished country-style bars with friendly, obliging staff, generously served food from an extensive menu and unobtrusive piped music; Badger Best and Tanglefoot; clean lavatories *(Richard Burton, Richard Dolphin)*

Charminster [A352 N of Dorchester; SY6793], *Three Compasses*: Popular new licensee, well kept Devenish Royal Wessex, good reasonably priced food; skittles alley, family-room with colour TV, plenty of locals; bedrooms *(Nigel Pritchard)*

Chesil [SY6873], *Little Ship*: Friendly local with Eldridge Pope beers and decent straightforward food such as ploughman's, ham and egg and apple and blackberry pie *(T R G Alcock)*

Chickerell [Lower Putton Lane; off B3157; SY6480], *Fishermans Arms*: Two small, comfortable bars with copper-topped tables, aquarium, maps and stuffed swordfish; friendly licensee, well kept Devenish Cornish Original tapped from the cask, restaurant *(Denise Plummer, Jim Froggatt)*; [East St;] *Turks Head*: Hotel-restaurant with huge helpings of attractively presented bar food such as massive sandwiches with interesting salads; ploughman's and hot dishes too *(Ian Phillips)*

Chideock [SY4292], *Clock*: Engaging mix of styles and furnishings in open-plan bar with popular food, well kept Devenish Wessex, table skittles, brightly lit pool-table; restaurant, simple bedrooms; nr GWG23 *(BB)*; [A35 Bridport–Lyme Regis] *George*: Thatched seventeenth-century pub with plush seats in dark-beamed lounge, wide choice of bar food from soup and sandwiches to steaks, well kept Palmers real ales, big log fire, family-room with pool, darts and other games; juke box, tables in back garden; nr GWG23; bedrooms *(LYM)*

☆ **Child Okeford** [Gold Hill; ST8313], *Saxon*: Comfortable and cosy village local tucked behind cottages and away from traffic, with friendly licensees, small spotless bar and separate, roomy eating area; well kept Bass and Charrington IPA, good choice of well prepared bar food, log fire and wood-burning stove; children welcome; two bedrooms *(Brian Chambers, WHBM, Mrs Sybil Baker, Mrs B M McHugh)*

☆ **Child Okeford** [on lane entering village from A357 Sturminster Newton–Blandford], *Union Arms*: Recent major extension giving restaurant (which seems a main interest now) and larger bar, with delicately patterned claret carpet, dark wood tables, claret-upholstered stools and chairs, though much of the original traditional core remains, with

high-backed settles huddling around wood-burning stove in a big stone fireplace; well kept Hook Norton Best and guest beers such as Batemans XXXB and Felinfoel on handpump, discreet piped music, lunchtime bar food, separate restaurant; pleasant licensees (new in 1988), calm alsatian called Zoe *(Nigel Paine, LYM)*

Christchurch [Church St; SZ1593], *Castle*: Friendly plush pub near priory, unobtrusive piped music, fine range of real ales including Bass, Ringwood Best, Fortyniner and Old Thumper, and a guest beer; usual pub food, upstairs folk nights; Norman wall, once part of castle, forms part of back kitchen; very busy July–Aug *(Lyn and Bill Capper, Roger and Kathy)*; *Royalty*: Large, clean, modern pub; Flowers Original, Wadworths 6X and Whitbreads Pompey Royal; food includes tremendous choice of filled baked potatoes and of puddings *(John Hayward)*

☆ **Church Knowle** [SY9481], *New*: Stripped stone and high rafters in spacious public bar of partly thatched pub looking over the Purbeck hills, cosy lounge, well kept Devenish real ales, decent wines, wide choice of good bar food including attractive dishes of the day, skittle alley and children's room in separate building; currently doing well – can get very busy in summer *(S J A Velate, Mrs P Powis, Steve and Carolyn Harvey, John Kirk, LYM)*

Corfe Mullen [away from town; SY9798], *Darleys Corner*: Huge helpings of excellent value food *(Mr and Mrs R Harrington)*

Dorchester [Monmouth Rd; SY6890], *Bakers Arms*: Bar dominated by tiled wall with two big steel-doored ovens used for previous owners' secondary occupation as bakers; good, simple home-made food, Eldridge Pope ales, friendly licensees *(Ian Phillips, Steve Huggins)*; [High East St] *Kings Arms*: Smart old-fashioned hotel with well kept Eldridge Pope ales and wide choice of freshly prepared and reasonably priced bar food including vegetarian dishes, in comfortably refurbished lounge bar; close associations with Nelson and Hardy's *Mayor of Casterbridge*; bedrooms *(LYM)*; [High West St] *Old Ship*: Externally attractive, but simply furnished inside – popular for reasonably priced simple bar food *(David Pearman)*; [20 High West St] *Royal Oak*: Good food at reasonable prices, excellent service *(R Blatch)*; [47 High East St] *Tom Browns*: Pleasant, unpretentious pub serving own-brewed Tom Browns and Flashmans Clout, bar food *(Stan Edwards)*; [A352 towards Wareham] *Trumpet Major*: Large pub in extensive grounds, public bar with sporting theme and adjacent dining-room, lounge and separate restaurant; well kept beer, extensive menu including excellent mixed grills; children's play area *(Stan Edwards)*; [53 High East St] *White Hart*: Friendly pub on edge of town centre, well kept Badger ales including Tanglefoot, good value bar food, wide variety of pub games, singing and juggling landlord *(S M House)*

East Knighton [A352 Wareham–Dorchester; SY8185], *Red Lion*: Well kept Badger ales, large menu, pleasant garden sheltered by trees and hedges; children's play area *(Stan Edwards)*

Easton [SY6870], *New*: Basic pub, but well decorated, with plenty of locals, warm welcome, helpful service (nothing too much trouble) and good bar food *(Richard Dolphin)*

☆ **Farnham** [off A354 NE of Blandford Forum; ST9515], *Museum*: Sympathetically refurbished cosy bar with inglenook fireplace, original bread oven, paintings by local artist, warm welcome, well kept Adnams, Badger Best and Palmers IPA on handpump, decent house wines, wide choice of particularly good bar food from sandwiches through unusual and decorative dishes such as mange-tout with prawns to steaks; four comfortable bedrooms in converted stableblock *(WHBM, John Kirk)*

Ferndown [A31; SU0700], *Smugglers Haunt*: A Roast Inn; seems to concentrate more on restaurant, though bar food (when available) good value; Whitbreads Pompey Royal *(Nigel Pritchard)*

Fiddleford [A357 Sturminster Newton– Blandford Forum; ST8013], *Fiddleford*: Pleasant and attractive old pub with vast flagstones in nicely furnished bar, wide choice of bar food (not cheap), interesting well kept real ales including guest beers, good garden with play area; bedrooms clean and comfortable, with substantial breakfasts *(WHBM, Kenneth Philpot, Richard Dolphin, LYM)*

Gillingham [turn off B3081 at Wyke a mile NW of Gillingham – pub 100yds on left; ST8026], *Buffalo*: Good local, friendly landlord and staff, good value bar food including first-rate minestrone *(Mea Horler)*

☆ **Gussage All Saints** [SU0010], *Drovers*: Old, partly thatched pub, open-plan inside with central fire; new licensees who really know their onions, Flowers Original, Gales BBB, Marstons Pedigree and Wadworths 6X, wide range of good bar food from sandwiches to T-bone steaks; jazz pianist Tues evenings *(WHBM)*

Hilfield [ST6305], *Good Hope*: Attractive pub in isolated, scenic spot, friendly licensees and attentive staff, unusual choice of excellent food in bar and restaurant *(Henry and Margaret Midwinter)*

Hinton St Mary [ST7816], *White Horse*: Excellent fish and wide choice of other fresh food in small lounge bar with tables, chairs and cushioned settles; darts in larger public bar, no piped music, Wadworths 6X; this quiet village has a superb manor house and medieval tithe barn *(Lyn and Bill Capper)*

Kingstag [ST7210], *Green Man*: Unpretentious pub, generous helpings of good home-made food, friendly licensees *(Mea Horler)*

Kingston [B3069; SY9579], *Scott Arms*: Well worth knowing for the superb view of Corfe Castle from the garden, and the rambling layout of the original part is interesting; this part is now largely devoted to fast food service for families, with drinks served in modern Barn Bar extension; on GWG25, in beautiful village; bedrooms comfortable *(Phil and Sally Gorton, Dr A V Lewis, R Inns, Mr and Mrs G J Lewis, C M Whitehouse, A P Carr, LYM)*

Knap Corner [B3092 S of Gillingham; ½ mile N of East Stour A30 Shaftesbury– Sherborne; ST8023], *Crown*: Small, delightful pub with gorgeous log fire in stone fireplace, friendly licensees and locals, two labradors, unobtrusive piped music, Wiltshire Stonehenge, Old Grumble and Old Devil on handpump and good choice of well prepared food *(Nigel Paine)*

Langton Matravers [SY9978], *Kings Arms*: Popular village pub with fine local marble fireplace in simple beamed main bar, well kept Whitbreads real ale, friendly locals and staff, good pub games including splendid antique Purbeck longboard for shove-ha'penny; children's room, seats outside; bedrooms *(Phil and Sally Gorton, LYM)*; [B3069 nr junction with A351] *Ship*: Robust basic local with well kept Whitbreads real ale, lively Purbeck longboard shove-ha'penny and very cheap bedrooms *(LYM)*

Longham [A348 Ferndown–Poole; SZ0698], *Angel*: Spacious traditional bar based on much smaller original core; open fires, nooks and corners, well kept Badger ales including Tanglefoot, wide choice of reasonably priced home-made food (not Mon evening – except maybe barbecued burgers in summer), pleasant staff, collection of foreign banknotes; big garden with well equipped play area including trampoline; children in good family eating room *(WHBM, Nigel Pritchard)*; [Ringwood Rd] *Bridge House*: More of a restaurant/hotel roadhouse than a pub, but worth knowing for good value carvery meals in pleasant surroundings *(Ken and Dorothy Worrall)*

Lyme Regis [Broad St; SY3492], *Royal Lion*: Old-fashioned many-roomed bar in traditional hotel – pleasant place for a weekend *(Prof S Barnett, LYM)*; [25 Marine Parade, The Cobb] *Royal Standard*: Friendly and popular little cottage pub leading to beach through sun-trap walled and partly canvas-roofed courtyard; well kept Palmers, quickly served home-made bar food including fresh crab sandwiches – but they may use paper plates and plastic cutlery *(R Fieldhouse)*

Maiden Newton [Main St; SY5997], *Chalk & Cheese*: Attentive licensees in refurbished pub with well kept Devenish beers, bar food, skittle alley *(Bill Hendry)*

Marshwood [SY3799], *Bottle*: Simple country

pub with well kept Ushers, traditional games and skittle alley; usually has reasonably priced bar food and is handy for pretty walking country *(David Pearman, Gordon and Daphne, LYM)*

Melplash [SY4898], *Half Moon*: Good value bar food including vegetarian dishes, wider evening choice *(Mrs R Thornton)*

Middlemarsh [A352 Sherborne–Dorchester; ST6607], *White Horse*: Decent bar food in dining area, also restaurant; obliging service; bedrooms *(Anon)*

☆ **Milton Abbas** [ST8001], *Hambro Arms*: Like the beautifully landscaped eighteenth-century village, this pretty inn is a powerful draw in the tourist season, but even then service in the airy opened-up bar is quick and friendly; wide choice of good bar food, well kept Devenish JD and Royal Wessex on handpump; on GWG24; neat bedrooms, including at least one four-poster *(A Cook, Derek and Sylvia Stephenson, WHBM, Shirley Pielou, LYM)*

Morden [off B3075, between A35 and A31 E of Bere Regis; SY9195], *Cock & Bottle*: Unpretentious, clean country pub with Badger ales and good food *(WHBM)*

☆ **Mosterton** [High St; ST4505], *Admiral Hood*: Wide range of food, especially fish, in civilised and popular dining pub with neatly furnished spacious L-shaped bar, well kept Watneys-related real ales on handpump, coal fire in handsome stone fireplace, quick service, simple skittle alley behind the thatched eighteenth-century stone building *(Nigel Paine, R A and D M Hill, Gordon and Daphne, BB)*

☆ **Mudeford** [beyond huge seaside car park at Mudeford Pier – OS Sheet 195 reference 182916; SZ1891], *Haven House*: Quaint old heart to much-extended seaside pub with Devenish ales and good value snacks and lunchtime meals; family cafeteria, tables on sheltered terrace; you can walk by the sea for miles from here *(WHBM, LYM)*

Osmington [A353 Weymouth–Wareham; SY7282], *Sunray*: Pleasant fresh décor, separate bar for families, good value bar food, good carvery, good service even in large garden; children's play area *(Alan Vere)*

Pamphill [OS Sheet 195 reference 995003; ST9900], *Vine*: Tiny, simple pub in rural surroundings run by same family for three or four generations; well cared for feel, Whitbreads Strong Country on handpump and simple bar food including fresh sandwiches and ploughman's; handy for NT Kingston Lacy *(WHBM)*

☆ **Piddlehinton** [SY7197], *Thimble*: Lovely old listed thatched pub, creeper-clad and quite small inside; pleasant landlady, glistening bar, real ale and good, varied choice of bar food from spick and span kitchen; homely good value bedrooms, with decent breakfasts *(Freddy Costello, WHBM)*

Pimperne [Salisbury Rd; off A354; ST9009],

Anvil: Sixteenth-century thatched inn with pleasant beamed bar and good home-cooked food from ploughman's to Dorset-landed plaice and baked crab; until recently it's had only a hotel licence, but in 1989 the new owners gained a full pub licence, adding more rooms and a new bar – a wider range of food, too; friendly staff; bedrooms, attractive surroundings *(JMW)*

☆ **Plush** [village signposted from B3143 N of Dorchester at Piddletrenthide, pub by Haselbury Bryan signposted turnoff; ST7102], *Brace of Pheasants*: On form, this charmingly placed thatched pub is hard to beat, with a good deal of character in its comfortable beamed bar, Bass and Hancocks HB and good choice of other drinks, real fires, good-sized garden and play area; food not cheap but can be very good indeed (as can service), giving a lot of pleasure to many readers – consistency seems a recurring problem, though; children in restaurant and family area, dogs around *(Gwen and Peter Andrews, K and D E Worrall, Cdr F A Costello, Dr A V Lewis, Mea Horler, Wayne Brindle, J M Watkinson, Mrs E M Thompson, K Leist, David and Eloise Smaylen, Mr and Mrs J D Cranston, LYM)*

Poole [Sandbanks Rd, Lilliput; SZ0489], *Beehive*: Old stripped beams and stripped pine furniture imported into large open-plan suburban family pub; Eldridge Pope Dorset and Dorchester on handpump, bar food from burgers to swordfish steaks, no-smoking area; tables on terrace and in garden, barbecues, play area with lots of climbing-frames and so forth *(S J A Velate, Mr and Mrs Edwicker)*; [Quay; SZ0190] *Lord Nelson*: Olde-worlde harbourside fisherman's haunt, full of character, with array of nautical bric-à-brac, interesting little corners, seats outside, well kept Badger Best and Tanglefoot on handpump *(R A Nelson – no relation)*; [Quay] *Poole Arms*: Magnificent green-tiled façade of waterfront tavern looking across harbour to Brownsea Island; handy for Poole Aquarium *(LYM)*; [West St] *Queen Mary*: Whitbreads pub with large open-plan bar, bar food including local cockles, hundreds of key-rings hanging from ceiling; tables outside *(WHBM)*

Portland [Reforne; SY6876], *George*: Dauntingly big helpings of good value food and Devenish real ales in low-beamed seventeenth-century stone-built pub mentioned by Thomas Hardy and reputed to have smugglers' tunnels running to the cliffs *(WHBM)*

☆ **Portland Bill** [SY6870], *Pulpit*: Pleasant and comfortably refurbished pub in interesting spot near Pulpit Rock, with great sea views; well kept Gibbs Mew real ales, friendly staff, piped music, food in bar and restaurant *(T R G Alcock, Denise Plummer, Jim Froggatt, Philip Whitehead)*

Shaftesbury [The Commons; ST8622], *Grosvenor*: Old wistaria-covered coaching-house converted into THF hotel, with small fish pond in front; public bar used by locals, serving cheap bar food including large ploughman's and help-yourself salads *(Heather Sharland)* [High St; *Mitre:*] Nice view from straightforward lounge bar with reasonably priced bar food including good fish and roast beef (service not always as quick as most readers have found it); piped pop radio; children allowed in restaurant; bedrooms *(S Watkins, JMW, LYM)*

☆ **Sherborne** [Cooks Lane (nr abbey); ST6316], *Digby Tap:* Simple, lively town-centre pub with plenty of character, popular for interesting real ales such as Smiles; farm cider, bar food, pub games, seats outside *(A J Ritson, D Pearman)*

Sherborne [Greenhill], *Antelope:* Generously served interesting home-cooked food in bar and restaurant *(SJE);* [Swan Passage] *Swan:* Long, low-beamed, historic pub with pleasant and relaxed atmosphere, real ales, friendly service; promising new chef-landlord 1989 *(Anon)*

Sixpenny Handley [B3081; ST9917], *Star:* Welcoming and well kept village pub, good real ales, bar food, seats outside *(Anon)*

Southbourne [Broadway – OS Sheet 195 reference 155914; SZ1591], *Saxon King:* Large and clean, with efficient friendly service, Eldridge Pope Dorchester, Dorset and Royal Oak, and Wadworths Old Timer; food including sandwiches and ploughman's as well as hot dishes, with separate dining-room; second bar with pool, darts and juke box; handy for Hengistbury Head *(Keith Widdowson)*

Stratton [SY6593], *Bull:* Friendly beamed local with well kept Eldridge Pope Dorchester and good range of bar food, separate restaurant *(Paul and Margaret Baker)*

☆ **Studland** [SZ0382], *Bankes Arms:* Wonderful peaceful spot above one of England's best beaches, giving excellent views of Poole Harbour and Bournemouth Bay; homely atmosphere in modest but friendly bar, good choice of simple bar food served very generously, pleasant, welcoming staff; nr start GWG26 and south-western Coast Path; bedrooms clean and comfortable *(E G Parish, Paul and Margaret Baker, Mrs H M T Carpenter, Alan and Audrey Chatting)*

Studland [Beach Rd], *Manor House:* Operates under a restaurant licence (you can't have a drink unless you eat), but this comfortable and charming old country-house hotel has a cheerful and homely atmosphere and is worth knowing for its good bar meals, including excellent sandwiches; King George VI and Montgomery watched the invasion fleet rehearse from here *(E G Parish)*

Sturminster Marshall [SY9499], *Black Horse:* Good, friendly service, pleasant atmosphere, well kept Badger ales, bar food; handy for NT Kingston Lacy *(Theo Schofield, W J Wonham)*

☆ **Sturminster Newton** [A357; ST7814], *Red Lion:* Delightfully cosy little pub with

welcoming atmosphere, friendly landlord, pleasant unhurried service, good reasonably priced food, log fire *(Mr and Mrs P W Dryland)*

Sutton Poyntz [SY7083], *Springhead:* Pleasant spot, friendly service, well kept beer at reasonable prices, good bar food *(Alan and Janet Pearson)*

Swanage [Durlston Rd; SZ0278], *Durlston Castle:* Endearing layout and style, like tea-room with added bar, in 1890 turreted 'castle' with stunning views over the Needles and sea; friendly welcome, bar food, well kept beer including Eldridge Pope Royal Oak and Dorset, dungeon lavatories; children allowed in recently refurbished games-room with three pool-tables, dogs welcome *(WHBM);* [Burlington Rd] *Grand:* Excellent lounge, prompt friendly service, good bar food; comfortable bedrooms *(Alan and Audrey Chatting);* [1 Burlington Rd] *Pines:* Good, reasonably priced bar food, courteous service and coffee-room overlooking bay; bedrooms with lovely sea views *(N M Glover)*

Swyre [B3157; SY5288], *Bull:* Warm welcome, friendly service, good food including locally caught plaice and sole; children welcome in family-room and dining area off main bar; play area, open-air swimming-pool *(Stan Edwards)*

☆ **Tarrant Gunville** [ST9212], *Bugle Horn:* Well furnished country pub with pleasant and welcoming new licensees, tasteful and comfortably furnished lounge bar, Ringwood and Wadworths 6X, usual bar food, seats in garden *(Brian Chambers)*

Three Legged Cross [SU0805], *Old Barn Farm:* Former early eighteenth-century thatched farmhouse with covered-over well in open-plan lounge, choice of real ales, wide choice of food (family dining-room), separate servery for big garden with barbecue terrace *(Anon)*.

Tolpuddle [SY7994], *Martyrs:* Large, tidy roadside pub, friendly staff, well kept Badger ales, good value varied bar food *(John Hayward)*

Trent [ST5918], *Rose & Crown:* Lovely converted farmhouse by beautiful old country church, relaxed atmosphere, books over the log fire; real ales such as Hook Norton and Wadworths 6X tapped from the cask, well cooked, good value food specialising in fresh local fish *(Dickie and Barbara Bird and friends, Michael Andrews, Nigel Paine, Freddy Costello)*

Uploders [SY5093], *Crown:* Good atmosphere quickly makes you feel at home; smallish cosy bar on right opens on to small back lawn *(Gordon and Daphne)*

☆ **Upwey** [B3159, nr junction A354 – OS Sheet 194 reference 666845; SY6684], *Masons Arms:* Fine atmosphere in largely unspoilt bar decorated with photographs of submarines and *Ark Royal*, fine collection of caps, shillelaghs and all sorts of plates, prints, foxes' brushes and oddments; Devenish ales, particularly good value bar food including fine salads, skittle alley; attractive garden, large children's play area *(Wendy and Ian Phillips)*

Upwey [A354 N of Weymouth, away from village], *Old Ship*: Old pub used by Thomas Hardy; character bar with large fireplace, skittle alley, well kept beer, good food, seats in garden *(John Hayward)*

☆ **Wareham** [South St; SY9287], *Quay*: Pub in charming quayside spot – until recently the New Inn; two spacious bars with stripped stone walls, open fire, friendly young bar staff, well presented bar food including vegetarian dishes, trendy music, good beer; parking nearby can be difficult *(Jackie and Jon Payne, T R Espley, WHBM)*

Wareham [41 North St (A351, N end of town)], *Kings Arms*: Flagstoned central corridor to back serving-counter divides the two traditional bars of this thatched town local; well kept Whitbreads Strong Country and Pompey Royal, bar food (not Fri–Sun evenings), back garden *(LYM)*

Waytown [between B3162 and A3066 N of Bridport; SY4697], *Hare & Hounds*: Seventeenth-century pub which also sells hard-to-find second-hand books (and offers a search service for these); Palmers real ales *(Anon)*

West Bay [SY4590], *George*: Overlooking the harbour at West Bay, Bridport's seaside village; well kept Palmers ales on handpump; good bar food including well filled crab sandwiches; nice mix of locals and holidaymakers *(David Fisher)*

☆ **West Knighton** [SY7387], *New*: Recently refurbished Devenish house, full of character, warm welcome; good value home cooking in bar and restaurant, skittle alley, garden; children's room *(Charles Bardswell)*

☆ **West Stour** [ST7822], *Ship*: Small and friendly well kept eighteenth-century local, with well kept Bass, Marstons Pedigree and Wadworths 6X on handpump, big log fire, good value nicely presented food in bar and intimate split-level restaurant, obliging attentive service, garden behind; bedrooms comfortable *(D A Ash, Nigel Paine and others)*

Weymouth [85 The Esplanade; SY6778], *Cork & Bottle*: Pleasantly old-fashioned and deceptively large cellar bar with bare boards and lots of interesting jugs and pots hanging from ceiling and walls; well kept Marstons Pedigree and Wadworths 6X, simple good value bar food including freshly prepared

pizzas, live bands Sun *(Peter Griffiths, S M House)*; [Barrack Rd, Nothe] *Nothe Tavern*: Big helpings of popular bar food and well kept Eldridge Pope ales in large local, sea views from back garden *(Mr and Mrs I M Howden, LYM)*; [Customhouse Quay] *Ship*: Spacious modern nautical-theme open-plan bar overlooking small, busy harbour; well kept Badger Best and Tanglefoot, good bar food including local crab salad, separate steak restaurant upstairs; children in lounge bar *(Stan Edwards, LYM)*

Wimborne Minster [The Square; SZ0199], *Kings Head*: Lunchtime food in well kept bar of THF hotel *(WHBM)*; [Uddens Cross (former A31, some way eastwards)] *Old Thatch*: Attractive thatched building in pleasant spot, recently renovated in Beefeater-style; open-plan, clean and modern, ample seating, no-smoking eating area, Flowers Original and Wadworths 6X, standard menu, pleasant service, piped music, seats outside; children's area *(Anon)*; [East St (A31)] *Rising Sun*: Clean and efficient pub, recently comfortably renovated, with large black-leaded kitchen range along one wall, full range of bar food including daily specials, Badger real ales, attractive streamside terrace *(Ian Phillips, Stan Edwards, BB)*; [Corn Market] *White Hart*: Alcoves and low seventeenth-century beams in old-fashioned bar with well kept Eldridge Pope Dorset, Dorchester and Royal Oak on handpump, bar food; in pedestrian precinct near north door of minster *(WHBM)*

☆ **Winterbourne Abbas** [A35 W of Dorchester; SY6190], *Coach & Horses*: Spacious recently refurbished pub, big on food, with reasonable prices and wide choice from rolls, sandwiches and ploughman's through good help-yourself salads to huge 20oz T-bone steaks and carvery with succulent joints; really welcoming atmosphere, brasses, hunting horns and pictures, stools with saddle seats, lots of barrel tables and comfortable chairs, also restaurant; generous helpings; attentive licensee, polite staff; bedrooms *(Mrs S A Bishop, T Muston, Sidney Drury, Jim Matthews)*

Yetminster [ST5910], *White Hart*: Popular, well run rural pub with well kept Bass and Oakhill Farmers, public and lounge bar and attractive exterior; beer garden *(A J Ritson)*

Durham   *see* Northumbria

Essex

A pub that didn't even figure in the Lucky Dip section in our last issue has soared straight into the main entries this year with a star award: it's the Cap & Feathers out at Tillingham, well worth tracking down for its good food and drink and, above all, splendid atmosphere and character. Other new main entries are the spaciously comfortable Old Anchor at Feering, the civilised and very ancient White Hart at Yeldham and the snug Red Lion at Lamarsh; and there are new licensees at the cosy Half Moon at Belchamp St Paul (the second change in just a year or two), the Generals Arms at Little Baddow (sadly, those interesting military tunics have gone, but it's as welcoming as ever) and the picturesque Bell at Woodham Walter. The county has a notable spread of interesting pubs, at least outside its big towns; among them, the Axe & Compasses at Arkesden (a happy place, currently doing very well), the stylish old Marlborough Head at Dedham, and the Eight Bells at Saffron Walden (with good wines by the glass, thanks to a new Cruover-style machine) are probably the pick of the bunch for food, though the Green Man at Toot Hill has its devotees – and with 40 champagnes and 100 still wines, including a fine choice by the glass, it's hard to beat on the wines side. For beers, the lively Hoop at Stock is outstanding. Other main entries particularly prominent in readers' affections at the moment are the friendly little Viper at Mill Green, the popular and relaxed Rose at Peldon and the cheerful Dolphin at Stisted. Among the Lucky Dip entries at the end of the chapter, Coggeshall has no fewer than three of particular promise, with another just outside; others to note include the Huntsman & Hounds at Althorne, Lion & Lamb at Canfield End, Cricketers at Clavering, Square & Compasses at Fuller Street, White Hart at Great Saling, Moreton Massey at Moreton, Ferryboat at North Fambridge, White Horse at Pleshey, Bear at Stock and Fleur de Lys at Widdington. Here and there in this chapter you'll come across things called huffers – a local name for very substantial filled soft rolls.

ARKESDEN   TL4834 Map 5
Axe & Compasses ★ 🍺
Village signposted from B1038 – but B1039 from Wendens Ambo, then forking left, is prettier; OS Sheet 154 reference 482344

An extremely happy, busy pub with consistently courteous, friendly service and a wide choice of appetising bar food. The rambling and comfortable carpeted saloon bar is distinctively furnished with cushioned oak and elm seats, quite a few easy chairs, old wooden tables, lots of brasses on the walls, and a bright coal fire. At lunchtime the food includes very good home-made soup such as tomato or minestrone (85p), generous wholemeal sandwiches (from 95p), various ploughman's (£1.75, the Stilton one is good), sausages, fish and grills with good, big chips, and home-made daily specials which the licensee and the chef dream up as they drive in to the pub each day – steak and kidney pie, beef and mushroom hot-pot, vegetarian dishes, a different roast three times a week, and so forth (£3.75), and puddings that include moist chocolate rum gateau, lovely lemon soufflé or home-made ice-cream specialities (£1.60). Each evening, there's a different 'theme': on Monday, a vegetarian menu (£4.25); Tuesday, fresh fish and scampi from Lowestoft (from £3.95); Wednesday, a £7.50 meal with steak or plaice as the main course, including a glass of wine or pint of bitter; Thursdays traditional English cooking – sausages, cottage pie, steak and kidney pie or lamb cutlets (from £2.75);

Fridays and Saturdays a grander range of full meals (£14) as well as bar snacks; Sundays, roast lunches (£9.35) and evening pasta (£4.25). Well kept Greene King Abbot, BBA ('Rayments') and IPA on handpump, good house wines, and several malts; part of the bar is set aside for non-alcoholic drinks. The smaller public bar, with cosy built-in settles, has sensibly placed darts, shove-ha'penny, dominoes, cribbage and a fruit machine. There are seats outside, on a side terrace with colourful hanging baskets; there's a popular barbecue here too on Saturday and Sunday lunchtimes – weather permitting. The village is pretty. *(Recommended by J S B Vereker, Dennis Royles, WTF, Mrs P Russell, R L Turnham, Joy Heatherley, Q Williamson, Gwen and Peter Andrews, S J A Velate)*

Greene King   Licensee Jerry Roberts   Real ale   Meals and snacks (not Mon evening) Restaurant tel *Saffron Walden (0799) 550272   Children in restaurant   Open 11–2.30, 6–11 all year; closed evening 25 Dec*

BANNISTER GREEN   TL6920 Map 5
Three Horseshoes

Village signposted with Felsted from A131 Chelmsford–Braintree opposite St Annes Castle pub; also signposted from B1417, off A120 Dunmow–Braintree at Felsted signpost

The chatty saloon bar on the right in this low dormer-windowed tiled white local has been extended to make more room for eating, though there's still the collection of pewter mugs hanging over the counter, horsebrasses, and big fireplace. They're also hoping – over the next year – to extend the bar on the left, which has a low seventeenth-century beam and plank ceiling, a high brown panelled dado, dark plush ribbed wall banquettes and spindle-back chairs around neat tables, and lots of brass and a musket decorating its fireplace; a separate games area may be created. The atmosphere is warm and relaxing, and the licensees particularly friendly. Good bar food includes pâté (£1.50), beef ploughman's (£1.90), ham and egg (£2.10), fisherman's pie, seafood platter (£2.50), gammon (£4.05) and chicken Kiev (£5.50); they do a cod or sausage and chips takeaway between 4–6pm on Fridays, and on Sunday there are nibbles such as roast potatoes and cheese and a late brunch; well kept Ridleys on handpump, decent wines by the glass and a good choice of whiskies; darts, shove-ha'penny, dominoes, cribbage, ring the bull (rare in Essex), fruit machine, and maybe unobtrusive piped late-1970s pop music. The neat side garden has picnic-table sets under cocktail parasols among fruit trees, with a summer weekend soft-drinks bar, and there are tables out on the big, quiet village green. *(Recommended by Graham Oddey, J H Walker, Gwen and Peter Andrews)*

Ridleys   Licensees John and Marcia Coward   Real ale   Meals and snacks (not Sun–Tues evenings)   Children in eating area   Occasional pie, mash and pianist nights   Open 10–3.30, 5.30–11; closed evening 25 Dec

BELCHAMP ST PAUL   TL7942 Map 5
Half Moon

Cole Green; Belchamp St Paul is on good back road Great Yeldham–Cavendish; the Belchamps are quite well signposted within the Sudbury–Clare–Sible Hedingham triangle

You can look out over the broad village green from the bow windows in this pretty white thatched pub. The neat lounge area has cushioned built-in wall benches and Windsor chairs on the dark red carpet, Elizabethan beams in its cream ceiling (steeply sloping under the low eaves), a glass-fronted solid-fuel stove, and a snug cubby by the serving counter. Bar snacks include sandwiches (95p, toasties £1.20), home-made soup (95p), ploughman's (£2.75) and scampi (£4.25), with more substantial meals such as vegetarian pancakes (£4.50), pork fillet in a creamy sauce with ham and cheese (£5.50), and peppered sirloin steak (£7.50); puddings (from £1.10); friendly service. Well kept Greene King IPA and Abbot, Nethergate Bitter and Old Growler on handpump from the temperature-controlled cellar; they also have Hackerpschorr, a full-flavoured real lager from Munich. The lively locals' bar has darts, dominoes, fruit machine and piped music. In summer a bar in the back beer garden serves soft drinks and so forth. *(Recommended by Gwen and Peter Andrews, J S Evans, NBM)*

Free house   Licensees Bob and Deni Horsfield   Real ale   Meals and snacks (12–2, 7.30–10; not Mon or Tues evenings)   Restaurant tel Clare (0787) 277402   Well behaved children welcome; not Fri or Sat evenings   Open 11.30–3, 7–11 all year; closed evening 25 Dec

BURNHAM-ON-CROUCH   TQ9596 Map 5

White Harte

The Quay

With its own private jetty, this hearty old inn is popular with boating people. There's a good view of the yachting estuary of the River Crouch from the window seat in the front bar, which also has old-fashioned, comfortably cushioned seats around oak tables on the polished parquet floor; other traditionally furnished, high-ceilinged rooms have sea pictures decorating the panelled or stripped brick walls. Attractively priced bar food consists of sandwiches or filled rolls (from 75p; toasties from £1.05, steak £2.50), and steak and kidney pie, boiled ham, lasagne and braised lamb chops (£2.50); service may not always be quick. Well kept Adnams and Tolly on handpump; dominoes. *(Recommended by Dave Butler, Lesley Storey, Graham Bush)*

Free house   Licensee John Lewis   Meals and snacks   Restaurant   Children in eating area of bar   Open 11–3, 6–11 all year   Bedrooms tel Maldon (0621) 782106; £18.15(£26.40B)/ £31.90(£44B)

CASTLE HEDINGHAM   TL7835 Map 5

Bell

B1058 towards Sudbury

Besides seats on a small terrace in the car park, there's a fine big walled garden behind the pub – an acre or so, with grass, trees and shrubs. Inside, the beamed and timbered busy saloon bar has Jacobean-style seats and Windsor chairs around oak tables, and there's a little gallery up some steps beyond standing timbers left from a knocked-through wall; a good mix of customers and maybe Lucia the Great Dane. Bar food includes ploughman's (£1.80), pâté (£2.20), half-pint of smoked prawns with garlic dip (£2.50), lasagne (£2.80), steak and Guinness pie or prawn Marsala (£3.30), trout (£4.30), and hot treacle tart (£1.40). Well kept Greene King IPA and Abbot tapped from the cask; brisk service; piped pop music. A games-room behind the traditionally furnished public bar has dominoes and cribbage. The twelfth-century castle keep is very striking. *(Recommended by Gwen and Peter Andrews, R M Sparkes, Tony Beaulah, Heather Sharland, J S Evans, Q Williamson)*

Grays (who no longer brew)   Licensee Mrs Sandra Ferguson   Real ale   Meals and snacks (12–2, 7–10 (9.30 Sun); not Mon evening exc bank hols)   Children welcome (not in public bar)   Open 11.30–2.30 (3 Sat), 6.15–11 all year; closed evening 25 Dec

CHAPPEL   TL8927 Map 5

Swan

Wakes Colne; pub visible just off A604 Colchester–Halstead

Standing oak timbers divide off side areas in the spacious carpeted lounge of this friendly 500-year-old rambling pub, with its low dark beams, banquettes around lots of dark tables, red velvet curtains on brass rings hanging from wooden curtain rails, and one or two swan pictures and plates on the white partly panelled walls; there are a few attractive tiles above the very big fireplace (log fires in winter, lots of plants in summer). Bar food includes filled French rolls (£1.20), sandwiches (from

£1.20), ploughman's (from £2), home-cooked ham (£2.50), basket meals (from £2.50), gammon steak and pineapple, fresh cod or home-made cottage pie (£2.95), home-made steak and kidney pie (£3.45) and sirloin steak (£6.50). Well kept Greene King IPA and Abbot, and Mauldons Bitter on handpump, and a good selection of wines by the glass; faint piped music; pool, dominoes, cribbage, pinball, fruit machine, space game, trivia and juke box in the biggish well furnished public bar. The very sheltered sun-trap cobbled courtyard has a slightly Continental flavour with its big tubs overflowing with flowers, parasols and French street signs; it's flanked on one side by the glass wall of the restaurant extension. The garden has picnic-table sets on grass stretching away from the big car park. The River Colne runs through the garden and below a splendid Victorian viaduct (which carries the Colne Valley Steam Railway, and steam enthusiasts will find the Railway Centre only ¼ mile away). *(Recommended by Gwen and Peter Andrews, John Evans, Quentin Williamson)*

Free house   Licensees Terence and Frances Martin   Real ale   Meals and snacks (11.30–2.30, 7–10.30; not 25 or 26 Dec)   Restaurant (no bookings)   Children in restaurant and eating area of bar   Open 11–3, 6–11 all year

DANBURY   TL7805 Map 5

Anchor

Runsell Green; just off A414 Chelmsford–Maldon

Probably originally a yeoman farmer's house, this listed building is largely fifteenth century. The more or less open-plan bar has heavy black oak beams, sturdy standing timbers, comfortable plush settles and stools around simple modern oak tables, masses of brass and copper around its fireplaces (including an engaging clock with a tinkling chime), and decorative plates on the cream walls. The conservatory/family-room – which also converts to an evening restaurant – is very popular. Big helpings of bar food include sandwiches (95p), soup (£1.35), ploughman's (£2.35), home-made chicken liver pâté with brandy (£2.25), pan-fried mussels in garlic butter or devilled whitebait (£2.65), hot Cromer crab Italian style (£3.50), scampi (£4.25), good steak, kidney and mushroom pie in Guinness or lamb cutlets grilled with Stilton (£4.95), steaks (from £6.75), Highland venison steak in a port and blackberry sauce (£7.75), and home-made puddings like blackberry and apple crumble (£1.75). Well kept Bass and Charrington IPA on handpump, 100 whiskies (including malts), and good dry white wine; efficient service, and a cheerful atmosphere (it can get crowded in the evening); fruit machine and juke box in side room. There are picnic-table sets on a raised front lawn with hollyhocks, roses and so forth, and swings behind. No dogs. *(Recommended by Tony Tucker, Gwen and Peter Andrews, Peter Griffiths, Roger Broadie)*

Charringtons (Bass)   Licensees C L and W E Abbott   Real ale   Meals and snacks (not Sun evening)   Evening restaurant tel Danbury (024 541) 2457; not Sun evening   Children in conservatory   Open 11–2.30, 6–11 all year; 11–11 Sat

DEDHAM   TM0533 Map 5

Marlborough Head 🏆

Opposite Constable's old school, this cheerful timbered inn has a wealth of finely carved woodwork in its central lounge; the refurbished beamed and timbered Constable bar is popular for eating, with many tables (which have a numbered pebble for ordering food) in wooden alcoves around its plum-coloured carpet. Bar food includes excellent soup (£1.10), sandwiches (from £1, £1.75 for sweet-cure ham with creamcheese, walnut and onion), baked potato with cheese (£1.10, with crunchy salad £1.50), ploughman's with home-made chutney or smoked salmon pâté (£2.50), bacon, mushroom and tomato quiche (£3.45), carrot and cashew-nut roulade (£3.50), turkey curry or flavoursome rabbit in mustard sauce (£4.35), Aga-roasted back bacon steak with peaches (£4.65), loin of pork with apple and brandy sauce (£4.65), excellent halibut and prawn bake (£4.75), English leg of lamb steak Longbow with creamy onion sauce (£5); puddings – such as home-made treacle tart (£1.60) or sherry trifle (£1.75) – are popular; get there early if you want a table; good value Sunday roast. Well kept Benskins Best and a guest beer on handpump; prompt, smiling service. There are seats in the garden behind. *(Recommended by Jan and Ian Alcock, M J Morgan, E J Knight, NIP, Gwen and Peter Andrews, J S Evans, Andy Tye, Sue Hill, Robert and Vicky Tod, Peter Griffiths, B K Scott, Alison Findlay)*

Ind Coope (Allied)   Licensee Brian Wills   Real ale   Meals and snacks   Children in family-room and Royal Square Room   Open 11–2.30, 6–11 all year; closed 25 and 26 Dec   Bedrooms tel Colchester (0206) 323250; £23S/£41S

FEERING   TL8720 Map 5
Old Anchor

B1024; take Kelvedon turn off A12 Chelsmford–Colchester and keep on right through Kelvedon

An old half-timbered village inn based on a pair of Tudor farm cottages, this has been extensively modernised inside to give a big rambling bar. It's comfortable and neatly kept, with plenty of bottle-green plush seats around black tables, various snug corners and alcoves – including one tiny cubicle like a confessional – and pictures of old Essex on the walls. Bar food includes filled French bread (from 80p), filled baked potatoes (from £1.20), a popular help-yourself salad bar (from £3.20) and a daily hot dish such as steak and kidney pie or fish pie (£3.40); Ruddles Best and County and Websters Yorkshire on handpump from the long serving-counter, and a reasonable choice of malt whiskies. There's a well lit pool-table around to the right, where the beams are heavier and lower, and where there's some black panelling and an attractive china cabinet; log fire, fruit machines, trivia machine; unobtrusive well reproduced piped music. There are tables in the sheltered garden. *(Recommended by Paul Barker, Alison Findlay, Heather Sharland, Brian Wood)*

Trumans   Licensees Mr and Mrs Martin Hopwood   Real ale   Meals and snacks   Restaurant   Open 11–2.30, 6–11 all year   Bedrooms tel Kelvedon (0376) 70684; £17.50/£25.50

FYFIELD   TL5606 Map 5
Black Bull

B184, N end of village

The several communicating but separate areas of the more or less H-shaped layout of this busy, tiled white village pub have low ceilings, big black beams, standing timbers, and cushioned wheel-back chairs and modern settles on the muted maroon carpet. It's particularly popular at lunchtime with businessmen and older people for its wide choice of good value food: guacamole (£2), smokies (£2.25), chicken tikka (£2.50), chilli con carne (£2.75), spinach and mushroom lasagne (£2.50), steak and kidney pie (£3), Mediterranean prawns (£5), shark steak (£5.35), pork (£5.40) and steaks (from £5.95); vegetables, salad or bread are extra; they have a policy that those who book get served first, even if they arrive later than those who haven't booked. Well kept Bass and Charrington IPA on handpump, piped music (unobtrusive, under the buzz of conversation), fruit machine; efficient service. By the car park, an aviary under a fairy-lit arbour has budgerigars and cockatiels, and there are picnic-table sets on a stretch of grass further back, and to the side of the building. *(Recommended by Alan and Ruth Woodhouse; more reports please)*

Charringtons (Bass)   Licensee Alan Smith   Real ale   Meals and snacks (12–1.45, 7–9.30)   Open 11–2.30 (3 Sat), 6–11

nr GREAT HENNY   TL8738 Map 5
Swan

Henny Street; A131 from Sudbury, left at Middleton road at foot of Ballingdon hill; OS Sheet
155 reference 879384

This small pub has a new Victorian-style conservatory leading on to a terrace in the
garden, where there's a pond and rustic benches among the willows on a delightful
riverside lawn; fishing permits are available, and barbecues are held on Sundays in
fine weather. Inside, the L-shaped lounge has well cushioned seats, timbered walls,
a big fireplace with a log-effect gas fire, and a cosy atmosphere. Bar food (with
prices virtually the same as last year) includes sandwiches (from 85p), good home-
made soup (95p), pâté (£1.80), scampi (£3.95), sole or trout (£5.90), steaks (from
£7.25), half a roast duck (£6.50), pheasant (in season, £8), and daily specials like
home-made steak and kidney pie, moussaka, crab salad, lamb curry or guinea-fowl
(from £2.50). Well kept Greene King IPA and Abbot on handpump; maybe Radio
Chiltern. *(Recommended by John Branford, Joy Heatherley, Gwen and Peter Andrews,
J S Evans, Alison Findlay)*

*Greene King   Licensee P A Underhill   Real ale   Meals (not Sun evening) and snacks
Restaurant tel Twinstead (078 729) 238 (not Sun evening)   Children in eating area of
bar until 9   Open 11–3, 6–11 all year; closed evening 25 Dec*

GREAT YELDHAM   TL7638 Map 5
White Hart

Poole Street; A604 Halstead–Haverhill

Samuel Pepys is said to have endorsed the licence application of this striking black
and white timbered and jettied tiled Tudor house; it's surrounded by well kept
lawns, where white cast-iron tables stand among lots of trees and shrubs. The oak-
panelled bar has very heavy beams, attractive antique Morland prints, winged easy
chairs, settees and wall settles; it opens into an extension, giving the feel of three
separate room areas. Genuine bar food consists of soup (£1.50), filled French bread
(from 90p), French bread with three sausages (£2.25), ploughman's with a choice of
English cheeses (£2.50), omelettes (from £2.50), a proper chilli con carne (£3,
winter), salads (from £3.25) and a dish of the day such as fresh Lowestoft cod or
locally smoked pork chops (£3.75); well kept Nethergate on handpump; log fire,
magazines to read, calm atmosphere. *(Recommended by Howard Gascoyne; more reports
please)*

*Free house   Licensee David Smillie   Real ale   Meals and snacks (not Sun evening)
Restaurant (not Sun evening) tel Great Yeldham (0787) 237250   Children welcome
Open 11–3, 6.30 (6 Sat)–11 all year*

HASTINGWOOD   TL4807 Map 5
Rainbow & Dove

¼ mile from M11 junction 7; Hastingwood signposted from exit roundabout

This popular rose-covered sixteenth-century cottage has a bar area with three small
low-beamed rooms opening off. The one on the left is particularly snug and beamy
with the lower part of the wall stripped back to bare brick and decorated with old
golf clubs, brass pistols and plates. Elsewhere, there are big brass platters, brass
horseshoes and so forth, with horse-collars, the odd halberd and boomerang, and
even a collection of garden ornaments in one fireplace. Simple bar food (popular
with businessmen at lunchtime) includes sandwiches, ploughman's (from £2.10),
sausages (£2.70), smoked haddock and prawn pasta or lasagne (£2.85), scampi
(£3.60) and eight-ounce rump steak (£7.50); it gets busy at weekends; maybe piped
radio. Picnic-table sets under cocktail parasols, on a stretch of grass hedged off

from the car park, are bordered by an 18-hole putting course and a paddock; there may be a children's summer bar out here at busy times, and there are summer Sunday evening barbecues. *(Recommended by Col A H N Reade, Joy Heatherley, Steve Waters, Jenny Cantle, Alan and Ruth Woodhouse)*

Ind Coope (Allied)   Licensee A R Bird   Meals (12–2, 7–10; not Mon evening)   Children welcome   Open 11.30–2.30, 6.30–11 all year

HIGH EASTER   TL6214 Map 5
Cock & Bell
The Easters signposted from the Rodings, on B184/A1060

Very much the focal point of the village, this listed medieval house has a warmly welcoming atmosphere and generously served food (which won them the *Pubcaterer* competition in 1988–9). This includes burger (£1.05), sandwiches (from £1.10), sirloin steak in French bread (£1.95), ploughman's (£2.75), pâté (£2.95), super home-made wholemeal quiche or home-cooked ham salad (£3.45), eggs caviare or lasagne (£3.95), scampi (£4.45), home-made steak and mushroom pie (£4.75), a cold plate of meat, cheese and fish (£4.95), and suprême of chicken poached in white wine and herbs with Stilton and brandy sauce (£7.25); home-made puddings like scrumpy apple pie (£1.75) and children's dishes (from £1.55); three-course Sunday lunch (£7.95). They have occasional Dickensian evenings in winter and barbecues with a marquee in summer (£10). Well kept Flowers IPA, John Smiths and Tolly on handpump; a good choice of house wines; piped music. The carpeted lounge bar has comfortably cushioned Windsor chairs, massive oak beams and vases of fresh flowers. The cheerful public bar has the oldest dragon-beam ceiling in Essex, a log fire and fruit machine. Outside this heavily timbered black and white house is a terrace and garden with a play area. They no longer do bedrooms. *(Recommended by E J Cutting, Jack and Dorothy Rayner, Alan and Ruth Woodhouse, Gwen and Peter Andrews, NBM, Roger Danes)*

Trumans (Watneys)   Licensee Barrie Day   Real ale   Meals and snacks   Children welcome   Restaurant   Open 12–2.30, 7–11 all year

HORNDON-ON-THE-HILL   TQ6683 Map 3
Bell
A quaint and charming country pub with a happy blend of locals and visitors. Seats in a bow window at the back of the open-plan bar have views over the fields, and there are some antique high-backed settles, plush burgundy stools and benches, flagstones or highly polished oak floorboards, and timbering and panelling; the fossilised objects hanging from the ceiling are hot-cross buns – collected, one a year, since 1900, though perhaps the wood carvings hanging from a block on the panelling and collected over much the same period are more edifying. Good bar food includes sandwiches, lasagne (£3.10), steak and kidney pie (£3.40), venison with herbs and blackcurrant (£3.50), and up to ten changing dishes, freshly made each day, are chalked up on a blackboard. Well kept Charrington IPA on handpump with Bass tapped from the cask. The sheltered back yard has picnic-table sets, pretty hanging baskets (which won a local flower competition), old mangles used as flowerpots, and a fountain. They do very much go in for sport; they have a ski club, a team in the London to Brighton cycle ride, and are coming up to their fourteenth year of the monthly Fun Runs every second Wednesday in summer (7pm start); the village cricket team were the Essex winners of the National Village Competition. *(Recommended by E G Parish, Graham Bush, Graham Oddey, Anne Heaton, Peter Griffiths)*

Charringtons (Bass)   Licensee John Vereker   Real ale   Meals and snacks (not Sun lunchtime)   Restaurant   Children in eating area of bar   Open 10.30–2.30, 6–11
Bedrooms in house two doors away tel Stanford-le-Hope (0375) 673154; /£40B

LAMARSH   TL8835 Map 5
Red Lion

From Bures on B1508 Sudbury–Colchester take Station Road, passing station; Lamarsh then signposted

In a relatively hilly part of the county, this looks down on the undulating fields and colour-washed houses of the Stour Valley; tables and small pews set by the front windows, in stalls with red velvet curtain dividers, make the most of the view. The quiet, timbered bar is softly lit, with a Turkey carpet, lots of timbering, and huge logs smouldering in a big brick sixteenth-century fireplace. Good value bar food shows some eclectic touches, such as a pea and bacon soup (95p) or the Greek-style tuna salad with feta cheese (£2.95); other things include sandwiches (from £1), filled baked potato (£1.35), ploughman's (from £1.95), spaghetti bolognese, ham and egg or pork loin and mushroom sauce (£2.95), a hefty double burger (£3.50), generous mixed grill (£4.95) and steaks (rump £6.95), with good rare roast beef on Sundays. Well kept Adnams and Greene King IPA on handpump, decent wines by the glass and good coffee; quietly friendly service – readers liked the moment when the landlady invited in a group of young hikers who'd been trying to eat their own sandwiches in pouring rain outside. A timbered-off area has pool and darts; maybe unobtrusive piped music. The restaurant is in a former barn. There are swings in the biggish sheltered sloping garden. Paradise Centre – on the left up Twinstead Lane – on the left after the church if you head towards Sudbury) is an interesting nursery. *(Recommended by Jenny Cantle, Gwen and Peter Andrews, Denis Korn, NBM)*

Free house   Licensees John and Angela O'Sullivan   Real ale   Meals and snacks (12–2, 7–10)   Restaurant (Thurs–Sat evenings, Sun lunch) tel Bures (0787) 227918   Children in eating area and restaurant (not after early evening)   Open 11–3, 6–11 all year

LEIGH ON SEA   TQ8385 Map 3
Crooked Billet

51 High Street; from A13 follow signpost to station, then cross bridge over railway towards waterside

Sympathetically redecorated this year, this unspoilt pub has a lounge bar with two big bay windows, cushioned seats facing into the room built in around the walls, shiny yellowing walls decorated with photographs of local cockle smacks, and a solid-fuel stove; on the left, the public bar has new bare floorboards, a huge log fire, more photographs, and sensibly placed darts, shove-ha'penny and cribbage. Well kept Ind Coope Burton, Taylor-Walker, and Tetleys on handpump; filled rolls (from 75p), and ploughman's, chilli con carne and hot-pots (from £2.50). They have picnic-table sets and long stoutly painted tables and benches out on a big terrace by the ancient wooden salt store and the sea wall – which itself is a nice place to sit on, looking down on the shellfish boats in the old-fashioned working harbour. Out here, they don't mind you eating cockles, shrimps or jellied eels from Ivy Osborne's marvellous stall just down the lane (it shuts at 10pm). *(Recommended by Graham Bush, R Inns)*

Ind Coope (Allied)   Licensee Alan Downing   Real ale   Meals and snacks (lunchtime, not Sun, and quiet evenings)   Open 11.30–3, 6–11 all year; longer afternoon opening in fine weather

LITTLE BADDOW   TL7807 Map 5
Generals Arms

The Ridge; minor road Hatfield Peverel–Danbury

New licensees have taken over this friendly pub, and tables have been added to the lounge bar and the children's room refurbished for functions and Sunday lunches.

There are original beams, attractively exposed brickwork, red plush button-back wall banquettes and dimpled copper tables, an interesting biography of the pub's namesake on the wall, and a very big collection of sailor hat ribands; log effect gas fires. Bar food includes filled baked potatoes or sandwiches (from £1.25), jumbo sausage (£1.75), ploughman's (from £1.95), lemon sole or lasagne (£3.50) and gammon (£3.95); as we went to press, they were hoping to open a restaurant. Well kept Bass and Charrington IPA on handpump; darts, dominoes, cribbage and fruit machine. There are picnic-table sets among neatly kept rose beds and three fine old holly trees on the big side lawn, and a children's play area with swings, climbing-frame and slide. *(More reports please)*

Charringtons (Bass)   Licensees Mr and Mrs K Surtees   Real ale   Meals and snacks   Open 11–3, 6–11 all year

LITTLE BRAXTED   TL8314 Map 5

Green Man

Kelvedon Road; village signposted off B1389 by NE end of A12 Witham bypass – keep on patiently

Tucked away on a very quiet lane, this pretty tiled brick house has picnic-set tables in the sheltered back garden. Inside, the cosy little traditional lounge has a collection of 200 horsebrasses and some harness, as well as mugs hanging from a beam, a lovely copper urn, an open fire, and a quiet, friendly atmosphere. Good value bar food includes sandwiches (from 80p, excellent steak), filled baked potatoes (from £1), hot locally baked French bread filled with ham off the bone, sardines, chicken, turkey, beef or even meaty haggis brought from Scotland (from £1.15), pâté (£1.50), ploughman's (from £1.95), lasagne, beef curry, or a very hot chilli con carne (£2.60), and big salads (from £4). Well kept Ridleys is dispensed from handpumps in the form of 40-millimetre brass cannon shells, and there are several malt whiskies; piped music. The tiled public bar leads to a games-room with darts, shove-ha'penny, dominoes, cribbage and fruit machine. *(Recommended by Alan and Ruth Woodhouse, Roger Huggins, Peter Griffiths, Gwen and Peter Andrews, Hope Chenhalls, Alison Findlay)*

Ridleys   Licensee Eion MacGregor   Real ale   Meals and snacks (12–2.15, 7.30–10) Children in eating area of bar   Open 11–3, 6–11 all year

LOUGHTON   TQ4296 Map 5

Gardeners Arms

2¼ miles from M11 junction 5; in Loughton, turn left on to A121, then right at war memorial and Kings Head on right; 103 York Hill

The atmosphere in the spacious open-plan bar here manages to stay relatively intimate, helped by the low lighting and ceilings (except in one place, where it soars up to the full height of the pitched roof). It's civilised and soberly decorated, with good prints, engravings and pencil drawings of this and other picturesque old inns (including some by Cecil Aldin), two or three Delft shelves, some figured plates on the walls, an aged kitchen clock, guns above the beam where the bar opens into the restaurant area, and a couple of open fires. Appealing bar food includes sandwiches (from £1, toasties from £1.20, steak £3.35), Scotch broth, a choice of ploughman's (£2.10), omelettes (£2.70), lasagne (£3.15), home-cooked ham and eggs (£3.45), salads (from £2.80, home-cooked meats from £3.40), steak, kidney and mushroom pie (£4.25), seafood pancake (£4.75), good liver and bacon, and eight-ounce rump steak (from £6.75); daily specials are chalked up on a blackboard; as it's all freshly cooked, they warn of delays of 20–30 minutes with some dishes. Well kept Ruddles County, Best and Websters Yorkshire on handpump; efficient friendly service; fruit machine, maybe piped music. Outside this tiled and weatherboarded house there's a little front verandah, and spreading views that include parts of Epping Forest from the picnic-table sets on the side terrace. *(Recommended by Joy Heatherley, Steve Evans, Stanley Matthews, Mr and Mrs G T Hunt)*

Watneys   Licensee Robert Worrell   Real ale   Lunchtime meals and snacks (not Sun) Restaurant tel 01(081)-508 1655; closed Sun evening   Open 11–3, 6–11 all year

MILL GREEN   TL6400 Map 5
Viper

Highwood Road; from Fryerning (which is signposted off *north-east bound* A12 Ingatestone bypass) follow Writtle signposts; OS Sheet 167 reference 640019

Idyllically set in an oak wood, with a bank of sweet chestnuts behind it, this homely cottage is popular with walkers. The parquet-floored tap-room (where booted walkers are directed) has simple shiny wooden traditional wall seats, and leads to a further room with country kitchen chairs and sensibly placed darts. The two little rooms of the lounge have a low ochre ceiling, pale hessian walls (the log fireplace is in a stripped brick wall), spindle-back seats, armed country kitchen chairs, and tapestried wall seats around neat little old tables, vases of flowers in summer, and maybe the pub cat. Bar snacks include soup (95p), sandwiches (from £1, toasties from £1.10), Hawaiian toast (£1.50), chilli con carne (£1.95) and ploughman's (from £2.20). Well kept Ruddles Best and County on handpump from the oak-panelled bar counter; shove-ha'penny, dominoes, cribbage, table skittles and a fruit machine. The garden is lovely – masses of nasturtiums, foxgloves, geraniums and lathyrus around the tables on a neat lawn, with honeysuckle and overflowing hanging baskets and window boxes on the pub itself. *(Recommended by Graham Oddey, Roy Clark, Nigel Paine)*

Trumans (Watneys)   Licensee Fred Beard   Real ale   Snacks   Open 11–2.30 (3 Sat), 6–11

NEWNEY GREEN   TL6507 Map 5
Duck

Village signposted off A414 W of Chelmsford

Attractively furnished, this popular country pub has dark beams and joists, ancient-looking pictures and old farm and garden tools on the partly dark-panelled and partly timbered walls, a wind-up gramophone, and a coal-effect gas fire in a big two-faced brick fireplace draped with hop-bines. Some of the many tables are tucked between high-backed booth seats, though most have wheel-back chairs, and there are one or two interesting seats such as the great curved high-backed settle in one of the alcoves. The atmosphere is almost cosy, even though the pub spreads extensively enough to cope with very considerable numbers of people; piped music. Food from a servery by the bar includes filled baps (from £1.25) and ploughman's (from £2 – both these at lunchtime only), vegetarian Stroganoff (£3.50), chicken hot-pot pie (£3.75), gammon and pineapple or salads (£4.50), whole lemon sole stuffed with crab (£4.75), venison casserole (£5.50), roast half duck (£6.50) and puddings like home-made pancakes (from £1.25); you're given a big wooden duck with your number on when you order. Well kept Adnams, Crouch Vale Best and Greene King Abbot and IPA, and Mauldons Bitter on handpump; also, several malt whiskies and cocktails. The garden by the huge car park has tables under cocktail parasols, lit by old street lamps; there are two big lily ponds (with anti-heron defences for the goldfish) in a rockery, and a hollow play tree for children with swings, a slide and a treehouse. *(Recommended by Gwen and Peter Andrews, John Baker, P Miller, Dave Butler, Lesley Storey, NBM, P J and S E Robbins)*

Free house   Licensee Gerald Ambrose   Real ale   Lunchtime snacks (not Mon) and meals (not Sun evening or Mon)   Open 11.30–3, 6.30–11; closed Mon and 25 Dec

Ring the bull is an ancient pub game – you try to lob a ring on a piece of string over a hook (occasionally a bull's horn) on the wall or ceiling.

PELDON   TL9916 Map 5
Rose

B1025 Colchester–Mersea, at junction with southernmost turn-off to Peldon

A large no-smoking conservatory in this busy, pink-washed house overlooks the garden (where there are good teak seats, a swing and a seesaw) and two ponds with ducks and geese. The bar has a cosy, relaxed atmosphere, mostly antique mahogany and sometimes rather creaky, close-set tables, one or two standing timbers supporting the low ceiling with its dark bowed oak beams, timbered cream walls, and chintz curtains in the leaded-light windows. Brass and copper decorate the mantelpiece of the gothick-arched brick fireplace, and there may be bunches of flowers. The food servery, beside a stripped pine dresser on an old-fashioned brick floor, does winter Dutch pea or Hungarian goulash soup, sandwiches, beef curry (£3.55), lasagne (£3.80), steak and kidney pie or Italian chicken (£3.85), steaks and Sunday roast beef (£5.25); other alcovey areas lead off here. Well kept Adnams on handpump and quite a few wines; attentive service – and a golden and a black labrador and a black and white cat. *(Recommended by Mr and Mrs T F Marshall, Gwen and Peter Andrews, D R Linnell, Alison Findlay, P J and S E Robbins)*

Free house   Licensees Ariette and Alan Everett   Real ale   Meals and snacks (12–2, 7–10)   Restaurant; only Fri and Sat evening   Children welcome (not in main bar) until 9   Occasional pianist in conservatory   Open 11–2.30, 5.30–11 all year   Bedrooms tel Peldon (020 635) 248; £20/£30

PURLEIGH   TL8401 Map 5
Bell

The rambling main bar in this clean, bright and friendly pub has heavy black beams and timbers, cushioned wall banquettes and Windsor chairs on the carpet, a huge log fire, and seats in the front bow window that look out over hedged flatlands to the Blackwater Estuary. Good simple food is made by the landlord's mother: sandwiches (from 80p, toasties 10p extra), pizza (£1.50), ploughman's (£1.60), ham and egg (£2), salads (from £2.30), plaice (£2.60) and scampi (£3); anyone not using the bar will have a 50p service charge added to the price of their food. Well kept Adnams and Benskins Best on handpump; dominoes, cribbage, trivia. Picnic-table sets on the side grass have estuary views; New Hall Vineyard is close by. George Washington's great-great-grandfather was rector in the neighbouring church until, in 1642, he was turned out for spending too much time in taverns. *(Recommended by Graham Bush, Quentin Williamson, Dr Paul Kitchener, John and Helen Thompson, Alison Findlay)*

Ind Coope (Allied)   Licensee Robert A Cooke   Real ale   Meals (not Fri–Sun evenings) and snacks   Open 11–3, 6–11 all year

SAFFRON WALDEN   TL5438 Map 5
Eight Bells 🏵

Bridge Street; B184 towards Cambridge

Reliably good food that changes every day continues to draw lots of people to this handsomely timbered black and white Tudor building: seafood, mostly fresh from Lowestoft, includes mussels marinière (£2.95), prawns (£2.55), good grilled fresh plaice or scampi (£4.95), baked fresh cod with cream, dill and lemon (£4.75), baked devilled crab (£4.95) and fresh skate or prawns thermidor (£5.25, also available as a vegetarian dish with mushrooms instead of prawns) both with garlic bread. Other dishes include omelettes (£3.95), home-made lasagne (£4.25), home-made steak and kidney pie (£5.50), good beef carbonnade, mixed grill (£5.95) and charcoal-grilled steaks (from £6.95); there's a popular summer cold buffet, lunchtime snacks such as home-made soup (£1.35), ploughman's (from £2.45), home-made pâtés (from £2.65) and fresh wholemeal pasta noodles with cream, mushrooms and garlic (£2.95), home-made puddings (from £1.95), daily specials and cream teas (£2.45). A good children's menu (from £1.40, including a drink, and quite a few things on the main menu are served in half portions). The neatly kept open-plan bar is divided up by the old timbers of a knocked-through wall, and has modern oak settles forming small booths around its tables; there's a family-room in the tiled-floor tap-room. Well kept Adnams, Benskins and Ind Coope Burton and Tetleys on handpump, and between six and ten wines by the glass from a Cruover-like cabinet; several coffees and teas; fruit machine. The restaurant, in a splendidly timbered hall with high rafters, has high-backed settles forming booths, and a very long refectory table. There are seats in the garden. Nearby Audley End makes a good family outing, and the pub is near the start of *Good Walks Guide* Walk 107. *(Recommended by R C Vincent, Joy Heatherley, Wayne Brindle, Gwen and Peter Andrews, Alison Findlay, Tony Gayfer, Tom, Lorna, Audrey and Alan Chatting, G and J Halphide, Gordon Theaker)*

Ind Coope (Allied)   Licensee Robin Moore   Real ale   Meals and snacks (noon–9.30; 12–2.30, 6–9.30 Mon)   Restaurant (not Sun evening)   Children in family-room and restaurant   Open 10am–11pm; 11–3, 6–11 Mon; closed 25–26 Dec   Bedrooms tel Saffron Walden (0799) 22790; /£33

STISTED   TL7924 Map 5

Dolphin

A120 E of Braintree

This friendly roadside pub has a heavily beamed and timbered room with comfortable banquettes on the black wood floor, an open fire, soft lighting, piped music – and darts, dominoes, cribbage, fruit machine and piped music; the other has a collection of chamber-pots. Bar food includes sandwiches (from 85p), home-made pies or roasts (£3), chilli con carne or curries (£3.50) and lots of puddings (90p). Well kept Adnams Extra and Ridleys PA are tapped from wooden casks behind the bar; chilled fresh orange juice; cheerful staff. The garden has an aviary with rabbits and cockatiels, a well equipped children's play area, and there are self-service barbecues; there's also a paddock with a pony and goats. *(Recommended by Gwen and Peter Andrews, Alison Findlay)*

Ridleys   Licensee John French   Real ale   Meals and snacks (not Tues evening)   Children in eating area of bar   Open 10.30–3, 5.30–11 all year; open 10.30am–11pm Sat

STOCK   TQ6998 Map 5

Hoop

B1007; from A12 Chelmsford bypass take Galleywood, Billericay turn-off

On the May Day weekend, this busy, cheerful little pub has a hundred real ales available. They normally have Adnams Bitter and Mild, Boddingtons, Hook Norton Old Hooky, Marstons Pedigree and Owd Rodger, Nethergate, Theakstons Old Peculier and Wadworths 6X on handpump or more likely tapped from the cask, with Timothy Taylors Landlord every fortnight, and two or three guest beers such as Brains Red Dragon, Robinsons Mild and Palmers Tally Ho. There are brocaded wall seats around dimpled copper tables on the left, and a cluster of brocaded stools on the right – where there's a coal-effect gas fire in the big brick fireplace; a new extension provides extra seating. Bar food includes sandwiches (from 70p), home-made soup (£1), filled baked potatoes (from £1), ploughman's (£1.50), omelettes (from £1.50), quiche or home-cooked ham and egg (£2), meaty grilled trout (caught by the licensee or his friends from their local reservoir) or steak and kidney pudding (£4), specials like rabbit stew or braised oxtail with dumplings or stuffed peppers (all £4), and puddings (£1); attentive staff. Sensibly placed darts (the heavy black beams are studded with hundreds of darts flights), cribbage and dominoes; farm cider, decent wines by the glass, and mulled wine in winter. The dog is called Misty and the cat Thomas (she has produced kittens since the last edition). There are lots of picnic-table sets in the big sheltered back garden, which is prettily bordered with flowers and where they have occasional summer barbecues and maybe croquet (or boules on the front gravel). *(Recommended by Graham Oddey, Gwen and Peter Andrews, Quentin Williamson, Nigel Paine, Dave Butler, Lesley Storey, Graham Bush)*

Free house   Licensee Albert Kitchin   Real ale   Meals and snacks (all day) Open 10am–11pm all year

TILLINGHAM   TL9903   Map 5

Cap & Feathers ★

B1027 N of Southminster

It's the delightfully warm and relaxed atmosphere which earns the star award here – though there are plenty of other really good points. Many people would put the drinks high on their list, including well kept Crouch Vale Woodham, Best, SAS, Essex Porter and in winter Willie Warmer, with Thatchers farm cider, decent wines by the glass, good coffee. Bar food features succulent and distinctively flavoured products of their own smokery – thinly sliced beef as a starter (£2.50), cod (£4.30), trout (£4.60) and specials such as pheasant (£4.60); the smoked mackerel is not local. Other home-cooked dishes include sandwiches (from 95p), burgers (from £1.30, vegetarian £1.40), ploughman's (from £2.75), fish pie (ingredients caught by the landlord, if he's been lucky – £3.95), a couple of vegetarian dishes (£3.95), steak and ale pie (£4.25), good steaks (from eight-ounce sirloin £5.80) and a generous mixed grill (£5.95); puddings are traditional – fruit crumble, rice pudding and so forth. The bar divides into three snug areas, with uneven low beams, timbers, sturdy wall seats (including a venerable built-in floor-to-ceiling settle), little wheel-back chairs with arms, a homely dresser and a formidable wood-burning stove; one parquet-floored part has bar billiards, sensibly placed darts, and table skittles – there's another set in the attractive family-room, and they have shove-ha'penny, cribbage and dominoes. Service is notably friendly and helpful. There are a few picnic-table sets under birch trees on a small side terrace; the village is quiet. *(Recommended by Gwen and Peter Andrews, Peter Seddon, P Cammiade, Simon Wilmshurst)*

Crouch Vale   Licensees Ollie and Carol Graham   Real ale   Meals and snacks   Children in family-room   Folk music first Thurs and Sun in month   Open 11.30–3, 7–11 all year

TOOT HILL   TL5103   Map 5

Green Man

Village signposted from A113 in Stanford Rivers, S of Ongar; and from A414 W of Ongar

A smallish and simply furnished area by the bar has mushroom plush chairs and pale mustard leatherette stools and settles, one or two hunting prints above the dark varnished wood dado, brass platters on a shelf just below the very dark grey-green ceiling, and an open fire. Well chosen wines from five wine merchants include forty different well served champagnes by the bottle (many pinks, including their doyenne, Veuve Clicquot), with one sold by the glass, and over a hundred wines (they have a wine of the week); there are also Beaujolais tastings. As well as sandwiches and good soup, the home-cooked food might include vegetable parcel (£2), fish stew or herring roes on toast (£2.50), quail with walnut stuffing (£2.60), wild rabbit with herb dumplings (£4), home-made steak and kidney pie (£4.50) and veal kidneys in Dijon mustard (£5). Well kept Ruddles Best and Websters Yorkshire on handpump; friendly service. There may be nibbles of Cheddar and cheesy biscuits; darts around the other side, shove-ha'penny, dominoes, cribbage and maybe piped Radio 1. The main emphasis is on the long dining lounge a step up from here, with candlelit tables, fresh flowers and attractively figured plates on a Delft shelf. In the evenings they take bookings for tables in here, but only for 7.30;

after that, when you turn up they put you on a queue for tables that come free. In summer there's a lovely mass of colourful hanging baskets, window boxes and flower tubs, prettily set off by the curlicued white iron tables and chairs. Many more picnic-table sets on the grass behind have a fine view over the quiet rolling fields and woods to North Weald. *(Recommended by MN, Joy Heatherley, Dave Butler, Lesley Storey, Alan and Ruth Woodhouse, Mr and Mrs Darlow, Roger Broadie, Gwen and Peter Andrews)*

Watneys   Licensee P J Roads   Real ale   Meals and snacks (not 25 Dec)   Restaurant tel North Weald (037 882) 2255   Children over 10 only   Open 11–3, 6–11 all year

WOODHAM WALTER   TL8006 Map 5
Bell

New licensees have taken over this lovely tiled and timbered Elizabethan building, with its memorable lounge bar: neatly kept, but friendly and informal, and divided into irregularly shaped alcoves on various levels, with old timbers and beams, comfortable seats and a log fire. The bar food is standard – sandwiches (from 75p), soup (£1.10), sausage in French bread (£1.20), ploughman's (from £1.75), salads (from £3.50) and daily specials; there's a prettily decorated dining-room in a partly panelled gallery up steps from the main bar. Well kept Benskins Best on handpump. *(Recommended by Gwen and Peter Andrews, Helen and John Thompson, Dave Butler, Lesley Storey, Alison Findlay)*

Ind Coope (Allied)   Licensee Bill Tuck   Real ale   Meals (not Sun evening) and snacks Well behaved children welcome   Restaurant (not Sun or Mon evenings) tel Danbury (024 541) 3437   Open 11–3, 6–11 all year

Cats

On back road to Curling Tye and Maldon, from N end of village

This black and white timbered cottage has a rambling traditional bar with bow windows, button-back red leatherette seats, black beams and timbering set off well by neat white paintwork, and a collection of china cats on the mantelpiece over the open fire. The food is very simple and straightforward, and the Adnams, Greene King IPA and Abbot and Mauldons on handpump particularly well kept; they have another real ale, brewed specially for them, called Cats Piss; friendly service. The well kept garden, looking out over quiet fields, makes this pretty cottage – its roof decorated with prowling stone cats – an attractive place in summer. *(Recommended by Gwen and Peter Andrews)*

Free house   Snacks   Real ale   Open 10.30–2, 6.30ish–11 all year; closed Mon, Tues, Weds, though may be only in winter

Lucky Dip

Besides the fully inspected pubs, you might like to try these Lucky Dips recommended to us and described by readers (if you do, please send us reports):

Abridge [TQ4696], *Maltsters Arms*: Crockery all over the ceiling, well kept Greene King and Youngs, basic lunchtime bar food; busy at weekends *(MN)*; [Market Pl] *White Hart*: Well kept Bass and Flowers IPA and good value well presented bar food *(R P Hastings)*
Aldham [Ford St; A604 2 miles W of A12; TL9125], *Queens Head*: Delightful pub with lots of whisky-water jugs hanging from beams; seven beers on draught, good food in bar (including marvellous toasties) and restaurant; piped music *(Paul Barker)*

☆ **Althorne** [TQ9199], *Huntsman & Hounds*: Popular country local – enlarged thatched cottage, long bar and L-shaped extensions at each end with open fire, low beams decorated with brasses, plates, mugs and foreign bank notes; well kept Greene King IPA and Abbot, good bar food, friendly staff, unobtrusive piped music, decent garden *(Alison Findlay, Peter Seddon, Gwen and Peter Andrews, LYM)*
Ardleigh [Harwich Rd; A137 – actually towards Colchester; TM0529], *Wooden*

Fender: Comfortably modernised open-plan beamed bar with usual pub food, well kept Adnams, Greene King IPA and Abbot and Marstons Pedigree on handpump, log fire, piped music, restaurant allowing children, a pool in back garden *(Gwen and Peter Andrews, LYM)*

Battlesbridge [Hawk Hill; TQ7894], *Barge*: Taylor-Walker cottage-type pub with more seating in outbuilding; simple but inviting bar lunches, barge pictures *(B R Wood)*; *Hawk*: Light and airy, with comfortable seats, friendly staff, Charrington ales, interesting generously served lunchtime bar food, garden – this bypassed village is attractive, with an antiques and crafts centre, old mills, sailing-barge mooring *(B R Wood, Jenny Cantle)*

Beaumont [byroad between B1035 and B1414; TM1724], *Swan*: Small pub off beaten track with reasonable bar food, Adnams real ale *(T Nott)*

☆ **Beazley End** [off B1053 N of Braintree; TL7428], *Cock*: Neat and spacious beamed lounge with good atmosphere, open fire and fascinating clock, village bar with pool and darts, restaurant decorated with corn dollies; well kept Adnams, Beazley (brewed for them by Mauldons) and Crouch Vale on handpump, farm cider, good choice of interesting bar food and unobtrusive piped music; no dogs, as the bar is ruled by their marmalade cat *(Gwen and Peter Andrews)*

Billericay [Sun St; TQ6794], *Rising Sun*: Friendly two-bar pub, reasonably plush lounge with fireplace, basic public bar with darts; Benskins Best on handpump *(Robert Lester)*

Birchanger [nr M11 junction 8 – right turn off A120 to Bishops Stortford; TL5022], *Three Willows*: Pleasant recently extended village pub with well kept Greene King Abbot and Rayments, good bar food (not Sun) including an enjoyable ploughman's, cricketing theme *(M J Morgan, T Nott, Frank Williams)*

Blackmore [The Green; TL6001], *Prince Albert*: Attractive pub in pleasant village, log fires, friendly landlord and bar staff, good bar food including vegetarian dishes and range of speciality baked potatoes named after eminent Victorians *(NBM)*

Bradfield [TM1430], *Lamb & Hoggit*: Trumans Best on handpump, good bar food, garden with waterfall, pond and fenced play area *(P J and S E Robbins)*

Bradwell on Sea [Waterside; TM0006], *Green Man*: Interestingly furnished flagstoned fifteenth-century pub with games-room and garden, close to sea *(LYM)*; *Kings Head*: Comfortable pub, clean and spacious, with pleasant fire, decent bar food, friendly staff and good children's play area *(K Leist)*

Braintree [Bradford St; Bocking; TL7524], *Old Court*: Nice atmosphere in Chef & Brewer with friendly service, good food

including some unusual dishes, well kept beer; bedrooms *(J S Evans)*

Brentwood [Ongar Rd; TQ5993], *Old Victoria*: Popular, open-plan town pub with Greene King ales *(Graham Bush)*

Broadley Common [Common Rd; TL4207], *Black Swan*: Small, cosy two-bar local with warm welcome and Ind Coope beer *(Robert Lester)*

Buckhurst Hill [Wellington Hill (nr A104/A121); TQ4193], *Duke of Wellington*: Friendly, one-bar pub on edge of Epping Forest with horsebrasses, plates, brass cask taps, real fire, darts, bar billiards, good atmosphere and Ind Coope Burton *(Robert Lester)*

Bumbles Green [Nazeing Common Rd; TL4004], *King Harolds Head*: Courage and John Smiths on handpump in comfortable single-bar pub with restaurant; good atmosphere, real fire *(Robert Lester)*

☆ **Canfield End** [TL5821], *Lion & Lamb*: Good no-expense-spared open-plan refurbishment (some might say the central red-brick fireplace is out of place – the imposing grandfather clock is an attraction, though) for welcoming and relaxed pub with well kept ale, good home-cooked bar food (especially huffers; also includes vegetarian and children's dishes), enlarged restaurant, efficient service, tables on terrace and in garden; beware the steps between the different levels in the bar *(T G Saul, Gwen and Peter Andrews, M J Morgan, S J Curtis)*

Chelmsford [Moulsham St; TL7006], *Black Horse*: Well kept Charrington IPA on handpump, sandwiches and simple lunches at check-clothed tables in carpeted bar *(E J Cutting)*; [Roxwell Rd] *Horse & Groom*: Popular mock-Tudor place, friendly and busy but relaxed, consistently good reasonably priced food including lots of salads (not Sun), Watneys-related real ales, reliable service, good furnishings and décor; benches outside *(Roy Clark, M J Morgan)*; [Lower Anchor St] *Orange Tree*: Cheerful, orderly pub with pleasant efficient service in spacious but cosy lounge and public bar with darts, both carpeted and with gas fires and unobtrusive piped music; excellent value lunchtime bar food (not Sun) including good huffers, pleasant terrace with climbing plants and waterfall; occasional live music; easy access for wheelchairs *(Brian Quentin)*; [Lower Anchor St] *Partners*: Well kept Adnams, Greene King, Ridleys and maybe guest beers; near county cricket ground – its popularity with players and supporters gives it rather an unusual sports-club atmosphere sometimes *(Ian Clark)*; [High St] *Saracens Head*: Worth watching having recently reopened with two new bars and refurbished restaurant *(Roy Clark)*

nr Chelmsford [Cooksmill Green – A414 5 miles W of Chelsmford; TL6306], *Fox & Goose*: Comfortable and spaciously extended well kept pub with lots of tables, lively but not boisterous evening atmosphere, well kept Watneys-related real ales on handpump, popular bar food, friendly efficient service *(Robert Lester, LYM)*

☆ **Chignall Smealy** [TL6711], *Pig & Whistle*: Taken over 1989 by an outgoing family, giving this country local with its coal fire, brasses and farm tools a pleasantly lively atmosphere; well kept Adnams on handpump, guest beers tapped from the cask, promising food – they plan to open up one end as restaurant *(Gwen and Peter Andrews)*

☆ **Clavering** [B1038 Newport–Buntingford, Newport end of village; TL4731], *Cricketers*: Enormous L-shaped bar, but low beams and two open fires give a cosy effect; well kept Flowers and Wethereds on handpump, wide choice of good well presented food including help-yourself salads and often roast beef carved from large dome-lidded trolley, separate restaurant, outside tables; accent very much on food – even bar tables can be booked; prices not low, but worth it *(Michael Prentice, Dorothy and Jack Rayner, Mr and Mrs E J Smith, Mrs B M Palmer)*

Cock Clarks [off B1010; TL8102], *Fox & Hounds*: Red-brick, refurbished pub under new young licensees (with young family); light, sunny and cheerful bar, popular with locals but welcoming to visitors, well kept Ridleys and Adnams Extra on handpump *(Gwen and Peter Andrews)*

☆ **Coggeshall** [West St (towards Braintree); TL8522], *Fleece*: Handsome Elizabethan pub next to Paycocke's (lovely timber-framed house open pm summer Weds, Thurs and Sun); grand fireplace, finely carved beams, well kept Greene King IPA and Abbot on handpump, decent wine, straightforward pub food (not Tues evening), warm and friendly local atmosphere with plenty of leg-pulling; play area in spacious sheltered garden; provision for children; has been open all day Mon–Fri *(Gwen and Peter Andrews, LYM)*

☆ **Coggeshall** [main st], *White Hart*: Fifteenth-century inn with lots of dark beams, library chairs and one or two attractive antique settles around oak tables, seats in bow windows, flower prints and fishing trophies on cream walls, well kept Adnams, freshly squeezed orange juice and decent wines and coffee from curving bar counter, good bar food with fish and seafood including their own smoked salmon often predominating; bedrooms comfortable *(Brian Wood, AE, Gwen and Peter Andrews, BB)*

☆ **Coggeshall** [91 Church St; turn off main st opp post office and Barclays Bank, then bear right], *Woolpack*: Handsome timber-framed Tudor inn with attractive softly lit period lounge, good value home-cooked bar food, well kept Ind Coope real ales and other decent drinks, log fire, friendly landlord,

maybe unobtrusive piped Radio 2; children welcome; bedrooms comfortable *(Gwen and Peter Andrews, D Jackson, LYM)*

Coggeshall [7 West St], *Cricketers*: Cosy and homely local, recently done up, with friendly and welcoming staff and good value simple home-cooked bar food *(Alison Findlay)*

☆ nr **Coggeshall** [Pattiswick (signposted from A120 about 2 miles W of Coggeshall – OS Sheet 168 reference 820247)], *Compasses*: Secluded country pub surrounded by farmland with comfortable and attractively decorated spacious rooms including restaurant, beams, flooring tiles, brasses; wide range of attractively priced agreeable bar food every evening and lunchtimes Weds-Sat, Greene King IPA and Abbot and Mauldons (named for the pub) on handpump, kept well under light blanket pressure; traditional pub games, fruit machine, piped music; lawns, orchard, play area *(Gwen and Peter Andrews, Martin and Debbie Chester, LYM)*

☆ **Colchester** [East St; TM0025], *Rose & Crown*: Carefully modernised handsome Tudor inn, timbered and jettied, parts of a former jail preserved in its rambling beamed bar, good value bar food, Tolly real ale ; comfortable bedrooms *(M J Morgan, LYM)*

Colchester [Trinity St], *Clarendon*: Wide choice of reasonably priced hot and cold food including good salads and vegetarian dishes; no-smoking area, friendly service and well kept beer (coffee too) *(Betty and Tony Croot)*; [Lexden Rd] *Hospital Arms*: Well kept pub with active staff and good value, plentiful food; home of Colchester Rugby Club, and popular with cricketers too *(A L Latham, M J Morgan)*; [High St] *Red Lion*: Vestiges of former Tudor grandeur survive in what is now a businessman's comfortable central hotel, with Greene King ales and a popular variety of eateries from coffee shop through burger and pizza bar to steakhouse *(LYM)*; [North Hill] *Wig & Pen*: Pleasant pub with Greene King IPA and good range of bar snacks; excellent staff; restaurant *(M J Morgan, JJM)*

Coopersale Common [TL4702], *Garnon Bushes*: Wide choice of good bar food in generous helpings *(Geo Rumsey)*

Copford Green [TL9222], *Alma*: Attractive recently refurbished brick pub with pleasant rather rustic atmosphere, well kept Greene King IPA and Abbot, decent wine and good value bar food *(Brian and Pam Cowling and others)*

Crays Hill [TQ7192], *Shepherd & Dog*: Well kept Benskins Best and Ind Coope Burton on handpump at prices that are relatively low for the area, recently added dining area serving limited range of good value food *(Helen and John Thompson)*

Cressing [TL7920], *Willows*: Quietly welcoming atmosphere in pub with airy country bar and smaller snug bar, well kept

Adnams Southwold and Extra, good bar food, attentive service, unusual brasses; live music Thurs, excellent floral displays *(Gwen and Peter Andrews)*

Debden Estate [41 Westall Rd (off A1168); TQ4398], *Clydesdale*: Spacious pub with pool-tables in both bars, Courage Best and Directors on handpump *(Robert Lester)*

Dedham [TM0533], *Sun*: Nicely carved beams and wood panelling in spacious and comfortably modernised Tudor pub, popular with locals; friendly, attentive staff, wide choice of bar food from hefty sandwiches and burgers to steaks, restaurant; bedrooms *(G B and J E Halphide, LYM)*

Duton Hill [pub signposted off B184 Dunmow–Thaxted, 3 miles N of Dunmow; TL6026], *Rising Sun*: Unspoilt traditional village local with Ridleys PA on handpump, bar food (only basket meals in the evening), piped music *(Gwen and Peter Andrews)*

☆ **Easthorpe** [village signposted from A12; TL9121], *House Without A Name*: Heavy standing timbers and low beams in recently extended Tudor pub with good choice of real ales including Mauldons (sold under the pub's name), log fire, usual pub food, friendly service, restaurant, seats in small garden; piped music may be loud; provision for children *(Alison Findlay, LYM)*

Eastwood [Eastwood Rd; TQ8488], *Bellhouse*: Courage pub/restaurant, warm and inviting, in beautiful building reached by small bridge over moat, surrounded by floodlit trees *(Jenny Cantle)*

Epping [High St; TL4602], *Duke of Wellington*: Friendly, comfortable one-bar pub with brass platters, good atmosphere, real fire, Ind Coope Best on handpump *(Robert Lester)*; [High St; nr police stn] *George & Dragon*: Welcoming 400-year-old pub – can get crowded in evening *(Robert Lester)*; [18 Lindsey St (B181)] *Globe*: Pleasant, one-bar local with pictures of pub in former times on walls and postcard captions over the bar; Ind Coope Best on handpump, unusually coloured pool-table *(Robert Lester)*; [Ivy Chimneys; TL4500] *Spotted Dog*: Friendly and quite spacious, bar food and restaurant, garden *(Robert Lester)*

☆ **Epping Forest** [coming from Harlow on B1393, turn right at 'City Limits' roundabout (A121) – pub on left after a mile; TQ4197], *Volunteer*: Nicely placed in centre of forest; very spacious – large open-plan bar, conservatory and outside seating; main attraction is authentic Chinese food prepared by Chinese landlady, in enormous helpings (they do other food, too); McMullens beer *(Alan and Ruth Woodhouse)*

Epping Forest [Bell Common – follow Ivy Chimneys signpost; TL4401], *Forest Gate*: Large one-bar pub with good mix of customers, well kept Adnams, good home-cooked bar food, even local fruit and veg for sale on the bar *(Alan and Ruth Woodhouse)*

Epping Green [B181; TL4305], *Travellers Friend*: Busy, friendly pub with good atmosphere, plenty of brasses and plates on walls, Ind Coope Best *(Robert Lester)*

Epping Upland [TL4404], *Cock & Magpie*: Small, smart one-bar pub with Courage Best on handpump and small restaurant *(Robert Lester)*

Fiddlers Hamlet [Stewards Green Rd; TL4700], *Merry Fiddlers*: Quiet, friendly pub with Benskins Best and Ind Coope Burton on handpump *(Robert Lester)*

Finchingfield [TL6832], *Fox*: Eighteenth-century pub with splendid pargeting, by well kept village green – spacious beamed bar caters comfortably for the many tourists, with coal fire, mainly Watneys-related beers, decent bar food and restaurant *(Gwen and Peter Andrews)*

Ford End [TL6716], *Swan*: Quaint little low-beamed Ridleys pub with simple, friendly atmosphere, well kept beer, home-made bar food, pool and darts, unobtrusive piped music *(Gwen and Peter Andrews)*

Frating [TM0822], *Kings Arms*: Warm welcome in seventeenth-century pub with obliging staff, bar food including good ploughman's, well kept Watneys-related real ales, warm red furnishings *(Peter Griffiths)*

☆ **Fuller Street** [The Green (off A131 Chelmsford–Braintree, towards Fairstead); TL7416], *Square & Compasses*: Old converted cottage with landlord's enthusiasm for folk music showing in the piped and sometimes live music and morris dancing; well kept Ridleys, good reasonably priced home-cooked bar food including popular pies; on Essex Way, very popular with CAMRA members *(Roy Clark, Ian Clark, John Gunby, Mr and Mrs M P Loy)*

Gestingthorpe [OS Sheet 155 reference 813375; TL8138], *Pheasant*: Simple country pub with attractive old-fashioned furnishings, popular and often interesting lunchtime food, Adnams, Greene King and a Mauldons beer brewed for the pub; children welcome *(LYM)*

☆ **Gosfield** [TL7829], *Green Man*: Spacious bar decorated with pictures of Second World War planes; warm welcome from licensees – both real characters, well kept Greene King IPA and Abbot on handpump, good wines by the glass, good coffee with real cream, wide choice of good home-made bar food from sandwiches to grills, lovely old brick fireplace, pet piranha; two restaurant areas leading off; garden; a good Christmas-time pub *(Gwen and Peter Andrews, Aubrey and Margaret Saunders)*

Gosfield [A1017 Braintree–Halstead; TL7829], *Kings Head*: Extraordinary collection of police uniforms on full-size dummies, truncheons, handcuffs, and so forth – well worth a look if you're nearby; decent bar food, coffee; good value bedrooms *(Tim Baxter, Gwen and Peter Andrews)*

Great Baddow [back rd to Galleywood (or off B1007 at Galleywood Eagle); TL7204], *Seabrights Barn*: Newly restored spacious sixteenth-century building of great character, with tables and chairs in gallery, carpeted bar decorated with interesting farming tools, family conservatory; Adnams Broadside and Greene King IPA, bar food, restaurant, big garden and farmyard with aviary, dovecote and pet animals such as two kid goats; definitely one to watch *(Gwen and Peter Andrews)*

Great Bardfield [TL6730], *Vine*: Simple pub with efficient staff, Ridleys and Adnams real ales, wide range of good value bar food; children allowed if eating *(Gwen and Peter Andrews)*

Great Chesterford [High St (2 miles E of M11 junction 9); TL5143], *Plough*: Fine old unspoilt village pub with open fire, original beams (with ancient coins in their cracks), cheerful licensees, well kept Greene King IPA tapped from the cask *(John Baker)*

☆ **Great Saling** [village signposted from A120; TL7025], *White Hart*: Attractive Tudor bar with ancient timbering and flooring tiles, easy chairs up in oak-floored gallery, good value huffers filled with first-class beef and other snacks, well kept Adnams Extra and Ridleys on handpump, friendly atmosphere – lounge quiet, bar noisier; seats outside – the pub's a real picture in summer *(A L and J W Taylor, J S Rowe, LYM)*

Great Sampford [TL6435], *Red Lion*: Friendly eighteenth-century village pub, hard-working licensees, spacious but cosy beamed bar decorated with brasses and framed music-hall song sheets; decent bar food, well kept Ridleys, pleasant service, small restaurant; five bedrooms *(Gwen and Peter Andrews)*

Great Stambridge [TQ9091], *Cherry Tree*: Watneys-related real ales and good value food, though pub's perhaps most notable for its big, well planted side conservatory *(Peter Griffiths)*

☆ **Great Waltham** [A130, about ¾ mile from Ash Tree Corner junction with A131; TL6913], *Free House*: Spotless sixteenth-century pub with well kept real ales including Boddingtons, Brakspears, Fullers ESB, Hook Norton, Eldridge Pope Royal Oak and King & Barnes Festive, and shelf full of malt whiskies; good lunchtime bar food, harmless ghost in gents' lavatory *(Mr and Mrs M Knowles)*

Great Warley Street [TQ5890], *Headley Arms*: Smart one-bar modernised pub, with good atmosphere, bellows, animal traps and so forth on the walls, Watneys-related real ales, Barnaby's Carvery upstairs (where a former room had a reputed highwayman's cupboard escape route to Warley Gap woods); by duck pond *(Robert Lester)*; *Thatchers Arms*: Pretty

pub beside village green, recently brightened up without spoiling its character; well kept beer, good food *(Quentin Williamson)*

☆ **Hadstock** [B1052; TL5544], *Kings Head*: Simple but remarkably friendly pub in historic village, original beams, tree-trunk table, well kept Tolly real ales, good bar food (not Mon) from snacks to steaks, bar billiards *(Geoff and Sarah Schrecker, Stuart Watkinson)*

Harlow [Three Horseshoes Rd; TL4510], *Cock*: Pleasant and attentive staff, good bar food *(Gerald Roll)*

Hatfield Broad Oak [TL5416], *Dukes Head*: Interesting and unusual food in old pub with friendly atmosphere, homely and attractive décor, well furnished conservatory; close to Hatfield Forest – and Stansted Airport *(Alan and Ruth Woodhouse, Gordon Theaker)*

☆ **Hatfield Heath** [overlooks biggest village green in Essex, junction of several roads; TL5215], *White Horse*: Friendly village pub on large green; dining area off main lounge opens on to pleasant lawn; solid wooden benches and a mix of interesting tables; well kept Greene King ales, decent wines by the glass, good bar food *(Alan and Ruth Woodhouse, Gwen and Peter Andrews)*

Henham [Chickney Rd; TL5428], *Cock*: Pleasantly placed family pub/restaurant, heavily timbered, with friendly landlord and staff, good value fresh food, real ales *(DJT)*

☆ **Herongate** [Dunton Rd – turn off A128 Brentford–Grays at big sign for Boars Head; TQ6391], *Old Dog*: Long traditional bar with dark-beamed ceiling, open fire, relaxed atmosphere, well kept Adnams Extra, Greene King IPA and Abbot, Ridleys PA and Ruddles County on handpump, lunchtime bar food popular with Ford staff (only snacks weekends) and evening meals, picnic-table sets on front terrace and in a neat sheltered side garden; the negotiations we reported in the 1989 edition for a Greene King takeover fell through *(Graham Bush, Dave Butler, Lesley Storey, LYM)*

Herongate [Billericay Rd, Ingrave; TQ6391], *Boars Head*: Busy Watneys food pub of Tudor origins, in attractive setting; popular with Ford staff *(Graham Bush)*

Heybridge Basin [TL8707], *Old Ship*: Really cheap bar food including baked potatoes and cottage pie – they don't mind if you just have a coffee; wonderful view of canal, lock and estuary *(Margaret and Trevor Errington)*

High Ongar [The Street, just off A414 Chipping Ongar–Chelmsford; TL5603], *Foresters Arms*: Delightful low-beamed bar, excellent range of real ales including Adnams Southwold, Greene King Abbot and Mauldons on handpump *(Robert Lester)*; [The Street] *Red Lion*: Small cosy local with real fire, one bar divided in two by dartboard, Ind Coope Best on handpump *(Robert Lester)*

High Roding [The Street (B184); TL6017],

Black Lion: Attractive building with friendly atmosphere, interesting food and well kept beer *(Dave Butler, Lesley Storey)*

Hockley [Main Rd; TQ8293], *Bull*: Recently extended local near Hockley Woods, very popular with families; wide choice of beers and whiskies, bar food, jolly licensee, big garden with own servery, animals, pond and play area *(Jenny Cantle)*

Horsley Cross [B1036; TM1227], *Hedgerows*: Free house with good choice of home-cooked food and of beers and wines, reasonable prices; children allowed by arrangement *(C H Fewster)*

Ingatestone [High St; TQ6499], *Bell*: Rather stylishly done up to look older than it is, with well kept Bass and Charrington IPA *(NBM, Dr and Mrs A K Clarke, Graham Bush)*; [High St] *Star*: Homely and unspoilt pub, with interesting collection of hats, friendly landlord, well kept Greene King IPA and Abbot *(Dr and Mrs A K Clarke)*

Knowl Green [TL7841], *Cherry Tree*: Delightful, unspoilt atmosphere under new, hospitable licensees; popular with locals; real ales, excellent home-made bar food and no piped music *(Mrs M Mackintosh)*

Leigh on Sea [Old Leigh; TQ8385], *Peter Boat*: Friendly, cosy pub by harbour, well kept beers and good, cheap bar food *(Quentin Williamson)*

☆ **Little Walden** [B1052; TL5441], *Crown*: Popular pub with homely furnishings, settles and chintzy cushions in spacious low-beamed open-plan bar; wide range of well kept beers on tap, excellent bar food specialising in seafood, friendly and caring staff; in peaceful place, handy for Linton Zoo *(Joy Heatherley, T G Saul)*

Littlebury [TL5139], *Queens Head*: Pleasant but very basic bar with new licensee; well kept Adnams, Batemans and Marstons Merrie Monk, and very good ploughman's *(Joyce and Norman Bailey)*

Loughton [Baldwins Hill; TQ4296], *Foresters Arms*: Cosy local near forest, Ind Coope Best and Burton on handpump, small garden *(Robert Lester)*; [Church Hill (A121)] *Plume of Feathers*: Small, cosy local with good atmosphere, well kept Ind Coope Burton on handpump *(Robert Lester)*

Magdalen Laver [Green Man Rd; TL5108], *Green Man*: Spacious open-plan pub with low ceiling, cosy atmosphere and Courage Directors, Greene King Abbot and Rayments BBA on handpump *(Robert Lester)*

Maldon [Silver St; TL8506], *Blue Boar*: Good atmosphere in Harness Bar, friendly staff, Adnams tapped from the cask, darts, fruit machine; a THF hotel, usual THF bar lunches *(Gwen and Peter Andrews)*; [The Quay] *Jolly Sailor*: Cosy old pub on quay beside medieval church; slightly elevated position gives views over stackies – Thames sailing barges once used to take hay stacks to London, with most of the survivors now moored here; snacks and bar meals, Watneys-related real ales *(Quentin Williamson)*

Manuden [TL4926], *Yew Tree*: Refurbished free house dating back to fifteenth century, with pleasant service, good bar food from sandwiches and ploughman's to steaks, evening restaurant, occasional Sun jazz nights ; two bedrooms in converted old forge adjoining *(T G Saul)*

Marden Ash [Brentwood Rd (A128); TL5502], *Stag*: Friendly country pub with well kept McMullens Bitter on handpump *(Robert Lester)*

Matching Tye [TL5111], *Fox*: Seventeenth-century pub in attractive countryside; welcoming licensees and staff, well cooked reasonably priced bar food; motor-cyclists, hikers and children welcome *(F W Folley)*

Monk Street [TL6128], *Greyhound*: Pleasant welcome in plushly refurbished beamed and red-carpeted bar, well kept Adnams and Greene King ales, good coffee, maybe decanted vintage port, standard bar food (not Sun evening) *(Gwen and Peter Andrews)*

☆ **Moreton** [TL5307], *Moreton Massey*: Large and attractive open-plan beamed pub, formerly the Nags Head; comfortably furnished and well run, with plenty of seating – though it's sensible to get there early for the good imaginative bar food ranging from smoked sprats and huge enterprisingly filled granary toasties to fish and steaks; well kept changing real ales such as Bass, Greene King, Marstons and Thwaites, good choice of wines including Chilean ones (the drinks don't stand out as cheap), restaurant *(Alan and Ruth Woodhouse, Geo Rumsey, Robert Lester)*

Mountnessing [TQ6297], *Prince of Wales*: Straightforwardly furnished pub with consistently well kept Ridleys, small but unusual selection of malt whiskies, well placed food bar, reasonably good-natured Dobermann *(J H Walker, Graham Bush)*

☆ **Navestock** [Horsemans Side (off B175); TQ5397], *Alma Arms*: Popular, comfortable, low-beamed free house with emphasis on the good food (some helpings not large), but also serving well kept ales such as Adnams, Greene King IPA and Abbot, Rayments BBA and Youngs Special; nice busy atmosphere, decent service *(R Houghton, Robert Lester)*

Navestock Side [TQ5697], *Green Man*: Pleasant spot by cricket pitch; Sun bar nibbles, well kept Ind Coope Burton and decent wines, cheerful lounge (may be closed for functions), darker middle bar, pricey restaurant (not Mon) in adjoining barn *(Gwen and Peter Andrews, Robert Lester)*

Nazeing [St Leonards Rd; TL4106], *Coach & Horses*: Unspoilt pub, bar with old Christie Brewery glasswork, lounge which was formerly a tea-room, Ind Coope Best on handpump *(Robert Lester)*

☆ **North Fambridge** [The Quay; TQ8597],

Ferryboat: Quaint little weatherboarded pub in remote riverside spot, with low beams, stone floor, old benches, old-fashioned atmosphere and lighting that gives a romantic feel; well kept Tetleys, cheap bar food and friendly mix of locals and (particularly in summer) Londoners and yachtsmen *(Quentin Williamson, Graham Bush)*

☆ **North Shoebury** [Frobisher Way (behind ASDA); TQ9485], *Parsons Barn*: Heavily refurbished former barn, though retains olde-worlde character, with five real ales on handpump and Adnams tapped from the cask; excellent, reasonably priced food, friendly service *(Peter Seddon, MN)*

Nounsley [Sportsman Lane – back road between those from Hatfield Peverel to Little Baddow; TL7910], *Sportsmans Arms*: Relaxing long open-plan bar with small dining-room at one end; Ind Coope ales on handpump, good toasted sandwiches *(Gwen and Peter Andrews)*

☆ **Paglesham** [TQ9293], *Plough & Sail*: Good value food pub – worth visiting even for the local oysters alone; attractive building with warm and friendly atmosphere, well kept Watneys-related beers, quick helpful service; can get crowded on warm summer evenings, but pleasant even then *(MN, Gordon Smith)*

Peldon [TL9916], *Plough*: Pretty little tiled and white-boarded village local, cheerfully busy in the evenings and at weekends *(BB)*

☆ **Pleshey** [TL6614], *White Horse*: Pleasantly refurbished fifteenth-century pub on several levels, doing well under new regime, with strong emphasis on enterprising and reasonably priced food including unusual dishes such as melon balls in port, seafood nibbles with tartare sauce, lamb Shrewsbury; newspapers and shelves of books for customers to read, well kept changing real ales such as Arkells or Crouch Vale, remarkable range of wines, unobtrusive piped music, friendly service, evening restaurant *(Gwen and Peter Andrews, Shirley Pielou)*

Purfleet [TQ5578], *Royal*: Beefeater steak-house with marvellous Thames views from tables on terrace, good range of lunchtime bar food, restaurant *(B R Wood)*

Rayleigh [High St; TQ8190], *Paul Pry*: Good local atmosphere without being unfriendly, cosy snugs, Watneys-related ales, large garden with barbecue; children welcome *(Graham Bush)*; [The Chase (off A1015)] *Rayleigh Lodge*: Interesting multi-level building that appears to be a converted country house, now a Watneys pub/restaurant; large gardens, barbecues; bedrooms *(Graham Bush)*

Rettendon [Southend Rd; A130 S; TQ7698], *Plough & Sail*: Much extended roadside pub with large conservatory, Watneys-related real ales with an outsider such as Greene King IPA, good value bar food and separate carvery; children's area *(M J Morgan)*

Rickling Green [B1383 Stansted–Newport; TL5029], *Cricketers Arms*: Brillant pub with friendly licensees, staff and even dogs; piped music catering for all tastes, Greene King IPA and Abbot, guest beer, excellent food with various specials and relaxed Sun lunches, and good service *(Caroline Wright)*

Ridgewell [A604 Haverhill–Halstead; TL7340], *Kings Head*: Simply furnished pub with Tudor beams and big brick fireplace, but otherwise much modernised, with good value bar food in dining area of small lounge, well kept Greene King IPA and Abbot on handpump, local Second World War memorabilia including Dambusters' print, signed James Stewart photograph, huge brass shellcases; pool and other games in airy public bar, piped music, a few tables in roadside garden *(Patrick Young, BB)*

Rochford [North St; TQ8790], *Golden Lion*: Intimate and friendly local with well kept Fullers London Pride, Greene King Abbot and three guest beers, warmly welcoming new licensee and improved bar food; can get crowded; outside lavatories *(Graham Bush, MN)*

Rowhedge [Quay; TM0021], *Anchor*: Splendid position overlooking River Colne with its swans, gulls and yachts; well kept Watneys-related real ales, fishing bric-à-brac, good atmosphere, ample helpings of good value food such as fresh plaice, restaurant *(J H Walker, Tony Tucker)*

Roydon [42 High St (B181); TL4109], *Crusader*: Large, smart one-bar pub with McMullens AK Mild and Bitter on handpump *(Robert Lester)*; [High St] *White Hart*: Pleasant, cosy bar with Greene King Abbot and Rayments BBA on handpump *(Robert Lester, Mrs E M Thompson)*

Saffron Walden [10–18 High St; TL5438], *Saffron*: Comfortably modern comfort and attractive décor – if you like aeroplanes; wide choice of good unusual waitress-served bar food, good service, tables on terrace; bedrooms *(K Howard)*

South Benfleet [High St; TQ7787], *Half Crown*: Fancy stools and curtains in gutted, extended and refurbished pub – still has pubby atmosphere, though, and worth knowing for lunchtime bar snacks and well kept Charrington IPA *(Brian Wood)*

South Weald [between Horsemanside and Sabines Green; TQ5793], *William IV*: Small, tucked-away clapboard pub, cosy and well decorated, with real fire, Thelwell pub-name cartoons, Watneys-related real ales, friendly atmosphere *(Quentin Williamson)*

Stanford Rivers [Toot Hill Rd; TL5300], *Drill House*: Worth knowing for its super summer salads and garden *(Anon)*

☆ **Stansted** [TL5124], *Kings Arms*: New licensees gaining local reputation for good food; simple dining-room with American-cloth tablecloths, but a Sun lunch included crab mousse made with fresh crab and plenty of sherry, and lamb cutlets with a good wine and rosemary sauce and crisp vegetables; good house wine *(Alison Graham)*

Stansted [Silver St], *Cock*: Pleasant atmosphere, good food at low prices *(Mrs C Wardell)*

☆ **Stanway** [London Rd; TL9324], *Swan*: Very large yet friendly local with well kept beer and several oak-beamed rooms including pretty restaurant (where children are allowed) used at lunchtime as servery for wide range of good hot and cold bar food; cheerful generous service, big open fire *(Alison Findlay, John and Ruth Bell)*

Stapleford Abbotts [Oak Hill Rd (B175); TQ5096], *Royal Oak*: Popular pub, especially in summer; good atmosphere *(Robert Lester)*

Steeple Bumpstead [TL6841], *Fox & Hounds*: Attractive and comfortable lounge with hunting pictures, friendly landlord, good bar food *(Mr and Mrs J Wilmore)*

☆ **Stock** [The Square (just off village street); TQ6998], *Bear*: Pleasant bars with warm and cosy atmosphere and lots of character, well kept Ind Coope-related beers, good bar food (the 'late breakfast' is popular), friendly landlord and helpful service; restaurant; sporting links include association with Essex CCC *(Graham Oddey, Dave Butler, Lesley Storey, Graham Bush, Michael Thomson)*

Stock [Common Rd (just off B1007 Chelmsford–Billericay)], *Bakers Arms*: Popular local with pleasant garden, good atmosphere, genial landlord, straightforward bar food and Watneys-related real ales; provision for children *(Graham Bush, Gwen and Peter Andrews, Graham Oddey)*

Stondon Massey [Ongar Rd; TL5900], *Bricklayers Arms*: Friendly, split-level pub with good atmosphere, darts in public bar, two moose-heads in lounge; Greene King IPA and Abbot on handpump *(Robert Lester)*

Thaxted [Mill End; TL6130], *Star*: Cheerful old beamed pub with pleasant service, wide choice of good food, well kept Ind Coope Burton *(Tom, Lorna, Audrey and Alan Chatting, Richard Houghton)*; [Bullring] *Swan*: Tudor inn with a good deal of potential, under new ownership and closed for very extensive renovation earlier in 1989 – may well be particularly worth watching *(Reports please)*

Theydon Bois [Station Rd (off B172); TQ4599], *Railway Arms*: Small, comfortable and rustic with friendly licensee; Flowers IPA and Original on handpump *(Robert Lester)*

Thornwood Common [B1393, nr M11 junction 7; TL4705], *Bull & Horseshoes*: Small, quiet pub with well kept Ind Coope beer *(Robert Lester)*

Tilbury [follow rd to Tilbury Fort; TQ6476], *Worlds End*: Unspoilt seventeenth-century waterside pub with interesting views of Gravesend across the water and of the docks up river; three fireplaces, original flagstones

throughout, Bass and Charrington IPA, very lively in the evening with darts, bar billiards and piped music; climbing-frame, slides and so forth in small garden behind, with cattle and horses wandering around *(Jenny Cantle)*

Tillingham [TL9903], *Fox & Hounds*: Warm and friendly welcome in well kept timbered bar with wooden benches, long tables, brick fireplace, eating area; brasses on wall, two fruit machines, darts and cribbage; Greene King IPA on handpump, good coffee *(Gwen and Peter Andrews)*

Tiptree [TL8916], *Maypole*: Welcoming Ind Coope local, unpretentious lounge bar with coal fire, hanging plants and unobtrusive local radio; reasonably priced simple bar food, pool in public bar *(Gwen and Peter Andrews)*

Toppesfield [TL7337], *Crawley Arms*: Formerly the Chestnut; friendly little pub in pretty, unspoilt village off the beaten track; nicely decorated, with fresh flowers and chintzy curtains *(Alison Findlay)*

Upshire [Horseshoe Hill; TL4100], *Horseshoes*: Friendly, comfortable local dating from 1800s, McMullens Bitter and AK Mild on handpump, garden *(Robert Lester)*; [Paternoster Hill] *Queens Head*: Young person's pub with plush lounge bar and impressive public bar; McMullens AK Mild and Bitter on handpump *(Robert Lester)*

Waltham Abbey [Honey Lane (A121); TL3800], *Green Man*: Friendly open-plan pub, modernised brickwork but old wooden beams, real fire and darts; Benskins Best *(Robert Lester)*; [Sewardstone Rd (A112)] *Sultan*: Good two-bar local on the outskirts; good atmosphere, panelling and stripped bricks in saloon, pool-table in public bar *(Robert Lester)*; [Skillet Hill, Honey Lane (at junction with Claypit Hill, ½ mile from M25 junction 26)] *Volunteer*: Good country local, with well kept McMullens Mild and Bitter, nice conservatory, tasty freshly made Chinese food; service can slow down on busy weekends *(Comus Elliott and others)*; [146 Crooked Mile (B194)] *Wheatsheaf*: Pleasant, comfortable open-plan pub with welcoming atmosphere and McMullens AK Mild and Country on handpump *(Robert Lester)*

Westcliff on Sea [West Cliff Parade; TQ8685], *West Cliff*: Attractively placed Victorian hotel, recently refurbished and redecorated – bar has comfortable chairs and settees, and fine estuary view from bow window; Youngers IPA on handpump, good bar food and service, terrace tables overlooking the water; bedrooms comfortable *(E G Parish)*

☆ **Widdington** [High St; TL5331], *Fleur de Lys*: Clean and unpretentious village pub, spacious and nicely decorated beamed bar, good log fire, well kept Adnams Broadside and Southwold, Greene King IPA, Mauldons and Nethergate on handpump, chatty but efficient young bar staff, small snooker- and darts-room, large choice of reasonably priced bar food, restaurant (children allowed here), tables outside; handy for Widdington Wildlife Park *(Gwen and Peter Andrews, Mrs A Dobson, Joyce and Norman Bailey)*

Witham [113 Hatfield Rd (B1389); TL8214], *Jack & Jenny*: Well run family pub with spacious L-shaped bar, pool-table at one end, good mix of customers, smiling and helpful staff, even when busy, and relaxing atmosphere; several real ales including Courage Directors on handpump, Symonds cider, standard bar food at reasonable prices, exuberantly decorated new conservatory, garden; has been open all day *(Gwen and Peter Andrews)*

Wivenhoe [TM0321], *Rose & Crown*: Very friendly, with good river views – great sitting out on the quayside; landlord's special cocktail is well worth trying *(Colin and Caroline)*

Woodham Mortimer [TL8104], *Hurdlemakers Arms*: Quiet tucked-away local looking like a cosy house, open fire in simply furnished flagstoned lounge with cushioned settles, low ceiling and timbered walls; well kept Greene King IPA and Abbot, good darts alley in public bar, picnic-table sets well spaced among trees and shrubs outside *(Gwen Andrews, J L Thompson, BB)*

Gloucestershire

One of the best parts of Britain for good pub food, this area includes as notable successes the Gardeners Arms at Alderton (especially in the evening), the Red Hart at Awre (one of the area's entirely new entries; the other is the interesting old Ragged Cot at Hyde), the Crown of Crucis at Ampney Crucis (its refurbishments and developments seem now to be complete), the Kings Head at Bledington (interesting fish dishes – another pub to have completed an ambitious programme of redevelopment), the stylish Crown at Blockley, the Bakers Arms at Broad Campden and Noel Arms in Chipping Campden (food all day, at least in summer, at both), the Slug & Lettuce in Cirencester (its kitchens now reopened), the Green Dragon near Cowley (a good range of real ales, too), the civilised Wild Duck at Ewen, the Plough at Ford (especially good at asparagus time), the Hunters Hall at Kingscote (a splendid cold table), the Hobnails at Little Washbourne (famous for its filled baps), the Black Horse at Naunton (particularly good meats), the Royal Oak in Painswick (good dishes of the day), the Crown at Shuthonger (surprisingly good food behind what it has to be admitted is an unassuming main-road façade), the Swan at Southrop (lunchtime bargains, though good in the evening too) and the Ram at Woodchester (imaginative home cooking including interesting vegetarian specialities). More and more pubs in the area are now doing bedrooms, with several of the main entries adding them this year – usually too recently for us to have been able to tell yet from readers' reports whether they merit our place-to-stay award. But there's already no shortage of these awards here, and in the Lucky Dip section at the end of the chapter many more pubs have been particularly praised for their bedrooms. Places in the Dip that are currently looking particularly promising for this or other reasons include the Craven Arms at Brockhampton, Seven Tuns at Chedworth, Cotswold in

The Gardeners Arms, Alderton

Cheltenham, Wyndham Arms at Clearwell, Ebrington Arms at Ebrington, Glasshouse at Glasshouse, Royal Spring at Lower Lydbrook and Golden Ball at Lower Swell.

ALDERTON   SP0033 Map 4

Gardeners Arms   🏮   [*illustrated on page 298*]

Village signposted from A438 Tewkesbury–Stow-on-the-Wold

There's an air of authenticity in this welcoming Tudor house, from the thatch and black beams outside, to the high-backed antique settles and other good solid seats in the L-shaped bar; there are also old mugs and tankards hanging from its sturdy beams, and a fine collection of interesting nineteenth-century prints on its cream walls – sporting, political, and scurrilous French literary ones by J-J Granville; good winter log fire, and a friendly labrador. The more straightforward public bar has sensibly placed darts, shove-ha'penny, dominoes, cribbage, fruit machine and juke box; well kept Whitbreads PA and Flowers Original on handpump. Readers continue to praise the lunchtime bar snacks, which include sandwiches (from 95p), soup (£1.50), ploughman's (from £2), pâté (£2.95) and salads (from £3.25); however, the landlord-chef saves most of his culinary energy for the evening restaurant, which specialises in local game and good meats. There are tables outside, where a partly covered crazy-paved back courtyard and a second terrace open on to a well kept garden. (*Recommended by PADEMLUC, Laurence Manning, Michael and Harriet Robinson, Dr F Peters*)

Whitbreads   Licensee Jack Terry   Real ale   Meals (Sun lunch only) and snacks (lunchtime, not Sun)   Evening restaurant tel Alderton (024 262) 257   Children welcome   Singer-guitarist Thurs   Open 10.30–2, 6.30–11 all year; closed evening 25 Dec

AMPNEY CRUCIS   SP0602 Map 4

Crown of Crucis   🏮

A417 E of Cirencester

The licensees have finally completed their ambitious programme of development and refurbishment of this old building. The spacious bar has been sympathetically modernised and redecorated, with new carpets and furnishings, and after some delays the substantial bedroom and function extension is now open. Fears that the enlargements would lead to overcrowding (it does get busy at weekends, particularly Sunday lunchtime) and a certain loss of character don't seem to have been realised, as the general feeling of readers testifies. The attractively priced bar food remains popular and includes sandwiches (from 80p), ploughman's (£1.75, lunchtime), a dish of the day (£2.25) and such meals as pancakes filled with mushroom, spinach and nuts (£2.50), home-made lasagne verde (£2.95), home-made steak and kidney pie (£3.25) and gammon (£3.35); children's dishes (from £1.10); the service, from a sprucely decorated side area, is friendly and efficient. Well kept Archers Village, Courage Directors and Marstons Pedigree on handpump. There are lots of tables on the grass at the back, by a stream with ducks and maybe swans. (*Recommended by Ewan McCall, Roger Huggins, Tom McLean, Patrick Freeman, Henry Midwinter, CEP, Peter Scillitoe, Michael and Alison Sandy, Alison Hayward, Nick Dowson, Lyn and Bill Capper, Norman Rose, Dorothy and Ken Worrall*)

Free house   Licensee R K Mills   Real ale   Meals and snacks (until 10 evenings)   Restaurant   No children under 12 in bar after 8   Open 11–2.30 (3 Sat), 6–11 all year; closed 25 Dec   Bedrooms tel Poulton (028 585) 403; £39B/£49B

Children: if the details at the end of an entry don't mention them, you should assume that the pub does not allow them inside.

AWRE   SO7108 Map 4

Red Hart 🏵

Village signposted off A48 S of Newnham

Tucked away in a remote Severnside farming village, this interesting and surprisingly tall pub dates back to the fifteenth century; the L-shaped bar has a deep glass-covered well, big prints on the walls, and a back area where a bale of straw swings from pitched rafters. Home-cooked bar food includes soup (£1.80), ploughman's (£3.25), cannelloni (£3.95), lamb kebab, plaice or well presented vegetable terrine (£4.95), chicken and mushroom en croûte (£5.50) and eight-ounce sirloin steak (£7.25), with a children's dish (£1.95), specials such as mussels (delivered fresh three times a week, £4.95), prawns with garlic bread (£5.95) or pheasant in madeira sauce (to be eaten round the corner, if you don't want to feel guilty under the eye of the stuffed one, on the mantelpiece over the good log fire). Vegetables are fresh and well cooked. Well kept Banks's on handpump, decent wines, good coffee, and (full marks) freshly squeezed orange juice; friendly service. The grand piano's played on Friday and Saturday evenings, and somehow they manage to squeeze in a six-piece jazz band on Mondays. There are a few picnic-table sets on the sheltered back lawn, with more out in front. (*Recommended by Gwynne Harper, Susi Joynes, E A George, Patrick Freeman and others*)

Free house   Licensees Martyn and Shirley Cocks   Real ale   Meals and snacks (12–2 (not winter), 7–10)   Restaurant tel Dean (0594) 510220; midnight supper licence   Children welcome   Open 12–2, 7–11ish all year; closed lunchtime (not Sun) Oct–Mar, closed Christmas week 1989

BARNSLEY   SP0705 Map 4

Village Pub

A433 Cirencester–Burford

The low-ceilinged communicating rooms in this popular and comfortable inn have plush chairs, stools and window settles around the polished tables on the carpet; the walls (some stripped back to bare stone) are decorated with gin-traps, scythes and other farm tools; several winter log fires. Well kept Flowers IPA and Wadworths 6X on handpump, and a range of country wines; piped pop music. Bar food under the new licensees includes sandwiches (£1.30), home-made soup (£1.40), ploughman's (£2.25), steak and kidney pie (£3.95), salads (from £3.95), half a chicken (£4.25), local pink trout (£4.95), ten-ounce charcoal-grilled sirloin steak (£6.75), and daily specials such as beef in elderberry wine or halibut in a prawn and crab sauce (around £4.50); puddings (from £1.20). The sheltered back courtyard has plenty of tables, and its own outside servery. (*Recommended by B and J Derry, P H King, Laurence Manning, Mrs J Oakes, John and Pat Smyth, Philip King, Dr M V Jones, V W Bankes, Aubrey and Margaret Saunders, Alison Hayward, Nick Dowson, Michael and Alison Sandy, Tom McLean, Ewan McColl, Roger Huggins; more reports on the new regime please, particularly on the food*)

Free house   Licensee S Stevens   Real ale   Meals and snacks   Restaurant   Children in eating area and restaurant   Open 11.30–2.30 (11–3 Sat), 6–11 all year; closed 25 Dec   Bedrooms tel Bibury (028 574) 421; £25B/£35B

BLEDINGTON   SP2422 Map 4

Kings Head 🏵 🛏

B4450

The extensive refurbishments which have finally been completed in this fifteenth-century Cotswolds inn have nevertheless left the bar very much as you'd hope for in such a prettily placed country village. The central main bar itself is largely unchanged and still has high-backed wooden settles, gateleg or pedestal tables, and some beams, including a heavy vertical one next to the serving-counter; there's a cheering log fire in the stone inglenook, in which hangs a big black kettle. The lounge looking on to the garden has been enlarged, and a decent car park built at the back; they've also added a large kitchen to cope with the demand – which is considerable – for bar and restaurant food. The bar menu varies twice daily; at lunchtime the range includes soup (£1.25), sausages (£1.95), hot roast beef sandwich or aubergine au gratin (£2.95), walnut bake, a good grilled red mullet or kidneys (£3.95) and steak and wine pie (£5.25); in the evening they typically serve pan-fried avocado and bacon (£2.25), black pudding and walnuts (£2.50), mushroom tagliatelle (£3.95), stuffed quail (£5.50) and grilled exotic fish (£7.50). Hook Norton, Tetleys and Wadworths 6X on handpump from the antique bar counter, and a good choice of malt whiskies; piped music. The public bar has darts, pool, bar billiards, shove-ha'penny, dominoes and fruit machine and space game, with Aunt Sally in the garden. There are tables on terraces at the front, looking over the attractive village green with its ducks and stream. *(Recommended by S V Bishop, David Pearmain, Laurence Manning, Stephen King, Mrs E M Thompson, C F Walling, Ted George, Simon Velate, Robert Olsen, John and Joan Wyatt, D Stephenson, Charles Turner, A J Hughes, Bridget Carter; in summer 1989 not all readers felt that the staff were as sympathetic as they might be – we'd like more reports on this aspect please)*

Free house   Licensees Michael and Annette Royce   Real ale   Meals and snacks (not Sun evening)   Restaurant   Children in garden-room   Open 11–2.30, 6–11 all year   Bedrooms tel *Kingham (060 871) 365; £24B/£39B*

BLOCKLEY   SP1634 Map 4
Crown ★ ✪
High Street

Over the past few years this golden stone Elizabethan inn has been going steadily up-market, with comfortably stylish refurbishments to match; though some yearn for the days when the atmosphere was simpler and more local, there's a consensus of approval for how things now stand, and particularly for the food and service. The entrance brings you straight into the public bar, which has an antique settle and more recent furnishings; off this is the snug carpeted lounge, with an attractive window seat, Windsor chairs around traditional cast-iron-framed tables, a winter log fire, and steps up into a little sitting-room with easy chairs. This in turn leads through into what used to be a skittle alley but has now become a spacious dining-room, in the ground floor of the Victoria Friendly Society building. Bar food includes sandwiches (from £1.40), steak and kidney pie (£4.25), a decent range of fresh fish such as tasty swordfish or monkfish (from £4.95) and steak (£5.25), with Sunday lunch; good puddings. Well kept Butcombe, Courage Directors and Wadworths 6X on handpump and a good selection of wines; you can sit out in front and have your drinks handed down from the window by the bar counter. Darts, bar billiards, dominoes, fruit machine, trivia and piped pop music or local radio. Close to Batsford Park Arboretum. *(Recommended by Mrs M E Lawrence, Dennis Royles, E V Walder, Laurence Manning, Derek and Sylvia Stephenson, G Eyre-Rodger, Mr and Mrs J M Elden, Robert and Vicky Tod, A C Watson and C J Lindon, PADEMLUC, S V Bishop, Jason Caulkin, A D Jenkins, S D Samuels)*

Free house   Licensees Jim and Betty Champion   Real ale   Meals and snacks (until 10 evenings)   Restaurant   Children in eating area   Open 11–3, 6–11 all year   Bedrooms tel *Blockley (0386) 700245; £49.50S/£62.50S*

BOURTON ON THE HILL   SP1732 Map 4
Horse & Groom 🛏
A44 W of Moreton-in-Marsh

The attractive little stripped stone, high-beamed lounge bar here has flowery-cushioned easy chairs, cricketing cartoons and steeplechasing photographs and a large log fire. There's a local atmosphere in the bigger, orthodoxly furnished public bar; sensibly placed darts, dominoes and fruit machine; Bass on handpump. Bar food includes soup (80p), sandwiches (from 80p), pâté (£2.15), ploughman's (£2.45), omelettes (£2.65), gammon (£4.35) and steak (£5.75). The inn is handy both for the Batsford Park Arboretum and for Sezincote. *(Recommended by Laurence Manning; more up-to-date reports please)*

Free house　Real ale　Meals and snacks (not Mon evening)　Restaurant (not Sun or Tues) Children welcome　Open 11–2.30, 6.30–11 all year　Double bedrooms tel Evesham (0386) 700413; /£30S

BRIMPSFIELD　SO9312 Map 4

Golden Heart

Nettleton Bottom; A417 Birdlip–Cirencester, at start of new village bypass

The range of real ales in this welcomingly old-fashioned cottage are proudly displayed behind the brass-topped, panelled serving-counter; they're all tapped from the cask and typically include Archers ASB and Headbanger, Bass, Buckleys Best, Hook Norton Best, Marstons Old Peculier, Ruddles County, Theakstons Old Peculier and Wadworths 6X; also Rosies cider. The red-tiled low-ceilinged bar has a big stone inglenook fireplace, stone-mullioned windows and traditional built-in settles; in the cosy parlour on the right there's china on the yellowing walls, flowers on the central table and a decorative Victorian fireplace. A plusher but still cosy room with yet another open fire on the left opens on to a sun-trap gravel terrace where hens and plump geese wander among rustic cask-supported tables. Highly praised home-made bar food includes steak sandwich (£2.50), ham off the bone in cider (£2.75), unusual casseroles such as chicken and peaches (£3.50) and rump steak (£4.50) – some tables through by the back have tablecloths and candles in the evening; summer barbecues; cribbage, dominoes. *(Recommended by Chris Payne, Ewan McCall, Rogger Huggins, Tom McLean, Simon Ward, Frank Cummins; more reports please)*

Free house　Licensees John and Jeanne Ashton　Real ale　Meals and snacks　Open 12–2.30, 6–11; closed Mon lunchtime in winter

BROAD CAMPDEN　SP1637 Map 4

Bakers Arms　✿

Village signposted from B4081 in Chipping Campden

This quietly welcoming country pub, strong on atmosphere, has walls stripped back to bare stone, dark brown beams in the dark ceiling, a log fire under a big black iron canopy at one end, a pleasantly mixed bag of tables and seats around the walls, and a big framed rugwork picture of the pub. A shoal of tropical fish shimmer in a tank on the attractive oak bar counter. Well kept Flowers IPA and Original and maybe Wadworths 6X on handpump; darts, cribbage, dominoes. Well presented food includes tomato soup (95p), garlic bread (a whole stick, £1.50), ploughman's (£1.50), omelette (from £2), salads (from £2.50, generous prawn £3.95), chilli con carne or chicken curry (£2.75), a selection of lasagnes (£2.95), chicken Kiev (£4) and good vegetarian dishes (sensibly marked out on the menu) such as chilli (£2.75) or mushroom and nut fettuccine (£2.95). There are white tables under cocktail parasols by flower tubs on a side terrace, some seats under a fairy-lit arbour, and yet more on grass behind, with a well provisioned play area and Aunt Sally. *(Recommended by Bernard Phillips, Mr and Mrs W Dermott, PADEMLUC, E V Walder, Mrs Margaret Dyke, Jill and Howard Cox, Maureen Hobbs)*

Flowers (Whitbreads)　Licensees Carolyn and Tony Perry　Real ale　Meals and snacks (noon–9.45 Easter–Oct, 12–2, 6.30–9.45 in winter; not 25 or 26 Dec)　Children in eating area　Folk music third Tues of month　Open 11.30–11 in summer; 11.30–2.30, 6.30–11 in winter; closed evening 25 Dec

CHIPPING CAMPDEN   SP1539 Map 4

Lygon Arms

The small bar here has a variety of horse photographs and hunting plates on its stripped stone walls, stripped high-backed settles and green plush stools around the dimpled copper tables on the flowery carpet, and a curious stone-slate roof over the stone-built bar counter. Bar food ranges from sandwiches (from 85p), sausage and egg (£2.25), pâté (£2.50), through salads (from £3, smoked salmon £5.50), home-made steak and kidney pie (£3.95), lemon sole (£4.25), gammon (£4.50), to steaks (from eight-ounce rump £6.95). Donnington SBA, Hook Norton Best, Ruddles Best and Wadworths 6X on handpump; some interesting wines by the glass. A few white cast-iron tables are set out in the sheltered inner courtyard. *(Recommended by E V Walder, Aubrey and Margaret Saunders; more reports please)*

Free house   Licensee I G Potter   Real ale   Meals and snacks (11.30–2.30, 6–10)   Evening raftered steak and wine bar   Children in family-room   Folk music Sun evening Open 11–11; 11–2.30, 6–11 in winter   Bedrooms tel Evesham (0386) 840318; £16/£28

Noel Arms   ⊗ ⇌

The new licensee at this charming Cotswold hotel was previously the manager for six years, so there's no indication of significant changes, beyond the welcome introduction of an all-day food service. The bar menu includes soup (£1.30), sandwiches (from £1.30), ploughman's (£2.60), filled baked potatoes (£2.95), good salads (£3.50) and beef and Guinness or turkey, chicken and peach pie (£3.95). The reception area is interestingly decorated with armour and leopard skins; the bare-stone bar itself is an atmospheric place, with casks hanging from its beams, and farm tools, horseshoes and gin-traps; there are attractive old tables, seats and settles among the Windsor chairs, and a coal fire; the small lounge areas are comfortable and traditionally furnished. Bass, Davenports and Ruddles Best on handpump; in the bar you can choose from the restaurant wine list. It's reputedly been licensed since 1360. There are seats in the coachyard. *(Recommended by Roy Bromell, S V Bishop, Lyn and Bill Capper, Heather Sharland and others; more reports on the new regime please)*

Free house   Licensee D M Feasey   Real ale   Meals and snacks (noon–9.30) Restaurant   Children in eating area   Open 11–11   Bedrooms tel Evesham (0386) 840317; £39.50B/£52.50B

CIRENCESTER   SP0201 Map 4

Slug & Lettuce   ★ ⊗

West Market Place

The atmosphere here is designedly old-fashioned, with a lot of stripped pine, stonework and flagstones, large rugs on bare boards, long cushioned pews or country kitchen chairs as well as a superannuated consulting couch, an enormous banqueting table, big log fires, shelves and cases filled with books, and old wine bottles or labels, claret case ends and vineyard charts (they keep decent wines). It's spacious and well kept, with several communicating areas and cosier side alcoves. They have a policy of not serving sandwiches or ploughman's, but the range otherwise includes chicken liver and brandy pâté (£2.50), tagliatelle (£3.25), home-made salmon fishcakes (£4.50) and chicken breast with avocado and garlic (£5.75); the kitchens re-opened last summer after being re-vamped to bring them into line with hygiene requirements. Well kept Courage Best and John Smiths on handpump; piped music. There are tables in a well protected central courtyard. The pub was called the Crown until a few years ago. *(Recommended by Ewan McCall, Roger Huggins, Tom McLean, Patrick Freeman, Joy Heatherley, Maggie Jo St John, Tony Dudley Evans, S V Bishop, Alison Hayward, Nick Dowson, Mike Hallewell)*

Courage   Licensee E O McCalley   Real ale   Meals (until 10 evenings)   Bookings tel *Cirencester (0285) 653206/652454   Children welcome   Open 11.30–2.30, 6–11 all year; closed 25 Dec*

COATES   SO9700 Map 4
Tunnel House

Village signposted off A419 W of Cirencester; in village follow Tarlton signposts, turning right then left; pub up track on right just after railway bridge; OS Sheet 163 reference 965005

As its name suggests, this isolated but lively Cotswold pub is close to the disused Thames and Severn Canal tunnel, which runs all the way to Sapperton, over two miles away. The decorations and furnishings in the bar show considerable attention to detail, with a well carved wooden fireplace for one of the several open fires, a haphazard mixture of easy chairs, a sofa, little spindle-back seats, massive rustic benches and seats built into the sunny windows, and lots of dried flowers, enamel advertising signs, race tickets and air travel labels hanging from its beams; there's also a python – called Pythagoras – secured in a glass case by the bar. Bar food includes bacon or sausage butties (£1.30), burger (£1.70), pork pie salad (£1.90), ploughman's (£2.30), half a pint of prawns (£2.50), chilli con carne (£3.10) and spare ribs (£3.20); popular weekend barbecues (from £1.50, steaks £5). Well kept Archers Best, Flowers, Wadworths 6X and a guest beer on handpump; darts, pinball, dominoes, space game, fruit machine and juke box (there may be a TV on). *(Recommended by Peter and Rose Flower, Rob and Gill Weeks, Julie Vincent, Patrick Freeman, Alison Hayward, Nick Dowson)*

Free house   Licensees V N Judd and C R Kite   Real ale   Meals and snacks (until 10 evenings)   Children welcome   Open 11–3, 7–11 (may open all day if demand); 11–11 Sat

COLD ASTON   SP1219 Map 4
Plough

Village signposted from A436 and A429 SW of Stow-on-the-Wold; beware that on some maps the village is called Aston Blank, and the A436 called the B4068

Generous helpings of bar food in this charmingly diminutive seventeenth-century stone village pub include home-baked filled rolls (from £1.25), ploughman's (from £2.30), nicely filled baked potatoes (from £2.50), cheese and onion quiche (£2.75), spring vegetables in cheese sauce or lasagne (£3.25) and home-baked ham salad (£3.50). The bar is divided into snug areas by standing timbers and by one built-in white-painted traditional settle facing the stone fireplace. There are simple old-fashioned seats on the flagstone and lime-ash floor, and low black beams; friendly, mixed clientele, from local farmers to day-trippers. Well kept Wadworths IPA on handpump, with Norburys farm cider; darts, cribbage, dominoes and piped easy-listening music. Service is friendly, the atmosphere gentle; small side terraces have picnic-table sets under cocktail parasols. *(Recommended by G and M Brooke-Williams, Craig and Suzanne Everhart, Alan Skull, G Wolstenholme)*

Free house   Licensee J A King   Real ale   Meals and snacks   Children in eating area   Open 11–2.30, 6.30 (6 Sat, 7 weekdays in winter)–11   Bedrooms tel *Cotswold (0451) 21459; £15/£30*

Please keep sending us reports. We rely on readers for news of new discoveries, and particularly for news of changes, however slight, at the fully described pubs. No stamp needed: *The Good Pub Guide*, FREEPOST, London SW10 0BR.

nr COWLEY   SO8319   Map 4

Green Dragon ★ ⊗

Cockleford; pub signposted from A435 about 1½ miles S of junction with A436; OS Sheet 163
reference 969142

There's a fine range of real ales well kept on handpump or tapped from the cask in
this attractive stone-fronted pub, including Bass, Boddingtons, Butcombe, Flowers
Original, Hook Norton, Marstons Pedigree, Theakstons Old Peculier and
Wadworths 6X. The bar has country kitchen chairs and tables, big flagstones as
well as some red carpet, a collection of foreign banknotes pinned to some of the
beams, logs burning all year in a spacious stone fireplace, and a wood-burning stove
in a big stone fireplace. The major draw for most readers continues to be the
extensive weekly menu, with, typically, good soup such as courgette and mint or
chicken and coriander (£1.50), baby sweetcorn with garlic butter (£2.25), garlic
snails (£2.50), three-bean casserole or spaghetti bolognese (£3.25), Irish stew or
lamb with redcurrant jelly, mushrooms and brandy (£3.75), veal goulash (£4.25)
and char-grilled steaks (from £7.50); puddings such as banoffi pie (particularly
popular) or apricot mousse (£1.50); it fills up quickly so it's best to get there early
for a table; efficient, helpful service (they ask customers to dress decently). A skittle
alley doubles as an overflow for weekend lunchers. There are seats outside on the
terrace opposite the car park. (*Recommended by Roger Huggins, Tom McLean, Ewan
McColl, Frank Cummins, Simon Ward, J S Taylor, Frank Gadbois, Laurence Manning, Patrick
Freeman, Ken and Barbara Turner, GCS, John and Joan Wyatt, Jill and Howard Cox, Graham
and Glenis Watkins, Catherine Steel-Kroon, Simon Velate, Joy Heatherley, I D Shaw, Michael
and Harriet Robinson, Mrs M E Lawrence*)

*Free house   Licensees Barry and Susan Hinton   Real ale   Meals and snacks (11–2, 6–10)
Children in restaurant   Jazz Mon, folk Weds evenings   Open 11–2.30, 6–11 all year*

nr ELKSTONE   SO9610   Map 4

Highwayman

Beechpike; A417 6 miles N of Cirencester (though we list this under Elkstone as it's the closest
place marked on most road maps, that village is actually some way off)

The sheltered rose lawn at the back of this surprisingly unbusy roadside pub has
recently made way for a restaurant extension, the Turpin's; during the week it has
its own menu, but on weekend lunchtimes it's used by families ordering from the
bar menu. The rest of the garden still has a slide and swings among young conifers.
The bar itself is well laid out – a rambling warren of low beams, stripped
stonework, small-paned bay windows, cushioned antique settles (as well as wheel-
backs and Windsor armchairs around the tables), with heartening log fires and
photographs of the pub cut off in a snowdrift. Arkells on handpump; piped classical
music at lunchtime, with more variety in the evening. Bar food includes soup
(£1.50), open sandwiches (from £2.50 – wider selection at lunchtime), lunchtime
ploughman's (from £2.75), home-made pizzas (from £3.50), salads (from £3.95),
gammon (£4.95) and steak (£6.95); there are children's dishes (from £1.95), and
puddings (from £1.75); friendly staff. (*Recommended by Ian and James Phillips, Jon
Wainwright, Simon Velate, Miss J A Harvey, Dr J R Hamilton, Donald Godden, Frank
Cummins; more reports on the food please*)

*Arkells   Licensees David and Heather Bucher   Real ale   Meals and snacks (12–2.15,
6–10.15)   Restaurant tel Miserden (028 582) 221   Children in two family-rooms, eating
area and restaurant   Open 11–2.30, 6–11 all year*

If you're interested in real ale, the CAMRA *Good Beer Guide* – no relation to us – lists
thousands of pubs where you can get it.

EWEN   SU0097 Map 4
Wild Duck   🚫 🛏

Village signposted from A429 S of Cirencester

Highly praised bar food in this small sixteenth-century hotel on the edge of the peaceful village includes clam chowder (£1.95), ploughman's (£2.95), home-made steak and mushroom pie with cauliflower cheese (£3.25), baked avocado with Stilton and walnuts (£3.45), lasagne (£4.25), peppered lambs' kidneys (£4.50), good tandoori chicken (£4.85) and steak (£7); efficient, considerate service. There's an attractively old-fashioned atmosphere in the comfortable high-beamed main bar, decorated with old guns, swords, horsebrasses and duck pictures on the walls, a fine longcase clock and a handsome stripped stone fireplace; Bass and Wadworths 6X on handpump, shove-ha'penny, gentle piped music. There are teak tables and chairs in the sheltered and well kept garden – always up among the leaders in a national pub garden competition. *(Recommended by M A and C R Starling, Laurence Manning, Roger Huggins, Tom McLean, Ewan McCall, M J Dyke, Peter and Rose Flower, Alan Skull, Gordon Theaker, Nigel Williamson, Alison Hayward, Nick Dowson)*

Free house   Licensee Martin Pulley   Real ale   Meals and snacks (until 10 evenings) Restaurant   Children in eating area   Open 11–11; 11–3, 6–11 in winter Bedrooms tel Kemble (0285) 770364; £43.50B/£58B

FORD   SP0829 Map 4
Plough   ★ 🚫

B4077

Bar food in this rambling and idiosyncratic but welcoming inn includes good asparagus feasts (April to June, £8.50), sandwiches (from £1), soup (£1.25), mushrooms on toast (£2.25), ploughman's (£2.75), home-made pies (£4.75), and winter pheasant (£7.50 or so), with seafood every other Thursday evening (around £7.50 depending on availability); it seems that at busy times there's still some progress to be made on the table-cleaning front. The beamed and stripped stone bar has log fires, old settles and benches around the big tables on its uneven flagstones and oak tables in a snug alcove; the atmosphere is frequently enlivened by Reg and his (not always well tuned) piano. Well kept Donnington BB and SBA on handpump; darts, shove-ha'penny, dominoes and cribbage. There are benches in front, with rustic tables and chairs on grass by white lilacs and fairy lights. The inn used to be the local court-house – and what's now the cellar was the jail. *(Recommended by E V Walder, Derek and Sylvia Stephenson, W L Congreve, Dr J M Jackson, PLC, Simon Ward, Dr M V Jones, Gwyneth and Salvo Spadaro-Dutturi, A T Langton, Denis Mann, M A and C R Starling, Mrs M J Dyke, Simon Velate, Hazel Church)*

Donnington   Licensee Leslie Carter   Real ale   Meals and snacks (11.30–2.30, 6.30ish–10)   Children welcome   Pianist   Open 10.30–3, 5.30–12 (may open longer Sat afternoon) all year   Twin bedrooms tel Stanton (038 673) 215; /£30

FOSSEBRIDGE   SP0811 Map 4
Fossebridge   🛏

A429 Cirencester–Stow-on-the-Wold

This ivy-covered Cotswolds inn, handy for Chedworth Roman villa, serves a good range of bar food, including Stilton and celery soup (£1.65), lunchtime filled French sticks (from £2.25) and ploughman's (£3.50), warm salads such as bacon and grated Parmesan (from £3.50), local faggots in madeira sauce (£4.25), stuffed aubergine with yoghurt and thyme (£4.50), steak and kidney pie or pan-fried lamb's liver (£5.25), steamed Dart salmon (£10.75) and Dover sole (£12.90); some dishes have two prices according to size. The delightful original fifteenth-century core houses two bars, linked by arches, with dark brown limestone walls and beams on the sloping ceiling, and simple but effective furnishings: oriental rugs on flagstones, traditional wooden chairs, wall benches and tables. There are prints, reproductions of old maps, decorative plates and copper pans on the walls, and a fine log fire up at the waist-high level of the original floor. A more modern area, with an attractive restaurant, leads off. Well kept Marstons Burton and Pedigree on handpump, and a useful choice of good malt whiskies and reasonably priced wines; sensibly placed darts and shove-ha'penny. There are tables out on the streamside terrace and a spacious lakeside lawn. The pub came on the market in the summer of 1989, and around that time, although we continued to get good reports on it, some readers mentioned lapses in service and to some extent in food quality; obviously we'd be grateful for more reports. *(Recommended by Aileen Mitchell, S V Bishop, Laurence Manning, Henry Midwinter, David Heath, Aubrey and Margaret Saunders, BKA, Mrs Margaret Dyke, Catherine Steele-Kroon, Alastair Campbell, Alun Davies, Mr and Mrs Wyatt, Ewan McCall, Roger Huggins, Tom McLean)*

Free house   Licensees Hugh and Suzanne Roberts   Real ale   Meals and snacks Restaurant   Children welcome   Open 11–2.30, 6–11 all year   Bedrooms tel Fossebridge (028 572) 721; £45B/£65B

FRAMPTON MANSELL   SO9102 Map 4

Crown

Village signposted off A419 Cirencester–Stroud

This pleasant and friendly Cotswold inn, attractively situated near a quiet wooded valley, has a main bar with stripped stonework, a dark beam and plank ceiling, little mullioned windows, a traditional settle alongside more up-to-date cushioned wall benches and ladder-back rush seats on the patterned carpet; there's a simpler public bar. Archers Village and Wadworths 6X on handpump, piped music. Bar food is served by uniformed waitresses from a good, though sometimes expensive cold buffet; there's a range of salads, from ham or chicken to beef (around £3–£5), as well as soup (£1.10) and ploughman's (£1.75). Good teak seats outside overlook the valley. *(Recommended by Mrs J Oakes, John Bowdler, NIP, Ewan McCall, Roger Huggins, Tom McLean, Alison Hayward, Nick Dowson; more reports please)*

Free house   Real ale   Meals and snacks   Restaurant   Open 11–3, 6–11 all year; closed 25 Dec   Bedrooms tel Frampton Mansell (028 576) 601; £35B/£50B

GREAT BARRINGTON   SP2013 Map 4

Fox

Village signposted from A40 Burford–Northleach; pub between Little and Great Barrington

This remote but popular inn, attractively positioned on an elbow of the tranquil River Windrush, has an atmospherically relaxed bar, with low ceilings, stripped stone walls, two good log fires, and rustic wooden chairs, tables and window seats; Donnington BB, SBA and XXX Mild on handpump; sensibly placed darts, dominoes, cribbage, fruit machine, and a skittle alley out beyond the sheltered yard. Bar food includes sandwiches (90p, toasted £1.20), soup (95p), ploughman's (£1.90), salads and steak and kidney or chicken and mushroom pie (£3). There are metal tables and seats on the concrete terrace by the river. We've had some mixed reports recently on food and service, so we'd appreciate some more up-to-date information. *(Recommended by Stephen King, Simon Ward, EML, Alan Skull, Graham Tayar, Simon Velate, Ewan McCall, Joan Olivier, Mr and Mrs Peter Gordon, Caroline Raphael, D Stephenson)*

Donnington   Real ale   Meals (not Sun) and snacks   Open 11–2.30, 6.30–11 all year Bedrooms tel Windrush (045 14) 385; £14/£27

'Space game' means any electronic game.

GREAT RISSINGTON   SP1917 Map 4

Lamb   🛏

Overlooking the village and the surrounding hills, this partly seventeenth-century Cotswold inn serves good bar food, including soup (£1.25) and home-made pâtés (£2.50), with main dishes like seafood platter, mild curry or chicken and mushroom pie (£5.45), local trout (£6.25), chicken breast filled with cheese and smoked ham (£6.90) and steaks (from £7.95); on Sunday the menu is limited to a roast lunch and ploughman's. The cosy two-room bar, decorated with plates, pictures and an interesting collection of old cigarette and tobacco tins, has wheel-back chairs grouped around polished tables on the carpet, and a log-effect gas fire in the stone fireplace. Well kept Flowers Original, Hook Norton, Wadworths 6X and guest beers such as Boddingtons or Marstons on handpump; piped pop music. The sheltered hillside garden has a play area and aviary. One of the chintzy bedrooms in the warren of small stairs and doors has a four-poster carved by the landlord; there's an indoor swimming-pool. *(Recommended by Patrick and Mary McDermott, Sarah and Jamie Allan, Simon Velate, BKA, Peter Griffiths, Mr and Mrs P W Dryland)*

Free house   Licensees Richard and Kate Cleverly   Real ale   Meals and snacks   Restaurant   Children welcome   Open 11.30–2.30, 6.30–11 all year   Bedrooms tel   Cotswold (0451) 20388; £21(£25B)/£32(£36B)

GUITING POWER   SP0924 Map 4

Olde Inne

Village signposted off B4068 SW of Stow-on-the-Wold (still called A436 on many maps)

The Danish licensee who caught readers' attention with her selection of national dishes has now left this snug stone cottage pub; all the signs are that the new licensees are continuing the tradition of hospitality, though obviously we'd appreciate more reports. Bar food now includes filled rolls, soup (£1.30), ploughman's (from £1.95), cod or haddock (£3.25), lasagne (£3.50), home-cooked ham or home-made steak and kidney pie (£3.95), with specials such as vegetable curry or butter-bean bake (£3.50), beef Stroganoff (£4.50) or baked trout (£5.75) and eight-ounce rump steak (£6.85). The gently lit bar has attractive built-in wall and window seats (including one, near the serving-counter, that's the height of the bar stools) and small brocaded armchairs. In winter logs burn in an unusual pillar-supported stone fireplace. Turkey carpet sweeps from here into a more spacious dining-room with winged settles and wheel-back chairs around neat tables. The public bar, with flagstones and stripped stone masonry but furnished like the main bar, has sensibly placed darts, bar billiards, dominoes and a fruit machine; Boddingtons, Hook Norton Best and Wadworths 6X on handpump, and a selection of malt whiskies. Tables on a strip of gravel in front (where they're planning to extend the patio) look over the quiet lane to a gentle slope of field. The pub's also known as Th' Ollow Bottom. *(Recommended by PADEMLUC, Simon Velate, Denis Waters)*

Free house   Licensees Kenneth and Paula Thouless-Meyrick   Real ale   Meals and snacks   Restaurant   Children in eating area and restaurant   Open 11.30–11

HYDE   SO8801 Map 4

Ragged Cot

Burnt Ash; Hyde signposted with Minchinhampton from A419 E of Stroud; or (better road) follow Minchinhampton, Aston Down signposted from A419 at Aston Down airfield; OS Sheet 162 reference 886012

Friendly and relaxed, this chatty old place under its stone-slab roof has a bar that rambles around a longish serving-counter, with a no-smoking restaurant area off to the right – we inspected just after it had been extended in summer 1989, and can report that it's been done well. In winter it's the traditional dark wood wall settle by the end fire that's most in demand; in summer the red-cushioned window seats overlooking the garden and its line of chestnut trees take over. Décor is mainly stripped stone and black beams. Attractively priced bar food, all home made, includes onion soup (£1.20), pizzas (£1.95), pâté (£2.50), salads (from £2.50), cauliflower cheese or omelettes (£2.95), sweet-and-sour pork or steak and kidney pie (£3.95), gammon (£4.75) and steaks (from £7.95); well kept Boddingtons, Marstons Pedigree, Theakstons Best, Uley Old Spot and Youngers IPA and No 3 on handpump. Service is kind and quick. There are picnic-table sets outside, and at holiday times a pavilion-like garden bar may be used; neat modern lavatories. *(Recommended by Frank Cummins, Ewan McCall, Roger Huggins, Tom McLean, Margaret Dyke, John Broughton, Patrick Freeman)*

Free house   Licensees Mr and Mrs M Case   Real ale   Meals and snacks (not 25 Dec) Restaurant tel Brimscombe (0453) 884643   Open 11–3, 6–11 all year; closed evening 25 Dec

KINETON SP0926 Map 4
Halfway House

Village signposted from B4068 and B4077 W of Stow-on-the-Wold

The bar in this small and pretty stone house, overlooking the valley, is unpretentiously traditional and functional, decorated with ancient farm tools and pictures at one end and beams at the other; attractively priced, well kept Donnington BB and SBA (fresh from the nearby brewery) on handpump; darts, dominoes, fruit machine and juke box. The simple bar food is good value, and includes sandwiches (from £1), ploughman's (from £2), salads (from £2.50), plaice (£2.75), steak and kidney pie (£3) and rump steak (£6). There may be cats and a lively dog wandering in from the narrow flagstoned front terrace, where you can sit separated from the slow, quiet village lane by tubs of bright flowers on top of a low stone wall. There are more tables, and children's swings, on the sheltered back lawn. *(Recommended by Mrs N Lawson, HNJ, PEJ, Simon Velate; more reports please)*

Donnington   Licensees Derek and Jean Marshall   Real ale   Meals and snacks (12–2, 6.30–9.30)   Restaurant   Children welcome lunchtime   Open 11–2.30, 6–11 all year; closed 25 Dec   Bedrooms tel Guiting Power (045 15) 344; £12/£24

KINGSCOTE ST8196 Map 4
Hunters Hall ★ 🏵

A4135 Dursley–Tetbury

This attractive, creeper-covered Tudor building is spacious and up-market inside; there's something to suit all tastes in the popular series of elegant high-beamed connecting rooms, which have a comfortable miscellany of easy chairs, sofas and a fine old box settle as well as some more elementary seats, velvet curtains, exposed stone walls and good winter log fires; there's more space to eat in the Gallery upstairs. The lower-ceilinged public bar has sturdy settles and oak tables on the flagstones in front of another big log fire. Bar food, generally served from a buffet in an airy end room, includes sandwiches, mussels in white wine, smoked trout, steak and kidney pie (£3.25), turkey and ham pie or seafood pancakes (£4.25), salads such as rare beef or mixed meats (£4.90), salmon (£5.50) and charcoal-grilled steaks (from £6.35). Bass, Hook Norton and Marstons Pedigree on handpump. The big garden has weekend summer barbecues; the outbuildings here have recently

---

You are now allowed twenty minutes after 'time, please' to finish your drink – half an hour if you bought it in conjunction with a meal.

been converted into bedrooms. *(Recommended by Peter and Rose Flower, Heather Sharland, BKA, Patrick Freeman, Mrs J Oakes, Dr M V Jones, Roger Huggins, Adrian Kelly, Dr James Haworth, Alison Hayward, Nick Dowson, J V Hayward, S Matthews, Alastair Campbell, Frank Cummins, Donald Godden)*

Free house   Licensee David Barnett-Roberts   Real ale   Meals and snacks   Restaurant   Children in eating and gallery area and restaurant   Open 11–3, 6–11; opens 7 in winter; closed 25 Dec   Bedrooms tel Dursley (0453) 860393; £35/£45

nr LECHLADE   SU2199 Map 4

Trout

St John's Bridge; 1 mile E of Lechlade on A417

New licensees at this riverside former almshouse have expanded the bar area and its menu, but preserved the atmosphere which attracts readers. A new snug area, which used to be the ground-floor cellar, now opens off the main bar area, and is furnished with wooden tables and settles, with fishing prints on the walls; the low-beamed main bar itself is partly panelled and decorated with trout and stuffed pike; a wrought-iron screen separates a carpeted area from the flagstoned part by the serving-counter, which has Courage Best and Directors and John Smiths on handpump; darts and maybe piped music. A third bar leads on to the spacious garden, which has plenty of tables by the old walnut tree, a summer bar and family marquee, with barbecues on fine summer Sunday lunchtimes; there are fine views from here over the meadows towards Lechlade. Bar food now includes soup (£1.50), pâté or whitebait (£2.25), home-made pizza (£3.25), lasagne or seafood crumble (£3.50), smoked prawns (£3.75), fresh trout (£5.95) and ten-ounce rump steak (£7.50), with a good selection of daily specials, and a vegetarian (from £2.50) and children's (from £1.10) menu. By an ancient royal charter the pub has two miles of coarse fishing rights. *(Recommended by Patrick Freeman, Frank Cummins, Lyn and Bill Capper, Mr and Mrs H W Clayton, John and Joan Wyatt; reports on the new regime please)*

Courage   Licensees Mr and Mrs Warren   Real ale   Meals and snacks   Restaurant tel Faringdon (0367) 52313   Children in restaurant and marquee   Open 11–2.30, 6–11

LITTLE WASHBOURNE   SO9933 Map 4

Hobnails ⚜

A438 Tewkesbury–Stow-on-the-Wold

There's an unchanging and thoroughly traditional atmosphere in this partly fifteenth-century long low building – not least because it's been with the same family for over 240 years. The snug little front bar has old wall benches by a couple of tables on its quarry-tiled floor, under low sway-backed beams hung with pewter tankards. There's more space in the carpeted back bar – more modern, with comfortable button-back leatherette banquettes. Flowers IPA and Original and Whitbreads PA on handpump; darts, shove-ha'penny, fruit machine, piped music. The primary feature of the bar menu continues to be the wide range of large and generously filled baps, which range from fried egg (50p), through sausage and grilled ham (£2.50), to steak with egg and mushrooms (£4.25), and burgers (from £1.75); there's also a choice of soups (£1.30) and other starters, a large bowl of salad (£1.60) and a wide range of home-made puddings including several based on liqueurs (from £1.50–£2.25); pleasant service. A separate skittle alley (for hire Monday to Friday evenings) has more tables. A terrace between the two buildings,

---

Children welcome means the pub says it lets children inside without any special restriction; readers have found that some may impose an evening time-limit – please tell us if you find this.

and beside a small lawn and flower bed, has good tables. *(Recommended by Derek and Sylvia Stephenson, G and M Hollis, Ted George, E V Walder, Frank Cummins, Catherine Steele-Kroon, PAB, Chris Cooke, B K Scott, Dr J R Hamilton)*

Flowers (Whitbreads)   Licensee Stephen Farbrother   Real ale   Meals and snacks (until 10.30 evenings)   Restaurant tel Alderton (024 262) 237   Children in eating area, restaurant and larger room at weekends   Open 11–2.30, 6–11 all year; closed 25 and 26 Dec

NAILSWORTH   ST8499   Map 4
Weighbridge
B4014 towards Tetbury

This Cotswolds pub, popular with walkers, has three little downstairs rooms, with attractive antique settles and small country chairs, and walls either crisply white or stripped to bare stone; the one on the left has its black beam and plank ceiling thickly festooned with black ironware – sheepshears, gin-traps, lamps, cauldrons, bellows; there are log fires in each. Steps lead up to a raftered loft with candles in bottles on an engaging mix of more or less rustic tables, and some unexpected decorations such as a wooden butcher's block. You can walk from here into the sheltered garden rising behind the pub, with swings and picnic-table sets under cocktail parasols. An unusual feature of the bar menu are the two-in-one pies with steak on one side and cauliflower cheese on the other, say (£3.70 large, £2.70 small), also shepherd's (£2.60), steak and mushroom or turkey and sweetcorn (£2.70); other bar food includes sandwiches (from 95p), filled baked potatoes (from 95p), ploughman's (from £1.95) and salads. Well kept Courage Best and Wadworths 6X on handpump. *(Recommended by BKA, Roger Huggins, Klaus and Elizabeth Leist, Frank Cummins, DE, Patrick Freeman, Steve Breame, E A George)*

Free house   Licensee J M Kulesla   Real ale   Meals and snacks   Children in two rooms away from bar   Open 11–2.30, 7–11 all year

NAUNTON   SP1123   Map 4
Black Horse   🏵 🛏
Village signposted from B4068 (shown as A436 on older maps) W of Stow-on-the-Wold

This L-shaped little inn on a quiet village lane serves a good range of food, including home-made soup (£1.25), pâté (£2), ploughman's (£2.25), salads (from £3.50), home-cooked ham, chicken breast or seafood platter (£4), succulent gammon (£5.50) and Scotch steak (£7.50), with specials such as marinated herring (£2), pork and pineapple casserole (£4), and half a roast duckling (£6.50). The bar is unpretentiously furnished, but still has a sophisticated atmosphere; there are flagstones and flooring tiles, black beams and some stripped stonework, simple country-kitchen chairs and built-in oak pews, polished elm cast-iron-framed tables and a big wood-burning stove. Well kept Donnington BB and SBA, sensibly placed darts, fruit machine and juke box; some tables outside. Note that they don't allow children. *(Recommended by Simon Ward, Henry Midwinter, Joy Heatherley, Dr F Peters, Jill Field, Simon Velate, Dr J M Jackson)*

Donnington   Licensees Adrian and Jennie Bowen-Jones   Real ale   Meals and snacks (not 25 Dec)   Restaurant   Open 11–2.30, 6–11 all year   Two bedrooms tel Guiting Power (045 15) 378; £15/£30

NORTH CERNEY   SP0208   Map 4
Bathurst Arms
A435 Cirencester–Cheltenham

On the edge of the little River Churn, this pink Cotswolds inn has a beamed and black-panelled bar, with high-backed antique settles and nice window seats, Windsor chairs on the Turkey carpet, pewter tankards above the serving-counter and a splendid stone fireplace; the quite separate Stables Bar has cribbage and dominoes. There's a good range of real ales, with Brains, Courage Best, Flowers, Gibbs Mew Bishops Tipple, Hook Norton Best, Ind Coope Burton, Tetleys, Wadworths 6X and Wethereds Winter Royal on handpump. The large choice of imaginative, restauranty food includes fresh salmon fishcakes in a cheese sauce (£3.95), pan-fried lemon sole (£4.25), pork fillets in a rich cherry and mushroom sauce (£4.50), smoked king prawns with a seasonal salad (£4.95) and steaks (from £6.75). They hold summer barbecues most weekends, lunchtime and evening on the pretty front lawn. *(Recommended by Russell and Christina Jones, Pamela and Merlyn Horswell, Mike Muston, Joy Heatherley, Alison Hayward, Nick Dowson, S V Bishop, Peter Wade, Mr and Mrs J M Elden)*

Free house   Licensees Mr and Mrs F A C Seward   Real ale   Meals and snacks Restaurant   Children in eating area   Open 11–3, 6–11 all year   Bedrooms tel North Cerney (028 583) 281; £25B/£30B

NORTH NIBLEY   ST7496 Map 4

Black Horse 🏠

B4060

This pleasantly welcoming stone-roofed building has a black-beamed bar, which is partly divided by standing timbers and surviving stub walls, and has some stripped stonework (including one particularly handsome fireplace with a wood-burning stove), wheel-back chairs and red cloth built-in wall and window seats around very sturdy rustic tables. It's decorated with black iron farm tools, heavy-horse harness and copper pans; darts, dominoes and fruit machine over on the right; Flowers Original and Whitbreads PA on handpump, with a guest beer. Good bar food includes sandwiches or filled rolls (from 85p), home-made soup (95p), hot pitta bread filled with steak (£1.60, prawn £2.25), salads (from £2.50), chilli con carne (£3.25), plaice or scampi (£3.50), gammon (£4) and steak (£5.85); decent range of puddings (from £1). Picnic-table sets on the grass behind look up to a steep wooded knoll and the Italianate monument on its crest. *(Recommended by JM, PM, Mr and Mrs Stevens, Dr and Mrs A K Clarke, Frank Cummins)*

Whitbreads   Licensees the Hamston family   Real ale   Meals and snacks (until 10 evenings)   Restaurant (Tues–Sat evenings and Sun lunchtime)   Open 12–2.30, 6–11 all year   Bedrooms tel Dursley (0453) 46841; £23.50(£26B)/£33(£37B)

New Inn ★ 🏠

Waterley Bottom, which is quite well signposted from surrounding lanes; inn signposted from the Bottom itself; one route is from A4135 S of Dursley, via lane with red sign saying Steep Hill, 1 in 5 (just SE of Stinchcombe Golf Course turn-off), turning right when you get to the bottom; another is to follow Waterley Bottom signpost from previous main entry, keeping eyes skinned for small low signpost to inn; OS Sheet 162 reference 758963

Part of the charm of visiting this peaceful rural brick inn is the adventure of actually tracking it down – many readers miss it first time round; but given the welcome, particularly from the cheerful landlady, the effort's well worth making. The good range of well kept real ales on handpump includes Cotleigh Tawny, Greene King Abbot, Smiles Best and Exhibition, Theakstons Old Peculier, and WB (a bitter brewed for the pub by Cotleigh); also Inch's cider and a good range of malts. The carpeted lounge bar is a cheerful place, with cushioned Windsor chairs and varnished high-backed settles against its partly stripped stone walls, a fine collection of breweriana – particularly antique handpump beer engines – and piped music. Picture windows look out on to a beautifully kept garden below the slopes of the hillside. The simply furnished public bar has sensibly placed darts, dominoes, shove-ha'penny, cribbage and quiz games. The home-made bar food is good value, with filled brown baps (from 45p), toasted sandwiches (from 75p), pâté (£1.65, smoked salmon £1.95), ploughman's (from £1.85), chilli con carne (£2.10), chicken and mushroom pie (£2.20), and beef or ham salad (£3.50); puddings (95p). To stay here (it's pleasant walking country) it's advisable to book a long way ahead. There are swings, slides and a timber tree-house in a small orchard beyond the garden.

(Recommended by Mr and Mrs J D Cranston, Cynthia McDowall, Dr and Mrs A K Clarke, Peter and Rose Flower, M E Dormer, Sue Cleasby, Mike Ledger, A C Watson and C J Lindon, Brian and Anna Marsden, Gill and Rob Weeks, Lynne Sheridan, Bob West)

Free house   Licensee Ruby Sainty   Real ale   Meals and snacks (not 25 Dec)   Open 12–3, 7–11 all year   Two bedrooms tel Dursley (0453) 3659; £12/£24

PAINSWICK   SO8609 Map 4

Royal Oak 🍺

St Mary's Street

The welcoming lounge bar here is divided in two by a massive chimney (with an open fire in winter), and has some walls stripped back to silvery stone, seats and copper-topped tables made from barrels, an elegant oak settle, and a lovely panelled oak door leading to a second bar on the left. A small sun lounge faces a sheltered sun-trap courtyard with wistaria and colourful pots of geraniums and calceolarias. The simple but highly praised food ranges from sandwiches (from 90p, fresh salmon £1.50), home-made soup (85p) and ploughman's (from £1.85), through home-made pâté (£1.95) and salads (around £4.50, salmon £4.95), to an enterprising range of hot dishes, changing every day but typically including good home-made lasagne (£3.50), lamb cutlets (£4.75), chicken Kiev (£4.95), fresh salmon and steaks (from £8); well kept Flowers Original and Whitbreads PA on handpump. The pub is well positioned in the centre of this charming small hillside town of old stone buildings (many of them now antique shops) in narrow alleys, and handy for St Mary's churchyard with its 99 yew trees. *(Recommended by Shirley Allen, Tom Evans, David and Ruth Hollands, Dr M V Jones, Helena and Arthur Harbottle, Ted Denham, G C Calderwood, C and J Cadbury, E J Alcock, Nigel Williamson)*

Flowers (Whitbreads)   Licensees Mr and Mrs Morris   Real ale   Meals and snacks (not Sun; until 10pm for snacks)   Children welcome   Nearby parking may be difficult   Open 11–3, 6–11 all year; closed 25 Dec

REDBROOK   SO5410 Map 4

Boat

Pub's inconspicuously signposted car park in village on A466 Chepstow–Monmouth; from here 100-yard footbridge crosses Wye (pub actually in Penallt in Wales – but much easier to find this way); OS Sheet 162 reference 534097

The walk across what was once a light railway bridge over the swirling Wye makes for the most unusual approach to any pub in this part of England. The bar itself is a relaxed place, and pleasantly spartan; a particular attraction is the range of well kept real ales, tapped straight from casks behind the long curved bar counter. There are usually three guest beers weekly, as well as the regular Bull Mastiff Best, Dorset IPA, Hook Norton Old Hookey, Marstons Pedigree, Theakstons Best, XB and Old Peculier and Wadworths 6X; also farmhouse cider and country wines; cribbage, dominoes and a space game. Bar food includes soup (£1.05), vegetable or Cornish pasty (£1.15), ploughman's (£1.90), steak roll (£2.30), vegetable curry or lasagne (£2.70), seafood pancakes (£2.95), chicken curry (£3), beef with cashew-nuts (£3.20) and salads (Parma ham £3.60, smoked salmon £3.80); additional winter dishes like lamb hot-pot or filled baked potatoes. There are splendid views of the valley from the steep terraced garden (prettily lit at night), which has tables among little waterfalls, and a pond cut into the rocks. The lavatories may not always be up to scratch. *(Recommended by R P Taylor, Paul S McPherson, Dave Braisted, P L Duncan, D Godden, Ian Clay, Barry and Anne, Maggie Jo St John, Dudley Evans, M A and W R Proctor, Gwynne Harper, Mr and Mrs G J Packer)*

Free house   Licensee Brian Beck   Real ale   Meals and snacks (12–2.30, 6–10)   Children in family-room   Folk music Tues, jazz Thurs   Open 11–3, 6–11 all year

ST BRIAVELS   SO5605 Map 4

George 🛏

Bar food here includes sandwiches (from 80p) and ploughman's (from £1.50) as well as hot dishes such as filled baked potatoes (from £1.20), vegetable, seafood or meaty lasagne (from £2.90), haddock, chilli con carne or chicken curry (£3) and home-made steak and kidney pie or a Sunday roast (£3.50); their speciality is what they call an oriental steamboat (£15 a head at 24 hours' notice). The bar is a three-roomed rambling affair, with toby jugs and antique bottles on black beams over the servery, green-cushioned small settles, old-fashioned built-in wall seats, some booth seating, and a large stone open fireplace. A Celtic coffin lid dating from 1070, discovered when a fireplace was removed, is mounted next to the bar counter. Badger Tanglefoot, Marstons Pedigree and Wadworths 6X on handpump; darts, cribbage, dominoes, fruit machine, trivia game, piped music. A 700-year-old tradition is enacted every Whitsun after evensong on the wall outside the neighbouring church, when a member of the local Creswick family throws down bits of bread and cheese to the poor in return for woodland and grazing rights in the woods that stretch to the west of the village. Outside the pub there are tables on a flagstoned terrace and among roses. *(Recommended by BKA, G B Pugh, J F and M Sayers, Nick Dowson, Barry and Anne, M A and W R Proctor)*

Free house   Licensee M E Day   Real ale   Meals and snacks   Open 11–11 all year Bedrooms tel Dean (0594) 530228; £18/£28

SAPPERTON   SO9403 Map 4

Daneway

Village signposted from A419 Stroud–Cirencester; from village centre follow Edgeworth, Bisley signpost; OS Sheet 163 reference 939034

The pub was built originally for the tunnel workers, who lived here in the four years in the 1780s that the tunnel of the Thames and Severn Canal (about 500 yards away) was being quarried through the stone, up to 250 feet below ground. It then became a popular bargees' pub, frequented particularly by 'leggers', men who lay on top of the canalboats and pushed them through the two-and-a-quarter-mile tunnel, using their legs against the tunnel roof. The heavy-horse harness and brasses in the traditionally furnished lounge recall those days – the canal fell into disuse around 1930, though it's now being partially restored by a canal trust. There's also a remarkably grand and dominating fireplace, elaborately carved oak from floor to ceiling, and racing and hunting prints on the attractively papered walls. Bar food includes filled rolls (70p, not Sundays; bacon and mushroom £1.30), ploughman's (from £1.70), filled baked potatoes (£1.70), tuna salad (£2.25), lasagne verde or chilli con carne (£2.85) and steak and kidney pie (£3.95); well kept Archers Best and a beer brewed for the pub on handpump and electric pump, Wadworths IPA on handpump, and 6X tapped from the cask, also regular guest beers; darts, dominoes and shove-ha'penny in the public bar, which has a big inglenook fireplace; friendly, attentive service. Lots of picnic-table sets on a sloping lawn bright with flower beds and a rose trellis look down over the remains of the canal and the valley of the little River Frome. The pub's car park is built over what used to be one of its locks – you can still see the cornerstone of the lock gates. It's on *Good Walks Guide* Walk 89.

(Recommended by Tom McLean, Ewan McCall, Roger Huggins, HNJ, PEJ, Patrick Freeman, Alison Hayward, Nick Dowson, Frank Cummins)

Free house   Managers Liz and Richard Goodfellow   Real ale   Snacks (not Sun) and meals   Children in small family-room off lounge   Open 11–2.30 (3 Sat in summer), 6.30–11

SHUTHONGER   SO8834   Map 4

Crown 🍺

A38 2 miles N of Tewkesbury, on W side of road (car park opposite)

Furnishings in the bar here are simple and modern, and there's quite a bit of nautical brassware against the plain cream walls – an Aldis lamp, engine-room telegraph, even two porthole hatches from the *Ark Royal*. Well kept Banks's, Bass and Marstons Pedigree on handpump; also Westons Old Rosie cider. Food is straightforward, but prepared and presented with great attention to detail – the local black pudding with mushrooms (£2.75) comes in for particular praise; other dishes include good spare ribs or avocado with prawns (£2.95), devilled kidneys (£3.25), lasagne (£3.50) and chicken cooked with pineapple, almonds and malibu (£8.50); they're served with good fresh vegetables such as fennel or baby beetroot in a creamy sauce. *(Recommended by Bernard Phillips, John and Joan Wyatt, Mr and Mrs Devereux)*

Free house   Licensee S G Bezani   Real ale   Meals and snacks   Restaurant tel Tewkesbury (0684) 293714   Children in restaurant   Open 11–2.30, 6–11 all year

SOUTHROP   SP1903   Map 4

Swan 🍺

Village signposted from A417 and A361, near Lechlade

The low-ceilinged front lounge in this creeper-covered stone-tiled pub has cottagey wall seats and chairs, and winter log fires; it's proving so popular with eaters that they're currently extending it. Beyond it is a spacious stripped-stone-wall skittle alley, well modernised, with plenty of tables on the carpeted part, and its own bar service at busy times; Morlands PA and Wadworths 6X on handpump, and a fair selection of wines by the bottle; darts. The choice of enterprising and home-made bar food is more restauranty in the evening, when it might include Stilton and onion or tomato, orange and mint soup (£1.80), deep-fried Camembert with cranberry and orange sauce or chicken liver pâté (£2.35), and a good range of main dishes such as moussaka (£5.25), tagliatelle with walnuts and mushrooms (£5.75), salmon and asparagus buckwheat pancakes or a whole spring chicken with red wine and bacon (£5.95) and fillet steak, ham and Stilton in puff pastry (£7); at lunchtime there's a bigger choice of light snacks and ploughman's (£2.65), as well as a selection of the evening dishes at markedly lower prices, such as moussaka at £3.65; tables in the sheltered garden behind. *(Recommended by Patrick Freeman, HNJ, PEJ, Alan Skull, Wg Cdr R M Sparkes, Ewan McCall, Roger Huggins, Tom McLean, Paul S McPherson)*

Free house   Licensee Patrick Keen   Real ale   Snacks (not evening) and meals (not Sun evening)   Restaurant tel Southrop (036 785) 205   Children welcome   Open 12–2.30, 7–11 all year

STANTON   SO0634   Map 4

Mount

Village signposted off B4632 (the old A46) SW of Broadway; Old Snowshill Road – take no through road up hill and bear left

This fine Cotswolds pub is particularly well positioned – up a steep, quiet lane looking back down over the lovely golden stone village; the best view is from the terrace, and on a good day you can see across to the Welsh mountains. The original central core of the bar, atmospheric and tranquil even when busy, has cask seats on big flagstones, a big fireplace, black beams, heavy-horse harness and racing photographs. There are also big picture windows in a spacious extension with comfortable oak wall seats, cigarette cards of Derby and Grand National winners, and an aquarium of goldfish and angel-fish; well kept, reasonably priced Donnington BB on handpump, and farm cider; darts, dominoes, shove-ha'penny, cribbage, fruit and space machine and piped music. Good bar food includes toasted sandwiches (£2), lunchtime ploughman's (from £2.50), their own cow pie (£3), steak and kidney pie, or ratatouille lasagne (£3), with extra dishes in the evening like chicken curry (£3) and sirloin steak (£4). You can play boules on the lawn; on *Good Walks Guide* Walk 88. *(Recommended by Laurence Manning, Michael and Alison Sandy, PADEMLUC, A C Watson and C J Lindon, Ian Blackwell, Wayne Brindle, Mrs E M Lloyd; more reports please)*

Donnington   Licensee Colin L Johns   Real ale   Meals and snacks (not Sun evening) Children welcome if well behaved   Open 11–11; 11–2.30, 6–11 in winter; closed 25 Dec

STOW-ON-THE-WOLD   SP1925 Map 4

Queens Head

The Square

The best place to sample the local atmosphere is in the spacious flagstoned back bar, which has a couple of attractive high-backed settles as well as wheel-back chairs, lots of beams, and a big log fire in the stone fireplace; pleasant piped music in here (not in front), darts, shove-ha'penny and fruit machine. The stripped stone front lounge is busier with a mixture of tourists and local businessmen, and is packed with small tables, little Windsor armchairs and brocaded wall banquettes. Bar food includes sandwiches (from £1.10), soup or filled baked potatoes (£1.50), broccoli flan (£2), ploughman's (£2.25), chilli con carne or faggots (£2.75) and steak and kidney pie (£3.25); Donnington BB and SBA are particularly well kept on handpump. There are some white tables in the back courtyard, and a green bench in front, under the climbing rose and the hanging baskets, looks across the square of charming buildings – of which this pub is undoubtedly one. Two puppies have recently replaced the elderly labrador, who has passed on to a more ethereal watering-hole. *(Recommended by Michael and Alison Sandy, David and Jane Russell, Mike Hallewell; more reports please)*

Donnington   Licensee Timothy Eager   Real ale   Meals and snacks (not Sun evening) Children in back bar   Occasional jazz Sun, sometimes guitarist in week   Open 11–2.30, 6–11 all year

nr STOW-ON-THE-WOLD   SP1925 Map 4

Coach & Horses

Ganborough; A424 2½ miles N of Stow; OS Sheet 163 reference 172292

They take great pride here in the fact that all the food is genuinely home made and home cooked; the attractive range includes sandwiches (£1.05; toasted £1.35), game soup (£1.20), basket meals (from £2.30), filled baked potatoes (from £2.10), ploughman's (from £2.30), chicken Kiev or steak and kidney pie (£3.90), local trout (£4.65), with specials such as roast rib of beef (£4.50) or pheasant (£4.95 in season); mixed grill (£5.95) and sirloin steak (£6.85); puddings (from £1.20); friendly service. The bar area has a welcoming atmosphere, and is decorated with good wildlife photographs and coach horns on its ceiling joists; there are leatherette wall benches, stools and Windsor chairs on the flagstone floor, and steps up to a carpeted part with high-backed settles around the tables; winter log fire in the central chimneypiece; darts, fruit machine, space game and juke box. Donnington XXX, BB and SBA, from the nearby brewery, are well kept on handpump. There are seats outside, on a terrace and a narrow lawn. *(Recommended by Joan Olivier, Simon Velate, Dr J R Hamilton; more reports please)*

Donnington   Licensees Andy and Sarah Morris   Real ale   Meals and snacks   Children in eating area   Open 11–2.30 (3 Sat), 6–11 all year; closed evening 25 Dec

WITHINGTON   SP0315 Map 4

Mill Inn   ★

Village signposted from A436 and from A40; from village centre follow sign towards Roman villa (but don't be tempted astray by villa signs *before* you reach the village!)

The best place to appreciate the beautiful isolation of this mossy-roofed pub is in the neat garden, from where one can see the little valley, empty but for the surrounding beech and chestnut trees. The rambling carpeted bar is full of little nooks and corners, with antique high-backed settles and big cut-away barrel seats under its beams, an attractive bay window seat, old china and pewter on a high Delft shelf, and good log fires in its stone fireplace; little side rooms open off it. It's frequently popular despite the location, though in quiet periods out of season the atmosphere may be slightly more subdued. Bar food, ordered at the bar and served by waitresses, includes home-made soup (75p), ploughman's (£2.20), basket meals (from £2.30), and main dishes like grilled trout, beef Stroganoff and curries (around £3–£5.50); summer salad bar; puddings (£1.35). Sam Smiths OB and Museum on handpump; darts, shove-ha'penny, table skittles, cribbage, dominoes, Trivial Pursuit and other board games, fruit machine and space game in the games bar; piped music. The site of the original mill from which the pub takes its name is now an island in the garden, connected by a stone bridge. The Roman villa is a good walk away. *(Recommended by M A and C R Starling, Graham and Glenis Watkins, Simon Ward, HNJ, PEJ, G and M Hollis, Leith Stuart, D J Cooke, Mrs J Oakes, John Branford, Ewan McCall, Roger Huggins, Tom McLean, Rob and Gill Weeks, Dr A Y Drummond, A C Watson and C J Lindon, Aubrey and Margaret Saunders, David Loukidelis, Mrs M J Dyke, Simon Velate, Ian and Liz Phillips, Patrick Freeman)*

Sam Smiths   Licensee David Foley   Real ale   Meals and snacks (until 10 evenings) Children welcome   Open 11–2.30 (3 Sat), 6.30–11 all year

WOODCHESTER   SO8302 Map 4

Ram   🏵

South Woodchester, which is signposted off A46 Stroud–Nailsworth

The attractive L-shaped bar here belies the more insignificant-looking exterior – there's a nice combination of crisp white walls, some stripped stonework, beams and three open fires; furnishings range from country-kitchen chairs to several cushioned antique panelled settles around a variety of country tables, and built-in wall and window seats; the atmosphere is particularly relaxed. The range of well kept real ales on handpump is enterprising, with Archers Village, Boddingtons, Holdens, Hook Norton Old Hookey, the local Uley Hogshead and Old Spot and two guest beers each week; sensibly placed darts, table skittles, fruit machine. The extensive bar menu includes rolls (£1.40) and ploughman's (from £2.15), with main dishes such as home-cooked pizza (£2.30), steak and kidney pie (£2.50), cottage pie (£2.60), baked avocado in a Stilton sauce (£3.95), beef and oyster pie (£4.05) and chicken stuffed with prawn and crab mousse (£5.95); also an interesting vegetarian choice, such as tasty walnut and orange or nut with chilli relish roast (£3.95). There are spectacular views down the steep and pretty valley from picnic-table sets on the terrace by tubs of flowers and an unusually big hibiscus. *(Recommended by Robert and Vicky Tod, Patrick Freeman, BKA, Mr and Mrs Wyatt, Catherine Steele-Kroon, Jonathan Williams)*

Free house   Licensees Stuart and Teresa Callaway   Real ale   Meals and snacks   Children welcome   Impromptu piano   Open 11–3 (4.30 Sat), 6–11 all year

Lucky Dip

Besides the fully inspected pubs, you might like to try these Lucky Dips recommended to us and described by readers (if you do, please send us reports):

Aldsworth [A433 Oxford–Cirencester; SP1510], *Sherborne Arms*: Welcoming country pub, friendly landlord and locals, rustic atmosphere, well kept beer, bar food, garden; handy for Bibury and Burford (*K R Harris, Mrs M Price*)

Alvington [SO6001], *Blacksmiths Arms*: Local free house with good range of beers and cider, friendly helpful staff, freshly prepared good value food including vegetarian dishes and good range of barbecued steaks; small candle-lit dining-room (booking advised); gardens, children's play area (*John Blake*)

☆ **Amberley** [SO8401], *Black Horse*: Quiet pub owned by syndicate of local customers; old stone building with recent extensions in keeping; two bars, one small, one long, with stripped walls, few pictures, good wooden tables and chairs, lamps, plants and good atmosphere; pleasant service, good range of real ales inc Mitchells, good simple bar food; attractive garden and back terrace with picnic-table sets; delightful Cotswold stone village (*Heather Sharland*)

Amberley , *Amberley Arms*: Impressive building in nice spot, with good atmosphere in public bar, pleasant service, decent food in bar and restaurant, well kept beer; bedrooms good value (*Mrs J Oakes, Patrick Freeman*)

Ampney Crucis [off main road at Crown of Crucis and veer left at triangle – OS Sheet 163 reference 069024; SP0602], *Butchers Arms*: Two newly refurbished rooms knocked into one, and now more of a dining pub, with good range of good value and well presented home-cooked bar food; well kept Flowers IPA and Original, warm friendly welcome, peaceful tables outside – nice spot (*John Savage*)

Andoversford [SP0219], *Royal Oak*: Old stone building with two large connected bars divided by open fireplace, back room with pool-table and seating area rather like a first-floor gallery; well kept Whitbreads beers, imaginative choice of food including Chinese dishes, simple bench seating, juke box; tables on terrace (*Maureen Hobbs, Ewan McCall, Roger Huggins, Tom McLean*)

Apperley [SO8628], *Farmers Arms*: Well run pleasant old beamed Cotswold family pub with wide choice of good food, well kept Flowers, open fire, garden; children welcome (*J H C Peters*)

Ashleworth [village signposted off A417 at Hartpury; SO8125], *Arkle*: Unpretentious and very welcoming one-bar Donnington pub; what could be front door of private house leads into big hall with skittle alley, darts and fruit machines, bar off with flock

wallpaper and mock stone decor, warm and clean atmosphere, well kept XXX, BB and SBA on handpump, bar billiards, bar food inc tasty freshly filled evening rolls (*Peter Scillitoe*)

Berkeley Road [A38; SO7200], *Prince of Wales*: Popular carvery restaurant overlooking big pretty garden, good service, real ales such as Marstons Pedigree, Theakstons Best, Wadworths 6X and Whitbreads PA; good value reasonable bedrooms (*Jill Field, Miss E R Bowmer*)

Berry Hill [SO5713], *Pike House*: Good home-cooked bar food and Sun lunches in country pub with Flowers Original and Whitbreads PA on handpump, friendly service (*John and Brenda Turner*)

Bibury [SP1106], *Catherine Wheel*: Busy atmosphere – staff can seem a bit functional – in village pub with good log fire, dauntingly generous helpings of good if not cheap food and well kept Courage Directors; pretty garden, handy for local walks along River Coln (*Martin and Debbie Chester, Roger Huggins, Tom McLean, Ewan McCall, Wayne Brindle*)

Birdlip [A417/A436 roundabout; SO9214], *Air Balloon*: Whitbreads pub with comfortable multi-level bar concentrating on varied choice of usual bar food (not cheap, but well presented) with good service, Flowers Original and IPA on handpump, lots of small areas, piped music; children welcome, and play area, maybe with pets, in one of the two garden areas; can be very busy, though (*Aubrey and Margaret Saunders, Tom McLean, Roger Huggins, Ewan McCall, Dr J M Jackson*)

☆ **Bisley** [SO9005], *Old Bear*: Interesting and welcoming landlord, excellent atmosphere and good beer in attractive and unusual sixteenth-century building; very pretty village (*Neville Burke, Ewan McCall, Roger Huggins, Tom McLean, Lady Quinny, Patrick Freeman*)

Bourton-on-the-Water [SP1620], *Duke of Wellington*: Food not traditional but rather good in pub with bar, garden and wine bar/dining-room, beers and décor good (*G C Hixon*)

☆ **Broadoak** [SO7013], *White Hart*: Spacious beamed and carpeted bar with upholstered banquettes, armchairs and stools; large evening restaurant, terrace with tables and chairs overlooking River Severn; Flowers and Whitbreads Pompey Royal, wide range of cold dishes, some hot food – good helpings; fruit machine and quiet piped music (not pop), quick friendly service, though busy at weekends; children welcome

(Lyn and Bill Capper, E A George, Paul McPherson)

Broadwell [off A429 2 miles N of Stow-on-the-Wold; SP2027], *Fox*: Pleasant village inn attractively placed opposite large village green, well kept Donnington beer and real cider; two comfortable double bedrooms *(Rob and Gill Weeks, Simon Velate)*

☆ **Brockhampton** [the one between Andoversford and Winchcombe – OS Sheet 163 reference 035223; SP0322], *Craven Arms*: Pleasant, comfortable and popular seventeenth-century pub, doing really well under newish owners, with several low-beamed and stone-walled but decidedly modernised rooms; efficient cheerful service, well kept Butcombe and Hook Norton on handpump, good bar food inc excellent Sun lunches, log fire; the kitchen extractor fan could perhaps be better placed for people in the garden *(Frank Cummins, PADEMLUC, WHBM, John Haig)*

Brockweir [village signposted just off A466 Chepstow–Monmouth; SO5401], *Brockweir*: Friendly local inn with stripped stonework, sturdy settles, snugger carpeted alcoves with brocaded seats, covered courtyard and sheltered terrace, limited choice of basic bar food, well kept real ales such as Boddingtons, Flowers Original and Hook Norton, games in public bar; good Wye Valley walks; children in eating area; simple bedrooms *(Keith and Sheila Baxter, LYM)*

Brockworth [A46; SO8816], *Brewers Fayre*: Friendly staff, extensive menu with well cooked food, Whitbreads ales and beer garden; children in separate dining area *(Mrs B E Asher)*

Cam [High St; ST7599], *Berkeley Arms*: Welcoming, friendly landlord, excellent service with good choice of beers *(Julian Jewitt)*

Cambridge [3 miles from M5 junction 13 – A38 towards Bristol; SO7403], *George*: Roomy and comfortable, with several cosy separate galleries set out mainly for dining – sewing-machine treadle tables and so forth – so atmosphere is not perhaps its strongest point; well kept Flowers Original, collection of matchbox and cigarette packets, friendly staff, interesting framed cartoon graffiti in gents; children's play area; handy for Slimbridge Wildfowl Trust *(Tom Evans, Jill Field, Neil Christopher, Joy Heatherley)*

Camp [B4070 Birdlip–Stroud, junction with Calf Way – OS Sheet 163 reference 914114; SO9109], *Fostons Ash*: Pleasant service and good value simple food in isolated Whiteways outlet with well kept Flowers Original and Whitbreads PA on handpump, gin-traps and man-trap over bar, fruit machine, darts and nickelodeon, pleasant small back garden *(Frank Cummins)*

Chaceley Stock [SO8530], *Yew Tree*: Spacious river-view dining-room in rambling country pub with choice of real ales and lots

of different bar areas inc skittle alley with three pool-tables; well kept Brains ales, attractive waterside lawns, Severn moorings *(John and Joan Wyatt, PADEMLUC, LYM)*

Chalford [France Lynch – OS Sheet 163 reference 904036; SO9002], *Kings Head*: Good country local with great views, friendly atmosphere, well kept beer, wide range of bar food even Sun lunchtime, garden *(Roger Entwistle)*

Charlton Kings [London Rd; SO9620], *London*: Good atmosphere in unpretentious local with good bar snacks and Flowers IPA and Original on handpump, lively helpful staff; large public bar with darts and quoits, small lounge bar, restaurant; festooned with flowers in summer, with tables under cocktail parasols in quiet courtyard; bedrooms *(JH)*

☆ **Chedworth** [OS Sheet 163 reference 052121; SP0511], *Seven Tuns*: Remote pub in delightful valley, with basic bar, adjoining games-room with pool and fruit machine (children allowed here), and pleasant, homely lounge with warm log fire; friendly welcome from licensees, quick friendly service, well kept Courage Best and Directors on handpump, original and varied bar food inc delicious steak and kidney pie, marinated chicken wings and profiteroles; some tables out in front, more over road and up bank beside tumbling stream; at start of GWG86 *(Roger Huggins, Simon Velate, Ewan McCall, Tom McLean, Dick Brown)*

☆ **Cheltenham** [Portland St; SO9422], *Cotswold Inn*: Handsome Regency pub, well preserved but up-to-date, and tastefully and comfortably furnished, with Victorian prints on flock-papered walls; well kept Wadworths IPA, 6X and Farmers Pride on handpump, variety of good home-cooked food inc Sun lunches, pleasant staff; open all day *(Simon Velate, Alan Skull, PADEMLUC)*

Cheltenham [Alma Rd], *Bass House*: Friendly estate pub with well kept Bass and good service *(G D Collier)*; [North Pl] *Duck & Pheasant*: Spacious interior and good choice of well presented bar food *(Shirley Pielou)*; [Portland St] *Evergreen*: Light and airy town-centre bar with good food (in bar and restaurant), good beer on handpump and quiet courtyard garden with tables under cocktail parasols; bedrooms *(JH)*; [Leckhampton Rd] *Malvern*: Suburban pub with one spacious bar, Flowers Original on handpump, good omelettes *(Mr and Mrs J H Wyatt)*; [37 High St] *Old Swan*: Very good town pub with generous helpings of well presented and good value lunchtime food; good, interesting beer brewed at the pub, plenty of space, friendly service *(Anon)*; [Montpellier Walk] *Rotunda*: Simply furnished public bar with sawdust on floor and colourful T-shirts and caps on walls and ceiling; separate area with basic seats and tables and panelled walls; six real ales inc Ind

Coope Burton, Smiles and Wadworths; burgers and pizzas in evening, when it's lively with quite loud music *(Simon Velate)*

Cherington [ST9098], *Cherington*: Sadly this pub recommended in last year's edition for good food and well kept Courage has been closed, and put up for sale as a private house *(Anon)*

☆ **Chipping Campden** [Main St; SP1539], *Kings Arms*: Civilised small hotel which has gone through various changes recently, but under its latest regime is reported to have good, well presented food at reasonable prices, exceptionally friendly staff and good log fire in its comfortable and old-fashioned bar; bedrooms stylish and comfortable *(Mr and Mrs W Dermott, LYM – more views please)*

Cirencester [Castle St; SP0201], *Black Horse*: Comfortable lounge bar in pleasant pub; bedrooms *(Roger Huggins)*; *Drillmans Arms*: Decent, friendly enough local with Archers Best and ASB, Flowers IPA and guest beer; licensees making real effort; children welcome *(Tom McLean, Ewan McCall, Roger Huggins)*; [Market Pl] *Fleece*: Flagstones and stripped wood in Shepherds food and wine bar, plusher hotel bar; bedrooms *(Keith Garley, BB)*; [Gloucester St] *Nelson*: Has been friendly, lively and comfortable, with ship theme in lounge, well kept Flowers IPA and Original; licensees retiring autumn 1989 *(Ewan McCall, Roger Huggins, Tom McLean)*

☆ **Clearwell** [B4231; SO5708], *Wyndham Arms*: Smart and well kept country inn dating back to fourteenth century, which has been very popular for good lunchtime bar food, well kept Hook Norton on handpump in stylish and carefully renovated beamed bar, evening restaurant, but came on the market as we went to press in summer 1989; attractive countryside near Wye and Forest of Dean; bedrooms comfortable, in new extension *(M A Watts, E J Knight, Mrs Eileen Webb, LYM – reports on new regime please)*

Clearwell [SO5708], *Lamb*: Free house with decent lunchtime and evening bar food *(Maggie Jo St John, Dudley Evans)*

☆ **Coberley** [A436 Brockworth–Andoversford, just SW of junction with A435 Cheltenham–Cirencester; SO9516], *Seven Springs*: An instant hit when first opened in late 1987 by its first owners (who had a tremendous track record at their previous pubs), this hasn't shone so brightly since being sold and coming under the Courage flag at the end of 1988; but it's still worth a visit to see the unusual approach – an imaginative and very spacious reworking of a big barn, thoroughly comfortable, with interesting side areas and a sloping pond-side garden; children allowed during daytime – has been open all day *(LYM)*

Coleford [Joyford, which is signposted off B4432 at Globe and Home Centre in Five Acres – OS Sheet 162 reference 579133; SO5813], *Dog & Muffler*: Remote, hospitable

free house with bar food, garden and spacious eighteenth-century cider press; children's play area *(Maggie Jo St John, Dudley Evans)*

Colesbourne [A435; SO9913], *Colesbourne*: Well refurbished pub with friendly landlord, huge log fire and good atmosphere; well kept beer and extensive range of good value bar food running up to fresh salmon and game *(Laurence Manning)*

Coln St Aldwyns [SP1405], *New Inn*: This prettily placed Cotswold inn, a former very popular main entry with a snug series of sixteenth-century rooms and comfortable bedrooms, was closed in late 1988, though a vigorous local campaign against plans to turn it into flats holds some promise that it may be reopened in at least some form *(LYM – watch this space)*

Cranham [SO8912], *Royal William*: Popular, spacious Whitbread Brewers Fayre pub with friendly staff, well kept Flowers Original and IPA, fair choice of bar food; nr Cotswold Way *(Neil and Anita Christopher)*

☆ **Ebrington** [SP1840], *Ebrington Arms*: Pleasant and cosy village free house under friendly and helpful new owners, with comfortable settles and farmhouse furniture, black beams, bare boards and flagstones, inglenook fireplace with log fire, no piped music or fruit machines, bay window overlooking the three oaks of its former name; well kept real ales inc Donnington SBA and Hook Norton, good choice of hearty home-cooked bar food inc enormous generously filled baked potatoes, good casseroles and ham and eggs; pretty garden; bedrooms, with excellent breakfasts *(E V Walder, Hugh Patterson, P J Brooks, D A Wilcock, Miss C M Davidson)*

Edge [A4173 N of Stroud; SO8509], *Edgemoor*: Modernised food pub included for the striking valley views through its back picture windows; Whitbreads-related ales under light carbon dioxide blanket, unobtrusive piped music, children in eating area *(Barry and Anne, LYM)*

☆ **Glasshouse** [by Newent Woods; first right turn off A40 going W from junction with A4136 – OS Sheet 162 reference 710213; SO7122], *Glasshouse*: Carefully preserved as basic country tavern, with decorative plates, fine British Match poster and open fires in cavernous hearth of kitchen bar, changing real ales such as Butcombe and Flowers or Theakstons tapped from a rack of casks, ploughman's and plain basket meals, seats on grass outside; fine nearby woodland walks *(Peter Scillitoe, Phil and Sally Gorton, LYM)*

☆ **Gloucester** [Bristol Rd], *Linden Tree*: Good atmosphere – almost that of a welcoming country pub; attractive inside, with friendly licensee and staff, good range of expertly kept real ales inc Butcombe, Hook Norton, Marstons Pedigree and Wadworths 6X, well prepared reasonably priced food *(Chris Payne)*

Gloucester [Southgate St; part of New County Hotel – between Greyfriars and Blackfriars], *County*: Panelling and solid furniture, with well kept Adnams, Ushers, Wadworths 6X and Whitbreads Pompey Royal, particularly good value bar food; bedrooms *(Tom Evans)*; [100 Westgate St] *Dick Whittingtons House*: Atmospheric Grade I listed building, largely fourteenth century and timber framed behind its early Georgian façade, though the connection with Dick Whittington is very tenuous; at least four real ales on handpump or tapped from the cask, some unusual furniture, log fire, friendly and helpful bar staff, fresh mainly home-made bar food generously served; separate downstairs bar, garden with barbecues; can be very quiet in the evening *(Alastair Campbell, Pamela and Merlyn Horswell)*; [A40 1 mile W of Gloucester] *Dog at Over*: A handy stop, much older and more interesting (and spacious) than it looks from the outside, with wide range of decent bar food, real ale, piped music; tables on side lawn *(John and Joan Wyatt, Paul McPherson, LYM)*

Gretton [SP0131], *Royal Oak*: Lovely spot, lively pub made from two cottages knocked together, super atmosphere, well kept real ales, extensive range of good bar food, pleasant little dining-conservatory, attractive garden *(Laurence Manning)*

Guiting Power [SP0924], *New Inn*: Pleasant lunchtime atmosphere, well kept beer, good reasonably priced bar food *(Dr A Y Drummond)*

Hardwicke [Sellars Bridge; SO7912], *Pilot*: Fine canalside position overlooking lock, buoyant atmosphere in pleasantly furnished long, busy bar with well kept Flowers Original, Wethereds and Whitbreads Pompey Royal, choice of wines by glass, smiling prompt service, bar food *(Gwen and Peter Andrews, Tom Evans)*

Hartpury [Ledbury Rd; SO7924], *Canning Arms*: Good atmosphere in attractive and cheerful pub with wide choice of well presented reasonably priced food, good garden great for children *(Mr and Mrs P Pitt, G T Doyle)*

Kilkenny [A436 near Cheltenham – OS Sheet 163 reference 007187; SP0019], *Kilkenny*: Small, comfortable country pub, pleasant atmosphere, lunchtime and evening bar food inc salad bar *(Neil and Anita Christopher)*

Lechlade [SU2199], *Red Lion*: Pleasant oak-beamed bar with well kept real ale, good value bar food, obliging service; attractive village – shame about the lorries thundering past *(John and Joan Wyatt)*

☆ **Leighterton** [off A46 S of Nailsworth; ST8291], *Royal Oak*: Old, charming free house, spacious and clean, in beautiful countryside; good, simple bar food at reasonable prices under new regime, running up to steaks and local trout; lots of real ales; quite handy for Westonbirt Arboretum *(Helen Maddison, Peter and Rose Flower, R G Cadman)*

Littledean [A4151 E of Cinderford; SO6714], *George*: Old-fashioned pub with rambling rooms, Whitbreads ales and bar food; garden with pleasant view of Forest of Dean and Severn Vale *(Dave Braisted)*

☆ **Longhope** [Ross Rd (A40); SO6919], *Farmers Boy*: Comfortable old pub with nice choice of good food, decent wines and beer, room for teenagers, pleasant owners *(John Miles)*

☆ **Lower Lydbrook** [Ventian Lane; SO5916], *Royal Spring*: In lovely setting, tucked away in a fold of the Forest of Dean with scenic views of Wye Valley and pretty garden with waterfalls; has gone from strength to strength over last couple of years thanks to hard-working licensees, with consistently well kept beer and improved range of good home-cooked bar food; they've opened up the adjacent former lime kilns and built a new adventure playground behind *(Sybil Baker, John Miles)*

☆ **Lower Swell** [B4068 W of Stow-on-the-Wold (sometimes still called A436 on maps); SP1725], *Golden Ball*: Neat and simple local inn – no pretensions to much atmosphere – with well kept Donnington BB, SBA and XXX Mild from the pretty brewery just 20 minutes' walk away, generously served plain bar food from soup, ploughman's and filled baked potatoes to steak, games area behind log fireplace, occasional barbecues, Aunt Sally and quoits in pleasant streamside garden; evening restaurant, no food Sun evening; very clean simple bedrooms, good value *(Derek and Sylvia Stephenson, B S Bourne, Mr and Mrs M V Cook, Jon Wainwright, PADEMLUC, John and Joan Wyatt, Simon Velate, LYM)*

Lower Swell, *Old Farm House*: Not strictly a pub, but lunchtime bar snacks are excellent; pleasant peaceful atmosphere *(Mrs E M Thompson)*

Lower Wick [ST7196], *Pickwick*: Fairly simple traditional country pub with large linoleum-tiled public bar and Butcombe, Theakstons and a changing guest beer; freshly cooked food *(Nigel Cant)*

Meysey Hampton [SU1199], *Masons Arms*: On the up-and-up under new regime with extended menu and real ales inc particularly well kept Ash Vine *(Tom McLean, Ewan McCall, Roger Huggins)*

☆ **Mickleton** [fairly handy for Stratford; SP1543], *Kings Arms*: Popular Cotswold-stone pub with delightful staff, well kept Flowers and first-class home-baked filled rolls; gets busy in summer *(Hope Chenhalls)*

Mickleton, *Butchers Arms*: Welcoming, comfortable pub with good atmosphere, in pleasant surroundings; well kept Flowers IPA, good range of bar food, fruit machine *(PADEMLUC)*; [Chapel Lane; A46, junction with Pebworth rd] *Three Ways*: Good, spacious bar with helpful staff; Fri night entertainment; bedrooms *(Paul McPherson)*

☆ **Minchinhampton** [SO8600], *Crown*: Typical Cotswold-stone building on market sq of historic village; popular, happy bars with welcoming landlord, open fires; well kept Flowers Original on handpump, choice of chilled wines, good hot and cold bar food; locals play darts and dominoes *(W H Bland, Gethin Lewis)*

☆ **Minchinhampton** [Minchinhampton Common; Nailsworth–Brimscombe – on common fork left at pub's sign], *Old Lodge*: Partly sixteenth century, superbly placed on high NT commons, with good range of interesting real ales inc local Uleys, friendly service, food which can be imaginative and good value, nice pub dog *(Patrick Freeman, Rob and Gill Weeks, Wilfred Plater-Shellard, LYM)*

Minsterworth [SO7716], *Apple Tree*: Attractive old pub with plenty of beams, unobtrusive piped music and pleasant, friendly service; well kept Flowers IPA, Original and Wadworths 6X, good bar food all sessions *(Neil and Anita Christopher)*

Miserden [OS Sheet 163 reference 936089; SE9308], *Carpenters Arms*: Cotswold-stone pub in attractive estate village; lots of wood inside, well kept Flowers Original, Whitbreads PA and Wethereds Winter Royal; good value serve-yourself summer buffet, ploughman's and casseroles at lunchtime, but in the evenings all tables are set for meals – main courses and puddings only (no cooked food Mon or Tues evenings); food good if not cheap, service efficient *(Frank Cummins, John and Joan Wyatt, Roger Bellingham)*

☆ **Moreton-in-Marsh** [SP2032], *Redesdale Arms*: Well renovated and comfortable bar and buttery in well furnished and old-fashioned country-town hotel; good bar food, lively atmosphere and lots of willing staff *(E V Walder, Wayne Brindle, Dr and Mrs A K Clarke)*

Moreton-in-Marsh [High St], *White Hart Royal*: Very comfortable THF hotel with Bass tapped from the cask and bar food in nice 'inn bar' – big inglenook with real roaster of a log fire in room off; bedrooms comfortable, though expensive *(Rob and Gill Weeks)*

Nailsworth [ST8499], *Egypt Mill*: New pub in converted mill with old, thick walls, central carpeted bar with small, solid wood table-tops on heavy, three-legged metal bases, piped music and fruit machine; two outer bars form L-shaped room, one with working millwheel and the other with static machinery; Ind Coope Burton and Wadworths 6X on handpump, good food inc

fisherman's pie, quick service and upstairs restaurant; occasional jazz evenings; children welcome, no dogs *(Roger Huggins)*

Newent Woods [SO7122], *Yew Tree*: Comfortable well laid out pub, well off beaten track with good bar food, good beer and friendly service; good restaurant *(Roy Clark)*

☆ **Newland** [SO5509], *Ostrich*: Lovely little seventeenth-century pub in charming old village close to River Wye; friendly and spacious bar with well kept Flowers IPA and Original, good food in bar and restaurant, open fire, wooden benches, Sun newspapers; bedrooms pleasant, with huge breakfasts *(Dr John Innes, M A and W R Proctor)*

Newport [A38; ST7098], *Stagecoach*: Traditional place with interesting fireplace, horsebrasses, beams, coach supports; well kept Flowers Original, Hook Norton, Marstons Pedigree, John Smiths and Wadworths 6X on handpump, variety of food in small bar and larger carvery restaurant; garden with children's facilities *(A C Lang)*

Oakridge Lynch [SO9102], *Butchers Arms*: Traditional low-beamed mainly eighteenth-century Cotswold-stone pub, attractively modernised; large roaring fire, fine choice of well kept beers inc Butcombe and Tetleys, very good reasonably priced bar food, up-market regulars; picturesque hillside village *(Ewan McCall, Roger Huggins, Tom McLean, John and Joan Wyatt)*

Oddington [Upper Oddington – OS Sheet 163 reference 222257; SP2225], *Horse & Groom*: Friendly and genuine staff, decent food inc enormous helpings of vegetables in the little restaurant, well kept Wadworths 6X, open fire; quietly attractive Cotswold village; bedrooms (winter breaks good value) *(BKA, Sir Nigel Foulkes)*

Overbury [SO9537], *Star*: Attentive licensees, well kept Flowers ales, well priced good bar food running up to steaks; bedrooms good value *(Ian Robinson)*

☆ **Parkend** [SO6208], *Woodman*: Pleasant pub with lots of character under new regime; well kept Flowers and Whitbreads Strong County on handpump, good food from extensive lunch menu inc children's helpings, welcoming and obliging staff; bedrooms *(R P Taylor, Paul and Heather Bettesworth)*

Paxford [B4479; SP1837], *Churchill*: Small Hook Norton pub, single bar made from two tiny rooms, flagstone floor, simple furnishings, large open fireplace and small darts alcove; welcoming licensees, well kept Best and Old Hookey, simple range of bar food from pre-packed sandwiches to steaks, small garden with picnic-table sets *(E V Walder)*

Perrotts Brook [A435; SP0105], *Bear*: Good Courage pub, friendly staff, doors wide enough for wheelchairs *(Ewan McCall, Roger Huggins, Tom McLean, HNJ, PEJ)*

Prestbury [Mill St; SO9624], *Plough*: Unspoilt thatched village pub, grandfather clock in corner, attractive wooden benches and tables, small side room with stone floor and large open fireplace; good range of Flowers and Whitbreads, good bar food, pleasant back garden *(B M Eldridge)*

Quedgeley [Bristol Rd; SO8014], *Little Thatch*: One of oldest buildings in Gloucestershire, good choice of food *(Julian Jewitt)*

Redmarley [A417 just off M50 exit 2; SO7531], *Rose & Crown*: Recently renovated at great expense with lovely dining-room in former skittle alley, charming licensees, good restaurant food *(B Walton)*

Sapperton [OS Sheet 163 reference 948033; SO9403], *Bell*: Well kept Courage Directors, Flowers Original and Whitbreads PA and reasonably priced bar food in roomy bar with wall and window settles and Windsor chairs; good games area, tables on small front lawn; fine walks from here – it's on GWG89 *(Frank Cummins)*

Selsley [just SW of Stroud; SO8304], *Bell*: Attractive pub on common, popular with walkers of the Cotswold Way; relaxed atmosphere, friendly staff and locals, large range of reasonably priced home-cooked bar food inc fine pies *(S Rochford)*

☆ **Sheepscombe** [village signposted from B4070 NE of Stroud, and A46 N of Painswick; SO8910], *Butchers Arms*: Cheerful atmosphere and low prices in simple village inn with well kept Flowers Original and Whitbreads PA under light carbon dioxide blanket, plain lunchtime bar food (only light ploughman's on Sun), fine views from bay windows and seats outside; the carved inn-sign is rather special; bedrooms very simple but good value in summer, with good breakfasts *(E J Knight, A C Watson, C J Lindon, Barry and Anne, LYM)*

Siddington [Ashton Rd, just outside Cirencester – OS Sheet 163 map reference 034995; SU0399], *Greyhound*: Efficient Wadworths pub – rare around here with good atmosphere in large brick-floored lounge and public bar; well kept IPA, 6X and Old Timer in winter, good well presented bar food *(Aubrey and Margaret Saunders)*

Slad [SO8707], *Woolpack*: Nice, unassuming Whitbreads pub – Laurie Lee's local *(Tom McLean, Roger Huggins, Ewan McCall)*

Sling [SO5807], *Montague*: Well run pub with well kept beer and good food in bar and restaurant; small, so be early or book *(Sybil Baker)*

☆ **Snowshill** [SP0934], *Snowshill Arms*: Well kept Donnington BB and SBA, open fire, efficiently served popular food (inc Tannoy system for back garden, which has a good play area – and a skittle alley); more airy inside than many Cotswolds pubs, with charming village views from bow windows;

cheery atmosphere, prices notably low for the Cotswolds; children welcome if eating *(Aubrey and Margaret Saunders, PAB, Mrs E M Thompson, Michael and Alison Sandy, Mr and Mrs W Dermott, LYM)*

Stow-on-the-Wold [SP1925], *Grapevine*: Beautiful conservatory with 120-year-old vine, good, cheap food and helpful staff; good value bedrooms *(Mr and Mrs W Dermott)*; [The Square] *Old Stocks*: Good value bedrooms in well run simple hotel with small comfortable bar, seats on pavement and in sheltered garden *(BB)*; [The Square] *White Hart*: Cheery atmosphere (it's next to the YHA) in front bar with heavy rustic furniture, some easy chairs and log-effect gas fire; green plush seats in plainer back lounge with tables set for bar lunches; clean and well kept; bedrooms *(G S Burrows, BB)*

Stroud [1 Bath Rd; SO8504], *Clothiers Arms*: Popular pub with one large bar divided into two areas, decorated with penny-farthing bicycle, spinning-wheels, weaving-frames, nineteenth-century bobbins and carding-combs, framed embroidered greetings cards, fish tank; old sewing-machine tables and two modern settles; decent bar food, well kept Archers ASB and Village, Smiles, and Wadworths *(BKA)*; [Nelson St; top of town, turn off before Police Stn] *Duke of York*: Local atmosphere in unpretentious town pub with good range of well kept real ales and decent if unsurprising food *(Jonathan Williams, BB)*; [Selsey Hill] *Ram*: Superb view of valley, good choice of real ales, bar food *(J C and D Aitkenhead)*

Tetbury [London Rd; ST8893], *Priory*: Tastefully done-up and welcoming newish pub with good well presented bar food (it's very much an eating house), and well kept beer; bedrooms clean and comfortable *(Dr and Mrs A K Clarke, Mrs S Curnock, N and J Matthews)*; [Market Pl] *Snooty Fox*: Modernised hotel lounge; welcoming, especially during happy hour *(Dr and Mrs A K Clarke)*; [A433 towards Cirencester] *Trouble House*: Popular low-ceilinged lounge with open fire, reasonable food, Wadworths beers, room off with bar billiards, darts, juke box *(Roger Huggins)*

Tewkesbury [52 Church St; SO8932], *Bell*: Comfortable plush lounge with some neat William and Mary oak panelling, black oak timbers, medieval leaf-and-fruit frescoes and big log fire; lunchtime food counter, garden above Severnside walk near lovely weir; bedrooms *(Wayne Brindle, BB)*; [High St] *Black Bear*: Rambling heavy-beamed rooms off black-timbered corridors, largely home-made simple but tasty food, well kept Flowers, riverside lawn *(Andrew Ludlow, LYM)*; *Plough*: Welcome and pleasant retreat from town bustle *(Wayne Brindle)*

Toddington [A46 Broadway–Winchcombe, junction with A438 and B4077; SP0432], *Pheasant*: Halls pub with lots of malt whiskies, choice of hot and cold bar food, friendly staff, garden; quite handy for Gloucs & Warwicks Rly; children's play area *(Joan Olivier)*

☆ **Twyning** [SO8936], *Village Inn*: Pleasant pub, particularly good atmosphere, interesting locals, good if not cheap bar food (may be limited Mon and Tues) *(Barry and Anne, J C Proud)*

Uley [The Street; ST7898], *Old Crown*: Simply furnished local with quite generous straightforward food, well kept Flowers, darts area; popular with young people at weekends – also known as the Upper or Top Crown, though the lower one has long since closed down *(Alan Frankland, Sarah Mellor, Alastair Campbell)*

Westbury-on-Severn [Popes Hill; SO7114], *White House*: Good pub with perfect views, but may be closed weekday lunchtimes; children allowed in restaurant *(Sybil Baker)*

Westonbirt [ST8589], *Hare & Hounds*: Family-run place next to Westonbirt Arboretum; good pubby atmosphere, good interesting food, well kept Wadworths Devizes and 6X and Websters Yorkshire; bedrooms good *(Gordon Theaker)*

Whitminster [nr M5 junction 13; SO7708], *Old Forge*: Pleasant old pub with small restaurant; friendly, welcoming licensees, good choice of beers and wines, good bar food *(M C and D H Watkinson)*

Winchcombe [High St; SP0228], *Corner Cupboard*: Typical welcoming Cotswolds pub, two simply furnished bars, pleasant atmosphere; friendly licensees, five real ales inc Flowers and Whitbreads, appetising but basic bar food inc good ploughman's, separate restaurant under different management *(David and Flo Wallington, AE)*; [37 North St] *Old White Lion*: Open, light and pleasant décor – basically a restaurant, but does have a bar *(Paul McPherson)*

Woolaston Common [off A48 at Netherend signpost – OS Sheet 162 map reference 590009; SO5900], *Rising Sun*: Rural pub on fringe of Forest of Dean, well kept Theakstons, good lunchtime bar food *(John and Joan Wyatt)*

Wotton under Edge [Haw St; ST7593], *Royal Oak*: Split-level pub with good toasted sandwiches, garden with play area *(Joan Olivier, Patrick Freeman)*

Hampshire

Two pubs here which changed their licensees last year have changed yet again – the Jolly Sailor near Fawley, right on Southampton Water, and the George up on the downs at Vernham Dean; in both cases, though, the new people have already shown themselves most sympathetic to their pub's special character. Other popular pubs here that have changed hands recently include the George at East Meon (it's kept its distinctive layout and food service arrangements), the Jekyll & Hyde at Turgis Green (no slackening in standards at this busy place), and the pretty little Boot just outside Vernham Dean (a wider range of food than before). A number of entirely new main entries, or pubs coming back into these pages after a gap of several years (usually with new licensees), include the Red Lion at Chalton (the county's oldest pub – considerable character), the Queen at Dummer (efficient food service just off the M3), the Royal Oak overlooking the water at Langstone (it now serves food all day in summer), the quaint and friendly Leather Bottle at Mattingley, the delightfully unspoilt little Travellers Rest at the Newtown that's north of Fareham (simple but good food, and don't be put off by the name – it's a tiny village), the White Lion at Soberton (long evening food service, and its restaurant stays open through Sunday afternoon; so much a family-run place that when we confirmed factual details with the licensees as we went to press, we had a long and very helpfully informative letter from their eight-year-old daughter Jodie), the formerly French-run Chequers at Well (very much reverting to a traditional country pub now) and the ancient Eclipse near the cathedral in Winchester. A change well worth noting is that the High Corner near Linwood (well, fairly near) has now opened bedrooms – one of the most remote places you can stay at in the New Forest; other good places to stay in the Forest are the smart Montagu Arms at Beaulieu and the New Forest Inn at Emery Down. Both these have particularly good food, as do the Red Lion at Boldre (full of character, very popular), the Chequers just in from the sea at

The Boot, nr Vernham Dean

325

Pennington, the idiosyncratic Coach & Horses at Rotherwick (lots of well kept real ales), the charming little old Harrow at Steep, the prettily thatched Tichborne Arms at Tichborne, and the Wykeham Arms in Winchester (an exceptional choice of well kept wines by the glass, and a nice place to stay at; but note that they've stopped allowing children). The Luzborough House outside Romsey, a fine example of careful recent refurbishment and extension, is notable for serving food throughout its all-day opening hours; it's not far from the M27. The delightful Bush at Ovington is a particular favourite with a great many readers, but the greatest appeal of all is that of the White Horse up on the Downs above Petersfield; people like this pub precisely because of the way it makes no concessions to current fashions in what pubs increasingly expect us all to like – it's just the epitome of a simple, unspoilt English pub. A good few of the Lucky Dip entries at the end of the chapter that have special appeal include the Carpenters Arms at Burghclere, Queens Head at Burley, Fox & Hounds at Bursledon, Flower Pots at Cheriton, Hampshire Bowman at Dundridge, Royal Oak at Fritham, New Inn at Heckfield, Osborne View at Hill Head, Cart & Horses at Kings Worthy, Shoulder of Mutton at Mattingley, Fish in Ringwood, Three Tuns in Romsey, Queens at Selborne, Grapes in Southampton, Cricketers near Steep, Three Lions at Stuckton, Bugle at Twyford, Thomas Lord at West Meon and Kings Head at Wickham.

ALRESFORD   SU5832 Map 2

Horse & Groom

Broad Street; town signposted from new A31 bypass

This is one of those rare open-plan bars which (while gaining in atmosphere from the way that everything's going on in the same area) preserves a pleasantly secluded intimacy, with various rambling nooks and crannies to suit different moods. There are neat settles and Windsor chairs, black beams and timbered walls partly stripped to brickwork, old local photographs and shelves of earthenware jugs and bottles. People particularly like the tables in the three bow windows on the right, looking out over the broad street. Good value bar food includes sandwiches (from £1.50; prawn £2.25), soup (£1.50), ploughman's (from £2.10), sausages (£2.95), salads (£3.50–£4.50), home-made steak and kidney pie (£3.75), home-cooked gammon (£5.25) and steaks (from £7); puddings (from around £1.50); they warn of some delays at busy periods. Well kept Flowers Original, Marstons and Whitbreads Strong Country and guest beers on handpump; welcoming service; coal-effect gas fire. *(Recommended by Bernard Phillips, Dr John Innes, BKA; more reports please)*

Whitbreads   Licensees Robin and Kate Howard   Real ale   Meals and snacks (until 10 evenings)   Open 11–2.30, 6–11 all year

BATTRAMSLEY   SZ3099 Map 2

Hobler

A337 a couple of miles S of Brockenhurst; OS Sheet 196 reference 307990

Bouncing with life, the black-beamed bar of this quaint sixteenth-century pub is dividied by the massive stub of an ancient wall – a great square pillar. The part on the left is particularly cosy: black-panelled, and full of books. The main area on the right is full of tables with red leatherette bucket seats, pews, little dining-chairs and a comfortable bow-window seat. Besides guns, china, New Forest saws and the odd big engraving, the dominant theme of the décor has been a mass of customers' snapshots – some perhaps rather indelicate (which we should warn would be a mild term to describe some of the jokes that have punctuated one at least of the changing menus). Bar food includes well filled baked potatoes or garlic bread with cheese (from £1.25), ploughman's (from £1.75), salads (from £2.95, prawn £5.95), chilli con carne (£3.50), steak and kidney pie or pork hock in an apricot sauce (£3.95), trout or a range of smoked fish (£4.95) and steaks (from £5.50), with weekly changing dishes such as liver (£3.95) or beef ragout (£4.95); vegetables are fresh and nicely cooked, helpings generous. Well kept Flowers Original, Gales HSB (called Hobler Special here) and Marstons Pedigree on handpump, and a good range of malt whiskies and wines (including some expensive bargains by the bottle); piped music, helpful and welcoming service, friendly golden labrador. It is very popular, so get there early for a table in the main building (many are booked in the evening). There are more out in a comfortable alpine-style log cabin with a hefty wood-burning stove, and in summer a spacious forest-edge lawn has a good few picnic-table sets, beside a paddock with ponies, donkeys and hens. Besides a summer bar and marquee out here, they should this year have completed a huge timber climbing-fort for the good play area. *(Recommended by Mr and Mrs D A P Grattan, Barbara Hatfield, Jon Payne, Daphne and Gordon Merrifield, Calum and Jane, Philip and Trisha Ferris; more reports please)*

Whitbreads   Licensee Pip Stevens   Real ale   Meals and snacks (11–2, 6–11)   Jazz Tues Open 11–2.30, 5–11 all year

BEAULIEU   SU3802 Map 2

Montagu Arms 🏠 🛏

A decent range of unusually interesting wines by the glass (around £2), in good condition, is a commendable feature of the spacious and relaxing Wine Press bar here. Divided into quiet separate areas by low curtain-topped partitions and sweeping arches, it has stylishly comfortable furnishings, an understated colour-scheme of cool greens, and a big Cecil Aldin hunting print as well as attractive little local landscapes. Quickly served bar food includes filled baked potatoes (from £1.25), soup (£1.40), ploughman's (from £2.25), mushroom pasta casserole or cheese and vegetable potato pie (£3), open sandwiches (from £3), beef goulash or navarin of lamb (£4.25), pork chops in cider or a daily roast (£4.50), salads (from £4.40), seafood platter (£4.60) and steak (£5.95). Well kept if not cheap Ruddles Best and Wadworths 6X and a guest beer such as Ruddles County on handpump, decent coffee; unobtrusive carefully chosen piped pop music (and loudspeaker food announcements). The inn, very solidly built in the early 1920s and decorously comfortable and well run, is off to one side. There are picnic-table sets in the front courtyard, looking down to the palace gates; hungry donkeys may stray past. *(Recommended by Mrs E M Thompson, E G Parish, H G and C J McCafferty, David Bland, B W B Pettifer; more reports please)*

Free house   Licensee N Walford   Real ale   Meals and snacks   Restaurant   Children in eating area lunchtimes   Open 11–11 July–Aug, 10.30–2.30, 6–11 rest of year   Bedrooms tel Beaulieu (0590) 612324; £54.58B/£65.98B

BEAUWORTH   SU5726 Map 2

Milbury's

Turn off A272 Winchester/Petersfield at Beauworth ¾, Bishops Waltham 6 signpost, then continue straight on past village

The Fox & Hounds when we first knew it, this high and remote downland pub takes its present name from a Bronze Age cemetery surrounding it – the Millbarrow, briefly famous back in 1833 when a Norman hoard of 6,000 silver coins was found here. It's an interesting building, carefully restored to show off its broad flagstones, sturdy beams, stripped masonry and massive open fireplaces (with good log fires in winter). In a side area overlooked by a little timber gallery (and safely grille-covered) is a remarkably deep medieval well, worked by a great side donkey-wheel; if you drop an ice cube into its spotlit depths, count the seconds until the surface of the water shatters into twinkling ripples, and if you know your physics you can work out that it's nearly 300 feet deep. Furnishings inside and out in the garden are in character with the pub's age. Bar food, served cheerfully and quickly, is largely home made using local ingredients. It includes sandwiches (from 95p), soup (£1.10), a choice of ploughman's (£2.25), salads (from £3.25), nut cutlet (£3.50), prawn and spinach pancake (£3.60), steak and mushroom pie (£3.65), gammon (£4.30) and steak (from £5.25), with children's dishes (£1.60), a good choice of home-made puddings (from £1) and Sunday roasts. Sunday brunch (£4.25, served 9.15–11.15) comes with Sunday papers. Well kept Courage Best and Directors, Gales HSB, Hermitage and John Smiths on handpump; some malt whiskies and a range of over 100 wines; weekend summer barbecues; friendly dog and cat. They're planning a skittle alley for this year. *(Recommended by HNJ, PEJ, Gordon and Daphne, Stephen Goodchild, Margaret Dyke, Bernard Phillips, Tom McLean, Ewan McCall, Roger Huggins, W A Gardiner, John and Margaret Estdale, HNJ, Keith and Sheila Baxter, WHBM, MBW, JHW, E U Broadbent, E Manley)*

Free house   Licensees Mr and Mrs L G Larden   Real ale   Meals and snacks (until 10.15 evenings)   Restaurant   Children in eating area and stable area   Open 11–3, 6–11 all year

BENTLEY   SU7844 Map 2
Bull

A31 Farnham–Alton, W of village and accessible from both directions at W end of dual carriageway Farnham bypass

For a main-road pub, this little tiled white cottage has an unusually homely and relaxing atmosphere (it's under the same management as the Hen & Chicken down the road at Froyle). Its two traditionally furnished and decorated rooms have low black beams and joists, small windows, and stripped timbered brickwork; there's a particularly snug alcove by the log-effect gas fire on the left. Well kept Courage Best and Directors on handpump; darts, shove-ha'penny, fruit machine, piped music. Bar food ranges from sandwiches, through lasagne (£3.45) and so forth, to steaks. There are picnic-table sets and a Wendy house outside. *(Recommended by Dr John Innes; more reports please)*

Courage   Licensees Peter and Mary Holmes   Real ale   Meals and snacks (until 10 Mon–Thurs evenings, 10.30 Fri and Sat)   Restaurant tel Bentley (0420) 22156 Children in restaurant   Open 11–2.30, 6–11 all year

BOLDRE   SL3298 Map 2
Red Lion ★ ☺

Village signposted from A337 N of Lymington

Judging by our postbag, the colourful front flower beds must catch the eyes of many who pass this pub, on the fringes of the New Forest near the Lymington River. And we've not heard of anyone, once enticed in, being disappointed. It's got a really warm and thriving yet very civilised atmosphere, thanks largely to friendly and efficient staff (the landlord, an escapee from Putney, is a cricket man). Its row of four black-beamed rooms has serving-bars at each end, and a pleasant and individual variety of seating – most snug in the central flagstoned sitting-room, with most tables down towards the right. Popular bar food includes home-made soup (£1.20), sandwiches (from £1.20), ploughman's or avocado and prawns (£2), smoked salmon (£2.80) and salads (from £3.50); for once even the basket meals are something special, and include marinated pork chops (£3.80) and half a duck with fresh orange soaked in wine (£4.10). The decorations include a profusion of chamber-pots, as well as hunting pictures and landscapes, heavy-horse harness, needlework, heavy urns and platters and daintier old bottles and glasses, farm tools, gin-traps and even man-traps. Well kept Eldridge Pope Dorchester and Royal Oak on handpump, good log fires; get there early for a table, particularly on weekend lunchtimes. *(Recommended by H K Dyson, P L Jackson, Bernard Phillips, Philip and Sheila Hanley, Mrs E M Brandwood, R M Sparkes, Jenny and Michael Back, Clifford Blakemore, Jon Payne, M C Howells, Drs S P K and C M Linter)*

Eldridge Pope   Licensees A E Fenge and J Bicknell   Real ale   Meals and snacks (12–2, 6–10)   Restaurant tel Lymington (0590) 673177   Open 10.30–3, 6–11 all year

BRAMDEAN   SU6128 Map 2

Fox

A272 Winchester–Petersfield

The spacious lawn which spreads among the fruit trees behind has a really good play area, with a trampoline as well as swings and a seesaw – and children like the hens in the neat run alongside. There are picnic-table sets under cocktail parasols, and weekend summer barbecues. The well kept black-beamed open-plan bar has tall stools with proper back rests around its L-shaped counter, and comfortably cushioned wall pews and wheel-back chairs; the fox motif shows in a big painting over the fireplace, and on much of the decorative china. Original touches lift the bar food out of the ordinary. It includes sandwiches (from £1.65), good soup (£2.15), ploughman's (from £2.45), locally smoked trout (£2.95), cold prawns with mayonnaise (£4.25), cod, lasagne, cauliflower cheese or mussels and prawns in sherry and garlic butter (£4.50), beef Stroganoff (£5.50) and fresh seafood platter (£6.75). Well kept Marstons Burton and Pedigree on handpump, decent coffee, friendly service; sensibly placed darts in the games-room, fruit machine, unobtrusive piped music. There's a new walled-in patio area at the back. *(Recommended by Anthony Willey, Gordon Smith, J A Calvert and others; more reports please)*

Marstons   Licensee Mrs Jane Inder   Real ale   Meals and snacks   Open 10.30–2.30 (3 Sat), 6–11 all year; closed 25 Dec

BURSLEDON   SU4809 Map 2

Jolly Sailor

2 miles from M27 junction 8; A27 towards Fareham, then just before going under railway bridge turn right towards Bursledon Station, keeping left into Lands End Road and bearing left past the station itself

It's the superb position which wins most friends for this old-fashioned pub, with tables out in the waterside garden under a big yew tree, and even on the wooden jetty, looking out over the picturesque bustle of this popular Hamble yachting harbour. There's a children's bar out here at busy times. Bow windows give the same view in the airy front bar, which has Windsor chairs and settles on its floorboards, and a nautical décor of ship pictures, nets and shells – though the beamed and flagstoned back bar, with pews and settles by its huge fireplace, is more authentically in the *Howards Way* mood. Well kept Badger Best and Gales HSB on handpump, with Old Timer in winter; darts, dominoes. Basic bar food includes filled rolls and hot dishes like lasagne, steak and kidney pie and chilli con carne. The path down to the pub from the lane is steep. *(Recommended by Peter Adcock, Leith Stuart, Ian Phillips, Keith Garley, Gwen and Peter Andrews, H G and C J McCafferty, SJC; more reports please)*

Free house   Real ale   Meals and snacks   Restaurant tel Bursledon (042 121) 5557   Children in eating area and restaurant   If parking in lane is full use station car park and walk   Open 11–2.30, 6–11

The initials GWG mentioned, for instance, as 'on GWG 22' stand for our companion Consumers' Association's book *Holiday Which? Good Walks Guide*, and show that the pub is on or near the walk numbered.

CHALTON   SU7315 Map 2

Red Lion

Village signposted E of A3 Petersfield–Horndean

Overlooking the South Downs, this pretty thatched village pub is Hampshire's oldest. It looks the part, with its quaint timbering and jettied upper floor. In the heavy-beamed and panelled bar logs burn in an ancient inglenook fireplace, and furnishings include high-backed traditional settles and elm tables. Well kept Gales BBB and HSB on handpump, and a variety of country wines; reasonably priced filling bar food such as toasted sandwiches or filled rolls, Stilton ploughman's and a good steak and mushroom pie (there's no really separate eating area); tables outside. This quiet downland hamlet is fairly close to the extensive Queen Elizabeth Country Park, which includes a working reconstruction of an Iron Age farming settlement. *(Recommended by Barry and Anne, A J Blackler, G B Longden, Diana Cussons, R Houghton, Charles Turner; more reports please)*

Gales   Real ale   Meals and snacks   Open 10.30–2.30, 6–11 all year

DUMMER   SU5846 Map 2

Queen

Half a mile from M3 junction 7; take Dummer slip road

Considerable care's been taken to give the much refurbished and extended open-plan bar a pleasantly alcovey feel, through the liberal use of timbered brick and plaster partition walls – and of course the open fire helps, as do all the beams and joists. There are built-in padded seats, cushioned spindle-back chairs and stools around the tables on its dark blue patterned carpet, and it's decorated with pictures of queens, old photographs, small steeplechase prints and advertisements. Quickly served good value food has included some magnificent sandwiches (from £1.50, going up to whoppers like their Chicago Waist-Breaker, £3.50), home-made soup (£1.75), pâté (£2.50), salads (from £4.95), and generous helpings of hot dishes such as chilli con carne or lasagne (£4.95), grilled plaice (£6.95) and char-grilled steaks (from ten-ounce rump £9.95). Well kept Courage Best and Directors and John Smiths on handpump; quick, friendly service; bar billiards and fruit machine in one corner, well reproduced pop music. There are picnic-table sets under cocktail parasols on the terrace and in a neat little sheltered back garden. *(Recommended by KC, Mrs C A B Johnson, Joy Heatherley)*

Courage   Licensee John Holland   Real ale   Meals and snacks (12–2, 6.30–10)   Restaurant area tel Dummer (025 675) 367   Children in restaurant area   Open 11–3, 5.30–11 all year

EAST MEON   SU6822 Map 2

George

Church Street; village signposted from A272 about 4 miles W of Petersfield, and from A32 Alton–Fareham in West Meon

The most unusual furnishings in the various cosy areas which loop around the stripped brick central serving-counter are sets of long curved tables and seats hewn from massive slabs of timber. The countryside mood runs on through scrubbed deal tables and chairs (both in the bar and in a charming adjoining candle-lit dining-room), up to three log fires, beams and some timber props, and a modicum of saddlery and harness. Bar food includes sandwiches (from £1.20), ploughman's (from £2.50), quiches such as Stilton and asparagus or mushroom (£3.50), a good range of home-made specials like steak pie, beef curry or spare ribs (£4), plaice or lemon sole (£4), salads (from £4), mixed grill (£7.50) and charcoal-grilled steaks (from £8). The spotless kitchen actually forms one end of the room, yet there are no cooking smells. Well kept Friary Meux, Gales BBB and HSB, Ind Coope Burton and a weekly guest beer on handpump; fruit machine. There are some picnic-table sets by the pretty village street, with more behind by the car park. *(Recommended by Mrs L Saumarez Smith, R Houghton, Charles Turner, Yvonne Healey, Colin Gooch, Peter Davies, A R Lord, HEG, SJC; more reports on the new regime please – particularly on service)*

Free house   Licensees Mike and Sue Young   Real ale   Meals and snacks   Restaurant tel *East Meon (073 087) 481   Children in restaurant   Open 11–3, 6–11 (may open longer afternoons) all year; closed evening 25 Dec*

EMERY DOWN   SU2808 Map 2

New Forest Inn ★ 🏵 🛏

Village signposted off A35 just W of Lyndhurst

The specials are getting so popular here that you have to come before one o'clock to be sure of a helping – giant prawns wrapped in bacon with cheese and garlic, say, salmon in champagne sauce or beef in Stilton and celery. There's a good choice of other food, such as soup (£1.50), various ploughman's with warm cottage loaves (from £2.25), smoked salmon pâté (£2.25), particularly good mushrooms in a garlic and tomato sauce (£2.25), Cumberland sausage (£2.75), chicken curry with poppadums or a daily pasta dish (£4.25), turkey, ham or prawn salad (£4.50), gammon (£5.25), venison in red wine (£6.25) and steaks (£7.25); puddings (£1.50). Even when busy, the big but softly lit open-plan bar is friendly and spotlessly clean, with good solid tables, russet plush settles and wall seats, smaller chairs, and a couple of log fires; it's decorated with antlers, foxes' masks, a big china owl and smaller china forest animals, country prints and old photographs of the area. Flowers Original, Whitbreads Strong Country and a guest beer tapped from the cask; good coffee; cheerful service; darts, shove-ha'penny, fruit machine. On the sloping back lawn you may, like us, hear a woodpecker drumming in the surrounding forest, though animal noises are likely to come from even closer – the white rabbits, the pony looking over the post-and-rails fence, maybe lambs or kids in the side stables, perhaps the Old English sheepdog's latest litter. *(Recommended by Sybil Baker, John Derbyshire, Roger Knight, Peter Adcock, Mr and Mrs D A P Grattan, Bernard Phillips, Heather Sharland, Ian Phillips, Nigel Pritchard, Norman Foot, Dick Brown, Clifford Blakemore, Andy Tye, Sue Hill, Roger Broadie, Roger and Kathy, Dr John Innes, Nigel Williamson, Nick Dowson, Alison Hayward, Roy McIsaac, C Williams)*

Whitbreads   Licensees Sue and Nick Emberley   Real ale   Meals and snacks   Children welcome   Summer string quartets in garden, morris dancing   Open 11–2.30, 6–11 (10.30 in winter)   Bedrooms tel *Lyndhurst (042 128) 2329; £20B/£40B*

nr FAWLEY   SU4503 Map 2

Jolly Sailor

Ashlett Creek; from A326 turn left into School Road, signposted Fawley ½; at Falcon pub crossroads take Calshot road, then fork left almost at once

Friendly and relaxed, this comfortably modernised waterside pub has a restaurant where big windows overlook the busy shipping channel – and at low tide the bustle of wading birds on the mud-flats. This view is shared by picnic-table sets on a long side lawn, with a dinghy park beyond. The carpeted bar is decorated with photographs of Southampton liners; it has soft banquettes, red velvet curtains and a central flame-effect fire. Well kept Flowers Original and Whitbreads Strong Country on handpump; shove-ha'penny, darts, cribbage, fruit machine, piped music. Bar food includes soup, open baps or sandwiches (from £1.95), baked potato filled with fresh baked salmon and prawns (£2.95), chilli con carne (£3.65), lasagne (£3.95), a selection of salads and sixteen-ounce T-bone steak (£8.75). The nearby rhododendron gardens at Exbury are well worth a visit in May or early

June, and now sell plants. *(Recommended by Bernard Phillips, Tony Triggle, Jon and Jacquie Payne, David Crafts; more reports on the new regime please)*

Whitbreads   Licensee Timothy Watton   Real ale   Meals and snacks (until 10 evenings)   Restaurant tel Fawley (0703) 891305   Children in restaurant and eating area   Open 11–11; may close afternoons in winter

FROYLE   SU7542 Map 2
Hen & Chicken

A31 Alton–Farnham

Though it dates back some 400 years, it's the Georgian rebuilding that's left most mark here – notably the coaching-days message rack above the huge fireplace, and the antique settles and oak tables in front of it. There's more modern furniture too in the dimly lit but cheerful open-plan bar, which seems bigger than you'd imagine from outside. The emphasis is very much on bar food, with many of the tables set out for eaters. A wide choice, served most professionally, includes sandwiches (from £2.40), ploughman's or omelettes (from £2.95), filled baked potatoes (from £3.25), salads (from £4.25), steak and kidney pie (£4.95), roast of the day (£4.95) and rump steak (£8.25) – daily specials might run, at a price, to lobster. It's essential to book for the good value family Sunday lunch. Adnams Broadside, Brakspears SB, Courage Best and Wadworths 6X on handpump, and a good choice of ciders and bottled beers; piped music. There are tables in the back garden, with boat swings, a climbing-frame and slide trampoline. More seats face the road in front. *(Recommended by E G Parish, Hazel Morgan, Quentin Williamson, E G Parish, R H Sawyer, KC, Martin, Jane, Simon and Laura Bailey)*

Free house   Licensees Peter and Mary Holmes   Real ale   Meals and snacks (until 10 evenings)   Small panelled restaurant tel Bentley (0420) 22115   Children in eating area and restaurant   Open 11–2.30, 5.30–11 all year; closed evening 25 Dec

HAMBLE   SU4806 Map 2
Olde Whyte Harte

3 miles from M27 junction 8; on B3397 (High Street)

In what tends to be expensive *Howards Way* territory, this is undeniably the place for value. Bar food prices seem a throwback to two or three years ago, with sandwiches and toasties from 70p, shepherd's pie at £1.10, ploughman's £1.45, omelettes and salads from £1.45, curry or chilli con carne at £1.60, fish £2.10 and scampi £2.40: no wonder the yachtsmen flood in at weekends. Yet the main attraction is the charm of the place itself; genuinely ancient, with settles and Windsor chairs on the flagstones of the main white-panelled low-ceilinged bar, a fine inglenook fireplace with the Charles I coat of arms on its iron fireback, Tudor ships' timbers serving as beams (you can still see some of their original fastenings), old maps and charts, rope fancywork, mugs and copper pans. The three-foot-thick back wall may even go back to the twelfth century. Well kept Gales BBB and HSB and XXX Mild on handpump, with XXXXX in winter; dominoes, shove-ha'penny, cribbage, fruit machine, maybe piped music. Besides barrel seats on the small front terrace, there is a back terrace by the sheltered lawn and garden. *(Recommended by Ian Phillips, MBW, JHW; more reports please)*

Gales   Real ale   Meals and snacks   Children in snug bar   Open 11–11 all year

IBSLEY   SU1509 Map 2
Old Beams

A338 Ringwood–Salisbury

Filling a clear need, this extensively refurbished dining pub specialises in quickly providing its large numbers of customers with a wide choice of well prepared popular food. It has similarities to other pubs owned by the same family – the Swans Nest at Exminster (Devon) and Bakers Arms near Lytchett Minster (Dorset), both also main entries in this *Guide*. The range includes soup (90p), sandwiches (from £1.55), ploughman's (from £2), and lots of hot dishes such as chilli con carne, scampi or lasagne (£3.55), rabbit casserole (£3.95), veal casserole (£4.35), lamb chops (£4.55), plaice or chicken Kiev (£4.70), pork chop in cider (£4.75), venison in red wine (£5.55) and braised steak (£5.75). The spacious oak-beamed main room has lots of varnished wooden tables and country-kitchen chairs, and it's divided by wooden panelling and a canopied log-effect gas fire. The U-shaped bar servery has Eldridge Pope Royal Oak, Ind Coope Burton, Gibbs Mew Bishops Tipple, Ringwood Best, Tetleys and Wadworths 6X, a decent choice of wines by the glass and some foreign bottled beers. The garden behind has picnic-table sets among its trees. *(Recommended by J M Norton, E M Brandwood, Roger and Kathy; more reports please)*

Free house   Licensees R Major and C Newell   Real ale   Meals and snacks   Restaurant tel Ringwood (0425) 475090   Children in eating area and restaurant   Open 11–2.30, 6–11 all year

LANGSTONE   SU7105 Map 2

Royal Oak

High Street; last turn left off A3023 (confusingly called A324 on some signs) before Hayling Island bridge

At high water swans come right up to the pub, whose waterside benches and seats in bow windows look out on a broad stretch of water forming a landlocked natural harbour. At low tide the saltings between here and Hayling Island fill with wading birds. Though it's the marvellous position which readers like most, the food counter dispenses a wide choice, with generous, well presented helpings, including home-made soup (£1), filled French sticks (£1.50), ploughman's (£2.75), home-made lasagne (£3.25), sweet-and-sour pork (£3.55), home-made chicken and ham pie (£3.85), rump steak (£5.95, evening only) and enterprising puddings (£1.50). Attractively simple furnishings include Windsor chairs around old wooden tables, there are rugs on wooden parquet and ancient flagstones, and two open fires in winter. The cream walls have old and informatively labelled prints of seabirds and fish. Well kept Flowers, Gales HSB, Wethereds SPA and Wadworths 6X on handpump; piped music; friendly smartly dressed staff. There's a sizeable pets corner at the back, with goats, ducks and rabbits – a popular draw for children. *(Recommended by J H Walker, J F Reay, Richard Houghton, L Walker, Charles Turner; more reports please)*

Whitbreads   Licensee Mr R G Wallace   Real ale   Meals and snacks (12–9.30 summer weekdays, 12–2.30, 7–9.30 in winter)   Restaurant tel Portsmouth (0705) 483125   Children in restaurant   Parking at all close may be very difficult   Open 11–11 all year; closed evening 25 Dec

LINWOOD   SU1810 Map 2

High Corner

Linwood signposted via Moyles Court from A338 (and also from A31); follow road straight up on to heath and eventually pub signposted left down a gravelled track; OS Sheet 195 reference 196107

In the heart of the New Forest, this gives a fine feeling of remoteness out of season, though at holiday times it can get very busy – even on the big neatly kept woodside lawn, which with well spaced picnic-table sets and a sizeable children's play area is such a summer attraction. Bar food includes home-made soup (£1.15), sandwiches (from £1.25), ploughman's (from £1.95), chicken (£3.10), plaice (£3.25), home-made steak, kidney and mushroom pie (£4.25), trout (£4.35), a choice of steaks (from £6.95), and children's dishes (from £1.50); service may sometimes be slow. There's an interesting series of rambling rooms beyond the main serving-bar; the atmosphere's perhaps most comfortable and intimate in the low-beamed bottom room with its aquarium and log fire. Other places include a family-room and a glazed verandah lounge. Well kept Flowers Original, Marstons Pedigree and Wadworths 6X on handpump; darts, dominoes, cribbage, fruit and trivia machine, unobtrusive piped music. In summer they have cook-yourself barbecues outside (or you can pay a little extra and they'll do the cooking); a separate stable bar, connected to the rest of the building by a new extension, may be open then. There's a squash court, and it's near *Good Walks Guide* Walk 40. They now do bedrooms. *(Recommended by Peter Adcock, Steve Dark, H W and A B Tuffill, Jill Cox, H G and C J McCafferty, Steve and Carolyn Harvey)*

Free house   Licensees Lin and Roger Kernan   Real ale   Meals and snacks Restaurant   Children in four eating areas   Open 11–11 (11–2.30, 7–10.30 in winter) Bedrooms tel Ringwood (0425) 473973; £39S/£58B

LONGPARISH   SU4344 Map 2

Plough

B3048 – off A303 just E of Andover

Good value food served most professionally is the main reason so many readers seek out the Plough, though it does have the feel of a restaurant more than a pub (and it's normally best to book). Even so, the rambling open-plan lounge has some comfortable easy chairs as well as its many tables set for food. Moreover, they keep their Flowers Original, Whitbreads Strong Country and a guest beer on handpump well. And the food itself includes properly pubby standbys such as crab sandwiches and a choice of ploughman's (around £2.70), as well as watercress soup (£1.25), smoked trout pâté (£2.35), chicken casserole, steak and kidney pie, gammon or baked trout (all £5.75), a choice of two or three fresh fish dishes (from £7), rump steak (£7.50) and puddings (£1.60). On Sunday there's either a three-course roast lunch (£7.95) or ploughman's; there can be a longish wait. The village is attractive. *(Recommended by J S Evans, S A Robbins, HNJ, PEJ, Joy Heatherley; more reports please)*

Whitbreads   Real ale   Meals and snacks (not Sun evening)   Restaurant tel Andover (0264) 72358   Children in restaurant   Open 11–2.30, 6–11 all year; closed evening 25 and 26 Dec

MATTINGLEY   SU7358 Map 2

Leather Bottle

3 miles from M3 junction 5; in Hook, turn right and left on to B3349 Reading Road (former A32)

Very pretty in summer with its tubs and baskets of bright flowers, riot of wistaria, honeysuckle and roses, and neat tree-sheltered garden, this old brick and tiled pub has good log fires in winter – two in great inglenook fireplaces. A popular move has been its conversion of the former back restaurant into a cottagey second bar room of quite some character, with country pictures on the walls (some stripped to brick), lantern lighting, lots of black beams, an antique clock, a red carpet on bare floorboards, and sturdy inlaid tables with seats to suit. The comfortable open-plan beamed front bar is more orthodox. Good value bar food includes sandwiches (from 90p, ham and egg £2, steak £3.15), minestrone (£1.25), ploughman's in variety (£2.10), sweetcorn and mushroom pizza (£3.40), salads (from £3.40), ham and egg (£4), eight-ounce burgers (£4.10), lemon sole (£4.35), char-grilled half-chicken (£5), lamb kebabs (£6.90) and steaks (from eight-ounce sirloin £7.60), with a dish of the day such as Wiltshire pie (£4). Well kept Courage Best tapped from the cask and Directors on handpump, coffee; friendly service; fruit machine, maybe unobtrusive piped music. *(Recommended by Jack Lalor, KC, Dawn and Phil Garside)*

Courage   Licensees Richard and Pauline Moore   Real ale   Meals and snacks (12–2, 7–10) Children in Cottage Room   Open 11–3, 6–11 all year

MINLEY   SU8357 Map 2
Crown & Cushion

From A30 take B3013 towards Fleet, then first left turn signposted Minley, Cove, Farnborough

For years, the 'sign' of this popular sixteenth-century tiled and timbered low-beamed pub has been the yew tree between it and the woodside cricket pitch: it's more or less shaped into a crown on a cushion. Though the pub itself is perfectly pleasant, it's the Meade Hall behind that's special. This is a rollicking pastiche of an ancient feasting place, with two very long communal refectory tables, smaller candle-lit tables in intimate side stalls, broad flagstones, a huge log fire, and a veritable armoury of scythes, pitchforks and other rustic ironmongery festooning its rafters and timbers (it also has anachronistic piped music and slot machines). A quick-service food counter does a wide choice of home-cooked meats and good fresh salads (around £2.75–£3.75), ploughman's (from £1.85), and at lunchtime roasts (not Sunday) and a couple of good hot dishes such as steak and kidney pie or lasagne (£3–£3.50). In the evening they add basket meals (from around £3) and dishes like gammon or plaice (£3.55) and steak (£5.50); on Sundays they do filled baked potatoes (from £2.10). Well kept Gales HSB, Ruddles County and Websters Yorkshire on handpump, with country wines, mead and a couple of draught ciders; prompt cheerful service. The separate original pub part is comfortable, and has darts, dominoes, cribbage and a fruit machine. There are picnic-table sets outside. *(Recommended by Dr R Fuller, John Baker, Ian Phillips, Alison Hayward, Nick Dowson, Ray Challoner)*

Phoenix (Watneys)   Real ale   Meals (not Sun) and snacks   Open 10.30–2.30, 5.30–11; Meade Hall opens noon and 7

MORTIMER WEST END   SU6363 Map 2
Red Lion

From Mortimer–Aldermaston road take turn signposted Silchester 1¾

Warm and friendly, this sheltered country pub has a good range of consistently well kept real ales on handpump: Adnams Bitter, Eldridge Pope Royal Oak, Fullers London Pride, Palmers IPA and Wadworths 6X. It's also popular for largely home-made food such as ploughman's (£2.50), salad niçoise (£3.85), chilli con carne (£4), steak and kidney pie (£5.25) and venison pie (£6.95). The spacious beamed and partly panelled main room has plenty of tables with upholstered stools, a good log fire in winter, and some stripped masonry and timbers. There are old-fashioned teak seats outside. The licensees have recently taken over the Lord Nelson at Brightwell Baldwin (see under Oxfordshire). *(Recommended by KC, DJ, JJ, Mayur Shah; more reports please)*

Free house   Licensee Peter Neal   Real ale   Meals and snacks (until 10 evenings) Restaurant (closed Sun) tel Silchester (0734) 700169   Open 12–3, 6–11 all year; closed evening 25 Dec

NEWTOWN   SU6113 Map 2
Travellers Rest ✿

Church Road – E of village, which is signposted off A32 N of Wickham

It's always so refreshing to find unpretentious country pubs where food counts for a lot, but isn't a cuckoo in the nest – where more traditional qualities haven't been submerged. This is a fine example: here, old virtues that are very much alive include a particularly chatty atmosphere warmly fuelled by locals and friendly licensees (and their black dog), unfussy old furnishings (well cushioned housekeeper's chairs, a winged settle, leatherette armed chairs, built-in cushioned wall seats), two small rooms not yet knocked into one, and a really pretty floodlit back garden where real trouble is obviously taken with the magnolia, roses, delphiniums, lilies, phloxes and so forth. They do their best to keep up a supply of their own vegetables for the dish of the day, which in winter is usually game (half a roast pheasant, say, at £4.20, or quail or venison) and in summer tends towards fresh seafood (running up to a whole lobster salad at £11.20). Other dishes include sandwiches, ploughman's and simple hot dishes such as ham and egg (£2.40) or plaice (£2.95). Well kept Gibbs Mew Wiltshire, Salisbury and Bishops Tipple on handpump (until recently, this was a Watneys pub); fruit machine, piano. (*Recommended by Melvyn Payne, J A Jones*)

Gibbs Mew   Licensee Peter Redman   Real ale   Meals and snacks (12–2, 7–10)   Occasional folk music or morris dancers   Open 11–3, 6–11 all year

OVINGTON   SU5531   Map 2

Bush ★

Village signposted from A31 on Winchester side of Alresford

Though so handy for the A31, the Bush seems deeply immersed in the peace of the Itchen valley. Outside, a tree-sheltered pergola dining-terrace has white wrought-iron tables by a good-sized fountain pool, and there are quiet walks along the river. The dimly lit low-ceilinged bar's deep-green walls are packed with old pictures in heavy gilt frames; the old-fashioned atmosphere is accentuated by cushioned high-backed settles, elm tables with pews and kitchen chairs, and the open fire on one side and antique solid-fuel stove opposite. It feels very unpretentious. Bar food includes home-made soup (£1.20), sandwiches, ploughman's (from £1.95), mussels in garlic butter (£2.95), steak and kidney pie (£4.50), trout (£5.25) and a hefty seafood platter (£7.25); puddings (from 95p) and a roast Sunday lunch (when the choice of other dishes may be more limited). It's worth booking on summer weekends. Well kept Badger Tanglefoot, Flowers, Gales HSB and Whitbreads Strong Country on handpump; a good selection of wines. (*Recommended by Gordon and Daphne, John Branford, Linda Duncan, W A Gardiner, Gwen and Peter Andrews, Dr John Innes, H G and C J McCafferty, BKA, Michael and Harriet Robinson, Sue Cleasby, Mike Ledger, H E G*)

Free house   Licensee G M Draper   Real ale   Meals and snacks   Evening restaurant (not Sun) tel Alresford (0962) 732764   Children in eating area (lunchtimes) and restaurant   Open 11–2.30, 6–11 all year

OWSLEBURY   SU5124   Map 2

Ship

This high downland village pub has kept its genuine local roots and unspoilt atmosphere, but visitors are treated with real friendliness, and good value food is served quickly. This includes lunchtime sandwiches and toasties (from £1.25), ploughman's (from £1.95), starters such as deep-fried mushrooms (£1.75), basket meals (from £2), home-made vegetable curry (£3.75) or beef in red wine (£4.25), seafood platter (£4.75) and eight-ounce sirloin steak (£6.35); children's helpings (£1.30). The knocked-through bar has simple built-in cushioned wall seats and wheel-back chairs around fairly close-set shiny wooden tables, and a big central fireplace. Those black oak beams and wall props were originally timbers salvaged from a seventeenth-century ship. Well kept Marstons Burton and Mercian Mild on handpump; sensibly placed darts, shove-ha'penny, dominoes, cribbage, fruit machine. There are picnic-table sets in two peaceful garden areas. One side looks right across the Solent to the Isle of Wight, the other gives a view down to Winchester. There are swings, climber and a slide, and occasional summer barbecues. Handy for Marwell Zoo. (*Recommended by N J Mackintosh, Y M Healey, Gordon and Daphne, Jenny and Michael Back, G C and M D Dickinson, JHW*)

Marstons   Licensee Robert O'Neill   Real ale   Meals and snacks (not Sun) Restaurant   Children in restaurant   Open 11–2.30, 6–11 (10.30 in winter)

PENNINGTON SZ3194 Map 2

Chequers ✿

Ridgeway Lane; marked as dead end at A337 roundabout in Pennington W of Lymington, by White Hart

Four hundred years ago, the tidal marshes just down the lane yielded salt which was marketed here; now, it's yachtsmen who make their way up to this unspoiled and prettily tucked-away white cottage. There are picnic-table sets out in its neat sheltered garden, with teak tables on a terrace below, and more tables in an inner courtyard. Inside is simple but stylish, with attractive local landscapes and townscapes and some yachting cartoons above the dark red dado, plain chairs and wall pews around wooden or cast-iron-framed tables, polished floorboards and crisp quarry tiles. Bar food changes daily, and even familiar dishes often show special thought. Besides home-made soup (£1.25) and ploughman's (around £2), the choice might include garlic prawns or citrus fruit, bacon and Stilton salad (£2.50), chilli con carne (£2.95), lasagne (£3.25), a half-pound burger (£3.50), grilled trout stuffed with avocado or plaice with parsley and lemon (£4.50), bream with tomato and herb sauce (£5.50), rack of lamb with mint and wine sauce (£5.95) and steak (from £5.95); the atmosphere may be smoky. Well kept Flowers Original, Gales HSB, Wadworths 6X, Wethereds Winter Royal and Whitbreads Strong Country on handpump; well chosen and reproduced piped pop music, cribbage, dominoes, darts and fruit machine. *(Recommended by Dr C S Shaw, Patrick Young, H G and C J McCafferty, R H Inns; more reports please)*

Free house   Licensees Michael and Maggie Jamieson   Real ale   Meals and snacks (until 10 evenings)   Restaurant tel Lymington (0590) 673415   Children in eating area   Occasional live entertainment   Open 11–2.30ish, 6–11 all year; 11–11 Sat

nr PETERSFIELD SU7423 Map 2

White Horse ★ ★ ★

Priors Dean – but don't follow Priors Dean signposts: simplest route is from Petersfield, leaving centre on A272 towards Winchester, take right turn at roundabout after level crossing, towards Steep, and keep on for four miles or so, up on to the downs, passing another pub on your right (and not turning off into Steep there); at last, at crossroads signposted East Tisted/Privett, turn right towards East Tisted, then almost at once turn right on to second gravel track (the first just goes into a field); there's no inn sign; alternatively, from A32 5 miles S of Alton, take road by bus lay-by signposted Steep, then, after 1¾ miles, turn off as above – though obviously left this time – at East Tisted/Privett crossroads; OS Sheet 197 coming from Petersfield (Sheet 186 is better the other way) reference 715290

The reason this isolated seventeenth-century downland pub rates so highly with us, and is reckoned by a great many readers to be such a special favourite, has nothing to do with food or drinks quality (though it has a fine range of well kept real ales, and lots of interesting country wines). And it's certainly not elegance, style or even conventional comfort: this wouldn't call itself a polished place, and some of the furnishings have seen decidedly better days. From outside it doesn't look special, either. Yet the two small bars have such a pronounced character that people who regularly travel many miles to get here wouldn't have a single thing changed. Indeed, that's an important part of the appeal – that so little does change here. If the old cat's not asleep on one of the oak settles, it'll probably be on the fireside rocking-chair. If the stuffed antelope heads were missing or the longcase clock

---

Real ale may be served from handpumps, electric pumps (not just the on-off switches used for keg beer) or, common in Scotland, tall taps called founts (pronounced 'fonts') where a separate pump pushes up the beer under air pressure. The landlord can adjust the force of the flow – a tight spigot gives the good creamy head that Yorkshire lads like.

stopped ticking, hundreds of people would feel they'd lost a friend. It simply wouldn't be the same without the dozing dog. The old pictures, farm tools, rugs and drop-leaf tables are there because they've always been there – not because an interior designer has just bought them from the Pub Bric-à-Brac Company. Above all, it's uncompromisingly a really unassuming country local: the cook does have to go home at two, so you won't be able to get something to eat then, and the folk up from London won't be treated with any more deference than the farmworker from a few fields away; on the other hand they've usually got local eggs for sale, including organic free-range ones, and in season pheasants too. On the practical side, there are a dozen or so good real ales, including their own very strong White Horse No Name, as well as Ballards, Bass, Courage Best, Eldridge Pope Royal Oak, Gales HSB, King and Barnes Mild, Bitter and Festive and Wadworths 6X; the country wines are tapped from small china kegs. Bar food includes sandwiches (from 70p, prawn £2.20), home-made soup (recommended – the stock's usually done overnight on the Aga), ploughman's (from £2.20), salads (from £3.25), and a selection of home-made hot dishes most days, such as hot-pot (£3.50; as Jack comes from Lancashire, it's genuine), vegetarian lasagne (£3.50), cheesy Cumberland cottage pie or beef and ale pie (£3.85); shove-ha'penny, dominoes, cribbage. There are rustic seats outside (including chunks of tree-trunk); these high downs can be pretty breezy. There are of course times (not always predictable, with Sundays – even in winter – often busier than Saturdays) when the place does get packed. This year we have to say that, alongside a continuing chorus of warm approval, there have been one or two readers who've found bar staff lacking Jack's own calm courtesy. And we trust that this description of the Pub With No Name (the nickname it gets from its lack of a sign) won't lead anyone to expect more from it than it aims to give; for most of its aficionados, its special appeal really is its utterly genuine simplicity and lack of airs and graces. There are caravan facilities in the nearby field. *(Recommended by Matt Pringle, Henry Midwinter, Ian Phillips, Tom McLean, Ewan McCall, Roger Huggins, Steve Dark, W A Gardiner, Mr and Mrs D M Norton, Chris Raisin, Graham Doyle, Gordon and Daphne, John Payne, Alison Hayward, Nick Dowson, Simon Collett-Jones, Roger Mallard, Richard Houghton, TOH, Alan Franck, Stuart Watkinson, Dr J L Innes)*

Free house   Licensees Jack and Margaret Eddleston   Real ale   Meals (sandwiches only Sun and bank hols) and snacks   Open 11–2.30 (3 Sat), 6–11; may open longer on demand, afternoons

ROCKBOURNE   SU1118 Map 2

Rose & Thistle

Village signposted from B3078 Fordingbridge–Cranborne

Though the choice of food may not be as wide as before, the new licensee has preserved this civilised pub's reputation for good seafood, fresh each day. It's the Dover sole which tends to get the warmest praise (big as well as tasty), though other fish dishes picked out recently have included lemon sole, plump moules marinière (£3.25), and the smoked salmon sandwiches. Other food ranges from home-made soup (95p) through taramosalata (£2.20), winter fish pie (£3) or steak and kidney pie (£4.60) to Dorset crab and lobster (around £8–£10). Tables are quite close set in both bars: the lounge with its prettily upholstered stools and small settles, old engravings, sparkling brass and good log fire; the public bar with tables arranged more in the style of booths. Well kept Whitbread Strong Country and Pompey Royal on handpump, piped music; ventilation could sometimes be better. The neat front garden has tables by a dovecote – thatched, like the seventeenth-century pub itself. The village is attractive. *(Recommended by E U Broadbent, J M Watkinson, Gordon Leighton, Dr R A L Leatherdale; more reports please)*

Whitbreads   Real ale   Meals and snacks   Open 10.30–2.30, 7–11; closed lunchtime 25 Dec

ROMSEY SU3720 Map 2
Luzborough House

3 miles from M27 junction 3; A3057 towards Romsey, but turn right at A27

It's the side rooms of this sympathetic 1986 conversion which are the most popular, especially an elegant cream-panelled eighteenth-century dining-room decorated with attractive landscapes, a neat conservatory with white cast-iron tables which opens off it, and a snugly low-beamed sixteenth-century country kitchen with a huge wood-burning stove in its inglenook fireplace. The spacious high-raftered main bar area at the front is more modern: attractively lit, with floral-print wall seats, a sofa and easy chairs, as well as high-backed stools by ledges around stripped-brick pillars. Bar food quickly served by neat staff includes soup (£1.10), pâté (£1.75), sandwiches (from £2.45), ploughman's (from £2.55), salads (from £2.95), home-made steak and kidney pie (£3.45), sirloin steak (£6.95), grilled salmon with a prawn sauce (£7.25) and a substantial mixed grill (£7.50). Well kept Flowers Original, Whitbreads Strong Country and Pompey Royal on handpump. A spacious walled lawn has well spread picnic-table sets under cocktail parasols, with a slide and sprung rockers, and there are more picnic-table sets in front. *(Recommended by Jackie and Jon Payne; more reports please)*

Whitbreads Licensees J Orritt and Valerie Orritt Real ale Meals and snacks (available during opening hours) Restaurant Children in conservatory and restaurant Open 11–11; 11–3, 5–11 in winter

ROTHERWICK SU7156 Map 2
Coach & Horses 🏵

4 miles from M3 junction 5; follow Newnham signpost from exit roundabout, then Rotherwick signpost, then turn right at Mattingley, Heckfield signpost; village also signposted from A32 N of Hook

This partly creeper-covered sixteenth-century village pub is bright with tubs and baskets of flowers in summer, and has rustic seats and picnic-table sets under cocktail parasols outside. It's attractively laid out inside, with two small beamed front rooms, one carpeted and the other with neat red and black flooring tiles, good log fires, interesting furniture including nice oak chairs and a giant rattan one, and a fine assortment of attractive pictures. The wide choice of well kept real ales on handpump from the servery in the parquet-floored inner area has been a special point of appeal – usually Arkells Kingsdown, Badger Best, Eldridge Pope Dorset and Royal Oak, Fullers London Pride, Marstons Pedigree, Palmers BB, Ringwood Old Thumper, Theakstons Old Peculier, a guest beer and one or two others. Well cooked, straightforward and good value bar food includes sandwiches (from 90p, open prawn £2.35), ploughman's (from £1.95), smoked trout pâté (£1.95), home-made burger (£2.25), a variety of home-made pizzas (from £2.15), chilli con carne (£2.75), gammon and egg (£4.45), mixed grill (£6.45) and steaks (from £6.25); welcoming and efficient service. *(Recommended by Ian Phillips, Gordon and Daphne, Gordon Theaker, G and M Stewart, Dr and Mrs Crichton, M Rising, R Houghton, TBB, R C Vincent, Joy Heatherley, Gary Wilkes, KC)*

Free house Licensee Mrs Terry Williams Real ale Meals and snacks (carvery only Sun lunchtime) Weekend carvery tel Rotherwick (0256) 762542 Open 11–2.30, 5.30–11 all year

SETLEY SU3000 Map 2
Filly

A337 Brockenhurst–Lymington

The beers on handpump here are not merely interesting – Ringwood Old Thumper, Wadworths 6X and Palmers IPA – but also notably well kept, and there's quite a good collection of whiskies. Yet it tends to be the food which takes first place in readers' recommendations, including sandwiches (from £1, toasted from £1.20), filled baked potatoes (from £1.50), home-made lasagne, chilli con carne or beef goulash (£2.50), steak and kidney pie (£3.50), seafood platter or scampi (£3.95), a wide choice of vegetarian dishes, such as cashew cutlets in mushroom sauce or nut roast (£3.95), and steaks (from £5.95); children's helpings (£2.25). Spacious but dimly lit and warmly if darkly decorated, one area has long cushioned antique settles and built-in pews, the other has spindle-back chairs around oak tables with a couple of cosy alcoves; there are big fireplaces. The décor is dominated by bric-à-brac hanging thick as Spanish moss from the beams; piped music, with a loudspeaker food-announcement system. The watchful alsatian's called Tess. There are a few picnic-table sets on neat grass at the back. *(Recommended by Trevor Rule, H G and C J McCafferty, Clifford Blakemore, Gary Wilkes)*

Free house   Licensees Tony and Lynn Bargrove, Manager Christophe Guay   Real ale   Meals and snacks (until 10 evenings)   Children in eating area   Open 11–2.30, 6–11 all year; closed 25 and 26 Dec

SOBERTON   SU6116 Map 2
White Lion
Village signposted off A32 S of Droxford

Looking over the quiet green to the tall trees of the churchyard, this seventeenth-century tiled and white-painted pub has picnic-table sets in a sheltered garden with swings, a slide and climbing-bars, and on a sun-trap fairy-lit terrace; they roast pigs on Bank Holidays out here (if it rains, there's an awning for the terrace), and may have children's entertainment in the afternoon then. Inside, the rambling carpeted bar on the right has red-cushioned pews, scrubbed tables, a picture of Highland cattle, a wood-burning stove and in a lower area a big photograph of HMS *Soberton* (replacing the pink elephant painted on the wall that, in the war, made the pub famous as the Pinky to WRENS from HMS *Mercury*). There are more pews with built-in wooden wall seats in the irregularly shaped public bar, which has darts. Carefully cooked and attractively presented bar food includes home-made soup (£1), filled French bread (from £1.25), ploughman's (from £2), filled baked potatoes (from £2.10), a wide variety of pasta (from £2.75), omelettes (from £2.90), steak and kidney pie (£3.75), poached trout (£4.25) and steaks (from £7.45), with dishes of the day such as corned beef hash (£2.50) and lamb cutlets done with tarragon (£3.75); there's a Sunday buffet. It can get very busy at weekends – lively then, much quieter weekday lunchtimes. Well kept Flowers, Fremlins, Whitbreads Strong Country and Pompey Royal, Wadworths 6X and a guest beer on handpump; friendly service, frequent theme nights. *(Recommended by J A Jones, J H Walker, ML, MBW, JHW and others)*

Whitbreads   Licensees Rod and Joanie Johnson   Real ale   Meals and snacks (12–2.30, 6–10.30)   Restaurant (open noon–10.30 Sun) tel Droxford (0489) 877346   Children in lounge and restaurant   Open 11–2.30 (3 Sat), 6–11 all year

SOPLEY   SZ1597 Map 2
Woolpack
B3347 N of Christchurch; village signposted off A338 N of Bournemouth

The new waterside conservatory makes an attractive place to watch the ducks dabbling about on the little chalk stream under the weeping willows, by the little bridge that leads over to a grassy children's play area with a swing and climbing-frame. The rambling low-beamed open-plan bar has a good local atmosphere, especially on the lively dress-up theme nights. It's furnished with red leatherette wall seats and simple wooden chairs around heavy rustic tables, and has both a wood-burning stove and a small black kitchen range. Bar food includes sandwiches (from 95p), filled baked potatoes (from £1.65), ploughman's (from £2), cottage pie (£2.35), prawn and cod pasta (£2.75), home-made curry (£2.85), pizza or various home-made casseroles (£3) and scampi (£3.30); well kept Whitbreads Strong Country and Pompey Royal on handpump, and a collection of unusual foreign beers; darts, dominoes, cribbage, juke box, space game, fruit machine, unobtrusive piped music. Short-sighted readers please note: that bird on the thatched roof is straw too. *(Recommended by Roger and Kathy; more reports please)*

Whitbreads   Real ale   Meals and snacks   Children in eating area and family-room Open 10.30–3ish, 5–11

SOUTHAMPTON   SU4212 Map 2
Red Lion

55 High Street; turning off inner ring road, in S of city

Walking in off the modern city street, it's a tremendous surprise to find this medieval hall, with dark Tudor panelling, lofty and steeply pitched oak rafters, and timbered walls decorated with arms, armour and even a flag reputed to have been presented to the city by Elizabeth I in 1585. Standard pub food, served generously in the lower-ceilinged back bar below the creaky upper gallery, includes filled rolls (from 55p) and sandwiches (from 65p), ploughman's (from £1.60), basket meals (from £1.90), home-made lasagne (£2.45), salads (from £2.75), cod (£2.95), home-made steak and kidney pie (£2.95), scampi (£4.45) and steak (eight-ounce rump £5.95); friendly service. Ruddles Best and County and Websters Yorkshire on handpump; fruit machine and trivia, piped music. *(Recommended by Steve Waters, Paul Corbett, Ian Phillips, Ben Wimpenny)*

Phoenix (Watneys)   Licensee Ian J Williams   Real ale   Meals and snacks (12–9.30) Restaurant tel Southampton (0703) 333595   Children in restaurant   Daytime parking nearby difficult   Open 10–11 all year; closed 25 Dec

STEEP   SU7425 Map 2
Harrow 🏵

Village signposted from A325 and A3 NE of Petersfield; then take road signposted Steep Church, and continue past church

Considering the size of the helpings and the quality of the simple home-cooked food, prices here are very alluring; some people even find it difficult getting through a whole round of sandwiches (from 95p) after a bowl of the excellent soup (£1.30). Other choices include outstanding home-made Scotch eggs (90p), ace ploughman's (from £2.30, home-cooked ham £4), lasagne or a marrow dish (£3.50), and salads (from £4 for an excellent home-made meat loaf); even the bread's normally baked on the premises. This distinctive pub has a terrific unspoilt old-fashioned style about it: recently the landlady hit the national papers with her banner proclaiming Britain's first grassroots anti-environmentalist protest – 'Keep Edward Thomas country free of ecologists, naturalists, tree-fellers, snailmen...' (the poet used to lodge with her aunt and uncle, until he moved next door). The little public bar conjures up those pre-1914 days, with its disdain for plushy rehabilitation: built-in wall benches around scrubbed deal tables, tiled floor, a good log fire in the big inglenook, stripped pine wallboards, summery cornflowers and drying wildflowers; dominoes. Flowers Original and Whitbreads Strong Country tapped from casks behind the counter, farm cider, country wines and a praiseworthy choice of soft drinks including locally made apple juice. Really too small to cope with crowds of outsiders (though there are plenty of tables in the big free-flowering garden), this is perhaps best visited during the week. Note that they don't take children.

If we know a pub has a no-smoking area, we say so.

(Recommended by Gordon and Daphne, Henry Midwinter, Chris Raisin, Graham Doyle, D Godden, Michael Simmonds, Jane Palmer; more reports please)

Whitbread   Licensee Edward McCutcheon   Real ale   Meals and snacks (until 10 evenings)   Open 10.30–2.30 (3 Sat), 6–11 all year; closed evening 25 Dec

STOCKBRIDGE   SU3535 Map 2

Vine

High Street (A30)

Reliably good value bar food, in decent helpings, includes sandwiches (from £1.05; open £2.95), soup (£1.10), ploughman's (from £2.50), omelettes (from £2.95), quiche (£2.95), lasagne verde (£3.65), gammon and egg or grilled fresh sardines (£3.95), local trout (£4.45), fresh plaice (£4.50) and seasonal fish specials. The relaxed and welcoming main bar has Windsor chairs around its many tables, gold velvet curtains, and a Delft shelf of china and pewter; Flowers Original, Marstons Pedigree and Whitbreads Strong Country on handpump; deft and friendly service. The garden behind runs down to a carrier of the River Test. Note that though people still enjoy the food on Tuesdays, that's been Mr Harding's day off; as he does the cooking, there have been no specials then. *(Recommended by Norman Foot, Joan and John Calvert, G A Gibbs; more reports please)*

Whitbreads   Licensees Michael and Vanessa Harding   Meals and snacks (12–3, 6–10; not Sun evening)   Restaurant   Children welcome   Open 11–3.30, 6–11 all year   Bedrooms tel Andover (0264) 810652; £15/£25

White Hart

Bottom end of High Street; junction roundabout A272/A3057

Long on local character and on that steady beat of warm-heartedness which distinguishes so many old coaching-inns, this irregularly shaped low-beamed bar has well divided tables with oak pews, wheel-back chairs and low rustic elm stools, small antique prints on the walls, and, as a prelude to all the china hanging from the beams of the small side restaurant, a collection of shaving mugs hanging over the bar counter. Bar food includes sandwiches (from £1), ploughman's or smoked local trout (£2.75), home-made curry or chilli con carne (£3) and steaks; good Sunday lunches, and cook-yourself summer barbecues. Bass and Charrington IPA on handpump and a range of country wines; shove-ha'penny. There's also a back wine bar; seats outside. *(Recommended by Jan and Ian Alcock, Barry and Anne, O E Hole, D Godden, J H C Peters, Gary Scott; more reports please)*

Free house   Licensee Peter Curtis   Real ale   Meals (in restaurant only, Sun lunchtime) and snacks (until 10 evenings)   Restaurant (not Mon)   Children in restaurant   Open 11–2.30 (3 Sat), 6–11 all year   Bedrooms tel Andover (0264) 810475; £20(£30B)/£35(£42.50B)

TICHBORNE   SU5630 Map 2

Tichborne Arms 🌣

Village signposted off A31 just W of Alresford

Though there's nothing fancy about the food in this pretty thatched pub, it scores both on honest value and on the freshness of the ingredients – often local, like the watercress they put in the bacon sandwiches (£1.20; others from £1). Other food includes home-made soup (£1), liver and bacon nibbles with a home-made dip (£1.50), ploughman's (from £1.80), baked potatoes with a fine range of fillings (from £2.60), salads (from £3.25), a range of home-made daily specials such as lasagne or cauliflower cheese (£3.65), pork and cider casserole or Hungarian goulash (£3.95) and plenty of home-made puddings such as golden syrup sponge with custard and fudge and walnut flan with cream (£1.25). Pictures and documents in the square-panelled room on the right recall the bizarre Tichborne Case – when a mystery man from Australia claimed fraudulently to be the heir to this estate. It's clean and comfortable, with wheel-back chairs and settles (one very long), latticed windows with flowery curtains, fresh flowers, and a log fire in an attractive stone fireplace. A similar room on the left has sensibly placed darts, shove-ha'penny, cribbage and a fruit machine; well kept Courage Best and Directors, Tetleys Bitter and Wadworths 6X tapped from the cask; friendly service. There are picnic-table sets in the big well kept garden. *(Recommended by SJC, Richard Parr, Dr C S Shaw, W A Gardiner, Gordon Hewitt, Gwen and Peter Andrews, Keith and Sheila Baxter, Michael and Harriet Robinson, MBW, JHW, G B Longden, G and M Stewart, J and J Measures)*

Free house Licensees Chris and Peter Byron Real ale Meals and snacks Open 11.30–2.30, 6–11 all year

TIMSBURY SU3423 Map 2
Bear & Ragged Staff

Michelmersh; on A3057 Romsey–Stockbridge, 1¼ miles on Stockbridge side of Timsbury

Well laid out to cope with a good many customers and yet stay cosy, this comfortable country pub has flowers on the rustic elm tables on its brick-tiled floor, brasses, black beams and a big log fire in winter. A separate food counter serves sandwiches (from £1.10), ploughman's (from £1.85), a decent choice of hot dishes such as plaice or cod (£2.75), ratatouille (£2.95), chilli con carne (£3.85) and rump steak (£7), and help-yourself salads (from £3.15); very popular with older people at lunchtime. Well kept Flowers Original, Whitbreads PA and Strong Country, and a guest beer on handpump; fruit machine. There are tables in a fairy-lit side garden (where they hold a September pumpkin competition), with more in front, some sheltering under a white awning. A play area has swings and hollow play trees. *(Recommended by Dr C S Shaw, H W and A B Tuffill, W A Gardiner; more reports please)*

Whitbreads Real ale Meals and snacks (not Sun evening) Open 10.30–2.30, 6–10.30 (11 Fri and Sat); closed evening 25 Dec

TURGIS GREEN SU6959 Map 2
Jekyll & Hyde 🏅

A33 Reading–Basingstoke

Daily specials in this rambling sixteenth-century pub might run up to a Dover sole that would run a fish restaurant close, and other food served quickly and cheerfully includes sandwiches (from £1, steak £3.25), home-made soup (£1), ploughman's (from £2), spinach and bacon Mornay (£2.55 – a special favourite with some readers), filled baked potatoes (from £2.85), good lasagne (£3.60), charcoal-grilled sardines (£3.65), salads (from £3.60), steaks (from eight-ounce sirloin £7.95, thirty-two-ounce T-bone £17.95), and plenty of puddings. The layout and furnishings are attractively individual, with the dining area up a few steps and looking down into the main bar area through timbered openings. A raised inglenook fire throws out lots of heat in winter, and is filled in summer with copper pans and brass platters; pewter mugs hang from the oak beam above it. Well kept Adnams, Badger Best and Tanglefoot, Gribble Reg's Tipple and Wadworths 6X on handpump. A back room has a fine winged and high-backed settle among more modern furnishings, and big Morland and Landseer prints. It leads out into a well sheltered and attractively planted garden, which has plenty of picnic-table sets under cocktail parasols, with swings, a slide and a climber behind. *(Recommended by Ian Phillips, R M Sparkes, E U Broadbent, KC, Roger Huggins, Gary Wilkes)*

Free house Licensees Tracy and David Hunter Real ale Meals and snacks Evening restaurant tel Basingstoke (0256) 882442 Children in eating area and restaurant Open 11–2.30 (3.30 Sat), 6–11 all year

VERNHAM DEAN　SU3456 Map 2

George

On the old coach road going NW from Hurstbourne Tarrant; follow Upton signpost from
A343; or from A338 5 miles S of Hungerford follow Oxenwood signpost and keep on

New licensees in this attractive brick and flint country pub appear to be
maintaining the relaxed, friendly feel you'd perhaps expect from the peaceful
surrounding downland village. The rambling open-plan beamed bar has a log fire in
its big inglenook fireplace, and besides more modern furniture includes a lovely
polished elm table, traditional black wall seats built into the panelled dado, and
some easy chairs. Good value bar food includes sizeable toasted sandwiches
(£1.50), a range of ploughman's (from £1.80), and daily hot dishes such as liver and
bacon with juniper berries or kidneys in sherry sauce (around £2–£3). Well kept
Marstons Burton and Pedigree on handpump; friendly service; cribbage and
dominoes. There are tables in the pretty garden behind. *(Recommended by H N and
P E Jeffery, L Walker, Gordon and Daphne, Neville Burke; more reports on the new regime
please)*

*Marstons　Licensees Mary and Philip Perry　Real ale　Meals and snacks (limited menu
Sun)　Well behaved children welcome; young children in family-room lunchtimes　Open
11–3, 6–11 all year*

nr VERNHAM DEAN　SU3457 Map 2

Boot [illustrated on page 325]

Littledown; on Upton side of Vernham Dean follow Vernham Street signposts

Tucked away on the downs, this little flint cottage is one of Hampshire's prettiest
pubs. And under its new licensees the choice of bar food has widened, with several
changing daily specials as well as sandwiches (from £1), ploughman's (from £1.75),
prawns (£3.25 the half-pint), seafood platter or scampi (£4.25) and steak (from
£7.25, not evenings); puddings (from £1, not evenings). Besides Badger Best,
Marstons Burton and Pedigree and Wadworths 6X tapped from casks on trestles,
they keep a good range of malt whiskies. Though there's more room nowadays in
the side extension, the pub still has the character of a really small place – especially
in the original low-beamed white-panelled bar, with barely space for a pair of tables
by the attractive inglenook fireplace; service is friendly and efficient. There's an
attractive collection of model boots and shoes in a corner cupboard. A conservatory
has darts, dominoes, cribbage and shove-ha'penny; the new people have put in
heating, so it's useful all year now. There are tables on a terrace, and in a well kept
garden with a climbing-frame and horse-drawn caravan. *(Recommended by Ewan
McColl, Roger Huggins, Tom McLean, Margaret Dyke, Mrs Maureen Hobbs, HNJ, PEJ,
Gordon and Daphne; more reports on the new regime please)*

*Free house　Licensees Neale and Helen Baker　Real ale　Meals and snacks (not Mon)
Restaurant (not Mon) tel Linkenholt (026 487) 213　Children in restaurant
and conservatory　Open 12–2.30 (3 Sat), 6–11; opens 7 in winter; closed Mon exc
bank hols*

WELL　SU7646 Map 2

Chequers

5 miles W of Farnham; off A287 via Crondall, or A31 via Froyle and Lower Froyle (easier, if
longer, than via Bentley); from A32 S of Odiham, go via Long Sutton; OS Sheet 186 reference
761467

In the quiet lanes below the North Downs, this tucked-away country pub has a
little, somewhat rough-and-ready low-beamed bar full of snug alcoves, antique
settles and heavily comfortable seats and stools. It's decorated with farm tools and

brasses, and has good log fires in winter. Until fairly recently, the pub was French-run, but food's now more what you'd expect from an English country pub, including grilled sardines (£3.50) and steak, kidney and Guinness pie (£4.50), though running up to fresh lobster salad (£9.50); Flowers Original and Marstons Pedigree. On a warm summer's evening the fairy-lit vine-covered front arbour is idyllic, and there are tables under cocktail parasols in the garden at the back. *(Recommended by GSS, Mr and Mrs P Wilkins, Dr John Innes, Michael Bareau, Phil and Sally Gorton, Gary Wilkes, Steve and Carolyn Harvey)*

Free house   Licensees Robert Collins and Bridget Buser   Real ale   Meals and snacks (not Mon or Sun evening)   Children in eating area   Restaurant tel Basingstoke (0256) 862605 Open 11–3, 6–11 all year

nr WHERWELL   SU3941 Map 2
Mayfly
Testcombe; A3057 SE of Andover, between B3420 turn-off and Leckford where road crosses River Test

From tables out by the River Test you can see the swirls, rings and eddies made by feeding trout, and on a still day maybe see the plump fish themselves. It's a very peaceful spot. Inside, the spacious beamed bar has lots of tables, with bow windows overlooking the water; it's decorated with fishing pictures and gear, and has two wood-burning stoves. You queue at a separate servery for the food, deservedly popular though not cheap; apart from soup (£1.50) and daily hot dishes, this consists of a selection of cold meats such as chicken tandoori or topside of beef, served with a good choice of attractive salads (which are charged extra, 60p each). The cheeses are a particularly strong point: a very wide choice, served with fresh crusty wholemeal bread (£2.50). Flowers Original, Whitbreads Strong Country and a guest beer on handpump. *(Recommended by TBB, Dr Peter Donahue, Mrs L Saumarez Smith, R M Young, Roy McIsaac, H W and A B Tuffill, WHBM, A T Langton)*

Whitbreads   Licensees Barry and Julie Lane   Real ale   Meals and snacks   Open 11–11; 11–2.30, 6–11 in winter

WINCHESTER   SU4829 Map 2
Eclipse
The Square; between High Street and cathedral

On a quiet corner just outside the cathedral close, this picturesque partly fourteenth-century pub has benches out on the pavement under the overhang of its jettied black and white timbered upper part. Though there's not much room in the heavy-beamed front bar, it's got a good-natured, pleasantly busy local atmosphere, with oak settles, mugs hanging from the ceiling, and timbers where walls have been knocked through – including one running vertically, to the right of the fireplace, and around which the original building was built. A wide range of good value home-made bar food includes sandwiches (from £1, toasted 15p extra), ravioli (£1.60), ploughman's (from £1.60), good filled baked potatoes (£1.85), plaice (£3), gammon (£3.25), steak and kidney or game pie (£3.45) and scampi (£3.55); the smaller back room's now been set aside for diners. Flowers, Marstons Pedigree and Whitbreads Strong Country tapped from the cask; friendly service, piped music. It was from an upper window of the pub that Lady Lisle was in 1685 led to the scaffold on which she was beheaded after being wrongly condemned of complicity in the Duke of Monmouth's rebellion; her ghost is said to haunt the top bedroom. *(Recommended by Joan and John Calvert, T C and A R Newell, Dr John Innes, A J V Baker)*

Whitbreads   Licensees Carol and John Baddock   Real ale   Meals and snacks (lunchtime) Children in back room if eating   Daytime parking nearby may be difficult Open 11–3, 5–11; 11–2.30, 6–11 in winter; all day Sat; closed 25 Dec, maybe 26 Dec

Wykeham Arms ★ ⊕ ⇔

75 Kingsgate Street (Kingsgate Arch and College Street are now closed to traffic; there is access via Canon Street)

The uncommonly good range of more than twenty wines by the glass is a special draw here, though their Eldridge Pope Dorchester, IPA and Royal Oak on handpump (under a light carbon dioxide blanket) are well kept too. Thoughtful bar food includes sandwiches (from £1, lunchtime only), soup (£1.25) and ploughman's (from £2.45), with changing evening dishes such as glazed local trout or medallions of pork (£6.95), skate (£7.25) and rack of lamb or sirloin steak (£7.95); puddings such as brown bread ice cream or rhubarb fool (£2.25). An attractive series of rooms, one panelled and each with its own log fire, radiates from a central bar area; one is no-smoking. Furnishings include nineteenth-century oak desks retired from nearby Winchester College, a redundant pew from the same source, kitchen chairs and candle-lit deal tables; the big windows have swagged paisley curtains, the prints are interesting (as are the antique tennis rackets), the piano carries quite a load of houseplants, and there are usually fresh flowers. Service is helpful. There are tables on a covered back terrace, with more on a small but sheltered lawn. Residents have the use of a sauna; the inn is very handy for the cathedral. *(Recommended by Steve Goodchild, Gordon Mott, H W and A B Tuffill, Dr C S Shaw, Patrick Young, GRE, AE, Dr John Innes, R G Ollier, Barbara Hatfield)*

Eldridge Pope   Licensees Mr and Mrs Graeme Jameson   Real ale   Meals and snacks (not Mon evening or Sun, and may be restricted end Dec)   If the small car park is full local parking may be difficult – don't be tempted to block up Kingsgate Street itself   Open 11–11 all year   Bedrooms tel Winchester (0962) 53834; £32.50(£42.50B)/£39.50(£49.50B)

Lucky Dip

Besides the fully inspected pubs, you might like to try these Lucky Dips recommended to us and described by readers (if you do, please send us reports):

Alresford [Broad St (extreme lower end); SU5832], *Globe*: Well kept Watneys-related real ales with a guest such as Gales, photographs of old Alresford, pleasant garden by neighbouring twelfth-century ponds with ducks – especially nice on a summer's day *(BKA, Dave Braisted)*; [West St] *Swan*: Comfortable with good, reasonably priced food; bedrooms *(R E Stratton)*
Alton [Church St; SU7139], *Eight Bells*: Low ceilings hung with bric-à-brac, particularly well kept Ind Coope Burton, related beers, and guest beers rotating monthly; can get very busy *(Dr John Innes, Olav Larsen)*; [Market St] *Kings Head*: Excellent welcoming atmosphere, friendly bar staff, cheap home-cooked bar food and fully enclosed garden with children's facilities *(Miss L Canham, M White)*
Ampfield [A31 Winchester–Romsey; SU4023], *Potters Heron*: Good value bar food in popular pub – one of the first to be done up to look old *(Tim Powell)*
☆ **Ball Hill** [Hatt Common; leaving Newbury on A343 turn right towards East Woodhay –

OS Sheet 174 reference 423631; SU4263], *Furze Bush*: Clean and airy décor, pews and pine tables, usual bar food, well kept Bass, Border Mild and Marstons Pedigree on handpump, decent wines by the bottle, tables on terrace by good-sized sheltered lawn with play area, restaurant; has had jazz Sun; well behaved children allowed, no-smoking area in dining-room *(LYM)*
Barton on Sea [SZ2393], *Red House*: Sadly this pub, popular for good food, beer and wines, closed early in 1989
Basing [Bartons Lane (attached to Bartons Mill Restaurant); SU6653], *Millstone*: Unusual, busy pub well placed by River Lodden; well kept real ale tapped from the cask, well cooked food *(Bernard Phillips)*
Basingstoke [A30 just W – visible from M3; SU6352], *Wheatsheaf*: Up-market refurbishment of a Georgian coaching-inn with panelled walls, beams, oak furniture, huge fireplace, whips, lanterns and so forth; Wadworths 6X and Wethereds Bitter on handpump; decent bar food from filled rolls to steaks (the counter's an old cast-iron

Children welcome means the pub says it lets children inside without any special restriction; readers have found that some may impose an evening time-limit – please tell us if you find this.

range); bedrooms comfortable, in recently added wing *(Patrick Young)*

☆ **Bentworth** [SU6640], *Sun*: Lovely old pub with brick and bare wood floors, open fireplace on right, inglenook on left and old pictures on walls; popular with students *(Gordon and Daphne)*

Binsted [SU7741], *Cedars*: Lively local with big public bar (and huge boar's head), quieter sitting-roomish lounge bar, well kept Courage ales, good freshly prepared food *(W A Gardiner, BB)*

Bishops Sutton [former A31 on Alton side of Alresford – now bypassed; SU6031], *Ship*: Friendly, pleasant and cosy local with relaxed atmosphere, good varied bar food quickly served, discreet piped music; village much quieter since Alresford Bypass *(G and M Stewart, LYM)*

Bishops Waltham [Church St; SU5517], *Bunch of Grapes*: Old-fashioned pub where conversation is the main source of entertainment (no music) and where the emphasis is on drinking, not eating; very friendly landlord and landlady (the pub has been in the same family for many years), well kept Courage Best tapped from the cask with Directors at Christmas; small garden *(Melvyn Payne)*; [The Square] *Crown*: Large, well run Whitbreads pub; children in restaurant area *(MBW, JHW)*

Bishopstoke [SU4619], *River*: Spacious pub with bric-à-brac on walls and ceiling, including a replica of the Crown Jewels *(Ben Wimpenny)*

Blacknest [OS Sheet 186 reference 798416; SU7941], *Jolly Farmer*: Enjoyable bar food, well kept Badger real ales, quiet piped music; food served outside too *(G and M Stewart, E U Broadbent)*

Botley [The Square; SU5112], *Bugle*: Well decorated beamed bar with Flowers and Whitbreads Strong County on handpump, excellent bar food including good fresh seafood, steaks, curries and so forth, quick pleasant service; restaurant *(A R Lord, C D Gill)*

Braishfield [Newport Lane; SU3725], *Newport*: Very unassuming – even rough-and-ready – place with well kept Gales, good value quickly served sandwiches, pleasant garden with various animals *(H W and A B Tuffill)*

Bransgore [Burley Rd; SZ1897], *Carpenters Arms*: Pleasant staff, good food and tables well spaced or in alcoves *(NIH)*; [Highcliffe Rd] *Three Tuns*: Open fire, friendly atmosphere, well kept beer, good bar food; service can be slow under pressure *(Gary Wilkes)*

Brockenhurst [Lyndhurst Rd; SU2902], *Snakecatcher*: Friendly local, Eldridge Pope Royal Oak and IPA, good bar food with some interesting dishes and daily specials *(WHBM)*

☆ **Bucklers Hard** [SU4000], *Master Builders*

House: Lovely spot by the water in carefully preserved Montagu-estate village; beamed and timbered bar with big log fire, adjoining buffet bar; friendly service, and recent reports suggest that bar food may be coming back into favour, with well kept Ind Coope Burton; you can't always forget that this is part of a substantial hotel complex (a good point is that using the hotel car park saves a hefty village parking fee) *(Leith Stuart, Y M Healey, Peter Hitchcock, TRA, MA, Barbara Hatfield, Keith Garley, LYM)*

☆ **Burghclere** [off A34 – OS Sheet 174 reference 462608; SU4761], *Carpenters Arms*: Well kept and friendly pub, small and busy, with big helpings of reasonably priced bar food including vegetarian dishes, Watneys-related real ales, unobtrusive piped music, fruit machine, garden; small evening fixed-price restaurant; opp Sandham Memorial Chapel (NT), Stanley Spencer's masterwork *(Dennis and Pat Jones, D J Cooke)*

☆ **Buriton** [OS Sheet 197 reference 735205; SU7420], *Five Bells*: Very wide choice of unusual food such as wholemeal spaghetti with courgettes and blue cheese dressing *(Glyn Edmunds)*

☆ **Burley** [on back rd Ringwood–Lymington; SU2003], *Queens Head*: Tudor pub with flagstones, low beams, timbering, panelling, good log fire and a swarm of bric-à-brac from assegais to divers' helmets and bespectacled animals' heads; usual bar food (not winter evenings), including a notable ploughman's; well kept Flowers Original and Whitbreads Strong Country on handpump, maybe piped music (which may be loud); gift/souvenir shop in courtyard – pub can get packed in summer, and standards may vary then; provision for children *(Ian Phillips, Gwen and Peter Andrews, LYM)*

☆ **Bursledon** [Hungerford Bottom; SU4809], *Fox & Hounds*: Popular for handsomely rebuilt ancient Lone Barn behind – long oak-trunk table, lantern-lit side stalls, jolly rustic atmosphere and lots of interesting farm tools and equipment, food bar, well kept Watneys-related real ales with a guest beer such as Gales, seats out in sheltered flagstone courtyard; games and juke box in main pub, which has sixteenth-century cooking spit; children in Lone Barn *(Patrick Young, Prof A N Black, H G and C J McCafferty, LYM)*

Cadnam [by M27 junction 1; SU2913], *Sir John Barleycorn*: Well kept Whitbreads Strong Country, generous helpings of good food and friendly staff, in traditional beamed bar of attractive old thatched pub *(Dennis and Pat Jones)*

Catherington [Catherington La; SU6914], *Farmer*: Very pleasant local where the emphasis is on darts; well kept Gales, friendly landlord, food lunchtime – a useful stop *(RH)*

☆ **Cheriton** [just off B3046 towards Beauworth

– OS Sheet 185 reference 581282; SU5828],
Flower Pots: Unspoilt village local with
homely parlourish bar, well kept Flowers
Original and Whitbreads Strong Country,
cheap sandwiches and ploughman's,
traditional games in public bar, old-
fashioned seats on front grass; bedrooms
good value, comfortable and homely;
excellent breakfasts *(Richard Parr, Ian
Phillips, Phil and Sally Gorton, LYM)*

☆ Crawley [village signposted from A272
Winchester–Stockbridge, and B3420
Winchester–Andover; SU4234], *Fox &
Hounds*: Striking building – sort of Bavarian
Tudor – with log fire in civilised oak-
parquet-floored small lounge, panelled black
wall benches and polished copper tables in
bigger beamed main bar, restaurant; in
attractive village; has been popular for well
kept real ales such as Flowers Original, Gales
HSB, Wadworths 6X and Whitbreads Strong
Country, and bar food including their good
Sparsholt Smokie; but we've had mixed
reports in 1989, and would like more news;
children in eating area; bedrooms *(Michael
Thomson, Dr R Fuller, Kate and Russell Davies,
Joan and John Calvert, LYM)*

Crondall [SU7948], *Hampshire Arms*:
Welcoming pub with good food *(Michael
Bareau)*; [Bowling Alley; N of village just off
A287 Farnham–Basingstoke – OS Sheet 186
reference 798502] *Horn*: Strikingly clean
pub, well kept Watneys-related real ales,
good food, courteous service *(D S Male)*

Denmead [Worlds End; SU6312],
Chairmakers Arms: Wide choice of bar food
and well kept Gales ales in knocked-together
rooms of popular, welcoming and
comfortable pub surrounded by paddocks
and farmland *(Colin Gooch, LYM)*;
[Southwick Rd, Bunkers Hill; SU6511]
Harvest Home: Delicious home-made food,
service always polite and friendly in pretty
and well decorated country pub with good-
sized garden *(Alan and Sharron Todd)*

Downton [SZ2793], *Royal Oak*: Well run,
with cheerful staff, consistently good food
including excellent pies, well kept
Whitbreads-related real ales, decent wine by
the glass, family atmosphere *(John Kirk)*

Droxford [SU6018], *Hurdles*: Friendly
service, well kept beer and good choice of
food including excellent vegetarian dishes at
reasonable prices in bustling fast-food pub,
small share-a-table bar, separate restaurant
(John and Margaret Estdale, TRA, MA); *White
Horse*: Rambling old inn with a great deal of
potential, which has had good choice of well
kept real ales, log fire, bar food; since a
management change last year it may be
looking up again; bedrooms *(LYM – more
reports please)*

☆ Dundridge [Dundridge Lane; off B3035
towards Droxford, Swanmore, then right at
Bishops Waltham 3¾ – OS Sheet 185
reference 579185; SU5718], *Hampshire*

Bowman: Simple isolated downland pub
which under the present landlord has
recovered its cosy, unspoilt friendliness, with
well kept Archers and Gales ales tapped from
the cask maybe under light blanket pressure,
good plain food; tables on spacious lawn
(ML, SJC, LYM)

Durley [Heathen St – OS Sheet 185 reference
516160; SU5116], *Farmers Home*:
Comfortable old-fashioned free house with
Whitbreads, very large and well equipped
children's play area *(MBW, JHW)*

East Meon [SU6822], *Izaak Walton*: Friendly
licensee and staff, particularly well kept
Watneys-related real ales with a guest beer
such as Gales HSB, bar food *(Richard
Houghton)*

East Tytherley [SU2929], *Star*: Comfortable
lounge with lots of atmosphere, well kept
Gales, good food in quaint restaurant *(Ian
Scrivens, H W and A B Tuffill)*

Emery Down [SU2808], *Green Dragon*: Busy
pub with good mix of customers, well kept
beer, bar counter surrounds interestingly
veneered with different woods from named
Forest localities, quickly served bar food,
garden; the headquarters of the commoners'
pony and cattle association *(WHBM, Philip
and Trisha Ferris)*

Emsworth [South St; SU7406], *Coal
Exchange*: Cheerful new licensee who makes
everyone welcome, friendly locals, basic
interior but plenty of character and
atmosphere, well kept Gales and good cheap
food including local cockles *(Richard
Houghton)*; [New Brighton Rd] *Fairfield*:
Substantial and discreet Regency building
with two comfortable bars, delightful
separate dining area and proper pub
atmosphere; well kept Gales, good
reasonably priced bar food, friendly service
(Richard Houghton); [North St] *Scalywags*:
Formerly the Railway; appearance and name
belie the pleasant, plush interior; well kept
Watneys-related real ales with a guest beer
such as Gibbs Mew, friendly, knowledgeable
staff; decent helpings of good value food
(Richard Houghton); [main st] *Ship*: Good
value simple food from sandwiches to local
crab and plaice, and well kept Bass and
Charrington IPA, in plain but comfortable
well kept pub with pretty little back yard
(LYM); [2 West St] *Town Brewery*: Village
local with well kept Whitbreads and very
friendly licensee; food, cooked by licensee's
wife, is very good value and generously
served; open all day *(Richard Houghton)*

Eversley [SU7762], *White Hart*: Good
atmosphere and beer and good traditional
crowd including the 'old boy' *(Sarah and
Jamie Allan)*

Eversley Cross [SU7861], *Chequers*:
Comfortably modernised (though in fact
partly fourteenth-century) Watneys pub with
quickly served bar food *(LYM)*

Everton [SZ2994], *Crown*: Good, traditional,

two-bar local with good service from hospitable licensees, Whitbreads-related real ales, decent bar lunches in eating area *(WHMB)*

Ewshot [A287 Farnham–Odiham; SU8149], *Queens Arms*: Attractive bar with lovely coal fires and good atmosphere, good service; good, well presented bar snacks, restaurant (not Sun lunchtime) *(Mrs J Ward)*

Exton [signposted from A32; SU6121], *Shoe*: Worth knowing for its pleasant riverside location, which gives the pub lots of potential; usual range of decent bar food, good puddings *(Mrs S A Bishop)*

Faccombe [SU3858], *Jack Russell*: Hilltop village free house opposite pond, with superb views; small but spotless bar, pleasant young licensees, usual range of bar food but including extras like home-cured ham and eggs and pheasant casserole; closed Tues; bedrooms *(HNJ, PEJ)*

Fareham [Trinity St/West St; SU5706], *Daniels*: Spacious, clean and efficiently run, good pastiche of 1930s cocktail bar with chrome bar stools, mirrors and elegant, comfortable sofas and banquettes in pastel colours; Whitbreads ales, well cooked and presented burgers, prompt service *(Ian Phillips)*

Farnborough [Rectory Rd (off A325); SU8753], *Prince of Wales*: Genuine local, no pretensions to poshness, with wide choice of splendidly kept real ales such as Badger Best and Tanglewood, Fullers London Pride, Eldridge Pope Royal Oak, King & Barnes and Wadworths 6X, also guest beers and reasonable choice of malt whiskies; good helpings of decent bar food, warm management and staff *(Dr R Fuller, R J Walden)*

☆ Farringdon [Crows Lane, Upper Farringdon (off A32 S of Alton); SU7135], *Rose & Crown*: Clean local with masses of bric-à-brac on walls and ceiling, good choice of well kept real ales, popular food in bar and restaurant, and lovely old cash till which sings up prices in pre-decimal money; bedrooms *(Gordon and Daphne)*

Fordingbridge [14 Bridge St; SU1414], *George*: Good choice of generously served good food, well kept beer and wine, attentive service *(JMW, Margaret and Geoffrey Tobin)*

☆ Fritham [SU2314], *Royal Oak*: Thatched New Forest pub, Flowers and Whitbreads Strong Country tapped from the cask for two quite unspoilt and decidedly basic – even untidy – bars, one with high-backed settles and stairs, pots and kettles hanging in wide old chimney; outside seats, tables, climbers and maybe a couple of friendly sheep, with cows, ponies and even pigs wandering nearby; no food beyond pickled eggs, but your own sandwiches welcome; children in back room; start GWG40 *(Roy McIsaac, Charlie Salt, WHBM, LYM)*

Frogham [SU1713], *Foresters*: Busy pub on edge of forest with wooden settles, good, friendly atmosphere and terrific choice of real ales including Hook Norton, Robinwood winter Old Fart and Theakstons, cider and bar food *(Charlie Salt)*

Froxfield Green [Alton–Petersfield rd; SU7025], *Trooper*: Exterior due for attention, but well kept Flowers and Wadworths, interesting choice of inexpensive wines and cheap, simple and freshly prepared bar food *(HEG)*

Grateley [SU2741], *Plough*: Attractive old pub in quiet village with small public bar with games, good-sized lounge, big open fire, good choice of local ales, pleasant, friendly staff and very good food served in small separate candle-lit dining area *(Mr and Mrs W C Waggoner, Mark Spurlock)*

Hambledon [SU6414], *Bat & Ball*: Good food, well kept Ind Coope real ales, relaxing atmosphere, interesting china and long cricketing history – lots of memorabilia in the restaurant which now dominates the pub and makes it very busy at weekend lunchtimes *(David Gaunt, LYM)*; *Horse & Jockey*: Perfect, remote spot but busy at lunchtimes; clean and civilised with good service, excellent food *(D S Male)*; [West St] *Vine*: Very welcoming well furnished pub with nice prints, farm tools, old banknotes and so forth; good food and wide choice of well kept real ales; shove-ha'penny (a big thing here), darts *(Ian and James Phillips)*

Hartley Wintney [B3011; SU7656], *Shoulder of Mutton*: Well kept Courage ales on handpump, wide choice of good value food (from humorous menu), pleasant staff, nice sunny garden looking out over countryside *(Aleister and Geraldine Martin)*

Havant [South St; SU7106], *Old House at Home*: Carefully enlarged Tudor pub, much modernised inside (electronic games, piped music); pleasant service, well kept Gales BBB and HSB *(LYM)*; [6 Homewell] *Robin Hood*: Wonderful old town pub just off the shopping mall with well kept Gales tapped from the cask and quickly prepared, reasonably priced good food; cosy atmosphere, caring pleasant staff *(Richard Houghton)*

Hawkley [Pococks Lane; SU7429], *Hawkley*: Interesting little pub, particularly friendly, with well kept Wiltshire Stonehenge Best; can be crowded, music may be loud *(Richard Houghton)*

Hayling Island [11 Rails Lane; SU7201], *Buccaneers*: Worth knowing for reasonably priced decent food; open fires in winter *(TRA, MA)*; [9 Havant Rd (A3023)] *Maypole*: Friendly and obliging licensee, well kept Gales ales, good bar food *(Richard Houghton)*

☆ Heckfield [B3349 Hook–Reading (still called A32 on some maps); SU7260], *New Inn*: Wide range of food in very extensive rambling open-plan bar, some traditional furniture and a couple of good log fires as well as the many well spaced dining-tables, warm welcome and friendly atmosphere, well kept Badger Best and Tanglefoot and Courage Best; restaurant (not Sun); bedrooms in comfortable and well equipped new extension (Dr R Fuller, DJ, JJ, LYM)

Highclere [Andover Rd (A343 S of village); SU4360], *Yew Tree*: Decent plain bar food from soup and sandwiches to shoulder of lamb and steaks in sprucely refurbished bar with big log fire, tables and chairs, plush button-back banquettes and velvet curtains; Flowers Original, Fremlins and Wadworths 6X on handpump; children in area off bar; bedrooms (R M Sparkes, LYM)

☆ **Hill Head** [Hill Head Rd; SU5402], *Osborne View*: Relaxed comfortably refurbished pub with superb view over Solent and Isle of Wight, and beach garden in summer where you can swim; full range of Badger real ales kept well, good range of well prepared and generously served bar food including enormous omelettes, friendly staff (SJC, Michael Bechley)

Hinton [A35 4 miles E of Christchurch; SZ2095], *East Close*: Large, friendly pub with variety of local beers including Ringwood Best and Gibbs Mew Bishops Tipple and large choice of hot and cold bar food in big helpings; children's area (Dr R B Crail)

Hinton Admiral [A35; SZ2196], *Cat & Fiddle*: Cosy and very popular, with unusual if not cheap bar food, friendly service (Mr and Mrs Edwicker)

☆ **Hook** [London Rd – about a mile E; SU7254], *Crooked Billet*: Spacious, recently refurbished pub with homely open fires; friendly licensee and staff, welcoming to all ages, good atmosphere, well kept beer and good range of soft drinks, good bar food served throughout the day including sandwiches, ploughman's and steaks; superb spot with stream, ducks, garden (some traffic noise out here); children welcome (Mrs Sue Mills, J S Rutter)

☆ **Horndean** [London Rd; SU7013], *Ship & Bell*: Quiet and relaxed, with a pleasant atmosphere (that of a town pub, rather than a country one); well run, with welcoming staff – virtually the tap to Gales Brewery, with their beers kept well; bedrooms (WHBM, R Houghton)

Horsebridge [about a mile SW of Kings Somborne – OS Sheet 185 reference 346303; SU3430], *John o' Gaunt*: Well prepared fresh food including first-rate home-made soup; positively pulses on fine weekends (H W and A B Tuffill)

Hursley [A31 Winchester–Romsey; SU4225], *Dolphin*: Well run, with bar food including good ploughman's (GSS); *Kings Head*: Polite, efficient service, Bass and other well kept real ales, wide range of good reasonably priced snacks; gets crowded at lunchtime with IBM staff – its décor rather matches that clientele (Gethin Lewis, Jon and Jacquie Payne, GSS)

☆ **Keyhaven** [SZ3091], *Gun*: Wide choice of good value simple bar food and well kept Whitbreads-related real ales in small but busy pub, dating from seventeenth century and overlooking boatyard; garden, good walk along spit to Hurst Castle with Isle of Wight views; only parking is in pay and display car park (Jenny Cantle, Barbara Hatfield, H G and C J McCafferty)

☆ **Kings Worthy** [A3090 E of Winchester, just off A33; SU4933], *Cart & Horses*: Big well kept rambling bar with cushioned settles, some milk churn seats, old enamel advertisements, various softly lit alcoves, and steps up to dining area with lots of well spaced rustic tables; can get crowded, with food from filled soft baps and ploughman's to hot dishes and popular salads; Marstons Burton, Pedigree and Owd Rodger, bar games, conservatory, tables outside, barbecues; children allowed in most areas, good play area outside with Wendy house; bedrooms (W J Wonham, Alan Vere, Ian Phillips, S Punchard, H G and C J McCafferty, LYM)

☆ **Kingsclere** [SU5258], *Crown*: Long comfortable partly panelled lounge with central log fire, Courage real ales, games in simpler public bar, pleasant atmosphere; very popular for somewhat pricey home cooking; children in family-room; bedrooms comfortable (J P Berryman, Gordon and Daphne, LYM); [A339 outside] *Star*: Attractive food, good quick service, nicely arranged bars – a popular busy main-road pub (G B Pugh)

Langstone [A3023; SU7105], *Ship*: Large pub in attractive spot by sea with excellent Gales, good friendly service and straightforward bar food (including good sandwiches) at reasonable prices (AJVB)

Lasham [SU6742], *Royal Oak*: Warm atmosphere, beam hung with toby jugs and steins, lintel above open fire with rack of pipes and horsebrasses and glowing wall lamps, good food and beer, tables out on lawn; may get crowded in gliding season (Prof and Mrs Keith Patchett)

nr **Liphook** [B3004 towards Alton; SU8331], *Passfield Oak*: Fine setting backing on to National Trust woodland, tables on front lawn and in big back garden, cheery bustling bar with simple rooms off; has had several real ales such as Ballards and Bunces, simple bar food, children's room, but new licensees 1989, with reports of plans to gut and remodel interior and add bedrooms (LYM)

Liss [A325; SU7728], *Spread Eagle*: Pleasant country pub overlooking square, friendly service in lounge bar, pool-table in plain public bar (Dr John Innes)

Liss Forest [SU7829], *Temple*: Refurbished local with friendy atmosphere, pool-table, well kept Gales HSB, reasonably priced bar food, good garden with play area and tree house; children's room (D C Bail)

Longstock [SU3536], *Peat Spade*: Friendly locals' bar, pleasant comfortable lounge, good choice of food, well kept real ale in straightforward Test Valley village inn (H W and A B Tuffill, LYM)

Lower Farringdon [Gosport Rd (A32); SU7035], *Royal Oak*: Big main-road pub with reasonably priced bar food served almost instantly; friendly staff, Courage real ale (Richard Houghton)

☆ **Lower Froyle** [SU7544], *Anchor*: Popular, clean and brightly lit pub with excellent service, good range of beers, piped music, friendly atmosphere, good if not exactly imaginative bar food; good restaurant (John and Heather Dwane, Dr John Innes, W A Gardiner)

Lower Wield [SU6340], *Yew Tree*: Remote pub well worth tracking down; family-run, with varied choice of bar food from ploughman's or baked potatoes through home-made pies to steaks (small kitchen, so food can be slow) (Anon)

Lyde Green [SU7057], *Fox*: Isolated country local – a real pub, with no frills, lively atmosphere, central fireplace, bar food; children's play area (Gordon and Daphne)

☆ **Lymington** [High St; SZ3295], *Angel*: Largely home-made bar food in comfortable and spaciously modernised hotel bar – we'd like more reports on the recent refurbishments; Eldridge Pope Dorchester, Dorset and Royal Oak on handpump – and reputedly a collection of ghosts that includes one of the very few Naval ones; children in Tuck bar; bedrooms (LYM)

Lymington [Quay Hill], *Kings Head*: Interesting display of pewter tankards and glasses suspended from beams of this attractive, cottagey bar with comfortable settles, good atmosphere, pleasant licensee and Whitbreads Strong Country and Pompey Royal (E G Parish); [High St] *Red Lion*: Small pub with bare floorboards, wooden chairs and nice atmosphere; very good beer and superb mussels (H G and C J McCafferty); [nr pier] *Wagon & Horses*: Well kept real ale and good choice of well cooked and presented food (J H C Peters)

Lyndhurst [High St; SU2908], *Fox & Hounds*: Lots of exposed brickwork, dried flowers in fireplaces, standing timbers dividing it into four areas, family-room beyond recently enclosed coach-entry arch, Fremlins real ale, usual bar food from ploughman's to steaks (Ian Phillips)

Lyndhurst Road Station [A35 Southampton–Lyndhurst, on edge of Ashurst; SU3310], *New Forest*: Large place that caters well for families: big garden (both grass area and terrace) with good children's facilities including bouncing castle, some goats and other animals; Courage Directors and

reasonable range of fairly priced food; children allowed in conservatory area (Nigel Pritchard)

Marchwood [Beaulieu Rd; off A326 Southampton–Fawley at Twiggs La; SU3810], *Bold Forester*: Quiet spot on border of New Forest; Watneys-related real ales, good food, darts, skittle alley and fruit machines (Paul Corbett); [Hythe Rd (also off A326)] *Pilgrim*: Immaculately sprightly décor in smart thatched pub with well kept real ales such as Bass and Courage Best and Directors, lunchtime bar food; neat garden (LYM)

☆ **Mattingley** [B3011 on Hazeley Heath; SU7459], *Shoulder of Mutton*: Popular pub well off beaten track, impeccable service, well kept Courage, excellent if not cheap food, pleasant atmosphere with quiet piped music; arrive early to get a table (Richard Houghton, G and M Stewart)

Meonstoke [SU6119], *Bucks Head*: Neat and clean middle-sized old pub in pleasant spot; warm and welcoming atmosphere, good value wholesome bar food (E Manning, Roger Mallard)

Milford on Sea [SZ2891], *Red Lion*: Good beer and great local atmosphere, especially on a Fri night; garden (H G and C J McCafferty)

Minstead [SU2811], *Trusty Servant*: Pleasant public bar; inn-sign said to have been painted by an Old Wykehamist (WHBM)

Monxton [SU3144], *Black Swan*: Pretty pub in village of thatched rose-covered cottages; the main part is a big back extension, with a wide range of pub food from sandwiches or baked potatoes to steaks, and Whitbreads beers; tables in courtyard and garden with play area, barbecue and slow-flowing stream (Ian Phillips)

☆ **Nether Wallop** [village signposted from A30 or B2084 W of Stockbridge; SU3036], *Five Bells*: Simple village inn with long cushioned settles and good log fire in beamed bar, good value bar food, well kept Marstons real ales on handpump including Mild, bar billiards and other traditional games in locals' bar, small restaurant, seats outside, provision for children; friendly welcome from licensee and resident goat who eats packets of polo mints whole; well kept Marstons (Alan Skull, John Tyzack, Mrs Ann Sugden, LYM)

New Milton [SZ2495], *Speckled Trout*: Good lunchtime food (R E Stratton)

Oakhanger [off A325 Farnham–Petersfield; SU7635], *Red Lion*: Small, cosy lounge with brasses and large log fire, separate dining area with good food, well kept Courage Directors, friendly service (John Atherton)

☆ **Odiham** [Church Sq; SU7450], *Bell*: Lovely little welcoming local attractively placed in pretty square opposite church and stocks; walls and ceiling festooned with banknotes, old iron, caps, American car number-plates; good food in bar and restaurant, well kept Courage Best and Directors (Ian Phillips)

Odiham [High St (A287)], *George*: Well kept Courage Best and Directors and John Smiths and bar food in well furnished and civilised old-fashioned bar; pleasant staff; bedrooms *(E G Parish, LYM)*

Pennington [Milford Rd; SZ3194], *White Hart*: Friendly, jolly landlord, good atmosphere, well kept beer, bar food, garden and terrace *(Philip and Trisha Ferris)*

☆ **Petersfield** [College St; SU7423], *Good Intent*: Welcoming and spotlessly kept sixteenth-century little pub, probably best in winter, with log fires; well cooked and presented bar food, small restaurant *(Gwen and Peter Andrews)*

Portchester [White Hart Lane; SU6105], *Wicor Mill*: Welcoming licensees, pleasant locals, well kept Bass, particularly good value food; building itself not special *(Richard Houghton)*

Portsea [84 Queen St; SU6400], *George*: One-room pub with bar atmosphere near entrance (panelling, leather seats), more comfortably plush at back; nautical theme throughout, glass-topped well, piano and two friendly cats; welcoming staff and regulars, well kept Flowers Original, Marstons Pedigree, Merrie Monk and Owd Roger on handpump, excellent fish dishes; handy for Naval Heritage Centre, open all day Thurs and Fri; bedrooms *(Matt Pringle)*

Portsmouth [Canber Dock; SU6501], *Bridge*: Included for its position on the busy quay of the old harbour, opposite Isle of Wight ferry and fishing-boat quay; recently 'aged' with pine tables and paving-slab floors, quite a good choice of help-yourself salads, baked potatoes and ploughman's, Marstons Pedigree *(Ian Phillips)*; [High St] *Dolphin*: Spacious, with Wadworths 6X and Whitbreads Strong Country on handpump, wide range of hot and cold bar food *(AE)*; [Portsdown Hill Rd, Widley; marooned on island in between A3 dual carriageways] *George*: Whitbreads pub with wonderful views of Hayling Island, Portsmouth, Southsea and Isle of Wight from terrace; hunting décor with guns, cartridges and stuffed birds; friendly, helpful service, Strong Country, bar food *(Ian Phillips)*; [High St, Old Town] *Sally Port*: Street full of character, opposite cathedral; well kept Gales HSB and Marstons Pedigree, good cold buffet and hot dishes, tables promptly cleared; lots of red banquettes and little tables, brass ship's lanterns with flickering electric candles, panelling like a boat's bows and so forth, but warm and welcoming atmosphere; children welcome; bedrooms being upgraded *(R G Ollier, K Sharp, Ian Phillips)*; [Bath Sq] *Still & West*: Marvellous waterside position, with upstairs windows and terrace seeming almost within touching distance of the boats and ships fighting the strong tides in the narrow harbour mouth; closed late 1988/early 1989 for extensive

refurbishment *(MBW, JHW, LYM – more news please)*; [Surrey St] *Surrey Arms*: Popular lunchtime pub serving well kept beer and good food; mixed but comfortable décor; bedrooms *(H G and C J McCafferty)*; [Copnor Rd] *Swan*: Large, ordinary pub but superb welcome, well kept Bass, small helpings of good cheap food *(Richard Houghton)*; [London Rd (North End)] *Tap*: Free house with eight well kept real ales which periodically change; lovely, busy lunchtime atmosphere, genuine service, good choice of bar food including king-sized sandwiches *(Richard Houghton)*; [London Rd (North End)] *Thatched House*: Old town-centre pub with fine welcome and relaxing atmosphere; full of bric-à-brac, good service, well kept beer including Whitbreads Pompey Royal; street parking difficult, but several car parks nearby *(Richard Houghton)*

Purbrook [SU6707], *Hampshire Rose*: Wide choice of food from ploughman's to steaks and friendly, helpful service in roomy, comfortable surroundings *(F Haworth)*

☆ **Ringwood** [A31 W of town – OS Sheet 195 reference 140050; SU1505], *Fish*: Friendly and comfortably modernised main-road Whitbreads pub with properly pubby atmosphere in clean, pleasant and restful bar with wood-burning stove and open fire burning three-foot logs, plain eating area where children allowed, lawn by River Avon; good value straightforward freshly prepared food; a useful stop for travellers *(Ian Phillips, Nigel Williamson, K and D E Worrall, WHBM, LYM)*

Rockford [OS Sheet 195 reference 160081; SU1608], *Alice Lisle*: Changed hands 1988; well kept Gales HSB, XXXXX and BBB, guest beers such as Ringwood Forty-niner and Wadworths 6X; bar food including good salads, large and popular conservatory-style eating area; log cabins, slides and so forth in garden; attractive position on green, on outskirts of New Forest *(H G and C J McCafferty, Jon and Jacquie Payne, BB)*

☆ **Romsey** [Middlebridge St; SU3521], *Three Tuns*: Cosy olde-worlde pub with good choice of reliably good modestly priced bar food, friendly and experienced staff, well kept Whitbreads ales, including Pompey Royal, and Marstons Pedigree *(WHBM, Chris Fluck, H W and A B Tuffill)*

Romsey [The Hundred], *Romsey*: Smart, bright central pub; attractive, clean and modern atmosphere, well kept range of beers, tasty food generously served *(Quentin Williamson)*

☆ **Sarisbury** [Sarisbury Green; 2½ miles from M27 junction 8 – left on A27; SU5008], *Bat & Ball*: Well laid-out family pub, spaciously and comfortably modern, with settees, library chairs, solid country dining furniture, efficient bar and food service, Legoland playroom and outdoor play area, tables on sheltered back terrace; well kept Flowers

Original and Whitbreads Pompey Royal on handpump, fruit machine, unobtrusive piped music; a Whitbreads Brewers Fayre pub, with afternoon teas too *(Keith Houlgate, J P Copson, BB and others)*

☆ **Selborne** [SU7433], *Queens*: Welcoming service and simple comfort including log fires; good bar food and afternoon teas from buttery, well kept Courage Best and Directors, relaxed attitude to children; children's area in garden, pleasant walks in picturesque countryside nearby; bedrooms good value, with decent breakfasts *(Yvonne Warren, Cdr G R Roantree, A T Langton, Gwen and Peter Andrews, Eric Locker, LYM)*

Selborne, *Selborne Arms*: Well kept Courage pub with friendly service, decent straightforward food *(Dr John Innes)*

Sherborne St John [SU6255], *Swan*: Thatched pub with attractive conservatory, terrace and big garden – good for families; bar food including good barbecued meats, decent wines *(Stephen Coverly)*

Sherfield on Loddon [SU6857], *White Hart*: Recent extensive renovations to long, low seventeenth-century inn, but interesting relics of coaching days, including message rack over big inglenook fireplace and attractive bow-window seat where ostlers and coachmen used to sit; wide choice of food (especially in the restaurant on the left), well kept Courage Best and Directors, big garden with play area *(Ian Phillips, Gordon and Daphne, LYM)*

Silchester [Silchester Common – OS Sheet 175 reference 625625; SU6262], *Calleva Arms*: Pleasantly placed, with attractive well kept garden including big adventure play area; big eating area with particularly good ham salad, well kept real ales – especially Gales HSB *(TOH)*

☆ **Southampton** [Oxford St; SU4212], *Grapes*: Roaring log fire, pianola played by dummy in tails, authentic Victorian prints and vases, small round tables with red-fringed tablecloths to the floor; well kept Flowers Original, quick, pleasant waitress service, good range of reasonably priced hot and cold food; live music some nights – not for sensitive ears; parking on nearby meters can be virtually impossible at lunchtime when pub is popular with local business people – it's busy in the evenings too *(Ian Phillips, Michael Bechley, JKW)*

☆ **Southampton** [Town Quay, by Mayflower Park and IOW ferry terminal], *Royal Pier*: Lofty building with upper floor reached by spiral staircase; relaxed atmosphere, well kept Flowers, good range of reasonably priced bar food, efficient and helpful service; sheltered sun-trap terrace, ample parking; children welcome *(Ian Phillips)*

Southampton [Commercial Rd], *Buds*: Very spacious modern pub with cool grey and beige furnishings, unobtrusive piped music and wide range of bar food with emphasis on

hamburgers *(Ian Phillips)*; [The Avenue] *Cowherd*: Prominent, butter-coloured, low and long Bass house pleasantly set on common, recently reopened; well re-styled to give numerous alcoves and rooms with individual décor, lots of Victorian photographs of Sunday-school outings and rustic scenes, carpets on polished boards, lots of fireplaces; simple bar food, separate restaurant, tables outside *(Ian Phillips)*; [45 St Mary St] *Masons Arms*: Small and friendly with Gales ales, good, basic bar food and live music from the landlord and his friends Sun lunchtime *(Peter Adcock)*; [Park Rd, Fremantle (off Shirley Rd)] *Wellington Arms*: Cosy pub with wide range of well kept real ales, lots of Wellington memorabilia *(Ben Wimpenny)*

Southsea [Eldon St; SZ6498], *Eldon Arms*: Well kept beer, fine atmosphere, good food in small back restaurant; popular with polytechnic students *(Charles Turner)*; [The Parade; SZ6498] *Parade*: Tiled pub with polished wooden floors, panels with engraved glass, wood and marble tables, brass footrail, immaculate décor; well kept Flowers, Wadworths 6X and Whitbreads Pompey Royal on handpump, good food – shame about the rock music *(A R Lord)*

Southwick [High St; SU6208], *Red Lion*: Popular with businessmen and locals, with well kept Gales, good choice of home-made bar food, prompt courteous service *(R Houghton, D S Male)*

Sparsholt [SU4331], *Plough*: Consistently good food with weekend menu concentrating on quickly prepared dishes as they are so busy; good facilities for young children and plenty of outside tables *(Joan and John Calvert)*

☆ **St Mary Bourne** [SU4250], *Coronation Arms*: Friendly neatly kept village local with welcoming landlord, well kept Marstons real ale, usual pub food, set lunches on Sun – when there may be free cockles and mussels; handy for Test Way walks; bedrooms *(Margaret Dyke, Maureen Hobbs, BB)*

St Mary Bourne, *Bourne Valley*: Pleasant, roomy pub with comfortable, airy bar, good seating and friendly bar staff; good range of standard bar food at moderate prices, small restaurant, large wild garden at back and smaller one at side; can get busy lunchtime *(HNJ, PEJ)*

☆ **Steep** [Church Rd; Petersfield–Alton, signposted Steep off A32 and A272; SU7425], *Cricketers*: Warm welcome in imaginatively refurbished main bar with light panelling, brass rails, biscuit-coloured upholstery and green carpet; busy at lunchtime for good value food, with particularly well kept Gales on handpump and good choice of decent malt whiskies; good service; piped music, garden – the only place children are allowed; families welcome; handy for walkers; comfortable bedrooms *(HEG, M G Rapley,*

Graham Dale, John Sterry)

Stockbridge [High St; SU3535], *Grosvenor*: Hotel with friendly bar service and good well served food; no piped music; bedrooms *(BB)*

Stratfield Saye [SU6861], *New Inn*: Remote, simple pub with wonderful atmosphere with plenty of banter between staff and customers, well kept ales that frequently change *(Richard Houghton)*

☆ **Stuckton** [village signposted S of Fordingbridge, by A338/B3078 junction; SU1613], *Three Lions*: Pub-restaurant with wide choice of interesting and unusual food, good wines and well kept Halls Harvest, Ind Coope Burton and Wadworths 6X on handpump; the general feeling is that this is now best thought of as a restaurant rather than a pub – which is why we no longer include it as a main entry, but there is a neat and airy bar with lots of fresh flowers, and a good choice of lunchtime snacks (not Mon); closed Sun evening and Mon in winter, maybe two weeks' summer hol *(P H F Hampson, R Reid, P L Leonard, R C Watkins, C N Cairns, LYM)*

Swanwick [Swanwick Lane; handy for M27 junction 9; SU5109], *Elm Tree*: Extended old pub, popular – even crowded – for wide range of good attractively priced bar food (especially steak and kidney pie), quick friendly service; restaurant *(R C Blatch, J H Walker)*

Sway [SZ2798], *Hare & Hounds*: Well spaced tables in comfortable and agreeable New Forest pub with real ales, decent food and service, big garden *(WHBM)*

Tangley [Tangley Bottom; towards the Chutes – OS Sheet 185 reference 326528; SU3252], *Cricketers Arms*: Extended village pub owned by MP for Romsey and now under new management, good cricketing prints and fine fireplace in stylishly simple small original bar, new L-shaped second bar with tiled fireplace, dark woodwork, colonial-style furnishings – cricketing theme here too; well kept Flowers Original and Whitbreads Strong Country on handpump, bar food including a couple of hot dishes, rustic seats outside *(LYM)*; *Fox*: Small pub with well kept Courage ale, extensive wine list, friendly licensees, good home-cooked food in bar and pleasant restaurant – booking needed here *(P M Wray, Dr A Y Drummond, Wg Cdr R M Sparkes)*

Thruxton [signposted off A303 flyover; SU2945], *White Horse*: Useful food bar and well kept beer in clean pub with sun-trap garden *(I Meredith)*

Totford [B3046 Basingstoke–Alresford; SU5738], *Woolpack*: Pleasant and interesting in attractive isolated spot, rambling comfortable bar with stripped brickwork and pitched ceiling, Gales HSB and Palmers IPA, bar food (not Sun or Mon), restaurant extension, skittle barn *(J and M Walsh)*

☆ **Twyford** [SU4724], *Bugle*: Plenty of widely

spaced tables in big U-shaped bar, lovely bustle of activity, very wide choice of food including unusual dishes of the day, lots of different pancakes and omelettes; a good many wines by the glass *(Ian Phillips, Joan and John Calvert)*

☆ **Upham** [Shoe Lane – village signposted from B2177 (former A333) and from Winchester– Bishops Waltham downs rd; SU5320], *Brushmakers Arms*: Comfortably modernised L-shaped bar with dark-red wall settles and other stools, good value bar food, well kept Bass and a guest beer such as Morlands Old Masters on handpump, big wood-burning stove, lots of ethnic brushes as decoration, tables in sheltered smallish garden, fruit machine *(JKW, Mrs J Fellowes, Tim Powell, BB)*

Upton [the one nr Hurstbourne Tarrant; SU3555], *Crown*: Spick-and-span comfortable country pub with flock wallpaper, dolls and china collection, home-cooked bar food and well kept Gibbs Mew ales; piped music *(BB)*

Upton Grey [SU6948], *Hoddington Arms*: Good local in very up-market village, popular food, well kept Courage Best and Directors *(H W and A B Tuffill)*

Wallington [1 Wallington Shore Rd; nr M27 junction 11; SU5806], *Cob & Pen*: Wide choice of reasonably priced good food in generous helpings including massive ploughman's, well kept Whitbreads-related real ales; plain but comfortable; large garden *(Gwilym and Joey Jones)*

Warsash [SU4906], *Rising Sun*: Good position, well kept beer, wide range of bar food *(SJC)*

Waterlooville [London Rd (old A3); SU6809], *Wellington*: Enlarged to include adjacent church hall with good décor, good bar food, unobtrusive juke box; if there's a problem parking, use large nearby public car park *(Keith Houlgate)*

☆ **West Meon** [High St; SU6424], *Thomas Lord*: Attractive village pub with cricketing theme, welcoming family atmosphere and generously served, tasty and inexpensive food, well kept Flowers and Whitbreads *(Mr and Mrs Whatley, Mr and Mrs C Knight, Dr and Mrs A K Clarke, C D Kinloch)*

West Wellow [nr M27 junction 2; A36 2 miles N of junction with A431; SU2919], *Red Rover*: Pleasant staff, good range of real ales and of well cooked and presented bar food *(K R Harris)*

☆ **Weyhill** [signposted off A303; SU3146], *Weyhill Fair*: Lively local popular for its Morrells and other well kept real ales including a weekly guest beer, and for swiftly served good value food; easy chairs around wood-burner, other solid furnishings, prints of stamp designs, old advertisements and poster for eponymous fair, pleasant atmosphere *(HEG, P M Wray, LYM)*

Whitchurch [Bell St; SU4648], *Bell*: Friendly

pub with basic, brightly lit bar, large open fire in nice back lounge bar, and steps up to attractive beamed room *(Gordon and Daphne)*; *Red House*: Ancient flagstones under heavy beams by inglenook fireplace, simple bar food, well kept Ind Coope Burton, games and juke box in saloon, sheltered seats outside; children in eating area and saloon *(LYM)*

Whitsbury [SU1219], *Cartwheel*: Horse-racing theme, good range of beers and well presented good food; children allowed in restaurant when not in use; start GWG37 *(R H Inns)*

☆ **Wickham** [Wickham Sq; SU5711], *Kings Head*: Interesting building with two main bars, Gales ales and over 130 whiskies, warm atmosphere with pleasant log fire, friendly and helpful licensees, good range of bar food – not many tables, so get there early; further bar behind skittle alley; opens 4.45 evening *(Barry and Anne, Keith Houlgate, J Clarke)*

Wickham [A32], *Roebuck*: Excellent food and beer *(Adrian Kelly)*

Winchester [Wharf Hill; SU4829], *Black Boy*: Wide range of real ales including interesting guest beers, usual lunchtime bar food (may be limited weekends), good juke box (or occasional discos) making it lively in the evening; bays of button-back banquettes in main L-shaped bar, separate rustic barn bar open busy evenings, seats outside *(HMM, LYM)*; [Southgate St] *Exchange*: Plain but comfortable with prints from old Winchester Breweries and smart young clientele; well kept Courage ales, well organised for food; open all day *(Matt Pringle)*; [Eastgate St] *Mash Tun*: Fairly unspoilt pub with scrubbed tables, entertaining customers, pool-table, well kept real ale *(Dr and Mrs A K Clarke)*; [34 The Square] *Old Market*: Good food and drink promptly served in

pleasant Whitbreads corner pub with soft piped music; handy for cathedral *(LYM)*; [Alresford Rd (Winchester exit from A31)] *Percy Hobbs*: Homely and warm with comfortable settles and chairs, well kept Flowers on handpump, good bar food including an authentic ploughman's and quiet, efficient service *(E G Parish)*; [14 Bridge St; continuation of High St, over river] *Rising Sun*: Timber-framed Tudor pub with friendly split-level low-beamed bar, generous helpings of food, well kept Courage Best and Directors, games-room with two pool-tables; apparently cellar was once a prison; handy for cathedral *(Dr and Mrs A K Clarke, BKA)*; [St Peters St] *Royal*: Up-market hotel bar and lounge, comfortably refurbished and very relaxing; good lunchtime bar food, spacious walled garden; bedrooms *(Keith Garley)*; [Royal Oak Passage; off pedestrian part of High St] *Royal Oak*: Cheerful town pub with well kept Whitbreads-related real ales and maybe a guest such as Wadworths 6X, good value straightfoward bar food (not winter evenings) including interesting range of open sandwiches; friendly staff, lots of snug seating in main bar – which can get crowded with young people in the evening, when music may be loud; the special feature is the no-smoking cellar bar (not always open in the evenings), with massive twelfth-century beams – and a Saxon wall which gives it some claim to be the country's oldest drinking spot *(Ian Phillips, LYM)*; [The Square] *Spys*: Well kept beer, lovely view of cathedral, comfortable bar downstairs *(Tim Powell)*

Woodgreen [OS Sheet 184 reference 171176; SU1717], *Horse & Groom*: Pleasant, cosy pub with real ale on handpump and eating area off lounge bar *(Phil and Sally Gorton)*

Hereford & Worcester

*This area is one of the richest in Britain for interesting pubs of great age.
Among them the Fleece at Bretforton stands out, scarcely changed over the
centuries – even down to its furnishings. Other delightfully antique places
include the cheerful Green Dragon at Bishops Frome, the truly cottagey
medieval Cottage of Content at Carey (doing particularly well at the moment –
and this year given not just a food award but a place-to-stay award and a star),
that curious little cider house the Monkey House just outside Defford, the
Pandy at Dorstone (back in this guide after a break – Herefordshire's oldest
pub, with a cheerful atmosphere and good food including gammon with
however many eggs you want), the imposing Green Man at Fownhope (a
comfortable place to stay at), the quaint Three Kings at Hanley Castle, the Old
Bull at Inkberrow (Ambridge, one is tempted to say), the fine old Talbot at
Knightwick (good food, a comfortable place to stay at), the Tudor Kings Arms
in Ombersley (good food, all through Sunday afternoon), the New Inn in
Pembridge (it hasn't really been new since around 1300), the rambling
Loughpool at Sellack, the cheery Olde Anchor in Upton upon Severn, the
Rhydspence at Whitney on Wye (good food and a fine place to stay at), and
the Butchers Arms down its quiet lane at Woolhope (another pleasant place to
stay at). As we've said, several of these have particularly good food. Soups
seem to be specially rewarding in this area – almost as characteristic as farm
ciders. Other places for really good bar meals include the engagingly nautical
Little Tumbling Sailor in Kidderminster (even the food fits the theme; it's a
brother pub of the extremely engaging Little Pack Horse in Bewdley), the
handsome Crown & Sandys Arms in Ombersley, the Swan by the river at
Upton upon Severn, the friendly Farriers Arms in Worcester, and the Ancient
Camp at Ruckhall Common – a real find, new to the Guide this year, with
good bedrooms and a fantastic position above the Wye. Two other new entries
well worth knowing are the Firs at Dunhampstead and the Huntsman near
Kempsey. And a good many Lucky Dip entries showing particular promise at
the end of the chapter include the Penny Farthing at Aston Crews, Roebuck at
Brimfield, March Hare at Broughton Hackett, Mug House at Claines, New
Harp at Hoarwithy, King & Castle in Kidderminster, Feathers in Ledbury,
Royal George at Lyonshall, Cliffe Arms at Mathon, Slip at Much Marcle, Boot
at Orleton, Chase at Upper Wyche, Boat at Whitney on Wye and Crown at
Woolhope.*

BEWDLEY   SO7875 Map 4

Little Pack Horse ★

High Street; no nearby parking – best to park in main car park, cross A4117 Cleobury road,
and keep walking on down narrowing High Street

Dark rambling rooms with low black beams are packed with entertaining bric-
à-brac from clocks and wood-working tools through Indian clubs, an old car horn,
a fireman's helmet and an incendiary bomb to a wall-mounted wooden pig's mask
that's used in the pub's idiosyncratic game of swinging a weighted string to knock a
coin off its ear or snout. There are lots of old photographs and advertisements. For

Pubs shown as closing at 11 do so in the summer, but may close earlier – normally 10.30 – in
winter unless we specify 'all year'.

all the oddities, this is the most traditional and perhaps the best of Mr O'Rourke's eccentric young chain of 'Little' pubs – with a fine relaxed and chatty atmosphere. Good value bar food includes soup (£1.10), large filled baked potatoes (£2.45), vegetarian samosa or lasagne (£2.95), prawns (half-pint £2.95), omelettes or chilli con carne (£3.25), the hefty Desperate Dan pie (£3.80) and sirloin steak (£5.25). Well kept Ind Coope Burton on handpump, the good value strong Lumphammer ale that's brewed for the chain (even non-beer-drinkers seem to like it), well made coffee; wood-burning stove; darts, cribbage, dominoes, fruit machine and sweet-box for children. Dogs allowed (one unfailing visitor is a good-natured alsatian cross called Pepper). This quiet riverside town is full of attractive buildings. *(Recommended by Jamie and Sarah Allan, Roger Taylor, Gordon and Daphne, Rob and Gill Weeks, Jon Wainwright, David Burrows, Miss E L Rogers; more reports please)*

Free house   Licensee Peter D'Amery   Real ale   Meals and snacks   Children in eating area   Open 11–3 (4 Sat), 6–11 all year

BISHOPS FROME   SO6648 Map 4
Green Dragon ★
Just off village centre, which is on B4214 Bromyard–Ledbury

Briskly basic, the furnishings of this heavily beamed old pub seem to encourage the lively atmosphere enjoyed here by many readers. Most have also found the notable range of real ales well kept: it's included Bass, Courage Directors, Hook Norton and Old Hookey, Robinsons Old Tom, Ruddles Best, Theakstons Best, Timothy Taylors Bitter, Landlord and Ram Tam in winter, and Woods. Good value basic bar food in helpings that are almost too generous includes sandwiches (from £1.05, steak £2.95), eight or nine starters (from around £1.30), ploughman's (£1.65), omelettes (from £2), salads (from £2.50) and hot dishes from curries (£3.25), through good home-cooked pies such as gammon and apple (£3.45) to steaks (from £6.35); service, normally notably friendly, could sometimes be quicker. The heavy-beamed main bar, with polished flagstones, flooring tiles and a good log fire in the big stone fireplace, is furnished with pews, settles and wall benches; a separate newer games bar has darts, dominoes, pool, cribbage, pinball and fruit machine; juke box. You can sit under apple trees on a small raised side lawn bordered by flowers. *(Recommended by R P Taylor, Derek and Sylvia Stephenson, David and Eloise Smaylen, G T Rhys, W L Congreve, Roger Huggins, Tom McLean, Ewan McCall, PADEMLUC, Jason Caulkin, Gordon and Daphne, Alan and Audrey Chatting)*

Free house   Licensees John and Anna Maria Pinto   Real ale   Meals and snacks   Restaurant tel Munderfield (088 53) 607   Children welcome   Open 12–2.30, 6.30–11 (all day Sat) all year; closed 25 Dec

BREDON   SO9236 Map 4
Fox & Hounds
4½ miles from M5 junction 9; A438 to Northway, left at B4079, then in Bredon follow To Church and River signpost on right

The comfortable main bar of this spaciously modernised old pub is popular for food such as soup (£1.35), ploughman's (from £2.25), savoury mushrooms (£2.75), braised faggots (£2.95), chicken breast or cottage pie (£3.25), chilli con carne (£3.50) steak, mushroom and onion pie (£3.75), mixed grill kebab or lamb cutlets (£4.95) and rump steak (£6.50); good puddings. The swirly white-plastered walls have stripped timbers and elegant wall lamps, with maroon plush and wheel-back chairs around attractive mahogany and cast-iron-framed tables. A smaller side bar has red leatherette wall seats, with more in its inglenook. Well kept Flowers IPA and Original and Marstons Pedigree on handpump; prompt friendly service; rather pervasive piped music, darts, shove-ha'penny, dominoes, cribbage, fruit machine and trivia machine. Beside the neatly thatched house with its colourful hanging baskets are picnic-table sets, some under Perspex, a barbecue and Wendy house. Dogs allowed – the pub has two terriers of its own. *(Recommended by PADEMLUC, M H Davis, Robert and Vicky Tod, M E A Horler)*

Flowers (Whitbreads)   Licensees Michael and Wendy Hardwick   Real ale   Meals and snacks (not Sat evening or Sun)   Restaurant   Children welcome   Open 11–3, 6.30–11 all year

BRETFORTON   SP0943 Map 4

Fleece ★ ★ ★

B4035 E of Evesham: turn S off this road into village; pub is in centre square by church; there's a sizeable car park at one side of the church

Readers who've driven right across the country just to find this glorious antique tell us they're really glad they've made the trip. It is the character of the building and what's in it that delights people so. A farm and then a farm-pub, it's been preserved as carefully by the National Trust and its tenants for the last dozen years – original furnishings and all – as it had for the preceding centuries by the family that had owned it for nearly 500 years. Mid-week or on a winter's day, it's usually quiet and roomy enough for you to see all the treasures inside. But the present licensees have also coped splendidly with its huge popularity in summer, making the most of the extensive orchard behind, by the beautifully restored thatched and timbered barn. Out here, besides an adventure playground, a display of farm engines, barbecues and goats cropping the grass, you may find anything from morris dancing, a vintage car rally or a sheep-shearing, spinning and weaving demonstration, to the merriment of their Friday to Sunday festival on the first weekend in July, with up to thirty real ales, bands and pony-rides. Inside, there are massive beams and exposed timbers, huge inglenooks with log fires, worn and crazed flagstones (scored with marks to keep out demons), and loads of striking antiques – from a rocking-chair and ancient kitchen chairs to curved high-backed oak settles, from the great cheese press and set of cheese moulds to the rare dough-proving table, from the fine grandfather clock to the dresser filled with Stuart pewter which is the pub's particular pride. Yet this 'museum' is still very much alive, with local regulars still playing darts, dominoes, cribbage, shove-ha'penny or quoits. Well kept Hook Norton Best, M&B Brew XI, Uley Pigs Ear and a guest beer on handpump are backed up by a choice of farm ciders and country wines, with mulled wine or hot toddy in winter, and a chilled summer punch. Food is appropriately simple, freshly prepared and good value, including sandwiches (from 80p), ploughman's (from £2), chilli con carne (£2.20), Gloucester sausages (£2.40), home-cured ham (£2.80), steak and kidney pie (£3.10) and locally cured gammon (£4). Service is pleasant and normally quick, though they warn of delays at busy times. *(Recommended by Dennis Royles, D Godden, Laurence Manning, Steve Mitcheson, Anne Collins, Steve and Carolyn Harvey, Peter and Rose Flower, Simon Ward, H K Dyson, Chris Raisin, Graham Doyle, J M M Hill, Mrs E M Thompson, G and M Hollis, Graham and Glenis Watkins, H W and A B Tuffill, M Rising, Nick Dowson, Alison Hayward, Pamela and Merlyn Horswell, Alan Skull, Denis Mann, Martin and Debbie Chester, Dennis Jones, Andrew Ludlow, Wayne Brindle, G Bloxsom, A Royle, WHBM, SH, SPH, Jason Caulkin, Bernard Phillips and many other readers)*

Free house   Licensees Dan and Nora Davies   Real ale   Meals and snacks (not 25 Dec) Children in room adjoining kitchen servery   Open 10–3ish, 6–11; may open longer afternoons

CAREY   SO5631 Map 4

Cottage of Content ★ 🍷 🛏

Village, and for most of the way pub itself, signposted from good road through Hoarwithy

The licensee who not so long ago took over this picturesque and beautifully placed medieval cottage has brought it firmly back into the ranks of the region's best pubs. Its two bar rooms, with dark beams, some timbering and panelling, and connected by an alcove with an antique settle, have been attractively and comfortably redone without losing nice old-fashioned touches like the rugs on the wooden floor, the open coal-burning range, more antique settles, and fresh flowers and plants; in the evening the atmosphere's pleasantly lively. Consistently good bar food includes soup (£1), sandwiches (from £1), mussels in garlic butter (£2), ploughman's (from £2.25), and hot dishes such as a fine vegetable crumble or vegetable croquettes in apricot sauce (£3), lasagne (£3), plaice (£3.25), good home-made pies (£3.75), gammon (£4.25) and ten-ounce rump steak (£7.25); breakfasts are excellent, and the small restaurant in the newer extension is praised by readers; attentive, friendly service. Well kept Hook Norton Mild, Best and Old Hookey and Marstons Pedigree on handpump, with good farm ciders; darts, dominoes and cribbage. One or two tables on a front terrace face a little stream and very quiet village lane; there are more on another terrace behind, with a spacious lawn sloping up beyond a rock wall. Some people who've stayed wish it were easier to get in before the 7pm opening time – and to get a drink before then. *(Recommended by Andrew Hudson, PB, HB, S J A Velate, David and Eloise Smaylen, PADEMLUC, John and Pat Smyth, Nick Dowson, Alison Hayward, Allan Slimming, M A and W R Proctor, M D Hare, John Hill, Richard Gibbs, Gordon and Daphne, Patrick Freeman, Jason Caulkin)*

Free house   Licensee M J Wainford   Real ale   Meals and snacks   Restaurant   Children welcome   Open 12–2.30, 7–11 (opens 6 Fri and Sat in summer)   Bedrooms tel Carey (043 270) 242; £27.50B/£35B

DEFFORD   SO9143 Map 4

Monkey House

Woodmancote; A4104 towards Upton – immediately after passing Oak public house on right, there's a small group of cottages, of which this is the last

A real curiosity, this traditional cider house doesn't have a bar – let alone an inn-sign. It's just a pretty black and white thatched cottage, set back from the road behind a small garden with one or two fruit trees. Beside the door, there's a hatch where very cheap Bulmers Medium or Special Dry cider, tapped from wooden barrels, is poured by jug into pottery mugs. In good weather you stand out here, with the bull terrier and the hens and cockerels that wander in from an adjacent collection of caravans and sheds. Or you can retreat to a small side outbuilding with a couple of plain tables, a settle and an open fire. They don't serve food (except crisps and nuts), but allow customers to bring their own. *(Recommended by Phil and Sally Gorton; more reports please)*

Free house   Licensee Graham Collins   Open 11–2.30, 6–10.30 (11 Sat); closed Mon evening, Tues

DORSTONE   SO3141 Map 6

Pandy 🍺

Pub signposted off B4348 E of Hay-on-Wye

Mainly fourteenth century, this out-of-the-way place dates back in part 800 years, and the main room – on the right as you go in – has broad worn flagstones, heavy beams in the ochre ceiling, stout timbers, a vast open fireplace, and a pleasant rambling layout with a number of alcoves. The food is often inventive (particularly in summer, when they have enough customers to allow a wider choice than in winter), and aromatic enough to recall for some readers meals in French country inns. It varies every day, but typically includes sandwiches, ploughman's, soup (£1.25), mussels (£2.95), vegetarian quiches or mackerel (£3.25), home-made steak and kidney pie (£3.95), rabbit pie (£4.25), lemon sole (£5.95), gammon with as many eggs as you want, and steaks (£6.45); the big helpings make the prices good value. Bass and Springfield on handpump are very well kept, and they have a good range of spirits and serve unlimited coffee; service is warmly friendly. A games area with stripped stone walls and a big wood-burning stove has pool, darts, quoits, juke box and fruit machine; a side extension has been kept more or less in character. There are picnic-table sets and a play area in the neat side garden. The pub is very much a focus for the village community – particularly on a Sunday afternoon in summer, when the cricket teams are in need of refreshment. The surrounding, partly wooded gentle hills are most attractive. *(Recommended by Patrick Freeman, David and Eloise Smaylen, Paul McPherson, Cdr J W Hackett, M E A Horler, Mr and Mrs P W Dryland, Mrs Nina Elliott; more reports please)*

Free house   Licensees Chris and Margaret Burtonwood   Real ale   Meals and snacks Children welcome   Visiting morris dancers, occasional piano singsongs or folk nights Open 12–3 (4 Sat), 7–11 all year; closed Tues lunchtime in winter

DUNHAMPSTEAD   SO9160 Map 4

Firs

3½ miles from M5 junction 6; A4538 towards Droitwich, first right signposted Offerton, Smite, then after Pear Tree first right signposted Oddingley, next left, next right signposted Dunhampstead, Trench Lane, then at T-junction right towards Sale Green; OS Sheet 150 reference 919600

The relaxed bar of this smartly refurbished country pub has two rooms partly divided by timber uprights, with flowers on the cast-iron-framed tables, Victorian prints over the dark pink dado, people reading newspapers or chatting by the bar; the inner part which leads through to a restaurant area has armchairs and settees around the open fire, as well as the bentwood chairs of the rest of the pub. Good bar food includes filled baked potatoes (£2.55), omelettes (from £2.65), lasagne (£3.35), steak and kidney pie (£3.95) and steaks (from eight-ounce rump £6.55), with lots of dishes of the day such as courgette soup (£1.25), hot garlic prawns (£2.20), pasta and Parmesan ratatouille (£4.25), home-cooked ham with cream cheese (£4.55), chicken and cheese roulade (£5.25), crown of lamb (£7.25), salmon (£7.95), and a wealth of puddings; well kept Bass on handpump, piped piano music, fruit machine in a dark-panelled side area (and juke box, rarely used). Pleasant service, with a discreet welcome from William (the dobermann) and a more effusive one from Oscar (less easily classified). A picture window with buff velvet curtains looks out on a pretty flower-filled terrace, with white tables under cocktail parasols; it's an interesting spot – out here, you hear the distant swish of motorway traffic, can see the humped bridge over the Worcester and Birmingham Canal, and occasionally have the rush of an express train speeding by. *(Recommended by R E and L J Rosier, Michael Thomson, Craig and Suzanne Everhart, Michael and Harriet Robinson)*

Free house   Licensees Mr and Mrs T S Forster   Real ale   Meals and snacks (12–2, 6.30–9.30)   Restaurant tel Droitwich (0905) 774094   Well behaved children allowed Open 11.30–2.30, 6–11 all year; closed 25 and 26 Dec

FOWNHOPE   SO5834 Map 4

Green Man 🛏

B4224

Known as the Naked Boy 500 years ago, this striking black and white Tudor inn still keeps mementoes of the days in the eighteenth and nineteenth centuries when court sessions were held here. The high-ceilinged beamed and timbered lounge bar has cushioned settles, window seats and comfortable armchairs, with brasses and small pictures on its ochre walls, and a good log fire. Good value bar food in generous helpings includes sandwiches (from 85p), soup (£1.10), ploughman's (from £2.20), salads (from £2.50), local chicken (£2.60), lasagne verde (£3.10), steak sandwich (£3.50), trout with almonds or gammon (£3.95), rump steak

(£5.50), puddings (£1.20) and children's portions (from £1.65). Well kept and attractively priced Hook Norton Best, Marstons Pedigree and Sam Smiths OB on handpump, and local ciders. Service is well organised and efficient. A second smaller but broadly similar bar has darts and dominoes; piped music. There are sturdy benches and seats around slatted tables among the trees and flower beds of the big back lawn, where they also serve coffee and afternoon tea in good weather; there's a play area out here. *(Recommended by Paul McPherson, S J A Velate, John and Helen Thompson, E M Lloyd, John Blake, Dennis Jones, Mike Muston, Dr R Fuller, Patrick Freeman, Gordon and Daphne, Hope Chenhalls, M A and W R Proctor; more reports please)*

Free house Licensees Arthur and Margaret Williams Real ale Meals and snacks (until 10 evenings) Two restaurants Children in eating area and restaurant Open 11–2.30, 6–11 all year Bedrooms tel Fownhope (043 277) 243; £27B/£36.50B

HANLEY CASTLE SO8442 Map 4

Three Kings

Pub signposted (not prominently) off B4211 opposite castle gates, N of Upton upon Severn

Tucked into the heart of a quiet and pretty hamlet, this picturesque old pub – a favourite of those who know it – has a marvellously traditional little tiled-floor tap-room, separated off from the entrance corridor by the monumental built-in settle which faces its equally vast inglenook fireplace. The hatch here serves well kept and low-priced Butcombe, Theakstons and Wadworths 6X tapped from the cask, with a guest beer such as Smiles Best or Boddingtons Mild, and Westons Old Rosie cider. The comfortable timbered lounge on the right has its own separate entrance; besides another antique winged and high-backed settle, this has little leatherette armchairs and spindle-back chairs around its tables, a neatly blacked kitchen range and an unchanging atmosphere. Good value home-cooked bar food includes soup (55p), sandwiches (from 55p), omelettes (£1.10), ploughman's (from £1.40), pork chop or gammon and egg (£3.55) and hefty steaks (£7.35), with more challenging specials which may take half an hour or so to do. A third room on the left, decorated with lots of small locomotive pictures, has darts and cribbage, and opens into a pool-room beyond. Bow windows in the three main rooms, and old-fashioned wood and iron seats on the front terrace, look across to the great cedar which shades the tiny green. *(Recommended by PADEMLUC, Derek and Sylvia Stephenson, Gordon and Daphne)*

Free house Real ale Meals and snacks Children in side room Singing duo Sun evening Open 11–2.30, 6–11 all year

INKBERROW SP0157 Map 4

Old Bull

A422 Worcester–Alcester; set well back down quiet side road, but visible from main road

The timbered lounge bar of this handsome black and white Tudor pub has flagstones, some stripped stonework, big log fires in huge inglenooks at each end, high-backed settles and rustic chairs among more modern seats, and an unusual high-raftered pitched ceiling, its oak trusses hung with posthorns and copper kettles. As photographs and clippings make clear, it's the model for the Ambridge Bull, in the BBC *Archers* radio serial. Good value home-made bar food, in decent helpings, includes filled rolls (£1.15), ploughman's (£1.95), bacon, sausage and egg or chilli con carne (£2.85), smoked trout fillets and salad, omelettes or lasagne (£2.25), beef curry (£2.65), and steak and kidney pie, prawn stir-fry or gammon and egg (£2.95); they do afternoon teas. Well kept Chesters Best Mild, Flowers IPA and Original on handpump; darts and fruit machine. There are tables on an

Pubs brewing their own beers are listed at the back of the book.

attractive flagstoned terrace. *(Recommended by PADEMLUC, H K Dyson,*
Dr J R Hamilton, Rob and Gill Weeks, Bernard Phillips, A Royle; more reports please)
Flowers (Whitbreads)   Licensee S G Pitcher   Real ale   Meals and snacks (lunchtime)
Children in eating area   Open 11–11 in summer; 11–3, 5–11 in winter

KEMPSEY   SO8548 Map 4

Huntsman

Green Street Village – signposted down Post Office Lane off A38 S of Worcester, in Kempsey;
OS Sheet 150 reference 869491

Cosy and unaffected, this welcoming and well kept village local does indeed have
horsy talk around the small corner bar counter, and if the landlord's out with the
local hunt you may have to settle for a less wide choice of the good bar food –
which normally includes sandwiches (from £1), soup (£1.10), various starters such
as pâté (£1.55), ploughman's (from £1.75), omelettes (£3), moussaka or lasagne
(£3.55), sole (£3.85), gammon and egg (£4.45) and steaks (from £5.05), with dishes
of the day such as chicken Cordon Bleu (£4.85), pork marsala and chicken with
leek and Stilton sauce (£5.25); there's a choice of chips, baked potato and salad, or
stir-fry vegetables. The two small rooms on the right have well cushioned oak seats
around attractive old waxed kitchen tables in window alcoves, and beyond is a
dining area appropriately named the Rookery Nook. On the left a lower room has
lots of little leatherette armchairs around its walls, and a trivia machine; there's a
full-size skittle alley. Well kept Banks's or Donnington on handpump, open fires,
horse and game pictures on the swirly plaster walls. There are rustic slabby benches
and picnic-table sets under cocktail parasols on the side lawn; the calmly friendly
great dane is called Sam. *(Recommended by PADEMLUC; more reports please)*
Free house   Licensees Neil and Pauline Harris   Real ale   Meals and snacks (not Sun or Mon
evenings)   Restaurant tel Worcester (0905) 820336   Children welcome   Open 12–3, 7–11
all year; closed 25 Dec, evening 26 Dec

KIDDERMINSTER   SO8376 Map 4

Little Tumbling Sailor ⊗

42 Mill Lane; from Mill Street, which is signposted off ring road by A442 Bridgnorth exit, fork
right at General Hospital up narrow lane

Connoisseurs of this small and idiosyncratic chain of 'Little' pubs reckon that this is
probably the one with the most interesting food, with readers particularly enjoying
seafood dishes such as whitebait (£2.20), plaice (£3.55, poached £3.75), Popeye pie
(a fish pie big enough for Olive too – £3.65) and salmon steak (£3.95). As you'd
expect, the pub is about as maritime as it could be, with even the licensee a long-
serving Navy man (his wife was in the WRENS). The spick and span bar's navy-blue
walls carry a particularly rich collection of naval photographs (with the relevant
sailor's hat riband for each ship), and there are masses of other ship pictures, ships'
badges, net-floats, hammocks, anchors, ships' wheels, oars, a naughty figurehead,
nautical brassware, model ships and rope fancywork. The several rooms that
radiate from the central servery have red and blue leatherette seats around cast-
iron-framed tables. Other food includes vegetarian dishes (from £1.95), filled baked
potatoes (from £2.40), omelettes (from £3), enterprising pies (from £3) including a
vegetarian one, and one-pound steak (£5.85). Well kept Ind Coope Burton and the
chain's own Lumphammer on handpump, a good range of rums, fruit machine,
trivia machine, piped pop music; charming service. They sell their own pink seaside
rock. The little sheltered garden has a trawler's deckhouse and a beached whaler
(called *Lucia and Mapp*) for children – and even a substantial mock-up of a

---

Soup prices usually include a roll and butter.

lighthouse. *(Recommended by Roy Bromell, Peter Scillitoe, E J Alcock, Rob and Gill Weeks, P J Hanson, Dave Braisted)*

Free house   Licensee Fred Trick   Real ale   Meals and snacks (11–2, 6–10)   Children welcome   Music night Mon (from '50s and '60s to folk and Irish)   Open 11–2.30, 6–11 all year; closed evening 25 Dec

KNIGHTWICK   SO7355 Map 4

Talbot 🔊 🍺

Knightsford Bridge; B4197 just off A44 Worcester–Bromyard

Smartened up outside, this fourteenth-century inn looks better than ever, in its pretty spot by the old bridge over the River Teme. The heavily beamed rambling lounge has a variety of interesting seats from small carved or leatherette armchairs to the winged settles by the tall bow windows, and its butter-coloured walls are decorated with entertaining and rather distinguished coaching and sporting prints and paintings. But what dominates the spacious room is the vast stove, plump as a hippopotamus, which squats in the big central stone hearth; there's another log fire, too – in cold weather it's best to get close to one or the other. The inventive food (the same as is served in the small restaurant) includes filled rolls (£1), fresh sardines or vegetable kebabs (£1.95), pork and prune pâté (£2.50), vegetable moussaka or strudel (£3.50), liver and bacon (£3.95), koftas or boiled mutton (£4.50), pork with melted cheese (£4.95), lamb noisettes with mint and honey (£5.25) and sirloin steak (£8.50); puddings are as enterprising (from £1.40). The well furnished back public bar has darts, dominoes, cribbage, pool on a raised side area, fruit machine, space game and juke box; well kept Bass and Flowers IPA on handpump – and, more cheaply, Banks's, though there may not be a visible label; well behaved dogs welcome. Some of the bedrooms, clean and spacious, are above the bar. There are some old-fashioned seats outside, in front, with more on a good-sized lawn over the lane (they serve out here too). *(Recommended by Jason Caulkin, Philip Riding, D S Fowles, PADEMLUC, Jill and George Hadfield, Verney and Denis Baddeley, M A and W R Proctor, Dr John Innes, Dave Braisted; more reports please)*

Free house   Licensee Derek Hiles   Real ale   Meals and snacks (limited Sun evening)   Restaurant   Children welcome   Open 11–11 all year; closed evening 25 Dec   Bedrooms tel Knightwick (0886) 21235; £18(£22B)/£30(£42B)

OMBERSLEY   SO8463 Map 4

It's remarkable that such a small village can boast not one but two pubs which have been giving so many readers so much pleasure. Currently food, a strong point in both, perhaps has the edge at the first; on character, it might just be the second which scores. We like both a great deal, and can't choose between them.

Crown & Sandys Arms 🔊

Coming into the village from A433, turn left at roundabout, into the 'Dead End' road

Don't skip the soup here: nourishing and appetising, and usually strong on good vegetables (£1 – help yourself to bread-and-butter). Other home-made bar food includes several more starters, sandwiches (from £1, dressed crab £1.85), ploughman's (from £1.95), quiche or lasagne (£3.65), steak and kidney pie (£4.10), gammon (£4.75) and ten-ounce local sirloin steak (£7.15), with up to half a dozen good value daily specials such as plaice with prawn sauce, pancakes filled with Stilton, walnuts and broccoli, or with salmon, and stir-fried beef (around £3–£4); besides children's dishes (£1.25) they do impressive puddings. Furnishings in the black-beamed, timbered and partly flagstoned bar are comfortable, individual and civilised, with antique settles, Windsor armchairs and even a couple of easy chairs as well as the plush built-in wall seats; it's decorated with old prints, maps and

ornamental clocks (which are for sale). Well kept Hook Norton Best and Old
Hookey and a range of guest beers like Adnams, Badger Tanglefoot, Bass, Brains
SA, Felinfoel Double Dragon and Wadworths 6X on handpump; good log fires;
friendly and efficient service; dominoes, cribbage. There are picnic-table sets in the
garden behind the attractive Dutch-gabled white house. The antique shop and
picture framer's in the back stables opens on Tuesday, Friday and Saturday. The
bedrooms have recently been refurbished. *(Recommended by E J Alcock, John Baker,
W C M Jones, PLC, Frank Cummins, David and Ruth Hollands, T H G Lewis, Laurence
Manning, Dr John Innes, Mike Tucker, Mrs Z A Fraser, A Royle, Mr and Mrs W H Crowther)*

*Free house   Licensee R E Ransome   Real ale   Meals and snacks (until 10 evenings)
Restaurant tel Worcester (0905) 620252   Well behaved children (not in prams or push-chairs)
until 8   Open 11–2.30, 5.30–11 (all day Sat) all year; closed 25 Dec*

Kings Arms 🏮

Charles II is reputed to have made this comfortable and very popular Tudor pub his
first stop, on the run from the Battle of Worcester in 1651 – hence his coat of arms,
decorating the ceiling of one room in the elaborately rambling bar. Other rooms
have black oak beams and timbers, and the jumble of nooks and crannies house
quite a gang of stuffed animals and birds, and a collection of rustic bric-à-brac. A
wide choice of enterprising home-made bar food includes sandwiches (from £1.20,
lunchtime), appetising soup (£1.25), pâtés, including a vegetarian one (£2.50), and
main dishes like salads (from £2.50; cold meat £4.25), steak and kidney pie or beef
chowder (£3.95), crab and asparagus or broccoli and Gruyère quiche, bouillabaisse
or turkey and leek pie (all £4.25), and juicy ten-ounce sirloin steak (£6.95), with
quite a few puddings (£1.50); well kept Bass on handpump; two good log fires (one
in an inglenook); quick friendly service; no dogs. A pretty tree-sheltered courtyard
has tables under cocktail parasols. *(Recommended by PADEMLUC, Brian Jones, PLC,
Mr and Mrs D M Norton, J Keppy, Chris Cooke, David and Ruth Hollands, Graham and
Glenis Watkins, GL, SL, M A and W R Proctor, Pamela and Merlyn Horswell)*

*Mitchells & Butlers (Bass)   Licensees Chris and Judy Blundell   Real ale   Meals and snacks
(all day until 8.30, Sun)   Children welcome until 8   Open 11–3, 6 (5.30 Sat)–11 all year*

PEMBRIDGE   SO3958 Map 6

New Inn

Market Square; A44

Black and white, like so many other buildings in the charming little town, this
ancient inn has not been overly done up, keeping its worn flagstones, aged oak peg-
latch doors, heavy beams and timbering, and elderly traditional furnishings
including a fine antique curved-back settle. Bar food includes sandwiches, deep-
fried Brie (£2.20), mussels in garlic or vegetable moussaka (£3), crispy duck salad
(£4.90) and puddings such as bananas in cider (£1). Flowers Original, Marstons
Pedigree and a guest beer on handpump, under light top pressure; substantial log
fire; darts, shove-ha'penny, dominoes and cribbage. There are tables on the
cobblestones between the pub and the open-sided sixteenth-century former wool
market behind it. *(Recommended by PLC, M E A Horler, Robert and Vicky Tod, Mrs
E M Lloyd, Alan and Audrey Chatting; more reports please)*

*Whitbreads   Licensee Jane Melvin   Real ale   Meals and snacks   Evening restaurant
Children away from bar until 9   Open 11–3, 5.30–11; 11–2.30, 6.30–11 in winter
Bedrooms tel Pembridge (054 74) 427; £12/£24*

Please keep sending us reports. We rely on readers for news of new discoveries, and
particularly for news of changes, however slight, at the fully described pubs. No stamp
needed: *The Good Pub Guide*, FREEPOST, London SW10 0BR.

ROSS ON WYE   SO6024 Map 4

Hope & Anchor

Riverside; entering town from A40 W side, first left turn after bridge

The waterside position is enviable, with flower-lined paths threading through the lawns to the banks of the Wye, and broad windows looking out on this from the small but airy family extension. The cheerful main bar, divided by arches, is decorated with old river photographs and boating bric-à-brac; it has a good coal fire. The upstairs parlour bar, its walls hung with Victorian prints, is cosier, with armchairs and old church pews; it opens into a pretty Victorian-style dining-room. Bar food includes home-made soup (£1.45), basket meals (from £2.40), open tuna salad sandwich (£2.50), filled baked potatoes (from £2.75), ploughman's (£2.95), pancakes with ratatouille (£3.25) and beef and Guinness casserole (£4.45); children's portions (£1.45). Well kept M&B Springfield and Marstons Pedigree on handpump; darts and fruit machine. A separate building has a conservatory-style wine bar with marble and cast-iron tables on herringbone pavers, and a cast-iron staircase leading up to a restaurant. *(Recommended by Wayne Brindle, JH, Byrne Sherwood, R W Clifford; more reports please)*

Free house   Licensee John Gardner   Real ale   Meals and snacks   Parlour restaurant tel Ross on Wye (0989) 63003; Conservatory restaurant tel 66184   Children in eating area Silver band Sun evening mid-May–Aug   Open 11–3 (4 Sat), 5–11 all year

RUCKHALL COMMON   SO4539 Map 6

Ancient Camp 🏮 🍽

Ruckhall signposted off A465 W of Hereford at Belmont Abbey; then pub signposted, down narrow country lanes and finally a rough track

Idyllically placed on a steep bluff looking down on a picturesque rustic landscape with the River Wye curling gently through the foreground and the Black Mountains in the distance, this quite remote small country inn is named for nearby Eaton Camp. It's sophisticatedly simple inside, with comfortably solid green-upholstered settles and library chairs around nice old elm tables in the central beamed and flagstoned bar. A green-carpeted room on the left has matching sofas around the walls, kitchen chairs around tripod tables, a good few sailing pictures, and a big Victorian architectural drawing of the imposing Ram Mills in Oldham (the family firm). On the right there's stripped stonework, and simple dining-chairs around stripped kitchen tables on a brown carpet. The food, all home made, is quite something, including sandwiches (from £1.35), soup (£1.40), ploughman's (from £2.50), taramosalata (£2.75), a vegetarian dish such as aubergine charlotte with a tomato and garlic purée, Greek shepherd's pie (£4.25), cannelloni, steak baguette or lamb kebab (£4.50), giant prawns (£6.25) and fine puddings (£1.95). On Sundays there's a cold buffet with original salads, and one hot dish such as pheasant casserole. Well kept Flowers Original and Woods Parish on handpump, decent wines and spirits, kind service; good log fires, maybe unobtrusive piped music. A long front terrace right on the edge of the bluff has white tables and chairs among roses; when you set off for a walk, Jack the hunt terrier may come part of the way. *(Recommended by Dr F E McAllister, PLC, Paul McPherson, RLB, Allan Slimming, David and Eloise Smaylen)*

Free house   Licensees David and Nova Hague   Real ale   Meals and snacks (not Sun evening, not Mon)   Children allowed lunchtime; over-10s if eating, evening   Open 12–2.30, 6–11 all year; closed Mon lunchtime (all day Mon Nov–Feb)   Three bedrooms tel Golden Valley (0981) 250449; £25B/£37.50B

Most pubs in this book sell wine by the glass. We mention wines only if they are a cut above the generally low average. Please let us know of any good pubs for wine.

SELLACK SO5627 Map 4

Loughpool ★

Back road Hoarwithy–Ross on Wye; OS Sheet 162 reference 558268

The simple but neat and careful décor of this popular country pub has a faintly Laura Ashley feel that appeals strongly to many readers. There are beams, flagstones, red flooring tiles, plain wooden tables, country chairs, a dresser of patterned plates, bunches of dried flowers and sporting prints, with log fires at each end of the main room, and several smaller rooms opening off. Dishes that have earned particular praise in this last year include stuffed mushrooms with home-made garlic mayonnaise (£2), deep-fried Brie (£1.95), kidneys in mustard sauce and chocolate and rum torte; other bar food includes home-made soup (£1.25), pâté (from £1.75), a vegetarian platter (£2.95), chilli con carne (£3.25), moussaka (£3.95), tagliatelle with ham, mushroom and garlic sauce (£4), seafood bake (£5.10) and trout or beef in red wine with walnuts (£5.75); they have sometimes specified that you have to be sitting at a table before you can order, and at busy times this has led to some frustration and delays. Well kept M&B Springfield on handpump; friendly family atmosphere. The neat lawn in front of the attractive black and white timbered cottage has plenty of picnic-table sets. *(Recommended by PLC, S J A Velate, B Walton, David and Eloise Smaylen, P L Jackson, Paul McPherson, Allan Slimming, M A and C R Starling, Mrs Nina Elliott, Nick Dowson, Alison Hayward, Graham and Glenis Watkins, Pamela and Merlyn Horswell, Phil and Sally Gorton, Richard Gibbs, Lynda Cantelo, Gordon and Daphne, M W Barratt, E M Atkinson, Miss J A Harvey)*

Free house   Licensees Paul and Karen Whitford and June Fryer   Meals and snacks Restaurant tel Harewood End (098 987) 236   *Children in restaurant   Open 12–2.30, 7–11 all year; closed 25 Dec*

UPTON UPON SEVERN   SO8540 Map 4

Olde Anchor

High Street

Quaintly picturesque, this black and white sixteenth-century timbered house has its upper floor jettied out over the pavement. It's unusual inside, too, with old black timbers propping up its low ceiling, old-fashioned settles and Windsor chairs around oak tables, a nice little corner bar, and even a copper mantelpiece among lots of other copper, brass and pewter. People like it chiefly for the warmth of the welcome and the buoyantly friendly atmosphere, with Ruddles County and Websters Yorkshire on handpump, and dominoes, cribbage, fruit machine, space game and piped music. There's an attractive summer servery on the back terrace, and a wide range of the usual bar food is served from the back carvery, including filled baps (65p), soup (£1.25), sandwiches (£1.50) and steak and kidney pie (£3.20). *(Recommended by E J Knight, Wayne Brindle, PLC, Laurence Manning, Alan Skull, Gordon and Daphne, P G Giddy)*

Free house   Real ale   Meals and snacks   Children in family-room   Live music weekends Open 11–2.30, 6–11 all year

Swan 🍷

Riverside

Overlooking the River Severn, the Swan's comfortable beamed lounge has been attractively refurbished in a civilised and even chintzy style, with sofas and easy chairs as well as antique settles and Windsor chairs. It has a big open fire at one end. From the side food bar, imaginative bar meals – reasonably priced considering the high quality – include dressed crab (£3.50), home-made lasagne (£3.95), seafood gratiné or home-made lamb and apricot pie (£4.50), smoked salmon (£4.95), home-cured gravadlax (£5.25) and other daily fresh local fish dishes. Well kept Butcombe and Wadworths 6X on handpump, and decent wines; piped music. There are tables on a waterside lawn (where the pub has its own moorings) across the quiet lane – with waitress service out here too. *(Recommended by Mrs Nina Elliott, Paul McPherson, Alastair Lang, J H C Peters, M A and W R Proctor, PADEMLUC)*

Free house   Licensees Peter and Sue Davies   Real ale   Meals (not Sun or Mon)   Evening bistro, Tues–Sat tel Upton upon Severn (068 46) 2601   Children over 12   Open 11.30–2.30, 7 (6.30 Sat)–11 all year; closed Mon lunchtime

WEATHEROAK HILL   SP0674 Map 4
Coach & Horses

Between Alvechurch and Wythall: coming S on A435 from Wythall roundabout, filter off dual carriageway so as to turn right about 1 mile S, then in Weatheroak Hill village turn left towards Alvechurch

The fine choice of well kept real ales on handpump brings a steady flow of people to this out-of-the-way country pub – a typical offering might be Banks's, Davenports, Everards Old Original, Flowers Original, Holdens Special, Hook Norton Old Hookey, Marstons Pedigree, Sam Smiths, Woods and Wadworths 6X. The big-windowed friendly lounge bar is on two levels, with plush wall seats, chairs and stools, though in good weather it's the spacious garden, with plenty of seats on lawns and an upper terrace, which gets most attention. Cheap simple food in big helpings includes sandwiches, soup (80p – or a large helping of main-course onion soup, £1.60), filled baked potatoes (from £1.30), pizza (from £1.40), ploughman's (from £1.80), home-made pies (£2.90), gammon (£3.20 or £4.20), lasagne, chilli con carne or moussaka (£3.40), and home-made puddings (from £1). The red-and-black-tiled public bar has sensibly placed darts, dominoes and a fruit machine (there's another in the lounge); piped music. *(Recommended by Mr and Mrs W H Crowther, Derek and Sylvia Stephenson; more reports please)*

Free house   Licensee Phil Meads   Real ale   Meals and snacks (12–2, 6–9)   Children in eating area   Open 11.30–2.30 (3 Sat), 5.30 (6 Sat)–11 all year

WHITNEY ON WYE   SO2747 Map 6
Rhydspence ★ 🏵 🍺

Pub signposted off A438 about 1½ miles W of Whitney

Cleverly combining the atmosphere of a country pub with the civilised comfort of a small hotel, the Glovers have also been winning warm approval for their food, served by friendly girls at the same price both in the bar and in a pretty cottagey dining room. Particularly popular have been the soup (£1.25), imaginative toasted sandwiches (£2.75), ploughman's (from £2.40), a variety of speciality sausages (£3.25), seafood dishes such as Mediterranean prawns in garlic and white wine (£3.75), moules marinière, avocado with crab, smoked fish pie or seafood pancakes (£4.50), steak and kidney pie (£6.50), well hung local steaks (from £8.95), and puddings such as hot meringue. Readers staying here have hardly dared eat out at night in case they miss something special, and we'd now say this is the best pub food in the county. But the building itself is a powerful attraction, too – striking Tudor timbering, with parts dating further back. The bar and rambling heavy-beamed rooms leading off have a relaxed old-fashioned atmosphere, with old library chairs and cushioned wall benches, a good log fire, well kept Hook Norton Best and Robinsons Best on handpump, decent wines, and magazines and newspapers set out. Darts, dominoes, shove-ha'penny and cribbage; no dogs. There are tables out on terraces and a sloping streamside lawn; this is an attractive part of the Wye

---

Pubs are not allowed to advertise the fact that they are included in *The Good Pub Guide* – for example, on their menu or brochure. Please let us know of any that infringe this rule.

Valley. Full marks for the get-you-home service for locals. *(Recommended by Frank Cummins, P Miller, George Atkinson, P L Jackson, G and M Brooke-Williams, Mrs E M Thompson, Ninka Sharland, John and Ruth Bell, Laurence Manning, John Baker, A Cook, Mrs Joan Harris, P and L Russell, Jonathan Williams, Dennis Jones, Mr and Mrs W Smurthwaite, Doug Kennedy, PLC, Gordon and Daphne, Mr and Mrs W H Crowther)*

Free house   Licensees Peter and Pam Glover   Real ale   Meals and snacks Restaurant   Children welcome   Open 11–2.30, 7–11 all year   Bedrooms tel Clifford (049 73) 262; £20B/£40B

WINFORTON   SO2947 Map 6

Sun

Pleasantly unpretentious and gleamingly clean, the two rather red-lit beamed areas which flank the central servery have an individual assortment of comfortable country-kitchen chairs, high-backed settles and good solid wooden tables. The walls, largely stripped to stone, are decorated with heavy-horse harness, brasses and old farm tools, and there are vases of fresh flowers in summer and logs burning in the two stoves in winter. Besides sandwiches, simple but well presented food includes soups such as savoury marrow or curried parsnip (£1.30), mushrooms à la grecque (£2.45), a popular cheese-topped devilled crab (£3), turkey and mushroom pie (£3.95), pizzas, local trout (£4.95), pigeon breasts with cranberry sauce (£6.28), veal with orange and ginger sauce (£7.75) and interesting puddings (£1.50). Felinfoel, Robinsons and Wadworths 6X on handpump; sensibly placed darts and table quoits. The neat garden, with some sheltered tables, also has a good timbery play area. *(Recommended by Frank Cummins, PLC, Alan and Audrey Chatting, C R Cooke)*

Free house   Licensees Brian and Wendy Hibbard   Real ale   Meals and snacks   Children in eating area   Open 11.30–2.30, 6–10.30 all year

WOOLHOPE   SO6136 Map 4

Butchers Arms ★ 🛏

Signposted from B4224 in Fownhope; carry straight on past Woolhope village

People staying in this quietly placed fourteenth-century inn like the bowl of fruit welcoming them to their spotless bedroom – pretty valley views, good big breakfasts. Twin low-beamed bars, each with a big sedately ticking clock and log fire, are attractively decorated with old pictures and engravings, and furnished simply but traditionally with Windsor armchairs and comfortable wall seats. Home cooking with good fresh ingredients includes lunchtime sandwiches (from £1), home-made soups (£1.35), ploughman's (from £1.95 – they do their own chutney, pickled onions and smoked ham), vegetarian lasagne (£3.55), mushroom biriani (£3.95), rabbit and bacon or steak and mushroom pie (£4.25), salads (from £3.75), gammon (£4.95), local rump steak (£6.55) and puddings (£1.35). Well kept Hook Norton Best and Old Hookey and Marstons Pedigree on handpump, Westons farm cider, Rombouts coffee; no dogs. Sliding French windows behind the tiled and timbered house lead out to a pretty little terrace by a tiny willow-lined brook. *(Recommended by John and Ruth Bell, Paul McPherson and Kat Wilson, S J A Velate, Henry Midwinter, David and Eloise Smaylen, John and Helen Thompson, John Baker, Graham and Glenis Watkins, Mrs Nina Elliott, Pamela and Merlyn Horswell, Patrick Freeman, Gordon and Daphne, Mrs E M Lloyd, Andrew Green, J S Evans, John Blake, Keith and Sheila Baxter, Mike Muston, M A and W R Proctor, Gordon Leighton, JAH, Tony Dudley-Evans, Maggie Jo St John)*

Free house   Licensee Bill Griffiths   Real ale   Meals and snacks (until 10 evenings) Restaurant (Weds–Sat evenings)   Children in restaurant   Open 11.30–2.30, 6–11; opens 7 in winter   Bedrooms tel Fownhope (043 277) 281; £20.50/£33

WORCESTER SO8555 Map 4

Farriers Arms 🏮

Fish Street; off pedestrian High Street, just N of cathedral

The happy atmosphere is a strong plus-point in both the snug little black-beamed lounge bar and the more rambling public bar of this bustling and well run seventeenth-century pub. But all readers who've tried it recently also pick out for praise the tasty and decidedly well priced home-cooked food. It includes soup (85p), pasty (95p), hummus with hot pitta bread (£1.20), ploughman's (£1.50), a vegetarian dish such as leek, potato and tomato bake or brown rice nut risotto (from £1.75), lasagne, quiche, pizza or their own-recipe pies (£2.25), and a daily special (from £2.25), with puddings such as tipsy trifle (95p) and treacle tart flavoured with lemon and ginger (£1). The Courage Best and Directors on handpump are well kept. It's worth seeing the grandfather clock carved with writhing lizards in the lounge, which has some copper-topped tables and attractive old seats (as well as supplies of the landlady's book on pressed flowers); piped music. The simpler public bar has sensibly placed darts, shove-ha'penny, dominoes, cribbage, an old penny arcade machine (which works with 2p pieces), pinball, a fruit machine, trivia game and juke box; dogs allowed. Tables on the sheltered terrace have their own summer servery. *(Recommended by Col G D Stafford, Klaus and Elizabeth Leist, Byrne Sherwood, A Royle, W L Congreve)*

Courage   Licensee Nona Pettersen   Real ale   Meals and snacks (12–2, 3–9) Open 10.30–11 all year

WYRE PIDDLE SO9647 Map 4

Anchor

B4084 NW of Evesham

In winter it's important to get here early for one of the handful of seats in the snug little lounge, with a good log fire in its attractively restored inglenook fireplace, and comfortably upholstered chairs and settles. On fine days though the action shifts to the back of the pub. There's a lovely view of the River Avon and the Vale of Evesham to the hills far beyond, from the big windows of the airy public bar – which has plenty of tables. And there are more out in the big floodlit garden, which steps prettily down to the water's edge and the barge moorings. Good value simple home-made food includes sandwiches (from £1.45), substantial soup (£1.10), an honest ploughman's (from £1.90), omelettes (£3.60), locally smoked chicken with their own apricot chutney, fresh plaice, gammon, home-baked honey-roast ham with cider jelly or Scotch beef salad (all £3.45) and steaks (from £6.40); puddings include good home-made meringue concoctions (£1.25) and hot stuffed peaches (£1.50). Well kept Flowers Original and Whitbreads PA on handpump; occasional unobtrusive Radio 2 or 4, dominoes, cribbage. The licensees have just celebrated their twentieth year here. *(Recommended by PADEMLUC, J C Proud, P Bramhall, Paul McPherson, PLC, G Bloxsom, Frank Cummins, R P Taylor, Wayne Brindle, Kit Read)*

Free house   Licensees G N and J Jordan   Real ale   Meals and snacks (not Sun evening) River-view lunchtime restaurant tel Pershore (0386) 552799   Children in eating area and restaurant   Open 11–2.30, 6–11 all year

Lucky Dip

Besides the fully inspected pubs, you might like to try these Lucky Dips recommended to us and described by readers (if you do, please send us reports):

Abberley [SO7667], *Manor Arms*: Well kept and comfortable hotel bar with open fires, which has been popular for friendly and helpful service and good, tasty bar food – though we've had no reports since it changed hands; lovely small village; Laura Ashley-style newish bedrooms good value *(Mrs D M Hacker – more reports on new regime please)*

Abbey Dore [SO3839], *Neville Arms*: Pleasant countryside location, good lunchtime bar food inc vegetarian dishes *(B Ratcliffe)*

Alvechurch [Red Lion St; SP0272], *Red Lion*: Pleasant friendly bar with good range of bar food, restaurant *(Sue Braisted)*

Ashton under Hill [Elmley Rd – OS Sheet 150 reference 997378; SO9938], *Star*: Village pub with pleasantly colourful bars and good range of straightforward home-cooked food generously served; well kept Flowers IPA, interesting wines, no machines *(PADEMLUC, P J Brooks)*

☆ **Aston Crews** [B4222 – village signposted off A40 at Lea; SO6723], *Penny Farthing*: Good value food, especially baked potatoes with wide range of imaginative fillings, in series of modernised rooms with rather bright carpet, some stripped stonework, easy chairs around low dimpled copper tables, one table formed from glass-topped floodlit deep well, and more orthodox dining tables; well kept Bass and Hook Norton Old Hookey on handpump, matter-of-fact service, rather muffled piped pop music; airy big-windowed restaurant, pretty valley views from garden tables, even better views from comfortable bedrooms *(John Miles, P L Jackson, Maggie Jo St John, Dudley Evans, BB)*

Aston Crews [just off B4222], *White Hart*: Hilltop village pub with easy chairs among other seats in low-beamed sloping bar dominated by huge fireplace, other rooms leading off; Banks's and Wadworths 6X on handpump, bar food, pub games, tables in attractive surroundings outside *(Mr and Mrs Wyatt, LYM)*

Badsey [2 miles east of Evesham on B4035; SP0743], *Round of Gras*: Plain pub with modern furnishings, Flowers real ale, log fire and locally popular home-cooked food – the name stresses connection with local asparagus growing and a visit in May or June will make the most of this; newish tenant is a cricketer, and there's a bat signposted by the 1988 team on the wall *(PLC, Steve Mitcheson, Anne Collins, BB)*

Barnards Green [SO7945], *Blue Bell*: Pleasant if unexceptional old-fashioned pub with limited range of good food and good Marstons Pedigree; welcoming atmosphere and not too noisy, though busy lunchtime *(PADEMLUC)*

Baughton [SO8741], *Gay Dog*: Well furnished free house with friendly atmosphere; two good value bedrooms *(T G Saul)*

Beckford [SO9735], *Beckford*: Good welcome, wide range of well kept beer and generous helpings of good bar food; skittle alley, steak restaurant *(L D Cartwright)*

Belbroughton [High St (off A491); SO9277], *Queens*: Comfortable and popular pub with friendly staff and well kept Marstons; good bar food – spaghetti, grilled plaice, puddings all praised *(Robert and Vicky Tod)*; *Talbot*: Dark, cool, inter-connecting rooms, well kept Hansons beer, good well priced bar food from sandwiches to steaks, friendly and helpful staff in beamified pre-war building; pleasant garden *(Ian Phillips)*

☆ **Berrow** [A438 Tewkesbury–Ledbury just E of junction with B4208; SO7934], *Duke of York*: Friendly pub, older than it looks from outside, with two connected bar areas, Flowers real ales, popular good value food especially Weds to Sun, from pâté through good salads to Severn salmon, attentive licensees, log fire in winter and big summer lawn *(B Walton, G and M Hollis, BB)*

Bewdley [50 Wyre Hill; off A456; SO7875], *Black Boy*: Immaculately kept, comfortable, quiet and welcoming pub in row of cottages, pleasant licensees, limited bar food, keg beers *(PADEMLUC, Gordon and Daphne)*; [A456 towards Kidderminster, just past railway arch] *Great Western*: Railway pictures, imaginative use of wall tiles and balcony, Banks's/Hansons ales; convenient for Severn Valley Rly *(Dave Braisted)*

Birtsmorton [off B4208; SO7935], *Farmers Arms*: Attractive black and white timbered village pub with outside skittles pitch, one picturesque and pleasant end with very low beams inside; decidedly a local *(Roger Huggins, Tom McClean, Ewan McCall, BB)*

☆ **Bishops Frome** [B4214; SO6648], *Chase*: Attractively decorated bar, warm welcome, well kept Hook Norton, limited range of good home-made bar food, restaurant; seats on terrace and in garden; children welcome; three comfortable bedrooms *(Dave Braisted, PLC)*

Bishopstone [Bridge Sollers; A438 about 6 miles W of Hereford; SO4142], *Lord Nelson*: Comfortable roadside pub with helpful staff, good value bar food and Sun roast lunch, well kept Flowers Original and Westons cider, some ceiling stripped away to show old timbers and pitched rafters, lots of tables by biggish side lawn; children allowed in restaurant, has had country and western music Thurs, closed Mon lunchtime in winter *(Gwen and Peter Andrews, Roger and Jenny Huggins, LYM)*

Bliss Gate [signposted off A456 about 3 miles W of Bewdley; SO7572], *Bliss Gate*: Small, cosy lounge bar with wood-burning stove, larger tiled public bar, well kept Marstons Burton and Pedigree, bar food from good value sandwiches up, good Sun lunch, enthusiastic young licensees *(Paul and Nicola Denham)*

Bodenham [just off A417 at Bodenham turn-off, about 6 miles S of Leominster; SO5351], *Englands Gate*: Welcoming pub with well kept real ales on handpump, good variety of bar food at reasonable prices *(J H C Peters)*

☆ **Bournheath** [Dodford Rd – OS Sheet 139 reference 935735; SO9474], *Gate*: Attractive and very popular food pub – good value in bar and restaurant, with good range of beer and friendly service; some Louisiana specialities; can get very busy, especially in summer *(Brian Jones, Dave Braisted, Colin Hall)*

Bradley Green [SP9862], *Red Lion*: Pleasant staff, good food at reasonable prices; handy for NT Hanbury Hall *(Denzil Taylor)*

Bransford [SO7852], *Bear & Ragged Staff*: Pleasant, freshly decorated interior with various connecting rooms and open fire; friendly, obliging licensees, well kept Flowers on handpump, the main attraction is the food, in bar and restaurant *(Elizabeth Lloyd)*; *Fox*: Generous helpings of good straightforward food at attractive prices inc good ploughman's with huge helping of cheese, and jokey friendly service; décor not its strongest point *(Anon)*

Bretforton [Main St; SP0943], *Victoria Arms*: Clean and well laid out, with friendly landlady, talkative cockatoo called Cocky, good pool-table and pleasant back garden *(Steve Mitcheson, Anne Collins)*

☆ **Brimfield** [off A49 near junction with A456; SO5368], *Roebuck*: Excellent imaginative home-cooked food – not cheap but worth it – in cosy beamed and oak-panelled lounge bar with no-smoking area, willow-pattern plates on Delft shelf, wider choice in adjoining modern restaurant (not Mon lunchtime or Sun); family connections with Walnut Tree at Llandewi Skirrid; perhaps more restaurant than pub really, now, though it does have Ansells Bitter and a genial and helpful licensee *(D Mayall, PLC, T Nott, Paul McPherson)*

☆ **Broadway** [Main St (A44); SP0937], *Lygon Arms*: Stately Cotswold hotel, owned by the Savoy group, well worth visiting for the strikingly handsome building itself, with interesting old rooms rambling away from the attractive if pricey oak-panelled bar;

sandwiches and maybe other snacks such as good cheese dips available all day, and in adjoining Goblets wine bar food is imaginative; tables in prettily planted courtyard, well kept gardens; children allowed away from bar; bedrooms smart and comfortable, but expensive; open all day in summer *(Brian and Rosemary Wilmot, Laurence Manning, M A and C R Starling, Mr and Mrs W H Crowther, LYM)*

Broadway [Collin Lane; marked Gt Collin Farm on OS Sheet; follow Willersey sign off A44 – OS Sheet 150 reference 076391], *Collin House*: Small hotel with well kept Donnington, good fresh lunchtime bar food, small evening restaurant; service aimed to please, not smother; bedrooms *(M A and C R Starling)*; *Horse & Hound*: Large and comfortable old Cotswold pub in busy village; carpeted lounge with lovely armchairs and quiet, modern piped music; good-sized public bars, pleasant helpful staff, Flowers IPA and Original and varied choice of good bar food from ploughman's to steaks, courteous service *(M R Williamson, Mr and Mrs W W Matthews)*

☆ **Broughton Hackett** [A422 Worcester–Alcester – OS Sheet 150 reference 923543; SO9254], *March Hare*: Quiet lounge bar with well cushioned stripped pews, country-kitchen chairs and tables, wing armchair, and rugs on tiled floor, glass-covered deep floodlit well; good bar food inc some unusual dishes such as the combination of taramosalata, hummus, tsatsiki and pitta bread, well kept Flowers Original, Hook Norton Best and Ruddles County on handpump; good public bar with games inc pool, big steak restaurant (not Sun evening), tables in garden with corner water feature, more with assault climber by car park; pleasant businesslike service, provision for children *(Chris Cooke, D S Foster, BB)*

Callow Hill [Elcocks Brook – OS Sheet 150 reference 010645; SP0164], *Brook*: Good food, friendly service in well kept pub *(A Royle)*

Chaddesley Corbett [SO8973], *Fox*: Pleasant, friendly staff, good carvery and bar food *(Mrs N W Neill)*; *Swan*: Worth knowing for its well kept Bathams Bitter *(Dave Braisted)*

Childswickham [signposted off A44 and A46 W of Broadway; SP0738], *Childswickham*: Pleasant pub, well kept Whitbreads ales, separate dining-room *(Dave Braisted)*

☆ **Claines** [3 miles from M5 junction 6; A449 towards Ombersley, then leave dual carriageway at second exit for Worcester; village signposted from here, and park in Cornmeadow Lane; SO8558], *Mug House*: Ancient place accurately known as The Pub In The Churchyard, decidedly plain and simple décor, low doorways, heavy oak beams, well kept cheap Banks's Bitter and Mild, minimal choice of basic but generous snacks (not Sun), sizeable garden merging into farmland with view of the Malvern Hills; children allowed in snug away from servery (E J Alcock, PADEMLUC, LYM)

Clifford [B4350 N of Hay-on-Wye; SO2445], *Castlefield*: Beautifully placed pub with friendly welcome, lovely atmosphere, good beer and food, log fire; children welcome (Mrs Sybil Baker)

Clows Top [Tenbury Rd (A456); SO7172], *Colliers Arms*: Tastefully modernised if restauranty dining-pub with open fire, Ansells beer, good food inc excellent dish of the day, pleasant service (BJT, G and M Hollis)

Colwall [SO7342], *Horse & Jockey*: Extremely friendly village pub with real fire, pool-table; well kept Ansells and Ind Coope Burton, bar food inc good plain low-priced sandwiches, small restaurant (Alastair Lang, D J Cooke)

☆ **Conderton** [southern slope of Bredon Hill – OS Sheet 150 reference 960370; SO9637], *Yew Tree*: Relaxing and unspoilt pub with stone floors, beams and so forth, well kept Marstons Pedigree and Westons farm cider on handpump, bar food (Derek and Sylvia Stephenson, Phil and Sally Gorton)

Craswall [SO2736], *Bulls Head*: Unspoilt, remote pub with ancient settles and chairs, stone floor, beams, Victorian cast-iron stove, original sentimental nineteenth-century prints on the wall; fruit machine, table skittles, Flowers and Greenalls served through hole in the wall, sandwiches and ploughman's; only modern touch a fruit machine (Phil and Sally Gorton, Salvo and Gwyneth Spadaro-Dutturi)

Crowle [SO9256]. *Old Chequers*: Comfortable, with good welcoming service, well kept Tetleys, good range of well prepared bar food (PADEMLUC, H E Panton)

Cutnall Green [SO8768], *Live & Let Live*: Small, unaffected pub with excellent home-made food which quickly fills the long, narrow bar with people in the know (they also do frozen takeaways); tables in pretty garden, where the Shed can be booked for parties (NWN)

Defford [SO9143], *Defford Arms*: Friendly and pleasant, particularly well kept Davenports, attractive bar food; family extension, nice big interesting garden (Derek and Sylvia Stephenson); *Oak*: Well kept reasonably priced Bass, good range of food (mainly Italian, like the owners – there's even a pizza parlour attached); reasonably comfortable, small and pleasant (PADEMLUC)

Drakes Broughton [A44 Pershore–Worcester; SO9248], *Plough & Harrow*: Large rambling lounge with lamps, flowers, settees, good choice of beer, extensive bar menu inc good sandwiches, friendly service (Laurence Manning)

☆ **Eardisland** [A44; SO4258], *White Swan*: Fine good value food, really pleasant friendly welcome in attractive pub with well kept Marstons Pedigree, log fire (H H Richards, Jane and Jerry Bevan, John Hicks, James and Marion Seeley)

Eardisland [A44], *Cross*: Friendly family-run simple old inn with simple food; bedrooms (LYM)

Eckington [in village centre on B4080; SO9241], *Anchor*: Very good value bar snacks and well kept real ales such as Banks's and Hansons (Mr and Mrs Devereux)

Elmley Castle [Mill Lane; village signposted off A44 and A435, not far from Evesham; SO9841], *Old Mill*: Former mill house in pleasant surroundings, under new regime, with promising bar food and well kept Hook Norton Best and Old Hookey and Marstons Pedigree on handpump; neat L-shaped lounge, children allowed in eating area; tables on well kept lawn looking over village cricket pitch to Bredon Hill (Dr J M Jackson, Lesley and Paul Compton, Derek and Sylvia Stephenson, H Bramhall, Mr and Mrs W H Crowther, LYM; more reports on the new regime please); *Plough*: Very old-fashioned and basic, even a bit spartan, full of atmosphere (and sheepdogs), with the local farmers telling jokes; beer, or very good cheap local cider, served in an odd assortment of china and metal tankards, from a shop-like counter; plain wooden tables (Jason Caulkin); *Queen Elizabeth*: Ancient pub with welcoming and lively atmosphere in attractive old-fashioned tap-room, in pretty village below Bredon Hill; well kept Marstons Burton (Chris Raisin, LYM)

Elsdon [SO3254], *Bird in Bush*: Well kept McEwans 80/- and good sandwiches, ordinary sliced bread but crammed with well cooked, tender meat (Mr and Mrs M D Jones)

Finstall [34 Alcester Rd; SO9869], *Cross*: Pine-panelled lounge and small timbered snug in local perched high above road, with good value bar food and well kept Flowers real ales; seats on sheltered lawn (A Royle, LYM)

Fladbury [OS Sheet 150 reference 996461; SO9946], *Chequers*: Comfortable pub with good local atmosphere and well done improvements; well kept Banks's, adequate range of good bar food pleasantly served, inc some things cooked on black-leaded oven range in bar; neat new bedrooms in former kitchen/stableblock (PADEMLUC)

Fownhope [SO5834], *Ferry & Forge*: Basic village pub with friendly landlord; well kept and rare Wye Valley Supreme real ale (John Baker)

Garway [SO4522], *Broad Oak*: This charming seventeenth-century pub, well recommended in previous editions, has recently been converted to a private house

Goodrich [SO5719], *Hostelrie*: Unusual,

turreted, Gothic-style extension, pleasant and friendly service, good choice of nibbles on bar, generous helpings of bar food, garden; décor not a prime attraction; close to Goodrich Castle and Wye Valley Walk *(Neil and Anita Christopher)*

Grafton [A49 2 miles S of Hereford; SO5038], *Grafton*: Nicely decorated bars, pleasant staff and above-average food *(G B Pugh)*

Grimley [A443 5 miles N from Worcester, right to Grimley, right at village T; SO8360], *Camp House*: Remote and basic Severnside pub with excellent atmosphere, farm cider and bar food *(HDC)*

Hadley [SO8664], *Bowling Green*: Comfortable pub with good bar food and beer *(A Royle)*

Hanbury [OS Sheet 150 reference 962649; SO9663], *Jinney Ring*: Though not a pub (part of local craft centre) worth knowing for wide range of good value snacks and meals in imaginative surroundings; wines and spirits licence *(Mr and Mrs W H Crowther)*

Harewood End [A49 Hereford–Ross; SO5327], *Harewood End*: Warm welcome, delicious steak and kidney pie and quick service in recently modernised likeable country pub *(Dawn Ross, S J Willmot)*

Hereford [Commercial Rd], *Hop Pole*: Very busy city-centre pub with good bar and restaurant food at reasonable prices *(S J Willmot)*

☆ **Hoarwithy** [signposted off A49 Hereford–Ross-on-Wye; SO5429], *New Harp*: Friendly and well kept, not pretentious, in attractive village below unusual Italianate church close to River Wye; nice bow-window seats, little country pictures on plain white walls, area around corner with pool, darts and fruit machine; good simple food at attractive prices from bacon and mushroom bap through good home-cooked ham to steaks, well kept Flowers Original and Whitbreads Castle Eden on handpump, picnic-table sets on yew-sheltered lawn beside pretty flower garden; children welcome; bedrooms good value, in cottage across road *(Richard Gibbs, S J A Velate, J H C Peters, R P Taylor, BB)*

Howle Hill [coming from Ross, fork left off B4228 on sharp right bend; left at X-roads after phone box – OS Sheet 162 reference 608207; SO6121], *Crown*: White painted, beamed old ramblers' pub, hidden away down an isolated lane through the Herefordshire hills, with welcoming landlord, cheerful and friendly atmosphere, well kept real ale and very good bar food inc vegetarian dishes and good puddings; simply renovated, neatly kept and clean, with skittles, darts, cribbage; tables outside overlooking hillside pastures *(Sara Nathan, Ikka Boyd)*

Kemerton [Bredon–Beckford; SO9437], *Crown*: Pleasant eighteenth-century pub with L-shaped lounge bar, panelled benches, horse-racing pictures, good atmosphere,

friendly and obliging landlady; well kept Flowers and fresh sandwiches attractively served *(Robert and Vicky Tod)*

☆ **Kidderminster** [Comberton Hill, in stn; SO8376], *King & Castle*: Good value food from wide menu, half a dozen well kept changing real ales, and railway memorabilia; what with its location by the Severn Valley Steam Railway, has very much the atmosphere of a 1920s station bar – a clean one *(Tony Tucker, Richard Sanders, SP, Mrs P Lawrence)*

Kingsland [SO4561], *Angel*: Old, beamed pub with inglenook fireplace, pleasant chairs, settles and tables, soft piped music and delightful atmosphere; standard bar food served generously with good daily specials and puddings; restaurant *(B H Stamp, Mrs Colbatch Clark)*

Kington [High St; note this is the Worcs one, at SO9855], *Lamb*: Refurbished sixteenth-century pub with some concentration on home-cooked food; real ale, Australian and Californian as well as French wines *(Anon)*

☆ **Kington** [Church Rd (A44); note this is the Herefs one, handy for Hergest Croft Garden and Hergest Ridge, at SO3057], *Swan*: Border town inn with ceiling fans in attractively redesigned airy bar overlooking square and main street; efficient and welcoming service, good value food (including well filled toasted sandwiches and excellent ploughman's), well kept Ansells and Tetleys, good evening restaurant; children welcome; at start of GWG93; bedrooms *(JAH, John Evans)*

Kington [also Church Rd], *Royal Oak*: Several bars, friendly landlord, Marstons ales, bar food and restaurant; seats in front and in back garden; camping available; bedrooms *(Tim Thomas)*

Kinnersley [Letton rd; off A4112 Hay–Leominster – OS Sheet 148 reference 341487; SO3449], *Kinnersley Arms*: Traditional country local, warm welcome from licensees and regulars; separate public bar (where dogs and boots allowed) and lounge, central bar serving both, large framed photographs of brewers' drays, cheerfully nondescript sturdy furniture, separate room for darts, fruit machine; well kept Bass on handpump, small restaurant, modern lavatories, large garden with picnic-table sets; bedrooms *(Frank Cummins)*

Kinnersley [SO8643], *Royal Oak*: Tastefully decorated and furnished – very clean, with warm friendly atmosphere and good bar food *(G Wolstenholme)*

☆ **Ledbury** [High St; A417; SO7138], *Feathers*: Elegantly timbered sixteenth-century inn, with attractively refurbished heavy-beamed Fuggles Bar – series of linked areas with pleasantly individual comfortable wall banquettes, armchairs, antique settles, good country tables, pale panelling, some stripped brickwork around log fire, soft lighting, big windows on narrow courtyard, civilised yet lively atmosphere; bar food from home-made ravioli or spinach, bacon and avocado salad to steaks (more reports on this, please), Bass and M&B Brew XI on electric pump; bedrooms now a successful blend of ancient appeal with modern facilities – a nice place to stay at; nr start GWG91 *(D J Cooke, J H C Peters, Ninka Sharland, S J A Velate, LYM)*

Ledbury [New St], *Olde Talbot*: Old building – an inn since 1595 – with quietly friendly atmosphere under newish licensees, no juke box, real fire, well kept beer and cider, good bar food; said to be haunted by a benign poltergeist; bedrooms *(J H C Peters, Tony Dudley-Evans, Maggie Jo St John, LYM)*; [down narrow passage to church from Town Hall] *Prince of Wales*: From outside looks deceptively small, but once inside rooms seem to stretch back for miles; friendly Scottish landlord, good atmosphere *(Gordon and Daphne)*

Leigh Sinton [SO7750], *Somers Arms*: Well kept Hook Norton Best and Youngers IPA and No 3 on handpump, wide choice of usual bar food done well *(J H C Peters)*

☆ **Leominster** [West St; SO4959], *Talbot*: Attractive hotel with carpeted and polished wood floors, heavy oak beams and gleaming copper everywhere, and delightful entrance bar – bay windows either side, armchairs, stools and settles (one impressively carved), and log fires in carved fireplaces at each end; well kept Marstons Burton and Pedigree, comprehensive bar menu attractively presented; bedrooms *(S J A Velate, David Wallington)*

Leominster [Broad St], *Grape Vaults*: Warm, clean and cheerful atmosphere in imaginatively refurbished old pub with quite a sparkle – two roaring fires, gleaming brass and copperware, and enchanting three-sided back bar cleverly decorated with old knick-knacks; agreeable staff, lunchtime bar food *(Ninka Sharland)*; [South St] *Royal Oak*: Rambling coaching-inn with good home-made bar food and real ales such as Woods; maybe due for some redecoration; simple bedrooms *(John Baker)*

Lingen [OS Sheet 149 reference 367670; SO3767], *Royal George*: Spacious and interesting interior, excellent value food from varied menu, Three Tuns and Woods ales, Westons cider; large garden with yew tree, tables and open views, first-class alpine nursery nearby *(Tim Thomas, Mr and Mrs C Crosthwaite)*

☆ **Lyonshall** [SO3355], *Royal George*: Spotlessly clean place, always bright and cheerful, with three bars opening off central servery; good standard bar menu supplemented by remarkable number of daily specials – excellent quality (especially meat) and quantity, and well presented; no-smoking dining area, well kept Flowers, friendly, helpful staff, no music *(F Else, CEP,*

D J Wallington, M E A Horler)

Malvern [British Camp, Wynds Pt; SO7641], *Malvern Hills*: Bass and good lunchtime buffet in comfortable oak-panelled lounge – a good pub for those who aren't normally keen on pubs, in that it's more hotelish; good bedrooms *(BKA)*; [Graham Rd] *Royal Malvern*: Friendly straightforward pub with interesting bar food inc range of vegetarian bar meals; Woods on handpump *(Chris Draper, Anna Jeffery)*

Malvern Wells [Wells Rd; A449 Malvern–Ledbury – OS Sheet 150 reference 772438; SO7742], *Railway*: Marstons Pedigree and Border Mild, separate skittles hall, pool-table, bar food and restaurant *(Alastair Lang)*

☆ **Mathon** [SO7345], *Cliffe Arms*: Impressive old black and white timbered pub in pleasant spot, cosy and spotless, with tiny low-beamed rooms full of nooks and crannies; well kept Flowers, Hook Norton and Marstons Pedigree, delicious food – ham off bone, vegetarian quiche, lasagne, good salads, braised pigeon, treacle tart all recommended; streamside garden, jolly landlord *(EML, Jason Caulkin)*

Much Birch [Ross Rd (A49 S of Hereford); SO5131], *Axe & Cleaver*: Good, clean pub under current regime, small bar with open fire leading to larger dining area; friendly staff, imaginative well cooked and presented bar food inc several daily specials, more formal and more expensive evening menu; well kept beer *(Horace Hipkiss, G and M Hollis)*

☆ **Much Marcle** [off A449 SW of Ledbury; take Woolhope turning at village stores, then right at pub sign; SO6633], *Slip*: Lovely flower garden around secluded country pub among the orchards of the Westons cider village; pleasantly chatty atmosphere, small choice of carefully cooked bar food inc specials such as home-made pizza and bacon chop with mushrooms, well kept Flowers Original and local cider; straightforwardly furnished neat lounge on left angling around to family area, fruit machine in public bar, very faint piped music; very popular with older people at lunchtime, more villagey in the evening; service can slow down at peak times *(Mr and Mrs W H Crowther, Sybil Baker, G and M Hollis, A T Langton, W L Congreve, BB)*

Much Marcle [just off A449 Ross-on-Wye–Ledbury], *Royal Oak*: Superb rural spot with magnificent views, pleasant lounge with stools around small round tables and open fire, bar with pool-table, large back dining area; Flowers IPA, Whitbreads West Country PA and – of course – Westons cider, bar food from sandwiches up *(S J A Velate)*

nr **Newnham** [A456 towards Tenbury Wells; SO6368], *Peacock*: Pleasant old pub – beamed bar, tables in nice side garden, well kept Flowers and Marstons, excellent ploughman's, window seats, variety of tables and chairs *(Robert and Vicky Tod)*

Newtown [A4103 Hereford–Worcester, junction with A417; SO6145], *Newtown*: Clean décor, attentive licensee, well kept beer and good food – especially lamb shanks; very popular with older people, not a lot of space though *(Maggie and Bruce Clarke, SJC)*

Oddingley [Smite Hill; nr M5 junction 6 – A4538 N, first right signposted Offerton, Smite, then follow bendy lane for 1½ miles – OS Sheet 150 reference 901589; SO9059], *Pear Tree*: Reliably good bar meals inc good choice of seafood dishes, in pleasant deceptively spacious surroundings with lots of divided areas, service pleasant and good, piped music not intrusive *(Mr and Mrs W H Crowther, E J Alcock)*

Old Swinford [Hagley Rd; SO9283], *Crown*: Interesting exterior, cosy Victorian-style interior with lots of bric-à-brac and large collection of hats and ties, good bar food *(E J Alcock)*

☆ **Orleton** [SO4967], *Boot*: Comfortable old black and white building, picturesque without being twee, with wide choice of excellent value freshly prepared food, both traditional and more unusual – puddings particularly good, especially home-made ices; good service, pleasant garden; the outbuildings and car park could be improved *(G Bloxsom, Lesley and Paul Compton, Chris Cooke)*

Penalt [SO5729], *British Lion*: Unspoilt throwback to 1950s on country lane, old wood-burning stove, well kept real ales, pretty side garden, campsite; friendly; bedrooms *(BB)*

☆ **Pensax** [B4202 Abberley–Clows Top; SO7269], *Bell*: Consistently good interesting food, well kept Everards, Hook Norton, Ruddles, Timothy Taylors and cheerful service; dining-room now extended – though character can't be said to be its strong point, it does have a pleasant view over hills towards Wyre Forest, opening on to wooden sun deck *(PLC, Tony Ritson)*

Peopleton [SO9350], *Crown*: Staggering array of flowers outside pretty Whitbreads pub with white tables and chairs out among them; good welcome inside, with fair atmosphere and good range of bar food under new regime; Flowers IPA *(PADEMLUC, Paul McPherson)*

Pershore [Bridge St; SO9445], *Millers Arms*: Cosy old beamed bar with sewing-machine treadle tables, well kept Wadworths IPA, Farmers Glory and 6X with a guest beer such as Badger Tanglefoot, good value pleasant food served very generously – omelettes, beef casserole and pork chop in cider all recommended; very much a young people's pub in the evening *(Andrew Ludlow, R J Yates, Derek and Sylvia Stephenson)*; [Newlands] *Talbot*: Pleasant local with guest beer and pub games *(Dr and Mrs A K Clarke)*

Pixley [SO6639], *Trumpet*: Pleasant old pub, popular at lunchtimes, with attractive timbers, rambling bars, bar food *(Gordon and Daphne)*

Rock Hill [SO9569], *Greyhound*: Well kept Flowers ales and excellent value bar food – lamb with apricots and turmeric recommended; atmosphere may grow as the recent refurbishment wears in *(Dave Braisted)*

Ross-on-Wye [High St; SO6024], *Kings Head*: Full of character; good lunchtime bar food inc vegetarian dish *(B Ratcliffe)*; [Owens Cross] *New*: Beautiful fifteenth-century coaching inn with warm welcome and good food; bedrooms (two) magnificent, with four-posters *(Gina Randall)*; *White Lion*: Very comfortable riverside pub, on the bank opposite the town, with seats on riverside lawn; wide choice of bar food, friendly staff *(Tim Brierly)*

Severn Stoke [A38 S of Worcester; SO8544], *Rose & Crown*: Old low-beamed building by green, with spacious inner room; wide choice of decent home-cooked bar food inc good pizzas, well kept Ansells, Banks's and Marstons, tables outside with play area for children *(Dave Braisted, P Giddy)*

Shenstone [off A450; SO8673], *Plough*: Real country pub with good food, Bathams beer and friendly service even at busy times *(John Baker)*

Spetchley [Evesham Rd; SO8953], *Berkeley Arms*: Pleasant pub with real ales, good range of home-cooked bar food and friendly, helpful staff *(K R Harris)*; *Berkeley Knot*: Comfortable and welcoming, with reasonable if rather restaurantish atmosphere; game machines not too much in evidence, well kept Bass, wide range of good bar food, pleasantly served by waitresses *(PADEMLUC)*

St Margarets [SO3533], *Sun*: Good local beer and cider in isolated rural setting, next to one of Betjeman's favourite churches and overlooking the Black Mountains *(N J Neil-Smith)*

St Owens Cross [SO5425], *New*: Completely renovated in the few years the licensees have been here; genuinely friendly staff and atmosphere, very good food inc sea bass; bedrooms *(Mrs Nina Elliott)*

Staplow [B4214 Ledbury–Bromyard; SO6941], *Oak*: Well kept Flowers Original and IPA, good range of imaginative bar food *(J H C Peters)*

Stiffords Bridge [SO7348], *Red Lion*: Very friendly small pub with good food in restaurant area – watercress and Stilton soup, chicken breasts in tarragon cream sauce, noisettes of pork in prune and port sauce and meringues all recommended *(Jason Caulkin)*

Stoke Lacy [A465 Bromyard–Hereford, just N of village; SO6249], *Plough*: Good value interesting home-made food including gravadlax and intensely flavoured ices, in modern main-road pub next to Symonds cider shop; skittle alley, quiet restaurant, keen and friendly young owners *(Anon)*

Stoke Prior [off A49 or A44 a mile SE of Leominster; SO5256], *Lamb*: Well kept Flowers IPA on handpump, good variety of bar food at reasonable prices *(J H C Peters)*

☆ **Stoke Works** [Shaw Lane; a mile from M5 Junction 5 – OS Sheet 150 reference 938656; SO9365], *Bowling Green*: Excellent drinking pub with well kept Banks's Bitter and Mild and friendly service – but also short choice of particularly good value food, well cooked and presented; attractive building with big garden and its own bowling-green (open to visitors for a small fee); very handy for Worcester– Birmingham Canal; railway adjacent *(Brian Jones, Dr R Hodkinson)*

Stourport-on-Severn [Canalside; SO8171], *Black Star*: Old-fashioned pub with warm welcome, friendly local atmosphere, well kept real ales, good value home-cooked food, occasional live music *(Paul and Sue Tanser)*; [Walshes Meadow; by swimming-pool just over bridge towards Gt Whitley] *Old Beams*: Delightful comfortable pub divided into areas by stub walls with arched timbered openings, smart food in eating area at one end, Flowers Original on handpump, piped music; has been open all day in summer *(Roger Huggins)*; [River Basin] *Tontine*: Large historic pub alongside Staffs & Worcs Canal basin, with gardens overlooking River Severn; good food, well kept Banks's *(Steve J Pratt)*

Symonds Yat [Symonds Yat West; SO5616], *Old Ferre*: Lively and attractive pub overlooking river – novel to arrive by its hand-pulled ferry; real ale, good value restaurant meals inc huge mixed grill; nr start GWG90; has small boat for 30-min river trips *(Ian Clay)*

Tardebigge [SO9969], *Tardebigge*: Recently reopened under new regime; mixed clientele (can be over-lively on Sat evening), well kept ale, good food *(Jim Whitaker)*

Tenbury Wells [Worcester Rd; A456 about 2 miles E; SO5968], *Peacock*: Friendly staff, cosy lounge with good open fire, side bar with pool-table, well kept Bass and Marstons Pedigree on handpump, good value lunchtime and evening bar food (Malaysian curry recommended), small restaurant, garden overlooking road *(SP, Jamie and Sarah Allan, A Cook)*; [High St] *Ship*: Lots of dark wood, Ansells bitter, wide range of good reasonably priced bar meals concentrating on seafood, rather nice semi-separate dining-room (smarter yet more intimate); back bar with pool and so forth; bedrooms comfortable *(Michael and Alison Sandy)*

Tibberton [Plough Rd; nr M5 junction 6, off A4538; SO9057], *Speed the Plough*: Pleasantly modernised old pub, good welcome, comfortable and not too noisy, well kept Banks's ales and good value bar food *(PADEMLUC, Dave Braisted)*

Upper Arley [nr stn; SO7680], *Harbour*: Cosy, compact old pub with considerable charm, good range of bar food, large dining-room where children welcome and good-sized garden with benches, play area and livestock; close to Severn Valley steam rly, and Worcester Way *(E J Alcock)*

Upper Sapey [On B4203 Bromyard–Great Witley; SO6863], *Baiting House*: Fine spot above road with good views; two small bars, friendly labrador, old fireplace, well kept Banks's and Flowers ales and good bar food – savoury pancakes recommended *(Dave Braisted)*

☆ **Upper Wyche** [from Walwyn Rd (B4218) heading W, first left turn after hilltop, on right-hand bend, on to Chase Rd; SO7643], *Chase*: Small country pub nestling on western side of Malvern Hills, well kept Donnington BB and SBA, Wye Valley and a guest beer such as Woods Special on handpump, limited but good bar food ranging from rolls through omelettes to steaks; good views from charming lounge; closed Tues *(Derek and Sylvia Stephenson, Nigel Winters)*

Upton Snodsbury [A422 Worcester–Stratford; SO9454], *Royal Oak*: Charming Ansells pub (also includes a wine bar), with hot dishes and large choice of cold food; chute-cum-Wendy house in trellised garden; handy for Spetchley Park gardens *(Hope Chenhalls)*

Upton-upon-Severn [SO8540], *Kings Head*: Pleasant riverside bar and lounge, well kept Flowers, good bar food and friendly service *(Robert and Vicky Tod)*; *White Lion*: Good food in popular hotel lounge with warm and lively atmosphere, comfortable sofas, stag's head and old old prints; bedrooms *(BB)*

☆ **Wadborough** [Station Rd; SO9047], *Masons Arms*: Friendly and unpretentious village pub with good food – particularly fine sandwiches – and well kept Banks's ales *(J S Walmsley, PADEMLUC)*

Walterstone [SO3425], *Carpenters*: Small, friendly public bar with lovely old-fashioned cast-iron fire hobs; lounge with table, piano and sideboard with mirror; cheerful and friendly landlady, Wadworths real ales; has been in same family for many years *(Gordon and Daphne)*

Wellington Heath [SO7141], *Farmers Arms*: Cleanly kept, comfortable place with welcoming licensee and staff; good range of well presented bar meals *(Mr and Mrs W H Crowther)*

Weobley [SO4052], *Olde Salutation*: Timbered and beamed pub in attractive village; friendly new licensees and good bar food, with fuller evening menu in restaurant area opening off comfortable inglenook lounge; tables in garden *(J Harvey Hallam, Andrew and Valerie Dixon, Mrs B Warburton)*; *Red Lion*: Striking though pricey fourteenth-century black and white timbered and jettied inn, separated from graceful village church by bowling-green; easy chairs, sofas, high-backed winged settles and huge stone fireplace in civilised heavily beamed lounge bar, well kept Flowers Original; lovely village; bedrooms comfortable *(LYM)*; *Unicorn*: Typical country pub, good food and welcoming atmosphere *(Mrs B Warburton)*

☆ **Whitney-on-Wye** [SO2747], *Boat*: Large and beautifully kept pub, well furnished, warm and friendly; big windows make the most of its delightful riverbank position; very ample home-cooked food, with fine puddings; bedrooms *(Peter Davies, Mrs B M Matthews)*

Wigmore [SO4169], *Olde Oak*: Olde-worlde front bar, more stylish back lounge with tables, candlelight and shelves decorated with collection of butter dishes; good choice of food running up to steaks, garden behind *(Shirley Allen)*

Wolverley [SO8279], *Lock*: Pleasant canalside pub with adventurous food menu in homely lounge bar; well kept Banks's, good wine choice *(Steve J Pratt)*

☆ **Woolhope** [just up rd from Butchers Arms; SO6136], *Crown*: Tastefully refurbished by newish licensees (son and daughter-in-law of former licensees of Cottage of Content, Carey), in mixture of bare brick, plaster and pine panelling; whole pub opened up, with bar in middle and attractive small area inside door – good balance of spaciousness and cosiness; well kept Hook Norton Best and Smiles Best on handpump, wide choice of enterprising food in bar and restaurant, good service; picnic-table sets on small front lawn; bedrooms *(Derek and Sylvia Stephenson, B H Stamp)*

Worcester [SO8555], *Bird in Hand*: Good ploughman's *(Prof A N Black)*; [Lowesmoor *Jolly Roger*: Unpretentious, roomy home-brew pub with random collection of comfortable furniture; good range of excellent beer and very good value straightforward bar food *(Geoffrey and Nora Cleaver)*; [London Rd, about ½ mile from centre] *Little Worcester Sauce Factory*: Formerly the Fort Royal, now part of the entertaining Little pubs chain, with strong Japanese influence on food – sushi and sea spinach soup; complimentary Dublin parking ticket for each customer, flamboyant décor majoring on sauce bottles *(Dave Braisted)*; [12 Cornmarket] *Slug & Lettuce*: Friendly staff, good food, well kept beer *(N and J D Bailey)*; [8–10 Barbourne Rd, The Tything] *Talbot*: Good atmosphere, good value bar food, friendly landlord; bedrooms *(Roy Clark)*

Wychbold [A38 towards Bromsgrove – OS Sheet 150 reference 929670; SO9265], *Thatch*: Good range of well cooked and presented snacks and meals in pleasant surroundings; though not a pub (part of Webbs Garden Centre, open 10–5, with wines licence) is worth noting for value for money *(Mr and Mrs W H Crowther)*

Yarpole [SO4765], *Bell*: Delightful village pub with impressive wood and brasswork; well kept Woods Special, usual bar food; good access for disabled people – there are riding stables for them behind; children's play area; in lovely village, nr Croft Castle and Berrington Hall *(Lynne Sheridan, Bob West, Norman Foot)*

Hertfordshire

Allied Breweries, through their Benskins wing, rather dominate this county, controlling a high proportion of its pubs. Fortunately, it's one of Allied's better areas, and a good many of their pubs here preserve a thriving individuality. Good examples are the Three Horseshoes by the duck pond at Letchmore Heath, the Bull at Much Hadham with its inglenook public bar and rambling garden, the bustling old Coach & Horses at Newgate Street (new to this edition), the Fighting Cocks in St Albans (new licensees concerned to make the most of its great antiquity), the quaintly old-fashioned and civilised Rose & Crown there, the warmly cheerful Sow & Pigs at Wadesmill (good sandwiches) and the Sword in Hand at Westmill (promising food under its new licensees – especially their pies). Among other pubs, food is a particularly strong point at the Fox & Hounds at Barley (which also brews its own beers – and seems to be getting better and better), the White Hart at Puckeridge (especially seafood) and the George & Dragon at Watton-at-Stone (particularly individual – and full marks here for the way that a truly pubby atmosphere has been preserved, with no signs of that scourge of so many once-good pubs, incipient restaurantitis). A particular favourite here is the highly individual old Brocket Arms at Ayot St Lawrence; and the atmosphere in the bar of the Two Brewers at Chipperfield is among the best we know of in any THF inn. St Albans has a bigger share of good pubs than most towns of its size – among them the Garibaldi, a new entry this year, is many people's favourite. It also has a goodish clutch in the Lucky Dip section at the end of the chapter. Other particularly promising places there include the Crooked Billet at Colney Heath, Two Bridges at Croxley Green, Candlestick at Essendon, Salisbury Arms in Hertford, Cabinet at Reed (we wish more readers would report on this charming old place) and Coach & Horses at Thorley Street.

The Fox & Hounds, Barley

ALDBURY   SP9612 Map 4

Valiant Trooper

Trooper Road (towards Aldbury Common)

Consistently popular, this friendly and pretty village pub has built-in wall benches, a pew and small dining-chairs around the attractive country tables in the lively red-and-black tiled room, as well as black beams and a wood-burning stove in its inglenook fireplace. The brown-carpeted middle room has some exposed brickwork and spindle-back chairs around its tables, and the far room – quiet even at weekends when young people crowd into the tiled part – has nice country kitchen chairs around individually chosen tables, and a brick fireplace; decorations are mostly antique prints of cavalrymen. The changing choice of bar food, though not wide, is good value – sandwiches, good home-made soup, filled baked potatoes (£2, the chilli is good), pork chop in a mushroom and wine sauce or gammon and pineapple (£3), roast lamb or beef (£3.20), fresh local trout (£3.40) and mixed grill (£3.50). Well kept Fullers London Pride and ESB, Greene King Abbot, Hook Norton, and Marstons Pedigree on handpump; farm cider and cheap spirits; darts, shove-ha'penny, dominoes, cribbage. There are some tables in the small garden behind the partly white-painted tiled brick building which has attractive front flower beds; good walks in nearby Ashridge, and the pub is on *Good Walks Guide* Walk 109. Dogs welcome. *(Recommended by Peter Adcock, BKA, Stephen King, Mrs M E Lawrence)*

Free house   Licensee Dorothy Eileen O'Gorman   Real ale   Meals and snacks (12–2, 6.30–8.30; not Mon or Sat evening, not Sun)   Restaurant (not Sun evening) tel Aldbury Common (044 285) 203   Children in eating area of bar   Open 12–3, 6–11; 12–11 Sat

AYOT ST LAWRENCE   TL1916 Map 5

Brocket Arms ★

This fourteenth-century tiled house has two old-fashioned rooms with a relaxed friendly atmosphere, orange lanterns hanging from the sturdy oak beams, a big inglenook fireplace, a long built-in wall settle in one parquet-floored room, and a wide choice of piped music from Bach to pop. Bar food includes soup, ploughman's or pâté (£2.75), salads, shepherd's pie, scampi (£3.30), and coq au vin, tagliatelle or fish pie (£4.18); winter Sunday roast lunch. Well kept Fullers London Pride, Greene King IPA and Abbot, Hook Norton Old Hookey, Marstons Pedigree, Wadworths 6X, and guest beers tapped from the cask; Rich's cider and several malt whiskies; darts and dominoes. The walled gardens behind the white-painted brick house – which hold some very romantic memories for some readers – are especially safe for children; on *Good Walks Guide* Walk 108. George Bernard Shaw's home is not far away, and just over the road are the romantic ivy-hung ruins of a medieval church. *(Recommended by Michael and Alison Sandy, Andy Blackburn, A J and M Thomasson)*

Free house   Licensee Toby Wingfield Digby   Real ale   Meals and snacks (not Sun or Mon evenings)   Restaurant   Children in restaurant   Open 11–2.30, 6–11 all year   Bedrooms tel Stevenage (0438) 820250; £30/£35

BARLEY   TL3938 Map 5

Fox & Hounds ★ 🅂   [illustrated on page 378]

A new conservatory has been added to this fifteenth-century white house (which will be no-smoking) to give more room for diners. The low-ceilinged rambling rooms have an enjoyable country atmosphere, and the various alcoves have an assortment of simple but comfortable furniture – one of the stripped wood tables has a brightly painted cast-iron base which used to be a wringer; there are substantial log fires on both sides of a massive central chimney, and a friendly cat. The dining area with its odd-shaped nooks and crannies was originally the kitchen and cellar. A big bonus is the fact that they brew their own beer – Nathaniels Special, as well as serving beers on eight handpumps from all over the country on continual rotation; farm cider, malt whiskies, and good house wine. Bar food (they now take bookings) from a huge menu of mostly home-made dishes includes sandwiches, garlic mushrooms (£1.95), spare ribs in home-made barbecue sauce (£2.25), lasagne, vegetable provençale or curries (£3.25), steak and kidney or lamb and apricot pies (£3.95), scallops, prawns and mushrooms in white wine or beef Stroganoff (£4.25), cold poached salmon and prawns (£4.60), whole plaice (£4.95), chicken Kiev (£5.25), honey-roast duck (£5.95) and steaks (from £5.95); service is efficient and friendly even when pushed. An excellent range of games includes darts (two league darts teams), bar billiards, shove-ha'penny, dominoes (two schools), cribbage, fruit machine and juke box. The pub also has a league football team. The garden was undergoing some heavy work as we went to press – they are installing new play equipment, moving the skittle alley, and hope to make more use of the barbecue area. They have a mini-bus which offers a get-you-home service. *(Recommended by Nigel Gibbs, Olive Carroll, Alan Whelan, R Wiles, Gordon Theaker, W H Cleghorn, Joy Heatherley, S Matthews)*

Own brew   Licensee Rita Nicholson   Real ale   Meals and snacks (12–2, 6.30–10) Children in eating area of bar (not too late Sats)   Very occasional live entertainment Open 12–2.30, 6–11 all year

CHIPPERFIELD   TL0401 Map 5
Two Brewers

This low white-tiled and neatly kept inn has some early nineteenth-century prints of bare-knuckle pugilists in the main bar (a reminder that Jem Mace, Bob Fitzsimmons and others trained in the back club-room), dark beams, cushioned antique settles, and a relaxed and genuinely pubby atmosphere. Lunchtime bar food is served in the comfortable bow-windowed lounge: home-made soup (£1.20), a good choice of ploughman's (£2.85), a daily hot dish (£3.25), an attractive buffet with excellent meats (£3.25), and puddings like home-made cherry trifle (from 95p). Tables in this room are spread with linen cloths at lunchtime, and there are easy chairs and sofas – get there early if you want a seat. Well kept Bass, Courage Best, Greene King IPA and Abbot, Marstons Pedigree, McEwans 80/-, Ruddles Best and Youngers Scotch on handpump. The building overlooks the pretty tree-flanked village cricket green – with pleasant walks in the woods beyond. *(Recommended by Lyn and Bill Capper, D L Johnson, Dr Mark Stocker, GP)*

Free house (THF)   Licensee Ian Towler   Real ale   Snacks (lunchtime, not Sun) Restaurant   Children in lounge and restaurant   Open 10.30–2.30, 5.30–11 all year; all day Sat   Bedrooms tel Kings Langley (092 77) 65266; £79B/£89B

GREAT OFFLEY   TL1427 Map 5
Green Man
Village signposted off A505 Luton–Hitchin

Even when this attractively situated pub is busy, the staff remain attentive and cheerful. The rambling bars have wheel-back and spindle-back chairs around simple country tables, stripped brick, low moulded beams, lots of antique farm-tool illustrations, and a wood-burning stove and fruit machine on the left. The larger and more airy right-hand room has lots of little countryside prints and one or two larger pictures, a cabinet of trophies, cushioned built-in wall seats as well as the chairs around its tables, another big wood-burner (with a row of brass spigots decorating the chimneypiece), and fruit machine. The quickly served bar food includes soup (95p), generous sandwiches and large filled rolls (from £1.40), filled baked potatoes (from £1.50), ploughman's (from £2), cottage or chicken and mushroom pie (£3.50), a good lunchtime spread of help-yourself salads (from

£4.50), and gammon with pineapple (£4.95); the meat is supplied by the local butcher and the turkeys come from a local farm. Well kept Flowers IPA and Original, Ruddles County, Websters Yorkshire and (unusual down here) Whitbreads Castle Eden on handpump, with a decent choice of wines by the glass; friendly cat, piped music. Curlicued iron tables and chairs on the flagstoned terrace (overlooked by a high-pillared comfortable restaurant) have a grand view beyond the lawn, with its rockery, pond and little waterfall, of the flatter land below, stretching for miles to the east. There's a mass of flowers, with lots of hanging baskets and tubs of flowers, and a couple of ponies may be stretching their necks over the stile at the end of the lawn. Children are asked to sit out in front instead, where there are swings and a slide. *(Recommended by David Shillitoe, Peter and Jacqueline Petts, Roger Broadie, D L Johnson, Rita Horridge, Lyn and Bill Capper, Michael and Alison Sandy)*

Free house   Licensee R H Scarbrow   Real ale   Meals and snacks (noon–11)   Restaurant tel Offley (046 276) 256   Children welcome   Open 10.30am–11pm all year; closed evenings 25 and 26 Dec

nr HARPENDEN   TL1314 Map 5
Three Horseshoes

East Common; from A1081 about 600 yds S of the S edge of Harpenden, follow sign towards Ayres End, Amwell, then turn left at Harpenden Common sign; OS Sheet 166 reference 144120

Tables on the side lawn and the terrace in front of this rather genteel pub are surrounded by a quiet common, with tracks off through it and a right of way over the golf course that's on the other side of the lane. Inside, there are some snug alcoves, cushioned rustic-style seats and stools around the many dark wood tables, horsebrasses, dividing timbers and beams of a partly knocked-through wall, and inglenook fireplaces with open fires in winter. The new licensee has changed the popular home-made food to include good soup (£1), filled French plaited roll with garlic dip (£1.60), baked potatoes (from £1.50), ploughman's (from £2), salads (from £2.75), several hot meals like steak and kidney pie, cod or chilli con carne, and daily specials such as Lancashire hot-pot or gamekeeper's pie. Well kept Brakspears, Flowers Original and Wethereds on handpump; sensibly placed darts, dominoes, cribbage, fruit machine and piped music. *(Recommended by Margaret and Trevor Errington, M Aston, BKA, John Atherton, J F Estdale, Stanley Matthews, Mrs M Lawrence)*

Whitbreads   Licensee Richard Jones   Real ale   Meals and snacks   Children welcome   Jazz Tues evening   Open 11–2.30, 5.30–11 all year; all day Sat

LETCHMORE HEATH   TQ1597 Map 5
Three Horseshoes

2 miles from M1 junction 5; A41 towards Harrow, first left signposted Aldenham, right at Letchmore Heath signpost

A well kept cottagey local opposite the duck pond on a serenely tree-shaded village green – quite a find for this part of the world. The tiny, low-ceilinged and carpeted main lounge has horsebrasses on the beams, a few olde-worlde prints on the walls, an old panelled settle as well as green-patterned plush cushioned wooden wall seats (some in a big bay window etched with the pub's name and emblem), and an open fire. A wide choice of bar food includes sandwiches (from 70p), ploughman's and a good many variants (from £1.60), hot snacks such as seafood pasta or turkey and ham hash (around £2.50), and changing dishes such as liver and bacon or chicken and leek pie (£3), with lots of vegetables or salad. Well kept Benskins Best and Ind Coope Burton on handpump; maybe faint piped music. There are a good many white tables on a side terrace beside the attractive house (covered in summer with pretty hanging baskets and window boxes), with more on the lawn; pretty quiet,

except for birdsong and the occasional scream of a neighbouring peacock.
(Recommended by Dr John Innes, M C Howells, Stanley Matthews, D L Johnson)
Benskins (Allied)   Licensee Ann Parrott   Real ale   Lunchtime meals and snacks (not Sun)
Open 11–3, 5.30–11 all year

MUCH HADHAM   TL4319 Map 5
Bull
B1004

This simple brick-built inn was licensed by 1727, and it was in the public bar in 1813 that the licensee locked the doors while two of his customers fought to the death. It's a friendly place now, with cafe seats and tables, a timber-propped inglenook with a very low beam, and sensibly placed darts, dominoes, cribbage, fruit machine, trivia and a decent juke box. Food here includes generous filled French sticks (£1.20), a choice of ploughman's (from £2.20), chilli con carne (£3.45) and steak and kidney pie (£3.95); on the other side, a much wider choice includes soup (£1.20) with lots of other starters (from £1.20), chicken and ham pie (£3.60), lasagne (£3.80), fish pie or fresh poached haddock (£3.85), salads (£3.95) and steaks (from £6.95), with rich puddings and children's helpings at half-price. The carpeted lounge bar has comfortable brocaded wall banquettes around neat tables, and is decorated with big blow-ups of old local photographs; it's supplemented by a cosy back family dining-room with brocaded seats around closer-spaced tables, and one or two old enamel advertising placards on its timbered white walls. Well kept Benskins Best and Ind Coope Burton on handpump, and several wines; piped music. There are rustic seats dotted around in the big informal back garden. *(Recommended by WTF, M and J Back, R C Vincent, SJC)*
Benskins (Allied)   Licensee Mike Wade   Real ale   Meals and snacks (12–2, 6–10; not 25 or 26 Dec)   Children in dining-room   Open 11.30–3, 6–11 all year; closed evening 25 Dec

NEWGATE STREET   TL3005 Map 5
Coach & Horses
1 mile N of Cuffley

The cheerful open-plan bar in this attractive old country pub has some surviving wall ends that create an illusion of separate little rooms, with a mellow mix of carpet and large flagstones, cosy built-in wall settles, good winter fires at either end, subdued lighting and perhaps piped music or Radio Essex. Good bar food includes a wide range of sandwiches or toasties (from £1; Reg's Special £2.25), potted shrimps (£2), ploughman's (from £2.75), chilli con carne or vegetable lasagne (£3), smoked haddock pasta (£3.20), and home-made specials like steak and kidney pie, macaroni cheese or beef in red wine sauce (£3.10). Well kept Benskins Best and Ind Coope Burton on handpump; fruit machine, trivia and piped music. There are tables on a lawn with high trees around it, and more on the forecourt of the densely ivy-covered tiled house. Handy for walks in nearby rolling fields (there are lots of paths), or in vast woods such as the Great Wood country park (from the Northaw road, take the B157 towards Brookmans Park). *(Recommended by John Day, Alan and Ruth Woodhouse, Gwen and Peter Andrews)*
Benskins (Allied)   Licensee Reg Newcombe   Real ale   Meals and snacks (not Sun)
Children in family-room   Open 11–3, 5.30–11 all year

PUCKERIDGE   TL3823 Map 5
White Hart ✿
Village signposted from A10 and A120

Under the heavy beams of the spreading bar is a medley of wooden armchairs, wheel-back chairs and button-back banquettes; the fireplace has a massive carved mantelbeam, and traditional decorations include pewter tankards, horsebrasses and coach horns. Good value food (which can be eaten in the bar or dining-room) includes seafood such as crab sandwich (£1.65), fresh prawns (from £1.75), spicy crab pâté (£1.95), seafood salad (octopus, squid, prawns and mussels, £2.25), Mediterranean prawns (from £4.50), delicious hot Arbroath smokies (£4.95), whole baked plaice stuffed with prawns (£5.50) and seafood platter (£5.75). Other food includes sandwiches (from 90p), ploughman's (from £1.75), home-made venison pâté (£1.95), home-made moussaka or fresh oven-roasted turkey (£4.95), lots of vegetarian dishes like country lentil crumble or home-made tomato pancakes (£4.95), steaks (from £7.50), and a children's menu. Well kept McMullens Bitter and AK Mild on handpump; darts, dominoes, cribbage, fruit machine, trivia and piped music. There are seats and swings in the floodlit garden by a paddock with chickens, roosters, ducks, goats, rabbits, sheep and ponies, and more under a thatched shelter built around a spreading tree. *(Recommended by Derek and Sylvia Stephenson, H Paulinski, Dave Wright)*

McMullens   Licensee Colin Boom   Real ale   Meals and snacks (12–2, 6.30–9.30) Restaurant (not Sun evening) tel Ware (0920) 821309   Children in eating area of bar and restaurant   Open 10.30–2.30, 5.30–11; closed evenings 25 and 26 Dec

ST ALBANS   TL1507 Map 5

Fighting Cocks

Off George Street, through abbey gateway (you can drive down, though signs suggest you can't)

Perhaps the most notable feature in the modernised bar of this almost circular-shaped pub is the small area down steps which used to be part of the Stuart cock-fighting pit which gave the pub its modern name – it was called the Round House when it first opened as an alehouse in 1600. There are some pleasant window alcoves, other nooks and corners, heavy low beams, and a good log fire in the inglenook fireplace. As we went to press the new licensee told us he was in the middle of changing the menu which he hoped would include sandwiches and other snacks and a range of hot daily specials. Well kept Benskins Best, Ind Coope Burton and Tetleys on handpump; fruit machine, trivia and piped music. The surroundings are very attractive: seats in the garden, then beyond that lots of ducks on the River Ver, a lakeside park, and the Roman remains of Verulamium. Some sort of building has been here since 795 when the abbey was founded, and by Norman times it served as a battlemented gatehouse (the upper fortifications were demolished in 1300). *(Recommended by David Goldstone, Michael and Alison Sandy, Wayne Brindle)*

Benskins (Allied)   Licensee J Capanella   Real ale   Lunchtime meals and snacks   Children in family-room   Open 11–3, 6–11 all year; open all day in summer

Garibaldi

61 Albert Street; off Holywell Hill below White Hart Hotel – some parking at end of street

Pulsing with life, this well kept and comfortably refurbished pub is bigger inside than its modest backstreet façade suggests. The carpeted bar encircles the island servery, with steps up to one little tiled-floor snug, and steps down to a separate food counter – which opens out into a neat little no-smoking conservatory. The style is softened Victorian, but the pub owes its character to the lively crowd of mainly youngish people – lots of T-shirts in warm weather. Good value home-made bar food includes sandwiches (from £1), soup (£1.20), ploughman's (£2.50), salads (from £2.75), their popular steak pie laced with ESB (£3.99), and other changing hot dishes such as spicy meatballs (£2.25), fresh vegetable and pasta bake (£2.60), Barnsley chop done with red wine and rosemary (£3.50) and chicken Kiev (£3.99); well kept Fullers Chiswick, London Pride and ESB; cribbage, dominoes, trivia machine, fruit machine, piped pop music – and a thirsty cricket team. Service is quick and friendly. There are a few picnic-table sets in the side yard. *(Recommended by John Baker, David Fowles, Michael and Alison Sandy, Andy Blackburn and others)*

Fullers   Licensee Gerry Combra   Real ale   Meals and snacks   Children allowed away from bar if quiet, until about 7.30   Open 11–3, 5–11 all year; all day Fri and Sat

Goat

Sopwell Lane; a No Entry beside Strutt and Parker estate agents on Holywell Hill, the main southwards exit from town – by car, take the next lane down and go round the block

Decorations in the network of linked rooms in this nicely refurbished old pub include stuffed birds, chamber-pots, books and prints. There's also a good range of real ales: Boddingtons, Fullers London Pride, Greene King Abbot, Hook Norton Best and Old Hookey, Marstons Pedigree and Wadworths 6X on handpump. Bar food includes soup (£1.10), sandwiches (steak £1.75), pizzas (from £2.25), steak and mushroom pie (£2.95), tagliatelle carbonara (£3.30), burgers (from £3.30), steaks (£5.75), and home-made puddings. Dominoes, fruit machine, trivia and piped music. Tables on the neat lawn-and-gravel back yard are sheltered by what, 200 years ago, used to be the most extensive stables of any inn here. *(Recommended by N Barker, David Goldstone, BKA, Richard and Dilys Smith, D C Bail, Nick Dowson, Stanley Matthews)*

Free house (though now owned by Inn Leisure/Devenish)   Licensee Anthony Ginn   Real ale   Meals and snacks (12–2, 6.30–9.30; not Sun evening)   Children in eating area of bar   Jazz Sun lunchtime   Nearby parking may be rather difficult   Open 11–2.30, 5.30–11 all year; 11–11 Sat; closed 25 Dec

Rose & Crown

St Michaels Street; from town centre follow George Street down past the abbey towards the Roman town

Hidden behind its elegant Georgian façade, this attractive and friendly old pub has unevenly timbered walls, old-fashioned wall benches, a pile of old *Country Life* magazines, and black cauldrons in the deep fireplace. Bar food includes plain or toasted sandwiches, cheesy potato pie (£2), ploughman's (from £2), quiches, casseroles or beef stew with dumplings (£2.95), and lots of home-made vegetarian dishes. Well kept Benskins Best, Ind Coope Burton and Tetleys on handpump, and farm ciders, country wines and winter hot punch; unusual crisps and a selection of snuffs. Darts (placed sensibly to one side), shove-ha'penny, dominoes, cribbage, fruit machine, video game and juke box. There's always a selection of books for sale – proceeds go towards buying guide dogs. *(Recommended by BKA, Sonia Elstow; more reports please)*

Benskins (Allied)   Licensee John Milligan   Real ale   Lunchtime snacks (11.30–2.15)   Folk music Thurs   Open 11.15–2.30 (3 Sat), 5.30 (6 Sat)–11 all year

WADESMILL   TL3517 Map 5
Sow & Pigs

Thundridge; A10 just S of Wadesmill, towards Ware

The central serving bar's a snug and warmly traditional little place, with a rustic cask-supported table in the bay of the comfortable window seat, an attractive wall clock, a small ship's wheel and binnacle under a collection of military badges, and dark glossy plank-panelling. It opens on either side into more spacious rooms, with big copper urns hanging from dark beams, antlers and prints above the dark dado, cosy wall seats and little spindle-back chairs around massive rustic or traditional cast-iron tables, log fires – and, throughout, the buzz of chatter and quiet enjoyment that marks a good, well run pub. They really know how to make sandwiches; from the wide choice, people pick out the roast beef done with dripping (£1.05), the smoked salmon (£1.60) and the steak (£2.40). Other well priced bar food includes a pauper's lunch (25p), soup (£1.05), ploughman's

(£1.50), steak and kidney pie (£2.30) and a bargain three-course steak lunch (£4.75). Well kept Benskins Best, Ind Coope Burton and Tetley Walker Best on handpump or tapped from the cask. There are picnic-table sets under cocktail parasols, with their own service hatch, on a smallish fairy-lit grass area behind by the car park, sheltered by tall oaks and chestnut trees. *(Recommended by R C Vincent, D L Johnson; more reports please)*

Benskins (Allied)   Licensee Willie Morgan   Real ale   Meals (not Sun evening) and snacks (any time during opening hours)   Restaurant tel Ware (0920) 463281   Children in restaurant   Open 11–2.30, 6–11 all year

WATTON-AT-STONE   TL3019 Map 5

George & Dragon ★ ⊗

High Street

Though the fresh, imaginative food here is well above pub standards, the place has stayed very much as a pub and hasn't been smartened up too much. The carpeted main bar has country kitchen armchairs around attractive old tables, dark blue cloth-upholstered seats in its bay windows, an interesting mix of antique and modern prints on the partly timbered ochre walls, and a big inglenook fireplace. A quieter room off, with spindle-back chairs and wall settles cushioned to match the green floral curtains, has a nice set of Cruikshank anti-drink engravings above its panelled dado. Bar food includes thick tasty soup (£1.10; Corsican fish soup £3), sandwiches (from 80p), ploughman's or an evening hot snack (£2.50), a lunchtime dish of the day (£3.25), salads (from £3.30), stuffed mushrooms or flaked smoked haddock topped with tomato concasse gratinated and grilled (£3.75), locally smoked salmon (£5.75), fillet steak in a bread roll (from £6), and puddings (£1.50); they also have seven dishes which change weekly, such as fresh Loch Fyne kipper (from £2), mussel and dill pâté (£3.30), diced rabbit cooked in a rich port wine sauce and served in a vol-au-vent (£3.50), and strips of pork fillet in a portugaise sauce (£4.50). Proper napkins, good house wines by half-pint or pint carafes, and a selected house claret. The Greene King beers are kept under pressure; friendly, efficient service, and daily papers are set out to read at lunchtime. There are picnic-table sets in a small shrub-screened garden. They like you at least to wear shirts with sleeves. The pub is handy for Benington Lordship Gardens. *(Recommended by Alan and Ruth Woodhouse, Harold Glover, Hope Chenhalls, Mr and Mrs S Pollock-Hill, Mr and Mrs A R Walmsley, Rita Horridge, C P Harris)*

Greene King   Licensee Kevin Dinnin   Meals and snacks (12–2, 7–10; not Sun, limited menu Sat lunchtime)   Restaurant (not Sun) tel Ware (0920) 830285   Children in restaurant   Open 11–2.30, 6–11 all year

WESTMILL   TL3626 Map 5

Sword in Hand

Village signposted W of A10, about 1 mile S of Buntingford

The friendly new licensee here is a classic car enthusiast and holds regular shows in the back garden in summer and meetings in the pub in winter. There are photographs of classic cars and local houses, and pictures of local scenes on the black and white timbered walls, comfortably cushioned seats and new tables on the Turkey carpet, and a log fire. A new menu with home-made food has been introduced: French onion soup (£1.35), pâté with Cointreau and orange (£1.95), ploughman's (from £1.95), smoked salmon mousse (£2.25), seafood or meaty lasagne (£3.75), pies with lovely flaky pastry (the speciality here – lamb and rosemary £3.75, steak and kidney or chicken, gammon and mushroom £3.95), lemon chicken (£5.95), stuffed baked trout wrapped in vine leaves (£6.50), steaks (from £6.95), jugged venison (£7.95), and puddings like caramel delight or spotted dick (£1.50). Well kept Benskins Best on handpump and Ind Coope Burton tapped

from the cask. Darts, shove-ha'penny, dominoes, cribbage, fruit machine, trivia and piped music. The little dog called Scuffy likes to do tricks. There are tables on a partly crazy-paved sheltered side garden under the pear tree. The pub takes its name from the crest of a local landowner – the first licensee, a blacksmith, used to make tools for his Caribbean sugar plantations. The village is particularly pretty.
(Recommended by R F Plater, Peter Storey; more reports please)

Benskins (Allied)   Licensees David and Heather Hopperton   Real ale   Meals and snacks Restaurant tel Royston (0763) 71356   Well behaved children welcome   Open 11–2.30, 6–11; they may stay open longer in afternoon if there are customers

Lucky Dip

Besides the fully inspected pubs, you might like to try these Lucky Dips recommended to us and described by readers (if you do, please send us reports):

Aldbury [SP9612], *Greyhound*: Simple old pub with Georgian refacing, by village duck pond below Chilterns beech woods; on GWG109 *(LYM)*

☆ **Amwell** [village signposted SW from Wheathampstead; TL1613], *Elephant & Castle*: Particularly nice in summer for its spacious and attractive floodlit gardens, with barbecues; low-beamed ancient pub with inglenook fireplace, panelling, stripped brickwork, 200-ft well shaft in bar; usual bar food (not Sun), well kept Benskins Best, Ind Coope Burton and Tetleys on handpump; restaurant; children in eating area *(Michael and Alison Sandy, David Shillitoe, LYM)*

Ardeley [OS Sheet 166 reference 310272; TL3027], *Jolly Waggoner*: Genuine, rustic and friendly pub with two unspoilt bars, one for eating which is extended into adjoining cottage – the extensive range of good bar food is cooked by licensee's wife; well kept Greene King ales *(Charles Bardswell)*

Ashwell [69 High St; TL2639], *Rose & Crown*: Good home-cooked bar food served quickly in friendly, welcoming pub with open fire and exceptionally attractive garden *(Anon)*

Ayot Green [TL2213], *Waggoners*: Pleasant, well kept pub with lots of mugs hanging from low ceiling, good bar food served on Wedgwood china, separate eating area, young and friendly staff; on GWG 108 *(GB, CH)*

Barkway [TL3835], *Chaise & Pair*: Plushly modernised small pub with bar food from sandwiches to steaks, real ale, restaurant *(LYM)*

Belsize [OS Sheet 176 reference 034009; TL0309], *Plough*: Pleasant country pub, central bar, barn-like beamed lounge with open fire; good friendly service, Benskins Best and Ind Coope Burton on handpump, good value bar lunches, unobtrusive piped music, picnic-table sets in garden *(Lyn and Bill Capper, Mr and Mrs F W Sturch)*

☆ **Berkhamsted** [Gravel Path; SP9807], *Boat*: Pleasantly decorated new Fullers pub by canal, friendly atmosphere, genial licensees who were very popular with readers at their last place (the Valiant Knight in Hampton Hill); good value lunchtime bar food, free seafood bar nibbles on Sun, well kept Fullers Chiswick, London Pride and ESB, tables on canalside terrace with shrubs and hanging baskets, loyal regulars *(Stephen King, John Wright, Michael Ansell, A D Clench)*

Berkhamsted [High St], *George*: Pleasant town pub with rambling rooms; saloon full of interesting prints and two large, comfortable leather chairs; well kept Ruddles Best and County and Wethereds, good cheap bar food, pinball machine unobtrusively placed in back room, no music *(Anon)*

☆ **Bishops Stortford** [Waterside; TL4820], *Five Horseshoes*: Friendly and attractive tiled-roof beamed pub overlooking cricket pitch, with tables in nice walled garden; Benskins ales, good food *(Anon)*

Bishops Stortford [Bedlars Green (so pub actually just over Essex border); just off A120 by M11 junction 8; TL5220], *Hop Poles*: Small friendly village pub with Benskins Best, Friary Meux Best and Ind Coope Burton on handpump; nr Hatfield forest *(Robert Lester)*

Bourne End [Winkwell – off Berkhamsted rd; TL0206], *Three Horseshoes*: Included primarily for its lovely setting by canal swingbridge; sixteenth-century, with stripped brickwork, harness, low lighting; Benskins Best, Ind Coope Burton and Tetleys on handpump, seats outside *(Gary Scott, Mr and Mrs J Wyatt)*

Bovingdon [Hempstead Rd; TL0103], *Halfway House*: Recently extended Benskins local with good value food all week in separate eating area; pleasant garden *(D C Horwood)*; *Wheatsheaf*: Cosy beamed pub with cushioned settles, horsebrasses, open fires, Whitbreads-related real ales, reasonably priced hot and cold food, friendly service; fruit machine, piped pop music and darts in upper extension *(Lyn and Bill Capper)*

Boxmoor [TL0306], *Fishery*: Big-windowed and airy open-plan upstairs bar has fine view of canal with brightly painted barges, as do waterside tables; usual bar food, Ind Coope-related real ales; music may be loud in evenings *(LYM)*

Braughing [B1368; TL3925], *Axe & Compasses*: Cricket-mad pub with pleasant seating in two lovely bars inc an unusual corner room; good bar food, especially generously served daily specials *(Alan and Ruth Woodhouse)*

Bricket Wood [School Lane; nr M1 junction 6; TL1202], *Old Fox*: Small, friendly and comfortable pub with well kept beers and good food; good walks nearby; children welcome *(Hugh Geddes)*

Bushey [High St; TQ1395], *Red Lion*: Friendly, competent service, Bass and Benskins Best on handpump, reasonable wine by the glass and good bar food *(D C Bail)*

Bushey [42 Sparrows Herne; TQ1395], *Royal Oak*: Congenial pub with wide choice of good bar food running up to steaks, well kept Charles Wells and Marstons Burton and Pedigree, pleasant service, mixed clientele; small play area in garden *(Stan Edwards, Richard Houghton)*

Bushey [25 Park Rd, off A411; TQ1395], *Swan*: Homely atmosphere in rare surviving example of single-room backstreet terraced pub, reminiscent of 1920s *(LYM)*

☆ **Chandlers Cross** [TQ0698], *Clarendon Arms*: Good atmosphere in large, popular bar with plenty of tables, friendly staff and locals, cheap plain bar food (not Sun) lunchtime – when it may be full of young people; Brakspears, Websters Yorkshire and Youngs, help-yourself coffee; best in summer for its nice setting and pleasant covered verandah *(BKA, D L Johnson)*

Chapmore End [off B158 Hertford–Wadesmill; TL3216], *Woodman*: Small village pub with good welcoming atmosphere, well kept Greene King, tables in garden *(Helen and John Thompson)*

Cheshunt [Turnford; TL3502], *Old Anchor*: Friendly, modernised pub with well kept McMullens real ale *(John Baker)*

Chipperfield [Tower Hill; TL0401], *Boot*: Neatly kept, with open fires, fresh flowers, simple range of good food, well kept Benskins Best and Friary Meux Best on handpump, lots of interesting regalia *(BKA)*; *Royal Oak*: Efficiently run and spotlessly clean with two small bars, log fire, soft piped music, no juke box and relaxed atmosphere; good bar food at reasonable prices *(Mrs Olive Way)*; *Windmill*: Simple pub, no piped music, well kept Ind Coope Bitter and Burton, good, plain, cheap bar food *(Dr M Quinton)*

☆ **Chipping** [off A10; TL3532], *Countryman*: Beams and timbering, traditional settles, open fire, farm tools, wide choice of bar food which recent reports suggest has been on a decided upswing, restaurant, well kept Adnams, Courage Best, Marstons Pedigree and Ruddles County from elaborately carved

bar counter, piped music; in summer (when the pub's been open all day Sats) the big pleasant garden is a plus; children in restaurant *(Alan and Ruth Woodhouse, Dave Butler, Lesley Storey, LYM)*

☆ **Chorleywood** [Long Lane – follow Heronsgate signpost from M25 junction 17 exit roundabout; TQ0295], *Land of Liberty, Peace & Plenty*: Spotlessly kept pub with good range of bar food (especially at lunchtime); friendly staff, well kept Courage and John Smiths, decent coffee, maybe unobtrusive piped music; children's play area, several pub dogs *(Lyn and Bill Capper, G and M Stewart, G S Landa)*

Chorleywood [Artichoke Dell, Dog Kennel Lane, the Common], *Black Horse*: Unpretentious building in pleasant walking country, nice seating under low dark beams in attractively divided room with open fire and children's area, good value food from generously filled buns and sandwiches upwards, including good salads; Benskins Best and Ind Coope Burton on handpump *(Hugh Wilson)*; *Garden Gate*: Food served from noon to 9.30 in friendly pub handy for walkers on well wooded common nearby; well kept Benskins Best and Ind Coope Burton on handpump; children welcome *(LYM)*; [Station Approach] *Sportsman*: Attractive late nineteenth-century hotel opposite railway stn; Huntsman bar with oak panelling, open fire, Bass, Charrington and Worthington tapped from the cask, good range of reasonably priced bar food inc children's dishes, friendly service; comfortably furnished garden bar on floor above with conservatory and terrace; family-room leading to garden with large children's play area, Toby Grill; pleasant walking area; bedrooms *(Lyn and Bill Capper)*

Codicote [High St; TL2118], *Bell*: Comfortably modernised old Whitbreads pub with terrace bar behind lounge, generous helpings of good bar food from separate counter (and handsome restaurant), well kept Flowers and Wethereds on handpump, piped music, fruit machine; short on atmosphere; bedrooms *(Lyn and Bill Capper, D L Johnson)*; *Goat*: Plushly renovated rambling old Benskins pub with full meals and smartly uniformed bar staff *(LYM)*

☆ **Colney Heath** [TL2005], *Crooked Billet*: Good range of well kept real ales and lots of unusual bottled beers in traditional tiled bar and comfortably modernised lounge – no frills, but friendly service, straightforward bar food, summer barbecues, pets' corner in garden, maybe children's ponies to ride in summer; partly covered terrace *(David Fowles, LYM)*

Cottered [TL3129], *Bell*: Recently rethatched Benskins pub under new licensee, whose wife cooks a wide range of good bar food; well kept Ind Coope Burton on handpump *(Charles Bardswell)*

☆ **Croxley Green** [Rickmansworth Rd; A412; junction Watford Rd/Baldwins Lane – OS Sheet 176 reference 087959; TQ0795], *Two Bridges*: Handsomely renovated roadhouse, with feel of well-heeled and relaxing solidity in the several decently and interestingly furnished areas of its spacious bar, attractive muted décor, sofas, easy chairs, books and so forth, with well kept Ind Coope-related real ales and efficiently served bar food inc good roast of the day *(Ian Phillips, Mr and Mrs F H Stokes, BKA, Lyn and Bill Capper, Mr and Mrs F W Sturch, TBB, Peter and Joy Heatherley, LYM)*

Dane End [Great Munden; from Dane End go two miles past the Boot – OS Sheet 166 reference 352234; TL3321], *Plough*: Included for the unique full-size Compton theatre organ in the comfortable and lofty lounge extension that's been built specially to house it; otherwise, usual bar food, well kept Greene King IPA and Abbot and Rayments, local atmosphere *(LYM)*

Datchworth Green [1 Watton Rd; TL2718], *Inn on the Green*: Large well refurbished lounge bar, plenty of room for eating in another bar; very good food, good choice of real ales such as Adnams, friendly atmosphere and good service *(D L Johnson, M Draper)*; *Plough*: Simple friendly pub with well kept Greene King real ales *(LYM)*

☆ **nr Datchworth** [Bramfield Rd, Bulls Grn; TL2717], *Horns*: Pretty fifteenth-century country pub decorated interestingly to show its age, with attractive rugs on brickwork floor, big inglenook, low beams or high rafters, seats out among roses on the crazy paving; good pub food worth waiting for, well kept Flowers Original and Wethereds on handpump, good cider and coffee *(LYM)*

☆ **Essendon** [West End Lane – off B158, which with Essendon and B1455 is signposted off A414 Hatfield–Hertford; TL2708], *Candlestick*: Friendly local alone in the countryside, plenty of seats outside; comfortable two-room mock-Tudor lounge, brightly lit public bar with games; generous helpings of good value simple food at low, low prices lunchtimes and Tues–Fri evenings, well kept McMullens Bitter and AK Mild, log fires, good service; note – still shuts 2pm Sun *(Robert Young, Alan and Ruth Woodhouse, D L Johnson, Lyn and Bill Capper, BB)*

Flamstead [High St; TL0714], *Three Blackbirds*: Pretty pub with low beams, two real fires, good value bar food inc unusual dishes, small restaurant *(David Shillitoe)*

☆ **Flaunden** [TL0100], *Green Dragon*: Neat and comfortably refurbished partly panelled pub with well kept Marstons Pedigree and Merrie Monk and Taylor-Walker on handpump, reasonably priced bar food; charmingly well kept garden with summerhouse and aviaries *(Capt and Mrs Gardner, LYM)*

Flaunden [Hogpits Bottom], *Bricklayers Arms*: Cottagey and low-beamed man's pub, with interesting choice of real ales, old-fashioned peaceful garden, sandwiches or ploughman's *(LYM)*

☆ **Frithsden** [TL0110], *Alford Arms*: A Whitbreads pub, brewing its own Cherry Pickers and other real ales (the tiny brewhouse is worth a look in daylight), and stocking well kept Brakspears, Flowers Original and Wethereds; simple bar food, attractive country surroundings which make it a splendid summer pub, local atmosphere *(BKA, LYM)*

Hailey [TL3710], *Galley Hall*: Warm, friendly atmosphere, well kept Benskins Best and Ind Coope Burton, good value food lunchtime and evening *(Dave Wright)*

Harpenden [469 Luton Rd; 2¼ m from M1 junction 10; A1081 (ex-A6) towards town, on edge; TL1314], *Fox*: Extremely friendly local, well kept beer and good food *(Douglas and Lorna Collopy)*; [High St/Station Rd] *Harpenden Arms*: Well decorated with Victorian-style wallpaper, pictures, tiles and plants, and plenty of small tables and chairs in the airy and spacious food area; well kept Fullers, wide range of interesting pub and car parking – a shade tight *(Michael and Alison Sandy, John Baker)*; [Marquis Lane] *Marquis of Granby*: Welcoming, pleasant atmosphere, good bar food *(Mr and Mrs F E M Hardy)*

Hatfield [89 Great North Rd; TL2309], *Wrestlers*: Busy, attractive and well kept bars with brassware and bric-à-brac; friendly staff and experienced licensee, well kept beer, good bar food, wide range of customers *(M Thompson)*

nr Hemel Hempstead [Briden's Camp; leaving on A4146, right at Flamstead/Markyate signpost opp Red Lion – OS Sheet 166 reference 044111; TL0506], *Crown & Sceptre*: Country pub which still has some character, with three rooms, roaring fire, well kept Greene King and Rayments BBA, friendly staff; basic food, and housekeeping/service no longer its strongest point, though it still has some character, with friendly staff, a mixed clientele and a good atmosphere *(Stephen King, D L Johnson, BKA, LYM)*

☆ **Hertford** [Fore St; TL3212], *Salisbury Arms*: Fine example of sedate English country-town hotel; though now under English management, it has the same Chinese chef as for the last quarter-century, with good Chinese food as well as outstanding sandwiches; well kept McMullens ales inc AK Mild, friendly waitress service, three very comfortable rooms – cocktail bar, public bar with machines, darts etc and lounge with lots of tables; bedrooms *(Ian Phillips, K and E Leist)*

Hertford [The Folly], *Old Barge*: Comfortably renovated canalside pub with good welcoming atmosphere, friendly and efficient staff, well kept Benskins Best and bar food inc tasty home-made ham or seafood baguettes; popular with young people *(Colin Dourish, LYM)*; [Old Cross] *Woolpack*: Large McMullens house next to brewery with bare floorboards, wooden tables and chairs and open fire; impressive range of good value home-made lunchtime bar food *(David Fowles)*

Hitchin [TL1929], *George*: Stylishly refurbished comfortable town-centre pub, friendly welcome *(Wayne Brindle)*; [Bucklersbury; just off Market Sq] *Red Hart*: Maybe town's oldest building – pretty little courtyard, well kept Greene King IPA and Abbot, simple bar food, comfortably modernised *(LYM)*

Hoddesdon [Spitalbrook; TL3709], *George*: Modernised roadside pub with coal fire, friendly attentive staff, Benskins Best on handpump, freshly cooked bar food from good range of toasted sandwiches up *(Mr and Mrs S Pollock-Hill)*

Ickleford [TL1831], *Old George*: Rambling heavy-beamed Tudor pub by churchyard, good value bar food and Greene King beers *(LYM)*

Kings Langley [A41 N of town; TL0702], *Eagle*: Simply furnished but friendly Benskins local with lunchtime bar food, Ind Coope-related real ales, seats outside, playground, maybe occasional jazz; bedrooms *(LYM)*; [60 High St] *Rose & Crown*: Under new management, recently refurbished; currently very popular in the evenings, with jazz/live bands four nights a week and Sun lunchtime; good beer range, obliging staff *(Gordon Leighton)*

☆ **Lemsford** [A6129 towards Wheathampstead; TL2111], *Crooked Chimney*: Roomy and comfortable open-plan bar with central feature fireplace, Ind Coope real ales, restaurant and garden by fields; it's been a popular dining pub, but two changes of management in the last couple of years leave us needing more reports before we can decide finally whether it should be a Dip or a main entry *(LYM)*

Lemsford, *Long Arm & Short Arm*: Friendly and well run, with popular food – especially Sun lunch (get there early) *(Margaret and Trevor Errington)*; *Sun*: Cheerful Courage pub close to River Lea, lots of beams and timbers, good filled rolls; where Joseph Arch's pioneer Agricultural Labourers Union used to meet *(LYM)*

Leverstock Green [TL0806], *Leather Bottle*: Popular pub, quick and efficient service, varied and reasonably priced straightforward bar food *(D L Johnson)*

Little Gaddesden [B4506; SP9913], *Bridgewater Arms*: Simple rather hotelish style, in place which used to be popular for own-brewed ales; big right-hand lounge now mainly used as family-room and for eating,

also comfortable middle lounge, and former public bar at far end which has been refurbished and decorated as additional lounge but keeps pleasantly local atmosphere; Greene King Abbot, IPA and Rayments, good bar food *(Michael and Alison Sandy, LYM)*

☆ **Little Hadham** [The Ford; TL4422], *Nags Head*: Well kept Greene King and Rayments real ales and good food using fresh ingredients in friendly sixteenth-century country local – the puddings are specially good; restaurant; children welcome *(Alan and Ruth Woodhouse, P Gillbe, LYM)*

Little Wymondley [TL2127], *Bucks Head*: Handy for A1(M), chintzy and friendly with well kept Wethereds beer; attractive garden *(LYM)*

☆ **London Colney** [Waterside; just off main st by bridge at S end; TL1704], *Green Dragon*: Immaculately kept pub, with friendly atmosphere, good value straightforward lunchtime bar food (not Sun), well kept Benskins Best, lots of beams and brasses, tables outside by quiet riverside green *(S Matthews, Mr and Mrs H L Malhotra, LYM)*

London Colney, *Bull*: Jolly, active pub with good atmosphere, lounge and lively bar, well kept beer and friendly, helpful staff *(Dr and Mrs A K Clarke)*

Long Marston [38 Tring Rd – OS Sheet 165 reference 899157; SP8915], *Queens Head*: Wide range of good value food from sandwiches up in three-sided bar with stone floors, open log fire and plenty of olde-worlde charm; ABC Best, Bass, Everards Tiger and Ind Coope Burton on handpump, wide range of bar food, small garden; children's room *(Margaret and Trevor Errington, Phil Cook)*

Markyate [TL0616], *Sun*: Recently refurbished pub with low beams and atmosphere, small range of simple lunchtime snacks, Benskins beer, inglenook log fire, garden *(LYM)*

Much Hadham [Hertford Rd, about ¼ mile outside; TL4318], *Jolly Waggoners*: Well furnished, good atmosphere, pleasant service and good if a little pricey bar food – worth it *(T G Saul)*

Pepperstock [nr M1 junction 10; TL0817], *Half Moon*: Lovely décor in very friendly and popular Brewers Fayre restaurant/pub with good range of reasonably priced bar food *(Margaret and Trevor Errington)*

Perry Green [TL4317], *Hoops*: Popular local with well kept McMullens and good bar food running up to steaks, in pleasant surroundings – nice gardens *(R C Vincent, Mrs C Wardell)*

Pirton [TL1431], *Cat & Fiddle*: Homely pub facing village green, well kept Charles Wells real ales, bar food, swing on back lawn *(LYM)*

Potten End [TL0109], *Red Lion*: Reliably good bar food at reasonable prices *(Mr and*

Mrs F W Sturch)

☆ **Potters Crouch** [leaving St Albans on Watford rd via Chiswell Green, turn right after M10 – OS Sheet 166 reference 116052; TL1105], *Holly Bush*: Small whitewashed pub with marvellous highly polished biggish tables and other dark wood furniture, walls covered with pictures, plates, brasses and antlers, and old-fashioned lighting; Benskins Best and Ind Coope Burton, reasonable simple food, efficient service, large garden with picnic-table sets; gets very popular *(Michael and Alison Sandy, D L Johnson)*

Puckeridge [High St; TL3823], *Crown & Falcon*: Pepys stayed here in 1662 – steep-roofed and friendly old inn, comfortably modernised; bar food, restaurant, good Sun lunch with big helpings, well kept Benskins Best and Ind Coope Burton; children in eating area; bedrooms *(H Paulinski, LYM)*

Redbourn [Redbourn Rd (A5183); nr M1 junction 9; TL1012], *Chequers*: Roomy old oak-beamed Chef & Brewer pub in attractive open countryside; popular for good atmosphere, food (inc wide choice of specials), well kept Watneys-related real ales and service; back terrace and big garden by stream, restaurant *(Mr and Mrs H L Malhotra, P Marsh)*

☆ **Reed** [High St; TL3636], *Cabinet*: Friendly and relaxed tiled and weatherboarded house, a pub for centuries; parlourish inside with spacious lounge extension, nice garden out, wide choice of well kept real ales such as Adnams, Greene King Abbot, Hook Norton, Mauldons and Nethergate tapped from the cask, reasonably priced bar food, children's summer bar in charming garden, warm welcome *(Dave Butler, Lesley Storey, Alan and Ruth Woodhouse, LYM)*

Ridge [Crossoaks Lane; TL2100], *Old Guinea*: Small and friendly with rustic atmosphere; tasty and reasonably priced bar food; helpful to customers in wheelchairs *(Mr and Mrs G Sparrow)*

☆ **Rushden** [village signposted off A507 about a mile W of Cottered; TL3031], *Moon & Stars*: Has been a great favourite – unspoilt and cottagey, with low heavy beams, big white-panelled inglenook fireplace, Windsor chairs around long scrubbed table, sandwiches and home-cooked hot dishes (not Sun), Greene King keg beers, playthings and tables in back garden; go-ahead new young licensee hopes to preserve charm while adding amenities inc new kitchen, wider range of food, small choice of wines *(Charles Bardswell, LYM; reports on the new regime please)*

Sarratt [The Green; TQ0499], *Boot*: Attractive early eighteenth-century tiled pub facing green, cosy rambling rooms, nice inglenook fireplace, well kept Benskins Best and Ind Coope real ales, lunchtime food *(LYM)*; [Church Lane] *Cock*: Attractively placed in country with unusual traditional two-room layout, inglenook fireplace and so forth *(BKA, LYM)*; [The Green] *Cricketers*: Pleasant comfortable atmosphere in popular low-beamed lounge bar with well laid-out eating area, quickly served good bar food from sandwiches up, Courage and John Smiths beers, fruit machine and darts in public bar, no piped music; tables out facing green *(Lyn and Bill Capper)*

Sawbridgeworth [West Rd; TL4814], *Three Horseshoes*: Well kept McMullens, good bar food at reasonable prices, outside tables and play area; service not noted for speed *(R C Vincent)*

☆ **St Albans** [Holywell Hill; TL1507], *White Hart*: Friendly but civilised hotel with considerable character and charm, and long and entertaining history; comfortable bar with antique panelling, handsome fireplaces and furnishings; bar food and accommodating restaurant, Benskins Best, Ind Coope Burton and Tetleys on handpump; bedrooms *(Gordon Mott, Michael and Alison Sandy, David Goldstone, Wayne Brindle, LYM)*

St Albans [Adelaide St; off High St on W side by Texas Homecare shop], *Adelaide Wine House*: Notable for staying open till very late Fri and Sat, three-floor pub with simply furnished upstairs bar, lunchtime bar food, downstairs wine bar and restaurant, real ale, top-floor discos and live bands *(LYM)*; [corner main st and Hatfield Rd] *Cock*: Comfortably modernised town pub with interesting history – it once had a floor of human bones, probably from second Battle of St Albans, 1461 *(LYM)*; [Lower Dagnall St] *Farriers Arms*: Friendly pub in no-frills old area of city; well kept McMullens *(David Fowles)*; [French Row] *Fleur de Lys*: Historic medieval building, though the best parts of it are now in a museum and it's been comfortably modernised *(LYM)*; [36 Fishpool St] *Lower Red Lion*: Adnams, Fullers, Greene King IPA and Youngs Special on handpump in beamed bars with gas-effect log fires, plenty of seating, and friendly atmosphere; widening range of good value interesting bar food from toasties and ploughman's to interesting savoury pancakes and big steak sandwiches; pretty garden; bedrooms reasonably priced, though share bathrooms; huge breakfast *(Michael and Alison Sandy, Neil Tallantire)*; [St Michaels] *Six Bells*: Comfortably well kept low-beamed Benskins pub with bar food and well kept real ales *(LYM)*

nr **St Albans** [Tyttenhanger Green – from A405 just under 2 miles E of A6/A1081 roundabout, take B6426 signposted St Albans, then first left turn; TL1805], *Barley Mow*: Spacious sunny-windowed modestly furnished modernised bar with home-cooked bar lunches, evening snacks, well kept Watneys-related real ales on handpump; tables outside overlooking paddocks; staff can come under pressure at busy times *(Mrs J Jelliffe and family, LYM)*

Stevenage [Old Town; TL2324], *Marquis of Lorne*: Friendly pub with good beer and food, exemplary lavatories, tables outside *(P Gillbe)*

Tewin [Upper Green Rd; TL2714], *Plume of Feathers*: Good Benskins pub with good bar food and popular restaurant – lots of the bar users are heading that way *(D L Johnson)*

☆ **Thorley Street** [A1184 Sawbridgeworth–Bishops Stortford; TL4718], *Coach & Horses*: Generous helpings of good value bar food and quick, pleasant service in tastefully furnished and extended dining area; Sun lunch especially popular; homely atmosphere, friendly welcoming staff, Benskins beer and generous glasses of decent wine; children's play area, maybe special bouncing castle bank hols *(R C Vincent, T G Saul, Alan and Ruth Woodhouse)*

Tring [Bulbourne; B488 towards Dunstable, next to BWB works; SP9313], *Grand Junction Arms*: Alongside Grand Union Canal, large grounds with free-range chickens and rabbits, tables outside; well kept Benskins, good choice of bar food including vegetarian dishes and children's helpings, restaurant; nr GWG110; children welcome *(Chris and Jacqui Chatfield)*; [King St] *Kings Arms*: Pleasant backstreet local with pine furniture inc pews and old chairs; well kept Greene King Abbot and IPA, King & Barnes, Wadworths 6X and guest beers such as Fullers, big helpings of cheap interesting bar food such as prawn crusties and mussels in garlic, pleasant garden *(Mark Evans)*

Walkern [TL2826], *White Lion*: Comfortable and welcoming old pub, sensitively restored outside, popular for bar food and small restaurant, cosy alcoves and low beams, nice inglenook *(LYM)*; [B1036] *Yew Tree*: Welcoming pub with clean bar, McMullens ale, well presented bar food from sandwiches up inc good puddings, separate tables for eating *(D L Johnson)*

Water End [B197 N of Potters Bar; TL2214],

Woodman: Two cosily decorated bars with traditional furniture and good fires at either end; well kept Adnams, Marstons and Sam Smiths, home-cooked specials *(Alan and Ruth Woodhouse)*

Welwyn [this is the old village – not the Garden City; TL2316], *Wellington*: Good choice of main courses at lunchtime; and, slightly higher prices, in the evenings *(Margaret and Trevor Errington)*

nr **Wheathampstead** [Gustard Wood; B651 1½ miles N; TL1713], *Cross Keys*: Benskins real ales and good value simple bar food in unspoilt and obliging open-plan pub alone in rolling wooded countryside, quiet midweek *(Margaret and Trevor Errington, LYM)*; [Gustard Wood; B651 1½ miles N of town, then potholed track; TL1712] *Tin Pot*: Good welcome from long-serving licensee; good, pubby atmosphere, decent choice of low- and non-alcoholic drinks, good food; service not always speedy, can get crowded *(D L Johnson, Mr and Mrs F E M Hardy)*; [Nomansland Common; B651 ½ mile S; TL1712] *Wicked Lady*: Now a good example of a Whitbreads Brewers Fayre pub – if that's your fancy – with long bar broken up into several areas inc a no-smoking one, separate food servery, pleasantly furnished family conservatory extension; fruit machines and piped music, well kept Boddingtons, Flowers, Wethereds and Whitbreads, waitress service, picnic-table sets on big lawn with play area *(Lyn and Bill Capper, Margaret and Trevor Errington)*

Whitwell [B651; TL1820], *Eagle & Child*: Cosy lounge with fine wooden lintel over inglenook fireplace, handsomely moulded beams with queen post, bar food, Whitbreads real ales, darts in snugly clubby public bar; good play area in back garden *(LYM)*

Willian [TL2230], *Three Horseshoes*: Good food and well kept Greene King real ales in warmly welcoming pub very handy for A1(M) – left after Letchworth turn-off *(LYM)*

Humberside

Though licensees in this area have in the past tended to stay put for quite a time – giving its pubs a degree of stability that other places might well envy – there have been more changes than usual recently. There are new people at the fine Olde White Harte in Hull (one of Britain's classic city pubs), the Queens Head in Kirkburn (they seem to be lining it up for serious consideration for a food award), the Three Cups at Stamford Bridge (bringing it into these pages after a bit of a break), and the St Vincent Arms at Sutton upon Derwent (another pub that's worth watching for food). But perhaps the most abrupt change here has been the fire which swept through much of the charming Pipe & Glass at South Dalton; Malcolm Crease, undeterred, has been getting it rebuilt very much as before. One of the best pubs here for food is the Gold Cup at Low Catton (a new entry this year, quietly friendly); but the crown must surely go to the Half Moon at Skidby, for its formidable Yorkshire puddings – usefully, they serve sandwiches all afternoon. Other pubs deserving a special mention are the Plough at Allerthorpe (a fine example of East Yorkshire friendliness), the White Horse at Beverley (something of a time capsule), the Minerva at Hull (brewing its own beer, with cheap food) and the Gate at Millington (unpretentiously family run). Among the more promising Lucky Dip entries at the end of the chapter are the Station at Barnetby Le Wold, Beverley Arms in Beverley, Altisidora at Bishop Burton, Black Swan at Brandesburton, Royal Dog & Duck at Flamborough, Star at North Dalton, Triton at Sledmere and Green Dragon at Welton. Hull – a revivified city, well worth getting to know if you've not been there recently – is a particularly rich hunting-ground for the pub-lover.

ALLERTHORPE   SE7847 Map 7

Plough

Off A1079 near Pocklington

This pretty pub has a delightful, friendly atmosphere in its two-room lounge bar: snug alcoves (including one big bay window), open fires, hunting prints and some wartime RAF and RCAF photographs (squadrons of both were stationed here). Good value, home-made bar food includes daily specials such as game pie, as well as soup or light Yorkshire pudding with onion gravy (£1), open sandwiches (from £1), spare ribs, beef and mushroom pie or salads such as home-cooked beef or ham (£3), roast chicken (£3.25), steaks (from £5.50), children's dishes (from £1.10), and puddings like very good home-made cheesecake (£1.25); Sunday roast lunch (best to book, £3.75). The games – pool, dominoes, shove-ha'penny, cribbage, fruit machine, space game and juke box – are in an extension. Well kept Theakstons Best, XB and Old Peculier, Youngers Scotch and occasional guest beers on handpump; piped music. There are tables on the gravel outside. The attractive lily-pond gardens and stuffed sporting trophies of Burnby Hall are nearby. *(Recommended by David Gaunt, M Suther, Eddie Palker, Derek Stephenson, Jon Wainwright)*

Free house   Licensee David Banks   Real ale   Meals and snacks   Restaurant tel *Pocklington (0759) 302349   Children welcome   Open 12–3, 7–11*

BEVERLEY   TA0340 Map 8

White Horse ('Nellies')

Hengate, close to the imposing Church of St Mary's; runs off North Bar Within

The small rooms in this fine unspoilt pub have a carefully preserved Victorian feel – quite without frills – with a gas-lit pulley-controlled chandelier, a deeply reverberating chiming clock, antique cartoons and sentimental engravings, open fires – one with an attractively tiled fireplace – and brown leatherette seats (with high-backed settles in one little snug) on bare floorboards. Well kept Sam Smiths OB and Museum on handpump, and remarkably cheap food – fish and chips (£1.40), chicken and mushroom pie (£1.40) and braised steak (£1.60); darts, dominoes and trivia. *(Recommended by T T Kelly; more reports please)*

Sam Smiths   Licensee Bruce Westaby   Real ale   Lunchtime meals and snacks   Restaurant tel *Hull (0482) 861973   Children welcome   Folk music Mon, jazz Weds   Open 11–3, 5–11; 11–11 Weds and Sat*

BRANDESBURTON   TA1247 Map 8

Dacre Arms

Village signposted from A165 N of Beverley and Hornsea turn-offs

The sixteenth-century cobbled yard outside this popular modernised posting-inn once had stabling for up to fifty horses. Inside, the rambling rough-plastered bar is comfortably and vividly furnished with plenty of tables, and the snug area on the right once housed the local Court of Justices. A wide range of reasonably priced bar food includes sandwiches, soup (85p), Yorkshire puddings (from £1.20 for onion gravy, £3.15 for beef), home-made pâté (£1.55), ploughman's (£2.25), salads (from £2.85), fried mixed seafood (£3.25), with specialities like steak and kidney pie (from £2), home-made lasagne (£3.45), fish bake (£4.25) and steaks (from £5.75). Well kept John Smiths, Theakstons Best and Old Peculier, and Youngers Scotch on handpump; fruit machine, piped music. *(Recommended by Stan Edwards, M A and W R Proctor, T T Kelly)*

Free house   Licensee B C Jefferson   Real ale   Meals and snacks (12–2, 7–10)   Restaurant tel *Leven (0401) 42392   Children welcome   Open 11–2.30, 6.30–11 all year; all day Sat*

ELLERTON   SE7039 Map 7

Boot & Shoe   *[illustrated on page 392]*

Village signposted from B1228

Low-tiled and sixteenth century, this large cottage has a comfortable, friendly bar with a nice bow window seat, low black beams, a butter-coloured ceiling, dark beige plush wall seats and wheel-back chairs around dimpled copper or wooden tables, and three open fires. Bar food includes soup (£1), cheese and herb pâté (£1.60), lasagne (£2.85), chicken and mushroom pie (£3.10), steak and kidney pie (£3.25), sirloin steak (£4.95), vegetarian meals, and puddings like home-made sherry trifle (£1); Sunday lunchtime roast beef (£3.50), children's menu (£1.20). Well kept Old Mill or Tetleys on handpump; darts, dominoes, fruit machine, trivia and piped music. There's a garden at the back. *(Recommended by Jon Wainwright; more reports please)*

Free house   Licensees Mrs Doreen Gregg and Patrick McVay   Real ale   Meals and snacks (evenings, not Mon, plus Sun lunch)   Restaurant tel Bubwith (075 785) 346   Children welcome until 9   Open 12–3, 7–11.30; closed weekday lunchtimes; closed Sat lunchtime Nov–Easter

FLAMBOROUGH   TA2270 Map 8

Seabirds

Junction of B1255 and B1229

The emphasis here is very much on seabirds – there's a whole case of stuffed ones along one wall. The public bar is full of shipping paraphernalia, scowling toby jugs, and old framed photographs of Flamborough. Leading off this is the lounge, which has pictures and paintings of the local landscape, a mirror glazed with grape vines, and a wood-burning stove. Good value bar food (the prices haven't changed since last year) includes sandwiches, soup (75p), rollmop herring (£1), ploughman's (£1.50), omelettes (from £2), good fresh local haddock (£1.80) or plaice (price according to season), scampi (£2), seafood platter (£2.50), a selection of fish salads (again price according to season) and sirloin steak (£5.50); daily specials such as mussels in garlic (£1.95), seafood pancakes (£3.50), fresh crab salad (£4), roast duckling or lobster thermidor (£6) and rack of lamb (£7). Over thirty wines; friendly staff. Darts, shove-ha'penny, dominoes, cribbage, space game and piped music. There's now an all-weather family-room in the garden. *(Recommended by TRA, MA, Dr and Mrs S G Donald, Prof S Barnett, Tony and Penny Burton, M A and W R Proctor)*

Free house   Licensee Barrie Crosby   Meals and snacks   Restaurant (not Sun evening) tel Bridlington (0262) 850242   Children in eating area of bar and restaurant if eating   Open 11–3, 6–11

HULL   TA0927 Map 8

George

Land of Green Ginger; park just outside town centre and walk in: Land of Green Ginger is a lane at far end of pedestrians-only Whitefriargate, which leads out of centre opposite City Hall

The long Victorian bar in this old shuttered coaching-inn has a copper and mahogany counter, high bar stools with sensible little back rests, high beams, squared oak panelling, and old latticed windows; at the far end, it opens out into an area with several more tables – come early if you want a place. The dining-room, furnished in traditional plush fashion, is upstairs. Good value food includes light snacks such as pork pies (50p) or home-made Scotch eggs (70p), as well as filled rolls and sandwiches (from 65p), burgers (from £1), ploughman's or home-made pâté with garlic bread (£1.80), and hot dishes such as lasagne, spaghetti bolognese, chilli con carne (£1.80), with salads such as home-cooked beef or ham (£1.90); well kept Bass and Stones on handpump; fruit machine and piped music. On your way in, look out for the narrow slit window just to the left of the coach entry; ostlers used to watch for late-night arrivals in case they were highwaymen. The pub is handy for the excellent Docks Museum. *(Recommended by M A and W R Proctor; more reports please)*

Bass   Licensee Paolo E Cattaneo   Real ale   Lunchtime meals and snacks   Restaurant tel *Hull (0482) 226373   Children in restaurant   No nearby parking   Open 11–11 all year*

Minerva

From A63 Castle Street/Garrison Road, turn into Queen Street towards piers at central traffic lights; some metered parking here; pub is in pedestrianised Nelson Street, at far end

A broad prettily paved pedestrian walkway separates this pub, just around the corner from the Pilot Office, from the Humber. This part of Hull's old waterfront is attractive, with interesting new or converted buildings, and a lively marina. The several rooms, rambling all the way around a central servery, have been thoughtfully refurbished: comfortable seats, interesting photographs and pictures of old Hull (with two attractive wash drawings by Roger Davis), a big chart of the Humber, a tiny snug with room for just three people, and a back room (which looks out to the marina basin, and has darts) with a profusion of varnished woodwork. The floor is raised a few feet above ground level though the windows are at normal height – so the view out is unusually good. Besides well kept Tetleys Mild and Bitter on handpump, the pub brews its own Pilots Pride (you can see into the microbrewery from the street). Lunchtime bar food includes sandwiches (from 90p), lasagne or curry (£2.30), beef cobbler or steak pie (£2.50) salads (from £2.50) and specials; in the evening there are burgers (from £1.60), plaice or scampi (£2.60), chicken Kiev (£3), gammon (£3.20) and steaks (from £4.20). Darts, dominoes and fruit machine. Piped music from the fine reproduction Wurlitzer juke box (the real 'works', with the records, are actually in a completely different place) is loud and clear. *(More reports please)*

Own brew (Tetleys – Allied)   Licensee John Harris McCue   Real ale   Meals (lunchtime) and snacks (not Sun evening)   Children in eating area of bar lunchtime only   Open 11–11 in summer; 11–3, 6–11 in winter

Olde White Harte ★

Off 25 Silver Street, a continuation of Whitefriargate (see George entry); pub is up narrow passage beside the jewellers' Barnby and Rust, and should not be confused with the much more modern White Hart nearby

Excellently preserved, this ancient tavern has carved heavy beams supporting black ceiling boards, attractive stained-glass windows over the bow window seat, polished flooring tiles, and brocaded Jacobean-style chairs in the inglenook by a fireplace decorated with Delft tiles; the new licensee was planning to re-upholster the furnishings as we went to press. The curved copper-topped counter serves well kept Youngers IPA and No 3, and simple, traditional bar food includes sandwiches (from 65p, hot beef £1.30), ploughman's (£1.50) and steak pie (£1.95); Sunday lunch (£4.25); courteous, speedy service. A handsome old oak staircase takes you up past a grandfather clock to a heavily panelled room where on St George's Day 1642 Sir John Hotham, the town's governor, decided to lock the gate at the far end of Whitefriargate against King Charles, depriving him of the town's arsenal – a fateful start to the Civil War. There are seats in the courtyard outside; dominoes and a fruit machine. *(Recommended by J D Shaw, Steve Waters, M A and W R Proctor)*

Youngers (S&N)   Licensees Gary and Anne Sowden   Real ale   Meals and snacks (not evening, Sun)   Lunchtime restaurant tel *Hull (0482) 26363   Children in restaurant   No nearby parking   Open 11–11 Mon–Fri, 11–4.30, 6–11 Sat all year*

KIRKBURN　SE9855　Map 8

Queens Head

Village signposted from A163 SW of Great Driffield; pub car park actually on A163

By spring 1990 the new licensees here will have extended the bar into the old kitchen to give more room for diners, and built a new kitchen. There are cushioned wheel-back chairs and wall settles, and prints of country scenes in the bar, with tapestries, embroidery and hand-painted plates in the galleried restaurant done by the licensee's wife. Home-made bar food includes soup (95p), pâté (£1.75), soused herring (£1.95), ploughman's (£2 – lunchtime only), breaded haddock (£2.75), chilli con carne (£2.90), lasagne or steak and kidney pie (£2.95), chicken curry (£3.10), goulash (£3.45), a lunchtime summer carvery with home-cooked meats (£3.95), and puddings such as wine and cream torte, savarin au fruite or cheesecakes (£1); efficient service. Ruddles Best and Websters Yorkshire on handpump, house wines and several fine wines; darts, dominoes, fruit machine, piped music. The labrador puppy is called Websters. The attractive garden, at the back by the car park, has new picnic-table sets and sturdy plain white seats and tables set among fruit trees, shrubs and flower beds. *(Recommended by Roger Bellingham, M A and W R Proctor, Dave Braisted, David Gaunt, Dr and Mrs J Biggs)*

Free house　Licensees Stewart Palmer and David Evans　Meals and snacks (12–2, 7–10)
Restaurant Sun lunchtime and Tues–Sat evenings tel Driffield (0377) 89261
Children welcome　Open 11–11; 11–3, 6–11 in winter

LOW CATTON　SE7053　Map 7

Gold Cup 🏅

Village signposted with High Catton off A166 in Stamford Bridge

The fat geese in the pub's back paddock came originally from the farm next door, and a neighbour's pony keeps them company. Inside, there's a relaxed and unforced atmosphere in the three communicating rooms of the comfortable lounge, with its red plush wall seats and stools around good solid tables, flowery curtains, some decorative plates and brasswork on the walls, soft red lighting and open fires at each end. People come out from York for the bar food, which includes sandwiches (from 95p), soup (95p), salads (from £2.50), curry, fish pie or steak and mushroom pie (£3.25), scampi or lasagne (£2.95), spicy ham (£3.50), chicken Kiev (£3.95) and good steaks (from £6.95); well kept John Smiths and Tetleys on handpump and maybe a guest such as Old Mill, good coffee with real cream, decent wines; efficient, unobtrusive service. The back games-bar is comfortable too, with a well lit pool-table, darts, space game, fruit machine and well reproduced pop music. The restaurant is very popular; best to book, particularly for Sunday lunch.
(Recommended by Ray Wharram, N P Hodgson, Roger Bellingham)

Free house　Licensee Geoffrey Gore　Real ale　Snacks (not Fri or Sat evenings) and meals (11.30–1.30, 7–9.30); no food Mon　Restaurant tel Stamford Bridge (0759) 71354　Open 11.30–3, 7–11 all year; closed 25 Dec

MILLINGTON　SE8352　Map 7

Gate

Village signposted from Pocklington

Though this engaging pub is sixteenth century, the age of the yew trees used in furnishing one of the rooms has been put at 1500 years. There are modern simple

---

Pubs shown as closing at 11 do so in the summer, but may close earlier – normally 10.30 – in winter unless we specify 'all year'. Often, country pubs don't open as early as we say at quiet times of the year.

furnishings as well as an antique settle with wings and a high back to keep the draught out, a big stone fireplace, and black beams supporting the ochre planks of the ceiling, with plates on the main beam over an opening through to another room (which has a set of antlers above its log fire). Cheap and well kept Bass and Tetleys on handpump; good value food such as sandwiches, home-made meat or rabbit pies, maybe pheasant, hare or wild duck in season, gammon (£3.50) and steaks (from £5); if you ring them the day before, they'll do a full dinner. Darts, pool and trivia in a back room; piped music. The pub is set in excellent walking country in the Wolds, within easy reach of remarkable views of East Riding. *(Recommended by Graeme Smalley, David Gaunt)*

Free house   Licensee Alan Moore   Real ale   Meals and snacks (not Thurs)   Restaurant under construction   Children in eating area of bar   Open 12–2.30, 6.30–12 all year Bedrooms tel Pocklington (0759) 302045; £8/£16

SKIDBY   TA0133 Map 8

Half Moon ✪
Main Street; off A164

One well travelled reader feels the Yorkshire puddings here are the largest and best he's ever eaten. The seemingly endless range is so popular that they're said to get through 60,000 eggs and 7,000 pounds of flour a year; they come in a variety of fillings (from £1.70 for onion and gravy, £2.25 with vegetarian gravy, £3.50 for roast beef); other food, efficiently served, includes soup (95p), four-ounce burgers (from £1.65), ploughman's (£2.20), chilli con carne (£2.80) and steak and kidney pie (£2.95); they serve sandwiches all afternoon; friendly staff. There's a rambling series of little bars and saloons: an old-fashioned partly panelled front tap-room has a tiled floor, long cushioned wall benches, old elm tables, a little high shelf of foreign beer bottles and miniatures, and a coal fire. The more spacious communicating back rooms have a lighter and airier atmosphere, and an unusually big clock. Dominoes, cribbage, fruit machine, piped music; possibly John Smiths on handpump. The landscaped garden area beside the car park has a children's play area with a suspended net maze, and there are plans for a family-room, terrace and barbecue area. A black and white windmill is nearby. *(Recommended by Philip Riding, PLC; more reports please)*

John Smiths (Courage)   Licensee Peter Madeley   Meals and snacks (12–2, 7–11, but see text)   Children welcome   Open 11–11

SOUTH DALTON   SE9645 Map 8

Pipe & Glass
Village signposted off B1248 NW of Beverley

This tiled white pub has had a pleasantly old-fashioned feel in its two bow-windowed bars, with beams, some high-backed settles and leather seats, old prints and log fires, and the entrance done up as a replica of a stage-coach door. In early 1989 there was a bad fire which affected the bars as well as the kitchen; as we went to press the pub was still being rebuilt in a way designed to reproduce its former character as closely as possible (and they are adding a conservatory). By the time this edition is published, the pub should have re-opened – back in business for the good value food which has made it so popular: sandwiches, Yorkshire pudding and gravy, nettle and lime soup, a substantial ploughman's with delicious oatmeal rolls, chicken piri piri (£3), duck and apricot pie or spaghetti marinara (£4), and char-grilled rump steak (£5). Besides the restaurant overlooking the lawn, the old separate stableblock has been converted into a weekend winter carvery bar. Ruddles County and Websters Choice on handpump; shove-ha'penny, table skittles, cribbage, fruit machine, piped music. In summer the hanging baskets are charming, and there are tables on a quiet lawn by the edge of Dalton Park, with a children's play area, flower borders, a very fine yew tree, ginger cats and maybe kittens. The village itself is best found by aiming for the unusually tall and elegant spire of the church, visible for miles around. *(Recommended by J C Proud, PLC, T Nott)*

Free house   Licensee Malcolm Crease   Real ale   Meals and snacks (not Sun evening) Restaurant (not Sun evening) tel Dalton Holme (0430) 810246   Children welcome Open 11.30–2.30, 7–11 all year

STAMFORD BRIDGE   SE7155 Map 7
Three Cups

A166, W end of town; as it's actually over the Derwent Bridge it is just inside the N Yorks border

Originally a farmhouse, this busy roadside pub has a spacious bar area with oak beams, extensive panelling, lots of bare ochre brick walls (including an arched stripped partition dividing the two rooms), and green banquettes, library chairs, stools and low armchairs around dark rustic tables. In the pleasant alcove at one end there are shelves of books, sepia photographs and an open fire with a hand-turned bellows machine. There's a rare annotated *Vanity Fair* cartoon of the nobs at Newmarket in 1885. Popular bar food includes a carvery (Tuesday to Sunday, £3.95) as well as soup (95p), filled rolls (£1.35), burgers (from £2.20), ploughman's (from £2.50), home-made lasagne, daily curry or vegetarian dish (£2.95), gammon with egg or pineapple (£3.95), steaks (from £5.95), and puddings (£1.35); children's meals (from £1.50). Well kept Bass and Stones on handpump. Rustic tables run along the front terrace, with more tables on the back lawn, swings and a big shoe house. *(Recommended by J C Proud, Ray Wharram, R C Watkins, S V Bishop, M A and W R Proctor)*

Bass   Licensees Ian and Gill McEnaney   Real ale   Meals and snacks (12–2, 6.30–10; not Sun)   Restaurant   Children in eating area of bar   Open 11–2.30, 6–11 all year; opens 6.30 in winter   Bedrooms tel Stamford Bridge (0759) 71396; /£25S

SUTTON UPON DERWENT   SE7047 Map 7
St Vincent Arms

B1228 SE of York

This cosy old pub is named after the admiral who was given the village and lands at the nation's bequest for his successful commands, and for coping with Nelson's infatuation with Lady Hamilton. The parlour-like, panelled front bar has traditional high-backed settles, a cushioned bow window seat, Windsor chairs, a massive old wireless set, quite a lot of brass and copper, a shelf of plates just under the high ceiling, and a coal fire. Another lounge and separate dining-room opens off here, and what was the games-room is now a new restaurant. Bar food includes sandwiches (from £1), daily home-made soups (£1.10), bacon and prawn pâté (£1.75), ploughman's (from £2.95), salads (from £3.25), steak and kidney pie (£4.50) and fillet steak with oyster or pepper sauce (£9.50). It's best to book a table if you want a full meal, especially at weekends; the friendly service makes up for the shortage of space. Well kept Courage Directors on handpump, and regularly changing guest ales such as John Smiths Magnet and Timothy Taylors Landlord; farm ciders and several malt whiskies. The wide choice of wines by the bottle is unusual for the area; piped music. The handsome and large garden has tables and seats. *(Recommended by T Nott, Graeme Smalley, Ray Wharram, N P Hodgson, Roger Bellingham)*

Free house   Licensees Steven and Rosemary Richards   Real ale   Meals and snacks (12–2, 7–10)   Restaurant tel Elvington (090 485) 349   Children welcome   Open 11–3, 6.30–11 all year; 11–11 Sat in summer

Lucky Dip

Besides the fully inspected pubs, you might like to try these Lucky Dips
recommended to us and described by readers (if you do, please send us reports):

Althorpe [SE8309], *Dolphin*: Friendly,
efficient staff and spacious, clean restaurant
with good cooking by landlord; good wines
(Peter H Clark)

Arnold [off A165 Hull–Bridlington;
TA1041], *Bay Horse*: Unspoilt, genuine
village local with single simple room;
friendly service, real fire in stone fireplace;
well kept Camerons Strongarm and maybe
Everards Old Original on handpump; basic
lavatories, animals tethered outside *(Lee
Goulding)*

☆ **Barnetby Le Wold** [close to M180 junction
8, opp rly stn; SE0509], *Station*: Comfortable
and congenial lounge with charcoal drawings
of steam locomotives and old railway train
prints; particularly well kept Wards
including Dark Mild on handpump;
interesting good value bar food lunchtime
and evening *(John Baker, D W Stokes)*

☆ **Beverley** [TA0340], *Beverley Arms*:
Comfortable and well kept THF hotel with
spacious and traditional oak-panelled bar,
well kept real ales, choice of several places to
eat including covered former coachyard, now
very much an internal part of the building
with an impressive bank of former kitchen
ranges; good bedrooms *(LYM)*
Beverley [15 Butcher Row (main pedestrian
st)], *Angel*: Bustling town-centre pub
popular with shoppers; hot and cold bar
food, sheltered back terrace with small
fountain *(Neil and Elspeth Fearn)*; [Hull
Bridge; A1035 towards Leven] *Crown &
Anchor*: Pleasant pub by River Hull with
outside tables and good, simple bar food –
worth knowing for the area *(Roger
Bellingham)*; [Saturday Mkt] *Kings Head*:
Large L-shaped bar in listed building,
opening into two smaller dining-rooms;
good choice of hot and cold food from buffet
display, fine puddings trolley, generous
helpings; Mansfield Riding and Marksman
on handpump; bedrooms *(G T Rhys)*;
[Saturday Mkt] *Push*: Old-fashioned (bare
boards), cosy and warm, with well kept
Stones and hot and cold bar food; lively in
the evening, with good music and friendly
chatter *(T T Kelly)*; [Flemingate] *Sun*: Next to
the minster, this cosy old pub is enjoying a
new lease of life under new licensees; well
kept Camerons real ales and outstanding
value bar food including bargain Sun lunch
(Michael Swallow)

☆ **Bishop Burton** [A1079 Beverley–York;
SE9939], *Altisidora*: Good value
straightforward food including big well filled
sandwiches, in low-beamed modernised
lounge with comfortable alcoves, games in
saloon bar, seats out by neatly kept flower
beds looking over to ducks on pretty

pond in lovely village green *(M A and W R
Proctor, Dr and Mrs S G Donald, G C and
M D Dickinson, T Nott, Jon Wainwright,
LYM)*

☆ **Brandesburton** [TA1247], *Black Swan*:
Spacious and attractively refurbished pub
with good choice of beers including
Batemans and Mansfield, popular at
lunchtime for bar food – good ordering
system and efficient staff *(Nick Dowson,
Alison Hayward, T Nott)*
Brantingham [southern edge; SE9429],
Triton: Spacious and comfortable
modernised pub with well kept Watneys-
related real ales, popular buffet in roomy and
airy sun lounge, restaurant, games-bar,
sheltered garden with children's play area;
near wooded dale *(BB)*

☆ **Bridlington** [184 Kingsgate (A165, just
outside); TA1867], *Broadacres*: Large,
popular Chef & Brewer pub with Websters
Yorkshire on handpump, good log fires, well
planned layout including snack bar, separate
restaurant and children's room; good food
including superb local haddock, excellent
service *(Roger Bellingham, John Gould)*
Bridlington [2 Flamborough Rd],
Beaconsfield Arms: Well laid out Bass pub
with comfortable lounge, airy lively public
bar, good service, bar food; near promenade
(LYM)
Burton Agnes [TA1063], *Blue Bell*: Pleasant
service, decent food, real ale *(Nick Dowson,
Alison Hayward, T Nott)*
Burton Fleming [TA0872], *Burton Arms*:
Solidly built, traditional pub in unspoilt
Wolds village; two cosy and cheerful bars
with down-to-earth friendliness – one mainly
for young people with darts, music and
conversational hubbub, the other more
sedate with a spacious, inglenooky
restaurant leading off *(G T Rhys)*
Cottingham [Parkway; TA0633], *Black
Prince*: Notable sandwiches and other food
including self-service salad trolley and good
evening steaks; reasonable wine list, pleasant
environment *(SY, T T Kelly)*; *Tiger*: Recently
refurbished Bass pub with well kept beer on
handpump and good reasonably priced food
including notable sandwiches *(Mr and Mrs
Harry McCann)*
Ellerker [SE9229], *Black Horse*: Cottagey
and cosy, low beams, candles, thick stone
walls, velvet curtains, well kept real ales, bar
food; has been good, but we've had no news
this last year *(LYM)*
Etton [3½ miles N of Beverley, off B1248;
SE9843], *Light Dragoon*: Wide range of bar
food including generous sandwiches, well
kept Youngers real ales; two roomy and
pleasantly renovated bars with inglenook

fireplace, garden with children's play area *(T Nott, LYM)*

☆ **Flamborough** [junction B1255/B1229; TA2270], *Royal Dog & Duck*: Warm and welcoming bar with cosy, homely atmosphere in snug back bar and several other rambling rooms; good food in efficient and popular restaurant, including well cooked fresh local fish; keg beers; children warmly welcomed, lots of amusements for them in courtyard; bedrooms *(Neil and Elspeth Fearn, Miss A Tress, G Smith)*

Great Driffield [TA0258], *Bell*: Popular for good value lunchtime food; good beer and service *(David Gaunt)*

Great Hatfield [TA1843], *Woggarth*: Cosy, friendly free house, well kept Camerons and Tetleys, comfortably furnished lounge, bar food and restaurant; children's room *(T T Kelly)*

☆ **Grimsby** [Brighowgate; TA2609], *County*: Good value popular bar with well kept Youngers and terrific breakfasts throughout the morning; bedrooms comfortable and reasonably priced *(Stephen Merson)*

☆ **Hedon** [TA1928], *Shakespeare*: Excellent village local, small L-shaped bar with beams covered by over 3000 beer-mats, old framed brewery advertisements, cosy atmosphere, especially by real fire; friendly service, at least five real ales including Darleys, Vaux Samson and Wards, juke box; gets very busy; bedrooms *(Lee Goulding)*

☆ **Hull** [150 High St (in Old Town to S of centre, quite near Olde White Harte; TA0928], *Olde Black Boy*: Historic pub associated with naval press gangs and slavers; little black-panelled low-ceilinged front smoke-room, lofty eighteenth-century back vaults bar (with juke box strong on golden oldies, fruit machine, TV); well kept Tetleys Mild and Bitter, bar food, friendly staff *(John Gould, BB)*

☆ **Hull** [alley off Lowgate; look out for the huge blue bell overhanging the pavement], *Olde Blue Bell*: Well kept Sam Smiths OB on handpump and good value simple lunchtime food including traditional Sun lunch, in old pub refurbished in traditional style, with three snug rooms; near market *(J D Shaw, BB)*

Hull [Castle St], *Marina Post House*: Comfortable modern THF hotel with well kept ale, good food including bar lunches, workout centre, indoor swimming-pool; fine position overlooking marina; bedrooms good though not cheap *(John Gould)*; [Princes Dock Rd] *Quayside*: John Smiths on handpump, lunchtime and early evening bar food *(John Gould)*

Langtoft [just off B1249, about a mile N of village – OS Sheet 101 reference 007680; TA0167], *Old Mill*: Quiet, remote pub, friendly service, John Smiths beer, well worth knowing for rather enterprising bar food; restaurant *(Dave Braisted)*

☆ **Market Weighton** [SE8742], *Londesborough Arms*: Relatively cheap bar food in elegant high-ceilinged Regency lounge with Cecil Aldin prints, flowers on tables, well kept real ales, friendly service, piped music – useful for area; bedrooms *(LYM)*

☆ **North Dalton** [SE9352], *Star*: Up-market village pub overlooking large pond, enthusiastically run by young licensees; well kept Tetleys on handpump, good food in bar and restaurant including excellent range of fixed-price meals; comfortable bedrooms *(J C Proud, PLC)*

☆ **North Newbald** [SE9136], *Tiger*: Attractively refurbished village pub on large green surrounded by rolling hills; generous helpings of excellent value bar food, upstairs restaurant *(Mrs P J Pearce, LYM)*

☆ **Pocklington** [SE8049], *Feathers*: Comfortable and popular open-plan lounge, good solid bar food, Youngers real ales, friendly service, children welcome; comfortable motel-style bedrooms *(Calvert C Bristol, LYM)*

Redbourne [Main St; SK9799], *Red Lion*: Well kept, with excellent atmosphere and good food; bedrooms *(B D Yates)*

Sewerby [High St; TA2069], *Ship*: Large, welcoming pub overlooking North Sea, real ale on handpump, games-room, good bar food and service, large garden; children's play area *(John Gould)*

☆ **Sledmere** [junction B1252/B1253, NW of Gt Driffield; SE9365], *Triton*: Small, traditional lounge with stately high-backed settles and a good log fire when it's really cold; well kept Youngers Scotch, simple but generously served bar food from sandwiches and soup to steaks, friendly licensees; games in public bar, piped music; eighteenth-century, in attractive spot; has been open all day; children welcome; bedrooms good value, with big breakfasts *(M A and W R Proctor, TRA, MA, LYM – more reports please)*

Snaithe [SE6422], *Downe Arms*: Good Sun summer barbecues in attractive courtyard *(PJP)*

South Cave [SE9231], *Fox & Coney*: Popular old white pub in large village with single traditional bar, old settles, treadle sewing-machine tables, lots of hunting bric-à-brac; Youngers real ale, bar food, good walks nearby including Wolds Way *(Lee Goulding)*

Sproatley [B1238; TA1934], *Blue Bell*: Welcoming village local, cosy lounge bar, John Smiths on handpump, friendly service, food in separate dining-room *(Lee Goulding)*

Stamford Bridge [SE7155], *Swordsman*: Well kept real ales in riverside pub with gruesome inn-sign and bar with half the tables laid for lunch *(G T Rhys)*

Ulceby [TA1014], *Brocklesby Ox*: Good atmosphere in old pub with well kept beer and good food including excellent fish and chips *(David Gaunt)*

☆ **Walkington** [B1230; SE9937], *Ferguson Fawsitt Arms*: Attractive mock-Tudor bars with wide choice of home-cooked hot dishes from buffet, including unusual puddings, in airy flagstone-floored food bar, tables on outside terrace, games bar with pool-table *(LYM)*

☆ **Welton** [village signposted from A63 just E of Hull outskirts; SE9627], *Green Dragon*: Spacious and comfortably refurbished, with good range of reasonably priced bar food including children's dishes, evening restaurant; notable as the real-life scene of the arrest of Dick Turpin *(T Nott, LYM)*

Isle of Wight

The island crowds into its relatively small area a surprising number of good pubs; and the fact that it has a value-conscious local brewery – Burts – has kept prices throughout the island's pubs for both drinks and food lower than they might otherwise have been, given transport costs from the mainland. Indeed, instead of simply putting up prices here, mainland brewers tend to pull out altogether when the local competition makes margins tighter than they are used to on the mainland. Whitbreads have recently closed two pubs here that have been popular with readers: the Jolly Brewer at Chale Green and the Chequers at Rookley. Fresh fish is often particularly worth looking out for, as for example in the New Inn at Shalfleet (a new landlord here, but he still gets some fish direct from the previous licensee's own trawler). Another good pub for food is the White Lion at Arreton. Perhaps the most lively place is the Wight Mouse Bar of the Clarendon Hotel in Chale; the best setting is that of the Fisherman's Cottage on the beach at Shanklin. Several particularly promising pubs among the Lucky Dip entries at the end of the chapter are the Bonchurch Inn at Bonchurch, Hare & Hounds at Downend, Red Lion at Freshwater, Chine at Shanklin and Crown at Shorwell.

ARRETON SZ5486 Map 2
White Lion
A3056 Newport–Sandown

The garden of this attractive old white house has a family Cabin Bar – full of old farm tools – and you can also sit out in front by the tubs of flowers. Inside, the communicating rooms of the spacious and relaxed lounge bar have beams or partly panelled walls decorated with guns, brass and horse-harness, and cushioned Windsor chairs on the brown carpet. The smaller, plainer public bar has dominoes and winter darts. Good, generous helpings of home-made bar food includes English cheeses and pâté, sandwiches, quiches, pies, curries, pasta and chilli con carne. Whitbreads Strong Country and Flowers Original tapped from casks behind the bar with an interesting cask-levelling device; pleasant staff, piped music. The pub is close to Elizabethan Arreton Manor (which houses the National Wireless Museum), the twelfth-century village church and the craft village. *(Recommended by Mr and Mrs P C Clark, Roger Broadie, Nick Dowson, Philip King; more reports please)*
Whitbreads   Licensees David and Maureen James   Real ale   Meals and snacks (12–2.45, 7–10.30)   Children in family-room and eating area of bar   Open 11–3.30, 6–11 all year; opens 7 in winter

CHALE SZ4877 Map 2
Clarendon/Wight Mouse ★
In village, on B3399, but now has access road directly off A3055

Over the last few years, this establishment has evolved into an unusual combination of three separate elements: the small hotel, comfortable and attractively furnished; a collection of family areas including a popular dining section that's open all afternoon; and – for most readers – the key ingredient – the Wight Mouse bar. This perky place, shaped a bit like a dumb-bell with the narrow bar-counter part joining two more spacious areas, has a huge collection of musical instruments hanging from the ceiling, and is full of life. Its special virtues include a fine collection of around 150 malts (and dozens of other whiskies), backed up by uncommon brandies, madeiras and country wines; live music every night of the week, pitched at a volume that still lets you chat companionably; good value home-cooked food. Well kept Burts VPA, Gales HSB, Marstons Pedigree and Whitbreads Strong Country on handpump; and above all a good relaxed atmosphere. Generous helpings of locally produced food includes sandwiches (from £1.10, fresh crab £2, toasties 20p extra), home-made soup (£1.20), ploughman's (from £1.75), burgers (from £2.65), ham and eggs (£2.80), salads (from £2.85), home-made pizzas (from £3.60), scampi (£3.65), wiener schnitzel (£3.95), fisherman's platter (£4.75), mixed grill (£5.45) and steaks (from £6.90); puddings such as home-made meringue nests filled with fruit, cream, ice-cream and nuts (£1.30). Darts at one end, dominoes, fruit machine, piped music; an adjoining games/family-room has pool, shove-ha'penny, space game, juke box, and, outside, pétanque. Picnic-table sets on a side lawn, many more on the big back lawn looking over the fields to the sea and, for children, swings, slide, seesaw, rabbits and chickens. A road now gives access from the main coast road. They run a pick-you-up and drop-you-home minibus service for four or more people (£2 per person). *(Recommended by Mr and Mrs P C Clark, Richard and Dilys Smith, M W Barratt, Alan Skull, Paul Sweetman, John Farmer, A Seatman, Roger Broadie, Nick Dowson, Alison Hayward)*

Free house   Licensees John and Jean Bradshaw   Real ale   Meals and snacks (all day – not 3–7 Sun)   Restaurant   Children in eating areas and three family-rooms   Live music every night   Open 11am–midnight   Bedrooms tel Niton (0983) 730431; £19(£21B)/£38(£42B)

nr COWES (EAST)   SZ5095 Map 2
Folly

Folly Lane – which is signposted off A3021 just S of Whippingham

Very much a yachtsman's pub, this comfortable place has a VHF radio-telephone, a wind speed indicator, a barometer and a chronometer, mail collection boxes, and even showers and a launderette. Big windows look out over the boats, as do picnic-table sets on the water's-edge terrace. There are old wood timbered walls and ceilings, venerable wooden chairs and kitchen tables, shelves of old books and plates, railway bric-à-brac and farm tools, old pictures and brass lights. Bar food includes sandwiches, cottage, fisherman's or home-made steak and kidney pies, burger or pint of prawns (all £3); Whitbreads Strong Country on handpump; darts, space game and piped music. There's a good children's play-room, and a new landscaped garden. *(Recommended by Alison Hayward; more reports please)*

Whitbreads   Licensee Peter Handtschoewercker   Real ale   Meals and snacks   Restaurant   tel Isle of Wight (0983) 297171   Children in family-room   Live entertainment Sun   Open 11–3, 6–11 all year

SHALFLEET   SZ4189 Map 2
New Inn ★ ✿

A3054 Newport–Yarmouth

Though this busy, cheerful dining-pub has new licensees, it still specialises in fresh fish – which they buy from the previous landlord who owns his own small trawler and lobster boat. Depending on what's been caught, this might include prawns (£1.55 a half-pint), prawn curry (£3.95), poacher's pie (£4.95), and Dover sole, cod, plaice, bass and fresh crab and lobster when available; in winter there are live mussels and oysters. The food's not all fish, of course, and as well as a daily changing blackboard menu there's soup (£1.10), sandwiches to order (from 80p, crab £1.95), five different ploughman's (from £2.10), lasagne (£3.25), red-hot chilli con carne (£3.50), crab salad (from £4.50), and eight-ounce sirloin steak (from

£6.60). The partly panelled public bar has a boarded ceiling, scrubbed deal tables on the flagstones, a cushioned built-in settle and Windsor chairs, and on cold days a roaring log fire in the big stone hearth, which has guns and an ale-yard hanging above it. The beamed lounge bar has stone walls, and Windsor chairs and wall banquettes around small tables. Well kept Flowers Original, Fremlins, Whitbreads Pompey Royal, and guests such as Gales HSB and Marstons Pedigree tapped from the cask; efficient staff. There are rustic tables outside by the road, and a garden. *(Recommended by H G and C J McCafferty, B S Bourne, R M Sparkes, Dr and Mrs R E S Tanner, Keith Houlgate, D Stephenson, Nick Dowson, Alison Hayward, Andy Tye, Sue Hill, Philip King)*

Whitbreads   Licensee Chris Vanson   Real ale   Meals (12–6, 7–10) and snacks (12–6) Restaurant tel Calbourne (098 378) 314   Children in restaurant   Open 11–11; may well close afternoons in winter

SHANKLIN   SZ5881 Map 2

Fisherman's Cottage

At bottom of Shanklin Chine

Marvellously placed, this thatched cottage has seats on a terrace which runs straight on to the beach, an outside bar, and barbecues on summer evenings. Inside, the low-beamed rooms have stripped stone walls, flagstones and bowls of fresh flowers. Bar food includes sandwiches (from 95p), sausages (£1.60), ploughman's (from £1.80), half-pint of prawns (summer only, £2.50), scampi (£2.65), crab salad (summer only, £4.25) and fish salad (summer only, £5.95). Coffee is served from 10.30; country wines. Darts, cribbage, dominoes and fruit machine. Though you can drive to the pub, there's a path zigzagging down the picturesquely steep and sinuous Chine. *(Recommended by Nick Dowson; more reports please)*

Free house   Licensees Mrs A P P Springman and Duncan McDonald   Lunchtime meals and snacks   Children in eating area   Open 11–3, 7–11 all year

YARMOUTH   SZ3589 Map 2

Bugle 🏠

St James' Square

The comfortable and relaxed Galleon Bar in this well kept seventeenth-century hotel has a serving-counter that looks like the stern of a galleon; also, captain's chairs, black plank walls and ceiling with a few burgees hung below it, pictures of ship and marine designs and a giant photograph of the harbour making up an entire side wall. Good home-made bar food includes sandwiches (from £1.40, open sandwiches from £1.65), filled baked potatoes (from £1.45), ploughman's (from £1.85), half-pint of prawns (£2.10), grilled sardines (£3.50), home-made lasagne (£3.95), grilled lamb or pork cutlet (£4) and crab or lobster salad (when available); children's meals (£1.50). Flowers Original and Marstons Pedigree on handpump; darts, pool, and snooker in winter. The sizeable garden (popular with families) has barbecued Italian-style whole roast pig, rolled in herbs, garlic and wine. The hotel – with its very fine street façade – is close to the Tudor castle, the pier, and *Good Walks Guide* Walk 40. *(Recommended by H G and C J McCafferty, Nick Dowson, Alison Hayward; more reports please)*

Whitbreads   Licensees R Perpetuini and Christopher Troup   Real ale   Meals and snacks (12–2.30, 7–9.30)   Restaurant   Children in own room   Singing duo Weds evenings and maybe Sat evenings   Open 10.30–3, 6–11 all year   Bedrooms tel Isle of Wight (0983) 760272; £20(£25B)/£40(£42B)

Lucky Dip

Besides the fully inspected pubs, you might like to try these Lucky Dips recommended to us and described by readers (if you do, please send us reports):

Bembridge [Forelands; off Howgate Rd – look for sign; SZ6487], *Crab & Lobster*: Bar food including good sandwiches and seafood, well kept Flowers Original and Whitbreads Strong Country from handpump; on cliffs by Foreland coastguard station *(Derek Stephenson)*

Bonchurch [Bonchurch Shute; from A3055 E of Ventnor turn down to Old Bonchurch opp Leconfield H; SZ5778], *Bonchurch Inn*: High-ceilinged public bar partly cut into the rocks of the Shute with furnishings that somehow conjure up image of shipwreck salvage, smaller saloon, usual bar food with several good Italian dishes too (their minestrone and zabaglione are particularly popular), Whitbreads Strong Country tapped from the cask, friendly and attentive licensees, games including pool, provision for children, piano Fri–Sat; cafeteria in splendidly arched converted stable across courtyard – which has summer tables; bedrooms *(D J Perry, HNJ, PEJ, LYM)*

Carisbrooke [B3401 1½ miles W; SZ4888], *Blacksmiths Arms*: Isolated, with good views from small garden, cosy front bar with a couple of leatherette sofas and heap of magazines, Flowers on handpump, children's room, pool-table in plain back bar *(Nick Dowson, Alison Hayward)*; [Clatterford] *Chute*: Real ales including Bass and Burts, juke box, bar food, tables outside *(Anon)*

☆ **Cowes** [25 High St; SZ4896], *Pier View*: Victorian pub with efficient pleasant service, fresh flowers on tables, unobtrusive piped music, prints of sailing-ships, plates and keys on the walls; well kept Flowers and Marstons Pedigree, good choice of house wines, original bar food such as fresh prawns with Greek salad or duck with morello cherry sauce *(Dr J R Hamilton)*

☆ **Downend** [B3056, at crossroads; SZ5387], *Hare & Hounds*: Excellent food and service in charming thatched Burts pub with interesting local bar and more orthodox modern extension behind *(Tony Bland, Nick Dowson, Alison Hayward)*

Fishbourne [Fishbourne Rd (from Portsmouth car ferry turn left into no through road); SZ5592], *Fishbourne*: Whitbreads pub with comfortable wall settles, bar food from ploughman's to grills, friendly staff *(Michael Bechley)*

☆ **Freshwater** [Church Pl; SZ3484], *Red Lion*: Delightful atmosphere, with flagstone floors and scrubbed kitchen tables; friendly and helpful licensees, impressive bar food including good daily specials such as smoked haddock pasta with mushrooms and prawns, and wide choice of filled baked potatoes *(W E Taylor)*

Hulverstone [B3399; SZ4083], *Sun*: Pretty pub with lots of flowers outside, patchwork-cushioned seats, Whitbreads Strong Country tapped from casks behind the bar *(Nick Dowson, Alison Hayward)*

Newchurch [SZ5685], *Pointer*: Pleasant two-bar pub with good local atmosphere, well kept Flowers Original and Whitbreads Strong Country *(Nick Dowson, Alison Hayward)*

Newport [High St; SZ4988], *Castle*: Behind the beamery, lattice-effect windows, log-effect gas fire and reproduction furniture and brasses, there's a genuinely ancient pub – as the flagstones and massive end wall show; but it's popular for more modern virtues, including lunchtime food such as a big good value ploughman's and well kept Whitbreads real ales including Wethereds Winter Royal; piped music *(Nick Dowson, Alison Hayward, IP)*

☆ **Niton** [off A3055, on village rd; SZ5076], *Buddle*: Beams, flagstones and stripped deal panelling in modernised smugglers' house with sandwiches, salads and hot dishes, Flowers Original, Wethereds, Whitbreads Pompey Royal and Strong Country and a guest beer; games in adjoining Smugglers Barn cafeteria; provision for children; good views from tables in garden with scale-model fort *(Nick Dowson, Alison Hayward, LYM)*

Niton, *White Lion*: Basic unpretentious village local with oak benches outside, rather a 1960s feel inside; Flowers and Whitbreads Strong Country on handpump, reasonably priced bar food, big family-room; a welcome even for muddy walkers and dogs *(Roger Broadie, Dr and Mrs R E S Tanner, HNJ, PEJ)*

Porchfield [off A3054, 2½ miles from Shalfleet; SZ4491], *Sportsmans Rest*: Cosy pub notable for its Whitbreads Pompey Royal and large children's play area *(Nick Dowson, Alison Hayward)*

Rookley [Niton Rd; SZ5084], *Chequers*: Formerly popular out-of-the-way local, sadly closed by Whitbreads a year ago *(LYM)*

Seaview [Esplanade; B3340, just off B3330 Ryde–Brading; SZ6291], *Old Fort*: Good value buffet, fine atmosphere with drinkers and diners mingling in an almost Continental way, fresh décor with natural wood furniture; Ind Coope Burton and Gibbs Mew Wiltshire, fine sea views from inside and tables outside *(A J Skull)*; [High St] *Seaview Hotel*: Edwardian-style furnishings, friendly atmosphere, lots of naval photographs, front terrace with Solent views, courtyard back garden, good range of bar food, Burts on handpump, restaurant; bedrooms *(John and Margaret Estdale)*

☆ **Shanklin** [Chine Hill; SZ5881], *Chine*:

Timbered pub in lovely wooded setting on side of chine with good views over chine, beach and sea; three bars and large conservatory family area with magnificent fruiting grapevine; wide range of straightforward bar food all week, well kept cheap Burts ales; no juke box, fruit machines or pool-table (darts in locals' bar); children allowed away from bar *(Glenn Thorpe, Nick Dowson, Alison Hayward)*

☆ **Shanklin** [High St, Old Town (A3055 towards Ventnor)], *Crab*: Picturesque thatched pub with low-beamed rambling bar, step up to part like inside of a sailing-ship, lunchtime sandwiches and hot dishes, well kept Flowers Original and Whitbreads Strong Country on handpump, games and children's room; has been open all day in summer, very popular with tourists *(W E Taylor, LYM)*

☆ **Shorwell** [SZ4582], *Crown*: Comfortable and attractively furnished old pub with pleasant atmosphere, unspoilt décor, wooden settles and tables, real fire, friendly staff, no piped music; consistently good food at reasonable prices including vegetarian dishes, well kept Flowers and Whitbreads Strong Country tapped from the cask, beautifully kept garden with trout stream and willow trees *(Lyn Jolliffe, Andrew Grant, HNJ, PEJ)*

Ventnor [Market St; SZ5677], *Hole in the Wall*: Basic two-bar local with good value simple food and one of the cheapest pints in Britain – Burts VPA, under top pressure; games-bar, tables in sheltered yard; on GWG42; children in Barn Bar family-room

(LYM); [Pier St] *Rose & Crown*: Old charming and spacious place with good food and an attractive outside area *(Miss E Waller)*

Whitwell [SZ5277], *White Horse*: Recently redecorated in country style, good busy atmosphere, friendly efficient staff, well kept Flowers Original and Whitbreads Strong Country, darts; popular in the evening with people from the nearby YHA *(Nick Dowson, Alison Hayward)*

Wootton [A3054; SZ5492], *Cedar*: Surrounded by cedar trees in garden; large public bar with darts and good-sized lounge bar with gas fireplace used for spit-roasting; Whitbreads Strong Country, with plans for a second real ale; good food; handy for Isle of Wight Steam Railway; children's room *(Keith Widdowson)*

Wootton Bridge [100 yds past Fishbourne Ferry; SZ5492], *Fishbourne*: Well cooked and presented bar food including ploughman's, delicious garlic mussels, grills, fish, salads and puddings; reasonable prices, friendly staff *(Roy and Margaret Johnston)*; *Sloop*: Simply decorated main bar done out boat-style with panelling, port-holes and curved ceiling, games-room with darts and billiards, plainer dining-room overlooking river; Flowers Original on handpump, good lunchtime bar food, children's room; riverside garden with galleon for children to climb on *(Roger Broadie)*

Wroxall [SZ5579], *Star*: Nice clean pub with reasonably priced Burts VPA, Mild and 4X, some seats outside; nr start GWG42 *(Nick Dowson, Alison Hayward)*

Kent

A lot of pubs here do fine food; good value fresh fish is a particular high-point of the area, as at the Brown Trout in Lamberhurst (a new main entry), the old-fashioned Black Pig at Staple, La Galoche in Tunbridge Wells (another new main entry; its cheeses are an outstanding draw, and it usually has over fifteen wines by the glass), Sankeys at the Gate there (useful changes here this last year), and Pearsons crab and oyster house in Whitstable (though there's a new licensee here, he did in fact manage it under the former regime). Other places particularly notable for food include the little King William IV in Benenden, the delightfully furnished George at Newnham, the Duck at Pett Bottom (can be quite a squeeze getting in), and the Ringlestone Inn at Ringlestone (speciality pies; the enthusiastic landlord keeps a good range of real ales). And a great many of the main entries that haven't quite made the grade of our new hard-to-get food award serve food that's a clear cut above average. The food at the Three Chimneys near Biddenden, for instance, which taken all round is normally the county's most enjoyable pub, can be delicious; and it looks as though the popular new licensees of the Flying Horse at Boughton Aluph are cantering it towards an award. In a county with so many pubs of real character, it's hard to pick out the classics, but any shortlist would have to include the peppy marshside Gate Inn at Boyden Gate, the unaffectedly 1940s-ish Mounted Rifleman in the orchards at Luddenham, the Shipwrights Arms down its seaside track at Oare, and the very popular (some would say too popular) Bell near Smarden with its fine choice of drinks. Other pubs on a

The Little Gem, Aylesford

decided up at the moment include the Wheatsheaf at Bough Beech, the friendly and simple Dove at Dargate (it has a 12.30 supper licence), the Crown at Groombridge (decent food in a lovely setting), the cosy and friendly Artichoke near Hadlow, the welcoming Dering Arms at Pluckley (a good place to stay at), and the very rural Tiger at Stowting. Among the Lucky Dip entries at the end of the chapter, particularly appealing prospects include the Walnut Tree at Aldington, Little Brown Jug at Chiddingstone Causeway, Ship at Conyer Quay, Sun in Faversham, Star & Eagle in Goudhurst, Gun & Spitroast at Horsmonden, Rose & Crown near Ivy Hatch, White Hart at Newenden, Bottle House near Penshurst, Black Horse in Pluckley, several pubs in or just outside Sevenoaks, both entries at Southfleet, Star at St Mary in the Marsh, Grove Ferry at Upstreet and New Flying Horse in Wye.

AYLESFORD   TQ7359 Map 3

Little Gem   [illustrated on page 407]

3 miles from M2 junction 3; A229 towards Maidstone, then first right turn, following signposts to village. Also 1¾ miles from M20 junction 6; A229 towards Maidstone, then follow Aylesford signpost; 19 High Street

A fine range of real ales in this ancient little pub – on handpump or tapped from the cask – includes Bass, Everards Old Original, Fullers London Pride, Greene King Abbot, Marstons Owd Rodger, Ruddles County, Theakstons Old Peculier, Wadworths 6X, Youngers IPA and a guest ale; local cider, and several whiskies. There's a cosy, friendly atmosphere, heavy timbers, a big open fire, interesting oddments including a history of the pub, and an unusual high pitched ceiling following the line of the roof; an open staircase leads to a mezzanine floor, a bit like a minstrels' gallery, with a few tables. Bar food includes sandwiches (from £1), ploughman's (from £1.50), sweet-and-sour chicken, lasagne or curry (£2), scampi (£2.50) and seafood platter (£2.75); piped music. It claims to be Kent's smallest pub. *(Recommended by Peter Neate, Peter Griffiths)*

Free house   Licensee Mrs Sandra Brenchley   Real ale   Meals and snacks (not Sun)   Children in eating area of bar   Open 11–3, 6–11 all year

BENENDEN   TQ8033 Map 3

King William IV ✪

B2086

Furnishings in this low-ceilinged village pub are carefully unsophisticated: half a dozen plain oak and elm tables (one or two behind a standing timber divider) with flowers on them, cushioned shiny pews, kitchen chairs, and an open fire in the carefully restored inglenook fireplace. Good, popular bar food includes toasted sandwiches, soup such as carrot and coriander or leek and watercress (£1.50), excellent duck liver pâté or ploughman's (£1.95), garlicky baked potted smoked trout with horseradish or egg and onion mousse on toast (£2.25), French onion tart served with salad and new potatoes or stuffed courgettes (£2.95), good chicken tandoori (£3.50), beef Stroganoff or sweet-and-sour pork (£4.25), Arabian-style lamb kebabs or swordfish steak with mashed garlicky potatoes (£4.50), and puddings such as apricot and almond cake with Cointreau (£1.45). Well kept Shepherd Neame and Mild on handpump, and a well made Kir. The public bar – popular with locals – has sensibly placed darts, fruit machine and juke box. You can sit out on the small but sheltered side lawn. *(Recommended by L M Miall, Joy Heatherley, Mrs M E Lawrence, Theodore and Jean Rowland-Entwistle)*

Shepherd Neame   Licensee Nigel Douglas   Real ale   Meals and snacks (not Mon evenings or Sun)   Open 11.30–2.30, 6–11 all year

nr BIDDENDEN   TQ8538 Map 3
Three Chimneys ★ ★
A262, 1 mile W of village

Appealing to a great many visitors, this pub's *forte* is its engaging atmosphere – that of a distinctive country pub of real character. Radiating from the central bar counter is a series of small, very traditionally furnished rooms with low oak beams, old settles, some harness and sporting prints on the walls, and good log fires in winter. At its best, the popular food is very good indeed, with a choice of at least four starters, four main courses and four puddings. The starters might include leek and bacon tartlet (£1.55), devilled crab soup (£1.85) or chicken and vegetable terrine (£2.40); main courses include a choice of quiches such as Brie and broccoli (£3.30), lamb casserole with prunes and raisins (£4.55), beef in Guinness with orange sauce (£4.65), and seafood pie (£4.75); there are puddings like fruit crumbles (£1.60) or banoffi pie (£1.65), all with Jersey cream. They always have two or three vegetarian dishes, such as haricot-bean casserole (£3.50). There is a useful overspill Garden Room, popular for families, where you can book tables (Biddenden (0580) 291472); as this part isn't licensed you have to carry your drinks in from the main bar. Besides a range of well kept real ales tapped from the cask, including Adnams Best, Fremlins, Goachers (from Maidstone), Harveys Best, Hook Norton Old Hookey and Marstons Pedigree (and in winter Harveys Old Ale), they keep local cider, several malt whiskies, and their sensible wine list includes several half-bottles; service good when not too pushed. The simple public bar has darts, shove ha'penny, dominoes and cribbage. The garden is another plus: careful plantings of flowering shrubs and shrub roses shelter the neatly kept lawn in a series of gentle curves. Just down the road from Sissinghurst. *(Recommended by Mr and Mrs D M Norton, Jill and Paul Ormond, Stephen Goodchild, Mrs E M Thompson, K Leist, Dr T H M Mackenzie, Mike Dixon, C Trows, Normon Foot, G Smith, Miss A Tress, Peter Hall, Paul Sexton, Sue Harrison, Theo Schofield, S A Robbins, Nigel Paine, Steve Dark, Mr and Mrs J H Adam, Barbara Hatfield, AE, GRE, David Crafts, J S Evans, Mr and Mrs G D Amos, Greg Parston, Robin and Bev Gammon, PLC; we'd like more reports on the service, please)*

Free house   Licensees C F W Sayers and G A Sheepwash   Real ale   Meals and snacks (11.30–2, 6.30–10)   Restaurant (see above)   Children in Garden Room   Open 11–2.30, 6–11 all year; closed 25 and 26 Dec

BOUGH BEECH   TQ4846 Map 3
Wheatsheaf
B2027, S of reservoir

Until 1963, when it got its first spirits licence, this handsome old pub was just a village alehouse. The smart bar has an unusually high ceiling with lofty timbers and a massive stone fireplace. A couple of lower rooms lead off and are divided from the central part by standing timbers. Decorations include cigarette cards, swordfish spears, a stag's head, and – over the massive stone fireplace which separates off the public bar – a mysterious 1607 inscription reading *Foxy Galumpy*. Bar food includes freshly cut sandwiches (from 90p, toasties 5p extra), soup (£1), home-made pâté (£1.10), jumbo sausage (£1.45), ploughman's or omelettes (from £1.95), home-cooked ham with egg (£2.90), deep-fried seafood platter (£2.95), salads with home-cooked meats (from £3.75) and steaks (£6.80); home-made puddings such as apple crumble or walnut, apple and raisin steamed pudding (£1.35). Well kept Fremlins and Flowers on handpump; sensibly placed darts, shove-ha'penny, dominoes, cribbage and fruit machine in the public bar (which has buffalo horns over its fire, and an attractive old settle carved with wheatsheaves); piped music. An attractive sheltered lawn with flower beds, fruit trees, roses, flowering shrubs and a children's rustic cottage stretches behind the building. *(Recommended by L M Miall, Joy Heatherley, K A Read, Alasdair Knowles, Patrick Freeman)*

Fremlins (Whitbreads)   Licensee Ron Smith   Real ale   Meals (not Weds evenings or Sun) and snacks (not Weds or Sun evenings)   Children in area set aside for them by public bar   Open 11–2.30, 6–11 all year

BOUGHTON ALUPH   TR0247 Map 3

Flying Horse 🏠

Boughton Lees; just off A251 N of Ashford

Attentive, friendly new licensees have taken over this old pub, and early reports from readers have been warmly enthusiastic. The comfortable open-plan bar has fresh flowers on many tables, upholstered modern wall benches, horsebrasses, stone animals on either side of the blazing log fire, and lots of standing space. Further inside, age shows in the shiny old black panelling and the arched windows (though they are a later Gothick addition). Good bar food includes sandwiches, deep-fried mushrooms with garlic dip (£1.80), home-made quiche Lorraine (£1.95), first-class cold meat salad, fresh fish (£3.50) and home-made steak and kidney pie (£3.60). Well kept Courage Best and Directors on handpump, a good wine list that includes their own-label house wine. Shove-ha'penny, cribbage, fruit machine and piped music. You can sit outside in the rose garden or watch cricket matches on the broad green opposite (weekly in summer). *(Recommended by Gwen and Peter Andrews, D N Lane, John McGee, Jenny and Brian Seller, L M Miall, David Gaunt, S V Bishop)*

Courage   Licensees Howard and Christine Smith   Real ale   Meals and snacks   Restaurant (not Sun)   Children in functions room   Open 11–3, 6–11 all year; 11–11 Sats in summer Bedrooms tel Ashford (0233) 620914; £18(£20S)/£28(£30S)

BOUGHTON STREET   TR0458 Map 3

White Horse 🏠

¾ mile from M2 junction 7; Boughton signposted off A2; note that this is the village shown on most maps as Boughton Street, though most people actually call it just Boughton – and note that it's a very long way from the Boughton of the previous entry!

This carefully restored medieval inn has a cosy dark-beamed bar with one table made from a massive highly polished smith's bellows, a sofa, tapestry-cushioned pews, a little glass-fronted bookcase, a brass-faced longcase clock, some sporting prints, and heavy-horse harness hanging on its stripped brick and timber walls. Beyond the servery another bar has a curved high-backed antique settle by a similar bellows table, and more formal tables and chairs, merging into a communicating restaurant area (with a live seafood tank). Bar food includes home-made soup (£1.20), sandwiches (from £1.20), a good choice of omelettes (from £2), ploughman's (£2.50), burgers (from £2.75), grilled sardines (£2.95), scampi (£3.95) and steaks (from £7.50); good breakfasts. Well kept Shepherd Neame on handpump; piped music. There are tables in the garden behind. *(More reports please)*

Shepherd Neame   Licensee John Durcan   Real ale   Meals and snacks (7am–10pm) Restaurant   Children welcome (though not sitting at bar)   Live jazz every third Sun of month   Open 11–11, though opens at 7 for breakfast   Bedrooms tel Faversham (0227) 751343; £35B/£45B

BOYDEN GATE   TR2265 Map 3

Gate Inn ★

Off A299 Herne Bay–Ramsgate – follow Chislet, Upstreet signpost opposite Roman Gallery; Chislet also signposted off A28 Canterbury–Margate at Upstreet – after turning right into Chislet main street keep right on to Boyden

There's a lazy, chatty atmosphere in the bar of this delightful country local, as well as pews with flowery cushions around tables of considerable character, hop-bines hanging from the beam, attractively etched windows, bunches of flowers in summer and a good log fire in winter (the fireplace serves both quarry-tiled rooms). The walls are covered in photographs, some ancient sepia ones, others new ('MCC' here stands for Marshside Cricket Club – the pub is a focus for many other games, too). Bar food consists of sausages on sticks (32p), sandwiches and enterprising toasties (from 75p), home-made soup (90p), a plate of prawns (£1.70), a good range of well presented ploughman's (from £1.80), home-made vegetarian or meaty hot-pot (£2.85), game pie (£3.30) and puddings (95p). Well kept Shepherd Neame Bitter, Mild, Best and Old tapped from the cask; sensibly placed darts, shove-ha'penny, dominoes, cribbage, trivia and lots of children's board games. The pub is perhaps at its best on a quiet summer's evening when you can sit at picnic-table sets on the sheltered side lawn, and in front, and the air seems to vibrate with the contented quacking of a million ducks and geese (they sell duck food inside – 5p a bag). *(Recommended by L M Miall, Frank Williams; more reports please)*

Shepherd Neame   Licensee Christopher Smith   Real ale   Meals and snacks (available during all opening hours)   Children welcome (family-room)   Piano Sun evening   Open 11–2.30 (3 Sat), 6–11 all year

CHIDDINGSTONE   TQ4944 Map 3
Castle

Signposted from B2027 Tonbridge–Edenbridge

Tile hung from roof to ground, this comfortable, busy village pub has a neatly modernised bar with well made settles forming booths around the tables on its partly carpeted oak floor, cushioned sturdy wall benches, an attractive mullioned window seat in one small alcove, beams, and latticed windows. Bar food includes home-made soup (£1.85), open sandwiches (from £2.25), baked potatoes with various fillings (£2.60), ploughman's (from £2.95), beef and ale pie or very hot chilli con carne (£3.95), hot king prawns with garlic butter (£4.50) and salads (from £5.95). Well kept King & Barnes Bitter and Festive, and Shepherd Neame Old on handpump, with Larkins Porter in winter; over 140 wines (including house wines) by the bottle, and local cider. The public bar has darts, shove-ha'penny, dominoes and cribbage. The garden behind is pretty, with a small pool and fountain set in a rockery, and tables on a back brick terrace and the neat lawn, surrounded by shrubs. The pub, like the rest of this beautiful village, is owned by the National Trust. *(Recommended by L D Glazer, Heather Martin, Mr and Mrs R C Abbott, Nick Dowson, Alison Hayward, Alasdair Knowles, Gethin Lewis, Robin and Bev Gammon, Jane Palmer, Steve Dark)*

Free house   Licensee Nigel Lucas   Real ale   Meals and snacks (11–2.30, 7–10.30) Restaurant tel Penshurst (0892) 870247   Children in eating area of bar   Open 11–3, 6–11 all year

CHILHAM   TR0753 Map 3
Woolpack 🏚

Best approached from signposted village road at junction A28/A252, which leads straight to inn

A cavernous fireplace with a big log fire dominates the busy, friendly bar of this comfortably renovated old timber pub. There are little brocaded armchairs, a sofa, pews and wall seats, lots of copper urns hanging from a high beam, and a row of jugs, flagons and kegs. Bar food includes sandwiches (from £1, the prawn is tasty), ploughman's (£2.25), hot food such as beef bourguignonne, steak and kidney pie or Woolpack platter (from £2.50), and an attractive separate carvery. Well kept Shepherd Neame Bitter and Best on handpump; friendly service; cribbage, unobtrusive piped music. The bedrooms are in an attractively converted former stable building behind, and the beautiful medieval square which has made the village famous is just up the lane. *(Recommended by Paul and Margaret Baker, Graham and Glenis Watkins, David Crafts, Col G D Stafford)*

Shepherd Neame   Licensee John Durcan   Real ale   Meals and snacks   Restaurant Children in eating area of bar   Open 11–11 all year   Bedrooms tel Canterbury (0227) 730208; £30(£40B)/£35(£45B)

CHIPSTEAD   TQ4956 Map 3
George & Dragon

1¼ miles from M25 junction 5: A21 S, then A25 towards Sevenoaks, then first left; 39 High Street

Upright timbers in the open-plan bar here divide it into smaller, cosier areas, two of which have open fires. The atmosphere is relaxed and friendly, and the furnishings, though modern, do tone in with the heavy black beams (some of them nicely carved), and the oak tables and Windsor chairs on the geometric carpet. Bar food (prices haven't changed since last year, though they don't include service charge) such as home-made soup (70p), sandwiches (from 75p, toasties 10p extra), pâté (£1.30), ploughman's (from £1.70), quiche (£1.40), salads (from £2.40), the 'special' (grilled bacon, tomato and cheese on toast, sausage and chips, £2.50), seafood platter (£2.75), ham and egg (£2.80), scampi (£3), gammon steak (£4.20), and steaks (from £7.50). Well kept Courage Best and Directors on handpump, and wines on tap; very good service, even when busy. Darts, dominoes, cribbage, piped music. There are tables on neatly kept grass beside roses and tall trees, behind the car park. *(Recommended by E G Parish, K Widdowson, Dave Braisted, S J A Velate)*

Courage   Licensee David Gerring   Real ale   Meals and snacks   Open 10–3, 5.30–10.30

COBHAM   TQ6768 Map 3
Leather Bottle

2½ miles from M2 junction 1; village signposted from A2 (towards London) on B2009

After strolling through the park of Cobham Hall, Dickens often used to end up at this ancient half-timbered house, and mentions it fondly in *Pickwick Papers*. In among all the decorations you'd expect, there are some truly interesting prints of Dickens' characters, including early postcards and teacards. The large, open-plan bar serves sandwiches, ploughman's (£3), cold meat salads (£3.60) and a daily hot dish, as well as Ruddles County, Trumans Bitter, Best and Sampson, and Websters Yorkshire; friendly staff. Tables are laid out on the extended back lawn, and in the orchard at the bottom there's a large fish pond with a children's play area and an outdoor summer tuck shop. The village itself is pretty, with medieval almshouses, and outstanding brasses in the church. *(Recommended by Michael and Harriet Robinson, M Rising, Peter Griffiths)*

Trumans (Watneys)   Real ale   Snacks (not Sat)   Restaurant   Children in eating area and restaurant   Open 11–3, 6–11 all year   Bedrooms tel Meopham (0474) 814327; £29/ £43(£58B)

DARGATE   TR0761 Map 3
Dove

Village signposted from A299

In a quiet hamlet, this pretty and friendly honeysuckle-clad brick house has a lovely garden with roses, lilacs, paeonies and many other flowers, and picnic-table sets under pear trees; there's also a dovecote – with white doves – and a swing. A bridlepath leads up into Blean Wood. Inside, it's carefully refurbished and well kept, with a good log fire; in winter well kept Shepherd Neame Old on handpump, which can be served by the jug; unobtrusive piped music. Good home-made food includes sandwiches (from 95p), soup (£1.20), pâté (£1.75), excellent lasagne (£2.45), vegetable Stroganoff (£3.50), salads (from £3.75), baked trout (£5.95), pork chop or swordfish steaks (£6.50), popular fresh salmon pie (£6.75), and daily specials like crispy duck with sweet-and-sour vegetables (£6.50) or chicken Kiev. *(Recommended by S D Samuels, Gary Scott, L M Miall, Dave Butler, Lesley Storey, Rob and Gill Weeks, Lyn and Bill Capper)*

Shepherd Neame   Licensees Peter and Susan Smith   Real ale   Meals (not Sun evening) and snacks (lunchtimes only)   Children in restaurant and eating area   Open 11–3, 6–11 all year; 12.30 supper licence; closed 25 Dec

EASTLING   TQ9656 Map 3

Carpenters Arms

Off A251 S of M2 junction 6, via Painters Forstal

The beamed front rooms in this old village pub have easy chairs and pews around simple, wooden tables of some character, hop-bines strung along some of the ancient beams, local and sporting prints and some equestrian and other decorative plates on the walls, and logs burning in a big brick inglenook fireplace. The two small back ones have country kitchen chairs, pews and oak tables with candles in bottles, rough-hewn oak beams, and a vast fireplace with well restored bread ovens. Bar food includes sandwiches (£1, toasted £1.50), pizza (£2.50), a large ploughman's (£3.50, with cheese and locally made sausage), scampi or a half-pound burger (£3.50), daily specials such as steak and kidney pie (from £3.50), and Sunday lunch (£7.50). Well kept Shepherd Neame Old on handpump, decent wines. Shove-ha'penny, table skittles, dominoes, cribbage and a fruit machine; piped music. In summer you can sit, sheltered by the steep-roofed inn's half-timbered brickwork and white clapboarding, by an outbuilding covered with jasmine, clematis and roses. *(Recommended by R Coe, Mrs V Vanderkar, TBB, Dave Braisted; more reports please)*

Shepherd Neame   Licensee Tony O'Regan   Real ale   Meals and snacks (12–2.30, 6.30–10.30; not Sun evening)   Restaurant (not Sun evening) tel Eastling (079 589) 234   Children in eating area of bar and restaurant   Folk music Weds evenings   Open 11–11 all year

FORDWICH   TR1759 Map 3

Fordwich Arms

Village signposted off A28 in Sturry, just on Canterbury side of level-crossing

Strikingly well built, this tucked-away building has small country prints and a few old local photographs on the dark-green hessian walls, an oak parquet floor, comfortable golden-yellow corduroy plush button-back banquettes that sweep in bays around the room, and brick mullions for the handsomely crafted arched windows; also, plates on a high Delft shelf, and copper pots (some with plants in), antique soda-syphons, pewter jugs and dried flowers. Dominoes, chess and draughts. Generous helpings of bar food include soup (£1.20), sandwiches (from £1.25), filled baked potatoes (from £1.65), ploughman's with really interesting English cheeses and home-made chutney (£2.45), salads (£3.95), and specials such as vegetable and lentil casserole (£3.80), beef goulash (£3.90) or trout with ginger and spring onions (£3.95). Well kept Flowers Original, Fremlins and Marstons Pedigree on handpump, quite a few wines by the glass or bottle, and mulled wine in winter; unobtrusive piped music, friendly service. There are white tables, chairs and cocktail parasols on the flagstoned terrace, and a spacious garden by the River Stour – in Roman times sea-going ships came up this far. The lovely little

We say if we or readers have seen dogs or cats in a pub.

herringbone-brick half-timbered medieval town hall opposite is said to be the smallest and perhaps the oldest in Britain. *(Recommended by L M Miall, P Poole, Lyn and Bill Capper; more reports please)*

Whitbreads   Licensee John Gass   Real ale   Meals and snacks (12–2, 6–10; not Sun) Children in family-room   Open 11–2.30, 6–11 all year

GROOMBRIDGE   TQ5337 Map 3
Crown
B2110

The most central of the small, old-fashioned rooms here – popular with drinkers – has a long copper-topped serving-bar, masses of old teapots, pewter tankards and so forth, logs burning in the big brick inglenook, and a relaxed, chatty atmosphere. The end room, normally for eaters, has fairly close-spaced tables with a variety of good solid chairs, a log-effect gas fire in a big fireplace, and an arch through to the food-ordering area. The walls, mostly rough yellowing plaster with some squared panelling and some timbering, are decorated with lots of small topographical, game and sporting prints (often in pretty maple frames), and a circular large scale map with the pub at its centre; some of the beams have horsebrasses. Quickly served on an entertaining assortment of plates old and new, the tasty food includes good value ploughman's, tortellini in Italian sauce (£3.10), chicken curry or steak and mushroom pie (£3.60), roast duck (£3.70), coronation chicken or Turkish-style spiced lamb and spinach (£3.80), smoked salmon and prawns (£4.20), paella (£4.50), and good puddings; excellent breakfasts. Well kept Flowers, Harveys and Marstons Pedigree on handpump, good value house wines; very efficient service, shove-ha'penny, cribbage. Picnic-table sets on the sunny brick terrace in front of the flower beds by this pretty tile-hung Elizabethan house look down over a steep, neatly kept village green. Behind is a big tree-sheltered lawn, with climbing-frame, slide and more picnic-table sets. *(Recommended by Dr T H M Mackenzie, S J A Velate, Mr and Mrs J H Adam, Philip and Sheila Hanley, Gwen and Peter Andrews, Alison Kerruish, Ashley Madden, J A Snell)*

Free house   Licensees Mr and Mrs W B Rhodes   Real ale   Meals and snacks (not Sun evening)   Children in eating area of bar and separate room off bar   Open 11–2.30 (3 Sat), 6–11 all year   Bedrooms tel Groombridge (0892 864) 742; £15/£30

nr HADLOW   TQ6349 Map 3
Artichoke
Hamptons; from Hadlow–Plaxtol road take first right (signposted West Peckham – the pub too is discreetly signposted, on an oak tree); OS Sheet 188 reference 627524

Partly tile hung and shuttered, this cosy and pretty thirteenth-century cottage has two softly lit rooms – one with an inglenook fireplace and decked out with jugs, kettles, pots, pans and plates, the other with a wood-burning range. There are beams in the low ceilings, cushioned high-backed wooden settles, wooden farmhouse-kitchen chairs, and upholstered wrought-iron stools matching unusual wrought-iron, glass-topped tables on its Turkey carpet. Decorations include lots of gleaming brass, country pictures (mainly hunting scenes), some antique umbrellas and old storm lamps. Bar food is good: ploughman's (£2.75), jumbo pork sausage (£2.75), home-made quiche Lorraine (£3.75), home-made lasagne or chilli con carne (£4.25), home-made steak and kidney pie or mixed grill (£4.75), prawn salads (from £5.25), chicken Kiev (£5.75), sirloin steak (£7.50) and daily specials. Fullers London Pride, Marstons Pedigree and Youngs Special on handpump, with a good range of spirits; friendly rather than speedy service. It's quiet during the day and on many evenings, but fills up quickly on weekend evenings. There are seats on a fairy-lit front terrace with a striped awning, and more built around a tall lime tree across the lane. *(Recommended by Norman Foot, Peter and Joy Heatherley, Peter Neate, S J A Velate)*

Free house   Licensees Terry and Barbara Simmonds   Real ale   Meals and snacks (not Sun evenings in winter)   Restaurant (Fri and Sat evenings) tel Plaxtol (0732) 810763   Children in eating area of bar   Open 11.30–2.30, 6.30–11 all year

IDE HILL   TQ4851 Map 3
Cock

On a lovely village green, this pretty, partly tile-hung pub is comfortably modernised: some Windsor chairs and cushioned settles on the polished floorboards and red carpet, lots of polished brass and copper, and a big hearth with an elaborate iron fireback. Bar food includes sandwiches (from £1.20, toasties from £1.80), home-made soup (£1.50), hot salt-beef in French bread (£2.30), ploughman's (from £1.60 for home-made rough pâté), local sausages and egg (£3), a range of meat or vegetarian burgers (from £3.50), salads (from £4), scampi (£4.50), tender steak (£7.50) and specials like good turkey curry; get there at 12.30 to get a seat (parking may be difficult too). Well kept Friary Meux, Ind Coope Burton and Gales HSB on handpump; cheerful service; shove-ha'penny, bar billiards, trivia and piped music. There are seats in front. Behind the pub you can get through to a public playing-field with swings, seesaw and slide, overlooking rolling fields and woodland. *(Recommended by Norman Foot, J A Snell, Miss M Byrne, M D Hare, Jenny and Brian Seller, Lt Col D J Daly, Dave Braisted, AE, GRE, Alison Kerruish, E G Parish)*

Friary Meux (Ind Coope)   Licensee Robert Arnett   Real ale   Meals (not Sun) and snacks (not Sun evening; 12–2, 6–8.30)   Open 11–2.30, 6–11 all year

LAMBERHURST   TQ6635 Map 3
Brown Trout ✪

B2169, just off A21 S of village nearly opposite entrance to Scotney Castle

It's the remarkable value daily specials which earn the warmest approval here: often from the main menu, but at bargain prices – say a plaice too big for its plate (£3.25), a tender steak (£4.25) or even half a lobster served with crab and prawns (£6.95); the normal menu is in fact strongest on fish, such as smoked sprats, cockles or soft roes on toast (£2.25), a heap of mussels (£3), six oysters (£4), trout with walnut and celery stuffing (£5.50) and crab (£5.95), but also includes dishes such as soup (£1.75), a half-chicken (£3.50) and other meat dishes. Though it is now primarily a dining pub, with place settings at all the tables, the serving-counter is still decidedly the centre of the bar; this pubby layout and the friendly staff preserve a thoroughly unstuffy and relaxed atmosphere. There are small country prints, mainly of trout fishing, on the russet hessian walls, and the beams are thickly hung with copper and brass. With only eight or nine tables in the small bar itself, in summer they certainly need the overflow into the biggish extension dining-room; on the way through, there's a big and remarkable well stocked aquarium. Well kept Fremlins on handpump, side fruit machine, faint piped music on Stevie Wonder lines. Even in winter the pub is bright with hanging baskets and tubs of pansies – and very pretty in summer, with picnic-table sets under cocktail parasols on the sloping front grass, opposite a big converted oast-house with unusually tall black-rendered brick kiln roofs. *(Recommended by Mr and Mrs R Harrington, S J A Velate, Mrs E M Thompson, E J and J W Cutting, P H Fearnley, P Gillbe)*

Fremlins (Whitbreads)   Licensee J Stringer   Real ale   Meals and snacks (bookings tel Tunbridge Wells (0892) 890312)   Open 11–3, 6–11 all year

If we know a pub does sandwiches we always say so; if they're not mentioned, you'll have to assume you can't get one.

LUDDENHAM   TQ9862 Map 3

Mounted Rifleman

3½ miles from M2 junction 6; follow Faversham signpost to A2, turn left on to A2, then follow Oare, Luddenham signpost; take first left turn (signposted Buckland, Luddenham), then turn right just before railway crossing; OS Sheet 178 reference 981627 – hamlet marked as Elverton

The two simply furnished, communicating rooms in this unspoilt, friendly old brick house have bare benches, kitchen chairs and the like on their bare floor-boards, and some hunting prints on the ochre walls; behind the bar is the former scullery with stone sink, Aga and kitchen table; darts. The well kept Fremlins is tapped in the cellar and brought up on a tray; sandwiches – with home-pickled onions and eggs – on request; darts, dominoes and cribbage. There are a couple of tables out behind, by the roses on the way to the vegetable patch. *(Recommended by Phil Gorton; more reports please)*

Whitbreads   Licensee Bob Jarrett   Real ale   Snacks   Open 11–3, 6–11

NEWNHAM   TQ9557 Map 3

George ★ ⊘

Village signposted from A2 just W of Ospringe, outside Faversham

Everything in this distinctive sixteenth-century pub seems individually chosen and cared for: the cabinet of fine rummers and other glassware, the early nineteenth-century prints (Dominica negroes, Oxford academics, politicians), the collection of British butterflies and moths, candle-lit tables, prettily upholstered mahogany settles, dining-chairs and leather carving-chairs, rugs on the waxed floorboards, and the table lamps and gas-type ceiling chandeliers; the flower arrangements are beautiful. Hop-bines hang from the beams, open fires warm each of the spreading series of rooms, there's well kept Shepherd Neame Old on handpump, and four wines by the glass, and the piped music is unobtrusive, well reproduced and interesting. A wide choice of bar food includes sandwiches (from 80p), soup (£1.20), a good variety of ploughman's and salads (from £2.50, crab £5.50), cheese-topped cottage pie (£2.50), pasta of the day (£3.50), steak and kidney pie or pudding (£4), with, in the evening, grills and fish, and a good many specials such as pheasant's egg and prawn cocktail (£2.75), Russian vegetable pie (£3.25), stuffed lambs' hearts (£4), veal chop with peppers and artichoke hearts in a white wine sauce (£6), and roast boned duck stuffed with orange and mint (£7.50). Another favourite is the 'Well' pudding – old-fashioned steamed suet, to a grandmother's recipe (£2); fresh speciality vegetables, salads, wild mushrooms and so forth are obtained through a local supplier who regularly buys in the Paris markets. Cribbage, dominoes, fruit machine and trivia. There are picnic-table sets in a spacious sheltered garden with a fine spreading cob-nut tree, below the slopes of the sheep pastures. *(Recommended by Ruth Humphrey, M Byrne, G Campion)*

Shepherd Neame   Licensees Simon and Ann Barnes   Real ale   Meals and snacks (not Sun evening, not Mon; 12–2, 7.30–10)   Children in eating area of bar   Occasional impromptu pianist   Open 10.30–3, 6–11 all year; closed 25 Dec

OARE   TR0062 Map 3

Shipwrights Arms ★

Ham Road, Hollow Shore; from A2 just W of Faversham, follow Oare–Luddenham signpost; fork right at Oare–Harty Ferry signpost, drive straight through Oare (don't turn off to Harty Ferry), then left into Ham Street on the outskirts of Faversham, following pub signpost

Reached down a long and extremely bumpy lane across the marshes (which are three feet below sea level), this isolated, white weatherboarded and tiled cottage has small front and back gardens leading up a bank to the path above the creek, where lots of boats are moored. This part of the shore is an Area of Special Scientific

Interest, and three Saxon walkways more or less join here. Inside, the original part
has three cosy and remarkably dimly lit little bars (there are no mains facilities –
lighting is by generator, and water is pumped from a well), separated by standing
timbers and wood part-partitions or narrow door arches. Decorations include
copper kettles, boating pictures, flags or boating pennants on the ceilings, and hops
and pewter tankards hanging over the bar counter. A medley of seats vary from
tapestry cushioned stools and chairs through some big Windsor armchairs to black
wood-panelled built-in settles forming little booths, and there are several brick
fireplaces – one with a wood-burning stove. Bar food, chalked up on a blackboard,
includes filled rolls (£1.35), various ploughman's (£2.85), cottage pie (£3.35), mild
lamb curry (£3.45) and fresh rainbow trout (£5.50); roast Sunday lunch (£3.75).
Well kept Adnams Best and Broadside, Fullers ESB, Shepherd Neame Old, and
Youngers IPA and No 3 tapped from casks behind the counter; farm ciders,
including their own called Looney Juice; cribbage and piped music. A larger room
with less atmosphere but considerably more light has a food hatch where a
loudspeaker tells you your food is ready. (*Recommended by Jill and Paul Ormrod, C
Trows, Ann and David Stranack, S A Robbins, A W Lewis, Quentin Williamson*)

*Free house   Licensees Mr and Mrs N Rye   Real ale   Meals and snacks   Children
welcome   Disco Fri and Sat nights, live guitarist Sun   Open 10.30–3, 6–11 all year; 11–11
Sat; closed evening 25 Dec*

PETT BOTTOM   TR1552 Map 3

Duck 🏅

From B2068 S of Canterbury take Lower Hardres turn; Pett Bottom signposted from there; OS
Sheet 179 reference 161521

It's the wide choice of interesting food which is the draw to this remote but busy
pub: besides sandwiches (from £2.25), ploughman's (from £2.60) and filled baked
potatoes (from £2.75), there's cauliflower cheese (£3.25), lasagne (vegetarian
£3.40, meaty £3.75), vegetable pie (£3.95), mussels in wine, cream and garlic
(£4.95), a good few pies such as seafood (£5.10) or steak and oyster (£6.20), one or
two changing dishes of the day such as hot spicy sausages (£3.95) or smoked
salmon quiche (£4.95), and more expensive specialities such as garlicky chicken en
croûte (£7.95), monkfish with a Dijon mustard and dill sauce (£8.95) and duck in a
ginger wine and honey sauce (£9.95); helpings and flavours are robust. Apart from
one sofa, a little stripped chest of drawers with a mirror on top, and a big fireplace
dating from the early seventeenth century, the furnishings and décor in the two tiny
bar rooms are very plain. Shepherd Neame and a couple of guest beers such as
Adnams Broadside, Greene King Abbot, Marstons Pedigree, Palmers, Wadworths
6X or Charles Wells Bombardier tapped from the cask; decent wines by the glass,
local cider, and maybe rather muffled piped pop music. There are some teak tables
in front of the tile-hung cottage, by a well and facing usable replica stocks, with
more in the sizeable garden; it's a peaceful, pretty valley (and Winston the barky
labrador/alsatian you may meet in the car park soon quietens down – especially if
you promise him a sip of Pedigree). (*Recommended by Paul and Margaret Baker, Serena
Hanson, Dr and Mrs R O Sadler, Comus Elliott*)

*Free house   Licensees Lorraine Brown and Ron Brown   Real ale   Meals and snacks
Restaurant (not Sun evening) tel Canterbury (0227) 830354   Children in left-hand bar and
restaurant   Open 11.30–3.30, 6.30–11 all year*

PLUCKLEY   TQ9243 Map 3

Dering Arms 🛏

Near station, which is signposted from B2077 in village

The bars in this striking old Dutch-gabled pub are simply but attractively
decorated, with a good variety of solid wooden furniture on the wood and stone

floors, log fires, and a relaxed, friendly atmosphere. Good bar food (prices haven't changed since last year) includes sandwiches (from 80p, toasties 10p extra), home-made soup (£1.65), pâté or various ploughman's with home-made chutney (£1.95), chicken (£2.45), home-made pie of the day (£3.65), local trout (£6.25), steak (£6.85), and puddings like fruit crumble (£1.95); a vegetarian dish and several fish specials are chalked up on a board – soft roes on toast (£1.95), marinated herring fillets with apple and horseradish sauce (£2.65) or whole crab salad (£7.95). They also have gourmet evenings every six weeks. Well kept Goachers Maidstone and a beer they brew for the pub, Harveys Best, Shepherd Neame Old and Youngs Special on handpump or tapped from the cask, a large wine list, and local cider; darts, bar billiards, dominoes and juke box. *(Recommended by Theo Schofield, Geoff and Sarah Schrecker, Geoffrey and Teresa Salt)*

Free house   Licensee James Buss   Real ale   Meals and snacks   Restaurant (closed Sun evening)   Open 11.30–2.30 (3 Sat), 6–11 all year   Bedrooms tel Pluckley (023 384) 371; £20/£32

RINGLESTONE   TQ8755 Map 3

Ringlestone 🏮

Ringlestone Road; village signposted from B2163; OS Sheet 178 reference 879558

This popular country pub – an ale-house since about 1615 – has a central room with a wood-burning stove and a small bread oven in an inglenook fireplace, farmhouse chairs and cushioned wall settles on the brick floor, tables with candle lanterns set into ropework centrepieces, and old-fashioned brass and glass lamps on the bare brick walls. An arch from here through a wall – rather like the *outside* of a house, windows and all – opens into a long, quieter room with cushioned wall benches, tiny farmhouse chairs, three old carved settles (one rather fine and dated 1620), similar tables, and etchings of country folk on its walls (bare brick too). Regulars tend to sit at the wood-panelled bar counter, or liven up a little wood-floored side room. Bar food includes a help-yourself hot and cold lunchtime buffet with dishes like sausages in cider (£2.45), lamb and coconut curry or garlic chicken (£3.45), as well as other things such as thick vegetable or meat soup with sherry and croûtons (£2), filled baked potatoes (£2.25), ploughman's (£2.85), crab pâté with lemon mayonnaise (£3), chilli con carne (£3.75), good speciality home-made pies (chicken and bacon, vegetarian or game with Madeira, from £4.50), filleted fresh trout in oatmeal (£5.95), rump steak (£6.75), and puddings like home-made cheesecake or fruit crumble (£2); no chips or fried food. Around eight changing well kept real ales are tapped from casks behind the bar and chalked up on a board: Adnams, Archers Headbanger, Batemans XXXB, Cotleigh Old Buzzard, Everards Tiger, Felinfoel Double Dragon, Fremlins, Flowers IPA, Gales HSB, Harveys, Marstons Pedigree, Shepherd Neame, Whitbreads Pompey Royal, Wiltshire Old Devil, and a beer from Goachers, the local brewers, called Ringlestone; they can be quite pricey; local cider, and over twenty country wines (some are chalked up on a beam over the bar counter). Cribbage and piped pop music. There are picnic-table sets on the large raised lawn with ponds and waterfalls, a rockery above the car park and troughs of pretty flowers along the pub walls. There's now another car park. *(Recommended by Robin and Bev Gammon, Mrs W Harrington; more reports please)*

Free house   Licensee Michael Buck   Real ale   Meals and snacks (12–2, 7–10)   Restaurant tel Maidstone (0622) 859207   Children welcome   Occasional morris dancers in summer   Open 11–3, 6.30–11 all year; may open longer in afternoon if trade demands; opens 7 in winter; closed evening 25 Dec   Bedrooms with self-catering facilities planned in house next door

We checked prices with the pubs as we went to press in summer 1989. They should hold until around spring 1990, when our experience suggests that you can expect an increase of a bit more than 10p in the £.

ST MARGARET'S AT CLIFFE TR3644 Map 3

Cliffe Tavern Hotel 🛏

High Street

Very handy for the Ramsgate or Dover ferry, this comfortable, friendly inn has a striking picture of a Second World War aerial dogfight above the village in the bar; there's also a larger open-plan lounge. Good, reasonably priced food includes sandwiches (from 95p, fresh crab £1.50), home-made carrot, orange and coriander soup (£1.90), vegetarian quiche (£2.75), home-made steak and kidney or chicken pies (£3.25), lots of vegetarian dishes like pistichio or stuffed pancakes (£4.25), fresh salmon and sorrel twist (£4.25), gammon steak with egg or pineapple (£4.85), steaks (from £5.30), and puddings (from £1.20); there's a dining area next to the back bar. Well kept Harveys, Ruddles County and Shepherd Neame on handpump; fruit machine. The staff are particularly helpful. On the quiet back lawn, sheltered by sycamores and a rose-covered flint wall, are some tables. Most of the bedrooms are in two little cottages across the yard from the main building. The inn is near *Good Walks Guide* Walk 43. *(Recommended by Bernard Phillips; more reports please)*

Free house Licensee Christopher Waring Westby Real ale Meals and snacks (12–3, 7–10) Well behaved children in eating area of bar and in restaurant Open 11.15–3, 6–11 all year Bedrooms tel Dover (0304) 852749 or 852400; £29B/£38B

SELLING TR0456 Map 3

White Lion

3½ miles from M2 junction 7; village signposted from exit roundabout; village also signposted off A251 S of Faversham

Tucked away in a small village among hop-gardens, this 300-year-old building has a friendly, homely atmosphere, with pews on stripped floorboards, an unusual semi-circular bar counter, and a working spit over the right-hand log fire. Generous helpings of bar food include sandwiches (from 75p), home-made soup (£1.50), delicious garlic and herb pâté (£2.25), ploughman's (from £2.30, the Stilton has been praised), salads (from £4), scampi (£3.95), chicken cocunut curry (£4.95), home-made vegetarian Stilton and sweetcorn quiche (£5), steaks (from £6.50), lunchtime specials such as traditional beef pudding (£3.60), puddings (£1.75), and Sunday roasts. Well kept Shepherd Neame Old on handpump, with decent wines by the glass; fruit machine, space game, maybe quiet piped music – the landlord's a trumpet-player. The garden has a thriving community of budgerigars, canaries, zebra finches, button quail, golden pheasants, rabbits and guinea-pigs, with their young – which generally seem to drive Timmy and Remi the cats indoors.

(Recommended by TBB, Quentin Williamson, Ted George, H P Chapman, Comus Elliott)

Shepherd Neame Licensee Anthony Richards Real ale Meals and snacks Restaurant (not Sun evening) tel Canterbury (0227) 752211 Children welcome (own room) Jazz Mon evening Open 11–3, 6.30–11 all year; closed 25 Dec

nr SMARDEN TQ8842 Map 3

Bell ★

From Smarden follow lane between church and The Chequers, then turn left at T-junction; or from A274 take unsignposted turn E a mile N of B2077 to Smarden

A fine range of real ales on handpump in this friendly, relaxed pub includes Flowers, Fullers London Pride, Goachers, Harveys, Shepherd Neame, and Theakstons Best and Old Peculier; also, six wines by the glass. The bars are all different in character: the snug little back rooms have bare brick or ochre plastered walls, brick or flagstone floors, low beams, pews and the like around the simple candle-lit tables, and an inglenook fireplace. The lively front bar has darts, pool, shove-ha'penny, cribbage, dominoes, fruit machine, trivia and juke box; part of it is partly set aside for families with children. Good bar food includes home-made soup (£1.10), sandwiches (from £1.20, toasties from £1.30, rump steak £2.75), home-made pâté (£1.80), ploughman's or pizza (from £1.95), home-made shepherd's pie (£2.50), basket meals (from £2.50), salads (from £3.55), good home-made steak and kidney pie (£3.75), gammon steak with pineapple (£4.25), steaks – including perfectly cooked fillet (from £6.55) – and daily specials such as fish Mornay or Cumberland pie; puddings like home-made chocolate crunch cake (£1.20). You can sit out at the side, among fruit trees and shrubs, admiring the pub, which is hung with fancy tiles and covered with roses. Every second Sunday in the month at midday, there is a gathering of vintage and classic cars (the pub is packed then). Basic continental breakfasts only. *(Recommended by Mr and Mrs J H Adam, Peter Scillitoe, J Maloney, Theo Schofield, Mr and Mrs R Gammon, Greg Parston, AE, GRE)*

Free house   Licensee Ian Turner   Real ale   Meals and snacks (12–2, 6.30–10)   Children in front family area of bar   Open 11.30 (11 Sat)–2.30, 6–11 all year; closed 25 Dec   Bedrooms tel Smarden (023 377) 283; £14/£22

SPELDHURST   TQ5541 Map 3
George & Dragon
Signposted from A264 W of Tunbridge Wells

It's said that Kentish archers returning from their victory at Agincourt in 1415 celebrated here. Based on a manorial great hall dating from 1212, there are heavy beams (installed during 'modernisation' in 1589 – until then the room went up to the roof), some of the biggest flagstones you can find anywhere, snug alcoves, panelling, antique cushioned settles and Windsor chairs, and a massive stone fireplace. Bar food includes sandwiches (from 90p), home-made soup, good generous ploughman's, cold meats with salad (£2.90, prawn £4.50), Speldhurst sausages, and a hot lunchtime dish (£3.60). Larkins and well kept Harveys, King & Barnes and Marstons on handpump, and lots of malt whiskies; cribbage. It can get very crowded at weekends, especially in the evenings. The striking first-floor restaurant under the original massive roof timbers serves good but expensive food and is served by a quite splendid wine cellar – a place for special occasions. There are white tables and chairs on the neat little lawn, ringed with flowers, in front of the building. *(Recommended by Brian and Jenny Seller, Nigel Williamson, Joy Heatherley, Alan Skull, Peter Neate, John Townsend, Alasdair Knowles, M J Masters, Richard Gibbs)*

Free house   Licensee Mrs Jennifer Sankey   Real ale   Meals and snacks   Restaurant (closed Sun evening) tel Langton (089 286) 3125   Children in eating area of bar   Open 11–2.30, 6–11 all year

STAPLE   TR2756 Map 3
Black Pig 🏮
Barnsole Road; follow signs to village hall; pub signposted from Wingham–Sandwich back road through Staple, on Sandwich side of village

An unusual fireplace in the rambling main bar here has a sort of semi-inglenook which may originally have been a smoking cabinet. There are comfortable chairs on the carpet, a heavy beam and plank ceiling, and a homely, friendly atmosphere. Home-made, freshly prepared, and generously served, the bar food includes sandwiches (from £1.75, crab £2.50), very good ploughman's with cheeses, home-made pâté, home-cooked ham, beef or turkey, very good fresh seafood or fresh poached salmon (from £2.50), lasagne or chicken curry (£3.50), salads (from £3.50), scampi (£3.75), superb fish pie, steak and kidney pie cooked in Guinness and red wine (£3.95), and half a roast duck (£7.50); daily specials like fresh plaice (£3.75), liver and onion casserole (£3.95), guinea-fowl in port (£4.75), and three-course Sunday lunch (£7.50). Well kept Bass, Ind Coope Burton and Tetleys on handpump, with a couple of guest ales such as Harveys Best or Wadworths Farmers Glory; darts, pool, dominoes, cribbage, trivia, juke box, bat-and-trap in the garden on Wednesday evenings in summer, and piped music. There's a big side garden with teak garden furniture, and more seats under an old yew by the quiet village lane. *(Recommended by John Knighton, Y Simon, L M Miall, Jack Taylor, Ted George, Mr and Mrs J H Adam)*

Free house   Licensees W Culver and J D O Wells   Real ale   Meals and snacks   Restaurant – with dance floor – tel *Dover (0304) 812361   Children welcome away from bar servery Open 11–2.30, 6.30 (6 Sat)–11 all year; closed evenings 25 and 26 Dec*

STOWTING   TR1242 Map 3

Tiger

The simplest route if coming from S is to turn left off B2068 signposted Stowting, straight across crossroads, then fork right after ¼ mile and pub is on right; coming from N, follow Brabourne, Wye, Ashford signpost to right at fork, then turn left towards Posting and Lyminge at T-junction

In lovely countryside, this seventeenth-century pub is a peaceful place with a background wash of sheep and farm animal noises outside, and contented chat inside. It's simply furnished with faded rugs on the dark floorboards, some floor-to-ceiling plank panelling, plain chairs and dark pews built in against the walls, and an open fire at each end of the main bar; decorations include an abundance of hop-bines draped from the high ceiling, candles stuck into bottles, and shelves of little kegs, stone jugs and copper pots. Good home-made bar food includes sandwiches (£1.25, steak in French bread £3.60), lovely soup (£1.75), a pint and a half of prawns (£2.60), duck liver pâté (£1.75), burger (£2.95), grilled local trout (£4.95), pies like cheesy smoked haddock and prawn or tasty steak and kidney pie (£4), and rump steak (£5.50). Well kept Everards Tiger, Gales HSB, Ind Coope Burton, Ruddles County, Tetleys and Wadworths 6X on handpump; darts, shove-ha'penny, dominoes, cribbage and table skittles. Outside, picnic-table sets and other tables sit on the front terrace, some under a thinly planted arbour. *(Recommended by D K and H M Brenchley, RWM, Brian and Jenny Seller)*

Free house   Licensees Alan and Linda Harris   Real ale   Meals and snacks (12–2, 7–10) Restaurant tel *Lyminge (0303) 862130   Children welcome   Jazz Mon evening Open 12–3, 6–11 all year*

TUNBRIDGE WELLS   TQ5839 Map 3

La Galoche 🏮 🛏

Mount Edgcumbe House Hotel, The Common

Although there's no problem finding good pubs out in the country in Kent, it's much more difficult in the bigger towns. This is a pleasant exception. It's actually the bar of a small, well run hotel on the Common, has a good deal of character, and is a friendly place to drop into for a drink. Converted eight years ago and built into the rock, it has a collection of shells by the entrance door, a tiny cavern-like area to one side, a long built-in slatted pine wall seat, little leatherette-cushioned chairs, solid pine tables, and bar stools against the slatted pine bar counter (where there may be prawns and mussels to pick at); decorations include bright modern prints and cartoons, and there are newspapers to read. The small two-roomed restaurant is most attractive and overlooks the Common. Good home-made bar food includes pâté (£1.90), fish soup with rouille (£2.20), insalata di mare with Japanese seaweed (£3.25), devilled shrimps (£3.75), pojarski smitane (meatballs with herbs and garlic and a sour cream, mushroom and white wine sauce) or aubergine bake (£4.50), properly made steak and kidney pie (£5), chicken in cream and ginger (£5.50), local game in season (around £5.50), several fish dishes such as seafood platter (£7.50), good minute steak (£7.75), and puddings (from £1.50). Their excellent cheeseboard

– which includes thirty different French cheeses – won them a national competition last year (£2.75 for French bread and as many as you want to taste). Well kept Bass on handpump, and seventeen wines by the glass. *(Recommended by Peter Neate, Patrick Stapley, RAB)*

Free house   Licensees David and Susan Barnard   Real ale   Meals and snacks (12–2, 7–10)   Restaurant   Children Sat and Sun mornings only   Open 12–2.30, 6.30–11 all year   Bedrooms tel Tunbridge Wells (0892) 26823; £36S/£61.87S

Sankeys at the Gate ✪

39 Mount Ephraim

The restaurant in this Victorian house has been moved upstairs, making the place more flexible. Downstairs is now more of a proper pub-like bar for drinks and bar snacks (there's a no-smoking area), with decorations such as *Vanity Fair* caricatures and fish prints, old maps and bottles, a relaxed atmosphere, and very friendly service. Bar food specialises in fish which is bought direct from source (wherever possible) or kept in their seawater tank: potted shrimps or fish soup (£3), home-made fishcakes or calamari salad (£3.50), stuffed Cornish clams (£4), hand-dived scallops or baby squat lobsters with home-made mayonnaise (£5), Mediterranean prawns (hot or cold £8), Loch Fyne salmon (en croûte, poached or cold £9.50), turbot (£11.50), fillet of bass or seafood platter (£12.50), whole Cornish crawfish (enough for two people, £16 per pound), and home-made puddings such as chocolate brandy cake or sorbets (£2.50). Well kept Harveys from an antique beer engine salvaged from the late-lamented Sussex Arms, and a decent wine list; piped music. A garden with seats for about forty is now open. *(Recommended by Heather Sharland, Isobel May, Patrick Stapley, RAB)*

Free house   Licensee Guy Sankey   Real ale   Meals and snacks (12–2, 7–10; not Sun)   Restaurant (closed Sun) tel Tunbridge Wells (0892) 511422   Children welcome   Open 12–11 weekdays, 11–3, 6–11 Sat; closed Sun, bank hol Mons and 25 and 26 Dec

WEALD   TQ5250 Map 3

Chequer Tree

Village signposted off A21 exit roundabout, at southernmost Sevenoaks exit; in village centre, turn left into Scabharbour Road

In summer, the garden here is the chief attraction: a new barbecue area, masses of space, fairy-lit terraces, a rambling pond, and young trees and shrubs among the older hawthorns, oaks and ashes; bat-and-trap. Inside, the open-plan carpeted bar is comfortably modernised, and a flagstoned games area has darts, pool, shove-ha'penny, cribbage, trivia and a fruit machine. Bar food served by neat young waitresses includes sandwiches (from £1.10), cauliflower cheese (£2), ploughman's or omelettes (from £2), lasagne (£2.50), ham and egg (£3) and steak and kidney pie (£3.75); well kept Ruddles Best and County and Websters Yorkshire on handpump. In 1989 eyebrows were raised over such service lapses as an evening meal served on paper plates – we hope things have settled down again. They have a minibus to collect/drop off pre-arranged parties. *(Recommended by K Widdowson, Michael Thomson; more reports please)*

Free house   Licensee J L Pocknell   Real ale   Meals and snacks (12–3, 7–10; not Sun or Mon evenings)   Restaurant (not Sun evening) tel Sevenoaks (0732) 463386   Children in eating area and restaurant   Open 11.30–3, 6–11 all year

WHITSTABLE   TR1166 Map 3

Pearsons ✪

Sea Wall; follow main road into centre as far as you can – then try to park!

Consistently good, very fresh seafood is the thing here: cockles (£1.10), rollmops or delicious crab sandwiches (£1.50p), prawn or smoked salmon sandwiches or smoked mackerel (£1.75), peeled prawns (£1.95), king prawns (£5.75), local oysters in season (three £3, six £6), and seafood platter (£6.95), with changing fresh fish or shellfish specials; also, other sandwiches (from 95p) and ploughman's (£1.95). In the downstairs bar, small areas are divided by stripped brickwork, and have mate's chairs, sea paintings and old local photographs, a ship's wheel, lobster pots, and rough brown ceiling planking; a lower flagstoned area gets most of its submarine light from a huge lobster tank. Well kept Flowers Original and Fremlins, and as we went to press a new experimental cask-conditioned version of Whitbreads Best on handpump; decent house wines, piped pop music, fruit machine. Upstairs, in two or three pleasantly close-packed dining-rooms, there's a wider choice (as well as a sea view from some tables – downstairs the sea wall gets in the way); service is kind and very quick. There are some picnic-table sets outside between the pub and the sea. *(Recommended by J Harvey Hallam, L M Miall, Theo Schofield, Barry Bawtree, Shirley Pielou, G T Rhys)*

Whitbreads   Licensee Michael Wingrove   Real ale   Meals and snacks (served all through opening hours)   Restaurant tel Whitstable (0227) 272005   Children in restaurant   Open 11–11; 11–3, 6–11 in winter

WYE   TR0546 Map 3
Tickled Trout
Signposted off A28 NE of Ashford

This renovated riverside pub is popular for its warm atmosphere and helpful service. It's open-plan, with comfortable wall banquettes around dimpled copper tables, and heavy timbers among the stripped brickwork; there's also a conservatory. Bar food includes sandwiches (from 75p), filled baked potatoes (from £1.20), good home-made soup (£1.25), ploughman's (from £1.80), seafood pie (£2.95), steaks (from £5.75), trout (£5.95) and daily specials. Flowers, Fremlins and Marstons Pedigree on handpump; maybe piped music. The lawn runs down under ash trees to the clear, shallow waters of the Great Stour (which have been restocked with carp and bream), with ducks paddling frantically around under the bridge. The pub is near the start of *Good Walks Guide* Walk 46. *(Recommended by Brian and Jenny Seller, L M Miall, TBB, Paul King, G and S L, Ted George, Robin and Bev Gammon, Mrs S Corrigan)*

Fremlins (Whitbreads)   Managers Betty and Jim Grieve   Real ale   Meals and snacks (12–2, 6.30–9.30)   Children in eating area and restaurant   Restaurant tel Wye (0233) 812227 Open 10.30–2.30, 6–11 all year

Lucky Dip
Besides the fully inspected pubs, you might like to try these Lucky Dips recommended to us and described by readers (if you do, please send us reports):

☆ **Aldington** [TR0736], *Walnut Tree*: Old smugglers' pub dating back to early fourteenth century with interestingly old-fashioned kitchen bar and lively local public bar, home-made bar food from sandwiches and ploughman's to hot dishes such as lamb and apricot pie or home-cured ham; well kept Shepherd Neame on handpump, sheltered garden with pool and summer barbecues; children allowed in eating area and restaurant; only reason it's not a main entry is lack of recent reports *(LYM – more*

reports please)
Appledore [Stn; TQ9529], *Railway*: Friendly atmosphere in real family pub with good log fires, wide choice of good food cooked by licensee's Italian/Swiss wife, choice of well kept real ales *(Gordon Smith)*; [The Street] *Red Lion*: Very friendly pub with partitioned eating area; good food (vegetarian dishes too), Courage beers, freshly squeezed orange juice, good coffee; comfortable bedrooms *(Sandra Kempson)*
Ash [High St (A257 towards Canterbury)];

TR2858], *Volunteer*: Friendly, welcoming landlord, well kept Adnams and Harveys and a varied menu with good home-made food *(Frank Williams, B Prosser)*

Ashford [Park St; TR0042], *Downtown Diner*: American-style bar with wide choice of well prepared food in ample helpings, pleasant staff *(B Prosser)*

Badlesmere [TR0054], *Red Lion*: Attractive, spacious country pub where time stands still, friendly landlord, Fremlins, Flowers Original and Wethereds Winter Royal; bar food, pleasant garden, paddock for caravans and tents *(Robert Caldwell)*

Barham [Elham Valley Rd (B2065); TR2050], *Dolls House*: Recently reopened as pub with restaurant after extensive refurbishment by new licensees; home-cooked food, closed Tues *(Anon)*; [The Street] *Duke of Cumberland*: Pleasant atmosphere and plenty of tables in two bars; Fremlins beers, large helpings of good value bar lunches; caravan site; bedrooms *(L M Miall)*

Bearsted [TQ7955], *Bull*: Hospitable pub with well kept beer and generously served bar snacks including sandwiches with tempting fillings; fruit machine *(J D Martin)*

Benover [B2162; TQ7048], *Woolpack*: Pretty tile-hung pub with well kept Shepherd Neame real ales, bar food in panelled and beamed lounge, games in public bar, summer barbecues on big lawn (Weds and Sat evenings); children in family-room or pool-room; bedrooms *(LYM)*

Biddenden [TQ8538], *Red Lion*: Old inn in a lovely village with good food, especially chilli con carne and cottage pie, and Fremlins and Whitbreads Castle Eden on handpump; done up with red plush furnishings, bright carpet *(Keith Walton, Alison Hayward, Nick Dowson)*

Birchington [Station Rd; TR3069], *Seaview*: Well run, friendly local with well kept Flowers IPA, good bar food *(P Garrad)*

Bishopsbourne [TR1852], *Mermaid*: Real friendly local in truly small village *(D P Green)*

Botolphs Bridge [Lower Wall Rd; TR1233], *Botolphs Bridge*: Excellent, well run pub overlooking Romney Marsh and fields of grazing sheep; pleasant and attentive licensees and enjoyable bar food including Sun roasts *(Peter Davies)*

☆ **Boxley** [nestling under M20; TQ7759], *Yew Tree*: Smart little Shepherd Neame pub tucked beneath Kentish downs; real ale, sandwiches and easy parking opposite; very pretty village and church *(Eileen Broadbent)*

Brabourne [Canterbury Rd (E Brabourne); TR1041], *Five Bells*: Good food and Courage ales in free house with comfortable atmosphere, log fire, tables in garden *(Alison Gurr)*

Bramling [A257 E of Canterbury; TR2256], *Haywain*: Well kept Courage Directors in spick-and-span pub, wide choice of good food, tables on lawn, children's playthings

(Ted George)

☆ **Brasted** [High St (A25 3 miles from M25 – Sevenoaks junction); TQ4654], *Kings Arms*: Nice traditional furnishings including huge carved armchair on parquet floor, inglenook fireplace with gleaming brass plates and other knick-knacks (but log-effect gas fire), antique tuba on the wall, maybe someone playing piano or electric organ (it's popular with musicians); bar billiards, shove-ha'penny and darts in other rooms, lunchtime food and evening snacks, well kept Shepherd Neame, friendly service *(Simon Velate)*

☆ **Brasted** [A25], *White Hart*: Friendly and efficient staff and relaxed weekday atmosphere in spacious lounge and sun lounge (it can get very busy at weekends); well kept Bass and Charrington IPA in Battle of Britain bar with signatures and mementoes of Biggin Hill fighter pilots, big neatly kept garden; generous helpings of reasonably priced bar food, restaurant; children welcome; bedrooms very clean if rather old-fashioned *(C A Holloway, LYM)*

Brasted [High St], *Bull*: Friendly, efficient service, good reasonably priced food, well kept Shepherd Neame Best, Old and Stock; shove-ha'penny and darts, garden with children's play equipment *(Keith Widdowson)*; [Church Rd] *Stanhope Arms*: Simple bar food and well kept Ind Coope Burton in unpretentious village pub near church, with relaxed atmosphere and traditional games (even bat-and-trap outside) as well as machines; children in eating area *(LYM)*

Brenchley [TQ6741], *Rose & Crown*: Sturdily timbered old inn with comfortable seats around rustic tables, straightforward home-made bar food including a good basic ploughman's and good home-cured ham, Fremlins, Harveys and Hook Norton real ales, friendly licensees, piped music; children in eating area, restaurant and family-room, seats on terrace, garden play area; bedrooms well equipped but not cheap *(Mr and Mrs G D Amos, LYM)*; [OS Sheet 188 reference 666417] *Walnut Tree*: Well decorated, warm pub with well kept beer, good bar food reasonably priced *(G C Saunders)*

Bridge [TR1854], *White Horse*: Smart pub in centre of pleasant village, tastefully decorated lounge with good collection of guns; Fremlins Bitter, good ham ploughman's, separate restaurant *(Brian and Jenny Seller)*

Brookland [pub just off and signposted from A259 about ½ mile out of village; TQ9825], *Woolpack*: Beautiful, low fourteenth-century beams, friendly and relaxed atmosphere, well kept Shepherd Neame on handpump, inglenook fireplace, good home-made lasagne and ploughman's; garden with stream at bottom *(Geoff and Sarah Schrecker)*

☆ **Burham** [Church St (near M2 junction 3); TQ7361], *Golden Eagle*: Good friendly atmosphere, welcoming landlord, impressive beams, well kept Flowers, Fremlins and Wethereds, inventive Malaysian-style and other bar food at reasonable prices; attractive North Downs view; seating rather 1960ish *(Geoff and Teresa Salt, Peter Griffiths)*

Burham [Burham Common, just W of Blue Bell Hill], *Robin Hood*: Lovely welcoming haven on undeveloped part of North Downs Way; neat and homely, Courage Directors, large garden with plenty of seating, bar food (maybe not in winter, unless local shoot meeting) *(Brian and Jenny Seller)*

☆ **Canterbury** [North Lane; TR1557], *Falstaff*: Good ploughman's and other reasonably priced weekday lunchtime bar food and well kept Flowers or Fremlins in clean and friendly old pub nicely refurbished with stripped panelling, hop bines and old coins; cheery staff, music can be a bit on the loud side; closed Sun lunchtime; note that this is different from the Falstaff Hotel in St Dunstans St – good, but decidedly not a pub *(A and J Whitley, Brian and Jenny Seller; hotel recommended by Gordon Mott, Paul and Margaret Baker)*

Canterbury [St Stephens], *Olde Beverlie*: Spacious, clean and warm with cheerful, comfortable atmosphere, attractive red stone floor; no food evenings *(TBB)*; [Old Dover Rd] *Phoenix*: Excellent value lunches, well kept real ales such as Adnams and Greene King *(R Coe, Richard Sanders)*; [Watling St] *Three Tuns*: Sixteenth-century, with comfortable beamed bar areas, sloping floors, conservatory, usual bar food, real ale, piped music, children's room; bedrooms generously sized; but they discriminate against the armed forces *(L Russell, Lyn and Bill Capper)*; [Castle Row, opp tree-shaded square off Castle St] *White Hart*: Friendly, courteous service; good variety of well cooked, reasonably priced bar food generously served *(W J Crust)*

Capel Le Ferne [A20 towards Folkestone; TR2439], *Valiant Sailor*: Big neatly kept roadside pub, warm welcome, well kept Flowers Original, good value lunchtime food; they ask for respectable dress; useful stop on North Downs Way *(Brian and Jenny Seller)*

Challock [Church Lane; TR0050], *Chequers*: Tastefully modernised country pub, and inn since 1700; reasonable range of good value bar food (Tues–Sat), nice spot, terrace *(R Coe, Miss M Byrne)*

Charing Heath [TQ9249], *Red Lion*: Splendid country pub, friendly and unspoilt with no juke box and well kept Shepherd Neame beers *(Comus Elliott)*

Chatham [Railway St; TQ7567], *Prince of Wales*: Town-centre pub, popular with business people at lunchtime, but more cosmopolitan in evenings; friendly welcome, cheerful staff, good lunchtime bar food and busy but clean upstairs restaurant *(A W Spencer)*

☆ **Chiddingstone Causeway** [B2027; TQ5146], *Little Brown Jug*: Good welcoming atmosphere in comfortably modernised

country pub, pleasant landlord (LSO trombonist – also plays jazz), at least six well kept real ales, wide choice of good bar food which can be eaten in restaurant, cheerful if not always speedy service; children allowed in one room; attractive garden with children's play tree and so forth; interesting to watch cricket balls being produced by hand at Duke's factory nearby *(W J Wonham, J A Snell, J M Price, Heather Martin, Mr and Mrs W Harrington)*

Chiddingstone Causeway [Charcott – off back rd to Weald], *Greyhound*: Clean Whitbreads local in quiet hamlet, with genuine welcome; well kept Flowers Original, Sun peanuts and cheese and biscuits on bar and all tables; bar food, barbecue and tables out in front *(Brian and Jenny Seller)*

☆ **Chilham** [TR0753], *White Horse*: Beautiful position on prettiest village square in Kent – with couple of tables out on the corner to make the most of it; lively lunchtime bustle in summer, good winter log fire, Fremlins real ale, good bar food including interesting vegetarian dishes *(C Trows, LYM)*

Chillenden [TR2653], *Griffins Head*: Rural and unpretentious with plenty of bar meals but only ploughman's as a bar snack *(L M Miall)*

Claygate [B2162 Yalding–Lamberhurst; TQ7144], *White Hart*: Clean, well kept pub with wide choice of good bar food and friendly service; children allowed in restaurant *(S Watkins)*

Cobham [TQ6768], *Ship*: Spaciously done up, with long bar, real ales such as Fremlins and Websters Original Mild *(R A Caldwell)*

☆ **Conyer Quay** [TQ9664], *Ship*: Rambling collection of cosily nautical little rooms in attractive creekside position, lots of traditional bar games, paperback exchange, groceries sold, cheery atmosphere; well kept Flowers Original and Fremlins on handpump, bar food including ploughman's, filled baked potatoes and basket meals, local oysters in the restaurant; tables outside facing waterfront; children allowed in restaurant; only reason it's not a main entry is lack of recent recommendations *(LYM – more reports please)*

Coopers Corner [TQ4849], *Frog & Bucket*: Popular pub near Bough Beech reservoir; friendly landlord, well kept Flowers IPA, farm cider, good bar food; pleasant garden with seats, tables and barbecue; live jazz Sun lunchtime, other live acts weekend evenings, when it can get crowded and noisy, popular with teenagers and bikers *(Jenny and Brian Seller, Alasdair Knowles)*

☆ **Cowden** [junction B2026 with Markbeech rd; TQ4640], *Queens Arms*: Clean and friendly with very old-fashioned atmosphere, well kept Whitbreads; landlady proudly displays sign outside saying 'No lager sold', and does mammoth helpings of bread, cheese and pickle at very old-fashioned prices *(Phil and Sally Gorton)*

Cowden [Holtye Common (A264 S of village

– actually just over border in Sussex)], *White Horse*: Old free house, tastefully enlarged, with King & Barnes and Pilgrims, and good value bar food *(Dave Braisted)*

Cranbrook [TQ7735], *Crown*: Friendly basic local with two real ales and exceptional value lunchtime specials with up to half a dozen vegetables *(R Coe)*; *Duke of York*: Unpretentious refurbished pub, with warm welcome and good food at very attractive prices *(Joy Hardwick)*

Crouch [TQ6155], *Olde Chequers*: Pleasant and friendly sixteenth-century pub with good choice of food and wines in bar and restaurant; special events; garden; good wooded walks nearby *(W J Wonham)*

Darenth [Darenth Rd; TQ5671], *Chequers*: Interesting black and white timbered pub, Courage Best, terrace and garden behind, bar food (Mon–Sat) and Sun lunch *(Anon)*

Dartford [3 Darenth Rd; TQ5373], *Malt Shovel*: Quiet old pub, unspoilt public bar and plush lounge with separate eating area; well kept Youngs, good choice of bar food from sandwiches, ploughman's and salads to hot meals and daily specials *(Paul Wyles)*

Deal [Manor House, Kingsdown Pk, Upper Street; TR3752], *Don Medi*: Place with a difference – cocktail bar, restaurant serving superb choice of Italian and English dishes at reasonable prices and with barbecue en suite, Julio Iglesias piped music; cars parked by stewards who will valet it on request *(J D Martin)*; [Strand] *Lifeboat*: Very much connected with the sea; congenial surroundings, good English pub food *(B Prosser)*

Denton [Canterbury rd (A260); TR2147], *Jackdaw*: Spotlessly clean, warm welcome, good value food *(C M Franks)*

Detling [TQ7958], *Cock Horse*: Friendly atmosphere, well kept Flowers Original and Fremlins, good value bar food, restaurant; pleasant outside seating areas *(Brian and Jenny Seller)*

Dover [opp Martin Mill BR stn; TR3141], *Ugly Duckling*: Popular real ale pub; welcoming landlord and landlady; good choice of bar food including seafood *(B Prosser)*

Dunton Green [London Rd; TQ5157], *Dukes Head*: Comfortably modernised listed building, with Benskins Best and other real ales, friendly licensee, bar food (not Sun), garden *(BB)*

Edenbridge [TQ4446], *Crown*: Cheerful local with Tudor origins and not over-modernised, popular for straightforward bar food, with good service, real ales such as Friary Meux Best; one of the last pubs to have kept its 'gallows' inn-sign stretching right across the road *(AE, GRE, LYM)*; [on edge] *Swan*: Popular pub with spectacular gardens overflowing with colour; unspoilt interior with stone fireplace, floral upholstery and curtains, copper and brasses, willow-pattern plates;

friendly attentive licensee, well kept Friary Meux Best and Ind Coope Burton, good bar food (limited on Sun) *(Heather Sharland)*

Elham [TR1743], *Kings Arms*: Friendly landlord and staff, well kept Whitbreads-related real ales, pleasant eating room/bar with good fire, bar food *(L M Miall)*; [B2065] *Palm Tree*: Good if not cheap real ales such as Flowers Original, Fullers ESB, Greene King Abbot, Ringwood Old Thumper, Theakstons Old Peculier and Wadworths, tasteful décor that includes fish tank and olde worlde atmosphere (but piped music); big garden *(Robert Caldwell)*; *Rose & Crown*: Good beer and food in very friendly inn, clean and tidy, with lots of old-world charm and efficient service; tables outside, attractive village; bedrooms *(Ted George)*

Etchinghill [TR1639], *New*: Large, fairly old pub, nicely laid out, helpful licensees, well kept Fremlins on handpump, well cooked locally caught grilled sole, small restaurant at one end *(Brian and Jenny Seller)*

☆ **Eynsford** [TQ5365], *Malt Shovel*: Popular Victorian local with interesting décor (and reputed ghost), well kept Courage Best and Directors, excellent value bar food with live lobsters in bar, friendly and prompt service; may not do bar food if restaurant busy eg Sun lunchtime *(Jenny and Brian Seller)*

☆ **Faversham** [10 West St; TR0161], *Sun*: Fascinating old-world fifteenth-century town pub with interesting rambling bar areas, good atmosphere, unpretentious furnishings and unobtrusive Radio 2; individually prepared and generously served good value lunchtime meals and snacks; well kept Shepherd Neame, friendly staff *(R Coe, Lyn and Bill Capper)*

Finglesham [TR3353], *Crown*: Free house, pleasant atmosphere, helpful and friendly bar staff; bar food, twelfth-century restaurant, huge car park *(M Roberts)*

Five Wents [A274 Maidstone–Sutton Valence, at B2163 crossroads; TQ8150], *Plough*: Spacious bar with good choice of food from nicely presented sandwiches through good value gammon and egg to steaks, with unusual specials; Courage ales, good coffee, piped music, restaurant area, seats in garden, quite handy for Leeds Castle *(TOH)*

Folkestone [North St; TR2336], *Lifeboat*: Friendly staff, half a dozen or more well kept and interesting real ales, tasty bar snacks; tables outside *(T R G Alcock)*

Fordcombe [TQ5240], *Chafford Arms*: Pretty inside and out, nr village cricket green *(David Gaunt)*

Fordwich [TR1759], *George & Dragon*: Tables on nice lawn by River Stour, and in covered outdoor area; comfortable inside, with good value bar lunches, Whitbreads-related real ales, subdued piped music, fruit machine; afternoon teas, Beefeater restaurant *(Lyn and Bill Capper)*

Frinstead [TQ8957], *Kingsdown Arms*: Welcoming atmosphere in free house with lots of swings, slides and so forth in large back garden, bar food even on Sun; out-of-the-way village *(Hazel Morgan)*

Gillingham [15 Garden St, Brompton; TQ7768], *Cannon*: Good polite service, relaxed atmosphere in snug bedecked with cartoons by local artist; well kept real ales including Ind Coope Burton, good bar food; local meeting point for sports clubs; good value bedrooms *(A W Spencer)*; [Court Lodge Rd] *Ship*: Pretty steep-tiled and weatherboarded pub, well modernised, with new conservatory extension and terrace, looking out over moorings and tidal flats; bar food from sandwiches to steaks, Ind Coope Burton and Tetleys on handpump *(Ian Phillips)*

Goathurst Common [TQ4952], *Woodman*: Lots of beams and much bare brickwork giving olde-worlde effect to extended split-level bar with several distinct areas; wide choice of real ales including Badger Best and Tanglefoot, Fremlins, Wem and Wethereds SPA, bar food and good steak restaurant, welcoming staff *(S J A Velate, W J Wonham)*

☆ Goudhurst [TQ7238], *Star & Eagle*: Striking medieval inn with settles and Jacobean-style seats in heavily beamed open-plan bar, well kept Flowers and Fremlins on handpump, decent bar food, polite staff, tables behind with pretty views; atmosphere could be warmer, piped music has been rather intrusive recently; children welcome; character bedrooms, well furnished and comfortable *(Mike Dixon, V H Balchin, J H Bell, LYM)*

☆ Goudhurst [A262 W of village] *Green Cross*: Good, interesting home-cooked bar food, good choice of real ales such as Adnams, Fremlins, Hook Norton and even Exmoor, beamed dining-room for residents; bedrooms light and airy, good value *(Sue Hallam)*

Gravesend [Queen St; TQ6473], *New*: Pleasant town pub with separate lounge and public bars and good local atmosphere; regular singsongs, well kept Fremlins *(Dave Webster)*; [Darnley Rd] *Somerset Arms*: Town pub worth knowing for its food, including speciality baked potatoes and home-made curries *(Anon)*

Greatstone [Coast Dr; TR0823], *Seahorse*: Very friendly sea-front pub with helpful staff, quick service, good choice of cheap bar food including children's meals; big sea-view terrace with play area *(Raymond Palmer)*

☆ Hadlow [Ashes Lane (off A26 Tonbridge Rd); TQ6349], *Rose Revived*: Good pub dating from 1515 though refurbished around 1980, with decent choice of well kept beers including Harveys and King & Barnes; well filled fresh sandwiches *(WHBM)*

Hadlow [Three Elms Lane – pub signposted from A26], *Carpenters Arms*: Delightful pub with very friendly atmosphere under new licensees; reasonably priced, large helpings of bar food served in attractive dining room; pretty garden with goat and other animals; convenient for Medway walks *(W J Wonham)*

Ham [Hayhill; TR3254], *Blazing Donkey*: Wide choice of good food, well kept beer, friendly staff; children welcome *(B Prosser)*

Harrietsham [Warren St; TQ8652], *Harrow*: Pleasant, relaxed and civilised atmosphere, choice of country wines, good food, very polite service, a nice place to stay at *(Mr and Mrs J R Graham)*

Harvel [TQ6563], *Amazon & Tiger*: In beautiful countryside, this very friendly place has a good choice of real ales (at a price) and good food; food Suns, too *(G F Scott)*

☆ Hawkhurst [A268 towards Rye; TQ7730], *Oak & Ivy*: Very friendly, quick service, reasonably priced food in comfortable and traditional pub with panelling, well kept Whitbreads-related real ales and roaring log fires; attractive restaurant *(Margaret and Trevor Errington)*

Hawkhurst [Highgate (A268)], *Royal Oak*: Unspoilt small hotel with comfortable bar and good value lunchtime food; bedrooms *(R Coe)*

Headcorn [North St; TQ8344], *White Horse*: Comfortable pub with friendly staff, good wide-ranging choice of reasonably priced bar food, pleasant garden complete with Wendy house *(Penny Mendelsohn)*

Herne [Herne Common; TR1865], *Fox & Hounds*: Excellent value bar lunches *(R Coe)*

Herne Bay [Sea Front; TR1768], *Bun Penny*: Friendly pub overlooking sea, three bars, well kept Shepherd Neame, good cheap bar food such as freshly boiled ham and attractive salads, outside seating; dogs on leads allowed *(Brian and Pam Cowling)*

Hever [TQ4744], *Henry VIII*: Country pub with pondside lawn and Boleyn connections, refurbished to cater with brisk friendliness for people visiting Hever Castle *(E G Parish, LYM)*

☆ Hildenborough [Stn; TQ5648], *Gate*: Friendly service, well kept Flowers and Fremlins, good though not cheap food – especially fish and seafood; the starters make good bar snacks – in pubby bar and restaurant; tables outside, good hillside spot with fine views over Downs *(Peter Griffiths, Barbara Hatfield, LYM)*

☆ Hildenborough [TQ5648], *Plough*: Country pub carefully extended, large open log fire; wide choice of real ales including Youngs, Flowers, Fremlins and Fullers ESB; good value bar food and carvery in the Barn *(J A Snell)*

☆ Hollingbourne [B2163, off A20 – OS Sheet 188 reference 833547; TQ8454], *Windmill*: Interesting and friendly pub with comfortable and welcoming bar – half a dozen different levels and nooks around the central servery; helpful staff, good food, well kept Whitbreads-related real ales, sunny garden with children's play area *(Roger Taylor, Mr and Mrs R Gammon)*

Hollingbourne [A20], *Park Gate*: Interesting and spacious old oak-panelled pub next to Leeds Castle, with good choice of well kept real ales, bar food (not Sun evening)

(R Houghton); *Pilgrims Rest*: Cosy, warm and inviting with good range of real ales including Adnams, Batemans XXXB, Everards Tiger and Shepherd Neame Old, bar food including good value ploughman's; right on North Downs Way *(Brian and Jenny Seller)*

☆ **Horsmonden** [TQ7040], *Gun & Spitroast*: Attractive up-market pub, overlooking village green, with very comfortable, spotless and spacious lounge, wide choice of good value bar food including generous hot or cold sandwiches carved in front of you, spit roasts on alternate days, well kept Ind Coope Burton; restaurant; friendly, smart and efficient service *(Gordon Smith, Capt R E G King, Eileen Broadbent)*

Ickham [TR2257], *Duke William*: Family-run free house, very friendly, with good value food and lots of well kept real ales such as Bass, Fullers, Shepherd Neame, Websters Yorkshire and Youngs *(D P Green)*

Ide Hill [TQ4851], *Crown*: Welcoming atmosphere, simple furnishings, pleasant cheerful atmosphere, bar food such as excellent cottage pie, log fire *(Ian Blackwell, P A Devitt)*

Iden Green [TQ8032], *Royal Oak*: Friendly pub, completely refurbished inside in attractive and pleasing 1920s style – soft, comfortable furnishings, ceiling fans; cheerful rather than speedy service and large helpings of very good reasonably priced food including vegetarian dishes *(W J Wonham, Mr and Mrs P Williamson)*

Ightham Common [Common Rd; TQ5755], *Harrow*: Small, modest-looking pub with comfortable, friendly bar and restaurant; quite substantial and varied reasonably priced food, fresh wherever possible *(Mr and Mrs P D O Liddell)*

☆ **nr Ivy Hatch** [Stone Street; TQ5754], *Rose & Crown*: Increasingly popular for good value bar food including outstanding puddings in pleasant bar with some stripped masonry and fine collection of jugs hanging from ceiling; well kept Flowers, decent wines, restaurant overlooking orchards; service not quite as quick as it might be; spacious garden with Fri evening summer barbecues, children's room in barn; on GWG49 *(Paul Evans, LYM)*

Kingsgate [Kingsgate Ave; TR3870], *Fayreness*: Excellent cliff-top sea views, well kept Youngs and pleasant bar food *(D S Fowles)*

Knockholt [Cudham Lane; TQ4658], *Tally Ho*: Cosy pub with Watneys-related real ales on handpump and reasonable food; may get rather smoky if crowded *(Alison Hayward, Nick Dowson)*

Lamberhurst [B2100; TQ6735], *Horse & Groom*: Good food in bar and dining-room; welcoming, even for just morning coffee, though they have well kept Shepherd Neame beers too; displays rotating selection of ties from massive collection *(Gordon Smith)*

nr Lamberhurst [Hook Green (B2169); TQ6535], *Elephants Head*: Ancient country pub near Bayham Abbey and Owl House, well kept Harveys, wide choice of food including good fresh sandwiches, polite service and friendly atmosphere; pleasant country views *(E G Parish, LYM)*

☆ **Larkfield** [New Hythe Lane (nr M20 junction 3); TQ7058], *Monks Head*: Olde-worlde low-beamed local dating from sixteenth century; three small bar areas downstairs, and another up the open staircase, two large fireplaces, one with huge log fire; well kept Courage Best and Directors on handpump, excellent range of food during week with dishes such as wild rabbit or Chinese spicy fish, more limited but still interesting menu at weekends *(Peter Griffiths, Keith Garley)*

Larkfield [London Rd], *Larkfield Inn*: Relaxing atmosphere in large, comfortable open-plan lounge, soft piped music, good lunchtime food and service; restaurant; bedrooms good value *(Keith Garley)*

Leeds [TQ8253], *George*: Pleasant village pub with compact and plainly furnished lounge and public bar, well kept Shepherd Neame on handpump, bar food *(S J A Velate)*; [A20] *Park Gate*: Sixteenth-century free house, spotlessly clean, oak-beamed lounge with welcoming roaring fire; usual bar food *(F J Robinson)*

☆ **Leigh** [Powder Mills – OS Sheet 188 reference 568469; TQ5446], *Plough*: Well kept and popular timbered country pub with cosy atmosphere, huge log fire, variety of seating places including huge old barn, efficient service, good range of real ales and of reasonably priced bar food; juke box (which can be loud) *(Peter Neate, Alison Kerruish)*

Little Chart [TQ9446], *Swan*: Isolated but comfortable seventeenth-century village inn with keen and obliging landlord and surprisingly good range of food *(Comus Elliott)*

Littlebourne [4 High St; TR2057], *King William IV*: Tastefully and traditionally decorated, comfortable, with sensible eating facilities and reasonable choice of good traditional hot or cold food, moderately priced; good service, good range of ales; bedrooms excellent value *(Mr and Mrs D P Millen, B Prosser)*

Longfield [TQ6068], *Wheatsheaf*: Long low thatched pub dating from fifteenth century, beamed bar with good oak settles, comfortable cask chairs, attractive brick fireplace, collection of cricket blazers and ties, brass milk dippers; simple food, well kept Courage, small games-bar *(Ian Phillips)*

Lower Hardres [TR1552], *Three Horseshoes*: Old-fashioned furnishings in country pub with Papas prints of Canterbury, choice of real ales, bar food *(Ian Phillips)*

Luddesdown [TQ6766], *Golden Lion*: Handy for M2 junction 2, yet in peaceful valley for walkers – classified as Area of Outstanding Natural Beauty and Special Landscape Area; simple pub with big wood-burning stove as well as open fire, Watneys-related real ales, bar food (not Sun, nor Mon–Thurs evenings) *(LYM)*

Maidstone [Penenden Heath Rd; ¼ mile from M20 junction 7, on Maidstone road; TQ7656], *Chiltern Hundreds*: Well kept and warm, with comfortable furnishings in airy well renovated lounge bar, good value hot dishes and filled crusty rolls, well kept Courage Directors, friendly efficient service, seats on terrace and in conservatory *(Geoff and Teresa Salt, BB)*; [9 Fairmeadow] *Drakes*: Excellent old-world feel in crab and oyster house with well kept Flowers and Fremlins, quiz machine, other food too *(Dr and Mrs A K Clarke)*

Marsh Green [TQ4345], *Wheatsheaf*: Friendly service, wide choice of enterprising lunchtime and evening bar food *(S J Bentley)*

☆ **Martin** [TR3346], *Old Lantern*: Ancient house in attractive gardens with cheerful, attentive service, good food at reasonable prices *(Mr and Mrs J H Adam, C M Franks)*

Matfield [TQ6541], *Wheelwrights Arms*: Attractive old building, part whitewashed brick and part weatherboarded, simple furnishings, lots of horsebrasses and yokes on walls and beams, attractive counter; Flowers and Fremlins on handpump, bar food from sandwiches (almost doorstep proportions) and ploughman's to steaks *(S J A Velate)*

Meopham [Meopham Green; TQ6466], *Cricketers*: Over 200 years the headquarters of the cricket club; bar food including very good sandwiches, friendly welcome *(David Gaunt)*

☆ **Minster** [2 High St; the one nr Ramsgate, at TR3164], *Bell*: Lots of character, comfortable old wooden settles, pleasant atmosphere, well kept Fremlins and Flowers, bar meals at attractive prices; can be crowded Sun lunchtime when customers' king-size dogs don't help (nor does their pipe smoke) *(Robert Caldwell, J D Martin)*

Minster [the same one – Monkton Rd], *Saddlers Arms*: Welcoming if narrow local, well kept Shepherd Neame on handpump, good reasonably priced bar food; ventilation could be better *(Robert Caldwell)*

New Romney [TR0624], *Plough*: Pub here since eighteenth century, long bar with log fires, games- and pool-room, cosy beamed restaurant, bar food including delicious puddings, barbecue and garden *(Rita Bray)*

☆ **Newenden** [A268; TQ8227], *White Hart*: Attractive sixteenth-century pub with low beams and timbers, inglenook log fire, good food from snacks to Scotch steaks in bar and restaurant, well kept beer, decent house wine, very helpful service *(David Gaunt, BB)*

Otford [TQ5359], *Bull*: Consistently good, with well kept Courage, good home-cooked bar food, pleasant young staff, attractive garden, good family-room; nr GWG47 *(K Leist, John McGee)*; [High St] *Horns*: Busy but quiet Tudor pub with fresh atmosphere and attentive service; well kept Harveys and King

& Barnes on handpump, big inglenook fireplace, good bar food including well filled sandwiches, inoffensive piped music; nr GWG47 *(GRE, AE and others)*

Pembury [TQ6240], *Black Horse*: Interesting combination of old and new, as the pub has a wine bar attached; good pub food, decent wine *(Brian Smith)*

Penenden Heath [TQ7656], *Bull*: Well run suburban pub with lots of games including outdoor ones such as boules; bar food, restaurant, summer barbecues *(BB)*

☆ **Penshurst** [Coldharbour Lane, Smarts Hill; following Smarts Hill signpost off B2188, bear right towards Chiddingstone and Cowden; TQ5243], *Bottle House*: Fine atmosphere in cosy and friendly family-run pub, wide choice of particularly good attractively priced food, attentive service; comfortable and attractive restaurant, garden *(Keith Walton, W J Wonham)*

Penshurst [Smarts Hill; following same Smarts Hill signpost, bear left towards Fordcombe and Tunbridge Wells], *Spotted Dog*: New licensees 1989, working hard to restore the popularity of this beautifully placed ancient pub with its heavy beams and timbers, handsome inglenook fireplace, some antique settles as well as more straightforward bar furnishings, rugs on the tile floor, and above all those idyllic summer views over Penshurst Place and the Medway Valley from the split-level terrace behind; food in bar and restaurant, well kept Whitbreads-related real ales – more reports on the latest regime please *(James Cross, LYM)*

Petham [Stone St; TR1251], *Slippery Sams*: Clean old beamed pub with friendly, cosy atmosphere; well kept Shepherd Neame, wide choice of excellently prepared food in candle-lit restaurant *(Paul and Margaret Baker)*

☆ **nr Plaxtol** [Sheet Hill; from Plaxtol, take Tree Lane from war memorial and church, straight through Yopps Green; from A227 nearly a mile S of Ightham, take unmarked turning beside lonely white cottage Bewley Bar, then right at oast-house signposted Plaxtol; TQ6053], *Golding Hop*: Secluded country pub with sun-trap lawn, real ales such as Adnams, King & Barnes Festive and Youngs Special tapped from the cask, choice of good farm ciders (it's even made its own; its own-brewed beer is served under heavy top pressure), simple bar food (not Mon evening), straightforward country furniture, maybe rather a take-it-or-leave-it atmosphere (they won't let children in even to get to the lavatory); music can be loud, may have spit-roast pig on bank hols – when it gets very busy *(Peter Griffiths, Joy Heatherley, Alasdair Knowles, LYM)*

☆ **Pluckley** [TQ9245], *Black Horse*: Cosy and busy old local with welcoming staff, low beams, really vast inglenook with unusual brazier-type fire, dark oak settles, huge friendly black cat, good if rather pricey home-made bar food including excellent puddings, well kept

Fremlins; large area given over to restaurant serving tasty business lunches; reputedly haunted, nice garden *(Geoff and Sarah Schrecker, Eileen Broadbent)*

Ripple [TR3449], *Plough*: Attractive olde-worlde pub with cosy flagstoned rooms, well kept changing real ales, decent bar food, friendly service *(Mr and Mrs J H Adam)*

Rochester [10 St Margarets St; TQ7467], *Coopers Arms*: Interesting old pub with quaint, friendly atmosphere; brisk lunchtime trade for tasty bar meals, well kept Courage and John Smiths real ales *(Dr and Mrs S G Donald)*; [16 High St] *Royal Victoria & Bull*: Complex of modernised bars opening off coachyard of substantial hotel, including back Great Expectations theme bar – the inn has many Dickens connections – and front real ale bar; wide choice of sensibly priced bar food, restaurant; children welcome; bedrooms *(LYM)*

Romney Street [TQ5461], *Fox & Hounds*: Quiet pub in lovely countryside with pleasant unpretentious bar, well kept Shepherd Neame Old, good value straightforward bar food, tables outside *(Jenny and Brian Seller)*

St Margaret's Bay [TR3844], *Granville*: A friendly place in a lovely clifftop position surrounded by NT land – on a clear day you can read the Town Hall clock in Calais through the U-boat binoculars on the bar terrace; interesting but limited bar menu, well kept Shepherd Neame ale; bedrooms; on GWG43 *(Lyn and Bill Capper)*

☆ **St Mary in the Marsh** [TR0628], *Star*: Delightful, remote, family-run pub, renovated 1989, with good bar food at moderate prices, friendly atmosphere, pleasant staff, Shepherd Neame tapped from the cask and other real ales on handpump; by small, attractive church; bedrooms attractive, with views of Romney Marsh *(Robert Crail, G A Trodd, Jim Froggatt, Denise Plummer)*

Sandgate [Brewers Lane; TR2035], *Clarendon*: Friendly new licensees and locals, consistently well kept Shepherd Neame, bar food, sparsely furnished bar *(Terry Buckland)*; [High St] *Ship*: Small unpretentious front bar with very friendly atmosphere and genuinely old furnishings; passage to another small back room; very good value home-made food including outstanding fish pie; good service, well kept Ind Coope Burton, seats outside *(Hugh Williams, Carron Greig)*

Sandhurst [Rye Rd; TQ7928], *Harrier*: Good value home-made bar food (not winter evenings Mon–Weds) inc children's menu, summer barbecues, Sun roasts; darts, round pool-table, fascinating parrot called Bonkers; children's play area *(Linda Barnes)*

Sandwich [Strand St; TR3358], *Admiral Owen*: Exceptionally clean and welcoming with characterful French licensee; interesting knick-knacks on walls and wonderful lunchtime and evening food *(Mr and Mrs A J Winthorpe)*; [The Quay] *Bell*: Comfortable carpeted lounge, soft pleasant piped music, usual choice of bar food including sandwiches, ploughman's and main dishes, with extra choice from restaurant; bedrooms *(Lyn and Bill Capper)*; [4 High St] *Crispin*: Fifteenth-century inn overlooking river with friendly atmosphere; good lunchtime menu; wide choice of beers and wines *(B Prosser)*

☆ **Sevenoaks** [Godden Green, just E; TQ5355], *Bucks Head*: Delightful pub in idyllic situation by duck pond on green, good food, prompt cheerful service, well kept Courage ales, decent wines, very cosy with pleasant atmosphere, copper and stags'-head decorations; nr GWG49, handy for Knole Park (NT) *(W J Wonham, Jenny and Brian Seller)*

☆ **Sevenoaks** [A225 just S (note that this is different from the next-door Royal Oak Hotel], *Royal Oak Tap*: Well presented and imaginative, reasonably priced food in pleasant bar with lively and genially welcoming atmosphere, good service, well kept Watneys-related and other real ales, restaurant; almost opp entrance to Knole Park *(PBK, Adam Loxley, Debbie Wilkinson, Mr and Mrs D I Baddeley)*

☆ **Sevenoaks** [Bessels Green, just off A21], *Kings Head*: Welcoming, friendly and clean, with reliably good food in bar and restaurant; dogs allowed, colourful garden *(WHBM)*

Shatterling [TR2658], *Green Man*: Good atmosphere, lively bar, restaurant with varied wholesome menu at reasonable prices *(J D Martin)*

Shepherdswell [TR2648], *Old Bell*: Pretty little pub on village green with photographs showing it in 1896; friendly licensee, well kept Flowers Original and Marstons, excellent value ploughman's, commemorative outside seat; on North Downs Way *(Brian and Jenny Seller)*

Shottenden [TR0454], *Plough*: Pleasant pub, good beer, no food, much cheer *(Anon)*

Smarden [TQ8842], *Chequers*: Pleasant atmosphere, Courage beers and good food, in beautiful village; bedrooms *(Comus Elliott)*; [B2077] *Flying Horse*: Small and spotless, very obliging landlord *(Ted George)*

Snargate [on Romney Marsh – OS Sheet 189 reference 990285; TQ9828], *Red Lion*: Fine old-fashioned pub, well kept Shepherd Neame, down-to-earth charm of another era *(T George)*

Sole Street [note – this is the one up above Wye; TR0949], *Compasses*: Largely unspoilt sixteenth-century country pub with big garden, rustic atmosphere, polite service, wide choice of good value bar food, Shepherd Neame real ales, choice of local farm ciders, log-effect gas fires, bar billiards, piped music *(Judy and Martin Corson, LYM)*

Sole Street [the other one, nr Cobham; TQ6567], *Railway*: Good food in bar decorated with railway memorabilia; pleasant atmosphere, excellent friendly service *(G F W Filtness)*

☆ **Southfleet** [Red St; coming from A2, left into Dale Rd, then left at Ship; TQ6171], *Black Lion*: Long, attractive, thatched pub, off the beaten track, rather smart but cosy inside, with warm welcome, log fire, massive helpings of interesting food (chilli prawns, steak and kidney pie and game casserole recommended), well kept Watneys-related real ales, summer barbecues; attractive restaurant *(Peter Griffiths, Elaine Pilkington, Geoffrey and Teresa Salt)*

☆ **Southfleet** [High Cross Rd, Westwood; coming from A2, keep on B262 into Betsham where you turn left], *Wheatsheaf*: Lovely thatched and beamed Tudor pub kept simple inside and out; barrel chairs, comfortable high-backed settles, inglenook with log fires, lots of interesting knick-knacks; well kept Courage Best and Directors, simple bar lunches (not weekends) such as ploughman's and fry-ups, occasional morris dancers *(Peter Griffiths)*

Staple [TR2756], *Three Tuns*: Warm, homely and well kept country pub with very reasonably priced, varied good food in bar and restaurant; bedrooms *(Clem Stephens)*

Stelling Minnis [Stone St (B2068); TR1446], *George*: Good food and service *(Mr and Mrs D B Allan)*

Stone in Oxney [TQ9427], *Ferry*: Former smuggling pub by what used to be the landing for the Oxney ferry – a simple, charming cottage with no fuss or frills; wide choice of fish, meat, pasta, curries and good puddings; big garden *(Peter Davies)*

Tenterden [main st; TQ8833], *Eight Bells*: Old building with friendly atmosphere, family-room and bar food *(Joan Olivier)*; [High St] *White Lion*: Early sixteenth-century building with great deal of atmosphere, pleasant bar and terrace by main street; good range of beers on handpump including Bass, wide choice of food in restaurant; bedrooms delightful – it's quite a substantial hotel *(Robert Crail)*

Teynham [Lewson St; TQ9562], *Plough*: Next to Guinness hop farm with very friendly, pleasant atmosphere, well kept Shepherd Neame beer and huge, fresh sandwiches *(Keith Widdowson)*

Tonbridge [High St; TQ5946], *Castle*: Modernised hotel, with small riverside terrace, busy atmosphere, friendly service, well kept Courage Directors; may be evening disc jockey; bedrooms *(Paul Evans)*

Toys Hill [OS Sheet 188 reference 470520; TQ4751], *Fox & Hounds*: Rustic unmodernised country pub with hotch-potch of motley furniture, in National Trust area; Ind Coope Burton on handpump, very limited food, log fire; nr GWG48 *(Alison Kerruish, S J A Velate; more reports please)*

Trottiscliffe [TQ6460], *Vigo*: Unspoilt, basic free house with Dadlums *(Phil Gorton)*

☆ **Tunbridge Wells** [Spa Hotel, Mt Ephraim; TQ5839], *Equestrian Bar*: Long, light and comfortable room with unusual equestrian floor-tile painting and steeplechasing pictures;

wicker and velveteen furnishings, friendly uniformed staff, good lunch snacks, well kept Fremlins and King & Barnes on handpump; bedrooms *(LYM)*

Tunbridge Wells [Little Mount Sion (off High St)], *Compasses*: Local with Victorian-style small rooms, open fires, Whitbreads-related real ales; has had imaginative good value bar food, but we've heard nothing of it this year *(Adam Loxley, Debbie Wilkinson, LYM)*; [Mount Ephraim] *Royal Wells*: Refurbished, well lit hotel bar with comfortable settees and chairs; Courage and Shepherd Neame Old on handpump; bedrooms *(Peter Neate)*; [Denny Bottom; TQ5739] *Toad Rock*: Pleasant and neatly kept little pub beside the Toad Rock itself; well kept Flowers Original and Fremlins, well cooked, good value bar food including vegetarian dishes, tables outside *(Brian and Jenny Seller)*

☆ **Ulcombe** [Fairbourne Heath, which is signposted from A20 – the best approach; TQ8548], *Pepperbox*: Friendly, relaxed pub with log fire, well kept Shepherd Neame ales tapped from the cask, wide choice of bar food including good fresh fish; big family garden *(B R Wood)*

Upnor [29 High St, Upper Upnor; TQ7571], *Tudor Rose*: Old-fashioned, friendly free house with good choice of well kept real ales including Youngs and others *(Comus Elliott)*

Upper Halling [TQ6964], *Black Boy*: Grade II listed building with new licensee a year or so ago; spotlessly clean with gleaming brass and John Smiths Bitter; bar food (not Sun, though you may get a sandwich then) *(Brian and Jenny Seller)*

☆ **Upstreet** [Grove Ferry; off A28 towards Preston; TR2263], *Grove Ferry*: Neatly kept riverside pub with nautical brass and copperware, full-length windows looking out on the water, ample helpings of well presented good bar food, carvery some days *(W P Ford, B Prosser)*

Walderslade [nr Bluebell Hill – and M2 junction 3; TQ7663], *Lower Bell*: Busy, old-fashioned pub with live music, Courage Best on handpump; bar food (not Sun) *(Jenny and Brian Seller)*

Waltham [TR1048], *Lord Nelson*: Attractive and welcoming village pub, open fires, Courage ales on handpump, generous helpings of good bar food, garden behind with South Downs views; children 's play area *(Victor Spells)*

Warren Street [just off A20 at top of North Downs; TQ9253], *Harrow*: Immaculate inside and out; extensive range of imaginative and well cooked and presented but rather pricey food makes it almost more of a restaurant than a pub, though they also have a good choice of well kept real ales; bedrooms *(Jane Palmer)*

Wateringbury [TQ6853], *Duke Without A Head*: Warm, friendly pub with three main areas; excellent service and generous help-ings of well prepared food – best to book if

you want a table; snooker room *(J D Martin)*
West Farleigh [TQ7152], *Chequers*: Locals'
pub hugely enlivened by flamboyant
decorations and entertaining licensee; well kept
Fremlins, straightforward sensible food, piano
some evenings, seats in garden; views over
upper Medway, with path down to the river
and good walks in both directions along it
(LYM)
West Kingsdown [TQ1763], *Horse & Groom*:
Good value bar lunches *(R Coe)*
Westerham [Market Sq; TQ4454], *George &
Dragon*: Chef & Brewer lounge bar full of
memorabilia including framed cinema
programmes and advertisements of the 1930s;
comfortable seating, pub atmosphere,
Watneys-related real ales on handpump, good
service, bar food including tasty sandwiches,
restaurant; this is a particularly pretty village,
with interesting houses to visit here and
nearby, and lots of walks *(E G Parish)*;
[Market Sq] *Kings Arms*: Elegant, civilised old
coaching-inn with comfortable lounge and
good bar food, restaurant *(AE, GRE)*;
[Westerham Hill; A233 to Biggin Hill]
Spinning Wheel: Recently refurbished free
house – though almost more of a restaurant –
with well kept John Smiths, comfortable
seating in lounge, rather sedate atmosphere,
wide choice of good bar food, good service
(E G Parish, WFL)
Whitstable [Borstal Hill; TR1166], *Four
Horseshoes*: Friendly licensees, jolly
atmosphere, well kept Shepherd Neame, no
food; can get crowded and smoky *(Robert
Caldwell)*
Wickhambreux [TR2158], *Rose*: Attractive
old building both inside and out, friendly
atmosphere, well kept beer; pretty village
(Q Williamson)
☆ **Wingham** [High St; TR2457], *Red Lion*:
Comfortably modernised inn – part of a
college founded here 600 years ago by
Archbishop of Canterbury; pleasant, friendly
atmosphere, neatly attractive décor, good
varied bar food, well kept Fremlins on
handpump; restaurant; bedrooms *(Ruth
Humphrey, LYM)*
Wingham [High St], *Anchor*: Traditional
beamed pub, cosy, with tasty, reasonably
priced bar food all week, warm service, well
kept Fremlins; garden *(L Russell, Q
Williamson)*
Wingham Well [TR2356], *Eight Bells*:
Comfortably modernised rambling beamed
pub, changing hands 1989 – with planning
permission for six motel bedrooms *(BB)*
Wittersham [B2082; TQ8927], *Ewe & Lamb*:

Romney Marsh country pub with simple
furnishings, wide choice of bar food, good
range of beers and wines; can be very quiet
lunchtimes; children welcome, adventure play
area *(C H Fewster)*
☆ **Worth** [The Street; TR3356], *St Crispin*:
Recently renovated old village free house
dating back to 1410, in pleasant spot close to
beach and golf courses; good value tasty bar
snacks and restaurant meals, attractive service,
relaxed atmosphere, well kept real ales
including guest beers *(Comus Elliott,
J D Martin)*
Worth [The Street], *Blue Pigeons*:
Comfortably refurbished Victorian country
pub with well prepared modestly priced bar
food and Sun lunch; good value bedrooms
(B Prosser)
☆ **Wrotham** [1¾ miles from M20 junction
2 – Wrotham signposted; TQ6159], *Bull*: In
the 1989 edition we asked readers to give their
views on an unusual experiment here – being
shown by a waitress to a linen-covered table as
you arrive, rather than going to a bar counter;
though it's still well worth knowing as an
interesting bar, with well kept Fremlins and (at
a quite considerable price) a wide choice of
truly enterprising food, readers' clear majority
vote on the experiment is that the changes do
really rule this out as a main-entry pub now;
decent piped music; children welcome; has
been open all day; bedrooms *(Jenny and Brian
Seller, TOH, LYM)*
Wrotham [The Square], *Three Post Boys*:
Simple, pleasant and friendly place with
generous helpings of straightforward,
wholesome food at very reasonable prices
– a proper pub *(Joy Heatherley)*
☆ **Wye** [Upper Bridge St; TR0546], *New Flying
Horse*: Pleasantly modernised seventeenth-
century inn, lots of beams, brass and
copperware but pleasantly light inside, good
seats, friendly atmosphere, locals at bar; wide
choice of substantial bar food, well kept
Shepherd Neame ales including Old, good
restaurant; attractive garden with Japanese
influence; bedrooms pleasant – especially those
in converted outbuildings – with good
breakfasts *(Heather Sharland, Alan Castle,
Stephen Goodchild)*
Yalding [Yalding Hill; TQ7050], *Walnut Tree*:
Cosy, characterful Whitbreads pub with beams
and inglenook, very popular for good bar food
including gorgeous home-made French onion
soup, home-cooked ham in sandwiches and
huge ploughman's; restaurant; bedrooms
(Eileen Broadbent)

Lancashire (including Greater Manchester and Merseyside)

A rich pattern of relatively powerful regional breweries (Greenalls, Boddingtons and their subsidiary Higsons, Thwaites and Robinsons) with a good few more local ones such as Lees, Holts, Hydes, Mitchells and Moorhouses, has done a great deal for this area's pubs. It makes for a more interesting choice both of drinks and of styles of pub than in most other places. It's done marvels for holding down the prices of both drinks and food – well below price levels in areas where the big national breweries have things more their own way. As we went to press in summer 1989 we could still find sandwiches for 60p, hot main dishes for under £2 (less than the price of a starter in many pubs in the south-east), steaks for £4.50 or less, puddings for 75p, and Holts pubs charging only 70p for a pint. Even the standardised dining arrangements now being introduced in some of their pubs by

Coal Clough House, Burnley

433

Boddingtons (Henry's Table) and Thwaites (Daniel's Kitchen) offer both value and some individuality. Though it has to be admitted that on the food side pubs here score more for generous value than for haute cuisine, *some pubs are outstanding for food: the Moorcock up at Blacko (including unusual Austrian and Italian dishes; its restaurant stays open through Sunday afternoon), the Bushells Arms at Goosnargh (unusual and imaginative, though the pub itself is straightforward), the Mark Addy and Royal Oak in Manchester (both amazing value for cheeses). Owd Nells at Bilsborrow (an entertaining thatched canalside pub – new in this year) and Old Rosins near Darwen usefully serve food all through the day, every day. On Sundays, pubs which serve food through the afternoon are the Black Dog at Belmont (until 5), Station at Broadbottom (another new entry – a splendid new reconstruction of a derelict building), Strawbury Duck at Entwistle (eight real ales), Harpers at Fence (a new licensee here) and Britannia near Oswaldtwistle (carefully refurbished this last year – one of the Daniel's Kitchen pubs). Changes to note this year include, after a long period of stability, new licensees at the Plough at Eaves near Broughton, Dunk Inn in Clayton le Moors, Duke of Wellington above Haslingden, that grand institution the Philharmonic in Liverpool (properly known as the Philharmonic Dining Rooms, to distinguish it from the other institution of the same name), Captains Cabin in Lytham and Tandle Hill Tavern outside Middleton (it's tied to Lees now); as we went to press the Hark to Bounty at Slaidburn was being sold to Scottish & Newcastle, who were to put in a manager (fingers crossed for this fine old inn). The Inn at Whitewell, one of the area's most interesting old inns, has been doing up its bedrooms with antiques and Victorian baths; full marks for keeping the same prices as before. But of course many of the area's best pubs owe much of their charm to the fact that by and large they* don't *change: the main entries are crowded with examples that positively bristle with character and individuality. And pubs to note particularly among the hundreds of Lucky Dip entries at the end of the chapter include the Rams Head at Denshaw, Diggle Hotel at Diggle, Egerton Arms above Heywood, Water Witch in Lancaster, Pump House among many promising Liverpool entries, Old Wellington and Britons Protection among even stiffer competition in Manchester, Ring o' Bells at Marple, Owd Betts near Rochdale, Duke of York at Romiley, Crown at Standish, Griffin in Stockport and Church at Uppermill.*

nr BALDERSTONE (Lancs)   SD6332 Map 7

Myerscough Hotel

2 miles from M6 junction 31; A59 towards Skipton

A quietly friendly new licensee has taken over this homely pub. There are creaky eighteenth-century oak beams, well made oak settles around dimpled copper or heavy cast-iron-framed tables, lots of brass and copper, soft lighting, ink and pen drawings of local scenes, and a painting of the month by a local artist. A fine padded elbow rest cushions the serving-counter, where you can order very good value, simple bar food: home-made soup (75p), sandwiches (from 85p), ploughman's (from £1.85), delicious grilled steak barm-cake (£2.25), home-made steak and kidney in gravy (£2.65), salads (from £2.85), a daily roast (£3.20), sirloin steak (£4.95), and specials such as beef in beer, quiches or sweet-and-sour pork (around £2.85); vegetables are fresh. Well kept Robinsons Best and Mild on handpump. The garden has been opened up and now has picnic-table sets, bantams and rabbits. *(Recommended by C J Parsons, George Hunt, Len Beattie, Dick Brown, Jon Wainwright, Roger Huggins, AE, GRE)*

Robinsons   Licensees John and Carol Pedder   Real ale   Meals and snacks (12–2, 6.30–8.30)   Children welcome until 8.30   Open 11.30–3, 5.30–11 all year

BELMONT (Lancs)   SD6716 Map 7

Black Dog

A675

The original part of this moorland pub has a collection of unpretentious small rooms with service bells for the sturdy built-in curved seats, rush-seated mahogany chairs, bygones from railwaymen's lamps to landscape paintings (along with more up-to-date collectables such as the bedpans and chamber-pots), and cosy coal fires; there are various snug alcoves, one of which contains what was the village court. Bar food includes sandwiches (from 80p), a winter home-made broth with suet dumplings or steak barm-cakes (£1), ploughman's (from £1.80), breaded cod (£2), lamb cutlets (£2.50), curries (£2.75), and six-ounce sirloin steak (£4.50). If you're in a hurry, make sure beforehand you know how long they'll take to serve you. The well kept Holts Bitter and Mild on handpump are among the cheapest you'll find anywhere; morning coffee. An airy extension lounge with a picture window has more modern furnishings; shove-ha'penny, dominoes, cribbage, fruit machine and piped classical music. There are two long benches on the sheltered sunny side of the pub, with delightful views of the moors above the nearby trees; from the village there's a track up Winter Hill and (from the lane to Rivington) on to Anglezarke Moor. There are also paths from the dam of the nearby Belmont Reservoir. *(Recommended by Denis Mann, G T Jones, Dr and Mrs A M Evans)*

Holts   Licensee James Pilkington   Real ale   Meals and snacks (not Mon or Tues evenings)   Restaurant tel Belmont (020 481) 218; open until 5 Sun   Children welcome   Ten-piece orchestra four times a year   Open 11–4, 6–11 all year; closed Sun evening   Bedrooms tel Belmont (020 481) 218; prices not set as we went to press

BILSBORROW (Lancs)   SD5139 Map 7

Owd Nells

St Michaels Road; at S end of village (which is on A6 N of Preston) take Myerscough College of Agriculture turn

This newish extensive white thatched canalside building has been well done out inside to give a cheerfully old-fashioned yet thoroughly family-minded feel, with plenty of space in its three or four communicating room areas. There are high pitched rafters at either end, lower beams (and flagstones) by the bar counter in the middle, and a mix of brocaded button-back banquettes, stable-stall seating, library chairs and other seats. A wide choice of efficiently served decent bar food, in big helpings, includes soup (90p), local potted shrimps (£1.90), hot beef sandwich (£2.20), six-ounce burger (£2.50), fresh Fleetwood fish and chips (£3.10), steak and kidney pie (£3.30) and minute steak (£4.45), with several dishes of the day such as black pudding (£2.65), liver and onion (£2.85) and beef salad (£3). They also do afternoon sandwiches (from £1.50), and late-evening snacks such as deep-fried courgette strips (£1.50), mussels casserole (£2) and fresh prawns (£2.60). Well kept Boddingtons, Chesters, Whitbreads Castle Eden and a beer named for the pub, with guest beers such as Flowers Original, Hartleys XB or Wethereds, and maybe good chunks of a cheese such as red Leicester as bar nibbles; decent wines including a bargain house champagne, tea, coffee, hot chocolate; space game, fruit machine and TV in one area, with unobtrusive piped pop music. There are colourful seats out on the terrace, part of which is covered by a thatched roof; a small walled-in play area has a timber castle. Lots of canalboats moor here. *(Recommended by Graham Bush, G J Lewis)*

Free house   Real ale   Meals (11–8) and snacks (all day)   Next-door restaurant (open all day inc Sun) tel Brock (0995) 40010   Children welcome   Open 11–11 all year

BLACKO (Lancs)   SD8541 Map 7

Moorcock 🏵

A682; N of village towards Gisburn

Even during a February snowstorm, this welcoming and spacious pub – high up on the moors – was busy. Truly home-made and generously served food is served willingly until very late in the evening, and includes an unusual range of garlicky Italian and Austrian dishes such as excellent bratwürst (£2.95), authentic goulash (£3.50) and schweinschnitzel (£3.95), as original as anything you're likely to find on the Continent; a wide choice of other food includes soup (£1.10), ploughman's (from £2.75), pâté (£1.95), burger, steak sandwich or home-cooked ham (£3), savoury pancakes (£3.25), steak and kidney pie or vegetarian lasagne (£3.50), halibut Mornay (£4.25), steaks (£7) and lots of daily specials; puddings such as cheesecake or good fruit pies (£1.25) and excellent fresh Sunday roasts (£3.50); friendly, speedy service (and dogs – one sheepdog has produced puppies). The comfortable bar is now refurbished, and has new carpets and furniture, and a new bar counter; the high cream walls are hung with brass ornaments, there's quite a lofty ceiling, and the views from its big picture windows are superb. Well kept Thwaites Bitter and Best Mild on handpump; juke box. The attractively landscaped back garden is very busy at weekends, though quieter during the week. *(Recommended by Geoff Wilson, Derek and Sylvia Stephenson, Alan and Marlene Radford, Len Beattie)*

Thwaites   Licensees Elizabeth and Peter Holt   Meals and snacks (12–2.30, 7–11; noon–11 Sun)   Restaurant   Children welcome, though very young children only until early evening Open 12–2.30, 6.30–12 (supper licence) all year; open all day Sun; closed 25 Dec   Bedrooms tel Nelson (0282) 64186; £12.50/£25

BLACKSTONE EDGE (Gtr Manchester)   SD9716 Map 7

White House

A58 Ripponden–Littleborough, just W of B6138

Popular with hikers and walkers, this friendly, isolated moorland pub has a cosy main bar area with a blazing coal fire in front of a Turkey carpet and under a large-scale map of the area; the snug Pennine Room opens off here, with brightly coloured antimacassars on its small soft settees. To the left, a spacious room has a big horseshoe window that looks out over the moors, comfortable seats around its tables, and coloured pins on a map of the world showing where foreign visitors have come from. Good bar food includes home-made vegetable soup (90p), sandwiches (from £1, steak £1.25), ploughman's (£1.80), Cumberland sausage with egg (£1.85), quiche Lorraine (£2), lasagne (£2.25), home-made steak and kidney pie (£2.50), salads (from £2.50),* and eight-ounce sirloin steak (£5); also, daily specials and home-made apple pie (75p). Well kept Exmoor Gold, John Smiths, Moorhouses Pendle Witches Brew, Robinwood Old Fart, and Timothy Taylors Landlord on handpump; fruit machine. *(Recommended by John Branford, Linda Duncan, G T Jones, Len Beattie)*

Free house   Licensee Neville Marney   Real ale   Meals and snacks (11.30–2, 7–10) Restaurant tel Littleborough (0706) 78456   Children welcome until 9   Open 11.30–3, 7–11 all year

---

Sunday opening is now 12–3 and 7–10.30 throughout England.

BROADBOTTOM (Gtr Manchester)   SJ9993 Map 7

Station

Just E of present end of M67; village signposted off A57 in Mottram; the train from
Manchester Piccadilly (every half-hour, more often in rush hours) takes 25 minutes

In 1988 the virtually derelict station building here was transformed into a
substantial and handsome stone pub, stylishly and imaginatively furnished. The
solidly comfortable bar, opening straight on to the platform, is full of Victorian
detail: the pattern of the carpet and wallpaper, prints large and small, elaborate
brass lamps, blue curtains on fat wooden rails, inset bookshelves, sturdy brass foot
rest and elbow rest for the bar counter, which has well kept Banks's Mild and Bitter
on handpump (and coffee or tea). The room is more or less divided into two by
stairs up to a galleried restaurant area, with banquette seating in booths, and a
striking art deco stained-glass ceiling. A second restaurant is done up as a dining-car
on the Orient Express, down to details like the curved and lofted carriage roof, tulip
lamps, masses of little vertical mirrors and a showy slave-lampholder. Bar food
includes soup (85p), sandwiches on request, onion bhajees with fresh minty yoghurt
(£1.45), ploughman's (£2.55), salads (from £2.75), pies (from chicken and
mushroom, £3.75), lemon sole stuffed with crab (£4.35) and steaks such as eight-
ounce sirloin (£6.95), with children's dishes (£1.95, including ice-cream after) and
lots of puddings such as home-made treacle tart (£1.10); smartly uniformed staff.
(Recommended by Steve Mitcheson, Anne Collins; more reports please)

*Free house   Licensees Peter Duffy and David Lamberton   Real ale   Meals and snacks
(12–2, 6.30–10, not Sat evening)   Restaurants tel Mottram (0457) 63327; open all day Sun
Children welcome   Live music Thurs evening   Open 11.30–3, 5.30–11 all year;
11.30–11 Sat*

nr BROUGHTON (Lancs)   SD5235 Map 7

Plough at Eaves

4½ miles from M6 junction 32: take M55 turn-off, then A6 N, then after about 1 mile N of
Broughton traffic lights, first left into Station Lane; after canal bridge bear right at junction,
then left at fork; pub on the right; OS Sheet 102 reference 495374

This tucked-away, spacious country pub has rush-seat chairs around dark wooden
tripod tables, lots of wooden casks, an antique oak linen chest and corner
cupboard, a couple of guns over one good copper-hooded open fire with a row of
Royal Doulton figurines above another, very low dark beams, and little latticed
windows; by the end of 1989 the pub should have been decorated. The food
arrangements here are what's known as Daniel's Kitchen – a branded set-up
introduced by Thwaites into a good few of their pubs in the last year or two: home-
made soup (80p), lunchtime sandwiches (from £1.10), ploughman's (£2.25), beef in
beer (£2.65), vegetarian dish (£2.85), chicken satay (£3.60), rack of lamb (£3.95),
and six-ounce sirloin steak (£4.25); daily specials, children's dishes (£1.35). Well
kept Thwaites Bitter on handpump; darts, dominoes, fruit machine, trivia and
piped music. Metal and wood-slat seats and cast-iron-framed tables run along the
front by the quiet lane, and there's a well equipped children's play area behind.
*(Recommended by Philip Riding, Derek and Sylvia Stephenson, L M Miall, Jon and Jacquie
Payne, Jon Wainwright, BKA, Sue Cleasby, Mike Ledger)*

*Thwaites   Licensee David Atherton   Real ale   Meals and snacks (12–2.30, 6.30–9.30)
Restaurant tel Rochdale (0706) 690233   Children in eating area   Open 12–3, 6.30–11
all year; may open longer afternoons in summer*

Stars after the name of a pub show exceptional quality. But they don't mean extra comfort,
and though some pubs get stars for special food quality it isn't necessarily a food thing either.
The full report on each pub should make clear what special quality has earned it.

BURNLEY (Lancs)   SD8332 Map 7

Coal Clough House   [*illustrated on page 433*]

Coal Clough Lane; between Burnham Gate (B6239) and A646; OS Sheet 103
reference 830818

This comfortable late-Victorian house has a spacious oak-panelled lounge with
antique prints, a lovely carved mantelpiece around the big open fireplace, and an
elaborately moulded high plaster ceiling; part of this room has been panelled off as
a place where people eating in the restaurant can have a drink before their meal.
There's also a popular front sun-lounge. Bar food from Mrs B's Farmhouse Pantry
includes soup (75p), meat and potato pie or plaice (£2.95), ham and eggs (£3.50),
steak and kidney pie (£3.95), sirloin steak (£5.75), and children's meals (£1.99); it's
popular with businessmen at lunchtime; fruit machine, maybe piped music. There
are tables outside on the terrace by the wistaria, and beside roses on the lawn.
(*Recommended by Len Beattie, Alan and Marlene Radford; more reports please*)

*Greenalls   Licensee Stephen Lucie   Meals (lunchtime, not Mon evening) and snacks (not Mon
evening)   Restaurant tel Burnley (0282) 28800   Children in restaurant and conservatory
Open 11–3, 6.30–11 all year*

CLAYTON LE MOORS (Lancs)   SE7430 Map 7

Dunk Inn 🍺

½ mile from M65 junction 7; A6185 towards Clitheroe, then first left (A678) towards Rishton,
then first left into Dunkenhalgh Hotel

In a converted stableblock and tucked away behind the low castellated stone hotel,
this thriving place spreads into cosy barrel-vaulted side sections (one with pool and
darts). There are lots of heavy brown beams and stonework, mate's chairs around
dark wooden tables on Turkey carpet, some big plates on a Delft shelf at the back of
the bar, and an airy feel helped by conservatory-style window bays looking out past
the sunken entry court to the sloping grass and shrubs beyond. Bar food includes
chicken (£2.35), pizzas (from £2.75) and scampi (£2.95); open fire; dominoes, fruit
machine and piped music. There are seventeen acres of grounds which the River
Hyndburn flows through. (*Recommended by Len Beattie; more reports please*)

*Free house   Licensee John Smith   Meals and snacks (not Sun evening)   Restaurant
Children in eating area of bar   Live disco or folk every night exc Mon   Open 11–11
all year   Bedrooms tel Accrington (0254) 398021; £53B/£63B*

nr DARWEN (Lancs)   SD6922 Map 7

Old Rosins

Pickup Bank, Hoddlesden; from B6232 Haslingden–Belthorn, turn off towards Edgeworth
opposite the Grey Mare – pub then signposted off to the right; OS Sheet 103 reference 722227

Down a steep narrow lane in an interesting moorland valley is this cosy, welcoming
pub. The big open-plan lounge has lots of mugs, whisky-water jugs and so forth
hanging from the high joists, small prints, plates and old farm tools on the walls,
and a blazing log fire in winter. It's furnished with comfortable red plush built-in
button-back banquettes, and stools and small wooden chairs around dark cast-
iron-framed tables; the big picture windows, which are heavily surrounded by
trailing plants, look out to the moors and wooded valley. Good value food includes
home-made soup (85p), sandwiches (from £1), ploughman's (£2.25), home-made
pizzas (£2.60), salads (£2.75), chicken tikka or home-made steak and mushroom
pie (£2.95) and gammon with egg or pineapple (£3.25). Matthew Browns Mild and
Bitter and Theakstons XB on handpump; pool, trivia, fruit machine and juke box.
There are picnic-table sets on a spacious crazy-paved terrace, with seesaws, swings
and a climber on the lawn; summer barbecues out here on Friday evenings and
Sunday lunchtimes. Watch out for sheep in the cark park. Bedrooms are under

construction. *(Recommended by Alan Holden, G J Lewis, Len Beattie, G T Jones, Carol and Richard Glover)*

Free house   Licensee Bryan Hankinson   Meals and snacks (12–10.30, 10 Sun) Restaurant evenings (not Mon) tel Darwen (0254) 771264   Children welcome   Open 11–11 all year

nr DELPH (Gtr Manchester)   SD9808 Map 7
Horse & Jockey

Junction of A62 and A670

Many would agree with the reader who suggested to us that the atmosphere in the two dimly lit, characterful rooms of this welcoming moorland pub lends itself to the telling of ghost stories. There are comfortable settees and easy chairs as well as Windsor chairs on the carpet, and (except in really warm weather) log fires; one room is panelled and served from a high hatch. A good range of well kept, changing real ales on handpump includes Clarks, Everards, Marstons, Mitchells, Moorhouses Pendle Witches Brew, Oak Best from Cheshire, Timothy Taylors and Vaux Sunderland. The wireless set at the back of the old-fashioned servery doesn't look as if it's moved since the 1940s. There are lovely views over the high moors, and good local walks including one down to the site of a Roman fort by Castleshaw reservoir; the Pennine Way is not far away. *(Recommended by Len Beattie, Gary Scott, Lee Goulding; more reports please)*

Free house   Real ale   No food   Open 7–11 all year; 1–2.30, 7.30–11 Sat

DOWNHAM (Lancs)   SD7844 Map 7
Assheton Arms

From A59 NE of Clitheroe turn off into Chatburn (signposted); in Chatburn follow Downham signpost; OS Sheet 103 reference 785443

This warmly welcoming, sixteenth-century pub sits on the lower slope of pasture hillsides, opposite the church. The rambling red-carpeted bar has beams and joists, olive plush-cushioned winged settles around attractive grainy oak tables, some cushioned window seats, and two grenadier busts on the mantelpiece over a massive stone fireplace (that helps to divide the separate areas). A wide choice of good, popular bar food includes soup (£1.05), sandwiches (from £1.65 – not Sunday lunchtime), Stilton or chicken liver pâté (£2.15), potted Morecambe Bay shrimps (£2.75), plaice or steak and kidney pie (£3.85), grilled ham with free-range eggs (£4.40), game pie (£4.95) and sirloin steak (£6.30), with several children's dishes (£1.65) and puddings (£1.95). Well kept Whitbreads Castle Eden and Trophy on handpump; Trivial Pursuit, unobtrusive piped music; kind, efficient service. There are picnic-table sets under cocktail parasols outside. The stone-built village, spread out along a pretty winding stream, is charmingly preserved. *(Recommended by Robert and Vicky Tod, P Booth, Mrs A Booth)*

Whitbreads   Licensees David and Wendy Busby   Real ale   Meals and snacks (12–2, 7–10)   Children welcome   Open 12–3, 7–11 all year   Adjoining cottage for hire tel Clitheroe (0200) 41227

EDGWORTH (Lancs)   SD7416 Map 7
White Horse

Bury Street

This cosy, friendly village pub is comfortably furnished with button-back wall banquettes curved around wooden or dimpled copper tables, lots of copper jugs and so forth hanging from the lacquered beams, and a brass ship's clock and barometer. There's also a profusion of highly lacquered dark brown oak panelling, much of it carved, and a couple of log fires (which may not always be lit). Bar food includes home-made half chicken (£2.20), plaice (£2.40), steak pie (£2.65), eight-ounce steak (£4.40) and home-made pies such as lamb and apricot or fisherman's (£3). Well kept Theakstons Old Peculier and XB and Youngers IPA on handpump; darts, pool, dominoes, fruit machine and juke box. *(Recommended by Roger Huggins, Wayne Brindle, Len Beattie; more reports please)*

Matthew Browns (S&N)   Meals and snacks (not Mon lunchtime)   Children welcome   Open 12–3, 7–11

ENTWISTLE (Lancs)   SD7217 Map 7

Strawbury Duck

Village signposted down narrow lane from Blackburn Road N of Edgworth; or take Batridge Road off B6391 N of Chapeltown and take pretty ¾-mile walk from park at Entwistle reservoir; OS Sheet 109 reference 726177

A fine range of well kept real ales in this lively, isolated pub includes Marstons Pedigree, Robinwood Old Fart, Ruddles County, Timothy Taylors Bitter, Mild and Landlord, and regular guest beers, all on handpump; also, Furstenberg Bavarian lager. The cosy flagstoned L-shaped bar has Victorian pictures on its partly timbered, partly rough-stone walls, a variety of seats, stools, little settees and pews, stuffed birds (and in the dining-room a stuffed mongoose struggling with a cobra), a mounted gun, and ceiling beams – the one over the servery is very low; one of the tables seems to be made from a big cheese press. Bar food includes sandwiches, soup (75p), filled baked potato (from £1.25), ploughman's (£1.95), steak and kidney pie or chilli con carne (£3.25), vegetarian dishes (£3.50) and steaks (£6.95). Darts, dominoes, fruit machine, juke box, and a pool-table in the tap-room (which now has flagstones). There are tables perched high over the cutting of the little railway line which brings occasional trains (and customers) from Blackburn or Bolton; plenty of nearby walks. *(Recommended by Sandra Kempson, Denis Mann, Keith Mills, K Sharp, Mr and Mrs Harry McCann, Ray and Jenny Colquhoun, Carol and Philip Seddon, Jon Wainwright)*

Free house   Licensee J B Speakman   Real ale   Meals and snacks (12–2, 7–10; 12–9.30 Sun; not Mon lunchtime)   Restaurant   Children welcome   Folk/jazz Thurs evening Open 12–11 (10.30 Sun); 12–3, 7–11 in winter; closed Mon lunchtime   Bedrooms tel Turton (0204) 852013; £28B/£35B

FENCE (Lancs)   SD8237 Map 7

Harpers

2¾ miles from M65 junction 12; follow Nelson, Brierfield sign, then right at roundabout, then at Brierfield's central traffic lights right again to pass station; cross A6068 following Fence, Newchurch signpost into Cuckstool Lane, turn right at T-junction, then first left into Harpers Lane; OS Sheet 103 reference 828376

The name of the village here goes back to the fourteenth century, when the local baron enclosed the forest of Pendle with a fence. Popular with families, this well kept and imposing stone-built house has a spaciously modernised lounge bar with pictures on the pale buffy pink flock wallpaper (including attractive prints by Vernon Ward), toby jugs on a high shelf, and red plush button-back banquettes curving around dimpled copper tables on the dark-red patterned carpet. The restaurant area is part of the same room, up steps and separated just by a balustrade; the atmosphere is thriving and friendly. Bar food includes home-made soup (90p), sandwiches (from 95p), lasagne or vegetarian dishes, steak and kidney pie (£3.25), gammon and egg, steak, and daily specials. Well kept Thwaites Mild and Bitter on handpump, and several wines; trivia, dominoes and piped music;

good friendly service. *(Recommended by Len Beattie, Carol and Richard Glover, Michael Heys, Comus Elliott)*

Free house   Licensee Kenneth Barlow   Real ale   Meals and snacks (11.30–2, 6.30–10; all day Sun)   Restaurant (open all day Sun) tel Nelson (0282) 66249   Children in eating area of bar   Open 11.30–3 (4 Sat), 6.30–11 all year

GARSTANG (Lancs)   SD4845 Map 7

Th' Owd Tithebarn ★

Church Street; turn left off one-way system at Farmers Arms

The big stone terrace out by the canal basin here has rustic tables overlooking the boats and ducks. Inside, this attractively converted barn has masses of antique farm tools, stuffed animals and birds, and pews and glossy tables spaced out on the flagstones under the high rafters. The dining area – more like a farmhouse kitchen parlour – has an old kitchen range, prints of agricultural equipment on the walls, and low beams. The atmosphere is jolly and the waitresses wear period costume with mob-caps. Popular, good value food includes home-made soup (£1.10), pâté (£1.25), ploughman's (£1.80), Lancashire hot-pot (£2.60), steak and kidney pie (£3.15), salads (from £2.10), a choice of roast meats (£3.60) and ham and eggs (£3.95); lots of puddings (£1.25), and a very good children's menu (from 55p). Country wines, bar billiards. It can get very busy at weekends. *(Recommended by Russell Hafter, John Branford, Linda Duncan, Mr and Mrs D J Nash, G A Worthington, M A and W R Proctor, Dr J K McCann, Sue Cleasby, Mike Ledger)*

Free house   Licensees Kerry and Eunice Matthews   Meals and snacks (12–2.30, 7–10; not Mon)   Children in dining area   Open 11–3, 7 (6 Sat)–11 all year; closed Mon (though not lunchtime bank hol Mons), 25 and 26 Dec, 1 Jan

GOOSNARGH (Lancs)   SD5537 Map 7

Bushells Arms ⊗

4 miles from M6 junction 32; A6 towards Garstang, right at Broughton traffic lights (the first ones you come to), then left at Goosnargh Village signpost (it's pretty insignificant – the turn's more or less opposite Whittingham Post Office)

The remarkably diverse and very wide choice of food is the main draw here: hummus or taramosalata with hot pitta bread (£1), falafel or crispy samosas (£1.80), duck pâté (£2), spicy chicken wings (£2.25), ploughman's or an authentic chilli con carne (£3.50), an elaborate fish pie or Malayan-style pork curry (£5), their very popular steak and kidney pie or chicken fillet with smoked bacon, asparagus, fresh chervil and hollandaise sauce in puff pastry (£5.50), local sirloin steak (£7), several dishes of the day and a good choice of vegetarian dishes (£3.50 – they also have rennet-free cream for the sumptuous puddings like strawberry Pavlova or sponge envelope filled with fresh fruit and cream £1.30). They will do sandwiches if they're not busy, serve some children's things (£1.75) or child-size helpings, and make the traditional local shortbread flavoured with caraway seeds and known as Goosnargh cakes (the place is pronounced Goozner, incidentally). Vegetables are fresh and crisp, and you may be given a choice of rice, chips, diced potatoes baked with cream and peppers, or tasty new potatoes; this year, the kitchen and cellar have been extended. Whitbreads Castle Eden on handpump, twenty-six wines (including house wines) and several malt whiskies. Walls or part-walls break the extensive modernised bar into snug bays, each holding not more than two or three tables and often faced with big chunks of sandstone (plastic plants and spotlit bare boughs heighten the rockery effect). There are soft red plush button-back banquettes and stools on the green Turkey carpet, with flagstones by the bar. Fruit machine, and maybe piped 1960ish music; service is neat and quick (though they warn of possible delays on busy Saturday evenings). *(Recommended by Miss E J Thickett, Col A H N Reade, Robert Gartery, John Atherton, AE, GRE)*

Whitbreads   Licensees David and Glynis Best   Meals and snacks (12–2.30, 7–10)   Children in eating area of bar   Open 12–3, 6–11 all year

HASLINGDEN (Lancs)   SD7522 Map 7
Duke of Wellington

Grane Road; B6232 signposted from Haslingden centre – OS Sheet 103 reference 767228

Not one for the traditionalist, this fills a real need with its sensible provision for families and its spacious layout – all too often such a glorious moorland position would mean saying goodbye to creature comforts. Balustered wood and black cast-iron screen dividers keep the softly lit main room in separate areas, and it's furnished with a lot of polished dark woodwork, the odd button-back leather sofa, button-back pink cloth settees and slat-back chairs around its tables, quiet country pictures on the muted pink-papered walls, art deco lamps, and bookshelves. The light and airy extension back dining-lounge has big picture windows looking over to the reservoirs nestling below the woods and sheep pastures of Rossendale. Bar food includes soup (80p), sandwiches (from £1.30), Cumberland sausage and egg (£2.55), steak and kidney pie (£2.80), cold platters with salad (from £2.75), gammon with egg or pineapple (£3.20), eight-ounce sirloin steak (£5.60) and daily specials. Well kept Boddingtons and Hartleys XB on handpump, good coffee. Picnic-table sets on neat grass face the views, and there's a well fenced and well equipped playground. *(Recommended by G T Jones, Carol and Richard Glover; more reports please)*

Whitbreads   Licensee Ian Cunningham   Real ale   Meals and snacks   Restaurant tel Rossendale (0706) 215610   Children in restaurant   Open 11.30–3, 6–11 all year; all day Sat

HEATON WITH OXCLIFFE (Lancs)   SD4460 Map 7
Golden Ball, *known as* Snatchems

Lancaster Road; coming from Lancaster on B5273, turn left by sandy wasteland where sign warns road liable to be under water at high tide (should also be signposted Overton, but sign may be removed by vandals)

From old-fashioned teak seats on a raised terrace in front of this friendly pub, there are views out over the broad River Lune and its boats. Inside, several cosy little rooms have low beams, cushioned antique settles, old-fashioned upright chairs (one attractively carved, with high arms), and built-in benches around cask tables; also, small flowery-curtained windows, a large collection of sporting rosettes, and fires in winter. Bar food includes baked potatoes (45p), home-made soup (50p), cheese and onion flan (70p), sandwiches (from 75p), steak or meat and potato pies with mushy peas (£1.05), steak sandwich or sausage and mash (£1.30), curry, bacon ribs or ploughman's (£1.55). Cheap well kept Mitchells Bitter and Mild, on handpump, served from a hatch; darts and dominoes, and a space game upstairs in the long, neat family-room. Because of the position, it can get crowded in summer. *(Recommended by Jon Wainwright, Jeff Cousins, Leith Stuart, Sue Cleasby, Mike Ledger, Dr and Mrs A K Clarke, AE, GRE)*

Mitchells   Real ale   Meals and snacks   Children upstairs   Open 11–3, 6–11 all year; opens 12 and 6.30 in winter

LIVERPOOL (Merseyside)   SJ4395 Map 7
Philharmonic ★

36 Hope Street; corner of Hardman Street

The mosaic-faced central serving-counter is the hub of this opulent gin palace:

heavily carved and polished mahogany partitions radiate out under the intricate plasterwork high ceiling, dividing off cosy little cubicles from the echoing main hall. This is decorated by a huge mosaic floor, rich panelling, and stained glass including contemporary portraits of Boer War heroes. The gents is a remarkable period piece (though not faultless), all marble and opulent glinting mosaics, and the copper panels illustrating musicians in the alcove of the fireplace are intriguing. A functions room – once set aside for coachmen to drink non-alcoholic drinks – is to open on the first floor. Home-made bar food that includes sandwiches, and main dishes such as chicken chasseur, liver and bacon, steak and mushroom pie or chilli con carne (all £2.50) is served in a splendid Grecian room decorated with half-naked art nouveau plaster goddesses reclining high above the squared panelling. Well kept Ind Coope Burton, Jennings Bitter and Tetleys Bitter and Mild on handpump; fruit machine, juke box and quizzes. There are two plushly comfortable sitting-rooms. *(Recommended by Steve Mitcheson, Anne Collins, D P Herlihy, Richard Saunders, Ian Phillips, Steve Waters)*

Tetley-Walkers (Allied)   Licensee John Draper   Real ale   Meals (not Sat or Sun) and snacks Metered parking nearby   Open 11.30–11 weekdays; 11.30–3, 6–11 Sat

LYTHAM (Lancs)   SD3626 Map 7
Captains Cabin
Henry Street; in centre, one street in from West Beach (A584)

Attractively decorated in Victorian style, this modest little pub has dark pink button-back plush seats and captain's chairs in bays around the sides, well chosen pictures – including local boats – on the muted bird-of-paradise wallpaper, and open fires. There's quite a bit of stained-glass decoration – in the solid wood screens which divide up the central area, and in the main windows, which have good freestyle stained inserts of fish and gulls; also, a coal-effect gas fire between two built-in bookcases at one end. Good value, simple bar food includes soup (60p), sandwiches (from 80p, toasties from £1.40), filled baked potatoes (90p) and cold platters (from £1.95), with hot daily specials like steak and kidney pie or quiche Lorraine (£2.10). Well kept Chesters Best Mild, Marstons Pedigree and Whitbreads Castle Eden and Trophy on handpump or tapped from the cask; friendly staff. Two fruit machines, juke box. *(Recommended by Carol and Richard Glover, D C Turner, Graham Bush, Peter Corris, Jon Wainwright)*

Whitbreads   Licensee John Rollo   Real ale   Lunchtime meals and snacks   Children welcome (not after 3)   Open 11–11 all year

MANCHESTER   SJ8398 Map 7
Lass o' Gowrie
36 Charles Street; off Oxford Street at BBC

The longish tall room in this lively, very busy home-brew pub is mainly stripped back to varnished bricks, with big windows in its richly tiled arched brown façade, hop-sacks draping the ceiling, and bare unsealed floorboards. First-comers get seats around lower tables on a cosier carpeted dais at one end, and there are quite high stools against ledges or unusually high tables. Brewed down in the cellar, the well made malt-extract beers are named for their original gravity (strength) – LOG35, which is quite lightly flavoured and slips down very easily, and the meatier LOG42, with well kept Chesters Mild and Bitter on handpump too; in one place seats around a sort of glass cage give a view down into the brewing room; Bulmers cider. Good value home-made food from a separate side servery includes moussaka or shepherd's pie (£1.95), and beef casserole, mince and onion pie, lamb hot-pot or savoury pork (all £2). Piped pop music can be very unobtrusive against the buzz of chatter, but it may be louder in term-time when students turn out on a Friday or

Saturday evening. The open gas lighting flares are a nice touch. *(Recommended by Steve Mitcheson, Anne Collins, Brian Marsden, Virginia Jones, Peter Race)*

Whitbreads/Own brew   Licensee Joe Fylan   Real ale   Lunchtime meals and snacks (no hot food Sat or Sun)   Children in small side room and raised area   Open 11.30–11 weekdays; 11.30–3, 6–11 Sat

Marble Arch

73 Rochdale Road (A664), Ancoats; corner of Gould Street, just E of Victoria Station

This friendly pub celebrated its centenary in October 1988 with more than a hundred real ales in one month. But there's always a wide, regularly changing range on handpump: Fullers London Pride, Hydes Anvil, Marstons Pedigree, Moorhouses Pendle Witches Brew, Oak Wobbly Bob, Ruddles and Timothy Taylors Landlord; a good choice of bottled beers and a selection of country wines. To add to the Victorian feel the walls are rag-rolled, the glazed brick lightly barrel-vaulted high ceiling has been magnificently restored, and there's extensive marble and tiling (particularly the frieze advertising various spirits, and the chimney breast above the carved wooden mantelpiece). The bar food includes filled barm-cakes (from 75p), huge ploughman's (£1.75) and hot dishes such as chilli con carne or hot beef curry; darts, dominoes, cribbage, chess, fruit machine, trivia and juke box. *(Recommended by Brian and Anna Marsden, Richard Saunders, Colin Dowse)*

Free house   Licensee Helene de Bechevel   Real ale   Meals and snacks (not Sun)   Children in eating area of bar   Open 12–11 all year; closed Sun and bank hol lunchtimes, 25 and 26 Dec

Mark Addy 🏵

Stanley Street, Salford, Manchester 3; look out not for a pub but for what looks like a smoked-glass modernist subway entrance

Originally waiting-rooms for boat passengers (and later the Nemesis Boat Club), the stylishly converted series of barrel-vaulted brick bays in this very smart waterside pub are furnished with russet or dove plush seats and upholstered stalls, wide glassed-in brick arches, cast-iron pillars, and a flagstone floor. Photographs around the walls show how it was in the nineteenth century: a sluggish open sewer from which the eponymous Mark Addy rescued over fifty people from drowning. Bar food includes an extraordinary range of cheeses – up to fifty at a time – from England, Scotland, Wales and several European countries, with granary bread (£1.90) – such is the size of the chunks that doggy-bags are automatically provided; there's also a choice of Belgian pâtés (£1.90), and soup in winter (£1). Well kept Boddingtons and Marstons Pedigree on handpump, and quite a few wines; piped music. Service stays efficient even when it gets so busy that there's a queue for food and it's hard to find a table. The canalside courtyard has tubs of flowers around its tables, from which you can watch the home-bred ducks. Dress rules are strict – too strict, say some readers: they may turn you away if you've got on a tie and proper trousers but no jacket, for example. *(Recommended by Len Beattie, Denis Mann, Steve Mitcheson, Anne Collins, Virginia Jones)*

Free house   Manageress Jill Chadwick   Real ale   Snacks   Children welcome   Open 11.30–11 all year

Peveril of the Peak

127 Great Bridgewater Street

The old-fashioned small-roomed layout in this particularly friendly, homely pub has three separate rooms opening off the central servery with various hatches and counters, a profusion of mahogany and stained glass, and framed Victorian song-covers and ancient prints of obscure village games such as sack-jumping. Furnishings are traditional – red leatherette built-in button-back wall settles, or sturdy red plush ones, and there's an interesting assortment of customers. Well kept Websters Yorkshire and Choice and Wilsons Original and Mild on handpump;

sensibly placed darts, pool, dominoes, cribbage, fruit machine, juke box and (rarity of rarities now) a bar football table. Food consists of sandwiches, hot pies such as steak and kidney or cheese and onion, and pork pie (all 55p). In summer there are some seats outside on the terrace. *(Recommended by Denis Mann, Steve Mitcheson, Anne Collins, Jon Wainwright)*

Wilsons (Watneys)   Licensee Teresa Swanick   Real ale   Snacks (not Sun)   Children welcome   Open 11–3, 5.30 (7 Sat)–11 all year; closed 25 Dec

Royal Oak 🏵

729 Wilmslow Road, Didsbury, Manchester 20

The full range of cheeses here is probably the widest you can find anywhere in the country, and one reader was amused to hear two elderly ladies asking for some without salad or bread which they put straight into their handbags; when asked why, they said it was far better value and there was a bigger range than the local Tesco's! There are pâtés too. It remains a mystery how they manage to heap your plate up with so much at the price (£1.90 – there are takeaway bags for what's left over). The atmosphere is warm and lively, and it's simply furnished with theatrical handbills, porcelain spirit casks, coronation mugs, and old-fashioned brass anti-spill rims around the heavy cast-iron-framed tables; there's a quieter snug bar. Well kept Marstons Burton, Pedigree and Mercian Mild on handpump; chatty, happy staff. There are some seats outside. *(Recommended by Richard Saunders, Jon Wainwright, David Wooff, Clarissa Ayman; more reports please)*

Marstons   Licensee Arthur Gosling   Real ale   Lunchtime snacks (not Sat or Sun)   Open 11–3, 5–11 all year; all day Sat; closed evening 25 Dec

Sinclairs Oyster Bar

Shambles Square, Manchester 3; in Arndale Centre between Deansgate and Corporation Street, opposite Exchange Street

The alcovey ground floor of this friendly, traditionally furnished, late eighteenth-century pub has small-backed stools that run along a tall old-fashioned marble-topped eating bar, squared oak panelling, and a low ochre ceiling. The second servery upstairs, which also serves lunchtime food, is in a quieter more spacious room with pictures of old Manchester, low old-fashioned wall settles, and a scrolly old leather settee. There's a decent range of bar food, served by neatly uniformed barmaids, such as ploughman's (£1.75), steak pie (£2.75), roast beef, gammon or turkey (£3), beef and oyster pie (£3.50), seafood platter (£3.70), and of course oysters (£4.50 the half-dozen), with sandwiches (hot gammon £1.50), rolls (75p) and side salads upstairs; the menu is limited on Bank Holidays. Sam Smiths OB and Museum on handpump kept under light blanket pressure, chess, fruit machine and piped music. There are picnic-table sets outside in a pedestrians-only square, in the middle of this huge modern shopping complex. *(Recommended by Steve Mitcheson, Anne Collins, P Miller, Brian and Anna Marsden)*

Sam Smiths   Licensee Mrs Coles   Real ale   Lunchtime meals and snacks (not Sun)   Nearby parking difficult   Open 11–11; closed 25 Dec

Tommy Ducks

East Street, Manchester 2

A striking sight, this pretty black and white Victorian pub is surrounded by towering new prestige office blocks and is convenient for the exhibition centre in the former Central Station. The street outside has been blocked off and there are picnic-table sets on the paving. Inside, there are plush button-back banquettes with gold fringes, antique theatrical posters, photographs and music hall cards on the mirrored walls, heavy swagged red curtains, and in one of its communicating rooms a big old-fashioned black cooking-range. An exuberant collection of knickers, donated by customers, is pinned on the red ceiling. Bar food includes sandwiches, beef in beer, curries, lasagne and sweet-and-sour chicken (all £2.50). Well kept Greenalls Local and Original on handpump, and a good few whiskies; fruit machine, juke box; very busy on weekday lunchtimes. *(Recommended by Howard and Sue Gascoyne, Steve Mitcheson, Anne Collins, Brian Marsden, Matt Pringle)*

Greenalls   Licensee Keith Shaw-Moores   Real ale   Lunchtime meals and snacks (not Sat or Sun)   Panama Jazz Band Sun evening   Children in eating area of bar – not evenings   Open 11.30–11 weekdays; 11.30–3, 7.15–11 Sat

MERECLOUGH (Lancs)   SD8332 Map 7
Kettledrum

302 Red Lees Road; from A646 Burnley–Halifax, quickest route is turn-off between Walk Mill and Holme Chapel, signposted Over Town, Worsethorne; OS Sheet 103 reference 873305

As we went to press we heard that this friendly, busy little pub was planning to extend the bar into the present dining-room (and move the existing one upstairs), extend the kitchen, move the lavatories, and decorate throughout. The interesting artefacts – we hope – will remain: wooden and copper masks, buffalo horns, gruesome-looking knives by the dozen, and sparkling brass – shovels, knockers, measures, corkscrews, keys, scales, weights, spigots, fancy boot-horns, imps, toasting-forks and warming-pans. A wide choice of food includes soup (95p), sandwiches (from £1.20, steak £3.95), omelettes (£2.45), ploughman's (£2.75), gammon with egg (£3.25), salads (from £3.25), home-made steak and kidney pie (£3.45), good home-made chilli con carne (£3.50), trout (£4.25), a massive mixed grill (£4.95) and sixteen-ounce T-bone steak (£6.95), with good home-made puddings. There's a good value set lunch (£6.25). Well kept Courage Directors, John Smiths Bitter and Magnet, Theakstons Best and XB, and a monthly guest beer on handpump; several malt whiskies; darts, fruit machine, space game and piped music. Seats outside look over a low stone wall beyond the quiet road to Burnley and its surrounding moors. *(Recommended by Len Beattie, Dr T H M Mackenzie, George Hunt, Michael Heys)*

Free house   Licensee Roy Ratcliffe   Real ale   Meals and snacks (12–2, 6–10.30; not 25 Dec)   Restaurant tel Burnley (0282) 24591   Children in eating areas until 7.30   Open 11–3, 5.30–11 all year; closed evening 25 Dec

MIDDLETON (Gtr Manchester)   SD8606 Map 7
Tandle Hill Tavern

Thornham Lane, Slattocks; this, with Thornham Old Road, is a largely unmade track between A664 and A671 just S of (but not quickly accessible from) M62 junction 20; OS Sheet 109 reference 899090

Actually part of a farm and surrounded by ducks, ponies and ageing tractors, this pub – under new licensees – is reached down a rough track with cavernous pot-holes. The two snug rooms have spindle-back chairs around dimpled copper tables, and lots of brass candlesticks on the mantelpiece above the coal fire. Bar food includes soup (50p), toasties (from 60p), pie (70p) and minute steak (£1.20). Well kept Lees ales on handpump; darts, cribbage, dominoes and piped music. There are some benches outside, and paths lead off on all sides. It's handy for the Tandle Hill Country Park. *(Recommended by Jon Wainwright; more reports please)*

Lees   Licensee Rita Rothwell   Real ale   Snacks (12–2, 7–10)   Children welcome   Open 12.30–3, 7–11 all year; 12–4, 7–11 Sat; closed weekday lunchtimes in winter

NEWTON (Lancs)   SD6950 Map 7
Parkers Arms   🏠

B6478 7 miles N of Clitheroe

In a surprisingly neat stone village, this black and white building, with its pretty window boxes and well spaced picnic-table sets on its big lawn, looks down towards the river and beyond to the hills. The well kept bar is brightly modernised, with one or two pictures on the white Anaglypta walls, lots of copper and brass kettles, candlesticks and an urn on the neat stone mantelpiece, and red plush button-back banquettes around dimpled copper tables on a flowery blue carpet. An arch leads through to a similar area with sensibly placed darts, pool, dominoes, fruit machine and trivia machine; discreet piped music, and an unobtrusive black labrador may wander in. Bar food includes soup (£1), sandwiches (from £1.50), burger, steak canadienne or ploughman's (£2.40), home-made steak and kidney pie (£3.40), gammon and egg (£3.90) and fresh salmon (£5.20); they do Sunday teas in the big, airy restaurant; good service. (*Recommended by Logan Petch; more reports please*)

Whitbreads   Licensee Henry Rhodes   Meals and snacks (12–2, 7–10)   Children welcome   Open 10.30–3, 6–11 all year   Bedrooms tel Slaidburn (020 06) 236; £15/£30

nr OSWALDTWISTLE (Lancs)   SA7327 Map 7
Britannia
Haslingden Old Road; junction of A677 with B6231

Though careful refurbishments here include a new Daniel's Kitchen restaurant in the old barn, the bar areas don't seem to have been affected much. There are curly brass lamps, old local photographs and brass platters on the butter-coloured walls, some panelling (particularly the waxed squared panelling screening another little bar area), boarded ceilings, and rugs on flagstones or stripped floorboards. Furnishings (which have been re-upholstered) are solidly traditional: sturdy plush-cushioned settles, wheel-back armchairs, well cushioned pews, cast-iron-framed tables and two fine log-burning black-leaded ranges. Bar food includes home-made soup (80p), lunchtime sandwiches (from £1.10), black pudding (£1.35), ploughman's (from £2.25), beef in beer (£2.65), gammon and pineapple (£2.75), daily vegetarian dishes such as cauliflower Mornay or spaghetti with provençale sauce (£2.85), six-ounce sirloin steak (£4.25), beef Wellington (£8.15), and specials with quite a lot of emphasis on fish such as freshly poached halibut in a white wine sauce (£5.25) or freshly poached Scotch salmon (£5.60); children's menu (£1.35). Well kept Thwaites and Mild on handpump; fruit machine, piped pop music and (the only false note) a brash free-standing cigarette machine by the stairs in the central area. There are old-fashioned slat-and-iron seats and picnic-table sets on a walled sun-trap back terrace, by a play area with a good climber under the nearby trees. (*Recommended by Wayne Brindle, Jon Wainwright; more reports please*)

Thwaites   Licensee William Stopford   Real ale   Meals and snacks (12–2, 6.30–10; all day Sun)   Restaurant tel Blackburn (0254) 679744   Children in family-room and restaurant   Open 11.30–3, 6.30–11 all year; all day Sun

RABY (Merseyside)   SJ3180 Map 7
Wheatsheaf
The Green, Rabymere Road; off A540 S of Heswall

This half-timbered, thatched and whitewashed cottage, built in 1611, has a central room with low beams and red tiles, an old wall clock and homely black kitchen shelves, and a nice snug formed by antique settles built in around its fine old fireplace. In a more spacious room there are upholstered wall seats around the tables, small hunting prints on the cream walls and a smaller coal fire. Well kept real ales on handpump include Flowers IPA, Higsons, Ind Coope Burton, Tetleys, Thwaites and Youngers Scotch and No 3, and there's a good choice of malt whiskies. (*Recommended by P Miller, Mr and Mrs J H Adam; more reports please*)

Free house   Real ale   Lunchtime meals and snacks (not Sun)   Open 11.30–3, 5.30–10.30

SLAIDBURN (Lancs)   SD7152 Map 7

Hark to Bounty

This large stone pub has plain cream walls in its cosy, comfortable lounge bar decorated with big Victorian engravings, a few Victorian fashion plates, and local photographs. Furnishings include an antique settee, a Victorian settle, one or two easy chairs, neat armed dining-chairs, and brass and copper over the open fire. Bar food has included home-made soup, sandwiches, ploughman's, Cumberland sausages, salads, home-made steak and kidney pie, and daily specials. Well kept Youngers Scotch, IPA and No 3 on handpump. There's lots of room to sit outside – on high days and feast days they may even have a fairground organ. Beyond the gently rolling wooded hills around here there are high fells and fly-fishing can be arranged on the nearby Stocks Reservoir. Some of the bedrooms are a good deal more spacious than others. This has been popular as a place to stay and for food, but Mrs Holt retired in summer 1989, selling to Scottish & Newcastle, who were putting in a manager just as we went to press – obviously far too soon to tell whether standards will change. But in any event, both the building and village have great appeal. *(More reports on the new regime, please)*

Free house   Real ale   Meals and snacks   Restaurant   Children in eating area and restaurant   Open 11–3, 6–11 all year   Bedrooms tel Slaidburn (020 06) 246; prices not fixed as we went to press

STALYBRIDGE (Gtr Manchester)   SJ9698 Map 7

Stalybridge Station Buffet

Done out in Victorian splendour, this lovingly kept and privately run place is still a working station buffet. It's full of railway memorabilia, including barge and railway pictures set into the red bar counter, with more railway pictures and some old station signs on the high walls; the beer-mats are interesting. As we went to press the conservatory room was being renovated. The atmosphere is friendly, with very well kept Moorhouses Premier and three guest beers (almost changing daily) from all over the country (including from home-brew pubs) on handpump, occasional farm ciders, tea (made fresh by the pot) and cheap snacks such as delicious black-eyed peas (30p), chilli beans (40p), sandwiches or hot or cold pies (45p). Proceeds from a paperback library on the piano beside the open fire go to a guide dog charity. *(Recommended by Dennis Jones, Steve Mitcheson, Anne Collins, Jon Wainwright, M A and W R Proctor)*

Free house   Licensee Ken Redfern   Real ale   Snacks (not Sun, Mon or Tues lunchtime)   Children welcome   Folk singers Sat evening   Open 12–3, 5 (7 Sat)–11; closed Sun, Mon, and Tues lunchtime

STOCKPORT (Gtr Manchester)   SJ8991 Map 7

Red Bull

14 Middle Hillgate; turn off A6 beside Town Hall following fingerpost towards Marple and Hyde into Edward Street; turn left at traffic lights – pub almost immediately on your left

Opening off the efficient central island serving-counter, the tucked-away, cosy rooms in this particularly friendly, old-fashioned pub are traditionally furnished: substantial settles and seats built into the partly panelled walls, beams, some flagstones, open fires, and lots of brassware, sketches and paintings. Good value, home-made food includes soup (90p), open sandwiches with home-cooked meats (from £1.65), cheesy plaice (£2.45), pork and ham pie (£2.65) and puddings (80p). Well kept Robinsons Best Bitter and Best Mild on handpump; dominoes and cribbage. It can get very crowded and hot in the evenings, but at lunchtime it's very handy for a quiet meal. The outside WC is typical of a Robbies pub. *(Recommended by Steve Mitcheson, Anne Collins, M A Robinson, Jon Wainwright)*

Robinsons Licensee Brian Lawrence Real ale Lunchtime meals and snacks (until 2.45 for sandwiches; not Sun) Open 11.30–3, 5–11 all year

THORNTON HOUGH (Merseyside) SJ3081 Map 7
Seven Stars

Church Road; B5136 in village centre

Most of the space in the spotless two-roomed bar here is given over to tables for diners, with cushioned wheel-back chairs and button-back wall banquettes; there are also easy chairs and a sofa by the fireplace. Served by friendly and neatly uniformed waitresses, the popular food includes soup (60p), sandwiches (from 70p), ploughman's (£1.70), pork saté (£1.75), a daily vegetarian dish (£3), gammon (£3.95) and steaks (from £4.95, T-bone £6.50); also, lunchtime daily specials like seafood pancakes (£1.85) or turkey pie (£2.25), and puddings (from 85p). Well kept Marstons Pedigree on handpump; plastic plants hang along the ceiling trusses, and there's gentle piped music. Seats outside on a terrace and in the small garden have a view of the neighbouring twin churches. *(Recommended by Alan and Marlene Radford, Mr and Mrs J H Adam; more reports please)*

Whitbread Licensee C E Nelson Real ale Snacks (lunchtime) and meals Restaurant tel 051-336 4574 Open 11.30–11 Tues–Sat; 11.30–3.30, 5–11 Mon; closed 25 Dec

TOCKHOLES (Lancs) SD6623 Map 7
Royal Arms

Village signposted from A6062 on S edge of Blackburn; though not signposted, good route on pretty moorland road about 1½ miles N of Belmont, just past AA telephone box (and on opposite side of road) – this is then the first pub you come to

This old-fashioned, popular country pub has four cosy and friendly little rooms with panelling-effect walls, cushioned wall settles, rustic decorations, and big log fires in handsome stone fireplaces. Bar food includes sandwiches (85p), ploughman's (£1.80), salads (from £1.80), home-made steak and kidney pie (£2.10), scampi (£2.20) and maybe steaks done over one of the open fires; well kept Thwaites Bitter and Best Mild on handpump, dominoes, fruit machine, juke box. Outside, there's a sheltered terrace (with a play area in the garden), white doves in a dovecote, geese in the field behind, and a nature trail opposite. Though the view is chiefly of the woods in the country that rolls away below the ridge, if you look hard on a clear day you can make out Blackpool Tower. *(Recommended by Denis Mann, Geoff Halson, Wayne Brindle, Jon Wainwright)*

Thwaites Real ale Meals and snacks Children welcome Open 12–3, 7–11 all year

UPPERMILL (Gtr Manchester) SD9905 Map 7
Cross Keys ★

Runninghill Gate; from A670 in Uppermill turn into New Street, by a zebra crossing close to the chapel; this is the most practical-looking of the lanes towards the high moors and leads directly into Runninghill Gate

Headquarters of the Oldham Mountain Rescue Team and various outdoor sports clubs, this lively, low-beamed hill pub has several rambling connecting rooms with pews, settles, flagstones, and an original cooking-range. The decent choice of bar food includes soup (65p), sandwiches (from 80p, good toasties from 90p), and a wide range of dishes such as liver and bacon casserole, Hungarian goulash, chilli con carne, scampi, Chinese spring roll and salads (all £2.50), with puddings like apricot crumble or apple and blackberry pancake (from 75p). Well kept Lees Bitter and Mild on handpump; darts, dominoes, cribbage and fruit machine, and a bridge school Monday and Friday evenings. There's a side terrace and a stylish flagstone back terrace with bright flowers sheltered by a dry-stone wall; next to it are swings, a slide and a climbing-frame. The sporting connections are strong: they're annual sponsors of the road running or fell races in the first week in June and on the last Saturday in August (there are lots of colourful photographs of these among the interesting older prints on the walls), and the Saddleworth Clog and Garland Girls practise regularly here. *(Recommended by Steve Mitcheson, Anne Collins, Pamela and Merlyn Horswell, M A and W R Proctor; more reports please)*

Lees   Licensee Philip Kay   Real ale   Meals (lunchtime) and snacks   Children in eating area of bar   Jazz and clog dancing Mon evenings, folk Weds evenings   Open 11–11; 11–3, 6.30–11 in winter, though open all day winter weekends and 25 Dec

WHARLES (Lancs)   SD4435 Map 7
Eagle & Child

Church Road; from B5268 W of Broughton turn left into Higham Side Road at HMS Inskip sign; OS Sheet 102 reference 448356

We were really pleased to find this new main entry. The very neatly kept and spacious L-shaped bar of this thatched country pub has part of the landlord's fine collection of antique oak seats, especially round the corner past the counter where a beamed area has a whole group of them, including a magnificent elaborately carved Jacobean settle which came originally from Aston Hall in Birmingham. Other treasures – there is a great deal to look at here – include the carved oak chimneypiece, and a couple of fine longcase clocks. Well kept Boddingtons on handpump, with several guest beers such as Mansfield Bitter and Old Baily and Wadworths 6X, on handpump; darts in a sensible side area; juke box. Even on our visit (in warm summer weather) there was a good fire burning in the elaborate cast-iron stove, and there's another open fire too. There are one or two picnic-table sets outside. *(Recommended by Jon Wainwright, John Atherton, Graham Bush; more reports please)*

Free house   Licensees Brian and Angela Tatham   Real ale   No food   Open 7–11 (plus 12–3 Sat; usual Sun hours) all year

WHEATLEY LANE (Lancs)   SD8338 Map 7
Old Sparrow Hawk

Towards E end of village road which runs N of and parallel to A6068; one way of reaching it is to follow Fence, Newchurch 1¾ signpost, then turn off at Barrowford ¾ signpost

Consistently polite, friendly service, a comfortable chatty atmosphere, and reliably good food draw readers to this busy pub. The big semi-circular bar has dark oak panelling, stripped stonework, an unusual stained-glass ceiling dome, studded leather seats and long button-back banquettes, and three stuffed sparrowhawks and an owl above the gleaming copper hoods of the log-effect gas fires. Served from an efficient food servery, the food includes a good range of sandwiches (from 90p, double-deckers £4.25; toasties from £1.10, steak £2.65), home-made soup (£1.15), ploughman's (£1.95), and lots of attractively presented salads or cold plates including smoked or roast ham, roast meats and smoked salmon, and a range of at least five hot home-made daily specials such as chilli con carne (£2.95), steak and kidney or chicken and leek pie (£3.50), and sirloin steak (£5.50). A mock-Tudor carvery serves good roasts (lunch, not Saturday, £8.45; three-course dinner £8.95). Well kept Bass Special and Mild on handpump; good coffee. Tables on a good-sized terrace give a view over to the moors behind Nelson and Colne, and Pendle Hill

Tipping is not normal for bar meals, and not usually expected.

rises behind the pub. *(Recommended by John Hayward, Len Beattie, Jon Wainwright, R Aitken)*

Bass   Licensee Don Butterworth   Real ale   Meals and snacks   Restaurant (12–2, 4.30–10.30 Sun) tel Burnley (0282) 64126   Children welcome until 9   Open 11.30–11 all year

WHITEWELL (Lancs)   SD6546 Map 7

Inn at Whitewell ★ ★ 🏠

Most easily reached by B6246 from Whalley; road through Dunsop Bridge from B6478 is also good

The atmosphere here is sometimes more that of an old-fashioned country house than a pub, with antique settles, oak gateleg tables, sonorous clocks, heavy curtains on sturdy wooden rails, old cricketing and sporting prints, and log fires (the lounge has a particularly attractive stone fireplace); one area has a selection of newspapers, local maps and guidebooks. Lunchtime bar food includes soup (£1.20), fish pâté (£3), ploughman's (from £3.50), Cumberland sausage, steak kidney and mushroom or fish pie (all £4), and salads (from £4.50); in the evenings there's spaghetti carbonara (£3.50), smoked chicken, ham and Roquefort cheese salad or seafood pancakes (£4), home-made gravadlax with dill mayonnaise or fillet steak sandwich (£5); also, popular home-made puddings like summer or bread-and-butter puddings, fresh fruit jellies and ice-creams (£1.50). They serve coffee and cream teas all day. Well kept Moorhouses Premier and Pendle Witches Brew on handpump; civilised, friendly service. The public bar has darts, pool, shove-ha'penny, dominoes, fruit machine, space game and juke box, with a 1920s game-of-skill slot machine; there's a piano for anyone who wants to play. Seats outside in front catch the afternoon sun. The inn has six miles of trout, salmon and sea-trout fishing on the Hodder, and can also (with notice) arrange shooting. It also houses a wine merchant (hence the unusually wide range of wines available), an art gallery, and a shop selling cashmere and so forth. They were renovating the bedrooms as we went to press and adding antiques and Victorian baths. *(Recommended by W D Horsfield; more reports please)*

Free house   Licensee Richard Bowman   Real ale   Meals and snacks (not Sat evening if a big function is on)   Restaurant   Children welcome   Pianist Fri and most Sat evenings   Open 11–3, 6–11 all year   Bedrooms tel Dunsop Bridge (020 08) 222; £25(£32B)/£39(£43B)

Lucky Dip

Besides the fully inspected pubs, you might like to try these Lucky Dips recommended to us and described by readers (if you do, please send us reports):

Affetside, Gtr Manchester [Watling St; SD7513], *Pack Horse*: Attractive moorland local on outskirts of Bolton *(Denis Mann)*
Altham, Lancs [Whalley Rd; SD7632], *Greyhound*: Good local, welcoming fire in winter, good Sam Smiths and pleasant sandwiches *(Len Beattie)*; [A678 Padiham– Clayton-le-Moors] *Martholme Grange*: Interesting creeper-clad former manor house with attractive panelled lounge bar, very popular with older customers; good Tetleys ales, carvery, cabaret room *(Wayne Brindle)*
Altrincham, Gtr Manchester [Stamford St; SJ7788], *Malt Shovels*: Lively, spacious, consistently good Sam Smiths house; focal staircase, large side games-room, Fri night jazz *(Jon Wainwright)*; [42 Victoria St] *Old Roebuck*: Pleasant pub with Watneys-related

real ales, good layout and plenty of seating *(Jon Wainwright)*; [Old Market Pl] *Orange Tree*: Handsome pub, central bar, cosy back room, pleasant furnishings, well kept Watneys-related real ales on handpump *(Jon Wainwright)*
Ashton Under Lyne, Lancs [Mossley Rd; SJ9399], *Heroes of Waterloo*: Clean, spacious and pleasant John Smiths house with friendly, conscientious licensee; local pictures for sale, good, old-fashioned bar food *(Steve Mitcheson, Anne Collins, N Hesketh)*; [52 Old St] *Witchwood*: Formerly the Gamecock, and recently renovated without losing all its former 'spit and sawdust' look; friendly atmosphere, Banks's, Holts, Marstons Pedigree, Old Mill Bullion, Theakstons XB and Old Peculier, and

Timothy Taylors Landlord with two guest beers; regular heavy metal rock band – customers reflect this *(Steve Mitcheson, Anne Collins)*

Audenshaw, Gtr Manchester [Audenshaw Rd (B6390); SJ8896], *Boundary*: Clean and friendly Wilsons pub with well equipped bar, stuffed owl and helpful licensee; good bar food including children's dishes served till late; two-hour horsedrawn boat trips, including meal, on adjacent Peak Forest Canal; handy for Guide Bridge railway station; children allowed in dining-room *(Steve Mitcheson, Anne Collins, N Hesketh)*

Aughton Park, Lancs [B5197; SD4006], *Derby Arms*: Excellent food inc good value steaks *(A A Worthington)*

Bamber Bridge, Lancs [main rd (former A6), nr M6 junction 29; SD5625], *Olde Hob*: A real rarity – a thatched pub in industrial Lancashire; pleasant food, small interconnecting rooms running the length of the pub *(Wayne Brindle)*

Barley, Lancs [SD8240], *Pendle*: Pleasant rather quiet pub in quiet village below Pendle Hill with friendly licensees, Bass and good ploughman's *(Len Beattie)*

Barnston, Merseyside [Barnston Rd (A551); SJ2883], *Fox & Hounds*: Nicely refurbished country pub with good food weekday lunchtimes, pianist Sun lunchtime, well kept Websters and Wilsons real ales *(Mr and Mrs J H Adam)*

Barrow, Lancs [OS Sheet 103 reference 735375; SD7338], *Dog & Partridge*: Always welcoming and chatty; good range of beers and generously served, home-made food *(Hugh Geddes)*; *Spread Eagle*: Spacious well kept pub with wide choice of generously served food and helpful staff, but busy weekends when service may be slow; no piped music *(KC)*

Barton, Lancs [A6 N of Preston, 200 yds from Barton Grange Garden Centre; SD5137], *Boars Head*: Nicely decorated pub with friendly staff and good value food bar *(I Wilson)*

Bashall Eaves, Lancs [SD6943], *Red Pump*: Character pub in beautiful Forest of Bowland countryside, overlooking Longridge Fell and filled with antique furniture; decent food, log fires, stoves, quite busy even on winter weekdays *(D Thornton)*

Belthorn, Lancs [SD7224], *Pack Horse*: The feel of an Italian restaurant with a moorland pub attached; Matthew Browns and Theakstons Old Peculier *(Anon)*

Bispham Green, Lancs [from B5246 N of Parbold, turn off at sharp T-junction signposted Chorley, Leyland, Mawdesley, Eccleston; pub beyond N end of village; SD4914], *Farmers Arms*: Pleasant, friendly Burtonwood house with several bars, family-room and separate dining-room; reasonable décor with traditional comfortable banquettes; decent food counter, well kept real ales; children's play area *(T Nott)*

Blackburn, Lancs [Exchange St; SD6828], *Borough Arms*: Cheerful, friendly, comfortable and almost always busy; cheap lunchtime food, good Bass, nice atmosphere *(Wayne Brindle)*; [Royal Oak Rd/Revidge Rd; near A6119 ring rd – OS Sheet 103 map reference 681302] *Royal Oak*: Remarkably peaceful surroundings considering its closeness to the ring road and town centre – eighteenth-century pub with some brass ornaments on beams, model of the pub over the fireplace, Matthew Browns beers, good sandwiches *(Len Beattie)*

☆ **Blackpool**, Lancs [35 Clifton St, just behind Town Hall; SD3035], *St Martins Tavern*: Stylish cafe-bar with marble, columns, statues, lofty coffered ceiling, good swivel seats, solid ash bar counter in central sunken area, tasty reasonably priced home-made lunchtime food, keg beers, espresso machine, rather assertive piped music; used to be a bank, now a popular evening meeting-place; open all day *(R H Sawyer, Graham Bush, I Coburn, John Hayward, LYM)*

☆ **Blackpool** [Whitegate Dr, Marton], *Saddle*: A rare find, a pub lifted out of the 1920s or 30s with original bar, etched and stained glass, tiles, snugs, open fires and interesting prints; good atmosphere though it gets very busy, well kept Bass Mild and Special on draught, no food *(Graham Bush, Brian and Anna Marsden)*

Blackpool [204 Talbot Rd], *Ramsden Arms*: The excellent pub atmosphere makes this local a real rarity in this particular area – a throwback to how pubs used to be; friendly licensee, well kept Jennings and other real ales on handpump *(Kenneth Wilkinson)*; [Vicarage Lane/Cherry Tree Rd] *Welcome*: Rather large pink and green holiday pub with excellent Burtonwood; conservatory, artificial plants, reasonably priced food *(Graham Bush)*

☆ **Blacksnape**, Lancs [Grimehills – Old Roman Rd; SD7121], *Crown & Thistle*: Isolated little moorland pub, on such a steep hill that its rooms are on different levels; excellent atmosphere *(Peter Corris)*

☆ **Blacksnape** [Old Roman Rd], *Red Lion*: Remarkable transformation under new enthusiastic regime; well kept Burtonwood ales and generous helpings of traditional bar food with interesting set menus each day *(Jeremy and Margaret Wallington)*

Bolton, Gtr Manchester [Pool St; SD7108], *Howcroft*: A little hidden gem, tucked away in modern housing development by old people's home; lots of small, screened-off rooms, plenty of games with pinball machine, darts, bar billiards, well kept Tetleys and Walkers, Addlestones cider, friendly local atmosphere, own bowling-green *(Jon Wainwright, Denis Mann)*

☆ **Bolton By Bowland**, Lancs [SD7849], *Coach & Horses*: Delightful neatly kept village pub in lovely spot, comfortable and clean with coal fires and excellent atmosphere; well kept Whitbreads Castle Eden, good home-made bar food (not usually Tues); get there early weekends for a table (*Dr and Mrs Gavin, E G Parish*)

Bowdon, Gtr Manchester [The Firs; by the church; SJ7686], *Stamford Arms*: Smart, lively, friendly pub, public bar with games and sedate lounge, first-class Boddingtons, good value food in restaurant (*Lee Goulding*)

Bramhall, Gtr Manchester [Redford Dr; towards Hazel Grove from Bramhall Lane, via Grange Rd; SJ8985], *Shady Oak*: Modern pub with good atmosphere and interesting design, several well kept real ales, welcoming staff, bar food, tables outside; can be packed weekends (*Paul Corbett*)

☆ **Brindle**, Lancs [B5256, off A6 from M6 junction 29; SD6024], *Cavendish Arms*: Attractive whitewashed pub by church, in pleasant village setting; tiny bar with TV, plushly furnished lounge, stained-glass windows, well kept Burtonwood real ales, darts (*Jon Wainwright, Wayne Brindle*)

Brookhouse, Lancs [3 miles from M6 junction 34; village signposted off A683 towards Settle; SD5464], *Black Bull*: Simple bar meals and well kept Thwaites real ales in comfortably modernised stone pub just below moors (*LYM*)

Burscough, Lancs [Martin Lane; SD4310], *Martin*: Free house with good friendly service, John Smiths real ale, imaginative good value food in bar and restaurant; handy for Peter Scott nature reserve; good value comfortable bedrooms (*JPS, EFS*)

Caton, Lancs [A683, E of M6 junction 34; SD5364], *Station*: Large, clean pub with two bars, games-room and family room; decent choice of good value food and well kept Mitchells ESB; bowling green; children welcome (*John Hayward*)

Chatburn, Lancs [SD7644], *Brown Cow*: Pleasant atmosphere, real ale, fine range of good bar food and courteous, attentive staff (*R Gostling*)

☆ *nr* **Chipping**, Lancs [Hesketh Lane Village; crossroads Chipping–Longridge with Inglewhite–Clitheroe – OS Sheet 103 reference 619413; SD6243], *Dog & Partridge*: Comfortable little lounge bar with easy chairs around low tables and log fire, very smooth and genteel, generous home-made bar food except Sat evening and Sun lunchtime, Tetleys on electric pump, restaurant; attractive country setting (*Wayne Brindle, G T Jones, LYM*)

Chipping [Windy St], *Sun*: Good atmosphere and decent beer (the cellar's cooled by a subterranean stream); in attractive village (*D J Cooke*)

☆ *nr* **Chorley**, Lancs [White Coppice; 2 miles from M61 junction 8; signposted from A674 towards Blackburn; SD6118], *Railway*: Simple comfort by the North-West Pennine Recreational Park, well kept Matthew Browns Bitter and Mild, bar food with half-price children's helpings; weekend cricket on the green, clay pigeon shoots winter Suns, fine cigarette card collection, Sat evening live entertainment in winter, monthly in summer (*G T Jones, LYM*)

nr **Chorley** [A674], *Red Cat*: Very friendly and popular, with Italian-style restaurant (*Sue Cleasby, Mike Ledger*)

Churchtown, Merseyside [off A565 from Preston, taking B5244 at Southport; SD3618], *Bold Arms*: Large, straightforward pub with well kept Ind Coope Burton (*Jon Wainwright*); *Hesketh Arms*: Attractive thatched pub sheltered by trees, spacious bar with central servery, Tetleys on handpump; close to botanic gardens (*Jon Wainwright, A T Langton*)

☆ **Churchtown**, Lancs [near church, off A586 Garstang–St Michaels-on-Wyre; SD4843], *Punchbowl*: Tetleys pub/restaurant in small and attractive peaceful village; stained glass, wood panelling, lots of stuffed animals in mock-Tudor pub with friendly staff, reasonably priced good food, well kept real ale, good fires; lavatory for disabled people (*Graham Bush, Wayne Brindle*)

Churchtown [the Lancs one again], *Horns*: Friendly, with good value food in very big helpings – very good choice of puddings despite being part of a chain (*M A and W R Proctor*)

☆ **Clayton Green**, Lancs [just off B5256, not far from M1 junction 29; SD5723], *Lord Nelson*: Friendly, busy local, nice and spacious inside with plenty of stripped stonework and pictures; good atmosphere, well kept Matthew Browns ales and good but limited bar food served quickly and cheerfully (*Col G D Stafford, Wayne Brindle*)

☆ *nr* **Clitheroe**, Lancs [Higher Hodder Bridge; nr Chaigley on old Clitheroe–Longbridge high rd, parallel to B6243 – OS Sheet 103 map reference 699412; SD7441], *Hodder Bridge*: Alone by the pretty River Hodder, with terraces looking down to the river – the hotel has its own fishing; panelled back lounge, bar food from home-made soup and sandwiches through steak and kidney pie and gammon and eggs to steaks, generous Sun carvery, Websters and Wilsons on handpump, river-view restaurant; has been open until 5 weekends; children welcome; bedrooms quiet and comfortable (*Dr T P Owen, Hugh Geddes, LYM*)

Cowan Bridge, Lancs [Burrow-by-Burrow; A65 towards Kirkby Lonsdale; SD6477], *Whoop Hall*: Spruced-up but comfortable décor and layout, quick food service at buttery bar, well kept Tetleys and Youngers Scotch and No 3 on handpump, tables outside with play area; children allowed in eating area (*LYM*)

Cowpe, Lancs [Cowpe Lane; SD8320], *Buck*:

Warm welcoming pub in terrace of houses with good choice of Timothy Taylors beers; strong local but friendly atmosphere, pool-table and juke box *(Jon Wainwright)*

Delph, Gtr Manchester [OS Sheet 109 reference 980070; SD9808], *Cross Keys*: Stylish food including very tasty beef pie with real French fries *(G C and M D Dickinson)*

☆ **Denshaw**, Gtr Manchester [2 miles from M62 junction 2; A672 towards Oldham, pub N of village; SD9710], *Rams Head*: Comfortable moorland pub, part of a farm; traditional settles, beams, panelling, log fires and small rooms, with well kept Theakstons and usually a guest beer, unobtrusive piped music and (a new development here) simple food; lovely views, good walking; closed lunchtimes (except Fri–Sun); a fine pub – only a lack of recent reports keeps it from the main entries; by the way, Major the dog is very fond of crisps *(Alan Holden, LYM – more reports please)*

Denshaw, Gtr Manchester [SD9710], *Junction*: Agreeable little pub with bar, lounge and back dining area; comfortable furnishings, roaring fire, pool-table, fruit machine, juke box, Lees Bitter and genuinely thoughtful landlady *(Jon Wainwright)*

Denton, Gtr Manchester [Stockport Rd; SJ9295], *Fletchers Arms*: Spaciously refurbished beamed bar with well kept Robinsons, decent wine and good plentiful food, large library and striking garden with coloured lighting and fountain, pond with lots of room for children to play *(Steve Mitcheson, Anne Collins, John Gould)*

☆ **Diggle**, Gtr Manchester [Diglea Hamlet, Sam Rd; village signposted off A670 just N of Dobcross; SE0008], *Diggle Hotel*: Three modernised open-plan rooms used mainly by diners – food from sandwiches or a choice of ploughman's through home-made steak and kidney pie to steaks, with children's dishes; well kept Boddingtons, Oldham Mild and Bitter and Timothy Taylors Golden Best and Landlord, decent wines, good choice of malt whiskies, good coffee, soft piped music, really welcoming service; rustic fairy-lit tables among the trees in front of this dark stone house – it's a nice spot just below the moors, by the mouth of the long railway tunnel (and the now-disused canal tunnel); opens noon *(Lee Goulding, BB)*

Dunham Woodhouses, Gtr Manchester [B5160 – OS Sheet 109 reference 724880; SJ7288], *Vine*: Busy unaffected local with well kept Sam Smiths on electric pump, straightforward cheap food *(Jon Wainwright)*

Eccles, Gtr Manchester [Church St (A57); SJ7798], *Duke of York*: Recently redecorated Victorian pub with open fires in two rooms and no-smoking room; well kept Chesters Best Bitter and Best Mild, Marstons Pedigree and Whitbreads on handpump, good value home-made weekday bar food from separate servery, unobtrusive piped music, darts and

juke box; open all dat Sat *(Mr and Mrs Harry McCann, Lee Goulding)*; [off A57, ½ mile from M602 junction 2] *Hare & Hounds*: Excellent very reasonably priced food in pub in pedestrianised central area, plenty of free parking nearby *(A A Worthington)*; [33 Regent St (A57)] *Lamb*: Large, friendly, four-roomed pub with good etched windows, bell tower and separate billiards room; excellent Holts beers at attractive prices, Victorian décor, middle-aged clientele *(Richard Sanders, J P Glew)*; [133 Liverpool Rd; Patricroft, a mile from M63 junction 2] *White Lion*: Busy, popular three-roomed street-corner pub with etched windows and passageway servery; well kept Holts *(Richard Sanders)*

Edenfield, Lancs [Bury Rd; SD7919], *Duckworth Arms*: Recently refurbished Whitbreads pub, lively and popular, with good food and service *(Carol and Richard Glover)*

Edgworth, Lancs [moorland rd N; SD7416], *Toby*: Friendly, isolated pub with pleasant views of surrounding countryside, modern-style renovations, well kept Tetleys, good adjoining Italian restaurant *(Wayne Brindle)*

Elswick, Lancs [High St; SD4238], *Ship*: Distinguished by its lovely Boddingtons and good garden for children *(Graham Bush)*

Fence, Lancs [Wheatley Lane Rd; SD8237], *Bay Horse*: Very good pub for food, garden, Matthew Browns real ale, attitude and surroundings *(Comus Elliott)*

☆ **Fence**, Lancs [300 Wheatley Lane Rd], *White Swan*: The fine collection of about a dozen well kept real ales is the main attraction of this friendly and lively village pub with simple comfortable furnishings and roaring fires in all three separate communicating areas; horsy decorations including jockey's silks, impressive collection of whiskies; landlord may not always be as welcoming as some readers have found, pub may not open before 1pm weekdays *(Derek and Sylvia Stephenson, John Hayward, Jon Wainwright, LYM)*

Forton, Lancs [A6 – OS Sheet 102 reference 492505; SD4851], *New Holly*: Warmly welcoming, with painstaking owners; bedrooms good value, with good breakfasts *(E Lee)*

Frankby, Merseyside [SJ2487], *Farmers Arms*: Recently extended, busy pub *(E G Parish)*

☆ **Freckleton**, Lancs [off A584 opp The Plough; towards Naze Lane Ind Est, then right into Bunker St; SD4228], *Ship*: Oldest pub on the Fylde, with big windows looking out over the watermeadows – and maybe fighters zapping close by from BAe's Warton aerodrome; has had strongly nautical theme in roomy main bar, with bar food including sandwiches, hot specials and salads (not Mon evening), Boddingtons on handpump, tables outside, airy upstairs carvery and buffet; as we went to press in summer 1989 there were plans for refurbishment, perhaps with more concentration on the food side; children provided for *(Brian and Anna Marsden, Jon Wainwright, LYM – more reports please)*

☆ **Garstang**, Lancs [on northbound section of one-way system; SD4845], *Wheatsheaf*: Small and cosy, low beams and creaky ceiling planks, gleaming copper and brass, little plush-cushioned black settles and dining-chairs, warm atmosphere, good service; food includes notable dishes of the day, from mussels in garlic butter to grilled halibut with prawn sauce or even lobster *(Wayne Brindle, Michael Williamson, M A and W R Proctor, BB)*

Gisburn, Lancs [SD8248], *White Bull*: Excellent atmosphere, good food quickly served *(A A Worthington)*

Godley, Gtr Manchester [signposted from A57, off Station Rd; SJ9595], *Godley Hall*: Low ceilings, plush seating, lots of brasses, lots of character and friendly, welcoming atmosphere *(Steve Mitcheson, Anne Collins)*

Goosnargh, Lancs [SD5537], *Grapes*: Pleasant village, reasonable beer and food *(Pamela and Merlyn Horswell)*

☆ **Greasby**, Merseyside [Greasby Rd; off B5139 in centre; SJ2587], *Greave Dunning*: Spacious revamp of eighteenth-century farm, lofty main lounge with upstairs food gallery, cushioned pews in flagstoned locals' bar with cosy snugs leading off, well kept Boddingtons, Tetleys and Websters Yorkshire, games-room *(Mr and Mrs J H Adam, E G Parish, LYM)*

Greasby [Frankby Rd], *Red Cat*: Comfortably refurbished Whitbreads local, polite service, lunchtime and evening bar food, tables on raised terrace *(E G Parish)*; *Twelfth Man*: Extensively renovated, good food *(E G Parish)*

Great Eccleston, Lancs [Market Pl; just off A586 – OS Sheet 102 reference 428402; SD4240], *White Bull*: Friendly, quiet village local with pleasant décor, two open fires, an old black range and comfortable seats; well kept Bass and Bass Special on handpump, simple bar food inc sandwiches, live music Weds, occasional quiz nights *(John Atherton)*

Great Mitton, Lancs [B6246 – OS Sheet 103 reference 716377; SD7139], *Aspinall Arms*: In pleasant surroundings on banks of River Ribble, plush seats in comfortable warm bars with soft piped music; Hartleys and Whitbreads Castle Eden on handpump, wide choice of bar food from sandwiches to steak, inc excellent salads *(Mike Tucker)*

Hambleton, Lancs [off A588 next to toll bridge; SD3742], *Shard Bridge*: Included for its lovely position overlooking the River Wyre; gets busy *(Wayne Brindle)*

Hapton, Lancs [outside village; nr M65 junction 9 – exit from eastbound only – OS Sheet 103 reference 803318; SD7932],

Bentley Wood Farm: Farmhouse recently converted to Beefeater steak house; busy and friendly with upholstered settles and wheel-back chairs, mixture of old and new décor, partly plastered walls and a few beams; Thwaites real ale *(Len Beattie)*; [2 Accrington Rd] *Hapton Inn*: Friendly atmosphere, pleasant staff, generously served good home-cooked food, well kept real ale *(K A Skilling)*

☆ **Hawk Green**, Lancs [SU9687], *Crown*: Extensive and popular food pub spreading into adjoining barn, lively atmosphere, well kept Robinsons, wide choice of food in bar and restaurant *(David Waterhouse, John Gould)*

Hawkshaw, Gtr Manchester [SD7615], *Red Lion*: Attractive, spotlessly clean pub under friendly new licensees with unusual bric-à-brac and no-smoking room; Boddingtons, Tetleys, Theakstons, Youngers Scotch; reasonable prices *(Mrs Copp)*

Helmshore, Lancs [Holcombe Rd (B6235); SD7821], *Robin Hood*: Strong local flavour with views of viaduct and tumbling river from back windows; table football, juke box and reasonably priced Wilsons; nr textile museum *(Jon Wainwright)*

Heswall, Merseyside [Pensby Rd; SJ2782], *Harvest Mouse*: Greenalls pub built as windmill, complete with sails; a galleried interior, reasonably priced food *(Peter Corris)*

☆ **Heywood**, Gtr Manchester [off narrow Ashworth Rd; pub itself signposted off B6222 on Bury side of N Heywood; SD8513], *Egerton Arms*: Alone by moorland church, with lovely views all around, especially from tables on terrace; comfortable sofas and easy chairs in plush lounge used mainly by people dining in the smart restaurant (which serves huge steaks), more simply furnished bar with cosy coal fire even in summer, big-windowed small extension, bar food from sandwiches and local black pudding through a variant on moules marinière to tagliatelle or steak and kidney pie *(David and Valerie Hooley, Carol and Richard Glover, Ian Briggs, BB)*

Higham, Lancs [Main St; SD8036], *Four Alls*: Pleasantly done-up Whitbreads pub, good beer, very cheap bar food, friendly welcome *(Wayne Brindle)*

Holden, Lancs [this is the one up by Bolton by Bowland – OS Sheet 103 reference 777494; SD7749], *Copy Nook*: Pleasant pub in lovely countryside with welcoming atmosphere and very adequate food *(G T Jones)*

Holme Chapel, Lancs [A646 Burnley–Todmorden; SD8829], *Ram*: Traditional old dark-beamed village pub with wide choice of bar food in back dining extension, well kept Bass, subdued lighting, juke box (not too loud), fruit machine; children in dining area *(George Hunt)*

Hornby, Lancs [SD5869], *Royal Oak*: Well decorated and run pub with fast efficient service, well kept beer and good range of cheap bar food *(P J Taylor)*

Hurst Green, Lancs [B6243 Longridge–Clitheroe; SD6838], *Eagle & Child*: Friendly roadside local in nice village with excellent Matthew Browns ales and views of the Ribble valley from lovely garden *(Wayne Brindle)*

Hutton, Lancs [A59 on roundabout by Longton turn-off, just S of Hutton; SD4826], *Anchor*: Popular pub with bar food including good value ploughman's *(R H Sawyer)*

Irby, Merseyside [Irby Mill Hill; SJ2684], *Irby Mill*: Eighteenth-century sandstone mill with real fires in two main lounges, flagstoned floor and dark oak furniture; cosy atmosphere, friendly bar staff and well kept Boddingtons and Higsons ales, food lunchtime (not Sun) and early evening; very popular *(Mrs Margaret Naylor)*

☆ **Lancaster** [Canal Side; parking in Aldcliffe Rd behind Royal Lancaster Infirmary, off A6, cross canal by pub's footbridge], *Water Witch*: Pitch-pine panelling, flagstones, bare masonry and rafters in simply furnished waterside pub with hearty bar food, summer barbecues on terrace, and hot beverages as well as cheap wines and Tetleys, Thwaites and McEwans 70/-; games-room, juke box; run as a Yates Wine Lodge; open all day Sat; children allowed in eating areas *(Peter Corris, Comus Elliott, G J Lewis, Keith Mills, LYM)*

☆ **Lancaster** [Green Lane – heading N on A6, last turn on right leaving speed restriction], *Howe Ghyll*: Neat and spacious conversion of former mansion in most attractive grounds on edge of town, well kept Mitchells real ales, efficient quick-service lunchtime food counter, games in public bar; children in family-room *(R P Taylor, LYM)*

Lancaster [Brewery Lane – next to Mitchells Brewery], *Golden Lion*: Traditional Matthew Browns house with no-smoking room, several small bars, good atmosphere, well kept Theakstons real ales and lunchtime pies *(Graham Bush)*; [Market St] *John of Gaunt*: Tetleys pub with fantastic beer-mat collection and well kept real ales with a non-Tetleys guest such as Jennings *(Peter Corris)*; [St Georges Quay] *Wagon & Horses*: Likeable atmosphere in relatively basic drinkers' pub, good choice of beers, good service *(Jon Wainwright)*

Laneshaw Bridge, Lancs [SD9240], *Emmott Arms*: Very friendly welcome, freshly cooked and nicely presented food from a varied menu *(Miss S Wild)*

Leigh, Gtr Manchester [78 Chapel St; SJ6699], *Eagle & Hawk*: Large, pleasantly refurbished pub, friendly staff *(Dr and Mrs A K Clarke)*

Littleborough, Gtr Manchester [A58 towards Halifax, on right; SD9316], *Rake*: Haunted pub – while we were there one of the ornaments fell to the ground after some shaking in the ghost's area *(John Branford,*

Linda Duncan); [Halifax Rd (A58), just through rly arches] *Red Lion*: Friendly, comfortable multi-roomed traditional pub with real fires, extensive range of ciders and well kept Wilsons and Websters; tables outside *(Dr Michael Clarke)*

☆ **Liverpool** [Albert Dock Complex], *Pump House*: Recent conversion, interestingly laid out and ideally placed by the water; lots of polished dark wood, marble counter with bulbous beer engines and brass rail supported by elephants' heads, tall chimney; bar food mainly very generous helpings of 10 cheeses and bread with sweet pickle, onion, gherkin and cucumber; some hot food; friendly, efficient service; preponderance of lagers and keg beers; tables outside overlook museum of shipping, dock and Liver building *(Ian Phillips, Jon Wainwright, Howard and Sue Gascoyne)*

☆ **Liverpool** [4 Hackins Hey, off Dale St], *Hole in Ye Wall*: Smallish Walkers pub, well restored, with several different areas in the pleasant panelled bar; friendly staff, beer unusually fed by gravity via pillars from upstairs cellar; side food servery popular at lunchtime with local businessmen; uncertain evening opening hours – may be closed by 7ish, always by 9 *(Richard Sanders)*

☆ **Liverpool** [67 Moorfields], *Lion*: Splendidly preserved pub with etched glass and serving-hatches in central bar, curious wallpaper, large mirrors, panelling and tilework, fine domed structure behind, well kept beer, cheap value lunchtime bar food, well kept Walkers Bitter and Mild *(Richard Sanders)*

☆ **Liverpool** [Ranelagh St; opp Central Stn], *Central Commercial*: Mahogany woodwork, sumptuous engraved glass, marble pillars and elaborately moulded domed ceiling in Victorian pub with attractively priced hot and cold buffet, well kept Ind Coope-related real ales, busy atmosphere, good but loud juke box *(Richard Sanders, Steve Mitcheson, Anne Collins, LYM)*

Liverpool [Regent Rd, Sandhills], *Atlantic*: Docks pub, plain and clean décor, live folk or jazz most nights *(Peter Corris)*; [Tarleton St] *Carnarvon Castle*: Spick-and-span city-centre pub next to main shopping area; fairly small with one main bar and back lounge; collection of Dinky toys in cabinet, well kept Higsons on handpump, lunchtime bar snacks *(P Corris)*; [Quarry St, Woolton] *Cobden*: Lively sporty bar, excellent cottagey atmosphere in lounge with toby jugs and lots of other ornaments; well kept John Smiths on handpump *(Peter Corris)*; [13 Rice St] *Cracke*: Basic studenty free house with bare boards, walls covered with posters for local events and pictures of local buildings – largest room devoted to Beatles; juke box and TV, well kept real ales including Marstons Pedigree *(Steve Mitcheson, Anne Collins)*; [25 Matthew St; page 66 of A–Z; SJ4395] *Grapes*: Friendly and lively city-centre pub, on atmospheric street close to the site of the former Cavern of Beatles fame, with reliably well kept Higsons and Boddingtons on handpump, good value cheap lunchtime bar food, good service, attractive unspoilt décor (though there have been recent rumours of impending refurbishment); closed Sun *(Peter Corris, Jon Wainwright)*; [Roscoe St] *Roscoe Head*: Small, clean Tetleys house, often very busy, with fine atmosphere and well kept Jennings too *(Peter Corris)*; [Wood St] *Swan*: One large bare-boarded room with no frills but well kept Marstons Owd Rodger, standard range of bar food including good Cumberland sausage; juke box, fruit machine; good escape from busy shopping area *(Steve Mitcheson, Anne Collins)*

Lowton, Lancs [Southworth Rd; SJ6198], *Bulls Head*: Well kept bitter and good bar food *(David Halton)*

Lowton, Gtr Manchester [Newton Rd; SJ6297], *Red Lion*: Clean and well furnished, well kept Greenalls, restaurant serving excellent steaks and good choice of home-made puddings *(E E Hemmings)*

Lydiate, Merseyside [Southport Rd; SD3604], *Scotch Piper*: Thatched pub with real fire, real ale, donkey and hens; claims to be oldest pub in Lancs, highly thought-of locally *(A V Fontes and others)*

Lytham, Lancs [Church Rd; SD3627], *County*: Large, pleasantly modernised pub with well kept Boddingtons and good value meals in Henry's Table restaurant *(Graham Bush, Ian Robinson)*; [Forest Dr] *Hole-in-One*: Comfortable modern Thwaites estate pub, close to golf course with appropriate décor; Bitter on handpump *(Peter Corris)*

☆ **Manchester** [Shambles Sq; behind Arndale off Market St in centre], *Old Wellington*: The only timber-framed building of its age to survive in the centre – flagstones and gnarled oak timbers, well kept Bass and Stones on handpump, oak-panelled bar; bar food (from noon, not Sun) with hot beef sandwiches a speciality, small upstairs Toby carvery (closed Mon–Weds evenings and all day Sun); often packed lunchtime *(Steve Mitcheson, Anne Collins, Brian and Anna Marsden, BB)*

☆ **Manchester** [50 Great Bridgewater St; corner of Lower Mosley St], *Britons Protection*: Fine tilework and solid woodwork in smallish rather plush front bar, attractive softly lit inner lounge with coal-effect gas fire, battle murals in passage leading to it; well kept Ind Coope Burton, Jennings and Tetleys, popular at lunchtime for its simple well prepared food, quiet evenings; handy for GMEX centre *(Brian Marsden, Steve Mitcheson, Anne Collins, BB)*

☆ **Manchester** [Cateaton St (nr cathedral and Arndale Centre)], *Chesters Pie & Ale House*: Whitbreads pastiche of Victorian ale-house,

large bare-boarded main bar and smaller area up steps; stripped walls, beams with anti-spitting notices, Victoriana such as clay pipes, old bottles, posters, plumbing taps – good period feel in spite of piped pop music; stools by counter overlooking street, Marstons Pedigree and Thwaites as well as Chesters, decent wines, pies and other well prepared food, reasonable prices, service friendly for city centre, often fairly quiet *(Lee Goulding, Steve Mitcheson, Anne Collins)*

Manchester [Albert Hill Rd; off Wilmslow Rd, Didsbury], *Albert*: Clean traditional layout, friendly service, well kept Hydes beers, simple food, collections of film-star photographs and caricatures, cigarette cards *(Lee Goulding)*; [Monton] *Bargee*: Canalside free house, well decorated and furnished, good range of real ales including Boddingtons, Hartleys Mild, Bitter and XB all on handpump, good bar food, restaurant upstairs *(Mr and Mrs Harry McCann)*; [1235 Chester Rd (A56), Stretford] *Bass Drum*: An architectural pun – it's not only a Bass house, but has been built just like a drum, completely circular with a flat roof; bar, lounge and outside tables under cocktail parasols *(Steve Mitcheson, Anne Collins)*; [6 Angel St; off Rochdale Rd] *Beer House*: Recently reopened as free house with up to ten regularly changing beers including Holts and Theakstons, ciders and good range of bottled foreign beers; lively atmosphere, bar food, unpretentious basic décor (beer prices not so basic); good juke box, housing part of the landlord's collection of blues records; very popular, especially with nearby Co-op Head Office workers, lunchtime and early evening *(Matthew Pringle, Lee Goulding, Richard Sanders)*; [Gt Ducie St] *Brewers Arms*: Boddingtons show pub, next to the brewery – so the beer's good; good really interesting bar food and salads including enormous helpings of beef goulash; very clean *(J A H Townsend)*; [86 Portland St] *Circus*: Tiny character pub with two cosy panelled rooms, wall seating, minuscule bar counter with well kept cheapish Tetleys; weekend evening opening 8 – so popular that they may shut the door when full *(Steve Mitcheson, Anne Collins)*; [Windsor Crescent (A6); opp Salford Univ] *Crescent*: Basic décor of panelling and plaster in four-room pub with three serving-bars, old mangle piled high with old magazines, good pubby atmosphere (not studenty – though so close to the university); growing range of real ales, mini beer festivals; piped laid-back 1970s rock music *(Lee Goulding, Richard Sanders)*; [41 Hilton St; off Newton St nr Piccadilly] *Crown & Anchor*: Smart pleasantly renovated Whitbreads pub, good choice of beers including Chesters Best Mild and guests such as Timothy Taylors Landlord and Ram Tam on handpump, efficient friendly service even when busy *(Brian and*

Anna Marsden, Graham Gibson); [Oldham Rd] *Crown & Kettle*: Ornate and brightly refurbished high-ceilinged Victorian pub with panelling from R100 airship in smaller room, breakfast served from 10am, well kept Watneys-related real ales on handpump, weekday lunchtime bar food, pool-table (*LYM*); [95 Cheetham Hill Rd (A665)] *Derby Brewery Arms*: Large two-roomed Holts brewery tap, reasonable bar food; children allowed lunchtime (*Richard Sanders*); [Collier St, off Greengate nr A604] *Eagle*: Seems untouched since the 1950s, absolutely no frills, well kept Holts ales at old-fashioned prices (*Richard Sanders*); [Portland St, nr Piccadilly] *Grey Horse*: Little Hydes pub with well kept beer, some unusual malt whiskies, popular for lunchtime food (*Steve Mitcheson, Anne Collins*); [47 Ducie St] *Jolly Angler*: Well kept Hydes ale brings real ale lovers considerable distances to this unpretentiously friendly little local, with its warm coal fire (*Richard Sanders*); [Hyde Rd, Gorton; nr Tan Yard Brown] *Lord Nelson*: Impressive cottagey pub set back from the busy traffic and looking quite out of place here; cosy, dimly lit lounge area and a plainer back overspill room; friendly welcome, Wilsons real ales, bar food (*Lee Goulding*); [5 Royce Rd] *Mancunian*: Loyal regulars highly praise the lunchtime food, service and atmosphere here (*John Povall, Stephen Napper*); [Wilmslow Rd, Didsbury] *Manor House*: Very friendly atmosphere for a town pub, good lunchtime food (*SY*); [Francis St] *Mawson*: Welcoming traditional multi-roomed pub with well kept Ind Coope Burton and Tetleys Mild and Bitter; haunt of university computer scientists (*Brian Marsden*); [Cross St] *Mr Thomas Chop House*: Comfortably refurbished Thwaites pub, well kept Mild and Bitter on handpump, good cheap bar food (*John Gould*); [Bloom St] *Paddys Goose*: Small pub with surprisingly ornate interior, well kept Websters, limited choice of food; handy for Charlton St coach stn so can be packed with travellers and their suitcases (*Wayne Brindle, Steve Mitcheson, Anne Collins*); [Park Lane, Whitefield] *Parkfield*: Whitbreads pub with lively atmosphere in split-level main bar and games-room (darts and two pool-tables); good food, reasonable beer, most efficient service; juke box not too obtrusive (*Hilary Robinson, Peter Maden*); [Honey St; off Red Bank, nr Victoria Stn] *Queens Arms*: Recently renovated, quiet but atmospheric and welcoming single bar with bar billiards, good juke box, bottle collection and old picture of Brakspears brewery; well kept Theakstons and three changing guest beers, simple lunchtime and evening bar food (*Lee Goulding*); [Sackville St] *Rembrandt*: Unusual modern furnishings, juke box and fruit machine; no bar food Sat; bedrooms (*Steve Mitcheson, Anne Collins*)[Leigh St, off

Oxford Rd] *Salisbury Ale House*: Cosy atmosphere, wooden floors; popular with young people (*Steve Mitcheson, Anne Collins*); [8 Corporation St, opp Marks & Spencer] *Seftons*: One large room decorated in dark wood and plush carpeting, some smaller tables overlooking bustling street, relaxing atmosphere, variety of tempting food, quick uniformed staff, juke box, upstairs restaurant called Granny's Attic (*Steve Mitcheson, Anne Collins*); [Bootle St, off Deansgate] *Sir Ralph Abercrombie*: Pleasantly refurbished Chesters pub with both Mild and Bitter on handpump, very popular in lunchtime for wide choice of good bar food; Australian landlord (*Brian and Anna Marsden, Yvonne and Don Johnson*); [35 Swan St] *Smithfield*: Terrific atmosphere on live music evenings – pub well laid out for these and gets packed at weekends when the music is among the best in town; at other times a quiet local, though distinguished by well kept Boddingtons and splendid young landlady; good juke box, pool on separate little railed-off dais (*BB*); [Back Hope St; Higher Broughton – just off Bury New Rd (A56)] *Star*: Cosy local, full of character, in timeless cobbled-street location; tiny bar with TV and good Robinsons including Old Tom, bigger lounge with piano, games-room with pool; regular folk music, otherwise usually very quiet (*Lee Goulding*); [Kirk St, Gorton] *Vale Cottage*: Three cosy rooms in almost country-type pub, full of interesting bits and pieces; friendly welcome, well kept Wilsons, big helpings of reasonably priced bar food, nice tree-lined terrace (*Lee Goulding*); [120 Regent Rd, Salford] *Wellington*: Clean and tidy, nice stained-glass windows, good value food (*T R G Alcock*)

☆ **Marple**, Gtr Manchester [130 Church Lane; by canal, Bridge 2 – OS Sheet 109 reference 960884; SJ9588], *Ring o' Bells*: Big welcoming village pub close to working Macclesfield Canal (trips arranged; 16 locks raise it 210ft through Marple); good helpings of good value food served very efficiently (it's becoming very much a dining pub), well kept Robinsons, reasonable wine, small garden with summer barbecues and tables overlooking canal – but piped music even out here; children welcome (*John Gould, K J Letchford, Dr and Mrs C D E Morris*)

☆ **Marple** [Ridge End; off A626 via Church Lane, following The Ridge signposts – OS Sheet 109 reference 965867], *Romper*: Comfortably furnished food pub with softly lit knocked-through oak-beamed rooms, well kept Fremlins, Ruddles County and Timothy Taylors Landlord, helpful staff, wide choice of food; superb setting alone on steep side of Goyt Valley (*David Waterhouse, John Gould, LYM*)

Marple Bridge, Gtr Manchester [Ley Lane; SJ9689], *Hare & Hounds*: Robinsons house with good country-pub atmosphere, open fire, shining brasses and beautiful setting; welcoming owner, varied bar snacks, garden behind; may be open all day bank hols *(Steve Mitcheson, Anne Collins)*

Mawdesley, Lancs [Croston–Eccleston rd, N of village; SD4915], *Robin Hood*: Well kept Chesters Best Mild and Whitbreads Castle Eden on handpump, good value food in recently extended lounge and restaurant, reasonably quick service despite being busy *(Peter Corris)*

Melling, Lancs [A683 Lancaster–Kirkby Lonsdale; SD6071], *Melling Hall*: Obliging service, good choice of several well kept real ales including Moorhouses, good home-cooked bar food including exceptional pizzas; bedrooms *(Derek and Sylvia Stephenson)*

☆ **Mellor**, Gtr Manchester [Longhurst Lane; this is the Mellor nr Marple; SJ9888], *Devonshire Arms*: Lovely well kept pub in attractive village, Robinsons real ale, good attractively priced food from interesting menu, open fire in each room, lots of antiques, friendly and efficient service *(Geoff Wilson)*

Mellor, [Shiloh Rd, same village], *Moorfield Arms*: Sandblasted former chapel, high in the hills, with beams, stonework and original panelling, good views all around, coal fire, well kept Boddingtons and decent wine; mixed views on the food, the pictures and the piped music, but clearly a good deal of promise *(John Gould)*

Mellor, Lancs [the other one, up nr Blackburn; SD6530], *Millstone*: Plush hotel with recently refurbished bars, in nice village; bedrooms *(Wayne Brindle)*

Middleton, Gtr Manchester [Long St; SD8606], *Old Boars Head*: Partly twelfth-century black and white timbered building of enormous potential, with cheap well kept Lees real ales, which has been undergoing piecemeal but very slow modernisation and renovation over the last four years, and this year has been closed – if reopened with even half the promise fulfilled, it will be well worth visiting *(Carol and Richard Glover, BB – progress reports please)*

Milnrow, Gtr Manchester [Newhey Rd; ¼ mile from M62 junction 21; SD9212], *Slip*: Cosy three-roomed pub with friendly welcome; well kept Sam Smiths, good bar food *(Dr Michael Clarke)*

Moreton, Lancs [Frankby Rd, Newton (A553 Birkenhead–West Kirby); SJ2589], *Ridger*: Good value for lunch, excellent décor, nice atmosphere *(Peter Corris)*

☆ **Mossley**, Gtr Manchester [Manchester Rd (A635 N); SD9802], *Roaches Lock*: Beautifully kept stripped stone free house, particularly welcoming licensee, well laid out interior with long bar, fans, hunting-horn, tropical fish; four real ales including well kept Marstons Pedigree, over a hundred

whiskies, food including good value three-course Sun lunch, quick service; tables out by Huddersfield Canal *(Steve Mitcheson, Anne Collins, Lee Goulding)*

Nether Burrow, Lancs [SD6275], *Highwayman*: Comfortably plush and spacious bar with well kept Tetleys, Theakstons and Youngers Scotch, usual range of bar food in generous helpings, restaurant, welcoming service, French windows to terrace with swing and climbing-frame beyond; children in eating area and restaurant *(Lee Goulding, LYM)*

Newburgh, Lancs [SD4710], *Red Lion*: Popular old village pub with cosy lounge bar, low beams, leaded windows, chequered tablecloths and friendly atmosphere; pool and games-room, Burtonwood on handpump, good range of reasonably priced bar food, separate upstairs restaurant, garden with swings; children welcome; bedrooms *(Howard and Sue Gascoyne)*

Newton, Lancs [this is the one on A583 Kirkham–Preston; SD4431], *Highgate*: Several spacious rooms including family-room in roadside pub geared to cheap and straightforward but good food; well kept Tetleys, pool, darts, machines *(Wayne Brindle and others)*

Oldham, Gtr Manchester [Hollins Rd; SD9305], *King George*: Pleasant and comfortable with good mix of customers, real ales including Boddingtons and Oldham, reasonably priced home-cooked bar food, restaurant *(Lee Goulding, Diane Hall)*

☆ **nr Oldham**, Gtr Manchester [Grains Bar (A672/B6197); SD9608], *Bulls Head*: Gleaming brass and copper in snug two-room moorland pub with cheap bar food, well kept Bass, Bass Special and Mild on handpump, and nostalgic singalongs to theatre organ played with gusto by Mr Wilson the landlord on Weds, Fri, Sat and Sun evenings *(LYM)*

Ormskirk, Lancs [Burscough St; SD4108], *Buck i' th Vine*: Very pleasant old Walkers pub with lots of rooms and nooks and crannies; food includes an excellent chilli con carne and handpumped beers are well kept; nice outside in summer *(Dave Cargill)*; [A59, S edge of town] *Royal Oak*: Well run pub with good service, Ind Coope Burton on handpump and wide range of bar food; landlord may show cellars in slack periods *(Gordon Smith)*

Osbaldeston, Lancs [Whalley Rd; SD6431], *Bay Horse*: Particularly well kept Thwaites real ales, straightforward choice of good value home-made food with lots of daily specials *(K A Skilling)*

☆ **Parbold**, Lancs [A5209; SD4911], *Wiggin Tree*: Former cafe, now a comfortable Whitbreads Brewers Fayre place, well thought of locally; pick a numbered table, order your starter and main course from one counter (not cheap but tasty and good value), drinks from another (well kept Chesters, Whitbreads Castle Eden and guests such as Boddingtons and Hartleys), and go back to order pudding (a particularly wide choice, especially ice-cream); good friendly service, magnificent view *(Comus Elliott, Geoff Halson)*

Parbold [Alder Lane], *Stocks*: Efficient service, well kept Tetleys, good bar food *(Philip and Carol Seddon)*

Pendleton, Lancs [SD7539], *Swan With Two Necks*: Friendly welcome in spotless village pub below Pendle Hill, good value homely food (though lunchtime service may stop before 1.40), well kept ale *(LYM)*

Port Sunlight, Merseyside [SJ3485], *Olde Bridge*: Mock Tudor beams, milk and butter churns, old bottles and a barrel or two; Tetleys and Walkers Best, limited choice of good food including salad bar *(Ian Phillips)*

Poulton Le Fylde, Lancs [Ball St; SD3439], *Thatched House*: Basically sound, open-plan pub with lively atmosphere and good mix of customers of all ages; well kept Boddingtons, bar snacks, good staff, fruit machine *(Graham Bush)*; [The Square] *Town Hall*: Busy, new pub in former town hall; friendly atmosphere, well kept beer, good sensibly priced food, efficient service *(G J Lewis)*

Preesall, Lancs [Park Lane; SD3647], *Saracens Head*: Friendly staff, well kept Thwaites, good simple bar food; bedrooms *(John Atherton)*

Preston, Lancs [Church St; SD5530], *Olde Blue Bell*: Decent Sam Smiths pub, worth knowing *(Jon Wainwright, Graham Bush)*; [London Rd] *Shaws Arms*: Good fairly plush games-room with big picture windows overlooking bridge over River Ribble *(Wayne Brindle)*

Rawtenstall, Lancs [Church St, Newchurch; SD8222], *Boars Head*: Friendly hilltop local with fine Pennine views, full of darts trophies; Bass Special *(Jon Wainwright)*

Ribchester, Lancs [Main St (B6245); SD6435], *Black Bull*: Utterly unpretentious, honest pub with good generous food; well kept Thwaites *(Sue Holland, Dave Webster)*; [outside village] *Halls Arms*: Welcoming, cottage-like atmosphere, well kept Whitbreads ales, good bar food *(Wayne Brindle)*; [Church St; sharp turn off B6245 at Black Bull] *White Bull*: Worth noting for the 1900-year-old Tuscan pillars supporting the porch - the second-oldest component of any pub we know *(LYM)*

Roby Mill, Lancs [not far from M6 junction 26; off A577 at Up Holland; SD5107], *Fox*: Nicely placed traditional pub serving a wide variety of good food; good food also at the Hungry Fox Eating House which is in the cottages belonging to the pub *(G T Kendal)*

☆ **Rochdale**, Gtr Manchester [470 Bury Rd; A6222, junction with A6452 continuation – OS Sheet 109 reference 881130; SD8913], *Cemetery*: Splendidly old-fashioned four-room pub, its tiled façade raising it well above the road; over half a dozen real ales and numerous bottled beers; good bare-boarded parlour, two comfortable little Victorian-style lounges, wide clientele from punks to beer hacks to smart townies *(Lee Goulding, Dr and Mrs A K Clarke)*

Rochdale, *Alpine*: Like a Swiss chalet, with old-fashioned balconies; soft piped music and good food including good value carvery *(Mrs J McCluskey)*

☆ nr **Rochdale** [Cheesden, Ashworth Moor; A680 – OS Sheet 109 reference 831161], *Owd Betts*: Isolated moorland pub with great views over Ashworth Reservoir and right across to Bury and beyond; cosy inside, with lots of tables in three communicating room areas, low beams, china cabinet, some oak-panelled dark settles, brasses gleaming around the open fires, some stripped stonework; well kept Greenalls Bitter and Mild on handpump, bar food from steak barm-cake to steak and kidney pie, pizza and plaice *(Carol and Richard Glover, Wayne Brindle, BB)*

☆ nr **Rochdale** [Oldham Rd, Thornham], *Yew Tree*: Stripped stone walls give the cosy feel of a moorland pub, without having to clamber up some mountainside to get there; well kept Sam Smiths, relaxed country atmosphere, good value food in bar and Pullman railway-carriage dining-room *(LYM)*

☆ **Romiley**, Gtr Manchester [Stockport Rd (B6104); SJ9390], *Duke of York*: Cheap John Smiths on handpump in older building with friendly atmosphere and character – lots of woodwork, some brasses, bar area opens into two smaller rooms, one of which, up a couple of steps, has creaky floorboards and is served by hatch; good value lunchtime and evening bar food, upstairs restaurant (not Sun in Advent); can get smoky when busy *(Simon Turner, Steve Mitcheson, Anne Collins)*

St Annes, Lancs [Church Rd; SD3129], *Victoria*: Worth knowing for its large airy bars, snooker room and pizza stall; originally designed by Mr Boddington the brewer as his own local – and it is very much a local *(GB)*

Slaidburn, Lancs [Woodhouse Lane; SD7152], *Parrock Head Farm*: Not a pub, but worth knowing as attractively furnished farmhouse alternative, relaxing atmosphere, friendly staff, excellent food from interesting menu including good English cheese choice, decent wines; in 200 acres; bedrooms *(RCR)*

Southport, Merseyside [Union St; SD3316], *Guest House*: In contrast with the previous entry and in spite of its name, this *is* a pub, with good art nouveau façade, lovely figured oak panelling in both main rooms and some of the original oak tables; Boddingtons and Higsons ales, no piped music and no food (though under new landlord this may change) *(Tony Harrison)*; [Kingsway] *Two Brewers*: Spacious, comfortable bar with interesting furniture and friendly atmosphere; well kept Tetleys, wide range of good bar food, restaurant with continental menu; open all day *(J H Adam)*; [Seabank Rd] *Windmill*: Nicely kept pub with plenty of antiques on walls; well kept Matthew Browns ales, bar food lunchtime and evening until 8; large outside area with relayed piped music from juke box *(Dave Cargill)*

Stalmine, Lancs [SD3745], *Seven Stars*: Real local with unpretentious roomy bar, bright and clean with good coal fire; well kept Greenalls and good bar food including meaty pies and well filled and presented sandwiches *(D J Cooke)*

Stalybridge, Gtr Manchester [Mottram Rd; SJ9698], *Hare & Hounds*: Tastefully redeveloped Bass house, well kept beer, good atmosphere *(Jon Wainwright)*; [Astley St] *Riflemans*: That's what everyone calls it – its actual name goes on for 55 letters; walls covered with old photographs and prints of regiment after which it's named; friendly locals, homely atmosphere, pool-table, juke box and well kept Wilsons *(Steve Mitcheson, Anne Collins)*

☆ **Standish**, Gtr Manchester [4 miles from M6 junction 27; A5209, straight on into B5239 as you go through Standish, then at T-junction turn left into Worthington, then left into Platt Lane; SD5610], *Crown*: Chesterfields, armchairs, panelling, fresh flowers and an open fire in comfortable pub with good value bar food and well kept real ales such as Bass and Bass Mild and Boddingtons on rather splendid handpumps; may be summer barbecues out by the pub's own bowling-green; kept out of the main entries only by a dearth of recent reports; children allowed away from bar *(J Pearson, LYM – more reports please)*

☆ **Stockport**, Gtr Manchester [552 Didsbury Rd (off A5145), Heaton Mersey; SJ9090], *Griffin*: Very popular with real ale enthusiasts for its remarkably cheap and well kept Holts Bitter and Mild, in unpretentious – even basic – surroundings and thriving local atmosphere; four Victorian rooms open off central servery with largely original curved-glass gantry; it's said that half of Manchester rioted when 'they' tried to demolish it; seats outside *(Brian and Anna Marsden, Derek and Sylvia Stephenson, Richard Sanders, Graham Bush, John Gould, Colin Dowse, C F Walling, Lee Goulding, BB)*

Stockport [Millgate], *Arden Arms*: Full of character but pleasantly quiet with two rooms, grandfather clocks, aquarium, old and restored wall seats and plants; well kept Robinsons served through doorway, lunchtime bar food, garden; parking difficult *(Lee Goulding, Diane Hall)*; [154 Heaton La, Heaton Norris] *Crown*: Pleasant town pub under arch of vast viaduct; partly open-plan but with several cosy areas, stylish modern décor; well kept Boddingtons Mild and Bitter

and Higsons Bitter, lunchtime bar food, open all day *(Lee Goulding, Diane Hall)*; [Heaton Moor Rd] *Elizabethan*: Was previously an old gentlemen's club, now a spacious pub with good well priced home-made food, well run bar, large garden and car park *(John Gould)*; [Wellington St; off Wellington Rd S (A6)] *Little Jack Horners*: Small pub on several levels with separate restaurant area; varied menu at reasonable prices *(Patrick Godfrey)*; [263 Newbridge Lane] *Midway*: Clean pub with striking grandfather clock, suit of armour, unusual brasses and copperware and beautifully carved settle; good home-cooked food generously served, pleasant garden with tree and wishing-well; children allowed in dining area *(Steve Mitcheson, Anne Collins)*; [King St W/Chatham St, nr back entrance Stockport Edgeley Stn] *Old Queen Vic*: Small, homely free house popular with locals; well kept Bass, Brains, Tetleys, Timothy Taylors Landlord and Wadworths 6X *(Keith Mills)*; [Market Pl] *Pack Horse*: Pleasant mock-Tudor pub with three bars including pool room, brasses, hunting prints; friendly welcome, well kept Tetleys, bar food *(Lee Goulding, Diane Hall)*; [82 Heaton Moor Rd, Heaton Moor] *Plough*: Completely refurbished, with new extension into old stables and former yard; antique furnishings, bric-à-brac, polished wood, comfortable seating, open fire, well kept Tetleys and Jennings, good bar food *(J C Gould)*; [Little Underbank] *Queens Head*: Attractively restored, with very sociable atmosphere and friendly efficient service under new landlady; long and narrow, 200 years old, with standing-room front bar (very lively on market day), small snug and back area used mainly by diners; well kept Sam Smiths on handpump, rare brass drinks fountain with over a dozen cordials on tap; the former gents (still in use alongside the new lavatories) is the smallest in Britain; no car park, but handy for bus and rly stn; formerly the Turners Vaults *(Steve and Sandra Hampson, John Gould)*; [Wellington Rd North, Heaton Chapel] *Rudyard*: Comfortably refurbished, with two spacious drinking areas, good choice of good, plentiful bar food at reasonable prices, Toby carvery, keg beer; great for children; bedrooms good value *(J C Gould)*; [Shaw Heath] *Swan*: Clean and friendly with good evening atmosphere, spacious modern layout, pleasant orange-tinted lights on brass stands, separate food servery *(Steve Mitcheson, Anne Collins)*

Thornton Hough, Merseyside [SJ3081], *Cheshire Cat*: Modern pub in grounds of country-house hotel, comfortable seats, discreet piped music, sedate atmosphere; smartly dressed and helpful staff, tempting bar food well presented, ample parking *(E G Parish)*

Timperley, Gtr Manchester [SJ7988], *Hare & Hounds*: Suburban pub with decent atmosphere, Marstons ales, frequent live music; restaurant locally popular *(G T Jones)*

☆ **Tockholes**, Lancs [Brokenstones Rd, Livesey; between Tockholes and Blackburn – OS Sheet 103 reference 666247; SD6623], *Black Bull*: Comfortably modernised food pub with good views from big windows; good straightforward bar food, well kept Thwaites Bitter and Mild on handpump, fine old slate-bed snooker-table in side room, some seats outside; dogs allowed, and children at lunchtime *(Philip Riding, Dennis Royles, LYM)*

☆ **Tockholes**, *Rock*: Comfortable atmosphere in well kept pub with plush seating, plenty of brass, friendly landlord, substantial helpings of good bar food from sandwiches to steaks, including Cumberland sausages made specially for them and daily specials cooked by the landlady, well kept Thwaites *(Len Beattie)*

☆ **Tockholes** [in village], *Victoria*: Good value bar food (not Mon evening) in comfortable and friendly moorland pub with tables in snug alcoves, partly stripped stone walls, wood-burning stove, well kept Matthew Browns; Italian-orientated restaurant with midnight supper licence; children welcome *(Len Beattie, Dennis Mann, LYM)*

Town of Lowton, Gtr Manchester [OS Sheet 109 reference 610962; SJ6096], *Travellers Rest*: Greenalls house with lots of alcoves, friendly and efficient service by uniformed staff, restaurant and garden; they sell bargain chiming clocks *(G T Jones)*

Tyldesley, Gtr Manchester [Elliott St (577); SD6802], *Mort Arms*: Real 'Rovers Return'-style pub popular with older locals, especially in lounge; rich in accents and character with crowds huddled around TV for Sat horse-racing; friendly landlord, good value Holts *(Jon Wainwright)*

☆ **Uppermill**, Gtr Manchester [Runninghill Gate, nr Dick Hill; SD9905], *Church*: Well kept Theakstons and other real ales and small range of well prepared generously served bar food in clean and comfortable partly stripped-stone old pub on steep moorland slope by isolated church, annual gurning championship, piped music; restaurant *(Steve Mitcheson, Anne Collins, LYM)*

Walshaw, Gtr Manchester [Hall St; SD7711], *White Horse*: Pleasant, tidy Thwaites pub with friendly customers, in quiet village *(Jon Wainwright)*

Warton, Lancs [Bryning Lane; off A584 Preston–Lytham; SD4028], *Birley Arms*: Rustic pub with large and lofty entrance hall, flagstones, good atmosphere, well kept Greenalls on handpump, cheap food and separate dining-room with large fire and hemispherical extension *(Graham Bush)*

Waterloo, Merseyside [Bath Rd; SJ3298],

Victoria: Popular real-ale local, good value lunchtime food; altered by Walkers without being spoilt *(Peter Corris)*

Weeton, Lancs [B5260; SD3834], *Eagle & Child*: Spacious and well kept village local *(Jon Wainwright)*

☆ **Werneth Low**, Gtr Manchester [Werneth Low Rd; from A560 Stockport Rd in Hyde take Joel Lane, turn right at top; SJ9592], *Hare & Hounds*: Large, popular hilltop pub in former farmhouse with good views; well kept Boddingtons, generous helpings of good value Henry's Table food in two eating areas (one no-smoking) *(John Gould, David Waterhouse)*

Westhoughton, Gtr Manchester [2 Market St (A58); SD6505], *White Lion*: Classic rough-and-ready pub with cheap Holts and low hatch service – you have to bend down to see barmaid's face *(Denis Mann)*

Wheelton, Lancs [SD6021], *Top Lock*: Very friendly renovated old pub on canal bank, with canal barge theme; shortish choice of generously served bar food; popular with locals in evening *(Col G D Stafford)*

Whitebirk, Lancs [SD7028], *Red Lion*: Quiet and friendly eighteenth-century pub with dimly lit alcoves, well kept Matthew Browns and Theakstons *(Len Beattie)*

Whittle Le Woods, Lancs [A6, not far from M61 junction 7; SD5721], *Sea View*: Yes, though it's nearly 20 miles from the sea and not particularly elevated, you can just make out the sea on a clear day – at least from across the road; small, cosy and well furnished, with food and well kept Matthew Browns *(Wayne Brindle)*

Wigan, Gtr Manchester [Wallygate; SD5805], *Raven*: Interesting traditional pub with variety of bars, rooms, alcoves etc – a contrast to the numerous fun pubs and theme pubs here *(Neil Barker)*; [Springfield Rd] *Springfield*: Large, spacious Walkers house with strong local flavour and lots of character, well kept beer including Winter Warmer at Christmas *(Jon Wainwright)*; [Wallgate, opp rly stn] *Swan & Railway*: Smashing pub by railway station that reverberates with passing trains; high ceilings, mosaic tiling depicting swan and railway train and lots of clocks give grandiose atmosphere; well kept Bass, Bass Mild and Stones *(Jon Wainwright)*

Woodford, Gtr Manchester [opposite BAe; SJ8982], *Davenport Arms*: Good traditional pub known as the Thieves Kneck – small rooms, coal fires, excellent games-room, good beer and food including choice of ten cheeses with the ploughman's; attractive garden with aviary, wandering ducks and chickens; well kept Robinsons real ales *(Peter and Carolyn Clark)*

Woodley, Gtr Manchester [A560 Stockport–Hyde; SJ9392], *White Hart*: Well run Bass house, recently renovated, with stripped pine, log fire, etched mirrors and eye-catching stained-glass ceiling creating apex; well kept Stones on handpump, darts, juke box and fruit machine *(Steve Mitcheson, Anne Collins)*

Worsthorne, Lancs [SD8732], *Crooked Billet*: Well preserved village pub with Victorian bar, panelling and well kept Tetleys *(Wayne Brindle)*

Wrea Green, Lancs [SD3931], *Grapes*: Old brick pub in picturesque spot on edge of village green, recently refurbished with former tap-room becoming part of restaurant; well kept Boddingtons, bar food *(Graham Bush)*

Wrightington Bar, Lancs [Highmoor Lane; 2 miles from M6 junction 27; SD5313], *High Moor*: Remote but comfortable and unpretentious, with good helpful service; to be thought of primarily as a restaurant, noted for good imaginative freshly cooked food, including excellent vegetables *(John Fairhurst and others)*; [Whittle Lane, High Moor] *Rigbye Arms*: Recently refurbished pub in pleasant spot, with oak beams, log fires, well kept Tetleys on handpump, good value lunchtime bar food (only sandwiches in evening), bowling-green *(John Fairhurst)*

Yealand Conyers, Lancs [not far from M6 junction 35A; SD5074], *New*: Main bar with good fire, friendly local atmosphere, pub cat, collection of knick-knacks including deer and foxes heads and two ancient cash registers; plainer back pool-room (which is where they normally expect children to go); well kept Hartleys XB, decent bar food *(Brian and Anna Marsden, A V Fontes)*

Leicestershire, Lincolnshire and Nottinghamshire

In this area, it's in Leicestershire that you're most likely to find particularly good food, as at the French-run Bell at East Langton (expensive now, but worth it), the White Horse at Empingham (a comfortable place to stay at, near Rutland Water), the Old Barn at Glooston (a delightfully refurbished inn, nice to stay at), the cheerfully unpretentious Bewicke Arms at Hallaton, the quaint Crown at Old Dalby (a special favourite of many readers) and the Black Horse at Walcote (the food's all genuinely Thai – and the pub's very handy for the M1). In Nottinghamshire, both Upton entries can be relied on for above-average food; the Cross Keys here gains a star this year, for all-round appeal. In Lincolnshire, the Red Lion at Newton stands out for its superb cold

The Wig & Mitre, Lincoln

carvery; and it's such an attractive pub in other ways that this year we've awarded it a star. In Lincoln itself, the attractive Wig & Mitre pioneered all-day pub food even before the licensing laws changed, and another place to serve good food all day is the distinguished old George in Stamford. The Old Kings Arms in Newark, a fine real ale pub and largely no-smoking, serves food right through the afternoon, and many pubs in the area serve it until later in the evening than elsewhere (but conversely, there's a tendency to open rather late in the country areas, and particularly in Leicestershire many of the foodier pubs close on Mondays). Though it's not necessarily their main attraction, food is by no means to be sniffed at in any of the new main entries here. These include the unusual Cotes Mill at Cotes (reopened not long ago after extensive changes), the Bell at Coleby (a comfortable dining pub), the quaint and friendly Nags Head in Heckington, the spacious and well run Three Horseshoes at Kibworth Harcourt, the George at Leadenham (masses of whiskies, and an interesting choice of other drinks too), the Fellows Clayton & Morton by the canal in Nottingham (brews its own real ales) and the Sir John Borlase Warren there (the nicest atmosphere we've found in any of this city's many fine pubs), the rambling White Hart at Tetford and the Angel in Wainfleet – not itself a Batemans pub, though this is the town producing these fine beers, which crop up in so many of the area's pubs. As well as the many other interesting main entries not so far mentioned, the Lucky Dip at the end of the chapter includes a lot of promise. We'd note particularly, in Leicestershire, the Sun at Cottesmore, Fox & Hounds at Exton, Black Horse at Grimston, Falcon at Long Whatton, Nevill Arms at Medbourne and Black Horse at Tugby; in Lincolnshire, the Tally Ho at Aswarby, Red Lion at Bicker, Hankerin at Brandy Wharf (unrivalled for its farm ciders), Blue Pig in Grantham, Nickersons Arms at Rothwell and Vine on the edge of Skegness; in Nottinghamshire, the extraordinary Coeur de Lion at Elston and the Grand Central in Nottingham itself.

BRAUNSTON (Leics)   SK8306 Map 4

Old Plough

Village signposted off A606 in Oakham

A typical Leicestershire duality is here expressed in the contrast between the stone-built stolidity of the traditional bars and the light elegance of the stylish modern conservatory dining-room at the back, with its cane furniture, neat tiles, cream-painted brickwork and frilled and swagged pastel curtains. A good variety of wholesome bar food includes filled rolls (from £1.35), ploughman's (£3), a large steak sandwich (£4.35), daily specials like chicken Kiev (£7.50), and Scotch salmon or fresh crab salad in season, and twenty-ounce T-bone steak (£9.50); cheerful service. The lounge bar has heavy leatherette seats around cast-iron-framed tables under its heavy and irregular back beams, brass ornaments on the mantelpiece, and well kept John Smiths on handpump, with Pimms by the jug in summer. The carpeted public bar has a fruit machine and winter darts; maybe piped pop music. Beside the conservatory picnic-table sets shelter among fruit trees, with a boules pitch. The inn-sign is attractive. *(Recommended by CEP, Peter L Astbury; more reports please)*

John Smiths (Courage)   Real ale   Meals and snacks   Restaurant tel Oakham (0572) 2714   Children in restaurant   Open 11–2.30, 6–11 all year; closed evenings 25 Dec, 26 Dec, 1 Jan

BURROUGH ON THE HILL (Leics)   SK7510 Map 7

Stag & Hounds

Village signposted from B6047 in Twyford, 6 miles S of Melton Mowbray

Much stronger than wine and with a taste more reminiscent of port than of ale, Baz's Bonce Blower here is the second-strongest handpump real ale we've ever come across, and not a beer to be trifled with. Like the pub's other 'own brews', Parish Bitter, Mild and Poachers, it's brewed just across the road (the pub's former owner has kept the brewery – one of Britain's smallest). To make the most of the beer, groups of ten or more can book an inclusive three-course dinner or cold buffet that includes a brewery tour and as much beer as you want all evening – £11.50, Monday to Thursday. But we shouldn't give the impression that the beers (which also include guests from other breweries) are the only distinguishing feature of this comfortably refurbished village pub – and it's reassuring to see most people there restricting themselves to half-pints. The landlord's strong point is cooking, and bar food includes sandwiches (from 65p), soup (95p), smoked mackerel in a Stilton sauce (£1.99), ploughman's (£1.95), local Rutland trout (£4.99), beef in one of the Parish ales (£5.25), and the landlord's personal special, duck in port and redcurrant sauce (£5.95), with a new emphasis on game; the three-course Sunday lunch is excellent value at £4.25. Fruit and trivia machines, juke box; there are seats in the garden, with a children's play area; not far from *Good Walks Guide* Walk 112. *(Recommended by Ian Blackwell, Rob and Gill Weeks, David Fisher, Tim and Lynne Crawford, Stewart Argyle, Richard Sanders, Julian Holland)*

Free house   Licensees Peter and Sue Ierston   Real ale   Meals and snacks (evenings) Restaurant tel Somerby (066 477) 375   Well behaved children welcome until 9 Live music every other Sun   Open 7pm–11, plus 12–3 Sat

COLEBY (Lincs)   SK9760 Map 8

Bell

Far Lane; village signposted off A607 S of Lincoln

Very much a dining pub, this is popular for its considerable range of food, particularly the cold carvery (meats from £4.25, including good salads). Other dishes include sandwiches (lunchtimes, not Sunday), basket meals (from £2.25), ten or so starters from home-made soup (£1.10) to grilled prawns (£2.50), lots of fish from haddock (£2.95) through cockles and mussels fried with bacon (£3.95) to swordfish (£6.25), three or four vegetarian dishes such as mushroom and nut pasta (£3.50), pies such as lamb and apricot or steak and kidney (£4.25) and sizeable steaks (from £7.50, one-pound T-bone £7.75). The row of three communicating carpeted rooms have low black joists, open fires, pale brown plank-panelling, and a variety of small prints. Well kept Camerons Strongarm, Marstons Pedigree and Tolly on handpump, decent wines, faint piped music or juke box, efficient service. There's a cosy and quite separate pool-room, and a couple of picnic-table sets outside. *(Recommended by Richard Trigwell, J D Maplethorpe, A and J Heaphy, Russell Wakefield)*

Melbourns (Camerons)   Licensees Mick and Gail Aram   Real ale   Meals and snacks (until 10 evenings, 10.30 Fri and Sat)   Restaurant tel Lincoln (0522) 810240   Children welcome Open 11–3, 7–11 all year

COTES (Leics)   SK5520 Map 7

Cotes Mill

A60 Loughborough–Nottingham

After standing empty for a while, this spacious converted watermill was reopened about three years ago. The watermill history is by no means drummed into you, though coming in by an iron stairway you get a good view of the rehabilitated waterwheel from the foyer. The airy and comfortably refurbished white-painted lounge bar looks out on meadows where cows may be grazing, and there are seats out by the former mill pond (fed by the River Soar and much enjoyed by the ducks). Decent bar food includes good cold pies, and Bass, Vaux and Wards on handpump are kept well; the popular upstairs restaurant does good value Sunday lunches. As we went to press we heard that the pub was up for sale yet again. *(Recommended by P A and J B Jones, Richard Sanders; more reports please)*

Free house   Real ale   Meals and snacks   Occasional live music   Open 11–2.30, 6–11 all year

DRAKEHOLES (Notts)   SK7090 Map 7

Griff Inn 🏠

Village signposted from A631 in Everton, between Bawtry and Gainsborough

Taking its name from the Griffiths family who in the 1980s transformed it from something forlorn and almost derelict into a remarkably civilised and stylish haven, this much refurbished eighteenth-century inn is doing just as well under its present owners. Like other pubs that are similarly tucked away but have a strong reputation in their area, it's sometimes virtually empty but sometimes (evenings especially) really humming with life. The neat and carefully colour-matched main lounge bar has small plush seats around its tables, and little landscape prints on silky-papered walls; besides the main restaurant, there's a more airy brasserie-style summer restaurant and a cosy cocktail bar. In summer people head for the well kept gardens, with their pretty view down over the Idle valley – and what was a loading basin, reached from the former Chesterfield Canal by tunnel under the road. Bar food includes soup (90p), sandwiches (from £1.25), ploughman's (£1.95), salads (from £2.85), scampi (£3.95), seafood platter (£4.95) and steak (£5), as well as a lunchtime carvery; Sunday lunch (£3.50). Tetleys and Whitbreads Castle Eden on handpump. The new bedrooms are attractively furnished and decorated, and breakfasts are substantial. *(Recommended by Col and Mrs L N Smyth, David and Ruth Hollands, Norman G W Edwardes, Frank Williams, ILP)*

Free house   Licensees Michael, Barbara and Norman Edmanson   Meals and snacks (until 10 evenings)   Restaurant; not Sun evening   Children welcome   Open 12–3, 7–11 all year Bedrooms tel Retford (0777) 817206; £30B/£40B

DYKE (Lincs)   TF1022 Map 8

Wishing Well

21 Main Street; village signposted off A15 N of Bourne

Knocking rooms together to make one big space often destroys the character of a village pub. Here, though, it's added an attractively almost-theatrical atmosphere to the long, rambling front bar – which does indeed have a wishing well up at the dining end. There's a cavern of an open fireplace, and throughout the dominant impression is of the darkness of stone walls and heavy beams set off cheerfully by candlelight and brasswork. There are green plush button-back low settles and wheel-back chairs around individual wooden tables; well kept Adnams, Greene King IPA and Abbot and Marstons Pedigree on handpump, and a friendly atmosphere. Good value home-cooked bar food includes toasted sandwiches (£1.35), ploughman's with Cheddar or Stilton (£1.65), cottage pie (£2.15), fish (£2.35), seafood platter, scampi, home-made lasagne or steak and kidney pie (£3), and a reasonably priced three-course Sunday lunch (£5.50). The quite separate public bar, smaller and plainer, has sensibly placed darts, pool, dominoes, fruit machine, space game and juke box. We'd suspect that this would be good value as a place to stay, though have not yet heard from enough readers to rate this aspect.

*(Recommended by Dr A V Lewis, R F Plater, M J Morgan, S A and P J Barrett,
D Stephenson, Nick Dowson, Alison Hayward; more reports please)*
*Free house   Real ale   Meals and snacks (not Sun)   Restaurant   Children welcome   Open
10.30–2, 6.30–11 all year; closed 25 Dec   Bedrooms tel Bourne (0778) 422970; £15B/
£22.50B*

EAST LANGTON (Leics)   SP7292 Map 4

Bell 🏮

The Langtons signposted from A6 N of Market Harborough; East Langton signposted from
B6047

Even more so than in the past, this is an eating- rather than a drinking-place
(though on a weekday lunchtime it's still possible to enjoy a chat over a quiet glass).
Stylish and civilised, it has rather the atmosphere of a bistro even in the bar, with its
stripped oak tables, cosy brown banquettes, bare stone walls, beams painted pink,
and a log fire in winter. The prices have now risen to restaurant levels, but people
still undoubtedly enjoy their meals here – cooking is clean and elegant, using good
ingredients, with starters such as gravadlax (£3.50) or melon and Parma ham
(£3.75), main dishes such as monkfish (£10), beef (£13) and Devon sole (£14), and
puddings with a continental flavour; they also do a ploughman's (£2.65, lunchtime
only). Sunday lunch (£9.50) is particularly popular; tables can be booked. Manns
and Websters Yorkshire on handpump are kept under light blanket pressure, coffee
is good, and the piped music carefully chosen from a repertoire that runs from
classical through jazz to heavy rock. The attractive village is set in peaceful
countryside. *(Recommended by R J Haerdi, Mel Bodfish, Patrick Freeman, R P Hastings)*
*Manns (Watneys)   Licensee Pascal Trystram   Meals (not Sun evening or Mon) and snacks
(not Mon)   Restaurant tel East Langton (085 884) 567   Children welcome   Open 12–3,
6.30–11 all year; closed Sun evening and Mon*

EMPINGHAM (Leics)   SK9408 Map 4

White Horse 🏮 🛏

Main Street; A606 Stamford–Oakham

Highly professional in the way it's laid out and run, this extensively refurbished inn
has distinctive bar food, sometimes with ingredients coming from the owners'
family farm. It includes soup (95p), pâtés (£1.85), ploughman's with a good choice
of cheese including local Stilton (£2.95), vegetarian burgers or pizza (£3.95),
kedgeree, Grimsby cod or stir-fried chicken (£4.45), a fine steak and kidney pie
(£4.50), salads (from £4.50), and lamb chops or pork with mushrooms, bacon and
cider (£4.95); puddings (from £1.35), and children's tastes, get careful attention
too. The main feature of the modernised open-plan lounge bar is the big log fire
below an unusual freestanding chimney-funnel; there are russet plush wall seats,
stools and armchairs with little silver scatter-cushions around dark tables. Friendly,
efficient service; well kept Courage Directors and John Smiths Magnet on
handpump; dominoes, fruit machine and piped music. They serve coffee and
croissants from 8am (£1.25) and cream teas (£1.75). Bedrooms include some in a
delightfully converted back stableblock, away from the main road; breakfasts are
good. The inn, handy for Rutland Water, has rustic tables outside in front, among
urns of flowers. *(Recommended by B R Shiner, M J Morgan, Janet and Gary Amos, Peter
Corris, Gordon Theaker, KC, Stanley and Eileen Johnson, D McD Wilson, M J Steward)*
*John Smiths (Courage)   Licensees Robert and Andrew Reid   Real ale   Meals and snacks
(until 10 evenings)   Restaurant   Children welcome   Open 11–midnight all year; open from
8am for breakfast, etc; closed exc for residents evening 25 Dec and 26 Dec   Bedrooms tel
Empingham (078 086) 221/521; £19.50(£29.50B)/£29.50(£39.50B)*

Pubs with attractive or unusually big gardens are listed at the back of the book.

GLOOSTON (Leics)   SP7595 Map 4

Old Barn ★ ⊘ ⇔

From B6047 in Tur Langton follow Hallaton signpost, then fork left following Glooston signpost

A gallon of quality squeezed into a pint pot, this splendid place typifies all that's best in the new wave of village-pub revitalisation: layout and furnishings that are interestingly individual but don't break too sharply with pub tradition, an inventive range of drinks and of bar food, and warmly committed staff that make light of the trickiest job of all – pleasing strangers while still nourishing the pub's essential local roots. Two bonuses here are comfortable new bedrooms (good breakfasts may include local ham), and a very small but *soigné* restaurant with its own little bar. Down behind this, the main bar has stripped kitchen tables and country chairs on its green Turkey carpet, an open fire, pewter plates on a beam, and Players cricketer cigarette cards; up steps, a snug corner has easy chairs and attractive country prints. The lighting's very sympathetic. Bar food, freshly made from fresh ingredients, includes sandwiches (from £1.25, hot beef £3.25), ploughman's (from £2.25), deep-fried avocado pear (£2.50), pasta provençale (£4.40), chicken curry (£4.75) and steak and Guinness pie (£5.25). For a country pub, the range of well kept real ales on handpump is tremendous; they serve only three or four at any one time, but from a selection of over a dozen: Adnams Broadside, Batemans XXXB, Brains SA, Greene King IPA and Abbot, Hook Norton Old Hookey, Marstons Pedigree, Mauldons Suffolk Punch, Theakstons XB and Old Peculier, Wadworths 6X and IPA and Youngs Special. There are a few old-fashioned teak seats in front, with picnic-table sets by roses under the trees behind. *(Recommended by Derek and Sylvia Stephenson, Mike Prentice, Gary Scott, Helen May, D R and J A Munford, M and J Black, Pamela and Merlyn Horswell, Roger Broadie, Dr John Innes, Mr and Mrs Jocelyn Hill, Dr John Innes, Dr A V Lewis, Rob and Gill Weeks)*

Free house   Licensees Charles Edmondson-Jones and Stuart Sturge   Real ale   Meals and snacks (not Sun evening)   Restaurant; not Sun evening   Well behaved children welcome Open 12–2.30, 7–11 all year; closed Sun evening (exc for residents)   Bedrooms tel East Langton (085 884) 215; £29.50B/£39.50B

GRANTHAM (Lincs)   SK9135 Map 8

Beehive

Castlegate; from main street turn down Finkin Street opposite the George Hotel

No pub connoisseur of the unusual should miss the unique inn-sign here. It's a hive, complete with live bees, set quite high up in a lime tree outside. Mentioned in a nineteenth-century rhyme –

Grantham, now two rarities are thine:
A lofty steeple and a living sign

– it's probably been the sign for two hundred years, making this one of the oldest populations of bees in the world. The pub itself, recently refurbished, is pleasantly straightforward, and serves a good value basic ploughman's with cheese or ham (from £1.70 – or a small version from just £1); the present licensee's father has a fair claim to have invented the ploughman's lunch, serving it first under this name nearly thirty years ago. Other attractively priced bar food includes a wide choice of freshly cut sandwiches (from 75p), soup (75p), filled baked potatoes (from £1), salads (from £1.80), and home-cooked ham and eggs (£1.70); Mansfield Riding and Old Baily on handpump, under light blanket pressure; fruit machine, space game and good juke box. *(Recommended by T Mansell; more reports please)*

Free house   Licensee John Bull   Real ale   Meals and snacks (lunchtime, not Sun)   Open 11–3 (4 Sat), 7–11 all year

HALLATON (Leics)　SP7896 Map 4

Bewicke Arms ★ ⊗

On good fast back road across open rolling countryside between Uppingham and Kibworth; village signposted from B6047 in Tur Langton and from B664 SW of Uppingham

The star award here is for the welcoming and vibrantly friendly atmosphere – as if, all year, some warm-heartedness lingers on from the village's cheery traditional Easter Monday 'bottle-kicking' race (they actually use miniature barrels). The cosy and unpretentious beamed main bar has wall benches, pokerwork seats and old-fashioned settles (including some with high backs and wings) around its stripped oak tables, with four copper kettles gleaming over the log fire in one of the two irregularly shaped rooms. Bar food includes soup (£1.30), ploughman's (from £2.30), smokies or avocado with Stilton and apples (£3.20), daily fish specials, lasagne or vegetarian dishes such as stuffed peppers or nut cutlets with sesame seeds (£3.80), steak and kidney pie (£5.20), a changing chicken dish such as a breast with bacon and mushrooms cooked in port, fresh rosemary and cream (£5.20), and steak (£6.95); bar meals can be booked on Saturday evening. Very well kept Marstons Pedigree, Ruddles Best and County and Websters Yorkshire on handpump; darts, and a fruit machine in the side corridor; piped music. Picnic-table sets on a crazy-paved terrace behind the thatched whitewashed pub look over the ex-stableyard car park to the hills behind; it's an attractive village. *(Recommended by Rob and Gill Weeks, Michael Prentice; more reports please)*

Free house　Licensee Neil Spiers　Real ale　Meals and snacks　Well behaved children welcome　Open 12–3, 7–11 all year

HECKINGTON (Lincs)　TF1444 Map 8

Nags Head

High Street; village signposted from A17 Sleaford–Boston

Low and white-painted, with steep red tiles, this picturesque seventeenth-century village inn has lots of shiny black woodwork in its snug two-room bar – particularly on the left, where one whole end of the room must once have been a gigantic inglenook. It has comfortably plush-cushioned seats, interesting ornaments like the attractive kitsch bronze lamp over one of the two open fires, and a gently sporting atmosphere (racing and other sporting pictures, maybe customers in glossy riding-boots). Bar food changes daily, and besides well filled sandwiches (£1.05) might typically give a choice of oxtail soup (£1.25), avocado and prawn hot-pot, gammon or chilli con carne (£2.75), broccoli and cheese pie (£2.75), lasagne (£2.85) and scampi (£3.50); well kept Ruddles Best and County and Websters Yorkshire on handpump, newspapers and magazines set out, fruit machine, obliging service. There are picnic-table sets in the garden behind. *(Recommended by Anthony Golds, Patrick Clarke)*

Manns (Watneys)　Licensees Bruce and Georgina Pickworth　Real ale　Meals and snacks (until 10 evenings)　Restaurant (Weds–Sat evening, Sun lunch)　Open 10.30–2.30, 6.30–11 all year　Bedrooms tel Sleaford (0529) 60218; £20/£32S

HOSE (Leics)　SK7329 Map 7

Rose & Crown

Bolton Lane

It's the interesting range of about half a dozen real ales which distinguishes this comfortably modernised village pub. Changing frequently, and mainly on handpump, they may all be unfamiliar even to the area's ale enthusiasts, drawn as they often are from smaller breweries in the West Country or up North as well as sometimes including more local heroes such as Batemans XXXB or Hoskins & Oldfields Old Navigation. Bar food is straightforward but sound – chiefly a good range of salads (from £5) and steaks (from six-ounce rump £4.70), though there should also be filled baps (from 90p), ploughman's (from £2.20, local Stilton £2.50), and vegetarian pie (£2.75); you can choose too from the larger main restaurant menu. The neat beamed lounge bar, separated into two areas by three broad steps, has green plush seats around dimpled copper tables. The simpler public bar has pool, a fruit machine, space game and juke box. There are tables on a fairy-lit sheltered terrace behind the building. *(Recommended by Derek and Sylvia Stephenson, Dave and Angie Parkes, D Frankland; more reports please)*

Free house   Meals and snacks   Restaurant tel Bingham (0949) 60424   Children in restaurant (lunchtimes) and eating area   Open 11.30–2.30, 7–11 all year

HOUGHTON ON THE HILL (Leics)   SK6703   Map 4
Rose & Crown

69 Uppingham Road; A47 Leicester–Uppingham

A useful stop, at lunchtime this comfortably plush main-road pub serves soup (£1), sandwiches, ploughman's (from £2.60), two or three home-made pasta dishes (from £3.20 – the place is Italian-run) and help-yourself salads (from £4.20). In the evening there are more hot dishes. The lounge bar, with gilt-trimmed panelling, has purple bucket armchairs and button-back wall banquettes, with Bass on electric pump. There are good summer weekend barbecues. Beware that lunchtime food service stops promptly at 2pm. *(Recommended by Howard and Sue Gascoyne, RJH; more reports please)*

M&B (Bass)   Licensees Tino and Elaine Vandelli   Real ale   Meals and snacks (not Sun or Mon evenings)   Well behaved children welcome   Open 11–2.30, 6–11 all year

ILLSTON ON THE HILL (Leics)   SP7099   Map 4
Fox & Goose

Village signposted off B6047 Market Harborough–Melton Mowbray, 3 miles S of A47

The most idiosyncratic pub we list in this area, this swarms with hunting and other sporting mementoes, and lots of other bric-à-brac such as gas-masks, gin-traps and a human skull; there are quite a few original McLachlan cartoons. The small and simple tiled-floor bar serves well kept Adnams Bitter and Everards Tiger on handpump; there's a warm winter coal fire in here, and in the cosy sitting-roomish front lounge; darts and piped music. They serve filled rolls and cobs at weekends. Both ourselves and readers have found the pub very quiet, but a poltergeist is said to liven it up from time to time. *(More reports please)*

Everards   Licensee Marilyn Kendall   Real ale   Snacks (not weekdays)   Open 7–11, plus 11–2 Sat and Sun, all year

KEGWORTH (Leics)   SK4826   Map 7
Cap & Stocking ★

Under a mile from M1 junction 24: follow A6 towards Loughborough; in village, turn left at chemist's down one-way Dragwall opposite High Street, then left and left again, into Borough Street

As delighted readers have pointed out, this has escaped the trap of becoming too twee or precious – often the fate of other pubs trying to re-create the past. That's no doubt because, here, the past hasn't been so much re-created as determinedly preserved despite extensions and discreet changes to bring housekeeping arrangements up to date. The two front rooms, each with a coal fire, are staunchly traditional: on the right are fabric-covered wall benches and heavy cast-iron-framed tables, lots of etched glass, big cases of stuffed birds and locally caught fish, and a cast-iron range; the vintage juke box is currently *hors de combat*. Well kept and reasonably priced Bass and M&B Mild and Thatchers cider are brought by jug from the cellar (on a rare quiet moment the friendly licensee may find the time to show you it). Bar food consists of individual sausages (25p), filled rolls (from 50p), home-made soup (75p), ploughman's (from £1.75), and hot dishes such as chilli con carne or vegetarian spaghetti (£2.25), Lancashire hot-pot or beef carbonnade (£2.50); dominoes, shove-ha'penny, cribbage, fruit machine. The new back room (with French windows to the garden) and most notably the lavatories are rather more Laura-Ashleyesque. *(Recommended by Neil and Elspeth Fearn, Richard Sanders, Jon Wainwright, Jane and Niall, Rob and Gill Weeks, Mr and Mrs P A Jones, S R Holman, Roger Bellingham, Dave Butler, Lesley Storey, TRA, MA, Stewart Argyle)*

Bass   Licensees Bil and Linda Poynton   Real ale   Meals and snacks (12–2, 7–8)   Open 11.30–3, 6–11 all year

KIBWORTH HARCOURT (Leics)   SP6894 Map 4
Three Horseshoes
Main Street; just off A6 in village centre

Behind the unassuming cream-painted brick façade is a spacious and comfortable bar, spick and span, with cheerful staff – and plenty of them. Open-plan, it has bays of tawny plush button-back built-in wall banquettes in the part by the serving-counter, and bookable tables set with wheel-back chairs in two side areas; decorations include illustrated maps of hunting territory, and several elaborate table paraffin lamps converted to electricity. A wide choice of popular and well priced bar food includes soup (£1), ravioli (£1.25), devilled whitebait or hot garlic prawns (£1.75), steak and kidney pie (£3.75), gammon and peaches (£4.25), salmon trout (£5.95), steaks (from £5.95) and several daily specials such as plaice (£2.75), pork escalope (£3.75) and game pie or fish and wine pie (£4.25); well kept Marstons Pedigree on handpump. You'd never guess that Smoky the amiable cat is getting on for thirteen. *(Recommended by C M Holt, Christopher Baker)*

Free house   Licensee Barrie Sutton   Real ale   Meals and snacks   Restaurant tel Leicester (0533) 793303   Open 11–2.30, 6.30–11 all year

LEADENHAM (Lincs)   SK5992 Map 8
George
High Street (A17 Newark–Sleaford)

Here's the best collection of whiskies in this part of England – not just a superb array of several hundred single malts ranged around the walls of both rooms of the bar, many from distilleries that no longer produce, but also some uncommon vatted malts, blends, rare Irish whiskeys, ryes and bourbons. Broad-mindedly, they also sell by the glass five or six German wines they import direct, and decent French house wines; and the Greene King IPA, Ruddles County and Theakstons Old Peculier on handpump are well kept. The quietly chatty bar is simply furnished, with red-cushioned wall settles and long stools around wood-effect or dimpled copper tables, and a coal fire in a fairy-lit stone inglenook; the busy hunt terrier is called Tia. Quickly served simple lunchtime bar food includes sandwiches (from £1), ploughman's (£1.50), a daily special (from £2.55), plaice and haddock (£2.75) and salads (from £2.95), with evening dishes such as devilled whitebait or Lincolnshire sausages (£1.75), smoked salmon sandwich (£2.20), goulash (£2.25), a quarter-chicken (£3.25) and steak (£4.95); rather indistinct piped pop music; fruit machines and space games in a side room. There are picnic-table sets on the sheltered back terrace. The bedrooms, plain but good value, are in a quiet cottage behind; breakfasts are good (and can be served to non-residents). *(Recommended by Rob and Gill Weeks)*

Free house   Real ale   Meals and snacks   Restaurant   Open 10–3, 6–11 all year   Bedrooms tel Loveden (0400) 72251; £15/£24

LEICESTER SK5804 Map 4

Tom Hoskins

131 Beaumanor Road; from A6 at Red Hill Circle (huge roundabout N of centre) follow
Motorway, Burton, Coventry sign into Abbey Lane (A5131), take second left into Wade Street
– pub on left at next crossroads

The main attraction of this backstreet pub is that it's the tap for the adjoining
Hoskins brewery, so of course has the full range of their beers on handpump –
Bitter, Mild, Penns and in summer Premium. You can arrange to be shown around
the late-Victorian brewhouse (telephone Leicester (0533) 661122), and the
brewery's former malt loft has been converted into a comfortable partly flagstoned
panelled lounge bar, decorated with old brewing equipment; piped music. The
original and much plainer wood-floored tap-room has a smokily masculine and
chatty atmosphere, with dominoes, darts and cribbage. A small range of
straightforward lunchtime bar food includes filled cobs (from 60p), ploughman's
(£1.95) and plaice (£2.25); beer prices (they also keep a changing choice of other
brewers' real ales) are low. *(Recommended by Graham Bush, Richard Sanders, Peter
Donahue, Dave Braisted, Alastair Lang, Lee Goulding, Mr and Mrs P A Jones, Michael
Cooke)*

*Hoskins Licensees Doug and Doris McPherson Real ale Meals and snacks (lunchtime, not
Sun; no hot food Sat) Open 11.30–2.30, 5.30 (6 Sat)–11 all year*

LINCOLN SK9872 Map 8

Wig & Mitre ★ 🏵 [illustrated on page 464]

29 Steep Hill; just below cathedral

Years before the 1988 licensing-law change which allowed pubs to serve drinks all
afternoon, this was pointing one way forward by serving food right through from
8am to midnight. It still is (even on Sundays) with last orders around 11pm. It's an
attractive conversion of a carefully restored fourteenth-century building on the
steeply picturesque alley that runs down from the cathedral towards the centre. The
upstairs dining-room is clubbily cosy, with settees, elegant small settles, Victorian
armchairs, shelves of old books and an open fire. It's decorated with antique prints
and more modern caricatures of lawyers and clerics, and by the stairs shows some
of the original medieval wattle and daub; the oak rafters are exposed, too. The
plainer and cheerier downstairs bar has pews and other seats around the tables on
its tiles. Food, changed twice daily, covers a remarkable range. Besides sandwiches
(from £1.35), ploughman's and all-day breakfast dishes (full fried breakfast £3.50),
there are usually two or three soups (£1.45), a choice of pâtés (£2.95), two or three
enterprising vegetarian or vegan dishes such as potato and cheese bake (£3.25), half
a dozen other main dishes like curry (£3.45), lamb with tomatoes (£3.85) and
gammon (£4.25), and good puddings (£2.25). You can also choose from the less
quickly changing restaurant menu, which includes more expensive dishes such as
chicken breast with Parma ham (£8.25) and steaks (from £9.95). A very wide
though not cheap choice of wines by the glass, many more by the bottle, Sam Smiths
OB and Museum on handpump, and freshly squeezed orange juice; newspapers and
magazines to read. The pub can get crowded on summer weekends. A small
sheltered back terrace has seats by a small pool and fountain. *(Recommended by Rob
and Gill Weeks, Peter Donahue, J D Maplethorpe, M A and W R Proctor, Michael Quine,
E Krakowska Smart, B Smart, Gary Scott, Guy Sowerby, Nick Dowson, Alison Hayward,
Geoff Wilson, ILP, B D Atkin)*

*Sam Smiths Licensees Michael and Valerie Hope Real ale Meals and snacks (8–midnight)
Restaurant tel Lincoln (0522) 535190/537482/523705 Children in eating area and
restaurant Open 8–midnight (with supper licence), inc Sun; closed 25 Dec*

LYDDINGTON (Leics)   SP8797 Map 4

Marquess of Exeter 🛏

Village signposted off A6003 N of Corby

Now part of a hotel group, this still has reasonably priced bar food in its rambling beamed lounge, plushly furnished in red, with a good log fire in its handsome stone fireplace. Served by neatly uniformed staff, it includes sandwiches (from £1, crab when available £2.20, steak £3.75), soup (£1.10), ploughman's (from £2.40), lasagne, moussaka or curry (£2.95), home-made specials like braised oxtail (£3.95) and pie or beef bourguignonne (£4.40), and sirloin steak (£4.95). Well kept Batemans XB and XXXB and Ruddles Best and County on handpump; piped music. The attractive stone-built village has for centuries been in the hands of the Burghley family, after whom the inn is named. There was a new manager in summer 1989. *(Recommended by Jamie and Sarah Allen, Derek and Sylvia Stephenson; more reports please)*

Free house   Manager Mr R M Morrell   Real ale   Meals and snacks   Restaurant   Children in eating area and restaurant   Open 11–11 all year   Bedrooms tel Uppingham (0572) 822477; £46B/£58B

MARKET BOSWORTH (Leics)   SK4003 Map 4

Olde Red Lion

1 Park Street; from centre, follow Leicester and Hinckley signpost

Another Hoskins pub (see Leicester entry), this keeps their Bitter, Mild, Penns, summer Premium and winter Old Nigel, with two or three beers from other breweries, such as Holdens Mild, on handpump. The beamed and L-shaped main bar has settles back to back to form booths around cast-iron tables; there's a cosy little traditional Victorian and a well equipped central children's room. Bar food includes filled cobs (80p), soup (£1.10), ploughman's (£2.15), omelettes (from £2.75), scampi or whitebait (£2.65), and steaks (from six-ounce rump, £2.80), with an excellent value three-course lunch (£4, not Sunday); bar billiards, fruit machine, piped music. The sheltered back courtyard has tables, swings, slides and a seesaw. *(Recommended by Ian Blackwell, W S Wright, T Nott, Richard Sanders; more reports please)*

Hoskins   Real ale   Meals and snacks (not Sun evening)   Children welcome   Easy-listening jazz Sun, trad jazz Thurs, pianist Sat   Open 11–11 all year   Bedrooms tel Market Bosworth (0455) 291713; £18.50(£23B)/£36(£42B)

MARKET DEEPING (Lincs)   TF1310 Map 8

Bull

Market Place

The interestingly convoluted layout of this market-town pub includes low-ceilinged alcoves, quaint corridors, and a strange but comfortable tunnel of a room down a few steps, with heavy black beams and roughly plastered walls made from enormous blocks of ancient stone – surely much older than the early-Georgian façade. They call this the Dugout, and down here tap well kept Adnams, Everards Tiger and Old Original and a guest beer from a fat row of casks. Decent bar food includes soup (£1.10), lunchtime sandwiches (from £1), ploughman's (from £2.25) and salads (from £3.25), as well as curry (£3.25), home-made steak and kidney pie (£3.45), with additional evening dishes such as king prawns (£4.95) and beef steaks (from sirloin, £5.50). There's a thriving local atmosphere; fruit machine, space

---

Places with gardens or terraces usually let children sit there; we note in the text the very, very few exceptions that don't.

game, piped music. There are seats in a pretty back coachyard. *(Recommended by Derek Stephenson, M J Morgan, Nick Dowson, Alison Hayward; more reports please)*

Everards   Licensees David and Shirley Dye   Real ale   Meals and snacks (11–2, 7–10; not Mon or Sun evening)   Restaurant   Children in eating area and upstairs room   Nearby daytime parking may be difficult   Open 11–2.30 (3 Sat), 5.30–11 all year   Bedrooms tel Market Deeping (0778) 343320; £18/£30

NEWARK (Notts)   SK8054 Map 7

Old Kings Arms

19 Kirkgate; follow To The Market Place signpost opposite Maltby agricultural engineers on A46

The bar, with its vaulted ceiling, plain stripped deal tables, traditional wall benches and so forth, gives a misleadingly spartan or even austere first impression. In fact, creature comforts rate highly here. Good helpings of wholesome food, served all day, include sandwiches (from £1.10), ploughman's (from £1.50), chilli con carne or lasagne (£1.60 or £2.40, depending on size of helping), ratatouille (£1.80 or £2.70), salads (from £2.60), with daily specials such as beef and tomatoes or mushrooms (£3) and steak and kidney pie (£3.20). The upstairs eating area has been refurbished and now has its own entrance; you can use it for morning coffee (available from 9.30) and afternoon teas. Marstons Burton, Merrie Monk, Pedigree and Owd Rodger on handpump are notably well kept, and service helpful. The atmosphere's warm and lively, and this very popular pub is largely no-smoking (though there is provision for smokers). Dominoes, cribbage, a fruit machine, trivia and juke box (which can be loud). The castle ruins are just a stroll away.

(Recommended by Brian and Genie Smart, Scott W Stucky, Richard Sanders, Graham Bush)

Marstons   Licensee Christopher Holmes   Real ale   Meals and snacks (11–8; not Sun or Mon evenings)   Children in eating area and upstairs   Trad jazz Mon night   Restricted nearby parking   Open 11–11 all year

NEWTON (Lincs)   TF0436 Map 8

Red Lion ★ ✿

Village signposted from A52 E of Grantham; at village road turn right towards Haceby and Braceby; pub itself also discreetly signposted off A52 closer to Grantham

Interesting things to look at, comfortable communicating rooms well laid out to give private corners without cutting people off, attractive and fairly priced wines as well as very well kept Batemans XXXB on handpump and good coffee, fresh flowers everywhere in summer, unobtrusive but well reproduced piped music (musician readers were sure the Vivaldi helped their digestion), seats in a neatly kept and sheltered back garden, and neat yet relaxed and cheerful service: hardly a surprise that readers rave about this country pub. Yet on top of all that, it's the imaginatively displayed and served food which is the highlight for most people. You choose as much as you like from an attractive and individual display of salads, with four different types of fish such as fresh salmon, cold meats, and pies; a small helping is £5, normal £5.50, and large £7, with children's helpings £1. The winter soups are also very good, as are the one or two local specialities such as stuffed chine of pork or spicy Lincolnshire sausages, and the rich puddings; they'll do sandwiches. Besides cushioned wall benches, there are old-fashioned oak and elm seats and a Gothick carved settle, and decorations range from farm tools and stuffed wildlife to a penny-farthing bicycle. Fruit machine, and during the day and at weekends two squash courts run by the pub can be used by non-members. Keep an eye open for Sam the floppy dog, when you're parking, as well as for the less

There are report forms at the back of the book.

active animal – a stuffed rat – hanging above the serving-counter. *(Recommended by Steve Dark, Tim and Lynne Crawford, Pete Storey, Neil and Angela Huxter, John Baker, Jane Palmer, David and Ruth Hollands, Brian and Anna Marsden, Dave Butler, Lesley Storey, Guy Sowerby, Amanda Rusholme, Frank Williams, Derek and Sylvia Stephenson)*

Free house   Licensee Bill Power   Real ale   Meals and snacks (12–2, 7–10; not Sun evening or Mon, exc bank hols, or 25 Dec)   Children in eating area and extension   Open 11–2.30 (3 Sat), 6–11 all year; closed Mon lunch, exc bank hols, and 25 Dec evening

NOTTINGHAM   SK5640 Map 7

Bell

18 Angel Row; off Old Market Square

Five hundred years old, this quaint building is reputed to have formed part of a Carmelite friary. It's pretty unspoilt inside; of the three downstairs bars, the cosiest is probably the low-beamed Elizabethan Bar, recently refurbished, with thickly cushioned banquettes forming booths around its tables. In the evenings it may be quieter upstairs in the Belfry (especially in term-time, when it can get really busy downstairs). Up here you can see the rafters of the fifteenth-century crown post roof at the back, or look down on the busy street at the front; at lunchtime, when there's a fairly priced hot and cold buffet, this functions as a family restaurant (currently being refitted); bar food includes filled cobs (from 45p), soup (85p), ploughman's (£1.85), plaice (£2.15), steak and kidney pie (£2.35) and steaks (from £4.25), as well as dishes, from a rotating menu, such as sweet-and-sour pork (£2.70) and sole Véronique (£2.95). Good value wines; Bass, Greene King Abbot, Marstons Pedigree, Ruddles County, Theakstons Best, Old Peculier and a weekly guest beer on handpump (from cellars thirty feet down in the sandstone rock – groups may be able to arrange tours); fruit machine, piped music. The pub's been in the same family since the end of the last century. In summer there's waiter service to the tables on the pavement outside. *(Recommended by BKA, P Miller, A C and S J Beardsley, Steve Waters, Richard Sanders, Graham Bush; more reports please)*

Free house   Licensees David, Simon and Paul Jackson, Manager Richard Jackson   Real ale   Meals (lunchtime, not Sun) and snacks (lunchtime)   Restaurant; closed Sun   Children in restaurant lunchtimes   Trad jazz Sun lunchtime and evening, Mon and Tues evenings   Open 10.30–11 all year

Fellows Clayton & Morton

Canal Street (part of inner ring road)

Well worn in now, this careful conversion of a former canal building (it's near the canal museum) has a cosy and quietly friendly pubby feel. It's softly lit, with dark blue plush seats built into its alcoves, copper-topped tables, some seats up two or three steps in a side gallery, screens of wood and stained glass, a dark wooden floor, and some bric-à-brac on the shelf just below the glossy dark green high ceiling. From the quarry-tiled glassed-in back area which looks towards the canal, cast-iron steps take you up to a big window into the brewery where they produce their own creamily malty gently hopped Samuel Fellows and stronger Matthew Claytons – well kept on handpump, as is the Whitbreads Castle Eden (they also have decent wines). Bar food includes soup (80p), filled cobs (including hot beef at lunchtime), chicken (£1.85) and scampi or home-made steak and kidney pie (£2); well reproduced nostalgic pop music, trivia machine. *(Recommended by Ian Phillips, BKA, Derek and Sylvia Stephenson; more reports please)*

Own brew   Licensee David Tipler   Real ale   Meals and snacks   Open 11–2.30, 5.30–11 all year

The opening hours we quote are for weekdays; in England and Wales, Sunday hours are now always 12–3, 7–10.30.

New Market Hotel

Lower Parliament Street, at junction with Broad Street; inner ring road passes the pub

Remarkably low drinks prices (still among the cheapest half-dozen in this book), perfectly kept Home Mild and Bitter and Youngers IPA and No 3 on handpump, and the affable ex-policeman tenant combine to make this archetypal town pub a favourite with value-conscious readers. There is a comfortable back lounge with curvy button-back banquettes, but the railway lamps, notices and engine number plates make the austerely practical high-ceilinged front bar worth a look too. Cheap home-made bar food includes filled cobs (50p, available all day), curry (£1.50), quiche with coleslaw, chilli con carne or pasta dishes (£1.75) and steak and kidney pie or fresh fish (£1.95). Darts, shove-ha'penny, table skittles, dominoes, cribbage, backgammon, card games, juke box, fruit machine and space game; seats on a back terrace. Dogs are allowed (rare for the area). *(Recommended by Richard Sanders, Stewart Argyle, Graham Bush, Guy Sowerby)*

Home (Scottish & Newcastle)   Licensee Tony (Dodger) Bill Green   Real ale   Meals and snacks (to order only, Sun)   Children welcome   Open 10 (10.30 Sat)–4.30, 5.30 (7 Sat)–11 all year

Olde Trip to Jerusalem ★

Brewhouse Yard; from inner ring road follow The North, A6005 Long Eaton signpost until you are in Castle Boulevard, then almost at once turn right into Castle Road; pub is up on the left

The star award here is for the outstanding curiosity value of the unique upstairs bar (often closed at lunchtime). This is carved into the sandstone castle hill: the walls soar steeply into a narrowing rock funnel that disappears into the shadows high above, with cosy simply furnished side alcoves. This may have served as cellarage for a medieval castle brewhouse there – the backing for the pub's prominent if otherwise tenuous claims to great antiquity (it's mainly seventeenth century). The rest of the place is unpretentiously quaint, with leatherette-cushioned settles built into the dark panelling, barrel tables on tiles or flagstones, more low-ceilinged rock alcoves, and passageways which may be thronged with friendly leather-jacketed youngsters. Reasonably priced and notably well kept real ales on handpump include Bass or Wards, Marstons Pedigree, Ruddles Best, Sam Smiths OB and a weekly guest beer on handpump; very friendly and helpful staff. Fruit machine, ring the bull; seats outside. They serve filled baps at lunchtime. *(Recommended by Ian Phillips, Richard Sanders, Jon Wainwright, M A and W R Proctor, Chris Raisin, Stewart Argyle, Barry, Graham Bush; more reports please)*

Free house   Real ale   Snacks (lunchtime)   Open 11–2.30, 5.30–11 all year; may open longer, weekends

Sir John Borlase Warren

Canning Circus (A52 towards Derby – pub faces you as you come up the hill from city centre)

Though this traditional pub is one of the city's most civilised, and placed opposite Georgian almshouses in an attractive area, its well kept beer is cheap – Shipstones Mild and Bitter on handpump. It has half a dozen communicating rooms, full of a friendly buzz of conversation, with all the old-fashioned trappings: swirly Victorian acanthus-leaf wallpaper, dark brown Anaglypta dado, sturdy brass lamps, Delft shelf, etched mirrors, engraved glass, swagged russet curtains with net lower curtains in the three big bay windows, comfortable parlourish seating, and pictures ranging from little Victorian cartoons to the big chromolithograph of Queen Victoria's Diamond Jubilee procession or the various prints commemorating Sir John, who defeated an attempted French invasion of Ireland off Kilkenna in 1798. Bar food, from a counter in the downstairs room, includes filled cobs (from 65p), soup (85p), ploughman's (£1.80, double-sized £2.45), salads (from £1.95), pizza

(£1.90), quiche (£2.25) and home-made steak and kidney pie (£2.50). Tables shelter under an old tree behind. *(Recommended by Ian Phillips, Stewart Argyle)*

Shipstones   Licensee Mr A W H Clark   Real ale   Meals and snacks (lunchtime and afternoon)   Open 11–11 all year

OLD DALBY (Leics)   SK6723 Map 7

Crown ★ ★ 🏮

By school in village centre turn into Longcliff Hill then left into Debdale Hill

Out on the village outskirts, this used to be a farmhouse, and has kept not only the small-roomed layout but also much of the style and atmosphere. Homely furnishings include easy chairs, one or two antique oak settles and Windsor armchairs; there are black beams, hunting and other rustic prints, fresh flowers and open fires, and the atmosphere is relaxed and unspoilt. The food, not cheap but well above the standard of the area, includes sandwiches (from £1.25), soup (£1.25), melted Stilton with crudités (£2.75), a bumper ploughman's (£3.95), stuffed whole peppers (£3.95), skate wings in a light beer batter with mint and watercress sauce, tagliatelle or carbonnade of beef (£4.50), and sirloin steak (£6.95), with good Sunday lunches. Service is efficient, though the place can get very full (especially in the evenings and at weekends), and bar food service may stop at 1.30. Adnams, Baileys Best, Batemans XXXB, Eldridge Pope Royal Oak, Greene King Abbot and IPA, Hardys and Hansons Mild and Best, Marstons Pedigree, Owd Rodger and Merrie Monk, Moorhouses Pendle Witches Brew and Maidens Ruin, Ruddles County, Theakstons XB and Old Peculier, and Wadworths Farmers Glory are tapped from the cask – a fine range, though quality has not always been as uniformly high as perhaps it could be if fewer beers were kept. One room has darts, dominoes, cribbage and table skittles. The two rooms of the restaurant area are as small and cottagey as the rest of the pub. There are plenty of tables on a terrace, with a big, sheltered lawn (where you can play pétanque) sloping down among roses and fruit trees. You'll have noted that there are one or two caveats in this year's entry, and there is now a school of thought holding that more needs to be done to deserve our two-star rating, though the majority of readers still feel it is justified. Obviously we'd like more views. *(Recommended by Ken and Barbara Turner, G and M Brooke-Williams, P Miller, A C and S J Beardsley, Tim and Lynne Crawford, Roger Entwistle, Richard Dolphin, Graham Oddey, Syd and Wyn Donald, Peter Donahue, A and J Heaphy, Steve Dark, Derek and Sylvia Stephenson, Stewart Argyle, Dave Butler, Lesley Storey, Guy Sowerby, Clifford Spooner)*

Free house   Licensees Lynne Bryan and Salvatore Inguanta   Meals and snacks (12–2, 6–9.45; not Sun evenings)   Restaurant tel Melton Mowbray (0664) 823134   Children away from bar   Open 12–2.30, 6–11 all year

SCAFTWORTH (Notts)   SK6692 Map 7

King William

Village signposted (not prominently) off A631 Bawtry–Everton

Like the rest of the village, this pub is part of a private estate – which perhaps helps towards its relaxed family atmosphere, with staff who really put themselves out for customers, bunches of flowers in summer, generous open fires in winter, amiable ginger cats, and chickens rootling around and peacocks preening themselves in the very big back garden. The three connecting rooms of the bar have hunting and other prints above the stripped dado, one wall filled with entertaining photographs, old farm tools, Delft shelves of knick-knacks, and masses of brasses. A pleasant variety of seats includes a sofa and high-backed settles, as well as plainer chairs around tables; the end room is no-smoking. Imaginative bar food includes soup (£1.20), a lunchtime fry-up (£2.75), ploughman's (£3.25), salads (from £3.50), casserole, chilli con carne or curry (£3.85), a good many interestingly flavoured pies such as Stilton and celery or steak and kidney pie (£4) and a mixed grill (£4.95); they do things like burgers late into the evening, and have local game in season. Well kept Camerons Strongarm, Everards Old Original, Marstons Pedigree and Whitbreads Castle Eden and Trophy on handpump, with a fine range of malt whiskies, decent wines and an espresso coffee machine; dominoes, cribbage, fruit machine, space game, unobtrusive piped music. Down a corridor a clean, light and airy family-room, with milk-churns as seats, leads through French windows to the sheltered garden. This runs down to the River Idle, with cows grazing beyond; it's sheltered and well planted with shrubs and young trees, with plenty of well spaced tables, swings, slides, a climber, and a covered barbecue area. *(Recommended by Derek and Sylvia Stephenson, Mrs I L Phillipson, RAB, William and Patrick Stapley)*

Free house   Licensee Michael Wright   Real ale   Meals and snacks (12–2.30, 7–10; not Mon–Weds lunchtime exc bank hols or Sun evening)   Children in dining-room   Morris men in summer   Open 12–2.30 (3 Sat), 7–11 all year; closed lunchtime Mon–Weds exc bank hols

SIBSON (Leics)   SK3500 Map 4
Cock

A444 N of Nuneaton

They tell Dick Turpin stories about this picturesque thatched and timbered black and white pub, which dates back in part to 1250 and was owned by the Church until just before the war (it got a Sunday licence only in 1954). The room on the right, with comfortable seats around cast-iron-framed tables, has built-in seats in a huge alcove which used to be a fireplace with a room-sized chimney above. The room on the left has country kitchen chairs around wooden tables. There are heavy black beams, ancient wall timbers, and genuine latticed windows; the doorways are unusually low. Good value bar food includes sandwiches (from 75p, smoked salmon £2.25), home-made soup (£1), ploughman's (from £1.75), omelettes (£2.45), salads (from £2.45), home-made steak and kidney pie or lasagne (£3.25) and steaks (from eight-ounce rump or sirloin £5.45), with children's dishes (£1.50). Well kept Bass and M&B Brew XI and Mild; friendly and efficient service; piped music. There are tables on the lawn behind. The restaurant (in a former stableblock) is popular. *(Recommended by Genie and Brian Smart, M A and W R Proctor, Jon Wainwright, W S Wright, Ian Blackwell)*

M&B (Bass)   Licensee John R McCallion   Real ale   Meals and snacks (until 10 evenings; not Sat evening or Sun)   Restaurant (not Sun evening) tel Tamworth (0827) 880357   Children in eating area and restaurant   Open 11.30–2.30, 7–11 all year

STAMFORD (Lincs)   TF0207 Map 8
Bull & Swan

High Street, St Martins; B1081 leaving town southwards

Shallow steps and wooden partition walls divide the comfortable bar of this old inn into three spacious but cosy areas – virtually separate rooms, each with its own log-effect gas fire. The one in the middle is perhaps the cosiest, with velvet-cushioned armchairs all around its walls, but there's a good atmosphere throughout, with low and heavy beams hung with lots of highly polished copper kettles and brassware. A wide choice of bar food, all home made, includes sandwiches (from 90p, steak £2.75), soup (£1), filled baked potatoes (£1), a choice of ploughman's (£2), steak and mushroom pie (£3.30), trout in a sweet-and-sour sauce (£3.50), a mixed grill (£5.60), a good few puddings (£1.40) and attractively priced daily specials such as seafood pancake (£2.60) and chicken and ham pie (£2.95). Well kept Camerons Strongarm and Tolly Original on handpump; good friendly service; unobtrusive piped music. There are tables in the coachyard behind. *(Recommended by Jamie and Sarah Allan, J D Maplethorpe, T Mansell, JFH; more reports please)*

Melbourns (Camerons)   Licensee Maurice de Sadeleer   Real ale   Meals and snacks (11.45–2, 6.30–10 (10.30 Sat); 7–9.30 Sun)   Restaurant   Children in separate room   Open 11–2.30, 6–11 all year   Bedrooms tel Stamford (0780) 63558; £28(£30B)/ £32(£38B)

George ★ ★ ✿ ⛉

71 St Martins

Many readers have particularly praised the way that this combines the amenities of what is after all a substantial and handsome hotel with bars that have a great deal of character and interest and are truly welcoming to the casual visitor. Perhaps best of all in summer is the cobbled courtyard at the back, with comfortable chairs and tables among attractive plant tubs and colourful hanging baskets, waiter drinks service, and an outstanding barbecue – fish and meat cooked deftly to make the most of open-air charcoal. Otherwise, the nicest place for lunch is the indoor Garden Lounge, with well spaced white cast-iron furniture on herringbone glazed bricks around a central tropical grove, and a splendidly tempting help-yourself buffet (£7.25). Bar food includes soup (£2.45), Danish open sandwiches (from £4.60), stir-fried vegetables in black-bean sauce (£4.85), lamb-burger with a yoghurt and mint dressing (£4.90), lasagne (£5.45), fritto misto (£6.95), grilled lemon sole with anchovy butter (£7.95) and a large seafood platter (£11.95); good puddings. The inn was largely built in 1597, but made use of much older material from the Norman pilgrims' hospice which had stood here before (the crypt under the cocktail bar may even be Saxon). Sturdy timbers, broad flagstones, heavy beams, and the massive stonework of the central lounge are signs of its Elizabethan days. The panelled front rooms are much more modern: eighteenth century, named after the London and York coaches, up to twenty a day each way, which changed horses here. Seats range from sturdy bar settles through leather, cane and antique wicker to soft settees and easy chairs. The best drinks are the Italian wines, many of which are good value (they don't sell real ales). Besides the courtyard, there's a well kept walled garden, with a sunken lawn where croquet and outdoor chess are often played. This is the headquarters of Ivo Vannocci's small but reliably good chain of Poste Hotels. *(Recommended by Dr and Mrs S G Donald, Gordon Theaker, T Mansell, F M Wand-Tetley, John Townsend, RMS, RLG, AE)*

Free house   Licensees Ivo Vannocci and Philip Newman-Hall   Meals and snacks (noon–11)   Restaurant   Children welcome   Open 11–11 all year   Bedrooms tel Stamford (0780) 55171; £62.50B/£86B

STRETTON (Leics)   SK9416 Map 7

Jackson Stops

From A1 follow village signposts

As you might guess from the inn-sign, this used to be called the White Horse, but got its present name years ago from an estate agent's sign, when it was waiting for a buyer. The lounge bar has a pleasantly informal and even idiosyncratic atmosphere, with its rustic décor of yokes, antlers and stuffed animal heads, and a homely collection of armchairs, country tables and chairs, and rugs. Most readers now go for the food, which includes lunchtime sandwiches (from £1) or ploughman's (from £1.80), soup (£1.10), salads (from £2), Somerby sausages (from £2.30), home-made pie (£3), lamb cutlets (£4.30), trout (£4.50), gammon and egg (£4.60), mixed grill (£5.30) and steaks (£7.60). They keep decent wines, as well as Ruddles Best and County and Sam Smiths OB on handpump in good condition. People who want just a drink may have to look for space in the small public bar, and the snug seems to be more or less a locals' preserve then. Dominoes, shove-ha'penny, nurdles and darts in a room off the public bar; open fires. The pub is handy for the A1. *(Recommended by Lyn and Bill Capper, Dr A V Lewis, Roger Bellingham; more reports please)*

Free house Licensees Frank and Sue Piguillem Real ale Meals and snacks Restaurant tel *Castle Bytham (078 081) 237 Open 11.30–2.30, 6.30 (6 Sat)–11 all year; closed 25 and 26 Dec*

SUTTON IN THE ELMS (Leics) SP5194 Map 4
Mill on the Soar 🍺

3¼ miles from M69 junction 2, but can leave motorway only southbound, rejoin only northbound – alternative access via junction 1, or via M1 junction 21; Coventry Road – junction B4114/B581

One of the biggest and busiest pubs we include in this area, this is a careful conversion of a substantial brick watermill. There are two big murals of barge and mill scenes, and you can see the restored waterwheel turning outside the serving end. But mostly, you're conscious more of the buoyant and friendly atmosphere than of the mill background. There are lots of tables in the recently refurbished spreading main bar, which has quite a few cheerful decorations on its stripped brick walls, some rugs and carpet on the flagstones, and brown beams and sturdy joists hung thickly with whisky-water jugs and some huge copper pans. Quickly served bar food includes sandwiches (from 75p), soup (90p), filled baked potatoes (95p), ploughman's (£1.85), simple but popular main dishes such as sausage, bacon and eggs (£2.30), quiche (£2.50), chicken and mushroom pie (£2.75), a good range of children's dishes on a separate menu (from 60p) and puddings (90p). The first-floor restaurant has attractive views of the River Soar. Everards Beacon, Tiger and Old Original and a monthly guest beer on handpump; fruit and cartoon machines, space game, trivia, maybe rather loud piped music. There are tables outside, with a good play area and occasional barbecues, as well as a rare-breeds farm, with its own fishing lake (50p adults, 25p children; lake £2.50). Popular with family parties at lunchtime, the inn can get very busy in the evenings and at weekends. *(Recommended by Theo Schofield, Roger Broadie; more reports on the new regime please)*

Everards Licensee Philip Cook Real ale Meals and snacks (until 10 evenings, 9.30 Sat) Restaurant Children welcome Open 11–11; 11–2.30, 5–11 in winter Bedrooms tel *Sutton Elms (0455) 282419; £34.50B/£44B*

SWITHLAND (Leics) SK5413 Map 7
Griffin

Village signposted from A6 Leicester–Loughborough

Though the great majority of customers in this modernised but well worn-in country pub are clearly regulars, there's a warm welcome for newcomers – who can rely on the quality of the Adnams Bitter and Everards Bitter, Mild, Tiger and Old Original on handpump, with usually a guest beer too. The three communicating rooms have beams, some modern panelling, carpet or parquet flooring, serviceable wall seats around dimpled copper tables, and hunting prints; the end one is usually quietest, with easy chairs by its fire. Good fresh bar snacks; darts, dominoes, cribbage, fruit machine and juke box, with a skittle alley in the quite separate back Stable Bar. Handy for Bradgate Country Park, with walks in Swithland woods. *(Recommended by Richard Sanders, Dave Butler, Lesley Storey, T Nott; more reports please)*

Everards Licensees Norman and Brenda Jefferson Real ale Meals and snacks (not Sun) Children welcome Open 11–2.30, 6–11 (11–11 weekends) all year

Bedroom prices normally include full English breakfast, VAT and any inclusive service charge that we know of.

TETFORD (Lincs)   TF3374 Map 8

White Hart

Village signposted from Greetham–Belchford road off A158 Horncastle–Skegness, and from Scamblesby–South Ormsby road between A153 and A16 S of Louth; inn near centre of this straggly village – OS Sheet 122 reference 333748

A wiggly corridor takes you through to the back of this early sixteenth-century inn, where there's a cosily traditional red-tiled bar with a high-backed curved oak settle by a big brick inglenook fireplace hung with brass plaques and horsebrasses. There are slabby elm tables, hunting-print cushions on other settles, china and pewter hanging from one black beam. Good value, home-made and appetising bar food includes soup (75p), pizza (£1.75), ploughman's (from £1.95), lasagne (£2.35), seafood platter (£2.70), goulash or gammon (£2.90), lamb cutlets or steak and kidney pie (£3.50), eight-ounce sirloin steak (£4.50), children's portions (£1.75) and puddings (£1.10); well kept Batemans XB and XXXB and Marstons Pedigree on handpump; darts, quiet piped music, a chatty welcome and friendly service. A bigger extension opening off is more simply furnished with plenty of tables and chairs. There's also a small snug. The sheltered back lawn has seats and swings. *(Recommended by Phil and Sally Gorton, Kevin and Mary Shakespeare)*

Free house   Licensee Stuart Dick   Real ale   Meals and snacks (12–2, 6.30–11, not Mon) Restaurant   Children in lounge and snug bar   Open 12–3, 6.30–11 all year; closed Mon lunchtime (exc bank hols) and evening 25 Dec   Bedrooms tel Tetford (065 883) 255; £21/£28

UPTON (Notts)   SK7354 Map 7

Cross Keys ★ 🍺

Main Street (A612 towards Southwell)

Distinctive bar food in this heavy-beamed seventeenth-century pub might include potted shrimps or chicken and brandy pâté (£2.25), smokies (£2.75), vegetarian dishes such as leeks in cream or cheese and courgettes baked in layers (£2.95), beef in ginger or casseroled (£3.10), fish pie (£3.30), lamb noisettes in port and redcurrant jelly (£3.65), as well as lunchtime sandwiches (from 90p) and ploughman's (£2.25); inventive puddings; they don't do chips, and the menu changes day by day. Fortunately, the new restaurant out in a former dovecote has not detracted from the quality of the pub side, where the careful choice of well kept beers consists of Batemans XXXB, Marstons Pedigree and Whitbreads Castle Eden on handpump, with a guest such as Yates. The bar rambles around a two-way log fireplace and in and out of various alcoves, with decorative plates and metalwork in one corner, and lots of pictures from sporting cartoons to local watercolours (one reader was so relaxed by the time he left that he bought one). A new extension room has carved pews from Newark church. Darts and dominoes; the dog's well behaved. Half a dozen tables are strung out in bays of the neatly plant-lined fence behind. *(Recommended by Dr Keith Bloomfield, J D Maplethorpe, Mike Tucker, Mrs M E Collins, Angie and Dave Parkes, Derek Stephenson, Douglas Bail, Peter Burton)*

Free house   Licensee Michael Kirrage   Real ale   Snacks (lunchtime) and meals (until 10 evenings)   Restaurant (Thurs–Sat evenings, Sun lunch until 4) tel Southwell (0636) 813269 Children in restaurant, lunchtimes too   Folk music winter Sun evening   Open 11.30–2.30, 6–11 all year; closed evening 25 Dec

French Horn 🍺

A612

This is another pub where a decent meal and good drink (well kept John Smiths on handpump, and a good choice of decent wines by the glass) may put you in the frame of mind to splash out as an art collector: they often have a show by local painters. The neat and comfortable open-plan bar has cushioned captain's chairs and wall banquettes around glossy tables; service is friendly and efficient. Generous helpings of home-made food include filled rolls (from 65p), soup (from 95p), chicken pâté (£1.95), ploughman's (from £1.95), salads (from £2.50), good vegetarian dishes (from £2.75), beef and red wine casserole or steak and kidney pie (£3.95), chicken Kiev (£4.95) and sirloin steak (£6.70), with lots of puddings (from £1.10); if Yorkshire pudding with onion gravy's on, try it (£1.75). The choice is wider in the upstairs brasserie. The big sloping back paddock, with picnic-table sets, looks over farmland. *(Recommended by Pat and Norman Godley, Derek Stephenson, PLC, RJH; more reports please)*

John Smiths (Courage)   *Licensees Graham and Linda Mills   Real ale   Meals and snacks Restaurant tel Southwell (0636) 812394   Children if eating   Open 11–2.30, 6.30–11 all year; closed evening 25 Dec*

WAINFLEET (Lincs)   TF5058 Map 8
Angel
High Street (A52 Skegness–Boston)

An inn since the eighteenth century, this Georgian-fronted building's neatly kept lounge bar has dark red plush-cushioned sturdy settles, smaller seats and stools on its red carpet, and traditional cast-iron-framed tables, with prints on its cream-painted walls. Reliably good bar food includes burgers or omelettes (£2.25), grilled fish (£2.95), lasagne (£3.95) and rump steak (£5.95); it's all home made, so there may be a wait. Well kept Adnams and Everards Beacon and guest beers from smaller breweries such as Uley or Linfit on handpump, and decent coffee; friendly young licensees, coal fire, juke box. A small communicating pool-room has one or two old enamel advertisements, and darts. *(Recommended by Mrs Karen Mitchell, C M Clements, D I Baddeley, Derek and Sylvia Stephenson, Richard Sanders)*

Everards   *Licensees Paul and Rosie Dicker   Real ale   Meals and snacks (not Mon)   Evening restaurant (not Sun) tel Skegness (0754) 880324   Well behaved children welcome   Open 12–2 (3 Sat), 7–11 all year; closed Mon (and has been closed winter weekday lunchtimes, though they tell us they plan to keep open in future)*

WALCOTE (Leics)   SP5683 Map 4
Black Horse 🏵
1½ miles from M1 junction 20; A427 towards Lutterworth

Bar food here is exclusively Thai – the landlady, who does the cooking, comes from Thailand. You can book a set evening meal (£8) with no menu, just four or five mystery courses, or you can choose one of about eight dishes, half spicy and half savoury, such as nasi goreng (fried rice with meat and egg), a Thai mixed grill, strips of beef in oyster sauce or khau mu daeng (marinated pork – all £3), and various Thai curries such as gaeng pak (vegetables) or gaen pla (fresh fish – £3–£3.50). Yet this is otherwise very much a proper unassuming English pub, with a quietly chatty atmosphere and a fine choice of drinks – well kept Flowers IPA, Hook Norton Best and Hoskins & Oldfields HOB with guests such as Brakspears SB and Hook Norton Old Hookey on handpump, an eclectic range of bottled beers that runs to Singha from Thailand, and country wines. It's furnished with russet plush button-back built-in wall banquettes, cast-iron and other heavy tables, more booth-like seats at the side, and pale mate's chairs in an airier section up steps; there's an open fire, and (for summer) seats out behind. *(Recommended by J C and D Aitkenhead, Dave Butler, Lesley Storey, Cdr Patrick Tailyour, W Rich; more reports please)*

Free house   *Licensee Mrs Saovanee Tinker   Real ale   Meals   Restaurant by arrangement only tel Lutterworth (0455) 552684   Children in eating area   Open 12–3, 5 (6 Sat)–11 all year*

WALTHAM ON THE WOLDS (Leics)   SK8024 Map 7
Royal Horseshoes 🛏
A607

Set in fine rolling Wolds country, this attractive stone-built Tudor village inn has comfortable, tidy and well equipped bedrooms. The knocked-through lounge bar has sturdy cushioned wall seats and plush stools around copper-topped tables, no fewer than three open fires, Vanity Fair caricatures and a substantial antique hunting painting, and a carvery and cold buffet built into the bar counter. Helping yourself from this costs around £4; other bar food includes soup (£1), pâté (£1.95), ploughman's (£2.30), a hot dish of the day such as steak braised in red wine (£3.35) and steaks (£6.25), with a four-course Sunday roast lunch (£6) and home-made puddings. Besides well kept John Smiths on handpump, they keep decent wines (though one or two readers would like a more generous glass of house wine) and a fair range of malts; piped music. The smaller public bar has darts and a fruit machine. There's a verandah seat outside, with more seats out behind. *(Recommended by G Smith, Miss A Tress, Mel Bodfish, RMS, RLG, John Oddey; more reports please)*

John Smiths (Courage)   Licensee Maurice Wigglesworth   Meals and snacks (12–2, 6–9; residents only, Sun evening)   Children in eating area   Open 11–2.30, 6–11 all year; closed 25–26 Dec   Bedrooms tel Waltham on the Wolds (066 478) 289; £21.75B/£37B

WEST LEAKE (Notts)   SK5226 Map 7
Star
Village signposted from A6006

Looking very picturesque from the outside, this old pub is still known as the Pit House from the distant days when it ran cockfights. Most people like the unpretentious beamed bar on the left best: sturdy settles around oak tables on the tiled floor, harness, whips, cockfighting prints and foxes' masks on the ochre walls, quite a collection of cats, and a warm welcome from behind the bar. The Bass and M&B Springfield on handpump are well kept (your money's just put in a wooden tray). The partly panelled lounge on the right has comfortable armed chairs and a good log fire. Good value simple food includes soup (65p), salads (from £2.95), a daily hot dish (around £3) and puddings (70p). There are picnic-table sets by the quiet lane in front. *(Recommended by John Wainwright, Richard Sanders, Jill and George Hadfield, Roger Broadie, Stewart Argyle)*

Bass   Real ale   Meals and snacks (lunchtime, not Sat or Sun)   Children in eating area Open 10.30–2.30, 6–10.30

WHITWELL (Leics)   SK9208 Map 8
Noel Arms
Though it's much the smallest part of this thatched inn, the most popular bar (and certainly the one the locals all go for) is the original part, furthest from the car park. It's got a really warm atmosphere, and the two tiny rooms have a good deal of character, what with things like the box for Rutland Water fishing catch returns, and the odd contraption in which they keep the pot plants (it's actually the local pattern of spit-roaster, turning on a vertical axis in front of the fire). There's much more room in the spacious and plushly comfortable back extension, where there may be piped music. Good waitress-served home-made bar food includes sandwiches (from 95p), soup (from £1.30), ploughman's or sausage and bread (£2.40), daily specials such as steak and kidney pie or a fish dish (£4.35) and pork fillet (£5.50), with steaks (from £6.50) and mixed grills in the evening, and interesting puddings (£1.90). Well kept Ruddles Best and County and Tetleys on handpump, and an extensive wine list; fruit machine; they do afternoon teas (not

Mondays). There are tables on the south-facing slope behind, with occasional barbecues. Residents have to book for the restaurant. *(Recommended by Rob and Gill Weeks, Jamie and Sarah Allan, Stewart Argyle, Malcolm Steward, Mrs J Stocks; more reports please)*

Free house   Real ale   Meals and snacks (until 10 evenings)   Restaurant   Children welcome   Open 11–2.30 (3 Sat), 6–11 all year   Bedrooms tel Empingham (078 086) 334; £20(£36B)/£32.50(£42.50B)

WILSON (Leics)   SK4024 Map 7
Bulls Head

On side road Breedon on the Hill–Melbourne; village signposted from A453 Ashby de la Zouch–Castle Donington

The buffet counter is a big attraction in this comfortably modernised country pub: a wide range of attractively presented salads using good fresh ingredients (from £3.25), with seafood such as dressed crab, cold fresh salmon or freshly sliced smoked salmon particularly popular. Other bar food, in generous helpings, consists of sandwiches (from 95p), soup (65p), ploughman's (from £1.75), a daily special (£3.50) and hot roast beef (£4.50). The beamed bar is a cheerful bustle at lunchtime, presided over by the smart and cheerfully efficient mature barmaids. With maroon plush banquettes and settles around neat black tables, it opens into several quieter alcoves, decorated with old sepia racing-car photographs (Donington racetrack is nearby) and some striking modern prints of immensely magnified insects; piped music. Well kept Ind Coope Burton on handpump. *(Recommended by Neil and Angela Huxter, Paul and Janet Waring, A C and S J Beardsley, T Nott, Chris Raisin, Michael and Alison Sandy, David Gaunt, M A and W R Proctor; more reports please)*

Ind Coope   Licensee Michael Johnson   Real ale   Meals and snacks (12–2, 6–10; not Sun or Mon evenings)   Children in eating area   Open 11–2.30, 6–11 all year

WING (Leics)   SK8903 Map 4
Kings Arms

Top Street

The friendly lounge of this simple early seventeenth-century stone inn has some engaging old-fashioned furnishings, such as the antique settle and the attractive window seat, among more conventional wheel-back chairs. It's been leaning more towards food recently: home cooking, with a wide choice including soup (£1), sandwiches (from £1.10), sausage and beans (£2.15), ploughman's (£2.50), daily specials with some emphasis on fish, omelettes (from £3.55), mixed grill (£6.55) and steak or jumbo prawns (£7.50). Well kept Batemans XXXB, Greene King IPA and Ruddles Best and County on handpump, with good log fires in the interesting copper-chimneyed central fireplace of this room as well as in the recently refurbished beamed back bar. The sunny yard has wooden benches; a medieval turf maze some seventeen yards across is just up the road. *(Recommended by Derek and Sylvia Stephenson, Jamie and Sarah Allan, Peter Hall, Dr A V Lewis, Geoff Lee)*

Free house   Real ale   Meals and snacks   Restaurant   Children welcome Open 10.30–2.30, 6–11 all year   Two-bedroom flat tel Manton (057 285) 315

WOODHOUSE EAVES (Leics)   SK5214 Map 7
Wheatsheaf

Brand Hill; follow Main Street straight through town off B591 S of Loughborough

Low-ceilinged and gently lit, this civilised open-plan country pub has comfortable brown plush seats in the two front rooms, with simpler tables and chairs in the area that opens off behind. There are good open fires, with foxes' masks and lots of hunting and other sporting prints. On warm evenings there's almost a continental feel to the floodlit area beyond the coach entry, with barbecues and picnic-table sets under cocktail parasols. Good value bar food includes sandwiches (£1.15), home-made soup (£1.30), chilli con carne or lasagne (£2.55), prawn salad (£2.75) and a four-ounce burger (£2.95); they do a special supper for couples on Monday nights. Well kept Bass, Marstons Pedigree and Ruddles County on handpump. Service is quick and friendly, even on busy evenings and weekends. No motor-cycles or leathers. *(Recommended by Tim and Lynne Crawford, Martin Aust, Richard Sanders, A J Leach; more reports please)*

Free house   Licensees Mr and Mrs Tony Marshall   Real ale   Meals and snacks (12–2, 7–10; not Sun evening)   Upstairs restaurant tel Woodhouse Eaves (0509) 890320   Children in restaurant   Open 11–2.30, 5.30 (6 Sat)–11 all year

---

Lucky Dip

Besides the fully inspected pubs, you might like to try these Lucky Dips recommended to us and described by readers (if you do, please send us reports):

Anstey, Leics [Bradgate Rd; SK5408], *Hare & Hounds*: Good local atmosphere under friendly and efficient new licensees, several tastefully refurbished rooms, wide range of home-made food, well kept Marstons Pedigree *(Paul and Janet Waring)*

Ashby de la Zouch, Leics [The Mews; SK3516], *Mews*: Wine bar rather than pub, but worth knowing for its food *(Jill Hadfield)*

☆ **Aswarby**, Lincs [A15 Folkingham–Sleaford; TF0639], *Tally Ho*: Small but imposing stone-built estate pub looking across the oak-tree park to the pretty slender-spired village church; two friendly rooms with country prints, big log fire and wood-burning stove, oak beams, simple traditional furnishings; well kept Adnams, Batemans XB and an interesting guest beer such as the fairly local Stanleys on handpump, straightforward bar food from soup and sandwiches to steaks; welcoming service; tables and timber play fort on grass behind, by sheep meadow; bedrooms comfortable and well equipped, in neatly converted block behind *(Angie and Dave Parkes, Mrs Pamela Dumenil, Jane Kingsbury, A and J Heaphy, Derek and Sylvia Stephenson, J D Maplethorpe, BB)*

Auboum, Lincs [SK9262], *Royal Oak*: Large helpings in pretty, very friendly country pub with garden *(Mr and Mrs Mark Smith, J D Maplethorpe)*

Awsworth, Notts [quite handy for M1 junction 26, via A610/A6096; SK4844], *Hog Head*: Huge helpings of good fresh traditional food and well kept beers in friendly family-run pub, very modern and clean *(John Balfour)*

Barholm, Lincs [TF0810], *Five Horseshoes*: Well kept Adnams, Batemans and guest beers in homely easy-going village local with horsy connections and paddocks behind the garden tables *(M J Morgan, LYM)*

Barkby, Leics [off A607 6 miles NE of Leicester; SK6309], *Brookside*: In pretty village with a brook running past the front

door; lots of toby jugs, brass and copper; well kept Ansells and Ind Coope Burton on handpump; try the beef puff – half a French loaf *(A C Lang)*

☆ **Barrow upon Soar**, Leics [Mill Lane, off South St (B5328); SK5717], *Navigation*: Picturesque two-roomed old split-level pub by Grand Union Canal, once used as stabling for barge horses; recently renovated and extended, and popular at weekends for good value straightforward lunchtime bar food and well kept John Smiths, Marstons Pedigree and Shipstones Mild and Bitter on handpump; skittle alley, small back terrace where boats are often moored; car park over small humped-back bridge *(P A and J B Jones, Richard Sanders)*

Barrow upon Soar, Leics, *Soar Bridge*: White-painted inn with collection of old cast signs, old local railway pictures and canalia; popular good value and well prepared food, well kept Everards Beacon and Old Original and lots of country wines; short walk through back to river *(P A and J B Jones)*

Bassingham, Lincs [High St; SK9160], *Five Bells*: Tucked in heart of village with immaculate interior, brimming with brass, beams and knick-knacks; warm and friendly atmosphere, roaring open fire, well kept Ind Coope and Tetleys, decent wine; bar food in separate raised eating area *(A and J Heaphy, Frank Williams)*

Baston, Lincs [Church St; TF1113], *Spinning Wheel*: Good choice of beers including Bass, particularly good value food in bar and restaurant *(M J Morgan)*

Beckingham, Lincs [off A17 E of Newark; SK8753], *Black Swan*: Well worth knowing for fine restaurant food such as duck breast tartlet, cheese soufflé with poached egg *(Anon)*

☆ **Belgrave**, Leics [Melton Rd (A607); edge of Leicester; SK6007], *Melton*: Large Asian-owned Victorian pub with interesting back Simba grill (Thurs–Sun), where chef from

Bombay, working in front of you and using recently installed tandoori oven, cooks good food inc tikkas, excellent nan, chilli dishes and kebabs with traditional sauces; no cutlery – use right hand for eating; well kept Marstons Burton, Pedigree and Border Mild on handpump *(P A and J B Jones)*

Belmesthorpe, Leics [Shepherds Walk; TF0410], *Bluebell*: Olde-worlde pub with lively atmosphere and entertaining landlord; well kept Marstons Pedigree and Ruddles County; good value lunchtime bar food (not Sun) *(C E Tyers)*

☆ **Bicker**, Lincs [A52 NE of Donnington; TF2237], *Red Lion*: Well kept Bass and Ind Coope Burton on handpump and wide range of good value simple bar food in comfortably modernised seventeenth-century pub with masses of china hanging from bowed black beams, huge fireplace, tables on terrace and tree-shaded lawn; interesting area – formerly a sea inlet, with remains of Roman sea dykes *(A V Lewis, J D Maplethorpe, David and Ruth Hollands, LYM)*

☆ **Blidworth**, Notts [SK5956], *Bird in Hand*: Particularly friendly local with probably the best view in Notts over Sherwood Forest; one large room with three-sided bar, well kept Mansfield Riding and Old Baily on handpump, good cheap bar food, large garden *(Angie and Dave Parkes, Stewart Argyle)*

Blyth, Notts [SK6287], *Angel*: Cheerful much-modernised coaching-inn with comfortable and quite lively lounge, well kept Hardys & Hansons real ales on electric pump, nice coal fire, piped music; public bar and pool-room, seats in garden; bar food straightforward (ham salad recommended), but usefully served on Sun too (rare around here) – so handy for A1; children welcome; bedrooms very simple, though OK for a stopover *(Jim Wiltshire, Roger Broadie, LYM)*; *White Swan*: Attractive pub, friendly landlord, well kept beer, good bar food *(C Elliott)*

☆ **Boston**, Lincs [Witham St; TF3244], *Carpenters Arms*: Traditional very friendly backstreet inn, vibrant with locals and young people (landlord's young too), well kept Batemans Mild and XB, enterprising home-cooked lunchtime food; bedrooms reasonably priced *(Richard Sanders)*

Boston, [High St (nr level crossing)], *Eagle*: Basic sparsely furnished bar and small lounge with fire, impressive choice of well kept beers (all available to take away) inc Timothy Taylors Landlord, Batemans XXXB, two weekly guest beers and annual beer festival; simple lunchtime bar food, roast lunch Sun *(Peter Donahue)*

Bramcote, Notts [Derby Rd; SK5037], *Sherwin Arms*: Lively and friendly roadside pub with rustic atmosphere, well kept beer, freshly prepared reasonably priced bar food *(B R Shiner)*

☆ **Brandy Wharf**, Lincs [B1205 SE of Scunthorpe; TF0197], *Hankerin*: Riverside pub with sense of space, popular with boating people as there are good moorings and slipways; jovial licensee, remarkable choice of dozens of farm ciders (with summer 'Sydre Shoppe'), standard choice of good cheap nicely served bar food inc excellent curry; the buildings look lucky to have survived, and the unusual décor is perhaps not the main attraction; closed Christmas, New Year and Mon winter lunchtimes *(Andy and Jill Kassube, T Nott)*

Branston, Leics [Main St; SK8129], *Wheel*: Friendly, 300-year-old two-roomed pub in beautiful area, well kept Batemans XB and John Smiths, reasonably priced bar food specialising in schnitzels and Stilton-based dishes; juke box, skittle area, boules piste *(Keith Bloomfield, Richard Sanders)*

Burbage, Leics [SP4294], *Cross Keys*: Good atmosphere in pleasant building with various snugs; well kept Marstons, cricket view from garden *(Graham Bush)*

Burton on the Wolds, Leics [Melton Rd (B676); SK5921], *Greyhound*: Redeveloped pub with friendly atmosphere, warm comfort and good value bar food *(R C Clark)*

Castle Bytham, Lincs [SK9818], *Castle*: Charming licensee and consistently good bar food (no food Tues) *(D R Uphill)*

☆ **Castle Donington**, Leics [90 Bondgate; B6504; SK4427], *Cross Keys*: Well kept Vaux Samson and Wards Best, attractive atmosphere, with good fire and good mix of customers *(Richard Sanders)*

☆ **Castle Donington**, Leics [Kings Mills; SK4427], *Priest House*: Unusual drinks and hearty snacks and grills in rambling beamed bars of inn with medieval tower in attractive spot by River Trent, which has been popular with young people for friendly service, well kept Watneys-related real ales, games-room with two pool-tables, darts and table football, though recent reports suggest that they may have been going to play up the restaurant side instead – more news of these please; children's play area; decent bedrooms *(Martin Aust, Richard Sanders, LYM)*

Clipstone, Notts [Old Clipstone; B6030 Mansfield–Ollerton – OS Sheet 120 reference 606647; SK6064], *Dog & Duck*: Comfortably modernised and friendly three-roomed pub with good home-made hot meals and well kept Home ales; not far from Center Parc at Rufford; children's room *(Alan and Marlene Radford)*

Coalville, Leics [SK4214], *Bull*: Friendly atmosphere with helpful, courteous service, good décor, well kept Burton and good food *(P Miller)*

Collingham, Notts [High St; SK8361], *Royal Oak*: Cheerful, rambling pub in pleasant village; well kept John Smiths served frothy, northern-style *(John Baker)*

Colston Bassett, Notts [SK7033], *Martins*

Arms: Idyllically placed rustic local in charming village with imposing, wood-carved fireplace and matching bar, mixture of old furniture inc settee opposite one of the fires, plenty of brasses, unusual scales – almost like someone's front room; Bass and Ruddles on handpump usually well kept, filled cobs sometimes, bowling-green; closed Sun (and opening times may vary); there may or may not be a warm welcome *(Chris Raisin)*

☆ **Coningsby**, Lincs [Boston Rd (B1192); TF2258], *Leagate*: Extensive and attractive oak-beamed pub with antique furnishings, wide choice of very good reasonably priced food, well kept beers – popular with servicemen from RAF Coningsby; big restaurant, garden with Koi carp pond, play area *(Neil and Elspeth Fearn, Peter Donahue, Kevin and Mary Shakespeare, J D Maplethorpe)*

Copt Oak, Leics [nr M1 junc 22; A50 towards Leics, then B587; SK4812], *Copt Oak*: Newly refurbished in 1920s-style with lush green plants in profusion and restaurant in new wing with stunning views over Charnwood Forest; good food at average prices, fast service *(J D Martin)*

☆ **Cottesmore**, Leics [Main St; SK9013], *Sun*: Very popular for bar food – soup, wrapped baps and several same-price hot dishes such as rabbit casserole or ham and egg; decent sporting prints and plush button-back banquettes in modernised bar with hot fire in stone inglenook, quieter side rooms, piped music and fruit machine, tables in garden; charge for cheque payment and if no drink bought; children welcome *(John Oddey, BB)*

☆ **Cropston**, Leics [Station Rd (B5328); SK5510], *Bradgate Arms*: Hoskins real ales with well kept guest beers and Weston's cider in gently refurbished traditional village pub with family area, skittle alley and garden; bar food; as we went to press we heard the pub was closed for refurbishment *(P A and J B Jones, Richard Sanders, LYM; more reports please)*

Dadlington, Leics [SP4097], *Dog & Hedgehog*: Extended dining pub popular for enormous grills; does have real ale *(Ken and Barbara Turner)*

☆ **Diseworth**, Leics [nr East Midlands Airport; SK4524], *Plough*: Delightfully refurbished Bass house with unique atmosphere, well kept beer and good range of bar food *(Harry Blood)*

Diseworth, *Bull & Swan*: Well kept Shipstones, good bar food *(Dave Braisted)*

East Kirkby, Lincs [OS Sheet 122 reference 334623; TF3362], *Red Lion*: Good, clean, cosy Batemans pub full of clocks that chime and ring for ten minutes around each hour; friendly and welcoming landlord *(Phil and Sally Gorton)*

Eastville, Lincs [TF4057], *Wheat Sheaf*: Clean and basic Fenland pub with particularly well kept Batemans; friendly, helpful licensees – they referred requests for

food to fish and chip shop (excellent and cheap) just down the road *(John Baker)*

☆ **Edenham**, Lincs [A151; TF0621], *Five Bells*: Friendly landlord, waitresses and locals, wide choice of usual bar food served quickly, well kept Camerons ales and log fire in busy but spacious modernised lounge with neatly ranged tables; piped music, soft lighting, good play area in garden; children welcome *(Geoff Halson, A and J Heaphy, LYM)*

☆ **Elston**, Notts [A47 S of Lincoln; SK7548], *Coeur de Lion*: Extraordinary building like a small Iberian summer palace – pinnacles, domes, lancet windows, steep roofs, tall chimneys, elevated terraces; decorous panelled bar with soft russet plush seats, country prints and engravings, neatly uniformed careful staff; good bar food served under domed silver covers, decent spirits, free peanuts; two candle-lit dining-rooms, one upstairs with soaring pitched and raftered ceiling *(David and Ruth Hollands, BB)*

☆ **Epperstone**, Notts [SK6548], *Cross Keys*: Particularly friendly village pub with well kept Hardys & Hansons on handpump, copious helpings of excellent value bar food *(David Carnill, Dr Keith Bloomfield, Stewart Argyle)*

Everton, Notts [SK6991], *Blacksmiths Arms*: Popular, well kept and comfortable, with good atmosphere *(ILP)*

Ewerby, Lincs [TF1247], *Finch Hatton Arms*: Imposing, country-house-type building in small village; tasteful décor, efficient staff *(A and J Heaphy)*

☆ **Exton**, Leics [The Green; SK9211], *Fox & Hounds*: Elegant high-ceilinged lounge in comfortable and attractive inn, in pretty surroundings; well kept Sam Smiths real ales, good value bar meals and Sun lunches, quite separate lively public bar, restaurant, pretty garden – it's an attractive village; children in eating areas; bedrooms *(Dr Keith Bloomfield, Ann Parker, E J and J W Cutting, T Nott, LYM)*

Fiskerton, Notts [SK7351], *Bromley Arms*: Popular local, especially for families and fishermen, by River Trent; well kept Hardys & Hansons, bar food including good sandwiches *(John Baker)*

Frampton, Lincs [signposted off A16 S of Boston; TF3239], *Moers Arms*: Attractive old free house with exposed beams throughout main lounge; well kept Adnams on handpump, simple home-made bar food from sandwiches up, big garden; busy weekends *(Peter Donahue)*

Frisby on the Wreake, Leics [Main St; SK6917], *Bell*: Bar food running up to steaks, inc good home-made fruit pies; obliging staff, fair range of wines, piped music, tables outside *(RJH)*

Gaddesby, Leics [SK6813], *Cheney Arms*: Once an eighteenth-century manor house, this two-roomed country local has genuine atmosphere and hasn't changed in character in the 15 years we've used it; racing prints and jockeys' silks, good Stilton cobs, well kept Everards and guest beers, open fire *(P A and J B Jones)*

Gainsborough, Lincs [Morton Terr; SK8189], *Elm Cottage*: An oasis in this part of the world – nice local atmosphere, comfortable cottagey interior, friendly staff, well kept Bass on handpump, good traditional pub food at anachronistic prices *(David and Ruth Hollands)*

Gedney, Lincs [Chapelgate; TF4024], *Old Black Lion*: Loyal regulars praise its food, homely atmosphere, service and real ale *(R Pinch)*

Glaston, Leics [SK8900], *Monkton Arms*: Good bar food in informal, very friendly surroundings; fresh fish and spare ribs in mammoth helpings, home-made puddings, real ales, good range of wines, unusual bar layout adding to atmosphere; can be busy in the evening; bedrooms being built *(B J A King)*

☆ **Grantham**, Lincs [High St; SK9135], *Angel & Royal*: The stone façade is quite unique, with carvings done 600 years ago to honour the visit by King Edward III to what was then a Commandery of the Knights Templar; the plush hotel bar on left of coach entry still has interesting oriel window, and high-beamed main bar opp has massive inglenook – tremendous potential for the historically minded; we've had very mixed reports on bar food recently; open all day; the hotel side is THF; bedrooms *(Rob and Gill Weeks, T Mansell, LYM; more reports please)*

☆ **Grantham** [Vine St], *Blue Pig*: Ancient, attractive half-timbered corner pub, with several cosy and atmospheric beamed drinking areas, lots of prints and photographs of old Grantham on the walls; well kept Flowers IPA and Whitbreads Castle Eden on handpump, bar food served quickly and in generous helpings, friendly staff; pretty hanging baskets in summer *(Howard and Sue Gascoyne, T Mansell, David and Ruth Hollands)*

☆ **Great Casterton**, Lincs [village signposted off A1; TF0009], *Crown*: High-backed booth seating in neat bar with walls stripped to bare stone above the white-painted wainscoting, good value bar food from soup, bacon sandwiches and ploughman's to hefty gammon and steaks with cheap daily specials, well kept Camerons and Tolly Original on handpump, log fire in inglenook, simpler back bar popular with the Young Farmers; old-fashioned seats in pretty little garden opposite attractive church; Post Office in car park *(A V Lewis, Stan Edwards, BB)*

☆ **Greetham**, Leics [B668 Stretton–Cottesmore; SK9214], *Wheatsheaf*: Good value bar food under new owners, usefully served until 11pm – soup, lunchtime sandwiches and ploughman's, cheap charcoal-grilled burgers, chops, gammon, grilled prawns, steaks; simply furnished L-shaped series of communicating rooms, coal fire, nautical charts, well kept Camerons Bitter and Strongarm Premium on handpump; pool and other games in end room, restaurant, tables on side grass; charge for cheques *(M and J Back, BB)*

Grimsthorpe, Lincs [A151; TF0422], *Black Horse*: Stripped stone, beams and blazing log fire in restaurant with good food; bedrooms *(Anon)*

☆ **Grimston**, Leics [SK6821], *Black Horse*: Well kept pub on edge of small village green in fine rolling farmland; spacious, but with several quiet, cosy corners, decent house wines, and particularly enjoyable freshly cooked bar food with good vegetables and superb puddings; efficient licensee keen on sport – hence the small TV for horse-racing and wealth of interesting cricket memorabilia *(Norman G W Edwardes, Jane Palmer, R J Haerdi)*

Halam, Notts [SK6754], *Wagon & Horses*: Immaculate dining pub popular, particularly in the evening, for good bar food; well kept Marstons Pedigree on handpump, open fire, some tables out in front *(Derek and Sylvia Stephenson, Tim and Lynne Crawford, Dr Keith Bloomfield)*

☆ **Halton Holegate**, Lincs [TF4165], *Bell*: Pretty tiled white-painted house with hanging baskets and passion-flower near the church in quiet village where the rolling Wolds slope down into the fens; simple but comfortable furnishings, aircraft pictures (the Lancaster bomber flying over the pub on the inn-sign commemorates 207 and 44 Squadrons, stationed nearby), decent home-made food from soup and sandwiches through chicken breasts and gammon to steaks; well kept Batemans XB on handpump, good coffee, friendly landlord (ditto Sam, the sleek black dog) *(Bert Dowty, BB)*

Hayton, Notts [Main St (B1403) – OS Sheet 120 reference 728852; SK7384], *Boat*: Picturesque spot backing on to quiet stretch of Chesterfield canal; friendly atmosphere, well kept Bass, Marstons Pedigree, Tetleys and Whitbreads Castle Eden on handpump, good value generously served carvery food; bedrooms with showers (and good breakfasts) in adjacent complex of cottages – good value *(Denise Plummer, Jim Froggatt)*

Hinckley, Leics [New Buildings; SP4294], *Greyhound*: Lively youngsters' pub with decently kept beer, trad jazz Weds, other jazz Thurs *(Graham Bush)*; [Coventry Rd (not far from M69 junction 1)] *Wharf*: Unspoilt many-roomed pub with collection of toby jugs in pleasant lounge, basic bar area, old-world snug with beams and brasses; well kept Marstons Burton and Pedigree *(G P Dyall)*

☆ **Horbling**, Lincs [4 Spring Lane (off B1177);

TF1135], *Plough*: Almost unique in being owned by Parish Council; good value bar food from toasted sandwiches to cheap mixed grills, well kept Greene King IPA and Abbot and guest beers on handpump, cosy and friendly comfortable lounge with log fire, darts and other games in lively public bar; children in eating area; bedrooms cheap but comfortable *(A B Barton, LYM)*

Horncastle, Lincs [TF2669], *Durham Ox*: Unspoilt pub with dark bar full of old cardboard drink advertisements, copper ornaments and stuffed animals *(Phil Gorton)*

Hose, Leics [Bolton Lane; SK7329], *Black Horse*: Particularly well kept Home Bitter and Mild in classic village local with three rooms – usually two in use, both with coal fires; settles on red-tiled floor, crisps kept in ancient Beeston Crisp Co tins (no proper bar food), back skittle alley and garden *(Richard Sanders)*

Hoton, Leics [A60; SK5722], *Packe Arms*: Spacious and comfortable Bird Bar and older front part in welcoming and well kept pub with decent bar food *(BB)*

☆ **Hough on the Hill**, Lincs [SK9246], *Brownlow Arms*: Attractive pub in peaceful picturesque village; sofas and comfortable chairs in relaxing lounge, separate bar, wide range of good value well cooked and presented food in bar and restaurant, friendly welcome, efficient service; attractive bedrooms with lovely breakfasts, reasonable prices *(Mrs Anne Brown, Andy and Jill Kassube)*

Hungarton, Leics [SK6807], *Black Boy*: Pleasant rustic local with lunchtime and evening bar food inc home-made specials, grills and filled cobs *(A R M Moate)*

Husbands Bosworth, Leics [A427 Market Harborough–Lutterworth, junction A50; SP6484], *Bell*: Pleasantly decorated L-shaped bar in clean pub with lots of brass, log fire, friendly helpful staff, Ansells Mild and Ind Coope Burton, freshly cooked and liberally served food from sandwiches to steaks *(A E Alcock)*

Ketton, Leics [SK9704], *Northwick Arms*: Very friendly and popular with locals; huge helpings of fish and chips *(Margaret and Trevor Errington)*

Kneesall, Notts [SK7064], *Angel*: Two roomy and comfortable recently refurbished connecting bars, well kept Whitbreads Castle Eden on handpump, interesting bar food at reasonable prices *(Denise Plummer, Jim Froggatt)*

Knipton, Leics [SK8231], *Red House*: Beautifully proportioned former hunting-lodge looking over pretty village close to Belvoir Castle; orthodox bar furnishings, but good value food from soup, bacon sandwiches and ploughman's through curries with basmati rice or venison and juniper pie to steaks; well kept Ind Coope Burton and Marstons Pedigree on

handpump, unobtrusive piped music, a welcoming tribe of dogs; restaurant *(BB)*

☆ **Lambley**, Notts [Church St; SK6245], *Woodlark*: Well preserved and interestingly laid out mining-village pub with a cheerful welcome for strangers and outstanding value cheap snacks, relaxing and quiet; well kept Home ales, navy memorabilia, wide range of pub games inc pool-room, table skittles and skittle alley; children in annexe *(Pete Storey, LYM – more reports please)*

Langham, Leics [Bridge St; SK8411], *Noel Arms*: Well kept Ruddles beers from the neighbouring brewery and bar food inc help-yourself buffet laid out on long table in comfortable low-ceilinged lounge divided by log fire; smart covered terrace, restaurant *(Rob and Gill Weeks, LYM)*

Laxton, Notts [High St; SK7267], *Dovecote*: Friendly, quiet and attractively furnished pub in attractive village, with medieval farming information centre next door; good choice of home-cooked bar food inc vegetarian dishes, well kept Whitbreads Castle Eden on handpump, pool-table; tables outside *(Alan Frankland, Sarah Mellor)*

☆ **Leicester** [Silver St; SK5804], *Globe*: Period features inc gas lighting and original woodwork, though the refurbishment has perhaps concentrated more on comfort than on preserving the original atmosphere; reasonably priced lunchtime food upstairs, well kept Everards real ale with a guest beer such as Adnams *(Mr and Mrs P A Jones, Richard Sanders, Steve Waters, LYM)*

Leicester [Welford Rd], *Bricklayers Arms*: Busy, lively pub with well kept beer *(Graham Bush, Richard Sanders)*; [London Rd] *Marquis Wellington*: Adnams, Everards and Sam Smiths in recently renovated pub which has kept old décor; popular at lunchtime for wide range of snacks and meals *(Alastair Lang)*; [Charles St] *Rainbow & Dove*: Large brightly decorated open-plan bar divided into two, with full range of Hoskins beers and a guest such as Holdens Mild, lunchtime bar food; popular with students, parking difficult *(Richard Sanders, Dave Butler, Lesley Storey)*; [Leire St/Harrison Rd] *Victoria Jubilee*: Real locals' pub with simple front bar (dominoes and darts) and comfortable lounge (occasional live music); consistently well kept Marstons Burton, Pedigree, Merrie Monk, Border Mild and winter Owd Rodger; no bar food, though Asian barbecues in summer in large flagstoned back yard – excellent value *(P A and J B Jones)*

Lincoln, Lincs [Steep Hill; SK9872], *Browns Pie Shop*: Not a pub as it's here for the food – variety of reasonably priced small casseroles with puff-pastry lids, and good puddings; but it does have well kept Everards Tiger, with helpful staff and pleasant atmosphere *(Derek and Sylvia Stephenson)*; [Alfred St (off High St)] *City Vaults*: Hatch service of well kept Wards ales, inc Mild, in simple friendly traditional town pub *(Richard Sanders, BB)*; [21 High St] *Golden Eagle*: Welcoming pub with well kept Batemans and decent bar food *(Richard Sanders)*; [Waterside North] *Green Dragon*: Noble waterside Tudor building – carved 16th-century façade gave it its homelier name 'The Cat Garret'; modernised but attractively timbered and beamed bar, John Smiths real ale, friendly staff (but somewhat regimented tables and chairs, fruit machines could be more discreetly placed, and it's become rather a noisily popular evening meeting-place for young people); restaurant *(Nick Dowson, Alison Hayward, LYM)*; [Moor St/Newland St West] *Queen in the West*: Delightful well kept family-run town pub, good Wards and Youngers No 3, home-cooked bar food, reasonably priced simple cooking *(David and Ruth Hollands)*; [83 Westgate] *Strugglers*: Cheap well kept Bass and Bass Mild on handpump in classic small two-room pub; very busy, nr castle *(Richard Sanders)*; [Union Rd] *Victoria*: Very busy two-room free house behind castle, with open fire in small front lounge, well kept changing real ales such as Everards Old Original, Old Mill and Timothy Taylors Landlord, country wines, good lunchtime bar food such as bacon buttie, ploughman's, kippers, curries; back children's area *(Richard Sanders, David and Ruth Hollands)*

Little Bowden, Leics [Kettering Rd (A6); SP7487], *Greyhound*: Pleasantly decorated bar, lounge and small smoking-room; well kept Watneys-related real ales on handpump, reasonably priced bar food, restaurant, terrace and garden *(A E Alcock)*

Little Steeping, Lincs [TF4362], *Eaves*: Well kept beer, nice premises, good value straightforward food *(Kevin and Mary Shakespeare)*

Long Sutton, Lincs [A17 Kings Lynn– Holbeach; TF4222], *Bull*: Unspoilt, old-fashioned hotel, 1920s décor; well kept Bass on handpump from servery divided from main passage by Victorian sash-window screen, bar food; bedrooms *(Phil Gorton)*; *Crown & Woolpack*: Small choice of well kept beers inc Bass, Sam Smiths and Stones, ample helpings of well cooked bar food at reasonable prices with daily changing specials, prompt friendly service, new restaurant (Thurs–Sat evenings, Sun lunch) *(Mr and Mrs Michael Back)*

☆ **Long Whatton**, Leics [SK4723], *Falcon*: Lounge has big comfortable bays of seats under a collection of stuffed animals and birds and other bric-à-brac; warm, relaxing atmosphere and friendly, efficient service, good choice of bar food from marvellous well filled cobs to superb steaks, well kept Everards Old Original and Tiger; good restaurant on raised level in back half of lounge (booking advisable), coffee lounge *(Howard and Sue Gascoyne, Jill Hadfield, Tony Gallagher, Paul and Janet Waring)*

Loughborough, Leics [canal bank, about ¼ mile from Loughborough Wharf; SK5319], *Albion*: Busy, welcoming, canalside local with friendly licensees, two rooms and central bar, whitewashed walls, brasses and mirrors; well kept Banks's Mild and Bitter, Hoskins & Oldfields HOB and Old Navigation, John Thompsons Lloyds Best and Shipstones Mild and Bitter; good value bar food inc steak and kidney pie, lovely home-cooked beef rolls and occasional barbecues; friendly staff; wonderful budgie aviary in big courtyard; children welcome *(Pete Storey, Richard Sanders)*; [Meadow Lane] *Gate*: Friendly, small three-roomed pub with open fires, popular darts and dominoes, well kept Marstons Pedigree and Border Mild, reasonable lunchtime food, weekend rolls, pleasant garden behind with Sat summer barbecues *(Richard Sanders)*; [The Rushes (A6)] *Swan in the Rushes*: Two-roomed, austerely furnished but friendly free house with particularly well kept real ales such as Batemans XXXB, Hardys & Hansons Mild, Marstons Pedigree and Tetleys, and weekend guest beers; good range of reasonably priced lunchtime and evening bar food, reasonably priced; coal fire, juke box, fruit machine; blues Weds, plans for bedrooms *(Richard Sanders, John Laing)*

Lount, Leics [A453 NE of Ashby de la Zouch; SK3819], *Ferrier Arms*: Consistently good even though building slightly over restored *(Dave Braisted)*

Mansfield, Notts [Nottingham Rd (a mile from centre); SK5561], *Talbot*: Extensively refurbished rather in Laura Ashley style, now open-plan with raised dining area, and popular with younger, trendier people, particularly as the evening wears on; not all former supporters approve, though there's still some character, with some quiet corners; good range of bar food inc casseroles and excellent puddings, particularly at lunchtime; well kept Shipstones *(Derek and Sylvia Stephenson)*

Maplebeck, Notts [signpost on A616/A617; SK7160], *Beehive*: Deep in the country, snug little beamed bar, clean and tidy but basic, with plain traditional furnishings; tables on small terrace with grassy bank running down to small stream; open fire, Mansfield real ale on handpump, free juke box; an idyllic spot *(Tim and Lynne Crawford, LYM)*

Mapperley, Notts [187 Plains Rd; SK6043], *Tree Tops*: Comfortably refurbished, with friendly service and very popular home-made lunches *(TWG)*

Mareham le Fen, Lincs [A115; TF2861], *Royal Oak*: Beamed interior with brasses, pleasant atmosphere and friendly staff; well kept Batemans XXXB and good if limited bar food served in small restaurant (Lincoln sausage in ale recommended) *(R F Plater)*

Marston, Lincs [2 miles E of A1 just N of Grantham; SK8943], *Thorold Arms*: Well kept beer inc Batemans, good value bar food; children welcome *(Stan Edwards)*

☆ **Medbourne**, Leics [SP7993], *Nevill Arms*: Interesting stone-built mullion-windowed arch-doored pub by village stream with vociferous ducks; wide range of decent bar food inc good value curries, well kept Adnams, Greene King, Hook Norton and Marstons Pedigree on handpump, fresh orange juice, log fires in two stone fireplaces, spacious back family dining-room with pews around its tables off the more traditional front bar; doesn't open till noon, and can then get very busy *(Dr A V Lewis, Brian and Genie Smart, Eric Locker, Dr Peter Donahue, BB)*

Minting, Lincs [The Green; off A158 Lincoln–Horncastle; TF1873], *Sebastopol*: Cosy, low-beamed pub with fish tank set into wall, good choice of hot food *(Frank Williams)*

Moorgreen, Notts [SK4847], *Horse & Groom*: Recent alterations tastefully completed; pleasant atmosphere, efficient staff, well kept Hardys & Hansons, particularly good bar food *(Alan Gough)*

Morton, Notts [SK7251], *Full Moon*: Pleasant atmosphere, relaxing décor, music in pool-room; good house wines, enterprising and reasonably priced bar food, good service *(Derek and Sylvia Stephenson)*

Nettleham, Lincs [The Green; TF0075], *Plough*: Friendly village pub in picturesque village centre, overlooking village green; well kept Batemans, RAF prints *(Frank Williams)*

Newark, Notts [Northgate; SK8054], *Malt Shovel*: Small, basic and old-fashioned local, green-tiled outside; recently comfortably refurbished, with friendly welcome, well kept Adnams Broadside, Timothy Taylors Landlord and Vaux and well kept food, especially Sun lunch *(Maureen and Steve Collins)*; [Riverside] *Navigation Co Brasserie*: Delightful warehouse conversion with genuine brasserie atmosphere and Everards Tiger *(Geoff Wilson)*

Newington, Notts [Newington Rd (off A614 at Misson signpost); SK6794], *Ship*: Unpretentious and friendly roadside pub with well kept Home ales and lively public bar *(LYM)*

Normanton on Soar, Notts [A6006; SK5123], *Rose & Crown*: Nicely laid out waterside pub with Watneys-related real ales on handpump and good value food; popular with boating crowd at lunchtimes *(Peter Corris)*

North Kilworth, Leics [4½ miles from M1 junction 20 – A427 towards Mkt Harborough; SP6183], *White Lion*: Well kept Marstons Pedigree, generous helpings of good bar food, restaurant *(Christopher Baker)*; *White Swan*: Pleasant canalside pub with good atmosphere, well kept Watneys-related real

ales on handpump, good range of bar food *(Gordon Theaker)*

☆ **North Muskham**, Notts [Ferry Lane; SK7958], *Muskham Ferry*: Lovely spot by River Trent, friendly efficient staff, good bar food, cold buffet and restaurant; garden with children's slide, own moorings, slipway, private fishing *(AE, GRE)*

☆ **Norton Disney**, Lincs [SK8859], *St Vincent Arms*: Lovely, quiet little country pub with real fire and traditional atmosphere; Adnams, Everards Old Original, Marstons Pedigree and maybe Batemans XXXB on handpump, good bar food (vegetarian dishes, lamb and apricot pie, mixed grills and steaks recommended), large back garden inc well equipped play area *(Andy and Jill Kassube, Derek Stephenson)*

☆ **Nottingham** [Gt Northern Cl; just off London Rd (A60), opp junction with Station Rd], *Grand Central*: Imaginative conversion of former railway building, good atmosphere in two roomy railway-arch areas – one cocktailish, one pubbier with cold but well conditioned Ind Coope Burton and Tetleys on handpump; steps up to little row of snug booths in mock-up of Orient Express, bar food and rather elegant side dining area, some interesting cigarette cards, well reproduced pop music, good mix of ages; tables on tank-engine terrace *(David and Ruth Hollands, BB)*

☆ **Nottingham** [Mansfield Rd], *Lincolnshire Poacher*: Recently reopened pub, formerly the Old Grey Nags Head, with several well refurbished bar areas inc small wood-panelled snug and conservatory; well kept Batemans and Marstons real ales, bar food; open all day; under same good landlord as Old Kings Arms, Newark – see main entries *(Richard Sanders)*

Nottingham [Parliament St], *Blue Bell*: Well run city-centre pub with well kept Home ales, good value food, pleasant staff, jazz nights *(Stewart Argyle, D Simmonite, Richard Sanders)*; [Clumber St] *Lion*: Thoroughly modernised open-plan city-centre pub, well kept Home Bitter, good cheap lunchtime bar food *(Angie and Dave Parkes)*; [Canal St] *Narrow Boat*: Large Shipstones pub, good beer, hot lunchtime bar food *(Richard Sanders)*; [Stony St] *Old Angel*: Well kept Home ales and lunchtime snacks in old two-room pub in Lace Market area; upstairs room, birthplace of several trades unions, still used as union chapel *(Richard Sanders)*; [Lower Parliament St] *Old Dog & Partridge*: Well kept Shipstones, good value ploughman's in variety *(Richard Sanders)*; [Mansfield Rd] *Peacock*: Well kept Home ales in refurbished city-centre pub which still has waiter-service bells in lounge, and maybe James Last-type piped music *(Stewart Argyle, Richard Sanders)*; [Maid Marion Way] *Salutation*: The ancient back part with heavy beams and flagstones is attractive (the front part is plush modern), and they've made a feature of the old rock cellars which can be visited at quiet times by arrangement; Whitbreads-related real ales and

Marstons Pedigree, reasonably priced bar food – including snacks even late in the evening; can get smoky when it's crowded *(Ian Phillips, BKA, Graham Bush, BB)*; [Market Pl] *Talbot*: Very large, popular Yates wine lodge with first-floor conservatory overlooking market place and basic, simple ground-floor bar; good lunchtime food, live music evenings *(Graham Bush)*; [402 Derby Rd] *Three Wheatsheaves*: Rambling old pub with flagstones, traditional furnishings, somewhat basic feel but good atmosphere; bar food, well kept Shipstones, summer lunchtime barbecues in big garden *(LYM)*; [Trent Bridge] *Trent Bridge*: Well kept Ind Coope and Tetleys and dining area with several decent hot dishes; one corner bar is the Larwood Library with a dozen or so cricket bats autographed by various teams, as well as a considerable number of cricketing books *(BKA)*; [Waverley Rd] *Vernon Arms*: Good value bar food in comfortable Italian-run suburban pub with tables on terrace and smart restaurant *(LYM)*

Oadby, Leics [Harborough Rd; A6 just SE of Leicester; SK6200], *Oadby Owl*: Attractive many-roomed ex-coaching-inn, good range of bar food, well kept Marstons, darts and fruit machine, garden behind *(Richard Sanders)*; [Harborough Rd; A6 just SE of Leicester, next to Wilkinsons] *Swinging Sporran*: Comfortably refurbished open-plan Scottish & Newcastle pub with pool-tables on left-hand side and quieter seating to the right; good mix of customers, friendly staff, good value food, big TV all day; children welcome *(Rona Murdoch)*

Oakham, Leics [North St; SK8508], *Wheatsheaf*: Town-centre pub with open fire and comfortable seats in lounge; well kept Adnams on handpump, changing menu of tasty food, friendly licensee *(Julian Holland)*; [Market Pl] *Whipper Inn*: Friendly old stone coaching-inn with oak-beamed and panelled lounge opening into cosy eating area, well kept Ruddles Best and County on handpump, restaurant; formerly the George, and now much more of a hotel – the bar is now really for residents; bedrooms *(LYM)*

☆ **Old Somerby**, Lincs [SK9633], *Fox & Hounds*: Attractive pub, warm welcome, well kept real ales such as Marstons Pedigree and Merrie Monk and Ruddles County on handpump, good range of reasonably priced bar food inc spectacular long filled rolls called submarines; several rooms with copper-topped tables and hunting-print wall banquettes *(Derek and Sylvia Stephenson, Rob and Gill Weeks)*

Ordsall, Notts [West Carr Rd; SK7079], *Market*: Very friendly – landlord's father ran it before him; well kept real ales inc Adnams, Batemans, Camerons and Timothy Taylors; good home-cooked simple bar food, restaurant *(Maureen and Steve Collins)*

Plumtree, Notts [just off A606 S of Nottingham; SK6132], *Griffin*: Popular for lunch, well kept Hardys & Hansons beer, interesting village church *(E Osborne)*; *Perkins*: Dining pub with good imaginatively prepared food using fresh ingredients, straightforward puddings, good range of wines (no real ales); not open Sun or Mon *(H J Stirling)*

Potterhanworth, Lincs [Cross St; TF0565], *Chequers*: Creamy Mansfield 4X and wide range of bar food inc superb gammon in village free house with cheerful landlady and landlord; piano in lounge bar *(Frank Williams)*

Preston, Leics [SK8602], *Fox & Hounds*: Tudor pub with plenty of character (inc reputed poltergeist) in attractive stone village; range of well kept real ales inc Adnams, very good food, usually with choice of three home-made soups, friendly service *(Eric Locker)*

Quorndon, Leics [Meeting St; SK5616], *Blacksmiths Arms*: Popular two-roomed old pub, low ceilings, well kept Marstons Pedigree, lunchtime bar food *(Richard Sanders)*; [corner Meeting St and A6] *Royal Oak*: Popular pub with small snug at front, particularly well kept Bass and M&B Mild, bar food *(Richard Sanders)*

Ratby, Leics [Boroughs Rd; SK5105], *Plough*: Cheerful unpretentious village pub with lively Fri night singalongs, well kept Marstons real ales, simple cheap lunchtime food and good play area in big back garden; decidedly a local, though *(LYM)*

Ravenshead, Notts [Main Rd (B6020); SK5956], *Little John*: Well organised modern pub with comfortable airy lounge, good value bar food, games in public bar, restaurant popular for lunch *(LYM)*

Rippingale, Lincs [High St; just off A15 Bourne–Sleaford; TF0927], *Bull*: Good value bar food and wide choice of restaurant dishes, friendly service, big children's play area *(Mrs M G Longman)*

☆ **Rothwell**, Lincs [Caistor Rd (A46); TF1599], *Nickerson Arms*: Very pleasant relaxed atmosphere in friendly and pleasantly decorated stone-built village local, excellent choice of well kept ales inc Batemans, Tetleys, Timothy Taylors Landlord and regular guest beers, simple but good weekday lunchtime bar food inc fine steak and kidney pie with fresh vegetables, and decent trifle; children's room, outside seating *(Andy and Jill Kassube, Mrs M E Lawrence, Derek and Sylvia Stephenson)*

Salmonby, Lincs [TF3273], *Crossed Keys*: Green leatherette banquettes in bays of simply decorated lounge extending back into bigger dining area, pool and other games in public bar, big windows, Ruddles Best on handpump, unobtrusive piped pop music, cheap simple food with bargain steaks Weds evening, friendly staff, tables and play area in garden behind; bedrooms cheap, clean and comfortable, with big breakfasts *(Kevin and Mary Shakespeare, BB)*

☆ **Scotter**, Lincs [High St; SE8801], *Gamekeeper*: Old, with five connecting rooms on different levels – beams, panelling, Delft shelves and abundant china, stuffed birds and animals, varied seating; well kept Darleys, Wards and Youngers on handpump; wide choice of food from sandwiches up *(David and Ruth Hollands)*

Scotter [The Green], *White Swan*: New owners of village-green pub with friendly staff, tasty bar food, big extension with restaurant and bedrooms above; jazz Mon *(J A Calvert)*

Scrooby, Notts [SK6591], *Pilgrim Fathers*: Cosy pub with plant-filled conservatory extension that's snug even in winter; small choice of good food *(Sue Cleasby, Mike Ledger)*

Sewstern, Leics [just off B767 Colsterworth–Melton Mowbray; SK8821], *Blue Dog*: Small but comfortable lounge bar, good range of home-cooked food, well kept John Smiths and Marstons Pedigree; bedrooms *(M and J Back)*

Sharnford, Leics [B4114; SP4791], *Falconer*: Well kept Ansells Mild and Bitter and Tetleys on handpump, wide choice of good value food, quieter tables in back area, well reproduced piped music *(Ted George, BB)*

Shawell, Leics [not far from M6 junction 1; village signposted off A5/A427 roundabout – turn right in village; SP5480], *White Swan*: Full of character with oak panelling, royal blue upholstery, coal fire and two log-effect gas fires in the bar, separate lounge and games-room; well kept Adnams Broadside and Banks's, well presented good food (which draws crowds at weekends), friendly staff *(Ted George)*

☆ **Sheepy Magna**, Leics [Main St (B4116); SK3201], *Black Horse*: Decently kept village pub with generous helpings of good value bar food inc good steaks and a very wide choice of cheeses for the ploughman's; well kept Marstons Pedigree, games in lively public bar, family area *(Jon Wainwright, Geoff Lee, M and J Back, LYM)*

Shepshed, Leics [6 Ashby Rd; SK4719], *Delisle Arms*: Warm, friendly pub with receptive locals; consistently high standard of food, live music Thurs fortnight *(Alex Slack)*

Shireoaks, Notts [SK5580], *Hewett Arms*: Attractively modernised barn by two carp lakes, welcoming licensee, plush blue sofas with contrasting white wood tables and chairs, Marstons Pedigree *(Anon)*

☆ **Sileby**, Leics [Swan St; SK6015], *White Swan*: Comfortable and welcoming book-lined dining-lounge with generous helpings of enterprising bar food (not Sun or Mon) inc home-made bread, hot crab gratin, good pies and casseroles, wonderful puddings, with a particularly wide evening choice; even the bread and chocolates are home-made *(Rodney R Elsley)*

☆ **Skegness**, Lincs [Vine Rd, Seacroft (off Drummond Rd); TF5660], *Vine*: Pleasant, relaxing bar with good atmosphere in well run seventeenth-century inn where Lord Tennyson stayed; well kept Batemans XB and XXXB, good but limited bar food from dining-room

(macaroni cheese, ham and turkey salad, fish pie, charlotte russe all recommended); pictures of variety artistes who've stayed here while playing Skeg; bedrooms *(Derek and Sylvia Stephenson, John Honnor)*

Skendleby, Lincs [Spilsby Rd; off A158 about 10 miles NW of Skegness – OS Sheet 122 reference 433697; TF4369], *Blacksmiths Arms*: Tiny village pub with low ceilings, open fire in black-leaded hearth, particularly well kept Batemans XB from small casks, no juke box or machines; talk of possible sale – news please *(Richard Sanders, Phil and Sally Gorton)*

Somerby, Leics [Main St; SK7710], *Stilton Cheese*: Good, friendly service, several well kept real ales on handpump, wide choice of imaginative food in ample helpings, inc good Sun lunch with special prices for children and OAPS *(Genie and Brian Smart, G I Carver)*

South Kilworth, Leics [Rugby Rd; SP6081], *White Hart*: Well kept, plain little pub with good, simple, home-cooked food at reasonable prices and well kept Banks's Bitter; separate small dining-room *(Cdr Patrick Tailyour)*

☆ **South Luffenham**, Leics [10 The Street; turn off A6121 at the Halfway House, then first right; SK9402], *Boot & Shoe*: Village inn with rambling stripped-stone bar, red plush easy chairs by the fire, lots of brass and copper; seats in neat small garden, games in lively public bar; formerly very popular with readers for thriving community atmosphere, good food, comfortable if simple bedrooms and well kept Camerons – but taken over early 1989 and being refurbished by new ex-footballer landlord, and not enough reports yet on this regime *(Christopher Knowles-Fitton, LYM – more news please)*

☆ **South Rauceby**, Lincs [Main St; TF0245], *Bustard*: Pretty village, attractive stone building with oddly church-like appearance but warm, friendly atmosphere inside; good wine, regular guest beer tapped from the cask, appealing choice of home-cooked bar food at moderate prices *(A and J Heaphy, Derek and Sylvia Stephenson)*

South Thoresby, Lincs [about 1 mile off A16; TF4077], *Vine*: Pleasant, welcoming pub, useful for this area where getting a reasonable meal is not easy; food reasonably priced with nice home-made pies; well kept Batemans XB and guests such as Timothy Taylors Landlord and Woodfordes Norfolk Pride on handpump; children in dining-room; bedrooms *(Derek and Sylvia Stephenson)*

☆ **Southwell**, Notts [SK6953], *Saracens Head*: Interesting old THF hotel (where Charles I spent his last free night), with well kept John Smiths on handpump, good value bar lunches in main beamed Smoke Room bar which has a good deal of character, pleasant helpful staff; children in eating area or restaurant; bedrooms comfortable and well kept, though some are small and none are cheap (but no extra charge for room service); bedrooms *(E J and J W Cutting, David and Ruth Hollands,*

Mr and Mrs Bill Muirhead, LYM)

Southwell [Church St (A612)], *Bramley Apple*: Unusual 3-D sign showing the fruit that originated here; comfortably furnished bar split into two by corridor, Batemans XXXB on handpump, good food *(Angie and Dave Parkes)*

☆ **Stamford**, Lincs [Broad St; TF0207], *Lord Burghley*: Popular and splendidly furnished town-centre pub with well kept Adnams, Greene King Abbot, IPA and Marstons Pedigree, good choice of bar food inc well filled lunchtime rolls, friendly staff, nice atmosphere, garden *(T Mansell, Dr A V Lewis)*

Stamford [High St, St Martins], *Anchor*: Old stone building next to town bridge with one long bar: bar food; popular with younger people at night; bedrooms *(T Mansell)*; *Hole in the Wall*: L-shaped bar with old tables, chairs and settles, friendly atmosphere; wide choice of drinks inc well kept Marstons Pedigree and Owd Rodger and reasonably priced wines, good food and service *(M J Morgan)*

Stanton under Bardon, Leics [Main St; 1½ miles from M1 junction 22, off A50 towards Coalville; SK4610], *Old Thatched*: Large, friendly open-plan thatched pub divided into various areas, one with open fire; well kept Marstons Pedigree and Border Mild on handpump, bar food inc good grills (Mon to Sat, Sun lunch by prior booking) *(Richard Sanders)*

Staunton in the Vale, Notts [SK8043], *Staunton Arms*: Attractively refurbished with interesting partitions and raised dining area and providing interesting partitions; well kept Tetleys, Whitbreads Trophy and guest beer, improved bar food (the soups are excellent) and service *(Derek and Sylvia Stephenson)*

☆ **Stoke Golding**, Leics [High St; SP3997], *Three Horseshoes*: Pleasantly roomy canalside bar with friendly staff, good value well cooked bar food even Sun evening, well kept Watneys-related real ales and Marstons Pedigree, cocktail bar and big restaurant; children welcome *(Mandy and Mike Challis)*

Stoney Stanton, Leics [Long St; SP4894], *Blue Bell*: Popular local with well kept Everards Bitter, Tiger and Old Original on handpump, good value straightforward food running up to hefty steaks lunchtime and early evening; busy at weekends *(Mike Tucker)*; *Farmers Arms*: Very local pub; bar/lounge packed out with almost too many curios and stuffed animals and curios, large bar with live rock music Fri, well kept Marstons beers *(Graham Bush)*

Stretton, Leics [Great North Rd (A1); SK9416], *Ram Jam*: Much refurbished old inn with well kept Watneys-related real ales and particularly good house wine in large comfortable bar; varied imaginative and sensibly priced food in bar and restaurant, inc good mushroom brioche, charcoal-grilled lamb strips with huge helping of Mediterranean braised vegetables and nut and treacle tart – breakfasts and simpler dishes served 7–11am,

main menu 11–11; good service, tables outside; bedrooms most attractively decorated and thoughtfully equipped *(Joy Heatherley)*; *Shires*: Welcoming and well run pub, of some character *(P F Dakin)*

Surfleet, Lincs [A16 nearby; TF2528], *Mermaid*: Family-run riverside inn with pleasant staff, well kept Shipstones, good bar food at reasonable prices, restaurant, garden with play area; bedrooms *(D A Green)*

☆ **Sutton Bonington**, Leics [3 miles from M1 junction 24; SK5025], *Old Plough*: Roomy, well run modern pub with new licensees; good value bar food, well kept Shipstones real ales and local atmosphere *(Richard Sanders, LYM)*

☆ **Sutton Cheney**, Leics [Main St; off A447 3 miles S of Market Bosworth; SK4100], *Hercules*: Always a pub to please some but not others, this is most notable for its extensive range of real ales, changing frequently and inc rarities as well as one or two brewed for the pub; cheerful refurbished bar (where piped music may be loud), friendly licensees, dining area *(Jon Wainwright, Ian Blackwell, W S Wright, T Nott, LYM)*

Sutton Cheney, Leics [Main St], *Royal Arms*: Friendly low-ceilinged village pub with central bar, three smallish rooms around it, conservatory for families, two open fires, well kept Marstons on handpump, wide choice of bar food inc masses of changing specials; can get smoky; restaurant *(Mandy and Mike Challis, Ken and Barbara Turner)*

Sutton in Ashfield, Notts [Alfreton Rd; off M1 junction 28; SK5059], *Duke of Sussex*: Consistently good value bar food (not Mon), especially steak sandwich, in friendly pub with quiet lounge and lively tap-room; Hardys & Hansons on electric pump *(Angie and Dave Parkes)*

Syston, Leics [SK6311], *Gate Hangs Well*: Large pub with several small, snug rooms, traditional bar, old-fashioned conservatory overlooking terrace, large garden with tables and background of Wreake Valley; well kept Everards Tiger, Old Original, Beacon and guest beer, large skittle alley in former stables by canal disused since 1920s *(Mr and Mrs P A Jones)*

☆ **Tattershall Thorpe**, Lincs [TF2259], *Blue Bell*: Attractive outside and in, very friendly landlord, good value bar food *(Kevin and Mary Shakespeare, J D Maplethorpe)*

Thurgarton, Notts [Southwell Rd; SK6949], *Red Lion*: Pleasant surroundings, friendly licensee, well kept John Smiths on handpump, good reasonably priced bar food *(E E Hemmings)*

☆ **Tugby**, Leics [Main St; village signposted off A47 E of Leicester, bear right in village; SK7600], *Black Horse*: Good value home-made evening meals in cosy and attractively traditional small rooms of picturesque black and white thatched village pub, Ansells on handpump, friendly service, log fire; children welcome; closed lunchtime *(LYM)*

Tur Langton, Leics [off B6047; follow Kibworth signpost from village centre; SP7194], *Crown*: Well kept Bass, Marstons Pedigree and Shipstones in distinctive pub with attractive furnishings from an antique curved settle to chintzy easy chairs; tables on pleasantly planted terraces and in sheltered back courtyard; restaurant; closed weekday lunchtimes *(T Nott, LYM)*

☆ **Upper Hambleton**, Leics [village signposted from A606 on E edge of Oakham; SK9007], *Finches Arms*: Perched above Rutland Water, with built-in button-back leatherette banquettes and open fire in knocked-through front bar, velvet curtain to restaurant extension with picture windows, tables on gravel terrace; bar food from sandwiches to devilled gammon with peaches, well kept Darleys Thorne, Wards Sheffield Best and Kirby and Vaux Samson on handpump *(Rob and Gill Weeks, M J Morgan, Mel Bodfish, Julian Holland, LYM)*

Uppingham, Leics [High St; SP8699], *Vaults*: Pleasant little pub on village square; exposed beams, a few tables and a separate eating area, which serves as overflow for bar; well kept Marstons Pedigree and Tetleys, reasonably priced decent food *(Dr John Innes)*; [High St West] *White Hart*: Friendly pub with pleasant front bar and plain back one, well kept John Smiths on handpump, piped music, wide range of reasonably priced food in comfortable dining area; bedrooms *(Dr M S Saxby)*

Wainfleet, Lincs [39 High St; TF5058], *Woolpack*: Friendly, obliging landlord, well kept Batemans Mild and XB, particularly good value bar food; a pub the Batemans themselves use *(Dr K Bloomfield)*

Washingborough, Lincs [TF0270], *Ferry Boat*: Friendly village pub with reconstructed millwheel; Watneys-related real ales, separate eating area with own bar and salad bar *(Frank Williams)*

Wellow, Notts [Eakring Rd; SK6766], *Olde Red Lion*: Small olde-worlde pub overlooking village green and famous maypole; Mansfield, Whitbreads Castle Eden and two or three guest beers, good bar food from sandwiches to steaks inc children's dishes *(Colin Wright)*

West Bridgford, Notts [SK5837], *Trent Bridge*: Old pub with associations with neighbouring Test cricket ground; good beer and bar food *(David Gaunt)*

Whitwick, Leics [SK4316], *Belfry*: Pleasant free house, nice spot *(Martin Aust)*

Wilford, Notts [Main Rd; SK5637], *Ferry*: Large, popular Shipstones pub by River Trent, plush lounge, pleasant main bar *(J L Thompson)*

Woodborough, Notts [Main St; SK6347], *Nags Head*: Delightful olde-worlde village pub with quiet, comfortable atmosphere, good service and wide choice of dishes, several home made *(TWG)*

Woodhall Spa, Lincs [Kirkstead; Tattersall Rd (B1192 Woodhall Spa–Coningsby); TF1963], *Abbey Lodge*: Attractively if rather darkly decorated warm and cosy food pub with good-sized tasty bar meals (presentation could be better and quicker) and separate restaurant *(A and J Heaphy, J D Maplethorpe, Patrick Godfrey)*

Woodhouse Eaves, Leics [SK5214], *Bulls Head*: Bright and cheerful, with quickly served good food; popular, especially with young people *(Jill Hadfield, Martin Aust)*

Woolsthorpe, Lincs [the one nr Belvoir; SK8435], *Rutland Arms*: Quite large welcoming pub on banks of disused Grantham Canal, with views of Belvoir Castle; family extension with old furniture, open fire, video juke box, bric-à-brac on walls and windows; quite good range of bar food, well kept Whitbreads Castle Eden on handpump, two pool-tables in annexe; play equipment on large lawn *(Howard and Sue Gascoyne)*

Lincolnshire   *see* Leicestershire

Midlands (Northamptonshire, Warwickshire and West Midlands)

This area has very few pubs that really stand out for exceptional bar food: the popular and spacious Bell at Alderminster, the civilised Falcon at Fotheringhay, the old stone-built Howard Arms at Ilmington (a new main entry, under relatively new licensees), and the Slug & Lettuce in Stratford-upon-Avon (serving food all through the day). But a great many others, if not outstanding, do give very good honest value eating. And it's much more common than usual to find pubs serving food relatively late in the evening here. Particularly on the west side of Birmingham you'll often find that delicious Black Country speciality, the hot roast pork sandwich. Besides the Howard Arms, new main entries this year (or pubs back after a break) include the Vine in Brierley Hill (newly refurbished at the back, but still typically old-school Black Country in front – the tap for Bathams brewery, with remarkably cheap good beer), the very civilised Red Lion at East Haddon (a nice place to stay at, if you don't mind not having your own bathroom, with good if rather pricey food), the Case is Altered at Five Ways (beautifully unspoilt), the Red Lion at Little Compton (also good value to stay at – with the same proviso; and the food's promising under the present licensees), and a third Red Lion, at Thornby (now a most attractive pub, with good home cooking). There are new licensees at the Bear at Berkswell (one of the nicest and most distinctive Chef & Brewers we know), the idiosyncratic Royal Oak at Eydon, the Butchers

The Bear, Berkswell

Arms at Farnborough (still a nice family dining pub, though the food's not been so individual), the Brewery at Langley (one of the Holt, Plant & Deakins beers is brewed here), the Marston Inn at Marston St Lawrence (no sign of its remarkably unspoilt traditional character changing... yet), the canalside Wharf at Old Hill (taken over by Scottish & Newcastle), the stylish White Swan in Stratford, and the Manor House, that curious survivor of medieval times in the suburbs of West Bromwich. The Holly Bush at Priors Marston, a popular main entry in previous editions, has closed, with plans for a housing scheme, and the Fox & Hounds at Great Wolford has stopped letting bedrooms – on the other hand, the attractive Rose & Crown at Charlton should have its new bedrooms ready this year. The latest episode of the saga of that distinctive old own-brew pub, the Old Swan in Netherton, is its takeover by Wiltshire. The area's really rich in canalside pubs, often more interesting than elsewhere, with nearly two dozen among the Lucky Dip entries at the end of the chapter; the Little Dry Dock at Netherton is probably the pick of the canalside main entries, though the Boat at Stoke Bruerne has the best position. A good few pubs in the Lucky Dip are showing particular promise at the moment, including the Kings Head at Aston Cantlow, Cottage of Content at Barton, Haywaggon at Churchover, Old Windmill and Greyhound in Coventry, British Oak (and indeed Bottle & Glass) in Dudley, Bell in Harborne, Navigation at Lapworth, Snooty Fox at Lowick, Shovel Inn in Lye, Black Horse at Nassington and Shakespeare Hotel in Stratford. Besides the several pubs in the lively and interesting Little Pub chain described in the main entries, there are good Lucky Dip ones in Cradley Heath, Halesowen and (perhaps the pick of the bunch) Tipton.

ALDERMINSTER (War)   SP2348 Map 4

Bell 🏆

A34 Oxford–Stratford

This friendly and attractively refurbished dining pub has several different communicating areas in the big rambling bar (one is no-smoking) that manage to keep an old-fashioned feeling of cosiness. There are small landscape prints and swan's-neck brass and globe lamps on the cream walls, plenty of stripped slat-back chairs around wooden tables (each with a plant on it), a panelled oak settle, little vases of flowers, a solid-fuel stove in a stripped brick inglenook, and bare boards and flagstones at one end, with a russet carpet at the other. From a menu that changes daily, the very good bar food might include sandwiches, soup such as bortsch (£1.95), various pâtés (£3), ploughman's (£3.25), seafood and mushroom scallop (£3.75), salads (from £4.75), and lots of changing specials such as red-hot pork spare ribs or braised sausage in red wine (£5), mouth-watering braised oxtail, crispy topped lamb in cider, chicken in tarragon or steak, kidney and oyster pie (all £6), calf's liver in cream and herbs (£6.95) and seafood platter (£8.95), with puddings such as banoffi pie (£2.50); they use only fresh produce and have no fried food at all. Flowers IPA and Original on handpump, and a good range of wines (from Berry Bros & Rudd); good service; dominoes. There are wooden tables under cocktail parasols on the sheltered grass of what must once have been a coachyard. *(Recommended by J Harvey Hallam, S V Bishop, John Knighton, John Bowdler, M A and C R Starling, Simon Turner, T Nott, Ian Phillips, S J A Velate)*

Free house   Licensee Keith Brewer   Real ale   Meals and snacks (12–2, 7–10; not Mon evenings in winter)   Restaurant tel Alderminster (078 987) 414   Children welcome   Open 12–2.30, 7–11 all year; closed Mon evenings in winter, 25 Dec, and evening 31 Dec

ASHBY ST LEDGERS (Northants)   SP5768 Map 4
Old Coach House

4 miles from M1 junction 18; A5 S to Kilsby, then A361 S towards Daventry; village signposted left

Describing this pub gives us more difficulty than almost any other, so sharply do readers divide into two camps. Some love the character and atmosphere of the place (and feel it should have a star), others have found the housekeeping seriously deficient. Our own inspections, indeed, have confirmed that both points of view are valid. People's views of food and friendliness seem to follow the trend of how they see the place as a whole: many find food appetising and staff friendly (and that's what we've found ourselves), though a minority have been disappointed. Several snug little rooms make up the lounge bar: high-backed winged settles on polished black and red tiles, old kitchen tables, harness on a few standing timbers, hunting pictures (often of the Pytchley, which sometimes meets outside), Thelwell prints, and a big log fire in winter. A front room has darts, and there is pool, and piped music (anything from Brahms to Tina Turner); the blind cat is called TC. Bar food includes giant prawns or slices of local pork pie, Danish herrings (£1.50), ploughman's, pâté (£2.25), turkey and game casserole, a wide choice of salads, herrings in madeira sauce, duckling (£6.25), and steak in pepper sauce (£6.50); also, vegetarian dishes, puddings (£1), children's reductions, and enormous breakfasts. Besides well kept Everards, Flowers and Sam Smiths on handpump, there are guest beers. They stock quite a grand collection of wines by the bottle, and do hot toddy in winter. In summer barbecues are held outside or in the conservatory/vinery, and there are seats among fruit trees and under a fairy-lit arbour, with a climbing-frame, slide and swings. The attractive village has thatched stone houses, with wide grass verges running down to the lane. *(Recommended by Richard Dolphin, Hilary Robinson, Peter Maden, J W Dixon, Wayne Brindle, Dr Paul Kitchener, Alan Skull, E J Alcock, Olive Carroll, Alan Whelan, H W and A B Tuffill, R C Watkins, H J Stirling, Clare Greenham, Bernard Phillips, BKA, M R Watkins, Jeremy and Margaret Wallington, Nick Dowson, Alison Hayward)*

Free house   Real ale   Meals (not Sun or Mon) and snacks (not Sun evening)   Children in family areas until 8   Landlady sometimes sings with guitar   Open 12–2.30 (3 Sat), 6–11 all year; opens 7 in winter; closed evening 25 Dec   Bedrooms (four-posters in all rooms) tel Rugby (0788) 890349; £27.50B/£35B

BERKSWELL (W Midlands)   SP2479 Map 4
Bear   [illustrated on page 498]

Spencer Lane; village signposted from A452

Popular with businessmen and couples, this picturesque timbered building has a friendly, unassuming atmosphere and good bar food: rolls (from £1), and five changing main dishes such as braised liver and onions, chilli con carne, steak and kidney pie, sweet-and-sour pork, lasagne, fish pie and roast loin of pork (£3.25); on weekday lunchtimes they have a cold table with quiches, cold meats and cheese and help-yourself salads (£3.10); Sunday roasts. Ruddles Best and County on handpump; piped music. There are tables and chairs out on the tree-sheltered back lawn. In the village, the church, in a very pretty setting, is well worth a visit. *(Recommended by Sheila Keene, J S Evans, J Harvey Hallam, Charles Gurney, Rob and Gill Weeks)*

Manns (Watneys)   Licensee C Bouhayed   Real ale   Meals and snacks (12–2, 7–10)   Restaurant tel Berkswell (0676) 33202   Children welcome if eating   Open 11–3, 6–11 all year

---

Though we don't usually mention it in the text, lots of pubs will now make coffee – always worth asking. And some – particularly in the North – will do tea.

BIRMINGHAM (W Midlands) SP0786 Map 4

Bartons Arms ★ ★

Birmingham 6; 2 miles from M6 junction 6; leave junction on A38(M) towards city centre but take first exit, going right at exit roundabout into Victoria Road, and left at next big roundabout into Aston High Street – A34 towards city centre; pub on next corner at Park Lane (B4144); car park just past pub on opposite side of road; pub also an unmissable landmark on A34 going N from town centre

A combination of magnificent Edwardian opulence with a lively up-to-date atmosphere. There is richly coloured and painted elaborate tilework (perhaps its most striking feature), a full set of painted cut-glass snob screens – little swivelling panels that you open when you want a drink and shut when you want privacy – lots of highly polished mahogany and rosewood, sparkling cut-glass mirrors and stained glass, plush seating, heavy brass hanging lamps, and a variety of rooms from palatial salons to cosy snugs. Bar food includes sandwiches (from 60p), ploughman's (£1.50), scampi (£1.95), daily specials like beef and Guinness pie, lasagne or chilli con carne (£2.50), and a cold table. Well kept M&B Mild and Brew XI on handpump; fruit machine and juke box. *(Recommended by Jon Wainwright, Rob and Gill Weeks, H G and C J McCafferty; more reports please)*

M&B (Bass) Licensee Stephen Lefevre Real ale Lunchtime meals and snacks (not Sat or Sun) Children welcome Free and easy Sun, big jazz band first Mon in month, rock Sat evenings, and other occasional events Open 11.30–2.30, 6–11

BRIERLEY HILL (W Midlands) SO9187 Map 4

Vine

Delph Road; B4172 between A461 and A4100, near A4100

Very popular (especially in the evenings and Friday lunchtimes), this straightforward Black Country pub – next to the brewery – has well kept Bitter and Mild (dark, unusually full-flavoured with a touch of hops) on handpump, with Delph Strong in winter, all at very wholesome prices indeed. It's been recently refurbished, with brass chandeliers, fresh Victorian-style wallpaper, newly covered seats and traditional cast-iron-framed tables in the very long back room, which has a piano and darts. The composition-floored front bar is much as ever, with wall benches and simple leatherette-topped oak stools; a snug on the left has solidly built red plush seats. Good, fresh snacks include old-fashioned sandwiches (from 85p), and salads with home-cooked ham (£1.70) or beef (£1.90). Darts, cribbage and space game; the side yard is now partly covered – you can get to the lavatories without getting wet. *(Recommended by Brian Jones, E J Alcock, Tony Gayfer)*

Bathams Licensee Yvonne Hunt Real ale Lunchtime snacks (not Sun) Children in own room Rock Sun, jazz Mon Open 11–3, 6–11 Mon–Thurs, 11–11 Fri and Sat

CHARLTON (Northants) SP5236 Map 4

Rose & Crown

Village signposted from A41 at W edge of Aynho, and from Kings Sutton

This very friendly neat thatched stone house has a civilised atmosphere, and a fine choice of real ales on handpump: Flowers IPA, Marstons Burton and Pedigree, Morlands Bitter and Old Masters, Wadworths 6X and a guest beer; also, some carefully chosen malt whiskies among the better-known ones, Dows Vintage Port, and good value wine. The walls in the beamed bar are mainly stripped to the carefully coursed masonry, and there are two or three good prints, a sofa and winged armchairs as well as seats that match the sturdy country-kitchen tables, and shelves of books by the big open fireplace; the quiet collie is called Boltby. Bar food includes sandwiches, Scotch smoked salmon (small £2.50, large £5), beef salad or home-baked ham (£3.50), lasagne (£3.75), gammon (£4), Barnsley chop (£4.25), excellent Angus rump steak (£6) and four-course Sunday lunch (£7.50 – bookings only). There are a couple of picnic-table sets on a small front terrace by the village lane, with a few more on gravel behind. *(Recommended by David and Jane Russell, Roy Bamford, M O'Driscoll, James Ogier, John Croft, P G M Connolly, Dr and Mrs A K Clarke)*

Free house   Licensees Peter and Brenda Reeves   Real ale   Meals and snacks (12–3, 7–10; not after 8.30 Mon evening)   Restaurant; open until 4.30 Sun   Children welcome in small room away from bar   Open 11.30–3, 5–11 all year   Bedrooms should be ready by 1990 tel Banbury (0295) 811317; £22.50B/£32.50B

EAST HADDON (Northants)   SP6668 Map 4

Red Lion   🛏

High Street; village signposted off A428 (turn right in village) and off A50 N of Northampton

The discreetly well kept lounge bar of this substantially built golden stone small hotel is most attractive, with oak panelled settles, library chairs, soft modern dining-chairs and a mix of oak, mahogany and cast-iron-framed tables. It has white-painted panelling, with recessed china cabinets, old prints and pewter, and the dark brown ceiling has a couple of beams hung sparingly with little kegs, brass pots, swords and so forth. There are sturdy old-fashioned red leather seats in the small public bar. Good bar food, well worth the higher-than-average prices, includes sandwiches (£1.60, fresh salmon and cucumber £3.25) and ploughman's (£3.25) – these are all they do in the bar in the evening – and at lunchtime home-made faggots (£3.95), fish pie (£4.25) and chicken chasseur (£4.50), with a popular cold table (from £2.95, bacon and sausage flan £3.95, dressed crab £5.75) and a good choice of home-made puddings (£2). Well kept Charles Wells Eagle and Bombardier on handpump, welcoming service. There are white tables under cocktail parasols on a small side terrace, well spaced picnic-table sets on the tree-sheltered neat lawn behind, and an attractively planted side walled garden. *(Recommended by David Gaunt, J M Norton, Cdr Patrick Tailyour, H W and A B Tuffill)*

Charles Wells   Licensees Mr and Mrs Ian Kennedy   Real ale   Meals (lunchtime, not Sun) and snacks   Pretty restaurant (evenings, Sun lunch)   Open 11–2.30, 6–11 all year   Bedrooms tel Northampton (0604) 770223; £30/£40

EASTCOTE (Northants)   SP6753 Map 4

Eastcote Arms

Gayton Road; village signposted from A5 3 miles N of Towcester

Conversation clearly takes precedence in this bustling and notably well run village pub with its two winter log fires, fresh flowers and simple traditional seats with cushions to match the flowery curtains. Above the dark brown wooden dado a profusion of individually chosen pictures includes cricket, fishing and other sports, militia, and many linked to the pub and its history. The well kept real ales include a fine fragrant beer brewed by Banks & Taylors especially for them (though now sold elsewhere too), as well as Adnams Extra, Marstons Pedigree, Sam Smiths OB and a guest beer changing monthly such as Brakspears SB. Good value food includes rolls (70p), soup (90p), sandwiches (from 95p), very good big home-made pasty with gravy (£1.55), ploughman's (£1.85) and daily specials like lasagne or excellent goulash (£2.45) or steak and kidney pie (£2.45); dominoes, cribbage and unobtrusive piped music. There are picnic-table sets and other tables in an attractive back garden, with roses, geraniums and other flowers around the neat lawn. *(Recommended by John Baker, Mrs M E Lawrence, Dr and Mrs A K Clarke, Nick Dowson; more reports please)*

Free house   Licensees Mike and Sheila Manning   Real ale   Lunchtime snacks (not Sun or Mon)   Open 12–2.30, 6–10.30; closed Mon lunchtime, exc bank hols

ETTINGTON (War)   SP2749 Map 4
Chequers
A422 Banbury–Stratford

Carefully cooked (and often enterprising) food here includes moussaka or prawns and mushrooms in garlic herb butter (£3.95), home-made chicken and asparagus pie with wholemeal puff pastry (£5.25), seasonal game dishes, several vegetarian specials (including a good vegetable bake), and home-made puddings like summer pudding or treacle tart; from Easter to September there's an hors d'oeuvre trolley with eighteen different dishes. They also do sandwiches. The main bar is at the back: brown leatherette wall seats and modern chairs, and attractive Ros Goody Barbour-jacket-era sporting prints; the shih-tzu is called Nemesis and the Hungarian vizsla is called Alex. Well kept Adnams, M&B Brew XI and Marstons Pedigree on handpump, thoughtful and friendly service; sensibly placed darts, shove-ha'penny, trivia machine and juke box in the simple front bar, and a pool-room. There are tables out on the neat back lawn and on an awninged terrace, with lots of hanging baskets. Dogs welcome in bar and garden (though not lounge). *(Recommended by Ted George, Frank Cummins, T Nott)*

Free house   Licensees Jan and Fred Williams   Real ale   Meals and snacks (12–2, 6–9.30; not 25 Dec)   Well behaved children allowed   Occasional live entertainment   Open 10.30–2.30, 6–11 all year

EYDON (Northants)   SP5450 Map 4
Royal Oak
Lime Avenue; village signposted from A361 Daventry–Banbury in Byfield, and from B4525

The room on the right as you go into this stone village pub has low beams, cushioned wooden wall benches built into alcoves, seats in a bow window, some cottagey pictures, flagstones and an open fire. A central corridor room, with its own serving-hatch, links several other small idiosyncratic rooms. Well kept Banks's Bitter, Hook Norton and Ringwood Fortyniner on handpump, with guest beers like Batemans or Hansons Black Country; friendly informal service. As we went to press we were told a new licensee would be moving in shortly; bar food has included lunchtime sandwiches and basket meals. Darts, dominoes, cribbage, fruit machine and piped music, with table skittles in a separate room. *(Recommended by Nick Dowson, Alison Hayward; more reports please)*

Free house   Real ale   Lunchtime meals and snacks   Children in lounge   Open 11–2.30, 6.30–11

FARNBOROUGH (War)   SP4349 Map 4
Butchers Arms

New licensees have taken over this creeper-covered dining pub. The farmhouse-style main lounge bar is furnished with simple, well made stripped deal pews and stout deal tables on the carpet; this opens into a barn-like extension with furniture made from old pine including a very long table, a flagstone floor, huge timbers, brass, copper and bric-à-brac on the walls, and lots of plants; at one end French windows overlook a colourful rockery. There is a carpeted front public bar. Bar food includes sandwiches (from £1), home-made soup (£1.50), ploughman's (from £2.25), quiche (£3.50), moussaka (£4.95), and good Stroganoff (£6.50); Sunday carvery (£4.95). Well kept Flowers IPA and Original and a guest beer that changes every couple of months; dominoes and piped music. The pub, with its matching

---

If a pub is on or near one of the walks described in *Holiday Which? Good Walks Guide*, also published by Consumers' Association, we mention this, giving the walk's number.

stableblock opposite, is set well back from the village road, and the safely fenced-in front lawn has climb-in toadstools, a sandpit, a sputnik with slide and so forth. There are tables and swings by a yew tree on another flower-edged lawn which slopes up behind. *(Recommended by Ken and Barbara Turner, Mrs E M Thompson, R F Plater, S V Bishop, Jon Wainwright, J C Proud; more reports on the new regime, please)*

Free house   Licensees Daphne and Tony Polglase   Real ale   Meals and snacks
Restaurant   Children welcome (not in public bar)   Restaurant tel Farnborough
(029 589) 615   Open 11–3, 6–11 all year; closed 25 Dec

FIVE WAYS (War)   SP2270 Map 4
Case is Altered

Follow Rowington signposts from A41 at junction roundabout with A4177 N of Warwick

Behind a wrought-iron gate is a little brick-paved courtyard with a stone table under a chestnut tree. A door at the back lets you into a simple little room, usually empty on weekday lunchtimes, with a rug on its tiled floor and a bar billiards table protected by an ancient leather cover (it takes pre-decimal sixpences). Here, the narrow door on the right lets you through into the small main bar – quite unspoilt, with a genuine welcome both from the landlady (probably sitting chatting to customers) and from Phil the barman (you'll know it's him if he calls you Squire, Chief or Boss). A couple of leather-covered sturdy settles face each other over the spotless tiles, with a few small tables. There's a fine old poster showing the Lucas Blackwell & Arkwright brewery (now flats), and a clock with its hours spelling out Hornleys, another defunct brewery. The separate door with the light on either side lets you into a homely parlourish lounge (usually open only on Friday and Saturday evenings). Well kept Ansells Mild and Flowers Original served by rare miniature pumps mounted on the casks that are stilled behind the counter, maybe good lunchtime sandwiches. A quite delightful place. *(Recommended by Rob and Gill Weeks, Gordon and Daphne, SP)*

Free house   Licensee Mary Jones   Real ale   Snacks (lunchtime)   Open 11–2.30, 6–11 all year

FOTHERINGHAY (Northants)   TL0593 Map 5
Falcon 🏵

Village signposted off A605 on Peterborough side of Oundle

A new terrace and conservatory have been added to this attractive stone pub, and the kitchen enlarged to make a separate still-room and pudding preparation area. The comfortable lounge has cushioned slat-back armchairs and bucket chairs, winter log fires in stone fireplaces at each end, antique engravings on its cream walls, and a hum of quiet conversation. There is a simpler public bar which the landlord prefers to keep for the locals. Good, imaginative bar food includes home-made soups like French onion or iced gazpacho (£1.60), home-made chicken liver pâté (£1.70), ploughman's (£1.90), sweet spiced herring salad (£2.10), bobotie or steak and kidney pie (£3.50), local trout with almonds or baked sugar-glazed ham with peaches (£4.80), roast duckling with apple and rosemary stuffing (£5.30), and steaks (from £6.80), and puddings (£1.60); prices are slightly cheaper at lunchtime. On weekend lunchtimes they only do a cold buffet. Well kept Elgoods Greyhound on handpump; darts, shove-ha'penny, dominoes, cribbage. Quietly welcoming service; magazines to read. There are seats in the neat side garden. The vast church behind is worth a visit, and the site of Fotheringhay Castle is nearby (where Mary Queen of Scots was executed in 1587). *(Recommended by Mrs E M Thompson, B M Eldridge, John Cox, T Nott)*

Free house   Licensee Alan Stewart   Real ale   Meals and snacks (not Mon evening)
Children welcome   Open 10–2.30, 6–11 all year

GREAT WOLFORD (War) SP2434 Map 4
Fox & Hounds

Friendly Cotswold stone inn with a dark, atmospheric open-plan bar: beams, flagstones, a pair of high-backed old settles and other comfortable armchairish seats around a nice collection of old tables, well cushioned wall benches and window seat, and old hunting prints on the walls, which are partly stripped back to the bare stone. There's a large stone fireplace with a good winter log fire by the marvellous old bread oven, and a small tap-room. Bar food includes sandwiches, soup (£1.05), pâté (£1.75), garlic mushrooms (£1.85), ploughman's (£1.95), lasagne (£2.95), salads (£3.45), steak and kidney pie (£3.95), Turkish-style lamb or sweet-and-sour pork (£4.25), sirloin steak in red wine sauce (£5.95), and puddings like spotted dick with custard or chocolate mousse (£1.50). Well kept Flowers IPA and Marstons Pedigree on handpump, quite a few malt whiskies and country wines; darts, shove-ha'penny, dominoes, chess, draughts, cards (all in the tap-room), with piped classical music in the main bar. Outside, there's a terrace with a well. Please note, they no longer do bedrooms. *(Recommended by Laurence Manning, Paul S McPherson; more reports please)*

Free house   Licensees David and Joan Hawker   Meals and snacks   Weekend restaurant tel Barton-on-the-Heath (060 874) 220   Children in eating area of bar   Open 12–2.30 (3 Sat), 7–11 all year

HIMLEY (W Midlands – though see below) SO8889 Map 4
Crooked House ★

Pub signposted from B4176 Gornalwood–Himley; OS Sheet 139 reference 896908; readers have got so used to thinking of the pub as being near Kingswinford in the Midlands (though Himley is actually in Staffs) that we still include it in this chapter – the pub itself is virtually smack on the county boundary

As a result of mining, this pub has subsided wildly – getting the doors open is an uphill struggle, the walls and floors slope very steeply, and on one sloping table a bottle on its side actually rolls 'upwards' against the apparent direction of the slope. At the back, there's a large (straight) back extension with local antiques. Bar food includes sandwiches, home-made faggots (£2), scampi (£2.50), home-made steak and kidney pie (£2.75) and rump steak (£3.50). Well kept cheap Banks's Bitter or Mild (on electric pump); dominoes, fruit machine and piped music. Tables out on an extensive terrace in surprisingly remote-seeming countryside. *(Recommended by Richard Sanders, Brian Jones, Pamela and Merlyn Horswell, E J Alcock, Rob and Gill Weeks; more reports please)*

Banks's   Licensee Gary Ensor   Real ale   Lunchtime meals and snacks   Children in eating area of bar 12–2 only   Open 11.30–2.30, 6–11 all year; 11.30–11 Sat

ILMINGTON (War) SP2143 Map 4
Howard Arms ✿

Village signposted with Wimpstone off A34 S of Stratford

In the two or three years they've been here, the Russons have gained a firm reputation for carefully prepared and presented bar food, generously served and changing from day to day; Mr Russon himself does the cooking. As we went to press current favourite dishes included sauté herring roes or Italian-style baked broccoli (£2.95), avocado filled with crab and prawns (£3.25), chicken stuffed with spinach and cream cheese (£5.50), grilled lemon sole or kidneys in red wine sauce with chipolatas and mushrooms (£5.95) and poached salmon with prawn and lobster sauce (£7.50); other things include soup (£1.45; iced summer soup £1.65), filled crusty French bread or ploughman's (from £2.25, lunchtime only), mushroom vol-au-vent (£2.95, large £4.95), omelettes (£4.50), steak and kidney pie (£4.95) and eight-ounce rump steak (£7.50), with good puddings using fresh fruit (£1.65). There's a genteel atmosphere in the neatly kept bar, with rugs on polished flagstones, dark heavy beams, and cushioned library chairs and window seats around the tables; one of the log fires is in a big inglenook, screened from the door by an old-fashioned built-in settle. Flowers Original on handpump, kept under light carbon dioxide blanket, and decent house wines; unobtrusive piped music. There are tables on a neat gravel terrace behind, with well spaced picnic-table sets on an attractive sheltered lawn. The golden stone tiled pub looks across the village green. *(Recommended by S V Bishop, E V Walder, Mrs J Oakes, P J Hanson)*

Flowers (Whitbreads)   Licensees David and Sarah Russon   Real ale   Meals and snacks (11.45–2, 6.45–9.45, not Sun evening)   Restaurant tel Ilmington (060 882) 226   Children allowed if eating (no under-tens evenings)   Open 11–2.30, 6.30–11 all year; closed Sun evening

KENILWORTH (War)   SP2871 Map 4
Virgins & Castle
High Street; opposite A429 Coventry Road at junction with A452

The inner flagstones-and-beams servery in this old-fashioned town pub has several rooms radiating off it. Down a couple of steps, a large room has heavy beams, a big rug on ancient red tiles, and matching seat and stool covers. A couple of simply furnished small snugs – one with flagstones and the other with rugs on its bare boards – flank the entrance corridor, and there's a carpeted lounge with more beams, some little booths, hatch service, a good warm coal fire and fruit machine (there's another in a lobby). Popular, good value bar food includes excellent filled rolls and sandwiches, ploughman's, salads and daily specials; well kept Davenports and Wem Special on handpump, and farm cider. Seats outside in a sheltered garden. *(Recommended by Brian Jones, Quentin Williamson, S J Curtis, Rob and Gill Weeks)*

Davenports (Greenalls)   Real ale   Meals and snacks   Live music Tues   Open 11–2.30, 6–11 all year

LANGLEY (W Midlands)   SO9788 Map 4
Brewery ★
1½ miles from M5 junction 2; from A4034 to W Bromwich and Oldbury take first right turn signposted Junction 2 Ind Estate then bear left past Albright & Wilson into Station Road

The cosy Parlour in this re-creation of a Victorian pub is on the left: nice dining-chairs or sturdy built-in settles around four good solid tables, plates and old engravings on the walls, a corner china cabinet, a coal fire in a tiled Victorian fireplace with china on the overmantel, and brass swan's-neck wall lamps. Shelves of Staffordshire pottery and old books divide this off from the similarly furnished red-tiled Kitchen, which has lots of copper pans around its big black range. The Tap Bar is more simply furnished, but on much the same general lines, and in a back corridor tractor seats give a view into the brewhouse (a charmingly think-small subsidiary of Allied Breweries, the Ind Coope empire) through a big picture window. They specialise in exceptional-value sandwiches, double-deckers, and tasty hot beef, pork or roast ham in thick doorsteps of bread (55p–£1), and there are faggots (£1); the beer to drink is the Entire brewed here, full-flavoured and quite strong, well kept on handpump – also Bitter and Mild, both brewed up in Warrington; friendly staff. Darts, dominoes, cribbage and piped music. *(Recommended by Brian Jones, Hugh Patterson, T R G Alcock, Richard Sanders, Brian Jones, Frank Cummins, Dave Braisted, E J Alcock, Roger Broadie, R M Sparkes, Mark and Caron Bernhoft, R P Taylor)*

Holt, Plant & Deakins (Allied)   Licensee Tony Stanton   Real ale   Lunchtime snacks (not Sun)   Children in eating area of bar lunchtime only   Open 11–3, 6–11 all year

LITTLE COMPTON (War)   SP2630 Map 4

Red Lion 🛏

Off A44

The lounge in this friendly Cotswold-stone village inn has snug alcoves, attractive etchings on the walls (mostly stripped stone), and a couple of nice little tables by the open fire, with a settee facing it; window seats look out on the garden – where a safely walled-off play area has a climber, swings and tunnels made from giant piping. Good bar food includes filled granary rolls (from £1.35), ploughman's (from £2.95), home-cooked ham and egg (£3.50), and steaks (from £6.85, 32-ounce £20.85 – the record stands at 48-ounce!), with changing home-made specials like soup (£1.25), chicken liver pâté with brandy and port (£2.05), smoked salmon and prawns creole (£2.95), beef curry (£4.20), casserole of beef in Guinness (£4.50) and marinated swordfish steak (£5.95). Well kept Donnington BB and SBA on handpump; piped music. The plainer public bar has darts, dominoes and fruit machine; also Aunt Sally. *(Recommended by Barry and Anne, B V Cawthorne, A Moggridge, Dr Fuller)*

Donnington   Licensee David Smith   Real ale   Meals and snacks (not 25 Dec)   Children in eating area of bar   Open 11–2.30, 6–11 all year   Bedrooms tel Barton-on-the-Heath (060 874) 397; £13/£24

MARSTON ST LAWRENCE (Northants)   SP5342 Map 4

Marston Inn

With vegetables growing in the front garden, it's sometimes tricky for readers to decide whether this isn't just another village house rather than the pub. It's quite unspoilt: a plain room by the serving-hatch has a winter fire and darts, there's a purple carpeted sitting-room with antique hunting prints and a TV, and a back room (with no bar counter), where the well kept Hook Norton Best, and winter Old Hookey splendidly cheap, are tapped from a cask; pool, shove-ha'penny, cribbage, dominoes and piped music. They do sandwiches. The back garden is a peaceful place to sit in summer, with interesting foreign birds in its aviary, and there are ducks and geese in the car park. Nicely placed near Sulgrave Manor with its George Washington connections; rolling countryside surrounds the village. *(Recommended by Jill and Ted George; more reports please)*

Hook Norton   Licensee Robert Fessey   Real ale   Meals and snacks (not Sun or Mon evenings)   Children in eating area of bar   Open 11–3, 6–11 all year

NETHERTON (W Midlands)   SO9387 Map 4

Little Dry Dock

Windmill End, Bumble Hole; you really need an A–Z street map to find it – or OS Sheet 139 reference 953881

Somehow a whole beached narrowboat has been squeezed into the right-hand bar of this red, white and blue painted pub and is used as the servery (its engine is in the room on the left). There's a curving green-planked ceiling with pierced ribs, a huge model boat in one front transom-style window, marine windows, winches and barge rudders flanking the door, and lots of brightly coloured bargees' water-pots, lanterns, jugs and lifebuoys; the atmosphere is busy and friendly. High point of the menu is the Desperate Dan Pie, complete with horns (£3.80), with other generous food served from the end galley such as soup (£1.10), sandwiches on request, pâté (£1.75), filled baked potatoes (from £2.35), vegetarian dishes (£2.95), omelettes or curry of the day (£3.25), home-baked ham with salad (£3.45), swordfish steak (£4.95) and daily specials. In common with the other pubs in the chain, they have their own Little Lumphammer ale as well as Ind Coope Burton, and their own wine,

Chateau Ballykilferret; catchy Irish piped music, fruit machine. Others in Mr O'Rourke's small young chain of Black Country pubs include main entries in Bewdley and Kidderminster (Hereford & Worcester), and several in the Lucky Dips. The Dudley Canal embankment is behind the pub. *(Recommended by David and Eloise Smaylen, Steve J Pratt, Peter Scillitoe, Brian Jones, Patrick and Mary McDermott, R P Taylor, E V Walder, Rob and Gill Weeks)*

Free house   Licensee Robin Newman   Real ale   Meals and snacks (available all opening hours)   Children welcome   Irish folk music Mon   Open 11–2.30, 6–11 all year

Old Swan

Halesowen Road; A459 towards Halesowen just S of Netherton centre

Since the death of Doris Pardoe – who gave impetus to the own-brew movement in pubs – the Swan has been through various transmogrifications, starting with the flotation of a company with strong support from CAMRA to keep the pub independent. The next stage was when Hoskins bought the pub from that company, and managed its brewing side (though the brewery is in formal terms still independent). Finally (will it be finally?) Wiltshire took over Hoksins' interest as we were going to press. The original bar has good solid traditional furniture, a lovely patterned ceiling with a big swan centrepiece, mirrors behind the bar engraved with the swan design, an old-fashioned cylinder stove with its chimney angling away to the wall, and an easy-going, unspoilt atmosphere. Ma Pardoe's Bar is decorated with 1920s bric-à-brac, though fitted out very much in keeping with the rest of the building, using recycled bricks and woodwork, and even matching etched window panels. The home-brewed beer is fresh, fragrant and very good value, and this year they've added a Mild; also, Wiltshire Stonehenge, Old Grumble and Old Devil. Bar food includes sandwiches (55p), black pudding and cheese (£1.50), and home-made pies, chilli con carne, or pork in cider (all £2.20); darts, fruit machine and piped music. A sizeable car park has been opened at the back of the pub. *(Recommended by Patrick and Mary McDermott, Steve J Pratt, E J Alcock, PLC)*

Own brew (Wiltshire)   Licensee Karen Jones   Real ale   Meals and snacks (not Sat or Sun) Children in smoke-room   Open 11–2.30 (3 Sat), 6–11

NEWBOLD ON STOUR (War)   SP2446 Map 4

White Hart

A34 S of Stratford

Stub walls and the main chimney slightly divide up the spacious beamed main bar in this well run pub without spoiling its fresh and open feel. There are seats set into big bay windows, reddish russet cord plush cushions for the modern high-backed winged settles, gleaming copper-topped tables, a gun hanging over the log fire in one big stone fireplace, brass twinkling here and there, and quarry-tiling throughout. Reliable bar food includes soup (£1.25), garlic mushrooms in cream and herbs (£1.95), prawn and asparagus mousse (£2.25), home-baked ham stuffed with spinach and topped with Stilton cheese sauce or lambs' kidneys with sherry, garlic and cream (£3.95), and curried prawns with fresh pineapple (£4.50). The roomy back public bar has darts, pool, dominoes, fruit machine and juke box; well kept Bass on handpump; there seems to be no objection to well behaved dogs. There are some picnic-table sets under cocktail parasols in front of the pub, which has well tended hanging baskets in summer. *(Recommended by T Nott, S V Bishop, Frank Cummins; more reports please)*

M&B (Bass)   Licensees J C and A M Cruttwell   Real ale   Meals and snacks   Restaurant (not Sun evening) tel Stratford-upon-Avon (0789) 87205   Children welcome   Open 11–2.30 (3 Sat), 6–11 all year

Waterside pubs are listed at the back of the book.

nr NORTHAMPTON SP7560 Map 4
Britannia

3¾ miles from M1 junction 15; A508 towards Northampton, following ring road, then take A428 towards Bedford; just after roundabout, turn right on Access Only road by trading estate

This beamed and flagstoned pub has an open-plan bar that rambles around several roomy alcoves, with stripped pine kitchen tables and pews, matching cupboards and shelves holding plates and books, Victorian prints and enamelled advertising placards on its stripped vertical plank panelling, and dim coloured lanterns. A side room is a converted eighteenth-century kitchen, and its cast-iron cooking-range and washing-copper are still intact. Bar food includes ploughman's (£1.95), lasagne, steak and kidney pie or curry (£3.15), and a carvery (£4.15), which can be eaten in a conservatory facing the River Nene. Well kept Ruddles Best and County on handpump. *(Recommended by Michael and Alison Sandy, M A and W R Proctor, Nick Dowson, Rob and Gill Weeks; more reports please)*

Manns (Watneys)   Licensee John Clark   Real ale   Lunchtime meals and snacks   Disco Tues and Thurs   Open 11–2.30, 5.30–11 all year

OLD HILL (W Midlands) SO9685 Map 4
Wharf

Station Road, which is off Halesowen Road (A459) in Cradley Heath; this entrance involves a hideously steep wooden canal bridge – the back way into the car park, from Grange Road off Waterfall Lane, is much easier

Reputed to be the oldest surviving farm building in the district, this pretty, cottagey, canalside pub has a quarry-tiled, neat front room with red leatherette settles, cribbage and a fruit machine. A carpeted back room has tapestry-cushioned mate's chairs around black tables, a plum-coloured fabric ceiling and well reproduced pop music. Stripped brick arches open between the two, as does a gas-effect coal fire, and there are old-fashioned little touches like the curly brass and etched glass wall lamps. A good range of well kept real ales chalked up on a board (with another board showing what will be available the following week) includes Home Bitter and Mild, Hoskins & Oldfields Navigation, Moles 97, Moorhouses Premier, Smiles Bitter, Youngers No 3, and one completely new to us – Maidens Ruin on handpump. Bar food at lunchtime includes sandwiches (65p), curry (£1.95), scampi (£2.75), steak and kidney pie (£2.85) and T-bone steak (£6.95). A chatty, friendly atmosphere (it can get lively at weekends); shove-ha'penny, dominoes, fruit machine, trivia, juke box and piped music. There are picnic-table sets in a sheltered side garden, which has a good children's play area with a fort and drawbridge. *(Recommended by Brian Jones, R P Taylor, Steve J Pratt, David and Eloise Smaylen, Roger Huggins, SP, Dave Braisted)*

Scottish & Newcastle   Licensee Janice Williams   Real ale   Meals and snacks (11.30–2, 6–9.30)   Children in snug   Occasional music Mon evenings   Open 11.30–3, 6–11 all year

PRESTON BAGOT (War) SP1765 Map 4
Olde Crab Mill

B4095 Henley-in-Arden–Warwick

There are lots of cosy nooks and crannies in the comfortable and attractive communicating rooms here, with cushioned antique carved settles, chintz-cushioned wicker easy chairs and other seats (similarly upholstered), and antique prints. Also, black beams in the low ochre ceilings, old-fashioned small-paned windows, and two log fires. Bar food such as steak sandwich (£2.95), steak and kidney pie (£3.50), salads (from £3.85), gammon and egg (£4.15) and rump steak (£7.25). Well kept Flowers IPA and Original, Marstons Pedigree and Wadworths

6X on handpump, several wines; fruit machine, piped music. Some seats shelter outside in an angle of the roadside house, and there's a children's tree-giant. *(Recommended by Brian Jones, David and Eloise Smaylen, Olive Carroll, M O'Driscoll, Roger Taylor, Wayne Brindle, HDC, J and M Walsh, Chris Cooke, S J A Velate)*

Whitbreads   Licensee A N Holden   Real ale   Meals and snacks (12–2, 7–10, and they do afternoon teas; not Sun evening)   Children in own area and no-smoking area   Open 12–11 all year

ROWINGTON (War)   SP2069 Map 4
Tom o' the Wood
Finwood Road; from B4439 at N end of Rowington follow Lowsonford signpost

When the previous owners were renovating the bedrooms here, they uncovered a magnificent Elizabethan ceiling – this floor is now the Windmill restaurant. The several comfortably modernised communicating bar rooms have Windsor chairs and cushioned rustic seats set around dark varnished tables, and log-effect gas fires. Good bar food includes sandwiches (from £1), jumbo steak bap, home-made chilli (£2.65), home-made lasagne (£2.95), large fresh plaice, lamb in rosemary sauce or beef in Guinness (£3.50) and good steaks. Well kept Flowers IPA and Original and Whitbreads Pompey Royal on handpump; fruit machine, piped music. There are picnic-table sets on a neat side lawn, with more on a terrace by the big car park. *(Recommended by Brian Jones, TBB, Bill Hendry, Mr and Mrs W H Crowther, Mandy and Michael Challis)*

Flowers (Whitbreads)   Licensee Peter Scoltock   Real ale   Meals and snacks (12–2, 7–10; until 9.30 Sun)   Restaurant tel Lapworth (056 43) 2252   Children in one bar, lunchtimes only   Open 11.30–3, 6.30–11 all year

SAMBOURNE (War)   SP0561 Map 4
Green Dragon
Friendly, pretty village-green pub with comfortably modernised, beamed, communicating rooms, little armed seats and more upright ones, some small settles, and open fires. Good value bar food, served by attentive staff, includes sandwiches (from 75p), soup (£1.05), pâté (£2), ploughman's (from £2.15), sausage and egg (£2.75), omelettes (from £3.10), home-made steak and mushroom pie (£3.25), gammon (£3.30), an excellent fish dish of the day (£3.85), salads (from £3.85) and steaks (£7.15); well kept Bass, M&B Brew XI and Springfield on handpump. There are picnic-table sets and teak seats among flowering cherries on a side courtyard, by the car park. *(Recommended by K and E Leist, Andrew Hudson, J E Rycroft, John Bowdler, Roger Broadie, S V Bishop, Richard Maries)*

Bass   Real ale   Meals and snacks (not Sun)   Restaurant tel Astwood Bank (052 789) 2465   Children welcome   Open 11–3, 6–11 all year

SHIPSTON ON STOUR (War)   SP2540 Map 4
White Bear
High Street

The rather narrow left front bar in this Cotswold-stone inn has massive stripped settles, attractive lamps on the rag-rolled walls, newspapers out for customers, and interesting pictures: charming pen and wash drawing of Paris cafe society, and sporting and other cartoons from Alken through Lawson Wood to bright modern ones by Tibb. On the right, a separate bar has a wood-burning stove in a big painted stone fireplace, with a fruit machine round at the back. The spacious back lounge, with rather plain but comfortable modern furniture, has bigger Toulouse-Lautrec and other prints of French music-hall life. Bar food includes soup (£1.10), mushrooms in coriander sauce (£2.20), lasagne (£2.95), vegetarian dishes like stuffed peppers (£3.20), home-made steak and kidney or cottage pie (£3.95), monkfish ragout (£6.75), shark steak (£7.50) and steaks (from £9.95). Well kept Bass and Springfield Bitter on handpump, with decent wines; darts, shove-ha'penny, dominoes. It can get very busy; there may be dogs. There are some white cast-iron tables in a small back yard, and benches face the street. *(Recommended by BKA, S V Bishop, Lyn and Bill Capper; more reports please)*

M&B (Bass)   Licensees Hugh and Suzanne Roberts, Manager John Gallagher   Real ale   Meals and snacks (not 25–26 Dec, nor bank hols)   Restaurant   Children in eating area and restaurant   Open 11–2.30, 6–11 all year   Bedrooms tel Shipston on Stour (0608) 61558; £30B/£41B

SHUSTOKE (War)   SP2290 Map 4
Griffin

5 miles from M6 junction 4; A446 towards Tamworth, then right on to B4114 and go straight through Coleshill; pub is at Church End, past Shustoke centre

This quaint little brick house has lots of old jugs hanging from the low beams in its L-shaped bar, an old-fashioned settle and cushioned cafe seats (some quite closely packed), sturdily elm-topped sewing trestles, log fires in both stone fireplaces (one's a big inglenook), and a relaxed atmosphere. Good value lunchtime bar food includes appetising sandwiches (from 75p), home-made steak and kidney pie (£2.30), salads (£2.50) and good local gammon and egg (£3.25 – they may have local fresh eggs for sale too); very well kept Everards Old Original, M&B Mild, Marstons Pedigree, Theakstons Old Peculier and Wadworths 6X on handpump, and about three other changing beers, say Arkells Kingsdown, Everards Old Bill and Gibbs Mew Bishops Tipple from a bar under a very low, thick beam; there are plans for a conservatory. Outside, there's a terrace, and old-fashioned seats and tables on the back grass by the edge of the playing-field. *(Recommended by Brian Jones, Ian Blackwell, E J Alcock, Clifford Spooner, Rob and Gill Weeks, John Baker)*

Free house   Licensees Michael Pugh and S Wedge   Real ale   Lunchtime meals and snacks (not Sun)   Children in planned conservatory   Open 12–2.30, 7–11 all year

SOUTHAM (War)   SP4161 Map 4
Old Mint

Coventry Street; A423 towards Coventry

Through the medieval arch of the back door there are tables and chairs in the sheltered, extended garden here, with more on the cobbles and laid bricks of a sheltered yard, which has clematis on a side wall and is fairy-lit at night. Inside, the interestingly shaped bar has two snug, heavy-beamed rooms, walls peppered with antique guns, powder flasks, rapiers, sabres, cutlasses and pikes, masses of toby jugs behind the serving-counter, sturdy old seats and settles, two cosy little alcoves, and an open fire. Good bar food includes sandwiches, soup (£1.10), filled baked potato (from £1), cheese and bacon flan (£1.80), ploughman's (£2), home-made curry (£2.50), steak and kidney pie, grilled gammon and pineapple or scampi (£3.50) and steaks. Well kept Adnams, Hook Norton, Marstons Pedigree, Sam Smiths OB, Theakstons XB and Old Peculier, Wadworths 6X and changing guest beers on handpump; friendly service. *(Recommended by Philip Orbell, Roy Bromell, B R Shiner, David and Ruth Hollands, Roger Broadie, Geoff Wilson, Dr J R Hamilton, Mrs P Fretter)*

Free house   Licensee Harry Poole   Real ale   Meals and snacks   Restaurant (not Sun evening) tel Southam (092 681) 2339   Children welcome   Open 12–2.30, 6.30–11 all year

Planning a day in the country? We list pubs in really attractive scenery at the back of the book.

STOKE BRUERNE (Northants)   SP7450 Map 4

Boat

3½ miles from M1 junction 15: A508 towards Stony Stratford, then Stoke Bruerne signposted on right

Included for its position by the neatly painted double locks of the Grand Union Canal, this popular, family-run place has an old-fashioned, low-ceilinged bar and tap-room which people like a lot: built-in wall benches, worn tiled floors, walls painted with simple, brightly coloured vignettes of barges and barge life, and a separate alley for the hood skittles. A spacious lounge at the back is perfectly comfortable though less special. Sandwiches (from £1), burgers (from £1.50), basket meals (from £1.45), ploughman's (from £1.50), vegetarian quiche (£3), home-made lasagne (£3.10), salads (from £3), mini-grill (£3.75) and steak (£5.95). Everards Old Original, Marstons Pedigree and Merrie Monk, Ruddles County and Sam Smiths OB on handpump; dominoes, cribbage, hood skittles, fruit machine, trivia and piped music; canalside tea-rooms serve the bar food all day from March to October. There are tables on the canal bank which look out on to the colourful narrowboats, and over to the other side where there's a handsome row of eighteenth-century warehouses (the canal museum here is interesting). It can get very crowded at peak times. A narrowboat is available for party or individual hire. *(Recommended by Mike and Sue Wheeler, Mrs M E Lawrence, Gordon Theaker, Sue Corrigan, Michael and Alison Sandy)*

Free house   Licensee John Woodward   Real ale   Meals and snacks (11.30–2.30, 7–9.30; not 25 Dec)   Restaurant (not Sun evening) tel Roade (0604) 862428   Children in lounge bar, restaurant and tea-room   Live entertainment Nov and Dec, and by arrangement at other times   Parking may be difficult at peak holiday times   Open 11–3, 6–11 all year, though may open longer in afternoon if trade demands; all day Sat

STRATFORD-UPON-AVON (War)   SP2055 Map 4

Garrick

High Street; close to Town Hall

The name Garrick originates from 1769 when the actor David Garrick visited Stratford and inaugurated the Stratford Festival, performing not Shakespeare's work but contemporary drama of the time. The small and often irregularly shaped rooms have heavy wall timbers, high ceiling beams, some walls stripped back to bare stone, with others heavily plastered with posters, sawdust on the wood floor, long upholstered settles and stools, and a talking mynah bird (Tuesday to Friday); the back bar has an open fire in the middle of the room with a conical brass hood. Bar food includes filled rolls, ploughman's (£2), steak and kidney pie (£2.10), game pie (£2.85) and cottage pie or lasagne (£3.40). Well kept Flowers IPA and Original on handpump, kept under light blanket pressure; a fruit machine and thoughtfully chosen piped music. The house next to this elaborately timbered building was the family home of Katherine Harvard, whose son founded America's best-known university. *(Recommended by David and Eloise Smaylen, Sheila Keene, S V Bishop, S J A Velate; more reports please)*

Flowers (Whitbreads)   Real ale   Lunchtime meals (not Sun or Mon) and snacks   Children in dining-room Tues–Sat lunchtimes only   Nearby daytime parking difficult   Open 10.30–2.30, 5.30–11 all year

Slug & Lettuce 🏵

38 Guild Street, corner of Union Street

At the back of this busy town-centre pub a small flagstoned terrace, with lanterns and floodlighting at night, has lots of flower boxes and sturdy teak tables under cocktail parasols, with more up steps. Inside, there are a few period prints on stripped squared panelling, sprays of flowers on the tables, pine kitchen tables and chairs on rugs and flagstones, a rack of newspapers for customers, and a solid-fuel fire. Enterprising bar food changes daily, and might include tomato and basil soup (£1.50), Burgundy mushrooms (£2.75), black pudding with tomatoes and cheese or leeks baked with prawns and eggs (£3.25), roast honey-glazed baby spring chicken or grilled pork chop with apples and calvados (£5.50), king prawns sauté in garlic butter (£6.25), half a roast guinea-fowl with port and bacon (£6.50), and fillet steak with a rich kidney sauce (£8); imaginative home-made puddings, good coffee. You can watch some food being prepared at one end of the long L-shaped bar counter. The young staff are friendly; if you tell them you're going to an RSC matinee they'll serve you quickly. Well kept Ansells, Ind Coope Burton, Tetleys, two other Ind Coope-related beers named for the pub, and guest ales on handpump; decent wine list, a good range of spirits, and they do a good Pimms. It can get very busy. (*Recommended by Brian Jones, Mrs E M Thompson, Roy Bromell, S J A Velate, Dr J R Hamilton, Maggie Jo St John, Tony Dudley Evans, Charles Gurney, V N Hill*)

Ansells (Allied)   Licensee Andrew Harris   Real ale   Meals and snacks (noon–10 Mon–Sat, ... Sun)   Children welcome   Jazz in courtyard summer afternoons   Open 11–11

White Swan

Rother Street; leads into A34

During renovations in 1927, a 1560 wall painting of Tobias and the Angel with the miraculous fish was discovered, hidden until then by the highly polished Jacobean oak panelling which covers much of the old-fashioned bar. It's a long quiet room with cushioned leather armchairs, carved ancient oak settles, plush smaller seats, a nice window seat and heavy beams; one fireplace has a handsomely carved chimneypiece, another smaller one an attractive marquetry surround. A staffed food counter outside serves home-made soup (£1.35), ploughman's (£2.75), a daily hot dish (£3.50), quiche (£3.95), cold meat platter (£4.25) and puddings (from £1.25). Well kept Bass, Marstons Pedigree and Wadworths 6X on handpump. (*Recommended by Wayne Brindle, S J A Velate; more reports please*)

Free house (THF)   Manager Ian Parfitt   Real ale   Lunchtime snacks   Restaurant Children welcome   Open 10.30–2.30, 6–11 all year   Bedrooms tel Stratford-upon-Avon (0789) 297022; £62B/£77B

THORNBY (Northants)   SP6775 Map 4

Red Lion

Welford Road; A50 Northampton–Leicester

What a pleasant change to ask for a fresh orange juice and actually get one, instead of the usual minuscule bottle at a grossly inflated price; two plump oranges juiced in front of you, for 50p – the Coopers are lucky to have deliveries from an enthusiastically helpful fruiterer. This is just one small but telling example of how much they've done, since taking over the Red Lion a couple of years ago, to turn a building which in itself had been relatively undistinguished into something really special. They've filled it with very carefully chosen furnishings, including for example the lovingly polished big golden table nestling between a couple of pews in one of the bay windows, the deep leather armchairs and sofa in one of two smallish areas opening off, and the individual old-fashioned lamps. There are fresh flowers, china jugs and steins on a shelf and hanging over the bar, pewter tankards hanging from a beam, and decorative plates densely covering the walls. Beside sandwiches (£1.50) and ploughman's (£2.25), good, honest home-made bar food, changing day by day, might include soup (95p), Stilton dip with fresh mayonnaise (£1.25), orange, tomato and cheese salad (£1.35), Cumberland sausage casserole (£2.95), chilli con carne (£3.25), curry or lasagne (£3.95), tuna and prawn salad (£3.95) and traditional puddings such as whisky syllabub or bread-and-butter (£1.50); a good value three-course Sunday lunch (served 12–1) is £8.50. Well kept Marstons Burton and Pedigree on handpump, decent wines kept fresh by the glass, good coffee, newspapers laid out, quietly friendly punctilious service, logs burning in an open stove. There are seats outside. *(Recommended by Roy Herbert, Cdr Patrick Tailyour)*

Free house Licensees Doug and Jen Cooper Real ale Meals and snacks (not Sun or Mon) Small restaurant (Fri and Sat evening, early Sun lunch) tel Northampton (0604) 740238 Open 11.30–2.30, 7–11 all year; closed Mon

THORPE MANDEVILLE (Northants) SP5344 Map 4

Three Conies

In village, just off B4525 Banbury–Northampton

Built in 1622, this stone pub has a cosy low-beamed and carpeted lounge bar with little hunting prints and polished brass on the walls (which are partly stripped to golden stone), tapestried built-in settles and spindle-back chairs and stone walls, (which may have fresh flowers), and horsebrasses around the ... is bought in) includes Beyond the servery, the public bar has bigger pictures ... and pool and fruit machine. Home-made bar sausages (£1.95), mushrooms in a sandwiches (from 95p), soup, ploughm.... chicken breast (£3.50), salads (£4), steaks and daily specials garlic and cream sauce, chicken breast (£3.50), salads (£4), steaks and daily specials such as chilli con carne or steak and kidney pie (from £2.95); puddings such as home-made ice-creams, sherry trifle or chocolate eclairs (from £1.50), and Sunday roast lunch. Well kept Hook Norton Best and Old Hookey on handpump, and a good selection of wines and spirits; friendly, efficient service. There are old-fashioned teak and curly iron seats on a lawn with a fruit tree; the pub is handily placed for Sulgrave Manor (George Washington's ancestral home) and Canons Ashby House (the Dryden family home). *(Recommended by Lyn and Bill Capper, Mrs E M Thompson, J E Rycroft, Dave Braisted, M O'Driscoll, G T Rhys)*

Hook Norton Licensee John Day Real ale Meals and snacks (11.30–2.30, 6.30–9.30) Restaurant (not Sun evening) tel Banbury (0295) 711025 Children in restaurant and eating area of bar Open 11–2.30 (3 Sat), 6–11 all year; may open longer in afternoon if trade demands

TWYWELL (Northants) SP9478 Map 4

Old Friar

Village signposted from A604 about 2 miles W of Thrapston

Most of the good plain wooden tables in this refurbished old pub are set out for eating (the dining area is no-smoking), and there are comfortable tub chairs and settles, and beams – like the brick fireplaces – that are decorated with wooden carvings of friars. Bar food includes sandwiches, soup, oriental parcels, fish dishes (from £3.45), lamb moussaka, vegetarian meals (£4.25), and steaks (from £5.95), a hot and cold carvery (£4.95, children's helping £2.45), and puddings such as spotted dick and treacle pudding. Well kept Ruddles Best and County, and Websters Yorkshire on handpump served from the brick bar counter; shove-ha'penny, dominoes, fruit machine and piped music. No dogs. *(Recommended by Frank Cummins, Comus Elliott, G W Judson; more reports please)*

Manns (Watneys) Licensee David Crisp Real ale Meals and snacks Restaurant tel Thrapston (080 12) 2625 Children welcome Open 11–2.30, 6–11 all year

WARMINGTON (War) SP4147 Map 4

Plough

Village just off A41 N of Banbury

This friendly, early seventeenth-century pub was quite new when Charles I marched through here towards Edge Hill with 18,000 men in October 1642; some of those men are buried in the churchyard here. The black-beamed and softly lit bar is largely stripped back to the stonework, and cosy seating includes a small settee, an old high-backed winged settle, leatherette-cushioned wall seats and lots of comfortable Deco small armed chairs and library chairs. There are old photographs of the village and locals, and good log fires in winter. Quickly served simple but good lunchtime bar food includes good minestrone soup, sandwiches, ploughman's, good minced beef pie, salads (from £3), flavoursome home-baked ham (£3.50), and home-cooked daily specials (from £2). Well kept Hook Norton Best, Marstons Pedigree and Merrie Monk, and Wadworths 6X on handpump, and several malt whiskies; good service, maybe faint piped pop music. This year, there's a new terrace and Aunt Sally shy. *(Recommended by Ted George, K and E Leist, Derek and Sylvia Stephenson, Gordon and Daphne)*

Free house   Licensees E J and D L Wilson   Real ale   Meals and snacks (lunchtime, not Sun)   Children in eating area of bar   Occasional live music   Open 11.30–2.30, 6–11 all year

WARWICK   SP2865 Map 4

Saxon Mill

Guy's Cliffe; A429 N of town

The centrepiece here is the great wheel turning slowly behind glass, and the mill race rushing under a glass floor panel – though it hasn't worked as a watermill since 1938. The rambling cottagey rooms have some beams and flagstones, pine cladding, open fireplaces, brasses, bookshelves, and fine views of the Avon weir. The standard range of bar food, well kept Courage Best and Directors on handpump, and gentle piped music. There are picnic-table sets on a terrace below and out under the surrounding trees, a fishing club (anyone can join), weekend barbecues – weather permitting – and a children's play area with slides, swings and so forth. This is a Harvester Family Restaurant. *(Recommended by Mr and Mrs Markham, Rob and Gill Weeks; more reports please)*

Free house (THF)   Real ale   Lunchtime meals and snacks   Restaurant tel Warwick (0926) 492255   Children welcome   Rock music Tues, jazz Thurs, country and western Sun   Open 11–11 Mon–Sat, 12–3, 7–11 Sun

WEEDON (Northants)   SP6259 Map 4

Crossroads ★ 🛏

3 miles from M1 junction 16; A45 towards Daventry – hotel at junction with A5 (look out for its striking clock tower)

The unusual and flamboyantly decorated main bar in this modern main-road hotel has shelves of plates, sets of copper jugs, antique clocks, and serving-counters made from the elaborate mahogany fittings of an antique apothecary's shop; there are various cosy alcoves, softly cushioned old settles and bucket seats, and a pastel-toned carpet. A cosy parlourish room leading off has soft easy chairs, and there's a light and airy coffee parlour that's open all day. Smartly served bar food includes home-made soup (£1.50), ploughman's with a selection of cheeses or smoked mackerel, prawns, home-cooked ham and pâté and salads (from £3.50), and fish bake or a hot dish of the day such as steak and kidney pie (£4.75). Well kept Bass, Ruddles County and Websters Yorkshire on handpump, freshly squeezed orange juice, and regular, organised wine tastings; shove-ha'penny. *(Recommended by Mrs C Smith, Dennis and Janet Johnson, Penny Zweep, H W and A B Tuffill, J C and D Aitkenhead, Rob and Gill Weeks, Alison Hayward, Nick Dowson, Robert and Vicky Tod)*

Free house   Licensee Richard Amos   Real ale   Meals and snacks (12–2, 6–10.30 – also see above)   Children welcome   Restaurant   Open 10–4, 6–11 all year; closed 25 and 26 Dec   Bedrooms tel Weedon (0327) 40354; £55B/£65B

WELFORD-ON-AVON (War) SP1452 Map 4

Bell

High Street; village signposted from A439

In an attractive riverside village, this well kept seventeenth-century pub has a comfortable, low-ceilinged lounge bar with beams, sober seats and tables that suit its dark timbering, and open fireplaces (which have an open fire in one and an electric fire in the other); the flagstoned public bar has another open fire. Flowers Original and IPA on handpump; efficient staff; darts, pool, dominoes, cribbage, fruit machine, trivia, juke box and piped music. A varied bar menu includes sandwiches (£1.20), cottage pie (£2.45), home-made steak and kidney pie (£3.35), liver and onions, fried plaice or chicken (£3.50), good gammon and eggs, and cold Scotch salmon (£4.25); good value Sunday lunch, and several types of liqueur coffee. You can sit in the pretty garden area and back courtyard. The lane leading to the village church has pretty thatched black and white cottages. *(Recommended by Paul and Margaret Baker, S V Bishop, S J A Velate; more reports please)*

Whitbreads Licensee Mike Eynon Real ale Meals and snacks (12–2.30, 7–10.30) Restaurant tel Stratford-upon-Avon (0789) 750353 Children in centrally heated and furnished, enclosed terrace Open 11–3, 6–11 all year

WEST BROMWICH (W Midlands) SP0091 Map 4

Manor House

2 miles from M6 junction 9; from A461 towards Wednesbury take first left into Woden Road East; at T-junction, left into Crankhall Lane; at eventual roundabout, right into Hall Green Road

The entrance through the ancient gatehouse to this remarkable moated and timbered small manor house is very picturesque – especially since the car park is sensitively tucked away behind some modern ancillary buildings. The main bar is a great hall, with twin blue carpets on its flagstones, and plenty of tables. Tremendous oak trusses support the soaring pitched roof (the central one, eliminating any need for supporting pillars, is probably unique), and a fine old sliding door opens on to stairs leading up to a series of smaller and cosier timbered upper rooms, including a medieval Solar, which again have lovely oak trusses supporting their pitched ceiling beams. Up here, there are comfortably cushioned seats and stools around small tables, with the occasional settle; a snug Parlour Bar is tucked in beneath the Solar. Bar food served from the efficient side food bar includes sandwiches, half a dozen home-made dishes (from £2.50) and roast pork or lamb (from £3.25). Well kept Banks's Bitter and Mild and Hansons on electric pump; friendly service, piped music, space game and fruit machines. A broad sweep of grass stretches away beyond the moat, towards the modern houses of this quiet suburb. The house is listed in the Domesday Book as being held by William Fitz Ansculph, Baron of Dudley. *(Recommended by E J Alcock, Dave Braisted, John and Pat Smyth, AE)*

Banks's Licensee John Walker Real ale Meals and snacks (12–2, 7–10.30) Restaurant (not Sun evening) tel 021-588 2035 Children in restaurant and eating area of bar Open 11–2.30, 6–11 all year

WHATCOTE (War) SP2944 Map 4

Royal Oak

Village signposted from A34 N of Shipston on Stour; and from A422 Banbury–Stratford, via Oxhill

In 1642 Cromwell used this very pretty stone-built pub as temporary quarters, and there's a very old tradition that he came back here after the Battle of Edgehill for drinks; when the Sealed Knots re-enact the battle around 20–30 October they come here in period costume for lunch. The small rooms of the original bar have some exceptionally low beams, a miscellany of stools, cushioned pews and other seats, old local photographs, brasses, a sword, and a stuffed peewit on the walls, and coins, bookmatches and foreign banknotes on the beams behind the high copper bar counter. The huge inglenook fireplace has rungs leading up to a chamber on the right – perhaps a priest's hiding hole, or more prosaically a smoking-chamber for hams. There's a more spacious (and more straightforward) bar on the left. A wide choice of bar food includes sandwiches (if they're not busy), home-made soup (90p), ploughman's (£2.20), cold ham (£2.90), trout (£3.30), chicken Kiev (£4.50), sirloin steak (£6.20) and specials such as vegetarian lasagne (£3), steak and kidney pie (£3.40), game dishes in season (from £3.50), shark steak (£4), and chicken with prawn and lobster (£4.50); puddings like treacle tart (£1.10). Well kept Marstons Pedigree, with guest beers tapped from the cask during the cooler months. Darts (winter), dominoes, fruit machine and piped music; Shadow the German shepherd is very welcoming – even to other dogs. The front terrace has some picnic-table sets, and there are more on grass at the side. (*Recommended by Mrs Nina Elliott, John Bowdler, M O'Driscoll, J S Evans*)

Free house   Licensee Mrs Catherine Matthews   Real ale (maybe not summer)   Meals and snacks (12–2, 6–10.30)   Children in eating area of bar   Occasional live music   Open 10.30–2.30, 6–11 all year

WITHYBROOK (War)   SP4384 Map 4

Pheasant

4 miles from M6 junction 2; follow Ansty, Shilton signpost; bear right in Shilton towards Wolvey then take first right signposted Withybrook – or, longer but wider, second right into B4112 to Withybrook

This friendly country pub is mainly popular for its wide choice of cheerfully served food: sandwiches (from 85p), soup (£1), ploughman's (£2.25), omelettes (from £3), home-made lasagne, steak and kidney pie, fresh quiches or braised liver and onions (all £3.50), salads (from £3.50), vegetarian dishes such as goulash (£3.95) or spinach and mushroom lasagne (£4.65), good stuffed sole (£4.25), braised guinea-fowl royale (£5.50), steaks (from £6.95) and puddings (£1.50); good Sunday lunch (£4.75 for one course; £6.95 in restaurant for four courses). They take your name when you arrive, and sit you down in order (a good idea), giving you time to relax with a drink beforehand. The extended lounge has lots of plush-cushioned wheel-back chairs and dark tables on the patterned carpet, good winter fires, and a few farm tools on its cream walls. The serving-counter, flanked by well polished rocky flagstones, has well kept Courage Best and Directors on handpump, with John Smiths on electric pump. A fruit machine in the lobby, and piped music. There are tables under fairy lights on a brookside terrace, and the bank opposite is prettily planted with flowers and shrubs. The Ankor Morris Men come a few times a year. (*Recommended by Ken and Barbara Turner, Graham Bush, Paul Wreglesworth, Wayne Brindle, Brian and Anna Marsden, Thomas Nott, Michael and Alison Sandy, Dr and Mrs B D Smith, Roy Bromwell, D P Cartwright, Mandy and Mike Challis, PLC*)

Free house   Licensees Mr and Mrs D Guy, Mr and Mrs A H Bean   Real ale   Meals and snacks (12–2, 6.30–10; not 25 and 26 Dec)   Restaurant tel Hinckley (0455) 220480 Children welcome   Open 11–3, 6.30–11 all year; closed evenings 25 and 26 Dec

Lucky Dip

Besides the fully inspected pubs, you might like to try these Lucky Dips recommended to us and described by readers (if you do, please send us reports):

Alcester, War [Stratford Rd; SP0857], *Cross Keys*: Pleasant atmosphere in small pub brightened up by new owner who has extended the choice of Ansells, Banks's Mild and Tetleys *(A J Woodhouse)*

Ardens Grafton, War [on edge of village, towards Wixford – OS Sheet 150 reference 114538; SP1153], *Golden Cross*: Pleasant carpeted and low-beamed L-shaped room with Victorian dolls, tables on one side set for substantial good value lunchtime bar food, served efficiently; well kept Flowers Original and Wethereds SPA on handpump, friendly staff, unobtrusive piped music, fruit machine; restaurant *(Frank Cummins)*

Armscote, War [SP2444], *Wagon Wheel*: Good interesting home-made food (not Sun) and well kept Bass in tastefully refurbished pub *(B S Bourne)*

☆ **Aston Cantlow**, War [SP1359], *Kings Head*: Beautifully timbered village pub not far from Mary Arden's house in Wilmcote, nicely restored with flagstones, inglenook, cheery log fire and settles; grandfather clock in low-beamed room on left, snug on right, well kept Flowers IPA and Original, good value home-made bar food *(Brian Jones, Chris Cooke, T George, S J A Velate, LYM)*

Atherstone, War [Long St; SP3097], *Cloisters*: Warm friendly atmosphere in bar with good range of drinks often including farm cider; nice staff and very reasonably priced lunchtime and evening food; folk music weekly *(Matthew Gough)*

☆ **Austrey**, War [Church Lane (A453); SK2906], *Bird in Hand*: Reputably one of the oldest pubs in the area, prettily thatched, and including old ships' timbers as beams; immaculately kept, with friendly atmosphere, well kept Marstons Pedigree on handpump, traditional games, pleasant coal fire *(C Davies, H S Harries)*

☆ **Aynho**, Northants [SP5133], *Cartwright Arms*: Neatly modernised lounge and bar in sixteenth-century inn, polite attentive service, good bar food, interesting restaurant with fish flown in daily from Jersey, a few tables in pretty corner of former coachyard; bedrooms comfortable *(Gordon Theaker, BB)*

Aynho [Wharf Base, B4031 W], *Great Western Arms*: Friendly bar staff, well kept beer on handpump and reasonably priced bar food including particularly good big ploughman's *(Graham Oddey)*

Badby, Northants [SP5559], *Maltsters Arms*: Character pub with interesting locals and pleasant service *(J V Dadswell)*; *Windmill*: Extensive refurbishments (amounting virtually to rebuilding) of this thatched stone village inn, completed in 1989, have left it very much more of a restaurant-with-bedrooms than a pub, though it still has a good, interesting choice of real ales, and as it was formerly a popular main entry we'd be grateful for more detailed views from readers who know it *(LYM)*

Baginton, War [SP3474], *Old Mill*: Converted watermill with gardens leading down to the River Sower; the oldest and most interesting part, with the river views and great millwheel, is given over to the restaurant and its cocktail bar (popular with businessmen), which seems the central feature here; the spacious beamed and panelled side bar has Watneys-related and maybe guest real ales, with old settles as well as its mainly modern seats *(LYM)*

Barford, War [SP2760], *Joseph Arch*: Well kept Flowers Original on handpump and good reasonably priced bar food; named after the founder of the agricultural workers union *(W H Bland)*

Barnacle, War [village signposted off B4029 in Shilton, nr M6 junction 2; SP3884], *Red Lion*: Lovely little pub with two rooms, one small, the other long with a leather bench seat around edge and collection of plates; Bass and M&B, ample unusually cheap bar food (not Sun lunchtime); covered area outside in front *(Ted George)*

☆ **Barnwell**, Northants [TL0484], *Montagu Arms*: Popular old pub with low beams and flagstones in original part, and a newly opened extension bar and restaurant which has eased the weekend pressure; well kept Greene King IPA, Marstons Pedigree and Charles Wells on handpump with guest beers such as Adnams, Batemans or Youngs, simple reasonably priced but imaginatively presented lunchtime bar food, more extensive evening menu – the food seems to be improving all the time; waitress service, good atmosphere *(M and J Back, Eric Locker)*

☆ **Barton**, War [pub signposted off B4085, just S of Bidford-on-Avon; SP1051], *Cottage of Content*: Cosy flagstoned bar with simple traditional furnishings, solid fuel stove in inglenook, low black beams, short choice of good simple bar food from soup and sandwiches through home-made pies to lemon sole, roast beef and summer salmon with good Weds evening specials, well kept Flowers IPA and Original on handpump, piped music, restaurant; picnic-table sets in front of the pretty house, touring caravan site with good play area behind; day fishing on River Avon here *(Elsie and Les Tanner, Andrew Ludlow, HDC, BB)*

☆ **Bearley**, War [A34 N of Stratford; SP1860], *Golden Cross*: Lovely old timbered bar with open fireplaces, soft lighting and lots of atmosphere; good generous bar food, pleasantly served; large range of beers, wine on tap; small restaurant *(Wayne Brindle, A J Woodhouse)*

Billesley, W Mid [SP0980], *Stags Head*: Interesting timbered old building with real ale and good value bar food *(Grahame Archer)*

Binley Woods, War [A428 Coventry–War; SP3977], *Cocked Hat*: Popular with businessmen during the week, nice relaxed atmosphere at weekends, with good food including vegetarian dishes in restaurant; comfortable bedrooms *(Sandra Kempson)*

Birmingham [Wheelers Lane, Kings Heath; SP0781], *Billesley*: Quiet and friendly with reasonably priced good food; bedrooms *(Anon)*; [Church St (nr Eye Hospital)] *Cathedral*: City-centre pub with friendly staff and very reasonably priced food; busy at lunchtime *(Roy Bromell)*; [Church Lane, Perry Barr; SP0692] *Church*: Large refurbished pub decorated with old-fashioned bric-à-brac, small panelled side room with open fire and serving-hatch, friendly bar, secluded and sheltered garden; outstanding chip butty, weekend barbecues *(E J Alcock)*; [Cambrian Wharf; Kingston Row, off Broad St] *Longboat*: Modern, city-centre pub overlooking canal, with terrace and balcony over the water; well kept beers, straightforward bar food and efficient service; juke box and fruit machines *(Colin Gooch)*; [Lea End Lane/Icknield St – so actually over the Hereford & Worcs border; SP0475] *Peacock*: Picturesque setting for small isolated pub with homely atmosphere, low ceilings and pub games; nice to sit quietly in summer at the picnic-table sets only a few minutes from city centre *(E J Alcock)*; [Edmund St] *White Swan*: Clean, smart, split-level M&B house with large front bar and back food area; Edwardian furnishings, gas lamps, heavy wallpaper, stained-glass screens creating small booths, pillars with shelf tables, comfortable banquettes; Brew XI, good sandwiches, ploughman's and pâté, sundae-type puddings; covered yard with white cast-iron tables and chairs; children welcome *(Ian Phillips, Dave Braisted)*

Blakesley, Northants [High St (Woodend rd); SP6250], *Bartholomew Arms*: Two cosy beamed bars cluttered with knick-knacks, well kept Marstons Pedigree and Ruddles on handpump, ready-made but well filled rolls and decent ploughman's; very popular Fri evening, calmer Sat lunchtime; sun-trap back garden with summerhouse *(Nick Dowson, Alison Hayward)*

☆ **Bodymoor Heath**, War [Dog Lane; SP2096], *Dog & Doublet*: Canalside pub which can get packed at weekends, and it's a shame that they let you eat only snacks in the pleasant garden, with its dovecote (children aren't allowed inside); but well worth knowing for its setting close to Kingsbury Water Park, for the reasonably priced good bar food including meals in a separate dining-room, and for the general character of the place – beams, brasses, bargees' painted ware, well kept M&B, comfortable seats, several open fires *(Colin Gooch, Mike and Sue Wheeler)*

Brackley, Northants [SP5837], *Bell*: Very good daily special such as home-made steak and kidney pie, plenty of tasty cheese and fresh salad with ploughman's, good beer, pleasant atmosphere *(Mrs M E Lawrence)*; [20 Market Sq] *Crown*: Classically refurbished, good value food in bar and restaurant; bedrooms very comfortable *(Lorna Hawkins)*

Braunston, Northants [on canal, about a mile from village; SP5466], *Admiral Nelson*: Large, modernised waterside pub with good atmosphere and piped music; Watneys-related real ales on handpump, good range of well cooked bar food *(Gordon Theaker)*; [A45 at canal junction] *Boatman*: Large pub in pleasant waterside spot, Watneys-related real ales on handpump, wide range of bar food, large back lounge, front games-room, small raised bar between the two, restaurant by canal; children in restaurant; bedrooms *(Mike and Sue Wheeler, Ted George)*

Bretford, War [A428 Coventry–Rugby – OS Sheet 140 reference 431772; SP4377], *Queens Head*: Open-plan bar with modern furnishings, plentiful helpings of reasonably priced good bar food, carvery, garden with play area *(Geoff Lee)*

Brierley Hill, W Mid [Delph Rd (B4172); SO9187], *Bell*: Cosy Holt, Plant & Deakins pub with their real ales kept well, roaring coal fires, lots of old knick-knacks, good value lunchtime bar snacks *(E J Alcock)*

Brinklow, War [Fosse Way; A427, fairly handy for M6 junction 2; SP4379], *Raven*: Friendly staff and customers, good value generously served bar food, well kept Ansells Mild and Bitter *(Geoff Lee)*

Bubbenhall, War [SP3672], *Malt Shovel*: Clean and tidy with plenty of olde-world charm; friendly staff, well kept Ansells and Tetleys, large range of bar food, tables in big garden, two bowling-greens *(Ted George)*

Buckby Wharf, Northants [A5 N of Weedon – OS Sheet 152 reference 607654; SP6065], *New Inn*: Simple food and Marstons real ale in several rooms radiating from central servery, hood skittles and other games, canalside terrace *(LYM)*

Chadwick End, War [A41; SP2073], *Orange Tree*: Well refurbished, comfortable and ingeniously laid out Whitbreads Brewers Fayre pub; Whitbreads-related real ales with a guest such as Marstons Pedigree, well prepared standard bar food with three or four daily specials, piped music; no-smoking family-room has high chairs, kids' menu, games, balloons, hats, even baby wipes *(Mr and Mrs M D Jones, Dave Braisted)*

☆ **Churchover,** War [handy for M6 junction 1, off A426; SP5180], *Haywaggon*: Carefully modernised old pub on edge of quiet village, now reorganised to provide a genuine bar and two small separate eating areas (before, it had been functioning solely as a restaurant on weekday lunchtimes); friendly pubby atmosphere, efficient staff, good range of beer including Badger Best, Bass, Courage Best and Directors, Marstons, Ruddles County and regular guest beers, good bar food such as lasagne and curry *(Ted George, Aleister and Geraldine Martin, BB)*

☆ **Claverdon,** War [SP1964], *Red Lion*: Spacious back saloon (where children allowed) opening on to garden with tables on terrace, playthings and country views; small plush front L-shaped lounge; popular for quickly served reliable food from ploughman's through dishes such as Arbroath smokies, lamb and leek or steak and kidney pie to attractively priced steaks; well kept Flowers IPA and Original on handpump, open fire *(Rob and Gill Weeks, Brian Jones, Geoff Lee, BB)*

Clay Coton, Northants [off B5414 nr Stanford Hall; SP5977], *Fox & Hounds*: Attractive country pub, tastefully furnished, with two log fires; well kept Adnams, Hook Norton Old Hookey, Marstons Pedigree and Theakstons XB, good generously served bar food (not Sun) *(Ted George)*

Clifton upon Dunsmore, War [B5414 NE of Rugby; SP5376], *Black Bull*: Popular, cosy village local, separate dining-room *(Wayne Brindle)*

Clipston, Northants [SP7181], *Bulls Head*: Clean and welcoming under new regime; over a hundred malt whiskies, well kept Watneys-related real ales, good bar food reasonably priced *(Cdr Patrick Tailyour)*

Coleshill, War [High St; not far from M6 junction 4; SP1989], *George & Dragon*: Well decorated and clean, well kept M&B on handpump, good bar food including daily specials and attractively priced steaks *(A E Alcock, T R G Alcock)*

Corley Moor, War [SP2884], *Bull & Butcher*: Off the beaten track, small lounge and two larger bars all with real fires, good choice of M&B ales, good bar food *(Clive Davies)*

Cosgrove, Northants [SP7942], *Barley Mow*: Well kept Watneys-related real ales and good home-cooked bar food *(Anon)*

Cottingham, Northants [Blind Lane; SP8490], *Royal George*: Wide range of usual bar food as well as six different curries at a variety of strengths *(Cdr Patrick Tailyour)*

☆ **Coventry,** W Mid [Spon St; SP3379], *Old Windmill*: Quaint and popular timber-framed sixteenth-century pub, all nooks and crannies with no large room; fine ancient fireplace, good atmosphere in lots of small

rooms, one of which has carved oak seats on flagstones; generous helpings of simple lunchtime food (chips and beans loom large), well kept Watneys-related real ales, friendly service, gets very busy Fri and Sat evening; one of the few buildings which started its life in this interesting street, to which other ancient survivors of wartime bombing have now been moved *(Syd and Wyn Donald, Rob and Gill Weeks, Geoff Lee, Dawn and Phil Garside, Dr J R Hamilton)*

☆ **Coventry,** W Mid [Sutton Stop, Aldermans Green/Hawkesbury; close to M6 junction 3, via Black Horse Rd off B4113 Coventry Rd; SP3684], *Greyhound*: Welcoming pub at junction of Coventry and Oxford Canals, good food at attractive prices including particularly good pies (already getting so popular that it may be best to book), well kept Bass and Brew XI on electric pump, waterside tables in delightful garden, interesting collection of ties; the new licensees were formerly popular at the Town Wall in central Coventry, and here too, as in that pub, there's a donkey-box (tiny snug) *(Mr and Mrs R Holroyd, Geoff Lee, C Davies)*

Coventry, W Mid [Craven St, Chapel Fields; SP3179], *Coombe Abbey*: Very friendly, with small busy lounge; well kept Bass and M&B Mild on handpump, good value bar food; occasional folk music, terrace *(Clive Davies)*; [Barnett Green] *Peeping Tom*: Free house with good choice of beers on handpump, including particularly well kept Marstons Pedigree; changing choice of good food *(Mr and Mrs M D Jones)*; [Foleshill Rd] *Saracens Head*: Pleasant pub with beams, feature fireplace and little private alcoves; well kept cellar and good value food; pool-table, juke box which may be loud *(Mr and Mrs N Beckett)*; [Bond St, behind theatre] *Town Wall*: Unspoilt compact Victorian pub, still much as it must have been in the 1940s, with original Atkinsons engraved windows, open fire in small lounge, plainer bar, tiny snug and flower-filled back yard; has had well kept Bass and remarkably cheap bar food (lunchtime and early evening) from hot filled rolls to steaks, though we've not heard since the licensees moved out to the Greyhound – see above *(Rob and Gill Weeks)*

☆ **Cradley Heath,** W Mid [St Annes Rd, Five Ways; SO9486], *Sausage Works*: Recent addition to Little Pubs chain, with good food featuring a variety of interesting sausage dishes – with décor to match; and don't miss the Little Lumphammer ale *(Steve J Pratt, E J Alcock, Dave Braisted)*

Crick, Northants [A428, a mile from M1 junction 18; A428; SP5872], *Old Royal Oak*: Lovely old village pub, two cosy log fires, very friendly licensees, good food in restaurant *(Ted George)*; *Red Lion*: Pleasant old village pub, good bar food including excellent steaks, well kept Watneys-related real ales, open fires, no piped music *(Gordon*

Theaker, Denis Waters)

Denton, Northants [SP8358], *Red Lion*: Small unpretentious pub in sleepy hollow of thatched stone houses, family atmosphere, spotless lavatories, locals playing skittles, bar food *(BB)*

Duddington, Northants [SK9800], *Royal Oak*: Outstandingly good food *(Mr and Mrs G Olive)*

☆ **Dudley**, W Mid [Black Country Museum; SO9390], *Bottle & Glass*: Friendly, old-fashioned atmosphere in Victorian pub reconstructed in village of Black Country Museum (well worth a visit – it also includes working trams and trip up canal tunnel); well kept Hansons on handpump, good sandwiches; open lunchtimes only *(Patrick and Mary McDermott, David Fisher, PLC)*

☆ **Dudley** [Salop St, Eve Hill], *British Oak*: Simply decorated pub, full of local characters and atmosphere; brews its own good value beers including Castle Ruin, Eve and maybe in winter Dungeon and Old Jones, has made its own cider; also Ansells, Tetleys and Wadworths on handpump, a good few whiskies, generous helpings of simple but good value food, piped music, fruit machine *(Ian Holden, T R G Alcock, E J Alcock, A E Alcock)*

Dudley [High St], *Lamp*: Notable for its superb collection of malt whiskies (also sells them by the bottle); loyal regulars also praise the Bathams Mild and Bitter, bar food and atmosphere *(T R G Alcock)*

☆ **Dunchurch**, War [very handy for M45 junction 1; SP4871], *Dun Cow*: Classic coaching-inn layout with big central courtyard, pubby front bars (linked by hallway with settles and antiques) have heavy beams, brasses, warm fires in inglenooks, old-fashioned furnishings, panelling; good atmosphere, particularly in evenings; bedrooms *(LYM)*

Dunchurch, *Green Man*: Pleasant village local, friendly licensees *(Wayne Brindle)*

Eathorpe, War [SP3868], *Plough*: Remote, with well kept Ansells and good food in restaurant *(Clive Davies)*

☆ **Edge Hill**, War [SP3747], *Castle*: Notable for terrific garden perched over steep slope of Edge Hill, with lovely views through the trees; and for the building itself, a battlemented folly (even the lavatories are all towers and turrets); internally, the bar is rather basic – the best room's now a restaurant; Hook Norton real ales, bar food *(T Nott, SP, Gordon and Daphne, LYM)*

Ettington, War [Banbury Rd (A422); SP2749], *Houndshill*: Traditional country pub with friendly service and large choice of good value bar meals *(R C Coates)*

Exhall, War [Coventry Rd, nr M6 junction 3; SP3385], *Black Bank*: Popular pub with Bass on draught, comfortable lounge, lunchtime bar food *(Clive Davies)*

Fenny Compton, War [SP4152], *George &*

Dragon: Friendly canalside pub with real ales, good bar food; piped music can be on the loud side *(Gordon Theaker)*

Frankton, War [about 1¼ miles S of B4453 Leamington Spa–Rugby; SP4270], *Friendly*: Friendly old low-ceilinged village pub with good value bar lunches, wooden settles, coal fire *(J C Proud)*

Gaydon, War [B4451, just off A41 Banbury–Warwick; SP3654], *Malt Shovel*: Modernised pub with pleasant atmosphere, good service, well kept Flowers IPA and Original, good value bar food *(Mark Evans, M J Morgan)*

Gayton, Northants [High St; SP7054], *Eykyn Arms*: Games inc hood skittles a particular attraction in this pub with former cockfighting connections; well kept Charles Wells Eagle on handpump, floral-patterned seating in comfortable lounge, plainer back bar; pretty flower baskets outside in summer *(Dr and Mrs A K Clarke, Nick Dowson)*; *Queen Victoria*: Refurbished village pub with hunting prints in comfortable back lounge, popular bar food running up to steaks from modern servery area, real ales, darts and hood skittles in lively front public bar, pool-room; they've introduced computerised barcode-reading guns to tot up both food and drinks bills – new to us *(LYM)*

Great Houghton, Northants [up No Through Road just before the White Hart; SP7958], *Old Cherry Tree*: Cosy low-beamed pub with single servery for two alcovey areas, Charles Wells Eagle and Bombardier on handpump, good value filled French bread *(Nick Dowson)*

Grendon, War [just off A5, NW end Atherstone bypass; SK2900], *Kings Head*: Small friendly two-roomed canalside pub with well kept beer on handpump, good value bar food including large filled Yorkshire puddings and Sun lunches *(Mike and Mandy Challis)*

☆ **Halesowen**, W Mid [Cowley Gate St; just off A458 to Stourbridge, at Cradley Heath – OS Sheet 139 reference 941847; SO9683], *Little White Lion*: A prime light-hearted example of the Little Pubs – bright red and blue paintwork, white lions all over the place, cask tables, six-foot papier-mâché bear, windows painted as if stained glass; good value freshly made bar food in massive helpings, and besides Ansells Mild and Ind Coope Burton has the group's Little Lumphammer real ale; live music Tues, otherwise quiet piped nostalgic pop music *(Dave Braisted, Brian Jones)*

Halesowen [Stourbridge Rd, next to Halesowen FC], *King Edward*: Popular lunchtime pub for good value home-cooked food and well kept Ansells *(Roger Huggins)*; [Hagley Rd, Hasbury] *Rose & Crown*: Pleasant, friendly pub, reasonable bar food, well kept Holt, Plant & Deakins real ales *(Dave Braisted)*

Halford, War [SP2545], *Halford Bridge*:

Large, modernised old hotel, Ruddles County on handpump, good bar food, restaurant; bedrooms (*Mr and Mrs J H Wyatt*)

Hampton in Arden, W Mid [High St; SP2081], *White Lion*: Though quite handy for National Exhibition Centre it successfully keeps village atmosphere; well kept M&B, good food including lunchtime buffet table and fine interestingly filled baps, quick friendly service, lots of atmosphere; children's room (*Dave Braisted, R Houghton*)

Hampton Lucy, War [SP2557], *Boars Head*: Pleasant, unspoilt village pub with log fire, brasses and friendly atmosphere; well kept Flowers, simple reasonably priced bar food and prompt service (*T Nott*)

☆ **Harborne**, W Mid [not far from M5 junction 3; SP0284], *Bell*: Lovely little pub in Botanic Gardens area, showing its origins as a private house, with servery by passageway at foot of stairs, much of snug (served by hatch) actually within chimney breast of former vast open fireplace; large, comfortable lounge, well kept M&B Mild, full range of reasonably priced lunchtime bar food; seats outside, wooden balcony overlooking bowling-green (*Ian and James Phillips*)

Harbury, War [SP3759], *Shakespeare*: Welcoming pub, well kept beer, good value bar food (*Anon*)

Harpole, Northants [High St; nr M1 junction 16; SP6860], *Bull*: Pleasant atmosphere in clean pub with good food – nothing too much for the licensees (*S Clarke*)

Hatton, War [SP2467], *Water Boatman*: Well placed next to Hatton flight of locks on Grand Union Canal, with big garden; wide choice of food, generous helpings (extra charge for eating in dining area); very popular Sun lunchtime; children welcome (*Patrick and Mary McDermott*)

Hawkesbury, W Mid [Blackhorse Rd, within a mile of M6 junction 3; OS Sheet 140 reference 358846; SP3684], *Boat*: One of Ansells Heritage Inns refurbishments, in interesting spot nr canal junction; well kept real ale, three coal fires, good mix of locals and canal people, traditional games, imaginative bar food; present licensee descended from the boatbuilder who originally built it around 1850 (*Geoff Lee*)

Henley in Arden, War [High St; SP1466], *Blue Bell*: Impressive timber-framed building with fine gateway to former coachyard, beamed inside, though furnishings modern; well kept Flowers, friendly service, good value straightforward food (*J Keppy*)

Hockley Heath, W Mid [Stratford Rd; A34 Birmingham–Henley-in-Arden; SP1573], *Barn*: Beefeater motel, tricked out with lots of beams and even brick and tile miniature houses and canopies over restaurant tables; worth knowing for decent food, well kept Whitbreads-related real ales on handpump and a really genuine welcome for children (*M T Casey*); [Stratford Rd] *Wharf*: Friendly,

spacious Chef & Brewer with gaily painted bargees' teapots, milk churns and trays; reasonably priced straightforward bar food from sandwiches up, garden and terrace overlooking Stratford Canal, Watneys-related real ales, piped pop music, fruit machines, lavatory for disabled people (*Joan Olivier, Grahame Archer*)

Islip, Northants [SP9879], *Woolpack*: Prints and brass rubbings on stripped stone, good furniture and carpet, weekday bar food, Sun restaurant lunch; Charles Wells real ales (*Tom Evans*)

☆ **Kenilworth**, War [High St; SP2871], *Clarendon House*: Painstakingly restored and interestingly decorated to make the most of its long history; good range of drinks including Flowers and Hook Norton real ales, reasonably priced lunchtime bar food, restaurant; bedrooms (*RW, GW*)

Kettering, Northants [Victoria St; SP8778], *Alexandra Arms*: Good value home-made lunchtime food and well kept Watneys-related real ales; interesting collection of ashtrays (*Tony Smith*); [Lower St] *Kings Arms*: Decent pub, worth knowing (*T N de Bray*); *Rising Sun*: Another place well worth knowing (*T N de Bray*)

Kilsby, Northants [A5; SP5671], *George*: Tastefully decorated oak-panelled lounge with hunting prints and green plush seating; Bass on handpump, darts and pool, good choice of bar food from sandwiches to steak, pleasant garden (*J H Adam*)

Ladbroke, War [A423 S of Southam; SP4158], *Bell*: Pleasant surroundings, well kept Davenports, well served good value bar food including cheap steaks, garden (*Charles Gurney*)

☆ **Lapworth**, War [SP1670], *Navigation*: Small but friendly pub with flagstone floors, beams and settles; well kept Bass, good generously served lunchtime bar food (only filled cobs Sun), good atmosphere and service, canalside garden with mendicant ducks; children welcome, with children's helpings (*Brian Jones, D P Cartwright*)

Leamington Spa, War [Sydenham Dr, Sydenham; SP3165], *Fusiliers*: Friendly, happy pub close to Grand Union Canal; two large bars with darts, pool and snooker, separate lounge, good bar food; children welcome (*Sarah Baker*); [Campion Terr] *Sommerville Arms*: Useful local with particularly well kept Ansells Bitter and Mild, Ind Coope Burton and Tetleys (*Graham Bush*)

☆ **Lilbourne**, Northants [Rugby Rd; 4 miles from M1 junction 18 – A5 N, then 1st right; SP5677], *Bell*: Spaciously comfortable modern lounge bar well worth knowing as a motorway stop-off, with low-priced quickly served good value simple bar food, seats outside (and climbing frame); children welcome (*Jill Hadfield, Tony Gallagher, Wayne Brindle, Graham and Glenis Watkins, LYM*)

Little Addington, Northants [SP9573], *Bell*: Popular village pub with beams and exposed stone in long lounge bar, Adnams, Ansells, Ind Coope Burton and Tetleys real ales, food in bar and restaurant, summer barbecues in pleasant garden *(Keith Garley)*

☆ **Little Brington**, Northants [also signposted from A428; 4½ miles from M1 junction 16; first right off A45 to Daventry; SP6663], *Saracens Head*: Old-fashioned village pub, harking back to an idealised memory of the 1950s – spick-and-span brass and copper, cosy seats by the lounge fireside, games in big L-shaped public bar (a log fire here too), tables in neat back garden overlooking quiet fields; friendly service and reasonably priced, well cooked and presented bar food, piano singalong Sat evening, Watneys-related real ale *(Dudley Fromant, LYM)*

Long Buckby, Northants [A428; SP6267], *Buckby Lion*: Friendly and plushly refurbished country pub with picture windows overlooking rolling wooded countryside, real ales, lunchtime bar food, restaurant *(LYM)*

☆ **Long Itchington**, War [off A423; SP4165], *Two Boats*: Friendly neatly kept canalside pub with good mooring on Grand Union Canal, well kept Flowers Original, good value food (trout, mixed grill and puddings all recommended), friendly youngish licensees; small, can be busy; children welcome *(Mike and Sue Wheeler, Dr R Hodkinson)*

Long Itchington, *Buck & Bell*: Fine old-fashioned pub, locals sit or stand in passage served through small hatch, with long benches and positively gleaming tables in another room which you may well have to unlock yourself *(T George)*; [Church Rd] *Harvester*: Well kept Hook Norton and Wadworths 6X on handpump, good value bar food, small restaurant *(T R G Alcock)*

Lower Boddington, Northants [A361 Banbury–Daventry – OS Sheet 151 reference 481521; SP4852], *Carpenters Arms*: Popular local, well kept beer, wide range of bar food including super fry-ups, cricketing landlord *(David Gittins)*

Lower Quinton, War [off A46 Stratford–Broadway; SP1847], *College Arms*: Whitbreads pub with large open-plan lounge, unusual table in former fireplace, stripped stone walls, heavy beams; separate bar; large range of bar food from sandwiches to old-fashioned ham and egg suppers or Japanese prawns *(E V Walder)*

☆ **Lowick**, Northants [off A6116; SP9780], *Snooty Fox*: Recently refurbished sixteenth-century or older pub, ornate lounge bar with stonework, panelling, oak beams, easy chairs, antique settle, and more upright dining-chairs, log fire, friendly smartly dressed barmaids, good value though not cheap bar food including interesting dishes, well kept Watneys-related real ales and

Adnams on handpump, garden with picnic-table sets; in fine walking country *(Richard and James Groome, N A Wood, T N de Bray, Michael and Alison Sandy, M J Horridge)*

Lowsonford, War [OS Sheet 151 reference 188679; SP1868], *Fleur de Lys*: Prettily placed old canalside pub with log fires, lots of beams and waterside garden, which has been popular for food including some unusual dishes, good range of beers on handpump including Flowers Original and Wadworths 6X and decent wines *(Brian Jones – more reports please)*

Ludstone, W Mid [Upper Ludstone; B4176 Dudley to Telford – OS Sheet 138 reference 802953; SO8094], *Boycott Arms*: Large, pleasant Banks's pub with good value home cooking *(Dave Braisted)*

☆ **Lye**, W Mid [Pedmore Rd; SO9284], *Shovel Inn*: Friendly refurbished town-centre pub with excellent range of changing well kept real ales such as Bathams, Everards Tiger and Old Original and Hook Norton Old Hooky, good value home-cooked bar food including good steaks; pleasant lounge, basic bar – small, can get very crowded *(Brian Jones, E J Alcock, Steve J Pratt)*

Meer End, W Mid [SP2474], *Tipperary*: Friendly comfortable pub with bar snacks, Davenports real ale, enormous goldfish in piano-aquarium, tables in garden *(LYM)*

Middleton, War [OS Sheet 139 reference 175984; SP1798], *Green Man*: Popular family pub with good value bar food (meals rather than snacks, though they do have filled cobs), helpful service; very attractive garden *(J M Norton, Dr and Mrs C D E Morris)*

Monks Kirby, War [Bell Lane; just off A427 W of Pailton; SP4683], *Bell*: Nicely decorated, with slabbed and cobbled floor, lots of brown beams, wood-burning stove; open-plan, but split into several areas; friendly new licensees end 1988 – he's Spanish, and the wide choice of good bar food, in big helpings, now shows a Spanish influence as well as traditional dishes, with some emphasis on fish; good restaurant *(Ted George, Roy Bromell, Geoff Lee)*; *Denbigh Arms*: Village pub tastefully decorated, well kept M&B beers on handpump, darts and pool-room, wide variety of good bar food including massive steaks, restaurant which is busy at weekends *(A E Alcock)*

☆ **Napton**, War [A425; SP4661], *Napton Bridge*: Busy canal pub with well kept Davenports and particularly good food from sandwiches to steaks, including outstanding pasta specials (landlord's wife is Italian); former stable for bargees' horses is now a skittle alley *(Bill Hendry)*

☆ **Nassington**, Northants [Fotheringhay Rd; TL0696], *Black Horse*: Has had particularly good if not cheap food including interesting and imaginative specialities, and well kept real ales such as Adnams, Greene King IPA and Wadworths 6X; two comfortable dining-rooms linked by bar servery, with striking stone fireplace, panelling from Rufford Abbey, beams, easy chairs and small settees; children allowed in eating area; restaurant; seats on sheltered lawn; sadly too few reports recently to keep its place among the main entries, and one reader with a complaint felt it wasn't handled kindly *(T Nott, PLC, LYM – more reports please)*

Nether Heyford, Northants [close to M1 junction 16; SP6558], *Old Sun*: Small, clean pub with amazing collection of old signs and brasses; good bar food generously served *(Jan and Ian Alcock)*

Netherton, W Mid [Woodside Rd; SO9387], *Woodside*: Welcoming art deco pub, not far from Merry Hill shopping centre; good home-cooked food, well kept Timothy Taylors ales *(SJP)*

Newbold-on-Avon, War [SP4777], *Barley Mow*: Pleasant, welcoming canalside pub with straightforward but good bar food and particularly attractive garden and terrace *(Mr and Mrs C H Stride, E J Alcock)*; [B4112] *Boat*: Clean and popular recently extended canal pub, busy at weekends, with well kept Davenports Mild and Bitter on handpump, good value basic bar food, open fire between eating area and bar; table skittles, darts *(T R G Alcock, J C Proud, E J Alcock)*

Newnham, Northants [SP5859], *Romer Arms*: Popular free house on green in large village; friendly, relaxed atmosphere, own-brew Romer beer, bar food *(Dr Paul Kitchener)*

Northampton [Wellingborough Rd; SP7560], *Abington Park*: Large town pub which brews its own Cobblers Ale, Abington Extra and in 1989 Headspinner (to celebrate Northants CCC centenary); food in bar and restaurant *(Anon)*; [11 Fish St] *Fish*: Town-centre pub with good value bar food and small, delightful restaurant; bedrooms comfortable *(Lorna Hawkins)*

Nuneaton, War [Bull St, Attleborough; SE of centre; SP3592], *Bull*: An Ansells traditional refurbishment, with real ales, freshly made bar food, coal fire, traditional games; present licensee's father ran it early this century *(I Blackwell)*; [Eastborough Way] *Crows Nest*: New one-room single-storey Banks's pub decorated with lots of old farm tools; bar food including very good filled rolls, well kept real ales, lively at lunchtime *(I Blackwell)*

Old Hill, W Mid [Waterfall Lane nr M5 junction 2; SO9685], *Waterfall*: Rejuvenated pub with enthusiastic licensees, range of ten well kept changing real ales, good choice of well prepared and served bar food; one to watch *(E J Alcock)*

Oxhill, War [just S of A422; SP3145], *Peacock*: Tidy, cosy bar with well kept Donnington on handpump, big lawn *(Nick Dowson)*

Pailton, War [SP4781], *Fox*: Clean pub, well kept M&B Brew XI, good reasonably priced bar food; bedrooms *(T R G Alcock)*

Pelsall, W Mid [Walsall Rd (B4154); SK0203], *Old House*: Pleasant, comfortable surroundings, well kept Banks's Mild and Bitter and limited but good value lunchtime bar food *(Paul Noble)*

Pensnett, W Mid [A4101 Dudley–Kingswinford; SO9188], *Fox & Grapes*: Holt, Plant & Deakins pub with their real ales, mixture of ancient and modern décor, bar food *(Dave Braisted)*

Potterspury, Northants [A5; SP7543], *Old Talbot*: Watneys-related real ales in brightly decorated bar with friendly staff, food in bar and small restaurant, simple public bar with darts and other games; bedrooms *(LYM)*

Princethorpe, War [junction A423/B4453; SP4070], *Three Horseshoes*: Popular roadside inn, with open fires and Flowers real ales, though most people are there for the big helpings of reasonably priced food; nice garden with lots of children's playthings *(Rob and Gill Weeks, J C Proud)*; [B4453 towards Cubbington] *Woodhouse*: Pleasant hotel lounge, well kept Watneys-related real ales, good help-yourself hot and cold buffet – take as much as you like; bedrooms *(Ted George)*

Priors Hardwick, War [SP4756], *Butchers Arms*: What was the lounge of this medieval stone inn is now attached to the up-market and tastefully kept restaurant (with lots of beams, oak panelling, antique furniture) doing ambitious food, with good wines; public bar something of a sideline, with big inglenook, beams, sloping floor, keg beers, piped music, limited bar food; attractive gardens *(Gordon Theaker, C Fisher Price, Graham Bush)*

☆ **Priors Marston**, War [from village centre follow Shuckburgh signpost, but still in village take first R by telephone box; SP4857], *Holly Bush*: A prominent main entry in previous editions, this rambling and unusual golden stone house with enterprising food, half a dozen interesting real ales and friendly staff closed in 1989, with proposals for conversion into private homes – our hope is that it will reopen as a pub, and we'd be glad of news either way *(LYM)*

☆ **Priors Marston**, *Falcon*: Pleasant well furnished sixteenth-century inn with charming efficient licensees (new 1988); well kept Bass, Everards and Hook Norton ales, imaginative bar food, restaurant *(David Gittins, CEP)*

☆ **Pytchley**, Northants [SP8574], *Overstone Arms*: Delightful pub and garden, friendly professional service, good changing choice of good food, excellent Pimms, Watneys-related real ales *(Dr Paul Kitchener, J M Norton, D M C Creighton Griffiths)*

☆ **Quarry Bank**, W Mid [Saltwells Lane; signposted off Coppice Lane, off A4036 nr Merry Hill Centre – OS Sheet 139 reference 934868; SO9386], *Saltwells*: Surprisingly modern hotel at end of rough lane – books on shelves in carefully refurbished main lounge, cheap straightforward bar food, Banks's and Hansons ales, play equipment in garden and family-room; a veritable haven in these industrial parts, in a nature reserve; bedrooms *(E J Alcock)*

Quarry Bank [High St (A4100)], *Church Tavern*: Homely, with welcoming landlord and excellent home cooking, Black Country style; well kept Holt, Plant & Deakins ales *(SJP)*

Ratley, War [OS Sheet 151 reference 384473; SP3847], *Rose & Crown*: Fine old building of golden Hornton stone, nr lovely church in small sleepy village, with two big fireplaces separating off dining-room, well kept Flowers Original and Hook Norton Best, lots of interesting brasses, small back terrace; steep steps from car park *(Gordon and Daphne, Pete Storey)*

☆ **Rockingham**, Northants [SP8691], *Sondes Arms*: Nice welcoming and civilised old pub with friendly service, good home-made food (sandwiches, mackerel bake, curries and puddings all praised) and well kept Charles Wells Bombardier and Eagle on handpump *(AE, EML, Derek Stephenson)*

Rugby, War [Hilmorton Wharf, Crick Rd; SP5075], *Old Royal Oak*: Popular canalside pub, especially with young people; comfortable interior, several softly lit alcoves, well kept beer, tasty bar food *(Wayne Brindle)*

☆ **Sedgley**, W Mid [Bilston St (A463); SO9193], *Beacon*: Particularly attractive restoration of Victorian pub with original fittings and furnishings in five distinct drinking areas, including a family-room, radiating from tiny serving area with hatches; they've even restored the small tower brewery at the back, to brew their own interesting and potent Sarah Hughes Dark Ruby Mild, and have other well kept real ales such as Bathams, Burton Bridge and Holdens; seats on terrace; good atmosphere, very mixed clientele *(Richard Sanders, E J Alcock, Colin Dowse, David Fisher)*

☆ **Shipston on Stour**, War [Sheep St; SP2540], *Bell*: Attractively placed old coaching-inn with relaxed lounge running front to back in place of the former coach entry, brocaded settles around tables in stripped-stone bar partitioned off on one side, pool in separate games-room, Flowers IPA and Original on handpump, bar food and restaurant; provision for children; a main entry in last edition, but changing hands 1989, too late for us to assess results; seven comfortable bedrooms *(G T Rhys, LYM – reports on new regime please)*

Shrewley, War [off B4439 Hockley Heath–Warwick; SP2167], *Durham Ox*: This otherwise straightforward pub gains its place for its spacious garden, with beer-barrel dovecotes on telegraph poles housing a flight of white doves – canal and railway nearby, and now the new M40; cheap basic snacks (not Sun lunchtime), M&B beers *(S R Holman, LYM)*

Shustoke, War [B4114 Nuneaton–Coleshill; SP2290], *Plough*: Cheap beer and good atmosphere in pleasant pub with friendly service *(Dave Braisted)*

Sibbertoft, Northants [SP6782], *Red Lion*: Simple village pub with well kept Flowers, upholstered bench seats, brightly patterned carpet, piano, darts and skittles; bar food, evening restaurant *(Anon)*

Smethwick, W Mid [SP0288], *New Chapel*: Welcoming landlord who talks to children, well kept beer, good hot roast pork sandwiches *(Roger Taylor)*; [Uplands/Meadow Rd] *Old Chapel*: Delightful little pub with timbered extension and timber effect in lounge; M&B Brew XI and Springfield on electric pump, well kept Mild on handpump, welcoming landlord, fresh food including fine hot pork sandwiches *(R P Taylor)*; [Waterloo Rd; A457/A4136/A4092] *Waterloo*: Decidedly unpretentious atmosphere, but if you enjoy exceptional pub architecture it's well worth a visit for the splendid Victorian tilework in the public bar and for the grandly decorated basement grill-room; cheap M&B and Springfield ales, more orthodox comfortable lounge *(LYM)*

Stourbridge, W Mid [Amblecote Rd (A491); SO8984], *Moorings*: Large, busy pub by canal spur; reasonably priced bar food, pleasant back terrace *(E J Alcock)*; [Church St] *Old Crispin*: Refurbished pub with sun lounge, good bar food including vegetarian dishes, good Flowers Original and Marstons Pedigree; popular with art students *(SP)*

☆ **Stratford-upon-Avon**, War [Chapel St; SP2055], *Shakespeare*: Smart THF hotel based on handsome lavishly modernised Tudor merchants' houses, stylish public rooms and accommodation, also comfortable Froth & Elbow bar with settles and armchairs, good choice of interesting and well kept real ales on handpump, bar food, pleasant and efficient service; tables in back courtyard; three minutes' walk from theatre; bedrooms comfortable and well equipped, though not cheap *(Frank Cummins, LYM)*

☆ **Stratford-upon-Avon** [Riverside], *Black Swan*: The star is for this sixteenth-century pub's delightful position, with an attractive terrace looking over the riverside public gardens, handy for the Memorial Theatre; bar food, Flowers IPA and Original, children allowed in restaurant *(S V Bishop, Philip King, Wayne Brindle, I J McDowall, LYM; more reports please)*

Stratford-upon-Avon, *Falcon*: Original core, with two bars and restaurant, is atmospheric and friendly though piped music can be monotonous; bedrooms (can be noisy in old part, functional in modern wing) *(John Evans)*; [Rother St; opposite United Reform

Church, handy for Fri Market] *Lamp-lighters*: Big pub with long bar, well kept if rather cold real ales such as Tetleys on handpump; no food Sun *(Sheila Keene)*; [Ely St] *Queens Head*: Well run genuine local, good atmosphere, real fire, good barman, well kept M&B, good toasted sandwiches inc Sun *(Sheila Keene)*

☆ **Studley**, War [Icknield St Dr; left turn off A435, going N from B4093 roundabout; SP0763], *Old Washford Mill*: The pretty waterside gardens are in summer perhaps the best part of this extensive and popular watermill conversion (and have a good play area); inside, there's old mill machinery, lots of different levels with various quiet alcoves, and a variety of catering; real ales, and in the past own-brewed beers and even their own English wines; provision for children *(LYM)*
Sudborough, Northants [SP9682], *Vane Arms*: Well kept real ales such as Greene King Abbot and Sam Smiths OB, and decent bar food (not Sun), in nice thatched pub; fine walking country *(T N de Bray)*
Sutton Bassett, Northants [SP7790], *Queens Head*: Under new management, with well kept Marstons Pedigree and a guest beer such as Hook Norton Old Hookey on handpump; very reliable food inc excellent value steaks; upstairs restaurant *(M B P Carpenter)*
Temple Grafton, War [1 mile E, towards Binton; SP1255], *Blue Boar*: Extended pub, popular for good food including fresh fish – same in softly lit stripped-stone bar and dining-room; well kept Flowers, open fire, darts in flagstoned area, friendly atmosphere *(HDC, S V Bishop)*
Thrapston, Northants [A604 to Kettering, just W of main bridge; SP9978], *Woolpack*: Substantial traditional inn with stripped stone in communicating bar rooms, bar food from sandwiches to steaks, wood-burning stove, pleasant service; upstairs evening restaurant *(C J Cowlin)*

☆ **Tipton**, W Mid [Hurst Lane, Dudley Rd; towards Wednesbury, junction A457/A4037 – look for the Irish flag; SO9592], *M A D O'Rourkes Pie Factory*: Currently one of the most popular of the Little Pubs, and one of the most spacious, with a newly opened upstairs bar; a pastiche of a pork butcher's, with a gloriously over-the-top meat-processing theme (all sorts of interesting ancient equipment, not to mention strings of model hams, sausages, pigs' heads and so forth), and the usual larger-than-life atmosphere; good value food from black pudding thermidor to gargantuan Desperate Dan cow pie, complete with pastry horns; traditional puddings, well kept Ind Coope-related real ales and their own powerful if a bit variable Lumphammer, regular jazz or folk music; children welcome if eating; when it's busy – maybe with a group from a Black Country coach tour staring around in a state of entertained shock – you may be warned of formidable delays for food *(R P Taylor, Brian Jones, PLC, Dave Braisted, James Billingham, Elaine Kellet, E J Alcock, Colin Dowse, M A and W R Proctor, E V Walder)*
Tipton [Lower Church Lane, opp Police Stn], *Old Court House*: Basic local – just a square bar with a wooden floor – popular with male beer-drinkers for a good choice of interesting real ales such as Glenny Wychwood, Hoskins Mild, Moorhouses Pendle Witches Brew, Premier Knightly, Thwaites and Wiltshire Old Grumble; bar snacks *(R P Taylor)*

☆ **Titchmarsh**, Northants [village signposted from A604 and A605, just E of Thrapston; TL0279], *Wheatsheaf*: Good value home-made bar food such as steak and mushroom pie, fresh fish and steaks in comfortably extended village pub with rocking-chairs as well as plush banquettes and cosy bucket seats; Ind Coope Best and Tetleys on handpump, friendly service, separate pool room, restaurant; children allowed in eating areas; closed Mon, and Tues–Fri lunchtimes; main entry standard, but too few recent reports to keep its place *(LYM – more reports please)*
Towcester, Northants [104 Watling St; SP6948], *Brave Old Oak*: Friendly and comfortable, well kept Watneys-related real ales, pleasant dining-room with good value straightforward food; bar can be crowded with young people in the evening; small basic bedrooms *(Douglas Bail)*; [Watling St] *Saracens Head*: Attractive building with strong *Pickwick Papers* connections, cavernous fireplace with cooking-range in the bar; bedrooms *(LYM)*
Tredington, War [SP2543], *White Lion*: Clean, comfortable pub, particularly good value bar food including home-made specials *(R G Watts)*
Ufton, War [White Hart Lane; just off A425 Daventry–Leamington, towards Bascote; SP3761], *White Hart*: Stone-built pub in pretty spot near top of hill overlooking Avon Vale; large main lounge, smaller bar on lower level, relaxed atmosphere, prompt service, well kept Davenports ales, good bar food lunchtime and evening, running up to steaks with traditional puddings *(Mike O'Driscoll, Dave Braisted)*
Upper Benefield, Northants [SP9889], *Wheatsheaf*: Well run up-market pub/hotel/restaurant with bar food including first-class home-made steak and kidney pie – pricey, but generously served and well worth it; comfortable bedrooms *(Cdr Patrick Tailyour)*

☆ **Upper Brailes**, War [SP3039], *Gate*: Attractive village pub with genuine old-world atmosphere, pleasantly free from pretentious over-decoration; good bar food inc wide range of sandwiches, good service, genial landlord, log fires, low beams, extensive gardens *(Sir Nigel Foulkes, D H Carr)*

Wakerley, Northants [SP9599], *Exeter Arms*: Pleasantly set out tables in bar, side room beyond fireplace with games and juke box; wider range of good well cooked food under new licensees, with well kept Batemans, Flowers, Youngers IPA and Youngs Special on handpump *(M and J Back)*

Walsall, W Mid [John St; SP0198], *Pretty Bricks*: Back-street pub, alias the New Inn, with well kept Ansells Mild and Best and Ind Coope Burton, good value bar food lunchtime and evening (not Sun) inc bargain Sun lunch; unobtrusive piped music *(Paul Noble)*

☆ **Warley**, W Mid [Church St, Oldbury; SO9987], *Waggon & Horses*: Authentically refurbished free house with superb Edwardian tiled bar, good range of well kept real ales inc Bathams on handpump; good bar food from sandwiches through omelettes, home-made pies and curries to steaks lunchtime and evening, inc weekends, friendly staff *(David and Eloise Smaylen, SP)*

Warmington, War [A41 towards Shotteswell], *Wobbly Wheel*: Warm welcome, attractive lounge and bar, enterprising food, real ales, pleasant situation *(M J Morgan, M S Hancock)*

☆ **Warwick** [11 Church St], *Zetland Arms*: Good value simple food, well kept Davenports on handpump, lively conversation around the bar but quieter areas too; delightful and well kept sheltered back garden *(Roger Taylor, Geoff Lee, LYM)*

☆ **Warwick** [St Nicholas Church St], *Barn*: Good bar food in converted barn with beams, exposed brickwork and flagstones, sewing-machine trestle tables with candles and fresh flowers, stripped wood chairs, tractor-seat bar stools, old farm tools, open fire; tables in courtyard with well; it does have a restaurant too, and the pub part has rather a restauranty feel Thurs–Sat evenings when most people seem to be eating *(Rob and Gill Weeks)*

Warwick [Birmingham Rd; A41, opp Sainsburys nr racecourse], *Black Horse*: Neatly kept lounge and public bar in welcoming pub with plentiful good food, well kept beers; bedrooms reasonably cheap, with decent breakfasts *(Patrick and Mary McDermott, Brian Jones, BB)*; [West St; between Lord Leycester Hospital and racecourse, towards Stratford] *Wheatsheaf*: Welcoming town pub with well kept Ansells, Ind Coope and Tetleys; bar food *(Dave Braisted)*

☆ **Weedon**, Northants [Stowe Hill; A5, S; SP6259], *Narrow Boat*: Spacious terrace and big garden with pheasants and peacocks sweeping down to Grand Union Canal, good canal photographs in main bar, high-raftered ex-kitchen family-room, home-made bar food, summer barbecues, Cantonese specialities in restaurant (Mon–Sat, traditional Sun lunch); well kept Charles Wells real ales; very busy in summer *(D C Horwood, Neil and Angela Huxter, LYM)*

Weedon [Watling St; junction A5/A45], *Globe*: Pleasant old pub in centre of village, good choice of beers, good lunchtime and evening bar food, occasional live music; bedrooms *(Mike and Sue Wheeler)*; [High St] *Wheatsheaf*: Friendly, welcoming, pleasantly fussy little pub jam-packed with brasses, substantial lunchtime baps *(Dr and Mrs A K Clarke)*

Welford, Northants [SP6480], *Shoulder of Mutton*: Friendly pub with well kept Watneys-related real ales on handpump, good bar food; about half a mile from canal *(Gordon Theaker)*

☆ **Welford-on-Avon**, War [Maypole; SP1452], *Shakespeare*: Very popular for food, with considerable concentration on this, and good range of wines; stunning displays of bedding plants and hanging baskets in summer *(J M Reading, S V Bishop)*

Wellesbourne, War [SP2755], *Kings Head*: Formerly a pub of considerable character, now rejigged and extended as Whitbreads Brewers Fayre operation with Laura Ashley-style décor, lots of iron embellishments, removal of internal walls (but retention of oak beams and big fireplaces), and neat rows of tables set for the well presented standard menu at competitive prices, with an inexpensive but limited wine list – worth knowing for what it is, but scarcely a real pub now; bedrooms *(LYM)*

West Bromwich, W Mid [High St (A41); SP0091], *Old Hop Pole*: Cosy Holt, Plant & Deakins pub with lots of old knick-knacks, roaring fire in black-leaded grate, their real ales kept well, superb doorstep sandwiches – especially the local speciality, hot pork *(E J Alcock)*; [High St, opp bus stn] *Sandwell*: Edwardian hotel with spacious bar inc no-smoking area by food counter; deep pink furnishings, cheerful efficient service, Springfield on handpump, good value waitress-served food; bedrooms *(Frank Cummins)*

West Haddon, Northants [about 3 miles from M1 junction 18; A428 towards Northampton; SP6272], *Wheatsheaf*: Very comfortable with snug and tasteful upstairs lounge, good bar meals and wide choice of courteously presented good food and wines in big candle-lit dining-room; pool-table in small cosy downstairs bar *(H W and A B Tuffill)*

Weston, Northants [SP5846], *Crown*: Good food and range of ales in warmly welcoming old pub with highwayman connections; handy for NT Canons Ashby *(David Gittins)*

Whilton, Northants [SP6365], *Locks*: Large, modern and comfortable, popular at lunchtime with local office people for its good range of bar food; back terrace with picnic-table sets, nr four locks of the Grand Union Canal (not touristy or picturesque here) *(Michael and Alison Sandy)*

Wilby, Northants [A45; SP8666], *George*: Comfortable Turkey-carpeted and partly panelled lounge with spacious beamed dining area, locally popular for food (not Tues evening or Sun); small front bar, basic public bar, Watneys-related real ales on handpump, big garden with seats looking on to farmland *(Michael and Alison Sandy)*

☆ **Willey**, War [just off A5, N of A427 junction; SP4984], *Sarah Mansfield*: Well run village pub, clean and comfortable, with polished stone floor, stone and plaster walls, open fire, copperware and horsebrasses and harness; well kept Banks's Bitter and Mild on handpump, good generously served bar food, piped music, fruit machine, darts; formerly the Plough; reports early summer 1989 that licensees might be moving on – more news please *(A E Alcock, Ted George)*

Wilmcote, War [Aston Cantlow Rd; SP1657], *Masons Arms*: Friendly, neat and snug pub with well kept Flowers IPA and Original, wide choice of good value bar food *(Andrew Ludlow, T George)*

Wixford, War [B4085 Alcester–Bidford – OS Sheet 150 reference 085546; SP0954], *Fish*: Tastefully refurbished roomy L-shaped bar and snug, beams, polished panelling, carpets over flagstones, well kept Bass on handpump, reasonably priced bar food, pleasant, efficient service *(Frank Cummins)*

Wollaston, W Mid [from Stourbridge on A458, 400 yds past shops, on left at hill brow; SO8984], *Forresters Arms*: Good food in friendly pub with well kept real ale *(Mr and Mrs W H Crowther)*

Wolston, War [Main Rd; SP4175], *Half Moon*: Friendly, olde-worlde pub notable for good value food; deep leather sofas by open fire, good range of beers, good if loud juke box, restaurant *(Mr and Mrs N Beckett)*

Wolverhampton, W Mid [Sun St; SO9198], *Great Western*: Busy, friendly town-centre pub next to preserved railway stn with lots of GWR memorabilia, local transport history, tie collection; well kept Holdens Mild, Bitter, Special and the fearsome Winter XL, good

bar food inc sandwiches *(Ian Holden)*; [Park Lane, Park Village] *Paget Arms*: Medieval-style dining-lounge with heavy oak refectory tables, two other rooms, well kept Flowers Original and Marstons Pedigree with interesting guest beers, very good value food such as chicken with garlic and cider, pork satay or full Sun lunch, traditional games *(Miss G L Paget – no relation)*

Wolvey, War [handy for M65 junction 1; SP4287], *Axe & Compass*: Very popular for really good food – because of this little room for casual drinkers *(Ken and Barbara Turner)*; *Blue Pig*: Friendly olde-worlde pub with nice atmosphere and reasonably priced bar food inc good chargrills; does get busy weekends *(Mandy and Mike Challis)*

☆ **Woodford Halse**, Northants [SP5452], *Fleur de Lys*: Typical old-fashioned stone-built village local with fairly large bar, basic furnishings, bench seats, wooden stools and wood-panelled counter; lively, friendly atmosphere, welcoming, efficient bar staff, well kept Hook Norton Best and Marstons Pedigree on handpump; at his last pub the licensee won a reputation too for interesting good value food, but he's not been here for long enough for us to hear about this aspect yet; children's room *(Mike O'Driscoll)*

Wootton Wawen, War [N side of village; SP1563], *Bulls Head*: Eighteenth-century or older black and white pub with massive timber uprights in low-ceilinged and heavily beamed L-shaped lounge, good bar food (there may be a wait), friendly staff, popular restaurant; keg beers *(S J A Velate, Geoff Lee)*

Yardley Gobion, Northants [30 High St; SP7644], *Coffee Pot*: Comfortable, friendly atmosphere with good value food counter *(H Rust)*

Yarwell, Northants [TL0697], *Angel*: Old village pub, lots of atmosphere in small cosy bar, friendly and welcoming licensees; well kept Batemans and Home Bitter, good bar food, friendly guinea-pig in garden with play area; children's room *(Andrew Taylor)*

Norfolk

In the last very few years we've added a number of new entries here, reflecting the current upsurge of individuality in the county's pubs. This year's crop includes the carefully demodernised Hare & Hounds at Baconsthorpe (interesting food), the waterside Ferry at Reedham Ferry with its good food and character back bar, the neatly kept and popular Gin Trap at Ringstead (again, good food), the very recently remodelled Manor Hotel near the bird reserve at Titchwell, the trend-setting Old Ram at Tivetshall St Mary (food all day, an interesting layout, a catholic approach to drinks including real fresh fruit juice), the stylishly simple Red Lion at Upper Sheringham (interesting food including special feasts, good malt whiskies), the Horseshoes at Warham with its little curio museum, and the busy Crown at Wells-next-the-Sea. Other main entries doing particularly well at the moment include the Kings Arms at Blakeney and Jolly Sailors at Brancaster Staithe (both serving food all day in the summer), the quaint Admiral Nelson at Burnham Thorpe (it's amazing all those TV films about Nelson ever got finished, once the crews discovered the potent Nelson's Blood made here), the Ostrich nicely placed at Castle Acre (good food), the Rose & Crown at Snettisham (very popular for food) and the atmospheric Lifeboat up at Thornham. Among the Lucky Dip entries at the end of the chapter there are a good few interesting prospects, including the Black Horse at Castle Rising, Spread Eagle at Erpingham, Berney Arms near Great Yarmouth (you can't get near it by road), Tudor Rose in Kings Lynn, White Horse at Neatishead, George at New Buckenham, Old Brewery House at Reepham, Hare Arms at Stow Bardolph, Green Man near Wroxham and, particularly, Darbys at Swanton Morley. It's not unexpected to find plenty of decent pubs in Norwich, but outsiders may be surprised at the rich choice in Wymondham.

BACONSTHORPE   TG1236 Map 8
Hare & Hounds

Hempstead Road; village signposted from A148 in Holt; OS Sheet 133 reference 115372 – ie, as we discovered to our cost on a first abortive inspection attempt, *not* the other Baconsthorpe down by Attleborough

Your initial reception here may be from Horace and Wilhelmina, a very vocal pair of white geese. Inside, the pub seems welcomingly and unchangingly old, but in fact has been carefully demodernised during the four years the landlord's been here. There's a casual mix of chairs and cushioned pews around plain deal or cast-iron-framed tables, rugs on old red flooring tiles, a big wood-burning stove in the broad low-beamed fireplace below a pendulum clock, several sets of Lawson Wood cartoons on the beige walls, dog-breed cigarette cards, pewter tankards hanging from one beam, and earthenware flagons on the deep sills of the small windows. Interestingly done bar food might include game pie, hot-pot, coq au vin, leek and bacon casserole and green bean and lentil pie (all £3.25), with ploughman's in variety at lunchtime (from £2); well kept Adnams and Old, Bass and Batemans on handpump, with a full-bodied and fragrantly fruity best bitter brewed for the pub by Woodfordes, and decent wines. There are some picnic-table sets on the side

If you see cars parked in the lane outside a country pub have left their lights on at night, leave yours on too: it's a sign that the police check up there.

grass, facing a new pond and rockery; also a children's play area. *(Recommended by Stuart Smith, David and Ruth Hollands)*

Free house   Licensee J M D Hobson   Real ale   Meals and snacks   Open 11.30ish–2.30, 6–11 all year

BLAKENEY   TG0243 Map 8
Kings Arms
West Gate Street

A large garden with lots of tables and chairs and a separate, equipped children's area has just been completed, two small rooms (one no-smoking) have been opened, and a new menu introduced. It's a lively place, and the licensees are both ex-theatricals – there are some interesting photographs of their careers on the walls (as well as framed reprints of old Schweppes advertisements). Three knocked-together rooms are simply furnished with a banquette facing the bar counter, and slat-backed seats around traditional cast-iron tables; the atmosphere is relaxed and friendly and the staff are helpful and efficient. Regulars tend to favour the red-tiled end room, where the flint walls have been exposed above low panelling. Tasty bar food includes very good fish, as well as sandwiches (from 90p, local crab in season £1.60), a wide choice of ploughman's (from £2.50, locally smoked ham £3.50), hot snacks (£2.95) and a daily special (£3.50), with evening dishes such as fresh cod (£3.60), gammon (£4.70), trout (£4.85) and steak (£7.10); also, puddings like fruit crumble or bread pudding (£1.75). Well kept Ruddles County and Websters Yorkshire on handpump, and freshly squeezed orange juice; darts, dominoes and fruit machine. There are picnic-table sets on the grass and gravel outside. It tends to get packed at busy times. *(Recommended by Mrs Russell Davis, Paul Sexton, Sue Harrison, L Walker, Wayne Brindle, Guy Sowerby, David and Ruth Hollands)*

Manns (Watneys)   Licensee Howard Davies   Meals and snacks (all day; 12–3, 6–9.30 in winter)   Children welcome   Open 11–11 all year

BLICKLING   TG1728 Map 8
Buckinghamshire Arms   🛏

This very popular (sometimes too much so), friendly and unpretentious place has a simply furnished little snug front bar with fabric cushioned banquettes, some brass tack above the open fire, and an antique seed-sowing machine in an alcove. The bigger lounge has neatly built-in pews, stripped deal tables, and landscapes and cockfighting prints. Bar food, though not cheap, is generously served: sandwiches (from £1.50, in French, brown or white bread; double-deckers from £2.50), home-made stockpot soup with croûtons (£1.75), ploughman's (£2.75), salads (from £3.50, roast rib of beef £4.50, smoked salmon £6.25), vegetarian hors d'oeuvre or home-made pâté (£3.30), and steak sandwich (£4.50), with specials like prawn risotto, steak and kidney pie or good curry. Well kept Adnams, Flowers, and Greene King IPA and Abbot on handpump; good service. Outside this civilised Jacobean inn, picnic-table sets shelter under cocktail parasols on the lawn (they serve food from an outbuilding here in summer), and there's a wide stretch of neatly raked gravel between the inn and a splendid Dutch-gabled stableblock; climbing-frame, slide and swing. Neighbouring National Trust Blickling Hall is open from April to mid-October only, and closed Mondays and Thursdays, though you can walk through the park at any time. *(Recommended by Joy Heatherley, Geoff Halson, Charles Bardswell, Jack Taylor, M A and W R Proctor, G and M Brooke-Williams, T Nott, Paul and Margaret Baker, Barbara Hatfield, Guy Sowerby, S V Bishop)*

Free house   Licensee Nigel Elliott   Real ale   Meals and snacks   Restaurant   Children in restaurant   Open 10.30–2.30, 6–11 all year; closed 25 Dec   Three double bedrooms tel Aylsham (0263) 732133; £43/£48

BRANCASTER STAITHE   TF7743 Map 8
Jolly Sailors ★

Popular with locals and visitors alike, this warmly friendly country pub has three bar rooms with some modern seats as well as a worn black oak settle, another with a roof and carved wings, and mainly stripped deal or mahogany tables on the red-tiled floor; the white-painted rough stone walls are hung with shorebird pictures and small but intricately detailed colour prints of Georgian naval uniforms, and there's a glass case with three stuffed albino birds. The log fire has one of those old-fashioned sturdy guards to sit on. The winter mussels, baked with garlic butter or white wine and cream, have the distinction of coming from the only natural harbour – just across the road – in England and Wales passed as pollution-free by a recent EEC survey. Other home-made bar food includes soup (from 80p), meat sandwich (£1.50), ploughman's (from £1.90), macaroni in a cream sauce with ham (£3.20), fresh plaice (£3.60), curry or chicken quarter in barbecue sauce (£3.80), popular lasagne or seafood pancake (£4.60), and six local oysters (£5.40); puddings (from £1) and children's dishes (£1.20). Service may be slow at peak times. Well kept Greene King Abbot and IPA on handpump, and an award-winning wine list; sensibly placed darts in one room; also shove-ha'penny, dominoes, table skittles and warri. There are seats by flowering shrubs on a sheltered lawn, or on a canopied side terrace, and there's a hard tennis court (which can be booked at the bar), and a children's play house and slides. The pub is on the edge of thousands of acres of National Trust dunes, salt-flats and Scolt Head Island nature reserve. *(Recommended by Geoff Halson, Joy Heatherley, Peter Griffiths, M A and W R Proctor, Charles Bardswell, James Cane, Michele and Andrew Wells, Guy Sowerby, S V Bishop)*

Free house   Licensee Alister Borthwick   Real ale   Meals and snacks (all day in summer; not 25 Dec)   Restaurant tel Brancaster (0485) 210314   Children in eating areas   Open 11–11; 11–3, 7–11 in winter; closed evening 25 Dec (no food that lunchtime)   Local bed and breakfast can be arranged

BRANDON CREEK   TL6091 Map 5
Ship

A10 Ely–Downham Market

The comfortable and spacious bar in this bow-windowed pink-washed pub has slat-back chairs and one or two upholstered settles, soft lighting, and an open fire at one end, with a wood-burning stove at the other – where steps drop down into a sunken area that was a working forge until not long ago (as the massive stone masonry and photographs on the walls show). The very long bar counter is decorated above with shepherds' crooks made from intricately plaited corn stalks. One menu serves both bar and restaurant and food can be eaten in either area (which means it isn't just restaurant diners who enjoy the river view). At lunchtime, food includes sandwiches (from £1.10), filled baked potatoes (from £1.65), ploughman's (from £2.20), poacher's pie (£3.30) and a roast of the day (£4.40); there are evening extras. Ruddles Best and County, and Websters Yorkshire on handpump. Besides shove-ha'penny, they have books on general knowledge, quizzes, short stories and so forth, and a winter quiz league. Outside, there are tables by the pub's own moorings at the junction of the creek with the high-banked Great Ouse. *(Recommended by Wayne Brindle, B R Shiner, R P Hastings)*

Manns (Watneys)   Real ale   Meals and lunchtime snacks   Restaurant tel Brandon Creek (035 376) 228   Children in eating area of bar until 8.30   Occasional Sun evening entertainment in summer   Open 10.30–4, 5–11 all year; closed after 2.30 Sun in winter

By law pubs must show a price list of their drinks. Let us know if you are inconvenienced by any breach of this law.

BURNHAM THORPE   TF8541 Map 8
Admiral Nelson

Village signposted from B1155 and B1355, near Burnham Market

There are some sixty pictures on show connected with Nelson in this unspoilt little pub, though this is just part of the knowledgeable licensee's fine collection of over two hundred items. These line the entrance corridor as well as the bar itself – a small room with well waxed antique settles on the worn red flooring tiles, a sheathed cutlass on one beam, and a cabinet of miniature bottles. Well kept Greene King IPA and Abbot are tapped from the cask in a back still-room, and the landlord makes a delicious potent rum-based concoction called Nelson's Blood; the glasses are simply stacked by the spotless sink, separated off from the rest of the room by two high settle-backs, below a window overlooking a lawn swarming with cats. It's well positioned by the village green. You are asked not to smoke. *(Recommended by Charles Bardswell, James Cane, M A and W R Proctor, Roger Huggins, C Elliott, Jonathan Williams)*

Greene King   Licensee Les Winter   Real ale   No food   Open 11.30–3, 7–11 all year

CASTLE ACRE   TF8115 Map 8
Ostrich 🍺

Stocks Green; village signposted from A1065 N of Swaffham; OS Sheet 144 reference 815153

There's a bustling, friendly atmosphere in this largely eighteenth-century ex-coaching-inn. The L-shaped front bar has a low ceiling, big photographs of the local sites on hessian walls, a huge old fireplace with a swinging pot-yard below its low mantelbeam (which may be used in winter for cooking soups and hams), and straightforward furnishings. The back room has a very high pitched ceiling with exposed oak beams and trusses, an end wall with exposed sixteenth-century masonry, a good log fire, and a strong local atmosphere. Good value, tasty bar food includes sandwiches (from 70p, a lovely crab and smoked salmon double-decker £2.45), various basket meals (from £1.25), pizzas (from £1.40), a wide range of ploughman's (from £1.70), omelettes (from £2), salads (from £3), rainbow trout (£4), inventive and eclectic daily specials such as braised duck in paprika and pineapple or squid and prawn salad (£3.50), and several vegetarian dishes, often outstanding (from £2.50). Well kept Greene King IPA, Abbot and XX Mild on handpump; fruit machine, piped music, and picnic-table sets in the sheltered garden, where you can play boules. The pub is on the tree-lined green near the ruins of a Norman castle, and there's a Cluniac monastery in the village. *(Recommended by Geoff Halson, Dave Braisted, Joy Heatherley, J D Maplethorpe, Graham and Glenis Watkins, L Walker, Mark Sheard, R P Hastings, Guy Sowerby, David and Ruth Hollands)*

Greene King   Licensee Ray Wakelen   Real ale   Meals and snacks (12–2, 7–10.30; not 25 Dec)   Children in decent adjacent family-room   Jazz every other Tues, folk/blues last Weds in month   Open 11–3, 6–11 all year; closed evening 25 Dec   Bedrooms (single only) tel Castle Acre (076 05) 398; £12

HUNWORTH   TG0635 Map 8
Bluebell

Village signposted off B roads S of Holt

Some of the comfortable settees in the cosy L-shaped bar here are grouped around the log fire, there are Windsor chairs around dark wooden tables, and Norfolk watercolours and pictures for sale hanging above the paneiling dado. Generous helpings of fresh bar food include sandwiches (from 90p), ploughman's (from £2), salads (from £2.50, local crab £3.50), plaice (£3), home-made steak and kidney pie or home-cooked ham (£3.25), gammon and pineapple (£4.25), sirloin steak (£6.50) and a daily special. Real ales include particularly well kept Woodfordes Wherry, as well as Adnams, Bass and Greene King Abbot; darts, fruit machine. In good weather there's bar service to the tables under cocktail parasols on the back lawn, where there are fruit trees – heavily laden in summer. *(Recommended by Charles Bardswell, Paul Sexton, Sue Harrison, R P Hastings, Brian and Anna Marsden)*

Free house   Licensee T P King   Real ale   Meals and snacks   Children in eating area of bar   Open 11–3, 6–11 all year

LETHERINGSETT   TG0538 Map 8
King's Head
A148 just W of Holt

This looks more like a small country house than a pub; it's set back from the road at the end of a short drive and surrounded by a spacious lawn with lots of picnic-table sets; park and paddock slope up beyond a post-and-rails fence. Inside, the main bar is decorated with lots of Battle of Britain pictures especially involving East Anglia, picturesque advertisements, a signposted John Betjeman poem, a panoramic view of Edward VII's first opening of Parliament, and jokey French pictures of naughty dogs. There's also a small plush lounge, and a separate games-room with darts, pool, dominoes, cribbage, pinball and fruit machines. Reasonably priced bar food includes sandwiches (from 90p, crab £1.50, evening toasties £1.50), soup (£1), home-made pasty (£1.50), burgers (from £2.25), home-cooked ham or steak and kidney pie (£3.50), salads (from £2.95, local crab £3.50), a huge and tasty pork chop, steaks (from £6.50, evening only), a daily special, and vegetarian dishes. Adnams, Bass and Greene King IPA and Abbot on handpump, and several wines. The church over the road has an unusual round tower. Two decorative cats, no dogs. *(Recommended by R C Vincent, Geoff Halson, Charles Bardswell, David and Ruth Hollands, Charles Turner, Guy Sowerby, R P Hastings, S V Bishop)*

Free house   Licensee Thomas King   Real ale   Meals and snacks   Restaurant tel Holt (0263) 712691   Children in eating area of bar   Country and western Mon   Open 11–3, 6–11 all year

NORWICH   TG2308 Map 8
Adam & Eve
Bishopgate; follow Palace Street from Tombland N of cathedral

Though the gables here are fourteenth and fifteenth century, the downstairs bar is some seven hundred years old, serving then as a refreshment house for the cathedral builders. The bars are cosy and traditionally furnished: old-fashioned high-backed settles, one handsomely carved, cushioned benches built into partly panelled walls, and tiled or parquet floors. The ghost of Lord Sheffield who was killed during Kett's Rebellion in 1549 is said to wander around. Generous helpings of good home-made bar food include sandwiches (from £1, excellent prawn), filled French bread (from £1), ploughman's (from £1.85), shepherd's pie (£2.55), vegetable bake (£2.40), salads (from £2.30), chicken curry (£2.65), casserole of pork in cider and rosemary (£2.85), tasty garlic prawns, fish pie (£2.95) and scampi (£3.10); puddings like home-made bread-and-butter pudding (95p), and daily specials. Ruddles Best and County, and Websters Yorkshire on handpump from a serving-counter with a fine range of pewter tankards, and around 34 different wines; efficient, friendly service. There are seats on the pretty quiet terrace, hung with clematis and baskets of flowers. *(Recommended by D I Baddeley, Paul Sexton, Sue Harrison, Geoff Lee, Tim Baxter, Gwen and Peter Andrews, G C Hixon, Ian Phillips, Colonel and Mrs L N Smyth, G and M Brooke-Williams, David and Ruth Hollands)*

Manns (Watneys)   Licensee Colin Burgess   Real ale   Lunchtime meals and snacks   Children in eating area of bar   Open 11 (10.30 Sat)–11 all year

REEDHAM   TG4101 Map 5

Ferry 🏮

B1140 Beccles–Acle; the ferry here holds only two cars but goes back and forth continuously until 10pm, taking only a minute or so to cross – fare £1.40, passengers or pedestrians 10p

Across the quiet lane, solid tables spaced well apart on the neatly kept grass look out over the River Yare – swans, Broads boats and the chain ferry itself. Inside, the long front bar fits well into that holiday scene, with comfortable banquettes lining the big picture windows, robust rustic tables carved from slabs of tree-trunk, and games and fruit machines. The back bar, secluded and relaxing, has a good deal of traditional character, antique rifles, copper and brass, and a fine log fire. The menu's not long, but the food is good and served generously: dishes winning approval recently have included the ploughman's, taramosalata with pitta bread, mushrooms au gratin with garlic bread, a homely fry-up (they make their own sausages), curries (from £2.95), pies such as chicken and mushroom (£3.35) or game (£3.65), beef in red wine (£3.55) and sirloin steak (£7.95); children's dishes, even arrangements for baby food (and changing facilities in the ladies lavatory). Well kept Adnams Bitter and Woodfordes Wherry on handpump, several whiskies, and country wines; good cheerful service, piped music. The moorings are good, and the fee is refundable against what you buy in the pub. The woodturner's shop next door is interesting. *(Recommended by R Aitken, Mr and Mrs J D Cramston, Q Williamson, G A Farmer, J E Rycroft, CDC)*

Free house   Licensee David Archer   Real ale   Meals and snacks   Children in front room Open 11–3, 6.30–11; opens 7 in winter; closed evening 25 Dec

RINGSTEAD   TF7040 Map 8

Gin Trap

Village signposted off A149 near Hunstanton; OS Sheet 132 reference 707403

A couple of man-traps hang above the main door of this attractive white-painted pub, and there's a handsome horse-chestnut tree in the middle of the car park. Inside, it's very neatly kept with lots more traps (some converted to electric candle-effect wall lights), copper kettles, carpenters' tools, cartwheels, and bottles hanging from the beams in the lower part of the bar, built-in window seats and captain's chairs with brocaded cushions and cast-iron-framed tables on the green and white patterned carpet, lots of toasting-forks above an open fire (which has dried flowers in summer), and a chatty, relaxed atmosphere; the tortoiseshell cat is called Whisky. The small dining-room has lots of chamber-pots hanging from the ceiling, and high-backed pine settles. Well kept Adnams Bitter, Charrington IPA, Greene King Abbot, Woodfordes Baldric and another beer brewed by Woodfordes for the pub on handpump; friendly, efficient staff. Good home-made bar food includes sandwiches (from £1.25), mushroom soup (£1.35), ploughman's (from £2.50), Norfolk pie (£3), lasagne or steak and kidney pie (£3.75), good home-cooked ham (£4.10), crab salad (£4.50), gammon with pineapple or egg (£5), pan-fried plaice (£5.75), steaks (from £6.35), and specials such as quiches (around £3), stuffed plaice (£5), or rump steak with scampi and chilli sauce (£6.50); on Fridays they do fresh fish dishes (from £3.50). There are free prawn croûtons, cheese, or cockles on the bar counter on Sundays. The walled back garden has picnic-table sets on the grass and a small paved area, and there are tubs of flowers. The pub is close to the Peddar's Way and welcomes hikers and walkers (but not their muddy boots). There's an art gallery next door. *(Recommended by David and Ruth Hollands, JMC, James Cane, Frank Cummins, Patrick Stapley)*

Free house   Licensees Brian and Margaret Harmes   Real ale   Meals and snacks (12–2, 7–9.30; 10 Fri and Sat; not Sun evenings in winter)   Well behaved children in upper part of bar   Open 11.30–2.30, 7–11 all year, though they will open earlier in evening if there are customers

SCOLE   TM1576 Map 5

Scole Inn ★ 🏠

One of only a handful of pubs or inns to have a Grade I preservation listing, this
stately seventeenth-century building – with its magnificently rounded Dutch gables
– was built for a rich Norwich merchant. It's a friendly place with a new licensee
this year, and the high-beamed lounge bar has a seventeenth-century iron-studded
oak door, a handsomely carved oak mantelbeam, antique settles, leather-cushioned
seats and benches around oak refectory tables on its Turkey carpets, and a big
fireplace with a coat of arms iron fireback. In the bare-boarded public bar there's
another good open fire, and stripped high-backed settles and kitchen chairs around
oak tables. Waitress-served bar food – popular with businessmen at lunchtime –
includes home-made soup (£1.05), sandwiches (from £1.25, crab £2.15), good
ploughman's (from £1.95), home-made pâtés – smoked mackerel or Stilton, celery
and port (£2.15) – chicken livers in herb butter (£3.15), salads (from £3.85, crab
£4.85), and charcoal-grilled steaks (from £7.85), with daily hot specials such as
grilled sardines in herb butter (£3.15) or steak and kidney pie (£3.95). Well kept
Adnams Bitter and Broadside, and Greene King Abbot on handpump; fruit
machine, piped music. The gate half-way up the great oak staircase was to stop
people riding their horses up and down (as John Belcher the highwayman is said to
have done). *(Recommended by E J Waller, Richard Fawcett, Geoff Halson, Rona Murdoch,
Paul Sexton, Sue Harrison, Michele and Andrew Wells, Barbara Hatfield, Brian and Anna
Marsden, Gavin May)*

*Free house   Licensee Ivor Wright   Real ale   Meals and snacks (12–2.30, 6–10)
Restaurant   Children welcome   Open 11–11 all year   Bedrooms tel Diss (0379) 740481;
£40B/£55B*

SNETTISHAM   TF6834 Map 8

Rose & Crown 🏴

Old Church Road; just off A149 in centre

This pretty white cottage has four popular bars. The cosy locals' bar at the back has
perhaps the nicest atmosphere, with tapestried seats around cast-iron-framed
tables, and a big log fire. At the front there's an old-fashioned beamed bar with lots
of carpentry and farm tools, cushioned black settles on the red-tiled floor, and a
great pile of logs by the fire in the vast fireplace (which has a gleaming black
japanned side oven). An airy carpeted room beside this has green plush seats around
tables with lacy tablecloths, and pictures for sale on the walls. Right at the back, an
extensive modern summer bar has a clean Scandinavian look, with bentwood chairs
and tractor seats with its tiled floor, bare brick walls, and narrow-planked ceilings.
Very good, quickly served bar food includes soup (£1.20), ploughman's (£2.40),
open baps (with home-cooked honey-roast ham £2.75, excellent rare topside of
beef £2.95 or large, juicy steak £3.25), gammon with pineapple or eggs or pork
chop (£5.25), salads (from £5.95), steaks (from £6.25), and cold seafood (£7.50);
there's a daily special, puddings like home-made apple pie (£1.50), children's dishes
(£1.40) and a barbecue menu (from £4.25, children from £1.40). Bass (called Rose
& Crown here), Adnams Bitter and Broadside, Greene King IPA and Abbot and
Woodfordes Wherry on handpump, with freshly squeezed orange juice (80p);
friendly service, even when pushed; an old-fashioned penny slot game. There are
picnic-table sets on a neat sheltered lawn and terrace. No dogs. *(Recommended by
Peter Corris, Peter Griffiths, L Walker, R J Haerdi, Angie and Dave Parkes, R P Hastings)*

*Free house   Licensee Margaret Trafford   Real ale   Meals and snacks (12–2, 6.30–10; not
Sun evenings in winter)   Restaurant (not Sun evening) tel Dersingham (0485) 41382
Children welcome   Open 11–3, 5.30–11 all year; closed 25 Dec*

We say if we know a pub has piped music.

THORNHAM TF7343 Map 8

Lifeboat ★ 🏵

Turn off A149 by Kings Head, then take first left turn

Though relatively isolated on the edge of coastal flats, this atmospheric old pub can get very busy, even out of season. There are no fewer than five fires in the small cosy rooms, and furnishings include romantic antique lamps hanging from the great oak beams (which are still lit), low settles, window seats, pews, carved oak tables, panelling, and rugs on the tiled floor; also, shelves of china, masses of guns, swords, black metal mattocks, reed-slashers and other antique farm tools. The atmosphere is chatty and relaxed. A simple conservatory (which is very popular with families) has benches and tables, an old-fashioned stove, a flourishing vine, and a hatch for ordering the popular, home-made food. This includes soup (£1.50), sandwiches (from £1.20), various ploughman's (£2.75), home-made brawn with pickled onions and gherkins (£1.95), potted shrimps (£2.75), salads with home-made mayonnaise (from £3.50, fresh crab £4.95, smoked chicken and prawns £5.35), lamb stew or mussels (£3.95), good smoked haddock in a cream and fresh herb sauce topped with puff pastry (£4.50), game pie (£4.95), sirloin steak (£7.95), and home-made puddings like ginger sponge (£1.35); children's dishes (from £1.50). The quaint and pretty little restaurant does a good value set menu with some choice (£13.95 including a glass of wine); booking recommended. Well kept Adnams, Greene King IPA and Abbot, and guest beers such as Badger Tanglefoot, Tetleys and Woodfordes Wherry on handpump, with a wide range of wines; efficient, helpful staff. Shove-ha'penny, dominoes and an antique penny-in-the-hole bench. Up some steps from the conservatory is a terrace with picnic-table sets, a climbing-frame and a slide. The pub is near *Good Walks Guide* Walk 116. Large car park.

(Recommended by WHBM, Peter Griffiths, Derek and Sylvia Stephenson, David and Ruth Hollands, M A and W R Proctor, James Cane, M J Morgan, Wayne Brindle, Angie and Dave Parkes, Michele and Andrew Wells, A T Langton, Frank Cummins, Deirdre Woodcock, R P Hastings, S V Bishop)

Free house Licensees Nicholas and Lynn Handley Real ale Meals and snacks (12–2, 7–10) Restaurant; not Sun lunch Children welcome Occasional folk singer Open 11–3, 5.30–11 all year Bedrooms tel Thornham (048 526) 236; £20/£30

TITCHWELL TF7543 Map 8

Manor Hotel 🛏

A149 E of Hunstanton

Looking over the coastal flats to the seaside salt-flats, this newly refurbished hotel is a draw for many people visiting the wildlife in the RSPB reserve there – particularly of course the birds – and the hotel keeps a good naturalists' record. Right over on the right, there's a room rather like a farmhouse kitchen with pine furniture, a Welsh dresser with unusual mustards and pickles on it, and a collection of baskets and bric-à-brac; children are allowed in here. In the main part of the building, a small bar has pretty patterned beige wallpaper, blue plush wall banquettes, small round tables, and Impressionist prints; beyond that, what had been the hotel bar and dining-room has very recently turned back into a restaurant, with soft pale mushroom, cream and pink furnishings, attractive flower and plant prints, and heavily swagged and pelmeted flowery curtains framing tall windows. French windows open from here on to a sizeable and sheltered neatly kept lawn with sturdy white garden seats. Bar food, served in the pine room, includes home-made soup (£1.35), sandwiches (£1.50, weekday lunchtimes), ploughman's (£2.50), quarter chicken, scampi or home-made steak and kidney pie (£3.95) and plaice (£4.60), with daily specials such as local trout or lambs' sweetbreads (£4); Greene King IPA and Abbot on handpump, piped music. *(Recommended by Dr and Mrs M Rayner, A T Langton)*

Free house   Licensees Mr and Mrs Snaith   Real ale   Meals and snacks   Children welcome   Open 12–2, 6.30–11 all year; closed 25 Dec   Bedrooms tel Brancaster (0485) 210221; £35.50B/£62B

TIVETSHALL ST MARY   TM1686 Map 5

Old Ram

A140 15 miles S of Norwich

This big well run main-road pub has been carefully refurbished to give several separate areas, all with a good deal of individuality and character, by John and Margaret Trafford who made such a success out of doing something broadly similar at the Rose & Crown, Snettisham. If anything, they've taken things further here – making for a good cheerful feeling of enjoyment. The spacious main room has brick floors, stripped beams and standing-timber dividers, a huge log fire in the brick hearth, a longcase clock, and lots of Lawson Wood 1920s humorous prints; it's ringed by cosier side areas, some carpeted, and other rooms ramble off. An attractive room with pews, an open wood-burning stove and big sentimental engravings leads through to an intimate dining room, with steps up to a gallery set out with pictures for sale, and sofas for idle contemplation. The emphasis is very much on food, with some tables (candle-lit at night) reserved. It includes filled rolls (from £1.25), burgers (from £2.50), ploughman's (£2.75), omelettes (from £3.25), aubergine and mushroom bake or lasagne (£3.50), steak and kidney pie (from £3.50), salads (from £3.95), twelve-ounce cod fillet or chicken curry (£4.25), gammon and pineapple (£4.95), rack of pork ribs (£5.50), steaks (from £7.50), and rumbustious puddings (£1.75); well kept Adnams, Greene King Abbot, Ruddles County, Websters Yorkshire and a guest beer such as Tolly Old, decent house wines, several malt whiskies, good coffee, freshly squeezed orange juice; unobtrusive fruit machine, jaunty piped music. There are seats on the sheltered terrace and lawn behind. It can get very busy at weekends. *(Recommended by Paul Cort-Wright, Dr R Fuller, R G Tennant, Mr and Mrs J E Rycroft)*

Free house   Licensees John and Margaret Trafford   Real ale   Meals and snacks (noon–10)   Children welcome   Open 9am–11pm all year

UPPER SHERINGHAM   TG1441 Map 8

Red Lion 🏮

B1147; village signposted off A148 Cromer–Holt

This part of Norfolk seems to be beginning to specialise in small pubs which initially strike you as very basic in an old-fashioned traditional way, but which prove to be considerably more sophisticated in style – particularly over food and drink. The two small bars of this flint village inn are indeed furnished very simply: stripped high-backed settles and country-kitchen chairs, a big wood-burning stove, plain off-white walls and ceiling, red tiles or bare boards on the floor. But a rack of newspapers includes the *Financial Times*, there are little bunches of country flowers, and on our visit food included a seafood bisque (£1.25), croûte à la grecque (£2.25), sauté of brains (£2.75), and moules marinière or salmon and cucumber vol-au-vent (£3.50), besides things like Scotch pie (£1), soup (£1.20), deep-fried mushrooms (£2.50), country pie (£3.25) and rabbit casserole (£3.50). They do a three-course meal every Wednesday evening (£5), a winter feast night every second Tuesday with roast duck, pheasant, Norfolk turkey or fresh fish (three courses around £6.50), Scottish steaks and fresh salmon on Friday or Saturday evenings (from £4.95), a home-baked glazed ham on Saturday lunchtime, and a traditional Sunday roast lunch (both around £3.95). They keep quite the best range of malt whiskies we've come across in this area (around 120), including a good few rarities;

also well kept Adnams Bitter and Broadside and a guest like Marstons Pedigree on handpump, and decent wines; cribbage, dominoes. There's an albino cockatiel in one room, and the atmosphere's good. Dogs welcome. *(Recommended by Heather Sharland, WHBM, J Bord, R P Hastings)*

Free house   Licensee Ian Bryson   Real ale   Meals and snacks   Children welcome   Open 11–2.30, 6–11 all year; opens 7 in winter   Bedrooms tel Sheringham (0263) 825408; £15/£30

WARHAM   TF9441 Map 8

Horseshoes

Warham All Saints; village signposted from A149 Wells-next-the-Sea–Blakeney, and from B1105 S of Wells

Gas lighting (with an electric lamp for the darts), an antique American Mills one-arm bandit still in working order, the big longcase clock with its clear piping strike, a small but cheerful log fire, the pianola pumping out old favourites on Saturday night, and prices that are pleasantly old-fashioned for North Norfolk – under its matter-of-fact new owner this plain two-room village pub is determinedly unspoilt. Furnishings are basic, lavatories outside, but there are decent house wines as well as the well kept Greene King IPA on handpump and Abbot and Woodfordes Wherry tapped from the cask (also, tea or coffee). Bar food includes soup (90p), sandwiches (from £1), potted meat on toast (£1.40), filled baked potatoes (£1.50), shrimps or local cockles in a cream sauce (£2), ploughman's (£2.25), local rollmops (£2.80), local crab salad (£3.80), specials such as chanterelles on toast (£1.10) or chicken and mushroom casserole (£3), and puddings like home-made fruit pie (£1.10). A separate games-room has darts, pool, shove-ha'penny, cribbage, dominoes, fruit machine and juke box, and one of the outbuildings houses a wind-up gramophone museum – opened on request. There are rustic tables out on the side grass. They are buying the house next door and plan to have letting bedrooms there. *(Recommended by R E Tennant, RCL, B Parkins, Peter Griffiths)*

Free house   Licensee I P Salmon   Real ale   Meals and snacks (not Sun–Weds evenings) Children in eating area of bar and games-room   Open 11–3, 7–11 all year Bedrooms plans – see above

WELLS-NEXT-THE-SEA   TF9143 Map 8

Crown 🛏

The Buttlands

Facing the long tree-lined central square of quiet Georgian houses, this bustling and well kept inn has a thriving local atmosphere – especially in the front part of the bar. The two rooms at the back are often quieter (that's where the black cat snoozes in front of the roaring log fire), and have some worthwhile pictures – including several big Nelson prints, maps showing the town in the eighteenth and nineteenth centuries, and local photographs a good deal more interesting than those decorating most pubs. Good value bar food served efficiently by neat waitresses includes sandwiches (from 95p), soup (£1.25), ploughman's (£2.50), ham and egg (£2.95), three-egg omelettes or vegetarian tagliatelle (£2.85), steak and kidney pie (£3.25), salads (from £3.25, crab £3.50) and rump steak (£8.50), with children's dishes (£1.75). Adnams, Marstons Pedigree and Tetleys on handpump; log fire; darts, fruit machine, space game and piped music. A neat conservatory with small modern settles around the tables looks over the back garden. Though the majority of readers have found this a good value place at which to stay, we'd like more reports

---

Soup prices usually include a roll and butter.

on this, please. *(Recommended by Gordon Pitt, Dr R Fuller, Sandra Kempson, M J Morgan, John Townsend)*

Free house Licensee Wilfred Foyers Real ale Meals and snacks Restaurant Children in eating area of bar Open 11–2.30, 6–11 all year Bedrooms tel Fakenham (0328) 710209; £30(£35B)/£40(£45B)

WINTERTON-ON-SEA TG4919 Map 8
Fishermans Return 🏠

From B1159 turn into village at church on bend, then turn right into The Lane

Much older than most of the expanded holiday village, this pretty and very friendly brick inn has a panelled public bar with low ceilings and a glossily varnished nautical air. The white-painted lounge bar, also panelled, has neat brass-studded red leatherette seats, a good winter log fire, and a cosy, relaxed atmosphere. There's also a separate serving-counter in the back bar, which opens on to a terrace and good-sized sheltered garden; more seats face the quiet village lane. Bar food includes toasted sandwiches (from £1), taramosalata with pitta bread or ploughman's (£2.25), burgers (from £2.50), chilli con carne (£3), salads (from £3), scampi or omelette (£3.50), Dover sole (£7.50) and steaks (from £7.50), with daily specials, children's dishes (£1.50) and puddings (£1.25); excellent breakfasts. Well kept Ruddles Best and Websters Yorkshire on handpump, and guest wines by the glass or bottle; darts, dominoes and cribbage. *(Recommended by W R Porter, M A and W R Proctor, M B Batley, Simon Tubbs, Michael Lawrence, David and Ruth Hollands, R P Hastings)*

Manns (Watneys) Licensee John Findlay Real ale Meals and snacks (11.30–2, 6.30–9.30) Children in eating area of bar Open 11–3, 5–11; 11–2.30, 7–11 in winter; closed evening 25 Dec Bedrooms tel Winterton-on-Sea (049 376) 305; £18/£30

Lucky Dip

Besides the fully inspected pubs, you might like to try these Lucky Dips recommended to us and described by readers (if you do, please send us reports):

Acle [A1064; TG3910], *Bridge*: Pink-washed Chef & Brewer pub on banks of River Bure with moorings; circular restaurant, unusual thatched inn-sign *(Peter Corris)*

Aylmerton [A148; TG1840], *Roman Camp*: Worth knowing for cheap good food such as home-made steak and kidney pie and sirloin steak; keg beers *(Anon)*

Banham [The Street; TM0687], *Red Lion*: Friendly atmosphere, good, reasonably priced food, juke box *(Miss J M Smith)*

Barford [TG1107], *Cock*: Good value well prepared bar food and Watneys-related real ales in straightforward pub with old drovers' quarters converted into restaurant *(IP)*

Bawburgh [TG1508], *Kings Head*: Pleasant smart lounge, beautiful attic room, real fire, good value food including vegetarian dishes; separate public bar can be noisy, with music and machines *(Lyn Jolliffe, Ian Phillips)*

Binham [TF9839], *Chequers*: Small, unspoilt village pub nr Binham Priory, with friendly atmosphere; well kept Batemans, Mitchells and Woodfordes on handpump, small but enterprising bar menu *(R P Hastings)*

Blakeney [The Quay; TG0243], *Blakeney Hotel*: Elegant economical variety of lunchtime bar food served in restaurant – good food, first-class service, delightful views over quay; bedrooms *(Kenneth Finch)*; *White Horse*: Good spot close to harbour; friendly little hotel bar with old advertisements, ships' crests and prints, Watneys-related real ales, bar food, restaurant; bedrooms; lease for sale 1989 *(Paul Sexton, Sue Harrison, S V Bishop)*

Bodham Street [TG1240], *Red Hart*: Real village pub with two small bars, Watneys-related real ales on handpump, bar food *(R P Hastings)*

Brancaster Staithe [TF7743], *White Horse*: Marvellous view across harbour and coastline to Scolt Head island from separate dining-room; Watneys-related real ales on handpump, long wine list, limited lunchtime menu but well cooked and generously served, more extensive evening bar food *(M and J Back)*

Brisley [TF9521], *Bell*: Just like someone's front room with no bar, large central table, armchairs, open fire and beer brought from the back; no food *(Stephanie Pattenden, MM)*

Briston [B1354, Aylsham end of village; TG0532], *John H Stracey*: Genial licensee, good choice of beers including local Reepham Rapier, good food in bar and restaurant – very popular for this *(R C Vincent)*

Broome [TM3491], *Oaksmere*: Country house converted into pub, with popular beamed bar in oldest part, well kept Adnams, excellent restaurant; the pub's actually over the border in Suffolk *(John Baker)*

Brundall [Station Rd – OS Sheet 134 reference 328079; TG3208], *Yare*: Busy, popular pub near river; wattled hurdles on ceiling, navigation lamps, ships' curios, good photographs of boats; John Smiths, Sam Smiths and Woodfordes ales, good bar food inc crab salads; children's room *(R Aitken)*

Burnham Market [The Green (B1155); TF8342], *Capt Sir William Hoste*: Comfortable bow-windowed inn overlooking green, interesting old-fashioned touches in lounge though also things like gun ports over the bar, bar food from soup through steak and mushroom pie or help-yourself salads to steaks, well kept Watneys-related real ales, attentive service; naval pictures in black-panelled side room, restaurant; children allowed in family-room; bedrooms *(David and Ruth Hollands, R C Vincent, Patti McNaught, M A and W R Proctor, LYM)*; *Lord Nelson*: Locally very popular for food *(Charles Bardswell)*

Castle Acre [A1065 nearby, at Newton; TF8315], *George & Dragon*: Pleasant surroundings and atmosphere, well kept Watneys-related real ales, wide range of reasonably priced hot and cold bar food; children in small restaurant area and games-bar; small caravan site *(Richard Fawcett, Richard Palmer, R P Hastings)*

☆ **Castle Rising** [TF6624], *Black Horse*: Well furnished and well run bar with central serving area, alcoves for diners, comfortable seats, house plants, map of Scotland on one ceiling; well kept Adnams and Charringtons IPA on handpump, wide range of good bar food from sandwiches and a notable ploughman's to local trout, pasta, fresh salmon, daily specials such as local seafood, children's dishes, cheerful smiling service, unobtrusive pop music; restaurant and carvery; children welcome *(M J Morgan, Frank Cummins, Kenneth Finch, Charles Bardswell)*

Cawston [OS Sheet 133 reference 144225; TG1323], *Ratcatchers*: Pleasant and friendly with well kept Adnams and Woodfordes, new wide range of most enterprising, reasonably priced bar food including handful of daily specials, separate restaurant; no food Tues *(R P Hastings)*

☆ **Cockley Cley** [TF7904], *Twenty Churchwardens*: Small and cosy pub in lovely setting, delightfully welcoming, good value food, good choice of well kept beers including Adnams; handy for Oxburgh Hall (NT) *(Derek Pascall)*

☆ **Colkirk** [TF9126], *Crown*: Well furnished Greene King pub in pleasant village, good bar food, friendly landlord, well kept real ales, own bowling-green behind *(Mrs Margaret Dennis, R G Tennant)*

Coltishall [Church St (B1354); TG2719], *Red Lion*: Attractive modernised pub with reasonably priced bar food (maybe not weekends), good friendly service, well kept Whitbreads-related real ales, decent coffee; doesn't seem to get as crowded as the waterside pubs; tables under cocktail parasols outside; bedrooms *(J D Cranston)*; *Rising Sun*: Superb spot on pretty bend of River Bure; well presented food inc good value ploughman's, courteous staff, Watneys-related real ales, waterside and other outside tables, family-room *(Col and Mrs L N Smyth, LYM)*

Cromer [Front; TG2142], *Bath House*: Welcoming seafront pub, friendly staff, real ales, upstairs eating area with bar food from good sandwiches to steaks *(T R G Alcock, Margaret and Roy Randle)*; *Red Lion*: Interesting bar, good real ale and food that's good value for the area *(R P Hastings)*

☆ **Dersingham** [Manor Rd (B1440 out towards Sandringham); TF6830], *Feathers*: Solidly handsome dark sandstone seventeenth-century inn with relaxed and comfortably modernised dark-panelled bars opening on to neatly landscaped garden with play area; well kept Charrington and maybe Adnams on handpump, reasonably priced bar food, restaurant (not Sun evening); can get very busy in season; children welcome; bedrooms – on which we've had mixed reports this last year *(Peter Corris, Charles Bardswell, LYM)*

Dilham [TG3325], *Cross Keys*: Olde-worlde pub, friendly atmosphere, pleasant licensees; well kept Watneys-related real ales, good cheap bar food, lovely bowling-green and garden *(Mr and Mrs G Hawksworth)*

Diss [9 St Nicholas St; town centre, off B1077; TM1179], *Greyhound*: Some handsome Tudor features such as the high moulded beams in otherwise comfortably refurbished carpeted lounge, with big brick fireplace, well kept Watneys-related real ales, popular bar food, games in public bar; children in eating area *(Louise Findlay, LYM)*

East Barsham [B1105 3 miles N of Fakenham on Wells rd; TF9133], *White Horse*: Large open fireplace with log fire, good choice of well kept beers including Woodfordes, good range of attractive reasonably priced bar food such as local fish *(M J Morgan, Mark Sheard)*

East Runton [A149; TG1942], *Fishing Boat*: Interesting interior, good real ale, limited choice of well cooked fairly priced food *(RPH)*

Edgefield [TG0934], *Three Pigs*: Friendly old pub which has had good beer and home-cooked food at reasonable prices; up for sale summer 1989 *(R P Hastings)*

Elsing [TG0516], *Mermaid*: Good value well presented steaks, well kept Adnams and Woodfordes in comfortably refurbished pub *(Mark Sheard)*

☆ Erpingham [OS Sheet 133 reference 191319; TG1931], *Spread Eagle*: Included particularly for the fine Woodfordes beers which they brew here, and enthusiasts will find it well worth the pilgrimage (though otherwise it's not so special, apart from terraced garden facing bowling-green); children allowed in games-room *(Reg and Marjorie Williamson, WHBM)*

Fakenham [Market Pl; TF9229], *Crown*: Friendly unpretentious front bar in Elizabethan inn with dimly lit front snug, nice carved oak furniture, Greene King ales, food in bar and separate dining-room inc good steaks, friendly and polite service; interesting former coachyard-gallery outside staircase (now glassed in); bedrooms *(S V Bishop, R C Vincent, AE, LYM)*

Foulden [TL7698], *White Hart*: Pleasant local with good home-cooked food and decent beer at reasonable prices *(Paul F Milner)*

☆ Framingham Earl [B1332; TG2702], *Railway*: Well kept open-plan modern pub with character and relaxing atmosphere; well kept Watneys-related real ales, reasonably priced well served food (advisable to book at weekends) *(Dr R Fuller, T Nott)*

Fritton [Beccles Rd (A143); TG4600], *Fritton Decoy*: Excellent atmosphere, courteous and helpful licensee, good variety of reasonably priced bar food, seats in garden, juke box *(M J and P Watts)*

Gayton [TF7219], *Crown*: Elegant old pub with unusual features, friendly and well kept, with well kept Greene King ales, decent food and open fire; children's facilities *(LYM)*

Geldeston [TM3991], *Locks*: Several real ales, home-made wine, usually bar food, summer evening barbecues in remote old pub (with big extension for summer crowds) by River Waveney; closed winter weekdays *(LYM)*

☆ Great Cressingham [OS Sheet 144 reference 849016; TF8501], *Windmill*: Friendly and cosy, with several rooms opening off either side of main bar area; good value food, quick service, Adnams, Ruddles and Sam Smiths, lots of farm tools; conservatory for families, well kept big garden *(Mark Sheard)*

Great Ryburgh [TF9527], *Boar*: Friendly, comfortable atmosphere, good food, well kept Adnams and Tolly *(Mrs Margaret Dennis)*

☆ nr Great Yarmouth [Berney Arms Stn; 8-min train trip from Gt Yarmouth – out 11.10 (not Sun) or 12, return about 3.45 (earlier Sun; OS Sheet 134 reference 464049; TG5207], *Berney Arms*: Only safe mooring between Reedham and Gt Yarmouth on River Yare, and accessible only by water or

by rail Gt Yarmouth–Norwich; interesting building with flagstone floors, wood-burning stove, fishing-nets and lamps, settles made from barrel staves; well kept Adnams and Courage, decent straightforward bar food inc excellent sausages, cheerful service; closed winter; nearby windmill worth visiting *(R Aitken, R P Hastings)*

nr Great Yarmouth [St Olaves; A143 towards Beccles, where it crosses R Waveney – OS Sheet 134 reference 458994], *Bell*: Attractive Tudor herringbone brickwork and heavy oak timbering in comfortably modernised Broads pub, with good range of bar food, well kept Flowers and Wethereds on handpump, two open fires, games in public bar; barbecues and good children's play area in riverside garden, free moorings; children in restaurant *(R Aitken, LYM)*

Gressenhall [TF9515], *Swan*: Friendly service with limited choice of well cooked bar food, popular with locals; well kept Flowers Original, tables outside *(M and J Back)*

☆ Happisburgh [by village church; TG3830], *Hill House*: Very pleasant pub with friendly atmosphere, doing particularly well under owner who took it over a couple of years ago; well kept Adnams and Woodfordes Best on handpump, well presented reasonably priced tasty bar food from sandwiches up, good restaurant Sun lunch; children's room separate from pub, well equipped with toys; bedrooms *(Derek and Sylvia Stephenson, Maj B G Britton)*

☆ Hempstead [TG1037], *Hare & Hounds*: Stripped beams, inglenook log fire, friendly atmosphere, well kept Bass, Woodfordes and guest beers, home-cooked food at reasonable prices *(R P Hastings)*

☆ Hethersett [TG1505], *Kings Head*: Homely and cheerful pub with enjoyable lunchtime bar food inc tasty gammon rashers cut from whole side, comfortable carpeted lounge, friendly and courteous welcome, traditional games in cosy public bar, attractive and spacious back lawn; well kept Watneys-related real ales *(Dr R Fuller, LYM)*

Hethersett [Henstead Rd], *Greyhound*: Traditional, simple village pub, strong on atmosphere; Watneys-related real ales, decent wines, good home-made bar food, good garden *(O C Winterbottom)*

☆ Heydon [village signposted from B1149; TG1127], *Earle Arms*: Where else can you find stabling still in use behind a pub that overlooks such a decidedly unpretentious village green? Flagstones, bare boards, well kept Adnams tapped from the cask and served through a hatch – and absolutely no pretensions or concessions to current fashions in pub design; readers who like it say proudly that 'basic' is an understatement, though others find it much too primitive for them; bedrooms (cheap and simple) *(Rena Myskowski, LYM)*

Hillborough [TF8100], *Swan*: Friendly and

welcoming with well kept Ridleys, tasty bar food; service can be slow when it's busy *(Joy Heatherley)*

☆ **Holkham** [A149 nr Holkham Hall; TF8943], *Victoria*: Several simply furnished but comfortable hotelish bar rooms in pleasantly informal coastal inn by entry to Holkham Hall, with bar food from generous sandwiches to sirloin steak, Tolly real ale; tables in former stableyard and on front terrace; handy for Holkham Hall, beaches and nature reserves a half-mile away; nr start GWG118; children welcome; bedrooms *(Derek Pascall, LYM)*

Holt [main st; TG0738], *Feathers*: Consistently warm atmosphere and welcoming service in well run Berni Inn with Watneys-related real ales on handpump, bar food with daily specials, separate attractive restaurant; bedrooms *(David and Ruth Hollands)*

☆ **Horning** [Lower St; TG3417], *Swan*: Perfect position on banks of Broads with lawn running down to river, and though building itself is nothing special it's been attractively and comfortably decorated; well kept Watneys-related real ales on handpump, rather pricey but decent bar food, pleasant service, nice restaurant; lawn runs down to river *(Peter Corris, R Aitken)*

Horning, *Ferry*: Riverside pub made special by well kept ales and friendly service, even when busy *(MN)*; *New Inn*: Old, well kept village pub with tile floors, panelled bar, lots of old farming tools, conservatory extension with terrace overlooking lawns to river; bar food cooked to order so can be slow, four separate eating areas *(R Aitken)*

Horsey [just visible down lane 'To The Sea' from B1159 in S bends; TG4522], *Nelsons Head*: Isolated pub nr coast and actually below sea level (Horsey Gap down the lane a weak part of sea defences), small and quaint; it's had well kept Adnams, rather limited bar food – and a great deal of potential; leasehold for sale summer 1989 *(RPH, BB)*

Hoveton [TG3018], *Black Horse*: Two comfortable, clean bars with friendly atmosphere, excellent home-cooked bar food at reasonable prices *(H R Edwards)*

☆ **Kings Lynn** [St Nicholas St; TF6220], *Tudor Rose*: Attractive fifteenth-century pub with large choice of wines, whiskies and beers (inc well kept Adnams, Bass and Batemans), excellent bar food inc vegetarian dishes, friendly atmosphere, efficient service *(Neil Colombe, N and J D Bailey)*

Kings Lynn [London Rd], *London Porterhouse*: Small, friendly and lively pub with good mix of customers and well kept Greene King IPA and Abbot tapped from the cask *(Nigel Paine)*

Lessingham [outside village; TG3928], *Victoria*: Well kept Adnams and Greene King ales, very friendly atmosphere, good food *(N F Doherty)*

Litcham [TF8817], *Bull*: Delightful, truly village pub with well kept Watneys-related real ales, bar food inc very good home-made game or ham and asparagus pie *(Robert Mitchell)*

Lyng [TG0617], *Fox & Hounds*: Very friendly local by River Wensum, huge helpings of bar food inc good gammon and outstanding steak pie *(Margaret and Trevor Errington)*

☆ **Mundford** [Crown St; TL8093], *Crown*: Ancient posting-inn rebuilt in eighteenth century, in charming village, good value food, very welcoming staff, happy atmosphere, well kept real ale; bedrooms good *(J A Flack, AAW)*

☆ **Neatishead** [TG3420], *White Horse*: Small, quiet and homely with lounge bar resembling one's own front room; Greene King, excellent reasonably priced home-cooked food; only a few minutes' walk from the staithe *(Tim and Anne Neale, Mrs M G Longman, J D Maplethorpe)*

☆ **New Buckenham** [TM0890], *George*: Former Watneys pub, now doing well as a free house under young new owners; well kept Courage Best and Directors, Flowers and Wethereds on handpump, generous helpings of decent bar food inc huge ploughman's and well cooked hot dishes in dining-room set out as restaurant; bar, lively games area with juke box; a pleasant place, on corner of the village green *(M and J Back)*

☆ **North Creake** [TF8538], *Jolly Farmers*: Recently taken over by new owners making promising effort to serve good local food, well cooked and genially served *(W F Coghill)*

North Walsham [B1150 a mile NW – OS Sheet 133 reference 292311; TG2730], *Blue Bell*: Modern but pleasant, well kept Watneys-related real ales, eating area with huge helpings of good value food – wide choice; play area in garden *(R P Hastings)*

☆ **Norwich** [King St; TG2308], *Ferryboat*: Traditional beamed old-fashioned front part, spacious raftered and flagstoned back area where you may find pianist in action, kitchen alcove complete with baking oven, well kept and attractively priced Greene King IPA and Abbot and Woodfordes, refurbished restaurant; slide and climbing-frame in riverside garden with barbecue (and industrial outlook beyond); children welcome *(Graham and Glenis Watkins, Brian and Anna Marsden, Rena Myskowski, LYM)*

Norwich [Timber Hill], *Bell*: Former ancient coaching-inn in good spot nr castle, now a thriving multi-bar Courage pub with briskly served good value bar food; opens into former uneven-flagged courtyard now fitted out with stall-style snugs *(Ian Phillips)*; *Buck*: Long building with four different roof levels, in front of church and across rd from River Yare; friendly atmosphere, good value food *(Peter Corris)*; [Tombland] *Edith Cavell*: Small, comfortable, friendly pub opposite cathedral with good value food (until 7pm); nicest at lunchtime – background music can be loud in evenings; Watneys-related real ales, extended opening hours *(WJGW)*; [Heigham St] *Gibraltar Gardens*: Well kept beer, good reasonable food and excellent gardens; good parking; children welcome *(P Gillbe)*; [Thorpe St Andrew (A47 towards Gt Yarmouth); TG2508] *Kings Head*: Attractive mixture of buildings all uniformly painted; welcoming bar with well kept Whitbreads-related real ales, bar food, amazing fish restaurant where chef cooks in view of diners, riverside garden, free moorings *(R Aitken)*; [Tombland] *Louis Marchen*: Named after founder of the first Round Table; civilised pub with cheap food, unobtrusive juke box and well kept Watneys-related real ales; quiet Fri lunchtime *(WJGW)*; [Prince of Wales Rd] *Prince of Wales*: Comfortable pub that usefully serves food until 8.45pm (unusual here); well kept Watneys-related real ales on handpump; piped music can be loud *(WJGW)*; [10 Dereham Rd] *Reindeer*: Own-brew pub producing Bills Bevy, Reindeer and Red Nose, and serving about five well kept guest beers; lively atmosphere, half-casks for tables, bare boards, occasional folk bands; can get crowded *(Matthew Pringle)*; *Rib of Beef*: Fairly attractive riverside pub in city centre, unpretentious, basic interior with room downstairs; splendid range of real ales inc Reepham, Woodfordes Headcracker and weekly-changing guest beers, informative and friendly staff *(William McKenzie)*; [Newmarket St/Bury St] *Unthank Arms*: Recently refurbished old pub in Victorian terrace with good atmosphere, open fires in winter, well kept real ales, choice of wines and good range of inexpensive food *(Dr Paul Conn)*; [St George St] *Wild Man*: Good well priced lunchtime bar food, well kept Tolly ales; not large, can get busy *(K R Harris)*

☆ **Ormesby St Michael** [TG4614], *Eels Foot*: Beautifully sited Whitbreads Broads pub with spacious waterside lawn, comfortably refurbished inside, with good bar food and civilised efficient service *(G D Crouch, LYM)*

Overstrand [High St; TG2440], *White Horse*: Good, honest, very friendly local with well kept Watneys-related real ales, limited choice of well cooked inexpensive meals *(RPH)*

Ranworth [village signposted from B1140 Norwich–Acle; TG3514], *Maltsters*: Included for its fine position across quiet lane from Ranworth Broad; rather nautical touristy décor, straightforward bar food, Watneys-related real ales *(Tim and Anne Neale, A T Langton, LYM)*

☆ **Reepham** [Market Sq; TG0922], *Old Brewery House*: Attractive Georgian house overlooking market sq with prominent sundial over door and wellhouse in adjacent yard; friendly and cosy but windowless bar, good choice of well kept beers inc Adnams,

helpful service, wide range of reasonably priced and generously served straightforward bar food in dining area, restaurant; bedrooms comfortable and attractive (the less well furnished ones at the back have been sold – and there's a new manageress) *(Ian Phillips, Geoff Lee, Guy Sowerby, R P Hastings, N Kirkby)*

Roydon [the one nr Kings Lynn; TF7022], *Three Horseshoes*: Quiet but welcoming simple bar and clean, cosy lounge with fires at each end; friendly staff, well kept Courage Directors, Flowers and John Smiths, decent wines, good home-made bar food, restaurant *(Joy Heatherley)*

Salhouse [Bell Lane; TG3014], *Bell*: Pleasant and friendly, with good real ales and limited choice of inexpensive food *(R P Hastings)*; [Vicarage Rd (off A1151)] *Lodge*: Pleasant rural pub, nicely set in its own grounds, with good range of well kept beers such as Greene King IPA and Abbot, Marstons Pedigree and Woodfordes Wherry and Phoenix; good range of efficiently served food, popular with older people; children tolerated in eating area; garden with play area and barbecue *(Brian and Anna Marsden)*

Sheringham [TG1543], *Crown*: Overlooks sea, with nice terrace; good bar food; nr start GWG117 *(N Kirkby)*; [Cromer Rd] *Dunstable Arms*: Two separate fires in lounge, Watneys-related real ales and good range of bottled beers, basic but tasty good value bar food *(R C Vincent)*; *Two Lifeboats*: Well kept beer and reasonably priced food inc excellent ploughman's; bedrooms *(R P Hastings)*

South Walsham [TG3713], *Ship*: Well kept Watneys-related real ales, good bar food inc good ploughman's, pleasant staff *(David and Genevieve Benest)*

South Wootton [Knights Hill Village; TF6422], *Farmers Arms*: Farming hamlet interestingly converted into pub, restaurant and hotel; the pub part is a huge old barn with lots of farm tools on the walls, church pews on very uneven stone floor; bedrooms *(Mr and Mrs T Scheybeler)*

Stalham [High St; TG3725], *Kingfisher*: Though this modern pub, part of a restaurant/motel complex with bedrooms overlooking industrial premises, does not have much atmosphere, it's worth knowing for well kept Adnams ale and cheap but well prepared bar food *(R P Hastings)*

☆ **Stokesby** [TG4310], *Ferry House*: Fairly basic traditional pub on River Bure with plenty of character, excellent service, generous helpings of good food, choice of real ales inc well kept Adnams Extra and Flowers on handpump; very popular with boating holidaymakers (free moorings); children welcome *(Peter Seddon, CDC)*

☆ **Stow Bardolph** [TF6205], *Hare Arms*: Pleasantly refurbished country pub opposite Stow Hall, with reasonably priced good lunchtime bar food, cheerful licensees, well kept Greene King IPA and Abbot, separate elegant evening restaurant (food then not cheap but good), conservatory for children *(R G Tennant, A E Clay, P Gillbe)*

☆ **Surlingham** [TG3206], *Coldham Hall*: Beautiful waterside setting on edge of Broads with attractive, well kept gardens; good bar food, well kept beer, pleasant service, family-room *(Sue Cleasby, Mike Ledger)*

☆ **Surlingham** [from village head N; pub on bumpy track into which both village roads fork; TG3206], *Ferry House*: Spaciously comfortable if dimly lit modernised bar with good views of the river (there's still a rowing-boat ferry); usual range of bar food from big filled granary rolls to steaks, several vegetarian dishes, Watneys-related real ales on handpump, traditional pub games, piped music, restaurant, free mooring for 24 hours; children welcome, with own menu; has opened 8pm winter *(LYM)*

☆ **Sutton Staithe** [village signposted from A149 S of Stalham; TG3823], *Sutton Staithe*: The great attraction is the position, in a particularly unspoilt part of the Broads; little alcoves, built-in seats and an antique settle among more modern furnishings, well kept Adnams and sometimes other real ales tapped from the cask, usual bar food from sandwiches to steaks including children's menu, restaurant; good nearby moorings; children allowed in eating areas; has been open all day summer; bedrooms *(Jason Caulkin, RPH, Brian and Anna Marsden, LYM)*

☆ **Swanton Morley** [B1147, E end of village; TG0216], *Darbys*: Exceptional bar food from ploughman's or duck in orange soup to fillets of baby Dover sole, with super side salads and corner table of home-made condiments, in cosy beamed country pub with tractor seats and potato sacks as cushions at bar, well kept Adnams and Broadside and Woodfordes Best, warm welcome with good service, winter log fire; children's room, special events in upstairs restaurant; under the licensees who took it over in 1988 it is by all accounts a real find, which we very much look forward to inspecting *(Mr and Mrs J D Cranston, Derek and Sylvia Stephenson)*

☆ **Thetford** [King St; TL8783], *Bell*: Clean, tidy and pleasant beamed and timbered Tudor bar with well kept Adnams and Greene King real ales and generously served bar food in THF hotel which is otherwise spaciously modern; bedrooms *(Quentin Williamson, BB)*

☆ **Thetford** [White Hart St], *Thomas Paine*: Well kept Adnams and Tolly Original in friendly, spacious and comfortable hotel lounge bar, good value bar food from fine range of sandwiches to hot dishes; excellent service, small fire in big fireplace; children welcome; bedrooms *(Ian Phillips, LYM)*

Thetford, *Ark*: Good range of bar food, separate restaurant and barbecues in garden; children's climbing area *(Anon)*

Thornham [TF7343], *Chequers*: Pretty pub in picturesque village with well kept beer, nicely presented good value food, friendly atmosphere *(Linda and Alex Christison, J F Stock)*; [Church St] *Kings Head*: Bar food lunchtime and evening inc a very generous ploughman's, Watneys-related real ales on handpump; nr GWG116; pleasant bedrooms *(A T Langton, Peter Corris)*

Titchwell [A149; TF7543], *Three Horseshoes*: Excellent food and drink in well run pub with good help-yourself carvery and friendly atmosphere; popular with locals *(Charles Bardswell)*

Toft Monks [TM4294], *Toft Lion*: Above-average village pub, clean and friendly, with good simple bar food *(A V Chute)*

Walpole St Andrew [TF5017], *Princess Victoria*: Sixteenth-century free house with Courage Bitter and Youngers Scotch, worth knowing for good bar food Tues–Sun; the former restaurant has been closed *(Anon)*

Walsingham [Friday Market Pl; TF9236], *Black Lion*: Fourteenth-century free house, pleasant lounge, wide choice of well presented good bar food; comfortable bedrooms *(Miss E Judge)* [Shire Hall Plain] *Bull*: Worth knowing as a good drinking-man's pub a short walk from the shrine – much used by pilgrims *(S V Bishop)*

West Beckham [Bodham Rd; TG1339], *Wheatsheaf*: Beamed pub comfortably done up with cottagey doors and banquettes, logs burning in feature fireplace, reasonably priced drinks inc well kept Greene King ales, friendly service, good value straightforward bar food – pies and hot-pots recommended; garden; children's room; bedrooms *(J D Cranston, Revd John Cooper)*

West Runton [TG1842], *Village Inn*: Beautifully placed spacious pub in village centre, olde-worlde bar with good often unusual bar food inc attractive lunchtime cold table; real ales on handpump, tables on front lawn, large garden which can accommodate campers *(Peter Corris, K R Harris)*

☆ **West Somerton** [B1159/B1152; TG4619], *Lion*: It's the genuinely warm and friendly welcome which pulls this airy and comfortable roadside pub out of the average; good value efficiently served bar food, well kept Greene King and guest real ales; handy for Martham Broad; children in family-room *(LYM)*

☆ **Wighton** [TF9340], *Sandpiper*: A real well-scrubbed modest East Anglian country pub with well kept Tolly and guest beers like Sam Smiths, bar food, friendly hardworking licensees; games-room; garden usefully equipped for children, and pony, donkey, goats as well as dogs and cats on green opposite; attractive village; children welcome; good value bedrooms *(John Baker, NBM)*

Wiveton [TG0342], *Bell*: Old pub

overlooking village green and church; much modernised inside with three well kept real ales and attractive if not cheap food; tables out in front, more in attractive back garden with views of church *(R P Hastings)*

Worstead [TG3025], *Rising Sun*: Worth knowing *(Mark Sheard)*

☆ *nr* **Wroxham** [Rackheath; A1151 towards Norwich; TG2917], *Green Man*: Notable for its beautifully kept bowling-green, but well kept and comfortable inside too – easy chairs, plush banquettes and other seats in open-plan bar, log fires, popular bar food such as French bread sandwiches and good steak and kidney pie (only fish in the evening), Watneys-related real ales, piped music; children allowed in eating area *(R P Hastings, LYM)*

Wymondham [Market Pl; TG1101], *Cross Keys*: Part-Tudor, part-Georgian timbered pub, attractively old-fashioned, with good value bar food, good service *(Mark Sheard, Quentin Williamson)*; [Town Green] *Feathers*: Lots of character, enthusiastic staff and a good few properly kept real ales (especially Tickler named for the pub by Woodfordes); interesting bar food *(John Baker)*; [Church St] *Green Dragon*: Fine seventeenth-century inn with solid beams in lounge bar, Tudor mantelpiece in quaint old snug; good value bar food, well kept Courage Directors, Flowers and John Smiths tapped from the cask; behind the abbey *(Frank Gadbois)*; [2 Bridewell St] *Queens Head*: Good varied choice of well prepared and beautifully presented food, at reasonable prices, in bar and restaurant *(Sharon Hall)*

Northumbria (including Durham, Northumberland, Cleveland and Tyne & Wear)

Several new entries here include two at Beamish: the Shepherd & Shepherdess just outside the main entrance to the Open Air Museum, so a useful place to eat at if you're visiting the museum; and the Sun, an actual part of the museum (like the other buildings in this fascinating place, a rescued relic of life early this century). If this is a successful re-creation of what town pubs were like some time ago, the Shakespeare in Durham is an active survival of those days – very full of life, still. The three new entries are all popular for food: the cosy Tankerville Arms in Eglingham, the Manor House at Carterway Heads – a real find under its new licensees and the Jolly Sailor at Moorsholm (back in these pages after a break, and now serving food all day). Compared with other relatively thinly populated parts of the country, an unusually high proportion of this area's better pubs do serve notably good bar food, among them the Fox & Hounds at Cotherstone, the Three Tuns at Egglestone (a good deal of fresh local produce at both of these), the smart Morritt Arms at Greta Bridge (a comfortable place to stay at), the Granby at Longframlington (another good place to stay at, with a friendly family atmosphere), the cheery Chain Locker in North Shields, the Olde Ship in Seahouses (the area's most interesting pub, with good value bedrooms), the Waterford Arms at Seaton Sluice (famous for

*fresh fish) and the Warenford Lodge at Warenford (imaginative cooking
– a valuable break from the A1). The Jolly Fisherman overlooking the sea at
Craster now serves its snacks (including good crab sandwiches) all through the
day, and there's food all day too at the altogether more substantial George at
Piercebridge (under new licensees this year; they've opened bedrooms here,
and are planning more). Two other inns with new licensees – both of them
buildings of considerable interest – are the Lord Crewe Arms at Blanchland
and the Rose & Crown at Romaldkirk. Among the Lucky Dip entries at the
end of the chapter, current front runners are the Miners Arms at Acomb, Blue
Bell at Belford, Meadow House just outside Berwick, Percy Arms at Chatton,
Swan & Three Cygnets in Durham, Milecastle at Haltwhistle, Devonport at
Middleton One Row, Kings Head at Newton, Tower at Otterburn,
Horseshoes at Rennington, Seven Stars at Shincliffe and Moorcock near
Stannersburn.*

BEAMISH (Durham)　NZ2254 Map 10

Shepherd & Shepherdess

By main gate of Open Air Museum

Spacious and well managed, this neatly refurbished pub's carpeted lounge spreads
comfortably around a substantial mahogany-fitted servery. There are plush button-
back built-in wall banquettes and small comfortable chairs, decorative plates and
pleasant reproductions of Victorian pictures on the walls, muted flowery wallpaper,
and an attractive Victorian fireplace. Efficiently served bar food includes filled rolls,
herby garlic bread (£1.10), plaice (£2.65), lasagne, chicken curry, cheese and onion
quiche, shepherd's or corned beef and potato pie (all £2.85), gammon (£3.50) and
rump steak (£4.85); well kept Vaux Samson and Wards Sheffield Best on
handpump; fruit machine, space game, piped 1970s pop music. There are tables
outside the slate-roofed white house. *(Recommended by Dr J K McCann, Mr and
Mrs M D Jones, Mr and Mrs J H Adam, Mr and Mrs G D Amos, John Oddey)*

*Vaux　Real ale　Meals and snacks (12–2.30, 7.30–10)　Children welcome　Open 11–3,
6.30–11 all year*

Sun

Open Air Museum; note that you have to enter the museum (1989 adult fee £4), and the pub is
then on the far side of the 260-acre site – so the point of going is to visit the museum, and not
just the pub

This was a redundant Victorian pub over in Bishop Auckland, and like the other
buildings in this remarkable living museum was moved here lock, stock and barrel,
opening in 1985. Its big etched and cut-glass windows look out over the cobbled
street (past the vintage tram and 1913 Daimler bus which can take you free around
the site) to a drapers' and Co-op moved here from nearby Annfield Plain, fitted out
inside with Edwardian goods, with shop assistants dressed to match and even a
working Edwardian upstairs cafe. The same little street includes a row of Georgian
houses fitted out with a 1920s dentist's, stationers' and solicitor's; other thoroughly
functional 'antiques' – the place is growing all the time – include a row of period
miners' cottages with busily house-proud 'miners' wives', a turn-of-the-century
station (with steam trains), a working colliery, smithy and farm (with a local
cheesemaker using traditional equipment to make Dales-type cheeses). Pervading
everything is that nostalgic pre-smokeless smell of burning coal fires. The pub itself,
happily bustling, has a real turn-of-the-century feel in its two smallish rooms, with
all the appropriate varnished woodwork, bare boards, wallpaper, sturdy settles,
antique coat rails, service bell-pushes, advertisements and even barmaids. It has
well kept McEwans 80/- and Youngers No 3 on handpump, bits of black pudding
as nibbles on the bar counter and filled barm-cakes – only the prices are today's. In

the yard behind you'll find the Scottish & Newcastle Clydesdale dray horses stabled, with an immaculate period tack-room. *(Recommended by Comus Elliott, Alan Bickley)*

Youngers   Licensee Michael Webster   Real ale   Snacks   Children welcome   Open 11–5 all year

BLANCHLAND (Northumberland)   NY9750 Map 10

Lord Crewe Arms   *[illustrated on page 547]*

In a magnificent moorland village near the Derwent Reservoir, this popular inn is a remarkable, partly Norman building, largely untouched for centuries; it was originally attached to the guest-house of a monastery, part of whose cloister still stands in the neatly terraced gardens, and one bar is down in a crypt – simply furnished, with pews against massive stone walls under a barrel-vaulted ceiling. Upstairs, the Derwent Room has old settles, low beams and sepia photographs on its walls. There's also a priest's hole next to a striking thirteenth-century fireplace. It's an austere place, and on a cold, quiet day may not seem at its most welcoming. Simple bar food includes soup (£1.10), sandwiches, ploughman's (£2.50), salads (from £2.80), chilli con carne (£3) and cod (£3.40); Vaux Samson on handpump, darts. The inn is named after an eighteenth-century aristocrat, the formidable Lord Crewe, Bishop of Durham. *(Recommended by Stephanie Sowerby, Mrs E M Thompson, TRA, MA, Sue Cleasby, Mike Ledger, Chris and Sandra Taylor, R F Moat; it changed hands in summer 1988 – more reports on the new regime please)*

Free house   Real ale   Meals (lunchtime, not Sun) and snacks (lunchtime)   Restaurant Children in restaurant   Open 11–3, 6–11 (all day in summer if very busy) all year Bedrooms tel Blanchland (043 475) 251; £45B/£66B

CARTERWAY HEADS (Northumberland)   NZ0552 Map 10

Manor House   🏵

A68 just N of B6278, near Derwent Reservoir

Don't be misled by the name: this is a simple stone building, looking south over moorland pastures. It's recently been taken over by a friendly and enthusiastic young couple – he was a farm manager (hence the big photographs of sheep, lambs and Muscovy duck), she did the imaginative cooking at the Feathers, Hedley on the Hill, which we highlighted a couple of years or so ago (she left there to have twins). Cooking here with her sister-in-law, who's in partnership with them, she's already made this a real oasis, changing the bar food daily: a typical choice might be fresh mushroom soup (£1), filled French bread (£1), pâté or cheese and ham croissant (£1.85), steak sandwich (£2.25), broccoli and Mozzarella tart (£2.75), smoked fish au gratin (£3.50), home-baked ham or duck casserole (£3.75), paprika chicken (£3.85) and rump steak (£4), with sticky toffee pudding or home-made ice-cream (£1.25). The straightforward lounge bar, with flowers and houseplants in its red-velvet-curtained windows, has red plush button-back built-in wall banquettes and other seats around its tables, and a locals' bar has leatherette wall seats and Formica tables; darts, dominoes, well kept Wards Sheffield Best, decent coffee. The newly reopened restaurant (evenings, not Sunday) has its own comfortable lounge, with sofas and so forth. Rustic tables out on a small side terrace and lawn have a pleasant view. *(Recommended by John Oddey, Graham Oddey, G G Calderwood)*

Free house   Licensees Anthony and Jane Pelly, Miss E J C Pelly   Real ale   Meals and snacks (12–2.30, 7–9.30)   Restaurant tel Consett (0207) 55268   Children in eating area   Open 11–3, 6–11 all year

---

Please tell us if the décor, atmosphere, food or drink at a pub is different from our description. We rely on readers' reports to keep us up to date. No stamp needed: *The Good Pub Guide*, FREEPOST, London SW10 0BR.

COTHERSTONE (Durham)   NZ0119 Map 10

Fox & Hounds 🏵

B6277 – incidentally a good quiet route to Scotland, through interesting scenery

On the edge of the picturesque little village green, this white-painted house serves an attractive range of imaginatively prepared bar food, including sandwiches, home-made beef and vegetable broth (£1.45), ploughman's with local cheese (£2.95), good home-made steak and kidney pie (£3.70), venison casserole (£4.50), local plaice or vegetable pancake (£4.20), chicken pieces with pineapple and walnuts in a light curry mayonnaise or dressed crab salad (£4.95), saddle of lamb (£5.20) and rib steak (£7.20); puddings (£2.25); attentive service. The same menu – with the same prices – is used in the restaurant. There are thickly cushioned wall seats in the various alcoves and recesses of the civilised L-shaped beamed bar, as well as local photographs and country pictures, and an open fire in winter. John Smiths on handpump. *(Recommended by the Atherton family, Margaret and Roy Randle, E R Thompson, Stephanie Sowerby, Dr P D Smart, TRA, MA, RAMS, Patrick Young)*

Free house   Licensees Patrick and Jenny Crawley   Real ale   Snacks (lunchtime, not Sun) and meals   Restaurant tel Teesdale (0833) 50241   Children in eating area and restaurant   Open 11.30–2.30, 6.30–11   Bedrooms planned

CRASTER (Northumberland)   NU2620 Map 10

Jolly Fisherman ★

Off B1339 NE of Alnwick

This is an unpretentious harbourside place, popular with workers from the kippering shed opposite and serving pleasantly simple (and cheap) food – hot pies, pasties, toasted sandwiches and beefburgers (70p), home-made pizzas (80p), and highly praised local crab and salmon sandwiches (95p); obliging service. The atmospheric original bar, particularly the snug by the entrance, is the place to sit, and there are good sea views from the big picture window in the airy extension. Tetley Bitter on handpump; wine from the wood; darts, shove-ha'penny, dominoes, cribbage, juke box, fruit machine and space game. It's close to a splendid clifftop walk – *Good Walks Guide* Walk 145 – to Dunstanburgh Castle. *(Recommended by Mr and Mrs G D Amos, Mike Tucker, A C and S J Beardsley, Sue Cleasby, Mike Ledger, Michael Thomson)*

Tetleys (Ind Coope)   Licensee A George   Real ale   Snacks (available during opening hours)   Children welcome   Open 11–11 in summer; 11–3, 6–11 in winter

DURHAM   NZ2742 Map 10

Shakespeare

Sadler Street

Readers' current favourite among the city's many interesting pubs, this half-timbered building is nicely placed on a pedestrians-only street between the old market square and the cathedral. It's small and cosy, with an almost vibrantly welcoming atmosphere in the busy, unpretentious main front bar, a charming panelled snug, and a further back room (both these tend to be popular with students – well behaved – in the evening). With a good range of well kept real ales that might typically include McEwans 80/-, Theakstons Best and Youngers No 3, simple good value bar snacks including good freshly made sandwiches, and friendly efficient service, it all adds up to a comfortable but basic reminder of what the best town pubs used to be like a few decades ago. *(Recommended by T J Maddison, Helen and Roy Sumner, John Tyzack, Sue Holland, Dave Webster, Jon Dewhirst, Philip Haggar)*

Scottish & Newcastle   Real ale   Snacks (lunchtime)   Open 11–11 all year

EGGLESTON (Durham)   NY9924 Map 10

Three Tuns 🍺

Facing the broad village green, this rustic and peacefully atmospheric stone pub serves a decent range of food, from cheese rolls (85p), home-made soup (£1), ploughman's (£1.95), through home-made cottage pie (£2.50), jumbo sausage (£2.65), omelettes (£2.95), trout (£3.50), duck (£4.25), to steaks (£6.25), with a couple of daily specials such as game casserole or local gulls' eggs with home-made mayonnaise; Sunday lunch (£9.50 – booking essential); puddings (£1.30); good house red. The beamed bar has old oak settles, one with amusingly horrific Gothick carving, as well as Windsor armchairs and the like, and a log fire. Big windows at the back look out past the terrace and garden to open fields, maybe with rabbits. The licensees celebrate twenty years at the Three Tuns this year. It's close to some fine moorland roads – the B6282, B6278 and B6279. *(Recommended by E R Thompson, Rosalind Russell, W A Harbottle, Hayward Wane, Margaret and Roy Randle)*

Whitbreads   Licensees James and Christine Dykes   Meals and snacks (not Mon, not Sun evening)   Restaurant (Sun lunch and Tues–Sat evenings, bookings only by previous day) tel Teesdale (0833) 50289   Children in eating area and restaurant   Open 11.30–2.30, 7–11; closed Mon (except bank hols) and 25 Dec

EGLINGHAM (Northumberland)   NU1019 Map 10

Tankerville Arms

B6346 NW of Alnwick

Very much a focus of local life, this long stone-built village pub is a chatty place in the evening: mainly Turkey-carpeted, with red plush banquettes and captain's chairs around cast-iron-framed tables, black joists, some walls stripped to bare stone, coal fires at each end; there's a snug (and, going by our own visit, much-needed) no-smoking area. Good well presented bar food includes sandwiches (£1.85), smoked fish or steak and kidney pies (£3.85), gammon and peaches or fresh smoked trout (£4.25) and Aberdeen Angus steaks (from £6.45); service, usually good and friendly, can get hurried at busy times. Well kept Stones and Tetleys on handpump, decent wines; fruit machine. *(Recommended by E R Thompson, Hazel Church, Richard Davies, John Oddey, Matthew Waterhouse)*

Free house   Real ale   Meals and snacks   Restaurant tel Powburn (066 578) 444   Provision for children   Open 11–3, 6–11 all year

ETAL (Northumberland)   NT9339 Map 10

Black Bull

Off B6354, SW from Berwick

An inviting, white-painted and thatched cottage, this pub has a roomy, modernised lounge bar with glossily varnished beams, and Windsor chairs around the tables on its carpet. The surrounding village is particularly picturesque, consisting mostly of cottages which are slightly smaller versions of the pub itself, and has the bare ruins of a castle on the banks of the River Till at the far end. Good value, straightforward bar food includes filled rolls and sandwiches (from 65p), soup (80p), ploughman's (£1.75), vegetarian choices like pizza, lasagne or curry (from around £2.75), haddock (£2.75), farm-cured gammon (£4.40), and Tweed salmon salad (£5.60); children's helpings. Well kept Youngers Scotch on handpump; darts, dominoes, cribbage, fruit machine; quoits pitch in front. It's well placed for Heatherslaw's working watermill (where you can buy flour ground on the premises), the restored Ford Castle and, half an hour's drive away, Berwick-upon-Tweed. The village's

---

If you have to cancel a reservation for a bedroom or restaurant, please telephone or write to warn them. A small place – and its customers – will suffer if you don't.

offspring, New Etal, a diminutive hamlet across the river, was originally conceived to replace Etal when it was destroyed by Border marauders. *(Recommended by Alan Hall, Mr and Mrs G D Amos)*

Vaux   Real ale   Meals and snacks   Children in eating area only, away from bar   Open 12–3, 7–11; closed 4–6 Sat

GRETA BRIDGE (Durham)   NZ0813 Map 10
Morritt Arms   ⊗   ⇔
Hotel signposted off A66 W of Scotch Corner

Dickens stayed in this well kept old-fashioned hotel on his way to Barnard Castle in January 1838 to begin his research for *Nicholas Nickleby*; these days a bar is named after him, and has a lively, lifesize Pickwickian mural which runs right the way round the room, done in 1946 by J V Gilroy (famous for the old Guinness advertisements – there are six here, signed by him). It's a civilised high-ceilinged room, with sturdy green-plush-seated oak settles and big Windsor armchairs around traditional cast-iron-framed tables, with big windows looking out on the extensive lawn. The adjacent green bar has dark grey leatherette wall seats, a stag's head and a big case of stuffed black game; there's also a fine big model traction engine in one of the lounges. Well kept Theakstons Best on handpump; good open fires; dominoes and a proper old shove-ha'penny board, with raisable brass rails to check the lie of the coins; darts, pool and a juke box in the separate public bar (the rest of the hotel is atmospherically quiet). Bar food includes sandwiches (from £1), home-made soup (£1.25), home-made pâté or ploughman's (£3) and salads from smoked mackerel (£3) to salmon (£5.75), with daily hot dishes such as rack of lamb with rosemary or pork cutlets. There are picnic-table sets and swings at the far end, and teak tables in a pretty side area look along to the graceful old bridge by the stately gates to Rokeby Park. *(Recommended by Mrs E M Thompson, Stephanie Sowerby; more reports please)*

Free house   Licensees David and John Mulley   Real ale   Meals and snacks (lunchtime; sandwiches and soup in evening)   Restaurant   Children welcome   Open 12–3, 6–10.30 (11 Sat) all year   Bedrooms tel Teesdale (0833) 27232/27392; £23(£31B)/£38(£48B)

HEDLEY ON THE HILL (Northumberland)   NZ0859 Map 10
Feathers
Village signposted from New Ridley, which is signposted from B6309 N of Consett; OS Sheet 88 reference 078592

The range of food in this idiosyncratic local is steadily increasing; although it's still only officially served at weekends, they'll rustle up some welcoming dish for the foot-weary traveller pretty much at any time, and we're hoping that the favourable noises being made by regulars will persuade the licensees to provide it on a more regular basis. It's all home made, and includes sandwiches (from 65p), watercress soup (95p), brandied pâté or ploughman's (£1.55), vegetarian flan (£2.55), smokies with salad (£2.75) and beef casserole with mushrooms and prunes (£3). All three welcoming, Turkey-carpeted bars have open fires, with beams, stripped stonework, solid brown leatherette settles, wood-burning stoves and country pictures. Well kept Marstons Pedigree, Ruddles Best and a regular guest beer on handpump; darts, shove-ha'penny, table skittles, dominoes and cribbage. *(Recommended by John Oddey, G Bloxsom; more reports please)*

Free house   Licensees Marina and Colin Atkinson   Real ale   Snacks (Sat and Sun, but see above)   Children in small room off lounge   Open 6–11 (plus 12–3.30 Sat, 12–3 Sun) all year

---

Looking for a pub with a really special garden, or in lovely countryside, or with an outstanding view, or right by the water? Such pubs are listed separately at the back of the book.

HIGH FORCE (Durham)   NY8728 Map 10

High Force Hotel 🍺

B6277 about 4 miles NW of Middleton-in-Teesdale

Popular with walkers, this fine inn is splendidly positioned in pine woods below high moors and near England's biggest waterfall, the High Force, which is best observed from the other side of the River Tees. The inn itself is more of a hotel than a pub, but it has a snug and cheerful public bar, with robustly simple furniture on its wood-block floor, piped music, darts and dominoes; the lounge and other rooms are comfortable. Bar food includes sandwiches, rolls and French bread (from 65p, toasted from 80p), soup (90p), ploughman's (£2.20, lunchtime only), home-made steak and kidney pie (£3.45), salads (from £3.80, good prawn £4.80), trout (£4) and steaks (from £6.50; wider range in the evening); puddings; a good range of malt whiskies. Incidentally it doubles as a mountain rescue post – so they know a thing or two about welcomes to foot-sore travellers. *(Recommended by Sue Carlyle, M J Lawson, Joy Heatherley)*

Free house   Licensees Barrie and Lilian Hutchinson   Meals and snacks (not Mon evenings, exc June–Sept)   Children welcome at lunchtime, in reception area and residents' dining-room only at other times   Open 11–3, 6–11 (opens 7 in winter)   Bedrooms tel Teesdale (0833) 22222/22264; £16/£28

LONGFRAMLINGTON (Northumberland)   NU1301 Map 10

Granby ⊗ 🍺

A697

There's something of a family atmosphere in this small modernised eighteenth-century inn – the woman who manages the food side is the sister-in-law of the licensee, who's the daughter-in-law of the previous one. The two rooms of the white-walled bar have red brocaded wall settles and stools around the walls and in the bay windows, brown wooden tables, a copper-covered little fireplace in one room, and copper and whisky-water jars and ushers' lamps hanging from the black joists; faint piped music. There's quite an emphasis on food, particularly in the evening when most people come to eat rather than to drink; the wide range includes soup (£1.20, not evenings), deep-fried Camembert (£1.95), sandwiches (from £1.95, steak £2.15), grilled asparagus with cheese (£2.55), home-made steak and kidney pie (£3.35, lunchtime only), a good range of seafood from cod (£3.15) to whole lobster (£15.15), salads (from £4.55, poached salmon £5.65), saddle of lamb (£5.95) and steaks (from £6.85); puddings (from £1.20); substantial breakfasts, with large kippers, for residents; friendly service. There are some picnic-tables on the small front terrace. *(Recommended by John Oddey, Richard Dolphin, Comus Elliott, R H Martyn, R A Hall, E R Thompson)*

Bass   Licensee Anne Bright   Meals and snacks   Restaurant   Children over eight in lounge lunchtime only   Open 11–3, 6–11 all year; closed 25 Dec   Bedrooms tel Longframlington (066 570) 228; £18.95(£19.95B)/£37.90(£39.90B)

LONGHORSLEY (Northumberland)   NZ1597 Map 10

Linden Pub ★ 🍺

Part of Linden Hall Hotel; down long drive, and past hotel itself

The airy feel in this comfortable, split-level family pub stems from its location in an ex-granary; the red-carpeted bar has lots of light-coloured woodwork, a log-effect gas fire in a large round central hearth and a notable collection of old enamel advertising signs on its largely stripped stone walls, with stairs to the galleried upper part. A flagstoned yard has tables under a Perspex roof. The good range of bar food, changing daily and served from a side counter, typically includes a couple of soups (95p), large filled baps (£1.50), salads with a choice of pâté or four meats (£3.25), nine or ten hot dishes such as turkey curry, steak pie, chicken Kiev, Northumberland sausage, leek and ham crumble, fisherman's pie or vegetarian lasagne (mostly around £3.95), and steak (£6.95); children's (£1.95) and senior citizens' (£2.50) portions; puddings (£1.25); helpful service. Ruddles County, Theakstons Best and Websters Best on handpump or tapped from the cask under a light blanket pressure; darts, pool (both sensibly placed), dominoes, cribbage, fruit machine and piped music. Quoits and garden draughts are played out in the yard, where barbecues are organised in good weather, and there is a good outdoor games area in the spacious grounds of the adjoining, handsomely restored country-house hotel, as well as the play area by the pub. *(Recommended by G Bloxsom, Sue Cleasby, Mike Ledger; more reports please)*

Free house   Licensees Jon Moore and Rod Tait   Real ale   Meals and snacks   Children upstairs   Open 11–11; 11–3, 6–10.30 (11 Fri and Sat) in winter   Bedrooms and restaurant in hotel tel Morpeth (0670) 516611, Telex 538224; £70B/£82.50B

MOORSHOLM (Cleveland)   NZ6914 Map 10
Jolly Sailor

A171 nearly 1 mile E of Moorsholm village turn-off

Alone on the moors, this is snug but spacious inside, with lots of cosy and comfortably upholstered little booths around the solid black tables of the long, welcoming bar – all beams, harness and stripped stone. Bar food includes sandwiches (from 85p, prawn £2.50), ploughman's (£2.80), a daily roast (£3.25), Whitby haddock (£3.65), home-made steak and kidney pie (£3.75), gammon (£3.80) and steaks (from £7.25); also a good range of vegetarian dishes such as spinach and mushroom lasagne, mushroom and nut pasta or lentil crumble (£3.75); Sunday lunch (£5.75, £3.50 children); children's menu (£1.75); friendly service. Well equipped family-room; juke box, darts on request. There are tables (and some children's playthings) outside, looking over the moorland pasture to heather and bracken rising beyond. *(Recommended by Alan and Ruth Woodhouse)*

Free house   Licensee Mrs Elaine Ford   Meals and snacks (served during opening hours) Restaurant tel Castleton (0287) 60270   Children in family-room   Open 11.30–3, 6–11 (all day Sat and bank hols); closed weekday lunchtimes Oct–Apr

NEWCASTLE UPON TYNE (Tyne & Wear)   NZ2266 Map 10
Bridge Hotel

Castle Square (in local A–Z street atlas index as Castle Garth); right in centre, just off Nicholas Street (A6215) at start of High Level Bridge; only a few parking meters nearby, but evening parking easy

The atmosphere in this Grade II listed building overlooking the Tyne varies from quiet and comfortable to bustling and noisy depending on the time of day or week, but the service remains friendly and welcoming. The bar is a well preserved Victorian affair, with a neatly kept and decorous lounge, which has high ceilings, a massive mahogany carved fireplace, a bar counter equipped with unusual pull-down slatted snob screens, decorative mirrors, and brown leather banquettes and elegant small chairs on its rust carpet. In the public bar, which has some cheerful stained glass, there's a good juke box, pool, dominoes and fruit machine (there's a second in the lounge lobby). Well kept Tetleys Bitter, Theakstons Best and XB and a weekly guest beer on handpump; simple bar snacks include toasted sandwiches (65p) and stottie cakes with meat and salad (70p). There are some picnic-table sets on the flagstoned back terrace by the remains of the city wall. The Thursday folk

---

club here is one of the country's oldest. *(Recommended by Graham Oddey, J F Thorndike, Perry Board and Andrew O'Doherty; more reports please)*

Free house   Licensee Dave Shipley   Real ale   Snacks   Blues club Tues, folk club Thurs Open 11.30–3, 5.30 (6 Sat)–11; closed 25 Dec, 1 Jan

Cooperage

32 The Close, Quayside; immediately below and just W of the High Level Bridge; parking across road limited lunchtime, easy evening

They always have seven real ales on handpump in this none-too-solid-looking Tudor house; as well as the regular Ind Coope Burton, Marstons Owd Rodger and Pedigree and Tetleys Bitter, there are three guests from an extremely extensive list, such as Adnams, Friary Meux, Fullers ESB, London Pride and Chiswick, Greene King Abbot, King and Barnes Festive, Ruddles County or Titanic Captain Smith; also Addlestones and Coates farm cider. There's a bustling atmosphere in the bar, which has heavy Tudor oak beams and exposed stonework, and there's extra seating in the lounge area by the pool-room; fruit and trivia machines, space game and juke box. Reasonably priced bar food includes soup (70p), burger (£1.60), cheese and tomato omelette (£1.70), filled baked potato or hot beef stottie (£1.80), grilled kipper fillets (£1.90), with specials such as braised rabbit pie (£2.75), steak and beer pie (£2.95) and pastry parcels of chicken and tarragon (£3.25). It's actually one of Newcastle's oldest buildings, and was indeed once a cooperage. *(Recommended by Michael Bolam, Comus Elliot; more reports please)*

Free house   Licensee Michael Westwell   Real ale   Meals and snacks   Restaurant tel Newcastle (091) 232 8286   Children in eating area   Open 11–11 all year; closed 25 Dec

NORTH SHIELDS (Tyne & Wear)   NZ3468 Map 10
Chain Locker ⊗

New Quay

This welcoming Tyneside pub, close to the pedestrian ferry landing area, is atmospheric in a straightforward way, with a wooden-ceilinged bar which has an open fire, navigational charts and nautical pictures on the walls, local literature and arts information, and stools and wooden wall benches around small tables – the one on your left as you go in, built over a radiator, is prized in winter. Well kept Ruddles Best and County, Websters Choice and Green Label and three guest beers on handpump; dominoes. For bar food they rely heavily on the nearby North Shields Fish Quay, and change the menu daily; typically it might include lunchtime sandwiches, ploughman's (from £1.80), cod and mushroom bake (£2.50), fish pie or fish and chips (£2.75) and poached salmon in white wine (£3.25); Sunday lunch (£4.95 – booking essential). *(Recommended by John Oddey, Graham Oddey, E V Walder, G Bloxsom, Grahame Archer)*

Free house   Licensees Sue and John Constable   Real ale   Meals and snacks (12–2.30, 6–8)   Restaurant (Thurs–Sat evening, Sun)   Children in restaurant   Folk music Fri evening   Open 11.30–3, 6–11 all year

PIERCEBRIDGE (Durham)   NZ2116 Map 10
George

B6275 just S of village

New licensees took over this attractively positioned (on the alternative, scenic route between Scotch Corner and Edinburgh), former coaching-inn last summer; but beyond some refurbishments inside and out, and the introduction of a new menu, relatively little seems to have changed, and we're confident that the welcome will be as good as ever. Three bars have plates, pictures and old farming equipment on the walls, solid wood furniture, and Chesterfields in the lounge (which overlooks the river); there are no fewer than five open fires in one room or another. Well worth a visit is the Ballroom Bar – just that, a bar inside a fully fitted ballroom (open only for special functions or during barbecues). The wide range of food includes soup (£1.25), sandwiches (£1.45), ploughman's (£2.95), curries, cod or scampi (£3.50), a separate vegetarian menu with such dishes as vegetable Stroganoff, green pepper risotto or mushrooms in Stilton (all £3.95), smoked trout (£3.95), a bacon and eggs breakfast (served all day) or chicken in mushroom sauce (£4.50), pork (£4.95) and steaks (from £7.95); puddings (£1.25). John Smiths and Caledonian Merman on handpump; fruit machine and piped music. They now do bedrooms, and are planning twenty more in the near future. A fine garden runs down to the River Tees. *(Recommended by Dr R H M Stewart, R F Plater, Mr and Mrs Norman Edwardes, Clare Greenham, TRA, MA, Bev Prentice, Bill Russell; reports on the new regime please)*

Free house   Licensees Mr and Mrs Wayne   Real ale   Meals and snacks (available all day) Restaurant (open all day)   Children in eating area   Occasional live entertainment Open 11–11 all year   Bedrooms tel Piercebridge (0325) 374576; £28B/£38B

RENNINGTON (Northumberland)   NU2119 Map 10

Masons Arms

Stamford Cott; B1340 NE of Alnwick

Such is the peaceful rural atmosphere in this coastal place that it's difficult to imagine that the road that runs past it was once the pre-A1 Great North Road – as you can see from the murals in the dining-room. The comfortable, atmospheric lounge bar has a solid-fuel stove at one end and a gas fire at the other, green leatherette stools and russet wall banquettes on the brown carpet, local newspapers set out to read, and photographs of heavy horses (and a locally beached whale) on the cream walls above the brown panelled dado. Tetleys Bitter on handpump, farm cider and a selection of malt whiskies; piped music; juke box, pool-table, darts, dominoes and fruit machine on the public side. Bar food includes sandwiches, home-made soup (65p), pâté (£1.50), chicken or vegetarian lasagne (£2.50), a good steak sandwich (£2.85), gammon (£3.25), three daily specials and steaks (from £5.50); children's dishes from £1.10. The small front terrace has sturdy rustic tables surrounded by lavender. You can arrange golfing breaks, which include full accommodation with breakfast and evening meal and a day's play on the course near Dunstanburgh Castle. *(Recommended by John Tyzack, A C and S J Beardsley, Mr and Mrs G D Amos, Sue Holland, Dave Webster, John Oddey, David Waterhouse, Mr and Mrs M D Jones, Sue Cleasby, Mike Ledger, Gill and Neil Patrick, G Bloxsom)*

Free house   Licensees George and Pat Beattie   Real ale   Meals and snacks Restaurant   Children welcome   Open 11–11 all year   Bedrooms tel Alnwick (0665) 77275; £12(£27B)/£24(£35B)

ROMALDKIRK (Durham)   NY9922 Map 10

Rose & Crown 🍺

Just off B6277

At their last inn, the Black Swan at Ravenstonedale, the Davys kept a tight ship – though they've taken over the Rose & Crown too recently for a reliable dossier of readers' reports to have built up yet, you can expect notably good housekeeping and thoughtful cooking; we won't be at all surprised if reports over the next year suggest that a food as well as a stay award is in order. The bar menu changes daily, lunchtime and evening, typically including home-made vegetable soup (£1.25), lunchtime sandwiches (from £1.25, served with marinated mushrooms) and ploughman's (£2.25), chilli con carne or sauté chicken livers in a cream, sherry and walnut sauce (£3.25), haddock in a fresh tomato sauce (£3.50), beef Stroganoff (£4), chicken breast in barbecue sauce (£4.85) and ten-ounce sirloin steak (£8.95); puddings such as walnut tart or profiteroles (£1.50). The inn itself is on the fine village green, where you can still see the original stocks and water-pump; the licensees have redecorated the bar, but it's still comfortably and traditionally furnished, with cream walls decorated with lots of gin-traps, some old farm tools and a large chiming clock, and old-fashioned seats facing the fireplace; the atmosphere has a certain timeless appeal, perhaps at its best in winter, when there are warm fires inside and rooks in the bare trees outside. Theakstons Best and Old Peculier and Youngers Scotch on handpump; dominoes, occasional piped music. The village is close to the Bowes Museum and the High Force waterfall. *(Recommended by Jim Whitaker, Rosalind Russell, Stephanie Sowerby, Sandra Kempson, Sue Carlyle, Mrs E M Thompson, H Bramhall; reports on the new regime please)*

Free house   Licensees Christopher and Alison Davy   Real ale   Meals and snacks Restaurant   Children welcome   Open 11–3, 5.30–11 all year   Bedrooms tel Teesdale (0833) 50213; £40B/£50B

SEAHOUSES (Northumberland)   NU2232 Map 10

Olde Ship ★ ★ 𝕊 ⛵

B1340 coast road

The collection of nautical memorabilia in this fine popular harbourside inn continues to grow – though at a slower rate now as the items sought after become rarer and more expensive; the latest addition is an anemometer, connected to the top of the chimney – a curious and mesmerising instrument. There's also a working radar which you can use to track the fishing boats coming in, good sea pictures and ship's models, including a fine one of the North Sunderland lifeboat, a knotted anchor made by local fishermen, and so much teak and mahogany woodwork, shiny brass fittings and small rooms throughout that the atmosphere is genuinely more like that of a ship than a building. The carpeted poop deck area contrasts with the bare floors elsewhere (it's actually ship's decking, and they may close for a day or two in early spring for sanding and rewaxing). There is another low-beamed snug bar, and a new family-room at the back. Pews surround barrel tables in the back courtyard, and a battlemented side terrace with a sun lounge looks out on the harbour. Many of the windows have stained-glass sea pictures, and the one that's clear looks out over the harbour to the Farne Islands. The atmosphere is authentically local, with sailors as many of the regulars. Bar food includes home-made soup such as crab (90p), filled rolls and sandwiches (from 80p), ploughman's (£1.55) and salads, with three or four lunchtime hot dishes, changing daily, such as popular mince and dumplings, rabbit, fresh sole, fish stew or salmon (around £2.50–£3); no chips. The hotel dining-room does a Sunday roast lunch (as well as good meals in the evening, when only sandwiches are served in the bar). McEwans Scotch and 70/- and Theakstons Best on handpump; also unusual blended whiskies, some uncommon bottled beers, and in winter mulled wine. Open fire, dominoes, fruit machine and trivia game. You can book boat trips to the Farne Islands Bird Sanctuary at the harbour, and there are bracing coastal walks, particularly to Bamburgh, Grace Darling's birthplace. *(Recommended by A C and S J Beardsley, Christopher Knowles-Fitton, Z Cumberpatch, E E Hemmings, Robert and Vicky Tod, T Nott, R F Moat, Sue Cleasby and Mike Ledger, Dave Butler, Lesley Storey, S V Bishop, Gill and Neil Patrick)*

Free house   Licensees Alan and Jean Glen   Real ale   Meals (lunchtime) and snacks (sandwiches only, evening)   Restaurant   Children in restaurant and lounge   Open 11–3, 6–11 all year   Bedrooms tel Seahouses (0665) 720200; £21(£23.50B)/£42(£47B)

SEATON SLUICE (Northumberland)   NZ3477 Map 10

Waterford Arms 𝕊

Just off A193 N of Whitley Bay

The profusion of local fish from the harbour just down the road is a considerable and popular attraction at this comfortably modern pub; it's all served in extravagantly large helpings, priced according to size – small, medium or large. This includes lemon sole (£3.25–£5.25), cod and haddock (£3.45–£7.95); other food includes sandwiches (from 90p), home-made soup (£1), sausage, mash and gravy (£2.75), leek pudding with mince (£3.35), home-made steak and kidney pie (£3.75), ploughman's (£3.95), a generous seafood platter (£7.80) and steaks (from £7.95); large breakfasts, with home-made jams, for residents. The bar has spacious green plush banquettes in its roomy bays, and bright paintings in one high-ceilinged room, and brown plush furnishings and a big children's rocking machine in another. Well kept Vaux Samson and Double Maxim on handpump; darts, pool, dominoes and a fruit machine in the back lobby. *(Recommended by Richard Dolphin, Helen and Roy Sumner, John Oddey)*

Vaux   Licensee Mrs Paddy Charlton   Real ale   Meals and snacks   Children in eating area   Open 11–3.30, 6.45–11 all year   Bedrooms tel Tyneside (091) 237 0450; £18.50S/£37S

TYNEMOUTH (Tyne & Wear)   NZ3468 Map 10

Tynemouth Lodge

Tynemouth Road (A193); a few minutes' walk from the Tynemouth Metro station

This clean little pub has largely a male clientele – attracted by the good range of very well kept real ales, including Belhaven 80/-, Marstons Pedigree, Robinsons Old Tom, Theakstons Best and Wards Sheffield Best on handpump. Bar food is straightforward, with stottie sandwiches (75p) and pot meals such as chilli con carne or lamb hot-pot (£1.90). The bar has copper-topped cast-iron tables, and button-back green leatherette seats built against the walls (which have stylish bird-of-paradise wallpaper); there's a winter coal fire in the neat Victorian tiled fireplace; tables beyond the car park. It's on the edge of Northumberland Park. *(Recommended by Grahame Archer, G Bloxsom, Jon Dewhirst; more reports please)*

Free house   Licensee Hugh Price   Real ale   Meals and snacks   Open 11–11 all year

Wooden Doll

103 Hudson Street; from Tyne Tunnel, follow A187 into town centre; keep straight ahead (when the A187 turns off left) until, approaching the sea, you can see the pub in Hudson Street on your right

The friendly, relaxed atmosphere inside this straightforward eighteenth-century place, overlooking the boats and warehouses of the harbour, belies its rather severe exterior; its simply decorated but comfortable front bar has been extended northwards and a new one added; a third one is similarly furnished with brown and green leatherette chairs, a brown plush long settle and Formica-topped cast-iron tables, with open fires in winter; fine views from the covered glassed-in verandah. There's an uncommonly good range of well kept real ales, with Halls Harvest, Ind Coope Burton, Mitchells ESB, Robinsons Best, Tetleys Bitter, Theakstons Best and Old Peculier and Youngers No 3 on handpump. Bar food includes filled rolls (around 70p, not evening), half a pint of prawns (£2.45), a strong chilli con carne (£2.95), mackerel salad (£3.50 – the mackerel is smoked on the quay which you can see from the balcony), local cod Mornay (£3.75) and seafood salad or steaks (£5.95); puddings (from £1). Shove-ha'penny, dominoes, fruit and trivia machines. *(Recommended by Graham Oddey, G Bloxsom, GB, Mr and Mrs G D Amos, Grahame Archer, Sue Cleasby, Mike Ledger)*

Free house   Licensee Mrs Pat Jones   Real ale   Meals and snacks (not Sun evening)   Children in eating area until 7.30   Live entertainment every evening, with classical quartet Sun evening, jazz Mon evening, quiz night Tues   Open 11–11; closed Mon–Thurs afternoons in winter

Most pubs kindly let us have up-to-date food prices as we went to press in summer 1989; with those that didn't – normally recognised by the absence of a licensee's name – we've assumed a 10 per cent increase.

WARENFORD   NU1429 Map 10

Warenford Lodge 🍴

Just off A1 Alnwick–Belford, on village loop road

Though quite old, the bar here looks modern, with some stripped stone walls, cushioned wooden seats and a big stone fireplace, with steps up to an extension which has comfortable easy chairs and settees around low tables, and a big wood-burning stove. The selection of home-cooked bar food is uncommonly good, consistently well prepared and attractively presented; the menu varies seasonally, but it might typically include soup or tomato salad (£1.10), grilled mussels or prawn fritters (£2.50), ham with pease pudding or grilled trout (£3.25), a hot-pot of lamb, onion, apple and potato or creamy cannelloni (£3.50), chicken curry (£4.50), a Northumbrian version of bouillabaisse or poached salmon with lime butter (£5.20) and a substantial sirloin steak (£7.50); puddings (from £1.50); decent selection of wines. *(Recommended by A H Doran, Dr J R Backhurst, T Nott, Dr P D Smart and others)*

Free house   Licensee Raymond Matthewman   Meals and snacks (not Mon lunchtime) Evening restaurant tel Belford (066 83) 453   Children in restaurant   Open 12–2, 7–11 all year; closed Tues lunchtime and all day Mon Oct–Easter

Lucky Dip

Besides the fully inspected pubs, you might like to try these Lucky Dips recommended to us and described by readers (if you do, please send us reports):

☆ **Acomb**, Northumberland [NY9366], *Miners Arms*: Charming old pub, small and friendly, with plenty of character, huge open fire and friendly welcome from licensee and locals; specialise in unusual and well kept real ales which suit wide span of tastes; home-cooked bar food; children in dining-room *(John Oddey, Matthew Waterhouse)*
Allendale, Northumberland [NY8456]: Keen competition among the five pubs and two inns round the square of this attractive town makes for a good choice of bar food *(Adrian Dodd-Noble)*
Allenheads, Northumberland [NY8545], *Allenheads*: Olde-worlde pub, in centre of delightful village, serving good home-cooked bar food; good walking area, has been open all day; bedrooms *(E R Thompson)*
Alnmouth, Northumberland [Northumberland St; NU2511], *Red Lion*: Traditional free house, warm welcome from licensees, happy and relaxed atmosphere, well kept McEwans 80/-, including good seafood platters; children welcome lunchtime, and in restaurant evening *(John Taylor)*
Alnwick, Northumberland [Narrowgate; NU1913], *Oddfellows Arms*: Pleasant and spotless lounge with coal fire and well kept Vaux Samson and Lorimers Best Scotch on handpump; nr start GWG142; bedrooms *(I T Glendenning)*; [Narrowgate] *Olde Cross*: Interestingly old, with ancient bottles in low window and story to suit, picturesque locals keen to display skill at dominoes, good beer on handpump, low-priced bar food –

friendly, unpretentious and fun *(WFL)*; [Market St] *Queens Head*: Unpretentious, but roomy and dignified, with good real ale and good value food, very friendly staff taking much trouble; bedrooms good value *(WFL)*; [Hotspur St] *Tanners Arms*: Small, one-roomed free house with friendly atmosphere and lots of character; flagstone floors, bare stone walls, excellent juke box, pleasant staff and licensee; well kept Belhaven 70/- and 80/- on handpump, maybe a guest beer *(Mr and Mrs P A Jones)*
Alwinton, Northumberland [NT9206], *Star & Thistle*: More a farm than pub – landlady had to leave bar to feed the lambs; basic seating in main room painted deep blue; good lunches; pool-table *(Dave Webster, Sue Holland)*
☆ **Bamburgh**, Northumberland [NU1835], *Lord Crewe Arms*: Relaxing and comfortable old inn, beautifully placed in charming coastal village below magnificent Norman castle; most interesting bar is the back cocktail bar, full of entertaining bric-à-brac, with winter log fire; generously served food in bar and grill-room, good service, children in side bar; bedrooms comfortable, good breakfasts and dinners *(Mrs J Roberts, Rosalind Russell, WTA, LYM)*
Bardon Mill, Northumberland [Military Rd (B6318); NY7864], *Thrice Brewed*: Large fell-walkers pub by Hadrian's Wall, now under keen new management; large range of real ales and malt whiskies, imaginative food and friendly bar staff; well placed for major sites; bedrooms rather spartan but warm and

cheap *(A Nelson-Smith)*

Barlow, Tyne & Wear [NZ1661], *Black Horse*: Welcoming pub on hill, tree-trunk stools, authentic décor, open fire, Theakstons ales, lounge with dining area *(Andrew and Sean O'Doherty, Perry Board)*

Barnard Castle, Durham [Market Pl; NZ0617], *Golden Lion*: Lovely old warm and comfortable pub with well stocked bar, well kept ale, good value food *(SS)*; [by Market Cross] *Kings Head*: Welcoming and pleasant, cheerful atmosphere, well kept John Smiths, good choice of well presented bar food *(Mr and Mrs J H Adam)*; [Startforth; Bowes rd, signposted to A67] *White Swan*: Dramatic setting on rocks above River Tees, opposite castle ruins; straightforward inside *(LYM)*

☆ **Belford**, Northumberland [Market Pl; village signposted off A1 S of Berwick; NU1134], *Blue Bell*: Comfortable and stylish lounge, plentiful and decent bar food at rather southern prices (the pleasantly old-fashioned dining-room overlooks the attractive garden, which produces some of the vegetables and fruit they use); a relaxing place, with polite and friendly service; recently opened family bar in former stables, with harness, saddlery and so forth, now has Theakstons Best on handpump, darts, pool and simpler food – filled baked potatoes, pancakes, basket meals, children's dishes; children in eating areas; comfortably refurbished bedrooms *(T Nott, Mr and Mrs G D Amos, G Bloxsom, LYM; more reports please)*

Belford, Northumberland, *Salmon*: Cheerful basic local with Vaux Lorimers Scotch, lively pool-room; simple bedrooms *(LYM)*

Bellingham, Northumberland [NY8483], *Black Bull*: Decent pub, good atmosphere *(Len Beattie)*; *Cheviot*: Good atmosphere, decent bar meals, well kept McEwans 80/-; five bedrooms *(M J Lawson)*; *Riverdale Hall*: Victorian hotel on River North Tyne, with salmon fishing; decent bar food can be eaten overlooking swimming-pool or cricket field, or out on the lawn; long-serving welcoming staff; bedrooms *(E R Thompson)*

Belsay, Northumberland [NZ1079], *Highlander*: Consistently good bar meals in very busy but comfortable and attractively decorated pub; evening restaurant *(Rosalind Russell, Ken Smith and others)*

☆ **Berwick Upon Tweed**, Northumberland [A1 N of town; NU0053], *Meadow House*: Friendly atmosphere, first-class service despite being busy, simple but excellent value bar food in large eating area, Vaux Lorimers Scotch on handpump *(A H Doran, David Waterhouse)*

Berwick Upon Tweed [The Green], *Pilot*: Small bar full of nautical knick-knacks with well kept Greenmantle, lunchtime snacks, comfortable lounge, welcoming landlord

(William Dryburgh); [Aller Dean] *Plough*: Remote pub on crossroads with farm, chapel and sheep fields, under new, attentive regime; old and comfortable, with open fire in small main bar, two Burmese cats, games-room, well kept beer, good value restaurant *(Mike Tucker)*

Boldon, Tyne & Wear [Front St (A184), E Boldon; NZ3661], *Black Bull*: Warm welcome from licensees, open-plan lounge bar with good-sized tables, well kept Vaux Samson and good whiskies, excellent lunchtime bar food; soft piped music, garden with children's play area *(E R Thompson)*

☆ **Bowes**, Durham [NY9914], *Ancient Unicorn*: Comfortably modernised open-plan bar, good bedrooms in well converted stableblock, in coaching-inn with *Nicholas Nickleby* connection *(LYM)*

Byrness, Northumberland [A68 Otterburn–Jedburgh; NT7602], *Byrness Inn*: Small bar, jolly atmosphere, good bar food; close to Pennine Way; bedrooms *(Len Beattie, M J Lawson)*

☆ **Chatton**, Northumberland [B6348 E of Wooler; NU0628], *Percy Arms*: Good value home-made food from soup and ploughman's through pies and local cod to evening steaks, with children's dishes, in comfortable carpeted lounge with brocaded seats and family area through stone-faced arch, neatly kept; well kept Theakstons XB on handpump, fair choice of malt whiskies, open fire, picnic-table sets outside; bedrooms *(T Nott, G Bloxsom, Dr P D Smart, BB)*

Chollerford, Northumberland [NY9372], *George*: Hotel in beautiful setting near Hadrian's Wall, with immaculate gardens running down to Upper Tyne; the pubby part is the Fisherman's Bar in what was the original smaller stone inn – simple food, Vaux Samson on handpump, pool, darts, etc. (closed winter mornings); children allowed in hotel part; bedrooms comfortable *(LYM)*

Coatham Mundeville, Durham [off A68, ¼ mile A1(M); NZ2920], *Foresters Arms*: Big pub with well kept John Smiths and Theakstons, bar lunches (not Sun) and pleasant, attentive staff *(John Tyzack)*; [part of Hallgarth Hotel; from A1(M) turn towards Brafferton off A167 Darlington rd on hill] *Stables*: Converted from stone outbuildings with high ceilings, lots of seating, well kept McEwans 80/- and Theakstons Best, Old Peculier and XB, bar food and Sun lunches, separate no-smoking eating area behind, conservatory at side for families; bedrooms *(Michael and Alison Sandy)*

Corbridge, Northumberland [Bridge End – OS Sheet 87 reference 998640; NY9964], *Lion*: Warm welcome in straightforwardly decorated bar with Theakstons beer and good value, home-made bar food including fresh fish; children welcome; bedrooms *(Mr and Mrs G D Amos)*; [about 3 miles N, at junction A68/B6318] *Errington Arms*: Landlord and staff most welcoming and friendly; good bar food, hot and cold, well organised and pleasant atmosphere *(Derek and Maggie Washington)*

Cramlington, Northumberland [NZ2777], *Plough*: Cavernous stone-built free house with wide range of beers including Stones and Youngers No 3, good value bar food including freshly made pizzas with thin bases, thick toppings and stiff lacings of garlic *(John Oddey)*

Crookham, Northumberland [A697 Wooler–Cornwall; NT9238], *Blue Bell*: Well kept McEwans 80/- on handpump and well presented food including fine steaks with tasty sauces and good seafood platter *(Mr and Mrs M D Jones)*

☆ **Durham**, Durham [Elvet Bridge; NZ2743], *Swan & Three Cygnets*: Excellent lunchtime meals have always been the draw in this beautifully placed pub – huge piles of cheese and pâté, doggy bags highly necessary and readily supplied; well kept Sam Smiths ales, very friendly *(T J Maddison, Wayne Brindle, Dave Braisted)*

Durham, Durham [A167 N of Nevilles Cross], *Duke of Wellington*: Big pub with several bars, one in grotesque Spanish style; main draw is varied, substantial and cheap food which includes a surprisingly good choice of vegetarian dishes and excellent Sun lunches; bedrooms comfortable *(T J Maddison, Philip Haggar)*; [Old Elvet] *Dun Cow*: Traditional town pub in pretty black and white timbered cottage; good value cheap snacks, well kept Whitbreads Castle Eden, maybe rapper dancing; children welcome *(G Bloxsom, LYM)*; [2 Sherburn Rd, Gilesgate Moor] *Queens Head*: Beam-effect bar with range of real ales on handpump, good bar food, friendly staff, nice warm fire; often folk group Thurs; bedrooms good value, with own bathrooms *(WFL)*; [86 Hallgarth St (A177)] *Victoria*: Unspoilt Victorian pub with family atmosphere, Theakstons and McEwans 80/-, over 60 whiskies, sandwiches and toasties all day (open 11–11); under same management as Sun at Beamish – see main entries; bedrooms *(Anon)*

☆ **Eastgate**, Durham [signposted from A689 W of Stanhope; NY9638], *Horsley Hall*: Lovely old manor house-type building, doing well under new regime; comfortable, modern bar and beautiful original restaurant; huge helpings of very good value food, splendid views – a place worth watching *(Shaun Burnley, John Tyzack)*

☆ **Egglescliffe**, Cleveland [663 Yarm Rd (A67); NZ4213], *Blue Bell*: Simple lunchtime bar food (not Sun) including good sandwiches in spacious big-windowed bar, seats on terrace by goat-cropped grass sloping down to the River Tees with fine view of the great 1849 railway viaduct – it's

the position that's the particular attraction; friendly service, restaurant; children welcome *(D J Cooke, TRA, MA, LYM)*

Egglescliffe, *Pot & Glass*: Popular local and enjoyable meeting-place *(Jon Dewhirst)*

☆ **Fir Tree**, Durham [A68; NZ1434], *Duke of York*: Good food in clean comfort – modern in style and service, with good solid furnishings by 'mouseman' Thompson; open land behind *(Mr and Mrs D B Allan, John Tyzack, Mrs Sue Johnson)*

☆ **Framwellgate Moor**, Durham [Front St; NZ2745], *Tap & Spile*: Refurbished Camerons pub run largely as free house (there are several similar ones under the same name in the region), simply but comfortably decorated in series of four main rooms, one used for pool and fruit machines, another for board games; friendly atmosphere, quickly changing choice of eight real ales and bar food; deservedly popular *(I W and P J Muir)*

Gateshead, Tyne & Wear [Eighton Banks, Low Fell; NZ2758], *Lambton Arms*: Consistently good food, staff and waitresses always pleasant and helpful, well kept Whitbreads Castle Eden, good coffee *(AKC)*

Great Stainton, Durham [NZ3422], *Kings Head*: Always full and deservedly popular with friendly locals' bar, lounge and restaurant, well kept Whitbreads Castle Eden and good, imaginative food *(Jon Dewhirst)*

Great Whittington, Northumberland [NZ0171], *Queens Head*: Good atmosphere, friendly service, good feel about the place, well kept Marstons Pedigree and Tetleys; neat village *(G Bloxsom, Drs S P K and C M Linter)*

Guisborough, Cleveland [Bow St (between A171 and A173, E of centre); NZ6016], *Fox*: Comfortably refurbished dining bar in modernised coaching-inn, good value quickly served bar food; children welcome; bedrooms *(LYM)*

☆ **Haltwhistle**, Northumberland [Military Rd; B6318 – OS Sheet 86 reference 715660; NY7164], *Milecastle*: Tastefully converted and comfortable – smart, even – with interesting bar food including salmon coulibiac, pheasant and claret pie, home-made venison sausages; atmospheric restaurant, warm and friendly bar with Watneys-related real ales and coal fire, where walkers are welcome *(David and Flo Wallington, E R Thompson, Kay Johnson)*

Haltwhistle, [further along B6318 – OS Sheet 86 reference 751668], *Twice Brewed*: Busy pub with well kept Marstons Pedigree, bar food; handy for Hadrian's Wall and Pennine Way *(Len Beattie, Patrick Young)*

Haverton Hill, Cleveland [NZ4923], *Queens Head*: Well run, with competitive prices and very civil clientele *(F E M Hardy)*

☆ **Haydon Bridge**, Northumberland [NY8464], *General Havelock*: Consistently good food and service; meat, seafood and pastry particularly good; the stripped stone dining-room overlooks the garden, River Tyne and hill sheep pastures *(Dr Kenneth Miller)*

Heighington, Durham [West Green; NZ2522], *Bay Horse*: Pleasant spacious lounge, conventionally decorated, in seventeenth-century pub with good range of food including particularly good trout; quick pleasant service, well kept real ale *(RHMS and others)*

Hexham, Northumberland [Priestpopple; E end of main st, on left entering from Newcastle; NY9464], *County*: Hotel rather than pub, but reliable for lunchtime bar food and friendly service; restaurant; bedrooms *(RHMS)*

Holmside, Durham [NZ2249], *Wardles Bridge*: Remarkable collection of whiskies in friendly country pub *(LYM)*

Holy Island, Northumberland [well worth visiting for the nature reserve; check tides before you cross to the island!; NU1343], *Crown & Anchor*: Excellent beer and quickly served food including good sandwiches in friendly bar with cheerful landlord; good décor including interesting rope fancywork *(Kenneth Finch)*; *Lindisfarne*: Friendly, cafe-like pub with good food in bar and dining-room including excellent crab sandwiches; welcoming licensees, well tended gardens, morning coffee, high teas and afternoon teas; children welcome; bedrooms excellent value *(Mr and Mrs G D Amos, Mr and Mrs Purcell)*

Holystone, Northumberland [NY9503], *Salmon*: Comfortably furnished Coquet Valley local, good value simple food and lively pool-room; in attractive countryside close to Holy Well *(LYM)*

Horsley, Northumberland [this is the one just off A69 Newcastle–Hexham; NZ0966], *Lion & Lamb*: Stone-built pub with comfortable bar, open fire and pleasant young staff; first-class Sun lunches served in two rooms *(Dr P D Smart)*

Hurworth, Durham [NZ3110], *Otter & Fish*: Attractive position, very good choice of well prepared food *(RHMS)*

Jesmond, Tyne & Wear [Osborne Rd; NZ2567], *Trotters*: Friendly and lively pub with lots of mementoes and knick-knacks such as Zurich car registration plates; several real ales including Robinsons and trivia quiz Mon evenings *(R P Taylor)*

Knarsdale, Northumberland [NY6854], *Kirkstyle*: Very friendly village pub, simple but nice, with good beer and good value food *(R A Hall)*

Langdon Beck, Durham [B6277 Middleton–Alston; NY8631], *Langdon Beck*: Like drinking in someone's parlour with a bell on the small bar in the corner of the room; good, cheap and filling basic bar food, well kept Youngers Scotch, popular with local farmers and those staying in nearby youth hostel; outside lavatories; Pennine Way half a mile away; bedrooms *(M J Lawson)*

nr **Langley on Tyne**, Northumberland [A686 S; NY8361], *Carts Bog*: Quickly served bar food and well kept Tetleys and Marstons Pedigree or Theakstons in cosy beamed bar and lounge allowing children; open fire, pool and other games, summer barbecues out by the moors; may be closed weekday lunchtimes *(LYM)*

Longframlington, Northumberland [Wheldon Bridge; NU1301], *Anglers Arms*: Rather dark and austere with lots of stuffed fish, well kept Wards Sheffield Best *(Comus Elliott)*; *New Inn*: Good drinking pub *(Comus Elliott)*

Lowick, Northumberland [NY0239], *Black Bull*: Well kept McEwans on handpump, nice quiet back snug, lively locals' bar, friendly atmosphere helped by landlord; bar food including good local salmon *(Mr and Mrs M D Jones)*

☆ **Marsden**, Tyne & Wear [signposted passage to lift in A183 car park, just before entering Marsden coming from Whitburn; NZ4164], *Grotto*: Notable for its unique position, partly built into cliff caverns: you take a lift down to the two floors – upper pink plush, lower brown varnish; Vaux Samson real ales, food in bar and restaurant *(John Oddey)*

Marske by the Sea, Cleveland [NZ6423], *Mermaid*: Plush and spaciously comfortable modern estate pub with good bar food, friendly, keg beers; family area/conservatory *(Alison Hayward, BB)*

Matfen, Northumberland [NZ0372], *Black Bull*: Country pub in idyllic surroundings facing village green, promising food, welcoming landlord *(D G Malkin)*

Middlesbrough, Cleveland [Grange Rd (central); NZ4919], *Strand*: Polite and friendly service, good bar food – particularly steak pie *(Robin White)*

☆ **Middleton in Teesdale**, Durham [Market Pl; NY9526], *Teesdale*: Wide range of customers in reliably welcoming, clean, comfortable and well furnished pub with well kept John Smiths and Tetleys and good food – sumptuously so in restaurant; occasional unobtrusive piped music; dishes particularly approved include generous cottage pie, pasta and poached salmon; bedrooms well equipped and comfortable *(Stephanie Sowerby)*

☆ **Middleton One Row**, Durham [NZ3612], *Devonport*: View from lounge bar over green and down to valley of river Tees, excellent sandwiches and hot and cold dishes, hard-working owners; bedrooms *(Mrs Shirley Pielou, John Oddey)*

Netherton, Northumberland [OS Sheet 81 reference 989077; NT9807], *Star*: Forbidding exterior and awesome interior with spartan service and drinking room pared to the essentials; no concessions to passing tourist trade and no food – what makes it all wonderfully worth while is the excellent Whitbreads Castle Eden tapped from the cask *(Dave Webster, Sue Holland)*

☆ **Newcastle Upon Tyne**, Tyne & Wear [The Side, by Dean St; NZ2266], *Crown Posada*: Privileged spot in city centre, imposing classical façade with huge stained-glass windows, authentic Victorian atmosphere with long, narrow bar, partly wood panelled with flowery wallpaper above, high, patterned ceiling, pleasant little mahogany tables by extra-long brown leather bench (a popular spot with locals for reading their newspapers); friendly and polite barmaid, sandwiches *(GB, CH)*

Newcastle Upon Tyne [Broad Chare – by river] *Baltic Tavern*: Spacious and comfortably converted warehouse, lots of stripped brick and flagstones or bare boards (as well as plusher carpeted parts) in warren of separate areas, good value bar food, well kept Whitbreads Castle Eden *(LYM)*; [City Rd, nr quayside] *Barley Mow*: Spruce-looking, white and green building with simple, fairly spartan interior and nostalgic gas streetlamps opposite bar counter, small garden overlooking quayside, wide range of real ales, food served through hatch, real fire; good juke box may be pumping out rock music at full volume, and big back area has frequent live music *(K A Topping, GB)*; [Clayton St W; Westmoreland Rd, nr Central Stn] *Dog & Parrot*: Busy pub, popular with students, with lots of seating and standing space, loud juke box, and beers which it brews on the premises (malt extract); had a notable beer festival Nov 1988 which it may repeat *(J F Thorndike)*; [Groat Mkt] *Maceys*: Recently renovated, clean bar with lots of stained glass, Camerons beer from tall founts, lunchtime food; happy hour 5.30–7.30 *(R P Taylor)*; [Pilgrim St] *Market Lane*: Very warm, welcoming pub with wide choice of beer and good food (especially good value lunchtime snacks); regular darts matches, good juke box in the back, happy hour until 8 Fri and Sat; known locally as the Monkey Bar *(K A Topping)*; [Groat Mkt/Bigg Mkt] *Robinsons*: Very friendly, clean bar with lots of pine; Camerons and Whitbreads ales and pop video screens on some walls; popular with young people *(R P Taylor)*; [Shields Rd, Byker] *Tap & Spile*: Popular Camerons theme pub with multi-roomed local feel; wide range of well kept real ales including Gladiator *(Jon Dewhirst)*; [Percy St] *Three Bulls Heads*: Busy, well laid out pub with central bar, well kept Bass and Stones, lunchtime bar food, wide range of customers *(John Thorndike)*; [off Groat Mkt] *Turks Head*: Recently refurbished airy bar with lots of pine furniture; bar food *(R P Taylor)*

☆ **Newton**, Cleveland [A173; NZ5713], *Kings Head*: Sprucely refurbished old pub with good value food from an extensive menu – pork casserole, beef salad, avocado with crab and tuna and hefty club sandwiches all recommended, with good value three-course

lunch (cut price for children); lots of alcoves in nicely furnished spacious lounge, good dining area with outside terrace, soft piped music, good service, John Smiths real ale; below Roseberry Topping, a beauty spot for walks *(E R Thompson, Eileen Broadbent)*

Newton Aycliffe, Durham [Main rd; NZ2825], *North Britain*: Good, cheap bar food, keg beer *(E E Hemmings)*

☆ **Newton by the Sea**, Northumberland [The Square, Low Newton; NU2426], *Ship*: Unspoilt, idyllic spot looking out to sandy beach with lots of wildlife and sailing-boats; 200-year-old pub with basic bar, friendly, helpful licensees, a wide choice of beers and local seafood specialities including good crab and salmon sandwiches; good ploughman's and soup too; keg Drybroughs, tea; children welcome *(Mrs Rina McIvor, Mr and Mrs G D Amos)*

☆ **Newton on the Moor**, Northumberland [NU1605], *Cook & Barker Arms*: A short detour from A1, for simple snacks and well kept McEwans 80/- and Youngers No 3 in unpretentious locals' pub, friendly and clean; landlord has superb sense of humour – but one has to dig a little to trigger it off; children in eating area *(John Oddey, Mrs Sue Johnson, LYM)*

☆ **North Hylton**, Tyne & Wear [Ferryboat Lane; N bank of River Wear almost under A19 bridge – OS Sheet 88 reference 350570; NZ4057], *Shipwright*: Riverside spot with excellent views, recently refurbished in olde-worlde style; homely welcome, bar with lovely coal fire, soft piped music, fruit machine; Vaux beer, extensive range of good bar food at reasonable prices, restaurant; open longer at weekends *(E R Thompson)*

☆ **North Shields**, Tyne & Wear [Burdon Main Row – by Appledore ship repair yard; NZ3470], *Wolsington House*: Unspoilt Edwardian docklands pub with thoroughly masculine big lofty-ceilinged bar, family lounge decorated in period style with two coal fires (children allowed here), cheap bar food lunchtime and early evening, well kept Hartleys XB, Warsteiner real Pilsener, farm cider; open all day, free live music most nights – reopened 1988 by the landlord of the Tynemouth Lodge (see Tynemouth main entries) *(More reports please)*

North Shields, Tyne & Wear [Preston Grange], *Pheasant*: Good food and excellent service, each meal seems to be individually prepared and served at table by assistant chef *(R Riccalton)*

☆ **Otterburn**, Northumberland [NY8992], *Tower*: Limited range of decent bar meals and morning coffee or afternoon tea in plush lounge of sprawling 1830s castellated hotel built around original thirteenth-century peel tower, well kept under present owners, unusual and imposing – something of a Hammer-horror atmosphere with suits of armour, crossbows and stuffed birds, but friendly, and customers genteel enough; limited range of tasty food; rather wildernessy stately grounds fun to explore; neat public bar, own fishing on 3½ mile stretch of River Rede; bedrooms comfortable and good value, with good breakfasts *(Syd and Wyn Donald, LYM and others – more reports please)*

Ovington, Northumberland [signposted off A69 Corbridge–Newcastle; NZ0764], *Highlander*: Good food including well presented smoked trout, tender steaks, pretty puddings, in pleasant and unostentatious dining-room of refurbished old village pub, warm welcome, relaxing atmosphere, calmly efficient service; seats in sloping garden *(Miss E G Tweddle)*

☆ **Rennington**, Northumberland [NU2119], *Horseshoes*: Clean and pleasant flagstone-floored pub, really welcoming, happy and helpful staff, good value freshly cooked food *(Alan Hall)*

Rochester, Northumberland [NY8398], *Redesdale Arms*: Well kept 80/- and reasonable bar food; a good base for the Kielder Forest and Borders area – bedrooms good value *(PLC)*

Rothbury, Northumberland [NU0602], *Queens Head*: Stone village-centre pub with comfortable and welcoming carpeted bars, well kept Vaux Samson on handpump and wide range of good bar food; comfortable bedrooms *(W H Bland)*

☆ **Saltburn by the Sea**, Cleveland [A174 towards Whitby; NZ6722], *Ship*: Magnificent position right on the beach with splendid sea views from original nautical-style black-beamed bars and big plainer summer dining-lounge; good range of speedily served bar food, friendly service, restaurant, children's room, seats on terrace by the beached fishing-boats *(Syd and Wyn Donald, John Tyzack, LYM)*

Seahouses, Northumberland [NU2232], *Bamburgh Castle*: Hotel superbly sited above harbour, looking out to sea and islands; friendly, good beers on handpump, good bar food, big warm fires, shelves of books; bedrooms comfortable and inexpensive *(WFL)*; *Lodge*: Welcoming bar in Scandinavian-style hotel with nice atmosphere, bar snacks specialising in seafood, restaurant; bedrooms *(Sue Cleasby, Mike Ledger)*

Shadforth, Durham [off B1283 Durham–Peterlee; NZ3441], *Plough*: Cosy pub, locals' bar, juke-box-free lounge with open fire; friendly new licensee, well kept Stones on handpump and good value simple bar food *(Jon Dewhirst)*

☆ **Shincliffe**, Durham [A177 1m S of Durham; NZ2941], *Seven Stars*: Delightful semi-rural pub at end of village street, small but comfortable, traditionally furnished in one half, with a remarkable fireplace in the other; friendly staff, amiable pug, quiet

atmosphere, good substantial food in bar and restaurant, well kept Vaux ales; attractive in summer, with some seats outside; bedrooms *(T J Maddison, John Tyzack, Patrick and Carole Jones, I W Muir)*

Shotley Bridge, Durham [NZ0953], *Raven*: Modern multi-level pub, well kept and comfortable, with valley views from picture windows – a real change from most pubs around here *(E J Alcock)*

Slaley, Northumberland [NY9858], *Rose & Crown*: Friendly welcome, well kept McEwans/Youngers ales, excellent home-made food in bar and restaurant including fine mid-week three-course special menu, efficient unobtrusive service; rather spartan décor *(John Oddey)*

South Shields, Tyne & Wear [South Foreshore – beach rd towards Marsden; NZ3766], *Marsden Rattler*: Made up of two railway carriages mounted on their tracks and joined by a bar; there's also a glass conservatory with plants; all-day tea, coffee and cakes, evening restaurant *(Gary Scott)*; [Mill Dam] *Steamboat*: Old-fashioned nautical pub full of photos and ship models, plenty of authentic atmosphere, Vaux ales, bar food *(John Oddey)*

☆ nr **Stannersburn**, Northumberland [Greystead; on Kielder Water road from Bellingham, past Birks – OS Sheet 80 reference 768856; NY7286], *Moorcock*: Plain and unspoilt but comfortable country pub on way to Kielder Water, welcoming landlord, well kept Tetleys, short choice of excellent lunchtime bar food – all home cooked; attractive old-fashioned fireplaces; children welcome, with sweets if they finish their food; well equipped bedrooms in new wing *(John Oddey, David Bolton, Matthew Waterhouse)*

Stannersburn, *Pheasant*: Good scenery, friendly licensees, excellent food, well kept McEwans 80/-; bedrooms comfortable *(John Haig)*

Stannington, Northumberland [NZ2279], *Ridley Arms*: Spacious open-plan bars with cosy furnishings, efficient food counter and well kept Whitbreads Castle Eden – useful stop-off from A1 *(LYM)*

Stockton on Tees, Cleveland [NZ4419], *Hardwick Hall*: Comfortable hotel bar, popular with locals; welcoming staff, good variety and quality of food; bedrooms *(John Tyzack)*; [Hartburn Village; southern outskirts] *Masham*: Four small rooms, each with its own character, well kept Bass, good cheap baps and sandwiches, and garden with aviary and children's play area backing on to paddock; children allowed *(Jon Dewhirst)*

Summerhouse, Durham [B6279 7 miles NW of Darlington; NZ2019], *Raby Hunt*: Pleasantly decorated pub in small village, very pleasant people, excellent food *(RHMS)*

Tantobie, Durham [NZ1855], *Oak Tree*: Excellent atmosphere, good unobtrusive service, very good food and a decent range of wines *(Jon Silkin)*

Thropton, Northumberland [NU0302], *Cross Keys*: Traditional stone-built three-bar village pub, handy for Cragside and Coquet Valley; open fires in cosy beamed main lounge, attractive garden with panoramic view over village to Cheviot, well kept Bass *(W H Bland, LYM)*; *Three Wheat Heads*: 300-year-old pub filled – perhaps overfilled – with bric-à-brac, but has open fires, and bar food can be good (game dishes recommended), though service may be slow; children's adventure play park; bedrooms comfortable *(E R Thompson, Richard Davies)*

Ulgham, Northumberland [NZ2392], *Forge*: Good range of food in comfortable and airy lounge opening on to terrace and sheltered neat lawn with croquet, quoits and play area; cheery high-ceilinged public bar used to be the village smithy *(T Nott, LYM)*

Waldridge, Durham [off A167; NZ2550], *Waldridge*: Dining pub with wide choice of good value food in lounge and restaurant, good service, Vaux beers, soft piped music but no machines; for eating, rather than just drinking *(E R Thompson)*

Wall, Northumberland [NY9269], *Hadrian*: Sixteenth-century house with cosy, comfortable atmosphere in Jacobean-style bars, good food and service; bedrooms *(Ken Smith)*

Warden, Northumberland [½ mile N of A69; NY9267], *Boatside*: Bass, McEwans and Stones, choice of wines and first-class food in bar or restaurant at reasonable prices, freshly prepared and generously served; spacious pub by River Tyne, closed Mon lunchtime *(E R Thompson)*

Warkworth, Northumberland [6 Castle Terr; NU2506], *Sun*: Homely, welcoming seventeenth-century hotel, obliging licensee most helpful with disabled people, extensive, reasonably priced menu including locally landed fish, McEwans and Theakstons; children welcome; bedrooms *(E R Thompson)*

West Auckland, Durham [A68; NZ1926], *Blacksmiths Arms*: Oak-beamed room with central bar counter, log fire and extensive range of bar food including sandwiches and home-made dishes *(Mike and Mandy Challis)*

West Woodburn, Northumberland [NY8987], *Bay Horse*: Comfortable bedrooms in refurbished inn with bustling unpretentious atmosphere in bar *(S C Beardwell, J Stacey, LYM)*

West Wylam, Tyne & Wear [off A695; NZ1163], *Falcon*: Attractive, modern Roast Inn with pleasant lounge, no piped music; well kept Whitbreads Castle Eden, excellent varied bar food, dining room, children's menu and OAP lunches, helpful service *(E R Thompson)*

Witton Le Wear, Durham [just E of A68, 5 miles N of West Auckland; NZ1531], *Victoria*: Comfortable and warm, good welcome, quick friendly service, varied menu *(Dr Peter Smart)*

Wolviston, Cleveland [NZ4526], *Wellington*: Pleasant local with good atmosphere, well kept Bass; pork pies and crisps, but no real bar food *(Jon Dewhirst)*

Wooler, Northumberland [High St; NT9928], *Black Bull*: Simple old town hotel with straightforward lunchtime bar food in season, McEwans real ale, games in public bar, quieter high-ceilinged knocked-through main bar; bedrooms *(LYM)*; [Ryecroft Way (off A697)] *Ryecroft*: Rather stretching a point to include this well run family hotel as a pub, but locals do drop into the busy lounge bar for the well kept real ales including Lorimers Scotch, Marstons Pedigree and Yates Bitter; imaginative restaurant food; bedrooms comfortable and good value *(Angie and Dave Parkes)*

Yarm, Cleveland [NZ4213], *George & Dragon*: Included as the place where the Stockton & Darlington Railway Co first met, to start modern mass transport; comfortably modernised; quickly served bar food *(LYM)*; [High St] *Ketton Ox*: One of village's oldest and most historic buildings, the windowless upper floor once being venue for cockfighting; friendly atmosphere, back pool-room, fruit machines, Vaux Samson and Wards on handpump; children welcome *(Martin Thomas)*

Nottinghamshire   *see* Leicestershire

Oxfordshire

This area has always been at the forefront of advances in pub food quality. One consequence is that, besides the dozen or so pubs here which have our new higher-standard food award, quite a number of other pubs have food so good that they are on the brink of award level. Wherever you go, it's quite hard to go wrong. At the top end, a problem is that some of the best pubs here for food are getting too restauranty. This not only tends to hoik up prices, but also brings the risk of losing an essential element of the appeal of eating out in pubs – the easy informality and lively natural charm of a true pub. Here, there's one insurance policy against that risk: the unchangingly natural and unspoilt nature of so many of the pubs tied to Brakspears, the Henley brewers. These do indeed cover the range from simple rusticity (as in the Fox & Hounds on Christmas Common) to relaxed elegance (as the White Hart in Nettlebed), but somehow always preserve an unforced easy charm. And one of the delights is that even in the easy-going surroundings of a low-ceilinged Chilterns walkers' pub such as the Five Horseshoes at Maidensgrove, the food can run to the finest steaks or prettily presented butterfly prawns; or there's the Chequers tucked away with its rabbits and sweet peas in a back lane in Watlington, and the prettily thatched and flagstoned Bottle Glass at Binfield Heath – other places to find fine food in unspoilt old-fashioned surroundings; and even when the pub itself's more modern – as in a new entry, the Butchers Arms at Sonning Common, which serves some of the best bar food around – the essential virtue of an honestly welcoming natural and unfussy warmth remains. The Three Tuns, an archetypal Brakspears pub in Henley itself, is serving food all through the day. All this, of course, is not to say that Brakspears have a monopoly on the combination of decent food with pubby charm. A very good non-Brakspears example is another new entry: the delightfully old-fashioned Home Sweet Home at Roke, well worth tracking down under its enterprising

The Elephant & Castle, Bloxham

567

*new owners. For all-round charm, the two most attractive places in the area –
both doing specially well at the moment – are the Lamb in Burford and
Falkland Arms at Great Tew. Among the many Lucky Dip entries at the end of
the chapter, places that are currently particularly promising include the
Abingdon Arms at Beckley, Mermaid in Burford, Hunters Lodge at Fifield,
White Horse at Forest Hill, Gate Hangs High near Hook Norton, Nut Tree at
Murcott, Lamb at Satwell, and Eagle & Child and Perch in Oxford (a rich
hunting-ground for good pubs, as is Woodstock).*

ADDERBURY   SP4635 Map 4
White Hart

Tanners Lane: off Hornhill Road (signposted to Bloxham) towards W end
of village

Refurbishments and rebuilding at the beginning of 1989 included the upgrading of
the restaurant, new indoor lavatories, and behind-the-scenes changes such as a
redesigned kitchen. The comfortable, friendly bar hasn't changed much: heavy
beams, eighteenth-century seats and other old-fashioned settles and armchairs,
paintings, antique prints, and a roaring log fire. Good home-made food includes
three starters such as soup, pâté or a mousse (£1.50), at least eight main courses like
hot chilli prawns, kidneys, a vegetarian dish, chicken and Hungarian goulash (all
£4), and four puddings like fruit pie, cheesecake, lemon mousse or Bakewell tart
(£1.50). Lunchtime sandwiches (from £1) and ploughman's (from £1.50) –
occasionally, this may be the only food then; winter Sunday lunch. Well kept Hook
Norton on handpump; helpful staff. Piped music. *(Recommended by Ian Phillips,
A T Langton, Andy Tye, Sue Hill, F M Steiner, R Simmonds, Hazel Church)*

*Free house   Licensee Andrina Coroon   Real ale   Meals and snacks (not Sun or Mon)   Open
12–2.30, 6.30–11 all year; closed evening 25 Dec*

BINFIELD HEATH   SU7478 Map 2
Bottle & Glass 🏠

Village signposted off A4155 at Shiplake; from village centre turn into
Kiln Lane – pub at end, on Harpsden Road (Henley–Reading back road)

Even when this thatched black and white timbered pub gets very busy, the staff
remain extremely helpful and pleasant. The low-beamed bar has fine old flagstones
and tiles, huge logs in the big fireplace, ancient tables (so scrubbed that one or two
are almost like silvery-grey driftwood), a bench built into black squared panelling,
and spindle-back chairs. The side room is furnished along similar lines, and one
window has diamond-scratched family records of earlier landlords. Bar food, often
imaginative, includes sandwiches (from £1.25), home-made pâté (£1.95),
ratatouille or cottage pie (£2.95), cauliflower with prawn sauce, chicken livers with
bacon, fresh grilled sardines, courgettes with prawns in a cheese sauce, seafood with
mushrooms, or fresh smoked trout (all £3.50) or rich wine casserole (£3.95), and
twelve-ounce rump steak (£8.50); well kept Brakspears Bitter, SB and Old on
handpump. In the garden there are old-fashioned wooden seats and tables under
little thatched roofs, and an open-sided shed like a rustic pavilion. *(Recommended by
Henry Midwinter, Ian Phillips, Lindsey Shaw Radley, Chris Raisin, Graham Doyle, Nick
Dowson, Jamie and Sarah Allan)*

*Brakspears   Licensee T C Allen   Real ale   Meals and snacks (not Sun)   Open 11–2.30,
6–11*

---

*Please keep sending us reports. We rely on readers for news of new discoveries, and
particularly for news of changes, however slight, at the fully described pubs. No stamp
needed: The Good Pub Guide, FREEPOST, London SW10 0BR.*

BLOXHAM SP4235 Map 4

Elephant & Castle [*illustrated on page 567*]

Humber Street; off A361

Much the most imposing building in this steep Cotswolds village street of thatched stone-built cottages, this friendly place has an attractively simple public bar with an elegant seventeenth-century stone fireplace and a stripped wood floor. The comfortable lounge has a good winter log fire in the massive fireplace in the very thick wall, which divides it into two rooms. The food prices here really are remarkably low: good sandwiches, ploughman's, sausage or ham with eggs, scampi or a daily special (£2.25), and rump steak (£4.50); the well kept Hook Norton Best and Old Hookey on handpump are well priced, too. Sensibly placed darts, dominoes, cribbage, a fruit machine and shove-ha'penny – the board is over a century old – and there's an Aunt Sally pitch up in the flower-filled yard, summer only. (*Recommended by Stephen King, Tom Evans, Sheila Keene; more reports please*)

Hook Norton   Licensee Chas Finch   Real ale   Lunchtime meals and snacks   Restaurant (closed Sun) tel Banbury (0295) 720383   Children welcome   Open 10.30–2.30, 6–11 all year

BRIGHTWELL BALDWIN SU6595 Map 4

Lord Nelson ✪

Brightwell signposted off B480 at Oxford end of Cuxham or B4009 Benson–Watlington

The new owners here, who also run the Red Lion at Mortimer West End in Hampshire, have introduced a new menu which covers the bar and restaurant (though in the evening the restaurant has its own menu): home-made soup (£1.75), duck liver and pork pâté (£2.50), garlic mushrooms with crispy bacon or prawn and peach cocktail with a brandy cocktail sauce (£3.25), popular lunchtime Welsh rarebit (£3.75), steak and kidney pie (£5.50), fettuccine al pesto (£5.75), salads (from £5.95), duck in orange pie or casserole of scallops, prawns and monkfish (£6.95), and puddings such as fruit crumble (£2.25) or raspberry meringue (£2.50). Sunday lunch (from £9.75). Tables are not bookable (except in the restaurant), so it's best to get here early at weekends. Brakspears PA on handpump, and a very decent wine list, including a good range of cheaper French wines. The left-hand bar has Nelson's influence very much in evidence: the plain white walls are decorated with pictures and prints of the sea and ships, there are some ship design plans, and a naval sword hangs over the big brick fireplace in the wall (which divides off a further room). It's comfortably modernised, with wheel-back chairs (some armed), country kitchen and dining-chairs around the tables on its Turkey carpet, candles in coloured glasses, orange lanterns on the walls, and pretty fresh flowers. Faint piped music, neat and friendly waitress service. There's a verandah at the front, and tables on a back terrace by the attractive garden or under its big weeping willow, beside the colourful herbaceous border. This listed seventeenth-century building was closed in 1905 by the squire, and then became the village shop and post office, though the previous owners still renewed its licence each year. (*Recommended by Henry Midwinter, AP, A T Langton, D L Johnson; more reports please*)

Free house   Licensees Peter Neal, Richard Britcliffe and Ann Neal   Real ale   Meals and snacks (12–2, 7–10; not Mon)   Restaurant (not Mon, not Sun evening) tel Watlington (049 161) 2497   Children over 9 in restaurant only   Open noon–3, 6.30–11 all year; closed Mon and evening 25 Dec

BURFORD SP2512 Map 4

Bull ✪

High Street

Divided by a central stone fireplace (with log fires on both sides), the main beamed and panelled bar in this now somewhat hotelish old inn is comfortably furnished with cushioned settees, Windsor chairs and other wooden seats; there's another adjacent room, as well as a dining-room. Imaginative food includes sandwiches (from £1.95, not Sunday), home-made soup such as carrot and coriander (£1.50), home-made chicken liver pâté (£2.30), chef's salad (£2.95), ploughman's (from £3.50), smoked duck breast with orange and cranberry sauce (£3.65), fish and chips (£4.75), smoked goats' cheese stuffed with mushroom and onion, covered with puff pastry and topped with tomato and basil sauce (£5.25), monkfish in a wine and cream sauce with bacon and chives (£5.55), a pie of the day such as good steak and kidney, fish or venison and smoked ham with redcurrants and port (£5.75), cassoulet (£5.90), good sirloin steak (£6.75), and puddings like fresh fruit crumble (£1.50); children's dishes (£2.50). Well kept Ruddles Best on handpump; darts, dominoes, cribbage and piped music. *(Recommended by G and M Brooke-Williams, Simon Collett-Jones, BKA, Jason Caulkin; more reports on the service please)*

Free house   Licensee M Cathcart   Real ale   Meals and snacks (12–3, 6.30–10)
Restaurant   Children welcome   Open 11–11 in summer; 11–3, 5.30–11 in winter
Bedrooms tel Burford (099 382) 2220; £28(£35B)/£47.50(£54.50B)

Lamb ★ ★ 🛏

Sheep Street

This 500-year-old Cotswold inn is a civilised, welcoming place with delightfully old-fashioned bars. The public bar is traditionally furnished with high-backed settles and old chairs on flagstones in front of its fire. The more spacious beamed main lounge has distinguished old seats including a newly upholstered chintzy high winged settle, ancient cushioned wooden armchairs, easy chairs, and seats built into its stone-mullioned windows, as well as bunches of flowers on polished oak and elm tables. There are oriental rugs on the wide flagstones and polished oak floorboards, attractive pictures, shelves of plates and other antique decorations, a grandfather clock, a writing desk, and a good winter log fire under its elegant mantelpiece. The rest of the building is decorated in similar style, with simple, old-fashioned, chintzy bedrooms. Bar lunches rotate on a daily basis, and should typically include soup (£1.50), sandwiches (from £1.15, smoked salmon £2.50), ploughman's (from £2.75), steak sandwich (£4.25), grilled sardines or potato and bacon hot-pot (£3.95), good liver with orange sauce, guinea-fowl casserole, navarin of lamb or goulash (all £4.50), smoked salmon salad (£5.95), and delicious puddings such as chocolate roulade with ginger or toasted hazel-nut mousse with chocolate (£1.75); free dips at Sunday lunchtime. Well kept Wadworths IPA and 6X from an antique handpump beer engine in a glassed-in cubicle, with winter Old Timer tapped from the cask down in the cellar. There's a real sun-trap of a garden, totally enclosed by the warm stone of the surrounding buildings, with a pretty terrace leading down to small neatly kept lawns surrounded by flowers, flowering shrubs and small trees. Dogs welcome. *(Recommended by Peter Scillitoe, J M M Hill, WHBM, Henry Midwinter, Patrick Freeman, Nigel Williamson, Stephen Goodchild, Roy Gawne, Simon Collett-Jones, Alan Skull, David and Jane Russell, Ewan McCall, Roger Huggins, Tom McLean, K A Read, Jason Caulkin, Neville Burke, BKA, M C Howells, Simon Velate)*

Free house   Licensees R M de Wolf and K R Scott-Lee   Real ale   Meals and snacks (lunchtime, not Sun)   Restaurant   Children welcome   Open 11–2.30, 6–11 all year
Bedrooms tel Burford (099 382) 3155; £27.50/£50(£58B)

nr CHINNOR   SP7500 Map 4

Sir Charles Napier 🏵

Spriggs Alley; from B4009 follow Bledlow Ridge sign from Chinnor; then, up beech wood hill, fork right (signposted Radnage and Spriggs Alley); OS Sheet 165 reference 763983

A favourite of ours, this totally individual establishment hangs on to its place in the *Guide* by the skin of its teeth. This is not because of doubts about its quality –

almost the reverse. The problem is that emphasis now is virtually wholly on the stylish and charmingly decorated restaurant which so surprisingly forms the major part of what from outside looks to be a plain little Chilterns pub. Indeed, at weekends, we'd say that there's no point in going unless you want a restaurant meal (which could easily cost you £50 a head). It's during the week that, with a bit of luck, you should find the place quiet enough to enjoy a drink and something much cheaper to eat, with room to sit in the original small front bar. There are homely armchairs, narrow spartan benches by the wall, highly polished tables, a plain woodblock or tiled floor, bare oak boards in the low ceiling, and a good winter log fire (with gleaming copper pipes running from the back boiler behind it); good music is well reproduced by the huge loudspeakers. The brief bar menu includes tomato soup with onions and herbs (£1.75), avocado, Mozzarella and tomato salad or moules marinière (£3), home-made sausages with mustard sauce or cold Scotch beef with new potatoes (£5), and braised lamb or baked haddock with parsley and lemon (£6). Champagne is served on draught at £2 a glass, they have well chosen wines by the bottle, well kept Wadworths IPA or 6X tapped from the cask, freshly squeezed orange juice, eight Russian vodkas and a few malt whiskies; friendly, unhurried staff. The decorations in the restaurant include works by two local artists – sketches of Francis Bacon by Claire Shenstone, commissioned by him to do his portrait, and sculpture by Michael Cooper; Sunday luncheon is possibly the most fashionable meal of the week, though it tends to work out at around £25 a head. In summer they serve lunch in a charming crazy-paved back courtyard with rustic tables by an arbour of vines, honeysuckle and wistaria (lit at night by candles in terracotta lamps), and there are peaceful views over the croquet lawn and the paddocks by the beech woods which drop steeply away down this edge of the Chilterns. (*Recommended by TBB, M A and C R Starling, Roger and Lynda Pilgrim, David and Flo Wallington, Dr J R Hamilton, Peter Hitchcock, John Tyzack, JMC*)

Free house   Licensee Mrs Julie Griffiths   Real ale   Lunchtime bar meals (not Sun or Mon) Restaurant (not Sun evening) tel Radnage (024 026) 3011   Children welcome lunchtimes; in evenings if over 8   Open 11.45–2.30, 6.45–11 Tues–Sat; closed Sun evening and Mon

CHIPPING NORTON   SP3127 Map 4

Crown & Cushion   🛏

High Street

Originally a coaching-inn dating back to 1497, this comfortably modernised hotel has a cosy, old-fashioned beamed bar. There are tapestried armed chairs around wooden tables on the red Turkey carpet with more in a snug low-ceilinged side alcove, chairs the height of bar stools by ledges set into timber partitions, some walls partly knocked through or stripped to bare stone, and a big winter log fire; the atmosphere is relaxed and the locals cheery. Well kept Donnington, Wadworths IPA and 6X, and changing guest beers on handpump from an attractive bar counter, which has warm-coloured ancient flagstones alongside it. The bar food is freshly prepared and includes double-decker sandwiches (from £1.50), home-made pâté or ploughman's (£1.95), omelettes (from £2.40), grilled rainbow trout or steak and mushroom pie (£3.20) and sirloin steak (£5.20); quiet piped music. Windows look out on the narrow brick-paved creeper-hung coach entry, which leads back to tables out on a sun-trap terrace. They are planning a back garden. (*Recommended by Michael and Alison Sandy, Lyn and Bill Capper, S V Bishop, Tom Evans, Margaret and Trevor Errington*)

Free house   Licensee Jim Fraser   Real ale   Meals (not Fri or Sat evenings) and snacks (not Sun lunchtime, not Fri or Sat evenings)   Restaurant; not Sun lunchtime   Children welcome Open 10.30–2.30, 5.30–11 all year   Bedrooms tel Chipping Norton (0608) 2533; £36B/£58B

Sunday opening is now 12–3 and 7–10.30 throughout England.

CHRISTMAS COMMON   SU7193 Map 4
Fox & Hounds

Hill Road from B4009 in Watlington; or village signposted from B480 at
junction with B481

Stepping in here is like going back thirty years or more. The tiny, simple beamed bar
on the left has three tables and wooden wall benches or bow-window seats, a
framed Ordnance Survey walker's map on one cream wall, a little carpet down on
the red-and-black flooring tiles, and two sturdy logs to sit on in the big inglenook –
which has a fire burning even in summer. A small room on the right (popular with
locals and for drinking only) is similar; the alsatian is friendly. Well kept Brakspears
PA, SPA and Mild are tapped from casks in a back still-room; efficient service.
Lunchtime food includes soup (80p), sandwiches (from 90p), ham and eggs (£2.15)
and scampi (£3.60); note that they do only soup and sandwiches on Sundays and
Mondays. Dominoes, cribbage. Outside there's a rampant Albéric Barbier rose
climbing the walls, old-fashioned garden seats and sitting-logs by the roses and
buddleja on the front grass beyond a small gravel drive, and picnic-table sets under
a sumac beside the house. There are fine Chilterns walks all around. *(Recommended
by Mayur Shah, Chris Raisin, Graham Doyle, Joan Olivier, Phil Gorton, Gordon and Daphne)*
*Brakspears   Real ale   Snacks (lunchtime)   Children in games-room off one bar   Open 11–2.30,
6–11 all year*

CLANFIELD   SP2801 Map 4
Clanfield Tavern
A4095

Friendly new licensees have taken over this pretty village inn and made a few minor
changes; they were hoping to add some bathrooms to the bedrooms as we went to
press. Off the carpeted main bar are several flagstoned small rooms with heavy
stripped beams, various chairs, seats cut from casks and settles around the tables,
brass platters and hunting prints on the old stone walls, and a handsome open stone
fireplace with a big log fire and a seventeenth-century plasterwork panel above it.
Home-made bar food includes good home-made soup (£1.20), sandwiches (from
£1.20), duck pâté (£2.50), ploughman's (£2.50), home-made burgers (from £3.55),
and rump steak (£5.45), specials like roast quail (£4.20) or medallions of pork in
kiwi sauce (£4.25), and puddings such as profiteroles or banoffi pie. Well kept
Hook Norton Best, Morlands Bitter and Morrells Varsity on handpump, and quite
a few bin-end wines; darts, dominoes, shove-ha'penny, cribbage, fruit machine and
trivia, and there is a proper skittle alley. There are tables and chairs on a small lawn
with a flower border and roses, and views across to the village green and pond.
*(Recommended by Patrick Freeman, Maj R A Colville, Andy Blackburn, Heather Sharland,
M E Lawrence, G B Pugh; more reports please)*
*Free house   Licensees Keith and Anne Gill   Real ale   Meals and snacks   Cottagey
restaurant   Children welcome (but not near bar servery)   Open 11.30–2.30, 6–11 all year
Bedrooms tel Clanfield (036 781) 223; £15/£30*

CLIFTON HAMPDEN   SU5495 Map 4
Barley Mow

Back road S of A415 towards Long Wittenham

The very low-beamed lounge in this 700-year-old building has old-fashioned
furnishings (including antique oak high-backed settles), and old engravings on the
walls. The black-flagstoned public bar is broadly similar, and there's a side family-
room with handsome squared oak panelling. Bar food includes ploughman's (from
£2.10), a buffet table (£3.25), daily specials, a roast of the day (£4.40), and
puddings like apple or fruit pies (£1.35). Ruddles County, Ushers Best and

Websters Yorkshire on handpump; dominoes, cribbage, fruit machine. There are rustic seats among the flowers on a well kept sheltered lawn, and the Thames bridge is a short stroll away. Beware the public car park some way down the road – there may be thefts. *(Recommended by M J Dyke, R Houghton, TBB, Gethin Lewis, Nancy Witts, Joan Olivier)*

Ushers (Watneys)   Real ale   Meals and snacks   Restaurant; closed Sun evening   Children in oak room   Open 11–2.30, 6–11 all year   Bedrooms tel Clifton Hampden (086 730) 7847; £29/ £46 (own lavatories)

CROPREDY   SP4646 Map 4

Red Lion

Off A423 4 miles N of Banbury

Part of a row of pretty thatched cottages, this old brown stone pub is simply furnished in a traditional style: high-backed settles under its beams, brasses on the walls, a fish tank, and a fine open fire in winter; the atmosphere is relaxed and friendly. Good home-made bar food includes sandwiches, garlic mushrooms (£2.25), pâté or terrine (£2.45), pork ragout (£3.75), vegetarian lasagne (£3.95), game or steak, kidney and Guinness pies (£4.95), half a honey-roast duck or excellent king prawns in garlic (£6.95), and puddings such as chocolate biscuit gateau or hot chocolate fudge cake (£1.45). In the last year Mr Hunt has branched out very considerably on the drinks side with well kept Arkells BBB, Tetleys, and Wadworths 6X on handpump, decent wines with special offers on a blackboard, properly mixed Pimms or bloody Mary, and summer and winter punches; friendly service. Darts, dominoes, cribbage, pool, fruit machine and juke box. There are seats in the back garden, a raised churchyard opposite, and the Oxford Canal a hundred yards away. Although it is generally very quiet, parking could be problematic at summer weekends. *(Recommended by David and Jane Russell, Graham Oddey, Jon Wainwright, Andrew Stephenson)*

Free house   Licensee Jeremy Hunt   Real ale   Meals and snacks   Children welcome   Open 11– 3.30, 6–11 all year; closes 2.30 afternoons in winter

CUMNOR   SP4603 Map 4

Bear & Ragged Staff

19 Appleton Road – village signposted from A420: follow one-way system into village, bear left into High Street then left again into Appleton Road – signposted Eaton, Appleton

Built in 1555, this twin gabled farmhouse has a spreading and comfortable bar: polished black sixteenth-century flagstones in one part and Turkey carpet elsewhere, easy chairs and sofas as well as more orthodox cushioned seats and wall banquettes, soft lighting, and a large open fire with a log basket. Good bar food is served in a no-smoking area and includes ploughman's (£2.50), salads with pâté (£3.65), locally smoked Eynsham trout (£4.25), or home-cooked beef or ham (£4.85), and hot dishes such as vegetarian flan or prawn and asparagus quiche (£3.50), lasagne (£3.95), veal and liver stir-fry (£4.25), a daily roast (from £4.25), lamb and mushroom casserole or fisherman's pie (£4.50), braised rib of beef (£4.75), and four or five puddings. Well kept Morrells and Varsity on handpump, and malt whiskies; friendly service. There's a children's play area, with a swing and climbing-frame at the back by the car park. This is part of Buccaneer Inns; it can get crowded at weekends. *(Recommended by Lynda and Howard Dix, Henry Midwinter, Dr C S Shaw, Mr and Mrs D A P Grattan, TBB, William Rodgers, Dr and Mrs S Pollock-Hill, John Tyzack)*

Morrells   Licensee Michael Kerridge   Real ale   Meals and snacks   Restaurant (not Sun evening) tel Oxford (0865) 862329   Children in eating area of bar   Open 11–2.30 (3 Sat), 5.30–11 all year

DORCHESTER   SU5794 Map 4

George 🛏

Village signposted from A423

This peaceful, civilised timber and tile inn was a posting- and then a coaching-inn, though it was actually built as a brewhouse for the Norman abbey which still stands opposite. Old-fashioned, comfortable furniture includes cushioned settles and leather chairs, and there are some beams, a big fireplace, and carpet on the wood-block floor of the bar. Lunchtime food includes home-made soup (£2.50), a little pot of prawns and mushrooms (£2.95), open sandwiches (from £3.25), lasagne or a daily special (£4.95), omelettes with free-range eggs (£5.25), Cornish fish pie (£6.15), grilled calf's liver and bacon (£7.25), and home-made puddings (£2.50). Brakspears on handpump, good wine by the glass; immaculate service. The pub is near *Good Walks Guide* Walk 96. *(Recommended by JMC, TBB; more reports please)*

Free house   Licensee Brian Griffin   Real ale   Lunchtime meals and snacks (not Sun)
Restaurant   Children in restaurant   Open 11–3, 6–11; closed Christmas week
Bedrooms tel Oxford (0865)   340404; £49B/£68B

EAST HENDRED   SU4588 Map 2

Wheatsheaf

Chapel Square; village signposted from A417

This popular sixteenth-century pub stands among thatched brick buildings behind a triangle of well kept grass. The friendly bar has some vertical panelling, high-backed settles and stools around tables on quarry tiles by a log-burning stove, a minute parquet-floored triangular platform by the bar, and cork wall tiles. Low stripped deal settles form booths around tables in a carpeted area up some broad steps. Good bar food includes sandwiches (from 90p, big baps from £1.50), home-made soup (£1.10), sausages (£1.95), vegetarian crêpes (£2.50), kedgeree (£2.95), gammon steak (£3.65), steaks (from £3.95), trout (£4.95), chicken stuffed with mushroom and asparagus (£5.10) and puddings (£1.75). Well kept Morlands Bitter and Old Masters on handpump, a few malt whiskies and country wines; darts, dominoes, Sunday quiz, Aunt Sally, piped music, and maybe Ben, the solidly built golden labrador. There are seats in front of the black and white timbered pub, and on the back grass among roses and other flowers, conifers and silver birches; there's a budgerigar aviary, and a new play area for children with swings and so forth. This attractive village is just below the downs, and its church has an unusual Tudor clock with elaborate chimes but no hands. *(Recommended by Lyn and Bill Capper, Dr Stewart Rae, Henry Midwinter, David Young, M J Dyke, A T Langton, Mrs Margaret Dyke)*

Morlands   Licensees Liz and Neil Kennedy   Real ale   Meals and snacks; not Mon evening   Children in restaurant   Open 11–3, 6–11 all year   Bedrooms tel Abingdon (0235) 833229; £18/£36

FARINGDON   SU2895 Map 4

Bell 🛏

Market Place

There's a seventeenth-century carved oak chimneypiece over the splendid inglenook fireplace in the old-fashioned bar of this comfortable, carefully run coaching-inn, as well as some unusual fragments of ancient wall painting, and Cecil Aldin hunting prints; it's attractively furnished with red leather settles, and still has the ancient glazed screen through which customers would watch the coaches trundling through the alley to the back coachyard – now the hallway. A side room has a modern panoramic mural by Anthony Baynes. Good bar food includes sandwiches or filled French bread (from £1.10), home-made soup (£1.75), home-made pâté (£2.75), Madras curry (£3.50), salads (from £3.50), omelettes or lasagne (£3.75), steak sandwich (£4.50), and a daily special such as liver and bacon, sausages with onion gravy or fish and chips (all £3); puddings (from £1.50). Well kept Badger Tanglefoot and Wadworths 6X and winter Old Timer on handpump, several malt whiskies; maybe Bess the charming labrador. The cobbled and paved yard, sheltered by the back wings of the inn, has wooden seats and tables among tubs of flowers. *(Recommended by Gordon and Daphne, B and J Derry, Dr and Mrs James Stewart, Joy Heatherley, Ewan McCall, Roger Huggins, Tom McLean, Frank Cummins, Patrick Freeman)*

Wadworths   Licensee William Dreyer   Real ale   Meals and snacks (10.30–2, 6–9.30) Restaurant; not Sun evening   Well behaved children welcome   Open 10.30–3, 5.30–11 all year   Bedrooms tel Faringdon (0367) 20534; £24(£32.50B)/£30(£37.50B)

FERNHAM   SU2992 Map 4

Woodman ★

The barn (which was the games-room) here is in the process of being converted to a gym – something the customers and staff are very keen to take advantage of; some other unusual touches include a big central log fire that sometimes has a hot-pot simmering over it in winter, hot saki, clay pipes ready-filled for smoking, and a collection of hats above the bar. The candle-lit tables in the heavily beamed rooms are made simply from old casks, cushioned benches are built into the rough plaster walls, and there are pews and Windsor chairs; decorations include milkmaids' yokes, leather tack, coach horns, an old screw press, and good black and white photographs of horses. The reasonably priced bar food, served at your table, includes filled baked potatoes (£1.75), ploughman's (£2), home-made steak and kidney pie (£3), and changing specials like mushroom quiche (£2.40), fennel and pasta in tomato sauce or moussaka (£3.20), beef and bitter cobbler (£3.75), and various puddings such as hot chocolate fudge cake (£1.25). Well kept Morlands PA and BB, Theakstons Old Peculier and Hook Norton Old Hookey or Gibbs Mew Bishops Tipple tapped from casks behind the bar – regular OAPs have been paying 30p a pint; country wines; friendly dog. *(Recommended by HNJ, PEJ, Gordon and Daphne, Ewan McCall, Roger Huggins, Tom McLean, Frank Cummins)*

Free house   Licensee John Lane   Real ale   Meals and snacks (not Mon evening)   Children in eating area of bar   Live music Fri or Sat every three weeks and every Sun   Open 11–2.30, 6–11 all year, though may open longer in afternoons if trade demands

FYFIELD   SU4298 Map 4

White Hart

In village, off A420 8 miles SW of Oxford

An enormous wooden door in this busy and very impressive medieval building leads to a fine rambling and sheltered back lawn with well tended flower borders (and quite a few cats), and the pub is not far from the delightful gardens of Pusey House. The main room is a hall with soaring eaves, huge stone-flanked window embrasures, and an attractively snug carpeted upper gallery looking down into it. A low-ceilinged side bar has an inglenook fireplace with a huge black urn hanging over the grate, and a framed history of the pub on the wall. The priest's room is now a dining area, as is the barrel-vaulted cellar. The impressive (if rather expensive) range of well kept real ales, which changes from time to time, typically consists of Boddingtons Bitter, Gibbs Mew Bishops Tipple, Morlands Bitter, Ruddles County, Theakstons Old Peculier, Wadworths 6X and Farmers Glory, and guest beers on handpump or tapped from the cask. Bar food includes soup (£1.25), pâté (£2.05), pan-fried sardines when available (£2.15), vegetarian lasagne (£3.25), chilli con carne (£3.45), Indonesian chicken or breaded plaice (£3.75), a range of home-made pies (from £3.45), and steaks (from £6.50); daily specials are usually available; good if sometimes casual service. Dominoes, cribbage, shove-ha'penny and fruit machine. *(Recommended by Roger Bellingham, Dick Brown, Margaret Dyke, Lyn and Bill Capper, Mr and Mrs G D Amos, H G Allen, Neville Burke, Anne Morris)*

Free house   Licensees Edward and John Howard   Real ale   Meals and snacks (12–2, 7–10)   Restaurant (closed Sun) tel Oxford (0865) 390585   Children in three or four rooms   Open 11–2.30, 6.30–11 all year; closed 25 and 26 Dec

GORING HEATH   SU6679 Map 2
King Charles Head
Goring Heath signposted off A4074 NW of Reading, and B4526 E of Goring

The garden by this isolated tiled-roof brick cottage meanders off into the tall beech woods which surround it – the woodland setting is very special, and no doubt contributes a lot to the warm, relaxed atmosphere inside. Here, small rooms ramble around a solidly built central servery, with comfortable floral-print wall banquettes and other seats, glossy plain tables, decorative plates and small country pictures on the white walls, and logs burning in a back stove and the open fire on the right. From the wide choice of well cooked popular food in generous helpings, readers have recently picked out for particular praise the attractively presented fresh salads, grilled sardines, lasagne, cannelloni and steak and kidney pie; well kept Adnams, Brakspears PA and Mild, Courage Directors, Glenny Hobgoblin, Hook Norton Best and Theakstons XB on handpump; darts, cribbage, fruit machine; friendly service. A more modern back extension opens into the garden, which has plenty of tables under cocktail parasols on a terrace and on the grass, with a timber climber and tyre swings. From just across the road you can walk down to Holly Copse and then the Thames, by Mapledurham Country Park. *(Recommended by James Cane, Sheila Keene, Steve Huggins, Henry Midwinter and others)*

Free house   Licensees David and Christine Lawton and A Glyn   Real ale   Meals and snacks (not Sun evening)   Children in eating area   Open 11.15–2.45, 6–11 all year; may close 25 Dec

GREAT TEW   SP3929 Map 4
Falkland Arms ★ ★ 🏠
Off B4022 about 5 miles E of Chipping Norton

It's extraordinary that we don't get more people complaining of crowdedness here – this little pub attracts so many readers, again and again, that we can't see how they all fit in. In a beautiful peaceful village, it is very much the classic country pub. The partly panelled bar has shutters for the stone-mullioned latticed windows, a wonderful inglenook fireplace, high-backed settles and a diversity of stools around plain stripped tables on flagstones and bare boards, one-, two- and three-handled mugs hanging from the beam and board ceiling, and dim converted oil lamps. The bar counter, decorated with antique Doulton jugs, mugs and tobacco jars, always serves several reasonably priced and well kept guest beers, as well as the regular Badger, Donnington, Hook Norton Best and Wadworths. They also keep country wines and farm ciders, do hot punch in winter, have clay pipes filled ready to smoke, some fifty different snuffs, and hankerchiefs for sale. Lunchtime bar food is home made and includes sandwiches, and six daily specials like mushrooms in Stilton and cider (£3.50), a vegetarian dish (£3.60), lamb and leek pie (£3.75), and Cotswold chicken (£3.80); friendly and cheerful service; darts, shove-ha'penny, dominoes, cribbage and table skittles. On a summer weekday, sitting on the wooden seats among the roses on the front terrace, with doves cooing among the lumpy cushions of moss on the heavy stone roof-slabs, can feel quite special. The pub is part of the manor of Great Tew which belonged to the Falkland family until the end of the seventeenth century; the fifth Viscount Falkland who was treasurer of the Navy in 1690 also gave his name to the Falkland Islands. The lavatories are a couple of doors down the lane – as the building is Grade I listed, the council will not let them build anything outside the back of the pub. *(Recommended by Denis Mann, Dennis and Pat Jones, David Young, Mr and Mrs J D Cranston, Richard Sanders, Nick Dowson, Mrs E M Bartholomew, HNJ, PEJ, Robert Gomme, Christopher Knowles-Fitton, Ian Phillips, Chris Raisin, Graham Doyle, John Bowdler, Simon Collett-Jones, Dr and Mrs James Stewart, Mr and Mrs J H Adam, Alan and Ruth Woodhouse, I R Hewitt, Richard Gibbs, Rob and Gill Weeks, H G Bown, T George, A and K D Stansfield, Julie Vincent, Lindsey Shaw Radley, Neil Barker, PADEMLUC, A E Loukidelis, Lady Quinny, Neville Burke, J E Rycroft, Wayne Brindle, M E Dormer, A J Hughes, Brian and Rosemary Wilmot, S V Bishop, Jason Caulkin)*

Free house   Licensee John Milligan   Real ale   Lunchtime meals and snacks (not Sun or Mon)   Children in eating area of bar   Folk music Sun evening   Open 11.30–2.30, 6–11 all year; closed Mon lunchtime   Three bedrooms tel Great Tew (060 883) 653; £20S/£28(£30S) (double rooms only)

HAILEY   SU6485 Map 2

King William IV ★

Signposted with Ipsden from A4074 S of Wallingford; can also be reached from A423; OS Sheet 175 reference 641859

Something of a rural museum, this friendly white house has beams in the glossy ruby-smoked ceiling and timbered bare brick walls festooned with well restored farm tools; everything has been researched to find its age, use and maker: root cutters, forks, ratchets, shovels, crooks, grabbers, man-traps, wicker sieves, full-size carts, ploughs, and a pitching prong. There's good sturdy furniture on the tiled floor in front of the big winter log fire with its original faggot oven, and two broadly similar carpeted areas open off. In winter the atmosphere is quiet and cosy, and in summer it's busy and friendly (when service may get a bit pushed). Well kept and reasonably priced Brakspears PA, SB, XXXX Old and Mild tapped from casks behind the bar, and good filled rolls such as ham, cheese and pickle, corned beef (from 50p – the only evening food), and pies, pasties or Stilton ploughman's with home-made soup (£2.40 – the soup alone, a winter thing, is £1.10). On the back lawn there are seats out among smartly painted veteran farm equipment, such as cake-breakers and chaff-cutters, looking down over a fine rolling stretch of wood-fringed Chilterns pasture. A friend of the landlord's operates horse and wagon rides from Nettlebed to the pub where you then have a ploughman's or supper and gently return through the woods and via Stoke Row back to Nettlebed (from £6 a head; telephone Ian Smith on 0491-641364). *(Recommended by Chris Raisin, Dr Stewart Rae, David Marshall, Graham Doyle, Dr J R Hamilton, Maureen Hobbs, Sharon Taylor, Tim Irish)*

Brakspears   Licensee Brian Penney   Real ale   Snacks   Children in eating area Open 11–2.30, 6–11 all year

HENLEY-ON-THAMES   SU7882 Map 2

Besides Lucky Dip entries listed under this town, you might like to see entries listed under Remenham – just over the Thames bridge and therefore in Berkshire

Three Tuns

5 Market Place

This popular and friendly pub's name refers to the three major vessels used in brewing beer. The layout is cosy and traditional, with two small rooms opening off a long tiled and panelled corridor (which leads to a small back terrace), and there are several cast-iron, pre-nationalisation railway company notices on the walls. The panelled front public bar has dominoes, cribbage, fruit machine and piped music; then, beyond the old-fashioned central servery, is a snug and unpretentious heavily beamed buttery, with a central chimney and log-effect gas fire dividing off its back part. There's an unusual pricing system that shows a complete disregard for the decimal system: soup with a sort of Vienna stick (70p), sandwiches (from 70p, two-rasher bacon, lettuce and tomato £1.54, hot salt beef £2.26), home-made chicken liver pâté (£1.55), filled baked potatoes (from £1.65), ploughman's (called boatman's or fisherman's here, from £1.88), vegetarian lasagne (£2.56), egg, bacon, sausage and tomato (£2.75), home-made lasagne (£2.93), a pie of the day (£3.56), gammon with egg or pineapple (£4.59), mixed seafood (£4.81), and six-ounce sirloin steak (£6.79). Besides chips, they also do croquettes. Well kept Brakspears PA and SB on handpump, with Mild and Old tapped from the cask, and cheap doubles; quick, polite service; piped music. The pub is near *Good Walks Guide* Walk 68. *(Recommended by Richard Sanders, David and Eloise Smaylen, D J Penny, Ian Phillips, Chris Payne, Sheila Keene, Gary Scott, Mrs Margaret Dyke, Quentin Williamson, D Stephenson, David Regan, TBB)*

Brakspears   Licensees Jack and Gillian Knowles   Real ale   Meals and snacks (10–9.30 Mon–Fri, noon–9 Sun)   Children in back part of buttery   Open 10–11 all year; closed evening 25 Dec

LITTLE MILTON   SP6100   Map 4
Lamb   🔾

3 miles from M40 junction 7; A329 towards Wallingford

Friendly and usually quiet (students don't get out this far), this thatched seventeenth-century pub has a softly lit carpeted bar with a few beams in its low cream ceiling, lots of tables with wheel-back chairs, and cottagey windows in its stripped stone walls that are so low you have to stoop to look out. A wide choice of quickly served, home-made food includes sandwiches (from £1.15, not weekends), ploughman's with warmed bread (£2.25), good fresh salads (£4.95), and hot main dishes such as rabbit and prunes, lamb and courgette casserole, oxtail braised in beer or grilled Portuguese sardines (all £4.95), venison in red wine (£5.35), guinea-fowl (£5.95) and steaks (from £6.65); there are lots of puddings such as lemon charlotte (from £1.20). Well kept Ind Coope Burton and Tetleys on handpump; fruit machine, piped music. This honey-coloured stone building is one of the reasons why the rolling farmland area is now a conservation area. It's decorated in summer with hanging baskets and tubs of flowers, and you can sit in the quiet garden, with swings, roses, a herbaceous border and fruit trees. *(Recommended by John Branford, D L Johnson, Dr J R Hamilton, A T Langton, SC)*

Halls (Allied)   Licensee David Bowell   Real ale   Meals and snacks (12–2, 7–10); bookings tel Great Milton (0844) 279527   Open 11–2.30, 6.30–11 all year

MAIDENSGROVE   SU7288   Map 2
Five Horseshoes   🔾

W of village, which is signposted from B480 and B481; OS Sheet 175 reference 711890

Remote on a lovely common among beech woods high in the Chilterns, this low-ceilinged, rambling pub is popular for its friendly welcome and stylishly prepared food. The main bar has mainly modern furnishings – wheel-back chairs around shiny dark wooden tables – though there are some attractive older seats and a big baluster-leg table, as well as a good log fire in winter. Bar food includes home-made soup (from £1.75), ploughman's (from £2.75), baked potatoes with interesting fillings (from £2.95), home-made pâtés like smoked trout or avocado and walnut (mostly £3.50), chilli con carne (£3.95), steak and kidney pie (£4.50), a casserole of the day, seafood lasagne (£5.95), stir-fried beef (£5.95), Scotch salmon (£6.50) and Scotch steak (from £9); specials include vegetable lasagne (£4.50), breaded butterfly prawns (£5.50) or giant New Zealand mussels (£6.50). Well kept Brakspears PA and SB on handpump; courteous, helpful service. It's popular with walkers, and there's even a separate bar in which boots are welcome. There are picnic-table sets on the sheltered lawn and under a fairy-lit Perspex arbour. Get there early to be sure of a table – it does get very busy indeed, with people waiting for seats at weekends. *(Recommended by Jane and Calum Maclean, Richard and Dilys Smith, Gordon and Daphne, Stephen King, J Roots, Alison Hayward, Nick Dowson, Don Mather, F M Bunbury)*

Brakspears   Licensees Graham and Mary Cromack   Real ale   Meals and snacks (not Sun evening)   Open 11–2.30, 6–11 all year

MINSTER LOVELL   SP3111   Map 4

Old Swan ★ 🏠

Just N of B4047; follow Old Minster signs

In a picturesque village, this beautifully placed old stone inn has three or four smartly modernised and attractive low-beamed rooms opening off the small central bar. There are Liberty-print easy chairs, good china in corner cupboards, an antique box settle, Turkey carpets on the polished flagstones, and big log fires in huge fireplaces. Lunchtime bar food includes soup (£1.25), sandwiches (from £1.25), home-made pâtés (from £2.25), ploughman's (£2.50), a slimmers' salad (£3), and prawns in a spicy dip (£3.50); well kept Ind Coope Burton and Tetleys on handpump pulled by a neatly dressed barman. The restaurant is housed in what used to be the brewhouse. On the way out to the garden there's a medieval well, and then a neatly kept lawn with seats, a lily pond, flowers and shrubs, and some shade from chestnut and sycamore trees. *(Recommended by C R Ball, Patrick Freeman, Capt and Mrs D S Kirkland, John Branford, Brian and Rosemary Wilmot, Chris Cooke, Nancy Witts, R P Taylor; more reports please)*

Halls (Allied)   Licensee Alan Taylor   Real ale   Lunchtime snacks (not Sun)   Restaurant; not Sun evening   Children welcome   Open 11–11 all year   Bedrooms tel Witney (0993) 75614; £37.50B/£59B

MOULSFORD   SU5983   Map 2

Beetle & Wedge 🏠 🏠

Ferry Lane; off A329, 1½ miles N of Streatley

For generations this has been the epitome of a Thames-side inn – the sort of place you'd make an expedition to, especially in summer, to eat and drink in relaxed surroundings, watching the ducks. And of course it's changed with the times. The latest development, in line with people's increasing expectations from food in pubs, is that it has been taken over by the people who have made the Royal Oak at Yattendon Berkshire's classiest food pub. So the style has changed here. Food has become the main thing, and a good deal more imaginative – as well as more expensive. They've moved the pubby part from what has now become much more of a hotel lounge bar into a new Boathouse bar down by the river. Here, as elsewhere, they've clearly got their sights set on re-creating a leisured feel that recalls the hotel's Edwardian heyday. Decorated in colours of tortoiseshell, greens and browns, there's a mix of old chairs, some armchairs, bar stools, a ten-foot Edwardian sofa, polished wooden tables, oak saddle-beams, a tiled floor, and flint and brick walls; you can also sit in the flagstoned conservatory. Food here includes leek and potato soup (£2.25), crispy duck with frisée salad (£3.75), cod's roe pâté or avocado salad with smoked chicken and prawns (£3.75 or £6.25), ploughman's with unpasteurised cheeses (£4), sirloin steak (£5), wing of skate with black butter and capers (£6.25), suprême of chicken with mushrooms and a creamy curry sauce (£7.85), and fillet of red mullet with queen scallops and saffron sauce (£8.75); they've installed a charcoal grill for steaks. Well kept Adnams Bitter, Badger Tanglefoot and Wadworths 6X on handpump; friendly service. The waterside lawn, flanked by roses, has robustly old-fashioned garden furniture. Moorings are available at £15 per boat per night, refundable on food in bar or restaurant, and the ferry which used to run from here will start again on summer weekends. The hotel is near the start of *Good Walks Guide* Walk 97. The bedrooms have all been redecorated. *(Recommended by Pat Jones, Dr Stewart Rae, John Knighton, Lyn and Bill Capper, A T Langton; more reports please)*

Free house   Licensees Richard and Kate Smith   Real ale   Meals and snacks (12.30–2, 7.30–10)   Restaurant   Well behaved children welcome   Occasional jazz nights Open 11–2.30, 6–11 all year   Bedrooms tel Cholsey (0491) 651381; £50B/£65B

NETTLEBED   SU6986 Map 2

Carpenters Arms

Crocker End; hamlet signposted from A423 on W edge of Nettlebed

New licensees here are planning to keep this little brick cottage as traditional as possible, with no fruit machines or juke box. The carpeted main room has flowery-cushioned dark small pews, wheel-back chairs, and country pictures on the cream walls. A partly panelled side saloon bar has a small settee, comfortable seats cushioned in plush deep red, and old prints on its walls; the hooks on the ceiling were once used to hang up hams smoked here – regulars were handed a knife with their pint and helped themselves. In winter there are three log fires. The bar food includes home-made soup (£1.35), ploughman's (from £2.45), lasagne (£3.50), vegetarian pie (£3.55), home-made steak pie (£3.95), steaks (from £6.95), and puddings (£1.25). Well kept Brakspears PA, SB and Mild on handpump; darts, shove-ha'penny, dominoes, cribbage and piped music. On the sunny front terrace white tables and seats stand by the climbing roses and shrubs. *(Recommended by Sheila Keene, Joan Olivier, Don Mather, G and S L)*

Brakspears   Licensees David and Debbie Taylor   Real ale   Meals and snacks (not Tues evenings)   Restaurant tel Nettlebed (0491) 641477   Open 11–3, 6–11 all year

White Hart

A423, in centre

There are cosy leather easy chairs, and other old-fashioned seats and settles in the civilised and beamed lounge bar of this big brick and flint ex-coaching-inn. It's been knocked through into an extensive series of sitting areas, with shallow steps between; one snug side area has a highly polished grand piano, another has a good winter log fire, and there's a big Act of Parliament wall clock. Bar food includes sandwiches, mushrooms in a Stilton sauce (£3), home-made charcoal-grilled burgers (£3.25), pies (£3.85) and nut cutlets or vegetarian salads (£4.35); children's helpings available. Brakspears PA and SB on handpump; shove-ha'penny, backgammon and chess. There are tables and benches outside. *(Recommended by Mike Tucker, Don Mather, Joan Olivier; more reports please)*

Brakspears   Licensee Gregory Leith   Real ale   Meals and snacks   Restaurant   Children welcome   Open 11–2.30, 6–11 all year   Bedrooms tel Nettlebed (0491) 641245; £20/£25

NEWBRIDGE   SP4101 Map 4

Rose Revived

A415 7 miles S of Witney

This spacious old stone inn is refurbished in Victorian style with rose-patterned wallpaper, lots of rose pictures, glass lamps and marble tables. The buffet bar serves sandwiches, ploughman's (£2.25), cold meat platter (from £2.25) and lasagne or steak and kidney pie (£3.25); well kept Morlands PA and Old Masters on handpump; fruit machine, trivia and piped music. The dining-room has a handsome sixteenth-century stone fireplace with an oak mantelbeam. Stretching along a quiet reach of the upper Thames, the lovely garden has a long lawn, crazy-paved paths, weeping willows, spring bulbs or a colourful summer herbaceous border, and is prettily lit at night by superannuated street lamps. *(Recommended by A T Langton, Paul Barker, GS; more reports please)*

Morlands Licensee Alan Jefferson Real ale Meals and snacks Restaurant Children welcome Jazz Sun evening Open 11–11 all year Bedrooms tel Standlake (086 731) 221; £30(£35B)/£40(£45B)

NOKE SP5413 Map 4
Plough

Village signposted from B4027, NE of Oxford

The three knocked-together rooms in the main bar have dark beams covered in brightly pictorial plates, settles and other closely spaced seats on the dark brown carpet, and several dogs and cats. Ordered through a hatch to the kitchen, the simple bar food includes sandwiches if they're not too busy, home-made French onion soup (95p), ploughman's (from £1.50), sausages and egg (£1.75), good value fry-up (£2.75), home-made steak and kidney pie or charcoal-roasted ham with egg (£2.75), home-made Lancashire hot-pot or lamb chops (£3), scampi (£3.50), steak braised in Guinness gravy (£3.75), and puddings such as good home-made fruit pie (from 95p); best to get there early on Sunday lunchtimes in summer. Well kept Courage Best and Directors on handpump; space game, piped music. In summer there are plenty of seats out in the pretty garden, which backs on to farmland, and walks in the nearby Otmoor wilderness. *(Recommended by Dr and Mrs James Stewart, Mrs E Ellis, M A and C R Starling, PAB, Roger Barnes, Helen Stanton; more reports please)*

Courage Licensee Peter Broadbent Real ale Meals and snacks (not Weds evening) Children at kitchen end of bar Country music Tues, folk third Sun of month Open 12–2.30, 7–11 all year

OXFORD SP5106 Map 4
Bear

Alfred Street

In its coaching heyday this used to stretch the whole way down the street, and parts of the surviving structure date back seven hundred years; even the handpumps – serving well kept Ind Coope Burton and Tetleys – are over a century old. The four low-ceilinged and partly panelled rooms have traditional built-in benches and plain tables, a collection of 7, 000 or so club ties, all neatly arranged behind glass (there are still regular additions), and an old-fashioned atmosphere that those who like call cosy and those that don't call cramped; fruit machine. Home-made bar food includes sandwiches, home-made pâté (£1.70), omelettes (from £1.75), ploughman's (from £1.75), home-made quiche (£1.80), steak and kidney pie (£2.20) and scampi (£2.65). The menu says welcome in five languages, giving some idea of the customers, though in term-time it gets very crowded with students from Oriel and Christ Church colleges, and often you'll find as many people drinking out on the street, by the tables on the side terrace. *(Recommended by Ian Phillips, Dr John Innes, Jon Wainwright, Graham Bush)*

Halls (Allied) Licensee M L Rusling Real ale Meals and snacks (12–2, 5.30–8.30) Nearby parking very limited Open 11–11; 11–2.30, 5.30–11 in winter; closed 25 and 26 Dec

Oxford Brewhouse ★

14 Gloucester Street; by central car park and Gloucester Green bus station

Steps in this well run place lead up to three linked mezzanines which look out into the main area and down into a two-level pit. It's largely done out in wood and stripped brick, and there are lots of basic junk-shop-style chairs, rocking chairs, pews and tables, with some benches let into the walls of the main area, and a big wood-burning stove. Decorations include big dark tuns perched on brick pillars, brass cask spigots, and an airborne brewers' dray laden with casks. Bar food includes sandwiches (from £1.50, large baps £1.75), soup with cheese and bread (£2.25), ploughman's (£2.70), and several hot meals like tagliatelle, a vegetarian dish, home-made quiche, curry or steak pie (all £3.20). The nine real ales might include Archers Village, Arkells BBB, Burton Bridge Porter, Fullers London Pride, Glenny Wychwood Best, Hook Norton Old Hookey and Wadworths 6X; piped music, good service. There are picnic-table sets in a small, neat back courtyard under a tall ash tree, and they are planning to open a side garden. It's quiet and cosy at lunchtimes, very lively and popular in the evenings. *(Recommended by RCL, Duncan and Lucy Gardner, David Fowles, Michael and Alison Sandy, P Miller, Roy Gawne, R H Inns, M O'Driscoll, John and Joan Wyatt, Jon Wainwright, Brian Marsden, Graham Bush)*

Halls (Allied)   Licensee Jo Hastings   Real ale   Meals and snacks (not Sat or Sun evenings) Children in upper levels   Live music once a month   Open 10.30–2.30, 5.30–11 all year

Turf Tavern

Bath Place; via St Helen's Passage, between Holywell Street and New College Lane

Buried in its hidden courtyard, and secluded from the modern bustle of the city by the high stone walls of some of its oldest buildings (including part of the ancient city wall), this medieval stone building is still much as Hardy described it when Jude the Obscure discovered that Arabella the barmaid was the wife who'd left him years before. There are dark beams and low ceilings, and flagstoned or gravel courtyards. Good bar food includes home-made soup (£1.05), vegetarian meals (from £2.95), beef and beer pie or lasagne (£3.35). Well kept Archers Headbanger, Flowers Original, Glenny Hobgoblin and Whitbreads Castle Eden on handpump, with mulled wine in winter; service can be slow on a busy weekend; trivia machine. The pub is popular with foreign visitors. *(Recommended by P Miller, Richard Sanders, R G Ollier, JMC, M O'Driscoll, Geoff Wilson, Charles Gurney, Ian Phillips)*

Whitbreads   Licensee Stephen Shelley   Real ale   Meals and snacks   Children welcome Jazz Sun evening   No nearby parking   Open 11–11 all year

PISHILL   SU7389 Map 2

Crown

B480 N of Henley

The three fine fireplaces in this ancient red brick and flint building use a ton of coal each week in winter. The friendly latticed-window bar has an elegant corner cabinet of decorated plates, old photographs on the partly panelled walls in the front area, and a central black-beamed and red-and-gold-carpeted part with little blocky country chairs and stools around wooden tables. The rear section is knocked through, with standing oak timbers. Good, home-made bar food includes sandwiches (weekday lunchtimes only), soup (£1.50), filled baked potatoes (from £2.25), ploughman's or deep-fried mushrooms with a garlic dip (£2.50), ratatouille topped with cheese (£2.95), lambs' kidneys turbigo or steak, kidney and mushroom pie (£3.95), creamy prawn curry or beef Stroganoff (£4.95), and sirloin steak (£6.50). Well kept Eldridge Pope Dorchester, Palmers BB and Ruddles Best and County on handpump. An attractive side lawn outside the wistaria-covered pub has picnic-table sets, and the surrounding valley is quiet and pretty. *(Recommended by Dick Brown, J P Day, M J Dyke, Derek and Sylvia Stephenson, Stephen King, Gary Wilkes)*

Free house   Licensee Jeremy Capon   Real ale   Meals and snacks (12–2, 7–10)   Restaurant tel Turville Heath (049 163) 364   Children in restaurant   Open 11.30–2.30, 6–11 all year Bedrooms in separate cottage tel Henley-on-Thames (0491) 63364; £65B(£65B)

Please tell us if any Lucky Dips deserve to be upgraded to a main entry, and why. No stamp needed: *The Good Pub Guide,* FREEPOST, London SW10 0BR.

ROKE SU6293 Map 2

Home Sweet Home 🏵

Village signposted off B4009 Benson–Watlington

Snugged away in its quiet hamlet, this pretty thatched and tiled old house has lots of flowers around the tables out by the well in its low-walled front garden. Inside, it's leisured and quietly civilised, with a great variety of good home-cooked food under the new owners – underlining the connection with their other pub, the Old Boot at Stanford Dingley. It includes a wide and unusual range of ploughman's, served generously but with packet butter (from £1.95), lots of filled baked potatoes (from £2.10), omelettes (£2.95), burgers (from £2.70), salads (from £3.25), creamy baked prawns (£3.60), ham and egg (£3.75), scallops provençale (£3.85), smoked beef fillet or steak sandwich (£3.95), with dishes of the day such as stuffed mushrooms with prawn and cream cheese salad (£3.50), cod (£3.95), chicken and Stilton en croûte (£4.25) and a well flavoured game pie with very light pastry (£4.25); vegetables are good and crisply cooked, and they have a notable range of vegetarian dishes (£1.50–£4.50); beside all that, you can eat in the bar from the more exalted restaurant menu – or vice versa. The main bar has two smallish rooms, with bare boards, heavy stripped beams, leather armed chairs, just a few horsy or game pictures such as a nice Thorburn print of snipe on its white-painted stone walls, and big log fires – one with a great high-backed settle facing it across a hefty slab of a rustic table. On the right, a carpeted room with low settees and armchairs, and an attractive corner glass cupboard, leads through to the neat and pretty restaurant. Well kept Ind Coope Burton, Tetleys and a guest beer such as Brakspears PA on handpump, a good choice of malt whiskies, interesting wines; unobtrusive piped nostalgic pop music, friendly service. *(Recommended by Lyn and Bill Capper, S Clark)*

Free house Licensees Jill Madle, Peter and Irene Mountford Real ale Meals and snacks (12–2.30, 5.30–10) Restaurant tel Wallingford (0491) 38249 Children in restaurant and snug Open 11–3, 5.30–11 all year; closed evening 25 Dec

SHENINGTON SP3742 Map 4

Bell

Village signposted from A422 W of Banbury

Looking very pretty across the narrow end of the green, this neatly kept, seventeenth-century pub has a lounge with heavy oak beams, old maps and documents on the cream walls, brown cloth-cushioned wall seats and window seats, and tables with vases of flowers; it's mainly carpeted, though on the left – where the wall is stripped to stone and decorated with heavy-horse harness – there are flagstones. On the right it opens into a neat little pine-panelled room (popular with locals) with decorated plates on its walls. The friendly new licensees have introduced a new menu: sandwiches (from £1.25) and home-made dishes like carrot and orange soup (£1.95), good pâté, avocado salad (£2.50), mushrooms on toast (£3.25), home-cooked gammon (£4.50), vegetarian hazel-nut roast or seafood quiche (£4.75), rogan josh curry (£5.25), good lamb and almond casserole or liver Stroganoff (£5.75), and puddings such as summer pudding or banoffi pie (from £1.95). Food was tremendously popular under the previous regime, though in the early days of new regime people who knew the pub before were not convinced that it was still as imaginative, but as summer progressed further reports suggested that the cooking was really getting into its stride. Well kept Flowers Original and IPA and Hook Norton Old Hookey on handpump, and a good choice of wines from Berry Bros; quick, efficient service; darts. The tortoiseshell cats are called Myrtle and Mittens (and they've added three of their own), the labrador is called Katie and the West Highland terrier Lucy. There are two or three tables out in front.

(Recommended by Ted George, Joy Heatherley, John Bowdler, G and M Brooke-Williams, M H Box, Bernard Phillips, I R Hewitt, Mr and Mrs M Pearlman; more reports please)

Free house   Licensees Jennifer and Stephen Dixon and Sylvia Baggott   Real ale   Meals and snacks (not Sun evening)   Restaurant (not Sun evening)   Children in eating area of bar only Open 12–3, 7–11 all year; closed Sun evening   Bedrooms tel Edge Hill (029 587) 274; £12/£24(£30B)

SHIPTON-UNDER-WYCHWOOD   SP2717 Map 4

Lamb ⊗ ⇔

Just off A361 to Burford

As we went to press this rather up-market, well kept place was up for sale; obviously a change of ownership might well affect our food award – we'd like news on this please. The atmosphere has been old-fashioned and relaxed, with newspapers on poles, a fine oak-panelled settle, long pews, beams, a solid oak bar counter, and flowery curtains in the small windows of the old partly bared stone walls. Well kept Hook Norton Best on handpump; good wines and several malt whiskies. Popular bar food has included an excellent cold buffet, home-made soup, duck and orange pâté (£2), Scandinavian hash or Cotswold pie (£5.50), seafood tart or duck in cherry sauce (£6.50), poached salmon and shrimp sauce (£7.50), and puddings such as treacle tart or strawberry Pavlova (£1.75). In summer you can sit at tables among the roses at the back. *(Recommended by Helen Crookston, Gwen and Peter Andrews, James Cane, Gordon Mott, Barbara Hatfield, Patrick Freeman, Gordon Theaker, S V Bishop, Nancy Witts)*

Free house   Real ale   Meals and snacks (12.15–2, 7–10)   Restaurant; not Sun evening Children in restaurant   Open 11.30–2.30, 6ish–11 all year   Bedrooms tel Shipton-under-Wychwood (0993) 830465; £30B/£48B (double rooms only)

Shaven Crown

The magnificent double-collar braced hall roof and front lounge here, with its lofty beams and sweeping double stairway down the stone wall, are part of the original Tudor building, which is said to have been used as a hunting-lodge by Elizabeth I. Bar food is served in the fine beamed bar at the back of the courtyard which has a relief of the 1146 Battle of Evesham, as well as seats forming little stalls around the tables and upholstered benches built into the walls. It includes sandwiches, soup (£1.25), ploughman's (£2.15), Canadian-style potato skins (£2.25), babotie (£3.95), lightly curried prawns (£4.85), sirloin steak (£6.25), and puddings like treacle tart (£1.50). Flowers Original and Hook Norton Best on handpump; friendly service. Surrounded by the heavily stone-roofed buildings, the medieval courtyard garden is a pleasant place to sit in summer, with a lily pool, roses and old-fashioned seats set out on the stone cobbles and crazy paving. It has its own bowling-green. *(Recommended by Frank Cummins, Stephen King, R G Bentley, Simon Velate)*

Free house   Licensee Trevor Brookes   Real ale   Meals and snacks   Restaurant   Children in eating area of bar only   Open 12–2.30, 7–11 all year   Bedrooms tel Shipton-under-Wychwood (0993) 830330; £24/£56B

SONNING COMMON   SU7080 Map 2

Butchers Arms ⊗

Follow Binfield Heath, Shiplake Row signpost into Blounts Court Road, from B481 Reading–Nettlebed on NE edge of Sonning Common – at car salesroom

The last time we saw Mr Banks was at the Old Crown in Skirmett (Buckinghamshire), which remained a thoroughly countrified and ancient place throughout the time that he was hauling it from obscurity into the front line of fine food pubs. His new venture here could hardly be more different – a 1920s-style brick building with a partly lino-floored games-bar, and a small lounge with brocaded wall banquettes and spindle-back chairs around shiny wood tables, a modern brick fireplace, and an opening into the bright big-windowed restaurant. Yet behind the modernity the essentials are still the same. First, the man himself, warmly welcoming, and going out of his way to make sure all the customers are happy; secondly, his way with the Brakspears PA, SB and Mild, so well kept on handpump. And then of course the food – a wide and changing choice, which might include soup (£1.25), Welsh rarebit (£1.75), pâté or boerewors (spicy sausage, £2.50), aubergine cheesecake, crispy lamb and mint rolls or Brie and mushrooms (£3), filled baked potatoes, pickled herring salad, mussels done in cream and Parmesan or moussaka (£3.50), baked crab (£3.75), haddock, prawn and mushroom pasta or steak and kidney pie (£4), salads (from £4.50), shark steak or braised venison (£6) and crêpes filled with smoked turkey and wild mushrooms (£6.50), with children's dishes and a good many puddings. There are white tables out on a terrace by the restaurant overlooking the woods of the common, with a little lamplit path winding down the grass slope to a duck pond; a garden on the other side, by a children's bar, has picnic-table sets under cocktail parasols, swings, a roundabout-swing, and a splendid helter-skelter. The public bar has darts, pool, cribbage, fruit machine, trivia machine (they're in a quiz league) and juke box. *(Recommended by Ian Phillips)*

Brakspears   Licensee Leon Banks   Real ale   Meals and snacks (until 10)   Restaurant
Children welcome   Open 11–2.30, 6–11 all year; all day Sat and bank hols
Bedrooms tel Kidmore End (0734) 723101; £15/£30

SOUTH LEIGH   SP3908   Map 4
Mason Arms
Village signposted from A40 Witney–Eynsham

This smart and neatly kept Cotswold-stone pub has a cosy lounge, separated into two halves by a wrought-iron divider, with built-in cushioned settles curving around the corners, a flagstone floor, an open fire with a stone hearth at one end, and a log-effect gas fire at the other. Good food includes home-made soup (£1.50), sandwiches (from £1.80), ploughman's (from £2.75), various filled pancakes (from £3.60), salads (from £4), steak, kidney and Guinness pie or grilled smoked gammon (£4.25), rump steak (£7.50) and specials like smoked salmon roulade (£6.75). Well kept Glenny Witney (from nearby Witney) and Hook Norton Best on handpump, a good range of cognacs and malt whiskies, and lots of wines. There may be peacocks and a couple of chickens in the big, pretty garden, where a small grove of what look like Balearic box trees shelter picnic-table sets. The small field beside the car park has Cotswold sheep. *(Recommended by Ian Phillips, Roger Taylor, Mrs M Lawrence, Edward Hibbert, D Stephenson)*

Free house   Licensee Geoff Waters   Real ale   Meals and snacks (not Sun evening, not Mon)
Restaurant (not Sun evening) tel Witney (0993) 702485   Children in restaurant
Open 11–2.30, 6.30–11 all year; closed Mon

SOUTH STOKE   SU5983   Map 2
Perch & Pike
Off B4009 2 miles N of Goring

The landlord of this friendly and unspoilt flint pub is an ex-professional guitarist and sings in the bar on Saturday evenings. There are low beams, a brick floor, stuffed perch and pike on its shiny orange walls, and a collection of plates painted with fish. A good choice of bar food includes French bread rolls (from £1.45), steak roll (£2.20), soup such as Stilton and watercress (£2.40), mixed ploughman's (£2.75), ham and egg (£2.95), cottage pie (£3), beef, Guinness and orange casserole (£5.75), chicken in tarragon and white wine (£5.95) and steaks. Brakspears PA, SB and Old on handpump; darts, bar billiards, shove-ha'penny, dominoes, cribbage, fruit machine, boules, Aunt Sally and piped music. There are benches by tubs of flowers and honeysuckle, and a spacious flower-edged lawn (past a black wooden barn) with a slide, seesaw and swings; summer barbecues. *(Recommended by M Rising, Gordon and Daphne, Jane and Calum Maclean, Col A H N Reade)*

Brakspears   Licensees Susie and Roy Mason-Apps   Real ale   Meals and snacks (limited Sun and Mon evenings in summer; no food then in winter)   Restaurant tel Goring (0491) 872415   Children in restaurant   Assorted guest musicians Thurs evening, singing guitarist landlord Sat evening   Open 10.30–3, 6–11 all year; may open longer in afternoon if trade demands

STANTON HARCOURT   SP4105 Map 4
Harcourt Arms
B4449 S of Eynsham

Attractively decorated, the three dining areas here are simply furnished with spindle-back chairs around wooden tables; in the annexe room there are Windsor-back chairs and framed Ape and Spy caricatures from *Vanity Fair*, and massive stone fireplaces. Bar food includes soup (£1.75), chicken satay (£2.95), grilled king prawns (£3.25), steak sandwich (£3.50), mussels in season, steak and kidney pie (£4.95), smoked haddock crumble (£6.75), liver and bacon (£7.95), sirloin steak (£8.25) and home-made puddings (£1.75). Ruddles and Websters Yorkshire on handpump, and around a hundred wines; piped music. There are tables on a neat side lawn. Please note, they have stopped doing bedrooms – so suddenly that one reader, having booked a holiday here, arrived to find they had failed to tell him that there was no accommodation. *(Recommended by Henry Midwinter, Lynda and Howard Dix, Mr and Mrs N W Briggs, Frank Cummins, D M Anderson, Nancy Witts)*

Free house   Licensee Peter Polhill   Real ale   Meals and snacks (11–3, 6–10.30) Restaurant tel Oxford (0865) 881931   Well behaved children welcome   Open 11–3, 6–11 all year

STANTON ST JOHN   SP5709 Map 4
Star
Pub signposted off B4027; village signposted off A40 heading E of Oxford (heading W, the road's signposted Forest Hill, Islip instead)

Up a flight of stairs (but on a level with the car park) is a characterful refurbished extension: old-fashioned dining-chairs and an interesting mix of dark oak and elm tables, shelves of good pewter, terracotta-coloured walls with just one portrait in oils, a stuffed ermine, pairs of bookshelves on each side of an attractive new inglenook fireplace, and rugs on flagstones. Lighting's thoughtful – like the crystal chandelier above a little group of tables on a small railed-in platform, and the atmosphere's chatty and relaxed. There's also an original couple of cheery little low-beamed rooms, one with ancient brick flooring tiles and the other with carpet and quite close-set tables. The pub's run spotlessly. Good home-made bar food includes pâté or crispy garlic mushrooms (£2), celery, Stilton and almond casserole (£3.25), cheesy tuna bake, corned beef hash or pork and cider casserole (£3.35), and puddings such as home-made bread pudding (95p) or baked fruit Alaska (£1.40); children's meals. Well kept Wadworths IPA, Farmers Glory and 6X on handpump, with Devizes (in summer) or Old Timer (winter) tapped from the cask, and a guest beer such as Badger Tanglefoot, hot toddies and hot chocolate; behind the bars is a display of brewery ties, beer bottles and beer-mats. Shove-ha'penny, dominoes, cribbage, piped music and Aunt Sally. The walled garden has picnic-table sets among shrubs, and swings and a sandpit. Several motoring clubs use the large car park as a monthly meeting point. *(Recommended by Dave Braisted, Michael Thomson, Ian Phillips, TBB, HMW, R M Sparkes, Joan Olivier, Edward Hibbert, Dr D A Sykes, V T Morgan)*

Wadworths   Licensees Nigel and Suzanne Tucker   Real ale   Meals and snacks (12–2, 7–10)   Children in public bar annexe   Open 11–2.30, 6.30–11 all year; closed 25 Dec

STEEPLE ASTON   SP4725 Map 4

Red Lion

Off A423 12 miles N of Oxford

The beamed bar in this civilised little village pub has a cheerful, homely atmosphere, a collection of rather crossword-orientated books, an antique settle among other good furniture, and dark hessian above its panelling. Good lunchtime bar food includes stockpot soup (95p), excellent sandwiches such as thickly cut rare beef (£1.25), ploughman's with local crusty bread (from £1.80), pâté or home-made taramosalata (£2), and in winter varying hot-pots, and summer salads such as fresh salmon (£3.90). Well kept Badger Tanglefoot, Hook Norton Best and Wadworths 6X on handpump, a choice of sixty or so malt whiskies, and around a hundred good wines in the restaurant (they ship their own wines from France). The terrace outside the stone house is a real sun-trap. *(Recommended by Nick Dowson, Alison Hayward, E J Waller, I R Hewitt, C Elliott, Peter Storey, Dr J R Hamilton)*

Free house   Licensee Colin Mead   Real ale   Lunchtime meals and snacks (not Sun) Restaurant (not Sun) tel Steeple Aston (0869) 40225   Open 11–3, 6–11 all year; closed 25 Dec

STEVENTON   SU4691 Map 2

North Star

The Causeway; central westward turn off main road through village, which is signposted from A34

Named after an 1837 steam engine, this simple village pub has a side tap-room (which has no bar counter) where Morlands Mild, Bitter and Best are tapped from the cask, and there are colourful stacks of crisps, bottles, barrels and so forth. The main bar – reached through a low-ceilinged tiled entrance passage – has a traditional snug formed by high cream-painted settles around a couple of elm tables by an electric bar fire. It's decorated with veteran steam engine pictures and there are interesting local horsebrasses. The small parlourish lounge has an open fire, and there's a very simply furnished dining-room; cribbage. Cheap bar food includes a celebrated so-called mini-ploughman's – two rolls, a thick slice of wholemeal bread, chunks of Cheddar, blue cheese and a soft plain cheese, a big slice of pressed beef, fresh tomato, cucumber, onion, spring onion, lettuce and chutney. A few large old-fashioned benches stand out on the side grass, by roses and cabbages, and the little wooden gate into the garden from the road goes through a small yew tree which is joined at the top. *(Recommended by Gordon and Daphne, Gordon Smith)*

Morlands   Real ale   Meals and snacks (weekday lunchtimes only)   Open 10.30–2.30, 6.45–11 all year

STOKE ROW   SU6784 Map 2

Crooked Billet

Newlands Lane

The little parlour is the real heart of this friendly seventeenth-century country pub. There's a big table under a single lamp hanging from the bowed beam, a log fire with an attractive rug in front of it, and a distinctively old-fashioned atmosphere; there's also a renovated lounge with another log fire, and a public bar with a couple of scrubbed deal tables in front of a vast open hearth. Well kept Brakspears PA, SB and Old tapped from casks down six cellar steps and served through doorways. Bar food includes platters such as salami or seafood (from £2.10), mushroom provençale or smoked salmon pâté (£2.35), steak and kidney pie (£3.95), Arbroath smokies, kidneys turbigo or jugged hare in season (£4.35), king prawns in garlic (£4.75), half a roast pheasant in season (£6.25), and Scotch sirloin steak (£6.75); puddings like bread-and-butter pudding or treacle tart (£1.50). Shove-ha'penny, cribbage, dominoes and trivia. A three-acre garden/paddock has picnic-table sets and tethered goats. From the pub, where there are benches in front by the very quiet lane (the only noise is from the geese and bantams in the back yard), you can walk straight into Chilterns beech woods. *(Recommended by Gordon and Daphne, Lyn and Bill Capper, Jane and Calum Maclean, Dick Brown, Phil and Sally Gorton)*

Brakspears   Licensee Ben Salter   Real ale   Meals and snacks; not Tues evening   Children in family/club-room until 8   Live music Weds evening, blue grass Sun evening   Open 11–2.30, 6–11 all year

SWINBROOK   SP2712 Map 4

Swan

Back road 1 mile N of A40, 2 miles E of Burford

A quiet and welcome retreat from the A40, this friendly and beautifully placed old inn is simply furnished with country benches, and a wood-burning stove on a simple flagstone floor. Good value lunchtime bar food includes prawn and Stilton toasted sandwiches (£1.75), delicious salmon and prawn sandwiches (£2.50), flaked white fish and prawns in a sauce topped with mushroom, potato and cheese (£2.85) or home-made steak and kidney pie (£3.30), with evening dishes like lemon sole with Calvados-flavoured sauce (£5.90) or brace of quail with a cream sauce (£6.25). Well kept Morlands Bitter and Wadworths 6X on handpump; darts, shove-ha'penny, dominoes, cribbage and trivia. It's close to the River Windrush and there are old-fashioned benches, a fuchsia hedge, and a smothering of wistaria on the seventeenth-century walls. Please note, they no longer do bedrooms. *(Recommended by Prof and Mrs Keith Patchett, Graham Tayar, Mrs E M Lloyd, Paul S McPherson, Nancy Witts; more reports please)*

Free house   Licensee H J Collins   Real ale   Meals and lunchtime snacks Open 11.30–2.30, 6–11 all year

TADPOLE BRIDGE   SP3203 Map 4

Trout

Back road Bampton–Buckland, 4 miles NE of Faringdon

This eighteenth-century place is one of the nicer upper Thames-side pubs. The smallish, single L-shaped bar has flagstones, attractive pot plants on the window sills and mantelpiece, a good pubby atmosphere, and friendly, efficient service. Reasonably priced food includes sandwiches, lasagne (£3), home-cooked ham (£3.40), scampi (£4.25), gammon (£4.80), rump steak (£5.95) and pies. Well kept Archers Village and Wadworths 6X on handpump; darts, dominoes and Aunt Sally. There are picnic-table sets among small fruit trees on an attractive side lawn, pretty hanging baskets and flower troughs, moorings for customers, and a 1¾-mile stretch of river where you can fish (the pub sells day tickets). There's a caravan and camping site for five. *(Recommended by Lyn and Bill Capper, Frank Cummins; more reports please)*

Free house   Licensee Roy Burton   Real ale   Meals and snacks   Restaurant tel Buckland (036 787) 382   Children in restaurant   Open 11–2.30, 6–11; closed all day Weds Nov–Apr

Ring the bull is an ancient pub game – you try to lob a ring on a piece of string over a hook (occasionally a bull's horn) on the wall or ceiling.

WATLINGTON   SU6894 Map 4

Chequers 🏵

2¼ miles from M40 junction 6; Love Lane – B4009 towards Watlington, first right turn in village

The pretty back garden of this red-tiled old white pub – cosily tucked away on a back lane – has picnic-table sets under apple and pear trees, and sweet peas, roses, geraniums, begonias and so forth; there may be rabbits too. Inside, the rambling, comfortable bar has low oak beams in a ceiling darkened to a deep ochre by the candles which they still use, a low panelled oak settle and character chairs such as a big spiral-legged carving chair around a few good antique oak tables, and rugs, red carpet and (in one corner) red and black shiny tiles on the floor; a pale grey cat dozes in front of one of the two open fires, and the atmosphere is quiet and relaxing. Interesting, carefully served home-made bar food includes toasted sandwiches (£1.40), pâté or ploughman's (£2.50), smoked fillet of beef or tagliatelle (£3.50), salads (from £4), prawn curry (£4.50), steak and kidney pie (£4.60), gammon steak (£5), pork fillet in herbs and cream (£6.20), veal T-bone valdostana (£6.40), steaks (from £6.90), and 24-ounce T-bone (£13.50); good home-made puddings. Brakspears on electric pump. On the right there are steps down to an area with more tables. *(Recommended by David Wallington, Henry Midwinter, Chris Raisin, Graham Doyle, P C Russell, TBB, HKR, SC, BKA)*

Brakspears   Licensee John Valentine   Real ale   Meals and snacks   Open 11.30–2.30, 6–11 all year

WYTHAM   SP4708 Map 4

White Hart

Village signposted from A34 ring road W of Oxford

The flagstoned bar in this picturesque stone pub has high-backed black settles built almost the whole way round its cream walls, wheel-back chairs, a shelf of blue and white plates, a fine relief of a heart on the iron fireback, and a homely atmosphere. At lunchtime there's a good self-service cold table, and in the evenings hot dishes such as chicken Kiev, veal Cordon Bleu and sirloin steak; get there early if you want a table, especially on Sundays. Well kept Ind Coope Burton and Tetleys on handpump. The new licensees have introduced a barbecue into the walled garden. *(Recommended by David Goldstone, Roy Gawne, Sheila Keene, Nancy Witts; more reports please)*

Ind Coope (Allied)   Licensees Rob Jones and Carole Gibbs   Real ale   Meals and snacks   Children in dining-room and conservatory   Open 11–2.30, 6–11 all year

---

Lucky Dip

Besides the fully inspected pubs, you might like to try these Lucky Dips recommended to us and described by readers (if you do, please send us reports):

☆ **Abingdon** [St Helens Wharf; SU4997], *Old Anchor*: Characterful Morlands pub in tucked-away riverside location with good mix of customers, flagstoned back bar with little shoulder-height serving-hatch, little front bar looking across Thames, bigger lounge and lovely little panelled dining-room overlooked the carefully clipped bushes of almshouse gardens; Morlands on handpump, usual range of bar food running up to steaks *(Ian Phillips, Graham Bush)*
Abingdon [21 Cornmarket], *Abingdon*

Arms: Self-effacing little pub, not noticeable until you are on top of it; lots of bare brick and old beams, open fireplace, nicely polished tables and truly warm welcome; newspapers and magazines in rack, chef and locals chatting, well kept Adnams and Theakstons; food inc excellent seafood platter, masses of doorstep sandwiches, even more filled baked potatoes *(Ian Phillips)*;
[Bridge] *Nags Head*: Friendly licensees, Ruddles County on handpump, good bar food lunchtime and evenings; good value

bedrooms, good breakfasts *(ST)*; [15 Oxford Rd] *Ox*: Consistently good, clean and well run pub, good value bar food inc superb salads *(V T Morgan)*

Appleton [SP4401], *Plough*: Gently refurbished pub under newish licensees, bar food (not Mon, no cooked food Tues), Morlands Bitter and Mild on handpump, live music Fri *(Joan Olivier)*

☆ **Ashbury** [SU2685], *Rose & Crown*: Friendly atmosphere and emphasis on good food in bar and restaurant, but real ales too; very busy at weekends but service prompt and friendly, quiet during the week; log fire, games-room; nr Ridgeway and Wayland's Smithy – good for walkers; bedrooms comfortable *(J M M Hill, F A Rabagliati, E Turner-Nedelev)*

☆ **Asthall** [just off A40 3 miles on Oxford side of Burford; SP2811], *Maytime*: Popular and friendly up-market food pub in old Cotswold-stone building; wide choice of dishes, reasonably priced Sun lunch, Morrells Varsity and Wadworths 6X, prompt service; in tiny hamlet – stunning views of Asthall Manor and watermeadows from car park *(R W B Burton, Nancy Witts, BB)*

Bampton [Bridge St; SP3103], *Romany*: Friendly atmosphere, good home-cooked bar food, restaurant; good value bedrooms *(Mrs D Farmer)*

Banbury [Parsons St; off Market Pl; SP4540], *Reindeer*: Good value bar food inc sandwiches, pasta and grills in much-refurbished Hook Norton pub with long history; its 'gallows' inn-sign, spanning street, is one of only half a dozen left *(LYM)*; [George St] *Wheatsheaf*: Small, lively pub with friendly landlord and bar staff; the young/fun atmosphere they generate attracts all ages; Bass *(Graham Bush)*

☆ **Barford St Michael** [Lower St; SP4332], *George*: New licensees in rambling thatched pub, modernised and open-plan inside, very pretty outside; well kept Adnams, Badger Tanglefoot and Wadworths 6X, home-cooked bar food, Aunt Sally, blues band Mon; a previous main entry – up-to-date reports please *(LYM)*

☆ **Beckley** [High St; SP5611], *Abingdon Arms*: Delightful little stone-built pub in lovely village on ridge overlooking Otmoor wilderness; very comfortable lounge with excellent if not cheap freshly prepared food inc Sun lunch – in summer it's normally cold food with soup and one hot dish, and they charge you extra if you eat but don't drink; well kept Arkells or Halls and Wadworths 6X on handpump, decent wines; service variable and may be slow but is usually friendly and efficient; tables and good summerhouse in orchard, attractive walks round about *(A T Langton, Mike O'Driscoll, Sir Nigel Foulkes, Annie Taylor, Henry Midwinter)*

☆ **Begbroke** [A34 Oxford–Woodstock; SP4613], *Royal Sun*: Clean and attractively decorated open-plan stone-built pub with good choice of quickly served and reasonably priced food, Ind Coope Burton on handpump, friendly quick service, tables out on terrace and in small garden; pleasant surroundings though on trunk road *(M V Fereday, Mrs H A Green)*

Benson [SU6191], *Three Horseshoes*: Welcoming free house, popular with locals; well kept Brakspears and weekly guest beer, wide choice of good value bar food *(Jane and Calum Maclean)*

Bix [A423; SU7285], *Fox*: Well kept creeper-clad brick pub with friendly atmosphere; well kept Brakspears, good variety of hot and cold bar food from sandwiches upwards *(Joan Olivier)*

☆ **Blewbury** [Chapel Lane; off Nottingham Fee – narrow turning N from A417; SU5385], *Red Lion*: Well kept Brakspears real ales and bar food from sandwiches and ploughman's to salads and changing hot dishes, often highly spiced, in downland village pub with beams, quarry tiles and big log fire; tables on back lawn; children in small restaurant *(H J Stirling, K G Latham, Col A H N Reade, LYM)*

Bodicote [Goose Lane; off A423 S of Banbury; SP4537], *Plough*: Comfortable, unassuming village pub notable for brewing its own beers (with takeaway sales); locals' bar with beams, darts, dominoes, bar billiards and juke box, lounge, friendly licensee and black cat called Sid; good helpings of simple food *(Matt Pringle)*

Brightwell [signposted from A4130 2 miles W of Wallingford; SU5790], *Red Lion*: Fourteenth-century building with low beams, large open fire and friendly atmosphere; choice of bar food inc filled baked potatoes and cold meats, tables on terrace *(Joan Olivier)*

Broadwell [SP2503], *Five Bells*: Small village pub with big garden, friendly atmosphere – it's had good food, though we've not heard since it changed hands; children welcome *(M J Dyke, F M Bunbury – news of the current regime please)*

Burcot [SU5695], *Chequers*: Lovely thatched pub, comfortably furnished with pretty gallery; well kept real ales on handpump, good landlord, pleasant atmosphere, with decent bar food such as lasagne – popular for Sun lunch; piano Fri and Sat *(Dawn and Phil Garside)*

☆ **Burford** [High St (A361); SP2512], *Mermaid*: Old beamed building with wide choice of particularly good food, not cheap but reasonably priced for the quality, inc good vegetarian dishes and interesting variations on familiar themes – you can eat downstairs in the softly lit lounge with red lamps on all the tables and toby jugs hanging from the ceiling, or up in the restaurant part;

quick and very attentive friendly service, well kept Courage Best and Directors *(E J Knight, Robert and Vicky Tod, Mike O'Driscoll, Jason Caulkin, Lindsey Shaw Radley)*

Cassington [SP4510], *Chequers*: Friendly atmosphere in recently refurbished pub with choice of good bar food, carvery, attentive staff, Morrells ales, tables in garden; children welcome *(Joan Olivier)*

Caulcott [SP5024], *Horse & Groom*: Isolated pub that fills up late; quiet and characterful, with good service, though we haven't yet heard how the food has settled in since its recent change of regime *(John and Margaret Estdale)*

☆ **Charlbury** [SP3519], *Bell*: Small seventeenth-century hotel, clean and smart, with comfortable bedrooms often used by people at nearby conference centres, quiet and civilised flagstoned area with stripped stone walls and enormous open fire, bar lunches inc good sandwiches, well kept Wadworths real ales, restaurant; children in eating area *(E G Parish, Hope Chenhalls, LYM)*

Charlbury [Sheep St], *Bull*: Friendly pub, cosy, clean and smart lounge with stone walls, red carpet, high-backed settles and log-effect gas fire; Bass and Worthington on handpump, pleasant reasonably priced wines, bar food *(Mike O'Driscoll)*; [Market St] *White Hart*: Large stone-built village local with friendly welcome and relaxing atmosphere; basic bar with pews, settles, benches, stone fireplace, Adnams Bitter and Hook Norton, darts, separate lounge with dining area *(Mike O'Driscoll)*

Chazey Heath [Woodcote Rd (A4074 Wallingford–Reading); SU6977], *Pack Horse*: Well kept and attractive old pub with big log fire in simply furnished lounge bar, very friendly; well kept Gales ales and country wines, good value home-cooked bar food, sizeable back garden with play area and fairy-lit barbecue terrace, family-room, Shetland ponies and boxers *(Sharon Taylor, Tim Irish, BB)*; [Woodcote Rd] *Pack Saddle*: Engagingly 1950s-ish pub with rather disjointed décor of alligator skins, African spears and masks, old rifles, Spanish bullfighting pictures, tartan-blanket carpet, fishing nets and floats, nostalgic pop music, cheery atmosphere, well kept Gales ales, country wines, bar food from ploughman's to hot dishes such as pork, scampi and gammon; pool in lounge bar *(Ian Phillips, BB)*

Checkendon [OS Sheet 175 reference 666841; SU6683], *Black Horse*: Great atmosphere in truly old-fashioned unspoilt three-room free house, well kept Brakspears tapped from the cask in a back room, 1950s armchairs, friendly licensees – two elderly sisters; lunchtime opening can be erratic *(Geoffrey Griggs, Phil Gorton, Richard Sanders)*; [OS Sheet 175 reference 663829] *Four Horseshoes*: Old, thatched and beamed, with spacious lounge and bar, very

welcoming atmosphere, friendly landlord, well kept Brakspears, huge helpings of good cheap food; summer barbecues *(Bill Ibbetson-Price)*

Chinnor [B4009; SP7500], *Royal Oak*: Roomy, comfortable and well set out though straightforward dining area, usual bar food inc big filled baguettes and home-made pies, Badger Tanglefoot and Wadworths 6X; popular with older people *(Jenny and Michael Back)*

Chipping Norton [High St; SP3127], *Blue Boar*: Large, comfortable bar area divided into several areas by arches and pillars; long conservatory behind, with white garden tables and chairs on the flagstones; this leads to a good bar/restaurant (on our visit an organist was here); wide range of well priced food, Courage Directors and Marstons on handpump, good cider *(Michael and Alison Sandy, Wayne Brindle)*; *Fox*: Ancient stone pub – rambling lounge comfortably furnished with antique oak settles, open fire, food in bar and restaurant, Hook Norton real ales *(LYM)*

Clanfield [SP2801], *Plough*: Substantial old stone inn with lovely Elizabethan façade, attractive gardens and civilised atmosphere; comfortable lounge bar, elegantly presented succulent restaurant food at a price, attentive service; bedrooms *(LYM)*

Claydon [SP4550], *Sun Rising*: Pleasantly run, slightly basic pub that's been functionally modernised, with well kept Hook Norton Best; picturesque outside, with historic preserved granary nearby *(John Baker)*

☆ **Clifton** [B4031 Deddington–Aynho; SP4831], *Duke of Cumberlands Head*: Thriving, popular and warmly welcoming thatched stone pub house under new regime, with large lounge, lovely fireplace and simple furnishings; good wines, friendly service, freshly home-made bar food – familiar things with one or two more continental touches from the French landlady, cosy restaurant; perversely got very busy in summer 1989 after advertising 'filthy ale and disgusting food'; ten minutes' walk from canal *(Mike O'Driscoll, Mr and Mrs C H Stride)*

Clifton Hampden [SU5495], *Plough*: Ancient low-ceilinged pub, not smart inside, with friendly licensee, Ushers ales, variety of bar food from sandwiches up, children's play area; said to be haunted by a benign presence that upturns empty glasses *(Joan Olivier, R Houghton, BB)*

Crawley [SP3412], *Lamb*: Splendid eighteenth-century pub with stone walls, heavy oak timbers and inglenook fireplace; Witney Glenny and Hook Norton, Australian wines; dining-room with food from sandwiches through Malaysian curry to steak (and piped music); darts *(Joan Olivier)*

Crays Pond [B471 nr junction with B4526, about 3 miles E of Goring; SU6380], *White*

Lion: Bar with open fire, darts and piped music, lounge with low ceilings, carpet, chairs and tables and pleasant, large conservatory extension; friendly licensee, well kept Courage and Websters Yorkshire, wide range of well presented bar food from snacks to hot meals inc vegetarian dishes (not Tues evening); children's play area *(Lyn and Bill Capper)*

☆ **Crowmarsh** [A423; SU6189], *Queens Head*: Cream-coloured pebble-dash building reopened 1988 with French licensees and chef; popular low-beamed bar, open fires, two fruit machines, piped music and friendly atmosphere; attractively priced straightforward bar food (not Sun evening) from sandwiches up, Watneys-related real ales on handpump; ambitious galleried medieval-style restaurant, garden *(Joan Olivier)*

Cumnor [Abingdon Rd; SP4603], *Vine*: Good reasonably priced food inc delicious salads in pretty pub with pleasant atmosphere and friendly, helpful service; nice garden *(Mr and Mrs Graham Stable, Joan Bowen)*

Cuxham [SU6695], *Half Moon*: Friendly and attractive old-fashioned beamed pub in pretty streamside village, expanded range of bar food from sandwiches to steaks, well kept Brakspears real ales, log fire, aquarium with minnows and the like, New Zealand pictures, bar billiards, darts, shove-ha'penny; seats outside, children welcome *(Joan Olivier, LYM)*

Deddington [Oxford Rd (A423); SP4631], *Holcombe*: Friendly licensees in seventeenth-century building with low-beamed stripped stone bar, well kept Hook Norton Best and fresh, well presented bar food; bedrooms large and comfortable (triple-glazed at the front) *(P Baker)*; *Kings Arms*: Friendly prompt service, well kept Marstons Burton and Pedigree on handpump, good variety of reasonably priced bar food from sandwiches and ploughman's up *(Mr and Mrs D Norton)*

Duns Tew [SP4528], *White Horse*: Flagstones, beams and thick stripped stone walls in former sixteenth-century farmhouse with two bars and well kept Courage Directors and Hook Norton *(Gwyneth and Salvo Spadaro-Dutturi)*

East Hendred [Orchard Lane; SU4588], *Plough*: Beamed village pub with Morlands ales, friendly licensees, food often using vegetables from the attractive garden – which has good play equipment; bar decorated with farm tools and so forth *(BB)*

☆ **Enslow** [Enslow Bridge; off A4095 about 1½ miles SW of Kirtlington; SP4818], *Rock of Gibraltar*: Rambling stone-built canalside pub with cosy nooks in spacious split-level bar, beams, stonework, open fire, bargee-style colourful paintwork; friendly newish licensees, comfortable atmosphere, games area downstairs overlooking large garden with barbecue; Watneys-related real ales on handpump, good choice of bar food from sandwiches to steaks; children's adventure playground *(E J Alcock, Mike O'Driscoll)*

Enstone [A34 Chipping Norton–Woodstock; SP3724], *Harrow*: Pleasant and friendly sixteenth-century inn with public bar and comfortably refurbished lounge bar; friendly, efficient service, real ales such as Morrells Varsity and Whitbreads and ciders on handpump; bar food from good filled rolls to steaks, inc help-yourself salads *(Lyn and Bill Capper, Neil and Angela Huxter)*

Exlade Street [SU6582], *Highwayman*: Rambling beamed pub dating back to fourteenth century, with unusual layout including sunken seats in central inglenook, good collection of ancient paintings; friendly staff, lively atmosphere, good food (service can slow when it's crowded), real ales such as Palmers Tally Ho, Theakstons Old Peculier and XB, Ushers and Wadworths 6X on handpump; children's bar (the pub itself is popular with young people) *(Gary Wilkes)*

☆ **Eynsham** [Newlands St; SP4309], *Newlands*: Pleasant, friendly atmosphere under most promising new licensees who've stripped the bar back to its flagstones, inglenook and early eighteenth-century pine panelling; good reasonably priced food inc produce from their own smokery at reasonable prices, Halls Harvest on handpump, decent wine, fairly unobtrusive piped music *(Mrs Pamela Dumenil, Edward Hibbert)*

Faringdon [Market Pl; SU2895], *Crown*: Well kept real ales such as Hook Norton, Glenny Wychwood, Morlands and Theakstons, decent bar food, friendly staff, flagstones, panelling, varnished wooden tables, roaring log fires in winter and lovely courtyard for summer; children welcome; bedrooms *(Mike Muston, Frank Cummins, D Stephenson, LYM – more reports please)*; [Coxwell (outside town)] *Plough*: Good range of beers such as Arkells, Halls Harvest, Wadworths 6X, fine choice of pub food; back restaurant; children in extension from bar *(Stan Edwards)*

☆ **Fifield** [A424; SP2318], *Hunters Lodge*: Isolated but warm and friendly stone inn, dating partly from thirteenth century, half-mile from pretty village; big helpings of bar food, well kept Donnington beers, tasteful refurbishments, warm welcome – especially from the dog; known as the Merrymouth until 1987; comfortably renovated clean bedrooms *(A T Langton, Joan Olivier, Tom Atkins, Helen Wright, LYM)*

Filkins [village signposted off A361 Lechlade–Burford; SP2304], *Five Alls*: Friendly free house with new licensees, comfortable lounge (open summer lunchtimes), bar and restaurant (open evenings, Sun lunchtime); Courage Best on handpump, good range of bar food from sandwiches up, garden; nearby working wool weaving mill in splendid eighteenth-century barn *(Joan Olivier)*; *Lamb*: Friendly free house, Morlands on handpump, wine by the glass, good choice of hot and cold bar food at reasonable prices; children's play area; bedrooms *(Joan Olivier)*

☆ **Forest Hill** [SP5807], *White Horse*: Cosy stone-walled pub with welcoming landlord, well kept Morrells on handpump, log fire, wide range of well presented food from particularly good ploughman's and spicy sausage-filled crusty rolls to salmon; tables in dining-room, Oxfordshire Way close by; children welcome *(Maureen Hobbs, Robert Gomme, Margaret Dyke, TBB)*

Fringford [SP6028], *Butchers Arms*: Remote village pub, well kept beer, good coarse pâté and granary bread, friendly service, boules played on roadside, seats outside *(Dr Paul Kitchener)*

☆ **Godstow** [SP4708], *Trout*: It's the marvellous position that makes this creeper-covered medieval pub special, with a lovely terrace by a stream clear enough to watch the plump trout, and peacocks in the grounds – one of the nicest summer spots in England; extensively commercialised inside, with far room knocked through into former stables, large snack room extension with children's area, garden bar and restaurant; Bass and Charrington real ale; very popular in summer *(Lyn and Bill Capper, Miss E Waller, Joan Olivier, Graham Bush, LYM)*

Goosey [SU3591], *Pound*: Nice little Morlands pub with lovely old brickwork opened up in bar; wide choice of decent food from sandwiches to steaks inc hefty burgers, well kept real ale, character Welsh landlord *(Gordon and Daphne)*

☆ **Goring** [Cleeve; off B4009 about a mile towards Wallingford; SU6080], *Olde Leatherne Bottle*: Overlooking a quiet stretch of the Thames from an unspoilt setting, unpretentious despite considerable refurbishments under new licensees, with what is now a more ambitious range of food from new kitchens; well kept Brakspears PA, XB and XXXX Old tapped from the cask, lots of window seats in the three connecting rooms (with some ancient masonry) *(Ian Phillips, Charles Gurney, LYM – more reports please)*

Goring, *Miller of Mansfield*: Double-fronted, homely looking corner pub with armchairs in large cosy bow-windowed bar, public bar on right divided from main bar by large brick fireplace with log-effect gas fire; well kept Courage Best and Directors, good bar food from sandwiches up inc good filled baked potatoes, back restaurant; children welcome *(Steve Huggins)*

Gosford [Gosford Hill; A43 Oxford–Bicester; SP4912], *Kings Arms*: Old Halls house with friendly atmosphere; beams, unobtrusive piped music, modern restaurant in keeping with style; good bar food inc filled French bread, terrace with tables and chairs *(Joan Olivier)*

Great Bourton [just off A423, 3 miles N of Banbury; opp church; SP4545], *Bell*: Friendly local with juke box, darts, lots of trophies and well kept Hook Norton ales *(Jon Wainwright)*; *Swan*: Thatched village pub, pretty outside, with good range of well kept Wadworths beers and enjoyable pizza-type bar food; bedrooms *(S V Bishop, Jon Wainwright, LYM)*

Great Milton [The Green; SP6202], *Bell*: Welcoming cottagey local, pleasant staff, friendly atmosphere; one quiet bar, one slightly more noisy; well kept Glenny Wychwood Best and Uley Old Spot, good choice of bar food *(R Houghton)*; *Bull*: Whitewashed sixteenth-century stone pub with small, cosy lounge, handful of tables, large stone fireplace; cordial welcome, relaxing atmosphere, prompt service, well kept Morrells Bitter, good varied bar food from ploughman's to steaks, restaurant; public bar with darts and fruit machine *(Mike O'Driscoll, Margaret and Trevor Errington)*

Hanwell [SP4343], *Moon & Sixpence*: Good bar food and efficient service in pleasantly refurbished pub, unusual for its Sicilian landlord *(T Nott)*

☆ **Headington** [London Rd; SP5407], *White Horse*: Large bars extensively and comfortably refurbished with exposed brickwork and beamery, mahogany and stained-glass screens separating areas, well kept Morrells beers; useful for its reasonably priced bar food served all day (separate children's menus – one for under-sevens, the other for under-twelves; prompt service; busy lunchtimes, piped music, fruit machines *(Mrs Margaret Dyke)*

☆ **Henley** [Market Pl; SU7882], *Argyll*: Well run pub with long tartan-carpeted lounge, Highland pictures; popular lunchtime food is good value (only roasts on Sun), well kept Morlands ales, seats on back terrace, handy parking behind; nr GWG68 *(LYM)*

Henley [Bell St], *Bell*: Small friendly bar, no-smoking room and dining-room; well kept Brakspears and good value food that includes a joint of pork or beef carved at the bar with up to five vegetables; ploughman's but no sandwiches; no car parking *(David Young)*; [Riverside], *Little White Hart*: Friendly and unpretentious but comfortable, with good value plain food; very useful location right on the river; bedrooms in recently refurbished hotel part *(Lindsey Shaw Radley)*

☆ **Henton** [a mile off B4009 Chinnor–Princes Risborough; SP7602], *Peacock*: Courteously run and smoothly modernised well kept thatched inn below the Chilterns, peacocks all around outside; well kept Brakspears and Hook Norton ales on handpump, mulled wine in winter, good log fires, popular if somewhat pricey food with duck and steak specialities; bedrooms in back block *(Lindsey*

Shaw Radley, B R Shiner, BB)

Highmoor [SU6984], *Dog & Duck*: Cosy two-bar Brakspears pub, cottagey-looking outside, with small comfortable bars, open fires, and good choice of food for dining area towards the back *(Gordon and Daphne)*

☆ **Hook Norton** [a mile N towards Sibford, at Banbury–Rollright crossroads; SP3533], *Gate Hangs High*: Snug and spotless pub with friendly efficient landlord, attractive inglenook, home-grown ingredients in generously served good value meals cooked by landlady, and salads inc good home-baked ham and rare beef; well kept Hook Norton Best and Old Hookey, country garden; isolated, quite near Rollright Stones *(Iain Hewitt, VL, Sir Nigel Foulkes, Brian and Rosemary Wilmot, LYM)*

☆ **Hook Norton**, *Pear Tree*: Popular for over 20 years with some readers, this welcoming pub has recently started letting a bedroom, with shower; delightfully friendly licensees, open fire, two small bars, lots of locals and (especially in summer) passing visitors; well kept Hook Norton ales from brewery a hundred yards away, freshly cut sandwiches (may not be available if busy, as it tends to be on summer weekends – though there's then plenty of room in the big garden, with a children's play area) *(Robert Gomme, Su and Andy Jones, J S Clements)*

Hook Norton, *Bear*: Theakstons and Davenports real ales, good choice of bar food, pleasant garden *(Dr A Y Drummond)*

Horspath [The Green; SP5704], *Chequers*: Friendly country pub, well kept Halls, good country-type meals; tables in big back garden, games inc Aunt Sally and pool in separate building behind *(Barry Shapley)*

Islip [B4027; SP5214], *Red Lion*: Very wide choice of well presented food including attractive buffet, Halls ales, nice bar with fantastic collection of drinking vessels; barn conversion behind with separate bar, skittle alley and dining area; lavatories for the disabled; garden *(Joan Olivier)*; *Swan*: Pretty country village pub, attractively refurbished, with long and narrow single bar; well kept Morrells Varsity on handpump, reasonably priced bar food, separate restaurant and outside eating area *(Derek & Sylvia Stephenson, BB)*

Kennington [off A4142 (Oxford eastern bypass); SP5202], *Tandem*: Morland real ale and good value bar food from sandwiches up in well kept pub with two bars, light and airy dining extension looking over meadows to river (with Cowley complex showing beyond); tables in garden, children in family-room *(Joan Olivier)*

Leafield [Lone End; SP3115], *Spindleberry*: Comfortable bar, Wadworths 6X, good if pricey bar food, up-market restaurant *(Dr A Y Drummond)*

☆ **Letcombe Regis** [follow Village Only sign as far as possible; SU3784], *Sparrow*: Relaxed

and unpretentious plain village-edge pub below prehistoric Segsbury hill-fort, well kept Morlands Bitter and Mild, simple lunchtime food from soup and sandwiches to fry-ups (not Sun); tables, swings and climbing-frame in safely fenced garden *(Dave Braisted, Derek and Sylvia Stephenson, LYM)*

Lewknor [SU7198], *Old Leathern Bottle*: Lovely country pub in small village with bustling atmosphere, well kept Brakspears and good bar food, generously served, such as barbecue ribs, stir-fried chicken with oyster sauce or curry; friendly efficient service *(Roger and Lynda Pilgrim)*

Long Hanborough [A4095 Bladon–Witney; SP4214], *Bell*: Small friendly pub, quaintly furnished with old treadle sewing-machine tables and stools like upholstered tree stumps; well kept Morrells, range of home-made country wines on tap, good value bar food inc interesting daily specials, open fires *(Margaret Dyke, MO)*; *George & Dragon*: Friendly old stone village pub, known on and off for 25 years; beams in low-ceilinged bar, Halls ales and bar food from sandwiches (not weekends) to steaks inc big filled baps; restaurant, tables outside, children's play area *(Joan Olivier)*

Long Wittenham [SU5493], *Machine Man*: The main thing which hits you is the good atmosphere created by the friendly and welcoming landlord – after a couple of hours strangers feel like popular regulars; several changing well kept real ales, maybe home-made cider *(David Fowles)*; *Plough*: Big riverside garden, rustic furniture in small low-beamed lounge, lots of horsebrasses around inglenook fireplace; bar food, Watneys-related real ales, games in public bar, children allowed in pool-room; bedrooms *(Joan Olivier)*; *Vine*: Morlands pub with two bars separated by fireplace, variety of hot and cold bar food from sandwiches to enormous steaks, real ales, garden with play area *(Joan Olivier)*

Longworth [A420 Faringdon–Kingston Bagpuize; SU3899], *Blue Boar*: Busy pub popular with locals and undergraduates alike; convivial log fires, welcoming and informal atmosphere, wide range of well prepared and generously served bar food running up to steaks *(Richard Fawcett)*; [Faringdon Rd] *Lamb & Flag*: Good value well kept Buccaneer Inn welcoming children, with sofa by open fire, Morrells real ales, home-cooked bar food, even breakfast 9.30–11; children welcome *(Joan Olivier)*

Lower Assendon [SU7484], *Golden Ball*: Reliable over the years for good bar food inc superb home-made pies; well kept Brakspears ales *(B H Pinsent)*

☆ **Marston** [Mill Lane, Old Marston – OS Sheet 164 reference 520090; SP5208], *Victoria Arms*: Notable above all for its position, as its large attractive garden with play area and picnic-table sets runs down to the River Cherwell, where there is a quay for punts; spacious and well decorated (Victorian prints, farm tools) bungalow extension to the original flagstoned and stone-built core, now mainly an eating area; good range of real ales – Badger Tanglefoot and Wadworths IPA, 6X, Farmers Glory and winter Old Timer; usual range of bar food from sandwiches and filled baked potatoes to steaks; good service, loudish piped music, children welcome *(Tim Brierly, Miss E Waller, Joan Olivier, Edward Hibbert, Ian Phillips, BB)*

Middle Assendon [SU7385], *Rainbow*: Friendly local with consistently very good plain food, well served in pleasant setting; well furnished with small tables, limited number of chairs as opposed to stools *(CGB, V P Prentice)*

Middle Barton [SP4325], *Carpenters Arms*: Friendly village pub, generous helpings of reasonably priced bar food; bedrooms *(Byrne Sherwood)*

Middleton Stoney [SP5323], *Jersey Arms*: Old inn with big log fires and good food in friendly beamed and panelled bar and restaurant; bedrooms large and well furnished, one with four-poster *(Henry Midwinter)*

Milton [SU4892], *Admiral Benbow*: Small friendly pub with friendly and obliging new licensees, well kept Morrells ales, reasonably priced simple bar food, quiet atmosphere; garden; by entrance to seventeenth-century Manor (open Sun afternoons Easter–Oct) *(A T Langton)*

Minster Lovell [B4070 Witney–Burford; SP3111], *White Hart*: White-fronted Cotswold-stone roadside pub with large, attractively laid-out bar, black beams, settles, comfortable chairs and hanging plates; polite welcome, good service, Courage Directors and Best, attractive food from ploughman's up; open all day *(Mike O'Driscoll)*

☆ **Murcott** [SP5815], *Nut Tree*: Immaculate white thatched pub with duck pond and interesting garden; particularly good range of drinks from Glenny Wychwood Best and a guest such as Burton Bridge kept under light carbon dioxide blanket to worthwhile whiskies and wines, welcoming service, and has been popular with readers for good if rather pricey bar food – particularly magnificent sandwiches and Scotch steaks – and for the way they look after their animals so well; more up-to-date reports please *(Dr Paul Kitchener, Charles Gurney, Joan Olivier, Mr and Mrs G Sparrow, LYM)*

Nettlebed [SU6986], *Sun*: Small friendly pub with collection of taps, 'time flies' clock, well kept Brakspears, good ploughman's, freshly made sandwiches, vegetarian and other food *(Dr J R Hamilton)*

Newbridge [A415 7 miles S of Witney; SP4101], *Maybush*: Low-beamed bar in unassuming Thames-side Morlands pub with waterside terrace *(LYM)*

Northmoor [off A415; SP4202], *Dun Cow*: Simple little pub with lovely gardens and well kept beer, run by the same family for 70-odd years *(Dr and Mrs A K Clarke)*

Osney [Bridge St; SP5005], *Hollybush*: Ten minutes' walk from Oxford centre and close to River Isis, this well run pub has a cosy atmosphere in lounge bar, separate panelled room and restaurant; fresh flowers, unobtrusive music, Courage Best and Directors, bar food, occasional live music; children welcome *(Jonathan Long)*;
Watermans Arms: On island by attractive stretch of canal, with Morlands ales and variety of reasonably priced and generously served bar food *(Nick Long, RCL)*

☆ **Oxford** [St Giles], *Eagle & Child*: Long and narrow pub, attractively refurbished with two four-person panelled snugs either side of the entrance, each with its own fireplace; further tiny area on right just before bar (itself small); modern extension beyond bar with open ceiling joists, leading to conservatory and finally a small, pretty terrace; tends to feel least cramped early in the week, and much enjoyed by readers for its friendly old-fashioned feel, also simple, well prepared and reasonably priced bar food such as pizzas and filled baked potatoes; well kept Ansells, Halls Harvest and Wadworths 6X on handpump, piped classical music, newspapers provided *(Ian Phillips, GL, SL, RCL, Dr and Mrs A K Clarke, Dr John Innes, BB)*

☆ **Oxford** [Binsey Lane; narrow lane on right leaving city on A420, just before Bishops Depository], *Perch*: Spacious thatched pub fronted by lovely riverside meadows; bare stone walls, flagstones, high-backed settles as well as more modern seats, log fires, bar meals inc a choice of hot dishes from filled baked potatoes to speciality steaks, help-yourself salads, maybe summer weekend afternoon teas; Arkells, Wadworths 6X and Ind-Coope-related real ales; big garden, play area, landing stage; has been live entertainment Sun; not all our older readers have taken kindly to the tone of the new licensees' stern notices about dogs in the garden, and people putting their feet on chairs; children allowed in eating area *(Jon Wainwright, LYM – reports on new regime please)*

Oxford [off Cornmarket St, in alley nr McDonald's, more or less opposite Boots], *Crypt*: Hardly a candidate for the main entries, as it's not a pub but a large underground restaurant with attached back-to-basics wine bar; but well worth knowing for its good atmosphere (sawdust on floor), smart service, good food inc excellent pies and nibbles on bar; numerous wines, ports, fresh orange juice and bottled beers *(S Matthews, Michael and Alison Sandy)*; [Little Clarendon St; just off St Giles] *Duke of Cambridge*: Well kept up-market popular place, more brasserie-cum-club than somewhere just to drop into, with flamboyant, efficient barmen; bottled beers from all over the world, a wide range of spirits, good cocktails and freshly squeezed juices; bar food inc scrambled eggs with smoked salmon and bangers and mash *(Stanley Matthews)*; [39 Plantation Rd; first left after Horse & Jockey going N up Woodstock Rd] *Gardeners Arms*: Friendly open-plan pub with mock beams, old local photographs, antique plates and brasses, home-made bar food, garden room; Morrells real ales *(G C Saunders, Jon Wainwright, LYM)*; [Holywell St] *Kings Arms*: Much the most studenty of Oxford's pubs, very full and lively in term-time; large and basic, with one main room (quite warehousey), two more comfortable and smaller ones at the back, no-smoking room just inside the Parks Rd entrance; good range of well kept real ales, dictionary provided for crossword buffs, decent bar food *(RCL, BKA, GL, SL, MKH, BB)*; [North Parade] *Rose & Crown*: Small unspoilt traditional pub with authentic Oxford feel, bar food inc lots of toasted sandwiches and good daily specials, well kept Halls and Ind Coope Burton; character landlord, who can be very welcoming *(M Quine, RCL)*; [Broad St] *White Horse*: Small, busy one-roomed Ind Coope pub somewhat below street level, sandwiched between parts of Blackwells bookshop; long bar with team photographs, oars on beams, oak furniture, well kept Wadworths 6X, reasonable bar food *(Dr John Innes)*; [272 Woodstock Rd] *Woodstock Arms*: Quiet, neat lounge with six small tables, bar with bar billiards and fruit machines, not usually too crowded even at busy times; obliging service, Morrells beer and good value, simple bar food with changing daily specials *(Mike O'Driscoll)*

Play Hatch [SU7476], *Shoulder of Mutton*: Real local with three small connecting bars with a fire in each; old-fashioned pubby atmosphere, friendly locals and licensee and well kept beer; no food at weekends; right on a wood with no pavement and very little parking *(Sheila Keene)*

☆ **Radcot** [Radcot Bridge; A4095 2½ miles N of Faringdon; SU2899], *Swan*: Unpretentious inn, delightful in summer for its riverside lawn, with Thames boat-trips from pub's camping-ground opposite – the boat has a powered platform to bring wheelchairs aboard; well kept Morlands Bitter, Best and Mild, pub games; children in eating area; bedrooms clean and good value, with hearty traditional breakfast *(Joan Olivier, Andy Blackburn, LYM)*

☆ **Russells Water** [up track past duck pond; village signposted from B481 S of junction with B480; SU7089], *Beehive*: Old-world pub with interesting collection of furnishings, big wood-burning stove, subdued red lighting, well kept Brakspears, Flowers Original,

Marstons Pedigree and Wadworths 6X, good food that includes imaginative dishes as well as tried favourites such as steak and kidney pie (not Mon); tables on rose-fringed terrace or under fairy-lit arbour, restaurant, has had trad jazz Tues or Weds evening; children in family-room *(M J Dyke, Mr and Mrs G A Evans, Dick Brown, LYM – more reports on new regime please)*

Sandford on Thames [SP5301], *Catherine Wheel*: Fifteenth-century pub run by friendly young couple – it's said to be harmlessly haunted by former landlord; garden with play area *(Joan Olivier)*

☆ **Satwell** [just off B481, 2 miles S of Nettlebed; follow Shepherds Green signpost; SU7083], *Lamb*: Unspoilt even after careful refurbishments – black-beamed farm cottage with tiled floors, low ceilings, huge log fireplace, simple bar food (though prices not as alluring as they were before the changes), well kept Brakspears, traditional games *(Gordon and Daphne, LYM)*

Shillingford Bridge [SU5992], *Shillingford Bridge*: Food good in friendly well furnished hotel bar and restaurant, idyllic spot with peaceful Thames-side lawn and outdoor swimming-pool; bedrooms good value for area *(BB)*

Shilton [SP2608], *Rose & Crown*: Fourteenth-century Cotswold-stone two-bar Courage house with low beams, soft piped music, fruit machine, darts and friendly atmosphere; wide choice of hot and cold food from sandwiches to steaks (inc pheasant at 24 hours' notice), small garden; close to Cotswold Wildlife Park *(Joan Olivier)*

☆ **Shiplake** [A4155 towards Play Hatch and Reading – OS Sheet 175 map reference 746768; SU7476], *Flowing Spring*: Well kept Fullers ales and decent bar food in three cosy but unpretentious rooms of small, sloping countrified pub with open fires and floor-to-ceiling windows overlooking the watermeadows; big attractive garden, occasional jazz and morris dancing *(John Hayward, TBB, LYM)*

Shiplake [by stn; SU7578], *Baskerville Arms*: Friendly landlord and customers, well kept beers and good choice of food; jazz Thurs evenings; good value clean bedrooms *(Ken Sharp)*

Sibford Gower [SP3537], *Wykham Arms*: Welcoming pub, worth knowing for impressive food *(John and Joan Wyatt)*

Sonning Common [Kingwood Common; SU6982], *Grouse & Claret*: Attractive free house, cosy interior with several intimate nooks; well kept Morlands Best, Ruddles County, bar food, attentive service, rather intrusive piped music *(Sheila Keene)*

Souldern [SP5131], *Fox*: Delightful Cotswold-stone pub with Flowers, Hook Norton and Sam Smiths real ales, bar food, most obliging licensees; comfortable bedrooms, good breakfasts *(Roy Bamford)*

South Moreton [SU5588], *Waterloo*: Clean, recently renovated outside and in, comfortable and spacious with good value home-made soup, ploughman's, sandwiches *(Anon)*

Stadhampton [signposted in village on A329; SU6098], *Bear & Ragged Staff*: Characterful free house bought a few years ago by a consortium of its regular customers; strong real ales on handpump, good interesting bar food inc giant burgers, music popular with young people *(Colin and Caroline)*

Steventon [SU4691], *Cherry Tree*: Seven well kept ales inc Hook Norton, good range of quickly served good value home-made food such as soup, ploughman's and pizzas *(Dick Brown, John Tyzack)*

☆ **Sutton Courtenay** [B4016; SU5093], *Fish*: Tastefully modernised pub which currently looks very promising under new owners who are moving it more up-market – particularly on the food side; well worth watching *(A T Langton, Mrs S Boreham)*

Tackley [SP4720], *Gardiners Arms*: Popular pub with good atmosphere, friendly and chatty staff; public bar with darts and soft piped music, lounge bar comfortably carpeted with settles, chairs, coal-effect gas fire, brasses on wall; well kept Ansells, Halls Harvest and Tetleys, well presented good value bar food inc bargain two-course steak meal with wine Sun–Thurs; two picnic-table sets in grassy car park *(Lyn and Bill Capper, Margaret and Douglas Tucker)*

Thame [High Street; SP7005], *Abingdon Arms*: Polite and friendly young staff in low-beamed old pub with tasty food and real ale inc unusual guest beers *(E G Parish)*; *Bird Cage*: Short reasonably priced bar lunch menu inc good sandwiches, ploughman's and home-made soup, and well kept Courage Best and Directors, in quaint black and white beamed and timbered pub, once a medieval jail; piped music *(LYM)*; *Black Horse*: Old-fashioned calm in panelled and chintzy back lounge, little sheltered courtyard, bar meals and restaurant; bedrooms *(LYM)*

Tiddington [SP6504], *Fox*: Neat and attractive low-beamed and stone-walled roadside pub, large softly lit lounge with comfortable chairs, many tables, big fire; lively and friendly atmosphere, efficient service; well kept Ind Coope Burton and Tetleys on handpump, good standard bar food, closely attentive service *(Mike O'Driscoll, Gwen and Peter Andrews)*

Toot Baldon [village signposted from A423 at Nuneham Courtenay, and B480; SP5600], *Crown*: Friendly village pub, popular at lunchtime for good food; benches and tables out on terrace *(Joan Olivier)*

Towersey [Chinnor Rd; SP7304], *Three Horseshoes*: Flagstones, old-fashioned furnishings and good log fire make for a warm country atmosphere; well kept ABC real ale, bar food, piped music, biggish

garden with playthings among fruit trees; children allowed at lunchtime *(Nancy Witts, TBB, Mike Tucker, LYM)*

Uffington [SU3089], *Fox & Hounds*: Limited space in small two-roomed local with beams and brasses; good atmosphere, friendly Jack Russell, wide choice of hot and cold bar food at reasonable prices; take-it-as-you-find-it garden with picnic-table sets *(Lyn and Bill Capper)*

Wallingford [SU6089], *George*: Much done-up series of bars and places to eat in hotel with spacious and attractive sycamore-shaded courtyard; bedrooms *(LYM)*

☆ **Wantage** [Mill St; past square and Bell, down hill then bend to left; SU4087], *Lamb*: Friendly and snugly comfortable family-run low-beamed and timbered pub with choice of attractively furnished seating areas, well kept Morlands, popular nicely presented freshly cooked bar food, good play area *(Stuart Ballantyne, LYM)*

Wantage [87 Grove St; just off market square], *Abingdon Arms*: Friendly atmosphere, traditional bar games, well kept Morlands, hot and cold bar food, garden *(David Gass)*; [Market Pl] *Bear*: Wide choice of food from home-made soup through sandwiches and baked potatoes to ham and eggs, meat salads and curries, well kept Ushers real ale, in big bustling bar with chintzy easy chairs and sofas; restaurant; bedrooms *(BB)*

☆ **Warborough** [The Green South; just E of A329, 4 miles N of Wallingford; SU5993], *Six Bells*: Low-ceilinged thatched pub with country furnishings, big fireplace, antique photographs and pictures, fairly priced bar food; tables in back orchard, cricket green in front, boules in summer; children in eating area *(LYM)*

West Hendred [Reading Rd, off A417 – OS Sheet 174 reference 447891; SU4488], *Hare*: Good local clientele, although strangers made very welcome; well kept beers and good choice of daily specials such as excellent leek and potato soup, delicious sandwiches *(A T Langton)*

Witney [17 High St; SP3510], *Royal Oak*: Cosy and welcoming with log fire and good lunchtime bar snacks; attractive courtyard *(Mrs F Abbot)*

☆ **Woodstock** [Market St; SP4416], *Feathers*: Traditional hotel with beautiful period furniture of all ages; stuffed birds, fish, watercolours and oils on walls – all of bygone days; food in sedate older-fashioned garden bar interesting, well priced and worth waiting for (smoked goose, game terrine, baked ham, salads all recommended); busy at lunchtime with tourists and locals; bedrooms *(G and M Brooke-Williams, G Heap)*

Woodstock [A34 leading out], *Black Prince*: Good atmosphere and prompt food service – not cheap, but good range inc ploughman's and Mexican dishes, and helpings plentiful *(B D Gibbs)*; [Park Lane] *Kings Head*: Pleasant atmosphere in consistently good pub with quick and friendly service, good value bar food inc enormous filled baked potatoes with salad; waitress service even in bar area *(Mrs Margaret Dyke, J M Norton)*; [Oxford St] *Marlborough Arms*: Courteous welcome in attractive lounge bar of Best Western hotel with cheerful fire, well kept beer and good value food; bedrooms warm and cosy, and worth it though not cheap and rather small *(E G Parish)*; *Punch Bowl*: Comfortable small-town pub with well kept Wadworths 6X and good food such as onion and cider soup and cheese-topped chilli with jalapenos *(Jason Caulkin)*; [59 Oxford St] *Queens Own*: Warm, one-bar pub with friendly licensees, good reasonably priced food and well kept Hook Norton ales; unobtrusive juke box; darts, dominoes *(Barry Shapley)*; *Woodstock Arms*: Friendly service and reasonably priced, simple bar food – a place for aficionados of artificial

flowers; bedrooms *(Syd and Wyn Donald)*

☆ **Woolstone** [SU2987], *White Horse*: Isolated partly thatched sixteenth-century pub in lovely spot, recently extended, with two big open fires in spacious beamed and partly panelled bar, prompt service, and well presented though not cheap bar food; Flowers and Wethereds real ales, children allowed in side eating area; fairly priced restaurant *(HNJ, PEJ, Dr A Y Drummond, Lady Quinny, Henry Midwinter)*

Wroxton [Church St; off A422 at hotel; pub at back of village; SP4142], *North Arms*: Popular thatched stone pub with plain but comfortable modernised lounge, bar food from good crusty sandwiches and ploughman's to trout, gammon and steaks, well kept Banks's on handpump, tables on idyllically placed front garden; no bar meals Sun (snacks only Sun lunch); restaurant, where children allowed; we have had too few reports since the Banks's takeover to be sure of the pub's rating *(I R Hewitt, S V Bishop, LYM – more reports please)*

Shropshire

For so long one of the quietest counties in this Guide – in the sense that little changed on the pub front – Shropshire's become one of the most active in the last two or three years. This edition yet again includes several interesting new main entries: the lively Hollyhead in Bridgnorth (good value as a place to stay at), the idyllically placed Stables at Hopesgate near Hope (one of our most delectable finds of the year – good food, too), the Church in one of the nicest positions in Ludlow (another good place to stay at), the attractively refurbished Lion of Morfe at Upper Farmcote, and two pubs brought back into the Guide by new licensees who've brought them back on form – the Crown at Hopton Wafers (good food, comfortable bedrooms) and the Ragleth in Little Stretton. Besides the many attractive main entries, promising prospects among the Lucky Dip entries at the end of the chapter include the Railwaymans Arms in Bridgnorth, Crown at Claverley, quaint Horse Shoe at Llanyblodwel, Feathers and Wheatsheaf in Ludlow, Crown at Munslow, and several pubs in the interesting Coalport/Ironbridge area, including one that's actually part of the Blists Hill open-air museum, and that archetypal own-brew pub the All Nations at Madeley.

BISHOP'S CASTLE   SO3289 Map 6
Three Tuns
Salop Street

Virtually unique and a Grade 1 listed building, the many storeyed towering Victorian brick brewhouse across the yard from this unspoilt and family-run pub has various stages of the brewing process descending floor by floor; the beers from it are XXX Bitter, Mild and an old-fashioned dark somewhat stoutish ale called Steamer; brewery tours can be arranged. The quaint public bar has a welcoming atmosphere, and home-made bar food includes soup (£1.25), baps, filled baked potatoes (from £1.25), hot beef and ham in French bread (£2.50), ploughman's or burger (from £2.50), ratatouille and cheese, chilli con carne and pitta bread or cottage pie (£2.85), lasagne (£3.75), steaks (from £7.60), and puddings such as fruit crumble, treacle tart or carrot cake (from £1.20). Halls and Westons ciders; malt whiskies. Darts, dominoes and cribbage. There's a garden and terrace, with a large selection of plants for sale. Plans are in hand for a restaurant. *(Recommended by Nick Dowson, Alison Hayward, Richard and Dilys Smith, BHP, Gwen and Peter Andrews, Derek and Sylvia Stephenson, T Nott)*

Own brew   Licensee Jack Wood   Real ale   Meals and snacks   Children welcome   Open 11.30–2.30, 6.30–11; 11.50–5, 6.30–11 Fri, Sat and bank hols in summer

BRIDGNORTH   SO7293 Map 4
Hollyhead 🛏
Hollybush Road; opposite station

Run by two friendly and attentive couples, this cheerful and unpretentiously well kept pub will this year be celebrating two centuries as a licensed house. The rambling, alcovey lounge has several areas – low chunky elm tables by the counter, high-backed modern winged settles and wheel-back chairs around sturdy dining-tables elsewhere; there are one or two hunting prints, swirly plastered timbered

---

Prices of main dishes usually include vegetables or a side salad.

walls, oak beams and joists, and logs burning in the big stone fireplace. A separate similarly furnished but smaller bar on the left has darts, dominoes, fruit machine and maybe pop videos. Simple good value bar food includes filled rolls (70p), burgers (£1.70), ploughman's (£1.95), home-made chilli con carne (£2.75), plaice, curry or vegetarian lasagne (£2.95) and steak and kidney pie (£3.25), with children's dishes (£1.25); they do new potatoes as an alternative to chips. Well kept Boddingtons and Courage Best on handpump, with a couple of frequently changing guest beers such as Timothy Taylors Landlord and Wadworths 6X. There are tables under cocktail parasols in a sun-trap roadside courtyard, as well as brown-painted slatted railway benches – appropriate enough, with the headquarters of the Severn Valley steam railway across the road. Breakfasts are good. *(Recommended by G B Pugh, G M K Donkin)*

Free house   Licensees D I Wilson and S Mellish   Real ale   Meals and snacks   Restaurant Children welcome   Open 12–3, 5.30–11 all year; all day Sat   Bedrooms tel Bridgnorth (074 62) 2162; £14/£28

CARDINGTON   SO5095 Map 4
Royal Oak

Village signposted off B4371 Church Stretton–Much Wenlock; pub behind church; also reached via narrow lanes from A49

Plainly very old indeed, this white stone house has been licensed as a pub for longer than any other in Shropshire. The more-or-less open- plan room has low beams, old standing timbers of a knocked-through wall, gold plush, red leatherette and tapestry seats solidly capped in elm, and a vast inglenook fireplace with its roaring winter log fire, cauldron, black kettle and pewter jugs. Good value, home-made lunchtime bar food includes soup (£1.20), sandwiches (£1.20, toasties £1.60), ploughman's (£2.20) and at least seven dishes – served without vegetables – such as macaroni cheese (£1.60), cauliflower cheese (£1.80), lasagne, cottage pie, steak and kidney or fidget pie or quiche (£2.20) and chicken curry or chilli con carne (£3). The choice in the evening (no orders after 8.30) is generally similar, and always includes plaice (£3), chicken cobbler (£3.50), gammon and egg (£4.25), rump steak (£5.25) and occasional evening specials. As we went to press we learnt that a new kitchen extension will mean an even more extensive choice of bar food. Well kept Ruddles County and Wadworths 6X on handpump, with Bass and Springfield, also on handpump, kept under light blanket pressure. Besides darts, dominoes and cribbage in the main bar, a brightly lit upstairs room has pool, a fruit machine, trivia machine and juke box. Tables beside roses in the front court look over to hilly fields, and a mile or so away, from the track past Willstone (ask for directions at the pub), you can walk up Caer Caradoc Hill which has magnificent views. *(Recommended by Gordon Mott, T Nott, James and Marion Seeley, A Royle, A B Garside)*

Free house   Licensee John Seymour   Real ale   Meals and snacks (not Sun evening) Children welcome lunchtime; only if eating in evening   Open 12–2.30, 7–11; closed Mon lunchtime Nov–Mar exc school hols   One self-contained double bedroom tel Longville (069 43) 266; £19.50S/£29S

CLUN   SO3081 Map 6
Sun

High Street; B4368 towards Clunton

Friendly and relaxed, the beamed lounge bar here has some attractive old tables and sturdy wall timbers, one or two high-backed winged settles, built-in cushioned wall benches, a carved antique oak armchair, and hop-bines around the beams; a sheltered back terrace opens off here with tables among pots of geraniums and other flowers. The L-shaped public bar has traditional settles on its flagstones, an enormous open fire, and dominoes, cribbage, chess, backgammon and tippet;

there's a friendly Scotty dog. Bar food includes sandwiches (from £1), home-made soup (£1.50), garlic and herb mushrooms or mackerel pâté (£2.50), with daily specials such as fabada (Spanish butter-bean stew £3), various curries (beef and lentil with fresh coriander £3.50; beef and cashew-nut £3.75), vegetarian dishes such as cassoulet (£3.75), and puddings like home-made apple and cinnamon pie or cheesecake (£1.50); evening dishes include more elaborate dishes such as rabbit with brandy, cream and raisins (£5.25) and seafood provençale (£6.50). Well kept Banks's and Woods Special on handpump. *(Recommended by Nick Dowson, Alison Hayward, Ninka Sharland, Lynne Sheridan, Bob West, Derek and Sylvia Stephenson, Paul McPherson, William Rodgers, Pete Storey, Hazel Ricketts)*

Free house   Licensee Keith Small   Real ale   Meals and snacks   Restaurant   Children in eating area and restaurant   Open 11–3, 6–11; 11–11 Sat all year   Bedrooms tel Clun (058 84) 277; £16/£32(£35B)

HOPE   SJ3401 Map 6

Stables 🏮

Drury Lane, Hopesgate; pub signposted off A488 S of Minsterley, at the Bentlawnt ¾, Leigh 1¾ signpost – then take first right turn

Just as the Hardings were building up a really enthusiastic following at the Fox at Broadwell over in the Cotswolds, they slipped away – with children, cats, and Corrie and Kelly the gruffly friendly mother-and-daughter cream-coloured labradors – to this remote little pub in utterly unspoilt countryside above the Hope Valley. They've already made it delightful. The black-beamed L-shaped bar, with logs burning in the imposing stone fireplace, has comfortably cushioned or well polished wooden seats around attractive oak and other tables, hunting prints of varying ages and degrees of solemnity, well chosen china, and in a back room (with copper-topped cask tables) some big prints of butterflies and herbs. Home-made bar food changes day by day, with soup (£1), ploughman's, snacks such as hot beef rolls, pasties, hot potted shrimps (£2) or smoked chicken Waldorf salad (£2.20), two or three hot dishes such as smoked haddock kedgeree (£3.20), Stilton and walnut pancake with spicy tomato sauce (£3.75) and beef and Beamish stout pie (£3.90), salads such as home-baked ham (£3), and good puddings (£1.30); vegetables are fresh. There tends to be a wider choice, running to lamb marinated in yoghurt, almonds and tandoori spices with a mint sambal (£3.80) or chicken breast with a mango, peach and pineapple sauce (£4.20), on Thursday to Saturday evenings, when the cottagey dining-room is open (only four tables, so booking's worth while). Well kept Ansells Best, Marstons Pedigree, Tetleys and Woods Special on handpump, with Westons and other farm ciders in summer, and decent wines and spirits (they do a good Kir). On summer Sunday evenings, when they have a boules knock-out, they do barbecues; darts, shove-ha'penny, cribbage, dominoes. There's a choice view from the front tables, over rolling pastures to the Long Mountain; behind, you look over the Hope Valley to the Stiperstones. *(Recommended by BOB; more reports please)*

Free house   Licensees Denis and Debbie Harding   Real ale   Meals and snacks (lunchtime, not Mon; Thurs–Sat evenings)   Restaurant tel Worthen (074 383) 344   Children welcome lunchtimes   Open 11–2.30, 7–11 all year; closed Mon exc bank hols

HOPTON WAFERS   SO6476 Map 4

Crown 🏮 🛏

A4117

Readers' reports this year indicate that this substantial and attractive creeper-covered stone building is now firmly back on course, with a wide choice of good bar food, well kept beer, and efficient, friendly service. The spreading bar has a relaxed atmosphere, fresh flowers, a variety of furnishings, flowery cushions on the black settles, oil paintings, silver band instruments hanging from the beams and a large inglenook fire as well as a wood-burning stove; unobtrusive piped music. Very good bar food includes sandwiches (from £1, prawn open £2.75), soup (£1.25), home-made pâté (£2.25), ploughman's (from £2.25), salads (from £2.45), meat or vegetarian lasagne (from £2.95), plaice or chicken curry (£3.50), chilli con carne (£3.60), steak and kidney pie or scampi (£3.65), steaks (£5.95), and daily home-made specials like baked mussels in garlic butter (£2.45), cauliflower cheese topped with crispy bacon, chicken curry with chappati and half a dozen side dishes, smoked trout salad (£2.75), liver, bacon and onion casserole (£3.50) or fresh Wye salmon with white wine, cream and prawns (£4.95); puddings range from hot syrup sponge and treacle tart to toffee cheesecake and filo pastry baskets filled with cream and fresh fruit; children's dishes (£1.50). There's a choice of real ales such as Flowers Original, Marstons Pedigree and Woods Bitter on handpump. There are tables under cocktail parasols on the terraces and in the streamside garden, with plenty of tubs of bright flowers; also, an adventure playground. *(Recommended by Mrs Nina Elliott, R C Parker, Mr and Mrs E J Rees, G and M Hollis, James and Marion Seeley, Alison Hayward, Ken and Barbara Turner, PLC, Paul McPherson, Ninka Sharland, Brian Jordan)*

Free house   Licensees Howard and Polly Hill-Lines   Real ale   Meals and snacks (12–2, 7–10)   Restaurant   Children in eating area of bar   Open 11–3, 6–11 all year   Bedrooms tel Cleobury Mortimer (0299) 270372; £25B/£35B

LINLEY   SO6998 Map 4

Pheasant

Pub signposted off B4373

This welcoming country pub has a low, black-beamed main bar with a stuffed pheasant and a collection of pheasant-decorated plates, a mixture of seats including a flowery-cushioned pew and big-backed country kitchen armchairs, rugs on red quarry tiles, and log fires at each end. Simple food includes sandwiches (from 70p, toasties 95p), good ploughman's with two cheeses (£1.85), cod, haddock or home-made lasagne (£2.95), scampi (£3.35), gammon with their own free-range eggs (£3.95) and rump steak (£4.75). Well kept Banks's, Marstons, Titanic Premium, Youngers Scotch and other guest beers on handpump; dominoes, fruit machine and juke box in a separate room. There are some picnic-table sets under damson trees on the side grass, by a pretty flower border. They can tell you a good circuit walk from here. *(Recommended by Jon Wainwright, A D Goff, Brian and Anna Marsden; more reports please)*

Free house   Licensee R S A Reed   Real ale   Meals and snacks (not Sun if busy)   Well behaved children in eating area if over 11 years old   Open 11.30–2.30, 6.45 (6 Sat)–11 all year; opens 7 in winter

LITTLE STRETTON   SO4392 Map 6

Green Dragon

Ludlow Road; village well signposted from A49

This pleasant creeper-covered white house has a well kept carpeted lounge bar with green plush banquettes and stools around the well spaced polished dark tables, and a relaxed atmosphere. Good value well presented bar food, served efficiently, includes soup (95p), filled rolls (£1 – or sandwiches on request), plaice or vegetarian lasagne (£3.50), scampi (£3.55), steak and kidney pie (£3.85), halibut (£5.20) and steaks (from sirloin £6.55). Well kept Manns, Ruddles County and Woods on handpump; maybe unobtrusive piped music. There are picnic-table sets

---

Pubs shown as closing at 11 do so in the summer, but may close earlier – normally 10.30 – in winter unless we specify 'all year'.

under cocktail parasols on the lawn of a prettily planted garden. *(Recommended by Nick Dowson, Alison Hayward, Paul McPherson, Mrs P Wilson, T Nott, A A Worthington)*

Free house   Real ale   Meals and snacks (not summer Sun evenings)   Restaurant tel Church Stretton (0694) 722925   Children in restaurant   Open 11.30–2.30, 6–11 all year; closed 25 Dec

Ragleth Inn

Ludlow Road

Close to Long Mynd (a spacious heather-and-bracken plateau owned by the National Trust, with fine views) this attractive pub has a pleasant, welcoming atmosphere. The comfortable bay-windowed lounge bar has built-in seats, a good winter fire, an unusual curved corner, and oak-topped bar counter. Good, reasonably priced home-made bar food includes sandwiches (£1.25), soup (£1.30), burgers (from £1.55), filled baked potatoes (from £1.85), chicken liver and brandy pâté (£2.45), cottage pie (£2.60), delicious ploughman's (from £2.65), salads (from £2.90), lasagne (£3.95), steaks (from £4.95); three daily specials might include pork stir-fry, chilli con carne or steak and kidney pie and a vegetarian dish like ratatouille pancakes (all £3.85); puddings like home-made cheesecake or chocolate and brandy mousse; good Sunday roast lunch (£7.25). The public bar has a huge inglenook fireplace, a brick and tiled floor, and darts, dominoes, fruit machine, space game and juke box. Well kept Bass, Courage Directors and John Smiths Bitter on handpump. Tables on the lawn (where there's a tulip tree) look across to an ancient-seeming thatched and timbered church (actually built in this century). The pub is near *Good Walks Guide* Walk 102. *(Recommended by T Nott, Mrs P Wilson, NWN, Mike Tucker, Nick Dowson, Alison Hayward, Dr P Webb, KC, Paul McPherson, Mr and Mrs M D Jones, Paul and Margaret Baker, A Royle, Robert and Vicky Tod, JH)*

Free house   Licensees Harford and Marion Ransley, Ted and Margaret Swift   Real ale Meals and snacks   Restaurant tel Church Stretton (0694) 722711   Children in bar Open 11–2.30, 6–11 all year; closed 25 Dec

LOPPINGTON   SJ4729 Map 6

Blacksmiths Arms

Village signposted from B4397 W of Wem

Neatly thatched, this heavily beamed village pub has a central bar with a collection of genuine horsebrasses, and farm and thatching tools, spindle-back chairs on its red tiled floor, and two seats by the inglenook fireplace. Off to the left there are dark plush built-in button-back banquettes around neat tables (with a vase of flowers), and country prints on the timbered walls. A smallish room on the right has more neat seats and tables and shooting prints. Good value home-made bar food includes home-made soup (£1), sandwiches (from £1), filled baked potatoes (from £1.50), ploughman's (£2), chilli con carne or vegetable pancake (£2.75), home-made pies (from £3.50), chicken Kiev (£4.50), steaks (from £5.95), and daily specials; various puddings such as apple and sultana pie or lemon and hazelnut cheesecake; Sunday roast lunch. Bass on handpump and large choice of malt whiskies; darts, shove-ha'penny and dominoes. There's a play area in the attractive garden, and picnic-table sets and other garden seats on the terrace. *(Recommended by Paul McPherson, William Rodgers, G E Rodger, R G Ollier)*

Free house   Licensee Mrs Jackie Brindley   Real ale   Meals and snacks (not Mon lunchtime)   Restaurant tel Wem (0939) 33762   Children welcome   Open 12–3, 7–11 all year; closed Mon lunchtime

Bedroom prices normally include full English breakfast, VAT and any inclusive service charge that we know of. Prices before the '/' are for single rooms, after for two people in double or twin (B includes a private bath, S a private shower). If there is no '/', the prices are only for twin or double rooms (as far as we know there are no singles).

LUDLOW   SO5173 Map 4

Church 🛏

Church Street, behind Buttercross; best chance of parking is in Broad Street

Neatly and comfortably modernised, this Georgian-stuccoed inn opens behind on to a decorous walk by the red sandstone church; the bedrooms on this side would be the quietest. Comfortably cushioned beige wall banquettes loop around the alcoves of its calm and airy bar, with attractively engraved old song title-pages, botanical prints and so forth on its cream walls. Good value bar food includes soup (95p), home-made quiche (£2.95), scampi or fresh plaice (£3.50), vegetarian dishes, fresh trout (£3.95), home-made lasagne or fisherman's pie (£4.20), steak pie (£4.50) and rump steak (£5.50), with lunchtime sandwiches (from £1.40), filled baked potatoes (from £1.50) and ploughman's (£2.95); well kept Flowers Original, Marstons Pedigree, Ruddles County and Websters Yorkshire on handpump, with guest beers. *(Recommended by A Cook, K and E Leist, Philip King, Nick Dowson, Alison Hayward)*

Free house   Licensees Brian and Carol Hargreaves   Real ale   Meals and snacks   Restaurant   Children in eating area and restaurant   Open 11–3, 6–11 all year   Bedrooms tel Ludlow (0584) 2174; £23B/£34B

MUCH WENLOCK   SJ6200 Map 4

George & Dragon

High Street

A collection of about one thousand water jugs hangs from the beams in the front bar here – the biggest pub collection in England; also, some George and the Dragon pictures, old brewery and cigarette advertisements, lots of bottle labels and beer trays, a few antique settles as well as conventional furnishings, and a couple of attractive Victorian fireplaces (with coal-effect gas fires). It can get smoky. The quieter snug old-fashioned rooms at the back have little decorative plaster panels, tiled floors, a big George and the Dragon mural as well as lots of smaller pictures (painted by local artists), black beams and timbering, a stained-glass smoke-room sign, and a little stove in a fat fireplace. A good choice of bar food at lunchtime includes sandwiches, home-made soup (£1.50), ploughman's with home-made chutney (from £2.25), home-made pâté (£2.75), lentils and vegetable gratin (£3), fisherman's pie or chicken in a lemon and tarragon sauce (£3.50), fresh trout stuffed with prawns, mushrooms and ginger or lamb curry (£3.75), and puddings like home-made sherry trifle (£1.50); evening meals are served in Eve's Kitchen, with starters such as Stilton and pear pâté (£2.25), and main courses such as lamb's liver (£6.50) or the house speciality, duck (£8.50). Well kept Hook Norton Best, Marstons Pedigree and guest beers on handpump; friendly service; music from a vintage wireless. *(Recommended by Colin Dowse, A M J Chadwick, Lynne Sheridan, Bob West, Maggie Jo St John, Dudley Evans, Derek and Sylvia Stephenson, M A and W R Proctor, Robert and Vicky Tod, N J Neil-Smith; more reports please)*

Free house   Licensees Eve and Brian Nolan   Real ale   Lunchtime meals and snacks   Evening restaurant tel Much Wenlock (0952) 727312; closed Sun and Mon evenings   Older children in restaurant if well behaved   Open 11–2.30, 6–11 all year; opens 7 in winter

Talbot 🍺

High Street

Several opened-together carpeted areas in this welcoming and very neatly kept old pub have low ceilings, comfortable green plush button-back wall banquettes around highly polished tables, walls decorated with prints of fish, and with shives, tuts, spices and other barrel-stoppers, lovely flowers, two big log fires (one in an inglenook decorated with a hop-bine), and you'll either like or loathe the 1920s plaster figurines around the bar. The atmosphere is welcoming and relaxed. Good, attractively presented home-made bar food includes soup (£1.25), pâté (£1.95), filled baked potatoes (£1.95), ploughman's (from £2.65), quiche (£3.25), omelettes (from £3.25), spicy pancake (£3.50), steak and kidney pie with first-class pastry (£3.75), locally produced sirloin steak (£5.75), specials such as lamb and apricot casserole or fish and prawn pie, and puddings like bread-and-butter pudding, blackberry and apple pie or lemon meringue pie; in the evening there's more concentration on main dishes such as grilled trout (£5.50), lamb chops (£6.25) or scampi provençale (£7.25), and specials such as pheasant in red wine sauce or breast of duck with apricot and ginger. They do a roast Sunday lunch (best to book). Ruddles Best and Websters Yorkshire on handpump; good value wines and good coffee; piped music. Through the coach entry, there are white seats and tables in an attractive sheltered yard. *(Recommended by Alison Graham, Steve Goodchild, Roy Bromell, Paul McPherson, T Nott, Kit Read)*

Free house   Licensee Timothy Lathe   Real ale   Meals and lunchtime snacks (not 25 Dec) Restaurant   Well behaved children welcome (no prams)   Open 10.30–2.30, 6–11 all year Bedrooms tel Much Wenlock (0952) 727077; £30B/£50B

NORTON   SJ7200 Map 4

Hundred House 🍺

A442 Telford–Bridgnorth

A lot of thought and energy have gone into designing the layout and furnishings of this comfortable pub. Three or four more or less separate areas have handsome fireplaces with log fires or working Coalbrookdale ranges (one has a great Jacobean arch with fine old black cooking-pots), old quarry tiles at either end and modern hexagonal ones in the main central part, which has high beams strung with hop-bunches and cooking-pots, a variety of interesting chairs and settles with some long colourful patchwork leather cushions, sewing-machine tables, and attractive lamps. Steps lead up past a little balustrade to a partly panelled eating area, where stripped brickwork looks older than that elsewhere. It's very up-market, with food prices to match – the kitchen has been enlarged and reorganised to enable them to offer a greater range of bar food: at lunchtime this will include soup (£1.90), chicken liver pâté with brandy and cream (£2.25), fresh fish goujons (£4.95), home-made steak and kidney pie (£5.25) and sirloin steak with parsley or Stilton butter (£8.75), while in the evening there are dishes such as garlic mushrooms topped with puff pastry (£2.50), marinated salmon with pink peppercorns (£3.95) and noisettes of lamb with onion and herb sauce (£6.50); herbs come from their own garden. They also serve breakfast (from £2.25) and afternoon teas. Well kept Chesters Mild, Flowers Original and a guest beer such as Wadworths 6X or Whitbreads Durham Mild, with Heritage (light and refreshing, not too bitter) and the stronger Ailrics Old Ale at the moment brewed for them by a small brewery. Darts, shove-ha'penny, dominoes and fruit machine; no dogs; seats out in a neatly kept and prettily arranged garden. The village bowling-green is next to the inn. *(Recommended by David and Flo Wallington, M A and W R Proctor, Laurence Manning, Derek Stephenson, Dave Butler, Lesley Storey, Eileen and Michael Brecker, Lynne Sheridan, Bob West)*

Free house   Licensees Henry, Sylvia, David and Stuart Phillips   Real ale   Meals and snacks (7.30–11.30 breakfast, 11.30–2.30 lunch, 2.30–6 tea, 6–9.30 supper)   Restaurant; not Sun evening   Children welcome   Open 11–11 all year   Bedrooms tel Norton (095 271) 353; £48B/£58B

If a service charge is mentioned prominently on a menu or accommodation terms, you must pay it if service was satisfactory. If service is really bad you are legally entitled to refuse to pay some or all of the service charge as compensation for not getting the service you might reasonably have expected.

PULVERBATCH SJ4202 Map 6

White Horse ✇

From A49 at N end of Dorrington follow Pulverbatch/Church Pulverbatch signposts, and turn left at eventual T-junction (which is sometimes signposted Church Pulverbatch); OS Sheet 126 reference 424023

A homely, rambling pub with plenty to look at: sturdy elm or cast-iron-framed tables in its several interconnected snug areas, unusual fabric-covered high-backed settles as well as the brocaded banquettes on its Turkey carpet, black beams and heavy timbering, an open coal-burning range with gleaming copper kettles, a collection of antique insurance plaques, big brass sets of scales, willow-pattern plates, and pewter mugs hanging over the serving-counter. The decided Scots influence extends to tasty cullen skink as a soup (95p), well hung proper steak in sandwiches (£2.95 – outstanding value) or on its own (from £5.75), and a good choice of malt whiskies as well as the well kept Wethereds SPA and Flowers Original or maybe Whitbreads Pompey Royal on handpump (and several decent wines by the glass); there's even a good Thorburn print of a grouse among the other country pictures. The wide choice of other bar food includes sandwiches (from 75p, their award-winning toasted roast beef and melted cheese £1.50), burgers (from £1.50), omelettes (from £1.80), ploughman's (from £1.95), fresh fish of the day (£2.50), gammon (£3.95), a popular fry-up or trout (£3.95), home-made curries (from £3.95), and children's dishes (from 75p); daily specials might include quiche (£2.25) or fresh poached salmon salad (£4.95); darts, juke box, friendly efficient service. The quarry-tiled front loggia with its sturdy old green leatherette seat is a nice touch. *(Recommended by PLC; more reports please)*

Whitbreads   Licensee James MacGregor   Real ale   Meals and snacks   Children welcome   Open 11.30–3, 7–11 all year; closed 25 Dec

SHREWSBURY SJ4912 Map 6

Boat House

New Street; leaving city centre via Welsh Bridge, follow Bishop's Castle A488 signpost into Port Hill Road

Right by the River Severn, this comfortably modernised pub has a summer bar on a sheltered and attractive terrace, a lawn with roses, and a footbridge that leads across to the park (where there are quite a few events). Inside, the long, quiet lounge bar has good views down over the river to the park – which, as you can see from a 1732 engraving that shares the panelling with rowing photographs and a collection of oars – hasn't changed much over the centuries. Generous helpings of bar food include filled rolls (£1.10), chicken and herb pâté (£2.55), ploughman's (from £2.70), lasagne (£2.85), pork and apricot or chicken and mushroom pie, vegetarian or meat quiches, chilli con carne or chicken curry, and specials like moussaka or prawn salad (all £2.95); afternoon teas and summer barbecues. Well kept Flowers Original and IPA on handpump; fruit machine, space game, trivia and piped music. *(Recommended by Wayne Brindle, M A Watts; more reports please)*

Whitbreads   Licensee Brian Branagh   Real ale   Meals and snacks   Open 11–11 all year; closed evening 25 Dec

UPPER FARMCOTE SO7792 Map 4

Lion of Morfe

Follow Claverley 2½ signpost off A458 Bridgnorth–Stourbridge

This country pub successfully combines a red-tiled traditional core (where broad-voiced local regulars chat around the coal fire or gravitate to the carpeted pool-room with its big black kitchen range) with an altogether smarter recently done lounge and conservatory. The brown-carpeted lounge bar has pink plush button-back built-in wall banquettes in curving bays, and a good log fire; it opens into the conservatory – no-smoking, with cushioned cane chairs around glass tables on the red-tiled floor. Outside, there are picnic-table sets under cocktail parasols on a terrace, and a lawn spreading out into an orchard with a floodlit boules piste. Attractively priced bar food includes sandwiches (from 75p for steak), filled baked potatoes (from only 75p), burgers (85p), ploughman's (£1.75), home-cooked hot dishes such as curry (£1.85), steak and kidney pie (£2), lasagne (£2.25) and a dish of the day such as Spanish-style chicken (£2.50), salads (from £2.30), and cheap banana splits and so forth. Well kept Banks's on electric pump and Woods Special on handpump; darts, pool, dominoes and fruit machine on the public side; friendly service. *(Recommended by Richard and Dilys Smith)*

Free house   Licensees Bill and Dinah Evans   Real ale   Meals and snacks (lunchtime) Children in eating area   Folk club Sat fortnightly   Open 11.30–2.30 (3.30 Sat), 7–11 all year

WENLOCK EDGE   SO5796 Map 4

Wenlock Edge Inn 🛏

Hilltop; B4371 Much Wenlock–Church Stretton; OS Sheet 137 reference 570962

Built originally around 1795 as a pair of quarrymen's cottages, this exceptionally friendly and carefully restored inn has two cosy low-ceilinged bar rooms with a door in between them. The one on the right has a shelf of high plates, a big wood-burning stove in its large inglenook, and leads into a little dining-room. The room on the left has pews that came from a Methodist chapel in Liverpool, a fine local oak bar counter, and an open fire. The licensee's interested in local ghosts and Chinese horoscopes. Good home-cooked bar food, using fresh ingredients and worth waiting for, includes soup (£1.30), pâté (£1.80), steak and mushroom pie (£3.25), scampi or honey-baked ham (£3.40), evening rump steak (£6.45, Tuesday to Saturday), and dishes of the day such as Elizabethan pork casserole (£4.75), Wedgie pie (beef and South Shropshire venison pie, £4.90), chicken breasts with apricots and cider sauce, and Shrewsbury lamb (£5.20); attractive puddings such as raspberry meringue (£1.60). Well kept Wem Best and Special on handpump, interesting whiskies, decent wines by both glass and bottle, and no music – unless you count the deep-throated chimes of Big Bertha the fusee clock. There are some tables on a front terrace and the side grass. The building is in a fine position just by the Ippikins Rock viewpoint, and there are lots of walks through the National Trust land that runs along the Edge. *(Recommended by Gordon and Daphne, Paul and Margaret Baker, Colin Dowse, Annette and John Kenny)*

Free house   Licensee Stephen Waring   Real ale   Meals and snacks (not Mon exc bank hols)   Restaurant   Children in restaurant (no under-10s after 8 Sat)   Open 11–2.30 (3 Sat), 6–11 all year; closed Mon lunchtime exc bank hols; closed 25 Dec   Twin bedroom tel Much Wenlock (074 636) 403; £17S/£29S

WHITCHURCH   SJ4947 Map 7

Willey Moor Lock

Pub signposted off A49 just under two miles N of Whitchurch

White tables under cocktail parasols on the terrace outside this low fairy-lit pub, which used to be the lockkeeper's cottage, let you watch the colourful narrowboats on the Llangollen Canal waiting to go into the lock. Inside, the several low-ceilinged carpeted rooms are neatly decorated – brick-based brocaded wall seats, stools and small chairs around dimpled copper and other tables, crisp black and white paintwork, red velvet curtains for the little windows, a decorative longcase clock, a shelf of toby jugs, and two winter log fires. Bar food includes good freshly cut sandwiches (from £1), steak and kidney pie (£2.50), scampi (£3), salads (from £3), gammon (£5) and T-bone steak (£6.75), with children's dishes (£1.50); well kept McEwans 70/- on handpump. Fruit machine and piped background music; friendly cat. *(Recommended by Neil and Elspeth Fearn, Laurence Manning)*

*Free house   Licensee Mrs E Gilkes   Real ale   Meals and snacks   Children in eating area
Open 12–3, 6–11 all year; closed some weekday lunchtimes in winter*

WISTANSTOW   SO4385 Map 6

Plough

Village signposted off A49 and A489 N of Craven Arms

This is the home of those fine Woods beers that crop up in so many pubs in
Shropshire and increasingly further afield. The brewery is actually separate, an
older building right by the pub, and the beers are among the best from any brewery
– Woods Parish, Special, the strong Wonderfull and the seasonal Christmas
Cracker. Food's a bonus too, good value and home made. At lunchtime it includes
fresh grilled sardines (£2), ploughman's with three English cheeses or pâté (£2.50),
lasagne or prawn curry (£3), steak and kidney pie (£3.20) and fresh salmon salad
(£5.80); evening meals might include lamb à la grecque (£4.95), duck in orange
sauce (£5.75), monkfish kebabs or halibut with prawns in a cream and sherry sauce
(both £5.95) and rump steak (£6.25); there's an attractive show of home-made
puddings. The décor is rather a surprise for a Shropshire village pub. The lounge
bar is high-raftered and airy, with high tables and chairs in the bay windows, green
velvet curtains, and many tables spread over its swirly patterned carpet. They keep
two farm ciders, and there's a useful choice of decent wines by the bottle or glass.
The games area has darts, pool, dominoes, cribbage, fruit machine, space game and
juke box; there may be piped music; one wall has a fine display cabinet of bottled
beers. There are some tables under cocktail parasols outside. *(Recommended by Paul
McPherson, James and Marion Seeley, Richard and Dilys Smith, Derek and Sylvia Stephenson,
SP, T Nott; more reports please)*

*Own brew   Licensee Robert West   Real ale   Lunchtime snacks and meals (limited choice
Mon lunchtime, none Mon evening)   Children in eating area   Open 11.30–2.30, 7–11 all
year*

Lucky Dip

Besides the fully inspected pubs, you might like to try these Lucky Dips
recommended to us and described by readers (if you do, please send us reports):

All Stretton [SO4695], *Yew Tree*: Friendly
and obliging staff, good value
straightforward bar food *(Gary Merrell)*
Aston Munslow [OS Sheet 137 reference
512866; SO5187], *Swan*: Ancient pub with
several bars, log fires, pool-room, well kept
Bass and other real ales, good bar food,
garden; lane beside leads to twelfth-century
White House (open summer) *(Lynne
Sheridan, Bob West)*
Baystonhill [A49 Shrewsbury–Hereford;
SJ4908], *Compasses*: Attractive, friendly pub
by old village common; naval influence on
decoration, well kept Bass, pleasant service,
big garden with summer barbecues *(Spencer
Roberts)*
Bridges [between the Long Mynd and
Stiperstones; SO3996], *Horseshoe*: Beautiful
spot, attractive old building with interesting
windows, clean and bright inside; Marstons
Pedigree on handpump, Westons cider, good
home-made bar food at moderate prices inc

ploughman's with Shropshire blue;
children's room *(D C Bail)*
☆ **Bridgnorth** [Stn; A458 towards
Stourbridge, opp the Hollyhead; SO7293],
Railwaymans Arms: A real curiosity,
recreating the atmosphere of bustling station
bars in the 1940s, and forming part of the
Severn Valley steam railway terminus (the
station car-parking fee is refundable against
either your train ticket or what you spend in
the pub); very basic amenities, basic snacks,
coal fire, fine range of well kept real ales
including Bathams, Timothy Taylors
Landlord, Woods Parish and good Milds;
children welcome *(Gordon Mott, Richard
Sanders, Jon Wainwright, Dave Braisted, LYM)*
Bridgnorth [High St] *Swan*: Attractive old
half-timbered pub, comfortable, with good
beer and food *(Quentin Williamson, Richard
Sanders)*
☆ **Brockton** [SO5894], *Feathers*: Friendly
atmosphere, wide choice of well presented

bar food inc children's dishes and well kept real ales in country pub with big collection of little china houses, huge set of bellows from local smithy as one table, pretty little covered back terrace *(P J Mathews, LYM)*

Cheswardine [Soudley; SJ7228], *Wheatsheaf*: Country local with good family atmosphere, good bar food – a nice place to stay at *(Mrs M H Shropshire)*

Chorley [SO6983], *Duck*: Village pub with good food – duck is the speciality – and well kept M&B ales; friendly owners *(Clifford Blakemore)*

Church Aston [A518 Newport–Wellington, outside village; SJ7418], *Red House*: Pleasant atmosphere, reasonable blend of modern decoration and old relics, Ansells real ale, good bar food *(Dave Braisted)*

☆ **Claverley** [High St; off A454 Wolverhampton–Bridgnorth; SO7993], *Crown*: A shame we don't get more reports on this ancient but comfortably furnished pub in one of the county's prettiest villages; heavy beams, open fires, good home-made bar food (not Sun–Weds evenings), well kept Banks's Bitter, pleasant service, and a particularly good garden with a play area, summer children's bar and barbecues; dogs allowed, long Sat opening; children allowed in eating area *(LYM)*

Claverley, *Plough*: Rambling old modernised pub with wide range of home-cooked bar food, restaurant in pleasantly converted barn (good Sun lunch), big garden behind with outdoor bar and children's play equipment *(SP)*

Clee Hill [track up hill off A4117 Bewdley–Cleobury, by Victoria Inn; SO6076], *Kremlin*: Claims to be Shropshire's highest pub with splendid view; pleasant rustic lounge; under new licensees has well kept Banks's beer, good value bar food *(Dave Braisted)*

Clun [SO3081], *Buffalo*: Happy, friendly bar staff, vivacious gang of customers *(Paul McPherson)*

☆ **Coalport** [Salthouse Rd; nr Mawes Craft Centre, over footbridge by chinaworks museum – OS Sheet 127 reference 693025; SJ6903], *Boat*: Cosy riverside pub at end of rough single-track road in Severn Gorge, with cheap well kept Banks's on electric pump, welcoming coal fire, friendly service, generous helpings of basic bar food, summer barbecues on idyllic riverside lawn; handy for the museums *(E J Alcock, Comus Elliott)*

☆ **Coalport**, *Woodbridge*: Pretty and well kept old inn with terraced Severnside garden overlooking the world's second iron bridge (1799); good food inc excellent steaks, cheap well kept real ales, small nooks and crannies, hops hanging from ceiling, friendly attentive staff; bedrooms *(G M K Donkin, Comus Elliott)*

☆ **Corfton** [B4368 Much Wenlock–Craven Arms; SO4985], *Sun*: Good value simple home cooking from soup and burgers

through gammon and pies to steaks and a monumental mixed grill, with children's dishes and a bargain Sun lunch (especially cheap for children) served till lateish in the evening, in pleasant lounge bar and lively and cheery locals' bar; tables on terrace and in good-sized garden with good play area including retired tractor; piped music *(S Pearce, John Mills, Mr and Mrs R A Gethen, BB)*

Harmer Hill [SJ4822], *Bridgewater Arms*: Very good food under new owners; restaurant being extended *(Kate Drakes)*

Hodnet [SJ6128], *Bear*: Sixteenth-century hotel, smartly done up fairly recently, with good range of reasonably priced and imaginative food and well kept John Smiths in big main bar (food service pleasant but not always quick); restaurant has small no-smoking area – with cocktail bar on far side housing former bear pit which now includes an interesting underfloor garden; opp Hodnet Hall gardens; four bedrooms, not large but comfortable *(MP, P J Taylor)*

☆ **Ironbridge** [11 High St at Blists Hill Open-Air Museum; SJ6703], *New Inn*: Well worth the museum entrance fee to sample what a pub of the 1880s could offer; it's very much a 'spit and sawdust' pub, with staff dressed in period style; well kept choice of real ales (you can pay in 'old money' from the museum bank), good sandwiches and ploughman's (an excusable anachronism – that pub staple wasn't really invented until the 1950s) and no juke box, fruit machines, cigarette machines or fancy drinks; open lunchtime – can be hired during the evening *(Patrick and Mary McDermott)*

Ironbridge [Wharfage], *Malt House*: Large, long room popular with tourists, bar at one end with well kept Davenports and Wem Special, good if not cheap food served from other end; across road from Severn, with view of the Iron Bridge and power station *(A Royle, Mr and Mrs J H Adam, Jon Wainwright)*; *Olde Robin Hood*: Good home-made food in carpeted lounge with comfortable pink plush seats, handsome collection of clocks and brasses; handy for the museums *(Ken and Barbara Turner)*; *Swan*: Cosy pub with good beer, simple food *(A Royle)*

Ketley [Holyhead Rd; nr M54 junction 6; SJ6810], *Unicorn*: Upon its sale late 1988 stopped brewing the wide range of its own real ales inc Old Horny which we mentioned in previous editions *(Anon)*

☆ **Leebotwood** [A49 Church Stretton–Shrewsbury; SO4898], *Pound*: Pleasant atmosphere in main-road pub with well kept beer, above-average bar food, helpful licensee *(T Nott, G B Pugh)*

Lilleshall [just off A518 2 miles SW of Newport; SJ7315], *Red House*: Big, well equipped pub with well kept real ales such as Boddingtons or Wilsons, good lunchtime bar food, restaurant *(A T Langton)*

Little Wenlock [SJ6507], *Huntsman*: Free house with friendly licensee and bar staff, well kept Davenports Wem, good food in bar and restaurant *(Colin Dowse)*

Llanfair Waterdine [village signposted from B4355 – turn left after crossing bridge; SO2476], *Red Lion*: Fine old riverside pub with rambling lounge bar and little black-beamed tap-room; new owners have extended bar menu; Marstons Pedigree on handpump; seats among roses in front of pub, with more on grass at the back; comfortable bedrooms *(T Nott, Mike Tucker, Gwen and Peter Andrews, LYM; more reports on the new regime please)*

☆ **Llanyblodwel** [village and pub signposted off B4396; SJ2423], *Horse Shoe*: Delightfully quaint black and white timbered Tudor inn by the River Tanat (where they have a mile of trout fishing), rambling low-beamed rooms, simple furnishings both traditional and more modern, bar food from sandwiches to steaks, pub games, piped music, tables outside; appeal is decidedly strongest for people who like the down-to-earth and easy-going; the village church is an exceptional piece of high Victoriana, well worth seeing; children in eating area until 9; bedrooms simple but cheap *(Paul McPherson, LYM)*

Llanymynech [A483 – OS Sheet 126 reference 267207; SJ2721], *Bradford Arms*: Elegant lounge, well kept Marstons Pedigree, good choice of bar food inc lots of puddings, restaurant, small garden *(Lynne Sheridan, Bob West)*

Longden [SJ4406], *Tankerville Arms*: Popular for imaginative bar food inc evening buffets (not Mon or Sat), game specialities as well as steaks and so forth Tues–Sun evenings, carvery Sun lunches (evening too); friendly staff, immaculate ladies' *(Kate Drakes)*

☆ **Longville** [B4371 Church Stretton–Much Wenlock; SO5494], *Longville Arms*: Well kept Bass and M&B Springfield and bar food from sandwiches, soup, baked potatoes and ploughman's to ham and eggs or lasagne, in plainly modernised big-windowed pub with sturdy elm or cast-iron-framed tables, leatherette banquettes and wood-burning stoves in left-hand bar, plusher furniture including some nice old oak tables in right-hand one; picnic-table sets and play area in neat garden *(Ted and Pat Samuels, BB)*

☆ **Ludlow** [Lower Bridge St; SO5175], *Wheatsheaf*: Particularly pleasant atmosphere in recently refurbished little pub spectacularly built into ancient town gate, well kept Bass and M&B on handpump, friendly welcome, good interesting food *(T Nott, Nick Dowson, Alison Hayward, Wayne Brindle)*

☆ **Ludlow** [Bull Ring/Corve St], *Feathers*: Famous for exquisitely proportioned and intricately carved timbered frontage, and a fine hotel inside – Jacobean panelling and carving, period furnishings; for the decent bar food or a casual drink you may well be diverted to a plainer more modern side bar; efficient pleasant service, well kept Flowers Original; artistically presented food in restaurant; bedrooms comfortable, if not cheap *(T Nott, Paul McPherson, Dr P Webb, LYM)*

Ludlow [Broad St], *Angel*: Attractive front in lovely architectural street; entrance via alley to long lounge with comfortable sofas; well kept Flowers Original and IPA, satisfactory bar food inc good value lunchtime baked potatoes; bedrooms *(A Cook)*; *Blue Boar*: Attractive, cosy rooms with pleasant prints, photographs and Ludlow Festival posters, good buffet; bedrooms impressively big, with good breakfasts *(Nick Dowson, Alison Hayward, Dave Braisted)*

Madeley [Coalport Rd; SJ6904], *All Nations*: Friendly unabashed local which for many decades has brewed its own beer; no food, nor any other concession to modernity *(Lynne Sheridan, Bob West)*

☆ **Market Drayton** [High St; SJ6734], *Corbet Arms*: Particularly good varied bar food inc fine buffet lunch at reasonable price, and wide choice of beers, in pleasant former coaching-inn with plenty of seating; sales are held here – they've two main halls for functions; bedrooms *(Mrs M H Shropshire, E G Parish)*

Marton [B4386 Chirbury–Westbury; SJ2902], *Lowfield*: Attractive fairly remote country pub, immaculate inside and out; restrained décor, with generous log fire in lounge, friendly and helpful landlord, M&B and Worthington beers, above-average bar food *(G W Tanner)*

Much Wenlock [SO6299], *Gaskell Arms*: Food and service excellent *(A J Woodhouse)*

☆ **Munslow** [B4368 Much Wenlock–Craven Arms; SO5287], *Crown*: Attractive old building in pleasant countryside with variety of tables and chairs in split-level beamed lounge with flagstones, bare stone walls, bottle collection, snug, bread oven, original cupboards and doors; eating area has small tables around central oven chimney – generous helpings of decent home-made food; reasonably priced Bass, Marstons Mild and Wadworths 6X *(Nick Dowson, Alison Hayward and others)*

Myddle [A528 7 miles N of Shrewsbury – OS Sheet 126 reference 468239; SJ4724], *Red Lion*: Clean and comfortable free house with pleasant spacious lounge, exposed beams and log fire, good value bar food, well kept Woods *(F and E Rossiter)*

Newcastle [B4368 Clun–Newtown; SO2582], *Crown*: Friendly, well kept and well furnished pub with attentive licensees, nicely presented good food including some interesting dishes, wide choice of well kept beer; tables outside, lovely countryside

(G Holliday, Mrs P J Hughes)
Newport [SJ7519], *Bridge*: Small, friendly pub with good bar food, restaurant *(M J St John, A M Dudley-Evans)*
Nordley [B4373 N of Bridgnorth; TQ4952], *Swan*: Friendly small country pub, warm welcome for strangers, good home-cooked food inc Sun evening, Davenports Wem real ales *(Simon Barber)*
Onibury [SO4579], *Hollybush*: Small, very friendly neatly kept pub with quiet and homely atmosphere – almost a blend of tea-room and pub; very good fresh home-made food such as curried parsnip soup and enormous helpings of roast beef with good Yorkshire pudding; children welcome *(Miles Kington)*
Pant [A483 Oswestry–Welshpool; SJ2723], *Cross Guns*: Pleasant and welcoming with good choice of well served food *(F A Noble)*
Pipe Gate [A51 Nantwich–Stone; SJ7441], *Chetwode Arms*: Friendly and comfortable family pub, recently refurbished to high standard; St Austells real ale from Cornwall, extensive range of decent bar food, superb carvery, evening restaurant *(Paul and Margaret Baker)*
Priorslee [SJ7109], *Lion*: Cosy, well run pub serving well kept Davenports Wem Best and Special, good value weekday lunchtime food with some interesting puddings *(Roger and Judy Tame)*
Shifnal [SJ7508], *White Hart*: Tastefully restored, comfortable, cosy village pub, well kept Ansells and related real ales, bar food inc good specials *(Bob Alton)*
☆ **Shrewsbury** [Wyle Cop; follow City Centre signposts across the English Bridge; SJ4912], *Lion*: Grand old inn with distinguished history, cosy oak-panelled bar and sedate series of high-ceilinged rooms opening off, comfortably refurbished by THF; obliging staff, Bass under light carbon dioxide blanket, bar food – which may be served in the restaurant if it's not busy; children welcome; bedrooms comfortable *(Colin Dowse, KC, LYM)*
Shrewsbury [16 Castle Gates], *Castle Vaults*: Town pub with well kept Boddingtons on handpump and good value Mexican restaurant called Panchos *(Nick Dowson, Alison Hayward)*; [Swan Hill/Cross Hill] *Coach & Horses*: Popular local with exposed brickwork, ships' timbers stripped back to original worn split grain, generous helpings of food, well kept Bass on handpump, unobtrusive piped music, cosy atmosphere *(Nick Dowson, Alison Hayward)*; [Mardol] *Kings Head*: Fifteenth-century timber-framed pub, carefully restored; popular with smartly dressed young people on weekend evenings *(Nick Dowson, Alison Hayward)*; [The Square] *Plough*: Town pub with varnished panelling, well kept Davenports Wem Special on handpump,

busy at lunchtime for good choice of reasonably priced food; full of teenagers, and inclined to be smoky, on weekend evenings *(Nick Dowson)*
☆ **Stiperstones** [village signposted off A488 S of Minsterley – OS Sheet 126 reference 364005; SO3697], *Stiperstones*: Folksy little friendly modernised lounge bar with leatherette wall banquettes, lots of brassware on ply-panelled walls, well kept Woods Parish on handpump, darts in plainer public bar, restaurant; at least in summer has been open all day, with good simple food inc excellent salads and maybe local whimberry pie right through until 10pm; picnic-table sets outside; on GWG100 *(J Phillips, BB)*
Stottesdon [SO6783], *Fighting Cocks*: Delightful old half-timbered pub in unspoilt countryside, low ceiling, open fire, equestrian pictures, good substantial simple food *(Anon)*
Telford [Foregate; SJ6710], *Telford Moat House*: Pleasant bar in modern hotel serving good value bar food; bedrooms *(Mrs H March)*
☆ **Tong** [A41 towards Newport, just beyond village; SJ7907], *Bell*: Friendly service and welcoming atmosphere in main-road pub busy at lunchtime for big helpings and good choice of decent hot food at reasonable prices, also cold table and good value Sun lunch; well kept Banks's real ales, big family-room, small dining-room, no dogs; nr Weston Park, in attractive area *(AE, Dave Braisted, Richard Fawcett)*
Upton Magna [SJ5512], *Corbet Arms*: Friendly spacious pub with good range of interesting food *(Gordon Theaker)*
Wellington [Church St; SJ6611], *Charlton Arms*: Antique carved grandfather clock, friendly atmosphere; courteous, helpful staff, good food, reasonable prices; bedrooms comfortable *(Dennys Wheatley)*
Wentnor [SO3893], *Crown*: Friendly and welcoming atmosphere, good food in bar and restaurant inc good choice of vegetarian food, good value wines, cosy and pleasant dining-room, decent wines, good coffee; bedrooms cheap and comfortable – also caravan/camping facilities *(Jackie Wynn)*
☆ **Whitchurch** [St Marys St; SJ5341], *Old Town Hall Vaults*: Small, charming and friendly eighteenth-century pub with well kept Marstons Border Mild and Pedigree on handpump, good value home-cooked lunchtime and evening food, friendly staff, refined rather than hearty atmosphere – piped Tchaikovsky; the birthplace of Sir Edward German *(G T Jones, Graham Gibson)*
Woore [Nantwich Rd; SJ7342], *Coopers Arms*: Pleasant, comfortable pub decorated with coopers' tools and beer engines; well kept Bass, good bar food, pleasant service *(K G S Adams)*

Somerset and Avon

A good many changes in this richly endowed area include interesting new entries in Axbridge (the rambling old Lamb), Barrow Gurney (the unpretentious Princes Motto), Bathford just outside Bath (the Crown – a splendid place under its new licensees), Blagdon (the snug New Inn, up above the lake), Cranmore (the handsomely extended Strode Arms – one of the best examples of sensitive refurbishment we've seen this year), Exford (the White Horse – a pleasantly relaxed place to stay at), Haselbury Plucknett (the Haselbury Inn, a comfortable dining pub), Rode (the quaint Red Lion) and Stanton Wick (the Carpenters Arms – another popular dining pub, with good bedrooms). New licensees have moved in at the Ashcott Inn at Ashcott (doing imaginative food, with lots of fresh fish), the Square & Compass near Ashill (doing well at the difficult task of replacing the Shepherds), the Ralegh's Cross up on the Brendon Hills, the Coronation Tap in Bristol (trying to give this cider pub a more general appeal), the busy Poachers Pocket at Doulting, the Windbound by the Severn at Shepperdine, the Greyhound at Staple Fitzpaine (which has been through several changes in recent years) and the snug Fox & Badger at Wellow. Pubs in the area that are doing particularly well at the

The George, Norton St Philip

moment include the Notley Arms at Monksilver (now the country's top pub
for bar food), the Wheatsheaf at Combe Hay (also outstanding for bar food),
the Bull Terrier at Croscombe (most welcoming, with wines that stand head
and shoulders above those of most pubs without being priced that high), the
New Inn at Dowlish Wake (everyone who's tracked it down really likes it), the
Anchor at Oldbury-upon-Severn (though they've not been there that long, the
present friendly licensees are very popular for their food), and the Crossways
at West Huntspill. And a good many of the Lucky Dip entries at the end of the
chapter are making quite a commanding appeal at the moment, most notably
the George at Abbots Leigh, George at Bathampton in Bath, Ring o' Bells at
Compton Martin, Crown at Exford, Inn at Freshford, Crown at Kelston,
White Hart at Littleton upon Severn, Volunteer at Seavington St Michael, Blue
Ball at Triscombe and Blue Bowl at West Harptree.

ALMONDSBURY (Avon)   ST6084 Map 2
Bowl

1¼ miles from M5 junction 16 (and therefore quite handy for M4 junction 20); from A38
towards Thornbury, turn first left signposted Lower Almondsbury, then first right down
Sundays Hill, then at bottom right again into Church Road

The long neatly kept bar in this tiled white house has a big winter log fire at one end
and a wood-burning stove at the other, traditional black-lacquered built-in seats as
well as mate's chairs and one or two Windsor armchairs, elm tables, low beams,
and walls stripped to bare stone. Good home-made bar food includes sandwiches
(95p; toasties from £1.10), soup (£1.20), ploughman's (£2.10), burgers (from
£1.75), good mushrooms in garlic sauce (£1.95), omelettes or salads (from £2.95),
quiche of the day (£3.55), cottage pie (£3.65), chilli beef with croûtons or cold
honey-roast ham (£3.85), steak and kidney pie (£4.65), puddings (£1.25), and daily
specials; grills and steaks Sunday evenings. Well kept Courage Bitter, Best and
Directors on handpump, some enterprising bottled beers, good value wines, tea or
coffee; friendly service. Fruit machine, piped music. There are picnic-table sets in
front of the building (which has very pretty hanging baskets in summer), and a
children's play area in the garden behind – though this is not open at quiet times.
(Recommended by Peter Adcock, Dennis Heatley, J L Cox, A D Jenkins, W A Harbottle;
more reports please)

Courage   Licensee John Alley   Real ale   Meals and snacks (12–2, 6–9.45; not 25 Dec)
Restaurant; not Sun evening   Children welcome   Open 11–3, 6–11 all year
Bedrooms tel Almondsbury (0454) 612757; £34B/£57B

APPLEY (Somerset)   ST0621 Map 1
Globe

Hamlet signposted from network of back roads between A361 and A38, W of B3187 and W of
Milverton and Wellington; OS Sheet 181 reference 072215

The chatter of locals fills the simple beamed front room in this unspoilt 500-year-
old country pub, the atmosphere is relaxed, and there are pictures of magpies,
benches and a built-in settle, and bare wood tables on the brick floor. The back
room has a pool-table, and yet another room has easy chairs and other more
traditional ones. An entry corridor leads to a serving-hatch where Cotleigh Tawny
(a local brew) and a guest beer are on handpump. Bar food includes filled rolls
(from 65p, fillet steak £1.25), soup (£1.25), ploughman's (from £2.25), chilli con
carne (£2.25), and salads such as home-cooked ham (from £2.95); darts, pool, alley

Pubs with outstanding views are listed at the back of the book.

skittles and fruit machine. The hilly pastures which surround this maze of twisting lanes are very pretty, and there are seats outside in the garden; the path opposite leads eventually to the River Tone. *(Recommended by Chris Raisin, Graham Doyle, Roger and Jenny Huggins)*

Free house   Licensees A W and E J Burt, R and J Morris   Real ale   Meals and snacks (not Mon lunchtime)   Restaurant (Tues–Sat evenings and Sun lunch) tel Greenham (0823) 672327   Children in eating area of bar and restaurant   Open 11–3, 6.30–11 all year; closed Mon lunchtime, exc bank hols

ASHCOTT   ST4337 Map 1

Ashcott Inn ✿

A39

After changing hands yet again, this attractive food pub still seems to tickle readers' palates in a most satisfactory way. Cooked by the new licensee's wife, the imaginative food includes filled baps (from £1), a meaty or vegetarian soup (£1.35), Greek salad or a selection of dips with crudités (£1.95), salmon mousse with tomato coulis or tasty devilled mushrooms (£2.80), pasta with smoked bacon, cream and cheese (£2.50), creamy fish pie (£3.85), moussaka (£3.85) and around six different fresh fish dishes each day (from Dartmouth or Port Isaac) such as plaice, halibut, turbot, monkfish, squid, king prawns or wild Dart salmon (from £6); puddings like steamed ginger pudding, treacle tart or meringues with clotted cream (from £1.75). There are good oak and elm tables, some interesting old-fashioned seats among more conventional ones, beams, stripped stone walls, and a gas-effect log fire in its sturdy chimney. Well kept Flowers Original and Marstons Pedigree on handpump; darts, shove-ha'penny, a fruit machine, alley skittles and piped music. There are seats on the terrace, and a pretty, newly created walled garden. *(Recommended by Maj and Mrs I McKillop, Dave Butler, Lesley Storey, K R Harris, John and Pat Smyth, Alan Carr)*

Heavitree (no longer brew)   Licensee Robert Porter   Real ale   Meals and snacks (12–2, 6.30–10)   Restaurant tel Ashcott (0458) 210282   Children in eating area of bar until 8 Open 11–2.30, 5.30–11 all year

nr ASHILL   ST3217 Map 1

Square & Compass

Windmill Hill; turn off A358 at Stewley Cross Garage

The Shepherds were a hard act to follow, so it's a surprise as well as a great relief to find that Fred and Eileen Balm who took over in August 1988 have succeeded in keeping up the quietly effervescent zing that makes people so pleased to find this rather out-of-the-way country pub. It's friendly and comfortable, and the cosy little bar (which has been refurbished) has upholstered window seats, and an open fire in winter; there's an extra room for eating. Bar food includes sandwiches (from £1, French bread toasties £1.50), home-made soup (£1.10), ploughman's (from £1.75), filled baked potatoes (from £2.25), savoury pancakes (£2.75), salads (from £3.10), home-made lasagne (£3.25), and honey-roasted ham with egg or pineapple (£3.50); also, vegetarian dishes and a children's menu. Well kept Exmoor Bitter and Gold on handpump. Darts, shove-ha'penny; piped music. The lavatories have been upgraded. Outside on the grass there are picnic-set tables, a swing, climbing-frame and bright blue hay wagon. There's also a touring caravan site. *(Recommended by S J Curtis, Shirley Pielou, the Barrett family, Mrs Crease, PLC, S J Edwards)*

Free house   Licensees Fred and Eileen Balm   Real ale   Meals and snacks   Children in restaurant   Restaurant tel Hatch Beauchamp (0823) 480467   Open 12–2.30 (3 Sat), 6.30–11 all year

Sunday opening is now 12–3 and 7–10.30 throughout England.

AUST (Avon) ST5789 Map 2

Boars Head

½ mile from M4 junction 21; village signposted from A403

The small rooms in this friendly village pub have some walls stripped back to the dark stone, old-fashioned high-backed winged settles in stripped pine, well polished country kitchen tables and others made from old casks, big rugs on dark lino, and decorative plates hanging from one stout black beam; the log fire in the main fireplace may, in summer, have a bunch of dried flowers in the opening of its former side bread oven. In another room with a wood-burning stove there's a little parakeet, and a pair of gerbils, and a third room has dining-tables. Good bar food, all cooked by the landlady, includes soup (£1.25), triple sandwiches (from £1.85), ploughman's (from £2.15), pâté (£2.40), cauliflower cheese and bacon or lasagne (£3.45), lots of omelettes (from £4.40), a cold buffet with a tremendous spread of up to thirty help-yourself salads (from £4.40, seafood platter £11.05), puddings such as home-made ice-cream or filled crêpes (from £1), and a blackboard showing daily specials and filled baked potatoes; children's helpings are available on request. Well kept Courage Best and Directors on handpump, and pleasant, attentive service; trivia. There's a medieval stone well in the pretty and sheltered garden, and a touring caravan site. *(Recommended by Pamela and Merlyn Horswell, B H Stamp, Dr P McCarthy, Jon Wainwright, Helena and Arthur Harbottle)*

Courage   Licensee Charles Broome   Real ale   Meals and snacks (not Sun)   Restaurant (Thurs, Fri and Sat evenings) tel Pilning (045 45) 2278   Children in two family-rooms until 9.30   Open 11–3, 6–11 all year; closed 25 Dec

AXBRIDGE (Somerset)   ST4255 Map 1

Lamb

The Square

In what must be one of England's most attractive small market squares, this ancient place faces a striking medieval house. An old-fashioned glazed partition divides the entrance hall from a big rambling bar full of heavy beams and timbers in butter-coloured plasterwork. There are red leatherette wall seats and small settles, with a coal-burning stove in one great stone fireplace, and a collection of tools and utensils including an unusual foot-operated grinder in another. A wide range of home-made bar food includes soup (£1), sandwiches (£1.20), pâté (£1.50), ploughman's (from £1.90), vegetarian pizza (£1.80), tripe and onions or lasagne (£2.30), filled crispy potato shells (£2.40), steak in ale pie (£3.45), gammon with egg or pineapple (£3.80) and eight-ounce rump steak (£5.75), with specials such as vegetarian stuffed tomato and cottage pie; children's menu (£1). Well kept Butcombe, Flowers Original and Fullers London Pride on handpump from a bar counter built largely of bottles, locally made wine, and Thatchers cider. Sensibly placed darts, table skittles, shove-ha'penny, dominoes, cribbage, alley skittles, fruit machine, an aquarium, and piped music; the atmosphere's friendly Somerset. Though the sheltered back garden's not big, it's prettily planted with rock plants, shrubs and trees; starlings in the square have learned to imitate the aviary's cockatiels. *(Recommended by Lyn and Bill Capper, Dr and Mrs A K Clarke)*

Butcombe   Licensees Simon Whitmore and Max Wigginton   Real ale   Meals and snacks (not Sun evening)   Children in eating area of bar until 9   Open 11–2.30 (3 Sat), 6.30–11 all year   Bedrooms tel Axbridge (0934) 732253; £16/£40B

BARROW GURNEY (Avon)   ST5367 Map 2

Princes Motto

Barrow Street; B3130 – linking A38 and A370 SW of Bristol

Specialising in Bass, this attractively laid out old pub also has Boddingtons,

Butcombe, and Marstons Pedigree on handpump, with Bass and Wadworths 6X tapped from casks behind the bar. Though very much an unpretentious and traditional local, it's that rare sort where strangers immediately feel they fit in. From the snug room by the bar, with a sentimental engraving of *Farewell to Nelson* over its log fire, steps lead up to an unusually long and narrow room behind. This has cosy winged high-backed settles at one end, and darts, shove-ha'penny and fruit machine towards the other; there are lots of horsebrasses on the beams. Good value bar snacks consist of filled rolls, toasted sandwiches and ploughman's, and there may be lots of nibbles. Picnic-table sets on the back grass have rustic views. *(Recommended by Peter Adcock, Dr and Mrs A K Clarke, S J A Velate, Michael and Harriet Robinson)*

Free house   Licensee Paul Bryant   Real ale   Lunchtime snacks   Open 11–2.30, 6–11 all year

BATHFORD (Avon)   ST7966 Map 2

Crown ★ ☺

2 Bathford Hill; signposted off A363 Bath–Bradford-on-Avon

A few years ago the Worralls made a Hampshire pub, the Crown at Kingsclere, outstandingly popular with readers. When they left it, we were by no means alone in wondering where they were going to turn up next. Here's the answer we've all been waiting for. Behind the handsomely classical façade of this substantial pub, they've created a really warm and relaxed chatty atmosphere. Four or five room areas spread around the central well manned bar, with a pleasant variety of furnishings from sensible tables and chairs for people who want to eat to Lloyd Loom-style chairs, large armchairs and comfortable button-back leather settees. There are rugs on stripped and polished floorboards, prints, old photographs and mounted butterflies on the attractively decorated walls, china, stoneware and so forth on Delft shelves, houseplants (even a sizeable palm), and careful lighting. Generously served home-made bar food includes big toasted sandwiches and filled baked potatoes (from £1.50), soup (£1.50), pâté (£1.95), chicken satay (£3.35), ploughman's with good cheeses (£3.75), chicken tikka in pitta bread (£3.95), steak pie (£5.50) and eight-ounce steak (£7.75), with lots of dishes of the day such as Cumberland sausage pie (£3.95), baked spaghetti maresca (£4.50), lentil nut casserole (£4.75) and chicken paprika (£5.65). They do half portions of several things for children (at less than half price), and nice puddings (£2.25). Well kept Ruddles Best and Ushers Best, decent wines including New Zealanders, non-alcohol cocktails, good cafetière coffee with fresh cream; kind and quick service, rack of newspapers and lots of magazines, very unobtrusive piped music, good log fire. The no-smoking garden-room on the left, with old nursery pictures among others, opens on to a terrace with tables under cocktail parasols; there's a small garden beyond its low retaining wall. *(Recommended by Deborah Frost, Roger Cunningham, D Heath, Marianne and Lionel Kreeger, Paolo Spyropoulos)*

Ushers (Watneys)   Licensees Gregg and Angela Worrall   Real ale   Meals and snacks (not Mon lunchtime, until 10 Tues–Sat)   Children in garden-room and burgundy room   Open 11–2.30, 6.30–11 all year; closed 25–26 Dec

BLAGDON (Avon)   ST5059 Map 2

New Inn

Church Street, off A368

Picnic-table sets on the grass behind look down over the fields to wood-fringed Blagdon Lake, and to the low hills beyond. Inside, the two rooms have a warm and welcoming atmosphere, and a good deal of individuality. There are some antique settles – one with its arm rests carved into dogs – as well as little russet plush armchairs, mate's chairs and so forth. Big logs burn in both stone fireplaces, the beams are decorated with horsebrasses and some tankards, and decorations include advertisements for Slades now-defunct ales from Chippenham. There's an elderly black labrador, and a plump cat (no dogs are allowed in the garden). Quickly and generously served food includes sandwiches (from £1.05, toasties from £1.40, open salad ones from £2.80), home-made soup (£1.10), ploughman's (from £2.30), salads (from £2.50), filled baked potatoes (£2.60), home-made steak and kidney pie (£2.65), platter of Scotch beef (£3.90), and evening grills like gammon with pineapple (£4.50), and steaks (from £5.95); home-made daily specials such as chilli con carne, curry and so forth. Bass and Wadworths IPA and 6X on handpump; darts, shove-ha'penny, trivia, and unobtrusive piped pop music. *(Recommended by Pamela and Merlyn Horswell, Miss M Byrne, M W Barratt)*

Wadworths Licensee M K Loveless Real ale Meals and snacks Open 11–2.30, 7–11 all year

BRADLEY GREEN (Somerset) SS0434 Map 1

Malt Shovel 🍺

Pub signposted from A39 W of Bridgwater, near Cannington

The family-room in this friendly little country pub has been redecorated this year, with new furniture to match the bar, black ceiling joists, and a door opening on to the garden. The main bar has some nice modern elm country chairs and little cushioned casks, window seats, sturdy modern winged high-backed settles around wooden tables, and a black kettle standing on a giant fossil by the wood-burning stove; there's also a tiny snug with red hessian walls. Good value food includes lunchtime sandwiches (from 50p, crusty French rolls from 60p) and ploughman's (from £1.70), as well as filled baked potatoes (from £2), smoked haddock cheesy bake (£2.25), salads (from £3), home-made pies such as steak and kidney (£3) or chicken and mushroom (£3.25), gammon with pineapple or egg (£3.50), chicken Kiev (£4.75) and steaks (from £5.95); also, starters and puddings chalked up on a blackboard, and children's meals on request (£1.50). Well kept Butcombe, Wadworths 6X and one guest ale on handpump, and Lanes and Rich's ciders; faint piped music, and a separate skittle alley. On the grass behind the pub there are picnic-table sets (an adjoining field may be used by touring caravans). West of the pub, Blackmore Farm is a striking medieval building. *(Recommended by R C Blatch, JM, PM, Mr and Mrs J Grebbell, Simon Barber, G Jones, Mr and Mrs P A Jones)*

Free house Licensees Robert and Frances Beverley Real ale Meals and lunchtime snacks Restaurant Children in family-room and restaurant Open 11.30–3, 6.30–11; 11.30–2.30, 7–11 in winter Bedrooms tel Combwich (0278) 653432; £15/£23; family-room £33

BRENDON HILLS (Somerset) ST0334 Map 1

Ralegh's Cross

Junction of B3190 Watchet–Bampton with unclassified but good E–W summit road from Elworthy to Winsford

On exceptionally clear days this isolated long white house has views right over the Bristol Channel to Wales. You can walk from the spacious lawns to Clatworthy Reservoir, or, from the road about a mile west, down the track of the railway that used to take iron ore from the mines here to Watchet harbour. Whippet-racing is held here on Sundays in summer. Inside, the new licensees haven't changed the spacious bar with its little red leatherette armchairs around the tables, button-back banquettes along the strip-panelled walls, good collection of photographs of the old mineral railway, and open fires in cool weather. Good bar food brought to your table includes sandwiches (from £1), soup (£1.10), pear and walnut starter or pâté (£1.50), salads (from £2.50), ploughman's (£2.75), omelettes (from £2.80), liver and bacon (£3.75), gammon and pineapple or local trout (£4.50), curries (£4.75), mixed grill (£6.75), steak (from £7.75, sixteen-ounce T-bone £7.95), and puddings such as Pavlova or apple pie (from £1.50); they do a salad and pudding (£4.75), summer cream teas, and children's menu (£1.50). Well kept Flowers Original and Exmoor Bitter on handpump; gentle piped music. *(Recommended by Richard Gibbs, Brian and Anna Marsden; more reports please)*

Free house   Licensees Roy and Wendy Guppy   Real ale   Meals and snacks   Restaurant Children in restaurant and family-room   Open 11–11 July–Sept; 11–2.30, 6–11 rest of the year   Bedrooms tel Washford (0984) 40343; £18B/£36B

BRISTOL (Avon)   ST5673 Map 2
Coronation Tap

Between Sion Place and Portland Street, Clifton

A new licensee has taken over this lively and friendly low-ceilinged place. He's refurbished it in a style which dilutes its heady uncompromising previous approach, making this old cider house more palatable to the casual visitor – of course there are people who knew it before who prefer the old, more severely traditional style. The only alcoholic drinks allowed on sale are ciders and beers, including well kept Courage Best and Directors on handpump, and Bulmers and Taunton ciders tapped from the cask. Good, reasonably priced bar food includes sandwiches (from £1), mixed grill (£1.75) and ploughman's (£2); dominoes and cribbage. Clifton Suspension Bridge is a stroll away. *(Recommended by David Pearman, Peter Adcock, Brian Jones, Alan Merricks)*

Courage   Licensee Les Green   Real ale   Lunchtime meals and snacks (not Sun) Open 11–3, 5.30–11 all year; closed 1 Jan

CATCOTT (Somerset)   ST3939 Map 1
King William

Village signposted off A39 Street–Bridgwater

A well kept, cottagey pub with friendly locals and traditional furnishings: kitchen and other assorted chairs, brown-painted built-in and other settles, window seats, stone floors with a rug or two, and Victorian fashion plates and other old prints. One of the big stone fireplaces has had its side bread oven turned into a stone grotto with kitsch figurines. A large extension at the back includes a skittle alley and a well. Good bar food includes sandwiches (from 70p), home-made soup (£1), filled baked potatoes (£1.50), ploughman's (from £1.75), salads (from £2.50), home-made meat or vegetable lasagne (£2.95), cheese and bacon flan (£2.85), beef curry (£3), scampi or home-made seafood pie (£3.40), pork in cider (£5.75), veal paprika (£6.50), duck in orange sauce (£7.85), and puddings (from £1.10). Well kept Bass, Eldridge Pope Dorchester and Royal Oak and Palmers IPA on handpump and good Wilkins farm cider; darts, dominoes, fruit machine, and piped music. *(Recommended by Ted George, Keith Walton, Mr and Mrs John Smyth, Jon Wainwright, S J Edwards)*

Free house   Licensee Michael O'Riordan   Real ale   Meals and snacks (12–2, 7–9) Children welcome   Open 11.30–3, 6–11 all year

CHISELBOROUGH (Somerset)   ST4614 Map 1
Cat Head 🏮 🍴

Village signposted off B3165 between A3088 and A30 W of Yeovil

Surrounded by small hills, this very friendly and comfortable old place has chairs and settles in Italian tapestry coloured to blend with the honey-coloured velvet curtains, a flagstone floor, a big solid-fuel stove, and an old-fashioned atmosphere. Good, popular bar food, mostly home made and using home-grown vegetables where possible, includes sandwiches (from £1.10), soup (£1.20), pâté (£1.25), Imam Bayildi (a Turkish dish with aubergine and a spicy filling, £2.15), ploughman's (from £2), home-made vegetable pie or butter-bean stew (£2.75), home-made fish pie or lasagne (£3.25), moussaka with Greek spices and herbs or ham salad (£3.85), chicken Kiev (£5.45), steaks (from £6.85), and puddings (from £1.20). Sunday roast lunch (main course £4.35). Well kept Gibbs Mew Wiltshire and Premium on handpump, and farmhouse cider. Sensibly placed darts, dominoes, cribbage, fruit machine, juke box and piped music. There is a separate skittle alley, and seats outside in an attractive garden. *(Recommended by John Nash, Mrs Mary Hallem, Nigel Paine, Rod and Christine Ward; more reports please)*

Gibbs Mew Licensees David and Rosemary Bowden Real ale Meals and snacks (not Sun evening) Restaurant; closed Sun evening Children in restaurant and eating area of bar Occasional live music Open 12–2.30 (3 Sat), 7–11 all year Bedrooms tel Chiselborough (093 588) 231; £13.50/£23

CHURCHILL (Avon) ST4560 Map 1
Crown

Skinners Lane; in village, turn off A368 at Nelson Arms

The small stone-floored and cross-beamed room on the right in this tucked-away old cottage has a lively local atmosphere, built-in wall benches, a wooden window seat, and an unusually sturdy settle; the left-hand room has a slate floor and a wood-burning stove, and some steps past the big log fire in a big stone fireplace lead to more sitting space. A good range of well kept real ales includes a nice light but well hopped bitter brewed for the pub by Cotleigh; also Cotleigh Tawny, Felinfoel Double Dragon, Fullers London Pride, Marstons Pedigree, Oakhill Farmers, Stout (under some top pressure), and Titanic – four on handpump, with others tapped from casks at the back; Gales country wines. Lunchtime bar food includes a home-made soup, good crab sandwiches, ploughman's, baked potatoes and steak and kidney pudding; there are picnic-table sets on a smallish back lawn, and the pub is near the start of *Good Walks Guide* Walk 1. *(Recommended by P Miller, Peter Adcock, WTF, Dorothy and Charles Morley)*

Free house Real ale Meals and snacks Open 11–2.30, 6–11 all year

CLAPTON IN GORDANO (Avon) ST4773 Map 1
Black Horse

4 miles from M5 junction 19; A368 towards Portishead, then B3124 towards Clevedon; village signposted in North Weston, then in village turn right at Clevedon, Clapton Wick signpost

On a country lane, this very prettily flower-decked white house is a friendly and unspoilt place. The partly flagstoned and partly red-tiled main room has lots of cigarette cards, no fewer than three competing wall clocks, winged settles around narrow tables, and a big log fire. A window in an inner snug is still barred, from the days when this room was the petty-sessions jail: high-backed settles – one a marvellous carved and canopied creature, another with an art nouveau copper insert reading *East, West, Hame's Best* – lots of mugs hanging from its black beams, and lots of little prints and photographs. The separate games-room has darts, pool, dominoes, cribbage and space game. Bar food includes sandwiches to order, home-made soup (£1.30), home-made pâté (£2.35), ploughman's (from £2.50), home-made pasty (£2.75), breaded haddock (£2.85), ham and egg or home-made steak and kidney pie (£3.65), and daily specials. Well kept Courage Bitter and Best tapped from the cask, and farm cider. There are old rustic tables out on the flagstones in front of the building, with more behind. The garden has swings and a climber. Paths from here lead up Naish Hill or along to Cadbury Camp. *(Recommended by Peter and Rose Flower, Helena and Arthur Harbottle, Peter Woods, Roger Huggins, Steve and Carolyn Harvey)*

Courage Licensee R A Womersley Real ale Lunchtime meals (not Sun) and snacks Children welcome Open 11–2.30, 6–11 all year

COMBE HAY (Avon)   ST7354 Map 2

Wheatsheaf 🏮

Village signposted from A367 or B3110 S of Bath

In a lovely spot, this country village pub is perched on the side of a steep wooded valley, with tables on the spacious sloping lawn that look down past the enterprising plunging garden to the church and ancient manor stables. Inside, the pleasantly old-fashioned rooms have low ceilings, brown-painted settles, pews and rustic tables, a very high-backed winged settle facing one big log fire, old sporting and other prints, and earthenware jugs on the shelf of the little shuttered windows. A wide choice of very good food includes dishes like home-made tomato and herb soup (£1.50), magnificent Stilton ploughman's (£2), very good pork and cider pâté (£2.25), quiche or garlic mushrooms (£2.50), vegetable chilli, hot-pot or squid and prawn vinaigrette (£3.50), vast gammon steak with pineapple (£4.25), braised lamb chop, chicken chasseur or pheasant (£4.50), pork chop in orange sauce (£4.60), grouse (£7), and a selection of fish specials like scallops in white wine (£4), lovely Cheddar-baked lemon sole or sole stuffed with asparagus and mushrooms (£4.50), Scotch salmon (£5.75), and whole fresh crab or lobster (from £6); summer barbecues. Well kept Courage Best and Directors tapped from the cask; courteous, friendly staff (and dogs); shove-ha'penny. *(Recommended by B H Hill, Barry and Anne, James Cane, Peter Adcock, M B P Carpenter, S J A Velate, Steve and Carolyn Harvey, M A and W R Proctor, Donald Godden, R Baskerville, Miss J Vincent)*

Courage   Licensee M G Taylor   Real ale   Meals and snacks   Restaurant tel Bath (0225) 833504   Children welcome   Open 11–3, 6–11 all year

CRANMORE (Somerset)   ST6643 Map 2

Strode Arms ★ 🏮

West Cranmore; signposted with pub off A361 Frome–Shepton Mallet

Successfully reworked and extended late in 1988, the Stroder Arms as it's misnamed on its engraved glass door is full of delights: charming country furnishings, fresh flowers and pot plants (on our visit, including lilies in a lovely Moorcroft vase), remarkable old locomotive engineering drawings and big black and white steamtrain murals in a central lobby, good bird prints, the pretty view through the stone-mullioned windows down to the lively village duck pond, newspapers to read, the grandfather clock on the flagstones.... And all that's without mentioning the more practical virtues. The kitchen has been reworked too, and though the pub's usually busy service is quick and pleasant, with generous helpings of really good home cooking: sandwiches (from 80p), game soup (£1.20), ploughman's (from £2), filled baked potatoes (from £2.30), steak and kidney and other home-made pies (£3.10), scallops with bacon or juicy ham and eggs (£3.25), nut cutlet (£4.25), rabbit done with lardons in a port sauce (£4.25), breast of chicken with cheese and a white wine sauce (£5.25), avocado and seafood platter (£5.50), filled steaks (from £6.25), wild duck (and other game in season) (£7.75), and puddings such as home-made meringue with raspberries, ice-cream, nuts and cream or treacle tart (from £1.25); daily specials and Sunday roast are chalked up on a blackboard. Well kept Bunces Best, Wadworths IPA and 6X and a weekly changing guest beer on handpump, an interesting choice of decent wines by the glass, quite a few ports, good log fires (in handsome fireplaces), shove-ha'penny, unobtrusive piped music. There's a front terrace with some benches and a back garden. On the first Tuesday of each month, there's a vintage car meeting. This is clearly a place that's run with real care and love. Handy for the East Somerset Light Railway. *(Recommended by J E Surridge, R M Morgan, P M Bisby)*

Free house   Licensees Rodney and Dora Phelps   Real ale   Meals and snacks (restricted Sun evening)   Cottagey restaurant (not Sun evening) tel Cranmore (074 988) 450   Children in restaurant and eating area of bar – if eating   Open 11.30–2.30, 6.30–11 all year

CROSCOMBE (Somerset)   ST5844 Map 2

Bull Terrier ★ 🕸 🍺

A371 Wells–Shepton Mallet

Readers have been so warmly enthusiastic about this neatly kept old village inn that this year we've decided to award it a star. The welcome from the licensee and his staff is particularly friendly, the food consistently good, and the choice of drinks wide. The lounge ('Inglenook') bar has attractively moulded fifteenth-century beams, cushioned wooden wall seats and wheel-back chairs around neat glossy tables, a red carpet on its flagstone floor, pictures on its white walls, and a log-effect gas fire in a big stone fireplace with a fine iron fireback. A communicating ('Snug') room has more tables with another gas-effect log fire, and there's a third in the parquet-floored 'Common Bar', by the local noticeboard; there's also a family-room. Bar food includes sandwiches (from 85p, steak bap £3.25), soup (£1.05), ploughman's (from £1.85), salads (from £3.05, home-cooked roast beef £4.25), spaghetti bolognese (£2.95), home-made Indian spiced beans (£3.25), home-made brazil-nut loaf (£3.50), excellent home-made steak and kidney pie (£3.50), Barnsley chop (£4.25), trout and almonds (£4.85), steaks (from £6.85), and home-made specials like ginger chicken with noodles, red-hot beef or lamb Shrewsbury; lovely puddings such as fudge cake with hot butterscotch sauce (£1.30). Well kept Butcombe, Palmers IPA and Bull Terrier Best Bitter (a strongish beer brewed for the pub) on handpump, with Greene King Abbot kept under light top pressure, and farmhouse cider and several wines both by the glass and by the bottle. They also have an off-sales pricelist. Dominoes, cribbage, shove-ha'penny and piped music. Originally called the Rose & Crown, this can claim to be one of Somerset's oldest pubs. It changed its name in 1976 and is a regular calling place for owners/breeders of bull terriers. *(Recommended by Duncan and Lucy Gardner, J B Greenhalgh, T C and A R Newell, Peter and Rose Flower, Margaret and Douglas Tucker, Roger Huggins, Gethin Lewis, Dr F Peters, Brian and Jenny Seller, Donald Godden, V Thomas, Major and Mrs D R C Woods)*

Free house   Licensees Stan and Pam Lea   Real ale   Meals and snacks (not Mon, not Sun evenings Nov–Mar)   Children in family-room   Open 12–2.30, 7–11; closed Mon lunchtime Nov–Mar   Bedrooms tel Wells (0749) 3658; £15/£32B

DOULTING (Somerset)   ST6443 Map 2

Poachers Pocket

Follow Chelynch signpost off A361 in village, E of Shepton Mallet

The atmosphere in this neatly kept little pub is especially warm and friendly, and there are some black beams, one or two settles, small wheel-back or captain's chairs, gundog pictures on the white walls, a crackling log fire in the end stripped stone wall, and flagstones by the bar counter (though it's mainly carpeted); the extension has created a lot more bar space. The new licensee has kept the very good value, popular food virtually unchanged: pâté (£1.10), sandwiches (from £1.20), ploughman's (from £1.95), home-made quiche Lorraine (£2.70), cauliflower cheese or home-cooked ham (£2.95), home-made steak and kidney pie (£3.05), scampi (£3.50), and pan-fried steak (£4.95); an evening charcoal grill serves a selection of lamb cutlets (£4.75), pork chops or gammon steak and pineapple (£4.95) and steaks (from £6.95); puddings like sherry trifle or cheesecake (£1.05) or meringue surprise (£1.60). Well kept Butcombe Bitter, Oakhill Farmers and Wadworths 6X on handpump, and Wilkins farmhouse cider. *(Recommended by Peter and Rose Flower, Ted George, Barry and Anne, D J Wallington, Pamela and Merlyn Horswell)*

Free house   Licensees Mike and Joyce Mock   Real ale   Meals and snacks (not Mon lunchtime)   Children welcome   Open 11.30–2.30, 6.15–11; closed Mon lunchtime

Please let us know of any pubs where the wine is particularly good.

DOWLISH WAKE (Somerset)   ST3713 Map 1
New Inn 🏮

Village signposted from Kingstone – which is signposted from A303 on W side of Ilminster, and from A3037 just S of Ilminster; keep on past church – pub at far end of village

It's rare to find a smallish pub that seems bound to please everyone, but this friendly and cosy village pub really should do just that. It's spotlessly clean, and the old-fashioned furnishings include a mixture of chairs, high-backed settles, attractive sturdy tables, dark beams which are strung liberally with hop-bines, and a stone inglenook fireplace with a wood-burning stove. The Swiss landlady does the cooking: as well as bar food including sandwiches (from 85p), soup (£1.15), good ploughman's (from £1.75), excellent spicy sausage (£1.95), ham and egg (£2.15), omelettes (from £2.25) and sirloin steak (£5.75), she's praised for dishes such as squid or soft roes (£2), raclette with authentic cheese (£4.50), seafood salad (£7.30), duck and pigeon breast (£7.50), whole shoulder of lamb (£9.75), and puddings like delicious apple and blackberry pancake with blackberry ice-cream. Besides well kept Butcombe, Wadworths 6X and a guest beer on handpump, and a decent choice of whiskies, there's a selection of Perry's ciders. These come from just down the road, and the thatched sixteenth-century stone cider mill is well worth a visit for its collection of wooden bygones and its liberal free tastings (you can buy the half-dozen different ciders in old-fashioned earthenware flagons as well as more modern containers; it's closed on Sunday afternoons). There may be piped music, and in a separate area they have darts, shove-ha'penny, dominoes, cribbage, table skittles as well as alley skittles and a fruit machine. There's a rustic bench in front of the stone pub, which is decorated with tubs of flowers and a sprawl of clematis. *(Recommended by K R Harris, Richard Dolphin, David Wallington, PLC, Graham and Glenis Watkins, Dr Stewart Rae, Brian and Pam Cowling, Jonathan and Helen Palmer)*

Free house   Licensees Therese Boosey and David Smith   Real ale   Meals and snacks (table bookings tel Ilminster (0460) 52413)   Children in family-room   Open 11–2.30, 6–11 all year, though may open all day if trade demands

DUNSTER (Somerset)   SS9943 Map 1
Luttrell Arms 🛏

A396

Until 1779, this fifteenth-century Gothic Hall was known as The Ship. It's now a comfortably modernised THF hotel, though it's kept a lot of character, especially in the back bar where there are old settles as well as more modern furniture, bottles, clogs and horseshoes hanging from the high beams, and a stag's head and rifles on the walls. Ancient black timber uprights glazed with fine hand-floated glass, full of ripples and irregularities, separate the room from a small galleried and flagstoned courtyard. Bar snacks include good sandwiches, an attractive cold buffet, plaice and a speciality mixed grill, as well as unusual evening meals; well kept Bass and Exmoor Bitter on handpump. In the gardens there are cannon emplacements dug out by Blake in the Civil War when – with Praise God Barebones and his pikemen – he was besieging the castle for six months. The town, on the edge of Exmoor National Park, is pretty. *(Recommended by W and S Rinaldi-Butcher, H W and A B Tuffill)*

Free house (THF)   Real ale   Meals and snacks   Restaurant   Open 11–2.30, 6–11 all year   Bedrooms tel Dunster (0643) 821555; £66B/£93B

EAST LYNG   ST3328 Map 1
Rose & Crown

A361 about 4 miles W of Othery

One reader feels this charming, friendly pub has hardly changed over the twenty years he's known it. The traditionally furnished, open-plan lounge bar has stacks of old *Country Life* on a bow window seat by an oak drop-leaf table, a corner cabinet of glass, china and silver, a court cabinet, beams, and a winter log fire in a modernised fine old stone fireplace; piped music. Good, freshly prepared food includes sandwiches (from 90p; steak £2.40), soup (£1.20), pâté (£1.50), ploughman's (from £1.95), home-cooked ham and egg (£2.40), omelettes (£3.45), salads (£3.20), scampi or trout (£4.10), mixed grill or very good duck (£7.25), steaks (from £7.75) and puddings (from £1.20). Well kept Butcombe, Palmers IPA and Eldridge Pope Royal Oak on handpump. The prettily planted back garden (largely hedged off from the car park) has picnic-table sets, and there's also a full skittle alley. (*Recommended by Patrick Young, Richard Dolphin, Alan Carr, J Harvey Hallam*)

Free house   Licensee P J Thyer   Real ale   Meals and snacks (12–2, 7–10)   Restaurant (not Sun lunchtime) tel Taunton (0823) 69235   Children in eating area of bar and restaurant Open 10.30–2.30, 6.30–11 all year

EXFORD (Somerset)   SS8538   Map 1
White Horse ⚑

B3224

Though the old coach road climbs from here up over Exmoor, the attractive village itself is sheltered – pretty in summer, with the river running past the inn. Unusually for the area, this is a tall building, creeper-covered, with its top storey half-timbered. It's got a friendly and casual atmosphere in its more or less open-plan bar, with Windsor and other country kitchen chairs, high-backed antique settle, scrubbed deal tables, hunting prints, photographs above the stripped pine dado, and a good winter log fire. A good range of home-cooked bar food includes filled rolls (from 90p), sandwiches (from £1.10), generous ploughman's (from £2), macaroni cheese (£1.65), lasagne (£3.95), tender duck (£6), steaks (from £6.95), lobster (around £9.65), and a dish of the day such as liver and bacon (£2.50) or venison pie (£4); the traditional puddings (£1.30) are popular. Well kept Bass, Cotleigh Tawny and Old Buzzard and a guest ale tapped from the cask; sensibly placed darts, tables outside. (*Recommended by Steve and Carolyn Harvey, Brian and Anna Marsden, T J Maddison, Sarah Vickers*)

Free house   Licensees Peter and Linda Hendrie   Real ale   Meals and snacks (12–2, 7–10) Children in eating area of bar   Open 12–3, 5.30–11 all year   Bedrooms tel Exford (064 383) 229; £28.75B/£57.50B

FAULKLAND (Somerset)   ST7354   Map 2
Tucker's Grave

A366 E of village

The smallest pub in the *Guide*, this unspoilt farm cottage pub has a flagstoned entry that opens into a tiny room with casks of well kept Bass and Butcombe Bitter on tap and Cheddar Valley cider in an alcove on the left. Two old cream-painted high-backed settles face each other across a single table on the right, and a side room has shove-ha'penny. There's a skittle alley, and seats outside. (*Recommended by Peter Adcock, Roger Huggins, Ewan McCall, Tom McLean; more reports please*)

Free house   Licensees Ivan and Glenda Swift   Real ale   Open 11–2.30, 6–11 all year

HASELBURY PLUCKNETT (Somerset)   ST4710   Map 1
Haselbury Inn ⊗

A3066 E of Crewkerne

In one half of the neatly kept bar, chintz armchairs and sofas relax around the fire and television set; in the other, candle-lit wooden tables have unusually heavy red-cushioned cask seats – there's a fire down here, too. A wide choice of bar food (though you can also choose anything from the à la carte menu) includes game soup (£1.50), home-made pâté or ploughman's with five cheeses (£2.40), good pasta such as spaghetti bolognese or lambs' kidneys and bacon fettucine (£2.80), beef curry (£3.80), charcoal-grilled steaks (from £6), coq au vin (£6.50), guinea-fowl (£7), local trout (£8), large Dover sole (£12), and daily specials like moules marinière in season (£3.50), Hungarian goulash (£3.80), or king prawns (£4.50); also, puddings such as apple strudel or raspberry and redcurrant pie (from £1.80), and barbecue menu (from £2.80). Vegetables are fresh, sauces home made, and service is friendly and helpful. Well kept Boddingtons, Butcombe Bitter, Exmoor Best, Hook Norton Best, Wadworths 6X, and Charles Wells Bombardier on handpump or tapped from the cask; care taken over wines and other drinks, including good espresso coffee. The most decorative thing here is undoubtedly the well behaved blue and yellow macaw, though other nice touches include plants in the windows, fresh or dried flowers, and the restrained collection of bric-à-brac on the rather lofty beams; piped music. Evening meals in the attractive back restaurant (around £14) should probably be booked on Fridays and Saturdays. There are picnic-table sets on the side grass. *(Recommended by Sue Hallam, CRS, MS, Mr and Mrs H Hearnshaw)*

Free house　Licensee James Pooley　Real ale　Meals and snacks　Restaurant Open 12–2.30, 7–11 all year; closed Mon

HUISH EPISCOPI　ST4326　Map 1
Rose & Crown
A372 E of Langport

The engaging rough and ready attitude to creature comforts here appeals very much to a number of readers, though it's not to everyone's taste. To get a drink, you just walk into the central flagstoned still-room and choose from the casks of well kept Bass and Butcombe or the wide choice of Somerset farm ciders and country wines which stand on ranks of shelves around it; prices are very low. This servery is the only thoroughfare between the casual little front parlours with their unusual pointed-arch windows, old rugs on stone floors, and seats which are inching into decrepitude. The pub has been in the family of the present licensee for 120 years or more, and, as you can see from the Sturgeon print in one front room, the pub hasn't changed externally much over the years, either. Food is simple and cheap: sandwiches (from 70p) and ploughman's (from £1.60). There's a fruit machine in one of the front rooms, and shove-ha'penny, dominoes and cribbage are available. A much more orthodox big back extension family-room has darts, pool, trivia and juke box; there's a skittle alley. Outside, there are tables and a lawn. *(Recommended by Chris Raisin, Graham Doyle, the Barrett family, Mrs Crease, Gordon and Daphne; more reports please)*

Free house　Licensee Mrs Eileen Pittard　Real ale　Snacks　Children welcome　Open 11.30–2.30 (3 Sat), 5.30–11 all year

KILVE (Somerset)　ST1442　Map 1
Hood Arms 🏮 🛏
A39 E of Williton

This very friendly well run village inn is popular for its good home-made bar food. At lunchtime this includes sandwiches (from 80p), good soup (£1.20), pâté or good ploughman's (£2), enormous salads (from £2.20), hot daily specials such as country-style chicken, steak and kidney pie, haddock and broccoli Mornay or National Trust pie (all £3.20), and puddings (from £1.10); in the evenings the main bar takes on much more the style of a restaurant, with full meals. The carpeted main bar is straightforwardly comfortable, and there's a wood-burning stove in the stone fireplace (decorated with shining horsebrasses on their original leathers). It leads through to a little cosy lounge with red plush button-back seats. Well kept Flowers Original and Marstons Pedigree on handpump, several malt whiskies, and they do tea and coffee; quick, attentive service; dominoes, cribbage, trivia, alley skittles and gentle piped music. A sheltered back terrace, by a garden with a prettily planted old wall behind, has white metal and plastic seats and tables. *(Recommended by E G Parish, Mrs Sue North, Mrs J M Gillman, David and Ruth Hollands, Derek and Jennifer Taylor, W G Davis, SC, T H G Lewis)*

Free house   Licensees Robbie Rutt and Neville White   Real ale   Meals and snacks (12–2, 6.30–10; not 25 Dec)   Restaurant Weds–Sat evenings   Children over 7 in restaurant   Open 10.30–2.30, 6–11 all year; closed evening 25 Dec   Bedrooms tel Holford (027 874) 210; £28B/£50B

LANGLEY MARSH (Somerset)   ST0729 Map 1
Three Horseshoes ★ ⊘

Village signposted off A361 from Wiveliscombe

A good range of well kept real ales in this friendly red sandstone pub includes Badger Tanglefoot, Bass, Butcombe Best, Fullers London Pride, Palmers IPA and Wadworths 6X on handpump or tapped from the cask; the guest ales change continually, and they keep Perrys farmhouse cider. Good value and entirely fresh home-made food from a constantly changing and imaginative menu includes baps (from £1), vegetable and lentil soup (£1.35), ploughman's (from £1.65), pheasant and liver pâté or garlic mushrooms (£1.80), salads, lovely courgette and mushroom bake (£3.10), leek croustade (£3.25), Somerset fish pie with perfect pastry or chicken and mushroom pie (£3.50), sliced lamb and cashew-nuts (£3.95), and spiced beef in ginger (£4.25); no chips or fried food, and the butter comes in little pots; puddings include good mincemeat, apple and brandy pancakes or excellent cheesecake with cherry topping. Quick, attentive service. The back bar has low modern settles, polished wooden tables with plants, dark red wallpaper, a piano, a local stone fireplace, banknotes papering the wall behind the bar and planes hanging from the ceiling; the lively front room with sensibly placed darts, shove-ha'penny, table skittles, dominoes, cribbage, piped music and the skittle alley is now finished. Guinness the pub alsatian has had puppies, two of which they've kept and called Mackeson and Murphy. You can sit on rustic seats on the verandah or in the sloping back garden, with a climbing-frame, swing and slide, and a view of farmland. In fine weather there are usually vintage cars outside. *(Recommended by Mrs Ann Spice, Alan P Carr, John Tyzack, Mr and Mrs Norman Edwardes, Heather Sharland, J L Simpson, S Matthews, D Stephenson, Mr and Mrs D A P Grattan, M C Howells)*

Free house   Licensee J Hopkins   Real ale   Meals and snacks   Well behaved children in eating area of bar   Singalongs Sat evenings and occasional spontaneous 'fiddle/squeeze box' sessions with local morris dancing musicians   Open 11–2.30, 6–11, though may stay open longer in afternoon if trade demands

MONKSILVER (Somerset)   ST0737 Map 1
Notley Arms ★ ⊘

B3188

Consistently popular with readers, this quiet village inn often adds interesting new dishes to the well established favourites on the menu. Regular dishes include soup (£1.10), sandwiches (from 90p), filled baked potatoes (from £1.75), excellent ploughman's (from £2), shepherd's purse (wholemeal pitta bread generously filled with garlicky lamb and salad, £2.50), home-made pasta or vegetarian curry (£2.75), lovely salads (local cured ham £3.75, generous prawn mayonnaise, delicious smoked mackerel), superb Chinese-style pork with stir-fry vegetables (£4.50), and correctly cooked vegetables; puddings like treacle tart or home-made ice-creams (£1.25), and evening extras such as fresh local trout (£5) and sirloin steak (£7). Well kept Ushers Best and Ruddles County on handpump, and country wines such as rhubarb or raspberry; hard-working, efficient staff. The L-shaped bar has beams, small settles and kitchen chairs around the plain country wooden and candle-lit tables, Old Master and other prints on the black-timbered white walls, a couple of wood-burning stoves, and a warm atmosphere; dominoes and alley skittles, well reproduced classical music, and a bright little family-room; dogs welcome. The charming, neatly kept cottage garden behind this quiet village inn runs down to a swift clear stream. *(Recommended by PLC, Steve Dark, Russell and Christina Jones, T H G Lewis, Pete and Mary Fintelley, P Miller, Mr and Mrs J D Cranston, Cynthia Pollard, Margaret Mawson, David and Ruth Hollands, Wayne Brindle, D H, M C Watkinson, Heather Sharland, M W Barratt, SC, Mr and Mrs R Gammon, M E Dormer, Mr and Mrs W A Rinaldi-Butcher, Joy Heatherley)*

Ushers (Watneys)   Licensee Alistair Cade   Real ale   Meals and snacks   Children in own room   Open 11–2.30, 6–11 all year; closed 25 Dec

MONTACUTE (Somerset)   ST4951 Map 2

Kings Arms

The atmosphere in this early Georgian inn is civilised yet friendly, and the lounge bar is comfortably furnished with grey-gold plush seats, soft armchairs, chintz sofas, a high curved settle, and towards the front – where parts of the walls are stripped back to the handsome masonry – plush seats around tables. Popular bar food includes soup with home-made bread (95p), a generous buffet, and daily specials such as steak and kidney pie, chicken chasseur or ham and asparagus bake (£3.45 or £3.95); best to book for Sunday lunch (when people tend to dress smartly). Bass and Gibbs Mew Wiltshire tapped from the cask; good wines and farm cider. The village includes the stately Elizabethan mansion of the same name, and behind the hotel the wooded St Michael's Hill is owned by the National Trust. *(Recommended by A M Kelly, Steve Huggins, Mrs E M Thompson, D K and H M Brenchley, Alan P Carr, Maggie and Bruce Clarke, G and S L, the Barrett family and Mrs Crease, C H Beaumont, Gwen and Peter Andrews)*

Free house   Licensee S D Price   Real ale   Meals and snacks (12–2, 7–10)   Children welcome   Restaurant   Open 11–3, 6–11 all year; closed 25 and 26 Dec   Bedrooms tel Martock (0935) 822513; £40B/£55B

NORTON ST PHILIP (Somerset)   ST7755 Map 2

George   *[illustrated on page 612]*

A366

Included for the character of its massive stone walls, high mullioned windows, and charming half-timbered and galleried back courtyard – which has an external Norman stone stair-turret – this was already working as an inn by 1397. Furnishings are simple: leather seats, square-panelled wooden settles, plain old tables, wide bare floorboards, and lofty beams hung with harness, copper preserving pans, and a magnificent pair of bellows; a long, stout table serves well kept Bass, and Wadworths Devizes and 6X on handpump. Bar food includes filled rolls (90p), home-made soup (£1), ploughman's (£2.40), and a couple of daily specials such as good pheasant casserole. A panelled lounge is furnished with antique settles and tables. Off the courtyard is the cellar Dungeon Bar (opened only at busy times), named to recall the men imprisoned there after the rebel Duke of Monmouth had been defeated. A stroll over the meadow behind the pub leads to an attractive churchyard around the medieval church, whose bells struck Pepys (here

---

Food details, prices, timing, etc. refer to bar food, not to a separate restaurant if there is one.

on 12 June 1668) as 'mighty tuneable'. *(Recommended by Gwen and Peter Andrews, H K Dyson, Peter Adcock, Barry and Anne, Mrs A M Viney, Mr and Mrs D M Norton, S J A Velate, Roger Huggins, Ewan McCall, Tom McLean)*

Wadworths Licensee M F Moore Real ale Meals and snacks (11.30–2, 6.30–10) Children in restaurant and two other rooms Restaurant tel Faulkland (037 387) 224 Open 11–2.30, 6–11 all year

OLDBURY-UPON-SEVERN (Avon) ST6292 Map 2

Anchor 🏮

Village signposted from B4061

This year, a separate restaurant decorated in new pine has been added, and there's now an indoor entrance to the lavatories. From a menu that changes daily, the consistently good waitress-served home-made food includes winter soup (from £1), good value ploughman's or pâté (from £1.35), Yorkshire pudding filled with roast beef (£2.95), beef in ale pie (£3.20), locally made pork and garlic sausages (£3.25), prawn and leek pancake (£3.65), seafood chowder (£3.75), beef Stroganoff (£4.65), particularly good charcoal-grilled steaks (from £6.25), and puddings such as rhuburb crumble, blackcurrant suprême, fruit sponge and so forth (from 95p); best to get there early if you want a seat. Bass tapped from the cask, with Butcombe, Hook Norton Best, Marstons Pedigree and Theakstons Best on handpump; friendly service. The beamed lounge is comfortably furnished with cushioned window seats, a curved high-backed settle facing an attractive oval oak gateleg table, winged seats against the wall, easy chairs, and a big winter log fire. Darts, shove-ha'penny, dominoes and cribbage. You can sit outside in the garden in summer. St Arilda's church nearby is interesting, on its odd little knoll with wild flowers among the gravestones (the primroses and daffodils in spring are lovely), and there are lots of paths over the meadows to the sea dyke or warth which overlooks the tidal flats. *(Recommended by Michael Watts, Russell and Christina Jones, Jon Wainwright, Barry and Anne, Helena and Arthur Harbottle, Tony Ritson, E and P Parkinson, John and Joan Wyatt, PLC, W D Horsfield, Pamela and Merlyn Horswell)*

Free house Manager Peter Riley Real ale Meals and snacks Restaurant tel Thornbury (0454) 413331 Children in dining-room Open 11.30–2.30 (3 Sat), 6.30–11 all year

OVER STRATTON (Somerset) ST4315 Map 1

Royal Oak 🏮

Village signposted from former A303 Yeovil–Ilminster through Seavington St Michael, which itself is signposted off A303 at E end of new Ilminster bypass

Decorations and furnishings in the cosy, extended dark-flagstoned bars of this popular thatched food pub are simple but careful, and the atmosphere is old-fashioned and relaxed. There are scrubbed deal farmhouse kitchen tables, a mixture of similar or dining-chairs, pews and settles, candles in bottles, plants in the windows, some hop-bines, and a stuffed pheasant. The beams have been prettily stencilled with an oakleaf and acorn pattern, the walls are stripped to bare stonework or attractively ragrolled red, and log fires burn, even in summer; maybe unobtrusive piped music. Bar food includes home-made soup (£1.50), salads (from £3.25, smoked salmon £5.50), filled baked potatoes (from £2.25), squid with lemon mayonnaise (£2.95), prawns in home-made yoghurt, mayonnaise, lemon and tomato sauce (£3.25), lasagne (£3.45), deep-fried local Brie with kiwi and peach jam (£3.75), filled pancakes (from £3.75), home-made burger (£4.25), beef in stout with a light orange sauce (£5.75), lamb in Greek pastry (£5.95), pheasant with green apples (£6.25), and Scottish steaks (from £7.50); good children's dishes (from £1.50). Well kept Butcombe, Hook Norton and Wadworths 6X on handpump, lots of malt whiskies and an extensive wine list. There are lots of picnic-table sets on a floodlit reconstructed-stone terrace sheltered by the back wings of the building, with more on a further sheltered gravel terrace with a barbecue; the play area is large and well equipped – there's even a big trampoline. *(Recommended by John and Pat Smyth, George Allardyce, Helena and Arthur Harbottle, Sue Hallam, Richard Dolphin, the Barrett family, Mrs Crease)*

Free house Licensees Derek and Claire Blezard Real ale Meals and snacks (12–2, 7–10) Restaurant tel Ilminster (0460) 40906 Children in restaurant Open 12–2.30, 7 (6.30 Sat)–11 all year

PORLOCK (Somerset) SS8846 Map 1

Ship ★ ⇥

A39

It's the low-beamed front bar that readers like most. Full of character and popular with the friendly locals, it has a sought-after window-ledge seat, traditional old benches on the tiled and flagstone floor, hunting prints on the walls, and an inglenook fireplace at each end. The carpeted back lounge has plush red banquettes, a Gothic settle, and a chimney seat. Bar food includes home-made soup (80p), venison sausages (£2.25), salmon and local curd cheese mousse (£3), and pheasant casserole, beef in Guinness or king prawns (all £3.50). Well kept Bass, Cotleigh Old Buzzard, Courage Best and a weekly guest beer on handpump from an air-conditioned cellar; Perrys cider and local country wines; attentive, cheerful licensees. Shove-ha'penny, dominoes, cribbage, bar billiards, and fruit machine, a separate pool-room (which has sensibly placed darts too, in winter), and a full skittle alley. You can sit outside this partly thirteenth-century thatched village cottage in the extended back garden, which is almost higher than the roof, with lovely views of the sea and moor; there's a children's play area. *(Recommended by P J Hanson, T J Maddison, P Miller, Henry Midwinter, Sarah Vickers, WHBM, Steve Dark, Pamela and Merlyn Horswell, B and J Derry, F A Noble, David Goldstone, Alan and Ruth Woodhouse, Wayne Brindle, Brian and Anna Marsden)*

Free house Licensee C M Robinson Real ale Meals and snacks Children in restaurant and eating area of bar Restaurant Open 10.30–3, 5.30–11 all year Bedrooms tel Porlock (0643) 862507; £14.50(£18.50B)/£29(£33B)

RODE (Somerset) ST8153 Map 2

Red Lion

Village signposted off A361 Trowbridge–Frome

A good many of our readers delight in hunting down real curiosities: here's one for the connoisseur's list. Once through the uncommonly wide front door, you find a warren of low-ceilinged, dimly lit and mainly bare-boarded small rooms, rather rough and ready but full of interest. There are lots of Royalty prints (particularly Edward VII and George V), and other old engravings and prints include an endearingly saucy one from the naughty nineties. The biggest collection is of enamelled advertising signs in all states of repair, many given by customers in the three years the landlord's been here; most of these (including a rare Raleigh bicycle one) are in the back skittle alley, which has a couple of pool-tables, various space games and a juke box. Well kept Ushers Best and Ruddles County on handpump, and farm cider; bar snacks are limited to toasties (£1); log fire, darts, fruit machine; friendly service. There are picnic-table sets out behind; this is an interesting village, with the Tropical Bird Gardens nearby. *(Recommended by Andy Mason)*

Ushers (Watneys) Licensee Mrs J Billington Real ale Snacks Children's room Open 11–2.30, 6.30–11 all year

It is illegal for bar staff to smoke while handling your drink.

SHEPPERDINE (Avon)   ST6295 Map 4

Windbound

From B4061 just N of Thornbury turn off at Oldbury signpost, then right at Shepperdine signpost, then next left into Shepperdine Lane; some maps and signposts spell it Sheperdine

It's the spacious and recently refurbished upper dining-lounge, laid out rather as a restaurant, which has extensive views over the Severn Estuary to the hills beyond. The downstairs bar (below the level of the sea dyke) has dining-chairs and straight-backed small settles forming booths around the tables, one or two local watercolours and prints with the wicker fish-traps on its walls, and a good winter fire. The new licensees have introduced some different dishes to the menu: home-made soup (90p), sandwiches (£1.20), grilled sardines or eggs Florentine (£1.95), ploughman's (£2.25), cold home-cooked ham (£2.95), salads (from £3.50), a home-made vegetarian dish (£3.50), grilled lamb kebabs (£5.25), steaks (from £6.50), and puddings (£1.50); also, daily specials such as prawn brochette (£4.45), tagliatelle carbonara (£4.40) or chicken Normandy (£4.95), children's menu (£1.75), Sunday lunch (£3.95), afternoon teas from June to September, and barbecues in fine weather. Darts, dominoes, cribbage and a separate skittle alley. Ind Coope Burton, Tetleys, Wadworths 6X and a guest beer on handpump, farm ciders such as Addlestones, and quite a few sherries. On the sheltered fairy-lit lawn outside this extended pub there are picnic-table sets among brightly coloured summer flowers, swings and slides, and more seats up on the dyke; you can walk along the banks of the Severn Estuary to Sharpness. It's popular with older people on weekday lunchtimes, though there's a much wider range of customers at weekends. *(Recommended by R F Warner, Gwen and Peter Andrews; more reports please)*

Halls (Allied)   Licensees Nigel and Josephine Wright   Real ale   Meals and snacks Restaurant tel Thornbury (0454) 414343   Children in eating area of bar   Open 11–3, 6–11 Mon–Thurs, 11–11 Fri and Sat; 11–3, 7–11 in winter

SOUTH STOKE (Avon)   ST7461 Map 2

Pack Horse

Village signposted opposite the Cross Keys off B3110, leaving Bath southwards – just before end of speed limit

Built by the priory as a hostelry for travellers, this ancient three-gabled stone house was rebuilt in 1489 with two rooms on both floors and a central alleyway leading to the church (which was used for carrying the dead to the cemetery). This entrance corridor – still a public right of way to the church – takes you to a central space by the serving bar where you get your well kept Courage Best on handpump and choice of ciders. The main room, popular with locals, has antique oak settles (two well carved), leatherette dining-chairs and cushioned captain's chairs on the quarry-tiled floor, a heavy black beam and plank ceiling, a cheery log fire in the handsome stone inglenook, some Royalty pictures, a chiming wall clock, and rough black shutters for the stone-mullioned windows (put up in the First World War); rather fine shove-ha'penny slates are set into two of the tables, and there are darts, dominoes and cribbage. There's another room down to the left. Very good value bar food includes home-baked cider ham in rolls (from 65p), mouth-watering home-made pasties (£1.10), sausage plait (£1.80), ploughman's, home-made lasagne or curries (£2), and fresh Cornish mussels (Thursday and Friday, £2.20); friendly staff. The spacious back garden looks out over the stolid old church and the wooded valley. *(Recommended by Peter and Rose Flower, Chris Raisin, Graham Doyle, Nick Dowson, Alison Hayward, Roger Huggins, Ewan McCall, Tom McLean)*

Courage   Real ale   Meals (lunchtime) and snacks   Children in eating area of bar lunchtimes only   Open 11–3, 6–11 all year

Waterside pubs are listed at the back of the book.

STANTON WICK (Avon)   ST6162 Map 2
Carpenters Arms 🏠
Village signposted off A368, just W of junction with A37 S of Bristol

Very popular for quickly served good value bar food, this long and low tiled-roof
country inn has managed to preserve a wholly relaxed and pubby atmosphere. This
is largely because drinking and chatting are still the main thing in the central area,
by the serving-counter, where there's a big log fire and a prettily stocked aquarium.
Diners are encouraged to step down into a snug inner room (lightened by mirrors in
arched 'windows'), or to go round to the sturdy tables angling off on the right
(where a pianist may be quietly vamping his way through Hoagy Carmichael and
other old favourites on Friday and Saturday nights). Note that most of these tables
get booked at weekends. The food ordering counter is round here: the wide choice
includes home-made soup (£1.25), filled baked potatoes (from £1.35), lots of
starters like pâté (£2.25), ploughman's (from £2.45), grilled fresh sardines (£2.75)
or devilled kidneys (£3.25), several vegetarian dishes such as ratatouille au gratin
(£2.65), home-cooked ham and egg (£3.75), fresh plaice fillet (£4.75), several
home-cooked cold roasts with salad (£5.25) and steaks (from £7.85); specials like
fresh asparagus or monkfish provençale, and home-made puddings (from £1.50).
It's red-carpeted throughout, with stripped stone walls, fresh flowers on the heavy
tables, and red-cushioned wall pews and other seats; there's a plump and rather
aloof ginger cat. Well kept Bass, Butcombe, Charrington IPA and Wadworths 6X
on handpump, and a good wine list, strong on medium-priced well-made wines.
The bedrooms are attractively furnished, and breakfasts are good. There are picnic-
table sets on the front terrace. *(Recommended by Steve Dark, Aubrey and Margaret
Saunders, Mr and Mrs F H Stokes, John Bell, Angus and Rosemary Campbell, Paul Evans)*

*Free house   Licensee Nigel Pushman   Real ale   Meals and snacks (12–2.15, 7–10)
Restaurant; closed Sun evenings   Children in eating area of bar   Piano Mon, Weds,
Fri and Sat   Open 11–3, 5–11 all year   Bedrooms tel Compton Dando (076 18) 202;
£32.50B/£39.50B*

STAPLE FITZPAINE (Somerset)   ST2618 Map 1
Greyhound
Village signposted from A358 Taunton–Ilminster at Hatch Beauchamp; or (better road) from
Shoreditch on B3170, just after crossing M5 S of Taunton

This popular creeper-covered country pub has flagstone floors, simple antique
furnishings, and log fires in attractive inglenooks. Reasonably priced food includes
home-made soup (£1.15), ploughman's (£2.25), cottage pie or lasagne (£2.95),
salads (from £2.95), grilled fillet of bream (£4.95), and evening charcoal grills like
gigot of lamb (£5.25), kebabs (£5.45) and steaks (from £7.45), with home-made
puddings such as treacle tart (£1.95) or profiteroles (from £2.35), Friday evening
fish specials, and Sunday lunch (£4.95). Well kept Exmoor Bitter, Eldridge Pope
Royal Oak, Flowers IPA and Marstons Pedigree on handpump, and lots of country
wines and a fair number of malt whiskies. Service is friendly, but can be rather
slow; piped classical music. There are some seats ouside in front of the pub among
troughs of flowers, with more in the gravelled stableyard behind; also, a children's
play area with a Wendy house and slide and a barbecue. Just to the south you can
walk in the hillside woods of Neroche Forest, which has a signposted nature trail.
The pub changed hands yet again in late 1988: though reports have not been
unanimous since, people who've known the pub a long time feel its essential

Though lunchtime closing time is now 3 on Sundays in England and Wales (with 20 minutes'
drinking-up time), some pubs hope to close a bit earlier; please let us know if you find this
happening.

character hasn't been affected much. We'd be grateful for up-to-date reports. *(Recommended by PLC, A B Barton, Mr and Mrs P J Barrett, John Tyzack, CED, Patrick Young, H W Clayton, Richard Dolphin, Julie Vincent)*

Free house Licensees Steven Watts and Mrs Audrey Watts Real ale Meals and snacks (12–2, 7–10) Children in garden and eating area Restaurant tel Hatch Beauchamp (0823) 480227 Jazz or rythmn and blues Thurs evenings Open 10.30–2.30, 5.30–11 all year; may open longer on weekend afternoons

STOGUMBER (Somerset)   ST0937 Map 1

White Horse

At the top of the closely huddled village and facing the red stone church stands this pleasant little pub. Inside, there's a long room with settles and cushioned captain's chairs around the heavy rustic tables on its patterned carpet, a coal fire in cool weather, and a red-tiled floor at one end with old-fashioned built-in settles. Well kept Cotleigh Tawny and Exmoor Bitter on handpump and Sheppys cider (summer only). Good, quickly served food includes sandwiches (from 70p), home-made soup (£1), salads (from £1.80), ploughman's (£1.90), omelettes (from £1.90), vegetable curry (£2.30), tasty Somerset pork (£3.10), steak and kidney pudding (£3.40), chicken with Stilton sauce (£4.60), trout (£4.20) and steaks (from £6.50); puddings such as home-made ice-creams or apple crumble (from 90p) and Sunday lunch (£6.50); friendly staff. A side room has sensibly placed darts and a fruit machine; shove-ha'penny, dominoes, cribbage, space game and soothing piped music; also, a separate skittle alley. The garden behind is quiet except for rooks and lambs in the surrounding low hills. *(Recommended by E G Parish, J F and M Sayers, WHBM, John Tyzack, K R Harris, Alan Carr, Wayne Brindle, Mrs J M Gillman, D Stephenson, M C Howells)*

Free house Licensee Peter Williamson Real ale Meals and snacks (11–2, 6–10.30) Restaurant Children in restaurant Open 11–2.30, 6–11 all year Bedrooms tel Stogumber (0984) 56277; /£30B

TINTINHULL (Somerset)   ST4919 Map 2

Crown & Victoria

Farm Street; from village, which is signposted off A303, follow signs to Tintinhull House

Even when this mellow stone pub is very busy, the welcome and service remain friendly. There are old-fashioned high-backed chairs, Windsor chairs, low modern settles, and a couple of easy chairs by the big winter log fire in one bared stone wall. Food includes sandwiches, lasagne (£2.20), scampi (£3.55), gammon (£4.10), steaks (from £6.05), and daily specials such as chicken in cream and cider (from £3). Well kept Bass, Flowers IPA, Wadworths 6X, Youngs Special on handpump; bar billiards, table skittles, alley skittles, dominoes, cribbage, fruit machine, trivia and piped music. The big lawn behind the pub is attractive and peaceful in summer, with cocktail parasols, white chairs, swings and a goldfish pool set in a rockery; there's a children's play area. Tintinhull House with its beautiful gardens is close by. *(Recommended by F A and J W Sherwood, Mrs E M Thompson, R Blatch, the Barrett family, Mrs Crease, E A George, J S Evans, Bernard Phillips)*

Free house Meals and snacks (not Sun) Children in eating area of bar (ask first) Open 10.30–2.30, 6–11 all year

TOLLDOWN (Avon)   ST7576 Map 2

Crown

Under 1 mile from M4 junction 18; A46 towards Bath; village not marked on many maps

Handy for the motorway, this popular Cotswold-stone pub has two comfortable little bars. A mixture of seats includes long cushioned settles and an antique carved armchair, and there are some heavy beams, open fires, a dresser with plates in one room, and dominoes, darts and a fruit machine. Efficiently served in generous helpings, the lunchtime bar food includes several ploughman's (from £2), chilli con carne (£3.25) or home-made pies; in the evening there's soup (£1.20), deep-fried plaice (£2.85), gammon with egg or pineapple (£4), pork loin with garlic cheese (£4.80), mixed grill (£6) and steaks (from £6.25). The restaurant has a no-smoking area. Well kept Wadworths IPA and 6X on handpump. The fenced-in garden – with equipped play area for children – has been extended. The National Trust's Dyrham House, with its large deer herd, is situated nearby. *(Recommended by Adrian Kelly, WFL, Mrs Margaret Dyke, M G Hart; more reports please)*

Wadworths   Licensee John Collins   Real ale   Meals and snacks   Restaurant   Children in restaurant and eating area of bar   Open 11–11; 11–2.30, 6–11 in winter   Bedrooms tel Bath (0225) 891231; £16/£28

TORMARTON (Avon)   ST7678 Map 2
Compass

Under 1 mile from M4 junction 18; A46 towards Stroud, then first right

The upper bar of this well run, busy roadhouse has stone walls, red plush chairs, red leatherette stools and cushioned settles, and is popular with locals; the lower bar – more set out for eating – has a glass cold food display cabinet, and leads out to the nicest room, the light and spacious conservatory. This has orange or green garden chairs around wooden-slatted tables, flowers and shrubs, and a vigorous climbing vine. Bar food includes home-made soup (£1.35), sandwiches (from £1.35, prawn £2.20), ploughman's (from £2.75), home-made cheese flan (£3.55), home-cooked meats (from £3.75), fresh poached salmon or dressed crab (£5.45), and hot specials. Archers Village, Bass and Wadworths 6X on handpump, country wines, and several malt whiskies; darts, dominoes, cribbage, fruit machine and piped music. Outside, the crazy paved terrace has bright flowers and some picnic-table sets. Badminton and Dodington are close by. *(Recommended by Dr Stephen Hiew, John Fazakerley, Mr and Mrs D A P Grattan, Michael and Alison Sandy, Helena and Arthur Harbottle, Aubrey and Margaret Saunders, Jenny and Brian Seller, Pamela and Merlyn Horswell, Sue Cleasby, Mike Ledger)*

Free house   Licensee P Monyard   Real ale   Meals and snacks (11–10, though limited menu in afternoon)   Restaurant; closed Sun lunchtime   Children in eating area of bar Open 11–11 all year   Bedrooms tel Badminton (045 421) 242/577; £42.50B/£54.75B

WELLOW (Avon)   ST7458 Map 2
Fox & Badger

Friendly new licensees had just moved into this fine old stone-built tavern as we went to press, and were in the process of building a new kitchen and creating a restaurant where the old kitchen had been. The flagstone-floored bar has flowers on the tables, seats built into snug alcoves, small winged settles with cushions to match the curtains, a handsome fireplace, and a pleasantly chiming clock. Good, fresh bar food includes sandwiches (from 85p), home-made pizza (£1.95), vegetarian dishes such as garlic, mushroom and courgette bake or vegetable gratin (£2.65), home-made quiche (£2.75), ploughman's with three cheeses (£2.75), honey-roast ham off the bone and salad (£2.95), sweet-and-sour pork (£3.25), steaks (from £4.25), and home-made crumbles (£1.40); Sunday roast lunch with a choice of two roasts (£3.95). Well kept Ruddles Best and Ushers Best on handpump. The cosy carpeted public bar has shove-ha'penny, dominoes, a juke box and fruit machine, and there's also a skittle alley. The inn-sign is rather striking, showing the two animals in

---

If we know a pub has an outdoor play area for children, we mention it.

Regency dress. *(Recommended by Barry and Anne, Peter and Rose Flower, BHP, S J A Velate, M A and W R Proctor, Roger Huggins)*

Ushers (Watneys)   Licensees Kevin and Maxine Spragg   Real ale   Meals and snacks Restaurant tel Bath (0225) 832293   Well behaved children welcome   Open 11–3, 6–11 all year

WEST HUNTSPILL (Somerset)   ST3044 Map 1

Crossways 🐌

2¾ miles from M5 junction 23 (A38 towards Highbridge); 4 miles from M5 junction 22 (A38 beyond Highbridge)

A happy mix of locals and visitors fills the various spreading bar areas in this popular food pub. The main part has good winter log fires, dining-room chairs, a mixture of settles, and seats built into one converted brick fireplace. At one end there's more of a dining-room, prettily decorated with old farm machinery engravings, Albert and Chic cartoons (chiefly about restaurants), and 1920-ish hunting prints, as well as neat red seats, and a brass colonial fan in its dark ceiling (Friday and Saturday bistro menu here). The other end has an area with big winged settles making booths, and there's a family-room with bamboo-back seats around neat tables (and a space game). A wide choice of good food includes various home-made soups (£1), sandwiches (from £1), chicken liver pâté (£2), ploughman's (from £2), tasty prawns by the half-pint (£2.60), salads (from £3.50), delicious quiche Lorraine (£2.80), vegetarian curried nut roast (£2.50), broccoli, chicken and ham Mornay or super local faggots with marrowfat peas (£3), home-made lasagne (£3.20), home-baked steak and kidney or lamb and apricot pies (£3.30), excellent gammon with egg or pineapple (£4.20), grilled fresh trout or poached salmon (£4.50), and steaks (from £5.50). The home-made puddings are good and served with double cream – treacle tart, bitter-sweet chocolate pudding or lemon cheesecake. Well kept Butcombe Bitter, Flowers IPA and Original, and Eldridge Pope Royal Oak on handpump, with a changing guest beer such as Cotleigh Old Buzzard; Rich's farmhouse cider, a few malt whiskies, and good wines (don't be put off by the name of the Australian Long Flat Red – it's excellent value); friendly, prompt service. Cribbage, pinball, dominoes, fruit machine and skittle alley. There are picnic-table sets among fruit trees in quite a big garden. *(Recommended by Tom Evans, C F Walling, Tessa Stuart, Dr Keith Bloomfield, K J Betts, Patrick Young, C F Stephens, W F Coghill, A V Chute)*

Free house   Licensees Michael Ronca and Tony Eyles   Real ale   Meals and snacks (12–2, 6.30–10)   Fri and Sat evening bistro   Children in eating area of bar, bistro and family-room   Jazz weekend in marquee in garden around Midsummer's Day   Open 10.30am–11pm; 12–3, 5.30–11 in winter; closed 25 Dec   Bedrooms tel Burnham-on-Sea (0278) 783756; £19.50B/£32.50B

WHEDDON CROSS (Somerset)   SS9238 Map 1

Rest & Be Thankful

Junction of A396 and B3224, S of Minehead

The central chimney in the comfortable lounge here divides the room in two, each side with a log fire in cool weather; decorations include plush burgundy built-in banquettes and chairs around modern wood tables, a graceful goldfish in a big aquarium, and a white plank ceiling; piped music. Bar food includes sandwiches (from 90p – not Sunday lunchtime), home-made soup (£1.20), home-made pâté (£1.25), three sausages (£2.45), ploughman's (from £2.10), home-made macaroni cheese (£2.85), salads with home-cooked meats (from £2.50), chicken and mushroom Kiev (£5.50), steaks (from £6.25) and puddings (from £1.10); children's meals (from £1.25), and they do tea, coffee and hot chocolate. Well kept Ruddles County and Ushers Best on handpump, and several malt whiskies; gentle piped music. A communicating games area has pool, darts, fruit machine, space game, juke box; there is a skittle alley and buffet bar. *(Recommended by T J Maddison, Sarah Vickers, Alan and Ruth Woodhouse, C F Stephens, PHF, Brian and Anna Marsden; more reports please)*

Free house   Licensee Michael Weaver   Real ale   Meals and snacks (12–2, 7–10) Restaurant tel Timberscombe (064 384) 222   Children in restaurant   Open 10.30–2.30, 6–11 all year; open 7 in winter

WINSFORD (Somerset)   SS9034 Map 1

Royal Oak 🏠

Village signposted from A396 about 10 miles S of Dunster

A well placed thatched Exmoor inn with plenty of nearby walks – up Winsford Hill for magnificent views, for example, or over to Exford. Inside, the cosy, partly panelled lounge bar has a cushioned big bay window seat looking across the road towards the village green and foot and packhorse bridges over the River Winn, which joins the Exe here. Also, Windsor armed chairs and cushioned seats on the red carpet, horsebrasses and pewter tankards hanging from the beam above the attractively panelled bar counter, a splendid iron fireback in the big stone hearth (with a log fire in winter), and a relaxed, friendly atmosphere. Another similarly old-fashioned bar has good brass, copper, wall prints and darts. Good bar food includes soup (95p), cold meat sandwiches (£1.25), traditional ploughman's (from £2.75), home-made pork, liver and orange pâté or home-made vegetarian quiche (£2.95), excellent game pie or home-baked soft bap with minute steak (£4.45), a hot or cold daily special (£4.45), and home-made puddings. Well kept Flowers IPA and Original on handpump; friendly staff. In the 1880s Ernest Bevin's mother worked in the kitchen here until she died, leaving him an eight-year-old orphan – which is no doubt how the foreign secretary came to be overheard, in the middle of the Palestine crisis, saying mysteriously on the telephone, 'You want to beat it and then put olive oil on it'. *(Recommended by P J Hanson, T J Maddison, Sarah Vickers, Heather Sharland, D Stephenson, Don Mather, Brian and Anna Marsden, Mr and Mrs W A Rinaldi-Butcher, Julie Vincent)*

Free house   Licensee Charles Steven   Real ale   Meals and snacks   Restaurant; not Sun evening   Children in eating area of bar   Open 11–11 all year   Bedrooms tel Winsford (064 385) 232; £50B/£60B

WITHYPOOL (Somerset)   SS8435 Map 1

Royal Oak 🏠

Village signposted off B4233

Tucked down below some of the most attractive parts of Exmoor, this busy country village inn has a cosy beamed lounge bar with a stag's head and several foxes' masks on its walls, comfortable button-back brown seats and slat-backed chairs, and a log fire in a raised stone fireplace; another quite spacious bar is similarly decorated. A wide range of good bar snacks includes sandwiches (from 80p, giant filled rolls from £1.40, steak and onions £2.60), filled baked potatoes (from £1.10), home-made soup (£1.25), home-made pâté (£2.40), ploughman's (from £2.60), good home-cooked ham (£3.25), two large sausages (a choice of pork and garlic, pork and herb, venison and bacon or spicy tomato £3.50), salads (from £3.75), good steaks (from £4.50) and large tasty Mediterranean prawns with garlic mayonnaise (£7). Well kept Ruddles County and Ushers Best on handpump, several vintage brandies, quite a few malt whiskies, and unusual wines; cheerful, pleasant service; shove-ha'penny, dominoes and cribbage. Outside on the terrace there are wooden benches and tables with parasols. Just up the road there are grand views from Winsford Hill and tracks lead up among the ponies into the heather past Withypool Hill. The River Barle runs through the village itself, with pretty bridleways following it through a wooded combe further upstream. For guests, they can arrange salmon and trout fishing, riding (stabling also), clay-pigeon shooting, rough shooting, hunting, sea-fishing from a boat and trips to see wild red deer. *(Recommended by W and S Rinaldi-Butcher, P Miller, John and Ruth Roberts, WTF, T J Maddison, Sarah Vickers, Ann and David Stranack, WHBM, Don Mather, Wayne Brindle, Dr and Mrs A R H Worssam, David and Ruth Hollands, B S Bourne, J C Smith)*

Free house   Licensee Michael Bradley   Real ale   Meals and snacks   Restaurant   Children over 10 in restaurant   Occasional jazz evenings in winter   Open 11–2.30, 6–11 all year; closed 25 and 26 Dec   Bedrooms tel Exford (064 383) 506; £25(£40B)/£40(£56B)

WOOLVERTON (Somerset)   ST7954 Map 2
Red Lion

A36, at N end of village on E side of road

Three hundred years ago, this attractively extended pub was a farm. The main area has lots of comfortably cushioned seats around decent elm tables, and an expanse of parquet flooring with oriental-style rugs. One older part has beams, flagstones, old panelling, cushioned farmhouse chairs, and a winged high-backed settle by the big stone hearth with a log-effect gas fire. Huge helpings of popular food include sandwiches (from £1), ploughman's (from £1.75), lots of interesting filled baked potatoes (from £2, prawn, ham and asparagus £3.10), original salad bowls such as garlic croûtons, walnuts, ham and cheese (£2.60), egg, tomato, smoked sausage, mushrooms and garlic croûtons (£3.15), or tuna, prawns, avocado, pineapple, sweetcorn and orange dressing (£3.75), chicken Korma (£4.95), seafood platter (£5.15), and daily specials. Well kept Bass, Wadworths IPA and 6X on handpump, with mulled wine in winter; good service; maybe piped music. You can eat outside, under the trees. *(Recommended by Roger Huggins, Dr Stewart Rae, Charlie Salt, Steve Dark, Mrs H Astley, John Baker, Mike Tucker, D Stephenson, Frank Cummins)*

Wadworths   Licensee Barry Lander   Real ale   Meals and snacks (12–3, 7–10)   Children welcome   Open noon–11 all year

Lucky Dip

Besides the fully inspected pubs, you might like to try these Lucky Dips recommended to us and described by readers (if you do, please send us reports):

Abbots Leigh, Avon [A369, between M5 junction 19 and Bristol; ST5473], *George*: Attractive pub with pretty hanging baskets and outside seating area, doing particularly well under newish licensees, with friendly and refreshingly unpompous old-fashioned atmosphere, consistently good interesting food inc impressive sandwiches, scrumptious Stilton soup, good value home-made pies; two lovely log fires, well kept Courage ales, no fruit machines *(A Borkowski, Barry and Anne, Barry Shapley)*

☆ **Bath** [Mill Lane, Bathampton (off A36 towards Warminster and A4 towards Chippenham); ST7766], *George*: Attractive canalside pub, busy (maybe very much so at weekends) but pleasant, with wide choice of well cooked and quickly served food inc vegetarian dishes, friendly welcome, good log fires (much loved by the black cat), well kept Courage Best and Directors; dining-room leads directly off the canal towpath; outside seats, garden bar; can be approached by peaceful three-mile walk from centre *(G G Calderwood, Chris Raisin, George Little, Hazel Morgan, T C and A R Newell, Wayne Stockton)*

☆ **Bath** [17 Northumberland Pl (off High St by W H Smith); ST7565], *Coeur de Lion*: Neat and tiny single-room pub in charming flower-filled pedestrian alley, well kept Devenish, good friendly atmosphere, big stained-glass window – perhaps Bath's prettiest pub, especially in summer *(Brian Jones, P Miller, LYM)*

☆ **Bath** [Lower Swainswick; Gloucester Rd (A46); ST7667], *Bladud Arms*: Friendly, simple pub notable for its wide choice of pub games, modern and traditional, including a skittle alley; good range of reasonably priced and well kept real ales including Bass, Butcombe, Marstons Pedigree, Wadworths 6X and Whitbreads, good value plain lunchtime food (not Sun) *(LYM)*

☆ **Bath**, [12 Green St], *Old Green Tree*: Small, crowded but friendly pub with unspoilt panelled bar, lounge and no-smoking room, nice traditional furnishings, paintings; well kept Ushers on handpump and generously served, good food – strong on cold dishes from crab rolls or ploughman's up *(Helena and Arthur Harbottle, M A and W R Proctor, H K Dyson)*

Bath [Abbey Green; ST7565], *Crystal Palace*: Big sheltered courtyard is chief attraction of modernised Georgian pub with Eldridge Pope ales under light top pressure, bar food, family area in pleasant heated conservatory *(Pamela and Merlyn Horswell, LYM)*; [central] *Grapes*: Lively, friendly pub with well kept Courage Directors; perhaps could do with some redecoration *(Brian Jones)*; [Lansdown Hill] *Hare & Hounds*: Notable for marvellous view over Charlcombe Valley from spacious well kept beer garden with long terrace, play area and conservatory; comfortable raj-style atmosphere (rather than that of a pub), with lots of cane chairs, elephant pictures and plastic palms; friendly staff, reasonably priced food, well kept Courage Best and Directors, family-room *(Mrs Gill Avis, Mrs E Pollard)*; [Sutton St] *Pultney Arms*: Three-sided bar with large three-sided lounge around it; well kept Watneys-related real ales, good choice of bar food, outside barbecue with some seating on pavement *(B R Woolmington)*; [central pedestrian area] *Roundhouse*: Interestingly shaped bar with Watneys-related real ales, reasonably wide choice of bar food from filled baps up, restaurant upstairs *(Alastair Campbell)*; [Saracen St, Broad St] *Saracens Head*: Spacious beamed bars with Courage ales and good value cold buffet lunches *(O Richardson, H K Dyson)*; [The Paragon; junction with Guinea Lane] *Star*: Particularly well kept Bass tapped from the cask and fresh filled rolls in interesting group of small rooms separated by part-glazed panelled walls; locals play cribbage on green baize table in one of back rooms; popular with local cricket and rugby teams *(W Bailey, Peter and Rose Flower)*; [150 London Rd West] *Wagon & Horses*: Large peaceful Courage house, pleasant views of Avon Valley from lounge, good food *(K R Harris)*

Bathford, Avon [Kingsdown; pub actually just over the Wilts border – OS Sheet 172 reference 809670; ST8067], *Swan*: Beautiful position perched on edge of one of the valleys around Bath – seems held to hill by chain; cosy, with log fires and Gibbs Mew real ales; bar food, though not a pub where everyone eats *(Roger Cunningham, Deborah Frost)*

Bayford, Somerset [ST7229], *Unicorn*: Former coaching-inn, spacious yet still intimate and welcoming local, one area with traditional settle and dark wood, fine choice of beers and wines, wide range of hot and cold food, small cheerful restaurant *(Major J A Gardner)*

Biddisham, Somerset [off A38 Bristol–Bridgwater; ST3853], *New Moon*: Busy but friendly main-road local with standard range of well cooked and reasonably priced bar food, good service *(K R Harris)*

☆ **Bishops Lydeard**, Somerset [A358 towards Taunton; ST1828], *Kingfishers Catch*: Pretty and cosily cottagey little rooms with really good reasonably priced simple food inc excellent Sun lunch; though it has a pub licence (and keg Eldridge Pope beer) it is really run much too much as a small restaurant now to be included as a main entry, but it's certainly up to main entry standard otherwise; until 1987 known as the Rose Cottage *(David and Ruth Hollands, Mrs Ann Spice, Shirley Pielou, G and L Owen, LYM)*

Bishops Lydeard, Somerset [Mount St; ST1629], *Bird in Hand*: Comfortable village local with carpeted bar, lounge window seats, low stools and sensible tables; young pleasant staff, Ushers Best on handpump, freshly baked pizzas and tasty sandwiches; garden *(E G Parish)*; *Lethbridge*: Cosy, good atmosphere, good value food, notable collection of Graham Clark prints, Whitbreads beers; live music weekends; bedrooms *(Elizabeth Lloyd)*

Blagdon, Avon [A368; ST5059], *Live & Let Live*: Cosy partly panelled back bar with log fire and sporting prints, plain but generous bar food, well kept Courage Bitter and Best, sensibly placed darts, pool and other pub games; bedrooms *(LYM)*

Blagdon Hill, Somerset [4 miles S of Taunton; ST2217], *Lamb & Flag*: Small pub, friendly landlord; decent range of snacks and larger meals; winter log fire *(Shirley Pielou)*

☆ **Brent Knoll**, Somerset [ST3350], *Red Cow*: Good choice of beers inc Flowers IPA and Whitbreads Trophy, wide choice of good food served throughout week to well spaced tables in lounge and (through separate hatch) delightful sheltered garden, with fields sloping beyond to Brent Knoll – lovely setting; friendly staff, good lavatories *(S J Edwards, John Cox)*

Bristol [off Boyce's Avenue, Clifton; ST5673], *Albion*: Friendly and unpretentiously old-fashioned pub with unusual flagstoned courtyard off cobbled alley, well kept Courage real ales *(LYM)*; [15 Small St] *Assize Courts*: Smart free house close to centre, on site of merchant's house with upstairs assembly room where Elizabeth I is said to have dined in 1574; piped music, Courage Best and Directors, Wadworths 6X, cheap bar food such as rolls, salads and home-made pies, small garden *(Carol Mason)*; [Prince St] *Bristol Clipper*: Old, beamed pub nr harbour with good, lively atmosphere (can get packed with businessmen at lunchtime when bar staff pressed to keep up), well kept ales, fairly good if rather pricey bar food; handy for Arnolfini Gallery *(P Miller)*; [Montpelier; ST5974] *Cadbury House*: Fascinating collection of 'antique' fruit machines/one-armed bandits; bar food, Courage beers *(Mark Spurlock)*; [Pembroke Rd; Clifton] *Channings Hotel*: Basement bar popular for wide range of good fresh bar food inc daily specials; bedrooms *(T R Norris)*; [15 Cotham Rd South; ST5874] *Cotham Porter Stores*: Lively cider pub – also well kept keenly priced Courage real ales – with benches along the panelled walls, cheap snacks, sensibly placed bars, dominoes, cribbage *(LYM)*; [St Thomas Lane; off Redcliff St and Victoria St] *Fleece & Firkin*: Eighteenth-century wool hall stripped back to flagstones, lofty ceiling, scrubbed butcher's tables; guest beers and own-brewed ales such as the hefty Rambow – owned by Halls (Ind Coope); lunchtime food (not Sun), live music Weds–Sat, children weekends *(Rob and Gill Weeks, LYM)*; [North St, Stokes Croft] *Full Moon*: Old, well restored, pleasant atmosphere, lots of electronic games *(Dr and Mrs A K Clarke)*; [Colston St] *Griffin*: Friendly, comfortable, old-fashioned free house; well kept Watneys-related real ales, good reasonably priced meals, piped music *(Barry Shapley)*; [St Michaels Hill] *Highbury Vaults*: Well kept real ales and good range of bar food (they don't play down the garlic) in only Smiles pub we know of here; covered garden *(Peter Adcock)*; [Bath Rd, Brislington; ST6171] *Kings Arms*: Well updated low-beamed pub with well kept Courage ales *(Dr and Mrs A K Clarke)*; [80 Victoria St] *Kings Head*: Lovely, unspoilt but well kept Victorian pub with warm atmosphere, well kept Courage ales, good lunchtime food, no juke box; the 'tramcar' is a small private snug in the main pub *(Mike Walters)*; [Hotwells Rd] *Mardyke*: Has an odd charm with interesting furniture, games, young and friendly staff; popular with motor-cycling fraternity *(Dr and Mrs A K Clarke)*; [St Georges Rd] *Myrtle Tree*: Small friendly pub with ss *Great Britain* just across water; well kept Bass and Wadworths 6X, lunchtime food *(Patrick Godfrey)*; [17–18 King St] *Naval Volunteer*: Simple but with considerable character *(Dr and Mrs A K Clarke)*; [King St] *Old Duke*: Duke Ellington inn-sign sets the tone – superb live trad jazz free every evening and Sun lunchtime, landlord sometimes joining in on trumpet; decent value food, reasonably priced Courage, warm atmosphere *(B R Woolmington, Barry and Anne)*; [Lower Guinea St] *Ostrich*: Very popular – and in summer busy – pub alongside docks, with waterside seats; well kept Courage *(B R Woolmington, BB)*; [Station Rd, Fishponds; ST6376] *Pecketts Flyer*: Halls pub with well kept Wadworths 6X and Smiles Best, good food, unobtrusive juke box, four pool-tables in separate section, lovely garden with children's play area *(Barry Shapley)*; [up very narrow steep rd off to left at top of Whiteladies Rd] *Port of Call*: Good pub with

good value bar food *(David Pearman)*; [Broad Plain, Old Market; nr *Evening Post* building] *Printers Devil*: Very friendly open-plan pub with good Courage ales and decent home cooking lunchtime and evening; popular with nearby office workers *(Mike Walters)*; [Merchants Rd] *Pump House*: Smartly converted imposing dockside building, charcoal-grey brickwork, grey tiles, high ceilings, real ales inc well kept Bass on handpump, decent wines; popular at lunchtime for bar food; waterside tables *(Gwen and Peter Andrews, LYM)*; [Prince St] *Shakespeare*: Lovely Georgian building backing on to floating harbour; varied, good value lunchtime bar food; can get busy lunchtime and early evening *(Barry and Anne)*; [Park Row] *Ship*: Consistently good pub with ten changing real ales such as Bass, Badger Tanglefoot, Boddingtons, Smiles Exhibition (it's a short walk from their brewery) and Wadworths 6X; lunchtime bar food from filled rolls or ploughman's to gammon; main bar upstairs with pine tables and chairs; juke box, downstairs pool-table *(Steve and Carolyn Harvey)*; [Princess Victoria St; Clifton] *Somerset Arms*: Well kept Watneys-related real ales, good food in separate bar, daily newspapers, no juke box; open all day *(Patrick Godfrey)*; [539 Fishponds Rd; ST6276] *Star*: Friendly roadside local with good décor and well kept beer *(Dr and Mrs A K Clarke)*; [off Whiteladies Rd, next to Clifton Down rly stn; ST5674] *Steam Tavern*: Appealingly remodelled pub in cobbled street; former rly station now has boats on roof and half a car through wall, but pleasant relaxed atmosphere, wide range of beers, Mexican food *(P Miller, Mark Spurlock)*
Broomfield, Somerset [ST2231], *Travellers Rest*: Attractive interior, wide range of fresh, well served bar food, garden tables *(Shirley Pielou)*
☆ **Bruton**, Somerset [High St; ST6834], *Castle*: Good solid food value – particularly inc well presented Indian food with proper side dishes, changing selection of well kept real ales, skittle alley with striking mural of part of town, tables in sheltered back garden; welcoming, with courteous service, but can get very full; children in eating area and skittle alley *(H F H Barclay, S V Bishop, LYM)*
Carhampton, Somerset [ST0042], *Butchers Arms*: Real ale and good food that includes children's menu; particularly elaborately equipped play area with two-storey house, helter-skelter, castle and so forth; children welcome *(Anon)*
Castle Cary, Somerset [South St; ST6332], *Countryman*: Good pub with Oakhill Farmers and bar food (slightly pricey) *(K Baxter)*; [Fore St] *White Hart*: Town-centre pub with well kept Courage, bar food, good family facilities *(Dr and Mrs A K Clarke)*
Charlton Adam, Somerset [just off A37

about 3 miles N of Ilchester; ST5328], *Fox & Hounds*: Freshly cooked and reasonably priced good food running up to sole stuffed with crabmeat or hefty mixed grill, also children's menu – and milk shakes *(Mrs P C Clark)*

Charlton Musgrove, Somerset [ST7229], *Smithy*: Smiling welcome and truly home-made food at very reasonable prices, with small restaurant behind bar; log fire, skittle alley *(Major and Mrs J V Rees, Nigel Paine; more reports on the new owners please)*

Chew Magna, Avon [back rd between Chew Magna and A358; ST5763], *Pony & Trap*: Delightfully rural spot with attractively decorated interior, warm, cosy atmosphere and cheerful customers *(Tom Evans)*

Chipping Sodbury, Avon [ST7282], *Dog*: One long bar with alcoves, Flowers Original and IPA, and guest beer such as Marstons Pedigree; it's the generously served food that really makes it *(BKA)*

Churchill, Avon [ST4560], *Stag & Hounds*: Enlarged and refurbished pub with large wooden stag in entrance, other interesting items on walls, efficient friendly staff, good food *(M W Barratt)*

Coalpit Heath, Avon [Causeway; ST6881], *Horseshoe*: Dimly lit split-level pub with friendly locals and well kept beer and cider *(Dr and Mrs A K Clarke)*; [Henfield Rd] *Ring o' Bells*: Refurbished local with friendly atmosphere and well kept beer *(Dr and Mrs A K Clarke)*

Cold Ashton, Avon [A420 Bristol–Chippenham ½ mile from A46 junction; ST7572], *White Hart*: Large, happy and very popular pub with crowds of tables, pleasant staff, well kept Ushers tapped from the cask, wide choice of bar food inc particularly good ploughman's (a shame about the way they call your number over the piped music); tables on lawn with swings; on Cotswold Way *(Mr and Mrs N Christopher, Theo Schofield)*

Combe Florey, Somerset [off A358 Taunton–Williton, just N of main village turn-off; ST1531], *Farmers Arms*: Neatly restored after 1985 thatch fire, with nice atmosphere, good winter log fire, picturesque beams, well kept Bass, good food served by dressed-up waitresses, and plenty of tables outside; enthusiastic local following *(B S Bourne, Mr and Mrs P W Dryland, BB)*

☆ **Combwich**, Somerset [ST2542], *Old Ship*: Attractive pub with welcoming and helpful newish landlord, wide choice of decent bar food *(Mr and Mrs J Talbot, Keith Walton, P and E Parkinson)*

☆ **Compton Martin**, Avon [A368; ST5457], *Ring o' Bells*: Well kept real ales such as Butcombe, Fullers London Pride, Marstons Pedigree and Wadworths 6X, good value bar food; snug traditional area with inglenook fire, rugs and flagstones, opening into extensive carpeted part with lots of tables;

cigarette card collection in public bar with darts, table skittles and fruit machine, family-room, good-sized garden with fruit trees, swings, climber and slide *(Tom Evans, Mark Spurlock, BB)*

☆ **Creech Heathfield**, Somerset [nr M5 junction 25; ST2827], *Crown*: Small seventeenth-century thatched pub with pleasant atmosphere, log fire and strong local following; wide range of bar food inc popular steaks and home-made specials changed twice daily, generous helpings, pleasantly served; well kept Watneys-related real ales *(Mrs Shirley Pielou, Richard Dolphin)*

Culbone Hill, Somerset [A39 W of Porlock; SS8247], *Culbone Stables*: One of the highest points on Exmoor; comfortable free house with well designed interior, pleasant atmosphere and good service; Bass on handpump, good bar food; children welcome; bedrooms good *(E G Parish)*

☆ **Ditcheat**, Somerset [village signposted off A37 and A371 S of Shepton Mallet; ST6236], *Manor House*: Most attractive frontage – and great views on the way down from Pye Hill on A37; particularly welcoming relaxed atmosphere in neat and simple communicating rooms, flagstones in public bar, unusual arched doorways, close-set tables, good attractively priced bar food; well kept Butcombe on handpump, open fires if cold; skittle alley, white rabbits by tables on back grass *(Col David Smiley, R C Blatch, BB)*

☆ **Doynton**, Avon [High St; ST7173], *Cross House*: Particularly pretty ivy-clad pub in idyllic village; good beer, pleasant bar lunches, olde-worlde charm *(Robert Freidus, Gill Avis)*

Dulverton, Somerset [SS9127], *Caernarvon Arms*: Friendly Butters Bar notable not for décor or layout but for good wines, imaginative bar food fairly priced and good service *(J S Evans)*

Dundry, Avon [Church Rd; ST5567], *Dundry*: Busy, recently redecorated village pub on hilltop overlooking Bristol; good food (esp what they call oggies), well kept Courage Best and Directors, big pleasant garden; children welcome *(Peter Adcock)*

Dunkerton, Avon [ST7059], *Prince of Wales*: One large room with eating area partitioned off, predominantly red décor, padded seats, piped music, Wadworths 6X on handpump and food such as good cold turkey and ham pie; atmosphere not such a strong point *(Roger Huggins)*

East Harptree, Somerset [ST5655], *Waldegrave Arms*: Two bars tastefully separating the young and noisy from their more sedate elders; pleasantly welcoming service, good food at bar and in dining-room *(J L Cox, Peter L Astbury)*

Easton in Gordano, Avon [Martcombe Rd; A369 about ½ mile from M5 junction 19; ST5276], *Rudgleigh Arms*: Especially nice in summer when there is weekend and evening cricket on the adjoining field – you can sit outside and watch; short choice of reasonably priced, really good food, well kept Courage beers; can be very busy at lunchtime *(Tom Evans, Paul and Joanna Pearson)*

Edington Burtle, Somerset [ST3943], *Olde Burtle*: Partly sixteenth-century pub with well kept beers inc Exmoor, good food in bar and restaurant, friendly landlord *(S J Edwards)*

Enmore, Somerset [ST2434], *Tynte Arms*: Free house with low beams and open fires, and pleasant dining areas; good range of well kept beers inc Flowers and Whitbreads, reasonably priced bar food, friendly service; restored well in car park wall *(B M Eldridge)*

☆ **Evercreech**, Somerset [A371 Shepton Mallet–Castle Cary; ST6438], *Pecking Mill*: Low-ceilinged stone-walled pub with ornate solid-fuel stove, long-barrelled rifles and harness on walls giving rustic atmosphere, comfortable furnishings, well kept real ales, good value bar food (not always in evening if restaurant busy), friendly staff; seats outside, live music Thurs *(John and Joan Nash, Ted George, BB)*

Evercreech [Evercreech Junction], *Natterjack*: Large well decorated roadside free house with good atmosphere, Butcombe Bitter, generous helpings of quickly served good bar food inc children's menu, separate dining area, garden *(Mrs Carol Mason, R C Blatch)*

☆ **Exebridge**, Somerset [SS9224], *Anchor*: Well furnished, clean, comfortable and friendly, with good food and attractive riverside garden; cheerful rather than speedy service; bedrooms pleasant *(CS, S Punchard)*

☆ **Exford**, Somerset [SS8538], *Crown*: Comfortable and traditional old pub in peaceful village, well kept ales, log fire, good bar food, friendly service, attractive garden with stream running through *(Wayne Brindle, P J Hanson, Alan Carr, T J Maddison, Sarah Vickers)*

Farleigh Hungerford, Somerset [ST8057], *Hungerford Arms*: Single long bar, separate dining area with splendid views over adjacent ruins of fourteenth-century castle; well kept Ushers, good bar food; children allowed in dining area *(Keith Walton)*

Frampton Cotterell, Avon [Ryecroft Rd; ST6683], *Rising Sun*: Wide range of well kept beers, friendly atmosphere *(Dr and Mrs A K Clarke)*

☆ **Freshford**, Somerset [OS Sheet 172 reference 790600; ST7859], *Inn at Freshford*: Comfortably modernised carpeted bar with obliging licensees, pleasant staff, good range of simple but good bar food in big helpings, well kept Watneys-related real ales, separate dining-room and pool-room in picturesque three-storey stone building; lots of pictures and plates, stone serving-counter with

built-in old bread oven – also milk-maid's yoke, coach-lamps, traps and so forth; picnic-table sets on secluded sloping back lawn with shrubs; quiet countryside by old stone bridge over the Avon, footpath walks *(Peter and Rose Flower, Frank Cummins, B R Woolmington, BB)*

☆ **Glastonbury**, Somerset [High St; ST5039], *George & Pilgrims*: Rambling medieval building with magnificently restored carved stone frontage, pleasant front bar with big open fire and fifteenth-century traceried bay window; bar food inc good sandwiches, clams and hash browns also recommended, consistently well kept Bass, children in restaurant and buffet; a shame that not all staff win plaudits from readers; bedrooms *(Mea Horler, Richard Dolphin, Joy Heatherley, Helena and Arthur Harbottle, W and S Rinaldi-Butcher, LYM)*

Glastonbury [27 Benedict St], *Mitre*: Jolly landlord running a proper pub (though lounge does not exactly throb with atmosphere), with good food inc specials like boiled ham with raisin sauce or lamb Benedict *(Barry and Anne)*

Green Ore, Somerset [A39 N of Wells; ST5750], *Plough Boy*: Smartly decorated pub, Courage beer, lunchtime and evening bar food (inc Sun), garden *(Mrs Carol Mason)*

Hardington Mandeville, Somerset [ST5111], *Mandeville Arms*: Local beer (used to be brewed on the premises) and bar food in friendly comfortable country pub *(LYM)*

Hardway, Somerset [off B3081 Bruton–Wincanton at Redlynch; pub named on OS Sheet 183 reference 721342; ST7134], *Bull*: Pleasant, remote inn with good choice of well kept beers, interesting chipless food in character dining-room, nice atmosphere, friendly landlord; handy for Stourhead Garden *(John and Joan Nash)*

Haselbury Plucknett, Somerset [A30 2 miles E of Crewkerne; ST4711], *Bent Tree*: Small, elegant, olde-worlde bar with good bar food; smart restaurant *(Norman Battle)*

Hatch Beauchamp, Somerset [ST3220], *Hatch*: Lots of copper and brass in carpeted lounge bar with pleasant bow-window seats; Bass, choice of ciders, pool-room behind yard *(BB)*

☆ **Hillesley**, Avon [ST7689], *Fleece*: Friendly pub in small Cotswolds village with decent food, well kept Whitbreads-related real ales, decent wines and interesting collection of malt whiskies; basic old-fashioned bar, busy lounge; beautiful surrounding countryside, close to Cotswold Way; bedrooms *(R G Cadman, Peter and Rose Flower)*

Hillfarance, Somerset [ST1624], *Anchor*: Popular local with good home-made bar food, willing friendly service and good range of beers *(John Tyzack)*

☆ **Hinton Blewett**, Avon [village signposted off A37 in Clutton; ST5957], *Ring o' Bells*: Simple country atmosphere in low-beamed stone-built village local with good value home cooking (not Sun evening), well kept Wadworths Devizes and 6X on handpump, pleasant view from tables in sheltered front yard; children welcome (*LYM*)

☆ **Hinton Charterhouse**, Avon [B3110; ST7758], *Stag*: Attractively furnished ancient pub with good range of well kept real ales such as Bass, Flowers Original and Ruddles County, log fire, often enterprising freshly cooked food at a price but usually worth it, in bar and restaurant; tables outside, children allowed in eating area; service not always as obliging as most readers have found it; bedrooms quiet and good value (*M A and W R Proctor, Steve Dark, Roger Huggins, Ted George, S J A Velate, Mr and Mrs G J Lewis, LYM – more reports please*)

Hinton Charterhouse, *Rose & Crown*: Good choice of well presented food, friendly atmosphere, log fire, range of well kept real ales (*John Davies*)

☆ **Hinton St George**, Somerset [ST4212], *Poulett Arms*: Olde-worlde local in charming village, which seems to be settling down under new owners, after succession of tenants; comfortable bar, friendly service and good value homely food running up to steaks; Watneys-related real ales, tables in garden (*Fiona Easeman, the Barrett family, Mrs Crease, AE*)

Holford, Somerset [A39; ST1541], *Plough*: Sixteenth-century pub with friendly locals, real ales, good bar food with charcoal specials in evening; what used to be the cold table now seems to be a pool-table; at start of GWG33 (*E G Parish*)

Holton, Somerset [ST6827], *Old*: Lots of key rings on beams and fire, flagstones, well kept real ales (*Dr and Mrs A K Clarke*)

☆ **Holywell Lake**, Somerset [off A38; ST1020], *Holywell*: Village pub with pleasant young licensees, above-average décor, very welcoming atmosphere, log fire, good value cold buffet with splendid spread of imaginative salads, sandwiches, interesting changing hot dishes such as rabbit pie, trout with garlic and honey, turkey risotto; magnificent evening menu in small dining-room; tables in peaceful garden (*Shirley Pielou*)

Horfield, Avon [Wellington Hill West; off A38 Gloucester Rd; ST5978], *Wellington*: Spacious, clean 1920s pub with comfortable bars and freshly cooked food from varied menu (*K R Harris*)

Horsington, Somerset [village signposted off A357 S of Wincanton; ST7023], *Half Moon*: Knocked-through beamed bars with neat tables, good log fires in big stone fireplaces, well kept Butcombe, Exmoor and Wadworths 6X on handpump, above-average house wines, friendly service (and dog); bar food (not perhaps the special feature that it used to be), weekend carvery and summer cold buffet; tables outside, inc

big back garden with good play area; has been open all day summer hols; restaurant; children welcome; bedrooms – most in recently converted ancient stableblock (*LYM*)

Horton Cross, Somerset [A303 W of Ilminster; ST3315], *Lamb*: Attractive one-bar pub with friendly staff and generously served appetising home-made food – wise to book; pretty hanging baskets (*Sue Hallam*)

☆ **Howley**, Somerset [ST2609], *Howley Tavern*: Pleasant pub, off the beaten track, praised by many loyal regulars for warm welcome, imaginative attractively presented bar food and well kept real ale and wines; restaurant (*Anon*)

Huish Champflower, Somerset [ST0429], *Castle*: Friendly village pub with Exmoor real ale, good value simple food, quiet country garden; children welcome (*LYM*)

Iron Acton, Avon [ST6884], *White Hart*: Good reputation for food cooked tandoori-style in a wood-burning clay oven, also excellent Stilton ploughman's; has changed little over past few years (*Barry and Anne*)

Keinton Mandeville, Somerset [off A37; ST5430], *Quarry*: Old quarrymaster's house with big clean and tidy front bar, back games-room, skittle alley and attractive restaurant; well kept reasonably priced Wadworths 6X and Oakhill Farmers, good value food (*Ted George*)

☆ **Kelston**, Avon [A431 Bristol rd, 4 miles from Bath centre; ST7067], *Crown*: Cosy, candle-lit, rustic free house, marvellously unspoilt, with low-beamed ceilings, flagstone floors, fresh flowers, coal fires; well kept Bass, Butcombe, Marstons Pedigree, Smiles and Wadworths 6X and winter Old Timer, good value bar food inc splendidly filled long brown rolls, also restaurant; back garden with occasional summer barbecues; dogs welcome, but beware of yuppies (*Carol Mason, J S Rutter*)

Keynsham, Avon [Bitton Rd; ST6568], *Lock Keeper*: Worth knowing for the big riverside garden, with weir, lock and marina; Courage Best and Youngers Scotch on handpump (*Tom Evans*)

Kingswood, Avon [Hill St; ST6473], *Highwayman*: Very friendly, updated early Victorian pub with reasonable food, good beer and gardens (*Dr and Mrs A K Clarke*)

☆ **Knapp**, Somerset [ST2925], *Rising Sun*: Recently reopened after major refurbishment, stripping back to beams and stonework; current owners have a fine track record as restaurateurs, and there's a wide choice of good home-made food in what's now rather a dining-room environment (attractively so), with Bass and Exmoor real ales; has been closed Mon and Tues lunchtimes (*Andrew and Michele Wells*)

Leigh on Mendip, Somerset [ST6847], *Bell*: Friendly helpful landlord, good if not cheap food such as garlic prawns and grilled kidneys (*Anon*)

Limington, Somerset [ST5322], *Lamb & Lark*: Pleasant, unpretentious village pub with homely atmosphere, caged parrot on bar, well kept Ind Coope Burton and good, simple bar food *(M K C Wills)*

☆ **Littleton upon Severn**, Avon [ST5990], *White Hart*: Interesting building in isolated village with good choice of well kept ales inc Smiles served from hatch, good busy atmosphere (esp on Weds evening when there's live jazz), generous helpings of good food, various games inc table football, genial bar staff; garden *(Jon Wainwright, A J Ritson, G and L Owen)*

Litton, Somerset [off A39 Bath–Wells; ST5954], *Olde Kings Arms*: Attractive fifteenth-century pub with olde-worlde décor and furnishings and two large open fires; well kept Butcombe, Wadworths 6X and another ale tapped from the cask, generous helpings of attractive food *(Alastair Campbell)*

Long Sutton, Somerset [A372 E of Langport; ST4625], *Lime Kiln*: Friendly pub with enormous chimney and log fire, horse tackle on walls, good bar food, skittle alley, restaurant *(Theo and Jean Rowland-Entwistle)*

Lopen, Somerset [Lopen Head; ST4214], *Poulett Arms*: Spotless, with quick friendly service, big helpings of good value food, well kept Bass and guest beers; busy weekends *(Anon)*

Lydford on Fosse, Somerset [A37/B3153; ST5531], *Cross Keys*: Excellent freshly cooked food with lovely new bread; spotless lavatories *(John and Pat Smyth)*

Mark, Somerset [ST3747], *White Horse*: Very popular old-world pub dating back to seventeenth century, with roomy attractive bars, wide choice of home-cooked food, well kept beer, good friendly service *(C F Stephens, A M Kelly)*

Marshfield, Avon [ST7773], *Lord Nelson*: Good atmosphere in pleasantly refurbished village pub with beams, open fires, well kept real ales, locals' games bar, ex-stables restaurant *(H K Dyson)*

Mayshill, Avon [A432 Coalpit Heath–Yate; ST6882], *New*: Attractive stone building, friendly and welcoming staff, unusual range of home-cooked bar food *(K R Harris)*

Mells, Somerset [ST7249], *Talbot*: Good country pub with well kept Bass, Boddingtons, Marstons Pedigree and Theakstons, cheap good bar food *(Ted George)*

☆ **Midford**, Avon [ST7560], *Hope & Anchor*: Open-plan L-shaped bar, comfortably furnished, in friendly and welcoming local with wide range of good beers, excellent value food in restaurant area (esp Sun lunch – booking advised), quick pleasant service; passage under road to derelict canal, also good walks along disused railway line through beautiful countryside *(Gordon Lane, S J A Velate, Wilfred Plater-Shellard)*

Milborne Port, Somerset [A30 E of Sherborne; ST6718], *Queens Head*: Simple country furnishings in beamed lounge, games in public bar, good choice of well kept real ales and farm ciders, skittle alley, tables in sheltered courtyard and garden with unusual playthings; bar food's always been popular here, and the new licensees who took over in 1989 are planning some concentration on this side; children welcome (except in bars); bedrooms *(LYM – reports on the new regime please)*

Minehead, Somerset [Blue Anchor Bay; ST0145], *Blue Anchor*: Well run split-level hotel bars with warm, friendly atmosphere, popular for wide choice of good food inc fresh hake, trout, steaks and mainly home-made puddings; smoothly painted beams, fruit machines, piped music; bedrooms clean, pretty and comfortable *(Mr and Mrs J Wright, Keith Houlgate)*

☆ **Monkton Combe**, Avon [ST7762], *Wheelwrights Arms*: Friendly and attractively laid out bar with lots of things on walls, attractive collection of chamber-pots, two baskets of reading materials (proceeds to charity), benches against stripped stone walls in front part with big open fire, more formal eating area, tiny darts-room at end, fruit machine, quiet piped music; Adnams, Flowers IPA and Original, impressive choice of bar food inc particularly good beef and smoked salmon sandwiches, and quite elaborate evening dishes; lovely surrounding countryside; bedrooms comfortable and well furnished, though not cheap, across narrow car-park lane *(Peter and Rose Flower, S J A Velate, Mrs M Finch, G C C Bartlett, H K Dyson, LYM)*

Nailsea, Avon [West End; ST4670], *Blue Flame*: Small free house with Bass tapped from the cask, farm cider, bar snacks, open fires, pub games, childrens' room, big garden *(Anon)*

☆ **Nether Stowey**, Somerset [Keenthorne – A39 E of village; not to be confused with Apple Tree Cottage; ST1939], *Cottage*: Big helpings of good value simple bar food, well kept Youngers Scotch on handpump (not that common around here), friendly service; comfortable dining-lounge with wood-burning stove, aquarium, interesting pictures; games-room with two pool-tables, juke box and machines (children allowed here); skittle alley, tables on terrace *(The Barrett family, Mrs Crease, LYM)*

North Cadbury, Somerset [ST6327], *Catash*: Warm and welcoming, real fires, hot fresh food which changes daily, Eldridge Pope Royal Oak on handpump; two bedrooms *(P H S Wettern)*

North Curry, Somerset [ST3225], *Rising Sun*: Very nice cosy pub with well kept beer and good Sun roasts *(G F Scott)*

North Petherton, Somerset [High St; nr M5 junction 24; ST2932], *Walnut Tree*: A hotel rather than a pub, but it has well kept

Wadworths – as well as welcoming and attentive staff, good value food, and beautiful comfortable bedrooms with walnut furniture (G Turner)

North Wootton, Somerset [ST5641], *Crossways*: Fairly large pub with good bar food, restaurant; bedrooms (Alan and Ruth Woodhouse)

Norton Fitzwarren, Somerset [ST1925], *Cross Keys*: Popular, with good service and well cooked good value food (John Tyzack); *Victory*: Nicely decorated free house with good beer (John Tyzack)

☆ **Nunney**, Somerset [11 Church St; village signposted off A361 Shepton Mallet–Frome; ST7345], *George*: Extensive rambling and much modernised open-plan pub with stripped stone walls, log fire, well kept Bass, Bunces Best and Benchmark and Butcombe on handpump, decent wines and good choice of other drinks, generous helpings of good value bar food, afternoon teas; rare 'gallows' sign spanning road, in interesting and attractive village with stream and ruined castle; bedrooms quiet, clean and well equipped (John Baker, Joy Heatherley, BB)

☆ **Old Sodbury**, Avon [Badminton Rd; ST7581], *Dog*: Very popular old pink building, carefully refurbished to keep stone and plasterwork and warm, attractive atmosphere; well kept Flowers Original and Marstons Pedigree, wide range of good bar food inc chicken Mexicano, well filled hot beef sandwiches and lots of fish and seafood; friendly efficient service; juke box can make itself heard; children 's room by bar with big log fire; on Cotswold Way; bedrooms (Peter Griffiths, John and Norma Loweth, Mr and Mrs N Christopher)

Old Sodbury, Avon [junction of A46 with A432; 1½ miles from M4 junction 18], *Cross Hands*: Comfortably done-up spacious inn with real ales, two restaurants; bedrooms (LYM)

Oldbury on Severn, Avon [ST6292], *Ship*: Friendly Turkey-carpeted long bar with two open fires, well kept Courage ales, bar food, piped music, skittle alley, children's play area (BB)

Olveston, Avon [ST6088], *White Hart*: Sandwiches, ploughman's and other food in carefully modernised and cleanly kept old pub with stripped stonework, beams, skittle alley (BB)

Panborough, Somerset [B3139 Wedmore–Wells; ST4745], *Panborough*: Good village pub, friendly, clean and comfortable with good food (K R Harris)

Paulton, Avon [Bath Rd; ST6556], *Somerset*: Small and attractively rustic pub with L-shaped bar, two open fires; well kept Courage, good fresh home-cooked lunchtime and evening bar food inc their own soda bread, big pleasant back garden, smaller one in front; wonderful view over Cam Valley (James Duthie, Mike Walters)

Pennsylvania, Avon [4 miles from M4 junction 18 – A46 towards Bath; ST7373], *Swan*: Modernised, stone-built row of cottages stepped downhill in tiny village which has developed quite a link with its US namesake, with Pennsylvania state flag and car registration plates decorating bar, locals' outing to USA; good live music Tues (Peter and Rose Flower)

Porlock, Somerset [SS8846], *Castle*: Friendly welcoming pub, good atmosphere, well kept beer, good well served bar food; bedrooms (Don Mather)

☆ **Porlock Weir**, Somerset [SS8547], *Ship*: Little thatched inn nr peaceful harbour, atmospheric original Ship Bar behind, with stone floor, well kept real ales inc Exmoor; this may be closed on some weekday evening May–Sept, when you can make do with the more modern front Mariners Bar; bar food, pleasant outside seating; children's room; bedrooms creaky and comfortably characterful, though not cheap, in Ship itself – the pub's run in tandem with neighbouring Anchor Hotel, sharing its reception and usually its restaurant (D H and M C Watkinson, Steve Dark, WHBM, Wayne Brindle, LYM)

Portishead, Somerset [West Hill; ST4777], *Royal Oak*: Clean pub with good atmosphere in lounge; skittles, dominoes and jazz twice a week in bar; good value bar food (Gerald Gilling)

☆ **Priddy**, Somerset [off B3135; ST5251], *New Inn*: Good no-fuss low-cost food in busy fifteenth-century former farmhouse with lovely fireplace, low beams, horsebrasses and so forth; well kept Eldridge Pope Royal Oak and Wadworths 6X, good local cider, friendly service; bedrooms very comfortable and homely (Mr and Mrs H Gaydon, R D Norman)

Priddy, *Queen Victoria*: Good cosy family pub with big garden and family-room (Dr and Mrs A K Clarke, Chris Raisin, Graham Doyle)

nr **Priddy** [coming from Wells on A39 pass hill with TV mast on left, then next left – OS Sheet 183 reference 549502], *Hunters Lodge*: Very unassuming – even basic and rather bare – walkers' and potholers' inn with good range of well kept real ales such as Badger, Bass and Butcombe tapped from casks behind the bar, log fire, flagstones; simple bar food, tables in garden; bedrooms clean and adequate for their low price (Mr and Mrs J M Elden, P Miller, LYM)

Queen Camel, Somerset [ST5924], *Mildmay Arms*: Consistently good; piped music in public bar (Jack Taylor)

Roundham, Somerset [A30 Crewkerne–Chard; ST4209], *Travellers Rest*: Comfortable and cosy main-road pub, welcoming bar staff and good value home-cooked bar food inc unique choice of puddings (K R Harris)

Rudge, Somerset [just off A36; ST8251], *Full Moon:* Fairly basic, old-fashioned pub which time seems to have passed by *(Dr and Mrs A K Clarke)*

Rumwell, Somerset [A38 Taunton–Wellington, just past Stonegallows; ST1923], *Rumwell:* Barren area, but comfortable pub with old beams, lots of tables, lively atmosphere, has been popular for hot and cold bar food from sandwiches up; taken over by Whitbreads summer 1989–reports on new regime please *(Major and Mrs I McKillop)*

☆ **Seavington St Michael,** Somerset [signposted from E side of A303 Ilminster bypass; ST4015], *Volunteer:* Dates from 1500s, but much modernised and comfortable; wide choice of good value straightforward food using local ingredients, well kept Badger Best, good local Perrys cider, friendly service; more relaxing now that the Ilminster bypass has opened *(R F Warner, B H Pinsent, AE, WAG, the Barretts, Mrs Crease, BB)*

Seven Ash, Somerset [A358 Taunton–Watchet; ST1433], *Stags Head:* Wide choice of good value home-cooked food with especially delicious puddings *(Miss C Scott)*

nr **Shepton Mallet,** Somerset [right off A37 N just before A37/A367 fork – pub 1½ miles on left; ST6445], *Wagon & Horses:* Well run classy pub with good view over Mendips from olde-worlde entrance, interconnecting rooms, large upstairs bar and small restaurant; well kept Courage Directors and Best, bar food *(Ted George)*

Shepton Montague, Somerset [off A359; ST6731], *Montague:* Pleasant and friendly licensees, warm atmosphere, good home cooking *(W M Elliott)*

Simonsbath, Somerset [SS7739], *Exmoor Forest:* Exmoor inn with several bar rooms inc games-room, straightforward furnishings (perhaps due for some refurbishment), log fires, lots of whiskies, well kept Whitbreads PA and a beer brewed for the pub; basic bar food; nr start GWG30; bedrooms – nine miles of good trout fishing for residents *(Wayne Brindle, LYM)*

Somerton, Somerset [Church Sq; ST4828], *Globe:* Popular local, hospitable licensees, comfortable atmosphere, good value lunchtime bar food, well kept Bass, big garden with terrace, skittle alley *(J S Wilson, the Barretts, Mrs Crease, Mrs Carol Mason)*; [opp Barclays Bank] *Red Lion:* Much improved over last few years with enlarged main bar and good bar food such as tremendous spare ribs *(S V Bishop)*; [Church Sq] *White Hart:* Smart and fairly large village-centre pub built on site of Somerton Castle, clean and well run; well kept Courage Best and Directors, excellent value bar food inc children's helpings in two small eating-rooms and airy, spacious and well furnished family-room *(Mrs Carol Mason, Roger Huggins, Ted George, K R Harris)*

Sparkford, Somerset [A303; ST6026], *Sparkford:* Pleasant service, reasonably priced food, decent beer; busy in summer *(G C C Bartlett)*

Staplegrove, Somerset [ST2126], *Staplegrove:* Well renovated roadside pub with good beer and bar food *(David Gaunt)*

Stathe, Somerset [ST3729], *Black Smock:* Lively local, especially Sat night; well kept Butcombe *(Mark Spurlock)*

☆ **Stoke St Gregory,** Somerset [Woodhill; ST3527], *Rose & Crown:* Charming old free house with glass-topped well in bar, helpful staff, pleasant wines, big helpings of decent food, soft piped music; bedrooms *(Graham Tayar)*

Stoke St Mary, Somerset [W of A358 Chard–Taunton; ST2622], *Half Moon:* Very roomy and attractive village local, much restored, with good service and choice of well priced food, wide range of Whitbreads-related real ales *(Shirley Pielou, Richard Dolphin)*

Stratton on the Fosse, Somerset [A367 towards Radstock, at junction with B3139; ST6550], *White Post:* Very clean, comfortable and well furnished country pub with good home-cooked food and Ushers real ale *(K R Harris)*

Tatworth, Somerset [ST3206], *Old Station:* Decent pub with comfortable bar, real ale, good choice of reasonably priced food, big coal-effect gas fire *(Alastair Campbell)*; *Olde Poppe:* Interesting old pub, two bars, one long with antiques, saddle-back chairs and plenty of tables for eating; wide choice of beers and bar food at reasonable prices, garden with barbecue *(Mrs Crease, the Barretts)*

Taunton, Somerset [ST2224], *County:* Pleasant lounge in big, bustling THF hotel, very good for bar lunches or afternoon tea; attractive service, well kept Exmoor ale; good parking for centre – get a token to get out; bedrooms *(W and S Rinaldi-Butcher)*; [Magdalene St] *Masons Arms:* Good old-fashioned free house with genial licensee, no piped music; well kept Exmoor and guest beers, good bar food; bedrooms clean and reasonably priced *(The Wyatts)*; [Middleway, Wilton; across Vivary Park from centre] *Vivary Arms:* Good interesting range of lunchtime bar food from sandwiches up, with several fish dishes – may not come quickly *(Shirley Pielou)*

Tickenham, Avon [B3130 Clevedon–Nailsea; ST4571], *Star:* Spacious pub with modern pine furniture in light and airy lounge, wide choice of bar food – filled baked potatoes and pies recommended; piped music can be loud *(Tom Evans)*

Timsbury, Avon [North Rd; B3115; ST6658], *Seven Stars:* Cheerful and brightly lit village local with big wood-burning stove, cheap well kept Courage Best and Directors, well reproduced juke box, pub games *(LYM)*

☆ **Triscombe,** Somerset [signposted off A358

Crowcombe–Bagborough; ST1535], *Blue Ball*: Thatched cottagey pub on slopes of Quantocks, peaceful relaxed atmosphere, simple but extensive and unusual choice of good value food from sandwiches to steaks and including Dutch dishes (there may be a wait), well kept real ales, local cider, friendly licensee; old open fire and settles in spruced-up bar with timbered ceiling and piped music; hens, chickens and goslings may hope to share your food out on the lawn *(P Bacon, T H G Lewis, Mrs M G S Finch, Mrs Shirley Pielou, G A Gibbs, SC)*

☆ **Trudoxhill**, Somerset [ST7443], *White Hart*: Very friendly landlord and staff in pub with good generously served food, farm cider and wide, unusual range of fruit and flower wines; the landlord has also ensured that the former Bishops brewery keeps going, under its new Ash Vine name – and of course sells that beer *(Andy Mason)*

☆ **Upton**, Somerset [OS Sheet 181 reference 006293; SS9928], *Lowtrow Cross*: Warm welcome in lonely country inn with well kept Cotleigh Tawny, nice low-beamed bar with enormous inglenook, simple good value bar food, skittle alley, provision for children *(CS, LYM)*

Upton Cheyney, Avon [ST6969], *Upton*: Refurbished village pub overlooking Avon Valley, with somewhat ornate and plush Edwardian-style elegance; well kept Bass and Wadworths 6X, bar food inc tasty steak and kidney pie, restaurant *(Tom Evans)*

☆ **Upton Noble**, Somerset [ST7139], *Lamb*: Small, comfortable bar with well kept beer and excellent value bar food, Sun roasts; small restaurant with extensive views beyond big garden; closed Mon *(P K Jones, W M Pinder)*

Vobster, Somerset [Lower Vobster; ST7049], *Vobster*: Well kept sensibly priced Bass, Ushers and Wadworths and good food in bar and restaurant; friendly and enthusiastic staff, good walking area *(James B Duthie)*

Wadeford, Somerset [ST3010], *Haymaker*: Bar friendly and pleasant (though appearance hasn't been the pub's strong point), with cheerful staff, well kept local beer, improving reasonably priced bar food, separate pool and billiards room; a firm rein on bad language here *(John Tyzack)*

Walton, Somerset [ST4636], *Royal Oak*: Well appointed, clean small pub with open fire, good bar food from sandwiches up, well kept Courage ales on handpump *(Mr and Mrs Harry McCann)*

Waterrow, Somerset [A361 Wiveliscombe–Bampton; ST0425], *Rock*: Friendly pub in small village, with log fire, wide choice of bar food, restaurant *(Jonathan and Helen Palmer)*

☆ **Wedmore**, Somerset [ST4347], *George*: Traditional furnishings in stripped-stone bar of rambling coaching-inn with real ale, bar food, lively locals' bar, sheltered lawn; bedrooms *(LYM)*

Wellington, Somerset [High St; ST1320], *Kings Arms*: Locally very popular, with well kept Ushers, famously big helpings of good food; bedrooms really good value, considering their very low price *(Alastair and Alison Riley)*

Wells, Somerset [Market Pl; ST5545], *Crown*: Good atmosphere in pleasant old multi-level coaching-inn close to cathedral, magnificent fireplace behind bar; well kept Wadworths ales tapped from the cask, good variety of decent if somewhat pricey bar food (though cathedral concert-goers have been disconcerted to find no early-evening quick snacks available) *(Ted George, S V Bishop, Gwen and Peter Andrews)*; [St Thomas St] *Fountain*: Friendly and comfortable, with good value food pleasantly served – especially in restaurant, popular for Sun lunch *(Mr and Mrs J H Adam, E F P Metters, G G Calderwood)*; [High St] *Kings Head*: Tudor inn with pleasant, friendly atmosphere and generously served reasonably priced good food; Courage Best and Directors and John Smiths on handpump *(Alastair Campbell)*; [High St] *Star*: Well run and comfortable, with two bars – one area sensibly earmarked for no-smokers; good attractive food, friendly service *(S V Bishop)*

☆ **West Harptree**, Avon [B3114, out of village towards Chew Lake; ST5657], *Blue Bowl*: Popular and efficiently run dining pub with wide choice of good value meals inc massive range of puddings; lots of bookable tables in a row of communicating rooms, with attractive family-room around corner; well kept Courage Best and Directors and John Smiths on handpump, friendly ginger cat, tables out on terrace and safely fenced lawn, surrounded by fields; bedrooms good value, with excellent breakfasts *(G J Brown, J P Alderson, BB)*

West Hay, Avon [OS Sheet 172 reference 435425; ST4663], *Bird in Hand*: Welcoming, small country free house with well kept Exmoor and Fremlins, reasonable bar food *(M E Wellington)*

West Monkton, Somerset [ST2728], *Monkton*: Peaceful spot; recently improved reasonably priced range of bar food (you need a real appetite to tackle their doorstep-sandwiches) *(Shirley Pielou)*

☆ **West Pennard**, Somerset [A361 E of Glastonbury; ST5438], *Red Lion*: Three neat dining areas opening off small flagstoned and black-beamed core with log fire in big stone inglenook; wide choice of bar food, particularly good children's menu (there's another log fire in the stripped stone family area); Ash Vine (carrying the pub's name), Badger Tanglefoot and Butcombe on handpump, maybe piped radio; bedrooms comfortable and well equipped, in neatly converted side barn *(Ted George, ACMM, BB)*

West Pennard, *Apple Tree*: Well kept, clean and spacious, with good furnishings and décor; well kept Watneys-related real ales, wide choice of good value lunchtime bar food, two restaurants *(Ted George, John and Pat Smyth)*

Westerleigh, Avon [ST7079], *Olde Inn*: Good value food and decent beers in cosy lounge and bar *(Ceri Jarr)*

Weston in Gordano, Avon [B3124 Portishead–Clevedon; ST4474], *White Hart*: Attractive cream-washed village pub, cheerful and cosy, with good furniture (some very fine small settles); no-smoking restaurant area, family-room and garden with children's play area *(Tom Evans)*

Weston super Mare, Avon [seafront, N end; ST3261], *Claremont Vaults*: Fine extensive views of bay and Brean Down from friendly seafront pub, helpful staff, friendly atmosphere, decent bar food *(Brian Barefoot, M W Barratt)*; *Grove*: Nr seafront with several levels and bar areas, library alcove and spiral staircase to rooftop bar area; good choice of ales, attractive food and lots of plants *(John Holmes)*

Westonzoyland, Somerset [Main Rd; ST3534], *Sedgemoor*: Small, cosy pub, reputedly where the king's officers slept before Battle of Sedgemoor; good atmosphere, many interesting mementoes inc reproduction of Monmouth's declaration of his illegitimacy; Flowers IPA, good bar food inc several vegetarian dishes, pleasant friendly service *(John Cox)*

Whatley, Somerset [ST7347], *Sun*: Good beer and bar food, particularly filled baked potatoes and curries; big helpings *(Andy Mason)*

Whitchurch, Avon [Court Farm Rd; ST6167], *Baccy Jar*: Very fine example of an estate pub, with excellent lounge *(Dr and Mrs Tony Clarke)*

Wick, Avon [ST7072], *Rose & Crown*: Good value food, olde-worlde charm, attractive location *(Mrs Gill Avis)*

☆ **Widcombe**, Somerset [OS Sheet 193 reference 222160; ST2216], *Holman Clavel*: Comfortably modernised Whitbreads pub named after its massive holly chimney-beam, good bar food, helpful service, nice country atmosphere; handy for Blackdown Hills and Widcombe Bird Garden *(John Tyzack, BB)*

Williton, Somerset [A39; ST0740], *Foresters Arms*: Comfortable and clean, with good mix of customers, well kept beer, good value bar food, pleasant garden *(Wayne Brindle)*; [on outskirts – B3191 towards Watchet] *Masons Arms*: Thatched village pub with cheerful atmosphere, good value bar food, quick friendly service, restaurant *(Wayne Brindle)*

Winterbourne Down, Avon [Down Rd, Kendleshire; just off A432 Bristol–Yate,

towards Winterbourne; ST6679], *Golden Heart*: Refurbished local that's kept its inglenook fireplace and good friendly atmosphere; good food inc toasted sandwiches and Stilton ploughman's, good gardens front and back; children's room *(Barry and Anne, Dr and Mrs Tony Clarke)*

nr **Withypool**, Somerset [Sandyway; 4 miles SW of Withypool on North Molton road; SS7934], *Sportsman*: Small, remote pub very high on the moor, with one of the most extensive views in the south – it does draw lots of visitors at weekends and in holiday times *(Anon)*

☆ **Wookey**, Somerset [B3139; ST5245], *Burcott Inn*: Friendly, pleasant and popular country local with well kept Butcombe, Cotleigh and a guest beer on handpump, at reasonable prices; good choice of wine and bar food, friendly service, restaurant, walled garden *(Phil and Sally Gorton, A J Ritson)*

Wookey, *Ring o' Bells*: Small, pleasant country pub with beamed ceiling, wooden tables, open fireplace, friendly landlord, well kept Bass, Charrington IPA and a guest beer such as Miners Arms Own, decent wine by glass, juke box (can be noisy) and fruit machine; good home-made bar food from sandwiches up, friendly service, new small extra restaurant area *(Helena and Arthur Harbottle)*

Wookey Hole, Somerset [ST5347], *Wookey Hole*: Friendly pub, good value bar food, children welcome in separate dining-room and games machine room; bedrooms *(Keith Walton)*

Wootton Courtney, Somerset [SS9343], *Dunkery*: Doing well under present regime, now locally popular for good choice of local dishes inc fine mixed grill and Dunkery Munchies – crispy granary bread topped with toasted prawns and Stilton; good value bedrooms *(Harold and Naydene Snodgrass)*

Wrington, Avon [High St; 2½ miles off A370 Bristol–Weston, from bottom of Rhodiate Hill; ST4662], *Plough*: Friendly, rural atmosphere, wide choice of tasty home-made food, good service, well kept beer *(H S Harries, Sybil Baker)*

Yate, Avon [Wellington Rd; ST7283], *Farmhouse*: Recently refurbished in old-fashioned style, split-level, lots of brick and beams *(Dr and Mrs A K Clarke)*

Yatton, Avon [High St; ST4365], *Butchers Arms*: Unspoilt fairly basic pub with well kept Courage Best and welcoming atmosphere *(Dr and Mrs A K Clarke)*

Yeovil, Somerset [Wine St; ST5516], *Wine Vaults*: Neat and popular town pub with well kept Bass, friendly atmosphere, rather wine bar-like décor *(LYM)*

Staffordshire   *see* Derbyshire

Suffolk

Among the county's most attractive pubs for food, the Beehive at Horringer always seems to have something fresh and new; the Kings Head in Orford, taken over this year by the son and daughter-in-law of the previous landlady, has excellent sources of local supply for its fresh fish; at the prettily tucked-away Plough at Rede it's the daily specials that are the thing; the stylishly civilised Golden Key at Snape seems as reliable as ever; the Crown in Southwold has a fine line in imaginative and delicately presented snacks – and wines that can't be beaten in this part of the country; the Angel at Stoke by Nayland, a new entry this year, combines delicious individual cooking with most attractive and comfortable surroundings (but get there early for a table); and the Crown by the green at Westleton is another pub that scores for really fresh fish. These last three are all particularly nice to stay at. Other good places to stay at include the Bull at Barton Mills (opening all day under its new licensees – and serving food from noon right through to 10), the elegantly restored Tudor Peacock at Chelsworth, the pleasantly traditional Crown overlooking the market square in Framlingham, the Crown at Great Glemham, and the handsome old Bull in Long Melford (doing particularly well at the moment – back in these pages after an absence). One or two other new entries to note (or places restored to the main entries after a break) include the hidden-away Crown at Buxhall, the cheerful Bell at Cretingham (popular newish licensees), and the Ship at Levington (some of its popular food comes from its own smokery). The Pickerel at Ixworth, highly praised for

The Swan, Hoxne

its seafood in our last edition, closed for a while but has now reopened under new management; too soon for us to tell yet whether the food will approach the former very high standards. There are new licensees too at the Bell at Kersey (now letting bedrooms), the Kings Head at Laxfield (they are determined to keep it as unspoilt as ever), and the beautifully placed Ramsholt Arms at Ramsholt. Pubs still in the same hands which seem to be doing particularly well at the moment include the friendly Queens Head at Blyford, the welcoming Victoria at Earl Soham (brewing its own good beers), and the Plough at Hundon (lots of improvements this year). And a number of particularly promising Lucky Dip entries at the end of the chapter include the Ship at Blaxhall, Queens Head at Erwarton, White Horse at Kersey, Swan at Lavenham, Volunteer at Saxtead Green and Plough & Sail at Snape – and Southwold's always a fine hunting-ground for the itinerant pub-lover, especially as the Adnams beers brewed here seem at their very best close to home. Another of the county's main breweries, Tolly of Ipswich, has been closed by its new owner (the Brent Walker property company), with brewing transferred to their other plant, Camerons of Hartlepool.

BARTON MILLS TL7173 Map 5

Bull 🍺

Just off A11 Newmarket–Thetford

Through the old coach entry here is a pretty seventeenth-century coachyard with a pigeon loft above its neatly converted high-doored stables. To the right is the comfortably modernised rambling bar, with beams and joists showing through the plasterwork, old and more recent panelling, big fireplaces, various cosy alcoves – one with attractive antique sporting prints on a Delft shelf – gold plush button-back built-in wall banquettes, and matching stools and studded seats; it's partly candle-lit at night. Well kept Adnams and Charringtons IPA on handpump, with a good selection of decent wines – particularly whites; on Sundays they may set out cheese cubes, nuts and crisps. Bar food includes home-made soup (£1.25), French bread rolls heaped with beef or ham (from £1.25), prawn sandwiches (£1.75), ploughman's (£2.25), salads, daily specials (£2.95) and gammon (£3.95); the restaurant does fine seafood. Dominoes, cribbage, a trivia machine and piped music. *(Recommended by Ian Phillips; more reports please)*

Free house Licensees Mark and Terry Rumsey Real ale Meals and snacks (noon–10) Grill-room and restaurant Children welcome Open 11–11 all year Bedrooms tel Mildenhall (0638) 713230; £25B/£40B

BLYFORD TM4277 Map 5

Queens Head

B1123

Cheerfully convivial, with an obvious long-standing appeal to local people as well as the many more occasional visitors who have tracked it down, this thatched fifteenth-century village pub has good, home-made food and well kept beer. It's attractively furnished with some antique settles, pine and oak benches built into its cream walls, heavy wooden tables and stools, low oak beams, and a huge fireplace with good brickwork. There are lots of photographs on the walls showing the damage caused by a fire in May 1988 and of the consequent rebuilding work. Home-made bar food from a menu that changes daily includes soup (£1.40), stuffed mushrooms (£2.25), garlic prawns (£2.50), chilli con carne, good lasagne or sausage and leek pie (all £3.45), stir-fried cod in soya and ginger (£3.95), and steak and kidney pie (£4.50); interesting lunchtime salad bar in the summer, home-made puddings such as strawberry suet pudding (from £1.40) and Sunday roast lunch (£3.95). A full range of very well kept Adnams on handpump; interesting wines; dominoes and piped music. There are seats on the grass outside, and a small village church opposite. *(Recommended by R M Sparkes, David Milner, Pete Storey, Alison Hayward, Nick Dowson, Derek and Sylvia Stephenson)*

Adnams   Licensee Paul Honeker   Real ale   Meals and snacks (12–2, 7–10 Mon–Sat; 12–2, 7–9 Sun)   Children welcome   Open 11–2.30 (3 Sat), 6–11 all year

BLYTHBURGH   TM4575 Map 5

White Hart

A12

New licensees have taken over this ancient place, an inn since 1548 (serving the drovers bringing sheep to auction outside). It's open-plan, with log fires at each end, some lovely curved oak beams, a fine Stuart staircase, and Elizabethan woodwork; between the bar and dining-room there's a large circular open fire. Good home-made food includes soup (£1.20), filled baked potatoes (from £2.50), lasagne (£3.50), fresh local fish (from £3.95, fresh salmon and broccoli au gratin £4.25), and various pies such as chicken and mushroom (£3.95) and steak and kidney (£4.25). Well kept Adnams Bitter, Broadside and winter Old on handpump; decent wines; table skittles, dominoes and cribbage. If you want a table in summer, turn up early. The spacious lawn behind has a pétanque pitch. The church down the lane on the other side of the main road is one of East Anglia's grandest. *(Recommended by Geoff Halson, Klaus and Elizabeth Leist, M J Morgan, A W Lewis, Derek Stephenson, David and Jocelyn Smith)*

Adnams   Licensee John Karaiossifoglou   Real ale   Meals and snacks (not Sun evening in winter)   Restaurant tel Blythburgh (050 270) 217   Children in eating area and restaurant   Open 10.30–2.30, 6–11 all year

BRANDESTON   TM2460 Map 5

Queens Head

Towards Earl Soham

The big open-plan bar in this well run, friendly country pub has some panelling, brown leather banquettes and old pews, and is divided into separate bays by the stubs of surviving walls. A new back bar has been opened just for drinking. Bar food is home made and good value: sandwiches (from 90p), ploughman's (from £1.95), steak and kidney pie (£2.70), and lamb and courgette bake, quiche or fisherman's pie (£2.95). Well kept Adnams on handpump; helpful staff; fruit machine, faint piped music, and (in a separate family-room) pool and table skittles. There's a big garden with tables on neatly kept grass among large flower beds and a play tree, climbing-frame and slide. The inn has a caravan and camping club site at the back. You can visit the nearby cider farm. *(Recommended by Paul and Rhian Hacker; more reports please)*

Adnams   Licensee Ray Bumstead   Real ale   Meals and snacks   Children in family-room   Open 11–2.30, 5.30 (6 Sat)–11 all year   Bedrooms tel Earl Soham (072 882) 307; £13/£26

BUXHALL   TM0057 Map 5

Crown

Mill Green; Buxhall signposted off B1115 in Great Finborough, about 3 miles W of Stowmarket; then turn left at Rattlesden signpost

Tucked away near a windmill down a quiet country lane, this is a real insiders' pub. The low-beamed main bar, on the left, has cushioned oak-cask stools and library chairs around low tables snugged into the tight space between the fire and the counter; it wriggles on round to give rather more room, with stripped pews lining more regular-height tables, locally painted pictures and piped music. A short choice of good value food includes ploughman's or cottage pie with ale (both £1.50), lasagne (£1.80), beef curry (£2.60), home-cooked ham with salad (£3.40), and rabbit casserole (£3.20); well kept Adnams Broadside and Greene King IPA and (their best-selling beer) KK Mild on handpump, decent house wines, Cona coffee, bowls of fresh flowers. The big-windowed public bar has little pews around deal tables, with darts, fruit machine, cribbage and dominoes and another fire; picnic-table sets on the side grass, with a swing and a slide. *(Recommended by Kevin and Mary Shakespeare, John Baker, Simon Reynolds)*

Greene King   Licensees Ian and Modwena Cutler   Real ale   Meals and snacks (12–2, 7–10; not Mon evening or Sun)   Live music Thurs evenings   Open 12–2.30, 7–11 all year

nr CHELMONDISTON   TM2037 Map 5

Butt & Oyster

Pin Mill – signposted from B1456 SE of Ipswich

Named for the flounders and oysters which used to be caught here, this unspoilt pub has a small, half-panelled smoke-room with high-backed and other old-fashioned settles on the tiled floor, and is decorated with model sailing-ships; spare a glance for the most unusual carving of a man with a woman over the mantelpiece. Good bar food includes sandwiches (from 65p; not on Saturday or Sunday lunchtimes, when there's a buffet), ploughman's (from £1.80), a choice of salads, home-made pies and quiches, and changing home-made hot dishes such as plaice or chicken fillet (£3.25), steak and kidney pie (£3.50), and giant prawns in garlic butter (£5); Tolly Bitter, Original and Mild on handpump with Old Strong in winter tapped from the cask; darts, shove-ha'penny, table skittles, dominoes and cribbage. There's a fine view of the big ships coming down the river from Ipswich, and it's interesting to see the long lines of black sailing-barges moored outside. One of the best times to visit the pub would be on the first Saturday in July for the annual Thames Barge race. *(Recommended by RCL, Martin and Jane Bailey, P J and S E Robbins, Margaret and Trevor Errington, Rob and Gill Weeks)*

Tolly   Licensees Dick and Brenda Mainwaring   Real ale   Meals and snacks (12–2, 7–10)   Children in two separate rooms   Open 11–11; 12–3, 7–11 in winter; closed evenings 25 and 26 Dec

CHELSWORTH   TL9848 Map 5

Peacock ★ 🏠

The Street; B1115

A partly open timbered partition divides the large beamed bar in this elegantly restored fourteenth-century inn into several areas, and there's a splendid stone inglenook fireplace. The cosy inner lounge has some exposed Tudor brickwork and the walls are decorated with local paintings for sale (there is a craft shop behind the garden). Home-made bar food includes soup (£1.25), sandwiches (from £1.25), burger (£1.50), ploughman's (£2.50), a good cold buffet in summer with quiche, home-cooked beef and so forth, as well as daily specials such as home-made lasagne or steak and mushroom pie, and fish dishes such as seafood Mornay or prawn chow-mein; home-made puddings from Pavlova and cherry and almond pie to bread-and-butter pudding; they also do afternoon teas. Well kept Adnams, Greene King IPA and Abbot and Mauldons on handpump, and sometimes there are nibbles such as stuffed olives or nuts on the tables; country wines. Polite staff; cribbage and piped music, and maybe a friendly Jack Russell. The rich parkland of Chelsworth

---

Waterside pubs are listed at the back of the book.

Hall is just over the bridge. *(Recommended by Gwen and Peter Andrews, P Miller, I S Wilson, D J Amery, J S Evans, Miss E T A Bennett, Dr Aristos Markantonakis, MBW, JHW)*

Free house   Licensees Mrs L R Bulgin and A F Marsh   Real ale   Meals and snacks (12–2.30, 6.30–10.30)   Children in eating area   Jazz Fri evenings, pianist Sun evenings Open 11–3, 6–11 all year; closed 25 Dec   Bedrooms tel Bildeston (0449) 740758; £18/£35

CLARE   TL7645 Map 5

Bell

An attractive timbered small hotel in the market place. The rambling lounge bar has splendidly carved black beams, panelling and woodwork around the open fire, armchairs on the green carpet and local notices on the hessian walls. Another room leads off, and to eat you go through to the wine bar with masses of prints – mainly to do with canals – on its walls: food here includes soup (£1.25), ploughman's (from £1.90), home-made lasagne (£3.25) and steaks (from £5.95); toasted sandwiches in the comfortable lounge bar. Well kept Nethergate Bitter and Old Growler on handpump; various malt whiskies; quick service. Fruit machine and piped music. There are some tables on a back terrace by the small, sheltered lawn. Several other striking buildings in the village include the remains of the priory and the castle (which stands on prehistoric earthworks). *(Recommended by Mrs R Wilmot, Rob and Gill Weeks, W T Aird; more reports please)*

Free house   Licensees Brian and Gloria Miles   Real ale   Meals and snacks (12–2, 7–9; 10 Fri and Sat evenings)   Restaurant (not Sun evening)   Children in eating area of bar   Open 11–11 all year   Bedrooms tel Clare (0787) 277741; £29.95(£37.50B)/£45(£52.50B)

CRETINGHAM   TM2260 Map 5

Bell

Converted from fifteenth-century cottages some twenty years ago, this cheerful place has exposed beams, standing timbers of a knocked-through wall, a large old fireplace, and a wall tapestry in its comfortably modernised lounge bar. Well presented, good bar food includes tasty tomato soup (£1.15), garlic mushrooms (£1.65), chicken in wine (£1.75), ploughman's (£2.35), Suffolk sausages (£2.95), chicken and vegetable pie (£3.55), haddock pie (£3.95), king prawns (£7.45) and daily specials such as lasagne (£3.45); popular Sunday roast lunch (£6.95). Well kept Adnams and Greene King Abbot on handpump; piped jazz. The quarry-tiled public bar has darts, shove-ha'penny, dominoes and cribbage. There are rustic tables and seats on the grass in front, which is sheltered by the buff-washed tiled building, with more on another lawn by rose bushes, and a fine old oak tree on the corner. The local harriers meet here each New Year's Day. *(Recommended by Donald Rice, C H Stride)*

Free house   Licensees Ron Blackmore, Tim and James Yeo   Real ale   Meals and snacks Restaurant tel Earl Soham (072 882) 419   Children in eating area and restaurant Open 11.30–2.30, 6.30–11 all year

DUNWICH   TM4770 Map 5

Ship

In summer this friendly and busy old-fashioned inn looks at its best, with bunches of grapes on the vine in the conservatory, a well kept garden with an enormous fig tree, and a sunny back terrace. The main bar has cushioned wall benches, pews, captain's chairs, wooden tables with candles, a dusky ochre ceiling, tiled floor, and a wood-burning stove (cheerfully left open in cold weather); the relaxed and easy-going style of management suits quieter times best. Good bar food, all home made, includes lovely soup (70p), ploughman's or cottage pie (£2.50), lasagne (£2.60), vegetarian dishes or excellent fresh local fish (£3), with evening dishes such as garlic mushrooms or pâté (£1.75), scampi (£5.25), steaks (£6.25), and puddings like home-made ice-cream. Well kept Adnams Bitter and Broadside, and Greene King Abbot on handpump; James White farm cider (very strong) at the handsomely panelled bar counter. The public bar area has darts, dominoes, cribbage, fruit machine, space game and piped music. *(Recommended by RCL, Geoff Halson, David Pearman, Helen Crookston, Jason Caulkin, Klaus and Elizabeth Leist, P Leeson and friends, Mrs S Burrows-Smith, Ian and Joanna Chisholm, Heather Sharland, Peter Bush, K Howard, Andy Tye, Sue Hill, Alison Hayward, Nick Dowson, Barbara Hatfield, David and Jocelyn Smith, Mr and Mrs O'Gorman)*

Free house   Licensees Stephen and Ann Marshlain   Real ale   Snacks (lunchtime) and meals   Restaurant (not Sun lunchtime)   Children welcome (not in Ship bar)   Open 11–3, 6–11 (will stay open longer afternoons if there are customers); opens 7 in winter; closed evening 25 Dec   Bedrooms tel Westleton (072 873) 219; £16/£32, not Christmas/New Year

EARL SOHAM   SM2363 Map 5
Victoria ★
A1120 Stowmarket–Yoxford

Warmly friendly, this little country pub has very good home-brewed beer (they do a takeaway service too), and tasty home-made bar food. The beer includes a Bitter, a mild called Gannet, another called Victoria and a stronger ale called Albert (you can visit the brewery). Reasonably priced, the food includes sandwiches, home-made soup, ploughman's, delicious chilli con carne or vegetarian lasagne (£2.50), pork with apple and cider, and beef curry (£3.25). The furnishings are nicely chosen – kitchen chairs and pews, plank-topped trestle sewing-machine tables and other simple country tables with candles, tiled or board floors, open fires, stripped panelling, a piano and an interesting range of pictures of Queen Victoria and her reign. Darts, shove-ha'penny, dominoes and cribbage; seats out in front and on a raised back lawn. The pub is close to a wild fritillary meadow at Framlingham and a working windmill at Saxtead. *(Recommended by RCL, Geoff Halson, P Miller, John Baker, Nigel Gibbs, Mr and Mrs J H Wyatt, A V Chute, N A Wood, Nick Dowson, Rob and Gill Weeks, E B Warrington)*

Own brew   Licensees Clare and John Bjornson   Real ale   Meals and snacks   Children in back bar only   Impromptu folk music   Open 11.30–2.30 (3 Sat), 5.30–11 all year

EASTON   TM2858 Map 5
White Horse
N of Wickham Market, on back road to Earl Soham and Framlingham

Attractively presented food which changes daily is still the main draw to this well run, smallish village pub: soup (£1.35), ploughman's (from £2.45), melon and Parma ham (£2.50), burger (£3.45), plaice (£3.75), steak and kidney pie (£4), sweet-and-sour pork (£4.25), lasagne (£4.50), chicken satay (£4.75), moussaka (£4.95), haddock pasta or gammon (£5.95), salmon steak (£7.25), vegetarian dishes such as celery and cashew-nut risotto (£4.50) or creamy vegetable pasta (£4.95), as well as a good cold buffet (from £4.50); puddings like chocolate fudge cake, banana créole or passion cake (from £1.95). Well kept Tolly Mild, Bitter and Original on handpump; good wines. The two enlarged rooms of the bar have country kitchen chairs, good small settles, cushioned stripped pews and stools, and open fires; new games-room. The terrace has barbecue facilities and the garden has a well equipped children's play area. Easton Farm Park is worth visiting. *(Recommended by Jason Caulkin, F J Lopez, Alan and Ruth Woodhouse)*

Tolly   Licensee Keith Pointer   Real ale   Meals and snacks   Restaurant (closed Sun) tel Wickham Market (0728) 746456   Open 11–2.30, 6–11; opens 6.30 in winter

FRAMLINGHAM   TM2863 Map 5

Crown 🍺

Market Hill

The cosy bar in this busy, friendly little black and white Tudor inn is popular with locals: high heavy beams, one or two settles (including an antique carved one), dark green plush armed seats, and a log fire, though perhaps the best place to sit is at the old windows overlooking the unusual sloping triangular market place (market day is Saturday, when nearby parking may be difficult). The comfortable lounge has wing easy chairs beside the fire, and there are more seats in the hall. Bar food includes home-made soup, sandwiches, home-made quiche, ploughman's, pâté, shepherd's pie and cold meat salads or a daily special. Adnams and Ruddles on handpump; piped music. Coaches once clattered through what is now a prettily planted flagstoned courtyard (with a cheerful winter-flowering cherry).
(Recommended by Heather Sharland, Gwyneth and Salvo Spadaro-Dutturi, A G Tucker; more reports please)

Free house (THF)   Meals and snacks   Restaurant   Children in restaurant   Open 11–4, 6–11 all year   Bedrooms tel Framlingham (0728) 723521; £59B/£76B

FRAMSDEN   TM1959 Map 5

Dobermann

The Street; pub signposted off B1077 just S of its junction with A1120 Stowmarket–Earl Soham

Photographs of and show rosettes won by the owner's dogs decorate the white walls of this cheerfully run and spotlessly kept thatched pub. It's been charmingly restored, with very low, pale stripped beams, and a central fireplace that divides the rooms – its log fire open to both sides. On one there's a big sofa (a favourite with the tabby cat), a couple of chintz wing armchairs, and by the big window a refectory table. The other side has a mix of chairs, plush-seated stools and winged settles around scrubbed rustic tables. Bar food includes sandwiches (from 95p, maybe hot beef £1.75), basket meals such as scampi (£2.95), Stilton ploughman's (£3.50), gammon grill (£4.95), trout in wine and almonds and home-made chicken and mushroom or steak and kidney pie (£5.50), and a special such as turkey fricassee (£2.50). Well kept Adnams Bitter and Broadside, Greene King IPA, a beer brewed for the pub, and a guest beer such as Charles Wells Bombardier, all on handpump, with a decent choice of spirits and malt whiskies; shove-ha'penny, dominoes, cribbage, and maybe piped Radio 1. They play boules outside, where there are picnic-table sets by trees and a fairy-lit trellis, with summer barbecues.
(Recommended by John Baker, Nick Dowson, Donald Rice; more reports please)

Free house   Licensee Susan Frankland   Real ale   Meals and snacks   Open 11.30–2.30, 7–11 all year   Bedroom tel Helmingham (047 339) 461; £15/£20

GREAT GLEMHAM   TM3361 Map 5

Crown 🍺

This popular and well kept old brick house has an open-plan lounge with beams, one or two big casks, brass musical instruments, button-back wall banquettes and captain's chairs around stripped and waxed kitchen tables, and an enormous double fireplace with a black wood-burning stove on one side and logs blazing on the other; there are local paintings and drawings on the white walls. A side eating-room has flowers and pot plants. Good, reasonably priced bar food includes sandwiches or soup (75p), ploughman's with good fresh ingredients or smoked mackerel (£1.50), chilli con carne (£2), omelettes, Suffolk ham and egg or fisherman's platter (all £2.50), salads (from £2.50), and steaks (from £5.50). Well kept Adnams Bitter, Broadside and winter Old, Greene King IPA and Abbot, and guest beers from old brass handpumps; good choice of malt whiskies; darts, shove-ha'penny, fruit machine and piped music. There's a neat, flower-fringed lawn, raised above the corner of the quiet village lane by a retaining wall; seats out here. *(Recommended by Patrick Young, John Baker, Chris Fluck, Jenny and Brian Seller, C Williams, Peter Griffiths, W J Wonham)*

Free house   Licensees Roy and Eve Wood   Real ale   Meals and snacks (not Mon evening) Restaurant – not Sun evening   Children in eating area of bar and restaurant   Open 11–3, 7–11 Mon–Fri; 11–11 Sat all year; closed evening 25 Dec   Bedrooms tel Rendham (072 878) 693; £15/£30B

HORRINGER   TL8261 Map 5

Beehive 🏵

A143

The particular attraction here is the very good, often unusual food: sandwiches (from £1, fillet steak £4.25), home-made fresh lobster bisque or parsley soup (£1.20), ploughman's, parsley omelette or home-made taramosalata (£2.50), lovely gravadlax, scrambled eggs with smoked salmon or smoked venison (£3.95), fillet of pork in a cream and apple brandy sauce (£6.50) and specials such as hot buttered asparagus (£2.95), and grilled, fresh lobster (£11.95); good puddings. The cottagey rooms have some very low beams in some of the furthest and snuggest alcoves, stripped panelling or brickwork, picture-lights over lots of nineteenth-century prints, deep brown velvet curtains on brass rails, a shiny ragged ochre ceiling, and a couple of quiet dogs including an aloof borzoi. There are carefully chosen dining and country kitchen chairs, one or two wall settles around solid tables, and a wood-burning stove. Well kept Greene King IPA and Abbot on handpump; decent house wines; young, cheerful service; fruit machine. A most attractively planted back terrace has picnic-table sets, with more seats on a raised lawn. *(Recommended by John Baker, Nigel Paine, Frank Gadbois, W T Aird, Derek and Sylvia Stephenson)*

Greene King   Licensee Gary Kingshott   Real ale   Meals and snacks (not Sun evening) Table bookings tel Horringer (028 488) 260   Children in eating area Open 11–2.30, 7–11 all year

HOXNE   TM1777 Map 5

Swan   [illustrated on page 647]

This carefully restored herringbone brick and timbered, late fifteenth-century pub has recently been upgraded to a starred grade II as a building of architectural and historical interest. There are heavy oak floors, the ancient timber and mortar of the walls is visible, and the front bar has two solid oak bar counters, as well as a deep-set inglenook fireplace. A fire in the back bar divides the bar area and snug, and the dining-room has an original wooden fireplace. Good bar food includes burgers (from 85p), sandwiches (£1.30, good ham), ploughman's (from £1.75), plate of salamis with black olives (£3.25), scampi (£3.95), rump steak (£4.95) and daily specials such as courgette and fennel soup (£1.25), garlic mushrooms (£1.65), smoked haddock fishcakes (£3.75), lamb's liver or pork satay (£3.95); puddings range from Cotswold apple cake to butterscotch meringue pie (from £1.45). Well kept Adnams tapped from the cask and Greene King Abbot on handpump; wine list; darts, shove-ha'penny, dominoes, pool and a juke box. The extensive lawn behind the inn used to be a bowling-green and is now used for croquet – a nice place to sit in summer on the hand-made elm furniture, sheltered by a willow and other trees and its shrub-covered wall; if you are eating outside, rather than use a tannoy they press a buzzer and then prop up scoreboard-type numbers on the roof to indicate your ticket number. The pub is close to the site of King Edmund's

---

We say if we know a pub has piped music.

Martyrdom on 20 November 870. *(Recommended by Mr and Mrs E J Smith, Nick Dowson, Gavin May, Robert and Vicky Tod, Mrs C O'Callaghan)*

Free house   Licensees Tony and Frances Thornton-Jones   Real ale   Meals (not Mon, not Sun evening) and snacks (not Mon or Sun)   Restaurant (not Sun evening, Mon or Tues) tel Hoxne (037 975) 275/652   Children in eating area of bar   Open 12–2.30, 7–11 all year; closed 25 Dec

HUNDON   TL7348 Map 5

Plough

Brockley Green; on Kedington road, up hill from village

Changes here this year include a new, Suffolk pink, pantiled extension housing a proper restaurant area, a real functions room instead of the marquee that has been something of a fixture in summer, and bedrooms. The two rooms of the neatly kept and friendly carpeted bar have a double row of worn old oak timbers to mark what must have been the corridor between them, and there are low side settles with Liberty-print cushions, spindle-back chairs, and sturdy low tables; most walls are stripped back to bare brick and decorated with striking gladiatorial designs for Covent Garden by Leslie Hurry, who lived nearby. Good bar food includes sandwiches (from 90p), home-made soup (£1.10), ploughman's (from £2.25), devilled whitebait in paprika or pâté (£1.95), seafood platter (£3.50), mushroom and nut fettuccine or trout with almonds (£3.95), very good steak and kidney pie (£4.50), steak (£5.25) and daily specials; puddings (from £1.25) and children's dishes (£1.75). Well kept Greene King IPA, Nethergate and a delicious house beer brewed by Mauldons ('Furrowed Brew') on handpump; choice of wines; shove-ha'penny, dominoes, trivia and cheerful piped music. The garden is due to be relaid as a result of the building work and a new terrace is planned. It's also a certified location for the Caravan Club, with a sheltered site to the rear for tourers. *(Recommended by Gwyneth and Salvo Spadaro-Dutturi, Frank Gadbois, Melvin D Buckner, Kevin Blick)*

Free house   Licensee David Rowlinson   Real ale   Meals and snacks (11–2, 7–9.30 Mon–Sat; 11–2, 7–9 Sun)   Restaurant   Children welcome   Open 11–11; opens 12 in winter   Bedrooms tel Hundon (0440) 86789; £35B/£45B

IXWORTH   TL9370 Map 5

Pickerel

Village signposted just off A143 Bury St Edmunds–Diss

Reopened after a six-month closure, this pub now has new licensees who have completely rebuilt the kitchen but hope to change very little in the bars. Leading off from the central servery, the small rooms have panelling that varies from ancient to eighteenth century, attractive brickwork, moulded Elizabethan oak beams, cushioned chairs and pews, big fireplaces, and a relaxed atmosphere. The emphasis on fish is not as strong as before, and while they aim to have quite a few fish dishes (the chef was previously second chef with Mortimers in Bury St Edmunds) there are more vegetarian and poultry meals: filled wholemeal baps (from £1.45), ploughman's (from £2.45), fruity chicken curry, chilli con carne or sirloin steak sandwich (£2.95), spicy spinach filos (£3.45), rump steak (£6.45), and blackboard specials. The pretty two-roomed dining-room has stripped pine tables and dressers, stripped pine dado, blue patterned wallpaper and a high shelf of plates. Well kept Greene King Abbot and IPA on handpump, and reasonable house wines. The public side has shove-ha'penny, table skittles, dominoes, cribbage and fruit machine. A small back sun lounge faces a sway-backed Elizabethan timbered barn across the old coachyard. There are picnic-table sets on a goodish stretch of grass, under a

It's against the law for bar staff to smoke while handling food or drink.

giant sycamore. *(Recommended by Nick Dowson, Alison Hayward; more reports on the new regime please)*

Greene King   Licensees Debbie Love and Martin Fincham   Real ale   Meals and snacks Restaurant tel Pakenham (0359) 30398   Open 11–2.30, 5.30–11

KERSEY   TL9944 Map 5
Bell

Village signposted off A1141 N of Hadleigh

Inside this old building – with its jettied upper floor and attractively carved black timbers – there are latticed windows, fine old timberwork, and doors off a worn brick-tiled corridor that open into a bar and lounge; these rooms are divided by a brick and timber screen decorated with copper and brassware. The low-beamed public side has simple seating on its tiled floor and a log fire, and the lounge side has comfortable red plush button-back banquettes and a swirly red carpet. Bar food includes sandwiches (from £1.10), home-made soup (£1.25), ploughman's (£2.50), salads (from £2.95), plaice (£3.50), home-made pies (steak and kidney £4.25, game and ale £4.50), eight-ounce rump steak (£6.95), and daily specials like home-made cottage pie (£3.25). Well kept Adnams, Flowers Original and Wethereds on handpump are regularly rotated with 32 other real ales. Out on the sheltered back terrace and under a fairy-lit side canopy, there are white cast-iron tables and chairs; steel quoits available. They now have bedrooms. *(Recommended by Geoff Halson, Mrs L Saumarez Smith, P Miller, John Evans, Mrs R Wilmot, J S Evans, Paul and Margaret Baker, Gordon Theaker)*

Free house   Licensees Alex and Lynne Cooter   Real ale   Meals and snacks   Restaurant Children welcome   Open 11–3, 6–11 all year; may open in afternoon for cream teas and barbecues   Bedrooms tel Ipswich (0473) 823229; £12.50/£25

LAXFIELD   TM2972 Map 5
Kings Head ★

Behind church, off road toward Banyards Green

The new licensees are hoping to keep this unspoilt, friendly Tudor pub very much as it was in Mrs Parsons' time, but are calling it locally the Lowhouse; eventually they hope to repaint and rethatch. The old-fashioned front room has a tiled floor and an open fire cosily surrounded by a high-backed built-in settle, and a couple of other rooms have pews, old seats, scrubbed deal tables, and a quietly ticking clock. Well kept Adnams Bitter and Broadside, and James White's farmhouse cider are tapped from casks in a back room; dominoes, cribbage, bridge and trivia. Bar food includes sandwiches, home-made soup such as Stilton and cauliflower (£1.25), farmhouse terrine with oatcakes or fish mousse (£2.25), vegetable crumble (£2.95), beef in ale or a rich seafood stew (£3.25), gammon baked in cider (£3.50) and rabbit pie (£3.80); Friday evening is traditionally 'kipper night', with oak-smoked kippers (£1.75); four-course evening meals if booked two days in advance. Going out past the casks in the back serving-room, you find benches and a trestle table in a small yard. From the yard a honeysuckle arch leads into a sheltered little garden and the pub's own well kept and secluded bowling- and croquet-green; occasional morris dancers on summer weekends. *(Recommended by Gwen and Peter Andrews, Pete Storey, Gavin May, Nick Dowson; more reports please)*

Free house   Licensee Nicholas Lockley   Real ale   Meals and snacks   Restaurant   Children welcome   Folk/jazz/string quartets/local theatre group Fri, Sat and Sun evenings Open 11–11 all year   Self-contained flat tel Ubbeston (098 683) 395; /£50B

The opening hours we quote are for weekdays; in England and Wales, Sunday hours are now always 12–3, 7–10.30.

LEVINGTON   TM2339 Map 5
Ship

Gun Hill; village signposted from A45, then follow Stratton Hall sign

The three cosy little rooms here have benches built into the wall, upholstered small settles (some of them grouped round tables, as booths), beams, ship prints, and photographs of sailing-barges. The middle one has a marine compass set into the serving-counter, which has a fishing net slung over it, a big black round stove, an energetic and talkative green parrot called Billy, and casks of well kept Tolly Bitter and Original. Good bar food, well served and presented, might include ploughman's (from £1.95), salads (from £3.60), chicken and broccoli lasagne or steak and kidney pie (£3.75); they home-smoke their own meat and fish including prawns, sausages (£3.25) and ham (£4.50); puddings such as date and toffee pudding or spicy apple and raisin crumble (£1.50). Benches out in front look over the quiet lane to the distant water. *(Recommended by John Baker, John Tyzack, K R Harris)*

Tolly   Licensee Mrs Wenham   Real ale   Snacks (lunchtime, limited Sun) Open 11.30–2.30, 7–11 all year; closed evening 25 Dec

LONG MELFORD   TL8645 Map 5
Bull 🛏

A134

On the right, as you go into the front lounge of this civilised and well kept black and white timbered building, is a woodwose – the wild man of the woods that figures in Suffolk folk-tales – supporting the beautifully carved high main beam; the room is divided by the remains of an oak partition wall, and has armed wing chairs around low tables with neat lacy tablecloths and flowers, a longcase clock from Stradbrook, a little writing-desk and chair in one corner alcove, a rack of daily papers, a huge brick fireplace with log fire, lots of black timbering, and big mullioned and leaded windows. A more spacious back bar has armed brown leatherette or plush dining-seats around characterful oak tables, dark heavy beams, and sporting prints on the white timbered walls. Bar food includes sandwiches (from £1.25), soup (£1.50), ploughman's (£2.50), cold meats and salads or steak and kidney pie (£3.95), seafood cassoulet (£4.05), scampi (£4.90) and steaks (from £5.95). Well kept Greene King IPA and Abbot on handpump. There are tables in the paved central courtyard. In 1648 a local man, arguing about Civil War politics, was murdered in a brawl just inside the front door (and buried in the yard of the magnificent church – look for the memorial to Richard Evered). Another murder was committed in 1739, and ghost-hunters hold these reponsible for the old brass and copper supposedly rising out of the fireplace and floating around the ceiling. The Elizabethan Melford Hall and moated Tudor Kentwell Hall are both fine buildings, in attractive grounds. *(Recommended by Heather Sharland, Gwen and Peter Andrews, Dave Butler, Lesley Storey, J S Evans)*

Free house (THF)   Manager Peter Watt   Meals and snacks (lunchtime, not Sun) Restaurant   Children welcome   Open 11–2.30, 6–11 all year   Bedrooms tel Sudbury (0787) 78494; £60B/£75B

ORFORD   TM4250 Map 5
Jolly Sailor   ★

An old-fashioned central cubicle in this waterside smugglers' inn serves the several cosy and cheerful rooms from counters and hatches. One main room, warmed in winter by a good solid-fuel stove, has an uncommon spiral staircase in the corner, another has a flagstoned floor, a small room is popular with the dominoes, darts and shove-ha'penny players; often, seats are pews. There are some curious stuffed Chinese muff dogs, about half the size of a chihuahua – said to be Tudor, though no one's sure. Well kept Adnams Bitter on handpump; friendly staff (and dogs); piped music. Bar food includes sandwiches, ploughman's or smoked mackerel (£1.90), scampi (£2.90), seafood (£3.20), steaks (£5.60) and a daily special such as fresh local cod, beef and vegetable or cottage pie (£2.50). The pub stands by a busy little quay on the River Ore, opposite Orford Ness and close to marshy Havergate Island, where avocets breed. *(Recommended by Jason Caulkin, Rona Murdoch, Heather Sharland, Gwyneth and Salvo Spadaro-Dutturi, Dave Butler, Lesley Storey, Angus Lindsay, Hugh Morgan, Pete Storey, A V Chute)*

Adnams Licensee Patrick Buckner *Real ale Meals and snacks Children welcome Live music most Sat evenings Open 11–2.30, 6–11 all year Bedrooms tel Orford (0394) 450243; £15.50/£26*

Kings Head ✿

Front Street

The busy main bar in this predominantly Tudor inn has carved black oak beams, one or two fine old wooden chairs, comfortable blue leatherette seats and cushioned wall benches grouped around the low tables on its carpet, and an open fire. Very good fresh fish at lunchtime in the bar includes fresh plaice (£2.85), home-made fish pie or monkfish and lobster soufflé with shellfish sauce (£4.75), scallops in sherry and mushroom sauce (£4.95), king prawns in garlic butter (£6.95), fresh local lobster (from £7.25); also, home-made soup (£1.50), ploughman's (from £2) and home-made pâté (£2.50); home-made puddings such as fruit sorbet or brown bread and honey ice-cream (from £1.30); good breakfasts often include grilled sole or poached whiting. Note that they don't do sandwiches. Well kept Adnams Bitter, Broadside and winter Old on handpump; large wine list; fruit machine. There are views from the well restored keep of the nearby twelfth-century castle. *(Recommended by Mrs H M T Carpenter, Jason Caulkin, Heather Sharland, Angus Lindsay, Andrew and Alison Beardwood, M C Howells, Geo Rumsey, D Stephenson)*

Adnams Licensees Alistair and Joy Shaw *Real ale Meals and snacks (not Mon evening) Restaurant (not Sun evening) Children in restaurant on certain days Open 11–2.30 (3 Sat), 6–11 all year; may stay open longer in summer; closed Jan Bedrooms tel Orford (0394) 450271; £18/£31*

RAMSHOLT TM3141 Map 5

Ramsholt Arms

Village signposted from B1083; then take turning after the one to Ramsholt Church

The setting here is so beautiful that just for that alone the pub is worth visiting. Surrounded by quiet pine woods, it's quite isolated by an old barge quay on the River Deben which winds past to the sea, and silent but for the distant noise of gulls, curlews and other waders. Simple furnishings include dark oak, tapestry-upholstered seats, red tiles or parquet flooring, some neatly nautical woodwork, tide tables and charts, and a big picture window. Well kept Adnams Bitter, Batemans XXX and Boddingtons on handpump; ploughman's (from £2.20), cold carvery in summer (from £3.95), and daily specials such as swordfish steak, pork or lamb kebabs, and various steaks. Sensibly placed darts, cribbage, dominoes, fruit machine; piped music. There is a riverside terrace bar and barbecue, and a lot of boating activity on summer weekends. *(Recommended by P A Bush, MBW, JHW; more reports please)*

Free house Licensees Liz and St John Girling *Real ale Meals and snacks Children in dining-room Steep longish walk down from car park Open 11–2.30, 7–11 all year*

Though English and Welsh pubs have to stop serving bar drinks between 3 and 7 on Sundays, they are allowed to serve drinks with meals in a separate dining-room all afternoon.

REDE TL8055 Map 5
Plough 🏮

Village signposted off A143 Bury St Edmunds–Haverhill

Even though there's a strong emphasis on food here, the atmosphere's truly warm and pubby. The simple and traditional cosy bar has red plush button-back built-in wall banquettes, copper measures and pewter tankards hanging from low black beams, and decorative plates on a low Delft shelf and surrounding the solid fuel stove in its brick fireplace. It's really the dishes of the day which earn our food award. On a typical day they might be pork chop baked with herbs, brewers' braise or rabbit and prune casserole (all £3.95), lamb with red cherries or traditional roasts (£4.25), and smoked sea-trout with unusual salad or delicious pan-fried whole plaice, with scrumptious puddings. They do a lot of game in season, such as roast partridge or pheasant casserole. There is a wide choice of other hot bar dishes, ploughman's and salads, and the little evening restaurant does things like moules au gratin, chicken stuffed with crabmeat and Swiss cheese (£7.50), poached salmon (£8.25), and steaks. The well lit pool-table is by no means relegated to some back area; also trivia machine, fruit machine, unobtrusive piped radio; keg Greene King beers. There are picnic-table sets in front of the pretty pink-washed partly thatched pub, with more in a sheltered cottage garden behind; it's a lovely quiet spot, with not much sound beyond the birds in the aviary (and the surrounding trees) or the burbling white doves in the dovecote. *(Recommended by Gwen and Peter Andrews, Mr and Mrs D E Milner; more reports please)*

Greene King   Licensees Brian and Joyce Desborough   Meals and snacks (not Sun evenings)   Restaurant (evenings, Sun lunch, bookings preferred) tel Hawkedon (028 489) 208   Children in eating area and restaurant   Open 11.30–2.30, 6.30–11 all year

SIBTON TM3669 Map 5
White Horse

Halesworth Road; village signposted from A1120

This well kept sixteenth-century inn is attractively furnished in an old-fashioned style: lots of tack, horsebrasses and plates on the yellowing walls, a big rug on the black and red tiled floor, cushioned settles, and little red plush armchairs by a wood-burning stove. Five steps take you up past an ancient partly knocked-through timbered wall into a carpeted gallery with comfortable armed seats around rustic tables. There's a parrot in a cage. Bar food includes sandwiches (lunchtimes only), soup (55p), ploughman's (£1.70), lasagne or chilli con carne (£2.95), rump steak (£4.85), duck à l'orange or lamb Shrewsbury (£5.40), daily specials such as seafood pie or gammon, and a selection of vegetarian dishes. Well kept Adnams Bitter on handpump and farm cider; darts, shove-ha'penny, dominoes, cribbage and piped music. There are tables under cocktail parasols out on the big garden where there's a children's play area and space for caravans. *(Recommended by N A Wright, Nick Dowson, Mr and Mrs J Wilmore, Peter Bush, Jeff Cousins, Mr and Mrs G P Bishop, Mr and Mrs M Johnson)*

Free house   Licensees Tony and Fay Waddingham   Real ale   Meals and lunchtime snacks (12–1.30, 7–9; not Sun evening)   Children in gallery and restaurant until 9 Open 11.30–2.30, 6.30 (6 Sat)–11; 11.30–2.15, 7–11 in winter; closed Mon lunchtime exc bank hols   Bedrooms tel Peasenhall (072 879) 337; £13B/£26B

SNAPE TM3959 Map 5
Golden Key ★ 🏮

Priory Lane

The small and sheltered, pretty garden in front of this civilised place has white tables and chairs on the gravel, and a lovely mass of summer flowers. Inside, the stylish lounge bar has nice pictures on the cream walls – pencil sketches of customers, a Henry Wilkinson spaniel and so forth, low beams, stripped modern settles around heavy Habitat-style wooden tables on a Turkey carpet, and a solid-fuel stove in its big fireplace. The serving end has an open log fire in winter, an old-fashioned settle curving around a couple of venerable stripped tables and a tiled floor; a brick-floored side room has sofas and more tables. Home-made food includes soup (£1.40), ploughman's with Cheddar, Stilton, Brie, rare beef or ham (from £2.45; pity about the little packs of butter), pâté with salad and French bread (£2.95), spinach and mushroom or smoked haddock quiche or sausage, egg and onion pie (£3.75), locally caught crab (£3.95), lobster (from £6.50), steak (£7.95), and daily specials such as excellent cottage pie or steak and kidney pie (£3.95); a choice of puddings such as fruit pies or lemon cake (£1–£1.75). Well kept Adnams Bitter and Broadside on handpump, with Old ale and Tally Ho in winter, and James White's cider; friendly staff. *(Recommended by Heather Sharland, Gwen and Peter Andrews, R M Sparkes, Peter Griffiths, Jenny and Brian Seller, Patrick Young)*

Adnams Licensee Max Kissick-Jones Real ale Meals and snacks Open 11–3, 6–11 all year, with afternoon and evening extensions during Aldeburgh Festival; closed evenings 25 and 26 Dec

SOUTHWOLD   TM5076 Map 5

Crown 🗫 ⛨

High Street

The new manager here is the son of Edric Hawkins (who made the Three Horseshoes at Elsted, Sussex, such a success before moving to the Halfway Bridge near Lodsworth, Sussex – one of this year's outstanding discoveries). The atmosphere is bustling and informal though not really pubby – falling very much into the same class as the Royal Oak, Yattenden, in Berkshire. The smart and attractive main carpeted bar has green-grained panelling, plain wooden tables with chairs and long settles and a carved marble and wood fireplace. A smaller back oak-panelled bar has brassy navigation lamps and a brass binnacle. Good bar food (not cheap – which has an obvious effect on the clientele) may include tomato and apple soup (£1.40), four or so starters (around £4) such as a warm salad of poached fish with soya and ginger or smoked breast of turkey, up to four main dishes at around £4.50, such as fillet of cod with chilli and black olives, loin of pork with apricots and hazel-nuts or lamb's liver with madeira and shallots, and puddings like baked apple with sultanas and apricots (£1.65) or marinated grapes in Grand Marnier (£1.75); cheeses are carefully chosen, and breakfasts are good. The eighteen wines or so, kept perfectly on a Cruover machine, are chosen monthly by Simon Loftus (so always interesting), and the Adnams Bitter, Broadside, winter Old and Tally Ho (Christmas only) on handpump are in superb condition – it's the nearby Adnams brewery's flagship. Shove-ha'penny and cribbage. There are some tables in a sunny sheltered corner outside. In winter they arrange wine tastings and other events such as classical music and jazz evenings; this coming summer they are planning a lunchtime theatre season. *(Recommended by RCL, Hope Chenhalls, Heather Sharland, Helen Crookston, Nigel Gibbs, A C and S J Beardsley, Quentin Williamson, Jason Caulkin, P Leeson and friends, M K Brown, Nigel Gibbs, Mr and Mrs J H Wyatt, Stephen and June Clark, Geo Rumsey, Derek and Sylvia Stephenson, Patrick Young, M C Howells, Rob and Gill Weeks, Gwen and Peter Andrews)*

Adnams Manager Simon Hawkins Real ale Meals and snacks (12.30–2, 7.30–9.45) Restaurant Children in eating area Live entertainment (see main text) Open 10.30–3, 6–11 all year Bedrooms tel Southwold (0502) 722275; £25.50B/£41B

If you're interested in real ale, the CAMRA *Good Beer Guide* – no relation to us – lists thousands of pubs where you can get it.

Harbour

Blackshore Quay; entering Southwold on A1095, turn right at Kings Head and go past golf course and water tower

A sort of unofficial clubhouse for working fishermen, this friendly old waterside place stands among the small black huts (where you can buy fresh fish), and has a ship-to-shore radio as well as a wind speed indicator in the bar. The back bar has model ships, lots of local ship and boat photographs, smoked dried fish hanging from a line on a beam, a lifeboat line launcher, cushioned built-in wooden wall benches, rustic stools, stripped panelling, and brass shellcases on the mantelpiece over a stove. The low-beamed, tiled and panelled front bar, with antique settles, is tiny. It specialises in good fish and chips, served in newspaper (from £1.70 – an extra 3p if you want a fork), and also serves sausages (£1.10), burgers (£1.20) and scampi (£2.20); cold food only on Sunday lunchtime with ploughman's, and chicken, Cromer crab or smoked mackerel salads. Well kept Adnams Broadside on handpump, attractively priced; darts; often locally smoked eel for sale, for your freezer. There is a somewhat unkempt garden with a couple of picnic-table sets behind the pub (where there are animals in pens and a children's play area), with more in front facing the jumbly waterfront bustle. There have been some disappointments in the service recently – we'd like more reports on this please. *(Recommended by RCL, Heather Sharland, Nigel Gibbs, Gavin May, Mr and Mrs J H Wyatt, Nick Dowson, N A Wood)*

Adnams   Licensee Ron Westwood   Real ale   Meals (not Tues or Thurs evening, not Sun lunchtime)   Open 11–3, 6–11 all year; opens 7 in winter

STOKE BY NAYLAND   TL9836   Map 5

Angel 🌣 🛏

B1068 Sudbury–East Bergolt; also signposted via Nayland off A134 Colchester–Sudbury

There aren't many tables here, and even on the winter Monday of our inspection all were filled shortly after noon. But people who have had to wait for one have stressed that the pleasant surroundings make that no hardship. One room has a low sofa and wing armchairs around its wood-burning stove, and Victorian paintings on the dark green walls. The main bar area, with a huge log fire, has handsome Elizabethan beams, some stripped brickwork and timbers, local watercolours and older prints, attractive table lamps, and a relaxed mixture of furnishings including more wing armchairs, mahogany dining-chairs, and pale library chairs which, like the tables, are lightly stained to bring out the grain. Round the corner is a little tiled-floor stand-and-chat bar – with well kept Adnams Bitter and Greene King IPA and Abbot on handpump, decent house wines and good coffee. But the main thing here is enterprising bar food such as interesting soups (£1.60), ploughman's (£2.50), a popular Greek salad (£2.95), fresh asparagus (£3.50), meat tartlet or ham and mushroom flaky-pastry pie (£4.25), moussaka, boiled gammon and parsley sauce or a daily roast (£4.50), a plate packed with three separate griddled fish (from £5.50), home-made gravadlax (£5.85), or chicken and king prawn brochette (£6.75); vegetables, side salads and bread are good – a shame about the plastic-tub butter. Piped classical music, businesslike service; cast-iron seats and tables on a sheltered terrace. *(Recommended by Gwen and Peter Andrews, Mr and Mrs Bill Muirhead, Sandra Kempson, Jim Matthews)*

Free house   Licensee P G Smith   Real ale   Meals and snacks (12–2, 6.30–9; last Sun orders 1.30)   Restaurant   Open 11–2.30, 6–11 all year; closed 25 and 26 Dec   Bedrooms tel Colchester (0206) 263245/6; £30B/£40B

If we know a pub does sandwiches we always say so; if they're not mentioned, you'll have to assume you can't get one.

SUTTON   TM3046 Map 5
Plough
B1083

A snug little front room in this tiled white house – surrounded by Sutton Common – has button-back wall banquettes, there's a more spacious room round the side, and service is friendly. Reliably good bar food includes sandwiches (from 75p, home-baked gammon 90p, toasties 5p extra), home-made soup (£1.20), ploughman's or burgers (from £1.85), salads (from £2.95), scampi (£3.95) and steaks (from £6.80). In the evening a rather grander choice concentrates more on fish, with starters like fresh crab or fried clams (£3.25) and main courses such as grilled halibut steak with prawns or garlic butter (£5.95) or Dover sole (£10.50); daily specials include steak and Guinness or ratatouille pie and there are house specialities (24 hours' notice) such as roast local pheasant in red wine sauce (£6.95) or chateaubriand (£9.40). Ruddles Best on handpump; jugs of Pimms or sangria (£2.45); darts, dominoes, cribbage, fruit machine and piped music. There are picnic-table sets in front and more by the fruit trees. *(Recommended by Martin Lowy, Dr F O Wells; more reports please)*

Watneys   Licensees Michael and Anne Lomas   Real ale   Meals and snacks (11.30–2, 6.30–9.30; not Sun evening or Mon)   Restaurant (not Sun evening) tel Shottisham (0394) 411785   Children in eating area and restaurant   Open 11–2.30 (3 Sat), 6.30–11 all year

THORNDON   TM1469 Map 5
Black Horse
Village signposted off A140 and off B1077, S of Eye

Before the River Dove was diverted, this quietly friendly, sixteenth-century pub was used by longboat traders. On one side of its central core (which has scrubbed ancient red flooring tiles and a glass-doored solid-fuel stove in the big fireplace) is a games-room with sensibly placed darts, well lit pool and juke box. On the other a carpeted area has small tapestried settles and country dining-chairs around stripped country tables or glossy darker ones; above a second huge fireplace a wall clock ticks ponderously between stuffed animal heads. There's quite a bit of stripped brick and studwork, dark low beams, and some standing timbers. A wide choice of attractively priced bar food includes soup (95p), sandwiches (from £1, steak £2.15), filled baked potatoes (from £1), burgers (from £1.45), omelettes (£2.15), several vegetarian dishes (from £2.20), salads (from £2.90), steak and kidney pie (£3.25) and charcoal-grilled steaks (from six-ounce rump £3.60). The restaurant (converted stables, with the original stalls) has a Friday seafood night, and good value three-course Sunday lunch. Adnams Extra, Courage Best and Greene King Abbot on handpump are kept well under light blanket pressure; well reproduced and interesting late-1950s and 1960s pop music; there are white metal and plastic tables on the lawn that spreads round to the back. *(Recommended by H D Boyden, E G N Alcock, Miss J M Smith; more reports please)*

Free house   Real ale   Meals and snacks   Restaurant tel Occold (037 971) 523   Children in eating area and restaurant   Monthly folk nights, morris dancing   Open 11.30–2.30, 6–11 all year

THORNHAM MAGNA   TM1070 Map 5
Four Horseshoes   🛏
Off A140 S of Diss; follow Finningham 3¼ signpost, by White Horse pub

Part of this popular thatched white pub is said to date back to the twelfth century. The extensive bar is well divided into alcoves and distinct areas, and there are low and heavy black beams, and some character seats such as tall Windsor chairs as well as the golden plush banquettes and stools on its spread of fitted Turkey carpet. The black-timbered white walls are decorated with country pictures and farm tools, and logs burn in big fireplaces. Generous helpings of good value, popular food, quickly served by uniformed waitresses, includes sandwiches (from £1.10, prawn £1.95), soup (£1.25), ploughman's (from £2.25), savoury rolls (£2.75), salads (from £2.90), lasagne (£4.20), seafood platter or a mild chicken curry (£4.25), steak and kidney pie or fisherman's hot pot (£4.50) and well hung steaks (£7.25); meat comes from the owners' own butcher's shop, most vegetables from their own market garden. Well kept Adnams Bitter, Ruddles Best and Websters Yorkshire on handpump; friendly helpful staff. Picnic-table sets stand by flower beds on a sheltered lawn and an even more sheltered back terrace. The Horseshoe Country Trail is a lovely pre-breakfast walk. *(Recommended by Mike and Jill Dixon, Stephen Goodchild, Mrs A Broderick)*

Free house   Managers Malcolm Moore and Caroline Ruth   Real ale   Meals and snacks (12–2, 7–10.30)   Restaurant   Children welcome   Open 12–2.30, 7 (6.30 Sat)–11 all year; closed 25 Dec   Bedrooms tel Occold (037 971) 777; £32.50B/£44B

TOSTOCK   TL9563 Map 5
Gardeners Arms
Village signposted from A45 and A1088

Warmly welcoming, this pretty sand-coloured house has low heavy black beams in the lounge bar, and lots of what used to be called carving-chairs (dining-chairs with arms) around the black tables. A wide range of good bar food includes sandwiches (from 85p), memorable home-made cream of mussel soup (£1), ploughman's with home-made granary rolls (£1.95), steak sandwich (£2.60), home-made vegetarian pizza (£2.75), cold salt beef (£3.50) and prawns (£3.75), with supper dishes (bookings only) like ratatouille with peanuts and cheese topping (£1.50), poached salmon steak (£6.50) and sirloin steak (£6.75); daily specials on the blackboard and puddings such as hot chocolate fudge cake (£1.35). Very well kept Greene King IPA and Abbot on handpump. The lively tiled-floor public bar has darts, pool, shove-ha'penny, dominoes, cribbage, juke box, fruit machine and a trivia machine. The sheltered lawn with its new terrace is a lovely place to sit at picnic-table sets among roses and other flowers, and watch the local team playing steel quoits on the pitch. *(Recommended by Charles Bardswell, Mr and Mrs G C Dickinson, Richard Fawcett, Nigel Paine, Andrew and Alison Beardwood, Nick Dowson)*

Greene King   Licensee R E Ransome   Meals and snacks (not Mon or Tues evenings or Sun lunchtime)   Restaurant tel Beyton (0359) 70460: Sun opening 8–10pm   Children in eating area of bar   Open 11–2.30, 7–11 all year

WALBERSWICK   TM4974 Map 5
Bell
Just off B1387

One reader was delighted to find the rambling oak-beamed bar here had changed little since his last visit a quarter of a century ago. The atmosphere is busy and happy, and there are curved high-backed settles on well worn flagstones, tankards hanging from oars above the bar counter, tiles and flooring bricks (that were here when this sleepy village was a flourishing port 600 years ago), and a wood-burning stove in the big fireplace; to one side there is a smarter and more conventionally comfortable area decorated with local photographs; maybe two friendly bull-mastiffs. Bar food includes sandwiches (95p), ploughman's (£2.15, ham £2.45), home-made fish pie, very good freshly caught plaice (£3), with a good choice of summer salads from smoked mackerel or home-made quiche (£3), scampi (£3.25) and prawns or crab (£3.75); in winter there are more hot dishes. If you eat outside you'll be given plastic knives and forks. Well kept Adnams and Mild from handpump. Shove-ha'penny, cribbage, fruit machine, space game. The big sheltered lawn here is a quiet place to sit at the seats and tables among roses and other flowers. The bedrooms all look over the sea or the river. *(Recommended by P Miller, Charles Bardswell, Mrs M Webster, RCL, Gwen and Peter Andrews, Mr and Mrs P A Jones, J H Walker, K Leist, Mr and Mrs O'Gorman, John Townsend, Gavin May)*

Adnams   Licensee Mark Stansall   Real ale   Meals and snacks (lunchtime)   Restaurant Children in small room off bar   Open 11–2.30, 6.30–11 all year; closed 25 Dec Bedrooms tel Southwold (0502) 723109; /£40(£44B)

WESTLETON   TM4469 Map 5

Crown 🏵 🛏

This quietly friendly and well kept village inn has a comfortably furnished bar with a couple of lobster-pots at one end, farm tools, a growing collection of old photographs and postcards of Westleton, pews, stools and settles, and a good open fire in winter. Good bar food includes sandwiches (from 85p), home-made soup (£1.50), ploughman's (from £2.25), salads (from £2.45, quiche £3.35), good fresh-caught local fish such as cod and sole (from £3.50), steak and kidney pie (£3.95) and sirloin steak (£5.95); lovely puddings such as home-made treacle pudding or apple pie (£1.65); children's menu and excellent breakfasts; efficient, courteous staff. Well kept Adnams Bitter and Broadside, Greene King Abbot, Marstons Owd Rodger and Wadworths 6X on handpump, and good dry white wine. Dominoes and shove-ha'penny. A conservatory was opened in the spring of 1989, and as we went to press we heard of plans to landscape the garden. The Minsmere bird reserve is a couple of miles away, and in that direction there are good walks (the 'Westleton Walks') – perhaps over to our Lucky Dip entry at Eastbridge. *(Recommended by RCL, Joy Heatherley, Heather Sharland, Gwen and Peter Andrews, Jenny and Brian Seller, Shirley Pielou, Richard Fawcett, Robert and Vicky Tod, Derek and Sylvia Stephenson, Amanda Rusholme)*

Free house   Licensees Richard and Rosemary Price   Real ale   Meals and snacks (lunchtime)   Evening restaurant (that doubles as an art gallery)   Children in restaurant Open 11–2.30, 6–11 all year; closed 25 and 26 Dec   Bedrooms tel Westleton (072 873) 273; £34.50B/£49.50B

Lucky Dip

Besides the fully inspected pubs, you might like to try these Lucky Dips recommended to us and described by readers (if you do, please send us reports):

☆ **Aldeburgh** [Crabbe St; TM4656], *Cross Keys*: Low-ceilinged sixteenth-century pub with massive central chimney (and two wood-burning stoves) dividing its two bar areas, lively and friendly local atmosphere out of season though touristy in summer, plain rather utilitarian furnishings, straightforward bar food such as sandwiches, ploughman's, crab salad and one or two hot dishes, well kept Adnams ales (the full range), traditional bar games and fruit machine, tables on back gravel which opens on to promenade and beach; nr start GWG120; children may be allowed in to eat if it's wet *(Joanna and Ian Chisholm, Heather Sharland, Chris Fluck, LYM)*
Aldeburgh [The Parade], *Brudenell*: Smart, comfortable THF hotel with large cocktail bar open to non-residents; reasonable bar meals, rather expensive drinks inc Adnams on

handpump and (if you're lucky) a table with spectacular sea views; pleasant, helpful staff; can get crowded at holiday times; children welcome; nr start GWG120; bedrooms; *(Heather Sharland)*
Aldringham [TM4461], *Parrot & Punchbowl*: Good food in cosy and unpretentious pub with uncommonly wide choice of wines by the glass, but could be more flexible with bar food service, and only dining-room meals Fri/weekend – when booking essential *(K R Harris)*
Badingham [TM3068], *White Horse*: Attractive and old-fashioned pub included particularly for its own neat bowling-green; well kept Adnams, wide choice of cheapish bar food including summer lunchtime cold buffet, vegetarian and children's dishes as well as usual pub food; more expensive busy restaurant, nice rambling garden *(LYM)*

Bardwell [The Green; TL9473], *Six Bells*: Free house with pleasant atmosphere, good food, extensive wine list and recently extended restaurant *(Terence May)*

Barham [TM1451], *Sorrel Horse*: Large, rambling local with exposed beams (some original, some cosmetic); friendly bar staff, well kept Tolly Original, well prepared food *(John Baker)*

☆ Blaxhall [off B1069 S of Snape; can be reached from A12 via Little Glemham; TM3657], *Ship*: Low beams, log fire and good basic local atmosphere in traditionally furnished public bar, more modern furniture in lounge, bar food from sandwiches and ploughman's through cod or a fry-up to steaks – the generous helpings make it good value, well kept Tolly Bitter and Mild and Marstons Pedigree on handpump, games in public bar; closed Mon lunchtime except bank hols, and except then no food Mon evening; children in eating area; bedrooms (just two); has been a real favourite but no recent reports *(Chris Fluck, Peter Bush, LYM – more reports please)*

Blundeston [from B1074 follow Church Lane, right into Short Lane, then left; TM5197], *Plough*: Handy for Jacobean Somerleyton Hall – smartly modernised Watneys pub which was the home of Barkis the carrier in David Copperfield *(LYM)*

☆ Boxford [Broad St; TL9640], *Fleece*: Promising and enterprising English home cooking and well kept Tolly in partly fifteenth-century pink-washed pub with cosy panelled bar on right, more spacious and airy lounge bar with big medieval fireplace, armchairs and some distinctive old seats among more conventional furnishings; if you see a girl in a mob-cap waving from the window of the upstairs restaurant, wave back – it's a ghost *(Gwen and Peter Andrews, LYM)*

Boxford, *White Hart*: Two-part bar with thick beams, fireplace and brasses; welcoming landlord, good atmosphere, well kept Ind Coope Burton and Taylor-Walker, home-cooked bar food *(Gwen and Peter Andrews)*

Bramfield [A144; TM4073], *Queens Head*: Handsomely refurbished high-beamed hall-house, clean and pleasant, with panel of original wattle and daub and large open fire; Adnams Bitter and Old on handpump, bar food, restrained atmosphere *(Nick Dowson)*

Brandon [by level crossing, A1065 N; TL7886], *Great Eastern*: Smart pub, well kept Adnams, bar food *(John Baker)*

Bromeswell [TM3050], *Cherry Tree*: Generous helpings of good bar food in straightforward local with comfortably modernised beamed lounge, open fire, velvet curtains; seats outside, charming inn-sign *(BB)*

Bures [TL9033], *Eight Bells*: Good and simple with pleasant atmosphere, friendly licensees, good bar food *(Nick Holmes)*

Bury St Edmunds [Angel Hill; TL8564], *Angel*: Thriving country-town hotel with good food in comfortable lounge, Regency dining-room and cellar grill-room; Adnams real ale, cheerful friendly service; bedrooms comfortable *(AE)*; [Eastgate St] *Fox*: Well kept and clean, with good service, good value food; close to centre, but adequate car parking *(Capt J Hurworth)*; [Station Hill] *Linden Tree*: Greene King beers, good choice of wines, enormous helpings of reasonably priced good bar food in conservatory *(Mrs M E Beard)*; *Masons Arms*: Relaxing Greene King pub with a good mix of customers, and old herbal remedies for sale *(John Branford)*; [Traverse, Abbeygate St; closed Sun and Holy Days] *Nutshell*: One of the smallest pubs in the country, with macabre cat and rat hanging from ceiling, Greene King Abbot and IPA on handpump *(Mr and Mrs P A Jones)*

Cavendish [TL8046], *George*: Smallish, intimate and well decorated, well kept beer, good value food cooked to order; lovely surroundings, pleasant helpful staff; children and dogs welcome in bar *(KH)*

Charsfield [off B1078; TM2556], *Three Horseshoes*: Friendly pub with reasonably priced and slightly different home-cooked food (not Sun), well kept Tolly ales, friendly and efficient owners; nearby Akenfield Garden worth a summer visit *(Geo Rumsey)*

☆ Clare [Callis St; TL7645], *Cock*: Hospitable host, pleasant atmosphere, good value food with good evening restaurant, well kept Adnams *(Melvin D Buckner, Tim Bell, Alison Krohn)*

Clare [Nethergate St], *Seafarer*: Wide choice of bar food, local Nethergate ale as well as Greene King and Websters Yorkshire, good small wine list, tables in garden; relaxing atmosphere, friendly young licensees; bedrooms *(LYM)*

Clopton Corner [Crown Hill; TM2254], *Crown*: Always friendly; good, well priced and presented bar food, much of it home made *(Miss V Johnston)*

☆ Coddenham [1¼ miles E of junction A45/A140; TM1354], *Dukes Head*: Well kept Tolly ales and good helpings of interesting food using fresh ingredients; stripped pine and simple atmosphere, welcoming landlady, pin-table in public bar, seats in steep garden behind; three bedrooms *(Col and Mrs L N Smyth, LYM)*

Dalham [TL7261], *Affleck Arms*: Good atmosphere in thatched village pub by stream, log fire in cosy low-beamed locals' bar, good value food in more comfortable and intimate rambling dining-bar on right; some tables outside *(LYM)*

Darsham [Darsham Stn; TM4169], *Stradbroke Arms*: Welcoming and pleasant staff in cheery high-ceilinged pub by level crossing with good value well presented bar food, Adnams real ale, high-backed settles, darts and bar billiards, restaurant; pretty garden under ash trees *(Peter Bush, BB)*

Debenham [High St; TM1763], *Red Lion*: Fine sixteenth-century plaster ceiling in nicely furnished lounge, pleasant landlord, good choice of bar food, Tolly ales, happy atmosphere *(E G N Alcock, BB)*

☆ **Dennington** [TM2867], *Queens Head*: Stylishly simplified beamed Tudor pub with good range of real ales, decent bar food; garden by village church *(Kevin and Mary Shakespeare, LYM)*

☆ **East Bergholt** [Burnt Oak – towards Flatford Mill; TM0734], *Kings Head*: Friendly attentive service in attractively decorated lounge with fine corner cupboard, comfortable seats, coal fire; reasonably priced home-cooked food inc good salads, well kept Tolly Bitter, Original and XXXX on handpump, decent coffee, juke box in uncarpeted public bar; pleasant garden with flower-decked hay wain *(Gwen and Peter Andrews, Mr and Mrs P W Dryland)*

Eastbridge [TM4566], *Eels Foot*: Simple local well placed for Minsmere bird reserve, Sizewell pebble beach (a good place to hunt for semi-precious stones) and heathland walks; crisp varnish, red leatherette, bright carpet or linoleum, well kept Adnams, friendly licensee, hefty helpings of basic home-made bar food (no winter evening meals); tables on quiet front terrace, children in eating area; start GWG122 *(Peter Griffiths, LYM)*

☆ **Erwarton** [TM2134], *Queens Head*: Good home-smoked Suffolk ham and other genuinely home-cooked food in unassuming sixteenth-century pub with old-fashioned furnishings; well kept Tolly (inc Mild and XXXX), picture window with fine view over the fields to the Stour estuary; seats in orchard behind *(Margaret and Trevor Errington, Rob and Gill Weeks, LYM)*

Eye [Castle St; TM1473], *Horseshoes*: Idiosyncratic décor with Christmas decorations all year round, huge log fire and vivacious bar staff; Adnams, Flowers, Whitbreads and Wethereds and good bar food; bedrooms comfortable and well equipped – video as well as TV *(Andrew Dawson)*

☆ **Felixstowe Ferry** [TM3337], *Ferry Boat*: Well kept Tolly real ales and simple bar food in neatly kept seventeenth-century pub close to sand-dunes, Martello tower and harbour *(LYM)*

Felsham [TL9457], *Six Bells*: Unpretentious grey flint building, one bar with two distinct areas; one carpeted with tables, chairs, attractive window seat, brasses and round brick fireplace; the other with tiled floor, more tables, darts; well kept Greene King IPA and Abbot, piped Radio 2 *(Gwen and Peter Andrews)*

Framlingham [TM2863], *White Horse*:

Doing very well under current management, with unusually good home-cooked food, especially fresh fish and seafood; promising restaurant *(M and W Williams)*

Great Barton [TL8967], *Flying Fortress*: Plenty of Second War World air force photographs – formerly farmhouse HQ of USAF support group, and on north edge of the airfield that was used in the film *Twelve O'Clock High*; perfectly kept Adnams and Greene King *(John Baker)*

Hartest [B1066 S of Bury; TL8352], *Crown*: A real village pub with two bars and pleasant licensee; simple lunchtime food, good beer, fine log fire (a shame the Hawkedon–Hartest rd is so dangerous) *(W T Aird)*

☆ **Haughley** [Station Rd; by level crossing towards Old Newton; TM0262], *Railway*: Warm-hearted country pub with plain traditional furnishings, log fire, good range of well kept real ales such as Adnams Old, Greene King IPA, Abbot and KK Mild and Mauldons Squire on handpump, good value simple food (not Mon pm), lots of labrador pictures, friendly Scots landlord; children in neat room at back *(John Baker, BB)*

Haughley, *Kings Arms*: Lots of dark tables in beamed lounge, log fire, wide choice of good value bar food from sandwiches to steak, Greene King ales, maybe loud but well reproduced piped pop music; pool and other games in comfortable saloon; tables and play house on back lawn *(Kevin and Mary Shakespeare, BB)*

Hawkedon [between A143 and B1066; TL7952], *Queens Head*: Sadly, the licensees who made this simply furnished village pub with its big open fireplace so popular for good home cooking left in summer 1989, and there's talk that the pub may be closed by the brewery *(Anon)*

Holbrook [Ipswich Rd; TM1636], *Compasses*: Beer has improved recently; good bar food *(G Smith, Miss A Tress)*

Hollesley [TM3544], *Fox*: Remote village pub with comfortable bar, somewhat cluttered with foxes (stuffed, ornaments or pictures); friendly welcome, separate pool room, good bar food *(K Leist)*

Huntingfield [TM3374], *Huntingfield Arms*: Friendly and imaginatively renovated pub on small green close to Heveningham Hall; bar food inc good ploughman's *(Anon)*

Icklingham [TL7772], *Red Lion*: Locally popular thatched pub with inglenook fireplace in comfortable lounge, restaurant section beyond wrought-iron divider, good value bar food, friendly efficient service, games in big public bar, seats outside; handy for West Stow Country Park and Anglo-Saxon village *(the Bailey family, LYM)*

Ipswich [Tavern St; TM1744], *Great White Horse*: Popular for good value lunch; comfortably well kept, with good Courage and Greene King ales; bedrooms *(Anon)*; [1 Fore St] *Spread Eagle*: Busy local with regulars' noticeboard and trophy cabinet, neat rooms, polite staff, well kept Tolly Bitter, Mild, XXXX on handpump *(Roger Broadie)*

Ixworth Thorpe [TL9173], *Oak*: Cheerful simply furnished pub with popular food, sensibly placed darts and pool-table, quite near Bardwell working windmill *(BB)*

☆ **Kersey** [The Street; TL9944], *White Horse*: Pretty pink-washed village pub with very friendly atmosphere, real fire in the public bar's open Victorian range, beams and timbering, wooden furniture, well kept real ales such as Adnams Extra and Old, Nethergate and perhaps a guest beer, good choice of well presented home-cooked food inc fine ploughman's and Suffolk ham, good service; children allowed in lounge bar – there's also a play area behind car park *(Mr and Mrs P W Dryland, LYM)*

☆ **Lavenham** [TL9149], *Swan*: Handsome and comfortable Elizabethan hotel, with in its heart a pubby little bar with leather seats on its tiled floor and well kept Adnams and Greene King; spacious overflow into numerous communicating but cosy seating areas and alcoves with beams, timbers, armchairs and settees; bar food, afternoon teas and so forth, lavishly timbered restaurant, seats in well kept garden, friendly and helpful staff; a magnet for American and other tourists; children welcome; pleasant if pricey bedrooms *(Geoff Halson, Barbara Hatfield, Mrs E M Thompson, Mrs R Wilmot, John Evans, AE, LYM)*

Lavenham, *Greyhound*: Friendly and simple pub in picturesque (if expensive) village, good bar food *(Tom, Lorna, Audrey and Alan Chatting)*

Leiston [Station Rd; TM4462], *White Horse*: More hotel than pub, but lively atmosphere, charming staff; good range of pub-priced hot dishes and salads in restaurant – serving late for this area, with generous helpings; bedrooms *(K R Harris)*

Lidgate [TL7257], *Star*: Attractive old building, partly an old cottage and hardly smart, with welcoming landlord, large open fire with Sun spit roasts, good bar food, lovely garden with indoor summer barbeques *(Mr and Mrs P W Dryland, Anthony Johnson)*

Long Melford [TL8645], *Crown*: Comfortable and quietly sedate, with pastel décor, rugwork 'pictures', easy chairs and sofas as well as smaller chairs and cushioned pews, bar food such as big filled rolls, sandwiches, ploughman's, gammon or scampi, good choice of real ales such as Adnams, Greene King IPA, Mauldons and Nethergate, morning coffee, afternoon tea, tables in walled garden with play area, restaurant open all day Sun; children allowed – nicely furnished back family-room; pub has been open all day; bedrooms *(Gordon Theaker, Robert and Vicky Tod, Gwen and Peter Andrews, LYM)*

☆ **Martlesham** [off A12 Woodbridge–Ipswich; TM2547], *Black Tiles*: Well kept and spacious roadhouse, included as a main entry when the A12 ran right outside; the village is now bypassed, so this is no longer quite such a convenient halt, but its standards have not fallen – quickly served fairly priced home-made food from lots of sandwiches, soup or a choice of ploughman's through steak and kidney pie and so forth to steaks, well kept Adnams Bitter and Broadside, garden tables; children allowed in restaurant; has been open all day *(LYM)*

☆ **Mendham** [TM2782], *Sir Alfred Munnings*: Cheery atmosphere in big open-plan bar of inn under promising new regime, with well kept Adnams, Charles Wells Bombardier and a weekly summer guest beer, bar food inc good value ploughman's and fresh mackerel served by neat waitresses, unobtrusive piped music, restaurant; children welcome, bedrooms, swimming pool for residents *(Gwen and Peter Andrews, LYM)*

Mildenhall [TL7174], *Bell*: Old hotel with pleasant atmosphere, friendly service, good value low-priced bar food *(K and E Leist)*

Newmarket [High St; TL6463], *Rutland Arms*: A welcome for strangers in well run and comfortable Georgian hotel, with decent food and beer; bedrooms *(W T Aird and others)*

North Cove [TM4789], *Three Horseshoes*: Pleasant pub with cosy atmosphere, bricks and rustic timberwork, open fire, tapestried seat coverings, piped music, horsebrasses and fruit machine; well kept Ruddles County on handpump, bar food and separate restaurant *(Nick Dowson)*

Pakefield [TM5390], *Jolly Sailors*: Excellent value carvery in comfortable well kept pub *(M J Morgan)*

Pakenham [TL9267], *Fox*: Recently cleaned up and very promising, with well kept Greene King IPA and good cheap food – sometimes original; largely unspoiled public rooms, local friendly staff *(John C Baker)*

Rattlesden [TL9758], *Brewers Arms*: Friendly and unpretentious village pub with lively public bar (pool, darts and so forth) *(LYM)*

Rickinghall [A143 Diss–Bury St Edmunds; TM0475], *Hamblyn House*: Sixteenth-century building, large lounge with copper and brassware and good atmosphere; well kept Adnams, Greene King and Abbot, good range of bar food; bedrooms have exposed timbers running down walls *(Roger Huggins)*

Saxmundham [High St; TM3863], *Queens Head*: Very reasonably priced good bar meals, with good choice and friendly surroundings; Whitbreads ales, aviary by car park; children's room *(Peter Bush)*

☆ **Saxtead Green** [B1119, opp old working windmill; TM2665], *Volunteer*: Light and airy lounge bar with reliable and popular bar food (they make their own pasties) and well kept Tolly ales; games in public bar, tables on pretty back terrace with small rockery pool; we've no reason to feel that this attractively placed pub's standards have fallen below main-entry level, but for some reason readers simply don't write recommending it; children allowed in corner bar *(Chris and Sandra Taylor, Mrs Olive Way, LYM – more reports please)*

☆ **Snape** [The Maltings; TM3959], *Plough & Sail*: Right by Snape Maltings complex so can get very full when there are concerts; but carefully modernised, with tiled floor, narrow L-shaped bar with alcoves and small restaurant leading off; good Adnams, interesting bar food, welcoming staff, lively atmosphere, open-air chess *(Gwen and Peter Andrews, Mr and Mrs J H Wyatt, John Baker, Heather Sharland)*

Snape [B1069], *Crown*: Front room supposed to be the model for the Boar in Britten's *Peter Grimes*, in much-done-up pub with well equipped bedrooms; well kept Adnams, but mixed views on food value – some have enjoyed it a lot *(Joanna and Ian Chisholm, Tony Gayfer, LYM)*

☆ **Southwold** [South Green; TM5076], *Red Lion*: Well kept Adnams ales and good snacks and salads in brown-panelled bar with big windows on to green, ship pictures, brassware and copper, elm-slab barrel tables; also welcoming family-room and summer buffet room *(Derek and Sylvia Stephenson, BB)*

☆ **Southwold** [7 East Green], *Sole Bay*: Good value simple lunchtime food (not Sun) and particularly well kept Adnams – this cheerful and delightfully relaxed Victorian local, its atmosphere scarcely changing over the years, is just across the road from the brewery, and only a stroll from the sea *(Derek and Sylvia Stephenson, W T Aird, LYM)*

Southwold, *Kings Head*: Pleasant proper pub with good food, decent house wines and helpful bar staff; children welcome; bedrooms *(Mr and Mrs J E Rycroft)*; *Swan*: Good prints and local pictures in Georgian hotel's lounge bar, Adnams ales – inc a full range of the interesting bottled ones; bar food; bedrooms *(LYM)*

Stoke by Nayland [TL9836], *Crown*: Spacious series of comfortably modernised room areas in lounge bar which has had reliable food and well kept Tolly on handpump, restaurant; changed hands twice – at notably high prices – in 1988, and in 1989 we've not yet heard how the latest regime is shaping up; bedrooms *(LYM – news please)*

Stradishall [A143; TL7452], *Cherry Tree*: Small country pub notable for its unusually big rustic garden, with very well spaced tables and a sizeable pond – friendly ducks and ducklings, moorhens, a side hen-run; two small low-beamed bars have big fireplaces and traditional furniture; bar food is a particular interest of the new licensees;

Greene King beers under pressure *(BB)*

Sudbury [North St; TL8741], *Four Swans*: Busy pub, good atmosphere, fair bar food; parking not easy; bedrooms clean, comfortable and good value *(Anon)*

Thurston [Barrells Rd; village signposted from A1108 N of Norton, then turn left by S-bend by Bayer Experimental Farm, then first right – OS Sheet 155 reference 939651; TL9365], *Black Fox*: Well kept Adnams, Greene King and Mauldons tapped from barrels in a back room and served in what still seems very much a converted house though in fact it started life as a drovers' tap-room and has always been a pub; good often hilarious atmosphere, quite unspoilt in spite of modest redecoration early 1989; open fire, frequent singsongs *(John Baker)*

Trimley St Martin [TM2736], *Hand in Hand*: Popular local, recently enlarged; warm welcome from licensee and staff, good pub food inc some of best steaks to be found round here *(C H Stride)*

Tunstall [TM3555], *Green Man*: Good value food inc fine burgers in comfortable and airily modern village inn close to RAF Bentwaters, well run, with well kept Tolly ales; pool, juke box and fruit machine in smaller bar; bedrooms *(Chris Fluck, BB)*

Wangford [A12 to Wrentham; TM4679], *Plough*: Good, clean, modern pub with neatly dressed customers, friendly reception, decent house wine and good food choice *(AVC)*

Washbrook [TM1042], *Brook*: Warm and cosy village pub with friendly service and good cheap food inc excellent steak cooked just as you ask *(Comus Elliott, Andrew Pye)*

Wenhaston [TM4276], *Star*: Basic friendly local with sun-trap small lounge, well kept Adnams ales, games in public bar, bar food, spacious lawn; simple bedrooms *(LYM)*

West Creeting Green [TM0758], *Red Lion*: Unusual and welcoming landlord – he feeds parrots by letting them take tidbits from between his lips; well kept Greene King beer *(D S Fowles)*

West Row [TL6775], *Judes Ferry*: Riverside free house with tables and chairs along bank; open fireplace, fruit machines, friendly landlord, good range of well kept ales on handpump which change weekly, wide choice of freshly prepared bar food *(Frank Gadbois)*

☆ **Westleton** [TM4469], *White Horse*: Friendly pub with well kept Adnams, good well presented bar food inc a children's menu, garden with climbing roses; has been open all day, and is handy for Minsmere RSPB reserve *(Joanna and Ian Chisholm, A T Langton, Geo Rumsey)*

Wetherden [TM0062], *Maypole*: Friendly village pub with strikingly beamed and timbered open-plan bar, usual bar food, well kept Adnams and Wethereds, live music Fri and Sat, disco Weds and Sun *(LYM)*

☆ **Wetheringsett** [TM1266], *Cat & Mouse*:
Fifteenth-century free house with friendly
licensees, several bars, fifteen well kept real
ales on handpump, bar food, barbecues by
stream, separate dining room, outside tables
(Frank Gadbois)

Wickhambrook [TL7554], *Cloak*: Has been
welcoming and friendly, with good beer and
food and a welcome for children; but found
closed as we went to press in summer 1989
(Steve Monk – more news please)

Woodbridge [Market Sq; TM2749], *Angel*:
Friendly pub with good, buzzing
atmosphere, low ceilings, interesting décor
and well kept Tolly *(Anon)*; [The
Thoroughfare] *Crown*: Reasonable priced
bar meals inc particularly good value daily
specials, fish and steaks; bedrooms; [Market
Sq] *Kings Head*: Friendly pub with scrubbed
kitchen tables around spacious bar and
inglenook fireplace; well kept Tolly and
good bar food *(Angus Lindsay)*; [Pytches Rd]
Melton Grange: Wide choice of reasonably
priced good bar meals in pleasant pub, well
kept Flowers and Stones; bedrooms *(Geo
Rumsey)*; [off Market Sq] *Olde Bell &
Steelyard*: Fascinating old local, derricks
from steelyard still in place over street, open
fires, well kept Greene King IPA and Abbot
on handpump *(Angus Lindsay)*

☆ **Woolpit** [TL9762], *Swan*: Neatly kept partly
panelled and beamed sixteenth-century bar
with open fires, low settles, seats in bay
windows, usual bar food but good value (not
Thurs–Sat evenings), well kept Watneys-
related real ales; good reasonably priced
modern bedrooms in converted outbuildings
*(Klaus and Elizabeth Leist, Mr and Mrs
G C Dickinson, LYM)*

Surrey

Here, as elsewhere, we've seen this year the start of a trend – allowed by the new licensing laws – for pubs to serve food throughout the day. It is so far only a tentative start, with just three of the main entries here doing it: the comfortably modernised but still traditional old Three Horseshoes not far from the Thames in Laleham (lots of sensible snacks), the Dog & Duck out in the country near Outwood, and the friendly Fox & Hounds in Walton on the Hill. But we expect to see this trend gather strength. It's only in the last few decades, since Great War emergency legislation first made them close for the afternoon, that pubs and inns had to abandon the tradition they'd formerly kept up over many centuries, of providing food as well as drink throughout the day. Now that they are at last allowed by law to get back to that tradition, we expect many more will do so. The Fox & Hounds, incidentally, is a new entry this year; other newcomers to the main entries include the Woodcock at Felbridge (good food, in most entertainingly unusual surroundings), the refreshingly unpretentious King William IV on its steep hillside at Mickleham

670

The Kings Head, Shepperton

(interesting vegetarian dishes), the Fox Revived in its spacious grounds out at Norwood Hill (good, quickly served food) and the Scarlett Arms at Walliswood (to everyone's relief as unspoilt as ever under its friendly newish landlord). Older stagers doing particularly well at the moment include the Plough at Blackbrook (good food, well kept beers, and exceptional wines), the Cricketers near Cobham (particularly popular with older people, but something for everyone), the Cricketers at Dorking (the newish licensee's had a much better year than some English cricketers we could name), the Crowns with its ever-changing menu at Haslemere, the spick and span Plough at Leigh, the civilised Punch Bowl near Ockley, the very foody Bell at Outwood, the idiosyncratic Skimmington Castle at Reigate Heath (its big new back car park makes it much more accessible), and the friendly Kings Head in Shepperton (it has an interesting variation on what has been this year's theme, the conservatory: detachable walls let it have more enclosed space in winter, more garden space in summer). Pubs currently looking particularly promising among the Lucky Dip entries at the end of the chapter include the Golden Grove in Chertsey, Sun at Dunsfold and Cricketers Arms at Ockley.

BATTS CORNER SU8240 Map 2
Blue Bell

Take road signposted Rowledge, Dockenfield, Frensham off A325 S of Farnham, by Halfway House pub at Bucks Horn Oak; after ¾ mile turn left into village lane; OS Sheet 186 reference 820410

Run in a very individual way, this civilised and friendly country pub has a cosy, low-ceilinged original room with bulgy white-painted stone walls, a big fireplace, and leatherette seats around low tables on the carpet. Other rooms open off: one, through an arch, has wheel-back chairs and settles on a tiled floor; another, with a high ceiling and more wheel-back chairs, opens into an airy big-windowed extension with button-back leatherette banquettes. Simple bar food includes substantial home-made sandwiches (from £1.05), soup (£1.15) and ploughman's (from £1.55). Well kept Ballards Best and Wassail, Brakspears SB, Courage Best and Fullers ESB tapped from the cask; darts, shove-ha'penny, dominoes and cribbage. Overlooking rolling countryside, the fine spreading garden has seats built around fairy-lit apple trees, tables on a terrace, tubs of flowers, and a tree-house and swings for children and toddlers. Large car park. *(Recommended by Mr and Mrs P Wilkins, W A Gardiner, Lyn and Bill Capper)*

Free house Real ale Lunchtime meals (not Sat or Sun) and snacks Open 11–2.30, 6–11 all year

BETCHWORTH TQ2049 Map 3
Dolphin

The Street

At the back of this flagstoned and gas-lit pub, the black-panelled and carpeted saloon bar has robust old-fashioned elm or oak tables, and a sonorous longcase clock; the front bar has kitchen chairs, plain tables and a big open fireplace. Well kept Youngs Bitter and Special on handpump; good toasted sandwiches, ploughman's, home-made shepherd's pie and some other hot dishes. There are some seats in the small laurel-shaded front courtyard, and more beyond the car park, opposite the church. *(Recommended by MKW, JMW, Phil and Sally Gorton; more reports please)*

Youngs Real ale Meals (not Sun or Mon evenings) and snacks (not Sun evening) Open 10.30–2.30, 5.30–11

BLACKBROOK   TQ1846 Map 3

Plough 🏆

On byroad E of A24, parallel to it, between Dorking and Newdigate, just N of the turn
E to Leigh

There's a risk that the brewery may replace by a manager the tenants who have
made this neatly kept, white-fronted pub pub so good; do keep your fingers
crossed! The airy saloon bar (which has a no-smoking area) has fresh flowers on the
tables, and large windows (with more fresh flowers on the sills) that look out on to
woods and open fields. Food is good and imaginative, with specials such as
Shropshire blue cheese and leek soup (£1.45), prawns with paw-paw (£2.95), cold
game pie (£4.50), ginger and orange lamb with onion rice (£4.95), beef and lime
curry, a grill such as ten-ounce rib-eye steak (£7.45), and sumptuous puddings like
blackcurrant bavarois or hot carrot pudding (£1.50); other food includes winter
filled baked potatoes (from £1.95), good ploughman's (£2.45), basket meals (from
£2.45), salads (from £2.95, fresh prawn £4.95), plaice (£3.75), lasagne, ratatouille
niçoise or ham steak (£3.95), prawn curry (£4.75), and steaks (from £6.25). Well
kept King & Barnes Bitter, Festive, Mild (in summer) and Old Ale (in winter) on
handpump; the pub regularly wins its brewery's annual best-kept cellar
competition. There are eighteen wines by the glass, including a wine of the month,
and vintage port by the glass; pleasant, friendly staff. Down some steps, the public
bar has brass-topped treadle tables, quite a formidable collection of ties as well as
old saws on the ceiling, bottles, flat-irons, and Tigger the tabby cat (Tess the black
labrador puts in an appearance after 10pm); shove-ha'penny, dominoes, cribbage
and piped music. You can sit outside on the grass or a small terrace at the back
(which in summer is full of tubs of flowers), or at the front under the fourteen
hanging baskets (based on red geraniums this year); they hope to extend the garden
facilities and possibly build a covered area. At Christmas time they hold annual
carol concerts and there are free mince pies and punch. Just south is a good stretch
of attractive oak wood with plenty of paths – and a big pond. (*Recommended by
Lindsey Shaw Radley, Chris Fluck, Peter Griffiths, George Key, Norman Foot, Mike Muston,
Mrs G Marlow, S A Lovett, Jason Caulkin, WFL*)

*King & Barnes   Licensee Robin Squire   Real ale   Meals and snacks (not Mon evening)
Open 11–2.30, 6–11; closed 25, 26 Dec and 1 Jan*

BLETCHINGLEY   TQ3250 Map 3

Whyte Harte

2½ miles from M25 junction 6; A22 towards East Grinstead then A25 towards Redhill

Dating partly from the thirteenth century, this busy pub has big, mostly open-plan
bars with dark low ceiling beams, rugs on the neat wood block floor, comfortable
old plush-covered settles and stools, old-fashioned prints on the walls, and an
inglenook fireplace with a heavily sagging chimney beam. Home-made bar food
includes sandwiches (from £1.20, smoked salmon £3), ploughman's (from £2.30),
ham and egg (£2.95), home-made steak and kidney pie (£3.50), salads (from
£4.50), beef Stroganoff (£5.50), steaks (from £5.95), and daily specials. On
Sundays they do only a roast lunch or ploughman's. Well kept Friary Meux, Ind
Coope Burton and Tetleys on handpump, and a fair range of wines; fruit machine,
trivia, and ring the bull. There are tables on a strip of lawn behind, sheltered by an
old stone wall and the backs of two of the Tudor cottages that are a feature of this
pretty village; you can also sit out in front, sharing the cobbles with tubs of flowers,
looking across the wide, sloping village street to the church. (*Recommended by
E G Parish; more reports please*)

*Friary Meux (Allied)   Licensees Helen and David Cooper   Real ale   Meals and snacks
(12–3, 6.30–10)   Children in dining-room   Open 11–3.30, 6–11; 11–11 Sat; closed
evening 25 Dec   Bedrooms tel Godstone (0883) 843231; £27.50(£31.50B)/£42(£48B)*

CHIDDINGFOLD SU9635 Map 2
Crown 🏠

In 1552 Edward VI, with a vast retinue, stayed in this lovely 700-year-old timbered building. It's the oldest licensed house in Surrey and has a splendid king-post roof, oak beams over two feet thick, fine oak panelling, a magnificently carved inglenook fireplace, massive chimneys, and a cabinet of coins going back some 400 years found here during renovations. The refurbished lower back area has a wood cooking fire with a central chimney dividing it into two separate rooms. Bar food includes sandwiches (from £1.50), home-made pâté (£1.75), ploughman's (from £1.75), lasagne (£2.50), steak, kidney and mushroom pie (£2.75), assorted cold meat salad (£2.85), and a hot daily special; they also do afternoon teas. Well kept Courage Best and Directors, Flowers, John Smiths, and Whitbreads Pompey Royal and Strong Country on handpump; piped music. The restaurant is panelled and tapestry-hung. There are seats outside looking across the village green to the church, which is much the same age, and other tables in a sheltered central courtyard. In early summer the inn is a marvellous sight with wood mullions, laburnum, lilac and wistaria. On 5 November there is a fireworks party on the village green. *(Recommended by Charles and Mary Winpenny, Gwen and Peter Andrews, Peter Griffiths, Hope Chenhalls)*

Free house   Licensees Peter Riley and John Lever   Real ale   Meals and snacks Restaurant   Children in restaurant and eating area of bar   Open 11–11 all year Bedrooms tel Wormley (042 879) 2255; £44B/£55B

Swan 🦢

Petworth Road (A283 S)

This well run tile-hung pub reflects the interests of the licensee in both the food and décor. The walls of the comfortable and spacious bar are hung with a good many hunting, shooting and fishing pictures and objects, and the game and game fish on the menu are probably bagged by him or his family. Other dishes (maybe using produce from the family farm) include sandwiches (from 95p), home-made soup (£1.10), filled baked potatoes (from £1.30), omelettes (from £1.35), ploughman's (from £1.95), squid with home-made garlic mayonnaise (£2.50), herby grilled sardines (£2.65), home-made steak and kidney pie (£3.40) and eight-ounce sirloin (£7.25); specials like marinated herring fillets (£2.50), lamb fillet with garlic and tarragon (£7.50), and grilled duck breast with cranberry port sauce (£8.75). The restaurant is strong on fish, local game and venison. Well kepts Benskins, Friary Meux and Gales HSB on handpump and decent wines. There are good winter log fires, a friendly pub atmosphere and a back den; fruit machine and trivia. Some seats outside. *(Recommended by Charles and Mary Winpenny, James Cane, Capt and Mrs L R Sowka; more reports please)*

Friary Meux (Allied)   Licensee Neil Bradford   Real ale   Meals and snacks   Restaurant tel Wormley (042 879) 2073   Children in restaurant   Open 11–3, 6–11 all year

CHIPSTEAD TQ2757 Map 3
Well House

3 miles from M25 junction 8; A217 towards Banstead, turn right at second roundabout following Mugswell, Chipstead signpost; can also be reached from A23 just W of Coulsdon

There is indeed a well outside this pretty country pub – on the sheltered back terrace (proceeds to charity). The garden is particularly attractive in summer, with hanging baskets, neat small flower beds, an old yew coppice then taller trees behind and masses of birdsong. Inside, there are big low fourteenth-century beams, inglenook fireplaces, and the central room (mainly used for standing) has a few tables and wheel-back chairs around the edge on the floral carpeting; a quieter room has many more tables and comfortable tapestried seats, and a side room has darts. Home-made bar food includes sandwiches, filled baked potatoes (from £1.60), ploughman's (£2), chilli con carne (£2.65), chicken curry, plaice or cod (£2.95), steak pie (£3.50) and puddings like apple, raspberry, apricot or blackcurrant pies with cream (£1.10). Well kept Bass, Charrington IPA on handpump, with winter Fullers ESB tapped from the cask; cribbage, dominoes, fruit machine and trivia; efficient service. *(Recommended by Mr and Mrs P Wilkins, Martin Aust, GRE, AE; more reports please)*

Charringtons (Bass)   Licensee W G Hummerston   Real ale   Meals and snacks (lunchtime, not Sun)   Children in eating area   Open 11–2.30, 5.30 (6 Sat)–11 all year

COBHAM   TQ1060 Map 3

Cricketers

Downside Common; from A245 on Byfleet side of Cobham follow Downside signpost into Downside Bridge Road, follow road into its right fork – away from Cobham Park – at second turn after bridge, then take next left turn into the pub's own lane

Some of the beams in this popular rambling country pub are so low they have crash-pads on them, and bar furnishings are simple and traditional. Also, there are some time-bowed standing timbers, places where you can see the wide oak ceiling boards and ancient plastering lathes, horsebrasses and big brass platters on the walls, and a good winter log fire. Good bar food includes sandwiches (from £1.35), lasagne, spare ribs, chicken breast in garlic or steak and mushroom pie (from £3.25), salads (from £3.75, including coronation chicken or fresh seafood), and vegetarian dishes. Well kept but pricey Ruddles Best and County, and Websters Yorkshire on handpump; young helpful service as a rule, though it can get very busy at weekends. The garden is neat and charming, with standard roses, dahlias and other bedding plants, urns and hanging baskets. *(Recommended by David and Eloise Smaylen, John Pettit, John Branford, R B Crail, Andrew and Michele Wells, MKW, JMW, Peter Griffiths, Mr and Mrs P Wilkins, P L Jackson, Norman Foot, I S Wilson, Alasdair Knowles, WFL)*

Watneys   Licensee B J W Luxford   Real ale   Meals and snacks (12–2.15, 7–10.30) Restaurant (not Sun evening) tel Cobham (0932) 62105   Children in stable bar Open 11–2.30, 6–11 all year

COLDHARBOUR   TQ1543 Map 3

Plough

Village signposted in network of small roads around Abinger and Leith Hill, off A24 and A29

There's been another change of licensees at this pretty black-shuttered white house in a quiet hamlet by Buryhill Woods. The two bars have timbering in the warm-coloured dark ochre walls, stripped light beams, quite unusual little chairs around the tables in the snug red-carpeted room on the left, little decorative plates on the walls and a big open fire in the one on the right – which leads through to the restaurant. Home-made bar food includes vegetable soup (£1.50), shepherd's pie (£3.25), steak and kidney pie, vegetarian quiche or lasagne (£3.75), curry (£4.20), mixed grill (£5.95), and puddings such as fresh strawberry Pavlova or spotted dick and ginger sponge pudding (£1.50). Well kept Adnams Broadside, Badger Best, Buckleys Best, Ringwood Old Thumper and Theakstons Old Peculier on handpump, a monthly guest such as Fullers London Pride and ESB, Greene King Abbot or Wadworths 6X, and country wines and farm cider. The games-bar on the left has darts, pool, cribbage, dominoes and piped music. There are picnic-table sets in front, with one or two tubs of flowers; the peaceful garden – with attractive views – has a fish pond with waterlilies, more picnic-table sets and is fairy-lit at night; a terrace with barbecue area is planned. Dogs (on a lead, though not in the restaurant) and walkers are welcome. *(Recommended by WFL, D J Penny, M B Porter, Jenny and Brian Seller, Ian Phillips, Ray Challoner, TOH)*

Free house   Licensees Richard and Anna Abrehart   Real ale   Meals and snacks (11.30–2.15, 7.30–9.30)   Restaurant tel Dorking (0306) 711793   Children in family-room and eating area of bar   Open 11.30–3, 6.30–11; 11.30–11 Sat in summer; closed evening 25 Dec

COMPTON   SU9546 Map 2

Harrow 🍺

B3000

Mainly popular for its unusual range of attractively presented food, this busy village pub has a cheerful, relaxed atmosphere and polite service. Listed on several blackboards, the food includes sandwiches such as smoked turkey and avocado or thickly cut beef (from £1.75), cream of leek soup, baked Brie with almonds, pasta with mussels and shrimps in a thick provençale sauce, baked trout with bacon, Delhi lamb with poppadums and chutney or Chinese lamb with noodles (all from around £3.50), and seafood platter (£12). Well kept Friary Meux Bitter, Ind Coope Burton and Tetleys on handpump. Some nice touches in the bars include brass horse-head coat hooks, photographs of the area, and a bas-relief in wood of the pub sign. The main bar has some interesting racing pictures below the ancient ceiling, mostly portraits of horses such as Nijinsky, jockey caricatures and signed race-finish photographs; other beamed rooms with latched rustic doors open off it. Piped music, space game. You can sit outside in summer, round by the car park but looking out to gentle slopes of pasture. In the pretty village the art nouveau Watts Chapel and Gallery are interesting, and the church itself is attractive; Loseley House is nearby too. *(Recommended by Philip King, Peter Griffiths, Dr John Innes, TOH, Charles and Mary Winpenny, Ian and Liz Phillips, Jenny Seller)*

Friary Meux (Allied)   Licensees Roger and Susan Seaman   Real ale   Meals and snacks (12–3, 5.30–10)   Children in eating area of bar   Open 11–3, 5.30 (6 Sat)–11 all year; closed 25 and 26 Dec

DORKING   TQ1649 Map 3

Cricketers

81 South Street; from centre follow signs to Horsham (A2003)

Friendly new licensees – who formerly ran the popular Beehive at Englefield Green, Surrey – have taken over this lively and informal town pub. They've changed very little, and the comfortably modernised, attractive bar still has stripped and sealed brick walls decorated with Spy cricketer caricatures and other cricketing pictures, library chairs around cast-iron-framed tables, well cushioned sturdy modern settles, and a central servery with a big modern etched-glass cricketers mirror; there's a log-effect gas fire. Very good value, home-made bar food includes sandwiches, filled baked potatoes, quiches or liver and bacon (£2), lamb hot-pot or chilli con carne (£2.10) and steak pie (£2.30). Well kept Fullers Chiswick, ESB and London Pride on handpump; darts, cribbage, dominoes and piped music. Up steps at the back there's a very pretty little sheltered terrace, interestingly planted with roses, a good red honeysuckle, uncommon shrubs and herbaceous plants, and gently floodlit at night. *(Recommended by Stephen King, Lindsey Shaw Radley, D J Penny, Tony Bland, Chris Payne)*

Fullers   Licensee Iain Anderson   Real ale   Meals and snacks (not Sat or Sun)   Nearby daytime parking difficult   Open 11–2.30, 5.30–11 Mon–Thurs; 11–3, 6–11 Sat

---

Though we don't usually mention it in the text, lots of pubs will now make coffee – always worth asking. And some – particularly in the North – will do tea.

nr EWHURST   TQ0940 Map 3

Windmill

Ewhurst–Shere back road; follow Shere signposts from E end of Ewhurst main street, or ask for Pitch Hill

It's the fine garden that draws people here – on a clear day you can see right across Sussex Weald to the South Coast, and the woods are marvellous for walking (the pub is on *Good Walks Guide* Walk 55). There are sheltered tables among flowers and shrubs that look out over the beautifully kept terraced lawns that drop steeply away below. Given the location, several people have been disappointed, though, that in winter provision for families isn't better. The main bar has easy chairs and a patterned carpet, and a sparser back bar, without the view, has darts, dominoes, shove-ha'penny, fruit machine, space game. Straightforward bar food – one reader arriving at 1.30 was surprised, after being told he was too late for food, to see a regular come in five minutes later and order a three-course lunch. Well kept King & Barnes Sussex and Youngs Special on handpump. *(Recommended by KC, Peter Griffiths; more reports, please)*

Free house   Real ale   Meals and snacks   Possible parking difficulties on sunny summer weekends   Open 10.30–2.30, 6–11; closed 25 Dec

FELBRIDGE   TQ3639 Map 3

Woodcock ✿

A22 N

You might easily speed past this on the main road, thinking that it's just another plush roadhouse. But it's been quite transformed by the Joneses, who made a name for themselves first at the Red Barn, Blindley Heath, in the 1970s, and then at the Spotted Dog near Penshurst in the 1980s. There's a crowded and companionable little flagstoned entrance bar (with Harveys PA, King & Barnes and Pilgrims Best on handpump, and decent wines and spirits). This opens on the left into a quieter carpeted room with unusual furniture from heavily upholstered chairs to finely lacquered oriental benches, interesting prints on the walls, oriental screens, occasional tables with copies of *Vogue*, a stuffed bird of paradise, attractive table-lamps – and lots of candles, in wall sconces and on tables. A handsome black spiral staircase leads up from here into the high eaves, where an almost entirely candle-lit gallery has low stools and sprawly cushions around a couple of low tables at one end, a fanciful crowd of decorative fans and parasols, and a flamboyant dressing-table which houses, among lots of other bird images elsewhere, the only woodcock in the place – but this one's a delicate skeleton. This in turn opens into a lovely old-fashioned Victorian dining-room with just one long, handsome table, used for bar meals (or you can book the whole room – a nice place for a private party of a dozen or so). On the right of the downstairs core, a few steps take you into a sumptuous Victorian parlour area filled with thickly cushioned chairs, settees and chaises-longues that would do credit to any seraglio; beyond that yet more candles glitter and flicker in the inviting restaurant. Bar food includes sandwiches (from £1.25), soup (£1.50), ploughman's (£2.75), a roast (£4.25) and steaks (from eight-ounce sirloin, £7.25), with quite a lot of fish fresh from Argyllshire – moules (£3.50), plate of mixed shellfish (£3.50), langoustines (£4.75) and grilled giant prawns with garlic sauce (£5.75); friendly service, maybe unobtrusive piped music. There are tables under cocktail parasols on the flagstones of a sunken front courtyard. *(Recommended by Bruce Poynter, A W Peters, Mrs V Newman)*

Free house   Licensees Peter and Valerie Jones   Real ale   Meals and snacks (12.30–2, 7–10)   Restaurant (not Mon lunchtime) tel East Grinstead (0342) 325859   Children welcome   Jazz duo in gallery Sun evening   Open 11–3, 6–11 all year

FICKLESHOLE TQ3860 Map 3
White Bear

Off A2022 Purley Road just S of its junction with A212 roundabout; at The Willows follow
Addington Court Golf Club signpost into Featherbed Lane and keep on

Converted from a row of old cottages, this attractive and friendly whitewashed pub
is quite a find for the outer fringes of London. As well as plenty of tables outside,
there's a big play area, and a walk-through paddock with hens, ducks, geese and
white doves, pheasants and rabbits in big pens, and a Nubian goat; other paddocks
have a donkey, ponies and sheep. Inside, a rambling series of dimly lit rooms dates
in parts from the fifteenth century. Some are very cosy and some quite spacious,
with low and heavy black beams, quarry tiles and oak parquet, polished flagstones,
bay windows inset with stained-glass panels, an attractive variety of seating
including some antique settles, and decorations ranging from china on Delft shelves
through halberds and pikes to a handsome Act of Parliament clock. There are open
fires and solid-fuel stoves. Lunchtime bar food includes soup (70p), quiches (from
£1.35), ploughman's (from £2.20), salads (from £3) and a few hot dishes; also,
Sunday lunch, and more substantial evening dishes. Well kept Fullers London Pride
and ESB on handpump; efficient service. Darts (winter), three fruit machines,
inoffensive piped music. *(Recommended by W J Wonham, Alan Skull, Michele and Andrew
Wells, Ray Challoner, Alasdair Knowles, AE, GRE)*

*Free house   Real ale   Meals and snacks   Children in eating areas   Open 11–2.30, 6–11 all
year; may open all day Sat*

GOMSHALL TQ0847 Map 3
Black Horse

A25 Dorking–Guildford

This biggish white hotel has a calm and relaxing spacious saloon bar with dark
squared panelling, Gothick dining-chairs and sideboard, open fire with copper hods
for logs and coal, old-fashioned leaded-light bar counter, and a decidedly
conversational atmosphere. Tasty food includes sandwiches (from £1.10), soup
(£1.25), ploughman's (£2.25), filled baked potatoes (£2.50), macaroni cheese (£3),
chicken curry (£3.50), steak and kidney pie (£4.25), seafood platter (£4.50) and
daily specials, with a special Friday fish menu; well kept Youngs on handpump. The
public bar on the other side has darts, shove-ha'penny, dominoes and cribbage.
There are tables under cocktail parasols on a back terrace and up on a spacious
sloping lawn with fruit trees – and good swings including a gondola one.
(Recommended by Michele and Andrew Wells, Chris Payne, P L Jackson, Don Mather, BMS)

*Youngs   Licensee Tony Savage   Real ale   Meals and snacks (12–2, 7–10)
Restaurant   Children in restaurant   Open 11–2.30, 6–11 weekdays, 11–11 Sat in summer;
closed evening 25 Dec   Bedrooms tel Shere (048 641) 2242; £19.95/£39.90*

HASCOMBE TQ0039 Map 3
White Horse

In an attractive spot, this rose-draped country pub is popular for its good range of
bar food. You can eat in the light and airy extension or in an inner beamed area
with quiet small-windowed alcoves. Best to get there early if you want a table as
people flock here from Godalming for business lunches: sandwiches (from £1.50
for good ham), whitebait (£2.25), home-made meaty burgers (£3 85), swordfish
steak (£4.25), fresh, interesting salads with vegetables like mange-tout or avocado
(from £4.25, prawn £6.25), poussin dijonnaise (£4.65), good beef curry with
apricots (£4.85), and puddings like treacle tart or fruit crumbles (£2.50). Well kept
Friary Meux Bitter, Ind Coope Burton and Gales HSB on handpump; quite a few
wines. Darts, shove-ha'penny, dominoes, fruit machine and piped music. There are

some tables in several places outside – on a little patio by the front porch, in a bower and under a walnut tree. Nearby, Winkworth Arboretum (B2130 towards Godalming) has walks among beautiful trees and shrubs. *(Recommended by Gordon Hewitt, W A Gardiner, Hilairie Miles-Sharp, Lyn and Bill Capper, R P Taylor)*

Friary Meux (Allied)   Licensee Susan Barnett   Real ale   Meals and snacks   Restaurant (not Sun evening) tel Hascombe (048 632) 258   Children welcome   Open 11–3, 5.30–11 all year

HASLEMERE   SU9032 Map 2

Crowns 🏅

Weyhill; B2131 towards Liphook, close to railway bridge

The interesting menu in this busy food pub changes all the time and may include mussels with garlic stuffing (£2.85), tagliatelle with cream, ham and herbs (£3.25), baked avocado with crab or cheesy leek and potato pie (£3.50), pork chop in a plum and red wine spicy sauce (£4.95), rabbit in mustard and marjoram (£5.25), peppered chicken in cream and Dijon sauce (£5.45), salmon steak with sorrel sauce (£5.95), and vegetarian dishes such as aubergine and mushroom lasagne made with wholewheat lasagne; they prefer to let people add their own salt. Well kept Friary Meux, Ind Coope Burton, King & Barnes Bitter and Tetleys on handpump, and around 46 wines. The pleasantly light and airy bar has comfortable chairs, shelves of books, unusual lamps, wall prints, flowers on the tables and piped music. There are tables outside, front and back; the pub is on *Good Walk Guide* Walk 53. *(Recommended by Maggie and Derek Washington; more reports please)*

Friary Meux (Allied)   Licensee Mrs Brenda Heath   Real ale   Meals and snacks (11–2.30, 6–10.30)   Restaurant tel Haslemere (0428) 3112   Children welcome at lunchtime   Open 11–3, 6–11; open for coffee from 9am; closed 25 Dec

HORLEY   TQ2842 Map 3

Olde Six Bells

3 miles from M23 junction 9: from Gatwick turn-off follow A23 towards Redhill and London, then Horley signpost at roundabout; after 600 yards pub signposted by sharp left turn into Church Road, which is first real left turn

Some changes here this year include the refurbishment of the saloon area (part of which is thought to have been a fourteenth-century or even older chapel – it certainly looks that way), and the building of an extension. The busy open-plan bar – which is a popular meeting-place for young people – has heavy beams, butter-coloured plaster walls and ceiling, a tiled floor and some copper measuring dippers for decoration. Upstairs is quieter, carpeted, with high rafters and heavy wall timbering: you can book tables up here for the home-made food, such as rolls (from £1.30), ploughman's (from £2), vegetable lasagne, turkey and ham pie or chilli con carne (all £3.10) and salads (from £3.25), with evening meals such as lamb marengo, pork normandie or veal korma (all £5.20). Well kept Bass and Charrington IPA on handpump; shove-ha'penny, dominoes, darts, fruit machine and piped music. Beyond a sheltered back flagstone terrace with jasmine on the wall is a sizeable garden beside the little River Mole. *(Recommended by Lindsey Shaw Radley, Jacquie Mundle, Comus Elliott, E G Parish)*

Charringtons (Bass)   Real ale   Meals and snacks   Restaurant tel Horley (0293) 782209   Children in restaurant   Open 11–11 all year

LALEHAM   TQ0568 Map 3

Three Horseshoes

B377

A conservatory extension is to be added on to this thirteenth-century building this year, and the comfortably modernised open-plan bar has had some refurbishment:

burgundy plush seats on the red carpet, lots of big copper pots and pans hanging from beams, interesting cock-fighting prints on the red walls, and blacksmiths' tools hanging over the main fireplace. One small alcove has high-backed settles. Good, reasonably priced bar food specialises in huge baked potatoes with hot or cold fillings (from £2.75, prawns £3.95), as well as an excellent choice of sandwiches (from £1.10, prawn with asparagus £1.80), ploughman's (£2.25), salads (from £4.25), and a selection of daily specials such as fresh mushroom quiche, lamb tikka masala or rump steak. Well kept Ruddles Best and County, Trumans Best Bitter and Websters Yorkshire on handpump; decent wines. The inn's façade is almost hidden by wistaria, hanging baskets and cartwheels, and the garden has some statues and plenty of tables – some under a cleverly rainproofed 'arbour' of creepers. The lane opposite leads down to a stretch of the Thames that is popular for picnics and sunbathing. *(Recommended by R B Crail, Richard Houghton, M Rising, Ian Phillips, Miss L Masolle, S Matthews, Simon Collett-Jones)*

Watneys   Licensee Philip Jones   Real ale   Meals and snacks (noon–9 Mon–Fri, 12–2, 7–9 Sat; not Sun evening)   Restaurant (not Sun evening) tel Staines (0784) 52617   Open 11–11 all year

LEIGH   TQ2246 Map 3

Plough

3 miles S of A25 Dorking–Reigate, signposted from Betchworth (which itself is signposted off the main road); also signposted from South Park area of Reigate; on village green

Cheerful and friendly, this pretty tiled and white-boarded cottage has beams in the lounge on the right that are so low they really do need their crash-pads; the timbered white walls are hung with a good many Cecil Aldin prints, and there are flowers on the tables. On the left the more local bar has a good bow-window seat, more Cecil Aldin prints on the yellowing walls (and darts, shove-ha'penny, dominoes, table skittles, cribbage, fruit machine, space game, trivia and piped radio). Lunchtime bar food, all made from fresh ingredients, includes sandwiches (from £1, rare beef in French bread £1.85), ploughman's (from £1.85), salads (from £2.90), very popular ham and eggs (£3.30) and dishes of the day such as deep-fried fresh cod, home-made steak, oyster and Guinness pie or Norfolk fish pie (£3.40); puddings like rhubarb crumble (£1.50). In the evenings (except at weekends) the food takes a turn towards dishes such as duck or lemon sole poached in wine with prawns, and steaks; best to get there early if you want a seat. Well kept King & Barnes Bitter, Festive, Mild and winter Old on handpump; Gales country wines, more sensible soft-drinks pricing than usual, and a good choice of crispy nibbles; helpful staff. Limited nearby parking. The pub is bright with geraniums in summer, and has picnic-table sets under cocktail parasols in an attractive side garden bordered by a neat white picket fence. *(Recommended by John Pettit, Reg Tickner, W M Elliott, J Crawford, Lindsey Shaw Radley, P L Jackson, Lyn and Bill Capper)*

King & Barnes   Graham and Geraldine Walker   Real ale   Meals and snacks; not Sun, not Mon evening   Restaurant tel Dawes Green (030 678) 348   Children in restaurant   Morris dancing/entertainment in summer   Open 11–2.30, 6–11 all year; closed evening 25 Dec

Seven Stars

Pretty country pub with a flower-filled garden and summer Sunday barbecues. Inside, the comfortable saloon bar has an early eighteenth-century sign painted on the wall, reading '...you are Wellcome to sit down for your ease, pay what you call for and drink what you please', and a 1633 inglenook fireback with the royal coat of arms in the smoke-blackened brick inglenook fireplace; also, lots of racing pictures and horsebrasses. The plainer public bar has an alley set aside for darts. Good bar food and well kept Ind Coope Burton Burton and Friary Meux. *(Recommended by Gwen and Peter Andrews, W A Lund, Jason Caulkin; more reports please)*

Ind Coope (Allied)   Real ale   Meals and snacks   Children welcome   Open 10.30–2.30, 6.30–11

MICKLEHAM   TQ1753 Map 3

King William IV

Byttom Hill; narrow steep track up hill off A24 Leatherhead–Dorking, just N of main B2289
village turn off; OS Sheet 187 reference 173538

Cut into the hillside, this unpretentious place is a steep climb up from the rough
track. There's a snug plank-panelled front bar looking down the hill, and a rather
more spacious quite brightly lit back bar with kitchen-type chairs around its cast-
iron-framed tables. The atmosphere's chatty and easy-going, with darts sensibly
placed in one corner, unobtrusive nostalgic piped pop music, and a serviceable
grandfather clock. In summer its garden is very popular, mainly brick-tiled, with
crazy paving in front, then grass below, and plenty of tables – some in a wooden
open-sided shelter. A path leads straight up into open country. Rather unusual bar
food includes filled baked potatoes or ploughman's (£2.75), several vegetarian
dishes such as tostados with tomato and bean sauce (£2.25), nut and tomato bake
(£2.95) or courgette and mushroom flan (£3.50), salads, chilli con carne or steak
and kidney pie (£3.25) and cod with prawns or rogan josh (£3.75); well kept
Adnams, Badger Best, Fullers London Pride and Marstons Pedigree on handpump;
informal, friendly service; cribbage, dominoes; good log fires. *(Recommended by
R P Taylor, Norman Foot, WFL)*

*Free house   Licensee Mr Beynon   Real ale   Meals and snacks (lunchtime, not Sun)
Occasional guitarist summer   Open 11–2.30, 6–11; 12–2.30, 7–10.30 in winter;
closed 25 Dec*

NEWDIGATE   TQ2042 Map 3

Surrey Oaks

Parkgate Road

The big attractive garden outside this family-run country pub has a large terrace, a
rockery with illuminated pools, fountains and waterfall, and a flock of pure white
doves; they also have sheep, a calf, and an aviary of budgerigars, and all sorts of
fowls. You can buy their free-range duck, hen and goose eggs from the bar. Inside,
the main lounge has tapestried seats in little partly curtained booths, and rustic
tables lit by lanterns hanging low from fairy-lit lowered beams. A much older part
on the right has a little snug beamed room by a coal-effect gas fire, then a standing
area with extraordinarily large flagstones and an open fire. Bar food includes
sandwiches or ploughman's, lasagne, bacon roly-poly, steak pie or pudding (£3.25),
vegetarian dishes, mixed grills and steaks, with puddings like treacle pudding
(£1.25); carvery Friday and Saturday evenings and Sunday lunchtime. Well kept
Friary Meux, Ind Coope Burton, King & Barnes and Taylor-Walker on handpump.
A separate games-room has a well lit pool-table, darts, shove-ha'penny, dominoes,
cribbage, a fruit machine, space game and juke box. *(Recommended by Norman Foot,
Mrs I Sears; more reports please)*

*Friary Meux (Allied)   Licensee Colin Haydon   Real ale   Meals and snacks (not Sun
evening)   Restaurant (not Sun evening) tel Newdigate (030 677) 200   Children welcome
Middle-of-the-road live music Sun evening   Open 11–3, 6–11 all year*

NORWOOD HILL   TQ2343 Map 3

Fox Revived

Leigh–Charlwood back road

Firmly cottage-revival in front, with broad bare boards, shelves of books, kitchen
tables, chairs, cushioned pews and an attractive stripped high-backed settle, and
decorative mugs on the beams, this spreads back into a similarly furnished and
comfortably informal dining area. Here, there's a wood-burning stove in a central

brick hearth, a set of sharply contrasty photographs in one alcove, and a pleasantly relaxed atmosphere. This part opens in turn into a double conservatory with its own stove, cane chairs and tables on shiny brown tiles, and some big plants. Hearty heaps of good food, served cheerily and with splendid celerity, might include smoked salmon or garlic prawns (£3.25) as starters, with evening main dishes such as chicken suprême or lamb kebab (£5.95), a hefty half-shoulder of lamb (£7.65), lemon sole (£7.95), seafood platter (£8.95) and Dover sole or steak with blue cheese sauce (£10.95); and at lunchtime giant sausages (£1.95), ploughman's (from £2.50), open sandwiches (from £2.60) and chilli con carne (£3.95). Good puddings; well kept Friary Meux Best and Ind Coope Burton on handpump, decent wines; daily newspapers; rather muffled piped pop music. Picnic-table sets are spread well through their big garden, which has a retired tractor among its weeping willow, apple and other trees, and backs on to paddocks. (*Recommended by D J Penny, Mrs H M M Tickner, J H Bell*)

Friary Meux (Allied)   Licensee Gary Kidd   Real ale   Meals and snacks (until 10)   Live music most Sun evenings   Open 11–2.30, 5–11 all year; 11–3, 6–11 Sat

nr OCKLEY   TQ1439 Map 3

Punch Bowl ★

Oakwoodhill (some maps and signposts spell it Okewoodhill); village signposted off A29 S of Ockley

Spotlessly kept, this friendly, partly tile-hung old house has a peaceful, homely bar with lots of beams, polished, big dark flagstones, some timbering, an antique settle among simpler country seats and scrubbed deal tables, an inglenook fireplace with huge logs smouldering gently on the vast round hearth, and maybe the two friendly cats – a tabby and a three-legged marmalade monster. Bar food includes sandwiches, ham and eggs (£3), chicken curry (£3.50), scampi (£4), and steak and kidney pie (£4.50). Well kept Badger Best, King & Barnes Bitter, Youngs Special and two guest ales on handpump; a good choice of malt whiskies, and efficient service. Another plainer bar has sensibly placed darts, a juke box and fruit machine. You can sit outside at tables on several different birdsong-serenaded terraces, with fields with oak trees and woods stretching away on all sides. (*Recommended by Shirley Fluck, WFL, Norman Foot, Jane Palmer*)

Free house   Licensee Robert Chambers   Real ale   Meals and snacks (12–2, 7–10; not Sun–Tues evenings)   Restaurant tel Oakwood Hill (030 679) 249   Children in special room for them   Open 11–3, 5 (5.30 Sat)–11 all year

OUTWOOD   TQ3245 Map 3

Bell ★ ✿

Just down the lane from the broad village green with its striking white windmill, this popular food pub has a carpeted front bar with low beams, elm and oak tables and chairs, some in Jacobean style, and a vast stone inglenook fireplace; there's another lounge bar at the back. Efficiently served bar food includes main dishes such as steak and kidney pie (£4.75), fresh whole plaice (£5.75), English rack of lamb (£6.25), char-grilled sirloin or rump steak (£6.50) or fillet steak topped with duck pâté (£9.50). They do sandwiches (from £1.50), ploughman's (£2.50), filled baked potatoes (from £2.75) and salads (£4.95) at lunchtime; also, morning coffee and an all-year barbecue (Sunday to Tuesday evenings) outdoors in summer. If you want a table, it's best to book in advance, especially in the evening (when drinking-only space is limited). Well kept Batemans XXXB, Charrington IPA, Fremlins, King & Barnes Sussex and Festive and Pilgrim Best on handpump. In summer the well managed garden is a peaceful place to sit in, among flowers and shrubs on the sheltered lawn, and look past its bordering pine trees to the fine view over rolling fields, dotted with oak trees and woods. *(Recommended by W J Wonham, I S Wilson, Sue Carlyle, Lindsey Shaw Radley, W A Gardiner, Mrs H M M Tickner, Mike Muston, Chris Fluck, GRE, AE, Alasdair Knowles, Andy Tye, Sue Hill, J H Bell)*

Free house   Licensee Harry Pam   Real ale   Meals and lunchtime snacks   Open 11–2.30, 6–11 all year

Dog & Duck

From A23 in Salfords S of Redhill take Station turning – eventually after you cross the M23 the pub's on your left at the T-junction; coming from village centre, head towards Coopers Hill and Prince of Wales Road

With far more space than you'd imagine from outside, this isolated partly tile-hung country cottage rambles through various rooms with ochre walls and stripped dark beams, comfortable settles and oak armchairs as well as more ordinary seats, rugs on the quarry tiles, a good log fire, and a cheerful, lively atmosphere. Bar food includes ploughman's in variety (£2.25), ham and egg (£3.50), mixed grill (£4.25), dressed crab salad (£4.50), a separate vegetarian menu, and children's dishes. In the evening the choice is more on the lines of soup with a puff pastry lid (£2.50), double egg mayonnaise (£3.50), and guinea-fowl with gooseberry sauce or poached fresh salmon (£7.50); they also do afternoon teas (£2) and Sunday roast lunch. Well kept Badger Best and Tanglefoot on handpump, with guest beers such as Adnams Best and Broadside, Everards Tiger, Gribble Reg's Tipple and Wadworths 6X (the specific gravities are listed on a blackboard); decent wines; newspapers out for customers, also shove-ha'penny, ring the bull, cribbage, Scrabble, backgammon, chess, trivia and unobtrusive piped music. The restaurant area, with another huge fireplace, really only functions separately in the evening – during the day it's more part of the bar that it communicates with. Picnic-table sets under cocktail parasols on the grass outside look over a safely fenced-off duck pond to the meadows. There's a pleasant walk to the old windmill in the village – the round trip's about an hour. *(Recommended by WFL, Lindsey Shaw Radley, BHP, Sue Corrigan, Alasdair Knowles)*

Badger   Licensee Amanda Buchanan-Munro   Real ale   Meals and snacks (noon–10pm) Evening restaurant tel Smallfield (034 284) 2964   Children in restaurant   Open 11–11 weekdays; 12–3, 7–10.30 Sat; closed evening 25 Dec

PIRBRIGHT   SU9455 Map 2

Royal Oak

Aldershot Road; A324S of village

Carefully kept, this tile-hung extended Tudor cottage is furnished with wheel-back chairs, tapestried wall seats and little dark church-like pews set around neat tables; also, ancient stripped brickwork, heavy beams and timbers, gleaming brasses set around the big low-beamed fireplace, and a rambling series of side alcoves. Bar food consists of sandwiches (from £1), ploughman's (from £2), pâté (£3), salads using produce from their own garden (from £3.75), gammon, lamb chops, or pork cutlets (£4) and rump steak (£5); no puddings. Very well kept Badger Best, Eldridge Pope Royal Oak, Marstons Pedigree, Shepherd Neame Old, Wadworths and Youngs Special on handpump, and several malt whiskies; the licensee firmly upholds the principle that a pub should be an alehouse – he doesn't serve coffee, and isn't keen to serve rounds of non-alcoholic drinks. A pleasant absence of games, machines and music. In summer the beautifully neat gardens are a mass of colour, and even in winter the many dwarf conifers keep them cheerful before the first spring bulbs show. *(Recommended by K Chenneour, Lyn and Bill Capper, J P Berryman, J T Alford, KC)*

Free house   Licensee Geoffry Walkling   Real ale   Lunchtime meals and snacks (not Sun) Open 11–2.30, 6–10.30 (11 Sat); closed evenings 25 and 26 Dec and 1 Jan

There are report forms at the back of the book.

PYRFORD LOCK   TQ0458 Map 3
Anchor

Lock Lane; service road off A3 signposted to RHS Wisley Gardens – continue past them towards Pyrford

Particularly popular with families, this open-plan modern country pub has a comfortable bar with a part-carpet and part-attractive brick floor, and big picture windows that give a fine view of the narrowboats on the canal leaving the dock and edging under the steeply hump-backed road bridge. The upstairs bar is full of narrowboat memorabilia and is mainly reserved for parents with small children. Bar food includes ploughman's (£1.85), steak and kidney pie (£2.95) and scampi (£3.25); Courage Best and Directors and John Smiths on handpump, and lots of bustle and noise from the tannoy system. Friendly, efficient staff; fruit machine, piped music. Outside on an extensive canalside terrace there are masses of picnic-table sets. The Royal Horticultural Society's nearby gardens are open every day (members only on Sunday mornings). *(Recommended by John Pettit, Ian Phillips, W A Gardiner, Dave Braisted, WTF, Peter Griffiths)*

Courage   Licensee Stephen Kerrawn   Real ale   Lunchtime meals and snacks   Children in own first-floor room   Open 11–3, 5–11 weekdays; 11–11 Sat; 11–2.30, 6–11 in winter

REIGATE HEATH   TQ2349 Map 3
Skimmington Castle ★

3 miles from M25 junction 8: through Reigate take A25 Dorking (West), then on edge of Reigate turn left past Black Horse into Flanchford Road; after ¼ mile turn left into Bonny's Road (unmade, very bumpy track); after crossing golf course fork right up hill

Old-fashioned and cottagey, this popular place has a small but efficiently run central serving-counter, framed in dark simple panelling, with a collection of oddly shaped pipes (and a skull among them) dangling over it. Leading off here, the bright main front bar has a miscellany of chairs and tables, shiny brown vertical panelling decorated with earthenware bottles, decorative plates, brass and pewter, a brown plank ceiling, and the uncommon traditional game of ring the bull. The back rooms are partly panelled too – cosy, with old-fashioned settles and Windsor chairs; one has a big brick fireplace with its bread oven still beside it. Bar food includes local sausages (30p), soup (75p), sandwiches (from 70p, cream cheese and prawn with walnuts £1.40, steak rolls from £1.70), basket meals (from £1.20, scampi £3), ploughman's (from £1.40), salads (from £3.20, crab £4.20), gammon steak with egg (£3.80), steaks (from £6) and daily specials. Friary Meux Best, Ind Coope Burton, King & Barnes Bitter and Tetleys on handpump, and Addlestones draught cider; the stuffed fox leering out of the crisp packets is commonly known as Derek. A small room down steps at the back has space games, and there are darts, shove-ha'penny, cribbage and dominoes. You can sit outside on the crazy-paved front terrace or on the grass by lilac bushes, and there's now a large rear car park; paths from here wind into the surrounding wooded countryside. *(Recommended by Andrew and Michele Wells, W A Gardiner, Mike Muston, John Day)*

Friary Meux (Allied)   Licensee Andrew Fisher   Real ale   Meals (lunchtime) and snacks Children in small back room until 9   Open 11–3, 5.30–11 all year

RUNFOLD   SU8747 Map 2
Jolly Farmer

A31 just E of Farnham

There's a warm welcome in this busy open-plan roadside pub, and comfortable furnishings include some massive rough-cut elm tables and chairs as well as more conventionally comfortable seats; the painted vineleaf dado around its cornices is unusual. Popular with businessmen at lunchtime, the bar food includes ploughman's (from £2.65), quiche (£4), meats (£6), puddings (£1.90) and a daily special; evening dishes tend to be considerably more ambitious. Well kept Courage Best and Directors on handpump, also children's cocktails (and adult ones); nibbles on the bar. Darts, shove-ha'penny, dominoes, cribbage, fruit machine and unobtrusive piped music. At one end of the pub, big windows look out on the back garden and terrace, where there are plenty of tables among some flowers and shrubs, and a good adventure playground. No dogs. *(Recommended by Michael and Harriet Robinson, Jenny and Brian Seller, Mr and Mrs P Wilkins)*

Courage   Real ale   Meals and snacks   Restaurant tel *Runfold (025 18) 2074   Children in restaurant   Open 11–2.30, 5.30–11 all year*

SHEPPERTON   TQ0867 Map 3

Kings Head   [illustrated on page 670]

Church Square; E side of B375

The new conservatory here has detachable outer walls which are removed in summer to give an airy covered area merging with the pretty terrace. It's an attractive pub with several small rooms full of dark panelling, oak beams, and oak parquet flooring, and there's an inglenook fireplace. Good, imaginative food includes sandwiches (from 95p), very good Welsh rarebit to a secret recipe (£2.25), herby sausages (£2.50), Shepperton pie or chilli con carne (£2.75), steak and kidney pie (£3.35) and scampi (£5.15). Well kept Courage Best and Directors on handpump and a good range of wines; fruit machine and juke box in the public bar. There are window boxes and black shutters, and a view of the brick and flint church. *(Recommended by Simon Collett-Jones, Ian Phillips; more reports please)*

Courage   Licensee David Longhurst   Real ale   Meals and snacks (12–2.15, 8–10.15; not Sun)   Lunchtime restaurant (closed Sun) tel *Walton-on-Thames (0932) 221910   Children in eating area lunchtimes only   Open 11–3, 5.30 (6 Sat)–11 all year*

SHERE   TQ0747 Map 3

White Horse

As this interesting old half-timbered pub is one of the pretty village's finest features, it can get very busy at weekends. The open-plan main lounge bar has antique oak wall seats, old manuscripts on the walls, massive beams, a huge inglenook fireplace, and elegant Tudor stonework in a second inglenook fireplace through in the Pilgrim's Bar. The floors are uneven – no foundations, just salvaged ships' timbers plunged into the ground some 600 years ago. Bar food includes sandwiches (from £1.40, prawn, avocado and mayonnaise £2.50), ploughman's (from £1.95), deep-fried goats' cheese and cranberry sauce (£2.75), steak, kidney and Guinness pie, fresh trout or sausage, Stilton, leek and tomato pie (£3.95), and sirloin steak (£6.75). Well kept Ruddles Best and County and Websters Yorkshire on handpump. There are seats outside on a sunny cobbled courtyard among carefully planted troughs of flowers and bright hanging baskets; good walking in the beech woods on the road north towards East Clandon. *(Recommended by John Evans, Mr and Mrs J H Adam, J M Caulkin, Gary Wilkes, Alasdair Knowles, J and M Walsh, Doug Kennedy)*

Watneys   Licensee M Wicks   Real ale   Meals and snacks (not Sun evening)   Children in eating area of bar   Open 11–2.30 (3 Sat), 6–11 all year; closed 25 Dec

STAINES   TQ0471 Map 3

Swan

The Hythe; south bank of the Thames, over Staines Bridge

It's the Thames-side setting that attracts readers to this carefully restored old inn. There's a charming sycamore-shaded terrace by the towpath with some tables protected by an overhanging upper balcony, and both the main bars have good riverside views. They're well run and pleasantly furnished, with upholstered settles, seats and armchairs, and carefully exposed original fireplaces. Bar food includes sandwiches (from £1.10), jumbo sausage or filled baked potatoes (from £1.95), ploughman's (from £2.25), lasagne, basket meals and chilli con carne (£3.25). Fullers London Pride and ESB on handpump; fruit machine, piped music. *(Recommended by A J Leach; more reports please)*

Fullers Licensee J Kothe Real ale Snacks and lunchtime meals Restaurant tel Staines (0784) 52494 Children in eating area of bar Open 11–11; 11–2.30, 5.30–11 in winter Bedrooms tel Staines (0784) 52494; £27/£37

WALLISWOOD   TQ1138 Map 3

Scarlett Arms

Village signposted from Ewhurst–Rowhook back road; or follow Oakwoodhill signpost from A29 S of Ockley, then follow Walliswood signpost into Walliswood Green Road

The old small-roomed layout is still preserved in this friendly and neatly kept sixteenth-century pub. Two communicating rooms have deeply polished flagstones and sparkling clean red lino, heavy black oak beams in the low brown ceiling, simple but perfectly comfortable benches, high bar stools with back rests, trestle tables, country prints, and open fires – one is an inglenook; there's also a pub dog. Bar food includes sandwiches (from 80p, toasties from £1.10), filled baked potatoes (from £1.10), ploughman's (from £1.70), a bowl of chilli con carne (£2.10), salads (from £2.50), breaded plaice (£2.95), gammon and egg (£3.20), and home-made daily specials. Well kept King & Barnes Bitter, Festive, Mild and winter Old on handpump; darts, shove-ha'penny, cribbage and dominoes in a small room at the end. There are old fashioned seats and tables in the garden. *(Recommended by D J Penny, Phil and Sally Gorton, WFL, Chris Payne)*

King & Barnes Licensee D S Haslam Real ale Meals and snacks Open 11–2.30, 5.30–11 all year

WALTON ON THE HILL   TQ2255 Map 3

Fox & Hounds

Walton Street

This comfortable village pub has a cheerfully thriving atmosphere at lunchtime and in the evenings – when you may have to wait to find a table. However crowded it gets, it always feels thoroughly good-natured, with pleasant and efficient service. A big attraction is the good value offered by their three dishes of the day (£3.95): roast lamb, tagliatelle with a spicy cheese sauce, or pork escalope done with brandy and mushrooms, say. A wide choice of other bar food includes a string of starters such as pâté (£2.25), avocado and prawns (£2.95), their popular char-grilled burgers (from £3.50), chilli con carne (£3.75), vegetarian bake, chicken and ham or steak and kidney pie (£4.25), gammon or prawn curry (£4.75) and steaks (from eight-ounce rump £6.75); at lunchtime they add good sandwiches (from £1.30), ploughman's (£1.70) and sausages (£3.25). Comfortable armed chairs and tables spread around the central bar of the low-ceilinged and partly dark-panelled pub; though the various areas open into one another, it's cosy and friendly, with three good coal fires. The restaurant area, over on the left of the serving-counter, has a separate menu. Well kept Bass, Charrington IPA and Highgate Mild on handpump, with quite a decent choice of wines; fruit machine. There are rustic picnic-table sets on a back terrace; if children want to run around, they're supposed to go instead to a freer area beyond the car park, with a timber climber and swing. *(Recommended by Mr and Mrs P Wilkins, B H Reeves, TOH, Jan and Ian Alcock)*

Charringtons (Bass) Licensees Mr and Mrs Hawkins Real ale Meals and snacks (noon–10) Open 11–11 all year

WARLINGHAM   TQ3658 Map 3
White Lion
B269

Shortly to be painted and refurbished, this unspoilt pub has a warren of dimly lit, black-panelled rooms with lots of nooks and crannies, wood-block floors, extremely low beams, deeply aged plasterwork, and high-backed settles by the fine Tudor fireplace. Bar food includes sandwiches, ploughman's (from £2), plaice (£3.15), steak and kidney pie or seafood Mornay (£3.20), and prawn salad (£3.50). Well kept Bass, Charrington IPA, and Youngs on handpump or tapped from the cask (from the central bar, by the door as you come in), and several wines. A side room with some amusing early nineteenth-century cartoons has darts, cribbage, fruit machine, space game and piped music. The back lawn is immaculate, and surrounded by a colourful herbaceous border; what was the goldfish pond is now a rockery, and there's some new garden furniture. *(Recommended by Alasdair Knowles; more reports please)*

Charringtons (Bass)   Licensee Catherine Duffy   Real ale   Lunchtime meals and snacks   Restaurant tel Warlingham (088 32) 1106   Children in eating area of bar   Open 11–3, 6–11 all year

---

Lucky Dip

Besides the fully inspected pubs, you might like to try these Lucky Dips recommended to us and described by readers (if you do, please send us reports):

☆ **Abinger Common** [Abinger signposted off A25 W of Dorking – then right to Abinger Hammer; TQ1145], *Abinger Hatch*: A great favourite for its position near the church in a clearing of the rolling woods; a good deal of character inside, with big log fires, heavy beams, flagstones, good range of well kept real ales inc Badger Best and Tanglefoot, Gibbs Mew Bishops Tipple, King & Barnes and Wadworths 6X, limited range of usual bar food but done well; restaurant, children allowed in area partly set aside for them; in summer the main attraction is the pair of attractive garden areas – with occasional visitors from the nearby duck pond; can get very busy indeed at weekends; more views on the latest management, please *(R B Crail, John Branford, Chris Payne, Lindsey Shaw Radley, WFL, LYM)*

Addlestone [Hamm Moor Lane; off A317 Addlestone–Weybridge, by canal; TQ0464], *Pelican*: Canalside pub with moorings, busy at lunchtimes, with river view from new garden-room; Ruddles Best and County and Websters Yorkshire on handpump, and good choice of cheap hot and cold food inc good value daily specials; children welcome *(R B Crail, Colin Chattoe)*; [New Haw Rd; corner A318/B385] *White Hart*: Cheerful local with attractive waterside garden, quickly served good value simple food, well kept Courage real ales, darts, bar billiards, juke box; pianist Sat *(Richard Houghton, LYM)*

☆ **Albury Heath** [Little London – OS Sheet 187 reference 065468; TQ0646], *William IV*: Particularly friendly little cottage with three picnic benches facing on to common; three low and genuinely beamed and flagstoned rooms with deep log fire, benches and tables; real ales such as Boddingtons and Fullers London Pride, steps up to eating-room – reasonably priced bar food from sandwiches up, inc generous ploughman's; darts, upstairs restaurant; occasional live music; favourite stop for walkers *(Ian and Liz Phillips, Phil and Sally Gorton)*

Alfold [B2133; TQ0334], *Crown*: Cheerful pub with pleasant, friendly service, well kept Courage Directors, home-made bar food (not Sun), several rooms, well kept garden, in quiet village *(John Evans, LYM)*; [Dunsfold Rd] *Three Compasses*: Remote country inn on quiet back lane with inglenook public bar and airy saloon *(LYM)*

Ashtead [The Street (A24); TQ1858], *Brewery*: Public bar and lounge that appeal to slightly older customers; well kept Friary Meux Best and Ind Coope Burton and good, straightforward bar food, with locally popular Sun roasts; nice garden with lots of wooden seats and tables and children's play area *(R P Taylor)*

Banstead [High St; TQ2559], *Woolpack*: Popular, roomy pub, decidedly a local but welcoming to strangers; pleasantly served good value varied bar food *(John Pettit)*

Beare Green [TQ1842], *Dukes Head*: Atmospheric public bar in pretty roadside Ind Coope pub with well kept real ales and pleasant garden *(LYM)*

Betchworth [TQ2049], *Red Lion*: Pleasant bar, well kept Bass, pretty garden, friendly staff, reasonably priced food well presented and quickly served *(Mrs Jenny Seller)*

Bishopsgate [OS Sheet 175 reference 979721; SU9871], *Fox & Hounds*: Largely restaurant, with most people in the bar on their way to a meal – food good though pricey by pub standards, but sandwiches too, well kept if pricey Courage Best, cheerful atmosphere, log fires; good location, with pleasant front garden *(Ian Phillips)*

Bisley [OS Sheet 175 reference 949595; SU9559], *Hen & Chickens*: Tudor pub (though only the beams show its great age), notable for pleasant efficient management, good lunchtime food; Courage *(WHBM)*

Bletchingley [2 High St; A25, on E side of village – all the pubs here are quite handy for M25 junction 6; TQ3250], *Plough*: Heavily modernised Benskins pub, bar food inc full evening meals, real ale *(Gordon Smith)*; *Prince Albert*: Relaxed pub with friendly Dutch owner; superb food – huge steaks and tasty fish – from regularly changing menu *(G Turner)*; [A25, Redhill side] *Red Lion*: Tudor pub, though heavily modernised, with warm and cosy atmosphere and reasonably priced bar food *(W J Wonham, BHP)*; [Little Common Lane; off A25 on Redhill side] *William IV*: Prettily tile-hung and weatherboarded country local with well kept Bass and Charrington IPA, darts, dominoes, cribbage and fruit machine in back bar, seats in nice garden with summer weekend barbecues; fair bar food lunchtime, not Sun *(John Kimber, E G Parish, LYM)*

☆ **Blindley Heath** [Tandridge Lane; TQ3645], *Red Barn*: Friendly country pub, still attractive in spite of modernisation, with jolly atmosphere, lovely inglenook fireplace, nicely furnished library bar, discreet piped music, good service, imaginatively presented bar food inc big tasty home-baked crusty rolls and good ploughman's; Flowers IPA and Fremlins on handpump, spacious pleasant garden; fills with its regulars at weekends *(E G Parish, Lindsey Shaw Radley, Jenny and Brian Seller)*

Bramley [High St; TQ0044], *Jolly Farmer*: Cheerful and lively atmosphere in Watneys pub with two log fires, very wide choice of well served and presented bar food, beer-mats on ceiling, big restaurant; just handy for Winkworth Arboretum and Loseley House; bedrooms *(W J Wonham, LYM)*

Brockham [Brockham Green; TQ1949], *Dukes Head*: Friendly place now concentrating heavily on its wide range of good, popular food – many tables booked; friendly, attentive landlord, Friary Meux Best on handpump, real log fire at one end and coal-effect gas fire at the other *(Mrs P J Pearce, R J Groves, JP)*; *Royal Oak*: Relaxed local atmosphere, open fire, friendly staff in idyllic village-green pub; licensee personally handles all cooking, well prepared and presented; enclosed lawn with tables; children's play area *(John Pettit, Peter Corris)*

☆ **Brook** [A286 – OS Sheet 186 reference 930380; SU9337], *Dog & Pheasant*: Pleasant atmosphere in busy and friendly character pub attractively placed opposite cricket green, with polished walking-sticks decorating low beams; well kept Benskins Best, Friary Meux Best, Ind Coope Burton and Tetleys, home-cooked food, restaurant with jazz piano Weds–Sun evenings; seats in garden, front and back *(Lyn and Bill Capper, David Gaunt)*

Byfleet [High Rd; TQ0661], *Plough*: Solid nineteenth-century building with lots of brass, copper and cosmetic beams in two comfortable bars; friendly, warm welcome, well kept Courage ales and good, basic bar food from sandwiches up *(Ian Phillips)*

Camberley [Park St; SU8759], *Carpenters Arms*: Tastefully improved local with friendly bar staff (almost entirely Antipodean), well kept Watneys-related real ales with a guest such as Gales HSB on handpump at moderate prices, darts, fruit machine, space game and juke box kept at reasonable level, traditional good value bar food *(M B Porter)*; [A30 W end of town] *Lamb*: Excellent Morlands beer, pleasant welcoming service, good atmosphere and very bright, modern décor in well extended pub with pleasant conservatory, flagstone floor; good choice of bar food *(Richard Houghton)*; [A30] *Staff*: Better inside than you'd think, with well kept beer, reasonable food and good mix of customers in pleasant lounge bar *(Richard Houghton)*

Caterham on the Hill [235 Stanstead Rd, Whitehill; TQ3354], *Harrow*: Busy pub with log fires, good choice of simple bar food, popular with young and old; garden nice in summer *(Gordon Smith, M D Hare – more news on new management, please)*

☆ **Charleshill** [B3001; SU8944], *Donkey*: Well run pub with pleasant bar and lounges, keeping its quietly civilised character though a new conservatory extension has increased dining area – good range of food from sandwiches up inc four good daily specials, excellent service, well kept Courage ales; big garden *(WAG, John and Heather Dwane)*

Charlwood [Church Rd; TQ2441], *Half Moon*: Plainly modernised old Friary Meux pub with good local atmosphere, freshly made sandwiches, bar billiards, shove-ha'penny, space game, darts and fruit machine *(BB)*

☆ **Chertsey** [Ruxbury Rd; St Anns Hill (nr Lyne); TQ0466], *Golden Grove*: Charming old pub on edge of St Anns Woods, with low beam and plank ceilings, plank-panelling walls, boarded floors; good, varied and reasonably priced home-cooked lunchtime food inc excellent salads, in generous helpings – there's a separate pine-tabled eating area; well kept Friary Meux Best, Gales HSB and Ind Coope Burton; attractive garden and playground for children (who are welcome in the pub too), with wooded pond *(Clem Stephens, Gary Wilkes, Rodney Coe, Tony Tucker, Ian Phillips)*

Chertsey [45 Guildford St (A317)], *George*: Friendly old pub with reasonably priced food; mentioned in H G Wells' *War of the Worlds*, said to be haunted – enjoyable, though the interior gives little hint of its history; well kept Courage ales *(Dr and Mrs A K Clarke, LYM)*; [Windsor St; on left heading towards Windsor] *Swan*: Friendly old pub under new regime; warm little lounge, with bar billiards being aimed at younger clients *(Dr and Mrs A K Clarke)*

Chobham [just N of village – OS Sheet 176 reference 970633; SU9761], *Four Horseshoes*: Useful Courage pub with decent choice of bar food (smoked salmon sandwiches and puddings recommended), facing village pump on green triangle of common reached by its own little lane; benches outside *(Ian Phillips)*; [B383 ½ mile towards Sunningdale, turn right into Red Lion Lane] *Red Lion*: Old, recently renovated and enlarged pub, a little off the beaten track; popular at lunchtimes with lots of tables, well kept Ind Coope Burton on handpump, reasonably priced bar food inc good pork chop, eager helpful staff *(R B Crail)*; [High St; 4 miles from M3 junc 3] *Sun*: Low-beamed lounge bar in quiet timbered Courage pub with decent bar food, friendly atmosphere, prompt service *(LYM)*

☆ **Cobham** [Plough Lane; TQ1060], *Plough*: Cheerful, bustling atmosphere in comfortably modernised low-beamed lounge bar, cheerful lively atmosphere (piped music may be on the loud side in the evening, when Porsches tend to crowd into the car park); straightforward popular food, well kept Courage real ales, traditional games in public bar, seats outside the pretty black-shuttered brick house *(MKW, JMW, LYM)*

Cobham [Pains Hill; TQ0960], *Little White Lion*: Well kept pub with Ruddles on handpump and good choice of hot and cold food *(Dr R B Crail)*

☆ **Compton** [Withies Lane; SU9546], *Withies*: Smart dining-pub with immaculate garden, good civilised atmosphere in tiny beamed bar with settles and inglenook, helpful landlady, some lunchtime bar snacks, well kept Bass, decent wines; children in restaurant *(J S Rutter, LYM)*

Cox Green [Station Yard; Baynards Lane (off B2128 just N of Rudgwick) – OS Sheet 187 reference 076349; TQ0934], *Thurlow Arms*: Rather isolated pub with excellent good value food and wide range of beers *(G J Lewis)*

Cranleigh [The Common; TQ0638], *Cranley*: Nicely decorated pub with good choice of reasonably priced food *(Anon)*; [Smithwood Common] *Four Elms*: Warm welcome and nice feel, with decent food and seats in back

garden *(Ian Phillips)*; [Bookhurst Rd; Parkmead estate – towards Shere] *Little Park Hatch*: Pleasant pub with well kept real ales, seats outside *(Anon)*

Dorking [Horsham Rd; TQ1649], *Bush*: A genuine free house – which makes it a really rare bird around here; comfortable and recently refurbished, with tables in terraced garden inc part covered (where landlord keeps vociferous budgerigars); well kept Fullers London Pride, Harveys BB, Marstons Pedigree, Charles Wells Bombardier *(D J Penny)*

☆ **Dunsfold** [TQ0036], *Sun*: Elegantly symmetrical eighteenth-century pub overlooking green, well kept Ind Coope real ales, friendly atmosphere, helpful service, comfortable seats, log fires, and beams; unusually varied good bar food inc interesting if not cheap dishes, casually smart young crowd, and separate cottage dining-room; children welcome *(Geoff Wilson, Prof and Mrs Keith Patchett, Dr John Innes, LYM)*

Dunsfold, *Rumpoles*: Well refurbished pub on village green with well kept Ruddles Best, bar food inc excellent sandwiches and three-course Sun lunch, pleasant staff; before the recent changes was called Hawk & Harrier *(D J Cooke)*

Eashing [SU9443], *Stag*: Attractive riverside pub by working mill, with several interconnecting rooms, comfortable traditional-style chairs, old legal documents on walls; well kept Tetleys, good range of bar food inc children's dishes, Sun roasts and handsome open sandwiches; small garden *(Ian Phillips)*

☆ **East Clandon** [TQ0651], *Queens Head*: Traditionally furnished half-timbered pub with big inglenook fireplace, fine old elm bar counter, relaxed atmosphere and tables outside; straightforward bar food, Friary Meux Best and Ind Coope Burton on handpump *(Dave Braisted, JSE, MKW, JMW, LYM – more reports on the current regime please)*

East Horsley [A246 Guildford–Leatherhead; TQ0952], *Duke of Wellington*: Busy pub at lunchtime with good food and atmosphere and winter log fires; good if not cheap food from open counter *(John Pettit, Mrs H Tickner)*; [Epsom Rd] *Thatchers*: Spacious, relaxing hotel lounge (not a pubby atmosphere), with efficient waiter service, drinks with coasters, daily papers, good food here and in restaurant; swimming-pool; bedrooms *(JSE, Stanley Matthews)*

East Molesey [Lion Gate; Hampton Court Rd; TQ1267], *Kings Arms*: Fine spot opposite entrance to Bushey Park; warm welcome in centre bar with lovely old panelling and stained-glass screens, separate bar with pool and fruit machines and, on left of entrance, eating area with good-sized tables; friendly staff, Adnams Broadside, Badger Tanglefoot, Gales BBB, Wadworths 6X and Old Timer, decent wines, good range of bar food from sandwiches to steaks *(Ian Phillips)*; *Paddock*: Large, attractive and comfortable open-plan bar with good carvery (not Sun evening) and well kept Watneys-related real ales *(Clem Stephens)*

☆ **Effingham** [Orestan Lane; TQ1253], *Plough*: Summer 1989 sold by Courage to Youngs – their beers now, kept well; food well above average too, imaginative and good value for area, with pleasant staff and tables outside; convenient for Polesdon Lacey *(WFL, MKW, JMW, TOH, JP – more news on the promising new regime please)*

Effingham, *Douglas Haig*: Decent pub, worth knowing *(WFL)*

☆ **Elstead** [SU9143], *Woolpack*: Good food from snacks to main dishes, changing daily, in picturesque old-world pub with wool-industry memorabilia in tastefully renovated oak-beamed lounge; well kept real ale tapped from the cask, decent wines, welcoming licensees, friendly dog, unobtrusive piped music, garden; parking can be a problem *(WAG, Mr and Mrs J C Dwane, Michael and Harriet Robinson)*

Epsom [East St; TQ2160], *Kings Arms*: Cheerful and friendly at lunchtime, with attractive (if softly lit) bar, handpump beer, simple honest food at moderate prices, willing polite service, picnic-table sets in small garden *(E G Parish)*; [West St (junction with High St)] *Marquis of Granby*: Comfortable pub with attractive wooden ceiling in bar, fresh flowers in lounge; very popular at lunchtime for good value bar food, especially sandwiches inc formidable hot salt beef ones; good service *(E G Parish)*

☆ **Esher** [82 High St; TQ1464], *Albert Arms*: Good range of real ales and sensibly priced French regional wines in lively Victorian pub/bistro with good value bar food inc interesting pâtés and well kept cheeses, friendly if rather unconventional service *(Richard Balkwill, LYM)*

Esher, *Bear*: Comfortable bar with good atmosphere, high-backed wooden settles and open fire in winter; no background music, friendly bar staff and updated choice of bar food inc good ploughman's *(Mrs J M Moore)*; [West End La; off A244 towards Hersham, by Princess Alice Hospice] *Prince of Wales*: Comfortable and spacious, slickly run, with Watneys-related real ales on handpump, good range of bar food (little cheap, though), piped music, coal-effect gas fire, pleasant conservatory, restaurant, well laid out sizeable garden *(Robert Crail, Mrs Clare Sack, Ian Phillips)*; [The Green] *Wheatsheaf*: Genuinely cosy bar running back from food counter with reliably tasty food, inc as many Yorkshire puddings as you like with the roast beef – one price for all main courses, another for the home-made puddings; Watneys-related real ales; they've put in fruit machine

and piped music now, but still pleasant, facing village green *(Ian Phillips, G T Rhys)*

Ewell [45 Cheam Rd; TQ2262], *Glyn Arms*: Still well worth knowing for its rambling series of rooms connected by lobbies and passages, reasonable range of well kept beer, reasonably priced food; the licensees who formerly made it particularly popular can now be found at the Fox & Hounds, Walton on the Hill (see main entries) *(Steve Waters, LYM)*; [Broadway, Stoneleigh; TQ2264] *Stoneleigh*: Spacious and lively, with friendly staff and good parking *(David Clare)*

Ewhurst [The Street; TQ0940], *Bulls Head*: Well kept and decorated pub with skittle alley, beer garden and decent food; start GWG55 *(Anon)*

Farley Green [Farley Heath; TQ0645], *William IV*: Very nice pub with lots of character, good wine, pleasant landlord *(C Gray)*

Farncombe [SU9844], *Ram*: Known locally as the Cider Hole as it has no beer, only draught cider; an interesting rural retreat in suburbia with discreet, simple rooms and a shaded garden *(Jon Dewhirst, WFL)*

Farnham [Middle Bourne La; SU8446], *Bat & Ball*: Free house under new regime, well kept real ales, good bar food and new restaurant; open all day *(Stuart Cunnell)*; [Castle St] *Nelsons Arms*: Wide choice of food inc good value triple-decker sandwiches in long low-beamed pub with polished tables and settles, Courage ales, and some naval mementoes; next to almshouses in fine Georgian st leading up to castle *(Liz Phillips)*; [West St] *Wheatsheaf*: Unpretentious, old-fashioned and spacious L-shaped bar with subdued lighting, interesting prints, open fire, comfortable banquettes, wide choice of good generously served traditional bar food inc wonderful array of salads and reasonably priced Sun roasts from side food counter, helpful smiling bar staff; unobtrusive juke box, fruit machine; handy for Farnham Maltings concert hall *(Jane Palmer)*; [Bridge Sq] *William Cobbett*: Cobbett's picturesque birthplace, now a lively and pleasantly laid-out young people's pub with good value cheap food, well kept Courage Directors and lots of amusements *(Gary Wilkes, LYM)*

Felbridge [Wiremill Lane; TQ3639], *Wiremill*: Beautiful lakeside spot, well kept beer, good bar food and service; piped music can be avoided by sitting outside *(BHP)*

Forest Green [nr B2126/B2127 junction; TQ1240], *Parrot*: Rambling bars in quaint old pub full of parrot designs, often in the most unlikely materials; real ales such as Courage Best and Directors on handpump, good food which is often interesting (the restaurant has a late supper licence), lots of room in nice surroundings outside; children welcome – so much so that it sometimes seems to have the atmosphere of a pleasantly unruly family dining-room *(N D Foot, Mr and*

*Mrs W Harrington, Gordon Hewitt, Mrs
H M M Tickner, LYM – more reports please)*
Frensham [A287; SU8341], *Mariners*: Small,
cosy bar, friendly and obliging service, well
kept beer, good bar food, occasional jazz
(R Houghton)
☆ **Godalming** [SU9743], *Inn on the Lake*:
Relaxed friendly atmosphere, consistently
good food and service, well kept Flowers and
Wethereds, winter log fire – welcoming for
families; gardens overlooking lake *(Mrs
Jeannette Simpson, Dr I J Thompson)*
Godalming [Ockford Rd], *Anchor*:
Comfortable, tastefully old-fashioned pub
with helpful and obliging staff, good range of
varying beers such as Brakspears, Courage
Directors and Fullers London Pride, and
straightforward choice of bar food inc
excellent soup and sandwiches; pleasant
garden and terrace *(P M Brooker, Derek and
Sylvia Stephenson)*; [High St (A3100)] *Kings
Arms & Royal*: Substantial eighteenth
century coaching-inn with cheap good value
lunches in busy but friendly warren of little
partitioned rooms and rather splendid Tsar's
Lounge; bedrooms *(BB)*; [off to right of top
end of High St] *Rose & Crown*: Well kept
pub with Watneys-related real ales on
handpump and bar food inc good choice of
sandwiches and tasty breaded cod *(R B Crail)*
☆ **Godstone** [128 High St; under a mile from
M25 junction 6, via B2236; TQ3551], *Bell*:
Spacious beamed and partly panelled main
bar of quite some character, with big fires at
each end, comfortable and individual seats;
also smaller timbered bar set out more for
eating; well kept Benskins Best, Friary Meux
Best, Ind Coope Burton and Tetleys on
handpump (but drinks prices high),
straightforward lunchtime bar food, more
main dishes and grills evening, restaurant;
good garden for children; bedrooms
*(E G Parish, Denis Gilder, Linda Egan,
W J Wonham, LYM)*
Godstone [Bletchingley Rd], *Hare &
Hounds*: Friary Meux pub opposite village
green, attractive exterior, heavily modernised
inside with mock oak beams but cosy nooks
and welcoming atmosphere, good bar food
and service; popular with young people in
the evening, when music may be loud
(E G Parish)
Grafham [Smithbrook; A281 Horsham Rd;
TQ0241], *Leathern Bottle*: Wide choice of
food and well kept King & Barnes ales; by no
means plush but a pleasantly pubby
atmosphere *(Lyn and Bill Capper)*
Guildford [Quarry St; SU9949], *Kings Head*:
Lots of beams and stripped brickwork in
large corner pub converted from former
cottages, lovely big inglenook, spacious
banquettes, lots of intimate nooks and
crannies, subdued piped music, well kept
Courage Best, full range of good value pub
food *(Ian Phillips)*; [Sydenham Rd] *Rats
Castle*: Wide range of interesting moderately

priced food – quite a haven away from the
High St bustle, though décor not striking *(Liz
and Ian Phillips)*; [Trinity Churchyard] *Royal
Oak*: Very friendly Courage pub with super
big log fires in winter, lots of stools around
small tables, good value simple bar food *(Liz
and Ian Phillips)*; [Chertsey St] *Spread Eagle*:
Glitzy-fronted pub with one bar on two
levels, friendly welcome, well kept Best,
Directors, and John Smiths on handpump,
stripped brickwork, good reasonably priced
lunchtime bar food, jazz Sat lunchtime *(Matt
Pringle, Ian Phillips)*; [Quarry St] *Star*: Split-
level old pub in centre, with good
atmosphere and well kept Ind Coope Burton
(Dr and Mrs A K Clarke)
Hersham [Queens Rd; TQ1164], *Bricklayers
Arms*: Happy atmosphere, good food, value
for money *(Mrs Clare Sack)*
Hindhead [SU8736], *Punch Bowl*:
Welcoming place with pleasant atmosphere
and quickly served food *(J A Uthwatt)*
☆ **Holmbury St Mary** [TQ1144], *Kings Head*:
Quietly spacious pub in beautiful spot, doing
well under newish landlord, with friendly
welcome, half a dozen well kept real ales on
handpump such as Badgers Tanglewood,
Batemans XXXB, Flowers Original, King &
Barnes, Ringwood Fortyniner and Tetleys,
sensible helpings of good food and large
garden *(Dr R Fuller, M D Hare, John Booth)*
Horley [TQ2842], *Farmhouse*: Although
relatively new as a pub, this building is 400
years old; beamed, connecting rooms with
good friendly atmosphere, well kept Courage
Best and Directors and John Smiths on
handpump, and good range of bar food inc
filled baked potatoes *(Roger Huggins)*;
[Victoria Rd] *Foresters Arms*: A surprising
find in this modern town centre – genuinely
old and unspoilt pub with high bar hatch for
tiny back rooms *(LYM)*; [42 High St]
Gatwick: Busy but comfortable town-centre
pub, well kept King & Barnes Sussex Bitter
and generously served bar food; named for
the racecourse, not the airport *(John Baker)*
Horsell Common [A320 Woking–
Ottershaw; SU9959], *Bleak House*: Warm,
friendly, Friary Meux pub isolated by
surrounding heath, real ales on handpump
and decent hot and cold bar food; décor not
to everyone's taste *(R B Crail)*
Irons Bottom [Irons Bottom Rd, off A217;
TQ2546], *Three Horseshoes*: Nice simple pub
out in the country; friendly, with several
changing well kept real ales, simple,
inexpensive and freshly cooked bar food, no
piped music, tables outside, and good new
lavatories (also recently enlarged car park)
(WFL)
☆ **Kenley** [Old Lodge Lane; left (coming from
London) off A23 by Reedham Stn, then keep
on; TQ3259], *Wattenden Arms*: One of very
few real country pubs on the outskirts of
London (and actually within London's
boundary, though by long tradition we list it

here under Surrey); cosy and friendly, with dark panelling, traditional furnishings, firmly patriotic décor, well kept Bass and Charrington IPA on handpump, big helpings of reasonably priced bar food (not Sun – and no children), prompt service, seats on small side lawn *(W J Wonham, LYM)*

Kingswood [Waterhouse Lane; TQ2455], *Kingswood Arms*: Popular, spacious open-plan bar with several more intimate sections within it, and conservatory-type light and airy dining extension – refreshingly non-smoky; variety of delicious bar food, quickly but matter-of-factly served, inc really doorsteppy sandwiches and good puddings; attractive if hilly garden *(Jane Palmer, Martin Aust)*

Laleham [TQ0568], *Feathers*: Lounge in old cottage with bar in single-storey front extension; well kept Courage Best and Directors, generous helpings of imaginative lunchtime and evening bar food inc fine well filled baps, steak sandwiches and good value hot dishes *(Peter Griffiths)*

Leatherhead [Chessington Rd; A243 nr M25 junction 9 – OS Sheet 187 reference 167600; TQ1656], *Star*: Big, popular pub – gets crowded, so rarely relaxed, but enjoyable, with cheerful service, particularly at table; generous helpings of good though not particularly cheap food *(John Pettit)*

Limpsfield Chart [TQ4251], *Carpenters Arms*: Pretty pub on delightful green, clean, well run and pleasantly laid out though heavily modernised inside; well kept Friary Meux Best and Benskins Best, good bar food inc vegetarian dishes *(Jenny and Brian Seller)*

Lingfield [TQ3843], *Hare & Hounds*: Friendly landlord cooks much of the imaginative, reasonably priced food himself, ringing the changes between cassoulet, curry, fish dishes, rabbit and so forth; attractive and unspoilt, good atmosphere *(Mrs Jensen)*

Little Bookham [TQ1254], *Windsor Castle*: Large, well laid out old pub, repeatedly but carefully extended; well kept Watneys-related real ales on handpump, friendly staff, wide choice of good reasonably priced lunchtime bar food (very much a dining pub), huge garden with tables and children's play area *(Roger Taylor, WFL)*

Long Ditton [5 Portsmouth Rd; TQ1666], *City Arms*: Basic little pub, central bar with old coal-burning kitchen range, tapestry-covered stools and banquettes, and separate food area with coal-effect gas fire; warm welcome, comfortable atmosphere, well kept Watneys-related real ales, good range of bar food from sandwiches to steaks inc children's helpings *(Ian Phillips)*

Lower Bourne [SU8544], *Spotted Cow*: Attractive rural pub in former sandpit now completely overgrown; well kept Courage ales, good food and good service, pleasant lunchtime clientele – currently on quite an upswing *(WAG)*

☆ **Merstham** [Nutfield Rd; off A23 in Merstham, or follow Nutfield Ch, Merstham 2 signpost off A25 E of Redhill – OS Sheet 187 reference 303514; TQ2953], *Inn on the Pond*: Pleasantly if not smartly refurbished pub with lots of tables in engagingly furnished and decorated back family conservatory, concrete path past herbaceous border and squash court to sheltered back terrace; front area rambles around central fireplace, with settles, pews, shelves of old books, decent prints; well kept Courage Directors, Flowers IPA and Original, Marstons Pedigree, Pilgrims Bitter and Whitbreads Pompey Royal on handpump, good choice of hot and cold bar food with big crusty sandwiches, good vegetarian dishes, daily specials and Sun morning breakfast; rather pervasive piped Capital Radio, staff can be a bit unbending; views over scrubland (and the small pond and nearby cricket ground) to the North Downs *(Jane Palmer, TOH, M Carrington, BB)*

Merstham [A23], *Jolliffe Arms*: Straightforward pub with well kept beer and excellent big ploughman's in variety *(Jenny and Brian Seller)*

Mickleham [London Rd; TQ1753], *Running Horses*: Straightforward pub in attractive village nr Box Hill, with well kept Friary Meux Best, bar food such as deep-fried cheese and ham sandwich or ham and eggs *(Paul Sexton, Sue Harrison)*

Mogador [coming from M25 up A217, pass second roundabout then follow signpost off – edge of Banstead Heath; TQ2452], *Sportsman*: Pleasant pub, all on its own down a country lane, yet near London and easily accessible: lots of character, good beer, quite friendly bar staff, bar food inc excellent ploughman's; darts and bar billiards *(John Day)*

☆ **Oatlands** [Anderson Rd; TQ0965], *Prince of Wales*: Most civilised, warm, pleasant and comfortable pub; well kept Fullers London Pride and Youngs ales; good bar food (sandwiches, liver and bacon, hot-pot all recommended), popular restaurant; HQ for local rowing clubs, and gets very busy in evenings *(Ian Phillips, Minda and Stanley Alexander)*

Ockham [Cobham Lane; on Effingham Junction crossroads a mile E of Hautboy; TQ0756], *Black Swan*: Old free house, fairly well extended, with well kept beers, bar food and garden; newish licensees *(WFL)*; [Ockham Lane – towards Cobham] *Hautboy*: Spectacular red stone Gothick building, given lots of potential by its unusual layout inc darkly panelled high-raftered upstairs area with minstrels' gallery; lots of seats outside *(LYM)*

☆ **Ockley** [Stane St (A29); TQ1439], *Cricketers Arms*: Flagstones, low oak beams and shinily varnished pine furniture in fifteenth-century stone village pub with good simple bar food, well kept real ales such as Badger Best, Fullers, King & Barnes and Pilgrims Progress, country wines, friendly staff, inglenook log fires, quiet piped music, darts area, small attractive dining-room decorated with cricketing memorabilia; seats outside, roses around the door *(Paul Sexton, Sue Harrison, M Webb, Chris Fluck, LYM)*

☆ **Ockley**, *Red Lion*: Decent choice of real ales in deceptively spacious former seventeenth-century coaching-inn, refurbished with stable/loose box theme under its genuine old beams; good value food, pleasant and efficient service *(Mr and Mrs R Harrington, BB)*

Outwood [Miller Lane; TQ3245], *Castle*: Good atmosphere, unpretentious décor; welcoming, friendly landlord; King & Barnes and Websters Yorkshire on handpump, good value bar food inc choice of ploughman's *(Jenny and Brian Seller)*

Pirbright [The Green; SU9455], *White Hart*: Popular cheap bar food, separate restaurant upstairs, good service, beautifully kept garden *(Shirley MacKenzie)*

☆ **Puttenham** [just off A31 Farnham–Guildford; SU9347], *Jolly Farmer*: An air of quiet prosperity in several attractively furnished rooms, with an overall Victorian feel and comfortable seats from cushioned wheel-back chairs to sofas and easy chairs; some concentration on Harvester restaurant, but bar food too, inc a good choice of ploughman's, well kept Courage Best and Directors, and quick service; picnic-table sets outside; children welcome *(LYM – more reports please)*

Ranmore Common [towards Effingham Forest, past Dogkennel Green – OS Sheet 187 reference 112501; TQ1451], *Ranmore Arms*: Deep in the country, and doing well under friendly new licensees, with wide range of well kept real ales, good bar food, huge log fire, no piped music, play area in big garden; children welcome *(WFL)*

Redhill [3 Redstone Hill (A25); TQ2650], *Home Cottage*: Nicely updated Youngs pub – not a cottage, but quite a big, multi-purpose pub with varying activities in lots of small areas; excellent service, wide mix of customers *(Dr and Mrs A K Clarke)*; [A25 towards Reigate] *Red Lion*: Popular at lunchtime for reasonably priced straightforward food *(BB)*

☆ **Ripley** [High St; TQ0556], *Ship*: Skilfully extended sixteenth-century pub with low beams, cosy nooks, comfortable window seats and real log fire; warm welcome from young licensees, good atmosphere, popular with locals, Courage and John Smiths on handpump, wide choice of reasonably priced home-cooked bar food from sandwiches up, interestingly converted courtyard garden *(E G Parish, Paul and Moira Entwistle)*

Ripley [High St], *Anchor*: Old-fashioned connecting rooms in Tudor inn with

lunchtime bar food, games in public bar, Ind Coope-related real ales, tables in coachyard *(LYM)*; [High St] *Half Moon*: Old and unpretentious free house with good range of beers inc Fullers ESB, friendly staff; bar food *(D J Penny)*

Row Town [off Addlestone–Ottershaw rd, sharp left past church up Ongar Hill – OS Sheet 176 reference 036633; TQ0363], *Cricketers*: Pleasant well run pub with Watneys-related real ales on handpump, good choice of reasonably priced food; clean and friendly *(Robert Crail)*

Rowledge [OS Sheet 186 reference 822434; SU8243], *Hare & Hounds*: Courage beer, reasonably priced bar food, lovely garden *(Dr John Innes)*

Send [TQ0155], *New Inn*: Charmingly placed by canal, cheerful staff, particularly well cooked and presented bar food – though the pub itself doesn't overflow with charm *(Jane Palmer)*

Sendmarsh [Marsh Rd; TQ0454], *Saddlers Arms*: Attractive, friendly and clean little pub well off beaten track; low beams, lots of horsebrasses; standard food but cheap, inc decent ploughman's, well kept Friary Meux Best *(Ian Phillips)*

Shackleford [SU9345], *Cyder House*: In spite of its name has a good choice of beers – and food; nice setting *(Dr I J Thompson)*

Shalford [The Street; TQ0047], *Sea Horse*: Large roadside pub with nice garden, opposite the ancient Shalford Mill; well kept Gales ales, friendly landlord, reasonably priced bar food inc decent ploughman's *(Anon)*

Shamley Green [B2128 S of Guildford; TQ0343], *Red Lion*: Surroundings of some character include handsome settles and other country furniture, antique clocks and old photographs, with well kept real ales inc Ind Coope Burton tapped from casks behind the bar; recent reports on the service and on the food (rather a narrower range than formerly) suggest an upturn in standards here *(Sue Corrigan, LYM – more reports please)*

☆ **Shepperton** [Shepperton Lock; Ferry Lane; turn left off B375 towards Chertsey, 100yds from Square; TQ0867], *Thames Court*: Large and busy 1930s riverside pub under new management (don't worry, the peanuts on the bar, missing at first, have reappeared), with lots of intimate nooks and crannies, panelled walls, Windsor chairs, roomy mezzanine and upper gallery looking out on to Thames and moorings; relaxed atmosphere, Bass and Flowers IPA, good home-cooked bar food inc Sun hot roast, pleasant service, large garden *(Ian and Liz Phillips, Minda and Stanley Alexander, Simon Collett-Jones)*

Shepperton, *Red Lion*: Age and character, spacious walls dripping with wistaria, good varied reasonably priced food; large outside area and lawn by river across the road, with gorgeous views *(Miss E Waller)*

Shortfield Common [SU8342], *Holly Bush*: Very pleasant village pub popular with locals (especially elderly ladies) who want a good lunch in nice surroundings *(Mr and Mrs K J V)*

Smallfield [Plough Rd; TQ3143], *Plough*: Friendly and busy, with efficient staff, generously served bar food inc huge ploughman's, bursting sandwiches and Fri fresh fish, large attractive garden *(Derek and Maggie Washington)*

South Godstone [Tilburstow Hill Rd; TQ3648], *Fox & Hounds*: Very old half-tiled black and white building with low-beamed bars, much modernised but still has high settles and old prints; big helpings of bar food, simple pleasant garden *(Mrs Pamela Roper)*

St Johns [Hermitage Rd; SU9857], *Capstans Wharf*: Converted from old canalside buildings and designed to benefit from the Basingstoke Canal's new connection to the Wey Navigation and thus the Thames; calls itself a wine bar though actually a rather nice little pub with Charrington ales, bar snacks and restaurant *(Ian Phillips)*

Staines [124 Church St; TQ0471], *Bells*: Attractive and pleasantly decorated local, comfortable and compact around central fireplace, welcoming atmosphere, well kept Courage Best, wide range of bar food from burgers and ploughman's up; darts and cribbage *(Ian Phillips)*; [Leacroft] *Old Red Lion*: Olde-worlde seventeenth-century pub overlooking green; warm welcome, well kept beer and wide choice of bar food *(Steve and Jane Mackey)*

☆ **Stoke d'Abernon** [Station Rd (off A245); TQ1259], *Plough*: Homely and comfortably modernised old pub with reasonably priced good sensible bar food in airy conservatory eating area; well kept Watneys-related real ales, big window seats, coal fire, helpful staff, sizeable garden *(John Pettit, BB)*

Sunbury [French St; TQ1068], *Jockey*: Unpretentious sidestreet Charringtons local, homely and comfortable, with lots of chamber-pots, family photographs, dogs and cat *(Ian Phillips)*

☆ **Sutton** [B2126 – this is the Sutton near Abinger; TQ1046], *Volunteer*: Attractively placed pub with charmingly intimate traditional interior, without the bustle of busier pubs – cosy on winter's evening, pleasant and quiet in the well tended garden in summer; food not geared to any substantial number of customers, but good value, with sandwiches, ploughman's and changing hot dishes; warm welcome, well kept Friary Meux Best and Ind Coope Burton, low beams and military paintings in their right historical context *(John Kimber, TOH)*

Tadworth [Box Hill Rd; TQ2256], *Hand in Hand*: Roomy red-brick pub in rural spot,

popular in summer; large bar with extension at one end, iron scrollwork, brassware, original paintings for sale and good seating with banquettes, stools and Windsor chairs; relaxed atmosphere, well kept Courage beers, good simple bar food, friendly staff, fruit machine, well spaced tables in big garden bounded by shrubs and trees *(John Pettit)*

Tandridge [Tandridge Lane; TQ3750], *Brickmakers Arms*: Pleasant though much modernised country pub with well kept Flowers IPA and Original, Fremlins and Wethereds Winter Royal and extensive choice of bar food *(Tim Powell, E G Parish)*

☆ **Thames Ditton** [Queens Rd; TQ1567], *Albany*: Consistently pleasant atmosphere, well kept Bass on handpump, three real fires, and good though not cheap lunchtime bar food; gets busy in summer, when the river terrace overlooking Hampton Court grounds is an attractive overflow *(I S Wilson, Ian Phillips)*

Thames Ditton, *Albion*: Busy Charringtons house with olde-worlde charm; well kept Bass on handpump, good value bar food, restaurant; close to Hampton Court Palace *(Jenny and Brian Seller)*; [Weston Green] *Cricketers*: Clean and attractive building with warm welcome and homely, friendly atmosphere; wide choice of good home-made bar food at reasonable prices, high standard of service *(Mr and Mrs Dobson and friends)*; [Summer Rd] *Olde Swan*: Civilised black-panelled upper bar overlooking quiet Thames backwater, bar food and restaurant *(LYM)*

Thorpe [Thorpe Green; TQ0268], *Rose & Crown*: Well kept, attractive pub covered in roses on one of Surrey's largest village greens; Courage ales and good home-cooked bar food lunchtime and evening, with pleasantly busy atmosphere and good staff; surrounded by gardens and lawns, with children's playground *(Clem Stephens, Richard Houghton)*

☆ **Thursley** [SU9039], *Three Horseshoes*: Dark and cosy, with lovingly polished furniture, well kept Gales HSB and a good range of other drinks, well made sandwiches and good hot dishes (not Sun lunchtime or Mon-Thurs evenings – at lunchtime they don't serve food until 12.30); very individual, owing a great deal to the personality of its landlord – if you like it, you'll love it *(Ray Challoner, C Gray, Ian Phillips, LYM)*

Tilford [SU8743], *Barley Mow*: Wonderful spot, well worth a visit – and the Courage Best, bar food and service are all good *(WAG, Sue Corrigan)*

Tilford Common [SU8742], *Duke of Cambridge*: Very rural, with climbing-frames and so forth in long garden, tables on high grassy terrace at one end – so you can keep an eye on the children *(Neil and Elspeth Fearn)*

☆ **Walton on the Hill** [Chequers Lane; TQ2255],
Chequers: Well laid out series of mock-
Tudor rooms rambling around central
servery, dark ochre walls, dark beams,
copper-topped tables, tapestry banquettes,
flowers and tropical fish; efficient good value
food bar, popular though not cheap
restaurant, well kept Youngs real ale, terrace
and neat garden with summer barbecues;
traditional jazz Thurs; children in restaurant
*(Patrick Young, Heather Sharland,
R C Vincent, LYM)*

☆ **West Clandon** [TQ0452], *Onslow Arms*:
Rambling beamed country pub, often busy,
with lots of bars and friendly service – but by
no means cheap; well laid out, with
comfortable seating in nooks and corners,
open fire, soft lighting, thick carpets; wide
choice of well kept real ales inc Brakspears,
Courage Directors and Youngs, bar meals
(rather than snacks), restaurant serving Sun
lunches, great well lit garden; children
welcome *(Roger Taylor, John Evans,
A R Lord, WFL, Lyn and Bill Capper, LYM)*

West Clandon [Clandon St], *Bull*: Small and
friendly country pub, split-level bars
tastefully refurbished with varied but
comfortable seating, keeping cosy
atmosphere; reliably good beer and food, not
overpriced; convenient for Clandon Park
(John Pettit)

West Horsley [TQ0753], *Barley Mow*:
Friendly, welcoming atmosphere; beamed
bars, traditional oak furniture, courteous
service; good, home-made food served in
separate dining-room *(Denis Waters)*

☆ **West Humble** [just off A24 below Box Hill
– OS Sheet 187 reference 170517; TQ1651],
Stepping Stones: Large, popular pub with
circular bar, real ale, good bar food –
especially pizzas and help-yourself salads –
and huge pool-table; terrace and garden with
summer barbecue; children's play area
(Roger Taylor, TOH)

Westcott [Guildford Rd; TQ1448],
Cricketers: Friendly, with good local
atmosphere, half a dozen real ales, food,
pool-table in sunken area *(Ray Challoner)*

☆ **Weybridge** [Bridge Rd; TQ0764], *Queens
Head*: Good friendly atmosphere in intimate
beamed bar with open fire, lots of stripped
brickwork, rugby football souvenirs, big
helpings of good bar food, well kept
Watneys-related real ales; spacious
restaurant with its own separate bar; benches
outside; can get very busy *(Ian Phillips, David
Clare, Gary Wilkes)*

Weybridge [Thames St], *Farnell Arms*:
Victorian pub with modestly priced
Watneys-related real ales on handpump, and
consistently good bar food cooked by
licensee and served by pleasant staff – get
there before 12.30, especially towards end of
week; good value big restaurant *(Dr
R B Crail)*; [Thames St] *Lincoln Arms*:
Oldish pub on river road, comfortably

refurbished and extended late last year, with
changing beers such as well kept Gales HSB,
as well as rather pricey Friary Meux Best, Ind
Coope Burton and Tetleys; large bar with
log-effect gas fires at either end, pleasant
staff and good mix of customers; picnic-table
sets on back lawn, other tables on little green
in front *(R Houghton, Robert Crail, Ian
Phillips)*; [Thames St] *Old Crown*: Attractive
seats in the little yard behind this
weatherboarded pub near the river; good
range of sandwiches and bar snacks, super
staff *(Ian Phillips)*

☆ **Windlesham** [Church Rd; SU9264], *Half
Moon*: Plain but popular (particularly with
younger people) with active atmosphere, fast
and friendly service, particularly good choice
of real ales such as Badger, Fullers ESB and
London Pride, Greene King Abbot, Marstons
Pedigree, Ringwood Old Thumper, Ruddles
County, Timothy Taylors Landlord,
Theakstons Old Peculier and Youngers No 3
(they may allow you samples if you're unsure
which to choose), straightforward lunchtime
food (not Sun); large attractive garden
overlooking nearby church and paddock
*(Gary Wilkes, Richard Houghton, Ian Phillips,
Dr M Owton)*

Windlesham [School Rd], *Bee*: Small local,
well kept Courage Directors, bar food and
large garden; open all day *(Dr M Owton)*;
[Chertsey Rd] *Brickmakers Arms*: Small and
friendly, with well kept Courage ales inc
Directors, and live music Sun; half of pub
devoted to restaurant, serving good food
(Dr M Owton)

☆ **Witley** [Petworth Rd (A283); SU9439],
White Hart: Largely Tudor, with good oak
furniture, pewter tankards hanging from
beams, inglenook fireplace where George
Eliot drank; Watneys-related real ales,
traditional games, unobtrusive piped music,
straightforward bar food; children in
restaurant and eating area, seats outside,
playground; village church well worth a visit
(W A Lund, LYM)

Woking [Arthurs Bridge Rd; TQ0159],
Bridge Barn: Large canalside Beefeater with
restaurant up in the roof beams of the barn
and bars with flagstone floors downstairs;
very welcoming and cheerful, good value all
round; lots of benches beside canal *(Liz and
Ian Phillips)*; [West End] *Wheatsheaf*: Genial,
friendly licensee, excellent value bar food,
pleasant garden with apple trees, ducks and
chickens *(S L Hughes)*

Wonersh [The Street; TQ0245], *Grantley
Arms*: Half-timbered sixteenth-century local,
popular – especially on Suns, with friendly
service, real ale, imaginative bar food *(J S
Evans)*; [Blackheath] take Sampleoak Lane
from Percy Arms, then left at crossroads]
Villagers: Popular pub off beaten track with
Watneys-related real ales on handpump,
good choice of moderately priced bar food,
pleasant service by young staff *(R B Crail)*

Wood Street [SU9550], *White Hart*: Good comfortably furnished free house with well kept real ales such as Brakspears, Flowers Original and Gales HSB, but after recent change of management food seems less extensive; in cul-de-sac off attractive village green, tables outside *(Lyn and Bill Capper)*

☆ **Woodmansterne** [High St; TQ2760], *Woodman*: Homely and easy-going country pub with plenty of room for children to play in splendid garden; often packed inside, with good Bass, Charrington IPA and a guest beer on handpump, comfortable settees and armchairs of some character (if you can get one), decent food, pleasant staff *(E G Parish, Martin Aust)*

Worplesdon [Worplesdon Stn rd off Guildford–Woking rd; SU9753], *Jolly Farmer*: Well kept real ales such as Badger Tanglefoot, Buckleys Best, Fullers ESB and Tetleys – at a price – in simply furnished L-shaped beamed bar of isolated country pub, bar food (also far from cheap, especially in the evening), piped music, pleasant staff, big sheltered garden; children in restaurant *(Ian Phillips, LYM)*

Wotton [A25 Dorking–Guildford; TQ1247], *Wotton Hatch*: Busy little low-ceilinged front bar, handsome cocktail bar, traditional games and fruit machine in tiled-floor public bar, well kept Fullers real ales on handpump, restaurant and tables with play area outside; after a change of landlord preliminary reports suggest that food and service in this nice pub may take a little while to settle down; children allowed in restaurant *(LYM)*

Wrecclesham [SU8245], *Bear & Ragged Staff*: Quite friendly Courage house with long, low bar and exposed beams; reasonable bar food; popular with older people *(Dr John Innes)*; [Sandrock Hill Rd] *Sandrock*: Unspoilt country pub with great atmosphere, exceptional choice of real ales inc guest beers from small breweries *(R G Watts)*

Sussex

Several changes here include new licensees at the prettily tucked-away Blue Ship near Billingshurst, the rather smart Swan at Fittleworth, and the cheerfully old-fashioned Three Cups near Punnets Town; the Swan at Dallington (a nice place to stay at, with decent food) has broken its tie with the brewery to become a free house, the Gribble at Oving has really got its own brewery going, and the Fox Goes Free in Charlton is serving food all through the day in summer. Lots of entirely new entries, or pubs back after a break, include the Bell at Burwash (doing very well under its new licensees, with rather good food), the Old House At Home at Chidham (the newish licensees here are doing some of their own brewing again), the pretty old George & Dragon in its big garden near Coolham, the Bull at Ditchling (fine old furnishings – a nice place to stay at), the quaint Juggs at Kingston Near Lewes, the Lickfold Inn at Lickfold (readers are really enthusiastic about the home cooking under the current regime), the Halfway Bridge at Lodsworth (a delightful find – good food and a fine atmosphere, charmingly made over by the family who originally made such a success of the Three Horseshoes at Elsted), the cleanly unpretentious Noahs Ark at Lurgashall, the welcoming Hope overlooking Newhaven's harbour mouth, the vibrantly idiosyncratic Lamb at Ripe, the Horse & Groom at Rushlake Green (very new licensees), the friendly Sloop at Scaynes Hill (generous helpings of good food), the flourishing Golden Galleon in its lovely position outside Seaford, the Horseguards perched over the village street at Tillington, and the Tudor Dorset Arms at Withyham. Other pubs currently doing particularly well here include the friendly little Rose Cottage at Alciston (simple but very popular food), the lively Six Bells at Chiddingly, the ancient Three Horseshoes at Elsted (particularly good food), the warm-hearted Anchor at Hartfield (good fish), the Rose & Crown in Mayfield (getting a place-to-stay award this year, to join its food award and star), the Bull at Ticehurst (very popular for its unpretentious food), the thriving New Inn in Winchelsea, and the Richmond Arms at West Ashling (perhaps the best range of uncommon bottled beers in

The Royal Oak, Wineham

the South, with a splendidly wide-ranging choice of real ales too). Among the Lucky Dip entries at the end of the chapter, pubs to mention particularly include the Sussex Ox at Berwick, Royal Pavilion in Brighton (the pub – not the other one), George & Dragon at Burpham, Royal Oak near Chilgrove, Old Vine at Cousleywood, Cherry Tree at Dale Hill, Sussex Brewery in Hermitage, William IV at Nutley, Jack Fullers at Oxleys Green, Oddfellows Arms in Pulborough, White Hart at Stopham, Crown at Turners Hill, Ram at West Firle and Three Crowns at Wisborough Green.

ALCISTON   TQ5103 Map 3

Rose Cottage 🏮

Village signposted off A27 Polegate–Lewes

Cosy and warmly welcoming, this well run little cottage has black joists in the bar that are hung with harness, traps, a thatcher's blade and lots of other black ironwork, and on shelves above its dark panelled dado or in the etched-glass windows there's a model sailing-ship, a stuffed kingfisher and other birds. There are perhaps half a dozen tables, with wheel-back chairs and red leatherette seats built in around them, a talking parrot (mornings only), open fires, and an atmosphere that stays relaxed and friendly even when it gets full. A small low-beamed and parquet-floored area by the bar counter has a wall bench and little side bench. At lunchtime (when you can also use the restaurant area for bar food), generous helpings of good simple food include wholesome soup (£1), good ploughman's (from £1.85), ham and egg (£2.50), big salads (from £2.50, prawn £3.75), Brie and asparagus quiche or first-class home-made pies such as rabbit or steak and kidney (£2.95), curried nut-loaf (£3.25), and steaks (from £6.95); in the evening there are extras like pâté (£1.75), smoked salmon cornet (£2.95), scampi (£3.25) and half a roast duckling (£6.85). Well kept Harveys and Ruddles Best on handpump; pleasant, efficient service; maybe cheap free-range eggs and local game. There are some seats outside by the tangle of wistaria, and a small paddock with a goat, chickens, and ducks on a pond. On the fence surrounding the car park there are quite a few enamel signs. *(Recommended by W J Wonham, Jane Palmer, S J A Velate, Geoff Wilson, D A Anderson, Theodore and Jean Rowland-Entwistle, J Caulkin, Heather Sharland, PAB, Patrick Young, Peter Corris)*

Free house   Licensee Ian Lewis   Real ale   Meals and snacks   Small evening restaurant (not Sun) tel Alfriston (0323) 870377   Children in eating area and restaurant   Open 11.30–2.30, 6.30–11 all year

ALFRISTON   TQ5103 Map 3

Market Cross ('The Smugglers Inn')

As a reminder of its smuggling history, this attractive, well run pub has a couple of cutlasses hanging over the big inglenook fireplace in the comfortably modernised L-shaped bar. There are low beams, Liberty print cushions on the window seats, Windsor chairs, and some brass on the walls (which have quite a lot of nautical-looking white-painted panelling). A cosier little room leads off, and in the conservatory at the back there's a hundred-year-old baker's table. Bar food includes sandwiches (from 90p, toasties from £1), ploughman's (£1.50), a vegetarian dish (£2.50), basket meals such as cod or scampi (from £2.50), gammon (£4.25), big trout (£4.75) and steaks (from £5.45). Well kept Courage Best and Directors on handpump; friendly staff. There's a beer garden behind. The cliff walks south of here are superb, though if you're feeling lazier Old Clergy, a house in the village, is

---

'Space game' means any electronic game.

worth visiting for its fine Elizabethan furniture. *(Recommended by John Hayward, John Knighton, S J A Velate, TRA, MA, Heather Sharland, Peter Corris, Nick Dowson, Alison Hayward)*

Courage   Licensee Maureen Ney   Real ale   Meals (not Sun lunchtime) and snacks   Children in eating area of bar and conservatory   Public car park only fairly close   Open 11–3, 6–11 all year

Star 🛏

Formerly belonging to Battle Abbey, this fifteenth-century inn was on the pilgrim route to the shrine of St Richard in Chichester. The front of the building is decorated with fine brightly painted medieval carvings; the striking red lion is known by local people as Old Bill – probably a figurehead salvaged from a seventeenth-century Dutch shipwreck. Inside, the elegant bar has handsome furnishings that include a heavy oak Stuart refectory table with a big bowl of flowers, antique Windsor armchairs worn to a fine polish, a grandfather clock, a Tudor fireplace, and massive beams supporting the white-painted oak ceiling boards (and the lanterns used for lighting). Lunchtime food includes home-made soup (£1.05), sandwiches (£1.35), ploughman's (from £2.30), a mixed meat salad (£3.65) and home-made dishes of the day such as chicken casserole or good steak and kidney pie (£3.55); puddings (from £1.05). Bass, John Smiths and Websters Yorkshire on handpump and English wines (drinks prices are very reasonable here, considering the style of the place). *(Recommended by S J A Velate, AE, GRE, Nick Dowson, Alison Hayward, WHBM)*

Free house (THF)   Manager Michael Grange   Real ale   Lunchtime snacks and meals (not Sun)   Restaurant   Children welcome   Open 11–11 all year   Bedrooms tel Alfriston (0323) 870495; £61B/£88B

ARUNDEL   TQ0107 Map 3

Swan 🛏

High Street

The spacious L-shaped Turkey-carpeted bar in this cosy, friendly inn has a relaxed, informal atmosphere, red plush button-back banquettes, red velvet curtains, and a good choice of well kept real ales: Badger Best and Tanglefoot, Courage Best and Directors, Harveys Best, King & Barnes Bitter, Marstons Pedigree and a guest bitter, all on handpump. Good, reasonably priced bar food, using fresh local produce, includes home-made soup (£1.25), sandwiches (from £1, home-cooked beef with horseradish £1.40, chicken, smoked bacon and mayonnaise £2, toasties 25p extra), filled baked potatoes, ploughman's (from £1.80), garlic mushrooms (£1.90), vegetarian curry, basket meals (from £2.20), bacon, sausages and eggs (£2.75), home-made burger (£3.25), salads with home-cooked meats, gammon with pineapple (£5.25) and steaks (from £8.50). Fruit machine, trivia machine and piped music. *(Recommended by R F Warner, P J Taylor, Norman Foot, D J Devey, Klaus and Elizabeth Leist, Simon Collett-Jones, A V Chute)*

Free house   Licensees Diana and Ken Rowsell   Real ale   Meals and snacks   Restaurant Children in eating area   Jazz first Sun night of month, 1950s/1960s/blues live music on other Sun nights   Open 11–11 all year   Bedrooms tel Arundel (0903) 882314; £35B/£45B

ASHURST   TQ1716 Map 3

Fountain

B2135 N of Steyning

The bar to head for in this friendly pub is on the right as you go in: a charmingly unspoilt sixteenth-century room with scrubbed flagstones, a cushioned pew built right around two sides, two antique polished trestle tables, a couple of high-backed wooden cottage armchairs by the brick inglenook fireplace, brasses on the black mantelbeam, and a friendly pub dog. Good value home-made bar food includes very good fresh tomato soup with a sprinkling of mint and cream, sandwiches (£1.10), ploughman's (from £1.65) and various daily specials such as tasty steak and kidney pie and pizza (£3); candle-lit suppers on Thursday and Friday evenings (booking advisable). Well kept Flowers Original, Fremlins, Whitbreads Castle Eden or Pompey Royal and a guest beer such as Wethereds SPA or Winter Royal on handpump or tapped straight from the cask; cheerful service. A bigger carpeted room (no dogs in this one) has spindle-back chairs around its circular tables, a wood-burning stove, and darts, shove-ha'penny, dominoes, cribbage and fruit machine. There are two garden areas, one with fruit trees, roses, swings, a seesaw and a tiled-roof weekend barbecue counter, the other with picnic-table sets on gravel by an attractive duck pond. *(Recommended by I W and P J Muir, Norman Foot, Gordon Smith, Mr and Mrs R Gammon)*

Whitbreads   Real ale   Meals (lunchtime, not Sun) and snacks (not Sun)   Children in eating area lunchtime only   Open 11–2.30, 6–11 (11–11 Fri and Sat) all year; closed evenings 25 and 26 Dec

nr BILLINGSHURST   TQ0925 Map 3

Blue Ship

The Haven; hamlet signposted off A29 just N of junction with A264, then follow signpost left towards Garlands and Okehurst

Understandably popular on summer evenings, this remote and friendly country pub has an unspoilt front bar served from a hatch, a snug bar down a corridor at the back, and another room furnished with kitchen chairs and post-war Utility tables. Good home-made bar food includes sandwiches (from £1), ploughman's (from £1.90), cottage pie (£2.75), cod (£2.95), lasagne (£3.25), and steak and kidney pie or scampi (£3.50). Well kept King & Barnes Bitter tapped from the cask, and Old in winter. A games-room has darts, bar billiards, shove-ha'penny, cribbage, dominoes and fruit machine. You can sit outside at the tree-shaded side tables or on benches in front by the tangle of honeysuckle round the door. It can get crowded with young people at weekends. The pub has its own shoot. *(Recommended by Sheralyn Coates, Kevin Ryan, Phil Gorton, N D Foot, Philip King; more reports please)*

King & Barnes   Licensee J R Davie   Real ale   Meals and snacks (not Sun or Mon evenings)   Children in eating area of bar and games-room   Open 11–3, 6–11 all year

BLACKBOYS   TQ5220 Map 3

Blackboys

B2192, S edge of village

Interesting odds and ends fill the charming series of old-fashioned small rooms in this partly black-weatherboarded fourteenth-century building: Spy cricketer caricatures and other more antique prints, a key collection hanging from beams, a stuffed red squirrel, a collection of ancient bottles on a high shelf, a snug armchair by the inglenook fireplace, and so forth. Good waitress-served food includes soup (£1.50), sandwiches (from £1.40, prawn £2), ploughman's or steak sandwich (£2.75), mussels in garlic butter seafood pancakes (£4.50), summer crab salad (£5.95) or lobster salad (from £6.95), rib-eye steak (£6.25) and lots of puddings (from £1). Well kept Harveys PA, BB and in winter XXXX on handpump; darts, shove-ha'penny, dominoes, table skittles, cribbage, fruit machine, space game and juke box. This year, eyebrows have been raised over the state of the lavatories. Seats among flowers and shrubs in front of the pub overlook a pond, and altogether there's about sixteen acres. The back orchard has rustic tables among apple trees, and a children's play area with two wooden castles linked by a rope bridge has quite a few animals; big well equipped playroom in the barn. *(Recommended by Philip and Sheila Hanley, Greg Parston, Comus Elliott, W P Ford, Alan Skull, Mrs E M Thompson)*

Harveys Real ale Meals and snacks (not Sun evening) Restaurant tel Framfield (082 582) 283 Children in restaurant Open 11–11 all year

BURWASH TQ6724 Map 3
Bell

Friendly new licensees have taken over this mainly seventeenth-century pub, opposite the church in this prettily conserved village. The comfortable dining-lounge has green plush button-back built-in banquettes and wheel-back chairs around the tables on the leafy green carpet, brass platters, Pickwickian prints and annotated old local photographs on the silky cream wallpaper, and a big open fireplace. A wide choice of food ranges from ploughman's (from £1.75), smoked salmon sandwich (£2.50) or Danish open prawn sandwich (£2.80), home-made pizzas (from £3.20 – these are also available to take away), beef curry (£4), breast of chicken in a leek and Stilton sauce (£4.85), whole grilled plaice (£4.95), halibut in lemon sauce (£5.50), king crab (from £6.50) and beef Wellington (£8.50). Well kept Brakspears, Fremlins, Harveys, Marstons and Charles Wells Bombardier on handpump. Newspapers on sticks for customers to read; darts, cribbage, ring the bull, toad-in-the-hole, and faint piped music. There are seats in front of the pub looking over the road to the church. Nearby parking may be difficult. Batemans (Kipling's home) is nearby. The pub is near the start of *Good Walks Guide* Walk 67. *(Recommended by H H Richards, Peter and Moyna Lynch, Lisa Freedman, G and M Brooke-Williams, Peter Corris)*

Beards (who no longer brew) Licensees David Mizel and Annick Howard Real ale Meals and snacks (not Sun evening) Restaurant Children in eating area of bar Small folk evening last Sun of month Open 11–2.30 (3 Sat), 6–11 all year Bedrooms tel Burwash (0435) 882304; £18/£28

BYWORTH SU9820 Map 3
Black Horse
Signposted from A283

Thought to have been a friary in the fifteenth century, this place is simply, even austerely furnished, with stripped pews and scrubbed tables on bare floorboards, candles in bottles, and decoration confined to a collection of old sepia photographs in the back part. In contrast to the simplicity of the décor, there's an elaborate choice of bar food: French onion soup (£1.95), ploughman's (from £2.75), shepherd's pie (£3.10), salads (from £3.20), courgette and prawn au gratin (£3.50), lambs' kidneys in sherry (£3.60), Mediterranean prawns in garlic (£4.30), beef curry (£4.99), monkfish in mustard sauce (£6.20), and steaks (from £8.50); lots of ice-creams and sorbets (from £1.35). Well kept Ballards and Youngs Bitter and Special on handpump. Last winter there were some serious doubts about service – more reports on this please. The garden is particularly attractive, dropping steeply down through a series of grassy terraces, each screened by banks of flowering shrubs (but still with a view across the valley to swelling woodland); a bigger lawn at the bottom is set beside a small stream and an old willow. *(Recommended by Mr and Mrs J H Adam, Stephen Goodchild, Miles Kington, WTF, M E A Horler, S J A Velate, Lyn and Bill Capper)*

Free house Licensees Mr and Mrs J Hess Real ale Meals and snacks (11.15–1.45, 6.30–9.45) Restaurant tel Petworth (0798) 42424 Children in restaurant if well behaved Open 11–2.30, 6–11; closed 25 Dec

---

Places with gardens or terraces usually let children sit there; we note in the text the very, very few exceptions that don't.

CHARLTON   SU8812 Map 2
Fox Goes Free

Village signposted off A286 Chichester–Midhurst just N of West Dean, also from
Chichester–Petworth via East Dean

The name comes from the legend that Sussex foxes by working in packs completely
bewilder the Charlton Hunt which has been meeting here for 300 years. It's a well
run and attractively reworked place, and the partly carpeted brick-floored main bar
has blond wood tables and mate's chairs, elm benches built against its yellowing
walls, a big brick fireplace, a small but entertaining hat collection, and a relaxed,
friendly atmosphere; a nice little low-beamed snug has a sturdy elm settle and a big
inglenook fireplace. The rustic-style extension gives extra eating space for bar
lunches, and becomes an evening restaurant (with the same menu as the bar). Good
bar food includes soup (£1.50), sandwiches (from £1.50), various ploughman's
(from £2.40), filled baked potatoes (from £2.55), lasagne or home-made steak and
mushroom pie (£3.65), chicken in provençale sauce (£3.95), and sirloin steak
(£6.95); they also have a 250-year-old recipe for local game marinated in port and
red wine. Well kept if pricey Ballards Wassail, Flowers Original, King & Barnes
Bitter, Mild and Festive and a guest beer such as Adnams, Greene King Abbot and
Whitbreads Castle Eden on handpump, decent house wines, country wines, and
local farm cider, piped music, fruit machine; they also have darts, shove-ha'penny,
dominoes, cribbage and some old-fashioned Victorian games. Tables among fruit
trees in the back garden looking up to the downs have a summer soft-drinks servery
and safe children's play area with sandpit and swings; the barbecue area can be
booked. Handy for the Weald and Downland Open-Air Museum. *(Recommended by
Norman Foot, Brian and Anna Marsden, Gwen and Peter Andrews)*

*Free house   Licensee Roger Waller   Real ale   Meals and snacks (noon–10 in summer)
Restaurant tel Singleton (024 363) 461   Children in eating area and restaurant
Singing duo and comedian last Sun in month   Open 11–11; 11–2.30, 6–11 in winter*

CHIDDINGLY   TQ5414 Map 3
Six Bells ★

Part of the elaborately carved bar counter in this warmly welcoming, old-fashioned
pub did service as a makeshift bridge over a stream for some years, after it was
removed from a nearby pub that closed down. Simply but attractively furnished,
there are tall Windsor armchairs, pews, scrubbed or polished tables, an antique box
settle, low beams, some panelling, old engravings, lots of prints and stuffed animals,
and a good winter fire. In the back bar there's a pianola with many rolls which can
be played with the landlord's permission. Consistently good home-made food
includes French onion soup (60p), filled French bread (70p), cheesy garlic bread
(£1.10), landlord's special (£1.25), steak and kidney, beef and vegetable or
shepherd's pies (£1.40), vegetarian or meaty lasagne (£1.60), chilli con carne
(£2.50), spicy prawns or spare ribs in barbecue sauce (£2.85), with generous
banana splits, treacle pie and other puddings (£1.20). Well kept Courage Best and
Directors on handpump, with Harveys tapped from the cask (winter only). Darts,
dominoes, cribbage. There's a fine collection of enamelled advertising signs in the
gents. Outside at the back, there are some tables beyond a goldfish pond.
*(Recommended by Lindsey Shaw Radley, Yvonne Woodfield, C R and M A Starling, Theo and
Jean Rowland-Entwistle)*

*Free house   Licensee Paul Newman   Real ale   Meals and snacks (not Mon)   Small
children's room and more room in music bar   Live bands Fri, Sat and Sun evenings, jazz Sun
lunchtime   Open 10–2.30, 6–11 all year; closed Mon exc bank hols*

Children: if the details at the end of an entry don't mention them, you should assume that the
pub does not allow them inside.

CHIDHAM   SU7903 Map 2
Old House At Home
Cot Lane; turn off A27 at Barleycorn pub

In a remote, unspoilt farm-hamlet, this friendly cosy cottage has low black joists in the white ceiling, timbered white walls, long wall benches, tables and Windsor chairs, and a winter log fire. A wide choice of bar food includes sandwiches (from 90p), soup (£1.20), filled baked potatoes (from £1.75), ploughman's (£2.25), vegetarian quiche (£2.45), omelettes (from £2.50), prawns in garlic butter (£2.75), salads (from £2.95), chicken casserole (£3.25), roast rib of beef with Yorkshire pudding or mussels in wine and garlic butter (£4.75), steaks (from £5.75), and a few dishes that can be served quickly for people in a hurry such as chilli con carne (£3), fisherman's pie (£3.20) or steak and kidney pie (£3.50); puddings (from £1.10) and children's meals (£1.75). Well kept Ballards, Ringwood Best and Old Thumper, guest beers, and they may sometimes brew their own beer, Old House, all on handpump; they also do farm cider, country wines, and tea and coffee. Behind the house, a sycamore tree shelters a cluster of picnic-table sets, and there are two more on the front terrace. (*Recommended by Richard Houghton, Brian and Anna Marsden*)

Free house   Licensees Terry and Phyllis Brewer   Real ale   Meals and snacks (12–2 (2.30 weekends), 6–10)   Children welcome   Open 11.30–2.30, 6–11 all year, though may open longer afternoons in summer

nr COOLHAM   TQ1423 Map 3
George & Dragon
Dragons Green; pub signposted off A272 between Coolham and A24

Popular with locals and visitors alike, this old tile-hung cottage has some unusually low and massive black beams in the cosy bar (see if you can decide whether the date cut into one is 1677 or 1577), as well as heavily timbered walls, a partly wood-block and partly polished tiled and carpeted floor, simple chairs and rustic stools, some brass, and a big inglenook fireplace with an early seventeenth-century grate. Reasonably priced bar food includes sandwiches (from 80p), ploughman's (from £1.80), salads (from £3), ham and egg (£3.80), home-made steak and kidney pie (£3.95), and cold topside of beef (£4.25); well kept King & Barnes Sussex Bitter and Festive on handpump, with Old Ale in winter. Darts and bar billiards. The big lawn which stretches away behind the pub is lovely in summer, with lots of rustic tables and chairs well spaced among fruit trees, shrubs and flowers, and a thirty-foot play caravan for children. (*Recommended by Hazel Morgan, Gwen and Peter Andrews, Norman Foot, T Nott, Theo and Jean Rowland-Entwistle, Dr and Mrs J Levi*)

King & Barnes   Licensee Ron Barber   Real ale   Meals and snacks   Children welcome Open 11–3, 6–11; 11–11 Sat

COWBEECH   TQ6114 Map 3
Merrie Harriers
Village signposted from A271

Once a farmhouse, this white clapboarded village pub still has something of the atmosphere of an old-fashioned farm parlour in the friendly panelled public bar: beams, pewter tankards hanging by the bar counter, a curved high-backed settle by the brick inglenook fireplace (with a log-effect gas fire now), pot plants in the window, and two friendly cats. The communicating lounge has spindle-back chairs around the tables on its flowery carpet. Popular lunchtime food includes home-made soup (£1.25), sandwiches (from £1, toasties £1.50, children's sandwiches 75p), filled cottage rolls (from £1.25), ploughman's (from £2.25), salads (from £3.50), steak and kidney pie (£4.50) and grilled lemon sole (£5.75); in the evenings there's salmon mousse or pâté (£2.25), fresh rainbow trout (£4.75), mixed grill (£5.95) and steaks (from £7.75). Flowers, Gales HSB and Harveys on handpump kept under light top pressure; also country wines and biscuits to nibble on the counter. Darts, shove-ha'penny, dominoes, cribbage. Outside the pub is a flower garden and a lawn with a swing and rustic seats. *(Recommended by Nancy and Grant Buck, D J Penny, Prof A N Black, AE; more reports please)*

Free house   Licensees G M and B J Richards   Meals and snacks (12–2, 7–10; not Sun evening)   Open 11–2.30, 6.30–11 all year

nr DALLINGTON   TQ6619 Map 3

Swan 🍺

Wood's Corner; B2096, E of Dallington

On a clear day you can see right across the soft country below this ridge to Beachy Head, either from the big picture windows in the simply furnished back bar or from the picnic-table sets in the neatly kept back flower garden. The main bar has well polished horsebrasses on the few beams and timbers in the cream walls, tapestry-cushioned stools and built-in wooden benches, sturdy wooden tables with little bunches of flowers, windows with more flowers and hanging copper saucepans, and a log fire. The menu changes day by day, serving mostly home-made dishes: sandwiches, vegetarian dishes (£3.50), beef stew with dumplings or prawn au gratin (£4.50), chicken, ham and mushroom pie (£4.65), and puddings like treacle tart (£1.50); good breakfasts. On Sundays little dishes of nuts, crisps and Cheddar cheese are put out on the bar counter. Well kept Harveys, King & Barnes Festive and Marstons Pedigree on handpump; decent house wines; friendly service. Bar billiards, shove-ha'penny, chess, trivia and unobtrusive piped music. From the bedrooms the nighttime view of the tiny distant lights of Eastbourne is stunning. Good woodland walks nearby, especially in Dallington Forest. *(Recommended by A C Earl, B R Shiner, S J A Velate, J M Shaw, J A H Townsend, V H Balchin, E G Parish, Philip King)*

Free house   Licensees John and Marie Blake   Real ale   Meals and snacks Restaurant   Children in bar lobby area and restaurant   Occasional folk nights Open 11–3, 6–11 all year   Two bedrooms tel Brightling (042 482) 242; £15/£28

DITCHLING   TQ3215 Map 3

Bull 🍺

2 High Street; B2112, junction with B2116

Attractive traditional furnishings in the heavily beamed and spotlessly kept main bar include polished oak chests and settles, handsome elm and mahogany tables, one sturdy central refectory table, dark oak floorboards, a longcase clock, and gundog prints and photographs over the wooden dado. A separate Turkey-carpeted corner bar has simpler, neater furnishings (no dogs allowed there). Good plain bar food, changing day by day, includes sandwiches, home-made winter soups, pies, half-shoulder of lamb roasted with rosemary, well hung steaks, local game, and a good deal of fresh local fish from mackerel to crab and lobster. Well kept Flowers Original, Marstons Pedigree, Whitbreads Strong Country and Pompey Royal on handpump and quite a few whiskies from the handsome linenfold panelling bar counter, and a quietly relaxed atmosphere; no fewer than three inglenook log fireplaces. There are picnic-table sets on a back sun-trap terrace, and in the spacious garden. This busy but charming old village is a good base for walking; a stroll past

---

Please keep sending us reports. We rely on readers for news of new discoveries, and particularly for news of changes, however slight, at the fully described pubs. No stamp needed: *The Good Pub Guide*, FREEPOST, London SW10 0BR.

the duck pond behind the church takes you up a little hill with a fine view of the South Downs, and the Jack and Jill windmills above Clayton. *(Recommended by Charles and Mary Winpenny, Mr and Mrs G Holliday, AE, John Knighton; more reports please)*

Whitbreads   Licensee R K Bryant   Real ale   Meals and snacks (not Sun evening – except for residents)   Restaurant   Children in eating area and restaurant   Open 10–2.30, 6–11 all year   Three bedrooms tel Hassocks (079 18) 3147; £28.50B/£38.50B

EASEBOURNE   SU8922 Map 2
Olde White Horse

A286 just N of Midhurst

Attractive and neatly kept, this stone pub has a friendly atmosphere and a snug little modernised lounge with Leech and other sporting prints on its white-painted partly panelled walls, and a small log fire. The bigger public bar, with wall settles on its woodstrip floor, has darts, dominoes and cribbage. One seat is the preserve of Guy the cat, even on those busy days when a shooting or polo party's in. Good value food that changes daily includes sandwiches (lunchtime only, except Sunday), haddock (£2.25), lamb chop in red wine with oranges (£3.25), fresh fish (Fridays), such as skate wing with capers, or steak and kidney pie topped with oyster (£3.45), and popular soufflé omelettes (£5.50); they have regular three-course specials such as artichoke soup, pike marinated in brandy and madeira with langoustine in puff pastry, and crêpes suzette (£8.25). Well kept Friary Meux and Ind Coope Burton on handpump, a few malt whiskies, and quite a few wines. There are tables out in a small courtyard, with more on the sheltered and well tended back lawn. *(Recommended by James Moller, Sylvia Matthews; more reports please)*

Friary Meux (Allied)   Licensee Alan Hollidge   Real ale   Meals and snacks   Evening restaurant tel Midhurst (073 081) 3521 (may be used as weekend lunchtime overflow)   Children over five in restaurant   Open 11–2.30, 6–11 all year; closed evening 25 Dec

EASTDEAN   TV5597 Map 3
Tiger

Pub (with village centre) signposted – not vividly – from A259 Eastbourne–Seaford

As the lane past the pub leads down to the coast at Birling Gap and then on to Beachy Head – much of the land between here and the sea is National Trust – this long low tiled white cottage is popular with walkers (and is on *Good Walks Guide* Walk 60). The setting is very pretty; it faces a quiet cottage-lined green, and has lots of window boxes, clematis and roses, some rustic seats and tables on the brick front terrace, and a big bright painting of a tiger on a branch. Inside, two rooms have low beams, ochre walls, low rustic tables, padded seats, housekeeper's chairs, old-fashioned tables, and (in the inner room) antique oak settles – one with a big bowed back and another attractively carved; decorations include photographs of the pub (often with a hunt meeting on the green), Victorian engravings, horsebrasses, pewter measures and china mugs hanging from beams, a big kitchen clock facing the bar, some handbells over the counter, and a stuffed tiger's head. Bar food includes toasted sandwiches in winter (from £1.20), pâté (£1.90), ploughman's (from £1.90), sausages (£2.50), salads (from £3), steak and kidney pie, macaroni cheese or excellent scampi (£3.50), gammon with pineapple (£4.50), eight-ounce sirloin steak (£5.50) and puddings like jam roly-poly (from 80p). Well kept Courage Best and Directors on handpump; good choice of wines by the glass, and hot toddies; fruit machine. *(Recommended by David and Ruth Shillitoe, Peter Corris, TBB, S J A Velate, Margaret Dyke, Jenny and Brian Seller)*

Courage   Licensee James Conroy   Real ale   Meals and snacks (not Sun evening)   Children in dining area   Open 10–3, 6–11

ELSTED   SU8119 Map 2
Three Horseshoes ★ ✦

Village signposted from B2141 Chichester–Petersfield

Set at the end of a hamlet, below the sweep of the South Downs, this pretty tiled house is popular for its good, imaginative food and friendly atmosphere. The four cosy connecting low-beamed rooms have oak benches, antique high-backed settles, studded leather seats, and good tables (candle-lit at night), attractive engravings and old photographs on the deep ochre walls, rugs on sixteenth-century bricks, on tiles or on bare boards, log fires, and simple latch and plank doors; there are newspapers on racks and two friendly cream retrievers. Changing food might include soup in winter (£1.50), ploughman's with a good choice of cheeses (from £2.50), butterfly prawns or tagliatelle with cheese and mushrooms (£2.75), baked potatoes with interesting fillings (£3.50), various quiches or chilli con carne (£3.75), dressed crab from Selsey (in season, £4), steak and kidney pie in Guinness (£4.50), whole Selsey plaice (£4.75), and salmon steak with cucumber mayonnaise (£6.50); Sunday lunchtime cold summer buffet from £2.75; youngish, helpful service. The pretty little rustic dining-room with candles in brass holders on its plain wooden tables serves the same food as the bar, though on Friday and Saturday evenings from October to March there's a set menu (three courses £9.95). Well kept changing ales tapped from the cask might include Adnams, Badger, Ballards Best and Wassail, Batemans, Boddingtons, Brakspears, Fullers London Pride, Gales HSB, Gibbs Mew Bishops Tipple, Harveys, Ringwood Old Thumper and Tetleys; Churchwards farm cider; dominoes, cribbage and shut-the-box. They sell local eggs. The biggish garden has picnic-table sets, a good herbaceous border, rose beds and a pets' corner with a lamb, goat, pigs and ornamental fowl. *(Recommended by Bernard Smalley, M Rising, Harriet and Michael Robinson, Norman Foot, Brian and Anna Marsden, W A Gardiner, John Evans, A J Skull, Shirley Fluck, Dr John Innes, Dr I J Thompson, HEG, Peter Hitchcock, Drs S P K and C M Linter, Gwen and Peter Andrews, M C Howells, Ian Phillips, Roger Mallard)*

Free house   Licensees Ann and Tony Burdfield   Real ale   Meals and snacks (12–2, 6.30–10)   Restaurant tel Harting (073 085) 746   Children in eating area and restaurant   Open 10–3, 6–11 all year; closed 25 Dec

FITTLEWORTH   TQ0118 Map 3
Swan

Lower Street; B2138

Perhaps the nicest place to sit in summer is at one of the well spaced tables on the big back lawn, sheltered by flowering shrubs and a hedge sprawling with honeysuckle; there are also benches by the village lane in front of this pretty tile-hung fifteenth-century inn. Inside, the main bar is comfortably furnished with Windsor armchairs on the patterned carpet, there are wooden truncheons over the big inglenook fireplace (which has good winter log fires), and a big collection of bottle openers behind the bar. Bar food includes sandwiches (from £1.05), soup (£1.20), baked potatoes (from £1.30), ploughman's (from £2.65), lasagne (£2.75), vegetarian dishes and curries (£3.30), steak and kidney (£3.95), salads (from £3.85), and puddings (from £1); children's meals (£1.95); good coffee. The attractive panelled room is decorated with landscapes by Constable's brother George. Well kept Ruddles Best and County, and Websters Yorkshire on

---

Real ale may be served from handpumps, electric pumps (not just the on-off switches used for keg beer) or, common in Scotland, tall taps called founts (pronounced 'fonts') where a separate pump pushes up the beer under air pressure. The landlord can adjust the force of the flow – a tight spigot gives the good creamy head that Yorkshire lads like.

handpump; piped music, and the smaller public bar has darts, pool, shove-ha'penny, cribbage, dominoes, trivia and fruit machine. There are good nearby walks in beech woods. *(Recommended by Dave Braisted, WTF, Charles and Mary Winpenny, Lyn and Bill Capper, Mr and Mrs W Harrington)*

Phoenix (Watneys)   Licensee Rod Aspinall   Real ale   Meals and snacks   Restaurant Children in eating area of bar   Open 11–3, 6–11 Mon–Weds, 11–11 Thurs–Sat all year Bedrooms tel Fittleworth (079 882) 429; £29.50(£33.50B)/£40.50(£46.50B)

FULKING   TQ2411 Map 3
Shepherd & Dog

From A281 Brighton–Henfield on N slope of downs turn off at Poynings signpost and continue past Poynings

As it's relatively small, this slate-hung cottage can get packed, especially at weekends. The low-ceilinged bar has an antique cushioned oak settle, stout pegged rustic seats around little gateleg oak tables, attractive bow-window seats, and a big log fireplace in one stripped wall hung with copper and brass; the partly-panelled walls are decorated with shepherds' crooks, harness, stuffed squirrels, mounted butterflies, and blue and white plates. There may be a long queue at the food servery: sandwiches (not Sunday, from £1, locally smoked salmon £2), various ploughman's (from £2.15), and salads (from £2.25), with evening dishes like beef and Guinness pie (£5.95), porterhouse steak (£7.60) or half a Sussex duck (£7.95). King & Barnes Festive, Ruddles Best and County, and Websters Yorkshire on handpump, kept under light top pressure; darts. The garden has a series of prettily planted grassy terraces, some fairy-lit, with an upper tree-sheltered play lawn, and a stream running through washes into a big stone trough. Eyebrows have been raised at the outside lavatories. *(Recommended by W J Wonham, Keith Walton, John and Heather Dwane, J Caulkin, Hugh Morgan)*

Phoenix (Watneys)   Licensees A Bradley-Hole and S A Ball   Meals and snacks (not Sun evening)   Open 11–2.30 (3 Sat), 6–11 all year

GUN HILL   TQ5614 Map 3
Gun

From A22 NW of Hailsham (after junction with A269) turn N at Happy Eater

Red curtains mark the openings between different rambling room areas in this neatly kept family-run pub. There are beams hung with pewter measures and brasses, small pictures on the cream walls, latticed windows with flowery curtains, several winter fires (one in an inglenook fireplace decorated with brass and copper), and some fifteenth-century flooring bricks and tiles, though it's mainly carpeted; one area, furnished more as a dining-room, has attractive panelling. Some of the bar food is still cooked on an ancient Aga in the corner of the bar, and might include soup, steak and kidney pie and several vegetarian dishes; there's also a help-yourself buffet. As food is cooked to order, there may be some delay at peak times. Well kept Charrington IPA and Larkins on handpump, a good choice of wines by the glass, and country wines; friendly service, with a good mix of age-groups among the customers. Outside the pretty tiled and timbered house – covered with clematis, honeysuckle, hanging baskets and heavy flower tubs – there are tables in the spacious garden, which has swings, fairy-lit trees and flower borders. *(Recommended by Neil Barker, Brian Smith, D L Johnson; more reports please)*

Free house   Licensee R J Brockway   Real ale   Meals and snacks (12–2, 6.30–10)   Children in eating area of bar   Open 11–3, 6–10.30 (11 Sat); closed 25 and 26 Dec   Bedrooms tel Chiddingly (0825) 872361; £20(£25B)/£25(£30B)

If we know a pub has a no-smoking area, we say so.

HALNAKER   SU9008 Map 2
Anglesey Arms
A285 Chichester–Petworth

Not far from the Weald and Downland Open-Air Museum, this well run roadside pub has picnic-table sets on the side grass, and white metal and plastic seats and tables by a fig tree in a sheltered back beer garden. The right-hand bar has flagstones, stripped deal settles and wall seats around candle-lit stripped deal tables, and modern paintings on the cream walls; at the back there's a rather more dining-roomish carpeted area. Generously served food includes sandwiches (from £1.10), toasties (from £1.20), ploughman's (£1.95), omelettes (from £1.50), and fry-up (£2.65), with more substantial dishes such as home-made watercress soup (£1.50), salads (from £3.50), lamb chops (£3.75), steaks (from £4.95) and Mediterranean prawns (£5.95), with blackboard specials such as home-made broccoli and cheese quiche (£3.50), fresh dressed Selsey crab (£3.95), and lobster when available; vegetables are extra and service is not included. Sunday roast lunch (when they'll also do sandwiches in summer). Well kept Friary Meux and Ind Coope Burton on handpump, and quite a few wines, especially from northern Spain. Dominoes, cribbage, fruit machine, yatzee, draughts, backgammon, chess and shut-the-box. *(Recommended by Neil and Elspeth Fearn; more reports please)*

Friary Meux (Allied)   Licensees C J and T M Houseman   Real ale   Meals and snacks (12–2, 7.30–10; limited Sun lunchtime; not 24–31 Dec and 1 Jan)   Restaurant tel Chichester (0243) 773474   Children in restaurant   Open 10.30–3, 6–11 all year

HARTFIELD   TQ4735 Map 3
Anchor 🏵
Church Street

Unlike many food pubs, you'd never mistake this one for a restaurant; although dining here would be the main reason for many a visit, drinkers aren't segregated, so there's the cheerful bustle of a proper pub. The heavy beamed and carpeted bar rambles around the servery, with cushioned spindle-back chairs and wall seats, old advertisements and little country pictures on the ochre walls, a brown panelled dado, and houseplants in the small-paned windows. Generously served, the bar food includes soup (£1.50), sandwiches (from £1.30), toasties (from £1.40), ploughman's (from £2.25), pâté (£2.50), salads (from £2.75), six escargots (£3), liver and bacon (£5) and sirloin steak (£6.50), though the emphasis is on seafood – crab sandwiches (£2.25), fresh plaice (£2.85), smoked trout, orange and walnut salad (£3.50), hot garlic prawns or crab and prawn curry (£4.00), skate with black butter and capers (£5.50), grilled Dover sole (£6), and a giant seafood salad (£30 for two); puddings (from £1) and children's meals (£1.75). The evening restaurant is used as a lunchtime overflow if the bar is full. Very well kept Adnams, Flowers Original, Fremlins, King & Barnes Bitter and Festive and a guest beer such as Whitbreads Pompey Royal on handpump. Service is notably friendly and prompt. Darts in a separate lower room; shove-ha'penny, dominoes, and unobtrusive piped music. A front verandah gets packed on warm summer evenings, and there are some seats outside behind. This pub is near the start of the *Good Walks Guide* Walk 62. *(Recommended by Philip and Sheila Hanley, Lindsey Shaw Radley, N D Foot, E G Parish, Jenny and Brian Seller, I D Shaw)*

Free house   Licensee Ken Thompson   Real ale   Meals and snacks (12–2, 7–10)   Restaurant (not Sun evening) tel Hartfield (089 277) 424   Children in eating area of bar   Open 11–3, 6–11; closed evening 25 Dec

---

Please let us know what you think of a pub's bedrooms. No stamp needed: *The Good Pub Guide*, FREEPOST, London SW10 0BR.

nr HEATHFIELD   TQ5920 Map 3

Star

Old Heathfield; from B2096 coming from Heathfield, turn right at signpost to Heathfield
Church, Vines Cross and Horam, then right at T-junction and follow lane round church
to the left

In a lovely position, this ancient pub has a pretty, well kept garden with good solid
furniture among the bright, well planted flower borders, or by the big fig tree with
its carpet of flowering balsam underneath. Children have a play area with an aviary
and drinks kiosk behind a hedge. There are peaceful views over the oak-lined sheep
pastures that roll down from this ridge in the Weald. Inside, the L-shaped bar has
fine heavy black oak beams, some panelling, close-set sturdy rustic furniture on its
dark brown patterned carpet, window seats, and a couple of tables in the huge
inglenook fireplace: get there early if you want a table. Bar food includes home-
made soup (£1.60), ploughman's (lunchtimes, £2.75), omelettes (lunchtimes,
£3.50), home-baked ham and eggs (£3.50), salad platters (from £3.95), home-made
pies such as steak and kidney (£4.25), chilli con carne (£3.95), sirloin steak (£6.95)
and daily specials; delicious home-made puddings such as banoffi pudding, apple
pie or chocolate mousse (from £1.50); there is waitress service to the garden.
They've opened a restaurant upstairs (bookings essential) where you can have the
same menu or more elaborate dishes such as lobster, Dover sole or guinea-fowl.
Well kept Gales HSB, Ruddles and Websters Yorkshire on handpump, and good
value wines; piped music. Parking is often such a struggle that it's best to stop on
the far side of the church and walk through the churchyard. *(Recommended by Mrs L
Curthoys, S J A Velate, V H Balchin; more reports please)*

*Phoenix (Watneys)   Licensees Chris and Linda Cook   Real ale   Meals and snacks (not Mon
evening)   Restaurant tel Heathfield (043 52) 3570   Children in eating area and restaurant
Open 11–3 (3.30 Sat), 6–11*

HOUGHTON   TQ0111 Map 3

George & Dragon

B2139

The new licensee has built a new kitchen in this ancient timbered building, which he
hopes will speed up food service, and the L-shaped bar, with its heavy beams,
attractive old tables, and big fireplace with handsome iron fireback, has been
extended; there's also a new side entrance. Bar food at lunchtime includes
sandwiches (from £1.15, prawn £3), home-made soup (£1.45), ploughman's (from
£2.30), vegetarian lasagne (£3.50), steak canadienne (£3.95), salads (from £4.25),
trout (£6.95), and sirloin steak; in the evenings there's pâté (£2.60), seafood platter
(£5.45), scallops with bacon and port (£5.75), spinach roulade (£5.95) and beef
Wellington (£11.50). Well kept Boddingtons, Huntsman Royal Oak, King and
Barnes, Larkins, and Tetleys on handpump, and English wine. There's a peaceful
country view from tables on the terrace behind the pub and on the lawn which
stretches down under fruit trees. *(Recommended by AE, Nigel Paine, N D Foot, Mr
Adams, Mrs M C Gray; more reports please)*

*Free house   Licensee David Walters   Real ale   Meals and snacks (12–2.15, 7–10)
Restaurant tel Bury (0798) 831559   Open 11–2.30, 6–10.30; closed 25 Dec*

KINGSTON NEAR LEWES   TQ3908 Map 3

Juggs

The Street; Kingston signposted off A27 by roundabout W of Lewes, and off Lewes–Newhaven
road; look out for the pub's sign – may be hidden by hawthorn in summer

Quaint both outside and in, this fifteenth-century tile-hung cottage, covered with roses in summer, has lots of quite closely set rustic teak tables and benches on the front brick terrace, with more tables under cocktail parasols in a neatly hedged inner terrace, and a timber climber and commando net by two or three more tables out on the grass. The beamed bar rambles engagingly around the central servery, with a motley décor full of interest, such as the battle prints and patriotic collage of the Lloyd George era at the back. Furnishings are a similar mix, from an attractive little carved box settle and Jacobean-style dining-chairs to the more neatly orthodox tables and chairs of the small no-smoking dining area under the low-pitched eaves on the right. Popular home-cooked bar food includes open sandwiches (from £1.95, salt beef £2.95), taramosalata (£1.95), a broccoli/sweetcorn/peppers/cheese vegetarian dish (£2), sausages (£2.25), spaghetti (£2.75), pitta bread with grilled ham, tomato, mushrooms and cheese (£2.95), salads (£3.50), sirloin steak (£5.50) and a dish of the day such as fresh crab (£5.75); good home-made puddings (from £1.50), and children's helpings. At Sunday lunchtime the choice is limited to cheese or pâté (maybe with paper plates and plastic knives). Well kept Harveys PA and Armada and King & Barnes Bitter and Festive on handpump; polite service; log fires, darts, shove-ha'penny. (*Recommended by Heather Sharland, Alan Skull, David Crafts, Theo and Jean Rowland-Entwistle, Margaret Dyke*)

Free house   Licensees Andrew and Peta Browne   Real ale   Meals and snacks (12–2, 6–9.30; limited Sun lunchtime)   Children in family area   Open 11–2.30, 6–11 all year; closed evenings 25, 26 Dec and 1 Jan

LICKFOLD   SU9225   Map 2

Lickfold Inn ⊗

Popular and very friendly, this fifteenth-century inn has an elegant and comfortable open-plan bar, divided into cosier areas by the huge central brick chimney: heavy oak beams, handsomely moulded panelling, Georgian settles (most of the seats are antique or well chosen to tone in), herringbone brickwork under rugs, and big log fires. Chalked up on a blackboard, the very good bar food might include sandwiches (from £1.50), winter soup (£1.80), lasagne, oxtail stew or very popular steak and kidney pie (£4), chicken and mushroom pie (£4.20), Barnsley chop (£4.25), steaks (from £5.50), and puddings such as home-made ginger pear dumplings or treacle and walnut tart (£1.50); good Sunday roast lunches. Well kept Badger Best and Tanglefoot, Ballards, Fullers ESB and London Pride, and changing guest beers on handpump; good coffee. The attractively landscaped garden has eleven separate sitting areas on six different levels, as well as an outside bar and a barbecue. The surrounding countryside is very attractive, with the National Trust woods of Black Down a couple of miles north, and more woodland to the south. (*Recommended by Gary Wilkes, Neil Lusby, M Rising, P J Taylor, Gwen and Peter Andrews, Mr and Mrs R Harrington, Mr and Mrs J C Dwane*)

Free house   Licensees Ron and Kath Chambers   Real ale   Meals and snacks   Open 11–2.30 (3 Sat), 6.30–11

LINDFIELD   TQ3425   Map 3

Bent Arms

98 High Street; B2028

The lounge bar of this old inn has an interesting collection of carefully gathered furnishings and objects such as Victorian stained glass, old metal pots and pans, spinning-wheels, ships' telegraphs, a red-lacquered grandfather clock, a stuffed bear, heavy chandeliers, and even a wheel-mounted cannon from the Afghan Wars. The spit-roast room is an eating area, and beef is cooked over the spit every lunchtime (not Wednesday or Sunday) for sandwiches, salads and roasts; other food includes mussels in garlic butter (£2.75), beef and Guinness pie (£3.50), guinea-fowl or fresh seafood platter (£5.50), and grouse (£6.50). Well kept Gales

HSB, King & Barnes, and Whitbreads Pompey Royal on handpump. The public bar has fruit machine, space game and piped music. There are seats in the attractive garden. *(Recommended by Philip King, Brenda Gentry, M C Howells, Aubrey and Margaret Saunders; more reports please)*

Free house   Licensee Rita Hoyle   Real ale   Meals and snacks (12–2.15, 6.15–10.15)   Two restaurants   Children in restaurant and eating area of bar   Open 11–2.30, 6–11 all year   Bedrooms tel Lindfield (044 47) 3146; £25S/£42S

LITLINGTON   TQ5201 Map 3
Plough & Harrow

This attractively placed, busy pub has pretty views across the Cuckmere Valley to nearby Alfriston, and there are rustic seats by a mass of clematis on the lawn beside the big back car park; a children's bar serves soft drinks, and there's an aviary. Inside, it's been refurbished, and the beamed and carpeted little original front bar has quite a few mirrors giving an illusion of space – get there early if you want a seat (especially at weekends). A back eating area is done up as a dining-car and decorated with steam railway models, pictures and memorabilia. Bar food, served both inside and outside, includes sandwiches (from £1.20, toasties from £1.90), home-made turkey broth (£1.90), ploughman's (from £2.55), lasagne (£2.85), quite a few salads (from £3.40, crab £6.20), and steaks (from £7.25), with a weekend special; there may be long delays at busy times. Well kept Adnams Best, Badger Best and Tanglefoot, Harveys BB, King & Barnes Festive, Wadworths 6X and two weekly guest real ales (summer only) on handpump; darts, shove-ha'penny, dominoes, cribbage and evening piped music. *(Recommended by A J N Lee, Joyce Robert-Smith, Anthony Willey, WHBM, Peter Corris; more reports please)*

Free house   Licensee Roger Taylor   Real ale   Meals and snacks (12–2.30, 7–10)   Restaurant tel Alfriston (0323) 870632   Children in restaurant   Live music Fri evening   Open 11–3, 6.30–11; 11–2.30, 7–11 in winter

LODSWORTH   SU9223 Map 2
Halfway Bridge ★ ✿
A272 Midhurst–Petworth

It was the Hawkins family that built up the original popularity of the Three Horseshoes over at Elsted; coming into their new venture here, we were immediately struck by the same personal warmth that made the Elsted pub such a hit with readers. This is perhaps more comfortable, and seems rather brighter and roomier. Several cottagey rooms ramble around the central bar: there are flowery-cushioned wall pews, nice oak chairs and a mixture of individual tables on the fitted flowery carpet, and little etchings of old buildings on the walls – which show some timbering. There are several log fires, one in a gleaming kitchen range, another in a remarkably broad old fireplace. Steps lead down to a pretty country dining-room with heavy tables, a longcase clock, a dresser and rose wallpaper between the dark oak ceiling trusses. A wide choice of home-cooked bar food includes sandwiches such as home-cooked ham (£2), ploughman's, crab pâté (£2.25), lots of interesting filled baked potatoes (from £2.50), tagliatelle bolognese (£3.50), steak and kidney pie (£4.25), poussin with cranberry sauce (£5.95), Mediterranean prawns in garlic butter (£6), salmon with mint and cucumber mayonnaise (£6.50) and duck with blackcurrants (£7.25); they offer you three different ways of doing the potatoes, and vegetables are good. Well kept Ballards Best, Flowers Original, Fremlins, Gales HSB, King & Barnes Festive, Wadworths 6X and a beer brewed for the pub on handpump, decent wines, unobtrusive piped classical music, thoughtful friendly service. There are sturdy tables and picnic-table sets on the grass and terrace in front. *(Recommended by A J Kentish, Mrs J A Blanks)*

*Free house   Licensees Sheila and Edric Hawkins   Real ale   Meals and snacks (12–2, 7–10)
Restaurant tel Lodsworth (079 85) 281   Children in restaurant and eating area of bar
Open 11–2.30, 6–11 all year*

LURGASHALL   SU9327 Map 2

Noahs Ark

Village signposted from A283 N of Petworth; OS Sheet 186 reference 936272

On the edge of the quiet village green, this interesting and secluded old pub has two
small bars – one with oak parquet, the other carpeted – with simple but attractive
furnishings, warm winter fires (the lounge on the left has a big inglenook, as well as
comfortable chairs and sporting prints), and fresh flowers in summer. Good bar
food includes sandwiches (from £1.30, toasties from £1.60, smoked salmon £1.95),
lasagne (£2.65), gammon and egg (£2.75), salads (from £2.75), winter steak and
kidney pie, lamb cutlets (£3.75), and calf's liver (£4.50). Friary Meux and King &
Barnes Bitter; friendly service. Sensibly placed darts and bar billiards, also shove-
ha'penny, dominoes, and cribbage. In summer the hanging baskets are lovely and
there are rustic seats and tables on the front grass. *(Recommended by Mr and Mrs
J C Dwane, John Knighton)*

*Friary Meux (Ind Coope)   Licensees Mr and Mrs Swannell   Real ale   Meals and snacks (not
Sun)   Children in own room and dining-room   Open 10.30–2.30, 6–11*

MAYFIELD   TQ5827 Map 3

Rose and Crown ★ ⊗ 🛏

Fletching Street; off A267 at NE end of village

A new terrace area has been created all around the front of this civilised and pretty
weatherboarded house, there are rustic wooden tables on the lawn beside the
building, and lots of hanging baskets and tubs filled with brightly coloured flowers.
Inside, the two cosy little rooms of the front bar have perhaps the most character:
low beams, ceiling boards with coins embedded in the glossy ochre paint, benches
built in to the partly panelled walls, an attractive bow window seat and a big
inglenook fireplace; the atmosphere is relaxed and friendly. Good home-made bar
food, served in generous helpings and varying from day to day, might include
starters like chicken liver and brandy pâté (£1.95), crab mousse (£2.15), fresh tuna
pâté (£2.25), and haddock and prawn mayonnaise or prawn and avocado aioli
(£2.50), with main dishes such as seafood pancake (£3.25), fresh fish from
Normans Bay (from £3.25), smoked ham with Cumberland sauce (£3.50), and
spiced and fried fillet of beef (£4.50). Well kept Adnams Best, Harveys Best and two
quickly changing guest beers on handpump from the small central servery; six
wines by the glass and Devonshire scrumpy; bar billiards, shove-ha'penny and
cribbage. *(Recommended by R Houghton, Alan Skull, Jeremy and Margaret Wallington, Peter
and Moyna Lynch, Mr and Mrs R J Welch, Mr and Mrs W Harrington, V H Balchin, Donald
Clay, Patrick Stapley, RAB)*

*Free house   Licensee Richard Leet   Real ale   Meals and snacks   Restaurant   Children in
restaurant   Open 11–3, 6–11; closed 25 Dec   Bedrooms tel Mayfield (0435) 872200;
£28B/£40B*

MIDHURST   SU8821 Map 2

Spread Eagle 🛏

South Street

Though part of this old place dates back to 1430, it was mainly built about 1650,
and the spacious lounge has a huge fireplace with a 1608 fireback (there's said to be
a secret room up one chimney, about six feet up). This room certainly has bags of

character – massive beams, big leaded windows, timbered ochre walls, oriental rugs on broad boards, old leather wing armchairs, Chesterfields, wicker settees, and original Victorian caricatures. Badger Best and Ballards on handpump (not cheap), decent wines by the glass, courteous service, shove-ha'penny and cribbage. A neat and cheerful barrel-vaulted cellar bar with crisp white paintwork, tiled floor and big oak cask seats or brocaded settles serves good value filled French bread or baked potatoes (£1.65), ploughman's (from £2) and salads (£3.25); darts in one bay, well reproduced piped music. Hilaire Belloc, who lived just around the corner from our editorial office, called this place 'the oldest and most revered of all the prime inns of this world'. *(Recommended by Keith Houlgate, Guy Harris; more reports please)*

Free house   Licensee George Mudford   Real ale   Bar meals and snacks (lunchtime) Restaurant   Children welcome in cellar food bar (lunchtime)   Open 11–2.30, 6–11 all year; closed evening 25 Dec   Bedrooms tel Midhurst (073 081) 6911; £58B/£60B

NEWHAVEN   TQ4502 Map 3
Hope
West Quay; follow West Beach signs from A259 westbound

From outside this looks like just another fairly modern coastal pub (though in fact it dates from the eighteenth century). Once through the door, you quickly find how much more pleasant it is. The lounge on the left has quite straightforward and unpretentious but comfortable modern furnishings – royal blue leatherette chairs around wood-effect tables, a parquet floor with memories of stiletto heels, and some nautical effects such as sailors' ribands, ropework and marine brassware decorating the false ceiling by the bar counter. The atmosphere, particularly warm and friendly, quickly makes people of all ages feel at home. And the home-cooked food, served generously, is good value. It includes several starters from soup (£1.20) to hot garlic prawns (£2.90), big well filled sandwiches (from £1.50, crab £2.20), ploughman's (from £1.90), omelettes (from £2.80), a wide choice of local fish (£3.15–£4.95), gammon (£4.30), large steaks (from £11) and daily specials such as bacon nuggets (£2.80) and steak and kidney pie (£3.50), with children's dishes (from £1.80); they'll do you a lunch box to take out. Well kept Flowers Original and Whitbreads Pompey Royal on handpump, decent house wine, friendly service; fruit machine, piped folk music; darts and pool in the separate equally airy public bar. The bars have big windows looking out on the neck of the busy harbour; sturdy teak tables in an upstairs conservatory look straight down on the coasters, yachts, fishing boats and maybe ferries as they pass, and there are slatted steamer benches and picnic-table sets under cocktail parasols out closer to the water, over the quiet lane down to the beaches. *(Recommended by Chris Fluck, G B Pugh, Mr and Mrs N E Friend)*

Whitbreads   Licensee Chris Haffenden   Real ale   Meals and snacks   Upstairs restaurant tel Newhaven (0273) 515389   Open 10–4.30, 6–11 all year; may close longer afternoons in winter; 10–11 Sat

NUTHURST   TQ1926 Map 3
Black Horse
Village signposted from A281 SE of Horsham

The friendly new licensee has hung the walls of the black-beamed bar with his fishing pictures and gundog sporting trial certificates, and there are a couple of armed Windsor chairs and a built-in settle on the big Horsham flagstones in front of the inglenook fireplace; one end of the room opens out into other carpeted areas with more seats and tables. Bar food includes home-made soup (£1.20), ploughman's (from £1.95), ham and egg (£2.25), beef or lamb curry (£3.95), vegetarian dishes (from £3.25), beef in ale pie (£3.95), grilled gammon (£3.95), and a popular twenty-ounce mixed grill (£6.25); children's meals (£1.50), and weekend evening barbecues (weather permitting). Well kept Badger, Harveys, King & Barnes Festive and Sussex, and a guest beer. A new upstairs restaurant should be open by the time this book is published. You can sit outside in front or in the attractive back garden by a little stream. There are good woodland walks nearby. *(Recommended by G T Rhys, Terry and Nicole Buckland, Norman Foot, Klaus and Elizabeth Leist, Peter Hall)*

Free house   Licensees Peter and Julie O'Hare   Real ale   Meals and snacks   Restaurant tel Lower Beeding (0403) 891272   Children in eating area   Live music Tues evenings   Open 11–2.30, 6–11 all year

OVING   SU9005 Map 2

Gribble

Between A27 and A259 just E of Chichester, then signposted just off village road; OS Sheet 197 reference 900050

Ten years ago there was no pub in Oving and hadn't been since the Second World War, but local farmer Peter Hague decided there should be and got all but six to sign his petition – which the council agreed not to oppose; when Rose Gribble died Mr Hague bought her cottage and spent eighteen months converting it. The lively bar has old heavy beams, timbered bare bricks, wheel-back chairs and cushioned pews around the old wooden country tables on its carpet, and a big log fire. On the left, a family-room with more pews and rugs on its oak parquet floor, has bar billiards and darts, and there's a no-smoking and an alcohol-free area; also shove-ha'penny, dominoes, cribbage, fruit machine. Besides Gribble Ale and Reg's Tipple, there's well kept Badger Best and Tanglefoot, Gales HSB and Palmers IPA and on handpump. Well presented bar food includes sandwiches (from £1, fresh Selsey crab £2.50, toasties from £1.20), soup (£1.25), home-made burgers including a vegetarian one (£1.75), ploughman's with five different cheeses (from £2.30), home-made cottage pie (£2.75), home-baked ham and eggs (£3.50), salads (from £3.25, Selsey crab £4.50), scampi (£3.50), sirloin steak (£6.95), and puddings like home-made apple and blackberry pie (from £1.50); specials such as cauliflower cheese (£3.50), good seafood lasagne or fresh trout (£4.50), and Sunday roast beef and fresh turkey (£4.50); a few smaller (and cheaper) portions for those with not much appetite. The lavatories have blackboards for graffiti. A small open-sided barn opens on to a garden with rustic seats under the apple trees. *(Recommended by M Rising, TOH, Henry Midwinter, Matt Pringle, Peter Griffiths)*

Own brew (pub leased to Badger)   Licensees Connie and James Wells   Real ale   Meals and snacks (not Sun evening)   Children in family-room   Open 11–2.30, 6–11 all year

nr PUNNETTS TOWN   TQ6220 Map 3

Three Cups

B2096 towards Battle

Comfortable plush cushioned seats in the bow window here look out over a spreading front green where bantams stroll between the picnic-table sets. The low-beamed bar has dark old plush chairs on its oak parquet floor (there are tiles by the door), fishing rods and mugs hanging from the low and heavy beams, lots of pewter tankards over the serving-counter, dark brown panelling, a large stone inglenook fireplace with a winter log fire, and a good local atmosphere. Reasonably priced bar food includes sandwiches, filled baked potatoes (£1.75), local prize-winning giant sausages, cottage pie or lasagne (£2.50), and trout or steak (£5.50). Well kept Courage Best and Directors and John Smiths on handpump, and a good range of fortified wines in cut-glass decanters; piped music. The family-room has darts, bar billiards, shove-ha'penny, dominoes, cribbage, fruit machine, space game and juke box. There is a small covered back terrace, seats in the garden beyond, and a safe play area for children (as well as ducks, chickens and geese). Clay pigeon shoots every alternate Sunday (by prior appointment), and three pétanque pitches; they have space for five touring caravans. *(Recommended by J A H Townsend, Mr and Mrs W Harrington; more reports please)*

Courage   Licensee Leonard Smith   Real ale   Meals and snacks   Children in eating area and family-room   Open 11–3.30, 6.30–11 all year

nr RINGMER   TQ4412 Map 3
Cock

Off A26, N of Ringmer turn-off

The A26 has now been diverted, leaving this white weatherboarded house in a very pleasant cul-de-sac, with virtually unlimited parking. Inside, there are heavy beams, small Windsor chairs, soft lighting, winter log fires in its inglenook fireplace, and a welcoming atmosphere; also, two lounges (one is no-smoking), and a black labrador. Waitress-served bar food includes open sandwiches (from £1.95), and quite a few main dishes such as home-cooked ham and egg (£3.50), fresh fish (from £3.75), moules marinière (in season, £4.25), and tandoori chicken kebab (£5.95); as the food is freshly prepared, there may be delays at peak times. Well kept Ruddles Best and County, and Websters Yorkshire on handpump, and a good selection of wines, including monthly specials; eclectic and enjoyable piped music. The sizeable fairy-lit lawn is attractively planted with fruit trees, shrubs, honeysuckle and clumps of old-fashioned flowers, and there are seats on a good terrace. *(Recommended by Charles and Mary Winpenny, Emilia Marty; more reports please)*

Phoenix (Watneys)   Licensee Brian Cole   Real ale   Meals and snacks (12–2, 7–10) Restaurant tel Ringmer (0273) 812040   Well behaved children in restaurant, lounge and no-smoking lounge   Open 11–11 all year, though may close afternoons if not busy; closed 25 Dec

RIPE   TQ5010 Map 3
Lamb

Signposted off A22 Uckfield–Hailsham at Golden Cross; and via Chalvington from A27 Lewes–Polegate

Redecorated in old-fashioned style with considerable verve – and masses of pitch-pine – this cheerful pub has lots to look at, in the various snug rooms radiating around its island serving-bar. Here there are old song-sheet covers ('Polly Perkins of Paddington Green', 'Did I Remember' – the Jean Harlow song – even 'Red Sails in the Sunset'); over there a string of eighteenth-century cartoons; on the left a big engraving of a farmyard scene by Herring; in a window alcove the tear-jerking Tommy Atkins' Friend. There are stripped old joists, pastel pink velvet curtains, plush-cushioned pews, eighteenth-century oak settles, stripped kitchen tables, red hessian wallcoverings above the stripped pine dado – a lively, enjoyable mix. Home-made bar food includes a particularly wide choice of good sandwiches and toasties (from £1), filled baked potatoes (£2), ploughman's (from £2.50), omelettes (from £2.80), cottage pie (£3), salads (from £3.20), steak and kidney pie (£3.20), savoury quiche (£3.50), plaice or gammon and egg (£4.20), eight-ounce sirloin steak (£6.40) and a good choice of children's dishes (£2.50). Well kept Courage Best and Directors and John Smiths on handpump, with a guest such as Harveys or Marstons Pedigree; two or three open fires; darts, cribbage, dominoes, fruit machine, space game, maybe piped music; interesting antique postcards in the gents. The little brick-floored dining-room is very pretty. The sheltered back garden has rustic tables and picnic-table sets under cocktail parasols, with a climber and swings. *(Recommended by Alan Skull)*

Free house   Licensees P A Wilkins and J R Bentley   Real ale   Meals and snacks (11–2, 6.30–9.30)   Restaurant tel Ripe (032 183) 280   Well behaved children welcome   Open 11–2.30, 6–11 all year; closed evening 25 Dec

ROWHOOK   TQ1234 Map 3
Chequers
Village signposted from A29 NW of Horsham

Sunny benches outside this sheltered pub overlook the quiet country lane, and there are picnic-table sets in the big, peaceful side garden among roses and flowering shrubs, and under cocktail parasols on a crazy-paved terrace. Inside, the snug front bar has upholstered benches and stools around the tables on its flagstone floor, an inglenook fireplace, and black beams in its white ceiling; up a step or two, there's a carpeted lounge with a very low ceiling. Home-cooked lunchtime food includes home-made soups and pâtés (from £1.35), chicken and onion tagliatelle or mushroom and bacon au gratin (£3.55) and home-cooked ham (£3.75); in the evening there's chicken satay (£4.25), king prawns with garlic butter (£4.75), chicken breast baked with avocado and garlic (£6.50) and steaks (from £7.50); home-made puddings (from £1.50); best to book at weekends. They do traditional roasts on Sunday lunchtimes and barbecues on Sunday evenings. Well kept Flowers Original, Fremlins and Whitbreads Strong Country on handpump, served from the elaborately carved bar counter; darts, shove-ha'penny, dominoes, cribbage and piped music; friendly service. *(Recommended by Mr and Mrs C H Kinnersly, Nick Dowson, Alison Hayward; more reports please)*

Whitbreads   Licensee Gyles Culver   Real ale   Meals and snacks   Children in supper bar until 9   Open 11–2.30 (3 Sat), 6–11 all year

RUSHLAKE GREEN   TQ6218 Map 3
Horse & Groom
Village signposted from B2096

New licensees had just taken over this old country pub as we went to press. They've opened up the two rooms on the left of the central serving-counter, putting in a mix of armchairs, stools, benches and wooden tables, and there's an adjoining Saddle Room. On the right the beamed and timbered Gun Room with its log fire in the big hearth is now more set out for diners. Home-made bar food includes hot roast beef in French bread (£1.75), ploughman's (from £2.50), spaghetti bolognese (£3.50), salads such as prawn (£5) or smoked salmon (£5.50), Mediterranean prawns in wine (£5.95), and steaks (from £5.95). Well kept Harveys BB and King & Barnes Festive on handpump; shove-ha'penny, dominoes and cribbage. There are tables on the lawn in front, doves from a dovecote, and visiting ducks from the village green. *(Recommended by Terry Buckland; more reports please)*

Free house   Licensees Jakki and Alan Perodeau   Real ale   Meals and snacks (12–2, 7–10) Restaurant tel Burwash (0435) 830320   Children in eating area of bar   Open 10.30–3, 6.30–11 weekdays; 11–11 Sat; closed evening 25 Dec

RYE   TQ9220 Map 3
Mermaid
On its steep cobbled lane, this black and white timbered Tudor inn looks extremely striking, and you can imagine the murderous Hawkhurst gang hauling kegs of smuggled rum up here, where they would drink with their loaded pistols beside their tankards. The back bar has interesting antique seats (one of them carved in the form of a goat) around its timbered walls, a huge fireplace with a halberd and pike mounted over it, some eighteenth-century carving, and a longcase clock; it's hardly changed over the last 65 years – as a picture there shows. Other rooms have panelling, heavy timbering and wall frescoes. Bar food includes sandwiches, home-made soup, ploughman's and a salad buffet; Bass and Fremlins on handpump.

Pubs with outstanding views are listed at the back of the book.

There are seats on a small back terrace. *(Recommended by Hazel Morgan, Sheila Keene, Jill and Paul Ormrod, Alison Hayward, Nick Dowson, Peter Corris, Richard Gibbs)*

Free house   Real ale   Snacks (lunchtime, not winter) and meals (lunchtime)
Restaurant   Open 11–3, 6–11 all year, but may be closed, particularly at lunchtime, in midweek out of season   Bedrooms tel Rye (0797) 223065; £40B/£66B

nr SCAYNES HILL   TQ3623 Map 3

Sloop

Freshfield Lock; at top of Scaynes Hill turn N off A272 into Church Lane, follow Freshfield signpost

This popular and friendly tile-hung pub has a neat and sheltered garden by the derelict Ouse Canal with tables, chairs, and a children's climbing-frame; there are benches in the old-fashioned brick porch. Inside, the long carpeted saloon bar has comfortable sofas, armchairs, and cushioned banquettes, and there may be pictures for sale. Generous helpings of good bar food includes filled warm cottage loaves (from £1.50, prawns in home-made mayonnaise £2.95), good smoked salmon soup in winter (£1.95), ploughman's (from £1.95), good home-made chicken liver pâté with sherry (£2.95), filled baked potatoes (from £2.25), and main dishes that change slightly each day and are chalked up on five blackboards such as fried cod (£3.75), smoked salmon and prawn quiche with lemon salad or beef and venison pie with puff pastry (£3.95), steaks (from £8.45) and a huge mixed grill (£10.95). Well kept Harveys BB and King & Barnes Festive on handpump, and 26 country wines; piped music. The simpler, airier public bar has a small games-room – sensibly placed darts, pool, dominoes, cribbage, fruit machine and space game. The pub is handy for the Bluebell steam railway, and not far from the great lakeside gardens of Sheffield Park. *(Recommended by Bernard Phillips, Theo Schofield, Jason Caulkin, W A Gardiner, T Nott, Chris Fluck)*

Beards (who no longer brew)   Licensee David Mills   Real ale   Meals and snacks
Restaurant (to stay open all afternoon weekends) tel Scaynes Hill (044 486) 219
Children in eating area of bar   Open 11–3, 6–11 all year

nr SEAFORD   TV4899 Map 3

Golden Galleon

Exceat Bridge; A259 Seaford–Eastbourne, near Cuckmere

Even in peak summer there's little feeling of crowdedness – but plenty of liveliness – in this spacious pub, with its neat rows of dining-tables under the high trussed and pitched rafters of its Turkey-carpeted main area. It's well organised to cope with masses of customers, with plenty of seats on the terraces and grass of the sloping garden outside. This looks out past the road to Beachy Head on the right, with the Seven Sisters Country Park just over the Cuckmere River, a ten-minute easy walk down to the beach, and walks inland to Friston Forest and the downs. The mass of flowers on the steep front slope, away from the tables, is very pretty. The cheerful summer bustle is slightly reminiscent of an Italian trattoria, with people collecting their own cutlery and waitresses searching for whoever wanted that tonno e fagioli. And in fact the young landlord, occasionally emerging from his kitchen to keep an eye on things, is Italian (his wife's English). Home-cooked bar food includes the starter mentioned, and a good few others such as an Italian seafood salad, sweet-cured herrings or pâté (all around £2–£2.50), ploughman's (£2.25), fresh local fish (from £4.40), a couple of daily specials such as lasagne (£4.25) or seafood pasta (£4.50), gammon (£6.50), pork tenderloin (£7) and steaks (from eight-ounce fillet, £8.75), with a good help-yourself salad counter (from £3.50), and half-portions of most things for children. Well kept Courage Best and Directors on handpump, decent wines; friendly service. At one side there's a nice little alcove, snugged in by an open fire. *(Recommended by Jenny and Brian Seller, Rosemary Dudley Lynch, Debbie Jellett)*

Courage Licensees Stefano and Lindsey Shaw Diella Real ale Meals and snacks (12–2, 6–9) Open 11–2.30, 6–11; closed 25 Dec, evening 26 Dec

SIDLESHAM SZ8598 Map 2
Crab & Lobster

Off B2145 S of Chichester, either Rookery Lane N of village (on left as you approach) or Mill Lane from village centre

Standing in a small group of houses right by silted Pagham harbour, this pub is comfortably well away from the main tourist places. The bar has been redecorated this year and has deep rose-pink or blue upholstered wall benches, wildfowl and marine prints on the freshly painted ochre walls, and a good log fire; there's also a plusher side lounge. The simple food's good value: crab or prawn sandwiches (£1.90), filled baked potatoes (from £1.90), toasties such as egg and bacon (£2.10), steak and kidney pie (£3.30), Selsey crab (£3.80), and home-made puddings (from £1.50). Well kept Friary Meux, Ind Coope Burton, and King & Barnes Bitter on handpump, and a decent choice of other drinks. The little back garden – with picnic-table sets – is filled prettily with sweet peas, gladioli, foxgloves, snapdragons, roses and so forth, and looks out across a meadow to the coastal flats. *(Recommended by Hope Chenhalls, Peter Griffiths, Mr Adams; more reports please)*

Friary Meux (Allied) Licensee Brian Cross Real ale Meals and snacks (not Tues evening) Open 11–2.30, 6–11 all year; closed evenings 25–26 Dec

nr TICEHURST TQ6830 Map 3
Bull 🏵

Three Legged Cross; coming into Ticehurst from N on B2099, just before Ticehurst village sign, turn left beside corner house called Tollgate (Maynards Pick Your Own may be signposted here)

Covered with climbing roses and clematis, this delightfully tucked-away fourteenth-century pub has several low-beamed rooms with heavy oak joined tables, kitchen seats, flowery cushions on benches and settles, flagstone, brick or oak parquet floors, and a big central fireplace (which the soft grey tabby heads for). Good lunchtime bar food includes home-made Stilton soup (£1.10), sandwiches (from £1, hot gammon £1.25, tasty steak £2.50), good ploughman's (£2.50), bubble and squeak, popular steak and kidney pie, gammon steak with mustard and demarara glaze or excellent venison stew, (£3.75), ten-ounce rib-eye steak (£4.50), a splendid summer buffet (£4.80), and home-made puddings like apple strudel, summer pudding or hokey-pokey ice-cream with honeycombe in it (£1.50). In the evenings (when they prefer bookings) they do more elaborate meals. Well kept Harveys BB and Shepherd Neame Master Brew, with regularly changing guests such as Badger Tanglefoot, Brakspears, Marstons Pedigree, and Charles Wells Bombardier on handpump; pleasant staff; darts, shove-ha'penny, dominoes and cribbage. The sheltered garden has old-fashioned seats, fruit trees, and a pool by a young weeping willow – all very pretty, and quiet but for birdsong. *(Recommended by Heather Sharland, Jason Caulkin, David and Ruth Shillitoe, Mrs E M Thompson, Mrs Jane Reid)*

Free house Licensee Mrs Evelyn Moir Real ale Meals and snacks (12–2.15, 7–10) Restaurant tel Ticehurst (0580) 200586 Well behaved children in eating area Open 11–3, 6–11 all year

TILLINGTON SU9621 Map 2
Horseguards

Village signposted from A272 Midhurst–Petworth

As this well kept and friendly pub is perched high over the lane opposite the 800-

year-old church, the big black-panelled bow window seat in the beamed front bar here gives a lovely view beyond the village to the Rother Valley. The comfortably refurbished bar has been recently redecorated and serves well kept King & Barnes Bitter, Festive and Mild, with Old in winter on handpump. Good value bar food includes sandwiches, tasty home-made fish soup (£1.15), ploughman's (from £1.45), beef curry or chilli con carne (£2.35), home-made steak and kidney pie (£2.80), beef bourguignonne, several vegetarian dishes, and steak (£4.95); Sunday roasts; prompt, cheerful service. Darts, bar billiards, shove-ha'penny, table skittles, dominoes, cribbage, a fruit machine, space game, and piped music. There's a terrace outside, and more tables and chairs in a garden behind. *(Recommended by R and S Bentley, S J A Velate, Norman Foot, Frank Cummins, Keith Walton, Chris Fluck)*

King & Barnes   Licensee Mike Wheller   Real ale   Meals and snacks   Children in family-room   Open 11–3, 6–11

WEST ASHLING   SU8107 Map 2
Richmond Arms
Mill Lane; from B2146 in village follow Hambrook signpost

Fourteen handpumps in this simple, out-of-the-way and very friendly village pub will have served 523 different real ales in just eight years: Boddingtons Bitter, Burts VPA, Greene King Abbot, Harveys XX, King & Barnes Festive and Bitter, Ringwood Old Thumper, and a regular selection of northern guest beers – notably Yates from Cumbria. They also have most bottle-conditioned English beers, and one of the best ranges of good foreign bottled beers in the South that includes beers from all five Trappist breweries (in summer there are fruity ones such as cherry, raspberry, blackcurrant, peach and mint) from Belgium, and some of the rarer German ales like Munich Weisse beer which has three grains of rice to maintain a creamy head and is served with a wedge of lemon; also, Thatchers cider. The real food fits in well: besides sandwiches (from £1.50, croque-monsieur £2.05), excellent ploughman's (£2.25), and five-ounce steak sandwich (£3.50), there are filled baked potatoes (from £1.95), home-made chilli con carne, curry, lasagne, tuna and mushroom or cottage pie (all £2.95), local trout (£3.95), and salads (from £2.25, with crab and lobster in summer). There are long wall benches, library chairs and black tables round the central servery, a fire in winter and numbered decoy ducks hanging on the wall (which are sometimes raced down the local stream); bar billiards, shove-ha'penny, dominoes, cribbage, and trivia and fruit machines. The old skittle alley has been renovated and doubles as a functions and family-room. There's a pergola, and some picnic-table sets by the car park. *(Recommended by Brian and Anna Marsden, Alan Skull, Nigel Paine, David and Sarah Gilmore, Ian Phillips, Richard Houghton, R Sims)*

Free house   Licensees Roger and Julie Jackson   Real ale   Lunchtime meals and snacks (evening food, if pre-booked, in skittle alley)   Children in eating area of bar and in skittle alley   Occasional folk music Sun or Thurs evenings in winter   Open 11–3, 5.30–11 all year

WEST HOATHLY   TQ3632 Map 3
Cat
Village signposted from either A22 or B2028 S of East Grinstead

This charmingly placed village pub is warm and comfortable, and the open-plan rooms of the partly panelled and partly beamed bar are separated by the massive central chimney (note the interesting ancient carving) with its big brick hearth and log-effect gas fire. Bar food includes tasty grilled sardines. Well kept Harveys BB, XX Mild and Old and King & Barnes on handpump. You can sit among roses on the small sun-trap terrace outside this old smugglers' pub and look across to the church nestling among its big yew trees (if you walk through the churchyard to the far side there's an even better view). The pub is near the start of *Good Walks Guide*

Walk 64. *(Recommended by TBB, Ian Phillips, James Cane, M C Howells; we'd be grateful for up-to-date food information, please)*
Beards (who no longer brew)   Real ale   Meals (not Sun) and snacks (not Sun evening)
Children in dining-room and entrance lobby only   Open 11–2.30, 6–10.30

WINCHELSEA   TQ9017 Map 3
New Inn 🍺
Just off A259

A pleasant buzz of conversation fills the three rather spacious rooms of the pleasantly old-fashioned rambling lounge bar here (one of them is no-smoking). There are wall banquettes, settles, sturdy wooden tables, masses of hop-bines hanging from the beams, and good log fires; the walls are painted a deep terracotta, and decorations include old local photographs, old farm tools, and china, pewter and copper on Delft shelves. Good, hearty bar food includes sandwiches (not Sundays or Bank Holidays), home-made soup (£1.55), garlic mushrooms (£2.25), ploughman's (from £2.25), home-cooked ham and egg (£3.25), a vegetarian dish (£3.95), salads (from £3.95), steak and kidney pie with good thick fluffy pastry or home-made curry (£4.50), a fresh fish dish, pork kebabs (£5.75), and steaks (from £7.50); children's meals until 7.30pm (from £1.25); efficient waitress service. Well kept Courage Best and Directors on handpump, decent wines by the glass. The wholly separate public bar has darts, well lit pool, cribbage, fruit machine and unobtrusive piped music. There are picnic-table sets and swings in a neat and good-sized orchard garden, and some of the pretty bedrooms look out on a charming medieval scene, with lime tree and swathes of bluebells around the church opposite. *(Recommended by K J Betts, F. G Parish, Theo and Jean Rowland-Entwistle, Cdr G R Roantree)*

Courage   Licensee Richard Joyce   Real ale   Meals and snacks (12–2, 6.30–9.30)   Children in no-smoking family area   Open 11–2.30, 6.30–11 all year; closed 25 Dec and evening 26 Dec   Bedrooms tel Rye (0797) 226252; /£27(£32S)

WINEHAM   TQ2320 Map 3
Royal Oak   [*illustrated on page 696*]
Village signposted from A272 and B2116

The enormous inglenook fireplace in this handsome black and white timbered pub carries the smoke-stains of centuries, and the brick floor in front of it is well worn. Above the serving-counter the very low beams are decorated with ancient corkscrews, horseshoes, racing plates, tools and a coach horn, and the furniture throughout is fittingly simple and old-fashioned. Well kept Whitbread Pompey Royal is tapped from casks in a still-room, on the way back through to the small snug; darts, shove-ha'penny, dominoes, cribbage; toasted sandwiches (80p). There are rustic wooden tables on the grass by a well in front, and on a clear day you can just see Chanctonbury Ring from the window in the gents, far beyond the nearby meadows and oak trees. *(Recommended by IAA; more reports please)*

Whitbreads   Real ale   Snacks (not Sat evening or Sun)   Open 10.30–2.30, 6–10.30; closed 25 Dec and evening 26 Dec

WITHYHAM   TQ4935 Map 3
Dorset Arms
B2110

Behind the tall white Georgian façade, there's an unusual raised L-shaped bar with beams, broad oak floorboards, simple furnishings, a stone Tudor fireplace with a winter log fire, and a relaxed atmosphere. Good bar food includes sandwiches (from 85p), huge filled rolls (£1.20), ploughman's (£1.80), whole avocado pear with curried prawns (£3.50), popular fresh plaice or trout or smoked trout salad (£3.75), and Scotch smoked salmon (£6), with daily specials such as steak and kidney pie, jumbo sausage and egg, braised steak or venison (from £2.50); on Sunday lunchtimes they do only rolls and ploughman's. Well kept Harveys BB and XX and winter XXXX on handpump; darts, dominoes, cribbage, fruit machine and piped music. Outside, there are white tables on a brick terrace raised well above the small green; the tree-lined lane past here leads to the village cricket ground. The grave of Vita Sackville-West (whose family owned Buckhurst Park here) is in the nearby church. *(Recommended by Richard Gibbs, Alan Skull, Leo and Pam Cohen)*

Harveys   Licensee David Clark   Real ale   Snacks and lunchtime meals   Restaurant tel Hartfield (089 277) 278   Children in restaurant and eating area of bar lunchtimes only   Open 11–11 weekdays; 11–3, 6–11 Sat

Lucky Dip

Besides the fully inspected pubs, you might like to try these Lucky Dips recommended to us and described by readers (if you do, please send us reports):

Adversane, W Sus [TQ0723], *Blacksmiths Arms*: Historic old pub, still cosy after recent enlargement, with pleasant atmosphere, good value though not cheap varied choice of food, friendly service; restaurant *(G Holliday)*
Albourne, W Sus [London Rd (A23); TQ2616], *Kings Head*: Unusual pub, interesting décor in Munster bar, 1940s-style juke box, Watneys-related real ales and King & Barnes Festive, good choice of one-price bar food *(John Hayward)*
Alfold Bars, W Sus[B2133 N of Loxwood – OS Sheet 186 reference 037335; TQ0333], *Sir Roger Tichbourne*: Ancient pub with open fireplace in large public bar, small snug saloon; cheerful staff serving good range of bar meals, well kept King & Barnes *(Reg Tickner)*
☆ **Alfriston**, E Sus [TQ5103], *Deans Place*: A hotel, but its pleasant lounge and bar serve reasonably priced drinks and good bar food such as steak and kidney pie or cold roast meats with help-yourself salads, lots of room in beautiful garden with croquet lawn; children welcome; bedrooms *(Heather Sharland)*
Alfriston [High St], *George*: Lots of beams and brass, pleasant staff; well kept Watneys-related and King & Barnes real ales, good bar and restaurant menus with fish caught locally; bedrooms *(Heather Sharland)*
☆ **Amberley**, W Sus [off B2139; TQ0212], *Black Horse*: Unspoilt, attractive and friendly family-run village pub, up a flight of steps, its beams festooned with sheep and cow bells and other downland farm equipment; flagstones, well kept Friary Meux Best and Ind Coope Burton, home-cooked bar food inc local shellfish, garden; children in eating area and restaurant, occasional folk music *(LYM)*
Amberley, [Houghton Bridge], *Bridge*: Neat and well kept pub which has had well kept Adnams, Flowers Original, Wethereds SPA and Youngers IPA and decent

straightforward bar food from good ploughman's to steaks, with free Sun nibbles, friendly and obliging staff and well tended garden with slide and climbing-frame, well enclosed for small children; restaurant up for sale early 1989; bedrooms *(Brian and Anna Marsden, Jenny and Brian Seller – more news please)*
Ansty, W Sus [2 miles from Ansty on A272 at junction with B2036; TQ2923], *Ansty Cross*: Popular local, modern bar, log fire, horsebrasses, darts and fruit machine, good straightforward hot dishes and more original salads, large garden *(C R and M A Starling)*
Apuldram, W Sus [Birdham Rd; SU8403], *Black Horse*: Comfortable, well run pub, well kept Friary Meux Best and Ind Coope Burton, good food at reasonable prices *(Peter Ames)*
☆ **Ardingly**, W Sus [Street Lane; TQ3429], *Oak*: Wide choice of good bar food, Watneys-related and guest real ales on handpump in fourteenth-century building with beams, antique furnishings and lovely log fire in magnificent old fireplace *(Norman Foot, Jenny and Brian Seller)*
Ardingly, *Gardeners Arms*: Attractive, olde-worlde interior with inglenook fireplace behind its plain façade, busy but not overcrowded; variety of good food individually cooked and well presented *(G Dudley)*
Arlington, E Sus [Caneheath; TQ5407], *Old Oak*: Pleasant atmosphere with good mix of customers; well kept beer tapped from the cask, good reasonably priced food *(R Houghton)*; *Yew Tree*: Neatly kept and comfortably modernised village pub with big garden, local atmosphere, usual range of bar food from sandwiches and filled baked potatoes through steak and kidney pie to steak; Courage Directors and Harveys on handpump *(Comus Elliott, BB)*
☆ **Arundel**, W Sus [Mill Rd; keep on and don't give up!; TQ0107], *Black Rabbit*: The lovely

location is the big attraction, with riverside tables looking across to bird-reserve watermeadows and castle; long bar with big windows and log fires, lots of spirits as well as Youngers Scotch and IPA, pub games, bar food (not Sun or Mon evening – and mixed views on its value), airy side restaurant; children in eating and family areas; bedrooms *(Mrs Val Rixon, Roger Taylor, Cyril Higgs, LYM)*

Arundel, *White Hart*: Huge improvements by new licensees, central bar serving two cosy lounges with old settles and ancient books; two well kept but pricey real ales (and plans for a third) along with three guests, reasonably priced fresh food and comfortable, separate dining area *(I W Muir)*

Balls Cross, W Sus [signposted off A283 N of Petworth; SU9826], *Stag*: Unspoilt King & Barnes pub with two rooms, one with flagstones and an inglenook fireplace, the other with a carpet *(Phil Gorton)*

Barcombe, E Sus [TQ4114], *Anchor*: Remote inn well worth knowing for charming gardens and boating on very peaceful river; small bar (sandwiches), restaurant and bedrooms; sadly we can't with reliability vouch for the welcome *(LYM)*

Barns Green, W Sus [TQ1227], *Queens Head*: Old pub in pretty village, pleasantly modernised with one large but cosy bar, several fires inc huge one in inglenook, piped music, fruit machine and friendly dobermanns; well kept Flowers and Whitbreads Strong Country, lunchtime bar food inc well filled sandwiches and huge filled baked potatoes; live music evenings, benches in front by quiet road, garden behind *(T Buckland)*

☆ **Battle**, E Sus [25 High St; TQ7416], *George*: Very friendly welcome at lovely old coaching-inn with L-shaped bar, part pine-panelled and with pine counter, up-market atmosphere, well kept Harveys on handpump, good lunchtime bar food inc salad buffet in restaurant, good teas; bedrooms *(S J A Velate, John Townsend, E G Parish)*

Battle [Mount St], *Olde Kings Head*: Straightforward town pub in ancient building with heavy beams; Courage Best and Directors, good value filled French bread *(Peter Corris)*

Beckley, E Sus [TQ8523], *Rose & Crown*: Old coaching-inn with plenty of character; has had friendly welcome, good food and service, but being sold 1989 *(Theodore and Jean Rowland-Entwistle; more news please)*

☆ **Berwick**, E Sus [Milton Street; TQ5304], *Sussex Ox*: Marvellous play area and big lawn outside country pub just below downs; can get very busy (and noisy in family-room), but good atmosphere, well kept beer, good bar food inc nourishing soups with thick crusty bread, pleasantly simple country furniture to match the brick floor and wood-burning stove *(R and S Bentley, Alan Skull, LYM)*

☆ **Berwick**, E Sus [by stn; TQ5105], *Berwick*: Excellent children's playground behind well run family pub with attractive Perspex-roofed garden bar, good choice of food and real ales *(Comus Elliott, LYM)*

Bexhill, E Sus [Cooden Beach Hotel, Cooden; TQ7407], *Sovereign*: Self-contained proper bar, popular with locals; warm and comfortable with wide choice of real ales on handpump, good range of bar food, excellent service; bedrooms *(E G Parish)*; [Egerton Park Rd] *Traffers*: Popular with all ages, well kept Harveys, King & Barnes Festive and Tetleys, friendly barmaids, good food in upstairs restaurant *(Nigel Paine)*

Billingshurst, W Sus [High St; A29; TQ0925], *Olde Six Bells*: Partly fourteenth-century flagstoned and timbered pub with well kept King & Barnes real ales, bar food, inglenook fireplace, pretty roadside garden; not everyone approves of the recent extension – and it still gets crowded in the evenings *(LYM)*

Binstead, W Sus [Binstead Lane; about 2 miles W of Arundel, turn S off A27 towards Binstead – OS Sheet 197 reference 980064; SU9806], *Black Horse*: Unpretentious pub with nice outlook over meadows behind, well kept Gales, sensibly placed darts, unusual food, special rack of tourist information; in quiet country lane; bedrooms *(Keith Houlgate)*

☆ **Birdham**, W Sus [B2179 a mile S of village; SU8200], *Lamb*: Attractive, comfortable and spotless, with lots of small rooms, good range of ales inc Harveys, King & Barnes, Tetleys, good reasonably priced choice of wines, interesting fairly priced food specialising in unusual toasted sandwiches, more choice evenings and weekends; lots of tables out in front and in sheltered back garden – good for children *(Ian Phillips, S Breame)*

Birdham [A286], *Black Horse*: Welcoming with good choice of well kept beer, interesting good value bar food *(SJC)*

☆ **Bodiam**, E Sus [TQ7825], *Curlew*: L-shaped bar with stable door giving airy atmosphere when half open; well kept Adnams and King & Barnes on handpump, sensibly priced decent wines, extensive range of food in bar and back dining area *(S J A Velate, John Townsend)*

☆ **Bodle Street Green**, E Sus [off A271 at Windmill Hill; has been shut Mon Oct–Easter, opens 7pm; TQ6514], *White Horse*: Cheerfully welcoming country pub, clean and well run, in small tucked-away village; airy and comfortably modernised bar with cushioned wheel-back seats and a long shiny settle (favoured by the pub's cat), well kept Harveys and King & Barnes Sussex and Festive on handpump, decent wines and malt whiskies, open fires, good value straightforward bar food from sandwiches and ploughman's to steaks (tables often booked), bar billiards, darts, cheery piped music; some tables outside – a helpful touch for walkers is the OS map framed outside *(J H Bell, John Townsend, BB)*

Bognor Regis, W Sus [3 The Steyne; SZ9399], *Elizabeth II*: Recently reopened under its new name – formerly the Chequers; bar food, pool, music and satellite TV *(Anon)*

Bosham, W Sus [High St; SU8003], *Anchor Bleu*: Lovely sea views from waterside pub with usual bar food, low ceilings and open fires; at its best out of season *(Charles Turner, LYM)*

☆ **Brighton**, E Sus [Castle Sq; TQ3105], *Royal Pavilion*: Efficient service from central food counter – good choice, good value; well laid out series of rooms attractively done up for old-fashioned look, inc intimate candle-lit wine-bar area (good big glasses), lots of panelling, successful pastiche full of character; ladies like the blackboards for graffiti in the lavatories – and there's now a popular first-floor nightclub *(Hazel Morgan, LYM)*

Brighton [The Lanes], *Bath Arms*: Pretty, heavy stone exterior in delightful Lanes area; basic décor in single bar with rugged, wooden furniture, fireplace, mirror and bookshelves; friendly bar staff, variety of customers inc some characters; Watneys-related real ales as well as its own-brewed Bathwater with malty taste *(Peter Griffiths)*; [175 Queens Rd] *Beaufort*: Bright, spacious but simple open-plan pub with warm welcome and comfortable atmosphere; open fire at one end and tables at other, particularly good value food generously served *(Christopher Portway)*; [Kings Rd Arches; on beach below prom, between the piers] *Belvedere*: Lively and youthful real-ale pub squashed into long arch below the road, right on the beach; with its similar next-door sister-pub the Fortune of War (which is lined with marine planking and may be a bit quieter) it has a good two-drinks-for-the-price-of-one happy hour, 7–8pm; live music *(BB)*; [15 Black Lion St] *Cricketers*: Attractive old-fashioned pub with chatty staff and good cheap bar food *(D Bates)*; [13 Marlborough Pl] *King & Queen*: Medieval-style main hall, straightforward food, good jazz most evenings, aviary in flagstoned courtyard *(LYM)*; [Trafalgar St] *Lord Nelson*: Good value unpretentious home cooking, well kept Harveys and farm cider, good mix of unaffected customers *(Alan Skull)*; [Queens Rd] *Queens Head*: Atmosphere not the strong point, but friendly staff, unobtrusive music, good value and imaginative bar food – and it's handy for stn *(Mrs Margaret Dyke)*; [Manchester St] *Star*: Immaculately kept pub with plenty of atmosphere, real ales, good food, lots of clowns in lounge, good food in cellar bar;

pianist twice a week *(Mrs M Openshaw)*

Broad Oak, E Sus [A28/B2089, N of Brede; TQ8220], *Rainbow Trout*: Recently refurbished, Fremlins on handpump and good bar food inc properly cooked fresh fish, and surprisingly reasonably priced lobster *(E J and J W Cutting)*

☆ **Bucks Green**, W Sus [TQ0732], *Queens Head*: Very pleasant olde-worlde village free house with well kept Badger, Courage Directors and King & Barnes; large pleasantly decorated single bar with log fires, nice atmosphere, friendly owners and extensive choice of good reasonably priced food *(Reg Tickner, Anthony Barreau)*

Bucks Green, *Fox*: Pleasantly unspoilt village pub with varied clientele, well kept King & Barnes, lunchtime sausages and sandwiches – a reminder of what pubs used to be like *(Stephen Goodchild)*

Burgess Hill, W Sus [TQ3118], *Top House*: Consistently good reasonably priced food *(Clifford Sharp)*

☆ **Burpham**, W Sus [Warningcamp turn off A27 outside Arundel: follow road up and up; TQ0308], *George & Dragon*: Decidedly on the up-and-up, this comfortably redone old pub near a Norman church, in a quiet village with good walks and fine views over Arundel Castle, has recently been gaining warm reports for its interesting food including refreshingly imaginative vegetarian dishes; airy and uncluttered lounge, friendly efficient service, well kept Courage Directors and Harveys; masses of window boxes outside, spotless lavatories *(Neil and Elspeth Fearn, Ian Phillips, David and Karina Stanley, BB)*

Burpham, *Green Man*: Harvester with usual rusticised atmosphere, but amiable bar service and good food *(D T Taylor)*

Burwash, E Sus [TQ6724], *Rose & Crown*: Friendly and pleasant local tucked away down side street in quaintly restored village, all timbers and beams, with wide choice of real ale such as Bass, Charrington IPA and Shepherd Neame, decent wines, quite enterprising bar food, restaurant; tables on quiet lawn; nr start GWG67 *(Comus Elliott, BB)*

Burwash Common, E Sus [Stonegate Rd; TQ6322], *Kicking Donkey*: Rustic old country pub by cricket field and hop garden, with good cheap bar food and adventure playground *(Brian Smith)*

Burwash Weald, E Sus [A265 two miles W of Burwash; TQ6624], *Wheel*: Friendly and well kept open-plan local with big fireplace, well kept real ales and good value straightforward food; some seats on small front terrace *(John Chapman, David and Marguerite Warner, BB)*

Bury, W Sus [A29 Pulborough–Arundel; TQ0113], *Black Dog & Duck*: Good bar food such as potato and leek soup and game pie, welcoming, courteous and efficient landlord, Gales ales on handpump *(R A Anderson)*

☆ **Chalvington**, E Sus [village signposted from A27 and A22; then follow Golden Cross rd – OS Sheet 199 reference 525099; TQ5109], *Yew Tree*: Isolated country local stripped down to bricks and flagstones inside, with elm seats built into the walls, low beams and inglenook fireplace; straightforward bar food (not Sun), well kept Harveys and Fremlins; popular with young people Fri and Sat evenings, and at other times atmosphere may be dominated by its regulars; attractive little walled terrace, and extensive grounds inc own cricket pitch (*M A and C R Starling, BB*)

Chichester, W Sus [St Pauls St; SU8605], *Rainbow*: Friendly, welcoming bar staff, good food and plenty of tit-bits at bar; small garden with aviary (*Mrs F Abbot*)

☆ **Chilgrove**, W Sus [Hooksway; off B2141, signposted Hooksway down steep hill – OS Sheet 197 reference 814163; SU8214], *Royal Oak*: Unspoilt pub in remote country setting with low ceilings, open fires in winter, piped classical music; real ales such as Gibbs Mew Bishops Tipple, Ringwood Old Thumper and Ruddles Best and County with free coffee for designated drivers of groups, country wines, good value bar food, restaurant (Tues–Sat evenings); garden with climbing-frame and timber fort; has been open all day Fri and Sat (*Brian and Anna Marsden, Neil Lusby, Prof A N Black, LYM*)

Chilgrove, *White Horse*: More restaurant than pub, and a smart one at that, with fine but expensive wines; but they do have good bar lunches inc a good choice of meats, seafood and help-yourself salads at reasonable prices; tables out in front and on green opposite; closed Sun and Mon, and not a place to drop in to just for a drink (*G Holliday*)

☆ **Cocking**, W Sus [A286 Midhurst–Chichester – OS Sheet 197 reference 878179; SU8717], *Cobden*: Low-beamed three-roomed eighteenth-century pub where new licensee is making promising start; well cushioned settles and other seats, open fire, good value bar food, well kept Badger Best and Tanglefoot, Ballards and Marstons Pedigree, warm welcome for locals and strangers; good steady walk from here up to South Downs Way; shut Mon lunchtime (*Frank Cummins*)

☆ **Colemans Hatch**, E Sus [signposted off B2026; or off B2110 opp church; TQ4533], *Hatch*: Simple but charming and welcoming traditional Ashdown Forest pub with lunchtime snacks, pub games, well kept Adnams and Harveys BB on handpump, tables on bluff of grass by quiet lane (*Chris Fluck, LYM*)

Compton, W Sus [SU7714], *Coach & Horses*: Friendly locals, well kept range of changing real ales, pleasant service, restaurant; walkers welcomed in one bar (*R Houghton*)

☆ **Cooksbridge**, W Sus [junction A275 with Cooksbridge and Newick rd; TQ3913], *Rainbow*: Pleasant atmosphere in attractive low-beamed pub with horsebrasses and old photos; efficient service, well kept beer inc King & Barnes Festive, huge choice of reasonably priced good bar food (*Chris Fluck, Philip Haggar*)

Copsale, W Sus [TQ1725], *Bridge*: Comfortable, rustic local with King & Barnes, good bar food (*I W and P J Muir*)

Copthorne, W Sus [A264 just E of village; TQ3139], *Abergavenney Arms*: Modernised, but with conservative furnishings, relaxed atmosphere, well kept real ale, popular lunchtime food, seats in garden (*BB*)

☆ **Cousleywood**, E Sus [TQ6533], *Old Vine*: Busy but attractive low-beamed lounge bar with Fremlins on handpump, wide choice of good bar food in small dining area, separate main restaurant and efficient service (*Peter Neate, Kit Read*)

Crowborough, E Sus [Mount Pleasant, off Walshes Rd; TQ5130], *Wheatsheaf*: Still a 'real' pub – rare for this town – with log fire in small lounge, two-room public bar (*Philip and Sheila Hanley*)

Cuckfield, W Sus [South St; TQ3025], *Kings Head*: Otherwise straightforward old and cosy pub in newly bypassed village, with surprisingly good subtle cooking using fresh ingredients in the two restaurant areas; bedrooms (*P S Simpson*); *White Harte*: Popular medieval pub close to church, comfortably modernised, with friendly licensees and good value usual pub food; well kept King & Barnes real ales, keen darts teams (*Terry Buckland, LYM*)

☆ **Dale Hill**, E Sus [by Dale Hill golf club; junction A268 and B2099; TQ6930], *Cherry Tree*: Generous helpings of good food, excellent pleasant service and friendly atmosphere in attractive building with well kept Youngs ales (*D A Benson*)

Danehill, E Sus [School Lane; off A275 opp the former Crocodile; TQ4027], *Coach & Horses*: Gently updated pub in attractive spot, with well kept Harveys, a weekly changing guest beer, decent house wine and attractively priced bar food in dining extension – formerly a small stables (*S D Sizen*)

☆ **Dell Quay**, W Sus [SU8302], *Crown & Anchor*: Modernised fifteenth-century pub on site of Roman quay, yacht-harbour views from bow window and garden, good generous food with local fish dishes, evening restaurant food mostly grills; log fire, plenty of tables outside overlooking water, Watneys-related real ales (*BB*)

Devils Dyke, W Sus [TQ2511], *Devils Dyke*: Perched on downs above Brighton, and well worth visiting for the views, which are staggering both night and day; basic bar food, upstairs carvery, and Bass, Charrington IPA, Harveys, Tetleys and a guest beer on handpump; but it is a very touristy place – reminding one reader of the cross-Channel ferry packed with duty-free shoppers; nr a hang-glider jumping-off point *(Keith Houlgate, Michael and Alison Sandy, LYM)*

Dial Post, W Sus [A24/B2244; TQ1519], *Crown*: Well kept friendly pub with good food in bar and reasonably priced restaurant; Badger beer *(Brenda Gentry)*

Duncton, W Sus [set back from A285 N of village; SU9617], *Cricketers*: Several attractive rooms on different levels, autographed cricket bats, good choice of well prepared bar food, service swift and attentive; well kept Friary Meux Best, Ind Coope Burton and King & Barnes *(P J Taylor)*

☆ **Eartham**, W Sus [SU9409], *George*: Country pub with cosy, uncluttered and restful lounge, and bar with games area; six well kept real ales, reasonably priced and generously served bar food, swift and courteous service; separate restaurant *(I W Muir, Mr and Mrs W Harrington)*

☆ **East Dean**, W Sus [village signposted off A286 and A285 N of Chichester – OS Sheet 197 reference 904129; SU9013], *Star & Garter*: Charmingly placed by peaceful green of quiet village below South Downs, with rustic seats and swing in pretty walled garden; bar food from sandwiches and home-made soup through omelettes and scampi to steaks, well kept Friary Meux Best and Ind Coope Burton, pub games, bank hol live music (lunchtime barbecues then); handy for South Downs Way, with pleasant walk to Goodwood; children in eating area *(R P Taylor, John Pettit, G B Longden, A V Chute, LYM)*

East Grinstead, W Sus [TQ3938], *Dunnings Mill*: Low-ceilinged three-roomed sixteenth-century mill cottage built right over stream (pretty garden), though the gas lighting and back-to-basics furnishings took a knock in a flood a few months ago, and we haven't yet heard that the pub's back to its old self – which included friendly service in a pleasant restaurant doing decent food inc Sun lunch; bar food, range of real ales, children welcome; handy for Standen (NT) *(Mr and Mrs K J V, Lindsey Shaw Radley, LYM; more reports please)*

Eastbourne, E Sus [Beachy Head; TV6199], *Beachy Head*: Excellent position, nice bars, good beer and bar food, very friendly atmosphere; very good restaurant with fine lunchtime carvery *(J H Bell)*; [The Goffs, Old Town] *Lamb*: Interesting Tudor building with attractive black-beamed interior, pleasantly quiet at lunchtimes; well kept beer, good bar food, open fires; close to art gallery, Gildredge Park and mile from seafront *(Bernard Phillips)*; [Terminus Rd] *Terminus*: Friendly, old-fashioned and busy town-centre pub with popular lunchtime

food and well kept Harveys; tables and chairs out in pedestrian precinct *(Roger Taylor, Peter Corris)*

Eastergate, W Sus [SU9405], *Labour in Vain*: Well kept, basic pub with part stone, part carpeted floor; popular with locals and visitors alike; Ballards Wassail, Harveys Bitter, Ringwood Old Thumper and Youngs Bitter and Special on handpump, good food; back car park small *(Keith Houlgate)*

Elsted, W Sus [Elsted Marsh; nearer to Midhurst than the Three Horseshoes, same road; SU8119], *Elsted*: Simple country local with straightforward food pleasantly served; formerly known as Ballards, but the microbrewery of that name has now moved a couple of miles away; new regime, with warm welcome for families *(Dr R Fuller, HEG, WFL)*

Fairwarp, W Sus [TQ4626], *Foresters*: Well sited by village green in Ashdown Forest; pleasant inside with welcoming and obliging landlord; well kept King & Barnes Festive, good value ploughman's, tables in garden *(Brian and Jenny Seller)*

Falmer, E Sus [Middle St; TQ3508], *Swan*: True free house with over half a dozen well kept real ales; locals' bar and more plush lounge with small drinking area between the two; friendly licensee, good value lunchtime food, morris dancing in summer *(Matt Pringle)*

Findon, W Sus [TQ1208], *Gun*: Large helpings of good standard food, well presented though not cheap, cheery service, and Flowers and Whitbreads Strong Country on handpump in comfortably modernised straightforward pub with attractive sheltered lawn, in quiet village below Cissbury Ring *(Jenny and Brian Seller, LYM)*; *Villager*: Interesting pub with well kept beer and good food *(Paul and Inge Sweetman)*

Fishbourne, W Sus [A27 Chichester–Emsworth; SZ8404], *Bulls Head*: Large bar with rustic décor and atmosphere, Watneys-related real ales and other beers such as King & Barnes on handpump, food in bar and restaurant with generous cook-your-own barbecue, and friendly service *(N E Bushby, W Atkins, A R Lord)*

☆ **Fletching**, E Sus [signposted off A272 W of Uckfield; TQ4223], *Griffin*: Pleasant, busy pub in attractive village with very welcoming barmaid, good food (freshly cooked – so there may be a wait; chicken, seafood pancakes, open sandwiches all recommended, with lots of fish Thurs evening); decent beers and wines, rewarding restaurant; quite handy for Sheffield Park; six attractive bedrooms – a really nice place to stay *(Miles Kington, TOH, Mr and Mrs P W Dryland, Derek and Maggie Washington)*

Gatwick, W Sus [Airport; TQ2941], *Country Pub*: Decent straightforward food – and reasonably comfortable, considering the number of people *(J S Rutter)*

Hammerpot, W Sus [A27 4 miles W of Worthing; TQ0605], *Woodmans Arms*: Very low-ceilinged single-bar pub with interesting prints and horsy décor, well kept Ind Coope real ales, massive helpings of usual pub food inc daily specials, friendly welcoming staff, comfortable seats inside and out, spotless lavatories *(Michael Bechley)*

Handcross, W Sus [TQ2529], *Red Lion*: Excellent value food in Barnabys Carvery, with very friendly staff and spotless surroundings, good coffee and good value wines; unusually good example of a chain pub/restaurant *(Dr Richard Neville, Chris Fluck)*; [Horsham Rd] *Royal Oak*: Pleasant atmosphere and well kept Ruddles and King & Barnes in spotless pub with decent bar food and rooms decorated in various themes – aircraft, Falklands memorabilia inc a white ensign from HMS *Intrepid*, Churchill *(TOH, Norman Foot)*

Hartfield, E Sus [Gallipot St; TQ4735], *Gallipot*: Useful friendly pub, with well kept Charrington and Flowers, wide range of bar food, good log fire, no music or machines; on GWG62, handy for Ashdown Forest *(Lindsey Shaw Radley)*; [A264] *Haywaggon*: Warm welcome, oak beams, good food in very clean bar and restaurant, quick and attentive service; nr start GWG62 *(Mr and Mrs G Turner, Roy and Shirley Bentley)*

Hastings, E Sus [Old Harbour; TQ8109], *Dolphin*: Pleasant with well furnished bar, Ruddles and good value locally caught fish, tables outside overlooking harbour *(Jenny and Brian Seller)*; [The Ridge] *Robert de Mortain*: Welcoming and comfortable bar with well presented, varying bar food *(Theo and Jean Rowland-Entwistle)*

Heathfield, E Sus [Horam Rd; TQ5821], *Prince of Wales*: Good choice of beers and wines, superb value lunchtime carvery, well cooked and generous helpings *(D Kayes-Knight)*

Henfield, W Sus [TQ2116], *George*: Olde-worlde pub in pretty village with pleasant atmosphere and good helpings of good value bar food; well kept Gales HSB and Ushers Best; restaurant *(Chris Fluck)*

☆ **Hermitage**, W Sus [36 Main Rd (A259); SU7505], *Sussex Brewery*: Peaceful, traditionally basic pub with rural furniture, sawdust on floors, no juke box or fruit machines, log fire, good mix of customers and pleasant atmosphere; friendly bar staff, choice of real ales inc Hermitage brewed on premises, food at reasonable prices inc occasional fresh local shellfish, pianist Sun night – a great escape from noisy, artificial, modern pubs *(James Adlington, Richard Houghton, M Hopton, P M Brooker, N A Lander)*

☆ **Heyshott**, W Sus [SU8918], *Unicorn*: Friendly welcome and helpful service in small pub with nice local atmosphere in L-shaped bar; well kept beer and quality bar food

generously served, particularly ploughman's with good range of help-yourself salads; restaurant, garden with barbecue; in attractive country at foot of downs *(R D Norman, J S Evans)*

Hollingbury, E Sus [Carden Ave; TQ3108], *Long Man of Wilmington*: Tastefully furnished and spotless, with well kept real ales and good food; collection of lions; pool and darts *(Mrs M Openshaw)*

Horsham, W Sus [Tower Hill; TQ1730], *Boars Head*: Well kept Wadworths 6X and good bar lunches *(D J P Dutton)*; [31 North St] *Hurst Arms*: Under new managament, pleasant bars with old-style armchairs and wood tables and well kept Watneys-related real ales with King & Barnes; good, reasonably priced food from ploughman's up *(Norman Foot)*

Horsted Keynes, E Sus [TQ3828], *Green Man*: Good pub atmosphere and a nice pint *(M C Howells)*

Hurstpierpoint, W Sus [High St; TQ2716], *New*: Old-fashioned pub with charming traditional back room, bar billiards in panelled snug, simpler public bar, well kept Bass and Charrington IPA *(LYM)*

☆ **Icklesham**, E Sus [TQ8816], *Queens Head*: Popular old pub with splendid view over Brede to Rye, good atmosphere, well presented varying home-cooked bar food at very reasonable prices (plenty of people waiting to sit in your seat when you've finished); good choice of beers, farm tool collection *(Theo and Jean Rowland-Entwistle, Alec Lewery, C H Fewster)*

Isfield, E Sus [TQ4417], *Laughing Fish*: Particularly well kept Harveys ales and lively local atmosphere in simple modernised village pub with good robust food; small garden, slide and swing in enclosed children's play area *(Alec Lewery, BB)*

Kingsfold, W Sus [Dorking Rd; A24 Dorking–Horsham, nr A29 junction; TQ1636], *Dog & Duck*: Useful stop – fairly extensive menu with good specials and lovely puddings *(Mrs H Tickner)*

Kirdford, W Sus [TQ0126], *Foresters*: Well run stone-floored bar with bench seats and tables, lounge with stools, upholstered benches and tables; well kept King & Barnes, limited choice of simple bar food prepared well by landlord's wife (inc lots of omelettes); restaurant *(Norman Foot)*

☆ **Lambs Green**, W Sus [TQ2136], *Lamb*: Cosy though extended plush bar with beams and open fire in welcoming pub with lively atmosphere; wide choice of quickly and generously served food (inc good value Sun roast) and several normally well kept real ales such as Badger Best, Gales HSB, King & Barnes and Ruddles County; big glass-walled garden room *(David and Sarah Gilmore, Norman Foot, Dr A V Lewis, Steve Goodchild, BB)*

Lavant, W Sus [Midhurst Rd; SU8508],

Hunters: Bright and attractive with extensive lunchtime and evening choice of attractively presented bar food, well kept beer, nice atmosphere; pleasant restaurant; bedrooms *(Shirley Pielon)*

Lewes, E Sus [22 Malling St; TQ4110], *Dorset Arms*: Seventeenth-century pub, recently well renovated to high standard; good bar food and well kept Harveys – it's within sight of the brewery; restaurant, outside terraces; children in well equipped annexe next to main bar; bedrooms *(Keith Walton, Alan Skull)*; [Castle Ditch Lane, Mount Pl] *Lewes Arms*: Friendly local with decent lunchtime food, wider weekend choice, well kept Harveys *(Neil Barker)*; [High St, St Anne's] *Pelham Arms*: Well kept town pub, locally popular for good value food, with friendly service and atmosphere; nr GWG61 *(Dr M D Wood, BB)*

Littlehampton, W Sus [westwards towards Chichester, opp railway stn; TQ0202], *Arun View*: Built out on to harbour edge, with extensive views of river – busy here with seagoing vessels; comfortable banquettes, accurate drawings of barges and ships worked into counter-top, Whitbreads-related real ales on handpump, wide choice of bar food and restaurant, flower-filled terrace; summer barbecues evenings and weekends *(Ian Phillips)*

Lodsworth, W Sus [SU9223], *Hollist Arms*: Small bar, games-room with pool, interesting licensee and good mix of customers; well kept King & Barnes Mild, well chosen wine list and good bar food culminating in huge trout caught locally by licensee *(P J Taylor)*

☆ **Lower Beeding**, W Sus [TQ2227], *Crabtree*: Large well run pub with public bar, snug and back bar with inglenook fireplace; good welcome, well kept King & Barnes, good bar food and dining-room *(Phil and Sally Gorton)*

Lower Beeding [Plummers Plain; TQ2128], *Wheatsheaf*: Popular; walls and ceiling decorated with military memorabilia; good food, well kept King & Barnes on handpump *(David Fisher)*

Lowfield Heath, W Sus [Charlwood Rd; TQ2740], *Flight*: Pictures and models of aircraft, good food; caters well for children in conservatory with view of planes taking off from Gatwick *(Charles Kingdon)*

☆ **Mayfield**, E Sus [TQ5827], *Middle House*: Olde-worlde Elizabethan hotel with attentive licensee and staff; chatty bar with lots of locals, well kept Harveys and Hoskins & Oldfields on handpump, darts and fruit machines at one end, wide choice of decent food, not cheap, inc lots of different ploughman's and maybe a spit-roast over the open fire; separate morning coffee/afternoon tea area with log-effect gas fire in ornate fireplace, big reddish leather Chesterfield, armchairs; pretty back garden with log house, slide, dovecote, picnic-table sets and pleasant views; bedrooms *(BB)*; [North St]

Angel: Old coaching-house with long-serving staff, well kept Gales, bar food, restaurant, large garden; bedrooms *(Doug Kennedy)*; [Petersfield Rd; A272 just W] *Half Moon*: Popular, cheerful and friendly well run pub, extensive range of bar food at reasonable prices; restaurant *(J F Deshayes)*

Midhurst, W Sus [A286 towards Chichester; SU8821], *Royal Oak*: Worth knowing particularly for the extensive garden, though the formerly quaint little farmhouse pub has recently been given a very thorough-going mock-Tudor refurbishment; good range of real ales and bottled beers, ploughman's and so forth; barbecues *(P J Taylor, LYM)*; [South St/Market Sq] *Swan*: Split-level Harveys pub with attentive licensees, interesting choice of freshly cooked and attractively served food *(Aubrey and Margaret Saunders)*

Milland, W Sus [A3; SU8328], *Fox*: Well kept beer, good cheap bar food, huge garden with animals and swings *(Ray Challoner)*; *Rising Sun*: Popular, with good choice of food, well kept Gales, decent coffee, interesting collection of jugs around dining-room; children welcome in family-room and dining-room; garden *(Anon)*

Netherfield, E Sus [Netherfield Hill; TQ7118], *Netherfield Arms*: Attentive, friendly licensees, quiet piped music; reasonably priced bar food inc good choice of vegetarian dishes *(Theo and Jean Rowland-Entwistle)*

New Bridge, W Sus [A272 W of Billingshurst; TQ0625], *Limeburners Arms*: Picturesque pub with simple food, well served in friendly atmosphere; rustic seats outside on lawn *(R Wilson)*

☆ **Normans Bay**, E Sus [TQ6805], *Star*: Extensively modernised family pub by caravan park in remote salt marshes, cushioned chairs in comfortable brick-pillared lounge, timber-effect walls and some paving-slab flooring besides the carpet, wide choice of generously and efficiently served food, cheerful atmosphere, piped music, fruit machines, games in children's room, seats on front terrace and in hawthorn-tree streamside garden, play area *(T G Saul, David Crafts, BB)*

Northchapel, W Sus [SU9529], *Half Moon*: Village pub with welcoming pleasantly rustic atmosphere, farm tools, subdued lighting, open fire; good value Sun lunch (best to book), pool-room; car park with goat tethered *(Charles and Mary Winpenny, Michael and Harriet Robinson)*

Northiam, E Sus [The Green; TQ8224], *Hayes Arms*: Civilised hotel overlooking village green; heavily beamed and comfortably furnished back Tudor bar with big brick inglenook fireplace; not a pub atmosphere, though Adnams tapped from the cask and lunchtime bar food from rare beef sandwiches up; bedrooms *(Anon)*

Nutbourne, W Sus [the one nr Pulborough; TQ0718], *Rising Sun*: Good atmosphere, friendly staff and good food inc vegetarian dishes *(Cathy Marsh)*

☆ **Nutley**, E Sus [A22; TQ4427], *William IV*: Spacious pub, consistently friendly staff and locals, wholesome and generously served bar food inc good value sandwiches, well kept King & Barnes and Ushers Best and decent wines, lovely log fires *(B Moran, Jan and Ian Alcock, Alan Bickley)*

☆ **Oxleys Green**, E Sus [TQ6921], *Jack Fullers*: Renamed from Fullers Arms summer 1989, underlining its move up market: two attractive rooms, with beams, brown velvet curtains, fresh flowers, two huge old fireplaces, mix of oak tables, plush-cushioned settles, dark kitchen chairs and dining-chairs; interesting food such as cashew and aubergine bake, salmon mousse, vegetables such as honeyed carrots, well kept Brakspears PA, Harveys and Youngs Special, good choice of other drinks inc good malts, decent French wines and a quite exceptional range of English wines by the bottle; charming garden, in attractive surroundings; fortnightly folk music; closed Mon, and may shut around 2.45; has a great deal going for it, and given decent welcoming service would be hard to beat; on GWG67 *(S J A Velate, Mrs D M Hacker, Bruce Wass, V F Ammoun, BB)*

Pease Pottage, W Sus [by M23 junction 11; TQ2533], *James King*: Comfortable bar, well kept King & Barnes, extensive bar food from ploughman's to steaks, cold buffet, restaurant *(Norman Foot)*

Peasmarsh, E Sus [TQ8822], *Horse & Cart*: Free house with well kept real ales such as Adnams and Websters Yorkshire, extensive but simple choice of good food – almost all home made, ample helpings, sensible prices *(E J Cutting)*

Pett, E Sus [TQ8714], *Two Sawyers*: Village pub with friendly staff and great dane, well kept beer and good range of well prepared reasonably priced waitress-served bar food *(Byrne Sherwood, Mr and Mrs E Hardwick)*

Petworth, W Sus [Angel Street; SU9721], *Angel*: Pleasant spacious pub with relaxed atmosphere and surroundings and friendly staff, straightforward decent bar food, Watneys-related real ales with a guest beer such as Gales, huge winter log fire; bedrooms *(Norman Foot)*; [A283 towards Pulborough] *Welldiggers*: Low-ceilinged food pub very popular for its good value restaurant-style meals – hardly a place for just a drink now – and attractive lawns and terraces *(LYM)*

Pevensey, E Sus [High St; TQ6304], *Priory Court*: Hotel in shadow of Pevensey Castle with refurbished plush-and-brasswork bar with some guns on the walls, welcoming log fire, Harvey and Flowers beer on handpump, bar food, extensive gardens with pond; bedrooms *(David Crafts)*

Plumpton, E Sus [Ditchling Rd (B2116); TQ3613], *Half Moon*: Popular nineteenth-

century pub with attractive rustic tables and benches outside looking out towards South Downs; prompt, friendly service, well kept Ruddles Best and County, good bar food specialising in ploughman's lunches; 1970s painting of a great crowd of its regulars *(Brian and Jenny Seller)*

Poundgate, E Sus [TQ4928], *Crown & Gate*: Character pub with warm, friendly licensees and wide range of good reasonably priced food (though food service stops at strictly observed times) *(Lisa Freedman)*

Poynings, W Sus [TQ2612], *Royal Oak*: Good varied bar food, esp fish; pleasant bar staff, attractive garden *(G B Pugh)*

☆ **Pulborough**, W Sus [99 Lower St; TQ0418], *Oddfellows Arms*: Attractive, friendly and comfortable well kept pub with good food inc good sandwiches with home-cooked meats, particularly fine generously served ploughman's, tasty daily specials; garden with children's slide/swing area *(Keith Walton, Guy Harris)*

Ringles Cross, E Sus [A22; TQ4721], *Ringles Cross*: Useful well kept roadside pub with reliable food inc good steaks, well kept real ale *(BB)*

Ringmer, E Sus [B2192; TQ4412], *Anchor*: Pretty from the outside, facing green in well tended flower garden, with side pigeon loft; very popular with older people for honest welcome, with flowers on tables and good value food from sandwiches to steaks; children in large garden with swings *(Ian Phillips)*

☆ **Rogate**, W Sus [A272; SU8023], *White Horse*: Old seventeenth-century coaching-inn with pleasant comfortable atmosphere, good red plush seats under low beams, wide choice of good food nicely served, several real ales, friendly service, notably clean lavatories *(Prof A N Black, R Groves)*

Rotherfield, E Sus [TQ5529], *Kings Arms*: Old and attractive pub with spacious bar, friendly service, good choice of reasonably priced hot bar food inc excellent liver and bacon, restaurant *(Miss P T Metcalfe, P H Fearnley)*

Rottingdean, E Sus [High St; TQ3702], *Coach House*: Attractive bow-windowed pub close to sea, with sedate atmosphere, real ales, attractively presented bar food at reasonable prices, more ambitious dishes in restaurant, good service *(E G Parish)*; [Marine Drive] *White Horse*: Pub side of seaside hotel (with separate cocktail bars), friendly and helpful staff, bar food and afternoon teas; clifftop Channel views; bedrooms *(E G Parish)*

☆ **Rudgwick**, W Sus [Church St; TQ0833], *Kings Head*: Refurbished pub backing on to lovely old church in attractive small village, always crowded, with pleasant atmosphere, generous helpings of good straightforward food at reasonable prices, no piped music; helpful, cheerful service – staff generally Antipodean or S African, don't pester for money before you eat *(Stephen Goodchild, Timothy Galligan, D J P Dutton)*

☆ **Rusper**, W Sus [village signposted from A24 and A264 N and NE of Horsham; TQ2037], *Plough*: Generous collection of real ales in seventeenth-century village pub with a big inglenook in its very low-beamed bar comfortably modernised partly panelled bar; good cheeses and help-yourself salads as well as other lunchtime bar food, fountain in back garden, pretty front terrace, bar billiards and darts in raftered room upstairs; children welcome *(Paul Sexton and Sue Harrison, Don Mather, LYM)*

Rusper [Friday Street (a mile or two from village)], *Royal Oak*: Country pub with good atmosphere and various nooks and crannies, very well kept by welcoming and genuine licensees, good honest-to-goodness pub food, decent beer, pleasant surroundings in quiet lane *(N D Foot, Roy Clark)*

Rye, E Sus [High St; TQ9220], *George*: Pleasant bar in THF hotel, friendly staff, lively with locals on Sat night; lounge more sedate with sofas and log fire; Fremlins on handpump; bedrooms *(Pamela and Merlyn Horswell, Alison Hayward and Nick Dowson)*; [Military Rd] *Globe*: Straightforward pub with pleasant atmosphere (though, facing E with its back to the cliff, it darkens early in winter), decent bar food inc good sandwiches and ploughman's, kind service, well kept Courage Directors *(Capt R E H King)*; [Landgate] *Queens Head*: Old Courage house with friendly atmosphere under new regime, and good food inc fresh Rye Bay fish and good puddings; bedrooms *(Leo and Pam Cohen)*; [The Mint] *Standard*: Busy, lively pub, juke box, King & Barnes Festive on handpump, reasonably priced bar food – a young person's pub *(Alison Hayward, Nick Dowson)*; [East St] *Union*: Clean and well kept split-level town pub with wide choice of usual bar food (not cheap), King & Barnes, Festive, Fremlins, Ruddles Best and Flowers Original on handpump, piped music, fresh flowers *(Sheila Keene, Mr and Mrs G D Amos, Alison Hayward, Nick Dowson)*; [Gun Garden; off A259] *Ypres Castle*: Unrefined, plain and rather dark but cosy local in pleasant situation, approached by steep flight of stone steps; friendly welcome, old yachting magazines for browsing through, local events and art exhibition posters, simple bar food from bread and cheese to steak, piped music *(WHBM, Hazel Morgan, Alison Hayward, Nick Dowson)*

Rye Harbour, E Sus [TQ9220], *William the Conqueror*: Functional pub with cheap food, well placed on undeveloped harbour edge *(BB)*

Sedlescombe, E Sus [TQ7718], *Queens Head*: Attractive pub in pretty village with three distinct areas, well furnished and decorated; Flowers on handpump, plain lunchtime bar food inc some freshly made sandwiches,

garden; usually very friendly, but may seem less than welcoming at very busy times *(S J A Velate)*

Selsey, W Sus [Albion Rd; SZ8593], *Lifeboat*: Good lunches in beautiful garden, very clean; friendly staff *(Stella Crist)*

☆ **Selsfield**, W Sus [Ardingly Rd; B2028 N of Haywards Heath, nr West Hoathly (its postal address); TQ3434], *White Hart*: Dark oak beams and timbers, big log fire dividing bar in two, half a dozen or more well kept real ales, popular bar lunches from ploughman's and omelettes through home-made steak and kidney pie to scampi and Sun lunches; restaurant in sensitively reconstructed sixteenth-century barn brought here from Wivelsfield, picnic-table sets on side lawn above steep wooded combe; handy for Wakehurst Place and Ingwersen's nursery; on GWG64; children welcome *(Chris Fluck, Norman Foot, LYM)*

☆ **Sharpthorne**, E Sus [Horstead Lane; TQ3732], *Ravenswood*: Spacious period bar with handsome panelling in converted Victorian house, Badger Best and Tanglefoot on handpump, restaurant; extensive grounds with tables outside, lake, summerhouse *(D J Penny)*

Sharpthorne [Station Rd], *Bluebell*: Pleasantly unpretentious pub on Sussex Border Path; wide choice of well kept beer inc Everards Old Original, bar food inc good value ploughman's *(Jenny and Brian Seller)*

Shoreham by Sea, W Sus [Upper Shoreham Rd; TQ2105], *Red Lion*: Lovely old pub with low beams, prompt cheerful service, Watneys-related ales, decent wines, good value bar food from sandwiches to steaks and fine salmon, Sun lunch, pretty sheltered garden *(I W and P J Muir)*

Shortbridge, E Sus [Piltdown – OS Sheet 198 reference 450215; TQ4521], *Peacock*: Attractive fourteenth-century country pub on high ground, some seats under cover in pleasant front garden and more behind; lots of character inside, with huge log fire; up-to-date reports please *(TOH)*

Singleton, W Sus [SU8713], *Horse & Groom*: Comfortable, relaxing pub with real fires and big helpings of good food – Sun also; within walking distance of Weald and Downland Open-Air Museum *(NHB)*

☆ **South Harting**, W Sus [B2146; SU7819], *White Hart*: Lovely old attractive place with large log fire, attentive licensees and staff, proper separate public bar for locals and young people; good fresh food – especially soup; decent coffee *(MCG)*

South Harting, *Coach & Horses*: South Downs village pub with open log fires, good food and drink, well equipped children's playroom, garden *(A J Blackler)*

☆ **Stopham**, W Sus [A283 towards Pulborough; TQ0218], *White Hart*: Friendly old beamed pub in lovely setting, with big lawn, play area, and grass walks by pretty junction of Arun and Rother rivers; open fire in one of the snug rooms, generous helpings of good freshly made bar food (not Sun evening), restaurant specialising in unusual fresh fish, well kept Flowers Original, Wethereds and Whitbreads Strong Country, unobtrusive piped music; children welcome *(Brian and Anna Marsden, Lyn and Bill Capper, LYM)*

Stoughton, W Sus [signposted off B2146 Petersfield–Emsworth; SU8011], *Hare & Hounds*: Much-modernised seventeenth-century brick-and-flint downs village pub, pine cladding, red leatherette, big open fires in dividing chimney, an airy feel; decent home-cooked bar food running up to steaks (served very early evening too – useful for families), well kept Gales ales, friendly young staff, winter restaurant, back darts room, pretty terrace; nr start GWG56; children in eating area and restaurant *(A J Blackler, LYM)*

Tismans Common, W Sus [TQ0732], *Mucky Duck*: Oak beams, timbers and flagstones in cheery well run country pub with simple home-cooked food, good choice of well kept real ales, lively evening atmosphere, play area and garden seats *(LYM)*

☆ **Trotton**, W Sus [OS Sheet 197 reference 837222; SU8323], *Keepers Arms*: Straightforwardly furnished L-shaped bar angling around into restaurant area, in beamed and timbered tile-hung pub standing on a little rise – country views from its latticed windows and from teak tables on a narrow terrace; real ales such as Badger Best and Tanglefoot, Ballards and Ruddles County on handpump, decent spirits, lots of non-alcoholic drinks, quietly chatty atmosphere, decent straightforward food cooked nicely and served quickly *(Steve Goodchild, J S Evans, J H Bell, Chris Fluck, BB)*

☆ **Turners Hill**, W Sus [East St; TQ3435], *Crown*: Attractively refurbished 1987 in rustic bookshelves-and-Staffordshire- china style, pictures inc Victorian oils, low settees as well as tables with dining-chairs, open fire, steps down to bookable dining area with lofty stripped beams and pitched rafters; well kept Friary Meux Best and Tetleys, wide choice of quickly served bar food from ploughman's through pies and marinated lamb to steaks, soft piped music; tables in garden, and in front; handy for Wakehurst Place, and Standen (NT); two bedrooms *(W J Wonham, NAC, Lindsey Shaw Radley, C F Stephens, John Pettit, Ruth Moynard, BB)*

Uckfield, E Sus [Eastbourne Rd (A22); 2 miles S, nr Framfield; on left going S; TQ4721], *Barley Mow*: Decent food, quick (almost too quick) service *(G B Pugh)*; *Brickmakers Arms*: Tiny old bar, unusual beers, wide choice of good cheap bar food *(Brian Smith)*; [Eastbourne Rd (A22)] *Highlands*: Good food under the current regime *(Brian Smith)*; [High St] *Olde Maidens Head*: Attractive old

coaching-inn under friendly new manager, with plans to upgrade it as a decent hotel; bedrooms have always been good value – should be even better; very promising – one to watch *(Patrick Young, Brian Smith)*

Udimore, E Sus [TQ8619], *Kings Head*: Small village pub with much character, open fire, low ceilings, attentive landlord, well kept Fremlins, bar food *(Michele and Andrew Wells)*

Upper Beeding, W Sus [A2037; TQ1910], *Rising Sun*: Fairly old pub just off South Downs Way, well laid out inside, with well kept Whitbreads Strong Country and Pompey Royal, bar food inc good ploughman's – not cheap but lavish; pleasant garden *(Jenny and Brian Seller)*

☆ **Upper Dicker**, E Sus [TQ5510], *Plough*: Fine country pub with three separate welcoming rooms, one with log fire in winter, friendly staff, wide choice of well prepared bar food, Watneys-related and King & Barnes real ales, good atmosphere – busy in the evenings; children's swings in big garden *(Peter Corris, J H Bell)*

Waldron, E Sus [Blackboys–Horam side road; TQ5419], *Star*: Wide choice of good plentiful food from sandwiches up; Charrington IPA and M&B Mild, friendly atmosphere, popular with locals and regular visitors; big garden, children's playground *(G and J U Jones)*

☆ **Warnham**, W Sus [Friday St; TQ1533], *Greets*: Incredible fifteenth-century rambling pub, beautifully restored but retaining its uneven flagstone floor and inglenook fireplace; friendly atmosphere, well kept Flowers and Whitbreads Strong County, imaginative home-cooking and pleasant garden *(Alison Anholt-White)*

Warnham [just off A24 Horsham–Dorking], *Sussex Oak*: Olde-worlde interior with large bar and eating area, big fire and darts corner; friendly welcome, warm atmosphere and well kept beer; no food Sat evenings *(Mayur Shah)*

Washington, W Sus [just off A24 Horsham–Worthing; TQ1212], *Frankland Arms*: Roomy pub with wide range of food, good choice of beers and pleasant, efficient staff *(M Sayer)*

☆ **West Firle**, E Sus [village signposted off A27 Lewes–Polegate; TQ4607], *Ram*: Village inn with vigorous local connections, which has been tremendously welcoming and popular under the Leisters, with good value simple bar lunches, well kept Charrington IPA and Youngs Special, traditional bar games, seats in big walled garden; near a fine stretch of the South Downs, close to Glyndebourne; as we went to press we heard that the Leisters might be moving on – if their successors are anything like as good, this pub will be very much worth knowing; bedrooms (three) good value, simple but with antique furnishings and clean, modern shower-room

(David Graves, Patrick Young, Lindsey Shaw Radley, Bernard Phillips, Jenny and Brian Seller, Chris Fluck, PB, HB, LYM)

West Marden, W Sus[B2146 2 miles S of Uppark; SU7713], *Victoria*: Pleasant rustic surroundings, well kept Gibbs Mew, decent house wines, good home-made food inc generous ploughman's and interesting hot dishes; quick friendly service *(Col and Mrs L N Smyth, R Houghton, R Sims)*

Westergate, W Sus [SU9305], *Wilkes Head*: Small, friendly pub with flagstones and open fire; well kept Friary Meux Best and Ind Coope Burton, good food, pleasant landlord *(C R T Low)*

Westfield, E Sus [TQ8115], *Plough*: Popular, well run local with good atmosphere, friendly landlord, bar food and restaurant; small garden with picnic-table sets *(Theodore and Jean Rowland-Entwistle)*

Wilmington, E Sus [TQ5404], *Wilmington Arms*: Does not have expected atmosphere of country pub – seems more like a converted private house – but is popular with locals, pleasant and comfortably furnished, and is useful for quiet civilised drink or bar meal *(PB, HB, WHBM)*

☆ **Wisborough Green**, W Sus [TQ0526], *Three Crowns*: Comfortable and spotless recently refurbished bar with oak beams, brick walls, parquet and carpeted floors; well kept Friary Meux Best, wide choice of bar food, good service – makes the busy pub seem

uncrowded *(Norman Foot, John and Heather Dwane, A Banister, Steve Goodchild, Mike and Sue Wheeler)*

Worthing, W Sus [32 Brighton Rd; TQ1402], *Egremont*: Friendly locals and staff, with good atmosphere, small evening restaurant, piano/organ music *(Tim Baxter)*; [High St, Tarring] *George & Dragon*: Spacious pub with cosy, friendly atmosphere – even if not very full; pleasant service, bar food from sandwiches up, attractive garden with water feature *(Sion Hughes)*; [Old Brighton Rd] *Royal Oak*: Large pub strategically placed next to Beach Hill Park, the mecca for bowls; very friendly to both locals and visitors, reasonably priced food, Watneys-related ales *(D L Johnson)*; [80–82 Marine Parade] *Wine Lodge*: Large, seafront free house, long bar, three pool-tables, many soft seats and plenty of standing room; pleasant staff, mixed clientele, Ruddles and Youngers IPA, wine from the barrel, good reasonably priced bar food generously served; quiet lunchtime, very busy weekend evening with disco music *(D L Johnson)*

Yapton, W Sus [North End Rd; SU9703], *Black Dog*: Good reasonably priced straightforward bar food, good variety of well kept beers such as Whitbreads Pompey Royal; particularly nice terrace with covered outdoor seating, large park, children's play area *(Anon)*

Wiltshire

Of the many things happening to the area's pubs, perhaps the most dramatic was the thatch fire early in 1989 which seriously damaged the Weight for Age at Alvediston – like the one five years ago. After that first fire, it changed its name from the Crown; now it's reopened after this time's rebuilding, it's changed its name back to the Crown. Another drama – sadder, as there's no happy end – was the closing of the delightfully placed Red Lion at West Dean by Whitbreads, its brewery; this popular entry of previous editions has been sold as a private house. Elsewhere, there are new licensees for the Waggon & Horses below Silbury Hill at Beckhampton, the marvellously placed Cross Guns near Bradford-on-Avon (they've stopped letting bedrooms), the civilised Crown at Everleigh (coming from the Hatchet at Lower Chute), the idiosyncratic Crown at Giddeahall (restaurant extensions, but bar areas unchanged), the busy Royal Oak at Great Wishford, the stylishly refurbished Carpenters Arms in Lacock, and the Vine Tree at Norton (already doing so well under the new people that we've given it a star award, to join its food award). The people at the Royal Oak at Wootton Rivers (one of the area's stars for food) have taken on the Pheasant just off the M4 at Great Shefford (Berkshire) – one of our most useful discoveries this year. Discoveries closer to home here (or pubs back among the main entries after a break) include the pleasantly countrified Cuckoo at Landford, the Wheatsheaf at Lower Woodford (a thriving food pub), the companionable Avon Brewery in Salisbury (one of the city's prettiest pubs, with a narrow riverside garden), the Antelope in Upavon (simple but good food, and good value as a place to stay at) and the canalside Barge at Seend (formerly virtually derelict, now positively shining with life after a marvellous job of refurbishment). Other pubs doing particularly well here at the moment include the beautifully kept Dove at Corton (good food), the thriving Bear in Devizes (a nice place to stay at), the civilised Lamb at Hindon (masses of favourable reports from readers – it has good food, and gains a star award this year), the Silver Plough at Pitton (probably the best pub food in the county, in lovely surroundings), and the very friendly and unspoilt Haunch of Venison in Salisbury (smashing atmosphere). Pubs currently looking particularly promising among the Lucky Dip entries at the end of the chapter include the Green Dragon at Barford St Martin, Ivy at Heddington, Bath Arms at Horningsham near Longleat, Hatchet at Lower Chute, Old Ship in Mere, Rose & Crown on the outskirts of Salisbury, Bell at Seend and Black Horse at Teffont Magna. Wanborough, handy for junction 15 of the M4, seems to have several places that are a cut above the average for the Swindon area, and Salisbury itself is a rewarding place to visit for pubs – as well as for so many other things.

ALVEDISTON   ST9723 Map 2

Crown 🏠

Though a bad fire gutted two-thirds of this building at the beginning of 1989, it's now been restored to its orginal form as a Grade II listed building and was opened again in spring 1989. It's also changed its name. Having been known as the Weight for Age for four years, it's reverted back to its original name, the Crown. The two open-plan beamed rooms are comfortably furnished in greens, pinks and browns, have brocaded seats, subdued lighting, and a fire at one end. An extension has been added which opens out on to the garden and is used as a family-room at lunchtimes and as a restaurant in the evenings. Home-made bar food includes sandwiches (from £1.10), soup (£1.50), baked potato with various fillings (from £2), ploughman's (from £2.20), home-made pâté (£2.25), steak and kidney pie (£3.95) and breaded plaice (£4); children's menu (£1.75) and Sun lunch (£5.25). Well kept King & Barnes, Palmers BB and Wadworths 6X on handpump; darts. On different levels around a thatched white well, the attractive garden here is nicely broken up with shrubs and rockeries among neatly kept lawns; it faces a farmyard with ponies and other animals, and there's a children's play area. *(Recommended by Trevor and Helen Greenfinches, WFL, Norman Rose, WHBM, Nigel Paine, Dr R Conrad; more reports please)*

Free house   Licensee Mrs Frampton   Real ale   Meals and snacks   Restaurant   Children welcome   Open 12–2.30, 7–11 all year; closed evening 25 Dec   Two bedrooms tel Salisbury (0722) 780335; /£40S

ANSTY   ST9526 Map 2

Maypole

Village signposted from A30 Shaftesbury–Salisbury

Dwarfed by England's tallest maypole (brought from Fonthill Abbey in October 1982, though there have been mapoles here since the fifteenth century), this white-shuttered brick and flint pub has spindle-back chairs, cushioned wall seats and winged settles around tables on the Turkey carpet, dark green hessian walls hung with old local photographs, drawings and hunting prints, and a welcoming, attentive landlord. Popular bar food includes sandwiches (from £1.10, home-cooked ham £1.35), soup (£1.25), filled baked potatoes (from £1.65), ploughman's (from £2.25), lasagne (£3.25), salads (from £3.25, topside of beef £4.75), seafood platter (£4.75), breaded chicken with cream cheese and pineapple filling or gammon steak with egg or pineapple (£4.95), fresh trout with almonds (£6.75), steaks (from £7.95), and enterprising puddings; Sunday roast (£4.25). Well kept Hook Norton Best, Marstons Pedigree and Wadworths 6X on handpump. There are seats in front and in the back garden. The manor house next door has a unique pond that is three feet above the road surface, is thirty-feet deep in places and stocked with trout for private fishing. The pub is near *Good Walks Guide* Walk 34. *(Recommended by J S Evans, Nigel Paine, V Thomas, Bob Smith)*

Free house   Licensees Brian and Pat Hamshere   Real ale   Meals and snacks (not Sun evening or Mon)   Restaurant (not Sun evening)   Children over five in eating area   Open 11–2.30, 6.30–11; closed Sun evening and Mon, exc bank hols (they then close the following day) Bedrooms tel Tisbury (0747) 870607; £20B/£35B

BECKHAMPTON   SU0868 Map 2

Waggon & Horses

A4 Marlborough–Calne; OS Sheet 173 reference 090689

In summer you can sit outside this lovely thatched inn at picnic-table sets among troughs of flowers on the big front cobbles, by the massive stone walls of the inn – a welcome sight to coachmen coming in from what was notorious as the coldest stretch of the old Bath road. Inside, the open-plan bar has beams in the shiny ceiling where walls have been knocked through, a large, old-fashioned high-backed settle on one side of the room, with a smaller one opposite, as well as red-cushioned Windsor chairs, leatherette stools and comfortably cushioned wall benches; the lounge is more cosy, but similarly furnished. A wide choice of bar food includes

Sunday opening is now 12–3 and 7–10.30 throughout England.

home-made soup (£1.25), lots of sandwiches (from £1), home-made pâté (£1.50), ploughman's (from £2.50), vegetarian lasagne (£2.95), salads (from £3.25), plaice (£4.95), gammon with pineapple (£5.25), steaks (from £6.75) and puddings like home-made fruit pie (£1.25); children's helpings on request. Well kept Wadworths IPA, 6X, Farmers Glory and in winter Old Timer on handpump. Fruit machine, trivia and piped music. Silbury Hill – a prehistoric mound – is just towards Marlborough, and Avebury stone circle and the West Kennet long barrow are very close too. Our tip for the new licensees, if they want to score quick popularity with readers, would be some modernisation of the gents. *(Recommended by Dennis Jones, Roger Cunningham, Deborah Frost, Frank Cummins, D H Voller, M C Howells)*

Wadworths   Licensees Bernie and Jackie Lucker   Real ale   Meals and snacks (not Mon evening)   Children in own room   Open 11–3, 6–11; closed evening 25 Dec

nr BRADFORD-ON-AVON   ST8060 Map 2
Cross Guns

Avoncliff; pub is across footbridge from Avoncliff Station (first through road left, heading N from river on A363 in Bradford centre, and keep bearing left), and can also be reached down very steep and eventually unmade road signposted Avoncliff – keep straight on rather than turning left into village centre – from Westwood (which is signposted from B3109 and from A366, W of Trowbridge); OS Sheet 173 reference 805600

This old-fashioned pub is popular in summer for its beautiful position with floodlit and terraced gardens overlooking the wide river Avon and a maze of bridges, aqueducts (the Kennet and Avon Canal) and tracks winding through this quite narrow gorge. We find it hard to draw firm conclusions about standards of service and so forth, as over the last few years no licensees have stayed here long enough to establish a clear pattern – and the pub changed hands again in the summer of 1989. The friendly new licensees are keen to make a go of things, so we're keeping our fingers crossed – let us know what you think. There's a large ancient fireplace with a smoking chamber behind it, stone walls, low seventeenth-century beams, and rush-seated chairs around plain sturdy oak tables. Bar food includes sandwiches (from 75p), home-made pâté, ploughman's (from £1.95), home-made steak and kidney pie (£2.99), various fish dishes including crab (£3.35), trout (£3.65) and lemon sole (£4.65), and steaks (from £4.95); well kept Badger Tanglefoot, Ruddles Best and County, Smiles Best and Ushers Best on handpump. Darts, dominoes, cribbage, fruit machine and piped music. Please note, they no longer do bedrooms. *(Recommended by Roger Cunningham, Deborah Frost, Chris Raisin, G Bloxsom, Philip King, Juliet Streatfield, Neil Evans, James and Susan Trapp, Nick Dowson, Alison Hayward, WHBM, Roger Huggins)*

Free house   Licensees Dave and Gwen Sawyer   Real ale   Meals and snacks   Open 11–2.30, 6–11 all year

CASTLE COMBE   ST8477 Map 2
White Hart

Village centre; signposted off B4039 Chippenham–Chipping Sodbury

In a lovely village, this friendly old stone pub is one of the most attractive buildings here (and is especially popular with summer visitors). The old-fashioned furnishings in the beamed and flagstoned main bar include an antique elm table as well as Windsor chairs, a traditional black wall bench built into the stone mullioned window, and a big winter log fire in the elegant stone fireplace. Bar food includes hot specials such as prawns in bacon, vegetarian dishes and a help-yourself salad bar in summer. Well kept Badger Best and Wadworths Farmers Glory on handpump, and a good range of country wines; darts, shove-ha'penny, dominoes and cribbage. A carpeted bar, decorated with copper and brass, leads off the main bar, there's a family-room, and more seats in a small central covered courtyard. You can also sit in the garden. *(Recommended by Lynne Sheridan, Bob West, Roger Huggins, H K Dyson, Len Beattie, Ted George, G Bloxsom, Rob and Gill Weeks, Roger Baskerville, W A Harbottle)*

Free house   Real ale   Meals (winter, not Sat or Sun) and snacks   Children in family-room   Parking nearby may be difficult; village car park is up steep hill   Open 10.30–2.30, 6–11

CHARLTON   ST9588 Map 2
Horse & Groom

B4040 towards Cricklade

The distinctive style in the left-hand lounge of this tiled stone pub includes attractive pine built-in stall seats and kitchen armchairs around scrubbed deal kitchen tables, a Turkey carpet, red velvet curtains, dark red Anaglypta walls (stripped to stone in some places), a pine-panelled bar counter and welcoming log fires in winter. A more spacious parquet-floored bar on the right has darts, dominoes and shove-ha'penny; friendly, chatty landlord. Bar food includes filled rolls (from 75p), soup (£1.45), filled baked potatoes (from £2.15), ploughman's (from £2.20), garlic mushrooms or smoked salmon pâté (£2.60), a half-pint of prawns with garlic mayonnaise (£2.80), and daily specials such as lasagne (£3.95), grilled pork chops with Dijon sauce (£4.85) or spring lamb casserole (£4.95); puddings such as treacle tart or orange and brandy chocolate mousse (£1.80). Well kept Archers Village, Moles and Wadworths 6X on handpump, good quality wines on a recently extended list. Tables with cocktail parasols are set out on the grass in front of the pub – the road doesn't carry much traffic. *(Recommended by Dick Brown; more reports please)*

Free house   Licensee Richard Hay   Real ale   Meals and snacks (not Sun evening or Mon) Restaurant (not Sun evening) tel Malmesbury (0666) 823904   Children over eight in restaurant   Open 12–2.30, 7–11; closed Sun evening, all day Mon

CHICKSGROVE   ST9629 Map 2
Compasses

From A30 5½ miles W of B3089 junction, take lane on N side signposted Sutton Mandeville, Sutton Row, then first left fork (small signs point the way to the pub, but at the pub itself, in Lower Chicksgrove, there may be no inn-sign – look out for the car park); OS Sheet 184 reference 974294

High-backed wooden settles form snug booths around tables on the mainly flagstone floor, the partly stripped stone walls are hung with farm tools, traps and brasses, and there are old bottles and jugs on the beams above the roughly timbered bar counter. A wide choice of reasonably priced, home-cooked bar food includes sandwiches, ploughman's, cod or plaice (£3), meat or vegetable chilli and lasagne (£3.25), steak and kidney pudding (£3.65), gammon and egg (£3.95) and steaks (from £6.75). Well-kept Adnams, Wadworths 6X and IPA on handpump; darts, shove-ha'penny, table skittles, dominoes and cribbage; prompt service. The lane past here carries very little traffic, and it's peaceful sitting out in the big garden or on the flagstoned farm courtyard. *(Recommended by Mr and Mrs R Marleyn, Nigel Paine; more reports please)*

Free house   Licensee P J Killick   Real ale   Meals and snacks   Restaurant   Children in eating area   Open 12–2.30 (3 Sat), 7–11 all year   Bedrooms tel Fovant (072 270) 318; £15/£30B

The opening hours we quote are for weekdays; in England and Wales, Sunday hours are now always 12–3, 7–10.30.

CORTON ST9340 Map 2

Dove ★ ⊗

Village signposted from A36 at Upton Lovell, SE of Warminster; this back road on the right bank of the River Wylye is a quiet alternative to the busy A36 Warminster–Wilton

Beautifully kept, this charming cottagey pub has attractive furnishings such as cushioned brick side benches, red bentwood cane chairs on the brick-tiled floor, a cane settle with colourful cushions by a pretty little chest-of-drawers in an alcove under the stairs, and a rug in front of the small log fire; some of the pictures are for sale. Tasty home-made food includes soup (£1.30), pâté (£1.85), variations on ploughman's with cheese, smoked loin of pork, home-cooked gammon, fish, quiche or pie (from £2.75), changing specials like herby lamb pudding and beef créole (£3.50) or Scotch salmon (£5.50), salad platters (£4.75), several vegetarian dishes and good puddings. Well kept Ushers Best on handpump and good wines; impeccable service. There are rustic seats on the grass behind the stone building, which has dovecotes by the climbing roses on its walls, and white doves on its tiled roof. Full marks for the charming ladies' lavatory here. *(Recommended by Mrs A Cotterill-Davies, B H Pinsent, Tony Gayfer, Dave Butler, Lesley Storey, Peter and Rose Flower, Norman Rose, DP, Mark Spurlock, K N Symons)*

Ushers (Watneys) Licensees Michael and Jane Rowse Real ale Meals and snacks (not Sun evening or Mon) Restaurant Children in restaurant Open 11–2.30, 6–11; closed Sun evening, Mon (exc bank hols), 2 weeks mid-Jan and first week Oct

DEVIZES SU0061 Map 2

Bear 🏠

Market Place

The big main bar in this imposing ex-coaching inn gives the striking impression of having been the centre of the town for three hundred years. Rambling through the central hall, it has old prints on the walls, muted red button-back cloth-upholstered bucket armchairs around oak tripod tables, black winged wall settles, fresh flowers here and there, and big logs on the fire in winter. An old-fashioned bar counter – with shiny black woodwork and small panes of glass – dispenses the well kept Wadworths IPA and 6X on handpump; it's brewed in the town, and from the brewery you can get it in splendid old-fashioned half-gallon earthenware jars. The Lawrence Room (named after Thomas Lawrence the portrait painter, whose father ran the inn), down steps from the main bar and separated from it by an old-fashioned glazed screen, has been attractively refurbished in a traditional style, with dark oak-panelled walls, a parquet floor, shining copper pans on the mantelpiece above the big open fireplace, and plates around the walls; it's useful for serving food until 10pm (11pm at the weekend) in the evening as well as at lunchtime: salads such as turkey and ham pie with cranberry topping (from £3.25) and daily hot dishes such as sausage plait with tomato, cheese and herbs or spicy meatloaf with tomato sauce (£3.25); evening extras include ratatouille lasagne (£3.95), a generous mixed grill (£4.25), chicken satay (£5.95) and steaks (from £6.50); tempting puddings. There is a special children's menu (from 60p, not after 8pm). Quick snacks, such as a good range of sandwiches (from 85p, vegetarian wholewheat crispbread sandwich £1.25, roast sirloin of beef with horseradish £1.65, bacon and tomato £1.55, smoked salmon with capers £3.25), ploughman's (from £1.40) and jumbo sausage and egg (£1.40), are served from the bar, with a wider choice ordered from the Lawrence Room waitress in the evening. Freshly ground coffee, Sunday roast lunches (£3.65), good breakfasts and afternoon teas;

Please tell us if any Lucky Dips deserve to be upgraded to a main entry, and why. No stamp needed: *The Good Pub Guide*, FREEPOST, London SW10 0BR.

cheerful, helpful service. *(Recommended by T J Maddison, P J Taylor, Dr J R Hamilton, Sarah Vickers, David Eversley, Gwen and Peter Andrews, Peter Burton, Doug Kennedy, Roger Broadie, Mr and Mrs G J Packer, Neal Clark, Kathleen and David Caig, Aubrey and Margaret Saunders)*

Wadworths   Licensees W K and J A Dickenson   Real ale   Meals and snacks Restaurant   Children in eating area   Frequent bar piano music   Open 11–11; closed 25 and 26 Dec   Bedrooms tel Devizes (0380) 2444; £40B/£55B

EBBESBOURNE WAKE   ST9824 Map 2

Horseshoe

The tables in this delightfully simple, homely downland pub are usually decorated with fresh flowers from the most attractive little garden where seats look out over the small, steep sleepy valley of the River Ebble. The spotless and carpeted public bar is a friendly parlour, its beams crowded with lanterns, farm tools and other bric-à-brac, and there's an open fire. Simple bar food consists of sandwiches, fresh trout pâté (£3), and ploughman's (£2.25) with other hot dishes such as home-made soup (90p), steak and kidney pie (£2.25, lunchtimes only) and lemon sole with crabmeat (£3.25); Sunday roasts. Well kept Adnams Bitter, Wadworths 6X and Farmers Glory drawn straight from the row of casks behind the bar; there may be guest beers – one reader found well kept Felinfoel Double Dragon on his visit; farm cider and malt whiskies. Darts and piped music. *(Recommended by Roy McIsaac, Prof H G Allen, Mr and Mrs F Hutchings, Byrne Sherwood, WFL, Nigel Paine, J Roots)*

Free house   Licensees Anthony and Patricia Bath   Real ale   Meals and lunchtime snacks Restaurant (evenings and Sun lunchtime only)   Children in eating area of bar   Open 11.30–2.30 (3 Sat), 6.30–11   Bedrooms tel Salisbury (0722) 780474; £18B/£30B

EVERLEIGH   SU2054 Map 2

Crown

New licensees have taken over this striking seventeenth-century building with its twin eighteenth-century wings, and as we went to press they were in the process of extensive restoration work. Home-cooked bar food varying from day to day might include ploughman's (from £2), cheese herbies (£2.50), hot peppered mackerel with horseradish or quails' eggs with celery salt (£2.75); vegetarian dishes; specialities are seafood in summer and game in winter. The well kept, airy bar has a mixture of upright rush-seated chairs, big Windsor armchairs and little easy chairs, lots of polished copper, sporting prints on the walls, fresh flowers, winter log fires and a restful, friendly atmosphere. Well kept Bass, Wadworths 6X and John Smiths Bitter on electric pump. There is a spacious walled garden which is safe for children. Dry-fly fishing for residents. *(Recommended by B and J Derry, Doug Kennedy, Stan Edwards, J B Whitley)*

Free house   Licensee Mrs Jacki Chapman   Real ale   Meals and snacks   Restaurant Children over five in restaurant   Open 11–3, 6–11   Bedrooms tel Collingbourne Ducis (026 485) 229; £25B/£45B

FORD   ST8374 Map 2

White Hart 🛏

A420 Chippenham–Bristol; follow Colerne sign at E side of village to find pub

This L-shaped, partly ivy-covered building has a cosy, friendly bar with heavy black beams supporting the white-painted boards of the ceiling, tub armchairs around polished wooden tables, small pictures and a few advertising mirrors on the walls, gentle lighting and a big log-burning stove in the old fireplace that's inscribed 1553. Good bar food includes sandwiches, home-made pâté (£1.95), curry (£3.10),

scampi or steak and kidney pie (£3.50), and gammon (£3.75); very good breakfasts. Well kept Badger Best and Tanglefoot, Fullers ESB and London Pride, Marstons Pedigree, Ruddles County, Smiles Exhibition, Tetleys Bitter and Wadworths 6X on handpump; efficient service. Dominoes, cribbage and – as some readers have particularly remarked on – piped music. In summer you can drink outside at the front of this little stone building, and there is another terrace behind, by a stone bridge over the By Brook, and for residents a secluded swimming-pool.
(Recommended by Dr Sheila Smith, Roger Cunningham, Deborah Frost, Alison Hayward, Nick Dowson, KC, Dr and Mrs B D Smith, Mr and Mrs J M Elden, Dennis Heatley, D S Rusholme, Frank Cummins, Neil and Elspeth Fearn, Pamela and Merlyn Horswell)

Free house   Licensee Bill Futcher   Real ale   Meals and snacks (12–2.15, 7–9.45) Restaurant   Children in eating area and restaurant   Open 11–3, 6–11 Mon–Fri; 11–11 Sat all year   Bedrooms tel Castle Combe (0249) 782213; £35B/£49B

GIDDEAHALL   ST8574   Map 2

Crown

A420 W of Chippenham

New licensees have taken over this sixteenth-century listed building, and the young couple who ran the pub for the previous people have since been working at the Fox & Badger in Wellow (a Somerset main entry). It is one of the most attractively laid out in the county, full of interesting details: a fluted stone plinth made from the base of an old column, little pillars holding up a velvet-fringed canopy, red plush wall seats (some in curtain-draped alcoves), Victorian ointment posters, two cases of small stuffed birds and a stuffed rough-legged buzzard, a crook and so forth over the mantelpiece, and a couple of wicker armchairs by the big log fireplace. A restaurant extension has been added. Good value food includes sandwiches (from 80p), platters of cheeses or mixed meats (from £2.10), three-egg omelettes (from £2.35) and steaks (from £7); puddings such as steamed golden roll or apple pie (£1.15); Sun lunch (£3.75). Well kept Marstons Pedigree, Moles, Smiles Exhibition, Wadworths 6X and Youngers Scotch and IPA on handpump; dominoes, cribbage and fruit machine. *(Recommended by Dr Sheila Smith, Gordon Hewitt, Roger Cunningham, Deborah Frost, Peter and Rose Flower, Aubrey and Margaret Saunders, Mr and Mrs G J Packer; more reports on the new regime please)*

Free house   Licensee Mark Grimshaw   Real ale   Meals and snacks   Restaurant tel Castle Combe (0249) 782229   Children welcome   Open 11–2.30, 6–11 all year; closed 25 and 26 Dec

GREAT WISHFORD   SU0735   Map 2

Royal Oak

In village, which is signposted from A36

The friendly main bar has cushioned pews, small seats and some easy chairs on its brown carpet, beams, and in winter a log fire at each end; a new lounge area is decorated with a multitude of antique fishing paraphernalia and there's a cheery family area with sturdy bleached wood tables. Well kept Ruddles County, Ushers Best and Websters on handpump, and country wines. The new licensees have changed the menu: home-made soup, sandwiches, a range of filled jacket potatoes (from £2.50), three-egg omelettes (from £3), burger (£3.75), Wiltshire ham and eggs (£3.85), lasagne (£4.50), steak and kidney pie (£4.95), vegetarian dishes such as vegetarian niçoise (£4) or mushroom and broccoli lasagne (£4.25) and steaks (from £6.50); fresh fish of the day is delivered five times a week; puddings like treacle roly-poly or bread-and-butter pudding (from £1.45). Children's menu;

Bar food is generally served 12–2 and 7–9 unless stated otherwise.

efficient, cheerful service. The garden behind the pub has swings. *(Recommended by Mr and Mrs F W Sturch, Helen Roe, Barry and Anne, Mr and Mrs C Austin, Gary Scott, Gordon Theaker, Mrs E M Brandwood, Keith Walton, Mr and Mrs D I Baddeley, Gwen and Peter Andrews, Roger Mallard)*

Ushers (Watneys)   Licensee Nigel Harding   Real ale   Meals and snacks   Restaurant tel Salisbury (0722) 790 229   *Children welcome   Live jazz Sun   Open 11–3, 6–11 all year; opens 8.30 for breakfasts*

HINDON   ST9132 Map 2

Lamb ★

B3089 Wilton–Mere

Over the last year we've had more favourable comments about this pub than any other in the county. It's quite clear that a star award is in order. The staff are friendly, the atmosphere relaxed and civilised, and the food and beer good. The two lower sections of the long bar are perhaps the nicest: one end has a window seat with a big waxed circular table, spindle-back chairs with tapestried cushions, a high-backed settle, brass jugs on the mantelpiece above the small fireplace, and a big kitchen clock; the middle – and main – area has a long polished table with wall benches and chairs, and a big inglenook fireplace. Up some steps, a third, bigger area has lots of tables and chairs. The varied choice of good bar food includes a very popular curry which comes with six side dishes (£4.25); soup (£1.30), sandwiches (from £1.40), toasties (from £1.60), home-made game pâté (£2.85), ploughman's (£2.95), fresh mussels (£3.25), home-made steak and game pie (£4.50), salads (from £4.95, poached salmon £6.50), grilled trout (£5.50); good Sun lunch (£9.50). Well kept Hook Norton and Wadworths 6X on handpump and a large choice of malt whiskies; good filter coffee. Shove-ha'penny; no dogs. There are picnic-table sets across the road (which is a good alternative to the main routes west).

(Recommended by J S Evans, J F and M Sayers, Henry Midwinter, Mrs P C Clark, S V Bishop, J S Rutter, Philip and Sheila Hanley, Sue Carlyle, P G Giddy, W A Gardiner, Mrs S A Bishop, K Baxter, Theo Schofield, HEG, Roger Broadie, John Townsend, Major and Mrs D R C Woods, A R Tingley, Mr and Mrs R Gammon, Mr and Mrs D I Baddeley, Major R A Colvile, Patrick Young, J and M Walsh)

Free house   Licensees A J Morrison and J Croft   Real ale   Meals and snacks (12–2, 7–10)   Restaurant   Children in eating area   Open 11–11 all year   Bedrooms tel Hindon (074 789) 573; £25(£30B)/£40(£50B)

KILMINGTON   ST7736 Map 2

Red Lion

Pub on B3092 Mere–Frome, 2½ miles S of Maiden Bradley

The bar in this 500-year-old pub has been extended, providing extra seating without losing the relaxed local atmosphere. The new area has a large window and is decorated with brasses, a large leather horse collar and hanging plates. The original part has flagstones, a curved high-backed black settle blocking off draughts from the door, red leatherette wall and window seats, lively photographs on the beams, a deep fireplace with a fine old iron fireback and a second, recently exposed large brick fireplace, both with log fires in winter. Home-made bar food includes three soups (£1), baked potatoes (from 65p), toasties (from 95p), open sandwiches (from £1.20), ploughman's (from £1.60), hot daily dishes such as game pie, vegetable lasagne or steak and kidney pie (£2.50) and salads (£2.50); food is now served in the evenings and includes ham and egg (£2.25), gammon steak (£2.75) and sirloin steak (£5.50). Well kept Bass under light blanket pressure and Butcombe Bitter on handpump, with quickly changing guest beers such as Adnams, Fullers London Pride, Marstons Pedigree and Ringwood Fortyniner; sensibly placed darts, dominoes, shove-ha'penny, spoofing and cribbage; friendly service. The black labrador is called Lady. Picnic-table sets in the large garden overlook White Sheet Hill (riding, hang gliding and radio-controlled gliders), and can be reached by a road at the side of the pub; the National Trust Stourhead Gardens are a mile away, and Longleat Safari Park is fairly handy too. *(Recommended by Lyn and Bill Capper, S V Bishop)*

Free house Licensee Christopher Gibbs Real ale Meals and snacks (not Mon and Tues eves) Children welcome until 9 Singer/guitarist every third Thurs evening Open 11–3, 6.30–11; closed lunchtime 25 Dec Bedrooms tel Maiden Bradley (098 53) 263; £10/£20

LACOCK ST9168 Map 2

Carpenters Arms

Made up of several buildings – the oldest dating from the 1500s – this attractively refurbished pub has several rambling cottagey areas. One room has a dresser filled with plates, and polished boards instead of the carpet elsewhere; another (on the way to the candle-lit raftered restaurant) has a plush porter's chair and a deep country-house sofa, and there are country wooden chairs unpainted or stripped to match the tables, as well as some older ones. It's decorated with old documents, bugles, trumpets, antlers, brass implements, old and modern prints, and lots of house-plants. Bar food includes home-made soup (£1.25), pâté (£2.25), ploughman's (from £2.50), omelettes or salads (from £3.25), mushroom Stroganoff (£3.75), steak and kidney pie (£4.50), steaks (from £7.75), daily specials and puddings (from £1.25); children's menu (£2.25). Well kept Ruddles County, Ushers Best and Websters Yorkshire on handpump; friendly service; piped music (may be rather loud). The bedrooms are by no means grand, but as we went to press we heard of plans to upgrade them. *(Recommended by W C M Jones, James Cane, Mrs E M Thompson, S V Bishop, G D Stafford, Mrs C Jennings, Philip King)*

Ushers (Watneys) Licensee Michael Duhig Real ale Meals and snacks (12–2, 7–10; limited menu during afternoon in summer) Restaurant (not Sun evening) Children in eating area Jazz Mon evening Open 11–11; 11–3, 6–11 in winter Bedrooms tel Lacock (024 973) 203; £25S/£35S (small shared lavatory)

George

The big central fireplace in this very friendly ancient inn has a three-foot treadwheel set into its outer breast, originally for a dog to drive the turnspit. There are upright timbers in the place of knocked-through walls making cosy corners, a low beamed ceiling, armchairs and Windsor chairs, seats in the stone-mullioned windows and flagstones just by the bar. Bar food includes sandwiches (from 90p), excellent Wiltshire ham, home-made dishes such as steak and kidney or cheese and onion pie, faggots or vegetarian dishes such as mushroom moussaka or spinach, mushroom and blue cheese crumble (all £2.95), and evening grills such as fresh trout or steaks (from £6.20). Well kept Wadworths IPA, 6X, and in winter Old Timer on handpump; good coffee. Darts, shove-ha'penny, dominoes, fruit machine and piped music. There are seats in the back garden, and a bench in front that looks over the main street. *(Recommended by Dr Sheila Smith, Tony Triggle, Alan Castle, Joan Olivier, Frank Cummins, David R Crafts)*

Wadworths Licensee John Glass Real ale Meals and snacks Restaurant tel Lacock (024 973) 263 Children welcome Open 11–11; 11–2.30, 6–10.30 in winter

Red Lion

High Street

Close to Lacock Abbey and the Fox Talbot Museum, this tall red brick Georgian inn has a friendly, pubby atmosphere in its long, friendly bar. It's divided into separate areas by cart shafts, yokes and other old farm implements, and decorated with branding irons hanging from the high ceiling, and plates, oil paintings, Morland prints, tools, and stuffed birds and animals on the partly panelled walls;

old-fashioned furniture includes a mix of tables and comfortable chairs, Turkey rugs on the partly flagstoned floor, and a fine old log fire at one end. Good home-made bar food includes soups (£1.90), ploughman's (£2.65), duck liver terrine and pickled damsons or smoked trout and garlic mayonnaise with home-baked bread (£2.95), filled baked potatoes (from £2.95), giant local sausages or home-made rissoles (£4.25), beef and orange casserole or chicken in tomato and tarragon sauce (£5.25) and puddings such as walnut and apricot crumble or sticky toffee pudding (£1.95); prices are slightly higher in the evening; good breakfast. Well kept Wadworths IPA, 6X, in summer Farmers Glory and in winter Old Timer on handpump; good wine by the glass; darts. They serve morning coffee from 10am. A stableblock is now used for teas, with fresh home-made scones. The pub is very popular in the latter half of the evening, particularly with younger people. *(Recommended by Gwen and Peter Andrews, Jean Morris, Mr and Mrs Maitland, Barbara Hatfield, L Walker, Nigel Williamson, Philip King, Joan Olivier, Jonathan Williams)*

Wadworths   Licensee John Levis   Real ale   Meals and snacks (11–2.30, 6.30–10) Children in eating area   Open 11–3, 6–11 (11–11 Sat in summer)   Bedrooms tel Lacock (024 973) 456; £25/£38(£45B)

nr LACOCK   ST9168 Map 2
Rising Sun   ★

Bowden Hill, Bewley Common; on back road Lacock–Sandy Lane

From the picnic-table sets among tubs of flowers on the two-level terrace outside this isolated little country pub, you can enjoy the magnificent view (especially at sunset) looking out over the Avon valley, some 25 miles or so. Inside, the L-shaped series of three rooms are refreshingly simple: one has a Victorian fireplace and sensible darts area; another has a mix of old chairs and a couple of basic kitchen tables on the stone floor, flowery cushioned wall benches, antlers on the wall, and dried flowers and plants in the windows; the third has a big case of stuffed birds, a stuffed badger, a grandfather clock, some old woodworking planes, a shotgun on the wall and a few country pictures. Bar food includes generous toasties (£1.20), sandwiches (from £1.25), smoked trout pâté (£2.05), ploughman's (from £2.10) and daily specials such as home-made leek and potato soup with Wiltshire bacon scone (£1.65), Wiltshire sausage or macaroni cheese (£2.65), home-made lasagne or moussaka (£3.25), lamb and apricot casserole (from £3.50) and home-made puddings such as chocolate fudge cake and apple strudel (from £1.15). Well kept Moles PA, Bitter, 97 and Landlord's Choice (brewed by Moles to the landlord's recipe) and Wadworths 6X on handpump, with several uncommon guest beers such as Bunces Best and Gibbs Mew Salisbury; friendly service. Dominoes, shove-ha'penny, cribbage and other card games; there are two Gordon setters and a friendly white and marmalade cat. *(Recommended by Peter and Rose Flower, Roger Cunningham, Deborah Frost, Joan Olivier, Frank Cummins; we're surprised to get so few reports here)*

Free house   Licensee Roger and Laura Catte   Real ale   Lunchtime snacks (not Mon or Sun)   Children welcome   Live music Weds evenings   Open 12–2.30 (11–3 Sat), 7–11; closed Mon lunchtime

LANDFORD   SU2519 Map 2
Cuckoo

Village signposted down B3079 off A36 Salisbury–Southampton; take first right turn towards Redlynch

Completely unspoilt, this thatched cottagey pub has a friendly little front parlour with lots of bird pictures on the papered walls, rustic seats and spindle-back chairs on its carpet, a stuffed cuckoo behind the bar, and a winter log fire. Two other rooms lead off, one with sensibly placed darts, dominoes and a juke box. Well kept

Badger Best and Tanglefoot, Bunces Best, and Wadworths IPA, 6X, Farmers Glory and winter Old Timer are tapped from casks down in a cool lower back room; food is confined to fresh filled rolls (from 55p), pies and Cornish pasties (85p), and ploughman's (£1.50); occasional weekend barbecues. The front lawn is patrolled by bantam cocks, and there are peacocks and rabbits in a pen at the side; there's a new pétanque pitch and a big play area has swings and a slide. *(Recommended by Dr and Mrs A K Clarke, WHBM)*

Free house   Licensees Derek and Jeane Proudley   Real ale   Snacks   Children in garden bar   Impromptu folk music gatherings Fri and Sat evenings   Open 11.30–3, 6–11 Mon–Fri; 11.30–11 Sat

LIMPLEY STOKE   ST7760 Map 2

Hop Pole

Coming S from Bath on A36, 1300 yds after traffic-light junction with B3108 get ready for sharp left turn down Woods Hill as houses start – pub at bottom; if you miss the turn, take next left signposted Limpley Stoke then follow Lower Stoke signs; OS Sheet 172 reference 781610

Part of this friendly pub dates back to 1350 when it was a monks' wine lodge, while partial rebuilding took place in 1580. The room on the right, with lots of dark wood panelling, has red velvet cushions for the settles in its alcoves, some slat-back and captain's chairs on its Turkey carpet, lantern lighting, a log fire, and the slow tick of a big kitchen clock. The spacious left-hand Avon Bar (with an arch to a cream-walled inner room) also has dark wood panelling, as well as pleasant furnishings, and a log-effect gas fire. Good value bar food includes burgers (from £1.30), Cumberland sausage and egg (£1.95), ratatouille with garlic bread or cauliflower cheese with mushrooms (both £2.25), good ploughman's or omelette (£2.45), salads, scampi, home-made fish pie or chicken and red peppers (£3.45); dishes only available in the evening include pork with apple and kiwi-fruit sauce, chicken and cider curry, poached cod fillet with Stilton and grape sauce or poached rainbow trout with almond and mushroom sauce (£4.50) and rump steak (£6.65); children's dishes (£1.75). Well kept Courage Best and Directors on handpump; darts, dominoes, cribbage, shove-ha'penny and piped music. Large, pleasant garden with chairs. *(Recommended by G J Lewis, M J Dyke, Chris Raisin, Peter and Rose Flower, Roger Cunningham, Deborah Frost, Nick Dowson, Alison Hayward, S J A Velate, M A and W R Proctor)*

Courage   Licensee Graham Claude Titcombe   Real ale   Meals and snacks (12–2, 7–9.30; 10 Fri and Sat)   Children in own room   Open 11–2.30 (3 Sat), 6–11 all year

LITTLE BEDWYN   SU2966 Map 2

Harrow

Village signposted off A4 W of Hungerford

Of the three rooms in this small but refreshingly light and airy village pub, the front one is the best for eating in. There's a mixture of country chairs and simple wooden tables on its well waxed boards (one table in the bow window), flowery curtains, pale walls with large-scale local Ordnance Survey maps and a big wood-burning stove. The two inner rooms are chattier; decorations include a fine brass model of a bull, and locally done watercolours and photographs for sale. From a regularly changing menu, the good, unpretentious, home-made food includes soup (£1.75), chicken liver pâté (£2.25), garlic mushrooms (£2.75), ploughman's with a choice of cheeses (£2.95), a vegetarian dish (£3.50), curry or chilli (£3.75), lasagne or moussaka (£3.95), pork cassoulet (£4.70), grilled trout (£5.25), shark and swordfish steaks or peppered rump steak (£7.95). Their puddings (£2.25) are good – especially the chocolate roulade. Well kept Hook Norton and Marstons Pedigree with two other guest beers such as Adnams, Arkells, Boddingtons, Exmoor and Youngs on handpump, with decent wines by the glass and a sensible small selection of malt whiskies. Service is quietly friendly and helpful, the atmosphere relaxed. On your way to the lavatories you'll go through what's recently become the village post office, with the original Victorian sit-up-and-beg counter. Bookings are encouraged, especially on Friday and Saturday evenings and for Sunday lunchtime; dominoes, cribbage, unobtrusive piped music. The long-haired Jack Russell is called Max. There are seats out in the garden, and the pub's a couple of hundred yards from the Kennet and Avon Canal. *(Recommended by Frank Cummins, D J Clifton, C H Pipe-Wolferstan, D Stephenson)*

Free house   Licensees Richard Denning   Real ale   Meals and snacks (12–1.45, 7–9.30; not Sun evening, not Mon exc bank hols lunchtime)   Restaurant (not Sun evening) tel Marlborough (0672) 870871   Children over ten allowed   Open 12–2.30, 5.30 (7 Sat)–11 all year; closed Mon lunchtime exc bank hols

LOWER WOODFORD   SU1235 Map 2

Wheatsheaf

Leaving Salisbury northwards on A360, The Woodfords signposted first right after end of speed limit; then bear left

The two main areas of the extensive dining-bar are linked by a miniature footbridge over a little indoor goldfish pond. Various rambling side areas include one with attractive William Morris wallpaper, and besides cushioned wall seats there are sturdy pale varnished tables and chairs on parquet or brown carpet. A massive choice of bar food includes a good few vegetarian dishes such as broccoli bake (£3.25), as well as home-made soup (£1.10), ploughman's (from £2.10), salads (from £2.40), local ham (£3.75), lasagne (£3.85), home-made steak and kidney pie (£3.95), steaks (from eight-ounce rump, £6.50) and Dover sole (£7.75); there are several children's dishes (£1.40) and daily specials. Badger Best and Tanglefoot on handpump, and a good open fire; service stays friendly even when it's busy. The snug separate Cabin Bar, with cask seats and an inglenook log fire, has darts, cribbage, dominoes and a fruit machine. There are tall trees around the big and peaceful walled garden, which has picnic-table sets, a climber and swings. *(Recommended by J A Simms, JMW, WHBM, Nigel Paine)*

Badger   Licensees Peter Charlton and Jennifer Falconer   Real ale   Meals and snacks (12–2, 7–10)   Children in eating area   Open 11–2.30, 6.30–11 (10.30 in winter)

MALMESBURY   ST9287   Map 2

Suffolk Arms

Tetbury Hill; B4014 towards Tetbury, on edge of town

A stone pillar supports the beams in the imaginative knocked-through bar here, leaving a big square room around the stairs which climb up apparently unsupported. There are soft lights among the copper saucepans and warming pans on the stripped stone walls, and comfortable seats such as a chintz-cushioned antique settle, sofa and easy chairs, captain's chairs, and low Windsor armchairs; there's also a lounge. Home-made bar food includes sandwiches (from £1), filled baked potatoes (from £2.25), ploughman's, salads (from £3.45), steak and kidney pie, chicken marsala, a range of fresh fish including swordfish steak (£4.25) and skate (£4.35); vegetarian dishes and home-made puddings. Wadworths IPA and 6X on handpump; large range of wines; obliging service. The neat lawns outside have some seats. *(Recommended by Alison Hayward, Nick Dowson, Mr and Mrs R Marleyn, P H Fearnley)*

Wadworths   Licensee John Evans   Real ale   Meals and snacks (12–2, 7–10)   Children over ten in eating area   Open 11–2.30, 6–11 all year

It's very helpful if you let us know up-to-date food prices when you report on pubs.

MARKET LAVINGTON SU0154 Map 2

Green Dragon

High Street; B3098, towards Upavon

Listed by the Department of Environment as a building of special architectural or historical interest, this early seventeenth-century pub is given a good deal of character by its landlord. The rambling bar has fancy Victorian wallpaper or stripped deal panelling, old kitchen chairs, smart dining-room chairs or massive boxy settles, a Spy cartoon of Sir Henry Irving, photographs of the town in the old days and Highland views, and corn dollies. Good home-made bar food, for which they won a local newspaper award, includes soup (95p), sandwiches, ham and eggs or liver and bacon (£3.50), mixed grill (£3.75), lasagne or lamb kebab (£4.15), steak and mushroom pie (£4.25), fresh plaice, and puddings such as lemon cheesecake or chocolate cream pie (from £1); they use home-cooked and locally bought meat and vegetables (when not grown in their garden); prices of some dishes may be slightly more in the evenings. Well kept Wadworths IPA and 6X on handpump and a wide range of wines. Darts and bar billiards in a raised, communicating section, also shove-ha'penny, dominoes and cribbage; classical piped music. There's a garden fenced off behind the car park. *(Recommended by Alan Curry, Dr and Mrs Crichton, S Leggate; more reports please)*

Wadworths   Licensees Gordon and Elaine Godbolt   Real ale   Meals and snacks (12.30–2, 8–9.30; not Sun, not 25 and 26 Dec)   Restaurant (closed Sun) tel Devizes (0380) 813235 Open 11.30–2.30, 6–11; closed evening 25 Dec

NORTON ST8884 Map 2

Vine Tree ★ 🍺

4 miles from M4 junction 17; A429 towards Malmesbury, then left at Hullavington, Sherston signpost, then follow Norton signposts; in village turn right at Foxley signpost, which takes you into Honey Lane

Remote in spite of the fairly handy motorway, this warm-hearted country pub has well kept Fullers London Pride, Wadworths 6X, a guest beer such as Devenish or Everards Tiger and a beer brewed for them by a Mr Kemp (a light well balanced taste reminiscent of Courage Bitter – good value), as well as decent wines. Home-made bar food includes soup, ploughman's (from £1.95), open prawn sandwiches or deep-fried courgettes (£2.50), burgers and nutburgers (£3.25), beef kebabs (£4.25), chicken cooked in white wine or gammon (£5.95) and steaks from ten-ounce rump (£6.95) to thirty-ounce whoppers (£15.95), with game in season; puddings are all home made and include lemon crunch, trifle and rhubarb and peach pie; pleasant, efficient service. The décor is almost like that of a successful city wine bar – yet the atmosphere is cosy and pubby, and clearly appeals to a very broad cross-section of the local community. The three smallish rooms, which open together, have lots of stripped pine, candles in bottles on the tables (the lighting's very gentle), some old settles, ochre or dark green walls, and lively decoration that includes plates and small sporting prints, carvings, hop-bines and a mock-up mounted pig's mask. There are picnic-table sets under under cocktail parasols in a vine-trellised back garden with young trees and tubs of flowers, and a well fenced separate play area with a fine thatched fortress and other goodies; they have stables at the back. *(Recommended by Julie Trott, Peter and Rose Flower, Miles Elwell, Ken Wright)*

Free house   Licensees Ken Camerier, Pete and Jean Draper   Real ale   Meals and snacks (12–2, 7–10)   Restaurant tel Tetbury (0666) 837654   Children in eating area of bar and restaurant   Open 12–2.30, 6.30–11; closed Tues

If you stay overnight in an inn or hotel, they are allowed to serve you an alcoholic drink at any hour of the day or night.

PITTON SU2131 Map 2

Silver Plough ★ 🍷

Village signposted from A30 E of Salisbury

Though they don't aim to serve many snacks in this well run, friendly pub, they do filled freshly baked rolls, fresh vegetable soup (£1.50), home-made pâté (£2.95), a good ploughman's with a handsome choice of cheeses (£3) and in the evening chilli con carne or lasagne (£3.50). Their more substantial bar meals, though, make this a place to eat out in style. With frequent variations, these might include wild boar terrine, marinated herring fillets (£3.95), green New Zealand mussels (£4.50), various pasta dishes such as spicy chicken with Greek yoghurt (£5.25), game pie (£6.50), halibut with cucumber, vodka and cream sauce (£7.50), lamb marinated in garlic and herbs or salmon with basil sauce (£8.50), lobster with wild mushroom sauce (£14.50), and excellent sea bass with ginger and soya sauce; their particular strengths are fresh fish and seafood, and game in season, and choice is best from Wednesdays onwards. The comfortable front bar has seats on the Turkey carpet that include half a dozen red-velvet-cushioned antique oak settles, one elaborately carved beside a very fine reproduction of an Elizabethan oak table. Its black beams are strung with hundreds of antique boot-warmers and -stretchers, pewter and china tankards, copper kettles, brass and copper jugs, toby jugs, earthenware and glass rolling pins, painted clogs, glass net-floats, coach horns and so forth. The timbered white walls have pictures that include Thorburn and other gamebird prints, original Craven Hill sporting cartoons, and a big naval battle glass-painting. The back bar is broadly similar, though more restrained, with a big winged high-backed settle, cased antique guns, substantial pictures, and – like the front room – flowers on its tables. Well kept Courage Best and Directors, Wadworths 6X and John Smiths on handpump, decent wines, good country wines, and a worthy range of spirits (Macallan on optic, for instance – always the sign of a licensee who knows his whiskies). The separate skittle alley has a fruit machine, and there may be unobtrusive piped music. There are picnic-table sets and other tables under cocktail parasols on a quiet lawn, with an old pear tree. *(Recommended by Mrs M Morawetz, Gordon and Daphne, TBB, Gavin Udall, John Derbyshire, N I Pratt, Alan Symes, Gordon Hewitt, Alan Skull, J M Watkinson, Ian Scrivens, Dr S P K and C M Linter, J B Whitley, Wayne Brindle)*

Free house Licensee Michael Beckett Real ale Meals and snacks Restaurant tel Farley (072 272) 266 Children in restaurant and skittle alley Occasional guitarist Open 11–2.30, 6–10 all year; closed 25 Dec

POTTERNE ST9958 Map 2

George & Dragon 🛏

A360 beside Worton turn-off

This fifteenth-century thatched cottage – extensively restored – was built for the Bishop of Salisbury. Of the original hall, you can still see the fireplace and old beamed ceiling – which is decorated with banknotes from around the world, box matches, and colourful toby jugs; furnishings include old bench seating and country-style tables. Bar food includes sandwiches (from 75p), home-made soup (£1), ploughman's (£1.50), filled baked potatoes (from £2), salads (from £2.55), four home-made daily specials such as lasagne (£2.60), home-made steak (£2.75), faggots and bacon (£2.80) or roast beef with Yorkshire pudding (£3), steaks (from £6.50), and various puddings such as peach or apple crumble (£1.40); good breakfasts. Well kept Wadworths IPA and 6X on handpump; friendly landlord. A separate room has pool and fruit machine; also, darts, shove-ha'penny, dominoes and cribbage, and there's a full skittle alley in the old stables. Through a hatch beyond the pool-room there's a unique indoor .22 shooting gallery. It opens on a twenty-five-yard shoulder-high tube, broad enough at its mouth to rest your elbows in, but narrowing to not much more than the width of the target. The small bull is an electric bell-push, which rings when hit. After your nine shots (two for practice), you pull a rope which lifts a brush from a whitewash bucket to whiten the target for the next marksman. A museum of hand-held agricultural implements has been opened at the pub. There's a pleasant garden and a sun-trap yard with a grapevine. The simple bedrooms are good value. *(Recommended by Gwen and Peter Andrews, Philip King, B K Plumb)*

Wadworths   Licensee Roger Smith   Real ale   Meals and snacks (not Mon)   Children in games-room   Open 12–2.30, 6.30–11 all year   Bedrooms tel Devizes (0380) 2139; £12.50/£23.50

RAMSBURY   SU2771 Map 2

Bell

Village signposted off B4192 (still shown as A419 on many maps) NW of Hungerford, or from A4 W of Hungerford

Separated by a chimneybreast with a wood-burning stove, the two bar areas in this well kept and civilised pub have polished tables, fresh flowers, and window settles in two sunny bay windows (one with Victorian stained-glass panels); no noisy machines or piped music. Bar food includes soup (£1.50), salads (from £3), spaghetti bolognese, toad-in-the-hole or ratatouille (£3.10) and speciality pies (£3.60). Well kept Wadworths IPA and 6X on handpump; charming service from the barmaid dressed in black and white. There are picnic-tables on the raised lawn. Roads lead from this quiet village into the downland on all sides. *(Recommended by GB, CH, Lyn and Bill Capper, Frank Cummins, Mr and Mrs W Smurthwaite; more reports please)*

Free house   Real ale   Meals and snacks (not Sat evening)   Restaurant tel Marlborough (0672) 20230   Children in room between bar and restaurant and in restaurant   Open 10–2.30, 6–11

SALISBURY   SU1429 Map 2

The pubs mentioned here are all within a short stroll of one another. The George, which used to be one of the country's finest old inns – Shakespeare probably performed in its yard – has now been rebuilt as a shopping arcade, but its façade is still well worth a look, and an upstairs coffee shop gives some idea of what it used to be like inside

Avon Brewery

Castle Street

Though the theatre next door is long gone and many customers now come instead from the neighbouring auction rooms, the law courts and the forces, the thriving atmosphere still seems vaguely theatrical. Outside, mosaic tilework and the elegant curved façade make it one of the city's prettiest pubs. Inside, the long narrow bar, divided by little balustered partitions, is attractively decorated with lots of pictures (often patriotic or military), framed ensigns, cigarette cards, decorative china and frilly wall-lamps. Behind, a narrow garden runs down to the River Avon. The atmosphere's very companionable. Good bar food includes sandwiches (from 95p, well filled crispy bacon £1.20, steak £2.15), hot dogs (£1.20), filling soups such as lentil with ham and sausage (£1.25), filled baked potatoes (£1.30), four lunchtime hot dishes such as home-made steak and kidney pie, vegetarian flan, seafood pancake or breast of chicken in filo pastry (£3) and specials such as venison sausages with a compote of green lentils, onions and garlic (with a suggested wine to accompany it); three-course supper menu (£8.95 – please note they don't take reservations). Well kept Eldridge Pope Dorset, Dorchester and Royal Oak on handpump; quite a few wines by the glass (and the bottle), and a nice idea is to have changing seasonal wines; good service. Fruit and trivia machines, shove-ha'penny, cribbage, a rack of newspapers and classical piped music. The bar broadens out at the back, with darts and a dainty Victorian fireplace. *(Recommended by Don Mulcock, R Inns, Byrne Sherwood, Col E Richardson)*

Eldridge Pope   Licensee Duncan Broom   Real ale   Meals and snacks (not Sat evening, not Sun)   Well behaved children welcome until 7.30   Occasional folk music   Open 11–11; 11–3, 4.30–11 in winter

Haunch of Venison ★

1 Minster Street, opposite Market Cross

Parts of this building date from about 1430, when it was the church house for the church of St Thomas, just behind. The chatty little downstairs bar has massive beams in the ochre ceiling, stout red-cushioned oak benches built into its timbered walls, genuinely old pictures, a black and white tiled floor, an open fire, an old-fashioned – and as far as we know unique – pewter bar counter with a rare set of antique taps for gravity-fed spirits and liqueurs, and an utterly genuine atmosphere of cheerful friendliness; a tiny snug opens off the entrance lobby. Well kept Courage Best and Directors on handpump; helpful, efficient staff. A quiet and cosy upper panelled room has a small paned window looking down on to the main bar, a splendid fireplace that dates back some 600 years, antique leather-seat settles, and a nice carved oak chair dating back nearly 300 years. In 1903 workmen found a smoke-preserved mummified hand holding some eighteenth-century playing-cards in here; it's now behind glass in a small wall slit. Lunchtime bar food – served in the lower half of the restaurant – includes sandwiches (from 90p, toasties 15p extra), delicious home-made soup (£1), baked potatoes (from £1.20), ploughman's (from £1.90), home-made pies such as tasty game, ham and mushroom or splendid steak and kidney (£1.70), savoury pancakes (£3), daily specials such as good chicken curry or peppered beef (£2), and good puddings (95p); attentive and friendly service. *(Recommended by Leith Stuart, Mr and Mrs K J V, Klaus and Elizabeth Leist, Ian Phillips, Gary Scott, Matthew Pringle, Gordon and Daphne, S J A Velate, Chris Fluck, J P Berryman, B S Bourne, Neville Burke, Dr A V Lewis, Nigel Paine, Dr John Innes)*

Courage   Licensees Antony and Victoria Leroy   Real ale   Snacks (not Sun evening) and lunchtime meals   Restaurant (closed Sun evenings Oct–June) tel Salisbury (0722) 22024   Children in eating area and restaurant   Nearby parking may be difficult   Open 11–11 all year

Kings Arms 🛏

St John Street; the main one-way street entering city centre from S

The dark-panelled bars in this creaky old inn have red leatherette benches built around their walls: one has attractive Windsor armchairs under its heavy beams, with carving around its fireplace and door; the other, more local, has a trivia machine and maybe piped music. The panelling in the heavily beamed restaurant, which has snug high-backed settles, is considerably older. There is Tudor timbering, and the fireplaces are of the same Chilmark stone as the cathedral, so may be as old as it. Well kept Ruddles County and Ushers Best on handpump; friendly staff. Bar food includes soup (£1), sandwiches (from £1.25, elaborate toasties £2.75), summer salad buffet (£2.75) and hot daily specials such as lasagne, pork chops in cider or steak and kidney pie (all £3.25). *(Recommended by Gary Scott, Dr John Innes; more reports please)*

Chef & Brewer (Watneys)   Real ale   Meals and snacks   Restaurant   Children welcome   Open 11–2.30, 6–11 all year   Bedrooms tel Salisbury (0722) 27629; £35B/£51B

SANDY LANE   ST9668 Map 2

George

A342 Chippenham–Devizes

More like a small manor house than a pub, this fine Georgian building has wooden benches and tables in front, with picnic table-sets on a side lawn; it overlooks a small green just off the main road. Inside, the neat, carpeted main bar has comfortable cushioned wall benches, decorative wall beams, horsebrasses, old pistols and photographs and a log fire; an arch leads through to the attractive back lounge. Good value, home-made food includes soup (£1), burgers (£1.60), ploughman's (£1.80), very good moussaka, fisherman's pie (£2.95), plaice (£3.20), steak and kidney pie, steak (£5.80), duck with home-made port and orange sauce (£7) and cold puddings. Well kept Wadworths 6X and IPA on handpump; darts and piped music; pleasant, friendly service. *(Recommended by Mary Rayner, John and Pat Smyth, Frank Cummins, S G Game, David R Crafts)*

Wadworths　Licensee T J M Allington　Real ale　Meals and snacks (12–2, 7–10.30) Children in eating area　Open 11–3, 6.30–11 all year

SEMLEY　ST8926　Map 2

Benett Arms ★ ⊨

Turn off A350 N of Shaftesbury at Semley Ind Estate signpost, then turn right at Semley signpost

Separated by a flight of five carpeted steps, the two cosy rooms of the bar in this very friendly and relaxed little village inn have deep leather sofas and armchairs, one or two settles and pews, ornaments on the mantlepiece over the log fire, a pendulum wall clock, carriage lamps for lighting, and hunting prints. Down by the thatched-roof bar servery, the walls are stripped stone; upstairs, there is hessian over a dark panelling dado. Attractively presented, good bar food served by a neat waitress includes home-made soup (£1.20), ploughman's (£2.30), omelette (from £2.50), deep-fried cod (£2.95), local ham and egg, lasagne or home-made steak and kidney pie (£3), salads (from £3), freshwater trout (£3.50), a variety of fresh fish delivered from Poole including lemon sole and salmon, gammon with pineapple (£4), scampi (£4.25), steak (£7), and home-made puddings such as apple pie or chocolate mousse with rum (£1.50); children's menu; Sunday roasts (from £6.50); good breakfasts. Gibbs Mew Premium and Salisbury on handpump and kept under light blanket pressure; good house wines and a wide range of spirits. Dominoes, cribbage and piped music. There are seats outside. Well behaved dogs welcome. *(Recommended by J M Smith, B and J Derry, John Nash, Philip King, Colin and Caroline, Nigel Paine)*

Gibbs Mew　Licensees Annie and Joe Duthie　Real ale　Meals and snacks (12–2, 7–10; not 25 Dec)　Restaurant (not Sun evening)　Children welcome　Open 11–2.30, 6–11; closed 25 Dec　Bedrooms tel East Knoyle (074 783) 221/469; £21B/£35B

SEEND　ST9461　Map 2

Barge

Seend Cleeve; signposted off A361 Devizes–Trowbridge, between Seend village and signpost to Seend Head

Closed at the end of 1986 and then virtually derelict, this tiled and stone-built canalside pub has now been extended and brilliantly rehabilitated by Wadworths. The bargee theme has been carried through with great panache, perhaps most memorably in the intricately painted Victorian flowers which cover the ceilings and run in a waist-high band above the deep green lower walls. More bargee paintwork includes some milkchurn seats among a distinctive mix of other attractive seats, including the occasional small oak settle among the rugs on the parquet floor. There's a pretty Victorian fireplace, big bunches of dried flowers, big sentimental engravings, a well stocked aquarium, and crushed red velvet curtains for the big windows. Bar food includes soup (£1), open sandwiches (from £1.50, prawn £2.95), filled baked potatoes (from £1.50), ploughman's (from £1.75), chilli (£1.95), plaice or haddock (£2.65), lasagne (£3.25), steak and kidney or game pie

(£3.50), eight-ounce rump steak (£5.25) and daily specials. Well kept Wadworths IPA and 6X on handpump, with Farmers Glory in summer and Old Timer in winter; friendly, attentive staff. The neat waterside garden, with moorings by a humpy bridge, has picnic-table sets among former streetlamps; besides a busy bird table, nice touches include the weatherdrake and the good inn-sign. This is a peaceful spot. *(Recommended by Roger Cunningham, Deborah Frost, B R Woolmington, Lord Johnston)*

Wadworths   Licensee Christopher Moorley Long   Real ale   Meals and snacks (12–2, 7–9.30; evening food until 10 Fri and Sat)   Well behaved children in eating area of bar   Open 11–2.30, 6–11 all year

UPAVON   SU1355   Map 2

Antelope 🏮 🛏

3 High Street; village on junction A345/A342

The simple but friendly lounge bar of this seventeenth-century village inn has an interesting antique wheel-driven water pump at one end, a good winter log fire at the other. It's not a big room: wall settles around dark tables, stools at the long bar counter, and a little bow-windowed games area with darts, cribbage, dominoes, bar billiards and a couple of fruit machines opening off. A very wide range of food includes soup (£1.10), fresh-baked filled French sticks (£1.50), ploughman's (from £1.95), a vegetarian dish or pitta bread stuffed with lamb and garlicky mushrooms (£2.50), steak and kidney pie (£2.95), poached tuna (£3.75), gammon and peaches (£3.95), salmon (£4.95), steaks (from £5.50), masses of puddings such as strawberry puffs with butterscotch sauce (mainly £1.50) and a good few interesting specials such as fresh oysters (£1 apiece), smoked salmon quiche (£3.25) and lamb biriani (£4.20); a good range of fresh fish on Fridays includes dressed crab, whole plaice and Dover sole, and on Wednesday evenings they have a vast array of cheeses. Food can also be eaten in an attractively decorated restaurant with another log fire. Well kept Wadworths IPA and 6X on handpump, mulled wine in winter, notably good service, piped music. *(Recommended by Mary Rayner)*

Wadworths   Licensees Derrick and Christine Bragg   Real ale   Meals and snacks Restaurant   Children welcome   Open 11–2.30 (3 Sat), 6–11 all year   Bedrooms tel Stonehenge (0980) 630206; £15/£28

WOOTTON RIVERS   SU1963   Map 2

Royal Oak 🏮

Village signposted from A346 Marlborough–Salisbury and B3087 E of Pewsey

By the Kennet and Avon Canal, this pretty sixteenth-century thatched pub is very popular for its wide choice of good value food. Lots of specials might include smoked salmon pâté (£3.25), vegetables with savoury dip (£3.95), pan-fried mackerel with gooseberry sauce (£4.75), home-made steak and kidney pie (£5; one reader thought it the best he'd ever eaten), roast lamb (£8.50) or grilled Dover sole (£11.50). Regular dishes run from soup or sandwiches (from £1) through ploughman's (£1.75), basket meals (from £1.75) and lots of salads to chicken Kiev (£6.75) and steaks (from £7.50); puddings such as very good fresh fruit Pavlova. The L-shaped dining lounge (where they take table bookings – people dress up to come and dine here) has a low ceiling with partly stripped beams, partly glossy white planks, slat-back chairs, armchairs and some rustic settles around good tripod tables, a wood-burning stove, and a friendly atmosphere; it's decorated with discreetly colourful plates and small mainly local prints, drawings, watercolours and photographs. Well kept Wadworths 6X tapped from the cask, decent wines (running up to some distinguished ones), and jugs of Pimms; good service. The timbered bar on the right is comfortably and more or less similarly furnished, though with fewer tables – so seems more spacious; it has darts, pool, dominoes, cribbage, fruit machine and juke box. There are tables under cocktail parasols in the back gravelled yard, by the car park. The thatched and timbered village is very attractive. *(Recommended by John and Pat Smyth, Mr and Mrs J D Cranston, Dr C S Shaw, Chris Raisin, HNJ, PEJ, Stan Edwards, Jim Gavin, Anna Jeffery, Jack Charles, Lady Quinny)*

Free house   Licensees John and Rosa Jones   Real ale   Meals and snacks (not Sun evenings Oct–June, nor 26 Dec)   Restaurant   Children in restaurant and area partly set aside until 8.30   Open 11–3 (3.30 Sat), 6–11; opens 7 in winter   Bedrooms (in adjoining house) tel Marlborough (0672) 810322; £17.50S/£27.50S

Lucky Dip

Besides the fully inspected pubs, you might like to try these Lucky Dips recommended to us and described by readers (if you do, please send us reports):

Aldbourne [SU2675], *Blue Boar*: Very small single-bar pub with few chairs; wonderful for warm evening with trestle tables overlooking the village green and fourteenth-century church in one of the prettiest villages in the county; stuffed boar's head over attractive fireplace, well kept Wadworths 6X, limited food *(Neville Burke, Mary Rayner)*; *Crown*: Pleasant, welcoming, slightly up-market pub with huge log fire, quiet piped music and pleasant, helpful licensee; standard range of bar food with several daily specials, all at reasonable prices *(HNJ, PEJ, Mary Rayner)*

Alderbury [SU1827], *Green Dragon*: Much-modernised fifteenth-century village pub with Courage real ales; Dickens, using it as the Blue Dragon in *Martin Chuzzlewit*, cheekily named its landlady Mrs Pugin after the wife of his friend the neighbouring grandee (who designed the Houses of Parliament) *(LYM)*

Amesbury [Church St; SU1541], *Antrobus Arms*: Quiet, comfortable and relaxed with good food, no piped music and beautiful garden with cedar tree; bedrooms *(Peter Burton)*; [High St] *George*: Rambling coaching-inn with unusually extensive surviving coach yard; well kept Gibbs Mew Salisbury, limited range of cheap bar food and quick, friendly service; fruit machine, piped music, pool in public bar; bedrooms – more reports please *(Robert Gomme, Roger Broadie, LYM and others)*; [Earls Court Rd] *Greyhound*: Well cooked and generously served food, friendly service and Ruddles County, Ushers and Websters ales *(Jenny and Michael Back)*

Atworth [ST8666], *White Hart*: Friendly pub in nice Cotswold village with very good three-course Sun roast and other food; very popular with locals *(Brian and Rosemary Wilmot, Roger Cunningham, Deborah Frost)*

Avebury [A361; SU0969], *Red Lion*: Right in the heart of the stone circles – much-modernised comfortable thatched pub with Whitbreads and other real ales, friendly staff, simple but good food inc steaks and apple pie

in interesting dining-room; children's room *(Joan Olivier, GB, CH, LYM and others)*

Axford [SU2370], *Red Lion*: Good place to wind up after a walk, with tables outside looking down over a field toward the Kennet, with the trees of Savernake on the hilltop by road; good value home-made soup and pleasant puddings *(Mrs A Sheard, Mary Rayner, HNJ, PEJ)*

Badbury [very near M4 junction 15 – A345 S; SU1980], *Plough*: Well kept Arkells, basic bar food *(R G Ollier)*

☆ **Barford St Martin** [junction A30/B3098 W of Salisbury; SU0531], *Green Dragon*: Old-fashioned panelled front bar with big log fire and larger games bar in pub; under friendly new management with reasonably priced good food and well kept Badger beer; bedrooms clean and simple; more news please *(Mr and Mrs R C Abbott, Colonel and Mrs L N Smyth, S G Game, LYM)*

Beckington [Bath Rd/Warminster Rd; ST8051], *Woolpack*: Used to be a stop-off for condemned men on the way to the gibbet for a last drink; one unfortunate individual refused this option, was taken up the hill and hanged; five minutes later his reprieve arrived from London; good food range *(Mark Spurlock)*

Berwick St John [ST9323], *Talbot*: Unspoilt heavy-beamed bar in friendly Ebble Valley pub, huge inglenook fireplace, well kept Badger real ales, sandwiches and ploughman's (summer), tables on back lawn with swings for children; warmly welcoming landlady; on start GWG35 *(LYM)*

Biddestone [ST8773], *Biddestone Arms*: Well kept village pub with simple but comfortable lounge, games in public bar, reasonably priced food such as steak and kidney pie, well kept Ushers Best and PA and Wadworths 6X, swings in fairy-lit garden *(Roger Cunningham, Deborah Frost, Mrs Carol Mason, Mr and Mrs John Smyth, BB)*; *White Horse*: Interesting, rambling pub overlooking village duck-pond in extremely picturesque village; friendly atmosphere, very good lasagne, casseroles such as

meatballs, chicken in garlic and beef in horseradish from blackboard, garden with tables; friendly service *(Roger Huggins, Roger Cunningham, Deborah Frost, Barry and Anne)*
Boscombe [Tidworth Rd; SU2038], *Plough*: Very enthusiastic licensee who is progressively upgrading and updating (tastefully); soon to have food and large garden; more news please *(Mark Spurlock)*
Box [off A4 E of junction with A365 – sharp narrow turn; ST8268], *Chequers*: Undeniably attractive building with ancient stonework, log fires, oak-parquet floor and traditional furnishings; Watneys-related real ales, traditional games, and featured as main entry in previous editions for good simple food and warm welcome; but food service stopped early 1989 and in spring pub closed altogether – more news please *(LYM)*; [A4, Bath side] *Northey Arms*: Friendly, relaxed pub recently reopened after several months redecorating with one large bar with deep red walls, wooden tables, chairs and window seats, homely décor; good wine list; young team of staff dressed in sweatshirts, small range of well cooked home-made bar food, children given Easter eggs on Easter Sun and made welcome; panoramic view of Box valley *(ADE, Roger Cunningham, Deborah Frost, Mr and Mrs E J Smith)*; [Box Hill; off A4 just W of Box] *Quarrymans Arms*: Pleasant, modernised hilltop pub with fine food such as tuna or cauliflower and mushroom bake; real ales include Butcombe, Moles Bitter and Wadworths 6X and guest beers such as Adnams Broadside and Oakhill Yeoman; new furniture, interesting photographs and tools linked to local stone quarries; major building developments taking place as we went to press inc addition of bedrooms – more news please *(Roger Cunningham, Deborah Frost, Peter and Rose Flower)*; *Queens Head*: Good local with lounge and bar, friendly staff and simple, adequate bar food *(Roger Cunningham, Deborah Frost)*
Bradford Leigh [ST8362], *Plough*: Previously run-down pub with fairly new licensees who are trying very hard; well kept beer and very good, reasonably priced bar food *(B R Woolmington)*
Bradford on Avon [35 Market St; ST8261], *Ancient Fowl*: Reasonably priced restaurant with bar *(Graeme Barnes)*; [Silver St] *Bunch of Grapes*: Converted shop, spotlessly clean with charming landlord; friendly, warm atmosphere and cheap food in big helpings *(Graeme Barnes)*; [top of Masons Lane] *Castle*: Good mix of people, mainly local but very friendly, and an interesting matchbox collection on the wall of the main bar; Ushers ales *(Andy Mason)*; [1 Church St; car park off A363 Trowbridge rd, beside bridge over Avon, in centre] *Swan*: Bar enlarged and improved in modernised coaching-inn; small car park immediately on the north end of the

town bridge and occasionally floods when the river breaks over its banks; bedrooms; recent reports have raised questions about food and service – more news please *(Ian Blackwell, GDPT, LYM and others)*; [55 Frome Rd; on bottom road out, by big car park by station] *Three Horseshoes*: Cosy, comfortable one-roomed Ushers house in coaching-inn style, close to canal bridge; Ruddles Best and County, separate restaurant *(Roger Huggins)*
Bremhill [ST9773], *Dumbpost*: Extremely good beer and food at low prices; long view from the bar, garden *(R Inns)*
Brinkworth [SU0184], *Three Crowns*: Food better and more interesting than most *(A H Bishop)*
Broad Chalke [SU0325], *Queens Head*: Modest frontage, real ales, good choice of bar food, efficient service; garden and car park; bedrooms *(Canon and Mrs G Hollis)*
Broad Hinton [A361 Swindon–Devizes; SU1076], *Bell*: Old country pub, beautifully kept and furnished, good bar food *(F E M Hardy)*; *Crown*: Big open-plan bar with good home-cooked bar meals, help-yourself salad bar and restaurant section, cheerful piped music, unusual gilded inn sign; bedrooms *(LYM)*
Brokerswood [ST8352], *Kicking Donkey*: Remote, spotless and friendly free house with several bars, shining brass-topped tables, stools, cushioned chairs and settles, and gentle piped music; John Smiths and Theakstons Best tapped from the cask and Hook Norton Old Hookey, Marstons Pedigreee, Theakstons Old Peculier and Wadworths 6X on handpump, good wine lists; reasonably priced bar food and à la carte menu served in restaurant with two log fires; children's play area; originally called Yew Tree in 1800s and was literally someone's front parlour with help-yourself service and biscuit tin kept on top of barrels for change *(Mr and Mrs S Binstead)*
☆ **Bromham** [ST9665], *Greyhound*: Superb building with tremendous atmosphere, amazing assortment of interesting items, attractively lit; friendly landlord; skittle alley, big garden, small intimate restaurant *(Lady Quinny)*
Broughton Gifford [ST8763], *Fox & Hounds*: Beautifully decorated with timbers, welcoming licensee and good quality bar food (not cheap) specialising in steaks, well kept real ales *(Roger Cunningham, Deborah Frost, Dave Marks, Tiff Wilson)*
Burbage [A338 Marlborough–Andover; SU2361], *Bullfinch*: Basic, but friendly roadside pub with simple, good value bar food; kitchen in process of being refurbished; children welcome *(Keith Walton)*
Burton [ST8179], *Old House at Home*: Main-street old pub with strong emphasis on excellent, generously served food with range of fresh fish such as monkfish on daily

changing blackboard; also frogs' legs and steaks; attractive dining recess *(Tony Triggle, C Davies)*; *Plume of Feathers*: Comfortable, friendly village pub, simply furnished with log fire and well behaved alsatian; good Ushers and acceptable house wine; unusually wide range of fine bar food inc Sinhalese dishes, lasagne, moussaka, award-winning steak and kidney pie; bedrooms *(Joy Heatherley)*

Castle Combe [The Gibb; B4039 Acton Turville–Chippenham – OS Sheet 173 reference 838791; ST8477], *Salutation*: Well restored, popular old pub augmented by new, barn-like restaurant; well kept Flowers and extensive range of good bar food inc daily specials such as chicken with ginger and lime sauce; attractive hanging baskets outside *(John and Pat Smyth, Patrick Godfrey, Peter and Rose Flower)*

Castle Eaton [High St; SU1495], *Red Lion*: Courage house under new regime with open log fire and pleasant riverside, at its best in summer *(Ewan McCall, Roger Huggins, Tom McLean)*

Chapmanslade [ST8247], *Three Horse Shoes*: Popular homely local, pleasant staff, Ushers, good food reasonably priced, separate restaurant, small garden *(Charlie Salt)*

Chilmark [B3089 Salisbury–Hindon; ST9632], *Black Dog*: Comfortably modernised fifteenth-century pub in attractive village; armchairs by the log fire in the lounge, fossil ammonites in the stone of another bar, and games in third bar; has had well kept Courage Best and Directors on handpump, and good value promptly served bar food (not Mon evening; also restaurant), but changed hands towards the end of 1988 – recent reports are favourable, but more news please; children have been welcome *(Nigel Paine, S V Bishop, Steve Huggins, LYM)*

Chilton Foliat [SU3270], *Wheatsheaf*: Friendly pub, good service, small selection of bar food inc highly praised home-made steak and kidney pie and chocolate crunchy-cake; piped music unobtrusive and you can get away from the loudspeakers *(J M Potter, John Hill)*

nr **Chippenham** [Pewsham; A4 towards Calne – OS Sheet 173 reference 948712; ST9173], *Lysley Arms*: Eighteenth-century free house completely refurbished with olde worlde bar and open fire, good choice of food inc menu for vegetarians and children *(Mr and Mrs D A P Grattan)*

Coombe Bissett [Blandford Rd (A354); SU1026], *Fox & Goose*: Separated from village green and silver-grey wooden barn by reedy stream; friendly, spacious open-plan pub with rustic wooden tables, coal fires and classical piped music, Ushers Best, wide choice of good bar food (though blackboards at lunchtime refer to evening restaurant) *(Ian Phillips, Canon G Hollis)*

Corsham [on A4 Corsham–Chippenham; ST8670], *Cross Keys*: Cosy atmosphere, well kept beer and friendly barman *(Roger Cunningham, Deborah Frost)*; [Pickwick] *Two Pigs*: Welcoming licensees and staff in very clean pub with attractive layout; constantly changing, very well kept real ales and efficient friendly service *(John Riggs)*

Corsley [A362 Warminster–Frome; ST8246], *White Hart*: Pleasantly furnished, well kept Bass, Huntsman Royal Oak and Palmers on handpump, emphasis on good lunchtime and (pricier) evening bar food; close to Longleat Safari Park *(Don Mather and others)*

Cricklade [SU0993], *Kings Head*: Good beer and sherry, popular food, very friendly staff and landlady *(JMW)*

Dauntsey [Dauntsey Lock; A420 – handy for M4 junctions 16 and 17; ST9782], *Peterborough Arms*: Particularly friendly welcome from landlord and his wife and a good selection of food and drink, inc several real ales *(P and K Davies)*

Derry Hill [ST9570], *Lansdowne Arms*: Wadworths house with unusual Victorian bar, separate restaurant and busy but friendly atmosphere; bar food inc speciality home-made pies (also sold in their shop in Colne); garden for children; near Bowood House *(David and Christine Foulkes, WHBM)*

Devizes [Long St; SU0061], *Elm Tree*: Welcoming, pleasant atmosphere, bedrooms *(Mr and Mrs F E M Hardy)*; [Nurseed Rd] *Moonraker*: Large, 1930s pub, comfortable lounge, Wadworths beer, good range of bar food and good bar service *(K R Harris)*; [Maryport St] *Three Crowns*: Friendly town pub with well kept local Wadworths real ales, George I backsword blade (found hidden in inn's ex-stables) decorating one hessian wall, seats in small sheltered yard *(BB)*

Dinton [SU0131], *Penruddocke Arms*: Spacious and comfortable country pub, good real ales, country wines, popular bar food, good pub games in public bar *(LYM)*

Downton [A338 Salisbury–Fordingbridge; SU1721], *Bull*: Very long bar in enlarged ex-fishing inn with food inc generous sandwiches, cold table and daily hot special, tables in many alcoves, brasses and ancient pistols on walls; dining area at one end (where juke box noise is muted); bedrooms *(LYM)*; *White Horse*: Fairly big place with Flowers IPA and outstanding value Sun lunches; beer garden; good parking facilities, children welcome *(Simon Turner, Caroline Bailey)*

East Chisenbury [SU1452], *Red Lion*: Unspoilt and basic country village pub where locals in the old-fashioned snug around the big winter fire function as a sort of gardeners' brains trust – a pub for devotees of times past, though they no longer keep real ale; play area on lawn *(LYM)*

Easterton [SU0155], *Royal Oak*: Attractive thatched pub, lovingly cared for by licensees;

good food drawing in people from far and wide *(A Triggle)*

Easton Royal [SU2060], *Bruce Arms*: One very basic room with bare floor, benches and tables, another full of old easy chairs and amaryllis plants; Whitbreads tapped from the cask *(Phil Gorton, J Maloney)*

Enford [SU1351], *Swan*: Interesting, thatched free house with two bars (one of which serves as family-room at lunchtimes), below-average beer and food prices, back garden and further trestle tables at front; children's play area *(R H Inns)*

Farleigh Wick [A363 Bath–Bradford; ST8064], *Fox & Hounds*: Well kept, clean pub with good Ushers and Websters, tasty food at reasonable prices *(B R Woolmington)*

Fonthill Bishop [ST9333], *Kings Arms*: Friendly, welcoming atmosphere with quiet side room off comfortable open-plan bar, darts and bar billiards; well kept Wadworths 6x and Worthington BB, beautifully cooked and generously served bar food; children welcome *(A J Bell)*

Fovant [A30 Salisbury–Shaftesbury; SU0128], *Cross Keys*: Fifteenth-century pub with wide range of tasty, low-priced bar food, separate restaurant, excellent service; bedrooms old and attractive *(Philip King, Canon G Hollis)*

Great Bedwyn [SU2764], *Cross Keys*: Good, fresh down-to-earth food and Wiltshire ales; bedrooms *(Chas and Dorothy Morley)*

Great Durnford [SU1338], *Black Horse*: Attractive pub under new management with pleasant service, excellent charcoal grills in restaurant and clean lavatories; children's outside room called London Transport Roadmaster *(Mr and Mrs George Ffoulkes)*

Ham [SU3362], *Crown & Anchor*: Free house with large selection of beers and draught cider; welcoming, cheerful landlord; well furnished, neat lounge bar; good variety of hot food at reasonable prices *(F A Rabagliati)*

☆ **Heddington** [ST9966], *Ivy*: Simple thatched village pub with good inglenook fireplace in low-beamed bar, timbered walls, well kept Wadworths real ales tapped from the cask, limited bar food such as rolls or pies, children's room; seats outside the picturesque house; ideal for walkers *(Maureen Hobbs, LYM)*

Heytesbury [Main St; ST9242], *Red Lion*: Nice comfortable pub, good Ushers and Websters Yorkshire, pleasant licensees *(Mr and Mrs D R Thornley)*

Highworth [Market Pl; SU2092], *Saracens Head*: Pleasant pub, well decorated, clean and relaxed; good bedrooms, large car park *(Dr and Mrs A K Clarke)*

Hindon [ST9132], *Grosvenor Arms*: Recently improved, but not spoilt old pub with pleasant terrace *(R H Inns)*

☆ **Horningsham** [by entrance to Longleat House; ST8141], *Bath Arms*: Comfortable pub in pretty village and at gates of Longleat,

good food with plenty of variety inc superb smoked trout; pleasant service; bedrooms *(Don Mather, Kathleen and David Caig, Mr and Mrs Maitland)*

☆ **Liddington** [a mile from M4 junction 15; just off A419; SU2081], *Village Inn*: Comfortable, clean and well furnished village pub; good range of real ales inc Fullers ESB and Marstons Pedigree, with Bulmers Traditional cider tapped from the cask, consistently good home-cooked lunchtime bar food; bedrooms *(K R Harris, Philip King, Chris Payne)*

Littleton Drew [B4039 Chippenham–Chipping Sodbury; ST8380], *Salutation*: Very friendly place with recently converted and newly furnished barn that provides a new bar and a very good range of bar food *(Mr and Mrs D A P Grattan)*

Lockeridge [signposted off A4 Marlborough–Calne just W of Fyfield – OS Sheet 173 reference 148679; SU1467], *Who'd A Thought It*: Three carpeted areas around small bar, with plush-cushioned Windsor and other chairs, wood-effect tables, fireplace with polished copper hood and fender; welcoming pleasant service, well kept Wadworths IPA and 6X on handpump, big helpings of well presented bar food – simple but good value; tables on back lawn, family-room *(Frank Cummins)*

☆ **Lower Chute** [the Chutes signposted via Appleshaw off A342 2½ miles W of Andover; SU3153], *Hatchet*: Neatly kept low-beamed thatched pub with huge log fire, good range of real ales such as Adnams, Ballards, Bass, Courage Directors and Wadworths 6X, and popular food running from soup or ploughman's through dishes such as braised steak in red wine to pricey steaks – also restaurant; seats on terrace and lawn; children in restaurant; has been open all day Tues, Thurs and Sat *(P M Wray, Henry Midwinter, Guy Harris, LYM and others)*

Lydiard Millicent [SU0985], *Sun*: Neat little pub with friendly service and well kept beer *(Dr and Mrs A K Clarke)*

Malmesbury [29 High St; ST9287], *Kings Arms*: Historic old coaching-inn with modest bars, lounge and restaurant; full of character with extensive and interesting range of home cooked food without chips: Wiltshire ham a speciality; cosy restaurant off lounge; real ales; bedrooms unpretentious *(RH Inns)*

☆ **Manton** [SU1668], *Up The Garden Path*: Small, pleasant and friendly village pub with well kept Archers BB, Flowers Original and Hook Norton Best, three farm ciders, decent traditional food, picnic-table sets on neat lawn by flower bed; in the process of extending, which has changed the outside 'cottage'appearance and may change the feel of the place – more news please *(Margaret Dyke, Neville Burke, T E Cheshire, Frank Cummins)*

☆ **Marlborough** [High St; SU1869], *Sun*:

Attractively furnished, friendly sixteenth-century pub, good lively atmosphere in bar on right with black panelling, heavy sloping beams, big fireplace, newspapers to read, well kept Ushers ale, bar food; plainer lounge on left, seats in small sheltered back courtyard; bedrooms rather basic, a do-it-yourself element in the breakfasts *(Chris Payne, Barry and Anne, Mary Rayner, Neville Burke, LYM and others)*

☆ **Marlborough** [High St], *Wellington Arms*: Friendly atmosphere in cosy well run pub with lots of commemorative and decorative mugs hanging from ceiling, newspapers on canes, steps down to eating area with wide range of good bar food inc soup, ploughman's, salads, omelettes, steaks and dishes such as ham or stuffed peppers; well kept Flowers on handpump, tables in courtyard; bedrooms *(HNJ, PEJ, Chris Payne, BB and others)*

Marlborough [High St], *Green Dragon*: Good menu with wide choice of lunch dishes; bedrooms *(F E M Hardy)*; [The Parade] *Lamb*: Local with excellent friendly atmosphere *(Chris Payne)*; [London Rd] *Roebuck*: New licensee took over in spring 1989 and so far has met with enthusiasm – more news please; bedrooms *(F E M Hardy and others)*

Marston Meysey [SU1297], *Spotted Cow*: Raised open fireplace, consistently good, civilised atmosphere; friendly, knowledgeable staff, well kept Ruddles County and Wadworths 6X; some US airmen as locals *(Ewan McCall, Roger Huggins, Tom McLean)*

Melksham [Semington Rd; ST9063], *New*: Unprepossessing exterior, but small, well renovated, one-roomed interior with annexe for darts and fruit machine; Liverpudlian, ex-merchant seaman licensee and wife run tight ship and create most welcoming atmosphere; good mix of lunchtime customers, well kept Watneys-related real ales, good value bar food, pleasant garden *(B R Woolmington)*

☆ **Mere** [Castle St; ST8132], *Old Ship*: Interesting sixteenth-century building with open fire in cosy, friendly hotel bar, spacious separate bar across coach entry divided into cosy areas by standing timbers and so forth, log fire here too, bar games; wide choice of bar food such as duck casserole, Badger Best under light blanket pressure; timber-walled restaurant; children allowed in eating area; bedrooms *(Bernard Phillips, Helen Roe, Mr and Mrs P W Dryland, E G Parish, LYM)*

Minety [SU0290], *White Horse*: Pleasant and friendly atmosphere, attractive home-cooked bar food inc fresh fish *(Mrs C Tuohy)*

Monkton Farleigh [ST8065], *Kings Arms*: Interesting pub with courtyard in sleepy village, very much a local; reasonably priced food *(Roger Cunningham, Deborah Frost, Mrs J Durnford, P G Walker)*

Netherhampton [SU1029], *Victoria & Albert*: Attractive beamed bars with lots of horsebrasses, well polished piano in one room and a Great Dane who has his own window seat (though they don't actually allow other dogs); friendly, young licensees and good, home-made bar food: soup, wholemeal bread, generous ploughman's and ham sandwiches *(Brigid Avison)*

Nettleton [ST8178], *Nettleton Arms*: Lovely old pub with good range of reasonably priced bar food *(Mr and Mrs D A P Grattan)*

Nunton [SU1526], *Radnor Arms*: Quaint and rustic place, friendly and efficient service, good wine list, good food such as fresh fish, pint of prawns, Stilton and broccoli quiche, vegetable pie; disabled toilet *(Barbara Want)*

Porton [just off Winterslow Rd; SU1936], *Porton*: Has had good range of Gibbs Mew beers and good, value-for-money food; satellite television in public bar, but new licensee recently – more news please; bedrooms *(Mark Spurlock)*

Poulshot [ST9559], *Raven*: Popular pub with small, intimate lounge and bar, well kept Wadworths 6X, friendly and efficient service; close to local common *(Roger Huggins)*

☆ **Salisbury** [Milford St; SU1429], *Red Lion*: Mix of antique settles, leather chairs and modern banquettes in knocked-through bar which opens into spacious old-fashioned hall, where interesting furnishings include amazing longcase clock with skeleton bellringers; well kept Bass, Courage Best, Ruddles Best and Wadworths 6X, with July beer festival; lunchtime bar food from sandwiches to cheap hot dishes, stylishly medieval restaurant, loggia courtyard seats; children in eating areas; bedrooms comfortable – a nice place to stay at *(Miss J A Harvey, LYM – more reports please)*

☆ **Salisbury** [Harnham Rd – at southernmost ring rd roundabout (towards A354 and A338), an unclassified rd not signposted city centre leads to pub], *Rose & Crown*: Worth a visit for the view – almost identical to that in the most famous Constable painting of Salisbury Cathedral; elegantly restored inn with friendly beamed and timbered bar, popular simple bar food (snacks only, Sun), Ruddles County and Ushers Best real ales, charming garden running down to River Avon, picture-window bedrooms in smart modern extension as well as the more traditional ones in the original building *(LYM and others)*

Salisbury [Bedwin St], *Arts Centre*: Not a pub, but indeed an arts centre which was formerly a church and has impressive stained glass windows and mini art gallery; Gibbs Mews and Wiltshire on handpump, simple food inc vegetarian dishes; beer festival in early June *(Matthew Pringle)*; [The Maltings] *Bishops Mill*: Tastefully decorated, very spacious, split-level place with pricey restaurant on upper level; wide range of bar drinks; views of River Avon *(Mark Spurlock)*; [Catherine St] *Cloisters*: Charming interior with low, beamed ceilings and spacious seating; local ales and good choice of food *(Mark Blundell)*; [Fisherton St] *Deacons*: Clean, basic free house (possibly converted from shop or house), small front bar and back games-room, wooden floorboards and jovial atmosphere; well kept Gales HSB, Ringwood Old Thumper and Wadworths 6X *(D J Penny)*; [New St] *New*: Creaky-beamed ancient timbered pub with good choice of simple food, Badger beers *(Gordon and Daphne, BB)*; [nr bus station] *Pheasant*: Old pub with well kept Courage *(Dr and Mrs A K Clarke)*; [Ivy St] *Queens Arms*: Really friendly, homely pub with comfortable atmosphere *(Dr and Mrs A K Clarke)*; [corner Ivy St/Brown St] *Star*: Basic pub with wooden floors, beams painted with canalboat patterns, pool and darts; gets noisy towards end of evening *(Dr and Mrs A K Clarke)*; [New St] *Wig & Quill*: Sixteenth-century building converted from antiques shop to pub in 1977 with low beams, wooden floors and ornate rugs, subtle lighting, real fire, leather chairs, stuffed birds and low arches to connecting rooms; Adnams and Wadworths, 1940s piped music; open all day Sat *(Matthew Pringle)*; [Estcourt Rd] *Wyndham Arms*: Basic, modern corner pub with small, cosy room opposite bar and friendly atmosphere; reasonably priced Hop Back beers brewed on premises inc Gilbert's First Brew (GFB), HBS, winter Entire Stout and summer Lightning; simple bar food *(Matthew Pringle, David Fisher)*

☆ **Seend** [ST9461], *Bell*: Traditional country pub with well kept beer and excellent food from soup and sandwiches to daily specials, prepared by the landlord's daughter; well kept Wadworths IPA and 6X; children in dining area; beautiful garden; ¼ mile from Kennet and Avon canal *(T C and A R Newell, T P Heavisides, BCL)*

Semington [A350 2 miles S of Melksham – OS Sheet 173 reference 898608; ST8960], *Somerset Arms*: Long room leading into another room where you can reserve tables; beams, carpets, chintz-upholstered wall settles and stools, cushions on tub chairs; quite attractive artificial flower displays, brassware; well kept Ruddles, Ushers BB and Websters Yorkshire; new licensees promoting food side, so now less of a place for a casual drink – more news please *(Roger Cunningham, Deborah Frost, Frank Cummins)*

Sherston [ST8585], *Carpenters Arms*: Good Whitbreads gravity fed from barrels behind bar in scrubbed-floored country pub, unusual choice of food in addition to the standard items; lounge is much more pleasant as the area set aside for eating, but music is more discreet in bar; very relaxing to sit down by the open fire and soak up the atmosphere; eating area in garden *(Roger Huggins)*; [B4040 Malmesbury–Chipping Sodbury – OS Sheet 173 reference 854859], *Rattlebone*: Seventeenth-century free house with two well furnished beamed and stone-walled bars; carpeted public bar with fruit machine, hexagonal pool-table, shove-ha'penny and table skittles, small central room; big dining-room with window settles, Windsor-back chairs, polished tables, big stone fireplace; well kept changing real ales such as Bass and Butcombe on handpump, good choice of lunchtime and evening bar food, pebbled terrace, attractive walled back garden; open all day Sat *(Frank Cummins, Roger Huggins)*

South Wraxall [ST8364], *Longs Arms*: Pleasant, cosy atmosphere in remote country pub, friendly and welcoming landlord, well kept Wadworths, good freshly cooked bar food *(J S Wilson, Roger Cunningham, Deborah Frost)*

Stockton [just off A36 Salisbury–Warminster, near A303; ST9738], *Carriers*: Refurbished pub with bar food and good choice of beer *(Mark Spurlock)*

☆ **Stourton** [Church Lawn; follow Stourhead signpost off B3092, N of junction with A303 just W of Mere; ST7734], *Spread Eagle*: Lovely setting at head of Stourhead Lake, and popular with mostly older customers; old-fashioned furnishings – some of which have seen better days (the possibility of a spring clean may come to mind); Bass and Charrington IPA kept under light blanket pressure, straightforward bar food, benches in back courtyard; restaurant; bedrooms *(S V Bishop, Hayward Wane, G Bloxsom, Pamela and Merlyn Horswell; more reports please)*

Sutton Mandeville [ST9828], *Lancers*: Good food and very pleasant service *(Heather Hodd)*

Swindon [Prospect Hill; SU1485], *Beehive*: Quaint little triangular pub with well kept Morrells ales, wooden floors, plain wooden counters, stools and benches around wall; made a national name for itself in late 1988 when it had philosophy sessions presided over by Czech refugee Dr Julius Tomin; most customers student-age, appropriately noisy *(Lady Quinny)*; [Cold Harbour Lane; Blunsdon, off A361] *Cold Harbour*: Useful big well decorated and comfortable Chef & Brewer, popular with businessmen for wide choice of good food served generously; Watneys-related real ales, restaurant *(M E A Horler)*; [Freshbrook; off A420 at first roundabout coming from M4 junction 16] *Cornflower*: Friendly atmosphere and good beer in estate pub of the current mock-rustic persuasion *(Dr and Mrs A K Clarke)*; [Wootton Basset Rd (main rd in from M4 junction 16)] *Running Horse*: Recently refurbished large pub with wood panelling, Arkells ales and quiet, relaxing atmosphere;

restaurant area at back and upstairs (Beefeater); beer garden with children's slide *(Paul Corbett)*; [Newport St] *Wheatsheaf*: Extended old pub with good potential and well kept Wadworths, with cheery local atmosphere in public bar *(Chris Payne, Lady Quinny, Neville Burke)*; [Oxford Rd] *White Hart*: Useful large, open-plan pub with plush lounge *(Dr and Mrs A K Clarke)*

☆ **Teffont Magna** [ST9832], *Black Horse*: Good food with frequently changing specials in pretty pub with comfortable and welcoming lounge; well kept real ales, limited but good value range of wines, more basic public bar; in attractive village *(H J Stirling, LYM)*

Trowbridge [7/8 Castle St; ST8557], *Peewees*: Live (mainly rock) bands most weekends, and the people who go with it – landlord is the singer of the local band; good range of beer and traditional cider *(Andy Mason)*; [Chilmark Rd; left off A363 Bath rd opp Citroen garage, then right then left] *Wiltshire Yeoman*: Big helpings of good value food and Watneys-related real ales on handpump in Chef & Brewer dining-pub – formerly a fine old stone farmhouse; looks out on open country, though surrounded by modern housing *(GDPT)*

nr **Trowbridge** [Strand, Seend; A361, near Keevil – OS Sheet 173 reference 918597; ST8557], *Lamb*: Popular eating pub, several rooms knocked together though still some attractive furnishings, good food, children welcome *(A J Triggle, LYM)*

☆ **Wanborough** [2 miles from M4 junction 15; B4507 towards Bishopstone; SU2083], *Black Horse*: A wide range of customers from businessmen to country locals, friendly landlord and staff in unpretentious country pub, generous helpings of well priced food weekday lunchtimes (only snacks Sun) inc fine ploughman's, well kept Arkells, separate homely dining room with own bar; fine views, with swings, climbing frame and assorted livestock in garden *(R G Ollier, HNJ, PEJ)*

☆ **Wanborough** [Lower Wanborough; also nr M4 junction 15], *Harrow*: Pretty thatched and oak-beamed pub with pear tree against the wall, seats out by flowers, wonderfully welcoming inside, with open fires, well kept Flowers IPA and Original and maybe Whitbreads Pompey Royal, good home-cooked food and friendly prompt service *(Mary Rayner and others)*

Wanborough [Lower Wanborough; SU2083], *Cross Keys*: Quaint pub despite being only 50 years old *(Dr and Mrs A K Clarke)*; [Upper Wanborough; from A419 through Wanborough, right at crossing, then 1½ miles on left] *Olde Shepherds Rest*: Remote pub, relaxed and comfortable, pleasantly presented reasonably priced bar food lunchtime and evening; décor not perfect, juke box in next bar may be noticeable *(Neil Barker, Mary Rayner)*

Warminster [High St; ST8744], *Old Bell*: Central country-town hotel where everyone goes to have a drink or a bar meal when they've come in to shop; olde-worlde setting, good service and well cooked and presented food inc excellent help-yourself salads and trout; good selection of wines; restaurant *(Maj and Mrs D R C Woods, K R Harris)*

West Dean [SU2527], *Red Lion*: Sadly this fine old English pub, a pub for two centuries, in its idyllic setting among trees, with village green leading down to river, was being sold to become a private house in 1989 *(LYM)*

Westbrook [A3102 about 4 miles E of Melksham; ST9565], *Westbrook*: Big helpings of good value food inc mild curries and vegetarian dishes are the main interest in this small and cleanly renovated pub, with farm tools and prints of seventeenth-century German towns on the walls; Watneys-related real ales on handpump, piped music; may be crowded *(Aubrey and Margaret Saunders, Frank Cummins, LYM)*

Westbury [Market Pl; ST8751], *Lopes Arms*: Friendly atmosphere, nice furnishings and decorations, good food, pleasant landlord; bedrooms *(Mr and Mrs D R Thornley)*

Westwood [main rd; ST8059], *New*: Cheerful pub with oak beams, friendly atmosphere and lovely open fires; well kept beer, good bar food *(Andy Mason)*

Whaddon [ST8761], *Three Crowns*: Useful well kept and cheerful modernised pub with children's play area *(Dr and Mrs A K Clarke)*

Whiteparish [Main St; SU2423], *Village Lantern*: Friendly and lively village pub, open-plan with central fireplace and sensibly placed pool and darts, well kept Gibbs Mew ales, good value bar food, well cooked and nicely presented *(Chris Fluck, Mark Spurlock)*

☆ **Wilcot** [SU1360], *Golden Swan*: Ancient steeply thatched village inn, very picturesque, with rustic tables on pretty front lawn; well kept Wadworths IPA and 6X in two small rooms of comfortable bar decorated with lots of china jugs and mugs hanging from beams; bar food, simple bedrooms, dining room; bedrooms *(BB)*

Wingfield [ST8256], *Poplars*: Friendly pub with well kept Wadworths ales and own cricket pitch *(LYM)*

Wootton Bassett [High St; SU0682], *Angel*: Pleasant sixteenth-century coaching inn, well kept Flowers, friendly atmosphere; lounge area leads back to bistro with wide choice of reasonably priced food; bedrooms *(Keith Garley)*

Wroughton [SU1480], *White Hart*: Straightforward bar food and Wadworths real ales in spacious lounge with old stone fireplace, lively public bar and skittle alley; handy for M4 junction 16 *(Mary Rayner, LYM)*

☆ **Wylye** [just off A303/A36 junction; SU0037], *Bell*: Well kept Wadworths IPA and 6X on handpump and local atmosphere in beamed front area with some stripped masonry, log fire in huge stone fireplace, wall seats and rustic benches around sturdy tables, piped music; bar loops right round past bar billiards area to dining area filled with tables and stall seating; good value food, country wines; bedrooms *(Stella Crist, Dorothy and Jack Rayner, BB)*

Yorkshire

Lots of changes here include extensive refurbishment, particularly on the hotel side, at the attractive Kings Arms at Askrigg (good food, and a nice place to stay at); refurbishments to the bedrooms, already popular, at the Fox Hall Inn at East Layton; plans for a bedroom extension at the Tempest Arms at Elslack (doing so well under its French landlord that this year we've awarded it a star, in addition to its food award); extensive additions to the Squinting Cat near Harrogate (on the whole a success, though there are those who hanker for the more crowded but cosier past); new bedrooms at the idiosyncratic White Bear in Masham; and a near doubling of space at the Moorings overlooking the Sowerby Bridge canal basin. The charming Star at Harome has widened its range of food beyond its popular sandwiches; it's doing particularly well in readers' ratings at the moment. A great many pubs with new licensees include the Rose & Crown at Bainbridge, the Buck at Buckden (in the year or so they've been there, they've been doing so well that we've given it a star award this year, and a food award), the White Lion at Cray (they're now letting bedrooms), the Ancient Shepherd at Cridling Stubbs, the Horse Shoe at Egton Bridge (gaining it our place-to-stay award) and the Postgate there, the Old Hall in Heckmondwike, the Chequers at Ledsham (currently very popular), the own-brew Fox & Newt in Leeds (bringing it back into these pages after a break), Whitelocks in Leeds (food all afternoon now in this most popular and interesting city-centre pub), the Boat at Sprotbrough (an interesting pub in a fine riverside spot, though we'd like more reports on the new regime), the Fox & Hounds at Starbotton (friendly, upgrading bedrooms and kitchen), both pubs at Wentworth (bringing one – the Rockingham Arms – back as a main entry after a spell in the Lucky Dip), the Pack Horse up at Widdop, and the White Swan at Wighill (adding a separate restaurant and bedroom block, but not changing the pub itself at all – a great relief). The Olde Starre in York has

The Fauconberg Arms, Coxwold

changed not only its licensee but also its brewer: firmly in the Watneys embrace now, it's as quaint as ever. Just as we go to press we hear that the people who've had the remote George at Hubberholme for the last decade or so are planning to retire; fingers crossed for this most popular of Wharfedale pubs. And there may also be a change at the Queens Arms just over the hill at Litton. The Malt Shovel at Oswaldkirk – which owed so much to the strong character of its former landlord – has changed hands; still a nice pub, but not of course the same. And sadly we have to report the death, at a fine old age, of Bessie Fletcher, who had so lovingly preserved the antique character of the Blue Lion at East Witton. Several new main entries, or pubs back after a break, include the welcoming Strines Inn up in the moors near Bradfield, the Cow & Calf at Grenoside (really friendly landlord), the quaint Blacksmiths Arms at Lastingham, the cheerful Bulls Head above Linthwaite (good food served all day), the Olde Punch Bowl at Marton cum Grafton (a relaxing break from the A1), the riverside Dawnay Arms at Newton on Ouse (a very popular outing from York), the spacious Cubley Hall just outside Penistone, the remarkably unspoilt and traditional Greyhound at Saxton, and the well run Scotts Arms at Sicklinghall. Besides pubs mentioned already, ones where the food is an outstanding attraction include the Lion up on Blakey Ridge (they serve it all day), the Angel at Hetton (a superb seafood platter), the smart Black Bull at Moulton (strong on smoked salmon, in various guises), the Nags Head at Pickhill, the civilised Sawley Arms at Sawley (a real family operation, with the cooking done by the landlady, her son and daughter-in-law), the Buck at Thornton Watlass (doing particularly well at the moment; a nice place to stay at), the stylishly refurbished Old Hall Inn at Threshfield and the Sportsmans Arms at Wath-in-Nidderdale (excellent cheeses and fish; and fine restaurant meals – another good place to stay at). There's a tremendous choice of fresh fish at the Frog & Parrot in Sheffield, though its chief claim to fame is its range of own-brewed beers, which include the most powerful we've come across. But the Sair in Linthwaite has the widest choice of all among own-brew pubs, and even does a genuinely cask-conditioned low-alcohol beer now. Though a good many Yorkshire pubs keep a fine range of malt whiskies, none approaches the remarkable collection of 700 kept by the Cragg Lodge at Wormald Green. Among Lucky Dip entries at the end of the chapter, pubs showing particular promise include the Ship at Aldborough, Craven Arms at Appletreewick, Birch Hall at Beck Hole, New Inn at Cropton, Hales in Harrogate, Tennant Arms at Kilnsey, Sandpiper in Leyburn, Windmill at Linton, Bridge at Stapleton, Royal Oak at Settle, Tan Hill Inn, Henry Boons in Wakefield, Agar Arms at Warthill, Fox & Hounds at West Burton and York Arms in York.

ARNCLIFFE (N Yorks)   SD9473 Map 7

Falcon

Off B6160

A welcome sight for walkers coming over the fells, this unpretentious, relaxing country pub stands at the head of a long village green, lined with a neat row of grey stone cottages. It's run by a family which has been here for four generations, with a fifth growing up, and hasn't changed much in that time: a small servery at the back taps the Youngers ales from the cask, and there's hatch service to a couple of functional little rooms with heavy settles and cast-iron tables, a fire (if you're lucky enough to get near it) and some old humorous sporting prints; there's also an airy conservatory-room behind, and a homely front lounge. Simple bar food includes baked potato with cheese (75p), soup (90p), sandwiches (from 90p) and good ploughman's (£2.40); enormous breakfasts; dominoes. The pub is on *Good Walks Guide* Walk 151. *(Recommended by Peter and Rose Flower, Jon Wainwright, Lynn Stevens, Gill Quarton, Neil and Angela Huxter)*

Free house   Licensee David Miller   Real ale   Lunchtime snacks   Children in conservatory (lunchtime only)   Open 12–3, 6.30–11 in summer; 12–2, 7–11 in winter   Bedrooms tel Arncliffe (075 677) 205; £17/£34 (may not be available in winter)

ASKRIGG (N Yorks)   SD9591 Map 10

Kings Arms 🏮 🛏

Village signposted from A684 Leyburn–Sedbergh in Bainbridge

Quite a few changes are to take place over the next year in this former Georgian manor house. As well as alterations and refurbishments to the hotel side (which includes adding and upgrading bedrooms), the bars are to be refurbished with antiques, horse-racing memorabilia (the inn was once a well known horse-racing stud), and photographs of the filming of James Herriot's *All Creatures Great and Small* (the inn itself, in the series, is the Drovers Arms), new lavatories are to be built, the courtyard re-paved and planted, new outside seating added, and more space created for car parking. The very high-ceilinged central room is warmly welcoming, and there's a real coaching feel with saddle-hooks still in place, a kitchen hatch in the panelling, hunting prints, a curving wall with high window that shows people bustling up and down the stairs, a huge stone fireplace, and nineteenth-century fashion plates and stag's head; an attractive medley of furnishings includes a fine sturdy old oak settle, and there's more oak panelling in a small low-beamed front bar that has brocaded wall settles in its side snugs and a fire in a lovely green marble fireplace. A simply furnished flagstoned back bar has yet another fire, and a fruit machine, trivia machine and juke box (that can be obtrusive); also darts, shove-ha'penny, dominoes, cribbage. Bar food includes sandwiches (from 95p), fine home-made soup (£1), filled baked potatoes (from 95p), burgers (£1.95), ploughman's (from £2.50), salads (from £3.50), steak and kidney pie (£3.95), gammon and egg (£4.50) and steak (£5.95); well kept McEwans 80/- and Youngers Scotch and No 3 on handpump, quite a few malt whiskies and wines, and good coffee (served before the bar opens, too); good, friendly service. *(Recommended by Alan and Ruth Woodhouse, Lee Goulding, Diane Hall, Roger Bellingham, Henry Midwinter, H K Dyson, Paul Newberry, Anthony Fernau, John H Jackson)*

Free house   Licensees Ray and Liz Hopwood   Real ale   Meals and snacks Restaurant   Children in eating area and restaurant (not under 10)   Occasional choral or brass band concerts   Open 11–4, 6.30–11 (11–5, 6–11 Sat) all year; closed weekday afternoons in winter   Bedrooms tel Wensleydale (0969) 50258; £22.50B/£35B

AUSTWICK (N Yorks)   SD7668 Map 7

Game Cock 🛏

The crags and screes of the Dales National Park and the Three Peaks rise above the green pastures around this quiet village of rose-covered stone houses – of which this friendly inn is part. The simply furnished but cosy back bar is popular with climbers and walkers, and has well made built-in wall benches and plain wooden tables, a few cockfighting prints on the butter-coloured walls, beams, and a good fire in winter; there is a more comfortable lounge. Well presented bar food includes sandwiches (ham £1.10, open prawn £2.50), crispy crab and vegetable parcels (£2.70), roast chicken (£3), steak and mushroom pie (£3.25), scampi (£3.60), and puddings such as apple and blackberry pie or chocolate and pear pudding (£1.30); good breakfasts. Well kept Thwaites on handpump; darts and dominoes. There are some seats in a glass-enclosed sun loggia, and outside. *(Recommended by Paul Newberry, J A Jack, Hilarie Miles-Sharp, A W Wallens)*

Thwaites   Licensee Alan Marshall   Real ale   Meals and snacks   Open 11–3, 6–11 Bedrooms tel Clapham (046 85) 226; £13.50/£27

BAINBRIDGE (N Yorks)   SD9390 Map 10
Rose & Crown 🍺
A684

New licensees have taken over this friendly old inn and early reports suggest that they've settled in very quickly. The beamed and panelled front bar has antique settles and other old furniture, a butterfly collection, flowers, and a cheerful fire; the spacious main bar has big windows overlooking the green. Good bar food includes home-made soup (£1.15), sandwiches (from £1.15, open sandwiches £3.50), good ploughman's (from £2.40), home-made sausages (£2.85), chilli bean pot or tuna-fish casserole (£3.25), lasagne (£3.45), home-made pie of the day (£3.50), sirloin steak (£6.95), daily specials, home-made puddings (£1.20) and children's menu (from £2). John Smiths, Theakstons and Youngers Scotch on handpump; extensive wine list; darts, pool, shove ha'penny, dominoes, fruit machine, juke box and piped music. *(Recommended by Henry Midwinter, Mr and Mrs J E Rycroft, Jenny Cantle, Helen and John Thompson, Mr and Mrs J H Adam, Dr and Mrs R J Ashleigh, G Jones, Dr and Mrs A K Clarke)*

Free house   Licensee P H Collins   Real ale   Meals and snacks   Restaurant   Children welcome   Open 11–3, 6–11 weekdays, 11–11 Sat   Bedrooms tel Wensleydale (0969) 50225; £26B/£48B

BLAKEY RIDGE (N Yorks)   SE6799 Map 10
Lion 🌓 🍺
From A171 Guisborough–Whitby follow Castleton, Hutton le Hole signposts; from A170 Kirkby Moorside–Pickering follow Keldholm, Hutton le Hole, Castleton signposts; OS Sheet 100 reference 679996

With spectacular moorland views in virtually every direction, this isolated and rambling old place has a cosy, friendly atmosphere and is popular with walkers and motorists alike. There are lots of small dining-chairs on the Turkey carpet, a few big high-backed rustic settles around cast-iron-framed tables, a nice leather settee, dim lamps and beams; on the stripped stone walls are photographs of the pub under snow (it can easily get cut off in winter – but there are good fires) and some old engravings. Bar food includes sandwiches (95p) or ploughman's (£2.65 – both these lunchtime only), steak sandwich (£2.05), home-made steak and mushroom pie, curry, home-cooked ham and egg or salads (all £3.55), steaks (from £5.55), special vegetarian menu, puddings (£1.35), children's menu (£2.05) and good Sunday roasts (£5.45, children £2.95); the award is for value as much as anything – the helpings are hugely generous. Well kept Tetleys and Theakstons Best, Old Peculier and XB on handpump; dominoes, fruit machine and piped music. Get there early for lunch at weekends or in summer. The two-room restaurant is smarter than you'd expect for this isolated spot. *(Recommended by Jane and Niall, Dr and Mrs R J Ashleigh, Lynn Stevens, Gill Quarton, Linda and Alex Christison, Bob Gardiner, Steve Dykes, G T Jones, Rob and Gill Weeks, F E M Hardy, Comus Elliott, T George, R A Hall)*

Free house   Licensee Barry Crossland   Real ale   Meals and snacks (11–10 Mon–Thurs, 11–10.30 Fri and Sat)   Restaurant; open all day Sun   Children welcome   Occasional live music Weds evenings   Open 11–11 all year   Bedrooms tel Lastingham (075 15) 320; £15/£30

Pubs with outstanding views are listed at the back of the book.

BOLTON PERCY (N Yorks)   SE5341 Map 7

Crown

Signposted with Oxton from Tadcaster – first real right turn after crossing the bridge, heading out from centre on York road

Tucked away by a striking medieval gatehouse behind the village church, this tiny, unpretentious and very friendly pub has two simply furnished rooms decorated with brass ornaments, a stuffed falcon, a Delft shelf of foxhunting plates and a big print of shire horses – very peaceful indeed on a weekday lunchtime, probably with just Teal the spaniel and Coot and Gipsy the labradors for company. The Sam Smiths OB on electric pump is in tip-top condition – the brewery is just over three miles away – and it's cheap, too. Bar food is freshly made and good value, including soup (75p), sandwiches (from 80p, toasties from 85p), burgers (£1.25), home-made steak and kidney pie (£2.40), ploughman's, chicken or scampi (£2.50), children's helpings, and there are summer barbecues on Saturday evenings. Darts and dominoes. Outside, the biggish terrace (with ornamental pheasants in a row of pens beside it) has picnic-table sets among fruit trees, and a very long wooden cat-walk footbridge that snakes out over a slow dark stream and its bordering nettle flats.
(Recommended by Syd and Wyn Donald, Tim Halstead, T Nott, JAH, HCH)

Sam Smiths   Licensees Geoff and Angela Pears   Real ale   Meals and snacks   Children in eating area and family-room   Open 10.30–3 (4 Sat), 6–11 all year

nr BRADFIELD (S Yorks)   SK2692 Map 7

Strines Inn 🏠

Strines signposted from A616 at head of Underbank Reservoir, W of Stocksbridge; or on A57 heading E of junction with A6013 (Ladybower Reservoir) take first left turn (signposted with Bradfield) then bear left

Local people know well that this corner of Yorkshire – virtually unknown to outsiders – can easily hold its own with the more familiar areas of the Peak District, the Dales and the North Yorkshire Moors. And here in its heart, looking out on the forests, the moorland pastures, the Dark Peak itself, and the glint of water from Strines Reservoir below, is a handsome stone-built inn. There's a sixteenth-century coat of arms over the door, but it probably dates back 300 years before that. Inside, the main bar seems most popular with outdoor people, with a good mixture of walkers and people who work on the moors – the landlord himself works a thriving hill sheep farm. There's a coal fire in the rather grand stone fireplace, homely red-plush-cushioned traditional wooden wall benches and small chairs, black beams liberally decked with copper kettles and so forth, and quite a menagerie of stuffed animals. A room off on the right has another coal fire, hunting photographs and prints, and lots of brass and china, and there's a simply furnished candle-lit room on the left, with an upstairs restaurant (Saturday evening, Sunday carvery lunch until 4pm). Though there's a wide choice of bar food, with a daily menu running up to roast pork (£4), we've only so far had commendations for the soup and sandwiches; Whitbreads Castle Eden on handpump, exceptionally good coffee (served from 10.30), decent wines and nearly four dozen malt whiskies; darts, cards and dominoes (winter), piped pop music. There are picnic-table sets outside.
(Recommended by Rob and Gill Weeks, Dennis D'Vigne)

Free house   Licensees Ken and Angie Slack   Real ale   Meals and snacks   Restaurant (see above)   Children welcome   Open 11–11 all year; a bit iffy Jan and Feb, as they can get snowed in   Bedrooms tel Sheffield (0742) 81247; £12/£24(£40B)

Bar food is generally served 12–2 and 7–9 unless stated otherwise.

BUCKDEN (N Yorks)   SD9278 Map 7

Buck ★ ⊗

B6160

It's long been very popular with readers, but since new licensees took over just as
we went to press last year people's reports on the Buck have been particularly
enthusiastic, so this year we've awarded it a star. There's a bustling, friendly
atmosphere in the modernised and extended open-plan bar which has upholstered
built-in wall banquettes and square stools around shiny dark brown tables on its
carpet – though there are still flagstones in the snug original area by the serving-
counter, decorated with hunting prints and willow-pattern plates. The wall by the
big log fire is stripped to bare stone, with others left buttery cream and decorated
with local pictures and the mounted head of a roebuck. Popular and good value bar
food (which can now be eaten anywhere) includes home-made soup (£1.20),
toasted sandwiches (£1.90, steak sandwich £3), giant Yorkshire puddings filled
with rich onion gravy or home-made smooth chicken liver pâté with cream, brandy
and garlic (£2.20), ploughman's (£3.15), vegetarian curry (£3.85), home-made
steak, mushroom and ale pie (£4.35), baked local trout Cleopatra style (topped
with prawns, toasted almonds and capers) or gammon steak and egg (both £4.95),
mixed grill (£6 – to suit the heartiest appetite), sirloin steak (from £7.15), and
blackboard specials which change twice daily; traditional Sunday lunch. Well kept
Tetleys Bitter, Theakstons Old Peculier and Youngers Scotch and regularly
changing guest beer on handpump served by uniformed staff; good choice of malt
whiskies and decent wines. Dominoes, video game, trivia and occasional piped
music. Seats on the terrace and beyond the sloping car park in the shelter of a great
sycamore have good views of the surrounding moors. The bedrooms have been
upgraded (prices are £2.25 a head higher on Friday and Saturday), and there's a
new residents' dining-room and lounge. (*Recommended by Peter and Rose Flower, David
Goldstone, Jenny Cantle, Jon and Jacquie Payne, J E Rycroft, Dr and Mrs T E Waine, Tim
Baxter, Prof S Barnett, Len Beattie, Lynn Stevens, Gill Quarton, Mrs D M Everard*)

*Free house   Licensee Trevelyan Illingworth   Real ale   Meals and snacks   Restaurant; not
Sun lunchtime   Children in eating area and restaurant   Open 11–3, 6–11 all year
Bedrooms tel Kettlewell (075 676) 227; £25.50B/£45B*

BURNSALL (N Yorks)   SE0361 Map 7

Red Lion

B6160 S of Grassington, on Ilkley road; OS Sheet 98 reference 033613

This pretty stone-built pub has a busy, friendly main bar with Windsor armchairs,
rugs on the floor, flowery-cushioned sturdy seats built into the attractively panelled
walls (decorated with pictures of the local fell races), and steps up past a solid-fuel
stove to a back area with sensibly placed darts (dominoes players are active up here,
too). The carpeted front lounge bar, which is served from the same copper-topped
counter through an old-fashioned small-paned glass partition, has a coal fire. Well
kept Tetleys and Theakstons on handpump. White tables on the cobbles in front of
the building look over the quiet road to the village green (which has a tall maypole)
running along the banks of the River Wharfe. (*Recommended by Tim Baxter, Jon
Wainwright, Prof S Barnett, Paul Newberry, J E Rycroft, Mike Suddards, Eileen Broadbent*)

*Free house   Licensee Patricia Warnett   Real ale   Snacks   Restaurant   Children welcome
until 9   Open 11–3, 6–11 all year   Bedrooms tel Burnsall (075 672) 204; £22(£30B)/
£30(£40B)*

Please keep sending us reports. We rely on readers for news of new discoveries, and
particularly for news of changes, however slight, at the fully described pubs. No stamp
needed: *The Good Pub Guide*, FREEPOST, London SW10 0BR.

BYLAND ABBEY (N Yorks)   SE5579 Map 7

Abbey Inn ⚲

The Abbey has a brown tourist-attraction signpost off the A170 Thirsk–Helmsley

The old-fashioned character in this refurbished pub – alone in a spectacular setting opposite the abbey ruins – has been preserved by leaving the rambling series of separate rooms more or less intact and by furnishing it very much in character. There are Jacobean-style dining-chairs, carved oak seats, oak and stripped deal tables, settees, and china cabinets, as well as polished boards and flagstones, big fireplaces, some discreet stripping back of plaster to show the ex-abbey masonry, decorative bunches of flowers among the candles, various stuffed birds, cooking implements, little etchings, willow-pattern plates and so forth. In a big back room this country theme rather runs riot – as well as lots of rustic bygones, an uptilted cart shelters a pair of gnomelike waxwork yokels. Though it's quiet in the early evening it quickly fills up with people after the food (all prepared by the licensee's Norwegian wife), which might include home-made pâté (£2.50), vegetarian dishes (£3.75), lamb curry or steak pie (£4), various casseroles (£4.25), breast of chicken with lemon and tarragon (£4.75) and lots of home-made puddings; it's also popular for Sunday lunch (from £4). Well kept Tetleys and Theakstons Best on handpump, interesting wines, efficient food service by neat waitresses, inoffensive piped music. No dogs. There's lots of room outside in the garden. (*Recommended by Roger Bellingham, M B Porter, Dr John Innes, Gill and Neil Patrick, Peter Race, Roger Barnes, Helen Stanton*)

Free house   Licensees Peter and Gerd Handley   Real ale   Meals and snacks (not Sun evening, not Mon)   Children welcome until 8.30   Open 10–2.30, 6.30–11 all year; closed Sun evening, all day Mon

CADEBY (S Yorks)   SE5100 Map 7

Cadeby Inn ★

3 miles from A1(M) at junction with A630; going towards Conisbrough take first right turn signposted Sprotbrough, then follow Cadeby signposts

The cheerfully efficient serving-bar is in the main lounge at the back of this busy 400-year-old place: a high-backed settle made in the traditional style to fit around one stone-walled alcove, comfortable seats around wooden tables, an open fire in the big stone fireplace, some silver tankards, caps of all seventeen County Cricket Clubs, a stuffed fox and pheasant and lots of house plants. There's a quieter front sitting-room, and, decently out of the way, a fruit machine (they also have a separate darts room, an old each-way horse-racing machine, shove-ha'penny, dominoes, cribbage and quiz evenings). Good bar food includes a lunchtime salad bar and generous carvery (both £3.50), as well as soup (65p), sandwiches (from 85p), ploughman's (from £1.95), home-made steak and kidney pie (£2.45), seafood platter (£3.25), gammon with pineapple and egg or scampi (£3.50), and good value steaks (from £4.75); their traditional Sunday lunches are exceedingly popular. Well kept Sam Smiths OB and Museum, and Tetleys Bitter on handpump, attractively priced, and over 150 whiskies. There are seats in the front beer garden, and in summer they have barbecues out here. (*Recommended by Steve Mitcheson, Anne Collins, KC, J A Edwards, J H Walker, Paul Newberry, Michael and Alison Sandy, M A and W R Proctor, T Nott, ILP, Rob and Gill Weeks*)

Free house   Licensee Walter William Ward   Real ale   Meals and snacks (12–2, 5–9.30)   Children in eating area of bar   Open 11–11 all year

COXWOLD (N Yorks)   SE5377 Map 7

Fauconberg Arms ★ 🛏 [*illustrated on page 758*]

Named after Lord Fauconberg – who married Oliver Cromwell's daughter Mary –

this well kept old stone inn has a comfortably furnished and civilised lounge bar made up of two cosy knocked-together rooms: cushioned antique oak settles, including one that's handsomely carved and another curved to fit the attractive bay window, an oak porter's chair, Windsor armchairs, matting on the flagstones, gleaming brasses on one beam, and on cold days a log fire in the unusual arched stone fireplace; some of the furniture has squirrels carved into it. Lunchtime bar snacks include soup (£1), sandwiches (£1.30), specials like fresh crab (£1.95), and hot dishes such as stew and dumplings (around £2.95); decent breakfasts. Well kept Tetleys, Theakstons and Youngers Scotch on handpump. The locals' spacious back public bar has a fruit machine and piped music. The pub is close to Shandy Hall, the home of Laurence Sterne the novelist. The broad, quiet village street is pretty, with tubs of flowers on its grass or cobbled verges. *(Recommended by Y Batts, Jane Palmer, Dr John Innes, Paul Newberry, Barbara Hatfield, Laurence Manning, Mrs Shirley Pielou, Syd and Wyn Donald, Wayne Brindle, John Adams, Hon G Vane)*

Free house   Licensee Richard Goodall   Lunchtime snacks (not Sun or Mon)
Restaurant   Open 10.30–2.30, 6–11; restaurant closed 2 weeks each Feb and Oct
Bedrooms tel Coxwold (034 76) 214; £22/£38

CRACOE (N Yorks)   SD9760 Map 7
Devonshire Arms
B6265 Skipton–Grassington

This very neatly kept and friendly pub has sturdy rustic or oak tripod tables, green plush cushioned dark pews and built-in wall settles, polished flooring tiles with rugs here and there, and white planks above the low shiny black beams; copper pans hang by the stone fireplace, and above the dark panelled dado are old prints, engravings and photographs, with a big circular large-scale Ordnance Survey map showing the inn as its centre. Good bar food includes sandwiches (from £1.10), carrot and orange soup (£1.20), ploughman's (£3.10), scrambled egg with smoked salmon (£3.20), salmon pâté (£3.45), fresh haddock (£4.30), steak and kidney pie (£4.60) and salads (£4.65); well kept Youngers Scotch and No 3 on handpump, decent coffee, friendly and attentive service. A fruit machine is tucked discreetly away by the entrance; there's a gentle old labrador; darts, maybe unobtrusive piped music. A terrace flanked by well kept herbaceous borders has picnic-table sets. *(Recommended by Jon Wainwright, Syd and Wyn Donald, G Milligan, David Burrows, Dr and Mrs A K Clarke, Wayne Brindle and others)*

Youngers (S&N)   Licensees M Jaques and Miss C Kurz   Real ale   Meals and snacks
Restaurant Tues–Sat evenings   Children welcome until 9   Open 11–3, 6.30–11 all year
Bedrooms tel Cracoe (075 673) 237; £18.50/£37

CRAY (N Yorks)   SD9379 Map 7
White Lion ★

In superb countryside, this welcoming and simply furnished little stone-built pub is popular with walkers. There's a lovely open fire (even in summer), a high dark beam and plank ceiling, seats around tables on the flagstone floor, shelves of china, iron tools and so forth, and a traditional atmosphere. Well kept Youngers Scotch and Moorhouses Premier on handpump. Bar food includes sandwiches (rare or well done beef £1.20, prawn £2.50), battered haddock or locally made Cumberland sausage (£2.75), Yorkshire pudding with lovely onion gravy, steak and kidney pie (£3.50), prawn salad (£4.20) and sirloin steak (£6.95); ring the bull. There are picnic-table sets above the very quiet, steep lane, and great flat limestone slabs (pleasant to sit on) in the shallow stream which tumbles down opposite. They now

We say if we or readers have seen dogs or cats in a pub.

have bedrooms. *(Recommended by Jon Wainwright, Peter and Rose Flower, KC, Paul Newberry, Lynn Stevens, Gill Quarton, Mark Sheard, Alan and Ruth Woodhouse)*

Free house   Licensee J C Outhwaite   Real ale   Snacks (lunchtime, limited Sun) and meals (not Sun)   Children in eating area of bar   Limited parking   Open 11–3, 5.30–11 Bedrooms tel Kettlewell (075 676) 262; £18.50S/£37S

CRAYKE (N Yorks)   SE5670 Map 7
Durham Ox

The old-fashioned lounge bar in this stylish old inn has antique seats and settles around venerable tables on the partly carpeted flagstone and tiling floor, pictures and old local photographs on its dark green walls, a high shelf of plates and interestingly satirical carvings in its panelling, and an enormous inglenook fireplace. Some of the panelling here divides off a bustling public area with a good lively atmosphere and more old-fashioned furnishings; darts. Bar food includes soup (£1.10), open sandwiches or omelettes (£2.50), Yorkshire pudding with a choice of fillings (£3) and salads (from £3); good Sunday lunch. Well kept Theakstons Best and XB on handpump. The tale is that this is the hill which the Grand Old Duke of York marched his men up. *(Recommended by David and Ruth Hollands, Jeremy and Margaret Wallington, Jon Wainwright, Syd and Wyn Donald; more reports on standard, and particularly speed, of service please)*

Free house   Real ale   Meals and snacks   Restaurant   Children in restaurant   Open 11–3, 5.30–11   Bedrooms tel Easingwold (0347) 21506; £20/£28

CRIDLING STUBBS (N Yorks)   SE5221 Map 7
Ancient Shepherd

4 miles from M62 junction 33: S of A1, first left signposted Cridling Stubbs; 3½ miles from M62 junction 34: S on A19, first right; pub signposted from village

The serving-bar in this carefully decorated pub is in an attractive flagstoned hall with swan's neck lamps and stone pillars: well kept Ruddles, Tetleys and Timothy Taylors on handpump. The comfortable lounge bar is decorated in soft browns, and there are sentimental engravings on the walls. Bar food includes home-made soup (£1.20), sausages (£2.10), vegetable curry (£3.10), gammon with fresh pineapple (£3.20), seafood vol-au-vent (£3.30), chicken in white wine (£3.70), and home-made puddings (£1.75). The public bar has darts and dominoes. *(Recommended by T Nott)*

Free house   Real ale   Meals and snacks (not Sat lunchtime, not Sun or Mon)   Restaurant (not Sat lunchtime, not Sun or Mon) tel Knottingley (0977) 83316   Children in eating area of bar   Open 12–3, 7–11 all year; closed lunchtime Sat, all day Mon

EAST LAYTON (N Yorks)   NZ1609 Map 10
Fox Hall Inn 🛏

A66

This tall roadside inn has a panelled bar decorated with prints covering a wide range of sporting pursuits, a high shelf of plates, and settles built in to make cosy booths around the tables; the back part is more open, with a big south-facing window (where maybe Sam, the friendly boxer, likes to sit). Good bar food includes home-made soup (£1.10), crispy mushrooms with garlic mayonnaise (£1.95), ploughman's or battered cod (£2.95), steak and kidney pie (£3.50), swordfish steaks in garlic butter (£4.25), spicy chicken marengo (£4.75), steaks (from £6.50, the T-bone is very popular, £6.75), honey-roast duckling (£6.95) and daily specials such as poached salmon steak with cream and horseradish sauce (£5.95) and fillet steak au poivre (£6.95); Sunday lunch (from £3.95); children's helpings; good service. Tetleys Bitter and Theakstons Best on handpump with Theakstons XB and

Old Peculier in summer; good range of malt whiskies and wines; dominoes, cribbage, sensibly placed darts, Trivial Pursuit, mah jong and piped music. There's a back terrace with tables and chairs. Down the nearby lane to Ravensworth (which climbs to fine views of the rolling countryside) is a ruined medieval castle. Be careful entering or leaving the pub's car park, as some of the traffic on this road is dangerously fast. Well behaved dogs welcome. The bedrooms have been redecorated and refurbished. *(Recommended by Mrs E Morgan, Hon G Vane; more reports please)*

Free house   Licensees Jeremy Atkinson and Susan Elvin   Meals and snacks (12–2.30, 6–10)   Evening restaurant (not Mon or Tues)   Children welcome   Open 11–3, 6–11 all year; opens 7 in winter   Bedrooms tel Darlington (0325) 718262; £15(£20B)/£25(£30B)

EAST WITTON (N Yorks)   SE1586 Map 10

Blue Lion

A6108 Leyburn–Masham

Alas, Mrs Bessie Fletcher died in the summer of 1989, at the age of ninety; for decades she had preserved this simple but charming old pub as it would have been long before the war – and run it in a way that delighted many readers as a true taste of the past. Obviously there will be changes, but as we went to press there were promising signs that the landowner who owned the pub was looking for some way of keeping continuity. So we're keeping our fingers crossed. The truly old-fashioned room has high-backed winged settles, glossy brown woodwork, ham-hooks in the high ceiling, an open fire (lit if there's a local shoot on or something, though not perhaps for a lone casual visitor), and a table full of house plants; a window seat looks out over the cobbled courtyard to the long village green lined neatly with stone cottages. Well kept and very cheap Theakstons Mild from an antique brass handpump in a back room. *(Recommended by Mrs Nina Elliott, Mrs V Carroll)*

Free house   Real ale   Open 11–3, 6–11; has been closed Sun

EGTON BRIDGE (N Yorks)   NZ8105 Map 10

Horse Shoe 🛏

Village signposted from A171 W of Whitby; via Grosmont from A169 S of Whitby

Cutting steeply through the moors, the River Esk provides shelter for this attractive stone house (which has new licensees). There are high-backed built-in winged settles, wall seats and spindle-back chairs around the modern oak tables, and a log fire; the walls are decorated with a big stuffed trout (caught near here in 1913), a fine old print of a storm off Ramsgate and other pictures. Well kept Tetleys, Theakstons Best, XB and Old Peculier on handpump; guest beer each weekend; occasional farm ciders. Darts, dominoes and piped music. A good range of bar food with daily specials includes sandwiches, local trout (£3.60), steak and kidney pie (£3.75) and ham and eggs (£3.80); barbecues in summer. Outside, by a little stream with ducks and geese, there are comfortable seats and tables on a quiet terrace and lawn; a footbridge leads to the tree-sheltered residents' lawn which runs down to the river. *(Recommended by P Bell, J Wiltshire, Derek and Sylvia Stephenson, G T Jones, Nick Dowson, Alison Hayward, M A and W R Proctor, Mr and Mrs Tim Crawford, Eileen Broadbent)*

Free house   Licensees David and Judith Mullins   Real ale   Meals and snacks   Restaurant; not Sun lunch   Children welcome   Open 11–3, 6–11, though they may stay open longer in afternoon if there is demand by trade   Bedrooms tel Whitby (0947) 85245; £18/£30

Postgate 🛏

In one of the prettiest parts of the moors, this friendly pub is named after Father Nicholas Postgate, hanged, drawn and quartered at York 300 years ago for baptising a child into the Roman Catholic Church. The well kept and carpeted lounge bar has upholstered modern settles and seats in a sunny window, Windsor chairs, a high shelf of cups and bottles, and an open fire. Good, home-made food from the daily changing menu might include sandwiches, home-made soup (£1.50), cold buffet (£3), vegetarian goulash (£3.25), whole fresh Whitby plaice, marinated lamb cutlets or pork chop with apple sauce (all £3.50) and home-made puddings. Camerons Lion and Strongarm on handpump. The public bar has darts (one ladies' team as well as three men's), dominoes (Monday evening) and cribbage. Seats outside on a sunny flagstoned terrace look down the hill. Salmon or trout fishing can be arranged, as can boat fishing. *(Recommended by Lynn Stevens, Gill Quarton, R D Jolliff, Robert Gartery, A W Wallens, Eileen Broadbent, Mr and Mrs G Olive, Nick Dowson, Alison Hayward, M A and W R Proctor)*

Camerons   Licensee David Mead   Real ale   Meals and snacks (11–3, 6–9.30)   Restaurant; not Sun evening   Children in eating area of bar   Open 11–11 (11–3, 6–11 in winter) Bedrooms tel Whitby (0947) 85241; £15/£30

ELSLACK (N Yorks)   SD9249 Map 7
Tempest Arms ★ ☺

Just off A56 Earby–Skipton; visible from main road, and warning signs ¼ mile before

The friendly welcome, consistently good, memorable food and warm atmosphere have earned this ancient, French-run pub a star this year. A series of quietly decorated areas have chintzy cushions on the comfortable built-in wall seats, small chintz armchairs, lots of carefully placed tables, quite a bit of stripped stonework, and a log fire in the dividing fireplace; the licensee flies the English flag (not the Union Jack) as well as the French tricolour. Bar food includes sandwiches (from £1.60, open prawn £2.95, steak £3.75), soups – including an exceptional French onion soup (from £1.20) – ploughman's (£2.75), liver and onion (£3.20), steak, kidney and mushroom pie, or gammon and egg (£3.75), an appetising low-calorie platter (£3.80), scampi (£4.25) and fresh salmon (£4.50); vegetarian dishes. Well kept Tetleys Mild and Bitter and Thwaites Bitter on handpump under light blanket pressure; darts, dominoes, fruit machine and piped music. Tables outside are largely screened from the road by a raised bank. As we went to press we heard that the licensees are planning an extension for ten bedrooms. *(Recommended by Syd and Wyn Donald, Russell and Christina Jones, G C and M D Dickinson, Dennis Royles, J Whitehead)*

Free house   Licensee Francis Boulongne   Real ale   Meals and snacks (11.30–2.15, 6.30–10)   Restaurant   Children welcome until 8.30   Open 11.30–3, 6.30 (7 Sat) –11 all year; closed evening 25 Dec   Bedrooms planned tel Earby (0282) 842450

GOOSE EYE (W Yorks)   SE0340 Map 7
Turkey

On high back road between Haworth and Sutton-in-Craven, and signposted from back roads W of Keighley; OS Sheet 104 reference 028406

This simply refurbished, cosy pub has comfortable button-back banquettes built into various snug alcoves, barrel tops set into the concrete floor, and a good old-fashioned copper-topped bar counter. Big End Piston, Ind Coope Burton and Tetleys on handpump – sadly, they no longer brew their own beer. Good value food includes winter soup, sandwiches (from £1.10), giant Yorkshire pudding (from £1.40), ploughman's (£2.50), chilli con carne (£2.40) and lasagne or vegetarian quiche (£2.50). A separate games area has darts, dominoes, various space games, juke box and fruit machine. The village is placed at the bottom of a steep valley with high-walled lanes. *(Recommended by Jon Wainwright; more reports please)*

Free house   Licensee Harry Brisland   Real ale   Meals and snacks   Children welcome   Jazz Tues evening   Open 12–3, 6–11 all year; all day Sat

GREAT AYTON (N Yorks) NZ5611 Map 10
Royal Oak
High Green; off A173 – follow village signs

This pleasantly bustling inn has a dark-panelled main bar with thick butter-coloured plaster on the humpy stone walls, beams supporting wide white ceiling planks, sturdy settles – some of them antique – and wheel-back chairs around traditional cast-iron-framed tables, and an inglenook fireplace (big enough to hold two of the tables); bow windows look out on the square of elegant houses around the village green. An adjoining longer room is set with more tables for the bar food, which at lunchtime includes hot beef baps (85p), soup (£1.05), smoked haddock in cheese sauce (£1.80), mushrooms in garlic mayonnaise (£2.15), salads (from £2.40), braised lamb cutlets (£2.70), steak and kidney pie and steaks (from £5.70); Sunday roast lunch (£3.25). Well kept Youngers No 3 on handpump. The public bar has darts, dominoes, a fruit machine and piped music. *(Recommended by Alan and Ruth Woodhouse, Laurence Manning, RB; more reports please)*

Scottish & Newcastle   Meals and snacks   Singer Weds evening   Restaurant   Children in eating areas   Open 11–11 all year   Bedrooms tel Great Ayton (0642) 722361; £25(£35B)/ £35(£45B)

GRENOSIDE (S Yorks) SK3394 Map 7
Cow & Calf
Skew Hill Lane, off A61 N from Sheffield; at traffic lights turn left following Oughtibridge, Grenoside Hospital sign 3 miles from M1 junction 35; on A629 towards Chapeltown, turn left to Ecclesfield on first minor road; at A6135 T-junction turn right, then shortly at multiple junction with B6087 go straight ahead on minor road to Grenoside

This handsomely converted old stone farmhouse has a particularly friendly and cheerful landlord. Several comfortably furnished interconnecting rooms, all in sight of the well manned bar counter, have a few dog or farmyard pictures on the plain white walls (just bare stone in one back room), some pieces of harness and so forth, and well made high settles. Good value bar food at lunchtime includes sandwiches (80p), Cumberland sausage, rabbit or steak and kidney pie (£2.25), and three-course roast lunch (£4); in the evening there are kidneys in red wine, pork à la crème, farmhouse grill and steak (£4.95), with puddings like home-made apple and blackberry pie (90p). Well kept Sam Smiths on electric pump; dominoes, cribbage, fruit machine and piped music. There is a family area opposite the main entrance, and a shop catering for children outside in the farmyard (where it's fun to sit among the various animals and enjoy the splendid views of Sheffield). *(Recommended by J C and D Aitkenhead, W P P Clarke, Paul Newberry)*

Sam Smiths   Licensee Geoffrey Hopkin   Real ale   Meals and snacks (12–2, 6–9; not Sat or Sun)   Children in family area   Open 11–3, 5.30–11

HARDEN (W Yorks) SE0838 Map 7
Malt Shovel
Follow Wilsden signpost from B6429

The three friendly rooms of the bar in this low building of dark stone have some panelling, red plush seats built into the walls, kettles, brass funnels and the like hanging from the black beams, horsebrasses on leather harness and stone-mullioned windows. Simple but good bar food includes sandwiches, ploughman's, steak and kidney pie and salads; well kept Tetleys Bitter and Mild on handpump; dominoes. From the other side of the bridge you can walk upstream beside the

Harden Beck. *(Recommended by J D Roberts, H K Dyson, Dr A V Lewis, Wayne Brindle, Syd and Wyn Donald)*

Tetleys (Allied) *Real ale* *Meals and snacks (not evening, Sun)* *Open 11.30–3, 5.30–11*

HAROME (N Yorks) SE6582 Map 10

Star ★ ☻

2 miles south of A170, near Helmsley

Almost a Yorkshire institution, this civilised thatched pub has a dark, bowed, beam and plank ceiling hung with ancient bottles (some pointed) and glass net floats, a copper kettle on the well polished tiled kitchen range (with a ship in a bottle on its mantelpiece), a very clean glass cabinet holding kepis, fine china and Japanese dolls, and a fox's mask with little spectacles and a lacy ruff. Bunches of fresh flowers decorate the heavy, deeply polished dark rustic tables, there are cushioned old settles on the Turkey carpet, and unobtrusive classical music. Home-made bar food includes marvellous Scotch broth (£1), lots of very good, generous sandwiches like chicken or prawn curry, good roast beef, ham, egg and cress, tuna, smoked salmon and so forth (from £1.40), salads with home-made horseradish and mayonnaise (from £3.50), a daily hot dish such as savoury pancakes or chicken marsala (£3.75), and puddings like orange cake, fresh strawberry sorbet or almond tart (£1.75); there's a coffee loft up in the thatch. Well kept Camerons Lion and Theakstons Best and Old Peculier on handpump. On a sheltered front flagstoned terrace there are some seats and tables, with more in the garden behind, which has an old-fashioned swing seat, fruit trees and a big ash. No animals. *(Recommended by Syd and Wyn Donald, M B Porter, Henry Midwinter, Patrick Clarke, S V Bishop, M A and W R Proctor, Laurence Manning, E Lee, Wayne Brindle, Rob and Gill Weeks, G Bloxsom, J C Proud, Sue Cleasby, Mike Ledger)*

Free house *Licensee Peter Gascoigne-Mullett* *Real ale* *Lunchtime meals and snacks* *Evening restaurant tel Helmsley (0439) 70397* *Children in dining-room or coffee loft* *Open 12–2.30, 6–11; closed Mon lunchtime and 25 Dec*

nr HARROGATE (N Yorks) SE3155 Map 7

Squinting Cat

Whinney Lane, Pannal Ash (which is signposted off B6162 W of Harrogate); OS Sheet 104 reference 296517

At last the long-heralded extensions to this very popular eighteenth-century pub have been completed. Bearing in mind one's natural preference to leave longstanding favourites unchanged, many people really like the results. They've taken a lot of care to keep the old-fashioned style and give rather the impression of stalls in a stable: a successful mix of pine chairs and tables in one part with re-covered armchairs in another, York stone walls (refashioned from an old railway bridge) hung with pictures, old grain sacks, barrels, bottles, and nautical wooden pulley systems radiating out from a minstrels' gallery complete with boat. The original part with its rambling rooms has changed little, apart from some smartening up. Bar food includes sandwiches (from £1), five home-made pâtés (from £1.95), home-made meaty or vegetarian lasagne or prawn omelette (£3), steak and kidney pie (£3.50), and a cold buffet (from £4.25); in the evening there are scallops of turkey in garlic, grilled gammon or chicken in cream (£4), and steaks (from £5.95). Barbecues, weather permitting (from £4). Well kept Tetleys Mild and Bitter on handpump; good red wine; friendly, courteous service; dominoes and fruit machine. There are tables outside. The North of England Horticultural Society's fine gardens on the curlew moors at Harlow Car are just over the B6162.

Children: if the details at the end of an entry don't mention them, you should assume that the pub does not allow them inside.

(Recommended by Jon Wainwright, A J Leach, G C and M D Dickinson, Richard and Carol Glover, Paul Newberry, Syd and Wyn Donald, George Hunt, Norman Hodgson)

Tetleys (Allied)   Licensee Ken Attewell   Real ale   Meals and snacks   Restaurant tel Harrogate (0423) 565650   Children welcome   Open 11–3, 5.30–11 all year, though may open longer in afternoon if trade demands; 11–11 Sat; closed 25 Dec

HATFIELD WOODHOUSE (S Yorks)   SE6808 Map 7
Green Tree
1 mile from M18 junction 5: on A18/A614 towards Bawtry

There's plenty of room in this well run, large pub even when it's busy. The series of connecting open-plan rooms and alcoves are comfortably modernised, with brown leatherette seats and Windsor chairs around the tables, an expanse of Turkey carpet, fresh flowers and a warm atmosphere. Good bar food includes soup (£1), sandwiches (from £1), ploughman's (£2.35), omelette or spinach roulade (£2.50), a pint of fresh prawns, fresh haddock or plaice from Grimsby (£3), home-made steak and kidney pie (£2.95), salads (from £3.25), grilled gammon (£3.45), mixed grill (£4), steaks (from £4.25), and puddings such as cherry and apple pie (£1). They do a seafood buffet on Friday and Saturday evenings, serving cockles, mussels, whelks and prawns. Well kept Darleys and Wards on handpump; friendly staff; fruit machine and piped music. *(Recommended by M A and W R Proctor, John Baker, ILP, Sue Cleasby, Mike Ledger, Jon Woodhouse)*

Wards (Vaux)   Licensee Trevor Hagan   Real ale   Meals and snacks (12–2.30, 6.30–10; not 25 Dec)   Restaurant (evenings and Sun lunch) tel Doncaster (0302) 840305   Children in eating area of bar   Open 11–3, 6–11 all year

HEATH (W Yorks)   SE3519 Map 7
Kings Arms
Village signposted from A655 Wakefield–Normanton – or, more directly, turn off opposite Horse & Groom

Sunny benches outside this very old-fashioned pub face the village green and you'd never believe that this is in the industrial heartland of West Yorkshire. The dark-panelled original bar has a fire burning in the old black range (with a long row of smoothing irons on the mantelpiece), plain elm stools and oak settles built into the walls, some heavy cast-iron-framed tables on the flagstones, a built-in cupboard of cut glass, and gas lighting. A more comfortable extension (with a fitted red carpet, even) has carefully preserved the original style, down to good wood-pegged oak panelling, a high shelf of plates, and more of the swan's-neck gas lamps. Quiet on weekday lunchtimes, it's more popular for an evening outing. The range of bar food changes daily, but typically should include soup (75p), Yorkshire pudding and gravy (80p), hot beef sandwich (£1.10), savoury mince pancake or chicken liver pâté (£2.20), savoury quiche (£2.40), rabbit pie (£2.75) and minted lamb chops, gammon steak or roast pork lunch (£3). Well kept Theakstons Bitter, XB and Old Peculier from antique hand-tap beer engines (or a tighter creamier head from the more orthodox handpumps in the new bar); dominoes. *(Recommended by Paul Newberry, Roger Huggins, Comus Elliott)*

Free house   Licensee David Kerr   Real ale   Meals and snacks (not Sun evening)   Restaurant (not Sun evening) tel Wakefield (0924) 377527   Children in eating area of bar   Open 11.30–3, 6.30–11

HECKMONDWIKE (W Yorks)   SE2223 Map 7
Old Hall
New North Road; B6117 between A62 and A638; OS Sheet 104 reference 214244

Once the home of the Nonconformist scientist Joseph Priestley, this carefully restored, fine old manor house has been partly knocked through inside, showing stripped old stone or brick walls (with pictures of Richard III, Henry VII, Catherine Parr and Priestley), lots of oak beams and timbers, and latticed mullioned windows with worn stone surrounds. Snug low-ceilinged alcoves lead off the central part with its high ornate plaster ceiling, and an upper gallery room, under the pitched roof, looks down on the main area through timbering 'windows'. Comfortable furnishings include cushioned oak pews and red plush seats, some with oak backs, on a sweep of Turkey carpet (there are flagstones by the serving-counter). Good bar food brought to your table by efficient staff includes sandwiches (from 85p), soup (£1.30), pâté (£1.30), scampi (£2.95), steaks (from £6.25) and unusual daily specials (£2.95); salad bar during the summer. Well kept Sam Smiths OB and Museum on handpump; unobtrusive piped music, and darts in a wall cupboard. *(Recommended by Mrs J McCluskey, Frank Cummins, Ian Robinson, M A and W R Proctor, PLC)*

Sam Smiths   Licensee Peter McCluskey   Real ale   Meals and snacks (12–2, 7.30–9.45; until 9.30 Sat)   Children welcome   Open 11–3, 6–11 all year

HELMSLEY (N Yorks)   SE6184 Map 10
Feathers
Market Square

There are heavy medieval beams and dark panelling in the low and cosy original pub part of this inn, as well as a venerable wall carving of a dragon-faced bird in a grape vine, a big log fire in the stone inglenook fireplace, and unusual cast-iron-framed tables topped by weighty slabs of oak and walnut. The main inn is a handsomely solid three-storey stone block with a comfortable lounge bar. Popular bar food includes lots of changing specials, as well as soup (£1.20), sandwiches (from £1.40), ploughman's (£2.25), good garlic mushrooms (£2.50), good Cumberland sausage, chilli, home-made quiche or deep-fried clams (all £3.50), fresh Scarborough haddock (£3.95), scampi (£4), home-made steak pie (£4.75) and steaks (£7.50). Well kept McEwans 80/- and Theakstons XB on handpump; large choice of wines; efficient service. Darts, dominoes, video game and juke box. There's an attractive back garden. This is a pleasant and relaxing town, close to Rievaulx Abbey (well worth an hour's visit). *(Recommended by M B Porter, Richard Dolphin, G Owens, Tony Pounder, E Lee, M A and W R Proctor, Jon Wainwright, Jane Palmer, Jon Dewhirst)*

Free house   Licensee Jack Feather   Real ale   Meals and snacks   Restaurant   Children welcome, but in small lounge between bars when busy   Open 10.30–2.30, 6–11; closes 10.30 in winter; closed 23 Dec–3 Jan   Bedrooms tel Helmsley (0439) 70275; £18.50(£28B)/ £37(£46B)

HETTON (N Yorks)   SD9558 Map 7
Angel ★ ⊘
The four rambling rooms in this attractively decorated and well run food pub have some beams, standing timbers and panelling, lots of cosy alcoves, comfortable country-kitchen chairs or button-back green plush seats, Ronald Searle wine snob cartoons, and older engravings and photographs; there are log fires, a solid-fuel stove, and in the main bar a Victorian farmhouse range in the big stone fireplace. Imaginatively presented food includes cream soups with fried croûtons or clear soups with cheese croûtes and a touch of wine or cognac (£1.35, provençale fish soup with garlic croûtons £1.80), sandwiches (from £1.85, open smoked salmon salad £3.85), home-made terrine (£2.95), a tasty plate of home-smoked and cured fish (£3.85), home-made steak, kidney and mushroom pie (£3.95), grilled gammon with egg or pineapple (£4.50), lamb cutlets with tarragon butter (£4.65), char-grilled calf's liver with sweet home-cured bacon (£6.50), cold Scotch salmon

(£5.95, when available), eight-ounce sirloin steak (£6.50) and home-made puddings (£1.50); also, daily fresh fish specials such as suprême of halibut with scallops, prawns, clams and mussels (£5.25), melody of seafood – mullet, king prawns, langoustine, salmon and sole fried in garlic butter and lemon juice (£8.75) and superb seafood platter (£9.55). It gets packed with families and walkers by 1pm (and can be hard to find a seat a quarter of an hour earlier) when there can be quite a long wait for food, and they may want to move you on when you've finished to make space for someone else. Well kept Theakstons Bitter, XB and Old Peculier, and Timothy Taylors Landlord on handpump, a decent choice of wines by the glass or bottle (chalked up on a blackboard, and often bin-ends), and quite a few malt whiskies; friendly service. Darts and dominoes. Sturdy wooden benches and tables are built on to the cobbles outside this pretty house. *(Recommended by Mr and Mrs J E Rycroft, E V Walder, Syd and Wyn Donald, G C and M D Dickinson, David and Flo Wallington, Alan and Marlene Radford, E Lee, Robert Gartery)*

Free house   Licensee Denis Watkins   Real ale   Meals and snacks (12–2, 7–10)   Restaurant (not Sun evening) tel Cracoe (075 673) 263   Children in eating area of bar and restaurant Open 11.30–2.30, 6–10.30 (11 Fri and Sat); closed evening 25 Dec

HUBBERHOLME (N Yorks)   SD9178 Map 7

George ★

Village signposted from Buckden; about 1 mile NW

In Yorkshire's smallest conservation area – which includes just the inn, bridge and church – this remote and unspoilt old Upper Wharfedale building has two small and well kept flagstoned bar rooms with walls stripped back to bare stone, dark ceiling boards supported by heavy beams, and simple seats around shiny copper-topped tables; an open stove in the big fireplace throws out plenty of heat. At lunchtime cheerful walkers crowd in for food, mainly fresh from the Aga, which includes home-made soup, delicious hefty warm rolls filled with big slices of juicy fresh ham, cheese or bacon (around £1.50), pâté (£1.90), steak and kidney or chicken and ham pie with the lightest of crusts (£3.30), and lovely chocolate fudge cake; very well kept Youngers Scotch and No 3 on handpump, and a good choice of malt whiskies; darts, dominoes and cribbage. The inn looks out on a lovely swirly stretch of the River Wharfe where they have fishing rights; they still let riverside land in aid of a church charity, and when they do (on the first Monday of the New Year), there's a licensing extension till nearly midnight. Seats and tables look up to the moors which rise all around. As we went to press we heard that the licensees were planning to retire. *(Recommended by Peter and Rose Flower, Jon Wainwright, Neil and Angela Huxter, Jane and Niall, Lynn Stevens, Gill Quarton, David Forsyth, Jacqueline Howard, Alan and Ruth Woodhouse, Rob and Gill Weeks, J E Rycroft; more reports on service please)*

Free house   Licensee John Fredrick   Real ale   Meals and snacks   Evening restaurant Children welcome   Open 11.30–3, 6.30–11 all year; opens 7 in winter; closed evening 25 Dec   Bedrooms tel Kettlewell (075 676) 223; £32 (twin only)

KILBURN (N Yorks)   SE5179 Map 7

Forresters Arms 🛏

Signposted from A170 E of Thirsk

Set in the Hambleton Hills with lovely countryside close by, this friendly stone and brick pub has white tables out on the front terrace looking across to pretty village gardens, which are interspersed with planked oak trunks weathering for the Thompson furniture workshop next door. Most of the sturdy yet elegant furniture here, usually oak, always has the trademark little carved mouse sitting, standing or running in some discreet corner of the piece. That's also the source of the fine bar counter and the great slab shelf along the wall of the inner room – lights beneath it throw the stripped stonework into striking relief. This inner room has tables for people eating; the smaller outer bar's chairs are much more for sitting and chatting by the log fire in its unusual rounded stone chimney breast. Well kept Tetleys Bitter on handpump, a good choice of popular bar food including sandwiches, lasagne or battered haddock (£3.45), home-made steak and kidney pie (£3.90), scampi (£3.70) and steaks (from £5.90); unobtrusive and pleasantly chosen piped music, and a quiz machine kept discreetly out of the way. Dogs welcome (James Herriot is in fact their vet). *(Recommended by Jenny Cantle, T George, Steve Breame and others)*

Free house   Licensees Brian and Kristine Livingstone   Real ale   Meals and snacks Restaurant   Children welcome, but no toddlers in restaurant in evenings   Open 11–11 (closed 3–5.30 weekdays in winter – summer too if not busy) all year   Bedrooms tel Coxwold (034 76) 386; /£35B

KIRBY HILL (N Yorks)   NZ1406 Map 10
Shoulder of Mutton 🍴

Signposted from Ravensworth road about 3½ miles N of Richmond; or from A66 Scotch Corner–Brough turn off into Ravensworth, bear left through village, and take signposted right turn nearly a mile further on

On the left of a communicating entry hallway, with a pretty 1880s watercolour of boats in a misty estuary, is the neat and comfortably modernised bar, with muted blues and reds for the carpet and the plush wall settles around simple dark tables, local turn-of-the-century photographs of Richmond, an open fire and a good welcoming atmosphere. The licensee came to the pub after thirty years in the Navy. Decent bar food includes ploughman's (£2.50), lasagne, chicken and bacon or steak and kidney pie (£2.60), a large plateful of haddock and chips (£3.50) and scampi (£3.75), and the stripped-stone restaurant is noted for its generous helpings; first-class breakfasts. Well kept Theakstons XB, Websters Choice and guest beers such as Exmoor or Ruddles County on handpump; darts, dominoes, with pool and juke box in a side room and a fruit machine around the back; piped music. The yard behind has picnic-table sets. This is a very quiet spot, looking out from a bluff over the ruin of Ravensworth Castle; the church clock opposite has an unusually tuneful bell. *(Recommended by Mr and Mrs Bill Muirhead, Hon G Vane and others; more reports please)*

Free house   Licensees Hylton and Shirley Pyner   Real ale   Meals and snacks (not Mon lunchtime)   Restaurant   Children welcome   Open 12–3, 7–11 all year; closed Mon lunchtime   Bedrooms tel Richmond (0748) 2772; £14(£17B)/£28(£34B)

LANGDALE END (N Yorks)   SE9491 Map 10
Moor Cock

Best reached from A170 at East Ayton (signposted Forge Valley, just E of bridge), or A171 via Hackness; OS Sheet 101 reference 938913

You can expect a cheery welcome in this unspoilt whitewashed stone terraced cottage, set in a beautiful valley. The neat little parlour has simple old settles around a scrubbed table, clean, red quarry tiles, a warm fire and one or two calendars on the wall. The beer is poured in a back room and brought out on a tray, and the sandwiches, with ham, cheese and tomato (75p), are freshly cut; there's even tea or coffee and biscuits if you wish. *(Recommended by T George; more reports please)*

Free house   Licensee Maud Martindale   Evening snacks (not Sun)   Open 10.30–3, 6–11 all year; closed Sun

---

People named as recommenders after the main entries have told us that the pub should be included. But they have not written the report – we have, after anonymous on-the-spot inspection.

LANGTHWAITE (N Yorks)   NZ0003 Map 10
Red Lion

Just off the Arkengarthdale road from Reeth to Brough

This warm, friendly and unpretentiously cottagey little pub is kept spick and span, and has comfortably cushioned wall seats, a few decorative plates on a Delft shelf, a fox's mask, flowery curtains, and a beam and plank ceiling; if you think that one's low, try the burrow-like side snug. They also have carved horn beakers, signed copies of books by Herriot and Wainwright, Ordnance Survey maps, and local paintings and books on the Dales for sale; dominoes. A sensibly short choice of simple good value bar food includes toasted sandwiches (from 90p), pizza (£1.30), lamb pie or various quiches (£1.60), ploughman's (£1.75), vegetarian goulash (£1.90), curries or Old Peculier casserole (£2.40), and puddings such as chocolate fudge cake or lemon meringue pie (80p); country wines. They very helpfully open at 10.30 for coffee on summer Sundays, keeping open for meals then until 2. There are some picnic-table sets out in the tiny village square. Footpaths from this charming cluster of houses thread their way along the Arkle beck and up the moors on either side. *(Recommended by Peter and Rose Flower, Alan Hall, TOH, G T Jones; more reports please)*

Free house   Licensee Mrs Rowena Hutchinson   Meals and snacks (11.30–2, 6.30–9; 10.30–2, 7–9 Sun)   Children in eating area until 8   Open 10.30–3, 6–11 all year

LASTINGHAM (N Yorks)   SE7391 Map 10
Blacksmiths Arms

There is lovely countryside all around this neat stone inn, below Spaunton Moor, with tracks through Cropton Forest. Inside, the comfortable oak-beamed bar has an attractive cooking-range with swinging pot-yards, some sparkling brass, cushioned Windsor chairs and traditional built-in wooden wall seats, and a good fire in winter. Good, reasonably priced bar food includes home-made Yorkshire pudding (from 60p), soup (from £1), sandwiches (from £1.10), ploughman's (£2), haddock (£2.80), lasagne (£3), salads (from £3.30), steak and kidney pie (£4), evening steak (£6) and home-made puddings. A simply furnished dining area opens off the main bar, with traditional Sunday roasts. Well kept Theakstons Best, XB and Old Peculier on handpump; a good range of malt whiskies; darts, dominoes, piped music. *(Recommended by Kelvin Lawton, Derek and Sylvia Stephenson, T George, G Bloxsom)*

Free house   Licensee Rodney Taylor   Real ale   Meals and snacks   Children in eating area of bar until 8.30   Open 11.30–3, 6.30–11; closed weekday lunchtimes in winter   Bedrooms tel Lastingham (075 15) 247; £15/£30

LEDSHAM (W Yorks)   SE4529 Map 7
Chequers

Opening off an old-fashioned little central panelled-in servery in this attractive, friendly pub are small, individually decorated rooms with lots of cosy alcoves, low beams, and log fires. Good, nicely presented bar food includes soup (80p), sandwiches (from £1.25), ploughman's (£1.95), tasty scrambled eggs and smoked salmon (£2.45), excellent chicken and mushroom pancake, lasagne (£2.95), steak pie (£3.65) and good ham and eggs (£3.95). Well kept Theakstons and Youngers Scotch, No 3 and IPA on handpump; cheerful service from the new licensees. A sheltered two-level terrace behind the creeper-covered stone village house has tables

If you enjoy your visit to a pub, please tell the publican. They work extraordinarily long hours, and when people show their appreciation it makes it all seem worth while.

among roses. *(Recommended by Christopher Knowles-Fitton, J E Rycroft, William Rodgers, Syd and Wyn Donald, Roger Bellingham, J C Proud, J H Tate, Brian Green, A V Lewis, John Oddey, M A and W R Proctor, PLC)*

Free house   Licensee C J Wraith   Real ale   Meals and snacks (12–2, 6–8.30)   Children in own room   Open 11–3, 5.30–11; 11–11 Sat; closed Sun

LEEDS (W Yorks)   SE3033 Map 7

Fox & Newt

9 Burley Road, Leeds 3; at junction with Rutland Street

Attractively done up as an old-fashioned tavern, this busy own-brew place has bright paintwork, green leatherette seats built into the dark panelling of the lower part of the walls (there's dark red embossed Anaglypta above) and dimpled copper-topped cast-iron tables on the bare floorboards of its main room; one or two steps lead up to a comfortable snug behind a wooden balcony. Well kept Abbey, Burley, Kirkstall's Ruin and Old Willow on handpump or by the four-pint jugs if you want. Bar food includes French bread sandwiches (from 70p), lasagne, chilli con carne or steak pie (£2), and moussaka (£2.20). Fruit machine, trivia and piped music; the What the Butler Saw machine is now just there for show. *(Recommended by Joy Heatherley, John Thorndike, Steve Waters, Graeme Smalley, Jon Wainright)*

Own brew/Whitbreads   Licensee Kevin Dixon   Real ale   Lunchtime meals and snacks Open 11–11 all year

Garden Gate ★

37 Waterloo Road, Hunslet; leaving Leeds centre on A61, turn right at traffic lights signposted Hunslet Centre P, Belle Isle 1½, Middleton 3, park in the public car park on your right, and walk through – the pub is obvious

Despite the unpromising surroundings (a mosaic of depressed areas and modern redevelopment), this lively pub has a marvellously preserved Victorian layout and décor. A tiled corridor panelled in mahogany and deep-cut glass links four old-fashioned rooms. The finest, on the left as you enter, has a lovely free-flowing design of tiles coloured in subtle tones of buff, cream and icy green, a mosaic floor, and a magnificent bar counter, the front of which is made from elaborately shaped and bowed tiles (with hatch service to the corridor too). Perfectly kept Tetleys Bitter and Mild on handpump – the brewery is just up the Hunslet Road. Ham or cheese salad sandwiches; darts, dominoes (very popular here), cribbage and fruit machine. It's very much a working men's pub (we saw no women here). *(Recommended by Denis Mann, J C Proud)*

Tetleys (Allied)   Real ale   Snacks (not Sat or Sun)   Open 11–3, 5.30–11 Mon–Thurs; 11–11 Fri and Sat

Whitelocks ★

Turks Head Yard; gunnel (or alley) off Briggate, opposite Debenhams and Littlewoods; park in shoppers' car park and walk

One reader remembers the days when, drinking here fifty years ago, he'd see all the top performers from the nearby Leeds Empire; another, even further back, remembers playing rugby football with a keg in the yard outside. But you don't need such a long memory to feel immediately touched by this lively pub's deep sense of times past. The long old-fashioned narrow room has grand advertising mirrors, a fine bar counter decorated with polychrome tiles, and stained-glass windows, with red button-back plush banquettes and heavy copper-topped cast-iron tables squeezed down one side. Good, reasonably priced lunchtime bar food includes bubble and squeak (40p), home-made Scotch eggs (60p), home-made quiche (£1), Yorkshire puddings (£1.20 with fillings), sandwiches, sausage and mash (£1.50) and meat and potato pie (£1.60), and jam roly-poly or fruit pie (70p); when it gets busy you may have to wait for your order. Well kept McEwans 80/- and Youngers IPA and Scotch on handpump; quiz evenings every Tuesday in the top bar. At the end of the long narrow yard another bar has been done up in Dickensian style.

(Recommended by P Miller, Steve Waters, J F Thorndike, Roger Taylor, J E Rycroft, Syd and Wyn Donald, Comus Elliott, Wayne Brindle, Jon Wainwright, Prof S Barnett, T Nott, Geoff Wilson, J C Proud)

Youngers (S&N)   Licensee Julie Cliff   Real ale   Meals and snacks (11–7.30; not Sun evening)   Restaurant tel Leeds (0532) 453950   Children in restaurant   Open 11–11 weekdays; 12–3, 7.30–10.30 Sat

LEVISHAM (N Yorks)   SE8391 Map 10
Horseshoe
Pub and village signposted from A169 N of Pickering

Originally, to be frank, we included this well kept pub chiefly for its position, but over the last few years it has built up a loyal following from readers for its friendly welcome and well presented, reasonably priced food. The extended and refurbished bar has plush seats around tables, a log fire in a stone fireplace, and darts, bar billiards, dominoes and piped music. Bar food includes soup (90p), sandwiches (from £1.25), ploughman's (from £1.95), popular sirloin sandwich (£2.85), home-made goulash (£2.95), attractive salads (from £3.15), good steak and kidney pie (£3.35), and good prawn thermidor (£3.65). Well kept Tetleys Bitter and Theakstons Best on handpump; good range of malt whiskies; service is pleasant, quick and efficient. Twice a day each way in spring and autumn, and four times in summer, steam trains of the North Yorks Moors Railway stop at this village.

(Recommended by Derek and Sylvia Stephenson, F Haworth, T George, R D Jolliff, M A and W R Proctor)

Free house   Licensees Roy and Marjorie Hayton   Real ale   Meals and snacks Restaurant   Children welcome   Open 11–3, 6–11, though they may stay open longer in afternoon if there are customers   Bedrooms tel Pickering (0751) 60240; £17/£32

LINTHWAITE (W Yorks)   SE1014 Map 7
Bulls Head ✿
31 Blackmoorfoot; Blackmoorfoot signposted from town centre, above A62 W of Huddersfield – head up past school towards moors, and bear right by dam

The most popular dish in this cheerful pub, transformed by the people who bought it in 1985, is a hefty Yorkshire pudding 'sandwich' packed with tender hot beef and gravy (£1.40); with a side order of succulent chips (30p), almost enough to defeat a drayman. Other very quickly served food – which changes from day to day – includes hot beef teacake (£1.10), cheese and spinach quiche or summer vegetable and nut crumble (£2.50), tagliatelle done creamily with mushrooms and ricotta (£2.75), a chicken, ham and asparagus pasta bake or liver done crisply with garlic butter (£2.95), beef casseroled with orange and Guinness, a prawn, courgette and tomato gratin or chicken breast stuffed with herby cream cheese (£3.20), and monkfish and bacon kebab (£3.25). On Mondays their steak 'n' bake night (now copied by several dozen other pubs in the area) is an outstanding bargain (£10.50 for two, including a bottle of wine). There are no pretensions here: two communicating rooms (one with Victorian-style wallpaper) furnished with sturdy brown-plush-upholstered wall benches and stools around cast-iron-framed tables, with coal fires, well reproduced piped music (Beatles on our visit), a fruit machine, and well kept Boddingtons Bitter and Mild and Stones on handpump. This being West Yorkshire, don't be surprised to see most of the girls here smoking. There are

---

If we know a pub does summer barbecues, we say so.

picnic-table sets in front of the dark stone pub. *(Recommended by Robert Gartery, H K Dyson, Connie Pearson)*

Free house   Licensee S L Head   Real ale   Meals and snacks (11–10; not after 3 Sat; permitted hours Sun)   Children welcome   Open 11–11 all year

Sair

Hoyle Ing, off A62; as you leave Huddersfield this is one of the only left turns in Linthwaite, and the street name is marked, but keep your eyes skinned for it – it burrows very steeply up between works buildings; OS Sheet 110 reference 101143

This place was an own-brew pub back in the last century, and one story is that the name Sair ('sour') dates back to a time around the turn of the century when the beer was off. Today, the remarkable range of ales produced by that compulsive brewer Ron Crabtree (previously one of the founders of the West Riding Brewery) are very well kept and include the laudably well balanced Linfit and Linfit Mild, Old Eli, Leadboiler, a Christmas ale that has a habit of turning up at the most unseasonable times, and the redoubtable Enochs Hammer. He even does stout (English Guineas) and a Hoyleingerbrau lager (just filtered – not pasteurised as we said in last year's edition), and this year has introduced a low-alcohol real ale. So there's masses of choice – not to mention his Causeway Sider. The quaint cluster of rooms have big stone fireplaces (in winter almost as many fires as beers), pews, more comfortable leatherette banquettes or smaller chairs, rough flagstones in some parts and carpet in others, bottle collections, beer-mats tacked to beams, and a happy, chatty atmosphere; as in many a Yorkshire pub, when it's busy the atmosphere isn't exactly mountain purity, in spite of the air cleaner. The room on the right has darts, shove-ha'penny, dominoes and a juke box (mainly golden oldies – and not noticed in the other rooms). There's a pub guinea-pig. *(Recommended by Steve Waters, N F Doherty, P Corris, Jon Wainwright, Mr and Mrs P A Jones, Rob and Gill Weeks)*

Own brew   Licensee Ron Crabtree   Real ale   Well behaved children welcome   Open 7–11 only on weekdays, plus 12–4 Sat and bank hols, all year; otherwise closed weekday lunchtimes

LINTON IN CRAVEN (N Yorks)   SD9962 Map 7

Fountaine

The licensees who took over here in summer 1988 had previously made themselves popular with readers at the Craven Arms, Appletreewick. They've clearly made a good start here: the atmosphere in the cosy and interestingly furnished little rooms is just what you want, looking down over the grass to the narrow stream that runs through this delightful hamlet. Good, popular bar food includes soup (£1.10), open sandwiches (from £1.45), black pudding with mild mustard sauce (£1.95), ploughman's (from £2.65), scampi (£3.50), salads (from £3.40), gammon with eggs or pineapple (£4.50), steaks (from £6.25) and mixed grill (£7.25); interesting home-made specials such as smoked mackerel baked in gooseberry sauce, braised oxtail, Yorkshire puddings topped with steak and kidney, parsnips 'Molly Parkin' or mussels in white wine and chilli sauce. They roast local beef or pork, and sausages are made specially for them with spices, herbs and walnuts. Well kept Theakstons Best and Old Peculier, and Youngers Scotch on handpump; darts, dominoes, ring the bull and fruit machine. *(Recommended by Jon Wainwright, Syd and Wyn Donald, Jenny Cantle, Mr and Mrs J H Adam, Dr and Mrs A K Clarke, Mr and Mrs M Tarlton)*

Free house   Licensees Gordon and Linda Elsworth   Real ale   Meals and snacks   Children in own room   Open 11.30–3, 6.30–11 all year

LITTON (N Yorks)   SD9074 Map 7

Queens Arms 🍺

As we went to press we heard that this friendly 300-year-old inn was up for sale – we hope things don't change too much. The main bar on the right has stools around cast-iron-framed tables on its stone and concrete floor, a seat built into the stone-mullioned window, stripped rough stone walls, a brown beam and plank ceiling, a large collection of cigarette lighters, and a good coal fire. On the left, the red-carpeted room has more of a family atmosphere, with varnished pine for its built-in wall seats, and for the ceiling and walls themselves, and there's another coal fire. Food at lunchtime includes home-made soup (90p), sandwiches (from £1), hot pork pie with mushy peas (£1.10), salads (£3); more substantial evening meals include local pork sausage with apple sauce and sage and onion stuffing (£2.30), ham with eggs or pineapple (£3.40) and rump steak (£6.10); excellent generous breakfasts. Well kept Youngers Scotch on handpump; darts, dominoes, cribbage and piped music. It's a lovely spot – a track behind the pub leads over Ackerley Moor to Buckden, and the quiet lane through the valley leads on to Pen-y-ghent. *(Recommended by Joan and John Calvert, Gary Melnyk, Jon Wainwright, Peter and Rose Flower, Neil and Angela Huxter, Jane and Niall, Hilaire Miles-Sharp, Mrs D M Everard, Andy Tyne, Sue Hill, C A Adams)*

Free house   Licensee Freda Brook   Real ale   Meals and snacks   Children welcome   Open 11–3, 6–11; opens 7 in winter   Bedrooms tel Arncliffe (075 677) 208; £15/£27

MARTON-CUM-GRAFTON (N Yorks)   SE4265   Map 7
Olde Punch Bowl

Village signposted from A1 3 miles N of A59

A cosy sense of individual rooms in the open-plan lounge bar of this well run village pub is preserved by the timber uprights, varying ceiling heights and heavy beams. Windsor chairs are set neatly around groups of tables on an expanse of Turkey carpet, and there are open fires. The lunchtime choice of good food includes home-made soup (95p), sandwiches (from 90p), ploughman's (£2.50), salads (from £2.30), and a range of hot dishes such as liver and onions (£2.50), home-made steak pie and gammon with egg or pineapple (£3.50); three-course business lunch (£4.95); there are evening main dishes, served in the dining-room, such as scampi, rack of lamb and steaks. Well kept Tetleys, Youngers Scotch, IPA and No 3 on handpump; piped music, darts, pool, dominoes, fruit machine, space game and juke box in the public bar. The large car park has a Caravan Club licence. The pub is convenient for the A1. *(Recommended by Sue Cleasby, Mike Ledger, Jane and Niall, Rob and Gill Weeks, Wayne Brindle)*

Free house   Licensee Christine Polson   Real ale   Meals and snacks   Restaurant   Children welcome   Occasional live music   Open 12–3.30, 6–11.30; opens 7 in winter

MASHAM (N Yorks)   SE2381   Map 7
White Bear ★

Signposted off A6108 opposite turn into town centre

The busy, traditionally furnished public bar here serves very well kept Theakstons Best, XB and Old Peculier on handpump – as you'd expect. The pub's part of Theakstons old stone headquarters buildings, though the brewery itself is on the other side of town (and of course Theakstons, taken over a few years ago by Matthew Browns, became part of Scottish & Newcastle two years ago). There's enough bric-à-brac to fill several antique shops: stuffed animals – including a huge polar bear behind the bar – copper brewing implements, foreign banknotes, harness, pottery and even an electric shock machine that's supposed to help rheumatism. A much bigger, more comfortable lounge has a Turkey carpet. Good bar food includes sandwiches, curries, trout and game dishes; no chips. Shove-ha'penny, dominoes, cribbage, fruit machine and juke box. In summer there are seats out in the yard. *(Recommended by Jenny Cantle, Paul Newberry, Dennis Jones, T Nott, Rob and Gill Weeks)*

Theakstons (S&N)   Licensee Neil Cutts   Real ale   Meals and snacks (not Sat or Sun evenings)   Children welcome   Live music Sat evenings   Open 11–11 all year   Bedrooms tel Ripon (0765) 89319; /£25

MOULTON (N Yorks)   NZ2404 Map 10
Black Bull 🏵

Just E of A1, 1 mile S of Scotch Corner

This very civilised, well run place has built-in red-cushioned black settles and pews, an antique panelled oak settle, and an old elm housekeeper's chair around the cast-iron tables (one has a heavily beaten copper top) on the dark grey carpet squares, black beams hung with copper cooking utensils, silver-plate Turkish coffeepots and so forth over the red velvet curtained windows, and a huge winter log fire. A nice side dark-panelled seafood bar has some high seats at the marble-topped counter; decorations include three nice Lionel Edwards hunting prints in the main bar, an Edwardian engraving of a big hunt meet, and a huge bowl of lilies. Bar snacks include excellent smoked salmon: sandwiches (£2), pâté (£2.25), smoked salmon and asparagus quiche (£3.50) and smoked salmon plate (£4.75); they also do a very good home-made soup served in lovely little tureens (£1), mushrooms in garlic butter (£1.50), lovely fresh salmon sandwiches (£2), avocado and prawns (£2.75), Welsh rarebit and bacon (£3.25), and memorable seafood pancakes (£3.50). In the evening you can also eat in the polished brick-tiled conservatory with bentwood cane chairs or in the Brighton Belle dining-car. Theakstons Best and Old Peculier served from the copper-topped panelled mahogany bar counter, good wine, several malt whiskies and decent coffee; quick, courteous service. There are some seats under trees in the central court. *(Recommended by Stephanie Sowerby, T Nott, SS, David Young, GB, Dr J R Hamilton, G L Archer, John Abel)*

Free house   Licensee Audrey Pagendam   Lunchtime meals and snacks (12–2; not Sun)   Restaurants (closed Sun) tel Barton (0325) 377289   Children over 7 if well behaved   Open 12–2.30, 6–10.30; closed 24–31 Dec

NEWHOLM (N Yorks)   NZ8611 Map 10
Beehive

Village signposted from A171

Almost the best thing about this well kept and notably friendly pub is how it looks – it's one of the prettiest pubs in the north, snug and low against winds from the North Sea coast, with a luxuriantly thatched roof, and seats on the grass outside. Inside, comfortable benches are built into the walls of its two rooms, there are heavy black beams in the low ceiling, rather narrow rustic tables, lots of horsebrasses, and some less common curios on ship-in-bottle lines. Well kept McEwans 80/- and Youngers Scotch on handpump, and food includes good local seafood; the restaurant upstairs has nice dormer windows in the tiled roof. *(Recommended by Jan and Ian Alcock, Sally Durnford, Mr and Mrs Tim Crawford)*

McEwans (S&N)   Real ale   Meals and snacks   Restaurant tel Whitby (0947) 602703   Open 11–3, 6.30–11

NEWTON-ON-OUSE (N Yorks)   SE5160 Map 7
Dawnay Arms

Village signposted off A19 N of York

The Ouse swirls past the moorings at the bottom of the neatly kept lawn, and there are picnic-table sets and other tables on the terrace, with a children's playhouse and seesaw. Inside is comfortable and spacious, with two red-carpeted room areas on either side of the entrance. On the right there are green plush wall settles and brown plush chairs around wooden or dimpled copper tables, with a good deal of beamery and timbering. On the left, red plush button-back wall banquettes are built into bays, and there's a good log fire in the stone fireplace. Popular good value bar food includes sandwiches (£1), soup (£1.20), their own duck pâté (£1.95), haddock (£2.75), ploughman's (£2.95), salads (£3.25), gammon and egg (£4.95) and steaks (from eight-ounce sirloin £6.95); dishes of the day are often beef curry (£3.50) and cod fresh from Whitby (£3.75), with Scotch salmon at weekends (£5.75). Well kept John Smiths and Tetleys and maybe Ind Coope Burton on handpump, decent house wines; an alcove has darts, fruit machine and trivia; maybe unobtrusive piped music; friendly service. *(Recommended by Mrs Shirley Pielou, Wayne Brindle)*

Free house Licensees John and Angela Turner Real ale Meals and snacks (12–2, 6.45–9.45; not Mon lunchtime) Restaurant tel Linton-on-Ouse (034 74) 345 Children in eating area and restaurant Open 11.30–2.30, 6.30–11 all year; closed Mon lunchtime

NUNNINGTON (N Yorks) SE6779 Map 7
Royal Oak

Church Street; at back of village, which is signposted from A170 and B1257

One of the walls in this well run old house is stripped back to the bare stone to display a fine collection of antique farm tools, and the high black beams are strung with earthenware flagons, copper jugs and lots of antique keys. The carefully chosen furniture on the Turkey carpet includes kitchen and country dining-chairs or a long pew around the sturdy tables, there's a lectern in one corner, and open fires. Good, popular bar food includes sandwiches (not Sunday lunchtime), home-made soup (£1), home-made pâté (from £1.50), ploughman's with several cheeses (from £2.50), plaice (£3.25), lasagne (£3.35), gammon with egg or pineapple (£4.25) and evening steaks (from £6.50), with home-made specialities such as ham and mushroom pasta (£3.25), steak and kidney casserole with herb dumpling (£3.95) or breast of chicken in orange and tarragon (£4.50). An extension is being built for a separate dining area. Near the car park there are a couple of tables on a little terrace with a good view. *(Recommended by Laurence Manning, Neil and Elspeth Fearn, E Lee)*

Free house Licensee Anthony Simpson Meals and snacks (not Mon lunchtime) Children welcome until 8.30 Open 11.45–2.30, 6.30–11 all year; closed Mon lunchtime Bedrooms tel Nunnington (043 95) 271; /£25

OSWALDKIRK (N Yorks) SE6279 Map 7
Malt Shovel

Village signposted off B1363/B1257, S of Helmsley

Towards the end of 1988 this pub – which has been a very special favourite of many readers – changed hands (the former tenant's personality was a prominent part of the pub's character). It's now to be a managed house; the new landlord (a former entertainer) used to run the Jug & Bottle in Huddersfield. The building itself has not been changed much, and still has its distinctive layout. The small heavily beamed bar has two big traditional settles (one curved), a rocking armchair and good winter fire. Other rooms lead off here (also with fires), including the quieter lounge down at the back facing the garden, with green-cushioned wall benches. Bar food includes sandwiches, home-made soup (£1.50), deep-fried Brie (£2.95), chicken livers and potato latkes (£3.25), crab-stuffed haddock with prawn sauce (£5.75) and hunter's chicken (£8.25); the licensee's wife, Kay, is a vegetarian herself and does several vegetarian dishes such as buckwheat pancakes filled with leeks, celery and almonds in a cheese sauce. Well kept Sam Smiths OB and probably Museum in winter on handpump; shove-ha'penny, cribbage, dominoes and piped music. There are seats out in the garden, which is floodlit at night. *(Recommended by Jan and Ian Alcock, M B Porter; more reports on the new regime please)*

Sam Smiths   Licensee Brian Hughes   Real ale   Meals and snacks   Restaurant   Children welcome   Open 11.30–2.30 (3 Sat), 6–11; closed Tues lunchtime   Three bedrooms tel Ampleforth (043 93) 461; £16.50/£33

nr OTLEY (W Yorks)   SE2047 Map 7
Spite

Newall-with-Clifton, off B6451; towards Blubberhouses about a mile N of Otley, and in fact just inside N Yorks

This neatly kept, welcoming and comfortable place has wheel-back chairs and plush or leatherette stools around the orderly tables, some wildfowl prints and a collection of walking-sticks on the plain white walls, Turkey carpet as you go in, with a blue and brown patterned one over by the bar, and a good log fire as well as central heating. Bar food includes soup (£1.50), sandwiches (from £1.75, open prawn £2.75), hot crusty mustard bread stuffed with sausages (£2.75), home-made quiche (£2.50), ploughman's (£5.50), hot specials such as steak and ale pie, and home-made puddings (£1.50). Beautifully kept Websters Yorkshire, Choice and Green Label on handpump; dominoes and unobtrusive piped music. There are white tables and chairs in a neat, well lit little rose garden. *(Recommended by Roger Bellingham, Richard and Carol Glover, Russell and Christina Jones, Tim and Lynne Crawford, Ned Edwards)*

Websters (Watneys)   Licensees Eric and Irene Law   Real ale   Meals and snacks (12–2, 7–9.45; not Mon, not Sun evening)   Restaurant (closed Sun evening) tel Otley (0943) 463063   Open 11–3, 7–11 all year; closed Mon lunchtime

nr PATELEY BRIDGE (N Yorks)   SE1966 Map 7
Half Moon

Fellbeck; B6265 3 miles E

Near a fat free-standing wood-burning stove in the spacious open-plan bar here are some easy chairs and a big sofa, with a spread of russet plush button-back built-in wall banquettes, light-wood country kitchen chairs and decent wooden tables set around the rest of the room; the cream walls have a Delft shelf. Well kept Timothy Taylors Landlord, Theakstons BB and Youngers Scotch on handpump; big helpings of simple but properly home-cooked bar food such as sandwiches (from 85p), home-made soup (90p), ploughman's (£2.50), omelettes (from £2.50), haddock or home-made steak and kidney pie (£2.90), chicken Kiev (£3.50), gammon (£3.95) and sirloin steak (£5.95). A back area has darts, pool, cribbage, dominoes, fruit machine and a juke box; there's a caravan park behind the pub. The bedrooms are in well equipped modern chalets; we've not heard from readers who have stayed here yet, though. *(Recommended by Chris Fluck; more reports please)*

Free house   Licensees David and Sheila Crosby   Real ale   Meals and snacks   Children welcome until 9.30   Open 12–3 (5 Sat), 6.30–11 all year   Bedrooms tel Harrogate (0423) 711560; £18B/£26B

PENISTONE (S Yorks)   SE2403 Map 7
Cubley Hall

Mortimer Road; outskirts, towards Stocksbridge

Originally a grand Edwardian villa and then a children's home, this imposing stone house in attractive gardens has been converted into a stylish and popular pub. The bar spreads through most of the ground floor, with mosaic tiling or Turkey carpet, elaborately plastered pink and cream ceiling, vast brass chandelier, panelling or red and gold flock wallpaper, and plenty of red plush chairs, stools and button-back built-in wall banquettes. Two snug rooms lead off the spacious main area, as does a side family sun lounge which gives a nice view beyond the neat tree-sheltered formal gardens to pastures in the distance; there's a second children's room, too. A wide choice of good value bar food served efficiently by neat waitresses includes noted chip butties (80p), soup (90p), sandwiches (from £1.05, steak £1.50), ham or vegetarian lasagne (£3.10), plaice, haddock (£3.50), omelettes (from £3.50, not Sunday lunchtime), eight-ounce porterhouse steak (£4.85) and mixed grill (£6.50), with a good few dishes of the day such as steak pie (£3.95) or rack of lamb done with honey and mint (£5.95), several children's dishes (£2.10) and Sunday lunch (£3.95; children £2.90); well kept Ansells Best, Clarks Garthwaite Special (from Wakefield), Ind Coope Burton and Tetleys on handpump, lots of malt whiskies and other spirits, a fair choice of wines, good coffee; cribbage, dominoes, fruit machines, space game, trivia, maybe piped music. There are tables out on the terrace, and the garden has a good children's playhouse. *(Recommended by W P P Clarke, SJC)*

Free house   Licensee John Wigfield   Real ale   Meals and snacks (12–2, 7–10.30)   Children welcome   Open 11–3, 6–11 all year

PICKHILL (N Yorks)   SE3584 Map 10
Nags Head 🏮

Village signposted off A1 N of Ripon, and off B6267 in Ainderby Quernhow

The busy, friendly tap-room on the left is comfortably furnished with muted pastel red plush button-back built-in wall banquettes around dark tables, and it's decorated with masses of ties hanging as a frieze from a rail around the red ceiling, with jugs, coach horns, ale-yards and so forth hanging from the beams. One table's inset with a chessboard, and they also have darts, pool, bar billiards, shove-ha'penny, dominoes, a silenced fruit machine and faint piped music in here, with pool in a separate room. A smarter bar with deep green plush banquettes and a carpet to match has pictures for sale on its neat cream walls. Bar food ingredients are bought carefully, and they have a changing choice of about fifteen dishes depending wholly on what looked good – maybe only a couple of helpings of some things (but their definition of a helping is pretty massive): mushrooms stuffed with ham and Stilton (£2.75), hot roast sirloin of beef sandwich (£3.75), hot lobster tails (£4.75), fresh crab salad (£5.25) and pan-fried hare fillet (£5.75); they will do sandwiches. Well kept Tetleys, Theakstons Best, XB and Old Peculier, and Youngers Scotch on handpump, decent wines by the glass. Creaky-boarded bedrooms, huge breakfasts. *(Recommended by PLC, Tim Halstead, Robert Gomme, Alan Bickley, Kevin Blick)*

Free house   Licensees Raymond and Edward Boynton   Real ale   Meals and snacks (12–2, 6–10)   Restaurant tel Thirsk (0845) 567391   Children allowed in eating area   Open 11–3, 5–11 all year   Bedrooms tel Thirsk (0845) 567570; £24B/£34B

RAMSGILL (N Yorks)   SE1271 Map 7
Yorke Arms 🛏️

Behind the warm stone façade and the stately stone-mullioned windows of this former shooting-lodge are comfortable sofas and easy chairs, as well as some fine older oak furniture including two or three heavy carved Jacobean oak chairs and a big oak dresser laden with polished pewter. Bar food includes sandwiches (from 85p), soup (90p), smoked haddock quiche or chilli con carne (£2.65), cottage pie (£2.70) and game pie (£3.65). The inn's public rooms are open throughout the day for tea and coffee, and spirits are served in cut glass. Dominoes and cribbage. You

Pubs brewing their own beers are listed at the back of the book.

can walk up the magnificent if strenuous moorland road to Masham, or perhaps on the right-of-way track that leads along the hill behind the reservoir, also a bird sanctuary. *(Recommended by Anthony Fernau, Paul Newberry, Wayne Brindle)*

Free house   Meals and snacks   Restaurant   Children welcome   Open 11–11 all year Bedrooms tel Harrogate (0423) 75243; £40B/£60B

REDMIRE (N Yorks)   SE0591 Map 10

Kings Arms

Wensley–Askrigg back road: a good alternative to the A684 through Wensleydale

A new dining conservatory – with good views of the Dales – was in the process of being built on to this friendly and unassuming thick-walled old pub as we went to press, and what was the dining-room will become a lounge for pre-dinner or after-dinner drinks. The long bar has a new mahogany-topped counter, simple furnishings that include a long soft leatherette wall seat and other upholstered wall settles, red leatherette cafe chairs or dark oak ones, round cast-iron tables, and a fine oak armchair (its back carved like a mop of hair); lots of interesting photographs include those of old local scenes (including folk-singers recording here in three-piece suits), of local filming for *All Things Great and Small*, of the licensee's RAF squadron, and of his steeplechasing friends such as John Oaksey. Home-made bar food includes sandwiches (from £1), home-made soup (£1.20), pâté (£1.90), omelettes (£2.85), meat or walnut and spinach lasagne (£3.75), grilled local trout (£3.85), steak and kidney pie or scampi (£3.95), venison in red wine (£4.95) and steaks (£6.95); Sunday roast lunch (best to book). Well kept Websters Yorkshire on handpump; 53 malt whiskies; cheerful, obliging service. Darts (under fluorescent light at one end), pool, trivia machine, dominoes, backgammon, chess and juke box or piped music. There are tables and chairs in the pretty garden, which has a superb view across Wensleydale; fishing nearby. Handy for Castle Bolton, where Mary Queen of Scots was imprisoned. *(Recommended by KC, Jenny Cantle, Stephanie Sowerby, Dr and Mrs B D Smith, Mr and Mrs M Tarlton, Patrick Young)*

Free house   Licensees Roger and Terry Stevens   Meals and snacks   Restaurant; closed Sun evening   Children in restaurant only   Singalongs every fourth Fri evening   Open 11–11 all year   Bedrooms tel Wensleydale (0969) 22316; £13/£22

REETH (N Yorks)   SE0399 Map 10

Black Bull 🏚

B6270

The wide sloping village green of this seventeenth-century market town is dominated by a big white coaching-inn. Inside, the cosy beamed L-shaped bar has high-backed wall benches, cheery fires and a relaxed atmosphere; more seats can be found in the lounge bar and outside. Good value bar food includes soup (80p), sandwiches (from 80p), home-made pâté (£1.40), ploughman's with three cheeses (£1.40), home-made cottage pie (£2.20), vegetarian dishes such as nut and fruit pilaff (£2.30), home-made pies like steak and kidney or chicken and ham (£2.60), and home-roasted ham salad (£2.95). Well kept McEwans 80/-, and Theakstons Best, XB and Old Peculier tapped from the cask; darts, pool, dominoes, cribbage, fruit machine, trivia and juke box. The hotel has its own fishing on the Swale. Readers have mentioned one or two hiccups in service – we'd be glad of more reports about this. *(Recommended by M J Lawson, E V Walder, ERT, Dr and Mrs R J Ashleigh, Helen and John Thompson, Dr and Mrs B D Smith, G T Jones, Richard Dolphin)*

Free house   Licensee R E Sykes   Real ale   Meals and snacks (12–2.30, 6–9.30) Restaurant   Children welcome until 8.30   Open 11–3.30 (4 Sat), 6–11 all year; may stay open if sufficient demand   Bedrooms tel Richmond (0748) 84213; £14.95/£29.90

RIPPONDEN (W Yorks) SE0419 Map 7

Old Bridge

Priest Lane; from A58, best approach is Elland Road (opposite Golden Lion), park opposite church in pub's car park and walk back over ancient hump-backed bridge

This carefully restored and well kept medieval house (which has been in the same hands for over 26 years) has three communicating rooms, each on a slightly different level. Comfortable furnishings include oak settles built into the window recesses of the thick stone walls, antique oak tables, rush-seated chairs, a few well chosen pictures and a big wood-burning stove; new carpets throughout. The fine structure has been carefully restored: plasterwork is stripped away just here and there to show the handsome masonry, and ceilings have been removed to show the pitched timbered roof. On weekday lunchtimes a popular cold meat buffet always has a joint of rare beef, as well as spiced ham, quiche, Scotch eggs and so on (£6, with salads). In the evenings, and at lunchtime on Saturdays (when you may have to wait some time for your food), good tasty filling snacks include home-made soup, breadcrumbed mushrooms with garlic mayonnaise, potted smoked trout with lime butter, chicken, ham and broccoli pancake, and pepperpot beef casserole, with frequently changing specials like smoked haddock pancakes (£2.50), locally smoked brook trout (£3.25) and goujons of plaice (£3.75). They will cut fresh sandwiches. Well kept Ruddles, Timothy Taylors and Youngers on handpump. The pub has a good restaurant, across the very pretty medieval bridge over the little river Ryburn. *(Recommended by Christopher Knowles-Fitton, Syd and Wyn Donald, Ian Blackwell, Brian and Anna Marsden)*

Free house Licensee Ian Beaumont Real ale Meals (evening, not Sun) and snacks (not Sun) (12–2, 7–10) Restaurant (closed Sun) tel Halifax (0422) 822295 Children tolerated in eating area Open 11.30–3, 5.30–11 all year

ROBIN HOOD'S BAY (N Yorks) NZ9505 Map 10

Laurel

The snug and friendly beamed main bar in this cosy white pub has a good local atmosphere, and is decorated with old local photographs, Victorian prints and brasses. Well kept Theakstons Best, XB and Old Peculier on handpump with many guest beers; darts, shove-ha'penny, table skittles, trivia machine, dominoes, cribbage, maybe piped music. In summer the hanging baskets and window boxes are lovely, and the pub is right at the heart of one of the prettiest and most unspoilt fishing villages on the north-east coast; *Good Walks Guide* Walk 160 is close by. The self-catering flat above the bar is enticing, and there's also a cottage (telephone Whitby (0947) 880400). Please note that they no longer do food. *(Recommended by Jane and Niall, Sally Durnford, Graeme Smalley, G T Jones, M A and W R Proctor, Nick Dowson, Alison Hayward, Mr and Mrs Tim Crawford)*

Free house Licensee M R Tucker Real ale Children in snug bar Folk club on Fri evenings Open 11.30–3.30, 6.30–11 all year

ROSEDALE ABBEY (N Yorks) SE7395 Map 10

Milburn Arms 🛏

Easiest road to village is through Cropton from Wrelton, off A170 W of Pickering

A snug area in the big, well run, refurbished bar of this busy, eighteenth-century stone inn has sentimental engravings (The Poor Poet, The Pensionist) by Karl Spitzweg, sporting prints with an emphasis on rugby and cricket, and black beams in the bowed cream ceiling by the log fire. Popular home-made food includes lunchtime wholemeal buns (from £1.20), soup (£1.25), lunchtime ploughman's (£2.65), good mariner's hot-pot (£2.95), spicy vegetable tagliatelle (£3.95), calf's liver, onion and bacon (£4.50), home-made steak and kidney pie (£5.25), home-made game pie with green ginger wine (£5.95), sirloin steak (£6.95), and puddings like treacle tart or hot sticky toffee sponge (£1.75). On Sunday there's also a range of cold meats, fish (the crab is excellent), quiche and cheese with salads, and roast lunch. Well kept Tetleys Bitter and Theakstons XB on handpump; quite a few malt whiskies, fresh ground coffee, and an impressive range on the wine list. Unobtrusive piped classical music at lunchtime; sensibly placed darts, with pool-table, shove-ha'penny, dominoes, cribbage and fruit machine in a separate balconied area with more tables, up a few steps; seats outside. The surrounding steep moorland is splendid. (*Recommended by Gary Melnyk, A C Lang, Jane Palmer, G Bloxsom, R G and A Barnes, F A Noble, G L Archer, Dr R Hodkinson*)

Free house   Licensee Stephen Colling   Real ale   Meals and snacks   Restaurant   Children in large family-room until 9   Occasional jazz, blues and country   Open 11.30–2.30, 6.30–11   Bedrooms tel Lastingham (075 15) 312; £32B/£50B

White Horse 🍺

Above village, 300 yards up Rosedale Chimney Bank – the exhilarating 1-in-3 moorland road over Spaunton Moor to Hutton-le-Hole

Warmly friendly, the cosy beamed bar in this isolated stone inn has red plush cushioned pews salvaged from a church in Wakefield, captain's chairs, wooden tables, several foxes' masks, a stuffed heron and peregrine falcon, various antlers, horns, and a reindeer skin, and a welcoming log fire. Good, generously served bar food includes soup (90p), sandwiches, home-made pâté (£1.95), ratatouille au gratin (£2.20), ploughman's (from £2.50), mussels in white wine (£2.50), salads (from £3.50), grilled plaice or local trout (£3.70), home-made pies or vegetarian nut roast (£3.90) and eight-ounce sirloin steak (£5.60), with children's dishes (from £2), puddings like home-made brandy-snaps and cream (from £1.20) and Sunday roast lunch (£4.30). Well kept John Smiths and Tetleys on handpump, good choice of malt whiskies and good choice of wines by the bottle; dominoes and piped background music. From the picnic-table sets on the stone front terrace the views of the high surrounding countryside (the inn itself has eleven acres with cattle, chickens and ducks) are marvellous. (*Recommended by Tim and Lynne Crawford, Paul Newberry, Linda and Alex Christison, Jytte Cumberland*)

Free house   Licensees Howard and Clare Proctor   Real ale   Meals and snacks (12–2, 7–10)   Restaurant   Children in bar if eating until 8.30   Monthly folk night and varied live entertainment all year   Open 11.30–2.30 (3 Sat), 6.30–11; may open longer in afternoons if trade demands; opens noon in winter; closed 25 Dec   Bedrooms tel Lastingham (075 15) 239; £26B/£42B

SAWLEY (N Yorks)   SE2568 Map 7

Sawley Arms 🏵

Village signposted off B6265 W of Ripon

All the interesting cooking in this civilised place is done by the family – Mrs Hawes (who has been here for twenty years), her son Robin and his wife: soups such as celery and apricot or mushroom with cumin, all made with proper stock (£1.20), good sandwiches (from £1.20), ham, spinach and almond pancake or ravioli done in red wine (£2.40), salmon mousse (£2.50), a Stilton, port and celery pâté (£2.60), egg, bacon and mushroom cocotte (£2.80), scampi (£3.80), freshly smoked trout (£3.10), steak pie with a fine buttercrust pastry (£3.90), salads (from £3.90) and sirloin steak (£7), with puddings like chocolate brandy mousse or strawberry marquise. A series of small and cosy Turkey-carpeted rooms have comfortable furnishings ranging from small softly cushioned armed dining-chairs and greeny-gold wall banquettes to the wing armchairs down a couple of steps in a side snug. Decent house wines (the beers are keg), and courteous service; also, log fires, unobtrusive piped piano music, passe-temps, and an engaging half-Siamese grey cat. The pub is handy for Fountains Abbey (the most extensive of the great monastic remains – floodlit on late summer Friday and Saturday evenings, with a live choir on the Saturday). An attractive and well kept small garden has two or three old-fashioned teak tables. *(Recommended by Tim and Lynne Crawford, E R Thompson, Mrs J H Vallance)*

Free house   Licensee Mrs June Hawes   Real ale   Meals and snacks (not Sun evening, not Mon)   Restaurant tel Ripon (0765) 86642   Open 11.30–3, 6.30–11 all year; closed Mon

SAXTON (N Yorks)   SE4736 Map 7
Greyhound

Village signposted off B1217 Garforth–Tadcaster; so close to A1 and A162 N of Pontefract

Quite unspoilt, this is the very picture of a traditional village pub – a little tiled white-painted cottage on the edge of the churchyard, bright in summer with a climbing rose, passion-flower and bedding plants. Inside on the left is a cosy and chatty tap-room, with a coal fire burning in the Victorian fireplace in the corner, ochre Anaglypta walls and a dark panelled dado; well kept Sam Smiths OB tapped from casks behind the counter. From here a corridor takes you past a small snug, with fancy shades on the brass lamps, browning Victorian wallpaper, a sturdy mahogany wall settle curving round one corner, and other traditional furniture; down at the end is another highly traditional room, with darts, shove-ha'penny, table skittles, cribbage and dominoes. There's a couple of picnic-table sets in the side courtyard. *(Recommended by Rob and Gill Weeks, J C Proud)*

Sam Smiths   Licensee Mrs Janette Romans   Real ale   Sandwiches (lunchtime)   Children welcome   Open 11–3, 6–11 all year; all day Sat

SHEFFIELD (S Yorks)   SK3687 Map 7
Fat Cat

23 Alma Street

Built in the second half of the nineteenth century, but run down by the early 1980s when Stones sold it as a free house, it was renovated with help from the City Council as it's in the heart of an industrial conservation area. The wide range of well kept real ales and foreign bottled beers (particularly Belgian ones) is what draws most people to this chatty, friendly pub: Brakspears SB, Huntsman Royal Oak, Ma Pardoes (from the Old Swan at Netherton, included in the Midlands chapter), Marstons Pedigree, Merrie Monk and Owd Rodger, Old Mill, Timothy Taylors Landlord and Woods Wonderful (from the Plough at Wistanstow, in the Shropshire chapter) on handpump. There are also country wines, several organically grown wines and farm cider. Cheap bar food includes big sandwiches (75p), soup (85p), quiche or chilli (£1.40), hot dishes, good vegetarian curry and ploughman's (£1.75); Sunday lunch; efficient service, cribbage. The two small downstairs rooms have simple wooden tables and grey cloth seats around the walls, with a few advertising mirrors and an enamelled placard for Richdales Sheffield Kings Ale; the one on the left is no-smoking and both have coal fires. Steep steps take you up to another similarly simple room (which may be booked for functions), with some attractive prints of old Sheffield; there are picnic-table sets in a fairy-lit back courtyard. Kelham Island Industrial Museum is close. *(Recommended by Matt Pringle, John Day, Richard Sanders, John and Helen Thompson, W P P Clarke, Lynn Stevens, Gill Quarton)*

Free house   Real ale   Meals and snacks (lunchtime)   Children allowed upstairs, if not booked, until 8   Open 11–3, 5.30–11 all year

Frog & Parrot

Division Street, corner of Westfield Terrace

Well laid out to take a lot of people and with a good conversational atmosphere, this popular pub has high stools at elbow-height tables, bare boards, a lofty brown ceiling and huge windows; one side (with an old neatly blacked kitchen range in a brick chimney breast) is carpeted, and an area up a few steps has blue plush button-back built-in wall banquettes. Up here, you can see down into the basement brewhouse where they produce the pub's speciality – Roger and Out, a hefty 1125OG ale (at nearly 17 per cent alcohol about five times the strength of an ordinary bitter), which they sell in third-pint glasses, restricting customers to one pint a session. The other beers here are Old Croak (by contrast very light and easy to drink), Reckless and Conqueror, with a winter Porter and occasional commemorative strong ales. In a splendidly spacious cage (though he's allowed to fly free on occasions) is a blue and yellow macaw, and there's a tank of large frogs; fruit machine, video game, piped music. As well as cheap bar food that includes soup (85p), Yorkshire puddings with onion gravy (£1.10), four or eight-ounce burgers (from £1.85), omelettes made with three free-range eggs (from £1.95), sweet-and-sour pork (£2.55) and roast beef (£3.25), there's a range of forty different types of fish every day – from haddock, ling, herring, cod and plaice to halibut, salmon, red mullet and swordfish, served in a variety of ways (from £2.25). *(Recommended by Steve Waters, Steve Mitcheson, Anne Collins, Jon Wainwright, J L Thompson, T T Kelly)*

Own brew (Whitbreads)   Licensee Roger Nowill   Real ale   Meals and snacks (lunchtime, not Sun)   Restaurant tel Sheffield (0742) 721280   Children in restaurant   Live music Sun evenings   Open 11–11 all year; closed Sun lunchtime

SICKLINGHALL (N Yorks)   SE3648 Map 7
Scotts Arms

Originally several cottages including a small inn (the settlement dates back to the Domesday Book), this well run place has a more-or-less open-plan main bar that keeps some sense of its original rooms with stubs of the old dividing walls left, and seats built into cosy little alcoves cut into the main walls. As well as a big inglenook fireplace, there's a curious sort of double-decker fireplace with its upper hearth intricately carved. On a shelf in the corner of the bar is a working model of a two-foot-high traditional Scotsman constantly raising and lowering his glass. Bar food includes home-made soup (£1.15), sandwiches (from £1.05), ploughman's (from £2.55), salads or filled French sticks (from £2.95), lasagne or large, fresh haddock (£2.95), good steak, kidney and mushroom pie (£3.25), scampi (£3.50), gammon with pineapple or egg (£3.75) and daily specials. Well kept Theakstons Old Peculier, and Youngers IPA and No 3 on handpump; darts, fruit machine, video game, juke box and unobtrusive piped music, and down steps a separate room has pool and another fruit machine. There are tables outside in summer. *(Recommended by Roy Bromell, S V Bishop, Lyn and Bill Capper, T Nott, Syd and Wyn Donald)*

Scottish & Newcastle   Licensee Carl Lang   Real ale   Meals and snacks   Restaurant tel Wetherby (0937) 62100   Children in eating area of bar and restaurant   Open 11.30–3, 5.30–11 all year

SOWERBY BRIDGE (W Yorks)   SE0623 Map 7
Moorings

Off Bolton Brow (A58) opposite Ash Tree

The big new bar extension in this attractively converted ex-canal warehouse has virtually doubled the ground-floor space, with an eating area up some steps, and a new food counter serving chilled salads. There are beams, stone walls, bare floorboards, big windows, a grain hopper, grain sacks and old pulley wheels. The lounge bar has big windows and a very high ceiling (giving a relaxed and airy atmosphere), and it's pleasantly furnished with fabric-covered seats built against the stripped stone walls (which are decorated with old waterways maps and modern canal pictures), rush-seated stools and tile-top tables. A new lobby leads to a family-room alongside, similarly furnished. Good, reasonably priced bar food includes home-made soup (95p), filled granary cobs (from 95p), chicken liver pâté (£1.70), haddock, Cumberland sausage or spinach and mushroom lasagne (£2.75), stir-fry duckling with peppers (£3.50), vegetable Stroganoff (£4.25), steak, kidney and mushroom pie (£4.50), steaks (from £7) and daily specials; help-yourself salad with all main dishes; home-made puddings (from £1.25) and children's dishes (£1.75); friendly, helpful service. Besides well kept Moorhouses Bitter, McEwans 80/-, Youngers Scotch and No 3 and a regularly changing guest beer on handpump, there is a range of sixty foreign bottled and canned beers (many Belgian bottle-conditioned real ales – also Dutch Lineboom which they import themselves), over eighty whiskies (including seven Irish), reasonably priced house wines, and cocktails – including children's specials. Dominoes and piped music. The pub overlooks the basin where the Calder and Hebble Canal joins the Rochdale Canal (part of which has been partially reopened, and there's now a circular walk), and there are tables out on a terrace with grass and small trees; other old canal buildings here are now crafts workshops and shops. *(Recommended by Steve Mitcheson, Anne Collins, Rob and Gill Weeks, Derek and Sylvia Stephenson, Wayne Brindle, G Bloxsom, Brian and Anna Marsden)*

Free house   Licensees Ian Clay and Andrew Armstrong   Real ale   Meals and snacks Restaurant tel Halifax (0422) 833940   Children in family-room until 8.30   Open 11.30–3, 5 (6 Sat, 7 Mon)–11; 11–11 Fri; closed 25 Dec

SPROTBROUGH (S Yorks)   SE5302 Map 7
Boat

2¾ miles from M18 junction 2; A1(M) northwards, then A630 towards Rotherham, then first right, signposted Sprotbrough, by Texaco garage; immediate left after crossing river

Three spacious room areas run together in this old pub (under new licensees this year), with open fires in rather portentous stone fireplaces, latticed windows, dark brown beams, prints of bygone scenes, a rack of guns, big cases of stuffed birds, a couple of longcase clocks, the odd bronze, and a pleasant mixture of comfort and character in the seating. Bar food includes rabbit casserole or steak and kidney pie (£2.75), salads (from £2.95) and a roast (£3.25); well kept Courage Directors, John Smiths Bitter and Magnet on handpump; noticeable piped music. A big enclosed brick-paved courtyard has picnic-table sets, and you can wander round to watch the barges and water-bus on the River Don (as the embankment's quite high you don't see much from the bar). *(Recommended by Tony Gayfer, Steve Mitcheson, Anne Collins, ILP, Alastair Lang)*

John Smiths (Courage)   Licensee Barrie Wastnage   Real ale   Meals (12–2, 6–9) Restaurant (Tues–Sat evening, Sun lunch) tel Doncaster (0302) 857188   Children in restaurant   Open 11–3, 6–11 all year; 11–11 Sat in summer

STANSFIELD MOOR (W Yorks)   SD9227 Map 7
Sportsmans Arms

Hawks Stones, Kebcote; on old packhorse road between Burnley and Hebden Bridge, high above Todmorden; OS Sheet 103 reference 928273

Originally a farm, this remote seventeenth-century building became a full public house around 1920. It's a very welcoming place, with a few toby jugs and other decorative china on a high shelf, beams hung with mugs and horsebrasses, and a comfortable mix of old and new furnishings such as big heavy russet plush settles facing the open fire in the back area, with mustard-coloured leatherette seats elsewhere; also, some dark squared panelling, swords, knives, assegais, heavy-horse harness, and stone-mullioned windows. The colour photographs of show horses and of a pony and trap are a clear clue to the licensee's interests. Good quality bar food includes sandwiches (from 85p), sausage and egg (£2.50), plaice (£2.75), steak pie (£2.95), lasagne (£3.25), trout (£4.25) and steaks (from £5.50). Well kept Ruddles County, and Websters Yorkshire and Choice on handpump, with quite a few decent malt whiskies; pool. Walkers welcome and dogs too, if on a lead. *(Recommended by Len Beattie, John Gumbley)*

Free house   Licensee Jean Greenwood   Real ale   Meals and snacks (12–2, 7–10; not Mon lunchtime)   Evening restaurant tel Todmorden (0706) 813449   Children welcome, but under-elevens until 8.30 only   Open 12–3, 7–11 all year; closed Mon and Tues lunchtimes

STARBOTTON (N Yorks)   SD9574 Map 7
Fox & Hounds

OS Sheet 98 reference 953749

Friendly new licensees have taken over this beautifully placed pub, and have upgraded the bedrooms and kitchen, and are planning to rearrange the dining-room (which is no-smoking) to give more space. There are high beams supporting ceiling boards, an antique settle and other solid old-fashioned furniture on the flagstones, a big stone fireplace (and enormous fire in winter), and saddles and country bric-à-brac. Lunchtime bar food includes home-made soup such as delicious cream of lettuce soup (£1), sandwiches (from £1), ploughman's or pâté (£2.25), and a winter hot dish. Well kept Theakstons Best and Old Peculier and Youngers Scotch on handpump; boardgames and dominoes. Outside, there are sturdy tables and benches in a sheltered corner where you can look out to the hills all around this little hamlet. *(Recommended by Carol and Richard Glover, A P Hudson, Jon Wainwright, Jenny Cantle, Richard Fawcett, Peter Race, Len Beattie, Mr and Mrs M Tarlton, Robert Gartery, Dr J C Barnes, J E Rycroft)*

Free house   Licensee Pam Casey   Real ale   Evening meals and lunchtime snacks Open 12–3, 7–11 all year; closed Thurs lunchtime and all day Mon Nov–May   Bedrooms tel Kettlewell (075 676) 269; /£40S

STAVELEY (N Yorks)   SE3662 Map 7
Royal Oak

Village signposted from A6055 Knaresborough–Boroughbridge

There's a genuine country atmosphere in this small tiled-floored pub with its dark settles and big check-clothed Victorian table in the broad bow window. A dark-beamed and carpeted inner room has small topographical prints on the walls, but is otherwise similar. Popular lunchtime bar food includes soup, sandwiches (from £1.75), ploughman's, salads and game pie (£4.25); in the evening the pub turns into a restaurant. Well kept Theakstons Best on handpump; darts, and the *Independent* or *Telegraph* for the rare customers who don't find themselves joining in the general conversation. Picnic-table sets under cocktail parasols on the neatly flower-bordered front lawn are dominated by the great lime tree standing over them, beside the village church. *(Recommended by Syd and Wyn Donald, Prof S Barnett)*

Free house   Licensee Peter Gallagher   Real ale   Snacks (lunchtime) and meals   Restaurant tel Harrogate (0423) 340267   Children welcome   Open 12–3, 7–11 all year; closed 25 Dec

SUTTON (S Yorks)   SE5512 Map 7
Anne Arms ★

From A1 just S of Barnsdale Bar service area follow Askern, Campsall signpost; Sutton signposted right from Campsall

An interesting and profuse collection of ornaments in this cosy and friendly creeper-covered stone house includes oak dressers filled with brightly coloured plates, fruit plates embossed with lifesize red apples, latticed glass cases thronged with china shepherdesses and the like, a throng of toby jugs collected over many years, lots of colourful five-litre and smaller Bavarian drinking steins, and wooden figures popping out of a Swiss clock when it chimes the quarter-hours. A separate room is filled with brass and copper, and there's a Victorian-style conservatory. Good value food includes a choice of six main dishes, a help-yourself salad buffet, and puddings such as trifles or meringues. (*Recommended by T Nott, D P Cartwright, Malcolm Steward, Sue Cleasby, Mike Ledger, Patrick Young, Richard Cole*)

John Smiths (Courage)   Meals and snacks   Children in buffet room/snug   Open 10.30–3, 6–10.30

SUTTON HOWGRAVE (N Yorks)   SE3279 Map 7
White Dog

Village signposted from B6267 about a mile W of junction with A1

In summer the upper windows of this pretty village cottage are almost hidden by the flowers in the window boxes and two clematis, and there are picnic-table sets among flower beds on the grass. Inside, the two main rooms are furnished with comfortably cushioned Windsor chairs, with flowers on the polished tables. On one side of the black-beamed bar there's an open kitchen range with a welcoming fire in cool weather; friendly cat. Good, popular bar lunches include sandwiches (from £1), French onion soup (£1.25), mariner's hot-pot (£2.85), salads (from £3.25), omelettes (from £2.95), fish pie, steak and kidney pie or chicken and mushroom casserole (all £3.25), sirloin steak (£6.95) and puddings (from £1.50). The pub stands at the end of a little farming hamlet by a peaceful green with field maples and sycamores. (*Recommended by Wayne Brindle, J E Rycroft; more reports please*)

Free house   Licensee Basil Bagnall   Lunchtime meals and snacks (not Mon)   Restaurant (closed Sun) tel Melmerby (076 584) 404   Open 12–2.30, 7–11 all year; closed Sun evening, all day Mon, 25 Dec and 1 Jan

THORNTON WATLASS (N Yorks)   SE2486 Map 10
Buck 🏠 🛏

Village signposted off B6268 Bedale–Masham

Looking past a grand row of sycamores to the village cricket green, this peaceful country pub (part of a row of low stone cottages) has two quoits pitches in the garden – with league matches on summer Wednesday evenings, practice Sunday morning and Tuesday evening – trout fishing on the Ure, and a children's play area. Inside, the bar on the right is pleasantly traditional, with handsome old-fashioned wall settles, cast-iron-framed tables, a high shelf packed with ancient bottles, and several mounted foxes' masks and brushes (the Bedale hunt meets in the village). Bar food includes soup (£1.20), bacon and tomato in French bread (£1.40), steak and kidney pie (£3.50), home-cooked ham (£3.95), fresh Whitby cod (£4 – picked out by several readers), baked avocado with prawns au gratin (£4.50), braised beef in ale (£4.90) and pork fillet topped with tomato and cheese (£5.50), with smaller helpings for OAPs; well kept Tetleys and Theakstons Best and XB on handpump; good choice of malt whiskies. A bigger plainer bar has darts, dominoes, pool, Trivial Pursuit and piped music. (*Recommended by E R Thompson, Gary Melnyk, Mr and Mrs K Hicks, William Langley, David Gaunt, A Sharp, JF*)

Free house   Licensees Michael and Margaret Fox   Real ale   Meals and snacks   Restaurant Children in functions room at lunchtime and in bar until 8.30   Organ singalong and dancing Sat and Sun evening   Open 11–2.30, 6–11 all year, all day for cricket matches and so forth   Bedrooms tel Bedale (0677) 22461; £13/£25

THRESHFIELD (N Yorks)   SD9763 Map 7
Old Hall 🏠

B6265, just on the Skipton side of its junction with B6160 near Grassington

The three communicating rooms in this friendly inn have cushioned pews built into the white walls, a high beam and plank ceiling hung with pots, a tall well blacked kitchen range, and simple, unfussy decorations – old Cadburys advertisements, decorative plates on a high Delft shelf. Imaginative bar food includes hot beef sandwich (£1.50), steak pie (£3.95), seafood lasagne or good Persian lamb curry with cream and almonds (£4.25), Indonesian-style lamb (£4.95), and roast monkfish with garlic or tasty halibut and prawn bake (£5.45). Well kept Timothy Taylors Bitter and Landlord, and Youngers Scotch on handpump. Darts, dominoes, fruit machine, maybe piped pop music. There are tables in a neat side garden, partly gravelled, with young shrubs, a big sycamore, and an aviary with cockatiels and zebra finches; a conservatory is planned. It's the back part – dating from Tudor times, and the oldest inhabited building in Wharfedale – which gives the inn its name; this ancient part is being turned into additional bedrooms. This is of course a fine base for dales walking, and the inn is on *Good Walks Guide* Walk 150. *(Recommended by Mr and Mrs M Tarlton, Prof S Barnett, Jon Wainwright, P Bramhall, J Whitehead, Wayne Brindle)*

Free house   Licensees Ian and Amanda Taylor   Real ale   Meals and snacks (12–2, 6.30–10)   Restaurant   Children in eating area and conservatory   Open 11–3, 5.30–11 all year   Bedrooms tel Grassington (0756) 752441; £15/£30

WATH-IN-NIDDERDALE (N Yorks)   SE1558 Map 7
Sportsmans Arms 🏵 🛏

To get the best of the young chef's excellent cooking in this friendly seventeenth-century country inn, you should really stay overnight and enjoy a good leisurely dinner. Bar lunches are good too: home-made soup (£1.80), chicken liver pâté (£3.20), locally made Coverdale and double Gloucester ploughman's (£3.20), fillet of fresh Scarborough woof in brown butter with prawns, almonds and capers (£3.25), locally made black pudding in creamed sherry and mushroom sauce (£3.50), rarebit with grilled bacon (£3.80), late breakfast (£4.50), fresh Nidderdale trout (£4.80), puddings or a tremendous range of cheese (£1.60); three course restaurant Sunday lunch (£8.50), and fresh fish daily from Whitby. There's a very sensible and extensive wine list, good choice of malt whiskies, and service is attentive. The comfortable blond-panelled bar has big gamebird prints on Madras cotton wallhanging, an open fire, dominoes and occasional piped music. Benches outside make the most of the charming valley setting. *(Recommended by Syd and Wyn Donald, Jane and Niall, Lynn Stevens, Gill Quarton, Geoff Wilson, Andy Tye, Sue Hill, K A Chappell)*

Free house   Licensee J R Carter   Lunchtime meals and snacks (not Sun)   Evening restaurant (not Sun)   Children welcome   Open 12–3, 7–11 all year; closed evenings 24, 25 and 26 Dec and 1 Jan   Bedrooms tel Harrogate (0423) 711306; £25(£27S)/£35(£40B)

WELBURN (N Yorks)   SE7268 Map 7
Crown & Cushion
Village signposted from A64 York–Malton

Close to Castle Howard and Kirkham Abbey, this pleasant old stone inn in a quiet village has a relaxed, carpeted lounge with two connecting rooms: wheel-back chairs and small cushioned settles around wooden tables, little pictures between strips of black wood on the cream walls, a collection of close to 500 water jugs, high shelves of plates, and open fires in winter. Bar food includes soup (£1.20), sandwiches (from £1.20), pâté (£1.90), ploughman's (£2.85), salads (from £3.25), haddock (£3.50), lasagne (£3.75), steak and kidney pie (£3.75), scampi (£4.40), gammon with pineapple (£4.50), steaks (from £6.55) and daily specials on a blackboard. Well kept Camerons Bitter and Strongarm on handpump; service may not be brisk. Darts, dominoes, fruit machine, juke box in the public bar; piped music. The back garden has been landscaped and includes a terrace with tables and chairs. Please note that they no longer do bedrooms. *(Recommended by J C Proud, Philip and Sheila Hanley, S V Bishop, Mr and Mrs F W Sturch, Bernard Phillips, Scott W Stucky)*

Camerons   Licensee David Abbey   Real ale   Meals and snacks (not Mon in winter) Restaurant tel Whitwell on the Hill (065 381) 304   Children in eating area of bar and restaurant   Open 11–2.30, 6.30–11; opens 7 in winter

WENTWORTH (S Yorks)   SK3898   Map 7
George & Dragon

3 miles from M1 junction 36: village signposted from A6135; can also be reached from junction 35 via Thorpe; pub is on B6090

Steps split the front area of the pleasantly rambling bar here into separate parts, and there's an assortment of old-fashioned seats and tables, with blue plates on the walls; a lounge (back by the little games-room) has an ornate stove. Good food includes sandwiches, venison burger (£1.25), meat and potato pie (£2.25) and salads (£2.95); Sunday roast lunch (£3.95). A wide range of well kept ales includes Oak Wobbly Bob, Timothy Taylors Bitter, Landlord and winter Porter, Tetleys Bitter, Theakstons Old Peculier and three different guest beers each week on handpump; also Symonds cider. Dominoes and piped music. There are benches in the front courtyard, where there's a barn and shop. *(Recommended by Tony Tucker, J A Edwards, Paul Newberry, M A and W R Proctor; more reports please)*

Free house   Licensee Steve Dickinson   Real ale   Meals and snacks   Children in dining area Open 12–3, 7–11 all year

Rockingham Arms

In summer it's lovely to sit outside this stone pub with its own bowling-green surrounded by mature trees. Inside, the new licensee hasn't changed much, and the comfortable main bar has hunting photographs and prints on its partly stripped stone walls, Windsor chairs around copper-topped tables, and a coal fire. A quieter little room with small pictures on its walls opens off this. Good bar food includes sandwiches (75p), very good Yorkshire puddings (£1.35 with gravy, £1.95 with roast beef), home-made quiche (£1.95), steak pie (£2.30) and daily specials; well kept Home Bitter, and Youngers Scotch, IPA and No 3 on handpump; dominoes, cribbage, space game. The Barn is popular and lively: black paintwork and whitewashed walls, high eaves, and neat barn stalls to make for some intimacy around the tables – but the main point here is the jazz (Wednesday), country and western (Thursday) and folk music (Friday). *(Recommended by M A and W R Proctor, Paul Newberry, J A Edwards)*

Free house   Licensee Murray Jameson   Real ale   Meals and snacks (not Sun evening)   Open 11–11 all year   Bedrooms tel Barnsley (0226) 742075; £19.50/£28.50(£32B)

WIDDOP (W Yorks)   SD9333   Map 7
Pack Horse

The Ridge; from A646 on W side of Hebden Bridge, turn off at Heptonstall signpost (as it's a sharp turn, coming out of Hebden Bridge road signs direct you around a turning circle), then follow Slack and Widdop signposts; can also be reached from Nelson and Colne, on high, pretty road; OS Sheet 103 reference 952317

This friendly, traditional walkers' pub (with new licensees this year) has sturdy furnishings, window seats cut into the partly panelled stripped stone walls that look out over the moors, and warm winter fires. Good, straightforward bar food includes sandwiches (from 85p, open sandwiches on French bread from £1.95), burger (£2.10), cottage hot-pot (£2.30), ploughman's (£2.65), gammon with two eggs or home-made steak and kidney pie (£4.25), steaks (from £6) and specials such as coq au vin or meat and potato pie (from £3); be prepared for a wait on summer weekends, when it's crowded. Well kept Thwaites, Youngers IPA and guests on handpump, and decent malt whiskies. There are seats outside. *(Recommended by Wayne Brindle; more reports please)*

Free house   Licensee Ron Evans   Real ale   Meals and snacks (not Mon evenings in winter, see note below)   Children welcome until 9   Open 12–3, 7–11 all year; closed weekday lunchtimes Oct–May

WIGHILL (N Yorks)   SE4746 Map 7
White Swan ★

Village signposted from Tadcaster; also easily reached from A1 Wetherby bypass – take Thorpe Arch Trading Estate turn-off, then follow Wighill signposts; OS Sheet 105 reference 476468

Though plans are afoot by the new licensees to house six bedrooms and a restaurant in the existing stableblocks, the unpretentious and remarkably relaxing pubby part won't change at all. Several attractively furnished separate rooms and a small lobby are served by the central bar; in a back room there are leather bucket seats and a curly armed mahogany settle, a very deep square-sided Second Empire cane sofa (in need of recaning), small sporting prints and a dark oil painting, a longcase clock and – as in all the other rooms – a coal fire. Lunchtime bar snacks include giant rolls filled with rare beef, prawns or ham (from £2.20) and home-made steak pie (£2.40); evening dishes range from scampi and fisherman's pot (£5.95) to large steaks (from £7.50, 32-ounce T-bone £9.50); three-course roast Sunday lunch (£5.95). Well kept John Smiths Magnet, Stones and Theakstons on handpump; piped music. French windows from an extension lead on to a patio area overlooking the garden, where there are lots of seats. *(Recommended by G Bloxsom, G C and M D Dickinson, AE, Graeme Smalley, T Nott, Jon Wainwright)*

Free house   Licensee Mrs Rita Arundale   Real ale   Lunchtime snacks (not Sun) and evening meals (not Sun, Mon and Tues)   Children in three rooms   Open 12–3, 6–11 all year; closed evening 25 Dec

WORMALD GREEN (N Yorks)   SE3065 Map 7
Cragg Lodge

A61 Ripon–Harrogate, about half-way

With well over 700 malt whiskies, this comfortably modernised roadhouse has probably the widest collection in Britain – maybe the world, including a dozen Macallans going back to 1937 (£2.30 – a remarkable bargain, smooth as silk yet glowing with deep character). They have sixteen price bands, between 80p and £7, depending on rarity – with a seventeenth 'by negotiation' for their unique 1919 Campbelltown; and happy-hour price cuts betwen 6 and 7. Not being too single-minded, they also have well kept John Smiths Bitter, Tetleys Bitter and Mild, and Theakstons Best, XB and Old Peculier on handpump, several distinguished brandies, and mature vintage port by the glass; friendly service. The extensive open-plan bar has horsebrasses and pewter tankards hanging from side beams, a dark joist and plank ceiling, little red plush chairs around dark rustic tables, and a coal fire. Good, well presented bar food at lunchtime includes home-made soup or sandwiches (from 80p), game and liver pâté (£1.40), curry (£2.90), gammon with egg or pineapple or country-style chicken (£3.95), steaks (from £5.50) and a daily roast; in the evenings there's a snack menu (from around £3), and a larger, more elaborate one (main courses around £6). Home-made puddings such as cheesecake (£1.50), children's meals, and morning coffee and snacks from 10am. Dominoes, cribbage, fruit machine and piped music. There are picnic-table sets under cocktail

---

If you report on a pub that's not a main entry, please tell us any lunchtimes or evenings when it doesn't serve bar food.

parasols on the side terrace. *(Recommended by R F Plater, T Nott, Mandy and Mike Challis, Barbara Hatfield, Audrey and Alan Chatting)*

Free house   Licensee Garfield Parvin   Real ale   Meals and snacks (11.30–2, 6–10) Restaurant   Children in eating area of bar   Open 11.30–3, 6–11 all year   Bedrooms tel Ripon (0765) 87214; £15(£27B)/£25(£35B)

YORK (N Yorks)   SE5951 Map 7

Black Swan

Peaseholme Green; inner ring road, E side of centre; the inn has a good car park

One reader remembers how in 1940 this very interesting, fifteenth-century building was used by the subalterns (senior officers went to the White Horse in Piccadilly). The splendid façade is timbered, jettied and gabled, and the lead-latticed windows in the twin gables are original (it was quite plain and plastered until complete restoration before the last war). Inside, there's a great deal of evocative character: the back bar has very heavy beams and a big log fire in a vast brick inglenook, while the panelled front bar, with its little serving-hatch, is more restful. The crooked-floored hall between the two has a fine period staircase (leading up to a room fully panelled in oak, with an antique tiled fireplace). Bar food includes sandwiches (from £1.40), home-made soup (£1), ploughman's (£2.80) and Yorkshire puddings filled with beef stew (£2.80). Bass and Stones on handpump; also, fruit wines; dominoes and piped music. *(Recommended by RCL, Stan Edwards, S V Bishop, Dr C D E Morris, Audrey and Alan Chatting, Graeme Smalley, J C Proud, Jon Wainwright, Chris Cooke, Nick Dowson, Alison Hayward)*

Bass   Licensee Robert Atkinson   Meals and snacks (lunchtime, though they will do evening food for party bookings)   Children welcome   Folk night Thurs   Open 11–11 all year Bedrooms tel York (0904) 625236; /£32B

Kings Arms

King's Staithe; left bank of Ouse just below Ouse Bridge; in the evening you should be able to get a parking space right outside, turning down off Clifford Street; otherwise there's a ¼-mile walk

In a fine spot by the river, this very busy ancient pub has some picnic-table sets on a cobbled riverside terrace. Flooding happens so often that its 'cellar' is above ground in an adjacent building, and there's a level meter on one of the walls recording some of the more severe deluges. Inside, there are bare brick and stone walls, a flagstoned floor, bowed black beams, and good thick cushions on stone window seats that look out over the river. Bar food includes burgers (£1), ploughman's (£1.80), prawn platter (£2), steak and kidney pie or home-made curry (£2.40), and scampi or plaice (£3); fruit machine, CD juke box. *(Recommended by Peter Race, RCL, S V Bishop, Graeme Smalley, Jon Wainwright, Andy Tye, Sue Hill, Nick Dowson, Alison Hayward)*

Sam Smiths   Licensee I C Webb   Meals and snacks (12–2, 5.30–8.30; not Sat or Sun evenings)   Open 11–11; 11–3, 5.30–11 in winter

Olde Starre

Stonegate; pedestrians-only street in centre, far from car parks

Off one of York's prettiest old streets, this very busy pub, which dates from 1644, has a Victorian layout: rambling, beamed rooms with some little oak Victorian settles, heavy cast-iron tables, an open fireplace and a stained-glass hatch servery with a copper-topped bar counter; the snug is now a wine bar. Bar food includes soup (90p), burgers (from £2.20), cod fillet (£2.60), ploughman's (£2.90), salads or scampi (£3), lasagne or moussaka (£3), and home-made beef curry or chilli (£3.20); children's menu (£1.65). Well kept Ruddles Best and County, and Websters Yorkshire on handpump. Fruit machine, day-time piped music and juke box in the evenings. Courtyard tables have a view up above the chimneys and tiled roofs of York's medieval Shambles to the minster's towers. The pub can get extremely crowded at weekends, when the main bar is the meeting-place for the young of York. (*Recommended by Tim and Lynne Crawford, S V Bishop, RCL, Dr Stephen Hiew, Jon Wainwright, Scott W Stucky, M A and W R Proctor*)

Websters (Watneys)   Licensees Bill and Susan Embleton   Real ale   Meals and snacks (11.45–3 Mon–Fri, until 4 Sat, 12–2.30 Sun; 5.30–7.30 Mon–Thurs; salad bar open until 7) Children in eating area of bar and family-room until 6.30   Open 11–11 all year

Lucky Dip

Besides the fully inspected pubs, you might like to try these Lucky Dips recommended to us and described by readers (if you do, please send us reports):

Acaster Malbis, N Yorks [SE5945], *Ship*: Not a great deal of atmosphere, but cheerful, with a riverside lunch which can include a pleasant river trip from York and back; simple bar food, restaurant; basic bedrooms (*Stan Edwards, David Young*)

Addingham, W Yorks [SE0749], *Craven Heifer*: Welcoming old pub, though conversion with reproduction furniture not to everyone's taste; good varied food (stops 2pm prompt) and decent Sun lunch (*Syd and Wyn Donald*)

Ainderby Steeple, N Yorks [SE3392], *Wellington Heifer*: Long low-ceilinged bar and lounge on two levels, with brown woodwork making no pretence at age; good choice of generously served bar food and beers, quick friendly service (*Anon*)

Ainthorpe, N Yorks [NZ7008], *Fox & Hounds*: Sixteenth-century country pub with oak beams, horsebrasses, real fires and homely atmosphere; well kept Theakstons, reasonably priced bar food, outside tables; bedrooms (*E R Thompson*)

Aislaby, N Yorks [A170 W of Pickering; SE7886], *Blacksmiths Arms*: Bar with original blacksmith's fire and bellows, used by diners in the good, smart restaurant; friendly welcome (*J F Derbyshire*)

☆ **Aldborough**, N Yorks [Low Rd; village signposted from B6265 just S of Boroughbridge, close to A1; SE4166], *Ship*: Fourteenth-century pub with heavy beams, stone inglenook, old-fashioned seats around heavy cast-iron tables, sentimental engravings and (in the back buffet) ship pictures; good value bar food including local gammon and egg, well kept John Smiths, Theakstons XB and Tetleys, traditional games, piped music, seats on back lawn; remains of Roman town beyond church; children if well behaved, in eating area; attractive bedrooms; has been open all day; enthusiastic new owners end 1988 – more reports please (*Richard Dolphin, LYM*)

☆ **Almondbury**, W Yorks [bear left up Lumb Lane; village signposted off A629/A642 E of Huddersfield – OS Sheet 110 reference 153141; SE1615], *Castle Hill*: Perched high above Huddersfield on site of prehistoric hill fort, with terrific views of the moors dwarfing the mill towns; lots of coal fires in the rambling partly panelled bar, sturdy traditional furnishings, well kept Timothy Taylors Best and Landlord and Tetleys, simple bar food (not Sun–Tues evenings), popular Sun lunch (*Rob and Gill Weeks, LYM*)

Ampleforth, N Yorks [SE5878], *White Swan*: Friendly staff, soft piped music, keg beer, darts, fruit machines; substantial helpings of good food (not that cheap), restaurant (*M B Porter*)

Appleton Roebuck, N Yorks [SE5542], *Shoulder of Mutton*: Good bar food, restaurant (*R C Watkins*)

☆ **Appletreewick**, N Yorks [SE0560], *Craven Arms*: Country pub in beautiful surroundings, with two bar rooms and dining area, roaring fires (one in old iron range), attractive settles and carved chairs, interesting decorations, fine relaxed atmosphere; jovial new landlord – with handlebar moustache – doing very well, with well kept Tetleys, Theakstons XB and Old Peculier and Youngers Scotch on handpump, good value bar food including good ploughman's and enterprising specials such as a tasty vegetable and bean stew, good service; lovely views across Wharfedale from outside tables, convenient for walkers (*Tim Baxter, Peter and Rose Flower, Jon Wainwright, Paul Newberry*)

Appletreewick, *New Inn*: Superb spot (especially at twilight), chatty landlord, well kept beer with interesting range of bottled beers, pub games; the stripped red brickwork is a curiosity for this area (*Jon Wainwright*)

Askrigg, N Yorks [SD9591], *Crown*: Good home-cooked bar food in pleasant pub, not large, in most attractive small village (*N Burrell*)

Austerfield, S Yorks [A614 N of Bawtry; SK6694], *Austerfield Manor*: Modern pub with spacious and comfortable L-shaped bar, picnic-table sets on terrace, quickly served bar food, Youngers No 3 on handpump; children welcome, restaurant; useful for the area (*LYM*)

Aysgarth, N Yorks [SE0088], *George & Dragon*: Attractive pub with pleasant atmosphere in large lounge divided into nooks and crannies; Websters real ale, good value bar food including interesting vegetarian dishes, seafood and Sun roast; friendly licensees, separate pool area *(Jenny Cantle, N Hesketh)*; *Palmer Flatt*: Moorland hotel near broad waterfalls and carriage museum, medley of largely modernised bars but some interesting ancient masonry at the back recalling its days as a pilgrims' inn, restaurant, seats outside, fishing rights; bedrooms *(LYM)*

Bardsey, W Yorks [A58; SE3643], *Bingley Arms*: Popular pub with fine food inc superb salmon pancakes in bar and restaurant, charming terraced garden *(George Little)*

Barkisland, W Yorks [SE0520], *Fleece*: Good choice of well kept real ales and bar food in comfortable moors-edge pub with good atmosphere and plenty of character; CD juke box in small cellar wine bar, bar billiards in another room, piano restaurant – open till small hours, maybe with disco/bar; trad jazz Sun afternoon, maybe Tues spit-roasts *(Steve Mitcheson, Anne Collins, Wayne Brindle, BB)*; [Stainland Rd] *Griffin*: Has been very popular in the past for timeless old-fashioned small rooms, particularly a cosy little oak-beamed parlour, with good value simple bar food and well kept ales; after two or three years of uncertainty it was sold and closed in 1989, with plans for building six houses on its car park *(LYM – more news please)*

Barwick in Elmet, W Yorks [Main St; SE4037], *Gascoigne Arms*: Cosy country pub with 200-ft maypole outside, well kept handpumped Tetleys and good food inc cheap steaks and grills (lunchtime not Sun and Weds–Fri evenings) *(T T Kelly)*

Beadlam, N Yorks [A170 Helmsley–Scarborough; SE6585], *White Horse*: Old, rustic pub with beamed ceiling, welcoming fires in bar and lounge and homely licensees; Youngers No 3 and reasonably priced straightforward bar food inc sandwiches and hot dishes *(E R Thompson)*

☆ **Beck Hole**, N Yorks [OS Sheet 94 reference 823022; NZ8202], *Birch Hall*: Really unspoilt and unusual pub by a bridge over the river in a beautiful village, in a steep valley near the steam railway and at the end of a delightful gentle walk (GWG159) on the old railway track to Goathland; keg beer and other drinks, home-made butties and hot pies served through a hole in the wall by friendly girl into small room with very simple furniture; ancient picture in glass frame on outside wall; up some steep steps at the side is a little beer garden with a nice view – lovely on a sunny afternoon; same couple run coffee lounge and village shop next door; close to Thomason Fosse waterfall *(Paul Newberry, Martin Parker, Mr and Mrs Tim Crawford, Roger Bellingham)*

Beckwithshaw, N Yorks [SE2753], *Smiths Arms*: Bright, friendly pub with good bar food and carvery *(Peter Race)*

Berry Brow, W Yorks [Robin Hood Hill; A616 S edge of Huddersfield; SE1314],

Golden Fleece: Good bar food inc fine Yorkshire pudding stuffed with roast beef, Stones ales *(David Waterhouse)*

Biggin, N Yorks [SE5435], *Blacksmiths Arms*: Pleasant beamed pub, John Smiths ale, locally popular bar food, character licensee *(J C Proud)*

Bingley, W Yorks [Ireland Bridge; B6429 just W of junction with A650 – OS Sheet 104 reference 105395; SE1039], *Brown Cow*: Small snug areas divide spacious open-plan bar of comfortable pub just below pretty bridge over River Aire; bar food (not Sun or Mon evenings) fairly robust – especially their Yorkshire pudding; good range of Timothy Taylors beers, summer barbecues, children in eating area and small snug; bedrooms in adjoining cottages *(LYM)*

Bingley, W Yorks [Otley Rd, High Eldwick; SE1240], *Dick Hudsons*: Busy food pub with good views over moors and dales to Bradford, local paintings for sale, friendly staff, well kept Tetleys, attractively priced food inc good Sun lunch *(Mike Tucker, J P Day)*; [Gilshead Lane] *Glen*: Very welcoming atmosphere, railway memorabilia, good sandwiches with lavish salad and other cheap food, Tetleys Mild and Bitter on handpump, play area; pleasant rural setting *(D Stokes)*

Birstwith, N Yorks [SE2459], *Station*: Interesting collection of porcelain and china and friendly staff in pleasant village pub; good real ale on handpump *(Chris Fluck)*

Bolsterstone, S Yorks [off A616, prettiest route just N of Wharncliffe Side – OS Sheet 110 reference 271968; SK2796], *Castle*: Attractive old stone-built local in small hilltop conservation-area village, almost 1,000 ft above sea level in spectacular surroundings by Ewden Valley and on edge of Peak Park; friendly and welcoming with plenty of atmosphere, good Stones Bitter on electric pump; prize-winning male voice choir rehearses Mon *(W P P Clarke)*

Booth Wood, W Yorks [3 miles from M62 junction 22, towards Halifax; opp reservoir – OS Sheet 110 reference 021162; SE0216], *Turnpike*: Isolated welcoming Pennine pub; three rooms, some panelling and flagstones, bar food, well kept Youngers real ales, good views to Deanhead *(Lee Goulding)*

Borrowby, N Yorks [A19 Middlesbrough–Thirsk; SE4389], *Wheatsheaf*: Simple, rustic free house in small village; well kept Tetleys, good sandwiches and bar food, small garden *(E J Cutting)*

☆ **Bradford** [Barkerend Rd; up Church Bank from centre, on left few hundred yds past cathedral; SE1633], *Cock & Bottle*: Notable Victorian décor in well preserved small rooms, good value cheap lunchtime snacks, unusually well kept Tetleys real ales, live music Fri and Sat evenings; down-to-earth atmosphere, no frills *(LYM)*

Bradford [Huddersfield Rd, Low Moor],

British Queen: Unspoilt unpretentious working-class pub kept by two friendly ladies, well kept Tetleys on handpump, coal fire in idyllic back room *(Kelvin and Janet Lawton)*; [Chapel St, Eccles Hill] *Cricketers Arms*: Once two stone cottages, now knocked into one with single bar, pool-table in annexe and Whitbreads Trophy; popular with young people weekend evenings *(Tim Baxter)*; [Preston St (off B6145)] *Fighting Cock*: Good traditional pub with many guest beers and good pies – you can phone in an order to be ready when you arrive *(J D Shaw)*; [Thornton Rd] *Great Northern*: Thwaites house with one large room and central bar, upstairs restaurant with wide choice of good value dishes *(Tim Baxter)*; [7 Stone St; off Manor Row] *Le Nouveau*: Downstairs wine bar with changing menu and very homely service, pleasant glass-enclosed upstairs restaurant; parking impossible *(Ronald Monjack)*

Bradshaw, W Yorks [SE0614], *Rose & Crown*: Attractive old stone pub with good views across moors and hills; well kept Tetleys, good bar food including gigantic Sun lunch (best to book) *(Chris Draper)*

Bramhope, W Yorks [SE2543], *Fox & Hounds*: Popular Tetleys pub with well kept Mild and Bitter, good hot and cold food *(J E Rycroft)*

Broughton, N Yorks [SD9351], *Bull*: Well kept real ale and varied, interesting well cooked bar meals in cosy pub, comfortable and smartly modernised, with pleasant atmosphere and friendly service; restaurant *(Mike Suddards, LYM)*

Burnlee, W Yorks [Liphill Bank Rd; just off A635 Holmfirth–Manchester; SE1307], *Farmers Arms*: Small, unspoilt pub in remote hamlet, with cheap lunchtime and evening bar food inc huge Yorkshire pudding sandwich; well kept Greenalls and Timothy Taylors; children welcome *(Robert Gartery)*

Burnt Yates, N Yorks [SE2561], *Bay Horse*: Pleasant spot, enthusiastic licensees, good if not cheap food; bedrooms in motel extension *(Peter Race)*

☆ **Calder Grove**, W Yorks [just off M1 junction 39; A636 signposted Denby Dale, then first right into Broadley Cut Rd; SE3116], *Navigation*: Well kept Tetleys and simple food in profusely decorated canalside pub with tables outside – very attractively placed for a pub so close to the motorway, though piped music can be loud *(Paul Newberry, LYM)*

Carlton, N Yorks [OS Sheet 93 reference 509044; NZ5104], *Blackwell Ox*: Atmosphere relaxed and friendly in low-beamed lounge overlooking quiet Georgian village street *(Anon)*

Carlton, N Yorks [Wensleydale; SE0684], *Foresters Arms*: Fascinating moorland pub in delightful spot with good, friendly atmosphere, well kept Theakstons beer and

good range of home-made bar food *(Anthony Fernau)*

Carlton Husthwaite, N Yorks [SE5077], *Carlton*: Good cheerful efficient service in friendly village pub with modernised décor, well kept Youngers on handpump, good varied food (even Sun evening) in bar and dining-room from vegetarian dishes to succulent steaks and salmon, with good vegetables *(W A Rinaldi-Butcher, G C and M D Dickinson)*

Carlton Miniott, N Yorks [A61 Thirsk–Ripon; SE3981], *Old Red House*: Close to BR station – good value well equipped bedrooms, real ale *(Alan Gough)*

Carperby, N Yorks [unclassified rd along N side of Wensleydale; SE0189], *Wheatsheaf*: Good atmosphere, well kept handpumped beer, friendly locals, bar food including good sandwiches; has avoided being a tourist trap *(KC)*

Carthorpe, N Yorks [off A1 N of Ripon, via Burneston and B6285; SE3184], *Fox & Hounds*: Popular dining pub, cosy inside, with good food in bar and restaurant; friendly service, well kept Camerons on handpump *(Peter Race, Tim Halstead)*

Castleton, N Yorks [NZ6908], *Moorlands*: Hotel with pleasant split-level bar, wide choice of good bar food at reasonable prices inc Fri evening steak specials and Sun lunch; friendly licensees; bedrooms good value *(Horace Hipkiss, Mr and Mrs F W Sturch)*

Chapel Le Dale, N Yorks [SD7477], *Old Hill*: Basic moorland pub with well kept Theakstons real ales, popular with walkers and climbers for its warm unfussy welcome and big open fire in the cosy back parlour; live music in barn most summer Sats; children welcome; bedrooms simple *(LYM)*

Cleckheaton, W Yorks [Highmoor Lane; nr M62 junction 26; SE1825], *Old Pack Horse*: Nice, busy pub where something always seems to be happening such as quiz or fun nights *(Ian Robinson)*

Clifton, W Yorks [Westgate; off Brighouse rd from M62 junction 25; SE1623], *Black Horse*: Attractive old pub with low ceilings, long corridors and exposed beams; popular for wide range of food in bar and dining-room; bedrooms *(Anon)*

Cloughton Newlands, N Yorks [TA0196], *Bryherstones*: Very pleasant position and atmosphere, good food and Youngers ales *(Prof S Barnett)*

Collingham, W Yorks [off A58; SE3946], *Barley Corn*: Spacious pub serving good value bar food and Sun lunches *(C Edwards)*; *Star*: Popular pub (can be crowded), with restaurant *(T Nott)*

Coneysthorpe, N Yorks [SE7171], *Tiger*: Fresh, sparkling pub with nice atmosphere, friendly service and wholesome, simple food *(Syd and Wyn Donald)*

☆ **Constable Burton**, N Yorks [SE1791], *Wyvill Arms*: Comfortably converted and attractively decorated farmhouse with elaborate stone fireplace and fine plaster ceiling in inner room; good value attractively presented bar food including ploughman's with three local cheeses, well kept Theakstons, obliging service *(Dr and Mrs B D Smith, LYM)*

☆ **Cropton**, N Yorks [SE7689], *New Inn*: Traditional stone village pub with pleasant modernised bar, pool-room, unobtrusive restaurant and very attractive garden; friendly staff (and Old English Sheepdog – easily mistaken for carpet), nice atmosphere, good range of bar food in substantial helpings, from soup and sandwiches to full meals; besides well kept Tetleys they brew their own good beers on the premises; bedrooms good value *(Maggie Goodwin, John Woolley, Brian and Pam Cowling, J H Tate)*

Cullingworth, W Yorks [Manywell Heights; B6429/A629 Halifax–Keighley; SE0636], *Five Flags*: Impressive hotel complex with comfortable and cosy lounge bar among striking theme bars, popular restaurant; bedrooms *(Wayne Brindle)*

Dalton, N Yorks [NZ1108], *Travellers Rest*: Old, rustic pub in quiet hamlet; pleasant, warm atmosphere, good range of bar food with specialities like duckling, friendly service *(Mr and Mrs Fraser)*

Darley Head, N Yorks [B6451; SE1959], *Wellington*: Small pub with warm, cosy atmosphere and log fires; well kept Tetleys on handpump, food in bar and restaurant extension *(Chris Fluck)*

Denby Dale, N Yorks [Wakefield Rd; SK2208], *Travellers Rest*: Good value hot or cold bar food in comfortable surroundings, Tetleys and Theakstons; open fires in winter *(A D and S A Gamble)*

Dishforth, N Yorks [nr junction A1/A168; SE3873], *Black Swan*: Good welcome, roaring fire, well kept John Smiths on handpump, home-cooked daily specials including vegetarian dishes *(Gill and Neil Patrick)*

Doncaster, S Yorks [St Sepulchre Gate West; Cleveland St; SE5703], *Corner Pin*: Cosy, pleasant little pub with well kept John Smiths *(J A Edwards)*; [Frenchgate; on edge of central pedestrian precinct] *White Swan*: Small front room so far below counter level that you need a high reach for your well kept Wards Sheffield Best; back lounge, bustling popular atmosphere, good value snacks *(J A Edwards, BB)*

East Keswick, N Yorks [Main St; SE3644], *Duke of Wellington*: Popular Victorian dining-room (no booking), with consistently good meals and snacks (not Mon); friendly and efficient service *(Tony and Penny Burton)*

East Marton, N Yorks [SD9051], *Cross Keys*: Interesting old-fashioned furnishings and good range of well kept ales in pub quite close to Leeds and Liverpool Canal; children's room *(LYM)*

☆ **East Witton**, N Yorks [towards Middleham; SE1586], *Cover Bridge Inn*: Unspoilt old pub with huge helpings of good food, well kept Theakstons and friendly welcome; could do with more attention, eg to sometimes messy garden *(David Gaunt, Anthony Fernau, Syd and Wyn Donald)*

Egton, N Yorks [NZ8106], *Horseshoe*: Warm welcome and good open fire in low-beamed moorland village pub popular for fried food and grills *(C Folkers, A Powell, LYM)*; *Wheatsheaf*: Popular and welcoming village local with plush lounge, smallish simple bar, attractive restaurant; wide choice of bar food, well kept McEwans 80/-, attractive outside – especially lit up in the dark *(Mr and Mrs Tim Crawford, Nick Dowson, Alison Hayward, Eileen Broadbent, M A and W R Proctor)*

Embsay, N Yorks [Elm Tree Sq; SE0053], *Elm Tree*: Village pub with open-plan bar and beams, brasses, old-fashioned prints and gas-effect log fire; pleasant landlord, bar food, locals' area with pool-table, darts, fruit machine, dominoes and TV; Whitbreads ales, juke box *(George Hunt)*

Emley, W Yorks [SE2413], *White Horse*: Village free house with well kept Tetleys *(Jon Wainwright)*

Escrick, N Yorks [SE6343], *Black Bull*: Pleasant atmosphere, comfortable surroundings, reasonably priced straightforward bar food; can get very full *(Roger Bellingham, T Nott)*

☆ **Fadmoor**, N Yorks [SE6789], *Plough*: Friendly landlord in traditionally furnished pub overlooking quiet village green, lunchtime bar food (when it can be very quiet) has included big filled Yorkshire puddings in winter but may be confined to soup and sandwiches, restaurant meals inc Sun lunch; Watneys-related real ales; comfortable bedrooms *(Peter Race, Bob Gardiner, T George, LYM)*

☆ **Farnley Tyas**, W Yorks [SE1612], *Golden Cock*: Dining pub with a bistro atmosphere and very good food in cosy bar, carvery and restaurant specialising in charcuterie and casseroles; well kept Bass, thoughtful wine list, very attentive landlord *(K A Chappell, Paul Wreglesworth)*

Felixkirk, N Yorks [SE4785], *Carpenters Arms*: Friendly old-world dining pub with good food and service in cosy bar and character restaurant; well kept John Smiths and Youngers Scotch, attentive licensees; children's high chair kept *(Mrs Irene Smith)*

Ferrybridge, W Yorks [SE4824], *Golden Lion*: Canalside pub below the power station, with well kept Tetleys and food in bar and restaurant inc particularly good value hot buffet Mon–Sun (except Mon and Tues evenings) *(Neil and Anita Christopher)*

Filey, N Yorks [TA1281], *Belle Vue*: Overlooks bay, well kept Tetleys *(Prof S Barnett)*

☆ **Follifoot**, N Yorks [OS Sheet 104 reference 343524; SE3452], *Lascelles Arms*: Welcoming pub with many cosy nooks and blazing fires; generous helpings of simple, tasty and inexpensive bar food; on the way up *(Syd and Wyn Donald)*; *Radcliffe Arms*: Well run attractive bar with friendly, pleasant atmosphere and good value, good food from a short menu *(Syd and Wyn Donald)*

☆ **Galphay**, N Yorks [SE2573], *Galphay Inn*: Good atmosphere and log fire in dining pub with food so good you may have to queue at opening time for a table *(Audrey and Alan Chatting)*

Gargrave, N Yorks [A65 W of village; SD9354], *Anchor*: Extensive canalside pub recently bought and redone in art deco style by Whitbreads as a Chef & Brewer; worth knowing as a useful family pub with a superb children's play area but has lost its individuality; bar food, competent service, Whitbreads-related real ales with a guest such as Marstons Pedigree; economically run bedrooms in modern wing *(LYM)*; *Masons Arms*: Typical dales village pub with dominoes in one of lounges, bowling-green behind, popular bar food *(Wayne Brindle)*

Garsdale Head, N Yorks [junction A684/B6259; nr Garsdale stn on Settle–Carlisle line; SD7992], *Moorcock*: Isolated in good walking country; good food, well and quickly produced, pleasant staff *(D T Taylor)*

Gayles, N Yorks [NZ1207], *Bay Horse*: Much done-up open-plan bar in friendly farm pub with small open fires, well kept McEwans 80/-, Newcastle Exhibition and Youngers Scotch on handpump, darts, straightforward food including good home-cooked ham; closed Weds *(Hon G Vane, BB)*

Giggleswick, N Yorks [SD8164], *Black Horse*: Seventeenth-century Tetleys pub crammed between churchyard and row of cottages, in quaint village; good food, well kept Timothy Taylors too *(Carol and Philip Seddon)*

☆ **Goathland**, N Yorks [opp church; NZ8301], *Mallyan Spout*: Good beer from Malton Brewery in very comfortable bar with good food including huge Yorkshire puddings with interesting fillings; popular restaurant; nr GWG159; bedrooms *(Anon)*

Goldsborough, N Yorks [two miles from A1; SE3856], *Bay Horse*: Traditional stone-built pub with good food in bar and restaurant; coal-effect gas fire, weaponry, massive cast-iron chandelier, Whitbreads Castle Eden and Trophy; bedrooms *(Rob and Gill Weeks)*

Grange Moor, W Yorks [A6142 Huddersfield–Wakefield; SE2216], *Kaye Arms*: Wide range of bar food from interesting soups, good beef sandwiches or ploughman's with home-made chutney to steaks; lots of whiskies *(K A Chappell)*

☆ **Grassington**, N Yorks [The Square; SE0064], *Devonshire*: Pleasant and popular inn with interesting pictures, attractive ornaments, open fires, good window seats overlooking attractive sloping village square; Youngers Scotch and No 3 on handpump, good range of food in separate eating area and well furnished dining-room, friendly staff and quick service; nr start GWG150; bedrooms reasonable, good breakfasts *(C M T Johnson, Mrs D Neilson, Jon Wainwright, George Hunt, LYM)*

Grassington [Garrs Lane], *Black Horse*: Good value bar food and well kept Theakstons ales in comfortable and friendly modern bar with darts in back room, open fires, sheltered terrace; bedrooms good value, looking over stone-slab rooftops to the moors, with maybe a glimpse of the cobbled square; nr start GWG150 *(Mrs D Neilson, BB)*

Great Barugh, N Yorks [off A169 Malton–Pickering – OS Sheet 100 reference 749790; SE7579], *Golden Lion*: Interesting country pub with well kept Tetleys on handpump, good reasonably priced bar food, helpful staff, piped light classics; separate dining-room with Sun lunch; beer garden; children welcome *(Mrs B E Asher, AE)*

☆ **Great Broughton**, N Yorks [High St; NZ5405], *Wainstones*: Well kept Bass and Stones on handpump and good home-made bar food inc Sun lunches in smartish bar; efficient service, restaurant; bedrooms *(Roger Bellingham, E J and J W Cutting, Lyn Marsay)*

Great Ouseburn, N Yorks [SE4562], *Crown*: Large white building with steep steps to main door; horseshoe-shaped bar with four spacious rooms, particularly friendly staff, huge helpings of good value freshly cooked food, big garden *(Jane and Niall)*

Grewelthorpe, N Yorks [SE2376], *Crown*: Friendly village pub with good bar food including giant local sausages *(Audrey and Alan Chatting)*; *Hackfall*: Lovely village pub with two light open-plan rooms, friendly welcome for strangers, well kept Tetleys and Theakstons and good food at reasonable prices; bedrooms warm and cosy *(P Battams, R S and E M Rayden)*

☆ **Gristhorpe**, N Yorks [off A165 Filey–Scarborough; TA0982], *Bull*: Spacious open-plan low-beamed bar with cushioned banquettes, lots of sporting pictures and village scenes; good value bar food including lunchtime cold buffet; games area; well kept Youngers Scotch and No 3 *(S Barnett, Margaret and Roy Randle, LYM)*

Gunnerside, N Yorks [SD9598], *Kings Head*: Classic dales pub with nice beer and food *(Jon Dewhirst)*

Haigh, S Yorks [M1 junction 38; SE2912], *Old Post Office*: Recently converted post office with pleasant bars upstairs and down and separate family-room with videos; well kept Tetleys and Whitbreads Castle Eden, good bar food including giant Yorkshire puddings and roast beef *(Ian Baillie)*

☆ **Halifax**, W Yorks [Paris Gates, Boys Lane – OS Sheet 104 reference 097241; SE0924], *Shears*: Superbly tucked away down narrow cobbled alleys, shut in by towering mills and the bubbling Hebble Brook; very dark inside, with décor reflecting sporting links with local teams, also collection of pump clips and foreign bottles; well kept Taylors, Youngers and unusual guest beers *(Jon Wainwright)*

Hampsthwaite, N Yorks [about 5 miles W of Harrogate; SE2659], *Joiners Arms*: Clean, warm and comfortable with good choice of well presented bar food; gets full quickly at lunchtime, children and dogs seem welcome *(Denis Waters)*

Hardrow, N Yorks [SD8791], *Green Dragon*: Garden access to Britain's highest single-drop waterfall, and on GWG147; bedrooms, and self-catering *(LYM – news of the new regime please)*

Harmby, N Yorks [A684 about 1½m E of Leyburn; SE1389], *Pheasant*: Comfortable two-roomed friendly local with well kept Tetleys on handpump and a genuine landlord keen on traditional values, with a sense of humour *(Jon Dewhirst, Jenny Cantle)*

☆ **Harrogate**, N Yorks [1 Crescent Rd; SE3155], *Hales*: Popular and atmospheric town local with gas lighting, well kept Bass and Stones, simple good value bar food; entertaining quiz nights Tues *(G T Jones, J Sheldrick, J E Rycroft, John Hayward)*

Harrogate [Montpellier Gdns], *Drum & Monkey*: Really an upmarket wine bar/restaurant excelling in seafood, though the downstairs part – friendly and quickly packed – is furnished rather in the style of a pub *(J E Rycroft, Syd and Wyn Donald)*; [6 Cold Bath Rd], *William & Mary*: Wine bar down stone steps in large Victorian house with interesting seating areas; very friendly prompt service, locally popular for lunch; upstairs restaurant *(B Pain)*

Hartoft End, N Yorks [SE7593], *Blacksmiths Arms*: Good home-made bar food from soup and fresh sandwiches to steak in spaciously extended modernised bars and lounges with log fires, well kept Tetleys on handpump, good wines by the glass and pleasant, friendly service; attractive dining-room; pool-table and fruit machine; tables in garden, lovely position at the foot of Rosedale in the N Yorks Moors National Park; bedrooms *(SS)*

Hatfield, S Yorks [High St; nr M18 junction 5; SE6609], *Bay Horse*: Olde-worlde pub on edge of village nr church; home-made individual pies such as chicken and mushroom, rabbit or steak and kidney *(Anon)*

Hawes, N Yorks [Main St; SD8789], *Board*: Friendly and welcoming pub in busy little dales town on the long-distance Pennine Way, and nr start GWG147; well kept Marstons Pedigree, adequate food *(Len*

Beattie, KC); [High St] *Crown*: Friendly, warm and welcoming pub, quite spacious, with well kept if cold Theakstons and popular good value bar food from generously filled giant wholemeal baps to full meals; seats out on front cobbled forecourt *(Helen Thompson, C and L H Lever, Peter Race, Len Beattie)*; *White Hart*: Tidy and spacious lounge bar with open fire, friendly licensees, generously served good food in bar and dining-room *(Peter Bedford, Anne Morris)*

☆ **Haworth**, W Yorks [Main St; SE0337], *Black Bull*: Splendid old Yorkshire pub in pretty village, now serving one of the biggest and best Yorkshire puddings you'll find anywhere; used to be Branwell Brontë's main drinking place, and the Museum bookshop opposite used to be the druggist where he got his opium; ideal stop before visiting the Parsonage, home of the Brontës; bedrooms *(AE, Roy and Margaret Randle)*

Haworth [Main St], *Fleece*: Good, friendly pub with flagstones, well kept Timothy Taylors and wholesome, good value food; morris dancers on bank hols, gets crowded in summer *(A and K D Stansfield)*; [West Lane] *Old White Lion*: Another Brontë-country inn with good, reasonably priced restaurant (vegetarian dishes); comfortable bedrooms *(Sandra Kempson)*

Hebden, N Yorks [SE0263], *Clarendon*: Well kept Timothy Taylors and Tetleys, good food – especially generous steaks; friendly service, laconic in typically Yorkshire way; bedrooms *(Mark Sheard, J D Maplethorpe)*

Hebden Bridge, W Yorks [Thistle Bottom; SD9927], *Stubbings Wharf*: Good friendly atmosphere in clean, bright pub with helpful, cheerful landlord, good choice of well kept beers and good cheap food *(R A Hall)*

☆ **Helmsley**, N Yorks [Market Pl; SE6184], *Black Swan*: Striking Georgian house and adjoining Tudor rectory included primarily as a place to stay; though the small saloon bar on the corner is quite ordinary, the beamed and panelled hotel bar (sharing the same servery, and the well kept real ale) has attractive carved oak settles and Windsor armchairs, and opens into cosy and comfortable lounges with a good deal of character; charming sheltered garden; bedrooms particularly well equipped and comfortable *(Laurence Manning, BB)*

☆ **Helmsley** [Market Sq], *Crown*: Good friendly atmosphere in simply but pleasantly furnished beamed front bar and bigger central dining bar with good value lunchtime snacks and home-made scones and biscuits for afternoon teas, friendly and efficient service, roaring fires, tables in sheltered garden behind with covered conservatory area; bedrooms nice *(Peter Race, Rob and Gill Weeks, M A and W R Proctor, BB)*

Helmsley [B1257], *Feversham Arms*: Worth knowing for decent bar food including good shellfish, with real ale; customers can include quite a strike force of smartly dressed ladies (SVB)

Heptonstall, W Yorks [SD9827], *White Lion*: Local atmosphere and well kept Whitbreads Castle Eden in quiet friendly pub, delightful Pennine village; simple bedrooms (LYM)

High Green, S Yorks [Packhorse La; SK3397], *Pickwick*: Well worth knowing for good, honest home cooking at attractive prices (Mrs E Sugden)

Higham, S Yorks [Higham Common Rd (off A628); SE3107], *Engineers*: Good Pennine views from well furnished dark-wood lounge with well kept Sam Smiths OB and well cooked attractively priced bar food from burgers to mixed grills, in generous helpings; juke box; children's play area (Roger Ollier)

Holmfirth, W Yorks [SD1508], *Rose & Crown*: Basic pub (more commonly known as 'the Nook') with low bar and flagstone floors, fine atmosphere, good range of real ales and riverside garden; don't expect any creature comforts in this drinkers' pub (Steve Mitcheson, Anne Collins); [Hinchliffe Mill; 1m SW on A6024] *Shepherds Rest*: Fairly unspoilt stone village pub with single modestly sized bar, tastefully yet comfortably furnished; well kept Thwaites Mild and Bitter on handpump, lunchtime bar food (not Mon or Tues), pie and mushy peas Fri evening (W P P Clarke)

Honley, W Yorks [SE1312], *Coach & Horses*: Good range of fresh, well presented bar food from sandwiches and ploughman's upwards, all good value and with friendly service (John and Jane Horn)

Hood Green, S Yorks [Stainborough; SE3103], *Stafford Arms*: Large pub dominated by superb old cooking-range; well kept John Smiths, good bar food – particularly steak and kidney pie with excellent chips; ample outdoor seating on lawn, pub backs on to pretty cricket pitch (Paul Newberry)

Hopperton, N Yorks [A59 Harrogate–York; SE4256], *Masons Arms*: Long-standing owners serving reliably good food including huge steaks (Anon)

Hovingham, N Yorks [SE6775], *Worsley Arms*: Good value bar food inc superb ploughman's and Tetleys and Theakstons on handpump in neat, plain but well kept locals' back bar with lots of Yorkshire cricketer photographs, especially of 1930s and 1940s; comfortable hotel with pleasant bedrooms, swifts and house-martins nesting under the eaves – a nice place to stay (S V Bishop, BB)

Huddersfield, W Yorks [New St; SE1416], *Jug & Bottle*: Interesting and attractive stone-built pub on city-centre pedestrian way, popular with wide range of ages for well kept Sam Smiths OB on handpump and good choice of food from separate section; licensee recently moved to the Malt Shovel at Oswaldkirk (Geoff Wilson, R G Ollier); [Lockwood (A616ish)] *Shoulder of Mutton*:

Warm and friendly atmosphere and good range of well kept beers such as Everards, Marstons, Tetleys and Theakstons (N F Doherty); [Bradford Rd] *Slubbers Arms*: Cheerful V-shaped local with coal fire in original range, well kept real ales such as Marstons Pedigree and Timothy Taylors, country wines, lively landlord, good value bar food inc good cheeseburger (Mr and Mrs P A Jones)

Hunton, N Yorks [SE1992], *Countrymans*: Friendly atmosphere and pleasant furnishings and décor; well kept Theakstons and good choice of good, generous, tasty bar meals; live music Sun (Mr and Mrs D C Leaman)

Hutton Le Hole, N Yorks [SE7090], *Crown*: Well placed Ryedale country pub with well kept Camerons, good interesting bar food inc evening steaks (E R Thompson)

Hutton Rudby, N Yorks [NZ4706], *Bay Horse*· Pleasant and roomy, choice of real ales, generous helpings of good bar food from sandwiches up inc good home-made pies (Mrs Shirley Pielou)

Hutton Sessay, N Yorks [off A19 S of Thirsk; SE4876], *Horsebreakers Arms*: Quite a bit of character, good atmosphere, well kept (Wayne Brindle)

☆ **Ilkley**, W Yorks [Stockel Rd; off Leeds–Skipton rd; SE1147], *Ilkley Moor*: Attractively refurbished, keeping its Victorian character with flagstones, open fires and so forth; popular even early in the evening, with good bar food inc giant lunchtime Yorkshire puddings, well kept Timothy Taylors and Tetleys; known locally as the Taps or the Vaults (J A Harrison, Pamela and Merlyn Horswell)

Ilkley [Skipton Rd], *Listers Arms*: Well kept beers and friendly service in solid inn with basement nightclub; may open late, winter evenings; bedrooms (LYM); [Ben Rhydding] *Wheatley*: Large, warm and friendly, generous helpings of good bar food inc Sun lunch; tables could be bigger (C Edwards)

☆ **Ingbirchworth**, S Yorks [Welthorne Lane; off A629 Shepley–Penistone; SE2205], *Fountain*: Neatly kept Tetleys Wayfarer Inn, with red plush banquettes in spacious Turkey-carpeted lounge, comfortable family-room, quite snug front bar, open fires; bar food from snacks such as pâté or lasagne to big helpings of gammon and egg or steaks, with several daily specials and children's helpings; well kept Bitter and Mild on handpump, well reproduced pop music, friendly service, tables outside with play area (Roger Huggins, W P P Clarke, BB)

Ingleby Cross, N Yorks [NZ4501], *Blue Bell*: Cosy, friendly with local atmosphere, well kept beer and interesting bar food; simple but well equipped bedrooms in former barn (Dr and Mrs R J Ashleigh)

Ingleton, N Yorks [SD6973], *Wheatsheaf*: Pleasant, relaxing décor with photographs of old Ingleton, friendly staff, Theakstons and bar food strong on good vegetarian dishes *(Anna Jeffery)*

Jackson Bridge, W Yorks [Scholes Rd; SE1607], *White Horse*: Bass pub with low-ceilinged small rooms and plenty of character – it's been in several episodes of *Last of the Summer Wine*; pool-room looking out on to charming waterfall behind, basic home-cooked bar food *(Steve Mitcheson, Anne Collins)*

Keighley, W Yorks [not a pub, but the buffet car on Keighley–Oxenhope steam trains; SE0641], *Worth Valley Railway*: Midland Rly buffet car with well kept Clarkes, Timothy Taylors and Youngers from handpump, and good sandwiches, as well as full range of other drinks; also occasional White Rose Pullman wine-and-dine trains; this is a fine way to reach Haworth, with marvellous views of Brontë and *Railway Children* country – you can simply change platforms from BR at Keighley; tel Haworth (0535) 43629 for talking timetable *(Charles Hall, Mr and Mrs P A Jones)*

Kettlesing, N Yorks [signposted 6 miles W of Harrogate on A59; SE2256], *Queens Head*: Has a staunch regular clientele, particularly older people, for bar food running up to good steaks, with well kept Theakstons and John Smiths; pleasant surroundings *(G Milligan, J E Rycroft)*

☆ **Kettlewell**, N Yorks [SD9772], *Bluebell*: Currently the most popular – at least among our readers – of this popular village's pubs, with a strong local flavour and lively atmosphere in its simple but pleasant knocked-through bar; friendly staff, decent bar food from home-cooked ham rolls up, well kept real ales and unusually fairly priced soft drinks, pool-room, tables on good-sized back terrace; bedrooms of typical old-fashioned-pub standard; nr start GWG151 *(Joan and John Calvert, Len Beattie, Jon Wainwright, Peter and Rose Flower, LYM)*

Kettlewell, *Racehorses*: Quiet and sedate open-plan hotel bar, consistently comfortable and well furnished, well kept Theakstons and other real ales; nr start GWG151; bedrooms – we have no current information on these or bar food *(Denzil Taylor, Len Beattie, Jon Wainwright, BB)*

Kilburn, N Yorks [SE5179], *Stone Trough*: New regime settling into this picturesque pub in superb spot; well kept Tetleys and Youngers *(J C Proud)*

☆ **Kilnsey**, N Yorks [Kilnsey Crag; SD9767], *Tennant Arms*: Friendly, clean and lively but relaxed Wharfedale pub; series of tasteful interconnecting rooms with beams, flagstones and open fires (one in an ornate carved fireplace), well kept Tetleys and Theakstons Best and Old Peculier, good value bar food (ploughman's, haddock, chicken, trout, beef and venison pie and children's dishes all recommended), piped

music; views over spectacular Kilnsey Crag from restaurant; on GWG150; comfortable bedrooms all with private bathrooms *(Peter and Rose Flower, Jon Wainwright, R F Plater, Peter Race, Len Beattie)*

Kirk Smeaton, N Yorks [2 miles from A1 Doncaster–Pontefract, at Wentbridge turn-off; SE5216], *Shoulder of Mutton*: Village local, unspoilt inside (except for the TV), with Whitbreads Trophy on handpump and character regulars; closed Mon, and not abounding in comfort, but worth knowing for being open all day Fri and Sat *(Alastair Lang)*

Kirkby Malham, N Yorks [SD8961], *Queen Victoria*: Pleasant, almost spartan village pub with good bar food inc excellent choice of vegetarian dishes, small terrace garden, well kept Tetleys and Theakstons; juke box – maybe duet with piped music; bedrooms *(J A Snell, Jon Wainwright)*

Kirkby Overblow, N Yorks [SE3249], *Star & Garter*: Popular local with cosy atmosphere and good choice of standard bar food *(Syd and Wyn Donald)*

Kirkbymoorside, N Yorks [Market Pl; SE6987], *Black Swan*: Picturesque and lively, wide choice of bar snacks, Camerons real ales; open all day at least on Weds; bedrooms simple *(LYM)*; *George & Dragon*: Cosy atmosphere, especially in winter with open fire, well kept Theakstons on handpump, good bar food *(R W K Gardiner)*

Knaresborough, N Yorks [Harrogate Rd; SE3557], *Yorkshire Lass*: Large, pleasant and clean with interesting décor from bicycles to Japanese sunshades; friendly licensees and staff, well kept Watneys-related real ales and good, interesting bar food inc incredible Yorkshire puddings; jazz Fri, pianist Sat; bedrooms good value *(John Hayward)*

☆ **Ledston**, W Yorks [SE4328], *White Horse*: Friendly pub, with well kept real ale and popular lunchtime food – regulars come from miles; in attractive village *(J E Rycroft, M A and W R Proctor)*

Leeds, W Yorks [Arkwright St; off new Armley Rd; SE3033], *Albion*: Splendid refurbishment of Victorian city pub, with well kept Tetleys *(Comus Elliott)*; [North St] *Eagle*: Pubgoers' pub with good range of Timothy Taylors real ales on hand-pump; bedrooms *(W P P Clarke, LYM)*; [Headrow] *Guildford Arms*: City-centre pub with wonderful freshly carved hot roast beef rolls lunchtime (get there early for these), well kept Tetleys *(Roger Taylor)*; [Roundhay Park; SE3131] *Mansion*: Cosy, warm atmosphere and wide choice of food at quite low price; well placed *(Christopher Edwards)*; [Burley Rd] *Queen*: Renovated Victorian pub with wide range of customers from nearby Yorkshire TV people and doctors, to students and workmen, all attracted by outstanding value bar food and well kept Tetleys *(Syd and Wyn Donald)*; [off Briggate –

alley opp Dixons] *Ship*: Cosy, friendly pub with old-fashioned atmosphere even though it's in middle of town; very good value Tetleys and bar food *(Quentin Williamson);* [Gt George St; just behind Town Hall] *Victoria*: Superbly opulent bar with high ceiling, ample alcoved plush seating, mirrors, soft lighting and great atmosphere, opening into side room and cosy back room; well kept Tetleys, efficient service, lunchtime bar food *(Graeme Smalley, Jon Wainwright);* [55 Wetherby Rd] *White House*: Good food at reasonable price, friendly atmosphere; spacious, with tables in pleasant garden *(Christopher Edwards);* [New Briggate] *Wrens*: Big, old-fashioned, city-centre pub with lots of bars, passages and nooks and crannies inc no-smoking room; wonderful Tetleys inc Imperial, dominoes *(Roger Taylor)*

Lepton, W Yorks [Paul Lane, Flockton Moor; SE2015], *Dartmouth Arms*: Good main dishes inc proper chips, brisk waitress service *(K A Chappell)*

☆ **Leyburn**, N Yorks [just off Market Pl; SE1191], *Sandpiper*: Pleasant atmosphere in cosy lounge area with comfortable seats around the fire, and large dining area on far side of the small bar – it doesn't feel cut off from main pub; well kept Theakstons Best, XB and Old Peculier (and they'll even make a ginger-beer shandy), cheerfully helpful and efficient service, moderately priced bar food from sandwiches up, and restaurant; sunny terrace and flower-surrounded floodlit back garden; Gemma the border collie's a celebrity for slip-catching beer-mats *(Jenny Cantle, Anne Morris, W M Sharpe)*

☆ **Leyburn** [Market Pl], *Golden Lion*: Homely, with benches around big pine tables, good value food from efficient food counter (ploughman's, home-made steak and kidney pie, crisp Yorkshire puddings, garlic chicken, fresh fish all recommended); good unusually flavoured Oliver Johns beer brewed here, decent house wines and malt whiskies, cheerful atmosphere; bedrooms good value – especially the bargain breaks *(Mrs V Carroll, Mr and Mrs Tarlton)*

☆ **Linton**, W Yorks [SE3947], *Windmill*: Polished charm, good bar food and pleasant atmosphere in carefully preserved small rooms with antique settles, oak beams, longcase clock, well kept Youngers Scotch and No 3 – where the Leeds millionaires go for Sun sherry *(J E Rycroft, T Nott, LYM)*

Lockton, N Yorks [A169 N of Pickering; SE8490], *Fox & Rabbit*: Bustling family pub on moors, well kept real ales, good value simple food, seats outside and in sun lounge; children's room *(LYM)*

Luddenden, W Yorks [SE0426], *Lord Nelson*: Cheerful modernised eighteenth-century local with interesting features, where Branwell Brontë borrowed books; attractive very steep streamside village *(LYM)*

Malham, N Yorks [SD8963], *Buck*: Enjoyed by readers chiefly for its position in awe-inspiring scenery nr Malham Cove and Gordale Scar, on the Pennine Way – it's the most prominent pub in the village; well kept Theakstons XB and Old Peculier in big lounge bar with comfortable old furniture, and busy hikers' bar; usual food inc decent ploughman's; nr start GWG152; children's area off main lounge *(Margaret and Roy Randle, Len Beattie, Jenny Cantle, Steve Waters);* *Lister Arms*: Large stone-built pub enjoying same position, Youngers Scotch and IPA on handpump, good helpings of bar food, steak restaurant; bedrooms *(Tim Baxter)*

Malton, N Yorks [Wheelgate; SE7972], *Crown*: Unspoilt place, in same family for generations, brewing its own good Malton beers, inc Double Chance and Owd Bob (named for the landlady's late husband); good value bedrooms *(Simon Feisenberger)*

☆ **Mankinholes**, W Yorks [SD9523], *Top Brink*: Lively, friendly moorland village pub, popular in evenings, with very good steaks; quite close to Pennine Way and nice walks to nearby monument on Stoodley Pike; midnight licence extension *(Len Beattie)*

Marsden, W Yorks [Manchester Rd (A62); SE0412], *Olive Branch*: Log fire in winter, Dutch landlord/chef doing good unusual bar food at reasonable prices, inc Weds bargain suppers *(Mr and Mrs G Hawksworth)*

Masham, N Yorks [Silver St, linking A6168 with Market Sq; SE2381], *Bay Horse*: Well kept John Smiths Bitter, Theakstons Old Peculier, XB and Best on handpump, good bar food inc ploughman's with three cheeses and German specialities, good friendly service *(Maggie Goodwin, John Woolley);* [Market Sq] *Kings Head*: Handsome stone inn with spacious and plushly comfortable lounge bar, attractively decorated, tables in courtyard and comfortable well equipped bedrooms; has had usual bar food (not Sat evening), restaurant usefully open through Sun afternoon, and well kept Theakstons Best, XB and Old Peculier on handpump, with a welcome for children, but was put on market in 1989 – more news please, particularly as the position on this broad square is so attractive *(LYM)*

Mexborough, S Yorks [S of A6023: follow 'waterbus' signs; SE4800], *Ferry Boat*: Old-fashioned with some traditional furnishings, lively friendly atmosphere, good welcome, well kept real ales inc Bass Special; quite near canal *(Steve Mitcheson, Anne Collins, LYM)*

☆ **Middleham**, N Yorks [SE1288], *Black Swan*: Attractive and comfortable olde-worlde pub in superb village with well kept Theakstons and good choice of generous bar food; quick, helpful service even though busy; pictures and poems reflect the local racehorse-training connection; mind your head at door; attractive back terrace, restaurant *(Mr and Mrs D C Leaman, Mrs V Carroll);* [Market Pl]

White Swan: Very friendly atmosphere, good plain cooking; bedrooms spotless and good value, big breakfast (no residents' lounge) *(Mr and Mrs M Tarlton)*

Midgley, W Yorks [signposted from Hebden Br; from A646 W of Halifax go straight through village, keep on high rd – OS Sheet 104 reference 007272; SE0326], *Mount Skip*: The outstanding view is really special – the ground drops so steeply that the opposite moorland and mill towns below take on a toy-like quality, with the streetlamps turned to twinkling golden necklaces at night; well kept Timothy Taylors Bitter, Landlord and Golden Best in simple modernised bar, usual bar food, restaurant, games inc pool, piped music, benches outside, good walks; children allowed (not late Sat evenings); opens 7 winter *(Wayne Brindle, Len Beattie, LYM)*

Minskip, N Yorks [SE3965], *White Swan*: Varied, reasonably priced good bar meals inc sirloin steak done to perfection; a John Smiths pub *(N Burrell)*

Mirfield, W Yorks [Dewsbury Rd (A644); SE2019], *Pear Tree*: Pleasing welcome in roadside pub with open fires, friendly and efficient licensee, well kept Websters, home-made bar food inc a particularly good steak and mushroom pie, back garden steeply sloping to river *(B D Gibbs)*; [just off A644 towards Dewsbury] *Ship*: Spacious pub, large restaurant *(Ian Robinson)*

Muker, N Yorks [SD9198], *Farmers Arms*: Friendly welcome, genuine and cosy atmosphere, well kept Theakstons, simple but well prepared bar food, good service; in attractive National Park surroundings, nr start GWG148 *(Dr and Mrs R J Ashleigh)*

Norland, W Yorks [Hob Lane; SE0723], *Hobbit*: Pleasant atmosphere, friendly staff, good value food, wide choice of beers; bedrooms comfortable and well equipped *(SM)*

North Rigton, N Yorks [SE2748], *Square & Compass*: Well kept beer, good food and service; up-market atmosphere evenings and Sun lunchtime *(J E Rycroft)*

Nosterfield, N Yorks [SE2881], *Freemasons Arms*: Friendly staff in pleasant pub with Tetleys and Theakstons ales and good value lunchtime bar snacks and evening meals; children welcome *(Alan Kelly)*

Nun Monkton, N Yorks [off A59 York–Harrogate; SE5058], *Alice Hawthorn*: Modernised beamed bar with dark red plush settles back to back around dimpled copper tables, open fire in big brick fireplace, keen darts players; on broad village green with pond, nr River Nidd *(BB)*

Ogden, W Yorks [SE0631], *Causeway Foot*: Spacious pub with several local beers and good bar food served till late evening *(Ian Robinson)*; [A629 Denholme–Halifax], *Moorland*: Free house smartened up well with lots of beams, dark woodwork, brasses, log-effect gas fire and subdued lighting;

Watneys-related real ales on handpump, juke box, pool-table; lunchtime bar food, small restaurant; children at lunchtimes *(George Hunt)*

☆ **Oldstead**, N Yorks [SE5380], *Black Swan*: Friendly inn in beautiful surroundings with pretty valley views from two big bay windows and picnic-table sets outside; engaging licensees (he's an American – and the dog's called Duke), decent bar food inc lots of grills, well kept John Smiths or Tetleys and Youngers IPA or No 3 on handpump, rather fuzzy piped music; children welcome; bedrooms in comfortable modern back extension, with huge breakfasts *(D B Delany, Greg Parston, BB)*

☆ **Osmotherley**, N Yorks [Staddlebridge; A172 towards Middlesbrough, just off its junction with A19 – OS Sheet 99 reference 444994; SE4499], *Cleveland Tontine*: Prosperous and attractive cellar bar with big log fire, good food and cheerful service – but prices decidedly in the restaurant bracket now, and at busy times most tables are reserved for diners *(Anon)*

Ossett, W Yorks [20 Horbury Rd (B6128); SE2820], *Crown*: Comfortably old-fashioned stone-built pub with masses of bric-à-brac inc attractive doll collection; good well cooked food, especially light and tasty Yorkshire puddings (choice more limited weekends but still includes them) *(Mrs K Chappell)*

Otley, W Yorks [Westgate; SE2045], *Crosspipes*: Pleasantly decorated, homely and friendly pub with well kept John Smiths on handpump, good bar food; bedrooms good value *(Tim Baxter and others)*

Overton, W Yorks [204 Old Rd; SE2617], *Reindeer*: Clean and tidy pub, thriving under new landlord, with happy and friendly staff and good, good value food *(Roger Allott)*

☆ **Oxenhope**, W Yorks [off B6141 towards Denholme; SE0335], *Dog & Gun*: Busy pub with plenty of character and atmosphere, doing well under current regime; well kept Timothy Taylors Landlord and Tetleys on handpump, good bar food inc sandwiches at reasonable prices and good value Sun lunches; bistro-style restaurant *(Mr and Mrs J E Rycroft, Wayne Brindle)*

Oxenhope, *Lamb*: Friendly landlord and family, real fires, well kept Websters and Wilsons, good reasonably priced bar food *(Charles Hall)*; [A6033 Keighley–Hebden Bridge *Waggon & Horses*: Moorside pub with fleeces on stripped stone walls, comfortable seats, good beer and bar food *(LYM)*

Pateley Bridge, N Yorks [SE1666], *Crown*: Cosy lounge with railed-off dining area alongside, stripped stonework and horsebrasses (but not too many), good choice of food inc good sandwiches, decent beer *(Anon)*

Patrick Brompton, N Yorks [SE2291], *Green*

Tree: Nicely refurbished, with well kept Theakstons, good cider and good fresh well cooked bar food varying from day to day *(Mr and Mrs W A Rinaldi-Butcher)*

☆ **Pickering**, N Yorks [Market Pl; SE7984], *White Swan*: Most inviting small bar run by enthusiastic hotel staff, good friendly locals, good chip-free bar food; bedrooms *(Jon Wainright)*

Pickering [Market Pl], *Bay Horse*: Warm welcome, good bar food (ploughman's and lasagne recommended), well kept Camerons, decent Soave, good log fire; can be smoky *(Anon)*; [18 Birdgate] *Black Swan*: Big old pub, fairly well modernised with John Smiths on handpump and limited range of decent food with generous helpings of vegetables; no dogs; bedrooms *(Dr John Innes)*; [Westgate] *Sun*: Small friendly local with seats around wall of central bar, well kept Tetleys on handpump *(Dr John Innes)*

Pickhill, N Yorks [SE3584], *Fox & Hounds*: True village local with main bar and small adjacent dining-room; well kept beer, good bar food inc lavish puddings cooked by landlady, friendly staff and customers *(Stan Edwards)*

Rainton, N Yorks [Village Green; under a mile from A1 Boroughbridge–Leeming Bar; SE3775], *Bay Horse*: Friendly village atmosphere with collections of blowlamps, bank notes and cigarette cards; generous helpings of good value food, very popular locally *(Gill and Neil Patrick)*

Reeth, N Yorks [Market Pl; SE0499], *Kings Arms*: Eighteenth-century free house overlooking sloping green in olde-worlde village; homely welcome in oak-beamed lounge, open fire, well kept Theakstons (and tea or coffee), good reasonably priced bar food, restaurant, obliging service; bedrooms *(E R Thompson)*

Richmond, N Yorks [Finkle St; NZ1801], *Black Lion*: Cosy and friendly pub with dark décor, well kept Camerons and Everards on handpump, good home-cooked cold meat salads as well as generous helpings of grouse, chicken pie and steaks; bedrooms reasonable *(Lorrie Marchington, Dr and Mrs R J Ashleigh)*

Ripon, N Yorks [SE3171], *Black Bull*: Old pub on market place (market day Thurs), with pleasant lounge and bar, well kept Theakstons, lunchtime bar food *(Lyn and Bill Capper)*; *Golden Lion*: Free house with generously served bar food inc huge helpings of Yorkshire pudding and big puddings, well kept Matthew Browns, Theakstons Best and XB, pool-table, darts, friendly licensees; small restaurant *(Geoff Hall)*

Robin Hood's Bay, N Yorks [The Dock, Bay Town; NZ9505], *Bay*: Well lit, busy pub with warm fire, welcoming staff, good bar food inc good steaks at moderate prices, well kept Camerons and Everards; only snag, it's a long walk back up to the car park; bedrooms *(Angela Nowill, Roger Bellingham)*; *Olde*

Dolphin: Fine Camerons ales, extensive menu *(Tony Pounder)*

Roecliffe, N Yorks [SE3766], *Crown*: Olde-worlde décor, friendly atmosphere, big helpings of good home-cooked food inc good value sandwiches, attentive family service, new back extension (in keeping with character) usefully gives more space *(Peter Race)*

Rotherham, S Yorks [Moorgate Rd; SK4393], *Belvedere*: Tastefully decorated horseshoe-shaped bar with bar food from sandwiches up in area sectioned off, Whitbreads beers, decent choice of wines *(David Tonkin)*

Rufforth, N Yorks [Main St; SE5351], *Tankard*: Reliable Sam Smiths pub in sleepy village, pleasantly decorated open-plan lounge and bar with well kept real ale, darts and welcoming licensee *(Jon Wainwright)*

☆ **Runswick Bay**, N Yorks [NZ8217], *Royal*: Cheerful and lively atmosphere, well kept John Smiths, welcoming staff, nautical back bar and lovely views down over fishing village and bay from big-windowed front bar and terrace *(M A and W R Proctor, LYM)*

Sandsend, N Yorks [NZ8613], *Hart*: Variety of good, home-cooked food, well kept Camerons Strongarm, good service, sea views, seats in good outside area *(Peter Kitson, Bridgett Sarsby)*

☆ **Scarborough**, N Yorks [Cambridge Terrace; TA0489], *Cask*: Decent choice of real ales in lively conversion of big Victorian house, often buzzing with young people *(J A Edwards, LYM)*

Scarborough [Vernon Rd], *Hole in the Wall*: Well kept ales with regular guest beers, graffiti blackboard in gents *(J A Edwards)*; [St Marys St] *Leeds Arms*: Well kept beers and pleasant relaxed atmosphere, pronounced nautical feel; interesting location in old part of town *(R A Hutson)*

Scawton, N Yorks [SE5584], *Hare*: Low and pretty, with simple wall settles, stools, little wheel-back armchairs and wood-effect or trestle tables, and inoffensive piped music; cheerful welcome, well kept John Smiths on handpump, decent straightforward food from sandwiches through steak and kidney pie to big steaks; new restaurant area; pool-table up steps, seats outside, nice inn-signs; fairly handy for Rievaulx Abbey *(Carole and John Rowley, BB)*

Scorton, N Yorks [B1263 Richmond–Yarm; NZ2500], *Royal*: Dark and cosy bar with bow window overlooking green; good well garnished sandwiches at quiet times, bigger menu when busier; cheerful service, big fire, pool-table, darts *(820)*

Scotch Corner, N Yorks [a couple of hundred yds up A66 past the big hotel; NZ2205], *Vintage*: Most attractive, homely pub with good bar meals from sandwiches to duck (with half-helpings for the elderly), real ale inc Websters Green Label, decent wine

cellar; bedrooms *(E R Thompson)*
Seamer, N Yorks [TA0284], *Copper Horse*:
Old pub in quiet village with beams, brasses,
bare stone, part wood-floored and part
carpeted, with gold plush bar stools and
wooden chairs around cast-iron-framed
tables; wide range of bar food inc good
sandwiches and outstanding generous
ploughman's *(Ian Blackwell)*
☆ **Settle**, N Yorks [SD8264], *Royal Oak*:
Fantastic value food late into evening from
popular turkey sandwich through traditional
hot dishes, fish, salads and children's dishes
to steak, in spacious dark-panelled hotel
entrance lounge (with rather restaurAnty
atmosphere); puddings include Yorkshire fat
rascals – a puff pastry and raisins concoction
served hot with cream; good choice of beers,
friendly service *(Brian Horner, Anne Morris,
Margaret and Roy Randle)*
Settle, *Golden Lion*: Easy chairs, sofas and
big Windsor armchairs in high-beamed
lounge bar, well kept Thwaites ales, games in
lively public bar, horses still stabled in
coachyard; bedrooms *(LYM)*
Sheffield, S Yorks [Abbeydale Rd; SK3687],
Beauchief: Attractively converted cellar bar
in hotel popular with older people at
lunchtime for good food inc good quiches
and delicious help-yourself salads; obliging
management; bedrooms *(Peggy Bramhall)*;
[Worksop Rd; just off Attercliffe Common]
Cocked Hat: Largely open-plan, tastefully
refurbished in dark colours, decorated with
breweriana and beer bottles; sewing-machine
treadle tables, well kept Marstons Pedigree
and Burton, lunchtime bar food; nr sports
complex being built for next World Student
Olympiad *(W P P Clarke)*; [400 Handsworth
Rd (A57)] *Cross Keys*: Ancient friendly pub
actually inside churchyard; well kept Stones,
open fires *(LYM)*; [195–199 Carlisle St]
Norfolk Arms: Large, multi-roomed Tetleys
pub amid the steelworks with striking
exterior and abundance of leather and wood
inside; strange, roundabout-style bar with
well kept beers, two pool-rooms and lively
Fri singalong *(Matt Pringle)*; [Packhorse Lane,
High Green] *Pickwick*: Wide range of
lunchtime and evening bar food, generously
served at reasonable prices *(Mrs E Sugden)*;
[18 Pitt St] *Red Deer*: Friendly locals in
comfortably furnished, tidy pub with
particularly well kept Tetleys; flowers
outside; gets packed *(Paul Newberry and
others)*; [Hollis Croft] *Red House*: Small,
backstreet, three-roomed Wards house,
recently redecorated and comfortably
furnished; well kept Darleys Best and Wards
Kirby and Sheffield Best, good lunchtime bar
food and often spontaneous folk music *(W
P P Clarke)*; [Charles St] *Red Lion*: Smart
town-centre pub with well kept Wards
Sheffield Best and conservatory *(W
P P Clarke)*; [off Cemetery Rd] *Royal Oak*:
Comfortable, welcoming opulent Edwardian

pub with heavy flock wallpaper, heavy velvet
curtains with fringes and deep banquettes in
a variety of side rooms; often shellfish on
bar, and well kept Whitbreads Castle Eden
(Ian and James Phillips); [Charles St]
Yorkshire Grey: Comfortably refurbished in
Victorian style with well kept Whitbreads
Castle Eden and Marstons Pedigree, good
lunchtime bar food inc Yorkshire puddings;
close to Crucible Theatre *(Allan Lloyd)*
Shelley, W Yorks [Royd House; SE2011],
Three Acres: Good range of real ales in
pleasant pub – if lacking real Yorkshire
character; food pricey, but includes good
steak and kidney pie *(Geoff Wilson,
K A Chappell)*
☆ **Shepley**, W Yorks [Penistone Rd; SE1909],
Sovereign: Open-plan, L-shaped dining
lounge with beamery, yucca plants and tables
neatly set for popular good value freshly
cooked unpretentious bar food inc
sandwiches, children's dishes, Yorkshire
puddings and plenty of other hot dishes,
generous salads and steaks; Bass and Stones
Best on handpump normally well kept,
moderately priced wines, cheerful and
efficient waitress service, garden; very busy
weekends *(Frank Cummins, Gillian Hamilton,
Geoff Wilson, K A Chappell)*
Sheriff Hutton, N Yorks [SE6566],
Highwayman: Friendly Tetleys pub with
welcoming licensees; just over road from
castle *(J C Proud)*
☆ **Skipton**, N Yorks [Canal St; from Water St
(A65) turn into Coach St, then left after canal
bridge; SD9852], *Royal Shepherd*: Friendly
local near canal with large bar, snug and
dining-room with open fires and old pictures
of town and canal; generously served simple
lunchtime food (inc Sun), well kept and well
priced Whitbreads-related real ales and a
guest beer, unusual whiskies, good mix
lunchtime customers, students in evening – it
has games and a juke box; Petrol the dog
isn't exactly chummy; tables outside;
children allowed in dining-room lunchtime
*(George Hunt, Pamela and Merlyn Horswell,
Lynn Stevens, Gill Quarton)*
Skipton, *Red Lion*: Cheerful and bustling
(next to the market), well furnished, with
pleasant food and Whitbreads ales; open for
most of the day on Suns *(Wayne Brindle)*
☆ **Slingsby**, N Yorks [Railway St; SE7075],
Grapes: Straightforward but popular good
value food and well kept Camerons in stone-
built village local with cast-iron-framed
tables on patterned carpet, children in room
off bar, helpful service; tables in garden
behind *(Tim Baxter, Carole and John Rowley,
BB)*
☆ **Snape**, N Yorks [SE2784], *Castle Arms*:
Friendly licensees, comfortable and homely
pub with cosy inglenooks and open fires, and
enterprising food; keg beer *(Jon Dewhirst,
Simon Feisenberger)*
South Anston, S Yorks [3 miles from M1

junction 31; SK5183], *Loyal Trooper*: Cheerful village local with well kept Tetleys and tables in lounge set at lunchtime for good value straightforward bar food; lively public bar *(LYM)*

Sowerby Bridge, W Yorks [Wharf St; main road, opposite entrance to canal basin; SE0623], *Ashtree*: The Indonesian bar food which makes this so popular has now taken over to such an extent that it's no longer a pub but has become part of the Java Restaurant; they do still have a (smart) bar, with real ales such as Moorhouses *(Anon)*

Soyland, W Yorks [OS Sheet 110 reference 012203; SE0423], *Blue Ball*: Unspoilt but adequately comfortable moorland pub; Theakstons ales, guest beers and straightforward bar food; music room with piano and organ; bedrooms *(G T Jones)*

Spennithorne, N Yorks [SE1489], *Old Horn*: Small, friendly, seventeenth-century pub with lunchtime bar food and good evening restaurant; bedrooms good *(Richard Fawcett)*

Sprotbrough, S Yorks [Melton Rd; SE5302], *Ivanhoe*: Large black and white mock-Tudor building with fine view of cricket ground; comfortable, smart lounge/dining area with conservatory extension, uniformed waitresses; strong emphasis on food (which is decent), well kept Sam Smiths OB; children's play area *(Steve Mitcheson, Anne Collins, J A Edwards)*

Stainforth, N Yorks [SD8267], *Royal Oak*: Useful village pub in good walking country serving well kept Thwaites Bitter *(Len Beattie)*

Stainton, S Yorks [SK5594], *Three Tuns*: Comfortable, clean pub with good choice of well presented bar food inc good help-yourself salads *(Richard Cole)*

Staithes, N Yorks [NZ7818], *Cod & Lobster*: Superb waterside setting for friendly local in unspoilt fishing village under dramatic sandstone cliff; well kept Camerons; parking nearby difficult *(M A and W R Proctor, Tony Pounder, LYM)*

☆ **Stanbury**, W Yorks [SE0037], *Old Silent*: Popular moorland village inn near Haworth, small rooms packed with bric-à-brac, four real ales, decent food in bar and restaurant served till late in the evening; good hill views, tables on attractive terrace; bedrooms old-fashioned but well equipped *(Robert Aitken, LYM)*

Stanley, W Yorks [Aberford Rd; SE3423], *British Oak*: Wilsons and Websters, good varied home-cooked bar food, good service, attentive licensee, restaurant; good facilities for disabled people, with helpful service for them *(A J Woodhouse)*

☆ **Stapleton**, N Yorks [NZ2612], *Bridge*: Exceptionally good food using top-quality fresh ingredients and showing real imagination and delicate preparation; service very pleasant, helpful and efficient, in cosy Victorian pub with heavy brown Anaglypta

walls and log-effect gas fire; restaurant; children allowed, with special helpings and prices, if they eat early *(K Baxter, Dr R C Keith, Mrs P Sachs)*

Steeton, W Yorks [Station Rd; SE0344], *Steeton Hall*: Warm welcome in very pleasant inn with good food; bedrooms comfortable *(Mr and Mrs Norman Morris)*

☆ **Stutton**, N Yorks [SE4841], *Hare & Hounds*: Popular old stone-built pub with pleasant atmosphere, well kept and priced Sam Smiths OB on handpump, good bar food (inc Yorkshire pudding with lots of dishes) in lounge or comfortable and well furnished restaurant; children allowed if eating *(Noel and Mo Tornbohm, Mr and Mrs M D Jones)*

Summer Bridge, N Yorks [junction B6451/ B6165; SE2062], *Flying Dutchman*: Village inn in beautiful Nidderdale setting, quiet relaxed atmosphere, well kept Sam Smiths; bedrooms good, with huge breakfast *(Chris Fluck)*

Sutton Bank, N Yorks [A170; SE5282], *Hambleton*: Conveniently near Cleveland Way and Sutton Bank, well kept Theakstons, wide choice of food *(Tony Pounder)*

Sutton under Whitestoncliffe, N Yorks [A170 E of Thirsk; SE4983], *Whitestoncliffe*: Busy pub, wide choice of good lunchtime and evening bar food at reasonable prices, restaurant used as extension to bar *(Mr and Mrs F W Sturch)*

Swainby, N Yorks [NZ4802], *Black Horse*: Good food, good service and tables outside with aviary and tree house; separate dining-room with Sun lunch; children welcome *(Mrs B E Asher)*

Swinton, N Yorks [the one near Malton, at SE7673], *Blacksmiths Arms*: Nice atmosphere in village roadside pub with good value food, decent beer, helpful landlord *(David Gaunt)*

☆ **Tadcaster**, N Yorks [Bridge St; SE4843], *Angel & White Horse*: The pub's coachyard has the stables for the Sam Smiths team of dappled grey shire horses – you can see them from the handsomely fitted and immaculately kept oak-panelled bar; cheap well kept Sam Smiths ales, good value weekday bar food, restaurant; brewery tours can be arranged – tel Tadcaster (0937) 832225 *(Gordon Mott, LYM)*

☆ **Tan Hill**, N Yorks [Arkengarthdale (Reeth– Brough) rd, at junction with Keld/W Stonesdale rd; NY8906], *Tan Hill*: Included for its remarkable position – at 1732 ft it's Britain's highest pub, some five miles from nearest neighbours, no mains electricity, often snowed in, and really needing its two big fires (a shame they sometimes light only one); a haven for walkers on the Pennine Way, and because of this its furnishings are simple, with flagstone floors and very few frills (apart from the juke box); well kept Theakstons Best, XB and Old Peculier, cheery food inc good soup and ploughman's, games-room, occasional singalong accordion sessions; housekeeping can be rather rough-and-ready; children welcome; bedrooms basic (*Len Beattie, Steve Dykes, Mr and Mrs D C Leaman, Wayne Brindle, G W Cheney, Peter and Rose Flower, TOH, PLC, LYM*)

☆ **Thirsk**, N Yorks [Market Pl; SE4382], *Golden Fleece*: Popular bar in attractive and comfortable THF hotel, with well kept real ales, good reasonably priced bar food, eager young staff; can get rather cramped; comfortable bedrooms (*Richard Dolphin, Prof S Barnett, Peter Race*)

Thirsk [Market Pl], *Black Bull*: Friendly welcome, well kept Camerons Mild and Bitter and good value Sun roast lunch; bedrooms good value (*Alan Gough*)

Thoralby, N Yorks [SE0086], *George*: Plain, comfortable, traditional local with friendly welcome, well kept Websters, good range of bar food (*Richard Fawcett*)

Thornton le Clay, N Yorks [SE6865], *White Swan*: Small country pub, one L-shaped room with central bar, brasses, tankards and corn dollies hanging from rafters; relaxed atmosphere, good value bar food inc Sun roast lunch (*S V Bishop*)

Thruscross, N Yorks [village signposted from A59 Harrogate–Skipton at Blubberhouses, or off B6255 Grassington–Pateley Bridge at Greenhow Hill; OS Sheet 104 reference 159587; SE1558], *Stone House*: Moorland pub with beams, flagstones, stripped stone, dark panelling and warm fires; straightforward bar food from sandwiches to steaks, and Tetleys Mild and Bitter (rather than Theakstons), under the latest regime; traditional games, sheltered tables outside; restaurant (not Sun evening); has been open all day; children welcome (*LYM*)

Thurlstone, S Yorks [A628 – OS Sheet 110 reference 230034; SE2303], *Huntsman*: Well run old stone-built pub with well kept real ales such as Greene King Abbot, Marstons Pedigree and Ruddles County on handpump, friendly landlord with taste for jazz records played quite loudly, good atmosphere, lunchtime bar food (*W P P Clarke*)

Todmorden, W Yorks [550 Burnley Rd, Knotts; look out for car park which is easy to overshoot on the steep A646 – OS Sheet 103 reference 916257; SD9324], *Staff of Life*: Old and eccentric pub formed from several cottages cut into slope of hill, full of bits and bobs, though can seem cold in winter; the special thing here is the wide range of real ales inc the pub's own Robinwood Bitter, XB and winter Old Fart brewed nearby; also superb cider, and good bar food (maybe no starters and only one pudding, and evening choice is on the pricey side) (*Wayne Brindle, Syd and Wyn Donald*)

Tosside, N Yorks [SD7755], *Dog & Partridge*: Old-fashioned cosy village free house with big log fire in lounge, good reasonably priced food, well kept Thwaites

Ulley, S Yorks [Turnshaw Rd; nr M1 junction 31 – off B6067 in Aston; SK4687], *Royal Oak*: Handsome stone country pub with Stable bar (beams with farm tools and horse tackle), garden lounge, family-room and dining-room; Sam Smiths on handpump, usual bar food inc children's helpings; as it's so near the motorway it could perhaps do with more staff; children's play area (*Helena and Arthur Harbottle*)

Upper Hopton, W Yorks [SE1918], *Travellers Rest*: Busy pub doing well under new licensees, with well kept Tetleys and good bar food at reasonable prices (*J E Rycroft*)

☆ **Wakefield**, W Yorks [Westgate; SE3321], *Henry Boons*: Large, attractive Victorian corner pub by rly stn; interesting décor with main open-plan bar actually thatched, full of breweriana such as sacks of hops and malt but comfortably furnished; separate room to one side used for live jazz, smaller room opposite wallpapered with local newspaper cuttings, library for customers, tables with inlaid chess boards (pieces available); well kept Clarks (it's the brewery tap for these beers) as well as Tetleys and Timothy Taylors Landlord on handpump, good choice of bottled foreign lagers, lunchtime bar food (*W P P Clarke*)

Wakefield, W Yorks [SE3321], *Harewood Arms*: Pleasantly refurbished with cheap, good beer and nice atmosphere for a city-centre pub (*Comus Elliott*); *Star*: Good reasonably priced food – especially the fish pie – in friendly and comfortable long room (*Roger Huggins*)

☆ **Warthill**, N Yorks [village signposted off A64 York–Malton and A166 York–Great Driffield; SE6755], *Agar Arms*: Steaks, steaks, steaks – that's what packs people into the L-shaped bar and further room of this prettily placed pub, opposite the duck pond; sizes go from twelve-ounce to 2lb, with all sorts of variations, often inc additions such as squid or chicken (they do other dishes, too, with lunchtime sandwiches and children's dishes); softly lit and nicely decorated, with open fires and well kept Sam Smiths on electric pump (*JAH, HCH, M Suther, Eddie Palker, J C Proud, BB*)

☆ **Weaverthorpe**, N Yorks [SE9771], *Star*: Neat litle village inn with pleasant relaxing atmosphere; front lounge, main back lounge, small pool-room and restaurant; open fires, well kept Tetleys and Theakstons Bitter and XB, extensive range of up-market food inc pheasant and so forth, very friendly licensees; bedrooms a little sparse but cheap, and very good value (*J A Edwards, DW*)

Wentbridge, W Yorks [off A1; SE4817], *Blue Bell*: Large pub with family-room, good choice of real ales, large helpings of bar food inc Sun lunch; service might be quicker (*Neil and Anita Christopher, T Nott*)

☆ **West Burton**, N Yorks [on green, off B6160

Bishopdale–Wharfedale; SE0186], *Fox & Hounds*: Unspoilt, basic pub in idyllic dales village where all the houses face a long green; small bar with extension, homely atmosphere, well kept John Smiths on handpump, reasonably priced decent home-cooked bar food inc children's dishes, good service from friendly staff *(Jenny Cantle, C M T Johnson, Anthony Fernau, NIH)*

☆ **West Tanfield**, N Yorks [A6108 N of Ripon – OS Sheet 99 reference 268788; SE2678], *Bruce Arms*: Traditional village pub with mixture of old-fashioned seats around the log fire in its snug front bar, second bar at the back, jaunty decorations, bar food – which may take a long while to prepare – from sandwiches to ham and eggs or steak (the ploughman's has been good), well kept John Smiths and Theakstons Best and XB, games, juke box, tables outside (the stables are still in use); restaurant; no bar food Mon, closed Mon lunchtime exc bank hols; children welcome lunchtime *(Mr and Mrs M Tarlton, Lyn and Bill Capper, Rob and Gill Weeks, LYM)*

☆ **West Witton**, N Yorks [A684 W of Leyburn; SE0688], *Wensleydale Heifer*: Comfortable rooms, good log fire, pleasant décor, interesting prints, chintz-upholstered furniture; pleasant service, well kept John Smiths, good helpings of bar food which can be good value (but if you want to eat you'll probably be put in a stall-style separate bistro); restaurant; attractive bedrooms *(Helen May, Dr and Mrs B D Smith, Mr and Mrs Bill Muirhead, C J Cuss)*

Wetherby, W Yorks [A1; SE4048], *Alpine*: Quick, well mannered service and an especially good fish pie *(Jill Hadfield)*

Whixley, N Yorks [SE4458], *Anchor*: Entertaining décor in stripped-brick separate rooms, good open fire, well kept John Smiths and Theakstons, good value food in bar and dining area; close to A1 *(Rob and Gill Weeks)*

☆ **Wigglesworth**, N Yorks [SD8157], *Plough*: Well run country inn with civilised atmosphere, bright and comfortable bar, and unusual choice of reliably good food in largish dining-room (former barn); friendly, efficient service, well kept Hartleys XB, good value white wine; popular with parents visiting nearby Giggleswick School; bedrooms *(Prof S Barnett and others)*

☆ **Winksley**, N Yorks [SE2571], *Countryman*: Pleasant pub off beaten track with friendly welcome, warm fire and imaginative bar food in separate dining-room; children welcome *(Mr and Mrs E F P Metters, Audrey and Alan Chatting)*

Worsall, N Yorks [NZ3909], *Ship*: Extended pub with good choice of well presented food inc excellent puddings *(RAMS)*

Yeadon, W Yorks [Nunroyd House; SE2141], *Inn on the Park*: Newly decorated pub in the centre of a park with value-for-money good food *(Tim Baxter)*

☆ **York** [26 High Petergate], *York Arms*: Good town-centre pub, partly no-smoking, only yards away from minster, with good atmosphere, well kept Sam Smiths and good value lunchtime and early evening bar food (soup, well filled crusty sandwiches, Yorkshire mince round, fish pie and seafood platter all recommended); friendly grey cat, cheerfully efficient service, cosy atmosphere in both small basic bar on left and more spacious back lounge areas *(H K Dyson, Tony Tucker, G G Calderwood, Nick Dowson, Alison Hayward, Jon Wainwright, S Barnett, Dr Stephen Hiew)*

☆ **York** [Merchantgate; between Fossgate and Piccadilly], *Red Lion*: Low-beamed rambling rooms with some stripped Tudor brickwork, relaxed old-fashioned furnishings, well kept John Smiths real ale, bar snacks and summer meals, tables outside, good juke box or piped music *(Jon Wainwright, Nick Dowson, Alison Hayward, LYM)*

☆ **York** [Walmgate], *Spread Eagle*: Fine range of well kept real ales, with admirable display of strength and price both inside and outside; good bar food inc huge sandwiches and luscious Yorkshire puddings, friendly staff, good atmosphere, pleasantly spartan décor *(David and Ruth Hollands, Jon Wainwright, Graeme Smalley)*

York [Goodramgate], *Anglers Arms*: Small friendly pub, nicer in than out, with log fire, plenty of atmosphere, unusual shape and décor; one of its ghosts is said to turn off the beer pumps *(Paul Corbett, Roy and Helen Sumner)*; [Blossom St] *Bay Horse*: Lots of nooks and alcoves in rambling rooms of Victorian local; can be smoky *(LYM)*; [23 Market St] *Hansom Cab*: Pleasant, comfortable pub with leather seats, panelling, old-fashioned carved tables, well kept Sam Smiths on handpump, well reproduced music – turned up at 7.30 *(T T Kelly)*; [High Petergate] *Hole in the Wall*: Very friendly recently refurbished and extended pub, cheerful and inviting, with well kept real ale and attractively priced bar food inc superb beef sandwiches – almost too generous; noticeable piped music *(Theo Schofield, Stan Edwards)*; [Layerthorpe; just outside walls, on road to Heworth, NE of centre] *John Bull*: Carefully neglected décor but apparently genuine 1930s memorabilia; friendly publican and wide range of interesting changing well kept real ales; not a family pub and can get very crowded *(RCL)*; *Red House*: Small hotel, worth knowing for courteous and helpful service, decent food and wines; bedrooms *(Jill Hadfield, Ann Roberts)*; [Micklegate] *Walkers*: Unusual layout with long bar at back, front more of an eating area for good bar food generously served; very friendly, with well kept Theakstons and some unusual features inc striking chandelier, peculiar artefacts, mynahs *(Stan Edwards, Jon Wainwright, Scott W Stucky)*

London

London

London

Given the five or six thousand pubs in the area, you might have thought that there would be many more really good ones here. Yet all too many London pubs take things too easy. In the centre, so many people are from out of town or even abroad – once-only customers, not people to lure back again and again – that lots of pubs don't seem even to try to stand out as places worth remembering as a repeat visit. And throughout, from city centre to suburbs, the distances involved are so short that dropping in to a local entails much less effort than elsewhere. London pubs can get by, just relying on their regulars' force of habit – whereas elsewhere pubs are increasingly doing much more to get people from further afield to make the greater effort involved in coming back again and again. There are precious few pubs in London whose customers regularly travel more than the length of a few streets to; in the country, a pub couldn't survive unless it was more attractive than that. This London pernicious-pub syndrome is particularly marked in the question of food. London of course stands out as magnificent for restaurants, which account for a massive chunk of restaurant guides. In the rest of the country, pubs have recently come forward strongly to challenge restaurants as places for eating out. This has scarcely happened in London. When people eat in pubs here, it's often a matter of necessity: offices empty thousands of people into the lunchtime streets, and with so little competition these hungry hordes crowd into indifferent locals to stand in line for their equally indifferent sausages, chicken curry, chilli con carne and lasagne. That's why, in contrast to elsewhere, so many London pubs do food only at lunchtime, when they can rely on this trade with their captive market. In the evening their perfunctory food bars – with no hope of attracting customers who've got more freedom of choice then – simply shut down. It's the wine bar, not the pub, which has

The Spaniards, Spaniards Road, NW3

developed the competitive edge to challenge the London restaurant. So, in the London section, we've made special efforts to find the few dozen pubs that really are worth hunting down. A handful do stand out for particularly good food, such as the Front Page (Central) and its brother pub the Sporting Page (West), the Orange Tree and the Ship (South), and the Dove, down on the Thames (West). Most others have food that's at least decent – including some that are now serving food all day, such as the charmingly traditional Lamb (Central), the nicely placed Museum (Central), that unaffected oasis the Compton Arms (North), the imposing Crown & Greyhound (South – a new entry), the Greyhound, with its own good built-in brewery (South – another new entry), and the Orange Tree, already mentioned; the Dove serves through the afternoon, but stops at 8. Pubs particularly memorable in other respects include in the Central area the flamboyant Black Friar, the big, bustling and very atmospheric Cittie of York (a new licensee here), the solid old George, the very lively back-to-basics Glassblower (a new manager here too), the low-ceilinged old Lamb & Flag (good cheeses), the densely decorated Old Coffee House (a new entry), and the countrified and delightfully spontaneous Olde Mitre; up North, the high-Victorian Crockers, the old-fashioned Flask (good new licensees), the accurately named Waterside (new manager here too, with an expanded food choice) and the relaxed White Lion of Mortimer with its splendidly cheap beer, in contrast to the sky-high prices elsewhere in London; and in South London (an area where there is indeed an increasingly wide choice of decent pubs) the refreshingly different Alma, the Angel with its lovely Thames views, the imposing new Horniman (also by the river) and that remarkable old coaching-inn, the George. In the Lucky Dip section at the end of the chapter, pubs looking particularly promising at the moment include, in the Central area, the Red Lion (Duke of York Street, SW1), Star (W1) and Salisbury (WC2); in North London, the George iv and Island Queen (N1); in South London, the Woodman (SW11), George & Dragon (Downe), Bishop out of Residence and Boaters (Kingston), Royal Oak (New Malden) and White Cross and Rose of York (Richmond); in West London, the Scarsdale Arms and Uxbridge Arms (W8), Green Man (Hatton) and Hare & Hounds (Osterley); and in East London, the Falcon & Firkin (fine children's room, E9) and House They Left Behind (E14).

CENTRAL LONDON

Covering W1, W2, WC1, WC2, SW1, SW3, EC1, EC2, EC3 and EC4 postal districts

Parking throughout this area is metered during the day, and generally in short supply then; we mention difficulty only if evening parking is a problem too

Antelope (Belgravia)   Map 13

Eaton Terrace, SW1

Not far from Sloane Square, this pleasantly old-fashioned pub has plenty of standing room round the central bar servery, with settles – old and modern – in the front part; the side room houses the fruit machine. Food is served from a counter in the smartly tiled back area and includes generous helpings of ploughman's, pâté or creamy taramosalata with granary bread, quiche, and hot dishes such as poached salmon in white wine and dill, half a roast duck or venison casserole (£4.50), and there is an upstairs wine bar. Well kept Adnams, Benskins, Ind Coope Burton and Wadworths 6X on handpump. It gets lively in the evening. There are a couple of long seats outside in the quiet street. *(Recommended by Dr and Mrs A K Clarke, Lee Goulding)*

Benskins   Licensee Geoff Elliott   Real ale   Meals and snacks (not Sat; by arrangement evening)   Restaurant tel 01 (071)-730 7781   Children in eating area   Open 11–11 all year

Black Friar (City) Map 13

174 Queen Victoria Street, EC4

The inner back room here has some of the best fine Edwardian bronze and marble art-nouveau décor to be found anywhere. It includes big bas-relief friezes of jolly monks set into richly coloured Florentine marble walls, an opulent marble-pillared inglenook fireplace, a low vaulted mosaic ceiling, gleaming mirrors, seats built into rich golden marble recesses, and tongue-in-cheek verbal embellishments such as Silence is Golden and Finery is Foolish. In the front room, see if you can spot the opium smoking-hints modelled into the fireplace. Good home-made food includes filled French bread (from £1.30), ploughman's (from £2.20), filled baked potatoes, a varied cold buffet (from £3), and three daily hot specials such as beef in red wine, coq au vin or cranberry lamb stew (around £3.20). Well kept Adnams, Arkells, Bass, Boddingtons Bitter, Tetleys and a guest beer on handpump. There's a wide forecourt in front, by the approach to Blackfriars Bridge. *(Recommended by Michael Bechley, Peter Griffiths, Chris Fluck, Nick Dowson, David Fowles)*

Nicholsons (Allied)   Real ale   Lunchtime meals (not Sat or Sun) and snacks (not Fri evening, not Sat or Sun)   Children in eating area of bar   Open 11.30–9 weekdays; closed weekends and bank hols

Cittie of Yorke (Holborn) Map 13

22 High Holborn, WC1; find it by looking out for its big black and gold clock

There's been a pub here since 1430, though it was reconstructed in Victorian times using seventeenth-century materials and parts, and the main back room has much of the fabric of the 1695 coffee house which stood here behind a garden. The bar counter is the longest in Britain with vast thousand-gallon wine vats (empty since prudently drained at the start of the Second World War) above the gantry, and a cat-walk running along the top of them. If you get there early enough (it can get packed, particularly with lawyers and judges), you can bag one of the intimate old-fashioned and ornately carved cubicles; there's an unusual big stove – uniquely triangular, with grates on all three sides, and big bulbous lights hanging from the extraordinarily high raftered roof. A smaller, comfortable wood-panelled room has lots of little prints of York and attractive brass lights. There's a lunchtime food counter in the main hall with more in the downstairs cellar bar: ploughman's, generously filled beef rolls, a good selection of cold dishes (from £2.50), with hot meals such as chilli con carne, curry, lasagne and daily specials (around £3.20). Well kept Sam Smiths OB and Museum on handpump – in a quiet moment you may be able to arrange with the manager to watch barrels being racked or tapped in the cellar; friendly service; darts, fruit machine and piped music. The ceiling of the entrance hall has medieval-style painted panels and plaster York roses. *(Recommended by Brian Jones, John Evans, R Inns, Ian Phillips, Nigel Paine)*

Sam Smiths   Licensee Stuart Browning   Real ale   Meals and snacks (not Sat evening or Sun)   Well behaved children welcome if sitting   Open 11–11 weekdays; 11.30–3, 5.30–11 Sat; closed Sun

Cross Keys (Chelsea) Map 12

Lawrence Street, SW3

Several interconnecting little rooms radiate off the walk-around island serving-counter in this friendly and popular Victorian pub. The décor is old-fashioned, there are military prints, a set of Cries of London prints and photographs of old London on the red or cream walls, high ceilings, and an open fire in winter. Good value food includes sandwiches, seven salads and home-made hot dishes like steak and kidney pie, salt beef, sweet-and-sour pork or chicken Kiev (£3). Well kept Courage Best and Directors on handpump, good mulled wine, a fine range of Irish whiskies, and quick and efficient service; shove-ha'penny, dominoes, cribbage and fruit machine. There are tables in a pretty little sunny back courtyard planted with creepers and tubs of brightly coloured flowers. *(Recommended by Patrick Stapley, Richard Gibbs; more reports please)*

Courage   Licensee Arthur Goodall   Real ale   Meals and snacks (not Sun)   Children in eating area   Open 11–3, 6–11 all year

Front Page ✪ (Chelsea) Map 12

Old Church Street, SW3

Light and airy, this popular pub – in an elegant part of Chelsea – has pews and benches around the panelled walls, heavy wooden tables, a wood-strip floor, big navy ceiling fans, huge windows with heavy navy curtains, and an open fire in one cosy area; lighting is virtually confined to brass picture-lights above small Edwardian monochrome pictures. Big blackboards at either end of the pub list the good value and nicely presented food: good soup of the day (£2), chicken liver pâté (£3), chicken satay with peanut sauce (£3.50), steak sandwich or avocado, Mozzarella and tomato salad (£3.95), vegetable stir-fry or sausage and mash (£4), smoked salmon with scrambled eggs or lamb cutlets (£4.50) and melon and prawn salad (£4.75), and puddings like baked bananas (£2.30). Well kept Ruddles Best and County and Websters Yorkshire on handpump; decent wines; quick, pleasant service. Fruit machine. Outside, there are big copper gas lamps hanging above pretty hanging baskets. *(Recommended by P Gillbe, S Matthews, Simon Turner; more reports please)*

Watneys   Licensees Christopher Phillips and Rupert Fowler   Real ale   Meals   Children in eating area of bar   Open 11–3, 5.30–11 (all day Sat); closed 25 and 26 Dec

George (West End) Map 13

55 Great Portland Street, W1

Popular with BBC regulars, this solid place has a good choice of well kept real ales on handpump that might include Adnams Bitter, Greene King IPA and Abbot, Charles Wells Bombardier and Wilsons. There are comfortable red plush high chairs at the bar, captain's chairs around traditional cast-iron-framed tables, heavy mahogany panelling, deeply engraved mirrors, equestrian prints, and etched windows. Bar food includes sandwiches (£1), ploughman's (from £1.75), hot salt beef (£2.20) and home-made steak pie (£3.50). *(Recommended by Peter Griffiths, Steve Waters, Dr John Innes)*

Free house   Real ale   Meals and snacks   Open 11–11 all year

Glassblower (Piccadilly Circus) Map 13

42 Glasshouse Street, W1

Just before this edition was published the Glassblower was due for a fairly thorough-going redecoration, but we've been assured that the character of the place won't be changed. The main bar, quite popular with tourists, has lots of untreated rough wooden beams with metal wheel-hoops hanging on them, plain wooden settles and stools, and sawdust on gnarled floorboards. An enormous copper and glass gas light hangs from the centre of the ceiling, flickering gently, and there are more gas light-style brackets around the walls, as well as lots of beer towels, framed sets of beer-mats and bottle-tops. A wide range of real ales on handpump includes Brakspears SB, Greene King Abbot and IPA, Marstons Pedigree, Ringwood Old Thumper, Ruddles County, Websters Yorkshire, Wiltshire Stonehenge and a couple of guest beers. Food includes large sandwiches (from around £2) and three or so daily hot dishes like beef and oyster or shepherd's pie or beef goulash (£3.75); fruit and trivia machines, space game and juke box. The upstairs lounge (closed on Sundays) has more standard decor, with carpets and comfortable chairs. There are hanging flower baskets outside. *(Recommended by Dr and Mrs A K Clarke, Peter Griffiths, I W and P J Muir, M B Porter, Steve Waters, GCS, Ian Phillips, Tom Hartman; more reports please)*

Whitbreads   Manager Rolan McLister   Real ale   Meals and snacks   Children in upstairs lounge   Open 11–11 all year

Grenadier (Belgravia)   Map 13

Wilton Row, SW1; the turning off Wilton Crescent looks prohibitive, but the barrier and watchman are there to keep out cars; walk straight past – the pub is just around the corner

Proud of its connection with Wellington, whose officers used to use it as their mess, this tucked-away little pub has a cramped front bar with a few stools and wooden benches, a shelf and a rare pewter-topped bar counter. It's popular with a wide variety of customers, and serves well kept Ruddles Best and County, and Websters Yorkshire on handpump – or if you'd prefer it, the licensee or Tom the very long-standing head barman will shake you a most special Bloody Mary. A corner snack counter serves very reasonably priced lunchtime food such as ploughman's (£2.20), and hot dishes like shepherd's pie or lasagne (£2.95) and steak sandwiches (£3.95); in the evenings bar food is limited to giant sausages (60p). *(Recommended by Dr and Mrs A K Clarke, TBB, Graham Oddey, Doug Kennedy, John Tyzack)*

Watneys   Licensee Raymond Dodgson   Real ale   Lunchtime meals and snacks   Intimate candle-lit restaurant tel 01 (071)-235 3074   Open 11–3, 5.30–11 all year

Kings Arms (Mayfair)   Map 13

2 Shepherd Market, W1

In a busy little patch of narrow streets just north of Piccadilly, this lively busy pub has a stripped-down décor of bare timbers and the textured concrete that is the South Bank's hallmark, with a dimly lit galleried upper area. A good choice of well kept real ales includes Charles Wells Bombardier, Everards Tiger, Wadworths 6X and Websters Yorkshire. Reasonably priced food includes large sandwiches (£2.60) and hot dishes such as beef and ale pie or sausages in cider (£4.15); CD juke box, fruit machines. *(Recommended by Quentin Williamson, Ian Phillips; more reports please)*

Clifton Inns (Watneys) – but run as free house   Real ale   Meals and snacks   Open 12–11 (12–3, 7–11 Sat) all year

Lamb   ★ (Bloomsbury)   Map 13

94 Lamb's Conduit Street, WC1

All the way around the U-shaped bar counter in this popular, friendly pub, there are cut-glass swivelling 'snob-screens', as well as traditional cast-iron-framed tables with neat brass rails around the rim, and on ochre panelling lots of sepia photographs of 1890s actresses; a small room at the back on the right is no-smoking. Good bar food includes sandwiches (not Sunday), ploughman's and salads, as well as hot dishes such as home-made pies or steak and kidney pudding, and daily specials like spinach and prawn crêpe or pork in cider casserole; three-course Sunday lunch in the room upstairs (£5.75); oyster evenings in season. Consistently well kept Youngs Bitter and Special on handpump; prompt service, and a good mix of customers. There are slatted wooden seats in a little courtyard beyond the quiet room which is down a couple of steps at the back; dominoes,

---

Real ale to us means beer which has matured naturally in its cask and is not pressurised or filtered. We name all real ales stocked. We usually name ales preserved under a light blanket of carbon dioxide too, though purists, pointing out that this stops the natural yeasts developing, would disagree (most people, including us, can't tell the difference!).

cribbage, backgammon. *(Recommended by Brian Jones, D A Parsons, Steve Waters, Peter Griffiths, R H Inns, Mr and Mrs D Norton, Brian Marsden, D J Cargill)*

Youngs　Licensee Richard Whyte　Real ale　Meals and snacks (11.45–11)　Open 11–11 all year

Lamb & Flag (Covent Garden) Map 13

33 Rose Street, WC2; off Garrick Street

This popular, friendly place is still much as it was when Dickens described the Middle Temple lawyers who frequented it when he was working in nearby Catherine Street – low ceiling, high-backed black settles and an open fire. The upstairs Dryden Room tends to be less crowded. There's a choice of ten well-kept cheeses and eight pâtés, served with hot bread or French bread (£2.20), as well as pasties (£1), quiche (£1.10), steak and kidney pie (£1.90), succulent roast beef baps (Monday to Friday), shepherd's pie, chilli con carne or curry (all £2.50). Very well kept Courage Best and Directors and John Smiths on handpump. Darts in the small front public bar. Dryden was nearly beaten to death by hired thugs in the courtyard outside. *(Recommended by Peter Griffiths, Steve Waters, Graham Oddey, Ian and James Phillips, Michael Bechley)*

Courage　Real ale　Meals (lunchtime only, not Sun) and snacks (not Fri evening)　Open 11–11 all year; closed evenings 24 and 31 Dec, all day 25 and 26 Dec and 1 Jan

Museum Tavern (Bloomsbury) Map 13

Museum Street, WC1

On a corner opposite the British Museum, this old-fashioned Bloomsbury pub has high-backed benches around traditional cast-iron pub tables, old advertising mirrors between the wooden pillars behind the bar, an 'Egyptian' inn-sign, and gas lamps above the tables outside. Bar food, served all day, includes ploughman's, cold pies and pasties, with hot dishes such as steak and kidney or shepherd's pie, beef in ale or pork in cider (all £4). Well kept Brakspears, Everards Tiger, Greene King IPA and Abbot, Ruddles County, and Websters Yorkshire on handpump, and a wide range of wines by the glass; piped music. *(Recommended by Prof A Barnett, Peter Griffiths, RHI, Brian Marsden)*

Free house　Licensee Michael Clarke　Real ale　Meals and snacks (11–9.30)　Open 11–11

Nag's Head (Belgravia) Map 13

53 Kinnerton Street, SW1

Near Belgrave Square and Knightsbridge, this tiny pub has a small old-fashioned front area with a wood-effect gas fire in an old cooking-range, panelling, and a low ceiling; a narrow passage leads down steps to an even smaller back bar with comfortable seats; piped music and a 1930s What-the-Butler-Saw machine. Benskins, Ind Coope Burton and Youngs pulled on attractive nineteenth-century china, pewter and brass handpumps. Food includes sandwiches, filled baked potatoes (from £1.75), salads, quiche (£2.75), chilli con carne (£2.75), good beef curry (£3.25) and steak and mushroom pie (£3.45). It can get crowded in the evening. *(Recommended by JA, M D and E M Fowler, Dr and Mrs A K Clarke, Mr and Mrs V Webster Johnson Jr)*

Benskins (Ind Coope)　Licensee Kevin Moran　Real ale　Meals and snacks　Children in eating area　Open 11–3, 5.30–11 all year

Old Coffee House (Soho) Map 13

49 Beak Street, W1

This was one of the first pubs in London to pile itself high with bric-à-brac – and has done it most enjoyably. Downstairs is a busy jumble of stuffed pike, stuffed foxes, great brass bowls and buckets, ancient musical instruments (brass and string sections both well represented), a good collection of Great War recruiting posters, golden discs, death-of-Nelson prints, theatre and cinema handbills, old banknotes, even a nude in one corner, and doubtless lots more that we failed to spot. Upstairs, the food room has as many prints and pictures as a Victorian study. Yet even though the place is small you can often find somewhere to sit. Food includes filled rolls, sandwiches and hot dishes – even ham and egg, alongside steak and kidney pie and so forth. Well kept Websters Yorkshire and Ruddles County on handpump. *(Recommended by Ian Phillips, Dr and Mrs A K Clarke, Peter Griffiths)*

Watneys Real ale Meals and snacks (lunchtime) Open 11–11

Olde Cheshire Cheese (City) Map 13
Wine Office Court; off 145 Fleet Street, EC4

The great cellar vaults date from before the Great Fire, though the present building is seventeenth-century, and over the years Congreve, Pope, Voltaire, Thackeray, Dickens, Conan Doyle, Yeats and perhaps Dr Johnson have visited this bustling, unpretentious place. The small rooms, up and down stairs, have bare wooden benches built in to the walls, sawdust on bare boards, and on the ground floor high beams, crackly old black varnish, Victorian paintings on the dark brown walls, and a big open fire in winter. Snacks include filled rolls (55p); the steak, kidney, mushroom and game pie (£6) in the busy little upstairs restaurant is something of an institution; Sam Smiths Old Brewery and Museum on handpump. *(Recommended by Steve Waters; more reports please)*

Sam Smiths Snacks (lunchtime, not Sat or Sun) Restaurant tel 01 (071)-353 6170/4388
Children welcome Open 11.30–11 all year; closed Sun evening

Ye Olde Mitre (City) Map 13
Ely Place, EC1; there's also an entrance beside 8 Hatton Garden

This carefully rebuilt pub with its quaint façade carries the same name of an earlier inn built here in 1547 to serve the people working in the palace of the Bishop of Ely, who actually administered the law here. The dark panelled small rooms have antique settles and big vases of flowers. Good bar snacks include filled rolls (60p), Scotch eggs and pork pies (60p), a good selection of sandwiches such as ham, salmon and cucumber or egg mayonnaise (from 80p, toasties 5p extra); well kept Friary Meux, Ind Coope Burton and Tetleys on handpump, reasonably priced for the area. There are some seats with pot plants and jasmine in the narrow yard between the pub and St Ethelreda's church. *(Recommended by M B Porter, John Roué, Quentin Williamson)*

Taylor-Walker (Allied) Licensee Don O'Sullivan Real ale Snacks (not Sat, Sun or bank hols) Open 11–11 all year; closed Sat, Sun, bank hols

Orange Brewery (Pimlico) Map 13
37 Pimlico Road, SW1

As well as a couple of guest beers on handpump in this lively, friendly pub, they brew over 300 gallons a week in the cellars – SW1, a stronger SW2, Pimlico Light and Pimlico Porter. The high ochre walls of the bar are decorated with sepia photographs and some decorative Victorian plates, there's a stuffed fox above a nicely tiled fireplace, and solid armed seats, a chaise-longue, and one or two Chesterfields on the bare floorboards. The cheery Pie and Ale Shop (open all day in summer) has lots more sepia photographs on the dark stained plank-panelling, plain wooden tables and chairs on pretty black and white tiles, and a shelf full of old flagons and jugs above the counter where they serve a range of home-made food: sandwiches, ploughman's, quiche (£3.70), and daily hot dishes, all in pie form, such as chicken and leek (£3.80) and steak and Stilton or lamb and apricot (£3.90). Fruit machine, trivia machine, juke box. There are seats outside facing a little concreted-over green beyond the quite busy street. *(Recommended by RCL, Mrs M E Collins, Peter Griffiths, S R Holman)*

Own brew (though tied to Clifton Inns, part of Watneys)   Licensee Bernadette Heneghan
Real ale   Meals and snacks   Children in eating area   Open 12–11 all year

Princess Louise (Holborn) Map 13

208 High Holborn, WC1

The elaborate décor in this old-fashioned gin-palace includes etched and gilt mirrors, brightly coloured and fruity-shaped tiles, and slender Portland stone columns soaring towards the lofty and deeply moulded crimson and gold plaster ceiling; the green plush seats and banquettes are comfortable. The magnificent gents is the subject of a separate preservation order. People cluster around the enormous island bar servery, eager for the fine range of regularly changing real ales, well kept on handpump. These include Boddingtons, Darleys Best, Greene King IPA and Abbot, Vaux Samson, Wards Best, and a beer brewed for the pub; quick, Antipodean staff in white shirts and red bow ties; fruit machine, piped music. Food, from a separate serving-counter still supplied by the original dumb-waiter, includes rolls, sandwiches and hot snacks (from 95p). Upstairs they have a wider range of food such as salads and lunchtime hot dishes, with lasagne, chilli con carne, cannelloni or Lancashire hot-pot (all £2.95); several wines by the glass – including champagne. *(Recommended by Steve Waters, Brian Jones, Peter Griffiths, M B Porter, G Cooper, Stephen R Holman, Ian Phillips, Tim Powell, Alan Mosley, Michael and Alison Sandy)*

Free house   Licensee Ian Phillips   Real ale   Lunchtime meals (not Sun) and all-day snacks
Jazz Sat evening   Open 11–11 (12–3, 6–11 Sat) all year

Red Lion (Mayfair) Map 13

Waverton Street, W1

The atmosphere in the little L-shaped bar of this stylish Mayfair pub is almost like that of a civilised country pub, with small winged settles on the partly carpeted scrubbed floorboards, old photographs of Sam Smiths' Tadcaster Brewery in the 1920s and London prints below the high shelf of china on its dark-panelled walls. Good food includes ploughman's, generous sandwiches, salads, and specials such as chicken bourguignonne, crab or salmon. Unusually for the area, food is served morning and evening seven days a week; Ruddles County and Websters Yorkshire on handpump. It can get crowded at lunchtime. There are cut-away barrel seats among the bay trees under its front awning. *(Recommended by Neil Barker, George Little; more reports please)*

Watneys   Real ale   Meals and snacks   Children in restaurant
Restaurant tel 01 (071)-499 1307   Open 11–3, 5.30–11 all year

Samuel Pepys (City) Map 13

High Timber Street, EC4; off 48 Upper Thames Street

Both bars in this converted tea warehouse (and the Toby grill restaurant on the floor between them) have their own river-view balcony. The top bar has lots of Pepysiana, prints of the river frontage over the past few centuries, chairs and high bar stools, and a vaulted brick ceiling. A few tables and chairs on the sheltered duckboarded upper balcony look beyond the river to the great mass of Bankside power station, with one or two attractive old houses surprisingly punctuating the vista of big blocks of flats and the Wilcox hose works. Home-made food served in the light-wood panelled and flagstoned lower bar (which is six feet below water level at high tide) includes steak and mushroom pie, moussaka, popular lamb curry or sweet and sour pork (all £3.50), beef and venison pie (£3.95) and puddings (from £1.30); bar billiards, fruit machine, trivia machine, well produced piped music.

Charrington IPA and Bass on handpump. *(Recommended by Chris Fluck; more reports please)*

Charringtons (Bass)   Manager Roger Coulthard   Real ale   Meals and snacks (not Sun) Restaurant tel 01 (071)-248 3048   Open 11.30–11 all year; closed Sun

NORTH LONDON
Parking is not a special problem in this area, unless we say so

Clifton 🐾 (St John's Wood) Map 12
96 Clifton Hill, NW8

The good range of bar food in this spacious pub includes sandwiches (from £1.25; smoked salmon with French bread £1.95), pâté or haddock and prawn chowder (£1.95), vegetable pie (£4.50), beef and Guinness stew with dumplings (£4.95), salads (from £5.25), shark steak (£5.50), char-grilled lamb chops (£5.95) or steaks (from £7.25); puddings (from £1.75); crisps, nuts and cheese on the bar on Sunday. The high-ceilinged, bare-boarded bar area is designed on more than one level, and the wooden balustrades create the impression of a series of small rooms; there are Edwardian and Victorian engravings and 1920s comic prints on the elegant wallpaper, panelling and other woodwork, unusual art-nouveau wall lamps, cast-iron tables, and fine brass and glass ceiling lights; relaxed, countrified atmosphere. Well kept Taylor-Walker and Ind Coope Burton and Tetleys on handpump; friendly staff; shove ha'penny, cribbage. Edward VII and Lily Langtry used to come here and there are quite a few prints of both of them (one signed by the king and his son – who became George V). A very leafy front terrace has attractive marble-topped tables, and the glass conservatory in the back courtyard is a lively, local place. *(Recommended by GB, L E May, G Berneck, C Herxheimer)*

Taylor-Walker (Allied)   Licensee John Murtagh   Real ale   Meals and snacks (11–3, 6.30–10.30)   Restaurant tel 01 (071)-624 5233   Children in eating area and restaurant Open 11–3, 5–11 (all day Fri and Sat) all year

Compton Arms (Canonbury) Map 12
4 Compton Avenue, off Canonbury Lane, N1

There's a good, friendly atmosphere in this diminutive pub, hidden away up a mews; the gently refurbished, low-ceilinged and cheerful rooms are simply furnished with wooden settles and assorted stools and chairs, with little local pictures on the wall. Bar food includes sandwiches and ploughman's, with hot dishes such as pies, chilli con carne, scampi, jumbo sausage and vegetarian dishes (around £2.50 to £2.95); Greene King IPA and Abbot and Rayments BBA on handpump; dominoes, cribbage. A quiet little crazy paved back terrace has benches around cask tables under a big sycamore tree. *(Recommended by M B Porter, Peter Griffiths; more reports on the new regime please)*

Greene King   Licensee Robert Burton   Real ale   Meals and snacks (11–10; not Sun)   Open 11–11 all year

Crockers ★ (Maida Vale) Map 13
24 Aberdeen Place, NW8

There's a fine range of real ales in this imposing Victorian pub, including Arkells, Boddingtons, Brakspears, Darleys Thorne, Greene King Abbot, Samson, Wards and Youngs; also Weizenbier from Wards – the only beer in the country brewed from wheat rather than barley. But the major attraction is architectural: the ceiling in the main room is possibly the most elaborately moulded of any London pub; marble pillars support arches inlaid with bronze reliefs, and there's a sweeping marble bar counter, with a vast pillared marble fireplace with a log-effect gas fire. A row of great arched and glazed mahogany doors opens into a similarly ornate but more spacious room. Darts, bar billiards, cribbage, dominoes, fruit machine, space game, trivia and juke box are in a less opulent room; also piped music. Bar food at lunchtime ranges from sandwiches (£1.20), home-made Scotch eggs (£1.30), through ploughman's (£1.40), to three hot dishes such as steak and kidney pie, lasagne or corned beef hash (£2.95); in the evening they do vegetarian dishes and grills such as burgers (£2.65) and rump steaks (£5.20). The pub is not far from Regent's Canal towpath. *(Recommended by Mrs M E Collins, Neil Barker, M C Howells, Gary Scott, George Little; more reports please)*

Vaux   Licensees Rosalind and Peter Cox   Real ale   Meals (11.30–2.30, 6–9.45) and snacks (all day)   Children in eating area   Occasional piano player   Daytime parking meters   Open 11–11 all year

Flask (Highgate) Map 12

77 Highgate West Hill, N6

Though this popular old inn has been extended, the partly panelled rooms in the lower, original part are little changed since its 1767 rebuilding; the bar counter is sash-windowed – so that you have to stoop below the sashes to see the barman. There are local historic pictures and prints on the walls, little wooden armchairs and a high-backed carved settle. The new licensees have started serving a wider range of bar food in the more spacious tile-floored extension, including filled baps (£1), soup (£1.50), cauliflower cheese (£2), quiche or steak and kidney pie (£3) and basket meals (£3.50); in the evenings they do only pizzas (£3.70 or £5.20). Ind Coope Burton, Taylor-Walker Bitter and Tetleys on handpump; fruit machine. Outside, there are sturdy wooden tables – one or two protected by a wood-pillared porch decorated with hanging baskets of geraniums and petunias. It was here that one of Hogarth's rowdy friends clobbered a regular with his tankard, and Hogarth himself nearly got clobbered back for sketching the result. *(Recommended by J P Day, M B Porter; more reports on the new regime please)*

Taylor-Walker (Allied)   Licensees Mr and Mrs Mather   Real ale   Meals (lunchtime; limited in evening) and snacks   Weekday lunchtime restaurant tel 01 (081)-340 7260   Well behaved children welcome   Open 11–3, 5.30–11 (all day Sat)

Holly Bush (Hampstead) Map 12

Holly Mount, NW3

There's an unchanging atmosphere in the front bar here, with its real Edwardian gas lamps, its dark and sagging ceiling, brown and cream panelled walls (which are decorated with old advertisements and a few hanging plates), and cosy bays formed by partly glazed partitions. The more intimate back room (named after the painter George Romney) has an embossed red ceiling, panelled and etched glass alcoves, and ochre-painted brick walls covered with small prints and plates. Bar food includes a good range of ploughman's (£2) and hot dishes such as chilli con carne, cauliflower cheese, duck and walnut or beef in ale pie and casseroles (around £2–£3.50); in winter, on the popular jazz evenings, they also serve hot-pots. Benskins and Ind Coope Burton, Tetleys and Youngs on handpump; fruit machine. *(More reports please)*

Taylor-Walker (Allied)   Licensee Peter Dures   Real ale   Meals and snacks (not Sun evening or Mon)   Children in eating area   Live music Weds, jazz Thurs evening   Nearby parking sometimes quite a squeeze   Open 11–3 (4 Sat), 5.30–11 all year

Olde White Bear (Hampstead) Map 12

Well Road, NW3

The dimly lit main room in this neo-Victorian pub has wooden stools, cushioned captain's chairs, a couple of big tasseled armed chairs, and a flowery sofa (surrounded by the excrescences of an ornate Edwardian sideboard), as well as lots of Victorian prints and cartoons on the walls, and a tiled gas-effect log fire with a heavy wooden over-mantel. A small central room – also dimly lit – has Lloyd Loom furniture, dried flower arrangements and signed photographs of actors and playwrights. In the brighter end room there are cushioned machine-tapestried ornate pews, marble-topped tables, a very worn butcher's table, dark brown paisley curtains and a food cabinet serving the standard selection of bar food, from sandwiches to main dishes including vegetarian specials; piped music, trivia machine. Adnams, Ind Coope Burton, Tetleys and Youngs on handpump, good range of malt whiskies. *(Recommended by Leo and Pam Cohen, M B Porter, George Little, David Fowles; more reports please)*

Nicholsons (Allied – but run as free house)   Licensee Miss Cheryl Warry   Real ale   Meals and snacks   Occasional quiz nights   Open 11–3, 5.30–11 (all day Sat in summer)

Spaniards Inn (Hampstead) Map 12   [*illustrated on page 813*]

Spaniards Lane, NW3

The atmosphere in this civilised old pub is lively and busy – in the evenings the upstairs bar is quieter. The main bar area (lit by candle-shaped lamps in pink shades in the evening) has genuinely antique winged settles, open fires, and snug little alcoves in the low-ceilinged oak-panelled rooms. Bass, Charrington IPA and Youngs Bitter on handpump; fruit machine. Home-cooked bar food includes ploughman's (from £2.15), quiche, vegetable curry (£3), vegetable moussaka (£3.15), chilli con carne (£3.55) and beef goulash (£3.80). The attractive sheltered garden has slatted wooden tables and chairs on a crazy-paved terrace which opens on to a flagstoned walk around a small lawn, with roses, a side arbour of wistaria and clematis, and an aviary. The pub is named after the Spanish ambassador to the Court of James I who is said to have lived here. *(Recommended by David Goldstone, Tim Powell, Ian Phillips; more reports please)*

Charringtons (Bass)   Meals and snacks   Children anywhere alcohol is not served   Open 11–11 all year

Waterside (King's Cross) Map 13

82 York Way, N1

Under the new management the good hot and cold food counter in this busy canalside pub has expanded, and includes ploughman's (from £2.75), lots of salads (from £3.75), and hot dishes like game pie (£3.95) and poached salmon or steak (£4.95), with vegetarian dishes. The bar is done out in traditional style, with latticed windows, stripped brickwork, genuinely old stripped timbers in white plaster, lots of dimly lit alcoves, spinning wheels, milkmaid's yokes, horse brasses and so on, with plenty of rustic tables and wooden benches; Adnams, Boddingtons and Brakspears on handpump, as well as wines on draught; fruit machine and trivia machine. The terrace (where there may be summer barbecues) overlooks the Battlebridge Basin, and the restaurant is out here in a converted barge. *(Recommended by E G Parish, Alison Hayward, Nick Dowson, Wayne Brindle, Neil Barker)*

Whitbreads   Manager Lawrence Heneage   Real ale   Meals and snacks (not Sun evening) Restaurant on barge (not Sun or Mon evening) tel 01 (071)-837 7118   Children in eating area and restaurant   Open 12–11 (12–3, 7–11 Sat) all year

White Lion of Mortimer (Finsbury Park) Map 12

Stroud Green Road, N4

Attractively converted from a garage showroom in 1986, this atmospheric and spacious place has a large etched front window, subdued gas lamp-style lighting throughout, and two full-size Victorian street lamps just inside the entrance. The carved island servery runs the length of the bar, which has cream tilework at the front, lion pictures on the partly panelled walls, and a medley of old tables. The cooking implements down the left-hand side contrast with the horse harness and farm tools on the right, which also has a public telephone with an old copper fireplace as its booth. Some alcoves have an old cast-iron fireplace and plush settees, and there's a relaxing conservatory area at the back, with hanging ivy plants, and a small fountain outside its door. A particular virtue is the emphasis on real ale; the range changes frequently, always with one beer offered at a price few other London pubs could match – Youngers Scotch at 83p, say; there's also typically Greene King Abbot, Marstons Pedigree and Wadworths 6X. Lunchtime bar food includes sandwiches and hot dishes such as spinach and mushroom pancakes or a courgette dish (£2.60), and stuffed lamb parcels, cod in parsley sauce or lamb cobbler (£2.90); cribbage, dominoes, chess, fruit machine and trivia machine. There are some cast-iron tables on the pavement outside. This is one of a chain of North London pubs set up a few years ago by Tim Martin as a reaction to the state of other establishments in the area – in his view, not enough real ale and too much loud piped music; other Wetherspoons pubs include the Old Suffolk Punch on the Grand Parade and the Mortimer Arms in Green Lane (both N4), and you'll find some mentioned in the North London Lucky Dip section at the end of the chapter. *(Recommended by Gary Scott, Gavin May)*

Free house　Managers Mr and Mrs Knipe　Real ale　Meals (lunchtime) and snacks (until 5)　Open 11–11 all year

SOUTH LONDON

Parking is bad on weekday lunchtimes at the inner-city pubs here (SE1), and at the Orange Tree in Richmond; it's usually OK everywhere in the evenings – you may again have a bit of a walk if a good band is on at the Bulls Head in Barnes, or at the Windmill on Clapham Common if it's a fine evening

Alma (Battersea)　Map 12

499 York Road

This stylish place is authentically done out as a French cafe-bar, with pintable and table footer, barmen in tight black waistcoats, a redundant wooden Frigidaire and, inevitably, bentwood chairs around cast-iron-framed tables. There's a lot of ochre and terracotta paintwork, gilded mosaics of the Battle of the Alma, an ornate mahogany chimneypiece and fireplace, bevelled mirrors in a pillared mahogany room divider, and in a side room a fine turn-of-the-century frieze of swirly nymphs. Service is careful and efficient, even when it's very full – which it often is. Besides Youngs Bitter and Special on handpump from the island bar counter, there are usually decent house wines, good coffee, tea or hot chocolate, newspapers out for customers, and bar food that includes sandwiches or French sticks (from 85p; generous toasted £1.85), onion soup (£1.85), kipper (£2.25), eggs and bacon (£2.65), a plate of cheeses (£3), moules marinière (£3.95), salad niçoise (£4.25) and steaks (£8.55). A thriving local atmosphere. The pub is under the same management as the Ship at Wandsworth (see below). *(Recommended by Richard Gibbs; more reports please)*

Youngs　Licensees Charles Gotto and Mrs P M Luckie　Real ale　Meals and snacks　Open 11–3, 5–11 (all day Sat) all year

Anchor (South Bank)　Map 13

Bankside, SE1; Southwark Bridge end

Carefully restored in the 1960s and dating back to about 1750 (when it was rebuilt to replace the earlier tavern), this was probably where Pepys went to watch the Great Fire burning London: 'one entire arch of fire above a mile long, the churches, houses, and all on fire at once, a horrid noise the flames made, and the cracking of houses at their ruine'. There's still a lot of atmosphere these days, and even when it's invaded by tourists it's usually possible to retreat to one of the smaller rooms. The rambling series of rooms have creaky boards and beams, black panelling and old-fashioned high-backed settles as well as sturdy leatherette chairs. Bar food includes ploughman's (£2.50), sandwiches cut to order (£2.95) and a hot dish of the day (£3.75). Well kept Courage Best and Directors on handpump, and a fair selection of wines by the glass and bottle; fruit machine, space game and trivia machine. A terrace overlooks the river. *(Recommended by Steve Waters, Nick Dowson, Alison Hayward, Graham Bush; more reports please)*

Free house   Licensee J W M Davidson   Real ale   Meals and snacks   Restaurant (all day Sun) tel 01 (071)-407 1577   Children in restaurant   Open 11.30–11 all year

Angel (Rotherhithe) Map 12

Bermondsey Wall East, SE16

This comfortably modernised, open-plan pub enjoys the distinction of an upstream view of Tower Bridge and the City – the classic perspective which it is now almost impossible to appreciate from anywhere else; certainly it makes it one of London's best riverside pubs. You can also look down the other way to the Pool of London. The bare-boarded balcony, on timber piles sunk into the river, is lit by lanterns at night. Bar food includes ploughman's (£2.25), game pie (£2.75) and steak, kidney and mushroom pie (£3.25); Courage Best and Directors on handpump; fruit machine and piped music. Pepys bought cherries for his wife at the jetty here. *(Recommended by Roger Huggins, Tom McLean, Ewan McCall; more reports please)*

THF – but tied to Courage   Licensee Peter Sutch   Real ale   Lunchtime meals and snacks Restaurant (until 9 Sun) tel 01 (071)-237 3608   Children in eating area   Open 11–11; 11–3, 5.30–11 in winter

Bulls Head (Barnes) Map 12

373 Lonsdale Road, SW13

The big draw to this riverside pub, just across from the Thames flood wall, is the live music – top-class modern jazz groups every evening, and weekend lunchtime big band sessions (practice on Saturday, concert on Sunday). Though admission to the well equipped music room is £2 to £3 the sound is perfectly clear – if not authentically loud – in the adjoining lounge bar. Alcoves open off the main area around the efficient island servery, which has Youngs Bitter and Special on handpump; darts, bar billiards, dominoes, cribbage, fruit machine and space game in the public bar. Bar lunches include soup with crusty bread, sandwiches, filled French bread, hot roast meat sandwiches, a pasta dish of the day, home-baked pies, and a carvery of home-roasted joints. *(Recommended by Doug Kennedy, C J Cuss, David Fowles; more up-to-date reports please)*

Youngs   Real ale   Meals and snacks   Restaurant tel 01 (081)-876 5241   Children in eating area of bar and in restaurant   Jazz nightly and Sun lunchtime   Nearby parking may be difficult   Open 11–11 all year

Crown & Greyhound (Dulwich) Map 12

73 Dulwich Village, SE21

An imposing landmark in the little village on the edge of Dulwich College, and therefore handy for walks through the park, this grand pub has lots of mahogany, etched glass and mirrors inside, with dark green velvet curtains swagged over the big windows looking out on the village road. The most ornate room is on the right, with its elaborate ochre ceiling plasterwork, fancy former gas lamps, Hogarth prints, good carved and panelled settles and so forth. It opens into the former billiards room, where kitchen tables on a stripped-board floor are set for the food, which includes doorstep sandwiches or toasties (£1.30), filled baked potatoes (£1.95), chicken curry (£3.95) and help-yourself salads (quiche £4.25, meats £4.50). A central snug leads on the other side to the saloon – brown ragged walls, upholstered and panelled settles, a coal-effect gas fire in the tiled period fireplace, and Victorian prints. A big two-level back terrace has a good many picnic-table sets under a chestnut tree, with summer weekend barbecues. Fairly quiet on weekday lunchtimes, it can be packed with young people in the evenings. Well kept Ind Coope Burton, Tetleys and Youngs on handpump, various fruit machines. *(Recommended by Alan Franck, Michele and Andrew Wells, EGP, Peter Griffiths)*

Tetley-Walkers (Allied) Licensees B P Maguire and N A Riding Real ale Meals and snacks (11–2.30, 5.30–9; 11–9 Sat) Restaurant tel 01(081)-693 2466 Children in restaurant Open 11–3.30, 5.30–11 all year; all day Sat

George ★ (Southwark) Map 13
Off 77 Borough High Street, SE1

This pub is one of those rare places which exudes genuine historicity and character. It was noted as one of London's 'fair Inns for the receipt of travellers' in 1598, and rebuilt on its original plan after the great Southwark fire in 1676. Jugglers, acrobats, conjurers, animal-trainers, musicians and even Shakespeare's strolling players used to perform here when Southwark was London's entertainment centre; this tradition is maintained in summer, when there may be morris men dancing or players from the nearby Globe Theatre performing in the courtyard. It is in fact the only coaching-inn in London to survive intact, with its tiers of open galleries looking down on the cobbled courtyard; these days it's carefully preserved by the National Trust. The row of ground-floor rooms and bars all have square-latticed windows, black beams, bare floorboards, some panelling, plain oak or elm tables, old-fashioned built-in settles, a 1797 Act of Parliament clock, dimpled glass lantern-lamps and so forth. It does of course attract quite a stream of tourists, and we'd recommend as the safest refuge from them the simple room nearest the street, where there's an ancient beer engine that looks like a cash register. Well kept Brakspears, Greene King Abbot, Marstons Pedigree and Wethereds on handpump; bar food includes sausage and beans, good Scotch eggs, quiche with three salads, and home-made steak and mushroom pie. A splendid central staircase goes up to a series of dining-rooms and to a gas-lit balcony. *(Recommended by Gary Scott, Steve Waters, Roger Bellingham, Chris Cooke, R G Ollier, G S B Dudley, Alison Hayward, Nick Dowson)*

Whitbreads Licensee John Hall Real ale Meals and snacks (not Sun evening) Restaurant tel 01 (071)-407 2056 Children in area by wine bar and restaurant Nearby daytime parking difficult Globe Players, morris dancers and Medieval Combat Society during summer Open 11–11 (11–3, 6–11 Sat) all year; closed 25 and 26 Dec

Greyhound (Streatham) Map 12
151 Greyhound Lane, SW16

The big side conservatory, with dark cushioned cane chairs, tall rubber plants and other plants on its tiles, rattan blinds and a curious row of side-sweeping cane ceiling fans, is quite an oasis for families, and the garden, with lots of picnic-table sets, comes in for hard wear. But the main attraction here is the product of the built-in brewery, a fine range of distinctively flavoured real ales: Special, Pedigree XXX Mild, Streatham Strong, occasional London Stout, a deadly Christmas Ale, and their hefty Streatham Dynamite – which on Bank Holidays may be replaced by the ambiguous GBH. The head brewer, Neil Allison (telephone 01 (081)-664 6694) may be able to arrange guided visits. The main bar has an elaborate high rounded-edge ceiling, with a decorative cornice above the pink striped wallpaper; there are pink button-back built-in wall banquettes, bentwood chairs, lots of smallish Victorian prints and quite a battery of fruit machines. A smaller middle bar, with souvenirs of the Streatham Redskins (the local ice-hockey team), has comfortable blue plush sofas, and a games-bar on the left has two pool-tables, CD juke box and space games. Quietly busy, with a good mix of mainly youngish people. Bar food includes generous salads from pasties or quiches (£2.85) to roast beef (£4.50), several hot dishes such as steak and ale pie, curry and lasagne (£3.20), and a good range of char-grills from veggieburgers (£3.20) to swordfish steak (£4.50) and ten-ounce rump steak (£5.50); decent wines, pleasant service. *(Recommended by Peter Griffiths, Hank Hotchkiss, Alan Skull, Nick Dowson)*

Own brew   Licensee G A Lane   Real ale   Meals and snacks throughout opening hours, until 10   Children in conservatory   Open 11–3, 5.30–11 all year; all day Fri, Sat, bank hols; closed evening 25 Dec

Horniman (Southwark) Map 13

Hays Galleria, Battlebridge Lane

Named after a tea merchant whose firm formerly operated from this wharf, this ambitiously designed waterside pub has above the bar the set of clocks made for Frederick Horniman's office, showing the time in various places around the world; the former activities here are commemorated by a tea-bar serving coffee, chocolate and other hot drinks, and Danish pastries and so forth; there's also a hundred-foot frieze showing the travels of the tea. But the range of stronger beverages is good too, with Adnams, Arkells, Boddingtons, Ind Coope Burton and Tetleys on handpump. The bar itself is spacious, elegant and neatly kept; the area by the sweeping bar counter is a few steps down from the door, with squared black, red and white flooring tiles and lots of polished wood. Steps lead up from here to various comfortable carpeted areas, with the tables well spread so as to allow for a feeling of spacious relaxation at quiet times but give room for people standing in groups when it's busy. From some parts there are good views of the Thames, HMS *Belfast* and Tower Bridge, as there are from the picnic-table sets outside. Bar food includes filled baps and hot dishes such as steak and kidney pie, and an upper carvery, within the same space, does full meals (around £15); in one place or another there's something to eat all day. Fruit machine, trivia machine, maybe piped music. The pub is at the end of a visually exciting development, several storeys high, with a soaring glass curved roof, and supported by elegant thin cast-iron columns; various shops and boutiques open off. *(Recommended by Richard Gibbs, Ian Phillips, David Fisher, Comus Elliott, Pete Storey, P Miller)*

Nicholsons/Taylor-Walker (Allied, but run as free house)   Licensee Colin Head   Real ale   Bar meals and snacks (lunchtime – and see above)   Children in eating area and restaurant   Open 11–11; closed Sat and Sun evening Jan–Feb, and 25 and 26 Dec

Market Porter (Southwark) Map 13

9 Stoney Street, SE1

There's a fine range of real ale in this lively place; the new licensee still brews the pub's own Market Bitter and Special, and there's also Boddingtons, Greene King IPA and Abbot, Sam Smiths, Youngs Bitter and Marstons Pedigree on handpump. The main part of the long U-shaped bar has rough wooden ceiling beams with beer barrels balanced on them, a heavy wooden bar counter with a beamed gantry, cushioned bar stools, an open fire with stuffed animals in glass cabinets on the mantelpiece, several mounted stags' heads, and 1920s-style wall lamps. Green and brown cushioned captain's chairs sit on the patterned green and brown carpet. At one end there's a glass cabinet for food, which includes sandwiches (steak £1.80), shepherd's pie (£2), lasagne or hot pot (£2.60), chilli con carne (£2.80), beef goulash (£2.90), a roast of the day (£2.95) and chicken Madras (£3.25); darts, fruit machine, pinball, space game and piped music. A small partly panelled room has leaded glass windows and a couple of tables. *(Recommended by M B Porter, Steve Waters, Iain McNair, Nick Dowson, Alison Hayward; more reports on the new regime please)*

Own brew   Licensee Andrew Bishop   Real ale   Lunchtime meals and snacks   Restaurant (not Sun evening) tel 01 (071)-407 2495   Open 11–11 (11–3, 7–11 Sat) all year

---

Please tell us if the décor, atmosphere, food or drink at a pub is different from our description. We rely on readers' reports to keep us up to date. No stamp needed: *The Good Pub Guide*, FREEPOST, London SW10 0BR.

Old Thameside (Southwark) Map 13

St Mary Overy Wharf, off Clink Street; from junction of Southwark Street and Borough High Street follow signpost to Southwark Cathedral

Looking out over the Thames to a cityscape punctuated by glimpses of the NatWest Tower, the Lloyd's building and the gilded sphere gleaming on top of the Monument, this fine pub is a local for many of the young bankers who flock in from the nearby ANZ building. In the main river-view bar there are dark floorboards and bare yellow brickwork, high stools by narrow dividing elbow rests with just about enough room for a well balanced plate, dark brown kitchen chairs, barrel tables, and some hefty wooden baulks serving as props and beams. Black-waistcoated bar staff serve Courage Best, Tetleys and Wethereds from handpump, and a food counter does filled French bread, good generously filled hot beef baps, pies, and crab salad; there's a wider choice of food, with several hot dishes, in the bigger but more intimate candle-lit downstairs bar, all dark beams, pews and flagstones. The waterside terrace has picnic-table sets, bya 1900 West Country schooner docked in a waterlocked inlet, and narrow alleys lead away from the modern development past Southwark Cathedral and the ruined shell of St Mary's church to the old-fashioned warren of Borough Market. *(Recommended by Peter Griffiths, GRE, AE, Heather Sharland; more reports please)*

Free house   Real ale   Meals and snacks   Restaurant (weekdays) tel 01 (071)-403 4253 Open 11–11 (11–3, 6–11 Sat) all year

Olde Windmill 🛏 (Clapham) Map 12

Clapham Common South Side, SW4

On the edge of Clapham Common, this large Victorian inn has a front room dominated by the substantial and heavily manned bar counter, and the domed and spacious main room has big prints of Dutch windmill pictures on the flowery black and brown wallpaper, and clusters of orange leatherette seats, sofas and small armchairs around elegant black tables; Youngs Bitter and Special on handpump; fruit machine, space game and trivia machine. Bar food includes sandwiches (from £1), ploughman's (from £2), salads (from £2.25, not winter evenings), home-made pizza (£2.50), chilli con carne (£2.75), seafood platter (£2.80), chicken Kiev (£4.50) and sirloin steak (£5.50). There are courtyards at each end with picnic tables, and one has a colonnaded shelter and tubs of shrubs. The inn can get packed in summer, when it seems to serve not just the pub but half the Common too. *(Recommended by Ian Phillips, Hazel Morgan; more reports on the new regime please)*

Youngs   Licensees Richard and Heather Williamson   Real ale   Meals and snacks (not Sun evening)   Restaurant   Children in restaurant   Open 11–11; may close Mon–Thurs afternoons in winter   Bedrooms tel 01 (081)-673 4578; £31S/£40S(£45B)

Orange Tree 🕸 (Richmond) Map 12

45 Kew Road

The spacious cellar bar here is attractively lit and has a wine-barish atmosphere, with old stripped brickwork walls and simple tables on a tiled floor. Bar food, served down here, includes chilli con carne (£3.75), steak and kidney pie (£4.10), beef salad (£4.25), steaks (from £6.45) and fondues (from £9.50 for two). On the ground floor there's a full range of lunchtime sandwiches (from £1), ploughman's (£1.60), sausage and egg and scampi. The main bar has an embossed ceiling with an unusual fruit and foliage pattern, and there are big coaching and Dickens prints, and the courtly paintings of the seven ages of man by Henry Stacy Marks – presented to the Green Room theatre club here in 1921; upstairs, the fringe theatre carries on the histrionic tradition. Youngs Bitter and Special on handpump; fruit

---

All *Guide* inspections are anonymous. Anyone claiming to be a *Good Pub Guide* inspector is a fraud, and should be reported to us with a name and description.

machine. *(Recommended by Raymond Palmer, Nigel Williamson; more up-to-date reports on the food please)*

Youngs Licensees Don and Chris Murphy Real ale Meals and snacks (all day) Restaurant (not Sun evening) tel 01 (081)-940 0944 Children in restaurant Nearby parking difficult Open 11–11 all year

Phoenix & Firkin ★ (Denmark Hill) Map 12

5 Windsor Walk

Perhaps the most striking of the Firkin own-brew pubs originally established by David Bruce (see also under Ferret & Firkin in the West London section, and *passim* in the Lucky Dips), this attractively renovated, palatial Victorian building has a vast lofty pavilion of a bar; the bar counter itself is made from a single mahogany tree, and there's solid wooden furniture on the stripped wooden floor, paintings of steam trains, old seaside posters, Bovril advertisements, old-fashioned station name signs, plants, big revolving fans, and a huge double-faced station clock, originally from Llandudno Junction, hanging by chains from the incredibly high ceiling. At one end there's a similarily furnished gallery, reached by a spiral staircase, and at the other arches lead into a food room; piped music. The building spans the railway cutting, and you can feel it throb when trains pass underneath. In the evenings it can get packed with a good mixed crowd. Straightforward food includes big filled baps (£1.30), portion of pie (£1.55), bread with a selection of cheeses (£1.85), salads (from around £2.10) and a daily hot dish. The beers include Phoenix, Rail and Dogbolter on handpump, as well as two changing guest beers kept under light blanket pressure. Outside there are some tables and chairs with parasols, and the steps which follow the slope of the road are a popular place to sit. *(Recommended by Greg Parston, Peter Griffiths, Norman Foot, Michele and Andrew Wells, Alison Hayward, Nick Dowson; more reports please)*

Own brew Real ale Meals and snacks Open 11–11 all year

Ship ✪ (Wandsworth) Map 12

41 Jews Row, SW18

This riverside pub is at its best in summer, when you can sample the food from the charcoal barbecue counter on the extensive terrace; changing daily, it includes burgers (£4), sausages or chicken (£4.25), Mediterranean prawns (from £5.25), lamb steak or kingfish (£5.50), seafood kebab (£6.50) and sirloin steak (£7); other food, served inside, includes sandwiches (from £1), ploughman's (£2.25), good peppered Brie and pork with bubble-and-squeak. The terrace itself is on two levels, partly cobbled and partly concrete, with picnic-table sets, pretty hanging baskets, brightly coloured flower beds, small trees and its own summer bar. Inside, most of the main bar is in a conservatory style, with only a small part of the original ceiling left. It's light and airy with a relaxed, chatty atmosphere, wooden tables (one a butcher's table), a medley of stools and old church chairs, and two comfortable leatherette Chesterfields on the wooden floorboards; one part has a Victorian fireplace, a huge clock surrounded by barge prints, and part of a milking machine on a table, and there's a rather battered harmonium, old-fashioned bagatelle, and jugs of flowers around the window sills; Youngs Bitter and Special on handpump. There are occasional theme evenings – such as a Last Night of the Proms, when people wear evening dress. The basic public bar has plain wooden furniture, a black kitchen range in the fireplace, and darts, pinball and a juke box. A Thames barge is moored alongside and can be used for private parties, although she may sail along

---

If a pub is on or near one of the walks described in *Holiday Which? Good Walks Guide*, also published by Consumers' Association, we mention this, giving the walk's number.

the East and South Coasts during the summer months. *(Recommended by G S B Dudley, Ian Phillips, M B Porter, Charles Gurney)*

Youngs   Licensee Charles Gotto   Real ale   Meals and snacks   You may have to park some way away   Open 11–11 all year

White Swan (Richmond) Map 12

25/26 Old Palace Lane

Readers praise the atmosphere in this little rose-covered cottage – exceptionally friendly and more like that of a village local than a busy London pub. An attractive place to sit in summer is the conservatory, looking on to the paved garden with its climbing plants, flowering tubs, flower beds and wooden tables and benches; summer barbecues out here on Tuesday and Thursday evenings. There are copper pots hanging from the dark beamed ceiling in the open-plan bar, old prints of London and china plates on the walls, captain's chairs, dark wood tables and plush banquettes on the green and terracotta patterned carpet. The good range of bar food includes sandwiches (£1.50), quiche (£2.75), salads (from £2.75), and hot dishes such as fish or steak and kidney pie, chilli con carne or lasagne (all £2.95). Courage Best and Directors on handpump. *(Recommended by Nigel Williamson, Sheila Keene, Ian Phillips)*

Courage   Licensee Anthony Savage   Real ale   Meals and snacks (12–2.30, 5.30–10.30)   Children in conservatory   Open 11–3 (4 Sat), 5.30–11 all year

WEST LONDON

During weekday or Saturday daytime you may not be able to find a meter very close to the Anglesea Arms or the Windsor Castle, and parking very near in the evening may sometimes be tricky with both of these, but there shouldn't otherwise be problems in this area

Anglesea Arms (Chelsea) Map 13

15 Selwood Terrace, SW7

This welcoming pub can get very full – particularly in the evenings and at weekends – when even the outside terrace (which has seats and tables) tends to overflow into the quiet side street. There's a good range of ales on handpump, including Adnams, Batemans XXXB, Boddingtons Bitter, Eldridge Pope Dorset, Greene King Abbot, Theakstons Old Peculier and Youngs Special. The bar itself has central elbow tables, leather Chesterfields, faded Turkey carpets on the bare wood-strip floor, wood panelling, and big windows with attractive swagged curtains; at one end several booths with partly glazed screens have cushioned pews and spindle-back chairs, and down some steps there's a small carpeted room with captain's chairs, high stools and a Victorian fireplace. The old-fashioned mood is heightened by some heavy portraits, prints of London, a big station clock, bits of brass and pottery, and large brass chandeliers; the atmosphere is relaxed and cheery. Food, from a glass cabinet, ranges from Scotch eggs or jumbo sausages (from 90p), through doorstep sandwiches (£1.65), ploughman's (£2.55) and salads, to a roast of the day or chicken Kiev (£3.30). *(Recommended by Ken Vostal, Howard and Sue Gascoyne; more reports please)*

Free house   Licensee Patrick Timmons   Real ale   Meals and snacks (12–2.30, 7–10)   Children welcome   Daytime parking metered   Open 11–3, 5.30–11 all year; closed 25 and 26 Dec

City Barge (Chiswick) Map 12

27 Strand-on-the-Green, W4

The place to head for in this fifteenth-century riverside pub is one of the two little low-ceilinged rooms of the cosy Old Bar, where there are cushioned wooden seats built into the ochre walls, an ancient fireplace raised above the quarry-tiled floor as protection against floods, a really worn old over-mantel, antique decorative mugs behind latticed glass and miniature bottles in a corner cupboard, and at least on weekday lunchtimes a relaxed local atmosphere. A more orthodox and more modern carpeted bar has some tables, lots of standing room (as well as elbow rests around central pillars), and reproduction maritime painted signs and bird prints. Straightforward bar food under the new managers includes pizzas (£1.90), ploughman's (£2.25), home-made steak and kidney pie (£3.25), a daily special such as coq au vin, and steak (£4.45); Courage Best and Directors; darts, fruit machine. There's also a warm white-walled conservatory with cane bentwood chairs around cast-iron-framed tables, a few houseplants and plastic ferns. On warm summer evenings people tend to crowd along the towpath outside, with many sitting on the low wall. *(Recommended by Mrs R Green, S C Collett-Jones, BKA; reports on the new management please)*

Courage   Managers Mr and Mrs Haynes   Real ale   Meals and snacks (not Sun)   Restaurant planned tel 01 (081)-994 2148   Open 11–3, 5.30–11 (all day Sat) all year

Dove ★ 🏵 (Hammersmith) Map 12

19 Upper Mall, W6

This old-fashioned riverside place is in the *Guinness Book of Records* for having the smallest bar room – the front snug, a mere 4 feet 2 inches by 7 feet 10 inches. The pub is at its best at lunchtime, when it's quiet and relaxed; but even when it's full (often predominantly of young people) there's still a good atmosphere. By the entrance from the quiet alley, the main bar has black wood panelling, red leatherette cushioned built-in wall settles and stools around dimpled copper tables, old framed advertisements, and photographs of the pub; very well kept Fullers London Pride and ESB on handpump. Up some steps, a room with small settles and solid wooden furniture has a big, clean and efficiently served glass food cabinet: sandwiches, sausage and beans or filled baked potatoes (£1.95), salads (from £3.10), shepherd's pie or moussaka (£3.25) and chicken chasseur or hot-pot (£3.55). From here, big windows open out on to a smallish terrace with a large vine; the main flagstoned area, down some steps, has lots of teak tables and white metal and teak chairs looking over the low river wall to the Thames reach just above Hammersmith Bridge. There's a manuscript of 'Rule, Britannia!' on the wall in one of the bars: James Thomson, who wrote it, is said to have written the final part of his less well-known 'The Seasons' in an upper room here, dying of a fever he had caught on a trip from here to Kew in bad weather. *(Recommended by Simon Collett-Jones, David Fowles, David Goldstone, Patrick Young, RCL, M C Howells, Doug Kennedy, Nick Dowson, Alison Hayward)*

Fullers   Licensee Brian Lovrey   Real ale   Meals and snacks (noon–8)   Open 11–11 all year

Eel Pie (Twickenham) Map 12

9 Church Street

You can sit at the front window of the simply furnished downstairs bar, decorated in Laura Ashley style, and look out to the quiet village street here. There's a good range of very well kept real ales, with Adnams, Badger Best and Tanglefoot, Everards Tiger, Ridleys, Wadworths 6X and guests such as Gribble Reg's Tipple and Wadworths Farmers Glory on handpump; prices approach central London levels. Bar food, served upstairs, includes toasted sandwiches (from £1.10), ploughman's (£2), salads (£2.70), cottage pie (£2.75), curry, goulash, chilli con carne or chicken chasseur (£2.85), and steak, kidney and Guinness pie (£2.90). Darts, fruit machine, juke box or piped music; a bench out on the pavement. It can be very popular at weekends, especially if there's a rugby match taking place.

Sunday opening is now 12–3 and 7–10.30 throughout England.

(Recommended by Ian Phillips, Nigel Williamson, A C and S J Beardsley, Peter Griffiths, CEO, P Miller)

Free house   Licensee Brendan Mallon   Real ale   Meals and snacks (not Sun)   Children in eating area of bar   Open 11–3, 5.30–11 (all day Weds–Fri) all year

Ferret & Firkin (Fulham) Map 12

Lots Road, SW10

Just around the corner from the *Guide* offices, this determinedly basic pub has unsealed bare floorboards, traditional furnishings well made from good wood, slowly circulating colonial-style ceiling fans, a log-effect gas fire, tall airy windows, and plenty of standing room in front of the long bar counter – which is curved, to match the green-painted front wall. Well kept own-brew ales include Ferret, Stoat, the notoriously strong Dogbolter, and usually a Bruce's; with 24 hours' notice you can collect a bulk supply. There are also two or three guest beers from other breweries, and a couple of real ciders. A food counter serves heftily filled giant meat-and-salad rolls, pies, ploughman's, salads, spare ribs and chilli con carne. The clientele tends to be young, easy-going, and very mixed – it's not unknown for Michael Caine to call in if he's staying in his flat in nearby Chelsea Harbour. The pub is another of the small chain of own-brew pubs started by David Bruce but sold by him in 1988 (see Phoenix & Firkin, South London); sister pubs we'd recommend in London follow much the same pattern as this, so have not all been described in detail. Seats outside. (Recommended by Charles Gurney, Nick Dowson)

Own brew   Real ale   Meals (not evening) and snacks   Daytime parking metered   Evening pianist or guitarist   Open 11–11 all year

Old Ship (Hammersmith) Map 12

25 Upper Mall, W6

The three bar areas in this spacious and comfortably modernised open-plan riverside pub are similarly decorated with a clutter of nautical bric-à-brac, including ship pictures and model boats, with racing skiffs, life-belts, rudders and oars on the beams; the wooden-floored end room has pool, fruit machine, space game and CD juke box. Bar food, served in the central area, ranges from ploughman's (£1.80) and salads (from £2.80) to hot winter dishes such as lasagne, shepherd's pie or moussaka (around £3); Ruddles County and Best and Websters Yorkshire on handpump. There's a wrought-iron balcony, wooden picnic-table sets and lots of hanging flowers on the terrace overlooking the river. The Dove (see above) is a short walk away. (Recommended by Ollie Raphael, Patrick Young; more reports please)

Watneys   Licensee Mary McCormack   Real ale   Meals and snacks (not Sun evening)   Open 11–3, 5.30–11 all year

Sporting Page 🏵 (Chelsea) Map 12

6 Camera Place, SW10

A fine, rather smart Chelsea local which seems as if it's always been as it is – but in fact was completely redone when the Front Page people (see Central London section) took it over in 1988. There are some obvious resemblances in the range of interesting bar food, which here includes soup (£2), garlic mushrooms and bacon (£2.50), kidneys in red wine sauce (£3.25), steak sandwich (£3.85), avocado, Mozzarella and tomato salad (£3.90), pasta (£4), smoked salmon with scrambled eggs, chicken tikka or smoked goose salad (£4.50) and good home-made salmon fishcakes (£5.50). Ruddles Best and County and Websters Yorkshire on handpump; decent house wines, espresso coffee; civilised service. The sturdy, cleanly cut tables around the walls leave plenty of room by the bar, and there's an airy feel from the big windows and light paintwork, with entertaining sporting decorations – old prints of people playing polo, rugby football, cricket and so forth, and big painted tile-effect murals of similar scenes; picnic-table sets outside. *(Recommended by Hank Hotchkiss)*

Watneys   Licensees Christopher Phillips, Rupert Fowler and Michael Phillips   Real ale   Meals and snacks (12–2.30, 7--10.15)   Children in eating area   Open 11–3, 5.30 (6.30 Sat in winter)–11 all year; closed 25 and 26 Dec

White Horse (Fulham) Map 12

1 Parsons Green, SW6

Opposite Parsons Green, this busy well run pub has a spacious U-shaped bar with a solid panelled central bar servery manned by a team of efficient barmen in matching dark blue shirts. The main part has big leather Chesterfields and plush stools on the green patterned carpet, wooden slatted blinds and brown hessian drapes over the huge windows, half-panelled and caramel-coloured Anaglypta walls with cheerful posters advertising wine tastings here, a central pillar with elbow rests, and a relaxed atmosphere. To one side is a plainer area with leatherette wall banquettes on the wood plank floor, green velvet curtains, a fruit machine, and a glass cabinet with tankards and sporting cups, and over on the other side is a small raised part reserved for non-smokers, a tiled Victorian fireplace with a marble over-mantel, and little plush seats and tables set out for eating. A glass food cabinet (with lots of healthy green plants hanging from a skylight above it) dispenses the truly home-made dishes: Scotch egg (£1.10), pâté (£1.50), ploughman's (£1.90), and cold meats (from 50p a slice) with carefully planned, really fresh salads (from 70p per helping); hot dishes such as carrot and feta cheese lasagne, liver and bacon, Italian meatballs or steak and kidney pie with pickled walnuts (around £3.30), puddings like apricot sponge with apricot sauce (£1.20), huge weekend breakfasts (£3.95), and Sunday roast lunch (£8 for two courses, best to book). Particularly well kept Adnams Bitter, Bass, Charrington IPA, Highgate Mild, and maybe even Traquair House Ale (brewed by the Laird of Traquair in a stately home in the Scottish borders) on handpump; a good, interesting and not overpriced wine list (with happy hour discounts), tutored wine and beer tastings, and seasonal festivals – the best known is for strong old ale held on the last Saturday in November. Outside, there are white cast-iron tables and chairs. It does get very crowded on weekend evenings. *(Recommended by RAB and others; more reports please)*

Charringtons   Licensee Sally Cruickshank   Real ale   Meals and snacks (12–2.55, 5.30–10; weekend breakfasts from 11)   Open 11.30 (11 Sat and Sun)–3, 5–11

Windsor Castle ★ (Holland Park/Kensington) Map 12

114 Campden Hill Road, W8

An attractive summer feature in this splendidly old pub is the big tree-shaded back terrace which has lots of sturdy teak seats and tables on flagstones, knee-high stone walls (eminently sittable-on) dividing them, high ivy-covered sheltering walls, and soft shade from a sweeping, low-branched plane tree, a lime and a flowering cherry. A bar counter serves the terrace directly, as does a separate food stall. The interior consists of a series of little dark-panelled, old-fashioned rooms, with sturdy built-in elm benches, time-smoked ceilings and soft lighting; a snug little pre-war-style dining-room opens off the bar. Bar food includes sandwiches (from £1.20, toasted from £1.30), ham or beef and chips (£2.95), salads (from £2.95, smoked salmon £5.10), bacon, egg and black pudding (£3.20), vegetarian dishes such as vegetable chilli or spinach and mushroom lasagne (£3.25) and eight-ounce steak (£6.10); Bass and Charrington IPA on handpump; no fruit machines or piped music. Usually fairly quiet at lunchtime, the pub is often packed in the evenings. Note that they

---

Stars after the name of a pub show exceptional quality. But they don't mean extra comfort, and though some pubs get stars for special food quality it isn't necessarily a food thing either. The full report on each pub should make clear what special quality has earned it.

don't allow children. *(Recommended by Patrick Young, Nick Dowson, Alison Hayward)*
Charringtons (Bass)   Licensee Anthony James Owen   Real ale   Meals and snacks (12–2.30,
5.30–10; not Sun evening)   Daytime parking metered   Open 11–11 all year

EAST LONDON

*Weekday daytime parking isn't too bad in this area, though you should expect quite
a walk to the Dickens Inn; there should be no real problems in the evening or at
weekends*

Dickens Inn (Docklands)   Map 12

St Katharine's Yacht Haven, off St Katharine's Way, E1

An unashamedly touristy pub which benefits from its fine dockland position, this
spacious place has timber baulks for pillars and beams, stripped brickwork, worn
floorboards, a very long polished brass bar counter, and a subdued atmosphere
emphasised by candles in bottles and by the partly glazed wooden partitions which
separate it into smaller areas. There's something of a cosmopolitan feel, with
clientele ranging from smartly dressed European tourists drinking tea or coffee,
through people from the nearby World Trade Centre or the Tower Hotel, to folk
who like at least to imagine themselves messing about in boats (the main bar
overlooks the lively yacht harbour); Courage Best and Directors, John Smith and
Dickens Own and Olivers, brewed especially for the pub just over the river in
Tooley Street; drinks are at Central London prices. Bar food includes sandwiches
and hot dishes such as bangers and mash (£1.95) and whole spring chicken (£4.25).
Doors open out on to the verandah (a mass of window boxes), and steps lead down
to the cobbled waterside terrace, though you can't take food or drink down here.
(Recommended by Nick Dowson, GB; more reports please)
*Courage   Licensees Eric Bingham, Paul Taylor, Louis Mazoi, Eddy Davis and Kevin
Malone   Real ale   Meals and snacks   Restaurant tel 01 (071)-488 9936   Open 11–11
all year*

Grapes (Limehouse)   Map 12

76 Narrow Street, E14

Fresh fish is a speciality in this relatively quiet little pub; in the long and narrow bar
they serve fish pasty (£2.15), seafood risotto (£2.20), and fish and chips or seafood
Mornay (£3.30); the upstairs fish restaurant (with fine views of the river) is highly
praised. The partly panelled bar, comfortably free of tourists, has lots of prints,
often of actors, and some elaborately etched windows. Ind Coope Burton and
Friary Meux and Taylor-Walker Bitter on handpump. The glass-roofed back
balcony is one of the most sheltered places for a riverside drink. Dickens used the
pub as the basis of his 'Six Jolly Fellowship Porters' in *Our Mutual Friend*.
(Recommended by Ian Phillips; more reports please)
*Taylor-Walker (Allied)   Real ale   Meals and snacks (not Sat or Sun, not Mon evening)
Restaurant tel 01 (071)-987 4396   Children in restaurant   Open 11–2.30, 5–11; may close
over Christmas*

Hollands (Stepney)   Map 12

9 Exmouth Street, E1

There's an unchanging atmosphere in this friendly little place – largely because
most of the decorations and furnishings are original early-Victorian. The heavy bar
counter has swivelling etched and cut-glass snob-screens, and there are antique
mirrors, *Vanity Fair* pictures, Victorian cartoons and photographs, as well as a
clutter of trumpets, glass and brass ornaments hanging from the ochre painted and
panelled ceiling in the main bar. Through an arched doorway and heavy velvet
curtains is the split-level, red-tiled lounge bar, with its panelled and velveteen-

cushioned bench seats, old sepia photographs, brass pots hanging from the ceiling and a big Victorian fireplace with large china ornaments on its mantelpiece. Bar food consists of freshly made sandwiches (from 90p; smoked mackerel £1.25); Wethereds on handpump; darts, cribbage. The pub was opened early in Queen Victoria's reign by the present landlord's great-grandfather. *(More reports please)*

Free house   Licensee J C Holland   Real ale   Lunchtime snacks (not Sat or Sun) Open 11–11 all year

---

Lucky Dip

Besides the fully inspected pubs, you might like to try these Lucky Dips recommended to us and described by readers (if you do, please send us reports). We have split them into the main areas used for the full reports – Central, North, and so on. Within each area the Lucky Dips are listed by postal district, ending with Greater London suburbs on the edge of that area.

CENTRAL

EC1

[56 Faringdon Rd] *Betsey Trotwood*: Green-painted building (inside and out), with lots of mirrors in one corner making it seem bigger than it really is; well kept Shepherd Neame Bitter and Best; popular with *Guardian* and other nearby office-workers; now known just as the Betsey *(Peter Griffiths)*

[Chiswell St] *Chiswell Vaults*: Subterranean, much-vaulted Whitbreads pub with plenty of space, reopened after long closure; very generous helpings of food, friendly well trained staff *(Joan Chenhalls, LYM)*

[Farringdon Lane] *City Pride*: Recently refurbished Fullers pub with two attractive downstairs rooms (though the rows of books in the overspill room by the bar are tantalisingly out of reach); well kept reasonably priced Chiswick, London Pride and ESB, imaginative excellent value food, fire in original fireplace, stained-glass windows with pub's name, extra seating for diners upstairs *(Anon)*

[362 St Johns St] *Empress of Russia*: Recently refurbished, small but pleasant Whitbreads pub with late nineteenth-century Russian theme, comfortable red banquettes and chairs in single semi-circular bar with eating annexe serving modest pub food all day *(Anon)*

[1 Middle St] *Hand & Shears*: Traditional Smithfield sixteenth-century pub with small-roomed feel though in fact only one partition wall still survives; often crowded and lively, one of London's least spoilt pubs with marvellously mixed clientele; well kept Courage real ales; open 11.30–11 Mon–Fri, closed weekends mid-afternoon *(Brian Jones, LYM)*

[33 Seward St] *Leopard*: Out-of-the-way free house with changing choice of up to half a dozen real ales such as Greene King Abbot and Thwaites; solid-looking square-cut Georgian building with back garden, varied

clientele, never crowded *(T J Maddison)*

☆ [166 Goswell Rd] *Pheasant & Firkin*: Good value ploughman's and other simple food, well kept own-brewed beers and guests such as Wadworths 6X; wooden stools, benches and tables on bare boards; popular with businessmen *(LYM and others)*

[Rising Sun Ct; Cloth Fair] *Rising Sun*: Cool, dark and lofty bar, looking on to church, with tall tables and high stools, coal-effect gas fire, friendly staff and calm atmosphere; well kept Sam Smiths, rolls and sandwiches; narrow room up steep stairs has more food including ploughman's, steak pie and quiche; very clean gents *(Ian Phillips)*

[1 Arlington Way] *Shakespeares Head*: Straightforward, friendly and busy local with hard-working licensees; some theatre posters; usual range of Whitbreads, simple food *(Anon)*

[56 Chiswell St] *St Pauls*: Recently done up by Whitbreads in country style, attractive décor with farm tools hanging from ceiling, stained pine tables and chairs, bare floorboards; good atmosphere *(Gavin May)*

EC2

[63 Charlotte Rd] *Bricklayers Arms*: Normally a dozen or more beers on tap including five real ales that change weekly – Adnams, Arkells, Greene King and so forth; very good lunchtime sandwiches and bar food *(Ken Vostal)*

[Foster Lane] *City Pipe*: Cellar ale-and-wine house with simple but good food from sandwiches to steaks, unusually good value Davy's wines and ports, and Old Wallop beer in pewter tankards or half-gallon copper jugs; tie required *(David Jones)*

[202 Bishopsgate] *Dirty Dicks*: Good substantial sandwiches with thick ham and other bar food, very good service and pleasant atmosphere in traditional ground-floor bar; barrel-vaulted cellar with good loud pop music, upstairs wine bar; the original tavern cultivated dirt and had five drink-encouraging rules, a common trick by early seventeenth century, such as No Person To Be Served Twice; all the original filth had gone by the 1930s *(LYM)*

EC3

[67 Fenchurch St] *East India Arms*: Well kept Youngs real ales; superb service even when it gets crowded at lunchtime *(David Fowles)*

EC4

[Cousin Lane] *Banker*: Fullers pub by River Thames and Cannon St Stn *(David Fisher)*
[22 Fleet St] *Cock*: Popular, with well kept real ale and retaining enough character to dare to stay basic in parts *(Dr and Mrs A K Clarke)*
[10 Creed Lane] *Davys*: More of a wine bar than a pub, atmospheric cellar bar with sensibly limited choice of good value food from pâté through dressed crab to sirloin steak; bar in front with standing areas, dining area behind, dim lighting, good Rioja and other wines, sherry in enormous glasses; good service; can be lively and noisy *(John Evans)*
[Charterhouse St] *Fox & Anchor*: Archetypal meat-workers' haunt, opening early for breakfasts; long, narrow bar with narrow tables; lunch served with very tender meat *(Timothy Powell)*
[6 Martin Lane] *Old Wine Shades*: One of the City's very few buildings to have escaped the Great Fire of 1666 – heavy black beams, dark panelling, old prints, subdued lighting, old-fashioned high-backed settles, antique tables and dignified alcoves; good value weekday lunchtime traditional bar snacks, a good range of wines (under same ownership as El Vino's); jacket and tie for men, no jeans or jump-suits for women; open weekdays 11.30–3, 5–8 *(LYM)*
[29 Watling St] *Olde Watling*: Well kept Bass and Charringtons IPA in heavy-beamed and timbered pub built by Wren in 1662 as a site commissariat for his new St Paul's Cathedral; lunchtime bar food served upstairs; closed Sat and Sun *(LYM)*
[Watling St] *Pavilion End*: Sky-blue ceiling with fluffy clouds and pavilion layout evoked summer cricket-match atmosphere – especially with Test broadcasts on TV; nice range of salads, often busy before noon with City dealers taking early lunches *(Tim Powell)*
[64 Queen Victoria St] *Sea Horse*: Small cosy City pub with very well kept Courage Best and Directors, limited range of food, well prepared and promptly served *(Chris Fluck)*
[Norwich St] *White Horse*: Quiet upstairs bar serving traditional hot food for eating in dining-room that evokes Anthony Powell novels; downstairs typical London businessman's pub *(Tim Powell)*

SW1

[Victoria St] *Albert*: Splendidly redecorated and commanding exterior, set off against bleak cliffs of modern glass; packed weekday lunchtimes, quiet otherwise; popular for bar food, a Scotland Yard local and used by some MPs and many civil servants *(BB)*
[104 Horseferry Rd] *Barley Mow*: Comfortable and well kept pub, handy for Royal Horticultural Society's Halls in Vincent Sq, with Watneys-related real ales, good value waitress-served food, a few pavement tables in side street; live entertainment Fri and Sat evening, Sun lunch *(John Booth, BB)*
[62 Petty France] *Buckingham Arms*: Pleasant, typical London pub with flowery wallpaper, stained glass and unusual long side corridor fitted out with elbow ledge for drinkers; massive helpings of food such as burger and chips, well kept Youngs, pleasant service; close to Passport Office and Buckingham Palace *(D J Cargill, LYM and others)*
[39 Palace St] *Cask & Glass*: A half-pint pub serving half-pints of Watneys-related beers, sandwiches; one small room (which used to be divided into two), overflowing into street in summer – when it's a riot of colour; handy for Queen's Gallery *(Ian Phillips)*
[16 Duke St] *Chequers*: Collection of Prime Minister pictures and very well kept Watneys-related beers with good basic rolls and sandwiches and cheap home-cooked hot dishes; very crowded 12.30–2 *(Ian Phillips)*
[53 Whitehall] *Clarence*: Popular with Ministry of Defence and other Whitehall folk as well as tourists for excellent range of real ales, including attractively priced weekly guest beers; food such as ploughman's, steak and kidney pie or stir-fried chicken; sawdust on floor, seats outside, good atmosphere *(Ian Phillips, Dr and Mrs A K Clarke)*
[Oxendon St] *Comedy*: Lively and welcoming, with lots of coming and going – interesting crowd constantly changing; well kept Marstons Pedigree and Ruddles County; good value imaginative food; stuffed birds, playbills, old prints and books in profusion, and not too hard to find a seat though always busy *(Ian Phillips)*
[63 Eaton Terr] *Duke of Wellington*: Friendly Whitbreads pub in elegant street not far from house where Mozart lived; real ales, cheap snacks including good sausage ploughman's *(John Tyzack, Quentin Williamson)*
[29 Passmore St] *Fox & Hounds*: Small and cosy with good atmosphere – glowing fire, friendly bar staff and good mix of customers including Chelsea pensioners; toasted sandwiches in evening *(Anon)*
[25 King St] *Golden Lion*: Rather distinguished bow-fronted building, opp Christies auction rooms; large downstairs bar with seats out in side passage *(Anon)*
[Dolphin Sq] *Lighthouse Bar*: Good selection

of worldwide beers, lively atmosphere *(Lord and Lady Graves and others)*

[58 Millbank] *Morpeth Arms*: Cheerful, very clean and busy Youngs pub handy for the Tate; nice comfortable feel; polite staff, good beer and food *(Dr and Mrs A K Clarke, P Garrad, Catherine Villals)*

☆ [Duke of York St] *Red Lion*: Veritable hall of mirrors, with chandeliers, windows, woodwork and reproduction Edwardian light fittings which merge totally; attractively priced food including smoked salmon sandwiches, ham rolls, giant sausage and hot meals; Ind Coope Burton, Taylor-Walker, quick friendly service; not large so gets crowded easily *(Ian Phillips, LYM)*

[44 Ebury Bridge Rd] *Rising Sun*: Popular, solidly decorated lunchtime pub with plenty of chairs and pews around the tables, wide choice of good value inexpensive food including home-made specials such as lamb rosemary or chicken chilli; well kept Youngs real ales, good quick service *(Peter Griffiths)*

[Parliament St] *St Stephens Tavern*: MPs' pub with elaborately old-fashioned high-ceilinged bar all etched glass and mahogany, basement food bar, upstairs restaurant *(LYM)*

☆ [Belgrave Mews West] *Star*: Real institution of a place with mixed crowd from workers with their racing pages to diplomats; stools by counter and window in small entry room which also has food counter serving good value food from ploughman's to dishes of the day such as gammon, salads, veg quiche and rib-eye steak; arch to side room which has swagged curtains, lots of dark mahogany, stripped mahogany chairs and tables, heavy upholstered settles, globe lighting, raj fans; back room similar but also has button-back green plush built-in wall seats; well kept Fullers Chiswick, London Pride and ESB; not too crowded lunchtime, can get packed evenings *(BB, LYM)*

[off Victoria Embankment] *Tattershall Castle*: Converted paddle steamer – great novelty value and marvellous vantage point for watching river traffic; canopied bar serveries, with barbecues and ice-creams too in summer, for both forward and aft decks with picnic-table sets; wardroom bar and nightclub below decks; keg beers, rather pricey *(Howard and Sue Gascoyne)*

[36 Panton St] *Tom Cribb*: One small bar in corner pub with lots of pugilistic prints, between National Gallery and Piccadilly Circus; comfortable banquettes in odd corners, quite low prices for sandwiches and decent Stilton or Brie ploughman's *(Anon)*

[39 Dartmouth St] *Two Chairmen*: Packed at lunchtime for good freshly cut meat sandwiches and well kept Watneys real ale, refurbished in old-fashioned style, in pretty Georgian street near St James's Park *(BB)*

[Warwick House St] *Two Chairmen*: Long narrow Courage house with very few seats, also elbow-shelf on one wall, claims built

1690 and pub 1787, reasonable snacks such as ploughman's; coffee *(Anon)*

[32 Duke St] *Unicorn*: Comfortable split-level downstairs bar in what amounts to a cellar pub, excellent food such as seafood risotto including octopus, mussels and langoustines, stuffed cabbage and half a dozen other appealing hot dishes, plenty of plate space, obliging staff, good range of real ales including Adnams, Marstons Pedigree, Tetleys and Wadworths 6X; wall covered with work by Ford Madox Brown, handy for Fortnums *(Peter Griffiths)*

[9 Storeys Gate] *Westminster Arms*: Good range of well kept real ales in two-floor pub, pleasant service, busy lively atmosphere, good choice of reasonably priced food; basement wine bar *(Anon, LYM)*

[71 Kinnerton St] *Wilton Arms*: Up-market little mews pub with good beer; well worth a visit *(Dr and Mrs A K Clarke)*

SW3

[17 Mossop St] *Admiral Codrington*: Good affluent atmosphere in attractive old-fashioned pub with wooden floor; well kept beer, pleasant conservatory seating area; unobtrusive piped music, restaurant *(RCL, B J Collins)*

[Milner St] *Australian*: Sensible wooden place with pubby atmosphere; can be Sloany *(RCL)*

[298 King's Rd] *Cadogan Arms*: Rough timber baulks, red-bulbed lanterns, impression of intimacy, well kept Combes and Watneys Stag, friendly atmosphere, Chef & Brewer food in waitress-service area *(BB)*

[43 Beauchamp Pl] *Grove*: Comfortable, split-level bar with Brakspears, Flowers and Wethereds real ales, lovely brown baps *(Anon)*

☆ [197 King's Rd] *Henry J Beans*: Though not a traditional pub, this spacious bar has – at a price – a splendid range of drinks and bottled beers and good value burger-style bar food; it's attractively laid out, with a fine collection of enamelled advertising signs, and has the most generously sized sheltered courtyard garden of any central London pub we know; open all day; the branch in Abingdon Rd W2 is run on similar lines; children in upper dining area *(LYM)*

[Cheyne Walk] *Kings*: Views of Thames and houseboats from smartly refurbished cocktail bar *(BB)*

[392 King's Road] *Man in the Moon*: Roomy pub with interesting man-in-moon tile frieze, good small theatre downstairs *(LYM)*

[23 Smith St] *Phoenix*: Tiny up-market pub with good range of well kept beers *(Dr and Mrs A K Clarke)*

[47 Denyer St] *Shuckburgh Arms*: Smart accents in simple pub with one long bar, conservatory-bar and video machine; popular with yuppies *(RCL)*

[200 King's Rd] *Trafalgar*: Smart and

spacious old-style Charringtons Vintage Inn with real ales and bar food *(BB)*

W1

[4 Conway St] *Adams Arms*: Smallish downstairs bar with Robert Adam pictures, designs and biographical pages, cabinet of carpenter's tools, autographed show-business photographs, good value home-cooked hot food, friendly staff; gets quite crowded lunchtime; upstairs restaurant *(Peter Griffiths)*

[37 Thayer St; bottom end of Marylebone High St] *Angel*: Well kept two-storey Sam Smiths pub, lively at lunchtime, quieter in the evening *(LYM)*

☆ [18 Argyll St; opp Oxford Circus tube side exit] *Argyll Arms*: Attractive façade increasingly covered with greenery, lovely cosy little bars with engraved glass and mirrors beautifully preserved, embossed ceilings and friezes, wide choice of real ales such as Adnams, Arkells, Boddingtons, Marstons Pedigree, Tetleys and Wadworths 6X, friendly obliging staff, good range of food including well filled sandwiches in pleasant back cafe-style area; open afternoons *(Peter Griffiths, Gary Scott)*

☆ [41 Mount St] *Audley*: Spacious and very well kept Mayfair pub with heavily ornamented mahogany panelling, generous (if pricey) helpings of food; upstairs restaurant, basement wine bar; choice of well kept real ales *(LYM)*

[8 Dorset St] *Barley Mow*: Eye-catching from the outside, has genuine-seeming snugs rather like pine box-pews in a church, supported by iron hoops from wall; decent bar food including good ploughman's (except for wrapped butter), bright welcoming staff, unobtrusive background music, couple of machines, Ind Coope-related beers with guests such as Adnams *(Ian Phillips)*

[18 Kingly St] *Blue Posts*: Usefully situated, pleasant enough little corner pub with Whitbreads-related ales; simply furnished; routine food choice *(Ian Phillips and others)*

[28 Rupert St] *Blue Post*: Large one-roomed Soho pub with Watneys-related beers and upstairs carvery; good sandwiches carved from big beef joint or roast turkey; often crowded; food such as sausage, bubble and squeak and baked potatoes *(LYM and others)*

[8 Mandeville Pl] *Boswells*: Up-market plush bar in New Mandeville Hotel – attractive surroundings *(Dr and Mrs A K Clarke)*

☆ [15 Bruton Lane; off Berkeley Sq] *Brutons*: Stylish – undoubtedly more wine bar than pub, but does have Courage Best and Directors and Websters Yorkshire on handpump; specialises in restaurany seafood showing considerable imagination, and attractively priced for the area; stained-wood booths on the left, small raised front dining area marked off by wood and glass

partition, interesting prints on pink ragged-look walls, service by waistcoated waitresses *(BB)*

[Old Compton St] *Comptons*: Popular spacious lunchtime pub with swivelling stools around tall tables; Bass, good value food; predominantly gay clientele *(Anon)*

[Denman St] *Devonshire Arms*: Corner pub stripped bare, basic wooden stools and tables, a few brasses and copper objects hanging from ceiling, reasonably priced Shepherd Neame real ale, mosaic coat of arms behind food bar *(Anon)*

[21a Devonshire St] *Devonshire Arms*: Decorously friendly and comfortable Edwardian pub with bar food and upstairs dining-room, good coffee *(LYM)*

☆ [18 Bateman St; corner of Frith St] *Dog & Duck*: Very pleasant, comfortable little Soho pub with two small adjoining bars, Tetleys and Ind Coope Burton on handpump; attractive décor of glass mirrors and green tiles showing dogs and ducks inside, plus bright dog-and-duck bas-relief high up outside *(Peter Griffiths, T J Maddison, LYM)*

[43 Weymouth Mews] *Dover Castle*: Smart pub in smart mews with attractive back room with blue-grey banquettes; choice of beers, decent food; business and professional clientele *(Peter Griffiths)*

[94a Crawford St] *Duke of Wellington*: Little local with very well kept Bass *(MH)*

[Rathbone St] *Duke of York*: Well kept Bass and Charrington IPA in old-fashioned welcoming local with popular and reasonably priced lunchtime home cooking *(LYM)*

[35 St James's Pl] *Dukes*: The bar of this hotel is a wonderful retreat, with good choice of spirits, copious titbits, and excellent sandwiches; bedrooms – at a price of course *(John Tyzack)*

[16 Charlotte St] *Fitzroy*: Historic place with photographs of Augustus John and Dylan Thomas, and George Orwell's NUJ card for *Tribune*, and so forth; Writers & Artists Bar feels quite villagey – bare floorboards, white-painted brickwork, new wooden settles, a couple of cubicles; the counter here's not always manned, so you may have to fetch your Sam Smiths BM or Museum from upstairs; good atmosphere up here too; piped music; decent food; plenty of outside seating, popular in summer *(Peter Griffiths, K A Topping and others)*

[55 Brewer St] *Glass House*: Straightforward London pub with brown ceiling, blackboard menu, fruit machine and Ind Coope-related beers; comfortable banquettes and stools, food and wine bar *(Anon)*

[Grafton Way] *Grafton Arms*: Very popular place; comfortable enough if you can get a seat, well kept Boddingtons, Brakspears, Flowers, Greene King Abbot, usual Central London food such as filled French sticks *(Anon)*

[57 Berwick St] *Green Man*: Bass and Charrington IPA in large, comfortable and smartly furnished pub; service always good even if it's busy; polished brass round central island servery, woodwork and light fittings look newly redecorated *(Michael and Alison Sandy)*

[30 Bruton Pl] *Guinea*: Partly fifteenth-century oak-panelled mews pub, well kept Youngs beer, smartly dressed customers overflow into the quiet mews – a long-standing part of traditional Mayfair; good no-nonsense atmosphere, but often very busy and smoky *(S R Holman, LYM and others)*

[5–6 Argyll St; in Sutherland House] *Handsel*: Very good value food from cheerful Italian chef in spacious, clean and comfortable bar (quite separate from adjoining Beefeater restaurant); well kept Greene King IPA and Abbot and Flowers Original *(Michael and Alison Sandy)*

[Broadwick St] *John Snow*: Easy-going pub with ornately framed and elaborately engraved glass, engravings of old London and Thames, interesting cast-iron-framed tables, lots of high stools, two stuffed ravens and documentation of Dr Snow who discovered in 1854 that cholera was water-borne – a pump outside was associated with the discovery; Watneys-related real ales, helpful West End and City map posted in window *(Peter Griffiths and others)*

[68 Gt Titchfield St] *Kings Arms*: Good reliable local with well kept Charrington IPA in long narrow bar, tables out on the corner of Riding House St; good freshly carved ham salad, hot meals such as pizza, turkey and ham pie, moussaka or chicken curry; where ITN staff come to escape the shop-talk in the Green Man; relaxed atmosphere *(Ian Phillips, LYM)*

[Poland St] *Kings Arms*: Lots of character in gas-lit pub with Everards Tiger and Old Bill, Charles Wells Bombardier and others; carved settle upstairs by window; full of American girls and tourists, sprinkling of businessmen *(I M Phillips)*

[44 Glasshouse St] *Leicester Arms*: Good range of real ales such as Charles Wells Bombardier, Huntsman Royal Oak and Palmers, efficient staff, plenty of comfortable seats; upstairs bookable for functions *(Michael and Alison Sandy)*

[Charing Cross Rd/Old Compton St] *Molly Moggs*: Small single-room Soho corner pub looking out on the Charing Cross Road bookworms; West End map, prints and theatre posters, friendly young staff, good mix of customers – young from St Martins School of Art, old Soho regulars; decent piped music (mainly jazz), well kept if pricey Flowers IPA and Original, Wethereds and Whitbreads Castle Eden, food such as pork and cider pie *(Peter Griffiths)*

[Tottenham Court Rd] *New*: Pine surrounds and frontage make it different, as do its three Youngers ales including IPA; decent food such as hot beef baps; attractive split-level layout *(Anon)*

[58–60 Goodge St] *One Tun*: Lively young person's pub with lots of games, lots of atmosphere *(Dr and Mrs A K Clarke)*

[22 Portman Sq] *Portman*: Charming welcome, pleasant service, fine Californian Cabernet Sauvignon on Thanksgiving Day; good choice of bar food with fancy puddings such as blackcurrant mousse; sitting at a window-table overlooking Portman Square feels very English *(GB, CH)*

[71 Marylebone High St] *Prince Regent*: Well kept Bass and Charrington IPA in pub whose food area is festooned with cheese dishes, as is the lunchtime dining room; interesting collection of attractive prints *(Michael and Alison Sandy)*

[Warren St] *Prince of Wales Feathers*: Used to have certain rough charm a few years ago with sawdust on floor – carpet has softened that; well kept Charrington IPA, leaded lights with inset fleur-de-lys, only a few benches and seats; good value doorstep sandwiches; a place to come for a quick drink *(Anon)*

[Kingly St] *Red Lion*: A relaxing 'brown pub' on two floors – brown panelling and seating, restful décor, though loudish music; big photograph of Sam Smiths brewery, grandfather clock on stairs; well kept Sam Smiths OB and Museum, food served upstairs *(Peter Griffiths, Michael and Alison Sandy, LYM)*

[Newman Street] *Rose & Crown*: Blue leatherette banquettes and stools, dark woodwork and good atmosphere, with well kept Sam Smiths OB, darts, piped music, fruit machine; food such as sandwiches, pasties and steak and kidney pie, mainly upstairs; picnic-table sets on pavement, with pretty flower baskets *(Ian Phillips)*

[5 Charles St] *Running Footman*: Small and often crowded, but doesn't feel uncomfortable; efficient staff *(Hank Hotchkiss)*

[29 Clarges St] *Samuel Pepys*: Very long refurbished bar with food and restaurant at far end; likely to be frequented by staff from nearby advertising agencies *(Anon)*

☆ [Langham Pl; take express lift in far corner of hotel lobby] *St Georges Hotel*: One of the finest views in London from the Summit Bar, which has floor-to-ceiling picture windows looking out over the city to the west (the gents, facing the other way, also has a splendid view); it's been a great favourite as a meeting-place, with comfortable well spaced settees, low gilt and marble tables, properly mixed cocktails (not cheap) and good fresh sandwiches and other bar food; usually a pianist at the grand piano (not Sun); there's been a question-mark over the service recently – more reports please; bedrooms *(Roy Bromell, Ian Phillips, JMC, LYM and others)*

☆ [Poland St] *Star & Garter*: Unspoilt, very friendly little Soho local with well kept Courage Best and Directors, handy for Oxford Street *(Dr and Mrs A K Clarke, LYM)*

[34 George St] *Westmorland Arms*: Deeply comfortable and welcoming, Tolly real ales, food bar *(LYM)*

[29 Crawford Pl] *Windsor Castle*: Very Royal-theme pub with lots of cuttings of the Abdication and so forth; friendly polite staff *(Dr and Mrs A K Clarke)*

W2

[28 Praed St] *Grand Junction Arms*: Rather grand corner pub worth a quick visit *(Dr A K Clarke)*

[31 Praed St] *Great Western*: Truly friendly crowded corner local with good atmosphere and welcoming young landlord *(Dr A K Clarke)*

[Water Gdns, Norfolk Cr] *Heron*: Tastefully updated, comfortable and well kept if a bit off the shelf *(Dr and Mrs A K Clarke)*

[66 Bayswater Rd] *Swan*: Attractively positioned looking across busy road to Kensington Gardens; comfortable banquettes and stools, clean WCs, lots of tree-shaded seats fenced off from pavement, many more under a glazed canopy; often popular; hot food lunchtime and evening; useful meeting-place *(Ian Phillips, LYM)*

WC1

[92 Southampton Row] *Bonnington*: Recently refurbished, plushly comfortable lounge bar in hotel owned by the same family as when it was built in 1911; Tolly Original on handpump, grill restaurant; bedrooms *(Robert Lester)*

[New Oxford St; other entrance top Shaftesbury Ave] *Crown*: Good range of beers including Adnams, Boddingtons, Ind Coope Burton; friendly young staff, comfortably padded banquettes and stools; tables and benches out on paved triangle at top of Shaftesbury Ave, can be very pleasant in summer *(Anon)*

[Lamb's Conduit Passage; between Red Lion Sq and Red Lion St] *Dolphin*: Rustic benches and flower-filled window-boxes outside, high stools and wide shelves around the walls with plenty of standing room inside; old photographs, copper pots, horsebrasses and so forth inside, with one or two unusual delicatessen items among the bar snacks, and real ales such as Marstons Pedigree, McMullens and Wethereds *(Peter Griffiths)*

[lower Tonbridge St/Bidborough St] *Dolphin*: Happy-go-lucky pub popular at lunchtime with local office-workers; Watneys-related beers, basic reasonably priced food *(R C Vincent)*

[31 University St] *Jeremy Bentham*: 'Welcome to Jeremy Bentham' picked out in seashells, with wax head of him and lots of captioned memorabilia – as well as pharmaceutical bottles and jars as reminder of UCH next door; discreet quietish clientele, cosy atmosphere, friendly efficient staff, oasis for area; upstairs restaurant *(Peter Griffiths)*

[Queen Sq] *Queens Larder*: Small and friendly pub with good choice of well kept real ales including Timothy Taylors and Wethereds, pleasant seating outside overlooking secluded square; upstairs dining-room *(Andrew Martin)*

[267 High Holborn] *Royal Connaught*: Useful retreat when other nearby pubs full; room to sit upstairs – maybe watching the ladies' darts teams in action *(T Nott)*

☆ [63 Lamb's Conduit St] *Sun*: Excellent choice of up to twenty usually well kept real ales, at a price – beer taken very seriously (tours of temperature-controlled cellar bookable for groups); can get very crowded with mixed clientele; sparsely furnished, with bare boards; straightforward bar food (not cheap) lunchtime and evening; if it gets too crowded you can sit out at tables in traffic-free street *(Peter Griffiths, Nick Dowson, Alison Hayward, David Fowles, Robin Armstrong, Kevin Macey, Michael and Alison Sandy)*

[Cosmo Pass] *Swan*: Well kept Watneys real ales and good choice of lunchtime food in pub given old-fashioned refurbishment, seats outside in pedestrian alley *(LYM)*

[22 Sandland St] *Three Cups*: Surprisingly mixed clientele from barristers to barrow-boys in big bar with good pre-war Charringtons mirrors, sandwiches and so forth *(Anon)*

[2 Theobalds Rd] *Yorkshire Grey*: Lively mixed clientele in pub which brews its own beers – the range is interesting and well served; nice atmosphere *(Dr and Mrs A K Clarke)*

WC2

[42 Wellington St] *Coach & Horses*: Nice small friendly pub with old-fashioned low copper-topped bar, lunchtime food, Watneys-related real ales; a contrast to bustling commercialised pubs in the area *(T T Kelly)*

[Long Acre] *Freemasons Arms*: Pleasant and relaxing upstairs with warm gas fire, reasonable choice of food including filled baked potatoes and ploughman's (not Sun), well kept Sam Smiths OB and Museum, acceptable draught wine *(Roy Bromell, S R Holman)*

[39 Bow St] *Marquis of Anglesea*: Lively and friendly Youngs pub with well kept ales on handpump; very busy, but friendly staff *(Tom Hartman)*

[10 James St] *Nags Head*: Plenty of seats in large lofty pub with old ceramic spirit barrels and stone jars on high gantry, masses of prints on walls; food reasonably priced for this tourist area, well kept McMullens real ales, cheapish wine by the bottle *(Ian Phillips, Prof S Barnett and others)*

[40 Covent Garden Market] *Punch & Judy*: Real reason for coming here is to stand on balcony overlooking piazza (familiar as backdrop in *My Fair Lady*) and heckle the jugglers, escapologists and acrobats who perform below – they love it but you have to be extra generous when they come round with the hat; pleasant and surprising atmosphere in cellar bar – old bricks, alcoves and two small rooms, juke box, darts and snack bar; Courage Best and Directors, straightforward bar food *(RCL, Ian Phillips, LYM and others)*

☆ [90 St Martins Lane] *Salisbury*: Fine Victorian interior, with copper-topped tables, brass lamps, deep red plush banquettes and velvet curtains, and superb cut glass; flamboyantly theatrical atmosphere; good food, Bass and Charrington IPA on handpump; close to theatres and antiquarian bookshops *(Peter Griffiths, Patrick Young, S R Holman, BB)*

[53 Carey St] *Seven Stars*: Old-style standing bar serving food, full of lawyers from the bankruptcy courts *(T Nott)*

[10 Northumberland St; Craven Pl] *Sherlock Holmes*: Good choice of well kept real ales such as Wethereds and Greene King Abbot, pleasant and clean; lots of convincing Sherlock Holmes memorabilia, including a re-creation of the Baker Street sitting-room (closed Sun); food always available *(Quentin Williamson, Nick Dowson, BB)*

[14 New Row] *White Swan*: Pleasant surroundin.... ...nusual rope-covered wrought-iron inner entry to small pillared front bar, unpretentiously plain seventeenth-century room behind, Bass and Charrington IPA on handpump; crowded at lunchtime with publishing people *(Peter Griffiths, BB)*

NORTH

N1
[Highbury Corner, next to entrance to Highbury and Islington Tube] *Cock*: Spacious bar with island servery; green plush stools and chairs, lots of wooden tables at one end; mixed clientele; CD juke box *(BB)*

☆ [60 Copenhagen St] *George IV*: Thwaites the Lancashire brewers developed this as a friendly pastiche of a northern pub, with lots of stripped woodwork, pine furniture and masses of old Burnley photographs; they've sold it now, but the pub still stocks their beers; good chatty atmosphere, lunchtime bar food including large sandwiches (not Sun), conservatory area, French windows to terrace and garden with play area; handy for Regent's Canal towpath *(Ian Phillips, Alison Hayward, Nick Dowson, Wayne Brindle, Neil Barker, LYM)*

☆ [87 Noel Rd] *Island Queen*: Giant Alice-in-Wonderland characters floating above bar, big mirrors with applied jungle vegetation, good choice of freshly made and often unusual food, well kept Bass, Charrington IPA and Springfield, pool in back room, good juke box, tables in front; theme evenings in upstairs dining-room (eg Titanic evening); a real welcome for children, close to Camden Passage antiques area *(H Paulinski, LYM)*

[Canonbury St; junction with Marquess Rd] *Marquess Tavern*: Large Youngs pub with comfortably plush domed back room, front bar with attractively stripped half-panelling, relaxed atmosphere, well kept real ales *(BB)*

N5
[26 Highbury Pk] *Highbury Barn*: One reader, with his son, celebrated attaining their ambition of visiting all 92 clubs in the English Football League with lunch in the dining-bar here – good helpings of reasonably priced simple food, with plenty of tables and own serving-counter; main bar oval-shaped, with good choice of real ales including well kept Greene King Abbot *(Roger Huggins)*

N7
[382 Holloway Rd] *Old Kings Head*: Reasonably tastefully refurbished pub, friendly and popular, with well kept Ind Coope Burton, Taylor-Walkers and Youngs, bar billiards, CD juke box, fruit machines and trivia, loud music Fri and Sat evenings; food filling but not cheap *(M B Porter)*

[162 Tufnell Park Rd] *Tufnell Park Tavern*: Big roomy pub, efficient courteous staff, popular for lively jazz, especially on Sun for the Crouch End All Stars – Wally Fawkes, Ian Christie and, on piano, their founder this recommender *(Graham Tayar and others)*

N14
[Bourne Hill] *Woodman*: Very small and civilised one-bar Whitbreads pub with warm, friendly and lively atmosphere, well kept Flowers, almost the air of a rural retreat; tables in garden behind *(Hilary Robinson, Peter Maden)*

N16
[Stoke Newington High St] *Tanners Hall*: Well kept Bass, many guest beers, country wines, interesting lagers in superbly decorated pub; good collection of well oiled locals *(Angus Lindsay)*

N20
[Totteridge Village] *Orange Tree*: Spacious pub by duck pond, plush décor, separate restaurant *(LYM)*

[310 Oakleigh Rd N; A109] *York Arms*: Watneys-related real ales in bright, clean and friendly two-bar local with lunchtime snacks and nice atmosphere *(Robert Lester)*

N21

[121 Hoppers Rd] *Salisbury Arms*: Friendly staff, well kept Bass on handpump, good atmosphere, table d'hôte menu known as Salisbury Supper is excellent value; decent wine list *(J S B Vereker)*

NW1

[35 Chalk Farm Rd] *Lock*: Large downstairs bar with fruit machine, big cold food counter (also hot food), Bass and Charringtons IPA, back terrace and smaller first-floor front roof garden *(BB)*

[Marylebone Rd; in Baker St Underground Stn] *Moriarty's*: Underground station bar with well kept Websters Yorkshire; very plain, slightly down-at-heel decorations; some Holmesian paraphernalia including prints and photographs; may not seem at its best on a quiet afternoon or early evening *(K A Topping, Michael Bechley)*

[Princes Rd] *Prince Albert*: Friendly, well run local, generous helpings of food, conservatory, well kept garden *(LYM)*

[49 Regent's Park Rd] *Queens*: Lots of mirrors downstairs, Victorian prints, stuffed birds, pictures of local personalities such as actor Robert Stephens, friendly staff, good view over Primrose Hill from balcony bar, decent food – the hot dishes are good value; stained glass in windows and outside lights; quietish clientele *(Peter Griffiths)*

[Marylebone Stn] *Victoria & Albert*: Huge range of real ales, wide choice of whiskies, attractively set out sandwiches in chill cabinet; immaculately kept plush chairs, reasonable prices *(Michael Bechley)*

[245 Baker St; by Regent's Park] *Volunteer*: Plush and black-panelled, popular with tourists, bar food, also restaurant and wine bar (good house wine); close to Regent's Park; pleasant ambience *(LYM)*

[Parkway] *Spread Eagle*: Good Youngs pub, well kept real ales and pleasant atmosphere *(Marshall Jones)*

NW3

[99 Heath St] *Coach & Horses*: Recently refurbished, with wooden floors, good lighting, beer garden and separate games-room; real ale *(Jonathan Warner)*

[14 Flask Walk] *Flask*: Attractively placed, snug Hampstead local, popular with actors and artists for 300 years – Pope, Steele and the Kit-Kat Club used to meet here; well kept Youngs, good value home-cooked food, village-pub atmosphere, no machines *(Miss K Haydon, Stephen Black, Michelle Davidson, BB)*

☆ [32 Downshire Hill] *Freemasons Arms*: Spacious garden right by Hampstead Heath with good arrangements for serving food and drink outside; skittle alley (one of only three in London) and unique lawn billiards court; cane-look chairs around well spaced tables in airy inner lounge, usually plenty of room in other bars too; well kept Bass and Charrington IPA; food seven days a week including good choice of pies and quiches with salads, attractive steak and kidney pie *(Michael and Alison Sandy, LYM)*

[79 Heath St] *Nags Head*: Very good choice of well kept real ales with for example Greene King Abbot as well as McMullens in refurbished open-plan bar; nice and peaceful on weekday lunchtimes, with real home-made soup and good salt beef, ham or cheese sandwiches, very friendly staff; very popular with younger people in the evening *(Leo and Pam Cohen, Jonathan Warner)*

[North End Way] *Old Bull & Bush*: Lively pub on traffic-busy hill, interesting history – and the home of that famous song *(LYM)*

[Rosslyn Hill] *Rosslyn Arms*: Maintains down-to-earth atmosphere though in a trendy area – used by working men; well kept Courage Best and Directors, friendly atmosphere *(G F Scott)*

[30 Well Walk] *Wells*: Comfortable, friendly and well kept Hampstead local *(Gil Johnson)*

NW5

[33 Dartmouth Park Hill] *Lord Palmerston*: Clean and tidy local, flowers on each table, good value doorstep sandwiches with weekday lunchtime hot food, licensees work hard raising funds for guide dogs and Gt Ormond St Children's Hospital *(Stuart Smith)*

NW8

[11 Alma Sq; off Hill Rd] *Heroes of Alma*: Good value freshly cooked food and well kept Watneys real ales in friendly little Victorian pub with tables outside *(LYM)*

[St John's Wood Rd] *Lords Tavern*: Good food counter and well kept real ales in attractively mocked-up pubby interior, tables outside *(BB)*

[2 Allitsen Rd; on corner of Townsend Rd] *New*: Really good value lunchtime food such as salads, fish and chips and cheap steak, in clean well kept pub with John Smiths and other beers; not too crowded, no juke box *(K Rooney)*

[29 Ordnance Hill] *Ordnance Arms*: Notable for massive helpings of really good fish and chips on Fri and Sat nights; lots of military paraphernalia including design drawings of guns and cannons, part of a heavy machine-gun; some leather Chesterfields, well kept Bass and Charrington IPA, modern conservatory area and terrace behind; loudish piped pop music *(Lyn and Bill Capper, LYM)*

☆ [23 Queens Grove] *Rossetti*: Good range of reasonably priced hot and cold lunchtime food including daily hot specials; open staircase up to cocktail bar and restaurant with mainly Italian food, no piped music or fruit machines, well kept reasonably priced Fullers London Pride and ESB; friendly service, food well priced for London; open noon–3, 7–12 *(Lyn and Bill Capper, Richard Sanders)*

BARNET
[133 East Barnet Rd] *Alexandra*: Tasty well priced hot and cold food, including good sandwiches, baps and ploughman's *(Mrs Rosemary Cunliffe)*
[Barnet Rd (A411); nr Hendon Wood Lane] *Gate at Arkley*: Civilised and well run pub with comfortable seats, good log fire in winter and lovely secluded garden for summer; good choice of food from sandwiches to hot dishes, and a better choice of whiskies than usual around London *(A J Silman, BB)*
[High St] *Mitre*: Friendly and unspoilt small-roomed friendly tavern with Dickens connections, well kept Benskins, Ind Coope Burton and Tetleys; usually remarkably uncrowded; food from roast to bread-and-butter pudding *(David Fowles, LYM)*
[193 High St] *Monken Holt*: Good home-cooked food and well kept Courage Best and Directors, pleasing olde-worlde interior; handy for Hadley Wood Common *(D S Fowles)*

EDGWARE
[Glengall Rd] *Sparrowhawk*: Lively two-bar pub with Whitbreads Castle Eden on handpump; private bar for functions and discos *(Robert Lester)*

ENFIELD
[179 Hertford Rd; Enfield Highway] *Black Horse*: Large and imposing single-bar Chef & Brewer set back from main road, with sandwiches as well as other food, Watneys-related real ales, live music and family entertainment, seafood stall on forecourt *(Robert Lester)*
[19 Chase Side Pl; off Chase Side] *Cricketers*: Much rebuilt and extended former cottage-style pub with comfortable lounge and basic public bar, lots of cricket ties above counter and other cricket memorabilia; McMullens on handpump *(Robert Lester)*
[Gentlemans Row] *Crown & Horseshoes*: Pleasant atmosphere in pub in attractive area next to canal with lots of ducks – big garden very popular on good summer days; extensive choice of bar food, helpful staff *(Helen Crookston)*
[320 Baker St; by rly stn] *Enfield Stores*: Watneys-related real ales in smart and lively one-bar pub; juke box may be rather loud *(Robert Lester)*
[5 The Town] *George*: Much-modified former coaching-inn with mock-Elizabethan black and white frontage – passage to back bar used to be the coach entry; Bass and Charrington IPA on handpump; good Toby grill-restaurant upstairs *(Robert Lester)*
[Market Pl (A110)] *Kings Head*: Fine 1898

building by Shoebridge & Rising, with original etched glass and ornate woodwork, Ind Coope Burton, Taylor-Walker and Tetleys on handpump; busy, particularly on Thurs–Sat market days *(Robert Lester)*
[Chase Side] *Moon Underwater*: Very plush recently opened free house with splendid range of well kept real ales such as Brains, Greene King Abbot, Marstons Pedigree, Wadworths 6X and Youngers IPA *(Robert Lester)*
[253 Southbury Rd; A110 just W of junction with A10] *Southbury*: Fine example of 1930s brewers' Tudor; large lively locals' bar, comfortable saloon, separate lounge, meals served until 10pm; opposite Enfield FC *(Robert Lester)*
[165 High St; A1010 Hertford Rd] *White Hart*: Imposing main-road pub with good public bar, old-style advertising mirrors in comfortable lounge, Ind Coope Burton and Taylor Walker on handpump; upstairs club-room for functions *(Robert Lester)*

HARROW
[West St] *Castle*: Pleasant in early evening (and popular then with couples), nice garden with talkative caged birds *(Denis Waters)*

HARROW WEALD
[Brookshill] *Hare*: Particularly good value bar lunches including fine open sandwiches, ploughman's and imaginative hot dishes, quickly and pleasantly served; comfortable bar with good atmosphere, nice garden; doing well under present management *(H W Wilson)*

NEW BARNET
[Albert Rd] *Builders Arms*: Good atmosphere in lounge of pleasant local – a rare Greene King tied house *(D S Fowles)*

PINNER
[High St] *Queens Head*: Attractive timbered building, well kept Benskins and Ind Coope Burton, friendly service, no piped music – just the pleasant murmur of conversation; fairly busy Sun lunchtime *(S C Collett-Jones, M C Howells)*

SOUTH

SE1
[Upper Ground; by Blackfriars Bridge] *Doggetts Coat & Badge*: Particularly good range of well kept beers such as Arkells, Boddingtons and Wadworths 6X in three-level modern pub; nice atmosphere with good service even when crowded at lunchtime, extensive range of food at a price – some tables reserved for diners; handy for South Bank arts complex *(R Houghton, BB)*
[Bankside] *Founders Arms*: Notable for the almost unobstructed view over the Thames of St Paul's, from the spacious glass-walled

modern bar and the big waterside terrace; Youngs Bitter and Special on handpump, green plush banquettes, elbow-rest screens; straightforward *(LYM, Nick Dowson)*

[47 Borough Rd] *Goose & Firkin*: Back-to-basics with bare boards, lots of tables and stools, high- backed benches at the tables around the sides; good cheapish popular food, mix of local businessmen, office types, South Bank Poly students from across road; no pretensions, but clean, tidy and friendly-feeling; Goose and Dogbolter on handpump, with guest such as Old Peculier; home-brew Dogbolter kits for sale *(Michael and Alison Sandy)*

☆ [5 Mepham St] *Hole in the Wall*: Immortalised by the Bonzo Dog Doo Dah Band, and a real London institution for many people; good choice of real ales; fine location, with Waterloo suburban trains shaking its railway-arch ceiling; somewhere to see the full range of society from City gents down; reasonably priced food; atmospheric *(David Fowles, R Houghton, Alan Skull, LYM)*

[320 Old Kent Rd] *St Thomas a' Becket*: Very lively atmosphere in young people's pub with heavily emphasised boxing theme – from motif on carpet to boxing-ring stage for live bands (Henry Cooper, John Conteh, Alan Minter, Terry Downes have all used its upstairs gym); large ex-boxing bouncers make sure there's no trouble so this is by far the safest place along the Old Kent Rd to drink *(Tim Powell)*

SE3

[1a Eliot Cottages] *Hare & Billet*: Nicely placed opposite pond, lovely views to south and east; refurbished by Whitbreads, with shelf of usual semi-antique props and old local photographs; Whitbreads-related and guest real ales, food such as ploughman's, sausage and mash, turkey and ham pie, beef stew, meat salads *(Anon)*

SE5

[149 Denmark Hill] *Fox on the Hill*: Newly refurbished, with good value well presented food in Toby Grill, polite service, good pub atmosphere; decent wines at fair prices, big car park *(E G Parish)*

SE9

[86 Eltham High St (opposite McDonald's)] *Greyhound*: Very big helpings of exceptionally good value food such as turkey and ham pie; nice atmosphere *(Neil Barker)*

SE10

[Lassell St] *Cutty Sark*: Attractive white-painted pub overlooking river to Docklands, with big upper bow window jettied out over the road – dates back nearly 300 years; long wooden bar counter, rough brick walls, wooden settles, barrel tables, big central

wooden staircase, narrow opening to tiny side rooms, low lighting; big food area serving omelettes, steak and kidney pie and so forth; small upstairs restaurant; jazz some nights, occasional morris men *(Alan Franck and others)*

[56 Royal Hill] *Fox & Hounds*: Very welcoming and friendly local with old photographs of the area, stuffed fox, heroic Victorian fireman picture over mantelpiece, Vanity Fair prints in back bar; simple bar food, real ale *(Anon)*

[19 Park Vista] *Plume of Feathers*: Dimly lit front bar with cosy winter fire, tables under two shady trees in enclosed back garden, benches in side yard and under front awnings; barbecues Mon; very efficient food area with large slices of gammon and egg, rolls and sandwiches *(Ian Phillips)*

[52 Royal Hill] *Richard 1*: Friendly and unpretentious South London pub with handsome deep bay windows and echoing boarded floor, sound local reputation for very well kept Youngs and good company; no music or gimmicks, serviceable old tables in yard; tasty cheese and onion rolls on Saturday; cheerful Cockney landlord *(Robert Gomme and others)*

[Park Row] *Trafalgar*: Panoramic Thames views from unusual wood-floored free house with pianola, model ship built into window, Ruddles, reasonably priced restaurant, jazz on Thurs and antique fairs upstairs *(M J Masters)*

[Crane St] *Yacht*: Refitted with light wood panelling and portholes instead of windows, photographs of famous yachts, quite cosy patterned grey banquettes and stools on the patterned red carpet, oval central bar; spacious conservatory-like upper room opening on to terrace overlooking river; decent open sandwiches, ploughman's, soup, chilli and so forth from food counter *(Heather Sharland and others)*

SE13

☆ [316 Lewisham High St] *Fox & Firkin*: Spacious and popular, no frills, good beer brewed here and well kept guest beers, straightforward good value food including big baps with any two of four meats; parking may be difficult *(Peter Griffiths, LYM and others)*

SE16

[117 Rotherhithe St] *Mayflower*: Carefully restored, atmospheric 18th-century pub with old-fashioned main bar and side room recalling days when Pilgrim Fathers' ship sailed from here in 1611; well kept Bass and Charrington IPA, bar food (not Sat lunchtime or Sun evening), upstairs evening restaurant and wooden jetty overhanging Thames; only English pub licensed to sell UK and US postage stamps *(Roger Huggins, Tom McLean, Ewan McCall, LYM)*

☆ [118 Lower Rd] *Prince of Orange*: Different jazz acts each night and weekend lunchtimes, with simple but good value food (especially pizzas), several Watneys-related real ales, fine collection of jazz photographs in one of the two smaller rooms off the main simply furnished bar; children allowed in eating area; open evening, and Sun lunchtime *(LYM)*

SE17

[Sutherland Sq] *Beehive*: A real locals' local, with good beer in friendly surroundings and splendid Sat hot beef sandwiches *(Anon)*

SE18

[Shooters Hill] *Bull*: Well kept Courage on handpump, friendly staff, very good value food, garden *(P Gillbe)*

[15 Thomas St] *Earl of Chatham*: Simple cheap food, excellent quick service even when busy, cheerful mixed clientele; refurbished inside, conservatory and terrace *(J B Simpson)*

SE19

[262 Beulah Hill] *Conquering Hero*: Good, busy Courage pub, customers range from football teams to OAPs, solicitors to plumbers; small selection of food *(Michele and Andrew Wells)*

[Anerley Hill] *Paxton Arms*: Attractively and elaborately refurbished by Allied, with old sporting prints in nicely painted and carpeted two front bars, and mementoes of Crystal Palace, old advertisements and ornaments and head-height books in back bar; popular local; good example of refurbishment improving rather than ruining the atmosphere *(Andrew and Michele Wells)*

[West Hill] *Royal Albert*: Small and unpretentious, with very congenial and spacious back lounge bar, well furnished including antiques; more than 300 jugs of varying sizes and ages hang from the beams; warm and friendly *(Michele and Andrew Wells)*

SE20

[Ridsdale Rd] *Anerley Arms*: Well kept and reasonably priced Sam Smiths OB and good value sandwiches and snacks in very comfortably refurbished pub with interesting posters and very friendly staff; on site of old Anerley Tavern and by rustic little station – both part of the old Pleasure Gardens *(Ian Phillips)*

SE21

[Park Hall Rd] *Alleyns Head*: Currently doing particularly well, with very good value, popular food including evening carvery, willing service and good pub atmosphere *(E G Parish)*

☆ [73 Dulwich Village] *Crown & Greyhound*: The most popular pub in the area with many readers, though it can get crowded; good cider as well as well kept Benskins served, décor has considerable character, and the big back garden, surrounded by beautiful mature trees, is a splendid feature in summer; restaurant food very good and not overpriced *(Alan Franck, Peter Griffiths, Michele and Andrew Wells and others)*

SE22

[522 Lordship Lane] *Grove*: The Harvester dining side has become very popular for lunches and dinners, and is open all day on Sun; very reasonable prices *(E G Parish)*

SE23

[Sydenham Hill] *Woodhouse*: Very pleasant Youngs pub, consistently good food *(Anon)*

SE25

[corner Albert Rd/Harrington Rd] *Albert*: Busy pub with strong cricketing traditions, pool, darts, well kept Courage Best and Directors and Youngs Special, friendly service by Don and Binny – a typical Gaelic pair *(R D Osmond)*

SE26

[39 Sydenham Hill] *Dulwich Wood House*: Comfortably refurbished suburban pub, with full range of Youngs real ales kept well, polite efficient service, good value food *(E G Parish)*

SW4

[Clapham High St] *La Rueda*: Very friendly welcoming licensee, 30 delicious inexpensive tapas, seats at bar (bottled San Miguel is the only beer – wine's the main thing, with bottles racked across the ceiling), exceptionally friendly atmosphere; restaurant next door *(Peter Griffiths)*

SW11

[60 Battersea High St] *Woodman*: Not to be confused with the original Woodman next door, this busy pub has lots of prints and a stag's head in its little panelled front bar, with a long Turkey-carpeted room decorated with dried flowers, baskets, a boar's head and even an aged wheelbarrow; there are brocaded stools and chairs, some big casks, and log-effect gas fires; well kept Badger Best and Tanglefoot and Wadworths 6X on handpump; bar billiards, darts and trivia machine at one end, picnic-table sets on raised terrace with barbecue area *(RAB, Richard Gibbs)*

SW12

[39 Balham High Rd] *Duke of Devonshire*: Large Victorian pub with magnificent glasswork, refurbished in typical Youngs style, with well kept Youngs beers on handpump *(David Fisher)*

[97 Nightingale Lane] *Nightingale*: Very

popular local, friendly prompt service, well kept Youngs *(C J Parsons)*

SW13
[2 Castelnau] *Red Lion*: Large restored pub with three connecting rooms – back one used mostly as a restaurant; decent reasonably priced bar food including vegetarian lasagne *(Richard Sanders)*

SW14
[Ship Lane] *Ship*: Pleasant Thames towpath pub with nautical décor, garden, Watneys-related real ales *(Anon)*
[West Temple Sheen] *Victoria*: Large and useful conservatory extension, yet place still retains its pubbiness; increasingly popular for good value food *(J P Berryman)*

SW15
[32 Waterman St; down cul-de-sac off Lower Richmond Rd nr Putney Bridge] *Bricklayers Arms*: Basic typical London pub, apparently unchanged for decades though now one bar with bare boards one side, carpet the other; staff bright and pleasant; Trumans on handpump (rare these days) *(Anon)*
[8 Lower Richmond Rd] *Dukes Head*: Good atmosphere, super position, and more effort now going into food, with good freshly cooked choice at lunchtime; better managed than before *(Doug Kennedy)*
[Wildcroft Rd] *Green Man*: On the edge of Putney Heath and always popular for that; cosy main bar, quiet sitting-room, friendly atmosphere, well kept Youngs Bitter and Special; has had good value simple bar food and quite elaborate barbecues in the pretty, sheltered garden (which has a play area) *(Doug Kennedy, Richard Houghton, LYM – reports on new regime please)*
[93 Lower Richmond Rd] *Half Moon*: Solid Youngs pub with spacious saloon and good beer; a particular attraction is the consistent programme of live folk, blues and rock music *(David Fowles)*

SW16
☆ [151 Greyhound Lane] *Greyhound*: Very pleasant high-ceilinged main bar with plenty of seats, though it and the adjacent extended, air-conditioned conservatory can get crowded; brewing visible from bar – Pedigree (Mild), Special, Strong and Dynamite; bar food includes good choice of generous ploughman's and popular Sun carvery/barbecue including swordfish and shark; nicely mixed clientele, a lot of youth some evenings *(Peter Griffiths, Hank Hotchkiss, Alan Skull, Nick Dowson)*
[498 Streatham High Rd] *Pied Bull*: Enormous Youngs pub overlooking Streatham Common *(David Fisher)*
[Streatham High Rd] *White Lion*: Rugged, slightly down-at-heel old coaching-inn with many attractive decorative features: dark wood, William Morrisish wallpaper, mirrors; doors taken off to connect bars but still a tiny snug; pews and high-stooled circular tables; seafood, cheese and onion snacks free Sun lunchtime; games machines, loud juke box *(Anon)*

SW18
[345 Trinity Rd] *County Arms*: Good Victorian décor, generally friendly service, good value filled rolls and other bar snacks; relaxed at weekday lunchtimes; crowded weekends; public grass area outside by dual carriageway is nice when it's sunny; well kept Youngs real ales *(Anon)*
[Wandsworth High St] *Kings Arms*: Characteristic Youngs pub, brown in and out, popular lunchtime and decent local; besides Youngs Ordinary and Special they have bottled Winter Warmer *(Anon)*

SW19
[Camp Rd] *Fox & Grapes*: Well run and spacious pub, with huge beams in high ceiling of main bar, dark wooden furniture on patterned carpet; friendly staff; good choice of fresh-cooked food, with big ploughman's and enjoyable seafood surprise; well kept Courage; not at its best on a Sat evening *(Doug Kennedy, Howard Pursey, Peter Griffiths)*
[6 Crooked Billet] *Hand in Hand*: Pretty and ancient exterior with outside tables on the grass, U-shaped bar, useful family-room; well kept Youngs real ales, Beamish stout; good ploughman's at a price; popular with students *(Peter Griffiths and others)*
[55 Wimbledon High St] *Rose & Crown*: Comfortably modernised Youngs pub, formerly a coaching-inn, with tables in former coachyard; well kept real ales on handpump, open fires, set of Hogarth's proverb engravings, green plush seats in alcoves, food from buttery; mixed clientele *(LYM and others)*

BECKENHAM
[Chancery Lane] *Jolly Woodman*: Small and friendly place with cheap beer, seats out in nice cosy garden; popular with older people *(SJM)*

BEXLEY
[Black Prince Interchange, Southwold Rd (A2)] *Black Prince*: Part of a hotel complex, but maintains reliably good standard of bar meals and service, with helpful bar staff; well kept Bass and Charrington IPA on handpump; bedrooms *(E G Parish)*

CARSHALTON
[High St] *Coach & Horses*: Very friendly local, good licensees, well kept Charrington, upstairs restaurant *(Roger Entwistle)*

– tea too *(E G Parish)*

CHISLEHURST

[Royal Parade] *Bulls Head*: Well kept Youngs and generous helpings of good reasonably priced bar food including a wide range of substantial individually prepared sandwiches as well as shepherd's pie, curries and so forth, in three large and comfortable bars; pleasant staff, restaurant *(Mea Horler)*
[just off Bickley Park Rd and Old Hill, by Summer Hill] *Ramblers Rest*: Most attractive tiled and weatherboarded cottage in excellent location by common, old-fashioned on right with big open-plan extension on lower level on left, Courage ale, food from noon; a couple of seats in front; said to have been built 1684 *(Ian Phillips)*

COULSDON

[Old Coulsdon] *Tudor Rose*: Spacious mock-medieval suburban pub with well kept Bass and Charrington IPA *(BB)*

CROYDON

[Laud St] *Bulls Head*: Very comfortable, in quiet area yet close to centre *(Neil Barker)*
[Southbridge Pl] *Cricketers Arms*: Attractive inside and out, unobtrusive piped music, simple good food, immaculately kept *(Ann and David Stranack)*
[Morland Rd] *Joiners Arms*: Dimly lit pub with lots of character and brass everywhere; well kept Allied-related beers, excellent doorstep steak sandwiches and other food on sensibly limited good menu; friendly and beautifully maintained, with tables in pretty little creeper-clad courtyard *(Ian Phillips)*
[Olde Market] *Le Refuge*: Wine bar really with the feel of a pub – especially at weekends, when it may have loud music and get packed with young people; good atmosphere, low ceilings, King & Barnes and Youngs Bitter and Special *(Alasdair Knowles)*

CUDHAM

[Cudham Lane] *Blacksmiths Arms*: Fine atmosphere in very popular country pub with summer barbecues in very pleasant garden, good reasonably priced food from ploughman's to steaks, well kept Courage beers *(Nick Dowson, Alison Hayward)*

DOWNE

[High St] *George & Dragon*: Cosy and recently refurbished in countrified style, with stuffed animals, rural pictures and so forth – done quite well, two bars instead of three; well kept and for the area relatively cheap Charrington IPA, good food; nice spot in small village; popular with walkers *(R J and F J Ambroziak, E G Parish, Dave Braisted)*
[High St] *Queens Head*: Homely and welcoming, with three compact lounges and separate children's room; good bar meals at reasonable cost, all week, and Friary Meux and Ind Coope Burton on handpump

KESTON

[Commonside] *Greyhound*: Spacious Courage pub with very good value bar food (especially hot-pot), Courage real ales, very friendly service, big garden with occasional barbecues and children's play area; handy for walks on common and in woods *(E G Parish)*

KEW

[Pond Corner] *Greyhound*: Very friendly small pub with comfortable settles, photographs of old Kew, red ceiling, reasonably priced food including good omelettes *(Ian Phillips)*
[Sandycombe Rd; close to tube stn] *Kew Gardens*: Pleasant atmosphere, good choice of ale, huge helpings of food including delicious Cheddar ploughman's and pate; roomy, attractive and relaxing *(Stephen R Holman)*

KINGSTON

[Tudor Rd] *Alexandra*: Straightforward, comfortable corner local with a few seats outside, coal-effect gas fire, some simple lunchtime food such as chilli con carne, Watneys-related real ale *(Anon)*
[Eden St] *Applemarket*: Remarkably large inside, with sage green banquettes and scattering of tables and chairs; pleasant swift service, congenial atmosphere, well kept real ale and good value simple food from sandwiches through ham and eggs to gammon or steak – prices kept down as this is the market traders' pub; loudish piped music; nearby parking difficult *(R Houghton, Ian Phillips)*
[2 Bishops Hall; off Thames St – down alley behind W H Smiths] *Bishop out of Residence*: Semi-circular bar facing river, Edwardian-style wallpaper, Coronation curtains; modern, but well kitted out to take advantage of Thames and bridge views; well kept Youngs real ales, good value bar food including sandwiches, ploughman's and hot dishes such as chilli or plaice segments; tables on terrace; handy for central Kingston *(Ian Phillips, Jenny and Brian Seller, A M Kelly)*
☆ [Canbury Gdns; Lower Ham Rd] *Boaters*: Excellent river views from recently refurbished pub with comfortable banquettes inside and floodlit tables in garden, real ales including Courage Directors, John Smiths and guests such as Wadworths 6X; permission granted for this development only on condition that it would continue to provide teas, ice creams and so forth for the people using the gardens *(Ian Phillips)*
[88 London Rd; corner Albert Rd] *Flamingo Brewery*: Large Edwardian corner pub recently taken over by Clifton Inns; bare boards, back room dominated by enormous brass chandelier, many tables around edges,

snugs and corners but lots of standing room too; three good real ales brewed on the premises, with guest beer; good value bar food including pitta and hummus, ploughman's, salads and several hot dishes such as steak and kidney pie; children in family-room with adventure playground and view into brewery *(Ian Phillips, R Houghton)*

[Portsmouth Rd] *Harts Boatyard:* Vast inside, with seven or eight dinghies tiered above bar area, place thick with all sorts of boating paraphernalia – even seats in the form of Peggoty-type upturned boats; external appearance would suggest a newly built weatherboarded place based loosely on tradition of Edwardian boat-builder's, but parts of the original building do survive – notably in the cellar; balconies overlooking Thames and Hampton Court grounds, upstairs Beefeater steakhouse; bags of character, varied seating in lots of nooks and crannies, lunchtime bar food, Flowers IPA on handpump *(Ian Phillips)*

[Fairfield Rd Sth; corner Villiers Rd] *Newt & Ferret:* Comfortable and friendly, with cases of decorative corks, cellar gear and so forth; well kept Badger Best, Tanglefoot and Old Timer, sandwiches and hot dishes such as liver and bacon, beef hot-pot and steak and kidney pie served by friendly staff and landlord *(Ian Phillips, R Houghton)*

LEAVES GREEN
Crown: Large and comfortable recently modernised bar, with well kept Shepherd Neame beers and large helpings of good food; tables and summer barbecues in garden; a favourite with local businessmen; children's room *(R J and F J Ambroziak)*

MITCHAM
[Mitcham Common] *Ravensbourne Arms:* Inter-war roadhouse improved a lot in recent years, good value help-yourself buffet at one end of U-shaped bar area, friendly staff, very popular summer Sundays with small side garden *(Anon)*

NEW MALDEN
[Coombe Rd] *Royal Oak:* Consistently good atmosphere, plenty of seating including one or two secluded areas in dining part; public bar with darts, excellent food, not overpriced considering quantity and quality, and well kept Benskins; car park not large *(Paul Sexton, Sue Harrison, G T Rhys, Paul Finan)*

RICHMOND
[5 Church Court; alley by Owen Owen] *Angel & Crown:* Old building down narrow alley, good atmosphere, well kept Fullers, sturdy and substantial pub food such as Lancs hot-pot, chilli, steak and kidney casserole *(David Fowles)*

[Upper Ham Rd] *Hand & Flower:* Watneys pub with spacious and comfortable lounge leading to lower floor levels with snugs and eating area with coal-effect gas fire and china on walls, smart tiled verandah with lots of foliage; piped pop music; public bar with mynah bird, beams festooned with soccer programmes *(Ian Phillips)*

[345 Petersham Rd; Ham Common] *New:* Comfortable brocaded banquettes and stools, log-effect gas fire in dining area, usual machines, Watneys-related real ale; friendly atmosphere and nice situation on Ham Common; good choice of main dishes in evening; very popular weekend lunchtimes; cosy in winter, comfortable and civilised *(Ian Phillips, Jenny and Brian Seller, Doug Kennedy, J P Berryman, P Gillbe)*

[130 Richmond Hill] *Roebuck:* Outstanding views from the wide sash windows of its two panelled front parlours, which are furnished with pine chairs and tables and brocaded banquettes; two intimate snug back areas with big fireplaces, discreet games machines, Youngers real ale; bar food from hot beef sandwiches and ploughman's to salads and steak and potato pie or moussaka *(Ian Phillips)*

[Petersham Rd] *Rose of York:* Vast place with oak panelling, pew-like stalls and softly lit cubby holes, discreet alcove for darts and pool, well kept Sam Smiths OB, food lunchtime and evening, with good Sun lunches; large garden, pleasant location – especially in summer *(Ian Phillips, Doug Kennedy, Michael Bolam)*

☆ [Cholmondeley Walk; riverside] *White Cross:* Still good despite its very popular position by the river; deep bay windows overlook Thames and Richmond Bridge, with large table in each and banquettes all round the window; as seats are quite close the ensuing contact makes for conviviality; reasonably priced lunchtime bar food, with overflow to upstairs dining room; well kept Youngs, friendly service *(Prof S Barnett, Ian Phillips, P Gillbe, S C Collett-Jones, Doug Kennedy)*

SIDCUP
[64 Blackfen Rd] *Jolly Fenman:* Produces own good Fenman Bitter and barley wine-like Explosive, though linked to Watneys; reasonable food *(Dave Braisted)*

[North Cray Rd] *White Cross:* Very good service, friendly, excellent food, well kept Courage *(P Gillbe)*

ST MARY CRAY
[Wellington Rd] *Beech Tree:* Considerable effort put into varied interesting bar food including sandwiches; Whitbreads-related real ale, warm atmosphere, unobtrusive piped jazz *(James Leigh)*

[Sevenoaks Way] *Broomwood:* Attractive bar food and reasonable prices, cheerful friendly staff, good atmosphere *(J S Quantill, J E Hillier)*

SURBITON
[1 Ewell Rd] *Railway*: Wide choice of consistently good real ales, fine bar service; children have good facilities indoors *(Roy Goldsmith)*

[Victoria Rd] *Victoria*: Huge U-shaped bar with two coal-effect gas fires, comfortable banquettes and stools in lots of nooks and crannies, and real local feel in evening – without being unfriendly; what was presumably the billiards hall is now used at lunchtime primarily for food; Youngs beers *(Ian Phillips, D J Cargill)*

THORNTON HEATH
[Pawsons Rd] *Lion*: Wide range of well kept ales such as Adnams, Everards Tiger, King & Barnes Mild, Bitter and Festive and Youngs Special, lots of bottled beers, good food served throughout the day, friendly well organised staff and a splendid mix of customers from solicitors to brickies' mates *(R D Osmond)*

[Bensham Gr; corner Beulah Rd] *Lord Napier*: Characteristic corner Youngs pub with well kept real ales, congenial landlord, large and popular jazz room opening straight off bar *(Peter Griffiths)*

WEST WICKHAM
[Pickhurst Lane] *Pickhurst*: Busy suburban pub popular for tasty well presented food (not cheap) lunch and evening, especially in spring and summer; two very big rooms very comfortably furnished with some deep armchairs; polite service; can get crowded in the evening, when it's necessary to book ahead for the restaurant *(E G Parish and others)*

WEST

SW6
[235 New King's Road] *Duke of Cumberland*: Big lavishly restored Edwardian lounge bar opposite Parsons Green; cheerful at weekend lunchtimes, relaxed for weekday lunchtime food *(GRE, AE)*

[577 King's Rd], *Imperial Arms*: Spacious, welcoming and scrupulously clean, Watneys-related real ales and good coffee including home-made biscuits; imaginative food includes tasty bangers and mash, liver and bacon, fresh fish including oysters in season, particularly good steaks; vegetables are fresh *(Conrad Russell, JBM)*

SW7
[127 Gloucester Rd; opp Hereford Sq] *Hereford Arms*: Good range of beers including Charles Wells Bombardier and Huntsman Royal Oak, Antipodean staff – very popular with Australians in the evening; at Christmastime may have a wandering minstrel *(Nick Dowson, Alison Hayward)*

[44 Montpelier Sq] *King George IV*: Considerate largely Australian staff, comfortable seats inside, a few picnic-table sets out, attractive prints; well kept Flowers, competitively priced food including excellent sandwiches, ploughman's, filled baked potatoes, quiche, beef or ham salad *(Liz and Ian Phillips)*

[Ashburn Place; in Gloucester Hotel, 4 Harrington Gdns] *Merrie Go Down*: A few real ales in uncrowded, slightly down-at-heel place *(Nick Dowson, Alison Hayward)*

[30 Queens Gate Mews] *Queens Arms*: Victorian pub with period furniture, heavy plush seating, massive mahogany bookcases, lithographs (including two of the nearby Albert Hall) and brass footrail round bar; Charrington IPA on handpump *(Gwen and Peter Andrews)*

W4
[72 Strand on the Green] *Bell & Crown*: Traditional riverside pub with lots of atmosphere, well kept Fullers Chiswick, ESB and London Pride; rather long and narrow, with conservatory behind and waterside terrace; large selection of cheap sandwiches; friendly customers *(Simon Collett-Jones, BKA)*

[15 Strand on the Green] *Bulls Head*: Little rambling rooms with black-panelled alcoves, simple traditional furnishings, well kept Watneys-related ales on handpump, reasonably priced lunchtime food from no-smoking food bar lunchtimes and Thurs–Sat evenings; back games-bar; right on Thames, with picnic-table sets by river; children allowed in Perspex-roofed back courtyard area *(S C Collett-Jones, LYM)*

[corner Chiswick Lane S and Gt West Rd, by Fullers Brewery] *Mawson Arms*: Excellent Fullers ales and really friendly staff; good parking facilities, not far from start of M4 *(Richard Houghton)*

[145 Chiswick High Rd] *Packhorse & Talbot*: Excellent choice of beers such as Brakspears, Everards Tiger and Felinfoel Double Dragon, with cheaper special; lunchtime food; very popular local in the evenings when it can get smoky; Weds folk club *(Doug Kennedy)*

W5
[Hanger Lane] *Fox & Goose*: Large pre-war pub with small public bar, spacious lounge divided into three areas, and conservatory; well kept Fullers London Pride and ESB, food served from separate counter *(Richard Sanders)*

[Elm Grove Rd; by Warwick Dene] *Grange*: Well kept Watneys-related real ales, very popular for good Sun roast lunch, tables on terrace behind, fairly slick service; cosy and comfortable, with pleasing décor in four drinking areas including small lounge, bar,

bigger lounge on higher level and conservatory with own bar (leading to garden) *(Simon Collett-Jones)*
[33 Haven Lane] *Haven*: Lovely rambling old pub with reliably good food at fair prices in conservatory buffet; friendly service, well kept Watneys-related real ales *(Simon Collett-Jones, P J and S A Barrett)*

W6

☆ [2 South Black Lion Lane] *Black Lion*: Very comfortable and cosy, with friendly, efficient staff, nice oil of A P Herbert over fireplace, photographs of Thames barges, tie collection over bar and so forth; excellent doorstep sandwiches, also hot dishes including good value curries Weds evening; healthy mix of customers, easy atmosphere, popular with families for Sun roast beef; Watneys-related beers *(Denis Waters, Ian Phillips, Simon Collett-Jones)*
[Lower Mall] *Blue Anchor*: Excellent riverside position, Courage real ales *(RCL)*
[57 Black Lion Lane] *Cross Keys*: Well kept simple local with good friendly atmosphere, not far from Thames *(BB)*
[13 Brook Green] *Queens Head*: Pleasantly placed off the Shepherds Bush Road, modernised but comfortable, decently kept beer, tasty and unusual Sun bar nibbles; piped music; can be fairly busy *(S C Collett-Jones, Alison Hayward, Nick Dowson)*
[15 Lower Mall] *Rutland Ale House*: Comfortable, cheery and efficient, with carefully cultivated layer of 'designer dirt' – peeling paint, contrived 'damp' plaster, new 'old' bookcases and so forth, even a couple of old clinker sculling boats hanging from high rafters in front bar; plethora of bric-à-brac from stone bottles to aged lacrosse sticks, wide range of good food includes dishes cooked to order such as omelettes; Watneys-related real ale *(Ian Phillips, RCL)*

W7

[Green Lane, Hanwell] *Fox*: Pleasant and friendly traditional local in very quiet spot close to Grand Union Canal *(Neil Barker)*

W8

[1 Allen St; off Kensington High St] *Britannia*: Real haven of comfort and peace, good food, well kept Youngs *(Prof S Barnett)*
[9 Kensington Church St] *Churchill Arms*: Comfortable and friendly, unusual here for doing evening bar food; well kept Fullers London Pride *(Ian Phillips)*
[71 Palace Gdns Terr] *Gaiety*: Good pastiche of Edwardian pub with attractive posters, good range of food, comfortable well spaced seating; Whitbreads-related real ales *(Ian Phillips)*
[84 Earls Ct Rd] *Hansom Cab*: Opulently refurbished pub with the cosy feel suggested by its name *(Dr and Mrs A K Clarke)*
[Hillgate St] *Hillgate*: Two communicating

bars full of knick-knacks and pictures, lots of intriguing little nooks and corners, nicely mixed clientele, benches outside among lots of plants and greenery; wide range of lunchtime food such as generous sandwiches and salt beef and ham; Watneys-related real ales, separate disabled person's lavatory *(Peter Griffiths)*
[25 Earls Ct Rd] *Princess Victoria*: Pleasant place to drop into, clean, with a nice friendly atmosphere *(Dr and Mrs A K Clarke)*

☆ [23a Edwardes Sq] *Scarsdale Arms*: Now a Chef & Brewer, up-market pub of basic design, partly gas-lit, with bare floorboards, flowers and winter fires in spacious bar; Ruddles and Combes on handpump; smoky atmosphere; convenient for Odeon Kensington High St *(Nick Dowson, LYM)*
[13 Uxbridge St] *Uxbridge Arms*: Comfortable, cosy and almost romantically dimly lit, tucked away in smart streets just behind Notting Hill Gate – with local clientele to match; well kept real ales such as Adnams, Brakspears, Greene King Abbot; pleasant exterior with hanging baskets – an exciting architectural contrast with the high-rise flats around it; can be crowded in the evening, and parking may be a problem *(Peter Griffiths, John Tyzack, Nick Dowson, Alison Hayward)*

W9

[6 Warwick Pl] *Warwick Castle*: Plenty of character in unspoilt high-ceilinged Victorian pub, big old cast-iron fireplace, friendly service, seats on quiet pavement; Morrells as well as Charrington IPA on handpump, reasonably priced bar lunches *(Howard and Sue Gascoyne, LYM)*

W11

[41 Tavistock Cres] *Frog & Firkin*: Interesting beers brewed here and well kept guest beers, reasonable food including big baps, enjoyable down-to-earth atmosphere with weekend singalongs *(Patrick Young, Nick Dowson, Alison Hayward, LYM)*
[95 Portobello Rd] *Portobello Gold*: Good food *(Patrick Young)*

W14

[187 Greyhound Rd] *Colton Arms*: Pleasant village-pub-like atmosphere and well kept Websters Yorkshire; little garden with rose canopy, next to Queens Club tennis courts *(M K C Wills and others)*
[253 North End Rd] *Seven Stars*: Excellent lunches, well kept Fullers and friendly service in small local *(C J Parsons)*

BRENTFORD

[Catherine Wheel Rd] *Brewery Tap*: Good atmosphere and particularly well kept Fullers – prices lower than nearby competitors; under new management, end 1988 – more news please *(C E Owens and others)*

[Brook Rd] *Griffin*: Splendid Fullers local, handy for Brentford FC – with a very good matchday atmosphere and no feeling of unease *(Jon Wainwright)*

[3 High St] *O'Riordans*: Pleasant inside, with wide range of well kept beer which isn't too expensive for London, nice atmosphere; husband-and-wife team do good home-made food such as rolls oozing with salad, ham and eggs or scampi and chips; opposite organ and piano museum and steam museum, by riverside footpath to Kew Bridge; parking can be difficult as this is a busy main road *(Richard Houghton, Ian Phillips)*

White Horse: Comfortable furnishings in popular Charringtons pub with conservatory and seats outside; weekday home-cooked food *(Miss E Waller)*

EASTCOTE

[High Rd] *Case is Altered*: Well kept Benskins, quiet setting, seats outside – a useful pub to know in this area *(M C Howells)*

FELTHAM

[High St; corner of Browells Lane, opp Sainsburys] *Red Lion*: Straightforward Chef & Brewer, keeping old pub layout and atmosphere, with well kept Watneys-related real ales; handy for shopping; acceptable town local *(Anon)*

HAMPTON

[122 High St] *Dukes Head*: Ordinary Courage pub, one-piece lounge with reasonable home-made food; little yard with tables under cocktail parasols; handy for Bushy Park *(Anon)*

[99 Higher Hampton Hill] *Valiant Knight*: The enthusiastic couple who made this very popular have moved out to the Boat at Berkhamsted in Herts – more news please *(Anon)*

[70 High St] *White Hart*: Good range of well kept real ales, friendly service, atmosphere building up as evening progresses; seats out on terrace; close to Thames, no car park *(R Houghton, C E Owens)*

HAREFIELD

[Shrubs Rd/Harefield Rd] *Rose & Crown*: Attractive low-ceilinged pub with Benskins Best and Ind Coope Burton on handpump, good choice of efficiently served food; favoured by staff from Harefield Hospital *(Stan Edwards)*

HARLINGTON

[High St] *Wheatsheaf*: Well kept (not cheap) beer and good choice of lunchtime food, lounge and public bar pleasant *(Anon)*

[High St] *White Hart*: Acceptable Fullers beer and reasonably priced hot and cold food in two popular big bars with heavy wooden furniture, friendly and efficient staff *(Anon)*

HATTON

[Green Man Lane; 30 yds from A30 crossroads at Bedfont] *Green Man*: Pretty little pub, now in the industrial area right under Heathrow Airport's main flight path but formerly a haunt of highwaymen on the Bath Road and Hounslow Heath – there's still a hidden compartment behind the deep fireplace in the low-ceilinged and dimly lit bar; boarded ceiling and walls, cases of bottle-stoppers, labels and clay pipes found here, plenty of room in sympathetic extension, decent food with day's special such as rib of beef, and good steak sandwiches; Ruddles County; seats in garden *(Ian Phillips)*

HOUNSLOW

[Bath Rd (A4/A30)] *Travellers Friend*: Decent Ruddles, pleasant staff, nice atmosphere, very good lunchtime food; close to Heathrow with good-sized car park *(Anon)*

ISLEWORTH

[183 London Rd] *Coach & Horses*: Very old Youngs pub recently thoughtfully refurbished, lunchtime bar food, well kept real ale, pleasant atmosphere; restaurant *(Stephen King)*

[Church St] *London Apprentice*: Long famous for its pretty Thames-side position, this spaciously comfortable Chef & Brewer pub does get very popular in summer and on winter weekends, especially with younger people; several Watneys-related real ales, young friendly staff, help-yourself salads and daily roast, upstairs restaurant (open all afternoon Sun); children welcome; open all day *(A C and S J Beardsley, LYM and others)*

NORWOOD GREEN

☆ [Tentelon Rd] *Plough*: A surprise for London – a real country-pub atmosphere, with two real fires, church pew in public bar and a bowling-green dating from 1349; fairly compact, with four Fullers real ales kept well; good value bar food from sandwiches to gammon and egg or savoury omelette *(Tom Evans, Simon Collett-Jones)*

OSTERLEY

☆ [Windmill Lane; B454, off A4 – called Syon Lane at that point] *Hare & Hounds*: Country-style suburban pub with mature garden with nooks and crannies to suit families of all ages; busy but relaxed atmosphere, good food, Fullers Chiswick, ESB and London Pride, no music; near Osterley Park *(Neil and Elspeth Fearn, Richard Houghton, GRE, AE and others)*

RUISLIP

[West End Rd, S Ruislip] *Tally-Ho*: Pleasant civilised pub with good bar food and well kept real ales *(Chris Fluck)*

SIPSON
[Sipson Rd; entrance next to Post House]
Plough: Lovely little pub with well kept
Watneys-related real ales and good food;
easy parking, and very convenient for M4
junction 4 *(Graham and Glenis Watkins)*

TEDDINGTON
[Broom Rd] *Anglers*: Spacious, with good
gardens running down to the Thames at
Teddington Lock, pleasant riverside walks,
footbridge to Ham Common, large awning-
covered terrace; inside has lots of glass-case
fish, three big paintings of the pub and lock,
lots of Thames and fishing prints and old
photographs, decent choice of bar food from
sandwiches and ploughman's to burgers and
salads, Tetleys on handpump, piped music
(Ian Phillips)
[High St] *Kings Head*: Comfortable bar with
fine atmosphere and good value food;
bedrooms *(Comus Elliott)*
[Broom Rd/Ferry Rd; close to bridge at
Teddington Lock] *Tide End Cottage*: Small,
intimate, cosy and friendly riverside pub, two
little rooms united by large log-effect gas fire;
back terrace and cabin sauna, Watneys-
related real ales; may be crowded with
people from nearby TV studios; food served
11–3 lunchtime *(Ian Phillips, Comus Elliott,
Hazel Morgan)*

TWICKENHAM
[London Rd] *Cabbage Patch*: Open fire,
good atmosphere and food, own parking –
and near station *(N L Westley)*
[Church St] *Fox*: Pleasant old exterior from
pretty village street; slightly artificial feel in
cosy single bar with imitation pillars and
plaster effect; plates and Victorian prints on
wall and shelf; fruit machines and juke box;
generous doorstep toasted sandwiches
(Anon)
[King St] *George*: Large old pub modernised
into one very long bar broken up by 18-inch-
high platforms with tables and chairs; warm
pale brickwork and plaster, usual range of
bar food from pine-clad kitchen area,
Whitbreads-related real ales; main attraction
elevated view down over pavement and busy
King St; open 11–11, but closed Sun
lunchtime *(Peter Griffiths)*
☆ [Cross Deep] *Popes Grotto*: Spacious and
well run Youngs pub with balustraded outer
area overlooking the stroll-around central
area; very helpful staff, good value bar food
from sandwiches through salads and steak
and kidney pie to roast beef carvery, well
kept Youngs real ale, good range of other
drinks, games in public bar; tables in own
garden, and attractive public garden opposite
(closed at night) sloping down to Thames;
children in eating area *(Simon Collett-Jones,
LYM and others)*

[Twickenham Green] *Prince Albert*: Good
value lunchtime food including outstanding
choice of sandwiches and ploughman's, well
kept Fullers ESB and London Pride, very
hard-working licensees – like a country pub
in town *(Stephen King)Prince Blucher*: Cosy
bustling bar with good food and beer,
interesting décor, friendly atmosphere *(Dr
and Mrs A K Clarke)*
☆ [Riverside] *White Swan*: Family pub
resolutely preserving its atmosphere, located
some 10–12 ft above road with pleasant
balcony overlooking river; plain and simple,
blazing fire, odd dining-tables and chairs,
minimal décor (style may not appeal to
everybody); riverside garden, can be very
crowded some evenings; licensee Mrs Sutton
still in charge despite on-going dispute with
brewery – considerable local support from
all walks of life and all ages; more news
please *(C E Owens, Ian Phillips and others)*

UXBRIDGE
[Hillingdon Hill] *Vine*: Attractively
refurbished, with good new licensees, very
friendly atmosphere, Ind Coope Burton,
Tetleys and Youngs on handpump, and fine
range of food *(Dennis Jones)*

WEST HYDE
[Coppermill Lane] *Fisheries*: Bright single-
bar layout with fresh panelling, good choice
of bar food, Benskins Best and Ind Coope
Burton; beside Grand Union Canal *(Stan
Edwards)*

EAST

E1
☆ [269 Whitechapel Rd] *Grave Maurice*:
Popular with staff from London Hospital,
quietly comfortable long lounge bar with
Victorian plush and polish, very well kept
Trumans real ales, friendly local atmosphere,
cheerfully run by Mrs H – a real oasis for
this area; well cooked and lovingly presented
food, including on Sat evening *(A L Latham,
Neil Barker, LYM)*
[36 Globe Rd] *Horn of Plenty*: Good
sidestreet local with well kept Trumans Best
and plenty of atmosphere *(Robert Lester)*
[285 Whitechapel Rd] *Lord Rodneys Head*:
Popular for live music each night, extrovert
staff; beer not a speciality but excellent range
of lagers; lunchtime bar snacks *(Judith
Denwood)*
[105 Globe Rd] *Prince Regent*: Large
modern two-bar pub with attractive pictures
in lounge bar, great atmosphere, Watneys-
related real ales; friendly landlady *(Robert
Lester)*
[124 Globe Rd] *Prince of Wales*: Small cosy
one-bar pub with very good atmosphere,
pool-table, Watneys-related real ale *(Robert
Lester)*
☆ [57 Wapping Wall] *Prospect of Whitby*:

Rollicking pub, popular with tourists now, done up old-style with cheerful evening live music, beams, panelling and flagstones, well kept Watneys-related real ales, superb river views (much appreciated by the painter Turner) from flagstoned waterside courtyard; has been a main entry for its very considerable entertainment value, but recent reports raise doubts about food and service – more news please *(LYM and others)*

☆ [62 Wapping High St] *Town of Ramsgate*: Long, rather narrow bar with squared oak panelling, green plush banquettes and captain's chairs, masses of bric-à-brac, old Limehouse prints, fine etched mirror of Ramsgate harbour, interesting old-London Thames-side setting; well kept Bass and Charrington IPA, usual bar food, has been open all day; it's only a shortage of reader reports that keeps this nice pub out of the main entries *(LYM – more reports please)*

E2

[89 Dunbridge St] *Lord Hood*: Federation beers from the North in lively pub with free music hall Weds, Fri and Sat, lunchtime food, occasional morris dancing *(David Cook)*

[211 Old Ford Rd] *Royal Cricketers*: Pleasant canalside pub with terrace, good views of canal and Victoria Park – a rural oasis in the East End *(Neil Barker)*

[13 Boundary St] *Ship & Blue Ball*: Small Shoreditch pub under same ownership as Pitfield Brewery, and notable for the good value interesting beers produced by them – Pitfield, Hoxton Best and Dark Star on handpump, with an unusual bottled London Porter of some distinction; simple post-war décor, good collection of mainly extinct beer-bottle labels strong on stouts and dinner ales, relaxed and chatty atmosphere *(BB)*

E3

☆ [104 Empson St] *Beehive*: Charming local with interesting range of well kept real ales such as Flowers, Greene King Abbot, Pitfield Dark Star and Theakstons Old Peculier; open fire, warmly hospitable licensees *(Andrew O'Doherty, Perry Board)*

[50 St Leonard St] *Imperial Crown*: Comfortable and friendly, interesting interior, close to walks along River Lee and Bow Back Rivers *(Neil Barker; reports on the food please)*

E4

[420 Hale End Rd] *County Arms*: Big and busy corner pub built solidly in 1908 by Herts & Essex Public House Trust (forerunner of THF), no cheap brass or stained glass; Watneys-related real ales, coffee too, food lunchtime and evening *(Robert Lester)*

[51 Sewardstone Rd; A112, by junction with A110 Lea Valley Rd] *Fountain*: Large single-bar pub with welcoming atmosphere, Ind Coope Burton and Taylor Walkers on handpump, darts, Weds disco *(Robert Lester)* [Kings Head Hill; next to police stn] *Kings Head*: Pleasant and comfortable one-bar pub with children's room and function room, food lunchtime and evening, Ind Coope-related real ales on handpump; photographs showing the pub in the 1880s *(Robert Lester)*

[Larkshall Rd] *Larkshall*: Comfortable pub with Victorian dining-room serving as saloon bar, old bar back salvaged from former Southwark Brewery; well kept Courage Best and Directors on handpump *(Robert Lester)*

[Mott St; off Sewardstone Rd – OS Sheet 177 reference 384983] *Plough*: Friendly roadside pub with bar billiards in smart public bar, good value food, genuine friendly atmosphere, well kept McMullens Country and AK Mild on handpump; tables outside; in spite of its London address this is really out in Essex – perhaps the most extreme example of the eccentricity of Post Office addressing *(Robert Lester, R P Hastings)*

[219 Kings Head Hill] *Royal Oak*: Small friendly pub owned by Terry Venables, manager of Tottenham Hotspur – pictures of when he was a player; Courage Best and John Smiths on handpump; known as Venners *(Robert Lester)*

E8

[90 Amherst Rd] *Pembury*: Friendly and lively tastefully refurbished Victorian pub with well kept Banks & Taylors real ales on handpump, as well as Ruddles; colourful bar staff especially at weekends, bands many evenings, high standard cabaret some Fri evenings – open late then *(Trevor Sizeland)*

E9

☆ [274 Victoria Park Rd] *Falcon & Firkin*: Vast fun room for children in own-brew pub with bare boards, lots of falconry memorabilia, good value cheap food – big filled baps, quiche, ploughman's, Cumberland sausages and daily specials such as cheese and onion pie or chicken and bacon flan; brews include Falcon Ale and Hackney Bitter, as well as guests; lively atmosphere, garden *(M A and W R Proctor, Robert Lester and others)*

E11

[31 Wanstead High St] *Cuckfield*: Recently smartly refurbished, with excellent atmosphere and Bass and Charrington IPA on handpump *(Robert Lester)*

[Nightingale Lane] *Duke of Edinburgh*: Tudor-fronted building where courts were once held upstairs (landlord said still to be a magistrate); Ind Coope Burton and Taylor Walker on handpump, three-course lunches in saloon, opens 10am for coffee *(Robert Lester)*

[24 Browning Rd] *North Star*: Genuine pub,

cosy and friendly, with well kept Bass and Charrington IPA, chippish food *(Simon Kleine)*

E14

☆ [27 Ropemakers Fields; off Narrow St, opp The Grapes] *House They Left Behind*: Renovated to catch the new Docklands feel (and customers) yet keeping a good local base; fine atmosphere, wine-barish at the edges, good value food cooked in front of you, including Sun lunchtime roasts and ploughman's, Watneys-related real ales, live music Thurs and weekends *(Judith Denwood, Ian Phillips)*

E17

[807 Forest Rd] *College Arms*: Pleasant atmosphere in small Wetherspoons pub with Greene King Abbot, Marstons Pedigree, Youngers Scotch and Wadworths 6X on handpump *(Robert Lester)*

BARKINGSIDE

[105 Fencepiece Rd (A123)] *Old Maypole*: Large pub with spacious lounge bar, three pool-tables and darts in carefully restored public bar, Ind Coope Burton and Tetleys on handpump; maypole outside *(Robert Lester)*

DAGENHAM

[New Rd (A13)] *Anglers Retreat*: Main-road pub by Fords with two panelled bars, three pool-tables, discos, Charrington IPA *(Robert Lester)*

HORNCHURCH

[189 High St] *Kings Head*: Small beamed and timbered pub with real fire and Watneys-related real ales on handpump; popular with young people *(Robert Lester)*
[Billet Lane] *Queens Theatre*: Though this is

a theatre bar rather than a pub, it's comfortable and handy, and has Greene King IPA on handpump *(Robert Lester)*

ILFORD

[645 Cranbrook Rd, Gants Hill] *King George V*: Courage Best and Directors and John Smiths on handpump in well decorated pub; darts popular *(Robert Lester)*

WANSTEAD

[High St; opp Underground] *George*: Large and friendly Berni Inn, with Watneys-related real ales in the bar *(Robert Lester)*

WOODFORD

[13 Cross Rd; just S of Manor Rd (B173)] *Crown & Crooked Billet*: Small and friendly pub overlooking village green, good food, Bass and Charrington IPA on handpump *(Robert Lester)*
[735 Chigwell Rd (A113)] *Three Jolly Wheelers*: Plush Mr Toby with a good friendly atmosphere in the bar *(Robert Lester)*

WOODFORD GREEN

[393 High Rd (A104)] *Castle*: Massive showpiece almost opposite the green, Watneys-related real ales, good food in upstairs Barnabys restaurant very popular, particularly at Christmas *(Robert Lester)*
[Hale End Rd/Oak Hill] *Royal Oak*: Good atmosphere in comfortable and spacious two-bar pub with bar billiards in saloon, Ind Coope Burton on handpump, disco Weds and Sun *(Robert Lester)*
[Chigwell Rd/Woodford Br] *White Hart*: Charming olde-worlde pub with posters of boxing bouts over the years, Ind Coope Burton and Taylor-Walker on handpump *(Robert Lester)*

Scotland

Scotland

The rising standard of Scottish bar food is even more noticeable this year than last. The stars for pub food are the Ardvasar Hotel on Skye, the Riverside Inn in Canonbie (moving towards more organic food; good wines and cheeses, too), the stylish Nivingston House at Cleish (back with a bang, after a rest from these pages), the Tweeddale Arms in Gifford, the Babbity Bowster in Glasgow, the Tormaukin in Glendevon, the Old Howgate Inn at Howgate (a new licensee, but even stern critics have not been able to fault the smorrebrod), the Hotel Eilean Iarmain at Isle Ornsay on Skye, Burts Hotel in Melrose, the Killiecrankie Hotel just outside Pitlochry (very hospitable new licensees – but the same well tried chef), the Crown at Portpatrick (a particularly fine inn that in spite of changing hands seems as good as ever, serving food all day), the rather grand Skeabost House Hotel at Skeabost Bridge on Skye, the Tayvallich Inn at Tayvallich, the Crook at Tweedsmuir (reintroduced to the Guide under go-ahead new licensees), the Morefield Motel in Ullapool (a new entry, included for its seafood), the Ailean Chraggan at Weem and another new entry – indeed, our food find of the year – the Wheatsheaf in Swinton. Many other main entries have notable food; the general strength is an increasing use of local fresh ingredients, particularly fish and seafood, but also game, cheeses, carefully chosen meats and even vegetables – long the Achilles heel of Scottish cooking. Besides those new entries already mentioned, other interesting newcomers (or pubs back among the main entries after a gap) include the

The Stein Inn, Stein

Cawdor Tavern not far from the castle in Cawdor, the Clachaig in a marvellous position in Glencoe (simple snacks all day), the Anchor overlooking the water at Kippford (doing well after a change of ownership since it was last in the Guide), the attractively placed Whistlefield by Loch Eck (another place doing well under new licensees), the useful Queens Head in Selkirk, the Tigh an Eilean at Shieldaig with its spectacular sea outlook (a nice place to stay at) and the trendy Ceilidh Place in Ullapool. A good few significant changes include above all the one we hope won't happen – the plan by the Next retailing chain to demolish the fine old Prince of Wales in Aberdeen; as we go to press they are still holding out. There are new licensees at the Salmon Leap in Drymen, the Claret Jug in Edinburgh (the new owners plan refurbishment in the new year), Jules there, the Ship in Elie (the new landlord, a local resident, firmly upholds the long-standing former licensee's view that this traditional place should stay traditional), the smart Taychreggan Hotel at Kilchrenan, and the Tibbie Shiels Inn on St Mary's Loch. In such a vast country, where distances are so great, it's often difficult for our inspection programme to pick up all the most worthwhile pubs and inns – which is why the Scottish Lucky Dip section at the end of the chapter is likely to hold a good few treasures. So this year, in the hope of focusing people's attention more easily on the areas they want, we've divided the Dip section into the various regions: places that look particularly promising include the Sherriff Muir Inn, Birds & the Bees on the edge of Stirling, Lion & Unicorn in Thornhill (all Central); Grange outside St Andrews (Fife); Thunderton House in Elgin, Towie at Turriff (Grampian); Old Inn at Gairloch, Ferry Boat in Ullapool (Highland); Cramond Brig at Cramond Bridge, Kays Bar in Edinburgh (Lothian); Fox & Hounds in Houston, George in Inveraray, Kilberry Inn at Kilberry (Strathclyde); and Granary in Perth (Tayside).

ABERDEEN (Grampian)   NJ9305 Map 11

Ferryhill House Hotel

Bon Accord Street (bottom end)

Kept in immaculate condition, the unusually wide choice of real ales and malt whiskies in this well run small hotel includes Belhaven 80/-, Broughton Greenmantle, Maclays 80/-, McEwans 80/-, Timothy Taylors Landlord and Youngers No 3, on handpump or electric pump. The bar food is wide-ranging: sandwiches, soup (80p), baked potatoes and ploughman's (£2) with main courses from fried scampi (£3.75) and chicken Kiev (£5) to fillet steak (from £7); daily changing set lunches (£4), cold buffet (£4.50). The spacious and airy communicating bar areas have plenty of seating, and there's a fruit machine and piped music. Outside, neatly kept, sheltered lawns have lots of well spaced tables; children's play area. *(Recommended by Leith Stuart; more reports please)*

Free house   Licensee Douglas Snowie   Real ale   Meals and snacks   Restaurant   Children in restaurant   Open 11–11 Mon–Weds, 11–11.30 Thurs–Sat, 12.30–11 Sun all year   Bedrooms tel Aberdeen (0224) 590867; £28(£30B)/£52B

Prince of Wales

7 St Nicholas Lane

As well as the longest bar counter in the city, this individualistic Aberdonian institution has a cosy flagstoned area with pews and other wooden furniture in screened booths, a log-effect gas fire, and a neatly refurbished main lounge. The staff are most friendly and welcoming. Popular good value lunchtime food includes soup (60p), filled rolls (65p), macaroni cheese (£1.70), lasagne, sweet-and-sour chicken, haddock and various home-made pies such as steak and kidney, gammon and leek or chicken and mushroom (all £2.30). Well kept Theakstons Old Peculier on handpump, Caledonian 80/- and Youngers No 3 on air-pressure tall fount, and two guest beers. Sensibly placed darts and fruit machine. It's reached down a Dickensianly narrow cobbled alley that twists right underneath Union Street. The plans for the Next retailing chain to demolish the pub for redevelopment are still pending. *(Recommended by Roger Danes, Nigel Paine; more reports please)*

Free house   Licensee Peter Birnie   Real ale   Lunchtime meals and snacks (not Sun)
No nearby parking   Open 11–11 all year

ARDFERN (Strathclyde)   NM8004 Map 11
Galley of Lorne
B8002; village and inn signposted off A816 Lochgilphead–Oban

In a lovely setting on Loch Craignish, this friendly and informal inn has views of the sea loch and yacht anchorage. Inside, the main bar has an easy-going assortment of chairs, little winged settles and rug-covered window seats on its lino tiles, big navigation lamps by the bar counter, and old Highland dress prints and other pictures. Generous helpings of cheap bar food might include home-made soup (£1.10), baked potato with cheese (£1.35), haggis with neeps or French bread filled with fresh salmon or crab (£2.25), moules marinière (£2.95), scampi (£3.75), Loch Craignish king prawns or Hungarian goulash (£3.95), beef Stroganoff (£4), home-made puddings and assorted Scottish cheeses; children's helpings. A wide choice of malt whiskies and bin-end wines; darts, space game and fruit machine. A spacious wine bar behind has a piano and dance floor, and big pool-table, and there are easy chairs in the entrance lounge with windows looking out over the sheltered terrace; the pub is at the start of *Good Walks Guide* Walk 178. *(Recommended by Patrick Stapley, Richard Gibbs)*

Free house   Licensee Tim Hanbury   Meals and snacks   Children in eating area of bar   Live Scottish music on Sat evenings   Open 12–2.30, 5–11 all year   Bedrooms tel Barbreck (085 25) 284; £20(£22B)/£40(£44B)

ARDUAINE (Strathclyde)   NM7911 Map 11
Loch Melfort Hotel 🏨

The light, modern bar in this comfortable hotel is papered with nautical charts and has a pair of powerful marine glasses which you can use to search for birds and seals on the islets and on the coasts of the bigger islands beyond. Low dark brown fabric and wood easy chairs surround light oak tables, and there's a free-standing wood-burning stove. At lunchtime the bar food includes home-made soup (£1), toasted sandwiches (£1.20), home-made pâté (£2.40), venison burger (£3), a pint of prawns (£4), locally smoked salmon (£7.50), fresh-caught langoustines (£8.50, weather permitting), and puddings (from £1.50); evening extras include pickled herring in mustard sauce (£2.20) and goujons of tuna (£4.30). Helpful service; darts and piped music. Wooden seats on the front terrace are a short stroll through grass and wild flowers (where five donkeys and a horse graze) to the rocky foreshore, though from late April to early June the best walks are through the neighbouring Arduaine woodland gardens. Some bedrooms are in a modern wing, some, older-fashioned, in the main house. *(Recommended by Stephanie Sowerby, Mrs Sue Johnson; more reports please)*

Free house   Licensees Colin and Jane Tindal   Meals and snacks   Restaurant   Children welcome   Open 11–2.30, 5–11; closed end Oct–Easter   Bedrooms tel Kilmelford (085 22) 233; £35B/£68B

There are report forms at the back of the book.

ARDVASAR (Isle of Skye)   NG6203 Map 11

Ardvasar Hotel ⊘ 🛏

Looking out across the Sound of Sleat to the fierce Knoydart mountains, the bars in this comfortably modernised eighteenth-century inn include the cocktail bar with crimson plush wall seats and stools around dimpled copper coffee tables on the red patterned carpet, and Highland dress prints on the cream hessian and wood walls; the locally popular public bar with stripped pews and kitchen chairs; and a room off the comfortable hotel lounge with armchairs around its open fire and a huge TV. Friendly and obliging young owners serve good fresh food in the dining-room, including local fish and shellfish, and the home-cooked bar food varies day by day. Typically, it might include lentil and carrot soup (90p), sweet pickled herring platter (£1.40), potted crab (£1.50), goujons of sole (£3.50), cold home-cooked gammon with cheese and pineapple (£3.60), home-made steak and kidney pie or roast shoulder of lamb with mint jelly (£3.80), cold poached Loch Eishort salmon (£4.60) and puddings such as hot apple and honey strudel (£1.30). The far side of the peninsula, by Tarskavaig, Tokavaig and Ord, has some of the most dramatic summer sunsets in Scotland – over the jagged Cuillin peaks, with the islands of Canna and Rhum off to your left. Near the Clan Donald centre. *(Recommended by S J A Velate, A H Doran, Janet and John Pamment, Miles Walton, Mrs E Higson)*

Free house   Licensees Bill and Gretta Fowler   Meals and snacks   Restaurant   Children in eating area of bar   Open 11–11 June–Sept; 11–2.30, 5–11 Oct–May; closed 25 Dec, 1 and 2 Jan   Bedrooms tel Ardvasar (041 14) 223; £20(£25B)/£38(£42B); not available Jan–Feb

BLANEFIELD (Central)   NS5579 Map 11

Carbeth Inn

West Carbeth; A809 Glasgow–Drymen, just S of junction with B821

Below the Kilpatrick Hills, this relaxed and well kept country pub has a cheerfully old-fashioned bar with heavy cast-iron-framed tables on the stone and tile floor, cushioned booths built from brown planking under a high frieze of tartan curtain (with a big colour TV peeping out) and a high ceiling of the same brown wood. At one end, under the mounted stag's head, there's an open fire, and at the other end a wood-burning stove. Generous helpings of good value bar food include home-made soup (90p), sandwiches (from £1, toasties from £1.20), filled baked potatoes (from £1.75), ploughman's (£2), burgers (from £2.10), salad with ham, prawns, cheese and egg (£2.60), chicken and bacon (£2.85), lasagne or scampi (£2.95), gammon with pineapple (£3.75) and steaks (from £5.50); also, daily specials such as vegetable curry (£3.50) or trout (£4.75), and children's meals (from £1). Well kept Flowers and Whitbreads Castle Eden on handpump; sensibly placed darts, fruit machine, trivia and piped music. A rather smarter carpeted bar – the Ptarmigan – and a pleasant panelled family-room both have old stone walls, open fires and bric-à-brac. On the front terrace outside there are lots of rustic benches and tables. *(Recommended by Ian Baillie, Nick Dowson, Alison Hayward)*

Whitbreads   Licensee Nigel Morrison   Real ale   Meals and snacks   Children in family-room, not after 9   Singer Weds, band Fri   Open 11–11 Mon–Thurs, 11–midnight Fri, Sat, 12.30–11 Sun; closed 25 Dec and 1 Jan   Bedrooms tel Blanefield (0360) 70382; £17/£30

BROUGHTY FERRY (Tayside)   NO4630 Map 11

Fisherman's Tavern

12 Fort Street; turning off shore road

A wide range of real ales in this small-roomed rambling pub includes Belhaven 80/-, Flowers, McEwans 70/- and 80/-, Maclays 80/-, Theakstons Best, Timothy Taylors Landlord, and a guest beer that changes weekly on handpump, with Youngers No 3 on air-pressure tall fount; there's also a goodish choice of whiskies, including distinguished single malts, on the dispensing optics. The cosy little snug has light pink, soft fabric seating on the brown carpet, basket-weave wall panels and beige lamps; the carpeted back bar has a Victorian fireplace and brass wall lights. Bar food includes sandwiches (50p), and hot dishes such as Finnan pie, beef olives, scampi, curry or lemon sole with prawns and mushrooms (from £2.50); friendly and professional service. Darts, dominoes, cribbage, two fruit machines. The nearby seafront gives a good view of the two long, low Tay bridges. *(Recommended by Alisdair Cuthil, JAH, HLH; more reports please)*

Free house   Licensee Robert Paterson   Real ale   Snacks and lunchtime meals   Children in snug bar until 6   Scottish folk music Mon   Open 11–midnight all year; closed evening 25 Dec and 1 Jan

CANONBIE (Dumfries and Galloway)   NY3976 Map 9
Riverside Inn ★ ★ 🕲 🛏
Village signposted from A7

Very good lunchtime bar food in this civilised and friendly inn includes home-made soups such as pea and broccoli or lovely mussel (£1.50), potted fresh trout, home-made kipper pâté or ploughman's with Blue Shropshire or Swaledale cheese (all £2.95), stir-fried chicken or home-made ham and mushroom pie (£4.25), lamb curry or casserole of pheasant and bacon in cider (£4.55), fresh plaice and sirloin steak. Puddings might include squidgy chocolate roulade or hot apricot crunch with apricot sauce (all £1.25). The food shows lots of careful small touches, like virgin olive oil for salad dressings, and they are concentrating more now on finding supplies of organic foods such as undyed smoked fish, wild salmon and naturally fed chickens; they also have a good range of English cheeses; thoughtful as well as substantial breakfasts, and most attractive bedrooms. The comfortable and restful communicating rooms of the bar have open fires, stuffed wildlife, local pictures, and good, sensitively chosen chintzy furnishings. Well kept Yates and regularly changing guest beer such as Adnams or Hook Norton on handpump, reasonably priced; they carefully look after a good range of wines and have Thatchers cider; sympathetic service. In summer – when it can get very busy – there are tables under the trees on the front grass. Over the quiet road, a public playground runs down to the Border Esk (the inn can arrange fishing permits). *(Recommended by Russell and Christina Jones, Paul Wreglesworth, PLC, Simon Ward, A C and S J Beardsley, Stephanie Sowerby, Timothy Galligan, David and Flo Wallington, J A H Townsend, Robert Olsen, John Hanselman, T Nott, Robert and Vicky Tod, Mr and Mrs E J Smith, Dave Butler, Lesley Storey, Tony Pounder, D H Nicholson, Jon Wainwright, David and Ruth Hollands)*

Free house   Licensee Robert Phillips   Real ale   Meals and snacks (Mon–Sat lunchtime, and Sun evening)   Children welcome   Restaurant; closed Sun   Open 11–2.30, 6.30–11 (12 Sat) all year; closed Sun lunchtime, 25 and 26 Dec, 1 and 2 Jan, 2 weeks Feb, 2 weeks Nov   Bedrooms tel Canonbie (038 73) 71512 or 71295; £40B/£50B

CARBOST (Isle of Skye)   NG3732 Map 11
Old Inn
This is the Carbost on the B8009, in the W of the central part of the island

Recently extended to include a new panelled bar, this busy and friendly old stone inn is simply furnished with red leatherette settles, benches and seats, and there are bare floorboards, walls part-whitewashed and part-stripped stone, and a peat fire. The popular bar meals – sandwiches, home-made soup (85p), basket meals (from £2.20), dish of the day such as beef curry (£3.20), fresh salmon salad or roast beef and Yorkshire pudding (both £3.50), and home-made puddings such as apple crumble – are served in helpings robust enough for climbers down from the fiercely jagged peaks of the Cuillin Hills; darts, pool-table (not available in summer), dominoes, cribbage, trivia machine, piped traditional music and the occasional ceilidh. The pub is beside the sea loch and near the Talisker distillery (where there are guided tours round the distillery, with free samples, most days in summer). *(Recommended by J Marshall, Roger Danes, M Shinkfield)*

Free house   Licensee Deirdre Cooper   Meals and snacks (12–2, 5.30–10)   Children in eating area of bar until 8.30   Open 11–11; 11–2.30, 5–11 in winter   Bedrooms tel Carbost (047 842) 205; £11.50/£23

CAWDOR (Highland)   NH8450 Map 11
Cawdor Tavern
Just off B9090; Cawdor Castle signposted from A96 Inverness–Nairn

The right-hand public bar has an imposing pillared serving-counter, elaborate wrought-iron wall lamps, chandeliers laced with bric-à-brac such as a stuffed mongoose wrestling a cobra, banknotes pinned to joists, a substantial alabaster figurine – not at all what you'd expect from a little Highland village pub. But then this is just a couple of minutes' drive from the castle. And it was the castle which furnished the squared oak panelling and chimney breast in the lounge, a substantial Turkey-carpeted room with green plush button-back built-in wall banquettes and bucket chairs, a Delft shelf with toby jugs and decorative plates (chiefly game), small tapestries and attractive sporting pictures. Besides sandwiches and home-made bar food such as lasagne, steak pie and fricassees, there's a sizeable formal restaurant with Liberty-print curtains and soft russet plush-upholstered chairs. Well kept McEwans 80/- and Theakstons Best on handpump, well over a hundred malt whiskies and some rare blends, a good choice of wines and decent coffee. Darts, pool, cribbage, dominoes, fruit machine in the public bar; piped music; no dogs. There are tables on the front terrace, with tubs of flowers, roses and creepers climbing the supports of a big awning; summer Saturday barbecues. *(Recommended by Dr John Innes, Neil and Angela Huxter, Brian and Anna Marsden)*

Free house   Licensee T D Oram   Real ale   Meals and snacks (not before 12.30) Restaurant tel Cawdor (066 77) 316   Children welcome   Open 11–11 (11.30 Sat) all year

CLEISH (Tayside)   NT0998 Map 11
Nivingston House ⊗ 🏠
1½ miles from M90 junction 5; follow B9097 W until village signpost, then almost immediately inn is signposted

Looking out over a lawn sweeping down to shrubs and trees, with hills in the distance, the relaxing L-shaped bar in this civilised country-house hotel has rust-coloured comfortable seats against sumptuous lotus-plant wallpaper. Interesting bar snacks might include delicious tomato and orange soup (£1.40), home-made pâté with oatcakes (£3.65), fine tagliatelle with smoked mackerel, mushrooms and parmesan cheese (£3.85), venison burger (£3.95), salad with fruit and Crowdie cream cheese or home-smoked trout with caper and horseradish sauce (£4.25), minute steak (£4.95), and specialities such as the croque Nivingston (French bread baked with ham, cheese, prawns and garlic, £4.65). Belhaven on handpump and a good choice of malt whiskies. Outside, there are picnic-table sets below the gravel drive. *(Recommended by T Nott)*

Free house   Licensee Allan Deeson   Real ale   Meals and snacks (not evenings)   Children in eating area of bar   Restaurant   Open 12–3, 6–12 all year   Bedrooms tel Cleish Hills (057 75) 216; £50B/£70B

CRAMOND (Lothian)   NT1876 Map 11
Cramond Inn
Cramond Glebe Road

The Firth of Forth is only a short walk away from this friendly, busy old pub in an attractively renovated fishing village. Back in its original place near the main door, the bar has brown button-back wall banquettes, wheel-back chairs and little stools, ceiling joists and an open fire. A long, white-clothed table is set out for lunch, and the daily changing bar menu may include home-made soup with soda bread (75p), ploughman's (£1.65), steak and kidney pie (£2.85), beef olives or mince and potato pie, fresh haddock in beer batter (£3), crayfish salad (£3.45) and home-made gateaux (£1.15). Five tall founts dispense Caledonian 80/-, Maclays 70/-, Marstons Pedigree, Timothy Taylors Best, and guests such as Broughton Merlins or Thwaites; reasonably priced spirits are measured in quarter gills; helpful service even when crowded. Darts, dominoes, card games and piped music. The pub's car park has some fine views out over the Forth; a small side terrace has seats and tables. *(Recommended by Roger Sherman, R P Taylor, Dr A V Lewis)*

Sam Smiths Real ale Snacks and lunchtime meals Restaurant tel 031-336 2035 Children in eating area of bar (if 14ft from serving-counter) until 7 Open 11–2.30, 5–11 weekdays, 11–midnight Sat; closed 25 and 26 Dec and 1 Jan

CRINAN (Strathclyde) NR7894 Map 11

Crinan Hotel ⇔

You can look down over the busy entrance basin of the Crinan Canal from the picture window in the stylish cocktail bar here, and watch the fishing boats and yachts wandering out towards the Hebrides. Seats in the cosy carpeted back part and the tiled front part are comfortable, and the décor includes sea drawings and paintings, model boats in glass cases and a nautical chest of drawers; the latest coastal waters forecast is chalked on a blackboard. The simpler public bar has the same marvellous views, and there's a side terrace with seats outside; fruit machine. Good bar food includes home-made soup (£1.50), Arbroath smokies or grilled fillet of Loch Awe trout (£2.75), freshly baked flan and salad (£2.95), Loch Sween mussels (£4.95), locally smoked salmon (£6.50), other locally caught fresh fish, and a weekend buffet lunch; large wine list. You can get sandwiches from their coffee shop or Lazy Jack's. The smart top-floor evening restaurant and associated bar, where jacket and tie are needed, look out to the islands and the sea. *(More reports please)*

Free house Licensee Nicholas Ryan Lunchtime meals Children welcome Evening restaurant Pianist in rooftop bar Fri, Sat, Sun evenings Open 11–2.30, 5–11 all year Bedrooms tel Crinan (054 683) 235; £37.50B/£70B

DRYMEN (Central) NS4788 Map 11

Salmon Leap

Established in 1759, this comfortable inn has a partly panelled L-shaped bar with harness on the walls, bric-à-brac hanging from the joists of the ceiling, and two good log fires. The plusher lounge, also L-shaped, is decorated with stuffed fish and birds and has a wood-burning stove. Bar food includes stuffed pitta bread (£2.15), lasagne, ploughman's or quiche (all £2.95), cold meat salad (£3.25), home-made steak pie (£3.75), pint of prawns (£3.95), scampi provençale (£5.75), poached salmon steaks (£6.50), puddings such as home-made apple pie (£1.10), and there are barbecues in summer; McEwans 80/- from tall founts, lots of malt whiskies; darts, dominoes, fruit machine, trivia and unobtrusive piped music. This year, some readers have put a question mark over the bedrooms. *(Recommended by M J Morgan, Mr and Mrs J H Adam, A Darroch Harkness, Hazel Morgan)*

Free house Licensee James Bryce-Lind Real ales Meals and snacks Restaurant, open 12.30–midnight Sun Children welcome Folk music Sun evenings and occasional ceilidhs Open 11.30–1am Mon–Sat, 12.30–midnight Sun Bedrooms tel Drymen (0360) 60357; £20B/£32.50B

DUMFRIES (Dumfries and Galloway)   NX9776 Map 9
Globe

High Street; up a narrow entry at S end of street, between Timpson Shoes and J Kerr Little (butcher), opposite Marks & Spencer

An inn since 1610, this old stone house has a little museum devoted to Burns in the room that he used most often, and on the wall of the old-fashioned dark-panelled Snug Bar there's a facsimile of a letter (now in the J Pierpoint Morgan Library in New York): 'the Globe Tavern here... for these many years has been my Howff' (a Scots word meaning a regular haunt). Upstairs, one bedroom has two window panes with verses scratched by diamond in Burns' handwriting (though not the touching verse he wrote for Anna Park, the barmaid here, who had his child). McEwans 80/- on handpump, very reasonably priced. A big plain public bar at the back has dominoes, a fruit machine, trivia and piped music. Good value simple bar food includes home-made soup or filled rolls (50p), quiche and salads, a three-course lunch at £2.75, and apple pie (50p). By the way, there's another pub of the same name in Market Street. *(More reports please)*

Free house   Licensee Mrs Maureen McKerrow   Real ale   Lunchtime meals and snacks (not Sun)   Restaurant (closed Sun) tel Dumfries (0387) 52335   Children in restaurant   Nearby daytime parking difficult; car park 5 mins away   Open 11–11 Mon–Sat all year

EDINBURGH (Lothian)   NT2574 Map 11

The two main areas for finding good pubs here, both main entries and Lucky Dips, are around Rose Street (just behind Princes Street in the New Town) and along or just off the top part of the Royal Mile in the Old Town. In both areas parking can be difficult at lunchtime, but is not such a problem in the evenings.

Abbotsford

Rose Street; E end, beside South St David Street

Quite an institution for generations of Edinburgh people, this pleasantly formal place has a heavily panelled Victorian island bar counter served by dark-uniformed waitresses and a remarkable mixture of customers. There are long deeply polished old tables, leather-cushioned seats and a handsome ceiling (a long way up – the elegantly panelled walls are tall). Good, reasonably priced food includes soup (60p), salads (from £2.30), grilled liver and bacon or haggis and neeps (£2.50), curried chicken or pork Stroganoff (£2.80), grilled gammon with pineapple (£2.90), rump steak (£3.60), mixed grill (£3.95), and puddings such as rhubarb crumble (85p). Caledonian 80/-, Greenmantle and Tennents 80/- on air-pressure tall founts, lots of malt whiskies; fruit machine tucked well away. Beware of the lunchtime crowds. *(Recommended by I R Hewitt, Richard Sanders, Mr and Mrs M D Jones, Scott W Stucky)*

Free house   Licensee Colin Grant   Real ale   Lunchtime meals and snacks (not Sun)   Restaurant tel 031-225 5276   Children in restaurant   Open 11–2.30, 5–11 all year; closed Sun

Athletic Arms

Angle Park Terrace; on corner of Kilmarnock Road (A71)

Because it was frequented by the gravediggers from the nearby graveyard, this very busy and quite unpretentious pub is known locally as The Diggers. A team of red-jacketed barmen works hard at the gleaming row of tall air-pressure founts to keep the throng of mainly young and very thirsty customers supplied with McEwans 80/- in tip-top condition; good bar food. Opening off the central island servery there are

Tipping is not normal for bar meals, and not usually expected.

some cubicles partitioned in glossy grey wood with Hearts and Scotland football team photographs – a side room is crowded with enthusiastic dominoes players. *(Recommended by J C Gould, Peter Corris, Richard Sanders; more reports please)*
Scottish & Newcastle   Real ale   Open 11–2.30, 5–11 all year

Bannermans Bar

212 Cowgate

This cellar-like bar up in the Old Town (and deep under some of its tallest buildings) has a warren of little brightly lit rooms with musty brick barrel-vaulted ceilings, massive bare stone walls and flagstones; it's furnished with old settles, pews and settees around barrels, red-painted tables and a long mahogany table. The front part has wood panelling and pillars, and rooms leading off have theatrical posters and handbills. A remarkably wide range of customers enjoy the well kept Arrols 70/- and 80/-, Caledonian 70/- and 80/- and Ind Coope Burton on handpump. There's an interesting choice of reasonably priced salads at lunchtime, and filled rolls in the evening (when it can get quite busy). The back area, open when busy, is no-smoking. *(Recommended by Richard Sanders; more reports please)*
Tennents (Bass)   Real ale   Meals (lunchtime, not Sun) and snacks   Open 11–2.30, 5.30–11 all year

Bennets Bar

8 Leven Street; leaving centre southwards, follow Biggar, A702 signpost

There are all sorts of treasures in this splendid Victorian bar: art nouveau stained-glass windows, arched and mahogany-pillared mirrors surrounded by tilework cherubs, Florentine-looking damsels and Roman warriors, and high elegantly moulded beams supporting the fancy dark maroon ceiling; red leather seats curve handsomely around the marble tables and there are old brewery mirrors. The long bar counter serves the pub's own blend of whisky from the barrel, as well as well kept McEwans 70/- and 80/- under air pressure. Bar food includes vegetarian dishes (from £2.20), curries and casseroles (£2.30), fresh haddock or seafood pie (both £2.40) and various salads and pasta dishes. *(Recommended by Richard Sanders, M C Howells; more reports please)*
Free house   Licensee Peter Davidson   Real ale   Meals (lunchtime, not Sun) and snacks   Children in eating area of bar   Open 11–11 Mon–Weds, 11–midnight Thurs–Sat, 7–11 Sun

Cafe Royal Circle Bar

West Register Street

Originally a showroom for the latest thing in Victorian gas and plumbing fittings, this handsome bar has a series of highly detailed Doulton tilework portraits of Watt, Faraday, Stephenson, Caxton, Benjamin Franklin and Robert Peel (in his day famous as the introducer of calico printing). The big island bar counter with hand-carved walnut gantry (a replica of the Victorian original) serves well kept Caledonian 70/-, McEwans 80/-, Youngers No 3 and weekly guest beer from air pressure tall founts; a good choice of whiskies. Simple bar food includes soup, pies (from 50p) or filled rolls (from 55p), and pizzas (from £1.90); fruit machine and trivia machine. *(Recommended by Gary Scott, Roger Huggins, Dewi and Linda Jones)*
Free house   Real ale   Snacks (12–7; not Sun)   Restaurant tel 031-556 4124   Children in restaurant   Open 11–11 Mon–Thurs, 11–12 Fri–Sat, 7–12 Sun all year

Claret Jug 🛏

Basement of Howard Hotel, 32–36 Great King Street

This hotel has recently changed hands, and although the L-shaped bar remains the same, we heard as we went to press that there were plans for refurbishment. At lunchtime the atmosphere is buoyantly clubby, though in the evenings it's peaceful and gently lit; there are prints of still lifes on the red-outlined panels of its walls – like the ceiling very dark brown, with russet velvet curtains, deep red, softly sprung leather chesterfields and library chairs, and wood-effect tables on the muted red patterned carpet. A smaller side room is similar. Well kept real ales on electric pump include McEwans 80/- and Websters Choice. The wide range of lunchtime bar food changes weekly and might include home-made soup (£1.20), home-made chicken liver pâté (£1.75), seafood salad with spicy tomato dressing (£2.25), roast of the day (£3.75), fried cod (£3.85), good steak and kidney pie (£4.20) and a cold buffet; on Sunday there's only roast beef, fish and chips or cold buffet; service is efficient and friendly. *(Recommended by JM, PM, Mr and Mrs M D Jones, Scott W Stucky)*

Free house Manager Trevor Laffin Real ale Lunchtime meals and snacks Restaurant (not Sun lunchtime) Children in eating area of bar Open 11–2.30, 5–11; closed 25 and 26 Dec, 1 and 2 Jan Bedrooms tel 031-557 3500; £52S/£75B

Guildford Arms

West Register Street

A snug little gallery bar here (closed on occasions – and there has been talk of it turning into a restaurant) gives a dress-circle view of the main one (notice the lovely old mirror decorated with two tigers on the way up). Under this gallery a little cavern of arched alcoves leads off the well preserved Victorian main bar. Its chief glory is the crusty plasterwork extending up from the walls, carefully painted in many colours. Other well preserved features include lots of mahogany, scrolly gilt wallpaper, big original advertising mirrors and heavy swagged velvet curtains for the arched windows. But this is no museum piece: the atmosphere is lively and welcoming, with the feeling that plenty is going on. Good basic pub food includes soup, mince pie, sausage, bacon, black pudding, egg and tomato, and scampi. Well kept Lorimers 80/- on handpump, and Lorrimers 70/-, McEwans 80/- and Youngers No 3 on air-pressure tall founts, friendly staff; lively piped music. *(Recommended by Patrick and Mary McDermott, Gary Scott, Richard Sanders, Dewi and Linda Jones)*

Free house Real ale Meals (lunchtime, not Sun) and snacks (lunchtime) Open 11–11 all year

Jules

Waterloo Place (top end)

Broken up into various areas and levels by round or curved elbow-height rests, this spacious bar has something of a conservatory feel: big orangery windows (with dusky pink swagged velvet curtains), masses of artificial plants and a high oval-ended ceiling. There are patchwork-pattern plush stools, chairs, settees and easy chairs, and decorations include stylish up-turned deco lamps, theatrical lighting gantries and lots of maroon-stained woodwork. Bar food includes filled rolls (60p), ploughman's, salads with pies and cold meats, chicken casserole, lamb curry or macaroni cheese (£2.75); coffee is served all day; McEwans 80/- on air-pressure tall fount, fruit machine in the lobby, piped pop music. *(Recommended by Quentin Williamson; more reports please)*

Free house Manager Alison Vallance Real ale Meals and snacks (noon–7, not Sun) Open 11–11 Mon–Thurs, 11–1 Fri and Sat all year

Peacock

Newhaven; Lindsay Road

Interesting photographs on the wall of this eighteenth-century place give some idea of what Newhaven used to be like before the new development (named after the pub) and other modern changes set in here. The main lounge is plushly comfortable, with lots of ply panelling and cosy seats, and the back room is well kept and cheerfully decorated with trellises and plants to seem like a conservatory (it leads on out to a garden). Bar food includes home-made soup or toasties (65p), pizzas (from

£1.40), fresh haddock or home-made steak pie (£2.45), good value carvery (three courses £7.95) and Sunday roast lunch (£2.95). (Best to book for evening food – dishes are more expensive then – as it gets very crowded). Well kept McEwans 80/- under air pressure. *(Recommended by I R Hewitt)*

Free house   Licensee Peter Carnie   Real ale   Meals and snacks   Children welcome Restaurant tel 031-552 5522   Open 11–11 all year

Sheep Heid

Duddingston; Causeway

The garden behind this old-fashioned ex-coaching-inn is a pretty place, with a goldfish pond and fountain, hanging baskets and clematis on the sheltering stone walls of the house, and a skittle alley – as far as we know, this is the only pub in Scotland that plays alley skittles; barbecues in fine weather – you can cook your own if you feel inclined. The main room has turn-of-the-century Edinburgh photographs, a fine rounded bar counter, seats built against the walls on the Turkey carpet, Highland prints and some reproduction panelling; the atmosphere is warm and relaxing and there's a good mix of customers. Tables in a side room are given some privacy by elegant partly glazed screens dividing them. Bar food includes soup, soused herring salad, mince pie, ploughman's and sirloin steak. Tennents 80/- on handpump; dominoes, a fruit machine, tv and piped music. The little village is lovely, and getting to the pub is a pleasant expedition, past Holyroodhouse, Arthur's Seat and the little nature reserve around Duddingston Loch. *(Recommended by W F Coghill, Gary Scott, R P Taylor)*

Tennents (Bass)   Real ale   Snacks and meals   Children in restaurant   Restaurant (closed Sun) tel 031-661 1020   Open 11–11 Mon–Sat, 12.30–2.30, 6.30–10 Sun all year

ELIE (Fife)   NO4900 Map 11

Ship

Harbour

As we went to press, Robin Hendry told us that he's moving on after seventeen years as landlord. The new licensee is a local and apparently has no intention of making any changes to this unspoilt little waterside pub. It has winged high-backed button-back leather seats against the partly panelled walls, beams in an ochre ceiling and a lively nautical atmosphere; there's a cosy, carpeted back room and open fires in winter. Bar snacks include soup or filled rolls (45p), and the Belhaven 80/- on handpump is well kept; darts, dominoes, cribbage and shut-the-box. Across the harbour lane sturdy seats and timber-baulk benches have an attractive view over the low sea wall. There's the pier and the old stone fish granary on the left, the little town on the right, and a grassy headland opposite. At low tide the bay is mostly sand, with oystercatchers and gulls shrilling over the water's edge.
(Recommended by JAH, HCH, T and A D Kucharski; more reports please)

Free house   Licensee Richard Philip   Real ale   Lunchtime snacks   Well behaved children in back room   Open 11–midnight, 12.30–2.30, 6.30–11 Sun all year

FINDHORN (Grampian)   NJ0464 Map 11

Crown & Anchor

Coming into Findhorn, keep left at signpost off to beach and car park

Several real ales in this lively and friendly old stone inn include Brakspears PA, Courage Directors and Wadworths 6X with regular guest beers such as Adnams, Badger or Timothy Taylors; they also have draught ciders (rare around here), and a good choice of spirits, including around a hundred malt whiskies. The lively public bar has an unusually big arched fireplace, old photographs of the area on the walls, and games (darts, dominoes, cribbage, fruit machine, trivia and juke box); the comfortable lounge bar is decorated with lots of pictures. Bar food includes sandwiches, soup (60p), burger (90p), and haddock (£2.40), with specials such as chilli con carne (£2.15), chicken curry (£2.50) and lasagne (£2.80). The inn still looks down to the jetty where Highlanders would have stayed before taking ship for Edinburgh or even London – people staying have the use of its boats – and sandy beaches are only a few moments' stroll away. (*Recommended by A Darroch Harkness, Vera Kelman; more reports please*)

Free house   Licensees Roy and Peta Liddle   Real ale   Meals and snacks   Children in eating area of bar until 9   Folk, 60s and jazz Sun evening   Open 11–11 all year; closes 11.45 Fri and Sat, opens 12 Sun   Bedrooms tel Findhorn (0309) 30243; £19S/£27S

GIFFORD (Lothian)   NT5368 Map 11
Tweeddale Arms ✍ ⇌
High Street

Facing an attractive long wooded green and the avenue to Yester House, this old white inn is a civilised place with a wide choice of good food. The comfortably relaxed lounge has big Impressionist prints on the apricot-coloured walls (there are matching curtains to divide the seats), modern tapestried settles and stools on its muted red patterned carpet, and brass lamps. Changing daily, the food includes soup (70p), sandwiches (from £1.50), pear and cheese salad (£1.95), omelettes (£2.80), lamb Madras (£2.95), steak and kidney pie, roast spring chicken and bacon or deep-fried haddock (£3), cold gammon salad (£3.50), scampi (£3.75), cold poached Tay salmon (£4), and home-made puddings like tropical fruit torte (from £1.25). The gracious dining-room has unusual antique wallpaper. McEwans 80/- on air-pressure tall founts; charming, efficient service. Darts, pool, dominoes, cribbage, fruit machine, juke box and piped music. The tranquil hotel lounge is a lovely place to sit over a long drink; there are antique tables and paintings, chinoiserie chairs and chintzy easy chairs, an oriental rug on one wall, a splendid corner sofa and magazines on a table. The B6355 southwards from here over the Lammermuirs, and its right fork through Longformacus, are both fine empty moors roads. (*Recommended by G Milligan, T Nott, Mr and Mrs Norman Edwardes, Eleanor Chandler*)

Free house   Licensee Chris Crook   Meals and snacks (not Sat evening)   Children welcome   Restaurant   Open 11–11 all year   Bedrooms tel Gifford (062 081) 240; £40B/ £52.50B

GLASGOW (Strathclyde)   NS5865 Map 11
Babbity Bowster ✍
16–18 Blackfriars Street

In a quiet pedestrian-only street this unusual pub/hotel – in a Robert Adam town house – has an almost continental atmosphere, and one where women on their own seem comfortable. There are pierced-work stools and wall seats around dark grey tables on the stripped boards, an open fire, and fine tall windows. A big ceramic of a kilted dancer and piper on the pale grey walls illustrates the folk song which gives the place its name – *Bab at the Bowster*; also, well lit photographs and big pen-and-wash drawings of Glasgow and its people and musicians; piped Scottish music (and occasional good-value musical dinners with folk like Dougie McLean). Well kept Maclays 70/- on air-pressure tall fount, a remarkably sound collection of wines, and even good tea and coffee. Enterprising food, usefully available from 8am until 9pm, starts with good breakfasts, then, after midday, includes soup (95p), haggis, neeps and tatties (from £1.85), traditional pies such as chicken and mushroom or spiced vegetable (£1.95), filled baked potatoes (from £1.95), fresh mussels in wine (£2.35), stovies (from £2.65) and several dishes of the day. Puddings range from chocolate and orange fudge cake to apple strudel with cream (from £1.15). A small terrace has tables under cocktail parasols. *(Recommended by WFL, Neville Burke, Martin Rayner)*

Free house   Licensee Fraser Laurie   Real ale   Meals and snacks   Restaurant; closed Sun   Children in restaurant   Open 11–midnight (and for breakfast); closed 1 Jan   Bedrooms tel 041-552 5055; £28.50S/£52S

Bon Accord

153 North Street

There are eighteen real-ale founts in this simply refurbished and stylishly neat place: Belhaven 80/-, Greenmantle, Ind Coope Burton, Marstons Pedigree, Theakstons XB and Old Peculier all on handpump, Caledonian 70/- and 80/-, McEwans 70/- and Maclays 70/- and 80/- on air-pressure tall founts, and guest beers as well (on handpump) – if the friendly landlord isn't too pushed he'll let you sample the beer before you make your choice; quite a few malt whiskies, too. A wide choice of bar food includes filled rolls (from 55p), home-made soup (£1), ploughman's, burgers (from £1.20), lasagne, seafood platter or beef stew in Belgian beer (£3.25) and mixed grill (£3.60). There are padded leatherette seats and little rounded-back chairs, the red hessian walls are decorated with beer-trays and the floor is partly carpeted, partly new quarry tiles; one side has quiet booth seating, with dominoes and cribbage, and there is a fruit machine and trivia game machine in a back lobby (a TV in the bar may be on for sport). It can get very busy on weekend evenings, when there's a pianist. *(Recommended by Tim and Lynne Crawford, Alastair Campbell, Ian Baillie)*

Free house   Real ale   Children in restaurant   Restaurant tel 041-248 4427   Occasional live music   Daytime parking restricted   Open 11–midnight all year

Horseshoe

17–19 Drury Street

From the horseshoe-shaped promontories of the enormous bar itself, the horseshoe motif in this Victorian monument spreads through a horseshoe wall clock to horseshoe-shaped fireplaces (most blocked by mirrors now); there's a great deal of glistening mahogany and darkly varnished panelled dado, a mosaic tiled floor, a lustrous pink and maroon ceiling, lots of old photographs of Glasgow and its people, antique magazine colour plates, pictorial tile inserts of decorous ladies, and curly brass and glass wall lamps. The bar counter, which still has pillared snob-screens, has old-fashioned brass water taps (and a house whisky blend); Broughton Greenmantle, Caledonian 70/-, Maclays 80/- and Tennents 80/- on handpump; fruit machines, a trivia machine and TV. The upstairs bar is less special, though popular with young people. The three-course lunch, with a wide choice of main dishes, is a steal at £1.40; evening hot dishes range from £1 to £1.50. *(More reports please)*

Tennents (Bass)   Licensee David Smith   Real ale   Meals and snacks   Children in eating area of bar   Live music every evening   Open 11–midnight all year

Pot Still

154 Hope Street

Crammed with several hundred malt whiskies – helpfully documented – the elegantly pillared and moulded bar gantry of this well run split-level pub includes several different versions of the great single malts in different ages and strengths, far more vatted malts than we knew of (these are blends, but malts only – no grain whisky), and a changing attractively priced malt-of-the-month. They sell by the bottle as well as the glass. It's attractively decorated, with comfortably upholstered banquettes in bays around heavy cast-iron-framed tables, photographs of old Glasgow on red baize walls, and slender pillars supporting the ornately coffered high dark maroon ceiling – with its two raj fans. Bar food includes home-made soup (75p), sandwiches (from 65p, toasties 10p extra), burgers (from £1.15), big ploughman's (£2.30), cold meat salads (£2.50), lasagne (£2.55) and lamb leg cutlet (£2.85). McEwans 80/- and Youngers No 3 on air-pressure tall fount. No jeans allowed, and the white-shirted barmen wear black bow ties. *(Recommended by Mr and Mrs J H Adam; more reports please)*

Free house   Licensee James Keenan   Real ale   Meals and snacks (12–10)   Open 11–11 all year; closed 25 Dec and 1 Jan

GLENCOE (Highland)   NN1058 Map 11

Clachaig

Inn signposted off A82; OS Sheet 42 reference 128567

Tucked by a little stream among sycamores and birch trees with the mountains soaring above, this slate-roofed white house shares its isolation with a discreetly tucked-away group of chalets. The back public bar is a biggish plain room kitted out for climbers and walkers (it serves as a mountain rescue post), with a nice big wood-burning stove in one stone fireplace and another in an opposite corner to thaw out the winter skiers; the atmosphere's lively and cheerful. On the other side, a big modern-feeling lounge bar has tables with green leatherette cushioned wooden wall seats and spindle-back chairs around its edges; decorated with good mountaineering photographs, it's usually quieter but can get very lively on folk nights. Simple but robust bar snacks include bridies and toasties (50p), home-made soup (85p), cheeseburgers (£1) and home-made shepherd's pie (£1.25) in summer, with even more substantial hot dishes added in winter – curries (£4.50 for a three-course meal), gammon, fish, steaks; well kept McEwans 80/- and Youngers Scotch and No 3 on air-pressure tall founts, a good range of malt whiskies; pool in the public bar. The friendly landlord is helpful with suggestions for walks. The inn has cheap bunkhouse beds as well as the more orthodox ones in the black clapboarded extension. *(Recommended by Steve Waters, A J Alcock, Alan Hall)*

Free house   Licensees Peter and Eileen Daynes   Real ale   Snacks (all day)   Children in lounge   Folk music Sat; winter lecturers eg Chris Bonnington and Tues mountain safety talks   Open 11–11 all year   Bedrooms tel Ballachulish (085 52) 252; £17/£26(£36B)

GLENDEVON (Tayside)   NN9904 Map 11

Tormaukin 🏵 🍺

A823

Ideally placed for walks over the nearby Ochils or along the River Devon which flows past the front of this cosy and neatly kept inn, and Loch and river fishing can be arranged with boats for hire; there are also said to be ninety golf courses within an hour's drive. Inside, all alterations are now complete – there's an extra, beamed eating area with an open log fire. The bar is softly lit and has plush seats against stripped stone and partly panelled walls. Ind Coope Burton on handpump, a good choice of wines (by the bottle or half-bottle) and malt whiskies, and gentle piped music. Very good bar food includes home-made soup (£1.10), char-grilled herring fillets (£1.45), spicy chicken winglets (£1.50), home-made pâté (£1.85), stovies or tagliatelle carbonara (£3.45), superb hand-made venison sausages with Cumberland sauce (£3.50), grilled whole fresh plaice (£3.45), home-made game pie (£4.30), salmon en croûte (£4.30), daily specials and puddings (from £1.45); they serve soup, cold meat and other salads and coffee throughout the day, and the breakfasts are very good. Four additional bedrooms have been created in the old stableblock. *(Recommended by G Smith, Mr and Mrs J H Adam, Miss A Tress, PLC, Syd and Wyn Donald, J N Fiell)*

Free house   Licensee Marianne Worthy   Real ale   Meals (12–2, 5–9.30 Mon–Sat; 12–9.30 Sun)   Children in restaurant until 7   Restaurant   Open 11–11 all year; closed 25 Dec, 1 Jan and two weeks mid-Jan   Bedrooms tel Muckhart (025 981) 252; £35B/£48B

HOWGATE (Lothian) NT2458 Map 11
Old Howgate Inn 🏆

The white-panelled bar in this civilised inn is airy and pretty with red plush window seats and nests of oak stools, a tiled floor and a stone fireplace; a couple of comfortable sitting-rooms have easy chairs and orange-red hessian walls. Interesting bar food includes a wide range of attractively presented, small Danish-style open sandwiches (they call them finger pieces): chicken liver pâté with mixed pickle (£1.55), Danish herring on rye bread, chicken with curry mayonnaise, prawn and lemon mayonnaise, dill-pickled salmon with mustard dressing or a selection of each (£1.75); they also do rib-eye steak sandwiches (£4.25) and a hot dish of the day such as spicy lamb casserole (from £3.50). Belhaven 80/-, McEwans 80/- and Theakstons Best on handpump, as well as a weekly guest beer, and frozen akvavit; friendly, helpful service. There are some teak tables on a small back lawn, edged with potentilla and herbaceous borders. *(Recommended by S J A Velate, David and Ruth Hollands, W F Coghill, Malcolm Ramsay)*

Free house   Licensees S Walsh and F D Arther   Real ale   Snacks   Restaurant tel Penicuik (0968) 74244   Children in restaurant   Open 11–2.30, 5–11; closed 25 Dec, 1 Jan

INVERARNAN (Central) NN3118 Map 11
Inverarnan Inn
A82 N of Loch Lomond

The barman in this old drovers' inn wears a kilt, and the long friendly bar is decorated with a horsecollar and a gun among the Highland paintings on the walls, bagpipes, green tartan cushions and deerskins on the black winged settles, and a stuffed golden eagle on the bar counter. Log fires burn in big fireplaces, there are stripped stone or butter-coloured plaster walls, small windows, red candles in Drambuie bottles if not candlesticks, and cupboards of pewter and china; piped Scottish traditional music. Sandwiches (toasties £1, steak £2.80), stags' broth (85p), Drovers' tart (£1), pâté (£1.30), herring with oatmeal (£3) and fresh salmon steak (£6). A range of good malts; peanuts 25p a handful. Lots of sporting trophies (such as a harpooned gaping shark), horns and so forth hang on the high walls of the central hall, where there's a stuffed badger curled on a table and a full suit of armour. Outside, in a field beside the house (also on a small back terrace), there are tables with cocktail parasols, a donkey, pony, and three aggressive geese; a stream runs behind. Worth knowing about, too, as a simple but decent place to stay at. *(Recommended by Gary Scott, E J Alcock, Nick Dowson, Alison Hayward, Roy Butler, Dr R Conrad)*

Free house   Licensee Duncan McGregor   Meals and snacks (12–2.30, 6–8.30) Restaurant   Children welcome   Impromptu live music   Open 11–midnight (11–10 in winter)   Bedrooms tel Inveruglas (030 14) 234; £14.50/£29

ISLE OF WHITHORN (Dumfries and Galloway) NX4736 Map 9
Steam Packet 🛏

The fine natural harbour here – sheltered by a long quay – is one of the most attractive in south-west Scotland; there are interesting buildings, little shops and always something to watch, such as people pottering in their yachts or inshore fishing boats, fishermen mending their nets and boys fishing from the end of the pier. Every 1½ to 4 hours there are boat trips from the harbour, and in the rocky grass by the harbour mouth are the remains of St Ninian's Kirk. The picture windows from this friendly and comfortably modernised inn have superb views, and it's naturally a popular place with locals and visitors alike. The low-ceilinged, grey carpeted bar has two rooms: on the right, plush button-back banquettes, brown carpet, and boat pictures; on the left, green leatherette stools around cast-iron-framed tables on big stone tiles, and a wood-burning stove in the bare stone wall. Good value bar food includes home-made soup (60p), filled rolls, fried haddock (£2), scampi (£2.75), steak au poivre (£6) and a daily special such as steak pie or quiche (£2). It may be served in the lower beamed dining-room, which has a big model steam packet boat on the white walls, excellent colour wildlife photographs, rugs on its wooden floor, and a solid-fuel stove; darts, pool and background music. The garden has white tables and chairs. *(Recommended by David and Flo Wallington, T Nott, Tony Pounder)*

Free house   Licensee John Scoular   Meals and snacks   Upstairs restaurant   Children welcome   Folk music alternate Weds evenings   Open 11–11 in summer; 11–2.30, 5–11 weekdays in winter   Bedrooms tel Whithorn (098 85) 334; £15B/£30B

ISLE ORNSAY (Isle of Skye)   NG6912 Map 11
Hotel Eilean Iarmain   ★   🚫   🛏
Signposted off A851 Broadford–Armadale

In a lovely spot, this sparkling white building has a big and cheerfully busy bar with a swooping stable-stall-like wooden divider that gives a two-room feel: leatherette wall seats, brass lamps and a brass-mounted ceiling fan, good tongue-and-groove panelling on the walls and ceiling, and a huge mirror over the open fire. If you hear the friendly staff and many of the customers speaking Gaelic, don't think it's to exclude you – it's just that that really is their everyday language (even the drinks price list and menus are in Gaelic – with translations). Bar food includes home-made soup (60p), sandwiches (from 60p), pâté (£1), haddock (£3), salmon steaks (£6.80), a hot daily special such as casseroled steak or curry (£3.25) and good local fish such as smoked mussels (£1.30) or fresh prawns (from £3). Dinners are served in the pretty dining-room, which has a lovely sea view past the little island of Ornsay itself and the lighthouse on Sionnach (you can walk over the sands at low tide). Well kept McEwans 80/- on electric pump, local brands of blended and vatted malt whisky (including their own blended whisky called Te Bheag and a splendid vatted island malt called Poit Dhubh, also bottled for them but seeping on to the mainland market), and a good wine list; darts, pool, dominoes and piped music. Some of the simple bedrooms are in a cottage opposite. This is an attractive part of Skye – less austere than the central mountains – where you will probably see red deer, and maybe otters and seals. *(Recommended by S J A Velate, Roger Danes, C A Holloway, Dr J R Hamilton, Vera Kelman, MJL, Mrs H Church, Colin Oliphant, AHNR)*

Free house   Licensee Sir Iain Noble   Real ale   Meals and snacks   Children welcome   Local folk or Scottish music Fri and Sat   Restaurant; not Sun lunch   Open 11–11 in summer; 11–2.30, 5–11 in winter   Bedrooms tel Isle of Skye (047 13) 332; £22(£25B)/£44(£50B)

KILCHRENAN (Strathclyde)   NS5285 Map 11
Taychreggan   🛏
B845 7 miles S of Taynuilt

In a beautiful spot, this civilised lochside hotel has an airy bar decorated with local photographs, stuffed birds, salmon flies and rods, and lots of stuffed locally caught fish – some of them real monsters; furnishings include turquoise cloth easy chairs and banquettes around low glass-topped tables. Attractively served lunchtime bar food includes sandwiches (from 80p), soup (£1), game terrine (£1.85), ploughman's (£2.40), home-made burger (£2.60), smoked Inverawe salmon (£3.20) and lots of salads (£3.80 for fresh salmon, £4.50 for Oban prawns). Neatly dressed waiters; unobtrusive piped music. Arched French windows open from the bar on to a cobbled inner courtyard which has slatted white seats and tables among bright hanging baskets, standard roses, and wistaria and clematis climbing the whitewashed walls. Well kept gardens run down to the water, where the hotel has fishing and hires boats on the loch. Some bedrooms overlook the loch. *(Recommended by E J Alcock, Heather Sharland; more reports please)*

Free house Licensee John Tyrrell Lunchtime meals and snacks Evening restaurant Children welcome Open 11–3, 6–11; closed Nov–Feb Bedrooms tel *Kilchrenan (086 63) 211; £39B/£78B*

KILMARTIN (Strathclyde)   NR8398 Map 11
Kilmartin Hotel   🛏

A816 Lochgilphead–Oban

This unassuming white-painted village inn has two snug and softly lit rooms decorated with old Scottish landscape, field sport and genre pictures, and a fine pre-war Buchanan whisky advertisement of polo-players; there are spindle-back armchairs, a settee, and a variety of settles including some attractive carved ones; some are built into a stripped stone wall snugged under the lower part of the staircase. Bar food, served generously, includes sandwiches (from 80p), home-made soup (70p), breaded beef cutlet (£2), home-cooked gammon salad (£3), smoked salmon quiche (£3.50), minute steak (£4.50) and venison in blackberry sauce (£6); vegetarian dishes and excellent breakfasts; good service. Sensibly placed darts, dominoes, maybe piped music. The inn is near the start of *Good Walks Guide* Walk 179. *(Recommended by C A Holloway)*

Free house Licensee Keith Parkinson Meals and snacks (12–2, 6–9) Accordion and fiddle Fri and Sat evenings Restaurant Children welcome until 9 Open 11–11 all year Bedrooms tel *Kilmartin (054 65) 244; £14(£16B)/£28(£32B); single occupancy of double rooms off season only*

KILMELFORD (Strathclyde)   NM8412 Map 11
Cuilfail

A816 S of Oban

Across the road from this Virginia-creeper-covered hotel is a very pretty tree-sheltered garden with picnic-table sets among pieris and rhododendrons (they serve afternoon tea here on request). The pubby bar has stripped stone walls, a stone bar counter with casks worked into it, foreign banknotes on the exposed joists, little winged settles around sewing-machine treadle tables on the lino floor and a wood-burning stove (open in cold weather). An inner eating-room has light wood furnishings, and the good choice of imaginative bar food includes soup (including a vegetarian one, 95p), sandwiches, sweet-cured herring, wine and nut pâté; main dishes such as haddock, mixed bean casserole, home-made burger, almond risotto with peanut sauce and steak and mushroom pie (from £2.25 to £4.50), with good puddings including sticky toffee pudding, honey and brandy cheesecake and fudgy nut and raisin pie (£1.25). Well kept Youngers No 3 on air-pressure tall fount (and served in jugs if you wish), and a good range of malt whiskies; darts, dominoes, cribbage and piped music. Though dogs are welcome, the owners warn that Heidi their St Bernard is large and noisy – they also have a labrador. *(Recommended by Ray Wainwright; more reports please)*

Free house Licensee James McFadyen Real ale Meals and snacks Evening restaurant Children in eating area of bar Open 11–2.30 (may close earlier if not busy), 5–11 all year; closed last two weeks Jan, first week Feb Bedrooms tel *Kilmelford (085 22) 274; £15(£21B)/£36(£42B)*

KIPPFORD (Dumfries and Galloway)   NX8355 Map 9
Anchor

Since changing hands in 1988, this well kept waterfront inn has recovered its former cheerful equanimity, and there's a warm welcome for everybody – whether you're in oilskins and yellow wellies or a visitor hoping for a decent meal in comfort. The traditional heart of the place has been in the back bar with its newly varnished panelled walls and ceiling, built-in red plush seats (some of them forming quite high booths around sturdy wooden tables), nautical prints and a coal fire. A lounge bar – mainly for eating in – has been opened up at the front; it overlooks the big natural harbour and has a tremendous variety of old and new prints on the walls of local granite, and dark blue plush banquettes and stools on the patterned carpet. Very good home-made bar food cooked by the licensee's wife includes soup (75p), good open sandwiches (from £1.75, prawn £2.95), filled baked potatoes (from £1.75), a half-pint of prawns (£2.15), fresh haddock (£2.80, when available), with daily specials chalked up on a blackboard such as curry or lasagne (£2.75), steak pie or roast beef (£2.95); children's dishes (from £1.20); well kept McEwans 80/- from air-pressure tall fount; cheerful, helpful staff. A games-room has a fruit machine, pool-table and video machine, and there's also dominoes and a juke box. Please note, they no longer do bedrooms. *(Recommended by John and Joan Dawson, Robert Wells, Stuart Murray, G A Worthington, NWN, David and Flo Wallington)*

Scottish & Newcastle   Licensees Simon and Margaret Greig   Real ale   Meals and snacks (12–2, 6–9)   Children welcome   Live music Sun evening   Open 10.30–midnight; 11–2.30, 6–11 in winter

LOCH ECK (Strathclyde)   NS1391 Map 11

Whistlefield

From A815 along lochside, turn into lane signposted Ardentinny; pub almost immediately to the right

Looking out over the loch and to the hills beyond, this isolated seventeenth-century house was once a drovers' inn. The cosy, low-ceilinged lounge bar has a fishing and shooting feel, with old guns, fishing rods and prints of sea trout and other fish on the bare stone or rough plaster walls, winged pine settles and stools upholstered in green and white tweed on the tartan carpet, and a log fire. A games-room has a pool-table, video game, two fruit machines, dominoes and cards; piped music. Well kept Tennents 70/- and 80/- and a good choice of bar food that includes soup (95p), filled baked potatoes (from £1.20), herring in dill (£1.75), various ploughman's (£2.40), haddock (£2.75), chilli con carne (£3.50), steak (£6.95), weekly specials such as stovies (£1), and home-made puddings (£1.75). Since the spring a new front terrace with tables and chairs, and a children's play area, have been added. There's a log cabin for hire, fishing boats for rent at £20 a day and fishing permits for £3 a day. *(Recommended by E J Alcock; more reports please)*

Free house   Licensee Ian Smith   Meals and snacks   Children in family-room   Open 11–11 all year; may close 2.30–6.30 if trade quiet   Bedrooms tel Strachur (036 986) 250; £13/£26

MELROSE (Borders)   NT5434 Map 9

Burts Hotel 🏆 🛏️

A6091

In perhaps the quietest and most villagey of all the Scottish Border towns, this welcoming, eighteenth-century inn has a comfortable L-shaped lounge bar with cushioned wall seats and Windsor armchairs on its Turkey carpet, and Scottish prints on the walls. A good range of waitress-served bar food includes soup (80p), two pâtés (£1.75), ploughman's (£2.50), haddock (£2.80), honey-baked ham or rare roast beef salads (£3), deep-fried breadcrumbed chicken (£3.40), scampi (£3.70), sirloin steak (£7), and puddings like home-made rhubarb crumble (£1); also, evening specials such as galantine of pheasant with whisky sauce or smoked breast of goose with lime sauce (£2.20), vegetable curry (£3.80), braised lamb in mustard sauce (£4.30) and braised venison in soft fruit sauce (£4.30). Belhaven 80/- on electric pump under light blanket pressure; a wide range of malt whiskies and wines; good service; snooker-room (residents only). There's a well-tended garden where there are tables in summer. *(Recommended by Mr and Mrs D M Norton, John Perry, Syd and Wyn Donald, Dr R Fuller, T Nott, Y Batts, John Spencely)*

Free house   Licensees Graham and Anne Henderson   Real ale   Meals and snacks (12–2, 6–9.30; 10.30 Sat)   Children welcome   Restaurant   Open 11–2.30, 5–11 all year Bedrooms tel Melrose (089 682) 2285; £28B/£50B

MOFFAT (Dumfries and Galloway)   NT0905 Map 9
Black Bull

1 Churchgate

Burns scratched a witty verse about one of his girlfriends and her mother on a window here (the only pub for miles) – but now the window, glass and all, is in a Moscow museum. Across a small courtyard from the main building the basic pubby bar has built-in benches, red panelling covered with metal station plates and other railway memorabilia, and well kept McEwans 80/- and Youngers No 3 on electric pump; a very good choice of malt whiskies. The softly lit cocktail bar is decidedly plusher and cosier, with soft piped music, plum-coloured walls, a pink ceiling and burgundy leatherette-upholstered seats. The tiled-floor dining-room has benches along a row of plastic tables set for food, and there are coaching notices and prints on the walls. Good lunchtime bar food includes tasty home-made soup (70p), pâté (£1.15), ploughman's (£2.50), salads (from £2.50), and hot specials such as excellent haggis, very good fresh plaice, shepherd's or fish pie (£2.50); children's helpings; quick service. There's a side room with darts, dominoes, a fruit machine, space game, trivia and piped music. Outside on the courtyard there are picnic-table sets. *(Recommended by Steve Waters, A E Alcock, Hazel Morgan, Cdr J W Hackett, G Smith, Miss A Tress, G A Worthington, Mr and Mrs J H Adam, Jill Hadfield, Tony Gallagher, Neil and Angela Huxter, David Fisher, Heather Sharland)*

Free house   Licensee Jim Hughes   Real ale   Meals and snacks   Children welcome until 9 Restaurant; not Sun evening   Open 11–11 Sun–Weds, 11–midnight Thurs–Sat all year Bedrooms tel Moffat (0683) 20206; £16B/£30B

MONIAIVE (Dumfries and Galloway)   NX7790 Map 9
George 🏠

Worth quite a detour, the endearing little flagstoned bar in this ancient white stone Covenanters' inn has a most welcoming atmosphere and relaxed, friendly and efficient staff. The butter-coloured timbered walls have good antique Tam O'Shanter engravings, and there are some small seats made from curious conical straight-sided kegs, high winged black settles upholstered with tartan carpet, dark butter-coloured ceiling planks and open fires in winter. Just off here is a pleasant, airy eating area with views of the nearby hills: home-made soup (70p), filled rolls (90p), delicious fresh sandwiches (from £1), home-made chicken liver pâté (£2), haggis (£2.50), haddock (£2.75), open sandwiches (from £2.50, prawn £2.95), home-made steak and kidney pie (£3.60) and venison in red wine (£4). Darts, pool-table, dominoes, cribbage, fruit machine, and juke box away in the public bar. The peaceful riverside village is surrounded by fine scenery. *(Recommended by Gethin Lewis, Mr and Mrs J H Adam, G Bloxsom)*

Free house   Licensees Alan, Marjorie and Richard Price   Meals and snacks   Children welcome   Restaurant (Fri–Sun evenings; Sun lunch)   Open 11–2.30, 5–11 Mon–Thurs; 11–midnight Fri and Sat   Bedrooms tel Moniaive (084 82) 203; £13.50/£27

Please tell us if the décor, atmosphere, food or drink at a pub is different from our description. We rely on readers' reports to keep us up to date. No stamp needed: *The Good Pub Guide*, FREEPOST, London SW10 0BR.

MONYMUSK (Grampian)   NJ6815 Map 11
Grant Arms
Inn and village sigposted from B993 SW of Kemnay

Below Bennachie, this handsome eighteenth-century stone inn has exclusive rights
to fifteen miles of good trout and salmon fishing on the River Don, eleven beats
with twenty-nine named pools, and there's a ghillie available. Inside, the lounge bar
is divided into two areas by a log fire in the stub wall, and there are some newly
upholstered, burgundy armchairs as well as other seats, a patterned carpet and dark
panelling, and it is decorated with paintings by local artists, which are for sale. Bar
food includes soup (85p), sandwiches, fried haddock or lemon sole (£2.95), fresh
crab (£3.95) and sirloin steak (£6). The simpler public bar has darts, dominoes,
cribbage, fruit machine, space game and piped music; Tennents 80/- and Youngers
No 3 on air-pressure tall founts. North of the village – spick and span in its estate
colours of dark red woodwork and natural stone – the gently rolling wooded
pastures soon give way to grander hills. *(More reports please)*

Free house   Licensee Colin Hart   Real ale   Meals and snacks (12–2.15, 6.30–9.30)
Restaurant   Children welcome   Open 11–2.30, 5–11 (midnight Sat) all year
Bedrooms tel Monymusk (046 77) 226; £25(£32B)/£42(£45B)

MOUNTBENGER (Borders)   NT3125 Map 9
Gordon Arms
Junction of A708 and B709

The cosy public bar in this little hotel has an interesting set of photographs of
blackface rams from local hill farms, there's a fire in cold weather and a local
'shepherd song' is pinned on the wall; a hundred and fifty years ago another
shepherd poet, James Hogg, the 'Ettrick Shepherd', recommended that this very inn
should keep its licence, which Sir Walter Scott, in his capacity as a justice and who
also knew the inn, subsequently granted. Good bar food includes lunchtime
sandwiches (from 75p), home-made soup (95p), lunchtime ploughman's (£1.75),
salads (£2.75), fresh Yarrow trout or home-made steak pie (£3.75); additional
evening dishes include lamb chops (£3.95), gammon (£4.95) and steaks (from
£7.50); children's dishes (from £1.25). Well kept Greenmantle on handpump
(brewed in Broughton, near Peebles) and Tennents 80/- on air-pressure tall fount;
large choice of malt whiskies. A lounge bar serves high teas – a speciality here – and
there's a games-room with pool, fruit machine and piped music. In addition to the
hotel bedrooms, they are building a bunkhouse with showers and drying facilities as
cheap accommodation for hill walkers and cyclists. The pub is a welcome sight
from either of the two lonely moorland roads which cross here: both roads take you
through attractive scenery, and the B-road in particular is very grand – indeed, it
forms part of a splendid empty moorland route between the A74 and Edinburgh
(from Lockerbie, B723/B709/B7062/A703/A6094). *(Recommended by Simon Ward,
Dave Butler, Lesley Storey; more reports please)*

Free house   Licensees Mr and Mrs H M Mitchell   Real ale   Meals and snacks
Restaurant   Children in eating area   Accordion and fiddle club third Weds every month;
folk club third Sat every month   Open 11–11; 11–2.30 Tues–Fri, 11–11 Sat and Sun, closed
Mon, in winter   Bedrooms tel Yarrow (0750) 82222/82232; £15/£26.50

NEWBURGH (Grampian)   NJ9925 Map 11
Udny Arms 🛏
The lounge bar in this hospitable and well kept place has carefully chosen furniture
that includes prettily cushioned stripped pine seats and wooden chairs around plain
wooden tables on the grey carpet, and bird prints, salmon flies, and a pictorial map
of the River Dee on the cream walls. Generous helpings of decent food in the

downstairs bar (open all day) include green-pea soup (90p), sausage bake (£1.95), cold roast meat or lasagne (£2.95), and sticky toffee pudding (£1.55); in the lounge bar, lunchtime food includes cheese and onion savouries with spicy dip (£3.65), tagliatelle with mushrooms in lemon and thyme sauce (£3.95) and steak and vegetable pie (£4.15). In the afternoon they serve tea and shortbread. Well kept McEwans 80/- on air-pressure tall fount, house wines, a selection of malt whiskies and bottled beers, and espresso coffee; friendly staff; piped music and pétanque. A sun lounge has green basket chairs around glass-topped wicker tables. On the sheltered back lawn there are lots of white tables, and from here a footbridge crosses the little Foveran Burn to the nine-hole golf links, the dunes and the sandy beach along the Ythan estuary. There are three good golf courses and Pitmedden Gardens nearby. *(Recommended by T and A D Kucharski, Chris France)*

Scottish & Newcastle   Licensee Alan Jappy   Real ale   Meals and snacks   Children welcome   Restaurant   Open 11–11.30 all year   Bedrooms tel Newburgh (Aberdeen) (035 86) 89444; £36B/£52B

OBAN (Strathclyde)   NM8630 Map 11
Oban Inn
Stafford Street

The downstairs beamed bar in this late eighteenth-century inn has a lively atmosphere and a good mix of local customers – harbour folk, fishermen, Navy divers, doctors, lawyers and so forth. There are small stools, pews and black winged modern settles on its uneven slate floor, blow-ups of old Oban postcards on its cream walls, and unusual brass-shaded wall lamps. Upstairs, a quieter and more decorous carpeted bar has button-back banquettes around cast-iron-framed tables, some panelling and a coffered woodwork ceiling; besides the real windows overlooking the harbour, it has little back-lit arched false windows with heraldic roundels in seventeenth-century stained glass. Bar snacks, served all day, include home-made soup (85p) and fresh mussels (£1), while lunchtime meals include filled baked potatoes (£1.95), haggis and neeps or salads (£2.95). Well kept McEwans 80/- and Youngers No 3 from tall founts, a large selection of whiskies, and hot toddies; dominoes, piped pop music. *(Recommended by Keith Mills, E J Alcock, Roy Butler)*

Scottish & Newcastle   Licensee Michael Hewitt   Real ale   Lunchtime meals (12–2.30) and snacks (11–1am)   Children in eating area of bar 12–2.30 only   Folk 9–midnight Sun Open 11–1am all year   Bedrooms being refurbished, prices not fixed as we went to press tel Oban (0631) 62484

nr PITLOCHRY (Tayside)   NN9458 Map 11
Killiecrankie Hotel   🏵 🍺
Killiecrankie signposted from A9 N of Pitlochry

Friendly, attentive new owners have taken over this comfortable country hotel – a far cry from the Swan in Stewkley, Buckinghamshire, which they ran before (earning praise from readers there). They plan to keep things much as they are – most notably the chef, but also the stuffed birds, a red squirrel holding some nuts, and good wildlife photographs. The bar (which opens into a front sun-lounge extension) has light armchairs and dimpled copper tables. Very good food includes home-made soup (£1.25), open sandwiches (crab and avocado £3.50), Swedish chicken mayonnaise salad (from £3.95), very good home-cooked ham salad, Highland game casserole or goujons of fresh sole with lemon mayonnaise (£4.50); there are evening main courses like a vegetarian dish (£3.55), smokies (£3.95), fresh trout in oatmeal (£4.50) and Angus sirloin steak (£6.50). The spacious grounds

Pubs with attractive or unusually big gardens are listed at the back of the book.

back on to the hills and include a putting course and a croquet lawn – sometimes there are roe deer and red squirrels. The views of the mountain pass are splendid. *(Recommended by R G Bentley, Helen and John Thompson, T Nott, RB, AHNR)*

Free house Licensees Colin and Carole Anderson Meals and snacks (12–2, 7–10) Children welcome, no infants in evenings Restaurant Open 12–2.30, 6–11; closed Nov–end Feb Bedrooms tel Pitlochry (0796) 3220; £27.50(£29.50B)/£53(£57B)

PLOCKTON (Highland)   NG8033 Map 11

Plockton Hotel

Village signposted from A87 near Kyle of Lochalsh

Strung out among palm trees along the seashore and looking across Loch Carron to rugged mountains, this low stone-built house has a comfortably furnished, partly panelled and partly bare stone lounge bar with green leatherette seats around neat Regency-style tables on a tartan carpet, an open fire, and a ship model set into the woodwork; window seats look out to the boats on the water. Bar food includes home-made soup (70p), filled rolls (from 70p, bacon 75p), sandwiches (from 70p, toasties 10p extra), home-made pâté or ploughman's (£1.95), vegetable pancake rolls (£2.25), fresh local prawns or smoked salmon quiche (£2.95), salads (from £2.95), with evening dishes like nut roast (£2.95), roast beef and Yorkshire pudding (£3.75), grilled sirloin steak (£5.95) and fresh wild salmon in season; children's dishes (£1.25), good breakfasts and first-rate service. Tennents 80/- on air-pressure tall fount and a good collection of whiskies. The separate public bar has darts, pool, shove-ha'penny, dominoes, cribbage and piped music; dogs welcome. The lovely village is owned by the National Trust for Scotland. *(Recommended by Paul King, Dr Q G Livingstone, Mr and Mrs R G Ing, Richard Gibbs)*

Free house Licensee Alasdair Bruce Meals and snacks (12.30–2, 6.30–8.30; basket meals until 9.30) Children in eating area of bar Open 11–2.30, 5–12 (11.30 Sat) all year Bedrooms tel Plockton (059 984) 250; £15.50S/£31S (twin rooms only)

PORTPATRICK (Dumfries and Galloway)   NX0154 Map 9

Crown ★ ✪ 🛏

A treasure is how one reader describes this delightful little harbourfront pub, under new licensees this year. The rambling old-fashioned bar has lots of little nooks, crannies and alcoves, and interesting furniture includes a carved settle with barking dogs as its arms and an antique wicker-backed armchair. There are shelves of old bottles above the bar counter, a stag's head over the coal fire, and the partly panelled butter-coloured walls are decorated with old mirrors with landscapes painted in their side panels; exceptional service and a really relaxing atmosphere. Food (the fish is caught by the chef) includes sandwiches (from 80p, toasties 95p, Danish open prawn sandwich £3), home-made soup (85p), smoked mackerel (£1.60), ploughman's £2, salads (fresh crab £4.30, prawn £5.70, lobster from £10), seafood kebab (£3), cod fillet (£3.80), whole grilled jumbo prawns (from £4.30), scallops (£5.70), steak (from £7), and seafood platter (from £13.75); excellent breakfasts. Piped music; sensibly placed darts in the separate public bar, and a fruit machine. An airy and very attractively decorated 1930s-ish dining-room opens through a quiet and attractively planted conservatory area into a sheltered back garden. Seats outside in front – served by hatch in the front lobby – make the most of the evening sun. Unusually attractive bedrooms have individual touches such as uncommon Munch prints. *(Recommended by David and Flo Wallington, NWN, T Nott; more reports please)*

Free house Licensee Curly Wilson Meals and snacks (noon–10) Restaurant Children welcome Open 11.30–11; 11–2.30, 5–11 in winter Bedrooms tel Portpatrick (077 681) 261; £26B/£46B

QUEENSFERRY (Lothian)   NT1278 Map 11
Hawes
In the quieter, older part of this old inn, there's still something of the atmosphere that made the inn so appealing to R L Stevenson – he used it as a setting in *Kidnapped*, and may even have been moved to start writing the book while staying here. The comfortable, airy lounge bar has a fine view of the Forth stretching out between the massively practical railway bridge and the elegantly supercilious road bridge. An efficient food counter serves soup (80p), four hot dishes which change daily such as burgers, chicken curry, pork chops or a pasta dish (from £3), and cold buffet with unusual salads (£3.15). Well kept Arrols 70/- and Tennents 80/- are served on handpump. The small public bar – more popular with younger people – has darts, dominoes, fruit machine and piped music. Tables outside overlook the Forth (where boat trips are available), and a back lawn with hedges and roses has white tables and a children's play area. *(Recommended by Roger Huggins, R P Taylor)*

Ind Coope (Allied)   Manager David Burns   Meals and snacks   Children in family-room until 8   Restaurant   Restaurant pianist Sat evenings   Open 11–11   Bedrooms tel 031-331 1990; £31/£45

ST ANDREWS (Fife)   NO5161 Map 11
Victoria Cafe
St Mary's Place; corner of Bell Street

Popular with young people – especially students in term-time – this attractive cafe has stripped panelling, tall green walls, a darker green ceiling with a colonial fan, bentwood chairs around marble-topped cast-iron tables on an oak floor, and brass lamps and potted plants; maybe piped modern jazz or juke box; a sunny roof terrace has three or four tables. Bar food, served throughout the day, includes good bacon rolls (£1), soup such as carrot and dill (80p), daily quiches such as broccoli and Brie (£1.05), filled baked potatoes (from £1.55), ploughman's (£1.80), steak sandwich (£2.15), salads (from £2.35, prawn £2.95; salad bar helpings from 50p), fried chicken (£2.95) and daily specials such as tortellini and a sauce topped with mozzarella (£2.65) or steak pie (£2.90). Maclays 80/- from an air-pressure tall fount, and good value fruit juices; fruit machine. A rather elegant oval room with waitress service is used as a family-room. *(Recommended by RCL, Alastair Campbell, Dr A V Lewis)*

Maclays   Licensee Peter Dickson   Real ale   Meals and snacks (11–9 in summer, 12–2, 7–9 in winter)   Summer restaurant tel St Andrews (0334) 76964   Children in snug and family-room   Occasional live music Thurs evening   Open 11–11 (midnight Thurs–Sat); closed one week Mar

ST BOSWELLS (Borders)   NT5931 Map 10
Buccleuch Arms
A68 just S of Newtown St Boswells

Opposite the village green and next to the cricket ground, this Victorian sandstone inn has a quiet, genteel atmosphere. The bar has reproduction Georgian-style panelling, pink plush seats, elegant banquettes, velvet curtains and something of a hunting theme; there may be dishes of nuts and other nibbles on the bar. The public bar is now called the Salmon Room and is for functions. Imaginative bar food (changed about three times a year) includes soup (85p), sandwiches, mushrooms in garlic butter (£1.25), chicken liver and whisky pâté (£1.50), ploughman's (£1.95), cold meat platter with salad (£3.25), scampi (£3.75), sugar-baked gammon with pineapple (£3.95) and sirloin steak (£6.25); daily specials such as steak and kidney pie, lamb korma, haggis and neeps or local trout; they serve sandwiches all day, do afternoon teas, and occasional speciality food nights such as Caribbean or

Moroccan. The inn is near *Good Walks Guide* Walk 162. *(Recommended by David Waterhouse, Robert and Vicky Tod, Syd and Wyn Donald)*

Free house   Licensee Mrs Lucy Agnew   Meals and snacks (12–2, 6–9 Mon–Thurs; 12–2, 6–10 Fri–Sat; 12.30–2.15, 6.30–9 Sun)   Restaurant   Children welcome   Open 11–11 all year   Bedrooms tel St Boswells (0835) 22243; £25(£30)/£45(£55B)

ST MARY'S LOCH (Borders)   NT2422 Map 9
Tibbie Shiels Inn 🛏

The cosy back bar in the original old stone part of this isolated and beautifully situated old inn (under new ownership) has well cushioned black wall benches or leatherette armed chairs, and a photograph of Tibbie Shiels herself: wife of the local mole-catcher and a favourite character of Age of Enlightenment Edinburgh literary society. Waitress-served food includes home-made soup (65p), sandwiches (from 70p), ploughman's (£1.50), home-made chilli con carne (£2.10), chicken curry (£2.30), tasty local trout or four-ounce rump steak (£3.10); daily specials such as bacon steaks in cider (£2.25), casseroled lamb (£3) or home-made steak and kidney pie (£4); home-made puddings like fruit pie, doughnuts or cloutie dumpling and cream (from 70p); coffee 50p. Bar food is served from noon to 9pm, and there are home-baked scones, cakes and shortbread at high tea. Well kept Belhaven 70/- and 80/- on handpump. There's a no-smoking dining area off the main lounge. Darts, cribbage, dominoes and piped music. The Southern Upland Way – a long-distance footpath – passes close by, the Grey Mares Tail waterfall is just down the glen, and the loch is beautiful (with day members to the sailing club welcome, and fishing free to residents; it's very peaceful – except when low-flying jets explode into your consciousness). *(Recommended by Willy Hendrikx, S J A Velate, Mark Shinkfield, Joy Marshall, E J Alcock)*

Free house   Licensees Jack and Jill Brown   Meals and snacks (12–9 Mon–Sat, 12.30–9 Sun)   Children welcome   Restaurant; open 12.30–9 Sun   Open 11–11 in summer; 11–2.30, 6.30–11 in winter; 12.30–11 Sun; closed 25 Dec and Mon Nov–Mar   Bedrooms tel Selkirk (0750) 42231; £13/£26

SELKIRK (Borders)   NT4728 Map 10
Queens Head
28 West Port

The big open-plan, low-beamed lounge bar in this cheerful and well run town pub has been recently refurbished by the new owners: navy blue banquettes and wheel-back chairs around copper-topped tables on the blue and silver speckled carpet, a gas-effect coal fire, prints of Sir Walter Scott and his family on the walls, and pretty dried flower arrangements; the red carpeted, simpler public bar has sensibly placed darts, dominoes, a fruit machine, trivia and juke box. Excellent home-made food (served until 9.30pm) includes soup (75p), sandwiches (from 90p, toasties from 95p), steak and kidney pie, lasagne, haddock, various salads and vegetarian dishes such as ratatouille (all £2.85) and scampi (£3.25). The Border country around Selkirk, with gentle hills rising to rounded heather tops, is particularly beautiful; nearby Bowhill is a stately home in lavish grounds. No dogs in the lounge. *(Recommended by David Waterhouse)*

Free house   Licensees Eric and Ruth Paterson   Meals and snacks (12–2.30, 5–9.30; not Sun evening)   Open 11–11 all year

SHIELDAIG (Highland)   NG8154 Map 11
Tigh an Eilean 🛏
Village signposted just off A896 Lochcarron–Gairloch

In a gorgeous position at the head of Loch Shieldaig, this grey-shuttered white house looks over forested Shieldaig Island to Loch Torridon and then the sea beyond – at certain times of summer, straight down the path of the late-setting sun. The basic bar at the side (used by locals, some speaking Gaelic) has red brocaded button-back banquettes in bays, with picture windows looking out to sea and three picnic-table sets in a sheltered front courtyard. Quickly served decent simple bar food includes soup (70p), sandwiches (80p), Scotch pie (£1.50), squid (may be called octopus, £2.50), home-made steak and kidney pie (£2.95) and fresh salmon salad (£4); keg beers, darts, fruit machine. The residents' side is quite a contrast, with easy chairs, books and a well stocked help-yourself bar in the neat and prettily decorated two-room lounge, and an attractively modern comfortable dining-room specialising in good value local shellfish, fish and game. Like the public rooms, the front bedrooms have the view. The well kept hotel, which is small and friendly, has private fishing and can arrange sea fishing. *(Recommended by David and Angela Tindall, Joan and John Calvert)*

Free house   Licensee Mrs E Stewart   Meals and snacks (not Sun evening)   Evening restaurant   Children in bar until 8.30   Open 11–2.30, 5–11 all year; all day summer; closed Sun in winter   Bedrooms tel Shieldaig (052 05) 251; £20.90/£39.80(£45B)

SKEABOST (Isle of Skye)   NG4148 Map 11
Skeabost House Hotel   ★   🏵   🛏

A850 NW of Portree, 1½ miles past junction with A856

In pleasant grounds at the head of Loch Snizort – perhaps Skye's best salmon river, with private fishing – this very civilised and friendly small hotel has a high-ceilinged bar with a new pine counter, red brocade seats on its thick red carpet and some in a big bay window which overlooks a terrace (with picnic-table sets) and the neatly kept lawn; this doubles as a putting course and runs down to the loch, bright with bluebells on its far side. The spacious and airy no-smoking lounge has an attractively laid out buffet table with soup (80p), generously filled sandwiches or rolls, lots of salads (smoked chicken or turkey £3.80, fresh salmon £4.20), a hot dish of the day (£2.60), and puddings (90p); coffee; note that service stops at 1.30 in the lounge bar. Lots of malt whiskies. A fine panelled billiards room leads off the stately hall; there's a wholly separate public bar with darts, pool and juke box (and even its own car park). The grounds around the hotel include a bog-and-water garden under overhanging rocks and rhododendrons, and a nine-hole golf course. The village Post Office here has particularly good value Harris wool sweaters, blankets, tweeds and wools. *(Recommended by S J A Velate, Richard Whitehead, Guy Harris, Stephen R Holman, MJL, Mr and Mrs D E Milner, Mrs H Church)*

Free house   Licensee Iain McNab   Meals and snacks (not Sun)   Evening restaurant Children in eating area of bar   Open 11–2.30, 5–11; public bar closed Sun; closed 23 Oct 1989–11 Apr 1990   Bedrooms tel Skeabost Bridge (047 032) 202; £24(£29B)/£44(£58B)

nr SPEAN BRIDGE (Highland)   NN2281 Map 11
Letterfinlay Lodge Hotel   🛏

7 miles NE of Spean Bridge on A82

Set well back from the road, this secluded and genteel family-run country house has attractive grounds running down through rhododendrons to the jetty and Loch Lochy. The spacious modern bar, with comfortable brown plush seats clustered around dark tables, has a long glass wall giving splendid lochside views over to the steep forests on the far side; there's a games area to one side with darts, pool, dominoes, cribbage and a space game. Good and popular lunchtime food is served buffet-style, and includes home-made soup (90p), sandwiches (£1.25, salmon £1.50 when available), pâté with oatcakes (£1.60), roast local meat salads (£3.25), fresh fillet of haddock (£3.50), roast sirloin of Aberdeen Angus beef or pheasant (£3.75), fresh Loch Ness salmon (£4.75), and puddings (£1.25); excellent breakfasts. Good wines and decent coffee; friendly, attentive service. Opening off one side of the main bar is an elegantly panelled small cocktail bar (with a black-bow-tied barman) furnished with button-back leather seats, old prints, and a chart of the Caledonian Canal; piped music. On the side gravel there are a couple of white tables under cocktail umbrellas. Fishing and perhaps deerstalking can be arranged, there are shower facilities for customers on boating holidays, and a small caravan club; dogs welcome. *(Recommended by S J A Velate, David and Christine Foulkes, Mark Shinkfield, Joy Marshall, Richard Whitehead, D M Bednarowska)*

Free house   Licensee Ian Forsyth   Lunchtime meals and snacks   Children welcome Restaurant; closed Sun lunch   Open 11–1am weekdays, 11–midnight Sat; closed mid-Nov–Mar   Bedrooms tel Spean Bridge (039 781) 622; £23B/£46B

STEIN (Isle of Skye)   NG2656 Map 11

Stein Inn   [illustrated on page 857]

Waternish; B886, off A850 Dunvegan–Portree; OS Sheet 23 reference 263564

Under new ownership, this dark little flagstoned inn won't seem quite the same to people who knew it before its 1987 closure: there are plans for extensions, with more bedrooms proposed, for instance. What won't change much is the traditionally furnished bar with its partly panelled bare stone walls, country chairs around good solid tables, a beam and plank ceiling, and an open fire in the stone fireplace. Bar snacks are limited to rolls (from 65p); there's a fine choice of malt whiskies. Darts, shove-ha'penny, dominoes, cribbage and piped music. What was the restaurant now houses the pool-table. The pub's waterside position in this time-stood-still village on the west coast of Skye is perfect for the glorious sunsets you get this far north (towards 10.30 or 11 in high summer). There's a watersports centre. *(Recommended by SJAV, A C Lang; more reports on the changes please)*

Free house   Licensee Len MacDonald   Snacks   Open 11–12 Mon–Fri, 11–11.30 Sat, 12.30–11 Sun   Bedrooms tel Waternish (047 083) 208; /£30

SWINTON (Borders)   NT8448 Map 10

Wheatsheaf ⊗ ⊨

A6112 N of Coldstream

Everyone who's recommended this attractive small sandstone hotel, facing the long village green, has particularly praised the outstanding bar food, and that's what virtually all the customers are here for. Alan Reid the chef/patron is particularly strong on fish, such as mixed Scottish seafood as an hors-d'oeuvre, prawn and cheese salad (£2.95), dilled Danish herring, moules marinière or baked avocado with seafood (£2.80), smoked fish pie (£3.40), fresh hake (£4.80), Tweed salmon smoked (£4.90) or freshly poached, scallops (£8.45) and langoustines done with garlic (£8.95). A wide choice of other dishes, generously served, includes soup (80p), sandwiches (from 85p), deep-fried Brie with real ale pickle (£2.45), gammon salad or spinach pancake (£2.75), lasagne or vegetarian tortellini (£3), asparagus in season (£3.25), beef bordelaise or bourguignonne (£3.45), curries (from £3.65), minute steak (£4.30), game in season, Barbary duck breast done with blackcurrant sauce (£7), sirloin steak (£7.65) and a good many puddings such as summer pudding with cream or poached fresh peaches with Cointreau syrup (£1.45). Booking is advisable, particularly from Thursday to Saturday evening. The main area has sporting prints and plates on the figured hessian wall covering, an attractive long oak settle and some green-cushioned window seats as well as the wheel-back chairs around the tables, and a stuffed pheasant and partridge over the log fire; a small lower-ceilinged part by the counter has pubbier furnishings, and small agricultural prints on the walls – especially sheep. Well kept Greenmantle on air-pressure tall fount; decent range of malt whiskies, good wines and coffee; warmly welcoming friendly service. A quite separate side locals' bar has darts, pool, dominoes and fruit machine. The Reids hope that by Easter 1990 they will have a new no-smoking front conservatory/sun lounge. *(Recommended by Grahame Archer, Alan Hall, Mrs B Crosland, W A Wright, Mr and Mrs M D Jones)*

Free house   Licensees Alan and Julie Reid   Real ale   Meals and snacks (12–2, 5.30–10; not Mon)   Restaurant   Children in eating area   Open 11–2.30, 5.30–11 all year; closed Mon, also one week Oct, one week Feb   Bedrooms tel Swinton (089 086) 257; £19/£30

TARBERT (Strathclyde)   NR8467 Map 11

West Loch Hotel 🏨

A83 1 mile S

The cocktail bar in this quiet modernised country inn has brown cloth upholstered easy chairs, little basket-weave chairs, and photographs of Tarbert; it opens into a lounge with Liberty-print easy chairs, a log/peat fire and piped classical music. The small public bar has a wood-burning stove and old fishing photographs. Good bar food includes Scotch broth (90p), venison sausages (£2.95), black pudding and apple pancake (£3.50), tripe and onions or rabbit casserole (£3.75), good salads, filo parcels of leek and cheese (£4.10), smoked salmon and scrambled duck eggs (£4.50), local seafood in a light curry mayonnaise (£4.60), grilled Argyll quail with orange wine butter (£4.95), and puddings (£1.75); set evening meals including local fish and game; friendly service. *(Recommended by Dr T H M Mackenzie, Richard Whitehead, Christa Grosse, D M Bednarowska)*

Free house   Licensee Mrs Sandy Ferguson   Meals and snacks (12–2, 6.30–7.30) Restaurant   Children welcome   Open 12–2, 5–11 all year   Bedrooms tel Tarbert (088 02) 283; £16/£32

TAYVALLICH (Strathclyde)   NR7386 Map 11

Tayvallich Inn 🏮

B8025, off A816 1 mile S of Kilmartin; or take B841 turn-off from A816 two miles N of Lochgilphead

Looking over the lane and the muddy foreshore to the very sheltered yacht anchorage, the small bar in this simple pub has cigarette cards and local nautical charts on brown hessian walls, exposed ceiling joists, and pale pine upright chairs, benches and tables on its quarry-tiled floor; sliding glass doors open on to a concrete terrace furnished with picnic-table sets (which share the same view). Bar food includes home-made soup (95p), ploughman's (£2.10), burgers (from £2.85), croûte Tayvallich (baked dish of bacon, potatoes, egg, peppers and cheese) or sweet-and-sour vegetables (both £3), Cajun chicken (£3.75), sirloin steak (£6.75) and home-made puddings (£1.50); there is a strong emphasis on local fish and, particularly, shellfish, with moules marinière (£1.50), haddock (£2.85), half a dozen Loch Sween oysters (£3.50), salads (crab claw £3.50, whole jumbo prawns £5), seafood platter (£5.50) and Sound of Jura clams (£6.50). Decent house wines, darts. *(More reports please)*

Free house   Licensee John Grafton   Meals and snacks   Restaurant   Children welcome Open 11–midnight (1am Sat); 11–2.30, 6–11 in winter; closed Mon Nov–Mar The landlady has one room available in her house (not summer) tel Tayvallich (054 67) 282; /£20

TWEEDSMUIR (Borders)   NT0924 Map 9

Crook 🏮 🏨

A701 a mile N of village

New licensees have taken over this ex-drovers' halt where Burns wrote his poem 'Willie Wastle's Wife'. Their home-made bar food, often interesting, includes soup (95p), sandwiches (from 95p), smoked trout mousse (£1.95), cruicket eggs (boiled egg on a bed of ham and Scottish mustard mayonnaise, £2.15), chicken liver pâté (£2.50), ploughman's (£2.75), omelettes (from £2.75), broccoli and Stilton quiche (£3.30), vegetarian bean casserole or smoked mackerel salad (£3.50), chicken fillet (£3.80), steak and ale pie (£3.99) and whole-tail scampi (£4.15); home-made puddings like Gaelic coffee meringues and apple pie (£1.15); children's dishes (from £1.15). The busy little back bar is warm and comfortable, with flagstones, local photographs, simple furniture, Greenmantle on handpump and a good choice of malt whiskies; one very thick wall, partly knocked through, has a big hearth with a log-effect gas fire. It opens into a big airy lounge with comfortable chairs around low tables, and beyond that is a sun lounge. A separate room has darts, pool, dominoes, cribbage, fruit machine and space games. The gents has superb 1930s tiling and cut design mirrors. There are tables on the grass outside, with a climbing-frame and slide, and across the road the inn has an attractive garden, sheltered by oak trees. There's seven miles fishing on the River Tweed, and two local lochs. *(Recommended by Paul Wreglesworth, Dr R H M Stewart, John and Joan Wyatt)*

Free house   Licensee Stuart Reid   Real ale   Meals and snacks (12–2.30, 6–9)   Children welcome   Open 12–3, 6–12 (12–12 Sat and Sun)   Bedrooms tel Tweedsmuir (089 97) 272; £26B/£40B

UDDINGSTON (Strathclyde)   NS6960 Map 11
Rowan Tree

60 Old Mill Road; in Uddingston High Street, turn into The Cut, which takes you into Old Mill Road with the pub almost opposite. A mile from M73 junction 6; leaving M73 from S, turn sharp right immediately at end of motorway, virtually doing a U-turn (permitted here) into A721, then following B7071 into village

Towering behind the high, heavily panelled serving-counter in the bar of this old-fashioned town pub are tall tiers of mirrored shelves, as well as gas-style chandeliers, Edwardian water fountains on the bar counter, interesting old brewery mirrors, and two coal fires. The shinily panelled walls have built-in bare benches divided by elegant wooden pillars which support an arch of panelling, which in turn curves into the embossed ceiling; there's also a lounge. Good, generously served, simple bar food includes soup (40p), filled rolls, egg mayonnaise or pâté (80p), home-made steak pie, lasagne or fried haddock (£2), and chicken chasseur or scampi (£2.30); well kept Maclays 70/-, 80/- and Porter on air-pressure tall fount. Darts, dominoes, fruit machine, trivia and quiet piped music. *(More reports please)*

Maclays   Licensee George Tate   Real ale   Lunchtime meals and snacks (not Sun)   Disc jockey with Golden Oldies Thurs and Sat, folk club Fri   Open 11–11.45 all year

ULLAPOOL (Highland)   NH1294 Map 11
Ceilidh Place

West Argyle Street

Unusual for the region, this airy and stylish cafe-bar has bentwood chairs and one or two cushioned wall benches among the rugs on its varnished concrete floor, spotlighting from the dark planked ceiling, attractive modern prints and a big sampler on the textured white walls, piped classical or folk music, CND and other magazines, Venetian blinds, houseplants, and mainly young up-market customers, many from overseas. Though the beers are keg, they have decent wines by the glass (and pineau de charentes), some uncommon European bottled beers, an interesting range of high-proof malt whiskies and a choice of cognacs that's unmatched around here. The side food bar – you queue for service – does a few hot dishes such as vegetarian curry or crumble (£2.85) and spaghetti bolognese (£3.25), with enterprising fresh salads (70p each); friendly service. There's a very up-to-date wood-burning stove, and they have dominoes. The hotel, which has an attractive conservatory dining-room, includes a bookshop. The white house, in a quiet side street above the small town, has climbing roses and other flowers in front, where tables on a terrace look over the other houses to the distant hills beyond the natural harbour. *(Recommended by Ian Baillie, Russell Hafter, Dr R Fuller, Ruth Humphrey, A Darroch Harkness)*

Tennents (Bass)   Meals and snacks   Evening restaurant   Children welcome   Frequent folk music   Open 11–2.30, 5–11 all year   Bedrooms tel Ullapool (0854) 2103; £30(£35B)/ £50(£60B)

Morefield Motel 🅪

North Road

Our most northerly main entry, this motel in a new estate on the outskirts of the small town draws people from far and wide for the exceptional fresh fish and seafood served in its bar and restaurant. The owners, ex-fishermen and divers, have first-class sources; the bar food, served with a generosity that overwhelms people used to southern ideas of seafood value-for-money, changes seasonally, and in high season might include poached or grilled mussels (£1.75), queen scallops marinière (£2.50), freshly smoked salmon from Achiltibuie or langoustine tails sauté in garlic butter (£3.25 – they judge the garlic very deftly), haddock baked with cheese sauce (£3.95), tender mussels done with white wine, onions and tomatoes or dressed crab (£4.95), mixed scallops, prawns and mussels or grilled fresh-caught salmon (£5.75), split-grilled langoustines (£6.95) and a high-heaped seafood platter which we've never heard of anyone finishing (£9.50). There are other dishes such as soup (85p), haggis (£1.95), steak pie (£2.95), beef olives (£3.50), salads (from £3.50) and steaks (from £7.25). In the restaurant, the shrimps flambé are exquisite, and the scallops with smoky bacon hard to beat. The lounge bar is squarely modern, with dark brown plush button-back built-in wall banquettes, colourful local scenic photographs, and a pleasant brisk atmosphere; in winter the packs of summer diners tend to yield to local people playing darts or pool, though there's bargain food then, including a three-course meal for £2.95. Keg beer (what else, this far north), but a very good range of malt whiskies, decent wines and friendly tartan-skirted waitresses; piped pop music, fruit machine. There are tables on the terrace. The bedrooms are functional. *(Recommended by Russell Hafter, Joan and John Calvert, Ian Baillie, Brian and Pam Cowling, D Goodger)*

Free house   Licensee David Smyrl   Meals and snacks (12–2, 5.30–9.30)   Evening restaurant   Children welcome   Open 11–11 (11.30 Sat) all year   Bedrooms tel Ullapool (0854) 2161; £16B/£30B

WEEM (Tayside)   NN8449   Map 11

Aileen Chraggan 🅪

B846

The comfortable modern lounge in this friendly inn has long plump plum-coloured banquettes, and Bruce Bairnsfather First World War cartoons on the red and gold Regency striped wallpaper. Big picture windows look across the flat ground between here and the Tay to the mountains beyond that sweep up the Ben Lawers (the highest in this part of Scotland). Bar food includes soup (£1.25), pâté (£2.25), lasagne (£2.95), omelettes (from £3.25), deep-fried plaice (£3.25), scampi or gammon and pineapple (£4.50), and good sirloin steak (£8.50), with specials that include first-class fish like Loch Etive mussels (£4.95), Tay salmon (£5.95) or Loch Etive prawns (£6.95). Winter darts, dominoes and piped music. There are tables on the large terrace outside. *(Recommended by W A Low; more reports please)*

Free house   Licensee Alistair Gillespie   Meals and snacks (12–2, 6.30–10)   Children welcome   Open 11–11 (12.30–2, 6.30–9 in winter); closed 25 and 26 Dec, 1–3 Jan Bedrooms tel Aberfeldy (0887) 20346; £21.50/£43

Lucky Dip

Besides the fully inspected pubs, you might like to try these Lucky Dips recommended to us and described by readers (if you do, please send us reports). Experimentally, we've split the country into regions – please let us know if you find this either a help or a hindrance:

BORDERS
Blyth Bridge [NT1345], *Old Mill*: Well run and attractive food pub with restaurant-style food *(SH)*
Chirnside [A6105 by church; NT8757], *Waterloo Arms*: Homely village inn with good value plain home cooking, well kept Belhaven 70/- and 80/-, entertaining pets; open all day summer weekends; children in eating area and bar lounge; bedrooms *(LYM)*
Clovenfords [off A72 Selkirk–Innerleithen, on N side; NT4536], *Thornielee House*: Converted farmhouse overlooking River Tweed and road; modern extension has bar with well kept Broughton ales and good bar food lunchtime and evening; adjacent restaurant, nearby caravan park; bedrooms comfortable, with tasty breakfasts *(Col and Mrs L N Smyth)*
Eddleston [A703 Peebles–Penicuik; NT2447], *Horseshoe*: Up-market old stone-built place with soft lighting, gentle music, comfortable seats and old-fashioned pictures; a popular main entry in previous editions, but after refurbishment 1989 (using quality materials and fittings) has reopened for dining only *(LYM)*
Gattonside [NT5435], *Hoebridge Inn*: Recently converted former cornmill overlooked by Eildon hills, with whitewashed stone walls, cool yet cosy; good interesting reasonably priced freshly prepared restaurant food with an Italian influence, good service *(Anon)*
Jedburgh [Abbey Dr; NT6521], *Carters Rest*: Modernised pub with friendly service, well kept Youngers, good food at reasonable prices *(W A Harbottle)*
Kelso [Bridge St (A699); NT7334], *Queens Head*: Welcoming eighteenth-century Georgian coaching-inn with particularly well kept Belhaven 70/- on handpump, big helpings of good food, good waitress service; bedrooms *(Mr and Mrs M D Jones)*; [signposted off A698 4 miles S] *Sunlaws House*: Elegant and expensive country-house hotel owned by Duke of Roxburghe, worth knowing for the superb bar food using local produce served in its handsome and interesting Library Bar; beautifully furnished and decorated, but the sort of place where you speak in hushed tones; bedrooms comfortable *(Syd and Wyn Donald, AE)*; *Waggon*: Pleasant atmosphere and surroundings in big if sometimes crowded bar with good choice of popular and reasonably priced food inc children's dishes, well kept beer, pleasant efficient service *(Mr*

and Mrs A Johnston, Robert and Vicky Tod and others)
Kirk Yetholm [NT8328], *Border*: Right at the end of the Pennine Way where you can claim a free half pint on completion of 270 miles; a well run and enjoyable pub with good food and beer *(Len Beattie)*
Lauder [A68], *Black Bull*: Dachshund photographs on plank-panelled bar of of pleasantly decorated seventeenth-century inn with wide choice of bar food; open all day; children welcome; bedrooms *(Ruth Humphrey, LYM)*; *Eagle*: Interesting serving-counter like Elizabethan four-poster in lounge bar, games in public bar, limited range of decent bar food, well kept McEwans 70/-, summer barbecues in old stableyard, children welcome, open all day; bedrooms; more reports on new regime, please *(Mr and Mrs M D Jones, LYM)*
☆ **Oxton** [A697 Edinburgh–Newcastle; NT5053], *Carfraemill*: Handily placed for the hill roads through the Borders, this substantial red sandstone hotel, taken over in 1989 by the owners of the Buccleuch Arms in St Boswells (see main entries), is being extensively refurbished, with the bar being enlarged and refurbished in period style – one to watch, especially as it's been worth knowing for good value bar food; bedrooms *(Hazel Church, E R Thompson, BB)*
West Linton [High St; NT1551], *Linton*: Comfortable lounge bar with two separate rooms, one smaller than the other, with upholstered seats and stools, well kept Theakstons Best on handpump, bar food; very much a local *(S J A Velate)*

CENTRAL
Ardeonaig [S side of Loch Tay; NN6635], *Ardeonaig*: Good food in wonderful lochside setting by a burn; McEwans under pressure; bedrooms *(Patrick Young)*
Brig o' Turk [A821 Callander–Trossachs; NN5306], *Byre*: Converted from old byre into bar with attached restaurant and high raftered roof with modern carved faces on beam ends, tractor-seat bar stools, very friendly service; McEwans on air-pressure tall founts, good bar food, spotless lavatories; open all day; children welcome; bedrooms *(Roger Danes)*
Callander [Bridge St; NN6208], *Bridgend House*: Handsome lounge full of leather armchairs, with waitress service, well kept Broughton Greenmantle, good bar food; bedrooms *(R G Ollier)*; *Myrtle*: Deceptively

ordinary pub with remarkably good, tasty and unusual food inc outstanding puddings *(Anon)*

Castlecary [NS7878], *Castlecary House*: Handily placed on Glasgow–Stirling route, cheerful main bar open all day (Sun afternoon high teas instead), good choice of well kept real ales, good value simple bar food, restaurant; bedrooms *(LYM)*

nr **Crianlarich** [down 10-mile single-track rd; NN3825], *Cozac Lodge*: Beautiful but remote spot, friendly welcome and excellent food, service and views *(Peter Jones)*

Dollar [NS9796], *Kings Seat*: Comfortable and clean, with friendly licensee, good civilised atmosphere and good food, reasonably priced *(Byrne Sherwood)*; [Chapel Pl] *Strathallan*: Great bar with pool, darts, fruit machine and juke box, quick friendly service, well kept beers, good food; bedrooms comfortable and inexpensive *(Elaine and Lyn Hamilton)*

Drymen [NS4788], *Buchanan Arms*: Welcoming, friendly pub with well kept beer and well cooked bar food, quickly served; children welcome *(D P Cartwright)*

☆ **Killearn** [Main St (A875); NS5285], *Old Mill*: Simple bar food in quietly friendly village pub with rustic cushioned built-in settles and wheel-back chairs around neat dark tables, open fire, piped music; open all day summer; fine views of Campsie Fells from behind; children in eating area and garden-room *(T and A D Kucharski, LYM)*

Kinlochard [3 miles W of Aberfoyle; NN4502], *Altskeith*: Beautifully placed on banks of Loch Ard, in Loch Lomond/Trossachs country; bar food and McEwans 80/- and Broughton Greenmantle real ales; open all day Sat *(David Fisher)*

☆ **Kippen** [NS6594], *Cross Keys*: Comfortably refurbished and friendly lounge with stuffed birds, well kept McEwans 80/-, decent waitress-served bar food, log fire; militaria in public bar; bedrooms *(Mr and Mrs J H Adam, LYM)*

☆ **Polmont** [Gilston Crescent; under a mile from M9 junction 7; A803 towards Polmont, then left; NS9378], *Whyteside*: Friendly and well run Victorian hotel with extensive comfortably furnished open-plan bar – most notable for its 300-plus whiskies, dozens of other spirits, over 60 bottled beers and well kept Archibald Arrols 70/- and Ind Coope Burton on handpump; children in eating area (not after 7.30), restaurant; organ music Tues, Thurs; closed 1 Jan; bedrooms *(LYM)*

☆ **Sherriff Muir** [back rd over the moors NE of Dunblane; NN8202], *Sherriff Muir Inn*: Glorious isolated spot, open-plan bar with panoramic views, simple wooden furniture and prints of local scenes, log fire, fine choice of whiskies, good varied reasonably priced bar food – welcoming haven in the wilderness *(Carol and Richard Glover, Miss C Haworth)*

☆ **Stirling** [Easter Cornton Rd, Causewayhead; off A9 N of centre; NS7993], *Birds & the Bees*: Interestingly furnished ex-byre, dimly lit and convivial, with Arrols 70/- and 80/-, Harviestoun 80/-, Maclays 80/- and Youngers IPA on handpump, reasonably priced bar food, loud piped music, live bands most weekends, restaurant; open all day until 1am – very popular with young people, reliably well run; children welcome *(Russell Hafter, LYM)*

Stirling [Castle Wynd], *Portcullis*: Next to castle, overlooking town and surroundings; very friendly service, pleasant atmosphere and reasonable, though limited, bar food; spacious bar with open fire and good choice of whiskies; bedrooms *(G and L Owen)*; [4 Melville Terr] *Terraces*: Refurbished, comfortable lounge bar decorated with Renoir prints, pleasant attentive service, Tennents 80/-, good reasonably priced bar food; bedrooms *(T Nott)*

☆ **Thornhill** [A873; NS6699], *Lion & Unicorn*: Attractive, cosy bar with very hot wood-burning stove, Maclays 80/- on handpump, decent wines and good range of spirits; friendly service, good bar food inc marvellous choice of home-made ice-creams, nostalgic atmosphere in evening restaurant with stone walls and open fires; own bowling green; children allowed in airy family lounge; bedrooms comfortable, with decent breakfast *(Russell Hafter, Carol and Richard Glover, LYM)*

DUMFRIES AND GALLOWAY

☆ **Auchencairn** [about 2 ½ miles off A711; NX7951], *Balcary Bay*: Bar and hotel with smuggling affiliations, much improved over the last few years and now very pleasant, with good bar food; bedrooms *(T Nott, NWN)*

Auldgirth [just E of A75, about 8 miles N of Dumfries; NX9186], *Auldgirth Inn*: Old, whitewashed stone frontage, comfortable lounge in side annexe with brasses, plates and pictures, varied bar food; bedrooms *(Anon)*

Beattock [NT0802], *Old Brig*: Interesting historical building, reasonable food *(T Nott)*

☆ **Dalbeattie** [1 Maxwell St; NX8361], *Pheasant*: Particularly useful for serving bar food until 10 in its comfortable upstairs lounge/restaurant, with the lunchtime choice maybe including Galloway beef and Solway salmon, and omelettes to steaks in the evening; lively downstairs bar, children welcome, open all day till midnight summer; bedrooms *(LYM)*

☆ **Drummore** [NX1336], *Queens*: Coastal village inn overlooking Luce Bay, the most southerly hotel in Scotland and fairly handy for Logan Gardens and Mull of Galloway; reopened 1988 after refurbishment, with good bar food, welcoming prompt service;

separate games-room, fishing parties arranged; bedrooms reasonably priced (*F S and N P Grebbell, BB*);

Drummore, *Ship*: By the shore; pleasant welcome, good beer and food inc fresh fish (*M H Box*)

Dumfries [English St; NX9776], *Cairndale*: Comfortable and substantial red sandstone hotel with Rotary Club lunches and plush hotel cocktail bar (*BB*)

Eskdalemuir [NY2597], *Hart Manor*: Desolate spot up in the hills, so this is an oasis with its cosy atmosphere, friendly licensee, well kept Greenmantle and good, varied, home-cooked food inc speciality puddings; pleasant dining-room overlooking valley; bedrooms (*Janet Rogerson*)

☆ **Gatehouse of Fleet** [NX5956], *Murray Arms*: Carefully rebuilt small seventeenth-century hotel with strong Burns connections; good buffet, usually with well kept real ales such as Broughton or Youngers, variety of mainly old-fashioned comfortable seating areas, games in quite separate public bar; open all day for food in summer; children welcome; bedrooms (*T Nott, LYM*)

☆ **Gatehouse of Fleet** [High St], *Angel*: Listed building with friendly, warm and cosy lounge bar, good value bar food, tasty dinner menu, McEwans ales; family run; bedrooms (*Tony Pounder, NWN*)

Glencaple [NX9968], *Nith*: Hotel on shore of Nith estuary, with spacious and comfortable lounge with ships' brasses and other maritime decorations; McEwans, varied bar food inc super smoked salmon sandwiches, pleasant quick service; bedrooms (*Anon*)

Isle of Whithorn [NX4736], *Queens Arms*: Friendly modernised lounge with popular bar food, pool-room, public bar, just up street from harbour; open all day; bedrooms (*BB*)

Kingholm Quay [village signposted off B725 Dumfries–Glencaple; NX9873], *Swan*: Busy, well looked after little hotel on banks of the River Nith; public and lounge bars, restaurant (only open at busy times during day), beer garden and embryonic adventure playground; very friendly staff despite being busy, wide range of food lunchtime and evening, also high tea; well kept McEwans 80/-; closes afternoon and 9pm weekdays, open all day till late Sat and Sun; children welcome; bedrooms (*G A Worthington*)

Kippford [NX8355], *Mariner*: Clean pub with 'ship' atmosphere, friendly staff, good value well presented food (vegetarian on request) (*Linda and Carl Worley*)

☆ **Kirkcudbright** [Old High St; NX6851], *Selkirk Arms*: Comfortable partly panelled lounge with good local flavour, in place that's been hotel since 1777, bar food, restaurant, evening steak bar, tables in spacious garden with summer live music (anda 1481 font); salmon and trout fishing; children in restaurant and lounge; good

value bedrooms, good service (*Jon Wainwright, LYM*)

Langholm [NY3685], *Eskdale*: Plain hotel bar, popular with locals; clean tablecloths on all bar tables and generous helpings of tasty bar food; bedrooms (*Syd and Wyn Donald*)

Moffat [High St; NT0905], *Moffat House*: Beautiful Robert Adam mansion with well kept McEwans 70/- and good choice of whiskies in grand, restful and clubby bar; bar food inc sandwiches – rather pricey; bedrooms (*Neil and Angela Huxter*)

☆ nr **Moffat** [hotel signposted off A74], *Auchen Castle*: Superb location with spectacular hill views, peaceful country-house hotel with delicious bar food, decent wines, good choice of malt whiskies, excellent service; trout loch in good-sized grounds; bedrooms (*Mr and Mrs Norman Edwardes*)

Newton Stewart [Minnigaff; NX4165], *Creebridge House*: Friendly atmosphere, excellent bar snacks and well kept Broughton real ale in comfortable country-house hotel; bedrooms (*Mr and Mrs J H Adam*)

Port Logan [NX0940], *Port Logan*: Good new licensee who does good reasonably priced bar food, and with friends provides great live music Sun evening (*L E Sculthord*)

Portpatrick [NX0154], *Portpatrick Hotel*: Comfortable bar in big hotel with heated pool and tennis, in striking position on bluff overlooking harbour; decent bedrooms (*BB*)

Sandhead [Main St; NX0949], *Tigh na Mara*: Pleasant atmosphere, satisfactory bar food (if you don't want mayonnaise in your crab sandwiches, warn them); bedrooms (*David and Flo Wallington*)

Springholm [A75 Crocketford–Castle Douglas; NX8070], *Reoch*: Small, pleasant, clean pub with friendly welcome; well kept McEwans, particularly good plain bar food, tables outside (*Col and Mrs J S Gratton*)

☆ **Stranraer** [George St; NX0660], *George*: Elegant and comfortable lounge bar with good value bar food, huge log fireplace, friendly staff; also wine bar/bistro with world-wide choice of bottled beers; open all day; children welcome; bedrooms most comfortable (*Michael Bechley, LYM*)

Stranraer [Church St], *Arkhouse*: Small, friendly local opposite old church with tiled floor in side bar; good collection of whiskies, unusual Chinese and Japanese drinks (*Michael Bechley*)

☆ **Thornhill** [NX8795], *Buccleuch & Queensberry*: Comfortably refurbished yet traditionally solid old red sandstone inn with sedate lounge bar, livelier public, average food; access to three miles of fishing on the River Nith; children welcome; bedrooms comfortable, with good breakfast (*John Spencely, LYM*)

Twynholm [Burn Brae; NX6654], *Burnbank*: Basic village local with cheerful licensees and cheap food; closed Mon lunchtime; fine

nearby coast and countryside; bedrooms
(LYM)

FIFE
Aberdour [A92 Inverkeithing–Kirkcaldy;
NT1985], *Aberdour*: Attractive hotel in
charming harbourside village; quietly lit bar
with wooden fittings, coal fire, darts and
dominoes; good friendly service, well kept
Belhaven 70/- and 80/- on handpump, good
value food in bar and restaurant; bedrooms
(N and M Gibbon); [Manse St] *Fairways*:
Small hotel with acceptable good value
home-cooked food from regularly changing
menu, friendly licensees; well equipped
newly refurbished bedrooms with good
views over Firth of Forth to Edinburgh *(Mike
and Mandy Challis)*; *Woodside*: Marvellous
original art nouveau ceiling in upper Clipper
Bar – a glass canopy with panelling rescued
from RMS *Orantes*; pleasant lounge, good
bar food, willing service; bedrooms *(T Nott)*
☆ **Anstruther** [High St; NO5704], *Smugglers*:
Good value straightforward bar food (fresh
scampi and mixed grill recommended) in
friendly old inn with rambling and attractive
upstairs lounge bar, busy downstairs games-
bar with good range of beers and whiskies,
summer barbecues on pretty terrace, popular
restaurant; children in eating area; bedrooms
small but immaculate *(Alastair Campbell,
LYM)*
☆ **Anstruther** [High St], *Dreel*: Cosy and
historic building in attractive double
overlooking Dreel Burn, locally popular for
well kept ale and reasonably priced well
cooked and presented bar food inc local
seafood and barbecues; open fire, pool area,
tables outside *(G Allen, Alastair Campbell)*
Anstruther [24 East Green], *Cellar*: Cosy
and attractive if simply decorated low-
ceilinged pub notable for its interesting
winter bargain dinners *(Anon)*; [Bankwell
Rd] *Craws Nest*: Good though pricey bar
food in straightforward lounge, inc freshly
caught haddock; Scottish entertainment
summer; bedrooms *(Rosalind Russell)*; [East
Shore] *Sun*: Snug harbourside tavern next to
Scottish Fisheries Museum, well kept
Tennents, summer weekend live music; has
had good local seafood, but recently pending
kitchen renovations there's been no food
(LYM)
Carnock [A907 Dunfermline–Alloa;
NT0489], *Old Inn*: Welcoming licensees in
low-beamed pub with neatly spaced tables in
tidy lounge, bar with pool-table well out of
way, well kept Maclays 60/-, 70/-, 80/- and
Porter, brass water tap on bar, good quickly
served bar food inc children's helpings;
children welcome *(Roger Huggins)*
Craigrothie [NO3710], *Kingarroch*: Small
but unusual pub with good bar food *(Mr and
Mrs N W Briggs)*
☆ **Crail** [4 High St; NO6108], *Golf*:

Comfortable village inn with neat and cosy
bar, tasty bar food (Scotch broth and local
fish recommended), well kept Youngers IPA,
good range of malt whiskies, coal fire;
bedrooms clean and comfortable, with good
breakfasts *(W F Coghill, JAH, HCH)*
Crossford [A994 W of Dunfermline;
NT0686], *Pitfirane Arms*: Small friendly bar,
comfortable lounge and separate eating area
– makes you feel really at home; McEwans
80/- and Youngers No 3, popular bar food
(Roger Huggins)
Cupar [NO3714], *Oastlers Close*: Well kept,
good atmosphere, decent food *(Mr and Mrs
N W Briggs)*
Dunfermline [Hospital Hill; NT0987],
Jardines: Modern, light and airy cafe-style
bar, good range of beers, freshly baked
pizzas *(Timothy Powell)*
Dysart [West Quality St; NT3093], *Old
Rectory*: Georgian building, friendly
licensees, good food and real ale *(Roger and
Kathy)*
Falkland [NO2507], *Covenanter*: Pleasant
pub in beautiful, historic village with
magnificent National Trust palace; attractive
service, average food; nr start GWG165;
bedrooms *(Leith Stuart)*
Limekilns [NT0783], *Ship*: Small and
welcoming, well kept Belhaven on
handpump, good value bar food *(Roger
Huggins)*
☆ **St Andrews** [Grange Rd – a mile S;
NO5116], *Grange*: Excellent atmosphere in
fine old building on outskirts; spotlessly
clean small bar with well kept beer and
decent wine; under current regime the food is
particularly good in bar and in restaurant,
which has changing set-price meals
lunchtime and evening, with interesting
dishes such as avocado with raspberry
vinaigrette and baked halibut with lobster
and brandy sauce *(A D Kucharska, Mr and
Mrs N W Briggs, Dr Stewart Rae, Dr
A V Lewis)*
☆ **St Andrews** [40 The Scores], *Ma Bells*:
Seafront pub by golf course, with popular
downstairs bar full of students during term-
time, and locals and tourists the rest of the
year; well kept Greenmantle and Watneys-
related real ales, over 75 different bottled
beers including all the Trappists, lots of malt
whiskies; open all day, with reasonably
priced bar food served through till 6pm, hot
pies in the evening; piped music, games
(Alisdair Cuthil, Dr T H M Mackenzie)
Strathmiglo [NO2110], *Strathmiglo*: Quiet
and simple but comfortable pub which has
been popular for good straightforward food
and pleasant service, with a welcome for
children; but we've had no news of it since it
came on the market towards the end of 1988
(LYM)
Upper Largo [NO4203], *Largo*: Food
helpings would satisfy Desperate Dan – and
cheap too; bedrooms *(Rosalind Russell)*

Wormit [Naughton Rd; NO4026], *Taybridge Halt*: Lounge overlooks Tay Bridge and estuary, tasteful railway-theme décor (picking up the motif supplied by the smoke-blackened former tunnel which is now part of the car park); pleasant prompt service, wide choice of good value food, well kept Tennents 70/- and 80/-; very relaxing (*JAH, HCH*)

GRAMPIAN

☆ **Aberdeen** [Dee St; NJ9305], *Gabriels*: Lofty converted chapel turned into showy and enjoyable bar without sparing expense; nightclub behind has most elaborate sound and lights system (*LYM*)

Aberdeen [Crown St], *Brentwood Hotel*: Comfortable lounge bar called Carriages has well kept Whitbreads-related real ales and popular choice of bar food from burgers to steaks; bedrooms (*Trevor Stearn*); [6 Little Belmont St] *Camerons*: Solid stone-built extended former coaching-inn, with many rooms inc original snug bar, and wide choice of well kept real ales such as Belhaven 80/-, McEwans 80/- and Whitbreads Castle Eden; open all day (*Richard Sanders*)

Aboyne [Charleston Rd; NO5298], *Boat*: Simple but friendly and comfortably remodelled inn with good value bar food, real ale and restaurant; games in public bar; bedrooms (*LYM*)

Banchory [NO6995], *Tor na Coille*: Lovely welcoming hotel with enterprising bar lunches inc four different kinds of home-baked rolls and imaginative salads; well kept Theakstons Best; bedrooms (*Mrs E Higson*)

Bieldside [North Deeside Rd; A93, W side of village; NJ8702], *Water Wheel*: Rather a trendy place, with carefully restored watermill main bar and plusher cocktail bar; bar food, well kept McEwans 80/- (*LYM*)

Braemar [NO1491], *Fife Arms*: Comfortable, attractive large lounge in big Victorian hotel with appropriate décor; friendly efficient service and good reasonably priced hot and cold bar food; nr start GWG166; children welcome (*Russell Hafter*)

Cabrach [A941; NJ3827], *Grouse*: Cheery family pub in fine scenery, with remarkable stock of whiskies (and staggering choice of whisky miniatures, with other souvenirs); adjacent cafeteria; open all day, handy stop on the splendid hill road from Braemar to Dufftown; bedrooms (*LYM*)

Craigellachie [NJ2845], *Fiddich*: Tiny pub in pretty spot on banks of River Fiddich at its confluence with River Spey, virtually unchanged over past 40 years with old bar and fireplace intact; good choice of malt whiskies, knowledgeable fishing talk in early evening (*Alastair Lang*)

☆ **Elgin** [Thunderton Pl; NJ2162], *Thunderton House*: Sympathetically restored and beautifully refurbished seventeenth-century

town-centre pub with fast and friendly service, real ale and wide range of good value bar food from filled rolls and baked potatoes to cheap steaks; busy and popular; children's room (*Leith Stuart, Mary and James Manthei, A Darroch Harkness*)

Fettercairn [NO6473], *Ramsay Arms*: Good bar food such as home-made steak and kidney pie and roast pheasant in pleasant village inn; bedrooms (and gymnasium/sauna) (*Mrs C S Smith*)

Fochabers [NJ3458], *Gordon Arms*: Real ale, snacks and meals in comfortable bars of town inn which can arrange stalking and fishing for residents; bedrooms (*LYM*)

Gartocharn , Strathclyde [A811 Balloch–Stirling; NS4286], *Gartocharn Inn*: Useful stop not far from the S end of Loch Lomond (there's a fine view over the loch, a quarter-mile up the hill), with leatherette banquettes in the modernised saloon, chintzy armchairs in a room off, a plainly furnished public bar (with a couple of shelves of paperbacks) and a pool-room leading off; tables on neat back terrace, generous helpings of decent straightforward bar food, coal fires, pampered bar cat, attractive service; open all day; bedrooms comfortable and inexpensive (*Dr A M Kerr, L Rowan, BB*)

Kincardine o' Neil [NO5999], *Gordon Arms*: Well kept beer at very reasonable prices, good bar food, friendly staff, log fire; bedrooms (*J Perry*)

☆ **Kinmuck** [turn on to B979 signposted Hatton of Fintray from A96 Aberdeen–Inverurie in Blackburn; in about 3½ miles turn left signposted Kinmuck; NJ8120], *Boars Head*: What it lacks in décor is more than made up for in remarkable warmth of landlord's welcome and superb choice of real ales; bar similar to a corridor, weekend lounge with pool-table and local musicians; basic bar food such as toasties and pickled eggs (*Alastair Campbell*)

Potarch [just off A93 5 miles W of Banchory; NO6097], *Potarch Inn*: Beautifully situated by River Dee; cosy, pleasant bar with tartan carpet, copper-topped tables and good, friendly service; real ales and good bar suppers, also good fresh salmon and steaks in restaurant; bedrooms (*Mrs E Higson*)

Stonehaven [Shorehead; NO8786], *Marine*: Superb views of Stonehaven harbour, bar downstairs with pool-table, lounge bar and restaurant upstairs; well kept McEwans 80/- and Timothy Taylors Landlord, coffee and tea, good value bar food; open all day, seven days; bedrooms (*Trevor Stearn*)

☆ **Turriff** [Auchterless; A947; NJ7250], *Towie*: Stylish and up-market, several cuts above the typical Scots hostelry but with a good friendly atmosphere; unvaryingly good food using fresh ingredients, well cooked, inc interesting vegetarian dishes – short choice at lunchtime, more extensive evening; quietly efficient service, no smoking or music in dining area; good choice of wines; children welcome; bedrooms *(Leith Stuart, A V Timmins, A Graham Mackenzie)*

HIGHLAND

Achnasheen [A832; NH2669], *Achnasheen Hotel*: It's the fantastic surroundings, in splendid Highland isolation, which earn a place for this plainly furnished establishment, which could do so much better on the food, beer (keg only) and service side; bedrooms *(LYM)*; [A890, just off A832] *Ledgowan Lodge*: Former shooting-lodge, now a country-house hotel, in similarly superb remote surroundings; enterprising bar food served in restaurant inc Scotch broth and interesting main dishes using good ingredients, also high teas and five-course dinners; bedrooms *(J D Cranston)*

Aultguish [NH3570], *Aultguish*: Isolated highland inn near Loch Glascarnoch, bar food; children welcome; bedrooms *(LYM)*

Aviemore [Loch Alvie; B9152, 2 miles S; NH8912], *Lynwilg*: Large old place backed by the mountains, giving a glimpse of loch across the fields; comfortable bar with hunting prints and skiing information, good range of whiskies and McEwans ale, new owners end 1988; bedrooms *(Roger Danes)*; *Macs*: Cheerful family pub with good well filled rolls and well kept Tennents 80/- and Youngers No 3 *(Neil and Angela Huxter)*; *Olde Bridge*: Warm and inviting with friendly staff and good, imaginative food *(Mrs A Hamilton)*; *Red McGregors*: Big open-plan functional bar with friendly staff, good simple food inc filling steak pie and good value pizzas all day, live music some evenings; steak bar next door *(Roger Huggins)*

Cononbridge [NH5455], *Conon*: Comfortably refurbished lounge bar, livelier public bar, usual bar food, restaurant; children welcome; bedrooms *(LYM)*

Dalwhinnie [NN6384], *Loch Ericht*: Modern Scandinavian-style hotel with comfortable and welcoming lounge bar; limited but interesting food and good views, inc waterfall immediately behind the bar; bedrooms *(Russell Hafter)*

Drumbeg [B869 Lochinver–Kylescu; NC1233], *Drumbeg*: Remote fishermen's hotel with bar which may have seen better days but mixes locals and visitors in a friendly way; inexpensive plain lunchtime bar meals, 180 single malts, pool-tables; evening restaurant; bedrooms *(Neil and Angela Huxter, HDC)*

Dulnain Bridge [A938 ½ mile W; NH9925], *Muckrach Lodge*: Secluded Victorian former shooting-lodge, now a hotel and decidedly not a pub, but notable for its good bar lunches inc interesting local cheeses and excellent substantial sandwiches; fine fresh local ingredients in restaurant meals, hearty breakfasts *(RB)*

Durness [NC4067], *Oasis*: Large, open and comfortable bar with pleasant, cheap restaurant attached *(Ruth Humphrey)*; *Sango Sands*: Welcoming bar, family-room with darts and pool, also cafe and restaurant *(Alastair Lang)*

Fort Augustus [NH3709], *Inchnacardoch Lodge*: Victorian former shooting-lodge in elevated position overlooking Loch Ness; bar meals, restaurant; bedrooms *(David Fisher)*

☆ **Fort William** [off A82 bypass, N end of town; NN1174], *Nevis Bank*: Friendly, bright and warming atmosphere in genteel lounge bar, courteous service, well kept Youngers IPA and No 3, decent bar food; pool in more basic back bar; bedrooms *(Mr and Mrs J H Adam, J A Edwards)*

Fort William, *Ben Nevis*: Beams and timbers, loch views, well kept Youngers No 3, cheap bar food, friendly competent staff, video juke box (and disco lights); good value food in nice upstairs restaurant *(A C Lang, Mary and James Manthei)*

☆ **Gairloch** [Fish Harbour; just off A832 near bridge; NG8077], *Old Inn*: Attractively priced bar food, well kept McEwans 80/-, a good few malts, unusually wide range of crisps etc; service friendly but can slow under pressure; dimpled copper tables and so forth in two small and rather dark rooms of lounge, newly refurbished public bar with pool-table and games, picnic-table sets attractively placed out by stream, splendid beach nearby; open all day; bedrooms *(Mr and Mrs J H Adam, J D Cranston, A C Lang, Steve Waters, Stephen R Holman, BB)*

Garve [A832; NH3961], *Garve*: Very friendly place with particularly good food – especially champion haggis; bedrooms *(Jon Payne)*

☆ **Glencoe** [off A82 E of Pass; NN1058], *Kingshouse*: Alone in a stupendous mountain landscape, with simple bar food including children's dishes, well kept McEwans 80/-; choose your bar carefully – the climbers' one at the back has very basic furnishings, loud pop music, pool and darts, the genteel modernised central cocktail bar has cloth banquettes and other seats around wood-effect tables; open all day ; good value bedrooms in inn itself, and in cheaper dormitory-style bunkhouse *(Philip Whitehead, Alan Hall, BB)*

Grantown on Spey [High St; NJ0328], *Tyree*: Pine-panelled walls with plush, comfortable furnishings; good home-cooked food with unusually carefully cooked fresh vegetables; bedrooms *(Janet Rogerson)*

Helmsdale [A9 about ¾ mile N; ND0315], *Navidale House*: Fishing/stalking hotel with good lunches from sandwiches to home-made game pie in cosy bar, and good restaurant dinners; bedrooms very comfortable, excellent breakfasts *(Guy Harris)*

Invermoriston [NH4117], *Glenmoriston Arms*: Lots of malt whiskies in cosy lounge of inn not far from Loch Ness, fishing and stalking by arrangement; also cheery stables bar; bedrooms *(Mary and James Manthei, LYM)*

Inverness [Church St; NH6645], *Criterion*: Three bars, the most interesting of which is the old-fashioned lounge/ diner; pleasing atmosphere and framed copies of old advertisements; straightforward bar food *(Ian Baillie)*; [41 Haugh Rd] *Haugh*: Nice pub just off centre by River Ness, with friendly atmosphere in panelled bar, well kept McEwans 80/- and Youngers No 3, simple lunchtime food such as good soup and mince and tatties at low prices, huge collection of beer-mats, friendly landlord, pleasant adjoining lounge *(AJVB)*; [Academy St] *Phoenix*: Decent food in pleasant back lounge *(AJVB)*

nr **Inverness** [Stoneyfield; A96 E], *Coach House*: Pretty stone-built former coach-house set well back from road, with nice views over the farmland around Culloden – particularly from the back terrace; simply furnished but spacious bar on right, McEwans 80/-, piped music; neatly plush lounge bar opening into spacious restaurant where children allowed (this also has the spreading view); bedrooms, nice little breakfast-room, neat residents' lounge; has been popular for good value food in bar and restaurant, but under new management 1989 – more reports please *(Ruth Humphrey, BB)*

Kingussie [NH7501], *Osprey*: Very comfortable and well run small hotel, with particularly good evening meals (and breakfasts), and good wines – but no bar food, and no proper bar; good bedrooms *(Jill and George Hadfield, T Gallagher, BB)*

Kinlochbervie [NO2256], *Kinlochbervie*: On hillside with superb views over busy little fishing harbour; simple public bar, opulent lounge, keg beers, limited choice of average food (the sort of place where they seem a bit surprised to have wine ordered); bedrooms in simple single-storey block *(Ian Baillie)*

Kylesku [A894; S side of former ferry crossing; NC2234], *Kylesku*: Particularly good bar food in unsurpassed scenic surroundings – fresh fish, scallops, large prawns in garlic butter, sandwiches and soup; also restaurant; five comfortable and peaceful bedrooms *(JDC)nr*

Lairg [13 miles N of Lairg on A836; NC5225], *Crask*: Welcome oasis, recently restored and reopened by new licensees; good bar food inc haggis and local prawns; bedrooms *(Anon)*

☆ **Lewiston** [NH5029], *Lewiston Arms*: Comfortable well kept lounge, games in friendly public bar, Youngers No 3, good filling bar food, restaurant, attractive garden; handy for Loch Ness (near ruined Urquhart Castle) and Glen Coiltie, with nice drive up to Glen Affric and back; bedrooms *(LYM)*

Lochailort [NM7682], *Lochailort*: Plain rather rough-and-ready bar and second room with big windows on to road, but cheery landlord, good atmosphere and promising bar food inc excellent fresh salmon sandwiches; bedrooms *(S J A Velate)*

Lochaline [NM6744], *Lochaline*: Friendly hotel in isolated village by Mull ferry landing; cheerful bar, good bar food; bedrooms *(HDC)*

Lybster [ND2436], *Portland Arms*: Built last century as staging-post on new 'parliamentary road', with two bars, large residents' lounge, restaurant; wonderful service, huge helpings of good food inc lightly soused herring, fresh salmon, excellent sorbets and puddings; nr spectacular cliffs and stacks, with local golf and ponytrekking; shooting and fishing can be arranged; reasonably priced bedrooms *(Hazel Church)*

Mallaig [side st up hill from harbour; NM6797], *Tigh-a-Chlachain*: Red leather settles, sea charts and pool-table; welcoming bar staff, relaxed atmosphere, mixed crowd, wide range of malts and good value bar food lunchtime and evening (toasties in between); they guarantee refund if you don't enjoy food *(Gary Scott)*

Melvich [NC8765], *Melvich*: Lovely spot with beautiful views of sea and coastline; friendly staff, leisurely atmosphere, peat fires and good food *(D A Wilcock, Miss C M Davidson)*

☆ **Nairn** [Viewfield St; NH8856], *Clifton House*: Charming and distinguished small hotel, wonderfully civilised, with delightfully furnished and sumptuously decorated lounge, delectable bar lunches made from the freshest and finest ingredients, fine restaurant, good wines and interesting spirits; was our highest-rated main entry in Scotland until its evolution into what's clearly no longer a pub even by our elastic definition; comfortable bedrooms *(LYM)*

Nairn [Marine Rd; coming from Inverness on A96, turn left at central roundabout], *Royal Marine*: Good reasonably priced meal-sized bar snacks and amazing views over Moray Firth from welcoming cocktail bar and terrace bar; bedrooms *(Peter Griffiths)*

North Kessock [NH6548], *North Kessock*: Decent bar food from sandwiches and ploughman's to baked chicken with oatmeal stuffing; puddings include lots of exotic ice-creams; bedrooms *(Hazel Church)*

Plockton [Innes St; NG8033], *Creag Nan Darach*: Small, homely hotel with friendly owners and good home-made food; comfortable bedrooms, very reasonably priced *(Peter Stratton)*

Poolewe [attached to Corriness Guest House; NB8580], *Choppys*: Worth knowing and repeatedly recommended by readers for

good plain bar food cooked to order, inc home-made soup and sandwiches as well as generous hot dishes; there is a simple modern bar as well, with pool, and the licensee is charmingly friendly, but this isn't a pub; bedrooms *(Keith Mills, BB)*; *Poolewe*: Plainly furnished bar and communicating lounge with big helpings of decent bar food served from noon until 8.30, well kept McEwans 80/-, good malt whiskies, piped folk music (live too, often), log fire; on quiet side road above sea loch, handy for the magnificent Scottish NT gardens at Inverewe; open all day; bedrooms *(W A Rinaldi-Butcher, BB)*
Scrabster [Harbourside; ND0970], *Upper Deck*: Good value food inc good fresh fish and steaks in large upstairs room, looking over harbour *(Hazel Church, Guy Harris)*
Tomatin [NH8029], *Tomatin*: Clean and well run, good atmosphere, friendly staff and keenly priced bar food; children welcome *(Mrs A Hamilton)*
☆ **Ullapool** [Shire St; NH1294], *Ferry Boat*: Closer to a real pub than our main entries here, and a really nice one at that, with a friendly atmosphere in its unpretentious bar and a fine view over the lively anchorage to the tall hills beyond; well kept McEwans 80/-, a decent choice of whiskies, unobtrusive piped pop music, good service, good value bar lunches, evening restaurant; incidentally the Frigate just along the road is also worth knowing, as a good seafood cafe/restaurant with decent drinks; bedrooms good value *(A C Lang, BB)*
Wick [ND3551], *Rosebank*: Unimpressive buildings and bars but super food inc good home-made soup, fresh scallops in Mornay sauce, salmon, daily roast; bedrooms *(Hazel Church)*

LOTHIAN

Aberlady [A198 towards Edinburgh; NT4679], *Waggon*: Well run and friendly, view over the salt-flats and Firth to Fife from big windows in the airy if somewhat incongruous high-ceilinged back extension, attractive front family-room, decent bar food, well kept McEwans 80/- (a better choice than the white wine); restaurant; nr GWG175 *(G Milligan, LYM)*
☆ **Cramond Bridge** [A90; NT1875], *Cramond Brig*: Good family stop with bar food all day, on main A90 N of Edinburgh; well kept McEwans 80/-, restaurant *(LYM)*
☆ **Dirleton** [village green; NT5184], *Castle*: Pleasant unpretentious lounge, generous helpings of well presented food inc well filled sandwiches, well kept McEwans 80/-, friendly service; restaurant; attractive spot, nr GWG175; bedrooms *(T Nott, Dr M I Crichton)*
Dirleton, *Open Arms*: Attractive rooms, good bar food, excellent service, fine spot opp castle; bedrooms *(Mr and Mrs N W Briggs)*
☆ **Edinburgh** [Jamaica St West; off India St], *Kays*: Charming mock-up of Victorian tavern with cosy mix of casks and red plush, and small rooms off; particularly well kept Belhaven 70/- and 80/-, Youngers IPA and No 3 on handpump and an uncommon guest beer such as Batemans or Fullers London Pride tapped from the cask, cheap and simple bar food, prompt courteous service; open all day but closed Sun; children in quiet panelled back room *(John Gould, LYM)*
☆ **Edinburgh** [55 Rose St], *Rose Street Brewery*: Worth visiting for the ales they brew here, Auld Reekie 80/- and potent 90/- – malt-extract brews, but considerable character; the downstairs saloon has been done up in beams-boards-and-flagstones style, and has loud but well reproduced pop music from its CD juke box; open all day, though not always the comfortable upstairs lounge, carpeted and partly panelled; bar food – ploughman's recommended *(Scott W Stucky, Dorothy Menzies, Alison Hayward, Nick Dowson, BB)*
Edinburgh [100 Rose St], *Auld Hundred*: Done up with peach plush furnishings and stripped stone – more comfortable now than older readers will remember it, though perhaps with less atmosphere *(BB)*; [12 Grassmarket] *Black Bull*: Comparatively new, but extremely popular; see-through front façade, bar well laid out with tiered levels leading up to servery, flamboyantly decorated with lots of red velour flock wallpaper, brass lamps and old oven in which bread is heated; good if sometimes studenty atmosphere, well kept Maclays 60/-, 70/- and 80/-, lots of malt whiskies, good bar food, juke box, live jazz Tues *(John Gould)*; [Victoria St] *Bow Bar*: Superbly restored and now most engaging, with particularly well kept real ale and very good service *(JM, PM)*; [142 Dundas St] *Clarks*: Well kept Youngers IPA in old-style Scottish bar, utilitarian yet relaxing, with good filled rolls *(BB)*; [Rose St, corner Hanover St] *Daddy Milnes*: Atmosphere particularly good, refurbishment well done in that the photographs of literati who used the pub really do bring back something of its atmosphere when it was a focus of Edinburgh literary life; comfortable and friendly *(WTA)*; [435 Lawnmarket] *Deacon Brodies*: Commemorates highwayman town councillor who was the model for Dr Jekyll and Mr Hyde, and hanged on the scaffold he himself had designed; expensively refurbished last year to make the most of this; fun for tourists, but worth knowing in its own right, with leather armchairs, period pictures and open fire in pleasant upstairs lounge, snug woodwork, settles and younger image downstairs, decent bar food, keg beers but coffee through till late *(T Nott, Graham Bush, BB)*; *East Port*: Central pub with

pleasant atmosphere, well kept Tennents, good filled rolls, back lounge bar, juke box, television, fruit machine *(Dorothy Menzies)*; [Grassmarket], *Fiddlers*: One of the pubbiest places in this well supplied area, full of locals; period feel, violins on walls, ornate wooden bar gantry; games-bar with pool *(Graham Bush)*; [Cowgate] *Gilded Balloon*: Unusual décor includes papier-mâché curtains and modern paintings, bare stone walls and wooden benches; well kept Whitbreads Castle Eden *(Dorothy Menzies)*; [34 Candlemakers Row] *Greyfriars Bobby*: Commemorates dog who stayed by his master's grave so loyally that eventually city paid for his upkeep; pleasant atmosphere, tartan décor *(BB)*; [James Court; by 495 Lawnmarket] *Jolly Judge*: Cosy and unusual tavern in base of sixteenth-century tenement, in secluded close just off Royal Mile; quickly served lunchtime bar food (not Sun), Ind Coope Burton on handpump, lots of whiskies, children allowed at lunchtime in eating area; note the characteristic antique fruit-and-flower decoration of the low beam-and-plank ceiling *(Graham Bush, LYM)*; [Rutland St] *L'Attaché*: Unusual pub/club (free entrance) with live folk or jazz nightly till 1am, cellar snugs in vaulted gated alcoves, leather wing armchairs in one corner, basic walls decorated with empty bottles and clocks; keg beers, daytime food *(Graham Bush)*; [Grassmarket] *Last Drop*: Gallows-theme bistro-pub with Arrols 70/-, popular with young people *(Graham Bush)*; [Cockburn St] *Malt Shovel*: Good friendly atmosphere, wide range of well kept real ales, good value bar food from a biggish menu – seafood, roasts, etc; popular in the evening *(Tad and Anna Kucharski)*; [Trinity Cres, Newhaven; off Starbank Rd] *Old Chain Pier*: Attractively restored old pier building jutting right out over the Forth with marvellous water views, friendly, good piped music, cosy upper gallery, well kept real ales, bar food *(LYM)*; [30 Wrights Houses] *Olde Golf Tavern*: Old golf prints and good cold buffet in famous old place with spacious main bar, cosy cocktail bar and upstairs restaurant; on edge of Bruntsfield Links, where golf first played here *(BB)*; [Queen St] *Oyster Bar*: Small cellar bar with friendly atmosphere and good helpings of unusual bar food from Scottish rock oysters or guacamole to venison casserole; Caledonian 80/- on air-pressure tall fount, several bottled Belgian Trappist beers *(Tad and Anna Kucharski)*; [202 Rose St] *Scotts*: Restrained modernisation in pleasantly traditional pub, low lighting, old-fashioned efficient service, well kept real ale *(LYM)*; [11 St Vincent St] *St Vincent*: Boasts one of longest continuous licences in city, dating back to 1830s; well looked after with low beams, nineteenth-century bar mirror, friendly service and no piped music; well kept Maclays, Rose Street

Auld Reekie 90/- and Tetleys on handpump; open all day Thurs–Sat *(Andrew Cottle)*; [67 Laverockbank Rd; by Starbank Gdns] *Starbank*: Marvellous view over the Forth (with a telescope too) in airy bar with fine collection of uncommon whiskies and a good few interesting and well kept guest beers as well as Belhaven ales – it's tied to them; sheltered back terrace, bar food, restaurant, maybe jazz Mon; open all day *(LYM)*; [Fairmilehead (A702)] *Steadings*: Long, low-ceilinged building with bar at one end, restaurant and food servery at other end on slightly lower level; smart interior, Ind Coope Arrols 70/-, 80/- and Burton, good bar food individually prepared, so not served quickly – more bar-restaurant than pub *(Peter Corris)*; [Drummond St] *Stewarts*: Easy-going traditional bar, open all day, very busy; good value sandwiches, Belhaven 80/- and Youngers IPA, blends own whisky; between 3 and 5pm would always give the lie to those who think Edinburgh is populated en masse by staid lawyers and stuffy shopkeepers *(LYM)*; [1 Cumberland St] *Tilted Wig*: Very civilised and well run, with grainy ply-panelling, flowery ceiling, well kept Maclays and Theakstons real ales, back food bar, attractive little sunken garden; open all day *(JM, PM, LYM)*; [The Vaults, 87 Giles St; Leith] *Vintners Room*: Perhaps more restaurant than pub, but does good bar lunches and admits drinkers as well as diners; imaginatively decorated, sophisticated atmosphere, in one of Scotland's oldest commercial buildings; the Scotch Malt Whisky Society is housed upstairs *(Leith Stuart)*; [The Grassmarket] *Watermans*: Small but popular refurbished pub, formerly the Carriers Rest; quiet at lunchtimes but lively in evenings with live jazz Thurs; well kept Belhaven and Theakstons, house wines, lunchtime salad table, juke box, open late *(John Gould)*

☆ **Gifford** [NT5368], *Goblin Ha'*: Warmly welcoming licensee, well kept McEwans 80/-, genuine home cooking, quick service; though the bar's big it's so popular it soon fills – chatty and jolly; boules in good garden; bedrooms *(K M McKelvey)*

☆ **Gullane** [A198; NT4882], *Golf*: Golf's the thing in this friendly easy-going inn with waitress-served bar food, restaurant, garden; open all day, nr GWG175; bedrooms *(LYM)*

☆ **Linlithgow** [65 High St; NS9976], *Four Marys*: Fine old furniture and setting, with tribute to Mary Queen of Scots who was born nearby; full range of well kept Belhaven real ales, good choice of malt whiskies, friendly, comfortable atmosphere, good bar food with waitress service; open all day Sat *(Mr and Mrs J H Adam)*

Pathhead [NT3964], *Foresters Arms*: Bright public bar with good range of whiskies and good food, particularly home-made pies *(W A Wright)*

nr **Penicuik** [Nine Mile Burn; off A702; NT2360], *Habbies Howe*: Attractively decorated lounge interestingly converted from stables, old-fashioned coaching-inn public bar; bedrooms *(LYM)*

Queensferry [Hopetoun Rd; NT1278], *Moorings*: Quiet and comfortable with interesting collection of naval memorabilia and good views of Forth Bridge from lounge; good bar food at reasonable prices, lounge/family-room *(Iain Montgomery)*

☆ **Ratho** [NT1370], *Bridge*: Extended eighteenth-century pub by canal, with good value food using local fresh ingredients, good choice of wine, open fires; own boats (doing trips for the disabled, among others) and waterside garden – play area with mock-up ship and retired tractor; open all day from noon *(GLA)*

STRATHCLYDE

☆ **Ardentinny** [NS1887], *Ardentinny*: Lovely views of Loch Long from well decorated waterside bars and back terrace, good but somewhat pricey choice of bar food, courtesy boat for guests; well placed for Younger Botanic Garden at Benmore; children in eating area; bedrooms; closed Jan/Feb *(LYM)*

Auchentiber [A736 Irvine–Glasgow; NS3647], *Blair*: Pleasant atmosphere and friendly, efficient staff; food good value *(AJVB)*

Bearsden [Station Rd; NS5471], *Beefeater*: Converted from former Bearsden railway station with well kept Whitbreads Castle Eden in attractive lounge bar full of railway memorabilia; good bar food, but the restaurant side predominates *(Ian Baillie)*

Cairndow [NN1810], *Cairndow*: Historic pub (Queen Victoria and Keats stayed here) with superb views over Loch Fyne and reasonable choice of good value bar food; by gardens containing tallest tree in UK; bedrooms *(E J Alcock)*; [just off A83] *Stagecoach*: Old pub with well kept beers, variety of generously served bar food at reasonable prices, friendly staff, pool-table and fruit machines, and separate dining-room with log fire *(A E Alcock)*

Cardross [NS3477], *Cardross*: Three bars, one with coal fire, another with snooker table; conservatory dining area with good home-cooked food at reasonable prices *(L Rowan)*

Colintraive [NS0374], *Colintraive*: Restful and friendly small family-run hotel in lovely spot overlooking the Maids of Bute; plain food inc nice puddings; bedrooms immaculate and attractive, with huge baths and good breakfasts *(A Darroch Harkness)*

Connel [NM9133], *Falls of Lora*: Well kept hotel on edge of village, across rd from Loch Etive: several spacious bar areas with sturdily comfortable cane armchairs, plush banquettes in bays, lots of brass and copper,

tubs of plants forming booths, 1920s-style lamps, big watercolour landscapes, and free-standing Scandinavian-style log fire; bedrooms comfortable and good value *(BB)*

Eaglesham [Polnoon St; NS5752], *Swan*: Recently refurbished, busy pub with well kept McEwans and good reasonably priced bar food inc high tea *(Alastair Campbell)*

Girvan [Dalrymple St; NX1897], *Kings Arms*: Unusual golf bar – serving-counter like giant golf ball, everything else has golf theme; also spacious lounge, bar food, real ale; open all day, children welcome; bedrooms *(LYM)*

Glasgow [India St, Charing Cross], *Baby Grand*: Continental-style cafe-bar, chatty and clattery with terrazzo or tiled floor, long grey marble counter, well kept McEwans 70/- and 80/- on tall founts, espresso machine, good hot chocolate and decent house wines; attractive bentwood furniture, baby pot palms, wide choice of French bread sandwiches and grills with enterprising specials such as herby mackerel, salt beef hash; jazz Sat evening, open all day *(BB)*; [George Sq] *Copthorne*: Lounge bar in city centre with good atmosphere and great decor, though a bit pricey *(Russell Hafter)*; [266 Bath St] *Griffin*: Consistently popular recently renovated smart bar with theatrical pictures; cheap bar food *(Ian Baillie)*; [Woodlands Rd] *Halt*: Old fashioned pub with basic furnishings in basic public bar and much smarter lounge bar – both popular with students; well kept real ales *(Alastair Campbell)*; [427 Dumbarton Rd] *Hayburn Vaults*: No-nonsense well renovated working man's pub, no fancy bar meals, no real ales, no foreign beers; good for quiet morning or evening drink, but uncomfortably busy afternoons *(Ian Baillie)*; [61 Renfield St] *Maltman*: Pleasant and very popular no-smoking bar with table service at quieter times, separate back areas for smokers; real ale inc Tennents 80/-, varied tasty bar food, friendly staff; downstairs restaurant *(Alastair Campbell)*; [formerly the Outside Inn; 1256 Argyle St, corner with Radnor St] *Montys*: Pleasant bar, well furnished with lots of dark wood; five well kept real ales inc Belhaven and Greenmantle, efficient amiable staff, bar food; the atmosphere's getting back to its old friendly self, now it's over the phase just after it reopened, when it was trendily popular with people sipping designer lagers; some form of entertainment most evenings, inc jazz and quizzes *(Alastair Campbell, Ian Baillie)*; [Highburgh Rd] *Rock*: Good choice of beer and bar food at reasonable prices, magnificently renewed Rock Garden section *(Ian Baillie)*; [47 West Nile St] *Smiths*: Smart and busy lunchtime pub, quieter in evenings; lovely airy décor in dark wood, Victorian-style bar; pricey Ind Coope Burton on handpump, good choice of foreign beers, decent wine, interesting bar food *(Alastair Campbell)*; [11 Saltmarket (corner of

Glasgow Cross)] *Tolbooth*: Caledonian real ales, good simple food and warm atmosphere, in solidly traditional surroundings *(Ian Baillie, LYM)*; [12 Ashton Lane] *Ubiquitous Chip*: Real ale, wide choice of malt whiskies and wines, daily changing home-cooked lunchtime food inc vegetarian dishes, peat fire, stained-glass windows and panels; popular with ex-pat sassenachs and linked to well established restaurant with attractive courtyard section *(A Darroch Harkness)*

☆ **Houston** [NS4166], *Fox & Hounds*: Genuine, pleasant place with plush lounge, comfortable seats by fire, attentive bar staff, wolf-whistling mynah, good choice of well kept real ales inc McEwans 70/- and 80/-; livelier bar with video juke box and pool; good popular food which can be eaten in either bar or restaurant; open all day *(Tom McLean, Roger Huggins, Linda and Alex Christison, Alison Hayward, Nick Dowson)*

☆ **Inveraray** [Main St E; NN0908], *George*: Go down corridor to stripped-stone bar with tiles, flagstones, exposed joists and log fire; Tennents 80/-, good choice of whiskies, bar games, food served noon to 9pm; nr GWG 180, and well placed for the Argyll woodland gardens that are at their best in May and early June; children welcome; bedrooms *(R G Ollier, Ray Wainwright, Mr and Mrs J H Adam, LYM; more reports please)*

Inveraray, *Argyll Arms*: Stately old-fashioned hotel overlooking Loch Fyne (especially spacious front conservatory), good choice of bar food and malts, well kept real ale, games in public bar, restaurant; well run, a nice place to stay at; open all day; bedrooms *(LYM)*

Irvine [NS3739], *Turf*: Imaginatively cooked, nicely presented and reasonably priced food; comfortable seating *(AM)*

☆ **Kilberry** [B8024; NR7164], *Kilberry*: Though so out-of-the-way, is very popular for constantly changing choice of delicious food, all home cooked using fresh ingredients (no food Sun evening, closed weekdays Oct-Easter); white-painted stone-built former post office, cosy inside, with friendly licensees, and views over the coastal pastures to the nearby sea and the island of Gigha beyond *(A H Doran and friends)*

Kilfinan [B8000; NR9379], *Kilfinan*: Sporting hotel half-way down Cowal Peninsula, close to shore of Loch Fyne; small public bar (used by locals) with communicating lounge, good beer and excellent food; bedrooms *(Paul Wreglesworth)*

Kilmory [NR8686], *Kilmory Rest*: Super wee place in heavenly surroundings, perfect food and drink served with such aplomb, husband-and-wife licensees make a great team; a nice place to stay at *(Anne Porter)*

Kilmun [NS1785], *Cot House*: Small, cosy lounge decorated with slabs of cedar, variety of pub dogs, well kept 80/-, good value bar food *(E J Alcock)*

Kirkmichael [NS3408], *Kirkmichael Arms*: Friendly and unpretentious, wide choice of good value food lunchtime and evening – cooked to order, so slight wait *(Linda and Carl Worley)*

Loans [NS3431], *Bruce*: Big modernised lounge with dimpled copper tables, wooden lanterns, piped music; friendly and well kept, open all day; Fri singalong *(BB)*

Loans [Old Loans Rd; NS3431], *Dallam Tower*: Note that this, a main entry in previous editions, has changed its name to the Highmore Hotel, with a more hotelish style and a reversion to keg beer; bedrooms *(LYM)*

Loch Eck [NS1493], *Coylet*: Friendly staff in cosy pub with well kept McEwans 80/-, good value bar food (choice rather limited if you don't like fish), real fires throughout, super views over the loch; bedrooms *(R G Ollier, E J Alcock)*

☆ **Lochaweside** [B840; NN1227], *Portsonachan*: Beautifully placed lochside fishing inn, which went through a rough patch in 1988 after losing its previous gifted licensees; it now seems to have been firmly taken in hand again, with most bedrooms, restaurant and dining lounge refurbished, good service from smartly dressed staff, enormous log fire in cosy hotel bar, fine choice of single malt whiskies, good food in bar and restaurant, small fishing-minded public bar; bedrooms simple but large, light and comfortable, with abundant hot water and exceptionally good breakfasts *(SS, A C Lang, LYM; more reports please)*

Luss [A82 about 3 miles N; NS3593], *Inverbeg*: Handy for its position across rd from Loch Lomond; food in busy lounge and restaurant, real ale, games in simple public bar; bedrooms *(Hazel Morgan, LYM)*

☆ **Port Appin** [NM9045], *Airds*: Friendly and notably well run inn with lovely shoreside position, particularly good food and charming attentive service; has been a main entry in previous editions but is now solely a hotel/restaurant – very much worth visiting; comfortable and well equipped bedrooms *(LYM)*

☆ **Strachur** [A815 N of village; NN0901], *Creggans*: Lovely position and views, by spot where Mary Queen of Scots landed 1563; tweedy hotelish lounge, conservatory, character locals' bar with games, bar food lunchtime and early evening, restaurant, McEwans 80/- on handpump, good range of malt whiskies, open all day; children welcome; you can walk for hours on the owners' land; comfortable well equipped bedrooms *(E J Alcock, LYM)*

☆ **Tarbert** [NR8467], *Tarbert Hotel*: Atmospheric and quaint hotel with lovely outlook over harbour, and very good value evening meals; bedrooms comfortable, with handsome breakfasts *(E J Alcock)*

☆ **Troon** [Troon Marina; Harbour Rd – from centre go into Temple Hill and keep bearing right; NS3230], *Lookout*: Comfortable plush and wicker-and-bentwood seats in smart first-floor bar of blocky modern building with lively sea and marina views from picture windows, and from barbecue terrace; reasonably priced separate dining area, well kept Greenmantle and Theakstons on electric pump, good espresso coffee, children welcome; open all day summer; sailing, windsurfing and waterskiing can be arranged in the marina *(LYM)*

TAYSIDE

Aberfeldy [Main St; NN8549], *Crown*: Comfortably modern well decorated comfortable lounge, generous helpings of reasonably priced bar food, well kept beer, polite staff; distillery and working watermill nearby; bedrooms good value *(E J and A E Alcock)*

Auchterhouse [NO3337], *Old Mansion House*: Pleasant small country hotel, good food in bar and dining room, good service; bedrooms *(Mr and Mrs N W Briggs)*

Ballinluig [NN9853], *Ballinluig*: Nice food and friendly efficient service; bedrooms *(Anon)*

Bridge of Cally [NO1451], *Bridge of Cally*: Beautiful, quiet setting by river with very warm welcome and excellent, value-for-money food; bedrooms clean, comfortable and well equipped *(P J Evans)*

Calvine [NN8066], *Bruar Falls*: Warm welcome, good value food in bar and restaurant, 70 malt whiskies; good value bedrooms *(K R and C E Watkins)*

Clova [NO3273], *Clova*: Very good welcoming bar, super fire if the weather's bad, decent food; keg beer *(D Pearman)*

Crieff [N, signposted off A85, A822; NN8562], *Glenturret Distillery*: Not a pub, but the whisky-tasting bar has very good value malt whiskies, full range of other drinks, and good self-service food – the haggis is a treat; terrace overlooks Scotland's oldest distillery, with very good visitors' centre and guided tours; open Mar–Dec Mon–Fri till 5.30, also Apr–Oct Sat until 4 *(T Nott)*

Dundee [16 Victoria Rd, about a mile N of centre; NO4030], *Ladywell Tavern*: No-frills small town pub with well kept McEwans 80/- and Youngers No 3, lively friendly atmosphere, sometimes crowded *(BB)*; [South Tay St, Old Hawkhill] *Tally-Ho*: Popular bar, fulsomely decorated with stuffed animals; well kept Timothy Taylors Landlord and Youngers No 3, good cheap bar food *(Alisdair Cuthil)*

Fortingall [NN7446], *Fortingall*: Pleasant pub with good bar lunches – soup and sandwiches, and summer buffet; bedrooms *(RB)*

Kenmore [NN7745], *Kenmore*: Civilised and quietly old-fashioned small hotel with long landscape poem composed here written in Burns' own handwriting on residents' lounge wall, friendly back bar and lively separate barn bar; gardens, good fishing; nr start GWG185; bedrooms *(LYM)*

Kinross [The Muirs; NO1102], *Windlestrae*: Attractive hotel with bar and restaurant; bedrooms *(T Nott)*

Loch Tummel [B8019; NN8460], *Loch Tummel*: Fine spot between the wooded mountains and the loch, with neat simple furnishings in long white-painted bar, big wood-burning stove, piped music, separate games bar, limited pub food and simple upstairs restaurant; children in eating area, open all day; bedrooms quiet and comfortable, with old oak furniture, though heating and hot water supply out of season could be improved; good breakfasts *(J Marshall, M Shinkfield, Helen and John Thompson, S R Holman, LYM; more reports on new regime please)*

☆ **Perth** [Canal Crescent; NO1123], *Granary*: Lovely building with lots of old farm equipment, stone walls and good character; friendly service, good food inc excellent open sandwiches, meaty steak pie and tasty fish; comfortable upstairs restaurant *(G and L Owen, Melvin D Buckner)*

Perth [South St], *Ewe & Lamb*: Small main-street pub with bar and upstairs restaurant; good value bar food and quick service; parking 50 yds away by River Tay *(A A Worthington)*

Scone [A94; NO1226], *Scone Arms*: Pleasant, comfortable surroundings; good, well presented bar food *(Mr and Mrs J H Adam)*

THE ISLANDS

Bute

Rothesay [NS0864], *Black Bull*: Friendly, comfortable three-roomed pub in town centre with good value bar food inc sizzling steaks (evening menu only on Fri and Sat); only pub we know on island with real ale – Broughtons Greenmantle *(P LLoyd, K Bamford)*

Islay

Bowmore [Shore St; NR3159], *Lochside*: Friendly efficient service, good food, good view from lounge; bedrooms *(Miles Walton)*

Port Charlotte [NR2457], *Port Charlotte Hotel*: Well run, with good atmosphere, reasonable local food; walls covered with nautical charts, underwater photographs, shipwreck salvage; bedrooms *(Paul Wreglesworth)*

Jura
Craighouse [NR5267], *Jura Hotel*: Next to the distillery and overlooking Small Isles Bay, with excellent home-cooked food using fresh local ingredients; the island is a paradise for walkers, birdwatchers and photographers; good value bedrooms *(Paul Wreglesworth)*

Lewis
Ness [NB5261], *Cross*: Friendly, relaxing haven with open peat fire in lounge, good value bar food and substantial evening meals; recently modernised bedrooms good value too *(Mr and Mrs J S Quantrill)*

Mull
Craignure [NM7136], *Craignure*: Excellent food in busy popular bar with good atmosphere; bedrooms *(Miles Walton)*

Seil
☆ **Clachan Seil** [island linked by bridge via B844, off A816 S of Oban; NM7718], *Tigh an Truish*: L-shaped panelled bar with wood-burning stove, prints and oil paintings, wheel-back chairs and stools, piano, tartan curtains, bay windows overlooking bridge and mainland; darts, well kept McEwans 80/- and Tennents 80/-, bar food from burgers to dressed crab and local giant prawns with home-made mayonnaise, restaurant; white chairs in small garden and also at side of building; bedrooms *(Patrick Stapley)*

Orkney
St Margarets Hope [Ronaldsway; ND4593], *Bellevue*: Good beer and other stronger liquids, very friendly staff and locals; on the edge of this small old village's harbour; bedrooms comfortable and inexpensive *(WFL)*

Shetland
Hillswick [HU2977], *Booth*: A favourite, with friendly service and good food; beware baby seals in the garden; bedrooms *(Denis Mann)*
Lerwick [central, by sea; HU4741], *Queens*: A nice place to stay at, though the bar's been revamped and is now a cafe/bar with video, TV, espresso machine and Grolsch at £2 a bottle; bedrooms *(Anon)*; [Docks] *Thule*: Bar rough and full of characters from local fishermen to Russians, upstairs lounge lively and best in town, with traditional music from time to time *(Denis Mann)*

Skye
Ardvasar [A851 towards Broadford;

NG6203], *Clan Donald Centre*: Not a pub but worth knowing for its very good food such as local scallops, fresh haddock and crisp vegetables *(Mrs H Church)*
Culnaknock [13 miles N of Portree on Staffin rd; NG5162], *Glenview*: Well cooked and reasonably priced bar food with original food such as honeyed lentil soup with soda scones or haddie buns (brioche filled with egg and smoked salmon) – and fresh local scallops, of course; evening restaurant good, too; comfortable bedrooms *(Mary and Bill Parsons)*
Isle Ornsay [NG6912], *Duisdale*: Comfortable lounge bar with striped flock wallpaper and deep brown leatherette settles, chairs and stools around dimpled copper-topped tables; ship's wheel on one wall with a smaller one as a light-fitting, and flags and pennants above the bar; bay window at front looks over croquet lawn/putting green to mainland hills and lovely side garden; appetising bar food; bedrooms *(S J A Velate)*
Sconser [NG5132], *Sconser Lodge*: The lovely view over to Raasay and the mainland is what distinguishes the basic locals' bar of this inn, handy for the Raasay ferry and the Red Hills – and we've had more promising reports on the bar food and service recently; children in eating area and family-room; bedrooms *(S J A Velate, LYM – more news please)*
☆ **Sligachan** [A850 Broadford–Portree, junction with A863; NG4830], *Sligachan*: Marvellously placed simple inn, remote in central Skye, with basic public bar full of wet and weary but elated walkers, climbers and others from the nearby campsite; plusher more sedate hotel bar with open fire, old prints of Skye, armchairs and sofas around low tables, bay window with views of the towering Red Hills; generous helpings of simple reliable food in bar and restaurant; bedrooms good value; closed winter *(S J A Velate, Steve Waters, BB)*
Uig [Pier; beside Ferry Terminal; NG3963], *Bakur*: Good no-nonsense bar in bungalow-style building right by ferry, pleasant people, usual simple bar food lunchtime and early evening, good choice of whiskies; pool, darts *(Stephen R Holman)*; *Ferry*: Well run unpretentious inn with decent simple food in cosy but sometimes rather cramped lounge, with leatherette seats around dimpled copper tables, flock wallpaper; bedrooms overlook pier and loch *(S J A Velate, BB)*;
Uig [closed Oct–Apr; NG3963], *Uig*: Lovely position overlooking sea, but no proper serving bar – sandwiches and a drink can be served to visitors in the hotelish lounge; bedrooms; closed winter *(BB)*
Ullinish [NG3138], *Ullinish Lodge*: Not a place to think of as a pub (plain lounge bar is accessible only through residents' dining-room and separate public bar is very basic), nevertheless a nice place to stay at; attractive

eighteenth-century building in superb position with fine views to the Cuillins; as it's relatively inexpensive you can forgive the occasional indifferent furnishings and rather hurried mealtimes; bedrooms *(S J A Velate)*

Wales

Wales

In the upsurge of quality which is vitalising pub food throughout Britain, it's often the outlying areas where this shows up most vividly. Wales is now a prominent example. Pubs and inns to note particularly for food include the atmospheric Olde Bulls Head in Beaumaris, the stylish Ty Gwyn on the edge of Betws-y-Coed, the friendly family-run Druidstone overlooking the sea at Broad Haven, the very individual old Bear in Crickhowell, the Old Black Lion in Hay-on-Wye (brought back into the Guide by new owners with a very up-front approach to freshly made imaginative food), the Queens Head at Glanwydden near Llandudno Junction, the delightfully tucked-away Leyland Arms at Llanelidan (as good as ever under its new licensees), the White Swan by the church at Llanfrynach, the Goat at Llanwnda (a new entry, in for its superb lunchtime cold table), the idiosyncratic Cerigllwydion Arms at Llanynys, the Griffin at Llyswen (increasingly a byword for easy hospitality), and the cheery Grapes at Maentwrog. Several of these are also nice places to stay at. Best of all for food is the Walnut Tree at Llandewi Skirrid, a unique though not cheap combination of Italian flair with top quality ingredients – often unusual. Some other new entries to mention particularly include the Parciau Arms at Marianglas (food all day, at least in summer), the Cottage Inn under the castle just outside Montgomery, the Red Lion on its steep hillside at Penderyn, the Ty Coch in a matchless position by the sea at Porth Dinllaen, and the Ship at Red Wharf Bay – another marvellous waterside spot. Other pubs particularly worth knowing for their seaside positions include the Harbourmaster in Aberaeron (promising new licensees in summer 1989), the Cresselly Arms at Cresswell Quay, the Sailors Safety near Dinas, the Bristol Trader in Haverfordwest, the Swan at Little Haven, the bustling Captains Wife near Penarth and the George III at Penmaenpool. Inland, magnificent

The Halfway Inn, nr Aberystwyth

903

surroundings count for a lot with the Halfway Inn near Aberystwyth (the owners plan to move to Canada, so to some extent we must keep our fingers crossed about this individualistic place), the Sportsmans Arms at Bylchau, the Olde Bull at Llanbedr-y-Cennin, the Pen-y-Gwryd across the mountains from Llanberis, the Glansevern Arms at Llangurig, the Abbey at Llanthony, the Brynffynon at Llanwonno and the Harp at Old Radnor. Lots of starred Lucky Dip pubs at the end of the chapter are jostling to get into the main entries, and many of these are of main-entry standard (particularly pubs with the give-away LYM initials that show they have been main entries in the past – often places that we simply haven't heard much of from readers recently); there just isn't room for them all in the book. Prospects here to note as specially promising are the Bush at St Hilary (S Glamorgan), Rock & Fountain at Clydach, Open Hearth near Pontypool and Royal in Usk (all Gwent), Ship in Porthmadog and Groes at Tyn-y-groes (both Gwynedd), and Radnor Arms at Llowes (Powys).

The Lleyn Peninsula and the District of Ceredigion (between Cardigan and the mouth of the River Dovey) are dry on Sundays. Pubs there are normally closed on Sundays, though hotels can sell drinks to their residents and may stay open for meals (there may be some blurring of the distinction between these two activities). We mention in the text any main-entry pubs that do close on Sundays.

ABERAERON (Dyfed)   SN4462 Map 6

Harbourmaster

Quay Parade

The new licensee, who took over this harbourside pub in August 1989, hopes to re-open the restaurant which closed under Mr Davies; but otherwise he has few plans to change anything – least of all the particularly welcoming and unpretentious atmosphere, partly created by the local fishermen. There are good local sea photographs above the green button-back banquettes of the dark-panelled bar; Bass, Hancocks and Worthington on handpump. As we went to press the bar menu hadn't yet been finalised, but there should be an emphasis on fish and French dishes. In fine weather the harbour wall outside is the place to sit, with its picture-book view over the yachts and boats to the row of colourfully painted houses opposite. *(Recommended by Lord Evans of Claughton, D S Rusholme, Doug Kennedy)*

Free house   Licensee Roland Morris   Real ale   Meals and snacks (not Sun)   Children welcome   Open 11.30–3ish, 7–11; may open all day summer if trade demands; closed Sun

nr ABERYSTWYTH (Dyfed)   SN5882 Map 6

Halfway Inn   ★   [*illustrated on page 903*]

Pisgah; A4120 towards Devil's Bridge, 5¾ miles E of junction with A487

In late 1988 this interesting pub perched prettily over the Vale of Rheidol once again got a new licensee; it's a great testimony both to the strong character of the place and to the discreetness of the takeover that its distinctive, even eccentric charm has survived pretty much intact. It went on the market again in summer 1989, but such is our confidence that history will repeat itself that we've kept its star. At the moment you're still trusted to tap your own interesting beer from the row of half a dozen well kept casks (unless you'd prefer a professional handpump job); Felinfoel Double Dragon is always on, and others might include Bass, Davenports, Smiles Exhibition, Wadworths 6X and Whitbreads Castle Eden. The food's kept its distance from chippiness, too: a wide but unfussy choice, including rich, thick home-made soup (£1.10), succulent turkey sandwiches (£1.20), a good few vegetarian and vegan dishes (£2.95), chilli con carne (£2.80) and good home-made pies such as steak and kidney (£2.95). The beamed and flagstoned bar has stripped deal tables and settles between its bare stone walls, with a wine bar/dining area opening off (the choice of wines is good – and they keep Symonds farm cider or perry too). Darts, cribbage and dominoes, maybe loudish piped music; no dogs. Outside, picnic-set tables under cocktail parasols have fine views of wooded hills and pastures; there's a play area, free overnight camping for customers, a paddock for ponytrekkers, and even free parking and picnic space for visitors – whether or not they use the pub. It gets particularly busy in summer. *(Recommended by Dr Stephen Hiew, Peter Scillitoe, E J Waller, G T Jones, Doug Kennedy, Peter Griffiths; more reports please)*

Free house   Licensees D L J and P A Allen   Real ale   Meals and snacks (not Sun) Restaurant tel Capel Bangor (097 084) 631; closed Sun   Children in restaurant and eating area (not Sun)   Open 12–3, 6–11 all year; closed Sun and maybe Mon lunchtime in Feb

BEAUMARIS (Anglesey)   SH6076 Map 6
Olde Bulls Head ★ ✿

Castle Street

Though it's the restaurant here which attracts the most mouth-watering praise, the lunchtime bar food in this charming partly fifteenth-century inn has gained an enthusiastic following over the last couple of years. Changing daily, it might include home-made soup (95p), sandwiches (from £1.15), ploughman's (£1.95), hot dishes such as chicken fricassee with mixed peppers or tagliatelle bolognese (£3), braised oxtail or venison sausages (£3.20) and roast leg of lamb, with home-made puddings such as walnut and treacle tart and cheesecakes (£1.20). The rambling low-beamed bar is interestingly quaint, yet comfortable too, with snug alcoves, low-seated settles, leather-cushioned window seats and a good open fire. Besides copper and china jugs, there's a bloodthirsty crew of cutlasses, a rare seventeenth-century brass water clock and even the town's oak ducking stool; very well kept Bass on handpump, good wine list; cheerful, friendly service, dominoes. The entrance to the pretty courtyard is closed by the biggest single hinged door in Britain. *(Recommended by Gordon Theaker, R L Theaker, Jon Wainwright, Gwen and Peter Andrews, C J McFeeters, Lynne Farrell)*

Free house   Licensee D I Robertson   Real ale   Meals and snacks (lunchtime, not Sun, and Sun evening)   Restaurant   Children in eating area until 9   Open 11–11 all year   Bedrooms tel Beaumaris (0248) 810329; £29.50B/£49.50B

BETWS-Y-COED (Gwynedd)   SH7956 Map 6
Ty Gwyn ✿ ⇌

A5 just S of bridge to village

Peaceful and cottagey, this relaxed seventeenth-century inn is protected against the overcrowding that's such an obvious risk even out here on the edge of this popular village both by its diminutive car park and by the terms of its licence – you have to eat, or stay overnight. Throughout, the furnishings and decorations reflect the fact that the owners run an antique shop next door. The beamed lounge bar has an interesting clutter of unusual antique prints and bric-à-brac, with an ancient cooking-range worked in well at one end; there are rugs and comfortable chintz easy chairs on its oak parquet floor. Quickly served bar food includes generous helpings of home-made soup (£1.25), sandwiches, pâté (£2.25), ploughman's (from

---

Sunday opening in now 12–3 and 7–10.30 in all Welsh pubs allowed to open on that day (we mention in the text the few that aren't).

£2.50), bulghur wheat and walnut casserole (£3.95), lasagne, gammon, trout, shark steak or home-made steak and kidney pie (all £4.50) and sirloin steak (£6.95); children's meals (£1.95); McEwans 80/- on handpump. *(Recommended by Brian Jones, R F Warner, Mr and Mrs Stevens, Lord Evans of Claughton, Mrs Colbatch Clark, C F Walling, Wayne Brindle)*

Free house   Licensees Jim and Shelagh Ratcliffe   Real ale   Meals and snacks   Restaurant with midnight supper licence   Children welcome   Open 12–3, 6.30–11 all year   Bedrooms tel Betws-y-coed (069 02) 383; £15/£30(£37B)

BISHOPSTON (W Glam)   SS5789 Map 6

Joiners Arms

50 Bishopston Road; village signposted from B4436, on the Gower Peninsula

Simple but comfortable, this truly hospitable local has been neatly restored to show off its stripped beams and stonework – underlining the point with quarry tiles, fitted carved oak benches, a massive solid-fuel stove and a copper-topped stone bar counter. But what strikes you most is the unusual spiral staircase. A short choice of good value simple home-made bar food includes filled rolls, chilli con carne (from £2), chicken curry (£2.50), chicken pie (£2.60), steak and kidney pie (£2.75) and children's meals (from £1.75); well kept Bass, Worthington BB and a guest beer such as Felinfoel Double Dragon on handpump; darts, cribbage, dominoes. The white-painted lounge bar is decorated with local paintings. *(Recommended by John and Helen Thompson, Mrs June Borrelli, Jenny and Brian Seller, Michael and Alison Sandy, M and J Back)*

Free house   Licensees Arthur and Gwyneth Mort   Real ale   Meals and snacks (12–2, 6–8)   Children welcome   Nearby parking can be difficult   Organist Sun evening   Open 11–11; 11–3.30, 5.30–11 Mon—Weds in winter

BODFARI (Clwyd)   SJ0970 Map 6

Dinorben Arms   ★

From A541 in village, follow Tremeirchion 3 signpost

Coping efficiently with its great popularity, this carefully extended old pub has enough seating areas to give plenty of quiet nooks. As much attention has been paid outside as in: carefully landscaped and prettily planted brick-floored terraces, with lots of tables, have attractive sheltered corners and charming views, and there's a grassy play area which – like the car park – is neatly sculpted into the slope of the hills. Inside, there are beams hung with tankards and flagons, high shelves of china, old-fashioned settles and other seats, and three open fires. Lunchtime bar food includes soup (£1), filled French bread (from £1.40), and a good value eat-as-much-as-you-like smorgasbord counter with three hot dishes as well as at least half a dozen cold meats, some ten fish dishes, and a couple of dozen salads (£6.25 for adults and from £1.50 for children). Evening main courses include curries or home-made steak and kidney pie (£3.95), salads, trout (£5) and gammon (£4.95), with two or three daily specials such as beef Stroganoff (£5.95) or langoustines (£6.25), and vegetarian dishes such as aubergine moussaka (£3.95). You choose starters and puddings from an attractive spread by a glassed-in well which may date from the seventh century. There's also an upstairs carvery on Wednesday to Saturday evenings, and a light and airy garden-room; over a hundred whiskies; maybe piped music. *(Recommended by Patrick Godfrey, KC, E G Parish, F A Noble, Mike Tucker, Steve Dark, C F Walling, BKA)*

Free house   Licensee Gilbert Hopwood   Real ale   Meals and snacks (12–2.30, 6–10.30) Restaurant tel Bodfari (074 575) 309   Children in garden-room and restaurant Open 12–3.30, 6–11 all year; closed 25 Dec

BROAD HAVEN (Dyfed)   SM8614 Map 6

Druidstone 🌣 🍺

From village, take coast road N and bear left, keeping on for about 1½ miles, then follow sign left to Druidstone Haven – after another ½ mile or so the hotel is a *very* sharp left turn; OS Sheet 157 reference 862168 (marked as Druidston Villa)

For most readers, the gloriously remote seaside setting and the unusually easy-going friendly informality of this family-run hotel combine to make it enjoyably memorable. Food – served generously – relies on fresh ingredients, including bread baked here. Bar lunches might include tomato and celery soup (£1.10), ploughman's (£2), salami platter (£2.20), watercress and creamcheese mousse (£2.40), big cold roast meat salads (£3.20 or £4.20), and whopping puddings (from £1.65). A seafood quiche turned out to be virtually all lobster, and vegetarian dishes can be imaginative – bean and fresh fennel pie, or aubergine and tomato crumble, for instance. Worthington BB is tapped from the cask in a flagstoned cellar bar with a strong folk-club feel, where old sofas and armchairs face a rough but lively mural of the beach below; darts and piped music. The rooms above (including simple but spacious bedrooms) have a clifftop view out to sea, and a steep path takes you down to the long and virtually private sandy beach. Outside, there are all sorts of sporting possibilities, from boules through archery to far more strenuous sports. We ourselves look forward to our visits here very much indeed. But we have been taken to task for not mentioning points which, though all part of the picture loved by its devotees, might strike you differently: the autocratic old plumbing, which may decide you've had enough hot water halfway through filling your bath; the very leisurely service; random eccentricities like the old ice-cream container which may be pressed into service to chill white wine (if it's not just served at cellar temperature). And it does help if you like dogs a lot. *(Recommended by Peter Griffiths, Steve Dark, Drs S P K and C M Linter, Janet and Gary Amos, Dr I J Thompson)*

Free house – hotel licence   Licensee Jane Bell   Real ale   Meals and snacks (12.30–2.30, 7.30–10)   Restaurant   Children welcome   Music weekends four or five times a year   Open 12.30–2.30, 6–11; closed, exc for party bookings, Nov, 7 Jan–9 Feb   Bedrooms tel Broad Haven (0437) 781221; £19.50/£39

BYLCHAU (Clwyd)   SH9863 Map 6

Sportsmans Arms (Tafarn yr Heliwr)

A543 3 miles S of village

This 400-year-old pub is where the Welsh-speaking people from the surrounding hills come to enjoy the company – not to mention the big helpings of good value bar food such as ploughman's, home-made steak and kidney pie (£3), plaice stuffed with mushrooms and in a wine, cream and prawn sauce (£4.95) and 10oz sirloin steak in a blue cheese sauce (£7.25), with a weekend hot and cold buffet with such dishes as Normandy pork and lasagne verde (£4.50); home-made puddings. The food is prepared to order, so there may be a wait if the pub is busy. They do a traditional three-course lunch on Sundays (£6), with filled rolls then as the alternative. The pub – the highest in Wales, and often snowed up in winter – is spectacularly isolated, with good moorland and forest views. It's comfortable, with both a log fire and a massive wood-burning stove to warm the old-fashioned high-backed settles and other more modern seats. Well kept Lees Best on handpump and Best Dark Mild under a light blanket pressure; darts, pool, fruit machine. Nearby Brenig reservoir has sailing, and walks in the forests around it include archaeological trails. *(Recommended by Mr and Mrs J H Adam, Philip Riding, Lee Goulding, Diane Hall, BKA; more reports please)*

Lees   Licensee Ioan Aled Evans   Real ale   Meals   Children in eating area   Organist and Welsh singing Sat evening   Open 11–3, 7–11; closed Tues lunchtime in winter

CARNO (Powys)   SN9697 Map 6

Aleppo Merchant 🍺

A470 Newtown–Machynlleth

Named after the sea captain who retired to open it in 1632, this has been simply but comfortably modernised and recently extended – red plush button-back banquettes around copper-topped tables, stripped stone and brassware in the beamed lounge bar, sofas and easy chairs in a small adjoining lounge, and a public bar with snooker, darts, dominoes, trivia machine and juke box. A wide choice of bar food includes an open prawn sandwich (£2.85), chilli con carne (£3.60), fish pie (£3.95), a good steak and kidney pie with new potatoes (£4.95) and steaks (£6.95); well kept Felinfoel Bitter and Double Dragon and guest beers on handpump; friendly service. *(Recommended by Mr and Mrs P W Dryland, A G Roby; more reports on the new regime please)*

Free house   Licensee John Carroll   Real ale   Meals and snacks   Restaurant   Children over 12 in eating area until 9   Open 11–3, 6–11   Bedrooms tel Carno (0686) 420210; £19/£30

CILCAIN (Clwyd)   SJ1865 Map 7

White Horse

Village signposted from A494 W of Mold; OS Sheet 116 reference 177652

Tucked away in a delightfully unspoilt hamlet of stone houses, this friendly and homely pub has a cluster of snug rooms – parlourish in the two by the serving-bar at the front, with exposed joists in the low ochre ceiling, mahogany and oak settles, Lloyd Loom chairs, brass, copper and decorative china on a high Delft shelf and around the little inglenook, and even a goldfish tank. Beyond a further little room with a piano (and a grandfather clock awaiting repair), there's one more conventionally furnished with tables and chairs. A separate quarry-tiled bar at the back allows dogs. Food includes filled rolls (from 80p), ploughman's (£2.30), omelettes (from £2.30), home-made steak and kidney pie (£3.60), home-made curries (from £3.60), home-baked ham (£3.80), ham and eggs (£4.50) and eight-ounce rump steak (£5.80). Well kept Ansells, Ind Coope Burton and Powells Bitter and Samsons on handpump, and Addlestones cider; darts, dominoes, cribbage, fruit machine, trivia machine. There are picnic-table sets at the side, with an attractively naive inn-sign in front of the creeper-covered flower-decked building. *(More reports please)*

Free house   Licensee Peter Jeory   Real ale   Meals and snacks (until 10 Fri and Sat) Open 12–4 (4.30 Sat), 7–11 all year

CILGERRAN (Dyfed)   SN1943 Map 6

Pendre

Village signposted from A478

This end of the village is top of the town (what the pub's Welsh name means); the other leads down to the River Teifi, with a romantic ruined castle on a crag nearby, and coracle races on the Saturday before the August Bank Holiday. The pub itself is an impressive blend of unpretentious comfort with great age – massive fourteenth-century stonework, broad flagstones; its sympathetic furnishings include armchairs and antique high-backed settles. Good value bar food includes sandwiches, home-made pâté or filled baked potatoes (£1.40), ploughman's (from £2.10), a late breakfast (£2.45), vegetable and cheese crumble (£2.75), home-made steak and kidney pie (£3.55) and beef or chicken curry with bhajee (£3.80). The public bar has a juke box, darts, pool and a fruit machine; Worthington BB on handpump, friendly service; an amiable parrot. There are seats outside, with an enclosed play

---

Bar food is generally served 12–2 and 7–9 unless stated otherwise.

area for small children. Near the village is a good local wildlife park. *(Recommended by John Branford, Wayne Brindle)*

Free house   Real ale   Meals and snacks   Restaurant tel Cardigan (0239) 614223   Children welcome   Open 11.30–3.30, 6 (6.30 Sat)–11

COWBRIDGE (S Glam)   SS9974   Map 6
Bear   🏨

Town signposted off A48

There's a reassuring feel of dependable solidity about this neatly kept old coaching-inn – still a lively focus of the life of this flourishing part of Glamorgan. On the left, an unusually heavy door opens into a bar with beams, flagstones, panelling, and attractively upholstered stools around cast-iron-framed tables; on the right there's carpet, and comfortable red plush armchairs. Bar food, served from the new bistro area (the lounge is now for residents), includes sandwiches, filled baked potatoes (from £1.30), soup (£1.35), gammon or curry (£3.25), steak and kidney pie (£3.50) and grilled sardines (£3.95), and there's a separate carvery. Well kept Bass, Brains Bitter and SA, Buckleys Best, Flowers Original, Hancocks HB, Marstons Pedigree and a weekly guest beer such as Hook Norton Old Hooky on handpump; log-effect gas fires, darts, maybe piped music. There's a rambling warren of quiet and comfortable beamed bedrooms, with more in a modern block behind; the breakfasts are good. *(Recommended by A Cook, Lyn and Bill Capper)*

Free house   Licensee J B Davies   Real ale   Meals and snacks (not Sat evenings) Restaurant   Children in eating area   Open 11.30–3 (3.30 Sat), 5.30–11 all year Bedrooms tel Cowbridge (044 63) 4814; £35B/£45B

CRESSWELL QUAY (Dyfed)   SN0406   Map 6
Cresselly Arms

Village signposted from A4075

So thoroughly traditional that its snacks are confined to sandwiches, this fine old creeper-covered pub can be reached by boat if the tides are right – one reader recently found the water lapping over the quay up to the pub's door. Inside the main rooms there's almost the feel of a sitting-room full of friends: red and black flooring tiles, a high beam and plank ceiling hung with lots of pictorial china, built-in wall benches, kitchen chairs and simple tables, an open fire in one room and a working Aga in another. A third red-carpeted room is more conventionally furnished, with red-cushioned mate's chairs around neat tables. Well kept and attractively priced Hancocks HB is tapped straight from the cask into glass jugs; friendly service, fruit machine, dominoes. Outside, picnic-set tables look out over the beautiful creek. *(Recommended by Janet Williams, Wayne Brindle, D P and M E Cartwright, Neil and Elspeth Fearn)*

Free house   Real ale   Sandwiches (lunchtime, not Sat or Sun)   Open 11–3, 5.30–11 all year

CRICCIETH (Gwynedd)   SH5038   Map 6
Prince of Wales

The Square; A497

The Lleyn Peninsula is not specially well served with good pubs, making this well kept and comfortable place all the more welcome. The food's good value, too: at lunchtime, filled rolls (65p), prawn sandwiches (£2), ploughman's (£2), cannelloni (£2.45), aubergine and mushroom lasagne (£2.55), steak and kidney or chicken and mushroom pie (£2.95); in the evening it's meals rather than snacks, with main dishes such as lemon sole (£4.75), vegetable Stroganoff or pie (£4.75), poached salmon (£4.95) and sirloin steak (£5.25). The spacious, modern open-plan bar, pleasantly redecorated recently, has cosy separate areas and alcoves, some nice panelling, attractive local and countryside prints, and open fires (one in a pretty tiled fireplace). Well kept Whitbreads Castle Eden on handpump; cribbage, dominoes and fruit machine. There's a piano for any customer who feels up to setting in motion impromptu sing songs. *(Recommended by Sue Holland, Dave Webster, Mr, Mrs and Miss Summerfield)*

Whitbreads Licensee Chris Johnson Real ale Meals and lunchtime snacks (12–2.30, 6–8; not Sun) Country and western or light pop music Tues evening Open 11–3, 6–11 (all day Sat in summer); closed Sun

CRICKHOWELL (Powys) SO2118 Map 6

Bear ★ 🅟 🛏

Brecon Road; A40

As one reader put it, the atmosphere seems built into the walls of this friendly and very civilised old coaching-inn. The heavily beamed lounge is packed with antiques including a fine oak dresser filled with pewter and brass, a longcase clock and interesting prints. Spread among the rugs on the oak parquet floor are lots of little plush-seated bentwood armchairs, along with handsome cushioned antique settles and, up by the great log fire, a big sofa and leather easy chairs. A window seat looks down the old market square. Snacks range from home-made soup (£1.20) and substantial sandwiches (from 85p), through a cheese platter (from £1.75) and pâté (£1.50) to cheese and asparagus pancakes (£2.75) or garlic prawns with granary bread (£2.95). Home-cooked main dishes might include faggots and peas (£2.25), omelettes (£2.95), an aubergine-based vegetarian dish (£3.95), steak and mushroom pie (£4.95), salmon béchamel pie (£5.25) and evening steaks (from £6.95), with a good choice of often original puddings (£1.50); efficient service. Bar food is served willingly until much later in the evening than usual for Wales. Well kept Bass, Ruddles County and Websters Yorkshire on handpump. There are seats on the sheltered back lawn. The back bedrooms – particularly in the new block – are the most highly recommended. *(Recommended by E J Waller, John and Helen Thompson, Mr and Mrs J H Adam, John Hayward, John Honnor, Angela Dewar, Gordon Theaker, Philip King, Nick Dowson, Stephen R Holman, TBB, Janet and Gary Amos)*

Free house Licensee Mrs Judy Hindmarsh Real ale Meals and snacks (until 10 evenings) Restaurant (closed Sun) Children in eating area Open 10–3, 6–11 all year Bedrooms tel Crickhowell (0873) 810408; £30B/£48B

DINAS (Dyfed) SN0139 Map 6

Sailors Safety

From A487 in Dinas Cross follow Bryn-henllan ½, Pwll Gwaelod 1 signpost

Perfect for its location on the edge of an isolated cove below windswept Dinas Head, this sixteenth-century pub has a no-nonsense medley of big scrubbed deal tables, pews and whisky-keg seats on its red tiles. It's got a friendly and buoyant atmosphere, and a lively nautical décor – its pride is the elaborate brass-inlaid counter, carved for the pub nearly seventy years ago. A brighter side bar has darts, pool, dominoes, cribbage, fruit machine, space game and video juke box, and they've opened a tiny French restaurant next door this last year. Bar food may now be limited to doorstep sandwiches and salads, and evidently they've stopped keeping real ale. Outside, seats huddle among the dunes that protect the pub itself; the cliff walks from here are very exhilarating. *(Recommended by G T Jones, Ian Evans, Janet Williams, Mike and Alison Blank, Wayne Brindle; more reports please)*

Free house Meals (restricted Sat lunchtime) and snacks Restaurant tel Dinas Cross (034 86) 207 Children welcome Occasional summer folk music weekends Open 11–3, 5.30–11; may be closed weekday winter lunchtimes

EAST ABERTHAW (S Glam) ST0367 Map 6

Blue Anchor ★

B4265

Over 600 years old, this pretty thatched and creeper-covered pub has a warren of low-beamed rooms all the way round the central servery, wriggling through massive stone walls – the doors are low enough to remind you that today everyone's a giant, compared to people in the days when the pub was built. It's mainly carpeted, with seats and tables worked into a series of chatty little alcoves, though the more open front bar has an old lime-ash floor, with antique oak seats built into the stripped stonework by the inglenook fire (there seem to be open fires everywhere). Brains Dark and SA, Buckleys Best, Marstons Pedigree, Theakstons Old Peculier and Wadworths 6X are kept carefully at a controlled temperature, and served by handpump or tapped from the cask. Good value lunchtime bar food includes soup (70p), tasty pasties or pie (60p), ploughman's (from £1.30), salads (from £2.10, fresh crab £2.75, fresh salmon £3), faggots or sausage and mash (£2.10), home-made cottage or steak and kidney pie (£2.25) and roasts (£2.75); darts, dominoes, and a sensibly isolated fruit machine. Rustic seats shelter among tubs and troughs of flowers outside, with more stone tables on a newer terrace. From here a path leads to the shingly flats of the estuary. The pub can get packed in the evenings and on summer weekends. *(Recommended by Patrick and Mary McDermott, Gary Scott, Dr John Innes, Gwynne Harper, TBB, Lyn and Bill Capper)*

Free house   Licensee J Coleman   Real ale   Lunchtime meals and snacks   Children welcome   Open 11–11 all year

GLASBURY (Powys)   SO1739 Map 6

Harp 🛏

A438 just N of village turn-off

It's the games bar which makes the most of the pub's position above the River Wye, with a good view from its big picture windows. This is an airy room, with pine kitchen tables on its wood floor, and pool, shove-ha'penny, dominoes, cribbage, quoits, juke box and space game. The red-carpeted lounge has small red-cushioned Windsor chairs around dark tables, and a log fire in its stripped-stone end wall; sensibly placed darts in here. Bar food includes filled rolls and sandwiches (from 80p), burger (80p), home-made soup (85p), filled baked potato (£1.40), steak and kidney or chicken and mushroom pie (£1.70), ploughman's (from £1.75), lasagne, chicken curry or hot-pot (£2.50), scampi (£3) and a choice of vegetarian dishes such as aubergine and mushroom lasagne (£2.50); they warn of delays at busy times, though the service remains friendly. Flowers IPA and Original and Robinsons Best on handpump, Rombouts coffee. At the price, the bedrooms are a real bargain. There are tables out on a crazy-paved terrace, with a lawn sloping down to the water. *(Recommended by Philip King, Keith Walton; more reports please)*

Free house   Licensees David and Lynda White   Real ale   Meals and snacks (until 10.30 evenings in summer, 10 in winter)   Children very welcome   Open 11–3 (4 Sat), 6–11; opens 6.30 in winter; closed evening 25 Dec   Bedrooms tel Glasbury (049 74) 373; £11.50B/£21B

HAVERFORDWEST (Dyfed)   SM9515 Map 6

Bristol Trader

Old Quay, Quay Street; coming into town from A40 E, keep left after crossing river and take first left turn

The massive walls are a clue to the great age of this pub: it's been open for over 600 years. Much modernised now, with green plush wall banquettes and stools around neat little round tables, and more tables up a couple of steps at one quieter end, it has the deep-down friendliness that often marks really old pubs, however much they've changed. Popular home-made bar food – they grow some of the ingredients themselves – includes sandwiches (from 65p), soup (£1.20, winter only), steak and kidney pie (£1.80), ploughman's (£1.90), curries (£2.40), lasagne (£2.65), salads and chicken (£2.90), scampi (£3.40) and gammon (£3.85); well kept Ind Coope Burton on handpump; maybe piped pop music. (*Recommended by Wayne Brindle, Steve Dark; more reports please*)

Free house   Real ale   Meals (lunchtime, not Sun) and snacks   Open 11–3, 5.30–11 all year; open all day Mon and Sat in summer; closed evening 25 Dec

HAY-ON-WYE (Powys)   SO2342 Map 6

Old Black Lion   🦁 🛏️

26 Lion Street

In the last year or so, after yet another change of owners, things have settled in well here, and from the toils of redecorations and rethinkings has emerged a fine, comfortable and neatly kept inn, with attentive service by the friendly new licensees. Even their eleven-year-old son may ask if you've liked your meal – it is indeed the wide choice of reasonably priced food, all home cooked, which seems the focus of interest in the bar now. Dishes which have been praised recently range from vegetable and mushroom soup (£1.35) or filled baked potatoes (£1.95) to the steaks (from £7.20); other dishes include home-made burgers (£1.95), pâté with hazelnuts and whisky (£2.15), ploughman's (from £2.20), lasagne (£3.55), home-made faggots (£3.75), a cold table (from £3.95) and a better-than-average selection of vegetarian dishes including neat laver-cake burgers and nut roast with their own horseradish sauce (£4.75); they use fresh local ingredients. The puddings can be very choice indeed – if their Tia Maria meringue is on, don't miss it. Besides well kept Bass and Flowers Original on handpump (the cellar's air-conditioned) they have good value well chosen wines and decent coffee. The low-beamed and partly black-panelled bar has recovered the poise that goes so well with this bookish town, its steep and twisty streets lined with antiquarian bookshops. There are tables on a sheltered back terrace. The pleasant bedrooms have been made very comfortable; the inn has Wye fishing rights, and can arrange ponytrekking. (*Recommended by WHBM, Mrs D M Hacker, Sheila Keene, Mr and Mrs C M Metcalf, Mrs P M Macaulay; more reports on the new regime please*)

Free house   Licensees John and Joan Collins   Real ale   Meals and snacks   Restaurant Children welcome   Open 11–11 all year   Bedrooms tel Hay-on-Wye (0497) 820841; £16.50/£33.50(£35.50B)

KENFIG (Mid Glam)   SS8383 Map 6

Prince of Wales

2¼ miles from M4 junction 37; A4229 towards Porthcawl, then right when dual carriageway narrows on bend, signposted Maudlam, Kenfig

In the twelfth century this was an important port with a castle, but over the next four or five hundred years a series of sandstorms engulfed it under the dunes which now stretch around here. The pub itself, just about the only survivor, still preserves the aldermen's mace upstairs (where, uniquely, they also hold Sunday school). The friendly main bar has a good deal of stripped stone, with an open fire, small storm windows, heavy settles and red leatherette seats around a double row of close-set cast-iron-framed tables. Well kept Bass, Fullers London Pride, Marstons Pedigree, Robinsons Old Tom, Theakstons Old Peculier and Wadworths 6X are tapped from the cask, with Worthington Dark Mild on handpump, and Worthington BB available either way – the best choice of ales in this area. Bar food is very simple, but home made, quickly served and very cheap: pasties, sandwiches and rolls filled to order (from around 65p: the home-roasted meat is well done), lasagne, cheese and potato pie or shepherd's pie (95p), steak and onion pie (£1.05) and faggots

(£1.15 – prices don't include potatoes or vegetables); the fresh eggs from their own hens are worth knowing of. Dominoes, cribbage and card games. The pub, close to Kenfig Nature Reserve, sells fishing permits during opening hours. *(Recommended by John and Joan Nash, TBB, Peter Griffiths)*

Free house   Real ale   Meals and snacks   Children in small lounge (daytime only)
Spontaneous music in side room   Open 11.30–4, 6–11 all year

LITTLE HAVEN (Dyfed)   SM8512 Map 6
St Brides

Note: the inn is in the village itself, *not* at the hamlet of St Brides further W; park in village car park opposite pub

If there's local fish or seafood on the menu here, go for it: crab sandwiches maybe (£1.40), crab pâté (£1.85), sewin or salmon (£3.50), perhaps crab salad (£3.75). Otherwise, the home-made bar food (spring and summer only) includes soup served with home-baked bread (85p), ploughman's (£1.75), sausage-meat tart or mushroom and cheese quiche (£2.40), locally smoked duck or ham salad (£2.80) and a daily special such as steak and kidney pie or chicken in a thyme and parsley sauce (£3). The cottagey atmosphere of the neat black-beamed bar is underlined by an unusually interesting collection of gleaming brasswork (the complete set of 1950s exhibition heavy-horse harness is a real museum piece); the well at the back may even be Roman and is at least medieval. Worthington BB on handpump is kept well in a new cellar in the barn across the road. Shove-ha'penny, dominoes, cribbage and a trivia machine; though the sea is a stroll through the village, the accurate tide-clock here is useful. *(Recommended by Geoff Wilson, Steve Dark, Peter Griffiths)*

Williams of Narberth (who do not brew)   Licensee Joan Giles   Real ale   Meals and snacks (not Mon or Sun evening; no food Dec–Feb)   Open 11–3 (4 Sat), 6.30–11 all year
Bedrooms tel Broad Haven (0437) 781266; £10/£20

Swan

This is one of the prettiest coastal villages in West Wales, lining a broad sandy cove sheltering between low hills. And this pub, perched on one side just above the beach, is beautifully placed for the view – especially if you can get a seat in the bay window, or if it's fine enough to sit out on the low sea wall in front. The two communicating rooms, with a winter open fire, are traditionally furnished with comfortable high-backed settles and Windsor chairs; the walls – partly stripped back to the original stonework – are decorated with old prints. Bar food includes soup (£1.05), ploughman's (£2), pâté (£2.15), sardine, spinach and egg bake (£2.45), lasagne, chilli con carne or curries (from £2.75), and good fresh fish or shellfish (£3.30); Courage Directors and Worthington BB on handpump from the heavily panelled bar counter. Mr Davies, who bought the pub a couple of years ago, is no stranger to it – he used to work here before taking over the Ship at Solva. *(Recommended by Geoff Wilson, Michael Morgan, Janet and Gary Amos, Mrs P Vereker)*

Free house   Real ale   Meals and snacks   Tiny restaurant tel Broad Haven (0437) 781256   Open 11–3, 6–11 all year; closed evening 25 Dec

LLANBEDR-Y-CENNIN (Gwynedd)   SH7669 Map 6
Olde Bull

Village signposted from B5106

One of those lively places that looks full even when it isn't, this sixteenth-century pub has a jaunty clutter of furniture and furnishings in its knocked-through rooms: antique settles (some elaborately carved), a close crowd of cheerfully striped stools, brassware, photographs, even Prussian spiked helmets. Massive low beams and good log fires (one in an inglenook) add to the cosy feel. Well kept Lees Bitter and

Mild on handpump or tapped from the cask; a wide choice of plain food such as soup (85p), burger (90p), sandwiches (from 90p, toasties from £1.20), cheesy baked potato (£1.10), bacon and egg flan or home-made pie (£2.20), salads (from £3.50) and grills (ten-ounce sirloin, £7); darts, dominoes, cribbage, fruit machine, trivia machine and piped music. There are tables out on a terrace by the car park; standing nearby gives you a sweeping view down over the Vale of Conwy to the mountains beyond. Dogs (except for guide dogs) have to be left in cars. *(Recommended by Verney and Denis Baddeley, Jon Wainwright, Lynda Brown, Mr and Mrs J H Adam; more reports please)*

Lees   Licensees Phillip and Brenda De Ville Forte   Real ale   Meals and snacks (12–3, 6.30–9.45)   Restaurant   Children in eating area and restaurant   Electric organ and Welsh singing Sun evening   Open 12–3, 6.30–11 (all day Sat in summer)   Bedrooms tel Dolgarrog (0492) 69508/65359; £12/£22

nr LLANBERIS (Gwynedd)   SH5860 Map 6
Pen-y-Gwryd

Nant Gwynant; at junction of A498 and A4086, ie across mountains from Llanberis – OS Sheet 115 reference 660558

A real mountaineers' inn, this seems the perfect romantic image of a remarkably solid and well equipped base camp: there's the rugged log-cabin feel of the slate-floored climbers' bar (which doubles as a mountain rescue post); the settles where residents sit down together in the panelled dining-room for the hearty and promptly served evening meal (check on the time when you book); the hatch from that room where you order bar food; the bedrooms (clean and sensible rather than luxurious); and all the climbing mementoes – signatures of the 1953 Everest team, who trained here, among the many others on the bar ceiling, a collection of boots that have done famous climbs (big feet, some mountaineers have had), and more climbing equipment in the smoke-room. At lunchtime there are good robust helpings of home-made food such as sandwiches, ploughman's using home-baked French bread (£1.65), quiche Lorraine (£1.85), cold meat or pâté salad or a home-made pie of the day (£2). They serve sherry from their own solera in Puerto Santa Maria; darts, pool and shove-ha'penny for residents (who have a charmingly furnished sitting-room too). The Edwardian bath and shower on the first floor is well worth a look. But of course the real reason for coming here is the magnificent surrounding mountain countryside – like precipitous Moel-siabod beyond the lake opposite, which you can contemplate from a snug little room with built-in wall benches and sturdy country chairs. *(Recommended by Gwen and Peter Andrews, Drs G N and M G Yates, Steve Dark, Peter Walker, Nick Dowson; more reports please)*

Free house   Licensees Mr and Mrs C B Briggs, Mr and Mrs B C Pullee   Meals and snacks (lunchtime)   Restaurant (evening)   Children welcome   Open 11–10.30 (11 Sat); closed early Nov to New Year, open weekends only Jan and Feb   Bedrooms tel Llanberis (0286) 870211; £15(£16B)/£30(£32B)

LLANCADLE (S Glamorgan)   ST0368 Map 6
Green Dragon

Village signposted off B4265 Barry–Llantwit just E of St Athan; OS Sheet 170 reference 038685

Popular for generously served home-made food, this thatched pub devotes a good deal of attention to the drinks side, too: besides Courage Best and Directors and John Smiths on handpump, they have three or four interesting and well kept guest beers tapped from the cask, an enterprising choice of spirits, and some formidable foreign bottled beers. The beamed and high-raftered main bar, its walls stripped to bare stone, is exuberantly decorated with masses of bric-à-brac including a fine collection of whisky-water jugs, an attractive dresser with willow pattern and other decorative plates, and a Llanelli wall clock. Bar food includes filled rolls (from 55p), home-made burgers (£2.20), home-made pies such as steak and kidney (£3.30), curries (£3.60), lasagne, scampi or faggots (£3.75), mixed grill (£5.90) and a few specials such as sweet-and-sour pork (£3.55) or shark steak (£3.85); filled baked potatoes (from £1.30) and ploughman's (from £1.75) at lunchtimes. There's a good wood-burning stove, with a log fire in the small hatch-served lounge; a sheltered back lawn has picnic-table sets. *(Recommended by Patrick and Mary McDermott, Gwynne Harper; more reports please)*

Free house   Real ale   Meals and snacks (not Mon or Sun evenings)   Open 11.30–3, 6–11; closed evening 25 Dec

LLANDEWI SKIRRID (Gwent)   SO3416 Map 6

Walnut Tree ★ 🏵

B4521

As we've explained before, this legendary Italian-run place is a far cry from a normal pub. Though there is a couple of token bar stools – and people using them for just a drink are treated kindly – this is decidedly a place to eat at. Food quality matches top restaurant standards; though prices are high for a pub, they're a good deal lower than what you'd expect to pay for similar quality in a restaurant. Particular strengths include fresh fish and shellfish, local lamb, game, home-cured meats, interesting fruity and/or herby sauces (orange with coriander has been one successful combination), prettily dressed salads, uncommon cheeses (Welsh and Italian), and the awesome range of imaginative puddings (around £4). They offer nearly twenty first courses that you might perhaps think of as snacks (from around £5), and even more main dishes (around £12). The small white-walled bar has some polished settles and country chairs around the tables on its flagstones, and a log-effect gas fire. It opens into an airy and relaxed dining-lounge with rush-seat Italianate chairs around gilt cast-iron-framed tables. The attractive choice of wines is particularly strong in Italian ones (they import their own); the house wines by the glass are particularly good value, as is the coffee. Service is efficient and friendly. There are a few tables outside in front. *(Recommended by MKW, Paul McPherson, Henry Midwinter, JMW, Angela Dewar, Peter Griffiths, Philip King, Col G D Stafford)*

Free house   Licensee Ann Taruschio   Meals and snacks (not Sun or Mon)   Restaurant tel Abergavenny (0873) 2797   Children welcome   Open 12–4, 7–12 all year; closed Sun and Mon and 4 days at Christmas

LLANDRINDOD WELLS (Powys)   SO0561 Map 6

Llanerch

Waterloo Road; from centre, head for station

Very relaxed and friendly, this sixteenth-century inn serves good value simple bar food such as home-made soup (£1), filled baps (£1), baked potatoes (from 80p), ploughman's (£1.95), omelettes (from £2), vegetarian pancakes (£2.50), chicken curry (£2.75), steak, kidney and mushroom pies (£2.95), salads (from £3.25), mixed grill (£6) and steaks (from £6). The squarish beamed main bar has old-fashioned settles snugly divided by partly glazed partitions; in summer the big stone fireplace is richly decorated with copper and glass. Well kept Bass, Hancocks HB and Robinsons Best on handpump; fruit machine and trivia machine, piped music; separate pool-room, with darts, dominoes, cribbage. There are more orthodox button-back banquettes in communicating lounges, and tables out on the back terrace which has a summer bar and leads on to a garden (where you can play boules in summer) and play area; there's an orchard in front, too. *(Recommended by Mike Tucker; more reports please)*

Free house   Licensee John Leach   Real ale   Meals and snacks   Restaurant   Children welcome   Open 11.30–3, 6–11 (all day Sat) all year   Bedrooms tel Llandrindod Wells (0597) 2086; £15(£18B)/£26(£32B) nr LLANDUDNO JUNCTION   SH7883 Map 6

Queens Head ⊗

Glanwydden; heading towards Llandudno on A546 from Colwyn Bay, turn left into Llanrhos
Road as you enter the Penrhyn Bay speed limit; Glanwydden is signposted as the first left turn
off this

Behind the little quarry-tiled public bar of this welcoming and well kept pub is a
spacious and comfortably modern lounge bar with brown plush wall banquettes
and Windsor chairs around neat black tables, divided by a white wall of broad
arches and wrought-iron screens. Generous helpings of beautifully prepared home-
made food include good soups such as French onion and blue cheese (95p), a fine
selection of specials (some award-winning) such as home-made lasagne (£3.75),
lamb cutlets with caper sauce or trout with raisin and orange butter (£4.25), steak
and mushroom pie (£4.50), fresh crab (£4.95) and Mediterranean prawns (£6.25),
with additional evening dishes like fillet of hake in a fennel cream sauce or ten-
ounce rump steak (£6.95). Fish and seafood are always a good bet here, as are the
puddings (£1.50). Well kept Ansells Mild, Burton and Tetleys on handpump or
tapped from the cask, a decent selection of malts, and good coffee maybe served
with a bowl of whipped cream; warm winter log fires, pleasant service – even when
things get very busy. There are some tables out by the car park. *(Recommended by Mr
and Mrs B Hobden, KC, H Geddes, R M Sparkes, David Millar)*

*Free house   Licensee Robert Cureton   Real ale   Meals and snacks   Children over 7
welcome   Open 11–3, 6.30–11 all year*

LLANELIAN-YN-RHOS (Clwyd)   SH8676 Map 6

White Lion

Village signposted from A5830 (shown as B5383 on many maps) and B5381 S of Colwyn Bay

This picturesque old place has two distinct parts, each with its own personality,
linked by a broad flight of steps. Up at the top is a neat and very spacious dining
area, while down at the other end is a traditional old bar, with antique high-backed
settles angling snugly around a big fireplace, Tudor beams hung with lots of toby
jugs, yellowing walls decorated with pictorial plates, and flagstones by the counter
where they serve well kept John Smiths Magnet from handpump. The new licensees
have expanded the bar menu, which now includes home-made soup (90p),
sandwiches and filled baps (from £1.25), ploughman's (£1.95), and a wide range of
hot dishes from pizzas (from £2.95) and meaty or vegetable lasagne (£3.25),
through fish dishes (from £3.40) and chicken (from £2.75) to steaks (from £5.95);
they do half-price children's portions on certain dishes; dominoes, piped music.
Outside, an attractive courtyard between the pub and the church has rustic seats by
tables under cocktail parasols; it's also used for parking. There's good walking in
the pasture hills around. *(Recommended by Dennis Royles, Mr and Mrs J H Adam, G
Owen; more reports on the new regime please)*

*Free house   Licensees the Cole family   Real ale   Meals and snacks (until 10 evenings)
Children in eating area   Open 11–3, 6–11 all year*

LLANELIDAN (Clwyd)   SJ1150 Map 6

Leyland Arms ★ ⊗

Village signposted from A494 S of Ruthin; pub on B5429 just E of village; OS Sheet 116
reference 110505

Idyllically placed by a peaceful country church, across fields from the village itself,
is a striking twin-gabled early nineteenth-century Gothick house that originally
carried this name, as the village inn. What in those days was its dairy, in the stable
quadrangle behind, is now a delightfully unusual pub – with uncommonly good

food. This might include soup (£1.20), sandwiches, chicken liver pâté (£1.75), lunchtime ploughman's (£1.95), various pies such as steak, mushroom and Guinness, rabbit or game (£4.25), seafood pancakes (£4.50), pork, cider and walnut casserole (£4.95) and salmon with herb butter or halibut steaks (£6.95); they have pheasant, venison, partridge and sea-trout in season, and when they're available the fresh Parkgate shrimps in a light garlic sauce with chunks of home-made bread have always gone down particularly well with readers. Furnishings are simple but neatly elegant, with little bunches of flowers on tables, and mugs hanging from the beams of the smaller room by the servery. Service is friendly, and there's good coffee (with cream) as well as Boddingtons Bitter; darts, dominoes. There are rustic seats on the grass outside, with a dozy background of bird and animal noises. Booking would be wise if you want a meal. Although there are new licensees, we haven't detected any changes. *(Recommended by Dennis Royles, Philip Riding, Mr and Mrs J H Adam, J E Sharp, KC)*

Free house Licensee Mrs C Topping Real ale Meals and snacks Children in eating area Open 12–3, 7–11 all year Bedrooms tel Clawdd Newydd (082 45) 207; /£20

LLANFRYNACH (Powys) SO0725 Map 6
White Swan 🗫

Village signposted from B4558, just off A40 E of Brecon bypass

Facing the churchyard across a very quiet village lane, this pretty black and white pub has stone and other tables on an unusual sheltered back terrace, attractively divided by roses and climbing shrubs and overlooking peaceful paddocks. The layout inside is well done too, with plenty of well spaced tables: the flagstoned lounge bar, with partly stripped stone walls and a big log fire, rambles back into a series of softly lit alcoves; an easy-going, never-changing atmosphere. The emphasis is very much on food – a wide choice, including soup (£1.65), light dishes such as ploughman's (from £2.65), lasagne or ratatouille au gratin (£3.20), and more substantial dishes such as chicken curry (£4.25), haddock and prawn pie (£5.25), beef and mushroom pie (£6.70), Welsh-style grilled trout with bacon, scampi or baked crab (£6.85) and well hung steaks (£7.50). They also do children's dishes (£2.35), and more egg cooking than most pubs. Service is friendly and efficient; Brains and Flowers IPA on handpump. The pub is handy for the Abergavenny–Brecon canal. *(Recommended by Col A H N Reade, David Wallington, M and P Rudlin, Dr I J Thompson)*

Free house Licensee David Bell Real ale Meals and snacks (not Mon, exc bank hols, or last three weeks Jan) Children welcome Open 12–2.30, 7 (6.30 Sat)–11 all year; closed Mon lunchtime (exc bank hols); closed lunchtime last three weeks Jan

nr LLANGURIG (Powys) SN9179 Map 6
Glansevern Arms Hotel 🛏

Pant Mawr; A44 Aberystwyth Rd, 4½ miles W of Llangurig; OS Sheets 135 or 136 reference 847824

Over 1,000 feet up, this quiet and civilised inn is a marvellously remote base for the steep hills and forests of the upper Wye Valley. The cosy bar has cushioned antique settles and captain's chairs, an open fire, and china mugs on its high beams, and the comfortable residents' lounge has a good supply of books (this really comes into its own as a place to stay). Besides consistently well kept Bass and Worthington Dark on handpump, the genial landlord stocks several good malt whiskies. Bar snacks are confined to home-made soup with home-baked and roasted meat and other sandwiches; the seven-course dinners (must book) are excellent value; very good

There are report forms at the back of the book.

breakfasts for residents. *(Recommended by Gavin May, Roger Entwistle, Lord Evans of Claughton, John Davidson)*

Free house   Licensee William Edwards   Real ale   Sandwiches (lunchtime, not Sun) Restaurant   Open 11–2, 6.30–11   Bedrooms tel Llangurig (055 15) 240; £27B/£42B

LLANGYNIDR (Powys)   SO1519 Map 6
Red Lion   🛏

Upper village, off B4558 (the quiet alternative to the A40 Crickhowell–Brecon)

The sheltered garden outside this creeper-covered old stone inn is as pretty as ever – neat and beautifully kept. Inside, it's comfortably up-market, with fox-brown leather armchairs, red-plush-cushioned settles, antiques and pictures in the old-fashioned bay-windowed bar. Under the new chef they've reduced the range of the bar menu, but increased the emphasis on daily specials, with such dishes as chicken livers with bacon, garlic and chicory (£2.65), scallops sauté in fennel and pernod (£3.20), trout (£6.50) and fillet steak (£7.60). The selection is similar to what's served in the restaurant, but often at much cheaper prices. Well kept Bass, Flowers Original and guest beers such as Greene King Abbot on handpump, and a decent range of malt whiskies; kindly service. The bedrooms are attractively decorated, and breakfast is said to be a real treat. *(Recommended by Jenny and Brian Seller, John Honnor, MKW, JMW, Geoff Wilson, Angela Dewar, Gordon Theaker)*

Free house   Licensee Ellie Lloyd   Real ale   Meals and snacks   Restaurant   Well behaved children welcome   Open 11–3, 6–11 all year   Bedrooms tel Bwlch (0874) 730223; £22.50(£27.50)/£40(£45B)

LLANGYNWYD (Mid Glam)   SS8588 Map 6
Old House

From A4063 S of Maesteg follow signpost Llan ¾ at Maesteg end of village; pub behind church

Dating back over 800 years, this very popular thatched pub is among the oldest in Wales. Wil Hopkin is said to have written *Bugeilio'r Gwenith Gwyn* here, and though it's been much modernised there are comfortably traditional touches in the two thick-walled rooms of its bar – such as the high-backed black built-in settles and lots of china and brass around the huge fireplace, the shelves of bric-à-brac, and the decorative jugs hanging from the beams. Generously served bar food includes soup (90p), chicken, ham or pork (£2.50), aubergine lasagne (£2.75), steak and kidney pie (£2.65), beef goulash (£3), gammon and eggs (£4.10), fresh fish such as hake (£4.40) or good salmon (£6.50), children's dishes (from 80p) and puddings such as raspberry charlotte (£1.10); our preference is for the well hung steak (sirloin £6.75 – even if it's not on the menu they'll usually do it for you). Well kept Flowers IPA and Original on handpump, and a relaxed but thriving local atmosphere. An attractive new conservatory extension leads on to the garden, which has a good play area; there's a soft-ice-cream machine for children. *(Recommended by John Nash, Alun and Eryl Davies; more reports please)*

Whitbreads   Licensee Mrs W E David   Real ale   Meals and snacks (until 10 evenings) Children in eating area and restaurant   Restaurant tel Maesteg (0656) 733310 Open 11–11; 11–4, 6.30–11 in winter

nr LLANRWST (Gwynedd)   SH8062 Map 6
Maenan Abbey Hotel   🛏

Maenan; A470 towards Colwyn Bay, 2½ miles N

Though this is first and foremost a comfortable hotel, don't let the solidity of the steep-gabled early-Victorian country house and the stately style of its grounds make you think there won't be a proper bar inside. There is indeed – a very welcoming place, with Windsor chairs around the tables on its oak parquet floor, tall stone-mullioned windows, Bass on handpump, and maybe Welsh singing on Saturday night; unobtrusive piped music. The elegant and airy back dining lounge has brocaded chairs, handsome drop-leaf tables, silky figured wallpaper and lots of house-plants. Bar food includes soup (95p), sandwiches (from £1.10, toasted £1.25), a cheese platter (£2.95), cannelloni (£3.95), trout, mixed grill or chicken (£4.95), steak (£6.95) and children's dishes (from £2.25). Outside, there are plenty of tables, with well kept lawns stretching beyond the terraces among topiary yews and tall trees; a good side play area has swings and a castle. Fishing on the River Conwy and nearby lakes, and rough or clay-pigeon shooting. *(Recommended by KC, Mike Tucker, Rita Horridge, Eileen Broadbent; it's had a star in previous editions – we'd like more reports so that we can confirm the award)*

Free house   Licensees Miss Ellis and Mr Hamilton   Real ale   Meals and snacks Restaurant   Children in bar until 9 and in coffee-room   Welsh singing Sat evenings Open 11–3, 6–11 all year; closed evening 25 Dec evening   Bedrooms tel Dolgarrog (049 269) 247; £34.50B/£49B

LLANSANNAN (Clwyd)   SH9466 Map 6
Red Lion
A544 Abergele–Bylchau

This pretty Welsh-speaking village, at the junction of several lonely hill roads, preserves a strongly traditional feel. So does its inn, here for over 700 years. Among other antiques in the delightfully old-fashioned (though too small for some readers' comfort), high-beamed central parlour is a great high-backed settle, draught-proofed by a curtain around its top, curving snugly around an inglenook with a warm kitchen range. Other bars are simpler and more up to date, with darts, pool, dominoes, cribbage, fruit machine, a juke box or maybe piped music, and there are seats in the garden behind. Bar food includes home-made soup (75p), sandwiches (65p), burgers (from £1.55), ploughman's (£2.20), steak and kidney pie or home-made cottage pie (£3) and salads (£3.30), with children's dishes (90p); cheap well kept Lees Bitter and Mild on handpump – and coffee, tea or hot chocolate. *(More reports please)*

Lees   Real ale   Meals and snacks   Children welcome   Open 11–3, 6–11 all year Bedrooms tel Llansannan (074 577) 256; £15/£30

LLANTHONY (Gwent)   SO2928 Map 6
Abbey Hotel
The reason for including this is its outstanding romantic setting – quite unique. The vaulted crypt bar is part of what used to be the prior's house, which now stands quite alone in the graceful ruins of the twelfth-century priory, with the broken arches that soar from sheep-clipped lawns framing gentle hill views. The bar is basic and simply furnished, but serves well kept Brains Bitter, Flowers Original, Ruddles County and a guest beer such as Buckleys on handpump or tapped from the cask, and Perry's farm cider. Bar food is simple too, with home-made soup or toasted sandwiches (£1.10) and ploughman's (from £2.50); the home-made meaty and vegetarian burgers (£2.95) have been praised, but service could sometimes be a good deal more welcoming; there may be a certain lack of atmosphere out of season. On *Good Walks Guide* Walk 201. *(Recommended by Gordon and Daphne, Paul McPherson, Helena and Arthur Harbottle, M and J Godfrey, Keith Walton, Alan Kilshaw, David and Eloise Smaylen; more reports please)*

Free house   Licensee Ivor Prentice   Real ale   Meals and snacks (not Tues–Sat evenings) Restaurant Tues–Sat evenings   Children welcome   Live music usually every other Sat evening   Open 11–3, 6–11 (all day Sat and holiday periods); closed some weekdays Dec–Feb   Bedrooms tel Crucorney (0873) 890487; £20/£35

LLANWNDA (Gwynedd) SH4758 Map 6

Goat 🕸 🛏

Village (a couple of houses or so) signposted as short loop off A499 just S of junction with
A487 S of Caernarfon

It's the lunchtime cold table in the room on the left which earns the food award here
– an excellent help-yourself cold table, with well over twenty fresh and attractive
dishes laid out on crisp linen (£4 for as much as you like, including starters such as
fresh melon in ginger wine and sherry-marinated grapefruit, then over half a dozen
fish, several cold meats and freshly baked quiche, and five different cheeses to
finish). They also do home-made soup, particularly good sandwiches, and
ploughman's; well kept Bass on handpump; piped music. The main bar area is at
the back, divided into two rooms by the almost circular bar counter, with its old-
fashioned small-paned rounded screen complete with serving-hatch, and an ancient
cash register. The Welsh speakers seem to gravitate to the red leatherette button-
back built-in wall banquettes around the four tables on the right; visitors go for the
bright red plush chairs by the coal fire on the left. There's also a genteel front room
on the right. In the evenings the buffet table's stripped down to reveal a pool-table,
and the dartboard comes into use; also dominoes, fruit machine, juke box. Tables
on the sunny front terrace, another under a sycamore down in the garden.
(Recommended by Ian Watson, Mrs Paddy Tilley)

*Free house   Licensee L Griffith   Real ale   Meals and snacks (lunchtime, not Sun)   Children
welcome   Open 11–4, 5.30 (6 Sat)–11 all year; closed Sun   Bedrooms tel Caernarfon
(0286) 830256; £15B/£30B*

LLANWONNO (Mid Glam) ST0295 Map 6

Brynffynon

From B4277 Porth–Aberdare in Ferndale, turn off down into valley at S-bend by Commercial
Hotel and Rhondda Independent Chapel; beyond the railway the road doubles so sharply back
on itself that you have to go further up the dead-end and do a U-turn before you can continue
uphill; also accessible from B4275 in Mountain Ash, and from Pontypridd via B4273 (keep
straight on beyond Ynysybwl, bear left a mile later); OS Sheet 170 reference 028956

Just what's wanted after a walk in the surrounding largely forested hills
– a genuinely warm and helpful welcome, well kept real ale, and good value
no-nonsense food. This includes cheap pasties, filled baked potatoes and
cheeseburgers, a couple of good home-cooked specials such as salmon rissoles
(£2.50) or chicken (£2.75), and a few hot dishes such as curry (£3.30), lasagne or
scampi (£3.90). The high-ceilinged bar on the left (favoured by the locals – and
their dogs) serves Flowers IPA from a massively built counter, and has comfortably
traditional turn-of-the-century seating and cast-iron tables, not to mention the
piano, and the art nouveau mirrored coat stand; darts, TV. The roomy saloon on the
right has a juke box and more modern furnishings, and there's a fruit machine in
the hall between. A fine place for walkers. *(Recommended by Julian Proudman, Dave
Braisted)*

*Whitbreads   Real ale   Meals and snacks   Children welcome until 9   Occasional live music,
quiz winter Weds   Open 11.30–4, 6–11; 12.30–4, 6–11 in winter*

LLANYNYS (Clwyd) SJ1063 Map 7

Cerrigllwydion Arms 🕸

Village signposted from A525 by Drovers Arms just out of Ruthin, and by garage in Pentre
further towards Denbigh

Set in a country backwater by an interesting church, this is so out of the way that
it's a real surprise to find such careful cooking of good fresh ingredients – besides
pheasant in season, bar food includes soup, sandwiches (weekday lunchtimes),

devilled crab (£2.95), home-made cottage pie (£3.50), fresh fish (from £3.50), asparagus wrapped in ham with a cream sauce (£4.40), filleted chicken breast in white wine sauce (£4.95) and half a fresh duckling (£7.25), with mouth-watering puddings. But this is no mere food pub. There's a splendidly friendly atmosphere, and the rambling building – which dates back nearly 600 years in part – has plenty of character, with old stonework, dark oak beams and panelling, and a cheerful décor with interesting brasses and other knick-knacks; seats range from green plush to older settles. Well kept Buckleys Best, Tetleys and Marstons Pedigree on handpump, good coffee; darts, dominoes, fruit machine, piped music; efficient service. Across the quiet lane there's a neat garden, with teak tables among fruit trees looking across the fields to low wooded hills. *(Recommended by David and Jill Roberts, Philip Riding, Mr and Mrs J H Adam; more reports please)*

Free house   Licensee Stephen Spicier   Real ale   Snacks (weekday lunchtimes) and meals (not Mon evening, Oct–Easter)   Restaurant tel Llanynys (074 578) 247   Children in restaurant Open 11.30–3, 7–11 all year; closed Mon lunchtime

LLWYNDAFYDD (Dyfed)   SN3755 Map 6
Crown

Coming S from New Quay on A486, both the first two right turns eventually lead to the village; the side roads N from A487 between junctions with B4321 and A486 also come within signpost distance; OS Sheet 145 reference 371555

The pretty tree-sheltered garden of this neat white-painted eighteenth-century pub has picnic-table sets on a terrace above a small pond among shrubs and flowers, with rides and a slide in a play area. The partly stripped stone bar – friendly and bustling, especially at weekends – has red plush button-back banquettes around its copper-topped tables, and a big wood-burning stove. Popular bar food includes decent sandwiches (from 70p), soup (£1.10), ploughman's (£2.70), pizzas (from £3.20), salads including home-made quiche (from £4), steak and kidney pie (£4.15), good grilled trout, gammon (£5.20) and steaks (from £6.60); the restaurant has more imaginative dishes. Well kept Flowers IPA and Original and Sam Whitbread; darts and piped music, with a fruit machine in the back pool-room (winter only). There's a good family-room. The side lane leads down to a cove with caves by National Trust cliffs. *(Recommended by Gordon Smith, Gwen and Peter Andrews, Wayne Brindle, D R Linnell, Denis Berry)*

Free house   Licensees D M Evans and K J Harper   Real ale   Meals and snacks (not Sun) Restaurant tel New Quay (0545) 560396   Children in eating area and restaurant Open 11–3, 5.30–11 all year; closed Sun

LLYSWEN (Powys)   SO1337 Map 6
Griffin ★ ⊗ ⛲

A470, village centre

Carefully detailed supervision by the Stocktons pays real dividends in this comfortably old-fashioned inn: high standards of housekeeping, good value food, well kept ales, and above all faultlessly welcoming service. The heavy-beamed Fishermen's Bar – decorated as you'd perhaps expect with old fishing tackle – has large Windsor armchairs, leatherette wall benches and padded stools around its low tables, and a big stone fireplace with a good log fire; at lunchtime there's extra seating in the restaurant for bar meals. These include noted sandwiches such as sugar-baked ham (£1.45), prawn (£2), and thick, tender slices of salmon, fresh or smoked (£2.35), as well as soup (£1.50), and main dishes which change daily, such as vegetarian crumble (£3.50), curry or home-made quiches (£3.75), cod and prawn pancakes or roast lamb (£4.25), braised pigeon in cider (£4.75) and rump steak (£7.50), with traditional home-made puddings like spotted dick (£1.95). Most days after Easter they serve brook-trout and salmon, caught by the family or by customers in the River Wye – just over the road; in season there's game such as roast pheasant (£4.95). Flowers IPA and Marstons Pedigree on handpump, with a guest beer; quoits played, dogs allowed. *(Recommended by Philip King, M and J Godfrey, MKW, JMW, L G and D L Smith, Anthony Land)*

Free house   Licensees Richard and Di Stockton   Real ale   Meals and snacks (not Sun evening)   Restaurant (evening)   Children welcome   Open 11–3, 6–11; 12–2.30, 7–11 in winter   Bedrooms tel Llyswen (087 485) 241; £19.50B/£35B

MAENTWROG (Gwynedd)   SH6741 Map 6

Grapes   ★ 🏵 🛏

A496; village signposted from A470

Cheerful and very popular, this bustling pub has log fires in all three bars – as well as in the great hearth of the restaurant, where there may be spit-roasts. It's also full of stripped pitch-pine – chiefly ecclesiastical salvage, not just pews and settles but pillars and carvings too. Home-made bar food comes in great variety – and quantity: dishes which have recently been found particularly good value include filled baps (from 65p), ploughman's (from £2.25 – these two lunchtime only), fried sliced beef with mushrooms in French bread (£2.50), burgers (£1.40), steak and kidney pie or spare ribs (£3.50) and gammon (£4.25 or £5.50), with specials running to lobster and local salmon; vegetarian dishes (from £2.75) and children's portions (£1.20); good coffee. Quick friendly service even at the busiest times, reliably well kept Bass and Stones on handpump and a decent selection of malts; piped music. Darts, dominoes, cribbage and juke box in the public bar, where there's also an interesting collection of brass blowlamps. There are tables on a good-sized and sheltered verandah (with a shellfish counter at one end). This catches the evening sunshine, and overlooks a pleasant back terrace and walled garden; there's a fountain on the lawn, and magnificent further views. Breakfasts are pretty monumental. At quiet times of year there have been one or two reports of barmen seeming to pay more attention to regulars than newcomers – we'd like more reports on this aspect please. *(Recommended by Tim and Lynne Crawford, David Wallington, Philip Riding, Mrs J S England, Tom Evans, Brian Jones, Patrick Godfrey, Gordon Theaker, Gavin May, Anthony Land, G A Worthington, Steve Dark, KC)*

Free house   Licensee Brian Tarbox   Real ale   Meals and snacks   Restaurant   Children in dining-room and restaurant   Open 11–11 all year   Bedrooms tel Maentwrog (076 685) 208/365; £19B/£38B

MARIANGLAS (Anglesey)   SH5084 Map 6

Parciau Arms

B5110

Attractively decorated rooms radiate out from the high-ceilinged inner bar area, which has local colour photographs on its dark red hessian walls, horsebrasses and leathers, miners' lamps and other bric-à-brac, and a mounted jungle fowl. The main seating area has comfortable rust-coloured plush built-in wall banquettes and stools around elm tables, a big settee matching the flowery curtains, antique coaching prints, and spears, rapiers and so forth on the elaborate chimney-breast over the coal fire. An airy family dining-room with little bunches of flowers on the tables has attractive Snaffles calendar cartoons. Good value bar food includes sandwiches (from £1.10, steak £3.10), home-made soup (£1.20), filled baked potatoes (£1.30), sweet-pickled herrings (£2.40), vegetarian dishes, cottage pie (£2.75), ploughman's (from £3.05), salads (from £3.10), all-day breakfast (£3.25), steak and kidney pie or a big slice of gammon and egg (£3.95), eight-ounce sirloin steak (£5.80), good children's dishes (from £1.10) and special dishes on request; well kept Ind Coope Burton and Tetleys on handpump with guest beers such as Banks's or Marstons

Pedigree, decent wines; good friendly service . There are picnic-table sets on a terrace and, with pews and other tables under cocktail parasols, in a good-sized garden with a good play area including a pensioned-off tractor, a camel-slide, a climber and so forth. *(Recommended by Jon Wainwright, David Waterhouse)*

Free house Licensee P H Moore Real ale Meals and snacks (all day until 9.30) Children in dining area Open 11–11 all year

MOLD (Clwyd) SJ1962 Map 7
We Three Loggerheads
Loggerheads; A494 3 miles towards Ruthin

One of the best recent refurbishments we've come across in Wales: plenty of space, quite a sense of style, yet a properly pubby atmosphere. The original part, which dates back to the eighteenth century, is quite snug. On the left a tiled-floor locals' bar has pool, dominoes, shove-ha'penny, table skittles and cribbage. On the right there are owl prints and other country pictures, stuffed birds and a stuffed fox, and lighting by pretty converted paraffin lamps. Steps lead up to the really spacious area: high-raftered, but pillars support a false ceiling holding farm machinery and carts. Here, in an attractive décor of deep greens and pinks, comfortable green cloth banquettes are set around tables in stripped-wood stalls. It's all well kept, with a thriving atmosphere. Bar food includes sandwiches (from £1, with more elaborate double- and triple-deckers), samosas (£2.10), Greek sausage with pitta bread (£2.95), a choice of ploughman's (£3.25), home-made chilli con carne (£3.45) and chicken and mango curry (£3.95), and steaks (from £8.25), with interesting daily specials, often charcoal grilled, such as fresh sardines or tandoori kebab; well kept Bass on handpump, loudish juke box, fruit machine. There are white tables and chairs on a side terrace. *(Recommended by Michele and Andrew Wells, KC, Mr and Mrs J H Adam; more reports please)*

Bass Licensee Gary Willard Real ale Meals and snacks (until 10 evenings) Children in eating area Open 12–3, 5.30–11 (all day Fri and Sat) all year; closed evening 25 Dec

MONTGOMERY (Powys) SO2296 Map 6
Cottage Inn
Pool Road; B4388 towards Welshpool, just off Newtown road

Below the wooded cliffs of ruined but massively imposing Powis Castle, this traditional place has a friendly and busy atmosphere in its several well kept small rooms, with their mix of carpets, soft lighting, heavy old-fashioned wooden-armed chairs and some dark marine-ply panelling. The cottagey old decorations are happily not overdone. Good bar food, all freshly made, includes soup (£1.25), several other starters from egg mayonnaise (£1.95) to smoked salmon (£3.45), haddock or chicken (£3.95), salads (from £3.95), curry (£4.75), gammon (£4.95) and steaks (from £6.25); prices are lower than this at lunchtime, when they also do sandwiches (from 80p) and ploughman's (from £2.25; the home-made duck pâté and smoked-salmon pâté versions are good). There are plenty of puddings such as home-made apple and blackcurrant tart (£1.25), and in the evenings they do some more expensive dishes such as salmon and lemon sole (£6.95). Well kept Boddingtons on handpump (they do make a change from time to time), decent wines and good coffee; unobtrusive piped music; good hospitable service. There are picnic-table sets on the neat grass behind. *(Recommended by T Nott, D H W Davies)*

Free house Licensees Brendan and Pauline Snelson Real ale Meals and snacks (12–2, 7–10) Restaurant tel Montgomery (068 681) 348 Children welcome Open 12–3, 7–11 all year; closed Mon lunchtime exc bank hols

---

Real ale to us means beer which has matured naturally in its cask, not pressurised or filtered.

MORFA NEFYN (Gwynedd)   SH2840 Map 6
Bryncynan
Junction A497/B4412

A useful haven, this serves local seafood in summer, including crab and lobster, as well as home-made soup (95p), quiche (£3.50), roast chicken or lasagne (£3.75), gammon (£5.25), king prawns (£6.75) and sirloin steak (£6.95); children's portions (£2.25) and puddings (£1). Service is quick and pleasant then, even with holidaymakers filling the simple rough-grained pews of the predominantly red-coloured bar, the back-to-back pews around cast-iron-framed tables in the next room, and the further dining-room. Well kept Tetleys and in summer Ind Coope Burton on handpump; fruit machine, space game, piped music; rustic seats outside. It's very quiet out of season. (*Recommended by Gavin May, J and J A Pearson; more reports please*)

Lloyd & Trouncer (Ind Coope)   Licensee Keith Jackson   Real ale   Meals and snacks Children in restaurant   Occasional live music   Open 11–11; 11.30–2.30, 7–11 in winter; closed Sun

NEVERN (Dyfed)   SN0840 Map 6
Trewern Arms ★ ⌂
B4582 – a useful short-cut alternative to most of the A487 Newport–Cardigan

The new bedroom wing, overlooking the lawn with its tables set among shrubs and trees, is a successful addition to this old inn (and breakfasts are huge). Its heart, though, is undeniably the stripped-stone slate-floored bar, its high rafters strung with nets, ships' lamps, ancient farm and household equipment, shepherds' crooks and cauldrons. Aside from a couple of high-backed traditional settles by the big log fire, it's fitted out with comfortable plush banquettes. Generous helpings of reasonably priced bar food include sandwiches (70p), ploughman's (£1.90), cod or cold ham (£2.90), chicken (£3), lasagne or cottage pie (£3.20), home-made steak and kidney pie (£3.40), scampi (£3.30) and steaks (from £6.10), with children's dishes (£1.50); well kept Bass, Flowers IPA and Original and a guest beer on handpump, maybe piped music; friendly, efficient service. A back games-room has sensibly placed darts, pool and dominoes; beyond is a more spacious lounge. Across the medieval bridge over the River Nyfer, the pilgrims' church has pre-Christian stones set into its windows, and a Celtic cross. (*Recommended by G T Jones, Stephen Dykes, Simon Ward, Gwen and Peter Andrews, Wayne Brindle, Steve Dark; more reports please*)

Free house   Licensee Mrs Molly Sanders   Real ale   Meals and snacks   Restaurant (not always open)   Children welcome   Open 11–3, 6–11 all year   Bedrooms tel Newport (0239) 820395; £18B/£36B

NOTTAGE (Mid Glam)   SS8178 Map 6
Rose & Crown ⌂
2 miles from M4 junction 37; A4229 towards Porthcawl, then signposted Nottage, Rest Bay

Refurbished by the present licensees, this comfortable and well kept pub just a stroll from the seaside has a good warm atmosphere. It shows its age in the thickness of the surviving walls that still divide the beamed bar into distinct areas, part flagstoned, part carpeted, with quite a feature made of the log-effect gas fire in the huge fireplace. There are well made traditional-style settles, plusher seats, and in the area on the right tables arranged more for eating: good value bar food includes steak sandwich (£1.05), ploughman's (£1.95), pizza (£2.45), plaice (£2.90), trout or gammon (£3.95) and steaks (from £5.95), with children's portions (from 99p). Well kept Ruddles Best and County and Websters on handpump; fruit machine, unobtrusive piped music, efficient service. The bedrooms are attractively decorated and equipped. *(Recommended by A A Worthington, Mrs J Frost; more reports please)*

Watneys   Licensees John and Christine Rout   Real ale   Meals and snacks   Restaurant
Children in eating area and restaurant   Open 11.30–4, 6–11 (all day Sat) all year
Bedrooms tel Porthcawl (0656) 714850; £34B/£45B

OGMORE (Mid Glam)   SS8674 Map 6

Pelican

B4524

Why do we hear so little of this well run and attractive pub, looking down on the ruins of Ogmore Castle? It does good value bar food, such as winter soup (£1.10), sandwiches (from £1.10), ploughman's (£1.80), and a sensibly short choice of hot dishes such as home-baked ham or home-made steak and onion pie (£2.95) and fresh fish (£3.25). The friendly bar, fairly functional on the left, has tables with pleasantly upholstered seats built into snug alcoves on the right. This part is given an almost luxurious air by its swagged pink curtains, harmonising carpet, curly wrought-iron wall lamps with pretty porcelain shades, and a shelf of decorative china. Well kept Courage Best and Directors on handpump, fruit machine, unobtrusive piped music. A side terrace has picnic-table sets, with swings beside it. *(Recommended by John and Helen Thompson; more reports please)*

Courage   Licensee Amanda Crossland   Real ale   Meals and snacks (until 10.30 weekend evenings)   Evening restaurant (Tues–Sat summer, Wed–Sat winter)   Children in restaurant Open 11–11; 11.30–4.30, 6.30–11 in winter

OLD RADNOR (Powys)   SO2559 Map 6

Harp ★ 🏠

Village signposted from A44 Kington–New Radnor just W of B4362 junction

Readers telling us about this lively hilltop inn launch into euphoric idylls that are a far cry from the very down-to-earth comments they make on other pubs. We hear about the squirrel eating in one of the oaks behind, the sunset colouring Radnor Forest and the Lugg valley spread out far below, the choirs of sheep lulling people to sleep.... But let's not forget the solid virtues here, too. The cosy slate-floored lounge has a handsome curved antique settle and a fine inglenook log fire. The old-fashioned brownstone public bar has high-backed settles, an antique reader's chair and other elderly chairs around yet another log fire; they play table quoits (matches winter Mondays, summer Tuesdays), darts (Friday) and tip-it. They've recently started serving real ales – a welcome and popular innovation – with Marstons Pedigree and Woods Special and Wonderfull on handpump or tapped from the cask. Good simple bar food might include sandwiches (from 85p), ploughman's with Stilton cut from the whole cheese (from £1.95), baked potato with prawns (£2.75), faggots (£2.85), lasagne (£3), chicken curry (£4 – very popular) and gammon and egg (£4). Evening main dishes in the snug and pretty dining-room are mostly £6.50. Service is first class, and breakfasts good. There's plenty of seating outside, under the big oak tree, on the green by the fifteenth-century turreted church, and on the side grass (where there's a play area). Near *Good Walks Guide* Walk 93. *(Recommended by Alan Franck, Philip King, Colin and Caroline, M J Steward; more reports please)*

Free house   Licensees Robert and Shirley Pritchard   Meals and snacks (not Tues lunchtime)
Children welcome   Open 11.30–2.30, 7–11 all year (closed Tues lunchtime)
Bedrooms tel New Radnor (054 421) 655; £20B/£32B

Cribbage is a card game using a block of wood with holes for matchsticks or special pins to score with; regulars in cribbage pubs are usually happy to teach strangers how to play.

PAINSCASTLE (Powys)   SO1646 Map 6
Maesllwch Arms

B4594 (off A470 Brecon–Builth Wells); village also signposted from Clyro on A438, near Hay-on-Wye

New licensees in this village inn have in general been praised by readers for preserving its atmosphere; on a quiet weekday lunchtime, the best bar is still probably the neat little public one – just three tables with small settles, a shelf of toby jugs on one stripped stone wall, a warm wood-burning stove, and sensibly placed darts. But at busier times there's a good deal more space in the airy and big-windowed carpeted lounge, with plush bucket armchairs around low tables, and black joists and wall-lathes setting off the crisp white paintwork. Generously presented bar food includes soup (£1), ploughman's or omelettes (£1.85), fish (£2.25), a couple of vegetarian dishes (£2.75) and home-made curry or prawn salad (£3.25); roast Sunday lunch (£3.25). Well kept Flowers Original and a guest beer tapped from the cask; dominoes, darts and cribbage. There are one or two tables outside in front. High in the border hills, this quiet village is surrounded by sheep pastures and higher moors criss-crossed with ancient tracks (useful now for ponytrekkers). *(Recommended by Paul McPherson, G and M Hollis, M and J Godfrey; more reports on the new regime please)*   .

Free house   Licensees Mr and Mrs G Wilson   Real ale   Meals and snacks (until 10 evenings)   Children welcome   Restaurant   Open 11–11; 11–3, 6–11 in winter   Bedrooms tel Painscastle (049 75) 279; £12.50/£25

nr PENARTH (S Glam)   ST1871 Map 6
Captains Wife

Beach Road, Swanbridge, which is signposted off B4267 at Penarth end of Sully

The food arrangements in this lively seaside pub seem to change from time to time, but one constant has been the charcoal grill in the upper gallery – reliable steak-bar standard; last summer people also enjoyed cheaper food in the cheery Smugglers Haunt, or at sturdy tables on the pretty back flagstoned courtyard, sheltered by low white former stable buildings. The main bar, with exposed stone walls and Turkey rugs and carpets on its broad bare boards, has several separate areas. Down at one snugly low-ceilinged end plush chairs and a high-backed traditional settle surround an old tile-surrounded kitchen range; towards the back Liberty-print-cushioned seats form stalls around tables under a glossy red plank ceiling. Brains Bitter, Flowers IPA and Original and a guest beer on handpump from the good long bar counter. Sitting on the low sea wall in front, you look out to Sully Island. *(Recommended by Patrick and Mary McDermott, Dr John Innes, TBB, Col G D Stafford; more reports please)*

Free house   Real ale   Lunchtime snacks (not Sun)   Two restaurants tel Penarth (0222) 530066; grill open 7 days a week, Mariners open Tues–Sun lunchtime and Tues–Sat evening   Children in room set aside for them and in restaurant   Open 11–11; 11.30–3.30, 5.30–11 in winter

PENDERYN (Powys)   SN9408 Map 6
Red Lion

From A4059 Aberdare–Brecon, turn off up hill at Lamb Inn, and keep left at T-junction; OS Sheet 160 reference 945085

Stripped stone walls, dark beams hung with flagons, flagstoned floors, traditional furnishings including bare antique settles – sounds austere, even with the open fires (one in a singularly big fireplace); but the atmosphere's pleasantly cheerful and lively – thanks both to the friendly staff and regular customers, and the good range of well kept real ales tapped from the barrel. Outside, sturdy seats and tables look down over the valley below, some built into the wall right on the brink of the pasture that drops away so steeply. There are good forest walks at Cwm Taf – back down the hill, keep straight across the main road at the Lamb. *(Recommended by Gwynne Harper, Tony Ritson; more reports please)*

Free house   Real ale   Open 1–3ish, 7–11ish all year

PENMAENPOOL (Gwynedd)   SH6918 Map 6

George III   ★ 🏠

Just off A493, near Dolgellau

The setting adds a great deal to the charm of this elegant seventeenth-century inn. It's on the Mawddach estuary, separated from the water by what used to be a shoreside railway but is now the inn's private drive. The waterside meadows, with a bird observation tower, are full of wildfowl (in spite of diligent culling by the resident otters). There are fine walks in the forested hills around, too, for example up the long ridge across the nearby toll bridge. The most attractive bar is upstairs – a civilised place, beamed and partly panelled, opening into a cosy lounge where armchairs face a big log fire in a stone inglenook; this has an interesting collection of George III portraits. In summer the downstairs bar is the busy place; it has heavy beams, flagstones, stripped stone walls and long green leatherette seats around plain varnished tables; darts, shove-ha'penny, dominoes and fruit machine. Home-made lunchtime bar food includes soup (£1), pâté (£2), steak and kidney pie (£3.25), roast spare rib of pork with barbecue sauce (£3.30), smoked trout (£3.95), Dublin Bay prawns (£5.75), and grilled Scotch sirloin steak (£7.25); maybe piped classical music. There's simpler food from Easter till October in the lower bar, such as toasted sandwiches (from £1), pizza (£1.60), and a self-service cold buffet (from £2.60); efficient service. The evening restaurant serves imaginative dishes, using good ingredients. Some bedrooms are in a very comfortable award-winning conversion of what used to be an adjacent station – the railway closed years ago. The hotel has estuary fishing just outside. It's the local police, not the landlady, who insist on enforcing the law against children in the bar. *(Recommended by A B Garside, David Wallington, F A and J W Sherwood, D S Rusholme, Eileen Broadbent, Alan Franck, Gordon Mott, Gavin May, Roger and Judy Tame, Rita Horridge)*

Free house   Licensee Gail Hall   Lunchtime meals (not Sun or Christmas and New Year fortnight) and summer snacks   Restaurant (closed Sun evening and May Day Mon)   Children in restaurant at lunchtime   Open 11–3, 6 (5.30 Sat)–11; closes 10.30 in winter   Double bedrooms (not Christmas and New Year fortnight) tel Dolgellau (0341) 422525; /£42(£70.40B)

PORTH DINLLAEN (Gwynedd)   SH2741 Map 6

Ty Coch

Beach car park (fee) signposted from Morfa Nefyn; 15-minute walk along beach or over golf links

In the long warm summer of 1989, one of the most idyllic days of all was 16 June – and on that day, the day of our inspection visit, one of the most perfect places in Britain must have been Porth Dinllaen. It's a small cluster of houses a mile from the nearest public road, on a curve of shallowly shelving beach backed by low grassy hills and the sand-cliffs where the martins nest, looking across what was on that day a quite Mediterranean expanse of tranquil water, boats anchored in the foreground, shadowy but dramatic hills across the sparkling bay. The pub, right on the beach and overlooking all this, is appropriately simple, with particularly cheerful service, and bar food such as filled rolls (from 80p), pies and pasties (85p), ploughman's with three cheeses, garlic mussels, home-made pizza, spare ribs, and meat or quiche salads from a cold display (£3); keg beers, decent coffee, a coal fire at each end. Its seventeenth-century black beams are hung with a mass of mainly nautical bric-à-brac, with more on the walls; the right-hand wall has a lot of RNLI photographs and memorabilia, and there's a Caernarfon grandfather clock. There are tables outside. *(Recommended by R L Nelson, Dewi and Linda Jones)*

Free house   Licensee Mrs B S Webley   Lunchtime snacks   Well behaved children welcome   Open 11ish–10.30; open 12–4 Sun, but no alcohol that day; closed end Oct–mid-Mar, but open Christmas and New Year   Nearby holiday cottages tel Pwllheli (0758) 720498

RED WHARF BAY (Anglesey)   SH5281 Map 6
Ship

Village signposted off B5025 N of Pentraeth

Looking out over ten square miles of treacherous tidal cockle-sands, this long and picturesque white-painted sixteenth-century house has lots of tables under cocktail parasols on the front terrace, and more rustic tables and picnic-table sets by an ash tree on grass by the side – where the view out past the anchorage is clearer. Inside is quite spacious, with a feeling of age and solidity in the two rooms on either side of the stone-built bar counter. There are long cushioned varnished pews built around the walls, glossily varnished cast-iron-framed tables, and quite a restrained décor including toby jugs, local photographs, attractive antique foxhunting cartoons and coal fires. Enterprising changing bar food includes sandwiches, ploughman's (£2.60), cockles in batter (£2.70), chicken and ham pie (£2.95), pork goulash with cider (£3.30), cottage pie (£3.40), beef casserole done with ginger or salmon done with sorrel in puff pastry (£3.80) and scampi (£4.70); there may be delays at busy times. The well kept Banks's, Sam Powells and Tetleys Mild and Bitter are drawn by handpump with a tight spray to give a northern-style creamy head; they also usually have Kenneallys, a beer brewed for them by the City Arms in Minera, and a wider choice of wines than usual for the area. Pool, darts and dominoes in the back room, and a summer family-room with space games; friendly service; piped music. *(Recommended by Jon Wainwright)*

Free house   Licensee Andrew Kenneally   Real ale   Meals and snacks (not Sun–Tues evenings out of season)   Restaurant tel Tynygongl (0248) 852568   Children in family-room   Open 11–3.30, 7–11 all year; 11–11 July–Sept

TALYBONT-ON-USK (Powys)   SO1122 Map 6
Star

B4558

It's the wide choice of real ales and ciders, unique for the area, which attracts people to this otherwise basic pub, unashamedly stronger on character than on creature comforts. The ales change regularly, but the list chalked up by the central servery usually runs to a dozen or so, such as Adnams, Felinfoel, Hook Norton, Marstons Pedigree and Owd Rodger, Ringwood Old Thumper and some that are rare around here, with two or three farm ciders such as Wilkins on handpump too. Several plainly furnished rooms radiate from this heart, including a brightly lit games area with darts, pool-table and fruit machine; also dominoes, cribbage, juke box, and cosy winter fires. Bar food includes filled rolls (80p), soup (£1.20), ploughman's (£1.80), giant sausage (£2), home-made pies (£4), steak (£6.25), and vegetarian dishes such as cashew and parsnip roast (£4.50). You can sit outside (the garden has potential), and the village, with both the Usk and the Monmouth and Brecon Canal running through, is surrounded by the Brecon Beacons National Park. The pub was up for sale in summer 1989, so there may be some changes. *(Recommended by Geoff Wilson, Gwynne Harper, M and P Rudlin, David Pearman)*

Free house   Licensee Mrs Joan Coakham   Real ale   Meals and snacks   Children welcome Open 11–3, 6–11 (all day Sat) all year

TREMEIRCHION (Clwyd)   SJ0873 Map 6

Salusbury Arms

Off B5429 up lane towards church

The civilised comfort of this immaculate country pub, looking out towards the coast, is reminiscent more of the smarter parts of Cheshire than of North Wales. The smallish beamed bar has thick carpet and richly upholstered seats; some of the timbering in the lower part, which dates back over six centuries and was originally the stables, is said to have come originally from St Asaph Cathedral. Meticulous attention to detail extends outside, too, where tables in the pretty gardens are set among flowers, shrubs and a little decorative stream, with goldfish and Koi carp in a pool. Bar food, carefully prepared from fresh ingredients and mostly home made, includes good soups (£1), sandwiches (from £1.20), ploughman's (£2.50), local sausages, steak and mushroom pie or curry (£2.95), grilled trout (£3.50), gammon and egg or pineapple (£4), steak (from £7), popular specials and children's meals (£1.20), with occasional Welsh and other theme menus. Well kept John Smiths on handpump, under light blanket pressure; dominoes, cribbage, and trivia. *(Recommended by Patrick Godfrey, Philip Riding, KC, E G Parish, Mr and Mrs John Mathews, Mr and Mrs J H Adam)*

Free house   Licensees Iain and Catherine Craze   Real ale   Meals and snacks (not Mon) Restaurant tel Bodfari (074 575) 262   Well behaved children welcome   Open 12–3, 7–11 all year; closed Mon

WOLF'S CASTLE (Dyfed)   SM9526 Map 6

Wolfe

A40 Haverfordwest–Fishguard

Service in this busy but friendly family food pub is efficient enough to trust even if you've a ferry to catch. Ever since this *Guide* first came out, readers have been finding the bar food reliable, too. It includes sandwiches (from 70p), soup (£1.25), ploughman's (£1.95), smoked trout pâté (£2.50), a good choice of salads (from £2.75), locally smoked trout or ham off the bone (£3.15), and scampi (£4.25); you can also choose from the many restaurant dishes, including steaks (from £6.75). And there's a wealth of home-made puddings such as gateaux, syllabubs, roulades, meringues and profiteroles (£1.60). Most readers eat in the neat but comfortable red-carpeted lounge, the garden room or the conservatory-restaurant; there's also a simpler tiled-floor public bar with darts, dominoes, fruit machine and piped music. Well kept Felinfoel Double Dragon on handpump. There are tables out among roses, hanging baskets, and banks of shrubs and trees. *(Recommended by Wayne Brindle, D P and M E Cartwright; more reports please)*

Free house   Licensees Fritz and Judith Neumann   Real ale   Meals and snacks (until 10 evenings; not winter Mon lunchtime)   Restaurant; closed Sun evening   Children welcome   Open 11–3, 6–11 all year; closed 25–26 Dec and Mon lunchtime Sept–Whitsun   One twin bedroom tel Haverfordwest (0437) 87662; £18S/£30S

Lucky Dip

Besides the fully inspected pubs, you might like to try these Lucky Dips recommended to us and described by readers (if you do, please send us reports). As this section has swollen so much in the last few years, we've experimented this time by splitting the country into its counties – please let us know if you find this either a help or a hindrance.

ANGLESEY

Beaumaris [SH6076], *Bishopsgate*: Though this has been popular for a wide choice of well presented good food it's now only a hotel, not doing bar lunches; bedrooms *(Mrs J Lloyd-Griffith)*; [Castle St] *Liverpool Arms*: Comfortably modernised, spacious, but well divided into smaller alcoves; good reputation locally, with variety of bar food; bedrooms *(R L Nelson, Mike Tucker)*

Brynefail [A5025; SH4887], *Pilot*: Pleasant, well decorated pub close to coast; handy for good walks *(Anon)*

Brynsiencyn [Foel Ferry; SH4867], *Mermaid*: Good choice of reasonably priced food under new owners; spacious bar, functions room, seats outside looking over Menai Straits to Caernarvon Castle *(W M Elliott, J Crawford)*

Llanddona [4 miles NW of Beaumaris; SH5879], *Owain Glendwr*: Very clean and friendly newly opened pub in old stone building; good value bar food from a wide menu, Youngers beer *(Paul and Margaret Baker)*

Menai Bridge [Glyngarth; A545, half-way towards Beaumaris; SH5572], *Gazelle*: Outstanding waterside situation looking across to Snowdonia, steep and aromatic sub-tropical garden behind, lively main bar and smaller rooms off; popular with yachtsmen, bar food and restaurants, well kept Robinsons Best and Mild; children allowed away from serving-bar; bedrooms comfortable *(Jon Wainwright, E J Waller, LYM; more reports on food and service, please)*

CLWYD

Afon Wen [SJ1372], *Pwll Gwyn*: Cheery and attractive beamed Tudor pub, prettily decorated outside with well tended flowers; pleasant restaurant with good food, particularly steaks; named for the White Pool (from marl clay behind); bedrooms *(Anon)*

Babell [SJ1674], *Black Lion*: Friendly, pleasant pub with warm atmosphere, remote and out of the way – but it pulls in regulars from far and wide for good lunchtime and evening food; a very considerable range of spirits and some excellent wine (the beer is keg) *(Lord Evans of Claughton)*

Bangor-is-y-Coed [SJ3945], *Royal Oak*: At foot of the old bridge with pleasant terrace; quiet pub with acceptable food and drink *(Neil and Elspeth Fearn)*

Bodelwyddan [A55 Abergele–St Asaph; SJ0076], *Fanol Fawr*: Handsome recently restored sixteenth-century manor house with comfortable bar area, good atmosphere, well kept Ruddles, imaginative bar food (not cheap, but worth it for ambience; separate restaurant with ambitious menu and wines; comfortable cottage bedrooms *(Hugh Geddes)*

☆ **Chirk** [SJ2938], *Hand*: Plushly furnished connecting bars in clean and spacious Georgian coaching inn, limited choice of decent straightforward food including children's dishes from buttery bar (not so attractive as main bar area), well kept Marstons Pedigree on handpump, friendly service, games area in public bar; bedrooms *(Mr and Mrs J H Adam, Gordon Theaker, R L Nelson, Pamela and Merlyn Horswell, Jenny and Brian Seller, LYM)*

☆ **Colwyn Bay** [Chapel St, Mochdre; off link road between A470 and start of A55 dual carriageway – OS Sheet 116 reference 825785; SH8578], *Mountain View*: Well kept Burtonwood Best and Mild and fine choice of salads with other dishes (seafood is a favourite) from popular food counter with good no-smoking area, in neatly kept, spacious and big-windowed pub a bit like a comfortable club-house; pleasant staff, pub games including pool *(KC, Dr R Hodkinson, LYM)*

Denbigh [SJ0666], *Bull*: Rambling bar with stylish Elizabethan staircase and old-fashioned furnishings, good robust range of bar food, real ale and bedrooms *(LYM)*

☆ **Erbistock** [village signposted off A539 W of Overton, then pub signposted; SJ3542], *Boat*: On a quiet day the position is enchanting – tables in a pretty partly terraced garden sharing a sleepy bend of the River Dee with a country church; the pub's mainly given over to food, with bar meals and snacks at lunchtime, more restauranty evenings (not Sun evenings, nor winter Mons); small flagstoned bar (used chiefly by people about to eat), comfortable beamed dining-room, bigger summer dining annexe; on a busy day it's not so nice outside, with cars coming to and fro and people trying to decide which of the three sections to go to – and in the last year or so there's not been unanimity about food value; children welcome *(Neil and Angela Huxter, Logan Petch, Mr and Mrs J H Adam, C F Walling, Gwynne Harper, Brian and Anna Marsden, AE, LYM – more reports please)*

Ffrith [B5101, just off A541 Wrexham—

Mold; SJ2855], *Poachers Cottage*:
Eighteenth-century pub refurbished by
newish owners concentrating on home
cooking – she's Danish, and does some
Danish dishes; careful choice of reasonably
priced wines (*Anon*)

Glyn Ceiriog [SJ2038], *Golden Pheasant*:
Comfortable country hotel in small hamlet,
with superb views; limited choice of good
bar food inc local trout in bar with stuffed
animals and open fire, changing imaginative
four-course dinners; nineteen roomy and
comfortable bedrooms (*Mrs J Gittings*)

Graianrhyd [B5430; village signposted off
A494 and A5104; SJ2156], *Rose & Crown*:
Small, bright, cosy country pub run by
enthusiastic young licensee, well kept
Marstons, good range of bar food inc
vegetarian dishes (*Mr and Mrs J H Adam*)

Gwernymynydd [SJ2263], *Plas Hafod*: Fine
views, lovely grounds, excellent Sun lunches
in classy dining-rooms (*Paula Devlin*)

Halkyn [SJ2172], *Britannia*: 500-year-old
former farmhouse with real fire and warm
welcome; well kept Lees real ales on
handpump, good bar food inc home-made
soups and big bacon and mushroom rolls
(*Andy and Jill Kassube*)

☆ **Hanmer** [SJ4639], *Hanmer Arms*: Good
relaxed pub atmosphere in popular bar with
food from sandwiches to steaks; attractive
manicured garden, with church nearby
making a pleasant backdrop; pretty village;
good sensibly priced bedrooms converted
from former stables, in courtyard (*Neil and
Elspeth Fearn, Keith Miller*)

Henllan [B5382 nr Denbigh; SJ0268],
Llindir: Pleasant pub in beautiful
countryside; good range of food, real ale (*Mr
and Mrs J H Adam*)

Higher Kinnerton [SJ3361], *Royal Oak*:
Village pub with friendly bar and cosy
lounge; Greenalls ales, good lunchtime and
evening bar food at reasonable prices; small
garden with aviary (*Peter Corris*)

Holywell [Greenfield Rd; SJ1876], *Royal
Oak*: Good choice of well cooked food,
presented nicely and served by waitress; lots
of beers (*L Allen*)

☆ **Llanarmon D C** [SJ1633], *Hand*: Very
civilised place, with atmosphere more
reminiscent of a French country inn than a
Welsh one, well run, with good value food,
quick friendly service, comfortably
cushioned chairs and sofas, log fire;
bedrooms comfortable – a nice place to stay;
this is a lovely spot (*Mr and Mrs B Hibbert, Mr
and Mrs A M Campbell, LYM*)

☆ **Llanarmon D C**, *West Arms*: Under same
ownership as the Hand, and as civilised –
though the back bar is a popular and often
lively meeting place for people from the
surrounding hills; interesting lounge bar inc
elaborately carved confessional stall as well
as sofas, antique settles and so forth; open
fires, bar food, lawn running down to River

Ceiriog (where residents of both places can
fish free); children welcome in both inns
(*LYM – we'd be very grateful for more reports
on both these places*)

Llanarmon yn Ial [B5431; SJ1956], *Raven*:
Basic country inn with well kept
Burtonwood Bitter and Dark Mild, simple
bar food, friendly staff and locals, pleasant
seats outside – this is an attractive village;
bedrooms (*LYM*)

Llanbedr D C [SJ1359], *Griffin*: Pleasant and
comfortably furnished roadside country pub
with lounge looking out on small, attractive
garden; Robinsons ale, good bar food,
restaurant; bedrooms (*Mr and Mrs J H Adam*)

☆ **Llandegla** [SJ1952], *Crown*: Very pleasant
and friendly atmosphere, good choice of
appetising bar food, well kept Lees real ale,
popular restaurant (*Mr and Mrs J H Adam,
DE*)

Llandegla, *Plough*: Attractive and busy, with
decent bar food, but piped music may be
loud (*KC*)

☆ **Llanferres** [A494 Mold–Ruthin; SJ1961],
Druid: Small soberly plush lounge with
attractive view over valley from bay window,
some oak settles as well as plainer more
modern furnishings in bigger saloon which
also looks over to the hills; well run, with
well kept Burtonwood Best, good food inc
vegetarian dishes, with emphasis on fresh
produce; good walking country; bedrooms
well furnished, with wide view (*Comus
Elliott, G T Jones, KC, Dennis Royles, Mr and
Mrs J H J Medland, BB*)

Llanfwrog [B5105 just outside Ruthin;
SJ1158], *Cross Keys*: Particularly good
atmosphere, really friendly, with good bar
food and well kept beer (*Wayne Brindle*)

☆ **Llangedwyn** [B4396; SJ1924], *Green*: Warm
and welcoming country inn in attractive
surroundings; bright and busy inside, with
oak settles and prints, pleasant service, good
choice of good bar food inc delicious
puddings, evening restaurant, Sun lunch;
fishing rights on the River Tanat (*Mrs J
Gittings, Miss S P Richards*)

Llangernyw [SH8767], *Stag*: Seventeenth-
century pub with beams, open fire, small
nooks and settles; two bars with interesting
collection of pottery jugs and mugs, stag and
fox heads, guns and other weapons; small TV
on wall, good range of bar food, Websters
real ale; bedrooms (*BKA*)

☆ **nr Llangollen** [Horseshoe Pass; A542
N – extreme bottom right corner of OS
Sheet 116 at overlap with OS Sheet 117
reference 200454; SJ2242], *Britannia*: Based
on fifteenth-century core, though much
extended and modernised, with good views,
generous helpings of good food in bar and
restaurant, pleasing efficient staff; gardens,
window boxes and hanging baskets are a fine
sight; bedrooms clean and good value (*Mr
and Mrs D W Payne*)

☆ **Llannefydd** [SH9871], *Hawk & Buckle*:

Cleanly run and comfortably modernised hill-village inn, decent food; good value bedrooms with remarkable views *(Mrs E M Thompson, LYM – more reports please)*

Llansannan [SH9466], *Saracens Head*: Pleasant atmosphere in nicely furnished pub with good bar food and well kept Robinsons real ale *(Mr and Mrs J H Adam)*

Nannerch [ST1669], *Cross Foxes*: Fine little village local where visitors are made as welcome as regulars; small attractive bar and lounge, well kept Youngers Scotch on handpump, nice fireplace *(Jon Wainwright)*

Pontblyddyn [just off A541 3 miles SE of Mold; SJ2761], *New Inn*: Friendly locally popular pub with well kept Watneys-related real ales, good bar food; darts, juke box and two pool-tables upstairs; licensee is trained cooper and will make you a barrel in his cellar workshop *(Alan Kilshaw)*

Rhesycae [SJ1771], *Miners Arms*: Pleasantly if unremarkably decorated pub with particularly good food and service; bedrooms *(John Davidson)*

Rhewl [OS Sheet 125 reference 176448; SJ1744], *Sun*: In small village on scenic north side of Dee Valley; whitewashed pub with two pleasantly furnished rooms, one with a piano, friendly landlord, Plassey Farmhouse real ale; close to Llangollen steam railway *(Jon Wainwright)*

Ruabon [Trevor; off A539 W, on N side of Pont Cysyllte aqueduct; SJ2742], *Telford*: Youngers pub on northern side of Pont Cysyllte aqueduct across the Dee; popular with barge users from adjacent canal, attractive views *(Jon Wainwright)*

St Asaph [SJ0475], *Red Lion*: Tetleys pub with red lion on porch, teapots hung from beams, old prints, bar food, good friendly service, wide choice of wines, piped music *(Gwynne Harper)*

Trofarth [B5113 S of Colwyn Bay; SH8569], *Holland Arms*: Cosy place with good food *(H Geddes)*

Wrexham [Mold Rd; ½ mile from centre, nr Wrexham FC ground; SJ3450], *Turf*: Friendly atmosphere, efficient service, well kept Marstons Pedigree on handpump, good reasonably priced home-cooked bar food *(John Rafferty)*

DYFED

Aberaeron [Queen St; SN4462], *Prince of Wales*: Cosy lounge bar with mantelpiece and high shelf display; bar food, restaurant with good fish and steaks *(Dr Stephen Hiew)*

Aberystwyth [Queens Rd, 50 yds from N end of prom; SN5882], *Boars Head*: Cheerful back lounge and lively front pool-room, freshly cooked bar food, well kept Felinfoel, restaurant *(BB)*; [Corporation St] *Unicorn*: A fun pub with lots of knick-knacks and atmosphere; Bass on handpump *(Doug Kennedy)*

nr **Aberystwyth** [Llanbadarn Fawr; SN5882], *Black Lion*: Cheerful evening atmosphere in well run local with spacious back lounge, games area, well kept Banks's real ales, good value simple food and splendid play area in big sheltered garden with summer evening barbecues *(LYM)*

Alltwalis [A485 about 7 miles N of Carmarthen; SN4431], *Masons Arms*: Good atmosphere and décor, great range of local real ales, good bar food, good-humoured licensee, occasional dances *(Frank Cain, Patricia Deegan)*

☆ **Amroth** [SN1607], *New Inn*: Sixteenth-century seafront pub with cushioned wooden chairs and settles and open fires in three-roomed beamed bar downstairs, upstairs lounge bar, separate games-room with pool-tables and machines; well kept Felinfoel, Flowers, Pembrokeshire Benfro and Tetleys ales, wide choice of bar food inc local shellfish and children's dishes, no piped music, friendly golden retriever; picnic-table sets out on grass; holiday flat to let *(Lyn and Bill Capper)*

Bosherston [SR9694], *St Govans*: Straightforward decently run pub with Worthington on handpump, included for its value in this attractively bleak spot near the coast; bar food, piped music, bar billiards, tables on terrace; the eponymous hermit's chapel overlooking the sea is worth getting to, as are the nearby lily ponds; nr start GWG190; bedrooms *(Canon and Mrs G Hollis, Neil and Elspeth Fearn, LYM)*

Brechfa [SN5230], *Forest Arms*: Big inglenook fireplace in main bar of simply furnished old stone inn in nice countryside, popular with locals; restaurant; bedrooms *(BB)*

Burry Port [Stepney Rd; SN4400], *George*: Comfortably plush lounge bar with wide range of hot and cold food (not sandwiches), well kept Buckleys, Felinfoel and Worthington ales, friendly service, lots about Amelia Earhart's historic Atlantic flight, discreet piped music; nr Pembrey Country Park and Welsh Motor Sports Centre; bedrooms, also self-catering *(Lyn and Bill Capper)*

Caio [SN6739], *Brunant Arms*: Good family atmosphere, reasonably priced home-cooked food inc home-made bread and good steak and kidney pie, entertaining licensees; children welcome *(Diana Jerman, Mrs M Ashwell)*

Cardigan [High St; SN1846], *Black Lion*: Well kept Flowers ale, quickly served bar food in spacious rambling lounge of seventeenth-century inn with stately Georgian façade; bedrooms *(Wayne Brindle, LYM)*

☆ **Carew** [A4075, just off A477; SN0403], *Carew*: Simple welcome in traditionally furnished country pub with well kept Worthington, snacks, friendly licensee, pleasant seats outside and play area; attractive position near river, tidal watermill and ruined Norman castle *(Janet Williams, LYM)*

Cenarth [SN2641], *White Hart*: Sixteenth-century white-painted pub with central bar and two rooms off, simple but pleasant furnishings, Courage Directors, good bar food generously served; nr pretty stretch of River Teifi, with mill being restored *(Joy Heatherley)*

Cilycwm [SN7540], *Neuadd Fawr*: Welcoming Welsh-speaking village pub with home-made food, simple furnishings, cheerful atmosphere *(BB)*

Cosheston [SN0004], *Cosheston Brewery*: Pretty, family-run village pub with well kept Ind Coope Burton, good imaginative food *(E O Stephens)*

Cross Inn [B4337/B4577 – not the Cross Inn near Newport; SN5464], *Rhos yr Hafod*: Friendly and traditionally furnished Welsh-speaking country pub with well kept Flowers IPA, good value specials and popular upstairs restaurant *(LYM)*

☆ **Cwm Gwaun** [Pontfaen; Cwm Gwaun and Pontfaen signposted off B4313 E of Fishguard; SN0035], *Dyffryn Arms*: Basic rough-and-ready village tavern known locally as Bessie's, run by same family since 1840 and quite untouched by time – plain deal furniture, well kept Bass and Ind Coope Burton served by jug through a hatch, sandwiches, draughtsboards inlaid into tables; nr start GWG193 *(Brigid Avison, LYM)*

Cynwyl Elfed [Llandeilo Rd; SN3727], *Bluebell*: Small country local with inglenook and log-burning stove, bar food *(S Watkins)*

Dinas [A487; SN0139], *Freemasons Arms*: Traditional cottage-style pub, part of a terrace, well modernised but keeping cosy character; good range of good home-cooked food in big helpings, two dining-rooms, open coal fires, real ale *(Simon and Ann Ward, Wayne Brindle)*; [A487] *Ship Aground*: Several rooms opening off servery, sea pictures and ship's brassware, portholes and low pitched ceiling give boat feel to long side gallery, softly lit back room; Felinfoel Double Dragon on handpump, plain good value bar food inc children's helpings *(BB)*

Dreenhill [Dale Rd (B4327 2 miles S of Haverfordwest); SM9214], *Masons Arms*: Friendly cottage pub where visitors are made to feel as welcome as locals; well kept Bass, Courage Directors and Worthington BB tapped from the cask, simple choice of good nicely presented food; children welcome *(Keith and Ann Dibble)*

Eglwyswrw [A487 Newport–Cardigan, at junction with B4332; SN1438], *Serjeants*: Antique high-backed settles in snug if basic bar with heavy black beams and capacious inglenook, Worthington BB on handpump, lounge and dining-room – and still a Petty Sessions court on the premises; promising reports on friendly and helpful new licensees – and their food; bedrooms clean and comfortable *(Mrs Joyce Reid, Rolf Kenton, LYM)*

Felingwmuchaf [SN5024], *Plough*: Stone-built country pub with delightful atmosphere in period bar with comfortable banquettes and open fire; very friendly service, smart and popular restaurant *(Richard and Betty Widder)*

Ffairfach [SN6221], *Torbay*: Busy, popular free house; small building, but surprisingly spacious inside; heavily beamed quarry-tiled bar with collection of jugs, brasses and darts trophies, smaller carpeted lounge; well kept Buckleys, Flowers and Worthington, good bar food specialising in seafood *(Joy Heatherley)*

☆ **Fishguard** [Lower Town – Trefin; SM9537], *Ship*: Well kept Worthington BB and Dark Mild in nautically-decorated and dimly lit fisherman's local nr old harbour; good atmosphere with a welcome for strangers, homely bar food inc filled rolls, friendly licensees, rugby talk; children welcome, with toys provided *(Dr S Fort, Keith and Anne Dibble, LYM)*

☆ **Fishguard**, *Fishguard Arms*: Friendly welcome in tiny terraced pub with well kept Felinfoel Double Dragon, Marstons Pedigree and Worthington BB served by jug at the elbow-high serving-counter; lots of rugby photographs, cheap snacks, open fire, traditional games and impromptu music in back games-room *(Dr S Fort, LYM)*

Glanaman [A474; SN6713], *Raven*: Newly decorated dual dining area with good value well cooked usual bar food in one part and restaurant meals running up to steaks in smarter part; well kept Buckleys Mild and Best, very friendly service – worth a wait in busy times *(M and J Back)*

Jameston [A4139; SS0599], *Swan Lake*: Good food, well kept real ales inc Bass and Courage Directors, but tends to get rather overrun with children in summer *(John Davidson)*

☆ **Landshipping** [SN0111], *Stanley Arms*: Attractive riverside pub, surprisingly well appointed, with good value well served bar food inc locally caught salmon and other fish, well kept Worthington tapped from the cask; restaurant *(Canon and Mrs G Hollis, E O Stephens)*

Lawrenny [SN0107], *Lawrenny Arms*: Attractively situated, paved terrace *(Janet Williams)*

Llanarthney [B4300 (good fast alternative to A40); SN5320], *Golden Grove Arms*: Stylishly furnished and interestingly laid-out inn which has been popular for its enterprising food, especially fish, but we've had no reports since its sale in 1988 – more news please; bedrooms *(LYM)*

Llandeilo [nr centre; SN6222], *Farmers Arms*:

Clean, very friendly pub with nice décor, quick efficient service and good ale; generous helpings of bar food from wide choice *(C and L H Lever)*

Llandybie [6 Llandeilo Rd; SN6115], *Red Lion*: Unusually shaped comfortable bar with local paintings and photographs for sale; well kept Flowers, wide choice of good lunchtime and evening bar food inc local salmon and fresh vegetables, enormous Sun lunches, restaurant; comfortable bedrooms *(Penny and Gwyn Jones)*

Llanfihangel Crucorney [village signposted off A465; SO3321], *Skirrid*: Among the oldest pubs in Britain, with parts dating from 1110 – and formerly where sheep-stealers were hanged; previously very popular with readers, but under the Courage flag the former interesting choice of real ales has narrowed, and the atmosphere has changed to 90 per cent restaurant (the food has changed too, but is still quite good) *(Neil and Anita Christopher, Gordon and Daphne, John Honnor, LYM)*

Llangadog [Gwynfe; this is the Llangadog up towards Llandovery; SN7028], *Three Horseshoes*: Lovely spot by stream, pleasant licensees, well kept Flowers, good home-made food *(E Kinnersly)*

Llangain [B4312 S of Carmarthen; SN3816], *Pantydderwen*: Comfortable pub with old settles and cushioned chairs; well kept Courage, good wines, good varied bar food (local fish, soups particularly good), friendly and attentive service *(Pete Storey)*

☆ **Llangranog** [SN3054], *Pentre Arms*: Nice old historic pub on seafront of beautiful fishing village, run by friendly landlord and family; well kept Buckleys Best on handpump, huge helpings of decent bar food, separate bistro; seven good value bedrooms, where you're lulled to sleep by the sound of waves on the beach *(Lord Evans of Claughton)*

Llangranog, *Ship*: On edge of beach, with real ales and expanding choice of home-cooked food under new licensees – two young families who plan renovations inc self-catering accommodation *(Tim and Ann Newell)*

Llanteg [SN1810], *Llanteglos Hunting Lodge*: Very good Pembrokeshire Benfro ale brewed here; attractive building with good value food *(Nigel Winters)*

☆ **Llanwnnen** [B4337 signposted Temple Bar from village, on A475 W of Lampeter; SN5346], *Fish & Anchor*: Snug bar with lots of stripped pine, well kept Greenalls on handpump, decent food (not Sun), pretty little country dining-room, views from garden with good play area; has been closed Sun; children allowed until 9pm if well behaved *(LYM)*

Llanwrda [A482, 2 miles towards Lampeter; SN7131], *Hafod Bridge*: Recently refurbished old free house with warm welcome, charming traditional lounge, food served all day inc breakfast, country and western evenings *(Gwen and Peter Andrews)*

Marloes [OS Sheet 157 reference 793083; SM7908], *Lobster Pot*: Warm welcome from licensee, well kept Felinfoel tapped from the cask, Hancocks HB on handpump, good food inc plenty of fish, large pool-table; a fine pub for walkers (and geologists), at start of GWG191 *(Gwyneth and Salvo Spadaro-Dutturi, D P and M E Cartwright)*

Mathry [off A487 Fishguard–St Davids; SM8732], *Farmers Arms*: Friendly atmosphere, with good bar food (home-grown mint for the sauce with the sweet, lean Welsh lamb), pleasant fire and collection of flatirons in lounge, well kept Worthington; darts, pool and juke box in extension bar, but plans for a restaurant here *(Gwen and Peter Andrews)*

Narberth [High St; SN1114], *Angel*: Friendly and efficient staff, well kept beer, extensive and reasonably priced bar food inc good salad bar *(E J Knight)*

Newcastle Emlyn [Sycamore St (A475); SN3040], *Pelican*: Well preserved seventeenth-century town pub with good choice of real ales, pews and panelling, and fireplace with bread oven still recognisable as the one where Rowlandson in 1797 sketched a dog driving the roasting spit; local atmosphere, games area on left; bedrooms in adjoining cottage *(Wayne Brindle, LYM)*

Newgale [main rd to St Davids; SM8422], *Duke of Edinburgh*: Simple pub just above splendid beach, lounge, public bar and pool room; bedrooms *(BB)*

☆ **Newport** [East St (A487 on E edge); SN0539], *Golden Lion*: Generous helpings of good value food inc very fresh fish and superb steak in seaside-town inn with interesting bar – stripped stone walls, distinctive settles, comfortable easy chairs; children allowed in eating area and own bar; bedrooms comfortable for the price, breakfasts huge *(Philip King, Wayne Brinde, LYM)*

Newquay [SN3859], *Black Lion*: Pleasant bar overlooking harbour, which usually has wide range of real ales such as Marstons Pedigree; bedrooms all with bath, most with sea view *(G T Jones)*

Pelcomb Bridge [SM9317], *Rising Sun*: Attractive and welcoming pub with generous helpings of bar food that's particularly good for the area *(W M Pinder)*

Pembroke [Main St; SM9801], *Old Kings Arms*: Good menu, modest prices, good service, real ale; bedrooms *(Canon G Hollis)*

Pembroke Dock [27 London Rd; SM9603], *Welshmans Arms*: Good pub, popular for evening meals and Sun lunch, with well kept Websters Yorkshire; bedrooms cheap, with enormous breakfasts *(E O Stephens)*

☆ **Pembroke Ferry** [at foot of bridge over estuary; SM9603], *Ferry*: Nice riverside setting, good range of decent bar food (especially imaginative fresh fish dishes), friendly helpful service; restaurant, good Sun carvery; children welcome *(A J and M Thomasson, Janet Williams)*

Pont-ar-Gothi [6 miles E of Carmarthen on A40 to Llandeilo; SN5021], *Cothi Bridge*: Popular bar food in comfortable bow-windowed plush lounge overlooking River Cothi, Courage ale, restaurant, riverside seats outside; bedrooms *(LYM)*; *Salutation*: Friendly jumble of rooms, with well kept Felinfoel Double Dragon on handpump, super food especially lobster, crayfish, steaks and puddings such as apricot praline roulade, with American-sized helpings – need to book; has been closed Mon; bedrooms large and comfortable, with big breakfasts *(Martin Thomas)*

Pontarsais [A485 Carmarthen–Lampeter; SN4428], *Stag & Pheasant*: Roadside pub with clean, well run bar, relaxing atmosphere, attentive staff, good food and restaurant *(K R Harris)*

Ponterwyd [A44 about quarter-mile W of A4120 junction – OS Sheet 135 reference 746806; SN7581], *George Borrow*: Lounges at front and back of bar with old copper objects; snooker room, bar food, restaurant; in fine spot by Eagle Falls and gorge, so gets lots of summer visitors; children and dogs welcome *(Dr Stephen Hiew)*

☆ nr **Ponterwyd** [A44 nearly two miles E of village – OS Sheet 135 map reference 774817], *Dyffryn Castell*: Good value bar food in lounge bar and dining-room, well kept Marstons Pedigree, John Smiths and Worthington BB in unpretentious but comfortable isolated inn dwarfed by the mountain slopes sweeping up from it; bedrooms clean, comfortable and good value *(Dr Stephen Hiew, LYM)*

Pontfaen [SN0134], *Gelli Fawr*: In wonderful setting, this is mixture of part pub, hotel, restaurant and self-catering place, with 18-hour service and family atmosphere; good value food, well kept Felinfoel, reasonable wines and comfortable bar; children welcome; bedrooms good value *(David Eversley)*

Rhandirmwyn [SN7843], *Royal Oak*: Straightforward food, friendly staff; bedrooms comfortable *(Steve Dark)*

☆ **Rhosmaen** [SN6424], *Plough*: Deep-cushioned comfort and good value bar food – especially puddings – in dining lounge with picture-window views, tiled front bar and separate restaurant; willing service *(K Wood, LYM)*

Solva [SM8024], *Harbour House*: Impressively placed by harbour, with good atmosphere and nice snacks *(Wayne Brindle)*; [OS Sheet 157 reference 806245] *Ship*: Unassuming exterior, but excellent atmosphere inside, with real home cooking *(Alan Castle)*

☆ **St Davids** [on rd to Porthclais harbour (and lifeboat); SM7525], *St Nons*: Hotel bar, but well worth a visit, with imaginative food (especially puddings), particularly well kept Hancocks HB and Bass, lots of life, cheery helpful staff, good restaurant popular for fresh fish; jazz Sat; bedrooms airy and reasonably priced *(Lord Evans of Claughton, D Pearman)*

St Dogmaels [SN1645], *Ferry*: Popular waterside family pub, simply furnished *(LYM)*

Talybont [A487; SN6589], *Black Lion*: Seats in sheltered back garden behind substantial stone village inn with comfortably modernised back lounge, games in and off front public bar, bar food and restaurant, Bass real ale; bedrooms *(Wayne Brindle, LYM)*; *White Lion*: Banks's Mild and Bitter and Hansons in pub next door to the above, comfortable lounge behind public bar, wide choice of bar food from sandwiches to steaks, friendly service *(M and J Back)*

Tegryn [SN2233], *Butchers Arms*: Said to be Pembrokeshire's highest pub; picturesque view, good Buckleys bitter and bar snacks, small restaurant *(BB)*

☆ **Templeton** [A478; SN1111], *Boars Head*: Good home-cooked food from filled baked potatoes upwards at reasonable prices, in friendly and appealing family-run local, clean and tidy, with lots of atmosphere, well kept Watneys-related real ales and helpful staff; restaurant; children allowed lunchtime *(Kate Lindsay, D P and M E Cartwright, P Corris)*

Tenby [Upper Frog St; SN1300], *Coach & Horses*: Cosy and clean, within the town walls, good value chip-free food, comfortable lounge, public bar, choice of beers; parking can be very difficult *(P Corris)*; [The Paragon] *Imperial*: Substantial hotel on cliffs, with tasty bar food from filled baked potatoes and hot beef sandwiches to main dishes; reasonably priced beer, superb view of Caldy Island from terrace; comfortable bedrooms *(Wayne Brindle)*

Trapp [OS Sheet 159 reference 653189; SN6518], *Cennen Arms*: Popular with Welsh-speaking locals, good bar food inc Sun roasts, small garden and terrace with seats; children welcome *(Keith Walton)*

Tregaron [SN6759], *Talbot*: Olde-worlde hotel bars, but with real pub atmosphere; most welcoming staff, well kept beer and attractive food; bedrooms *(Gwyneth and Salvo Spadaro-Dutturi)*

Velindre [A487 Newport–Cardigan; SN1039], *Olde Salutation*: Pleasantly restored eighteenth-century inn, good value bar snacks and nice garden; in attractive spot, with fishing in nearby River Nevern; bedrooms *(Wayne Brindle)*

GLAMORGAN – MID

Aberdare [Heads of the Valleys Rd; SO0002], *Baverstocks*: Spacious comfortably furnished lounge with one-price lunchtime hot and cold buffet; bedrooms *(Lyn and Bill Capper)*

Bryncethin [SS9184], *Masons Arms*: Pleasant spot, well kept Brains, wide range of bar food inc good popular sandwiches *(Helen and John Thompson)*

Caerphilly , [Cardiff Rd; ST1587], *Courthouse*: Newish pub with outstanding views across lake to castle from terrace and conservatory restaurant; good if not cheap range of food, inc its own Caerphilly cheese, friendly licensees and staff; children allowed in restaurant *(Paul and Rhian Hacker, Keith Walton)*

☆ nr **Caerphilly** [Watford; nr M4 junction 30 via mountain rd from Tongwynlais and Bwlch-y-cwm – OS Sheet 171 reference 144846], *Black Cock*: Beautifully placed well modernised country pub, with extensive garden and play area; particularly well kept Bass, good range of good value snacks and meals, especially at lunchtime, open fire in winter; open later in the afternoon than most pubs around Cardiff *(Dr A P M Coxon)*

Llangeinor [SS9187], *Llangeinor Arms*: Remote hill-top pub by church with excellent Bristol Channel view from conservatory; two bars with fine collection of antique artefacts and porcelain; real fires, choice of real ales, good bar food with adjacent fifteenth-century restaurant *(D Salt)*

Merthyr Tydfil [SO0709], *Crown*: Good food pleasantly served in huge helpings by helpful chef, well kept Flowers on handpump – a refreshing change for a town with so many 'locals only' pubs *(J F Thorndike)*

Pen-y-Fai [SS8982], *Pheasant*: Large, comfortable pub with good atmosphere and welcoming staff; well kept Courage Best and Directors on handpump, popular range of lunchtime bar food inc traditional puddings such as jam roly-poly and spotted dick *(John and Helen Thompson)*

Pontneddfechan [SN9007], *Old White Horse*: Small, comfortable, recently refurbished pub close to Ystradfellte Waterfalls; friendly welcome, good service, well kept Courage Best and Brains SA, good cheap bar food; can get busy weekends *(Alun and Eryl Davies, Pamela and Merlyn Horswell)*

☆ **Rudry** [ST1986], *Maenllwyd*: Comfortably furnished traditional lounge in low-beamed Tudor pub with well kept Whitbreads, popular bar food, spacious restaurant with midnight supper licence *(LYM)*

Southerndown [SS8873], *Three Golden Cups*: Near a particularly attractive stretch of the coast and locally popular for meals, views to Devon when it's clear; bedrooms *(LYM)*

GLAMORGAN – SOUTH

☆ **Cardiff** [Custom House St], *Golden Cross*: Victorian pub carefully and expensively restored by Brains, and now a showpiece of

conservation; much ornate tilework inside and out, cast-iron tables and fireplace, glittering glass, glossy woodwork and scrubbed floors; friendly licensees, Brains real ales and lunchtime bar food – all main dishes home made; live music Thurs *(A J Ritson)*

Cardiff [St Mary St], *Albert*: Good atmosphere, back lounge, well kept Brains Dark, Bitter and SA, bar food *(Alun Davies)*; [same st as Howells dept store] *Cottage*: Well laid out city-centre pub with well kept Brains Dark and SA at reasonable prices, good lunchtime home cooking from ploughman's up *(John Thorndike)*; [Wharton St] *Glassworks*: Great place rather like French brasserie with pleasant bar area, real ale and fine range of both bar snacks and restaurant meals *(Geoff Wilson)*; [Church St] *Old Arcade*: Well renovated city-centre pub with traditional atmosphere and wide mix of customers; well kept Brains, good bar meals, evening live music, lots of rugby mementoes *(A J Ritson)*; [St Mary St] *Philharmonic*: Old-fashioned, dark and busy, popular at lunchtime for bread and huge chunks of good value cheeses in variety, also wide range of good value club sandwiches in downstairs food bar; well kept Felinfoel and Websters, video juke box *(Michael and Alison Sandy, A Cook)*; [Westgate St] *Queens Vaults*: Well run Victorian-style pub with well kept Ansells and Tetleys from square central bar, efficient friendly service, good value bar food; close to law courts and Cardiff Arms Park *(Dave Braisted, S Watkins)*

☆ **Dinas Powis** [Station Rd; ST1571], *Star*: Well decorated and efficiently run village pub with stripped stone walls or panelling and heavy Elizabethan beams; eating areas, two with welcoming fires, and a no-smoking room; friendly licensees, good bar food, well kept Brains ales *(Mrs E P Hird, LYM)*

☆ nr **Lisvane** [follow Mill Rd into Graig Rd, then keep on; ST1883], *Ty Mawr Arms*: Country pub with several comfortable rooms, good lunchtime food (not Sun), unusually good choice of real ales such as Butcombe, Hook Norton, Robinsons and Smiles, all well kept; friendly service, big attractive garden with spectacular view over Cardiff to the Severn Estuary – useful for families and children *(Tony Ritson, LYM)*

☆ **Llancarfan** [signposted from A4226; can also be reached from A48 from Bonvilston or B4265 via Llancadle; ST0570], *Fox & Hounds*: Locally popular for attractively presented reasonably priced food (though some things on menu may not be available) and well kept Brains, Felinfoel Double Dragon, Wadworths 6X and a guest beer, in rambling and comfortable bar; tables out on terrace in pretty surroundings; children in eating area *(Patrick and Mary McDermott, TBB, LYM)*

Llandaff [Cardiff Rd; A4119; ST1578],

Maltsters Arms: Local atmosphere in cheerful and spacious downstairs bar, easy chairs upstairs, well kept Brains real ales, quickly served food *(LYM)*

Llantwit Major [SS9668], *Old Swan*: Unusual medieval building housing straightforward pub with lively public bar and busy juke box, also restaurant *(LYM)*

☆ **Monknash** [follow Marcross, Broughton signpost off B4265 St Brides Major–Llantwit Major, turn left at end of Water St – OS Sheet 170 reference 920706; SS9270], *Plough & Harrow*: Unspoilt and untouched isolated country pub – flagstones, old-fashioned stripped settles, logs burning in cavernous fireplace with huge side bread oven, good value plain food, Flowers IPA and Original on handpump; pool, juke box and fruit machine in room on left, picnic-table sets on grass outside the white cottage; nr start GWG195 *(BB)*

☆ **Morganstown** [Ty Nant Rd (not far from M4 junction 32); ST1281], *Ty Nant*: Exceptionally well run and usually busy, with beamed lounge and popular basic bar; consistently well kept real ale, pool-table, usual bar food, seats outside *(A J Ritson, Dr A P M Coxon)*

Pendoylan [2½ miles from M4 junction 34; ST0576], *Red Lion*: Friendly pub in pretty vale, well kept Flowers IPA and Original on handpump, good bar food, restaurant *(Alun Davies)*

☆ **Penllyn** [village signposted from A48; SS9776], *Fox*: Neatly kept and surprisingly smart village pub with well kept Flowers Original on handpump, good value house wines and decent malt whiskies; very popular for its enterprising food under the former licensees (no bar food Sat evening or Sun, restaurant open Mon–Sat evenings and Sun lunch); more reports on the current regime, please; children welcome *(LYM)*

Porthcawl [Newton; SS7277], *Jolly Sailor*: Very friendly pub full of nautical brassware; well kept Brains beer, good atmosphere, straightforward bar food *(P L Duncan)*

Roath [Newport Rd; ST1978], *Royal Oak*: Large Victorian pub with public bar of unspoilt character, sporting mementoes going back to 1900; noisy, smoky and busy but informal and friendly – to our knowledge the only Brains tied house with SA tapped straight from the cask *(Dr A P M Coxon)*

☆ **Sigingstone** [SS9771], *Victoria*: Beautifully kept pub with antiques, fresh flowers, fast service and very good reasonably priced bar lunches; out of the way, but always busy *(Vera Davies, Mrs H March, E J Knight)*

☆ **St Hilary** [ST0173], *Bush*: Thatched village pub nestling behind church, old settles in traditional flagstoned public bar, comfortable low-beamed lounge with warm atmosphere, well kept Bass, Hancocks and Worthington, generous helpings of good bar food inc some Welsh dishes such as laver bread with bacon and boiled ham with parsley sauce, cheerful service, restaurant with long menu in Welsh and English *(G T Rhys, D S Morgan, Pamela and Merlyn Horswell, LYM)*

St Mellons [A48; TT2281], *Fox & Hounds*: Beautifully kept and clean Brains pub with friendly service and good reasonably priced meals *(Vera Davies)*

Treoes [SS9478], *Star*: Friendly, relaxed and tasteful village pub with polished pine furniture and church pews; Crown real ales, table skittles, separate pool-room; good food *(D Salt)*

Ystradowen [A4222 Llantrisant–Cowbridge; ST0177], *White Lion*: Pleasant village pub with open fire, pleasant service and good bar food *(A A Worthington)*

GLAMORGAN – WEST

Bishopston [Murton; off B4436 Bishopston–Swansea; SS5889], *Plough & Harrow*: Good choice of food in well run village pub with well kept real ales *(E J Knight)*

Gowerton [by traffic lights junction B4296/B4295; SS5896], *Welcome*: Spacious pub with cheery atmosphere and lots of comfortable plush seats; well kept Buckleys, good value generously served bar lunches with some imaginative dishes, restaurant *(Michael and Alison Sandy)*

Killay [Gower Rd; SS6092], *Commercial*: Recently refurbished, with pleasant atmosphere, real ales, piped music, good range of reasonably priced bar food *(E J Knight)*

Llangyfelach [B4489 just S of M4 junction 46; SS6498], *Plough & Harrow*: Smoothly comfortable modernised lounge bar with big helpings from food counter, well kept Courage Best and Directors and John Smiths on handpump *(Michael and Alison Sandy, LYM)*

Llanrhidian [SS4992], *Welcome to Town*: Formerly basic, cheerfully traditional and much loved for its unpretentious simplicity, this charmingly placed pub has changed hands and now been knocked into one open-plan plushly decorated bar, with piped music and so forth *(LYM)*

Mumbles [Newton Rd, Oystermouth; SS6287], *White Rose*: Well organised pub, with ship's wood panelling in extension; good value bar food promptly served, well kept Bass and Worthington BB and Dark; popular at weekends *(Pamela and Merlyn Horswell, M C Howells, Michael & Alison Sandy)*

☆ **Oldwalls** [SS4891], *Greyhound*: Spacious and comfortable lounge bar with well kept Bass, Hancocks HB and interesting guest beers, reasonably priced bar food, restaurant very popular at weekends for good fish such as flounder, mussels salad and hake; good

coal fire; can get very busy *(Gwynne Harper, Pamela and Merlyn Horswell)*
Parkmill [SS5489], *Gower:* Busy and pleasant pub, spacious, light and airy, with art deco décor, above-average bar food from ploughman's to steaks inc choice of vegetarian dishes; well kept Bass, Hancocks HB and Worthington BB real ale on handpump, some tables outside; mixed views on service *(M Saunders, Jenny and Brian Seller)*
Penclawdd [Berthlwyd; B4295 towards Gowerton; SS5495], *Berthlwyd:* Large, plushly refurbished open-plan pub popular with wide range of age groups, giving fine views across Loughor estuary; well kept Courage Best, John Smiths and Felinfoel, attentive staff, some picnic-table sets on lawn by road *(Michael and Alison Sandy)*
Resolven [A465, just S of junction with B4434; SN8202], *Farmers Arms:* Lounge bar like Victorian parlour with brass-topped tables, red plush seats, mock gas lighting, plants, walls adorned with plates and polished brass; cosy atmosphere, good staff, wide choice of good value bar food *(Karen Bettesworth, Chris Down)*
Swansea, *Dragon:* Good value bar food in lively and popular pub *(Anon)*; [Kingsway] *Hanbury:* The licensee who took over this spacious pub in early 1989 previously did very well at the Roebuck in Marlborough, for good value food and a welcoming atmosphere in a well run pub *(F E M Hardy)*; [Uplands Cres, Uplands] *Streets:* Interesting trendy décor with shopfronts around the walls, central bar with integral Pizza Hut counter and separate seating areas balustraded off, good choice of reasonably priced beer; popular with students in the evening when the pop music's loud, with frequent discos *(Bryan Drew)*; [seafront] *Woodman:* Popular, with good value carvery (need to book Sun lunch), well kept Bass *(Jenny and Brian Seller)*

GWENT
Abergavenny [Market St; SO3014], *Greyhound Vaults:* More of a pub at lunchtime than evenings, when it gets more restaurany; good food, industrious owners keen to please *(Merlyn and Pamela Horswell)*; [Flannel St] *Hen & Chickens:* Unspoilt old pub with fairly friendly atmosphere, new licensees fiercely proud of their Bass, good bar food inc first-class sandwiches; children allowed at lunchtime (busy then) *(Gwyneth and Salvo Spadaro-Dutturi)*; [Raglan Rd (old A40, 2 miles SE)] *Horse & Jockey:* Pleasant, clean and well furnished, with good staff and wide range of good value freshly cooked pub food *(K R Harris, Pamela and Merlyn Horswell)*; [The Bryn (old A40, 3 miles SE] *King of Prussia:* Going from strength to strength under new regime; recently refurbished with

two large, warm bars, clean and friendly atmosphere, well kept beer inc Courage on handpump, enjoyable food in separate dining area *(Graham Watkins)*
Caerleon [ST3490], *Bell:* Promising food in pleasant and well organised surroundings *(Pamela and Merlyn Horswell)*; [Uskside] *Hanbury Arms:* Pleasant old pub by river with friendly licensee, well kept Bass, restaurant; bedrooms *(A C Lang)*
☆ **Clydach** [Old Rock Rd; SO2213], *Rock & Fountain:* Old free house with superb stone walls and archways, doing particularly well under newish owners – the transformation's really quite dramatic; outstanding food in delightful recently extended side restaurant (it even has a fountain); well kept Watneys-related real ales, very friendly welcome; three bedrooms should be ready by the time this edition is published *(John Hayward, Graham and Glenis Watkins, Pamela and Merlyn Horswell)*
☆ **Grosmont** [SO4024], *Angel:* Carefully modernised seventeenth-century village pub with welcoming atmosphere, reasonably priced straightforward home-cooked food from sandwiches to steaks, hospitable licensees, cheap Whitbreads real ale; nice to sit out in the attractive single street, next to ancient market hall; they don't allow children; bedrooms *(D W Beecher, H W H Outfin, BB)*
☆ **nr Grosmont** [B4347 N – OS Sheet 161 reference 408254], *Cupids Hill:* Tiny homely pub, alone on very steep hill in pretty countryside; a quaint survivor – not at all olde-worlde, just basic and homely; bottled beers only (stood on sawn-off former bagatelle table with plyboard top), plain old settles by fire, low white ceiling; table skittles, dominoes, cribbage; landlord who doubles as local undertaker born here and took over from father *(Gordon and Daphne, BB)*
Llandogo [SO5204], *Old Farmhouse:* Lovely spot, several bars, pool-tables; delicious food inc home-made rolls with superb, friendly table service in pretty dining-room; bedrooms in motel accommodation *(Mrs A Sheard)*; *Sloop:* Also in this lovely Wye Valley setting, with warm welcome, well kept Smiles and bar food inc good value Sun lunches; children welcome *(Gwyneth and Salvo Spadaro-Dutturi)*
☆ **Llangwm** [B4235 S of Raglan; SO4200], *Bridge:* Relaxed atmosphere in well run pub, varnished pews in bright and airy dining extension with very wide choice of good enterprising food, at a price; well kept Bass in separate pubbier bar with beams, nooks, crannies and traditional furnishings; has been closed Sun evening and Mon lunchtime; children in dining area *(Col G D Stafford, Gwyneth and Salvo Spadaro-Dutturi, LYM)*
Llanishen [SO4803], *Carpenters Arms:* A 'real' pub in unspoilt spot with friendly

owners and staff, real ale, good reasonably priced bar food, restaurant; children welcome; a nice place to stay at *(Gwyneth and Salvo Spadaro-Dutturi)*

Llanthony [SO2928], *Half Moon*: Simple country inn with lots of nearby ponytrekking centres and walks, welcoming cheerful service, real ales, limited choice of decent food; shows its bones a bit in the winter; bedrooms with mountain views *(U W Bankes)*

☆ **Llantilio Crosseny** [SO3915], *Hostry*: Fifteenth-century pub (oldest in Gwent, though with recent extension), in pretty village; welcoming staff, well kept Smiles and good choice of home-cooked bar food inc vegetarian dishes; children allowed in lounge; bedrooms comfortable *(Gwyneth and Salvo Spadaro-Dutturi, Ian Campbell, Neil Christopher)*

Llantilio Crosseny, *Halfway House*: Small tastefully decorated sixteenth-century pub with lots of beams, log fire, friendly licensees, good range of drinks inc particularly well kept Bass; good home-cooked bar food inc some tasty vegetarian dishes and tempting puddings *(R N Harris)*;

Llanvihangel Gobion [A40 on Usk turning, about 3½ miles from Abergavenny; SO3509], *Chart House*: Smoothly modernised with nautical memorabilia and soothing piped music, current owners doing good food in bar and popular restaurant, distant hill views, Watneys-related real ales *(Pamela and Merlyn Horswell, BB)*

Machen [ST2288], *Royal Oak*: Warm welcome, friendly landlord and staff, pleasant atmosphere, good value bar food, restaurant *(Philippa Hawkins)*

Mamhilad [SO3003], *Horseshoe*: Cheap, plentiful food, well kept Brains and Felinfoel real ales; busy at lunchtime at ICI and Health Authority nearby *(Pamela and Merlyn Horswell)*

☆ **Monkswood** [SO3503], *Beaufort Arms*: Notable not just for its own cricket pitch, but also – particularly since being taken over by its chef – outstanding food changing daily, such as delicious carrot and coriander soup, fresh bream, pigeon breast in red wine, even lobster; welcoming atmosphere, Courage Directors and Best tapped from the cask *(David Gittins, Gwyneth and Salvo Spadaro-Dutturi)*

☆ **Monmouth** [Agincourt Sq; SO5113], *Kings Head*: Lovely period building with open, inviting atmosphere, flowers everywhere, good food in up-market dining-room with attentive service, decent wines; bedrooms comfortable *(DB)*

Monmouth [outside town], *Gockett*: Friendly staff and imaginative, freshly cooked and generously served food *(Anon)*; [junction A466/A4196] *Queens Head*: Good food, not expensive, no-smoking area *(Dr D M Forsyth)*

Parkhouse [SO5003], *Parkhouse*: Small,

comfortable village pub away from tourist route; two bars, small restaurant, and particularly generous pub food inc good ploughman's with four different cheeses *(Dr John Innes)*

Penallt [SO5211], *Boat*: We list this fine pub under Redbrook, in the Gloucs section – though it is actually on this side of the border river *(LYM)*

☆ **Pontypool** [The Wern, Griffithstown, nr Sebastopol; SO2901], *Open Hearth*: On bank on Brecon–Newport Canal – very popular particularly at lunchtime for this location, and for good changing range of well kept real ales inc rarities here like Boddingtons and Davenports, and moderately priced, well prepared and promptly served bar food *(A J Ritson, Pamela and Merlyn Horswell, Dr R Fuller)*

Raglan [SO4108], *Beaufort Arms*: Comfortable and roomy hotel bars with piped music, well kept Courage and John Smiths, bar food, good restaurant, friendly service; children welcome; bedrooms *(Lyn and Bill Capper)*

Rogerstone [ST2688], *Rising Sun*: Comfortable pub, recently modernised with attractive dining conservatory; good value lunchtime and evening bar food; children's room downstairs, outside play area *(Penny and Gwyn Jones)*

☆ **Shirenewton** [in village signposted off B4235 just W of Chepstow; ST4893], *Tredegar Arms*: Usual reasonably priced bar food, well kept Hancocks PA, Smiles, Wadworths 6X and guest beers and very good choice of malt whiskies in welcoming and cosy village pub; games in public bar, seats outside; children in eating area; good value new bedrooms *(C G A Kearney, Joy Heatherley, AE, LYM)*;

Shirenewton [on B4235], *Carpenters Arms*: Lots of little rooms, warm and welcoming, good food, wide range of well kept beers inc Bass and Marstons *(Graham and Glenis Watkins)*

St Brides Wentlooge [ST2982], *Church House*: Friendly and informal country pub on quiet road between Cardiff and Newport, with well kept Brains on handpump, meals and snacks (not Sun), garden and play area *(A J Ritson)*

Tintern [Devauden Rd (off A466 Chepstow–Monmouth); SO5301], *Cherry Tree*: Unspoilt old pub in pretty spot, pleasant licensee, excellent Hancocks PA and cider tapped from cask; a 'real' pub; children welcome *(Gwyneth and Salvo Spadaro-Dutturi)*; [A466 Chepstow-Monmouth] *Moon & Sixpence*: Good atmosphere, usual food, real ale, friendly service *(Steve Dark)*

Tredunnock [ST3896], *Newbridge*: Friendly and helpful licensees, well kept beer, good bar food, separate restaurant with fixed-price menu *(G L Carlisle)*

☆ **Trelleck** [B4293 6 miles S of Monmouth;

SO5005], *Lion*: Quiet and unpretentious backwater country pub with unusually good and reasonably priced food in very pleasant lounge bar *(J F and M Sayers)*

☆ **Usk** [New Market St; SO3801], *Royal*: Pleasant country-town inn with traditional fixtures and fittings, old crockery and pictures on the walls, old-fashioned fireplaces, comfortable wooden chairs and tables, and lots of atmosphere; good bar food lunchtime and evening, when there's a wider choice (get there early for Sun lunch, esp in summer), well kept Bass, Hancocks, Worthington and esp Felinfoel, friendly service *(Gwyneth and Salvo Spadaro-Dutturi, A J Ritson, Lyn and Bill Capper)*
Usk [Old Market St], *Kings Head*: Interesting food, choice of well kept real ales and decent comfortable lounge; bedrooms *(Pamela and Merlyn Horswell)*; [The Square] *Nags Head*: Consistently good décor, service, beer and food *(Col G D Stafford)*

GWYNEDD

☆ **Aberdovey** [opp Penhelig rly stn; SN6296], *Penhelig Arms*: Attractive building in fine position overlooking sea, still unspoilt though recently refurbished by new owners who are doing good home-cooked food – no chips; well kept Burton ale, warm atmosphere; bedrooms good *(A J Billingham, J R Saunders)*

☆ **Aberdovey**, *Britannia*: Well kept Bass, good bar food and superb view over Dovey estuary to mountains of N Cardigan, with balcony open in summer; hard to imagine a better situation *(Anon – more reports please)*
Abergynolwyn [SH6807], *Railway*: Friendly staff, well kept Tetleys tapped from the cask, good home-prepared food inc huge club sandwiches; not a great deal of intrinsic character, but in tiny ex-mining village in beautiful countryside, convenient for Tal-y-Llyn Railway *(SJC)*
Bala [High St; SH9336], *Olde Bulls Head*: Oldest inn in town – comfortably refurbished, with well kept Whitbreads, and straightforward bar food even in the evening; bedrooms *(LYM)*; [61 High St] *White Lion Royal*: Old coaching-inn, character beamed bar with inglenook fireplace, well kept Youngers No 3 on handpump, bar meals, dinners, Sun lunches; comfortable bedrooms all with private bathroom *(Dougal Bannerman)*
Bangor [Garth Rd; SH5973], *Union*: Multi-roomed pub close to pier, full of nautical bric-à-brac; mixture of Welsh and English-speaking customers, good bar meals and snacks, well kept Burtonwood beers, good service *(Jon Wainwright)*

☆ **Beddgelert** [SH5948], *Prince Llewelyn*: Quietly civilised plush bar with raised dining area, simpler summer bar, good value straightforward bar food, well kept Robinsons, cheerful and helpful staff, rustic seats on verandah overlooking village stream and hills; nr GWG206; gets busy at peak holiday times; children if eating when not too busy; bedrooms pleasant, with excellent breakfasts *(Michael and Alison Sandy, R L Nelson, Drs G N and M G Yates, KC, BB)*
Beddgelert, *Tanronen*: Simply furnished main bar, small but pleasant separate lounge bar, well kept Robinsons real ale, simple food; not a great deal of atmosphere, but friendly, and used by locals as well as tourists; nr GWG206; bedrooms simple but clean – good value *(Gordon Theaker, Michael and Alison Sandy, BB)*
Betws-y-coed [A5, next to BP garage and Little Chef; SH7956], *Waterloo*: Wide choice of bar food inc good salads, quick service even early Sat evening, in comfortable modern lounge bar; bedrooms comfortable *(KC)*

☆ **Capel Garmon** [signposted from A470 just outside Betwys-y-coed, towards Llanrwst; SH8255], *White Horse*: Comfortable and cosy, with very friendly homely atmosphere, magnificent views, good value simple home-made food, pleasant staff; in delightful countryside; bedrooms very reasonably priced and well equipped – marvellous breakfast *(KC)*
Conwy [Castle St; SH7878], *George & Dragon*: Neatly restored old pub in attractive position, garden backing on to town wall; well presented food, particularly puddings *(Wayne Brindle)*

☆ **Corris** [village signposted off A487 Machynlleth–Dolgellau; SH7608], *Slaters Arms*: Reliably good Banks's Bitter and Mild at attractive prices in classic welcoming local with high-backed antique settles and lots of character; open fire in slate inglenook, good value simple bar food, friendly service; interesting ex-slate-mining village, with railway museum and nearby forest walks *(Dr M Owton, W P P Clarke, LYM)*
Deganwy [SH7880], *Deganwy Castle*: Plushly comfortable lounge with fine views, and pleasantly pubby rambling back bar with fat black beams, stripped stone, flagstones and lots of nooks and crannies; good choice of bar food, well kept Websters and Wilsons on handpump; bedrooms (this is a big hotel) *(LYM)*
Dinas Mawddwy [SH8615], *Llew Coch*: Traditionally furnished village inn with hundreds of sparkling horse brasses, food in simple dining area inc trout or salmon from River Dovey just behind, well kept Bass and lively Sat evening music; surrounded by plunging fir forests *(LYM)*
Fairbourne [SH6213], *Fairbourne*: Neatly kept and quite spacious bar that would be a credit to many big city suburbs, well kept Bass and McEwans real ale, maybe fudge pork scratchings; grey stone hotel in holiday village near sea; bedrooms *(BB)*

☆ **Ganllwyd** [SH7224], *Tyn-y-Groes*: Sixteenth-century Snowdonia inn owned by National Trust, oak beams, appropriate furniture, log fires, snug atmosphere, good freshly prepared bar food using local produce, Victorian restaurant, lots of malt whiskies, good service; fine forest views, salmon and sea-trout fishing, sun lounge; bedrooms comfortable *(Kenneth Bowden, LYM)*

Llanbedr [A496; SH5827], *Victoria*: Pleasant riverside pub with attractive gardens; smartly refurbished, but it's kept a fine old-fashioned inglenook in the back bar, and has well kept Robinsons, popular range of food in lounge bar, children's play area; bedrooms *(Tim and Lynne Crawford, SJC, LYM)*

Llanbedrog [Bryn-y-Gro (B4413); SH3332], *Ship*: Friendly local, recently extensively refurbished, with well kept Burtonwood Mild and JBA, lively family lounge, good range of popular straightforward food; pretty in summer, with lots of hanging baskets, window boxes and good outside seating area; dry on Sun *(Tim and Lynne Crawford, LYM)*

☆ **Llandudno** [Old St; SH7883], *Kings Head*: Friendly and spacious open-plan bar with variety of areas inc bistro-style part for huge range of good food, not cheap but with many dishes unusual for such an otherwise traditional pub; well kept Tetleys and Ind Coope Burton, pool area, interesting position by Great Orme Tramway station *(Richard Fawcett)*

Llandudno [West Shore], *Gogarth Abbey*: Fine views across bay to Puffin Island and Anglesey, bar food, open fire, morning coffee, afternoon teas, restaurant, waitress service; bedrooms *(Graham Gibson)*; [Mostyn St] *London*: Excellent local where strangers welcome; lots of bric-à-brac inc chamber pots, miniature London taxi and red telephone box which used to be on Chester station; well kept Burtonwood Mild and Bitter on handpump, lunchtime and evening bar food in summer, quiz nights, folk music, fancy dress competitions; bedrooms *(Graham Gibson)*

Llanwnda [SH4758], *Stables*: Pleasant, welcoming atmosphere, good food and service *(Mrs J Lloyd-Griffith)*

☆ **Porthmadog** [Lombard St; SH5639], *Ship*: Attractively renovated old pub known as Y Llong to its local regulars, with huge open fireplace and comfortable seats in lounge, wide choice of well kept real ales inc Ind Coope Burton, friendly efficient staff and really welcoming landlord; wide choice of particularly good lunchtime food cooked by his wife, served generously at reasonable prices, well appointed and popular upstairs evening restaurant; pool-table in comfortable public bar; children's room *(R L Nelson, Dewi and Linda Jones, Anthony Niner, David Millar)*

Rhyd-Ddu [the one on A4085 N of Beddgelert; SH5753], *Cwellyn Arms*: Lively stone-built pub with fine Snowdon views and good value food (baked potatoes, home-made pies, salad bar, vegetarian dishes and puddings all recommended); log fires, friendly staff, a welcome for walkers and children, restaurant, garden with barbecue *(Gordon Theaker and others)*

Rhydyclafdy [SH3235], *Tu Hwnt I'r Afon*: Charming building in pleasant countryside off the main routes, comfortable inside, with friendly landlord, well kept Whitbreads Castle Eden, wide choice of attractively presented inexpensive bar food *(R L Nelson)*

Tal-y-Bont [B5106 6 miles S of Conwy, towards Llanrwst; SH7669], *Y Bedol*: Well kept, friendly and reasonably comfortable village local in Vale of Conwy, well kept Tetleys on handpump, dark beams, winter open fire; curious TV room *(Jon Wainwright, BB)*

Tal-y-Cafn [A470 Conway–Llanrwst; SH7972], *Tal-y-Cafn*: Handy for Bodnant Gardens, cheerful and comfortable lounge bar with big inglenook, simple bar meals from sandwiches up, Greenalls on handpump, seats in spacious garden *(Paul S McPherson, LYM)*

Talsarnau [SH6236], *Caerffynnon Hall*: Very attractive entrance courtyard with water garden and tables; interesting bar with raised area overlooking sea, good range of good value meals, esp puddings, from buttery bar, well kept Bass and M&B Mild on handpump; bedrooms, and self-catering *(Tim and Lynne Crawford)*

Talyllyn [SH7209], *Ty'n y Cornel*: Pleasant fishing with big lounge looking out on lake and moorings; helpful service, good bar food; bedrooms decent *(Lord Evans of Claughton)*

Trefriw [B5106; SH7863], *Fairy Falls*: Well kept real ales such as Banks's and Ind Coope Burton, wide range of food generously served *(Jon Wainwright)*; *Princes Arms*: Good bar meals, attractive view, enthusiastic and welcoming licensees; children allowed; bedrooms *(H Geddes)*

Tremadog [The Square; SH5640], *Golden Fleece*: Attractive stone-built inn with simply furnished but interesting rambling beamed lounge bar (serving area gives appearance of a cave), nice little snug, games in public bar, tables in sheltered inner courtyard under Perspex roof – even a solarium/sauna; wide choice of decent food from side food bar, well kept Marstons Pedigree tapped from the cask; service can be somewhat leisurely; children in bistro or small room off courtyard; closed Sun *(Tom Evans, Tim and Lynne Crawford, LYM)*; [The Square] *Union*: Old stone pub, clean, tidy and very friendly, with good, generously served and reasonably priced food inc vegetarian dishes *(Tim and Lynne Crawford, Gordon Theaker)*

☆ **Tyn-y-Groes** [B5106 N of village; SH7672], *Groes*: Pleasant atmosphere in rambling series of dimly lit low-beamed medieval rooms with miscellany of furnishings, log fires, friendly and helpful newish owners doing good food inc fresh local fish in bar and tastefully furnished new Victorian-style dining-room – service can come under pressure when busy; bedrooms lovely, overlooking valley *(Paul Yeoman, Alan Franck, D M Moss, Hugh Geddes, LYM)*

POWYS

Bleddfa [A488; SO2168], *Hundred House*: Free house with good ales and good choice of reasonably priced, generously served food with fresh vegetables *(Joy Heatherley)*

Brecon [SO0428], *Three Horseshoes*: Incredible attention to detail and watchful service in cosy pub with good bar food and well kept beer *(P Miller)*

Bwlch [A40; SO1522], *Farmers*: Wide choice of good food – not cheap but often imaginative – in a smartly rejuvenated plush pub with big log fires and a good choice of real ales on handpump; primarily a dining place *(LYM)*; [A40] *Morning Star*: Unexpectedly wide range of bar food in friendly eighteenth-century former coaching-inn with well kept Courage Best and Directors; has been closed Mon *(Gordon Smith)*

Crickhowell [New Rd; SO2118], *Bridge End*: Has had lively, friendly atmosphere, pleasant decor, choice of well kept Worthington real ales, well served good value food – more reports on the new licensees, please *(Nick Dowson)*; *Corn Exchange*: Comfortably refurbished pub with good value bar food *(Pamela and Merlyn Horswell)*; [two or three miles NW, by junction A40/A479; SO2118] *Nantyffin Cider Mill*: Popular food pub in handy main-road position, attractive surroundings, enormous log fire in end dining area, good choice of consistent food, keg beers, decent ciders *(Warren Marsh, John and Joan Wyatt, PLC)*; *Riverside*: Nice position on River Usk, deservedly very popular for wide and imaginative choice of bar food *(Tim Brierly)*

☆ **Defynnog** [SN9228], *Lion*: Carefully restored roadside pub with good value home cooking, well kept Flowers real ales, pleasant service, good atmosphere, witty and enthusiastic landlord *(M and P Rudlin, LYM)*

☆ **Derwenlas** [A487 – OS Sheet 135 reference 723992; SN7299], *Black Lion*: Very old beamed cottage pub with huge log fire, friendly service, cottagey furnishings, well kept Marstons Pedigree on handpump, basic choice of decent wines, unobtrusive piped music; good home-cooked bar food in dining area divided off by oak posts and cartwheels, full vegetarian menu as well as standard one (all-day breakfast recommended),

imaginative puddings inc Greek ones; garden up behind, with good adventure playground and steps up into woods *(D J Wallington, Mr and Mrs P A Godley, G T Jones)*

Dolfor [inn signposted up hill from A483 about 4 miles S of Newtown; SO1187], *Dolfor*: Much modernised inn high in the hills, with easy chairs in beamed lounge opening into neatly modern dining area, Davenports and Tetleys on handpump, unobtrusive piped music; food's been priced more as meals than as bar snacks; bedrooms comfortable and good value *(John Davidson, LYM – more reports on new regime please)*

Dylife [off B4518 Llanidloes–Llanbrynmair – OS Sheet 135 map reference 863941; SN8694], *Star*: Free house with resolute cheerfulness amid desolate ruins of eighteenth-century lead-mining village, food running up to steaks *(Dr Stephen Hiew)*

Felindre [sometimes spelled Velindre: the one on the hill rd Hay-on-Wye–Talgarth; SO1836], *Three Horseshoes*: Pleasant pub popular with ponytrekkers, canoeists and walkers; well kept Courage Best and Directors on handpump, good pub food with wide choice, pleasant service, attractive dining-room *(M and J Godfrey)*

Frankwell [SN9696], *Swan*: Decent, busy town-centre pub with well kept Ansells, Ind Coope Burton and Wadworths 6X; snooker-room, restaurant (good fish Thurs–Sat, good value Sun lunch); tables outside *(Colin Dowse)*

☆ **Gladestry** [SO2355], *Royal Oak*: Unpretentious inn on Offa's Dyke, pleasant and welcoming new licensees, good home-cooked bar food inc fine ham ploughman's, newly refurbished lounge, separate bar; bedrooms lovely – sparkling clean, well equipped and excellent value, with good breakfasts *(Mrs J S England)*

Glangrwyney [A40 Crickhowell–Abergavenny; SO2416], *Bell*: Pleasant old building with oak beams, cheap bar food, Davenports ales, helpful staff, open fire; games-room, restaurant, fishing available for residents; bedrooms comfortable and good value *(John Hayward)*

Gwystre [A44 about 7 miles E of Rhayader – OS Sheet 136 map reference 066657; SN0666], *Gwystre Arms*: Friendly small local, a free house, with basic food, garden for children *(Dave Braisted)*

Hay-on-Wye [Bear St; SO2342], *Kilvert*: Small hotel bar with wooden benches, outside tables overlooking small town square, relaxed atmosphere, friendly barman smartly dressed complete with bow tie, well kept Fullers ESB on handpump *(D J Penny)*

Hundred House [SO1154], *Hundred House*: Wide range of good food inc imaginative specials and excellent vegetarian dishes, served in huge helpings in the two relatively spacious rooms off the cosy and low-beamed small main bar; popular Sun lunches, children's dishes and even takeaways; well kept Hancocks HB; has been closed Mon lunchtime, Tues, no food Mon evening *(Joy Heatherley, M E A Horler)*

Llanbadarn Fynydd [A483 Newton– Llandrindod Wells; SO1078], *New Inn*: Built like an octagonal theatre, with bar surrounded by two rooms and well used play-room; good value bar food, service friendly and helpful if a little slow, delightful lawned garden behind *(Tom Evans)*

Llanbrynmair [A470/B4518 E of Machynlleth; SH8902], *Wynnstay Arms*: Stripped stone and big fireplace in recently refurbished lounge, good choice of nicely cooked bar food up to big gammon and steaks, well kept Ansells and Powells Samson on handpump; bedrooms *(Brian Jones)*

Llanfair Caereinion [High St, off A458; SJ1006], *Goat*: Settees, easy chairs and warm inglenook in comfortable lounge, good value straightforward bar food, well kept Hancocks HB and Felinfoel Double Dragon on handpump, friendly service; public bar, tables outside *(Brian Jones)*

Llangadfan [A458 Welshpool–Dolgellau; SJ0111], *Cann Office*: Spacious roadside hotel, said to have been known to the Tudors, with lounge, cocktail and public bars, dining-room, children's room and garden; good value bar food inc children's helpings, well kept Marstons Pedigree on handpump; bedrooms *(G A Worthington, Dave Braisted)*

Llangattock [A4077 (village signposted from Crickhowell); SO2117], *Vine Tree*: Well run small and simple pub with efficient pleasant service and good interesting bar food – most of what space there is is given over to this, and it can get crowded, though calms down as the evening wears on *(John Honnor, Pamela and Merlyn Horswell, LYM)*

Llangenny [SO2417], *Dragons Head*: Busy and lively pub with good beer and reasonably priced food – has been a favourite *(Graham and Glenis Watkins; more reports on newish owners please)*

Llangurig [SN9179], *Blue Bell*: Cheerfully basic country inn; bedrooms *(LYM)*

Llangynidr [B4558; SO1519], *Coach & Horses*: Worth knowing for its sloping canalside lawn, safely fenced – a particular attraction for families; spacious inside, with Watneys-related real ales, open fire, pub games, straightforward bar food from sandwiches to light grills in front dining area, more substantial meals in restaurant (mixed views on value, and may not be quickly served); children welcome *(Mr and Mrs J H Adam, LYM)*

Llanwddyn [SJ0219], *Lake Vrnwy*: Hotel in superb position on hill giving breathtaking panoramic view of reservoir and backdrop of hills, especially from continental-style balcony; well kept Marstons Pedigree, good value sturdy common-sense bar food; bedrooms *(Robert A Caldwell)*

☆ **Llowes** [A438 Brecon–Hereford – OS Sheet 161 reference 192416; SO1941], *Radnor Arms*: Small, modest and very old, with log fire in bar, very prettily furnished quaint dining room, and tables in pleasant garden looking out over fields towards the Wye; particularly wide choice of food from beautifully filled big rye rolls or spicy pea soup to good but restaurant-priced dishes such as tender duck in apricot sauce, tasty if a bit chewy grouse, and calorific puddings such as hazelnut meringue – all these recently particularly recommended by readers; most competent attractive service, jovial licensees, well kept Felinfoel Double Dragon and Devenish Newquay Steam, spotless lavatories; closed Sun pm, all day Mon; at weekends it's wise to book *(David Wallington, Eileen Broadbent, PLC, Paul McPherson)*

Llyswen [B4350 towards Builth Wells; SO1337], *Boat*: Simple country pub with charming, spacious garden overlooking River Wye tumbling through steep valley *(LYM)*

☆ **Montgomery** [The Square; SO2296], *Dragon*: Friendly lounge bar with good food, also real ale, in hotel at top of town; enthusiastic new owners doing good food; bedrooms very comfortably refurbished, good value *(Mr and Mrs R H Martyn)*

Newbridge on Wye [SO0158], *New Inn*: Friendly village inn in upper Wye Valley, cold meats and fish with wide variety of salads at lunchtime, good home cooking in evening restaurant; well kept Flowers IPA, spacious carpeted back lounge with button-back banquettes in big bays, good bookmatch collection in public bar with TV, snug Cabin Bar with cushioned wall benches, welcoming licensees; bedrooms *(Mr and Mrs D A P Grattan, BB)*

Old Church Stoke [SO2894], *Oak*: Welcoming sixteenth-century pub, well kept Powells Bitter and Samson, good bar food attractively priced, small restaurant serving good Sun lunch *(David and Daphne Margetts)*

☆ **Presteigne** [SO3265], *Radnorshire Arms*: Picturesque rambling timbered THF inn with decent food in panelled bar, well kept Bass, good service, well spaced tables on sheltered lawn *(Mrs Joan Harris, LYM)*

Rhayader [Aberystwyth Rd; SN9768], *Crown*: By clock tower in town centre, good helpings of bar food from ploughman's to steaks, several well kept real ales on handpump inc Bass and Hancocks HB *(Patrick Godfrey, M and J Back)*

☆ **Talgarth** [from S take first turn into town; 50 yds walk from first car park; SO1534], *Radnor Arms*: Has been marvellously preserved old-fashioned tavern with antique settles and roaring log fire in gleaming kitchen range of flagstoned parlour bar and well kept Flowers Original and Whitbreads brought in the jug to your table; but with the long-serving landlord's retirement change (if not closure) is virtually inevitable *(Roy and Pamela Wade, LYM)*

Three Cocks [A438 Talgarth–Hay-on-Wye; SO1737], *Old Barn*: Long, spacious converted barn with choice of areas for games, quiet chats, drinking well kept Hancocks, or eating generous helpings of simple bar food; seats outside with good play area and barbecues on fine Fri evenings; the separately run parent inn across the road, the Three Cocks itself, is a traditional stone-built country inn with a good restaurant taking real trouble over the food, and comfortable bedrooms *(LYM)*

Trecastle [SN8729], *Castle*: Comfortably refurbished former coaching-inn with simple pleasant bar, tables outside, and wide choice of reasonably priced bar food; bedrooms *(Mr and Mrs J H Adam)*

Welshpool [High St; SJ2207], *Mermaid*: Very friendly old-world fifteenth-century pub with dominoes played in cosy low-beamed little front bar (cathedral glass in the windows), spacious pleasantly furnished back bar, well kept Banks's beer; very good atmosphere *(Pauline Watt, Stuart Smith)*; [Raven Sq] *Raven*: Pleasant rooms, log fire, unobtrusive piped music, fruit machines and separate pool room; friendly staff, well kept Banks's, good buffet and other dishes *(M A Watts)*

Ystradfellte [SN9213], *New Inn*: Charming homely whitewashed pub in tiny whitewashed village near pretty valley with a string of waterfalls; spacious and attractive, with most agreeable smiling landlord and cat, polished brass, well kept Flowers Original, good bar food and Sun lunch *(Tim Brierly, Jenny and Brian Seller)*

Channel Islands

Channel Islands

On Jersey, the Old Court House overlooking the water at St Aubin can be a delightful place to stay at, with a busy seafood restaurant, a pubby cellar bar and a smarter upstairs cocktail bar with views across the bay. If a really genuine local is what you want, the intriguing back locals' bar of Les Fontaines in St John couldn't be more unspoilt. These in their very different ways have been among the island's most outstanding pubs. A new entry, the Moulin de Lecq (a converted watermill at Grève de Lecq), is now pushing hard on their heels, though, with an unrivalled choice of real ales. For food, fresh fish and seafood is the thing to go for – at prices that strike mainlanders as absurdly low (do make sure it is fresh, though – surprisingly, frozen has made great inroads here). Anther Jersey place particularly worth noting for fish is the Dolphin in Gorey. On Guernsey, the top place to try is the civilised Hougue du Pommier, inland in Castel (a relaxed and comfortable place to stay at), though for a relaxed pubby atmosphere the Lamplighter in St Helier is hard to beat. Good places for fish are the Rocquaine Bistro looking out over beautiful Rocquaine Bay, and the bustling Ship & Crown in St Peter Port (taken over this year by the son of the previous long-serving landlord). On both islands, drinks prices are marvellously low compared with the mainland – on Jersey, beer, wine and spirits cost only about half what they do in London. Guernsey and Sark, though not as cheap, are still a good deal cheaper than the mainland.

The OS numbers we give after placenames in Jersey (except in St Helier) are six-figure map references to the Ordnance Survey official leisure map of Jersey. A useful illustrated booklet is Jersey Pubs & Inns, written by the landlord of the Old Smugglers at Ouaisné on Jersey – one of the best pubs in the Lucky Dip section (listed under St Brelade) at the end of the chapter. Others to note on the islands include the Georgian House on Alderney; La Trelade at St Martin on Guernsey; and Le Hocq at Le Hocq and La Folie in St Helier on Jersey. It's well worth knowing that there's a decent pub on Herm, too. Please note that a much higher proportion of the Lucky Dip entries here than on the mainland have been personally inspected by us, often proving a clear cut above the usual Lucky Dip run. We've described these more fully than usual – the BB initials signify which they are.

BEAUMONT (Jersey)   OS613498   Map 1

Foresters Arms

This whitewashed, tiled house can lay claim to being the oldest pub on the island – its licence dates from 1717; before that it served as the parish bakery, and parts of the building are fifteenth century. A more unusual claim to fame is the tombstone in the public bar, the result of a bet between a stonemason and an earlier landlord – we gather that the current licensee may be able to fill you in on the tale; there are also darts, dominoes, cribbage, space game and juke box here. The main low-beamed bar is quarry tiled, and has cushioned wheel-back chairs and black wooden seats built into bays, small windows with heavy curtains in the thick walls, and a winter log fire in the big stone fireplace; there's a good local atmosphere. The carpeted side lounge, with lots of shiny black woodwork, has blue plush stools and cushioned seats, and in winter a snooker table. In summer bar food is served from a side servery, and includes sandwiches (60p), filled baked potatoes (from £1),

947

ploughman's (£1.70) and some simple hot dishes such as chicken (£1.80). In winter the menu is more restricted, with home-made soup (60p) and some hot dishes. There are picnic-table sets on the front terrace, just across the road from Street Aubin's Bay. *(Recommended by Comus Elliott; more reports please)*

Ann Street   Licensee Colin Veitch   Meals and snacks (lunchtime, not Sun)   Children in lounge   Open 10–11 all year

CASTEL (Guernsey)   Map 1

Hougue du Pommier 🛏

Route de Hougue du Pommier, off Route de Carteret; just inland from Cobo Bay and Grandes Rocques

This elegant eighteenth-century hotel, peacefully set on the west coast of the island, serves good bar food, including home-made soup (80p), ploughman's (from £1.70), sandwiches (from £1.15; open from £1.90), vegetarian dishes (from £2.40), salads (from £2.90) and hot dishes such as omelettes (£2.80), gammon and egg or steak and kidney pie (£3) and rump steak (£4.40), with several children's dishes (£1.70), a day's special such as grilled whole plaice (£4.40) and a couple of carvery roasts (from £3.25). The roomy, red-carpeted and oak-beamed bar has leatherette armed chairs around wood tables, old game and sporting prints, hare and stag heads, guns, a stuffed falcon, pewter platters on a high shelf, good brass candelabra, and a nice snug area by a big stone fireplace surrounded by bellows and copper implements. The oak bar counter is attractively carved, with some mellowed oak linenfold panelling; piped music. There are good leisure facilities in the grounds, such as a pitch-and-putt golf course (for visitors as well as residents), a swimming-pool in a sheltered walled garden (tables beside it for drinks or bar meals in summer), a tree-shaded courtyard with lots of flowers, and a neat lawn with white tables under fruit trees. The hotel was originally a cider farm. *(Recommended by J S Rutter, Mr and Mrs G H Williams)*

Free house   Licensee J H Henke   Meals and snacks (lunchtime; limited menu Sun) Restaurant   Children in eating area and restaurant   Country and western music Mon and Thurs evening   Open 11–2.30, 6–11.45; closed Nov–Mar   Bedrooms tel Guernsey (0481) 565311; £29B/£58B

GOREY (Jersey)   OS714503   Map 1

Dolphin ✿

This cheerful waterside pub is most popular at lunchtime for its straightforward but fine selection of local fish, including stuffed clams (£3.10), grilled sardines (£3.60), moules marinière (£3.70), local plaice (£4), a dozen oysters (£4.80) and scallops poached in white wine (£6.80). But at other times the preoccupation is likely to be with the splendid setting – nestling beneath the medieval Mont Orgueil castle, the pub faces towards the harbour and the sweep of the bay; it's well worth climbing the steep rise on the opposite side of the harbour for the view. The bar itself has big bow windows overlooking the busy road, cushioned wheel-back and mate's chairs around the tables, and brown nets and the odd lobster-pot hung from its high black beams and woodwork; many of the high stools, with comfortable back rests, along the long bar counter are reserved for diners. In the evening there may be a strolling minstrel. Rather loud piped pop music. *(Recommended by Comus Elliott, Ewan and Moira McCall; more reports please)*

Free house   Manager Mario Dauru   Meals and snacks   Open 10–11 all year

---

Most pubs kindly let us have up-to-date food prices as we went to press in summer 1989; with those that didn't – normally recognised by the absence of a licensee's name – we've assumed a 10 per cent increase.

GREVE DE LECQ (Jersey)   OS583552   Map 1

Moulin de Lecq

On the way down to one of the only north-coast beaches, this black-shuttered pink granite building looks taller than it is wide, and is indeed a former mill. Outside there's still a huge working waterwheel, and inside it's not just children who are fascinated by the way its massive black gears turn perpetually in their stone housing behind the bar, between the neatly ranked bottles and glasses. Though the mill theme does extend to a pretty miller's-daughter costume for the barmaid, this is a thoroughly proper pub, with good bar food; in summer there's a cold table with ploughman's (£2) and salads (from £3.95, crab or prawn £4.50), as well as a popular barbecue outside, with grills running up to T-bone steak (£6.50); in winter they serve traditional Jersey dishes such as bean crock, rabbit casserole and beef in red wine (£3.25), with special puddings like carrot pudding (£1.50). It's also the only pub we know of in Jersey which serves four real ales: Bass, Guernsey Mild and Bitter and a guest such as Gales or Ringwood, kept well on handpump. There are red plush cushioned black wooden seats against the white-painted walls, little low black chairs and tables, and a huge stone fireplace with a good log fire in cool weather; service is welcoming and helpful; piped music. The terrace has picnic-table sets under cocktail parasols, with swings and a climber in the paddock. The valley and nearby coast have pleasant walks. The licensee ran the Foresters Arms at Beaumont until a couple of years ago. *(Recommended by Iain Anderson, Comus Elliott, Dr C S Shaw, Ewan and Moira McCall, Jonathan Warner)*

Ann Street   Licensee Gary Healey   Real ale   Meals and snacks   Restaurant planned (with all-day Sun licence)   Children in upstairs bar   Occasional morris dancing and folk music Open 11–11 all year

ROCQUAINE BAY (Guernsey)   Map 1

Rocquaine Bistro 🏵

On W of island

For some readers this is the best place at which to drink in Guernsey – and, from the location alone, you can see why: from the terrace you can look down to the bay, with its sand-brightened water and the vivid sails of the windsurfers dancing across, and beyond to the castle, floodlit at night; at low tide you can walk out to a great rock pool. But the pub has its own virtues too – particularly the substantial range of fresh fish, displayed prominently on crushed ice in the bar so that you can select exactly what you want; dishes include fish soup (£2.50), half a dozen oysters (£3.95), prawn tails in garlic or seafood pizza (£4.25), crab salad (£7.50), lobster thermidor (£13) and a substantial seafood platter (£20). The cool and quarry-tiled bar has pale bentwood and cane chairs, red gingham tablecloths, a lazy brass fan in the dark green ceiling, and big antique engravings on its swirly cream plastered walls. Decent wines by the glass, half-litre or bottle, bucks fizz, and coffee; piped music. *(Recommended by David and Jane Russell, J S Rutter)*

Free house   Licensees J R and E S Tautscher   Meals and snacks (not Mon in winter) Restaurant tel Guernsey (0481) 63149   Children in eating area   Open 12–2, 7–11 all year; closed Mon in winter

SARK   Map 1

Stocks Hotel 🛏

Dixcart Lane

There's an attractive balance between civility and liveliness in the stone-walled snug bar of this comfortable granite house; beneath the beam and plank ceiling there are cushioned easy chairs and small settees as well as red leatherette button-back wall banquettes, and stormy sailing-ship prints on the walls. Bar food, efficiently served in a separate buffet, includes sandwiches, soup (£1.30), ploughman's (£2.50), burger or quiche (£3.25), home-baked pie or vegetarian lasagne (£3.95), seafood pancake (£4.25) and steaks (from £4.25), with a good selection of salads from the cold table. In summer there are rustic seats by an attractive fine-grit, sheltered courtyard, and, beside the swimming-pool, a terrace for which you can book a table. *(More reports please)*

Free house   Licensees the Armorgie family   Meals and snacks   Restaurant   Children welcome   Open 12–2.30, 6–9.30; closed Oct–Apr   Bedrooms tel Sark (048 183) 2001; £26(£29B)/£52(£58B)

ST AUBIN (Jersey)   OS607486   Map 1

Old Court House Inn 🛇 🛏

This fifteenth-century inn has fine sea views across the tranquil harbour to St Aubin's fort. The upstairs cocktail bar is elegantly (and cleverly) crafted as the aft cabin of a galleon, with a transom window, a mast king post at one end and bowed varnished decking planks on the ceiling. The main basement bar has cushioned pale wooden seats built against its stripped granite walls, low black beams and joists in a white ceiling, heavy marble-topped tables on a Turkey carpet, a dimly lantern-lit inner room with an internally lit rather brackish-looking deep well, and beyond that a spacious cellar room open in summer and at busy times (when service can falter, and when it can seem as if half the morning's flight from Gatwick are there). Bar food includes soup (£1), lasagne or pâté (£3.25), salads (from £2.50), moules marinière (£3.50), dish of the day (£3.50) and grilled prawns (£4.50). The front part of the building was originally a merchant's homestead, storing privateers' plunder alongside more legitimate cargo. The bedrooms, individually decorated and furnished, are comfortable though not large; there can be noise from the popular restaurant at night, so ask for one well away from here if you're not a late-to-bed person. *(Recommended by Roger Mallard, Miss J A Harvey, Simon Turner; more reports please)*

Free house   Licensee Jonty Sharp   Meals and snacks (not Sun)   Restaurant   Children welcome   Nearby parking may be difficult   Open 11–11 all year   Bedrooms tel Jersey (0534) 46433; £37.50B/£75B

ST HELIER (Jersey)   Map 1

La Bourse

Charing Cross

Just beyond the main tourist shopping area of the island, this old-fashioned, one-roomed place has nineteenth-century French coloured cartoons behind a plate of glass on one purple wall, framed junk bonds, and comfortable, red leatherette tall stools at the bar counter and the ledge opposite it. Bar food includes onion soup (£1), sandwiches (from £1.30, steak £2.20), home-made pâté (£1.85), pizza, lasagne, escargots and a good selection of seafood; decent juke box. The bar is at its best on a quiet afternoon, when the atmosphere is truly relaxing, with discreetly friendly service. *(More reports please)*

Free house   Licensee Sue Fernandes   Meals and snacks   Upstairs restaurant (closed Sun) tel Jersey (0534) 77966   Children in restaurant   Open 11–11 all year

Lamplighter

Mulcaster Street

For one reader at least the atmosphere here is the most pubby of any of Jersey's watering-holes; a particular bonus is the notably well kept real ale (very rare for the area) – Bass on handpump. The décor is in back-to-basics style, but comfortably so, with captain's and kitchen chairs, pews and tables all done out in stripped wood; there's also grainy panelling, heavy timber baulks, real gas lamps on swan's-neck brass fittings, and old newspapers recording historic Jersey moments and photographs of old packet boats on the walls. Bar food includes sandwiches (from 70p), ploughman's (£1.40), sausages (£1.60), home-made shepherd's pie (£1.70), chicken or plaice (£2.10), salads (from £2.20) and scampi (£2.30); darts and piped music. The ornamental façade is attractive, with its elegantly arched windows and proudly carved Britannia on top. *(Recommended by Comus Elliott, Simon Turner)*

Randalls   Licensee David Ellis   Real ale   Meals and snacks (lunchtime, not Sun)   Morris men, Jersey Lilies, folk music or jazz on occasion   Open 10–11 all year

ST JOHN (Jersey)   OS620564   Map 1
Les Fontaines
Le Grand Mourier, Route du Nord

This traditional locals' pub is attractively set on the northernmost tip of the island, where the 300-feet high granite cliffs face the distant French coast. The main bar is clean and carpeted, with plenty of wheel-back chairs around neat dark tables, and a spiral staircase up to a wooden gallery under the high pine-raftered plank ceiling. But the place to head for is the distinctive public bar – and particularly the unusual inglenook by the large fourteenth-century stone fireplace. There are very heavy beams in the low dark ochre ceiling, stripped irregular red granite walls, old-fashioned red leatherette cushioned settles and solid black tables on the quarry-tiled floor, and for decoration antique prints and Staffordshire china figurines and dogs; look out for the old smoking chains and oven by the granite columns of the fireplace. The only problem is finding the place; either look for the worn and unmarked door at the side of the building, or as you go down the main entry lobby towards the bigger main bar slip through the tiny narrow door on your right, which is marked, but barely visibly. Pool, bar billiards, pin-table, shove-ha'penny, three space games, trivia machine, juke box or piped music in the main bar, and darts, dominoes, and cribbage in the original bar. Bar food includes soup (£1), sandwiches (£1), ploughman's (£2.50), burgers (£2.40), steak and kidney or chicken and bacon pie (£2.50), trout (£3) and eight-ounce sirloin steak (£3.95); Bass on handpump, and cheap house wine. *(Recommended by Ewan and Moira McCall, Brian Barefoot, Simon Turner)*

Randalls   Licensee Malcolm Shaw   Real ale   Meals and snacks (not Sun)   Children in eating area   Open 11–11 all year

ST MARTIN (Guernsey)   Map 1
Auberge Divette
Jerbourg; near SE tip of island

There are particularly fine views down past St Peter Port to the top of Guernsey (with Herm lying off to the right) from the lawn of this slightly down-market country pub. In the picture-window bar there are dark navy button-back banquettes in bays around low tables; a small carpeted lounge beyond folding doors has more banquettes and bucket seats. There's also a high-ceilinged back public bar, with sensibly placed darts, bar billiards, dominoes and cribbage; piped music. Guernsey Bitter and LBA Mild on handpump; sandwiches (from 75p, crab £2.20), ploughman's (£1.75), bacon, egg, sausage and chips (£2.20), salads (from £2.20), gammon or scampi (£3.30), steaks (£4.40) and children's dishes (from £1.30). *(More reports please)*

Guernsey Brewery   Real ale   Meals and snacks (not Sun)   Children in small side room (after 7) and eating area   Open 10.30–11 all year; closed Sun

ST PETER PORT (Guernsey)   Map 1
Ship & Crown   🏵

Opposite Crown Pier, North Esplanade

Just over the road from the harbour, this very lively old locals' pub has a distinctly nautical theme: it shares a building with the Royal Guernsey Yacht Club, and many of the local ship photographs on the cream Anaglypta walls above the dark maroon built-in seats date from the war years when this was the Naval HQ of the occupying German forces; there are others of local wrecks, sea disasters and RN and passenger liners which have visited the island. The quieter back area has drawings of tall ships. Popular bar food includes sandwiches (£1), ploughman's (£2), home-made lasagne (£2.70), home-made steak and mushroom pie (£2.80), gammon and egg, scampi or chicken Kiev (£3), good fresh fish (£3.20) rump steak (£3.20), and salads (from £3, local crab £6.50); Guernsey Bitter on handpump, and a decent selection of malts. The pub is family-run – the current licensee took over recently from his father. *(Recommended by J S Rutter; more reports please)*

Guernsey Brewery   Licensee Glen Pontin   Real ale   Meals (lunchtime, not Sun) and snacks (not Sun)   Open 10.30–11 all year; closed Sun

Taylors

The Arcade; behind Town Church, off High Street

The new licensee who took over in late summer 1989 is planning to transform the upstairs bar (closed for the past six years) into a plush restaurant-cum-lounge; otherwise things seem to be much as ever in this airy cafe-style local bar, which has cafe chairs on its bare boards, a very long bar counter decorated with tulip-style tall brass lamps, cream-painted brick walls, a pretty tiled Victorian open fire, and punka fans circling in the high brown Anaglypta ceiling. Straightforward bar food includes sandwiches (75p), filled rolls (95p), filled baked potatoes (from £1.50) and salads from a buffet counter (from £1.75); a good choice of wines by the glass; piped music (sometimes too loud for readers' comfort). It's in an area of small smart shops. *(Reports on the new regime please)*

Free house   Licensee Geoff Warren   Meals and snacks (not Sun)   Children upstairs   Open 10.30–11 all year; closed Sun

TRINITY (Jersey)   OS669545   Map 1
Waters Edge Hotel   🛏

Bouley Bay

Although this partly seventeenth-century building is far more of a very comfortable hotel complex (complete with spacious grounds and a heated swimming-pool) than a pub, its bar is popular with visitors and local fishermen. Called the Black Dog in honour of Bouley Bay's ghost, it's decorated in tranquil neutral colours and has mock-Tudor beams, a bare stone fireplace, stripped granite walls, attractive cushioned captain's chairs and wall seats around cast-iron-framed tables on the Berber carpet, and a relaxed atmosphere; there's gentle piped background music, and red-bow-tied barmaids in neat uniforms. Bar food includes sandwiches (from £1, crab £2.25, steak £3.50), salads (from £2.50), chicken curry or gammon (£2.75), moules marinière (£3), and Jersey lobster or crab, priced according to size. Whitbreads under air pressure, and a very good selection of wines. The residents' lounge, like the restaurant, has big picture windows looking out to sea. The back bar, the Picnic Hamper, has sea views from tables on its terrace in summer. *(Recommended by Comus Elliott, Miss J A Harvey)*

Free house   Manager Mr B Oliver   Meals and snacks (lunchtime, not Sun)   Restaurant   Children in restaurant   Open 10–11 all year   Bedrooms tel Jersey (0534) 62777; £43.50B/£79B

Lucky Dip

Besides the fully inspected pubs, you might like to try these Lucky Dips recommended to us and described by readers (if you do, please send us reports):

ALDERNEY

☆ **St Anne** [Victoria St], *Georgian House*: Very relaxing and welcoming, friendly bar with good food, restaurant excellent; can get very busy, with frequent live music; bedrooms comfortable *(Mark Higson, Jon Wainwright)*

Newtown, *Harbour Lights*: Varied choice of good bar food at very reasonable prices in welcoming, clean and well run hotel/pub in a quieter part of this quiet island; pleasant garden; caters particularly for families with children; well kept Guernsey Bitter; bedrooms *(Jon Wainwright, Donald Godden)* Other pubs here worth noting are the Albert (interesting interior, navigational charts), Campania (table skittles, darts, TV), Coronation (quite basic – old bookshelves, well kept Bobby Best tapped from the cask), Divers (sand on floor, lively, view over sandy bay), Belle Vue (near island cricket pitch, interesting bank-notes) and Sea View (splendid picture-window view of ships and boats entering harbour) *(Jon Wainwright)*

GUERNSEY

Castel [Rue Cohu], *Hotel de Beauvoir*: Spacious surroundings, pleasant service, no piped music, good bar food decent cold beef, help-yourself salad table; no-smoking area in lounge bar; bedrooms *(J S Rutter)*; [Cobo Coast Rd] *Rockmount*: Verandahed small hotel with thickly cushioned leatherette seats around American-cloth-covered tables in carpeted lounge; adequate seafood bar lunches, efficient service; picture windows overlook attractive beach with windsurfing school in pretty rock channels – and face the sunsets; bedrooms *(J S Rutter, BB)*

Erée Bay, *L'Erée Hotel*: Cosy bar popular with locals and fishermen *(David and Jane Russell)*

Grande Havre [Rte de Picquerel (part of Houmet du Nord Hotel)], *Houmet*: Big picture windows overlook rock and sand beach, though not a great deal of atmosphere in the high-ceilinged saloon with its cushioned library chairs, heavy rustic oak tables, bar billiards, space game; collect bar food from sandwiches to steaks from hatch; bedrooms *(BB)*

☆ **Kings Mills** [Kings Mills Rd], *Fleur du Jardin*: Swings and a rope swing in neat quiet garden with unusual flower tubs, outside pretty steep-tiled inn with square bar – open fire, lots of flowery-cushioned seats around tables, good range of Guernsey beers; popular with young professional people; bedrooms *(BB)*

☆ **St Martin** [Forest Rd], *La Trelade*: Reliable bar food in generous helpings, at attractive prices – often excellent fresh fish such as plaice, hake, conger eel, Dover or lemon sole; other good recent dishes have included cheese and avocado salad, curry, roast beef, chicken suprême with Brie; brisk and efficient service even on busy weekend evenings and holiday times; well kept Guernsey Bitter, surroundings comfortable if not particularly individual; children allowed in lounge; comfortable bedrooms *(J S Rutter)*

St Martin [Les Hubits], *Green Acres*: Pleasant surroundings in large country hotel, bar snacks popular – particularly Sun lunchtime (when pubs are closed); bright interior, well kept Guernsey Bitter, excellent service; good bedrooms *(J S Rutter)*; [La Fosse] *Les Douvres*: Pleasant food inc seafood in bar and restaurant, useful cellar, good service; not too crowded though in most beautiful part of the island; bedrooms good *(J S Rutter)*; [La Grande Rue] *Queens*: Surprisingly luxurious, with consistently well kept beer and reasonable service; bar snacks; bedrooms *(J S Rutter)*; [Idle Rocks Hotel, Jerbourg] *Raffles Pavilion*: Fabulous views over all the islands, helpful and energetic manager, good Bobby Best, good bar food *(J S Rutter)*

☆ **St Peter Port** [Albert Pier], *Buccaneer*: Much nicer inside than it looks from out – dim-lit bars with lots of woodwork and alcoves, sea and ship prints, model ships, nautical brassware; food such as quiche, chilli con carne, curries, omelettes, salads – also restaurant with harbour view; well kept Guernsey real ale; pool, darts and space game in bare-board public bar; some seats outside facing harbourside car park *(BB)*

☆ **St Peter Port** [South Esplanade; by bus stn], *Harbour Lights*: Spacious upstairs dining lounge looking past trees to harbour, locally very popular for lunch – neat waitresses bring sandwiches, ploughman's, salads, omelettes, home-made pies and fish; Guernsey Bitter chilled, under pressure; darts in downstairs bar *(BB)*

St Peter Port [Rte de Sausmarez], *Fermain*: Attractive local with masses of interesting foreign banknotes on the dark brown walls of its parquet-floored saloon; also biggish brightly lit public bar with pool, sensibly placed darts, space game *(BB)*; [Rohais Rd (part of St Pierre Hotel)] *Pierrots*: Pricey cocktail bar with cool décor, dark bentwood cane-seat chairs and broad marble-topped tables, well reproduced pop music, small sunken corner dance floor for live music; opens into airy tiled-floor brasserie, and into broad terrace by neat lawn running down to pretty pool and fountain, with tennis courts beyond; part of well run St Pierre Hotel, with comfortable bedrooms; open all day high season, but closed Sun except for residents *(BB)*

St Sampsons, *English & Guernsey*: Spacious lounge with green glass-and-brass chandeliers, leatherette cushioned blond captain's chairs, big brass clock, French windows to tables on sheltered lawn; also small snug bar, big plain harbourside public bar with darts, pool and side games-room with pin-table and space game *(BB)*; *Mariners*: Locals' harbourside bar not much changed – 1860s polychrome tiled floor, knotty veneer panelling, sensibly placed darts, cafe seats and leatherette wall benches, local punters watching horse-racing on tv; comfortably refurbished lounge *(BB)*; [Les Capelles] *Pony*: Plush lounge done up in shades of brown, with russet plush armchairs and smart booth seats; well kept Guernsey Mild and Bitter; public has two dart boards, space game, tv and juke box (maybe on together); rather rough-and-ready local atmosphere; tables out by front car park *(BB)*

St Saviour [rue de la Perelle, Perelle Bay], *Atlantique*: Pleasant spot with sea views; adequate service, consistently well kept Guernsey ale and excellent coffee; bedrooms *(J S Rutter)*

HERM
Mermaid: Charming pub in magic spot *(J S Rutter)*

JERSEY
Bonne Nuit Bay, *Bonne Nuit*: Hotel bar with superb stone fireplace and marvellous views over sea to France from terrace; bedrooms *(Ewan and Moira McCall)*

Grève De Lecq [OS reference 582554], *Prince of Wales*: Huge lounge with three well lit pool-tables, lots of games machines and juke box has picture windows looking over roof terrace with tables and aviary to small pretty sandy bay in pink granite cove; restaurant; live bands; bedrooms *(BB)*

Jersey Airport, *Horizon Bar*: Up in the lift to glass-walled view of the Flying Banana and other uncommon propeller aircraft which buzz around busily; very wide choice of reasonably priced spirits, conventional airport décor *(BB)*

☆ **Le Hocq** [St Clements Coast Rd; OS reference 685466], *Le Hocq*: The most southerly pub in the British Isles, just over road from interesting rocky sand beach; green plush button-back seats, Turkey carpet, heavy cast-iron-framed tables, ship pictures on gold Regency wallpaper – very popular for quickly served filled rolls, ploughman's, home-made fish soup served

with lashings of garlic bread, fish, burgers, scampi, steaks etc; some tables on front terrace, side lobby with tortoise rocker; pool, darts and space game in tiled public; on a clear day you can see France from the upstairs restaurant and cocktail bar; children's room *(Miss J A Harvey, BB)*

Rozel, *Rozel Bay*: Snug little inn near quiet and pretty bayside village (geese paddle along the pebbly beach); old prints and local pictures above dark brown plush wall seats in small back bar, plain public bar, poolroom; well kept Bass, bar lunches, toby jugs over bar, and 'Guinness es bouan por te' says the clock in the local patois; tables out behind by attractive steep terraced gardens *(BB)*

☆ **St Brelade** [Ouaisné Bay – OS reference 595476], *Old Smugglers*: Genuine local atmosphere in friendly and comfortable thick-walled black-beamed pub just above Ouaisné beach and slipway, sensibly placed darts, cosy black built-in settles, little sun porch, well kept Bass on handpump, good value quickly served bar food; the name refers to Second World War smuggling; pretty public gardens further along beach; children in central lounge *(Ewan and Moira McCall, BB)*

☆ **St Brelade** [Portelet Bay – OS reference 603472], *Old Portelet*: Extensive series of bars in stone pub above fine distant-view climb down to sheltered cove; well kept Bass, neatly kept lounge bar, well equipped children's room, buffet dining-room, upstairs 1920s bar, partly covered flower-bower terrace, spacious garden, pervasive pop music; children welcome *(BB)*

St Brelade [le Boulevard – OS reference 581488] *La Marquanderie*: Spacious and comfortable roadside pub alone on well wooded hill, dark shiny tables with cushioned mate's chairs and wall seats, ploughman's, salads, hot dishes, some spit roasting in restaurant (they may shut down on bar food out of season); lots of rustic benches on paved yard among lots of roses and cistuses *(BB)*; [St Ouen rd – OS reference 562488] *La Pulente*: Across road from the island's longest beach; popular with older local people for lunch, with sandwiches, ploughman's, filled baked potatoes (fillings may include scallops and fish), scampi, salads; more main dishes in evening, inc steaks; well kept Bass on handpump; green leatherette armchairs in smallish lounge, sailing-ship prints, leatherette-topped tables; fairy-lit side terrace *(BB)*

☆ **St Helier** [The Quay; between English and French Harbour – OS reference 649478], *La Folie*: A real harbourman's pub – three little rooms with simple seats, lots of brightly varnished woodwork, big pictures of fish and ships, chart, nautical brassware; cheerful and clean; on harbour though no views *(BB)*

St Helier [Halkett St], *Dog & Sausage*:

Comfortable and neatly refurbished town pub, handy for shops; some snug small rooms *(BB)*; [Royal Sq] *Peirsons*: Friendly and traditionally furnished old town pub with green plush button-back seats, Turkey carpet, cast-iron-framed tables, old prints, some black panelling, well kept Bass on handpump, upstairs food bar; in quiet chestnut-shaded square nr shops – the scars on one outside wall are from the 1871 Battle of Jersey *(John and Margaret Harvey, BB)*

St Peter [part of small hotel complex nr airport – OS map reference 592507], *Mermaid*: Pretty creeper-covered pub, separated by pond and swimming-pool from modern hotel; black beams, plank ceiling, Spanish-style cream flooring tiles, some seats cut into thick walls, wheel-back chairs around black lacquered tables, big fireplace in end stone wall; darts, juke box, space games, and pool-room with pin-table and space game; plain food, functional service; bedrooms *(BB)*; [St Peters Mill – OS reference 595540] *Windmill*: Neatly rebuilt windmill in attractive setting, with partly galleried lounge bar – cushioned milk churns, pews built into stable-stall-like alcoves, food such as sandwiches, salads, fish and chips, steak, country music; pool, juke box and sensibly placed darts in quarry-tiled public bar; restaurant and diners' cocktail bar in mill tower; tables in neat garden *(BB)*

Trinity [OS reference 663539], *Trinity Arms*: Cheery local with spacious and comfortable lounge, rambling quarry-tiled public bar with pool, space game and juke box; keg beers, straightforward bar food, piped music *(BB)*

SARK

Bel Air: Pretty cottage, where the tractors drop you at the end of the steep climb from the jetty; big wood-burning stove, plank ceiling, comfortable easy chairs and settees, model ship, boat-shaped counter; old boat pictures in simpler Harbour Bar; darts, piped pop music, tables on terrace *(BB)*; *Mermaid*: A real country local, basketwork chairs and cloth wall seats in lino-floor entrance bar, large and friendly games bar, paperback charity sales, snacks such as sandwiches and ploughman's, keg beers (not too fizzy or chilly), tea and coffee; seats on side terrace; welcoming *(BB)*

Overseas *Lucky Dip*

We're always interested to hear of good bars and pubs (or their local equivalents) overseas. Readers have recently recommended the following (we start with ones in the British Isles, then go alphabetically through other countries):

IRELAND

Ballinskelligs, *Sigersons Arms*: Lovely view from garden, though partly obscured by windbreak hedges; very friendly service, with pleasant lounge and area partitioned away from pool-table, also long narrow basic bar with TV; can easily walk down on to Ballinskelligs beach *(Roger Huggins)*

Belfast [Gtr Victoria St; opp Europa Hotel], *Crown Tap*: Beautiful nineteenth-century National Trust pub – tile, glass, mosaic, carved wood, great comfortable snugs with bell to bring barman or barmaid, lovely old-fashioned atmosphere, lunchtime food – a unique cultural experience *(D P Herlihy, Diane Duane)*

Chapeltown [Valentia Island], *Bostons*: Long thin bar with tables running parallel to it; at the end of the room it leads to another with a pool-table, TV and a games machine; live music from about 10pm *(Roger Huggins)*

Gap of Dunloe, *Kate Kearneys Cottage*: More of a tourist souvenir shop with somewhere to drink; wonderful scenery with horse and carts ready to take you up through Gap of Dunloe *(Anon)*

Glencar, *Climbers*: Not just for climbers, with pulpit and pew seating in lounge giving wonderful atmosphere; reasonably priced food, and Murphys as well as Guinness; pool-table in bar, friendly staff; a couple of alsatians – father and son; magnificent scenery in this area *(Roger Huggins)*

Hillsborough [21 Main St], *Hillside*: Popular meeting-place with cosy atmosphere, friendly service and very good, varied food *(F S and N P Grebbell)*

Kenmare, *Kingdom*: Extremely friendly people, great on Sat or Sun evenings with dancing – locals perform the Kerry sets; no food *(E O Stephens)*

Kinsale, *Armada*: Old pub on main street with connections with Battle of Kinsale; comfortable, good food and a quaint, delightful atmosphere; Murphy's, Guinness *(E O Stephens)*

Lisburn [Balinderry Rd], *Down Royal*: Large, rather dark pub with tables and chairs in alcoves around the walls; friendly service, own-brewed beer, incredible choice of lunchtime bar food including large filled baked potatoes and tasty prawn omelettes *(John Hayward)*

Strangford, *Lobster Pot*: Traditional, spacious old Irish pub, well kept ales, friendly staff, superb restaurant (last orders here 9.30) serving fresh, local fish and oysters, small garden *(John Hayward)*

Waterville, *Bay View*: Very friendly staff, whoever is serving, and basic though good value food such as sausage or fish and chips *(Roger Huggins and others)*; *Fishermans*: At the back of the Butler Arms Hotel and owned by the same people; comfortable and relaxing seats, ceiling beams and TV in one corner; picture of their most famous patron (Charlie Chaplin) on wall, along with a complete section of fishing flies; bedrooms *(Roger Huggins)*; *Strand*: Live entertainment most nights – can still be heard in the quieter conservatory; owned by Mick O'Dwyer, County Kerry hurling player and coach; also used for receptions and parties, and readers have had problems getting admitted on such occasions *(Anon)*

Wexford, *Bohemian Girl*: Swivel top bar stools, some barrel tables and a partitioned area in the corner make it all very cosy; charismatic, friendly licensee and lots of customers of all ages *(Roger Huggins)*

Youghal, *Ahernes*: Very busy place with delicious fresh fish in generous helpings; taped music has been replaced by pianist playing light classics from about 8pm; bar walls lined with awards *(Anon)*

ISLE OF MAN

Castletown [Market Sq; SC2767], *George*: Very comfortable town square hotel with good, home-made food; bedrooms *(Simon Turner)*

Douglas [North Quay; SC3876], *Bridge*: Good, modernised pub with fresh crab or lobster salad and well kept Okells Castletown; has a no-smoking section *(Simon Turner)*; [Drumgold St; known as the Dogs Home] *Victoria*: Excellent, panelled pub with ornate ceiling and interesting bar; friendly staff *(Dr and Mrs A K Clarke)*

Glenmaye [S of Peel – OS Sheet 95 reference 236798; SC2480], *Waterfall*: At the head of one of the island's beautiful glens leading to a sea cove; clean and cheerful place with seats outside; on *Good Walks Guide* Walk 141 *(Dr and Mrs C D E Morris)*

Laxey [New Rd – OS Sheet 95 reference 433846; SC4484], *Bridge*: Comfortable lounge in little hotel near to the Laxey Wheel; bedrooms *(Dr and Mrs A K Clarke)*; [Tram Station] *Mines Tavern*: Unique situation in historic electric tram/mountain railway station with interesting pictures, maps and photographs on the walls and an enormous waterwheel; Okells beer and straightforward food; service can be slow when busy; seats outside – watch out for wasps *(Dr and Mrs C D E Morris and others)*

Onchan [Avondale Rd; SC4079], *Archibald Knox*: Newly refurbished pub with an extension being added; very comfortable chairs (pub is popular with older people), Okells ales and standard lunches, though it can get very smoky *(Simon Turner)*

Peel [Station Pl; NX2484], *Creek*: Harbourside pub with friendly landlord, Okells ales and good bar lunches *(Simon Turner)*

Ramsey [Market Pl; SC4595], *Royal George*: Neatly kept old pub modernised next to harbour, with art-deco-style furnishings; good efficient staff, well kept Okells Castletown ales; readers particularly praise the fresh cod; quiet at lunchtime – music quiet too *(Dr and Mrs C D E Morris, Simon Turner)*

Union Mills [Peel Rd; A1 W of Douglas; SC3578], *Railway*: Basic and bare, but full of character; Castletown and Okells tapped from the cask, dominoes, three albino cats; landlady's beehive hair-style is not to be missed *(Matt Pringle)*

LUNDY

Marisco: Reached only by two-hour voyage from mainland, this one-room tavern is attached to the island shop and is social centre of permanent inhabitants (population 20) and holidaymakers; bar snacks and evening meals such as pasties, fish and curries; open 12–2, 6–11 & when ship in; children welcome; bedrooms tel 0628-825920 *(Brian Barefoot)*

AUSTRALIA

Adelaide [Pultney St; corner with Carrington St], *Earl of Aberdeen*: One of a growing number of own-brew pubs here – the brewery is visible through the end wall, and the Scotch Ale is fairly authentic; pleasant brewery memorabilia on wall, wooden bar counter (which is not something you can take advantage of here) *(Nick Dowson)*

Fremantle [64 South Terr; W Australia], *Sail & Anchor*: Well done replica of an English pub in pleasantly airy turn-of-the-century hotel, with English-style beer brewed by Matilda Bay Brewing Co; helpful staff take time to explain the different types of beer they do, even giving small free tastes *(Richard Houghton, Nick Dowson)*

Perth [William St, Northbridge], *Brass Monkey*: Replica of an English pub, even with English-style beer (much stronger than Australian equivalents) brewed by Matilda Bay Brewing Co; very friendly staff, and the re-creation of an English pub has been done particularly well *(Richard Houghton)*

Wilmington [Main St], *Wilmington*: Very pleasant, with nice staff and friendly locals – one of the few country pubs where women might feel comfortable; serve Coopers Stout, and bottled real ales *(Richard Houghton)*

AUSTRIA

Seefeld, *Britannia*: English-theme pub in the Tyrol – cribbage, dominoes, shove-ha'penny, draught beer, bottled Guinness, good choice of whiskies, simple food including Heinz beans, even a red telephone box; express waitress service *(Steve Mitcheson, Anne Collins)*

BARBADOS

St Philip, *Sams Lantern*: Nice relaxed informal atmosphere in small bar on the right, and further drinking area past the restaurant; good martinis and rum-based cocktails, modest but good snack menu such as flying-fish sandwiches, with reasonably priced main dishes in the evening such as grilled chub; wide windows, bright colours and fans make it seem cool; small drinking area outside; just outside the gates of Sam Lords Castle *(J S Evans)*

BELGIUM

Antwerp [Kleine Markt], *Kumulator*: A must for beer enthusiasts – they stock 550, either off the shelf or from the cellar; even the English bottled beers include ones that are very rare here (Courage Russian Stout) or virtually unobtainable (Bass Kings Ale), and the Belgian and other continental ones are quite remarkable *(Graham Gibson)*

Brussels [Grand Place], *Roy d'Espagne*: Spectacular located, particularly when the square is floodlit; large room with tables around central fire, further tables in gallery upstairs and outside; wide range of beers – and one of the few pubs in the world to contain a stuffed horse *(Dr John Innes)*

CANADA

Ashton [Ottawa], *Old Mill*: Very pleasant if a little self-consciously British, run by British couple who do good fish and chips, steak and kidney pie, Cornish pasties, ploughman's and salads; closed Tues *(John Roué)*

Toronto [123 Queen St W], *Good Queen Bess*: Fake English pub in Sheraton Hotel –

but there's a good atmosphere and interesting beer *(Dr and Mrs A K Clarke)*

GREECE

Santorini [Kamari], *Banana Moon*: Stylish cocktail bar, rustic and pretty, with old waggon-wheels built into décor on terrace; helpful English bar staff, amazing range of good if pricey cocktails – try their special made with fresh bananas, banana liqueur, vodka and cream *(Jo and Neil Davenport)*; [Kamari] *Hook Bar*: Small cosy sea-front bar, nothing fancy but plenty of atmosphere with dark wood, candles in bottles, old barrels – one of the cheapest bars on the island, even if the very friendly barman doesn't decide he likes your face and then pours them on the house *(Jo and Neil Davenport)*

LUXEMBOURG

Luxembourg [Rue Albert Unden], *George & Dragon*: Comfortable traditionally furnished large room with friendly atmosphere, range of British and other beers including the delightful local Bofferding; the local wines, notably the sparkling, are worth sampling; appeals to a wide range of tastes including the Luxembourg RUFC – the largest gnomes in international finance *(Thomas Nott)*

SINGAPORE

Singapore [19 Tanglin Rd], *Excalibur*: Straightforward, unpretentious and very friendly, popular with locals and Europeans, draught Tiger, good choice of spirits, bottled Belgian Trappist beer (which has travelled well) *(Mr and Mrs T S C Kucharski)*

SPAIN

Torremolinos [Parcela C; La Nogalera; C/SKAL S/N Local 2306], *Pink Panther*: Pink décor, with soft mauve seats, keeps a cool feel; small dance floor and really friendly welcome from Judy (from England) and Issac *(V N Carr)*

SWITZERLAND

Basel [Rheingasse 45; Route 8 tram from SBB stn], *Fischerstube*: Own-brew pub serving three Ueli beers – Hell (a lager), Dunkel (brown) and superb Spezial; food also excellent, more Baden-Wurttemberg than Swiss; faultless friendly service, and of course the place is spotless; closed Sun *(John C Baker)*
Cery, *Fleur de Lys*: One of the select few pubs that give their names to railway stations (in this case a halt on the Lausanne–Echallens line); good, basic, freshly prepared food – neither Tourist-twee nor French *haute*

cuisine; Boxer beer (perhaps the best in the Suisse Romande) *(John C Baker)*

THAILAND

Phuket [Paradise Beach], *Paradise Bar*: Air stirred by old-fashioned ceiling fans; Singha beer, bar snacks; one of the few bars where a single unchaperoned male is not targeted by the ladies of the town *(G T Jones)*

USA

Berkeley [1 Bolivar Dr; California], *Golden Gate Brewery*: Unusual among US brew-pubs for its ambitious food; simple décor dominated by glass-wall view of the gleaming microbrewery which produces their own ale, porter and light wheat beer; closed Mon, and lunchtimes *(Anon)*; [1920 Shattuck Ave] *Roaring Rock*: High-ceilinged rather cavernous place with own-brewed light ale and porter, very young owners, rock music *(Joel Dobris)*
Cape May [Washington Mall; New Jersey], *Ugly Mug*: Lager served in frozen mugs in this home of the Froth Blowers' Union, who meet here for annual froth-blowing world championships – their hundreds of mugs hang from the ceiling (and are turned towards the sea when they die); tasty seafood, especially fresh tuna *(Ed Hamill)*
Captiva Island [Sanibel; Florida], *Mucky Duck*: Good range of beers from around the world, nice friendly atmosphere, good range of mainly seafood, reasonable prices; a few stools by serving-counter in bar more restaurant than British pubs – in spite of the prints, signs and so forth trying to anglicise it *(J S Evans)*
Carmel [California], *Bully III*: Very good dependable food, pleasant staff, cricket bats on the wall *(PLC)*; *Hogs Breath*: Though more a restaurant than a pub it's worth a visit; owned by Clint Eastwood *(PLC)*
Chicago [901 West Jackson Bvd], *Tap & Growler*: Good choice of character beers brewed on the premises *(Joel Dobris)*
Cleveland [2516 Market Ave; Ohio], *Great Lakes Brewing Co*: Newish brew-pub with big window into brewing-room which produces two or three real ales including a light lager and dark amber beer; simple home-made food *(Anon)*
Clifton [River Rd; nr Route 3; New Jersey], *Rutts Hutt*: Started as a 1930s road stand – has original knotty pine décor; best hot dogs on the East Coast, cold fresh lager, handy for New York City via Lincoln Tunnel *(Ed Hamill)*
Davis [132 E St; California], *Mansion Cellars*: Wide range of bottled beers including dozens of imports, tables outside, snacks *(Joel Dobris)*; *Pistachios*: Serious wine and beer bar with terrace – popular college hang-out; nearly 100 bottled beers including

lots from Europe and the new dry Japanese beers; about three dozen keg beers, again including many Europeans *(Joel Dobris)*

Hancock [New Hampshire], *Hancock Inn*: Low beams and booth seating gives eighteenth-century English pub atmosphere; snacks, meals and wide choice of bottled beers *(Stephen McNees)*

Los Angeles [536 East 8th St; California], *Gorkys*: Airy cafe-bar with food including good Russian pastries and hot dishes; now brewing its own beers, including an Imperial Russian Stout, and has a branch in Hollywood (1716 N Cahuenga Bvd); open all day and night *(Joel Dobris)*

Muir Beach [from Highway 101 take Stinson Beach/Highway 1 exit; California], *Pelican*: Perfect replica of a British pub, nothing jarring or out of place, and no Ye Olde Tea Shoppe feeling: sixteenth-century low-beamed Tudor bar, big inglenook fireplace, cottage pie, rack of lamb and other English dishes; draught Bass, Courage, Watneys and Guinness, bottled Belhaven, Ruddles County and Theakstons Old Peculier; bedrooms with half-tester beds and old English furnishings *(Alan Franck and others)*

New York [93 South St Seaport; New York], *North Star*: In the centre of South Street Seaport – a group of restored warehouses and quays with a couple of full-rigged ships as background; a good imitation of an English pub with dark green lincrusta ceiling, wall mirrors, oak furniture, handpumps for the Bass and Watneys, good choice of English bottled beers, and real English food including fish and chips, steak and kidney pie, and delicious bangers and mash *(Patrick Young)*

North Conway [New Hampshire], *Scottish Lion*: Tartan walls and carpet, varied beer, excellent mixed drinks with free munchies; the restaurant specialises in good Scottish food *(Stephen McNees)*

Philadelphia [Head House Sq; 2nd and Pine Sts; Pennsylvania], *Dickens*: Dickens beer from Tooley St, London, with Bass and Guinness on tap, bottled Fullers ESB, London Pride, Sam Smiths and other English ales, friendly British pub atmosphere, good bar food including Cornish pasties, pâté, ploughman's, toad-in-the-hole, shepherd's pie, beef and mushroom pie; darts, good restaurant, shop selling scones and so forth as well as takeaway bar food; remarkably good English-style chips *(Paul Weinberg)*

Sacramento [1001 R St; California], *Fox & Goose*: Landlord from Yorkshire, good food using fresh ingredients and including English specialities, serving several types of tea and coffee as well as a good choice of English and other beers *(Joel Dobris)*; [2004 Capitol Ave; California] *Rubicon Brewing* Co: Pleasant noisy brew-pub with blonde furniture and hi-tech industrial-style décor, producing their

own attractive Pale and Amber ales, Steed summer wheat beer, delicious Summer Stout and dark steely Ol Moeller; sandwiches, snacks, salads; popular with the thirty-somethings *(Joel Dobris)*

San Francisco [Van Ness/Geary; California], *Jimmy's Joynt*: Imported beers from all over the world, vary daily, great atmosphere and conversation (on the macho side), very good cafeteria-style food specialising in buffalo-meat stew and Sloppy Joes *(PLC, Ed Hamill)*; [3848 Geary; California] *Pat O'Shea's Mad Hatter*: Busy Irish sports saloon with good, unusual beers and interesting beers including draught English beers and good bottled ones – the Palo Alto Brewery beers, brewed to English ale recipes, are always worth looking out for in the Bay area *(PLC)*

Santa Rosa [99 6th St; California], *Xcelsior Brewery*: Not a pub but a small brewery which can be visited (tel 707–578–1497); their Acme Beer is brewed additive-free to Reinheitsgebot purity standard *(Anon)*

Saratoga [Big Basin Rd; California], *English Pub*: English food such as fish and chips and steak and kidney pie – even a couple of cricket teams *(PLC)*

Savanna [Georgia], *Crystal Beer Parlor*: Archetypal American long bar with fine Southern hospitality, good beer, fine food served with freshly baked corn loaves including outstanding seafood gumbo *(Ed Hamill)*

Seattle [The Market; Washington], *Pikes Place*: Worth a visit for its collection of British beers – over 40 when I was last there *(Cyril Aydon)*

Sunnyvale [next to Hilton Hotel; California], *Rusty Scupper*: Usual range of American beers in pleasant surroundings, food specialising in seafood and including outstanding gazpacho served in attractive multi-level area; in the heart of Silicon Valley, British voices often heard *(PLC)*

Washington [1523 22nd St, NW], *Brickskeller*: Amazing choice of beers from nearly 50 countries – claims to be the world's largest range, with dozens each from Britain and Germany and numerous US microbrewery beers; games-bar a bit like a successful contractor's recreation room; food from burgers to buffalo steaks in bare brick, stone-floored and gingham tablecloth dining-room *(Joel Dobris)*

White River Junction [58 South Main St], *Catamount Brewing* Co: Not a pub but a small brewery which can be toured (at least in summer) 11am Tues–Sat; brews strong and interesting Amber and Gold, to exacting additive-free standards *(Anon)*

VENEZUELA

Caracas [Av Rio de Janeiro; Las Mercedes], *Dog & Fox*: Half-timbered English pub with jettied upper floor, a few hunting prints looking a little lost inside, local cowboys mixing with young Brits, local blue-collar workers and trendier types; loud piped music *(John Roué)*

WEST GERMANY

Cologne [100 yds from cathedral], *P J Fruhs*: Famous for brewing its own elegant Kolschbier, served from a barrel by the door and delivered by specially dressed waiters; busy and lively big drinking hall with snugs opening off, good restaurant food; friendly atmosphere *(Graham Bush)*; [Waterfront] *Papa Joes*: Lively jazz pub *(Graham Bush)*
Gluckstadt [Am Fleth 4], *Millieways*: English-run bar with darts, smoked Cumberland sausage, Guinness and bottled Charles Wells Bombardier as well as more continental food, drink and amusements *(Anon)*
Heidelberg [main st, below Schloss], *Sepp'l*: Panelled student pub with lots of college photographs, liberated road signs, names and so forth carved by customers on tables, walls and even ceiling; Bitburger or Heidelberger Pils, 'boots of beer' drinking contests, singalong piano – even English folk songs *(Graham Bush)*
Wiesbaden [Michelsberg 9], *Stortebeker*: First-class food and prompt service in scrupulously clean 'pub' in pedestrian shopping area, maybe free jazz 11am Sun (even free Sun brunch for small children); very reasonable prices *(L V Nutton)*

Special interest lists

Pubs with good gardens

The pubs listed here have bigger or more beautiful gardens, grounds or terraces than are usual for their areas. Note that in a town or city this might be very much more modest than the sort of garden that would deserve a listing in the countryside.

BERKSHIRE
Aldworth, Bell; Four Points
Hampstead Norreys, New Inn
Hamstead Marshall, White Hart
Holyport, Belgian Arms
Hungerford, Bear
Hurley, Dew Drop
Marsh Benham, Red House
West Ilsley, Harrow
Wickham, Five Bells
Winterbourne, New Inn

BUCKINGHAMSHIRE
Akeley, Bull & Butcher
Amersham, Queens Head
Bledlow, Lions of Bledlow
Bolter End, Peacock
Chesham, Black Horse
Fawley, Walnut Tree
Fingest, Chequers
Hambleden, Stag & Huntsman
Hawridge Common, Full Moon
Lacey Green, Pink & Lily
Little Horwood, Shoulder of Mutton
Marsh Gibbon, Greyhound
Marsworth, Red Lion
Northend, White Hart
Penn, Crown
Skirmett, Old Crown
The Lee, Old Swan
West Wycombe, George & Dragon
Whitchurch, White Swan
Worminghall, Clifden Arms

CAMBRIDGESHIRE AND BEDFORDSHIRE
Bolnhurst, Olde Plough
Chatteris, Crafty Fox
Coton, Plough
Eltisley, Leeds Arms
Fowlmere, Chequers
Heydon, King William IV
Horningsea, Plough & Fleece
Southill, White Horse
Swavesey, Trinity Foot
Wansford, Haycock

CHESHIRE
Alvanley, White Lion
Brereton Green, Bears Head
Goostrey, Olde Red Lion
Lower Peover, Bells of Peover
Lower Whitley, Chetwode Arms
Sutton, Sutton Hall

CORNWALL
Helford, Shipwrights Arms
Manaccan, New Inn
Philleigh, Roseland
Trebarwith, Mill House

CUMBRIA
Barbon, Barbon Inn
Bassenthwaite, Pheasant
Eskdale Green, Bower House
Grasmere, Wordsworth
Warwick-on-Eden, Queens Arms

DERBYSHIRE AND STAFFORDSHIRE
Alrewas, George & Dragon
Birch Vale, Sycamore
Burton on Trent, Albion
Buxton, Bull i' th' Thorn
Grindleford, Maynard Arms
Grindon, Cavalier
Little Longstone, Packhorse
Melbourne, John Thompson
Onecote, Jervis Arms
Rowsley, Peacock
Tutbury, Olde Dog & Partridge

DEVON
Blagdon, Barton Pines
Doddiscombsleigh, Nobody Inn
Exminster, Turf
Haytor Vale, Rock
Newton Abbot, Two Mile Oak
Sidford, Blue Ball
South Zeal, Oxenham Arms
Torbryan, Old Church House

DORSET
Chedington, Winyards Gap
Christchurch, Fishermans Haunt
Hurn, Avon Causeway
Lytchett Minster, Bakers Arms
Nettlecombe, Marquis of Lorne
Osmington Mills, Smugglers
Sandford Orcas, Mitre
Shave Cross, Shave Cross
Stoke Abbott, New Inn
Tarrant Monkton, Langton Arms
West Bexington, Manor Hotel

ESSEX
Bannister Green, Three Horseshoes
Castle Hedingham, Bell
Chappel, Swan
Great Henny, Swan
Great Yeldham, White Hart
Hastingwood, Rainbow & Dove
Mill Green, Viper
Newney Green, Duck
Peldon, Rose
Stock, Hoop
Toot Hill, Green Man
Woodham Walter, Cats

GLOUCESTERSHIRE
Alderton, Gardeners Arms
Ampney Crucis, Crown of Crucis
Ewen, Wild Duck
Fossebridge, Fossebridge Inn
Great Rissington, Lamb
Kingscote, Hunters Hall
Lechlade, Trout
North Nibley, New Inn
Redbrook, Boat
Sapperton, Daneway
Southrop, Swan
Withington, Mill

HAMPSHIRE
Battramsley, Hobler
Bramdean, Fox
Emery Down, New Forest Inn

Fawley, Jolly Sailor
Linwood, High Corner
Longparish, Plough
Newtown, Travellers Rest
Ovington, Bush
Owslebury, Ship
Pennington, Chequers
Petersfield, White Horse
Romsey, Luzborough House
Steep, Harrow
Stockbridge, Vine
Tichborne, Tichborne Arms
Timsbury, Bear & Ragged
   Staff
Turgis Green, Jekyll & Hyde

HEREFORD &
   WORCESTER
Bretforton, Fleece
Fownhope, Green Man
Ross on Wye, Hope &
   Anchor
Sellack, Loughpool
Weatheroak Hill, Coach &
   Horses
Woolhope, Butchers Arms

HERTFORDSHIRE
Ayot St Lawrence, Brocket
   Arms
Great Offley, Green Man
Letchmore Heath, Three
   Horseshoes
Much Hadham, Bull
Newgate Street, Coach &
   Horses
Puckeridge, White Hart

HUMBERSIDE
Kirkburn, Queens Head
South Dalton, Pipe & Glass
Sutton upon Derwent, St
   Vincent Arms

ISLE OF WIGHT
Chale, Clarendon (Wight
   Mouse)

KENT
Biddenden, Three Chimneys
Bough Beech, Wheatsheaf
Chiddingstone, Castle
Cobham, Leather Bottle
Dargate, Dove
Groombridge, Crown
Newnham, George
Pett Bottom, Duck
Ringlestone, Ringlestone
Smarden, Bell
Stowting, Tiger
Weald, Chequer Tree

LANCASHIRE
Burnley, Coal Clough House
Clayton le Moors, Dunk Inn
Darwen, Old Rosins

Haslingden, Duke of
   Wellington
Newton, Parkers Arms
Uppermill, Cross Keys
Whitewell, Inn at Whitewell

LEICESTERSHIRE,
   LINCOLNSHIRE AND
   NOTTINGHAMSHIRE
Drakeholes, Griff Inn
Newton, Red Lion
Old Dalby, Crown
Scaftworth, King William
Stamford, George of
   Stamford
Sutton in the Elms, Mill on
   the Soar
Upton, French Horn

MIDLANDS
Ashby St Ledgers, Old
   Coach House
Berkswell, Bear
East Haddon, Red Lion
Eastcote, Eastcote Arms
Ettington, Chequers
Farnborough, Butchers
   Arms
Ilmington, Howard Arms
Stratford-upon-Avon, Slug
   & Lettuce
Thorpe Mandeville, Three
   Conies
West Bromwich, Manor
   House

NORFOLK
Brancaster Staithe, Jolly
   Sailors
Brandon Creek, Ship
Letheringsett, Kings Head
Reedham, Ferry Inn
Titchwell, Manor

NORTHUMBRIA
Blanchland, Lord Crewe
   Arms
Greta Bridge, Morritt Arms
Longhorsley, Linden Pub
Piercebridge, George

OXFORDSHIRE
Binfield Heath, Bottle &
   Glass
Brightwell Baldwin, Lord
   Nelson
Burford, Lamb
Chinnor, Sir Charles Napier
Clifton Hampden, Barley
   Mow
Fyfield, White Hart
Goring Heath, King Charles
   Head
Maidensgrove, Five
   Horseshoes
Minster Lovell, Old Swan

Moulsford, Beetle & Wedge
Newbridge, Rose Revived
Noke, Plough
Shipton-under-Wychwood,
   Shaven Crown
Sonning Common, Butchers
   Arms
South Leigh, Mason Arms
South Stoke, Perch & Pike
Stanton Harcourt, Harcourt
   Arms
Stanton St John, Star
Stoke Row, Crooked Billet
Tadpole Bridge, Trout
Watlington, Chequers

SHROPSHIRE
Bishop's Castle, Three Tuns
Upper Farmcote, Lion of
   Morfe

SOMERSET AND AVON
Ashcott, Ashcott Inn
Axbridge, Lamb
Brendon Hills, Raleghs
   Cross
Combe Hay, Wheatsheaf
Dunster, Luttrell Arms
Monksilver, Notley Arms
Over Stratton, Royal Oak
Shepperdine, Windbound
South Stoke, Pack Horse
Tintinhull, Crown &
   Victoria
Tormarton, Compass
West Huntspill, Crossways

SUFFOLK
Blythburgh, White Hart
Brandeston, Queens Head
Easton, White Horse
Hoxne, Swan
Laxfield, Kings Head
Rede, Plough
Walberswick, Bell

SURREY
Batts Corner, Blue Bell
Chipstead, Well House
Coldharbour, Plough
Ewhurst, Windmill
Fickleshole, White Bear
Hascombe, White Horse
Horley, Olde Six Bells
Laleham, Three Horseshoes
Leigh, Seven Stars
Mickleham, King William IV
Newdigate, Surrey Oaks
Norwood Hill, Fox Revived
Outwood, Bell; Dog & Duck
Pirbright, Royal Oak
Pyrford Lock, Anchor
Warlingham, White Lion

SUSSEX
Blackboys, Blackboys

Byworth, Black Horse
Charlton, Fox Goes Free
Coolham, George & Dragon
Elsted, Three Horseshoes
Fittleworth, Swan
Fulking, Shepherd & Dog
Gun Hill, Gun
Heathfield, Star
Houghton, George & Dragon
Lindfield, Bent Arms
Ringmer, Cock
Rowhook, Chequers
Rushlake Green, Horse & Groom
Seaford, Golden Galleon
Sidlesham, Crab & Lobster
Winchelsea, New Inn
Wineham, Royal Oak

WILTSHIRE
Alvediston, Crown
Bradford-on-Avon, Cross Guns
Chicksgrove, Compasses
Everleigh, Crown
Lacock, Rising Sun
Landford, Cuckoo
Lower Woodford, Wheatsheaf
Norton, Vine Tree
Seend, Barge

YORKSHIRE
Bolton Percy, Crown
Egton Bridge, Horse Shoe
Harrogate, Squinting Cat
Penistone, Cubley Hall
Threshfield, Old Hall
Wentworth, Rockingham Arms

LONDON, CENTRAL
Cross Keys, SW3
Red Lion, W1

LONDON, NORTH
Flask, N6
Spaniards, NW3
Waterside, N1

LONDON, SOUTH
Crown & Greyhound, SE21
Ship, SW18
White Swan, Richmond

LONDON, WEST
Dove, W6
Old Ship, W6
Windsor Castle, W8

SCOTLAND
Aberdeen, Ferryhill House Hotel
Ardfern, Galley of Lorne

Arduaine, Loch Melfort Hotel
Cleish, Nivingston House
Gifford, Tweeddale Arms
Kilchrenan, Taychreggan
Kilmelford, Cuilfail
Newburgh, Udny Arms
Pitlochry, Killiecrankie Hotel
Skeabost, Skeabost House Hotel
Spean Bridge, Letterfinlay Lodge Hotel
Tweedsmuir, Crook

WALES
Aberystwyth, Halfway Inn
Bodfari, Dinorben Arms
Crickhowell, Bear
Dinas, Sailors Safety
Llandrindod Wells, Llanerch
Llanfrynach, White Swan
Llanrwst, Maenan Abbey
Llanthony, Abbey
Llwyndafydd, Crown
Marianglas, Parciau Arms
Nevern, Trewern Arms
Old Radnor, Harp
Tremeirchion, Salusbury Arms
Wolf's Castle, Wolfe

CHANNEL ISLANDS
Castel, Hougue du Pommier
Sark, Stocks Hotel
St Martin, Auberge Divette

Waterside pubs

The pubs listed here are right beside the sea, a sizeable river, canal, lake or loch that contributes significantly to their attraction.

BERKSHIRE
Great Shefford, Swan
Hungerford, Bear
Kintbury, Dundas Arms

CAMBRIDGESHIRE AND BEDFORDSHIRE
Cambridge, Boathouse
Holywell, Olde Ferry Boat
Sutton Gault, Anchor
Wansford, Haycock

CHESHIRE
Wrenbury, Dusty Miller

CORNWALL
Bodinnick, Old Ferry
Helford, Shipwrights Arms
Malpas, Heron
Mousehole, Ship
Mylor Bridge, Pandora
Polkerris, Rashleigh

Polperro, Blue Peter
Port Isaac, Port Gaverne Hotel
Porthleven, Ship
St Mawes, Rising Sun

CUMBRIA
Biggar, Queens Arms
Sandside, Ship
Ulverston, Bay Horse

DERBYSHIRE AND STAFFORDSHIRE
Cheddleton, Boat
Consall, Black Lion
Onecote, Jervis Arms
Rowsley, Peacock
Shardlow, Malt Shovel

DEVON
Ashprington, Watermans Arms

Burgh Island, Pilchard
Combeinteignhead, Coombe Cellars
Dartmouth, Royal Castle
Dittisham, Ferry Boat
Exeter, Double Locks
Exminster, Turf
Lynmouth, Rising Sun
Topsham, Passage
Torcross, Start Bay

DORSET
Chesil, Cove House
Chideock, Anchor
Lyme Regis, Pilot Boat

ESSEX
Burnham-on-Crouch, White Harte
Chappel, Swan
Great Henny, Swan
Leigh on Sea, Crooked Billet

GLOUCESTERSHIRE
Fossebridge, Fossebridge Inn
Great Barrington, Fox
Lechlade, Trout
Redbrook, Boat
Withington, Mill

HAMPSHIRE
Bursledon, Jolly Sailor
Fawley, Jolly Sailor
Langstone, Royal Oak
Ovington, Bush
Wherwell, Mayfly

**HEREFORD &
WORCESTER**
Knightwick, Talbot
Ross on Wye, Hope &
Anchor
Upton upon Severn, Swan
Wyre Piddle, Anchor

HUMBERSIDE
Hull, Minerva

ISLE OF WIGHT
Cowes, Folly
Shanklin, Fishermans
Cottage

KENT
Fordwich, Fordwich Arms
Oare, Shipwrights Arms
Whitstable, Pearsons Crab
& Oyster House
Wye, Tickled Trout

LANCASHIRE
Bilsborrow, Owd Nells
Garstang, Th'owd Tithebarn
Heaton with Oxcliffe,
Golden Ball
Manchester, Mark Addy
Whitewell, Inn at Whitewell

**LEICESTERSHIRE,
LINCOLNSHIRE AND
NOTTINGHAMSHIRE**
Cotes, Cotes Mill

MIDLANDS
Netherton, Little Dry Dock
Northampton, Britannia
Old Hill, Wharf
Stoke Bruerne, Boat
Warwick, Saxon Mill

NORFOLK
Brandon Creek, Ship
Reedham, Ferry

NORTHUMBRIA
North Shields, Chain Locker
Piercebridge, George

OXFORDSHIRE
Moulsford, Beetle & Wedge
Newbridge, Rose Revived
Tadpole Bridge, Trout

SHROPSHIRE
Shrewsbury, Boat House
Whitchurch, Willey Moor
Lock

SOMERSET AND AVON
Shepperdine, Windbound

SUFFOLK
Chelmondiston, Butt &
Oyster
Orford, Jolly Sailor
Ramsholt, Ramsholt Arms
Southwold, Harbour

SURREY
Horley, Olde Six Bells
Pyrford Lock, Anchor
Staines, Swan

SUSSEX
Newhaven, Hope

WILTSHIRE
Bradford-on-Avon, Cross
Guns
Salisbury, Avon Brewery
Seend, Barge

YORKSHIRE
Newton on Ouse, Dawnay
Arms
Sowerby Bridge, Moorings
Sprotbrough, Boat
York, Kings Arms

LONDON, CENTRAL
Samuel Pepys, EC4

LONDON, NORTH
Waterside, N1

LONDON, SOUTH
Anchor, SE1
Angel, SE16
Bulls Head, SW13
Horniman, SE1
Old Thameside, SE1
Ship, SW18

LONDON, WEST
City Barge, W4
Dove, W6
Old Ship, W6

LONDON, EAST
Dickens, E1
Grapes, E14

SCOTLAND
Ardfern, Galley of Lorne
Arduaine, Loch Melfort
Hotel
Carbost, Old Inn
Crinan, Crinan Hotel
Elie, Ship
Findhorn, Crown & Anchor
Isle of Whithorn, Steam
Packet
Isle Ornsay, Hotel Eilean
Iarmain
Kilchrenan, Taychreggan
Kippford, Anchor
Plockton, Plockton Hotel
Portpatrick, Crown
Queensferry, Hawes
Shieldaig, Tigh an Eilean
Skeabost, Skeabost House
Hotel
Spean Bridge, Letterfinlay
Lodge Hotel
St Mary's Loch, Tibbie
Shiels Inn
Stein, Stein Inn
Tarbert, West Loch
Tayvallich, Tayvallich Inn

WALES
Aberaeron, Harbourmaster
Broad Haven, Druidstone
Cresswell Quay, Cresselly
Arms
Dinas, Sailors Safety
Little Haven, Swan
Nevern, Trewern Arms
Penarth, Captains Wife
Penmaenpool, George III
Porth Dinllaen, Ty Coch
Red Wharf Bay, Ship

CHANNEL ISLANDS
Rocquaine Bay, Rocquaine
Bistro
St Aubin, Old Court House

Pubs in attractive surroundings

These pubs are in unusually attractive or interesting places – lovely countryside, charming villages, occasionally notable town surroundings. Waterside pubs are listed again here only if their other surroundings are special, too.

BERKSHIRE
Aldworth, Bell
Frilsham, Pot Kiln
Hurley, Dew Drop
Littlewick Green, Cricketers

BUCKINGHAMSHIRE
Bledlow, Lions of Bledlow
Brill, Pheasant
Hambleden, Stag & Huntsman
Hawridge Common, Full Moon
Ibstone, Fox
Little Hampden, Rising Sun
Northend, White Hart
Turville, Bull & Butcher

CAMBRIDGESHIRE AND BEDFORDSHIRE
Barrington, Royal Oak
Chatteris, Crafty Fox
Dullingham, Kings Head

CHESHIRE
Barthomley, White Lion
Bottom of the Oven, Stanley Arms
Great Budworth, George & Dragon
Langley, Leathers Smithy
Lower Peover, Bells of Peover

CORNWALL
Boscastle, Cobweb
Chapel Amble, Maltsters Arms
Lamorna, Lamorna Wink
Lerryn, Ship
Morwenstow, Bush
Polperro, Blue Peter
St Kew, St Kew Inn
Trebarwith, Mill House

CUMBRIA
Bassenthwaite, Pheasant
Biggar, Queens Arms
Boot, Burnmoor
Coniston, Sun
Dent, Sun
Elterwater, Britannia
Hawkshead, Drunken Duck; Kings Arms
Langdale, Old Dungeon Ghyll
Little Langdale, Three Shires
Loweswater, Kirkstile
Melmerby, Shepherds
Mungrisdale, Mill Inn

Scales, White Horse
Ulverston, Bay Horse
Wasdale Head, Wasdale Head Inn

DERBYSHIRE AND STAFFORDSHIRE
Alstonefield, George
Brassington, Olde Gate
Consall, Black Lion
Froggatt Edge, Chequers
Grindon, Cavalier
Hardwick Hall, Hardwick
Little Hucklow, Old Bulls Head
Little Longstone, Packhorse
Monsal Head, Monsal Head Hotel
Over Haddon, Lathkil
Rowarth, Little Mill

DEVON
Branscombe, Fountain Head
Burgh Island, Pilchard
Countisbury, Exmoor Sandpiper
Exminster, Turf
Haytor Vale, Rock
Holne, Church House
Horndon, Elephants Nest
Horsebridge, Royal
Knowstone, Masons Arms
Lustleigh, Cleave
Lydford, Castle
Lynmouth, Rising Sun
North Bovey, Ring of Bells
Peter Tavy, Peter Tavy
Postbridge, Warren House
Rattery, Church House
Sandy Park, Sandy Park
Slapton, Tower

DORSET
Askerswell, Spyway
Chedington, Winyard's Gap
East Chaldon, Sailors Return
Osmington Mills, Smugglers
Powerstock, Three Horseshoes
Rampisham, Tigers Head
Sandford Orcas, Mitre
Worth Matravers, Square & Compass

ESSEX
Bannister Green, Three Horseshoes
Belchamp St Paul, Half Moon
Leigh on Sea, Crooked Billet

Mill Green, Viper
Purleigh, Bell

GLOUCESTERSHIRE
Bledington, Kings Head
Coates, Tunnel House
Cold Aston, Plough
Great Rissington, Lamb
Guiting Power, Olde Inne
Nailsworth, Weighbridge
North Nibley, New Inn
Painswick, Royal Oak
Sapperton, Daneway
St Briavels, George
Stanton, Mount
Stow on the Wold, Queens Head

HAMPSHIRE
Beaulieu, Montagu Arms
East Meon, George
Emery Down, New Forest Inn
Hamble, Olde Whyte Harte
Linwood, High Corner
Ovington, Bush
Pennington, Chequers
Petersfield, White Horse
Soberton, White Lion
Tichborne, Tichborne Arms
Vernham Dean, Boot
Winchester, Eclipse

HEREFORD & WORCESTER
Hanley Castle, Three Kings
Knightwick, Talbot
Ruckhall Common, Ancient Camp
Sellack, Loughpool
Woolhope, Butchers Arms

HERTFORDSHIRE
Chipperfield, Two Brewers
Harpenden, Three Horseshoes
Letchmore Heath, Three Horseshoes
St Alb . , Fighting Cocks
We: .l, Sword in Hand

HUMBERSIDE
South Dalton, Pipe & Glass

ISLE OF WIGHT
Chale, Clarendon (Wight Mouse)

KENT
Boughton Aluph, Flying Horse
Chiddingstone, Castle
Cobham, Leather Bottle
Groombridge, Crown
Lamberhurst, Brown Trout
Luddenham, Mounted Rifleman
Newnham, George
Pett Bottom, Duck
Stowting, Tiger

LANCASHIRE
Blacko, Moorcock
Blackstone Edge, White House
Downham, Assheton Arms
Entwistle, Strawbury Duck
Haslingden, Duke of Wellington
Middleton, Tandle Hill Tavern
Newton, Parkers Arms
Slaidburn, Hark to Bounty
Tockholes, Royal Arms
Uppermill, Cross Keys
Whitewell, Inn at Whitewell

LEICESTERSHIRE, LINCOLNSHIRE AND NOTTINGHAMSHIRE
Glooston, Old Barn
Hallaton, Bewicke Arms
Lyddington, Marquess of Exeter

MIDLANDS
Himley, Crooked House
Warmington, Plough

NORFOLK
Blickling, Buckinghamshire Arms
Brancaster Staithe, Jolly Sailors
Castle Acre, Ostrich
Thornham, Lifeboat

NORTHUMBRIA
Beamish, Sun
Blanchland, Lord Crewe Arms
Craster, Jolly Fisherman
Eggleston, Three Tuns
Etal, Black Bull
High Force, High Force
Moorsholm, Jolly Sailor
Romaldkirk, Rose & Crown

OXFORDSHIRE
Brightwell Baldwin, Lord Nelson
Chinnor, Sir Charles Napier
Christmas Common, Fox & Hounds
Clifton Hampden, Barley Mow
Cropredy, Red Lion
Goring Heath, King Charles Head
Great Tew, Falkland Arms
Hailey, King William IV
Maidensgrove, Five Horseshoes
Minster Lovell, Old Swan
Oxford, Turf
Pishill, Crown
Shenington, Bell
Shipton-under-Wychwood, Shaven Crown
Stoke Row, Crooked Billet
Swinbrook, Swan

SHROPSHIRE
Cardington, Royal Oak
Hope, Stables
Wenlock Edge, Wenlock Edge

SOMERSET AND AVON
Appley, Globe
Ashill, Square & Compass
Axbridge, Lamb
Blagdon, New Inn
Brendon Hills, Ralegh's Cross
Combe Hay, Wheatsheaf
Cranmore, Strode Arms
Exford, White Horse
Stogumber, White Horse
Winsford, Royal Oak

SUFFOLK
Blythburgh, White Hart
Chelsworth, Peacock
Dunwich, Ship
Easton, White Horse
Kersey, Bell
Long Melford, Bull
Ramsholt, Ramsholt Arms
Sutton, Plough
Walberswick, Bell

SURREY
Batts Corner, Blue Bell
Blackbrook, Plough
Chiddingfold, Crown
Cobham, Cricketers
Ewhurst, Windmill
Mickleham, King William IV
Ockley, Punch Bowl
Outwood, Bell
Reigate Heath, Skimmington Castle
Shere, White Horse

SUSSEX
Billingshurst, Blue Ship
Burwash, Bell
Dallington, Swan
Ditchling, Bull
Eastdean, Tiger
Fulking, Shepherd & Dog
Heathfield, Star
Lickfold, Lickfold Inn
Lurgashall, Noahs Ark
Seaford, Golden Galleon
Sidlesham, Crab & Lobster
West Hoathly, Cat
Wineham, Royal Oak

WILTSHIRE
Alvediston, Crown
Bradford-on-Avon, Cross Guns
Castle Combe, White Hart
Ebbesbourne Wake, Horseshoe
Lacock, Rising Sun
Landford, Cuckoo
Wootton Rivers, Royal Oak

YORKSHIRE
Arncliffe, Falcon
Askrigg, Kings Arms
Bainbridge, Rose & Crown
Blakey Ridge, Lion
Bolton Percy, Crown
Bradfield, Strines
Buckden, Buck
Burnsall, Red Lion
Byland Abbey, Abbey
Cray, White Lion
Heath, Kings Arms
Hubberholme, George
Kilburn, Forresters Arms
Kirby Hill, Shoulder of Mutton
Langdale End, Moor Cock
Langthwaite, Red Lion
Lastingham, Blacksmiths Arms
Levisham, Horse Shoe
Linton in Craven, Fountaine
Litton, Queens Arms
Ramsgill, Yorke Arms
Robin Hood's Bay, Laurel
Rosedale Abbey, Milburn Arms; White Horse
Stansfield Moor, Sportsmans Arms
Starbotton, Fox & Hounds
Sutton Howgrave, White Dog
Thornton Watlass, Buck
Wath-in-Nidderdale, Sportsmans Arms
Widdop, Pack Horse

LONDON, CENTRAL
Olde Mitre, EC1

LONDON, NORTH
Spaniards, NW3

LONDON, SOUTH
Crown & Greyhound, SE21

Horniman, SE1
Old Thameside, SE1
Olde Windmill, SW4

LONDON, EAST
Dickens, E1

SCOTLAND
Arduaine, Loch Melfort
  Hotel
Crinan, Crinan Hotel
Edinburgh, Sheep Heid
Glencoe, Clachaig
Kilchrenan, Taychreggan
Loch Eck, Whistlefield
Mountbenger, Gordon Arms

Pitlochry, Killiecrankie
  Hotel
St Mary's Loch, Tibbie
  Shiels Inn
Tweedsmuir, Crook

WALES
Abery :twyth, Halfway Inn
Broad Haven, Druidstone
Bylchau, Sportsmans Arms
Cilcain, White Horse
Dinas, Sailors Safety
Kenfig, Prince of Wales
Llanbedr-y-Cennin, Olde
  Bull
Llanberis, Pen-y-Gwryd

Llanelidan, Leyland Arms
Llangurig, Glansevern Arms
Llanthony, Abbey
Llanwonno, Brynffynon
Maentwrog, Grapes
Old Radnor, Harp
Penderyn, Red Lion
Penmaenpool, George III
Porth Dinllaen, Ty Coch
Red Wharf Bay, Ship

CHANNEL ISLANDS
Sark, Stocks Hotel
St John, Les Fontaines
Trinity, Waters Edge

Pubs with good views

These pubs are listed for their particularly good views, either from inside or from a garden or terrace. Waterside pubs are listed again here only if their view is exceptional in its own right – not just a straightforward sea view, for example.

BERKSHIRE
Chieveley, Blue Boar

BUCKINGHAMSHIRE
Brill, Pheasant
Great Brickhill, Old Red
  Lion
Penn, Crown

CHESHIRE
Higher Burwardsley,
  Pheasant
Langley, Hanging Gate;
  Leathers Smithy
Overton, Ring o' Bells
Rainow, Highwayman

CUMBRIA
Cartmel Fell, Masons Arms
Hawkshead, Drunken Duck
Langdale, Old Dungeon
  Ghyll
Loweswater, Kirkstile
Mungrisdale, Mill Inn
Sandside, Ship
Ulverston, Bay Horse
Wasdale Head, Wasdale
  Head Inn

**DERBYSHIRE AND
  STAFFORDSHIRE**
Foolow, Barrel
Monsal Head, Monsal Head
  Hotel
Over Haddon, Lathkil

DEVON
Blagdon, Barton Pines
Burgh Island, Pilchard
Hennock, Palk Arms
Postbridge, Warren House

DORSET
Chedington, Winyard's Gap
West Bexington, Manor
  Hotel
Worth Matravers, Square &
  Compass

ESSEX
Purleigh, Bell

GLOUCESTERSHIRE
Stanton, Mount
Woodchester, Ram

HAMPSHIRE
Owslebury, Ship

**HEREFORD &
  WORCESTER**
Ruckhall Common, Ancient
  Camp
Wyre Piddle, Anchor

HERTFORDSHIRE
Great Offley, Green Man

LANCASHIRE
Blacko, Moorcock
Blackstone Edge, White
  House
Darwen, Old Rosins
Entwistle, Strawbury Duck
Mereclough, Kettledrum
Tockholes, Royal Arms
Uppermill, Cross Keys

NORTHUMBRIA
Eggleston, Three Tuns
Seahouses, Olde Ship
Tynemouth, Wooden Doll

SHROPSHIRE
Hope, Stables

SOMERSET AND AVON
Blagdon, New Inn
Brendon Hills, Ralegh's
  Cross

SUFFOLK
Hundon, Plough
Levington, Ship

SURREY
Ewhurst, Windmill

SUSSEX
Dallington, Swan
Houghton, George &
  Dragon

WILTSHIRE
Lacock, Rising Sun

YORKSHIRE
Blakey Ridge, Lion
Bradfield, Strines
Grenoside, Cow & Calf
Kirby Hill, Shoulder of
  Mutton
Litton, Queens Arms
Rosedale Abbey, White
  Horse

LONDON, SOUTH
Angel, SE16

SCOTLAND
Ardvasar, Ardvasar Hotel
Crinan, Crinan Hotel
Glencoe, Clachaig

Isle Ornsay, Hotel Eilean
  Iarmain
Pitlochry, Killiecrankie
  Hotel
Shieldaig, Tigh an Eilean
St Mary's Loch, Tibbie
  Shiels Inn
Weem, Ailean Chraggan

WALES
Aberystwyth, Halfway Inn
Bodfari, Dinorben Arms
Broad Haven, Druidstone
Bylchau, Sportsmans Arms
Llanbedr-y-Cennin, Olde
  Bull
Llanberis, Pen-y-Gwryd
Old Radnor, Harp

Penmaenpool, George III
Porth Dinllaen, Ty Coch

CHANNEL ISLANDS
Rocquaine Bay, Rocquaine
  Bistro
St Aubin, Old Court House
St Martin, Auberge Divette
Trinity, Waters Edge

Pubs in interesting buildings

Pubs and inns are listed here for the particular interest of their building – something
really out of the ordinary to look at, or occasionally a building that has an
outstandingly interesting historical background.

BERKSHIRE
Cookham, Bel & the Dragon

BUCKINGHAMSHIRE
Forty Green, Royal Standard
  of England

CHESHIRE
Sandbach, Old Hall

CORNWALL
Morwenstow, Bush

DERBYSHIRE AND
  STAFFORDSHIRE
Buxton, Bull i' th' Thorn
Derby, Abbey

DEVON
Dartmouth, Cherub
Harberton, Church House
Rattery, Church House
Sourton, Highwayman
South Zeal, Oxenham Arms

HAMPSHIRE
Beauworth, Milbury's
Southampton, Red Lion

HEREFORD &
  WORCESTER
Bretforton, Fleece

HUMBERSIDE
Hull, Olde White Harte

LANCASHIRE
Garstang, Th'owd Tithebarn
Liverpool, Philharmonic

LEICESTERSHIRE,
  LINCOLNSHIRE AND
  NOTTINGHAMSHIRE
Nottingham, Olde Trip to
  Jerusalem
Stamford, George of
  Stamford

MIDLANDS
Birmingham, Bartons Arms
Himley, Crooked House
West Bromwich, Manor
  House

NORFOLK
Scole, Scole Inn

NORTHUMBRIA
Blanchland, Lord Crewe
  Arms

OXFORDSHIRE
Fyfield, White Hart

SOMERSET AND AVON
Norton St Philip, George

SUFFOLK
Long Melford, Bull

SURREY
Chiddingfold, Crown
Shere, White Horse

SUSSEX
Alfriston, Star
Rye, Mermaid

WILTSHIRE
Salisbury, Haunch of
  Venison

LONDON, CENTRAL
Black Friar, EC4
Cittie of York, WC1

LONDON, NORTH
Crockers, NW8

LONDON, SOUTH
George, SE1
Phoenix & Firkin, SE5

LONDON, EAST
Hollands, E1

SCOTLAND
Dumfries, Globe
Edinburgh, Bennets Bar;
  Cafe Royal; Guildford
  Arms
Glasgow, Horseshoe

WALES
Llanthony, Abbey

Pubs that brew their own beer

The pubs listed here brew their own brew on the premises; many others not listed
have beers brewed for them specially, sometimes to an individual recipe (but by a
separate brewer). We mention these in the text.

CORNWALL
Helston, Blue Anchor

DERBYSHIRE AND
  STAFFORDSHIRE
Melbourne, John Thompson

Shraleybrook, Rising Sun

DEVON
Ashburton, London
Horsebridge, Royal

Newton St Cyres, Beer
  Engine

HERTFORDSHIRE
Barley, Fox and Hounds

HUMBERSIDE
Hull, Minerva

LANCASHIRE
Manchester, Lass o' Gowrie

LEICESTERSHIRE,
LINCOLNSHIRE AND
NOTTINGHAMSHIRE
Burrough on the Hill, Stag &
Hounds
Leicester, Tom Hoskins
Nottingham, Fellows
Clayton & Morton

MIDLANDS
Brierley Hill, Vine
Langley, Brewery
Netherton, Old Swan

SHROPSHIRE
Bishop's Castle, Three Tuns
Wistanstow, Plough

SUFFOLK
Earl Soham, Victoria

SUSSEX
Chidham, Old House At
Home
Oving, Gribble

YORKSHIRE
Leeds, Fox & Newt
Linthwaite, Sair
Sheffield, Frog & Parrot

LONDON, CENTRAL
Orange Brewery, SW1

LONDON, SOUTH
Greyhound, SW16
Market Porter, SE1
Phoenix & Firkin, SE5

LONDON, WEST
Ferret & Firkin, SW10

Open all day (at least in summer)

We list here all the pubs that have told us they plan to stay open all day, even if it's
only on a Saturday. We've included the few pubs which close just for half an hour
to an hour, and the many more, chiefly in holiday areas, which open all day only in
summer. The individual entries for the pubs themselves show the actual details.
Some pubs in England and Wales, allowed to stay open only since summer 1988,
are still changing their opening hours – let us know if you find anything different
from what we say.

BERKSHIRE
Brimpton Common,
Pineapple
Cookham Rise, Swan
Uppers
Knowl Hill, Bird in Hand
Littlewick Green, Cricketers

BUCKINGHAMSHIRE
Amersham, Kings Arms
Chalfont St Peter,
Greyhound
Marlow, Ship
Northend, White Hart
Penn, Crown
Stoke Green, Red Lion
The Lee, Old Swan
West Wycombe, George &
Dragon

CAMBRIDGESHIRE AND
BEDFORDSHIRE
Etton, Golden Pheasant
Fowlmere, Chequers
Woburn, Black Horse

CHESHIRE
Chester, Boot
Ollerton, Dun Cow
Plumley, Smoker
Wrenbury, Dusty Miller

CORNWALL
Boscastle, Cobweb
Crows Nest, Crows Nest

Lamorna, Lamorna Wink
Lanner, Fox & Hounds
Lanreath, Punch Bowl
Mousehole, Ship
Mylor Bridge, Pandora
Pendoggett, Cornish Arms
Penzance, Turks Head
Polkerris, Rashleigh
Polperro, Blue Peter
Porthleven, Ship
St Mawes, Rising Sun
St Merryn, Cornish Arms

CUMBRIA
Ambleside, Golden Rule
Barbon, Barbon Inn
Coniston, Sun
Elterwater, Britannia
Hawkshead, Kings Arms
Keswick, Dog & Gun
Kirkby Lonsdale, Snooty
Fox; Sun
Langdale, Old Dungeon
Ghyll
Little Langdale, Three Shires
Warwick-on-Eden, Queens
Arms
Wasdale Head, Wasdale
Head Inn

DERBYSHIRE AND
STAFFORDSHIRE
Bamford, Derwent
Birch Vale, Sycamore
Castleton, Castle

Derby, Abbey; Brunswick
Grindleford, Maynard Arms
Monsal Head, Monsal Head
Hotel
Rowarth, Little Mill
Shardlow, Malt Shovel
Shraleybrook, Rising Sun
Wardlow, Three Stags
Heads

DEVON
Cockwood, Anchor
Combeinteignhead, Coombe
Cellars
Dartmouth, Royal Castle
Dittisham, Ferry Boat
Exeter, Double Locks
Exminster, Turf
Hatherleigh, George
Kingston, Dolphin
Lustleigh, Cleave
Newton St Cyres, Beer
Engine
North Bovey, Ring of Bells
Paignton, Inn on the Green
Postbridge, Warren House
Sandy Park, Sandy Park
Slapton, Tower
Stoke Gabriel, Church
House
Topsham, Globe; Passage

DORSET
Abbotsbury, Ilchester Arms
Bourton, White Lion

Bridport, George
Cerne Abbas, New Inn;
  Royal Oak
Chesil, Cove House
Chideock, Anchor
Langton Herring, Elm Tree
Osmington Mills, Smugglers
West Lulworth, Castle

ESSEX
Danbury, Anchor
Leigh on Sea, Crooked Billet
Saffron Walden, Eight Bells
Stisted, Dolphin
Stock, Hoop

GLOUCESTERSHIRE
Broad Campden, Bakers
  Arms
Chipping Campden, Lygon
  Arms; Noel Arms
Coates, Tunnel House
Guiting Power, Olde Inne
St Briavels, George
Stanton, Mount

HAMPSHIRE
Beaulieu, Montagu Arms
Fawley, Jolly Sailor
Langstone, Royal Oak
Linwood, High Corner
Pennington, Chequers
Romsey, Luzborough House
Soberton, White Lion
Southampton, Red Lion
Wherwell, Mayfly
Winchester, Wykeham Arms

HEREFORD &
  WORCESTER
Inkberrow, Old Bull
Knightwick, Talbot
Ombersley, Crown &
  Sandys Arms
Ross on Wye, Hope &
  Anchor
Worcester, Farriers Arms

HERTFORDSHIRE
Aldbury, Valiant Trooper
St Albans, Fighting Cocks;
  Garibaldi; Goat

HUMBERSIDE
Beverley, White Horse
Brandesburton, Dacre Arms
Hull, George; Olde White
  Harte
Sutton upon Derwent, St
  Vincent Arms

ISLE OF WIGHT
Chale, Clarendon (Wight
  Mouse)
Shalfleet, New Inn

KENT
Boughton Aluph, Flying
  Horse
Boughton Street, White
  Horse
Chilham, Woolpack
Eastling, Carpenters Arms
Tunbridge Wells, Sankeys at
  the Gate
Whitstable, Pearsons Crab
  & Oyster House

LANCASHIRE
Bilsborrow, Owd Nells
Blacko, Moorcock
Broadbottom, Station
Clayton le Moors, Dunk Inn
Darwen, Old Rosins
Entwistle, Strawbury Duck
Fence, Harpers
Haslingden, Duke of
  Wellington
Liverpool, Philharmonic
Lytham, Captains Cabin
Manchester, Lass o' Gowrie;
  Marble Arch; Royal Oak;
  Tommy Ducks
Uppermill, Cross Keys
Wheatley Lane, Old
  Sparrow Hawk

LEICESTERSHIRE,
  LINCOLNSHIRE AND
  NOTTINGHAMSHIRE
Empingham, White Horse
Lincoln, Wig & Mitre
Lyddington, Marquess of
  Exeter
Newark, Old Kings Arms
Nottingham, Bell; Sir John
  Borlase Warren
Stamford, George of
  Stamford
Sutton in the Elms, Mill on
  the Soar

MIDLANDS
Brierley Hill, Vine
Himley, Crooked House
Preston Bagot, Olde Crab
  Mill
Stoke Bruerne, Boat
Stratford-upon-Avon, Slug
  & Lettuce

NORFOLK
Blakeney, Kings Arms
Brancaster Staithe, Jolly
  Sailors
Norwich, Adam & Eve
Scole, Scole Inn
Tivetshall St Mary, Old Ram

NORTHUMBRIA
Beamish, Sun

Blanchland, Lord Crewe
  Arms
Craster, Jolly Fisherman
Durham, Shakespeare
Longhorsley, Linden Pub
Newcastle upon Tyne,
  Cooperage
Piercebridge, George
Rennington, Masons Arms
Tynemouth, Tynemouth
  Lodge; Wooden Doll

OXFORDSHIRE
Henley-on-Thames, Three
  Tuns
Minster Lovell, Old Swan
Newbridge, Rose Revived
Oxford, Bear; Turf
Sonning Common, Butchers
  Arms

SHROPSHIRE
Bridgnorth, Hollyhead
Clun, Sun
Norton, Hundred House
Shrewsbury, Boat House

SOMERSET AND AVON
Ashill, Square & Compass
Combe Hay, Wheatsheaf
Shepperdine, Windbound
Tolldown, Crown
Tormarton, Compass
West Huntspill, Crossways
Winsford, Royal Oak
Woolverton, Red Lion

SUFFOLK
Barton Mills, Bull
Chelmondiston, Butt &
  Oyster
Clare, Bell
Great Glemham, Crown
Hundon, Plough
Laxfield, Kings Head

SURREY
Bletchingley, Whyte Harte
Chiddingfold, Crown
Coldharbour, Plough
Gomshall, Black Horse
Laleham, Three Horseshoes
Outwood, Dog & Duck
Pyrford Lock, Anchor
Staines, Swan

SUSSEX
Alfriston, Star
Arundel, Swan
Charlton, Fox Goes Free
Coolham, George & Dragon
Elsted, Three Horseshoes
Fittleworth, Swan
Newhaven, Hope
Ringmer, Cock
Withyham, Dorset Arms

WILTSHIRE
Ford, White Hart
Hindon, Lamb
Lacock, Carpenters Arms;
    George; Red Lion
Landford, Cuckoo
Salisbury, Avon Brewery

YORKSHIRE
Askrigg, Kings Arms
Blakey Ridge, Lion
Bradfield, Strines
Cadeby, Cadeby Inn
Egton Bridge, Horse Shoe;
    Postgate
Kilburn, Forresters Arms
Ledsham, Chequers
Leeds, Fox & Newt;
    Whitelocks
Linthwaite, Bulls Head
Masham, White Bear
Redmire, Kings Arms
Saxton, Greyhound
Sheffield, Frog & Parrot
Sprotbrough, Boat
Starbotton, Fox & Hounds
Thornton Watlass, Buck
Wentworth, Rockingham
    Arms
York, Black Swan; Kings
    Arms; Olde Starre

LONDON, CENTRAL
Antelope, SW1
Front Page, SW3
George, W1
Glassblower, W1
Lamb, WC1
Lamb & Flag, WC2
Museum, WC1
Old Cheshire Cheese, EC4
Old Coffee House, W1
Olde Mitre, EC1
Orange Brewery, SW1
Princess Louise, WC1
Samuel Pepys, EC4

LONDON, NORTH
Clifton, NW8
Compton Arms, N1
Crockers, NW8
Flask, N6
Olde White Bear, NW3
Spaniards, NW3
Waterside, N1
White Lion of Mortimer, N4

LONDON, SOUTH
Alma, SW18
Anchor, SE1
Angel, SE16
Bulls Head, SW13
Crown & Greyhound, SE21
George, SE1
Greyhound, SW16
Horniman, SE1
Market Porter, SE1
Old Thameside, SE1
Olde Windmill, SW4
Orange Tree, Richmond
Ship, SW18

LONDON, WEST
Dove, W6
Eel Pie, Twickenham
Ferret & Firkin, SW10
Windsor Castle, W8

LONDON, EAST
Dickens, E1
Hollands, E1

SCOTLAND
Aberdeen, Ferryhill House
    Hotel; Prince of Wales
Ardvasar, Ardvasar Hotel
Blanefield, Carbeth
Broughty Ferry, Fishermans
    Tavern
Carbost, Old Inn
Cawdor, Cawdor Tavern
Cramond, Cramond Inn
Drymen, Salmon Leap
Dumfries, Globe
Edinburgh, Bennets Bar;
    Cafe Royal; Jules;
    Peacock; Sheep Heid
Elie, Ship
Findhorn, Crown & Anchor
Gifford, Tweeddale Arms
Glasgow, Bon Accord;
    Horseshoe; Pot Still;
    Babbity Bowster
Glencoe, Clachaig
Glendevon, Tormaukin
Inverarnan, Inverarnan Inn
Isle of Whithorn, Steam
    Packet
Isle Ornsay, Hotel Eilean
    Iarmain
Kilmartin, Kilmartin Hotel
Kippford, Anchor
Loch Eck, Whistlefield
Moffat, Black Bull
Moniaive, George

Mountbenger, Gordon Arms
Newburgh, Udny Arms
Oban, Oban Bar
Queensferry, Hawes
Selkirk, Queens Head
Shieldaig, Tigh an Eilean
Spean Bridge, Letterfinlay
    Lodge Hotel
St Andrews, Victoria Cafe
St Boswells, Buccleuch Arms
St Mary's Loch, Tibbie
    Shiels Inn
Stein, Stein Inn
Tayvallich, Tayvallich Inn
Tweedsmuir, Crook
Uddingston, Rowan Tree
Ullapool, Morefield Motel
Weem, Ailean Chraggan

WALES
Beaumaris, Olde Bulls Head
Bishopston, Joiners Arms
Cowbridge, Bear
Criccieth, Prince of Wales
East Aberthaw, Blue Anchor
Hay on Wye, Old Black Lion
Llanbedr-y-Cennin, Olde
    Bull
Llanberis, Pen-y-Gwryd
Llandrindod Wells, Llanerch
Llangynwyd, Old House
Llanthony, Abbey
Maentwrog, Grapes
Marianglas, Parciau Arms
Mold, We Three
    Loggerheads
Morfa Nefyn, Bryncynan
Nottage, Rose & Crown
Ogmore, Pelican
Painscastle, Maesllwch Arms
Porth Dinllaen, Ty Coch
Red Wharf Bay, Ship
Talybont-on-Usk, Star

CHANNEL ISLANDS
Gorey, Dolphin
St Aubin, Old Court House
St Helier, La Bourse;
    Lamplighter
St John, Les Fontaines
St Martin, Auberge Divette
St Peter Port, Ship & Crown;
    Taylors
Trinity, Waters Edge

Pubs close to motorway junctions

The number at the start of each line is the number of the junction. Detailed directions are given in the main entry for each pub. In this section, to help you find the pubs quickly before you're past the junction, we give in abbreviated form the name of the chapter where you'll find them in the text.

M1
5: Letchmore Heath
   (Herts)
   2 miles
15: Northampton
   (Midlands)
   3¾ miles
   Stoke Bruerne
   (Midlands)
   3¾ miles
16: Weedon (Midlands)
   3 miles
18: Ashby St Ledgers
   (Midlands)
   4 miles
20: Walcote (Leics etc)
   1½ miles
24: Kegworth (Leics etc)
   under a mile
   Shardlow (Derbys/
   Staffs)
   3½ miles
29: Hardwick Hall (Derbys/
   Staffs)
   4½ miles
35: Grenoside (Yorks)
   3 miles
36: Wentworth (Yorks)
   3 miles

M2
1: Cobham (Kent)
   2½ miles
3: Aylesford (Kent)
   3 miles
6: Luddenham (Kent)
   3½ miles
7: Boughton Street (Kent)
   ½ mile
   Selling (Kent)
   3½ miles

M3
5: Mattingley (Hants)
   3 miles
   Rotherwick (Hants)
   4 miles
7: Dummer (Hants)
   ½ mile

M4
5: Colnbrook (Bucks)
   1¼ miles
9: Holyport (Berks)
   1½ miles
   Littlewick Green
   (Berks)
   3¾ miles

13: Chieveley (Berks)
   3½ miles
14: Great Shefford (Berks)
   ⅓ mile, 2 miles
   Wickham (Berks)
   3 miles
   Hungerford (Berks)
   3 miles
18: Tormarton (Somerset/
   Avon)
   ½ mile
   Tolldown (Somerset/
   Avon)
   ¾ mile
19: Clapton in Gordano
   (Somerset/Avon)
   4 miles
21: Aust (Somerset/Avon)
   ½ mile
37: Nottage (Wales)
   2 miles
   Kenfig (Wales)
   2¼ miles

M5
2: Langley (Midlands)
   1½ miles
5: Dunhampstead
   (Hereford/Worcs)
   3½ miles
9: Bredon (Hereford/
   Worcs)
   4½ miles
16: Almondsbury
   (Somerset/Avon)
   1¼ miles
23: West Huntspill
   (Somerset/Avon)
   2¾ miles
27: Sampford Peverell
   (Devon)
   1 mile
30: Topsham (Devon)
   2 miles
   Woodbury Salterton
   (Devon)
   3½ miles
   Exeter (Devon)
   4 miles

M6
2: Withybrook (Midlands)
   4 miles
6: Birmingham (Midlands)
   2 miles
9: West Bromwich
   (Midlands)
   2 miles

14: Seighford (Derbys/
   Staffs)
   3 miles
   Sandon Bank (Derbys/
   Staffs)
   4½ miles
15: Whitmore (Derbys/
   Staffs)
   3 miles
16: Barthomley (Cheshire)
   1 mile
   Shraleybrook (Derbys/
   Staffs)
   3 miles
17: Sandbach (Cheshire)
   1¼ miles
   Brereton Green
   (Cheshire)
   2 miles
19: Plumley (Cheshire)
   2½ miles
   Great Budworth
   (Cheshire)
   4½ miles
31: Balderstone (Lancs etc)
   2 miles
32: Goosnargh (Lancs etc)
   4 miles
40: Stainton (Cumbria)
   3 miles
   Askham (Cumbria)
   4½ miles
43: Warwick-on-Eden
   (Cumbria)
   2 miles

M11
5: Loughton (Essex)
   2¼ miles
7: Hastingwood (Essex)
   ¼ mile
13: Coton (Cambs/Beds)
   ¾ mile

M18
2: Sprotbrough (Yorks)
   2¾ miles
5: Hatfield Woodhouse
   (Yorks)
   2 miles

M23
9: Horley (Surrey)
   3 miles

M25
5: Chipstead (Kent)
   1¼ miles

6: Bletchingley (Surrey)
2¼ miles
7: Chipstead (Surrey)
3½ miles
8: Reigate Heath (Surrey)
3 miles
Betchworth (Surrey)
4 miles
10: Cobham (Surrey)
3 miles
13: Staines (Surrey)
2 miles
19: Chipperfield (Herts)
2¼ miles

M27
3: Romsey (Hants)
3 miles
8: Bursledon (Hants)
2 miles
Hamble (Hants)
3 miles

M40
2: Forty Green (Bucks)
3½ miles
5: Ibstone (Bucks)
1 mile

Bolter End (Bucks)
4 miles
6: Watlington (Oxon)
2¼ miles
7: Little Milton (Oxon)
2½ miles

M50
1: Shuthonger (Gloucs)
1 mile

M55
1: Broughton (Lancs etc)
3½ miles

M56
10: Higher Whitley
(Cheshire)
1¼ miles
Lower Whitley
(Cheshire)
2¼ miles
Little Leigh (Cheshire)
4½ miles
12: Overton (Cheshire)
2 miles
14: Alvanley (Cheshire)
2½ miles

M62
34: Cridling Stubbs (Yorks)
3½ miles
M65
7: Clayton le Moors
(Lancs etc)
½ mile
12: Fence (Lancs etc)
2¾ miles

M69
2: Sutton in the Elms
(Leics etc)
3¼ miles

M73
6: Uddingston (Scotland)
1 mile

M90
5: Cleish (Scotland)
1½ miles

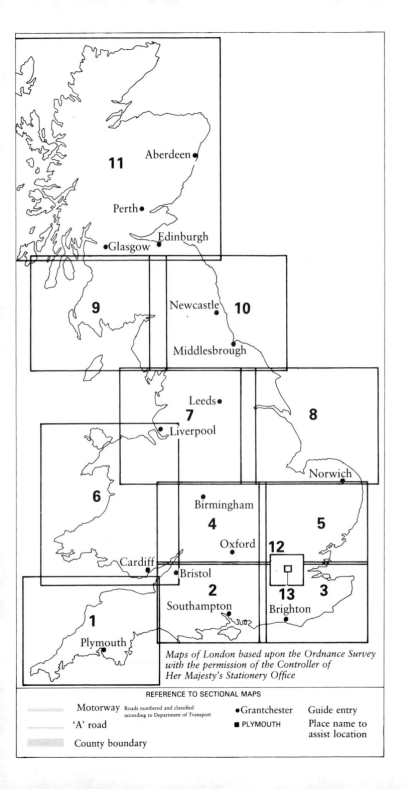

Aberdeen •

11

Perth •

Edinburgh •
• Glasgow

9

Newcastle • **10**

Middlesbrough •

Leeds •

7

• Liverpool

8

Norwich •

6

Birmingham •

4

5

Oxford •

12

Cardiff •
• Bristol

2

Southampton •

Brighton •

13

3

1

Plymouth •

*Maps of London based upon the Ordnance Survey
with the permission of the Controller of
Her Majesty's Stationery Office*

REFERENCE TO SECTIONAL MAPS

	Motorway	Roads numbered and classified according to Department of Transport	• Grantchester	Guide entry
	'A' road		■ PLYMOUTH	Place name to assist location
	County boundary			

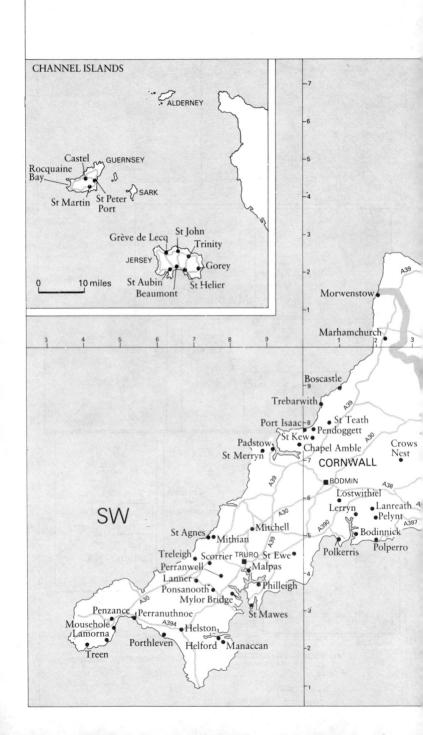

CHANNEL ISLANDS

ALDERNEY

GUERNSEY
Castel
Rocquaine
Bay
St Martin
St Peter
Port
SARK

Grève de Lecq
St John
Trinity
JERSEY
Gorey
St Aubin
St Helier
Beaumont

0   10 miles

3   4   5   6   7   8   9

Morwenstow

Marhamchurch
1   2   3

Boscastle
9

Trebarwith

Port Isaac
8   St Teath
Pendoggett
St Kew
Padstow
Chapel Amble
St Merryn
CORNWALL

BODMiN
Lostwithiel
6
Lerryn   Lanreath 4
Pelynt
SW
Bodinnick
Polperro
St Agnes   Mitchell
5
Treleigh   St Ewe
Mithian   Polkerris
Scorrier   TRURO
Perranwell   Malpas
Lanner   Philleigh
Ponsanooth   4
Mylor Bridge
Penzance   St Mawes
3
Perranuthnoe
Mousehole   Helston
Lamorna   A394
Porthleven   Helford   Manaccan
Treen   2

Crows
Nest

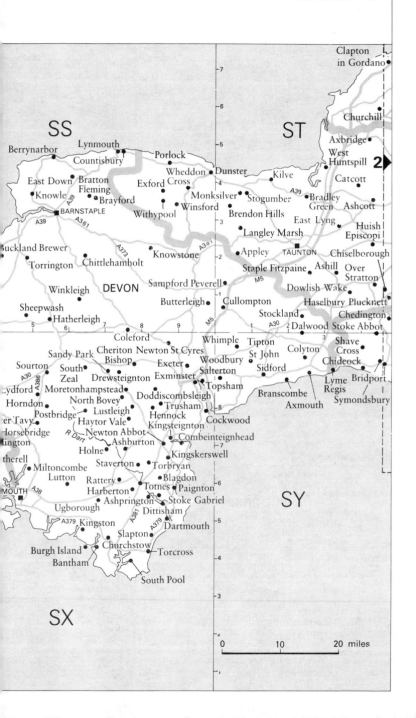

MAP 1

SS

ST

2

Clapton in Gordano●

Churchill●

Axbridge●

West Huntspill●

Catcott●

Berrynarbor●
Lynmouth●
Countisbury
Porlock●

Wheddon Cross
Dunster●
Kilve●

East Down●
Bratton Fleming●
Exford●
Monksilver●
Stogumber●
Bradley Green●
Ashcott●

Knowle●
Brayford●
Winsford●
Brendon Hills●
East Lyng●

BARNSTAPLE■
A39
A361
Withypool●

Langley Marsh●
Huish Episcopi●

●uckland Brewer
A373
Knowstone●
Appley●
TAUNTON■
Chiselborough●

Torrington●
Chittlehamholt●
Staple Fitzpaine●
Ashill●
Over Stratton●

Winkleigh●
DEVON
Sampford Peverell●
Dowlish Wake●
Haselbury Plucknett●

Sheepwash●
Butterleigh●
Cullompton●
Stockland●
Chedington●

Hatherleigh●
Stoke Abbot●

5
6
7
8
9
Coleford●
Whimple●
Tipton St John●
Colyton●
Shave Cross●

Sandy Park●
Cheriton Bishop●
Newton St Cyres●
Woodbury Salterton●
Chideock●

Sourton●
South Zeal●
Exeter●
Sidford●

●ydford
A386
Drewsteignton●
Exminster●
Lyme Regis●
Bridport●

Horndon●
Moretonhampstead●
Topsham●
Branscombe●
Axmouth●
Symondsbury●

●r Tavy
North Bovey●
Doddiscombsleigh●

●orsebridge
Postbridge●
Lustleigh●
Trusham●
Cockwood●

●ington
Haytor Vale●
Hennock●
Kingsteignton●

●therell
Newton Abbot●
Combeinteignhead●

Miltoncombe●
Holne●
Ashburton●

●OUTH
Lutton●
Staverton●
Kingskerswell●

A38
Rattery●
Torbryan●
SY

Harberton●
Blagdon●

Ugborough●
Ashprington●
Totnes●
Paignton●
Stoke Gabriel●

A379
Kingston●
Dittisham●

Slapton●
Dartmouth●

Burgh Island●
Churchstow●
Torcross●

Bantham●
South Pool●

SX

0   10   20 miles

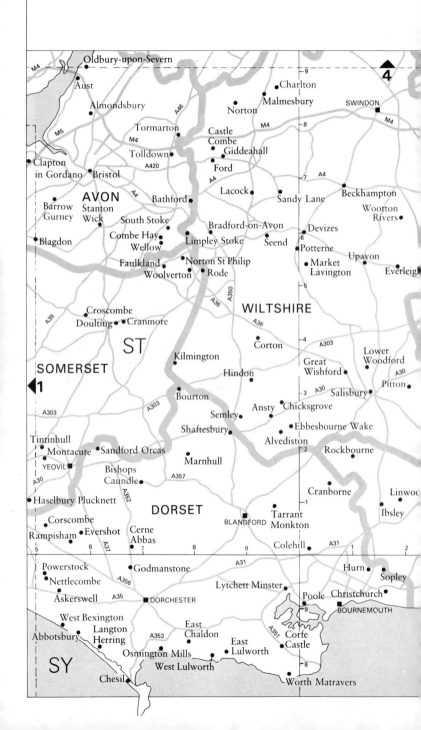

MAP 2

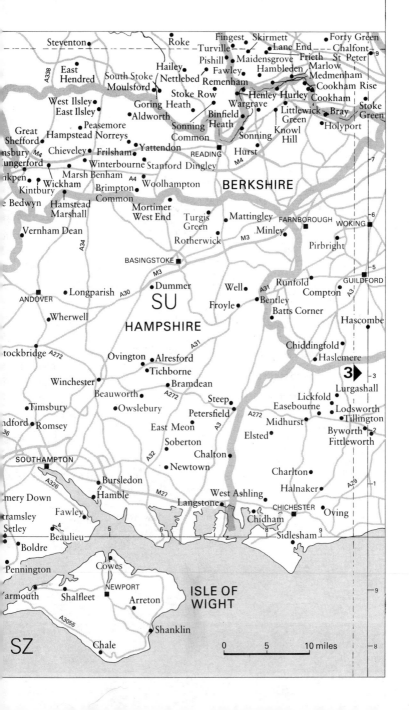

Steventon •   Roke •   Fingest • Skirmett •   • Forty Green

Turville • Lane End   Chalfont St Peter

Pishill • Maidensgrove   Frieth

Hailey •   Fawley • Hambleden   Marlow   Medmenham

East Hendred •   South Stoke   Nettlebed   Remenham   Cookham Rise

Moulsford • Stoke Row   Henley Hurley   Cookham

West Ilsley •   Goring Heath   Wargrave   Stoke Green

East Ilsley •   Aldworth •   Binfield Heath   Littlewick Green   Bray

Peasemore •   Sonning Common   Holyport

Great Shefford • Hampstead Norreys   Sonning   Knowl Hill

nsbury   Chieveley • Frilsham • Yattendon   Hurst

ungerford •   Winterbourne Stanford Dingley   READING

nkpen • Wickham   Marsh Benham   Woolhampton   **BERKSHIRE**

Kintbury • Brimpton Common

e Bedwyn   Hamstead Marshall

Vernham Dean •   Mortimer West End   Turgis Green   Mattingley   FARNBOROUGH   WOKING

Rotherwick   Minley

BASINGSTOKE ■   Pirbright

ANDOVER   Longparish   Dummer   Well •   Runfold   GUILDFORD

SU   Froyle •   Bentley •   Compton

Wherwell •   **HAMPSHIRE**   Batts Corner

Hascombe

tockbridge   Ovington • Alresford   Chiddingfold •   Haslemere

Tichborne   **3▶**   Lurgashall

Winchester •   Bramdean   Lickfold •

Beauworth •   Steep •   Easebourne   Lodsworth

Timsbury •   Owslebury •   Petersfield   Midhurst   Tillington

dford • Romsey   East Meon   Elsted •   Byworth

Soberton   Fittleworth

SOUTHAMPTON   Chalton •

Newtown •   Charlton •

mery Down   Bursledon •   Halnaker •

Fawley   Hamble •   West Ashling   Oving

ramsley   Langstone   CHICHESTER ■

Setley   Beaulieu   Chidham   Sidlesham

Boldre •

Pennington •   Cowes

armouth •   Shalfleet •   NEWPORT   Arreton •   **ISLE OF WIGHT**

SZ   Chale •   Shanklin •

0   5   10 miles

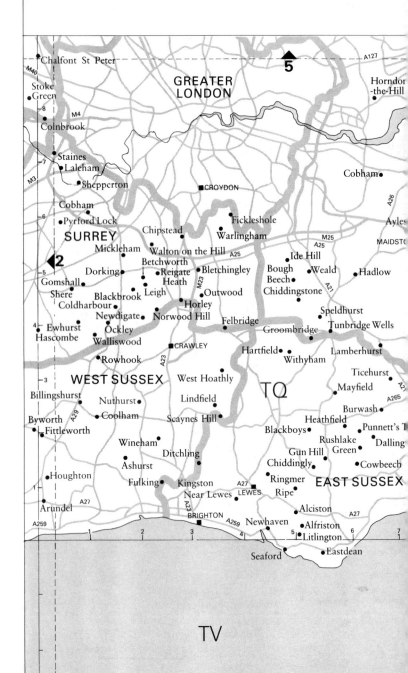

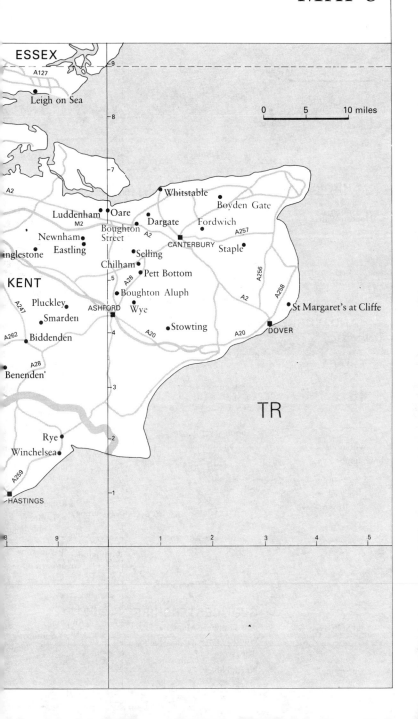

MAP 3

ESSEX

A127

Leigh on Sea

0   5   10 miles

A2

Whitstable

Boyden Gate

Luddenham • Oare

M2

Dargate Fordwich

Boughton A257

Newnham• Street A2

inglestone Eastling CANTERBURY Staple•

Selling

Chilham• A28 Pett Bottom A256

KENT A258

A247 Pluckley •Boughton Aluph A2

ASHFORD Wye St Margaret's at Cliffe

Smarden

A262 Biddenden Stowting A20 DOVER

A20

A28

Benenden'

TR

Rye •

Winchelsea•

A259

HASTINGS

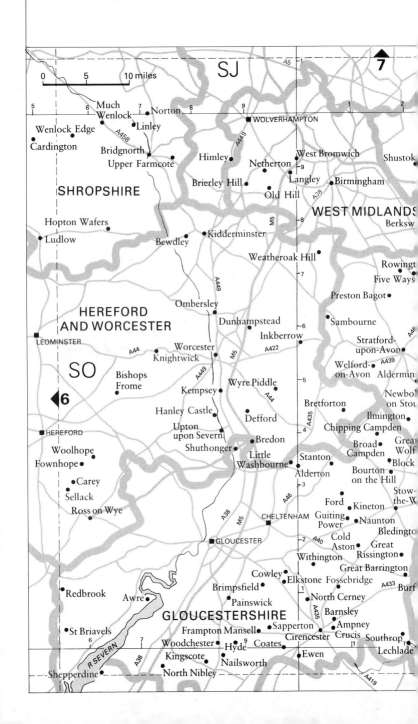

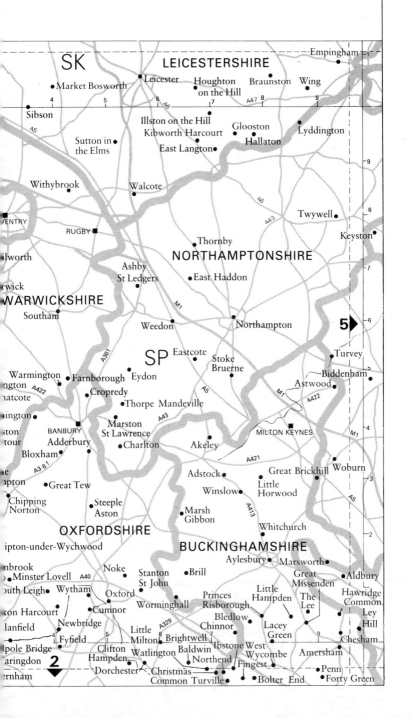

MAP 4

SK

LEICESTERSHIRE

Empingham

Market Bosworth • Leicester • Houghton on the Hill • Braunston • Wing

Sibson

Illston on the Hill
Kibworth Harcourt
Sutton in the Elms
East Langton • Glooston • Hallaton • Lyddington

Withybrook • Walcote

VENTRY

RUGBY

Thornby

NORTHAMPTONSHIRE

Twywell

Keyston

lworth

rwick

WARWICKSHIRE

Southam

Ashby St Ledgers • East Haddon

Weedon • Northampton

5

SP Eastcote • Stoke Bruerne

Turvey • Biddenham

Warmington • Farnborough • Eydon
ngton • Cropredy
hatcote
ington • Thorpe Mandeville
ston • Marston St Lawrence
tour • Adderbury • Charlton
BANBURY
Bloxham

Astwood

MILTON KEYNES

Akeley

Woburn

A361

Great Tew

Chipping Norton • Steeple Aston • Marsh Gibbon

Adstock • Great Brickhill • Little Horwood

Winslow

Whitchurch

OXFORDSHIRE

ipton-under-Wychwood

BUCKINGHAMSHIRE

Aylesbury • Marsworth

nbrook • Minster Lovell
uth Leigh • Wytham
on Harcourt
lanfield • Newbridge
pole Bridge • Fyfield
aringdon
rnham

Noke • Stanton St John • Brill

Oxford

Cumnor

Worminghall

Little Milton • Brightwell

Watlington • Baldwin

Clifton Hampden

Dorchester

Christmas Common

Princes Risborough

Bledlow • Chinnor

Lacey Green

Northend • Ibstone • West Wycombe

Turville • Bolter End

Great Missenden • Aldbury

The Lee • Hawridge Common

Ley Hill

Chesham

Little Hampden

Fingest

Amersham

Penn • Forty Green

2

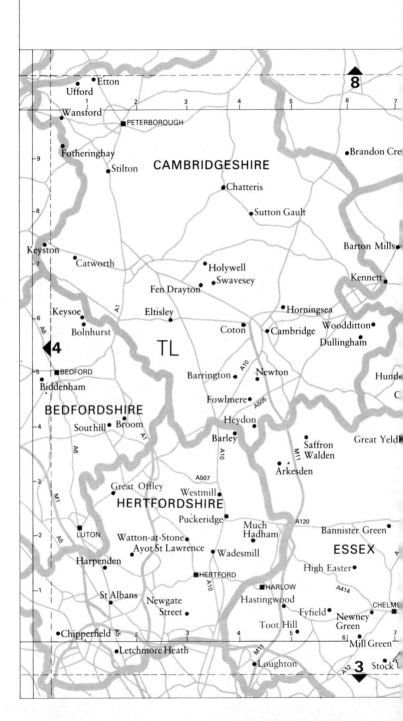

Etton
Ufford
1
Wansford
■ PETERBOROUGH

Fotheringhay
9
Stilton

CAMBRIDGESHIRE

● Brandon Cre

Chatteris

8
Sutton Gault

Barton Mills●

Keyston
7
● Catworth

Holywell
Swavesey
Fen Drayton

Kennett

Keysoe
6
Bolnhurst

Eltisley

Horningsea
Woodditton ●

Coton
Cambridge
Dullingham

TL

A1

● BEDFORD
5
Biddenham

Barrington ●
A10
Newton

Hund
C

BEDFORDSHIRE
4
Southill ● Broom

Fowlmere ●
A505

Heydon
Barley

Great Yeld

A6
A1

3
Great Offley

A507
Westmill ●

A10

Saffron
Walden

M11

Arkesden

HERTFORDSHIRE

Puckeridge ●

A120

M1

2
■ LUTON

Watton-at-Stone ●
Ayot St Lawrence ●

Much
Hadham

Wadesmill

Bannister Green ●

ESSEX

A5

Harpenden

■ HERTFORD

A10

High Easter ●

A414

1
St Albans

Newgate
Street ●

■ HARLOW
Hastingwood

Fyfield ●
Newney
Green

CHELMS
■

● Chipperfield
A5

2
● Letchmore Heath

3

Toot Hill

4

M11

5

6
Mill Green

7

● Loughton

A12 ▼ 3

Stock ●

Keysoe
A6
◀ 4

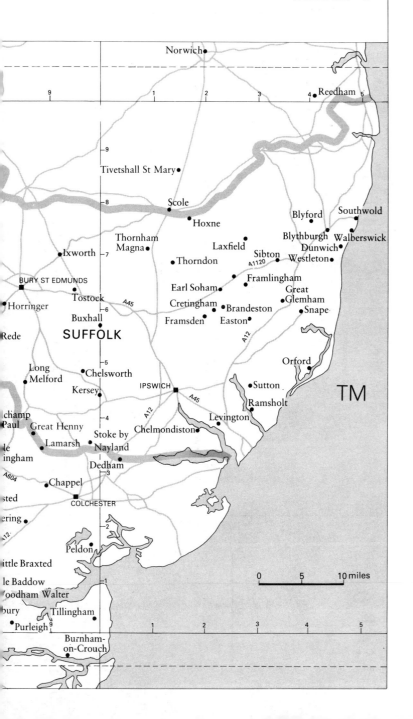

MAP 5

Norwich
Reedham

Tivetshall St Mary

Scole
Hoxne
Blyford
Southwold
Blythburgh
Walberswick
Thornham
Magna
Laxfield
Sibton
Dunwich
Ixworth
Thorndon
A1120
Westleton

BURY ST EDMUNDS
Earl Soham
Framlingham
Horringer
Tostock
A45
Great
Glemham
Cretingham
Brandeston
Rede
Buxhall
Framsden
Easton
Snape
SUFFOLK
A12

Long
Chelsworth
Orford
Melford
Kersey
IPSWICH
A45
champ
Paul
Great Henny
A12
Sutton
Ramsholt
le
Lamarsh
Stoke by
Nayland
Levington
TM
ingham
Chelmondiston
A604
Dedham
Chappel
sted
COLCHESTER
ering
A12
Peldon
ittle Braxted

le Baddow
0   5   10 miles
oodham Walter
bury
Tillingham
Purleigh
Burnham-
on-Crouch

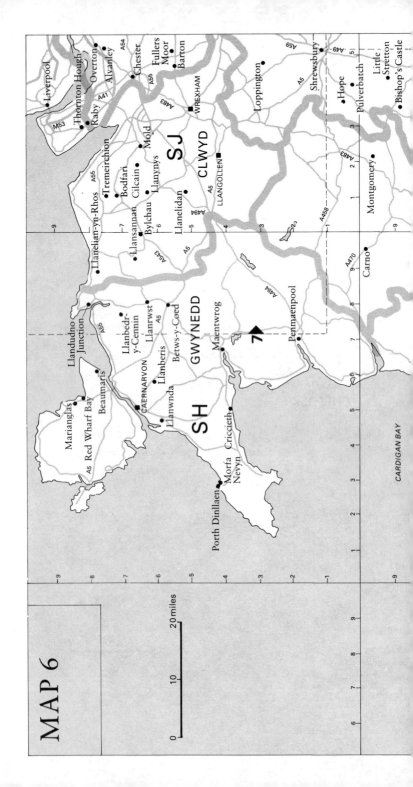

MAP 6

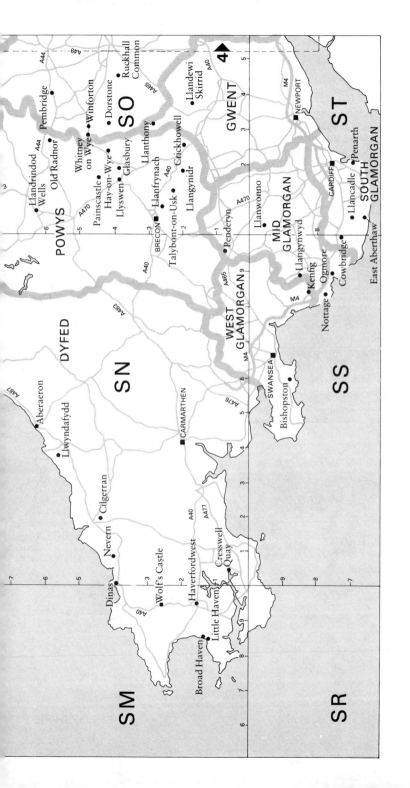

MAP 7

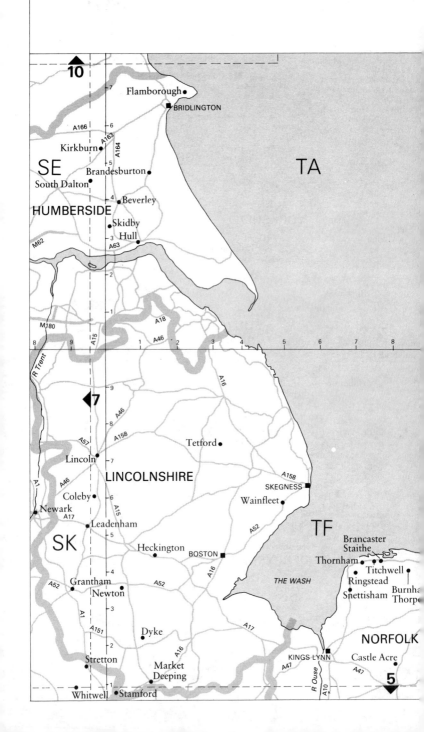

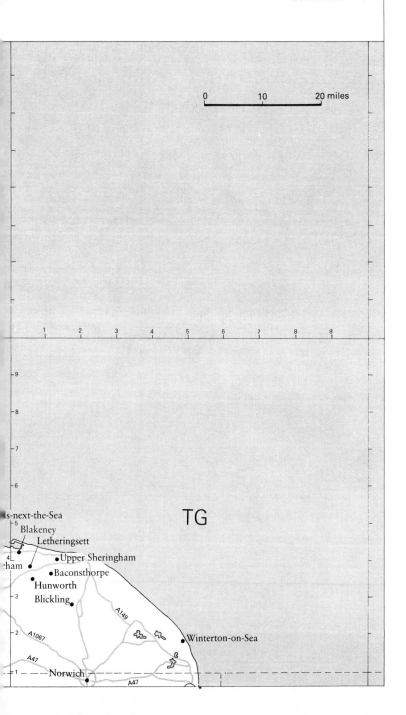

MAP 8

0   10   20 miles

1   2   3   4   5   6   7   8   9

9

8

7

6

TG

s-next-the-Sea
5
Blakeney
Letheringsett
4
•Upper Sheringham
ham
•Baconsthorpe
Hunworth
3
Blickling
A149
2
A1067
Winterton-on-Sea
A47
1
Norwich
A47

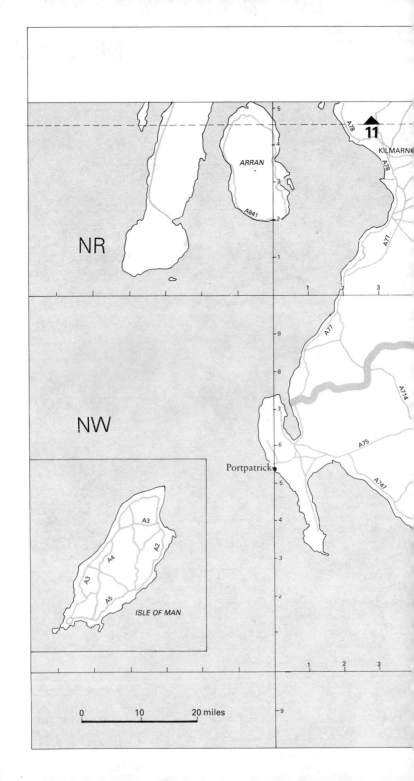

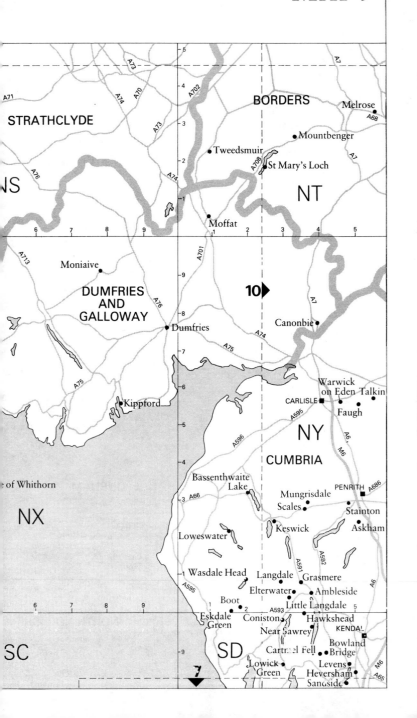

MAP 9

STRATHCLYDE

BORDERS

Melrose

Mountbenger

Tweedsmuir

St Mary's Loch

NT

Moffat

NS

Moniaive

DUMFRIES
AND
GALLOWAY

10▶

Canonbie

Dumfries

Kippford

Warwick
on Eden · Talkin
CARLISLE · · Faugh

NY

CUMBRIA

e of Whithorn

NX

Bassenthwaite
Lake

Mungrisdale
Scales · PENRITH
Stainton
Askham

Loweswater

Keswick

Wasdale Head
Langdale · Grasmere
Elterwater · Ambleside
Boot · Little Langdale
Eskdale
Green · Coniston · Hawkshead
Near Sawrey · KENDAL

SC

SD

Cartmel Fell · Bowland
Bridge
Lowick · Levens
Green · Heversham
Sandside

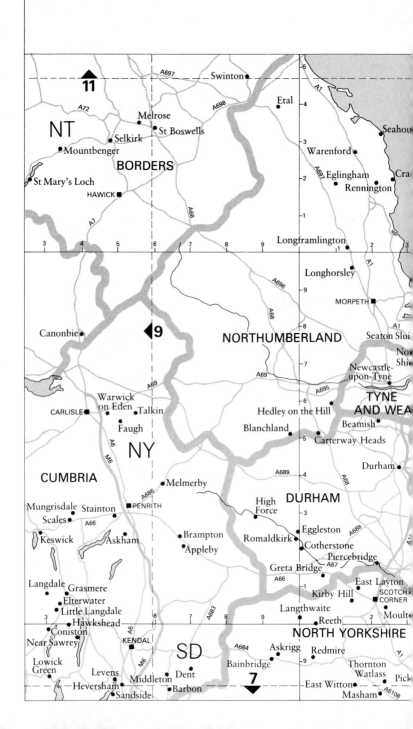

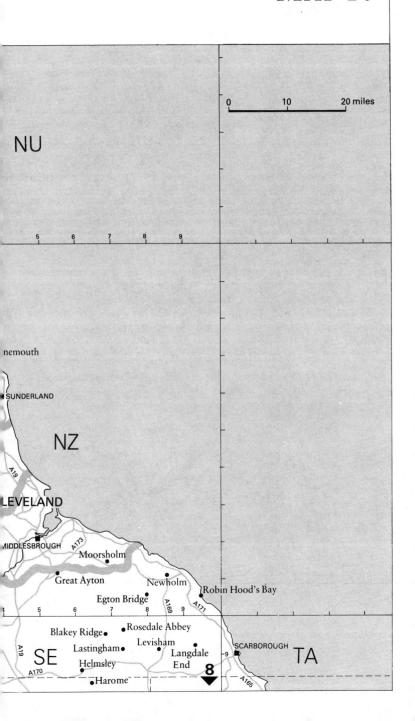

MAP 10

0   10   20 miles

NU

5   6   7   8   9

nemouth

SUNDERLAND

NZ

A19

LEVELAND

MIDDLESBROUGH

A173

Moorsholm

Great Ayton

Newholm

Robin Hood's Bay

Egton Bridge

A169

A171

1   5   6   7   8   9

Blakey Ridge

Rosedale Abbey

A19

Lastingham

Levisham

SCARBOROUGH

TA

SE

Langdale
End

9

Helmsley

A170

8

Harome

A165

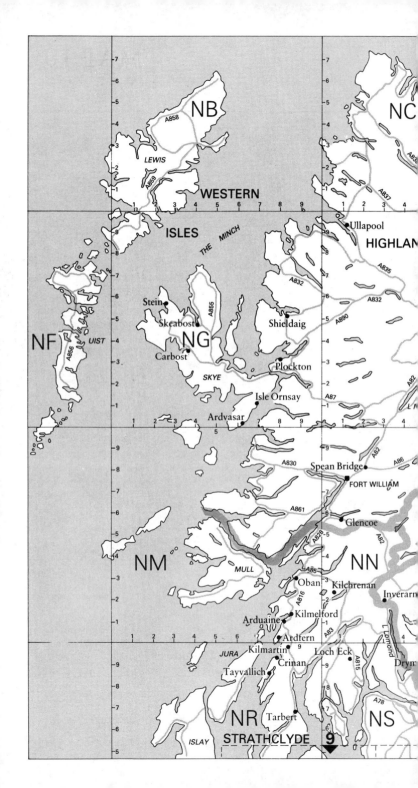

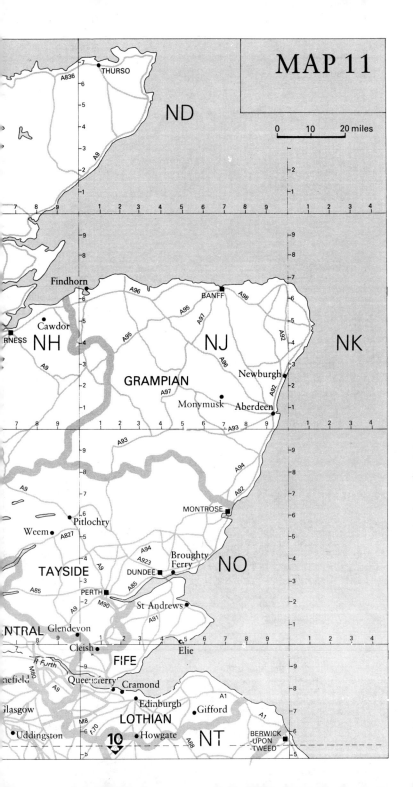

MAP 11

0　　10　　20 miles

ND

NH

NJ

NK

NO

ND

THURSO
A836

Findhorn
A96
BANFF
A98
A96
A97
Cawdor
A95
NESS
A9
GRAMPIAN
A96
Newburgh
A97
Monymusk
A93
Aberdeen
A92

A93

A94
A9
A92
Pitlochry
MONTROSE
Weem
A827
A94
A923
Broughty
Ferry
TAYSIDE
A9
DUNDEE
A85
A85
PERTH
M90
St Andrews
A9
A91
NTRAL
Glendevon
Cleish
Elie
R Forth
FIFE
nefield
M80
Queensferry
Cramond
A9
Edinburgh
A1
Gifford
lasgow
M8
LOTHIAN
A1
Uddingston
M74
Howgate
NT
A68
BERWICK-
UPON-
TWEED

10

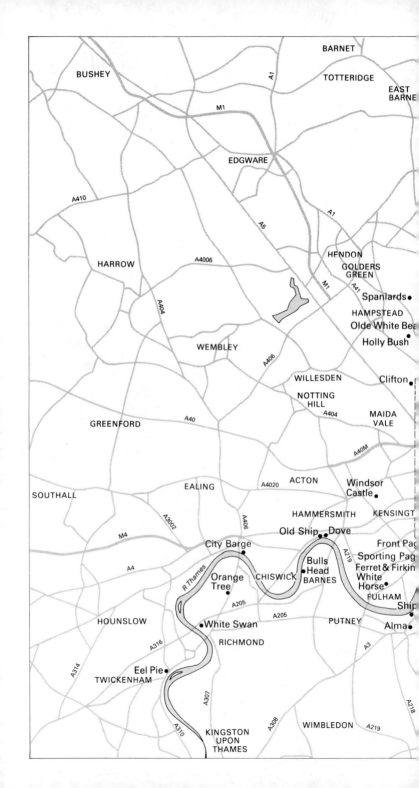

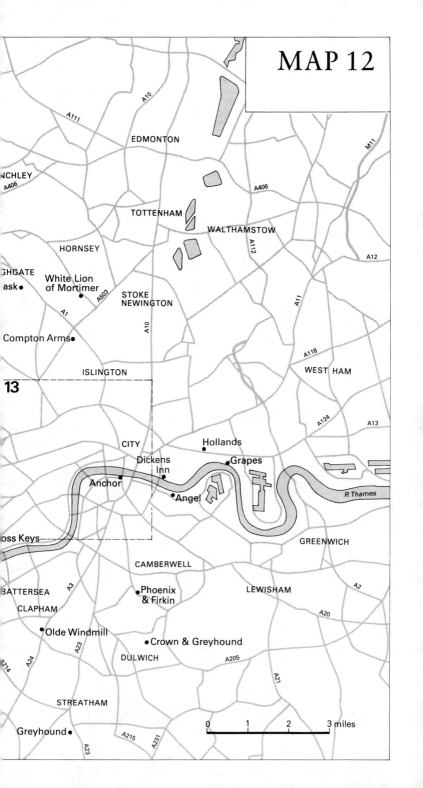

MAP 12

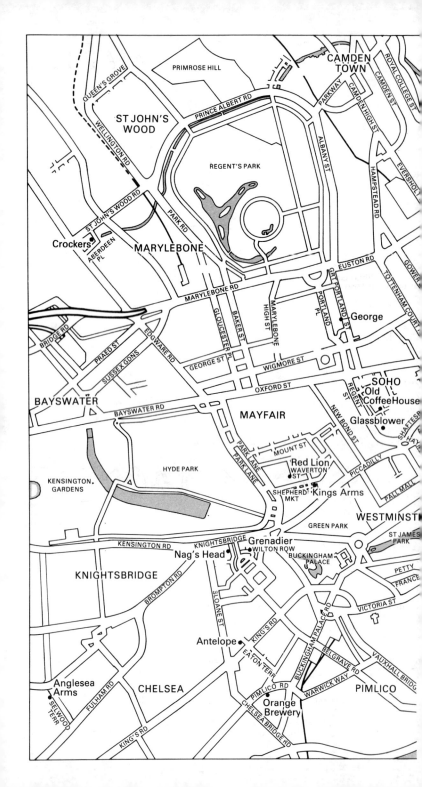

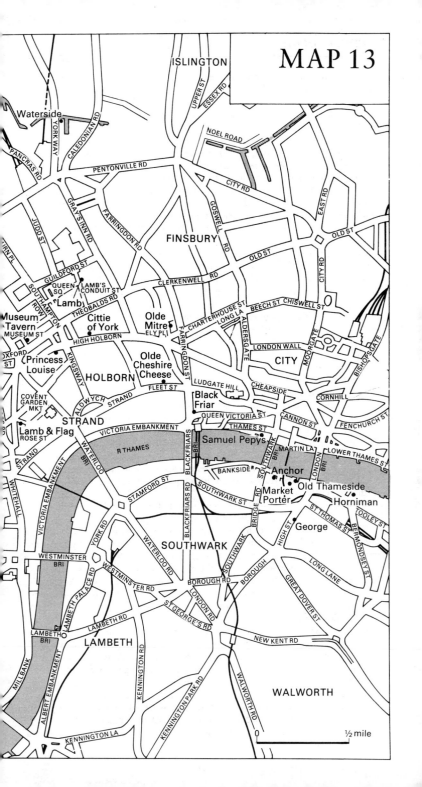

MAP 13

ISLINGTON

Waterside

FINSBURY

CITY

Museum Tavern
'Lamb
Cittie of York
Olde Mitre
Princess Louise
Olde Cheshire Cheese
HOLBORN
Black Friar
STRAND
Lamb & Flag
Samuel Pepys
Anchor
Market Porter
Old Thameside
Horniman
George
SOUTHWARK
LAMBETH
WALWORTH

½ mile

Report forms

Please report to us; you can use the tear-out forms on the following pages, the card in the middle of the book, or just plain paper – whichever's easiest for you. We need to know what you think of the pubs in this edition. We need to know about other pubs worthy of inclusion. We need to know about ones that should not be included.

The atmosphere and character of the pub are the most important features – why it would, or would not, appeal to strangers. But the bar food and the drink are important too – please tell us about them.

If the food is really quite outstanding, tick the FOOD AWARD box on the form, and tell us about the special quality that makes it stand out – the more detail, the better. And if you have stayed there, tell us about the standard of accommodation – whether it was comfortable, pleasant, good value for money. Again, if the pub or inn is worth special attention as a place to stay, tick the PLACE-TO-STAY AWARD box.

Please try to gauge whether a pub should be a main entry or is best as a *Lucky Dip* (and tick the relevant box). In general, main entries need qualities that would make it worth other readers' while to travel some distance to them; *Lucky Dips* are the pubs that are worth knowing about if you are nearby. But if a pub is an entirely new recommendation, the *Lucky Dip* may be the best place for it to start its career in the *Guide* – to encourage other readers to report on it, and gradually build up a dossier on it; it's very rare for a pub to jump straight into the main entries.

The more detail you can put into your description of a *Lucky Dip* pub that's only scantily described in the current edition (or not in at all), the better. This will help not just us but also your fellow-readers to gauge its appeal. A description of its character and even furnishings is a tremendous boon.

It helps enormously if you can give the full address for any new pub – one not yet a main entry, or without a full address in the *Lucky Dip* sections. In a town, we need the street name; in the country, if it's hard to find, we need directions. Without this, there's little chance of our being able to include the pub. And with any pub, it always helps to let us know about prices of food (and bedrooms, if there are any), and about any lunchtimes or evenings when food is not served. We'd also like to have your views on drinks quality – beer, wine, cider and so forth, even coffee and tea.

If you know that a *Lucky Dip* pub is open all day (or even late into the afternoon), please tell us – preferably saying which days.

When you go to a pub, don't tell them you're a reporter for *The Good Pub Guide*; we do make clear that all inspections are anonymous, and if you declare yourself as a reporter you risk getting special treatment – for better or for worse!

Sometimes pubs are dropped from the main entries simply because very few readers have written to us about them – and of course there's a risk that people may not write if they find the pub exactly as described in the entry. You can use the form at the front of the batch of report forms just to list pubs you've been to, found as described, and can recommend.

When you write to *The Good Pub Guide*, FREEPOST, London SW10 0BR, you don't need a stamp in the UK. We'll send you more forms (free) if you wish.

Though we try to answer letters, there are just the two of us, with only part-time help – and with other work to do, besides producing this *Guide*. So please understand if there's a delay. And from June to August, when we are fully extended getting the next edition to the printers, we put all letters and reports aside, taking as much account of their contents as we can, but not answering them until the rush is over (and after our post-press-day late summer holiday).

We'll assume we can print your name or initials as a recommender unless you tell us otherwise.

I have been to the following pubs in The Good Pub Guide *in the last few months, found them as described, and confirm that they deserve continued inclusion:*

PLEASE GIVE YOUR NAME AND ADDRESS ON THE BACK OF THIS FORM

Your own name and address (*block capitals please*)

REPORT on   *(pub's name)*

Pub's address:

☐ YES MAIN ENTRY   ☐ YES *Lucky Dip*   ☐ NO don't include
Please tick one of these boxes to show your verdict, and give reasons and descriptive comments, prices etc:
.

PLEASE GIVE YOUR NAME AND ADDRESS ON THE BACK OF THIS FORM

☐ Deserves FOOD award   ☐ Deserves PLACE-TO-STAY award   90:1

. . . .

REPORT on   *(pub's name)*

Pub's address:

☐ YES MAIN ENTRY   ☐ YES *Lucky Dip*   ☐ NO don't include
Please tick one of these boxes to show your verdict, and give reasons and descriptive comments, prices etc:

PLEASE GIVE YOUR NAME AND ADDRESS ON THE BACK OF THIS FORM

☐ Deserves FOOD award   ☐ Deserves PLACE-TO-STAY award   90:2

Your own name and address (*block capitals please*)

DO NOT USE THIS SIDE OF THE
PAGE FOR WRITING ABOUT PUBS

. . . .

Your own name and address (*block capitals please*)

DO NOT USE THIS SIDE OF THE
PAGE FOR WRITING ABOUT PUBS

REPORT on   *(pub's name)*

Pub's address:

☐ YES   MAIN ENTRY   ☐ YES *Lucky Dip*   ☐ NO don't include
Please tick one of these boxes to show your verdict, and give reasons and descriptive comments, prices etc:

PLEASE GIVE YOUR NAME AND ADDRESS ON THE BACK OF THIS FORM

☐ Deserves FOOD award   ☐ Deserves PLACE-TO-STAY award   90:3

. . . .

REPORT on   *(pub's name)*

Pub's address:

☐ YES   MAIN ENTRY   ☐ YES *Lucky Dip*   ☐ NO don't include
Please tick one of these boxes to show your verdict, and give reasons and descriptive comments, prices etc:

PLEASE GIVE YOUR NAME AND ADDRESS ON THE BACK OF THIS FORM

☐ Deserves FOOD award   ☐ Deserves PLACE-TO-STAY award   90:4

Your own name and address (*block capitals please*)

. . . .

Your own name and address (*block capitals please*)

REPORT on (pub's name)

Pub's address:

☐ YES MAIN ENTRY ☐ YES *Lucky Dip* ☐ NO don't include
Please tick one of these boxes to show your verdict, and give reasons and descriptive comments, prices etc:

PLEASE GIVE YOUR NAME AND ADDRESS ON THE BACK OF THIS FORM

☐ Deserves FOOD award ☐ Deserves PLACE-TO-STAY award   90:5

. . . .

REPORT on (pub's name)

Pub's address:

☐ YES MAIN ENTRY ☐ YES *Lucky Dip* ☐ NO don't include
Please tick one of these boxes to show your verdict, and give reasons and descriptive comments, prices etc:

PLEASE GIVE YOUR NAME AND ADDRESS ON THE BACK OF THIS FORM

☐ Deserves FOOD award ☐ Deserves PLACE-TO-STAY award   90:6

Your own name and address (*block capitals please*)

DO NOT USE THIS SIDE OF THE
PAGE FOR WRITING ABOUT PUBS

....

Your own name and address (*block capitals please*)

DO NOT USE THIS SIDE OF THE
PAGE FOR WRITING ABOUT PUBS

REPORT on   *(pub's name)*

Pub's address:

☐ YES MAIN ENTRY   ☐ YES *Lucky Dip*   ☐ NO don't include
Please tick one of these boxes to show your verdict, and give reasons and descriptive
comments, prices etc:

PLEASE GIVE YOUR NAME AND
ADDRESS ON THE BACK OF THIS FORM

☐ Deserves FOOD award   ☐ Deserves PLACE-TO-STAY award   90:7

. . . .

REPORT on   *(pub's name)*

Pub's address:

☐ YES MAIN ENTRY   ☐ YES *Lucky Dip*   ☐ NO don't include
Please tick one of these boxes to show your verdict, and give reasons and descriptive
comments, prices etc:

PLEASE GIVE YOUR NAME AND
ADDRESS ON THE BACK OF THIS FORM

☐ Deserves FOOD award   ☐ Deserves PLACE-TO-STAY award   90:8

Your own name and address (*block capitals please*)

· ·

Your own name and address (*block capitals please*)

REPORT on   *(pub's name)*

Pub's address:

☐ YES MAIN ENTRY ☐ YES *Lucky Dip* ☐ NO don't include
Please tick one of these boxes to show your verdict, and give reasons and descriptive comments, prices etc:

PLEASE GIVE YOUR NAME AND ADDRESS ON THE BACK OF THIS FORM

☐ Deserves FOOD award ☐ Deserves PLACE-TO-STAY award   90:9

. . . .

REPORT on   *(pub's name)*

Pub's address:

☐ YES MAIN ENTRY ☐ YES *Lucky Dip* ☐ NO don't include
Please tick one of these boxes to show your verdict, and give reasons and descriptive comments, prices etc:

PLEASE GIVE YOUR NAME AND ADDRESS ON THE BACK OF THIS FORM

☐ Deserves FOOD award ☐ Deserves PLACE-TO-STAY award   90:10

Your own name and address (*block capitals please*)

. . . .

Your own name and address (*block capitals please*)

REPORT on   *(pub's name)*

_____

Pub's address:

_____

☐ YES MAIN ENTRY ☐ YES *Lucky Dip* ☐ NO don't include
Please tick one of these boxes to show your verdict, and give reasons and descriptive comments, prices etc:

PLEASE GIVE YOUR NAME AND ADDRESS ON THE BACK OF THIS FORM

☐ Deserves FOOD award ☐ Deserves PLACE-TO-STAY award   90:11

· ·

REPORT on   *(pub's name)*

_____

Pub's address:

_____

☐ YES MAIN ENTRY ☐ YES *Lucky Dip* ☐ NO don't include
Please tick one of these boxes to show your verdict, and give reasons and descriptive comments, prices etc:

PLEASE GIVE YOUR NAME AND ADDRESS ON THE BACK OF THIS FORM

☐ Deserves FOOD award ☐ Deserves PLACE-TO-STAY award   90:12

Your own name and address (*block capitals please*)

DO NOT USE THIS SIDE OF THE
PAGE FOR WRITING ABOUT PUBS

· ·

Your own name and address (*block capitals please*)

DO NOT USE THIS SIDE OF THE
PAGE FOR WRITING ABOUT PUBS

REPORT on   *(pub's name)*

Pub's address:

☐ YES   MAIN ENTRY   ☐ YES *Lucky Dip*   ☐   NO don't include
Please tick one of these boxes to show your verdict, and give reasons and descriptive comments, prices etc:

PLEASE GIVE YOUR NAME AND ADDRESS ON THE BACK OF THIS FORM

☐ Deserves FOOD award   ☐ Deserves PLACE-TO-STAY award   90:13

. . . .

REPORT on   *(pub's name)*

Pub's address:

☐ YES   MAIN ENTRY   ☐ YES *Lucky Dip*   ☐   NO don't include
Please tick one of these boxes to show your verdict, and give reasons and descriptive comments, prices etc:

PLEASE GIVE YOUR NAME AND ADDRESS ON THE BACK OF THIS FORM

☐ Deserves FOOD award   ☐ Deserves PLACE-TO-STAY award   90:14

Your own name and address (*block capitals please*)

DO NOT USE THIS SIDE OF THE
PAGE FOR WRITING ABOUT PUBS

. . . .

Your own name and address (*block capitals please*)

DO NOT USE THIS SIDE OF THE
PAGE FOR WRITING ABOUT PUBS

REPORT *on*   *(pub's name)*

Pub's address:

☐ YES   MAIN ENTRY   ☐ YES *Lucky Dip*   ☐   NO don't include
Please tick one of these boxes to show your verdict, and give reasons and descriptive comments, prices etc:

PLEASE GIVE YOUR NAME AND ADDRESS ON THE BACK OF THIS FORM

☐ Deserves FOOD award   ☐ Deserves PLACE-TO-STAY award   90:15

. . . .

REPORT *on*   *(pub's name)*

Pub's address:

☐ YES   MAIN ENTRY   ☐ YES *Lucky Dip*   ☐   NO don't include
Please tick one of these boxes to show your verdict, and give reasons and descriptive comments, prices etc:

PLEASE GIVE YOUR NAME AND ADDRESS ON THE BACK OF THIS FORM

☐ Deserves FOOD award   ☐ Deserves PLACE-TO-STAY award   90:16

Your own name and address (*block capitals please*)

DO NOT USE THIS SIDE OF THE
PAGE FOR WRITING ABOUT PUBS

. . . .

Your own name and address (*block capitals please*)

DO NOT USE THIS SIDE OF THE
PAGE FOR WRITING ABOUT PUBS

REPORT on   *(pub's name)*

Pub's address:

☐ YES   MAIN ENTRY   ☐ YES *Lucky Dip*   ☐   NO don't include
Please tick one of these boxes to show your verdict, and give reasons and descriptive comments, prices etc:

PLEASE GIVE YOUR NAME AND ADDRESS ON THE BACK OF THIS FORM

☐ Deserves FOOD award   ☐ Deserves PLACE-TO-STAY award   90:17

....

REPORT on   *(pub's name)*

Pub's address:

☐ YES   MAIN ENTRY   ☐ YES *Lucky Dip*   ☐   NO don't include
Please tick one of these boxes to show your verdict, and give reasons and descriptive comments, prices etc:

PLEASE GIVE YOUR NAME AND ADDRESS ON THE BACK OF THIS FORM

☐ Deserves FOOD award   ☐ Deserves PLACE-TO-STAY award   90:18

Your own name and address (*block capitals please*)

....

Your own name and address (*block capitals please*)